"Jonathan Raskin's *Psychopathology and Mental Distress* is a one-of-a-kind textbook that fills a major gap in the literature on mental disorders. First, it is the only textbook on the market that successfully covers a wide range of approaches, including biological, psychological, and sociological perspectives, in a fair-minded way which carefully examines the strengths and weakness of each approach. The sections on the psychological approaches also provide a rare survey of a broad range of theories of psychopathology, including psychodynamic, cognitive, behavioral, and humanistic approaches. In addition, Raskin brings an unparalleled expertise in various nosologies of psychopathology, and he expands the reader's appreciation of a wide range of diagnostic practices that go beyond the usual focus on the DSM-5. The textbook is written in a lucid style that lends itself to use in undergraduate classes as well as more advanced graduate courses in psychopathology. Raskin's text is one that I will be using in my doctoral-level course in psychopathology, because it provides the broadest possible scope to the study of mental distress and offers essential conceptual tools to help students think critically about conventional approaches to diagnosis."

– **Dr. Brent Dean Robbins**, Point Park University, USA

"What I like best about Raskin's new text is that it moves beyond the typical DSM-V-TR presentation and discussion. The inclusion of the ICD-10-CM codes and other international ideas is refreshing. The *Contrasting perspectives* are the strongest aspect of this text."

– **Dr. Dallas M. Stout**, Brigham Young University, Idaho, USA

"Dr. Raskin's book will be the new standard psychopathology text in the education and training of mental health practitioners. This is the best review of the history, theories, diagnostic systems, measures, and case examples of the various mental disorders currently available. No other text covers so much ground in such an interesting and readable manner."

– **Dr. Robert M. Gordon**, Ph.D., ABPP

"This textbook uniquely offers diverse perspectives on and understandings of mental distress, allowing the reader to come to their own informed conclusions. I have used it in all of my classes dedicated to the topic, and it is one of my favorite teaching tools."

– **Dr. Sarah Kamens**, Clinical Psychologist and Author

"Instructors have numerous choices when selecting a textbook for a course on psychopathology and mental disorders. Fortunately, their choices are considerably narrowed when considering Raskin's remarkable achievement in this volume. Every key area of psychopathology is covered thoroughly, but that is just the beginning. Rather than being solely tethered to classical classificatory rubrics, Raskin brings in the latest perspectives in the field, such as the Hierarchical Taxonomy of Psychopathology (HiTOP). This new edition of Raskin's scholarly and progressive textbook is most welcome, and very likely to have a considerable impact on the training of the next generation of students and professionals in diverse mental health disciplines."

– **Dr. Robert F. Krueger**, Hathaway Distinguished Professor of Clinical Psychology,
Distinguished McKnight University Professor, University of Minnesota, USA

"Raskin's writing style is both enjoyable to read and accessible to students, without sacrificing a comprehensive presentation of the current data on psychopathology. His strong appreciation of the socio-historical context, infused throughout the text, is incredibly important for students in the field."

– **Dr. Deborah Pollack**, Utica University, USA

"This up-to-date and comprehensive textbook offers multiple perspectives on psychopathology and mental distress, including those of people with lived experience. This textbook does not shy away from some of the trickier contemporary debates and questions about mental distress. A valuable resource for psychology students – or anyone interested in mental health!"

– **Dr. Alyson Dodd**, Northumbria University, UK

PSYCHOPATHOLOGY AND MENTAL DISTRESS

CONTRASTING PERSPECTIVES

Second edition

JONATHAN D. RASKIN
STATE UNIVERSITY OF NEW YORK AT NEW PALTZ, USA

BLOOMSBURY ACADEMIC

LONDON • NEW YORK • OXFORD • NEW DELHI • SYDNEY

BLOOMSBURY ACADEMIC
Bloomsbury Publishing Plc
50 Bedford Square, London, WC1B 3DP, UK
1385 Broadway, New York, NY 10018, USA
29 Earlsfort Terrace, Dublin 2, Ireland

BLOOMSBURY, BLOOMSBURY ACADEMIC and the Diana logo
are trademarks of Bloomsbury Publishing Plc

First edition published in 2019 by Red Globe Press
First edition reprinted by Bloomsbury Academic in 2022
This edition published 2024

Cover design: Terry Woodley
Cover image © EschCollection /Getty Images

A catalogue record for this book is available from the British Library.

A catalog record for this book is available from the Library of Congress.

ISBN: HB: 978-1-3503-3043-6
         PB: 978-1-3503-3038-2
       ePDF: 978-1-3503-3153-2
      eBook: 978-1-3503-3154-9

Typeset by Integra Software Services Pvt. Ltd.
Printed and bound in India

To find out more about our authors and books visit www.bloomsbury.com
and sign up for our newsletters.

BRIEF CONTENTS

TABLE OF CONTENTS

LIST OF FIGURES

LIST OF TABLES

LIST OF DIAGNOSTIC BOXES

LIST OF FEATURES

TOUR OF THE BOOK

Accomplishing the goals outlined above is a difficult task! So, how does this book do so? Key features are outlined below. Each one helps students master the material while offering instructors ways to assist them in the learning process.

- A Perspectives Approach: Chapters are organized by perspectives, allowing students to "try on" each way of looking at problems in the field. The perspectives typically covered in comparable textbooks (e.g., neurochemical, genetic, cognitive-behavioral, and classic psychoanalytic) are given extensive attention, but so are perspectives that often receive less consideration (e.g., immunological, evolutionary, modern psychodynamic, humanistic, social justice, cross-cultural, and systems). Further, rather than presenting traditional mental disorder categories as givens that other perspectives unquestioningly treat, they too are framed as perspectival products—hence the grouping of DSM and ICD as diagnostic perspectives. This subtle shift allows mental disorder categories to be explored more fully and fairly without enshrining them as universally accepted (after all, the other perspectives covered have widely divergent opinions about them). The idea is to place all perspectives side by side, presenting them (as well as critiques lodged against them) in a dispassionate and even-handed manner. In so doing, students should come to understand each perspective's strengths and weaknesses while also developing their own educated points of view.
- Numbered Sections: Chapters are divided into numbered sections. Instructors can assign these sections in the order provided or in whatever order they deem best. Specific numbered sections can easily be assigned for different class dates (e.g., "Read Chapter 1, Sections 1.1–1.3"). This gives instructors latitude to spend more than one class on a chapter, mix and match material across chapters, or omit material from chapters they don't have the time or inclination to cover.

Learning Objectives

Each chapter begins with clearly defined learning objectives. By the time they finish studying each chapter, students should be able to fulfill these objectives.

LEARNING OBJECTIVES

After reading this chapter, you should be able to:

1. Explain why contradictory perspectives are common when studying mental distress.
2. Define psychopathology, mental illness, harmful internal dysfunction, deviance, and social oppression.
3. Summarize common criteria for making judgments about what is "abnormal."
4. Describe historical perspectives on mental distress from the Stone Age to the present day.
5. Distinguish and explain the many types of quantitative and qualitative research perspectives.

Case Examples

Each chapter presents one or more case examples. Typically introduced at the beginning of the chapter, these cases are regularly revisited to provide concrete instances of the theories and interventions discussed.

Sara and Brian

In the marriage counseling of Sara and Brian, Sara insists that her mother-in-law is "out to get her" by putting her down and manipulating Brian to spend more time with her than Sara. Brian sees no evidence of this, arguing that his mother only wants what is best for him and Sara. Whose perceptions of reality are correct? If we could determine this, would it matter? Is the person whose perceptions are less correct more psychologically disturbed? Finally, who is the ultimate authority on reality? Is it Sara, Brian, Brian's mother, their therapist, or someone else altogether?

In Depth

This feature zeros in on interesting topics to provide detailed explorations of areas currently garnering attention. Going in depth on select topics affords students the chance to gain a richer appreciation for the kinds of clinical and research explorations occurring in the field.

In Depth: Ignorance and Psychology

A 2015 *New York Times* opinion piece by Jamie Holmes advocates acknowledging that we often know less than we claim. In other words, ignorance is a lot more rampant than most of us wish to admit—even in academic subjects where we usually are told otherwise. Holmes describes how, in the 1980s, University of Arizona surgery professor Professor Marlys H. Witte created controversy when she began teaching a class called "Introduction to Medical and Other Ignorance." She wanted to include ignorance in her class because she believed we often ignore or minimize how little we know about many topics (J. Holmes, 2015b). In Witte's view, textbooks often contribute to the problem. For example, she pointed out that surgery textbooks usually discuss pancreatic cancer without ever mentioning that our present understanding of it is extremely limited. Her goal? Helping students appreciate that questions are as important as answers (J. Holmes, 2015b).

Some might deem it foolish of me to share Holmes' opinion piece at the very start of a textbook on psychopathology and mental distress. Yet my experience teaching this course over the years fits nicely with Holmes' thesis. I once had a student who, several weeks into the class, said she was going back to being a math major. "At least in math, there are clear right answers," she exclaimed. "In studying psychology, there are so many conflicting viewpoints that it's hard to know what the right answer is." Admittedly, despite all the attempts to combine rigorous research into an integrative perspective, all too often most psychology textbooks overstate how much we know. But acknowledging our ignorance up front potentially opens, rather than closes, possibilities. Holmes notes that we often think of ignorance as something to be eliminated, viewing it as simply lack of knowledge. Yet answers don't put an end to questions. They simply give rise to new questions (J. Holmes, 2015b)! As you read this text, here's to the many questions you will hopefully begin to ask.

Critical Thinking Questions

1. Do you think Witte's contention that ignorance is more rampant than we usually admit applies to the field of psychology?
2. Does recognizing the limits of our knowledge about psychopathology and mental distress help us? If so, how?

Controversial Question

Posing controversial questions invites students to grapple with issues that have often bedeviled researchers and clinicians. The goal is to expose students to prominent and ongoing debates about pathology and distress.

Controversial Question: Should There Be Warning Labels on Unrealistic Images in Fashion Magazines and on Social Media?

Fashion magazines and social media are filled with unrealistic photos. These snapshots are digitally altered, airbrushed, and tweaked to present an idealized (and often unattainable) image of the perfect body. Because exposure to images that celebrate unrealistically thin bodies is positively correlated with body dissatisfaction and eating disorders, it has been suggested that warning labels be added to them to educate people about their damaging impact. Unfortunately, there is little evidence this works. Research consistently finds that warning labels or disclaimers on unrealistic fashion magazine images are ineffective in reducing body dissatisfaction—and sometimes might even make things worse (Bury et al., 2017; Di Gesto et al., 2022; Fardouly & Holland, 2018; Kwan et al., 2018; Naderer et al., 2022; Tiggemann & Brown, 2018; S. Weber et al., 2022). Studies on warning labels exemplify how research can test whether commonsense ideas hold up to scrutiny. Disclaimers on altered media sound like they should work, but they don't. For better or worse, most researchers have reluctantly concluded that warning labels are ineffective at countering the negative impact of unrealistic images in magazines and on social media—and that it is time to explore and assess other solutions.

Critical Thinking Questions

1. Are you surprised by the results of research on warning labels? Why or why not?
2. Irrespective of the effectiveness of warning labels, is it ethical for advertisers to digitally alter ads? Should they be prevented from doing so?
3. What other interventions might we develop to reduce the negative impact of unrealistic magazine and social media images? How might you go about testing their effectiveness?

The Lived Experience: Grief Ten Years Later

This September, it will be ten years since my mother died of cancer. It seems as if it were a lifetime ago and it seems as if it were yesterday. That is the nature of grief; it has its own rhythm. It is both present and in the past and it appears that it continues to stay that way no matter how much time has gone by.

A few years ago when my friend Meghan O'Rourke and I published a series of articles on grief and loss in *Slate* magazine, some criticized the findings because some of the respondents had experienced a loss many years before taking the survey. In psychology we call this phenomenon "recall bias," where people filling out surveys wrongly or incompletely remember experiences from the past.

Memory is certainly pliable, and it is possible that people made errors in recalling what their grief was really like for them. Methodologically and intuitively that makes sense, but as a griever, I am not so sure.

The idea that the more years have passed since a loss, the less likely someone is to recall their grief rests on the assumption that grief is a static event in time that will eventually fade. This view is aligned with what many researchers in the field of psychology and psychiatry believe: that grief has a starting point, a middle point, and an end point. The heated debates in the media and in the field about when grief becomes pathological rest on the assumption that at some point, grief becomes "too much" and needs to be treated with medication or a mental health professional. If grief is a static event in time, then it certainly makes sense that it would be hard for people to remember what their experience was like five or ten years after a loss.

Having spent years studying grief, and being a griever myself now entering her tenth year of loss, I know that grief does not work this way. It is not an event in time. It is not even just an emotional response to a loss. It is a process that changes us permanently but also constantly as we ourselves change and grow. In this sense, grief is just like love. It is not something that happens once and goes away—it is something that evolves, expands and contracts, and changes in shape, depth, and intensity as time goes on.

Grief is a lifelong, ever-changing companion. It is both in the present and in the past. Moments of intense yearning and pain for the deceased can come and go even ten or twenty or thirty years after a person we love has died. It is cliché to say it, but it is also true: Grief is the price we pay for love. Grief is still with me because my mother is still with me. To deny one is inevitably to deny the other.

Interestingly, between mothers and children, there is a biological correlate to "the being with and in each other" called fetal microchimerism. It is an amazing phenomenon where fetal cells from the baby make their way into their mother's bodies and vice versa, mother's cells become intertwined into the baby's body. In other words, my mother is literally part of me biologically and emotionally and my cells were with, and in her when she died.

To be sure, microchimerism is just a metaphor—this being with and part of each other is not just for biological mothers and children. It is for everyone who has loved and lost. When I present my professional work, I often say I am a grief researcher, but actually, grief is just a stand in for what I am really studying—love and attachment. One cannot come without the other. Just like love, grief is an experience that evolves and changes with time; but one thing is for sure, it is not forgettable, because it never goes away.

By Leeat Granek, Ph.D. Reprinted with permission.

Diagnostic Box 6.2 Social Anxiety Disorder

DSM-5-TR and ICD-11
- Disproportionate fear and avoidance of social situation(s) where the person might be scrutinized.
- Overly concerned about behaving anxiously and being evaluated negatively for it.
- Symptom duration:
  - **DSM-5-TR**: At least six months.
  - **ICD-11**: At least several months.

Information from American Psychiatric Association (2022, pp. 229–230) and World Health Organization (2022a).

CHAPTER SUMMARY

Overview

- *Feeding problems* involve concern over food preferences.
- *Eating problems* are characterized by disturbed body image.

Diagnostic Perspectives

- DSM-5-TR and ICD-11 identify three eating disorders (anorexia nervosa, bulimia nervosa, and binge-eating disorder) and three feeding disorders (avoidant/restrictive food intake disorder, pica, and rumination disorder).
- PDM-2 links eating disorders to the psychological need for care and affection, HiTOP locates them on its "Somatoform" spectrum, and PTMF reframes them as responses to mistreatment and trauma.

Historical Perspectives

- The term "anorexia" has Greek origins and means "without appetite" and was first used to describe patients in 1873.
- Bulimia was first described in the 1950s but did not gain attention until the 1970s.

NEW VOCABULARY

1. Abnormal psychology
2. Analogue experiment
3. Antipsychiatry
4. Biological perspectives
5. Bodily humors
6. Case study
7. Common criteria of "abnormality"
8. Confounding variable
9. Control group
10. Correlation
11. Correlational research
12. Deinstitutionalization
13. Demonological perspective
14. Dependent variable
15. Deviance
16. Double-blind studies
17. Empirically supported treatments (ESTs)
18. Epidemiological research
19. Experiments
20. External validity
21. Grounded theory methods
22. Harmful internal dysfunction
23. Harmfulness to self or others
24. Hypothesis
25. Hysteria
26. Incidence
27. Independent variable
28. Internal validity
29. Lobotomy
30. *Malleus Maleficarum*
31. Medicalization
32. Mental disorder
33. Mental distress
34. Medical model
35. Mental illness
36. Mixed methods
37. Moral therapy
38. Phenomenological methods
39. Placebo control group
40. Placebo effect
41. Population
42. Presenting problems
43. Prevalence
44. Psychological perspectives
45. Psychopathology
46. Purposive sampling
47. Qualitative methods
48. Quantitative methods
49. Quasi-experiment
50. Random assignment
51. Random sample
52. Randomized controlled trial (RCT)
53. Sample
54. Single-subject experiments
55. Snowball sampling
56. Social oppression
57. Sociocultural perspectives
58. Trepanation
59. Trustworthiness
60. Variables
61. Violation of social norms and values
62. Wandering womb theory

ONLINE LEARNING AND TEACHING RESOURCES

Accompanying this book is a full suite of supportive resources to help both students and lecturers get the most out of their learning and teaching.

Access the digital resources here: **bloomsbury.pub/psychopathology-and-mental-distress-2e**

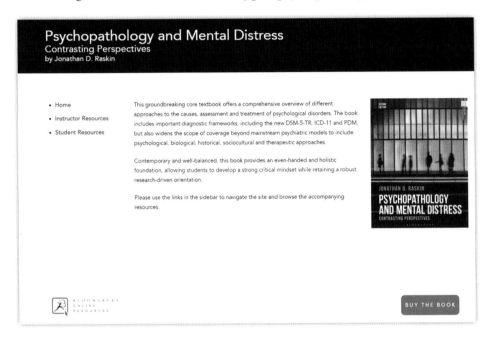

Resources for lecturers include:

- Test Bank: Includes multiple-choice, matching, and essay questions. In devising the test bank, the goal was to create materials that target key ideas in the book. As a long-time instructor aware of how often test banks disappoint, much effort was put into providing test items that effectively discriminate student understanding of key concepts.
- Instructor's Manual: For each chapter, detailed lecture notes are provided, along with PowerPoint slides to accompany them.
- Lecture Slides: MS PowerPoint slides for instructors to use during class lectures.

Resources for students include:

- Knowledge Checks: Each chapter has an accompanying online "knowledge-check" quiz that students can complete to quickly assess their understanding. Results can easily be sent to instructors.
- Videos: Relevant YouTube videos and video lectures by the author are available on the online companion website.
- "Try It Yourself" Activities: This online feature offers activities that students are invited to complete. The techniques, methods, exercises, and other activities provided let students apply what they are learning in a more personal way.
- Online Study Guide (for students): The online companion site includes a study guide, consisting of questions to help students develop study materials. By sketching answers to study guide questions, students will be able to concisely summarize content from the chapters as they prepare for exams.

PREFACE

THE CHALLENGE OF CONTRASTING PERSPECTIVES

When it comes to psychopathology and mental distress, we can probably agree that there isn't much agreement. On the contrary, there are many contrasting perspectives—different lenses that, when looked through, inevitably shape our definitions of psychopathology and mental distress, the research questions asked about them, and the clinical interventions undertaken to alleviate them. Are pathology and distress mainly attributable to neurochemical imbalances or other brain disorders, genetic inheritance, immune system reactions to stress, evolutionary mismatches between our ancestral environments and modern society, unconscious conflicts, faulty attachment relationships, irrational thinking, conditioned learning, a failure to self-actualize, cultural differences, economic adversity, social oppression, or some combination thereof? To students' dismay, the number of explanations can be dizzying!

As we shall see, those advancing these contrasting perspectives on psychopathology and mental distress are passionate about their divergent outlooks. This book tries to capture that passion by examining how advocates of contrasting perspectives often strongly and loudly disagree. The idea is to present these disagreements fully and thoroughly—but without being disagreeable! To accomplish this, the book adopts a *credulous approach* (Kelly, 1955/1991a), in which—rather than immediately judging the contrasting perspectives presented—students are encouraged to understand and appreciate every perspective on its own. To that end, it sympathetically discusses each perspective's theoretical rationale for viewing various problems in certain ways, and how this gives rise to specific intervention strategies. It also examines research on each perspective to help students make comparisons. However, rather than me—as your humble guide in this endeavor—declaring some perspectives as winners and others as losers, my goal is more modest: to provide the necessary information, pose challenging questions, and encourage you to draw your own conclusions.

Some might question this approach. "Aren't you the expert? Shouldn't you be informing students about which perspectives are most correct?" The trouble with offering definitive answers is that, in my experience, different students inevitably draw different conclusions about the material, no matter how hard (or not) I advocate for some perspectives over others. This is so even when exposed to the same theories, research, and practice aspects of these perspectives. In many respects, this isn't surprising. Deciding what is pathological and determining what to do about it are not simply dry academic endeavors. They touch on people's core beliefs about what it means to be a person and to live a healthy and productive life. They also tap into students' ideas about themselves and their own personal problems. In this regard, student disagreements about what counts as mental distress, what should be done about it, and what the research recommends mirror fundamental disagreements in the field. This book proposes a modest and exciting (but challenging) goal: After digesting the relevant information and trying to understand each perspective fairly and openly, students are encouraged to decide which perspectives on psychopathology and mental distress they most agree with and why.

PEDAGOGICAL FEATURES OF THE BOOK

Accomplishing the goals outlined above is a difficult task! So, how does this book do so? Key features are outlined below. Each one helps students master the material while offering instructors ways to assist them in the learning process.

- **A Perspectives Approach**: Chapters are organized by perspectives, allowing students to "try on" each way of looking at problems in the field. The perspectives typically covered in comparable textbooks (e.g., neurochemical, genetic, cognitive-behavioral, and classic psychoanalytic) are given extensive attention, but so are perspectives that often receive less consideration (e.g., immunological, evolutionary, modern psychodynamic, humanistic, social justice, cross-cultural, and systems). Further, rather than presenting traditional mental disorder categories as givens that other perspectives unquestioningly treat, they too are framed as perspectival products—hence the grouping of DSM and ICD as diagnostic perspectives. This subtle shift allows mental disorder categories to be explored more fully and fairly without enshrining them as universally accepted (after all, the other perspectives covered have widely divergent opinions about them). The idea is to place all perspectives side by side, presenting them (as well as critiques lodged against them) in a dispassionate and even-handed manner. In so doing, students should come to understand each perspective's strengths and weaknesses while also developing their own educated points of view.

- **Numbered Sections**: Chapters are divided into numbered sections. Instructors can assign these sections in the order provided or in whatever order they deem best. Specific numbered sections can easily be assigned for different class dates (e.g., "Read Chapter 1, Sections 1.1–1.3"). This gives instructors latitude to spend more than one class on a chapter, mix and match material across chapters, or omit material from chapters they don't have the time or inclination to cover.

- **Learning Objectives**: Each chapter begins with clearly defined learning objectives. By the time they finish studying each chapter, students should be able to fulfill these objectives.

- **Case Examples**: Each chapter presents one or more case examples. Typically introduced at the beginning of the chapter, these cases are regularly revisited to provide concrete instances of the theories and interventions discussed.

- **In Depth**: This feature zeros in on interesting topics to provide detailed explorations of areas currently garnering attention. Going in depth on select topics affords students the chance to gain a richer appreciation for the kinds of clinical and research explorations occurring in the field.

- **Controversial Questions**: Posing controversial questions invites students to grapple with issues that have often bedeviled researchers and clinicians. The goal is to expose students to prominent and ongoing debates about pathology and distress.

- **The Lived Experience**: This feature brings topics to life by providing first-hand (and often deeply personal) accounts from clients and clinicians alike of their lived experiences dealing with the presenting problems the book explores.

- **Diagnostic Boxes**: Appearing in most chapters, these succinctly present DSM and ICD definitions of disorders, helping students grasp their similarities and differences.

- **Chapter Summaries**: Brief summaries are provided at the conclusion of each chapter that highlight the main themes covered. These summaries review what students have read and guide them as they begin to study.

- **New Vocabulary and Glossary**: New vocabulary terms are bolded in each chapter and defined in the margins. A comprehensive glossary containing all new vocabulary items is also provided at the end of the book. Lists of these terms are available online too.

- **Online Knowledge Checks**: Each chapter has an accompanying online "knowledge-check" quiz that students can complete to quickly assess their understanding. Results can easily be sent to instructors.

- **Online Videos**: Relevant YouTube videos and video lectures by the author are available on the online companion website.

- **Online "Try It Yourself" Activities**: This online feature offers activities that students are invited to complete. The techniques, methods, exercises, and other activities provided let students apply what they are learning in a more personal way.

- **Online Study Guide** (for students): The online companion site includes a study guide, consisting of questions to help students develop study materials. By sketching answers to study guide questions, students will be able to concisely summarize content from the chapters as they prepare for exams.

- **Online Test Bank** (for instructors): Includes multiple-choice, matching, and essay questions. In devising the test bank, the goal was to create materials that target key ideas in the book. As a long-time instructor aware of how often test banks disappoint, much effort was put into providing test items that effectively discriminate student understanding of key concepts.

- **Online Instructor's Manual** (for instructors): For each chapter, detailed lecture notes are provided, along with PowerPoint slides to accompany them.

ABOUT THE AUTHOR

Jonathan D. Raskin earned his undergraduate degree in psychology from Vassar College and his Ph.D. in counseling psychology at the University of Florida. He completed his doctoral internship at Emory University's Counseling Center. Dr. Raskin is a professor at the State University of New York at New Paltz, where he is chair of the Department of Psychology and teaches psychology and counselor education courses. In addition to his academic work, Dr. Raskin maintains an active private practice as a psychologist.

Dr. Raskin's scholarship addresses constructions of mental distress, attitudes toward and alternatives to psychiatric diagnosis, and meaning-oriented approaches to psychotherapy. He has also co-edited six books: *Constructions of Disorder: Meaning-Making Frameworks for Psychotherapy* (published by the American Psychological Association) and all five volumes of the *Studies in Meaning* series (published by Pace University Press). He is currently working on a book and video on constructive psychotherapies for the American Psychological Association Press. A past president of the Society for Humanistic Psychology (Division 32 of the American Psychological Association), Dr. Raskin is coeditor of the *Journal of Constructivist Psychology* and serves on several journal editorial boards. He is a fellow of the American Psychological Association, as well as a recipient of the SUNY Chancellor's Award for Excellence in Scholarship and the SUNY Research Foundation Research and Scholarship Award.

ACKNOWLEDGMENTS

Writing a book is an enormous undertaking and I am indebted to so many people who helped me on the long and arduous journey of doing so. I wish to express heartfelt thanks to Jenna Steventon, my commissioning editor, whose brilliance helped me navigate not only the revision process but also the change in publisher to Bloomsbury. Jenna has been supportive and caring throughout, providing invaluable insight and guidance—and as a bonus, she knew exactly where to get the best cinnamon bun in Iceland (and perhaps the world). In addition to Jenna, I wish to acknowledge my past commissioning editors Paul Stevens and Luke Block. Their support getting the book rolling was invaluable to me. I also am thankful and deeply indebted to Emily Wood, Emily Lovelock, and Lauren Zimmerman for their work as development editors. Their feedback on chapters was invaluable at improving them, and their enthusiasm and support during the review process was very much appreciated. Speaking of reviews, I am thankful to the many unsung anonymous reviewers, whose comments on draft chapters were extremely helpful. Finally, I wish to thank Kanji Rodriguez, for her stellar work on supplementary materials.

Professionally, there are too many colleagues to thank, so I'll just name a few. First and foremost, I would like to dedicate this edition of the book to my doctoral advisor, Franz Epting, who passed away in June 2023. Franz was a great advisor, mentor, and friend. He taught me a lot, and I will miss him. In many respects, this book is a culmination of his many years of mentorship.

Thanks also to Sara Bridges, Mark Burrell, Don Domenici, Valerie Domenici, Jay Efran, Mike Gayle, Jack Kahn, Sarah Kamens, Justin Karter, the late Chuck Lawe, Spencer McWilliams, Bob Neimeyer, Greg Neimeyer, Amberly Panepinto, Mark Paris, Brent Dean Robbins, Donna Rockwell, Caroline Stanley, David Winter, and my many colleagues at SUNY New Paltz.

I'd also like to thank the following people close to me (1) because their love and support has been invaluable and (2) just because: My amazing daughters, Ari, Noa, and Evelyn; my parents, Paula and Sherman; my brother, Daniel; my sister-in-law (and fellow psychologist) Kayoko Yokoyama; my nephew, Taro; my friend, Mike Rozett; and my caring and kind partner, Tessa Killian. I am deeply grateful to all of them.

Okay, now go read the book.

CONCEPTUAL, HISTORICAL, AND RESEARCH PERSPECTIVES

1

Photo 1.1
We Are/Getty Images.

OVERVIEW

1.1 Getting Started: Psychopathology and Mental Distress

Basic Definitions

This book examines the field of **psychopathology**, which studies dysfunctions or disorders that lead to cognitive and emotional upset—that is, **mental distress**. Sad, anxious, or angry thoughts and feelings, sometimes accompanied by physical symptoms, are examples of mental distress. Mental distress can be caused by psychopathology, but it doesn't have to be. For instance, mental distress over missing a train is expected—there is nothing "wrong" with experiencing it, and we don't see those who do as suffering from a disorder. On the other hand, distress over believing the government is monitoring us via radio transponders in our breakfast cereal does seem pathological to most people. Nonetheless, in most cases distinguishing psychopathology from normal and expected mental distress is no easy task. To illustrate this, consider the case examples below. Which ones do you believe are good examples of psychopathology? Of mental distress? Of neither?

Psychopathology:
Attributes mental distress to internal dysfunction or sickness inside the individual.

Mental distress:
Cognitive and/ or emotional upset; considered expected/ normal in some cases and a sign of psychopathology in others.

Case Examples

Jim

Jim is a 20-year-old university student studying psychology. Though he is a good student with excellent grades, Jim begins to behave erratically a few months before graduation. He claims to hear voices, which tell him that his professors are spying on him. He insists that the university police have planted listening devices in his bedroom to monitor his activities. He stops bathing and combing his hair. His friends start to worry about him and so does one of his instructors, who alerts the campus health center. Jim is diagnosed with schizophrenia, sent home to his parents, and placed on antipsychotic drugs. After six months on the drugs, Jim gets a part-time job while living at home with his parents but does not feel ready to return to his university.

Michelle

Michelle, a 14-year-old girl, has always been outspoken, but recently she has become downright rebellious. She initiates arguments with her parents and refuses to obey their eleven o'clock curfew. In fact, Michelle stays out all night and when she comes home she ignores her parents entirely or yells at them about how unfair they are to her. Exasperated, her parents take Michelle to a local psychiatrist, who diagnoses her with oppositional defiant disorder. Michelle is briefly hospitalized, and her behavior temporarily takes a turn for the better after she is released. However, within a month she returns to her rebellious ways, much to the chagrin of her overwhelmed parents.

Sam

Sam, who is 13 years old and was born biologically female, has recently come out as transgender. Sam has stopped using the name assigned them at birth (Sandra) and begun using they, them, and their pronouns. Sam's parents have refused to pay for hormone therapy that will give Sam a more masculine appearance, lamenting that their "beautiful daughter" is too young and immature to "decide to become a boy."

Mary

Mary is a 70-year-old grandmother of three. Her husband of thirty years, Phil, recently passed away. Mary feels isolated and depressed. She increasingly spends time alone in her apartment, has trouble sleeping, and loses her appetite. After several months, Mary tells her family doctor about her sadness, and he writes her a prescription for antidepressants. Mary does not fill the prescription and instead seeks psychotherapy to talk about her loneliness and depression. The therapy raises her spirits some and she establishes a more active daily schedule and social life. However, though she is happier than before therapy, her mood remains tinged with occasional sadness, as she continues to miss her husband. Her doctor keeps encouraging her to try the antidepressants, but she doesn't want to.

Jesse

Jesse is a 37-year-old Black man living in an urban area of the United States that has recently been rocked by racial tension over police profiling and mistreatment of people of color. Jesse goes to see a psychotherapist and states that he is worried that the police are monitoring his movements. "They're out to get me," he says. "I know they're watching." Jesse's therapist, a white woman, is unsure what to make of Jesse's assertions.

Some of the cases above may seem obviously pathological, while the very inclusion of others may offend you. Although they all reflect situations viewed, at one point or another, as pathological by mental health professionals or the public, do not assume that sharing them here means endorsing such interpretations. Rather, the cases are offered to get you thinking about what you consider psychopathology versus reasonable distress. Your reactions are welcome and important—and something to discuss (sensitively and respectfully) with your instructor and fellow students. As you read this book, you will regularly be asked to distinguish psychopathology (disorder in the person) from normal and expected mental distress. But realize that not everyone will agree with your assessments—and vice versa.

The Challenge: Experts often Disagree

This lack of consensus isn't just confined to students. Experts in the field regularly disagree. For example, consider the notion of **mental illness**. Despite this term's ubiquity in daily life, its definition is hotly debated. For instance, the American Psychiatric Association (APA), the professional organization of American psychiatry, says:

Mental illnesses are health conditions involving changes in emotion, thinking or behavior (or a combination of these) …. Many people who have a mental illness do not want to talk about it. But mental illness is nothing to be ashamed of! It is a medical condition, just like heart disease or diabetes. And mental health conditions are treatable. We are continually expanding our understanding of how the human brain works, and treatments are available to help people successfully manage mental health conditions. (American Psychiatric Association, 2018, para. 7)

The APA defines mental illnesses as *medical* conditions. This sounds quite definitive and that may be comforting. The problem is that not all professionals agree with this view. Consider the perspective of the Division of Clinical Psychology of the British Psychological Society (BPS), the professional association of psychologists in the United Kingdom. It takes a very different stance on mental illness, worrying about the **medicalization** of everyday problems (British Psychological Society, 2011). Medicalization occurs when we inappropriately classify non-medical issues as medical. The BPS directly challenges the APA's medical conception of mental distress:

It is often assumed that there is a straightforward dividing line between "mental health" and "mental illness" (normality and abnormality) and that discrete, identified disease processes (for example "schizophrenia") are responsible for experiences such as hearing voices. However, recent research suggests that this is not the case. Viewing experiences as symptoms of illnesses is only one way of seeing them, and one that not everyone finds helpful. (British Psychological Society, 2017a, p. 18)

What's going on here? We have two mainstream organizations taking completely different—and contradictory—positions on mental illness! One group says that mental illness is a medical condition. The other group says just the opposite, namely that many of the things we call mental illnesses are instead reasonable responses to challenging life circumstances and oppressive social conditions—and we often incorrectly classify them as medical problems.

At this point, I wouldn't be surprised to find you flipping a few pages ahead to figure out which view is the right one. Realizing that a definitive answer isn't provided, you might ask your instructor. But this merely gives you one person's opinion (albeit a person who has a big say over your grade!). It doesn't resolve the fact that we have two prominent groups with extensive mental health expertise holding seemingly irreconcilable views. While textbooks and professors can (and often do) offer their opinions, on many issues there is admittedly no clear consensus. What constitutes "pathology" or "distress," how to best identify each, and how to deal with them effectively are questions that receive different answers depending on who is asked. In other words, when it comes to psychopathology and mental distress, there are many *contrasting perspectives*. The goal of this book is to help you make sense of them all, so you can decide which you believe are best. Let's define some basic terms to get you started with this task.

Mental illness: Defined by the American Psychiatric Association as an illness affecting or located in a person's brain that affects how a person thinks, behaves, and interacts with other people.

Medicalization: Inappropriately classifying non-medical problems as medical.

1.2 Basic Terms

Some of these terms are mainly descriptive. Others have assumptions about psychopathology and mental distress embedded within them that reflect broader perspectives encountered throughout the book. All are important for navigating the terrain ahead.

Psychiatry vs. Psychology

Students are often confused about the difference between psychiatry and psychology, two of the major mental health professions. Psychiatry is a medical specialty concerned with mental disorders and their treatment. *Psychiatrists* are physicians who have completed specialized training in psychiatry (American Psychiatric Association, n.d.-d). Not surprisingly, because they are medical doctors, psychiatrists generally adhere to a **medical model**, which views psychiatric problems as illnesses (B. J. Deacon, 2013; Huda, 2021; Joyce, 1980; Patil & Giordano, 2010).

Unlike psychiatrists, *psychologists* don't have medical degrees. Instead, they have graduate degrees (usually doctorates) in psychology, a discipline that studies mental processes and behavior. Clinical psychologists and counseling psychologists conduct *psychotherapy*, which involves talking with clients/patients about their problems as a means of remediating their distress. *Clinical psychologists* are typically trained to see mental distress as a dysfunction in the individual, usually of a psychological nature (G. J. Neimeyer et al., 2011). Like psychiatrists, many but not all clinical psychologists adopt a medical model. This "places a premium on assessment, diagnosis, and treatment within a broad range of hospital and community contexts" (G. J. Neimeyer et al., 2011, p. 44). *Counseling psychologists* differ from clinical psychologists in that their training tends to focus less on pathology and more on the everyday problems of otherwise well-adjusted people (G. J. Neimeyer et al., 2011; Norcross, 2000; Society of Counseling Psychology, n.d.).

In practice, clinical and counseling psychologists are often hired to do the same kinds of jobs, sometimes making it difficult to discern the difference between them (G. J. Neimeyer et al., 2011). Compared to clinical psychology, counseling psychology generally places less emphasis on assessment and diagnosis and more on the emotional strengths and positive aspects of client functioning (G. J. Neimeyer et al., 2011; Norcross, 2000). Like clinical psychologists, counseling psychologists work in private practice and mental health agencies. They are somewhat less likely to work in hospitals than clinical psychologists and more likely to be employed at university counseling centers and other sites where client issues are deemed less severe (G. J. Neimeyer et al., 2011).

Mental Illness and Mental Disorder

As alluded to earlier, mental illness and **mental disorder** are terms rooted in the psychopathology perspective. Both imply something wrong inside the person being diagnosed. However, distinguishing between them can prove difficult. In public discourse, mental illness usually has a more biological connotation than mental disorder. Recall APA's (2018) definition of mental illness as "a medical condition, just like heart disease or diabetes." This is decidedly more medical than the definition of mental disorder that APA gives in its *Diagnostic and Statistical Manual of Mental Disorders* (DSM), a comprehensive book that lists and describes all APA-recognized disorders (see Chapter 3). The DSM defines a mental disorder as "a syndrome characterized by clinically significant disturbance in an individual's cognition, emotion regulation, or behavior that reflects a dysfunction in the psychological, biological, or developmental processes underlying mental functioning" (American Psychiatric Association, 2022, p. 14). Though this definition defines mental disorder as psychopathology (i.e., a dysfunction in the person), it leaves room for those who do not see all mental disorders as brain diseases. However, as we shall see, even the broader DSM definition is sometimes controversial (A. Frances, 2013a; Paris, 2015).

Medical model: Views psychiatric problems as categorical syndromes reflecting underlying biological illnesses that must be accurately diagnosed before they can be effectively treated.

Mental disorder: Defined by the American Psychiatric Association as a syndrome characterized by clinically significant disturbance in a person's cognition, emotional regulation, or behavior reflecting a dysfunction in psychological, biological, or developmental processes.

Harmful Internal Dysfunction

The notion of **harmful internal dysfunction** is central to the psychopathology perspective on mental disorder. It holds that mental disorders are best viewed as having two components: (a) a mental mechanism that fails to operate according to its naturally designed function (i.e., an internal dysfunction), and (b) behavior society deems harmful that is caused by the internal dysfunction (J. C. Wakefield, 1992a, 1992b, 1999). Importantly, both harm and dysfunction are necessary conditions for something to be a disorder. For example, "a dysfunction in one kidney often has no effect on the overall well-being of a person and so is not considered to be a disorder" (J. C. Wakefield, 1992b, p. 384). At the same time, social deviance in the absence of internal dysfunction is also insufficient for something to qualify as a disorder. A biological or psychological mechanism inside the person must be malfunctioning—that is, operating in a way nature did not intend. Requiring both social judgment and an internal dysfunction is supposed to protect against incorrectly labeling social deviance as psychopathology:

The requirement that a disorder must involve a dysfunction places severe constraints on which negative conditions can be considered disorders and thus protects against arbitrary labeling of socially disvalued conditions as disorders .... Diagnoses such as "drapetomania" (the "disorder" of runaway slaves), "childhood masturbation disorder," and "lack of vaginal orgasm" can be seen as unsound applications of a perfectly coherent concept that can be correctly applied to other conditions .... [T]he harmful dysfunction view allows us to reject these diagnoses on scientific grounds, namely, that the beliefs about natural functioning that underlie them—for example, that slaves are naturally designed to serve, that children are naturally designed to be nonsexual, and that women are naturally designed to have orgasms from vaginal stimulation in intercourse alone—are false. (J. C. Wakefield, 1992b, p. 386)

Though influential, the harmful internal dysfunction model hasn't been explicitly incorporated into the DSM definition of mental disorder. Further, some people complain that it doesn't consistently identify disorder in everyday life (S. O. Lilienfeld & Marino, 1995, 1999). One explanation for this is that it relies on social judgments about harmfulness. When these judgments change, so does what counts as a disorder (Sadler & Agich, 1995). Additionally, the concept of "mental mechanism" strikes some critics as fuzzy (Houts, 1996; D. Murphy & Woolfolk, 2000). These critics contend that the model treats a mental mechanism as something biologically broken in the brain (G. R. Henriques, 2002), even though what is "mental" is by definition not physical and therefore can't literally be found in someone's brain. Something mental also cannot be scientifically observed or measured. If a mechanism is mental rather than physical, we can't see it. Consequently, we can never know if mental mechanisms truly exist (Houts, 1996).

Deviance

Not everyone subscribes to the internal dysfunction/psychopathology perspective. Some prefer the notion of deviance instead. **Deviance**, a word often used by sociologists, refers to socially unacceptable behavior—but, like the term mental distress, without presuming the behavior is disordered (Endleman, 1990). Deviant behavior does not necessarily stem from pathology inside individuals. In fact, sociologist Thomas Scheff (1999) famously (and controversially) argued that what gets called mental illness is more a product of society labeling behavior as deviant than it is a product of internal psychopathology. From this viewpoint, how different social groups define suitable behavior is central in determining who is considered pathological. For example, in some conservative Muslim countries a woman who does not veil her face in public may be acting in a socially deviant manner, but most people would not consider her behavior a sign of psychopathology.

Harmful internal dysfunction: Definition of mental disorder that has two components: (a) a mental mechanism that fails to operate according to its naturally designed function (i.e., an internal dysfunction), and (b) behavior that society deems harmful which is caused by the internal dysfunction.

Deviance: Behavior that violates social norms and values.

Social Oppression

Those emphasizing **social oppression** attribute mental distress to unjust societal conditions. Sometimes they accept the notion of individual psychopathology, but they believe it is caused by social oppression (i.e., prolonged exposure to economic inequality and discrimination produces ongoing stress, which fosters illnesses inside people). However, other times they contend that ongoing oppression merely produces deviant behavior (i.e., oppressed people act out not because they are ill, but because they can no longer abide by the norms of a tyrannical society). The key point to those emphasizing social oppression is that mental distress originates in social conditions, not individuals. From this perspective, we too often conceptualize distress as an individual, rather than social, problem:

Oppression contributes to mental health problems in the form of depression, suicidal ideation, learned helplessness, surplus powerlessness, emotional isolation, and other difficulties. Although the link between oppressive societal conditions and psychological health may seem obvious to us now, this has not always been the case. Historically, psychology and psychiatry ascribed mental health problems to internal mechanisms that were thought to be quite independent from the social circumstances in which the person lived. (Prilleltensky, 1999, p. 107)

Photo 1.2 The English National Opera's Production of Atwood's *The Handmaid's Tale* at The London Coliseum. We can read *The Handmaid's Tale* as a representation of oppressed people acting out and being perceived as "ill" because they can no longer abide by the norms of a tyrannical society.
Robbie Jack/Getty Images.

Some who emphasize social oppression reject the idea of individual psychopathology entirely. They question attributing mental distress to disorders inside people. In this view,

services should be based on the premise that the origins of distress are largely social. The guiding idea underpinning mental health services needs to change from assuming that our role is to treat "disease" to appreciating that our role is to help and support people who are distressed as a result of their life circumstances, and how they have made sense of and reacted to them. (Kinderman, 2014b, para. 14)

Others take a middle ground position in which internal dysfunctions are accepted as real but greatly influenced by social and cultural factors like gender, race, and class (López & Guarnaccia, 2020; Winstead & Sanchez-Hucles, 2020). The degree to which mental distress is caused by internal dysfunction versus social oppression is a question we return to repeatedly. The "Lived Experience" feature examines the sharp rise in mental distress among teens and young adults and its connection to social adversity.

The Lived Experience: "Generation Disaster"

People in the United States born between 1990 and 2001 have lived through the 9/11 attacks, prolonged wars in Afghanistan and Iraq, the 2008 economic crisis, an ongoing and worsening climate crisis, regular school shootings, a society rife with political and racial divisions, and—to top it all off—the lengthy COVID-19 pandemic. That's a lot to handle! Psychologist Karla Vermeulen (2021), who researches this age group, refers to them as "Generation Disaster." She argues that the historical circumstances they faced while growing up have shaped their psychological development. Vermeulen (2021) points out that in 2017 (before the COVID-19 pandemic exacerbated things), nearly 9 million Americans ages 18 to 25 were coping with some type of mental distress or substance use issue—a huge number of young people!

Photo 1.3 People in the United States born between 1990 and 2001 have lived through a lot—including the 9/11 attacks, rampant school shootings, and the COVID-19 pandemic. Some call them "Generation Disaster."
Yoav Aziz/Unsplash.

What sorts of things do members of "Generation Disaster" tell us about their life experiences? A sampling of relevant first-hand accounts from Vermeulen (2021) offers insights into their psychology. A male born in 2000 complained that his generation is too often misconstrued as lazy, when in fact they are merely struggling: "We are not lazy—we live in a scary and hard time" (p. 108). Building on this, one of his peers contended that the current generation of college students has had to face continual anxiety over things prior generations did not, like terrorism and school shootings:

> Things like terrorist attacks and school shootings are extremely real and extremely possible to happen to us .... I hear kids talk about how when they are bored in class sometimes they think about what they would do if a school shooter came into the building. I don't think that is something my parents ever thought about. And I think it really has an effect on our mental health. (p. 77)

Also affecting Generation Disaster's mental health is a sense that prior generations have decimated the environment and are bequeathing the mess to them: "Climate change does worry me and impact my daily life .... I have had nightmares about it and I try not to read any of the apocalyptic articles because I don't want to stress myself out" (p. 152). This sentiment was echoed by a female born in 1999 who lamented that "a big part of the challenges of younger generations is having to deal with the greed and mistakes of the previous generations not thinking or caring about the future" (p. 119). But Generation Disaster's difficulties do not end there. Beyond the horrors of terrorism, school shootings, and climate change, many of them feel that the fast-paced interconnected world they reside in has only amplified their distress: "With access to the Internet, and having been raised throughout this mess, I feel hyperconnected and hypersensitive to what the world holds" (p. 112). A trans man born in 1993 perhaps summed it up best:

> My generation is exhausted. We overwork, overstress, and abuse substances to cope. We can't afford therapy no matter how much we all need it .... We are saddled with debt and half the time aren't sure when our next real meal will be .... Our country is dying and has been dying .... You have to be born rich to survive at this point and it's going to kill us all. (p. 181)

In reflecting on the challenges of Generation Disaster, Vermeulen concludes that "today's emerging adults are indeed demonstrably more anxious, depressed, and addicted than current older groups" but it is unclear "whether these rates reflect an increase in distress over previous cohorts moving through this same stage or if this is a developmental rite of passage that all groups go through as they move into adulthood" (p. 109). Although the psychological issues of Generation Disaster cannot be directly attributed to the grievous events they have endured (because correlation doesn't prove causation), advocates of sociocultural perspectives are likely to maintain that these events have played an important role in their increased levels of anxiety, depression, and mental distress. Do you agree or disagree?

Are you a member of Generation Disaster? If so, what has your experience been? Has the era you were raised in contributed to whatever mental distress you and your peers have faced? If so, what—if anything—can or should be done about it?

"Abnormal Psychology"

Until recently, psychopathology and mental distress were referred to as **abnormal psychology**. This phrase is still sometimes used. It might even be the name of the course in which you are reading this book. However, many consider abnormal psychology a problematic term due to its negative associations—which is why the *Journal of Abnormal Psychology* changed its name to the *Journal of Psychopathology and Clinical Science*. As the editors explained, "human diversity is too broad to be contained—or constrained—by the metaphor of abnormality" (MacDonald et al., 2021, p. 2). Ironically, "abnormal psychology" has become pejorative for the very reason the phrase has also been

Abnormal psychology: Alternative name for the study of psychopathology and mental distress that is increasingly considered pejorative.

useful. Calling something abnormal makes judgments about it explicit in a way that using the terms psychopathology and mental distress does not. Although it is critical to acknowledge the negative connotations that the word "abnormal" carries, considering common criteria of "abnormality" can help students clarify their judgments about psychopathology and mental distress. So, let's turn to those criteria next.

1.3 Common Criteria of "Abnormality"

Common criteria of "abnormality":
Statistical deviation, violation of social norms and values, behavior that disturbs others, harmfulness to self or others, emotional suffering, and misperception of reality; used to make judgments of "abnormality."

It may be becoming apparent that psychopathology and mental distress do not come readily labeled and identified for all to see. People use **common criteria of "abnormality"** to distinguish them. Though many of these criteria have overlapping elements, each is important on its own. None are necessary and sufficient, but all are useful. As you read about them, consider previously introduced concepts like psychopathology, deviance, and social oppression. How do criteria for "abnormality" help us judge when mental distress is expectable, socially deviant, or triggered by an internal dysfunction?

Statistical Deviation

Statistical deviation identifies abnormality by comparing people to statistical norms. For example, most of us live with other people, not by ourselves. Anyone who does live alone is, statistically speaking, abnormal. Of course, just because something is statistically deviant doesn't necessarily mean it's pathological. For instance, only a small percentage of people earn doctoral degrees. This makes doing so statistically abnormal, but few would argue that holding a doctorate is a sign of psychopathology! The "Controversial Question" feature offers another example of the uncertain link between statistical deviation and disorder.

Controversial Question: Is Shortness a Disorder?

In 2003, an advisory panel for the Food and Drug Administration in the United States recommended genetically engineered human growth hormone be approved for use in otherwise healthy children (mostly boys) identified as being idiopathically short. *Idiopathic* illnesses are ones that arise unexpectedly without a known cause. Although these very short children were at the bottom of the normal growth curve, they showed no hormonal deficiencies (Angier, 2003). The FDA approved the advisory panel's recommendation and now growth hormone can be prescribed for children diagnosed with *idiopathic short stature (ISS)* (P. Cohen, Rogol, et al., 2008; Inzaghi et al., 2019; M. Morrison, 2015). The rationale for this? American men under the average height of 5′ 9″ are more likely to drop out of school, drink excessively, date sporadically, get sick, or experience depression (Angier, 2003). In other words, short men develop psychosocial problems more often than their taller friends—although whether they are at risk for more serious psychopathology remains unclear (P. Cohen, Rogol, et al., 2008).

Consider shortness in relation to the common criteria of "abnormality" discussed in this chapter. A case for shortness as abnormal, even pathological, can be made using four of the criteria: statistical deviance, violation of social norms and values, internal dysfunction, and emotional suffering:

- Shortness is *statistically deviant*. Only a small percentage of men are under the 5′ 3″ height targeted by the FDA.
- Shortness *violates social norms* requiring men to be imposing and strong. This perhaps explains why short men earn less money, date less often, and have a lot less luck getting elected to higher office (in U.S. presidential elections, for example, the shorter candidate usually loses).
- Shortness is due to an *internal dysfunction*. Due to hormonal dysfunctions, what some medical specialists call a "growth failure" occurs.
- Shortness is associated with *emotional suffering*. As mentioned above, short men drink more, date less, get sick, and feel depressed more often than tall men.
  Of course, the criteria used to discern shortness as "abnormal" can also be challenged.
- *Statistical deviance* is not always viewed negatively. LeBron James' extreme height is statistically deviant but is generally credited as helping make him a spectacular basketball player. Singer Bruno Mars is quite short but is often considered a sex symbol.
- *Social norms and values* change. Sometimes they are foolish or shallow. In the past, social norms led people to see many things as pathological that today we do not. For instance, enslaved people in the United States who ran away from their masters were once diagnosed as suffering from a disorder called *drapetomania* (Cartwright, 1851).

- The idea of shortness as *internal dysfunction* can be challenged, especially given the FDA's recommendation that short boys with no discernible growth hormone deficiency be medicated to cure their shortness. If there is no discernible hormone deficiency, what is the internal dysfunction? Maybe it's not that short people necessarily have an internal dysfunction, but rather that in Western cultures "short stature itself is often regarded as an inherently undesirable state" (M. Morrison, 2015, p. 310).

Almost everyone has something about their looks they don't like. How much emotional suffering must one experience about being short before it becomes a problem? Regardless of your opinion, the example of shortness highlights something fascinating, namely that almost anything can be talked about in a way that makes it seem functional or dysfunctional. Criteria for "abnormality" can help us in thinking about what we consider normal or pathological, but these criteria can never resolve the issue once and for all.

Author disclaimer: I'm 5' 3" tall. Check out this online list of short statured men (all better known than I am) who may or may not have suffered from idiopathic shortness: http://shortguycentral.com/gallery.php. For more general information and support for short people, see http://www.supportfortheshort.org.

Critical Thinking Questions

1. Using the criteria for "abnormality" discussed in this chapter, do you believe that idiopathic short stature is a disorder? Why or why not?
2. Choose another physical difference between people besides shortness and apply the criteria for "abnormality" to it. Using the criteria as a guide, do you see this difference as a disorder or as normal human variation? Explain.

Statistical deviation is pertinent to prevalence and incidence estimates that tell us about the frequency of mental disorders. **Prevalence** refers to the percentage of people in the population currently believed to have a specific disorder, while **incidence** is the number of new cases reported over a specified period (N. Pearce, 2012). Prevalence and incidence rates make clear that mental disorders are statistically deviant. For example, the lifetime prevalence rate of schizophrenia has been reported to be between 0.3 and 0.7 percent of people (American Psychiatric Association, 2022; N. Pearce, 2012). Its annual incidence rate has been estimated to be anywhere between 14 and 42 out of every 100,000 people (Esan et al., 2012; J. J. McGrath, 2005). This means that a little less than 1 percent of the world's population is thought to have schizophrenia and that 14 to 42 people out of 100,000 are expected to develop it in any given year. While statistical deviance alone does not guarantee something will be identified as "abnormal," the things that mental health professionals consider disordered are statistically atypical.

Prevalence: Percentage of people in the population believed to currently suffer from a specific mental disorder.

Incidence: The number of new cases of a mental disorder that are diagnosed within a specified period.

Violation of Social Norms and Values

Sara and Brian

Sara and Brian seek marriage counseling because their marriage is on the rocks. Brian was raised in a family where feelings were rarely discussed. Conflict was considered unpleasant, and people's differences were usually ignored or minimized to maintain congenial relationships. Sara, by comparison, grew up in a home where people freely expressed emotions; even negative feelings were readily communicated, often with a great deal of yelling and screaming. As each blames the other for their marital problems, it quickly becomes clear to their marriage counselor that Sara and Brian's different family norms and values lead them to see each other as abnormal.

"Something's definitely wrong with him," Sara says of Brian. "He doesn't seem to have feelings. That's not normal unless he's a robot!"

"It's not me, Doc," Brian retorts. "Sara's just out of control, always yelling or crying or getting upset. Last week she got so mad that she threw a stapler across the room at me. It's like she's a crazy person!"

Sara and Brian's assessments of one another demonstrate how *violation of social norms and values* play into judgments of abnormality. Different people have different ideas about how others should behave, what is socially appropriate, and what is morally acceptable. Even though violation of social norms seems readily applicable to socially deviant behavior, we often infer internal pathology in those who consistently violate values we hold dear. Perhaps this is because across families and cultures, varied social norms and values influence what people deem out of the ordinary. Not surprisingly, this means that what mental health professionals consider pathological is often controversial—and can change over time.

Sexuality is one of the most obvious areas where we see this. Medical experts once considered masturbation and other forms of non-procreative sex clear indicators or causes of psychopathology (Bullough, 2002). The eighteenth-century Swiss physician S. A. D. Tissot (1728–1797) labeled those who masturbate as having a mental disorder called *onanism*, which he defined as "all non-procreative sex" (Bullough, 2002). He described the dangers of those suffering from it:

Onanism … led to (1) cloudiness of ideas and sometimes even madness; (2) decay of bodily powers, resulting in coughs, fevers, and consumption; (3) acute pains in the head, rheumatic pains, and an aching numbness; (4) pimples on the face, suppurating blisters on the nose, breast, and thighs, and painful itchings; (5) eventual weakening of the power of generation as indicated by impotence, premature ejaculation, gonorrhea, priapism, and tumors in the bladder; and (6) disordering of the intestines, resulting in constipation, hemorrhoids, and so forth. (Bullough, 2002, p. 29)

While Tissot's eighteenth-century ideas about masturbation strike most people today as outdated, social norms continue to change, often rapidly. Until 1973, the DSM considered homosexuality to be a mental disorder (Drescher, 2012; A. V. Horwitz, 2021). However, as homosexuality became more socially accepted, people began to question its deviant status and eventually the American Psychiatric Association stopped classifying it as a disorder (Drescher, 2012; A. V. Horwitz, 2021). Importantly, even when social norms change, it doesn't mean that everyone agrees. Though the American Psychiatric Association (1998, 2000b) and American Psychological Association (2012) reject homosexuality as a mental disorder and cite extensive research that therapies to convert homosexuals into heterosexuals are ineffective and damaging, a small number of rogue mental health professionals stubbornly (and controversially) insist that homosexuality is pathological and can be successfully treated (Higbee et al., 2022; Morrow & Beckstead, 2004). Social norms and values are one way to determine what is "abnormal," but conflict always remains because people and cultures differ in what they see as acceptable and appropriate.

An important question to ask is whether at least some social norms and values are universal. Do certain values cut across all people and cultures—such as taboos against murder and incest? Some people maintain that while many social values are relative to time, place, and culture, at least some norms are universal. Does this mean that certain forms of psychopathology and mental distress are problematic regardless of when and where they occur? Are social values and norms about them always culturally relative or at least sometimes universal?

Behavior that Disturbs Others

Behavior that disturbs others is often judged abnormal. For example, people riding in elevators usually face toward the doors. Next time you get on an elevator, see what happens when you face away from the doors and toward those riding with you. Your fellow passengers may consider your actions strange, and a significant number of them may feel uncomfortable. Behavior that disturbs others often violates social norms and values, too. Creating a scene in a restaurant, loitering on a street corner while talking to oneself, dressing in atypical fashion, and expressing emotions generally considered inappropriate to a situation (e.g., laughing during a funeral) violate social norms and, consequently, tend to disturb others.

Our responses to people differ depending on how we interpret why they engage in disturbing or disruptive behavior. When we conclude that such behavior is a product of mental disorder, we often excuse it. In this line of thought, mentally disordered people are suffering from internal psychopathology and cannot be accountable for their disturbing behavior. A contrary line of thinking holds that those engaging in disturbing behavior freely choose it, thus they are responsible for the consequences of their conduct. The "illness versus responsibility" debate occurs prominently in the legal arena because the legal system generally presumes that people are responsible for behaving in ways consistent with social norms and laws, whereas the mental health system contradicts this by arguing that sometimes disturbing or illegal behavior is a byproduct of mental illness. More on this when we discuss competency to stand trial and the insanity defense in Chapter 16.

Another difficult question arises: When someone else's behavior disturbs us, does this tell us more about us or them? For instance, protesters who engage in civil disobedience may disturb us by disrupting our routines and forcing us to examine issues we would rather ignore. However, this does not make them mentally disordered.

Harmfulness to Self or Others

Sue repeatedly cuts her arms with a razor blade. Jorge gambles away his life savings. Miwa overdoses on painkillers. Gerald abuses his wife. These are examples of behavior that appears maladaptive or causes *harmfulness to self or others*. Harmful behavior is often implicitly assumed to indicate psychopathology. So, we might diagnose Sue as suffering from borderline personality disorder (see Chapter 12), Jorge as having gambling disorder (see Chapter 11), Miwa as experiencing major depressive disorder (see Chapter 5), and Gerald as having intermittent explosive disorder (see Chapter 13). Of course, there are also many cases in which harmful behavior might not be attributed to mental disorder. For example, Bill smokes cigarettes, Goran never puts on sunscreen, Isabella skydives, Cai drives fast on the freeway, and Gina likes to rock climb without safety gear. In these cases, there is clearly potential harm to self or others. However, are these people suffering from psychopathology?

Harmfulness to self or others as an indicator of pathology seems most clear in situations where there is agreement that the potential harm in a behavior outweighs any possible benefits. In psychology, this often applies to circumstances where people are an imminent threat to themselves or others—such as in attempted suicide, assault and battery, or attempted murder. Consistent with this, most mental disorders explicitly include criteria indicating that impaired social, occupational, or other functioning is required before a disorder can be diagnosed (American Psychiatric Association, 2022). That is, people's symptoms must harm or interfere with their lives. Harm to self or others is important in judgments about pathology and distress, even though people often disagree about what constitutes harm or how much is necessary.

Emotional Suffering

Excessive *emotional suffering* and unhappiness are often judged abnormal. Consistently appearing depressed, anxious, angry, or ambivalent is both socially deviant and often thought to imply internal pathology. As with other criteria, however, agreeing on how much emotional suffering is pathological can prove challenging. Most of us would concur that a suicidally depressed person is suffering, but what about less extreme instances? For example, is feeling emotionally down for an extended period psychopathological if it does not significantly affect work or relationships? Further, do the reasons why someone is suffering matter?

Neil and Sharon

Consider Neil, a successful businessman and husband who suddenly and inexplicably becomes extremely depressed. There appear to be no specific environmental triggers for Neil's sadness and only after he is briefly hospitalized and medicated does he begin to feel better. Neil is suffering, but for no apparent reason—which leads him and his doctors to view his suffering as due to an internal dysfunction rather than life circumstances.

Compare Neil with Sharon, a middle-aged woman who feels extremely depressed, anxious, and angry after her 19-year-old son is killed while serving in the military. Sharon clearly is experiencing emotional suffering, but does having a good reason for it make it an understandable reaction to terrible life circumstances rather than a sign of mental disorder? Or is any extreme emotional suffering, even in response to difficult life events, a form of psychopathology?

It is easy to see emotional suffering as a form of mental distress but less clear when it rises to the level of psychopathology. This begs two important questions. First, how do we decide what constitutes a good reason for suffering? Second, how much suffering is appropriate? Can we be confident in a case like Neil's that there is no reason for his suffering, as opposed to simply not being able to find the reason? When and how does suffering indicate psychopathology?

Misperception of Reality

When Burt tells us that the CIA is monitoring his actions via microchips secretly embedded in his brain, we are likely to feel he has lost touch with reality and therefore suffers from psychopathology of some kind. *Misperception of reality* is often attributed to faulty perceptions and interpretations. Those who misperceive reality are usually considered to be irrational or suffering from some sort of perceptual defect (Dryden & Ellis, 2001). The ability to accurately perceive reality is commonly considered a critical component of psychological well-being. Conceptually, as with some of the other criteria we have been reviewing, misperception of reality is most useful in extreme cases. After all, few would question that Burt's perceptions do not match what is going on around him. But what about other situations in which people's perceptions of reality conflict? Assessing reality misperception helps us make judgments about psychopathology and distress—especially in cases where someone's perceptions diverge extensively from most everyone else's. However, there is often disagreement about such determinations and who has the authority to make them.

> **Sara and Brian**
> *In the marriage counseling of Sara and Brian, Sara insists that her mother-in-law is "out to get her" by putting her down and manipulating Brian to spend more time with her than Sara. Brian sees no evidence of this, arguing that his mother only wants what is best for him and Sara. Whose perceptions of reality are correct? If we could determine this, would it matter? Is the person whose perceptions are less correct more psychologically disturbed? Finally, who is the ultimate authority on reality? Is it Sara, Brian, Brian's mother, their therapist, or someone else altogether?*

Biological perspectives: Attribute mental distress to illnesses that afflict people.

Psychological perspectives: Attribute mental distress to psychological conflicts involving problematic thoughts, feelings, and behaviors.

Sociocultural perspectives: Attribute mental distress to social causes (e.g., socioeconomic conditions, cultural influences, and social oppression).

1.4 Three Contrasting Perspectives

The contrasting perspectives on psychopathology and mental distress reviewed in this book are divided into three types. **Biological perspectives** emphasize malfunctioning physiology and focus on mental illnesses as medical conditions that afflict people. **Psychological perspectives**, by contrast, conceptualize psychopathology in psychological terms as involving problematic thoughts, feelings, and behaviors. Finally, **sociocultural perspectives** attribute mental distress to social causes, with factors like socioeconomic conditions, cultural influences, and social oppression as the root causes of people's emotional upset. Your task is to master these perspectives and figure out what you agree or disagree with about each as you develop your own personal perspective.

HISTORICAL PERSPECTIVES

1.5 From Stone Age to Greek and Roman Perspectives

Stone Age Perspectives

Disagreement about mental distress and what to do about it is not new. Humans have tried to understand "madness" since the beginning of recorded history (R. Porter, 2002). The first evidence of people trying to manage it goes back to the Stone Age. Prehistoric skulls from around the world show evidence of **trepanation** (also called *trephination*), a process by which holes were drilled in them (Sturges, 2013). Historians often view trepanation as evidence of the **demonological perspective** (also called the *supernatural perspective*), which attributes psychopathology to possession by evil spirits (Vadermeersch, 1994). From a demonological perspective, drilling a hole in the skull allowed possessing spirits to escape (R. Porter, 2002). At the same time, trepanation has also been viewed as an early biological approach (Millon, 2004; Sturges, 2013). After all, drilling a hole in the skull constitutes a biological intervention. Trepanning was used for many centuries. There is evidence of it during the Greek and Roman periods, the Middle Ages, and the Renaissance (Dreher, 2013; Missori et al., 2015; J. Weber & Czarnetzki, 2001).

Trepanation: Prehistoric treatment of abnormal behavior in which holes were drilled in the skull to free evil spirits; also called *trephination*.

Demonological perspective: Views abnormal behavior as due to possession by evil spirits; also called the *supernatural perspective*.

Greek and Roman Perspectives
Hippocrates' (Mostly) Biological Perspective

The Greek physician Hippocrates (460–367 BCE) is considered the founder of a scientific approach to medicine and neurology (Breitenfeld et al., 2014). Many of his views about mental distress therefore reflect an early biological perspective (J. R. Matthews & Matthews, 2013; Millon, 2004). Hippocrates believed that the world was made of four substances: earth, air, fire, and water. These elements were characterized by heat, cold, moisture, and dryness, which through a variety of factors (including the weather, heredity, and diet) combined inside each person to form four **bodily humors**: *black bile* (combining cold and dryness), *yellow bile* (combining hot and dryness), *phlegm* (combining cold and moisture), and *blood* (combining heat and moisture) (J. R. Matthews & Matthews, 2013). Hippocrates maintained that psychopathology resulted when these bodily humors were out of balance. His effort to categorize types of madness based on bodily humor imbalances anticipates later attempts at diagnostic classification (Millon, 2004). In keeping with his rejection of supernatural explanations in favor of biological humors, many of Hippocrates' recommended treatments were medicinal. Peppermint leaves were used to relieve depression, the herb St. John's wort was used to ward off evil spirits, and peony was worn around the neck to prevent epilepsy (J. R. Matthews & Matthews, 2013).

Hysteria and the Wandering Womb

Hippocrates' view of **hysteria**—a malady involving numerous psychological and physical symptoms that the Greeks diagnosed exclusively in women—also reflects a biological viewpoint in that he attributed it to a woman's uterus detaching from its natural location and wandering around her body (Ng, 1999; Palis et al., 1985; C. Tasca et al., 2012). This explanation—the **wandering womb theory**—seems silly today, but it represents an early effort to understand psychological distress in biological (rather than supernatural) terms. Many sociocultural theorists see hysteria as a sexist term. They argue that women from Hippocrates' days onward have often been unfairly diagnosed as hysterical (C. Tasca et al., 2012; Ussher, 2013).

Socrates, Plato, and Aristotle

Whereas Hippocrates saw psychopathology as stemming primarily from brain processes, the philosopher Socrates (470–399 BCE) and his student Plato (429–347 BCE) focused less on the brain and more on the soul. Their perspectives incorporate supernatural and biological elements, as well as psychological ones. Socrates believed that when human passions run amok, emotional distress results. His famous plea, "Know thyself," makes it clear that introspective self-knowledge is the key to overcoming our passions (Millon, 2004). Plato offered a similarly psychological perspective, arguing that psychopathology originates when there is a problem in the part of the soul that controls reason (J. R. Matthews & Matthews, 2013). Interestingly, he distinguished madness instilled by the Gods (which is desirable because it endows us with special abilities, such as being able to predict the future) from madness caused by disease (which isn't desirable and requires treatment) (J. R. Matthews & Matthews, 2013).

Plato's student Aristotle (384–322 BCE) adopted a more naturalistic perspective like Hippocrates, but he saw the heart rather than the brain as the central organ responsible for mental functioning. Aristotle influenced modern cognitive-behavioral therapy (CBT) (defined in Chapter 2 and revisited throughout the book). His emphasis on using reason and logic to overcome emotional difficulties has a cognitive flavor (J. R. Matthews & Matthews, 2013), while his view of learning as the association of ideas anticipated classical conditioning (described in Chapter 2), in which learning results from repeatedly pairing stimuli so that they become associated with one another.

1.6 Perspectives during the Middle Ages

Avicenna's Biological Perspective and Early Hospitals
Avicenna

The Middle Ages roughly cover the period from the fall of the Western Roman Empire in 476 CE to Columbus' arrival in North America in 1492 (Papiasvili & Mayers, 2013). The Greeks' scientific perspective flourished most fully in the Islamic Middle East, where the bodily humors

Bodily humors: Four biological substances identified by the Ancient Greeks and long considered important in understanding mental distress; the four humors were *black bile, yellow bile, phlegm,* and *blood.*

Hysteria: A malady involving numerous psychological and physical symptoms that the ancient Greeks diagnosed exclusively in women.

Wandering womb theory: The ancient Greek physician Hippocrates' biological theory that attributed hysteria to a woman's uterus detaching from its natural location and wandering around her body.

theory maintained influence (Millon, 2004; Papiasvili & Mayers, 2013; R. Porter, 2002). The Islamic philosopher and physician Avicenna (980–1037 CE) described mania, melancholia, insomnia, and hallucinations (Papiasvili & Mayers, 2013). He adopted Hippocrates' biological perspective, hypothesizing that the middle part of the brain is responsible for intellectual dysfunction and the frontal areas control reason and common sense (Millon, 2004). Avicenna also noted a relationship between emotional states and health (Millon, 2004).

Early Hospitals

Hospitals were established in Baghdad, Cairo, Damascus, and Aleppo between the eighth and thirteenth centuries and provided services to those considered mad (Papiasvili & Mayers, 2013). During this period, various psychological and biological treatments were developed. For instance, Cairo's Mansuri Hospital employed something that resembles today's *bibliotherapy*: Patients were encouraged to read books and discuss their emotional reactions in groups. Other techniques common in the era included hydrotherapy, music, and activities (Papiasvili & Mayers, 2013).

Demonological Perspectives in Europe

In Christian Europe during much of the Middle Ages, Hippocrates' biological perspective held less sway than in the Islamic Middle East. Theological approaches dominated, increasing the influence of demonological explanations. Christian theology saw madness as a moral struggle (Papiasvili & Mayers, 2013). Strategies for overcoming it often involved punishment for sinful behavior. Fasting, prayer, and various types of exorcism to expel the devil were employed. Many of those deemed possessed were labeled as witches. Two monks, Heinrich Kramer (1430–1505) and Jacob Sprenger (~1435–1495), authored the **Malleus Maleficarum** (also known as the *Hammer of Witches*), a book in which they systematically examined witchcraft and demonic possession (Elkins, 2016; H. Kramer et al., 1486/2021; Papiasvili & Mayers, 2013; R. Porter, 2002). This book served as an early "diagnostic manual" but from a demonological perspective.

Malleus Maleficarum: Popular book during the Middle Ages that examined witchcraft and demonic possession; reflected a demonological perspective.

The Influence of Cultural Context: Dancing Mania

Some of the syndromes identified during the Middle Ages strike us as strange today. For instance, *dancing mania* was a form of "mass madness" in which people felt an unstoppable urge to dance. For instance,

dozens of mediaeval authors recount the terrible compulsion to dance that, in 1374, swept across western Germany, the Low Countries, and northeastern France. Chronicles agree that thousands of people danced in agony for days or weeks, screaming of terrible visions and imploring priests and monks to save their souls .... On a far larger scale was the outbreak that struck the city of Strasbourg in 1518, consuming as many as 400 people. One chronicle states that it claimed, for a brief period at least, about 15 lives a day as men, women, and children danced in the punishing summer heat. (J. Waller, 2009, p. 624)

Dancing mania illustrates the idea that how people express "madness" is at least partly determined by historical context and culture (J. Waller, 2009).

1.7 Renaissance Perspectives

The Renaissance as One of Europe's Most "Psychically Disturbed" Periods

The Renaissance in Europe, which lasted roughly from the late 1400s until the early 1700s, is considered a period of intense scientific and artistic achievement. However, the changes it brought resulted in substantial social upheaval. Consequently, some historians have argued that the Renaissance was one of Europe's most "psychically disturbed" periods, with *melancholia* (or *melancholy*, an early and somewhat more inclusive term for what today we might call depression) the condition warranting the most attention (Dreher, 2013). Long-established and new explanations of mental distress flourished, including those that attributed it to "the influence of the moon, the stars, weather, earwigs in the head, and an imbalanced life involving excessive or insufficient drink, diet, sleep, exercise, passions, and humors, along with witchcraft and the devil himself" (Dreher, 2013, p. 36). Treatments were as varied as the explanations: whipping, chaining, bloodletting, laxatives, exorcisms, herbal medicines, diets of various sorts, and even near-drowning were all employed as remedies for madness (Dreher, 2013).

Early Asylums in Europe
Geel

The Church often took on caring for "mad" people, providing them food and shelter. One of the best-known examples of humane religious treatment occurred in Geel, Belgium, where rumors circulated of miraculous cures of madness (Aring, 1974; J. L. Goldstein & Godemont, 2003). Pilgrims from all over Europe descended on the town to receive nine days of religious treatment. At the request of the church canons, area residents housed pilgrims before and after their treatments. To this day, Geel continues to offer community support services for those diagnosed with mental disorders—although no longer under the auspices of the Church (Aring, 1974; J. L. Goldstein & Godemont, 2003).

Bedlam

Not all Renaissance treatments for madness were as pleasant as Geel. *Asylums* for housing mad persons began to appear throughout Europe. Despite being founded to treat madness, these institutions usually wound up serving more of a custodial function for vagrants, criminals, the sick, people without housing, and those who today likely would be identified as psychotic or demented (Shorter, 1997). One of the more notorious asylums was Bethlehem Hospital in London. Begun as a Church institution, Bethlehem was acquired by the city of London in 1547. During the Renaissance and into the 1700s and 1800s, it was known for its deplorable conditions. Treatments included cold baths, bloodletting, and rotating patients in chairs for hours at a time (often resulting in vomiting) (Devlin, 2014; Elkins, 2016). Many patients were kept in chains and displayed to sightseers visiting the gallery (J. C. Harris, 2003). In 1733, the artist William Hogarth famously portrayed these horrific conditions as part of his work, *A Rake's Progress* (J. Andrews, 2007a; J. C. Harris, 2003). Over time the hospital's nickname, "Bedlam," became synonymous with "a scene or state of wild uproar and confusion" (Dictionary.com, n.d.-a). Interestingly a modern version of the institution, now called Bethlehem Royal Hospital, remains an active psychiatric hospital, albeit in a different location and minus the notoriety.

1.8 Perspectives during the Eighteenth and Nineteenth Centuries

Moral Therapy
Alienists and the Development of Moral Therapy

Historical accounts of eighteenth- and nineteenth-century approaches to mental distress often focus on several interrelated themes: efforts toward more humane care, the development of biological and psychological perspectives, and the increasing reliance on asylums. In the late 1700s and early 1800s, the first psychiatrists (called *alienists* back then because they worked with people experiencing "mental alienation") began to see the asylum as critical to effective treatment (R. Porter, 2002). They generally viewed psychopathology in biological terms, but many of their interventions had a psychological flavor. These interventions often involved talking to inmates about their difficulties and providing them a structured schedule and mild discipline within the asylum. Even though they hypothesized about biological causes of psychopathology, these alienists were simultaneously contributing to the development of **moral therapy**, an early version of psychotherapy with a clear psychological bent—especially compared with more biological perspectives (Elkins, 2016; R. Porter, 2002). Moral therapy did away with physical coercion. Early alienists—most famously Philippe Pinel (1745–1826) in France—began viewing the asylum as a place where gentler treatment would allow for more effective therapy. Unchained inmates became "part of a supportive social environment" in which they were treated kindly while being asked to participate in activities

Moral therapy: An early treatment for mental distress in which providing a warm and nurturing environment was used to help people overcome madness.

(such as group discussions, chores/work, art, music, reading, and writing) that were "designed to enhance their physical, mental, and emotional well-being" (Elkins, 2016, p. 79).

The York Retreat

The traditional asylum was not the only setting where moral therapy blossomed. Independently of Pinel and the other European asylum administrators, the English Quaker William Tuke (1732–1822) developed a version of moral therapy at the *York Retreat* that grew less from a biological perspective and more from a religious one—although it intermingled both (Charland, 2007). Tuke was not a doctor, and the York Retreat was a very different kind of asylum—one that emphasized Quaker values (such as benevolence, charity, discipline, self-restraint, and temperance) more than medicine (Charland, 2007; Elkins, 2016). As Tuke himself wrote, "medicine, as yet, possesses very inadequate means to relieve the most grievous of human diseases" (Tuke, as cited in Charland, 2007, p. 66). Moral treatment spread throughout Europe and the United States. Unlike larger, more traditional institutions, asylums providing Tuke's version of moral therapy were typically small, rarely restrained patients, allowed them to wear their own clothes, and tried to foster a family-like atmosphere (J. Andrews, 2007b; "Moral Treatment in America's Lunatic Asylums," 1976). They also encouraged patient participation in activities such as arts and crafts, carpentry, domestic tasks, and farming—all consistent with the Quaker emphasis on living a healthy and meaningful life (Charland, 2007).

Critics of Moral Therapy

Historians generally view moral treatment as a benevolent movement that treated patients kindly and was a clear improvement upon previous practices (Bockoven, 1972; Charland, 2007; Elkins, 2016). However, in its day moral treatment did have its critics. Members of the Alleged Lunatics' Friends Society, a group concerned with the rights of those deemed mad, attacked moral treatment "as an imposition of society's values on the individual"; they "expressed suspicion of the tranquility so frequently admired by the Commissioners in asylums," suggesting that "patients were first crushed, 'and then discharged to live a milk sop existence in society'" (Hervey, 1986, pp. 253–254). The issue of whether involuntary hospital treatment is an act of kindness or oppression isn't unique to thinking about moral treatment. It remains something we struggle with to this day (see Chapter 16). Nineteenth-century critics notwithstanding, historians still tend to conclude that "moral treatment was a new and more humane way of working with the insane" (Elkins, 2016, p. 84).

Why Did Moral Therapy Decline?

The reasons for the decline of moral therapy in the second half of the nineteenth century have been hotly debated. Some historians argue that the movement spread too quickly. They contend that, in addition to uninspired leadership after its founders passed on (Bockoven, 1972), the moral treatment movement led to the rapid proliferation of asylums, resulting in overcrowding and staff shortages. Consequently, asylums became unable to offer the personalized attention moral treatment required. This problem was compounded in the United States, where immigration produced a more diverse population and the prejudices of those running the asylums interfered with the provision of compassionate care (Bockoven, 1972). Other historians assert that moral treatment failed because it simply wasn't effective. In this interpretation, many patients required more stringent, medically based treatments than moral treatment provided. This contradicts historians who argue that moral treatment was highly successful (Bockoven, 1972)—so successful that physicians turned against it because it showed how lay people could cure madness better than doctors could (Elkins, 2016). In this analysis, moral therapy disappeared because medical doctors reasserted their authority and instituted a more strictly medical model that restored them as the ultimate authorities on mental illness and its treatment (Elkins, 2016; Vatne & Holmes, 2006).

Larger Asylums and Their Reform

Moral treatment all but disappeared in the latter 1800s and was replaced by custodial care—warehousing patients for long periods of time without providing much in the way of treatment. As asylums became larger and more custodial in nature, the focus shifted from best treatments to a more basic question: How do we ensure inmates have adequate basic living conditions? Thus, the latter 1800s focused on reforming oppressive conditions in asylums and other institutions such as jails. The most famous asylum reformer was Massachusetts school teacher Dorothea Lynde Dix (1802–1887), who for forty years investigated, reported on, and tried to improve the settings where mad people were housed (T. J. Brown, 1998; Gollaher, 1995; Millon, 2004; Parry, 2006). In a petition she brought before the Massachusetts Legislature in 1843, Dix (1843/2006, p. 622) forcefully made her case: "I proceed, Gentlemen, briefly to call your attention to the present state of Insane Persons confined within this Commonwealth, in cages, closets, cellars, stalls, pens! Chained, naked, beaten with rods, and lashed into obedience!" Through her advocacy efforts in both the United States and Europe, over thirty mental hospitals were founded or expanded during the latter half of the nineteenth century (Parry, 2006; Viney & Bartsch, 1984). Though Dix was a heroic social advocate whose forty-year crusade to build mental hospitals to house and care for the mentally ill marked a humane historical turning point, some historians blame her for the rise of large, state-sponsored mental institutions that warehoused the mentally ill without providing sufficient treatment (Bockoven, 1972).

1.9 Perspectives in the Twentieth and Twenty-first Centuries

Early Twentieth-century Mental Hospitals

The first half of the twentieth century saw an expansion in the size of mental hospitals in the United States and Europe—partly because collectively housing patients in hospitals was viewed as most efficient and effective, but also because families and communities welcomed having hospitals relieve their burden of care (M. Knapp et al., 2011). In the United States, for instance, over 400,000 mental patients were institutionalized by 1940, mainly in large state psychiatric hospitals (Grob, 1994). Patients were often housed for long periods of time with little treatment provided. Funding was lacking, staff shortages were common, and the physical conditions of the hospitals were deteriorating (Grob, 1994).

Of the treatments employed, some don't hold up well to historical scrutiny, though they were used because they sometimes worked and few alternatives were available (Lieberman, 2015). Controversial twentieth-century treatments include malarial therapy, convulsion therapy, and psychosurgery. *Malarial therapy* was rooted in the assumption that a high fever improves symptoms of psychopathology; thus, patients were injected with the malaria virus as a treatment for their ills (Elkins, 2016; Lieberman, 2015). *Convulsion therapy* was used to treat schizophrenia; epileptic-like convulsions were induced by injecting patients with insulin *(insulin coma therapy)* or administering electric shocks to their brains *(electroconvulsive therapy [ECT])* (Endler, 1988; R. M. Kaplan, 2013; Lieberman, 2015; Shorter, 1997). Lastly, *psychosurgery* (brain surgery for mental disorders) severed connections between the prefrontal lobes and other parts of the brain; this was known as **lobotomy** (J. Johnson, 2014; Swayze, 1995). Except for ECT, these treatments are rarely (if ever) used anymore. Many of them are revisited in future chapters (e.g., when we discuss psychosis in Chapter 4).

Antipsychiatry and Desinstitutionalization

Antipsychiatry

The second half of the twentieth century saw the birth of an **antipsychiatry** movement that challenged the hegemony of biological perspectives. R. D. Laing (1927–1989) and Thomas Szasz (1920–2012) are two figures associated with this movement. Laing (1965, 1967) challenged the idea that "mental illness" is best explained in biological terms. He saw "madness" as a meaningful and important response to oppressive life circumstances and believed people should be provided an opportunity to delve into the meaning of their mental distress instead of simply being prescribed drugs to remove their symptoms.

Similarly, Szasz (1974) argued that biological perspectives conflate mind and body. He claimed that *minds*, which are non-physical, can't be biologically diseased; only *brains* can be physically sick. This explains why the notion of a brain tumor makes sense but a mind tumor doesn't. Minds can't get tumors because minds aren't physical things! Therefore, in Szasz's view, the concept of "mental illness" (illnesses of the mind) makes no sense—logic that, interestingly, also applies to the term mental distress. Despite rejecting the label "antipsychiatrist," Szasz spent his career

Lobotomy: Historical form of *psychosurgery* used mainly for schizophrenia in which the prefrontal cortex was surgically disconnected from the rest of the brain; also called a *leucotomy.*

Antipsychiatry: Movement that challenged the medical model of psychiatry, arguing that mental illnesses are better viewed as everyday problems in living.

critiquing biological psychiatry (T. Szasz, 2008). He argued that mental disorder diagnoses describe objectionable behavior (social deviance), not brain diseases (T. S. Szasz, 1963, 1974, 1987, 1970/1991, 1996). He believed that what we call mental disorders are better conceptualized as *problems in living*. Szasz maintained that psychological upset due to problems in living—such as not having sufficient housing, being in an unhappy relationship, dealing with family problems, disliking one's job, or feeling dissatisfied in life—are part of human experience, not sicknesses. By calling them disorders, Szasz believed that we increasingly and incorrectly medicalize everyday life.

Deinstitutionalization

Deinstitutionalization:
Release of patients from mental hospitals; widespread in the latter twentieth century at mental institutions across North America and Europe.

Partly due to the influence of thinkers like Szasz, who were opposed to involuntary commitment (see Chapter 16), the second half of the twentieth century saw a large-scale deinstitutionalization movement at mental hospitals throughout North America and Europe (Dumont & Dumont, 2008; Grob, 1994; Hamlin & Oakes, 2008; Krieg, 2001; Torrey, 2014). **Deinstitutionalization** involves releasing people from mental hospitals and other institutional settings. The intent was to replace large public institutions with local *community mental healthcare* that provides an integrated array of outpatient services (medication management, therapy, family support, job training, etc.), often via government-funded programs. The reasons behind deinstitutionalization are numerous and ripe for debate. Among those most often given are (a) growing criticism of mental hospitals as ineffective institutions that dehumanized and mistreated mental patients, (b) the advent of psychotropic drugs that allowed patients to be medicated and managed outside a hospital setting, and (c) economic pressures, mainly cuts in funding for mental health services that led to the closing of hospitals (usually without replacing them with the community mental health centers that had been promised).

As they have for many centuries, different perspectives continue to compete for influence. Today some clinicians strongly advocate for biological perspectives, others for psychological and/or sociocultural perspectives. Although there have been regular attempts to integrate these perspectives, history suggests a fundamental and ongoing struggle between them:

Psychiatry has always been torn between two visions of mental illness. One vision stresses the neurosciences, with their interest in brain chemistry, brain anatomy, and medication, seeing the origin of psychic disturbance in the biology of the cerebral cortex. The other vision stresses the psychosocial side of patients' lives, attributing their symptoms to social problems or past personal stresses to which people may adjust imperfectly …. Yet even though psychiatrists may share both perspectives, when it comes to treating individual patients, the perspectives really are polar opposites, in that both cannot be true at the same time. Either one's depression is due to a biologically influenced imbalance in one's neurotransmitters, perhaps activated by stress, or it stems from some psychodynamic process in one's unconscious mind …. This bifurcation was present at the very beginning of the discipline's history. (Porter, 2002, pp. 26–27)

RESEARCH PERSPECTIVES

1.10 The Scientific Method

One of the ways people try to distinguish which perspectives are best is through research. Understanding how researchers study psychopathology and mental distress is important because it provides a way to sift through all the conflicting perspectives to distinguish which are best. However, there are lots of different ways to conduct research. Just as there are many perspectives on psychopathology and mental distress, there are also competing perspectives on conducting research. Understanding different research perspectives is important if one hopes to comprehend, critique, and use research findings effectively.

Quantitative methods:
Research methods in which numerical data and statistical analyses are used to test hypotheses.

Researchers typically rely on the *scientific method*, in which they systematically collect data through various means of observation and measurement. Exactly which methods are used depends on the problem being studied and the perspective of the researcher. When using **quantitative methods**, the researcher uses mathematical statistics to test hypotheses (Stockemer, 2019). Data is systematically collected and statistically analyzed, with the goal of discovering universal laws or truths. When using **qualitative methods**, on the other hand, the researcher gathers data about subjective experience or sociocultural phenomena, usually with the goal of comprehending the specific worldviews reflected in what is being studied. Qualitative researchers tend to see their findings as constructed understandings that are true within a particular context or time-period, but not necessarily universal (N. Frost, 2011). Let's briefly review quantitative and qualitative research perspectives.

1.11 Quantitative Research Perspectives

Correlational Method

Positive and Negative Correlations

Correlational research looks at the relationship between two variables to see whether changes in one are systematically tied to changes in the other (D. T. Campbell & Stanley, 1963; W. E. Martin & Bridgmon, 2012; M. L. Smith & Glass, 1987). **Variables** are aspects of the world that can change; they must have two or more values (M. L. Smith & Glass, 1987). Gender, age, level of depression, and marital status are examples of variables. A **correlation** occurs when two variables are related (D. T. Campbell & Stanley, 1963; M. L. Smith & Glass, 1987). As one fluctuates, so does the other. As a hypothetical example, we might ask whether there is a relationship between how much time people spend on Facebook and their level of emotional well-being. We could gather data from people about how many hours a day they spend on Facebook and then ask them to complete an emotional well-being inventory. There are three possible results (M. L. Smith & Glass, 1987):

- The first possibility is a *positive correlation*. In such a correlation, as one score increases, so does the other. Look at the positive correlation in Figure 1.1. Note that as the number of hours on Facebook increases so does emotional well-being. If this were the data our correlational study yielded, we'd conclude that Facebook time is positively correlated with emotional well-being.
- The second possibility is a *negative correlation*. In this kind of correlation, as one score increases, the other decreases. In Figure 1.2, as the number of hours on Facebook increases, emotional well-being scores decrease. In this example, emotional well-being and time on Facebook are negatively correlated.
- The third possibility is *no correlation*. That is, we might find that the amount of daily time spent on Facebook is unrelated to emotional well-being scores. As you can see in Figure 1.3, there is no pattern to the scores. They show no signs of being related to one another and are therefore uncorrelated.

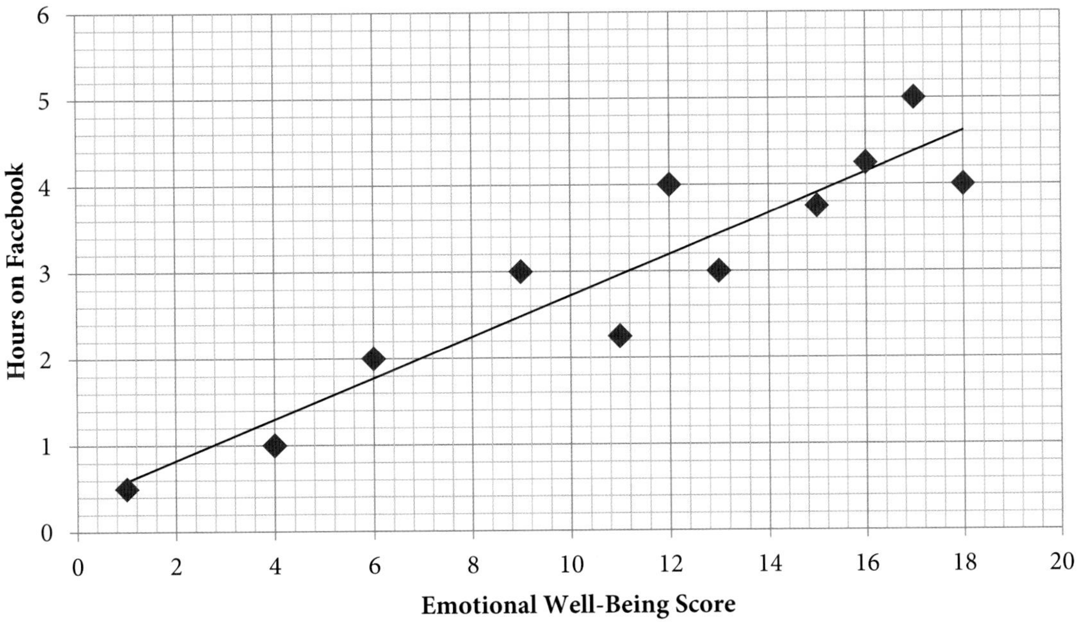

Qualitative methods: Research methods in which accounts of subjective experiences or sociocultural phenomena are collected, with the goal of comprehending worldviews about what is being studied.

Correlational research: Looks at the relationship between two variables to see whether changes in one are systematically tied to changes in the other.

Variables: Aspects of the world that can change; measured in correlational and experimental research studies.

Correlation: When two variables are related; changes in one systematically are associated with changes in the other; correlations can be *positive* (as one variable increases, so does the other) or *negative* (as one variable increases, the other decreases).

Figure 1.1 Positive Correlation. Positive correlations are indicated by a scatterplot of scores through which a line going upward to the right can be drawn. The stronger the correlation, the steeper the line.

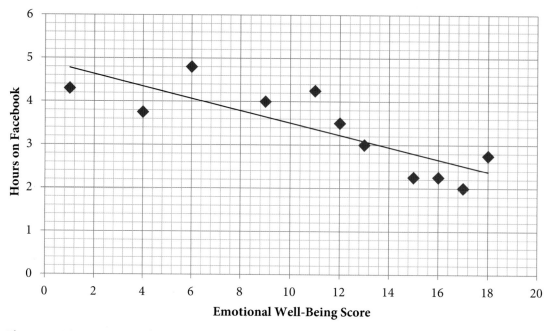

Figure 1.2 Negative Correlation. Negative correlations are indicated by a scatterplot of scores through which a line going downward to the right can be drawn. The stronger the correlation, the steeper the line.

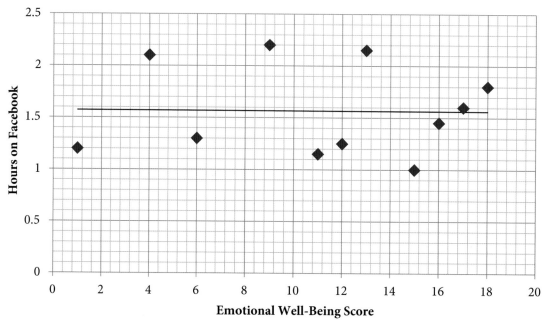

Figure 1.3 No Correlation. No correlation is indicated by a scatterplot of scores through which a horizontal line can be drawn. This shows there is no relationship between the variables.

Some variables are more strongly correlated than others. The strength of a correlation is expressed using a *correlation coefficient*, a statistically calculated number between −1.0 and +1.0 (M. L. Smith & Glass, 1987). Positive correlations are closer to +1.0, while negative correlations are closer to −1.0. When two variables are uncorrelated, the correlation coefficient hovers around 0. Correlation coefficients are symbolized by the letter *r*. So, from now on when you overhear instructors casually discussing *r*-values, you'll know they are talking about a correlation.

We made up the Facebook and emotional well-being data discussed earlier just to illustrate positive and negative correlations. But for the record, frequent Facebook use has been negatively correlated with self-esteem (Vogel et al., 2014). However, don't make the classic mistake and infer that Facebook use causes low self-esteem! Correlations only tell us there is a relationship between two variables. They don't tell us if one variable causes the other (D. T. Campbell & Stanley, 1963). Sure, low self-esteem might cause Facebook use. Of course, using Facebook might also cause low self-esteem. However, there's a third possibility, namely that neither of these things causes the other. A third variable could potentially explain any relationship between them. The same researchers who found the negative correlation between self-esteem and Facebook usage did a follow-up experiment showing that it is the kind of profiles looked at on Facebook that makes a difference; self-esteem only suffers if you are looking at profiles of people who you negatively compare yourself to (Vogel et al., 2014). The takeaway message: Correlational data merely tells us there is a relationship between two variables, not why such a relationship exists. If we want to infer cause, we need to do an experiment (discussed shortly).

Epidemiological Research

Correlational data is used in **epidemiological research**, which studies the prevalence and incidence of various disorders in a population (N. Pearce, 2012). As we discussed earlier, prevalence rates report the percentage of people in the population currently believed to have a given disorder, while incidence rates refer to the number of new cases reported over a specified period (N. Pearce, 2012). For example, one study examined prevalence rates for alcohol use disorder among Americans up to age 30. It found that 27.6 percent of women and 42.9 percent of men qualified for an alcohol use disorder diagnosis (Seeley et al., 2019). Note that these prevalence data are correlational; they report relationships between being a U.S. male or female under 30 and meeting the criteria for alcohol use disorder. However, no causal relationship can be inferred.

This same study also looked at the incidence rates (the number of new cases) of alcohol use disorder up until age 30. It found these rates increased the most between ages 18 and 25—with a 16.3 percent incidence rate for women and a 29.4 percent rate for men. By comparison, incidence rates were much lower between ages 14 and 18 (6.4 percent for women and 8.1 percent for men) and ages 25 and 30 (3.2 percent for women and 4.9 percent for men) (Seeley et al., 2019). This tells us that alcohol use issues most often appear between ages 18 and 25. Once again, these results are correlational in nature. We don't know what causes alcohol use disorder to first occur most frequently in 18- to 25-year-olds. Incidence data only tells us there is a relationship between being in this age cohort and developing an alcohol problem—a relationship future experimental research can explore.

Epidemiological research can be quite useful in understanding and responding to changing patterns of mental distress in the population. For instance, incidence rates for depression and anxiety have sharply increased in a variety of countries during the COVID-19 pandemic; that is, the number of new cases spiked after the pandemic hit (Mencacci & Salvi, 2021). Knowing this provides a basis for responding, perhaps by allocating additional resources to mental health and other relevant policies and services.

Experimental Method
Hypotheses and Variables

The goal of **experiments** is to uncover causal relationships among variables (D. T. Campbell & Stanley, 1963; J. J. Kennedy & Bush, 1985; W. E. Martin & Bridgman, 2012; M. L. Smith & Glass, 1987). By carefully manipulating one variable, we can see its effect on another. For instance, let's imagine we are interested in knowing whether psychodynamic or cognitive-behavioral therapy (CBT) is more effective in alleviating depression (these therapies are described in greater detail in Chapter 2). We might design an experiment to find out. Type of therapy (psychodynamic or CBT) and level of depression are our variables. Once we settle on these variables, we need to develop a **hypothesis**, a prediction we make about how the variables will affect one another (J. J. Kennedy & Bush, 1985; M. L. Smith & Glass, 1987). We might hypothesize that psychodynamic therapy and CBT will be equally effective in reducing depression compared with no therapy at all.

Epidemiological research: Form of correlational research used to study the prevalence and incidence of disorders.

Experiments: Research studies in which controlled variables are manipulated to identify causal relationships among variables.

Hypothesis: A prediction we make about how variables will affect one another.

Independent variable: Variable the researcher controls; its manipulation should cause the result in the dependent variable.

Dependent variable: Variable that depends on the manipulation of the independent variable; the observed result in an experiment.

Population: All people of a given class; for instance, all people suffering from depression.

Sample: Members of a population chosen to participate in a study.

Random sample: A sample that is chosen arbitrarily from the population; choosing participants randomly gives us the best chance that the sample will be representative of the larger population.

Random assignment: The practice of assigning an experiment's participants to different independent variable conditions at random.

Confounding variable: Any variable in an experiment that interferes with the independent variable manipulation.

Control group: A group of experimental participants who do not receive the treatment; gives us something with which to compare the treatment group.

Placebo control group: A control group that gets an activity that is comparable to the treatment, but is not the treatment.

Next, we need to design our study. This involves identifying the independent and dependent variables. The **independent variable** is the variable that we, as the researchers, control (J. J. Kennedy & Bush, 1985; M. L. Smith & Glass, 1987). In our hypothetical experiment, we control what kind of therapy participants receive (psychodynamic, CBT, or none). The **dependent variable** is the observed result (J. J. Kennedy & Bush, 1985; M. L. Smith & Glass, 1987)—in this case, how depressed our participants feel after undergoing psychodynamic or cognitive-behavioral therapy. For the dependent variable in our study, we might use participants' scores on the *Beck Depression Inventory (BDI)*, a self-administered instrument used to measure levels of depression (see Chapters 3 and 5) (Dozios & Covin, 2004). If an experiment is constructed well, the outcome on the dependent variable will *depend* on the manipulation of the independent variable. In our study, the kind of therapy participants receive (the independent variable) should determine how much less depressed they are (the dependent variable).

Participants, Populations, and Sampling

Of course, before we can conduct our experiment, we need *participants* (also called *subjects*). The more participants we have, the more confident we can be in our results. In fact, in a perfect world we'd be able to include every depressed person out there—the entire **population** of depressed people (M. L. Smith & Glass, 1987). But that's obviously not feasible, so instead we select a **sample** of people to participate in our study (M. L. Smith & Glass, 1987). Ideally, we'd choose our sample from the population of all depressed people in the world, but in real-life circumstances researchers often have populations of convenience. In our case, maybe we have access to a large mental health clinic that provides outpatient psychotherapy. All the patients who go to this clinic who qualify for a DSM diagnosis of major depressive disorder (discussed in Chapter 5) would be our population for the study. Those we select as participants would be our sample. How should we choose our sample? Randomly! As its name implies, a **random sample** is chosen arbitrarily from the population (M. L. Smith & Glass, 1987). This gives us the best chance that the group of participants selected is representative of the larger population. If we choose people non-randomly, we are more likely get a non-representative sample (based on whatever biases influence how we pick participants) and therefore our experiment's results might not reflect trends in the broader population.

Not only should we sample randomly, but we should also assign participants to different independent variable conditions randomly—a practice known as **random assignment** (J. J. Kennedy & Bush, 1985; M. L. Smith & Glass, 1987). Random assignment minimizes the chance that our respective treatment groups differ from one another in ways that could potentially influence our results. Any variable that interferes with our independent variable manipulation being responsible for results on our dependent variable is called a **confounding variable** (J. J. Kennedy & Bush, 1985; M. L. Smith & Glass, 1987). If, for example, we let our participants choose for themselves whether to receive psychodynamic therapy, CBT, or no therapy, we might wind up with skewed results; maybe people who choose CBT are different in some way from those who choose psychodynamic therapy and this factor, not the kind of therapy they receive, is what determines how much less depressed they feel after treatment. Using random sampling (to select participants) and random assignment (to decide which treatment participants receive) is critical to limiting the potential effects of confounding variables on experimental results.

Control Groups

Did you notice that in our proposed experiment, we included a group that doesn't get any therapy at all? This is a **control group**, a group of participants who do not receive the treatment. A control group gives us something with which to compare our treatment groups (M. L. Smith & Glass, 1987). Without a control group, it would be hard to know whether our treatments are effective. In our experiment, we want to compare psychodynamic therapy and CBT with each other, but we also want to know if these therapies are more helpful than no therapy. That's what a control group is for. Of course, if our control group does nothing and winds up more depressed than either of our treatment groups after the experiment, it will be difficult to tell whether it is therapy or simply engaging in a weekly activity that determined how depressed participants were. Therefore, we might implement a **placebo control group** instead of a traditional control group. A placebo control group gets an activity that is comparable to the treatment, but is not the treatment (Chiodo et al., 2000;

M. L. Smith & Glass, 1987; Vickers & de Craen, 2000). In our therapy study, we might have control group participants do something that takes the same amount of time as therapy but isn't therapy. For instance, our placebo control participants might simply play cards with a friendly adult for an hour each week. We would then compare these participants' levels of depression with those of the treatment participants who received either psychodynamic or cognitive-behavioral therapy.

Placebo control groups are commonly used in studies testing antidepressants and other psychotropic drugs (which are discussed in many chapters throughout the book). In these studies, the placebo control group is given a sugar pill (rather than no pill at all) and compared with the experimental group that is given the antidepressant. This way the researchers control for whether it is the antidepressant drug itself or simply knowing you are taking a pill that is responsible for the results. Interestingly, taking a placebo pill (or being in a placebo control group of any kind) often results in improvement on its own. This is called a **placebo effect** (Kirsch, 2010, 2014; F. G. Miller & Rosenstein, 2006; M. L. Smith & Glass, 1987). For a treatment to be considered effective, experimental research must show that its effectiveness goes above and beyond any placebo effect.

Internal and External Validity

We want our experiment to have high internal validity. **Internal validity** involves the degree to which results are caused by the manipulation of the independent variable (M. L. Smith & Glass, 1987). Random assignment and use of control groups both help to ensure internal validity. However, researchers sometimes control for other variables that they think might influence their results. In our imaginary experiment gender, socioeconomic status, and being on antidepressants are all variables we might wish to control for. In doing so, we improve the likelihood that it is the type of therapy participants receive, and not these extraneous variables, that determines our results. Researchers also like to conduct **double-blind studies** to improve internal validity. In a double-blind study, neither the participants nor the researchers testing them know which treatment group participants belong to (M. L. Smith & Glass, 1987). In drug trial studies, for example, participants typically don't know whether they are receiving the experimental drug or a placebo pill. Further, those evaluating the degree to which participant symptoms improve aren't privy to this information either. To keep our participants blind, we would not inform them about what kind of therapy they are receiving. To ensure the experiment is double-blind, we would also keep the researcher who administers the Beck Depression Inventory in the dark about which therapy group participants belong to. In doing so, we hope to neutralize any biases in how the inventory is administered so that internal validity is assured.

We also want our experiment to have high external validity. **External validity** is the extent to which we can generalize our results to everyday life (M. L. Smith & Glass, 1987). Researchers must balance the demands of internal and external validity. A study in a tightly controlled environment where the experimenter can control potentially confounding variables is high in internal validity. However, the cost may be a study that has so little resemblance to everyday life that its results may not generalize beyond the laboratory. Psychology students often have a sense of this issue when they are asked to be participants in research themselves (something most of them are asked to do given how hard it can be for psychology professors to round up participants for their experiments!). I have often heard psychology students complain that the tasks they are asked to do in psychology experiments (such as memorizing nonsense syllables or clicking a button whenever they see a dot on a screen) are so far removed from activities people do in the real world that whatever results are found couldn't possibly generalize beyond the laboratory. When students make complaints like this, they are raising issues of external validity. If the way that psychodynamic and cognitive-behavioral therapies are administered in our experiment doesn't reflect how these therapies are conducted in daily life, we might have an external validity problem. By the way, overreliance on undergraduate psychology students as experimental participants is one of the most common threats to external validity. After all, can we really generalize to the wider population based on how undergraduate students respond?

Randomized Controlled Trials

Mental and physical health researchers often conduct a certain kind of experiment called a **randomized controlled trial (RCT)**, in which participants are randomly assigned to different

Placebo effect: When a placebo control group activity induces results like those expected from a treatment group.

Internal validity: The degree to which experimental results are caused by the manipulation of the independent variable.

Double-blind studies: Experiments in which neither the participants nor the researchers testing them know which treatment group participants belong to.

External validity: The extent to which experimental results can be generalized to everyday life.

Randomized controlled trial (RCT): A kind of experiment designed to compare different therapies' effectiveness in treating specific presenting problems.

treatments, whose efficacy is then compared (Hollon, 2006; MacGill, 2018; Sibbald & Roland, 1998). RCTs are commonly used to evaluate the effectiveness of different psychotherapies in treating specific presenting problems. The experiment outlined above in which we wanted to compare psychodynamic and cognitive-behavioral therapies is an example of a randomized controlled trial. An RCT much like our hypothetical experiment compared the effectiveness of cognitive-behavioral and interpersonal therapies for depression (Lemmens et al., 2015). The researchers randomly assigned patients diagnosed with major depression to receive either CBT or interpersonal therapy. They also used a control group, but not a placebo control group (control group participants didn't receive a comparable activity; they simply remained on a waitlist for therapy). Using scores on the Beck Depression Inventory-II as the dependent measure, the study found both CBT and interpersonal therapy to be more effective than no therapy but equally effective to one another.

Because they ostensibly reveal cause and effect relationships, randomized controlled trials are considered the "gold standard" by many psychotherapy researchers (Nezu & Nezu, 2008). **Empirically supported treatments (ESTs)** are those that have been found effective for specific presenting problems in randomized controlled trials (Norcross et al., 2006). Some clinicians argue that it is ethically questionable to use any therapy that hasn't been shown effective in RCT research (T. B. Baker et al., 2008). Other researchers strongly disagree, arguing that RCTs don't always capture the nuances of therapy (T. A. Carey & Stiles, 2015), focusing too much on treatments and not enough on the relationship between therapist and client (Wampold & Imel, 2015). As we will see in upcoming chapters, therapists from cognitive-behavioral and biological perspectives have generally been more supportive of RCTs than those from psychodynamic and humanistic perspectives. This makes sense, given some of the traditional theoretical commitments adherents of these perspectives hold.

Quasi-Experiments

Sometimes researchers are unable to randomly assign participants to groups. For example, imagine we want to follow up on correlational research that suggests living in a war zone affects psychological functioning (Mugisha et al., 2015). We can't randomly assign participants to live in a war zone, insist they remain there, and keep the area in a state of sustained battle. Doing so wouldn't be practical or ethical! So, we simply need to find participants who have lived in a war zone for a long time and compare them with those who haven't. This kind of experimental design, one without random assignment, is called a **quasi-experiment** (D. T. Campbell & Stanley, 1963; M. L. Smith & Glass, 1987). The problem is that without random assignment, quasi-experiments increase the risk of confounding variables affecting the results. People unable to escape a war zone might be poorer, less educated, and more likely to belong to ethnic groups that other countries don't want as immigrants—and it's possible that our experimental results are due to these factors, not prolonged exposure to a war zone. To compensate for this, quasi-experiments often employ *matched-control groups*, in which people comparable to experimental group participants (on various confounding variables like age, sex, socioeconomic status, ethnicity, etc.) are chosen to be in the control group (M. L. Smith & Glass, 1987).

Analogue Experiments

Sometimes we can't conduct certain experiments because they are too expensive, impractical, or unethical. In such cases, experimenters often rely on analogue experiments. An **analogue experiment** is one in which researchers create laboratory scenarios similar (or *analogous*) to those they want to study and use them to draw inferences about the situation they are interested in but can't practically study (Abramowitz & Jacoby, 2014a; Cook & Rumrill, 2005). Sticking with a previous example, we can't simulate prolonged exposure to war, but we can create an analogous laboratory experience. Perhaps participants watch a documentary about surviving a war or play a realistic video game in which they are exposed to the horrors of war. We could measure participants' stress levels while they are watching the documentary or playing the video game. The advantage of analogue experiments is that they usually have good internal validity because the experimenter has tight control over the laboratory environment. However, external validity can be an issue. Remember earlier when we discussed your experiences as a research participant in studies that seemed to bear little resemblance to everyday life? Many of those studies are analogue experiments. So, the advantage of analogue studies is strong internal validity, but the weakness is the potential for poor external validity.

Empirically supported treatments (ESTs): Treatments that have been found effective for specific presenting problems in randomized controlled trials.

Quasi-experiment: Variation on an experiment in which the researchers are unable to randomly assign participants to groups; often uses *matched-control groups* in which control participants are selected who are demographically comparable to the experimental group.

Analogue experiment: Uses laboratory scenarios similar (*analogous*) to situations that cannot be practically studied; *animal studies*, which use animals as analogues for humans, are an example.

Animal studies are one of the best-known examples of analogue studies. In animal studies, the animal participants serve as analogues for human beings (Abramowitz et al., 2014). Many drug studies use animals as human analogues. These studies test the effectiveness of experimental drugs by giving them to animal subjects. For example, analogue studies on potential treatments for Alzheimer's disorder (see Chapter 14) often use mice and rats as subjects (Ilieva et al., 2021; Krivinko et al., 2020; L. Wang et al., 2020; Z.-J. Wang et al., 2020).

Animal studies aren't limited to drug development and testing. Behavioral researchers have long used animal research to study human learning processes. In a series of classic studies, psychologist Martin Seligman tested the notion that learned helplessness (see Chapter 5) is a central component of depression in research using dogs (S. F. Maier & Seligman, 1976; Overmier & Seligman, 1967; M. E. Seligman et al., 1968; M. E. Seligman & Maier, 1967). The dogs were placed in an experimental situation in which they were unable to avoid an electric shock. After a while, the dogs stopped trying to avoid the shock because they learned they couldn't. Once the dogs learned this, they gave up trying to avoid the shock—even when the situation changed, and escape was again possible. The idea that depression is partly about learning to feel helpless and ineffective has been generalized from dogs to humans and used to advance cognitive-behavioral therapy techniques in which attributions that produce helplessness can be challenged and modified.

As you can see from these examples, animal studies often provide important information about human functioning. Still, some people object to conducting research on animals, seeing it as cruel. Defenders counter that animal research is necessary and that without it we would be hard-pressed to make advances in psychology and other areas of scientific inquiry.

Photo 1.4 A protest against animal testing in 2022.
Chuko Cribb/Unsplash.

Single-Subject Experiments

A **single-subject experiment** is conducted on just one person (D. T. Campbell & Stanley, 1963; M. L. Smith & Glass, 1987). It is an experiment because it involves actively manipulating an independent variable to determine its effect on a dependent variable. However, only one subject is tested. The most common type of single-subject experiment is probably an *ABAB design* (also called a *reversal design*). We might use such a design when we are testing a new therapy for the first time and don't think the expense of an RCT is justified yet. We might also use an ABAB design when an RCT is untenable because we don't have access to a lot of participants. For example, let's imagine using an ABAB design to test the effectiveness of a new relaxation technique to treat the rare problem of *lycanthropy* (the belief that one is possessed by or has been transformed into a wolf or other animal). We would alternate between A and B options, as follows:

Single-subject experiment: Experiment conducted on just one person; most common type is the ABAB design, which alternates between presenting and removing the independent variable manipulation to see its effect on the single participant.

- *A*: Measure our single subject's symptoms over a period of two weeks to establish baseline symptom levels.
- *B*: Have our participant practice our new relaxation technique each day for two more weeks and measure symptom levels daily.
- *A*: Have our participant stop using our new relaxation technique for an additional two weeks while continuing to measure daily symptom levels.
- *B*: Reinstate the participant's use of the new relaxation technique for a final two weeks while still measuring symptoms each day.

This ABAB design would let us test whether symptoms of lycanthropy decrease when we use the new relaxation technique, increase again when the technique is stopped, and return to lower levels when the technique is reinstituted. Despite not having access to lots of participants, an ABAB design lets us infer causal relations between the independent variable (in this example whether the participant is practicing our new relaxation technique) and the dependent variable (symptoms of lycanthropy). Internal validity can be an issue in ABAB designs because we can't always know if any changes we observe are due to our intervention or due to other factors, such as time passing, the subject maturing, and the subject being tested repeatedly (D. T. Campbell & Stanley, 1963; M. L. Smith & Glass, 1987).

An ABAB design can also lack external validity because it is hard to generalize from one participant to larger populations. Our single lycanthropy client might do well with our new therapy technique, but others with the same symptoms might not. Further, sometimes we can't use an ABAB design because once we go from A to B we can't always go back. If we were testing the effectiveness of a new antibiotic drug on infections, the subject might no longer have an infection after initially receiving the drug. Therefore, we'd be unable to return to the baseline condition.

1.12 Qualitative Research Perspectives

Most psychology texts still don't include qualitative methods, so it isn't surprising that students are often unfamiliar with qualitative research perspectives. Compared with quantitative approaches, qualitative methods constitute a fundamentally different "way of knowing." Whereas quantitative methods test objective theories using statistical analyses to infer relationships among variables, qualitative methods focus more on studying people's subjective experiences, aiming to explore and understand "the meaning individuals or groups ascribe to a social or human problem" (Creswell & Creswell, 2018, p. 4). Whether one uses quantitative or qualitative methods depends on the research question being asked because some questions lend themselves better to one approach or the other.

For instance, the question "Does being exposed to television violence result in higher levels of aggression in people diagnosed with schizophrenia?" is clearly best answered using quantitative methods. Doing so, we might expose people with and without schizophrenia (discussed in Chapter 4) to a violent or non-violent program and then objectively measure their level of aggression using a standardized aggression scale. Our goal at the end of the study is to be able to make general statements about the effect of violence on aggression in those diagnosed with schizophrenia. Now consider another research question: "What is it like to experience auditory hallucinations?" This is a different kind of question entirely. Rather than looking to uncover universally true causal relationships among variables, this question asks about the subjective experience of hallucinations. As such, it lends itself to qualitative inquiry. Approaching this research question qualitatively, we might ask people with schizophrenia about their hallucinatory experiences to understand what these experiences are subjectively like for them—and in doing so we might learn about what sorts of experiences are common among those who hallucinate.

Unfortunately, one of the challenges in reviewing qualitative methods is that there are many approaches that operate from somewhat different theoretical assumptions. However, Giorgi (1997, p. 245) notes that all qualitative methods require the following steps: "(1) collection of verbal data, (2) reading of the data, (3) breaking of the data into some kind of parts, (4) organization and expression of the data from a disciplinary perspective, and (5) synthesis or summary of the data for purposes of communication to the scholarly community." There are many different qualitative methods, including case studies, grounded theory methods, phenomenological analysis, discursive methods, and narrative methods. Let's briefly review the first three of these methods.

Case Studies

Because many psychology texts don't review qualitative methods, case studies (which generate qualitative data) are usually discussed alongside quantitative methods. When presented this way, case studies are often portrayed as precursors to experimental studies. At the same time, despite yielding qualitative data, case studies—perhaps because they go back a long way and originated independently of other qualitative methods—are often overlooked in texts about qualitative research (Yin, 2014). Thus, in many ways case studies are caught betwixt and between quantitative and qualitative approaches, not quite fitting easily within either approach. This has led one prominent case study researcher to comment on "the separateness of case study research from other social science research methods" (Yin, 2014, p. 210). Despite this separateness, case studies are presented here because the qualitative (as opposed to quantitative) data they provide is often highly valuable.

In a **case study**, a specific instance of something is examined in depth, often using a theoretical perspective to organize the data gathered and to generalize to other instances (Yin, 2014). The subject of a case study can vary widely. Its focus can be on a person, a small group, an organization, a partnership, a community, a relationship, a decision, or a project (Yin, 2014). For instance, an organizational case study might scrutinize a particular psychiatric unit in depth to examine

Case study: Qualitative design that examines a specific instance of something in depth; its focus can be a person, small group, organization, partnership, community, relationship, decision, or project.

issues facing such units. As another example, a community case study might look at the specific neighborhood street where a community mental health center has recently been established to document the responses of residents. Most familiarly, an individual case study would focus on a given individual in depth—examining his or her upbringing, education, career, personal relationships, and current situation.

Various forms of data can be used in constructing a case study (Yin, 2014):

- *Documents* (using letters, e-mails, diaries, calendars, minutes of meetings, new clippings, administrative documents, etc., as sources of data)
- *Archival records* (using census data, organizational records, maps or charts of the geography of a place, etc.)
- *Interviews* (speaking directly with case study subjects or other important people in their lives)
- *Direct observation* (observing meetings, activities, classrooms, therapy sessions, etc.)
- *Participant observation* (participating in the situation being studied; for example, moving to the street where the community mental health center has been established as a way of learning first-hand what the experience is like)

Case studies have the advantage of providing a rich and thorough examination of the situation or person being studied. One of the most famous individual case studies in psychology is that of Phineas Gage, an American railroad worker who suffered a terrible injury in 1848 when an explosion sent a tamping iron through his skull, taking a large portion of his brain's frontal lobe with it (Yin, 2014). Gage survived, but reportedly underwent a noticeable personality change. Whereas before his injury he was responsible, cordial, and an excellent worker, afterwards he was irreverent, temperamental, and stubborn (J. M. Harlow, 1848). Gage was a perfect subject for a case study. Where else could someone with this kind of brain damage be studied?

The case of Phineas Gage is but one famous case study related to psychopathology. Sigmund Freud relied almost exclusively on case studies in developing psychoanalytic theory (see Chapter 2). For example, his case study of "Little Hans" served to illustrate how unresolved Oedipal feelings in children can produce phobias (again, see Chapter 2) (Rolls, 2015). Though perhaps most often associated with them, psychoanalysis isn't the only theoretical perspective to have made use of case studies. John Watson's infamous work teaching "Little Albert" to fear a white rat served as a powerful case study of classically conditioned fear (Rolls, 2015; J. B. Watson & Rayner, 1920)—so powerful, in fact, that it has been argued that the strength of its findings are often exaggerated in the behavioral literature (B. Harris, 1979). More on Little Albert in Chapters 2 and 6.

As noted, quantitative researchers often see case studies as limited because they don't reveal causal relationships. In this view, case studies best serve as a means for generating formal hypotheses that can then be tested using experimental methods. That is, although qualitative in nature (they don't usually involve statistically analyzing data), case studies have often been treated as precursors to quantitative research. However, case study researchers object to viewing case studies as less valuable than experiments, arguing that case studies are different from, but not inferior to, quantitative methods (Yin, 2014).

Grounded Theory Methods

Grounded theory methods help researchers develop conceptual theoretical models of the topics they study that are *grounded* in the data collected. This is very different from what occurs in quantitative experiments, where the researcher begins with a theory and then tests it to see if it withstands scrutiny. In contrast, grounded theory researchers build their theories from the ground up while conducting their research. Many variations on grounded theory have been developed. Some are more *positivist-postpositivist* in assuming grounded theory allows researchers to build theories that approximate objective reality, while other approaches are more *constructivist* in maintaining that grounded theories are human constructions that help us understand something from a specific perspective at a given juncture in time (Charmaz, 2014; Levitt, 2021; Morrow et al., 2012).

There are numerous steps in conducting a grounded theory research project. The process begins by developing a research question. Using a relevant example, Singh (2003, 2004) employed a grounded theory method to examine the question, "How do mothers and fathers experience parenting boys

Grounded theory methods: Qualitative methods that attempt to help researchers develop *grounded theories*— conceptual theoretical models of the topics they study; data collected via participant observation, interviewing, and reviewing documents/archives, and then qualitatively coded.

diagnosed with attention deficit hyperactivity disorder (ADHD)?" This question in part was devised using the grounded theory technique of *theoretical sensitivity* in which the researcher's knowledge and experience informs the question being asked. In this case, Singh (2004) had extensive experience with ADHD (a topic examined in Chapter 13)—including attending ADHD conferences and support groups, following how ADHD is portrayed in the scientific literature and by the media, observing clinical evaluations for ADHD, and talking to people affected by ADHD. She used this experience to formulate her research question.

Once a question is posed, a grounded theory researcher begins gathering data. This can be done several ways: through *participant observation*, conducting *interviews*, and examining *documents and archives* (N. Frost, 2011). In Singh's (2003, 2004) work, she interviewed thirty-nine mothers and twenty-two fathers of boys diagnosed with ADHD. Grounded theory often relies on *theoretical sampling*, which entails devising and revising strategies for recruiting participants as the research project goes along; the tactics used may change as the researcher learns more about the topic being studied and figures out what kinds of additional data are needed (Charmaz, 2014; N. Frost, 2011; Morrow et al., 2012). Participants in Singh's research were recruited using **purposive sampling**, in which people are asked to participate because they have characteristics that allow the research question to be examined in depth (N. Frost, 2011). Sometimes purposive sampling is supplemented with **snowball sampling**, where initial participants are asked if they know anyone else with similar experiences (N. Frost, 2011). Thus, a researcher interviewing parents of boys with ADHD might locate additional interviewees by asking participants if they know of other parents who also have boys with ADHD.

Once participants are recruited and interviewed, the data gathered is used to refine and further focus the research question. For instance, Singh (2003, 2004) initiated interviews by having participants look at magazine materials related to ADHD. Their reactions were used to begin a conversation with them. She then asked participants how they felt about using stimulant medications to treat ADHD. Singh used data from these early interviews to refine her research question. This helped her focus later interviews on emerging concepts and hypotheses. As hopefully is becoming clear, a key feature of grounded theory research is that the researcher tacks back and forth between data collection and analysis, using budding hypotheses about existing data to determine what additional information should be obtained.

In analyzing data, the grounded theory researcher uses several techniques (Charmaz, 2014; N. Frost, 2011; Levitt, 2016). *Coding* involves going through data (e.g., interview transcripts or archival documents) line-by-line, jotting down relevant phrases and codes; the goal is to distill key ideas. *Categorizing* is when the researcher examines the codes created and looks for links among them, eventually sorting them into categories that seem to best fit. Throughout the entire research process, the grounded theory researcher also utilizes *memo writing*, in which analytical reactions to the data are written down to help shape the researcher's evolving understanding of the topic. Codes, categories, and memos are examined to devise a *theoretical coding*, where latent links among them are sought and an integrated conception of the topic being studied starts to materialize. Theoretical coding and sorting are often arrived at using the method of *constant comparison*, which involves comparing instances highlighted in various codes, categories, and memos. That is, "the researcher continually moves from comparing data to other data in the early stages, data to emerging codes, codes to codes, codes to categories, and back again" (Morrow et al., 2012, p. 100).

For example, as Singh used constant comparison throughout the process of her research, she began to realize that mothers and fathers experienced their sons' ADHD quite differently. Mothers tended to endorse the ADHD diagnosis as a medical explanation that relieved them of blame for their sons' problems. Fathers, by comparison, were generally skeptical (if often quietly tolerant) of medical explanations and treatments of ADHD, identifying with many of their sons' symptomatic behaviors (I. Singh, 2003, 2004).

Phenomenological Analysis

Phenomenological methods are rooted in the phenomenological philosophical tradition, which can be traced back at least as far as the work of philosopher Edmund Husserl. The idea is to describe the essence of something by setting aside our biases and preconceptions to "study conscious experience" in its most basic form and identify "the building blocks of subjectivity" (Levitt, 2016,

Purposive sampling: Sampling technique in which participants are recruited to participate in a study because they have characteristics that allow the research question to be examined in depth; often used in grounded theory research.

Snowball sampling: Sampling technique in which additional participants are recruited by asking initial participants if they know anyone else with similar experiences; often used in grounded theory research.

Phenomenological methods: Qualitative research approaches in which the goal is to describe the essence of something by setting aside one's biases and preconceptions and studying conscious experience; requires bracketing preconceptions and allowing the world to "present" itself to us so we can interpretively describe and make sense of it.

p. 340). Conscious experience is characterized by *intentionality*, the idea that mental events always refer to or "intend" something in the world (Morrow et al., 2012). Thus, by setting aside our biases and carefully studying conscious experience, we can describe the essences of things in the world and (more interestingly for psychologists) subjective experiences. Numerous phenomenological research approaches have been developed. Here we briefly summarize Amedeo Giorgi's version as a representative example. Giorgi (1997) breaks down the phenomenological method into three steps.

The Phenomenological Reduction

The first step is the *phenomenological reduction*, which consists of two parts. First, the researcher must bracket his or her preconceptions. *Bracketing* involves laying aside one's taken-for-granted beliefs about what is being studied (Z. C. Y. Chan et al., 2013; Tufford & Newman, 2012). For instance, if we were to conduct a phenomenological study of the experience of hallucinations, bracketing would require us as the researchers to set aside any previous beliefs about the phenomenon of hallucinations (e.g., they are only experienced by "crazy" people and are meaningless byproducts of neurochemistry). While some question whether researchers can ever fully bracket their experience, the idea is to let the thing being studied (instead of our biases and preexisting mindsets about it) influence our results. The second component of the phenomenological reduction can be a bit difficult for newcomers to grasp. It entails shifting from the view that our understandings accurately mirror the world to the view that objects in the world "present" themselves to us and we interpretively make sense of them. Another way to think about this is that we shouldn't naïvely accept the commonplace belief that our experience shows us the world as it is. Thus, in our phenomenological study, the assumption that our everyday experience reflects what hallucinations really are must be bracketed and replaced with the idea that hallucinations present themselves for us to interpret and understand.

Description

The second step involves *description*, in which the researcher obtains descriptions of what is being studied from participants. As with grounded theory, we likely use purposive sampling in which we seek and select individuals who are experiencing hallucinations to be our participants. In our study, we solicit vivid and detailed descriptions from these participants of what the experience of hallucinations is like. Bracketing our biases, we record these descriptions and attempt to understand the participants' experiences as best we can.

The Search for Essences

The third step involves the *search for essences*. The researcher breaks participants' descriptions down into meaningful units, looking for commonalities across participants. The results constitute the essence of the experience of hallucinating. Phenomenological analysis is a challenging method to learn because it requires a lot of the researcher. However, its emphasis on understanding lived experience makes it an interesting approach for understanding what it is like to experience psychological distress.

Trustworthiness, Mixed Methods, and the Status of Qualitative Methods

Postpositivist qualitative researchers, who use qualitative methods to generate accounts approximating external reality as accurately as possible, tend to view validity similarly to how quantitative experimental researchers view it (Morrow, 2005). They judge their research based on how well it controls for biases and answers the question "Do results accurately reflect the world as it is?" More constructivist qualitative researchers, by comparison, argue that because subjective bias can't be eliminated, it is important for researchers to acknowledge it by highlighting (rather than obscuring) their role in the research process (Charmaz, 2014). These qualitative researchers shift how they judge the validity of their studies. They examine the **trustworthiness** of qualitative research—evaluating it by looking at its social validity, whether it acknowledges its biases, and whether it provides adequate data (evaluated using criteria such as number of participants, variety of data sources, richness of analysis, and adequate searching for disconfirming evidence) (Morrow, 2005).

Although tensions between qualitative and quantitative research perspectives remain unresolved, many researchers are increasingly emphasizing **mixed methods**, in which quantitative

Trustworthiness:
Characteristic of good qualitative research; evaluated by looking at the study's social validity, whether it acknowledges its biases, and whether it provides adequate data.

Mixed methods:
Combine qualitative and quantitative methods to study a specific issue.

and qualitative work is combined in studying a specific issue (Creswell & Creswell, 2018; Fetters et al., 2013; Heyvaert et al., 2013). For better or worse (depending on your viewpoint), qualitative methods have not gained parity with quantitative methods and philosophical differences between these approaches remain (M. R. Jackson, 2015). Nonetheless, both quantitative and qualitative research can inform our understanding of mental distress.

An adequate grasp of different research methods is critical in this course. Just because research is cited throughout the book doesn't mean you should unquestioningly accept what is reported. Being a good consumer of research requires continually improving your ability to read and evaluate research studies so that you can determine for yourself whether the findings are convincing. This is one of the ongoing challenges any good student faces in learning about mental distress and the many perspectives that define, explain, and treat it. Sometimes the more we learn, the less we know for sure—something explored further in the "In Depth" feature.

In Depth: Ignorance and Psychology

A 2015 *New York Times* opinion piece by Jamie Holmes advocates acknowledging that we often know less than we claim. In other words, ignorance is a lot more rampant than most of us wish to admit—even in academic subjects where we usually are told otherwise. Holmes describes how, in the 1980s, University of Arizona surgery professor Professor Marlys H. Witte created controversy when she began teaching a class called "Introduction to Medical and Other Ignorance." She wanted to include ignorance in her class because she believed we often ignore or minimize how little we know about many topics (J. Holmes, 2015b). In Witte's view, textbooks often contribute to the problem. For example, she pointed out that surgery textbooks usually discuss pancreatic cancer without ever mentioning that our present understanding of it is extremely limited. Her goal? Helping students appreciate that questions are as important as answers (J. Holmes, 2015b).

Some might deem it foolish of me to share Holmes' opinion piece at the very start of a textbook on psychopathology and mental distress. Yet my experience teaching this course over the years fits nicely with Holmes' thesis. I once had a student who, several weeks into the class, said she was going back to being a math major. "At least in math, there are clear right answers," she exclaimed. "In studying psychology, there are so many conflicting viewpoints that it's hard to know what the right answer is." Admittedly, despite all the attempts to combine rigorous research into an integrative perspective, all too often most psychology textbooks overstate how much we know. But acknowledging our ignorance up front potentially opens, rather than closes, possibilities. Holmes notes that we often think of ignorance as something to be eliminated, viewing it as simply lack of knowledge. Yet answers don't put an end to questions. They simply give rise to new questions (J. Holmes, 2015b)! As you read this text, here's to the many questions you will hopefully begin to ask.

Critical Thinking Questions

1. Do you think Witte's contention that ignorance is more rampant than we usually admit applies to the field of psychology?
2. Does recognizing the limits of our knowledge about psychopathology and mental distress help us? If so, how?

CLOSING THOUGHTS

1.13 Caveats before Proceeding

Having a basic grasp of conceptual, historical, and research perspectives provides the foundation for discussions throughout this text. In ensuing chapters, we continually revisit major perspectives on psychopathology and mental distress as they relate to different **presenting problems**—the issues that people present when they enter a clinical setting. As you read the chapters that follow, bear several things in mind. First, not every perspective speaks as fully to every possible problem, so depending on the presenting problem, some perspectives may receive more attention than others. Second, it is common for various perspectives to be used in conjunction with one another. For instance, diagnostic perspectives are often, though not always, combined with various other perspectives in working to address presenting problems. When this happens, efforts are made to differentiate each perspective's contribution and to make clear the ways in which the perspectives complement and contradict one another. Third, disagreement is common. The perspectives presented sometimes fit together nicely, but just as often are at odds. One goal of this chapter has been to highlight clashing and difficult to reconcile perspectives. Fourth, even though this text endeavors to give each perspective a fair and even-handed hearing, biases are inevitable. It is impossible not to privilege some perspectives over

Presenting problems: The problems that clients request help for when consulting with mental health professionals. Presenting problems may or may not ultimately be the primary focus of treatment.

others sometimes, so students are encouraged to look at what it being presented with a skeptical eye. What are the author's biases, blind spots, and theoretical preferences? How might the material have been organized and presented differently? Might conveying the information in other ways change reader reactions to it? If so, how? Reflecting on what you see as the strengths and limitations of the text as you read it is encouraged.

Finally, you should remain aware that it's very common (we might even dare say, normal!) for students reading a textbook like this one to start feeling like everything they are reading about applies to them, their families, and their friends. "Oh no! That's me!" is a common refrain as students learn about various presenting problems, which they then worry that they might have. When not seeing themselves as suffering from every syndrome reviewed throughout the text, some students start engaging in the unfortunate habit of diagnosing friends and family—who don't always appreciate the free consultation. The good news is that learning about mental distress encourages people to reflect on their own experience and, in some cases, seek help for their problems. The bad news is that students often worry they have problems that they probably don't. Regardless, appropriate self-awareness about whether you need help is never something to dismiss. You are encouraged to speak with your instructor or seek mental health services should anything you read about in the text raise concerns. After all, studying about mental distress often confronts us with issues we have encountered in our own lives. That is what makes it both challenging and interesting.

CHAPTER SUMMARY

Overview

- Basic terms include *psychopathology, mental distress, psychiatry, psychology, mental illness, mental disorder, deviance,* and *social oppression*.
- The three main contrasting perspectives covered in this text are *biological, psychological,* and *sociocultural perspectives*.
- Using *common criteria for "abnormality"* can be helpful but does not eliminate disagreement because people differ in which criteria they emphasize and why.

Historical Perspectives

- During the Stone Age, *demonological perspectives* were influential, and *trepanation* was a common "treatment."
- The ancient Greeks emphasized *bodily humors* as causes of psychopathology, and (incorrectly) saw a wandering womb as causing hysteria.
- In the Middle Ages, early hospitals were established throughout the Middle East, while in Europe the *Malleus Maleficarum* was used to determine who was a witch or demonically possessed.
- The Renaissance saw the development of early asylums such as Geel and Bedlam to care for "mad" people; Bedlam was an asylum infamous for its terrible conditions.
- The eighteenth and nineteenth centuries saw more humane treatment of people in asylums and the rise of *moral therapy*. By the latter nineteenth century, asylums grew increasingly large, impersonal, and oppressive. Dorothea Dix was among the activists who campaigned to reform such institutions.
- The size of mental hospitals grew during the first half of the twentieth century, leading the antipsychiatry movement to rail against involuntary treatment. As drug treatments were developed in the second half of the twentieth century, *deinstitutionalization* occurred.

Research Perspectives

- In scientific method, researchers systematically collect data through various means of observation and measurement.
- Quantitative methods include *correlational research, experiments, quasi-experiments, analogue experiments,* and *single-subject experiments*.
- Qualitative methods include *case studies, grounded theory methods,* and *phenomenological methods*.
- Some researchers use *mixed methods* that combine quantitative and qualitative studies.

Closing Thoughts

- Future chapters focus on different *presenting problems,* the issues people present with when entering a clinical setting.

NEW VOCABULARY

1. Abnormal psychology
2. Analogue experiment
3. Antipsychiatry
4. Biological perspectives
5. Bodily humors
6. Case study
7. Common criteria of "abnormality"
8. Confounding variable
9. Control group
10. Correlation
11. Correlational research
12. Deinstitutionalization
13. Demonological perspective
14. Dependent variable
15. Deviance
16. Double-blind studies
17. Empirically supported treatments (ESTs)
18. Epidemiological research
19. Experiments
20. External validity
21. Grounded theory methods
22. Harmful internal dysfunction
23. Harmfulness to self or others
24. Hypothesis
25. Hysteria
26. Incidence
27. Independent variable
28. Internal validity
29. Lobotomy
30. *Malleus Maleficarum*
31. Medicalization
32. Mental disorder
33. Mental distress
34. Medical model
35. Mental illness
36. Mixed methods
37. Moral therapy
38. Phenomenological methods
39. Placebo control group
40. Placebo effect
41. Population
42. Presenting problems
43. Prevalence
44. Psychological perspectives
45. Psychopathology
46. Purposive sampling
47. Qualitative methods
48. Quantitative methods
49. Quasi-experiment
50. Random assignment
51. Random sample
52. Randomized controlled trial (RCT)
53. Sample
54. Single-subject experiments
55. Snowball sampling
56. Social oppression
57. Sociocultural perspectives
58. Trepanation
59. Trustworthiness
60. Variables
61. Violation of social norms and values
62. Wandering womb theory

THEORETICAL PERSPECTIVES

2

Photo 2.1
Klaus Vedfelt/Getty Images.

LEARNING OBJECTIVES

1. Describe biological perspectives on psychopathology that emphasize brain chemistry, brain structure, genetics, evolutionary theory, and the immune system.

2. Summarize biological perspective assumptions and evaluate the strengths and weaknesses of the biological perspective.

3. Describe the following psychological perspectives: psychoanalytic/psychodynamic, cognitive-behavioral, and humanistic.

4. Summarize the assumptions of psychodynamic, behavioral, cognitive, and humanistic perspectives and evaluate their respective strengths and weaknesses.

5. Describe the following sociocultural perspectives: multicultural and social justice perspectives, consumer and service user perspectives, and systems perspectives.

6. Summarize sociocultural perspective assumptions and evaluate the strengths and weaknesses of the sociocultural perspective.

OVERVIEW

2.1 Getting Started: The Importance of Theoretical Perspectives

Case Examples

Seth and Lillian

Seth is a 21-year-old university student who seeks therapy complaining about angry outbursts that keep getting him into trouble. He has a long history of getting into fights. In his view, people purposely provoke and disrespect him, although he doesn't know why. Seth has had a string of girlfriends, all of whom he eventually loses interest in right before they break up with him. Seth's current girlfriend, Lillian, a 20-year-old student attending the same university as Seth, reports that their relationship has been deteriorating. Seth and Lillian have been arguing a lot lately because Lillian suspects Seth has a crush on Lillian's best friend, Abigail. Seth says problems in the relationship have led Lillian to recently become quite depressed; she hasn't been eating or sleeping and seems tearful much of the time. The precipitating event that led Seth to seek therapy occurred recently when he was arrested for assaulting a fellow student in the library after an argument about who was in line first to use the copy machine. Seth reports a reasonably normal childhood, although his parents always argued a lot and were quite strict with Seth and his younger brother. These days, he often argues with his father, who doesn't understand why Seth is studying art rather than accounting. His father has been threatening to stop paying for Seth's education unless Seth reconsiders his "poor choices."

Perspectives as Frameworks for Understanding People's Problems

What makes Seth and Lillian behave as they do? What is the cause of their problems and how can we best help them? The answers depend on one's theoretical approach. This chapter reviews theoretical approaches to psychopathology and mental distress, dividing them into biological, psychological, and sociocultural perspectives.

BIOLOGICAL PERSPECTIVES

2.2 Introducing Biological Perspectives

When we look at psychopathology and mental distress using biological perspectives, we view them through a medical model lens. Presenting problems are organized into categories thought to reflect underlying biological illnesses (Huda, 2021). Patients are viewed as physically sick. Recall the American Psychiatric Association's assertion from Chapter 1 that "mental illnesses are health conditions … just like heart disease or diabetes" (2018, para. 7). This reflects a biological perspective.

Researchers and clinicians look to four basic kinds of biological explanations of mental distress: brain chemistry, brain structure, genetics, evolution, and the immune system. These explanations aren't mutually exclusive. For example, genetics can influence brain structures and brain chemistry, just as germs and a compromised immune system can impact gene expression. Biological factors are interrelated in ways we are only beginning to comprehend. See Table 2.1 for a summary of biological perspective assumptions.

2.3 Brain Chemistry Perspectives

Brain chemistry perspectives emphasize how brain chemistry (and the psychiatric drugs we develop to alter it) influences cognition, emotion, and behavior. How does brain chemistry work? Well, the brain consists of billions of cells called *neurons*, which communicate with one another both electrically and chemically (see Figures 2.1–2.2). When a neuron is at rest, its inside has a negative electrical charge (usually around −70 millivolts) compared with its outside. It also has receptors at the end of its dendrites, the tree-like branches that extend from its cell body. These dendrites are responsive to **neurotransmitters**—brain chemicals involved in neural communication. A neuron "fires" when enough neurotransmitter chemicals released by other neurons bind with the receptors on its dendrites. This chemical bonding rapidly shifts the neuron's electrical charge from negative to positive. When this happens, an **action potential** occurs in which an electrical impulse is sent along the neuron's axon (see Figure 2.1). This causes the neuron to release neurotransmitters from its axon terminals into the synapses (open spaces) between it and surrounding neurons (see Figure 2.2). When these neurotransmitters bond with receptors on the dendrites of other nearby neurons, they

Brain chemistry perspectives:
Biological approaches to psychopathology that focus on neurotransmitters (chemicals in brain) and how they influence cognition, emotion, and behavior.

Neurotransmitters:
Brain chemicals involved in neural communication.

Action potential:
When an electrical impulse is sent along a neuron's axis; occurs when neurotransmitters bond with receptors on a neuron's dendrites, causing the electrical charge in the neuron to shift from negative to positive; central process in neural communication.

Table 2.1 Five Biological Assumptions

1. *Human experience can be reduced to and explained in biological terms.* Thoughts, feelings, and behaviors are ultimately best understood as mental illnesses caused by underlying biological processes.
2. *Many mental disorders are brain diseases.* Because human experience can be reduced to and explained in terms of underlying biological processes, many of the problems identified as mental disorders will eventually be revealed to be brain diseases.
3. *Scientifically studying the brain will yield an understanding of mental illness.* Our understanding of the human brain is in its infancy. As we learn more about how the brain works, we will begin to discover the biological causes of mental illness.
4. *Biological processes are central in understanding mental illness, but social and contextual factors have a secondary influence.* While life experiences and environmental circumstances may affect the course of mental illnesses, their primary cause is rooted in biological processes (e.g., from a biological perspective, posttraumatic stress disorder is triggered by events in the environment, but will only occur if the person suffering a tragedy is biologically predisposed to it).
5. *Mental disorders can be caused by malfunctions in brain chemistry, brain structures, genetics, and even viruses.* Sometimes more than one of these explanations must be used to explain a disorder; a person's genetic makeup may make one susceptible to brain chemistry, brain structure, or immunity-related causes of mental illness.

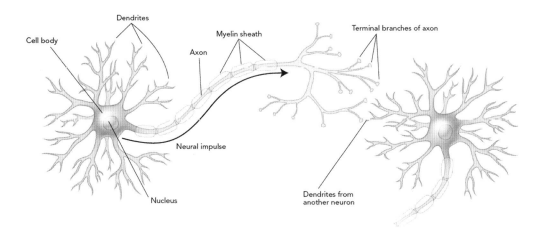

Figure 2.1 Parts of a Neuron. The brain consists of billions of neurons, cells that communicate electrically and chemically. When an electrical impulse travels along the axon to the terminal branches, neurotransmitters are released that trigger surrounding neurons to fire.

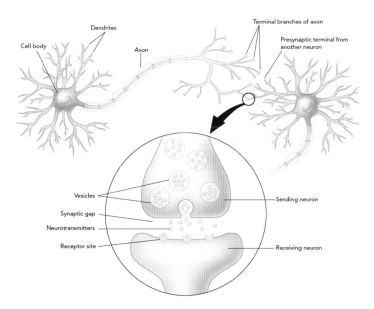

Figure 2.2 Neurotransmission across a Synapse. Upon firing, a neuron releases neurotransmitters from its terminal branches into the synapse between it and surrounding neurons. When the released neurotransmitters bind with the receptors on surrounding neurons, these neurons fire.

trigger similar electrical reactions in those neurons. Neural transmission involves neurons firing and triggering other neurons to fire in rapid succession.

There are a few important things to remember. First, action potentials are all-or-none; a neuron either fires or it doesn't. Second, some neurotransmitters send excitatory signals while others send inhibitory ones. The former stimulate the brain (causing surrounding neurons to fire) and the latter calm it (preventing surrounding neurons from firing). **Gamma-aminobutyric acid (GABA)** is the brain's primary inhibitory neurotransmitter, while **glutamate** is its main excitatory neurotransmitter (Littrell, 2015). Third, extra neurotransmitter chemicals remaining in the synapse after neurons fire are either broken down or reabsorbed by the neurons that released them. Some prescription drugs work by affecting the reabsorption process.

There are many neurotransmitters—so many that we haven't discovered them all (Sukel, 2019; Valenstein, 1998). Neurotransmitters are significant to psychopathology and mental distress because of their roles in mood and cognition. A few examples: **Norepinephrine** (an excitatory neurotransmitter) and **serotonin** (an inhibitory neurotransmitter) are associated with depression and anxiety; too much **dopamine** (an inhibitory neurotransmitter implicated in memory, motivation,

Gamma-aminobutyric acid (GABA): The brain's primary inhibitory neurotransmitter.

Glutamate: The brain's main excitatory neurotransmitter.

Norepinephrine: An excitatory neurotransmitter associated with anxiety and depression.

Serotonin: An inhibitory neurotransmitter associated with depression and anxiety.

Dopamine: An inhibitory neurotransmitter implicated in memory, motivation, and reward/pleasure; too much is associated with psychosis.

and rewards/pleasure) with psychosis; and too little GABA with fear and anxiety (Itoi & Sugimoto, 2010; Littrell, 2015; Möhler, 2013). Many prescription drugs used to alleviate depression, psychosis, and anxiety affect these neurotransmitters. However, methods for measuring neurotransmitters remain cumbersome or in development (Ceccarini et al., 2020; Kharrazian, 2011; Marc et al., 2011; Ou et al., 2019). Therefore, we almost always prescribe drugs based on people's reported moods rather than tests of neurotransmitter levels.

Certain neurotransmitters are grouped together due to their chemical similarities. GABA and glutamate are *amino acids* (chemical compounds consisting of carbon, hydrogen, nitrogen, and oxygen), whereas norepinephrine, serotonin, and dopamine are *monoamines* (chemical compounds derived from ammonia). The monoamines can be further divided into *catecholamines* (dopamine and norepinephrine) and *indoleamines* (serotonin).

Seth and Lillian

In the case of Seth and Lillian, a psychiatrist might assess them and diagnose Seth with intermittent explosive disorder (see Chapter 13) and Lillian with persistent depressive disorder (see Chapter 5). Both disorders are often treated using antidepressant drugs. The psychiatrist might prescribe selective serotonin reuptake inhibitors for each of them.

2.4 Brain Structure and Function Perspectives

Brain structure and function perspectives: Biological approaches that stress how the functioning (or malfunctioning) of different brain regions influences psychopathology.

Brain structure and function perspectives examine how the functioning (or malfunctioning) of areas in the brain influences psychopathology. For example, one brain region of interest to psychopathology researchers is the *limbic system*, which developed early in human evolution and is associated with motivation, emotional regulation, and long-term memory (MacLean, 1985; Ploog, 2003). The limbic system contains several important structures discussed in future chapters—including the *amygdala* (an almond-sized area deep in the brain linked to basic emotions such as fear and anger), the *hippocampus* (important in memory), the *orbitofrontal cortex* (involved in decision-making), and the *nucleus accumbens* (implicated in addictive behavior).

Remember that brain structure and brain chemistry explanations are deeply interrelated. Different brain regions communicate via the neural processes described earlier. So, whenever we suspect a brain structure is malfunctioning, there are also potential problems with neural communication. Given the neurally interconnected nature of the brain, psychopathology researchers increasingly emphasize *brain circuits*, networks of brain structures that work together. For example, the *hypothalamic-pituitary-adrenal (HPA) axis* is a brain circuit that links several brain structures. It has been implicated in numerous forms of mental distress discussed in future chapters, such as depression and posttraumatic stress.

2.5 Genetic Perspectives

Genetic perspectives: Focus on the role of genes in explaining the origins of presenting problems.

Genetic perspectives focus on the role of genes in psychopathology. *Genes* can be thought of as biological instructions for building a person. The complete set of genetic information for each human (its *genome*) consists of twenty-three sets of *chromosomes*, which are made out of *DNA* (*deoxyribonucleic acid*) (C. Baker, 2004). DNA consists of chemical compounds known as *nucleotides*. Nucleotide sequences are instructions for how you will mature over time. DNA nucleotides are coiled up inside each cell's nucleus in the well-known *double helix* shape. DNA's blueprint for development gets copied into *RNA (ribonucleic acid)*, which carries out DNA's genetic instructions (C. Baker, 2004). Figure 2.3 provides a visual illustration of the structure of DNA and RNA.

Genes are found at random intervals on a chromosome's DNA. The exact number we have isn't known, but estimates range from 50,000 to 100,000 (Salzberg, 2018). We have two versions of every gene (called *alleles*)—one inherited from our mother and the other from our father. Usually, one allele in a pair is dominant. Dominant alleles take priority in influencing how particular characteristics genetically unfold, while recessive alleles are carried from generation to generation but only displayed in rare instances when a person inherits two of them (one from each parent).

Thus, only some genetic information displays itself in the organism. A person's *genotype* is their entire genetic makeup. It includes all alleles, even non-dominant ones not reflected in the individual's physical and psychological makeup. In contrast, a person's *phenotype* consists of their actual properties, the physical and psychological traits a person has developed because of genetic and environmental influences.

Heritability refers to the percentage of phenotypic variation attributed to genes, as opposed to environment (C. Baker, 2004). *Heritability studies* estimate how much a given psychological trait or disorder is influenced by genetic, rather than environmental, factors. These studies yield *heritability estimates*, scores from 0.0 to 1.0. For example, research on autism (see Chapter 13) has yielded a heritability estimate of .83 (Sandin et al., 2017). To correct a common misconception, this doesn't mean that any given individual's autism is 83 percent caused by genes and 17 percent by environment. It just means that 83 percent of phenotypic variation across all people with autism is estimated to be influenced by genes. Importantly, heritability estimates are controversial (Tenesa & Haley, 2013). For instance, it has been argued that autism heritability is grossly inflated and should only be estimated as 37 percent (J. Joseph, 2012). While many researchers continue to value and refine heritability estimates (H. Zhu & Zhou, 2020), others question their accuracy (J. Joseph, 2012; Rose, 2006).

Heritability makes clear that biological processes alone don't determine gene expression. The environment also plays a role. That fern you forget to water and place in the sun looks quite different from the one your botany major friend meticulously tends to. These two plants might be genetically the same (they have the same genotype), but their different environments trigger how their genes express themselves, influencing what each looks like (its phenotype). To further complicate things, gene expression isn't just influenced by the environment. It is also *polygenic* (C. Baker, 2004; Bouchard & McGue, 1981; Lisik, 2014), meaning that multiple genes often work together to produce a trait or disorder. Only when environmental conditions and multiple gene expression align does something like schizophrenia or autism result.

Lillian

Lillian may have a genetic predisposition toward depression, but her life circumstances are what could have caused it to emerge. Had she grown up under different environmental circumstances, the multiple genes responsible for depression might simply never have been "triggered."

2.6 Evolutionary Perspectives

Evolutionary perspectives use Charles Darwin's (1872/2021) evolutionary theory to explain how and why different presenting problems evolved. Evolutionary theory maintains that whether an organism survives and reproduces (passing on its genes) depends on its *fitness*, which reflects how well it is adapted to its environment. Fish are adapted to their environment (i.e., they are fit) because their gills let them extract oxygen from the water in which they live. However, what counts as fitness depends on the environment. If the lake dries up, all the fish will die because they no longer are adapted to their surroundings. *Survival of the fittest* refers to the idea that only organisms suited to an environment reproduce and keep their species alive. Of course, different organisms are fit in different environments. As environments change, species that can adapt are the ones to survive,

DNA and RNA structure

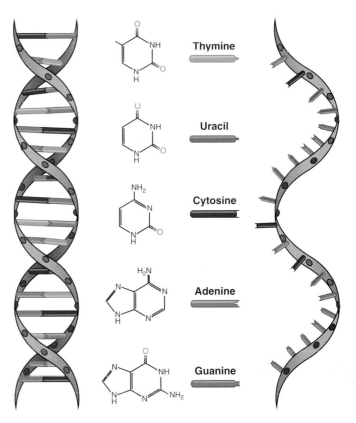

Figure 2.3 DNA and RNA Structure. Chromosomes are made of DNA, which consists of four nucleotides (chemical compounds) called adenine, cytosine, guanine, and thymine. DNA gets copied into RNA, which carries out its instructions for building a person. RNA is made of three of the four DNA nucleotides (adenine, cytosine, and guanine) plus a fourth nucleotide called uracil.

Heritability: Percentage of phenotypic variation attributed to genes, as opposed to environment; *heritability estimates* (scores from 0.0 to 1.0) estimate the degree to which a trait is genetic (e.g., .60 attributes 60 percent of phenotypic variation to genes and 40 percent to environment).

Evolutionary perspectives: Use Darwin's evolutionary theory to understand how presenting problems evolved, seeing them as both genetically inherited and adaptive in early human history.

reproduce, and pass on their genes. Those that can't adapt die off. Evolutionary changes in species are slow, occurring over many millions of years. Further, it is sometimes mistakenly assumed that evolution produces more "advanced" and "higher evolved" human beings. This isn't so. Evolution has no direction, purpose, or endpoint. How organisms evolve is only a matter of what is adaptive at a given time in each environment.

Evolutionary perspectives apply evolutionary principles to understanding psychological problems (Adriaens & De Block, 2010). They often posit that traits previously adaptive in our early ancestors' environments no longer work in modern society. For instance, few people today die from poisonous spider bites or falling from great heights but many die from car accidents. However, our evolutionary heritage makes us much more likely to develop phobias of spiders or heights than automobiles. That is, evolution has biologically prepared us to easily develop conditioned fears to certain kinds of things (like spiders and heights), even though this is no longer as threatening as other things in our environment (like Fords and Hondas). According to evolutionary perspectives, behaviors and experiences considered disordered—such as psychosis (Burns, 2006, 2009; Scheepers et al., 2018), depression (N. B. Allen & Badcock, 2006; Gałecki & Talarowska, 2017), and obsessive-compulsive rituals (Feygin et al., 2006; Schalkwyk & Leckman, 2017)—may have origins in what was adaptive in ancestral environments.

2.7 Immune System Perspectives

**Immune system
perspectives:** Emphasize
the importance of the
immune system (cells and
biological processes
to fight off pathogens)
in understanding
psychopathology.

Immune system perspectives have been rapidly gaining attention from researchers. The immune system consists of cells and biological processes used to fight off *pathogens* (foreign bodies that cause disease, such as viruses, bacteria, parasites, and cancer cells). Prolonged stress taxes the immune system and has an extremely powerful (usually negative) impact on physical health and emotional well-being (Dhabhar, 2014; R. Glaser, 2005). Understanding the complex connections among the immune system, psychological factors, and physical health holds much promise for understanding psychopathology and mental distress.

Germ theories:
Hypothesize that
psychological disorders
can be caused by viruses,
bacteria, fungi, or parasites
that attack the immune
system.

Germ theories hypothesize that psychological disorders can be caused by four types of germs that attack the immune system: viruses, bacteria, fungi, and parasites (National Library of Medicine, 2021). The most famous historical instance of a germ theory explanation of mental distress occurred with a disorder we don't see much anymore called *general paresis* (Wallis, 2012). People with general paresis show a progressive decline in mental functioning—exhibiting mania, psychotic delusions, physical deterioration, and eventually death. It turns out general paresis is caused by the syphilis bacterium (Wallis, 2012). If treated with antibiotics, the symptoms disappear. General paresis is the best example of mental distress being explained biologically. Treating general paresis with psychotherapy is pointless because its psychological symptoms are not caused by irrational beliefs or childhood conflicts. They are due to a syphilis infection. Treat the infection and the problem is cured. Discovering that a bacterium caused general paresis advanced the medical model view that mental distress could be explained entirely in biological terms.

Inspired by their success with general paresis, biological researchers have developed germ theories for other presenting problems. For example, mothers who contract viral infections during pregnancy are more likely to have children who develop schizophrenia or autism (Fatemi, Folsom, et al., 2012; H. Jiang et al., 2016; Kneeland & Fatemi, 2013). These and other immune system explanations of psychopathology are generating growing interest from researchers and clinicians.

2.8 Evaluating Biological Perspectives

Biological models are viewed as having the following strengths:

1. *Mental phenomena explained in terms of biological processes.* Biological perspectives hold promise that complex and elusive behaviors can be explained in physiological terms.
2. *Scientific.* Biological perspectives have generated an enormous amount of research into the relationship between physical and mental functioning.

3. *Development of psychiatric drugs and other biological interventions.* Biological researchers have developed many psychiatric drugs and related interventions for problems ranging from depression to psychosis to anxiety.

Biological models also are prone to the following criticisms:

1. *Reductionistic.* Some critics complain that complex psychological phenomena cannot be explained in purely biological terms.
2. *Everyday problems become "medicalized."* Critics argue that some presenting problems aren't illnesses, and that biological perspectives view too many life problems as brain diseases. Medicalization occurs when non-medical problems are inappropriately classified as medical (A. Frances, 2013a; Pridmore, 2011).
3. *Overreliance on psychiatric drugs.* A common criticism of biological perspectives is that by equating psychological distress with illness, they have contributed to the over prescription of psychiatric drugs.

PSYCHOLOGICAL PERSPECTIVES

2.9 Introducing Psychological Perspectives

Psychological perspectives stress thoughts, feelings, and behaviors in explaining psychopathology and mental distress. Although they sometimes endorse a medical model that emphasizes disorders, the interventions they offer are psychological in nature—things like discussing and processing upsetting feelings, analyzing and changing troublesome thoughts, and teaching new and more adaptive behaviors to replace problematic ones. Psychological perspectives often advance psychotherapy, which relies on conversation between a professional helper (the therapist) and the person being helped (the client or patient, depending on the preferred term). Although many people seek therapy, myths about it remain widespread (see "In Depth"). To dispel common misconceptions, "The Lived Experience" feature explains what the first session of therapy is like. After that, we review common psychological perspectives.

In Depth: Myths about Therapy

These myths about therapy are reproduced from HelpGuide (M. Smith & Segal, 2021):

1. *I don't need a therapist. I'm smart enough to solve my own problems.* We all have our blind spots. Intelligence has nothing to do with it. A good therapist doesn't tell you what to do or how to live your life. He or she will give you an experienced outside perspective and help you gain insight into yourself so you can make better choices.
2. *Therapy is for crazy people.* Therapy is for people who have enough self-awareness to realize they need a helping hand, and who want to learn tools and techniques to become more self-confident and emotionally balanced.
3. *All therapists want to talk about is my parents.* While exploring family relationships can sometimes clarify thoughts and behaviors later in life, that is not the sole focus of therapy. The primary focus is what you need to change unhealthy patterns and symptoms in your life. Therapy is not about blaming your parents or dwelling on the past.
4. *Therapy is self-indulgent. It's for whiners and complainers.* Therapy is hard work. Complaining won't get you very far. Improvement in therapy comes from taking a hard look at yourself and your life, and then taking responsibility for your own actions. Your therapist will help you, but you're the one who ultimately must do the work.

Critical Thinking Questions

1. How many of these myths have you adhered to?
2. How many of these myths have your friends and families adhered to?
3. Should we try to debunk these myths and, if so, how?

The Lived Experience: What Will Happen in My First Therapy Session?

Many people who have never participated in a therapy session wonder what it will be like. Will the therapist ask you a lot of questions about your feelings? Will you be asked to discuss your fears? Will you have to talk about your childhood? The truth is that different therapists handle their first therapy sessions differently. They may even encourage you to ask them questions about their lives, training, or experiences in the first session. Three therapists explain below what goes on in their first sessions with new clients.

Valerie Domenici, Ph.D.

In our first meeting, I have two goals. First, I'd like to get to know you, hear about the kinds of things you'd like help with, and to decide if I can be helpful with those things. Second, I'd like you to get to know me, so that you can decide if I'm the kind of person you'd be comfortable working on those things with. To accomplish these goals, I will start by making you as comfortable as possible. I will explain how our conversation is confidential, and describe the exceptions to that rule. You will get some paperwork ahead of time that explains all of this, but we'll go over it again so that you can ask any questions that you may have about it. You can also ask me anything about me or my practice that would make you more comfortable sharing about yourself. If you want to know whether I've worked with a particular problem before, or how many years I've been in practice, or what my feelings are on a particular issue, I'll invite you to do that right up front. Often, people feel a bit more at ease when they know something about the person they are speaking with, and I'm happy to help.

Photo 2.2 Valerie Domenici.
Simply Well/Eric Klinedinst.

In getting to know you, I like to get to a couple of different areas. First, what is the current problem, feeling, or situation that brings you to therapy? Second, what is the history of that problem? For example, how long has it been going on? What has made the problems better or worse? And third, it can be extremely helpful to gather some family history. Sometimes we can get through all of this in one session, but often it takes two or three. It's ok if this all comes out in a jumbled mess. It's part of my job to help you put it all together in a way that makes sense. I will repeat back to you what I've heard you say, to make sure I have it right, and ask questions to fill in any blanks in my understanding of the situation.

You will likely get to know some things about me by the questions that I ask, or the way that I react to what you've said. I will also describe for you what my typical approach to therapy is like, and how that might apply to the specific issues you want to work on. I will ask you what you hope therapy will be like, and how you would not want it to be. If you've had any experience with therapy before, I can describe how my approach might be similar to or different than that one.

By the end of our first meeting (or after several), I will either say "yes, I think I can be helpful!" or I will suggest another colleague or type of service that might better fit your needs. Sometimes, I can give you a sense of how long therapy might take to address your concern, but often this is unpredictable. I will make a recommendation about how often to meet, which is usually based on the severity of the problem. Hopefully, at this point, you have a good sense of how comfortable you feel with me and my office, and it's up to you to decide whether to move forward with therapy!

Jonathan Rust, Ph.D.

When you first contact me, I will schedule a brief, ten- to twenty-minute phone consultation with you. During this consultation, I'll ask you to tell me a little about yourself, what your major concerns are, and how long you've been experiencing these issues. I'll also ask how you heard about me and what your main goal or expectation for therapy might be. Finally, I will explain my fee structure and payment options. I find these brief phone interactions to be extremely helpful for myself and you as a potential client, as I'm able to determine (with your help) if we may be a good fit to work together. If we both decide that we'd like to proceed, I will schedule an initial appointment with you, which is usually an hour in length.

Photo 2.3 Jonathan Rust.
With permission from Jonathan Rust.

It is important to keep in mind how the COVID-19 pandemic has affected the provision of psychotherapy. As a result, *telehealth* (health services delivered online) has moved from being a rarely thought of alternative to a vital necessity by which most psychotherapy has occurred over the last few years. Whether we choose to meet in person or virtually by *teletherapy* (see Chapter 16), the essential aspects of our meeting and working together will be the same. However, there are specific and important differences, as well. If we choose to work in person, when you arrive for the initial appointment, I'll meet you in the waiting area with an informed consent document, which explains in writing what you can expect from therapy. This document explains how long our sessions will be, our respective roles as therapist and client, my fee and cancellation policies, and your rights as a client—especially privacy, confidentiality, and their limits. After you've read and signed the informed consent, I'll ask you to come into my office and I'll answer any questions or concerns you may have about information on the form.

If we've decided to work virtually, in addition to a standard informed consent form, I'll forward an informed consent form addressing issues specific to teletherapy, including how it may affect issues such as confidentiality and privacy. I'll ask you to sign both forms and send them back to me by the time we meet for our first session. I'll also forward you a link to a HIPPA approved video conferencing platform that we'll use to meet.

From this point, whether meeting in person or virtually, the content and process of our work together will be the same. I'll invite you to continue telling me about yourself and your concerns, with no particular instructions or directions on what to talk about. As I listen, I may ask questions or make comments to encourage you to tell me more about yourself and to make you feel comfortable with the therapy process. The purpose of the initial session is to gather as much relevant information about you as possible—including your current issues and their history—to assist me in understanding you. Usually, we will just brush the surface in terms relevant information, but we will form the basis of a productive working relationship. At the end of the initial session, I will ask if you have any questions or concerns and how you felt about the session. If we both feel we can work together, I'll schedule another session for you. Then, I'll give or forward to you an "intake" form to complete before our next session. The reason I give the intake form to you at this point is to save you time filling it out if you did not want to continue working with me. The intake form gives me supplemental information that may not come out initially in our work together. If either of us feels it better for you to work with someone else, I will do my best to find an appropriate referral for you.

Jay S. Efran, Ph.D.

When you first arrive, I would ask the following question: "What can I do for you?" Your answer would help me understand why you are there and what you hope to get out of our meetings. Even if you could not give a very specific answer—and many individuals cannot—the question helps determine an appropriate starting point, including what I might need to explain about the therapy process and our work together.

Usually, I also want to know about "the final straw" that motivated you to pick up the phone and make an appointment. People often suffer for a long time before asking for help. Knowing why they are now ready to take action often provides important insights into the nature of the problem. Similarly, it helps to hear about any steps you previously took to solve the problem or reduce your distress. Even partially successful solutions can provide clues to useful approaches, and past failures may suggest approaches that might best be avoided.

Photo 2.4 Jay S. Efran.
With permission from Jay S. Efran.

Obviously, during this first session, I want to learn many details about what is bothering you. This is important information for me to have, but such exchanges can also increase your confidence that your situation is being understood. During this first meeting, I will check to see if we agree on an initial set of goals as well as the criteria we will use to determine if we are achieving those goals. We can add or subtract goals later, but it is important that we have at least a preliminary working agreement. Also in this first session, we will attempt to identify some fundamental beliefs about yourself that may be getting in your way and keeping you stuck. It will be part of my job to propose some alternatives to those ways of looking at the world.

Printed with permission of Valerie Domenici, Jonathan Rust, and Jay S. Efran.

2.10 Psychodynamic Perspectives

Psychodynamic perspectives originate in the work of Viennese neurologist Sigmund Freud (1856–1939). It helps to distinguish *psychodynamic* from *psychoanalytic*. The latter term refers to Freud's original theorizing, whereas the former is broader and includes both "classic" Freud, as well as later approaches that build on Freud but diverge from some of his central ideas. Table 2.2 summarizes core assumptions of psychodynamic perspectives.

> **Psychodynamic perspectives:** Theories that trace their origins to Freud's work; early life attachments and unconscious processes are emphasized.

Freud's Original Psychoanalytic Theory
Drive Theory

Freud conceptualized human psychology as a kind of energy system. He said each person was born with a set amount of *psychic energy*, which must be expressed. This makes psychoanalytic theory a *drive theory* (Bornstein et al., 2013; Eagle, 2011). Drive theories see people as psychologically motivated (i.e., driven) to think, feel, and act certain ways. Some psychic energy takes the form of *libido*, or sexual instinct (Freud, 1923/1960), which can be framed broadly as a drive to seek pleasure and avoid pain (R. B. Miller, 2015). Freud's drive theory roots human psychology in biological instincts. It also embraces *psychic determinism*, the idea that all mental events have underlying causes. In psychoanalytic theory, every mental event derives from psychic drives building up and then being expressed. Mental actions aren't freely chosen. They always have underlying (often multiple) causes.

Table 2.2 Five Psychodynamic Assumptions

Psychodynamic theories uphold all or most of these assumptions:

1. *The centrality of the unconscious.* The *unconscious* can be defined as mental experiences that a person is unaware of and cannot easily make conscious.
2. *The importance of early life experiences in shaping personality and psychopathology.* What happens in childhood is very important in both adaptive and pathological psychological development.
3. *Every mental event is caused.* Freud referred to this as *psychic determinism.* Psychological experiences never happen by accident and often have multiple causes.
4. *The importance of defense mechanisms.* Defense mechanisms are partly unconscious strategies people use to avoid anxiety and cope with emotionally upsetting experiences.
5. *The ability of the therapeutic relationship to address and resolve unconscious conflicts.* Psychodynamic therapies use their relationships with patients to make them aware of how their unconscious conflicts lead to problematic ways of dealing with others. In the process, patients come to learn new relational patterns.

Repression:
Unacceptable ideas and impulses are pushed out of awareness (i.e., made unconscious).

Id: Unconscious psychoanalytic personality structure consisting of the infant's aggressive, selfish, and sexual desires; motivated by the *pleasure principle* (desire for immediate pleasure/gratification).

Ego: Partly conscious/partly unconscious psychoanalytic personality structure that tries to satisfy id impulses while considering superego demands and constraints in the external environment; motivated by the *reality principle* (considering what is practical and possible).

Superego: Partly conscious/partly unconscious psychoanalytic personality structure that houses moral beliefs.

Conscious and Unconscious Experience

An emphasis on both conscious and (especially) unconscious experience is central to psychoanalytic theory. *Conscious* experience concerns the rational and adult component of the mind that the person is cognizant of, whereas *unconscious* experience reflects the childish and irrational part that is out of awareness but influences thoughts, feelings, and behavior. The conscious mind pushes unacceptable ideas and feelings out of awareness and into the unconscious through the psychological process of **repression**. Repressed memories are prevented from entering conscious awareness. Of course, not everything out of awareness is unconscious (i.e., repressed). *Preconscious* experience may not be conscious at a given moment but can easily be made conscious if focused on (e.g., that time you had fun at the beach with a friend). By contrast, unconscious memories can't be made conscious because they are repressed (e.g., parental abuse that a person is unable to recall).

Psychic Structures

Psychoanalytic theory emphasizes three psychic structures: the id, ego, and superego. The **id** is the entirely unconscious part of the personality from which aggressive and self-serving drives originate. The ego and superego are partly conscious and partly unconscious. The **ego** is the part of the personality that must express id impulses in acceptable ways. The **superego** houses the person's moral beliefs. The relationships among these three structures determine personality and mental experience. This is visually illustrated by comparing the mind to an iceberg (Figure 2.4).

Seth

From a psychoanalytic perspective, Seth's fights are caused by angry id impulses that are triggered when people challenge him. His ego expresses these impulses by getting into physical altercations with others, while his superego causes him to feel guilty for hurting them. His anger and guilt aren't freely chosen. They are psychically determined.

Psychosexual Stages

Freud's (1923/1960, 1905/1962) **psychosexual stages** have always been (and remain) controversial. They emphasize early childhood development, holding that personality is formed during the first five or so years of life. The stages combine nature (instinctual drives that must be expressed) and nurture (the effect of childrearing on personality development). What happens during the first five years of life determines how psychic energy is distributed across id, ego, and superego.

The first stage is the *oral stage* (from birth to roughly 1½ years old). At birth, all psychic energy is contained in the id. In fact, you could say that newborns are "pure id"—no egos or superegos just yet! The id consists of the infant's aggressive, selfish, and sexual desires. It is ruled by what Freud called the *pleasure principle*—the yearning for immediate pleasure and gratification while avoiding pain. During the oral stage, psychic energy is most easily expressed through oral activities (involving the mouth). Effective caregivers provide their infants with the optimal amount of oral gratification, feeding them when they are hungry. Too much or too little gratification leads to *fixation* (getting stuck at the stage). A fixated child can't move to the next stage. Freud believed children fixated at the oral stage develop issues around *autonomy* and *dependence*. As adults, they are ambivalently attached to others. Some feel overwhelmed by people and desire distance from them, while others become clingy and dependent.

The second stage is the *anal stage* (roughly 1½ to 3 years old), during which toilet training serves as the basis for ego development. The ego monitors environmental demands and constraints. It is ruled by the *reality principle*, the need to consider requirements of the external world when expressing id impulses. The ego emerges primarily during toilet training because such training requires *delay of gratification*—holding off expressing id impulses until circumstances allow it. Learning to delay gratification during toilet training generalizes to other situations where external demands must be considered in deciding when and how to express id impulses. If caregiving is too lax or strict during toilet training, the child becomes fixated in one of two ways. *Anal-retentive* individuals are overly ego-regulated, priding themselves on their ability to delay gratification. They are rigid, neat, stingy, stubborn, and highly organized (that student who organizes her bookshelf alphabetically by author and doesn't let you touch her books). *Anal-expulsive* individuals, on the other hand, rebel against demands to delay gratification. They are unregulated, messy, reckless, disobedient, and disorganized (that roommate who is a huge slob, overwhelming you with his mess). Importantly, both anal-retentive and anal-expulsive people have control issues. The former wish to exert control over the environment, while the latter refuse to be controlled by it.

The third stage is the *phallic stage* (roughly 3 to 5 years old), which results in the development of the superego. It is famous for Freud's controversial *Oedipus complex* (boys) and *Electra complex* (girls). These complexes differ because in psychoanalytic theory *anatomy is destiny*, by which Freud meant that having or lacking a penis affects superego development. In the *Oedipus complex*, the little boy desires mom for himself and wishes to get rid of dad. These feelings persist until the boy starts worrying that if dad discovers his desires, dad will become so angry that he might castrate the boy. *Castration anxiety* is so terrifying that the boy represses his Oedipal feelings for his mother and—to avoid being found out—identifies with his father. This results in the boy internalizing his father's moral beliefs. When this occurs, the superego is formed, and the Oedipus experience repressed (which is why you don't recall it). For girls, the *Electra complex* goes a bit differently. Freud said it begins with castration anxiety. Once a girl realizes she has nothing to castrate, she experiences *penis envy*. Little girls develop weaker superegos, according to Freud, because their castration anxiety isn't as powerful as that experienced by boys. Consequently, they don't identify as strongly with their mothers as boys do with their fathers—and this leads to weaker internalization of moral beliefs. The Electra complex has been widely criticized as sexist. Freud said people fixated at the phallic stage are narcissistic, proud, competitive, and vain. They are also overly sexualized in how they deal with others.

By the end of the phallic stage, the structure of the child's personality is in place. It consists of the ego trying to balance the demands of *three harsh taskmasters*: the id (unconscious self-serving drives), the superego (moral beliefs about acceptable behavior), and external reality (constraints and consequences the world imposes) (Freud, 1933/1965). Sometimes people mistakenly think of the ego as opposing the id, but this is not so. The ego serves the id. It must find outlets for id impulses,

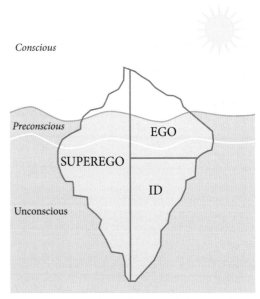

Figure 2.4 Freud's Iceberg Model of Mind. Freud's psychoanalytic theory envisions the mind as an iceberg. Everything below the water line is unconscious. Note how the id is fully unconscious, while the ego and superego have both conscious and unconscious parts.

Psychosexual stages: Developmental stages that determine id, ego, superego patterns in adult personality; the stages are *oral* (birth to 1½ years old), *anal* (1½ to 3 years old, ego develops), *phallic* (3 to 5 years old, superego develops via Oedipal/Electra complexes), *latency* (6 years old to pre-adolescence), and *genital* (adolescence onward); *fixation* at one or more of the first three stages leads to symptoms at the genital stage.

but in a way that satisfies the superego and accommodates external reality. This is a difficult task. *Neurosis* is Freud's term for when the ego feels overwhelmed in balancing the demands of its three harsh taskmasters.

Seth

Seth finds himself sexually attracted to his girlfriend Lillian's best friend, Abigail. Psychoanalytically speaking, Seth's ego must find a way to express this id impulse. However, both social norms and Seth's superego object to cheating on one's girlfriend—especially with her best friend! Neurosis occurs when Seth's ego struggles to balance the need to express his sexual attraction to Abigail while keeping his superego and girlfriend Lillian at bay.

Photo 2.5 A female reporter demonstrated the dangers of the "Freudian slip" when commenting on Tiger Woods in the wake of his affair.

Kevin C. Cox/Getty Images.

Psychoanalysis: Freud's original therapy in which patients lie on couch facing away from analyst; employs *free association* (patient says whatever comes to mind), *dream analysis* (unconscious wish fulfillments expressed in dreams are identified), and examination of *transference* (ways patients transfer feelings about important others onto their analysts); *catharsis* (emotional release) and *working through* (psychological integration of what has been made conscious) are goals.

After the phallic stage, there are two more stages. The fourth stage is the *latency stage* (6 years old to pre-adolescence), a period of relative calm and quiet. The fifth stage is the *genital stage* (adolescence onward), during which fixations at the first three stages fully emerge. Freud developed psychoanalysis to uncover and resolve the unconscious conflicts behind these fixations.

Psychoanalysis

Freud's brand of psychotherapy is called **psychoanalysis**, and it aims to transform the basic structure of personality (Freud, 1933/1965, 1900/1965). Patients attend hourly sessions with their analysts three to five times per week. They lie on a couch facing away from their analysts, who rely on two main techniques to help bring unconscious conflicts to the fore.

The first technique is *free association*, during which patients are instructed to say whatever comes to mind without censoring themselves. The goal is to have unconscious conflicts leak out, often through *slips of the tongue* (also called *Freudian slips*) in which the person accidentally uses wrong words and, in so doing, expresses unconscious feelings or thoughts (Freud, 1914). For example, "soon after the adulterous Tiger Woods complained of a neck injury, a female reporter blurted that the golfer withdrew from the 2010 Players tournament due to 'a bulging di**' in his back" (Pincott, 2012, para. 5).

The second psychoanalytic technique is *dream analysis*. During dream analysis, patients share their dreams, and the analyst analyzes them. Freud believed every dream contains a *wish fulfillment*, an unconscious desire that is often disguised by the ego to satisfy superego and external reality constraints (Freud, 1900/1965).

Seth

When it comes to Seth's repressed sexual wish to have sex with his girlfriend Lillian's best friend Abigail, his ego may disguise this wish and allow it to be expressed in a dream about sex with a famous movie star—who reminds him of (and is a stand-in for) Abigail.

Another important element of psychoanalysis is analyzing transference. *Transference* occurs when patients transfer feelings about important people in their lives onto their analysts. For instance, a patient hostile toward her father may come to interact with and treat her analyst the same way. Another patient who feels deferent and weak when dealing with his mother may start feeling that way with his analyst, too. Transference provides analysts with information for understanding patients' repressed conflicts. Psychoanalysis encourages transference by having patients lie facing away from their analysts during sessions. With their analysts out of view, they are more likely to begin treating them like important people in their lives (e.g., their parents).

Seth

Imagine Seth sees a psychoanalytic therapist. Over the course of the first few sessions, transference would develop, in which Seth feels the same kind of anger toward his therapist that he feels toward his father. "You're just like my dad!" Seth might exclaim in session. "You don't respect my choices and you don't understand me!"

Unlike transference, *countertransference* isn't desired. Countertransference occurs when analysts project their own feelings onto patients. This interferes with analysts' grasp of patient behavior. To minimize countertransference, psychoanalytic trainees go through their own analysis to work through issues likely to interfere with them accurately reading patients.

Seth

If Seth's psychoanalyst is a middle-aged woman with a teenage son, she might notice herself starting to feel the same frustration with Seth that she sometimes feels toward her son. To address this, she would hopefully seek consultation with another therapist, who could help her work through these countertransference feelings.

As analysts come to understand the repressed conflicts behind patients' symptoms, they begin offering interpretations. The goal is to bring repressed conflicts into consciousness. *Resistance* initially occurs, with patients rejecting their analysts' interpretations and relying on **defense mechanisms** (partly unconscious mental processes used to ward off or reduce anxiety; see Table 2.3). However, if all goes well, patients eventually accept these interpretations and consciously recall previously repressed conflicts. When this fully occurs, patients experience *catharsis*, a strong emotional release of pent-up feelings. Psychoanalysis doesn't end with catharsis. Afterwards, there is a long *working through* period, during which patients integrate what has been uncovered into their lives and begin engaging others in new ways. Psychoanalysis is a long-term project that takes many years.

Defense mechanisms:
In psychodynamic theories, partly unconscious mental processes used to ward off or reduce anxiety and cope with emotionally upsetting experiences.

Table 2.3 "The Best Offense Is a Good Defense!" Defense Mechanisms

DEFENSE	DEFINED	IN ACTION
Denial	Refusing to acknowledge an impulse or desire.	Bill insists he doesn't have a crush on Hillary, even though he clearly does.
Displacement	Redirecting one's feelings for one person toward someone else.	Pedro is mad at his boss, so he goes home and kicks his cat.
Identification	Becoming like someone else by incorporating their beliefs into one's own sense of self.	Donald starts dressing and acting like his professor, whom he admires very much.
Intellectualization	Logic and reason are used to minimize powerful emotions resulting from upsetting events.	After barely surviving a violent battle, a soldier describes it in emotionally detached terms as "a necessary evil" and "not a big deal."
Projection	Attributing one's own unacceptable feelings and thoughts to others.	Aparna feels her colleague dislikes her, even though it is she who dislikes her colleague.
Rationalization	Logic and reason are used to justify or explain away one's own behavior.	Sidney plagiarizes her term paper; when confronted about it she shrugs and remarks how "everyone does it."
Reaction formation	Transforming one's underlying feelings into their opposite	A preacher who rails against homosexuality is discovered having gay sex.
Regression	Reverting to an earlier stage of behavior and development.	Sally coos and whines like a 5-year-old when her partner isn't attentive.
Repression	Keeping unacceptable impulses unconscious.	Someone sexually abused in childhood has no recollection of it.
Sublimation	Directing aggressive and unacceptable impulses in socially approved ways.	Steven's aggressive impulses are channeled into football, where he becomes a celebrated player.

Psychodynamic Theories

Psychodynamic offshoots of Freud include the Neo-Freudians, ego psychology, object relations theory, interpersonal theory, and self-psychology (Eagle, 2011; A. Elliott, 2015). Below we describe two examples of psychodynamic approaches, both of which stress relationships over instinctual drives.

Object Relations Therapy

Object relations therapy focuses on how pathological relationship patterns in adulthood are tied to lessons learned in early attachment relationships with caregivers (Caligor & Clarkin, 2010). The term *object* can seem odd and confusing. It is any person or thing, real or imagined, for which an infant develops an *introjection*, or internal mental representation (Cashdan, 1988; A. Elliott, 2015; M. Klein et al., 1952). Your internal representation of your mother might not be accurate, but you use it in relating to her and others who remind you of her. Early childhood relationships with caregivers are critical in developing internal object representations. When infants experience anger toward their caregivers, those with consistently loving and nurturing caregivers learn that both they and their caregivers have positive and negative qualities. This is psychologically healthy. However, infants whose caregivers respond inconsistently or in a rejecting manner learn that their angry feelings aren't acceptable. These infants grow up isolating and repressing these feelings in a process called *splitting*, where the offending object is divided into "good" and "bad" parts (Cashdan, 1988; A. Elliott, 2015; M. Klein et al., 1952). Psychopathology develops when relational patterns learned in childhood—including splitting off unacceptable feelings—impact relationships in adolescence and adulthood. People who rely on splitting cannot experience the good and bad aspects of others simultaneously. They alternate between seeing others as all good or all bad. This leads to relational difficulties.

Just as they do with other people in their lives, patients project unwanted and split-off feelings about themselves onto their therapists. This is called *projective identification* (Cashdan, 1988; M. Klein et al., 1952). For instance, a projective identification of *dependency* occurs when patients project onto their therapists longstanding feelings of helplessness (learned in childhood relationships with caregivers). They might repeatedly ask their therapists to tell them what to do. A *power* projective identification, on the other hand, results in a relational pattern where patients dominate and control others to avoid being hurt (Cashdan, 1988). Object relations therapists uncover patients' projective identifications by examining countertransference feelings—distinguishing "good" from "bad" countertransference. The "bad" kind is what Freud spoke of: therapists transferring their own issues onto patients. This is to be avoided. The "good" kind occurs when therapists are induced to act and feel certain ways because of their patients' behavior. This sort of countertransference is "good" because it provides insight into patients' projective identifications. The therapist who feels helpless with patients who project power or bossy with patients who project dependency can use these feelings to inform therapy. By talking with patients about their projective identifications and refusing to abide by them, object relations therapists provide a *corrective emotional experience* (Alexander & French, 1946)—a new kind of relationship in which patients learn to assess others more realistically so that projective identifications are no longer necessary.

Seth

Consider what might happen were Seth to work with an object relations therapist. After a few sessions, the therapist might feel intimidated by Seth and fear doing anything to provoke his anger. She would eventually begin sharing these feelings with Seth. By processing Seth's projective identification and conveying caring toward him while also refusing to tiptoe around him as others do, Seth would have a corrective emotional experience in which he explores what it's like to interact with his therapist without resorting to the familiar pattern of browbeating her into submission to avoid emotional injury. After developing this new way of relating to his therapist, Seth would hopefully start to generalize it to others in his life, as well.

Time-Limited Dynamic Psychotherapy (TLDP)

Time-limited dynamic psychotherapy (TLDP) exemplifies a briefer, contemporary form of psychodynamic therapy (Levenson, 2017). It shares the object relations emphasis on identifying and revising problematic interpersonal patterns, but—by establishing clear therapeutic goals and addressing them in twenty to twenty-five sessions—it accommodates modern contexts that don't permit long-term therapy. Like object relations therapy, TLDP holds that people develop internal working models of relationships based on early experiences with caregivers, usually parents (Levenson, 2017). From a TLDP perspective, people generalize relationship patterns learned as children into their adult relationships, even when this is counterproductive. Therapy remedies these *cyclical maladaptive patterns* by providing clients with a *corrective emotional experience* (a new and healthier relationship pattern with the therapist) (Levenson, 2017).

Time-limited dynamic psychotherapy (TLDP): Short-term psychodynamic therapy that shares object relations therapy's emphasis on using therapy to identify and revise problematic interpersonal patterns (*cyclical maladaptive patterns*) but does so more quickly by establishing clear therapeutic goals and addressing them in twenty to twenty-five sessions.

Seth

A time-limited dynamic therapist working with Seth would notice how Seth behaves in assertive and intimidating ways with others. This keeps him from being taken advantage of but prevents him from experiencing intimacy; hence, his long string of girlfriends who have broken up with him because they found him bossy and hard to talk to. After all, who wants to confide in someone intimidating? TLDP therapy would see Seth's cyclical maladaptive pattern as involving relating to others in intimidating ways that keep them deferent and at a distance. Therapy would identify this pattern, which inevitably would get reproduced in Seth's interactions with the therapist. The therapeutic relationship would be used to help Seth develop more effective ways of relating to others.

Evaluating Psychodynamic Perspectives

The following are cited as strengths of psychodynamic perspectives:

1. *Clinically rich and engaging.* Freud and later psychodynamic therapists illustrated their ideas though compelling case studies. Their rich clinical descriptions of intriguing cases continue to attract newcomers to psychodynamic therapy.
2. *Emphasis on childhood origins of psychopathology.* We take the importance of early life events for granted due to Freud's influence. While some question Freud's emphasis on the centrality of early experiences (Efran & Fauber, 2015), an emphasis on childhood remains central to many theories of psychopathology.
3. *Attention to irrational and unconscious aspects of human functioning.* Psychodynamic perspectives remind us that reason often has less influence over behavior than irrational emotions and drives we aren't aware of.
4. *Psychoanalysis as the first fully articulated form of psychotherapy.* Dubbed the "talking cure" by an early patient (Breur & Freud, 1893–1895/2013), psychoanalysis legitimized the idea that discussing problems with a trained professional could help.

Psychodynamic theories are also criticized on the following grounds:

1. *Not very scientific.* Freud relied on case studies, not controlled experiments. His concepts don't lend themselves to experimental inquiry because unconscious material can't be directly observed or measured. However, modern psychodynamic therapists have undertaken more rigorous research on the effectiveness of their approach, with some promising results (Lindegaard et al., 2020; Steinert et al., 2017).
2. *Sexist and culture biased.* Freud's views on female psychology have been widely criticized (Balsam, 2013; Horney, 1924; Mead, 1974). Early psychoanalysis also rejected patient reports of sex abuse, seeing them as "projected fantasies" (Masson, 1984). Finally, the psychosexual stages, in assuming a traditional nuclear family, have been criticized as culture biased—although there have been efforts to adapt them to non-nuclear families (A. Parsons, 1970).

3. *Deterministic view of people.* Not everyone likes Freud's notion of psychic determinism, the idea that mental events have underlying causes. Theorists who emphasize choice and free will are especially critical.

4. *Overly pathologizing.* Psychoanalytic theory has been criticized for pathologizing everything. Of course, psychoanalysts view this as a strength, not a weakness. Freud (1914) did, after all, write a book called *The Psychopathology of Everyday Life*. Nonetheless, his notions that everyone is a bit neurotic and that every little thing a person does potentially betrays unconscious conflicts rub some people the wrong way. To these critics, sometimes a cigar is just a cigar!

2.11 Cognitive-Behavioral Perspectives

Cognitive-behavioral therapy (CBT) combines two distinct perspectives often blended in clinical practice: cognitive and behavioral perspectives. Because behavioral perspectives developed first, we begin there, then move on to cognitive perspectives. We finish with ways cognitive and behavioral perspectives have been combined.

Behavioral Perspectives

Whereas Freud endorsed psychic determinism, **behavioral perspectives** embrace a different kind of determinism, one in which environmental conditioning shapes behavior. Students and practitioners often fail to grasp that behaviorists (especially old-time *radical behaviorists*) challenge the notion of psychopathology as residing inside people. To them, speculation about internal disorders is unnecessary and unscientific (Andersson & Ghaderi, 2006). Instead, we should stick to what can be observed. From a strict behavioral stance, "psychopathology" is not something we "have" inside us. It is something we do, consisting of undesirable conditioned behaviors. In the behavioral perspective, simply change the environment to recondition behavior—and voilà! Problem solved. Table 2.4 presents behavioral assumptions.

Classical Conditioning

The most important early behaviorist was John B. Watson (1878–1958). Watson drew on the work of Russian physiologist Ivan Pavlov (1849–1936) in developing **classical conditioning**. In classical conditioning an *unconditioned stimulus* is paired repeatedly with a *neutral stimulus* to turn the latter into a *conditioned stimulus* that elicits the same response as the unconditioned stimulus (Craske, 2017). Let's unpack this. Pavlov gave his dogs food, and they began salivating. The food was an unconditioned stimulus and the salivation an unconditioned response. Neither required learning; dogs just instinctually salivate in response to food. After Pavlov repeatedly rang a bell every time he fed his dogs, the bell elicited the same response as the food—even when no food was given. The bell had become a conditioned stimulus, capable of evoking the same salivation response as food. Salivating after the bell rang was a conditioned response. The dogs had learned to associate food with the sound of a bell.

Cognitive-behavioral therapy (CBT): Therapy that combines elements of *cognitive therapy* and *behavior therapy*.

Behavioral perspectives: View mental distress as caused by environmental conditioning and social learning, not internal psychopathology.

Classical conditioning: An *unconditioned stimulus* (no learning required) is paired with a *neutral stimulus*, which turns the neutral stimulus into a *conditioned stimulus* that evokes the same response as the unconditioned stimulus, even when the unconditioned stimulus isn't present.

Table 2.4 Five Behavioral Assumptions

Purely behavioral theories historically have made these assumptions:

1. *Psychology as the scientific study of observable behavior.* To be scientific, psychology must rely on empirical observation. It should limit its focus only to what can be directly observed. Mental concepts that cannot be observed (e.g., id, self, mind, cognitions) have no place in a scientific psychology.
2. *Behavior as determined by conditioning.* The environment conditions human behavior, mainly through classical and operant conditioning.
3. *Most behavior is learned.* While people are born into the world with some basic emotions, most human behavior is learned through conditioning. People are born as *blank slates.*
4. *Dysfunctional behavior as conditioned behavior.* The environment has conditioned behaviors deemed dysfunctional. We can use conditioning to replace these undesirable behaviors with more desirable ones.
5. *We can learn a lot about dysfunctional behavior in humans by studying non-human animals.* Conditioning processes are the same for humans and non-human animals. Studying the latter can provide insight into dysfunctional behavior in people.

The early behaviorists quickly realized that classical conditioning could explain undesired behavior. Watson notoriously tried to illustrate this by classically conditioning fear in Little Albert, the 9–12-month-old infant discussed in Chapter 1 (J. B. Watson & Rayner, 1920). By clanging loud steel bars whenever he presented Albert with a white rat, Watson taught Albert to fear the rat. Rather than seeing phobias as symptoms of repressed internal conflicts (as psychoanalysts do), behaviorists view them as classically conditioned behaviors.

Operant Conditioning

Operant conditioning, most associated with B. F. Skinner (1904–1990), focuses on how reinforcement and punishment influence future behavior (Bolling et al., 2006). Whereas classical conditioning focuses on conditioned stimuli that precede behavior, operant conditioning focuses on the consequences that follow it. **Reinforcement** consists of consequences that increase the likelihood of a behavior, while **punishment** consists of those that decrease its likelihood (Bolling et al., 2006). There are two ways to reinforce and two ways to punish (McConnell, 1990):

- *Positive reinforcement* is when something desirable is added after a behavior. A teacher who praises a student for speaking in class positively reinforces the student. Something desirable (praise) is added that increases the likelihood of the student speaking again next class.
- *Negative reinforcement* is when something undesirable is removed after a behavior. Taking aspirin for a headache is negatively reinforced if the headache goes away. Something undesirable (a headache) is eliminated, making it more likely you will take an aspirin again the next time your head hurts.
- *Positive punishment* is when something undesirable is added after a behavior. Parents who scold their children for misbehaving at the grocery store are positively punishing them. By adding something undesirable (verbal criticism), they are making it less likely the children will misbehave during the next grocery store visit.
- *Negative punishment* is when something desirable is removed after a behavior. Parents who take away their children's Internet access for rudely talking back are negatively reinforcing them. By removing something desirable (time on the Internet), they are making it less likely the children will be rude the next time.

Students often mistake negative reinforcement as a form of punishment because they incorrectly equate "positive" and "negative" with "good" and "bad" rather than with "adding" or "subtracting." When we remove something undesirable (negative reinforcement), we provide a reward that makes behavior more likely—that's why, for instance, removing stress by completing your homework reinforces doing homework! Reinforcement (positive or negative) always increases the likelihood of the behaviors it follows, while punishment (positive or negative) always decreases the likelihood of the behaviors it follows (McConnell, 1990).

Seth

A behavioral therapist would note how Seth has often received reinforcement for behaving aggressively. By getting angry with people, he usually gets what he wants. Others have inadvertently rewarded him by backing down when he becomes belligerent. His recent arrest for assaulting Jorge is the first time that Seth recalls receiving any kind of serious punishment for his angry behavior.

Social Learning

Not all behavior is conditioned directly. **Social learning theory** holds that learning often occurs through observation and modeling. Observation involves watching others. Modeling is when others behave in ways we can imitate. Psychologist Albert Bandura (1925–2021) famously showed how children who observed adults acting aggressively towards an inflatable "Bobo" doll later imitated what they saw (Bandura et al., 1961, 1963c, 1963b, 1963a). Interestingly, the children were less likely to imitate if the adult was punished. However, even then, observational learning still occurred: The children didn't spontaneously imitate the adult but were quite able to when given a reward for doing so (Bandura, 1965)!

Operant conditioning: Behavioral approach focused on how the consequences of behavior (reinforcement of punishment) influence whether it is likely to be repeated.

Reinforcement: Consequences that increase the likelihood of the behavior they follow; can be *positive* (add something desirable) or *negative* (remove something undesirable).

Punishment: Consequences that decrease the likelihood of the behavior they follow; can be *positive* (add something undesirable) or *negative* (remove something desirable).

Social learning theory: Behavioral approach that focuses on how observation and modeling contribute to learning.

Seth

In therapy steeped in social learning theory, Seth might recall seeing his father get in fights while Seth was growing up. This earned his father the respect of his male friends who worked with him at the loading dock but resulted in Seth's mother becoming increasingly fed up with Seth's father for losing his temper too often. Seth and his therapist could discuss what Seth may have learned from seeing his father model aggressive behavior.

Behavior Therapy

Behavior therapy uses classical and operant conditioning, as well as social learning, to alter undesired behavior. Classical conditioning techniques often involve exposure that leads to extinction of the conditioned response (Craske, 2017). **Extinction** works by no longer pairing the unconditioned and conditioned stimuli. Consequently, the conditioned stimulus loses its ability to evoke a conditioned response. If we stopped ringing the bell before presenting Pavlov's dogs with food, extinction would occur. The bell would stop eliciting salivation as its association with food weakened. In **exposure therapies**, the client is placed in the presence of the conditioned stimulus to extinguish the old response and condition a new one (Zalta & Foa, 2012). Through this exposure, the client learns that nothing bad happens when in contact with the stimulus.

Evaluating Behavioral Perspectives

The following are cited as strengths of behavioral perspectives:

1. *Scientific.* Behaviorists have extensively researched their approach. Many studies have been conducted that support behavioral perspectives.
2. *No speculation about hard-to-prove mental entities.* By focusing exclusively on behavior, speculation about unobservable processes inside the person becomes unnecessary.
3. *Highly practical therapy approach.* Reconditioning behavior is straightforward and easy for clients to understand. It is effective for many behavioral problems.
4. *Optimistic.* By seeing distressing behavior as caused by environmental circumstances that can be changed, behaviorists paint an optimistic picture in which undesirable behavior can be reconditioned.

At the same time, behavioral perspectives have also been criticized for several reasons:

1. *Too deterministic.* Their insistence that behaviors are little more than conditioned responses to the environment is sometimes seen as limited and simplistic; humanistic critics argue that people have some say in how they behave.
2. *Internal processes ignored.* While supporters like behaviorism's exclusion of unobservable mental concepts, critics see an impoverished view of the person. Just because scientists can't directly observe internal mental processes doesn't mean they don't exist or that we should give up studying them.
3. *Biological influences minimized.* Because they see almost all behavior as learned, behaviorists are accused of ignoring or minimizing biology. Critics contend that some forms of psychological suffering—such as schizophrenia—are caused by brain disease, not conditioning.
4. *Animals are limited in what they teach us about human psychology.* Some critics believe people are psychologically more complex than the non-human animals used in behavioral research. They feel that drawing conclusions about mental distress based on animal research is limited in what it can teach us.

Cognitive Perspectives

Cognitive perspectives emerged during the 1950s and emphasize thoughts and beliefs as the root causes of psychopathology and mental distress. Early cognitive therapists were intrigued by advances in computer technology and began conceptualizing people as sophisticated information processors. Cognitive approaches stress *cognitive restructuring*—techniques to help people overcome

---

Extinction: When a conditioned stimulus is no longer paired with an unconditioned stimulus, the conditioned stimulus stops eliciting a conditioned response.

Exposure therapies: Behavior therapy techniques in which the client is placed in the presence of the conditioned stimulus to extinguish the old response and condition a new one.

Cognitive perspectives: Emphasize thoughts and beliefs as the root causes of mental distress.

Table 2.5 Five Cognitive Assumptions

These assumptions are adapted from Reinecke and Freeman (2003):

1. *How people interpret events influences how they feel or behave.* Events do not determine our responses; what we think of them does.
2. *People actively interpret events.* We are always actively making sense of events.
3. *People develop their own unique belief systems.* We not only develop unique belief systems; we then selectively attend to events in ways that fit with these belief systems. We become sensitive to specific stressors based on our beliefs about them.
4. *People become functionally impaired when they respond to stressors based on problematic belief systems.* Stressors we believe to be important lead us to respond to situations in maladaptive and self-fulfilling ways: "the person who believes ... that 'the freeway is horribly dangerous' might drive in such a timid manner ... that he causes an accident, thus strengthening his belief in the danger of freeways" (Reinecke & Freeman, 2003, p. 229).
5. *Mental disorders can be distinguished based on their specific cognitive content and processes.* This is the *cognitive specificity hypothesis,* and it holds that each disorder has a unique way in which its sufferers cognitively interpret events.

Source: Adapted from Reinecke and Freeman (2003).

their problems by thinking more rationally (Leahy & McGinn, 2012; van Bilsen, 2013). The Stoic philosopher Epictetus anticipated cognitive perspectives when he famously quipped, "What upsets people is not things themselves but their judgments about the things .... So when we are thwarted or upset or distressed, let us never blame someone else but rather ourselves, that is, our own judgments" (Epictetus, as cited in Reinecke & Freeman, 2003, p. 225). Cognitive therapy and rational emotive behavior therapy exemplify cognitive perspectives. Assumptions made by cognitive therapists are listed in Table 2.5.

Cognitive Therapy

Psychiatrist Aaron Beck (1921–2021) founded **cognitive therapy**, which attributes psychopathology to dysfunctional thinking (J. S. Beck, 2011). Successful treatment involves evaluating one's beliefs and thinking more realistically and adaptively. Cognitive theorists identify four levels of cognition (J. S. Beck, 2011):

1. *Automatic thoughts* are spontaneous thoughts (e.g., "I'm not good enough to win the race," "I'm hungry for ice cream," "Why am I always the one who must take care of everything?"). Automatic thoughts, not events themselves, are what trigger emotional responses.

Cognitive therapy: Aaron Beck's therapy approach, which focuses on correcting the client's dysfunctional thoughts; focuses on four levels of cognition: *automatic thoughts, intermediate beliefs, core beliefs,* and *schemas.*

Seth and Lillian

Seth is waiting to make copies in the library and Jorge cuts in front of him. Seth has the automatic thought "I'm being disrespected!" and, consequently, he feels angry. In response to his anger, he yells at Lillian, who has the automatic thought, "I wound up with the sort of boyfriend I deserve" and feels sad.

2. *Intermediate beliefs* are general rules and beliefs that influence automatic thoughts. Problems arise when intermediate beliefs become rigid.

Seth and Lillian

Seth's intermediate belief, "Deferring to others in social situations is a way of showing them respect," helps us understand why he thinks Jorge's line cutting is disrespecting him. Lillian, on the other hand, maintains the intermediate belief that "Only valuable people deserve to be well treated."

3. *Core beliefs* are basic philosophies or mindsets we hold about ourselves that influence intermediate beliefs and automatic thoughts.

Seth and Lillian

One of Seth's core beliefs is "I may not be good enough to warrant respect," whereas one of Lillian's may be "I am not valuable to others."

4. *Schemas* are mental structures used to organize information. Broader than core beliefs, schemas are generalized scripts about how the world works that we use to anticipate different situations (Reinecke & Freeman, 2003). We have schemas for mundane events such as what to expect when we go to a restaurant, but we also have schemas for relationships. When relational schemas are negative or rigid, we get into psychological trouble. We often attend to information that confirms our schemas and overlook information that doesn't (Reinecke & Freeman, 2003).

Seth and Lillian

One of Seth's schemas holds that "I may not be good enough to warrant respect, but to ensure I get it I must stand up for myself and demand that others treat me properly. When they don't, the only way to win is to get angry." Lillian maintains a very different schema: "I am unimportant, unattractive, and invisible. Other people know this and will eventually come to ignore and mistreat me. Life will be a series of disappointments in which I won't get what I want or need."

Cognitive distortions:
Errors in thinking that lead to emotional distress.

Cognitive therapy focuses on the client's belief system, which is often riddled with **cognitive distortions** (see Table 2.6). The goal is to identify errors in logic (A. T. Beck et al., 1979; J. S. Beck, 2011; Leahy & Rego, 2012; van Bilsen, 2013). Therapy challenges the illogic of automatic thoughts and replaces them with more reasonable beliefs and responses.

Table 2.6 "Do You Really Believe That?" Common Cognitive Distortions

DISTORTION	DEFINED	IN ACTION
All-or-nothing thinking	Interpreting everything as either "all good" or "all bad" with no middle ground.	"If I don't do this perfectly, then I am a complete failure."
Catastrophizing	Expecting the worst to always come true even though it is unlikely.	"I have a headache. It's probably a brain tumor."
Emotional reasoning	Relying on feelings to make judgments, even when they aren't supported by evidence.	"I feel unattractive, therefore I must be unattractive."
Filtering	Focusing exclusively on negative events and discounting positive ones.	"When I won the game, it was due to luck; when I lost it was because I'm dumb."
Jumping to conclusions	Reaching a conclusion despite little evidence for doing so.	"They haven't replied to the job application I submitted last week; they definitely aren't going to."
Magnification	Overemphasizing negative events.	"This pimple is hideous! Nobody is going to talk to me until it goes away."
Mind reading	Assuming one knows what others are thinking.	"He didn't return my text. He must not like me."
Minimization	Underemphasizing positive events.	"Sure I got an 'A' this time, but usually I don't."
Overgeneralization	Taking one instance and applying it too broadly to explain other instances.	"She rejected me for a date. Nobody will ever date me!"
Personalization	Assuming others' behavior is necessarily about you.	"When the professor said in class that some students ask too many questions, she had to mean me."

Rational Emotive Behavior Therapy (REBT)

Psychologist Albert Ellis (1913–2007) developed **rational emotive behavior therapy (REBT)**, which—like cognitive therapy—presumes that beliefs determine emotions and behavior (Craske, 2017; Dryden & Ellis, 2001). In REBT, eliminating irrational thinking is the way to remedy mental distress. To accomplish this, REBT relies on the **ABCDE model** (Dryden & Ellis, 2001; Trower et al., 1988). In this model, "A" is an _activating event_ that occurs in a person's life, "B" is a _belief_ that determines how the person interprets the event, and "C" is the _emotional consequence_ of the belief. Therapy involves "D," _disputing irrational beliefs_, and "E," _replacing irrational beliefs with effective new beliefs._

Lillian

Lillian is reprimanded by her professor for not doing her math homework correctly. This is an activating event, which triggers a specific belief ("I'm incompetent"). The emotional consequence is that Lillian feels depressed about her ability to succeed at school. An REBT therapist might ask Lillian to examine whether her belief system is supported by evidence. If it isn't, then the therapist would dispute Lillian's illogical beliefs. For example, he might help her replace her irrational belief ("I'm incompetent") with a more realistic and effective belief ("I may not always do everything well at school, but I am able to learn and improve my performance").

REBT works to prevent _awfulizing_, the irrational tendency to interpret things as more awful than they are (Dryden & Ellis, 2001). It also ties to eliminate _musterbating_, Ellis' humorously named term for the irrational belief that things must be a certain way or life can't go on (Dryden & Ellis, 2001). The REBT therapist challenges whether events—even those we don't like—are as bad as they seem. By changing our irrational beliefs about events, we can change our responses to them.

Lillian

An REBT therapist might address Lillian's awfulizing by asking her to consider the worst thing that could happen if her math skills are lacking. Perhaps she'd have to pursue a different course of study—and that wouldn't be the end of the world or as awful as she thinks. Her therapist would also address Lillian's musterbating—her belief that she must succeed at math or life will be awful. This belief isn't true. Lillian's life after dropping math could be enjoyable in ways she can't yet appreciate. She might take a literature class and find that she enjoys and is good at writing poetry.

Evaluating Cognitive Perspectives

Cognitive perspectives are viewed as having several strengths:

1. _Scientific._ Cognitive perspectives are well grounded in science. Many studies on the effectiveness of cognitive therapy for problems like depression and anxiety have been conducted. Cognitive approaches have substantial research support.
2. _Straightforward and intuitive._ Cognitive therapies are praised for offering logical and intuitive solutions to problems. Clinicians can learn how to do cognitive therapy easily because—compared with psychodynamic and humanistic therapies—it offers concrete procedures. Its well-defined therapy techniques are intuitive, clear, and broken into discrete steps.
3. _Adaptable._ Cognitive therapies are adaptable enough that they can readily be combined with other approaches—most often, behavioral approaches.

Cognitive perspectives have also been criticized:

1. _Logic and reason overemphasized._ Critics believe cognitive perspectives overemphasize logic and reason. Many say the mind-as-computer metaphor overlooks the importance of emotion.

> **Rational emotive behavior therapy (REBT):** Albert Ellis' cognitive therapy, which focuses on disputing clients' irrational beliefs.
>
> **ABCDE model:** REBT model of how psychological problems originate and how to fix them; A = activating event; B = beliefs; C = emotional consequences of beliefs; D = disputing beliefs; and E = more effective beliefs that replace those that were disputed.

2. *Biology minimized and mind–body dualism instituted.* From a biological perspective, cognitive therapists minimize physiological influences (e.g., brain chemistry) and reinstitute a mind–body dualism that sees thinking as a psychological product of mind rather than a biological product of brain.

3. *Mentalistic explanations.* From a behavioral perspective, cognitive approaches are no better than psychodynamic and humanistic approaches because they rely on speculation about mental entities that cannot be scientifically observed (Skinner, 1985, 1987, 1990).

Combining Cognitive and Behavioral Perspectives

Despite objections from radical behaviorists like Skinner, cognitive and behavioral therapies are so often combined that cognitive-behavioral therapy (CBT) is considered its own distinct perspective. Obviously, CBT is less theoretically "pure" than behavioral or cognitive perspectives alone. In CBT, how people think and how they are conditioned by their environments are both stressed. Due to a shared emphasis on concrete and direct interventions that lend themselves to traditional scientific inquiry, behavioral and cognitive perspectives fit nicely together.

2.12 Humanistic Perspectives

Humanistic perspectives include humanistic, existential, and constructivist approaches. These perspectives place personal meaning front and center. They maintain that people are proactive meaning-makers who strive to develop their full potential. Psychological problems result when they are prevented from doing so. Building on the work of pioneers like Abraham Maslow (1968) and Carl Rogers (1959), classic humanistic theories advance a positive view of human nature. They view people as naturally constructive and growth-oriented when provided a supportive environment. By contrast, existential and constructivist theories are less optimistic about human nature. They see no inherent meaning or purpose in life but hold people responsible for inventing and living by their own meanings. All humanistic perspectives reject *reductionism*, the idea that we can break complex human experience into component parts—such as thoughts, behaviors, and drives (when theorizing psychologically) or genes, neurochemicals, and brain parts (when theorizing biologically). They resist reducing complex human difficulties to mental disorder categories that overlook each person's unique experience. Instead, humanistic approaches emphasize the whole person. They also challenge the notion that all human behavior is caused, believing instead that people have free will. See Table 2.7 for humanistic assumptions.

Humanistic perspectives: See people as proactive meaning-makers who strive to develop their full potential; include humanistic, existential, and constructivist perspectives.

Table 2.7 Five Humanistic Assumptions

1. *People as growth-oriented.* Humanistic approaches stress *self-actualization*, the process of developing one's full potential. Existential and constructivist approaches stress how people continually revise the meaning systems they use to guide their lives.

2. *People as meaning-makers.* Humanistic perspectives see people as meaning-makers. People must invent and be responsible for their own meanings.

3. *People as in process.* Humanistic theorists see people as forever changing and growing as they actualize. Existentialists stress *existence over essence.* People change as they make choices. They can't be reduced to static qualities:

   Human existence is irreducible to a set of essential components. That is, even if I could list every one of your essential qualities—for instance, your level of extraversion, your "Intelligence Quotient," the neurochemicals passing through your brain—I would still not be describing *you*, because the actual, concrete *you* that you are is more than all these essential components put together. (M. Cooper, 2003, p. 10)

4. *People as free.* Humanistic and existential theorists believe people have free will. They reject the idea that mental distress is *entirely* caused by internal drives, environmental conditioning, irrational thinking, or biological processes. Constructivists also emphasize human agency, though some say psychological and physical structures both limit and inform human meaning making.

5. *"Psychopathology" as self-inconsistency.* Humanistic-existential theorists see psychological difficulties as arising from a failure to be true to oneself. Humanists explain this in terms of interference with the self-actualizing process, while existentialists focus on people lying to themselves about certain human truths and denying responsibility for their choices. Constructivists say that "psychopathology" results from a failure to revise one's meanings, even when there is a lot of evidence that they are no longer working very well.

Rogers' Person-Centered Therapy

Carl Rogers' (1902–1987) **person-centered therapy** (or *client-centered therapy*) starts from the humanistic assumption that people are born with an *actualizing tendency*, an innate motivation to fulfill their full potential—to be all they can be, which humanists call *self-actualization* (Cain, 2010; Murphy & Joseph, 2016; Rogers, 1951, 1959, 1961). When provided with love, support, and understanding from others, people naturally develop in ways consistent with their actualizing tendency. To help them actualize, people rely on what Rogers called the *organismic valuing process*. Through this process, people seek experiences that enhance their personal growth and avoid those that don't.

In addition to an innate need to actualize our potential, people also have a need for acceptance and love from others—what Rogers called positive regard. There are two ways to obtain positive regard: unconditionally or conditionally. When others provide *unconditional positive regard*, they love us as we are, even when we behave in ways they don't like. This allows us to stay true to our actualizing tendency because there are no conditions that we must meet to maintain others' affection. When your best friend conveys acceptance and approval for you as a person even when you disagree about the next election, that's unconditional positive regard. Unfortunately, sometimes people don't accept us unconditionally. Instead, they provide *conditional positive regard*—loving and supporting us only if we abide by certain conditions. A good example is those teenagers at school who only liked you if you dressed a certain way and listened to certain music. Psychopathology occurs when there is a conflict between our need for positive regard and our need for *congruence* (i.e., *self-consistency*, the need to be true to our actualizing tendency). When positive regard is conditional, people lose touch with their organismic valuing process. They struggle to know whether they are doing something because it is enhancing or because it sustains conditional positive regard. When people behave self-inconsistently for conditional positive regard, they are in a state of psychological *incongruence*.

When it came to therapy, Rogers disliked the medical model. He preferred the term "client" to "patient" because he did not see the people he worked with as ill. His goal was to help clients reconnect with their organismic valuing process and return to a self-actualizing path. He accomplished this by providing clients with three *core conditions for change*: unconditional positive regard, empathy, and genuineness. Unconditional positive regard allows clients to feel safe and be themselves in therapy; providing it means being warm and caring toward clients and accepting them no matter what. Empathy involves understanding clients; it requires therapists to actively listen to what clients say and reflect what is heard back to clients. This ensures that therapists correctly grasp each client's unique experience. Genuineness requires therapists to be self-consistent (i.e., congruent); they can't expect their clients to be genuine if they aren't.

When therapists provide the core conditions, clients reconnect with their actualizing tendency. Person-centered therapy is non-directive in that it assumes that therapists shouldn't tell clients what to talk about or what to do because, quite frankly, they don't know what is right for clients. Instead, therapists simply need to provide the core conditions. When they do, clients will get back in touch with the actualizing tendency and figure things out for themselves.

Person-centered therapy: Rogers' humanistic and non-directive therapy in which therapists provide *core conditions for change* (empathy, genuineness, and unconditional positive regard) to get clients back on a path toward self-actualization.

Lillian

A person-centered therapist working with Lillian would aim to provide her the core conditions necessary for change. When Lillian says that she feels undeserving of a nice boyfriend and feels inept at math, the therapist would endeavor to empathically understand her perspective by nonjudgmentally reflecting her thoughts and feelings back to her to make sure he comprehends them correctly. He would also convey unconditional positive regard by continuing to be kind and caring toward Lillian, even when she expresses negative feelings about herself. Lastly, he would behave genuinely; when Lillian puts herself down, he would let her know that it is difficult for him to hear her talk that way about herself. From a person-centered perspective, a safe and supportive therapeutic environment in which she is listened to and accepted would allow Lillian to rediscover what future directions might be best for her. She would begin reconnecting with her own organismic valuing process and actualizing tendency. Consequently, Lillian might realize that she doesn't want to date Seth anymore. She might also start feeling like she wants to drop math class; she was only taking it because her parents wanted her to.

Existential Therapy

There are numerous **existential psychotherapies**—such as logotherapy, daisenanalysis, American humanistic-existential therapy, and British existential therapy (M. Cooper, 2003). Without delving into the specifics of each, let's review commonalities across these approaches. Existential therapies view people as free to make choices. At the same time, human freedom has its limits. From an existential vantage point, life is inherently meaningless and full of givens we can't control—things like death, suffering, guilt, and anxiety (M. Cooper, 2003). Each of us is thrown into the world at a certain time and place with a unique combination of physical and cultural characteristics over which we have no say. You don't get to choose your family, ethnic background, or hat size! However, how you fashion a life within the constraints of these givens is up to you. Bearing the responsibility of meaningfully creating a life from the lot you are handed constitutes the existential dilemma. Psychological problems develop when people become overwhelmed by the existential anxiety that accompanies this kind of burdensome responsibility. In the words of the famous existential philosopher Jean-Paul Sartre: "Man is condemned to be free: condemned, because he did not create himself, yet nonetheless free, because once cast into the world, he is responsible for everything he does" (Sartre, 1947/2007, p. 29). Because the burden of being responsible for our lives provokes anxiety, we sometimes lie to ourselves and act as if we have no say over our behavior.

> **Seth**
>
> *What might happen if Seth worked with an existential therapist? In discussing the violent outbursts that repeatedly land him in trouble, Seth might claim "I had to punch Jorge because he disrespected me." The existential therapist would likely challenge Seth on whether punching Jorge was something he "had" to do or something he "chose" to do.*

Seth's statement exemplifies *inauthenticity*, the denial of responsibility for one's choices. Seth didn't "have" to punch anyone, but by convincing himself he was forced to behave a certain way by circumstances, he avoids responsibility for his actions. The existential therapist sees psychopathology as a product of inauthentic living: "Inauthenticity is illness, is our living in distorted relation to our true being" (Bugental, 1987, p. 246). By contrast, *authenticity* involves awareness of one's responsibility for creating meaning and living by it. In other words, "authentic living is about being able to make clear and well-informed choices in accordance with the values one recognizes as worth committing oneself to" (van Deurzen, 2012, p. 61). Existential therapy helps people gain awareness of themselves and their experience so they can live more authentic lives.

Constructivist Perspectives

Although sometimes considered a variant of the cognitive perspective, **constructivist perspectives** are included here as humanistic-existential approaches because they emphasize people as active meaning-makers responsible for the meanings they create. There are numerous constructivist perspectives, such as *personal construct theory* (G. A. Kelly, 1955/1991a, 1955/1991b), *radical constructivism* (Glasersfeld, 1984; Maturana & Varela, 1992), and *narrative therapy* (M. White & Epston, 1990). All focus on how people create meaningful ways of understanding themselves, their world, and their relationships, which they then use to guide their lives. From a constructivist perspective, difficulties occur when people mistake their constructed meanings for reality itself and get locked into meanings that no longer work well (Chiari & Nuzzo, 2010; R. A. Neimeyer, 2009; R. A. Neimeyer & Raskin, 2000; Procter & Winter, 2020; Raskin, in press). Constructivist therapy helps people revise their meanings to generate new possibilities.

Narrative therapy is a type of constructivist therapy that emphasizes the stories (or narratives) that we create to account for and understand our experiences (Madigan, 2019; Monk et al., 1997; M. White & Epston, 1990). Although creating meaningful stories is necessary, sometimes our stories limit us and lead to unhappiness. Narrative therapists argue that in the Western world, we tell highly individualistic stories that locate problems inside people. To counter this, narrative therapists use **externalizing the problem**, a technique in which they ask clients to talk about their problems as distinct from themselves rather than as internal defects (Madigan, 2019; Tomm, 1989; M. White & Epston, 1990). In so doing, clients begin to tell a different kind of story about the problem, one in which it is viewed as something separate from them that gets the best of them (rather than a disorder they "have"). When problems are externalized, it allows clients to look for exceptions—times the problem was resisted successfully. This helps clients to replace narratives in which they are disordered or defective with ones where they can overcome the influence of problems.

Seth

Seth lives by the narrative that he was born with a bad temper. He considers himself an inherently angry and explosive person. However, a narrative therapist would challenge this story. She might ask Seth to externalize his temper by talking about it as something distinct from him that sometimes gets the best of him. In doing so, Seth would start to map his temper's influence. He'd learn that his temper often gains sway when others criticize him, which is when he tends to lash out angrily. Seth's therapist would encourage him to recall exceptions, times when his temper didn't get the best of him. Seth might remember several exceptions—times when his temper didn't goad him into getting into altercations with others—and realize that when he surrounds himself with supportive friends, he can resist his temper's invitations to attack those who criticize him. Seth therefore would begin to revise his narrative, shifting it from "I am an inherently temperamental and angry person" to "I am someone able to resist the influence of my temper when I make sure to seek out people to support and care for me during challenging times in my life."

Evaluating Humanistic Perspectives

The following are viewed as strengths of humanistic perspectives:

1. *Emphasis on the whole person as free and responsible.* The humanistic-existential emphasis on human agency can seem highly refreshing compared with more deterministic approaches that see people as ill or as victims of circumstance.
2. *Emphasis on people as unique.* Careful attention to the uniqueness of each person's problems and a disinclination to placing people into diagnostic categories are often seen as strengths of the humanistic-existential viewpoint.
3. *Impact on therapy.* Humanistic approaches have greatly influenced therapy. Their use of face-to-face weekly sessions quickly eclipsed the psychoanalytic practice of daily sessions on the couch. The humanistic emphasis on a supportive and safe therapeutic environment has become a staple of most therapies.

Criticisms of humanistic perspectives include:

1. *Unscientific.* The humanistic emphasis on free will runs counter to scientific determinism. Critics say humanistic-existential perspectives reject traditional scientific inquiry, though humanists counter that alternative human science methods are needed when studying people (Giorgi, 1970).
2. *Inadequate for treating serious disorders.* Some critics see humanistic-existential approaches as fine when working with everyday problems-in-living, but inadequate for conceptualizing and treating serious mental disorders like schizophrenia and bipolar disorder (Cain, 2010).
3. *Too individualistic.* Humanistic perspectives have been critiqued for overemphasizing individualism and inadvertently encouraging self-absorption and ethnocentrism (Cain, 2010). Some complain that an emphasis on fulfilling one's potential reflects the individualistic bias of Western cultures and may be inappropriate when working with clients from communal cultures.

SOCIOCULTURAL PERSPECTIVES

2.13 Introducing Sociocultural Perspectives

Sociocultural perspectives focus on how social and cultural factors influence psychological functioning. They view social, familial, and cultural factors as affecting the development of people's presenting problems. Some sociocultural theorists accept the idea that psychopathology stems from biologically or psychologically based disorders while highlighting cultural variations in how people express symptoms. Other sociocultural theorists go further, arguing against biological and psychological perspectives that emphasize defects inside people (Bassett & Baker, 2015). A pure sociocultural orientation reframes understanding of human suffering almost entirely in social terms.

We discuss three kinds of sociocultural perspectives: multicultural/social justice perspectives, consumer/service user perspectives, and systems perspectives. Multicultural and social justice perspectives argue that mental distress is the product of culture and social oppression, not biological disease. Adherents of such perspectives believe that intervening at the societal level, rather than sticking to interventions at the individual level, is key (Aldarondo, 2007; R. C.-Y. Chung & Bemak, 2012; Prilleltensky et al., 2007). From a somewhat different vantage point, service user perspectives focus on the experiences of those receiving services for mental distress. They highlight how society and health professionals treat people diagnosed with mental disorders. Finally, systems perspectives shift from working with individuals to working with "systems" (i.e., groups, communities, and families). They differ from psychological perspectives by locating pathology in systems, not individuals.

Importantly, sociocultural theorists move beyond what they see as the behaviorists' narrow focus on environmental conditioning and instead stress broader influences on mental distress like social norms, cultural customs, family dynamics, economic disparities, racism, sexism, and social oppression. Sociocultural approaches often emphasize community mental healthcare, which provides patients with support, guidance, and in some cases housing. Common sociocultural perspective assumptions are in Table 2.8.

2.14 Multicultural and Social Justice Perspectives

Multicultural Perspectives

Multicultural perspectives: Hold that what is considered psychopathology is often a function of culture and that clinicians must be aware of how cultural differences impact their work with clients.

Multicultural perspectives hold that culture is critical in shaping understandings of psychopathology and mental distress. *Culture* can be defined as the values, beliefs, and practices of any ethnic or cultural group (American Psychological Association, 2017a; López & Guarnaccia, 2020). Multicultural perspectives maintain that human behavior and our judgments about it take place within a cultural context influenced by communal values. Therefore, "psychopathology should be examined within the context of culturally embedded worldviews, norms, and practices"

Table 2.8 Five Sociocultural Assumptions

1. *Mental distress is primarily explainable in familial and social terms.* It is caused by family dynamics, cultural influences, and social factors such as racism, sexism, and economic inequality.
2. *What we call mental disorders are social, cultural, and family problems.* Many of the problems we attribute to mental disorder are better understood as social problems.
3. *Changing family dynamics or social systems is the key to reducing emotional suffering.* Clinicians need to rely less on adjusting people to their situations and more on helping them to address oppressive family dynamics and social conditions.
4. *Move beyond working with individuals.* Family systems therapists work with families rather than individuals because they see mental distress as emerging from recurrent family patterns, not individual pathology. Social justice therapists view social action as a supplement to individual therapy.
5. *Therapists should be advocates for social change.* A social justice perspective maintains that working with individual clients is insufficient. Advocating for social change is also essential.

(Krigbaum, 2013, p. 234). Multicultural perspective clinicians emphasize cultural differences that impact client behavior and clinician understanding of it (Causadias, 2013; Fields, 2010; Krigbaum, 2013; López & Guarnaccia, 2020). They resist evaluating patients from minority cultures using research and interventions of the dominant culture. That is, they "advocate that mental health providers avoid the tendency to infer diagnoses and psychopathology based on a unilateral cultural understanding or use of psychometric assessments normed outside of the clients'/patients' culture" because doing so "can distort the clinical facts" and risk finding "too much or too little psychopathology" (Krigbaum, 2013, p. 236).

Thus, multicultural perspectives often view mental disorders not as culturally universal (true across times and cultures), but as culture-bound (true within a given historical time and context) (Bassett & Baker, 2015). *Culture-bound syndromes* reflect shared cultural values (Isaac, 2013). For example, rather than seeing "dependent personality disorder" (see Chapter 12) as a universal affliction, multicultural theorists reframe it as reflecting Western culture's view that people should be autonomous and independent. In a different historical and cultural context, the same behavior might not be pathologized. Hence, a dependent personality diagnosis—in being tied to a specific set of social norms and values—can be viewed as culture-bound.

As noted, not all multicultural theorists reframe psychopathology entirely in social terms. Some see psychopathology as biologically and psychologically based but influenced by social factors (Bassett & Baker, 2015; López & Guarnaccia, 2020). These theorists are interested in cross-cultural data that looks at variations in incidence and prevalence of disorders in different countries and cultures, as well as in distinctive ways of effectively remediating mental disorders across cultural contexts (López & Guarnaccia, 2020). Other multicultural theorists endorse a more fully social view, reframing mental disorders as understandable distress with cultural and social origins (Kinderman, 2014a, 2017). Such theorists often view ideas about psychopathology and mental distress as socially constructed. A *social construction* is any socially shared way of defining, talking about, and understanding something that influences how people experience it (Burr, 2015; Gergen, 2015). From a social constructionist viewpoint, mental disorders are not universal things but socially invented and context-dependent ways of talking about people (Gergen & McNamee, 2000; Maddux et al., 2020; C. M. Stanley & Raskin, 2002). As such, behavior socially understood to be disordered in one culture may not even raise eyebrows in another.

Social Justice Perspectives

Social justice perspectives view mental distress as the product of social inequalities. They maintain that presenting problems aren't caused by disorders inside people but are attributable instead to economic inequality, racism, sexism, and other forms of social oppression (Aldarondo, 2007; R. C.-Y. Chung & Bemak, 2012). Many social justice perspectives adopt a *critical psychology* position that challenges Western definitions of mental health, seeing them as reflecting Eurocentric biases that marginalize Indigenous groups and people of color (A. J. Joseph, 2015; Sundararajan et al., 2013). These perspectives seek "alternatives to the Western traditional independent and autonomous model of the self" that has dominated psychology and related disciplines, "resulting in context-free explanations of behavior on the basis of the dispositions, traits, characteristics, and styles of the individual" (Sundararajan et al., 2013, p. 71). They wish to raise awareness of how Western cultural conceptions of "mental health" reflect taken-for-granted discourses that have had disastrous consequences when imposed on marginalized people, serving as mechanisms of "dominance, oppression, and exploitation" (A. J. Joseph, 2015, p. 1038). From a social justice perspective:

Structural features of society are seen as systematically marginalising and disempowering some people and not others; and psychology itself is viewed as part of an ideological dimension which shapes how we think and feel about ourselves. Importantly, this includes what is regarded as acceptable or deviant behaviour, such as what is seen as mental "ill health." In fact, the very notion of psychological experience as indicative of a state of "health" is a pervasive and questionable assumption. (McClelland, 2014, p. 121)

For instance, social justice perspectives view schizophrenia and other psychotic experiences as primarily caused by social factors such as inequality, poverty, racism, and economic disadvantage

Social justice perspectives: View mental distress as the product of social inequality; aim to reduce mental distress by eliminating oppressive social conditions.

(British Psychological Society, 2017a). Despite acknowledging that genetics, neurochemistry, and brain structure play roles, they point to evidence that people who hear voices often have been sexually abused in childhood. They also cite research that being poor and living in densely populated urban areas constitute major risk factors for psychosis. Therapy involves helping people gain insight into how their psychotic symptoms are meaningful responses to extremely difficult and stressful social circumstances—and then altering those circumstances through social reform (British Psychological Society, 2017a).

Feminist therapy is an excellent example of a social justice perspective. Feminist therapy holds that *patriarchy* (the structuring of society so that men are in charge) is the root cause of many problems labeled as mental disorders. In a feminist conception, individuals aren't sick; society is. A famous phrase used to exemplify the feminist stance is that "the personal is political" (Hanisch, 1970/2006), meaning that individual problems always occur in a social context. Instead of viewing people as "having" mental illnesses that are primarily attributed to individual psychology and biology, feminist and other social justice therapists view people as reacting in understandable ways to social injustices such as trauma, socioeconomic disadvantage, and sexism. Therapy is reconceptualized from a treatment that fixes disturbed individuals to a collaborative relationship between therapist and client, one in which both work for social reform:

The very word "therapy" is obviously a misnomer if carried to its logical conclusion. Therapy assumes that someone is sick and that there is a cure, e.g., a personal solution. I am greatly offended that I or any other woman is thought to need therapy in the first place. Women are messed over, not messed up! We need to change the objective conditions, not adjust to them. Therapy is adjusting to your bad personal alternative. (Hanisch, 1970/2006, para. 2)

One of the impediments to social reform, according to feminist and other social justice therapists, is that therapy clients often live in a state of false consciousness. When living in such a state, oppressed people fail "to recognize their own economic and political interests by internalizing the values of their oppressors" (K. M. Perkins & Cross, 2014, p. 98).

Lillian

Lillian has internalized the unfair idea that as a female she must defer to men in positions of power. A social justice view maintains that holding this attitude keeps Lillian oppressed. Similarly, Seth opposes increased government taxation even though it would fund his university education. From a social justice vantage point, he has internalized an anti-tax perspective that is false and not in his own best economic interests.

Social justice therapies focus on *consciousness-raising*, which involves educating clients about racism, sexism, and other economic and social inequalities that they have unwittingly accepted and which lead to emotional distress (L. A. Goodman et al., 2004; Morrow et al., 2006; Toporek & Williams, 2006). Clients are encouraged to challenge the status quo and work toward a more just world, often with their therapists' assistance. Social justice therapists step outside the therapy room and into the social world where they actively advocate for their clients because, from their perspective, traditional therapies too often adjust clients to oppressive social conditions rather than helping them fight for a more just society (Prilleltensky et al., 2007). From a social justice orientation, the most direct way to alleviate human suffering is not to change people but to change society.

Lillian

Lillian grew up in a poor family. Her parents held very traditional ideas about the role of women in a family. If she were to see a therapist adopting a social justice perspective, the therapist might employ consciousness-raising by encouraging Lillian to examine social and cultural factors that have given rise to her current difficulties—specifically the detrimental effects of having been born into a male-dominated society and having been raised in a socioeconomically poor family

Feminist therapy:
Holds that patriarchy (the structuring of society so that men are in charge) is the root cause of many problems labeled as mental disorders; sees therapy as a collaborative relationship between therapist and client, one in which both work for social reform.

that espoused traditional gender roles. As her consciousness is raised regarding ways she's been oppressed, Lillian might begin to stand up for herself more as she starts to question the attitudes she was taught about male and female roles by her parents and by the wider culture. She might begin to view her deference to Seth as due to her having internalized traditional gender roles. As therapy progresses, she might eventually break up with Seth. Her therapist would potentially encourage Lillian to become politically involved. Lillian might do so and gain further self-confidence as she fights for economic justice and equal treatment for women.

2.15 Service User Perspectives

Service user perspectives focus on "what it is like to be on the receiving end of the mental health system" (P. Campbell, 2013, p. 141). In considering service user perspectives, we must distinguish the consumer movement from the service user/survivor movement. Much of the **consumer movement** accepts psychiatric views of mental disorder and finds traditional treatments helpful (Adame, 2014; Forbes & Sashidharan, 1997; Hölling, 2001). The movement's activism is "largely directed toward reducing the stigma of mental illness, reform of policy and practices, and generating more treatment choices within the mental health field" (Adame, 2014, p. 458). *Stigma* can be defined as society's negative and often hostile responses to people carrying certain marks or labels, in this case those related to mental disorder (Corrigan & Kleinlein, 2005). The consumer movement's goal is to better understand the needs and experiences of those stigmatized by mental disorders, thereby allowing professionals and society to deal with them more compassionately and effectively. The consumer movement aims to improve traditional psychiatric practice by improving social attitudes and practices. Two of the most well-known consumer groups are the National Alliance for the Mentally Ill (NAMI) in the United States and the Mental Health Foundation in the United Kingdom.

By contrast, the **service user/survivor movement** (also called the *psychiatric survivor movement*) rejects mainstream psychiatric perspectives, contending that many interventions—especially prescription drugs and involuntary treatments—are inhumane, abusive, and fail to consider the desires of the people forced to endure them (Bassman, 2001; P. Campbell, 2013; Crossley, 2004; Oaks, 2006). Those who identify as psychiatric survivors argue that the problems identified by psychiatry as mental disorders are better viewed as psychosocially caused problems in living. Therefore, they reject medical model psychiatric perspectives. Consider the words of Matthew, a psychiatric survivor who spurned his diagnosis and the mental health system that assigned it to him:

It was just like they had all bought into this pathologizing model of mental illness. And they tried to inculcate you with that. And you were made to feel as if you were irreparably damaged inside your brain. And that you couldn't trust yourself anymore because you might become ill again. That was the message. And it was extremely *damaging. (Adame, 2014, p. 460)*

Psychiatric survivor groups openly defy psychiatric authority. For example, the Hearing Voices Network (HVN) advances a psychosocial (rather than medical) view of auditory hallucinations. Present in more than twenty countries, HVN advocates for "an alternative approach to coping with emotional distress that is empowering and useful to people, and does not start from the assumption that they have a chronic illness" (Hearing Voices Network USA, n.d., para. 1). Another survivor group, MindFreedom International, fights for people labeled with psychiatric disabilities "who have experienced human rights violations in the mental health system" (MindFreedom International, n.d., para. 6). Not surprisingly, the psychiatric survivor movement and professional psychiatry have an uneasy relationship. According to critics of the survivor movement, "organized psychiatry has found it difficult to have a constructive dialogue with" survivor groups because they see such groups as opposing psychiatry and spreading "disinformation on the use of involuntary commitment, electroconvulsive therapy, stimulants and antidepressants among children, and neuroleptics among adult" (Rissmiller & Rissmiller, 2006, p. 866). However, survivor groups see things differently, contending that critics unfairly dismiss their critiques of psychiatric diagnosis and treatment (Oaks, 2006).

Service user perspectives: Focus on the experience and concerns of people receiving psychiatric services.

Consumer movement: Movement of consumers of psychiatric services that accepts psychiatric views of mental disorder and often finds traditional treatments helpful; largely directed toward reducing stigma and increasing access to services.

Service user/survivor movement: Rejects mainstream psychiatric perspectives, contending that many interventions—especially prescription drugs and involuntary treatments—are often inhumane and abusive; also called the *psychiatric survivor movement.*

2.16 Systems Perspectives

Systems perspectives look at how individuals are influenced by and function within "systems" of relationships. What constitutes a *system* varies, ranging "from small groups such as the family to the largest, called civilization" (von Bertalanffy, 1969, p. 44). The main idea is that individuals combine into systems (such as families) that establish recurring patterns. The functioning of individuals therefore reflects the broader system of relationships in which they exist (Fife, 2020). Because "systems are integrated wholes whose properties cannot be reduced to those of smaller units," systems theories locate dysfunction not in individuals but in patterns of relationships (G. Mitchell, 2015, para. 4).

One system of interest to mental health professionals is the family. *Family systems therapy* looks at couple and family dynamics in understanding and remediating mental distress. There are many different family systems theories, but all place recurring family patterns front and center. From a family systems viewpoint, problems exist within a family's dynamics, not within its individual members (Dallos & Stedmon, 2014). The *identified patient* (the family member outwardly displaying symptoms) bears the burden of "carrying" the family's pathology. Instead of seeing individual family members as disordered, the family itself is diagnosed as dysfunctional in perpetuating problematic relationship patterns. Let's examine how two family systems approaches shift pathology from person to family.

Minuchin's Structural Family Therapy

Salvador Minuchin's (1921–2017) **structural family therapy** focuses on unspoken family rules that influence family members' behaviors (Minuchin, 1974). Structural family therapists emphasize problems with *boundaries* between members—for instance, in *enmeshed families* the boundaries between members are blurred. Dysfunctional families also often form *coalitions*, in which some members are aligned with one another against other members. This leads to problematic *power hierarchies* in which some coalitions dominate others in detrimental ways. The key becomes establishing appropriate boundaries, addressing unspoken rules, and helping the family to communicate better so it can more flexibly adapt to external demands.

Bowen's Multigenerational Family Therapy

Murray Bowen's (1913–1990) **multigenerational family therapy** focuses on the *multigenerational transmission process*, in which families pass down dysfunctional patterns from

---

Systems perspectives: Look at how individuals are influenced by and function within "systems" of relationships.

Structural family therapy: Minuchin's family therapy, which emphasizes how the structure of a family system—including its rules, boundaries, coalitions, and power hierarchies—contributes to its dysfunction.

Multigenerational family therapy: Bowen's approach to family therapy, which stresses how families pass dysfunctional patterns down across generations.

Photo 2.6 HBO's show *Succession* is a good example of a dysfunctional family dynamic, rife with conflict and problematic family patterns.
LANDMARK MEDIA/Alamy Stock Photo.

generation to generation (M. Bowen, 1978). Disturbed families engage in problematic behaviors such as *triangulation*, in which two family members deal with conflict between them by pulling a third family member into the mix. The inevitable "two versus one" interaction creates further family conflict. *Emotional cutoff* is another hallmark of dysfunctional families. It occurs when family members place emotional or physical distance between one another to avoid conflict. Bowen maintained that to overcome family dysfunction, *differentiation* must occur. That is, family members must distinguish their own thoughts and feelings from those of others in the family so that they can resist and eliminate problematic family patterns.

Seth

Seth's parents often aligned against Seth and his younger brother. This familial power hierarchy made it rare for Seth and his brother to have their feelings and opinions listened to. Seth's brother spent a lot of time during childhood with his friends and away from the family. He eventually moved to Nevada to get away from his controlling parents—an example of emotional cutoff. When it came to Seth, his parents identified him as the family "troublemaker" with an "explosive temper." Thus, Seth became the identified patient even though his parents often displayed angry outbursts too, as did Seth's grandparents before them. From a family systems perspective, Seth's angry behavior reflects longstanding family patterns passed down via a multigenerational transmission process. Were Seth to undergo family systems therapy, he might start to differentiate his own thoughts and feelings from those of his parents. If effective, he'd begin thinking and behaving in new ways less influenced by past family patterns.

2.17 Evaluating Sociocultural Perspectives

Strengths of sociocultural perspectives include:

1. *Social, cultural, and familial factors highlighted.* With its focus on the mental processes of the individual, psychology has often overlooked social, cultural, and family influences. Sociocultural perspectives counter this.
2. *Cultural differences accounted for.* Social justice perspectives emerged from the multicultural psychology movement, which emphasizes attending to how cultural assumptions play a strong role in what kinds of issues cause mental distress and how people express that distress.
3. *Social change encouraged by attributing human suffering to oppressive social systems rather than blaming individuals.* Social justice perspectives avoid blaming individuals for their problems. Instead, they see family patterns, cultural norms, and unfair social conditions as the things that must be changed to alleviate mental distress.
4. *The experience of people diagnosed with mental disorders is highlighted.* Consumer and service user/survivor approaches encourage us to pay attention to the voices of those experiencing psychological distress.

Noted weaknesses of sociocultural perspectives include:

1. *Difficulty establishing causal connection between mental distress and social factors.* Those who see mental disorders as individual afflictions contend that social factors like poverty and racism are correlated with emotional suffering, but whether they cause such suffering remains unclear. Critics see social and cultural factors as exacerbating mental disorders but not as their primary cause.
2. *Familial and social conditions do not always produce mental distress.* Two different people facing the same oppressive familial and social conditions may not both experience mental distress. Sociocultural perspectives cannot account for this. Biological critics argue that sociocultural factors exacerbate or trigger individual disorders but do not entirely explain them.
3. *Tied to a political agenda.* Critics argue that social justice perspectives impose a left-wing political ideology on clients by objecting to the status quo of Western capitalism and demanding that

clients and therapists adopt progressive positions on fair trade, unions, prison reform, education reform, environmental issues, and the minimum wage (S. Johnson, 2001; Raskin, 2014; S. D. Smith et al., 2009).

4. *Service user perspectives are too extreme or not extreme enough.* Psychiatric survivor groups are often considered extreme in their views. On the other hand, consumer groups may be too wedded to traditional medical model views of mental illness and, consequently, fail to see how traditional approaches can have damaging consequences for patients.

CLOSING THOUGHTS

2.18 So Many Perspectives!

Each perspective makes different assumptions about mental distress, its origins, and what to do about it. However, clinicians often integrate perspectives in practice. This makes sense. Consider psychological and biological perspectives. Early childhood experiences, failure to self-actualize, irrational thinking, and environmental conditioning influence a person's biology—and vice versa! That is, biological and psychological factors mutually influence one another, making biological and psychological perspectives incomplete on their own. The same is true of psychological and sociocultural perspectives. Sociocultural ideas about what it means to be a person—highly individualized in the Western world (where most of this book's ideas originate)—affect the kinds of psychological theories that make sense to us. Freud, Skinner, Beck, Rogers, and most of the other theorists in this chapter developed their theories within a Western social context—and in turn have had an unmistakable impact on it. Lastly, biological and sociocultural perspectives are also interconnected. Researchers increasingly combine them in studying the relationship between social circumstances and physical health. They find that people under socially stressful circumstances are at higher risk for physical illness. Racism, socioeconomic and educational disadvantage, and undergoing military training all correlate with both physical illness and psychological distress (Grzywacz et al., 2004; Paradies et al., 2015; N. B. Schmidt & Lerew, 1998; D. R. Williams et al., 1997). Biological and social factors influence one another when it comes to mental distress.

The point is that taking all perspectives into account contributes to an integrative understanding of presenting problems. However, this does not reconcile their contradictory assumptions. Sure, early childhood experiences influence brain development, but in most respects psychodynamic and biological perspectives remain at odds. Yes, stress affects emotional well-being and physical health, but this doesn't change the fact that—at their core—biological and sociocultural perspectives hold fundamentally different views about mental distress. Your challenge is to balance understanding each perspective on its own while appreciating efforts to integrate them. To help you with this task, we close with a "Controversial Question" feature that asks how (or whether!) different theories should be combined in clinical practice.

Controversial Question: Is Theoretical Integration a Good Idea?

As seen in this chapter, there are many compelling theories of psychopathology and mental distress. You may find it hard to choose among them. You might even ask, "Can't I simply combine the best elements of each theory as I see fit?" Asking such a question means you've stumbled into an ongoing and complex debate that has plagued the psychotherapy field—namely, whether theoretical integration is a good idea.

What Is Psychotherapy Integration?

Numerous definitions of *psychotherapy integration* have been offered. In the broadest sense, integrating different psychotherapy approaches involves "ongoing rapprochement, convergence, and complementarity not only at the conceptual level but also at the clinical and empirical level" (Fernández-Álvarez et al., 2016, p. 820). That's a fancy way of saying that links among different theories are identified and used together to develop effective therapy interventions. There are many reasons why integration is a contentious topic. Below we briefly identify two of them.

How Important Are Common Factors?

One of the more well-known integrationist positions is the *common factors* perspective. Common factor advocates argue that all effective therapies share certain features—such as a supportive and caring client–therapist relationship; they contend that these "common factors" are much more important in predicting therapy outcomes than specific interventions (Wampold & Imel, 2015). From a common factors standpoint, identifying what all effective therapies share is key to theoretical integration. The power of common factors is compelling—and consistent with humanistic therapies such as Carl Rogers' person-centered approach, which holds that core conditions are all that is necessary and sufficient for transformative change. However, critics of the common factors approach argue that it overlooks differences in the kinds of problems people bring to therapy. To these critics, specific interventions must be tailored to specific presenting problems (T. B. Baker et al., 2008). Many of the less relationally oriented therapies (such as CBT) hew toward the view that different clinical strategies—organized into empirically supported treatments (ESTs) consisting of a concrete series of standardized steps—must be devised depending on the presenting problem at hand (for more on ESTs, revisit Chapter 1). Debate over whether psychotherapy effectiveness studies best support common factors or ESTs continues to rage within the field (T. B. Baker et al., 2008).

Does Integrating Theories Lead to a Theoretical Mess?

Even if there are common factors that cut across all effective therapies, when we combine different theories rooted in different assumptions, do we risk producing theoretical muddle? Without attention to the theoretical challenges integration produces, some critics think so. Such critics argue that *technical eclecticism* (combining the use of whatever techniques are shown to work) results in therapist confusion (Fernández-Álvarez et al., 2016). Without a clear theoretical base to guide decision-making, how does the technically eclectic therapist know what counts as a good outcome? To these critics, theoretical integration must be done carefully; when different ideas from different therapies are used together, it is necessary to think through the implications of combining them (Fernández-Álvarez et al., 2016). Along these lines, advocates of *assimilative integration* argue that when therapists operating from one theoretical perspective incorporate a technique from another theoretical perspective, they must be careful to think about how the theory they are using and the theory they are coopting a technique from are both changed (Messer, 2001). However, to the technically eclectic therapist, the only thing one needs worry about is whether a technique works in practice.

Critical Thinking Questions

1. What risks and benefits do you see in psychotherapy integration?
2. Do you believe common factors that cut across all therapies are the most important in therapy outcomes? Or are specific ESTs necessary to address different problems? If unsure, what evidence would you need to seek out to answer these questions?
3. Do you prefer technical eclecticism or assimilative integration? Why?

CHAPTER SUMMARY

Overview

- Perspectives provide frameworks for understanding presenting problems. Biological, psychological, and sociocultural perspectives each stress different causes of mental distress.

Biological Perspectives

- *Brain chemistry perspectives* stress how brain chemistry influences cognition, emotion, and behavior. In the brain, neurons communicate electrically and chemically; chemical transmission involves *neurotransmitters*. Prescription drugs for mental distress affect neurotransmitters.
- *Brain structure and function perspectives* focus on how different parts of the brain influence psychopathology.
- *Genetic perspectives* emphasize the importance of genetic inheritance in understanding psychopathology; the *heritability* of mental disorders concerns the extent to which they are attributable to genetic and environmental factors.
- *Evolutionary perspectives* use Darwin's theory to explain how different presenting problems evolved and at one time might have been adaptive.
- *Immune system perspectives* focus on how people's immune systems respond to prolonged stress and explore the impact of physical ill health on emotional well-being.

Psychological Perspectives

- Psychological perspectives focus on thoughts, feelings, and behavior in understanding mental distress.
- *Psychodynamic perspectives*, such as *object relations therapy* and *time-limited dynamic psychotherapy* (*TLDP*), derive from Sigmund Freud's original *psychoanalytic* theory.
- *Behavioral perspectives* view presenting problems not as dysfunctions inside people, but as conditioned behaviors.
- *Cognitive perspectives* focus on thoughts and beliefs. Associated therapies alleviate mental distress by correcting irrational thinking.
- *Cognitive-behavioral perspectives* (*CBT*) combine behavioral and cognitive theories.
- *Humanistic perspectives* stress self-actualization, meaning, and the narratives people construct. They challenge the medical model.

Sociocultural Perspectives

- Sociocultural perspectives emphasize social and cultural factors in mental distress.
- *Multicultural perspectives* see cultural influences as shaping understandings of mental distress.
- *Social justice perspectives* view mental distress as originating in social inequality and oppression, not individual dysfunction. *Feminist therapy* is an example.
- *Service user perspectives* focus on the experience of mental distress and what it is like to receive a mental disorder diagnosis or use mental health services.

Closing Thoughts

- Many people combine perspectives but doing so does not necessarily reconcile their fundamentally different assumptions.

NEW VOCABULARY

1. ABCDE model
2. Action potential
3. Behavioral perspectives
4. Brain chemistry perspectives
5. Brain structure and function perspectives
6. Classical conditioning
7. Cognitive distortions
8. Cognitive perspectives
9. Cognitive therapy
10. Cognitive-behavioral therapy (CBT)
11. Constructivist perspectives
12. Consumer movement
13. Defense mechanisms
14. Dopamine
15. Ego
16. Evolutionary perspectives
17. Existential psychotherapies
18. Exposure therapies
19. Externalizing the problem
20. Extinction
21. Feminist therapy
22. Gamma-aminobutyric acid (GABA)
23. Genetic perspectives
24. Germ theories
25. Glutamate
26. Heritability
27. Humanistic perspectives
28. Id
29. Immune system perspectives
30. Multicultural perspectives
31. Multigenerational family therapy
32. Narrative therapy
33. Neurotransmitters
34. Norepinephrine
35. Object relations therapy
36. Operant conditioning
37. Person-centered therapy
38. Psychoanalysis
39. Psychodynamic perspectives
40. Psychosexual stages
41. Punishment
42. Rational emotive behavior therapy (REBT)
43. Reinforcement
44. Repression
45. Serotonin
46. Service user perspectives
47. Service user/survivor movement
48. Social justice perspectives
49. Social learning theory
50. Structural family therapy
51. Superego
52. Systems perspectives
53. Time-limited dynamic psychotherapy (TLDP)

DIAGNOSIS, FORMULATION, AND ASSESSMENT

Photo 3.1
Finn/Unsplash.

OVERVIEW

3.1 Getting Started: Defining Diagnosis

Case Examples

Jill

Jill is a 20-year-old student who arrives in therapy feeling anxious and lacking the motivation to complete her schoolwork. She is studying medicine, something her parents always wanted her to do. However, she complains that she cannot focus on her work and regularly feels fidgety and short-tempered. In addition, she reports difficulty sleeping, daily stomachaches, and occasional shortness of breath. Growing up, Jill danced ballet. However, she gave up dancing because her parents were concerned that it interfered with her medical studies. Jill appears touchy and tense during her first session, as well as a bit sad and helpless over her situation.

Photo 3.2
Yaroslav Shuraev/Pexels.

Perspectives on Diagnosis

Before we can assist someone like Jill, we need to evaluate the situation and identify what the problem is. In a nutshell, this is what diagnosis, formulation, and assessment are about. The challenge for students is that mental health professionals hold contrasting opinions about them and, consequently, go about them in a variety of ways. This chapter introduces some of the main approaches to diagnosis, formulation, and assessment.

The word "diagnosis" came into modern use in the late seventeenth century. It is a Latin application of the ancient Greek words *dia* ("through") and *gignoskein* ("to know"). In modern phrasing, it simply means "to know thoroughly" or to "discern or distinguish" (Online Etymology Dictionary, n.d.). What confuses students is that some mental health professionals adopt a definition that defines **diagnosis** as a medical procedure for determining the "nature and circumstances of a diseased condition" (Dictionary.com, n.d.-b). However, others opt for a non-medical definition, viewing diagnosis as merely seeking "the cause or nature of a problem or situation" (Dictionary.com, n.d.-b). This means the term "diagnosis" can be (and often is!) used in a variety of ways.

> **Diagnosis:** In medical terms, a procedure for determining the nature and circumstances of a diseased condition; in psychological and social terms, seeking the cause or nature of a problem or situation.

Jill

If we think of diagnosis in medical terms, we might diagnose Jill as suffering from an underlying mental disorder such as generalized anxiety disorder. If we think about diagnosis in psychological terms, we might diagnose Jill as failing to self-actualize or as engaging in overly negative and irrational thinking. Finally, if we think in sociocultural terms, we shift away from diagnosing the problem as something medically or psychologically wrong inside Jill. Instead, we might diagnose her difficulties as due to deficits in her surroundings, such as insufficient social support to succeed in her studies. All three "diagnoses" posit a cause of Jill's presenting problem but in very different terms (as mental disorder, illogical thinking, or lack of social support).

Different approaches to diagnosis are found in competing diagnostic *nomenclatures*—a term referring to any system of names used in a field of study (Merriam-Webster Dictionary, n.d.). We now turn to some of the more influential ones.

DIAGNOSTIC PERSPECTIVES: DSM AND ICD

3.2 DSM and ICD

The ***Diagnostic and Statistical Manual of Mental Disorders*** (**DSM**) and the mental, behavioral, and neurodevelopmental disorders section of the ***International Classification of Diseases*** (**ICD**) are the two most prevalent psychopathology diagnostic systems. They are generally referred to as forms of psychiatric diagnosis because even though every kind of mental health practitioner uses them, primarily psychiatrists develop them. Given that psychiatrists are medical doctors, it should come as no surprise that both DSM and ICD use a medical model in which clusters of symptoms are organized into distinct *syndromes* consisting of *symptoms* (presenting complaints) and *signs* (physical changes) (Kawa & Giordano, 2012; Paris, 2015). In this respect, they utilize *categorical diagnosis*, where similar patterns of symptoms and signs are grouped into categories and distinguished as distinct disorders.

By grouping observable symptoms and signs into categories, DSM and ICD also exemplify *descriptive psychopathology*, in which diagnoses are made using descriptions of how people think, feel, and act rather than measures of underlying *etiology* (a medical term for "cause") (Zachar, 2009). Why are DSM and ICD diagnoses merely descriptive when the medical model assumes disorders reflect dysfunctions (i.e., psychopathology) inside people? Because, despite all the research being done, we still don't know the etiology of DSM and ICD disorders. We therefore lack the ability to make diagnoses based on underlying causes (A. V. Horwitz, 2021; Paris, 2015). Descriptive psychopathology is currently the best we can do!

DSM and ICD are the diagnostic systems most often employed in clinical practice throughout the world. In the United States, DSM remains dominant, though ICD has made inroads (Goodheart, 2014). In the United States these manuals play a central role in getting mental health services covered by health insurance (Goodheart, 2014). Given their dominance in practice, it is important to understand how DSM and ICD are used to conceptualize and diagnose disorders.

Who Writes Them?
ICD

ICD is an international classification system authored by the World Health Organization (WHO), which is part of the United Nations (G. M. Reed, 2010). Its scope is broader than mental health. ICD catalogs all internationally recognized "diseases, disorders, injuries, and related health problems" (Goodheart, 2014, p. 13). Currently, 194 WHO member countries (https://www.who.int/countries/) have signed an international treaty that commits them to using ICD's coding system for reporting health information (Goodheart, 2014; G. M. Reed, 2010; M. C. Roberts & Evans, 2013). This makes ICD "the clinical and research standard for the world, for both physical and mental disorders" (Goodheart, 2014, p. 13; M. C. Roberts & Evans, 2013). Mental health professionals focus mainly on one section of ICD: the classification of mental, behavioral, and neurodevelopmental disorders (World Health Organization, 1992, 2022a).

DSM

While ICD is developed internationally under the auspices of the U.N.'s World Health Organization, DSM is a purely American product. Nevertheless, some consider DSM (rather than ICD) the global standard for research and practice (Paris, 2015). It is written and published by the American Psychiatric Association, the professional organization of American psychiatry. In other words, psychiatrists (not psychologists) author it. Psychologists and other mental health professionals use it, but psychiatrists publish it, making DSM the official diagnostic system of American psychiatry—a medical specialty with a medical identity (Kawa & Giordano, 2012). Importantly, whereas ICD is free and can be accessed online, DSM must be purchased. DSM-5-TR currently sells for between $170 and $220 in the United States, £126 and £163 in the UK, and $223 and $288 in Canada (depending on whether you opt for paperback or hardcover). An abridged desk reference and an app for phones and tablets sell for less.

Diagnostic and Statistical Manual of Mental Disorders (DSM): Diagnostic manual of the American Psychiatric Association.

International Classification of Diseases (ICD): Diagnostic manual of the World Health Organization.

Historical Perspectives on ICD and DSM
ICD

ICD's origins predate those of the WHO. In 1893, the International Statistical Institute developed the first edition of the *International List of Causes of Death*. This manual went through numerous revisions. When the WHO was established in 1948, it was charged with overseeing the manual, its name now changed to the *International Classification of Diseases, Injuries, and Causes of Death*. That year, ICD-6 was published, and it included a section on mental disorders—although technically mental disorders first appeared in ICD-5 even though there wasn't a separate section for them (Halter et al., 2013). There have been six versions of ICD since the WHO began overseeing it, and these days its name has been shortened to the simpler *International Classification of Diseases*. ICD-11 was approved in May 2019 and took effect January 1, 2022 (World Health Organization, 2018, 2019).

DSM

Modern DSM diagnosis is heavily influenced by the work of the late nineteenth-century German psychiatrist Emil Kraepelin (1856–1926), who was among the first to catalog psychological disorders (Decker, 2013; Halter et al., 2013). Kraepelin examined groups of symptoms and organized them into categories of disorder in the hope that eventually their causes would be uncovered (Decker, 2013; Kirk & Kutchins, 1992).

In the United States, the first efforts at diagnostic classification were devised to count "abnormal" people for the census (Halter et al., 2013; Kawa & Giordano, 2012; Kirk & Kutchins, 1992). For the 1840 census, there was only one category (idiocy), which included people considered insane. By 1880, the census contained seven categories: mania, melancholia, paresis, monomania, dementia, epilepsy, and dipsomania (Kirk & Kutchins, 1992). The census was no longer the focus in 1918 when the American Medico-Psychological Association (a precursor to today's American Psychiatric Association) developed its *Statistical Manual for the Use of Institutions for the Insane*, which included twenty-two diagnostic categories. By 1942, this manual—a forerunner of DSM—had gone through ten different editions (Kawa & Giordano, 2012; Kirk & Kutchins, 1992). Because it focused on serious disorders found mostly in inpatient settings, its utility in addressing concerns more typical of the general population was limited. Therefore, during the Second World War, the U.S. Army and Surgeon General developed *Medical 203*, a classification system that included less acute problems common in soldiers and veterans. Medical 203 is considered the immediate predecessor to DSM (Halter et al., 2013; A. V. Horwitz, 2021).

The American Psychiatric Association published DSM-I, with 106 categories, in 1952; the 182-category DSM-II appeared in 1968 (Decker, 2013). Neither was especially influential (Shorter, 2013). Both were seen as having a psychoanalytic bent (A. V. Horwitz, 2021). It was DSM-III in 1980 that really changed psychiatric diagnosis (Decker, 2013; A. V. Horwitz, 2021; Kawa & Giordano, 2012; Kirk & Kutchins, 1992; Paris, 2015). Heralded as a triumph of science over ideology, DSM-III tried to rely on scientific data more than previous editions to determine what belonged in the manual (Kawa & Giordano, 2012). Its 265 categories added two features now essential to DSM diagnosis: diagnostic criteria and diagnostic codes (both discussed below). DSM-III-R ("R" for "revised"), with 292 categories, appeared in 1987. It was replaced in 1994 by DSM-IV, with 297 categories. DSM-IV was republished in slightly revised form as DSM-IV-TR ("TR" for "text revision") in 2000, but without changes to DSM-IV diagnostic categories (A. V. Horwitz, 2021; Paris, 2015). DSM-5, containing 541 diagnoses, appeared in 2013. A text revision edition, DSM-5-TR, was published in 2022.

Current Versions
ICD

Countries are switching to ICD-11 at their own pace (Dx Revision Watch, 2019; World Health Organization, 2022b). Some say the United States will switch between 2025 and 2027 (American Academy of Professional Coders, 2019). Others aren't so sure (Dx Revision Watch, 2019). It took the United States over twenty years to adopt ICD-10. The United States takes a long time because it modifies ICD for insurance reimbursement and statistical recording purposes. During the switch to ICD-10, there was worry the change would produce insurance claim errors (Friedan, 2015; Kirkner, 2015). It will be interesting to see how long the United States takes to adopt ICD-11.

DSM

DSM-5-TR (again, "TR" for "text revision") was published in 2022. One new diagnosis was added to it (for a total of 542). Criteria for seventy others were updated. DSM-5-TR is organized into three sections. Section I is "DSM-5-TR Basics," which introduces the manual and reviews how to use it. Section II is "Diagnostic Criteria and Codes." The bulk of the manual, it contains criteria, codes, and additional information for officially recognized mental disorders. Section III is "Emerging Measures and Models." It includes assessment measures, cultural information, an alternative proposal for personality disorders, and conditions for further study. This section is where not yet officially recognized proposals for new measures and disorders appear.

Definition of Disorder

The ICD-11 and DSM-5-TR definitions of mental disorder are nearly identical. ICD-11 defines a disorder as "a clinically significant disturbance in an individual's cognition, emotional regulation, or behaviour that reflects a dysfunction in the psychological, biological, or developmental processes that underlie mental and behavioral functioning" (World Health Organization, 2022a). Similarly, the DSM-5-TR definition sees a disorder as "a syndrome characterized by clinically significant disturbance in an individual's cognition, emotion regulation, or behavior that reflects a dysfunction in the psychological, biological, or developmental processes underlying mental functioning" (American Psychiatric Association, 2022, p. 14). Both manuals define disorders as internal dysfunctions that impact how we think, feel, and behave. However, what is broken isn't necessarily biological. Dysfunctions viewed as psychological or developmental count too. As descriptive manuals, DSM and ICD take no position on what causes the disorders they contain. They merely specify that mental disorders disrupt social, occupational, or other functioning. Importantly, these manuals distinguish social deviance from mental disorder. For example, civil disobedience (during which people may violate social norms) or culturally expected responses to everyday stressors (such as mourning the death of a loved one) are not mental disorders (American Psychiatric Association, 2022).

Guidelines, Criteria, and Codes

Diagnostic Guidelines

ICD provides **diagnostic guidelines** to help clinicians make diagnoses. Diagnostic guidelines include *essential features* required to make a diagnosis. Although essential features are intended to be clear and measurable, ICD guidelines still place great emphasis on clinical judgment (First et al., 2015). Clinicians impressionistically use the guidelines to decide whether a patient's presentation approximates (or looks enough like) the disorder at hand (Maj, 2015; Paris, 2015; D. J. Stein et al., 2013). As an example, Table 3.1 contains diagnostic guidelines for generalized anxiety disorder (GAD; see Chapter 6).

Diagnostic guidelines: Descriptors used to make ICD diagnoses; written broadly for diagnostic flexibility, they include *essential features* of each diagnosis.

Diagnostic Criteria

DSM uses **diagnostic criteria**, which tend to be stricter and more precise than diagnostic guidelines in specifying the number and duration of symptoms. Table 3.2 shows DSM-5-TR diagnostic criteria for generalized anxiety disorder. Compare these with the ICD-11 guidelines in Table 3.1, then think about what kind of information you need to determine if Jill (the case study in this chapter) qualifies for a diagnosis. Note how DSM criteria—in being more precise in specifying what is needed to make a diagnosis—leave less room for clinical judgment than ICD guidelines. For generalized anxiety disorder, DSM is more specific about how many symptoms are required (three of six) and how long these symptoms must be present (six months, as opposed to "several months" in ICD). The specificity of diagnostic criteria is intended to reduce errors in clinician judgment and enhance diagnostic reliability (discussed below).

Diagnostic criteria: Symptom lists used to make DSM diagnoses; they tend to be strict and discourage clinical judgment.

Table 3.1 ICD-11 Diagnostic Guidelines for Generalized Anxiety Disorder

- Marked symptoms of anxiety that persist for at least several months, for more days than not, manifested by either:
  - general apprehensiveness that is not restricted to any particular environmental circumstance (i.e., "free-floating anxiety"); or
  - excessive worry (apprehensive expectation) about negative events occurring in several different aspects of everyday life (e.g., work, finances, health, family).
- Anxiety and general apprehensiveness or worry are accompanied by characteristic additional symptoms, such as:
  - Muscle tension or motor restlessness.
  - Sympathetic autonomic overactivity as evidenced by frequent gastrointestinal symptoms such as nausea and/or abdominal distress, heart palpitations, sweating, trembling, shaking, and/or dry mouth.
  - Subjective experience of nervousness, restlessness, or being "on edge."
  - Difficulties maintaining concentration.
  - Irritability.
  - Sleep disturbances (difficulty falling or staying asleep, or restless, unsatisfying sleep).
- The symptoms are not transient and persist for at least several months, for more days than not.
- The symptoms are not better accounted for by another mental disorder (e.g., a Depressive Disorder).
- The symptoms are not a manifestation of another health condition (e.g., hyperthyroidism), are not due to the effect of a substance or medication on the central nervous system (e.g., coffee, cocaine), including withdrawal effects (e.g., alcohol, benzodiazepines).
- The symptoms result in significant distress about experiencing persistent anxiety symptoms or result in significant impairment in personal, family, social, educational, occupational, or other important areas of functioning. If functioning is maintained, it is only through significant additional effort.

Source: Reproduced from World Health Organization (World Health Organization, 2022a).

Table 3.2 DSM-5-TR Diagnostic Criteria for Generalized Anxiety Disorder

A. Excessive anxiety and worry (apprehensive expectation), occurring more days than not for at least 6 months, about a number of events or activities (such as work or school performance).
B. The individual finds it difficult to control the worry.
C. The anxiety and worry are associated with three (or more) of the following six symptoms (with at least some symptoms having been present for more days than not for the past 6 months). Note: Only one item is required in children.
  1. Restlessness or feeling keyed up or on edge.
  2. Being easily fatigued.
  3. Difficulty concentrating or mind going blank.
  4. Irritability.
  5. Muscle tension.
  6. Sleep disturbance (difficulty falling or staying asleep, or restless, unsatisfying sleep).
D. The anxiety, worry, or physical symptoms cause clinically significant distress or impairment in social, occupational, or other important areas of functioning.
E. The disturbance is not attributable to the direct physiological effects of a substance (e.g., a drug of abuse, a medication) or a general medical condition (e.g., hyperthyroidism).
F. The disturbance is not better explained by another mental disorder.

Source: Reproduced from American Psychiatric Association (2022, pp. 250–251).

Diagnostic Codes

Diagnostic code: An alphanumeric key assigned to disorder categories.

Every ICD diagnostic category has a unique **diagnostic code**, an alphanumeric key assigned to it (O'Malley et al., 2005). The generalized anxiety disorder code is F41.1 in ICD-10 and 6A70 in ICD-11 (World Health Organization, 1992, 2022a). Diagnostic codes are useful for record-keeping, making it easier to track incidence and prevalence. Importantly, diagnostic codes originate in ICD, not DSM (Goodheart, 2014; O'Malley et al., 2005). However, DSM appropriates and uses ICD codes (O'Malley et al., 2005). This allows for "harmonization," with the goal being to make the manuals as consistent and similar as possible (Goodheart, 2014). Results of this harmonization are mixed

(Blashfield et al., 2014). Differences remain, but ICD and DSM diagnoses are more alike now than in past decades (First et al., 2021).

Including ICD diagnostic codes in DSM is important for a very practical reason: In the United States, these codes are used for insurance billing (O'Malley et al., 2005). To collect insurance payments, American clinicians must assign each patient a reimbursable diagnostic code. As awareness has grown that the codes in DSM are adopted from ICD, some U.S. mental health professionals have questioned whether purchasing and using DSM is necessary (Gornall, 2013). After all, ICD's codes (and very similar "harmonized" diagnoses) are freely available online.

Reliability

By providing standardized rules for making diagnoses, diagnostic guidelines and criteria aim to enhance **reliability**. Reliable measures yield similar results each time. A diagnostic category has good *interrater reliability* when different raters using the same criteria or guidelines reach the same diagnosis much of the time. Without diagnostic criteria and guidelines, clinicians making a diagnosis must decide for themselves whether specific behaviors count. This potentially yields poor reliability, with different clinicians assigning different diagnoses for the same presenting problem. You can see why this is bad. If one psychologist diagnoses a client with generalized anxiety disorder, a second diagnoses bipolar disorder, and a third diagnoses narcissistic personality disorder, this creates confusion. DSM-5 Task Force member Helena Kraemer explained the problem this way: "If two clinicians give a patient two different diagnoses, you know at least one of them has to be wrong …. And the clinician who was wrong may have given the patient a treatment that was unnecessary for a condition the patient didn't have" (Moran, 2012, para. 3).

When DSM-III was published in 1980, it was hailed for improving diagnostic reliability (Decker, 2013; A. V. Horwitz, 2021; Kirk & Kutchins, 1992). All DSMs since have generally had a good reputation for reliability. A solid body of research suggests that DSM-5-TR categories such as posttraumatic stress disorder, schizophrenia, autism spectrum disorder, and bipolar disorder can be reliably diagnosed (Clarke et al., 2013; Freedman et al., 2013; Narrow et al., 2013; Regier et al., 2013). However, the research also shows mediocre to poor reliability for other categories—including widely used diagnoses such as major depression and generalized anxiety disorder (Freedman et al., 2013; A. V. Horwitz, 2021). For ICD-11, field trials found strong reliability for some diagnoses (e.g., schizophrenia, bipolar I disorder, recurrent depressive disorder, and panic disorder) and solid to good reliability for others (e.g., schizoaffective disorder, generalized anxiety disorder, agoraphobia, and social phobias (G. M. Reed et al., 2018). Among "high burden" diagnoses, only dysthymic disorder yielded mediocre reliability (G. M. Reed et al., 2018).

Critics contend that standards for reliability have often been lowered to make DSM and ICD appear more reliable than they are (A. V. Horwitz, 2021; K. D. Jones, 2012; Lacasse, 2014; Obiols, 2012; Spitzer et al., 2012; Vanheule et al., 2014). They challenge interpretations of the *kappa statistics* used to make judgments about reliability in field trials. They argue that DSM and ICD authors regularly change what counts as a strong kappa score, and that there is no agreed upon threshold for determining good reliability (R. Cooper, 2014; A. V. Horwitz, 2021; Kirk & Kutchins, 1992). However, ICD and DSM authors believe such criticisms are unfair, and say they have paid greater attention to reliability than specialists in other areas of medicine (Kraemer et al., 2012; Moran, 2012).

Validity

Diagnostic **validity** is concerned with whether a diagnostic measure is accurate in measuring what it is supposed to (Paris, 2015). There are numerous kinds of validity relevant to diagnosis: *descriptive validity* (does a diagnosis accurately describe what is being observed?), *face validity* (on the face of it, does a diagnosis seem accurate?), *predictive validity* (does a diagnosis allow us to predict outcomes?), *construct validity* (does a diagnosis correlate with other measures that we think are getting at the same thing?), and *concurrent validity* (is the diagnosis consistent with other measures assessing the same disorder and given concurrently—that is, at the same time?). Each type of validity is important to DSM and ICD categories.

Validity for mental disorders has proven elusive because there isn't agreement about what a mental disorder is. Without a widely accepted definition, it is hard to know what is or isn't a disorder (A. V. Horwitz, 2021; Kirk & Kutchins, 1992; Paris, 2015). This may be why DSM focuses more on reliability

Reliability: Regarding diagnosis, the degree to which a diagnostic system yields similar results each time it is used; *interrater reliability* is high when different clinicians independently arrive at the same diagnosis much of the time.

Validity: Degree to which a diagnostic system or assessment instrument measures what it claims to; types include *descriptive validity* (does a measure accurately describe what is being observed?), *face validity* (on the face of it, does a measure seem accurate?), *predictive validity* (does a measure predict outcomes?), *construct validity* (does a measure correlate with other measures measuring the same thing?), and *concurrent validity* (are a measure's results consistent with other measures given at the same time?).

than validity (Kirk & Kutchins, 1992). However, reliable measures aren't always valid. Notably, efforts to address validity in psychiatric diagnosis go back a long way. In a classic paper, psychiatrists Eli Robins and Samuel Guze (1970) proposed five criteria for establishing diagnostic validity. They argued that valid diagnoses should (a) provide precise clinical descriptions, (b) have measurable biological lab tests, (c) clearly distinguish disorders from one another, (d) have good construct validity to help distinguish disorders, and (e) be supported by genetic evidence. This is a tall order!

For DSM and ICD, Robins and Guze's criteria remain aspirational (A. V. Horwitz, 2021; Paris, 2015). This is partly because we still lack biological or other tests to distinguish mental disorders from one another (A. V. Horwitz, 2021; Obiols, 2012; Paris, 2015). Even when disorders have good diagnostic reliability, there is still a problem with **comorbidity** (multiple disorders co-occurring or being diagnosed at the same time). Comorbidity means the boundaries between disorders often remain fuzzy (Paris, 2015). Therefore, critics contend that DSM and ICD have not yet solved the validity problem (A. V. Horwitz, 2021; Kirk & Kutchins, 1992; Obiols, 2012).

To address validity, critics argue that DSM must define disorder in clear, measurable, and etiological (causal) terms. DSM's authors acknowledge that validity is a challenge, and that focusing on diagnostic reliability doesn't solve the problem: "Although the use of explicit 'operational criteria' is essential for obtaining reliable clinical assessments, the reliability of such criteria does not guarantee that they are the most valid representation of an underlying pathological process" (Regier et al., 2013, p. 59). As you read about DSM and ICD disorders throughout the book, remain aware that these categories still have questionable validity, despite our best efforts. Sadly, the late psychologist David Rosenhan was so intent on illustrating validity problems in psychiatric diagnosis that he rigged his now infamous pseudopatient study. See the "In Depth" feature for details.

Comorbidity: When multiple disorders co-occur (i.e., are diagnosed at the same time).

In Depth: Sane People, Insane Places, Dishonest Researchers

In the early 1970s, psychologist David Rosenhan (1973) conducted his pseudopatient study on the validity of psychiatric diagnosis. In a famous article in the prestigious journal *Science*, Rosenhan described how eight people (three women, five men—including Rosenhan) with no history of mental illness posed as *pseudopatients* and presented at twelve different psychiatric hospitals in the United States. Rosenhan indicated that the pseudopatients were instructed to feign auditory hallucinations, telling hospital staff that they heard voices saying "empty," "hollow," and "thud." Rosenhan wondered how many of the pseudopatients would be correctly turned away as imposters. Shockingly, he reported that none were, and that all were hospitalized—seven with schizophrenia diagnoses and one with a manic-depressive psychosis diagnosis. When eventually released from the hospital, they were all supposedly labeled as "in remission" rather than identified as imposters.

Rosenhan's pseudopatient study was one of the most well-known and talked about studies in the history of psychology. For years, it was regularly cited (including in the first edition of this book) as evidence for the argument that mental health professionals cannot truly differentiate "sane" from "insane." However, in 2019 it was revealed that Rosenhan didn't just fake insanity. He also faked much of his data. A reporter investigating the history of the Rosenhan study found that most of the pseudopatients could not be identified or tracked down. It appears that Rosenhan made them up (Cahalan, 2019). One pseudopatient who was located said that his experience in the hospital ward was misrepresented by Rosenhan. Rather than finding the hospital experience alienating and isolating, this pseudopatient found the staff helpful and the overall experience a humane and positive one. However, Rosenhan excluded this account from his article, perhaps because it did not fit his larger narrative that mental hospitals arbitrarily admit and drug people without being able to accurately determine who warrants such treatment.

Rosenhan's unethical behavior has misled a generation of psychologists (including psychology students, who have been dutifully taught about his pseudopatient study for the past half century). More is said about research ethics in Chapter 15, but for now suffice to say that Rosenhan's work no longer holds the important place in the field it once did. Rosenhan died in 2012, so he did not live long enough to see his duplicity come to light. Sadly, someone who was a hero to a generation of psychologists turned out to be a charlatan who unethically faked one of the most well-known psychology studies of all time.

Critical Thinking Questions

1. Why do you think Rosenhan made up his results?
2. Does Rosenhan's dishonesty necessarily mean that his hypothesis that mental health professionals have difficulty distinguishing "sane" from "insane" people is incorrect?
3. What consequences should there be for psychologists who engage in fraudulent research? If Rosenhan were alive today, what penalties—if any—would you want him to face?
4. Are there larger consequences to scientific psychology when researchers engage in unethical research practices? If so, what are they?

Evaluating DSM and ICD
Success and Influence

In many respects, DSM and ICD have been remarkably successful. They have introduced two major innovations that we now take for granted: diagnostic criteria and diagnostic codes (Decker, 2013; Kirk & Kutchins, 1992; Paris, 2015). They have also tackled the challenging issue of diagnostic reliability (Regier et al., 2013). The success of these manuals is reflected in their widespread use. Although ICD is free, DSM and the many supplemental books published alongside it sell many copies and have a mass readership (R. Cooper, 2014; Halter et al., 2013)—an impressive feat for a dry and technical manual aimed at clinicians and researchers. DSM's influence has extended to both practice settings (where it is used for clinical and insurance purposes) and research settings (where grant agencies, journals, and medical schools have used it) (Halter et al., 2013; A. V. Horwitz, 2021; Kawa & Giordano, 2012; Paris, 2015; Shorter, 2013).

Advantages

Supporters of DSM and ICD point to these advantages:

- *DSM and ICD provide a common language for professionals.* ICD and DSM offer professionals a shared language that facilitates easy and quick communication (J. L. Sanders, 2011). A diagnosis can convey a lot of information readily and efficiently without having to explain the details of a patient's situation.
- *DSM and ICD help get people treatment.* Without a diagnosis, it can be hard to know how to help someone. A DSM or ICD diagnosis can be the first step in determining the best course of action. That is, treatment follows diagnosis. Patients diagnosed with social anxiety disorder receive different interventions from those diagnosed with schizophrenia. Put another way, when operating within a medical model, accurate diagnosis is critical to choosing the correct treatment. More practically, a DSM or ICD diagnosis is also a practical necessity because many agencies and insurance companies won't cover services without one. Diagnoses are often required for treatment eligibility.
- *DSM and ICD advance scientific understanding of mental disorders.* Having a shared language aids researchers. For example, having shared DSM criteria for schizophrenia allows researchers to diagnose and then study the causes of schizophrenia, as well as treatments for it. Therefore, many people argue that these manuals, despite their drawbacks, have improved the understanding and treatment of mental disorders (Decker, 2013).
- *DSM and ICD give patients names for their problems and decrease stigma.* Those diagnosed with mental disorders face a great deal of social stigma (Corrigan, 2005). Supporters say ICD and DSM diagnoses bring mental illness out of the shadows. By attaching names to problems, they help people to (a) better understand what is happening to them, (b) receive effective treatment, (c) find a community of fellow-sufferers who share their experience, and (d) reduce stigma by seeing themselves as having an illness from which recovery is possible (Angell et al., 2005).

Disadvantages

Despite (and perhaps because of?) their success and widespread use, ICD and DSM have received substantial criticism. Commonly cited disadvantages include:

- *DSM and ICD have reliability and validity problems.* As noted, DSM and ICD have been criticized for inadequately addressing reliability and validity issues. Critics contend that these issues are reflected in high levels of comorbidity (Widiger, 2020). According to critics, if a client fits numerous categories, then it is uncertain whether we are reliably or validly identifying distinct disorders.
- *DSM and ICD "medicalize" everyday problems.* Whereas supporters believe ICD and DSM diagnoses reduce stigma, critics see these same diagnoses as dehumanizing. They worry about the dangers of recasting everyday human struggles as diseases (C. E. Dean, 2021; A. Frances, 2013a; Gambrill, 2014; Kinderman, 2017). They believe DSM and ICD encourage medicalization— inappropriately classifying non-medical problems as medical (see Chapter 2). For example, some critics have complained that disruptive mood dysregulation disorder (DMDD), characterized

by recurrent temper outbursts, turns an everyday problem (childhood temper tantrums) into a medical disorder (A. Frances, 2013a). Critics also worry that the thresholds for some disorders have been lowered, qualifying too many people for diagnoses (A. Frances, 2013a; G. Greenberg, 2013; Kamens et al., 2017; Kinderman & Cooke, 2017; Paris, 2015; B. D. Robbins et al., 2017). Table 3.3 compares DSM-IV-TR and DSM-5-TR categories that critics believe have had their diagnostic thresholds improperly lowered. DSM defenders say these revised criteria simply capture more people who warrant a diagnosis. What do you think?

- *DSM and ICD have increased the use of pharmacological interventions.* Critics maintain that DSM and ICD's medical model approach has significantly increased the number of prescriptions written (C. E. Dean, 2021; A. Frances, 2013a; A. V. Horwitz, 2021). Whether this is good or bad depends on whether you tend to view the problems in these manuals as medical disorders or everyday problems in living. Critics generally see them as the latter, while pro-DSM and ICD folks see them as the former.

- *DSM and ICD do not explain the etiology of disorders.* These manuals remain descriptive rather than etiological. Efforts to identify *biomarkers* (biological measures used to make diagnoses) are ongoing, but as of now mental disorders are still diagnosed using behaviors rather than biological indicators (A. V. Horwitz, 2021; Paris, 2015). To critics, this raises questions about the validity of DSM and ICD categories.

- *DSM and ICD rely on political consensus more than science and are culturally imperious.* Ever since homosexuality was removed from DSM-III based on a vote by the American Psychiatric Association membership (see Chapter 10 for a detailed account), critics have complained that DSM and ICD are more influenced by political considerations than science (Decker, 2013; A. V. Horwitz, 2021; Kirk & Kutchins, 1992). Additionally, critics complain that these manuals are culturally imperious, imposing a Western view of mental disorder on the rest of the world (Bredström, 2019; Nadkarni & Santhouse, 2012). To address this, DSM includes a cultural formulation interview that can be used in the diagnostic process; details in Table 3.4. Whether DSM and ICD are culture-bound remains hotly debated, a topic explored in the "Controversial Question" feature.

Table 3.3 DSM and the Lowering of Diagnostic Thresholds. DSM-5 (and now DSM-5-TR) lowered diagnostic thresholds for some disorders, allowing more people to meet the criteria for a diagnosis. Some argue this is a bad thing, continuing the DSM trend of pathologizing normal behavioral variations. Others contend that when more people qualify for diagnoses, more people become eligible for much-needed treatment. This table summarizes some instances where thresholds are lower in DSM-5-TR compared with DSM-IV-TR.

DISORDER	DSM-IV-TR	DSM-5-TR
Attention-deficit hyperactivity disorder (ADHD)	Symptoms must be present before age 7.	Symptoms must be present before age 12.
Major depressive disorder	Not diagnosed for symptoms lasting less than two months following the death of a loved one (i.e., the bereavement exclusion).	Bereavement exclusion eliminated; someone grieving death of a loved one can be diagnosed if clinician deems it appropriate.
Agoraphobia, specific phobia, and social anxiety disorder (social phobia)	Individuals over 18 must recognize their anxiety is excessive.	Individuals over 18 no longer need to recognize their anxiety is excessive.
Bulimia nervosa	Frequency of binge eating and inappropriate compensatory behavior: at least twice weekly.	Frequency of binge eating and inappropriate compensatory behavior: at least once weekly.
Oppositional defiant disorder	Must exclude conduct disorder in making a diagnosis.	Exclusion criterion for conduct disorder eliminated.
Intermittent explosive disorder	Physical aggression required.	Physical aggression or verbal aggression and non-destructive/noninjurious physical aggression required.

Table 3.4 DSM-5-TR's Cultural Formulation Interview

In DSM-5-TR's *cultural formulation interview (CFI)*, clinicians inquire about cultural factors potentially impacting the presenting problem. The CFI assesses four domains (American Psychiatric Association, 2022, pp. 864–867):

1. *Cultural definition of the problem* (3 questions); sample question: "Sometimes people have different ways of describing their problem to their family, friends, or others in their community. How would you describe your problem to them?"
2. *Cultural perceptions of cause, context, and support* (7 questions); sample question: "Are there any aspects of your background or identity that make a difference to your [PROBLEM]?"
3. *Cultural factors affecting self-coping and past help-seeking* (3 questions); sample question: "Often, people look for help from many different sources, including different kinds of doctors, helpers, or healers. In the past, what kinds of treatment, help, advice, or healing have you sought for your [PROBLEM]?"
4. *Cultural factors affecting current help-seeking* (3 questions); sample question: "Sometimes doctors and patients misunderstand each other because they come from different backgrounds or have different expectations. Have you been concerned about this and is there anything we can do to provide you with the care you need?")

DSM-5-TR encourages mental health professionals to "integrate the information obtained from the CFI with all other available clinical material into a comprehensive clinical and contextual evaluation."

Source: American Psychiatric Association, 2022, pp. 864–867.

Controversial Question: Are DSM and ICD Culture-Bound?

Despite efforts to incorporate culture into assessment, DSM and ICD have been accused of assuming their categories are *culturally universal* rather than *culture-bound* (a distinction introduced in Chapter 2). Some mental health professionals pointedly ask whether DSM and ICD, despite being used globally, are culture-bound documents. They note that "the cross-cultural portability of diagnoses is limited" and using these manuals in non-Western countries contributes to "overdiagnosis and misdiagnosis" (Nadkarni & Santhouse, 2012, p. 118). From this perspective, gathering cultural information when diagnosing is insufficient because it doesn't address whether the diagnostic categories being used are—in and of themselves—biased entities lacking cross-cultural validity. DSM and ICD presume their disorders cut across cultures, while those from other cultures are culture specific. Therefore, many syndromes identified in non-Western countries aren't recognized as disorders in DSM or ICD. These syndromes "have been seen largely as curiosities occurring outside Western concepts of mental health, and imply that the Western classification of diseases is the reference point, with any experiences outside its domain being culture bound" (Nadkarni & Santhouse, 2012, p. 118). Examples of these "culture-bound syndromes" (a term popularized by DSM) include the following:

Photo 3.3 The DSM has gone through numerous editions since it first appeared in 1952. The most recent edition, DSM-5-TR, was published in 2022.

- *Dhat syndrome*, common in India and southern and southeast Asia, is diagnosed when "a patient complains of semen loss" and displays symptoms such as "sleepiness, loss of concentration, heart palpitations, headache, and stomach pain" (Martín-Santos et al., 2017, p. 236).
- *Brain fag syndrome* is found in Nigeria, Uganda, Liberia, and Malawi. It is characterized by "crawling sensations in the head and body" and "unpleasant cranial symptoms (pain, burning, heat in the head, feelings of vacancy)"—as well as visual disturbances, cognitive difficulties, weakness, dizziness, and other pains (Ebigbo et al., 2017, p. 199).
- *Koro* "describes a patient's conviction that his genitals or, rarely, another body part, are shrinking and retracting into the body" (Garlipp, 2017, p. 168). It is found in Malaysia and China, as well as South Asia more broadly; it also sometimes occurs in Europe and North America (Garlipp, 2017).

These diagnoses illustrate how expressions of mental distress are impacted by cultural contexts. Some argue that DSM and ICD are as culture-bound as the diagnoses just described because they originate from within American culture and its historically Eurocentric viewpoint. In other words, "European ethnocentric concepts have been widely and uncritically adopted in intercultural therapy with non-Western patients because they are believed to have universal applicability and philosophical value" (Lazaridou & Heinz, 2021, p. 9). Critics contend the Eurocentric viewpoint is often blind to its colonialist and imperialistic assumptions, which dehumanize and oppress people of color (Azibo, 2016; A. J. Joseph, 2015; Lazaridou & Heinz, 2021). If so, then DSM and ICD diagnoses aren't only problematic when imported into non-European countries but also when used to diagnose people of non-European descent living in Europe and North America. Consistent with this sentiment, the African-centered *Azibo Nosology II (AN-II)* identifies fifty-five mental disorders that it claims afflict people of African descent, including:

- *Alien-self disorder*, which involves "an active rejection of one's personal self (me-myself-I) as meaningfully African beyond mere lip service" (Azibo, 2014, p. 53).
- *Negromachy*, characterized by "confusion and doubt of self-worth in an African-U.S. person due to dependency on or the use of standards and definitions from White American culture" (Azibo, 2014, p. 56).
- *Psychological dissemblance*, "defined as a defeatist response to Eurasian hegemony" exemplified by symptoms such as "muting of one's Africanness/Blackness" and "behaving using Eurasian cultural and linguistic forms, aesthetics, and standards" (Azibo, 2014, p. 70).

Supporters of AN-II contend it is a "more culturally suitable diagnostic system for people of African heritage" than DSM or ICD (Jamison, 2014; Kwate, 2005; Lazaridou & Heinz, 2021, p. 9). However, AN-II has been criticized for including misogynistic and homophobic diagnoses (Lazaridou & Heinz, 2021). How do we balance encouraging culturally grounded nosologies while avoiding the prejudices and biases of the cultures responsible for them? It is not easy! While "local non-Western knowledge should be appreciated," we must also "be wary of assuming that all local values must be honoured" (Lazaridou & Heinz, 2021, p. 9). Any diagnostic nosology can oppress if its cultural biases aren't accounted for. This holds for DSM, ICD, and all other diagnostic systems—something to keep in mind going forward.

Critical Thinking Questions

1. How important is culture bias in diagnosis, formulation, and assessment?
2. How can culture bias best be reduced?
3. Are DSM and ICD disorders better viewed as culturally universal or culture-bound?
4. What do you think of the Azibo nosology?

Trends and Future

Here are some current DSM and ICD trends worth noting:

- *Move toward dimensional diagnosis.* DSM remains mainly a book of diagnostic categories (A. V. Horwitz, 2021). So does ICD. However, they have incorporated some aspects of *dimensional diagnosis*, in which disorder severity of is mapped along continua (Blashfield et al., 2014; Widiger, 2020). The idea behind this shift is that people don't always neatly fit into mutually exclusive categories; sometimes pathology comes in degrees. Dimensions let us chart gradations in depression, anxiety, and overall dysfunction. Whereas DSM used to have multiple autism and substance abuse diagnostic categories, it now has one for each and assesses severity as mild, moderate, or severe—a slight shift in a dimensional direction (see Chapters 11 and 13) (American Psychiatric Association, 2013, 2022; Paris, 2015). For personality disorders, ICD has gone even further, fully adopting a dimensional model by instituting personality dimensions and eliminating previously used categories (see Chapter 12) (Bagby & Widiger, 2020; G. A. McCabe & Widiger, 2020).
- *The search for biomarkers.* DSM and ICD have shifted toward a more biological view of mental disorders. DSM-III through IV-TR claimed to be "atheoretical" regarding etiology; they described disorders but took no stance on their causes (American Psychiatric Association, 1980, 1987, 1994, 2000a). By comparison, DSM-5 and 5-TR stopped identifying as atheoretical and more openly speculated about biomarkers for diagnosis (Bredström, 2019; Carroll, 2013). However, as mentioned, mental disorder biomarkers remain elusive (A. V. Horwitz, 2021; Paris, 2015). Thus, neither DSM-5-TR or ICD-11 use them.

- *Rise of ICD in the United States?* Clinicians in the United States overwhelmingly use DSM but have begun taking an interest in ICD (Gayle & Raskin, 2017; Raskin et al., 2022; Raskin & Gayle, 2016). The American Psychological Association brought attention to ICD, publishing resources on using it (Goodheart, 2014; G. M. Reed et al., 2022). Practically, this makes sense. The U.S. government, like all countries that belong to WHO, is required to use ICD codes, so even though most American clinicians still use DSM, technically "the official U.S. diagnostic system for mental illness is the ICD" (M. C. Roberts & Evans, 2013, p. 72). In instances where DSM diagnoses do not correspond to ICD diagnoses (because not all categories are "harmonized" across the manuals), the "DSM diagnoses must be recoded or translated via computerized 'crosswalks' into ICD codes" (M. C. Roberts & Evans, 2013, p. 72). Even if ICD eventually eclipses DSM in the United States (and it isn't certain it will!), many believe a role for DSM remains because it contains more information and detail than ICD ("ICD vs. DSM," 2009).
- *Lengthy transition to ICD-11?* One thing holding back ICD is how long it takes countries to transition to the latest version. Many clinicians are reluctant to use the outdated ICD-10 (which is over three decades old) but cannot adopt ICD-11 until their home country switches to it. Although ICD-10 is still the official nomenclature in some places, it is a product of the past. ICD-11, by comparison, is better harmonized with DSM and reflects current thinking and research in the field. Given this, subsequent chapters present ICD-11 guidelines when covering ICD disorders.
- *Ongoing controversy but sustained influence.* The DSM-5 revision process was rife with controversy (Blashfield et al., 2014; A. V. Horwitz, 2021). Nonetheless, DSM remains preeminent in its field. In fact, it is often referred to as the "psychiatric bible" (Decker, 2013; A. V. Horwitz, 2021). Not everyone appreciates this nickname (R. Friedman, 2013). However, it fits because DSM is arguably the most influential diagnostic system today (A. V. Horwitz, 2021; Paris, 2015). In thinking about its tremendous impact, one DSM historian remarked that it's "not completely unthinkable to call it a Bible for the millions it affects, an actual holy book, whose verses guide professional authorities in many fields" (Decker, 2013, p. 330). Amen.

DIAGNOSTIC PERSPECTIVES: ALTERNATIVES TO DSM AND ICD

3.3 Psychodynamic Diagnostic Manual (PDM)

Distinguishing PDM from DSM and ICD

The ***Psychodynamic Diagnostic Manual* (PDM)**, currently in its second edition (PDM-2), is an explicitly psychodynamic diagnostic system that serves as an alternative or supplement to DSM or ICD. Unlike DSM and ICD diagnoses, which provide descriptive criteria for disorders but remain mute about their causes, PDM diagnoses are overtly theoretical. They are grounded in psychodynamic conceptualizations of psychopathology and mental distress (Lingiardi & McWilliams, 2017).

> ***Psychodynamic Diagnostic Manual* (PDM):** Diagnostic manual of the American Psychoanalytic Association.

PDM Axes

PDM diagnoses are made along three axes. Different versions of these axes are tailored to adults, children, adolescents, and the elderly. The first axis is the *P-Axis (Personality Syndromes)*. It is used to map healthy and disordered personality functioning. PDM defines *personality* as "relatively stable ways of thinking, feeling, behaving, and relating to others" (Lingiardi & McWilliams, 2017, p. 71). When using the P-Axis, clinicians dimensionally assess the patient's *level of personality organization*, which ranges from healthy to psychotic; see the first part of Table 3.5. The clinician then identifies *personality syndromes* and their underlying psychodynamics—including the patient's *central tension/preoccupation* (usually the presenting problem), *central affects* (i.e., emotions), *characteristic pathogenic beliefs about self and others*, and *central ways of defending* (see defense mechanisms in Chapter 2). Personality syndromes for common presenting problems are presented in the second section of Table 3.5. The P-Axis is discussed further when reviewing personality disorders in Chapter 12.

Table 3.5 The P-Axis in PDM-2

Levels of Personality Organization (1–10 scale, with 1 most pathological and 10 least pathological)

Psychotic level (1–2): Break with reality; poor sense of identity; highly defensive; difficulty distinguishing fantasy and reality.
Borderline level (3–5): Have difficulty with emotional regulation; often overwhelmed by intense depression, anxiety, and rage.
Neurotic level (6–8): Respond to certain stressors with rigidity, despite having many functional capacities overall.
Healthy level (9–10): Have preferred coping style, but it is flexible enough to accommodate challenges of everyday life.

Personality Syndromes

SYNDROME	TENSION/ PREOCCUPATION	CENTRAL AFFECTS	PATHOGENIC BELIEF ABOUT SELF	PATHOGENIC BELIEF ABOUT OTHERS
Depressive	Self-critical, self-punishing, overly concerned with relatedness and/or loss	Sadness, guilt, shame	"I am bad or inadequate" or "Something I need for well-being has been lost."	"Others will reject me once they get to know me."
Dependent	Maintaining relationships	—	"I'm inadequate, ineffective, and need others."	"I need powerful others to care for me, but I resent it."
Anxious-avoidant and phobic	Staying safe vs. avoiding danger	—	"I am always in danger and must keep myself safe."	"Others are dangerous or able to protect me."
Obsessive-compulsive	Submitting to vs. rebelling against the control or authority of others.	Anger, guilt, shame, fear	"Feelings are dangerous, so I must control them."	"Others are less careful and controlled than I am, so I must control them and resist them controlling me."
Schizoid	Fearing intimacy vs. wanting intimacy	Emotional upset when overstimulated; emotions so strong they must be repressed.	"It is dangerous to depend on or love others."	"Others overwhelm me, impinge on me, and engulf me."
Somatizing	Integrity vs. fragmentation of the physical body	General distress; implied anger or rage; difficulty identifying and acknowledging emotions	"I am fragile and in physical danger of dying."	"Others are powerful and healthy but indifferent to me."
Hysteric-histrionic	Unconscious devaluing of own gender while being envious and fearful of opposite gender	Fear, shame, guilt	"My gender and its meaning are somehow problematic."	"Others are best understood in terms of gender binaries and conflicts."
Narcissistic	Inflating vs. deflating self-esteem	Shame, humiliation, contempt, envy	"I must be perfect to be okay."	"Others are okay and have good things; I must have more of those things to feel better."
Paranoid	Attacking vs. being attacked by others	Fear, rage, shame, contempt	"I am always in danger."	"Others will attack and use me."
Psychopathic	Manipulating others vs. being manipulated by them	Rage and envy	"Anything I want to do, I can do."	"Others are selfish and weak and are going to try to manipulate me."
Sadistic	Suffering humiliation vs. imposing humiliation	Hatred, contempt, sadistic pleasure	"I am permitted to humiliate and hurt others."	"Others are there for me to dominate."
Borderline	Coherent vs. fragmented sense of self; enmeshed attachment vs. despair at abandonment	Intense and shifting emotions, especially rage, shame, and fear.	"I am unsure who I am; I have many disconnected emotional states rather than an integrated sense of self."	"Others are defined only by their effect on me, rather than as complex individuals with their own unique psychological features."

Source: Levels of personality organization PDM-2 material adapted from Gordon and Bornstein (2018, p. 284).
Personality syndromes material curated from Lingiardi and McWilliams (2017, pp. 780–814).

PDM's second axis is the *M-Axis (Profile of Mental Functioning)*, used to assess mental functioning in four basic areas: *cognitive and emotional processes, identity and relationships, defenses and coping,* and *self-awareness and self-direction.* The M-Axis evaluates aspects of functioning that often lie outside of conscious awareness (Etzi, 2014). PDM lists numerous established assessment instruments that clinicians can use to make M-Axis appraisals.

The third and final axis of a PDM-2 diagnosis is the *S-Axis (Subjective Experience).* The S-Axis places common symptom patterns into diagnostic categories. It takes the major DSM disorders and describes, in psychodynamic terms, what it is like to have them. PDM provides diagnostic codes for each S-Axis symptom pattern. Table 3.6 shows Jill's PDM diagnosis.

Table 3.6 Jill's PDM Diagnosis

P-Axis

Level of Personality Organization 1–10 scale (with 1–2 psychotic level, 3–5 borderline level, 6–8 neurotic level, and 9–10 healthy level)	Rating = 5 (high functioning end of borderline level)
P-Axis Select from twelve personality syndromes	Anxious-Avoidant and Phobic / Somatizing

M-Axis

Rate each of the twelve mental functions on this 1–5 scale:
1 (severe deficit), 2 (major impairment), 3 (moderate impairment), 4 (mild impairment), 5 (healthy)

COGNITIVE AND AFFECTIVE PROCESSES	
Capacity for regulation, attention, and learning	4
Capacity for affective range, communication, and understanding	4
Capacity for mentalization and reflective functioning	3
IDENTITY AND RELATIONSHIPS	
Capacity for differentiation and integration (identity)	3
Capacity for relationships and intimacy	3
Self-esteem regulation and quality of internal experience	3
DEFENSE AND COPING	
Impulse control and regulation	4
Defensive functioning	3
Adaptation, resiliency, strength	3
SELF-AWARENESS AND SELF-DIRECTION	
Self-observing capacities (psychological mindedness)	3
Capacity to construct and use internal standards and ideals	3
Meaning and purpose	3
TOTAL	35

Healthy functioning (54–60), appropriate functioning with some difficulties (47–53), mild impairments (40–46), moderate impairments (33–39), major impairments (26–32), significant impairments (19–25), severe impairments (12–18)

S-Axis

S41.1. Adjustment disorder (DSM-5 diagnosis: Adjustment disorder with mixed anxiety and depressed mood)

Source: Psychodiagnostic Chart-2 (PDC-2) format adapted from Lingiardi & McWilliams (2017, pp. 950–956).

Evaluating PDM

PDM has been praised for mapping the internal meaning systems of clients (Bornstein, 2011; Etzi, 2014; McWilliams, 2011)—something DSM and ICD, in sticking to objective descriptions of disorders, don't do. Many psychodynamic psychotherapists believe that PDM nicely supplements DSM, or can be used in lieu of it (E. B. Davis & Strawn, 2010; McWilliams, 2011; Polychronis & Keyes, 2022; Wallerstein, 2011). Others have criticized PDM for adopting the style and language of

DSM in a way that reifies diagnosis (*reification* is when we treat invented categories as if they are real) and oversimplifies psychodynamic theories by homogenizing them into a single diagnostic system (I. Z. Hoffman, 2009; McWilliams, 2011).

With a few exceptions, PDM codes aren't widely accepted for health insurance reimbursement in most places (Lingiardi & McWilliams, 2017). Nonetheless, both psychodynamic and non-psychodynamic psychologists seem to like PDM (R. M. Gordon, 2009). It has had a significant impact on some clinicians yet remains virtually unknown by others (Lingiardi et al., 2015; Raskin et al., 2022). Some believe its length and depth deter clinicians from adopting it (A. Frances, 2018). Others value it as a psychological alternative to DSM and ICD.

3.4 Research Domain Criteria (RDoC)

Toward a Diagnostic System Based on Biomarkers

Research Domain Criteria (RDoC): U.S. National Institute of Mental Health (NIMH) research initiative to devise a diagnostic system that uses biological measures (i.e., biomarkers) to diagnose mental disorders.

The **Research Domain Criteria (RDoC)** project is an initiative by the United States' National Institute of Mental Health (NIMH) to devise a diagnostic system that uses biological measures (i.e., biomarkers), rather than observable behaviors, to diagnose mental disorders. It is rooted in three assumptions: (a) mental illnesses are brain disorders that "can be addressed as disorders of brain circuits," (b) "dysfunction in neural circuits can be identified with the tools of clinical neuroscience," and (c) "data from genetics and clinical neuroscience will yield biosignatures" that can be used to diagnose and treat disorders (Insel et al., 2010, p. 749). When it comes to searching for the bases of psychopathology, RDoC's developers view DSM and ICD categories as impediments to research due to their questionable validity (Cuthbert & Kozak, 2013; Kozak & Cuthbert, 2016). Consequently, the NIMH is no longer funding studies that rely exclusively on such categories (Winerman, 2013). Instead, it is asking investigators to focus on the neural and behavioral aspects of six *research domains* related to different presenting symptoms (Cuthbert, 2014, 2022; National Institute of Mental Health, n.d.-a).

RDoC's Six Domains

RDoC's six domains are:

1. *Negative valence systems* (things like fear, anxiety, threat, loss, and frustration);
2. *Positive valence systems* (response to rewards, learning, and habit creation);
3. *Cognitive systems* (attention, perception, memory, and language skills);
4. *Social processes* (emphasizing development of attachment, social communication skills, and understandings of self and others); and
5. *Arousal and regulatory systems* (concerned with arousal, emotional regulation, and sleep-wake cycles);
6. *Sensorimotor systems* (oversee motor behavior and its development).

The goal is to start from scratch by identifying brain mechanisms, mapping their functions, and seeing which behavioral domains they affect. RDoC researchers contend that only once this is done can valid mental disorder categories—diagnosable via measurable dysfunctions in the biological domains underlying them—be devised. Thus, the RDoC project is about developing a biomarker-based diagnostic scheme from the ground up.

RDoC has been surrounded by confusion over whether it is a research initiative or a diagnostic system. It currently considers itself a research initiative, with the eventual goal of developing into a diagnostic system based on biological and other assessments in the six domains. Bruce Cuthbert, director of the NIMH, nicely explains RDoC's present status:

What does RDoC involve? The official statement of the RDoC goal—"Develop, for research purposes, new ways of classifying mental disorders … "—could be inferred to mean that NIMH has created a fully-fledged new nosology that is now ready for field trials. This is misleading. In fact, the goal of RDoC is to foster research to validate dimensions defined by neurobiology and behavioral measures that cut across current disorder categories, and that can inform future revisions of our diagnostic systems. In other words, RDoC is intended to support research toward a new classification system, but does not claim to be a completed system at the current time. (Cuthbert, 2014, p. 29)

Evaluating RDoC

Critics say RDoC mistakenly assumes that mental disorder can be reduced mostly to brain function even though emotional difficulties are often meaningful psychological, situational, or spiritual conflicts as much as they are biological issues (Maj, 2015; McLaren, 2011). RDoC developers reply that they don't prioritize biology but instead aim to balance the biological, psychological, and social (Cuthbert, 2022). Critics disagree, countering that five of seven RDoC units of analysis privilege the biological over the psychosocial (Lilienfeld & Treadway, 2016). Some also worry that RDoC is being imposed on investigators seeking NIMH grant funding, regardless of whether they wish to use it and despite questions about its validity (B. S. Peterson, 2015; C. A. Ross & Margolis, 2019). Nonetheless, RDoC has garnered significant attention. Its developers hold out hope that RDoC can "reconcile and integrate separate research traditions (e.g., phenomenology, behaviorism, neurobiology, and genetics) into a coherent view of mental disorders supported by empirical research" (Cuthbert, 2022, p. 112). Time will tell if RDoC succeeds, but it constitutes the latest in a long line of historical efforts to define, diagnose, and treat mental disorders primarily in biological terms (Harrington, 2019).

3.5 Hierarchical Taxonomy of Psychopathology (HiTOP)

Defining HiTOP and Distinguishing it from DSM and ICD

The **Hierarchical Taxonomy of Psychopathology (HiTOP)** breaks with DSM and ICD by rejecting their longstanding practice of dividing problems into diagnostic categories—noting that the supposedly discrete categories these manuals contain all-too-often overlap (reflecting the problem of comorbidity, described earlier) (C. C. Conway et al., 2022; C. C. Conway & Krueger, 2021; Kotov et al., 2017, 2021; Ruggero et al., 2019). Instead, HiTOP offers a dimensional and hierarchical approach to diagnosis. It is dimensional by plotting pathology along dimensions of severity, rather than organizing it into all-or-none categories. It is hierarchical in that its dimensions are divided across different levels. Dimensions at the top of the hierarchy offer more general assessments of pathology (e.g., social anxiety broadly defined), while dimensions lower in the hierarchy measure distinct ways the higher-level dimensions manifest (e.g., performance anxiety or social interaction concerns, as specific instances of social anxiety) (C. C. Conway et al., 2022). Higher and lower-level dimensions that are strongly correlated are linked in the hierarchy because they measure overlapping aspects of an area of mental functioning (American Psychological Association, 2017c; Gambini, 2017; Kotov et al., 2017, 2021).

Figure 3.1 shows HiTOP's six hierarchical levels, each consisting of one or more dimensions used to measure and diagnose psychopathology. Atop the hierarchy is the *superspectrum* level. It contains just a single dimension, the *general dimension of psychopathology* (*p*), which represents "dysfunction, distress, or demoralization common to all forms of mental disorder" (C. C. Conway et al., 2022, p. 156). Below superspectrum is the *spectra* level, consisting of these six basic dimensions of psychopathology:

1. *Internalizing* (or *negative affectivity*) *spectrum*, characterized by negative emotions inside the person, such as social withdrawal, loneliness, depression, anxiety, and difficulty concentrating.
2. *Thought disorder spectrum*, which ranges from eccentric thinking to florid *psychosis* (a broad term to describe people whose thoughts, behaviors, and perceptions are so strange that they appear to have lost contact with reality; see Chapter 4).
3. *Disinhibited externalizing spectrum*, which assesses acting out behaviors attributed to lack of self-control (e.g., impulsivity, irresponsibility, risk taking, substance use).
4. *Antagonistic externalizing spectrum*, which assesses acting out behaviors attributed to antagonizing others (e.g., callousness, deceitfulness, rudeness, physical aggression).
5. *Detachment spectrum*, entailing disengagement from others (e.g., intimacy avoidance, interpersonal passivity, withdrawal).
6. *Somatoform spectrum*, characterized by displaying physical symptoms (e.g., headaches, gastrointestinal complaints, converting psychological stress into physical symptoms); a "provisional" spectrum because it needs further research support.

Hierarchical Taxonomy of Psychopathology (HiTOP): Offers a dimensional (rather than categorical) approach to diagnosing mental disorders.

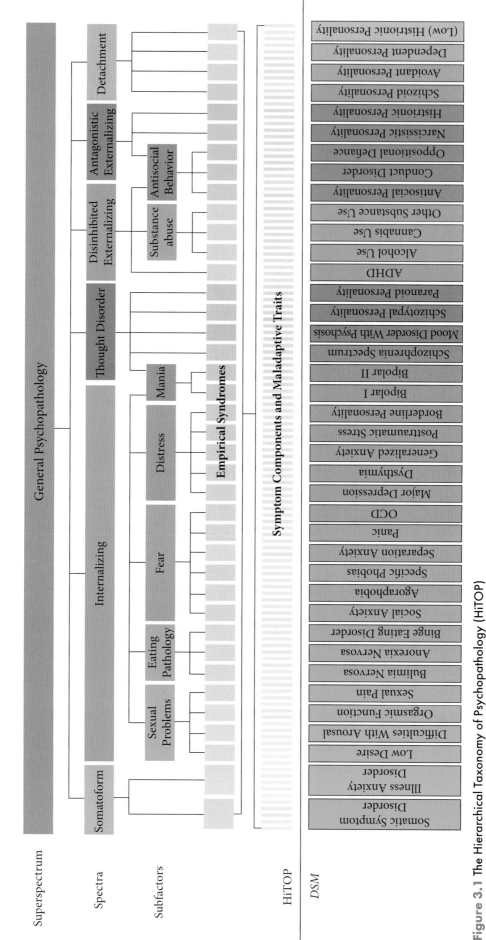

Figure 3.1 The Hierarchical Taxonomy of Psychopathology (HiTOP)

Conway, C. C., & Krueger, R. F. (2021). Rethinking the diagnosis of mental disorders: Data-driven psychological dimensions, not categories, as a framework for mental-health research, treatment, and training. Current Directions in Psychological Science, 30(2), 151–158.

Below the spectra level in the hierarchy is the *subfactors* level. The subfactors further divide the spectra above them. Subfactors are in turn separated into *empirical syndromes*, comprised of even more finely differentiated clusters of *symptom components and maladaptive traits*. Thus, each level of the hierarchy measures narrower and more focused aspects of the level above it.

Importantly, note how Figure 3.1 lists DSM diagnoses below a solid line (after symptoms and maladaptive traits). The solid line indicates that these diagnostic categories are not part of the HiTOP system; they are listed to illustrate how HiTOP transforms them (C. C. Conway et al., 2022). While HiTOP admits that DSM categories are recognizable ways of naming presenting problems, it does not view them as discrete disorders, but merely as diverse expressions of the dimensional levels above them in the hierarchy. Returning to Figure 3.1, for example, generalized anxiety disorder (GAD) and major depressive disorder (MDD) are merely two ways of exhibiting pathology on the internalizing spectrum dimension.

How does a clinician arrive at a HiTOP diagnosis and what might one look like? Rather than using diagnostic criteria to arrive at DSM categories, a clinician using HiTOP identifies assessments that measure its six spectra and their corresponding lower-level symptom and trait dimensions. HiTOP does not currently provide a definitive list of assessments for this, so clinicians must familiarize themselves with what is available. After administering the chosen assessments, the clinician distinguishes spectra with problematically high scores (Ruggero et al., 2019). For example, a DSM diagnosis of major depressive disorder might be reframed in HiTOP terms as an elevated score on the internalizing spectrum, with specific symptoms identified (e.g., loss of appetite, insomnia, and suicidal ideation) (Ruggero et al., 2019). Likewise, as an alternative to DSM's social anxiety disorder, HiTOP would list high scores on the antagonistic externalizing spectrum, perhaps with manipulativeness as a recurring maladaptive trait (Ruggero et al., 2019). In other words, instead of using diagnostic categories, HiTOP diagnosis employs personality assessments to pinpoint inflated scores on spectra dimensions, as well as relevant symptoms and traits.

HiTOP and RDoC

Besides challenging DSM, HiTOP also distinguishes itself from RDoC's heavy focus on neurobiology (American Psychological Association, 2017c). Although HiTOP does attend to genetic and biological factors (Waldman et al., 2020), it has a broader and more inclusively psychological flavor than RDoC. Further, unlike RDoC—which is currently just a research initiative—practicing clinicians can already use HiTOP to make diagnoses. Differences notwithstanding, HiTOP's creators hope that when RDoC eventually develops diagnostic applications, the two systems can complement one another (Kotov et al., 2017). Both are dimensional systems that aim to transform diagnosis, so they potentially can enhance one another (Michelini et al., 2021).

Evaluating HiTOP

HiTOP researchers argue that their system's hierarchical dimensions make it easier to identify genetic correlates of mental disorder, and that they are successfully doing so (Waldman et al., 2020). They point out that genetic studies using DSM and ICD yield confusing and difficult to replicate results, with the same genetic markers correlated with many different diagnostic categories. However, they believe this problem can be rectified by switching from categories to hierarchical dimensions—especially if one of their central predictions is correct, namely that certain genes correlate with HiTOP's general dimension of psychopathology (*p*), while others are associated only with particular spectra or subfactors lower in its diagnostic hierarchy (Kotov et al., 2021; Waszczuk, 2021; Waszczuk et al., 2020).

HiTOP researchers also contend that their system is more *parsimonious*—meaning that it accounts for psychopathology equally or better than DSM and ICD while relying on fewer concepts (Kotov et al., 2017). A general dimension of psychopathology, six basic spectra dimensions, and various syndromes consisting of correlated symptoms and traits offer a leaner assessment system than the many hundreds of DSM and ICD categories. Finally, HiTOP's authors suggest that their system explains why the same treatments (such as SSRIs) work for many different DSM and ICD diagnoses. How so? Well, in the HiTOP system, supposedly discrete DSM and ICD disorders that inexplicably respond to the same treatment are reframed as simply different expressions of dysfunction along the same spectra. This makes their responsiveness to similar treatments understandable.

Turning to weaknesses, HiTOP is new and requires further study. Its somatoform spectrum, especially, lacks research support (Kotov et al., 2017). Critics argue that HiTOP, like DSM and ICD, remains descriptive rather than etiological (Haeffel et al., 2022). They assert that HiTOP can't specify what causes people to score high or low on its dimensions, or whether such scores indicate specific disorders (Haeffel et al., 2022). For example, two people might score high on the internalizing spectrum but the underlying reasons why (i.e., the disorders behind these scores) might be different. Equally as worrisome, HiTOP assumes its spectra dimensions are distinct, but it is unclear that the lines between them are any less fuzzy than those of the DSM and ICD categories they hope to replace (Haeffel et al., 2022).

More practically, clinicians familiar with DSM and ICD might find it challenging to transition from diagnostic categories to spectra dimensions. Critics have challenged the contention that HiTOP is ready for use, arguing that it doesn't provide an approved list of its own assessment instruments, nor does it offer criteria for determining pathological scores on whatever assessments are used (Haeffel et al., 2022). Further, quick communication about presenting problems—for tracking incidence and prevalence or greasing the wheels of insurance reimbursement—remains a real-world issue that HiTOP must address if it hopes to be widely embraced. For better or worse, beyond being reliable and valid, diagnostic systems must meet the administrative demands of everyday practice. Diagnostic categories, for all their limitations, do this quite well. Whether HiTOP can meet this practical requirement remains to be seen.

3.6 Power Threat Meaning Framework (PTMF)

A Psychosocial Framework for Identifying and Assessing Mental Distress

Power threat meaning framework (PTMF): Psychosocial alternative to traditional diagnosis, which attributes distress to economic and social injustice, not individual disorders; emphasizes *power* (what happened to a person), *threat* (response to what happened), and *meaning* (sense made of what happened).

Although grouped here with other diagnostic alternatives to DSM and ICD, the **Power Threat Meaning Framework (PTMF)** is technically an "alternative nondiagnostic conceptual system" (Johnstone & Boyle, 2018). Developed by clinical psychologists from the British Psychological Society (BPS), it rejects attributing mental distress to psychiatric disorders. Instead, it offers a psychosocial alternative to the medical model of DSM and ICD (Johnstone et al., 2018). PTMF holds that mental distress originates in economic and social injustices that affect psychosocial functioning (Harper & Cromby, 2022; Johnstone et al., 2018; Read & Harper, 2022). These injustices limit caregivers' ability to provide their children the secure relationships necessary to cope with adversity. Difficulty coping with adversity, in turn, leads to mental distress and the development of problematic and counterproductive behaviors. PTMF maintains that this cycle is perpetuated so long as the original economic and social injustices remain unaddressed. Instead of assuming something is "wrong" with clients, PTMF assesses three intertwined constructs—*power*, *threat*, and *meaning*:

- *Power* emphasizes what has happened to clients (M. Boyle, 2022; Johnstone et al., 2018). When assessing the role of power, clinicians look at social circumstances that have impacted clients— such as physical power (e.g., war, assault, bullying), legal power (e.g., arrest, imprisonment, hospitalization), economic and material power (e.g., lack of access to employment, housing, medical care), ideological power (dominant social discourses that disadvantage them), interpersonal power (e.g., abandonment or neglect by others), and biological power (mistreatment due to one's physical and intellectual attributes).
- *Threat* focuses on people's responses to how power impacts them (Johnstone et al., 2018). People respond differently to what happens to them, but certain responses are common. Table 3.7 presents common threat responses identified in PTMF.
- *Meaning* concerns itself with how people make sense of what happens to them (Cromby, 2022; Johnstone et al., 2018). Does a client who has faced economic discrimination make sense of her situation in a way that leads her to feel hopeless, alienated, outraged, ashamed, isolated, defeated, etc.? PTMF maintains that we must understand client meanings to comprehend their emotional distress.

Although PTMF eschews diagnostic categories, it does describe general patterns of response to particular social and economic inequalities (Johnstone, 2022). These patterns describe common reactions to things like rejection, entrapment, and invalidation; disrupted attachment relationships and adversity in childhood; separation and identity confusion; defeat, disconnection, and loss;

Table 3.7 PTMF's Functional Groupings of Threat Responses

Regulating overwhelming feelings	E.g., by dissociation, self-injury, memory fragmentation, bingeing and purging, differential memory encoding, carrying out rituals, intellectualisation, 'high' mood, low mood, hearing voices, use of alcohol and drugs, compulsive activity of various kinds, overeating, denial, projection, splitting, derealisation, somatic sensations, bodily numbing
Protection from physical danger	E.g., by hypervigilance, insomnia, flashbacks, nightmares, fight/flight/freeze, suspicious thoughts, isolation, aggression
Maintaining a sense of control	E.g., by self-starvation, rituals, violence, dominance in relationships
Seeking attachments	E.g., by idealisation, appeasement, seeking care and emotional responses, use of sexuality
Protection against attachment loss, hurt and abandonment	E.g., by rejection of others, distrust, seeking care and emotional responses, submission, self-blame, interpersonal violence, hoarding, appeasement, self-silencing, self-punishment
Preserving identity, self- image and self-esteem	E.g., by grandiosity, unusual beliefs, feeling entitled, perfectionism, striving, dominance, hostility, aggression
Preserving a place within the social group	E.g., by striving, competitiveness, appeasement, self-silencing, self-blame
Meeting emotional needs/self-soothing	E.g., by rocking, self-harm, skin-picking, bingeing, alcohol use, over-eating, compulsive sexuality
Communication about distress, elicit care	E.g., by self-injury, unusual beliefs, voice-hearing, self-starvation
Finding meaning and purpose	E.g., by unusual beliefs, overwork, high moods

Source: Reproduced from Johnstone and Boyle (2018) with permission of the British Psychological Society through PLSclear.

social exclusion, shame, and coercive power; and single threatening events (e.g., natural disasters, accidents, assaults, bereavement, medical issues). Importantly, PTMF sees these general patterns as not only common, but as expected and reasonable responses to troublesome social circumstances. As an example, consider PTMF's description of common responses to *surviving or witnessing domestic abuse as a child/young person*:

These children may be particularly likely, especially if boys, to pass on violence (cruelty to animals, aggression and temper outbursts, delinquency, fighting, bullying, threatening, poor peer relationships, disrespect for women, domestic abuse as an adult). This may involve a process of "identifying with the aggressor." Alternatively they (mainly girls) may resort to compliance, withdrawal, and feel great responsibility for the abused parent, as shown in high levels of guilt, anxiety, and separation anxiety. Later, adolescents and adults may seek affection through risky and indiscriminate sexual behaviour. The worse the violence in the home, the more severely children are affected. (Johnstone et al., 2018, p. 229)

Evaluating PTMF

Like HiTOP, PTMF is new and research on it is in the early stages. PTMF is highly consistent with formulation (discussed next) in that, unlike the purely descriptive DSM and ICD, it aims to provide a psychosocial explanation for clients' presenting problems. Consistent with RDoC, PTMF is skeptical of existing diagnostic categories. However, unlike RDoC, it does not seek to identify biological markers for presenting problems because—in direct contrast to RDoC—it sees mental distress as originating from social conditions, not brain diseases. Social and economic disparities, not biomarkers, are privileged in PTMF.

PTMF has been praised for placing the social origins of mental distress front and center (Strong, 2019). It challenges the medical model view of distress as attributable to problems with the individual (rather than society) (Johnstone et al., 2019; Read & Harper, 2022). Perhaps because of this, mental health professionals holding a more conventional perspective worry that PTMF downplays biological and psychological factors (G. Phillips & Raskin, 2021). Other critics have complained that PTMF's notions of power, threat, and meaning are vague and need clarification (M. Larkin, 2018; Raskin, 2021). Finally, some have criticized PTMF for lacking research support (M. Larkin, 2018; Raskin, 2021), though PTMF's authors see this criticism as reflecting a bias for quantitative over qualitative (and other less traditional) research methods (Johnstone et al., 2019). Regardless, PTMF offers a provocative alternative to traditional diagnosis worthy of consideration—one grounded in a sociocultural rather than medical model.

FORMULATION

3.7 Formulation vs. Psychiatric Diagnosis

> **Formulation:** A hypothesis about a person's difficulties, which draws from psychological theory.

A **formulation** is a "hypothesis about a person's difficulties, which draws from psychological theory" (Johnstone & Dallos, 2014b, p. 5). In Chapter 2 we reviewed prominent psychological and sociocultural perspectives on mental distress—such as psychodynamic, cognitive-behavioral, humanistic, social justice, and family systems. Quite simply, a formulation is when a practitioner uses concepts from one of these perspectives to *conceptualize* (i.e., think about in the theory's terms) what is happening with a client and then uses this conceptualization to plan what to do about it (Bolton, 2014; Eels, 2015; R. N. Goldman & Greenberg, 2015a; Johnstone & Dallos, 2014a). Formulation differs from psychiatric diagnosis in that it relies on psychological and sociocultural theories, not medical model disorder categories. While a DSM or ICD diagnosis can be used in conjunction with formulation (Eels, 2015), not all psychologists support doing so (Johnstone & Dallos, 2014b). Formulation doesn't require diagnoses because built into any formulation is a hypothesis about what is going wrong with the client—and such a hypothesis stands on its own, with or without an accompanying diagnosis. In psychoanalysis, formulations frame client problems in terms of underlying unconscious conflicts; in cognitive-behavioral therapy (CBT), formulations posit issues with how the client interprets information; in person-centered therapy, formulations emphasize disruptions in self-actualizing; and in social justice perspectives, formulations tie mental distress to socioeconomic inequality, discrimination, and other forms of societal oppression.

Thus, a formulation can be made using any theoretical perspective without necessitating the use of DSM or ICD diagnoses because each formulation has its own built-in theory of psychological function and dysfunction. However, formulations share core features. All formulations: (a) summarize the client's central problem; (b) draw on psychological theory to understand how the client's issues are interrelated; (c) use psychological theory to explain why the client has developed these issues; (d) develop a plan for alleviating the difficulties that is rooted in the psychological theory applied; and (e) must be revised and updated as needed (Johnstone & Dallos, 2014b). Let's examine two examples of formulation: one that incorporates psychiatric diagnosis and one that doesn't.

Two Examples of Formulation
Integrative Evidence-Based Case Formulation

> **Integrative evidence-based case formulation:** Four-step model of formulation in which the steps are: (1) create a problem list; (2) make a diagnosis; (3) develop an explanatory hypothesis; and (4) plan treatment.

Integrative evidence-based case formulation is an example of formulation that includes psychiatric diagnosis (Eels, 2015). Its four steps are as follows (Eels, 2015):

- *Step 1: Create a problem list.* Problems are defined as discrepancies between perceived and desired states. Four kinds of problems are distinguished: *red flags* (problems demanding immediate attention, such as substance use issues, dangerousness to self or others, and neglect), *self-functioning* (problems involving troublesome behavior, thinking, moods, physical illnesses, or existential issues), *social/interpersonal functioning* (difficulties in relationships), and *societal functioning* (legal, financial, or employment problems).

- *Step 2: Diagnose.* DSM diagnoses are made, but with the caveat that any diagnosis is a social construction that "does not 'exist' in the sense that some general medical conditions exist" (Eels, 2015, p. 103; see Chapter 2 for a definition of a social construction). Thus, diagnostic categories are viewed as merely one source of useful information in developing a formulation. They aren't treated as medical entities to be taken literally, nor are they viewed as explanations for why clients behave as they do.
- *Step 3: Develop an explanatory hypothesis.* Theories (e.g., psychodynamic, CBT, humanistic) and evidence (e.g., assessment data, observations of the client, research on therapy effectiveness) are used to arrive at explanatory *core hypotheses* of clients' problems. Core hypotheses might explain client difficulties in psychodynamic or humanistic terms as due to having desires accompanied by feared negative consequences (e.g., a client wants to establish social connections but fears rejection). However, they might also offer cognitive or behavioral explanations (e.g., a client relies on cognitive distortions in making assessments about job prospects or is negatively reinforced for avoiding social situations because avoiding them reduces anxiety). Whatever the explanation, it is theoretically grounded.
- *Step 4: Plan treatment.* Therapists work with clients to develop shared goals and then employ interventions consistent with the theory used to make the formulation.

4P Model of Case Formulation

The **4P model of case formulation** typically excludes psychiatric diagnoses, rejecting them as static and unhelpful labels: "The act of giving a diagnosis conveys a sense of finality"—in direct contrast to the theoretically grounded act of formulating a provisional (and thus revisable) formulation (Bolton, 2014, p. 182). In other words:

Diagnosis encourages the clinician to see the person or the person's problem as a type of problem; formulation encourages the clinician to see the person or problem as something unique, complex, and situated. Diagnosis is a label; formulation is a map. It is a map of the extensions and connections of a problem and a map for action. (Bolton, 2014, p. 181)

There are four areas of the 4P model that clinicians must consider in devising a formulation. Each begins with the letter "P" (hence, the name of the model). The four areas are (Bolton, 2014; S. W. Henderson & Martin, 2014):

> **4P model of case formulation:**
> Model of formulation in which clinicians gather information about four areas: (1) preconditions; (2) precipitating factors; (3) perpetuating factors; and (4) protective factors.

- *Preconditions*: What preconditions made the client vulnerable to the current presenting problem? Depending on the theoretical perspective(s) being used, what biological, psychological, and sociocultural factors contributed to or were required for the development of the problem? Was the person genetically vulnerable? Did past relationships or learned ways of thinking and behaving influence the problem? Are there social conditions—poverty, discrimination, social norms—that made the problem possible?
- *Precipitating factors*: What events or factors triggered the current problem or led the client to seek help now? Emotional upset, developing physical symptoms, getting arrested, being unable to pay the rent, or being served with divorce papers are examples of precipitating factors. Knowing what elicited the problem or prompted the request for assistance is important for understanding the problem in context.
- *Perpetuating factors*: What factors maintain the problem and prevent it from being resolved? Are there things keeping the person from getting help or effectively addressing the problem? Without addressing these factors, improvement is unlikely.
- *Protective factors*: What factors have prevented the problem from being worse? What client strengths have kept the problem from having an even more detrimental impact? Identifying client strengths (e.g., emotional resilience, physical health, social resources) provides a foundation for building solutions to the problem.

Evaluating Formulation

While many clinicians are attracted to the nuanced and individualized conceptualizations of each client that formulation provides, debate continues over whether diagnostic categories should be retained in case formulation. Those who think they should say diagnosis provides a shared professional

Table 3.8 Three Formulations of Jill's Presenting Problem

Humanistic Formulation

Jill is experiencing psychological *incongruence* because her parents haven't provided her with *unconditional positive regard*. Because Jill's parents only have provided *conditional positive regard*, she has lost touch with her *actualizing tendency*. Therapy should provide Jill with the core conditions for change—*empathy*, *genuineness*, and *unconditional positive regard*. Once provided, Jill should begin to reconnect with her actualizing tendency, become more *self-consistent*, and begin figuring out what future course is right for her.

Cognitive-Behavioral (CBT) Formulation

Jill's *self-schema* is one in which she sees herself as requiring guidance to make decisions and as only being likable if she defers. She employs cognitive distortions such as *mind reading* ("Others will disapprove if I pursue ballet over medical school."); *"should" statement* ("I should study medicine to not disappoint others."), and *catastrophizing* ("If I don't study medicine, it will be the end of the world."). Further, Jill's deferent behavior has been negatively reinforced; when behaving deferentially, she experiences relief from anxiety about displeasing others. Therapy should focus on challenging Jill's cognitive distortions and changing her self-schemas, as well as helping her have new experiences that reinforce less deferential behavior.

Narrative Formulation

Jill has internalized a *problem-saturated narrative* in which she has come to see herself as suffering from anxiety, sadness, and lack of motivation. Therapy should *externalize the problem* by talking about "anxiety," "sadness," and "lack of motivation" as external entities that influence her, rather than internal maladies she "has." Through externalizing the problem, Jill may start to identify *sparkling moments* when "anxiety" and "lack of motivation" failed to get the best of her. This will help Jill start telling a new story about who she is and what she wants from life.

language that allows for efficient communication among clinicians. To these supporters, "diagnosis helps with treatment selection since an enormous amount of treatment research has been conducted on the basis of selecting individuals according to diagnostic categories" (Eels, 2015, p. 100). Others disagree. To them, incorporating diagnosis is theoretically inconsistent with formulation because "it introduces an extra layer of confusion to use *medical/psychiatric* concepts in order to describe something that is actually being conceptualised in *psychological terms*" (Johnstone, 2014, p. 273). In everyday practice, it isn't always possible to discard psychiatric diagnosis because sometimes diagnoses are required for administrative or economic reasons. Setting that issue aside, Table 3.8 presents provides examples of humanistic, cognitive-behavioral, and narrative formulations in the case of Jill.

ASSESSMENT

3.8 Introducing Assessment

Assessment: Gathering information to understand or diagnose a person's difficulties.

Diagnosis and formulation often rely on **assessment**, which involves gathering information to understand or diagnose a person's difficulties. Clinical interviews, personality tests, intelligence tests, neuropsychological tests, and neurological tests are examples of assessment. Most, but not all, assessment involves *standardization*, in which clearly defined rules for how to administer and interpret a test instrument are developed. Standardization ensures that an instrument is used the same way regardless of who is administering it. As with diagnosis, reliability and validity are important in thinking about assessment. Reliable assessment measures yield similar results each time they are administered, whereas valid measures measure what they are supposed to. Various types of validity are relevant to assessment, including *descriptive validity* (does an assessment accurately describe the individual?), *face validity* (on the face of it, does the assessment seem accurate and sensible?), *predictive validity* (does an assessment allow us to predict future behavior?), and *concurrent validity* (are the assessment results consistent with other assessments measuring the same thing and given concurrently—that is, at the same time?). We discuss different types of assessment below.

3.9 Clinical Interviews

Clinical interview: Assessment procedure in which clinician talks to client to gather information about the presenting problem; can be *structured* (clinician employs a clearly defined and predetermined set of questions) or *unstructured* (clinician asks client open-ended questions).

In a **clinical interview**, the clinician talks to the client about the problem. Interviews are useful in learning the client's history. They also allow for direct observation of behavior—noticing the client's demeanor, style of speech, and mannerisms can provide useful insights (Anastasi & Urbina, 1997; K. D. Jones, 2010; Sommers-Flanagan et al., 2020).

Unstructured Interviews

In an *unstructured interview* the clinician asks the client open-ended questions. Because there is no clear script, the information gleaned depends on what a clinician chooses to ask. The advantage of unstructured interviews is that they are open-ended, allowing clients to share what they deem important. The disadvantage is that such interviews lack standardization and important areas may get overlooked (Anastasi & Urbina, 1997). Vital questions may not get asked and reliability and validity may suffer.

Jill

An unstructured interview with Jill might involve the clinician inquiring about what brings her to therapy. The direction the interview takes depends on Jill's responses and the clinician's follow-up questions.

Structured Interviews

In a *structured interview* the clinician employs a clear set of questions. Structured interviews vary from *semi-structured* (where clinicians retain some latitude in how they respond) to *highly structured* (where the interview is akin to a questionnaire administered verbally). When conducting a structured interview, the clinician asks a scripted set of questions in precise order. This guarantees that everyone undergoing such an interview receives the exact same questions. Spontaneity is removed, but greater reliability and validity are potentially gained.

One well-known structured interview is the **mental status exam**, which assesses cognitive and behavioral functioning. When conducting a mental status exam, the clinician observes and asks about the client's *appearance, behavior, motor activity, speech, mood, affect, thought processes, thought content, perceptions, cognition, insight,* and *judgment*. Mental health and medical professionals often assess mental status when first examining new patients. The areas assessed are clear, unambiguous, and generally asked about in a standardized manner.

Mental status exam: Structured clinical interview to assess current mental status; data is gathered about appearance, attitude, and activity; mood and affect; speech and language; thought processes, thought content, and perception; cognition; and insight and judgment.

Jill

A mental status exam with Jill reveals that she appears neat and well groomed, seems lethargic but also deferent to the assessor, talks slowly and methodically, thinks clearly for the most part except when discussing family and career issues, lacks insight into why she has been feeling anxious, and shows questionable judgment in decision-making.

Interviews in DSM Diagnosis

When making DSM diagnoses, unstructured interviews appear to be less accurate than more structured ones (R. W. Baker & Trzepacz, 2013). Therefore, many clinicians use the **Structured Clinical Interview for DSM Disorders (SCID)**, a well-known semi-structured interview for making DSM diagnoses (First, 2015; First & Gibbon, 2004). A clinician administering the SCID asks a series of structured questions and then—depending on the client's responses—uses decision-trees to ask follow-up questions and arrive at a DSM diagnosis. The latest version, the SCID-5, was published in 2015 and is based on DSM-5 categories (First, 2015). A SCID interview might help a clinician arrive at a generalized anxiety disorder diagnosis for Jill.

Structured Clinical Interview for DSM Disorders (SCID): Semi-structured interview for making DSM diagnoses.

3.10 Personality Tests

A **personality test** measures emotions, interpersonal relationship patterns, levels of motivation and interest, and attitudes (First & Gibbon, 2004). Personality tests are often used to understand and diagnose psychopathology and mental distress. There are many kinds of personality tests. Self-report inventories and projective tests are the most common personality assessments, but other approaches are also used.

Personality test: Any test that measures emotions, interpersonal relationship patterns, levels of motivation and interest, and attitudes; includes objective tests (e.g., self-report inventories) and projective tests.

Objective Tests

An **objective test** uses standardized items with limited response choices (e.g., multiple-choice, "true/false," or "yes/no") (Anastasi & Urbina, 1997). *Self-report inventories*, which are filled out by the person being assessed, are the best-known type of objective tests. They are easy to administer and score because they have clear answer choices and scoring schemes. However, by limiting responses, important issues the test doesn't ask about may be overlooked. Additionally, test-takers can minimize their concerns or interpret items in ways the test-constructors did not intend.

The best-known *self-report personality inventory* is the **Minnesota Multiphasic Personality Inventory (MMPI)**, an assessment consisting of statements to which respondents answer "true," "false," or "cannot say." The MMPI was first published in 1943. The original version is no longer in use, but three later versions are: the 567-item MMPI-2 (published in 1989), the 338-item MMPI-2-RF (Restructured Form, published in 2008), and the 335-item MMPI-3 (published in 2020) (Ben-Porath et al., 2020; Ben-Porath & Tellegen, 2020; J. R. Graham, 2011). The MMPI's norms—the data used to determine how to score test items—were established by seeking responses to many true–false sample statements from people with different mental disorder diagnoses. The statements that most reliably distinguished people in the different diagnostic groups became the items included on the inventory.

There are ten general clinical scales on the MMPI-2, nine on the MMPI-2-RF, and eight on the MMPI-3. The MMPI-2's ten clinical scales are *hypochondriasis, depression, hysteria, psychopathic deviate, masculinity–femininity, paranoia, psychasthenia* (symptoms such as phobias, obsessions, compulsions, and anxiety), *schizophrenia, mania,* and *social introversion* (J. R. Graham, 2011). To some clinicians' satisfaction and others' frustration, the MMPI-2-RF and MMPI-3 significantly overhauled these scales out of concern that they lacked *discriminant validity* by overlapping with one another too much (R. J. Cohen & Swerdlik, 2018). The MMPI-3's eight updated clinical scales are *demoralization* (general unhappiness), *somatic complaints, low positive emotions, antisocial behavior, ideas of persecution, dysfunctional negative emotions, aberrant experiences* (unusual perceptions associated with thought disorder), and *hypomanic activation* (aggression, impulsivity, and grandiosity).

Besides the primary clinical scales, each version of the MMPI also contains additional scales that assess specific problems. These scales measure things like anxiety, depression, psychoticism, compulsivity, substance abuse, stress, self-doubt, cynicism, and social avoidance. Further, a number of validity scales help identify test-takers who lie, respond randomly, or try to appear more or less troubled than they are (Ben-Porath et al., 2020; Ben-Porath & Tellegen, 2020). As with the general clinical scales, the specific problem and validity scales have been revised significantly in the MMPI-2-RF and MMPI-3.

Jill

On the MMPI-3, Jill scored high on Demoralization (which assesses general unhappiness and dissatisfaction) and Dysfunctional Negative Emotions (which assesses anxiety, anger, and irritability). She also registered elevated scores on specific problem scales measuring aggression, cynicism, worry, stress, self-doubt, helplessness/hopelessness, anger proneness, and social avoidance. Her scores on the ten validity scales—particularly the Adjustment Validity Scale, which identifies efforts to appear more adjusted—suggest that at times Jill might be downplaying her level of distress. Jill's MMPI-3 profile supports a diagnosis of generalized anxiety disorder.

Another of the many established personality inventories is the **Sixteen Personality Factor (16PF) Questionnaire**. The 16PF consists of 185 multiple-choice items and yields scores on sixteen primary personality factors (*warmth, reasoning, emotional stability, dominance, liveliness, rule-consciousness, social boldness, sensitivity, vigilance, abstractedness, privateness, apprehension, openness to change, self-reliance, perfectionism,* and *tension*), as well as on the **Big Five** global personality traits (*extraversion, anxiety* [*neuroticism*], *tough-mindedness* [*openness*], *independence* [*agreeableness*], and *self-control* [*conscientiousness*]) (Cattell, 2004). The 16PF has fewer items than the MMPI-2, so it doesn't take as long to complete. A free online adaptation of the 16PF is available at https://openpsychometrics.org/tests/16PF.php.

Objective test: Test that uses standardized items with limited response choices (e.g., multiple-choice, "true/false," or "yes/no"); self-report personality inventories are objective tests.

Minnesota Multiphasic Personality Inventory (MMPI): Objective self-report personality inventory; contains clinical scales plus validity scales to determine if test-taker is faking good or bad.

Sixteen Personality Factor (16PF) Questionnaire: Multiple-choice self-report personality inventory yielding scores on sixteen primary personality factors (warmth, reasoning, emotional stability, dominance, liveliness, rule-consciousness, social boldness, sensitivity, vigilance, abstractedness, privateness, apprehension, openness to change, self-reliance, perfectionism, and tension), plus the "Big-Five" global personality traits (extraversion, anxiety, tough-mindedness, independence, and self-control).

Big Five: The five traits measured by the Five-Factor Model (FFM) of personality: extraversion, agreeableness, conscientiousness, neuroticism, and openness.

Some inventories assess an aspect of functioning rather than the entire personality. The most famous example is the *Beck Depression Inventory (BDI)*, a 21-item self-administered inventory for measuring depression (Dozios & Covin, 2004). Other inventories that assess a specific area of functioning include the *Child Abuse Potential (CAP) Inventory* (J. S. Miller, 2004), the *State-Trait Anxiety Inventory (STAI)*, and the *State-Trait Anger Expression Inventory (STAXI)* (Spielberger & Reheiser, 2004).

Projective Tests

When taking a **projective test**, the individual engages in some form of artistic representation that is used to infer aspects of psychological functioning (Leichtman, 2004). Whereas objective tests require discrete answers, projective assessments are more ambiguous and open-ended (Leichtman, 2004). Many but not all projective tests have psychodynamic origins. There are many projective tests. Two well-known ones are discussed here.

Projective test: Uses responses to artistic representation to infer aspects of psychological functioning.

Rorschach Inkblot Method (RIM)

The **Rorschach Inkblot Method (RIM)** is perhaps the best-known projective test. Originally developed by Hermann Rorschach in 1921, it consists of ten inkblots on 6¾ by 9¾ inch cards (Searls, 2017; I. B. Weiner, 2004). People taking the Rorschach are asked what they see in each inkblot, and to explain what about the blot makes it look that way (e.g., the shape, color, or texture). Figure 3.2 offers an example of an inkblot like those used in the Rorschach. Numerous procedures for administering the Rorschach have been devised. Classic ones often employ psychodynamic perspectives (Lerner, 1998). The most well-regarded administration and scoring system today is the *Rorschach Performance Assessment System (R-PAS)* (Gurley, 2017; G. J. Meyer & Eblin, 2012; Mihura & Meyer, 2018). R-PAS improves on the *Comprehensive System (CS)*, which became popular several decades ago because it *normed* the Rorschach (Searls, 2017). Norming the test involved administering the Rorschach to many people and identifying which kinds of responses distinguished diagnostic groups from one another. The CS (which is no longer being updated) and the R-PAS (a replacement for the CS) employ research-based norms (the most common answers given by each diagnostic group) (Mihura & Meyer, 2018). These norms inform scoring (Gurley, 2017; Mihura & Meyer, 2018). Norms differentiating diagnostic groups allow the Rorschach to be used in making DSM diagnoses.

Rorschach Inkblot Method (RIM): Projective assessment technique in which test-taker responds to ten inkblots.

Critics of the Rorschach not only complain that it is difficult to administer and score, but that the Comprehensive System isn't valid (Lilienfeld et al., 2000; J. M. Wood et al., 2001; J. M. Wood & Lilienfeld, 1999). However, the newer R-PAS system has quieted much of the controversy by establishing more scientifically supported norms (Mihura & Meyer, 2018; Searls, 2017). Nonetheless, debate continues over the Rorschach's utility in court settings (Erard et al., 2014; Gacono & Smith, 2021; Gurley et al., 2014). With the R-PAS's scientific improvements, some critics now concur that the Rorschach can be useful in identifying cognitive ability and impairment (J. M. Wood et al., 2015). Regardless, the test remains controversial. The Rorschach is widely used in some settings and not at all in others.

Figure 3.2 An Inkblot like the Ones Used on the Rorschach
Note: A sample inkblot is shown to protect real Rorschach cards from exposure outside of an assessment setting.
spxChrome/iStock.

Thematic Apperception Test (TAT)

The **Thematic Apperception Test (TAT)** is another projective technique. It contains thirty cards, all of which contain illustrations of vague scenes—except for one that is blank (Moretti & Rossini, 2004). Depending on age and gender, test-takers are presented with twenty of the cards, usually in two separate fifty-minute sessions (Moretti & Rossini, 2004). For each card, test-takers are asked to tell a story with a beginning, middle, and end. Many TAT administrators score and analyze test-takers' stories by identifying thematic content, often from psychodynamic and narrative perspectives (Cramer, 1999). However, critics complain that the TAT lacks standardization and that administrators use different scoring systems—or sometimes none at all, instead relying on their own subjective interpretations (Garb, 1998; Lilienfeld et al., 2000). Some TAT supporters counter that clinical interpretations are often more valid and useful than reliance on strict scoring schemes (Karon, 2000; Rossini & Moretti, 1997), while others have worked to develop the *Social Cognition and Object Relations Scale-Global Rating*

Thematic Apperception Test (TAT): Projective assessment technique in which test-taker tells stories about pictures on twenty cards (determined by age and gender).

The Lived Experience: Two of Jill's TAT Stories

These are the imagined responses to when Jill is shown the cards described below.

Card 3: Woman standing next to open door with hand to downcast face

Jill: A woman woke up and her husband yelled at her for not cleaning up properly. Her kids were running around and making her crazy. The dog ran through, and the kids spilled fruit punch. Her mail was full of bills. So, she called a babysitter, bought an airline ticket to Bermuda on her husband's credit card, and left. In Bermuda, she fell in love with a sexy Bermuda guy and never returned.

- HERO: woman
- OUTCOME: runs away to escape
- THEMES: responsibility, frustration, need to escape, familial relationships

Card 6: Young woman on sofa with older man smoking cigar behind her

Jill: A 15-year-old girl's father refuses to let her meet her boyfriend for a date because she isn't 16. The girl sneaks out of the house to meet him anyway. She has a wonderful time, but while kissing her boyfriend on the porch she is caught by her father. The father calls the boyfriend a cradle robber, then lectures the girl while smoking a cigar. The mother comes downstairs and tells the father to leave the girl alone because they were dating at her age. The mother also makes the father put out the cigar. The girl calls the boyfriend for a date the next night.

- HERO: the girl
- OUTCOME: positive; can see boyfriend, but without resolving father conflict
- THEMES: control, rebellion against authority, father–daughter relationship

Method (SCORS-G), a scientifically derived approach to assessing cognitive and relational pathology using the TAT (Siefert et al., 2016; M. Stein et al., 2011; M. B. Stein et al., 2014, 2015; Westen et al., 1990). See the "The Lived Experience" feature for two of Jill's TAT stories, along with an analysis of their thematic content.

Cognitive-Behavioral Assessment
Behavioral Assessment

Because purely behavioral perspectives reject speculation about processes inside people, their understanding of dysfunction almost exclusively emphasizes how the environment influences behavior (Hadaway & Brue, 2016; Heiby & Haynes, 2004; Ollendick et al., 2004; Strosahl & Linehan, 1986). Therefore, **behavioral assessment** focuses on identifying conditions in the environment that sustain undesirable behaviors (Hadaway & Brue, 2016; Haynes, 1998; Heiby & Haynes, 2004; Strosahl & Linehan, 1986). Once these conditions are understood, the environment can be altered to encourage preferred behaviors. Behavioral assessment uses a variety of techniques—including *behavioral observation*, *clinical interviews*, and *self-reports*—to arrive at a *functional analysis*, which consists of judgments about relationships between environmental conditions and client behavior, along with estimates of how these relationships might be modified (Hadaway & Brue, 2016; Ollendick et al., 2004). Let's briefly examine several behavioral assessment techniques.

Behavioral observation is just what it sounds like: direct observation of behavior. For instance, *ABC recording* involves directly observing and recording client behaviors ("B"), while writing down their antecedents (what comes before them, or "A") and their consequences (what comes after them,

Behavioral assessment: Identifies conditions in the environment that sustain undesirable behaviors; uses techniques such as behavioral observation, clinical interviews, and self-reports.

Jill

A behavior therapist employing ABC recording might observe Jill during a day at school while narratively recording her behavior. This would allow data to be gathered that reveals patterns among Jill's behavior, its antecedents, and its consequences. In so doing, the behavior therapist can identify how Jill displays more anxiety during and after pre-med classes and less anxiety during and after dance classes.

or "C") (Gable et al., 1999; Lanovaz et al., 2013; R. H. Thompson & Borrero, 2011). By doing this, the clinician identifies reinforcement patterns that maintain undesired behaviors.

The goal of behavioral assessments is to identify environmental patterns that sustain undesired behaviors. Once functional relations between environment and behavior are understood, the environment can be altered to condition preferred behaviors. While critics complain that behavioral assessment fails to get at underlying meanings that may not be readily observable, its main appeal is that by limiting itself to observable behaviors, it locates the source of problems in the environment rather than in individuals.

Cognitive Assessment

Cognitive assessment measures evaluate clients' ways of thinking. For example, self-report measures have been developed to assess clients' *self-efficacy* (their cognitive estimates of how likely they are to succeed in performing tasks) (Luszczynska et al., 2005; Scholz et al., 2002; Sherer et al., 1982). This sort of data tells us how a client's cognitive attributions influence their psychological functioning.

Most cognitive assessments focus on measuring negative thinking or cognitive distortions. Two well-known examples are the *Daily Record of Dysfunctional Thoughts (DRDT)* (see Chapter 5) and the *Beck Depression Inventory (BDI)* (discussed earlier). The DRDT is a form with five columns. In these columns, the client records the situation, any accompanying emotions, automatic thoughts the situation triggers, a more rational response, and the outcome of the situation (A. T. Beck et al., 1979; J. S. Beck, 2011; van Bilsen, 2013). The goal is to identify negative automatic thoughts, which are then targeted in therapy. In assessing problematic thoughts, the DRDT and the BDI keep with the cognitive emphasis on psychopathology as a product of dysfunctional thinking.

Humanistic Assessment

Humanistic perspectives on assessment focus on the underlying meanings that clients assign to their symptoms, with an emphasis on using everyday (rather than diagnostic) language to describe client problems. Rather than arriving at static categorical diagnoses, they aim to understand the problem in terms of the client's ever-changing experience. Below are two examples of humanistic assessment, the Q-sort and the role construct repertory test.

Q-sort

The **Q-sort** is a person-centered assessment that uses everyday descriptors to understand psychological functioning (Rost, 2021). In the *California Q-sort*, test administrators sort 100 cards, each with a descriptor on it, into nine sets containing 5, 8, 12, 16, 18, 16, 12, 8, and 5 cards. This is done using their clinical impressions of the client. In the first set, assessors place the five cards most descriptive of the person; in the second set, they place the eight cards next most descriptive of the person; and so on until reaching the last five cards, which are least descriptive of the person. Three examples of descriptors are: "Is fastidious, meticulous, careful and precise," "Initiates humor; makes spontaneous funny remarks," and "Feels cheated and victimized by life; self-pitying; feels sorry for self" (Block, 2008). The idea is to describe personality using everyday descriptions rather than DSM or ICD diagnostic categories. Q-sort researchers have tried to identify sorting patterns that indicate paranoia, hysteria, ego-resiliency, and optimal functioning. While the Q-sort has been criticized for assuming all assessors interpret descriptors similarly and for forcing assessors to sort cards into nine predetermined piles, the test is interesting in its humanistic effort to understand clients using ordinary language (Block, 2008). Some humanistic therapists don't sort the cards themselves. Instead, they have clients do it. This provides therapists with a sense of how clients understand themselves.

Role Construct Repertory Test

The **role construct repertory test (rep test)** emerges from George Kelly's (1955/1991a, 1955/1991b) personal construct theory (mentioned in Chapter 2). When using the rep test, clients are provided a list containing sets of three people in their lives. For each set, they must identify how two of the people are similar to and different from the third (Fromm, 2004; Jankowicz, 2003). Each result constitutes a *personal construct*. Analyses can be done to map the relationships among a client's personal constructs. While this can be time-consuming, personal construct therapists argue that the

Q-sort: Person-centered assessment in which 100 cards with descriptors written on them are sorted into piles to describe client personality using everyday language.

Role construct repertory test (rep test): Personality test in which a client's *personal constructs* (bipolar dimensions of meaning created by the client) are elicited and their relationships mapped; allows for an assessment using the client's personal meanings rather than the clinician's diagnostic categories.

Intelligence tests:
Assessment measures used to evaluate intelligence.

Intelligence quotient (IQ): Mental age (a score reflecting level of performance on an intelligence test) divided by chronological age (how old one is) multiplied by 100.

Neuropsychological tests: Psychological tests used to evaluate perceptual, cognitive, and motor skills; often used to infer underlying brain dysfunction.

Neurological tests: Physiological tests that measure brain functioning directly.

Bender Visual Motor Gestalt Test: Neuropsychological test consisting of nine cards with geometrical designs; test-takers are asked to examine the designs and draw them from memory; difficulty doing so is often interpreted as an indicator of brain damage.

Halstead-Reitan Neuropsychological Test Battery (HRB): Neuropsychological battery that assesses visual, auditory, and tactile functioning; verbal communication; spatial and sequential perception; ability to analyze information; motor ability; and attention, concentration, and memory.

Luria-Nebraska Neuropsychological Battery (LNNB): Neuropsychological inventory consisting of clinical scales assessing areas such as reading, writing, math, memory, language, and motor function.

personal constructs elicited during a rep test help clinicians understand presenting problems using the client's meanings rather than the clinician's diagnostic categories (Procter & Winter, 2020).

Jill
On a rep test, Jill might be asked about her mother, best friend, and favorite professor. She indicates that her mother and favorite professor are "powerful," while her best friend is "influenced by others." "Powerful vs. influenced by others" is one of Jill's personal constructs, which she uses to make sense of events.

3.11 Intelligence Tests

Definitions of *intelligence* vary across cultures, but psychologists typically view their instruments as measuring "general cognitive ability" (Drozdick & Puig, 2020, p. 135). Most theorists see intelligence as stable over time, even though they disagree about how many different abilities intelligence consists of. Psychologists have devised many different **intelligence tests**—a difficult task because intelligence cannot be observed directly and must be inferred from performance. Another challenge is distinguishing intelligence from achievement. Whereas intelligence is often assumed to consist of innate abilities, *achievement* describes successful performance following learning. Intelligence and achievement are related but not the same (F. Kaya et al., 2015; M. C. Ramsay & Reynolds, 2004). Debate over how well intelligence tests predict academic achievement or other life outcomes is ongoing, though they do have some predictive power (Borghans et al., 2016; Čavojová & Mikušková, 2015; Gygi et al., 2017).

Among the most popular intelligence tests are the *Weschler Adult Intelligence Scales (WAIS)* and the *Weschler Intelligence Scales for Children (WISC)* (Drozdick & Puig, 2020). Both can be used to arrive at an **intelligence quotient (IQ)**, calculated by dividing *mental age* (performance score on an intelligence test) by *chronological age* (how old you are) and multiplying the result by 100. An IQ between 130 and 145 is considered gifted; 120–129, superior; 110–119, high average; 90–110, average; 80–89, low average; and 70–79, borderline (School Psychologist Files, 2021). Scores lower than 70 may indicate an intellectual disability (Bhaumik et al., 2016). IQ is a popular but crude means for communicating something as complex as intelligence. Still, intelligence tests are considered one of professional psychology's greatest achievements and are widely used to predict school performance and diagnose intellectual and learning disabilities, discussed in Chapter 14 (J. Zhu et al., 2004).

3.12 Neuropsychological and Neurological Tests

The medical model assumes psychopathology is tied to brain function. Two kinds of tests to assess brain functioning have been devised: neuropsychological tests and neurological tests. **Neuropsychological tests** are psychological tests in which someone completes perceptual, cognitive, and motor tasks to assess things like *learning and memory*, *attention and concentration*, *perception*, *language skills*, *visuospatial skills* (ability to understand spatial relationships among objects), *sensorimotor skills* (ability to receive sensory messages and produce an appropriate motor response), and *executive functioning* (cognitive processes involving attention, planning, decision-making, and goal-directed behavior) (Suhr & Angers, 2020). Based on performance, hypotheses about potential brain dysfunction are inferred. In contrast, **neurological tests** are physiological tests that measure brain functioning directly. To clarify, let's discuss examples of neuropsychological and neurological tests.

Neuropsychological Tests

The **Bender Visual Motor Gestalt Test** is a neuropsychological test consisting of nine cards with geometrical designs printed on them. Test-takers are asked to examine the designs and then draw them from memory. Difficulty doing so is viewed as an indicator of brain damage. One of the weaknesses of tests like the Bender Gestalt is that they only assess one area of neuropsychological functioning (Benson, 2003; Martínez & Nellis, 2020). To counter this drawback, standardized *test* *batteries* of various tasks intended to assess the full range of neuropsychological functioning have been developed.

Two examples of neuropsychological test batteries are the **Halstead-Reitan Neuropsychological Test Battery (HRB)** and the **Luria-Nebraska Neuropsychological Battery (LNNB)**. The HRB consists of eight tests that assess the following domains: visual, auditory, and tactile functioning; verbal communication; spatial and sequential perception; ability to analyze information; motor ability; and attention, concentration, and memory ("Halstead-Reitan Battery," n.d.). It is used to assess brain damage, as well as to hypothesize about causes of lost function (e.g., stroke, Alzheimer's disease, alcohol use, and head injury) (Anastasi & Urbina, 1997; G. Goldstein, 2017). The LNNB is a 269-item inventory that takes less time to complete than the HRB. It has eleven clinical scales assessing areas such as reading, writing, math, memory, language, and motor function ("Luria-Nebraska Neuropsychological Battery," n.d.; Reitan & Wolfson, 2004).

Neurological Tests

Among neurological tests, psychologists commonly use the *electroencephalogram (EEG)*, a device that records the electrical activity of neurons firings, known as *brain waves*. The EEG is one way to measure brain activity. *Neuroimaging techniques* are more advanced (and expensive!) neurological measures that photograph brain activity.

Positron emission topography (PET scan) is a powerful neuroimaging technique in which radioactive isotopes are placed into the bloodstream (B. Kim et al., 2021; Portnow et al., 2013; Weingarten & Strauman, 2015). The PET scan detects the location of these isotopes using gamma rays and generates images reflecting changes in cerebral blood flow. Areas with increased blood flow are more active, so if we ask someone to complete a task and take a PET scan, we can see which brain areas "light up" during the task.

Magnetic resonance imaging (MRI) is another neuroimaging technique, which creates an x-ray-like picture of the brain using the magnetic activity of hydrogen atoms (B. Kim et al., 2021; Weingarten & Strauman, 2015). One kind of MRI, *functional magnetic resonance imaging (fMRI)*, can be used to measure blood flow in various brain areas while the person is thinking, feeling, or completing a task (B. Kim et al., 2021). The fMRI maps brain blood flow activity by tracking the amount of oxygen in the brain's hemoglobin (Weingarten & Strauman, 2015). From fMRI data, researchers can infer which areas of the brain are associated with different psychological experiences. The fMRI has eclipsed the PET scan in psychopathology research, though both are still used.

Despite impressive advances in brain imaging, mental disorders cannot yet be diagnosed using neurological tests. Some argue that existing neurological tests are only able to assess lower-level aspects of brain functioning (such as brain blood flow), with neuropsychological tests currently the "only rigorous and objective method of assessing higher-level aspects of brain functions" (Reitan & Wolfson, 2004, p. 107). Regardless of whether you agree with this sentiment, diagnosing underlying brain pathology remains an elusive if widely sought-after goal (think RDoC) that neuropsychological and neurological assessments aim to reach.

CLOSING THOUGHTS

3.13 Beware of Culture Bias

As discussed in this chapter's "Controversial Question" feature, clinicians increasingly emphasize how diagnostic and assessment tools are always developed within a cultural context. Therefore, many researchers warn against **culture bias**, which occurs when diagnosis, formulation, or assessment reflects cultural assumptions and, consequently, provides misleading results that disadvantage members of certain groups. Assessment tests, for example, might be biased in their construct validity, content validity, or predictive validity.

Positron emission topography (PET scan): Neuroimaging technique in which radioactive isotopes are placed in the bloodstream and gamma rays used to generate images reflecting changes in cerebral blood flow; identifies brain areas active during a given task.

Photo 3.4 At the Brain Electrophysiology Laboratory in Oregon, Research Laboratory Manager Shijing Zhou wears a Geodesic Head Web with 280 electrodes that does standard EEG collection used in research that is ongoing in the lab.
The Washington Post/Getty Images.

Magnetic resonance imaging (MRI): Neuroimaging technique that creates an x-ray-like picture of the brain using the magnetic activity of hydrogen atoms; one kind, the fMRI (functional MRI), tracks oxygen levels in the brain's hemoglobin, allowing assessment of blood flow in various brain areas while the person is thinking, feeling, or completing a task.

Culture bias: Occurs when diagnostic, formulation, or assessment approaches reflect the cultural assumptions of those devising them.

- *Construct validity bias* occurs when a test fails to measure what it purports to. For instance, an intelligence test that uses English words unfamiliar to those from certain cultures may be measuring language skills, not intellectual ability.
- *Content validity bias* occurs when members of some cultural groups don't perform as well on a test because they (a) haven't been exposed to necessary information, (b) give answers that make sense from their cultural perspective but are considered "wrong" by the test developers, or (c) are asked questions in a manner that culturally doesn't make sense to them. For instance, old intelligence tests used to ask people to match a cup with a saucer; those who did not scored lower on intelligence. However, people of lower socioeconomic status (SES) or from cultural groups where they had never seen a saucer didn't know to match it with a cup. The test developers' lack of cultural sensitivity led to a test that was biased against members of certain groups—and in so doing, yielded inaccurate assessments of intelligence!
- *Predictive validity bias* occurs when a test fails to predict outcomes for members of a certain culture. An "unbiased" test should predict outcomes for different groups equally well. While culture bias can probably never be avoided entirely (no measure can ever truly be "culture free"), attending to it allows clinicians and researchers to minimize its impact as much as possible. In the example above about cups and saucers, test-takers from cultural groups unfamiliar with saucers would score lower on intelligence and therefore the test might not accurately predict their future academic success as well as it could if it were more culturally sensitive.

The approaches to diagnosis, formulation, and assessment discussed in this chapter are revisited throughout the rest of the book as we discuss various presenting problems. Keep in mind that the choices clinicians make about which approaches to use both reflect and shape their perspective. Every diagnostic and assessment strategy has advantages and disadvantages. Hopefully these will become clearer as we discuss them in subsequent chapters.

CHAPTER SUMMARY

Overview

- *Diagnosis*, which translates as "to know thoroughly," can have medical or non-medical connotations.

Diagnostic Perspectives: DSM and ICD

- The two dominant systems of psychiatric diagnosis are the *Diagnostic and Statistical Manual of Mental Disorders* (*DSM*) and the mental, behavioral, and neurodevelopmental disorders section of the *International Classification of Diseases* (*ICD*).
- DSM uses *diagnostic criteria* and ICD uses *diagnostic guidelines*. Each diagnosis also has a *diagnostic code* that can be used for administrative purposes.
- The DSM and ICD have been praised for providing a common language for diagnosis, helping people get treatment, advancing the science of mental disorders, and giving patients names for their problems. They have been criticized for having reliability and validity problems, medicalizing everyday problems, encouraging reliance on psychiatric drugs, and being influenced by politics.

Diagnostic Perspectives: Alternatives to DSM and ICD

- The *Psychodynamic Diagnostic Manual (PDM)* is a diagnostic system grounded in psychodynamic theory. It reformulates DSM diagnoses in psychodynamic terms. A PDM diagnosis is made along three axes—the P-Axis (Personality Syndromes), M-Axis (Profile of Mental Functioning), and S-Axis (Subjective Experience).
- The *Research Domain Criteria (RDoC)* are a U.S. National Institute of Mental Health (NIMH) research initiative to develop a diagnostic system that relies on biological measures (i.e., biomarkers) to identify and diagnose disorders. RDoC is currently in the research and development stage.

- The *Hierarchical Taxonomy of Psychopathology (HiTOP)* replaces diagnostic categories with dimensions organized in a hierarchy. Its advocates see it as more parsimonious than DSM and ICD. However, some worry about its ease of use.
- The *Power Threat Meaning Framework (PTMF)* rejects diagnosis of mental disorders and instead attributes distress to economic and social injustices. It has been praised for attending to the social causes of mental distress but criticized for lacking research support.

Formulation

- *Formulation* uses psychological theory to generate hypotheses about mental distress. In contrast to diagnostic labels, formulations provide detailed conceptualizations of cases.
- In *integrative evidence-based case formulation*, the formulation is used in addition to a DSM or ICD diagnoses. In the *4P model of case formulation*, formulation is designed for use instead of a DSM or ICD diagnosis.

Assessment

- In *assessment*, clinicians collect information to understand or diagnose a person's presenting problem. Types of assessment include clinical interviews, personality tests, intelligence tests, neuropsychological tests, and neurological tests.
- In *clinical interviews*, clinicians assess client problems by talking to them. These interviews can be unstructured or structured.
- *Personality tests* assess emotions, interpersonal relationship patterns, levels of motivation, and attitudes; they can also assist in making diagnoses.
- *Behavioral assessment* focuses on identifying environmental conditions that maintain undesired behaviors. Cognitive-behaviorists supplement behavioral assessments with cognitive data.
- *Intelligence tests* attempt to measure "general cognitive ability" and can be used to calculate an *intelligence quotient (IQ)* score to sum up people's intelligence in a number. They can help predict school performance and diagnose intellectual and learning disabilities.
- *Neuropsychological tests* employ perceptual, cognitive, and motor tasks to assess learning and memory, attention and concentration, perception, language skills, visuospatial skills, sensorimotor skills, and executive functioning.
- *Neurological tests* directly measure brain functioning. Although they can measure brain activity, they cannot currently be used to diagnose specific mental disorders.

Closing Thoughts

- There is always a risk of *culture bias* when diagnosing, formulating, or assessing clients.

NEW VOCABULARY

1. 4P model of case formulation
2. Assessment
3. Behavioral assessment
4. Bender Visual Motor Gestalt Test
5. Big Five
6. Clinical interview
7. Comorbidity
8. Culture bias
9. Diagnosis
10. *Diagnostic and Statistical Manual of Mental Disorders* (DSM)
11. Diagnostic code
12. Diagnostic criteria
13. Diagnostic guidelines
14. Formulation
15. Halstead-Reitan Neuropsychological Test Battery (HRB)
16. Hierarchical Taxonomy of Psychopathology (HiTOP)
17. Integrative evidence-based case formulation
18. Intelligence quotient (IQ)
19. Intelligence tests
20. *International Classification of Diseases* (ICD)
21. Luria-Nebraska Neuropsychological Battery (LNNB)
22. Magnetic resonance imaging (MRI)
23. Mental status exam
24. Minnesota Multiphasic Personality Inventory (MMPI)
25. Neurological tests
26. Neuropsychological tests
27. Objective test
28. Personality test
29. Positron emission topography (PET scan)
30. Power Threat Meaning Framework (PTMF)
31. Projective test
32. *Psychodynamic Diagnostic Manual* (PDM)
33. Q-sort
34. Reliability
35. Research Domain Criteria (RDoC)
36. Role construct repertory test
37. Rorschach Inkblot Method (RIM)
38. Sixteen Personality Factor (16PF) Questionnaire
39. Structured Clinical Interview for DSM Disorders (SCID)
40. Thematic Apperception Test (TAT)
41. Validity

PSYCHOSIS

Photo 4.1
Soulful Pizza/Pexels.

OVERVIEW

4.1 Getting Started: What Is Psychosis?

Case Example

Luke

Luke is a 21-year-old university student studying chemistry. He has always been a strong student academically who also did well socially. However, a noticeable change occurred in Luke as he approached graduation. He became increasingly focused on how the university administration was intruding into student privacy. He often spoke about university officials monitoring student e-mail accounts and placing security cameras around campus to keep an eye on students. Eventually, he started complaining that the government was spying on him via a radar device secretly implanted in fillings in his teeth. He also reported hearing voices telling him that he was the Messiah and that he needed to go around campus blessing his fellow students. Luke's personal hygiene deteriorated, and his speech became hard to follow. He began using made up words that others didn't understand and sometimes strung words together in a way that made no sense to others. These days Luke has stopped going to class and spends long periods alone in his room. When he does go out, he walks around town alone muttering to himself or trying to bless those he encounters. The university has recently placed Luke on leave and has contacted his family to request that they come take him home.

Psychosis and Reality Contact

Psychosis is a broad term to describe people who appear to have "lost contact" with reality. Those identified as psychotic think and perceive in ways that strike us as grossly inappropriate or strange. Their manner of talking, thinking, and communicating seems bizarre or off the mark. Individuals labeled as psychotic often appear the most stereotypically "mad" or "insane" (Beer, 1996; Lobel, 2013). Psychosis evokes strong reactions from others (including clinicians and researchers). As you read the chapter, notice how different perspectives sometimes appear at odds, yet other times they are integrated to comprehend psychosis.

DIAGNOSTIC PERSPECTIVES

4.2 DSM and ICD

DSM and ICD define psychotic disorders as involving one or more of the following symptoms: delusions, hallucinations, disorganized thinking and speech, abnormal motor behavior, and negative symptoms. Let's examine these symptoms one at a time.

Five Symptoms of Psychosis
Delusions

Delusions are false beliefs that the person won't give up, despite overwhelming evidence against them. *Non-bizarre delusions* don't seem outlandish; they just seem false. In contrast, *bizarre delusions* are unrealistic and, to be blunt, just plain odd. It isn't always easy to tell when non-bizarre delusions are false. Are those conspiracy theories you keep reading about on the Internet true or the product of delusional thinking? Determining what is a false belief can be challenging!

Psychosis: A broad term used to describe people whose thoughts, behaviors, and perceptions are so strange that they appear to have lost contact with reality.

Delusions: False beliefs that a person won't give up, despite overwhelming evidence against them; specific types include *bizarre delusions, erotomanic delusions, grandiose delusions, jealous delusions, non-bizarre delusions, persecutory delusions,* and *somatic delusions.*

Luke

A non-bizarre delusion occurs when Luke thinks the university is spying on him even though there is no evidence of this. A bizarre delusion is when Luke believes that the university is monitoring him via radio waves broadcast through the fillings in his teeth. This belief isn't simply false. It is downright strange and all-but impossible.

Photo 4.2 In *Stranger Things,* Winona Ryder's character Joyce exhibits what the rest of the characters perceive as delusions when she thinks her missing son is communicating to her through light bulbs. The show frequently examines the lines between delusions and reality.
Theo Wargo/Getty Images.

Still other delusions are grandiose. In *grandiose delusions,* people view themselves as important or special in some way. Grandiose delusions can be non-bizarre or bizarre.

Luke
If Luke thinks the university is spying on him because he alone understands the degree of its corruption, this would be a non-bizarre but grandiose delusion. If Luke believes the university is monitoring him because he will soon be revealed as the Messiah, this would be a bizarre grandiose delusion.

In both these delusions, not only is Luke special (which is what makes the delusion grandiose), but he is also being persecuted (for knowing about university corruption or being the Messiah). These are therefore not just grandiose delusions; they are also *persecutory delusions* (sometimes called *paranoid delusions*) because they include the idea that Luke is being unfairly treated or pursued by others.

Hallucinations: Sensory experiences in the absence of sensory stimulation; can be auditory (hearing things), visual (seeing things), olfactory (smelling things), gustatory (tasting things), or tactile (feeling things touching you).

Disorganized thinking: Thinking pattern in psychosis characterized by disturbances in the form of thought; *loose associations* (leaping from topic to topic during conversation) and *tangential responding* (responding to something other than what was asked) are common, as is incoherent or disrupted language use (e.g., *word salad*); also called *formal thought disorder.*

Abnormal motor behavior: A symptom of psychosis in which the person seems physically agitated/restless or catatonic (unresponsive to surroundings).

Catatonia: Form of abnormal motor behavior that sometimes occurs in psychosis; characterized by decreased responsiveness to one's surroundings as evidenced by reduced movement, holding oneself in a rigid posture, or a *catatonic stupor* (ceasing to respond verbally or physically).

Positive symptoms: Additions to the personality that occur in psychosis; hallucinations and delusions are examples.

Negative symptoms: Subtracted from the personality in psychosis; symptoms such as *diminished emotional expression, flattened affect, avolition* (decreased motivation), *alogia* (poverty of speech), *anhedonia* (loss of pleasure), and *asociality* (disinterest in social contact).

Hallucinations

Delusions involve thinking, whereas hallucinations involve perceiving. Quite simply, **hallucinations** are sensory experiences in the absence of sensory stimulation.

Luke

Luke hears voices that nobody else hears instructing him, as the Messiah, to bless his fellow students. These are hallucinations.

Luke's hallucinations are auditory because they involve hearing things. Although auditory hallucinations are most common in psychosis, hallucinations can also be visual (seeing things), olfactory (smelling things), gustatory (tasting things), or tactile (feeling things touching you). Hallucinations and delusions often occur together. In Luke's case, his belief that he is the Messiah is a delusion, while his hearing voices telling him to bless people is a hallucination. Delusions contain false beliefs. Hallucinations involve false sensory perceptions.

Disorganized Thinking and Speech

Disorganized thinking—also called *formal thought disorder*—can't be observed directly. It must be inferred from how people talk and what they say. People whose thinking is disorganized display *loose associations* in which they leap from topic to topic during conversation. Their responses to questions tend to be *tangential*, or unrelated to what was asked. Sometimes their language use is so incoherent that their speech seems like a jumble of random words—a phenomenon known as *word salad*. DSM and ICD assume that by listening for word salad and other peculiarities in speech, we can infer oddities in thought.

Luke

Luke's word salad speech confuses others. For instance, he walks up to a cashier in the store and says, "Rain from whence the blue owl sings." The cashier doesn't understand what Luke means and experiences him as strange and frightening.

Abnormal Motor Behavior

Abnormal motor behavior can be reflected in physical agitation or restlessness, difficulties performing daily activities, and—in some cases—catatonia. **Catatonia** is characterized by a decreased responsiveness to one's surroundings. Sometimes this involves reduced movement, holding oneself in a rigid posture, or ceasing to respond at all either verbally or physically. Catatonia can also involve agitated or extreme movement. The person might stare, scowl, or verbally repeat what's just been said (a behavior called *echolalia*). Catatonia is associated primarily with schizophrenia but is also diagnosable in other psychotic disorders.

Luke

Luke exhibits catatonia when he remains completely still and does not speak at all. This is an example of a catatonic stupor. Luke also engages in echolalia when someone says to him "Why do you think the university is monitoring your e-mail?" and he replies verbatim, "Why do you think the university is monitoring your e-mail?"

Negative Symptoms

The symptoms described so far are chiefly **positive symptoms**, which are additions to the personality (Jablensky, 2010). Hallucinations and delusions, for example, are added to the personality in psychosis. So are disordered thought and speech. By comparison, **negative symptoms** are things subtracted from the personality (Jablensky, 2010). *Avolition* is a common negative symptom in schizophrenia. It is a fancy term for decreased motivation; such a person stops initiating goal-directed behavior. Another negative symptom is *diminished emotional expression*; for instance, the person may exhibit *flattened affect*, in which they speak in an unemotional voice with few inflections and little expressive body language. Alogia, anhedonia, and asociality are other negative symptoms. *Alogia* involves reduced verbal communication (also called *poverty of speech*); the individual just doesn't say much. *Anhedonia* is when a person gets little pleasure from previously entertaining activities. Finally, *asociality* refers to a lack of interest in social contact. Positive and negative symptoms are typically identified in schizophrenia, but they can also be seen in other psychotic disorders. Luke's negative symptoms involve diminishment of his personality.

Luke

Luke displays various negative symptoms. He sits for long periods doing nothing and shows little interest in work, school, or social activities. When he does speak, it is in an unexpressive monotone—even when he is discussing emotionally loaded topics such as being dismissed from school. The amount of talking Luke does has steadily decreased over the past few months, and his interest in previously enjoyed activities has plummeted. He used to love going to the theater, but now he gets little enjoyment from it and has stopped going. Luke mostly sits in his room and declines invitations from visitors.

Specific Psychotic Disorders in DSM and ICD

Schizophrenia

Schizophrenia is the most well-known and severe psychotic disorder in DSM-5-TR and ICD-11. To be diagnosed with it, a patient must actively display at least two symptoms of psychosis for a month or more. DSM criteria are narrower than ICD guidelines. First, DSM says at least one of the two symptoms must be hallucinations, delusions, or disorganized speech, while ICD says one of the two symptoms can also include feeling influenced or controlled by one's thoughts. Second, DSM specifies that if positive symptoms (e.g., hallucinations and delusions) last only a month, ongoing signs of the disorder (e.g., evidence of negative symptoms or odd thinking and perceiving that doesn't rise to the level of positive symptoms) must continue for at least six months. ICD doesn't require this, making its guidelines more inclusive and leaving more to clinical judgment. In most other respects, DSM-5-TR and ICD-11 are closely harmonized on schizophrenia (Gaebel et al., 2015). See Diagnostic Box 4.1.

DSM-5-TR estimates a 0.3 percent to 0.7 percent chance of developing schizophrenia during one's lifetime. The manual also notes that age of onset is usually between the late teens and mid-thirties. Once diagnosed, the prognosis is not very good. According to DSM-5-TR, the median proportion of people who recover from schizophrenia is only 13.5 percent. The odds after first-episode schizophrenia are better, with remission occurring in 56 percent of cases. Schizophrenia

> **Schizophrenia:** The best known and perhaps most severe psychotic disorder in the DSM and ICD; characterized by hallucinations, delusions, and disorganized speech.

Diagnostic Box 4.1 Schizophrenia

DSM-5-TR
- Two or more for at least one month: (1) delusions, (2) hallucinations, (3) disorganized speech, (4) disorganized or catatonic behavior, (5) negative symptoms; at least one symptom must be (1), (2), or (3).
- Additional signs for at least six months: negative symptoms or milder symptoms such as odd thinking and perceiving.
- Functional impairment in one or more areas (e.g., work, relationships, self-care).

ICD-11
- Two or more for at least one month: (1) delusions, (2) hallucinations, (3) disorganized thinking, (4) feeling as if one's thoughts or actions were being controlled from outside oneself, (5) negative symptoms, (6) disorganized behavior, (7) psychomotor disturbances; at least one symptom must be (1), (2), (3), or (4).
- There is often functional impairment in one or more areas (e.g., work, relationships, self-care).

Information from American Psychiatric Association (2022, pp. 113–115) and World Health Organization (2022a).

tends to be chronic, with many diagnosed people needing ongoing assistance with daily living. Because schizophrenia is the most researched and discussed psychotic disorder, we spend more time on it than other psychotic disorders.

Delusional Disorder

Delusional disorder is diagnosed when symptoms are limited to delusions (see Diagnostic Box 4.2). In DSM-5-TR, these delusions must last one month or more. In ICD-11, the delusions must persist a bit longer—at least three months, making ICD more conservative than DSM in how many people qualify for a diagnosis. The disorder is often characterized by grandiose and persecutory delusions. However, other types of delusions are also possible, including *erotomanic delusions* (incorrectly insisting that a person is in love with you), *jealous delusions* (preoccupation with the idea that your partner is cheating despite no evidence of this), and *somatic delusions* (falsely believing that you have a disease). DSM-5-TR indicates the lifetime prevalence for delusional disorder is 0.2 percent. Although the jealous type is more common among men than women, delusional disorder is diagnosed about equally in males and females.

Diagnostic Box 4.2 Delusional Disorder

DSM-5-TR

- One or more delusions for at least one month.
- Has never met criteria for schizophrenia.
- Besides the delusion, functioning not seriously impaired.

ICD-11

- One or more delusions for at least three months.
- No hallucinations, thought disorder, or negative symptoms (as in schizophrenia).
- Besides the delusion, functioning not seriously impaired.

Information from American Psychiatric Association (2022, pp. 104–106) and World Health Organization (2022a).

Brief Psychotic Disorder/Acute and Transient Psychotic Disorder

Brief psychotic disorder is the DSM-5-TR diagnosis for people whose psychotic symptoms only last a short time: at least a day but no more than a month. The ICD-11 equivalent goes by a different name—*acute and transient psychotic disorder (ATPD)*—and has a longer maximum duration (up to three months, though symptoms usually remit by one month). If symptoms last longer than one month (DSM-5-TR) or three months (ICD-11), the diagnosis is changed to a different psychotic disorder (depending on the symptoms). DSM-5-TR indicates that 2–7 percent of first-onset psychoses are classifiable as brief psychotic disorder. Like schizophrenia, it often first appears in the teens or twenties, with average onset by the mid thirties. Diagnostic Box 4.3 summarizes DSM criteria and ICD guidelines.

Schizophreniform Disorder

Schizophreniform disorder only appears in DSM. ICD doesn't include it. Its criteria are like schizophrenia but with a shorter duration (see Diagnostic Box 4.4). Schizophreniform symptoms last from one to six months, while signs of schizophrenia remain for six months or longer. A person can be diagnosed with schizophreniform disorder and then, if symptoms persist beyond six months, the diagnosis can be changed to schizophrenia. DSM-5-TR notes that about a third of people diagnosed with schizophreniform disorder recover within six months, but most of the remaining two-thirds wind up with a schizophrenia or schizoaffective diagnosis.

Diagnostic Box 4.3 Brief Psychotic Disorder/Acute and Transient Psychotic Disorder

DSM-5-TR: Brief Psychotic Disorder

- One or more, with at least one being (1), (2), or (3): (1) delusions, (2) hallucinations, (3) disorganized speech, (4) disorganized or catatonic behavior.
- Lasts one day to less than one month, with eventual return to regular functioning.

ICD-11: Acute and Transient Psychotic Disorder

- From non-psychotic state to psychotic state within two weeks.
- Can include (1) delusions, (2) hallucinations, (3) disorganized thinking, (4) feeling as if one's thoughts or actions were being controlled from outside oneself, and (6) psychomotor disturbances.
- Lasts one day to three months, but one day to one month most common.

Based on American Psychiatric Association (2022, pp. 108–109) and World Health Organization (2022a).

Diagnostic Box 4.4 Schizophreniform Disorder

DSM-5-TR

- Two or more for at least one month but less than six months: (1) delusions, (2) hallucinations, (3) disorganized speech, (4) disorganized or catatonic behavior, (5) negative symptoms; at least one symptom must be (1), (2), or (3).

ICD-11

- This diagnosis is not included.

Information from American Psychiatric Association (2022, pp. 111–112).

Schizoaffective Disorder

Schizoaffective disorder combines elements of psychosis and depression. In addition to showing signs of schizophrenia, the person must concurrently experience a manic or depressive *mood episode* (discussed in Chapter 5). This mix of psychotic and depressive symptoms has made schizoaffective disorder a notoriously unreliable diagnosis (Jonathan et al., 2013; D. L. Peterson et al., 2019). See Diagnostic Box 4.5 for criteria and guidelines. DSM-5-TR notes that lifetime prevalence for schizoaffective disorder is 0.3 percent, but that incidence is higher for females, probably because depressive disorders are more common in women. Age of onset is usually early adulthood, but the disorder can occur anytime from adolescence until old age. Because of the depressive symptoms, there is a higher risk of suicide than with some psychotic disorders. DSM-5-TR places the lifetime suicide risk for both schizoaffective disorder and schizophrenia at 5 percent.

Schizoaffective disorder: DSM and ICD disorder in which the person displays aspects of psychosis and depression.

Schizotypal Disorder

ICD-11 includes one additional psychotic disorder, **schizotypal disorder**. It is characterized by a longstanding pattern of odd and eccentric talking, perceiving, and behaving that doesn't rise to the level of schizophrenia, schizoaffective disorder, or delusional disorder. Because of its milder and more enduring nature, DSM-5-TR classifies schizotypal disorder as a personality disorder rather than a psychotic disorder and calls it *schizotypal personality disorder (STPD)*. We don't discuss schizotypal disorder further in this chapter. Instead, we examine it when reviewing personality disorders in Chapter 12.

Schizotypal disorder: ICD psychotic disorder diagnosis for people with eccentric thoughts, perceptions, and behaviors accompanied by difficulty forming close relationships; equivalent to DSM's *schizotypal personality disorder (STPD)*.

Diagnostic Box 4.5 Schizoaffective Disorder

DSM-5-TR
- Two or more for at least one month: (1) delusions, (2) hallucinations, (3) disorganized speech, (4) disorganized or catatonic behavior, (5) negative symptoms; at least one symptom must be (1), (2), or (3).
- Major mood episode (depressive or manic) accompanies the above most of the time symptoms present.
- Delusions or hallucinations for two or more weeks during a time when no major mood episode is present.

ICD-11
- Simultaneously meet criteria for schizophrenia and a mood episode (depressive [moderate or severe], manic, or mixed).
- Psychotic and mood episodes develop at the same time or within a few days of each other.
- Symptoms last at least one month.

Information from American Psychiatric Association (2022, pp. 121–122) and World Health Organization (2022a).

Evaluating DSM and ICD Perspectives

Categorical vs. Dimensional Diagnosis

Both DSM-5 and ICD-11 field trials found the revised criteria for schizophrenia yielded strong reliability (specifically, *test–retest reliability*—the degree to which a test yields similar results each time) (G. M. Reed et al., 2018; Regier et al., 2013). Nonetheless, these manuals have been criticized for sticking with diagnostic categories rather than shifting toward dimensional diagnosis (Reininghaus et al., 2013). Critics argue that questionable DSM and ICD categories interfere with identifying biological mechanisms behind psychotic symptoms. That is, people lumped together in a category like schizophrenia vary widely in their symptoms, which might better be understood if measured along dimensions—without any need to assume they are part of a broader schizophrenia diagnostic category. One researcher summarized the concern about ICD and DSM diagnostic categories this way:

Despite sustained effort, the mechanism of schizophrenia has remained elusive. There is increasing evidence that the categorical diagnosis of schizophrenia and other psychotic disorders contributes to this lack of progress …. The current diagnoses do not accurately capture the considerable variability of symptom profile, response to treatment, and most importantly, social function and outcome. As a result, there is increasing pressure to change the structure of psychiatric nosology, in order to accelerate better treatment, prevention, and ultimately cure …. The 5th edition of the DSM does not represent such a paradigm shift. (Heckers et al., 2013, p. 11)

Postmodern vs. Medical Views

Critiques of DSM can be divided into two kinds: *postmodern* and *medical* (N. Ghaemi, 2014). Postmodern critiques hold that mental disorder categories are not medically and scientifically established diseases but instead are social constructions (socially shared ways of defining, talking about, and understanding behavior identified as pathological, which influence how people come to experience it). They throw "into doubt the biological and scientific validity of diagnoses such as manic-depressive illness and sometimes even schizophrenia" (N. Ghaemi, 2014, p. 78). Postmodern critics support a less medical orientation toward psychotic disorders given what they see as a lack of evidence that ever-changing DSM and ICD categories are biologically based. By contrast, medical critiques contend that DSM makes decisions about what to include or exclude based on pragmatic and political motives (what is best for clinicians, insurers, and drug companies) rather than scientific evidence (N. Ghaemi, 2014). Consistent with the Research Domain Criteria approach introduced in Chapter 3, those offering medical critiques want to see DSM and ICD move toward diagnoses that can eventually be made using biological markers. Keep postmodern and medical critiques in mind as you read the rest of this chapter, with an eye toward how they inform your own perspective. As a final example of the controversy over DSM and ICD conceptions of psychotic disorders, see the "Controversial Question" feature for a discussion of the debate over DSM's proposed **attenuated psychosis syndrome (APS)**.

Attenuated psychosis syndrome (APS): Proposed DSM diagnosis characterized by odd or eccentric behavior that does not qualify as full-blown psychosis.

Controversial Question: Should Attenuated Psychosis Syndrome Be in DSM?

Controversy has surrounded a proposed DSM category called attenuated psychosis syndrome (APS). The syndrome is "characterized by psychotic-like symptoms that are below a threshold for full psychosis" (American Psychiatric Association, 2022, p. 138). In other words, attenuated psychosis syndrome is a diagnosis for people whose behavior is odd or eccentric and might eventually develop into full-blown psychosis—but doesn't yet qualify. Advocates for including attenuated psychosis syndrome in DSM have argued that doing so would allow clinicians to provide early treatment (most likely antipsychotic drugs) for high-risk patients, preventing full-blown psychosis from ever occurring (W. T. Carpenter, 2020; W. T. Carpenter & van Os, 2011; Tsuang et al., 2013; Zachar et al., 2020). The logic behind this is that all too often treatment for psychotic disorders is initiated too late, when the prognosis is not as good. The argument for adding APS to DSM holds that "the best hope for secondary prevention of the often devastating course of psychotic disorders resides in early detection and intervention when individuals first develop symptoms" (W. T. Carpenter & van Os, 2011, p. 460).

DSM critics, however, have expressed concern over the diagnosis. Some worry about high false positive rates for the diagnosis—meaning people will be diagnosed who don't have the disorder (Salazar de Pablo et al., 2020; Zachar et al., 2020). Others are concerned about prescribing powerful antipsychotics to people before they display serious psychotic symptoms (A. Frances, 2013c; Kamens et al., 2017; Zachar et al., 2020). To critics, APS is an example of DSM pathologizing normal human variations. They argue that being odd or eccentric doesn't make someone mentally ill. Further, it is difficult to predict which APS patients will eventually develop full-blown psychosis (Fusar-Poli et al., 2017; Fusar-Poli & Yung, 2012; B. Nelson, 2014; A. E. Simon et al., 2013; Zachar et al., 2020). This view was somewhat supported by disappointing DSM-5 field trials, which—besides having too few participants—suggested clinicians might not be able to reliably diagnose APS (Yung et al., 2012; Zachar et al., 2020). This isn't surprising; diagnoses with mild and subtle symptoms are more difficult to consistently spot. Because of its poor showing in reliability trials and concerns that a psychotic diagnosis for people with mild symptoms could be unnecessarily stigmatizing, APS was relegated to Section III of DSM (where proposed but not officially accepted disorders in need of further study are placed) (Tsuang et al., 2013; Yung et al., 2012; Zachar et al., 2020).

However, the controversy doesn't end there. Even though attenuated psychosis syndrome isn't an officially approved disorder, it was "slipped" back into DSM under the awkwardly named *other specified schizophrenia spectrum disorder and other psychotic disorder* (A. Frances, 2013c; Kamens, 2014; A. E. Simon et al., 2013). DSM encourages clinicians to use this diagnosis for patients whose symptoms don't meet criteria for any other psychotic disorder but who nonetheless are believed to be psychotic, including those thought to be suffering from attenuated psychosis syndrome! Thus, despite the controversy surrounding it and its technically not being an official disorder, DSM instructs clinicians to diagnose attenuated psychosis syndrome using the "other psychotic disorder" category. DSM authors defended this decision by claiming that no reasonable person closely examining the manual could conclude that APS was anything but a disorder for further study (W. T. Carpenter et al., 2014). However, DSM-IV chair turned DSM-5 critic Allen Frances (2013c) expressed outrage over letting clinicians diagnose APS using the "other psychotic disorder" diagnosis, arguing it could result in a large number of teens and young adults who won't ever develop schizophrenia being improperly told they have a scientifically suspect "other specified" form of it. Still, advocates contend that the ability to diagnose and treat APS will get many people the early intervention they need to avoid long-term problems (W. T. Carpenter et al., 2014; W. T. Carpenter, 2020; W. T. Carpenter & van Os, 2011). Whether attenuated psychosis syndrome eventually becomes an official DSM disorder remains to be seen. Until then, debate over its merits as a diagnosis is likely to continue.

Critical Thinking Questions

1. Do you think attenuated psychosis syndrome is a sound proposal for a new DSM disorder? Why or why not?
2. What do you see as the risks and benefits of adding attenuated psychosis syndrome to DSM?
3. Should attenuated psychosis syndrome be added to the next version of DSM? If yes, why? If not, why not?
4. Did DSM do something improper by allowing clinicians to diagnose attenuated psychosis syndrome using the "other psychotic disorder" category? Explain your reasoning.

4.3 Other Diagnostic Perspectives on Psychosis

PDM

The S-Axis of the *Psychodynamic Diagnostic Manual* (PDM-2) describes psychotic disorders in psychodynamic terms. It tries to capture "the internal world of someone suffering from any of these conditions" (Lingiardi & McWilliams, 2017, p. 146). According to PDM-2, people with psychotic disorders struggle to differentiate thoughts, feelings, and perceptions. Their "self-environment" and "self-other" boundaries become fuzzy, which leads them to be hyper-reflexive: "For example, instead of simply enjoying the redness of a rose, a psychotic man might reflexively ask himself, 'Why is it called "red"?' … Nothing is assumed; everything has to be considered" (Lingiardi & McWilliams, 2017, p. 147). Due to repeated interpersonal disappointment and mistreatment (discussed in the psychodynamic section of this chapter), "the psychotic person withdraws from consensual reality and ordinary contact into a solitary delusional world" (Lingiardi & McWilliams, 2017, p. 151). PDM-2's focus on subjective experience offers a vivid and refreshing alternative to the descriptive approach of ICD and DSM, but non-psychodynamic clinicians and researchers may find it abstract and difficult to relate to.

HiTOP

In response to criticism of DSM and ICD as wedded to problematic diagnostic categories, the Hierarchical Taxonomy of Psychopathology (HiTOP) offers a dimensional way to diagnose psychosis. Two HiTOP spectra dimensions, "Thought Disorder" and "Detachment," have been linked to psychotic disorders, with the former generally corresponding to positive symptoms and the latter to negative symptoms. (Kotov et al., 2020). HiTOP researchers say psychosis can be diagnosed using these two spectra (plus fourteen narrower dimensions below them in the HiTOP hierarchy) (Kotov et al., 2020). They prefer this to using DSM and ICD because it avoids the problem of comorbid diagnostic categories while improving diagnostic reliability and predictive power. They also contend their model is more acceptable to clinicians, who often ignore DSM criteria and ICD guidelines when diagnosing (Kotov et al., 2020). It remains unclear whether clinicians will embrace using dimensions to make a diagnosis, as doing so is more time and labor intensive than selecting a DSM or ICD label.

PTMF

The Power Threat Meaning Framework (PTMF) challenges the legitimacy of traditional diagnosis. In keeping with its view that *power* (what happened to you) leads to *threat* (your response) and *meaning* (the sense you made of what happened), it sees psychosis as tied to social oppression and adversity (Johnstone, 2022; Read & Harper, 2022). Thus, PTMF acknowledges the distress and difficulties of people who experience what gets called psychosis, but it does not see them as suffering from disorders. The material in the sociocultural section of this chapter is consistent with a PTMF perspective on psychosis. Of course, critics might argue that PTMF minimizes biological contributions to psychosis. Your take likely depends on whether you favor biological or sociocultural explanations.

HISTORICAL PERSPECTIVES

4.4 From Dementia Praecox to Schizophrenia

Morel, Kraepelin, and Dementia Praecox

The Greek origins of the word psychosis mean "an abnormal psyche, or mind" (Lobel, 2013, p. 15). Although descriptions of extreme madness can be traced to the ancient Greeks, the concept of schizophrenia (the most well-known form of psychosis) is relatively new, arising after 1800 (Tueth, 1995). The French psychiatrist Bénédict-Augustin Morel (1809–1873) is credited with first describing schizophrenia. He used the term **dementia praecox**, which means "premature dementia." Morel defined dementia praecox as involving "mental degeneration with acute episodes of 'madness' that begin in the young"; such a definition "is central in subsequent accounts of what we now call 'schizophrenia'" (Hunter & Woodruff, 2005, p. 2).

Emil Kraepelin (1856–1926), an early developer of psychiatric diagnosis (see Chapter 3), included Morel's dementia praecox category in his classification system. However, he expanded it to include symptoms of *catatonia* (defined previously), *paranoia* (characterized by persecutory delusions), and *hebephrenia* (inappropriate affect with fleeting hallucinations and delusions) (Hunter & Woodruff, 2005; Tsoi et al., 2008). Kraepelin also distinguished dementia praecox from

Dementia praecox:
Early term used to describe what is today called schizophrenia; it means "premature dementia."

manic-depressive psychosis (Lavretsky, 2008). Importantly, he identified dementia praecox as an endogenous disorder—meaning he thought it originated in the body and had a physical cause (Beer, 1996; Lavretsky, 2008). Kraepelin's views on dementia praecox "profoundly influenced European and American psychiatry" (Lavretsky, 2008, p. 4).

Bleuler Coins the Term "Schizophrenia"

The Swiss psychiatrist Paul Eugen Bleuler (1857–1939) coined the term "schizophrenia" in 1911. Bleuler thought of schizophrenia in more psychological terms than did Kraepelin and the name he chose for the disorder literally means "a mind that is torn asunder" (Lavretsky, 2008, p. 4). Unfortunately, because the term has also been interpreted as "split mind," many people incorrectly assume that people with schizophrenia have "multiple personalities"—but talk of multiple personalities belongs in discussions of dissociative identity disorder, an entirely different presenting problem discussed in Chapter 8. Although DSM and ICD conceptions of schizophrenia have become narrower and more fully operationalized since Bleuler, the basic concept is similar (Lavretsky, 2008).

4.5 Early Twentieth-century Treatments

Early twentieth-century treatments for schizophrenia are often considered odd and/or abusive today, though the alternative to them was generally long-term incarceration in a hospital setting (A. Gibson, 2014). Let's review four such treatments (the first three of which were introduced in Chapter 1). *Insulin coma therapy* involved bringing patients in and out of comas daily over several weeks. It reduced symptoms, but nobody knows why (R. M. Kaplan, 2013; Lobel, 2013; Shorter, 1997). *Electroconvulsive therapy (ECT)*—modern forms of which are still used for schizophrenia (S. Grover et al., 2019)—was thought to neutralize psychotic symptoms by administering electric shocks to the brain that induced epileptic-like seizures (Endler, 1988; Lobel, 2013; Tueth, 1995). *Lobotomy*, a psychosurgery technique also known as *leucotomy*, disconnected the prefrontal cortex from the rest of the brain. It decreased aggression but seriously impaired cognitive and emotional functioning (J. Johnson, 2014; Lobel, 2013; Swayze, 1995). Finally, *hydrotherapy* entailed wrapping patients in wet sheets of varied temperatures for several hours at a time. The goal was to alleviate toxic impurities in the body thought to influence psychotic symptoms (Lobel, 2013). These historical treatments for schizophrenia enjoyed popularity prior to the advent of antipsychotic drugs in the 1950s, after which they generally fell into disrepute and stopped being used (Lavretsky, 2008). The take home message is that there have been many treatments for psychosis, but most look archaic in retrospect. Although today's treatments seem eminently reasonable, time will tell whether they stand up to the retrospective gaze of history.

BIOLOGICAL PERSPECTIVES

4.6 Brain Chemistry Perspectives

Dopamine Hypothesis of Schizophrenia

Since the late 1960s and early 1970s, the **dopamine hypothesis of schizophrenia** has been the most influential brain chemistry perspective on schizophrenia. In its most basic form, it holds that schizophrenia and other forms of psychosis result from too much of the brain neurotransmitter dopamine (Bloomfield & Howes, 2021; Kendler & Schaffner, 2011). **Antipsychotics** (also called *neuroleptics* and—as explained in Chapter 6—*major tranquilizers*) are prescribed to treat psychosis. This is consistent with the dopamine hypothesis because antipsychotic drugs decrease dopamine receptivity. Yet these drugs were in use before the dopamine hypothesis was formulated (Kendler & Schaffner, 2011). The hypothesis emerged because these drugs alleviated positive symptoms of schizophrenia.

Dopamine hypothesis of schizophrenia: Hypothesis that schizophrenia results from too much of the brain neurotransmitter dopamine.

Antipsychotics: Drugs used to alleviate psychotic symptoms; *first-generation antipsychotics* reduce dopamine transmission, while *second-* and *third-generation antipsychotics* reduce dopamine and serotonin transmission; also called *neuroleptics* and *major tranquilizers.*

Distinguishing the Dopamine Hypothesis from Antipsychotic Use

Because antipsychotic drugs were developed first and then efforts to explain how they work came later, it can be helpful to distinguish the clinical use of antipsychotics from research into the dopamine hypothesis of schizophrenia. Regardless of whether we accept the dopamine hypothesis, antipsychotic drugs reduce positive symptoms of psychosis such as hallucinations and delusions (R. Tandon et al., 2010). Unfortunately, evidence supporting the dopamine hypothesis itself (which potentially explains why these drugs help) is far less conclusive (O. D. Howes et al., 2015; Kendler & Schaffner, 2011; Keshavan et al., 2008; Moncrieff, 2009). This may be because we can only measure dopamine levels indirectly via neuroimaging, postmortem analysis of patient brains, or metabolites that remain in cerebrospinal fluid after the body breaks down dopamine. While imaging and postmortem studies provide evidence of excessive dopamine production in the brains of patients with schizophrenia (O. D. Howes et al., 2015), these results are confounded by the fact that most of the subjects in them were on antipsychotic medications for much of their lives, which could explain the results (Kendler & Schaffner, 2011).

Dopamine Hypothesis and Amphetamine Psychosis

Some argue that the most compelling evidence for the dopamine hypothesis comes from studies on amphetamines and psychosis (Kendler & Schaffner, 2011). In large doses, amphetamines induce psychotic symptoms. This is called *amphetamine psychosis*. The fact that amphetamines can cause psychosis is important for the dopamine hypothesis because we know that amphetamines increase dopamine levels. We also know that antipsychotic drugs relieve symptoms of amphetamine psychosis. Therefore, it is reasonable to infer that psychosis results from abnormally high dopamine levels. Research studies looking at the effect of amphetamines on psychosis provide some support for the dopamine hypothesis. However, it is difficult to conclude with certainty that excess dopamine is the sole cause of psychotic symptoms because amphetamines affect other neurotransmitters besides dopamine (O. D. Howes et al., 2015). Given the mixed research support, the trend has been towards a more skeptical view of the dopamine hypothesis, with many researchers questioning whether it alone is sufficient to explain schizophrenia and other psychotic disorders (O. D. Howes et al., 2015; Kendler & Schaffner, 2011).

Aberrant Salience

Aberrant salience hypothesis: Ascribes psychosis to over activity of the *mesolimbic dopamine pathway*; this results in excess dopamine, which leads to over-attributing meaning (i.e., salience) to extraneous and irrelevant events.

In light of evidence that excessive dopamine alone may not explain psychosis, some researchers now view dopamine as fueling the experience of psychosis rather than being its sole cause (O. D. Howes et al., 2020; O. D. Howes & Nour, 2016; Kapur, 2003, 2004; Kapur et al., 2005; Winton-Brown & Kapur, 2021). These researchers offer the **aberrant salience hypothesis**, which starts with the observation that dopamine is important in making attributions of salience. When something is experienced as salient, it is viewed as important or noticeable; it catches our attention and influences our behavior because it is associated with reward or punishment (Kapur, 2003; Winton-Brown & Kapur, 2021). The aberrant salience hypothesis holds that psychosis results when the *mesolimbic dopamine pathway* (a dopamine-mediated brain circuit implicated in rewards and pleasure) is overactive, leading to excessive dopamine. This is believed to cause over-attributing meaning (i.e., salience) to extraneous and irrelevant events, potentially explaining delusions and hallucinations: Delusions reflect efforts to interpret and make sense of the experience of salience, while hallucinations constitute responses to abnormally salient perceptions and memories that are treated as externally (rather than internally) generated phenomena (O. D. Howes & Nour, 2016; Kapur, 2003, 2004). While there is evidence of aberrant salience in schizophrenia (O. D. Howes et al., 2020; Kapur et al., 2005; Roiser et al., 2009), the hypothesis is difficult to test because our ability to directly measure dopamine remains limited and study participants are typically on antipsychotic drugs that affect dopamine transmission (O. D. Howes & Nour, 2016; Roiser et al., 2009).

Dopamine and Antipsychotic Drugs
First-Generation Antipsychotics

Despite problems with the dopamine hypothesis, antipsychotic drugs mostly target dopamine. They are more effective at reducing positive symptoms than negative symptoms (J. Dunlop &

Brandon, 2015; Leucht et al., 2021). The development of the original *first-generation antipsychotics*—known as *phenothiazines*—was accidental. Early phenothiazines were developed as industrial dyes and later used as antihistamines (Frankenburg & Baldessarini, 2008). However, once their efficacy for positive symptoms was established, they became the primary biological treatment for psychosis. *Chlorpromazine* (trade name *Thorazine*) was the first phenothiazine employed to treat psychosis. It was initially synthesized in 1950 and used as a sedative (Frankenburg & Baldessarini, 2008). However, it was soon found to relieve hallucinations, delusions, and mania. Consequently, it began to be prescribed for schizophrenia (W. T. Carpenter & Davis, 2012; Frankenburg & Baldessarini, 2008).

Despite the mixed research evidence for the dopamine hypothesis, we know antipsychotic drugs decrease dopamine receptivity. They do this mainly by binding to the dopamine receptors of neurons, preventing dopamine from doing so. When dopamine doesn't bind to these receptors, the neurons don't fire. Brain researchers have located five different dopamine receptors in the brain. Antipsychotic drugs impact *D2 dopamine receptors* (O. D. Howes et al., 2015; Keshavan et al., 2008; M. V. Seeman & Seeman, 2014; P. Seeman, 2011, 2013; I. A. Thompson et al., 2020). We don't know if this is because people with psychotic symptoms have too many D2 receptors, their D2 receptors are too sensitive, or their brains produce too much dopamine (O. D. Howes et al., 2015; Kendler & Schaffner, 2011; P. Seeman, 2011), but *D1 receptors* may also be important (S. Yun et al., 2023).

First-generation antipsychotics are still used, but less often due to their severe side effects (Ling Young et al., 2015). These side effects, known as **extrapyramidal side effects**, produce Parkinson's disease-like symptoms such as muscle tremors, a shuffling gait, and drooling. Patients sometimes experience muscle-rigidity (*dystonia*), involuntary muscle movements that affect the legs, lips, and fingers (*dyskinesia*), and a tendency to fidget and have difficulty remaining still (*akasthesia*). When antipsychotic drugs are taken for many years, these symptoms can develop into an irreversible syndrome known as **tardive dyskinesia**, which involves repetitive and involuntary muscle movements (Vasan & Padhy, 2022). Other symptoms include lip smacking, tongue wagging, and repeated eye blinking.

Second- and Third-Generation Antipsychotics

Second-generation antipsychotics were developed in the 1990s. The first one, *clozapine*, was originally used in treatment-resistant cases (Mortimer et al., 2010). Second-generation antipsychotics differ from their first-generation predecessors by binding more loosely with dopamine receptors while also blocking serotonin (a neurotransmitter implicated in depression). Similarly, *third-generation antipsychotics*, developed in the 2000s, also impact both dopamine and serotonin—but in an even more targeted manner (Limandri, 2019a). Because newer antipsychotics affect both dopamine and serotonin, it is unclear exactly how they reduce psychotic symptoms (Moncrieff, 2009). Due to their unique chemical makeup, second- and third-generation antipsychotics are sometimes referred to as *atypical antipsychotics*. Table 4.1 lists common first-, second-, and third-generation antipsychotics.

Newer antipsychotics are often deemed equally or more effective than the older first-generation drugs, especially in (a) improving cognitive functions such as memory and attention (Buchanan et al., 2007; S. K. Hill et al., 2010), and (b) alleviating negative symptoms (W. T. Carpenter & Davis, 2012; Limandri, 2019a; Mortimer et al., 2010; Orsolini et al., 2020). Despite optimism about newer antipsychotics, some researchers contend that they are no more effective than the older drugs (F. Cheng & Jones, 2013; Leucht et al., 2017; L. A. Lin et al., 2015; Nielsen et al., 2015; Rosenheck, 2013). This has led to debate over whether the increased cost of newer antipsychotics is worth it (L. M. Davies et al., 2007; Nielsen et al., 2015).

Besides their positive effects on cognition and—perhaps—on negative symptoms (a matter of intense debate) (Leucht et al., 2021), newer antipsychotics are viewed as less likely to cause extra-pyramidal side effects and tardive dyskinesia, but the evidence is mixed (Dibben et al., 2016; Ling Young et al., 2015; A. O'Brien, 2016; Peluso et al., 2012). The U.S. Food and Drug Administration hasn't allowed pharmaceutical companies to remove warnings about tardive dyskinesia from the labels of second-generation antipsychotics (Rosenheck, 2013). Additionally, the newer drugs have their own unpleasant side effects, such as weight gain and increased diabetes risk (Ling Young et al.,

Extrapyramidal side effects: Side effects of antipsychotic drugs that include muscle tremors, a shuffling gait, and drooling.

Tardive dyskinesia: Irreversible syndrome from prolonged use of antipsychotics; involves repetitive and involuntary muscle movements; symptoms such as lip smacking, tongue wagging, and repeated eye blinking are common.

Table 4.1 Common Antipsychotic Drugs

FIRST GENERATION	SECOND GENERATION / ATYPICAL	THIRD GENERATION / ATYPICAL
• Chlorpromazine (Thorazine, Largactil) • Fluphenazine (Prolixin, Permitil) • Haloperidol (Haldol, Peridol) • Thiothixene (Navane) • Trifluoperazine (Stelazine)	• Clozapine (Clorazil, Denzapine) • Lumaperone (Caplyta) • Lurasidone (Latuda) • Olanzapine (Zyprexa) • Paliperidone (Invega) • Quetiapine (Seroquel) • Risperidone (Risperdal) • Ziprasidone (Geodon)	• Aripiprazole (Abilify, Aristada) • Brexpiprazole (Rexulti) • Cariprazine (Vraylar)

Common trade names in parentheses.

2015)—although third-generation side effects may be fewer than second-generation ones (Orsolini et al., 2020). Given their side effects, many patients stop taking antipsychotics and experience *discontinuation symptoms* that resemble drug withdrawal (a topic revisited in Chapter 5 when discussing antidepressants) (C. Salomon & Hamilton, 2014; Stonecipher et al., 2006).

Antipsychotics may be the best drugs we currently have for psychosis, but their effectiveness is limited. Although twice as many patients improve when given antipsychotics versus placebo pills, only a small percentage (23 percent) have a "good response" and are "much improved" (Leucht et al., 2017). By some estimates, antipsychotics lead to full remission of symptoms in less than 35 percent of patients (Papanastasiou et al., 2013) and have little to no effect at all in nearly one-third of patients (Mortimer et al., 2010; J. M. Stone, 2011).

Luke

A psychiatrist at the university health center places Luke on the antipsychotic drug Risperdal. He also arranges for Luke to withdraw from his courses and go home to his family. When Luke arrives home, he sees a local psychiatrist who, after a few months, decides that the Risperdal isn't sufficiently relieving Luke's psychotic symptoms. He takes Luke off the Risperdal and prescribes Clozapine instead.

Glutamate Hypothesis

Glutamate hypothesis of schizophrenia:
Hypothesizes that deficient glutamate transmission is behind many symptoms of schizophrenia.

Uncertainty about the dopamine hypothesis has fueled research on other brain chemistry hypotheses. The **glutamate hypothesis of schizophrenia** holds that deficient transmission of the excitatory neurotransmitter glutamate is implicated in schizophrenia (Egerton et al., 2020, 2021; Javitt, 2021). Supplementing the glutamate hypothesis are additional hypotheses about the inhibitory neurotransmitter GABA. Some researchers suspect that glutamate dysfunction is related to both GABA and dopamine issues in psychosis (T. Chen et al., 2017; Egerton et al., 2017; Hjelmervik et al., 2018; Swanton, 2020; S. Weber et al., 2021). The same kinds of evidence sought for the dopamine hypothesis are now being sought for glutamate and GABA hypotheses, but measuring these neurotransmitters remains as challenging as measuring dopamine. There are currently no antipsychotic drugs focused primarily on glutamate or GABA instead of dopamine. However, besides impacting dopamine and serotonin, the third-generation antipsychotic *lumateperone* also indirectly affects glutamate (D. Cooper & Gupta, 2022; Orsolini et al., 2020).

4.7 Brain Structure and Function Perspectives

Whereas dopamine is associated with positive symptoms, brain structure abnormalities are often linked to negative symptoms (Asami et al., 2014; Chuang et al., 2014; Metzak et al., 2020).

For schizophrenia, brain structure and function perspectives tend to emphasize the roles of brain ventricle size and brain volume. These factors seem potentially related to one another.

Ventricle Size

Human brains have four *ventricles*, which are empty spaces filled with cerebrospinal fluid. This fluid serves as a pathway to remove waste material and transport hormones; it also protects the brain by cushioning it (Juuhl-Langseth et al., 2015). Research has consistently found a correlation between schizophrenia and enlargement of these four brain ventricles, especially the third ventricle (Haijma et al., 2013; Juuhl-Langseth et al., 2015; Rosa et al., 2010; Sayo et al., 2012; Svancer & Spaniel, 2021; van Erp et al., 2014). Having larger ventricles suggests that schizophrenia patients have fewer brain cells. That is, their overall brain volume is decreased, leaving more ventricle space. Why this is remains unclear.

Decreased Brain Volume

Given that larger ventricles imply less brain matter, it makes sense that schizophrenia brain research has found decreased volume of *gray matter* (important in movement, memory, and emotions) (Mercadante & Tadi, 2022; Svancer & Spaniel, 2021). Specifically, there may be abnormalities in the *prefrontal cortex* and in and around the *temporal cortex*—including the *hippocampus* (important in memory), *amygdala* (implicated in basic emotions like fear and rage), and *caudate nucleus* (important in goal-directed activity) (Cahn et al., 2009; Ebdrup et al., 2010; El-Sayed et al., 2010; Haijma et al., 2013; S. W. Lewis & Buchanan, 2002; Niznikiewicz et al., 2003; H. E. H. Pol et al., 2012; Radulescu et al., 2014; Sugranyes et al., 2015; van Erp et al., 2014; Veijola et al., 2014; Yüksel et al., 2012). The prefrontal cortex is important in decision-making, emotional-regulation, goal-oriented behavior, and speech, whereas the temporal cortex plays a part in language, emotion, and memory. Thus, decreased brain volume in these areas could influence deficits in speech, emotion, and planning common in schizophrenia.

The challenge with brain volume studies is their correlational nature. It is difficult to know whether decreased brain volume and larger ventricles are caused by schizophrenia. Research studies have identified other factors associated with changes in brain volume and schizophrenia, including childhood trauma (A. S. Brown, 2011; du Plessis et al., 2020; Ruby et al., 2017), cannabis use (De Peri et al., 2021; Koenders et al., 2015; Malchow et al., 2013; Rapp et al., 2013; Scheffler et al., 2021), socioeconomic status (SES) (A. S. Brown, 2011; Yeo et al., 2014), and being on antipsychotic medication (Fusar-Poli et al., 2013; D. A. Lewis, 2011; Moncrieff & Leo, 2010; Veijola et al., 2014; Zhuo et al., 2020). However, even when accounting for these factors, there still appears to be a relationship between brain volume and schizophrenia. We just don't know exactly what the relationship is.

4.8 Genetic Perspectives

Various types of genetic studies look at the degree to which susceptibility to schizophrenia is inherited. Twin studies, family studies, and adoption studies estimate the overall degree of heritability for schizophrenia but don't focus on specific genes. Genetic marker studies, on the other hand, do focus on specific genes. They try to identify chromosome defects associated with schizophrenia. Let's examine twin studies, family studies, adoption studies, and genetic marker studies one at a time.

Twin Studies

Twin studies examine **concordance rates** in twins—the percentage of the time that both twins in a twin pair are diagnosed with schizophrenia. These studies compare concordance rates of identical twins with those of fraternal twins. Identical twins are *monozygotic twins*. Having come from a single fertilized egg that split in two, monozygotic twins share all the same genes. In contrast, fraternal twins are *dizygotic twins*—they come from separate fertilized eggs, making them siblings who share only half their genes despite being in utero at the same time. Twin studies assume that schizophrenia has a genetic influence if pairs of genetically identical monozygotic twins develop schizophrenia at higher rates than pairs of more genetically different dizygotic twins.

Twin studies: Studies in which identical twins, who are genetically the same, are compared to see if both develop a trait or disorder.

Concordance rates: Percentage of time both twins in a pair develop a trait or disorder.

Averaging across studies, the concordance rate for schizophrenia is typically estimated to be between .45 and .50 for identical twins and .10 and .15 for fraternal twins (Cardno & Gottesman, 2000; Gejman et al., 2010; Glatt, 2008; Gottesman, 1991; D. F. Levinson & Mowry, 2000; S. W. Lewis & Buchanan, 2002; Prescott & Gottesman, 1993). This means that both identical twins wind up with schizophrenia 45–50 percent of the time compared with only 10–15 percent of the time for non-identical twins—suggesting a genetic influence on the development of schizophrenia, or at least a genetic vulnerability to it. Twin studies are used to argue that some people have a genetic susceptibility to schizophrenia, which the environment may or may not elicit (Glatt, 2008; Gottesman, 1991; Green, 2001; S. W. Lewis & Buchanan, 2002; Shean, 2004).

While genes do seem to play a role in schizophrenia, an identical twin concordance rate of 45–50 percent means that 50–55 percent of the time when one identical twin develops schizophrenia, the other one doesn't. This is half the time or more! So even if schizophrenia is partly genetic (as twin studies imply), the environment matters a lot too. Genes tell part of the story, not the whole story. They may predispose some people to schizophrenia, but environmental factors play a key role in how and whether genes are expressed (Karl & Arnold, 2014).

Critics of twin studies point to problems with them. First, many of these studies are old, having been done in the mid-twentieth century when the criteria for schizophrenia were not standardized across studies or based on current definitions of the disorder. These older studies might overestimate concordance rates (Shean, 2004). Second, some critics argue that schizophrenia concordance rates are inflated. Rates of 45–50 percent for identical twins and 10–15 percent for fraternal twins are often arrived at by averaging concordance rates across twin studies (Shean, 2004). This can be misleading because concordance rates vary widely from study to study, and averaging them doesn't adequately account for methodological differences across studies (J. Joseph, 2004, 2015; Shean, 2004). More conservative estimates of concordance are around 28 percent for monozygotic twins and 6 percent for dizygotic twins (Torrey, 1992). This still implies a genetic influence on schizophrenia but far less of one. Third, environment is a confounding variable in twin studies. These studies assume that identical twins aren't treated more similarly to one another than non-identical twins. That is, twin studies make the *equal environments assumption* that the environments of monozygotic twins and dizygotic twins are identical (Fosse et al., 2015; Henriksen et al., 2017; C. A. Ross, 2014). Critics challenge this assumption, arguing that identical twins likely receive more similar treatment than non-identical twins and this explains their higher concordance rates (Fosse et al., 2015; J. Joseph, 2004, 2015; C. A. Ross, 2014).

Family Studies

Family studies: Study how often the relatives of those with a trait or disorder also develop it.

Family studies look at how often relatives of those with schizophrenia are also diagnosed with it. They assume that the closer you are genetically to someone with schizophrenia, the more likely you are to develop it too. Many studies support this hypothesis (Gottesman, 1991; Gottesman et al., 2010; Green, 2001; Shean, 2004). A seminal review concluded that first-degree relatives of those with schizophrenia were much more likely to develop it than second- or third-degree relatives (Gottesman, 1991). Even among the first-degree relatives, the closer someone was genetically to the patient, the more likely that person was to also have schizophrenia. For instance, an identical twin (who shares all the genes of the person with schizophrenia) was estimated to have a 48 percent chance of developing schizophrenia, but a fraternal twin (who only shares half the genes) was estimated to have only a 17 percent chance of developing it. Non-twin siblings developed schizophrenia just 9 percent of the time and parents merely 6 percent of the time. These findings suggest a role for genes in susceptibility to schizophrenia.

Despite their tantalizing results, family studies have limitations. For one thing, lots of schizophrenia patients have no close relatives with schizophrenia. In that seminal review, 89 percent of those diagnosed with schizophrenia didn't have a parent with schizophrenia and 65 percent didn't have any first- or second-degree relatives who suffered from it (Gottesman, 1991). For another thing, it is difficult to determine the relative influence of genetics versus the environment in family studies. Genetically close relatives (e.g., siblings and their parents) are more likely to share similar environments compared with less genetically close relatives (e.g., aunts, uncles, and cousins) (J. Joseph, 2004). The former usually live together, the latter don't. Thus, it could be shared environment, as much or more than genetics, that accounts for what is found in family studies. Genes may not always explain the results:

Schizophrenia may run in families, but not all traits that run in families are genetic. Drinking red wine runs in Italian families, but it takes considerable mental acrobatics to attribute this behavior to anything other than environmental influences. In searching for explanations for this behavior we do not feel compelled to invoke a red-wine-drinking gene that lurks in the Italian blood. We have a much simpler explanation: If you are raised with red wine at dinner, odds are good that you will maintain this custom when you get older. (Green, 2001, p. 54)

Adoption Studies

Adoption studies look at schizophrenia rates among siblings adopted early in life and reared separately. The idea is to control for environmental influences. If siblings raised by different adoptive families develop schizophrenia, then the cause should be genes rather than environment. Numerous studies support this assumption. Let's mention three. In one, 7.9–8.7 percent of biological relatives of adoptees with schizophrenia were on the schizophrenia spectrum compared with only 1.9 percent of biological relatives of adoptees without schizophrenia (Kety, 1988). In another, kids whose biological (but not adoptive) parents had schizophrenia were more often on the schizophrenia spectrum than those whose adoptive (but not biological) parents had it (18.8 percent versus 4.8 percent of the time) (Wender et al., 1974). Finally, in a third study, adopted children of biological parents with schizophrenia were at higher risk for developing schizophrenia themselves, but the risk was greater when the adoptive families were dysfunctional; being raised in an emotionally healthy family protected genetically vulnerable children from schizophrenia, nicely illustrating how genes and environment potentially interact (Tienari et al., 2006).

Critics say adoption studies artificially inflate results by using overly broad criteria for schizophrenia (Fleming & Martin, 2011). Further, adoption studies cannot use random assignment to place children with adoptive families. This confounds results because families that adopt children whose parents have schizophrenia might differ from other adoptive parents (J. Joseph, 2004). Moreover, children are rarely adopted immediately after birth, creating another confound for adoption studies—namely that the children in them were likely raised by their biological parents for at least a while, which could influence later development of schizophrenia (J. Joseph, 2004).

Genetic Association Studies

Once researchers mapped the genome, they could do more than just study if mental disorders run in families. They became able to search for specific genes correlated with disorders. To do this they run **genetic association studies**, which aim to identify genetic markers (DNA sequences on chromosomes) associated with the disorder or trait being studied (C. M. Lewis & Knight, 2012). For instance, in *candidate gene studies*, genetic markers on genes of interest are examined to see if they are more common among case subjects than controls; such studies focus on a small number of genes already suspected of being related to the disorder at hand. By comparison, in *genome-wide association studies (GWAS)*, researchers don't limit themselves to candidate genes. Instead, they examine all genes in the genome to see which have markers associated with a given disorder. GWAS requires a lot of participants to obtain statistically significant results, but some researchers prefer GWAS because candidate gene studies have a poor track record in selecting the best genes to focus on (L. E. Duncan et al., 2019).

Genetic association studies of schizophrenia have identified a variety of genetic markers correlated with the disorder. The list of implicated genes is long (S. J. Allen et al., 2021). However, the exact roles of these genes remain unclear because (a) genetic association studies are correlational, (b) many of the implicated genes are also associated with other mental disorders, and (c) findings have proven difficult to replicate (Guang et al., 2014; E. C. Johnson et al., 2017; Ripke et al., 2013; C. A. Ross, 2013a; van Os et al., 2014). Relationships of some kind between the many candidate genes and schizophrenia are suspected, but we currently can't stipulate what they are—not surprising given how schizophrenia consists of complex symptoms linked to multiple genes. Importantly, gene expression is apt to be significantly impacted by the environment (P. J. Harrison, 2015; Sallis et al., 2021; van Os

Adoption studies: Compare rates of traits or disorders among siblings adopted early in life and reared in separate environments.

Genetic association studies: Aim to identify genetic markers (DNA sequences on chromosomes) associated with the disorder or trait being studied; *candidate gene studies* focus on specific genes while *genome-wide association studies (GWAS)* analyze the entire genome.

et al., 2014; Zwicker et al., 2018). If so, genetic vulnerability and environmental stressors combine to induce psychosis. In light of this *"dual hit" model*, identifying gene–environment interactions has become a central goal of genetic research on schizophrenia (Bloomfield & Howes, 2021; Karl & Arnold, 2014; Smigielski et al., 2020; van Os et al., 2014; Zwicker et al., 2018).

4.9 Evolutionary Perspectives

Schizophrenia as Evolutionarily Advantageous

Evolutionary perspectives hypothesize that schizophrenia and other psychoses have been retained by evolution (Adriaens, 2008; Kelleher et al., 2010). They posit that, despite obvious disadvantages, schizophrenia also confers benefits that keep it in the gene pool (Nichols, 2009). For example, some researchers contend that creativity, which often accompanies psychosis, is a desirable trait—one that helps psychotic-prone creative types (e.g., artists, musicians, authors, performers) attract mates and pass on their genes (Del Giudice, 2014). In this conception, psychotic behaviors constitute a high-risk mating strategy whose downside is full-blown schizophrenia or related disorders (Del Giudice, 2014).

It has also been theorized that psychotic individuals are charismatic leaders who often become inspirational politicians or religious figures. Consequently, they attract and inspire others, cultivating social unity. This benefits the group by enhancing its chances of survival (Brüne, 2004; Burns, 2006; Nichols, 2009). If so, the higher risk for psychosis in charismatic leaders gets transmitted (rather than eliminated) by evolution because it accompanies compelling traits that foster social cohesiveness and survival (Brüne, 2004; Burns, 2006; Nichols, 2009).

As a last example, some say psychosis results from an excessively hypersensitive perceptual system that helps identify and eliminate environmental threats. In this conception, the hypervigilance that often accompanies psychosis is adaptive; being perceptually sensitive to threats prevents being taken by surprise (Dodgson & Gordon, 2009). However, when this adaptive perceptual hypersensitivity becomes extreme, it morphs into psychosis. Hallucinations are one pathological byproduct of having an extremely sensitive, evolutionarily adaptive perceptual system: In highly stressful situations, some people's auditory perceptual sensitivity leads them to hear things that aren't there. When this becomes habitual, we consider them psychotic (Dudley et al., 2014).

Not everyone agrees with these theories. They have mixed research support across both gender and culture (Adriaens, 2008; Nichols, 2009). Some see little evidence that psychosis is evolutionarily advantageous (Nesic et al., 2019). Like many evolutionary hypotheses, theories of schizophrenia as evolutionarily beneficial are difficult to verify (Nichols, 2009). Objections notwithstanding, the idea that psychosis might be maintained by evolution remains intriguing.

Schizophrenia and Theory of Mind

Theory of mind:
Evolved human ability to view the world through others' eyes and generate interpretations of why others behave as they do, as well as to infer and comprehend one's own mental states and behavior.

Some researchers believe that people with schizophrenia suffer from impaired **theory of mind**—the evolved human ability to view the world through others' eyes and generate interpretations of why they behave as they do, as well as to infer and comprehend one's own mental states and behavior (Brüne, 2005; Frith, 2004). Good theory of mind skills are highly adaptive; they let us accurately predict others' behavior by mentally placing ourselves in their shoes. People experiencing psychosis struggle with theory of mind, leading to behavior that seems strange or disconnected from reality (Bora et al., 2009; Brüne, 2005; Brüne & Brüne-Cohrs, 2006; Frith, 2004; Frith & Corcoran, 1996; Pickup & Frith, 2001; Popolo et al., 2016). When they attribute intentions to themselves and others, they do so badly and are often wrong (Frith, 2004).

How does psychosis potentially impair theory of mind? It can reduce *affective empathy*, the ability to perceive others' emotions (Bonfils et al., 2016; Frith, 2004). This leads to behavior that seems odd or psychotic because it isn't informed by a grasp of other people's feelings and experiences. Impaired theory of mind also makes it difficult to identify *socially relevant information*; people in a psychotic state attend to extraneous stimuli, leading to bizarre and confusing behavior (Brüne, 2005). Finally, theory of mind impairment can affect *subjective representations*; as such, schizophrenia often involves mistaking subjective experiences for reality itself, resulting in delusional beliefs (Brüne, 2005).

Luke

Luke, for instance, mistakes his subjective worry that others may harm him as a feature of the objective world, thereby coming to believe that the government is monitoring him.

Research links the largest theory of mind deficits to patients displaying mainly negative symptoms (Frith & Corcoran, 1996; U. M. Mehta et al., 2014). This makes sense given that negative symptoms are characterized by emotional withdrawal and social disengagement. Comparatively, patients with more positive symptoms—especially paranoid delusions—perform better on theory of mind tasks but still worse than non-psychotic people (Frith, 2004; Pickup & Frith, 2001); their attributions about others' behavior are often wrong (Frith & Corcoran, 1996). It is possible that theory of mind is overdeveloped, not underdeveloped, in patients with positive symptoms. These patients overinterpret things and incorrectly attribute intentions to themselves and others, leading to delusional inferences and behavior that seems out of touch with reality. The **cliff-edge fitness theory** of psychosis holds that some people cross the line, shifting from being exceedingly sensitive in reading others to over interpreting their behaviors. This subtle shift may explain the difference between highly attuned social sensitivity and psychosis:

It is only one step further, over the cliff's edge of psychotic cognition, as it were, to finding secret meanings and evidence for conspiracies in other people's most casual gestures, to believing idiosyncratic grand theories and religions, and to thinking that others are controlling your thoughts. (R. M. Nesse, 2004, p. 862)

4.10 Immune System Perspectives

The **inflammatory hypothesis** postulates that many psychiatric disorders are tied to immune system inflammation. For psychoses, this inflammation is often associated with viral infections before or after birth (Kulaga & Miller, 2021). As mentioned in Chapter 2, people whose mothers contract viruses while pregnant with them are at higher risk for schizophrenia—a phenomenon predicted by the **viral theory of schizophrenia** (Boksa, 2008; A. S. Brown & Derkits, 2010; Crow, 1988; Kneeland & Fatemi, 2013; U. Meyer, 2013; R. M. Murray & Lewis, 1987; D. R. Weinberger, 1987). This may explain why those with schizophrenia are more likely to be born during winter months, when pregnant mothers stand a greater chance of immune system disruptions from influenza, the herpes simplex 2 virus, or the toxoplasma gondii parasite (A. S. Brown & Derkits, 2010; Torrey et al., 2015). The resulting prenatal inflammation is believed to influence fetal development and increase an infant's chances of later developing psychosis. However, the inflammatory hypothesis isn't limited to prenatal maternal infections. It's also supported by evidence linking psychosis to viral infections *after* birth. Risk for schizophrenia increases in some people after these infections—especially if they occur during formative developmental periods such as childhood or adolescence (Kulaga & Miller, 2021). The novel coronavirus pandemic that began in 2020 only heightened concerns about viral infections, with researchers worried that SARS-CoV-2 (the virus that causes COVID-19) places certain individuals at greater risk for psychosis and other psychiatric disorders (Kulaga & Miller, 2021).

The inflammatory hypothesis of psychosis extends beyond viral infections. Other immune system-activating conditions may also be at play. Along these lines, psychosis has been positively correlated with autoimmune diseases, gastrointestinal disorders, and infections following hospitalization (Benros et al., 2011; Jeppesen & Benros, 2019; Severance et al., 2016). Consistent with this, elevated levels of inflammatory *cytokines* (soluble peptides in the immune system whose presence suggests past viruses and infections) are found in many patients with schizophrenia, suggesting a role for prolonged immune activity (Bowcut & Weiser, 2018; Fond et al., 2020; P. D. Harvey, 2017; A. P. McLaughlin et al., 2021; B. J. Miller et al., 2011; Mondelli & Howes, 2014; Potvin et al., 2008).

Evidence for the inflammatory hypothesis is increasing. Analogue studies in rats and mice indicate that maternal viral infections affect offspring in ways applicable to understanding schizophrenia (Boksa, 2008; A. S. Brown, 2011; A. S. Brown & Derkits, 2010; Kneeland & Fatemi,

Cliff-edge fitness theory: Proposes psychosis occurs when theory of mind ability shifts from exceedingly sensitive to over interpretive.

Inflammatory hypothesis: Postulates that many psychiatric disorders (psychosis, anxiety, mood problems, etc.) are tied to immune system inflammation.

Viral theory of schizophrenia: People whose mothers had a virus while pregnant with them are at higher risk for schizophrenia.

2013; U. Meyer, 2013; B. J. Miller, Culpepper, et al., 2013; Moreno et al., 2011; Purves-Tyson et al., 2021). Studies also report heightened levels of immune system inflammation among schizophrenia patients (Feigenson et al., 2014; P. D. Harvey, 2017; Leboyer et al., 2016; B. J. Miller et al., 2011; B. J. Miller, Gassama, et al., 2013; Mondelli & Howes, 2014; Mongan et al., 2020; Tomasik et al., 2016). It has even been suggested that antipsychotic drugs relieve symptoms of psychosis in part by reducing inflammation (Kelsven et al., 2020; Leza et al., 2015; Mondelli & Howes, 2014).

Despite these promising findings, much remains unknown. Elevated cytokines are associated with presenting problems besides psychosis—most commonly depression (see Chapter 5). Teasing apart interrelationships among elevated cytokines, psychosis, and depression can be tricky, although efforts to do so can yield promising results (E. E. Lee et al., 2017). That said, research tying psychosis to inflammation is correlational, so direct causal links currently elude our grasp. Nonetheless, the inflammatory hypothesis is gaining traction. We revisit it often when discussing other presenting problems in later chapters. Interestingly, given that inflammation is associated not just with physical illnesses but also with environmental stressors, immune system hypotheses may help bridge biological and sociocultural perspectives—with immune system dysfunction and social adversity (discussed later in the chapter) mutually influencing the development of psychoses and other forms of mental distress (P. D. Harvey, 2017).

4.11 Evaluating Biological Perspectives

Biological perspectives on psychosis dominate current research and treatment. Adopting a medical model, they conceptualize psychoses as bodily diseases. When evaluating biological perspectives, remember that even though neurochemical, structural, genetic, and viral/immunological explanations seem distinct, researchers seek linkages among them—such as how genetics might make patients with schizophrenia susceptible to neurochemical brain imbalances. Also keep in mind that despite many promising research avenues, the primary biological intervention for psychosis remains neurochemical: the use of prescription drugs.

Despite their influence, biological perspectives do have detractors. Some critics complain that biological research tends to treat schizophrenia as a single disorder even though many researchers view the diagnosis as an unfortunate catch-all for people with a variety of severe but not-always-similar symptoms. Consistent with this view, the Research Domain Criteria (RDoC) movement is changing how researchers study psychoses; it discourages taking traditional diagnostic categories for granted and then casting about for evidence of their biological bases (Cuthbert & Morris, 2021; Fanous, 2015; Shepard, 2014). Instead, RDoC argues that we must begin with basic biological research that uncovers underlying mechanisms behind psychotic symptoms (W. T. Carpenter, 2013; Insel, 2013). Only then can we construct valid disorder categories capable of being diagnosed via biological tests (Insel, 2013). The RDoC approach fits with the growing belief among many researchers that what we now call schizophrenia will ultimately turn out to be various different disorders, or "biotypes" (Arnedo et al., 2015; Cuthbert & Morris, 2021; Fanous, 2015; S. E. Morris et al., 2021).

Other critics feel that the search for biological markers is ultimately a dead end. They question whether the concepts of psychosis and schizophrenia are scientifically valid, reliable, and best thought of in biological terms (M. Boyle, 2002; M. Pearson et al., 2023; Read, 2013b; T. S. Szasz, 1976/2004; R. Whitaker, 2002). In so doing, they challenge the assumption that schizophrenia is indisputably a brain disease by pointedly reminding us that it is diagnosed behaviorally, not biologically (T. S. Szasz, 1976/2004; S. E. Wong, 2014). Why isn't schizophrenia diagnosed biologically? Because we have yet to identify biological mechanisms that let us do so. To biological perspective opponents, this implies that the "schizophrenia-as-proven-brain-disease" position is asserted more conclusively than the evidence justifies (R. P. Bentall, 2013). According to these detractors, by privileging the biological we overlook psychological and sociocultural factors (S. E. Wong, 2014). Consequently, we lean too much on drug treatments and not enough on psychosocial interventions (L. Mosher et al., 2013; R. Whitaker, 2002, 2010).

Of course, not all critics take such a strong stance against the biological model. Many simply argue for a more integrated **biopsychosocial model** that sees biological, psychological, and social factors all contributing to schizophrenia (Corradi, 2011; Kotsiubinskii, 2002; Zipursky et al.,

Biopsychosocial model: Holds that presenting problems arise from an interaction among biological, psychological, and social factors.

2013). Nonetheless, the biological view has clearly taken precedence over psychological and social explanations in recent decades (Read & Dillon, 2013; R. Whitaker, 2002; Zipursky et al., 2013). Whether this is defensible depends on your perspective.

PSYCHOLOGICAL PERSPECTIVES

4.12 Psychodynamic Perspectives

Classic Psychoanalytic and Psychodynamic Views of Schizophrenia
Freud: Ego Turned Inward

Sigmund Freud (1924/1959) believed psychosis occurs when the ego is overwhelmed by the id and turns inward, away from the external world. Recall that the ego is motivated by the reality principle, the idea that what is practical and possible must be considered when satisfying unconscious id impulses. If a person regresses to a pre-ego state, then there is minimal contact with the practical realities of the conscious world. Consequently, the person seems out of touch with reality—that is, psychotic. Freud saw the psychotic patient's efforts to reestablish ego control and reengage the social world as generally ineffective, merely exacerbating symptoms. Psychotic patients often rely on the defense mechanism of projection: They project their confused and unacceptable feelings onto the world, resulting in symptoms like paranoia (A. J. Lewis, 2008). Freud doubted that psychosis could be treated with psychoanalysis (Saks, 2021).

Interpersonal View: Relational Origins of Psychosis

More interpersonally oriented psychodynamic thinkers such as Frieda Fromm-Reichmann (1889–1957) and Harry Stack Sullivan (1892–1949) were more optimistic than Freud regarding psychosis. They saw schizophrenia as having relational origins and believed it could be effectively treated using psychotherapy (Fromm-Reichmann, 1939, 1954; Silver & Stedman, 2009; H. S. Sullivan, 1962). Sullivan viewed schizophrenia as an extreme anxiety response to difficult relationships in infancy and childhood. Fromm-Reichmann also emphasized the importance of early relationships. She described **schizophrenogenic mothers** as cold, demanding, and domineering and believed this fostered schizophrenia in their children (Fromm-Reichmann, 1948). Sullivan and Fromm-Reichmann were both skilled therapists who saw the therapeutic relationship as a means for understanding and treating schizophrenia (Fromm-Reichmann, 1939; H. S. Sullivan, 1962). However, as biological perspectives gained influence, interpersonal and other relational approaches to schizophrenia increasingly became seen as misguided (Vahia & Cohen, 2008). Fromm-Reichmann's notion of schizophrenogenic mothers has received strong criticism on the grounds that it overlooks biology and is sexist in erroneously blaming mothers for their children's schizophrenia (Hartwell, 1996; Willick, 2001).

Schizophrenogenic mothers: Fromm-Reichmann's term for cold, demanding, and domineering mothers whose parenting style she blamed for their children's schizophrenia.

Modern Psychodynamic Therapy for Schizophrenia

Modern psychodynamic therapists view psychotic symptoms as reactions to extreme anxiety and terror, usually in response to intense abuse that prevents the formation of secure attachment relationships (Hertz, 2016; Karon, 2003; Koehler et al., 2013; B. Rosenbaum, 2019; Searles, 2013; Shean, 2004). Although psychodynamic clinicians often supplement therapy with medication (Iannitelli et al., 2019; Saks, 2021), many feel that "too often, mental health professionals attend minimally to the content of a client's psychotic processes, not recognizing that they may be internally logical and rational to the client" (Hertz, 2016, pp. 345–346). From a psychodynamic perspective, psychotic symptoms aren't mere byproducts of disease but meaningful defenses against anxiety:

For people with schizophrenia, the heavy reliance on denial, projection, introjection, and externalization helps to manage chaotic and intrusive thoughts, and to avoid the experience of unbearable loss and frightening contact with others. These defenses are attempts at a solution, and on some level "work"— but at an enormous price. Painful thoughts and feelings are disavowed, but reality becomes distorted. (Hertz, 2016, p. 349)

During sessions, patients' utterances are treated as subjectively true to them regardless of whether what they say seems "normal" or "pathological" (B. Rosenbaum, 2019). By exploring transference and countertransference in the therapeutic relationship (see Chapter 2), psychodynamic therapists help patients work through past traumas and establish more effective ways of relating that do not require withdrawing from reality contact when emotionally overwhelmed (R. Horowitz, 2002; Karon, 2003, 2008b, 2008a; B. Rosenbaum, 2019; Searles, 2013).

Luke

A psychodynamic therapist working with Luke would try to understand Luke's psychotic symptoms as meaningful defenses against overwhelming terror.

Perhaps the therapist would uncover something similar to what psychodynamic therapist Bertram Karon (1992, p. 201) did when working with a patient diagnosed with schizophrenia who stuttered and spoke in Latin. In this case, a seemingly meaningless psychotic symptom—odd and incoherent speech—turned out to be a meaningful response to an intensely terrifying and abusive experience:

The patient's terrible stutter was ... revealed to have an extraordinary cause. In the middle of his stutter there were words in Latin. When asked if he had been an altar boy, he said, "You swallow a snake, and then you stutter. You mustn't let anyone know." He was extremely ashamed and guilty. Apparently, he had performed fellatio on a priest.

Psychodynamic therapists contend that their approach to schizophrenia is supported by research (Karon, 1992, 2003; Koehler et al., 2013), but others challenge this claim on the grounds of poor methodology and few randomized controlled trials (RCTs) (T. M. Lincoln & Pedersen, 2019; Strupp, 1986; Summers & Rosenbaum, 2013). Defenders point to evidence that psychodynamic therapy combined with drug treatment can be more effective than drugs alone at reducing psychosis (Duggins & Veitch, 2013; B. Rosenbaum et al., 2012). Still, psychodynamic therapy for psychosis has mixed research support, at best (R. E. Cooper et al., 2020; T. M. Lincoln & Pedersen, 2019). Consequently, it is regularly overshadowed by biological approaches (Koehler & Silver, 2009). While some see psychodynamic therapy as blaming parents and being clinically vague, psychodynamic therapists counter that drug treatments often don't help and that environmental factors—including upbringing and childhood adversity—are implicated in psychosis (Larsen, 2009; Read, 2013a; B. Rosenbaum, 2019). Therefore, they continue developing and researching psychodynamic interventions for it.

4.13 Cognitive-Behavioral Perspectives

Cognitive and Behavioral Assumptions about Psychosis

Cognitive perspectives attribute psychosis to problematic thinking that leads to abnormal perceptions (A. T. Beck & Rector, 2000). Indeed, cognitive misinterpretations seem to play a role in psychotic experience. For example, people diagnosed with paranoid schizophrenia are especially attuned to threat-related stimuli, while those with auditory hallucinations often misinterpret printed words and garbled sounds as voices (A. T. Beck & Rector, 2000). Further, negative beliefs about others combined with social adversity can lead to paranoid thinking (O. D. Howes & Murray, 2014; A. P. Morrison et al., 2015). Paranoid people often attribute negative events to others rather than themselves or their surroundings (A. T. Beck & Rector, 2000; S. Sullivan et al., 2013). Put simply, cognitive approaches assume that cognitive processes influence psychotic symptoms.

Behavioral perspectives conceptualize psychosis as learned behavior. Historically, behaviorists viewed psychosis as produced and maintained by often-subtle reinforcement contingencies while arguing that behavior therapy reconditions more suitable responses (Lindsley, 1956, 1960; Rutherford, 2003; Skinner, 1954; S. E. Wong, 2006). Psychosis, then, occurs when socially appropriate behavior isn't reinforced, resulting in individuals no longer attending to typical social cues and instead gaining attention for bizarre behavior and other psychotic symptoms. To the lament of some behaviorists (S. E. Wong,

2006; Wyatt & Midkiff, 2006), a strictly behavioral view of psychosis is rejected today in favor of biological perspectives (J. C. Wakefield, 2006). However, combined cognitive-behavioral therapies are widely used, often as a supplement to drug treatment.

Cognitive-Behavioral Therapy for Psychosis (CBTp)

Cognitive-behavioral therapy for psychosis (CBTp) combines cognitive and behavioral perspectives. It looks at how thought processes and behavioral conditioning influence psychotic behavior. CBTp incorporates many different CBT techniques. The techniques used are continually evolving, and there isn't always agreement on which ones fall under the CBTp umbrella (T. Lincoln & Brabban, 2021). Still, let's review some common CBTp techniques.

Photo 4.3 Mathematician and Nobel Prize winner John Nash was famously diagnosed with schizophrenia, and his experiences became the basis for the 2001 film *A Beautiful Mind.*
Gary Miller/Getty Images.

Common CBTp Techniques

CBTp relies on many cognitive techniques. In *Socratic questioning*, the therapist asks questions designed to help therapists and clients better understand the client's experiences (Carona et al., 2021; T. Lincoln & Brabban, 2021). With psychosis, Socratic questioning might gently call into question the client's hallucinatory perceptions and delusional beliefs. *Evidential analysis* involves client and therapist identifying evidence for and against the client's psychotic beliefs (A. P. Morrison, 2001). *Normalization* is when the therapist explains that what the client is experiencing is more common than the client believes. For example, psychotic clients usually don't know that in the United States alone nearly 15 million people hear voices, but many of them go about their lives just fine and never receive psychiatric services (A. P. Morrison, 2001). Finally, CBTp therapists often invite clients experiencing psychosis to engage in *behavioral experiments* in which they test the reality of their delusional beliefs (Combs & Tiegreen, 2007; T. Lincoln & Brabban, 2021). Table 4.2 illustrates how CBT techniques could be used with Luke.

CBTp also incorporates behavioral techniques. For instance, **social skills training (SST)** helps those with schizophrenia interact more effectively in social settings. Complicated social scenarios—such as making friends, dating, ordering food in a restaurant, or going for a job interview—are broken down into concrete steps that are taught to the client (Tenhula & Bellack, 2008). SST incorporates various behavioral techniques, including **modeling** of appropriate behavior by the therapist and **behavioral rehearsal** in which the client role-plays how to act in specific social situations. During SST, "participants are first taught to perform the elements of the skill, then gradually learn to combine them smoothly through repeated practice, shaping, and reinforcement of successive approximations" (Tenhula & Bellack, 2008, p. 242). SST is effective with psychosis, but more studies are needed (Brando et al., 2021; Granholm et al., 2022; D. T. Turner et al., 2018).

> **Luke**
>
> *As Luke improves, he begins to think about finding a job. Luke's therapist could use social skills training to help Luke develop job interview skills. If so, the therapist would model how to behave during a job interview, then Luke would practice job interviewing in role-plays. Concrete behaviors such as dressing professionally, giving the interviewer a firm handshake, making eye contact with the interviewer, and smiling at appropriate moments would be practiced individually. Once mastered, these individual skills could be integrated into a broader role-play experience.*

Syndrome vs. Symptom Approaches in CBTp

There is tension in CBTp between syndrome and symptom approaches. In the *syndrome approach*, schizophrenia and other psychoses are viewed as bodily diseases for which CBTp serves as a secondary treatment to antipsychotics (Brockman & Murrell, 2015). The syndrome approach employs a **stress-vulnerability-coping skills model** in which a biological vulnerability to psychosis is triggered by environmental stress. The degree to which someone has sufficient cognitive coping skills then influences whether this stress triggers a biological vulnerability that, once triggered, allows the resulting psychotic symptoms to be dealt with effectively (Muesser, 1998). From a stress-vulnerability-coping skills perspective, combining drug treatment with cognitive-behavioral interventions makes

Cognitive-behavioral therapy for psychosis (CBTp): Uses cognitive and behavioral therapy techniques (e.g., *Socratic questioning, evidential analysis, normalization,* and *behavioral experiments*) to challenge the psychotic patient's perceptions and behavior.

Social skills training (SST): CBT technique in which complicated social scenarios (e.g., making friends, dating, ordering food in a restaurant, or going for a job interview) are broken down into discrete steps and taught to clients.

Modeling: Indirect form of exposure in which the therapist models the aversive behavior for the client, demonstrating that the fear is unjustified.

Behavioral rehearsal: Behavioral technique in which the client role-plays how to act in specific social situations.

Stress-vulnerability-coping skills model: Says a *biological vulnerability* to psychosis is triggered by *environmental stress;* the degree to which someone has sufficient cognitive coping skills influences whether stress triggers the biological vulnerability or, once triggered, allows the resulting psychotic symptoms to be dealt with effectively.

Table 4.2 CBTp for Psychosis with Luke

Socratic Questioning

Luke: The government is spying on me by using radar signals sent through the fillings in my teeth.

Therapist: How long have they been doing this?

Luke: Since last May.

Therapist: Why are they doing this?

Luke: Because they are afraid of me. I may be revealed soon as the next Messiah.

Therapist: How do you know they are doing this?

Luke: The voices told me. Sometimes my teeth hurt.

Therapist: Is there any other reason your teeth might hurt?

Luke: I guess I could have a cavity.

Evidential Analysis

Evidence for "The government is spying on me by using radar signals sent through the fillings in my teeth."	*Evidence against* "The government is spying on me by using radar signals sent through the fillings in my teeth."
• The voices tell me it is true. • The government has spied on other people before. • My teeth hurt sometimes and that could be from the radar device implanted in them.	• The voices could be wrong. • The government hasn't moved against me; nobody's been sent to arrest me. • I might have a cavity and that's why my tooth hurts.

Behavioral Experiment

Luke's therapist asks him to go the dentist to see if the radar device in his teeth can be found and removed. Luke is skeptical and says he might not be able to trust just any dentist. He only agrees if he can go to his family's long-time dentist, who Luke believes the government would be unlikely to corrupt. After giving Luke a thorough check-up, the dentist tells Luke that there is no radar device in his teeth. Luke remains skeptical but agrees to discuss the issue further with his therapist during their next session.

Source: Reproduced from Johnstone and Boyle (2018) with permission of the British Psychological Society through PLSclear.

sense. Consistent with this, some practitioners use CBT to improve medication compliance (Sudak, 2011). There is research to justify doing so; it often (but not always) finds adding CBT to drug treatment for psychosis is more effective than drug treatment alone (Dickerson, 2000, 2004; Dickerson & Lehman, 2011; A. P. Morrison et al., 2018). This fits with the syndrome approach view of CBTp as a supplementary intervention for psychotic illness best used in conjunction with drug treatment.

By comparison, the *symptom approach* questions the wisdom of conceptualizing psychosis using medical model diagnoses such as schizophrenia and points to preliminary evidence that CBTp reduces psychosis even in the absence of antipsychotics (A. P. Morrison et al., 2012, 2014). Rather than trying to figure out which DSM or ICD psychotic disorder someone suffers from, the symptom approach looks at each patient's symptoms one at a time and figures out how best to address them (Brockman & Murrell, 2015). Symptom approach therapists don't reject biological aspects of psychosis, agreeing that some people are innately predisposed to interpret events in psychotic ways (R. Bentall, 2013). However, they maintain that assigning psychotic people to stigmatizing and scientifically questionable diagnostic categories isn't advisable (R. Bentall, 2013; R. P. Bentall et al., 1988). A symptom approach uses CBTp to target specific psychotic symptoms without privileging diagnosis and medication.

Evaluating CBTp

Some research supports using CBTp with psychosis, both as a supplement and alternative to medication (T. Lincoln & Brabban, 2021; A. P. Morrison et al., 2014, 2018; Naeem et al., 2016). Accordingly, CBTp is recommended as an evidence-based psychosocial treatment for schizophrenia by the American Psychiatric Association, the UK National Health Service, and the German Association of Psychiatry, Psychotherapy, and Psychosomatics (Brockman & Murrell, 2015; Dixon et al., 2009). However, not everyone is convinced. Some studies and *meta-analyses* (in which data from many previous studies are combined and analyzed) find CBTp to be ineffective or only slightly effective for psychosis (Garety et al., 2008; Jauhar et al., 2014; C. Jones et al., 2012; Lynch et al., 2010; McKenna & Kingdon, 2014; L. Wood et al., 2020). CBTp has been also criticized for requiring highly trained clinicians—consequently, in many settings there are few professionals able to competently deliver it (N. Thomas, 2015). CBTp therapists need to (a) undertake more research showing that their strategies are effective and (b) find ways to train enough clinicians to administer these therapies (T. Lincoln & Brabban, 2021).

4.14 Humanistic Perspectives

Psychosis as a Meaningful Extreme State

Humanistic perspectives challenge medical model conceptions of mental distress. They view the retreat into psychosis as a meaningful effort to maintain a sense of self or identity in the face of overwhelming invalidation and mistreatment. Through the prism of his person-centered therapy, humanistic psychologist Carl Rogers (1967) attributed psychosis to extreme incongruence and invalidation, which he felt could be addressed by providing clients a secure and supportive relationship consisting of empathy, genuineness, and unconditional positive regard. Rogers' more existential colleague, psychiatrist R. D. Laing, saw schizophrenia as a sane response to an insane world. Laing (1965, 1967) didn't see schizophrenia as a disease, but as the person's best efforts to respond to exceedingly pathological family and social conditions.

Today's humanistic therapists build on the work of Rogers and Laing, viewing psychosis as an *extreme state* rather than a disordered one (Cornwall, 2019a). From a humanistic perspective, people in extreme states are trying to make sense of and cope with difficult problems such as poverty, abuse, neglect, bullying, rape, assault, racism, trauma, and spiritual crises (Breggin, 2019; C. Knapp, 2019; Longden, 2017; Lukoff, 2019; Read, 2019; Sedláková & Řiháček, 2019; Unger, 2019). What they need is acceptance, love, and not having their experience explained away as a permanently debilitating brain disease (Cooke & Kinderman, 2018; Cornwall, 2019b; Unger, 2019). Humanistic therapists worry about psychiatric drugs being used to suppress symptoms, and instead believe the path to overcoming extreme states requires grasping the purpose and meaning of symptoms (Cooke, 2017; Read, 2019; Sedláková & Řiháček, 2019). Despite being criticized for their anti-medical view of psychosis (Torrey, 2013) and insufficient research support for their perspective (T. M. Lincoln & Pedersen, 2019), humanistic therapists maintain that psychiatry too often reduces psychotic symptoms to byproducts of brain disease rather than seeing them as meaningful responses to extremely difficult circumstances (Cooke, 2017; Read, 2019). Let's examine two humanistic approaches to psychosis: pre-therapy and narrative therapy.

Pre-therapy

In the 1960s, Carl Rogers and his colleagues were optimistic that person-centered therapy could help those with schizophrenia, but their study of its effectiveness provided middling results (Prouty, 2002; C. R. Rogers, 1967). However, Garry Prouty developed **pre-therapy**, a version of person-centered therapy for use with psychotic individuals (Prouty, 1994, 2002, 2007; Van Werde & Prouty, 2013). The logic of pre-therapy is that before people experiencing psychosis can engage in full-fledged psychotherapy, their therapists must make *psychological contact* with them, which traditional person-centered therapy doesn't always do given how hard it is to establish psychological contact with someone in an extreme state. In pre-therapy, the therapist makes contact by reflecting the client's experiences in a variety of concrete ways such as restating the client's bizarre language word for word, describing what the client is doing in the moment, reflecting the client's emotions, and imitating the client's body language and facial expressions (Barker, 2015; Prouty, 1994, 2002, 2007; Van Werde & Prouty, 2013). Once contact is established, genuine therapy can begin in which client and therapist explore the meaning behind the client's psychotic symptoms.

Pre-therapy: Version of person-centered therapy for use with psychotic individuals; goal is to make *psychological contact* with the psychotic client as a pre-condition for effective therapy.

Luke

Imagine Luke is brought to the hospital during a psychotic episode, during which he keeps insisting that the government is spying on him via the fillings in his teeth and that he can feel the fillings monitoring him because they are vibrating. The psychiatric nurse admitting him might use pre-therapy to help Luke reestablish reality contact. When Luke cowers in the corner, points to his jaw, and screams "They're watching me!" the nurse—in keeping with the active listening approach of pre-therapy—simply reflects what she observes: "You're here at the hospital. You're in the corner, pointing at your jaw, and screaming." When Luke turns toward the wall and yells "Must hide! Can't let them get me!" the nurse again offers a concrete reflection, stating "You're facing the wall and trying to hide." Luke responds in a tearful voice, "I had to hide." "You had to hide," reflects the nurse. "Yes," says Luke, turning toward the nurse and looking her right in the eye for the first time while tears stream down his face. "My teacher hurt me. He hurt me!" The nurse embraces Luke while he sobs. Psychological contact has been made.

Prouty (2002) cites a variety of small research studies suggesting that pre-therapy is effective for psychosis. However, a lot of this research consists of pilot studies with few participants. More recent qualitative research provides support for pre-therapy (Courcha, 2015; Erskine, 2015; Traynor, 2019; Traynor et al., 2011), but quantitative research is lacking—perhaps because humanistic clinicians often value qualitative over quantitative research. Nonetheless, additional quantitative studies could more fully assess pre-therapy's effectiveness.

Narrative Therapy

Narrative therapy (described in Chapter 2) encourages clients to question the dominant social narrative in which they are "afflicted by" psychosis. In this pathologizing narrative, psychosis is a part of them. Thus, their essential identity is that they "are" psychotic. Instead, by using the narrative technique of externalizing the problem (defined in Chapter 2), clients are encouraged to view psychosis as something separate from them that negatively influences their lives (Hewson, 2015). Once externalized, questions can be asked to map the influence of psychosis, such as: "How does psychosis get the best of you?" "When does psychosis have the most influence over you?" "Are there times when you are able to neutralize psychosis?" The goal is to encourage clients to view schizophrenia as something distinct from them (rather than a disorder that they "have"). Ideally, externalizing psychosis helps clients devise new life narratives that highlight *exceptions*—times they did not give in to schizophrenia's influence. Clarifying exceptions provides clients with clear ideas about how to avoid letting psychosis get the best of them (Hewson, 2015).

Luke

A narrative therapist might ask Luke to "externalize" schizophrenia by talking about it not as a disease he "has" but as a separate entity that often gets the best of him. In so doing, Luke might realize that schizophrenia has the firmest grip on him when he is alone and has nothing to do. However, Luke might also identify several exceptions—times when schizophrenia and the voices it uses against him aren't as powerful. As he identifies these exceptions, an alternative narrative might be developed in which schizophrenia loses much of its influence over Luke when he is busy with other people (e.g., on a lunch date, at a movie, or playing Dungeons and Dragons at the local community center). Luke might find that, when he becomes engaged in social activities, the voices are quieter and Luke's urge to obey them is weaker. Luke might begin to adopt this new, less pathologizing narrative about himself—coming to view himself not as a "schizophrenic" but as a person distinct from schizophrenia with the tools to evade its influence over him when he plans accordingly.

Impoverished Narratives and Difficulty with Metacognition

Paul Lysaker and colleagues have developed a narrative approach in which they conceptualize schizophrenia as occurring when biological and environmental conditions combine in ways that lead people to have impoverished personal narratives and difficulty with reflecting on their own thinking (Lysaker et al., 2010, 2013, 2019; Lysaker & Lysaker, 2006). From this perspective, people with schizophrenia have trouble constructing meaningful stories about their lives—hence the assertion that they have impoverished narratives (Lysaker et al., 2001, 2013). They also struggle with *metacognition*, the ability to think about their thinking. As a result, they aren't very adept at reflecting on their own thought processes or those of others (Lysaker et al., 2013, 2019, 2020). Lysaker's narrative therapy for schizophrenia helps clients revise or replace problematic stories they live by. This is accomplished through the therapeutic relationship. Clients are encouraged to not only pay attention to their own and their therapists' thinking (as they might in cognitive therapy), but also to reflect on their personal narratives. Where did these narratives originate? What purposes do they serve? Are there other (more helpful) stories? Lysaker has developed rating scales that clinicians can use to measure the coherence of client narratives (Lysaker et al., 2002, 2003). Despite needing more research support, Lysaker sees much promise in therapy focused on metacognition (Lysaker et al., 2020).

4.15 Evaluating Psychological Perspectives

As noted, because schizophrenia and other psychoses are so often viewed through the prism of the biological illness model, psychological perspectives have often been relegated to the sidelines—an afterthought to supplement the effects of antipsychotic drugs. Early psychodynamic therapies for schizophrenia didn't perform well in clinical research trials and for a long time afterwards therapy was generally viewed as ineffective (Hamm et al., 2013; Lysaker et al., 2010). However, advocates of psychotherapeutic approaches contend that over the last two decades there has been a significant shift, with psychotherapy again being looked at as a viable intervention for schizophrenia. Much of the shift has been due to the limitations of antipsychotic drugs (they often don't work, have unpleasant side effects, and patients often stop taking them). The shift can also be attributed to the emergence of a recovery-oriented approach in which schizophrenia is viewed as something from which people can successfully recover (E. R. Carr et al., 2018; Hamm et al., 2013; Lysaker et al., 2010; Ridenour et al., 2019). A growing body of research suggests that psychotherapy, rehabilitation, and other psychosocial interventions are effective in addressing psychosis (Bourke et al., 2021; Brus et al., 2012; R. E. Cooper et al., 2020; Dickerson & Lehman, 2011; T. M. Lincoln & Pedersen, 2019)—especially during early onset (Armando et al., 2015; Goldsmith et al., 2015; Kane et al., 2016). Some researchers are even looking at how psychotherapy might biologically alter brain processes associated with schizophrenia and other psychoses (Bomba & Cichocki, 2009; Kumari et al., 2011; Matsuda et al., 2019). In other words, biological and psychological approaches to schizophrenia are increasingly being integrated.

SOCIOCULTURAL PERSPECTIVES

4.16 Cross-Cultural and Social Justice Perspectives

Inequality and Adversity

Social justice perspectives point out that psychosis is correlated with social inequality and adversity. Those who experience psychosis are much more likely to have been physically or sexually abused as children (DeRosse et al., 2014; H. L. Fisher et al., 2010; Vaskinn et al., 2021). This suggests that even if there is a genetic predisposition to psychosis, environmental factors often elicit it (Husted et al., 2010, 2012; Karl & Arnold, 2014; Popovic et al., 2019; van Os et al., 2014). Other sociocultural factors frequently associated with psychosis and schizophrenia are cannabis use, low socioeconomic status, and living in an urban environment (Fett et al., 2019; Luo et al., 2019; S. Patel et al., 2020; Wainberg et al., 2021). Because the data on sociocultural factors is correlational (just as it is with a lot of biological research), we can't conclude that social factors such as abuse and neglect cause psychosis. However, we do know that they are important variables that can predict who is at risk.

Ethnic and Racial Factors

Ethnic and racial factors are also important. Research spanning the United States, Canada, and Europe has found that belonging to an ethnic or racial minority group and experiencing discrimination places one at higher risk for psychosis (D. M. Anglin et al., 2021; Oh et al., 2014; J. Pearce et al., 2019; M. V. Seeman, 2011). Given this, it isn't surprising that immigrants and those living in neighborhoods where they are a clear minority are more likely to be diagnosed as psychotic (DeVylder et al., 2013; Henssler et al., 2020; Veling & Susser, 2011). Being from an ethnic or racial minority group can lead to extreme psychological stress that potentially increases the chances of psychosis. At the same time, there is also evidence that members of ethnic and racial minority groups are often viewed as more disturbed than other people. This implies that higher rates of psychotic disorders may be due—at least in part—to culture bias in diagnosis. In the United States, for instance, Black Americans are much more likely to be diagnosed with schizophrenia than white Americans (Gara et al., 2019; E. K. Schwartz et al., 2019; R. C. Schwartz & Blankenship, 2014). Is this because of racial bias in diagnosis or because Black Americans often face stressful environmental conditions such as poverty and discrimination, which predispose them to psychosis? It may turn out to be a bit of both.

4.17 Service User Perspectives

Stigma of Psychosis

Service user perspectives stress how psychosis has a significant impact on people's lives. Qualitative studies have identified various things that people with schizophrenia commonly experience. First, they experience a change in social roles; their work, social, and family relationships are impacted. Many things they could do before their symptoms developed are no longer easy for them (S. Gibson et al., 2013). Second, they think of themselves differently, needing to incorporate "schizophrenia" into their sense of self (Gumber & Stein, 2013; L. Howe et al., 2014; Jansen et al., 2015). Some do this by coming to see themselves as suffering from a chronic illness, while others resist the medicalization of their difficulties. One patient who accepted the schizophrenia diagnosis commented: "It was like a relief in a way that at least they knew now what I already knew, that I'd got this schizophrenia" (L. Howe et al., 2014, p. 157). Third, they often must deal with the challenges of hospitalization and taking antipsychotic drugs. Drug side effects are unpleasant, and patients often grapple with whether the tradeoffs are worth it. As one patient described it:

Because of the side effects, I gained nearly 80 pounds, developed severe acne, and tried to fight the involuntary jaw movements and painful oculogyral reactions brought on by the medications. These side effects added to the visible stigma of having a mental illness and consequently contributed to the ostracism by my peers at school. (Bjorkland, as cited in Gumber & Stein, 2013, p. 190)

Finally, people diagnosed with schizophrenia encounter social stigma (L. Howe et al., 2014), which often leads them and their caregivers to avoid seeking services (Dockery et al., 2015). For instance, one patient remarked, "I couldn't tell anyone what was happening [related to my illness] because I was so afraid of being labeled as 'crazy'" (Jordan, as cited in Gumber & Stein, 2013, p. 190). Stigma is commonly accompanied by discrimination, with patients simultaneously dealing with their own feelings of shame and the unfair treatment they receive from others. Another patient stated:

You're just kind of afraid of being stigmatised by other people … you just know there are prejudices about all these things; I used to be like that myself … and so in order to avoid that people were thinking badly of me, I thought I'd better put on a façade. (Jansen et al., 2015, p. 90)

Overcoming stigma is an important achievement. According to one patient, "Though I still plan to keep a low profile as far as my psychosis goes, I will never again allow stigma to guide my life, at least not to a significant extent" (BGW, as cited in Gumber & Stein, 2013, p. 190). Coping with psychosis requires not just dealing with the experience of psychosis itself but also with the stigma that accompanies it.

Consumer Groups vs. Survivor Groups
Consumer Groups

Consumer groups such as the Mental Health Foundation and the National Alliance for the Mentally Ill (NAMI) campaign against stigma. For instance, the Mental Health Foundation (n.d.) contends that "there is more media misinformation about schizophrenia than about any other type of mental health problem …. Sensational stories … tend to present people with schizophrenia as dangerous, even though most people diagnosed with schizophrenia don't commit violent crimes." NAMI integrates medical and recovery models that see schizophrenia as a treatable illness that people can overcome or manage (Duckworth, 2015). For a personal story about living with schizophrenia that is consistent with the illness and recovery model, see the first "The Lived Experience" feature.

The Lived Experience: Living with Schizophrenia: Jamie's Story

In September 2014, I remember feeling particularly strange I was really suspicious of everyone and experienced a lot of paranoia, and I would constantly switch the light on and off.

After an altercation with my mum's boyfriend, I was admitted to a mental health inpatient facility in Northamptonshire where I was diagnosed with schizophrenia. When I was diagnosed with schizophrenia, I was not happy. I tried to break out of the hospital by kicking the doors. I was given some medication to help calm myself down when I was in there. I started to feel a bit better after taking the medication, and soon I moved into a Rethink Mental Illness Supported Accommodation Service.

I arrived at Selsey House, Corby, in August 2015 aged 30. To be honest, at that time I barely spoke. If I did, it was only to answer questions. When I was first introduced to Rethink, I felt trapped in hospital and found it a huge relief that I had found a place in Corby where I came from. I was happy to move in and staff were excellent in helping me settle into the new accommodation. They helped by starting my folder and making sure all my needs were met and I had input into what I wanted from my time here.

The move into a new home is never easy, but over time, I started to feel more confident and I was more sociable with the other tenants in Selsey House. After settling in, I started going to The Green Patch community allotment to lend my hand as a volunteer. When I started at Green Patch, I was always accompanied by a member of staff from Rethink Mental Illness, but over time I felt confident enough to travel on the bus on my own. I still go to this day, and the time I spend there really helps me manage my schizophrenia. I love it. A typical day at Green Patch is varied. I do help a lot with making the lunch, like soup and sandwiches. We plant a lot of bulbs and flowers especially over the winter months, and in the summer we do a lot of garden maintenance like watering the plants. This makes me feel nice and peaceful when I am doing this, and it helps calm me down. I like the social aspect of it too, because I enjoy spending time with other like-minded people.

At Selsey House, I loved taking part in the various activities put on by staff there. I really enjoyed playing pool, doing arts and crafts or going to the cinema. I now regularly leave the house with other tenants to play pool or go and watch a film, and I even went go-karting too! These events really made me feel like a part of the team, and enabled me to feel confident enough to sit on an interview panel and help decide who the new Mental Health Recovery Worker at Selsey House would be. It felt great to be trusted with this responsibility.

Staff at Selsey House have helped me with a lot of things. In fact, they have helped me so much that I am now able to live my life independently. I live with my brother in a flat close to Selsey House. I can do my own cooking, I clean up after myself and I'm able to keep my flat tidy. Those may sound like small things, but it is a huge transformation in comparison to what I was able to do before I arrived. Being close to the House means it is easy for me to still be involved in activities and to see staff, too.

My family also played a big part in my recovery. Whilst at Selsey House, my dad would visit a few times a week, and my brother would also come to visit too. The support of my family has really helped with my recovery as I know I am valued and loved. Without them, I feel my recovery may have taken longer. It's with their support that I have been able to change my story, and indeed change my life.

Reprinted with permission from https://www.rethink.org/news-and-stories/blogs/2021/07/jamies-story/.

Survivor Groups

Whereas consumer groups like NAMI and the Mental Health Foundation try to reduce stigma and enhance services while supporting a medical model perspective, service user/survivor groups such as the Hearing Voices Network (HVN) challenge traditional psychiatric conceptions of psychosis. HVN (2022) is a peer support group that helps "voice hearers to find ways of accepting and making sense of their experiences and to provide frameworks for coping and recovery" (Branitsky et al., 2021, p. 555). Its website states that "the majority of people who hear voices have no mental health issue at all," while noting that diagnoses such as schizophrenia "are a hotly contested area"— useful to some people but a "barrier to healing" for others (Hearing Voices Network, 2022). HVN (2022) maintains that with insight and understanding, many patients learn to cope with their voices. A small body of research supports the utility of hearing voices groups (Branitsky et al., 2021; Longden et al., 2018), although a UK study found that mental health professionals questioned the strength of the evidence despite holding positive attitudes overall toward such groups (B. Jones & Jacobsen, 2021). The second "The Lived Experience" feature provides a personal account of someone who, like many in the Hearing Voices Movement, rejected the medical model.

You may be confused because "The Lived Experience" features in this chapter endorse contradictory viewpoints on psychosis. One author embraces the medical model while the other prefers a psychosocial approach. This may frustrate your desire for definitive answers about psychosis, but it nicely reflects enduring tensions in the field.

The Lived Experience: "The Schizophrenist"

Reshma Valliappan (also known as Val Resh) is an artist and mental health activist from India. She is the subject of the award-winning documentary film, "A Drop of Sunshine," which recounts her controversial recovery from schizophrenia without taking psychiatric drugs. Her autobiographical book, "Fallen, Standing: My Life as a Schizophrenist," provides further insights into her experiences as someone who recovered from schizophrenia while rejecting the medical model. In this brief piece, she explains what she means when she refers to herself as "The Schizophrenist."

Photo 4.4 Reshma Valliappan (also known as Val Resh).
Val Resh.

My story of psychosis revolved around bad vampires trying to kill me because I was the prophesied good vampire who needs to save the world. The voices told me "If you are true, change will happen." I was obsessed with trying to decode the messages I received from the radio and television. I would make journal entries dated to every second and in mirrored writings. I felt I was living in a mirror, stuck and cursed to be inside forever. Thus, when I was told I had schizophrenia, I agreed that I was indeed mad. My life had reached a roadblock and there was no turning back or moving forward. It was the end; a really frightening place to be.

My adult mind was experiencing something horribly wrong (so it appears). It was reflecting the reality of the adults around me through voices and visions because I couldn't accept that people could be dishonest, cruel, and greedy. I was scared of people, including my parents. Stepping beyond my room was not a possibility because another set of commanding voices sat in my living room, urging me to do things I didn't want to do. There were dead people lined up outside my house looking in all the time. When they saw me, their hands would extend towards my windows and they would try to grab me. And so, I would yell and tell my family members to shut all the windows. Over the next few years, life wasn't worth living. Doctors told me there were no known cases of people with schizophrenia returning to "normalcy." They said I would have to be on medications my entire life, with no guarantee of recovery. In other words, "no hope, lost cause, live with it."

The medications failed to work for me after a while. At 14 pills a day, I was still hearing voices and seeing people, but the drugs prevented me from responding or reacting to them. This kept everyone else happy and comfortable, but not me. The socio-bio-political world considered this recovery. I did not.

I soon figured the problem wasn't with me or this thing called schizophrenia. I didn't survive my schizophrenia; I survived the mockery, labelling, insults, humiliations, and degradation of a psychiatric system and a world that thinks it knows what schizophrenia is without experiencing it. My "cure?" I learnt to live with my schizophrenia.

The concept of recovery that has been laid out by Western constructs of normalcy has also influenced the concept of surviving, of healing, of creating balance in one's life. Those know-it-all authorities who "treated" me told me not to listen to the voices in my head. They wanted me to listen to them instead, so they numbed me and told me what to do, how to live, what to say, how to behave, what to eat and read, and whom to sleep with. What a paradox!

Hi, I'm Ganesh. I have BIG EARS because I need to HEAR billions of VOICES who need my blessings everyday. My father had a PANIC ATTACK after cutting my human head in anger. So he replaced it with that of an Elephant's.

I have a Big Belly cause I carry the WHOLE UNIVERSE in it.

My rat is my vehicle. He takes me all over the world.

thegodsarecrazy(c)ValResh 2014

Photo 4.5 Lord Ganesh from Val Resh's *The Gods Are Crazy* series
©Val Resh 2014.

Schizophrenia to me is a communication of the visions and voices I hear while interpreting the metaphors and symbols I experience. I have learnt to experience the visions and voices with confidence. My "symptoms" haven't changed, but my reaction to them and my ability to translate them for others has—through my writing, art, and public speaking engagements. Such is the way of the world. Until we learn to say things in a way that others can understand, we remain mad. The schizophrenia label has made my life difficult at every stage, even after carving my own way out of it through artistic pursuits and my own spiritual practices.

Today people see my "schizophrenic" experiences as normal because, being from India, I tell them I'm the spiritual daughter of an Aghora (a Hindu ascetic), whose tantric mysticism was practiced by my biological father, his father, and his father's father. So, when I now present my story of vampirism as the worship of the Goddess Kali, it is accepted and admired. People don't tell me to consult shamans anymore after I tell them I've received my initiation in the path.

Most people call my experience schizophrenia; I call it waking up to life's many uncertainties. When they pray to gods and goddesses and believe in a person long dead who commands their spiritual evolution, they consider it personal growth; when I hear voices in my head, they consider it a mental sickness. While they market my metaphors under the label of "schizophrenia," I practice the art of what I call "schizophrenistry," which involves challenging stereotypes about madness and misconceptions about atypical life experiences like mine. So, I call myself "The Schizophrenist" and my job is to demystify "madness" by reframing it as a way some people absorb meaning from the world using all their different senses.

In my religion of Hinduism, there is a God named Lord Ganesh, who is easily identifiable by his elephant head and pot-belly. Ganesh is a God who helps people remove life's obstacles. I try to do the same. However, because I do not possess male genitalia, an elephant head, or a pot-belly, I am reduced to a mental disorder. I do wonder who truly are the mad ones. *wink

By Reshma Valliappan. Printed with permission.

4.18 Systems Perspectives

Family Systems and Psychosis
Double Binds

Systems perspectives view psychosis as occurring within a social context, often the family. One early family-oriented theory was Gregory Bateson and colleagues' *double bind theory of schizophrenia*. A **double bind** occurs when someone is placed in a situation where there are two contradictory demands, neither of which can be satisfied or avoided (Bateson et al., 1956). Bateson and his colleagues theorized that children who grow up in families where double binds are the norm are at higher risk for developing schizophrenia.

> **Luke**
>
> *In therapy, Luke discusses his parents, who mean well but have long sent him two contradictory messages: "You cannot succeed on your own" and "Why don't you grow up already and leave us alone?" In addition, his parents make it difficult for him to avoid this contradictory dilemma because they also tell him "We're not going to let you move away from us because you need us to keep a roof over your head." Thus, from a very early age, Luke has been in a double bind that has proven quite difficult to escape.*

The double bind theory has been criticized for blaming parents and lacking research support (Koopmans, 2001; Ringuette, 1982; Schuham, 1967). However, its supporters argue that those who use it to blame families for their children's schizophrenia are "less skilled theorists, given to dull and reductive readings of complex work" (Gibney, 2006, p. 51). There have been efforts to update double bind theory and integrate it with a vulnerability stress model in which biological factors influence susceptibility to double bind family dynamics (Koopmans, 2001).

Expressed Emotion

Extensive research has been conducted showing that the amount of **expressed emotion** in the family is related to outcomes in cases of schizophrenia. Expressed emotion is defined as the degree to which family members respond to a person diagnosed with schizophrenia in hostile, critical, or emotionally overinvolved ways (Amaresha & Venkatasubramanian, 2012; Kymalainen & Weisman de Mamani, 2008). There is substantial research showing that the more expressed emotion in a family, the worse the outcome in cases of schizophrenia (Amaresha & Venkatasubramanian, 2012; Breitborde et al., 2010; Cechnicki et al., 2013; Hashemi & Cochrane, 1999; Kohler et al., 2010; Kymalainen & Weisman de Mamani, 2008; O'Driscoll et al., 2019). The form of expressed emotion often varies by culture (Hashemi & Cochrane, 1999; O'Driscoll et al., 2019), and more of it tends to be expressed when the individual with schizophrenia consistently violates the family's cultural norms and expectations (Kymalainen & Weisman de Mamani, 2008). Problems associated with expressed emotion in families may be compounded given that people diagnosed with schizophrenia are not very good at perceiving others' emotions (Kohler et al., 2010). The takeaway is that how families respond to a member diagnosed with schizophrenia matters quite a bit in how well that member fares over time.

Community Care Approaches

Community care approaches integrate people experiencing psychosis into the social environment, often by housing them in group homes or other shared living situations. Community care also emphasizes continuity of care, independence, and advocacy to ensure patients receive necessary services and are treated properly (Bowl, 1996; Thornicroft, 1994). Let's examine several community care approaches.

The Soteria Model

The **Soteria model** is a community-based approach that applies humanistic-existential ideas to therapeutic communities for people diagnosed with schizophrenia. The Soteria model owes a lot to the nineteenth-century moral therapy movement discussed in Chapter 1 (Elkins, 2016). "Soteria"

Double bind: Occurs when someone is placed in a situation where there are two contradictory demands, neither of which can be satisfied or avoided; children in families where double binds are the norm have been hypothesized to be at greater risk for schizophrenia.

Expressed emotion: Degree to which family members respond to a patient in a hostile, critical, or emotionally overinvolved way; associated with poorer patient outcomes.

Community care: Care that integrates people with chronic mental health issues into the social environment, often by housing them in group homes or other shared living situations; emphasizes continuity of care, encouraging independence, and advocacy that ensures patients receive necessary services and are treated properly.

derives from a Greek term meaning "salvation" or "deliverance" (L. R. Mosher, 1999). In the Soteria model, people with schizophrenia are housed in a small and supportive environment with minimal or no use of antipsychotic drugs and a staff of mainly non-professionals (Ingle, 2019; L. Mosher, 2015; L. R. Mosher, 1991, 1999; Prouty, 2002). The Soteria model is skeptical of the brain disease view of schizophrenia. Instead, schizophrenia is conceptualized as a meaningful existential crisis best overcome in a caring, reassuring environment. In keeping with the humanistic tradition, Soteria caregivers aim to "develop a true human connection based on honesty" and an "inherent ability to be with another human being who is in distress" (Jacobs, 2019, p. 684). The Soteria model is named after the original but now-defunct Soteria House in the San Francisco area during the 1970s. Several therapeutic communities based on Soteria can be found across Europe, as well as in Israel; the only Soteria House currently open in the United States is in Vermont (Ingle, 2019).

Soteria researchers conclude the model is equally effective as traditional medical treatment, if not more so, for first-episode psychosis. However, critics see Soteria as misguided in its hostility toward antipsychotics and its rejection of schizophrenia as a brain disease (Bola et al., 2006; Bola & Mosher, 2003; Calton et al., 2008; W. T. Carpenter & Buchanan, 2002; Lindgren et al., 2006; L. R. Mosher et al., 1975, 1995; L. R. Mosher, 1999). Defenders contend that the medical establishment purposely sabotaged the original Soteria House because it threatened to show that psychosis could be effectively treated outside of medical settings without heavy reliance on drugs (Bola & Mosher, 2003; R. Whitaker, 2002). The debate over Soteria is ongoing. The mainstream healthcare system continues to view it with suspicion, but humanistic clinicians celebrate it as a notable achievement (Elkins, 2016).

Assertive Community Treatment (ACT)

Assertive community treatment (ACT): A way to organize services for those diagnosed with schizophrenia and other severe psychological disorders in which team members from a variety of professions work together to coordinate services for outpatients with schizophrenia and other chronic mental disorder diagnoses.

Developed during the 1970s, **assertive community treatment (ACT)** is not a treatment itself, but rather a way to organize services for those diagnosed with schizophrenia and other severe psychological disorders (DeLuca et al., 2008). ACT embraces a medical model view of schizophrenia as a manageable illness. In the model, team members from different professions coordinate services for outpatients with schizophrenia and other chronic mental disorders. They conduct home visits, encourage medication compliance, and focus on everyday problems patients encounter. The service is long-term, provided consistently over many years to those who need it. ACT seeks to reduce homelessness, substance abuse, incarceration, and hospitalizations of patients while improving drug compliance (DeLuca et al., 2008). There is substantial empirical support for ACT (DeLuca et al., 2008; Karow et al., 2012). However, not all studies have found it to be effective (C. C. Lee et al., 2015). In many U.S. states the availability of ACT is limited and few treatment programs fully implement it (Spivak et al., 2019). Still, numerous agencies and organizations—including NAMI—consider ACT an evidence-based program for chronic mental illness (Ellenhorn, 2015).

Open Dialogue

Open Dialogue: A community-care approach rooted in narrative and dialogical theories that aims to create a support network that can intervene and assist the person experiencing psychosis.

Open Dialogue, developed in Finland during the 1990s, is a community care approach rooted in narrative and dialogical theories (Seikkula et al., 2001a, 2001b; Van Rensburg, 2015). It creates a support network to assist the person experiencing psychosis. This network consists of the patient, mental health professionals, and significant people in the patient's life (friends, relatives, romantic partners, employers, etc.). Treatment meetings include all members of the support network, who engage in dialogue that fosters decisions intended to help the patient. Medication is sometimes used, but the idea is to rely less on drugs and more on the relational network to help the patient recover from the psychotic episode in ways that frame it more relationally and less medically. Open Dialogue's developers have conducted studies providing support for their approach (Aaltonen et al., 2011; Bergström et al., 2018, 2021; Seikkula et al., 2001b, 2006, 2011). However, the quality of these studies has been criticized (A. M. Freeman et al., 2019). Open Dialogue has spread rapidly in recent years and the approach is now practiced at locations across the United States (Olson, 2019). Given the large number of people involved, Open Dialogue programs can be challenging to implement and administer (Buus et al., 2021). However, their advocates see them as advancing human rights by treating people experiencing psychosis with dignity and respect (S. von Peter et al., 2019).

NAVIGATE Program

Another promising community intervention for first-episode psychosis is the **NAVIGATE program**, a product of the U.S. National Institute of Mental Health's "Recovery After an Initial Psychotic Episode" (RAISE) initiative. NAVIGATE is a team-based approach that stresses four areas of intervention: individualized medication management (intended to keep doses of antipsychotics as low as possible), **psychoeducation** about psychosis (to educate patients and their families about psychosis, encourage medication adherence, and help patients and families cope), resilience-focused psychotherapy, and employment training (Mueser et al., 2014, 2015). A treatment team works together to provide these services (Mueser et al., 2014, 2015). A randomized controlled clinical trial found NAVIGATE to be a more effective for first-episode psychosis than the usual more drug-focused approach (Kane et al., 2016). Efforts to implement and evaluate the program continue in the United States and Canada (Kozloff et al., 2020; Mueser et al., 2019). The NAVIGATE program is one example of how adding psychosocial interventions to traditional drug treatments might improve outcomes for psychosis.

4.19 Evaluating Sociocultural Perspectives

There is a compelling body of evidence that sociocultural factors influence the development and course of psychosis (Vespia, 2009). It is generally agreed that people in developing nations tend to have a better chance of recovery from schizophrenia than those in developed nations. Further, women fare better in dealing with the disorder than men. Additionally, symptoms are displayed somewhat differently across cultures and socioeconomic status, and this is relevant in thinking about outcomes. Although there is **social drift** among those diagnosed with schizophrenia (they tend to slide down the socioeconomic ladder, which makes sense given how their symptoms impede their ability to function and earn a living), this doesn't account for the fact that low SES places people at higher risk for schizophrenia in the first place. Taken in combination with the fact that family dynamics are also associated with course and outcome, the evidence that sociocultural factors influence psychosis is strong (Vespia, 2009).

That said, many argue that psychosis can't be understood in terms of sociocultural factors alone. Just as not everyone genetically vulnerable to psychosis develops it, not everyone at social risk develops symptoms either. In fact, most people at social risk never become psychotic. This suggests that the biological perspective emphasis on physiological susceptibility is at least as important as sociocultural factors—and that in many ways, these two seemingly contradictory ways of understanding psychosis need to be better integrated. Recent efforts to integrate biological, cognitive, and sociocultural perspectives have led to an integrated **sociodevelopmental-cognitive model of schizophrenia**, examined in the "In Depth" feature.

NAVIGATE program: Community intervention program for psychosis that stresses individualized medication management, psychoeducation, resilience-focused psychotherapy, and employment training.

Psychoeducation: Technique in which clients are taught about the problem they are diagnosed with to help them better cope with it.

Social drift: Tendency of those diagnosed with severe mental disorders such as schizophrenia to slide (or drift) down the socioeconomic ladder.

Sociodevelopmental-cognitive model of schizophrenia: Says schizophrenia emerges from a circular and mutually influencing interaction among biological, cognitive, and sociocultural factors; genetic vulnerability and social disadvantage/adversity lead to dopamine dysregulation, which produces cognitive misattributions of salience, which yields psychosocial stress, which further impacts dopamine transmission, and so on in an ongoing cycle.

In Depth: The Sociodevelopmental-Cognitive Model of Schizophrenia

Should biological, cognitive, and sociocultural perspectives be combined into an integrated model of schizophrenia? Researchers Oliver D. Howes and Robin M. Murray (2014) believe so and have proposed just such a model. Their model views schizophrenia as a neurodevelopmental disorder, one that typically develops in early adulthood. It integrates the following independent lines of research evidence previously discussed in this chapter:

- Dopamine dysregulation is commonly correlated with psychosis and schizophrenia.
- Vulnerability to schizophrenia seems to have a genetic component.
- Schizophrenia is associated with progressive neurodevelopmental brain deterioration, as evidenced by decreased brain volume.
- Psychosis is characterized by cognitive impairments, most notably problems with aberrant salience (attributing meaning to irrelevant events)—a problem believed to be related to dopamine dysregulation.
- Social disadvantage (e.g., being a minority group member, an immigrant, being low in socioeconomic status) and social adversity (e.g., being physically or sexually abused in childhood or experiencing parental neglect) are predictors of psychosis and schizophrenia.

The integrated sociodevelopmental-cognitive model of schizophrenia assimilates these research findings into a multifactorial explanation of how schizophrenia develops and persists. It asserts that schizophrenia only emerges when a genetic vulnerability combines with social disadvantage and/or adversity to elicit problems with dopamine transmission in the brain. The resulting dopamine dysregulation leads to excessive dopamine, which yields cognitive difficulties—the over-attribution of meaning posited by aberrant salience theory. This, in turn, produces psychological stress, which further amplifies dopamine dysregulation by causing more dopamine to be released. A vicious cycle ensues. As more dopamine is released in response to stress, aberrant salience continues or worsens, leading to increasingly paranoid and psychotic cognitive processing and further stress—and so on and so on. Continuing symptoms of schizophrenia, therefore, occur due to a repetitive and self-perpetuating sequence of mutually influencing genetic, social, and cognitive factors. Figure 4.1 portrays this ongoing circular process visually.

The strength of Howes and Murray's model is that there is already substantial research on the genetic, neurodevelopmental, neurochemical, and sociocultural components that the model integrates. However, the proposed dynamic relationship between social disadvantage/adversity and dopamine dysregulation remains somewhat speculative (especially in humans) and it's not clear how much neurodevelopmental changes in the brain (such as decreased brain volume) are due to stress versus ongoing treatment with antipsychotic drugs. Nevertheless, the integrated sociodevelopmental-cognitive model is noteworthy for trying to account for what often seem like contradictory findings. It entertains the audacious (and increasingly commonsensical) idea that psychosis—rather than being singularly biological, cognitive, or sociocultural—is a complex phenomenon that materializes from the mutual interaction of all three factors.

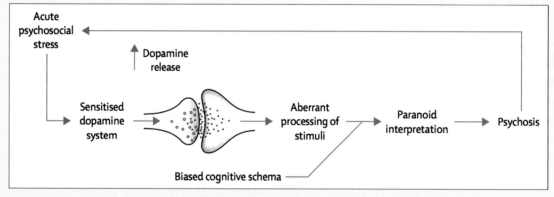

Figure 4.1 **The Onset of Psychosis in the Integrated Sociodevelopmental-Cognitive Model.** The integrated sociodevelopmental-cognitive model posits that biological factors (sensitized dopamine system), cognitive factors (aberrant processing of stimuli), and social factors (acute psychosocial stress) interact with one another to foster psychosis.
Source: Howes, O. D., & Murray, R. M. (2014). Schizophrenia: An integrated sociodevelopmental-cognitive model. The Lancet, 383(9929), 1677–1687. https://doi.org.10.1016/S0140-6736(13)62036-X

Critical Thinking Questions

1. Do you think Howes and Murray's model overcomes longstanding disagreements about whether schizophrenia and other forms of psychosis are mainly biological, cognitive, or sociocultural problems?
2. What research studies might you design to further test the Howes and Murray model?
3. Are there factors that you believe Howes and Murray have not accounted for in their model? If so, what are they?

CLOSING THOUGHTS

4.20 Caring for Those Experiencing Psychosis

Caring for seriously impaired people suffering from psychoses is costly and difficult. Theoretically, the advent of antipsychotic drugs has allowed for the deinstitutionalization of many psychotic patients, which involves releasing them from psychiatric hospitals and placing them in community care settings—something that would generally be celebrated except for the fact that funding for community care has historically been lacking (Torrey, 2014). This has often contributed to widescale homelessness and lack of support for people experiencing psychosis, especially those low on the socioeconomic ladder. Caring for people with chronic psychosis is a sociopolitical issue that requires thoughtful deliberation and careful planning.

This is complicated by the fact that professionals differ in how they define psychosis and think it should be addressed. Should we primarily rely on medication, therapy, or social change to deal with it? Even if we take an integrated path and combine these approaches, the question of which should take precedence remains. Although brain disease perspectives continue to dominate, we still diagnose schizophrenia behaviorally—and it remains unclear when, if ever, we will be able to diagnose it biologically. Given this difficulty, it isn't surprising that researchers and clinicians debate whether schizophrenia is a single disorder or a catch-all category for people who act the most "mad." This debate matters because the stigma of schizophrenia is significant—so much so that some researchers recommend retiring Bleuler's more than 100-year-old name "schizophrenia" in favor of something more modest such as "salience syndrome" or "psychosis susceptibility syndrome" (George & Klijn, 2013; van Os, 2009b, 2009a). A name change for schizophrenia is increasingly supported by clinicians, patients, and other stakeholders (Lasalvia et al., 2021; Mesholam-Gately et al., 2021). In fact, it has already occurred in Japan (van Os, 2009b). The desire for a name change stems from a belief that the term "schizophrenia" confuses more than clarifies (J. J. Miller, 2022). As one researcher put it:

The complicated, albeit ultimately meaningless, greek [sic] term suggests that schizophrenia really is a "thing", i.e. a "brain disease" that exists as such in Nature. This is a false suggestion, however, as schizophrenia refers to a syndrome of symptom dimensions that for unknown reasons cluster together in different combinations in different people with different contributions of known risk factors and dramatically different outcomes and response to treatment; no knowledge exists that may help decide to what degree schizophrenia, for example, reflects a single or 20 different underlying diseases—or none at all. Nevertheless, the way mental health professionals use the medical diagnosis of schizophrenia in clinical practice and communication inevitably results in its "reification"—or becoming a "thing." (van Os, 2009b, p. 368)

Whether or not you agree with this quote, it illustrates how—when it comes to categorizing, comprehending, and treating psychosis—many different perspectives remain in play. Psychosis is an area where, despite noble efforts to integrate contrasting perspectives, we still have more questions than answers.

CHAPTER SUMMARY

Overview

- *Psychosis* involves strange or grossly inappropriate ways of thinking, communicating, and behaving.

Diagnostic Perspectives

- In DSM and ICD, psychotic disorders involve one or more of these: delusions, hallucinations, disorganized thought/speech, abnormal motor behavior, and negative symptoms.
- Specific psychotic disorders include *schizophrenia, delusional disorder, brief psychotic disorder* (DSM)/*acute and transient psychotic disorder* (ICD), *schizophreniform disorder* (DSM only), *schizoaffective disorder, schizotypal disorder* (ICD only).

Biological Perspectives

- The *dopamine hypothesis of schizophrenia* says schizophrenia results from excess dopamine. *Antipsychotics* reduce dopamine transmission, mainly reducing positive symptoms.
- Enlarged ventricles, decreased brain volume, and abnormalities in the *prefrontal cortex, hippocampus,* and *amygdala* are linked to schizophrenia.
- Twin studies yield estimated schizophrenia concordance rates of 45–50 percent for identical twins and 10–15 percent for fraternal twins. *Family studies* suggest that first-degree relatives of those with schizophrenia are more likely to develop schizophrenia than second- or third-degree relatives.
- Evolutionary perspectives say schizophrenia is associated with desirable traits that keep it in the gene pool.

- The *inflammatory hypothesis* proposes that mental disorders such as schizophrenia are associated with immune system inflammation, including high levels of *cytokines*.
- *Biopsychosocial* models combine biological views with psychological and sociocultural explanations.

Psychological Perspectives

- Early interpersonal therapists saw schizophrenia as tied to extreme anxiety from traumatic early life relationships and offered the controversial *schizophrenogenic mother* theory.
- Modern psychodynamic perspectives connect psychosis to anxiety and terror, commonly from abusive relationships.
- Cognitive perspectives attribute psychosis to problematic information processing; behavioral perspectives see it as conditioned learned behaviors.
- *Cognitive-behavioral therapy for psychosis (CBTp)* uses *Socratic questioning, evidential analysis, normalization, behavioral experiments,* and *social skills training.*
- Humanistic perspectives see psychosis as a meaningful *extreme state* rather than a brain disease.
- There is growing evidence for psychological interventions for psychosis, and they are increasingly combined with drug interventions.

Sociocultural Perspectives

- Psychosis is correlated with social inequality, environmental adversity, physical and sexual abuse, cannabis use, low socioeconomic status, living in an urban environment, belonging to a racial minority group, and experiencing discrimination.
- Minority group members are often rated as more disturbed than others, suggesting biased assessment.
- Consumer groups educate people about psychosis to reduce stigma and survivor groups challenge traditional psychiatric conceptions of psychosis as brain disease.
- Systems perspectives see psychosis as occurring within contexts such as the family. They stress how *expressed emotion* affects people diagnosed with psychoses.
- The *Soteria model, Assertive Community Treatment (ACT), Open Dialogue,* and the *NAVIGATE program* are community care approaches aligned with traditional psychiatric approaches to greater or lesser degrees.

Closing Thoughts

- Chronic care for psychosis is expensive. Deinstitutionalization has contributed to homelessness and lack of social support.
- The best ways to help people with psychosis remain debated.

NEW VOCABULARY

1. Abnormal motor behavior
2. Adoption studies
3. Antipsychotics
4. Assertive community treatment (ACT)
5. Attenuated psychosis syndrome (APS)
6. Behavioral experiments
7. Behavioral rehearsal
8. Biopsychosocial model
9. Brief psychotic disorder
10. Catatonia
11. Cliff-edge fitness theory
12. Cognitive-behavioral therapy for psychosis (CBTp)
13. Community care
14. Concordance rates
15. Delusional disorder
16. Delusions
17. Disorganized thinking
18. Dopamine hypothesis of schizophrenia
19. Double bind
20. "Dual hit" model
21. Evidential analysis
22. Expressed emotion
23. Extrapyramidal side effects
24. Family studies
25. Genetic association studies
26. Glutamate hypothesis of schizophrenia
27. Hallucinations
28. Inflammatory hypothesis
29. Modeling
30. Negative symptoms
31. Normalization
32. Open Dialogue
33. Positive symptoms
34. Pre-therapy
35. Psychoeducation
36. Psychosis
37. Schizoaffective disorder
38. Schizophrenia
39. Schizophreniform disorder
40. Schizotypal disorder
41. Social drift
42. Social skills training
43. Sociodevelopmental-cognitive model of schizophrenia
44. Soteria model
45. Stress-vulnerability-coping skills model
46. Tardive dyskinesia
47. Theory of mind
48. Twin studies
49. Viral theory of schizophrenia

DEPRESSION AND MANIA

5

Photo 5.1
Francesco Carta fotografo/Getty Images.

LEARNING OBJECTIVES

After reading this chapter, you should be able to:

1. Differentiate depression from mania.

2. Distinguish types of mood episodes, define the depressive and bipolar disorders in DSM and ICD, and summarize critiques of these disorders.

3. Outline historical antecedents of modern mood problems, including defining terms like melancholia, acedia, and neurasthenia.

4. Review and appraise biological perspectives on mood problems—including the monoamine and glutamate hypotheses, the use of antidepressants and mood stabilizers, brain structures implicated, non-drug biological treatments, genetic and evolutionary explanations, and the role of inflammation.

5. Discuss and critique the following psychological perspectives on mood problems: psychodynamic, cognitive-behavioral, and humanistic approaches.

6. Explain and evaluate sociocultural perspectives stressing the following issues in understanding and alleviating mood problems: socioeconomic inequality, gender issues, relationship problems, expressed emotion, and systems conceptualizations and interventions.

OVERVIEW

5.1 Getting Started: The Highs and Lows of Mood

Case Examples

Shirley

Shirley, a 34-year-old accountant, comes to therapy feeling extremely depressed. Depression is not new for her. She has had bouts of sadness before. However, this time the feelings came on abruptly and out of the blue. Shirley says that for the last six weeks she has felt despondent, having to fight back tears throughout the day. Besides having lost her appetite, she reports feeling listless and tired, with no energy to get out of bed in the morning. She has been sleeping fourteen hours per night, but despite so much rest, is having difficulty concentrating at work. Because she feels so tired and depressed, Shirley has been frequently absent from work the past few weeks and is on the verge of being fired. Her fiancé Ralph is threatening to break up with her unless she gets help. When asked about her situation, Shirley just shrugs and says, "Things are bad because, when it comes down to it, I'm a worthless loser that nobody could ever truly love." She has thought about suicide but says doing so requires too much effort.

Don

Don is a 25-year-old freelance writer with a history of depression who comes to therapy after being arrested for drunk driving. He doesn't believe he needs help because, for the past two weeks, he has felt highly energetic and excited about life—so inspired, in fact, that he has been working non-stop on the "greatest novel of the last decade." When asked when he last slept, Don waves his had dismissively and notes that he has little need for sleep or food. Instead, he has been staying up twenty-two hours per day working on his novel. The night he was arrested Don went on a shopping spree for the new wardrobe he would need now that he was going to be an acclaimed author. Afterwards, he went to a bar to celebrate. Don was pulled over on the way home for speeding and driving erratically. A breath test showed him to be legally intoxicated. The judge mandated that Don seek treatment immediately. Don thinks it's all a plot to sabotage his budding career as a novelist. "They always undermine the truly great ones," he quips as he rambles on incessantly during his first session.

Depression and Mania

Depression involves feelings of intense and often debilitating sadness and melancholy, along with a generally pessimistic worldview and loss of interest in previously enjoyed activities. *Mania* is the quite the opposite, characterized by euphoric mood, boundless energy, and a sometimes-distorted sense of one's capabilities. Disturbed moods are easy to relate to because everyone experiences emotional ups and downs in life. This makes us all rather opinionated on the subject. Take depression, for instance. How often is it okay to feel depressed? How long is it acceptable to feel that way? What are justifiable reasons for depression? What causes it? Different perspectives answer these questions differently.

DIAGNOSTIC PERSPECTIVES

5.2 DSM and ICD

Types of Mood Episodes

Depressive episode: In DSM and ICD, at least two weeks of intense sadness and depressed mood or loss of interest in daily activities; other symptoms include change in appetite, sleep disturbance, tiredness, indecisiveness, feelings of worthlessness, lethargy or restlessness, and suicidal feelings.

In DSM and ICD, depression and mania occur in discrete *episodes*. A **depressive episode** is characterized by two weeks or more of either (a) intense sadness and depressed mood or (b) loss of interest in daily activities. It can also involve changes in appetite (with weight gain or loss), changes in sleep habits (sleeping more or having trouble sleeping), tiredness and fatigue, indecisiveness and trouble concentrating, feelings of worthlessness, physical lethargy or restlessness, and suicidal feelings or overtures (see Diagnostic Box 5.1). Depressive episodes are intense and debilitating. The person might stop going to work, stay in bed all day, give up leisure activities, be consistently teary-eyed and weepy, display very low energy levels, and seem sluggish and unmotivated.

Shirley

Shirley's extremely sadness, lack of energy, loss of appetite, and difficulty concentrating meet the criteria for a depressive episode.

Diagnostic Box 5.1 Depressive Episodes

DSM-5-TR
- One of these: (1) depressed mood, (2) loss of interest or pleasure in activities.
- At least three additional symptoms: (1) increased or decreased appetite or noticeable weight change, (2) insomnia or hypersomnia (difficulty sleeping or excessive sleep), (3) physically agitated/restless or lethargic, (4) tiredness or reduced energy, (5) feeling worthless or guilty without reason, (6) hard time concentrating or making decisions, (7) focus on death or a suicidal plan/attempt.
- Lasts at least two weeks.
- Use clinical judgment if bereavement present.

ICD-11
- One of these: (1) depressed mood, (2) loss of interest or pleasure in activities.
- At least three of these: (1) trouble concentrating or difficulty making decisions, (2) feelings of low self-worth or excessive guilt, (3) hopelessness, (4) focus on death or a suicidal plan/attempt, (5) disrupted or excessive sleep, (6) increased or decreased appetite or noticeable weight change, (7) physically agitated/restless or lethargic, (8) tiredness or reduced energy.
- Lasts at least two weeks.
- Symptoms not due to bereavement.

Information from American Psychiatric Association (2022, pp. 141–142) and World Health Organization (2022a).

Whereas depression entails intense sadness and loss of interest, a **manic episode** is characterized by one week or more of persistently elevated mood accompanied by high energy and intense goal-directed activity (see Diagnostic Box 5.2). It often involves inflated self-esteem or *grandiosity* (the idea that one is very important), a decreased need for sleep, extreme talkativeness, racing thoughts, distractibility, and impulsive or risky behavior (e.g., shopping sprees, poor financial choices, unsafe or indiscreet sexual activity, drug abuse). Extreme cases can include distortions in thinking and perceiving that cross into psychosis (see Chapter 4).

Don
Don, who grandiosely believes he is writing the next great American novel while sleeping just two hours a night and behaving impulsively, is experiencing a manic episode.

A **hypomanic episode** is a shorter and milder version of a manic episode. DSM-5-TR specifies that symptoms must last four days to one week, but ICD-11 merely says symptoms must last several days (see Diagnostic Box 5.2). ICD also includes a **mixed episode**, in which manic and depressive symptoms rapidly alternate or co-occur for at least two weeks. DSM no longer includes mixed episodes. Instead, it has clinicians specify "with mixed features" when diagnosing bipolar and depressive disorders. Differentiating depressive, manic, hypomanic, and (if using ICD) mixed mood episodes is crucial in diagnosing the disorders discussed next.

Manic episode:
In DSM and ICD, one week or more of persistently elevated mood accompanied by high energy and intense goal-directed activity; often involves inflated self-esteem, grandiosity, decreased need for sleep, extreme talkativeness, racing thoughts, distractibility, and impulsive/risky behavior.

Hypomanic episode:
In DSM and ICD, a shorter and milder version of a manic episode, lasting just a few days.

Mixed episode:
ICD-only mood episode in which manic and depressive symptoms rapidly alternate or co-occur for at least two weeks; replaced with "with mixed features" specifier in DSM.

Diagnostic Box 5.2 Manic, Hypomanic, and Mixed Episodes

DSM-5-TR
- Inflated or irritable mood with extremely intensified energy and activity levels.
- At least three (four if mood only irritable): (1) exaggerated self-esteem or grandiosity, (2) diminished need for sleep, (3) talkativeness or urge to talk, (4) rapidly fluctuating ideas or racing thoughts, (5) easily distractible, (6) excessive activity (goal-directed or unfocused), (7) risky, impulsive, or dangerous behavior.
- *Manic*: Lasts at least one week.
- *Hypomanic*: Lasts at least four days but less than one week; milder symptoms.
- *Mixed*: Not included in DSM-5-TR; use "mixed features" specifier as needed.

ICD-11
- Euphoric, irritable, inflated, or rapidly changing mood with intensified energy and activity levels.
- Several of these: (1) talkativeness or urge to talk, (2) rapidly fluctuating ideas or racing thoughts, (3) exaggerated self-esteem or grandiosity, (4) diminished need for sleep, (5) easily distractible, (6) risky, impulsive, or dangerous behavior, (7) enhanced sexual desire, feelings of sociability, or goal-oriented behavior.
- *Manic*: Lasts at least one week.
- *Hypomanic*: Lasts several days but less than one week; milder symptoms.
- *Mixed*: For at least two weeks, rapid shifting among depressive, manic, and hypomanic symptoms (often within hours).

Information from American Psychiatric Association (2022, pp. 140–141) and World Health Organization (2022a).

Specific Mood and Bipolar Disorders
Major Depressive Disorder/Single-Episode or Recurrent Depressive Disorder

Major depressive disorder (MDD): DSM disorder diagnosed in those who experience one or more major depressive episodes; divided into *single episode depressive disorder* and *recurrent depressive disorder* in ICD.

In DSM-5-TR, **major depressive disorder (MDD)** (also called *major depression*) involves one or more depressive episodes. People who only experience one depressive episode are diagnosed with *major depressive disorder, single episode*. Those with more than one are diagnosed with *major depressive disorder, recurrent*. ICD-11 doesn't use the term "major depressive disorder" but covers the same ground with two diagnoses, *single episode depressive disorder* and *recurrent depressive disorder*. Importantly, to qualify for either DSM or ICD versions of these disorders, there must be no history of manic or hypomanic episodes. If there is, then a form of bipolar disorder is diagnosed instead. See Diagnostic Box 5.3.

Depression accounts for the highest percentage of mental disorders (GBD 2019 Mental Disorders Collaborators, 2022). Its prevalence is alarmingly high. In 2021, depression is thought to have affected 251–310 million people worldwide, which is 2–6 percent of the global population (World Population Review, n.d.). The World Health Organization (2021d) estimates global incidence at 3.8 percent—including 5 percent of all adults and 5.7 percent of adults over age 60. However, incidence varies by country. In 2017, the United States was tied with Australia and Estonia for the second highest incidence

Diagnostic Box 5.3 Major Depressive Disorder/Single-Episode or Recurrent Depressive Disorder

DSM-5-TR: Major Depressive Disorder
- One or more major depressive episodes.
- Has never had a manic or hypomanic episode.

ICD-11: Single-Episode or Recurrent Depressive Disorder
- **Single-Episode:** Only one depressive episode
- **Recurrent:** Two or more depressive episodes.
- Has never had a manic, hypomanic, or mixed episode.

Information from American Psychiatric Association (2022, pp. 183–185) and World Health Organization (2022a).

of depression (5.9 percent), just behind Ukraine (6.3 percent) and ahead of Brazil (5.8 percent) (World Health Organization, 2017a); DSM-5-TR estimates twelve-month U.S. prevalence at 7 percent. Though some evidence suggests prevalence remained roughly the same between 1990 and 2019 (GBD 2019 Mental Disorders Collaborators, 2022), other evidence points to increasing prevalence—especially in the past few years, with the COVID-19 pandemic among the contributing factors (Ettman et al., 2022; Iranpour et al., 2022; Q. Liu et al., 2020; Moreno-Agostino et al., 2021; Santomauro et al., 2021).

DSM-5-TR notes big differences by age group. Depressive episodes can occur at any age but people in their teens or twenties are at greatest risk, with 18–29-year-olds at three times the risk of those over 60. There are gender differences, too. Women are twice as likely to be diagnosed as men. There is also variability in course of symptoms. Some people have long breaks between depressive episodes while others are almost continually depressed. However, it is common for depressive episodes to spontaneously lift within three months of onset even without intervention. The more time since a depressive episode, the less the likelihood of having another one.

Bipolar Disorders: Bipolar I and II

DSM-5-TR and ICD-11 divide bipolar disorder (sometimes still called *manic depression*) into two basic kinds. **Bipolar I disorder** is diagnosed in anyone who has ever had a full-blown manic episode. People who meet the criteria for bipolar I may also experience hypomanic and depressive episodes, but these aren't required for a diagnosis. **Bipolar II disorder** is less severe than bipolar I. It is diagnosed in people who have experienced both hypomanic and depressive episodes but have never had a manic or (if using ICD) a mixed episode. If someone diagnosed with bipolar II undergoes a full-scale manic episode, the diagnosis is changed to bipolar I. Prevalence for bipolar disorders is lower than for depression, estimated between 0.3 and 1.2 percent (Dattani et al., 2021). DSM-5-TR reports twelve-month U.S. prevalence rates of 1.5 percent for bipolar I and 0.8 percent for bipolar II. Because DSM-5-TR criteria for mania and hypomania are stricter than ICD-11 guidelines, more people qualify for bipolar diagnoses in ICD than DSM (Angst et al., 2020). For criteria and guidelines, see Diagnostic Box 5.4.

Bipolar I disorder: DSM and ICD disorder diagnosed in those who experience one or more manic episodes.

Bipolar II disorder: DSM and ICD disorder diagnosed in those who have experienced hypomanic and depressive episodes but have never had a manic episode.

Diagnostic Box 5.4 Bipolar Disorder

DSM-5-TR
- **Bipolar I Disorder**
  - At least one lifetime manic episode: Required.
  - Hypomanic and depressive episodes: Common but not required.
- **Bipolar II Disorder**
  - At least one lifetime hypomanic episode: Required.
  - At least one lifetime major depressive episode: Required.
  - There has never been a manic episode.

ICD-11
- **Bipolar I Disorder**
  - At least one lifetime manic or mixed episode: Required.
  - Hypomanic and depressive episodes: Common but not required.
- **Bipolar II Disorder**
  - At least one lifetime hypomanic episode: Required.
  - At least one lifetime major depressive episode: Required.
  - There has never been a manic or mixed episode.

Information from American Psychiatric Association (2022, pp. 140–143, 150–153) and World Health Organization (2022a).

Cyclothymic Disorder

The **cyclothymic disorder** diagnosis is for people who consistently have hypomanic and depressive symptoms, neither of which rise to the level of a hypomanic or depressive episode. These symptoms must be present at least half the time for two or more years. Details are available in Diagnostic Box 5.5. According to DSM-5-TR, the twelve-month prevalence rate for cyclothymic disorder in the United States and Europe ranges between 0.4 and 2.5 percent.

Cyclothymic disorder: DSM and ICD diagnosis for those with hypomanic and depressive symptoms that do not rise to the level of hypomanic and depressive episodes.

Diagnostic Box 5.5 Cyclothymic Disorder

DSM-5-TR

- Hypomanic symptoms that do not meet criteria for a hypomanic episode.
- Depressive symptoms that do not meet criteria for a depressive episode.
- Symptoms at least half the time for two years (one year in children and adolescents) and never absent for more than two months.
- Has never had a full-blown depressive, manic, or hypomanic episode.

ICD-11

- Hypomanic symptoms that may not qualify as a hypomanic episode.
- For first two years, depressive symptoms do not meet criteria for a depressive episode.
- Symptoms for at least two years without being absent for an extended period.
- No manic or mixed episodes.

Information from American Psychiatric Association (2022, pp. 159–160) and World Health Organization (2022a).

Persistent depressive disorder (PDD): DSM disorder for chronic depression that lasts two years or more, either with or without also meeting criteria for a depressive episode; related to but different in important respects from ICD's *dysthymic disorder.*

Dysthymic disorder: ICD disorder for ongoing depression lasting two years or more that is milder than a depressive episode; related to but different in important respects from DSM's *persistent depressive disorder.*

Persistent Depressive Disorder/Dysthymic Disorder

Prior to DSM-5, *dysthymia* referred to mild but ongoing depression. However, as criteria were broadened to include severe cases of chronic depression, DSM changed the name to **persistent depressive disorder (PDD)**. Individuals diagnosed with PDD experience long-term depressive symptoms but may or may not ever meet criteria for a full-blown major depressive episode. The same kinds of symptoms found in major depression occur. However, they are considered chronic because they last for a minimum of two years (one year for children and adolescents) and never remit for more than two months at a time (see Diagnostic Box 5.6). If severity rises to the level of a major depressive episode, the PDD diagnosis is given a "with major depression" specifier. If not, then it is given a "with dysthymia" specifier.

ICD has not adopted the name PDD or expanded its corresponding **dysthymic disorder** diagnosis to include more severe depression. Instead, it still adheres to the classic definition of dysthymic disorder as a milder, long-term depression that doesn't include depressive episodes—at least for the first two years. After two years, a single or recurrent depression diagnosis can be added to a dysthymic disorder diagnosis, but before that it would replace it. Importantly, both PDD and dysthymic disorder preclude ever having had a manic, hypomanic, or (if using ICD) mixed episode. If these occur, the diagnosis is changed to bipolar I or II disorder.

Diagnostic Box 5.6 Persistent Depressive Disorder/Dysthymic Disorder

DSM-5-TR: Persistent Depressive Disorder

- Major or mild depression for at least two years, with symptoms never absent for more than two months.
- Two or more of these symptoms: (1) change in appetite, (2) change in sleep habits, (3) tiredness or reduced energy, (4) decreased self-esteem, (5) trouble with concentration or decision-making, (6) feels hopeless.
- There has never been a manic episode, hypomanic episode, or cyclothymic disorder.
- Various specifiers indicate role, if any, of major depressive episodes over last two years.

ICD-11: Dysthymic Disorder

- Persistently depressed mood most days for at least two years.
- For first two years, depressive symptoms don't meet criteria for a depressive episode.
- Symptoms such as: (1) loss of pleasure in activities, (2) tiredness or reduced energy, (3) trouble with concentration or decision-making, (4) feeling guilty and unworthy, (5) suicidal thoughts, (6) change in sleep habits, (7) change in appetite, (8) physically agitated/restless or lethargic.
- No history of manic, hypomanic, or mixed episodes.

Information from American Psychiatric Association (2022, pp. 193–194) and World Health Organization (2022a).

DSM-5-TR reports a 1.5 percent U.S. prevalence rate for PDD with major depressive episodes, but only a 0.5 percent prevalence rate for PDD without them. It also indicates that PDD tends to start in childhood, adolescence, or young adulthood and is often comorbid with anxiety disorders, personality disorders, and substance use. Separation from or loss of parents is a risk factor.

Premenstrual Dysphoric Disorder and Disruptive Mood Dysregulation Disorder

Premenstrual dysphoric disorder (PMDD) is diagnosed in women who consistently show depressive symptoms during the week before their menstrual periods. PMDD is included in ICD-11 but grouped with diseases affecting genital organs rather than with mental disorders. **Disruptive mood dysregulation disorder (DMDD)** (mentioned in Chapter 3) is a diagnosis for children and adolescents who show depressive symptoms combined with temper outbursts. ICD-11 doesn't include DMDD, but it can be coded as a form of oppositional defiant disorder (discussed in Chapter 13). For more on PMDD and DMDD, see Diagnostic Boxes 5.7 and 5.8.

Premenstrual dysphoric disorder (PMDD): DSM and ICD disorder diagnosed in women who show depressive symptoms during the week before their menstrual periods.

Disruptive mood dysregulation disorder (DMDD): DSM disorder diagnosed in children and adolescents who show depressive symptoms combined with temper outbursts.

Diagnostic Box 5.7 Premenstrual Dysphoric Disorder (PMDD)

DSM-5-TR
- During menstrual cycles for the last year, at least five symptoms.
- At least one symptom must be: (1) mood swings, (2) touchiness, anger, relational conflicts, (3) sadness, hopelessness, self-denigrating thoughts, (4) anxiety, tension, edginess.
- At least one symptom must be (1) loss of interest in activities, (2) feeling distracted, (3) tiredness or low energy, (4) changes in appetite, (5) insomnia or hypersomnia, (6) sense of being overwhelmed, (7) physical symptoms (tender breasts, muscle pain, bloating, gaining weight).

ICD-11
- During most menstrual cycles, at least one mood symptom (e.g., depressed, anxious, irritable)
- Additional physical symptoms (e.g., joint pain, fatigue, overeating, sleeping excessively, tender breasts) and/or cognitive symptoms (e.g., trouble concentrating and remembering).

Information from American Psychiatric Association (2022, p. 197) and World Health Organization (2022a).

Diagnostic Box 5.8 Disruptive Mood Dysregulation Disorder (DMDD)

DSM-5-TR
- Verbal and behavioral temper outbursts roughly three times per week that are developmentally inappropriate.
- Consistently irritable mood most days.
- Symptoms last at least a year and are never absent for three or more months.
- Onset before age 10; shouldn't be diagnosed before age 6 or after age 18.

ICD-11
- Not in ICD-11.
- Can be coded as "oppositional defiant disorder with chronic irritability-anger."

Information from American Psychiatric Association (2022, p. 178) and World Health Organization (2022a).

Postpartum Depression and Seasonal Affective Disorder

Photo 5.2 "I also just didn't think it could happen to me. I have a great life ... But postpartum does not discriminate," model Chrissy Teigan wrote about her experience of postpartum depression for *Glamour* magazine. https://www.glamour.com/story/chrissy-teigen-postpartum-depression.
CBS Photo Archive/Getty Images.

Postpartum depression: Depression that develops in women who are pregnant or have given birth within the last four weeks.

Seasonal affective disorder (SAD): Depression that occurs during the winter months when there are fewer hours of daylight.

Postpartum depression is depression in women who are pregnant or have given birth during the last four weeks. **Seasonal affective disorder (SAD)** describes those who become depressed during the winter when there are fewer hours of daylight. Neither is a stand-alone DSM or ICD diagnosis. However, DSM-5-TR provides postpartum or seasonal onset specifiers that can be added to mood and bipolar diagnoses. ICD-11 includes a catch-all diagnosis for mental disorders associated with pregnancy and childbirth. As for SAD, ICD-11 considers it a type of recurrent depressive disorder, with a distinct code to indicate seasonal onset.

Evaluating DSM and ICD Perspectives
Threshold and Comorbidity Issues

DSM and ICD conceptions of depression and mania have been criticized for threshold and comorbidity issues (Bebbington, 2013). *Threshold problems* involve uncertainty over how severe mood symptoms must be to rise to the level of disorder. We already mentioned how difficult it is for laypeople to agree about this. Creators of DSM and ICD haven't always been able to, either. As for comorbidity, it occurs when patients meet criteria for more than one disorder. Mood disorders are highly comorbid—not only with one another but also with anxiety disorders, trauma and stress-related disorders, substance use disorders, and impulse-control disorders (Cummings et al., 2014; Hasin et al., 2018; R. M. A. Hirschfeld, 2001; Horesh et al., 2017; Kalin, 2020; R. C. Kessler et al., 2003, 2010; Klein Hofmeijer-Sevink et al., 2012; Stander et al., 2014). Critics says this proves that DSM and ICD can't distinguish different disorders. Others feel this is criticism is unfair. They say depression's ubiquity shouldn't be held against it, especially given that it isn't just comorbid with other mental disorders but also with physical illnesses like cancer, stroke, and coronary disease (S. M. Gold et al., 2020; H.-J. Kang et al., 2015).

Assessing the Reliability of Depressive and Bipolar Diagnoses

Despite its frequent use as a diagnosis, major depressive disorder showed questionable reliability in DSM-5 field trials—meaning that clinicians didn't consistently agree on which patients warranted a diagnosis (Regier et al., 2013). However, its ICD equivalents (single episode and recurrent depressive disorders) showed markedly better reliability during ICD-11 field trials (G. M. Reed et al., 2018). Similarly, in both DSM and ICD trials, bipolar I and (to a lesser extent) bipolar II disorders yielded fairly strong reliability (G. M. Reed et al., 2018; Regier et al., 2013). However, the reliability of DSM-5's DMDD was quite poor (Regier et al., 2013). Why might reliability for some depressive disorders be low? Perhaps because depression is a *heterogeneous* diagnosis—meaning that people given it often have dissimilar symptoms and circumstances (S. N. Ghaemi & Vöhringer, 2011; Lieblich et al., 2015). Thus, clinicians are unclear about what counts as depression. In fact, in DSM-5 field trials "highly trained specialist psychiatrists under study conditions were only able to agree that a patient has depression between 4 and 15% of the time" (Lieblich et al., 2015, p. e5).

Harmonization Issues: PDD, DMDD, and the Bereavement Exclusion

Despite efforts at harmonization, DSM and ICD don't define all mood disorders identically (First et al., 2021; Maj, 2013). Several areas where DSM diverges from ICD have been criticized. For instance, DSM's PDD diagnosis has been accused of conflating dysthymia and major depression (Uher et al., 2014). However, defenders say DSM was right to blur the line because a firm distinction between dysthymia and chronic depression is scientifically suspect (Gotlib & LeMoult, 2014). DSM has also been attacked for adding DMDD, which performed poorly in diagnostic reliability trials (Regier et al., 2013). Critics say DMDD turns a normal part of childhood (temper tantrums) into a mental disorder, leading to inappropriately prescribing medication to young children (R. Cooper, 2014; A. Frances, 2012; Raven & Parry, 2012).

Finally, many have decried DSM's elimination of the **bereavement exclusion**, which ICD kept. The bereavement exclusion is a guideline that discourages diagnosing depressive episodes in people grieving the loss of a loved one (A. V. Horwitz & Wakefield, 2007; Zachar et al., 2017). Its supporters argue that bereavement looks like a depressive episode but is really an expectable and normal reaction to grief. From their perspective, removing the bereavement exclusion pathologizes normal human sadness following loss (A. J. Frances & Nardo, 2013; J. C. Wakefield, 2013b; J. C. Wakefield & First, 2012). Opponents disagree, asking why there should be an exception for bereavement when other situations such as divorce or job loss don't disqualify people from a depressive episode. In their view, depression is depression regardless of circumstances (A. M. D. Iglewicz et al., 2013; Karam et al., 2013; Pies, 2014; Zisook et al., 2012). The dispute over the bereavement exclusion is ongoing—and reflected in DSM and ICD's different rules about it. When a patient's symptoms are due to bereavement, DSM-5-TR suggests clinicians use their judgment in diagnosing depression, while ICD-11 instructs them not to diagnose it. Should a depressive episode diagnosis depend on whether a clinician supports or opposes the bereavement exclusion?

Bereavement exclusion: DSM-IV criterion for major depressive disorder that discouraged clinicians from diagnosing major depression in people grieving the loss of a loved one; removed starting with DSM-5.

Should Premenstrual Dysphoric Disorder (PMDD) Have Been Added?

Premenstrual dysphoric disorder (PMDD) became an official disorder for the first time in DSM-5 and ICD-11 but remains controversial. Critics say PMDD is a sexist category that reinforces stereotypes about women being emotionally unstable during menstruation (Caplan, 1995; Offman & Kleinplatz, 2004; J. C. Wakefield, 2013a). By contrast, supporters argue that PMDD is legitimate but should only be diagnosed in extreme cases requiring treatment (American Psychiatric Association, 2022; Gotlib & LeMoult, 2014). They add that the diagnosis relieves stigma and facilitates treatment (Osborn et al., 2020; Parameshwaran & Chandra, 2018). To further reduce stigma, ICD-11 considers PMDD a disease affecting genital organs rather than a mental disorder. However, critics see menstrual distress as a normal part of being female and believe it is wrong to consider it a disorder (T. K. Browne, 2015). What do you think?

5.3 Other Diagnostic Perspectives on Mood Problems

PDM

Depression

PDM-2 complements DSM and ICD by describing the psychodynamics behind mood problems, emphasizing the importance of personality patterns (measured on the P-Axis) in how depression manifests. PDM's S-Axis describes the subjective experience of depression as "complex," often masked by physical symptoms, and divisible into two basic types (Lingiardi & McWilliams, 2017). The first type, *anaclitic depression*, is characterized by feeling helpless, weak, guilty, and depleted—often due to problematic early relationships with caregivers. The second type, *introjective depression*, involves feeling inferior, worthless, inadequate, and self-critical; these individuals crave approval and recognition but behave in ways that lead to criticism and rejection rather than support (Lingiardi & McWilliams, 2017).

Mania

According to PDM, the subjective experience of mania in bipolar disorder involves irritability, grandiosity, restlessness, and impulsivity (Lingiardi & McWilliams, 2017). Manic individuals are likely to feel invincible or all-powerful while craving fame or recognition, having boundless energy, and needing little sleep. Interpersonally, relationships tend to be chaotic, unpredictable, and hypersexualized. Therapists often are befuddled by manic clients, finding it difficult to keep up with their rapid shifts in mood. Consequently, establishing a productive psychotherapy relationship can be difficult (Lingiardi & McWilliams, 2017).

HiTOP

Rather than trying to fit people into DSM and ICD's comorbid mood disorder categories, HiTOP assesses depression and mania dimensionally (Kotov et al., 2017, 2021). Many symptoms of depressive and bipolar symptoms fall along HiTOP's "Internalizing" spectra dimension, characterized by negative thoughts and feelings inside the person (such as depression, loneliness, and social withdrawal). Internalizing symptoms don't manifest in easily observed behaviors—the spectrum name reflects that such symptoms are experienced internally. HiTOP researchers have been developing assessment instruments, such as the *Inventory of Depression and Anxiety Symptoms (IDAS)*, to measure depressive and bipolar patterns on the "Internalizing" spectrum (Barendse et al., 2022; De la Rosa-Cáceres et al., 2020; Sellbom et al., 2021; D. Watson, Forbes, et al., 2022). Of course, depressed individuals may also score higher on other spectra, including "Detachment" (withdrawal and social disengagement) and "Somatoform" (physical symptoms are common among depressed people). Those with bipolar disorders may score high on "Disinhibited Externalizing" (impulsive and risky behaviors), "Antagonistic Externalizing" (aggressive behaviors), and "Thought Disorder" spectra (grandiose thinking and, in extreme cases of mania, psychosis). Research is ongoing (Barendse et al., 2022; F. Conway, 2012; De la Rosa-Cáceres et al., 2020; Eubanks & Hunter, 2020). HiTOP advocates believe their approach maps depressive and bipolar experience in a manner that overcomes DSM and ICD's comorbidity problems (C. C. Conway & Krueger, 2021).

PTMF

As it does with nearly all presenting problems, PTMF (somewhat controversially) rejects the medical view of "depression" as an illness (Johnstone et al., 2018). Instead, it contends that what we consider "symptoms" of "depression"—things like self-blame, hopelessness, helplessness, social withdrawal, and avoidance—are better viewed as threat responses to social adversity and oppression. PTMF aims to identify how societal power structures have elicited threat responses in service users, which in turn has led them to make sense of events in ways that aren't always productive. While PTMF can be used in conjunction with DSM or ICD, it is fundamentally at odds with them philosophically (Johnstone et al., 2018).

HISTORICAL PERSPECTIVES

5.4 Ancient Greece through the Renaissance

Melancholia in Ancient Greece

Depression and mania have been identified throughout the ages (Baldessarini et al., 2015; Shorter, 2019). Ancient Greek medicine divided madness into three kinds: *frenzy*, *mania*, and *melancholy* (Lawlor, 2012). Its definitions of mania and melancholy don't correspond precisely to our current conceptions (Lawlor, 2012). For instance, melancholy—or *melancholia*—was broader than what today we call depression. It involved not just baseless sadness and fear, but sometimes included other symptoms such as hallucinations (Lawlor, 2012). Ancient Greek humoral theory blamed melancholia on imbalances in (and sometimes overheating of) black bile, one of the four bodily humors (see Chapter 1) (Azzone, 2013; Lawlor, 2012; Sani et al., 2020; Telles-Correia & Marques, 2015). Melancholia was also often attributed to unrequited love (Lawlor, 2012). Treatments for mania and melancholia included bloodletting and leeching, intended to correct the humoral imbalances (Lawlor, 2012).

Acedia and Melancholia in the Early Christian Era and Renaissance

Later, during the early Christian era, the term *acedia* was used to describe the low mood, boredom, and longing among isolated monks living in the Egyptian desert during the fourth century (Benvenuto, 2018; K. Kennedy, 2017). Acedia also involved despair over the pressure to avoid temptation. Although rarely used today, the term was reintroduced during the COVID-19 pandemic to describe the boredom and disenchantment people felt in lockdown (Zecher, 2020).

Historically, elements of acedia became incorporated into Western conceptions of melancholia. Perhaps the most prevalent form of madness during the Renaissance, melancholia was broader than today's depression (Dreher, 2013). Symptoms included

overwhelming anxiety, fearfulness, sadness, and gloom, restlessness, dissatisfaction, emotional instability, suspicion, weeping, complaining, ill-tempered and aggressive behavior, withdrawal from social life, disturbed sexual relations, torpor, the inability to feel pleasure, lethargy, oppression with a sense of guilt and unworthiness, inability to sleep, delusions, hallucinations, profound weariness with life, and suicidal tendencies. (Dreher, 2013, p. 41)

Renaissance thinkers attributed melancholy to various factors, including supernatural causes (e.g., God or the devil), natural causes (e.g., astrological influences or biological factors such as imbalances in the digestive system), and external causes (e.g., conflicted interpersonal relations with others or unfortunate life circumstances like financial loss, poverty, or grieving) (Dreher, 2013). Importantly, the Renaissance romanticized melancholy, with feelings of sadness and despair seen as natural accompaniments of genius—a view sometimes still held today (Lawlor, 2012).

5.5 Evolving Views during the Nineteenth and Twentieth Centuries

Industrialization, Depleted Nervous Systems, and Neurasthenia

During the late nineteenth and early twentieth centuries in Europe and North America, melancholy became associated with the oppressive consequences of industrialization (Lawlor, 2012). Interestingly, some modern ways of describing depression are traceable to the industrial era's emphasis on harnessing energy (for instance, DSM and ICD cite loss of energy as a key symptom). In this vein, people began attributing depression and mania to extreme variations in energy (or overly stimulated or depleted nervous systems). The energy-system metaphor influenced a host of important thinkers, including Emil Kraepelin (1856–1926; see Chapter 4) and Sigmund Freud (1856–1939; see Chapter 2) (Lawlor, 2012).

Sticking with the energy metaphor, *neurasthenia* was a popular diagnosis during the latter 1800s and early 1900s. Coined in 1869 by neurologist George Miller Beard (1839–1883), the diagnosis was given to sad and anxious people whose nervous systems were thought to be exhausted from the stresses of modern life (Beard, 1869; J. Beck, 2016; Bhola & Chaturvedi, 2020; Flaskerud, 2007; Jewell, 2003; Lipsitt, 2019; Overholser & Beale, 2019). Just like current diagnoses, neurasthenia reflected the cultural biases of its time; it was frequently identified in women and the lower classes (J. Beck, 2016; Bhola & Chaturvedi, 2020). Although more or less a defunct diagnosis, neurasthenia remained in ICD until ICD-11 (Bhola & Chaturvedi, 2020). And its influence continues. For example, neurasthenia has similarities to "burnout," a more recent term describing people exhausted and overwhelmed by demanding careers (Lipsitt, 2019). Echoes of neurasthenia can also be seen in modern diagnoses like chronic fatigue syndrome and fibromyalgia (Overholser & Beale, 2019). Neurasthenia is a historical leftover that bridges ancient conceptions of melancholia and modern notions of depression (Lawlor, 2012).

From Kraepelin to Modern Conceptions of Depression and Mania

In 1899, diagnostic pioneer Emil Kraepelin placed depression and mania along a *manic-depressive illness continuum*—greatly influencing modern understandings (Baldessarini et al., 2015; Shorter, 2019). Mania involved overactivity and the flight of ideas, while depression entailed feelings of sadness accompanied by slowed down physiology and cognition (Lawlor, 2012). Although Kraepelin treated manic-depressive illness as a single diagnostic category, by the mid-twentieth century it was divided it into "bipolar" and "unipolar" types—the former characterized by alternating "poles" of mania and depression; the latter restricted to one "pole" of "pure depression" (Shorter, 2019). Incorporated into DSM, the unipolar–bipolar distinction remains integral to modern diagnostic terminology (Shorter, 2019). This terminology also owes a great deal to psychiatrist Adolf Meyer (1866–1950), who advocated replacing the more inclusive concept of "melancholia" with the more focused word "depression" (Lawlor, 2012). We have Meyer to thank for the narrower definition of depression taken for granted today.

BIOLOGICAL PERSPECTIVES

5.6 Brain Chemistry Perspectives

Monoamine Hypothesis of Depression and Antidepressants

Monoamine hypothesis: Hypothesis that depression is due to a shortage of the monoamine neurotransmitters serotonin, norepinephrine, and dopamine.

Antidepressants: Drugs used to alleviate depression and many other presenting problems; they work by affecting monoamine neurotransmitters in the brain.

MAO inhibitors (MAOIs): Antidepressants that work by inhibiting monoamine oxidase (MAO), a brain enzyme that breaks down excess monoamine neurotransmitters; this leaves more monoamine neurotransmitters available.

Tricyclics: Antidepressants that mainly affect norepinephrine and serotonin; they inhibit reabsorption of these neurotransmitters, leaving more available.

Selective serotonin reuptake inhibitors (SSRIs): Antidepressants that prevent reuptake or reabsorption of serotonin by neurons that release it; this leaves more serotonin available.

Serotonin and norepinephrine reuptake inhibitors (SNRIs): Antidepressants that block reuptake of serotonin and norepinephrine, leaving more of both available.

Atypical antidepressants: Antidepressants that are chemically unrelated to the four main types of antidepressants (SSRIs, SNRIs, MAOIs, and tricyclics). *Bupropion*, *trazodone*, and *mirtazapine* are examples.

The **monoamine hypothesis** holds that depression is due to a shortage of the monoamine neurotransmitters serotonin, norepinephrine, and dopamine (Cosci & Chouinard, 2019; Filatova et al., 2021; Hillhouse & Porter, 2015; R. M. Hirschfeld, 2000). Just as the dopamine hypothesis was devised after the fact to explain why antipsychotics reduce schizophrenia symptoms (see Chapter 4), the monoamine hypothesis was developed in the 1960s after early **antidepressants** were found to alleviate depression. The earliest antidepressant drugs were the MAO inhibitors and the tricyclics. In more recent decades, the SSRIs and SNRIs have become popular. All work in ways consistent with the monoamine hypothesis. Let's examine them more closely.

MAO Inhibitors and Tricyclics

As with antipsychotics, the first antidepressants were discovered serendipitously (Di Benedetto et al., 2010; Hillhouse & Porter, 2015; Hyman, 2014; López-Muñoz & Alamo, 2009). *Iproniazid*, a drug originally developed to treat tuberculosis, became the first successful antidepressant during the 1950s when it was accidentally found to reduce depressive symptoms (France et al., 2007; Hillhouse & Porter, 2015; López-Muñoz & Alamo, 2009; Shorter, 2009). It belongs to a class of drugs called **MAO inhibitors (MAOIs)**. MAOIs do exactly what their name suggests: inhibit *monoamine oxidase (MAO)*, a brain enzyme that breaks down excess monoamine neurotransmitters in the synapses between neurons. Inhibiting the action of monoamine oxidase leaves more serotonin, norepinephrine, and dopamine available, thus increasing the chances these neurotransmitters will bind with surrounding neurons and cause them to fire. Around the same time, researchers developed another class of antidepressants, the **tricyclics**, which mainly affect norepinephrine and serotonin (usually with more impact on norepinephrine) (Di Benedetto et al., 2010; Hillhouse & Porter, 2015). The tricyclics work by inhibiting the synaptic reabsorption of serotonin and norepinephrine, leaving more available to trigger neuronal firing. One of the first tricyclic drugs was *imipramine* (France et al., 2007).

Tricyclics and (especially) MAOIs are used less today because of unpleasant side effects such as dry mouth, constipation, weight gain, and drowsiness. Those taking MAOIs must avoid cheese and other dairy products or run the risk of increased heart rate, sweating, and high blood pressure that can culminate in a hypertensive crisis that damages internal organs (Bauer et al., 2013; Hillhouse & Porter, 2015). Though less concerning than MAOI side effects, tricyclics can cause dizziness and memory problems (Bauer et al., 2013; Hillhouse & Porter, 2015).

SSRIs, SNRIs, and Atypical Antidepressants

The 1980s and 1990s saw the rise of a new class of antidepressants, the **selective serotonin reuptake inhibitors (SSRIs)** (Carlsson, 1999). As with the MAOIs, the name of the SSRIs describes how they work. SSRIs selectively block the reuptake of serotonin. The term "selective" is used to make clear that the SSRIs affect only serotonin. Because their effect is more focused, they are commonly seen as having fewer side effects than MAOIs and tricyclics. The most famous SSRI is probably *fluoxetine* (often marketed as *Prozac*), but many others have been developed.

Starting in the 1990s, **serotonin and norepinephrine reuptake inhibitors (SNRIs)** began appearing on the market (Hillhouse & Porter, 2015). These drugs work similarly to SSRIs except instead of only targeting serotonin, they prevent the reuptake of both serotonin and norepinephrine. *Venlafaxine* (trade name *Effexor*) was the first SNRI marketed in the United States (Hillhouse & Porter, 2015; Sansone & Sansone, 2014).

Finally, **atypical antidepressants** are chemically unrelated to SSRIs, SNRIs, MAOIs, and tricyclics (Bruty et al., 2012; Mental Health America, n.d.; Sheffler & Abdijadid, 2022). Each is unique and works in a novel way. For instance, *bupropion* (sold as *Wellbutrin* and *Zyban*) is a *norepinephrine-dopamine reuptake inhibitor (NDRI)* (Bruty et al., 2012). It blocks reuptake of norepinephrine and dopamine, leaving more available. However, it has little to no effect on serotonin. *Mirtazapine* (trade name *Remeron*), another atypical antidepressant, is an *alpha-2 antagonist*; it blocks alpha-2 receptors

Table 5.1 Common Antidepressants

MAO INHIBITORS	TRICYCLICS	
• Isocarboxazid (Marplan) • Phenelzine (Nardil) • Selegiline (Emsam) • Tranylcypromine (Parnate)	• Amitriptyline (Vanatrip, Elavil, Endep) • Amoxapine (Asendin, Asendis, Defanyl, Demolox) • Desipramine (Norpramin) • Doxepin (Deptran and Sinequan)	• Imipramine (Tofranil) • Nortriptyline (Pamelor) • Protriptyline (Vivactil) • Trimipramine (Surmontil)
SSRIS	**SNRIS**	**ATYPICAL ANTIDEPRESSANTS**
• Citalopram (Celexa, Cipramil) • Escitalopram (Lexapro) • Fluoxetine (Prozac) • Paroxetine (Paxil, Pexeva, Seroxat) • Sertraline (Zoloft, Lustral)	• Desvenlafaxine (Pristiq, Khedezla) • Duloxetine (Cymbalta, Irenka) • Levomilnacipran (Fetzima) • Venlafaxine (Effexor XR)	• Bupropion (Wellbutrin, Zyban) • Mirtazapine (Remeron) • Trazadone (Desyrel, Oleptro) • Vortioxetine (Trintellix, Brintellix)

Note: Common trade names in parentheses.

in the sympathetic nervous system, which increases serotonin and norepinephrine (Bruty et al., 2012). Like mirtazapine, *trazadone* (sold as *Desyrel* and *Oleptro*) and *vortioxetine* (sold as *Trintellix* and *Brintellix*) also block reuptake of serotonin; distinct from other antidepressants, exactly how they work remains unknown (Bruty et al., 2012; D'Agostino et al., 2015). See Table 5.1 for a list of common antidepressants by type.

The Rapid Rise in Antidepressant Usage

The advent of SSRIs and SNRIs has coincided with a sharp increase in the number of people taking antidepressants. Simply put, these drugs are very popular. Depressed U.S. outpatients who received antidepressants increased from 37.3 percent in 1987 to 74.5 percent by 1998—with three quarters being given SSRIs (Shorter, 2009). Since then, the prevalence of antidepressant usage in the United States—for both depression and other presenting problems—has steadily increased (Brody & Gu, 2020; Medco, 2010; L. A. Pratt et al., 2017). As Figure 5.1 shows, from 2015 to 2018 in the United States, 13.2 percent of adults reported taking antidepressants during the past month. Further, from 2009–10 to 2017–18, the total percent of adults on antidepressants jumped from 10.6 percent

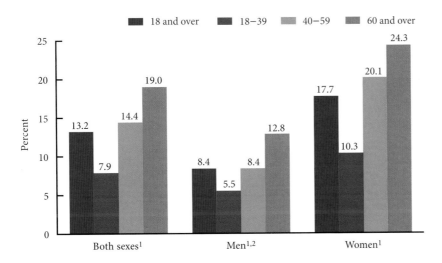

[1]Significant increasing trend by age.
[2]Significantly lower than women in the same age goup.
NOTE: Access data table for Figure 1 at: https://www.cdc.gov/nchs/data/databriefs/db377-tables-508.pds#1.
SOURCE: National Center for Health Statistics, National Health and Nutrition Examination Survey, 2015–2018.

Figure 5.1 Percentage of Persons Aged 12 and over Who Took Antidepressant Medication in the Past Month, by Age and Sex: United States, 2011–2014. U.S. data suggests that older people and women are more likely to be taking an antidepressant.
Source: Brody, D. J., & Gu, Q. (2020). Antidepressant use among adults: United States, 2015–2018 (No. 377; NCHS Data Brief). National Center for Health Statistics. https://www.cdc.gov/nchs/products/databriefs/db377.htm

to 13.8 percent (Brody & Gu, 2020). This increase wasn't significant among men (7.1 percent to 8.7 percent) but was among women (13.8 percent to 18.6 percent), who take antidepressants more in the first place (Brody & Gu, 2020). In the United States, adolescent antidepressants use has seen an especially steep upsurge, with prevalence between 2015 and 2019 rising from 5.7 percent to 7.9 percent, a 38.3 percent increase (Express Scripts, 2020).

Rising antidepressant use isn't limited to the United States. Rates more than tripled in England between 1998 and 2018 (Bogowicz et al., 2021), and the number of antidepressant hospital prescriptions in China was nearly 43 percent greater in 2018 than just five years earlier (Z. Yu et al., 2020). Further, the COVID-19 pandemic only increased antidepressant use (R. Henderson, 2021; Rabeea et al., 2021). Curiously, an unexpected benefit of antidepressants may be prevention of severe disease in COVID-19 patients, perhaps due to these drugs' anti-inflammatory properties (Hoertel et al., 2021; Oskotsky et al., 2021). More research is needed.

Which country consumes the most antidepressants? According to the Organization for Economic Cooperation and Development (OCED), it's Iceland. OCED data doesn't include the United States. If it did, the United States would likely rank second. For use by country, see Figure 5.2.

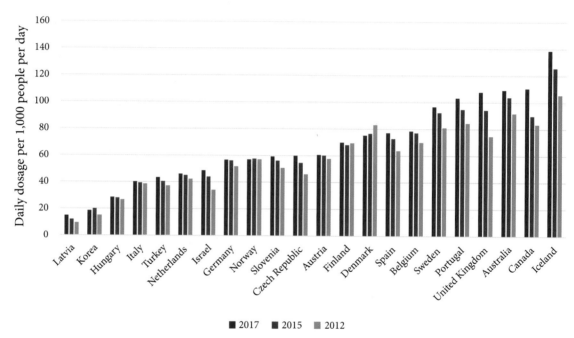

■ 2017　■ 2015　■ 2012

Figure 5.2 Antidepressant Use around the Globe. Your chances of being on an antidepressant vary depending on what country you live in. This graph doesn't include the United States, but it would probably rank second.
Source: Based on data downloaded from OECD, https://www.oecd.org/els/health-systems/health-data.htm

Effectiveness of Antidepressants

Despite widespread use, the benefits of antidepressants are debated. Researchers often conclude these drugs work, estimating them effective 50 percent to 75 percent of the time (Bauer et al., 2013; A. Cipriani et al., 2018; A. J. Rush et al., 2006). However, others conclude the evidence is lacking (Munkholm et al., 2019). Even when research finds antidepressants work, they often don't work as well as we'd like. One study indicated that only 28 percent of depressed people experienced full remission of symptoms (Hyman, 2014; M. H. Trivedi et al., 2006). Another found antidepressants do not improve people's health-related quality of life (Almohammed et al., 2022). It has been estimated that between 33 percent and 50 percent of depressed people are resistant to the effects of antidepressants (N. J. Wolf & Hopko, 2008). Further, many who initially respond to them later redevelop symptoms (S. N. Ghaemi et al., 2013). The "Controversial Question" box discusses the provocative (and much disputed) view that antidepressants are no better than placebos.

Although SSRIs and SNRIs are easier to tolerate than older antidepressants, they still have adverse effects—including headaches, insomnia, weight gain, and sexual dysfunction (Santarsieri &

Controversial Question: Antidepressants as Placebo?

When researchers study a drug's effectiveness, they often compare it with a placebo pill. Placebo pills typically cause improvement on their own due to patient expectations that they will get better. For a drug to be considered effective, it needs to improve symptoms more than a placebo pill does.

To study the placebo effect in the treatment of depression, psychologist Irving Kirsch (2010, 2014, 2019) used meta-analysis (the statistical technique that pools the results of many studies to identify overall effects). Kirsch reached a controversial conclusion, namely that antidepressants aren't noticeably more effective than placebo pills! This finding rocked the psychiatric establishment. Kirsch wound up being interviewed repeatedly in the media about his stunning finding. After all, given the billions of dollars that pharmaceutical companies generate selling antidepressants, could it be possible that they are no more effective than sugar pills?

Critics—and even Kirsch himself—note that there does seem to be a small effect for antidepressants compared with placebo pills. However, upon conducting further meta-analyses, Kirsch (2010, 2014, 2019) concluded that this difference probably has a lot to do with whether subjects can guess if they are getting the antidepressant or the placebo pill. Being able to figure this out is called *breaking blind*. Participants who break blind and realize they are getting the real drug improve more than those who get the real drug but don't know it; think of this as a placebo effect on top of the drug effect. Oddly, one of the ways participants break blind is by identifying drug side effects. If they experience side effects, then they must be getting the real drug! If they don't, they're probably taking the placebo pill. Kirsch found that some studies account for this by using active, as opposed to passive, placebos. An active placebo is designed to cause side effects, making it harder to break blind. In studies where an active placebo was used, Kirsch found no difference between antidepressants and placebos. Based on his research, all the money we spend on antidepressants is for naught; a sugar pill each day might work just as well.

Not everyone buys Kirsch's conclusions, and numerous researchers have presented evidence challenging his contention that antidepressants are little better than placebos (A. Cipriani et al., 2018; Fountoulakis et al., 2013; Fountoulakis & Möller, 2011; Hieronymus et al., 2018; Holper & Hengartner, 2020). Psychiatrist Peter Kramer (2011) has argued that many of the studies Kirsch looked at were sloppily done and include too many people who don't really qualify for a depression diagnosis, thereby potentially washing out any effect of the drugs. Kramer (2011) also points to evidence that taking antidepressants can be helpful in a variety of specific situations—including recovering from a stroke, dealing with depression due to neurological problems, and alleviating anxiety in children. To Kramer, Kirsch's conclusion that antidepressants are mainly placebos is dangerous because it encourages people to stop taking drugs that Kramer believes can help them.

But Kirsch isn't convinced and stands by his findings. He notes that meta-analyses on therapy, antidepressants alone, antidepressants with therapy, and alternative treatments such as acupuncture all show equal effectiveness in alleviating depression. Kirsch concludes: "There is a strong therapeutic response to antidepressant medication. But the response to placebo is almost as strong;" therefore, if antidepressants "are to be used at all, it should be as a last resort, when depression is extremely severe and all other treatment alternatives have been tried and failed" (Kirsch, 2014, p. 132).

Critical Thinking Questions

1. How is it that Kirsch and Kramer draw such different conclusions about the effectiveness of antidepressants?
2. Are you more sympathetic to Kirsch's or Kramer's view of antidepressants? Why?
3. Antidepressants currently are dispensed quite readily and are used more often than psychotherapy to treat depression. Do you agree with Kirsch that these drugs should only be used as a last resort? Why or why not?

Schwartz, 2015; Settle, 1998; Stahl et al., 2005). SSRIs sometimes also cause nervousness, insomnia, and gastrointestinal distress, while SNRIs can lead to dry mouth, nausea, and high blood pressure (Cappetta et al., 2018; Santarsieri & Schwartz, 2015). Due to side effects, many people stop taking these drugs (Balsikci et al., 2014; S. N. Ghaemi et al., 2013; Hotopf et al., 1997; Settle, 1998).

Shirley

Shirley discusses her depressed mood with her family physician. He prescribes Zoloft, an SSRI. Several weeks after starting on Zoloft, Shirley reports feeling less depressed. However, she also complains about trouble sleeping and lack of interest in sex.

Black Box Warning on Antidepressants

Controversy surrounds whether antidepressants raise the risk of adolescent suicide, with some evidence suggesting they do (K. Li et al., 2022). Since 2004, the United States has included a hotly debated *black box warning* on antidepressants. This warning, printed on the outside packaging, states that antidepressants may increase suicidal tendencies in teens. Some applaud the warning as warranted, especially in a culture they feel overprescribes to children and adolescents (A. C. Leon, 2007; Sparks & Duncan, 2013; Spielmans et al., 2020). Others lament this warning, arguing that the benefits of giving depressed teens antidepressants outweigh any risks (Fornaro et al., 2019; R. A. Friedman, 2014; Nagar et al., 2010).

Discontinuation Syndrome

Discontinuation syndrome: Occurs when antidepressants are discontinued; includes flu-like symptoms, dizziness, insomnia, nausea, diarrhea, irritability, nightmares, and depressive symptoms due to stopping the drug.

Those on SSRIs and SNRIs often encounter **discontinuation syndrome** when they stop taking them. Discontinuation can induce flu-like symptoms, dizziness, insomnia, nausea, diarrhea, irritability, nightmares, and depressive symptoms due to stopping the drug (rather than a return of the depression that precipitated drug use in the first place) (Fava et al., 2015, 2018; Hameed et al., 2020; B. H. Harvey & Slabbert, 2014; Rizkalla et al., 2020). Given the severity of discontinuation symptoms and the difficulty many people have getting off antidepressants, it has been argued—albeit controversially within psychiatry—that "discontinuation syndrome" should be renamed "withdrawal syndrome" (Fava et al., 2015, 2018). Discontinuation symptoms, side effects, and debates over effectiveness notwithstanding, depressive symptoms are sometimes worse than the negative consequences of antidepressants. Therefore, these drugs are recommended by the American Psychiatric Association, American Psychological Association, and World Federation of Biological Psychiatry (Bauer et al., 2013, 2015; Guideline Development Panel for the Treatment of Depressive Disorders, 2019; Work Group on Major Depressive Disorder, 2010).

Shortcomings of the Monoamine Hypothesis

The monoamine hypothesis has several shortcomings. First, antidepressants quickly impact monoamine levels but don't affect mood until people have been taking them between two and four weeks (Boku et al., 2018; Malhi, Hitching, et al., 2013; N. P. Nair & Sharma, 1989). Why this is remains a mystery. However, promising research suggests that to work, SSRIs must accumulate in the "lipid raft" area of neuron cell membranes, and this takes time (Erb et al., 2016). Second, there is evidence that long-term SSRI use lowers rather than raises serotonin levels (Moncrieff et al., 2022). The proposed explanation for this is that the brain compensates for increased availability of serotonin by synthesizing less of it (Bosker et al., 2010; Siesser et al., 2012). Third, not all drugs that enhance monoamine levels—such as cocaine and amphetamines—have antidepressant effects (Di Benedetto et al., 2010; N. P. Nair & Sharma, 1989). Fourth, monoamine levels are difficult to assess and typically measured indirectly via brain scans or metabolites in urine (N. P. Nair & Sharma, 1989; Niyonambaza et al., 2019; Valenstein, 1998). Fifth, depleting monoamine levels in non-depressed people doesn't induce depression, so depression can't be about depleted monoamines alone (Hillhouse & Porter, 2015; R. M. Salomon et al., 1997). Based on these challenges, many researchers suspect that depression can't be fully explained by the monoamine hypothesis. It is now often hypothesized that low monoamine levels interact with other neurobiological systems in triggering depression (Di Benedetto et al., 2010; J. S. Goldberg et al., 2014; Hillhouse & Porter, 2015). However, one thorough research review provocatively concluded that low serotonin and depression are not consistently linked (Moncrieff et al., 2022). Given the mixed evidence, investigators are exploring other biological explanations of depression.

Glutamate Hypothesis of Depression and New Kinds of Drug Treatments

Glutamate hypothesis of depression: Proposes that depression is associated with high levels of glutamate, the brain's main excitatory neurotransmitter.

Ketamine: Anesthetic drug that inhibits glutamate and has antidepressant and anti-anxiety effects; ketamine and a derivative of it, *esketamine*, are used to treat depression.

The **glutamate hypothesis of depression** proposes that depression is associated with high levels of glutamate, the brain's main excitatory neurotransmitter (Hashimoto, 2009; C.-T. Li et al., 2019; Sanacora et al., 2017; Tokita et al., 2012). Consequently, **ketamine**, an anesthetic that decreases glutamate by inhibiting glutamate receptors in the brain, has become a new drug treatment (Krystal et al., 2013; C.-T. Li et al., 2019; Skolnick et al., 2009; Tokita et al., 2012; Walsh et al., 2022). In 2019, *esketamine* (a derivative of ketamine) was approved in the United States and Europe for treatment-resistant depression (Mahase, 2019; U.S. Food and Drug Administration, 2019). It is administered by nasal spray (trade name *Spravato*) as a supplement to antidepressants. Treatments can be twice weekly, weekly, or biweekly for several months—with frequency often decreasing over time. Though only esketamine nasal spray is approved for depression, some doctors and clinics administer ketamine intravenously or provide prescriptions for home use via telehealth appointments (Hamby, 2023; Meltzer & Blum, 2022). Such practices are controversial because they don't limit use to treatment-resistant depression, run the risk of side effects and addiction, and occasionally rely on slick marketing campaigns. For instance, one pricey New York City clinic (founded not by a mental health professional, but by a former fashion designer) touts itself as providing "a spa day for your brain" (Meltzer & Blum, 2022).

One big advantage of ketamine and esketamine is their speed. They take effect within twenty-four hours, much faster than the two to four weeks needed for monoamine antidepressants (Dutta et al., 2015; Kavalali & Monteggia, 2015; Musazzi et al., 2012). However, they also wear off within a week and must be given repeatedly; they are more treatment than cure (Carboni et al., 2021). Administration is conducted under close medical supervision at a doctor's office or clinic because ketamine is highly addictive with hallucinatory properties. Illegally sold as "Special K," it is one of the most abused drugs in China (Hillhouse & Porter, 2015; Levi King, 2021); illicit use in the United States, while rare, is increasing (Palamar et al., 2021). Effectiveness studies of ketamine/esketamine for depression are promising so far, but additional research is needed (Anand et al., 2023; R. L. Dean et al., 2021; Walsh et al., 2022).

Other glutamate-blocking drugs are on their way. In August 2022, the United States approved a rapid-acting antidepressant, *dextromethorphan-bupropion* (tradename *Auvelity*). It is the first oral pill for depression to target glutamate (Brooks, 2022; Iosifescu et al., 2022).

Herbal Remedies for Depression

Despite skepticism in mainstream medicine, using **herbal remedies for depression** has grown in popularity. Examples include St. John's wort, Rhodiola rosea, omega-3 fatty acids, ginkgo biloba, valerian, melatonin, S-adenosyl methionine (SAMe), lavender, passionflower, saffron, black cohosh, chamomile, and chasteberry (Mischoulon, 2018; K. S. Yeung et al., 2018). Let's discuss the first two. It's not entirely clear how St. John's wort works; like many antidepressants, it potentially fosters serotonin transmission (Mischoulon, 2018). Rhodiola rosea's mechanism of action isn't fully understood either, but it seems to impact serotonin and glutamate (Panossian et al., 2014). Research support for both is mixed. Some studies find they reduce mild and moderate depression but others don't (Apaydin et al., 2016; Deltito & Beyer, 1998; Gahlsdorf et al., 2007; Hypericum Depression Trial Study, 2002; Konstantinos & Heun, 2020; Linde et al., 2005; J. J. Mao et al., 2015; Pilkington et al., 2006; Qureshi & Al-Bedah, 2013; Randløv et al., 2006).

Herbal treatments have fewer side effects than traditional antidepressants (Mischoulon, 2018). However, it is safest to use them under medical supervision to avoid interactions with other medications. For instance, combining herbal remedies with antidepressants can produce excessive serotonin levels, resulting in a life-threatening condition called *serotonin syndrome* (Mischoulon, 2018). Although not discussed much in future chapters, herbal remedies aren't limited to depression. Supporters recommend them for all sorts of mental health problems, including anxiety, insomnia, and dementia (Mischoulon, 2018; Sarris et al., 2011; K. S. Yeung et al., 2018). Such remedies aren't typically approved by government testing agencies as sanctioned treatments.

Mood Stabilizers and Bipolar Disorder
Types of Mood Stabilizers

The drugs used to treat the manic symptoms of bipolar disorder are called **mood stabilizers**. "Mood stabilizer" is broad and doesn't specify the exact mechanism by which these drugs work—which is why this term applies to several different classes of drugs (Hirschowitz et al., 2010). The best-known mood stabilizer is **lithium**, a metallic mineral salt that can reduce mania (G. Curran & Ravindran, 2014; K. Gao et al., 2015; Hanwella, 2020; Hirschowitz et al., 2010; Keck et al., 2015). How lithium works is not entirely clear, but research suggests it affects second-messenger neurotransmitter systems, circadian rhythms, and a protein known as CRMP2 (Alda, 2015; Geddes

Herbal remedies for depression: Herbs used to treat depression that are not approved by mainstream medicine; most notably *St. John's wort* and *Rhodiola rosea*.

Mood stabilizers: Various types of drugs used to treat mania.

Lithium: Metallic mineral salt used as a mood stabilizer.

Table 5.2 Common Mood Stabilizers

LITHIUM	ANTICONVULSANTS	BENZODIAZEPINES
• Lithium (Eskalith, Lithobid)	• Carbamazepine (Tegretol) • Gabpentin (Neurontin) • Lamotrigne (Lamictal) • Valproic acid (Depakote)	• Alprazolam (Xanax) • Clonazepam (Klonopin) • Diazepam (Valium) • Lorazepam (Ativan)
ANTIPSYCHOTICS (FIRST GENERATION)	**ANTIPSYCHOTICS (SECOND GENERATION)**	**ANTIPSYCHOTICS (THIRD GENERATION)**
• Haloperidol (Haldol) • Loxapine (Adasuve or Loxapine)	• Asenapine (Saphris) • Olanzapine (Zyprexa) • Quetiapine (Seroquel) • Risperidone (Risperdal) • Ziprasidone (Geodon)	• Apriprazole (Abilify) • Lurasidone (Latuda)

Note: Common trade names in parentheses.

& Miklowitz, 2013; Malhi, Tanious, et al., 2013; Tobe et al., 2017). The genetics of lithium response are also being studied (Papiol et al., 2018).

Besides lithium, three other kinds of drugs are used as mood stabilizers: **anticonvulsants** (initially developed to treat seizures), *benzodiazepines* (more often considered anti-anxiety drugs, but also used to stabilize mood; see Chapter 6), and *antipsychotics* (because, as mentioned, mania can include psychotic symptoms). As with lithium, exactly why these drugs stabilize mood remains unclear. Table 5.2 lists common mood stabilizers.

Anticonvulsants: Drugs initially developed to treat seizures, but also used for various psychiatric conditions; they enhance GABA activity.

Side Effects of Mood Stabilizers

Lithium levels must be closely monitored via regular blood tests. If doses are too low, then there is no effect. If they are too high, then lithium poisoning can occur—with symptoms like nausea, vomiting, tremors, kidney malfunction, and (in extreme cases) death. Lithium is also associated with weight gain, cognitive difficulties, tremors, and feelings of sedation (Gitlin, 2016; Keck et al., 2015; Mago et al., 2014). Long-term lithium use (twenty or more years) puts people at risk for renal failure (Schoot et al., 2020; Werneke et al., 2012). Anticonvulsants can also have serious side effects, causing a variety of stomach, liver, or kidney problems (Hamed, 2017; Leo & Narendran, 1999; National Center for Biotechnology Information, 2019). As for antipsychotics, they have extrapyramidal side effects such as muscle tremors, shuffling gait, and drooling (discussed in Chapter 4). Side effects from mood stabilizers may partly explain why many patients stop taking them (Gitlin, 2016; Mago et al., 2014; Öhlund et al., 2018).

Effectiveness of Mood Stabilizers

Although most research concludes that lithium is the gold standard drug for bipolar disorder (Volkmann et al., 2020), its use has declined in favor of other mood stabilizers (Karanti et al., 2016; Y. Lin et al., 2020; Pérez de Mendiola et al., 2021). Lithium use does need to be closely monitored to avoid lithium poisoning. This may lead to negative perceptions of it, along with a preference for less effective mood stabilizers that require less monitoring (Rybakowski, 2018; Tondo et al., 2019). Nonetheless, lithium is generally considered the most effective mood stabilizer, helpful in roughly two-thirds of patients (Tondo et al., 2019). Of course, this means that 33 percent of patients don't respond well. Mood stabilizers are also sometimes combined with antidepressants because mood stabilizers don't always help bipolar patients with their depressive episodes (Baldessarini et al., 2010). Mixing mood stabilizers and antidepressants can be complicated, as it is not always clear how each drug contributes to symptom improvements (Geddes & Miklowitz, 2013). Further, findings are mixed regarding which mood stabilizers are best for long-term maintenance (Coryell, 2009; G. Curran & Ravindran, 2014; Gigante et al., 2012; Miura et al., 2014). This sheds light on the fact that mood stabilizers, like antidepressants, are a way to manage bipolar symptoms over the long term, rather than a cure.

Don

After a judge mandates treatment following his drunk driving arrest, Don sees a psychiatrist who diagnoses him with bipolar disorder and prescribes him two mood stabilizers: Latuda (an antipsychotic approved to treat bipolar disorder) and Depakote (an anti-seizure drug also approved for bipolar disorder). Don begins taking these drugs. Although he complains the drugs make him feel dizzy, within a week or two his wild mood swings appear to level off. However, Don says he feels "out of it" when taking the drugs and he isn't sure he wishes to take them for an extended period.

5.7 Brain Structure and Function Perspectives

Brain Areas Linked to Depression and Bipolar Disorder

Hippocampus

The hippocampus is a limbic structure involved in forming memories. In both depression and bipolar disorder, hippocampal volume may decrease—that is, the hippocampus becomes smaller and takes up less space (Arnone et al., 2012; Espinoza Oyarce et al., 2020; Lener & Iosifescu, 2015; Lorenzetti et al., 2009; Nolan et al., 2020; Santos et al., 2018; Treadway & Pizzagalli, 2014). There is more evidence of this in depression than bipolar disorder (Haukvik et al., 2022; Otten & Meeter, 2015). However, shrinkage doesn't occur in all depressed patients (T. C. Ho et al., 2022; Malykhin & Coupland, 2015; Roddy et al., 2019). It is most common among the chronically depressed (Lorenzetti et al., 2009; Nolan et al., 2020; Treadway & Pizzagalli, 2014). Antidepressants may slow or prevent hippocampal shrinkage (Lorenzetti et al., 2009; Malykhin & Coupland, 2015; M. A. Rogers et al., 2016; Sapolsky, 2001).

Amygdala

The amygdala, which regulates basic emotions, has been implicated in depression. Amygdala activity, shape, and volume often decrease in depressed and anxious individuals (T. C. Ho et al., 2022; Lener & Iosifescu, 2015; Sacher et al., 2012; J. R. Swartz et al., 2015). However, findings vary. Further, when depression and anxiety are comorbid, amygdala size might increase rather than decrease (Espinoza Oyarce et al., 2020). In bipolar disorder, some but not all studies show increased amygdala responsiveness in those diagnosed with mania (Maletic & Raison, 2014; M. R. Schneider et al., 2012). Amygdala volumes appear smaller in bipolar children and teens but larger in bipolar adults (D. Cui et al., 2020; Garrett & Chang, 2008; López-Jaramillo et al., 2017; Maletic & Raison, 2014; M. R. Schneider et al., 2012). How mood stabilizers affect this pattern isn't clear. Perhaps amygdala changes occur after the onset of bipolar symptoms.

Frontal Lobe

The **frontal lobe** (important in mood, attention, decision-making, immunity, and executing behavior) is another brain region tied to depression. Depression is associated with reduced frontal lobe volume, especially in severe cases (Lorenzetti et al., 2009; F.-F. Zhang et al., 2018). Whether frontal lobe activity increases or decreases in depression isn't clear (Lemogne et al., 2010, 2012; Vialou et al., 2014). Frontal lobe volume loss is a problem in bipolar disorder, too (Abé et al., 2021; M. R. Schneider et al., 2012). This volume loss may be related to decreased synaptic connections to other brain areas (Maletic & Raison, 2014).

Hypothalamic-Pituitary-Adrenal (HPA) Axis

The **hypothalamic-pituitary-adrenal (HPA) axis** plays a role in managing stress, and it is associated with depression—especially when there is evidence of early life stress (Ceruso et al., 2020). The HPA axis is integral in the release of **cortisol**, the primary stress hormone (**hormones** are chemical messengers in the *endocrine system*, a collection of glands that regulate sexual functioning, sleep, mood, and metabolism). Cortisol counters bodily substances that cause physical inflammation. High cortisol levels are linked to depression, though it is not clear whether cortisol levels go up due to prolonged stress or a malfunctioning HPA axis (H. M. Burke et al., 2005; Ceruso et al., 2020; Dedovic & Ngiam, 2015; Lamers et al., 2013; Varghese & Brown, 2001; Zajkowska et al., 2022). The HPA axis and elevated cortisol levels are also implicated in mania (Bauer & Dinan, 2015; Belvederi Murri et al., 2016).

Frontal lobe: Brain region important in executing behavior.

Hypothalamic-pituitary-adrenal (HPA) axis: Interconnected brain structures that play a role in managing stress and releasing cortisol (the primary stress hormone).

Cortisol: Primary stress hormone of the *endocrine system*; high levels correlated with problems like depression and mania, while low levels may occur in response to posttraumatic stress.

Hormones: Chemical messengers of the endocrine systems.

Non-Drug Brain Treatments for Depression
Electroconvulsive Therapy (ECT)

Electroconvulsive therapy (ECT): Treatment in which electrical volts are delivered to the brain to produce a seizure; used mainly for treatment-resistant depression, but sometimes also used for bipolar disorder and psychosis.

Electroconvulsive therapy (ECT) is sometimes used to treat depression, especially when antidepressants don't work (Degerlund Maldi et al., 2021; Lisanby, 2007). In this treatment (introduced in Chapter 1), electrical current is delivered to a patient's brain, inducing a seizure. ECT is typically administered two to three times per week for six to twelve sessions in total, unless more are needed (C. H. Kellner et al., 2020). In the early days of ECT, the current was sent bilaterally through the entire brain without anesthesia. However, today anesthesia is used, and the shocks are more localized—with current usually delivered only to the non-dominant hemisphere (C. H. Kellner et al., 2020). Although we don't know why ECT alleviates depression, there are numerous hypotheses—including that it activates neurotransmission, triggers brain structure growth, fosters HPA axis hormone release, and reduces immune system inflammation (M. Li, Yao, et al., 2020; A. Singh & Kar, 2017). Despite its immediate effectiveness, many people who receive ECT become depressed again (McClintock et al., 2011). By one estimate, relapse rates are 37 percent within six months and 51 percent within a year (Jelovac et al., 2013). Consequently, some severely depressed patients undergo ECT repeatedly over many years.

ECT is seen as especially helpful in cases of psychotic depression (Fink, 2009). It is also used for bipolar disorder (C. H. Kellner & Fink, 2015; Liebman et al., 2015; Salik & Marwaha, 2022) and postpartum depression (Gressier et al., 2015). ECT's main side effects are confusion and memory loss (Breggin, 2007; Fink, 2009; Semkovska et al., 2011). Given its impact on memory and the fact that we don't fully understand why it works, ECT is controversial (I. M. Anderson, 2021; Cleare & Rane, 2013). Supporters argue it is a proven and safe treatment for chronic and intense depression (Ferrier et al., 2021; C. H. Kellner et al., 2020; Trifu et al., 2021; J. Zhang, Wang, Yang, et al., 2021). Detractors contend it is brutal, imprecise, and damages the brain (I. M. Anderson, 2021; Breggin, 2007, 2009, 2010; Read & Arnold, 2017).

Transcranial Magnetic Stimulation (TMS)

Transcranial magnetic stimulation (TMS): Treatment for depression and sometimes bipolar symptoms in which magnetic energy is sent through the brain via electromagnetic coils placed on the scalp.

Transcranial magnetic stimulation (TMS) is another technique used with depressed (and sometimes bipolar) patients who are unresponsive to drug treatments and psychotherapy (Berlim et al., 2014; Rizvi & Khan, 2019; A. G. Yip & Carpenter, 2010). In TMS, magnetic energy is sent through the brain via electromagnetic coils placed on the scalp. As with ECT, we don't know how TMS works, but stimulating the cerebral cortex seems to enhance synaptic transmission (S. Hardy et al., 2016; Janicak & Carpenter, 2014). Side effects of TMS, which tend to be less severe than those from ECT, include headaches, drowsiness, face twitches, excessive eye tearing, and in rare cases seizures (S. Hardy et al., 2016; Janicak & Carpenter, 2014; R. Taylor et al., 2018). Existing studies support TMS for depression and suicidal ideation, although it is less effective (and more labor intensive) than ECT (Berlim et al., 2014; Y. Cui et al., 2022; Fitzgerald, 2019; Somani & Kar, 2019). Consequently, it is less often chosen as a treatment (Cleare & Rane, 2013; Y. Cui et al., 2022; Somani & Kar, 2019).

Deep Brain Stimulation (DBS)

Deep brain stimulation (DBS): Treatment in which electrodes are permanently implanted in the brain and then low levels of electrical current are sent to these electrodes using a transmitter the person wears; used to treat Parkinson's disease and Tourette's syndrome, as well as chronic depression that does not respond to antidepressants.

Finally, **deep brain stimulation (DBS)** is another technique being explored for chronic depression that doesn't respond to antidepressants (Delaloye & Holtzheimer, 2014). It is an already established treatment for movement disorders such as Parkinson's disease (Blomstedt et al., 2011). In DBS, electrodes are permanently implanted in the brain and then low levels of electrical current are sent to these electrodes using a transmitter the person wears (Delaloye & Holtzheimer, 2014). The evidence for DBS's effectiveness in depression is promising but preliminary, and it is considered an experimental treatment (Dandekar et al., 2018; Morishita et al., 2014; Mosley et al., 2015; Y. Wu et al., 2021; Yager, 2019). Research on DBS, including which brain areas to target, continues (Crowell et al., 2019; Drobisz & Damborská, 2019).

5.8 Genetic Perspectives

Family and Twin Studies

Family studies find that individuals diagnosed with major depression run three times the risk of having a first-degree relative who is also depressed (E. C. Dunn et al., 2015; P. F. Sullivan et al., 2000).

There is also evidence that bipolar symptoms recur in families (Perlis, 2015). Of course, to what extent these findings are attributable to genetics or shared environment remains unclear.

Twin studies have yielded heritability estimates in the .37 to .38 range for major depression (Shadrina et al., 2018; P. F. Sullivan et al., 2000). This means that 37 percent to 38 percent of phenotypic variation among people diagnosed with major depression can be attributed to genetic factors. Heritability estimates for bipolar disorders are considerably higher: 73 percent for bipolar I disorder, 56 percent for bipolar II disorder, and 71 percent for cyclothymic disorder (Edvardsen et al., 2008). Across all bipolar diagnoses (types I, II, and unspecified), heritability has been estimated at 60.4 percent (Johansson et al., 2019). As discussed in Chapter 2, heritability estimates can be controversial and difficult to interpret, especially because they don't always account for gene–environment interactions (J. Joseph, 2012). Nonetheless, genetics researchers remain confident that depression and mania are heritable disorders, with bipolar more heritable than major depression.

Photo 5.3 "Struggle and pain is real. I was devastated and depressed." Dwayne Johnson has discussed struggling with depression, especially after his mother's attempted suicide. Unfortunately, depression and mania are common in many families. https://www.express.co.uk/celebrity-news/939767/Dwayne-the-rock-Johnson-secret-battle-with-depression
Tristan Fewings/Stringer/Getty Images.

Genetic Association Studies

Genetic association studies (both candidate gene and GWAS studies) have identified many different genes as potentially important in depression and bipolar disorders (Almeida et al., 2020; J. R. I. Coleman et al., 2020; Direk et al., 2017; Guglielmo et al., 2021; D. M. Howard et al., 2018b, 2018a, 2019; Janiri et al., 2021; Liebers et al., 2021; Pereira et al., 2018; Shadrina et al., 2018; Wray et al., 2018; H. Zhang et al., 2018). However, results have often been difficult to replicate (Alam et al., 2021; Border et al., 2019). Consequently, depression and bipolar disorder can't currently be diagnosed using genetic markers. Still, some researchers remain highly optimistic, noting that after a long drought without much progress, recent findings "brought back the excitement that had evaporated during the years of negative GWAS findings" (Ormel et al., 2019, p. 1). Others are less sanguine, concluding that "the large number of associations reported in the depression candidate gene literature are likely to be false positives" and that "the genetic underpinnings of common complex traits such as depression appear to be far more complicated than originally hoped" (Border et al., 2019, pp. 376, 385). Clearly, there is much disagreement on how close we are to zeroing in on specific genes tied to mood problems.

Two findings do seem to recur in the existing literature. First, genes associated with depression and mania cut across not only DSM and ICD depressive and bipolar disorder diagnoses but are often associated with other psychiatric diagnoses. For instance, depression-linked genes also are tied to anxiety and stress-related disorders (Forstner et al., 2021; Mei et al., 2022; Warrier, 2020). Similarly, genes connected to bipolar disorder overlap with those associated with schizophrenia (Corponi et al., 2019; Prata et al., 2019). Second, genes and environment are both important. When it comes to fostering depression, research often (but not always) finds that genes interact with adverse environmental conditions such as childhood maltreatment, early life stress, and parental criticism (M. Li, Liu, et al., 2020; Nelemans et al., 2021; Normann & Buttenschøn, 2020; Peyrot et al., 2018; Q. Wang et al., 2018). Nature–nurture debates over the genetics of depression and mania can be expected to continue for some time.

5.9 Evolutionary Perspectives

Depression as Evolved Adaptation

Evolutionary perspectives can be divided into **adaptationist versus dysregulation models**. According to adaptationist models, depression is adaptive for several reasons. It can help people avoid social risks, minimize losses, ruminate about problems they need to address, fight infection and recover from sickness, conserve energy, give in when socially defeated, and solicit resources by encouraging others to help them (N. B. Allen & Badcock, 2006; Anders et al., 2013; P. W. Andrews & Thomson, 2009; Badcock et al., 2017; Durisko et al., 2015; R. M. Nesse, 2000; Tavares et al., 2021; P. J. Watson & Andrews, 2002). Controversially, advocates of adaptationist models contend that if their perspective is correct, then widescale antidepressant use interferes with depressed feelings that

Adaptationist versus dysregulation models: Adaptationist models say depression serves adaptive purposes (e.g., avoiding social risks, minimizing losses, conserving energy, soliciting assistance), whereas dysregulation models say the adaptive mechanism behind normal sadness is broken and runs amok in severe and recurrent depression.

people need to ruminate about and resolve problems (P. W. Andrews & Thomson, 2009; Durisko et al., 2015). Instead, adaptationists argue for psychotherapy to help people address life situations that give rise to depression (Durisko et al., 2015). Not surprisingly, some have challenged adaptationist arguments that antidepressants should be withheld (Kennair et al., 2017; McLoughlin, 2002; Sinyor, 2012). According to one critic: "Even if it has adaptive underpinnings, depression is clearly a source of true suffering and its theoretically adaptive value is an insufficient argument for withholding antidepressants or other treatments that may provide relief" (Sinyor, 2012, p. 336). The adaptationists counter that antidepressants stop people from experiencing the adaptive feelings necessary to help them remedy pressing life problems.

Shirley

Imagine Shirley goes to an adaptationist evolutionary psychotherapist. He might question whether she needs to be on Zoloft, noting that Shirley became depressed after losing a power struggle with a colleague, which resulted in Shirley getting demoted. The therapist could view Shirley's depression as an adaptive strategy that serves two purposes. First, it is a way of socially giving in after being defeated by her colleague. Second, it is a signal to herself that she needs to think about what her next steps should be professionally.

Dysregulation models disagree that depression is adaptive, and instead hold that the adaptive mechanism behind normal sadness is broken and runs amok in severe and recurrent depression (Nettle, 2004; Rantala et al., 2018). The main difference between adaptationist and dysregulation models is that the former sees depression as a normal and evolutionarily adaptive response to trying circumstances (P. W. Andrews & Thomson, 2009; Badcock et al., 2017; Durisko et al., 2015), whereas the latter says it is a disorder caused by the malfunctioning of evolved mechanisms for handling sadness and loss (Nettle, 2004; Rantala et al., 2018). The main criticism of all evolutionary perspectives on depression is that they are speculative, positing hypothetical "mental mechanisms" that are difficult to test (Faucher, 2016; Hagen, 2011).

Circadian Rhythms and Bipolar Disorder

One intriguing but still minimally researched hypothesis of bipolar disorder is that it evolved among people living in cold climates as an adaptation to extreme changes in light and dark throughout the year (Sherman, 2001, 2006, 2012). This is consistent with findings of circadian rhythm disruptions in people diagnosed as bipolar (Abreu & Bragança, 2015; Takaesu, 2018; Tal & Primeau, 2015; Walker et al., 2020). *Circadian rhythms* are mental and behavioral changes in alertness and energy that people experience throughout the day that are tied to levels of light and dark in the environment (R. G. Foster, 2020). The theory of bipolar disorder as a circadian rhythm disorder that developed among people in cold climates is similar to theories explaining seasonal affective disorder (SAD) (Abreu & Bragança, 2015; Takaesu, 2018; Walker et al., 2020). **Light therapy**, in which a person sits next to a box that projects bright light, is used to treat SAD (P. D. Campbell et al., 2017). If bipolar disorder is also tied to light levels, then combinations of light therapy and **dark therapy** (in which patients are kept in the dark for several hours) may help stabilize circadian rhythms (A. K. Gold & Kinrys, 2019; Tal & Primeau, 2015). Research on light therapy for depressive and bipolar disorders offers promising but inconclusive results (P. D. Campbell et al., 2017; R. W. Lam et al., 2020; S. Wang et al., 2020).

5.10 Immune System Perspectives

The inflammatory hypothesis (introduced in Chapter 4) postulates that—like various other psychiatric disorders—depression and bipolar disorder may be tied to immune system inflammation (Benedetti et al., 2020; Karabulut et al., 2019; C.-H. Lee & Giuliani, 2019; R. Mao et al., 2018; Osimo et al., 2019; Rosenblat et al., 2014, 2015; N. A. L. Ruiz et al., 2022; Troubat et al., 2021). In testing this hypothesis, cytokine levels are often measured. Cytokines (mentioned in Chapter 4) are small proteins produced by immune system cells that are important in healing. However, large amounts can cause swelling. Studies find elevated cytokine levels in depressed people, suggesting their immune systems are highly active (Felger & Lotrich, 2013; C.-H. Lee & Giuliani, 2019; N. A. L. Ruiz et al.,

Light therapy: Therapy for seasonal affective disorder in which patient sits next to a box that projects bright light.

Dark therapy: Treatment sometimes combined with light therapy for bipolar disorder; patient kept in the dark for several hours to correct circadian rhythm disruptions suspected of causing mania.

2022; J. J. Young et al., 2014). There is also evidence that for bipolar patients, immune inflammation is linked to cognitive impairment (Rosenblat et al., 2015). The data is correlational, so we can't specify cytokines' precise relationships with depression and bipolar disorder. Immunological stress might lead to depression and mania, but depression and mania might also trigger the immune system. It is also possible depression and inflammation mutually influence one other (Beurel et al., 2020).

If immune system inflammation is involved in mood problems, then one potential treatment is anti-inflammatory drugs—especially for the 30–40 percent of depressed people who don't respond to antidepressants (J. J. Young et al., 2014). Researchers are studying the use of **nonsteroidal anti-inflammatory drugs (NSAIDs)** for depression and mania. NSAIDS are pain-relieving drugs such as *aspirin*, *ibuprofen* (trade names *Advil*, *Motrin*, and *Nuprin*), *naproxen* (trade names *Aleve* and *Naprosyn*), and *celecoxib* (trade name *Celebrex*). Research so far has yielded mixed results (S. Bai et al., 2020; Baune et al., 2021; Halaris et al., 2020; Husain et al., 2020; Kapulsky et al., 2021; Köhler-Forsberg et al., 2019; Rosenblat et al., 2016). Further, while NSAIDs are generally safe, they can cause serious side effects such as dyspepsia and gastrointestinal bleeding when taken along with SSRIs (R. Anglin et al., 2015; S. Bai et al., 2020).

Nonsteroidal anti-inflammatory drugs (NSAIDs): Anti-inflammatory pain relief drugs such as aspirin and ibuprofen.

5.11 Evaluating Biological Perspectives

A major criticism of biological approaches is that even though they regard mood problems as physical illnesses, depression and mania currently can't be diagnosed using physical measures (Strawbridge et al., 2017). In other words, despite regular use of medical metaphors, the biology of depression and mania remains ambiguous (Patten, 2015). Diagnoses are based on behavior, not underlying biological defects or chemical imbalances. This doesn't mean biological interventions don't help. However, their helpfulness isn't sufficient to conclude an underlying disease-state is being corrected. Feeling better after taking a mood-altering drug doesn't prove the original mood was caused by an underlying chemical imbalance. For instance, people often feel calm after smoking marijuana, but this doesn't mean they were pathologically anxious in the first place! In other words,

response to antidepressants is not by itself proof that an imbalance of brain chemicals causes depression. Psychotherapy can alleviate depression … therefore (using the above logic), a deficiency of psychotherapy causes depression (of course, we are unaware of any serious assertions to this effect). (France et al., 2007, p. 412)

Furthering this critique, it's been noted that "the most serious conceptual problem with the neurochemical deficiency hypothesis … is that no adequate contextually grounded standard exists for normal versus disordered levels of serotonin or other amines" (A. V. Horwitz & Wakefield, 2007, p. 169). Not only are we unable to directly measure monoamine levels, but we also have no idea what constitutes "normal" amounts of these neurotransmitters—just as we don't know how active one's amygdala, hippocampus, or frontal lobe should be or what the "healthiest" constellation of mood-related genes truly is. More broadly, it's been argued that the biological model's endless quest to subsume more and more mood problems has resulted in the loss of normal sadness (A. V. Horwitz & Wakefield, 2007). In this line of thinking, by recasting so many mood variations as a physical illness, the biological perspective pathologizes ordinary grief and melancholy. This leads us to stop seeing them as customary and expected experiences that play roles in every person's life. Consequently, normal forms of sadness and loss get inappropriately "treated" with drugs and other medical interventions.

PSYCHOLOGICAL PERSPECTIVES

5.12 Psychodynamic Perspectives

Classic Psychoanalytic and Attachment Perspectives
Classic Psychoanalytic Perspectives

Early in his career, Freud (1917/1953) saw depression as tied to grief and loss. He believed real losses (such as the death of a loved one) or symbolic losses (such as failing at work or in a relationship) trigger depression. In his model, the difference between simple grief and depression is that depressed people redirect repressed anger toward the lost object onto themselves—hence the psychoanalytic idea of depression as *anger turned inward*. Freud (1917/1953) said that mania, on the other hand, is caused by the ego asserting itself to counter depression; grandiosity and an inflated sense of self are defenses against internally directed anger. In his later writings, Freud (1923/1960) attributed depression more to an overly stern superego than to grief and loss. Nonetheless, modern psychodynamic perspectives retain an emphasis on attachment and loss in depression and mania.

Attachment Perspectives

The importance of attachment issues in mood problems has ample research support. In his famous studies of *contact comfort*, psychologist Harry Harlow raised baby monkeys in an environment where their biological mothers were replaced with fake surrogate mothers made of wire, foam, and terry cloth. The baby monkeys formed strong attachments to the surrogate mothers and became alarmed and depressed when separated from them (H. F. Harlow, 1958; H. F. Harlow & Suomi, 1974).

Additional support for the role of attachment can be found in John Bowlby's attachment theory (introduced in Chapter 2)—an approach compatible with and influenced by psychodynamic theory. Attachment theory emphasizes how early childhood relationships affect later psychological functioning (Ainsworth et al., 1978; Bowlby, 1980, 1988). It holds that children of attentive and emotionally responsive parents develop *secure attachments*. They become emotionally hardy, see themselves in a positive light, and can safely establish relationships with others (Ainsworth et al., 1978). By comparison, children of parents who are inconsistently attentive and emotionally unresponsive develop *insecure attachments*. Consequently, they experience others as untrustworthy and undependable; they worry about being abandoned and struggle to regulate negative emotions in relationships with others (Ainsworth et al., 1978). Research on attachment theory has found that insecurely attached infants are at increased risk for later emotional upset—including moodiness and depression (Blatt & Homann, 1992; Fonagy, 2001). In the past, the term **anaclitic depression** (mentioned when discussing PDM) was used for depression in young children caused by separation from their caregivers. In more recent times, it refers to attachment-related depression in adults who are clingy, helpless, dependent, and fear abandonment (S. Reis & Grenyer, 2002).

Short-Term Interpersonal and Psychodynamic Therapies for Depression
Short-Term Interpersonal therapy (IPT)

Interpersonal therapy (IPT) for depression, developed by psychiatrist Gerald Klerman, is a modern short-term relational therapy influenced by the works of early interpersonal therapists such as Harry Stack Sullivan, Frieda Fromm-Reichmann, and Karen Horney (Klerman et al., 1984). IPT is time-limited (usually twelve to sixteen weeks) and focuses on four relational problem areas associated with depression: *role disputes* (interpersonal disagreements with others), *role transitions* (important life changes—e.g., moving, getting married, breaking up, or starting a new job), *grief* (death of an significant life figure), and *interpersonal deficits* (difficulties beginning or maintaining relationships) (Klerman et al., 1984; Markowitz, 2013). IPT helps patients build the relational skills needed to deepen or repair existing relationships and develop new ones. Although CBT is usually considered the "gold standard" therapy for depression, research consistently finds IPT to be equally or nearly as effective (Cuijpers et al., 2011, 2013, 2016; de Mello et al., 2005; Duffy et al., 2019).

Short-Term Psychodynamic Therapies

IPT has been criticized for being insufficiently psychodynamic and lacking theoretical elaboration (de Jonghe et al., 2013; Law, 2011; Lemma et al., 2010). As alternatives, more explicitly psychodynamic therapies have been developed. One example is **intensive short-term dynamic psychotherapy (ISTDP)**, a time-limited intervention for various presenting problems, including depression (Davanloo, 1995). Consistent with a psychodynamic worldview, ISTDP assumes that patients cope with hidden emotions (i.e., unconscious conflicts) via anxiety and defense mechanisms. In ISTDP, the therapist points out patients' anxiety and defense mechanisms

---

Anaclitic depression: Historically used to describe depression in young children, but now refers to attachment-related depression in adults who are clingy, helpless, dependent, and fear abandonment.

Interpersonal therapy (IPT): Short-term therapy that focuses on improving relationships to alleviate depression and other presenting problems.

Intensive short-term dynamic psychotherapy (ISTDP): Short-term psychodynamic therapy that helps patients identify anxiety and defenses that interfere with the experience of hidden emotions; used for depression and other presenting problems.

(T. Schröder et al., 2016). As patients learn to identify their anxiety and defenses, they are better able to experience and integrate hidden emotions. Research—including randomized controlled trials—supports ISTDP for depression (Town et al., 2017, 2020). A systematic review and meta-analysis provided further evidence that short-term dynamic therapy is effective for depression (Caselli et al., 2023).

Shirley

If Shirley sought short-term supportive ISTDP for her depression, her therapist would point out defense mechanisms she uses to ward off anxiety when dealing with her fiancé, Ralph. For instance, she uses projection by attributing to Ralph her own anger and disappointment over her career choices. Were Shirley to gain awareness of her defenses and the conflicts behind them in ISTDP, her depression should wane.

Interpersonal and Social Rhythm Therapy for Mania

Interpersonal and social rhythm therapy (IPSRT) uses IPT's interpersonal problem-solving techniques to help clients regulate their sleep habits. The idea is to manage disrupted circadian rhythms suspected of playing a part in bipolar symptoms. Clients accomplish this by resolving interpersonal problems and establishing regular social routines (E. Frank, 2007; Reilly-Harrington et al., 2015). IPSRT uses interpersonal therapy techniques to help clients identify mood states, regulate levels of stimulation, minimize emotional ups and downs, manage grandiosity, and attend to risks of drug abuse (H. A. Swartz et al., 2012). Although IPSRT research finds it effective for bipolar disorder, results are mixed and it tends to be viewed as an adjunct to mood stabilizers (Gottlieb et al., 2019; Inder et al., 2015; C. Lam & Chung, 2021; Miziou et al., 2015; Reilly-Harrington et al., 2015; Reinares et al., 2014; Steardo et al., 2020).

Interpersonal and social rhythm therapy (IPSRT): Short-term therapy for bipolar symptoms that uses interpersonal therapy (IPT) techniques to help clients regulate sleep habits and overcome suspected circadian rhythm disruptions.

5.13 Cognitive-Behavioral Perspectives

Beck's Cognitive Theory of Depression
The Cognitive Triad

Aaron Beck's cognitive therapy famously attributes depression to the **cognitive triad**—a thought pattern consisting of negative beliefs about *self, experience,* and *future* (A. T. Beck et al., 1979; A. J. Rush & Beck, 1978). *Negative beliefs about the self* involve thinking one is unworthy and lacks the attributes necessary for happiness. *Negative beliefs about experience* emphasize how current, ongoing life circumstances are negative and unpleasant. Finally, *negative beliefs about the future* presume that the future will be bleak.

Cognitive triad: Negative beliefs about self, experience, and future that cognitive therapists believe result in depression.

Shirley

It isn't hard to see how the cognitive triad leads to Shirley's depression:

- *Shirley thinks she is unlikable and incapable of being valued and loved by others. These negative beliefs about self are why she thinks she was demoted at work and why her fiancé Ralph has threatened to leave her.*
- *When Shirley laments how awful and unbearable her employment and personal situations are, she is focusing on negative beliefs about experience.*
- *Shirley's insistence that she will be stuck in her current dead-end job forever and that her relationship with her fiancé Ralph is doomed exemplify negative thinking about the future.*

If Shirley believes she (a) is unlikable and lacks the personal qualities to succeed, (b) faces terrible ongoing circumstances, and (c) will continue to be unhappy indefinitely, then how could we expect her to feel anything but depressed?

Schemas and Cognitive Distortions

In addition to emphasizing the cognitive triad, Beck's approach to depression also stresses the role of cognitive schemas. Recall from Chapter 2 that schemas are mental structures we use to organize information—scripts we rely on to navigate daily interactions.

Shirley

Shirley's schema for relationships goes something like this:

The more people know about me, the less they will like me. Therefore, I shouldn't open myself up emotionally—even with those I wish to be closest to. Of course, keeping quiet and avoiding intimacy will only delay the inevitable because eventually everyone realizes just how unlovable I am, and they leave me. Thus, working too hard to preserve a relationship is pointless.

When people hold negative schemas, they distort information to fit their expectations. They engage in faulty information processing, which reinforces negative schemas and fosters depression. Said another way, depressed individuals fall prey to cognitive distortions (See Table 2.6 in Chapter 2) such as *absolutistic thinking, arbitrary inference, magnification, minimization, overgeneralization, personalization,* and *selective abstraction* (A. T. Beck et al., 1979).

Criticisms of Cognitive Therapy

Critics contend Beck's approach overemphasizes logical thinking and practical problem-solving while insufficiently attending to emotional experience and relational dynamics (D. A. Clark, 1995; Giacomantonio, 2012; Gipps, 2013, 2017). They question whether irrational feelings are best altered via logic and reason, while also wondering if what is deemed "logical" often reflects unexamined social norms (Gipps, 2013; Kantrowitz & Ballou, 1992). Advocates of cognitive perspectives counter that interventions at the level of thinking are essential for emotional transformation and point to a large body of research support for their approach (A. C. Butler et al., 2006; Gautam et al., 2020; Hofmann et al., 2012; Moorey, 2017; Tolin, 2010). See Table 5.3 for examples of how cognitive distortions contribute to Shirley's depression.

Learned Helplessness
Seligman's Original Theory

Learned helplessness:
Conditioned response in which an organism learns its behavior has no effect on its environment so it stops engaging in behavior and endures unpleasant situations—even when they can be avoided.

Martin Seligman's work on **learned helplessness** was introduced in Chapter 1. Learned helplessness results when operant conditioning teaches an organism that its behavior has no effect on its surroundings. In Seligman's initial research, he created learned helplessness in dogs by shocking them repeatedly and not allowing them to escape the shock. After a while, the dogs didn't bother trying to avoid getting shocked—even when the situation was altered so they could escape (Overmier & Seligman, 1967; M. E. Seligman et al., 1968; M. E. Seligman & Maier, 1967). Seligman analogized learned helplessness in dogs to depression in people, arguing that depression is about learning to feel helpless. Thus, learned helplessness is a behavioral way to understand depression, one that contends people learn to be depressed when their behavior has little or no effect on their surroundings. For instance, many people in abusive relationships learn that their actions are irrelevant. They become depressed due to learned helplessness and stop trying to get out of their situation—even overlooking opportunities to do so when circumstances change.

Shirley

Shirley might not look for a new job because she has learned her actions have no effect on her current job. This is an example of learned helplessness.

Table 5.3 Shirley's Depression-Producing Cognitive Distortions

DISTORTION	DEFINED	IN ACTION WITH SHIRLEY
Absolutistic thinking	Dividing experience into one of two opposite categories; like "all or nothing" thinking from Chapter 2.	"I must be perfect at work or else I am a complete failure."
Arbitrary inference	Drawing a specific conclusion without sufficient evidence; like "jumping to conclusions" from Chapter 2.	"My fiancé doesn't like seeing me sad, which must mean he wants to break up with me."
Magnification	Overemphasizing negative events.	"Losing that power struggle at work tells me everything I need to know about my ability to advance in my profession."
Minimization	Underemphasizing positive events.	"Yes, I have previously succeeded at work, but that was a fluke."
Overgeneralization	Taking one instance and applying it too broadly to explain other instances.	"I was demoted at work. I'll never succeed at my job again."
Personalization	Assuming others' behavior is necessarily about you.	"The secretary at work didn't say hello this morning. She did that on purpose to let me know she dislikes me."
Selective abstraction	Taking a detail out of context and ignoring other more relevant aspects of the situation.	"Ralph has complained about me being depressed, which—even though he recently proposed and keeps buying me wedding planning magazines—must mean he wants to break up."

Source: Cognitive distortions in the first column are derived from the work of Aaron Beck et al. (1979).

Attribution Style and Hopelessness Theory

Despite its behavioral origins, researchers have extensively studied the kinds of cognitive attributions that contribute to learned helplessness. By attributions, they mean how people explain their behavior and experiences. **Hopelessness theory** predicts that depressed people tend to make *stable*, *global*, and *internal* attributions (Abramson et al., 1978, 1989; T. Hu et al., 2015; R. T. Liu et al., 2015). Stable attributions don't change, global attributions apply globally across most or all situations, and internal attributions assign responsibility for an outcome to oneself. People typically feel depressed when they make negative attributions that are stable, global, and internal. The opposite of stable, global, and internal attributions are unstable, specific, and external attributions—which hopelessness theory posits don't produce depression. Table 5.4 maps Shirley's attribution style, with examples of stable–unstable, global–specific, and internal–external attributions.

Negative attributions, especially global and stable ones, are positively correlated with depression (T. Hu et al., 2015). However, their impact can vary by age and gender (T. Hu et al., 2015). Global attributions only seem to correlate with depression in adults, not children or adolescents. Further, all three attributions—stable, global, and internal—are more strongly associated with depression in females than in males (T. Hu et al., 2015). This may mean that men who make negative attributions

Hopelessness theory: Predicts that people who make stable, global, and internal attributions will experience depression.

Table 5.4 Learned Helplessness and Shirley's Attribution Style

ATTRIBUTIONS LEADING TO DEPRESSION	POTENTIAL ALTERNATIVE ATTRIBUTIONS
Stable: "My job situation will never change."	*Unstable*: "It's possible there are better jobs out there."
Global: "The work world is terrible no matter where you work."	*Specific*: "Working here stinks, but it might be better elsewhere."
Internal: "My problems at work are my own fault; I'll be dissatisfied no matter where I work."	*External*: "My problems at work are because my workplace is toxic; I'll be more satisfied in a different job."

don't become depressed as often as women who do so. If so, this is consistent with research showing women are at greater risk for depression than men. We will revisit this when discussing sociocultural perspectives.

Criticisms of Learned Helplessness

The learned helplessness model of depression has been criticized for relying too extensively on animal research; this partly led to hopelessness theory's emphasis on attributions over conditioning (Abramson et al., 1989). Because animals don't make cognitive attributions the same way people do, generalizing from Seligman's dogs to human beings is questionable. Most people's life circumstances and meaning-making capabilities are more complex than what a shocked dog in a controlled lab setting experiences. Learned helplessness theory has also been critiqued for assigning too much importance to individual attributions while insufficiently attending to socially constructed societal norms that shape ideas about depression (Stam, 1987). Failure to challenge cultural assumptions that depression is due to faulty attributions rather than oppressive social structures may unwittingly encourage people to bring their attributions into sync with dominant social norms instead of challenging such norms. Whether hopelessness theory inappropriately encourages people to accept social limits by viewing attributions that don't fit dominant social norms as "unrealistic" is an argument that those who don't care for learned helplessness theory will find compelling, but those who like it will probably dismiss.

Shirley

Is Shirley's learned helplessness less about her making unrealistic negative attributions and more due to ongoing societal discrimination against women in the workplace?

CBT Assessment and Therapy for Depression

Beck Depression Inventory (BDI)

Beck Depression Inventory (BDI):
21-item self-administered inventory for measuring depression.

The cognitive part of CBT assesses and works to change people's thinking. It identifies the negative beliefs, schemas, and cognitive distortions that lead to depression (Power, 2013). As part of assessment, clients might be administered the **Beck Depression Inventory (BDI)**, introduced in Chapter 3. Currently in its second version, the BDI-II is a 21-item self-administered scale that measures depression by assessing thinking patterns. Items ask respondents to rate statements about their experience over the past two weeks using 4-point scales (Dozios & Covin, 2004). Scores range from 0–63, with 14–19 deemed "mild depression," 20–28 "moderate depression," and 29–63 "severe depression"—although recommended cutoffs vary (Dozios & Covin, 2004; von Glischinski et al., 2019). The BDI can be completed in five to ten minutes, making it an efficient way to quickly assess depressive feelings. Advocates point to the BDI's strong psychometric properties, including *test–retest reliability* (the degree to which a test yields similar results each time) (Y.-P. Wang & Gorenstein, 2013). Nonetheless, BDI scores often change over time, sometimes because the person no longer feels depressed (Dozios & Covin, 2004; Y.-P. Wang & Gorenstein, 2013). BDI developers warn that depression shouldn't be diagnosed based solely on a BDI score. It is also worth noting that women tend to score higher than men (Dozios & Covin, 2004). It is unclear whether this means the test is gender biased, women are more depressed than men, or women are more willing to report depression.

Daily Record of Dysfunctional Thoughts (DRDT)

Daily Record of Dysfunctional Thoughts (DRDT): A form used by cognitive therapists to help clients track events, their emotional reactions, their automatic thoughts, their behavioral response, and their errors in logic.

After taking the BDI-II, clients might be asked to complete a **Daily Record of Dysfunctional Thoughts (DRDT)**. This is a form on which they keep track of events, their emotional reactions to these events, their automatic thoughts about these events, how they responded to these events, and the outcomes of the events. The data generated helps identify dysfunctional thinking patterns. Beck's cognitive therapy or Ellis' rational emotive behavior therapy (REBT) can then be used to revise and replace depression-related beliefs (A. T. Beck et al., 1979; J. S. Beck, 2011; A. Ellis & Ellis, 2019; Power, 2013).

Behavioral Activation, Exercise, and Problem-Solving Therapy

The behavioral component of CBT supplements the cognitive part by actively changing what people do (Power, 2013). One of the most common behavior-based techniques in CBT is **behavioral activation**, which involves asking clients to schedule activities—such as taking a walk or calling a friend (Martell et al., 2022). The idea is to encourage behaviors that bring positive reinforcement. Depressed people have usually stopped regularly engaging in such behaviors. Behavioral activation counters this by assigning these behaviors as homework. Research suggests behavioral activation may help reduce depression (Mazzucchelli et al., 2009; Sturmey, 2009; Uphoff et al., 2020). It can be used on its own or in combination with other types of cognitive therapy—including **problem-solving therapy**, an empirically supported CBT approach in which therapists help clients to define specific problems and then generate and implement concrete solutions (A. C. Bell & D'Zurilla, 2009; Cuijpers et al., 2007; Martell et al., 2022).

One specific behavior that therapists encourage in depressed clients is physical exercise. Comprehensive reviews of existing research usually conclude, with some notable exceptions, that exercise has antidepressant effects (Al-Qahtani et al., 2018; Chalder et al., 2012; G. M. Cooney et al., 2013; S. B. Harvey et al., 2018; M. X. Hu et al., 2020; S. Hu et al., 2020; Krogh et al., 2017; Wegner et al., 2020; Xie et al., 2021). Given this and its other health benefits, most mental health professionals enthusiastically recommend exercise to depressed patients.

Behavioral activation: Behavioral technique in which client schedules activities that bring positive reinforcement.

Problem-solving therapy: Cognitive-behavioral therapy (CBT) approach in which therapist helps client define specific problems and then generate solutions that can be implemented.

Shirley

How might Shirley's therapist combine cognitive-behavioral therapy techniques to treat her depression? Cognitively, he might administer the Beck Depression Inventory, which would likely reveal her to be quite depressed. He could then help map Shirley's negative thought processes by asking her to complete a dysfunctional thought record between sessions. Behaviorally, he might use behavioral activation. He could ask Shirley what things she likes to do when not feeling depressed. If she says she likes to go to the movies with friends and go to the gym, the therapist might assign these behaviors as homework between sessions. Later sessions with Shirley would involve more directly challenging her irrational beliefs and cognitive distortions. When Shirley tells her therapist that she is unlovable and will never be happy, her therapist might highlight the lack of evidence that happiness isn't possible. Regarding work, he could point out that Shirley has had many past successes and her recent demotion is an aberration. He also might note that Shirley's fiancé, Ralph, wants to salvage his relationship with her despite her insistence that he is bound to leave her. By identifying cognitive distortions and negative attributions, the therapist would be encouraging Shirley to think about how she thinks about things—and to evaluate how this contributes to her sadness. Over a dozen sessions or so, Shirley would hopefully revise her negative beliefs, thereby improving her mood.

CBT Effectiveness

CBT is perhaps the most studied therapeutic approach to depression, with extensive evidence for its effectiveness (Cuijpers et al., 2013; C. Vasile, 2020). Research reviews suggest that CBT for depression is helpful with adults (Cuijpers et al., 2013; López-López et al., 2019), adolescents (Oud et al., 2019), postpartum women (Buck et al., 2019; L. Huang et al., 2018), older adults with cognitive deficits (S. S. Simon et al., 2015), and people experiencing treatment-resistant depression (J.-M. Li et al., 2018). Given its effectiveness, you might wonder how CBT compares with antidepressants. Some research finds it equally as effective as antidepressants, or more so, for depression (DeRubeis et al., 2008; Roshanaei-Moghaddam et al., 2011; N. Singh & Reece, 2014; Whiston et al., 2019). However, other research finds antidepressants alone or combined with CBT to be more effective (Boschloo et al., 2019; Cuijpers et al., 2013). It has been argued that CBT has longer-lasting benefits than antidepressants (DeRubeis et al., 2008; Wiles et al., 2016). Another potential advantage CBT has over antidepressants is lack of side effects (Elkins, 2016).

Photo 5.4 Three mindfulness practices

DrAfter123/Getty Images.

Mindfulness

Mindfulness-based cognitive therapy (MBCT) combines cognitive therapy with mindfulness training (Z. V. Segal et al., 2004). In *mindfulness training*, influenced by Zen Buddhist traditions, people are taught to observe and be aware of their thoughts (as opposed to trying to stop or change them) (Baer, 2003; Langer, 1989). The logic of MBCT is that observing our depressive thoughts alters our relationship to them, often decreasing their influence (Z. V. Segal et al., 2013). Rather than getting upset about being depressed, mindfulness encourages simple acceptance of feelings. By not resisting depressed feelings, they run their course and dissipate on their own rather than become more intense as we ruminate about them. Despite some methodological shortcomings, existing research finds MBCT reduces depression (Frostadottir & Dorjee, 2019; M. B. MacKenzie et al., 2018; Musa et al., 2020; Schanche et al., 2020; Z. V. Segal et al., 2020; Tickell et al., 2020). There is evidence that MBCT can also alleviate bipolar symptoms, but more and better studies are needed (Lovas & Schuman-Olivier, 2018; Xuan et al., 2020).

CBT and Mania

CBT is often used to increase medication adherence among bipolar patients (Popovic et al., 2015). However, it can also be used to change irrational thinking patterns common during mania. CBT attributes mania to overly optimistic thinking and helps manic individuals monitor and reality-test their irrationally optimistic beliefs (Geddes & Miklowitz, 2013; Schwannauer, 2013). Some researchers are hopeful that individual and group CBT interventions can help with bipolar symptoms, but others are skeptical (Bond & Anderson, 2015; Geddes & Miklowitz, 2013; Henken et al., 2020; Miziou et al., 2015; Novick & Swartz, 2019; Schwannauer, 2013).

Mindfulness-based cognitive therapy (MBCT): Therapy that combines *mindfulness training* (learning to observe and be aware of thoughts) with *cognitive therapy*.

> **Don**
>
> *Once he begins taking mood stabilizers, Don seeks psychotherapy. The therapist might use CBT to challenge Don's contention that he needs little or no sleep. Don's belief that he is writing the greatest novel ever written would be explored—especially how Don's grandiose expectations in this regard have made it difficult for him to accept feedback from others about his writing. CBT might prove most helpful once Don has been taking mood stabilizers for a while and has become calmer, more coherent, and more rational.*

5.14 Humanistic Perspectives

Person-Centered Therapy

Humanistic perspectives often question the medical model view of depression. For instance, rather than seeing depression strictly as a disease-state, person-centered therapists view it as a form of psychological incongruence that arises when people don't receive empathy, unconditional positive regard, and genuineness from key relationships (Haimerl et al., 2009; D. Murphy, 2019). Sadness results from being self-inconsistent to maintain love from others; this leads to self-devaluation, self-dissatisfaction, distorted self-perception, and guilt (Haimerl et al., 2009). By providing core conditions for change in therapy, the person-centered therapist fosters a space for clients to reestablish self-consistency and move toward self-actualization. As this occurs, depression lifts (D. Murphy, 2019). There is less research on person-centered therapy for depression than other therapies we have discussed, but one noteworthy randomized controlled trial found it as effective as CBT at six months but—especially for more severely depressed individuals—less effective than CBT at twelve months (Barkham et al., 2021).

Emotion-Focused Therapy (EFT)

Emotion-focused therapy (EFT) is a short-term (eight- to twenty-session) humanistic psychotherapy that combines person-centered, Gestalt, and constructivist ideas (R. N. Goldman & Greenberg, 2015b; L. S. Greenberg & Goldman, 2006). EFT emphasizes *process diagnosis*, not *person diagnosis*. The former stresses understanding how the client makes sense of experience in ways that produce depressed mood, while the latter is more about assigning people to diagnostic categories and seeing them as mentally ill (a practice humanistic therapists generally don't like) (R. N. Goldman & Greenberg, 2015b; L. S. Greenberg & Goldman, 2006). EFT challenges the primacy that CBT places on thinking in depression, and instead stresses emotion as more central (L. S. Greenberg & Watson, 2006). EFT holds that depressed people experienced unsupportive environments growing up—especially in their teens, when they may not have felt liked, attractive, or athletically competent. They also may have lacked peer and/or parental support. In adulthood, the feelings of inadequacy they developed as teenagers become supplemented with feelings of shame for not being able to deal more effectively with negative social interactions (L. S. Greenberg & Watson, 2006). Thus, in the adult EFT model of depression, disappointing life events activate primary emotions of sadness and disappointment. In response to these primary emotions, the person feels fear and shame and then concludes, "I'm weak, worthless, and unable to cope." This triggers hopelessness. Out of this hopelessness comes depressive behavior and thinking that makes the person even more vulnerable to experiencing future events as disappointing. In the EFT model, feelings take precedence over thoughts, with the emotional organization of the self being critical to how vulnerable someone is to depression (L. S. Greenberg & Watson, 2006).

> #### Shirley
>
> *If she were working with an emotion-focused therapist, Shirley would be encouraged to share and process her feelings. The therapist would listen intently and empathize with Shirley's plight. As Shirley trusted the therapist more and more, he would steer the conversation toward Shirley's feelings about herself. Shirley often felt unsupported and ridiculed growing up. Now, as an adult, she feels ashamed whenever social interactions don't go well. EFT would endeavor to explore her feelings of disappointment, shame, and hopelessness about how things have gone recently at work and in her relationship with her fiancé. Shirley would be encouraged to experience her negative emotions to better get in touch with them. Her therapist would help her transform these negative feelings into more positive, productive ones by processing his relationship with her, so she has a new relational experience different from past unsupportive relationships. EFT would help Shirley identify her needs and goals, while encouraging her to construct new ways of understanding herself that lead to different and more positive emotions.*

Humanistic therapists often struggle to have their perspective recognized as empirically supported. Their reluctance to use DSM and ICD diagnoses and their location on the margins of the academic research world likely don't help in this regard. Even if non-humanistic therapists aren't always convinced, a small group of researchers tout a growing body of evidence suggesting EFT and other humanistic therapies are effective for depression (Angus, 2012; Barkham et al., 2021; R. Elliott, 2016; R. Elliott et al., 2013).

5.15 Evaluating Psychological Perspectives

While psychological interventions are often praised for being as good as or better than biological ones for depression (Cuijpers et al., 2014), they are usually seen as inadequate on their own for managing mania. Thus, they tend to be used as a secondary—albeit often effective—treatment for bipolar disorder (Miklowitz et al., 2021; Salcedo et al., 2016). They often incorporate psychoeducation, in which they teach patients to accept their disorder as an illness and to develop skills to manage it (Bond & Anderson, 2015; Buizza et al., 2019; Joas et al., 2020; Miziou et al., 2015; Reinares et al., 2014).

Emotion-focused therapy (EFT): Brief humanistic psychotherapy that combines person-centered, Gestalt, and constructivist ideas.

Psychedelic-assisted therapy: Combines hallucinogenic drugs like psilocybin, MDMA, or LSD with talk therapy for issues like depression and trauma.

Despite their effectiveness for depression, psychological approaches have limits. Roughly half of those who improve from psychotherapy become depressed again within a year or two (Steinert et al., 2014). Further, even though research finds up to 62 percent of people with major depression no longer meet diagnostic criteria for the disorder following therapy, neither do 43 percent of control patients who don't receive therapy (Cuijpers et al., 2014). This implies that while therapy helps, depression often lifts on its own with the simple passage of time. Given that drugs and therapy both have their limits, it makes sense that they are often combined. As the "In Depth" feature explains, **psychedelic-assisted therapy** is one area where drugs and therapy are increasingly being combined to treat depression and other presenting problems.

In Depth: Psychedelic-Assisted Therapy for Depression

Psychedelic drugs, long ridiculed as "dangerous dalliances of the counterculture," are rapidly gaining acceptance as a psychotherapeutic tool in the treatment of depression and trauma (Tullis, 2021, p. 506). We have already discussed a ketamine derivative, esketamine, as a new treatment for depression. However, psychedelic-assisted therapy differs from esketamine treatment in that it combines the use of hallucinogenic drugs like psilocybin, MDMA, or LSD (see Chapter 11) with talk therapy. The rationale behind psychedelic-assisted therapy is that depression and trauma are intransigent problems requiring a fundamental overhaul in longstanding beliefs about self and experience. Why would taking psychedelics help with this? It's suspected that "the receptive state that the drug confers opens the door to fresh ideas about how to think about the past and future, which the therapist can reinforce" (Tullis, 2021, p. 508). Here's what psilocybin-assisted therapy for depression can look like:

> A 2021 psilocybin trial for treatment-resistant depression required 6 to 8 hours of preparatory talk therapy about mental health issues and what to expect during the dosing session, which can be quite intense, emotional, and even scary. The dosing session itself took about 8 hours and required two psychotherapists in a closed room with a nurturing physical environment to ensure full safety and support. Later, there were three sessions of "integration," where a therapist helped participants process their psychedelic experience in order to get the most out of it. (Frysh, 2022)

So, does it work? Research on using psilocybin for treatment-resistant depression and MDMA for trauma has increased rapidly, in part because the U.S. Food and Drug Administration (FDA) felt psilocybin held sufficient promise that they designated it a "breakthrough therapy" for depression, fast-tracking the research and approval process. Since then, a variety of studies have concluded that the effects of psilocybin-assisted therapy for depression are quick and long-lasting (Carhart-Harris et al., 2018; COMPASS Pathways, 2021; A. K. Davis et al., 2021; S. B. Goldberg et al., 2020; G. M. Goodwin et al., 2022; Gukasyan et al., 2022; N.-X. Li et al., 2022; Stroud et al., 2018; A. S. Vargas et al., 2020). Research on psychedelic-assisted therapy for trauma using MDMA is also encouraging (J. M. Mitchell, 2022; Tullis, 2021).

Promising as it is, psychedelic-assisted therapy faces several obstacles. First, it's difficult to research because (a) control groups aren't always used and when they are, participants usually know if they have been given a hallucinogen, making it easy for them to guess if they are in the experimental or control group; and (b) it's hard to tease apart the effects of the drug from the effects of the therapy (Barnby & Mehta, 2018; Frysh, 2022)—something made more difficult because different studies use different therapy approaches (Carhart-Harris et al., 2018; Guss et al., 2020; M. Wolff et al., 2020). Second, patient safety is a concern. Although the drugs used are administered under strict medical supervision to protect patients, some patients still have "bad trips" that can be frightening or even harmful (Bienemann et al., 2020). Some people also worry that moving too quickly to promote psychedelics for mental health encourages dangerous recreational use outside supervised environments (Pilecki et al., 2021; Pollan, 2019; Rucker & Young, 2021). Thus, despite a great deal of promising research, mental health professionals hold contrasting opinions on psychedelic-assisted therapy, with some seeing it as a safe and effective new treatment that should be quickly approved and others recommending a more deliberate approach that reserves judgment until further efficacy and safety studies are completed.

Critical Thinking Questions

1. Is psychedelic-assisted therapy for depression ready for approval? If yes, why do you think so? If not, what additional evidence is needed?
2. In anticipating research on the relative effects of the drugs versus the therapy components of psychedelic-assisted therapy, what do you predict their relative contributions to outcomes will be?
3. Would you be willing to undergo psychedelic-assisted therapy? Why or why not?

SOCIOCULTURAL PERSPECTIVES

5.16 Cross-Cultural and Social Justice Perspectives

Context and Culture in Mood Problems

Sociocultural perspectives emphasize context and culture in the development and maintenance of mood difficulties. They view depression and mania as tied to social, cultural, and environmental factors. For example, a growing research literature highlights the relationship between materialism and depression, suggesting that capitalist culture and its emphasis on compulsive buying over social interest contributes to depressive experience (Azibo, 2013; Claes et al., 2010; N. Gupta & Singh, 2019; Mueller et al., 2011; Muñiz-Velázquez et al., 2017; Otero-López & Villardefrancos, 2013, 2013; Richardson & Manaster, 2003; D. C. Watson, 2015; Wegemer, 2020). This sort of analysis—where social influences are placed front and center in trying to understand mood problems—typifies sociocultural approaches. Rather than seeing people as biologically sick, a purely sociocultural viewpoint views mood disturbances as originating in social oppression, family dynamics, cultural factors, and environmental conditions. However, most sociocultural perspectives take a somewhat integrative view. They acknowledge the relevance of biological and psychological processes but see sociocultural factors as critical in eliciting and shaping the course of these processes (R. A. Gordon, 2010).

Socioeconomic Inequality and Depression

Social justice perspectives contend that depression doesn't occur in a vacuum. It is tied to, and perhaps caused by, unfair social conditions. For example, depression has been linked to lower earnings and socioeconomic status (SES) (A. Freeman et al., 2016; Hoebel et al., 2017; Schlax et al., 2019; Zou et al., 2020), as well as to living in a poor neighborhood (Dawson et al., 2019; Fone et al., 2014; Joshi et al., 2017; Kowitt et al., 2020). In recent years, the COVID-19 pandemic placed an additional social stressor on lower-SES individuals, putting them at even greater risk for depression and anxiety (L. R. Hall et al., 2021). Importantly, research on SES and depression tends to be correlational, so it isn't clear whether economic adversity leads to depression or vice versa. However, some people still maintain that the best way to remedy depression among lower-income individuals is to advance social policies promoting economic equality (Butterworth et al., 2012; Raymond, 2019).

Gender and Depression

Gender Differences in Diagnosis and Treatment

Research finds gender differences in rates of depression. Women are much more likely to be diagnosed with depression than men. In 2019, there were an 279.6 million suspected cases of depression around the globe, 61 percent of them women (GBD 2019 Mental Disorders Collaborators, 2022). Past estimates suggest an even greater disparity, with women diagnosed perhaps twice as often as men (Norman, 2004; Ussher, 2011). A similar pattern extends to antidepressants. As seen in Figure 5.3, prevalence of antidepressant use among U.S. women in 2019 was more than double that of men (15.1 percent to 7.0 percent) (Express Scripts, 2020). Results of a more comprehensive study of U.S. rates between 1995 and 2015 were even more lopsided, with women accounting for 70 percent of adult major depression antidepressant use (Luo et al., 2020). UK data for 2019 shows a similar but less stark disparity, with women only on antidepressants 1.5 times as often as men (Public Health England, 2020). It is unclear if these gender differences are because (a) women truly are more depressed, (b) there is gender bias in diagnosis, or (c) men are socialized to exhibit depression through displays of irritability, hostility, and acting out rather than sadness (Jack & Ali, 2010; Norman, 2004; Ogrodniczuk & Oliffe, 2011; Ussher, 2011; Wilhelm, 2009).

Those stressing gender bias note that women are socialized to show vulnerable emotions more openly than men. Thus, socialized gender differences in expressing depression could lead to women being more readily diagnosed than men (Norman, 2004). Women also face certain social barriers more frequently than men—such as higher poverty rates, domestic violence, unequal pay, being

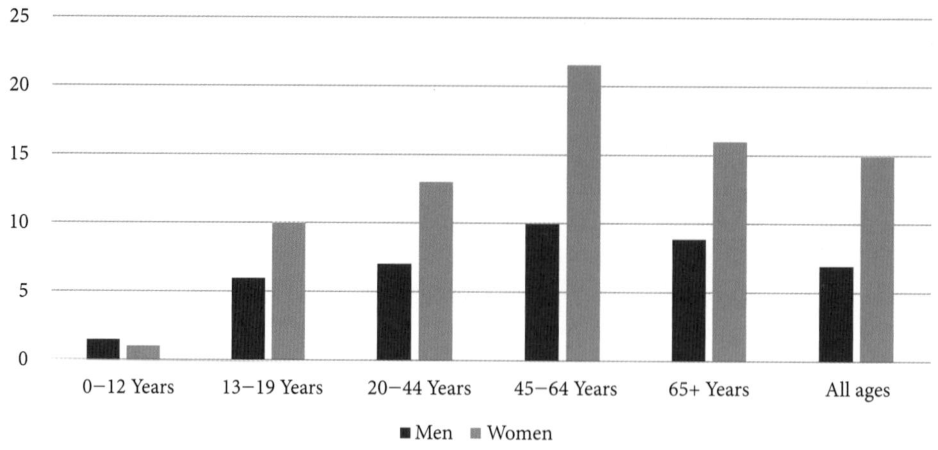

Figure 5.3 Percentage of U.S. Patients Taking Antidepressants by Age and Gender, 2019.
Source: Created using information originally available at: Express Scripts. (2020, April). America's state of mind report. https://www.express-scripts.com/corporate/americas-state-of-mind-report

denied educational opportunities, and disproportionate household responsibilities (Astbury, 2010; Ussher, 2011). Such obstacles could lead to higher rates of depression, making gender differences in depression attributable to cultural and social factors. From a social justice perspective, women aren't necessarily more inherently predisposed to depression. Rather, they become or are identified as depressed more than men primarily due to gender bias and inequality. Social justice therapists cite evidence that "women who experience frequent sexism, or who perceive themselves to be subjected to personal discrimination, report higher levels of depression than those who experience little sexism or low levels of discrimination" (Ussher, 2011, p. 38).

Silencing the Self Theory

Silencing the self (STS) theory proposes that depression in women is a product of deeply rooted cultural assumptions that direct women to silence or suppress certain thoughts and feelings to satisfy the demands of a male-centered world (Jack, 1991; Jack & Ali, 2010). STS theory holds that women are raised in a society that demands they be pleasing, unselfish, and loving. This leads them to be compliant and deferent in ways that result in them silencing themselves, which results in depression (Jack, 1991; Jack & Ali, 2010; Maji & Dixit, 2019). STS theory implies that medicalization causes depressed women to be seen as sick patients suffering from brain diseases rather than as oppressed individuals responding to social subjugation in expectable ways. In this line of thinking, antidepressants too-often become a form of social control, further silencing women by accommodating them to unjust social conditions.

5.17 Service User Perspectives

The Experience of Depression

The experience of depression itself can be extremely intense regardless of whether the depression is considered mild or severe. One patient described depression this way: "I was in a terrible state … I would simply break down and cry and you know feel absolutely useless" (Louch et al., 2005, p. 113). Another depressed person stated bluntly: "Personally I can say that in my experience being depressed is worse than knowing that I will die of cancer" (M. Deacon, 2015, p. 458). As these quotes illustrate, knowing the symptoms of depression doesn't convey its intensity. The "The Lived Experience" feature offers another first-hand account of depression.

Stigma

Those experiencing mood disturbances often face stigma and discrimination (Aromaa et al., 2011; Louch et al., 2005)—although this stigma may be decreasing in the United States (Pescosolido et al., 2021). A qualitative study in which almost 70 percent of participants were diagnosed with a

Silencing the self (STS) theory: Sees depression as a product of deeply rooted cultural assumptions that direct women to silence or suppress certain thoughts or feelings to satisfy the demands of a male-centered world.

The Lived Experience: Healing from Depression

My journey with depression began very early, when I was 10 years old. My parents had separated and through my adolescence I slowly lost my brightness, my brilliant creative energy and all round can do attitude.

It was never so extreme when I was a young child that I couldn't get out of bed in the morning. For the most part my days were filled with melancholy and I turned inward.

I had some good years. Like, when I moved school after the junior cert. It was the best thing I ever did and my depression eased off and life started to fill with joy.

Then, at 23, I relapsed. I was stuck in a job for two years that I hated, a relationship ended, there was illness in the family. I cried every day for two months and couldn't leave the house for weeks. I felt like a potted plant.

Taking Ownership

My body felt so heavy, I couldn't move. I decided I needed help. Nobody can make that decision for you. You need to come to that realisation for yourself and take ownership of your life. So that's exactly what I did. For months I went to counselling and went on medication.

My days began to fill with colour. Colours and nature around me seemed more vibrant. I never realised how gray the world had become in my darkest days.

When I started seeing beauty in the mundane, I turned to art for healing. Painting was something I loved as a child but was something that I turned away from in the past. I rediscovered art and my creative side during my healing process.

The Artist's Way

Writing became my knight in shining armour. It's always something I fall back on and recommend to anyone going through tough times. Currently I've set myself a goal I've taken from Julia Cameron's book, the *Artist's Way* and get up every morning and write three pages before I do anything else.

It helps process my thoughts, feelings, the world or whatever is on my mind. This morning I got up and wrote three haikus. This may sound weird, but I had a laugh writing them. The more entertaining you make life, the more fun you will have.

Taking Ownership of my Mental Health

Now, a year after my relapse, my life is filled with vitality. I've taken ownership of my mental health. I take my medication every morning, I meditate every day.

I try to do yoga every day and I fill my time by seeing people who make every moment feel special. It's a journey trying to figure out what your individual antidote is to depression but it's worth trying everything under the sun to figure it out.

It can be fun too! I tried so many new hobbies and found new and old passions.

It can and it will be okay. In fact, I believe your life will be great.

Reprinted with permission from https://turn2me.ie/personal-story-healing-from-depression/.

depressive or bipolar disorder found that 38 percent of participants believed that discrimination led to their feeling suicidal and 20 percent felt it contributed to an actual suicide attempt (Farrelly et al., 2015). Another qualitative study found that, when it comes to treatment, many depressed people worry about getting caught in a "drug loop" that makes it difficult to get off medication; they appreciate antidepressants when in a crisis, but once the crisis is over they are ambivalent about remaining on the drugs long-term (Bayliss & Holttum, 2015).

5.18 Systems Perspectives

Relationship Problems and Expressed Emotion

Depression and mania are both strongly associated with relationship problems. Divorce, for instance, places people at higher risk for depression and suicide (Hiyoshi et al., 2015; Sbarra et al., 2014; Stack & Scourfield, 2015). Although bad relationships may lead to mood problems, people with mood problems may also have a harder time sustaining effective relationships. That is, mood problems likely both lead to and result in relational and family difficulties.

Couple and family therapists often try to reduce expressed emotion in partners and relatives of clients with mood problems. Recall from Chapter 4 that expressed emotion involves the extent to which partners or family members express hostility and criticism toward the identified patient—in this case the person displaying depression or mania. There is evidence that high expressed emotion in families of people diagnosed with mood problems correlates with worse outcomes (Division of Clinical Psychology, 2010). This may be because high levels of expressed emotion provoke dysfunctional thinking that undercuts interventions to improve the identified patient's mood (Bodenmann & Randall, 2013; K. Wright, 2013).

Shirley

Shirley's depression is negatively impacting her fiancé, Ralph. He has increasingly taken on responsibility for paying bills, doing household chores, and taking care of Spot (the dog they co-own) because Shirley has been too depressed to attend to these issues. Further, as Shirley has sunk into depression, their sex life has deteriorated and conflict between them increased. This, in turn, has led to Ralph also feeling depressed.

Family Therapies

Family-focused therapy (FFT):
Family therapy approach emphasizing psychoeducation, improving communication skills, and problem-solving.

Attachment-based family therapy:
Integrates attachment theory into family therapy to strengthen parent-child attachment relationships in depressed and suicidal adolescents.

Couple and family therapies often use **family-focused therapy (FFT)** with depression and mania. FFT is a 21-session, nine-month treatment program emphasizing psychoeducation, improving communication skills, and problem-solving (Reilly-Harrington et al., 2015). The goal is to help patients, their partners, and their family members to communicate and support one another more effectively. FFT seems to be helpful for depression and mania (Reilly-Harrington et al., 2015), but some research has found it no more helpful than less time-intensive psychoeducation programs for bipolar disorder (Miklowitz et al., 2014; H. A. Swartz, 2014). Another approach that has shown promise is **attachment-based family therapy**, which integrates attachment theory into family therapy to help strengthen parent–child attachment relationships in depressed and suicidal adolescents (Diamond, 2014; E. S. K. Ewing et al., 2015; Waraan, Rognli, Czajkowski, Aalberg, et al., 2021; Waraan, Rognli, Czajkowski, Mehlum, et al., 2021). Although couple and family approaches are often used in conjunction with prescription drugs, conceptually they expand our understanding of mood difficulties beyond the biological to the relational realm. They contend that depression and mania do not simply emerge from within broken individuals; they emerge systemically from a network of problematic relationships.

5.19 Evaluating Sociocultural Perspectives

Sociocultural perspectives highlight the importance of social factors in mood problems, yet social factors alone don't always account for depression or mania. Many people facing oppressive social conditions or dysfunctional family environments don't develop mood difficulties, while many others from advantaged backgrounds and "happy" families do. Thus, social conditions alone can't explain all depression and mania. For instance, biologically oriented researchers and clinicians contend that sex differences in depression are rooted in physiological differences between men and women. To them, social considerations are important but disorders like MDD and PMDD are equally if not more influenced by genetic, neurochemical, hormonal, and immunological factors (Altemus et al., 2014; Baller & Ross, 2019; Filatova et al., 2021; Pérez-López et al., 2009). That said, sociocultural perspectives provide a strong counterweight to individualistic biological and psychological viewpoints, which tend to ignore or downplay the role of social factors in mental distress. When mood issues are portrayed as originating mainly inside the broken biology or psychology of individuals, social reform takes a backseat, and we risk using psychiatric drugs and psychotherapy to adjust people to oppressive social conditions. Of course, agreeing on which social conditions are oppressive and how they should be changed is not easy, but that doesn't mean we shouldn't try. Sociocultural interventions at family and social levels are important components of helping those with mood problems.

CLOSING THOUGHTS

5.20 The Wide-Ranging Relevance of Mood

Chapters on depression and mania often discuss *suicide*, the act of intentionally ending one's own life. After all, people who experience mood disturbances are at increased risk for attempting or completing suicide (Cai et al., 2021; L. da S. Costa et al., 2015; World Health Organization, 2014). However, suicide isn't linked exclusively to mood problems. People with other diagnoses—notably substance abuse, schizophrenia, trauma, and anxiety—are also at higher risk for suicide (Bachmann, 2018). Although depression greatly increases this risk (Bachmann, 2018), "many people who complete suicide or attempt suicide are not depressed and the overwhelming majority of depressed people will not attempt or complete suicide" (A. K. MacLeod, 2013, p. 413). Suicide is discussed more fully in Chapter 16.

In closing, mood disturbances often accompany—or, in medical terms, are comorbid with—other presenting problems. This is not surprising. If you are struggling with eating issues, trauma, obsessions and compulsions, drug abuse, or sexual performance, then there is a good chance you will also feel depressed. Thus, mood problems are revisited in future chapters.

CHAPTER SUMMARY

Overview

- *Depression* involves intense and often debilitating sadness and melancholy, a pessimistic worldview, and loss of interest. *Mania* includes euphoric mood, boundless energy, and at times a distorted sense of one's abilities.

Diagnostic Perspectives

- DSM includes *major depressive disorder* (*single episode* or *recurrent depression* in ICD), *bipolar I*, *bipolar II*, *cyclothymic disorder*, *persistent depressive disorder* (*dysthymic disorder* in ICD), *premenstrual dysphoric disorder*, and *disruptive mood dysregulation disorder*.
- DSM and ICD have been criticized for threshold and comorbidity problems, mixed reliability, harmonization issues, and adding new disorders.
- A PDM mood diagnosis maps personality patterns (P-Axis) and subjective experience (S-Axis).
- HiTOP assesses depression on its "Internalizing," "Detachment," and "Somatoform" spectra; bipolar symptoms correspond to its "Externalizing" spectra.
- PTMF views depressive experiences as threat responses to adversity and oppression.

Historical Perspectives

- The ancient Greeks divided madness into *frenzy*, *mania*, and *melancholy*.
- *Neurasthenia* was a nineteenth- and twentieth-century diagnosis for people exhausted by the stress of modern life.
- Emil Kraepelin proposed the *manic-depressive illness continuum*.

Biological Perspectives

- The *monoamine hypothesis* attributes depression to monoamine neurotransmitter deficiencies.
- Antidepressants include *MAO inhibitors*, *tricyclics*, *SSRIs*, *SNRIs*, and *atypical antidepressants*.
- Antidepressant effectiveness is debated, but their use has risen rapidly.
- *Ketamine* treatment is based on the *glutamate hypothesis of depression*.
- Herbal remedies are sometimes used for depression.
- *Mood stabilizers* such as *lithium* are common drugs for bipolar disorder, although *anticonvulsants*, *benzodiazepines*, and *antipsychotics* are also prescribed.
- Brain regions implicated in depression and mania include the *hippocampus*, *amygdala*, *frontal lobe*, and *HPA axis*.

- *Electroconvulsive therapy (ECT)*, *transcranial magnetic stimulation (TMS)*, and *deep brain stimulation (DBS)* are non-drug interventions for treatment-resistant depression.
- Depression and mania run in families; gene–environment interactions play key roles.
- *Adaptationist models* view depression as evolutionarily adaptive. *Dysregulation models* see it as disordered, occurring when adaptive mechanisms malfunction.
- Mood problems may be related to *circadian rhythm* problems. *Light therapy* and *dark therapy* are resulting treatments.
- Immune inflammation is associated with depressive and bipolar disorders. *Nonsteroidal anti-inflammatory drugs (NSAIDs)* are sometimes prescribed.
- Biological perspectives are criticized for lack of biomarkers, not knowing if antidepressants cure an underlying chemical imbalance, and pathologizing sadness.

Psychological Perspectives

- Classic psychoanalytic perspectives attributed depression to grief and loss; they saw manic grandiosity as a defense against self-directed anger.
- Attachment perspectives traced depression to problematic attachments to caregivers and discussed *anaclitic depression* in children.
- Modern psychodynamic therapies for depression include *interpersonal therapy (IPT)*, *dynamic interpersonal therapy (DIT)*, and *short-term psychoanalytic supportive therapy (SPST)*.
- *Interpersonal and social rhythm therapy (IPSRT)* uses IPT principles to address circadian rhythms disruptions in bipolar patients.
- Cognitive therapy emphasizes the *cognitive triad*, *cognitive distortions*, and dysfunctional *cognitive schemas* in depression.
- Behaviorists explain depression as *learned helplessness*. *Hopelessness theory* links learned helplessness to *stable*, *global*, and *internal* attributions.
- The *Beck Depression Inventory (BDI)* and the *Daily Record of Dysfunctional Thoughts (DRDT)* are cognitive instruments for assessing mood problems.
- *Behavioral activation* and *problem-solving therapy* alleviate depression by encouraging novel behavior and tackling life problems.
- *Mindfulness-based cognitive therapy (MBCT)* has clients observe and accept their thoughts.
- For mania, CBT is used to improve medication adherence and change overly optimistic beliefs characteristic of grandiosity.
- *Person-centered therapy* attributes depression to psychological incongruence and provides core conditions to foster self-consistency.
- *Emotion-focused therapy (EFT)* ties depression to unsupportive environments during childhood and adolescence, and helps clients work through feelings and establish new relational patterns.
- Evidence supports psychological interventions for depression, but recurrence often occurs.

Sociocultural Perspectives

- Sociocultural perspectives highlight the relationship between depression and socioeconomic inequality.
- There are gender differences in rates of depression. Antidepressant use is higher in women than men.
- *Silencing the self (SST)* theory says depression results from women being socialized to be deferent and pleasing.
- The personal experience of depression for service users can be debilitating, overwhelming, and stigmatizing.
- Systems perspectives see depression as produced and sustained by social and relational patterns.
- Family therapies reduce *expressed emotion* in the family of depressed clients.
- *Family-focused therapy (FFT)* helps patients, partners, and family members to communicate more effectively.
- *Attachment-based family therapy* integrates attachment theory into family therapy for adolescents experiencing depression.
- Sociocultural perspectives cannot always explain mood problems but their emphasis on overlooked social factors discourages adjusting individuals to oppressive social conditions.

Closing Thoughts

- Mood problems place people at greater risk for *suicide*.
- Mood problems are comorbid with many other presenting problems.

NEW VOCABULARY

1. Adaptationist versus dysregulation models
2. Anaclitic depression
3. Anticonvulsants
4. Antidepressants
5. Atypical antidepressants
6. Attachment-based family therapy
7. Beck Depression Inventory (BDI)
8. Behavioral activation
9. Bereavement exclusion
10. Bipolar I disorder
11. Bipolar II disorder
12. Cognitive triad
13. Cortisol
14. Cyclothymic disorder
15. Daily Record of Dysfunctional Thoughts (DRDT)
16. Dark therapy
17. Deep brain stimulation (DBS)
18. Depressive episode
19. Discontinuation syndrome
20. Disruptive mood dysregulation disorder (DMDD)
21. Dysthymic disorder
22. Electroconvulsive therapy (ECT)
23. Emotion-focused therapy (EFT)
24. Family-focused therapy (FFT)
25. Frontal lobe
26. Glutamate hypothesis of depression
27. Herbal remedies for depression
28. Hopelessness theory
29. Hormones
30. Hypomanic episode
31. Hypothalamic-pituitary-adrenal (HPA) axis
32. Intensive short-term dynamic psychotherapy (ISTDP)
33. Interpersonal and social rhythm therapy (IPSRT)
34. Interpersonal therapy (IPT)
35. Ketamine
36. Learned helplessness
37. Light therapy
38. Lithium
39. MAO inhibitors (MAOIs)
40. Major depressive disorder (MDD)
41. Manic episode
42. Mindfulness-based cognitive therapy (MBCT)
43. Mixed episode
44. Monoamine hypothesis
45. Mood stabilizers
46. Nonsteroidal anti-inflammatory drugs (NSAIDs)
47. Persistent depressive disorder (PDD)
48. Postpartum depression
49. Premenstrual dysphoric disorder (PMDD)
50. Problem-solving therapy
51. Psychedelic-assisted therapy
52. Seasonal affective disorder (SAD)
53. Selective serotonin reuptake inhibitors (SSRIs)
54. Serotonin and norepinephrine reuptake inhibitors (SNRIs)
55. Silencing the self (STS) theory
56. Transcranial magnetic stimulation (TMS)
57. Tricyclics

ANXIETY, OBSESSIONS, AND COMPULSIONS

6

Photo 6.1
Guille Pozzi/Unsplash.

LEARNING OBJECTIVES

After reading this chapter, you should be able to:

1. Distinguish anxiety from fear and obsessions from compulsions.

2. Define and critique the major anxiety and obsessive-compulsive disorders contained in DSM and ICD.

3. Summarize historical perspectives on anxiety, obsessions, and compulsions.

4. Outline and appraise biological perspectives on anxiety, obsessions, and compulsions—including neurochemical conceptions and interventions, brain structure hypotheses, genetic and evolutionary explanations, and the suspected roles of inflammation and the gut.

5. Distinguish and evaluate psychodynamic, cognitive-behavioral, and humanistic approaches to anxiety, obsessions, and compulsions.

6. Explain and critique sociocultural accounts of and interventions for anxiety, obsessions, and compulsions—including the roles of culture, economics, gender, stigma, expressed emotion, accommodation, and family systems.

OVERVIEW

6.1 Getting Started: Anxiety, Fear, Obsessions, and Compulsions

Case Examples

The Steadman family consists of Theresa, 35; her husband Gary, 36; and their daughter Tammy, 8.

Theresa
Theresa feels anxious almost every day, but usually can't pinpoint specific concerns that worry her. In addition to being generally anxious most of the time, Theresa has recently become nervous about speaking in front of groups—a real problem given that she is a pharmaceutical representative who often gives presentations to health professionals about new drugs on the market.

Tammy
Theresa's 8-year-old daughter, Tammy, also has been experiencing a lot of anxiety. Over the last few months, she has begun to fret whenever her parents leave for work, often crying and expressing

worry about when she will see them again. She often gets so upset that her parents let her miss school and instead take her to work with them.

Gary

Gary has many rituals that he must complete before leaving the house in the morning—such as repeatedly making sure the gas on the stove is turned off and the security alarm on the house is properly programmed. If he doesn't attend to these tasks, he feels extremely anxious and cannot stop worrying. He is also highly anxious about dirt and repeatedly washes his hands throughout the day. Gary's rituals take up so much time that he is chronically late for work—and his boss has noticed.

Defining Anxiety, Fear, Obsessions, and Compulsions

Anxiety and Fear

This chapter focuses on anxiety, obsessions, and compulsions. The American Psychological Association defines **anxiety** as "an emotion characterized by feelings of tension, worried thoughts and physical changes like increased blood pressure" (American Psychological Association, n.d.-a, para. 1). Those experiencing it worry a lot and feel fear, uneasiness, or dread (A. A. Shah & Han, 2015). While everyone worries sometimes, intense anxiety can be debilitating.

Anxiety: Emotion characterized by feelings of tension, worried thoughts, and physical changes like increased blood pressure; involves cognitive appraisals related to more basic fear responses.

Theresa and Tammy

Theresa Steadman and her daughter Tammy are both overwhelmed by anxiety.

Whether anxiety is unitary or divisible into different types has long been debated: "Some researchers emphasize the similarities of all anxieties and postulate the unity of all anxiety disorders. Others stress the differences between different kinds of anxiety, positing several distinct disorders, each with its own etiology, phenomenology, and treatment" (I. M. Marks & Nesse, 1994, p. 249). Consistent with the latter view, many clinicians and researchers distinguish anxiety from **fear**. They define fear as a basic emotion in response to perceived danger. It has distinct physiological symptoms that are universal, automatic, and brief. Anxiety, by contrast, involves cognitive appraisals related to more basic fear responses. To illustrate this, phobias are considered fear-based problems (there's something specific that causes an immediate fear reaction) compared with generalized anxiety (in which the person's thoughts about a variety of life situations lead to pervasive and global feelings of unease). Because they include thinking and reflection, anxiety reactions are often considered less biologically "hard-wired" than fear reactions (Hofmann et al., 2002).

Fear: Basic emotional response to something specific that is perceived as dangerous with distinct physiological symptoms that are universal, automatic, and brief.

Obsessions and Compulsions

Sometimes fear and anxiety are accompanied by obsessions and compulsions. **Obsessions** are persistent thoughts, images, or urges that are hard to dismiss or stop thinking about. **Compulsions** are behaviors or mental acts that a person feels driven to perform, often in response to obsessions. One way to keep them straight is to remember that obsessions are thoughts and compulsions are actions.

Obsessions: Persistent thoughts, images, or urges that are hard to dismiss or stop thinking about.

Compulsions: Behaviors or mental acts that a person feels driven to perform.

Gary

Gary Steadman could be diagnosed with OCD. His endless ruminating about whether the stove is off or the security system is properly programmed exemplify obsessive thinking. His repeated checking the stove and reprograming the security keypad constitute compulsive behavior.

Photo 6.2 The emotions provoked by a scary film are usually automatic, universal and brief, making this reaction fear rather than anxiety.
Steven Weeks/Unsplash.

We all know what it's like to experience anxiety or to occasionally obsess or get compulsive about certain issues. After all, anxiety is highly common in the Western world. By one estimate, the lifetime prevalence for an anxiety disorder diagnosis is 33.7 percent (Bandelow & Michaelis, 2015). This chapter discusses perspectives on anxiety, obsessions, and compulsions.

A Caveat: We All Feel Anxious Sometimes

Given how many people qualify for a diagnosis, it suffices to say that anxiety is a common human response to challenging circumstances. We all have experienced it and know that it can motivate us. Without anxiety, you might not have read this chapter by the date your instructor told you to! You also might not prepare as well for exams without anxiety to spur you on. Yet how much anxiety is too much? When does it become a problem? Is it primarily due to biological, psychological, or sociocultural causes? Because anxiety is so prevalent in the modern world, answering these questions remains a challenge.

DIAGNOSTIC PERSPECTIVES

6.2 DSM and ICD

Anxiety Disorders
Specific Phobia

Specific phobia: DSM and ICD disorder characterized by fear associated with a given object or situation; the fear is focused on something specific.

When most of us use the word "phobia," we are describing what DSM and ICD categorize as **specific phobia**, namely fear associated with a given object or situation (see Diagnostic Box 6.1). The fear is focused, with the phobic individual afraid of something in particular—such as heights, flying, enclosed spaces, a kind of animal, getting an injection, or going to the dentist. The feared object or situation is actively avoided and provokes immediate anxiety. However, when the person isn't near the phobic object, anxiety isn't present. Cross-national one-year and lifetime prevalence rates for specific phobia have been estimated at 5.5 percent and 7.4 percent, respectively—with higher rates for females (7.7 percent and 9.8 percent) than males (3.3 percent and 4.9 percent) (Wardenaar et al., 2017). In 60.5 percent of lifetime cases, specific phobias are accompanied by (i.e., comorbid with) other mental disorders—most often anxiety disorders (41.2 percent) or mood disorders (34.3 percent) (Wardenaar et al., 2017).

Diagnostic Box 6.1 Specific Phobia

DSM-5-TR and ICD-11
- Disproportionate fear and avoidance of a specific object or situation that occurs upon exposure to it.
- Symptom duration:
  - **DSM-5-TR**: At least six months.
  - **ICD-11**: At least several months.

Information from American Psychiatric Association (2022, pp. 224–225) and World Health Organization (2022a).

Social Anxiety Disorder

Social anxiety disorder: DSM and ICD disorder diagnosed in people who become anxious and fear embarrassing or humiliating themselves in social situations where they might be scrutinized.

Social anxiety disorder is diagnosed in people who become anxious and fear embarrassing or humiliating themselves in social situations where they might be scrutinized—such as when meeting people, having social conversations, eating in a restaurant, asking someone on a date, or making a speech (see Diagnostic Box 6.2). This disorder used to be called "social phobia" but has been renamed "social anxiety disorder." DSM-5-TR estimates twelve-month U.S. prevalence at 7 percent. Cross-nationally, twelve-month prevalence is believed to be 2.4 percent and lifetime prevalence 4 percent—with higher risk for younger, female, and unemployed individuals, as well as for those with lower household incomes and less education (D. J. Stein et al., 2017). Social anxiety disorder is highly comorbid with anxiety disorders (59.8 percent), mood disorders (47 percent), substance use disorders (26.7 percent), and impulse-control disorders (19.3 percent) (D. J. Stein et al., 2017).

Diagnostic Box 6.2 Social Anxiety Disorder

DSM-5-TR and ICD-11
- Disproportionate fear and avoidance of social situation(s) where the person might be scrutinized.
- Overly concerned about behaving anxiously and being evaluated negatively for it.
- Symptom duration:
  - **DSM-5-TR**: At least six months.
  - **ICD-11**: At least several months.

Information from American Psychiatric Association (2022, pp. 229–230) and World Health Organization (2022a).

Panic Disorder

Panic disorder is characterized by recurrent and unexpected **panic attacks**. A panic attack is an intense anxiety reaction that comes on abruptly and include symptoms like a pounding heart, trembling, shortness of breath, chest pain, nausea, dizziness, feeling chilled or hot, tingling sensations, and detachment from oneself or the world. Those experiencing panic attacks often feel like they are dying, so it isn't surprising that panic attacks can be mistaken as heart attacks, strokes, or other sudden life-threatening events. Unfortunately, the term "panic attack" has entered our everyday vocabulary in a way that doesn't fit with DSM and ICD definitions. It is common to hear people describe mild anxiety as a "panic attack," but a genuine panic attack is more than just run of the mill worry. It is severe, debilitating, and terrifying. Notably, having a panic attack doesn't mean one has panic disorder. A diagnosis is only made when the attacks are recurrent (they happen repeatedly) and unexpected (the person has no idea when or why they occur). There must also be persistent worry about further panic attacks—for at least one month (DSM) or several weeks (ICD) (see Diagnostic Box 6.3). This explains why twelve-month cross-national prevalence rates for panic attacks (4.9 percent) are higher than for panic disorder (1 percent) (de Jonge et al., 2018). Lifetime panic disorder prevalence is 1.7 percent, but significantly greater in high-income countries (2.2 percent) than low- and lower-middle-income countries (0.8 percent); other risk factors include being female, smoking and alcohol issues, having a comorbid mental disorder, and low socioeconomic status (de Jonge et al., 2018).

Panic disorder: DSM and ICD disorder characterized by recurrent and unexpected panic attacks.

Panic attack: Intense and sudden anxiety reaction; symptoms include pounding heart, trembling, shortness of breath, chest pain, nausea, dizziness, feeling chilled or hot, tingling sensations, and detachment from self or world.

Diagnostic Box 6.3 Panic Disorder

DSM-5-TR and ICD-11
- Regular and unanticipated panic attacks.
- Following one or more of these attacks, either or both these symptoms: (a) worrying about further panic attacks, or (b) dysfunctional alteration of behavior in response to the attacks (e.g., avoiding novel situations).
- Symptom duration:
  - **DSM-5-TR**: Worry about further panic attacks for one month or longer.
  - **ICD-11**: Worry about further panic attacks for several weeks or longer.

Information from American Psychiatric Association (2022, pp. 235–236) and World Health Organization (2022a).

Agoraphobia

Agoraphobia literally translates as "fear of the marketplace." It is a DSM and ICD diagnosis for people who dread situations where they may have an intense and embarrassing fear reaction and won't be able to escape. Those with agoraphobia may worry about using public transportation, going to the movies, or being in a crowd because they might experience anxiety or a panic attack and be unable to flee the situation easily or without feeling humiliated. Because panic attacks are common in agoraphobia, panic disorder is often diagnosed concurrently (see Diagnostic Box 6.4). DSM-5-TR indicates that approximately 1 percent to 1.7 percent of adolescents and adults meet agoraphobia criteria, with

Agoraphobia: DSM and ICD disorder diagnosed in people who fear being in situations where they may have an intense and embarrassing fear reaction (such as a panic attack) and won't be able to escape.

females twice as likely to receive a diagnosis as males. The diagnosis is rare in older adults, with only 0.4 percent to 0.5 percent of Europeans and North Americans over age 55 estimated to qualify. Roughly 90 percent of people with agoraphobia concurrently meet criteria for other mental disorders—most often other anxiety disorders, depression, posttraumatic stress, and alcohol use problems.

Diagnostic Box 6.4 Agoraphobia

DSM-5-TR and ICD-11

- Disproportionate fear and avoidance of two of these: (1) public transportation, (2) open spaces like parking lots, public markets, and bridges, (3) enclosed spaces like theaters or stores, (4) crowds or lines, (5) being away from home by oneself.
- These situations are feared or avoided because escape might not be possible and panic or other embarrassing anxiety symptoms might ensue.
- Feared situations typically provoke fear and anxiety and are avoided or anxiously tolerated.
- Symptom duration:
  - **DSM-5-TR**: At least six months.
  - **ICD-11**: At least several months.

Information from American Psychiatric Association (2022, p. 246) and World Health Organization (2022a).

Generalized Anxiety Disorder

Generalized anxiety disorder (GAD):
DSM and ICD diagnosis characterized by excessive and consistent worry that is global rather than specific.

Whereas specific phobias and social anxiety disorder involve focused anxiety that occurs in very particular circumstances, **generalized anxiety disorder (GAD)** is epitomized by excessive and consistent worry that is global rather than specific (see full GAD criteria and guidelines in Chapter 3). Those who qualify for this diagnosis experience persistent anxiety not limited to anything specific. They are just continually anxious in general (see Diagnostic Box 6.5). ICD merely indicates that symptoms must continue for several months, but DSM stipulates a minimum of six months before a diagnosis can be made. DSM-5-TR reports twelve-month U.S. prevalence is 0.9 percent among teens and 2.9 percent among adults. Cross-nationally, estimated lifetime prevalence and 12-month prevalence are 3.7 percent and 1.8 percent. Being female, unmarried, and less than 60 years old are risk factors and, as with many anxiety disorders, GAD is much more prevalent in higher-income than lower-income countries (Ruscio et al., 2017). Context matters, too: At the height of the COVID-19 pandemic in 2020, prevalence among U.S. adults jumped from 1.8 percent to a whopping 17.9 percent (Cordaro et al., 2021)!

Diagnostic Box 6.5 Generalized Anxiety Disorder

DSM-5-TR

- Undue, hard to control, and ongoing anxiety and worry that occurs almost every day.
- Three or more of these symptoms: (1) restlessness, (2) easily tired, (3) trouble concentrating, (4) irritability, (5) muscle tension, (6) sleep difficulties.
- Symptoms last at least six months.

ICD-11

- General worry or "free floating" anxiety about several areas of life that is not restricted to specific situations.
- Three or more of these symptoms: (1) restlessness, (2) physiological indicators (gastrointestinal problems, heart racing, sweating, trembling, dry mouth), (3) trouble concentrating, (4) irritability, (5) muscle tension, (6) sleep difficulties.
- Symptoms last for at least several months.

Information from American Psychiatric Association (2022, pp. 250–251) and World Health Organization (2022a).

Theresa

Theresa's ongoing daily anxiety, which is not tied to specific events but is broad and all-encompassing, might warrant a diagnosis of generalized anxiety disorder.

Separation Anxiety Disorder

People diagnosed with **separation anxiety disorder** show excessive anxiety about being separated from people they are attached to. According to DSM-5-TR, this presenting problem is much more prevalent in children (roughly 4 percent) than teens (1.6 percent) and adults (0.9 percent to 1.9 percent). Separation anxiety is often comorbid with specific phobia and generalized anxiety. See Diagnostic Box 6.6 for criteria and guidelines.

Separation anxiety disorder: DSM and ICD disorder in which one shows excessive anxiety about being separated from significant attachment figures.

Diagnostic Box 6.6 Separation Anxiety Disorder

DSM-5-TR and ICD-11

- Disproportionate worry about being separated from or losing important attachment figures—usually parents or close relatives in children and significant others or children in adults.
- Symptom duration:
  - DSM-5-TR: At least four weeks in children and usually six months in adults.
  - ICD-11: At least several months.

Information from American Psychiatric Association (2022, p. 217) and World Health Organization (2022a).

Tammy

Eight-year-old Tammy Steadman, who experiences intense anxiety whenever she is apart from her parents, might be diagnosed with separation anxiety disorder.

Selective Mutism

Selective mutism is diagnosed mainly in children who consistently fail to speak in social situations where it is expected (see Diagnostic Box 6.7). Note that the failure to speak is not due to inability. For example, the child might speak at home to parents and grandparents, but not in school or with strangers. Selective mutism appears to be rare, occurring in just 0.03 percent to 0.79 percent of children; of those diagnosed, 80 percent are diagnosed with another anxiety disorder, most often social anxiety (69 percent) (Driessen et al., 2020).

Selective mutism: DSM and ICD disorder diagnosed mainly in children who fail to speak in social situations in which it is expected.

Diagnostic Box 6.7 Selective Mutism

DSM-5-TR and ICD-11

- Not speaking when socially expected, even though speaks in other situations.
- Failure to speak not due to inability or lack of comfort speaking the language required.
- Interferes with achievement at school or work.
- Symptoms last at least one month (excluding the first month of school).

Information from American Psychiatric Association (2022, p. 222) and World Health Organization (2022a).

Obsessive-compulsive disorder (OCD): DSM and ICD disorder marked by the presence of obsessions and compulsions.

Obsessive-Compulsive and Related Disorders
Obsessive-Compulsive Disorder

Obsessive-compulsive disorder (OCD) is marked by the presence of obsessions and compulsions. People with an OCD diagnosis spend inordinate amounts of time engaging in obsessive thinking and compulsive behavior. For details, see Diagnostic Box 6.8. DSM-5-TR estimates that 1.2 percent of people in the United States meet criteria for OCD. It gives a prevalence range of 1.1 percent to 1.8 percent for the rest of the world. Females are believed to develop OCD symptoms slightly more often than males, but males develop OCD in childhood more than females. Average age of onset in the United States is thought to be 19.5 years old, with almost 25 percent of cases developing before age 14. OCD is highly comorbid with anxiety disorders, mood disorders, and eating disorders. Many people with OCD (up to 30 percent) also qualify for a tic disorder (see Chapter 14).

Body dysmorphic disorder (BDD): DSM and ICD disorder in which people display obsessional preoccupation with one or more perceived physical flaws in their appearance.

Diagnostic Box 6.8 Obsessive-Compulsive Disorder

DSM-5-TR and ICD-11
- Obsessions and/or compulsions.
  - *Obsessions* are persistent, distressing, invasive, and unwelcome thoughts, impulses, or images that are difficult to ignore or eliminate; they are often counteracted by engaging in compulsions.
  - *Compulsions* are recurring behaviors or mental acts that the person feels compelled to engage in to decrease anxiety associated with obsessions (even though doing so has no effect).
- The obsessions and compulsions take up enormous amounts of time.

Information from American Psychiatric Association (2022, pp. 265–266) and World Health Organization (2022a).

Hoarding disorder: DSM and ICD diagnosis for people who have a hard time giving up possessions, even when they have too many or the possessions are no longer useful or valuable.

Other Obsessive-Compulsive Related Disorders

DSM-5-TR and ICD-11 contain several other OCD-related diagnoses. People with **body dysmorphic disorder (BDD)** display obsessional preoccupation with one or more perceived physical flaws in their appearance. As examples, they might think their nose is too big, their ears are lopsided, their chin is shaped funny, or their hips are too wide. Some people even worry about not being muscular enough, a form of BDD that DSM-5-TR gives the specifier "with muscle dysmorphia." **Hoarding disorder** is a diagnosis for people who have difficulty giving up possessions, even when they have too many or the possessions are no longer useful or valuable. As a result, living space becomes cluttered and congested. Finally, **trichotillomania (hair-pulling disorder)** describes those who compulsively pull out their hair, while **excoriation (skin-picking disorder)** involves compulsive picking at the skin, resulting in lesions. Diagnostic Box 6.9 provides details about other OCD-related disorders.

Trichotillomania (hair-pulling disorder): DSM and ICD disorder describing those who compulsively pull out their own hair.

Excoriation (skin-picking disorder): DSM and ICD disorder that involves compulsive picking of the skin.

Evaluating DSM and ICD Perspectives
Diagnostic Reliability

DSM-5 diagnostic reliability trials found questionable reliability for generalized anxiety disorder (Regier et al., 2013). This isn't surprising, as generalized anxiety is broad in its very definition; getting clinicians to agree on how much amorphous anxiety is too much has proved challenging. The field trials also found unacceptable reliability for a proposed diagnosis called **mixed anxiety and depressive disorder**, reserved for people who display symptoms of both depression and anxiety for two weeks or more, but whose symptoms don't qualify them for other mood or anxiety disorders. This disorder wasn't included in DSM-5 due to its poor showing in reliability trials—clinicians couldn't consistently distinguish it from major depressive disorder (MDD) or generalized anxiety disorder (Regier et al., 2013). However, it does appear in ICD-11 (as a mood, not anxiety, disorder). Difficulties distinguishing anxiety from depression are revisited throughout the chapter.

Mixed anxiety and depressive disorder: Proposed DSM and official ICD diagnosis for people who display symptoms of both depression and anxiety for two weeks or more, but whose symptoms don't qualify them for other mood or anxiety disorders.

Diagnostic Box 6.9 Other Obsessive-Compulsive Related Disorders

Body dysmorphic disorder (BDD)
- **DSM-5-TR**: Excessive focus on at least one perceived physical defect or flaw that is not noticeable or significant. Includes (a) repetitive behaviors like checking appearance, grooming excessively, picking at skin, or asking to be reassured, or (b) mental acts like comparing appearance to others.
- **ICD-11**: Excessive focus on at least one perceived physical defect or flaw that is not noticeable or significant. Characterized by self-consciousness and concern about being judged. Person repeatedly checks appearance, tries to hide perceived flaws, or avoids social situations.

Hoarding disorder
- **DSM-5-TR**: Anxiety and worry about disposing of possessions, even ones no longer of value; results in accumulating possessions that clutter living space.
- **ICD-11**: Excessive collection of possessions and distress over getting rid of them due to their emotional, not monetary, value; leads to cluttered and/or dangerous living space.

Trichotillomania (hair-pulling disorder)
- **DSM-5-TR**: Frequent pulling out of one's own hair (causing hair loss) with ongoing efforts to stop.
- **ICD-11**: Regular pulling of one's own hair, leading to hair loss; there are unsuccessful attempts to stop.

Excoriation (skin-picking disorder)
- **DSM-5-TR**: Frequent skin-picking leading to injuries accompanied by ongoing efforts to stop.
- **ICD-11**: Regular picking at one's skin, leading to injuries; one specific subtype focuses on recurrent picking at acne pimples.

Information from American Psychiatric Association (2022, pp. 271–272, 277, 281, 284) and World Health Organization (2022a).

Other Controversies

Let's examine three other anxiety and OCD-related diagnostic controversies. First, starting with DSM-5 (and continuing in DSM-5-TR), several anxiety disorders were relocated elsewhere. Posttraumatic stress disorder (PTSD) and acute stress disorder (see Chapter 7) were moved to a new "trauma- and stressor-related disorders" section of DSM, and OCD to a new "obsessive-compulsive and related disorders" section. Some objected, arguing the reorganization made no sense because anxiety is central to all these disorders (Abramowitz & Jacoby, 2014b; L. A. Zoellner et al., 2011). Nonetheless, a similar reorganization was incorporated into ICD-11. Second, panic disorder and agoraphobia, which used to be yoked together, have been separated in both DSM and ICD. Some believe this makes it easier to meet criteria for either one (Asmundson et al., 2014). This potentially qualifies more people for services, but people with mild symptoms may be diagnosed unnecessarily. Third, comorbidity is a challenge for diagnoses like GAD, OCD, and hoarding disorder (Abramowitz & Jacoby, 2014b; R. O. Frost et al., 2011; D. Nutt et al., 2006; Pertusa et al., 2008). Too much comorbidity can raise reliability and validity concerns.

6.3 Other Diagnostic Perspectives

PDM-2

PDM-2 frames anxiety in psychodynamic terms, viewing it as a response to four basic danger situations: (1) "loss of a significant other"; (2) "loss of love"; (3) "loss of bodily integrity or functioning"; or (4) "loss of affirmation and approval by one's own conscience" (Lingiardi & McWilliams, 2017, p. 165). Cognitively, anxious people exhibit "poor concentration, difficulty focusing, easy distractibility, and poor memory" (Lingiardi & McWilliams, 2017, p. 166). Somatic symptoms are common (e.g., feeling tense, sweaty palms, shortness of breath, stomach "butterflies"). In relationships, anxiety manifests as fearing rejection, being clingy, seeking reassurance, feeling guilty, and alternating between desiring closeness and distance from others (Lingiardi & McWilliams, 2017). PDM-2 provides several clinical illustrations of the subjective experience of anxiety, including this one:

My mind is deluged with all sorts of frightening thoughts and images. My body is all nerves. I can't sit down for any period of time; I'm constantly up and down. I feel like I'm going to crack up. At my job, I can't do a thing; I just feel I can't go on. (Lingiardi & McWilliams, 2017, p. 167)

HiTOP

Instead of trying to overcome anxiety disorder comorbidity, HiTOP embraces it, reorganizing co-occurring categories into hierarchically nested dimensions and subdimensions (see Chapter 3, Figure 3.1 for a visual refresher) (C. C. Conway et al., 2022). At the spectra level, anxiety disorders load on the "Internalizing" dimension that captures all negative thoughts and feelings (not just anxiety, but also depression, loneliness, and social withdrawal). "Fear" constitutes a narrower subdimension beneath internalizing; it subsumes anxiety, obsessions, and compulsions. As Figure 6.1 illustrates, "social anxiety" is an even more specific syndrome located under "fear," which divides into narrower "performance" and "social-interaction" types, each further separated into distinct experiences. HiTOP assessment maps these experiences while acknowledging that, at the spectra level, they reflect different incarnations of the same pathology (and not discrete disorders, as DSM and ICD imply). Of course, sometimes psychopathology spans multiple spectra. For instance, OCD loads not only on the "fear" subfactor of the "Internalizing" dimension but also on the "Thought Disorder" spectra (Faure & Forbes, 2021).

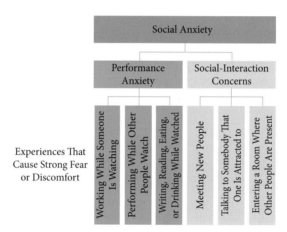

Figure 6.1 Hierarchical Structure of Social Anxiety Symptoms in HiTOP.
Source: Conway, C. C., & Krueger, R. F. (2021). Rethinking the diagnosis of mental disorders: Data-driven psychological dimensions, not categories, as a framework for mental-health research, treatment, and training. Current Directions in Psychological Science, 30(2), 151–158. https://doi.org/10.1177/0963721421990353

PTMF

PTMF rejects pathologizing anxiety, seeing it is an understandable response to social threats. From a PTMF perspective, children who refuse to go to school don't have "separation anxiety disorder." Their school avoidance is meaningful, perhaps "a way of escaping bullies or trying to ensure a parent's safety" (Johnstone & Boyle, 2018, p. 109). Likewise, "social anxiety" stems not from internal dysfunctions but from social origins, such as undependable parenting. In other words, PTMF views anxiety and panic as comprehensible reactions to adversity, not as mental disorders. When using PTMF, client and clinician identify threats in clients' lives. "Symptoms" are reframed as effective, yet sometimes limiting, responses to these threats.

HISTORICAL PERSPECTIVES

6.4 Ancient Greece through the Renaissance

As with many forms of emotional distress, the ancient Greeks attributed anxiety to imbalances in bodily humors (Gee et al., 2013; A. V. Horwitz, 2013). This early physiological view remained influential until the Renaissance (Gee et al., 2013). Courage (as opposed to fear and anxiety) was considered a moral virtue among the Greeks and its development was instilled, but only in men: "Men act bravely, not because they are compelled to but because it is noble for them to do so and they have developed this nobility. Women were of such low social status that such considerations did not apply to them" (A. V. Horwitz, 2013, p. 31). This illustrates how attitudes about anxiety have been gender biased throughout history.

During the Middle Ages, humoral theory remained influential but, with the rise of Christianity, spiritual explanations of anxiety became prominent. Faith in the teachings of Jesus were seen as a remedy, but Christian dogma sometimes produced anxiety: "Fear of perpetual damnation in the afterlife was a particular source of terror that persisted through the Reformation in the sixteenth century" (A. V. Horwitz, 2013, p. 37). Spiritual and medical explanations of anxiety existed side by side throughout this period. While anxiety was discussed from ancient Greek times through the Middle Ages, Renaissance, and into the 1800s, it was not usually considered a distinct disorder (M. H. Stone, 2010): "Before the 19th century, symptoms of anxiety were grouped with the melancholic states (e.g., depression) or considered to be the cause of other mental disorders, including insanity; however, rarely was anxiety considered a disease in its own right" (Gee et al., 2013, p. 31).

6.5 Eighteenth through Twentieth Centuries

That began to change over the course of the eighteenth century as anxiety increasingly was distinguished from melancholia (a historical precursor to modern notions of depression; see Chapter 5) and identified as a key component of the "nervous disorders" (A. V. Horwitz, 2013; M. H. Stone, 2010). This trend continued into the nineteenth century, with the medical model of anxiety eclipsing moral and religious perspectives. However, depression and anxiety still were more interconnected in nineteenth-century diagnostic categories than they are today. Neurasthenia (discussed in Chapter 5) was commonly diagnosed in people exhibiting both sadness and anxiety. This diagnosis was broader than today's more focused DSM and ICD anxiety disorders (M. H. Stone, 2010):

Neurasthenics complained of numerous yet amorphous physical pains, including headache, stomachache, back pain, fatigue, skin rashes, insomnia, asthma, and poor general health …. Although symptoms of anxiety were not among the most prominent aspects of neurasthenia, irrational concerns, various phobias, and fears of contamination were explicitly part of this condition. (A. V. Horwitz, 2013, p. 65)

As the nineteenth and early twentieth centuries unfolded, anxiety was increasingly distinguished in its own right—even though neurasthenia remained a popular catch-all diagnosis (A. V. Horwitz, 2013; R. B. Miller, 2015; M. H. Stone, 2010). For example, while obsessions and compulsions have been discussed for centuries, it wasn't until the 1830s that the early French alienist Jean-Étienne-Dominique Esquirol (1772–1840) provided the first detailed clinical descriptions of patients who today would be diagnosed with OCD: "Esquirol described a 34-year-old woman who feared retaining money in her hands when giving change to a customer, and who would vigorously shake her hands despite not having touched anything, in order to make sure nothing remained on her hands" (Gee et al., 2013, p. 37). Later, the French neurologist Édouard Brissaud (1852–1909) described "paroxystic anxiety," which today we would call a panic attack. Similarly, in 1901 another Frenchman—the psychiatrist Paul Hartenberg (1871–1949)—offered an early account of social anxiety disorder (Gee et al., 2013). He observed "how the presence of other humans precipitated in some people feelings of intense anguish, sweating, and heart palpitations" (A. V. Horwitz, 2013, p. 70). As one last example, German psychiatrist and neurologist Karl Friedrich Otto Westphal (1833–1890) coined the term "agoraphobia" to describe his male patients who "feared and avoided being alone in wide streets and open space" (Gee et al., 2013, p. 35). He was also the first to distinguish obsessions (recurrent thoughts) from delusions (demonstrably false thoughts) (W. K. Goodman et al., 2014).

In the twentieth century, DSM eventually reflected the move to distinguish anxiety from other presenting problems. DSM-I and -II both used the word neurosis, a psychodynamic term with anxiety at its center. However, it was with the appearance of DSM-III in 1980—with its strong emphasis on distinct diagnostic categories exhibiting high interrater reliability—that anxiety disorders as we now know them became fully differentiated from depression and other issues (A. V. Horwitz, 2013, 2021). Some historians and theorists have suggested a firm cleavage between anxiety and depression is unwise, as these experiences are interrelated (A. V. Horwitz, 2013; R. B. Miller, 2015). This explains modest support for the mixed anxiety and depression diagnosis (J. Fawcett et al., 2010), which is included in ICD-11 but not DSM-5-TR. Whether we will return to an approach where anxiety, depression, anger, and other emotions are less differentiated as separate disorders remains unclear, but it seems unlikely in an era that stresses discrete and reliable categories (A. V. Horwitz, 2013).

BIOLOGICAL PERSPECTIVES

6.6 Brain Chemistry Perspectives

Anxiety

Benzodiazepines and GABA

Anxiolytics: Drugs used to relieve anxiety; usually refers to benzodiazepines.

Benzodiazepines: Anxiolytic drugs that enhance the functioning of the inhibitory neurotransmitter GABA to reduce anxiety; sometimes also used as mood stabilizers.

With their emphasis on neurochemistry, brain chemistry perspectives are intertwined with the use of psychiatric drugs. The drugs used to relieve anxiety are called **anxiolytics**. **Benzodiazepines** are probably the most well-known anxiolytic drugs, although antidepressants are prescribed more often for anxiety. Benzodiazepines enhance the ability of gamma-aminobutyric acid (GABA) (the brain's primary inhibitory neurotransmitter; see Chapter 2) to bind with GABA-A receptors in the brain. This slows or stops neurons from firing and is believed to reduce anxiety (Gbemudu, 2021; C. Taylor & Nutt, 2004). Thus, it is sometimes hypothesized that a problem with GABA or its receptors is involved in anxiety disorders (Nuss, 2015). Unfortunately, it's not clear whether GABA inactivity leads to anxiety or anxiety leads to GABA inactivity. Regardless, benzodiazepines boost GABA.

Benzodiazepines were first introduced in the late 1950s as a safer and less addictive alternative to *barbiturates*, which are discussed in Chapter 11 (A. V. Horwitz, 2013; López-Muñoz et al., 2011). Marketed as *minor tranquilizers*—as opposed to major tranquilizers, another name for antipsychotics—benzodiazepines were once very popular, peaking at over 103 million prescriptions in 1975 (A. V. Horwitz, 2013). While generally deemed effective at reducing anxiety (Garakani et al., 2020), their use has steadily decreased over concerns that they are habit-forming; this trend is ongoing, with use dropping 12.1 percent between 2015 and 2020 (Express Scripts, 2020). Some research suggests that a fifth to a quarter of people on them for extended periods show signs of dependency (C. Taylor & Nutt, 2004). Further, when people stop taking them, anxiety often rebounds (Hearon & Otto, 2012). Such findings led to tighter regulation of benzodiazepines. The United Nations Commission on Narcotic Drugs, at the bequest of the World Health Organization, declared them controlled substances in 1984 (López-Muñoz et al., 2011). While some clinicians feel that concern over prescribing benzodiazepines is exaggerated (López-Muñoz et al., 2011; J. F. Rosenbaum, 2020; E. Silberman et al., 2021), the current consensus seems to be that they do pose an addiction risk with some patients—usually those with a history of drug abuse (Gandra et al., 2019; Hearon & Otto, 2012; Nash & Nutt, 2007; K. R. Tan et al., 2011). Additional side effects include memory loss, drowsiness, and impaired balance (Nash & Nutt, 2007). These days, benzodiazepines are most often prescribed for generalized anxiety disorder, panic disorder, and social anxiety disorder (Balon & Starcevic, 2020; Griebel & Holmes, 2013). However, to avoid dependency, clinicians are advised to only keep patients on these drugs for short periods when anxiety is most intense (Penninx et al., 2021; C. Taylor & Nutt, 2004). Table 6.1 lists common benzodiazepines prescribed for anxiety.

Table 6.1 Common Benzodiazepines Prescribed for Anxiety

- Alprazolam (Xanax)
- Bromazepam (Lectopam, Lexotan)
- Chlordiazepoxide (Librium)
- Clonazepam (Klonopin, Rivotril)
- Clorazepate (Tranxene)
- Diazepam (Valium)
- Lorazepam (Ativan)
- Oxazepam (Serax, Serapax)

Antidepressants and Monoamine Neurotransmitters

Antidepressants have overtaken benzodiazepines as the drugs of choice for anxiety. The rationale for prescribing them is that the same monoamine neurotransmitters implicated in depression (primarily norepinephrine and serotonin) are also associated with anxiety (Garakani et al., 2020; Nash & Nutt, 2007; A. A. Shah & Han, 2015). SSRI and SNRI antidepressants are considered first-line drug treatments for anxiety, though tricyclics, MAOIs, and atypical antidepressants are used too (Garakani et al., 2020; Griebel & Holmes, 2013; Nash & Nutt, 2007; A. A. Shah & Han, 2015). Due to unpleasant side effects like weight gain, sexual problems, dizziness, insomnia, and nausea, many patients stop taking them (Balsikci et al., 2014). Further, as noted in Chapter 5, some parents may hesitate to give their children SSRIs for anxiety problems such as selective mutism and separation anxiety due to controversial black box warnings about possible suicidal behavior (Fornaro et al., 2019; R. A. Friedman, 2014; Sparks & Duncan, 2013).

Other Drugs Prescribed as Anxiolytics

Several other drugs are used to relieve anxiety. **Buspirone** is an anxiolytic drug that increases serotonin activity—but it doesn't do so by blocking serotonin reuptake, so it isn't classified as an SSRI (Garakani et al., 2020; T. K. Wilson & Tripp, 2022). Buspirone is not habit-forming like the benzodiazepines, but it takes several weeks to take effect. Besides buspirone, numerous other drugs are occasionally used to address anxiety. *Antipsychotics* (which affect not only dopamine, but also block serotonin receptors), **beta blockers** (blood pressure reducing drugs that block norepinephrine receptors), and *anticonvulsants* (which enhance GABA activity) are all sometimes prescribed as anxiolytics—though evidence for their effectiveness is mixed or lacking and so they are usually deemed secondary treatments (Garakani et al., 2020; Nash & Nutt, 2007; C. Taylor & Nutt, 2004).

In addition to monoamines and the inhibitory neurotransmitter GABA, the excitatory neurotransmitter glutamate has drawn attention for its potential role in anxiety (Nasir et al., 2020; Sanacora et al., 2012). The anesthetic ketamine (which reduces glutamate levels and is approved for treatment-resistant depression; see Chapter 5) is being researched as a potential drug for anxiety. Results so far suggest it may be somewhat helpful for anxiety but less so for panic, with more studies needed (Dougherty et al., 2018; Glue et al., 2017, 2018; Silote et al., 2020).

Buspirone: An anti-anxiety drug that decreases serotonin levels, but not by blocking serotonin reuptake; thus, it is not classified as an SSRI.

Beta blockers: Blood pressure reducing drugs that block norepinephrine receptors; used to relieve anxiety.

Theresa and Tammy
Theresa Steadman's family doctor prescribes her Paxil, an SSRI antidepressant, for her anxiety. Despite Theresa's concerns about black box warnings over potential suicidal behavior in kids, her daughter Tammy is also prescribed an SSRI for her separation anxiety—Prozac. After a month or so on these drugs, both notice some improvement.

Obsessions and Compulsions
SSRIs and Serotonin

Prior to the mid-1970s, OCD was typically considered unresponsive to drug interventions (W. K. Goodman et al., 2014). However, trial and error use of antidepressants found them to be helpful. Therefore, researchers began to hypothesize that serotonin is implicated in OCD and related disorders (W. K. Goodman et al., 2014). SSRIs, which boost serotonin, are the most common antidepressants used to ameliorate obsessive-compulsive symptoms (Bandelow et al., 2012; Pittenger & Bloch, 2014; M. T. Williams et al., 2014). The SSRIs fluvoxamine (Luvox), fluoxetine (Prozac), sertraline (Zoloft), and paroxetine (Paxil) are frequently prescribed (M. T. Williams et al., 2014). SSRIs are also used for OCD-related problems such as body dysmorphia and hair-pulling (D. Castle et al., 2021; Fang et al., 2014; Sani et al., 2019). Interestingly, when used for OCD (compared with major depression), SSRIs take longer to fully impact symptoms (eight to twelve weeks) and usually require high doses. Why this is remains unknown (Pittenger & Bloch, 2014; Reddy & Arumugham, 2020).

Research has found that SSRIs reduce obsessions and compulsions (Del Casale et al., 2019; W. K. Goodman et al., 2014; Kotapati et al., 2019; E. W. Miller et al., 2019; Reddy & Arumugham, 2020).

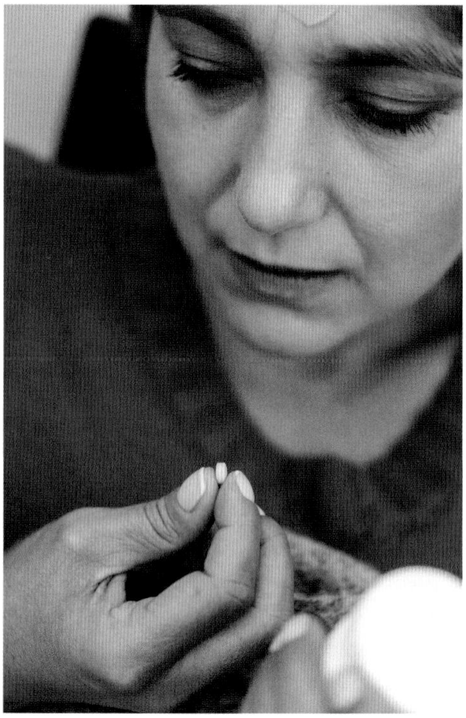

Photo 6.3 SSRIs reduce obsessions and compulsions for some people but not others.
Karolina Grabowska/Pexels.

Yet they are not cure-alls. Between 25 percent and 60 percent of OCD patients do not respond to them (M. T. Williams et al., 2014). Further, they tend to work best in conjunction with cognitive-behavioral interventions (W. K. Goodman et al., 2021; Romanelli et al., 2014). OCD patients who benefit from antidepressants are urged to remain on them for at least a year and preferably indefinitely because 80 percent to 90 percent of those who stop taking them relapse (Bystritsky, 2004; M. T. Williams et al., 2014). However, convincing people to stay on these drugs is difficult due to their side effects. Because SSRIs tend to have fewer side effects than other antidepressants, they are usually tried first. If they prove ineffective, an older tricyclic antidepressant (typically *clomipramine*) is usually prescribed (M. T. Williams et al., 2014). Side effects notwithstanding, clomipramine is as effective as SSRIs for OCD (Pittenger & Bloch, 2014; Reddy & Arumugham, 2020; M. T. Williams et al., 2014).

Augmenting Agents

Because SSRIs alone are often not that helpful, OCD patients are sometimes given other drugs at the same time. Secondary drugs used to improve the impact of primary drugs are known as *augmenting agents*. Benzodiazepines, mood stabilizers, atypical antipsychotics, and glutamate-modulating drugs are all used as augmenting agents to improve the effect of SSRIs for OCD (Pittenger & Bloch, 2014; Reddy & Arumugham, 2020; M. T. Williams et al., 2014). Not everyone supports all the augmenting agents used for OCD. For instance, some say the benefits of antipsychotics are offset by their long-term side effects (Reddy & Arumugham, 2020).

Glutamate Hypothesis of OCD

Glutamate hypothesis of OCD: Contends that obsessive-compulsive disorder (OCD) results from excess glutamate.

As with anxiety, glutamate has increasingly gained attention for its possible role in obsessions and compulsions (Dougherty et al., 2018; W. K. Goodman et al., 2021). The **glutamate hypothesis of OCD** (reminiscent of the glutamate hypothesis of depression) contends that OCD results from excess glutamate. Researchers are studying glutamate's role and the potential of glutamate-inhibiting drugs such as *topiramate* (a seizure disorder drug) and *riluzole* (a drug for amyotrophic lateral sclerosis [ALS]) (Dougherty et al., 2018; W. K. Goodman et al., 2021; Reddy & Arumugham, 2020).

> **Gary**
> *Gary Steadman is prescribed Zoloft for his OCD. He remains on it for a few months, but it doesn't relieve his symptoms. His doctor switches him to Prozac and eventually—when that doesn't help either—to Luvox. The Luvox improves Gary's symptoms, but only after he takes it for ten weeks. Had the Luvox not worked, the doctor's next plan would have been to augment it with a benzodiazepine or switch to the tricyclic antidepressant clomipramine.*

6.7 Brain Structure and Function Perspectives

Anxiety and Fear

In Chapter 5, we noted that the amygdala (important in emotional memory) tends to be highly active in depressed people (J. R. Swartz et al., 2015). The same is true for anxiety and fear. The amygdala has been identified as a central structure in the brain's *fear circuit*, which stores classically conditioned fear-related associations (LeDoux, 2015). Consistent with this, brain scan research has repeatedly linked anxiety to high levels of amygdala activity (Bas-Hoogendam & Westenberg, 2020; Kolesar et al., 2019; Linsambarth et al., 2017; Madonna et al., 2019). It is also tied to activity in the *insula*, a small area deep within the cerebral cortex believed to play a role in socio-emotional processing (Alvarez et al., 2015; Brühl et al., 2014; Kolesar et al., 2019; Madonna et al., 2019; C. K. Schmidt et al., 2018; L. Q. Uddin et al., 2017). Thus, one theory of anxiety disorders is that they result from excessive reactivity of the amygdala and insula (Etkin, 2012; Etkin & Wager, 2007; M. G. Newman et al., 2013). Interestingly, these two brain structures aren't only implicated in anxiety disorders. They are also linked to PTSD, which DSM and ICD no longer consider an anxiety disorder. From an RDoC perspective (see Chapter 3), this exemplifies how DSM and ICD don't always use biological data to inform their decision-making. More on PTSD in Chapter 7.

Obsessions and Compulsions

Given that compulsions reflect impulse-control problems, prefrontal brain regions involved in executive functioning and goal-directed behavior might be implicated. The **cortico-striatal-thalamo-cortical loop (CBGTC) hypothesis** proposes that OCD involves dysfunction in circuitry linking the *orbitofrontal cortex* (important in goal-directed behavior), *anterior cingulate cortex* (implicated in decision-making, anticipating rewards, emotion, and impulse control), *thalamus* (relays sensory information), *striatum* (part of the brain's reward system), and *basal ganglia* (important in voluntary motor movement) (Maia et al., 2008; Saxena et al., 2001). OCD might result when CBGTC loop activity gets out of balance. Although questions remain, this hypothesis is generating a lot of research (Beucke et al., 2020; Dogan et al., 2019; Dong et al., 2020; K. Dunlop et al., 2016, p. 2016; Kubota et al., 2019; T. W. Robbins et al., 2019; J. Wood & Ahmari, 2015; T. Xu et al., 2021; Q. Zhao et al., 2021).

OCD brain structure research often yields inconsistent or inconclusive results (Menzies et al., 2008; T. W. Robbins et al., 2019). Why? In keeping with the RDoC model, perhaps OCD isn't one disorder, but numerous disorders—each with its own brain pathology (Mataix-Cols, 2006; Mataix-Cols et al., 2004). Along these lines, it has been proposed that different types of OCD symptom patterns—"symmetry/ordering," "contamination/wishing," and "harm/checking"—show distinct patterns of brain structure activity and volume (Leopold & Backenstrass, 2015; van den Heuvel et al., 2009). Hopefully, future research will clarify current understandings.

Cortico-striatal-thalamo-cortical loop (CBGTC) hypothesis: OCD involves dysfunction in the circuitry linking the *orbitofrontal cortex* (important in goal-directed behavior), *anterior cingulate cortex* (implicated in decision-making, anticipating rewards, emotion, and impulse control), *thalamus* (relays sensory information), *striatum* (part of the brain's reward system), and *basal ganglia* (important in voluntary motor movement).

6.8 Genetic Perspectives

Anxiety

Anxiety appears to run in families, perhaps because some people are genetically predisposed to an anxious temperament (S. Taylor et al., 2010). Research has consistently found first-degree relatives of people with generalized anxiety disorder, panic disorder, specific phobia, social anxiety disorder, and agoraphobia are at increased risk for these same problems (Hettema et al., 2001; Schumacher et al., 2011; Shimada-Sugimoto et al., 2015; Telman et al., 2018). Likewise, twin studies also suggest a genetic influence on anxiety (Ask et al., 2021; M. N. Davies et al., 2015; Skre et al., 1993; Torgersen, 1986). Such studies have generated low to moderate heritability for anxiety disorders, with 20 percent to 60 percent of phenotypic variation attributed to genetic influences (Ask et al., 2021). These estimates are comparable to those for major depression and imply that anxiety is partly due to genetics. Of course, there is debate over the trustworthiness of heritability estimates and how they should be interpreted (J. Joseph, 2012, 2013). When it comes to identifying specific genes in anxiety disorders, candidate gene studies have yielded mixed results, making it difficult to draw conclusions (Shimada-Sugimoto et al., 2015). The largest number of gene association studies have been done on panic disorder. Though there are several promising candidate genes, results have not always been consistent or replicated (A. S. Howe et al., 2016; Maron et al., 2010).

Obsessions and Compulsions

Family studies support the contention that OCD and related disorders have a genetic influence (Cath et al., 2019). One review reported that 12 percent of first-degree relatives of those with OCD also met the criteria for it, compared with only 2 percent among relatives of control families (Nicolini et al., 2009). Another found that 6.7 percent to 15 percent of first-degree relatives of children diagnosed with OCD also had it (Mundo et al., 2006). Family members of people with OCD are not only at increased risk of being diagnosed with OCD but are also more likely to be diagnosed with generalized anxiety disorder, separation anxiety disorder, panic disorder, agoraphobia, tic disorders, and attention-deficit hyperactivity disorder (Cath et al., 2019; Nicolini et al., 2009). While family studies don't control for shared environment, they nonetheless provide imperfect evidence that people with similar genetic backgrounds may be predisposed to obsessive-compulsive symptoms and other forms of anxiety.

Many but not all twin studies on OCD also suggest a genetic contribution (H. A. Browne et al., 2014; Cath et al., 2019; Nicolini et al., 2009; Pauls, 2012). One review concluded that identical twin concordance for OCD ranges from 62 percent to 87 percent (M. Wolff et al., 2000). Because twin studies often suffer from methodological limitations, more conservative estimates of identical twin concordance are between 18 percent and 87 percent (Pauls, 2012). Yes, this is a wide range! However, one large twin study provided a more precise concordance rate of 52 percent for identical twins compared with 21 percent for fraternal twins; heritability estimates ascribed 48 percent of variance to genetics (H. A. Browne et al., 2014). These results imply that genes matter, but so does environment.

Given that monoamines (serotonin, norepinephrine, and glutamate) and glutamate are implicated in OCD and related disorders, it is not surprising that genes related to these neurotransmitters have been linked to obsessions and compulsions (Grünblatt et al., 2014; Zai et al., 2019). As one example, a region of the serotonin transporter (*5-HTT*) gene known as 5-HTTLPR has garnered a lot of attention for its potential role in OCD (Grünblatt et al., 2014; S. Taylor, 2013; Zai et al., 2019). Genes related to glutamate (e.g., *SLC1A1*), dopamine (e.g., *COMT*), and GABA (e.g., *BDNF*) have also been associated with OCD, but findings vary (Zai et al., 2019). There is particular interest these days in the glutamatergic system genes. This fits with previously discussed theorizing about the CBGTC loop, which involves glutamate transmission (Grünblatt et al., 2014; Rajendram et al., 2017).

Like other mental disorder categories, OCD involves a complex set of behaviors, cognitions, and feelings. Thus, susceptibility to it is impacted by many different genes, making it unlikely we will ever discover a single "OCD gene." Not only are multiple genes probably involved, but environment matters too. In other words, "a heterogeneous disorder such as OCD cannot fully be explained by a simple one-gene cause and effect model. This lends support to not only a polygenic [multiple gene] model but also to the possible role of environment-gene interactions" (Mak et al., 2015, p. 440).

6.9 Evolutionary Perspectives

Anxiety as Adaptive

From evolutionary perspectives, fear and anxiety are "part of an elaborate menu of defensive, adaptive processes that have evolved over millions of years in us humans and our mammalian ancestors" (Hofmann et al., 2002, p. 317). These emotions alert us to danger, which improves our odds of surviving and reproducing. However, if they become too intense or interfere with daily living, then anxiety disorders are diagnosed. Said another way, "everyone recognizes that anxiety is a useful trait that has been shaped by natural selection. Even good things, however, cease to be good when they become excessive" (I. M. Marks & Nesse, 1994, p. 247).

Prepared Conditioning

Prepared conditioning:
Conditioning that is easier to accomplish because the organism is evolutionarily predisposed to it.

Evolutionary psychologists critique behaviorists for attributing fear and anxiety reactions entirely to environmental conditioning. They point to **prepared conditioning**, the idea that some phobias are easier to condition than others because our species' evolutionary history physiologically predisposes us to them (M. E. P. Seligman, 1971). Thus, we are biologically primed to develop phobias of some things (like heights, rats, bugs, and blood), even though other things (like cars and planes) are more dangerous to us in modern society (Hofmann et al., 2002; Mineka & Öhman, 2002; Zafiropoulou & Pappa, 2002). As noted in Chapter 2, lots of people are phobic of bugs, but very few of automobiles.

Malfunctioning Mental Mechanisms

More broadly, evolutionary theorists contend that problems with anxiety, obsessions, and compulsions occur when evolved mental mechanisms (or *adaptations*) meant to keep people safe malfunction (Feygin et al., 2006; Glass, 2012; Hofmann et al., 2002; I. M. Marks & Nesse, 1994; J. S. Price, 2013; D. J. Stein & Bouwer, 1997; D. J. Stein & Nesse, 2011). For example, *escape or avoidance* responses are often highly adaptive because they help people elude threatening situations (I. M. Marks

& Nesse, 1994). However, an overly responsive escape or avoidance mechanism leads to problems such as generalized anxiety, phobias, and social anxiety. Similarly, *freezing/immobility* responses evolved to let people conceal themselves and assess dangerous situations (I. M. Marks & Nesse, 1994). Yet if the apparatus behind such responses becomes maladaptive, then it provokes so much inhibition that one can't engage with the world—as happens in cases of selective mutism, for example. Finally, *submission/appeasement* is also adaptive, especially in helping people get along peaceably with others in their own social group (I. M. Marks & Nesse, 1994). However, like freezing/immobility, when it leads to too much inhibition, problems like social anxiety and selective mutism may result.

Group Selection

Group selection is a hypothesized process by which different members of a species or social group evolve specialized functions that benefit the larger community (Polimeni et al., 2005). Among honeybees, for example, we find workers, drones, and a queen—each with distinct and important jobs that contribute to and strengthen the hive. The **group selection theory of OCD** proposes that checking, cleaning, and hoarding behaviors are adaptive and important but also time-consuming (Polimeni et al., 2005). If everyone did them, it would place too many members of the group at risk. However, by having specific individuals focused on these vital tasks, the entire group benefits without everybody needing to expend energy on them. Unfortunately, inheriting a tendency toward checking, cleaning, and hoarding may not be adaptive in modern society. Those who have it may be diagnosed with OCD.

Group selection theory of OCD: OCD behaviors developed via group selection; having some group members partake in time-consuming behaviors (e.g., checking, cleaning, and hoarding) benefits the entire group without everyone needing to expend energy on them.

Evaluating Evolutionary Perspectives

Evolutionary perspectives are criticized for relying on the idea of evolved mental mechanisms, or adaptations. Detractors maintain that such mechanisms are assumed, not proven (Chrisler & Erchull, 2011; Gannon, 2002; B. M. Peters, 2013; Raskin, 2013). That is, we can't directly observe the mental mechanisms that supposedly control human anxiety responses—which makes evolutionary accounts hypothetical and impossible to test (Feygin et al., 2006). Further, the notion of evolutionary mechanisms provides something of a circular argument: People behave anxiously because these mechanisms exist, and we know these mechanisms exist because people behave anxiously. Nonetheless, the evolutionary perspective is compelling and continues to influence how we think about anxiety, obsessions, and compulsions.

6.10 Immune System Perspectives

Inflammation

As with psychosis and mood problem (see Chapters 4 and 5), immune system inflammation is correlated with anxiety, obsessions, and compulsions—although research results haven't always confirmed this (Dell'Osso et al., 2016; Furtado & Katzman, 2015; S. T. H. Lee, 2020; Marazziti et al., 2015; Najjar et al., 2013; C. Parsons et al., 2020; W. A. van Eeden et al., 2021; Zainal & Newman, 2022). Inflammatory cytokines—the small immune-system produced proteins that aid healing but cause swelling in large amounts—are often increased among people diagnosed with anxiety and obsessive-compulsive disorders (Fluitman et al., 2010; Furtado & Katzman, 2015; Hou et al., 2017; Marazziti et al., 2015; Najjar et al., 2013; C. Parsons et al., 2020; N. P. Rao et al., 2015; M. Uddin & Diwadkar, 2014; Zainal & Newman, 2022). Altered levels of cortisol (sometimes increased, sometimes decreased) have also been found, occasionally with gender differences (Furtado & Katzman, 2015; Hou & Baldwin, 2012; Kische et al., 2021; Kluge et al., 2007; Yousry Elnazer & Baldwin, 2014; Zorn et al., 2017). Anxiety may sometimes produce an upsurge in the release of cortisol, the body's main stress hormone (after all, anxiety is stressful), but other times may result in physiological adjustment to anxiety (resulting in lower cortisol levels) (Furtado & Katzman, 2015).

The Gut

Anxiety/OCD researchers are increasingly interested in the **gut–brain axis**, the system of biochemical connections between the gut and brain (Crumeyrolle-Arias et al., 2014; J. A. Foster & McVey Neufeld, 2013; Rutsch et al., 2020; Turna et al., 2016). The *gut* (or *gastrointestinal tract*)

Gut–brain axis: System of biochemical connections between the *gut* (or *gastrointestinal tract*) and brain; imbalances in gut bacteria (*gut microbiome*) are suspected of playing roles in anxiety, OCD, depression, autism, psychosis, and other presenting problems.

is the tube extending from the mouth to the anus through which food is taken in and digested. The gut contains *bacteria* (also known as *gut microbiome*) necessary for digestion and health (P. Ho & Ross, 2017; Turna et al., 2016). Gut microbiomes help absorb nutrients, prevent bad bacteria from accumulating, and are important in the release of cytokines. Thus, they are intimately tied to inflammation and immune system function (P. Ho & Ross, 2017). Researchers are exploring the relationship between anxiety/OCD symptoms and gut microbiome imbalances (J. A. Foster & McVey Neufeld, 2013; Rutsch et al., 2020). The gut's influence isn't limited to anxiety and OCD. Researchers are studying its role in other forms of mental distress—including depression, autism, nonsuicidal self-injury, and psychosis (Burokas et al., 2017; J. A. Foster & McVey Neufeld, 2013; P. Ho & Ross, 2017; Rutsch et al., 2020; Turna et al., 2016).

Despite the promise gut–brain research holds for understanding anxiety and other presenting problems, the exact relationship among the gut, the immune system, neurotransmitters, and brain circuity remains unclear (Turna et al., 2016). Some researchers suspect that dietary supplements containing healthy gut bacteria can reduce anxiety and depression, but more evidence is needed (Bear et al., 2020; M. I. Butler et al., 2019; Larroya et al., 2021). Still, this emerging area of research may clarify why anxiety is often felt in the stomach. Perhaps those butterflies before a big exam have a biological basis after all!

6.11 Evaluating Biological Perspectives

It surprises many people that antidepressants are a mainline treatment for anxiety, obsessions, and compulsions. However, once it is understood that these symptoms are highly comorbid with depression, the widespread use of antidepressants becomes more understandable. Consider, for instance, that 90 percent of people diagnosed with OCD are thought to have another comorbid mental disorder—with 40 percent suspected of having a depressive disorder and 75 percent an anxiety disorder (M. T. Williams et al., 2014). Do high levels of comorbidity mean that people are suffering from distinct anatomical disorders, or does it reflect our current inability to distinguish these problems at a biological level? Critics of biological models of anxiety contend it is the latter. In their view, using the same drugs for all these problems suggests that our knowledge of what is going on biochemically across presenting problems remains basic and undifferentiated.

While numerous brain structures and genes have been implicated in anxiety, problems with replicating findings combined with the fact that most of this research is correlational provide ample reason to pause before concluding that anxiety can be explained primarily in biological terms. Critics contend that biological approaches to anxiety, obsessions, and compulsions sometimes minimize the important roles of psychological and sociocultural factors—especially considering evidence that therapy may be as or more effective for such issues (Bandelow et al., 2015; Öst et al., 2015). We next turn to psychological and sociocultural conceptions of anxiety.

PSYCHOLOGICAL PERSPECTIVES

6.12 Psychodynamic Perspectives

One of the challenges for psychodynamic therapies is that, "unlike CBT" they are "traditionally not tailored to single mental disorders or specific symptoms" (Leichsenring & Salzer, 2014, p. 226). Instead, they focus "on core underlying processes" that cut across all disorders (Leichsenring & Salzer, 2014, p. 226). Thus, psychodynamic perspectives tend to see all presenting problems generally—and various anxiety disorder categories specifically—as having similar origins in unconscious conflicts.

Classic Freudian Case Studies

The psychodynamic interest in unconscious meanings can be traced to Freud himself. His cases of Little Hans and the Rat Man provide vivid examples of a psychoanalytic approach to anxiety, obsessions, and compulsions (Freud, 1909/1955a, 1909/1955b). *Little Hans* was a 5-year-old boy who developed an intense fear of horses, worrying that one might fall on him or bite him. Hans' father asked Freud for advice in understanding this peculiar phobia. Freud (1909/1955a) hypothesized that

Hans' phobia reflected an unresolved Oedipus complex (see Chapter 2), with Hans displacing Oedipal-anger toward his father (including fear of being castrated by him) onto horses. Thus, Hans' phobia symbolically expressed castration anxiety. By achieving insight into this unconscious conflict, Hans' phobia of horses was eliminated.

The *Rat Man* was an attorney in his late twenties whose main symptom was fear that something terrible might befall his father and fiancée—even though his father was already dead. More specifically, the Rat Man experienced obsessions about rats boring into the anuses of his father and fiancée. He also felt a compulsion to slit his own throat with a razor. Freud (1909/1955b) tracked these symptoms back to childhood sexual abuse of the Rat Man by his governesses. The Rat Man worried about his father finding out about these experiences and developed an unconscious conflict: "If I have this wish to see a woman naked, my father will be bound to die" (Freud, 1909/1955b, p. 163). When he became an adult with a fiancée he was attracted to, this conflict reemerged. Freud's nearly yearlong psychoanalysis with the Rat Man made the conflict conscious so it could be resolved, eliminating the obsessions and compulsions.

Unconscious Impulses and Anxiety

Like Freud, modern psychodynamic therapies "conceptualize anxiety disorders as developing from wishes, feelings, and fantasies, often unconscious, that are experienced as frightening or intolerable" (Busch et al., 2010, p. 125). Chronic worry emerges from either unacceptable repressed wishes or inconsistent parenting in early life. In the former case, powerful but problematic unconscious impulses overwhelm the person, resulting in an "ongoing threat and struggle with unacceptable feelings and fantasies"—hence the emergence of anxiety (Busch & Milrod, 2015, p. 155). In the latter case, the anxious person lacks secure attachments in childhood (Guo & Ash, 2020). Inconsistent parenting leads to "perceptions that the child will be rejected by the parent, cannot depend on the parent for care, or must take care of a fragile or incompetent parent" and this "chronic fear of disruption in attachments" exacerbates prolonged worry (Busch & Milrod, 2015, p. 155).

Insecure Attachments and OCD

Problematic attachment relationships are also implicated in psychodynamic notions of OCD. Psychodynamic therapists argue that people are at risk for OCD when intrusive thoughts threaten "core perceptions of the self" (Doron et al., 2015, p. 202). In this interpretation, OCD develops in people whose parents are emotionally ambivalent or superficially supportive but subtly rejecting. As a result, the person lacks secure attachment to others and becomes extremely sensitive and self-doubting about things such as job and school performance, morality, and relationship success. Intrusive thoughts or events related to these areas negatively affect feelings of self-worth and trigger efforts to compensate for or correct such feelings—often in the form of compulsive behaviors. Ironically, the compulsive behaviors often produce more intrusive negative thoughts, which only worsens the original problem. Unfortunately, the only randomized controlled trial of psychodynamic therapy for OCD to date did not find it effective (Maina et al., 2010).

Photo 6.4 Freud and his grandson Stephen Gabriel Freud, 1922.
Wikimedia Commons.

Gary

Gary Steadman's parents were often subtly critical and rejecting of Gary, although outwardly they appeared supportive. As he grew up, Gary felt unsure of himself and his abilities. Despite succeeding in his career, he experienced himself as incompetent; many of his obsessions and compulsions centered on his uncertainty about whether he had done something correctly ("I can't trust myself to remember to turn off the stove, set the thermostat, or meet my boss' expectations"). He also worried he wasn't smart or attractive enough for his wife, Theresa—and often found himself obsessing about whether he belonged with her. Psychodynamic therapy would focus on addressing Gary's self-doubt and insecure attachments to significant people in his life.

Unified Psychodynamic Protocol for Anxiety Disorders (UPP-ANXIETY)

Unified psychodynamic therapy protocol for anxiety disorders (UPP-ANXIETY):
Psychodynamic protocol for all anxiety disorders; therapy is broken into concrete steps (or "modules"), each with empirical support for its effectiveness.

Although psychodynamic therapies are sometimes criticized for lacking research evidence, the **unified psychodynamic protocol for anxiety disorders (UPP-ANXIETY)** integrates empirically supported treatment principles into a therapy useable with all anxiety disorders (Leichsenring & Salzer, 2014). The therapy is divided into concrete steps, or "modules." After being socialized into therapy, treatment goals are set. Patients explore their relationship patterns, map underlying conflicts that produce anxiety, and examine the strategies they use to ward off anxiety. As they gain insight into these conflicts and the defenses that they use to cope with them, patients begin to alter longstanding relational patterns and overcome their anxiety. Because UPP-ANXIETY psychodynamic therapy has strong empirical support and can be tailored to each patient, its developers see it as an effective method for treating anxiety and related emotional disorders (Leichsenring & Salzer, 2014; Leichsenring & Steinert, 2018, 2019). Critics still view cognitive-behavioral therapy as more effective and having a stronger evidence base than psychodynamic therapy (Bandelow et al., 2014, 2015, 2021; A. A. Shah & Han, 2015). However, supporters point to studies showing psychodynamic therapies for anxiety can be as effective as CBT (Bögels et al., 2014; Leichsenring & Steinert, 2019; F. Monti et al., 2014).

Theresa

If Theresa Steadman underwent psychodynamic therapy, she would be encouraged to talk about past relationships. These conversations would reveal that while growing up, she had a younger sister who had many emotional and behavioral problems that consumed her parents' attention. Thus, Theresa came to believe she could make her parents' lives less stressful by not causing them additional grief beyond that caused by her sister. Being a well-behaved and compliant high achiever shielded her parents from further stress. However, this also placed pressure on Theresa. Any time she didn't live up to her high standards, she felt like she was hurting her parents. Further, she lost track of what mattered to her. Psychodynamic therapy would focus on the unconscious conflict "I must always succeed to spare others stress—regardless of my own feelings about what I'm doing." This would explain why, after being promoted at work and asked to do more public speaking (something she didn't want to do), she began experiencing social anxiety. The promotion triggered an internal conflict in which she either had to succeed at an unwanted task (public speaking) or feel like she massively disappointed others who—like her parents—she believed had more important problems to worry about. Psychodynamic therapy would help Theresa understand this unconscious conflict, its origins, and the strategies she has relied on to keep it at bay. Consequently, it would be expected that her anxiety (both about public speaking and in general) would resolve. She eventually might even speak to her boss about a career trajectory more in keeping with her interests.

6.13 Cognitive-Behavioral Perspectives

CBT Conceptualizations of Anxiety and Panic
Conditioning and Social Learning of Anxiety

According to strictly behavioral perspectives, anxiety is caused by environmental conditioning. A phobia, for example, is classically conditioned. Recall the case study of Little Albert, in which John Watson and Rosalie Rayner (1920) took a white rat (a neutral stimulus that Albert wasn't initially scared of at 9 months old) and repeatedly paired it with a loud noise—an unconditioned stimulus (US) that naturally evoked fear. After the white rat was associated with the loud noise, it became a conditioned stimulus (CS) that caused anxiety on its own. Consequently, Albert began showing a phobic response to the rat—even though initially it hadn't frightened him. Behaviorists contend that all anxiety reactions are conditioned in this manner.

Although anxiety responses are often conceptualized as classically conditioned, operant conditioning is important in sustaining them. Because their anxiety decreases when they avoid situations that scare them, people are negative reinforced for doing so (Mowrer, 1939, 1947). Given that they do not test their fears, anxious people don't have an opportunity to learn that their fears aren't as bad as they think. Thus, the anxiety never extinguishes.

Of course, anxiety doesn't have to develop from first-hand experience. According to social learning theory (introduced in Chapter 2), people often take cues from others when it comes to anxiety. *Observational learning*—in which people learn behavioral and emotional reactions by watching other people model responses to situations—is integral to this process.

Gary, Theresa, and Tammy

Theresa and Gary Steadman have modeled many anxiety reactions for their daughter, Tammy. Tammy has observed her father Gary's anxiety when he calls his wife Theresa at work, and she fails to answer her phone. Gary becomes very agitated, breaks out in a sweat, and frantically dials Theresa again and again until he reaches her. In so doing, Gary has inadvertently modeled anxious behavior, which Tammy—through the process of observational learning—repeats when her parents leave for work.

Cognitive Explanations of Anxiety

Cognitive models of anxiety hold that anxiety results from faulty thinking. For example, cognitive therapy founder Aaron Beck proposed that pathologically anxious people make exaggerated threat appraisals and believe themselves unable to handle dangerous situations (D. A. Clark & Beck, 2010). Other cognitive models of generalized anxiety build on Beck's idea that pathological anxiety is tied to faulty cognitive processing. Consider these four examples:

- The *avoidance model of worry* maintains that people often are anxious about negative events befalling them in the future (Behar et al., 2009; Borkovec et al., 2004; P. L. Fisher & Wells, 2011; R. Warren, 2020). Because the events haven't happened yet, fight or flight responses aren't possible. The only alternative is to worry, which is negatively reinforced because thinking about anxiety-provoking possibilities is less stressful than experiencing more intense physiological symptoms of anxiety.

- The *intolerance of uncertainty model* posits that ongoing anxiety occurs in those who have difficulty handling uncertainty (Carleton, 2012, 2016; Dugas et al., 1997). Such people tend to have a negative problem orientation, seeing challenges as threatening and insurmountable—thus, problems are avoided. They also hold positive beliefs about worry, viewing it as essential in motivating problem-solving.

- The *metacognitive model* focuses on how people think about worrying (A. Wells, 1995, 2010). It hypothesizes that people hold both positive and negative beliefs about worry. Examples of positive beliefs are "worrying helps me to cope" and "worry helps me to deal with problems more effectively" (P. L. Fisher & Wells, 2011, p. 129). Negative beliefs see worry as uncontrollable and harmful. When such beliefs become powerful, there is a tendency to begin worrying about how much one is worrying.

- The *emotional dysregulation model* contends that anxious people have difficulty regulating their emotions and therefore find strong emotions highly aversive (Mennin et al., 2004). They experience their emotions very intensely and have a difficult time identifying and understanding their feelings. Consequently, they respond poorly to their emotions and attribute negative consequences to experiencing them.

Cognitive Explanations of Panic and Agoraphobia

From a cognitive standpoint, people susceptible to panic disorder and agoraphobia tend to be extremely sensitive and attuned to subtle physiological variations—such as increased heart rate, altered blood pressure, or fluctuations in breathing rate. The **catastrophic misinterpretation model of panic disorder** holds that people prone to recurrent, unexpected panic attacks catastrophically misinterpret bodily sensations (D. W. Austin & Richards, 2001; D. M. Clark, 1986; D. M. Clark & Ehlers, 1993). The more they interpret sensations in an anxious way, the stronger the sensations become—eventually resulting in a full-blown panic attack.

The sensations which are misinterpreted are mainly those which are involved in normal anxiety responses (e.g. palpitations, breathlessness, dizziness etc.) but also include some other bodily sensations. The catastrophic misinterpretation involves perceiving these sensations as much more dangerous than

Cognitive models of anxiety: Hold that anxiety results from faulty thinking processes; besides Beck's model, other well-known cognitive models include the *avoidance model of worry*, the *intolerance of uncertainty model*, the *metacognitive model*, and the *emotional dysregulation model*.

Catastrophic misinterpretation model of panic disorder: People prone to recurrent, unexpected panic attacks catastrophically misinterpret certain bodily sensations; the more they interpret sensations in an anxious way, the stronger the sensations become—eventually resulting in a full-blown panic attack.

they really are. Examples of catastrophic misinterpretations would be a healthy individual perceiving palpitations as evidence of impending heart attack; perceiving a slight feeling of breathlessness as evidence of impending cessation of breathing and consequent death; or perceiving a shaky feeling as evidence of impending loss of control and insanity. (D. M. Clark, 1986, p. 462)

Research generally supports the catastrophic misinterpretation model (Ohst & Tuschen-Caffier, 2018, 2020). Cognitive therapy for panic disorder focuses on changing clients' interpretations of bodily events (D. M. Clark & Salkovskis, 2009; Roy-Byrne et al., 2006; Salkovskis, 2007). Psychoeducation is employed to teach clients about their tendency to catastrophically misinterpret bodily feedback. This is combined with cognitive interventions to correct faulty beliefs about panic symptoms. Behavioral activation (introduced in Chapter 5) is also used to disconfirm client predictions that certain situations will produce panic attacks. A client who avoids elevators because she thinks they will make her panic might be taken on an elevator ride. When panic doesn't occur, the client's previous predictions are disconfirmed and her beliefs about elevators are apt to change. Finally, exposure therapies (discussed below) are employed in which bodily changes such as dizziness, heart palpitations, and shortness of breath are induced to show clients that these events don't necessarily lead to panic attacks.

CBT Conceptualizations of Obsessions and Compulsions
Behavioral Conditioning

Behavioral perspectives invoke both classical and operant conditioning to explain obsessions and compulsions (Mowrer, 1939, 1956, 1960). The trouble begins when neutral stimuli become classically conditioned through repeated pairings with threatening objects or events; consequently, they elicit anxiety and fear. People with OCD respond to the resulting anxiety by obsessing about it. To cope, they also engage in mental or behavioral rituals. These rituals—what we have been calling compulsions—bring temporary relief from anxiety, which negatively reinforces them. It becomes a never-ending vicious cycle.

> **Gary**
>
> *For Gary, the stove and security systems in his home have become anxiety-producing conditioned stimuli that lead to obsessive thinking. To alleviate his anxiety, Gary engages in compulsive rituals. He repeatedly checks whether the stove is on and the home security system off. From a behavioral standpoint, these rituals are negatively reinforced because when Gary does them his anxiety is momentarily relieved. Gary's compulsive behavior is maintained by the ongoing, if temporary, reinforcement he receives.*

Cognitive Explanations

Cognitive models of OCD maintain that everyone periodically has intrusive thoughts, but obsessive patients overestimate the importance of such thoughts (Salkovskis, 1985). This increases their risk for OCD, especially during times of stress (Rachman, 1997, 1998). In cases of OCD, intrusive thoughts trigger upsetting (and erroneous) automatic thoughts. For example, people with OCD often interpret their intrusive cognitions as indicating they "may be, may have been, or may come to be, responsible for harm or its prevention" (Salkovskis et al., 1998, p. 57). They also engage in *thought–action fusion* (in which they mistakenly believe that thinking something is the same as doing it) and *inferential confusion* (in which they conflate imagined events with actual events). In all these instances, OCD is attributable to faulty thinking.

Common CBT Interventions for Anxiety, Obsessions, and Compulsions
Exposure plus Response Prevention

For anxiety and OCD, exposure therapies are considered first-line, research-supported behavioral interventions (Ferrando & Selai, 2021; Hezel & Simpson, 2019; Kaczkurkin & Foa, 2015). As discussed in Chapter 2, exposure therapies involve placing clients in the presence of conditioned stimuli to extinguish old responses and condition new ones. In **exposure plus response prevention** (also called *flooding and response prevention*), the client is placed in direct contact with the anxiety-

Cognitive models of OCD: Maintain that everyone periodically has intrusive thoughts, but obsessive patients overestimate the importance of such thoughts—especially during times of stress.

Exposure plus response prevention: Exposure technique in which client is thrust into contact with the conditioned stimulus and prevented from leaving the situation; client learns nothing bad happens when in contact with the stimulus; also called *flooding and response prevention*.

provoking stimulus and prevented from leaving the situation (Baum, 1970; L. A. Zoellner et al., 2008). For example, someone afraid of cats might have a cat placed in her lap. When nothing bad happens, she will calm down and form a new association between the cat and feeling calm. Exposure plus response prevention is often used to address anxiety, obsessions, and compulsions.

Gary

Imagine a behavior therapist uses flooding and response prevention with Gary. Gary would be placed in the heart of an anxiety-provoking situation—for instance, getting ready for work in the morning. While getting ready, he would inevitably feel compelled to check the stove and house alarm but would be prevented from doing so. At first, this might cause Gary's anxiety to increase, but after a few minutes he would realize that nothing bad has happened even though he hasn't gone through his lengthy checking rituals. Gary would therefore begin to calm down. After numerous sessions of flooding and response prevention, Gary would feel calm rather than anxious while preparing for work, even when he doesn't compulsively check. Why? Because a new emotional response has been conditioned!

Systematic Desensitization

The danger in flooding is that sometimes the person being flooded panics rather than calms down when placed in the heart of the feared situation, and this strengthens the association between anxiety and the feared object. To avoid this risk, many behavior therapists instead use **systematic desensitization** (Head & Gross, 2008; Wolpe, 1961, 1968). Systematic desensitization consists of two parts: a *fear hierarchy* and *relaxation training*. In conjunction with their therapists, clients develop a fear hierarchy that ranks potential experiences with the feared object or situation from least to most scary. Clients also undergo relaxation training—usually *progressive relaxation*, wherein they learn to alternately relax and tense body muscles so they can become completely relaxed. Then, clients proceed through each step of the fear hierarchy while in a state of progressive relaxation. When they reach the top of the fear hierarchy and can stay calm when exposed to the dreaded object or situation, the anxiety is extinguished. Note how systematic desensitization conceptualizes anxiety in purely behavioral terms: Tense muscles constitute anxiety, while relaxed muscles equal calmness. The idea is that one cannot be tense and relaxed simultaneously.

Systematic desensitization: Exposure technique that combines *relaxation training* and use of a *fear hierarchy* (ranking potential experiences with the feared object or situation and from least to most scary); the client is gradually exposed to the conditioned stimulus while in a relaxed state, with the goal of conditioning a new response.

Theresa

Theresa's fear of speaking in front of groups could be addressed using systematic desensitization. If so, her therapist would help her develop a fear hierarchy related to public speaking—with sitting on stage in front of a group (but not talking) at the bottom of the hierarchy and standing at a lectern giving a prepared speech to her colleagues at the top of the hierarchy. Theresa would be taught progressive relaxation and asked to practice it while role-playing each step of her fear hierarchy. After a few sessions, she would hopefully be able to stay relaxed even while standing at the lectern and giving a speech to an audience.

Modeling

Modeling (introduced in Chapter 4) is an indirect form of exposure in which the therapist models the aversive behavior for the client, demonstrating that the fear is unjustified. A client who fears dogs might observe his therapist petting a Labrador, while a client phobic of heights might watch on a webcam as her therapist rides an elevator to the top of a skyscraper. In **participant modeling**, clients are invited to partake in the anxiety-provoking activity with the therapist (Bandura et al., 1974; Denney et al., 1977; Ritter, 1968).

Participant modeling: Variety of modeling wherein the client is invited to partake in anxiety-provoking the activity with the therapist.

Theresa and Gary

If Theresa's therapist were to use modeling to help her overcome her social anxiety about speaking in front of a crowd, he might invite her to come with him to a nearby conference where he is giving

In vivo exposure:
Exposure technique in which client is exposed to the actual anxiety-provoking object or situation to condition a new, non-anxious response to it.

Imaginal exposure:
Exposure technique in which client is asked to imagine the feared scenario to condition a new, non-anxious response to it.

Virtual reality exposure: Exposure technique in which client is exposed to the anxiety-provoking object or situation using computer-generated virtual reality experiences to condition a new, non-anxious response to it.

Thought stopping: CBT technique in which clients are taught to stop their thoughts, often by saying or thinking "Stop!" whenever an intrusive thought occurs.

a presentation. Similarly, Gary's therapist could model getting her hands dirty but not immediately washing them. She might then encourage Gary to join her in the activity and if—after initial reluctance—he did so, he might be surprised when his anxiety about having dirty hands starts to dissipate.

In Vivo vs. Imaginal Exposure

Ideally, exposure therapies are done in real life with direct exposure to the actual anxiety-provoking objects or situations. This is called ***in vivo* exposure** (Hazlett-Stevens & Craske, 2008; J. S. Kaplan & Tolin, 2011). However, real-life exposure isn't always practical or possible. In such cases, clinicians use **imaginal exposure**, in which people are simply asked to imagine the feared scenario (J. S. Kaplan & Tolin, 2011). Although imaginal exposure may not always be as powerful as *in vivo* exposure, there is evidence both work (Foa et al., 1985; Hecker, 1990). Clinicians have also developed **virtual reality exposure**, which uses computer-generated virtual reality experiences to help clients face their fears. Like other forms of exposure, it is also effective (Fodor et al., 2018).

Thought Stopping

Thought stopping is a CBT technique in which clients are taught to stop their thoughts, often by saying or thinking "Stop!" whenever an intrusive thought occurs (Lombardo & Turner, 1979; D. M. Ross, 1984). It is often used to reduce anxiety, obsessions, and compulsions. However, some CBT practitioners—especially those emphasizing a mindfulness approach (see below) in which clients are encouraged to accept rather than resist upsetting thoughts—are skeptical of any approach they see as encouraging thought suppression (Beevers et al., 1999). In their view, resisting unwanted thoughts only strengthens them. Defenders of thought stopping counter that it isn't the same as thought suppression. Rather, it is a cognitive self-control technique for overcoming dysfunctional thinking, one they believe has a strong evidence base for treating anxiety disorders and OCD (Bakker, 2009).

Traditional Cognitive Therapies

Cognitive therapies for anxiety and OCD change patients' faulty beliefs. For anxiety, cognitive therapy employs a variety of techniques—including *psychoeducation* (patients are taught about fear and anxiety, so they understand such feelings are normal and expected), *self-monitoring* (patients identify and evaluate their anxious thoughts), and *cognitive restructuring* (patient beliefs about anxiety are challenged and changed via therapy strategies such as evidence gathering, identifying thinking errors, and testing irrational beliefs in real life) (D. A. Clark & Beck, 2010). For OCD, some of these same techniques are used. Therapy helps patients identify distorted and negative beliefs and assumptions tied to their obsessions, construct alternative interpretations, and use self-monitoring to map and modify obsessional thinking. Behavioral interventions such as behavioral experiments and exposure therapy are often incorporated, as well (Salkovskis et al., 1998).

Mindfulness and Acceptance Cognitive Therapies

Some cognitive therapists apprehensive about thought stopping emphasize mindfulness and acceptance-oriented approaches to anxiety. Such approaches incorporate mindfulness training (see Chapter 5), in which clients are taught to observe and accept upsetting thoughts and feelings without trying to squelch or eliminate them. Certain types of mindfulness training involve *meditation techniques* (in which clients consciously focus on observing their mind's processes and thoughts), while other types encourage more informal means of nonjudgmentally observing and accepting thoughts and feelings (A. R. Norton et al., 2015).

Two examples of mindfulness-oriented approaches are mindfulness-based cognitive therapy (MBCT) and **acceptance and commitment therapy (ACT)**. As discussed in Chapter 5, MBCT combines cognitive therapy with mindfulness meditation techniques, helping clients observe and acknowledge anxiety-provoking thoughts (Hofmann & Gómez, 2017; Z. V. Segal et al., 2004; Teasdale, 2004). The idea is that calmly observing thoughts changes clients' relationship to them, reducing the thoughts' negative emotional impact. In a similar vein, ACT emphasizes accepting, rather than banishing or taking literally, stressful cognitions that lead to anxiety (S. C. Hayes,

Acceptance and commitment therapy (ACT): CBT intervention designed to help people stay focused and in touch with the present moment; acceptance of negative emotions encouraged as a method to defuse them.

2004). As with MBCT (and in contrast to traditional cognitive therapies), ACT doesn't try to change client thoughts. Rather, it assumes that accepting those thoughts as they occur in the moment decreases their power and negative influence. Consequently, the thoughts cause less anxiety. Despite the need for additional research, evidence is mounting that MBCT and ACT are effective in treating anxiety disorders and OCD (Hale et al., 2013; Khusid & Vythilingam, 2016; Landy et al., 2015; Manjula & Sudhir, 2019; A. R. Norton et al., 2015). One especially promising study found mindfulness-based stress reduction worked as well as medication for anxiety disorders (Hoge et al., 2022). Good news for those concerned about drug side effects.

Effectiveness of CBT

Research on CBT generally finds it reduces anxiety, obsessions, and compulsions—with exposure therapies deemed especially effective (Ferrando & Selai, 2021; Hezel & Simpson, 2019; Kaczkurkin & Foa, 2015; Öst et al., 2015). Some evidence even suggests it can be more effective than antidepressants for OCD (Öst et al., 2015). However, there is room for improvement. CBT leads to long-term remission only about half the time, according to one meta-analysis (Springer et al., 2018). Interestingly, CBT increasingly looks at anxiety-related issues through a *transdiagnostic* prism—an issue explored in the "In Depth" feature.

Photo 6.5 Illustration demonstrating a mindfulness technique in which someone (in this case a mother) would observe and accept stressful or overwhelming thoughts and feelings without trying to eliminate them. *Magnilion/Getty Images.*

In Depth: Transdiagnostic Therapy

A primary justification for dividing mental distress into distinct diagnostic categories is so that researchers can devise specific interventions for each disorder. However, not everyone sees this as the best approach. In recent times, interest has surged in *transdiagnostic therapies*, which "apply the same underlying treatment principles across mental disorders without tailoring the protocol to specific diagnoses" (McEvoy et al., 2009, p. 21). Transdiagnostic therapies assume that, when it comes to something like anxiety, the underlying psychological processes are the same regardless of the specific diagnosis (Dalgleish et al., 2020; McEvoy et al., 2009; McManus et al., 2010; P. J. Norton & Roberge, 2017; Sauer-Zavala et al., 2017).

Given the comorbidity of anxiety disorders, CBT therapists have been vocal in advocating a transdiagnostic approach (P. J. Norton & Paulus, 2017; P. J. Norton & Roberge, 2017). *Transdiagnostic CBT (tCBT)* holds that there are "common transdiagnostic mechanisms" that occur across all anxiety disorders (including OCD and related disorders)—things such as negative affect, intolerance of uncertainty, and anxiety sensitivity (P. J. Norton & Paulus, 2017, p. 131). From a tCBT perspective, effective therapy must address these common mechanisms. In a transdiagnostic framework, commonalities in the psychological processes behind various anxiety diagnoses outweigh any differences among them. Therefore, the same therapy interventions can be used effectively with all forms of anxiety. Advocates of tCBT have been busy developing unified protocols that cut across diagnoses, finding substantial evidence to support their transdiagnostic approach (D. H. Barlow et al., 2017; D. L. Ewing et al., 2015; Ito et al., 2022; McEvoy et al., 2009; P. J. Norton & Paulus, 2017). Supporters of transdiagnostic approaches embrace newer diagnostic approaches such as HiTOP and RDoC, which move beyond comorbid DSM and ICD diagnoses (Dalgleish et al., 2020); tCBT can also be used with PTMF, which discards diagnoses entirely.

Transdiagnostic themes are not new to CBT. Aaron Beck espoused them long ago in his approach to cognitive therapy (Sauer-Zavala et al., 2017). However, transdiagnostic thinking did not originate with Beck or CBT. Transdiagnostic values have been implicit in psychodynamic and humanistic therapies from the start. You might have picked this up in our previous discussions of these therapies, when we noted that they apply the same basic therapy strategies across presenting problems. Specific diagnoses notwithstanding, psychodynamic therapies "focus on exploring self-concept and personality features, with a particular emphasis on resolving psychic conflicts" (Sauer-Zavala et al., 2017, p. 131). In other words,

the psychotherapeutic prescription for how patients should be treated is the resolution of these conflicts, using strategies such as increased attention to affect and emotion expression, identification of recurring themes or patterns, discussion of past experiences, and exploration of avoidance related to upsetting thoughts or feelings, interpersonal relationships, and fantasy life.

(Sauer-Zavala et al., 2017, p. 131)

The UPP-ANXIETY protocol discussed earlier in the chapter is an example of a transdiagnostic psychodynamic approach to anxiety (Leichsenring & Salzer, 2014). As for humanistic therapists, their suspicion of mental disorder categories combined with their emphasis on core conditions of change irrespective of diagnosis seems fundamentally transdiagnostic:

Humanistic psychotherapy provides a compelling illustration of universally applied therapeutic principles. Rather than being developed to target specific mechanisms of psychopathology, this collection of approaches follows from central tenets of human capacity and need .... Client-centered therapy, perhaps the best known type of humanistic psychotherapy, is structured around the universally applied therapeutic principles of empathy, genuineness of the therapeutic relationship, and unconditional positive regard. These strategies represent the humanistic tool-kit applied to all patients.

(Sauer-Zavala et al., 2017, pp. 130–131)

Among humanistic therapists, only emotion-focused therapists have developed a transdiagnostic approach to anxiety (Timulak & Keogh, 2020, 2022). More generally, although our focus in this chapter has been on anxiety, transdiagnostic conceptualizations are being applied to many presenting problems. We will encounter them again in later chapters. Be on the lookout.

Critical Thinking Questions

1. Do you like transdiagnostic approaches? Why or why not?
2. Is treatment effectiveness improved by tailoring interventions to specific disorders, or are transdiagnostic therapists on to something by shifting in a more general direction?
3. Is there a double-standard in which CBT earns praise for moving in a transdiagnostic direction, even though psychodynamic and humanistic perspectives have long been criticized for their transdiagnostic skepticism of disorder-specific interventions? If so, why?

6.14 Humanistic Perspectives

Person-Centered Therapy

Person-centered perspectives see anxiety as caused by incongruence. When people can only obtain positive regard from others by being inconsistent with their true selves, then anxiety and other emotional difficulties result (Cain, 2010; R. Elliott, 2013; D. Murphy & Joseph, 2016; C. R. Rogers, 1951, 1959). In other words, "psychological distress in general and anxiety in particular derives from discrepancies between different aspects of self, variously referred to as 'actual/organismic,' 'perceived,' and 'ideal' or 'ought' selves" (R. Elliott, 2013, p. 20). Person-centered therapy for anxiety is no different from therapy for any other presenting problem: The therapist avoids medical model diagnostic labels while providing a safe and supportive environment containing person-centered therapy's core conditions for change (empathy, genuineness, and unconditional positive regard). This allows clients to reconnect with their self-actualizing tendencies. As they start behaving in more psychologically congruent ways, their anxiety should lift (R. Elliott, 2013).

Tammy

In therapy for 8-year-old Tammy Steadman, a person-centered therapist would empathize with Tammy and accept her unconditionally—even when Tammy gets extremely anxious. Over time, Tammy could be expected to share that her parents like it when she performs before others. She might even recount how they made her sing in the third-grade talent show, although she told them she didn't want to. Tammy would also likely confide that she prefers to draw or do math puzzles in a workbook they have at school. The therapist would reflect Tammy's feelings back to her. He would also keep paper, pencils, and puzzles in his office and encourage Tammy to use them whenever she wants during sessions. Over several months, Tammy would hopefully become less and less anxious, especially in therapy. Tammy and her therapist might discuss inviting her parents to a session so Tammy could share her feelings with them about what kinds of activities she enjoys most.

Existential anxiety:
Normal and expected anxiety that motivates people to construct meaningful lives for themselves; emerges from the four basic existential givens: death, freedom, isolation, and meaninglessness.

Existential Perspectives
Existential Therapy

Existential psychotherapies (see Chapter 2) contend that although anxiety is often seen as a "medico-psychological problem," it is also a "metaphysical and spiritual problem" (Costello, 2011, p. 65). Existential therapists distinguish existential anxiety from neurotic anxiety. **Existential anxiety** is a normal and expected part of human existence. It emerges from four basic *existential givens* that none of us can avoid or escape (Yalom, 1980). These givens are:

- *Death*: We are all going to die—a fact none of us can avoid, but one that understandably causes us anxiety.

- *Freedom*: While we usually think of freedom as a good thing, it is often terrifying because it means that we are responsible for our choices. Yet we often don't want to bear such responsibility. Sometimes we deny our freedom and act as if the way we are living our lives has been foisted upon us and we have no say in the matter.
- *Isolation*: We are all ultimately alone in the world, trapped inside our bodies and never fully able to move beyond that fact. While we may seek out social relations and connections with others, our aloneness is an inevitable and unavoidable fact of existence.
- *Meaninglessness*: There is no inherent meaning in life. The only meaning it has is whatever meaning we imbue in it. A lot of existential anxiety stems from our struggle to invest life with meaning, which we must create ourselves.

Although not always pleasant, existential anxiety is healthy and adaptive. Awareness of mortality and need for connection motivates people to take responsibility for constructing meaningful and rich lives for themselves. However, sometimes people experience **neurotic anxiety**, which occurs when they refuse to acknowledge existential givens that demand they invest their lives with meaning (M. Cooper, 2003; Iacovou, 2011; Temple & Gall, 2018).

Neurotic anxiety: Pathological anxiety that occurs in people who refuse to acknowledge existential givens that demand they invest their lives with meaning.

Logotherapy

An example of the existential approach to anxiety is the work of psychiatrist and psychotherapist Victor Frankl (1959, 1968), a Holocaust survivor who was able to find meaning in the horrible circumstances he faced in a Nazi concentration camp at Auschwitz. This led him to develop an existential treatment method called **logotherapy**. Frankl's approach stresses how failure to make meaning can lead to a variety of symptoms—including anxiety, obsessions, and compulsions. For Frankl, when people don't face their responsibility to make meaning in an inherently meaningless world, they are at risk for neurotic anxiety. To cope with the overwhelming anxiety caused by their lack of meaning, they focus on insignificant things:

Logotherapy: Existential treatment method developed by Victor Frankl that emphasizes helping clients find meaning in life.

The phobic focuses on some object that has caused him concern in the past; the agoraphobic sees her anxiety as coming from the world outside her door; the patient with stage fright or speech anxiety focuses on the stage or the podium. The anxiety neurotic thus makes sense of his or her discomfort with life. (Boeree, 2006)

Frankl (1968) explained OCD similarly. He argued that, in the absence of having constructed personal meaning, people who experience obsessions and compulsions demand perfect certainty about minor details, something that is impossible. In logotherapy, clients with anxiety neuroses are taught not only to accept uncertainty, but also encouraged to find meaning in life because only by doing so can they overcome anxiety. Finding meaning in relationships, work, and even through accepting one's own suffering are all ways to overcome neurotic anxiety (Frankl, 1959, 1968). The evidence base for existential therapies is relatively small, but the research that has been done provides encouraging if limited support (Shumaker, 2012; S.-Y. Tan & Wong, 2012; J. Vos et al., 2015; J. Vos, 2019).

Gary

Gary Steadman regularly obsesses about whether he properly programmed the security system in his house. By preoccupying himself with such an insignificant event, he avoids the larger existential questions behind his obsessive-compulsive anxiety. If a logotherapist were to work with Gary, the goal would be to help Gary gain awareness of his neurotic anxiety. Consequently, Gary might realize that he has been unwilling to risk taking a leave of absence from his job as an accountant so that he can pursue an interest in creative writing. Logotherapy would try to help Gary see how he has rationalized this decision as something beyond his control by telling himself "I need to earn a living for my family" and "There's always tomorrow." If logotherapy were effective, Gary would begin accepting responsibility for creating his own future—a future that might involve him incorporating creative writing into his life in meaningful and rewarding ways. As a result, his obsessions and compulsions would be expected to recede.

Emotion-Focused Therapy (EFT)

As discussed in Chapter 5, emotion-focused therapy (EFT) theorizes that addressing emotional conflicts (rather than reconditioning behavior or learning to think logically) is at the heart of resolving psychological problems. According to EFT, emotional conflicts originate in difficult or painful past experiences. EFT helps anxious clients gain awareness of emotional conflicts that cause them to be fretful or avoidant in everyday interactions. The goal is to provide a supportive therapeutic environment in which they can learn to tolerate and accept (rather than fear and avoid) painful and difficult feelings. Reducing avoidance allows clients to face and resolve emotional conflicts, which frees them to better identify their own needs and cope more effectively in situations that previously caused anxiety. For instance, the EFT formulation of social anxiety holds that socially anxious people experience shame due to "repeated experiences of being bullied, criticized, rejected, or neglected" (Shahar, 2014, p. 538). Socially anxious situations are those that elicit these feelings of shame. Similarly, people experiencing generalized anxiety feel as if they are under constant threat because almost all situations trigger painful past emotions for them (Timulak & McElvaney, 2016).

Effectiveness of Humanistic-Existential Therapies

Although humanistic-existential therapies can often be helpful (Angus et al., 2015), they appear to be somewhat less effective for relieving anxiety than more directive approaches such as CBT (Angus et al., 2015; R. Elliott et al., 2013). EFT is a notable exception. Not only has it has shown promise in relieving social anxiety and generalized anxiety (R. Elliott, 2013; R. MacLeod et al., 2012; Priest, 2013; Shahar et al., 2012, 2017), but one study directly comparing EFT with CBT for generalized anxiety found the two therapies worked equally well (Timulak et al., 2022). Additional studies are necessary to draw firmer conclusions. Regarding obsessions and compulsions, there simply isn't much research on humanistic therapies besides a recent case study intended to jumpstart theory and practice in this area (Ralph & Cooper, 2022).

6.15 Evaluating Psychological Perspectives

Because CBT has the most established evidence base, treatment guidelines usually recommend it as the first-line psychotherapy for anxiety issues (G. Andrews et al., 2018; Bandelow et al., 2021; Katzman et al., 2014; NICE Guidance, 2019). Psychodynamic therapies are typically considered a second-line therapy if CBT doesn't work. This is because, compared with CBT, the evidence for psychodynamic therapies is deemed not as strong. However, just as there are studies indicating EFT can compete with CBT for anxiety, there are also studies suggesting the same for psychodynamic therapies (Maljanen et al., 2014; F. Monti et al., 2014). Additional research on this would be helpful.

The area where psychodynamic and humanistic therapies currently lack support is in treating obsessions and compulsions. Here, CBT remains the most recommended therapy, with reviews and meta-analyses consistently finding it effective (Franklin et al., 2012; Lewin, Wu, McGuire, & Storch, 2014; Olatunji et al., 2013; Öst et al., 2015). CBT seems to work not only for OCD, but also related disorders such as hoarding, skin-picking, and hair-pulling (Keuthen et al., 2015; Lochner et al., 2017; Snorrason et al., 2015; Tolin et al., 2015). However, even when improvement occurs, therapy does not always succeed in eliminating obsessions and compulsions; unfortunately, symptoms often return (Springer et al., 2018).

The long-term impact of therapy for anxiety and OCD remains unclear. For instance, although CBT moderately improves symptoms, its effects dissipate over time, and are small to non-existent twelve months after treatment (van Dis et al., 2020). In sum, although therapy is beneficial for anxiety, obsessions, and compulsions, there is substantial room for improvement.

SOCIOCULTURAL PERSPECTIVES

6.16 Cross-Cultural and Social Justice Perspectives

Cultural Differences in the Expression of Anxiety

Sociocultural perspectives view presenting problems through a cultural lens, seeing mental disorders as culture-bound syndromes that emerge and are defined within social contexts (D. J. Stein &

Williams, 2010). In keeping with this idea, research consistently shows that cultural background influences how people exhibit anxiety. For example, a small but compelling body of evidence suggests that symptoms of panic attacks vary by culture—with higher rates of dizziness in Asian cultures, burning or skin-pricking sensations among African Americans, trembling in Caribbean Latinos, and fears of death in African American and Arab populations (Lewis-Fernández et al., 2010). Similarly, some Chinese and Japanese patients diagnosed with social anxiety disorder don't avoid social situations out of concern about embarrassing themselves (as DSM and ICD suggest). Instead, they worry about embarrassing or offending others—a form of social anxiety referred to in Japan as *taijin kyofusho (TKS)* (Arimitsu et al., 2019; Hofmann et al., 2010; Lewis-Fernández et al., 2010; X. Zhu et al., 2014). There are many other ways that anxiety looks different cross-culturally. Three more examples:

- In non-Western societies, generalized anxiety is much more likely to involve somatic (physical) complaints (Lewis-Fernández et al., 2010). For example, in Cambodian culture it is common to believe that an internal air-like substance called *khyâl* flows through the limbs and body. Thus, physical symptoms like sore necks, weak or cold limbs, and panic attacks about neck pain or gastrointestinal symptoms are common ways of displaying anxiety (Hofmann & Hinton, 2014).
- *Ataques de nervios* is a culturally specific syndrome found in Puerto Rico and the Dominican Republic (Hofmann & Hinton, 2014). In addition to fear and anger, an *ataque* often includes tightness in the chest, feeling one is losing control, sensations of heat in the body, feeling faint, heart palpitations, and shaking that affects the arms and legs. Patients often feel like they are dying or fret that their impending loss of control could lead to hurting themselves or others (Hofmann & Hinton, 2014).
- Anxiety disorders are least prevalent in Asia and Sub-Saharan Africa and most prevalent in Latin America and the Caribbean (Santomauro et al., 2021). Regional differences notwithstanding, the COVID-19 pandemic led to dramatic increases in anxiety around the globe (Santomauro et al., 2021). The "Controversial Question" feature explores whether COVID-19 anxiety should be considered a mental disorder.

It is important for therapists to be aware of how anxiety presents differently across cultural contexts. Without such awareness, cultural misunderstandings that lead to ineffective or harmful interventions can result. Notions of anxiety have evolved through history, which is why some theorists see them as social constructions—socially shared ways of defining, talking about, and understanding what we collectively label as "anxiety" (Dowbiggin, 2009; Gergen & McNamee, 2000; C. M. Stanley & Raskin, 2002). You must decide the extent to which you believe the experience of anxiety is universal across cultures versus socially and culturally constituted.

Controversial Question: Is COVID-19 Anxiety a Mental Disorder?

The COVID-19 pandemic has been stressful for everyone. Some people exhibited so much distress that researchers have proposed a "COVID-19 anxiety syndrome (CAS)" (Nikčević et al., 2021; Nikčević & Spada, 2020; S. Taylor et al., 2020). CAS has been characterized as involving the following symptoms:

(1) avoidance (e.g., of public transport because of the fear of contracting COVID-19); (2) checking (e.g., of symptoms of COVID-19); (3) worrying (e.g., imagining what could happen to loved ones if they were to contract COVID-19); and (4) threat monitoring (e.g., paying close attention to others displaying possible symptoms of COVID-19). (Nikčević & Spada, 2020, p. 2)

CAS combines aspects of several DSM and ICD disorders—not only generalized anxiety and OCD (both addressed in this chapter) but also posttraumatic stress disorder (PTSD) and illness anxiety disorder (see Chapters 7 and 8). Researchers have developed a variety of scales for measuring CAS, and these have shown strong psychometric properties (Akbari et al., 2021; Albery et al., 2021; Nikčević et al., 2021; Nikčević & Spada, 2020; S. Taylor et al., 2020). Those who see CAS as an empirically supported diagnostic entity believe that naming it allows therapists to research it and identify the most effective treatments. Their aim is to discover "important new empirical findings on the nature of reactions to COVID-19 in particular and future pandemics in general" (S. Taylor et al., 2020, p. 6).

However, not everyone is enamored with turning COVID-19 anxiety into a new mental disorder diagnosis. Sociocultural critics of CAS warn that doing so medicalizes and pathologizes reactions that are entirely appropriate under certain circumstances. During a pandemic, "being too scared to leave the house for fear of contracting a fatal disease, and spending most of the day washing our hands and wiping down doorknobs, are not signs of 'OCD' but of a responsible citizen" (Johnstone, 2020, p. 278). How much pandemic anxiety is "normal," and should we view justifiable (if sometimes counterproductive) distress as disordered? These are questions you must answer for yourself.

Critical Thinking Questions

1. When, if ever, is COVID anxiety a form of mental disorder?
2. What do you see as the strengths and weaknesses of the syndrome versus sociocultural approaches to thinking about COVID anxiety?
3. Do the advantages of medicalizing COVID anxiety outweigh the disadvantages? Why or why not?

Economic Conditions and Anxiety

Since the middle of the twentieth century, it has been common for social critics to contend that we live in what poet W. H. Auden dubbed the "age of anxiety" (Dowbiggin, 2009). The term refers to our ever-present awareness of the perils of modern times. The age of anxiety has continued for many decades now, as we continually worry about terrible things—including environmental destruction, nuclear waste, drug addiction, pornography, violence, religious fanaticism, terrorist attacks, loss of privacy in an Internet age, and global health pandemics (Santomauro et al., 2021; D. Smith, 2012). The idea that we live in an age of anxiety is consistent with perspectives that see anxiety as emerging from sociocultural factors such as socioeconomic, gender, and racial inequality. Along these lines, depression and anxiety correlate with lower socioeconomic status (SES) and current financial strain (Dijkstra-Kersten et al., 2015; K. A. McLaughlin et al., 2011; Pulkki-Råback et al., 2012; Ridley et al., 2020). This suggests that economic disadvantage—lacking the means to manage life's challenges—makes it more difficult to harness the resources necessary to ward off anxiety and depression.

In seeming contradiction to this, studies consistently find that anxiety is most prevalent in high-income countries and least prevalent in low- to lower-middle-income countries (Ruscio et al., 2017; Santomauro et al., 2021; D. J. Stein et al., 2017). What explains this pattern, and how do we reconcile it with findings that lower-SES predicts higher levels of anxiety? First, culture bias might influence anxiety prevalence estimates; in countries where anxiety carries greater stigma, people might report it less or present it in less typically Western ways—for example, as physical symptoms (Sheridan, 2017). Second, people in low/lower-middle income countries might feel as much or more anxiety as people in high-income countries but not identify it as "excessive" because it seems warranted given their stressful socioeconomic circumstances (Sheridan, 2017). Third, prevalence rates might not capture anxiety's more severe impact in poorer versus wealthier nations; for instance, in low- and middle-income countries, depression and anxiety are accompanied by alarmingly high mortality rates among older people (Y. Wu et al., 2020). What other reasons can you think of to explain higher prevalence rates of anxiety in higher- versus lower-income countries?

Gender and Anxiety

For most anxiety disorders, women are diagnosed more often than men—in many cases, twice as often (American Psychiatric Association, 2022; Asher et al., 2017; Bandelow & Michaelis, 2015; Christiansen, 2015; Vanderminden & Esala, 2019; Vesga-López et al., 2008). Women also seem to be more burdened by anxiety, as indicated by more doctor visits and missed days from work (McLean et al., 2011; Vesga-López et al., 2008). Some attribute gender differences in rates and intensity of anxiety to genetic, neurochemical, and hormonal differences between men and women (Altemus, 2006; Altemus et al., 2014; Maeng & Milad, 2015; A. A. Marques et al., 2016; McHenry et al., 2014). However, others contend that women face social disadvantages men don't, and this better explains higher rates of female anxiety. For instance, physical abuse, sexual abuse, and trauma place women at greater risk for anxiety issues (Hossain et al., 2021; Oram et al., 2017; Ranta et al., 2009; Ussher, 2011). Further, studies find that people (mostly women) who have been bullied by peers during childhood are more likely to experience anxiety (Kaloeti et al., 2021; R. E. McCabe et al., 2010; Pontillo et al., 2019; Ranta et al., 2009). Unfortunately, the negative consequences of bullying aren't limited to childhood. Workplace bullying in adulthood is tied to anxiety, as well (Verkuil et al., 2015; T. Xu et al., 2019).

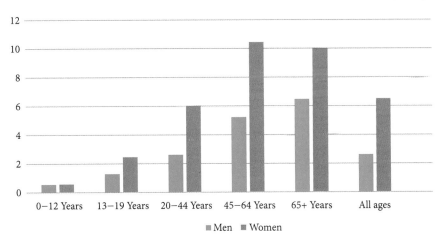

Figure 6.2 Percent of U.S. Patients Taking Benzodiazepines by Age and Gender, 2019.
Created using information originally available at: Express Scripts. (2020, April). America's state of mind report.
https://www.express-scripts.com/corporate/americas-state-of-mind-report

Somewhat controversially, women are more likely than men to be given drugs for their anxiety. Although benzodiazepine use has dropped precipitously over the years, longstanding gender differences remain, with U.S. women receiving more than twice as many benzodiazepine prescriptions in 2019 as men (roughly 6 percent compared with slightly more than 2.5 percent; see Figure 6.2) (Express Scripts, 2020).

When you also consider that women take antidepressants more than twice as often as men (15.1 percent vs. 7.0 percent) and that antidepressants are the most commonly prescribed drugs for anxiety (with almost half of those on benzodiazepines also taking them), it becomes clear that women are medicated for anxiety much more than men (Express Scripts, 2020). Given this data, feminist critics contend that women's emotional difficulties are too often attributed to mental illnesses rather than deeply ingrained societal discrimination. These critics argue that the solution is not to medicate women into submission (as they feel we too often do), but to reform social institutions that oppress women and produce their anxiety in the first place (Ussher, 2011). From a social justice perspective, addressing women's mental distress at the individual level is best accomplished by political reform at the societal level. This involves a shift away from individual treatment and towards community action. An example of such action occurred in the state of Kerala in India:

Since the beginning of the century, women in this poor state began to organize into social movements that demanded tenant protection, nutrition programs for children, land reform, and community development. Through the organizing process women experienced a psychological sense of empowerment. But solidarity resulted not only in enhanced personal control and a sense of mastery; it also led to meaningful social change. Public health indices such as literacy, infant mortality, and longevity have been higher in Kerala than in the rest of India for many years. (Prilleltensky et al., 2007, p. 24)

Photo 6.6 Feminist therapists have critiqued pharmaceutical ads marketing anti-anxiety drugs to women. This ad is from 1967. Disclaimer: This advertisement is being used to represent the general attitudes of this era in relation to anxiety drugs and gender and is not in any way representative of the current views or attitudes of Pfizer.
© Pfizer.

6.17 Service User Perspectives

What is the service user's experience of being diagnosed with anxiety? Mainstream research literature on anxiety, obsessions, and compulsions focuses on problems related to stigma. Although the public views anxiety less negatively than depression or schizophrenia (L. Wood et al., 2014), having an anxiety disorder diagnosis can still be quite stigmatizing, especially because it is often viewed as a personal weakness (Curcio & Corboy, 2020). For instance, simply describing someone as experiencing social anxiety can be equally as stigmatizing as identifying someone as mentally ill (K. N. Anderson et al., 2015). Further, it is common for people to blame those with anxiety for their problems (Curcio & Corboy, 2020; L. Wood et al., 2014). This has egregious consequences because, as with other mental health problems, people with anxiety diagnoses often internalize negative attitudes others hold about them, and this can reduce the effectiveness of treatment (Ociskova et al., 2018). To combat stigma, many researchers advocate educating people by exposing them directly or indirectly (e.g., via the media) to individuals diagnosed with anxiety disorders (Batterham et al., 2013; Curcio & Corboy, 2020; L. Wood et al., 2014).

OCD and related disorders also carry significant stigma (Akyurek et al., 2019; Fang et al., 2014; Fennell & Boyd, 2014; Ponzini & Steinman, 2022). A survey of psychiatrists found that even though they reported having a compassionate attitude toward those with OCD, they also "thought that OCD patients talk too much, waste a lot of time, and need more patience when compared with other psychiatric disorder sufferers" (Kusalaruk et al., 2015, p. 1703). Interestingly, stigma toward those with OCD varies based on the types of obsessions and compulsions. OCD related to harm and aggression is the most stigmatizing (people see such individuals as dangerous and don't wish to be near them); social distance is also strongly desired when obsessions and compulsions are sex-related (Ponzini & Steinman, 2022). Service providers must keep in mind how stigmatizing OCD can be, as it often results in people not seeking help or dropping out of treatment. "The Lived Experience" feature provides one service user's story of how she overcame her OCD.

The Lived Experience: A True Story of Living with Obsessive-Compulsive Disorder

The underlying reasons why I have to repeatedly re-zip things, blink a certain way, count to an odd number, check behind my shower curtain to ensure no one is hiding to plot my abduction, make sure that computer cords are not rat tails, etc., will never be clear to me. Is it the result of a poor reaction to the anesthesiology that was administered during my wisdom teeth extraction? These aggravating thoughts and compulsions began immediately after the procedure. Or is it related to PANDAS (Pediatric Autoimmune Neuropsychiatric Disorder Associated with Streptococcal infection) which is a proposed theory connoting a strange relationship between group A beta-hemolytic streptococcal infection with rapidly developing symptoms of obsessive-compulsive disorder in the basal ganglia? Is it simply a hereditary byproduct of my genetic makeup associated with my nervous personality? Or is it a defense tactic I developed through having an overly concerned mother?

The Consequences Associated with My OCD

Growing up with mild, in fact dormant, obsessive-compulsive disorder, I would have never proposed such bizarre questions until 2002, when an exacerbated overnight onset of severe OCD mentally paralyzed me. I'd just had my wisdom teeth removed and was immediately bombarded with incessant and intrusive unwanted thoughts, ranging from a fear of being gay to questioning if I was truly seeing the sky as blue. I'm sure similar thoughts had passed through my mind before; however, they must have been filtered out of my conscious, as I never had such incapacitating ideas enter my train of thought before. During the summer of 2002, not one thought was left unfiltered from my conscious. Thoughts that didn't even matter and held no significance were debilitating; they prevented me from accomplishing the simplest, most mundane tasks. Tying my shoe only to untie it repetitively, continuously being tardy for work and school, spending long hours in a bathroom engaging in compulsive rituals such as tapping inanimate objects endlessly with no resolution, and finally medically withdrawing from college, eventually to drop out completely not once but twice, were just a few of the consequences I endured.

Seeking Help

After seeing a medical specialist for OCD, I had tried a mixed cocktail of medications over a ten-year span, including escitalopram (Lexapro), fluoxetine (Prozac), risperidone (Risperdal), aripiprazole (Abilify), sertraline (Zoloft), clomipramine (Anafranil), lamotrigine (Lamictal), and finally, after a recent bipolar disorder II diagnosis, lurasidone (Latuda). The only medication that has remotely curbed my intrusive thoughts and repetitive compulsions is lurasidone, giving me approximately 60 to 70 percent relief from my symptoms.

Many psychologists and psychiatrists would argue that a combination of cognitive behavioral therapy (CBT) and pharmacological management might be the only successful treatment approach for an individual plagued with OCD. If an individual is brave enough to undergo exposure and response prevention therapy (ERP), a type of CBT that has been shown to relieve symptoms of OCD and anxiety through desensitization and habituation, then my hat is off to them .... In the majority of cases of severe OCD, I believe pharmacological management is a must.

How I Conquered My OCD

So, what does a person incapacitated with OCD do? If, as a person with severe OCD, I truly had an answer, I would probably leave my house more often, take a risk once in a while, and live freely without fearing the mundane nuances associated with public places. It's been my experience with OCD to take everything one second at a time and remain grateful for those good seconds. If I were to take OCD one day at a time, well, too many millions of internal battles would be lost in this 24-hour period. I have learned to live with my OCD through writing and performing as a spoken word artist. I have taken the time to explore my pain and transmute it into an art form which has allowed me to explore the topic of pain as an interesting and beneficial subject matter. I am the last person to attempt to tell any individuals with OCD what the best therapy approach is for them, but I will encourage each and every individual to explore their own pain, and believe that manageability can come in many forms, from classic techniques to intricate art forms, in order for healing to begin.

By Tiffany Dawn Hasse in collaboration with Kristen Fuller, MD. Reprinted with permission. This is Tiffany's personal story. Reproduced from Hasse and Fuller (2017).

Source: Hasse, T. D., & Fuller, K. (2017, April 3). A true story of living with obsessive-compulsive disorder [Psychology Today]. Happiness Is a State of Mind. https://www.psychologytoday.com/us/blog/happiness-is-state-mind/201704/true-story-living-obsessive-compulsive-disorder

6.18 Systems Perspectives

Expressed Emotion and Accommodation

Family context plays a role in anxiety, obsessions, and compulsions. Among people diagnosed with such disorders, interpersonal relationships are often strained—especially with parents and significant others. The problem is often circular: "The considerable burden of living with a person with a severe anxiety disorder may strain relationships, but relationship dysfunction, in turn, plays a role in exacerbation of anxiety problems and affects response to treatment" (Chambless, 2012, p. 548). Higher levels of expressed emotion—relatives and significant others being hostile, critical, or emotionally overinvolved—are associated with worse treatment outcomes (Chambless et al., 2001, 2007; De Berardis et al., 2008; Ozkiris et al., 2015; Przeworski et al., 2012; Steketee & Chambless, 2001). We saw that this was true for both psychosis and mood issues (see Chapters 4 and 5), and it is also true for anxiety. When people close to us respond to our difficulties with criticism or hostility, it simply makes matters worse.

Theresa and Gary

When Theresa Steadman gets angry with her husband Gary for having to repeatedly check the stove and is contemptuous and critical about it, she hampers his recovery. Couples therapy might help Theresa better understand how this kind of strong expressed emotion is counterproductive in helping Gary overcome his obsessive-compulsive issues.

Accommodation:
Process by which patients' relatives or significant others collude with them to help them avoid anxiety-provoking situations or repeatedly reassure them that everything is okay; associated with poorer patient outcomes.

Accommodation—the process by which patients' relatives or significant others collude with them to help them avoid anxiety-provoking situations or repeatedly reassure them that everything is okay—also correlates with poorer outcomes (Cherian et al., 2014; E. Lebowitz et al., 2013; E. R. Lebowitz et al., 2012, 2016; Macul Ferreira de Barros et al., 2020; Peris, Sugar, et al., 2012; Peris, Yadegar, et al., 2012; B. M. Rudy et al., 2015; Shimshoni et al., 2019; Thompson-Hollands et al., 2014). This makes sense because accommodating anxious family members allows them to continue their problematic behavior patterns.

Tammy

Eight-year-old Tammy Steadman repeatedly seeks reassurance from her parents that everything will be okay if she goes to school. She also regularly asks them if she can stay home from school; when they accommodate her in this way to prevent her from feeling anxious, they inadvertently encourage her anxious behavior.

In cases of OCD, some family members are so accommodating that they end up performing rituals on the patient's behalf.

Theresa and Gary

When Theresa Steadman, at her husband Gary's request, checks whether the stove is off, she accommodates his obsessive-compulsive tendencies. Besides allowing him to perpetuate his problematic behavior patterns, it also leads Theresa to feel put upon and, over time, resentful and angry. This, in turn, generates more expressed emotion from her. Her accommodating behavior, combined with the resulting expressed emotion, only hampers Gary's recovery.

A goal of family therapy in such cases is to help significant others and relatives better understand how expressed emotion and accommodation interfere with their loved one's improvement. Changing these family dynamics ostensibly enhances treatment outcomes. Educating family members about better ways to respond to their anxious loved ones, as well as helping them gain insight into the problematic family dynamics that perpetuate the problem, are the focus of many family interventions.

Structural Family Therapy for Generalized Anxiety

Bowen's structural family therapy, which has long viewed anxiety as a problem in family and couple relationships (K. G. Baker, 2015; M. Bowen, 1978), has been adapted to specifically address generalized anxiety (Priest, 2015). This adapted model exemplifies how family systems perspectives conceptualize anxiety. It contends that people with generalized anxiety often experience high levels of tension in their romantic relationships because their capacity to differentiate is poor. Recall from Chapter 2 that differentiation is the ability to distinguish one's own thoughts and feelings from those of others. From a structural family therapy perspective, anxious people—due to trauma or abuse in their families of origin—have a hard time with differentiation. When anxious, they either fuse with other people to gain comfort and reassurance, or they emotionally cut themselves off from others as a form of self-protection. Their relational boundaries therefore become too loose or too rigid, and they often respond to significant others in emotionally impulsive and defensive ways. Not surprisingly then, their romantic relationships suffer. Structural family therapy helps couples develop more differentiated boundaries, allowing for more effective communication and support (K. G. Baker, 2015; M. Bowen, 1978). Research is needed to determine how effective such an approach is for alleviating anxiety, but other preliminary systems therapy research is encouraging. For example, a randomized controlled pilot study found manualized family systems therapy superior to CBT for social anxiety (Hunger et al., 2020). A more general review concluded that systemic therapies are by and large effective for anxiety issues (A. Carr, 2014).

Theresa and Gary

Were Theresa and Gary Steadman to seek structural family couples therapy, the therapist would work to help them better understand the dynamics of their relationship. Over time, it would become clear that whenever Gary asks about Theresa's ongoing anxiety, Theresa emotionally withdraws. In response, Gary becomes more solicitous of Theresa, which in turn only elicits further emotional distance from her. Structural family couples therapy would try to help Theresa gain insight into how her childhood family dynamics inform how she deals with Gary. Her parents always fussed over her when she felt anxious, which only made Theresa feel like she couldn't handle things. Today, when Gary asks about Theresa's anxiety, it elicits self-doubt and withdrawal. Couples therapy would teach Theresa and Gary to understand how patterns in their respective families of origin often recur in destructive ways in their marriage. As they come to better understand these dynamics, they would hopefully begin to change their communication patterns and improve their relationship.

6.19 Evaluating Sociocultural Perspectives

Sociocultural perspectives emphasize family, social, and cultural influences on anxiety. Their main advantage is that they remind us how emotions like anxiety are shaped by context. Family perspectives aim to reduce expressed emotion and accommodation, while also helping people alter family patterns to minimize anxiety. Social justice perspectives stress not simply treating anxiety as an individual problem, but addressing economic, racial, and gender inequality. The question is whether social justice perspectives alone can account for anxiety issues. Not everyone who faces challenging social circumstances experiences anxiety, leading many to conclude that biological and psychological approaches are needed to supplement a sociocultural viewpoint.

CLOSING THOUGHTS

6.20 Anxiety and Fear as Uniquely Human

Joseph LeDoux is a neuroscientist who has conducted groundbreaking research on the underlying fear circuitry of the brain. His work has been essential in identifying the amygdala as a key component of the brain's fear circuit (discussed earlier). However, despite his neuroscience underpinnings, LeDoux (2015) is skeptical of a strictly biological account of anxiety and fear. On the contrary, he has provocatively argued that anxiety and fear are uniquely human emotions that emerge from, but can't be fully reduced to, brain processes. His ideas provide a nice way of trying to integrate biological, psychological, and sociocultural perspectives.

LeDoux (2015) believes he made a mistake when he called the brain circuitry implicated in fear and anxiety the "fear circuit." In reflecting on this error, he explains that "the mistake I made was a semantic one—the mistake was to label the amygdala as part of the 'fear circuit.' And that has led to all kinds of bad consequences in the field" (C. Schwartz, 2015, para. 9). Why? Because by calling it this, people erroneously concluded that anxiety and fear arise directly from this circuit being activated. But this is incorrect, contends LeDoux. What happens is that the fear circuit (which LeDoux now thinks he should have named the "threat detection circuit") is activated whenever people sense a threat to their safety (LeDoux, 2015; C. Schwartz, 2015). Anxiety and fear, as emotional experiences, only result from our interpretations of threat detection system data. That is, "fear and anxiety are not wired into the brain as basic responses to the world around us—rather, the responses that lead to them are, and they only coalesce into fear when the brain interprets them as such" (C. Schwartz, 2015, para. 7).

Thus, anxiety and fear are uniquely human emotions because humans are thought to be alone among animals in being able to interpret their own bodily sensations. Other animals experience threat when the fear circuit is activated, but because they can't reflect on it and interpret what it means, they never truly experience the more complex emotions of anxiety or fear. LeDoux nicely highlights the integrative aspects of complex emotions like anxiety and fear: They are a combined product of basic brain circuitry and psychological reflection influenced by socially shared definitions and understandings of various emotions. However, his ideas also have therapeutic implications. When we express disappointment that psychiatric drugs for anxiety are limited in their helpfulness, LeDoux (2015) points out that they are merely doing what we designed them to do, namely target and subdue threat detection circuitry. However, because anxiety and fear aren't reducible to that circuitry (cognitive interpretation is necessary before people feel these emotions), drugs alone are unlikely to fully eliminate them. LeDoux (2015)—a neuroscientist—is arguing that talk therapy may be essential in remediating anxiety and fear. As we move on to other presenting problems, it may be helpful to keep in mind LeDoux's contention that complex human emotions are attributable to a combination of biological, psychological, and sociocultural processes—suggesting that an integrative framework is helpful for a comprehensive understanding.

CHAPTER SUMMARY

Overview

- *Fear* is a basic emotion in response to something perceived as dangerous. *Anxiety* involves cognitive appraisals in response to basic fear responses and is less hard-wired.
- *Obsessions* are persistent thoughts, images, or urges that are hard to dismiss or stop thinking about. *Compulsions* are behaviors or mental acts that a person feels driven to perform, often in response to obsessions.

Diagnostic Perspectives

- DSM and ICD include these anxiety disorders: *specific phobia, social anxiety disorder, panic disorder, agoraphobia, generalized anxiety disorder, separation anxiety disorder,* and *selective mutism.*
- DSM and ICD include these obsessive-compulsive and related disorders: *obsessive-compulsive disorder (OCD), body dysmorphic disorder, hoarding disorder, trichotillomania (hair-pulling disorder),* and *excoriation (skin-picking disorder).*
- DSM and ICD perspectives have been criticized for reliability problems, splitting OCD and anxiety disorders, and comorbidity issues.
- PDM sees anxiety as a response to four basic danger situations and assesses how anxiety manifests in relationships.
- HiTOP assesses anxiety on its "Internalizing" spectra dimension and uses subdimensions to further divide it into distinct but related manifestations.

Historical Perspectives

- Historically, anxiety was conceived in both spiritual and medical terms.
- Between the eighteenth and twentieth centuries, anxiety was distinguished from depression and increasingly viewed in medical terms.

Biological Perspectives

- *Benzodiazepines* and *antidepressants* are commonly prescribed as *anxiolytics.*
- *SSRIs* and *tricylics* are prescribed for OCD; *augmenting agents* are also used.
- *Glutamate* is implicated in OCD, leading to drug research on *topiramate* and *riluzole.*
- Excessive *amygdala* and *insula* reactivity have been linked to anxiety. The *cortico-striatal-thalamo-cortical loop (CBGTC) hypothesis* ties OCD to dysfunctional circuitry.
- Anxiety and OCD have low to moderate *heritability.*
- Evolutionary perspectives emphasize anxiety as either *adaptive* or due to malfunctioning mental mechanisms (*adaptations*).
- Immune approaches to anxiety, obsessions, and compulsions stress *inflammation* and the *gut–brain axis.*
- Biological perspectives are criticized for difficulty replicating findings and overlooking psychological and sociocultural factors.

Psychological Perspectives

- *Little Hans* and the *Rat Man* are classic Freudian case studies of phobia and OCD, stressing unconscious conflicts.
- Modern psychodynamic therapies (such as *UPP-ANXIETY*) attribute anxiety to unacceptable repressed wishes or inconsistent parenting in early life; they link OCD to insecure parental attachments.
- CBT attributes anxiety, obsessions, and compulsions to conditioning, social learning, and faulty thinking processes. CBT interventions for anxiety, obsessions, and compulsions include *exposure plus response prevention (flooding), systematic desensitization, modeling, in vivo and imaginal exposure, thought stopping, traditional cognitive therapies,* and *mindfulness and acceptance cognitive therapies.*
- *Person-centered therapy* attributes anxiety to psychological incongruence and provides core conditions to foster self-consistency.
- Despite room for improvement, evidence supports CBT, psychodynamic, and humanistic therapies for anxiety. CBT fares best for OCD.

Sociocultural Perspectives

- There are cross-cultural differences in conceptions and expressions of anxiety. Poorer people suffer more from anxiety, but high-income countries have higher prevalence rates.
- Women are diagnosed with and medicated for anxiety more than men.
- *Structural family therapy* and other systemic therapies have been adapted for generalized and other forms of anxiety.
- Sociocultural perspectives are critiqued on the grounds that not everyone who faces challenging social circumstances experiences anxiety.

Closing Thoughts

- Neuroscientist Joseph LeDoux argues anxiety and fear are uniquely human emotions that emerge from, but can't be fully reduced to, brain processes.

NEW VOCABULARY

1. Acceptance and commitment therapy (ACT)
2. Accommodation
3. Agoraphobia
4. Anxiety
5. Anxiolytics
6. Benzodiazepines
7. Beta blockers
8. Body dysmorphic disorder (BDD)
9. Buspirone
10. Catastrophic misinterpretation model of panic disorder
11. Cognitive model of anxiety
12. Cognitive models of OCD
13. Compulsions
14. Cortico-striatal-thalamo-cortical loop (CBGTC) hypothesis
15. Excoriation (skin-picking disorder)
16. Exposure plus response prevention
17. Existential anxiety
18. Fear
19. Generalized anxiety disorder (GAD)
20. Glutamate hypothesis of OCD
21. Group selection theory of OCD
22. Gut-brain axis
23. Hoarding disorder
24. Imaginal exposure
25. *In vivo* exposure
26. Logotherapy
27. Mixed anxiety and depressive disorder
28. Neurotic anxiety
29. Obsessions
30. Obsessive-compulsive disorder (OCD)
31. Panic attack
32. Panic disorder
33. Participant modeling
34. Prepared conditioning
35. Selective mutism
36. Separation anxiety disorder
37. Social anxiety disorder
38. Specific phobia
39. Systematic desensitization
40. Thought stopping
41. Trichotillomania (hair-pulling disorder)
42. Unified psychodynamic protocol for anxiety disorders (UPP-ANXIETY)
43. Virtual reality exposure

TRAUMA, STRESS, AND LOSS

LEARNING OBJECTIVES

After reading this chapter, you should be able to:

1. Define trauma, stress, bereavement, grief, and dissociation.

2. Describe and evaluate DSM and ICD conceptualizations of posttraumatic and acute stress, adjustment disorder, and prolonged grief.

3. Explain historical perspectives on trauma.

4. Summarize and critique biological perspectives on trauma, stress, and loss—including neurochemical theories and treatments, brain structures implicated, genetic and evolutionary theories, and immune system explanations.

5. Review and assess psychodynamic, cognitive-behavioral, and humanistic approaches to trauma, stress, and loss.

6. Discuss and evaluate sociocultural approaches to trauma, loss, and stress that emphasize the importance of gender, culture, socioeconomic status, stigma, and expressed emotion; explain group interventions and couple/family system therapies.

Photo 7.1
Mike Labrum/Unsplash.

OVERVIEW

7.1 Getting Started: The Impact of Trauma, Stress, and Loss

Case Examples

Joe

Joe is a 30-year-old single man who recently survived an earthquake. The apartment complex where he lives was severely damaged in the quake and the roof collapsed, killing neighbors in several adjacent apartments. Joe himself was trapped in the rubble for six hours until rescuers could get him out safely. Miraculously, Joe escaped the building unharmed. Still, he has been having a difficult time psychologically in the six months since the event. Joe feels perpetually anxious and has nightmares about the roof collapsing on him. He also finds it difficult to concentrate at work or in social situations. When asked about this he merely replies, "I'm not quite myself lately." Joe also finds many things remind him of the quake. His office is near a metro station and whenever a train rumbles by, he gets anxious and jumpy because the sound is like the loud noise the apartment roof made just before crashing down on him. When asked what it was like to be trapped in the debris after the roof collapsed, he says, "It was like I was outside my own body watching it happen to someone else." Despite feeling grateful he survived the event, Joe is not getting much sleep, is worried about another earthquake, feels guilty that he survived while others perished, and can't seem to move past the incident. His relationships with others—especially his girlfriend Carol—are starting to suffer, so he decides to seek professional help.

Marigold

Marigold is a 55-year-old woman whose husband Harry passed away three years ago. Since that time, she has had a difficult time functioning. She feels sad and weepy much of the time. She even complains that time seems slower, and food hasn't tasted the same to her since Harry died. She desperately yearns to be reunited with her deceased husband and thinks about him much of the time. Reminders of Harry, however, rarely produce positive feelings of reminiscence and appreciation. Instead, they usually result in Marigold becoming tearful, upset, or angry over the loss. Marigold reports feeling emotionally numb and says she has lost interest in many things she previously enjoyed. For instance, her work as an attorney—which she used to love—now holds little interest for her and instead feels like a chore. Marigold has cut herself off from most of the friends and family with whom she and Harry used to associate. She is in a great deal of emotional pain and decides to seek out a psychotherapist.

Defining Trauma, Stress, Bereavement, Grief, and Dissociation

Trauma, stress, and loss are common presenting problems. They are so common, in fact, that a lot of the words that clinicians use when talking about them—terms such as trauma, stress, bereavement, grief, and dissociation—are used in everyday life by non-professionals, but often imprecisely. Therefore, before proceeding it seems important to define how clinicians and researchers typically use these terms.

Trauma

Let's start with **trauma**. Just like "panic attack" (discussed in Chapter 6), the term "trauma" is used more loosely in casual conversation than it is by most helping professionals. It is common to hear non-professionals identify events such as taking a difficult exam or having a favorite sports team lose a key game as "traumatic." This imprecise use of the term causes confusion because in clinical situations a "traumatic event" is typically limited to something severe, life threatening, and intense. For example, the DSM defines a trauma as involving "exposure to actual or threatened death, serious injury, or sexual violence" (American Psychiatric Association, 2022, p. 301). Taking a difficult exam clearly doesn't qualify! According to the ICD-11, events that do qualify include

natural or human-made disasters, combat, serious accidents, torture, sexual violence, terrorism, assault or acute life-threatening illness (e.g., a heart attack); witnessing the threatened or actual injury or death of others in a sudden, unexpected, or violent manner; and learning about the sudden, unexpected or violent death of a loved one. (World Health Organization, 2022a)

Less disruptive events may be upsetting and cause for concern, but don't fit the clinical definition of trauma.

Joe

Joe's life-threatening accident constitutes a traumatic event.

Stress

Stress is another term we often use imprecisely, probably "because it is such a highly subjective phenomenon that it defies definition" (Marksberry, n.d., para. 1). Stress is often defined in exceedingly broad terms as "a feeling of being overwhelmed, worried or run-down" (European Society of Preventative Medicine, n.d.; Mental Health Foundation, 2015), or as "the physiological or psychological response to internal or external stressors" (American Psychological Association,

Trauma: Exposure to actual or threatened death, serious injury, or sexual violence.

Stress: A feeling of being overwhelmed, worried, or run-down.

n.d.-h). The **general adaptation syndrome (GAS)** divides stress into three stages: *alarm* (the immediate fight or flight reaction to a stressor), *resistance* (the way the organism adapts physically and psychologically to the stressor), and *exhaustion* (the effects of long-term stress on physical and emotional well-being) (Selye, 1950). Although prolonged stress has deleterious effects, stress itself isn't always bad. It accompanies not just negative events (e.g., trauma and loss) but also positive ones (e.g., graduating college, getting married).

Bereavement and Grief

One common stressor people face is **bereavement**, defined as "the situation of having recently lost a significant person through death" (M. Stroebe et al., 2007, p. 1960). Bereaved individuals often undergo intense suffering and are vulnerable to emotional problems and physical illnesses (M. Stroebe et al., 2007). **Grief** is the primary emotional response to bereavement, consisting of both emotional and physical reactions (M. Stroebe et al., 2007). *Bereavement grief*, defined as grief over the loss of a close loved one, is extremely common. In one study, 96 percent of participants had experienced it at least once, and 78 percent (nearly four out of five participants) were still experiencing some degree of it at the time they were interviewed, which suggests that "bereavement grief is a major but largely unrecognized public health issue" (D. M. Wilson et al., 2018, p. 466). The numbers may be even higher than this because the study was conducted before the COVID-19 pandemic left so many people around the world grieving loved ones, including an estimated 1 in 450 children who lost a parent (R. M. Kumar, 2021; Lehrer-Small, 2021; Slomski, 2021; Unwin et al., 2022).

Elisabeth Kübler-Ross's well-known **five-stage theory of grief** posits that mourners progress through stages of *denial, anger, bargaining, depression,* and *acceptance* (Kübler-Ross, 1970; Kübler-Ross et al., 1972). While stage theories of grief enjoy widespread popularity, they have also been criticized for being simplistic, assuming people neatly move from one stage to the next in an orderly fashion, overlooking cultural differences, and lacking research support (M. Stroebe et al., 2017). Further, stage models assume that grief has a finite end point. But does it? Although we often speak of "getting over" grief, this is probably a misnomer because losses we experience in life typically continue to affect us indefinitely. Past losses may no longer be fresh or raw, but they can remain influential the rest of our lives (Arizmendi & O'Connor, 2015). Thus, some argue that grieving is best viewed as a lifelong process.

Dissociation in Response to Trauma, Stress, and Bereavement

In response to upsetting events such as trauma, stress, and bereavement, people sometimes dissociate. **Dissociation** is difficult to explain because the experience of it isn't logical or easily conveyed in words. Even clinical researchers often disagree on the particulars, offering varied definitions—including ones that stress narrowed consciousness, altered consciousness, and disengagement or separation from aspects of everyday experience (E. R. S. Nijenhuis & van der Hart, 2011). Despite some differences in emphasis, most definitions hold that dissociation involves detaching from experience, usually by separating, or *compartmentalizing*, emotions from one another so that when experiencing one emotion, other emotions are out of awareness (E. R. S. Nijenhuis & van der Hart, 2011). For example, when feeling extremely angry with your best friend, it is difficult to recall positive feelings you also have about this person; in that moment, those feelings are dissociated. Two commonly discussed aspects of dissociation are derealization and depersonalization (Holmes et al., 2005). In **derealization** the world seems remote, altered, or unreal. In **depersonalization**, the self (rather than the world) seems unreal or changed. Those who are depersonalizing disconnect from themselves and their emotions.

Marigold and Joe

Examples of derealization include Marigold's complaints that since her husband's death food hasn't tasted the same and time has slowed down. To Marigold, it is as if her physical surroundings have changed since her loss. By contrast, a good example of depersonalization involves Joe's recollection that, "It was like I was outside my own body watching it happen to someone else." He feels detached from his own experience.

In addition to depersonalization and derealization, people who are dissociating sometimes also experience **amnesia** (memory gaps), especially about emotionally charged issues (E. A. Holmes et al., 2005). For instance, someone who has been sexually assaulted may not be able to recall the event later.

The terms discussed above obviously are interrelated. Trauma and bereavement, for instance, can cause stress and dissociation. This chapter and Chapter 8 focus specifically on trauma, stress, loss, and dissociation. However, other presenting problems (depression, anxiety, and psychosis, among others) often involve these issues too, but without them necessarily being the prime focus of clinical attention. That is, problems like anxiety, depression, and psychosis often are associated with a history of trauma (DeRosse et al., 2014; H. L. Fisher et al., 2010; Kinderman et al., 2013)—something explored in the sociocultural sections of each chapter.

Amnesia: Memory gaps; sometimes occurs in dissociation.

DIAGNOSTIC PERSPECTIVES

7.2 DSM and ICD

There are some important differences in how DSM and ICD catalog trauma and stress disorders. DSM-5-TR includes posttraumatic stress disorder (PTSD), acute stress disorder, prolonged grief disorder, adjustment disorder, reactive attachment disorder, and disinhibited social engagement disorder. ICD-11 differs from DSM-5-TR by classifying acute stress as a "reaction" rather than "disorder," as well as by including a complex PTSD diagnosis.

Trauma- and Stressor-Related Disorders
Posttraumatic Stress Disorder (PTSD)

To receive a diagnosis of **posttraumatic stress disorder (PTSD)**, a person must experience a traumatic event (traumatic in the clinical sense, as described above). This makes PTSD "distinctive among psychiatric disorders in the requirement of exposure to a stressful event as a precondition" (Pai et al., 2017, p. 2). However, trauma alone isn't sufficient. PTSD is only diagnosed in people who experience significant psychological difficulty after the traumatic occurrence. Symptoms include distressing and intrusive memories of the incident, intense emotional upset about what happened, avoidance of things that remind them of the event, and reliving the event through bad dreams and *flashbacks* (experiences in which a person feels and acts as if the traumatic event is happening again). Ongoing and exaggerated anxiety is common, as is a tendency to dissociate. (Note that although DSM classifies PTSD as a trauma- and stressor-related disorder, it includes dissociative elements.) To qualify for a diagnosis, the DSM-5-TR requires that symptoms last one month or longer. In DSM-5 reliability field trials, PTSD was among the most reliable diagnoses (Freedman et al., 2013).

In response to concerns that PTSD is too inclusive, ICD-11 divided it into two diagnoses: PTSD and complex PTSD. The ICD-11 guidelines for PTSD focus more narrowly on fear circuitry than in the past (Bryant, 2019). They restrict the diagnosis to three core symptoms, which must persist for at least several weeks: reexperiencing the trauma, avoiding reminders of the event, and a sense of heightened threat and arousal. In addition to these core symptoms, **complex PTSD** also requires (a) difficulty managing emotion, (b) a sense of worthlessness plus feelings of shame, guilt, or failure, and (c) trouble maintaining relationships. By dividing PTSD into basic and complex types, ICD diverges from DSM, where a single PTSD category is used regardless of whether one displays these additional symptoms. Diagnostic Box 7.1 spells out these differences.

Posttraumatic stress disorder (PTSD): DSM and ICD disorder diagnosed in people who experience significant psychological difficulty for an extended period following a traumatic event.

Complex PTSD: ICD diagnosis for PTSD patients who have difficulties managing emotions, negative beliefs about themselves as worthless, and trouble maintaining relationships.

Joe
Joe reexperiences his accident in nightmares, actively avoids thinking about what happened because it upsets him, and feels an exaggerated sense of danger anytime there is a loud noise (such as a train rumbling by). He clearly qualifies for a PTSD diagnosis—and might even qualify for a complex PTSD diagnosis given that he is struggling to regulate his feelings and is encountering relational difficulties with his girlfriend, Carol.

Diagnostic Box 7.1 Posttraumatic Stress Disorder (PTSD)

DSM-5-TR

- Exposure to a traumatic event (actual or threatened death, physical injury, or sexual violation that is experienced, witnessed, or happened to a close friend or family member).
- At least one *intrusive symptom*: (1) invasive and upsetting recollections of the event, (2) dreams related to the event, (3) dissociative re-experiencing of the event (like flashbacks), (4) psychological or physical distress when reminded of the event.
- Avoids thoughts, feelings, memories, and reminders of the event.
- Has altered thoughts and feelings about the event (e.g., struggles to recall it, has distorted beliefs about it, blames self for it, feels negative emotions, loses interest in important activities, feels alienated from people, is unable to feel positive emotions).
- Regularly feels aroused and reactive (e.g., feels irritable and angry, engages in irresponsible and self-destructive actions, is easily alarmed startled, has trouble concentrating and/or sleeping).
- Symptoms last more than one month and can develop up to six months after the event.

ICD-11

- Response to an extremely threatening or catastrophic event (disaster; war; serious accident; witnessing someone die; being tortured, raped, assaulted, etc.).
- Displays three core symptoms: (1) re-experiences the trauma through memories, flashbacks, and dreams accompanied by strong emotions, (2) intentionally avoids reminders of the event, (3) experiences an ongoing sense of exaggerated threat.
- Symptoms last at least several weeks.
- *Complex PTSD*: Diagnosed instead of PTSD if the person also displays (1) difficulties regulating emotions, (2) the belief that one is worthless plus feelings of shame, guilt, or failure, (3) impaired interpersonal relationships.

Information from American Psychiatric Association (2022, pp. 301–304) and World Health Organization (2022a).

DSM-5-TR estimates lifetime prevalence for PTSD in the United States to be between 6.1 percent and 8.3 percent, with one-year prevalence at 4.7 percent. Although we might expect the highest rates of PTSD among people from poor countries (where poverty, malnutrition, and civil war run rampant), prevalence is actually greater in high-income than low-income countries (Benjet et al., 2016; Dückers et al., 2016; Dückers & Brewin, 2016; Dückers & Olff, 2017; Heir et al., 2019; Koenen et al., 2017). This has been described as a *vulnerability paradox*, in which countries better able to protect their citizens from trauma (e.g., Australia, Canada, the Netherlands, New Zealand, and the United States) have much higher PTSD prevalence than countries less equipped to do so (e.g., Colombia, Israel, Lebanon, Mexico, and South Africa); one pre-COVID-19 study found lifetime PTSD prevalence of 7.4 percent in the former countries but only 2.1 percent in the latter (Dückers et al., 2016)! Perhaps people in wealthy and more sheltered countries expect to live a trauma-free life, so when they encounter something traumatic, they are more likely to experience it as a serious and life-changing event, which places them at high risk for PTSD (Dückers et al., 2016; Heir et al., 2019). However, it is also possible that in wealthy countries where mental health issues have become less stigmatized, people are simply more likely to report traumatic events (Heir et al., 2019). The vulnerability paradox remains puzzling and not fully understood.

Variations by country notwithstanding, DSM-5-TR notes that the highest rates of PTSD are found among people who have faced terrible traumas such as rape, imprisonment, or war. DSM reports lower prevalence for children and adolescents following trauma, but this may reflect problems with diagnostic criteria. Further, those who have experienced prior psychological difficulties are at higher risk for PTSD, which makes sense given that the less well-adjusted one is the more difficult it will be to deal with a traumatic event. Childhood adversity, lack of social support, being of lower socioeconomic status, and belonging to minority racial or ethnic groups are also associated with developing PTSD. What all these factors have in common is that they involve social hardships that make coping with trauma more difficult.

Acute Stress Disorder/Reaction

DSM and ICD use the term **acute stress** to describe PTSD-like symptoms that don't last long enough to constitute full-blown PTSD. They posit nearly identical acute stress symptom durations—three days to one month in DSM-5-TR and a few hours to one month in ICD-11. The critical difference is that DSM classifies acute stress as a mental disorder, whereas ICD does not. ICD considers acute stress a "reaction" rather than a disorder; it assigns it a diagnostic code but views it as a normal response to traumatic events. This change addressed criticism that by including acute stress as a disorder, any reaction to trauma—even a brief and expected one—is unfairly deemed pathological. Diagnostic Box 7.2 outlines DSM criteria and ICD guidelines.

Acute stress: DSM and ICD term for PTSD-like symptoms that do not last long enough for a PTSD diagnosis; considered a disorder in DSM ("acute stress disorder") but normal and expected in ICD ("acute stress reaction").

Diagnostic Box 7.2 Acute Stress Disorder/Acute Stress Reaction

DSM-5-TR: Acute Stress Disorder

- Exposure to a traumatic event (actual or threatened death, physical injury, or sexual violation that is experienced, witnessed, or happened to a close friend or family member).
- Symptoms of intrusion, negative mood, dissociation, avoidance, and arousal like those found in PTSD.
- Symptoms usually occur right after the trauma and persist for three days to one month.

ICD-11: Acute Stress Reaction

- NOTE: Not considered a disorder, but still can be diagnosed.
- Normal and expected response to an extremely threatening or catastrophic event (disaster; war; serious accident; witnessing someone die; being tortured, raped, assaulted, etc.).
- Person may appear dazed, anxious, depressed, angry, despairing, overactive, or withdrawn—all symptoms considered normal given the intensity of the event.
- Symptoms occur within minutes of the event and last no more than a few days; when stressor or event continues, symptoms usually decrease within one month.

Information from American Psychiatric Association (2022, pp. 313–315) and World Health Organization (2022a).

Because of its shorter duration, more people encounter acute stress than PTSD after a traumatic event. Consistent with this, DSM-5-TR reports that half of people with PTSD previously experienced acute stress. DSM-5-TR also indicates that acute stress is more common following interpersonal traumatic events (such as rape or assault) than non-interpersonal traumas (such as car or other accidents).

Adjustment Disorder

Whereas PTSD and acute stress are responses to intense, often life-threatening, traumatic events, **adjustment disorders** are emotional reactions to milder life circumstances. People who receive adjustment disorder diagnoses are having a hard time coping with stressful life events—things like breaking up with someone, starting a new job, getting married, moving to a new home, starting a new business, retirement, or dealing with an ongoing health situation (the list is endless, really). It is common for such experiences to affect conduct and mood so long as the stressful situation is ongoing. Adjustment disorders are commonly used as catch-all categories for people who are facing continuing life stress but otherwise aren't especially disturbed and don't meet criteria for any other major mental disorder (Grubaugh, 2014; Strain & Diefenbacher, 2008). This allows clinicians to use adjustment disorder codes to diagnose people in a relatively non-stigmatizing way. Diagnostic Box 7.3 clarifies how ICD guidelines emphasize preoccupation with and worry over the stressor, while DSM criteria are more general but retain subtypes not in ICD (O'Donnell et al., 2019)—a definitional difference that potentially impedes adjustment disorder research (Zelviene & Kazlauskas, 2018).

Adjustment disorders: DSM and ICD diagnoses used to identify emotional reactions to ongoing stressors.

Diagnostic Box 7.3 Adjustment Disorder

DSM-5-TR
- Emotional and behavioral symptoms due to one or more life stressors.
- Disproportionate distress and/or impaired functioning.
- Symptoms not due to bereavement or another mental disorder.
- Symptoms develop within one month of the stressor, but once the stressor is eliminated symptoms resolve within six months.
- Specific types of adjustment disorder are diagnosed depending on whether the main symptoms are depression, anxiety, disruptive conduct, or some combination thereof.

ICD-11
- Emotional distress due to major life changes or stressful circumstances (e.g., divorce or break-up, job loss, receiving an illness diagnosis, work conflicts, family conflicts).
- The person is preoccupied with the stressor and worries excessively about it.
- Once the stressor is eliminated, symptoms disappear within six months.

Information from American Psychiatric Association (2022, pp. 319–320) and World Health Organization (2022a).

Prolonged Grief Disorder

Prolonged grief disorder: DSM and ICD diagnosis for people who experience intense and disruptive grief for an extended period following the loss of a loved one.

DSM-5-TR and ICD-11 both introduced a new diagnosis called **prolonged grief disorder**, intended for clients who feel intense grief for an extended period and have difficulty moving on with their lives. These clients yearn for and seem preoccupied with the lost loved one, feel intense sorrow, and experience a great deal of emotional distress over the loss that interferes with their daily functioning. It has been estimated that 10 percent of bereaved adults are at risk for prolonged grief (Lundorff et al., 2017). However, DSM-5-TR reports that its prevalence is unknown. Some studies suggest prevalence might be higher in women, but this remains debated. Due to cultural differences in how people display grief, it can be difficult to identify prevalence differences across ethnic groups. Diagnostic Box 7.4 shows how DSM-5-TR and ICD-11 conceptualize prolonged grief disorder.

Diagnostic Box 7.4 Prolonged Grief Disorder

DSM-5-TR
- After the death of someone close, one or more: (1) yearning for the lost person, (2) immense grief and emotional upset over the loss, (3) fixation on the lost person, (4) overly focused on how the person died.
- Experiences both (1) *reactive distress* (e.g., trouble accepting the death, incredulity about the loss, difficulty reminiscing positively, angry or bitter feelings, avoids reminders of the loss); and (2) *social/identity disruption* (e.g., wants to die and be reunited with dead person, doesn't trust others, feels detached, feels life is meaningless without the lost person, lack of interest in planning for the future).
- Reactive distress and social/identity disruption last at least 12 months (six months in children).

ICD-11
- Ongoing and extensive grief response involving longing for and fixation on the lost person, intense emotional upset (e.g., anger, guilt, denial, blame, numbness), and trouble participating in social interactions.
- Symptoms last at least six months, though cultural differences should be considered in making a diagnosis.

Information from American Psychiatric Association (2022, pp. 322–323) and World Health Organization (2022a).

Marigold
Marigold, who has been overwhelmed with unbearable grief since her husband's death three years ago, could be diagnosed with prolonged grief disorder.

Reactive Attachment Disorder and Disinhibited Social Engagement Disorder

There are two trauma- and stressor-related diagnoses reserved specifically for children. **Reactive attachment disorder** is diagnosed in kids who have experienced severe environmental neglect, often with regular changes in who is taking care of them. Consequently, they do not develop an ability to form attachments. Children with this diagnosis are emotionally withdrawn and inhibited around caregivers. They don't seek comfort when distressed and, when comfort is provided, they aren't especially responsive to it. Episodes of sadness, irritability, and fear are also common. Children with **disinhibited social engagement disorder** also have a history of neglect or deprivation, with frequent changes in and failure to establish strong attachments to primary caregivers. Yet rather than becoming withdrawn and disengaged, they are overly comfortable and familiar with strangers; they seem perfectly willing to approach, engage with, or even wander off with unfamiliar adults. DSM-5-TR says the prevalence of these two disorders is unknown but that they are rare. Criteria and guidelines appear in Diagnostic Box 7.5.

Evaluating DSM and ICD Perspectives

Various concerns and controversies have surrounded the DSM and ICD approaches to PTSD, acute stress, and adjustment disorders. A few of these are highlighted below.

Reactive attachment disorder: DSM and ICD diagnosis given to children who have experienced severe environmental neglect and do not develop the ability to form attachments; they are withdrawn and inhibited around caregivers.

Disinhibited social engagement disorder: DSM and ICD diagnosis given to children who have experienced severe environmental neglect and show a lack of reticence and/or overly familiar behavior around adult strangers.

Diagnostic Box 7.5 Reactive Attachment Disorder and Disinhibited Social Engagement Disorder

Reactive Attachment Disorder: DSM-5-TR and ICD-11
- There is a history of neglect or maltreatment from primary caregiver(s).
- Inhibited and withdrawn around adult caregivers when upset; unresponsive when caregivers offer comfort during times of distress.
- Develops by age 5 but cannot be diagnosed before age 1 (or in those with a developmental age less than 9 months).

Disinhibited Social Engagement Disorder: DSM-5-TR and ICD-11
- There is a history of neglect or maltreatment from primary caregiver(s).
- Lack of reticence and/or overly familiar behavior around adult strangers.
- Minimal or absent checking back with caregivers in unfamiliar situations.
- Minimal or absent hesitation about wandering off with adult strangers.
- *DSM-5-TR:* Developmental age of 9 months or older.
- *ICD-11:* Develops by age 5 but cannot be diagnosed before age 1 (or in those with a developmental age less than 9 months).

Information from American Psychiatric Association (2022, pp. 295–296 and 298–299) and World Health Organization (2022a).

Separating Trauma- and Stressor-Related Disorders from Anxiety Disorders

DSM-5 created controversy by placing PTSD, acute stress disorder, adjustment disorder, and (more recently, in DSM-5-TR) prolonged grief in a new trauma- and stressor-related disorders chapter (Pai et al., 2017)—a step also taken by ICD-11. Regarding PTSD specifically, there has long been discussion about where to locate it in DSM. It was classified as an anxiety disorder for over thirty years, from its first appearance in DSM-III through DSM-IV-TR. However, even when PTSD was grouped with the anxiety disorders, some wondered whether it belonged elsewhere—as a dissociative disorder, for instance (R. D. Marshall et al., 1999). It has been debated whether grouping PTSD as a trauma- and stressor-related disorder (rather than as an anxiety disorder) undermines researchers working to identify its underlying fear mechanisms (M. W. Miller et al., 2014; L. A. Zoellner et al., 2011). The takeaway is that PTSD—with its mix of anxiety, fear, and dissociation—has similarities to a variety of other presenting problems. This might explain disagreement over where to house it in DSM and ICD.

PTSD as an Expectable Reaction, Not a Disorder

PTSD has also been criticized for something more serious: violating the very definition of mental disorder. How so? Well, many consider the symptoms of PTSD—even if they last notably longer than acute stress reactions—to be reasonable reactions to unreasonable and understandably traumatizing events (Burstow, 2005; Prescod, 2020; M. Thompson, 2011). If such distress is expected, then how is PTSD a disorder? After all, according to DSM-5-TR, a mental disorder cannot be an "expectable or culturally approved response to a common stressor or loss" (American Psychiatric Association, 2022, p. 14). Thus, critics maintain that we are on shaky ground when we classify PTSD as a disorder.

Adjustment Disorder as a "Waste-Basket" Diagnosis

Adjustment disorder has been criticized for being nebulous, perhaps because it was purposely devised to lack specificity (Strain & Friedman, 2011). The reason for this ambiguity appears to be so that people experiencing ongoing stress, who don't meet criteria for more serious disorders such as depression or anxiety, can be diagnosed and receive services (Casey & Bailey, 2011). Because of its flexible and vague criteria, critics complain that "adjustment disorder is one of the most ill-defined mental disorders, often described as the 'waste-basket' of the psychiatric classification scheme" (Maercker et al., 2013, p. 198). Perhaps even more than PTSD and acute stress, adjustment disorder has been criticized for improperly turning expectable forms of everyday emotional distress into mental disorders (Casey & Bailey, 2011). However, despite conceptual disagreement over its legitimacy, adjustment disorder serves a highly practical purpose in the United States, where diagnoses are required for health insurance to pay for services: Without adjustment disorder diagnostic codes, many people who don't meet criteria for any other disorder couldn't afford psychotherapy (Casey & Bailey, 2011). Whether this practical goal justifies including adjustment disorder in DSM and ICD depends on whether you prioritize insurance coverage or avoiding the medicalization of mental distress.

Should Prolonged Grief Be a Disorder?

Designating prolonged grief as a mental disorder has been controversial. Supporters say it is a clearly identifiable problem that can be reliably distinguished from normal bereavement (Prigerson, Boelen, et al., 2021; Prigerson, Kakarala, et al., 2021). They contend that recognizing it as a mental disorder raises awareness and encourages research into new treatments (Barry, 2022). They also argue that DSM-5-TR criteria and the *PG-13-R assessment scale* (used to help make prolonged grief diagnoses) constitute "reliable and valid measures for the classification of bereaved individuals with maladaptive grief responses" (Prigerson, Boelen, et al., 2021, p. 105). However, critics object to making prolonged grief a disorder. They think doing so medicalizes and pathologizes grieving (Bandini, 2015; Granek, 2017; Wada, 2022). As one critic put it, "the medicalization of grief narrows the criteria of what is considered 'appropriate grief,' both in the duration and magnitude of depressive feelings, turning much of normal grief into a psychiatric disorder in need of treatment" (Bandini, 2015, p. 351). In "The Lived Experience" box, a critic of prolonged grief shares her personal experience to argue that grief is a lifelong process, not a disorder.

The Lived Experience: Grief Ten Years Later

This September, it will be ten years since my mother died of cancer. It seems as if it were a lifetime ago and it seems as if it were yesterday. That is the nature of grief; it has its own rhythm. It is both present and in the past and it appears that it continues to stay that way no matter how much time has gone by.

A few years ago when my friend Meghan O'Rourke and I published a series of articles on grief and loss in *Slate* magazine, some criticized the findings because some of the respondents had experienced a loss many years before taking the survey. In psychology we call this phenomenon "recall bias," where people filling out surveys wrongly or incompletely remember experiences from the past.

Memory is certainly pliable, and it is possible that people made errors in recalling what their grief was really like for them. Methodologically and intuitively that makes sense, but as a griever, I am not so sure.

The idea that the more years have passed since a loss, the less likely someone is to recall their grief rests on the assumption that grief is a static event in time that will eventually fade. This view is aligned with what many researchers in the field of psychology and psychiatry believe: that grief has a starting point, a middle point, and an end point. The heated debates in the media and in the field about when grief becomes pathological rest on the assumption that at some point, grief becomes "too much" and needs to be treated with medication or a mental health professional. If grief is a static event in time, then it certainly makes sense that it would be hard for people to remember what their experience was like five or ten years after a loss.

Having spent years studying grief, and being a griever myself now entering her tenth year of loss, I know that grief does not work this way. It is not an event in time. It is not even just an emotional response to a loss. It is a process that changes us permanently but also constantly as we ourselves change and grow. In this sense, grief is just like love. It is not something that happens once and goes away—it is something that evolves, expands and contracts, and changes in shape, depth, and intensity as time goes on.

Grief is a lifelong, ever-changing companion. It is both in the present and in the past. Moments of intense yearning and pain for the deceased can come and go even ten or twenty or thirty years after a person we love has died. It is cliché to say it, but it is also true: Grief is the price we pay for love. Grief is still with me because my mother is still with me. To deny one is inevitably to deny the other.

Interestingly, between mothers and children, there is a biological correlate to "the being with and in each other" called fetal microchimerism. It is an amazing phenomenon where fetal cells from the baby make their way into their mother's bodies and vice versa, mother's cells become intertwined into the baby's body. In other words, my mother is literally part of me biologically and emotionally and my cells were with, and in her when she died.

To be sure, microchimerism is just a metaphor—this being with and part of each other is not just for biological mothers and children. It is for everyone who has loved and lost. When I present my professional work, I often say I am a grief researcher, but actually, grief is just a stand in for what I am really studying—love and attachment. One cannot come without the other. Just like love, grief is an experience that evolves and changes with time; but one thing is for sure, it is not forgettable, because it never goes away.

By Leeat Granek, Ph.D. Reprinted with permission.

7.3 Other Diagnostic Perspectives

PDM-2

In discussing PTSD and complex PTSD, PDM-2 notes that psychodynamic approaches have long emphasized the "shock, helplessness, vulnerability, and terror specific to trauma" (Lingiardi & McWilliams, 2017, p. 187). PDM views the patient–therapist relationship as a mechanism for patients to "work through" trauma and warns about the risk of secondary traumatization when therapists aren't prepared to handle the magnitude of their patients' traumas. PDM-2 notes that the trauma and neglect of complex PTSD, in particular, "are essentially relational, and so the therapeutic relationship itself becomes the principal vehicle of change" (Lingiardi & McWilliams, 2017, p. 191). We revisit the relational nature of psychodynamic approaches to trauma later in the chapter.

HiTOP

PTSD symptoms are associated with high scores on HiTOP's "Internalizing," "Thought Disorder," and "Externalizing" spectra dimensions; these symptoms are also correlated with personality dimensions related to negative affect, detachment, and psychoticism (Somma et al., 2022). HiTOP researchers argue that DSM and ICD posttraumatic stress diagnoses miss nuances that cut across symptomatic trauma survivors. For instance, reexperiencing unpleasant memories may not be as unique to PTSD as DSM and ICD indicate (Levin-Aspenson et al., 2021). By assessing trauma along its spectra and related dimensions, HiTOP aims to provide a more accurate clinical picture than what it views as the flawed categorical approach of DSM and ICD.

PTMF

Because PTMF places oppressive and challenging social conditions front and center, trauma is central to its conception of mental distress. Its emphasis on *power* ("what happened to you") and *threat* ("how you responded to it") reflect this. Although PTMF sometimes uses the term "trauma," its developers prefer the word "adversity" to avoid the medical connotations that "trauma" conveys. PTMF identifies many examples of adversity (often but not always in childhood) that cause mental distress—including bullying, neglect, sexual and physical abuse, violence at home, and emotional abuse (Johnstone et al., 2018).

HISTORICAL PERSPECTIVES

7.4 Early Clinical Descriptions of Trauma

We limit our historical discussion to trauma. Accounts of what today we call posttraumatic stress are found throughout history. For example, six months after surviving the 1666 Great Fire of London, renowned diarist Samuel Pepys reported ongoing emotional symptoms, including panic and nightmares (Tehrani, 2004). Some of the earliest clinical descriptions of posttraumatic stress can be traced to the U.S. Civil War, when soldiers experienced heart palpitations, exhaustion, and excessive alcohol and tobacco use. Their condition was alternately referred to as *disordered palpitation of the heart, irritable heart,* or *soldier's heart* (DiMauro et al., 2014; van der Kolk, 2007). Combatants exhibiting these symptoms were often stigmatized and viewed negatively as either having a constitutional weakness or simply being malingerers (DiMauro et al., 2014).

7.5 Traumatic Neurosis

By the 1880s, the German neurologist Hermann Oppenheim (1858–1919) coined the term *traumatic neurosis* and argued it had an organic cause originating in the central nervous system (Tehrani, 2004; van der Kolk, 2007). In the UK, the idea of traumatic neurosis was applied to people who experienced emotional difficulties following railway accidents, a condition known as *railway spine* (Gasquoine, 2020; E. Jones & Wessely, 2007). Oppenheim's emphasis on physiology anticipated current biological theories of PTSD. However, not everyone shared his biological perspective. Those coming from a more psychological orientation saw trauma and stress—including sexual abuse—as central to cases of *hysterical neurosis* (a broad diagnostic category reserved for people who displayed a variety of physical and psychological symptoms). Jean-Martin Charcot, Pierre Janet, and later Sigmund Freud all gravitated toward this more psychological way of understanding trauma. Yet they weren't always accurate in their assessments. Freud, for instance, incorrectly predicted that soldiers' war neuroses would disappear when the fighting ended (van der Kolk, 2007). He also focused too much on patients' projected fantasies, downplaying the psychological impact of real traumas such as sexual abuse (Tehrani, 2004). However, in connecting posttraumatic stress to repression and avoidance of painful memories, Freud and his colleagues planted the seeds for a psychodynamic model of trauma that remains influential (van der Kolk, 2007).

7.6 War Neurasthenia and Shell Shock

Diagnostically, the term *war neurasthenia* became popular in the late 1800s and early 1900s. It constituted a variation on neurasthenia, the diagnosis given to sad and anxious people (see Chapters 5 and 6). War neurasthenia was a vague disorder attributed to a weak nervous system deemed unable to handle the challenges of combat (DiMauro et al., 2014). During the First World War, war neurasthenia gave way to *shell shock* (Crocq & Crocq, 2000; Linden & Jones, 2014). Like soldier's heart before it, shell shock included symptoms such as "chest pain, heart palpitations, tremors, fatigue, and even paralysis" (DiMauro et al., 2014, p. 777). The condition was called shell shock because it was thought to originate from repeated exposure to exploding artillery shells (Andreasen, 2010).

After the First World War, psychoanalyst Abram Kardiner (1891–1981) wrote extensively about shell shock (Kardiner & Spiegel, 1947). Kardiner preferred Oppenheim's term traumatic neurosis, as he combined Oppenheim's biologically based explanations with Freud's emphasis on repressing traumatic memories (E. Jones & Wessely, 2007; van der Kolk, 2007). In describing traumatic neurosis, Kardiner noted that many soldiers exhibited exaggerated startle responses, irritability and aggression, nightmares, and a fixation on the trauma—all symptoms today considered part of PTSD. Given how well he anticipated current understandings, it has been argued that "more than anyone else, Kardiner defined PTSD for the remainder of the 20th century" (van der Kolk, 2007, p. 26). However, his impact wasn't immediate. At the start of the Second World War, many of Kardiner's insights went unheeded and had to be learned anew as many soldiers began displaying signs of trauma (van der Kolk, 2007). Awareness was greater by the end of the war, with one study predicting that 98 percent of surviving soldiers would suffer from emotional exhaustion, anxiety, and depression (E. Jones & Wessely, 2007).

7.7 The Emergence of PTSD as a Diagnosis

Both before and after the Second World War, a variety of diagnostic names went in and out of fashion before clinicians settled on PTSD. Besides *traumatic war neurosis*, other diagnoses for combat-induced posttraumatic stress included *combat fatigue*, *battle stress*, and *gross stress reaction* (Andreasen, 2010). Gross stress reaction was the term in 1952's DSM-I (American Psychiatric Association, 1952). It was a milder and more general diagnosis than today's PTSD. Its symptoms were viewed as temporary reactions to exceptional mental or physical stress (DiMauro et al., 2014). Surprisingly, gross stress reaction was removed from 1968's DSM-II. This might have occurred because DSM-II was developed during a period of relative peace when few soldiers were returning from war in a damaged emotional state (Andreasen, 2010). Regardless of why, from 1968 until 1980, DSM contained no diagnosis specifically for trauma.

Posttraumatic stress disorder—originally developed using names like *post-Vietnam syndrome* and *delayed stress syndrome*—debuted as a diagnosis in 1980's DSM-III (E. Jones & Wessely, 2007). The category was added mainly in response to Vietnam War veteran groups, which lobbied to have it recognized as a disorder. However, although the proposal for PTSD was originally intended for veterans, it soon broadened to encompass similar symptoms in response to other threatening life events (S. A. Baldwin et al., 2004). For instance, researchers studying what was then informally called *rape trauma syndrome* (Burgess, 1983; Burgess & Holmstrom, 1974)—a reaction to being sexually assaulted characterized by similar symptoms to those displayed by returning war vets—began using the PTSD diagnosis. In the end, PTSD came to include not just trauma from war and rape, but also from accidents, natural disasters, physical assaults, terrorism, and genocide.

Regardless of whether one sees PTSD as having become too inclusive, an important point in thinking about its history is that—despite its preeminence today—PTSD is a relatively recent diagnosis and our ways of understanding and talking about it continue to change with the times. Within the last few years alone, ICD-11 revised "classic" PTSD, added complex PTSD, and demoted acute stress from disorder to reaction. As one PTSD historian warned, "research on mental disorders reflects the historical period and associated cultural values in which the research is conducted" and therefore "what we today call PTSD is quite different from both what started out as PTSD and from previous war-related problems" (S. A. Baldwin et al., 2004, para. 30). Some historians believe this makes PTSD a culture-bound syndrome that mirrors societal ways of defining and responding to trauma (E. Jones & Wessely, 2007). From a historical perspective, evolving notions of PTSD reflect how ideas about mental distress shift across time.

Photo 7.2 Rapper G Herbo has lost dozens of friends to gun violence and has reflected on the pain of this loss in his music. His album *PTSD* examines his own experience of the diagnosis and the prevalence of PTSD in his community in Chicago.
Prince Williams/Getty Images.

BIOLOGICAL PERSPECTIVES

7.8 Brain Chemistry Perspectives

Posttraumatic Stress

Both serotonin and norepinephrine transmission are suspected of playing roles in posttraumatic stress (Bryant et al., 2010; X. Pan et al., 2018; Southwick et al., 1999). Consistent with this, SSRIs (which increase serotonin) and SNRIs (which increase serotonin and norepinephrine) are commonly prescribed for PTSD, although evidence for them is mixed and their effects are often small (Bryant, 2019; M. D.

Hoskins et al., 2021; Merz et al., 2019). The best supported SSRIs for PTSD are *paroxetine* (trade name *Paxil*), *sertraline* (trade name *Zoloft*) and *fluoxetine* (trade name *Prozac*); there is also a strong body of evidence for the SNRI *venlafaxine* (*Effexor*) (M. D. Hoskins et al., 2021). At this time, only paroxetine and sertraline are approved by the U.S. FDA for PTSD (Bryant, 2019). Part of the reason SSRI and SNRI antidepressants are used is because PTSD is highly comorbid with depression (Bryant, 2019).

Other drugs are sometimes used for PTSD, even though there isn't always much evidence for doing so. Although some researchers suspect they are as effective as SSRIs, tricyclic and MAOI antidepressants aren't usually prescribed for PTSD because (a) they have more serious side effects and (b) drug companies have few economic incentives to further research and market them (Davidson, 2015; Friedman & Davidson, 2014). The anti-seizure drug *topiramate*, the antipsychotics *aripiprazole* (Abilify) and *risperidone* (Risperdal), and the high blood pressure medicine *prazosin* (an alpha-adrenergic drug, which blocks norepinephrine at alpha receptors) are occasionally used with PTSD (alone or combined with antidepressants); they can alleviate certain symptoms (for instance, prazosin reduces nightmares) but lack extensive research support (Britnell et al., 2017; Guideline Development Panel for the Treatment of Depressive Disorders, 2019; M. D. Hoskins et al., 2021; Z.-D. Huang et al., 2020). *Benzodiazepines* are explicitly not recommended for PTSD, as they sometimes make symptoms worse (Guina et al., 2015).

Although a variety of drugs are prescribed for PTSD, they are often (but not always) considered inferior to psychological therapies (D. J. Lee et al., 2016; Merz et al., 2019; Sonis & Cook, 2019). While SSRIs are the most highly regarded drugs for posttraumatic stress, not everyone views them as a first-line treatment. One review concluded that "pharmacological interventions for PTSD can be effective, but the magnitude of effect unfortunately is small, and the clinical relevance of this small effect is unclear" (M. Hoskins et al., 2015, p. 98). When it comes to PTSD, drugs are often a second line treatment after psychotherapy.

Joe

In the first few months after the earthquake, when Joe's posttraumatic stress symptoms were at their worst, his family physician prescribed him the antidepressant paroxetine (Paxil). Joe took it (along with prazosin for his nightmares) for six months, despite his girlfriend Carol's misgivings. However, Joe eventually weaned himself off the paroxetine. He thinks taking it helped him somewhat but feels that seeking psychotherapy to come to terms with what happened will prove more beneficial in the long run.

Adjustment

Given that adjustment disorder tends to be diagnosed in generally well-adjusted people dealing with ongoing life stress, research into brain chemistry and psychopharmacology has not been very extensive or of high quality (O'Donnell et al., 2018). Nonetheless, drugs are sometimes prescribed for adjustment difficulties—including benzodiazepines, antidepressants, and even antipsychotics (Greiner et al., 2020; D. J. Stein, 2018). These drugs are used to alleviate symptoms such as depression, anxiety, or sleep difficulties. Prescribing drugs for adjustment problems is controversial—with particular attention on the appropriateness of benzodiazepines, which (as already noted) are contraindicated for PTSD, another trauma- and stressor-related disorder; this has led some to suspect that benzodiazepines might also do more harm than good for adjustment disorder (D. J. Stein, 2018).

Prolonged Grief

Even with the addition of prolonged grief to DSM and ICD, few studies have examined drug treatment for it, and many suffer from small sample sizes (Bui et al., 2012; A. H. Jordan & Litz, 2014). What evidence there is suggests that antidepressants—both SSRIs and tricyclics—can reduce signs of bereavement-related depression (Bui et al., 2012). However, many researchers distinguish bereavement-related depression from prolonged grief. For the latter, there is some evidence for use of *paroxetine* (Paxil) and *escitalopram* (Lexapro), especially when combined with talk therapy (Bui et al., 2012; A. H. Jordan & Litz, 2014; Mancini et al., 2012; Shear & Mulhare, 2008; N. M. Simon, 2013). However, overall evidence for medication is ambiguous (Bui et al., 2012; Doering & Eisma, 2016). Critics of prescribing drugs worry that doing so reflects the inappropriate trend toward medicalizing grief (Bandini, 2015). Medication supporters counter that when grief goes on for a long time, drugs provide much needed assistance.

7.9 Brain Structure and Function Perspectives

Hippocampus

People diagnosed with PTSD encounter a variety of memory-related symptoms. They ruminate about the trauma, relive it through flashbacks, and have trouble recalling it. Many studies have found that the hippocampus (the limbic structure involved in storing and recalling long-term memories) shows reduced volume in people with PTSD (Ahmed-Leitao et al., 2016; Bremner, 1999; Casale et al., 2022; Chao et al., 2014; L. W. Chen et al., 2018; O'Doherty et al., 2015; Sala et al., 2004; Sapolsky, 2000; Shin et al., 2006; Villarreal et al., 2002; Woon et al., 2010). SSRIs or exposure therapy may reverse or stall hippocampal shrinkage, but more evidence is needed (L. L. Davis et al., 2006; Rubin et al., 2016). Also unresolved is whether smaller hippocampus volume makes people vulnerable to posttraumatic stress or whether posttraumatic stress leads to reduced hippocampus volume (Gilbertson et al., 2002; Sherin & Nemeroff, 2011; van Rooij et al., 2015; Wignall et al., 2004; Woon et al., 2010). Perhaps it's both: smaller hippocampal volume might place one at risk for PTSD, but trauma could also affect the size of the hippocampus.

Amygdala and Medial Prefrontal Cortex

Two other brain structures implicated in posttraumatic stress are the amygdala (part of the limbic system, like the hippocampus) and the medial prefrontal cortex (not part of the limbic system, but closely connected to it). The amygdala, which is involved in emotional memory, is not just very active in depressed people (see Chapter 5). It is also highly active in acute and posttraumatic stress (Forster et al., 2017; Kredlow et al., 2022; Reynaud et al., 2015; Shin et al., 2006). While the amygdala appears to be over responsive, the *medial prefrontal cortex* (important in memory and decision-making) appears under-responsive in PTSD (Kredlow et al., 2022; Shin et al., 2005, 2006). It is suspected that the underactive medial prefrontal cortex and hippocampus fail to inhibit the amygdala (Forster et al., 2017; Koenigs & Grafman, 2009; D. Sun et al., 2020). Researchers are also exploring whether the amygdala and medial prefrontal cortex have decreased volumes in PTSD. Existing evidence is mixed but suggests posttraumatic stress may be associated with smaller volumes in these two brain regions (Casale et al., 2022; L. Li et al., 2014; R. A. Morey et al., 2012; Shin et al., 2006).

Autonomic Nervous System and HPA Axis

The **autonomic nervous system (ANS)** is implicated in posttraumatic stress. The ANS is responsible for regulating automatic biological functions affected by stress—things like heart rate, blood pressure, and emotional arousal. It has two branches: the sympathetic and parasympathetic nervous systems. The *sympathetic nervous system (SNS)* is activated when a person is under stress, causing physiological changes such as increased breathing and heart rate, pupil dilation, inhibition of appetite, and higher blood pressure. The *parasympathetic nervous system (PNS)* counters the SNS, slowing down breathing and heart rates, normalizing pupils, reestablishing hunger, and lowering blood pressure. The **fight or flight response** (in which an organism decides whether to flee from danger, engage it, or freeze) is controlled by the sympathetic nervous system. People experiencing posttraumatic stress appear to be in a perpetual "fight or flight" state—perhaps due to decreased activity of the medial prefrontal cortex, which helps suppress the sympathetic nervous system (Williamson et al., 2013).

Also noteworthy is the hypothalamic-pituitary-adrenal (HPA) axis (discussed in relation to depression in Chapter 5). The HPA axis consists of the hypothalamus, as well as the pituitary and adrenal glands. It is involved in stress, immunity, mood regulation, and sex drive. The HPA axis oversees production of the anti-inflammatory stress hormone cortisol (again, see Chapter 5). It

Autonomic nervous system (ANS): Regulates automatic biological functions affected by stress; consists of *sympathetic nervous system* (during times of stress, activates increased breathing and heart rate, pupil dilation, inhibition of appetite, and higher blood pressure) and *parasympathetic nervous systems* (following stress, slows down breathing and heart rates, normalizes pupils, reestablishes hunger, and lowers blood pressure).

Fight or flight response: Controlled by the sympathetic nervous system; process by which organism decides whether to flee from danger, engage it, or freeze.

is suspected that after initial hypersensitivity, the HPA axis becomes inhibited in PTSD (Lehrner et al., 2016). This should result in lower cortisol levels, but research support for this is mixed (de Kloet et al., 2006; Ironson et al., 2007; Lehrner et al., 2016; Meewisse et al., 2007; Olff et al., 2006; Pace & Heim, 2011). Although the exact roles of the HPA axis and cortisol still require clarification, researchers are testing low doses of *hydrocortisone* (an anti-inflammatory drug that replicates the effect of cortisol) as an immediate posttraumatic stress intervention. Unfortunately, the hydrocortisone must be administered within six hours of the trauma to have an effect (Amos et al., 2014; Astill Wright et al., 2019).

7.10 Genetic Perspectives

Heritability of Trauma and Stress

Only 20 percent to 30 percent of those exposed to trauma develop full-blown posttraumatic stress; when it comes to PTSD risk, heritability accounts for 30 percent to 40 percent of the variance (Almli et al., 2014). This suggests some people have a genetic predisposition to mental distress after trauma. However, given that PTSD is a response to environmental (rather than genetic) events, most researchers believe gene–environment interactions are key to understanding it. Genetic predispositions make people vulnerable to PTSD, but nothing comes of it unless there are trauma-inducing circumstances (Hawn et al., 2019; Koenen et al., 2008, 2009; D. Mehta & Binder, 2012; Sheerin et al., 2019). Nonetheless, parsing gene–environment interactions in PTSD is difficult.

Candidate Genes in Trauma and Stress

Candidate gene studies have identified numerous genetic markers that seem to correlate with stress, trauma, and depression. Given that impaired serotonin transmission is thought to play a role in posttraumatic stress, it makes sense that variations in the serotonin transporter gene (*5-HTT*)—such as having the short rather than long allele in the 5-HTTPLR region—have been tied to posttraumatic stress (Bryant et al., 2010; Caspi et al., 2003; L. Liu et al., 2018; McGuffin et al., 2011; Zerbinati et al., 2021; M. Zhao et al., 2017). Genome-wide association studies (GWAS) have implicated a large number of genes in PTSD (L. E. Duncan et al., 2018; Nievergelt et al., 2019; M. B. Stein et al., 2021). Heritability and genetic markers vary somewhat by sex (with women more vulnerable to PTSD than men) (L. E. Duncan et al., 2018; Nievergelt et al., 2019; J. Wang et al., 2022). Additionally, some genes linked to PTSD are also tied to schizophrenia (L. E. Duncan et al., 2018), as well as internalizing (e.g., mood and anxiety) disorders (M. B. Stein et al., 2021). Unfortunately, genetic marker studies have yielded inconsistent results (L. E. Duncan et al., 2018; M. B. Stein et al., 2016). Perhaps genetic vulnerability to PTSD varies by the type of trauma someone experiences (M. B. Stein et al., 2021).

Bereavement

There isn't much research on genetic correlates of prolonged grief. A small pilot study found that having the longer allele on the monoamine oxidase gene (*MAO-A*) increased the likelihood of prolonged grief (Kersting et al., 2007). Other research suggests that for some bereaved people, certain genetic markers correlate with higher levels of inflammation (Schultze-Florey et al., 2012). Of course, gene–environment interactions are likely important in all this. As with PTSD following trauma, some people appear to be genetically vulnerable to prolonged grief following loss (O'Connor et al., 2014; Seiler, von Känel, et al., 2020).

7.11 Evolutionary Perspectives

Trauma and Stress

Evolutionary perspectives look at how trauma and stress responses aid in survival and reproduction (Cantor, 2009). Fight or flight reactions are viewed as evolved mechanisms that help people cope with stress and danger (D. V. Baldwin, 2013). When operating properly, these mechanisms yield normal and expected emotional upset following trauma. In most cases, this upset eventually fosters personal growth—an idea surprisingly consistent with the humanistic view discussed later. The end result is greater emotional resilience, deeper and more intimate relationships with others, and a transformed philosophy of life (e.g., changed priorities, enhanced personal meaning, and a heightened appreciation for what life has to offer) (Christopher, 2004).

Psychopathology only occurs when evolved stress and trauma coping mechanisms malfunction (D. V. Baldwin, 2013; Christopher, 2004). PTSD results when there is "a failure to adequately modulate the normal adaptive trauma response, resulting in symptoms that include severe dissociation, intrusive re-experiencing of events, extreme avoidance, severe hyperarousal, debilitating anxiety, severe depression, problematic substance use, and even psychotic breaks with reality" (Christopher, 2004, p. 86). Because people have evolved as social animals with advanced cognitive abilities, providing those experiencing posttraumatic stress with social support and opportunities to transform their interpretations of the traumatic event are the best ways to help them (Christopher, 2004). Evolutionary theories of trauma and stress are compelling, but empirical support for them can be hard to come by.

Bereavement and Grief

It has been argued that grief doesn't initially seem adaptive because it appears to decrease fitness (the likelihood of reproducing and passing on one's genes; see Chapter 2); the emotional and physical health deficits that bereaved individuals encounter make them less likely to attract a mate (Archer, 2001). Yet grief might be adaptive in a different way by reflecting a strong ability to form attachments to others (Archer, 2001; Reynolds et al., 2015; C. White & Fessler, 2017; Winegard et al., 2014). This ability increases social cohesion, which enhances survival rates of all group members. That is, being part of a socially cohesive group bound by strong attachments provides safety and protection, making survival and reproduction more likely. In this conception, grief is the downside of an evolved tendency to form strong, mutually supportive attachments with others (Archer, 2001). Interestingly, there isn't clear evidence that grief negatively affects fitness (R. M. Nesse, 2005b). Research finds that high grievers are deemed trustworthy, loyal, and nice—which potentially increases their fitness by signaling an ability to form strong attachments (Reynolds et al., 2015). What to conclude from this? Despite theoretical disagreements, evolutionary psychologists remain focused on exploring the adaptive functions of grief.

7.12 Immune System Perspectives

Like many presenting problems, trauma, stress, and loss are associated with immune system inflammation. There is growing evidence of inflammation in cases of posttraumatic stress (Michopoulos & Jovanovic, 2015; Neylan & O'Donovan, 2019; Passos et al., 2015; Y. Sun et al., 2021; J.-J. Yang & Jiang, 2020), as well as grief (Brew et al., 2022; M. Cohen et al., 2015; C. Fagundes et al., 2019; C. P. Fagundes et al., 2018; Hopf et al., 2020). Research is needed to determine if inflammation is a biomarker for prolonged grief (C. Fagundes et al., 2019; J. M. Holland et al., 2014). Of course, inflammation is correlated with many presenting problems (not just trauma, stress, and loss), so perhaps all adverse experiences tax the immune system and compromise physical health. If so, it isn't surprising that survivors of trauma and loss are at increased risk for illness and death (Z. Chen et al., 2020; Jankowski, 2016; Klest, Freyd, Hampson, et al., 2013; Prior et al., 2018; Schultze-Florey et al., 2012; M. Stroebe et al., 2007).

Photo 7.3 An earthquake like the one Joe survived would undoubtedly be traumatic, but survivors could also suffer bereavement and grief in an accident involving many deaths. In huge natural disasters, these concepts would be closely linked. The February 2023 earthquake in Turkey and Syria affected 14 million people, and caused over 55,000 deaths. This image shows a man praying in front of the rubble in Hatay, Turkey. *Aksel Anıl/Pexels.*

7.13 Evaluating Biological Perspectives

The main challenge for biological researchers studying the physiological underpinnings of trauma, stress, and loss is that there are many biological hypotheses, but the evidence for them is often contradictory or inconclusive. For instance, PTSD is often attributed to low cortisol levels, but research support for this hypothesis isn't clear (Speer et al., 2019). Similarly, studies linking hippocampal volume to PTSD are correlational, so it remains unknown whether hippocampal deterioration contributes to or results from PTSD (G. M. Rosen & Lilienfeld, 2008). Until these kinds of questions can be answered, biological perspectives have a long way to go.

More broadly, from the perspective of RDoC (the initiative to build a diagnostic system from the ground up by studying basic biological and psychological processes; see Chapter 3), biological research on trauma, loss, and stress often falls into the same trap affecting much psychiatric research: It hunts for causes of taken-for-granted diagnoses rather than building diagnoses based on research into symptom etiology (Cuthbert, 2014, 2022; Insel et al., 2010; B. S. Peterson, 2015; U. Schmidt, 2015). That is, DSM and ICD start with what RDoC considers scientifically questionable diagnostic categories such as PTSD, acute stress disorder, and prolonged grief disorder, and then researchers cast about trying to uncover the biological bases of these empirically suspect disorders. RDoC believes this is backwards and discourages using existing diagnostic categories as the departure point for brain research. Instead, we should begin by studying normal physiological responses to trauma, stress, and loss. Not until we understand such responses can we map what happens psychologically and behaviorally when these responses go awry (U. Schmidt, 2015). Only then can we construct diagnostic categories tied to measurable biological markers. We aren't there yet, but RDoC trauma research is pushing in that direction (U. Schmidt & Vermetten, 2018; G. Young, 2014; Zambrano-Vazquez et al., 2017).

PSYCHOLOGICAL PERSPECTIVES

7.14 Psychodynamic Perspectives

Personality Factors Associated with Posttraumatic Stress

Research consistently finds that people who display a lot of *negative emotionality (NEM)*—the tendency toward negative moods such as anger, anxiety, and depression—are more likely to struggle with posttraumatic stress (Jakšić et al., 2012; E. C. Meyer et al., 2020; M. W. Miller, 2003; M. W. Miller et al., 2012; J. S. Robinson et al., 2014; Sadeh et al., 2015). However, negative emotions aren't the only factors correlated with PTSD. Being interpersonally cold and domineering are good predictors of chronic PTSD. The hypothesized reason for this is that a cold and domineering style prevents people from obtaining social support for coping with their posttraumatic stress, thus it lingers (K. M. Thomas et al., 2014). Although modern psychodynamic approaches emphasize personality factors, these findings are also relevant to other psychological perspectives.

Freud and Breuer's Influence on Modern Psychodynamic Perspectives

Sigmund Freud and Josef Breuer's early psychoanalytic work in the late 1800s was among the first to highlight the impact of trauma, stress, and loss on mental health. Freud and Breuer felt that having patients recall past traumatic and stressful events while reexperiencing the emotions that accompanied them could eliminate symptoms (Breuer & Freud, 1893–1895/2013; Kudler et al., 2009). Today's psychodynamic perspectives continue to uphold the view that psychological symptoms reflect underlying emotional conflicts originating in past trauma, stress, and loss. Given that there are many different psychodynamic and interpersonal perspectives on trauma and stress, it is helpful to consider what they share. In the broadest sense:

Psychodynamic treatment seeks to reengage normal mechanisms of adaptation by addressing what is unconscious and, in tolerable doses, making it conscious. The psychological meaning of a traumatic event is progressively understood within the context of the survivor's unique history, constitution, and aspirations .... The therapist-patient relationship itself is a crucial factor in the patient's response. (Kudler et al., 2009, p. 364)

Posttraumatic Stress

Short-term dynamic therapy of stress response syndromes is one example of a psychodynamic treatment for posttraumatic stress (M. J. Horowitz, 1973, 1991; M. J. Horowitz, Wilner, Kaltreider, et al., 1980; M. J. Horowitz, Wilner, Marmar, et al., 1980). This twelve-session therapy helps people navigate the following phases that occur in the aftermath of trauma: (a) *initial outcry* and awareness that the trauma has occurred; (b) *denial and numbness*, including dissociation from self and world; (c) *intrusive thoughts and feelings* about what has happened; (d) *working through* the trauma, so that thoughts and feelings about it are integrated into the self, and (e) *completion* of the process, in which the person comes to terms with the trauma and moves past it (Brewin & Holmes, 2003; M. J. Horowitz, 1973, 1991). During this therapy, underlying emotional conflicts and counterproductive patterns of relating to others are examined: "For example, individuals who place great value on being able to control their emotions and their capacity to endure life's adversity might see themselves as weak and vulnerable when they cannot control their tears after a violent assault" (Krupnick, 2002, p. 923). Ideally, such patients undergo a *corrective emotional experience* (see Chapter 2) with their therapists, in which they share vulnerable feelings about the trauma or loss without being judged or critiqued. The goal is for them to generalize the new interpersonal patterns they learn to relationships outside the therapy room.

Research on psychodynamic therapies for posttraumatic stress often finds them effective, even if the evidence isn't as strong and voluminous as it is for CBT (C. Ho & Adcock, 2017; Levi et al., 2016, 2017; Paintain & Cassidy, 2018). Nonetheless, the American Psychological Association does not include psychodynamic therapies in its *Guideline* of recommended PTSD treatments, presumably due to insufficient research support (American Psychological Association Guideline Development Panel for the Treatment of PTSD in Adults, 2017). This has angered psychodynamic therapists who believe the omission reflects a bias against their more relational (and less medical model) approach (Dauphin, 2020; Shedler, 2017). As one psychodynamic defender complained, "the *Guideline* implicitly frames psychotherapy as an activity that therapists *do to* patients instead of one they *do with* them" (Dauphin, 2020, p. 121). However, defenders of the *Guideline* maintain psychodynamic therapies overemphasize non-specific relationship factors, and this leads to too few randomized controlled trials on specific interventions for problems like PTSD (Lilienfeld et al., 2018; D. McKay, 2011; D. McKay & Lilienfeld, 2017). As one critic put it, "until psychodynamic researchers identify mechanisms associated with psychopathology on the basis of the specific theory guiding treatment, the ability to approach treatment will continue to be less a scientific enterprise and more an art form" (D. McKay, 2011, p. 148). This debate over common factors versus specific interventions is one you will eventually have to wade into should you pursue a career as a psychotherapist.

Adjustment and Attachment

There is not much research on psychodynamic therapies for people diagnosed with adjustment disorders. However, two studies found short-term psychodynamic therapies had positive effects (Domhardt & Baumeister, 2018). More research is recommended.

For reactive and socially disinhibited attachment, psychodynamically inclined clinicians invoke Bowlby's attachment theory (introduced in Chapter 2), which emphasizes early caregiver–child interactions in the development of attachment styles. However, attachment theory does not easily translate into attachment therapy—leading some to advocate retiring these sometimes confusing terms (B. Allen, 2016; L. T. Hardy, 2007). One integrated therapy for attachment issues that combines psychodynamic and object relations therapies with cognitive-behavioral interventions has shown promise as a therapy for attachment issues (Lawson et al., 2021). Interestingly, even without therapy, children exhibiting problematic attachment behavior due to neglect typically recover when placed with loving caregivers (B. Allen, 2016).

Short-term dynamic therapy of stress response syndromes: Psychodynamic therapy that addresses five phases of trauma and grief: (a) initial outcry; (b) denial and numbness; (c) intrusive thoughts and feelings; (d) "working through;" and (e) completion.

Bereavement

In his classic paper, "Mourning and Melancholia," Freud (1917/1953) argued that grieving requires *decathexis*, the process of divesting psychic energy from the lost love. This is a fancy way of saying that id energy must be withdrawn from memories of the loved one before it can be redirected towards others. In even simpler terms, we must detach from the deceased person before we can move forward (Berzoff, 2003; G. Hagman, 2001). This classic Freudian view framed grief as a restorative process, one that plays out in a person's private psychological experience rather than in relationships with others (G. Hagman, 2001).

Short-term dynamic therapy of stress response syndromes was designed not only for trauma but also prolonged grief (M. J. Horowitz, 2014). People who successfully move through its four phases (initial outcry, denial and avoidance, intrusive feelings and thoughts, "working through," and completion) complete the mourning process and incorporate the loss into their identities. This enables them to form new attachments. In cases of prolonged grief, patients get stuck before reaching the completion phase (M. J. Horowitz, 2014). Short-term dynamic therapy for grief involves addressing patients' underlying (often unacknowledged) feelings about the loss and challenging interpersonal ways of coping that prevent successful navigation of the mourning process.

Marigold

If a therapist used short-term dynamic therapy to help Marigold with her prolonged grief, he would attend to how Marigold avoids reminders of her late husband because she finds them painful and upsetting. He'd also note that, at the same time, Marigold often cannot stop thinking about her husband. Marigold's therapist would therefore work to form a strong interpersonal relationship with her. As she comes to trust him, he would gently encourage her to share her memories of her husband. Although Marigold might initially find this difficult, she eventually would feel safe enough to do so. In sharing her memories, she would likely find herself less preoccupied with thoughts of her husband between sessions. She would have begun successfully "working through" her grief.

7.15 Cognitive-Behavioral Perspectives

Behavioral Perspectives

Exposure Therapies for Posttraumatic Stress

Chapter 6 examined how exposure therapies are used to alleviate environmentally conditioned anxiety. Exposure therapies include behavioral techniques like *exposure plus response prevention*, *systematic desensitization*, and *modeling* (all discussed in previous chapters). In these procedures, people are exposed to anxiety-provoking stimuli to condition new, non-anxious emotional responses to them. Because anxiety is an important element of posttraumatic stress, exposure therapies are used for it too. In fact, exposure therapies are well supported by research and typically recommended as a first-line intervention for posttraumatic stress (Cusack et al., 2016; Deng et al., 2019; Eshuis et al., 2021; Kothgassner et al., 2019; McLean et al., 2022; S. A. M. Rauch et al., 2012). Some research even suggests that exposure therapy improves amygdala, hippocampal, and prefrontal cortex brain functioning in PTSD patients (M. J. Roy et al., 2014; Stojek et al., 2018; X. Zhu et al., 2018). Exposure therapy for PTSD is often done using imaginal exposure or virtual reality exposure (see Chapter 6) (Deng et al., 2019; Eshuis et al., 2021; Kothgassner et al., 2019). This is because it is often impractical, impossible, or unethical to recreate traumatic situations like accidents, wars, and natural disasters *in vivo* (in real life). Imaginal and virtual reality exposure are often the only options.

Interestingly, therapists don't widely use exposure therapies despite strong evidence of their effectiveness. When asked why, therapists report that exposure is impractical and strenuous to implement, while expressing worry about it backfiring and causing distress to them and their clients (C. B. Becker et al., 2004; J. A. Jaeger et al., 2010; Pittig et al., 2019; van Minnen et al., 2010). Given these concerns, therapists often wrongly assume that clients are reluctant to try exposure therapy, but clients who believe talking about problems is important and necessary are actually quite open it (J. A. Jaeger et al., 2010). Thus, exposure therapy advocates encourage clinicians to overcome their hesitance about using it, especially considering its demonstrated effectiveness.

Joe

If exposure techniques were used to address Joe's posttraumatic stress, his therapist might begin with imaginal exposure, in which Joe would be asked to practice relaxation techniques while recalling the earthquake and building collapse. Then, Joe and his therapist could move on to in vivo exposure. They would slowly expose him to increasingly anxiety-provoking situations related to the trauma. For instance, at one point Joe's therapist might accompany him to the location of the building collapse—a part of town that Joe has actively avoided since the quake. Joe would initially feel distressed and panicked, but after a few minutes these feelings should dissipate as he realizes that nothing bad is likely to happen. Joe's anxiety would decrease as he is gradually exposed to reminders of the trauma.

Exposure Therapies for Prolonged Grief

When using exposure therapies for prolonged grief, the client gradually confronts the loss by focusing on the most painful parts of the loved one's passing, sometimes by making a brief recording recounting the story of the loved one's death (Boelen et al., 2013; Wetherell, 2012). The goal is to stop people from avoiding feelings about the loss and instead face its reality (Boelen et al., 2007). Exposure for prolonged grief differs from exposure for PTSD in that instead of eliminating fear and anxiety, the focus is on reducing feelings of longing and sadness (N. M. Simon, 2013). Incorporating exposure into therapy for prolonged grief appears to improve outcomes (Bryant et al., 2014, 2017).

Behavioral Activation for Posttraumatic Stress

Behavioral activation (discussed in Chapters 5 and 6) is another behavioral intervention for PTSD. As with depressed clients, those experiencing posttraumatic stress often stop engaging in previously enjoyed activities and become increasingly isolated. In behavioral activation, they are instructed to engage in rewarding activities. The reinforcement they receive helps them overcome patterns of avoidance and social isolation that are central symptoms of PTSD (Cukor et al., 2009; Etherton & Farley, 2020; Jakupcak et al., 2010).

Cognitive and CBT Perspectives on Posttraumatic Stress

Cognitive Processing Therapy (CPT)

Cognitive processing therapy (CPT) holds that PTSD results when dysfunctional cognitions interfere with making sense of traumatic events. These cognitions are often about issues besides danger and safety—beliefs about things like self-esteem, competence, or emotional intimacy. The trauma usually violates or conflicts with such beliefs, and this is what produces psychological upset (Resick et al., 2017; Resick & Schnicke, 1992). Originally developed for work with rape survivors, CPT consists of twelve sessions administered in individual or group formats. The goal is to reduce the tendency to overgeneralize beliefs about the traumatic event to other situations, while also challenging cognitions that result in self-blame and avoidance. For example, CPT might help someone who survived a violent assault revise the belief that "because I didn't fight harder, it is my fault I was assaulted" (Watkins et al., 2018, p. 4). CPT is often recommended as a research-supported therapy for trauma (Chard et al., 2012; Cusack et al., 2016; Watkins et al., 2018).

Cognitive processing therapy (CPT): Cognitive therapy for PTSD that combines exposure therapy with a more primary focus on having clients examine and revise their cognitions about the traumatic event.

Joe

Imagine Joe's therapist used CPT to challenge the automatic thoughts that cause Joe to feel anxious and avoid certain situations. Recall that Joe fears another earthquake trapping him inside a collapsing building. A cognitive therapist would educate Joe that it is common for natural disaster survivors to worry about it happening again. However, the therapist would emphasize that the probability is very low and that life is inherently risky. She might point out that no matter how many precautions Joe takes, it is impossible to guarantee one's safety. Joe would hopefully become more aware of his automatic negative thoughts and notice when they occur. He'd replace irrational beliefs (e.g., "I can't tolerate the fear that this building may collapse") with more logical ones (e.g., "While it is possible the building could collapse in an earthquake, the chances are low and spending time worrying about such an unlikely event interferes with enjoying my job"). Joe would be asked to write a story describing what happened during the earthquake, which he would read aloud to himself at home and to his therapist during a session. As therapy progressed, the expectation would be for Joe to become better at resisting the anxiety provoked by his automatic thoughts.

Cognitive Therapy for PTSD

Cognitive therapy for PTSD: Therapy for PTSD that works to (1) eliminate *negative appraisals* that produce an ongoing sense of threat, (2) reduce re-experiencing of the trauma by helping people elaborate memories of it and identify triggers, and (3) eliminate dysfunctional cognitive and behavioral strategies used by trauma survivors.

Cognitive therapy for PTSD says that people experience posttraumatic stress when they make *negative appraisals* about traumatic events, producing an ongoing sense of threat (Ehlers et al., 2005; Ehlers & Clark, 2000). They interpret the external world as dangerous and come to see themselves as damaged and no longer able to function effectively (Ehlers & Clark, 2000). Examples of such negative appraisals are beliefs like "Nowhere is safe," "I attract disaster," "I deserve the bad things that happen to me," "I'll never be able to relate to people again," and "I will never be able to lead a normal life again" (Ehlers & Clark, 2000, p. 322). Cognitive therapy for PTSD has three goals (Ehlers et al., 2005):

1. *Alter negative appraisals of the trauma.* For example, a client deeply traumatized following a rape found herself regularly reacting emotionally to having been called ugly by her assailant. After the attack, she developed negative appraisals of herself as unattractive and undesirable. Consequently, she began engaging in casual sex to convince herself otherwise. Cognitive therapy helped her develop an alternative interpretation, namely that her assailant said she was ugly because he could only get aroused by abusing women (Ehlers et al., 2005).

2. *Reduce re-experiencing of the trauma by elaborating memories of it and identifying triggers.* To fully articulate what happened to them, clients write a detailed narrative of the event, imaginally reliving the experience. This helps them construct a more coherent story about what happened and make clear that the event is in the past. Clients also learn to identify triggers that provoke intrusive thoughts and feelings about the trauma. For example, a man traumatized by a nighttime car accident came to realize that bright lights (like the headlights from the wreck) triggered upsetting memories. However, "once this became clear, the patient discriminated between 'then' and 'now' … by telling himself that he was reacting to a past meaning of the light" (Ehlers et al., 2005, p. 418).

3. *Eliminate dysfunctional cognitive and behavioral strategies.* Certain strategies used by trauma survivors are beneficial in the short-term but have long-term negative consequences. For instance, avoiding reminders of the trauma or refusing to discuss it prevents immediate upset but interferes with challenging negative appraisals and constructing a coherent narrative that places the event in the past. Therefore, cognitive therapy for PTSD teaches clients about the harmful consequences of avoidance strategies (Ehlers et al., 2005).

Cognitive therapy for PTSD appears to reduce posttraumatic stress (Ehlers et al., 2005, 2014; Watkins et al., 2018). A randomized controlled trial found that 73 percent to 77 percent of PTSD clients who were provided it recovered, compared with 43 percent of clients who underwent supportive therapy and just 7 percent of clients who received no therapy (Ehlers et al., 2014). This is impressive, but roughly 25 percent of clients didn't recover—a reminder that even highly effective interventions don't help everyone. Interestingly, the principles of cognitive therapy for PTSD have also been applied to persistent grief (Ehlers, 2006).

Trauma-Focused CBT (TF-CBT)

Trauma-focused CBT (TF-CBT) is geared to children and adolescents. It consists of eight to twenty-five therapy sessions that combine behavioral techniques (such as exposure therapy and relaxation) with cognitive techniques (such as cognitive restructuring, affect modulation skill training, trauma narration, and psychoeducation about the effects of trauma) (J. A. Cohen et al., 2018; J. A. Cohen & Mannarino, 2015). Parents are included in the treatment, unless they are the source of the trauma (J. A. Cohen & Mannarino, 2015). Helping parents correct their own irrational beliefs (e.g., they didn't do enough to protect their child from the trauma) can be as important as helping their children do so. Like many other CBT approaches to posttraumatic stress, it has a good deal of research support and is recommended as a first-line treatment (J. A. Cohen et al., 2018; J. A. Cohen & Mannarino, 2015; Mavranezouli et al., 2020).

Emotional Processing Theory

Emotional processing theory attributes posttraumatic stress (as well as other fear and anxiety responses) to dysfunctional *fear structures* (Foa et al., 2006; Foa & Kozak, 1991; Foa & McLean, 2016; S. A. M. Rauch et al., 2012; S. Rauch & Foa, 2006). A fear structure consists of closely associated thoughts, feelings, beliefs, and behaviors that occur simultaneously in response to threatening events (S. Rauch & Foa, 2006). For instance, a gun might trigger a fear structure consisting of behavioral and physiological elements (e.g., running away, hiding, heart racing, sweating, etc.), as well as meaning elements (e.g., the belief that "I am going to die"). Fear structures in PTSD are characterized by two dysfunctional beliefs, namely: (a) "I am not safe in the world" and (b) "I am crazy and incapable of managing distress" (Foa & Kozak, 1991; S. A. M. Rauch et al., 2012; S. Rauch & Foa, 2006). Emotional processing theorists have clients undergo exposure therapy while their fear structures are active and new information incompatible with those structures is available. This results in "emotional processing, the process by which corrective, realistic information is incorporated into the fear structure," modifying its pathological elements (Foa & McLean, 2016, p. 3). There is research evidence for emotional processing theory, but more is needed to tease apart the precise role of emotional processing (E. Alpert et al., 2021; S. A. M. Rauch et al., 2012; S. Rauch & Foa, 2006).

Stress Inoculation Training (SIT)

Stress inoculation training (SIT) combines a variety of CBT techniques to decrease avoidance and anxiety related to the trauma (Meichenbaum, 2007, 2019). As the therapy's name implies, the goal is to inoculate the client against the destructive consequences of stress. SIT uses CBT techniques to build resilience—including psychoeducation, self-monitoring, behavioral activation, behavioral rehearsal, mindfulness, role-playing, relaxation training, *in vivo* exposure, and thought stopping (Cahill et al., 2009; Meichenbaum, 2019). SIT has been used with military veterans and is often recommended for PTSD (Hourani et al., 2016; S. Jackson et al., 2019; Watkins et al., 2018).

Mindfulness and Acceptance Approaches

Mindfulness-based cognitive therapy (MBCT) and acceptance and commitment therapy (ACT) (discussed in Chapters 5 and 6) are additional CBT interventions that train PTSD clients to focus on the current moment (rather than being preoccupied with past traumatic memories). The idea is to accept one's present reactions without letting them become overwhelming. Mindfulness meditation training, for instance, teaches clients to observe their experience in the moment without being emotionally triggered by it (Mulick et al., 2011; Orsillo & Batten, 2005). The assumption is that being mindful and accepting upset feelings—however unpleasant—helps people cope with posttraumatic stress. As the old saying goes, "What we resist persists." Acknowledging rather than avoiding anxious feelings about traumatic events weakens the power of these feelings. Mindfulness-based treatment and ACT have growing bodies of support for reducing posttraumatic stress

Trauma-focused CBT (TF-CBT): Brief trauma therapy for children and adolescents that combines behavioral techniques (e.g., exposure therapy and relaxation) with cognitive techniques (e.g., cognitive restructuring, affect modulation skill training, trauma narration, and psychoeducation about the effects of trauma).

Emotional processing theory: Cognitive theory that attributes trauma, fear, and anxiety responses to dysfunctional *fear structures*; contends that for exposure therapy to be most effective, fear structures must be activated during exposure.

Stress inoculation training (SIT): Uses CBT techniques to decrease avoidance and anxiety (e.g., education, relaxation training, breathing retraining, role-playing, covert modeling, guided self-dialogue, graduated *in vivo* exposure, and thought stopping).

(J. E. Boyd et al., 2018; Bremner et al., 2017; Fortuna et al., 2018; Hopwood & Schutte, 2017; Jasbi et al., 2018; Pohar & Argáez, 2017; Polusny et al., 2015; Schure et al., 2018). One caveat is that in certain instances, mindfulness approaches can inadvertently trigger negative reactions because they reduce avoidance of traumatic memories—the very same reason they are often helpful. Clients with severe PTSD symptoms who lack emotional regulation skills might not be ready to mindfully observe and accept their experiences (J. E. Boyd et al., 2018).

Eye Movement Desensitization and Reprocessing (EMDR)

Eye movement desensitization and reprocessing (EMDR):
Therapy technique in which people imagine anxiety-provoking or traumatic events while engaging in bilateral stimulation.

Eye movement desensitization and reprocessing (EMDR) combines cognitive, behavioral, and neuroscience perspectives (F. Shapiro & Maxfield, 2002; R. Shapiro & Brown, 2019). In EMDR, clients recall traumatic or upsetting events while engaging in *bilateral stimulation*, which involves rhythmically exposing them to alternating stimulation on their left and right sides. Bilateral stimulation is usually visual and involves moving a stimulus in front of clients' faces so their eyes move back and forth (hence the "eye movement" part of EMDR). However, it can also be auditory (alternating sounds between left and right ears) or tactile (back and forth tapping of the right and left sides of the body). Still, visual stimulation is most common, with clients asked to track the movement of their therapists' fingers while recounting a traumatic event. Before and after each set of eye movements, clients rate their anxiety on a scale of 1 to 10. They also rate positive and negative statements about the trauma. When EMDR works, anxiety ratings decrease with each set of bilateral eye movements. The following case example illustrates the use of EMDR with a mother mourning the death of her infant daughter:

A baby was killed in the Oklahoma City bombing. The mother was not allowed to see the remains, but was told that the baby had died of a head wound. For the next two months, the only image the mother had of her child was an imagined one of her baby with a severe head wound. She had no access to other memories. Further, this negative image was easily triggered and disrupted her ability to function. Two months later, after an hour assessment, EMDR was provided. The negative vicarious image of the baby was targeted. After the first set of eye movements, a memory of the baby with her husband came to mind. With further sets of eye movements, more memories came to mind—the baby with her, family interactions, and finally the memory of handing her baby to the daycare worker and saying "Good-bye" and "I love you." At that moment, she wanted to stop the EMDR because she felt a sense of peace and closure. This memory was then installed by having her keep the positive image and feelings in mind during sets of eye movements. (R. M. Solomon & Rando, 2007, pp. 111–112)

Despite some methodological concerns, a large body of research finds EMDR effective in reducing posttraumatic stress (Cuijpers et al., 2020; M. S. K. Ho & Lee, 2012; Manzoni et al., 2021; McGuire et al., 2014; Moghadam et al., 2020; Natha & Daiches, 2014; Opheim et al., 2019; E. Shapiro, 2012; F. Shapiro, 2012; G. Wilson et al., 2018). Nonetheless, EMDR has been surrounded by debate and controversy, probably because the reasons it works aren't clear. Various psychological and neurobiological explanations for why eye movements help people integrate and resolve traumatic memories have been proposed (Elofsson et al., 2008; Gunter & Bodner, 2008; Landin-Romero et al., 2018; Oren & Solomon, 2012). Many clinicians remain skeptical of EMDR, contending it too often employs unreliable verbal reports from clients about whether they feel less anxious (Lohr et al., 1998, 1999; Sikes & Sikes, 2003). Some critics also suspect that EMDR's effectiveness isn't due to bilateral stimulation but because of overlooked commonalities with exposure therapies (J. D. Herbert et al., 2000; Lohr et al., 1999). Others say that any dual attention task while discussing traumatic memories is effective, not just those involving bilateral stimulation (Landin-Romero et al., 2018; van den Hout & Engelhard, 2012). EMDR advocates counter that research shows eye movements are essential to EMDR's effectiveness (Jeffries & Davis, 2013). They maintain that critics misinterpret the research and unfairly reject EMDR despite much evidence for it (Oren & Solomon, 2012; B. R. Perkins & Rouanzoin, 2002; R. Shapiro & Brown, 2019). Debate over EMDR will likely continue given ongoing disagreement about the role of bilateral stimulation in processing trauma. Though its strongest research support is for PTSD, EMDR has also been adapted for addressing grief, including assisting those who lost loved ones to COVID-19 (R. M. Solomon, 2018; R. M. Solomon & Hensley, 2020; R. M. Solomon & Rando, 2007). It remains a popular, if hotly debated, clinical approach.

7.16 Humanistic Perspectives

Person-Centered Therapy

Humanistic therapists contend that person-centered therapy's core conditions for change (empathy, congruence, unconditional positive regard) are an underutilized method for alleviating posttraumatic stress and grief. Like psychodynamic clinicians, humanistic therapists view the therapeutic relationship as the key mechanism for healing following trauma and loss (Larson, 2013; A. Quinn, 2008). There is not much research on person-centered therapy for posttraumatic stress, but it has fared well in a couple of studies comparing it with prolonged exposure. Although prolonged exposure performed a bit better, person-centered therapy was also effective (McLean et al., 2015; Zandberg et al., 2016).

Meaning Reconstruction following Trauma and Loss

Chapter 2 described constructivist perspectives as humanistic approaches emphasizing how people invent (i.e., "construct") meaningful ways of understanding themselves and their worlds, which they use to make sense of events in their lives (Chiari & Nuzzo, 2010; R. A. Neimeyer, 2009; R. A. Neimeyer & Mahoney, 1995; R. A. Neimeyer & Raskin, 2000). Constructivist therapists have been especially interested in trauma and loss because these events often invalidate people's core assumptions about the world, requiring them to revise their understandings in order to move forward effectively (R. A. Neimeyer, 2001a). Thought of another way, trauma and loss can destroy the personal stories—or *self-narratives*—by which people live (R. A. Neimeyer, 2001b; R. A. Neimeyer et al., 2014). From a constructivist perspective, posttraumatic stress and prolonged grief occur when people have difficulty "constructing a plausible account of important events, a story that has the ring of narrative truth, regardless of whether it corresponds to a historical truth that would be endorsed by a disinterested observer" (R. A. Neimeyer, 2001b, p. 263).

Constructivist approaches maintain that we can never know if the stories we tell ourselves about trauma and loss are objectively correct (i.e., historically accurate accounts of what "really" happened). All that matters is whether these narratives are internally coherent, personally meaningful, and permit us to move forward with our lives. Constructivist therapists have developed numerous assessment instruments and meaning-focused therapy techniques for posttraumatic stress and loss (R. A. Neimeyer, 2001b, 2005; R. A. Neimeyer et al., 2023; Sewell & Williams, 2001). Research support for constructivist grief and loss interventions is growing (R. A. Neimeyer, 2019).

Posttraumatic Growth

According to the old saying, "what doesn't kill us makes us stronger." This captures the spirit of humanistic perspectives on trauma and loss. Although most people who have undergone traumatic crises would undo what has happened if they could, many nevertheless report that coping with the event transformed them in unexpected ways. That is, many people experience **posttraumatic growth (PTG)**—positive changes following crises, traumas, losses, and other stressful events (Calhoun & Tedeschi, 2006; Tedeschi & Calhoun, 2004).

Posttraumatic growth (PTG): Positive changes following crises, traumas, losses, and other stressful events.

Posttraumatic growth describes the experience of individuals whose development, at least in some areas, has surpassed what was present before the struggle with crises occurred. The individual has not only survived, but has experienced changes that are viewed as important, and that go beyond what was the previous status quo. Posttraumatic growth is not simply a return to baseline—it is an experience of improvement that for some persons is extremely profound. (Tedeschi & Calhoun, 2004, p. 4)

Research suggests that being extraverted, open to experience, and optimistic predict posttraumatic growth; having a strong social support system helps too (Tedeschi & Calhoun, 2004; T. Zoellner & Maercker, 2006b). Interestingly, posttraumatic growth is also associated with the propensity to think a lot about the traumatic event—that is, to ruminate about it (Tedeschi & Calhoun, 2004; T. Zoellner & Maercker, 2006b). This is notable because ruminating is often viewed negatively and taken as a sign of psychopathology. However, PTG research implies that being preoccupied—even distressed— after a traumatic event may be essential to the growth process (Na et al., 2021; Tedeschi & Calhoun, 2004). The "symptoms" sometimes turn out to be beneficial. Psychotherapy within a posttraumatic growth framework assumes that trauma and loss shatter people's previous worldviews. Humanistic therapies guide trauma and loss survivors through the arduous process of making meaning of what they have been through (S. Joseph & Linley, 2006; R. A. Neimeyer, 2001b; T. Zoellner & Maercker, 2006a).

The study of posttraumatic growth is relatively new, and many questions remain. Research on rumination fails to clearly distinguish intentional and deliberate thinking about a trauma from intrusive and obsessional thinking that can't be controlled (T. Zoellner & Maercker, 2006b). Further, reported growth isn't the same as actual growth. People sometimes say they have grown after trauma but they haven't; they might even be covering up their suffering (Frazier et al., 2009). Of course, suffering and growth aren't mutually exclusive. People can experience posttraumatic growth and depreciation simultaneously (Zięba et al., 2019).

Joe

Although Joe has encountered many challenges since surviving the building collapse, he feels he has grown in unexpected ways. "I appreciate things much more since the quake," he says, "because I am much more attuned to how precious life is." He no longer lets little things bother him, is closer to and more open with loved ones, and feels wiser and more mature. "If I could undo what happened, I would," he reports, "but in many ways I've become a more patient, understanding, and kind person."

7.17 Evaluating Psychological Perspectives

Evaluating psychological interventions for grief is difficult because "loss is universal and permanent" and the grief that results rarely fully resolves (N. M. Simon, 2013, p. 419). What we assume is essential to overcoming grief may not be. For example, it isn't clear that emotional disclosure helps people experiencing normal bereavement (W. Stroebe et al., 2005). Additionally, until recently, when DSM and ICD added the prolonged grief diagnosis, it was difficult for researchers to know which clients to include in therapy effectiveness studies (Jordan & Litz, 2014). Nevertheless, there is evidence that cognitive-behavioral and other grief-specific therapies are more effective than more general interventions (A. Iglewicz et al., 2020; A. H. Jordan & Litz, 2014; N. M. Simon, 2013; Wittouck et al., 2011). However, the research on therapy effectiveness for prolonged grief remains in its early stages.

Like prolonged grief, there isn't much research on adjustment disorder therapies either. There is some evidence that various therapeutic approaches to adjustment disorder can be helpful—including psychodynamic, CBT, person-centered, and EMDR (Domhardt & Baumeister, 2018). There are calls for more studies that use a clearer and more consistent definition of adjustment disorder (M. A. Morgan et al., 2021).

There is strong evidence that psychotherapy for posttraumatic stress is safe and effective (Hamblen et al., 2019; Hoppen et al., 2022), but disagreement remains over which types are best. Exposure, EMDR, and trauma-focused cognitive interventions are usually viewed as having the strongest evidence base compared to other therapies (American Psychological Association Guideline Development Panel for the Treatment of PTSD in Adults, 2017; Ehlers et al., 2010; Hamblen et al., 2019; Mavranezouli et al., 2020; McLean et al., 2022; N. P. Roberts et al., 2015; Steenkamp et al., 2015; Watkins et al., 2018). However, not everyone shares this view, with some concluding all bona fide therapies for PTSD are more or less equally effective (Benish et al., 2008). The most reasonable conclusions are that (a) trauma-focused therapies such as exposure, EMDR, and cognitive therapy appear to be effective (even if we disagree about which is best and why), and (b) passionate debate over the effectiveness of other therapeutic approaches continues. The "In Depth" feature concludes our discussion of therapy effectiveness by discussing **critical incident stress debriefing (CISD)**—a formerly popular but now controversial PTSD treatment that researchers and practitioners increasingly agree does not work—and comparing it with a newer approach called **psychological first aid (PFA)**.

Critical incident stress debriefing (CISD): Extended single session post-trauma intervention during which trauma victims are asked to recall the event in vivid detail shortly after it occurs; controversial because some research suggests CISD can be harmful.

Psychological first aid (PFA): Less invasive intervention than CISD that builds on research showing most people are resilient in the face of trauma; offers help to victims in the aftermath of a traumatic event in a non-intrusive way.

In Depth: Critical Incident Stress Debriefing versus Psychological First Aid

Critical incident stress debriefing (CISD) is an extended single session post-trauma intervention during which trauma survivors are asked to recall the event in vivid detail shortly after it occurs (A. M. Mitchell et al., 2003; J. T. Mitchell, 1983). It was originally developed in 1983 to help workers in high-risk occupations (such as firefighters and police officers) cope with trauma; over time its use has expanded to anyone exposed to a traumatic event and is often part of a larger model of pre- and post-incident training, debriefing, and counseling known as *critical incident stress management (CISM)* (A. M. Mitchell et al., 2003; J. T. Mitchell, 1983; Swab, 2020). CISD is based on the rationale that actively and aggressively intervening as quickly as possible with trauma survivors (ideally within 24–72 hours after the event) hastens the recovery process. CISD is typically delivered as a structured group session lasting between one and a half and three hours, during which trauma survivors are (a) asked to describe their experience of the traumatic event and process their feelings about it, (b) provided psychoeducation about normal and expected trauma responses, and (c) encouraged to return to their regular routines.

Although initially popular, controversy engulfed CISD when various researchers found it ineffective and possibly even harmful (Bisson et al., 2009; Bledsoe, 2003; Litz et al., 2002; van Emmerik et al., 2002). Critics assert that CISD coerces trauma victims to process what has happened to them even if they prefer not to and this can be psychologically damaging. These critics also complain that CISD incorrectly assumes that most trauma survivors will have difficulty handling the event and consequently require a preventative intervention. However, research suggests most people are resilient in the face of trauma, making it is questionable to impose a treatment on them when they haven't shown clear signs of psychological distress. CISD advocates counter that research on it isn't as damning as critics say, but merely offers mixed results—with some studies finding it helpful and others not (P. R. Clark et al., 2019; A. M. Mitchell et al., 2003; Pack, 2013). Supporters also maintain that in instances where CISD proved harmful, it wasn't being used as intended. They argue that when CISD is generalized beyond homogenous groups, used with individuals, or used with people who haven't been screened for previous trauma issues, it is being implemented improperly in a manner inconsistent with its theoretical underpinnings (Aucott & Soni, 2016; Cantu & Thomas, 2020). Nonetheless, many researchers and clinicians consider CISD ineffective at best and harmful at worst (Bledsoe, 2003; Burchill, 2019). However, it continues to have defenders and remains, by one estimate, the most used intervention for assisting first responders following trauma exposure (Swab, 2020).

An alternative to CISD is psychological first aid (PFA), a less invasive intervention that builds on research showing that most people are resilient in the face of traumas (Brymer et al., 2006; Vernberg et al., 2008). Thus, contact and engagement with trauma survivors is handled in a non-intrusive but compassionate manner; unlike CISD, it is not pushed on those who aren't interested or ready. Broad goals of PFA include "(a) promoting sense of safety, (b) promoting calming, (c) promoting sense of self- and community efficacy, (d) promoting connectedness, and (e) instilling hope" (Vernberg et al., 2008, p. 383). PFA is a relatively new intervention and the evidence base for it remains preliminary; questions about training and implementation of PFA remain, but guidelines for doing so have been developed. The World Health Organization (2011) provides a guide to PFA for field workers. More recently, PFA has been adapted for use during the COVID-19 pandemic (Feinstein, 2021; Minihan et al., 2020). In sum, PFA tries to avoid the problems associated with CISD. After all, the first rule for all interventions is to do no harm.

Critical Thinking Questions

1. Do you agree with critics of CISD that it should be avoided because it can harm vulnerable people? Or do you concur with those who believe people are more resilient than CISD critics claim?
2. We know that avoidance is not an especially effective strategy for dealing with trauma, but we also have evidence that pushing people to talk when they aren't ready can be counterproductive. How can we best address this in clinical practice?

SOCIOCULTURAL PERSPECTIVES

7.18 Cross-Cultural and Social Justice Perspectives

Sociocultural Factors and Posttraumatic Stress

Gender

Women are diagnosed with PTSD two to three times more often than men, even though men have a higher lifetime risk for trauma exposure than women (Dückers & Olff, 2017; Kimerling et al., 2014; Olff, 2017; Seedat et al., 2005). Why? One explanation posits that even though women encounter fewer traumas than men, the traumas they face more often (such as sexual assault and child sexual abuse) are not only socially stigmatized, but also highly correlated with increased risk of posttraumatic stress (Kimerling et al., 2014; Tolin & Foa, 2008). Further, the traumas women experience often occur within a *traumatic context*—a set of circumstances in which there is prolonged and intense exposure to trauma. Spending a lot of time in such a context makes developing PTSD more likely (Kaysen et al., 2003; Kimerling et al., 2014). Sexual assault and child abuse often happen within the ongoing traumatic context of an abusive home. Thus, when it comes to gender differences in PTSD "some of what appears to be excess vulnerability among women" may be "partially a function of chronicity and context" (Kimerling et al., 2014, p. 317).

Race, Ethnicity, and Socioeconomic Status

Race, ethnicity, and socioeconomic status (SES) are also relevant to posttraumatic stress. Being poor or belonging to certain ethnic or racial minority groups is associated with higher rates of PTSD (Bonanno et al., 2007; Klest, 2012; Klest, Freyd, & Foynes, 2013; Klest, Freyd, Hampson, et al., 2013; N. Pole et al., 2005; Sibrava et al., 2019; T. Weiss et al., 2011; Xue et al., 2015). Teasing apart how much of the increased risk is due to poverty as opposed to racial and ethnic discrimination is challenging, but at the very least it appears these factors influence one another and together enhance the likelihood of posttraumatic stress following trauma. Members of minority groups often face ongoing racial discrimination, which might increase their susceptibility to posttraumatic stress (see the Controversial Question Box for more).

Controversial Question: Can Racism Cause Posttraumatic Stress?

Can racism cause posttraumatic stress? Prominent mental health professionals argue it can (Butts, 2002; Carter, 2007; Comas-Díaz et al., 2019; Corley, 2015; Helms et al., 2012; S. B. Holliday et al., 2020; Sibrava et al., 2019; M. T. Williams et al., 2018, 2021). They maintain that individual and institutional discrimination are too often overlooked as triggers of posttraumatic stress. *Race-based traumatic stress* has been proposed as term to help clinicians better identify and understand the traumatizing impact of racism on members of minority groups (Carter, 2007; Comas-Díaz et al., 2019). As an example, consider the following vignette:

> A light-skinned Hispanic male was treated courteously when he made application for an apartment in New York City. However, when he returned with his African-American wife, the renting agent became aloof and informed them that the apartment was rented. In response to the denial of the apartment, the wife immediately became depressed, insomniac, and hypervigilant. She had repeated nightmares. At the time of the alleged discrimination, she noticed that her hair had begun to fall out, that her skin was dry, and she was constipated. There were no hallucinations, delusions or ideas of reference, and there was a mild paranoid trend. All of her symptoms were causally related to the discrimination. (Butts, 2002, p. 338)

Evidence of racism as a source of trauma is growing. Researchers are finding that discrimination predicts PTSD diagnoses among Black Americans and Latinos; advocates of recognizing race-based trauma argue that police brutality, racial profiling, immigration detention, and other forms of discrimination have significant psychological consequences (R. E. Anderson et al., 2018; Chavez-Dueñas et al., 2019; S. B. Holliday et al., 2020; Sibrava et al., 2019). Members of other racial and ethnic groups are impacted by discrimination, as well. The incarceration of Japanese Americans in internment camps during the Second World War, the genocide and forced removal of Native Americans throughout U.S. history, and ongoing prejudice against people of Middle Eastern and North African (MENA) descent are further examples in which oppression based on race or ethnicity has been implicated in trauma reactions (Awad et al., 2019; Nagata et al., 2019; Skewes & Blume, 2019).

Photo 7.4 Black Lives Matter protests and civil unrest in 2020 against police brutality and systemic racism in the wake of George Floyd's murder. George Floyd was a 46-year-old African American man who was murdered by a police officer.
Colin Lloyd/Unsplash.

Social justice advocates contend DSM and ICD definitions of trauma should be expanded to recognize (and encourage interventions to counteract) racial oppression (Comas-Díaz et al., 2019; Corley, 2015; Saleem et al., 2020; M. T. Williams et al., 2021). Some even argue that, at times, Western society's emphasis on individual rights fosters and tolerates trauma-inducing racism. Citing rallies by the Ku Klux Klan and Neo-Nazis as examples, they argue that "it is often the case that social policies (e.g., freedom of speech) legitimize the rights of the perpetrators while disregarding the possible mental health consequences to the victims" (Helms et al., 2012, p. 68). Whether speech rights should be curtailed to curb trauma-inducing racism is bound to provoke debate. Regardless, the notion of race-induced trauma demands further theory and research. Those seeking the recognition of racism as a source of trauma conclude:

> Failure to recognize or acknowledge the mental health relevance of the sociopolitical, racial, and cultural factors that intersect with trauma experiences for the survivors of trauma as well as for the service providers will greatly inhibit one's ability to provide effective treatment programs or to conduct meaningful trauma research. (Helms et al., 2012, p. 72)

Critical Thinking Questions

1. Should the experience of racism be considered a form of trauma, akin to natural and human-made disasters? Why or why not?
2. Does research on racism as a traumatic stressor suggest that our definition of trauma is too narrow? Explain your reasoning.
3. Should the free speech rights of hate groups be restricted to protect members of racial and ethnic minority groups from being traumatized?
4. How might we research the question of whether racism can induce trauma?

Cultural awareness is critical in helping those experiencing posttraumatic stress. Along these lines, some mental health professionals advocate making **cultural adaptations** to empirically supported trauma interventions (Mattar, 2011). Such adaptations modify the treatment to account for cultural differences. Because interventions developed within one ethnic, racial, or cultural context may not work in another, "trauma education and training must integrate cultural considerations in order to remain relevant for demographically and culturally diverse groups" (Mattar, 2011, p. 263). Efforts to culturally adapt PTSD treatments are ongoing, but more transparent and systematic approaches are needed (Ennis et al., 2020; M. Williams et al., 2014; A. Wright et al., 2020).

Cultural adaptations: Modifying empirically supported treatments to account for cultural differences.

Social Support

People who lack social support don't handle trauma, stress, and loss as well as those who have such support (Bonanno et al., 2007; Brewin et al., 2000; Neria et al., 2008; J. Platt et al., 2014; N. Simon et al., 2019; I. H. Stanley et al., 2019; Y. Wang et al., 2021; Xue et al., 2015; Zalta et al., 2021). This is understandable. Family, friends, co-workers, and community provide needed assistance to those going through difficult times; without them, even the most resilient person won't fare as well. Importantly, while social support protects against posttraumatic stress, suffering from PTSD erodes social support. People experiencing it "lose interest in interpersonal activities, become estranged and irritable and thus find it difficult to accept and value others' support" (Y. Wang et al., 2021, p. 2). In the United States, those in their late teens and early twenties (Gen Z) appear most in need of social support, as they have faced various stress-inducing challenges (e.g., COVID-19 and political discord) throughout their formative years (American Psychological Association, 2020). See Figure 7.1.

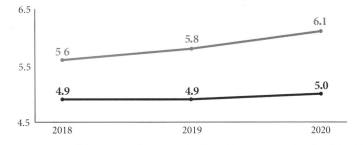

Figure 7.1 Average Reported Stress Level during the Past Month, on a Scale of 1–10

Source: American Psychological Association. (2020). *Stress in America*TM *2020: A national mental health crisis.* *https://www.apa.org/news/press/releases/stress/2020/sia-mental-health-crisis.pdf*

Cross-Cultural Differences in Bereavement

From a cross-cultural perspective, bereavement research has too often overlooked the role of culture in shaping the experience of grief, thinking of mourning mainly in terms of individual deficits distinct from social context. However, this may be changing. According to one culturally focused researcher, although the bereavement field "continues to develop a substantial literature that is oblivious to culture … it also is developing a substantial literature about the connections of culture and grief" (Rosenblatt, 2008, p. 207). In the mental health professions, conceptions of healthy grief are often shaped by distinctly Western ideas about when life ends, how long it is okay to grieve, how one should properly express grief, and what the goal of grieving is (Rosenblatt, 2008). Yet when it comes to mourning there are extensive differences cross-culturally in death rituals, customs, gender expectations, and spiritual/religious beliefs (J. D. Morgan et al., 2009; Parkes et al., 2015). For example, Chinese and American grievers show certain differences in how they mourn. Chinese bereaved often display more intense grief immediately after the loss but recover from it more quickly, while the grief of American bereaved tends to be less acute initially but lasts longer (Bonanno et al., 2005; Pressman & Bonanno, 2007). Even though some aspects of grief may be universal, culture and context influence the experience: "The context (relational, social, cultural) in which the loss and subsequent mourning behaviors occur will impact the type and amount of grief processing engaged in by bereaved individuals" (Pressman & Bonanno, 2007, p. 730). Mental health practitioners must be aware of cultural differences in bereavement to avoid pathologizing people from other backgrounds whose grieving differs from their own.

7.19 Service User Perspectives

Posttraumatic Stress

Part of the impetus for adding PTSD to the DSM was to bring attention to the plight of combat veterans who struggled upon returning home. PTSD's inclusion in 1980's DSM-III was influenced by the political lobbying of service users and service providers during the Vietnam War, when "activists began to note the inequity created by sending men to war without recognizing the psychiatric consequences and the need to provide adequate treatment for them" (Andreasen, 2010, p. 68). Some have gone so far as to provocatively argue that many who advocated the addition of PTSD to the DSM-III were motivated by an anti-war political agenda. According to this line of thinking, authenticating PTSD was a means of

undermining the US government's pursuit of the war. If it could be shown that the conflict caused long-term and widespread psychological injury to US servicemen, then this was further reason to call the campaign to a close. Hence … PTSD was one of the few politically driven psychiatric diagnoses. (E. Jones & Wessely, 2007, p. 171)

Obviously, not everyone accepts this interpretation. Regardless, while recognizing PTSD as a mental disorder raised awareness about the mental health needs of combat veterans, the stigma associated with the diagnosis discourages some veterans from seeking services (J. R. Smith et al., 2020). Research with UK and U.S. veterans returning from combat reveals that soldiers pursuing treatment for posttraumatic stress—especially men—hold a lot of stereotypes about PTSD and worry about being labeled as "dangerous/violent" or "crazy" (Mittal et al., 2013; Osório et al., 2013; J. R. Smith et al., 2020). Overcoming internal stigma is a daunting obstacle to these soldiers requesting help (D. Murphy et al., 2014).

Stigma research offers insight into why some veterans oppose the idea of PTSD as a disorder. In the words of U.S. Staff Sergeant and Medal of Honor winner Ty Carter, "If you just call it stress, what it really is, it explains the fact that it's a natural reaction to a traumatic experience …. It's our body's and mind's natural reaction to try and remember and avoid those situations" (Timm, 2013, para. 2). In keeping with this sentiment, there is an ongoing consumer-based movement to change the name of PTSD to PTSI (*posttraumatic stress injury*) (Fayed, 2021; Keynan & Keynan, 2016; Ochberg, 2013). The implications aren't merely semantic. U.S. military veterans with PTSD diagnoses are ineligible for the Purple Heart (awarded for injuries received in combat). Some argue that "replacing the term *disorder* (PTSD) with *injury* (PTSI)" would help "deconstruct the term" and "facilitate the eligibility of traumatized veterans" for Purple Hearts (Keynan & Keynan, 2016, p. 3). Those advocating a name change to PTSI are motivated "by a conviction that there are many who deserve help, including benefits, and they closet themselves due to stigma and fear" (Ochberg, 2013, p. 99). So far, DSM and ICD have not changed the name.

Adjustment Issues

Because adjustment disorder is considered a "transient condition between the normal and pathological," it is considered less stigmatizing than other mental health diagnoses (Zelviene & Kazlauskas, 2018, p. 378). For instance, 55 percent of child psychiatrists reported diagnosing patients with adjustment disorders (as opposed to something more serious) to avoid stigmatizing them (Setterberg et al., 1991). Similarly, a study of labor outcomes found that, unlike people with other mental disorder diagnoses, employment rates for people diagnosed with adjustment disorders are no different than for people with no mental disorder diagnosis (M. L. Baldwin & Marcus, 2007). The reason offered for this is that "adjustment disorders are typically time-limited, stress-related disorders occurring in otherwise normally functioning individuals. These would be expected to confer relatively little long-term impairment in productivity, and also relatively little stigma" (M. L. Baldwin & Marcus, 2007, p. 506). Still, any diagnosis carries stigma risk. Caution is warranted given the minimal research on adjustment disorder and stigma.

Prolonged Grief

Researchers are studying whether the new prolonged grief diagnosis is stigmatizing. There is evidence that it is—with people having strong negative reactions to and desiring greater social distance from people diagnosed with prolonged grief (H. Dennis et al., 2022; Eisma, 2018; Eisma et al., 2019; Gonschor et al., 2020). The stigma appears to generalize "across cultures and languages" (H. Dennis et al., 2022, p. 203). While its addition to DSM and ICD brings awareness of prolonged grief to the wider public (and encourages developing interventions to alleviate it), the stigma the diagnosis carries might discourage some people from seeking help. Diagnoses inevitably have advantages and disadvantages.

Marigold

Marigold reads about a new diagnosis called prolonged grief disorder. "That describes me!" she thinks to herself. Awareness of this diagnosis helps Marigold realize she isn't the only person who has ever had difficulty dealing with the death of a close loved one. However, she also feels shame at the prospect of "having" this new disorder, increasing her reluctance to seek therapy.

7.20 Systems Perspectives

Group Therapy for Posttraumatic Stress

Group therapy is one of the most common PTSD interventions and considered a treatment of choice by many clinicians (Harney & Harvey, 1999; Shea et al., 2009). Various group interventions have been developed, several of which are mentioned here. **Psychodynamic PTSD groups** aim to make members' traumatic memories conscious so feelings about them can be worked through in the group setting. Similarly, **interpersonal PTSD groups/PTSD process groups** emphasize helping group members gain awareness of their feelings and patterns of relating to others; the group setting provides an excellent forum for members to give one another interpersonal feedback. **Supportive PTSD groups** focus more broadly on having group members provide each other with emotional support and encouragement; by fostering supportive relationships, those coping with trauma can assist one another. Psychodynamic, interpersonal, process, and supportive groups are usually less structured than **trauma-focused cognitive-behavioral groups**, which educate group members about trauma and use exposure and relaxation techniques to reduce anxiety. Therapy groups are often tailored to specific types of trauma: There are groups for combat veterans, substance users, disaster workers, automobile-accident survivors, sexual assault survivors, child-abuse survivors, and disaster survivors (B. H. Young & Blake, 1999).

Psychodynamic PTSD groups: Aim to make members' traumatic memories conscious so feelings about them can be worked through in the group setting.

Interpersonal PTSD groups/PTSD process groups: Emphasize helping group members gain awareness of their feelings and patterns of relating to others; the group setting provides an excellent forum for members to give one another interpersonal feedback.

Supportive PTSD groups: Group members provide each other with emotional support and encouragement; by fostering supportive relationships, those coping with trauma assist one another.

Trauma-focused cognitive-behavioral groups: Structured group approach that educates members about trauma and uses exposure and relaxation techniques to address anxiety.

Joe

Let's envision Joe joining a supportive therapy group for trauma survivors led by a local therapist. The group would likely consist of roughly eight trauma survivors and meet once a week for ninety minutes. Members would share their stories and support one another as they cope with their posttraumatic stress. In session, Joe might share that he has been feeling anxious and jittery at work. In response, other members would empathize and share similar difficulties that they have had. As a result, Joe would feel like others understand what he is going through. Members of the group would share strategies they use to overcome their difficulties at work and Joe, listening intently, would be encouraged to think about how he could adopt similar strategies.

Although group therapy is often a "go to" treatment for trauma, especially in agency settings, evidence for it remains limited. Research suggests that cognitive-behavioral, psychodynamic, interpersonal, and process-oriented group therapies can be effective (Bisson et al., 2007; Ehlers et al., 2014; Harney & Harvey, 1999; Levi et al., 2017; Schwartze et al., 2019; Shea et al., 2009; van Reekum & Watt, 2019). However, the quality of the evidence is mixed, with CBT groups having a larger and more compelling body of research support than other approaches (Schwartze et al., 2019). So, although groups are often used to treat posttraumatic stress, we don't know that much about their effectiveness (J. G. Beck & Sloan, 2014; Schwartze et al., 2019). This doesn't mean groups don't help. It simply means more studies are needed—especially for psychodynamic and interpersonal groups, which remain promising but under researched. (Schwartze et al., 2019).

Couples and Family Therapy Approaches

Posttraumatic Stress

Cognitive-behavioral conjoint therapy (CBCT) is a fifteen-session manualized treatment to teach conflict management to couples in which one partner suffers from PTSD (Monson & Fredman, 2019). It teaches the couple about the toxic role of avoidance in sustaining posttraumatic stress. It also helps them experiment *in vivo* with overcoming PTSD (e.g., they might be asked to go to a restaurant, even though they have typically avoided being in public due to fears of the PTSD-diagnosed partner). CBCT also teaches communication skills while helping the couple make meaning of the trauma. Problematic appraisals of what happened are examined and more productive ones developed.

Emotionally focused couples therapy (EFCT) combines humanistic, narrative, attachment, interpersonal, and family systems elements into a therapy for trauma survivors and their partners (Greenman & Johnson, 2012; S. M. Johnson, 2002). It restructures the couple's relationship by encouraging acceptance and communication of feelings. The PTSD-identified partner learns to reach out when in need, and the non-PTSD partner becomes better able to provide emotional support.

A small number of randomized controlled trials on CBCT and EFCT suggest they are helpful (Conradi et al., 2018; L. W. Davis et al., 2021; Ganz et al., 2022; Ghochani et al., 2020; Kugler et al., 2019; Pukay-Martin et al., 2017; Pukay-Martin et al., 2015; Shnaider et al., 2014). A self-help online adaptation of CBCT, known as *Couple HOPES* (Helping Overcome PTSD and Enhance Satisfaction), also shows promise (Monson et al., 2021, 2022). Interestingly, efforts are underway to incorporate psychedelics into CBCT and EFCT. As discussed in Chapter 5, psychedelic-assisted therapy uses hallucinogenic drugs like psilocybin, MDMA, and LSD (all discussed in Chapter 11) to facilitate talk therapy. It is being developed for issues like depression and trauma. Initial studies on incorporating MDMA into CBCT and EFCT couple interventions show promise (Almond & Allan, 2019; Monson et al., 2020; A. C. Wagner et al., 2019).

Grief and Loss

Family-focused grief therapy exemplifies a family approach to bereavement (Kissane et al., 2006; Kissane & Lichtenthal, 2008). This ten-session group treatment teaches families to communicate and share emotions more effectively to assist members with the mourning process. A randomized controlled study found evidence of improvement (albeit modest) among families who underwent family-focused grief therapy (Kissane et al., 2006; Kissane & Lichtenthal, 2008). More research is called for. In the meantime, this approach encourages us to think about grief not as an individual affliction, but as a family problem (Kissane & Lichtenthal, 2008).

Cognitive-behavioral conjoint therapy (CBCT): Fifteen-session manualized PTSD treatment for couples and families in which cognitive therapy techniques are used to teach conflict management.

Emotionally focused couples therapy (EFCT): Combines humanistic, narrative, attachment, interpersonal, and family systems elements into a therapy for trauma survivors and their partners.

Family-focused grief therapy: Ten-session therapy that teaches families to communicate and share emotions more effectively to help with the mourning process.

7.21 Evaluating Sociocultural Perspectives

Trauma, stress, and loss are problems especially intertwined with the social world. When people present with them, the emotional upset they experience is directly attributable to events in their social surroundings. Wars, disasters, and death—as well as less dramatic, more run-of-the-mill everyday stressors—exemplify the kinds of external, socially embedded events that produce posttraumatic stress, prolonged grief, and adjustment issues. Yet even though sociocultural factors set off these problems and influence how we define and treat them, such factors alone can't fully explain these experiences. Not everyone who faces trauma, stress, and loss responds the same way. Individual differences interact with social context in shaping our reactions to these kinds of events. Nonetheless, we tend to disproportionately attribute human distress to individual dysfunctions at the expense of social influences. Trauma, stress, and loss remind us that people's mental distress is deeply intertwined with their cultural surroundings.

CLOSING THOUGHTS

7.22 Erase Trauma, Loss, and Grief?

Memories related to trauma, stress, and loss are unpleasant. Nobody enjoys them and most of us wouldn't mind forgetting them. What if we could erase such memories? Researchers are exploring precisely this possibility (Lu, 2015). Analogue experiments using rodents and snails have met with some success in eradicating memories (Clem & Huganir, 2010; J. Hu et al., 2017; Kida, 2019; Meloni et al., 2014; Rafiq et al., 2020; Redondo et al., 2014). Among the possible ways to accomplish this is by blocking specific molecules related to an enzyme essential for long-term memory, *protein kinase M (PKM)* (J. Hu et al., 2017). In a related vein, the beta blocker *propranolol* (among other substances) is being researched as a possible drug to alter or eradicate traumatic memories in humans (Brunet et al., 2018; M. J. Friedman, 2018). Medications may not be the only way to erase memories. One study found that sounds played during sleep could reduce associative recall of certain previously learned word pairings—suggesting the possibility of non-drug interventions for removing unpleasant memories (Joensen et al., 2022).

If we do develop the ability to eliminate or change traumatic or distressing memories, should we? Every one of us will face stress and loss in our lives and almost all of us will be touched—directly or indirectly—by trauma, too. To this point in our species' history, these arduous experiences have simply been part of being human. The ongoing challenge for researchers, clinicians, and service users has been determining how much upset over these events is called for, when intervention is necessary, and whether what people gain from such experiences is worth the sacrifice of what is lost. When (if ever) might it be appropriate to erase grief over a loved one's death or preoccupation with surviving a rape, assault, war, accident, or natural disaster? Regardless of what you conclude, hopefully this chapter has helped you grasp current perspectives on the difficult issues of trauma, loss, and stress.

CHAPTER SUMMARY

Overview

- *Trauma* involves exposure to actual or threatened death, serious injury, or sexual violence; *stress* is feeling overwhelmed, worried, or run-down.
- *Bereavement* involves losing a significant person through death; *grief* is the primarily emotional response to bereavement.

Diagnostic Perspectives

- DSM and ICD trauma- and stressor-related disorders are *posttraumatic stress disorder (PTSD), acute stress disorder/reaction, adjustment disorder, prolonged grief disorder, reactive attachment disorder,* and *disinhibited social engagement disorder.*

- DSM and ICD critics question whether (a) trauma/stressor-related disorders are distinct from anxiety disorders, (b) posttraumatic stress is a reaction or disorder, (c) adjustment disorder is a "wastebasket" diagnosis, and (d) prolonged grief should be a disorder.
- PDM frames PTSD/complex PTSD as a relational problem in which therapists must avoid inflicting secondary trauma.
- Trauma is assessed along HiTOP's "Internalizing," "Thought Disorder," and "Externalizing" spectra dimensions.
- As part of moving away from a medical model, PTMF prefers the term "adversity" to "trauma."

Historical Perspectives

- Descriptions of trauma are found throughout history.
- Past trauma terms include *traumatic neurosis, war neurasthenia, shell shock, combat fatigue, battle stress,* and *gross stress reaction.*
- PTSD emerged as a diagnostic term in 1980's DSM-III.

Biological Perspectives

- *SSRIs* and *SNRIs* are the drugs most often prescribed for PTSD.
- Various drugs are prescribed for adjustment issues, but research on them is lacking.
- Despite limited research, *SSRIs* and *tricyclics* are prescribed for prolonged grief.
- *Limbic system* structures (e.g., *hippocampus, amygdala,* and *hypothalamus*) are implicated in posttraumatic stress; so is the *medial frontal cortex.*
- The *autonomic nervous system (ANS)* is tied to PTSD.
- The *HPA axis* may be inhibited in PTSD. *Hydrocortisone* is being studied as a treatment.
- Gene–environment interactions are key to posttraumatic stress.
- Evolutionary perspectives see trauma, stress, and grief responses as adaptive. PTSD only occurs when evolved trauma and stress coping mechanisms malfunction.
- *Inflammation* is associated with trauma, stress, and grief.
- There is mixed evidence for biological perspectives.

Psychological Perspectives

- *Negative emotionality (NEM)* is associated with vulnerability to posttraumatic stress.
- Psychodynamic perspectives view symptoms as reflecting past trauma, stress, and loss; unconscious conflicts, maladaptive interpersonal patterns, and problematic relationship beliefs are emphasized.
- Psychodynamic therapies for trauma, stress, and loss often rely on attachment theory.
- Classic psychoanalytic perspectives on bereavement/grief emphasize *decathexis,* while modern psychodynamic address interpersonal issues.
- *Exposure therapies* are effective interventions for trauma- and stressor-related disorders. They have also been adapted for prolonged grief.
- Cognitive-behavioral interventions for posttraumatic stress include *behavioral activation, cognitive processing therapy (CPT), cognitive therapy for PTSD, trauma-focused CBT (TF-CBT), emotional processing theory* approaches, *dual representation theory* approaches, *stress inoculation training (SIT), mindfulness-based cognitive therapy (MBCT), acceptance and commitment therapy (ACT),* and *eye movement desensitization reprocessing (EMDR).*
- *Person-centered therapy* views the therapeutic relationship as central to helping people cope with trauma, stress, and grief.
- *Constructivist perspectives* address trauma and loss by fostering the revision of invalidated meanings (or *self-narratives*).
- *Posttraumatic growth* involves positive changes following trauma and loss.
- CBT has the most research support for trauma, stress, and loss, but other approaches might be comparably effective.
- *Critical incident stress debriefing (CISD)* is a controversial post-trauma intervention; *psychological first aid (PFA)* is an alternative to it.

Sociocultural Perspectives

- Women, low SES people, and members of racial minority groups have higher rates of PTSD.
- *Cultural adaptations* are adjustments to therapy to account for cultural differences.
- Lack of social support predicts worse outcomes following trauma.
- There are cross-cultural differences in how people experience bereavement.
- PTSD and prolonged grief diagnoses carry stigma but foster awareness and research.
- Group therapies are common PTSD interventions.
- *Cognitive-behavioral conjoint therapy (CBCT)* and *emotionally focused couples therapy (EFCT)* are couple therapies for posttraumatic stress.

- *Family-focused grief therapy* addresses how family dynamics impact grief.
- Sociocultural perspectives do not always account for individual differences in responses to trauma, stress, and loss.

Closing Thoughts

- Researchers are studying ways to erase traumatic memories, but the ethics and wisdom of doing so are debated.

NEW VOCABULARY

1. Acute stress
2. Adjustment disorders
3. Amnesia
4. Autonomic nervous system (ANS)
5. Bereavement
6. Cognitive-behavioral conjoint therapy (CBCT)
7. Cognitive processing therapy (CPT)
8. Cognitive therapy for PTSD
9. Complex PTSD
10. Critical incident stress debriefing (CISD)
11. Cultural adaptations
12. Depersonalization
13. Derealization
14. Disinhibited social engagement disorder
15. Dissociation
16. Emotionally focused couple therapy (EFCT)
17. Emotional processing theory
18. Eye movement desensitization and reprocessing (EMDR)
19. Family-focused grief therapy
20. Fight or flight response
21. Five-stage theory of grief
22. General adaptation syndrome
23. Grief
24. Interpersonal PTSD groups/PTSD process groups
25. Posttraumatic growth (PTG)
26. Posttraumatic stress disorder (PTSD)
27. Prolonged grief disorder
28. Psychodynamic PTSD groups
29. Psychological first aid (PFA)
30. Reactive attachment disorder
31. Short-term dynamic therapy of stress response syndromes
32. Stress
33. Stress inoculation training (SIT)
34. Supportive PTSD groups
35. Trauma
36. Trauma-focused CBT (TF-CBT)
37. Trauma-focused cognitive-behavioral groups

DISSOCIATION AND SOMATIC COMPLAINTS

8

Photo 8.1
esraa gamal/Unsplash.

LEARNING OBJECTIVES

After reading this chapter, you should be able to:

1. Define dissociation, somatic complaints, and the posttraumatic model commonly used to explain them.

2. Describe DSM and ICD dissociative and somatic symptom diagnostic categories, as well as discuss debates about these categories.

3. Recall historical antecedents of dissociative and somatic symptom complaints.

4. Discuss biological perspectives on dissociation and somatic symptom complaints, including those looking at brain chemistry, brain structure, genes, evolution, and the immune system.

5. Distinguish psychodynamic, cognitive-behavioral, and humanistic perspectives on dissociative and somatic complaints.

6. Describe the sociocognitive model of dissociative identity disorder, the false memories debate, the role of stigma in dissociation and somatic symptoms, and family systems perspectives on dissociation and somatic symptoms.

OVERVIEW

8.1 Getting Started: Dissociation, Somatic Symptoms, and Stress

Case Examples

Lauren

Lauren is a 25-year-old woman who seeks therapy at a local health clinic. Meek and quiet in demeanor, her primary complaint concerns gaps in her memory. She reports periods of several days (including the previous two) that she can't recall and is befuddled as to why. She knows that she must be doing something during these times because she finds her food eaten and her clothes in the laundry. Although her childhood memories are also spotty, Lauren recollects being raised in a poor family that moved around a lot. When asked about how her parents treated her, her body language and demeanor shift abruptly; she now speaks in a louder and more aggressive voice, with a distinctly different accent. She tells the therapist her name is "Bix" and that she doesn't want to talk about Lauren's family but does know what has been going on the last two days. She reports going to a local bar and picking up a man, whom she took to a hotel for a one-night stand. When asked about Lauren, it becomes clear that Bix sees Lauren as a different person. "She doesn't know about me," Bix says, "but I look out for her."

Paul

Paul, a 35-year-old man, is referred to therapy after seeking treatment for a thyroid condition. "I don't know why the doctor sent me to you," Paul tells the therapist. "I just need her to figure out what's wrong with my thyroid." It turns out that Paul has a long and complicated medical history. He has previously been treated for a variety of digestive issues, ongoing headaches, and arthritic-like pain in his hands. His doctors haven't identified the biological origins of Paul's complaints. However, in the past he has received medical treatments for his many different symptoms.

Tiiu

Tiiu is a military pilot who has run over 100 bombing missions. She has won numerous commendations and is well respected by her peers and superiors. Recently, however, Tiiu began experiencing numbness in her hands. This has resulted in her being grounded from flying. Oddly, physical exams have found no medical reason for her hand numbness. Because Tiiu has been grounded, her commanding officer recently reassigned her to a base near her home and family. Tiiu seems calm about it all. "They'll just have to run more tests and figure it out," she says unemotionally just before being sent home.

Isabel

Isabel is a 39-year-old businesswoman who works at a large investment firm. She works long hours and is expected by her boss to bring in new business for the company. The pressure at work has started taking a toll on Isabel's health. At her last doctor's visit, she was told she has high blood pressure. Isabel isn't surprised. "If you had my job, you'd have high blood pressure, too!" she exclaims. In addition to blood pressure medication, Isabel seeks psychotherapy to cope with the stress she feels at work and at home.

The Posttraumatic Model

As seen in Chapter 7, trauma and loss often produce mental distress. This chapter examines dissociation and somatic symptoms, two other psychological problems linked to stressful life events. Given this link, it isn't surprising that many perspectives on dissociation and somatic symptoms adhere to a **posttraumatic model** (also called the *traumagenic position*). This model holds that somatic and dissociative issues are usually tied to stressful or traumatizing life events (Lynn et al., 2019, 2020; Meganck, 2017). More on this throughout the chapter.

Posttraumatic model: Links somatic and dissociative symptoms to stress or trauma; also called the *traumagenic position.*

Defining Dissociation and Somatic Complaints

Dissociation and somatic complaints differ. The former are mainly about disconnection from experience. The latter are characterized by physical symptoms with some underlying psychological connection. However, both are responses to stress that involve emotional or physical detachment from psychological upset. Thus, despite the DSM and ICD doing so, not all clinicians draw a firm distinction between dissociation and somatization; the boundary between them can appear arbitrary and artificial (Espirito-Santo & Pio-Abreu, 2009; Lewis-Fernández et al., 2007; C. A. Ross, 2008). Dissociative and somatic symptoms are strongly correlated (Lewis-Fernández et al., 2007). They are slightly different but interrelated ways of avoiding emotional anguish—by disconnecting from it, expressing it in physical terms, or both.

Dissociation

Chapter 7 described how dissociation involves disconnecting from feelings and experiences or separating (i.e., *compartmentalizing*) different feelings from one another (E. R. S. Nijenhuis & van der Hart, 2011). A dissociating individual might feel nothing during an emotionally charged situation. Or, if in a state of extreme anger, the person might be unable to simultaneously experience other feelings because dissociation often involves separating different feeling states; while experiencing one, others aren't consciously accessible. Everyone dissociates sometimes, but—as discussed in Chapter 7—severe dissociation often produces a sense of disconnection from or unreality about self (*depersonalization*) and/or world (*derealization*) (Şar, 2014). Dissociation can also result in *amnesia* (memory loss) about upsetting events. When dissociative compartmentalization is very extreme, **identity confusion** and **identity alteration** may even occur (Şar, 2014). The former involves confusion about and/or a hard time recalling one's identity, while in the latter a new identity is established in lieu of the old one.

Identity confusion and alteration are less common than depersonalization, derealization, and amnesia. For example, during an intense argument with a friend, depersonalization occurs when you feel like you're watching the proceedings from outside your own body. By contrast, in derealization reality appears altered—for instance, during the argument, it seems like time is standing still. Finally, you encounter amnesia to the extent that, after the argument, you have difficulty recalling precisely who said what to whom!

Dissociation can seem strange and dramatic, but keep in mind that most dissociation is mild and mundane (R. J. Brown, 2006; L. D. Butler, 2004, 2006; R. Herbert, 2013). Losing track of time due to getting absorbed in a task can be considered a minor form of dissociation. So can daydreaming, fantasizing, listening to music, and *highway hypnosis* (in which people drive long distances without paying conscious attention to what they're doing) (M. R. Barlow & Freyd, 2009; Cerezuela et al., 2004; R. Herbert, 2013). These examples are considered "normal" forms of dissociation. They are distinguished from the more "pathological" forms mentioned above (derealization, depersonalization, amnesia, and identity confusion/alteration). Besides being more severe, dissociation deemed pathological is commonly (and, as we shall see, controversially!) viewed as a response to highly traumatic events such as assault or abuse (M. R. Barlow & Freyd, 2009; Lanius, 2015; van der Hart, 2021). Given this trauma-oriented perspective on dissociation, it is no wonder that distressing events such as wars, natural disasters, and sexual assaults are believed to produce it—and why dissociation is a criterion for posttraumatic stress disorder (PTSD) (see Chapter 7). However, dissociation is just one component of PTSD, perhaps explaining why DSM and ICD don't classify PTSD as a dissociative disorder. In this chapter, we focus on presenting problems in which dissociation itself is identified as the primary issue.

Somatic Complaints

A **somatic complaint** involves experiencing or worrying about physical symptoms. Having a stomachache, feeling pain in one's chest, and spells of dizziness are all somatic complaints. Over the last few decades (until DSM-5 in 2013), somatic complaints were often distinguished using the terms *psychosomatic* and *somatization*. According to this distinction, a complaint is **psychosomatic** (or *psychophysiological*) when prolonged psychological stress results in or exacerbates a real medical condition (Bransfield & Friedman, 2019; R. Kellner, 1994; H. Nisar & Srivastava, 2018; Samaran & Vivek, 2020).

Isabel

Under a lot of pressure at work, Isabel develops high blood pressure. Her high blood pressure is physiologically real but caused or made worse by ongoing psychological tension. It is a psychosomatic symptom.

Somatization, on the other hand, traditionally refers to the process of expressing psychological problems in physical terms (Bransfield & Friedman, 2019; Rohlof et al., 2014). In this classic definition, somaticized symptoms are medically unexplained—they are viewed as excessive and/or as physical representations of underlying emotional conflicts (De Gucht & Fischler, 2002; R. Kellner, 1994). As we shall see, DSM and ICD have moved away from this classic view of somatization.

Tiiu

Somatization occurs when Tiiu develops medically inexplicable hand numbness and can no longer fly bombing missions. The numbness in her hands conveys psychological conflict over bombing people. She is expressing her emotional distress through a physical symptom, but her hand numbness can't be explained by any known physical impairment.

Identity confusion: Form of dissociation in which there is confusion about or difficulty recalling one's identity.

Identity alteration: Form of dissociation that sometimes accompanies identity confusion, in which a person establishes a new identity in lieu of the old one.

Somatic complaint: Presenting problem that involves experiencing or worrying about physical symptoms.

Psychosomatic: Term for when prolonged psychological stress results in or exacerbates a real medical condition; sometimes also referred to as *psychophysiological*.

Somatization: The process of expressing psychological problems in physical terms.

Although the psychosomatic–somatization distinction goes back a long way, it isn't always firmly adhered to. DSM and ICD include numerous diagnoses that combine or blur the line between psychosomatic and somatization problems. This sometimes makes it difficult to differentiate various kinds of somatic symptom complaints.

DIAGNOSTIC PERSPECTIVES

8.2 DSM and ICD

DSM-5-TR and ICD-11 both include sections on "Dissociative Disorders" but use different titles for their sections on somatic complaints: "Somatic Symptom and Related Disorders" in DSM-5-TR and "Disorders of Bodily Distress or Bodily Experience" in ICD-11. To further confuse matters, DSM and ICD don't always include the same disorder names—and these names have frequently changed over the years. Table 8.1 provides clarification.

Table 8.1 The Many Names of Dissociative and Somatic Symptom Disorders

DSM-5-TR	CLOSEST ICD-11 EQUIVALENT	CLOSEST ICD-10 EQUIVALENT	ALSO KNOWN AS
Dissociative amnesia (with or without dissociative fugue)	Dissociative amnesia (with or without dissociative fugue)	Dissociative amnesia and dissociative fugue (considered distinct diagnoses)	—
Depersonalization/ derealization disorder	Depersonalization/derealization disorder	Depersonalization/derealization syndrome	—
Dissociative identity disorder	Dissociative identity disorder	Multiple personality disorder	—
Somatic symptom disorder	Bodily distress disorder	Somatization disorder	Briquet's syndrome
Functional neurological symptom disorder (conversion disorder)	Dissociative neurological symptom disorder	Dissociative disorders of movement and sensation	Psychogenic movement disorders
Illness anxiety disorder	Hypochondriasis	Hypochondriacal disorder	Hypochondria
Psychological factors affecting other medical condition	Psychological or behavioral factors affecting disorders or diseases classified elsewhere	Psychological and behavioral factors associated with disorders or diseases classified elsewhere	Psychosomatic illness
Factitious disorder (distinguish if imposed on self or imposed on another)	Factitious disorder (distinguish if imposed on self or imposed on another)	Intentional production or feigning of symptoms or disabilities, either physical or psychological (factitious disorder)	Munchhausen's syndrome (Munchhausen's syndrome by proxy if imposed on another)

Dissociative Disorders

Dissociative Amnesia

People diagnosed with **dissociative amnesia** have difficulty recalling important autobiographical information. The information that can't be remembered is usually of a traumatic nature, and the memory loss is not due to simple forgetting. For example, a violent sexual assault survivor later reports no memory of the attack and doesn't recall being hospitalized afterwards or attending the trial of the perpetrator. In rare cases, the amnesiac individual leaves home, travels somewhere new, and establishes a new identity. When this occurs, *dissociative amnesia with dissociative fugue* is diagnosed. See Diagnostic Box 8.1.

Prevalence rates for dissociative amnesia and dissociative fugue are hard to come by. DSM-5-TR notes that the twelve-month prevalence rate for dissociative amnesia among adults in a U.S.

Dissociative amnesia: DSM and ICD dissociative disorder that involves difficulty recalling important autobiographical information; diagnosed as *dissociative amnesia with dissociative fugue* if there is intentional travel or confused wandering from home.

Diagnostic Box 8.1 Dissociative Amnesia

DSM-5-TR and ICD-11

- Unable to recall information about oneself and one's life.
- Forgotten information is typically associated with trauma or stress and is more than just everyday forgetfulness.
- Specify *with fugue* is there is intentional travel or confused wandering from home.

Information from American Psychiatric Association (2022, p. 337) and World Health Organization (2022a).

community study was 1.8 percent. Dissociative amnesia prevalence estimates for other countries range between 0.2 percent and 7.3 percent (Staniloiu & Markowitsch, 2014). Data for dissociative fugue are even scarcer. One study from China estimated prevalence at 1.3 percent; another from Turkey 0.2 percent (Şar et al., 2007; Staniloiu & Markowitsch, 2014).

Depersonalization/derealization disorder: DSM and ICD dissociative disorder diagnosed in those who experience *depersonalization* (disconnection from self), *derealization* (disconnection from world), or both.

Depersonalization/Derealization

As its name implies, **depersonalization/derealization disorder** is diagnosed in people who experience depersonalization, derealization, or both (see Diagnostic Box 8.2). DSM-5-TR estimates that half of adults will experience an episode of depersonalization/derealization during their lifetimes. Exact prevalence rates are hard to come by, but DSM-5-TR estimates one-month prevalence in the UK to be 1 percent to 2 percent. Depersonalization/derealization is a good predictor of other mental health problems, such as anxiety and depression (Schlax et al., 2020).

Diagnostic Box 8.2 Depersonalization/Derealization Disorder

DSM-5-TR and ICD-11

- Repeated depersonalization, derealization, or both.
- *Depersonalization*: Feeling disconnected from or outside one's thoughts, emotions, and behavior; one's experience seems altered or unreal.
- *Derealization*: Feeling disconnected from or outside one's environment; world seems altered or unreal.

Information from American Psychiatric Association (2022, p. 343) and World Health Organization (2022a).

Dissociative Identity Disorder

Dissociative identity disorder (DID): DSM and ICD dissociative disorder describing people who have two or more distinct "personalities" (or "alters"); ICD-11 includes *partial dissociative identity disorder* for cases where the non-dominant personalities are intrusive but don't seize executive control.

Dissociative identity disorder (DID) is one of the more controversial DSM and ICD categories (Paris, 2019). It used to be called *multiple personality disorder*, but the name has been changed. The hallmark of DID is having two or more distinct "personalities," with only one present at any given time. Patients diagnosed with DID experience amnesia and can't recall personal information or past trauma. When one personality (or *alter*) is in conscious control, the person may not remember information about the other personalities—or even be cognizant of their existence at all. People with this diagnosis vary in how aware they are of their multiple identities. Many of them minimize their amnesias even though they often experience quite odd things—such as not remembering their names, their family, what happened yesterday, or how they arrived at a given location. Despite its seemingly dramatic symptoms, personality shifts can be subtle, and patients often don't know of their various alters, making DID hard to detect. Symptoms typically persist for five to twelve years before a diagnosis is made (Mitra & Jain, 2021; Spiegel et al., 2013). "The Lived Experience" box illustrates what it is like to have dissociative identities and how challenging it can be for therapists to recognize them.

Lauren

Lauren, who appears to have several distinct "personalities," was diagnosed with DID—but only after having seen many therapists who did not identify it.

The Lived Experience: Living with Dissociative Identity Disorder

Rachel took a deep breath and grabbed her coffee cup to prevent herself from going into a full-blown panic attack, hoping that it would quiet the overwhelming surge of voices in her head, all fighting to be heard. Dr. Jones, sensing her distress, said encouragingly, "You can share anything here and it will be kept strictly confidential. I know it's hard to open up, but I really want to hear your story." That reassurance seemed to be exactly what Rachel needed.

Well, I guess I'm here because I don't know what to do anymore. I've been dealing with some really difficult things for a long time. Lately, things have just started to unravel. Weird things have been happening to me and I feel like I'm losing control of my life. I just don't know how to handle things anymore. My doctor recently diagnosed me with depression and anxiety and put me on medication for that, but it's not really helping all that much. I kind of feel like I'm at the end of my rope.

"You mentioned that weird things happening recently," Dr. Jones commented. "Can you tell me more?"

Rachel's heart started racing, and she began gulping in deep breaths. Peering up at her doctor's kind face, she quickly looked back down. I can do this. I have to tell her! I can't do this on my own anymore. Without looking up, Rachel began speaking very quietly, voice shaking.

Sometimes ... I can be talking to someone and all of a sudden I get this really weird far away and foggy feeling ... like I am way back in my head somewhere ... The next thing I know I'll "come back," but things just aren't right. For instance, I'll be in the house doing housework, then the next thing I know I'm back in the house but three hours have passed and there are grocery bags on the counter, but I don't remember going to the store. One time I all of a sudden was sitting on my couch and I realized my ankle was hurting like crazy and I looked down and I had a cast on it! But I couldn't remember getting hurt.

I'll get this odd sensation like I'm in my body, but I'm not "me" ... like I'm behind someone looking through their eyes, or I'll look at my hands touching something and know that it's me, but it's someone else's hands that are touching the object. Or I'll hear myself having a conversation with someone but I don't know how because I'm not talking.

I have nightmares and flashbacks. Sometimes I see pictures of things in my head that are familiar yet I don't know what they are or where they are from. Other times, sights, sounds, smells, they'll send me into a panic and scare me silly, but I don't know why. They always seem familiar but again, for no reason. And sometimes, and I know this will make me sound completely nuts, but sometimes I'll hear voices, two, three ... having a conversation and I'm listening to it ... only the voices are having a conversation inside my head, but I'm not a part of it.

Stuff like this, well, it's been happening my whole life. And up until a while ago I managed to cope with it pretty well, you know, I developed ways to cover up dealing with people who knew me that I didn't seem to know, and I managed to create explanations for why I suddenly had groceries or a new item of clothing that I couldn't remember buying. I just faked my way through life, you know?

Rachel finally looked up, tears streaming down her face. "Can you please help me understand what's happening to me? Am I crazy? Please tell me honestly, because I'd rather know and deal with it than continue living my life like this. I just can't do it anymore. For the first time I can remember, I'm really scared. I don't know what to do anymore."

Dr. Jones looked compassionately at Rachel and spoke very gently, "I'm so sorry to hear about how much you've been struggling. You must have felt so alone." Rachel nodded shakily as Dr. Jones continued,

Thank you for your courage to be honest with me, Rachel. I don't want you to feel alone dealing with these symptoms, so I'm glad you've told me what's going on for you so I can help you. And no, you're not crazy, I have a feeling your mind is trying very hard to deal with trauma that's happened in your life, and it's just coping the best way it can right now.

At the word "trauma," Rachel stiffened and a visible shudder ran through her body. The tears continued streaming down her face, and that was when it happened, one of those weird things Rachel had hoped wouldn't happen while she was here with her doctor. As Dr. Jones was asking her questions Rachel felt the like the room was getting more and more distant ... things were fading and her head felt fuzzy and distant ...

"Daddy says we can't talk about dat cause I could get a whoopin'. He says bad men will take me away from him cause Mommy went to heaven so I can't say nuthin'." Right before Dr. Jones' eyes, Rachel slumped back into the couch and sat cross legged. She started to nervously pick at the sore on her arm, scratching as she talked.

As she continued talking in a high-pitched lisp, Dr. Jones reached for a squeeze ball on her desk and handed it to Rachel, who took it and started playing with it. "Rachel," she coaxed gently, "Rachel, please come back. Listen to the sound of my voice, and feel the squeeze ball in your hand. Feel the rubbery spikes on the ball and just let my voice bring you back."

Rachel found herself coming out of the fog that had enveloped her brain so suddenly. The distant feeling she had had the moment before was fading and she again was able to focus on the fact that she was sitting in the doctor's office. For some reason though, she couldn't remember anything that she and Dr. Jones had been talking about before her space-out happened. Even more startling to her was the realization that she was holding a squeeze toy in her hands, and she couldn't remember how it got there.

Panic rose up inside of her and she caught her breath ... not this again! Not here! With hands that shook slightly, Rachel reached over and put the squeeze toy on the therapist's desk. "I'm sorry," Rachel said, "Um, I seem to have forgotten your question. Would you mind repeating it?"

The therapist took a deep breath herself and carefully considered how to explain her diagnosis. "Rachel, have you ever heard of Dissociative Identity Disorder?"

Reprinted with permission of Dr. Merry C. Lin.

Diagnostic Box 8.3 Dissociative Identity Disorder

DSM-5-TR
- Presence of two or more discrete personality states; in some cultures, may be described as an experience of possession.
- Difficulty remembering daily events, personal information, or past traumas that is more than simple forgetfulness.

ICD-11
- Divided into two diagnoses:
  - *Dissociative identity disorder*: Presence of two or more discrete or not-fully integrated personality states that alternately take control of the person's functioning.
  - *Partial dissociative identity disorder*: Presence of two or more discrete or not-fully integrated personality but the non-dominant states do not alternately take control of the person's functioning.

Information from American Psychiatric Association (2022, p. 330) and World Health Organization (2022a).

Photo 8.2 *United States of Tara* is a 2009–2011 American television series that offered a fictionalized account of Tara (played by Toni Collette), a suburban wife and mother grappling with dissociative identity disorder. The show was praised for its sensitive and humane portrayal of dissociation and mental distress.

AJ Pics/Alamy Stock Photo.

ICD-11 added a *partial dissociative identity disorder* diagnosis for cases where one or more non-dominant personalities are present and intrusive but, unlike in "classic" DID, never seize executive control. Some clinicians believe partial DID is more common than the classic variety. See Diagnostic Box 8.3 for details. Notably, ICD-11 includes two other new disorders not discussed in this chapter, but which must be distinguished from DID: *trance disorder* (identity is lost and awareness narrowed, as in a trance) and *possession trance disorder* (identity is lost and the person feels influenced by a spirit, deity, or higher power).

Prevalence of DID is difficult to assess, in part because the disorder is controversial and many clinicians don't believe in it (Gleaves et al., 2001). International prevalence estimates range from 1 percent to 5 percent (Mitra & Jain, 2021). Not surprisingly, DID rates are significantly higher among people with other mental disorders (Sar, 2011; Sar et al., 2014). This may be because DID is associated with trauma—and those who have faced extensive trauma may lack the emotional resources to cope with additional adversity, making them more susceptible to anxiety, sadness, and other presenting problems.

Somatic Symptom and Related Disorders
Somatic Symptom Disorder and Bodily Distress Disorder

DSM and ICD have turned away from classic views of somatization, in which symptoms were often viewed as expressions of psychological conflict without a medical basis. Instead, they have adopted a more agnostic stance on whether psychologically influenced somatic symptoms have a biological basis. In this vein, DSM-5-TR's **somatic symptom disorder (SSD)** is diagnosed in people who display one or more somatic symptoms that they think and worry about excessively. These symptoms might be biologically based, but they also might not be. This reflects a shift from assuming somatic symptoms are only in people's heads and not real. The ICD-11 equivalent of somatic symptom disorder eliminates the term "somatic" (and its negative connotations) entirely, speaking instead of **bodily distress disorder** (Gureje & Reed, 2016). Because it is a new diagnosis, prevalence of somatic symptom/bodily distress disorder isn't clear, although DSM-5-TR reports prevalence estimates between 6.7 percent and 17.4 percent. See Diagnostic Box 8.4 for more on somatic symptom disorder and bodily distress disorder.

Paul

Paul qualifies for a somatic symptom disorder or bodily distress disorder diagnosis, depending on whether his therapist uses DSM-5-TR or ICD-11.

Somatic symptom disorder (SSD): DSM diagnosis for people who have one or more somatic symptoms that they think and worry about excessively; roughly equivalent to *bodily distress disorder* in ICD.

Bodily distress disorder: ICD disorder characterized by physical symptoms that the person finds distressing and pays excessive attention to; roughly equivalent to the DSM's *somatic symptom disorder*.

Diagnostic Box 8.4 Somatic Symptom Disorder and Bodily Distress Disorder

DSM-5-TR: Somatic Symptom Disorder
- One or more upsetting and disruptive somatic symptoms.
- At least one of these: (1) ongoing and excessive thinking about the symptom(s); (2) extreme anxiety about the symptom(s) or one's health; (3) lots of time and attention focused on the symptom(s) or one's health.
- Continuous symptoms of some kind persist, usually for six months or more.

ICD-11: Bodily Distress Disorder
- Physical symptoms that the person finds distressing and pays excessive attention to.
- Even when the symptoms have a physical explanation, worry about them is excessive and the person cannot be reassured, even by doctors.
- The physical symptoms are present for several months or more.

Information from American Psychiatric Association (2022, p. 351) and World Health Organization (2022a).

Functional Neurological Symptom Disorder (Conversion Disorder)

DSM-5-TR's **functional neurological symptom disorder** (often still called by its old name, *conversion disorder*) involves loss or alteration of physical symptoms for which there is no known neurological or medical explanation (see Diagnostic Box 8.5). In other words, someone with this disorder literally converts psychological conflict into a physical symptom. Such a person displays symptoms related to *motor functioning* (e.g., weak limbs, paralysis, physical tremors) or *sensory loss* (e.g., blindness, hearing impairment), but these symptoms aren't easily explained medically and seem to be related to stressors in the person's life. ICD-11 uses the name **dissociative neurological symptom disorder**; as the name indicates, ICD considers this a dissociative disorder, but DSM groups its version as a somatic symptom disorder. Clearly, disagreement remains over the boundaries between somatization and dissociation. DSM-5-TR notes that the prevalence of functional neurological symptoms isn't known, but it estimates annual incidence between 4 and 12 out of every 100,000 people.

Functional neurological symptom disorder: DSM diagnosis that involves physical loss or alteration for which there is no known neurological or medical explanation; also called *conversion disorder* or, in ICD, *dissociative neurological symptom disorder*.

Dissociative neurological symptom disorder: ICD disorder in which there is lost or altered sensory, motor, or cognitive functioning inconsistent with any known disease or health condition; DSM equivalent is *functional neurological symptom disorder*.

Diagnostic Box 8.5 Functional Neurological Symptom Disorder and Dissociative Neurological Symptom Disorder

DSM-5-TR: Functional Neurological Symptom Disorder (Conversion Disorder)
- One or more physical symptom involving lost or altered motor or sensory functioning.
- Incompatibility between the symptom(s) and known neurological/medical conditions.
- Subtypes: *with weakness or paralysis; with abnormal movement; with swallowing symptoms; with speech symptom; with attacks or seizures; with anesthesia or sensory loss; with special sensory symptoms; with mixed symptoms.*
- Specify *acute* (less than six months) or *persistent* (more than six months); specify *with psychological stressor* or *without psychological stressor.*

ICD-11: Dissociative Neurological Symptom Disorder
- Lost or altered sensory, motor, or cognitive functioning inconsistent with any known disease or health condition.
- Subtypes: *with visual disturbance; with auditory disturbance; with vertigo or dizziness; with other sensory disturbance; with non-epileptic seizures; with speech disturbance; with paresis or weakness; with gait disturbance; with movement disturbance; with cognitive symptoms.*

Information from American Psychiatric Association (2022, pp. 360–361) and World Health Organization (2022a).

Tiiu

Tiiu, the military pilot experiencing numbness in her hands after repeatedly flying bombing missions, qualifies for a functional neurological symptom disorder (conversion disorder) diagnosis.

Illness Anxiety Disorder and Hypochondriasis

Hypochondriasis: ICD diagnosis describing excessive worry about being physically ill, traditionally with the assumption that there is little or no basis for such concern; *illness anxiety disorder* is its closest DSM equivalent.

Illness anxiety disorder: DSM somatic symptom diagnosis for people who worry about having one or more physical illnesses; differs from ICD's *hypochondriasis* by not requiring that those diagnosed aren't sick.

ICD still uses the term "hypochondriasis," but DSM doesn't. **Hypochondriasis** involves excessive worry about being physically ill, with the assumption that there is little or no basis for such concern. Thus, hypochondriasis is diagnosed in people who worry about having one or more physical illnesses and can't be reassured that they don't—even though there is nothing seriously wrong with them medically. In DSM, this disorder is called **illness anxiety disorder**. Like somatic symptom disorder, illness anxiety disorder does not require that patient complaints lack a physical basis. The main difference between these diagnoses is that the former involves prominent somatic symptoms, while the latter does not. DSM-5-TR estimates the prevalence of illness anxiety to be between 1.3 percent and 10 percent.

While DSM-5-TR classifies illness anxiety disorder as a somatic symptom disorder, ICD-11 groups hypochondriasis with obsessive-compulsive disorders. The ICD's logic is that, unlike bodily distress disorder, hypochondriasis involves few or no physical symptoms. However, the excessive concern about symptoms involves obsessive thinking and compulsive checking (van den Heuvel et al., 2014). Illness anxiety disorder and hypochondriasis are presented in Diagnostic Box 8.6.

Diagnostic Box 8.6 Illness Anxiety Disorder and Hypochondriasis

DSM-5-TR: Illness Anxiety Disorder
- For six months or more, preoccupied with being or becoming ill.
- No physical symptoms or mild physical symptoms; if ill, disproportionate concern about it.
- Excessively anxious/alarmed about health.
- Checks symptoms constantly or avoids doctors and hospitals.
- Classified as a "somatic symptom and related-disorder."

ICD-11: Hypochondriasis
- Consistent preoccupation with having one or more serious illnesses.

- Checks symptoms constantly or avoids doctors and hospitals.
- Catastrophically misinterprets bodily feedback as indicating illness.
- Classified as an "obsessive-compulsive or related disorder."

Information from American Psychiatric Association (2022, p. 357) and World Health Organization (2022a).

Psychological Factors Affecting Other Medical Conditions

Psychological factors affecting other medical conditions is the DSM-5-TR diagnosis for people who have a known medical symptom brought on or made worse by ongoing psychological stress. The ICD-11 uses the even wordier name, **psychological or behavioral factors affecting disorders or diseases classified elsewhere**. The DSM and ICD versions of this diagnosis can be viewed as psychosomatic problems because they involve real medical conditions impacted by emotional conflict. However, in including "psychological factors affecting other medical conditions" in the same chapter as somatic symptom and functional neurological symptom disorders, DSM-5-TR has challenged the traditional psychosomatic versus somatization distinction. This change—not found in ICD-11, which doesn't group this disorder with any others—has generated much debate and receives more attention below. According to DSM-5-TR, prevalence rates for psychological factors affecting other medical conditions aren't clear. See Diagnostic Box 8.7 for concise criteria and guidelines.

Isabel

Isabel, whose emotional stress seems related to her high blood pressure, probably qualifies for a diagnosis of psychological factors affecting other medical conditions.

Psychological factors affecting other medical conditions: DSM diagnosis for people who have a known medical symptom that is brought on or made worse by ongoing psychological stress. Called *psychological or behavioral factors affecting disorders or diseases classified elsewhere* in ICD.

Psychological or behavioral factors affecting disorders or diseases classified elsewhere: ICD equivalent to the DSM diagnosis of *psychological factors affecting other medical conditions*.

Diagnostic Box 8.7 Disorders in which Psychological Factors Impact Medical Conditions

DSM-5-TR: Psychological Factors Affecting Other Medical Conditions
- The patient has a medical condition (besides a mental disorder).
- Psychological factors adversely impact the medical condition by influencing its course or treatment, endangering the person's health, or making the symptoms worse.

ICD-11: Psychological or Behavioral Factors Affecting Disorders or Diseases Classified Elsewhere
- Psychological or behavioral factors influence a physical disorder.
- Psychological factors adversely impact the medical condition by influencing its course or treatment, endangering the person's health, or making the symptoms worse.

Information from American Psychiatric Association (2022, pp. 364–365) and World Health Organization (2022a).

Factitious Disorder

Factitious disorder is an ICD and DSM diagnosis that isn't easily classified as either psychosomatic or somaticizing. DSM-5-TR groups it with somatic symptom and related disorders, but it is housed it in a separate "Factitious Disorders" section of ICD-11. Factitious disorder is diagnosed in those who physically tamper with themselves or otherwise exaggerate or simulate symptoms to produce signs of illness and convince others they are sick (see Diagnostic Box 8.8). The goal is to get medical attention. Factitious disorder is usually distinguished from *malingering*, a fancy word for "just faking"—although the dividing line between them can be difficult to discern (Bass & Halligan, 2014; Galli et al., 2018). One way of differentiating them is to see the malingerer as faking to gain something, such as disability insurance payments or being relieved of burdensome responsibilities at work. The factitious disorder patient, by comparison, has a deep psychological need for medical attention (Carnahan & Jha, 2022; McCullumsmith & Ford, 2011).

Factitious disorder: DSM and ICD diagnosis for people who physically tamper with themselves or otherwise exaggerate or simulate symptoms to produce signs of illness and convince others they are sick, with the goal being to get medical attention; can also be done to others; sometimes called *Munchausen's syndrome*.

DSM-5-TR and ICD-11 distinguish *factitious disorder imposed on self* from *factitious disorder imposed on another* (previously called *factitious disorder by proxy*). In the former, the focus is on one's own health; in the latter, there is interference with the health of someone else—often by surreptitiously doing things to spouses or children to make them ill, such as slipping toxins into their food. Factitious disorder is also sometimes known as *Munchausen's syndrome*. Because of the deceptiveness involved in this disorder, prevalence rates for factitious disorder are hard to determine, but DSM-5-TR estimates that nearly 1 percent of general hospital inpatients referred for psychiatric consultations meet criteria for it.

Diagnostic Box 8.8 Factitious Disorder

DSM-5-TR and ICD-11
- Faking, falsifying, or tampering with self to produce injury or illness.
- Misleadingly presents to others as sick, damaged, or hurt.
- Not motivated by external rewards (e.g., financial gain, disability benefits).
- Not accounted for by another mental disorder (e.g., not delusional or psychotic).
- Two types:
  - *Factitious disorder imposed on self*
  - *Factitious disorder imposed on another* (previously *factitious disorder by proxy*).

Information from American Psychiatric Association (2022, p. 367) and World Health Organization (2022a).

Evaluating DSM And ICD Perspectives
Doubts About Dissociation and Dissociative Identity Disorder

Dissociation has been criticized for being an overly broad concept that is imprecisely defined (E. R. S. Nijenhuis & van der Hart, 2011). According to some research, many clinicians are skeptical of dissociation and unconvinced that dissociative disorders should be accepted as legitimate diagnoses (Lalonde et al., 2001; Pope et al., 1999, 2006). Part of the issue is that, like the Freudian notion of repression, dissociation can't be scientifically observed. After all, if an experience is compartmentalized and out of awareness, it isn't overtly visible. This means we must rely on abstract theoretical definitions. Consequently, many scientists and practitioners doubt whether dissociation is scientifically testable, leading them to challenge its validity.

Although all the dissociative disorders attract criticism, the debate gets especially intense around dissociative identity disorder. Psychiatrists critical of DID don't believe it exists, seeing it as a "fad" diagnosis propagated by misguided mental health professionals (Paris, 2012, 2019; Pope et al., 2006). They have called for its removal from DSM and ICD, arguing that it is an **iatrogenic condition**—meaning that mental health professionals who believe in it subtly encourage their patients to see themselves as having multiple personalities and that, in response, these patients start acting as if they do because they don't wish to displease their therapists (Piper & Merskey, 2004a, 2004b). Some critics add that not only is DID scientifically suspect, but that there are no randomized controlled trials (RCTs) of effective therapies for DID and that so-called treatments make patients worse (Paris, 2012; Piper & Merskey, 2004a, 2004b). Defenders counter that critics ignore data showing that DID can be reliably diagnosed using assessment methods such as the *Structured Clinical Interview for Dissociative Disorders (SCID-D)* (Dorahy et al., 2014). They also contend that DID is a genuine disorder found throughout the world and that critics ignore a large research literature that has established its scientific legitimacy (B. Brand et al., 2013; B. L. Brand et al., 2014; Loewenstein, 2018; C. A. Ross, 2009, 2013b). Other key aspects of the debate over DID—especially disagreement about whether child abuse causes it—are examined later in the chapter. The main point for now is that dissociation and DID are highly controversial concepts.

Iatrogenic condition: A condition or disorder induced when mental health professionals subtly (and usually inadvertently) encourage their patients that they have it.

Debate over Somatic Symptom Disorders in DSM

Some clinicians criticized the new somatic symptom disorders chapter when it debuted in DSM-5. In particular, they questioned the new somatic symptom disorder diagnosis for its more inclusive definition of somatic symptoms. The diagnosis that somatic symptom disorder replaced (called *somatization disorder*) confined itself to bodily symptoms that lacked a clear biological basis and seemed to have psychological origins. Critics worried that the new somatic symptom disorder, with its agnosticism about whether bodily concerns have a biological basis, was too broad and would result in over diagnosis (A. Frances, 2013b; A. Frances & Chapman, 2013). The danger, in their view, was that somatic symptom disorder pathologizes normal worry about being physically sick:

There are serious risks attached to over-psychologizing somatic symptoms and mislabeling the normal reactions to being sick—especially when the judgments are based on vague wording that can't possibly lead to reliable diagnosis. DSM-5 as it now stands will add to the suffering of those already burdened with all the cares of having a medical illness. (A. Frances & Chapman, 2013, p. 484)

Those in favor of somatic symptom disorder challenged such characterizations, pointing to research supporting the reliability and validity of the diagnosis (Dimsdale et al., 2013; Löwe et al., 2022). Additionally, SSD supporters argued that older diagnoses like somatization disorder and hypochondriasis were stigmatizing in falsely suggesting that nothing was wrong with patients, implying their suffering wasn't justified or legitimate. Advocates of the new somatic symptom disorder believed it would reduce stigma because "it offers greater acknowledgement of patients' suffering and avoids questioning the validity of their somatic symptoms" (Dimsdale et al., 2013, p. 227). While downplaying medically unexplained symptoms may avoid stigma, it is easy to see how taking a more neutral stance on the biological basis of somatic symptoms blurs the old psychosomatic–somatization distinction. In so doing, it could make diagnosing somatic symptom disorder confusing to clinicians and patients alike.

8.3 Other Diagnostic Perspectives

PDM-2

PDM-2 emphasizes the subjective experience of dissociative disorders, especially the separation of affect (i.e., emotion) into disconnected parts. As PDM-2 explains it: "In the absence of dissociation, thoughts and ideas are invested with different affects that help determine their meaning, and these affectively meaningful cognitions are all integrated into a sense of self" (Lingiardi & McWilliams, 2017, p. 106). Situations can elicit mixed feelings, but these feelings are integrated sufficiently to be "experienced as connected" (Lingiardi & McWilliams, 2017, p. 107). In dissociative disorders, by contrast, "such processes, which seem automatic to individuals without dissociative tendencies, cannot be taken for granted; any of them can be split off and experienced as alien" (Lingiardi & McWilliams, 2017, p. 107). For instance, in depersonalization, patients disconnect from affect related to bodily sensations; in amnesia, they disengage from affect tied to painful memories. One other point worth noting: PDM-2 groups dissociative identity disorder with personality (rather than dissociative) disorders and prefers to call it *dissociative personality disorder*. PDM-2 also includes *somatizing personality disorders* in which psychic conflicts are expressed in or contribute to physical symptoms; as with most presenting problems, PDM-2 links presenting complaints to ingrained personality styles.

HiTOP

Research into dissociation's location on HiTOP's spectra dimensions remains in its early stages (Kotov et al., 2021). Limited evidence to date suggests dissociation falls on HiTOP's "Thought Disorder" spectrum, which makes sense because dissociative and psychotic experiences are often linked (Cicero et al., 2022; Kotov et al., 2020). HiTOP investigators have been developing subscales to measure dissociation (Cicero et al., 2022). They also have been developing measures for the somatoform spectrum, HiTOP's least established dimension (Sellbom et al., 2022). Research is ongoing.

PTMF

PTMF conceptualizes dissociation as a response to threat. Many people resort to it when faced with violence, bullying, and intimidation (A. Griffiths, 2019; M. Reis et al., 2019). Even if it has a significant downside, PTMF views extreme dissociation as a reaction to oppressive conditions rather than an indicator of psychopathology. It goes from being a symptom of disorder to an understandable, if sometimes problematic, response to persistent and overwhelming threat.

HISTORICAL PERSPECTIVES

8.4 Hysteria and the Wandering Womb

Modern understandings of dissociation and somatic complaints trace their origins to the classic term hysteria (North, 2015). Throughout much of history, hysteria was a broadly defined diagnosis that included symptoms such as emotionality, nervousness, and physical complaints. It was diagnosed almost exclusively in women in ancient Egypt and Greece, as well as during later eras (da Mota Gomes & Engelhardt, 2014b; C. Tasca et al., 2012). Given its highly gendered history, it is not surprising that the wandering womb theory (introduced in Chapter 1) was a widely accepted explanation of hysteria from ancient times until the 1800s. This theory attributed hysteria to a wandering uterus (da Mota Gomes & Engelhardt, 2014b; van der Feltz-Cornelis & van Dyck, 1997). The famous Greek philosopher Plato vividly referred to the womb of the typical hysterical patient as a "sexually and socially frustrated animal" (van der Feltz-Cornelis & van Dyck, 1997, p. 119). Might the historical tendency to blame hysteria on disordered female anatomy be because the people diagnosed with it—particularly women—have often lived in ways that challenge traditional notions of gender and sexuality (Dmytriw, 2015)?

8.5 Sydenham, Briquet, and Charcot on Hysteria

Sydenham, Briquet, and Briquet's Syndrome

The wandering uterus theory finally began losing influence between the seventeenth and nineteenth centuries. The famous British physician Thomas Sydenham (1624–1689) felt that hysteria was best understood as a disease of the nervous system that occurred in men as well as women (Boss, 1979; da Mota Gomes & Engelhardt, 2014a; Lamberty, 2007). Two centuries later, the French physician Paul Briquet (1796–1881) shared Sydenham's view that men could have hysteria, even though his research found it much more prevalent in women (Mai & Merskey, 1980). Briquet's greatest contribution to modern understandings of hysteria may have been to destroy once and for all "its historical association with physical pathology of the female genitalia" (Mai, 1983, p. 420). In his 1859 treatise on the subject, Briquet described hysteria in detail and attributed it not to sexual pathology, but to brain dysfunction (Mai, 1983; Mai & Merskey, 1980, 1981). He wasn't able to specify precisely where in the brain the dysfunction was, except to say that "affective" rather than "intellectual" brain regions were impacted (Mai, 1983). Briquet's work greatly influenced later conceptions of *somatoform disorders*, the pre-DSM-5 term for somatic complaints that saw them as mainly psychological without a physical basis. In the early 1970s, what DSM and ICD later began to call somatization disorder was even named after Briquet (Guze et al., 1972). To this day, somatization disorder is still sometimes referred to as Briquet's syndrome (as previously shown in Table 8.1).

Charcot, La Belle Indifférence, and Hypnosis

Jean-Martin Charcot (1825–1893), a neurologist at the Salpêtrière Hospital in Paris during the latter nineteenth century, was a seminal figure in the history of dissociative and somatic symptom problems. As noted in Chapter 7, Charcot worked with patients diagnosed with hysteria. These patients often displayed medically unexplainable symptoms. Nonetheless, Charcot believed that hysteria had biological origins, even though precisely what the ailment was remained a mystery. He did, however, also hypothesize that in addition to a constitutional susceptibility, hysteria usually requires the experience of trauma (Havens, 1966)—clearly incorporating a psychological aspect into his conceptualization. One of the interesting observations Charcot made about his hysterical patients is that they seemed unconcerned about their symptoms (the French term for this is *la belle indifférence*) (J. Stone et al., 2006). Being indifferent to symptoms implies they serve a psychological purpose for hysterical patients.

Charcot used **hypnosis** to treat hysteria (Havens, 1966; Teive et al., 2014). Hypnosis is best understood as combining deep relaxation (often referred to as a *trance* state) with suggestion (requests that hypnotic subjects can follow if they wish to). Because hypnosis was considered scientifically suspect in Charcot's day, he was criticized by his colleagues for using it (Teive et al., 2014). However, his work deeply influenced Sigmund Freud, who later developed the term "conversion disorder" to explain hysterical symptoms (Nydegger, 2013).

Hypnosis: Combines deep relaxation (a *trance* state) with suggestion (requests that hypnotic subjects can follow if they wish to).

8.6 Janet and Dissociation

The modern concept of dissociation can be traced to one of Charcot's protégées, Pierre Janet (1859–1947) (Dorahy & van der Hart, 2006; Heim & Bühler, 2006; Janet, 1886; LeBlanc, 2001; van der Hart & Horst, 1989). Like Charcot, Janet employed hypnosis to study hysteria. With a case study participant named Lucie, Janet used *post-hypnotic suggestion*—wherein a suggestion made during hypnosis is obeyed while no longer hypnotized (Janet, 1886; LeBlanc, 2001; van der Hart & Horst, 1989). Janet gave Lucie the post-hypnotic suggestion that she would be able to write down things he said while simultaneously talking to others and not consciously paying attention to him. She was able to do so, even though she couldn't recall Janet asking her to write anything. Janet took this as evidence of "double consciousness," the idea that people could have separate and distinct conscious experiences that were split off from one another (LeBlanc, 2001; van der Hart & Horst, 1989). In 1887 he began calling this phenomenon dissociation (LeBlanc, 2001). He argued that dissociation could be used to understand hysteria, which he believed was caused by dissociated memories of traumatic events (Heim & Bühler, 2006). Thus, "in working out his solution to the problem of post-hypnotic suggestion, Janet had arrived at the ideas of the traumatic memory and, in a rudimentary way, the cathartic cure" (LeBlanc, 2001, p. 62). Many current ideas (and controversies) about dissociation are traceable to Janet's pioneering work.

BIOLOGICAL PERSPECTIVES

8.7 Brain Chemistry Perspectives

Dissociation

The excitatory neurotransmitter glutamate has been implicated in dissociation, but its exact role remains unclear (Loewenstein, 2005; Packard & Teather, 1999; Roydeva & Reinders, 2021). When it comes to pharmacological interventions, many different kinds of drugs are prescribed for dissociative symptoms—including antidepressants, anxiolytics, and even antipsychotics (Gentile et al., 2013, 2014; Sutar & Sahu, 2019). However, these drugs don't appear to have much direct effect on dissociation itself (Maldonado & Spiegel, 2014). Rather, they are typically used to address accompanying depression, anxiety, psychosis, and PTSD (Gentile et al., 2013, 2014; Loewenstein, 2005). The International Society for the Study of Trauma and Dissociation (2011) indicates that "psychotropic medication is not a primary treatment for dissociative processes, and specific recommendations for pharmacotherapy for most dissociative symptoms await systematic research" (p. 205). It notes that, despite minimal evidence, medication remains a common treatment for DID.

The small body of research on pharmacotherapy for dissociation has mainly focused on SSRIs and **opioid antagonists**. The latter are a class of drugs traditionally used to treat substance addiction; they bond to opioid receptors, preventing other opioid substances (such as heroin) from doing the same (see Chapter 11). There is slight evidence that the SSRI *paroxetine* (trade name *Paxil*) and the opioid antagonist *naloxone* (trade names *Narcan* and *Evzio*) improve depersonalization and dissociative symptoms (Sutar & Sahu, 2019). Another opioid antagonist, *naltrexone* (trade names *Vivitrol* and *Revia*), the anticonvulsant *lamotrigine* (trade name *Lamictal*), and various other SSRIs have also been studied, but there currently isn't much evidence for their effectiveness (Gentile et al., 2013; Sutar & Sahu, 2019).

Why might opioid antagonists reduce dissociative symptoms? The body's kappa and mu opioid systems appear to mediate depersonalization and *stress-induced analgesia* (pain suppression that occurs when exposed to frightening or possibly traumatizing situations) (B. L. Brand et al., 2012).

Opioid antagonists: Drugs used to treat substance addiction and dissociation; they bond to opioid receptors, preventing other opioid substances (such as heroin) from doing the same; examples include *naloxone* (trade names *Narcan* an *Evzio*) and *naltrexone* (trade names *Vivitrol* and *Revia*).

Giving dissociative clients opioid antagonists may interfere with opioid system activity, thereby reducing dissociation. However, as noted in Chapter 11, such drugs are controversial because of their potential for abuse (Rosenblum et al., 2008).

Lauren

What might happen were Lauren—our case example client experiencing dissociative identities— referred to a psychiatrist for medication? There is a good chance she'd be prescribed an SSRI antidepressant like paroxetine. This might reduce some of her mood symptoms, but it probably wouldn't have much effect on her multiple personalities. If the SSRI alone didn't prove helpful, naloxone or naltrexone might also be prescribed. Lauren might find that these two drugs help her to some extent, but she also might view them mainly as supplements to weekly psychotherapy sessions.

Somatic Symptoms

A variety of drugs are given to people with somatic symptoms—including antidepressants, antipsychotics, anticonvulsants, and herbal remedies such as St. John's Wort; however, antidepressants are the most common drugs used (Kleinstäuber et al., 2014; Somashekar et al., 2013). Unfortunately, research on the effectiveness of drug treatments for somatic symptoms is meager (Holster et al., 2017; Kleinstäuber et al., 2014; Kroenke, 2007; Somashekar et al., 2013). A small amount of research has tied somatic symptoms to diminished serotonin and norepinephrine transmission (Bresch et al., 2016; Y. Liu et al., 2019; Rief et al., 2004). This fits with the limited evidence that antidepressants, which increase serotonin and/or norepinephrine, are sometimes effective in reducing somatic symptoms (Fallon, 2004; Holster et al., 2017; Kleinstäuber et al., 2014; Kroenke, 2007). All kinds of antidepressants appear beneficial, with SSRIs (which impact only serotonin) preferred for hypochondriasis and SNRIs (which impact norepinephrine and serotonin) for pain symptoms (Holster et al., 2017; Somashekar et al., 2013; Sumathipala, 2007). Beyond traditional antidepressants, a limited number of studies point to St. John's wort (see Chapter 5) as a potentially effective herbal remedy for somatization (T. Müller et al., 2004; Sumathipala, 2007). Finally, the few studies that have been done on antipsychotics and anticonvulsants have found these drugs reduce somatic and pain symptoms, respectively (Holster et al., 2017; Somashekar et al., 2013; Sumathipala, 2007). Looking at the overall picture, there isn't sufficient research on somatic symptom drug treatments to draw firm conclusions. Consequently, doctors employ a trial-and-error approach to finding drugs that work for specific patients.

8.8 Brain Structure and Function Perspectives

Dissociation

People prone to dissociation show enhanced activity of the *hippocampus* and the *posterior parietal cortex*, which are associated with encoding and recall of negative information (de Ruiter et al., 2007). Dissociation has been connected to reduced parietal lobe activity, as well as decreased volume of the hippocampus (important in memory) and amygdala (important in basic emotions) (Blihar et al., 2020; García-Campayoa et al., 2009; Reinders, 2008; Vermetten et al., 2006). Additionally, it has been linked to dysfunction along the *hypothalamic-pituitary-adrenal (HPA) axis* (Chalavi et al., 2015). As discussed in Chapters 5 and 7, the HPA axis is also important in depression and posttraumatic stress—both problems in which dissociation is common. Given the HPA axis' role in stress responses, it makes sense that cortisol, the primary stress hormone, has also been implicated in dissociation (Boulet et al., 2022; H. S. Lee et al., 2022; E. R. S. Nijenhuis & den Boer, 2009; Simeon, 2001; Simeon et al., 2007). As with PTSD, there is disagreement among researchers about whether cortisol levels are increased or decreased among trauma survivors who dissociate (E. R. S. Nijenhuis & den Boer, 2009).

Decreased hippocampal and amygdalar volumes have been correlated with dissociative identity disorder (Blihar et al., 2020; Chalavi et al., 2015; Vermetten et al., 2006). Many other brain regions also appear related to DID—including the *orbitofrontal cortex* (part of the fear network connecting perception and emotion) and *anterior cingulate cortex* (important in problem-solving during early learning) (Blihar et al., 2020). Those who believe DID is a legitimate disorder point to the growing body of brain structure evidence. However, many of the same brain differences implicated in DID are also found in research on other disorders (such as depression, borderline personality disorder, and PTSD). This makes it difficult to know whether DID is a distinct disorder or a variant of other forms of mental distress. Researchers using an RDoC framework (introduced in Chapter 3) caution that DSM diagnostic categories can confuse as much as clarify. They advocate studying brain structures involved in dissociation without worrying whether findings comport with preexisting diagnoses such as DID and PTSD; in their view, as data accrues we will likely need to discard taken-for-granted categories and devise new ones based on emerging knowledge (Indelli et al., 2018).

Somatic Symptoms

Somatic symptoms aren't limited to people with somatic symptom disorders. Those with other diagnoses—especially depression and anxiety—often display somatic symptoms too (Fu et al., 2019). Studies have found increased limbic system and frontal lobe activity, as well as decreased gray matter density, in the brains of people with somatic diagnoses (Browning et al., 2011; D. A. Nowak & Fink, 2009). Similarly, high-stress somatic symptoms have been linked to reduced gray matter volume in numerous brain regions—including the *ventral medial prefrontal cortex* (which prompts emotional distress when physiological changes in the body are perceived), *anterior insula* (activated in response to various things, including pain), *somatosensory cortex* (important in processing sensory information), *hippocampus* (important in memory), and *amygdala* (important in experiencing emotion) (D. Wei et al., 2020). When it comes to somatic symptom disorder specifically, the *medial prefrontal cortex* and *anterior cingulate cortex* show anomalies; the former "integrates both emotional and cognitive information," while the latter "plays an important role in the evaluation, processing, and integration of sensory, motor, cognitive, and emotional aspects" (Q. Li et al., 2016, p. 3). Although research on brain structures tied to somatic symptoms is growing, currently "the neuropathology underlying somatization symptoms in psychiatric disorders remains unclear" (Fu et al., 2019, p. 1).

While conversion (functional neurological symptom disorder) is tied to activity in the left *dorsolateral prefrontal cortex* (important in decision-making, working memory, and planning), malingering and factitious symptoms are associated with activity in the *right anterior prefrontal cortex* (suspected of helping people perform tasks related to one goal while simultaneously keeping information about a different goal in working memory) (Chahine et al., 2015; Kaufer, 2007; Leong et al., 2015; Ramnani & Owen, 2004). This difference might help distinguish genuine cases of conversion from malingering and factitious disorder (F. P. de Lange et al., 2010; D. A. Nowak & Fink, 2009). Conversion symptoms have also been tied to increased blood flow to the *left inferior frontal gyrus* (important in language comprehension) and left insula (Czarnecki et al., 2011), as well as to gray matter abnormalities (Kozlowska et al., 2017).

Though more research is being called for, transcranial magnetic stimulation (TMS) (in which magnetic energy is sent through the brain; see Chapter 5) shows promise as a treatment for functional neurological symptom and somatic symptom disorders (Oriuwa et al., 2022). It is hypothesized that TMS works by stimulating motor areas of the brain that have been inhibited, perhaps in response to limbic activity (D. A. Nowak & Fink, 2009). The controversial technique of electroconvulsive therapy (ECT) (described in Chapter 5) is also occasionally used to treat somatic symptom disorders (Sarma et al., 2021). Researchers theorize ECT fosters long-term changes to the limbic system and prefrontal cortex (Leong et al., 2015)—a claim in need of further study.

8.9 Genetic Perspectives

Genetics of Dissociation

Adoption and Twin Studies

There aren't many studies on the genetics of dissociation, but genetic perspectives maintain that the tendency to dissociate is innate and not dependent on trauma to bring it out (Dorahy, 2006). A study comparing biological siblings with adopted siblings concluded that there is a considerable genetic influence on dissociation, even if environmental factors are also relevant (Becker-Blease

Photo 8.3 A Norwegian twin study found that even among identical twins, environment plays a major role in somaticizing, despite the importance of genes.

Frank Mckenna/Unsplash.

et al., 2004). Likewise, twin studies suggest genetics plays a role in dissociative experiences—with heritability estimated at 62 percent (Domozych & Dragan, 2016; Jang et al., 1998). Agreement isn't universal, however. Investigators examining twin data in another study concluded that dissociation is almost exclusively tied to environmental events (N. G. Waller & Ross, 1997). When it comes to genetic versus environmental influences on dissociation, researchers disagree.

Genetic Marker Research

Turning to genetic markers for dissociation, some evidence points to the *5-HTT* (serotonin) gene. One interesting study found that the presence of the S/S allele on the *5-HTT* gene predicted higher levels of dissociation among people diagnosed with obsessive-compulsive disorder (OCD); however, environmental neglect also predicted dissociation (Lochner et al., 2007). One twin study suggested a gene–environment interaction. In this study, the SS allele on the *5-HTT* gene predicted greater levels of dissociation. However, environmental factors were critical too, explaining over half (55 percent) the variation in dissociative symptoms (Pieper et al., 2011). It seems like both genetic and environmental factors contribute to dissociative experiences.

Beyond the *5-HTT* gene, a recent genome-wide association study (GWAS) identified two genes worthy of further attention when it comes to dissociation: *ADCY8* and *DPP6* (E. J. Wolf et al., 2014). Unfortunately, the study's results didn't quite reach statistical significance. Whether this is because large sample sizes are needed to obtain significant results in genome-wide association studies or because these two genes don't play a role in dissociation requires additional research.

Genetics of Somatic Symptoms
Family, Adoption, and Twin Studies

A classic U.S. family study concluded that somatization runs in families (Guze et al., 1986). However, family studies can't easily control for environmental influences. To address this, a Swedish adoption study tried to tease apart gene–environment interactions in somatization. It attributed an association between frequent somatization and alcohol abuse to genetic inheritance, noting that the male biological relatives of adopted women with somatic symptoms were more likely to abuse alcohol and commit violent crimes (Bohman et al., 1984). However, in some cases the adoptive environment was also extremely relevant. The adopted fathers of daughters with somatic symptoms were more likely to be unskilled workers, petty criminals, and alcohol abusers (Bohman et al., 1984). Family environment seems to matter. In further studies, children of parents who reported frequent somatic symptoms were more likely to show somatic symptoms themselves (T. K. J. Craig et al., 2002; Gilleland et al., 2009).

The renowned psychiatric geneticist Kenneth Kendler concluded that somatization is mainly genetic, with family and environmental factors having little influence (Kendler et al., 1995). However, a Norwegian twin study contradicted this. It found higher concordance rates among identical twins (29 percent) compared with fraternal twins (10 percent)—implying that even among identical twins, environment plays a major role in somaticizing despite the importance of genes (Torgersen, 1986). More recent twin research supports this idea, pointing to both genetic and environmental influences on somatic complaints (Gillespie et al., 2000; Vassend et al., 2012). Interestingly (but perhaps not surprisingly), parental criticism appears to be an especially important environmental influence on somatic symptoms among adolescents (B. N. Horwitz et al., 2015). Why are some people more impacted by environmental factors than others? Perhaps genetically influenced personality traits foster susceptibility to somatic complaints (Ask et al., 2016). In this vein, obsessional thinking, body dysmorphia, and social anxiety—all traits tied to genes—seem to predict health anxiety (López-Solà et al., 2018). More research is needed.

Genetic Marker Research

Because low serotonin levels are suspected of playing a part in somatization (just as they are with depression), genetic marker research has focused on serotonin-related gene pathways (Espiridion & Kerbel, 2020; Y. Liu et al., 2019). Somatic symptoms have been associated with serotonin receptor (*HTR2A*) and tryptophan hydroxylase (*THP1* and *TPH2*) genes (important in synthesizing serotonin) (K. L. Holliday et al., 2010; Koh et al., 2011). However, most serotonin gene variations don't seem to place people at higher risk for somatoform problems (Koh et al., 2011). Genetic marker research is correlational, so we can't infer that genes cause somatic symptoms.

8.10 Evolutionary Perspectives

Evolutionary Explanations of Dissociation
Dissociation as Adaptive

Although we tend to think of dissociation negatively, evolutionary perspectives counter that dissociation "may be an evolutionarily adaptive mechanism designed to prevent overwhelming flooding of consciousness at the time of trauma" (Leigh, 2015, p. 260). For example, becoming too emotional during a stressful situation such as a house fire isn't helpful. It is better to temporarily disconnect from strong emotions and to calmly determine the best way to escape the flames. A little bit of dissociation is adaptive! It only becomes pathological from an evolutionary standpoint when generalized to too many non-traumatic situations (J. G. Allen & Smith, 1993; Leigh, 2015).

Dissociative Identity Disorder

An intriguing evolutionary explanation of DID holds that people displaying multiple personalities avoid further trauma by convincing others they are ill (Beahrs, 1994). To successfully pull this off, they themselves must believe their own symptoms. In other words, successful DID patients not only convince others that their symptoms are real; they deceive themselves too (Beahrs, 1994). This evolutionary interpretation can be used to counter concerns about DID being an iatrogenic condition. However, it lacks research support.

Evolutionary Explanations of Somatic Symptoms
Unexplained Somatic Symptoms

Evolutionary theorists suspect unexplained somatic symptoms such as pain are adaptive. Shared pain might bring people together and foster social cooperation. However, a study that found group cohesion and survival are enhanced when members go through something painful together has not been replicated (Bastian et al., 2014; Prochazka et al., 2022). However, other research finds that displaying pain to others elicits empathy and assistance from them; in this way, pain serves as an evolutionarily based form of communication designed to help people obtain support from others (Hadjistavropoulos et al., 2011). Perhaps, then, people with inexplicable medical symptoms are, like chronic dissociators, overgeneralizing the use of an otherwise evolutionarily adaptive behavior. This hypothesis is speculative but understandably inferred from research on the social benefits of conveying pain to others. Importantly, how people express pain is influenced by cultural, as well as individual, differences. Failing to keep this in mind can lead to racial and ethnic stereotypes that negatively affect how we respond to people's chronic pain (Tait & Chibnall, 2014).

Psychophysiological Disorders

At the core of psychosomatic (psychophysiological) disorders is the idea that when individuals feel run down and tired, they are more likely to get sick. However, all people don't come down with the same illness. What they get sick with depends on inherited biological vulnerabilities. Whether you develop acne, backaches, stomach issues, ulcers, high blood pressure or something else is contingent on where you are constitutionally weakest. In other words, from the standpoint of evolution, people break down where they are most susceptible. This is consistent with the **diathesis-stress model of psychosomatic illness**, which maintains that psychosomatic illnesses emerge from a combination of *diathesis*—a "predisposing organic or psychological condition" (Flor et al., 1992, p. 452)—and *stress*. The stress slowly takes a toll on the predisposing organic susceptibility, eventually resulting

Diathesis-stress model of psychosomatic illness: Psychosomatic illness emerges from a combination of *diathesis* (a predisposing biological vulnerability) and *stress*.

in illness. Diathesis-stress models have been used to understand a variety of psychophysiological issues, including hypertension (high blood pressure) and chronic pain (Coulon, 2015; Flor et al., 1990, 1992; Flor & Turk, 1989; Turk, 2002; Vaessen et al., 2021).

8.11 Immune System Perspectives

Psychoneuroimmunology, Stress, and Vulnerability to Illness

Psychoneuroimmunology (PNI): Discipline that studies how psychological stress influences the central nervous system, endocrine system, and immune system.

Psychoneuroimmunology (PNI) is the field that studies how psychological stress influences the central nervous system, endocrine system, and immune system (Danese & Lewis, 2017; R. Glaser, 2005; Slavich, 2020). PNI research consistently links psychological stress to weakened immune responses and poorer health (Seiler, Fagundes, et al., 2020; Slavich, 2020). For instance, people under stress are more likely to catch colds and other illnesses (including COVID-19) (Ayling et al., 2022; P. Cohen, Rogol, et al., 2008). They heal more slowly, respond less quickly and robustly to vaccines, and have more difficulty fighting off the progression of severe illnesses such as cancer (R. Glaser, 2005; Madison et al., 2021). Put simply, chronic stress is bad for your health. Of course, some of us are more prone to stress than others. The "Controversial Question" box explores whether your basic temperament—that is, your core personality traits—increase your risk of high blood pressure and coronary heart disease.

Controversial Question: Can Your Personality Give You a Heart Attack?

You've probably heard of the *Type A personality*—that driven, impatient, and competitive style with which some people aggressively engage the world. Type A individuals are highly achievement-oriented, want recognition for their accomplishments, and have a heightened sense of time urgency (i.e., they like to get things done quickly) (M. Friedman & Rosenman, 1959). The Type A behavior pattern is usually contrasted with the *Type B personality* (easygoing folks who lack drive, ambition, and urgency) and the *Type C personality* (people who seem Type B, but are anxious and insecure) (M. Friedman & Rosenman, 1959). It's common to hear that being Type A makes you more likely to have a heart attack. Where did that idea come from? And is it true? Let's consider these questions.

The Type A style first gained attention in the late 1950s and early 1960s, when cardiologists Meyer Friedman and Ray H. Rosenman conducted research suggesting a positive correlation between Type A behavior and coronary heart disease (M. Friedman, 1977; M. Friedman & Rosenman, 1959; Rosenman & Friedman, 1961). Being too intense, it appeared, might literally place you at higher risk of having a heart attack! Friedman and Rosenman's work marked an early effort to link psychological stress with physical health. It garnered so much attention that the lay public often takes it for granted that being Type A is bad for your health.

But is it? While research between the 1950s and 1970s generally found a relationship between coronary disease and Type A behavior, later studies often did not (Khayyam-Nekouei et al., 2013; P. Lin et al., 2018; Šmigelskas et al., 2015). Why the inconsistent results? Some investigators contend personality style is difficult to measure, making Type A research challenging (Šmigelskas et al., 2015). Consequently, what we call the Type A personality contains various traits—only some of which predict heart disease. Being Type A alone doesn't place one at risk for heart disease. What poses the risk seems to be *hostility*, something some (but not all!) Type A individuals display. Angry, hostile, time-urgent, and stressed people are the ones more likely to have coronary issues (R. J. Burke, 1985; Khayyam-Nekouei et al., 2013; Šmigelskas et al., 2015). Being driven, ambitious, and competitive may be fine, so long as these characteristics aren't accompanied by hostility. Consistent with this, recent studies emphasize the *Type D personality*, characterized by emotional negativity and social inhibition. Some but not all research has linked Type D with heart and other health problems (Enatescu et al., 2021; Grande et al., 2012; S. Howard & Hughes, 2013; Kupper & Denollet, 2018; Oliva et al., 2016; Staniute et al., 2015). Type D individuals' high stress levels, negativity, and hostility potentially put them at greater health risk.

Rather than relying on Type A–D personality types, some investigators prefer to research the relationship between physical health and the Big Five personality traits (introduced in Chapter 3). For example, people who score high on neuroticism (characterized by mood swings and negative emotions) appear to be at increased coronary heart disease risk (Armon, 2014; Čukić & Bates, 2015; Medda et al., 2020). Neuroticism doesn't only predict coronary heart risk. Individuals high in neuroticism (and, in some cases, low in conscientiousness) show increased rates of psychosocial health problems in general (Hengartner et al., 2016). Interestingly, while neuroticism predicts coronary heart disease, extraversion (another Big Five trait) often predicts stroke risk (Jokela et al., 2014). Thus, researchers increasingly have taken interest in how Big Five personality traits can predict coronary heart problems specifically and other health problems more broadly.

Of course, all this talk of personality style as a predictor of heart disease potentially overlooks that people's behavior patterns are highly responsive to their environmental circumstances. *Environmental stressors* likely interact with personality in fostering heart disease and other health problems. Low socioeconomic status, lack of social support, and stress tied to work and family all predict coronary heart disease (Albus, 2010; Hamad et al., 2020; Schultz et al., 2018). Other common environmental risk factors for cardiac disease include "pollutants in the air, noise exposure, artificial light at night, and climate change" (Münzel et al., 2022, p. 2880). Therefore, when we focus so heavily on biological aspects of personality, do we overlook the impact of social conditions on physical health? Although psychological, biological, and social factors all play a role in who does or doesn't experience coronary issues, sorting out the exact relationships can be quite challenging!

Critical Thinking Questions

1. To what extent do you think personality style impacts physical health? Explain.
2. When it comes to coronary heart disease and other health issues, what is the relative contribution of personality style and environmental stressors?
3. What future research do you think needs to be done to clarify the influence of personality style on physical health? What methodological challenges do researchers who are interested in this topic face?

The Negative Effect of Stress on Lymphocytes

How does psychological stress compromise the immune system? Various types of **lymphocytes** (white blood cells important in fighting off illness) appear to be affected by stress. For instance, some PNI studies find that people experiencing stressful life events and loneliness lack *natural killer (NK) cells* (a lymphocyte important in fighting off viral infections and tumors) (R. Glaser, 2005; Maydych et al., 2017). This fits with previously mentioned studies suggesting stress negatively affects our ability to combat viruses and cancer. Other lymphocytes known as B cells and T cells also are impacted by stress. *B cells* produce *antibodies* that attack invading viruses and bacteria to stop them from entering cells, while *T cells* work to kill viruses and bacteria once they have entered cells (Cano & Lopera, 2013). Some T cells produce cytokines, the small proteins important in healing that can also cause inflammation. Research over the past few decades has repeatedly found that lymphocyte number and functioning can be negatively affected by stress (Coe & Laudenslager, 2007; Dhabhar, 2014; Esterling et al., 1994; R. Glaser, 2005; Kemeny & Schedlowski, 2007; Kiecolt-Glaser & Glaser, 1992; McGregor et al., 2016; Moynihan & Santiago, 2007; O'Leary, 1990; Segerstrom & Miller, 2004; E. V. Yang & Glaser, 2002; Zakowski et al., 1992).

Lymphocytes: White blood cells important in fighting off illness; *natural killer (NK) cells, B cells,* and *T cells* are lymphocytes.

Although in many instances stress negatively impacts the immune system, its exact influence depends on the circumstances. Acute but short-lasting stress boosts immune system functioning (an adaptive feature that, evolutionarily speaking, enhances survival), but chronic stress depletes it (Segerstrom & Miller, 2004). As noted when discussing dissociation, the hypothalamic-pituitary-adrenal (HPA) axis plays a role in immune system responsiveness to stress, mainly through releasing steroid stress hormones like cortisol and non-steroid stress hormones like *adrenaline* and *dopamine* (yes, the brain neurotransmitter dopamine also serves as a hormone in the endocrine system). Thus, there is a clear link between brain structures such as the HPA axis and immune system responsiveness to stress. Although many questions about how the immune system responds to stress remain, PNI investigations of psychosomatic illnesses constitute one of the more researched areas related to somatic symptoms.

8.12 Evaluating Biological Perspectives

Compared with some other presenting problems (e.g., psychosis, mood issues, posttraumatic stress), there is less biologically oriented research on dissociative and somatic symptoms—apart from research on the immune system and psychosomatic illnesses. Many different medications are prescribed on a trial-and-error basis, mainly because there is not much consensus on the biochemistry of dissociative and somatic symptoms. Serotonin is suspected of being involved, but the evidence remains sketchy. Numerous brain areas are implicated in dissociative and somatic symptoms but, again, the research is meager compared with that on other presenting problems, and results remain preliminary. Genetic and evolutionary explanations are intriguing, but also still need additional research.

Because biological research is often correlational, causal relationships can't be inferred. For example, we don't know if low serotonin leads to dissociation and somatic symptoms, if somatic and dissociative symptoms negatively impact serotonin production, or if there is some other undiscovered relationship between these symptoms and serotonin. Overall, the strongest biological research has been in psychoneuroimmunology—with studies repeatedly pointing to a powerful relationship between psychological stress and immune system functioning. Future investigations should expand on existing PNI research findings, as well as flesh out burgeoning biological research on dissociative and somatic symptoms.

PSYCHOLOGICAL PERSPECTIVES

8.13 Psychodynamic Perspectives

Psychodynamic perspectives conceptualize dissociative and somatic symptoms as expressions of unconscious conflicts and/or attachment difficulties, often of a traumatic or upsetting nature (M. J. Kaplan, 2014; Kluft, 2000; Luyten et al., 2019; Luyten & Fonagy, 2020; Sinason & Silver, 2008; W. C. Tomlinson, 2006). In other words, they adhere to the previously mentioned posttraumatic model (Lynn et al., 2020). The psychodynamic emphasis on unconscious memories of trauma is traceable to Breuer and Freud's (1893–1895/2013) early psychodynamic work on hysteria.

Primary vs. Secondary Gain

Primary gain: The reason for a symptom; the central (or *primary*) conflict the symptom is intended to address.

Secondary gain: Any other advantages a symptom provides beyond the original unconscious conflict that it expresses.

Before proceeding, let's clarify the psychodynamic distinction between primary and secondary gain. **Primary gain** is the reason for a symptom; it is the central (or primary) conflict the symptom addresses (Fishbain, 1994; van Egmond, 2003). The primary gain from a dissociative or somatic symptom is to manage an unconscious conflict and prevent it from entering awareness. **Secondary gain** involves any other advantages the symptom provides (Fishbain, 1994; van Egmond, 2003). It is not about the original unconscious conflict that the symptom expresses. Instead, it is the other good stuff the patient gets from having the symptom. This makes it secondary to the original conflict.

Tiiu

Tiiu's primary gain from her hand numbness is that she avoids and remains oblivious to her conflicted feelings about dropping bombs on people. Getting shipped home and being near her family are secondary gains. These are additional benefits of being symptomatic, but they aren't the reason she developed hand numbness in the first place.

One way to distinguish malingerers from people with legitimate (if unexplained) somatic symptoms is that there is no primary gain for the malingerer. Why? Because for malingerers, there is no underlying psychological conflict that their deliberately feigned symptoms express. Instead, the entire goal is secondary gain. For malingerers, such gain is primary. That's why they fake their symptoms. Recall that time from childhood when you faked having the flu so you could stay home from school. You didn't have a somatic symptom problem. You were just malingering (how sneaky!).

Tiiu

Tiiu isn't a malingerer. She really has an involuntary somatic symptom that represents her emotional upset about bombing people. By contrast, a malingerer pretends to have a somatic symptom. He wants to go home, so he feigns hand numbness to trick his superiors into sending him. What constitutes a secondary gain for Tiiu is the primary goal of the malingerer.

Dissociation as Response to Trauma

Dissociation and Splitting

Psychodynamic approaches maintain that people often cope with trauma by repressing it or disconnecting from memories of it. In this respect, dissociation involves psychologically splitting off painful memories and emotions by compartmentalizing them to keep them out of conscious awareness, thereby muting their impact. That is, "dissociation is a defensive response to severe physical, sexual, or emotional abuse and/or other highly aversive events that often date to childhood" (Lynn et al., 2020, p. 365). Psychodynamic explanations of dissociative amnesia, dissociative fugue, conversion disorder, and dissociative identity disorder are therefore rooted in a posttraumatic model. There is evidence for such a model, with one study finding that people who dissociate often are more likely to have experienced past traumas (Dalenberg et al., 2012). Critics, however, point to other research suggesting that the link between trauma and dissociation may not be as strong as commonly believed (Lynn et al., 2020).

Reintegrating Dissociated Experiences into Awareness

Traditional psychodynamic therapies for dissociation aim to make unconscious conflicts conscious so that dissociated feelings and memories can be reintegrated into awareness. However, more recent psychodynamic approaches sometimes conceptualize dissociated experiences not as repressed, but as *unformulated* (D. B. Stern, 2009, 2017, 2020). In this way of thinking, dissociation isn't about placing clearly formed memories out of awareness. Rather, it is about failing to coherently articulate (usually in words) perceptions about a traumatic event. Until the trauma is properly articulated, it is difficult to integrate it into one's life. Consequently, dissociative perceptions of what happened unconsciously influence behavior. In therapy, patients must verbally articulate their experiences to become aware of and make sense of them.

Regardless of the type of dissociative disorder being treated, psychodynamic approaches use the therapeutic relationship to help patients gain insight into their unconscious conflicts and integrate dissociated parts of the personality (Spermon et al., 2010). As noted, critics skeptical of psychodynamic theory question whether traumatic memories can be dissociated from awareness (Lynn et al., 2020). These critics not only doubt recovered memories of past trauma, but—as mentioned—they also contend that dissociation itself is a dubious concept. However, supporters of psychodynamic perspectives counter that traumas really occur, people often respond by dissociating, and therapy must help people gain insight into feelings about these past traumas.

Self-Hypnosis and Dissociative Identity Disorder

In keeping with the posttraumatic model, psychodynamic approaches generally conceive of DID as occurring in people who (a) have been severely abused as children, and (b) are very susceptible to hypnosis. Patients diagnosed with DID are thought to be especially good at **self-hypnosis**, the ability to enter a hypnotic trance on their own without guidance from others (Bliss, 1984; Kihlstrom et al., 1994; Loewenstein & Ross, 1992). Self-hypnosis can be thought of as dissociative because it involves mentally going elsewhere while facing highly stressful and traumatic circumstances. Psychodynamically speaking, people who develop DID are highly creative and use self-hypnosis to invent alternate "personalities" that offer a psychological escape from the terrible abuse they have endured (Bliss, 1984; Kihlstrom et al., 1994; Loewenstein & Ross, 1992).

Self-hypnosis: Ability to enter a hypnotic trance one one's own without guidance from others.

Somatic Symptoms due to Unconscious Conflicts and Problematic Attachments

Sometimes people dissociate by isolating their negative feelings somatically. According to psychodynamic theorists, when this occurs the unconscious conflict is set aside and expressed indirectly via somatic symptoms.

Tiiu

Tiiu's hand numbness prevents her from running bombing missions. If medical exams reveal nothing wrong with her nervous system, a psychodynamic therapist might conclude that the numbness represents an unconscious conflict about dropping bombs on innocent civilians.

Psychodynamic therapy operates from the assumption that eliminating somatic symptoms requires bringing their underlying meaning into conscious awareness and working through the resulting emotions. Some psychodynamic approaches see somatic symptoms as intricately tied to problematic attachment relationships. Therapy provides clients insight into attachment patterns and allows them to develop more secure and trusting relationships, resulting in the elimination of the symptoms (Luyten et al., 2019). Does psychodynamic therapy for somatic symptoms work? A meta-analysis of seventeen randomized controlled trials on short-term psychodynamic therapy found it effective at reducing functional somatic symptoms (A. Abbass et al., 2020). See the "In Depth" feature for an example of psychodynamic therapy for conversion. A psychodynamic approach could also be used in the case of Paul, who meets criteria for somatic symptom disorder.

In Depth: Psychodynamic Therapy for a Case of Conversion (Functional Neurological Symptom Disorder)

Kaplan (2014) presents the case of "Mr. A," a 28-year-old man who was having tonic clonic seizures in which he would lose consciousness and have rapid muscle convulsions. A thorough medical examination at an epilepsy-monitoring unit revealed no biological basis for the seizures, so Mr. A was referred for psychodynamic psychotherapy. Although Mr. A told the therapist that he often felt depressed as a child, he denied ever having been physically or sexually abused. After two sessions, Mr. A's mother contacted the therapist and told him that Mr. A had been a normal and happy child until age 7, when he developed *encopresis* (involuntary defecation; see Chapter 15). At age 8, Mr. A made his first suicide attempt; after the third attempt, he was admitted to a psychiatric unit, where he admitted to having been bullied by other kids because of his involuntary defecation problems. The therapist asked Mr. A about this in the next session, which led to a discussion in which Mr. A tearfully recalled having been repeatedly sexually abused as a child by his older cousin in the loft of the family barn. The abuse only stopped after Mr. A began attempting suicide, probably because at that point the cousin worried about the abuse being discovered. Mr. A never told anyone about the abuse because he didn't think his family would believe him or respond sympathetically.

Soon after telling the therapist about the abuse, Mr. A had a seizure in church. In the next session, the therapist wondered aloud whether "if having had to hold all this pain and anger inside all these years, and having no way to ever express the bad feelings meant it could only come out this way, through the seizures" (M. J. Kaplan, 2014, p. 605). This interpretation resonated with Mr. A, who shortly thereafter told his parents about the abuse. To Mr. A's surprise and relief, they responded supportively. As of a year later, no additional seizures had occurred. Kaplan (2014, p. 609) concludes:

> When previously well-functioning individuals develop conversion symptoms, it is safe to assume that an old conflict related to childhood traumatic experience has been revived by more recent trauma that cannot be addressed with conscious thought .... With help from a psychotherapist to develop a narrative about one's life experiences and the current experience of an old conflict, the conversion symptom is no longer necessary and forward development is again possible, albeit with the acceptance and mourning necessary for progress in any form of psychoanalytic psychotherapy.

Obviously, this quote reflects commitment to psychodynamic principles. The assumption is that conversion symptoms are a way of expressing an underlying unconscious conflict. Once Mr. A gains insight into the conflict and works through his feelings about it, his conversion symptoms disappear. Those who question psychodynamic theory are likely to be skeptical of the therapeutic outcome described above, but supporters of psychodynamic approaches will inevitably appreciate the emphasis on unconscious meanings behind symptoms.

Critical Thinking Questions

1. Do you agree with the psychodynamic assumption that Mr. A's seizures stopped because he gained conscious insight into his past abuse? Explain.
2. How confident should doctors be before assuming that the symptoms of someone like Mr. A are better explained psychologically than medically? What sort of evidence is required?

Paul

If Paul underwent psychodynamic therapy for his somatic symptoms, the focus would be on his childhood. His parents rarely talked about their feelings, but Paul's father often lost his temper and became violent. Throughout childhood, Paul was unable to express fear of his father's temper because that only further angered his father. It was while young that Paul began to make somatic complaints, with his mother often taking him to the doctor. Psychodynamic therapy would help Paul recognize his pattern of somaticizing anxiety into physical symptoms, tracing it to his childhood trauma. Paul and his therapist would relate this to how Paul currently copes with anxiety. While initially Paul might struggle to identify or express how he feels, over time he would become better at accessing previously unacknowledged feelings. A psychodynamic perspective assumes that if Paul accesses unconscious conflicts, his somatic complaints will decrease.

8.14 Cognitive-Behavioral Perspectives

Cognitive and Behavioral Perspectives on Dissociation
Dissociation as Conditioned Response

According to behavioral perspectives, dissociation is learned through classical and operant conditioning (Casey, 2001; C. V. Ford & Folks, 1985; E. Nijenhuis et al., 2010; E. R. S. Nijenhuis & den Boer, 2009; E. R. S. Nijenhuis & van der Hart, 2011). According to a classical conditioning perspective, dissociation involves internal and external stimuli that become conditioned to evoke not just physical, but also mental, avoidance responses (E. R. S. Nijenhuis & den Boer, 2009). From an operant conditioning perspective, forgetting painful and traumatic memories provides emotional relief—hence doing so is encouraged and maintained via negative reinforcement.

A strictly behavioral conception of dissociative identity disorder sees different "personalities" as conditioned responses. Therapeutically, it employs reinforcement contingencies to extinguish "behavioral variability" and reinforce "behavioral stability"—with the goal to literally "shape one personality" (Kohlenberg, 1973; Phelps, 2000, p. 245). The research literature on behavioral approaches to dissociation is small and much of it goes back many years (R. Barr & Abernethy, 1977; C. V. Ford & Folks, 1985). Today cognitive perspectives typically supplement behavioral views.

Dissociation and Cognitive Encoding

From a cognitive perspective, dissociation reflects problems with encoding and retrieval of upsetting information. People who rely on dissociation as a strategy fail to encode, consolidate, and store integrated recollections of stressful events (Dorahy, 2006; Dorahy et al., 2014). To illustrate this, consider the case of Mr. X, an emergency services worker haunted by memories of a horrible auto accident (Dorahy, 2006). His visual memory of the event was vivid. He recalled the exact positions of the dead bodies and destroyed cars. However, he was unable to remember any of the onlookers or the smell of burning blood; this information had not been encoded alongside aspects of the event that he recalled (Dorahy, 2006). Cognitively speaking then, dissociation occurs when multiple streams of sensory information fail to be combined into an integrated memory. Instead, they are recalled separately under different circumstances. People experiencing dissociative amnesia, for instance, are unable to retrieve certain memories, while those having flashbacks (see Chapter 7) struggle with involuntary memory retrieval—they can't stop painful memories from intruding into awareness at inopportune moments (Dorahy, 2006).

Photo 8.4 A hyperassociating patient discussing a difficult memory could quickly shift into a joyful recollection, like a memory of a beloved pet, without seeming aware of these disjointed associational threads. *Mario Beqollari/Unsplash.*

Dissociation and Hyperassociativity

Cognitively, dissociation might also reflect problems with **hyperassociativity**—the tendency for upsetting memories to readily activate other tangentially related (and often emotionally out-of-sync) memories (Lynn et al., 2019, 2020). For example, a hyperassociating patient discussing

Hyperassociativity: Cognitive tendency in dissociation in which upsetting memories readily activate other tangentially related (and often emotionally out-of-sync) memories.

"how her father harshly disciplined and berated her when she did not complete homework" might quickly shift to recalling "a joyful interaction with a beloved pet with accompanying changes in her demeanor appropriate to these seemingly disparate associational threads" (Lynn et al., 2019, p. 5). Perhaps due to these rapid cognitive shifts, people who hyperassociate report not experiencing or attending to emotions; they often feel detached from self and surroundings, rapidly shifting from one set of memories and emotions to another—all key components of dissociation.

Dissociation and State-Dependent Learning

A related cognitive-behavioral explanation of dissociation suggests it results from **state-dependent learning**—the idea that people's ability to recall something is affected by their psychological or emotional state. Studies with both rats and humans have found that recall can be affected by the state in which learning occurs (Arkhipov, 1999; G. Bower, 1994; G. H. Bower, 1981; Gill et al., 1986; Kanayama et al., 2008; Lowe, 1983; Oberling et al., 1993). In humans, for example, memories encoded while angry may be easier to remember when angry, while those encoded while frightened may be easier to remember when frightened. This potentially explains amnesia and related dissociative experiences (Radulovic et al., 2018). Perhaps multiple personalities—the most dramatic example of dissociation—reflect an extreme form of state-dependent learning in which, when emotional states shift, the "personality" and its specific memories shift too (G. Bower, 1994; E. K. Silberman et al., 1985).

Cognitive-Behavioral Therapy for Dissociation

Various cognitive-behavioral therapy (CBT) techniques have been adapted to treat dissociation—including cognitive restructuring, self-monitoring, exposure therapy, and EMDR (Kennerley, 1996; Pruthi, 2018; van Minnen & Tibben, 2021; Varese et al., 2021). CBT prevents dissociation by teaching clients to deliberately avoid or distract themselves from trigger events that remind them of the trauma; in addition, cognitive restructuring helps clients alter irrational beliefs that upset them and lead to dissociation (Kennerley, 1996). Consider the case of Linda, a rape survivor who dissociated in the presence of unfamiliar men (Kennerley, 1996). Cognitive restructuring enabled Linda to revise one of her automatic thoughts from "all men are rapists" to "some men are safe and decent." This allowed her to overcome the tendency to dissociate when encountering men whom she hadn't met before.

Cognitive and Behavioral Perspectives on Somatic Symptoms/Bodily Distress
Behavioral Conditioning and Cognitive Misinterpretation

From a CBT perspective, somatic symptoms involve both behavioral conditioning and cognitive misinterpretations of bodily symptoms. Behaviorally, somatic symptoms are reinforced. For instance, people with illness anxiety concerns receive negative reinforcement (removal of something unpleasant) for seeking assurance that they are okay. Their worry temporarily decreases when others tell them that they aren't sick, and carrying out safety behaviors also momentarily reduces worrying (Bouman, 2014). Cognitively, people prone to somatic symptoms misinterpret bodily changes, misreading minor aches and pains in catastrophic ways that lead to symptoms or excessive worry about becoming ill (Bouman, 2014).

CBT for Somatic Symptoms

Behaviorally, CBT practitioners often use techniques such as relaxation training (in which clients are taught how to calm themselves) and exposure plus response prevention (first introduced in Chapter 2). For instance, teaching people relaxation techniques is sometimes effective in helping them reduce high blood pressure (Chicayban & Malagris, 2014; Dusek et al., 2008; Yen et al., 1996). Similarly, there is research support for using exposure-based CBT with somatic symptom and illness anxiety disorders (E. Hedman, Lekander, et al., 2016).

Cognitively, CBT for somatic issues employs cognitive therapy to prevent catastrophic misinterpretations of minor physical changes that lead to or exacerbate physical symptoms (or anxiety associated with these symptoms). As one example, stress inoculation training (SIT)—previously discussed in Chapter 7—assists with pain management by helping people eliminate negative thoughts that make pain harder to handle (P. Gupta, 2020; Meichenbaum, 2007; Milling &

Breen, 2003; M. J. Ross & Berger, 1996). As a second example, **mindfulness-based stress reduction (MBSR)**—a version of mindfulness-based cognitive therapy (introduced in Chapter 5)—facilitates maintaining awareness of one's thoughts without trying to influence or stop them. MBSR reduces stress associated with psychosomatic and unexplained somatic symptoms (Aktaş et al., 2019; Fjorback et al., 2013; Grossman et al., 2004). SIT and MBSR are excellent examples of how CBT techniques aim to change people's cognitive responses to somatic symptoms.

Research supports using CBT—both in person and via Internet-delivered treatment—for somatic symptoms and illness anxiety (L. A. Allen & Woolfolk, 2010; Bleichhardt et al., 2004; Buwalda et al., 2007; Greeven et al., 2009; Gropalis et al., 2013; E. Hedman, Axelsson, et al., 2016; Hennemann et al., 2022; Kleinstäuber et al., 2019; J. Liu et al., 2019; D. K. Marcus et al., 2007; Markert et al., 2019; Neng & Weck, 2015; Newby et al., 2018; Newby & McElroy, 2020, 2020; Olatunji et al., 2014; A. Schröder et al., 2013; Shirotsuki et al., 2017; Verdurmen et al., 2017; Weck et al., 2015; Woolfolk & Allen, 2012). There is not much evidence for using CBT to treat functional (conversion) symptoms (L. A. Allen & Woolfolk, 2010; Markert et al., 2019; Woolfolk & Allen, 2012). However, overall CBT approaches are considered reasonably effective for somatic complaints.

Paul

If Paul pursued CBT for his unexplained somatic complaints, cognitive interventions would help him reinterpret bodily feedback more realistically. Instead of thinking about his symptoms in overly negative ways ("My thyroid symptoms are unbearable and mean I am severely ill!"), he would be taught more reasonable interpretations ("My symptoms are uncomfortable, but I can manage them; the doctor and I will figure out what's wrong and take care of it"). To supplement cognitive interventions, exposure plus response prevention might be used. Paul would be exposed to educational information about thyroid issues, which ordinarily would upset him and lead him to repetitively check his symptoms. However, he would be prevented from checking symptoms and, as a result, realize that doing so isn't necessary or helpful. Finally, Paul would be taught relaxation techniques so he could relax in situations where he ordinarily becomes anxious.

Biofeedback for Psychosomatic Illnesses

Biofeedback is a behavioral intervention often used with people suffering from psychosomatic illnesses. In this technique, patients are hooked up to a machine that measures one or more biological functions (e.g., heart rate, breathing rate, muscle tension, or temperature). Patients are reinforced for desired changes to these biological functions—for instance, lowering the heart rate line on the biofeedback monitor. Thus, biofeedback rewards patients (through positive reinforcement) for altering biological functions they typically presume to have little control over. It can be quite effective at reducing biological symptoms caused or made worse by ongoing psychological stress. Biofeedback is used with a variety of psychosomatic complaints, such as hypertension (high blood pressure), migraine headaches, tension headaches, asthma, ulcers, and irritable bowel syndrome (Khazan, 2013). Evidence suggests it is especially helpful with headaches and hypertension (Nanke & Rief, 2004; J. B. Newman, 2013).

Isabel

Biofeedback training could help Isabel manage her hypertension (high blood pressure). Isabel would be taught a deep breathing relaxation technique. She would then be attached to a monitoring device that measures her blood pressure. A tone would sound more often as Isabel's blood pressure rose and less often as it dropped. Isabel would be instructed to use deep breathing to decrease the frequency of the tone. In operant conditioning terms, this reinforces her for lowering her blood pressure. Isabel would hopefully learn how to practice deep breathing and lower her own blood pressure.

Mindfulness-based stress reduction (MBSR): Variation of mindfulness-based cognitive therapy that facilitates awareness of one's thoughts without trying to influence or stop them.

Biofeedback: Technique that provides patients feedback on one or more biological functions (e.g., heart rate, breathing rate, muscle tension, or temperature) and reinforces them for desired changes to these functions.

8.15 Humanistic Perspectives

Dissociation as Meaningful and Adaptive Strategy

Although those coming from humanistic perspectives have not devoted much attention to dissociation, when they have their focus has often been on its positive aspects (Krycka, 2010; Richards, 1990). This is consistent with the humanistic emphasis on adjustment, meaning-making, and personal growth. One qualitative humanistic study found that when asked to reflect on their bodily experience, people who often dissociate found the experience quite meaningful:

Meaning is freshly made from dissociative experiences when the bodily felt sense process is invited. Even when emotions of fear, confusion, or excitement accompany it, new meaning begins to form, ushering in a multiplicity of new engagements and reflections. This very human activity frees up dissociation to be one in which the capacity to further the lives of those experiencing it is possible. (Krycka, 2010, p. 153)

Despite highlighting the adaptive aspects of dissociation, humanistic therapists have otherwise generally adhered to the same posttraumatic model of severe dissociation espoused by their psychodynamic peers (Humphreys et al., 2005; M. S. Warner, 1998, 2013). Psychotherapist Margaret Warner (1998, 2013) developed a person-centered therapy approach to dissociation (particularly DID), one in which clients are provided person-centered therapy's core conditions for change—empathy, genuineness, and unconditional positive regard (see Chapter 2). From a person-centered standpoint, when such conditions are provided, clients naturally reconnect with their own dissociated experiences and start to share them with their therapists. Through this process, clients become more aware of their own dissociated "parts" and the trauma responsible for them. As awareness grows, the need to dissociate decreases. Person-centered therapy's nondirectedness may be advantageous in working with DID clients because it avoids the pitfall of pressuring clients into accepting that they have multiple personalities (M. S. Warner, 1998, 2013). Consequently, a person-centered approach may be less likely to iatrogenically induce DID. There is little experimental research support for the humanistic approach to DID, but its emphases on empathy and not trying to convince clients that they have DID seem intuitive and worthy of further study.

Somatic Symptoms and the Need to Integrate Bodily Awareness

Practitioners who employ **body-oriented psychotherapies** challenge the traditional mind–body distinction that sometimes ensnares our thinking about somatic symptoms (Marlock & Weiss, 2015). They contend that physical and psychological states are deeply interconnected; understanding the whole person (a goal in humanistic approaches) requires overcoming the artificial division of mind and body (Criswell & Serlin, 2015). Body-oriented therapies incorporate dance, meditation, martial arts, yoga, and awareness through movement techniques (Criswell & Serlin, 2015; Marlock & Weiss, 2015; Tarsha et al., 2020). Their origins are often traced to clinicians such as Wilhelm Reich (1945) and Alexander Lowen (1971). Reich (1945) held that people often establish **character armor** (or *body armor*), the physical postures they adopt—including how they walk, talk, breathe, and carry themselves (Moss, 2015). Body armor tells us a great deal about people's psychological functioning.

Although used for various presenting problems, body-oriented therapies are especially relevant for somatic symptoms. People who somaticize express emotional conflicts physically because they experience **alexithymia**—difficulty in expressing emotions verbally. Consequently, "they use body language (symptoms) instead of talking about problems" (Röhricht, 2009, p. 144). Body-oriented therapies help people get back in touch with their emotions by reintegrating awareness of bodily sensations (Ben-Shahar, 2014; Criswell & Serlin, 2015; Marlock & Weiss, 2015; Röhricht et al., 2014; Tarsha et al., 2020). There is not much research on body-centered therapies, perhaps because many body-centered practitioners work outside of academic institutions where research can more readily be conducted (Röhricht, 2009). However, a few studies provide preliminary evidence supporting it (Bloch-Atefi & Smith, 2015; Nickel et al., 2006; Röhricht et al., 2019; Röhricht & Elanjithara, 2014; Tarsha et al., 2020). For instance, **bioenergetics exercises** (breathing and other exercises intended to enhance bodily awareness) potentially ease chronic somatic symptoms (Nickel et al., 2006), while **functional relaxation** can reduce psychosomatic symptoms associated with asthma, tension

---

Body-oriented psychotherapies: Incorporate dance, meditation, martial arts, yoga, and awareness through movement techniques into the therapeutic encounter.

Character armor: Physical postures (how one walks, talks, breathes, and carries oneself) that provide insight into one's psychological functioning; also called *body armor*.

Alexithymia: Difficulty naming, describing, or expressing emotions verbally.

Bioenergetics exercises: Breathing and other exercises intended to enhance bodily awareness.

Functional relaxation: Body-oriented relaxation technique to increase body awareness.

headaches, and irritable bowel syndrome (Lahmann et al., 2009, 2010; Loew et al., 2000; Röhricht, 2009, 2015; Tarsha et al., 2020). Functional relaxation is a body-oriented technique to increase body awareness. It is like progressive relaxation in that the muscles of the body are systematically relaxed.

8.16 Evaluating Psychological Perspectives

Research on psychological interventions for dissociation has generally been limited to case studies, *naturalistic observations* (observing people in their natural environment), and *nonrandomized studies without control groups*. The lack of randomized controlled trials (RCTs) has been blamed on funding difficulties and the complexity of studying something as elusive as dissociation (B. L. Brand, 2012). Studies that have been done find psychodynamic, cognitive-behavioral, and various other therapies to be effective for reducing dissociation, improving quality of life, and limiting the cost of inpatient and outpatient care (B. L. Brand, 2012; B. L. Brand et al., 2009; Myrick, Webermann, Langeland, et al., 2017; Myrick, Webermann, Loewenstein, et al., 2017). Establishing a strong therapeutic patient–therapist alliance is considered especially important (Cronin et al., 2014)—not surprising if dissociation results from abuse that leaves people lacking trust in others. Without RCTs to confirm these findings, however, many researchers remain skeptical of them.

There has been a bit more research on therapy effectiveness for somatic symptoms, although the total number of studies is still relatively small. A meta-analysis of ten randomized and six nonrandomized trials found that psychotherapy had a large effect on reducing physical symptoms and a medium effect on improving health, life satisfaction, interpersonal problems, and maladaptive cognitions and behavior; however, therapy didn't have much effect on reducing psychological symptoms such as depression, anger, and anxiety (Koelen et al., 2014). In another meta-analysis, CBT fared best among psychological interventions for illness anxiety and somatic symptoms (Maass et al., 2020). When it comes to psychosomatic illnesses, supplementing physical treatments with psychotherapy is often helpful (R. Kellner, 1994; Matheny et al., 1996). Relaxation, hypnosis, exercise, classical conditioning, biofeedback, self-disclosure, cognitive-behavioral therapy, mindfulness and other forms of meditation, and exposure techniques are all used to help people manage psychological stress and relieve psychosomatic illnesses (Grossman et al., 2004; Kiecolt-Glaser & Glaser, 1992; J. B. Newman, 2013; G. Tan et al., 2015).

SOCIOCULTURAL PERSPECTIVES

8.17 Cross-Cultural and Social Justice Perspectives

Cross-Cultural Differences and the Risk of Culture Bias

The precise boundaries of dissociation and somatization differ cross-culturally (Janca et al., 1995; Lewis-Fernández et al., 2007; Sirri & Fava, 2014). For instance, U.S. clinicians make a stronger distinction between dissociation and somatization than do their European and Turkish counterparts; they also more firmly differentiate psychosis from dissociation—even though both are associated with trauma and can involve auditory hallucinations and delusions of control (Lewis-Fernández et al., 2007). How people display dissociative and somatic symptoms also varies by culture. For example, a classic study found Chinese patients presented with somatic (rather than psychological) complaints more often than Westerners (Kleinman, 1977). Why? Perhaps Chinese cultural norms encourage people to present psychological concerns less directly—that is, somatically (Zaroff et al., 2012). From a sociocultural standpoint, the types of somatic symptoms seen in different countries reflect socially and culturally influenced ways of communicating mental distress (Lipowski, 1987).

In a similar vein, in many non-Western countries people diagnosed with DID experience themselves as being possessed by spirits or as supernatural beings—and not as having multiple personalities (American Psychiatric Association, 2022; Dorahy et al., 2014; Krüger, 2020). Debate over spirit possession being a cultural variant of DID (versus something distinct from it) recalls questions about whether DSM and ICD are culture-bound (see "Controversial Question" in Chapter 3). Those who view them as culture-bound say the DSM/ICD worldview overlooks the

Double dissociation:
Term to explain how African Americans (and other marginalized groups) often experience themselves in two distinct but incompatible ways (positively and through the prejudiced views of the dominant culture).

socioculturally induced experience of **double dissociation**. Double dissociation is a term to explain how African Americans (and other marginalized groups) often experience themselves in two distinct but incompatible ways. In addition to positive feelings, they also measure themselves through the prejudiced views expressed toward them by the dominant culture (Krüger, 2020; T. O. Moore, 2005; Pittman, 2016). In double dissociation, "double consciousness arises from the difference between how others see you (negatively) versus how you see yourself (positively). This distinction then gets internalized as two alternate and co-existing views of oneself" (Krüger, 2020, p. 6). Double dissociation's self-protective compartmentalization of experience—its "complex feeling of 'two-ness'" consisting "of disparate and competing 'thoughts', 'strivings', and 'ideals'" (Pittman, 2016, para. 8)—sounds a lot like DSM and ICD dissociative disorders. However, by not accounting for the social circumstances that produce double dissociation, DSM and ICD appear culture blind, pathologizing the mental distress of marginalized persons without attending to social context.

The Sociocognitive Model of Dissociative Identity Disorder

Sociocognitive model:
Maintains there is no such thing as dissociative identity disorder; media accounts and therapists who believe in DID iatrogentically induce it; also known as the *fantasy model* and the *iatrogenic position*.

The **sociocognitive model** of dissociative identity disorder (sometimes referred to as the *fantasy model* or *iatrogenic position*) stands in direct opposition to the previously discussed posttraumatic model (Lynn et al., 2012, 2020; Spanos, 1994). It maintains that there is no such thing as DID because DID is a purely social invention—a false diagnosis made up by society and then imposed on patients by misguided but well-meaning psychotherapists who hold questionable cultural assumptions about personality and the effect of abuse on memory (Lilienfeld et al., 1999; Lynn et al., 2004, 2012, 2020; Spanos, 1994). Sociocognitive theorists argue that DID's popularity is spread by media accounts that incorrectly portray it as real. Therapists who accept these accounts then iatrogenically induce DID in their fantasy-prone patients through various suggestive means, encouraging these patients to reinterpret their symptoms as evidence of multiple personalities (Lilienfeld et al., 1999; Lynn et al., 2020; Spanos, 1994). Perhaps the most controversial aspect of the sociocognitive model is its doubt about the suspected child abuse (especially sexual) that the posttraumatic model considers the root of most dissociative problems. From a sociocognitive perspective, therapists often use hypnosis, dream analysis, guided imagery, symptom interpretation, and self-help books to persuade patients that abuse happened (Lynn et al., 2004).

Lauren

Sociocognitive theorists would argue that Lauren began attributing her difficulties to multiple personalities only after being induced into doing so by previous therapists.

Sociocognitive theorists point to substantial research (much of it by renowned memory researcher Elizabeth Loftus) showing that memory is malleable (Loftus, 1979, 2005). Consequently, they argue that encouraging people to recall past sexual abuse or see themselves as having DID creates self-fulfilling prophecies (Loftus & Ketcham, 1994). From their vantage point, society's unquestioning acceptance of scientifically suspect concepts like repression, DID, and dissociative amnesia encourages false memories of sexual abuse (Lilienfeld et al., 1999; Otgaar et al., 2019, 2020). When this leads to erroneous abuse accusations lodged against family members, social injustice results (Lindsay, 1998; Loftus, 2011; Otgaar et al., 2019).

Opponents of the sociocognitive model also make strong social justice claims. They argue that the only way to obtain justice for child sex abuse victims is to acknowledge the abuse and bring it out of the shadows. They also cite research supporting their hypothesis that dissociation is caused by trauma, not fantasy-proneness (Dalenberg et al., 2012, 2014). From their point of view, the sociocognitive model unfairly accuses therapists of uncritically encouraging false memories (Dell, 2013; Gleaves, 1996). Detractors believe the sociocognitive model dangerously asserts "that an extremely debilitating, chronic disorder such as DID … can be caused by mere exposure to media portrayals of the disorder" (Dell, 2013, p. 438). They refute the sociocognitive model by arguing that good therapists must remain open to the possibility their clients were really abused (L. S. Brown, 1997). Rather than disbelieving clients, ethical therapists should validate them while remaining careful not to suggest or plant memories.

Lauren

From a posttraumatic model perspective, Lauren's emerging recollections of past abuse during therapy sessions should be believed. From a sociocognitive perspective, these recollections could be false memories unwittingly encouraged by the therapist and media.

To sociocognitive model detractors, questioning recovered memories sustains power hierarchies that oppress the abused. To them, social justice demands that clients be believed when they re-experience previously dissociated memories of past abuse. Despite efforts to move beyond it (Lynn et al., 2019; Meganck, 2017), debate over the posttraumatic versus sociocognitive models continues. Where do you stand?

8.18 Service User Perspectives

The false memory debate isn't only important to clinicians. It is also significant to service users. Service users who believe they have been abused fall on one side of this debate, while those who say they have been falsely accused of abuse fall on the other. However, in addition to the false memory debate, service users are also deeply concerned about potential stigma that accompanies dissociative and somatic symptom diagnoses. We turn to that issue next.

Dissociation, Abuse, and Stigma

While there has been little examination of the connection between dissociation and stigma, research bears out the intuitive notion that child abuse (the trigger for dissociation, according to the posttraumatic model) is strongly stigmatized (Theimer & Hansen, 2018). Survivors of childhood sexual abuse dissociate more than others and experience stigma over what happened to them—especially feelings of shame and self-blame (Feiring et al., 2010). This isn't surprising, given that many cultures blame abuse victims for what happened to them and unfairly view them as "damaged goods" (Follette et al., 2010). The resulting stigma can make it much more difficult for survivors to come to terms with the abuse and disclose it to others (Follette et al., 2010). Avoiding what happened because of stigma only encourages continued dissociation of traumatic memories.

Stigma and Somatic Symptoms

Research finds somatic symptom disorder diagnoses are stigmatizing, but less so than diagnoses such as depression (Aydogmus, 2020; von dem Knesebeck et al., 2018). If somatic symptoms do carry less stigma than psychological problems, this might explain the previously noted finding that Chinese patients often present psychological issues somatically, potentially avoiding the stigma in Chinese culture associated with having a psychological problem (Zaroff et al., 2012). Something similar has been found in India, with somatic symptoms being less stigmatizing because of their similarity to typical illnesses that everyone encounters (Raguram et al., 1996; Raguram & Weiss, 2004).

This doesn't mean somatic symptom issues are stigma-free—especially when the symptoms are unexplained. For instance, greater stigma accompanies medically unexplained somatic syndromes (fibromyalgia, chronic fatigue syndrome, and irritable bowel syndrome) than comparable medically explained conditions (rheumatoid arthritis, multiple sclerosis, and inflammatory bowel disease) (Looper & Kirmayer, 2004). Experiencing unexplained somatic symptoms does carry stigma, just not as much as more transparently psychological concerns.

8.19 Systems Perspectives

Family Systems Perspectives on Dissociation
Caution Before Using Family Therapy for Dissociation

Clinicians operating from a posttraumatic model urge caution before using family therapy for dissociation. They encourage therapists to keep in mind any history of abuse in the family and consider whether the dissociative client is ready to handle a family session in which an abusive relative is present (Pais, 2009). At the same time, sessions with members of the client's family who weren't part of past abuse can educate those family members about the client's dissociative issues (Pais, 2009).

Internal Family Systems Therapy (IFS)

Internal family systems therapy (IFS) applies systems theory to the psychological functioning of individuals, including those who dissociate. IFS conceptualizes human personality as a series of "parts" that relate to one another (R. C. Schwartz et al., 2009; Sweezy & Ziskind, 2013). Just as every family has members who play specific roles in maintaining family patterns, everyone has different parts (or subpersonalities) that play certain roles in individual functioning. The goal of therapy is not to eliminate these parts but to help them communicate and work together. Three particularly common parts are exiles, managers, and firefighters (R. C. Schwartz et al., 2009; Sweezy & Ziskind, 2013; Twombly, 2013). *Exiles* are "young" parts that have experienced trauma; they are often separated from other parts to avoid terror and other negative trauma-related emotions. *Managers* direct daily activities, trying to control situations and ward off trouble. Finally, *firefighters* work to extinguish the emotional pain of exiles; they might push the individual to take drugs, impulsively shop, binge eat, or pursue sexual activities in response to exile distress.

In extreme dissociation, parts are especially isolated from one another. IFS therapy aims to get parts communicating and cooperating (TheOneInside Podcast, 2021; Twombly, 2013). As cooperation increases, traumatic memories are processed, the trauma becomes less influential, and parts of the personality work together more effectively (TheOneInside Podcast, 2021; Twombly, 2013). The relevance of IFS for DID and other forms of dissociation is obvious—multiple personalities are parts that don't communicate; each deals with (or avoids) past trauma in its own way. Despite the compelling nature of IFS, it has mainly been described theoretically and in case vignettes without much research into its effectiveness.

Family Systems Perspectives on Somatic Symptoms

Systems perspectives focus on how somatic symptoms are fostered or exacerbated by family dynamics. Research points to lack of family coherence and parental criticism as familial predictors of childhood somatic complaints (Bafiti, 2001; B. N. Horwitz et al., 2015; K. Williams et al., 2018). Conversion symptoms specifically correlate with lack of psychological sophistication, low socioeconomic status, lack of education, and living in a rural setting (Scher et al., 2014).

Structural Family Therapy

Salvador Minuchin's structural family therapy (see Chapter 2) exemplifies a family systems approach to psychosomatic complaints. It views psychosomatic and related symptoms—including asthma, diabetes, and eating disorders—as emerging from dysfunctional family patterns (Minuchin et al., 1975). Structural family therapy speaks of **psychosomatic families** in which there is a great deal of *enmeshment* (blurred boundaries between family members), *rigidity, overprotectiveness*, and *difficulty with conflict* resolution (Kog et al., 1985; Minuchin et al., 1975; S. Rousseau et al., 2014). In such families, somatic symptoms are believed to be more likely. To address them, structural family therapists work with the entire family to help members strengthen boundaries, reduce rigidity and overprotectiveness, and learn to resolve conflicts. Unfortunately, concepts such as enmeshment, rigidity, and overprotectiveness have not held up to empirical scrutiny (Kog et al., 1985). Instead, research finds that adolescents from "chaotic" families (which report an exceptional number of problems) and "average" families (which report an average number of problems) display significantly more somatic symptoms than those from families with few functioning problems (S. Rousseau et al., 2014). This might be because marital problems and poor parental functioning are more common in chaotic and average functioning families—and these two factors predict somatic symptoms (S. Rousseau et al., 2014).

Family Resistance to Psychological Aspects of Somatic Symptoms

One challenge in working with families is that they sometimes resist the idea that their members' somatic symptoms are in any way psychological (Kozlowska et al., 2013). Given that people often develop somatic symptoms to avoid psychological issues, this lack of insight into psychological factors isn't that surprising. However, it is important to make sure that medical explanations of symptoms are fully investigated before concluding that unexplained symptoms are primarily psychological (Kozlowska et al., 2013). Otherwise, there is a risk of dismissing legitimate medical concerns and denying patients essential treatments. For instance, research shows that doctors are less likely to take women's medical complaints seriously and more likely to attribute them to psychological causes compared with men's complaints (Claréus & Renström, 2019; Colameco et al., 1983; Daniel et al., 1999; M. T. Ruiz & Verbrugge, 1997). Clinicians must be careful not to mistakenly attribute physical illnesses to psychological causes.

Isabel, Anna, and Malcolm

Besides her own somatic symptom of high blood pressure, Isabel's 9-year-old daughter, Anna, experiences asthma attacks. What might structural family therapy for Isabel, her husband Malcolm, and her daughter Anna look like? Initially, we might expect Isabel to be annoyed that the therapist is interpreting Anna's asthma as "all in her head" and "due to Malcolm and I being bad parents." Family therapy sessions would reveal that Isabel and Malcolm have a lot of conflict in their marriage. They also communicate poorly with one another and Anna. One problem that might come to light is how Isabel and Malcolm often complete Anna's homework for her (Isabel: "We must! In today's world children require help to get ahead."). Therapy would improve family communication and strengthen boundaries—including differentiating rigid overprotectiveness from supportive help when it comes to issues like Anna's homework. As boundaries are firmed up and communication improves, Anna should experience fewer and milder asthma attacks.

8.20 Evaluating Sociocultural Perspectives

As with trauma, stress, and loss, presenting problems involving dissociation and somatic symptoms are deeply tied to social factors. Research supports aspects of both posttraumatic and sociocognitive theories of dissociation, but debate over the reality of child sexual abuse remains a simmering area of disagreement in professional circles, with both sides claiming the mantle of social justice. Family systems perspectives for both dissociation and somatic symptoms are interesting and have generated a lot of case studies but little in the way of experiments (Hulgaard et al., 2019; Sumathipala, 2007). Future research should explore the effectiveness of family systems therapies, try to reconcile posttraumatic and sociocognitive theories of dissociation, and continue to unpack the role of culture in how people experience and display dissociative and somatic symptoms.

CLOSING THOUGHTS

8.21 Dissociation and Somatic Symptoms as Elusive yet Intriguing

Dissociation and somatic symptoms are among the more controversial topics in this book. They are difficult to define and differentiate from other issues because they typically accompany (i.e., show comorbidity with) anxiety, depression, and posttraumatic stress (J. G. Allen & Smith, 1993; Bozkurt et al., 2015; Gray et al., 2020; Kienle et al., 2017; Kratzer et al., 2021; Kroenke, 2003; Luoni et al., 2018; Lyssenko et al., 2018; Spiegel et al., 2013). To further complicate matters, some clinicians doubt the legitimacy of concepts like dissociation, so there are fewer studies on dissociation and dissociation-related somatic symptom issues compared with other presenting problems. Debate over the reality of dissociation is unlikely to be resolved soon.

Dissociative and somatic symptom issues highlight the mind–body relationship. When something upsets us psychologically, it frequently affects physical health. Further, when we dissociate from the pain of traumatic events, we often express the conflict physically. The relationships among psychological stress, dissociation, and physical health are complex and our grasp of them remains tenuous. Even in our own lives, we often fail to make the connection between physical and psychological well-being. The elusive (and at times controversial) nature of dissociation and somatic symptom problems might be why so many of us find them thoroughly intriguing.

CHAPTER SUMMARY

Overview

- The *posttraumatic model* ties somatic and dissociative issues to traumatic events.
- *Dissociation* involves disconnecting from feelings and experiences; *depersonalization, derealization, amnesia, identity confusion,* and *identity alteration* can occur.
- *Somatic complaints* involve experiencing or worrying about physical symptoms.

Diagnostic Perspectives

- DSM and ICD dissociative disorders are *dissociative amnesia (with or without fugue), depersonalization/derealization disorder,* and *dissociative identity disorder (DID).*
- DSM and ICD somatic symptom disorders are *somatic symptom disorder* (bodily distress disorder in ICD), *functional neurological symptom disorder (conversion disorder), illness anxiety disorder* (hypochondriasis in ICD), *psychological factors affecting other medical conditions,* and *factitious disorder (imposed on self or another).*
- Some view dissociative disorders (especially DID) as *iatrogenic* conditions.
- PDM uses the terms *dissociative personality disorder* and *somatizing personality disorder.*
- Dissociation is located on HiTOP's "Thought Disorder" spectrum.
- PTMF views dissociation as a threat response to oppression/trauma.

Historical Perspectives

- Modern notions of dissociation and somatic complaints can be traced to the term *hysteria.*
- In the late 1800s, Charcot found hysterical patients were indifferent to their symptoms; he treated them using *hypnosis.*

Biological Perspectives

- Glutamate might be important in dissociation; drug treatments include SSRIs and *opioid antagonists.*
- Drug treatments for somatic symptoms lack research support; SSRIs, SNRIs, and other drugs are prescribed.
- Brain areas implicated in dissociation: *hippocampus, posterior parietal cortex, amygdala,* an *HPA axis.* DID is linked to the *orbitofrontal cortex* and *anterior cingulate cortex.*
- Somatic symptoms are associated with the *ventral medial prefrontal cortex, anterior insula, somatosensory cortex, hippocampus,* and *amygdala.*
- Genes have been associated with dissociation and somatic symptoms, but environment also plays a role.
- Dissociation might be adaptive by preventing emotional overload.
- Somatic symptoms might be adaptive by eliciting empathy and assistance from others.
- The *diathesis-stress model of psychosomatic illness* says stress leads to biological breakdown in areas of biological vulnerability.
- *Psychoneuroimmunology (PNI)* studies how stress affects immunity and health.

Psychological Perspectives

- Psychodynamic perspectives differentiate *primary gain* from *secondary gain.*
- Psychodynamic approaches view dissociation as defense against upsetting memories; therapy reintegrates these memories into awareness.
- Psychodynamic approaches see somatic symptoms as representing unconscious conflicts.
- CBT attributes dissociation to classic and operant conditioning and to difficulties with encoding/retrieval of upsetting information.
- CBT employs *behavior therapies, cognitive therapies,* and *mindfulness-based stress reduction (MBSR)* to treat dissociation and somatic symptoms; biofeedback is used with psychosomatic illnesses.
- Humanistic therapists emphasize positive aspects of dissociation, including its potential meaning.
- *Body-oriented psychotherapies* view physical and psychological states as connected and reintegrate bodily sensations into people's experience.

Sociocultural Perspectives

- How people display dissociative and somatic symptoms varies cross-culturally.
- *Double dissociation* explains how African Americans (and other marginalized groups) experience themselves in both positive and negative ways taught by the dominant culture.
- The *sociocognitive model* views DID as an iatrogenic condition.
- Dissociation and somatic symptoms carry stigma.
- *Internal family systems therapy (IFS)* applies a systems approach to conceptualizing the compartmentalized "parts" of people experiencing dissociation.
- *Psychosomatic families* are hypothesized to show *enmeshment*, but research support is limited.
- Families of people with somatic symptom diagnoses often deny psychological conflicts related to the symptoms.

Closing Thoughts

- Dissociative and somatic symptoms highlight mind–body connections.

NEW VOCABULARY

1. Alexithymia
2. Bioenergetics exercises
3. Biofeedback
4. Bodily distress disorder
5. Body-oriented psychotherapies
6. Character armor
7. Depersonalization/derealization disorder
8. Diathesis-stress model of psychosomatic illness
9. Dissociative amnesia
10. Dissociative identity disorder (DID)
11. Dissociative neurological symptom disorder
12. Double dissociation
13. Factitious disorder
14. Functional neurological symptom disorder
15. Functional relaxation
16. Hyperassociativity
17. Hypochondriasis
18. Hypnosis
19. Iatrogenic condition
20. Identity alteration
21. Identity confusion
22. Illness anxiety disorder
23. Internal family systems therapy (IFS)
24. Lymphocytes
25. Mindfulness-based stress reduction (MBSR)
26. Opioid antagonists
27. Posttraumatic model
28. Primary gain
29. Psychological or behavioral factors affecting disorders or diseases classified elsewhere
30. Psychological factors affecting other medical conditions
31. Psychoneuroimmunology (PNI)
32. Psychosomatic
33. Psychosomatic families
34. Secondary gain
35. Self-hypnosis
36. Sociocognitive model
37. Somatic complaint
38. Somatic symptom disorder (SSD)
39. Somatization
40. State-dependent learning

FEEDING AND EATING PROBLEMS

Photo 9.1
Spencer Davis/Unsplash.

OVERVIEW

9.1 Getting Started: Feeding vs. Eating Problems

Case Examples

Marta

Marta, a 16-year-old female, is extremely underweight due to continuous dieting and a refusal to eat enough. Since she was 14, Marta has consistently complained about being "too fat." She goes to the gym for intense daily workouts and is exceedingly careful about what she eats—often skipping lunch entirely and limiting her dinner to a single piece of toast, three pieces of lettuce without salad dressing, and a glass of water. Occasionally, when she thinks she's eaten too much, Marta forces herself to throw up. Marta's friends and teachers have become increasingly alarmed at how dangerously thin she is. When they ask her about it, she dismisses their concerns. Marta, a champion on her school debate team, recently passed out during a tournament. Apparently, she hadn't eaten anything all day. Her doctor repeatedly warns her that she must eat enough to have sufficient energy. He tells her that not getting her period in recent months is a symptom of starvation.

Zayna

Zayna is a 24-year old woman who comes to therapy at the request of her live-in boyfriend, Emmanuel. "He's unnecessarily worried about my eating," Zayna tells the therapist with a roll of her eyes. Emmanuel complains that Zayna often secretly locks herself in the bedroom for several hours and eats large stashes of food that she's hidden throughout their apartment. Zayna denies this, though she admits that Emmanuel has periodically found evidence that she has thrown up what she has eaten, or—in at least one case—that she drank large amounts of laxative to clear her system. "It's not a big deal," Zayna says. "Everyone overeats sometimes." The rest of the time, Zayna is quite careful about what she eats, avoiding junk food while exercising regularly. Zayna is of average weight for her height and build but doesn't like her body shape: "I look like a bloated pear!" Ashamed and embarrassed, Zayna only reluctantly shares that she has had eating and body image issues on and off since she was a teen.

Daemyn

Daemyn is a 22-year-old male computer programmer who is extremely overweight. He seeks therapy because he is unhappy with his weight and wants to do something about it. Daemyn admits that he sometimes feels compelled to eat large amounts of food. Several times per week he gathers numerous boxes of his favorite cookies, a pint of chocolate ice cream, and whatever other sweets he finds around the house and eats them all in one sitting. This has been going on for a few years. Daemyn is distressed and ashamed about his eating and weight and wants to address them because he is starting to have associated health problems.

Wendy

Wendy is an 8-year-old girl who is an extremely picky eater. Other than the occasional dessert, Wendy has restricted her diet to essentially two foods: fried chicken fingers and plain pasta. She refuses to eat anything else. When asked why, she says that she doesn't like the taste of other foods or "how they feel in my mouth." He parents are frustrated because they feel obliged to always make Wendy a different meal from what everyone else in the family is eating. They also worry that Wendy's restricted diet may prevent her from growing and developing properly.

Alastair

Alastair, a 6-year-old boy, is taken for medical attention by his parents because he keeps eating things that aren't food. First, it was the chalk from his chalkboard set. Then, it was soap from the bathtub. Alastair recently began eating pebbles from the driveway outside his home. He has previously been diagnosed with an intellectual disability and his parents wonder if that has anything to do with his odd feeding habits.

Simone

Simone is a 13-year-old girl whose parents are concerned because she brings up food she has previously eaten and then re-chews and re-swallows it. Like Alastair, she has also been diagnosed with an intellectual disability. Simone's parents want her to stop engaging in regurgitating and re-chewing food because they find it disgusting. Simone says it is a harmless habit that she finds comforting.

Can We Distinguish Feeding from Eating Problems?

It is common to distinguish *feeding* from *eating* problems. What is the difference? **Feeding problems** are discussed less often than eating problems (C. Howard, 2016). They tend to be diagnosed in children and involve not eating enough to meet nutritional requirements—sometimes for biological reasons (e.g., breathing or swallowing difficulties) and other times for psychological reasons (e.g., fussy or faddish eating in which certain foods are avoided or refused because of taste, texture, or a basic dislike for them) (Goday et al., 2019; C. Howard, 2016; Rybak, 2015; Uher & Rutter, 2012). Feeding disorders can also involve eating inappropriate, non-food substances such as dirt, chalk, paper, clay, coins, or paint chips (C. Howard, 2016; Mishori & McHale, 2014); or regurgitating and re-chewing one's food (Bryant-Waugh et al., 2010; A. S. Hartmann et al., 2012). Many, but not all, people with feeding problems also suffer from developmental disabilities (American Psychiatric Association, 2022; Bryant-Waugh et al., 2010; A. S. Hartmann et al., 2012).

Feeding problems: Characterized by concern over food preferences; involve fussy or faddish eating habits in which certain foods are avoided or refused because of taste, texture, or a basic dislike for them.

Eating problems:
Characterized by disturbed body image; involve concerns about being overweight or experiencing one's body negatively or in ways that appear distorted.

Eating problems, on the other hand, are characterized by disturbed body image. They often involve concerns about being overweight or experiencing one's body in negative or distorted ways (C. Howard, 2016; Uher & Rutter, 2012). Eating problems are more commonly diagnosed in adolescents and adults. Unfortunately, the distinction between feeding and eating problems is a fuzzy one at best. Many of the eating problems identified in adolescents and adults are preceded by feeding issues in childhood, which means that dividing presenting problems into feeding versus eating problems might not always be valid or useful (Uher & Rutter, 2012).

Photo 9.2 *Heathers* is a dark comedy about teenage girls that approaches body issues, including eating disorders like bulimia, with humor. Whether this portrayal is problematic or sensitive is very much up for debate. What do you think?
Archive Photos/Stringer/Getty Images.

DIAGNOSTIC PERSPECTIVES

9.2 DSM and ICD

DSM-5-TR and ICD-11 identify six diagnoses as feeding and eating disorders: anorexia nervosa, bulimia nervosa, binge-eating disorder, avoidant/restrictive food intake disorder, pica, and rumination disorder. The first three are generally identified as eating disorders. The latter three are usually viewed as feeding disorders.

Anorexia and Bulimia

Anorexia and bulimia are the two most well-known eating disorder diagnoses. Because they are often confused with one another, let's discuss them together to clarify their similarities and differences.

Anorexia

Anorexia nervosa:
DSM and ICD disorder involving seriously low body weight due to restricted food intake.

The key element of **anorexia nervosa** is significantly low body weight due to restricted food intake. People diagnosed with anorexia have an intense fear of gaining weight. They also have a distorted sense of their own body shape, which negatively affects how they feel about themselves. Anorexic clients don't recognize that they are extremely underweight or the health risks this poses. The key component of anorexia is a *failure to maintain minimum body weight*. Diagnostic Box 9.1 contains diagnostic criteria and guidelines.

Marta
Marta, who diets and sees herself as needing to lose weight despite being dangerously thin, qualifies for an anorexia diagnosis.

Diagnostic Box 9.1 Anorexia Nervosa

DSM-5-TR

- Limits food intake, resulting in extremely low body weight (less than minimally normal or expected).
- Fears gaining weight or becoming fat, or regular behavior that prevents weight gain even though notably underweight.
- Has a distorted sense of one's own body shape. Body weight or shape excessively influences sense of self, or low body weight not acknowledged as a serious problem.
- Subtypes: *restricting type* (no binge eating or purging during last three months); *binge-eating/purging type* (recurrent binge eating or purging during last three months).
- Specify: *mild* (BMI ≥ 17), *moderate* (BMI = 16-16.99), *severe* (BMI < 15).
- Use the "other specified feeding or eating disorder" code for "atypical anorexia," in which weight loss criterion not met.

ICD-11

- Exceedingly low body weight (adults: BMI < 18.5; children/teens: below fifth percentile BMI-for-age), or rapid weight loss (more than 20 percent in six months); not due to a medical condition or lack of food.
- Recurrent behaviors to lose weight (e.g., fasting; eating little or slowly; hiding or spitting out food; forced vomiting; use of laxatives, diuretics, or enemas; excessive exercise).
- Preoccupied with body weight/shape; overvalues being thin or has a distorted sense of own body weight and shape.
- Patterns: *restricting pattern* (no binge eating or purging during last three months); *binge–purge pattern* (recurrent binge eating or purging during last three months).

Information from American Psychiatric Association (2022, p. 381) and World Health Organization (2022a).

Bulimia Nervosa

By comparison, **bulimia nervosa** is characterized by binge eating followed by compensatory behavior. **Binge eating** is a form of overeating in which a person eats a huge amount of food in a single sitting—much more than most people would eat during a comparable period. During a binge, there is a sense of being unable to control or limit how much one eats. **Compensatory behavior** is behavior to counteract having binged. People often equate compensatory behavior with *purging*, in which the person who has binged actively removes the food from his or her body through self-induced vomiting or misuse of laxatives, diuretics, or other drugs. However, while purging is a type of compensatory behavior, compensatory behavior is broader than just purging. It can also involve behaviors that don't involve removing the food from one's system, but which are still meant to counteract having binged. Fasting and excessive exercise are non-purging compensatory behaviors. Importantly, people with bulimia diagnoses—such as Zayna, one of the cases presented at the start of the chapter—aren't excessively underweight. Unlike anorexic clients, they don't appear strikingly thin. Diagnostic Box 9.2 outlines bulimia criteria and guidelines.

Bulimia nervosa: DSM and ICD disorder characterized by binge-eating followed by compensatory behavior.

Binge eating: Overeating in which a huge amount of food is eaten in a single sitting—much more than most people would eat during a comparable period.

Compensatory behavior: Behavior a person engages in to counteract having binged; includes *purging, fasting*, and *excessive exercise*.

Diagnostic Box 9.2 Bulimia Nervosa

DSM-5-TR

- Regular binge eating (eats more food in a distinct period than most others would and feels unable to control the eating).
- Regular compensatory behavior (e.g., forces self to vomit; takes laxatives, diuretics, or other drugs; fasts, or exercises excessively).
- Binging and compensatory activities occur once a week or more for three months.
- Self-assessments are disproportionately based on body shape and weight.
- Does not occur only when experiencing symptoms of anorexia.
- Specify: *mild* (compensatory behavior 1–3 times weekly), *moderate* (compensatory behavior 4–7 times weekly), *severe* (compensatory behavior 8–13 times weekly), *extreme* (compensatory behavior more than 14 times weekly).
- If some or none of the symptoms are no longer present for an extended time, can specify "in partial remission" or "in remission."

ICD-11

- Regular binge eating (e.g., once a week or more for one month or more).

- Regular compensatory behavior (e.g., once a week or more for one month or more); forced vomiting most common compensatory behavior but may also use laxatives or enemas; take diuretics; fast, or exercise excessively).
- Overly attentive to weight and body shape.
- Distress or impairment due to the symptoms.
- Doesn't meet criteria for anorexia.

Information from American Psychiatric Association (2022, pp. 387–388) and World Health Organization (2022a).

Zayna
Zayna, who alternatively binges (eating a huge amount in one sitting) and purges (compensates by making herself throw up or exercising excessively), could receive a bulimia diagnosis.

Distinguishing Anorexia from Bulimia

DSM-5-TR and ICD-11 identify two types, or patterns, in anorexia: the *restricting type* and the *binge-eating/purging type*. Restricting types lose weight mainly by dieting, fasting, and exercising excessively, but they don't binge or purge. Binge-eating/purging types, on the other hand, do engage in bingeing and purging; they binge and then make themselves vomit or use laxatives or diuretics to rid their bodies of what they've eaten. The binge/purge type of anorexia is often confused with bulimia—especially cases of bulimia where compensatory behaviors don't involve purging. To confuse matters, anorexia can include binges and purges, so knowing if someone purges doesn't determine whether they have anorexia or bulimia. The key to distinguishing anorexia from bulimia is to not worry about whether there is bingeing or purging and instead to focus on body weight. *If the person isn't maintaining minimal body weight, then the diagnosis must be anorexia.* In fact, if someone with a bulimia diagnosis becomes excessively thin and refuses to maintain body weight, the diagnosis is changed to anorexia.

According to DSM-5-TR, lifetime prevalence for anorexia is higher among women (0.9–1.42 percent) than men (0.12–0.3 percent). The same pattern holds for bulimia (0.46–1.5 percent among women; 0.05–0.08 percent among men). Cross-culturally, anorexia and bulimia are much more common in high-income post-industrialized countries like the United States, Australia, New Zealand, Japan, and many European nations. However, DSM notes that rates are increasing in low- and middle-income countries across Asia and the Middle East. Within the United States, prevalence is lower among Black and Latinx Americans compared with white Americans; exactly why isn't clear. The African American author of "The Lived Experience" shares her journey with anorexia, along with her concern that people of color are underrepresented in media portrayals of eating disorders.

The Lived Experience: When You Don't Fit the "Eating Disorder" Mold as an African American

The first time I heard about eating disorders, I was in middle school. Our health class watched a film on the dangers of extreme dieting, and the implications it could have on mental and physical health. I watched intently as the film portrayed the typical narrative of a middle-class Caucasian girl who was on a dangerous path toward starvation. At the time, it was inconceivable to me that I could ever develop an eating disorder. I was just an average sized African American girl who loved food.

In high school and college, like many adolescent girls, I began to feel increasingly inadequate about my body. I fell victim to society's glorification of the thin and athletic body, and I internalized these messages. I quickly developed an unhealthy relationship with food, body image, and exercise. Unbeknownst to me, I had an eating disorder. I felt inadequate in many aspects of my life, and these feelings fueled my fractured relationship with my body. I never felt happy.

It took me a long time to seek help for my eating disorder. When I eventually realized I had a problem, I felt extremely self-conscious. There were many barriers that prevented me from seeking treatment. First, I thought had to be "thin enough." My mind flashed back to PSA posters that lined the hallways of my school, and documentaries I had seen about eating disorders. I believed that if I didn't look thin, fragile, or skeletal, that I was unworthy of treatment. Additionally, I never saw African American people portrayed as having eating disorders. I felt as if I was an anomaly. I feared people wouldn't take me seriously, or that it was impossible for me to have an eating disorder because I didn't fit the "eating disorder mold."

When I eventually sought help, none of my concerns about being thin enough or looking like the typical eating disorder client mattered. I was met with understanding, compassion, and empathy by all the clinicians who helped treat me. I learned that there is no stereotypical eating disorder patient, and that everyone can be helped whether or not you feel worthy of treatment.

Today, I am still fighting for recovery. What I know now is that I am enough. I can ask for help when I need it, and no one will turn me away. I work with a treatment team, and I feel heard and supported. What I hope is that everyone who is struggling can receive the care they need to recover regardless of being "enough."

I believe the mental health advocacy community needs more accurate representations and portrayals of people who struggle with eating disorders. The reality is that people of all ages, gender identities, races, ethnicities, abilities, and sizes can develop eating disorders. If people don't see themselves represented, it may become an obstacle to seeking treatment.

If the media highlighted the struggles of marginalized voices, I feel that more people would be comfortable coming forward to receive help. What I want people who are struggling to know is that even if you feel you are not thin enough, sick enough, or the right ethnicity to seek treatment, you are wrong. There is a place for everyone in recovery.

By Celeste Saddler. Reproduced with permission from https://www.nationaleatingdisorders.org/blog/when-you-dont-fit-eating-disorder-mold-african-american.

Binge-Eating Disorder (BED)

Binge-eating disorder (BED) is characterized by recurrent binge-eating episodes. These episodes must occur at least once a week for three months or more. Binge-eating disorder differs from bulimia in that there is no compensatory behavior to counteract having binged. Thus, it shouldn't surprise you that people who seek treatment for binge eating are often overweight or obese.

Binge-eating disorder (BED): DSM and ICD disorder characterized by recurrent binge eating.

Daemyn
Daemyn's pattern of frequent bingeing followed by feelings of shame and remorse is consistent with criteria and guidelines for BED.

BED was first added to DSM-5 and more recently to ICD-11. As with anorexia and bulimia, DSM-5-TR estimates lifetime prevalence of BED to be higher among females (1.25–3.5 percent) than males (0.42–2.0 percent). Prevalence is roughly equal across high-income post-industrialized countries, and similarly high in certain areas of Latin America. In contrast to anorexia and bulimia, DSM-5-TR says BED prevalence in the United States doesn't vary by ethnic or racial background. See Diagnostic Box 9.3 for diagnostic information.

Diagnostic Box 9.3 Binge-Eating Disorder (BED)

DSM-5-TR
- Regular binge eating (eats more food in a distinct period than most others would and feels unable to control the eating).
- Binge eating involve at least three of these: (1) eats much faster than usual; (2) eats until overly full; (3) eats a lot even if not hungry; (4) eats alone due to shame about amount being eaten; (5) feels revolted, despondent, or remorseful after bingeing.
- Experiences great distress about bingeing.
- Bingeing occurs approximately once a week for at least three months.
- Does not occur only when experiencing symptoms of anorexia or bulimia.
- No compensatory behaviors.

ICD-11
- Regular binge eating (e.g., once a week or more over three months); eats more than usually does and feels like can't stop.
- No regular compensatory behaviors.
- Distress or impairment due to the symptoms.

Information from American Psychiatric Association (2022, pp. 392–393) and World Health Organization (2022a).

Avoidant/Restrictive Food Intake Disorder (ARFID)

Avoidant/restrictive food intake disorder (ARFID): DSM and ICD disorder characterized by extremely picky eating and failure to eat enough to meet basic nutritional needs.

Avoidant/restrictive food intake disorder (ARFID) is a diagnosis reserved for extremely picky eaters who fail to eat enough to meet basic nutritional requirements. People given this diagnosis tend to suffer from malnutrition and often must rely on dietary supplements (or in extreme cases, an eating tube) to compensate for their poor eating habits. ARFID usually begins in childhood but can persist into, or even develop during, adolescence or adulthood. ARFID is a new diagnosis (it first appeared in DSM-5), so prevalence estimates remain in flux (Coglan & Otasowie, 2019). DSM-5-TR reports ARFID is equally common in males and females. It is believed to show comorbidity with anxiety disorders, obsessive-compulsive disorder (OCD), autism (especially in males), attention-deficit/hyperactivity disorder, and intellectual disability. Criteria and guidelines are in Diagnostic Box 9.4.

Wendy

Wendy's parents view her as a "picky eater" but, according to DSM-5-TR and ICD-11, she is a likely candidate for an ARFID diagnosis.

Diagnostic Box 9.4 Avoidant/Restrictive Food Intake Disorder (ARFID)

DSM-5-TR
- Disinterested in eating or food; avoids food due to sensory characteristics; concern about unpleasant consequences of eating.
- Doesn't meet nutritional needs, with one or more of the following: (1) substantial weight loss (fails to meet expected weight gain goals or reduced growth in children); (2) inadequate nutrition; (3) requires a feeding tube or nutritional supplements; (4) psychosocial functioning negatively impacted.
- Not due to lack of food or cultural practices.
- Does not experience body weight and shape in a distorted manner.
- Does not occur only when experiencing symptoms of anorexia or bulimia.

ICD-11
- Restricted food intake or food avoidance that leads to one or both: (1) not meeting nutritional requirements (resulting in weight loss, failure to gain weight, inadequate nutrition, need for nutritional supplements/feeding tube, or negative health consequences); or (2) impaired functioning.
- Not due to a preoccupation with body weight/shape, lack of food, or another medical condition/mental disorder.

Information from American Psychiatric Association (2022, p. 376) and World Health Organization (2022a).

Pica

Pica: DSM and ICD disorder involving the eating of non-food substances.

Pica is diagnosed in people who consistently eat non-food substances. Such substances include things like "paper, soap, cloth, hair, string, wool, soil, chalk, talcum powder, paint, gum, metal, pebbles, charcoal or coal, ash, clay, starch, or ice" (American Psychiatric Association, 2022, p. 372). DSM-5-TR estimates prevalence among school-age children at 5 percent, and ICD-11 notes that pica occurs about equally among males and females. It usually begins in childhood, but adolescent or adult onset also occur. Pregnant women are prone to pica—especially those facing food scarcity; DSM-5-TR says worldwide prevalence during pregnancy is 28 percent. For diagnostic information, see Diagnostic Box 9.5.

Diagnostic Box 9.5 Pica

DSM-5-TR
- For at least one month, regularly eats non-nutritious substances that are not food.
- The behavior is developmentally inappropriate.
- The behavior is not due to cultural or other social norms.

ICD-11
- Regularly eats non-nutritious substances (e.g., clay, chalk, dirt, paint chips, paper, plaster, metal).
- The eating of non-nutritious substances poses a risk to physical health or daily functioning.
- The person is developmentally old enough to distinguish what is and is not edible (usually older than age 2).
- Not due to another medical condition, such deficient nutrition.

Information from American Psychiatric Association (2022, pp. 371–372) and World Health Organization (2022a).

Alastair

Alastair—the 6-year-old boy who eats pebbles, soap, and chalk—qualifies for a pica diagnosis.

Rumination Disorder

Rumination disorder (*rumination and regurgitation disorder* in ICD-11) describes those who regularly re-chew, re-swallow, or spit out food after intentionally regurgitating it. They don't find this disgusting or nausea-inducing. Instead, they tend to experience it as an uncontrollable habit. It can occur in infancy, childhood, adolescence, or adulthood—and when it occurs, it can lead to medical emergencies or even death (especially among infants). DSM-5-TR cites prevalence rates for rumination disorder of 1–2 percent for grade-school-age children. Rumination is highly comorbid with neurodevelopmental disorders, especially intellectual development disorder; individuals with these diagnoses often find it soothing. See Diagnostic Box 9.6.

Rumination disorder: DSM disorder characterized by re-chewing, re-swallowing, or spitting out food after intentionally regurgitating it; called *rumination and regurgitation disorder* in ICD.

Simone

Simone, the 13-year-old girl who brings up, re-chews, and re-swallows her food, meets the criteria for rumination disorder.

Diagnostic Box 9.6 Rumination Disorder

DSM-5-TR
- For at least one month, habitually regurgitates food; regurgitated food; may re-chew food or spit it out.
- Not due to a gastrointestinal or other medical condition.
- Does not occur only when experiencing symptoms of anorexia, bulimia, binge-eating disorder, or ARFID.

ICD-11
- Called "rumination-regurgitation disorder" in ICD-11.
- Purposely brings swallowed food back up into mouth (regurgitation), then either re-chews and re-swallows it (rumination) or spits it out.
- Occurs at least several times per week for at least several weeks.
- Individual has a developmental age of 2 years or older.
- Not due to a medical condition.

Information from American Psychiatric Association (2022, p. 374) and World Health Organization (2022a).

Evaluating DSM and ICD Perspectives
Impact of Revised Anorexia and Bulimia Criteria on Prevalence

Since DSM-5, anorexia and bulimia criteria have been more inclusive, potentially increasing prevalence rates. For bulimia, the minimum frequency of binge eating with compensatory behavior has been loosened from twice to only once per week. For anorexia, patients no longer must weigh 85 percent or less than what is expected for their height and build; instead, *body mass index*

(BMI)—a weight by height index to measure if people are underweight, normal, or overweight—is used (American Psychiatric Association, 2022; T. A. Brown et al., 2014). Further, *amenorrhea* (loss of period) from lack of nutrition has been eliminated as an anorexia criterion, allowing those menstruating or not menstruating to more easily be diagnosed (Attia & Roberto, 2009). These changes were expected to increase anorexia and bulimia prevalence while also yielding fewer diagnoses of **other specified feeding or eating disorder (OSFED)**, the DSM and ICD category for those who don't qualify for any other feeding or eating disorder (C. Call et al., 2013; Flament et al., 2015; J. J. Thomas et al., 2015). However, just the opposite may have occurred; one meta-analysis found anorexia and bulimia prevalence have decreased since 2013 while OSFED prevalence has increased (Qian et al., 2013, 2022). The researchers who conducted this meta-analysis nonetheless believe that the prevalence of all eating disorders is likely underestimated (Qian et al., 2022). Researchers appear less worried about inflated prevalence rates for eating disorders and more concerned that so many patients only seem to fit the "other specified" diagnosis.

Other specified feeding or eating disorder (OSFED): DSM and ICD diagnosis for those who don't meet criteria for other feeding or eating disorders but warrant a diagnosis; used to diagnose *purging disorder, night eating syndrome, atypical anorexia,* and *atypical bulimia.*

Misuse of the "Other Specified Feeding and Eating Disorder" Diagnosis?

Is the "other specified feeding and eating disorder" diagnosis for cases that don't qualify for any other feeding or eating disorder overused? DSM-5-TR encourages use of the OSFED diagnosis for cases of *purging disorder* (where someone recurrently purges but doesn't binge) and *night eating syndrome* (in which a person wakes up during the night and eats excessively). Clinicians are also told to use it for "atypical" anorexia and bulimia. *Atypical anorexia nervosa* is diagnosed when all other criteria for anorexia are met but the person is normal weight or overweight, while *atypical bulimia nervosa* is diagnosed when bingeing and compensatory behaviors occur less than once a week and/or for fewer than three months. Whether these two atypical "other specified" diagnoses exemplify the improper lowering of diagnostic thresholds or simply allow clinicians to diagnose and treat people who don't quite meet the stringent criteria for anorexia and bulimia is a matter of ongoing debate. Does requiring people to be underweight for an anorexia diagnosis incorrectly prevent normal-weight and overweight people who show symptoms of starvation (i.e., "atypical" anorexics) from being diagnosed as anorexic (Freizinger et al., 2022; Siber, 2022)? Some say yes, but others argue no. What do you think?

Issues Facing the Binge-Eating Disorder Diagnosis

Binge-eating disorder was one of the most discussed additions to DSM-5, with many believing its inclusion was overdue (Attia et al., 2013; C. Call et al., 2013; L. L. Myers & Wiman, 2014; Striegel-Moore & Franko, 2008). However, some complained that it pathologizes normal variations in eating and could lead to overdiagnosis (A. J. Frances & Widiger, 2012; Paris, 2015). Nonetheless, DSM-5 field trials concluded BED has good interrater reliability (a concept introduced in Chapter 2) (L. L. Myers & Wiman, 2014; Regier et al., 2013). Disagreement remains over what should count as a binge (an issue for the bulimia diagnosis too). Some researchers want the definition to focus on lack of control over eating more than how much is eaten (L. L. Myers & Wiman, 2014). Concerns have also been raised about the clinical utility of DSM severity criteria for BED, which focus on how often people binge; evidence suggests overvaluing weight and shape might be a better way to ascertain severity—not just for BED, but also for anorexia (Dang et al., 2022). Finally, discussion continues about the relationship between BED and **obesity**, defined by the World Health Organization (2021a) as having an extremely high BMI (30 or greater). Many BED patients are obese, but not all obese individuals meet BED criteria.

Obesity: According to the World Health Organization, extremely high body mass index (greater than 30).

Should Orthorexia Be Added to DSM and ICD?

Interest is increasing in **orthorexia nervosa**, a possible new eating disorder characterized by a preoccupation with healthy eating (Bratman, n.d.; T. M. Dunn & Bratman, 2016; D. Vasile & Vasiliu, 2022). First proposed in the late 1990s, it entails eating a nutritionally unbalanced diet, excessive worry and guilt about eating unhealthy foods, rigid avoidance of foods considered unhealthy, inordinate time and money spent on researching and thinking about eating healthily, and intolerance of other people's dietary habits (T. M. Dunn & Bratman, 2016; Koven & Abry, 2015; D. Vasile & Vasiliu, 2022). Orthorexia is not in DSM or ICD, and whether it should be added is a matter of debate. Some mental health professionals caution that orthorexia overlaps (i.e., is comorbid) with anorexia and bulimia, as well as with obsessive-compulsive disorders (Bhattacharya et al., 2022; Brytek-Matera, 2012; Koven

Orthorexia nervosa: Proposed mental disorder characterized by a preoccupation with healthy eating.

& Abry, 2015). They warn that creating a new diagnostic category is premature and contend that anorexia, bulimia, and orthorexia are different expressions of the same core psychopathology. For instance, all three diagnoses are tied to perfectionism, concern with body image, and attachment issues (Barnes & Caltabiano, 2017). Other professionals believe that orthorexia is distinct enough that it warrants its own diagnostic category (Bratman, n.d.; T. M. Dunn & Bratman, 2016; Koven & Abry, 2015; Ryman et al., 2019). Time will tell if DSM and ICD decide to add it.

9.3 Other Diagnostic Perspectives

PDM-2

PDM reports that eating disorders are often associated with stressful life events (e.g., starting college, family issues, grief, or loss). It goes on to note that people with eating disorders often feel "starved for care and affection" (Lingiardi & McWilliams, 2017, p. 215). Guilt and shame are common, as are feelings of inadequacy, worthlessness, and weakness. PDM also indicates that those with eating disorders are afraid to express anger because they equate emotional expression with losing control, something they dread. Further, PDM views anorexic patients as wishing to remain childlike and avoid growing up. This potentially sheds light on these patients' puberty-disrupting self-starvation. Because those with eating disorders tend to keep their issues secret, PDM describes their relationships as superficial, unstable, and marked by immaturity. They crave being protected and cared for by others, but their eating and relationship patterns often elicit negative responses instead.

Photo 9.3 One recent study suggests that as many as 28 percent of athletes are affected by orthorexia.
Jonathan Chng/Unsplash.

HiTOP

Eating disorders have been connected to several HiTOP spectra, but recent work groups them under the "Somatoform" spectrum (Sellbom et al., 2022). HiTOP researchers are developing subscales that they believe differentiate six elements of eating disorders—"Body Image and Weight Concerns, Restricting and Purging, Cognitive Restraint, Binge Eating, Excessive Exercise, and Muscle Building" (Sellbom et al., 2022, p. 71). Future studies to refine these preliminary subscales are underway. The aim is to clarify the location of eating pathology along HiTOP's six spectra, especially "Somatoform" and "Internalizing" (Sellbom et al., 2022).

PTMF

In keeping with its rejection of the medical model, PTMF reframes "eating disorders" as "eating problems" and conceptualizes them as meaningful threat responses to mistreatment and trauma (Caplan & Watson, 2020; Johnstone et al., 2018). Eating (or not eating) becomes a means to emotionally self-soothe, regulate overwhelming feelings, or maintain a sense of control (Johnstone et al., 2018). PTMF rejects the tendency to pathologize eating problems as disorders, instead arguing that such issues "should be understood not as a symptom of an illness but as a reaction to difficult experiences, as a threat response, a way of surviving the intolerable, that will on every level make sense" (Caplan & Watson, 2020, para. 17).

HISTORICAL PERSPECTIVES

9.4 Anorexia, Bulimia, and Binge Eating

Reports of disturbed eating and self-starvation are found throughout Western history—from ancient Greece to the Roman Empire to the Middle Ages to the Renaissance (Dell'Osso et al., 2016; J. M. S. Pearce, 2004; Shafter, 1989). It has been posited that numerous historical figures suffered from anorexia—including Saint Catherine of Siena and Joan of Arc (Dell'Osso et al., 2016; Moncrieff-Boyd, 2016). However, labeling such cases as anorexia or bulimia is problematic because "instances of self-starvation and food abstinence are essentially culture-bound and cannot be separated from their sociocultural context" (Moncrieff-Boyd, 2016, p. 115). Applying present-day eating disorder diagnoses to historical figures is tricky because these diagnoses reflect today's worldview rather than the worldviews of past eras.

Perhaps the first medical account of something resembling modern notions of anorexia was provided in 1694 by the British physician Richard Morton (1637–1698) (Breathnach, 1998; Caparrotta & Ghaffari, 2006; J. M. S. Pearce, 2004). Morton observed that symptoms included "a want of Appetite, and a bad Digestion, upon which there follows a Languishing Weakness of Nature, and a falling away of the Flesh every day more and more" (Morton, 1694/2011, Vol. 3, p. 4). Some years afterwards, in 1764, Scottish physician Robert Whytt (1714–1766) provided additional descriptions of patients who today would probably be considered anorexic or bulimic (Silverman, 1987). In 1859, nearly a century later, the French doctor Louis-Victor Marcé (1828–1864) offered even more detailed portrayals of anorexia-like behavior (Blewett & Bottéro, 1995; Silverman, 1989). He described

young girls, who at the period of puberty and after a precocious physical development, become subject to inappetency carried to the utmost limits. Whatever the duration of their abstinence they experience a distaste for food, which the most pressing of want is unable to overcome. (Marcé, as cited in Silverman, 1989, p. 833)

The term "anorexia" has Greek origins and means "without appetite" (Moncrieff-Boyd, 2016). It was first applied to patients in 1873 by two physicians—Britain's Sir William Gull (1816–1890) and France's Charles Lasègue (1816–1883) (Caparrotta & Ghaffari, 2006; Gull, 1874/1954; J. Lock & Kirz, 2008; Moncrieff-Boyd, 2016; Soh et al., 2010; Vandereycken & Van Deth, 1989). Gull (1874/1954) described anorexia as a "disease occurring mostly in young women, and characterized by extreme emaciation" (p. 173). Because it was considered a variant of hysteria, Gull called the condition "anorexia hysterical," while Lasègue used the term "anorexia hystérique" (J. Lock & Kirz, 2008).

By 1914, the German pathologist Morris Simmonds (1855–1925) offered a purely medical account of anorexia, attributing it to underactive pituitary glands—a hypothesis that was refuted after the Second World War (Caparrotta & Ghaffari, 2006; J. Lock & Kirz, 2008; J. M. S. Pearce, 2004). Early psychodynamic theories (discussed more later) conceptualized anorexia and bulimia as related to **oral impregnation**—the unconscious Oedipal wish to become pregnant by oral means (Caparrotta & Ghaffari, 2006; J. Lock & Kirz, 2008; Zerbe, 2010). These psychodynamic explanations notwithstanding, it wasn't until the 1960s and 1970s that anorexia began truly receiving extensive attention (J. Lock & Kirz, 2008), in part due to the groundbreaking work of psychiatrist and psychoanalyst Hilde Bruch (1904–1984). Bruch outlined many of the characteristics of anorexia discussed elsewhere in this chapter—particularly distorted perceptions about body image and problematic family dynamics (Bruch, 1962, 1963, 1971, 1978/2001).

Bulimia first received widespread attention in the late 1970s—although American psychiatrist Albert Stunkard (1922–2014) described symptoms resembling binge eating as early as the 1950s. However, the binge/compensate pattern of bulimia nervosa wasn't formally recognized as a disorder until 1979 when British psychiatrist Gerald Russell (1928–2018) coined the term (G. Russell, 1979; G. F. M. Russell, 2004). Thus, despite eating problems being seen throughout history, current notions of anorexia, bulimia, and binge-eating disorder are relatively recent historical developments. While anorexia has been in DSM since 1952, bulimia didn't appear until 1980 and binge-eating disorder wasn't added until 2013.

9.5 Pica

Pica has been documented throughout history, although depending on the time and place "it has been regarded as a psychiatric disease, a culturally sanctioned practice or a sequel to poverty and famine" (Woywodt & Kiss, 2002, p. 143). Between the sixteenth and twentieth centuries, it was often considered a symptom of other disorders more often that a disorder unto itself (Parry-Jones & Parry-Jones, 1992). The most identified type of pica in historical descriptions is **geophagia**, the intentional eating of dirt, soil, or clay (Mishori & McHale, 2014; Woywodt & Kiss, 2002). Accounts

Oral impregnation: Psychodynamic conceptualization of eating disorders in which patients have an unconscious Oedipal wish to become pregnant by oral means.

Geophagia: Form of pica in which a person intentionally eats dirt, soil, or clay.

of geophagia were recorded in ancient Greece (by Hippocrates himself), the Roman Empire, sixth-century Turkey, the Middle Ages, and throughout the sixteenth through nineteenth centuries (Woywodt & Kiss, 2002).

9.6 Rumination

Although rumination in animals—especially regurgitation and re-chewing of food by cows ("chewing the cud")—has been written about since ancient Greece, the first historical attention to it in humans didn't occur until the seventeenth century (Parry-Jones, 1994). The Italian anatomist Fabricius ab Aquapendente (1537–1619) believed that human ruminators were somehow descended from cows; that is, they had some sort of bovine ancestry (Parry-Jones, 1994). By the eighteenth century, **mercyism** (another name for rumination in humans) was beginning to be studied as a digestive disorder (Parry-Jones, 1994). Medical accounts of mercyism expanded in the nineteenth century; some of the patients described used their ruminating abilities to get out of military service or earn a living by performing in side shows and circuses (Parry-Jones, 1994). By the twentieth century, discussions of rumination focused increasingly on its frequency among infants and adults with intellectual disabilities; however, it was recognized that some anorexics or bulimics also ruminated (Parry-Jones, 1994). Interestingly, the term "rumination"—which emphasized obsessional regurgitating, re-chewing, and re-swallowing of food—also came to refer to obsessional mental reflection. This might be why earlier editions of ICD classified rumination as both an aspect of obsessive-compulsive disorder (OCD) and as a somatic disorder of digestive origins (Parry-Jones, 1994).

> **Mercyism:** Another name for rumination in humans; used in past historic eras.

BIOLOGICAL PERSPECTIVES

9.7 Brain Chemistry Perspectives

Monoamine Neurotransmitters

Neurotransmitters important in regulating mood, emotion, memory, and anxiety are also relevant to weight and feeding—including the monoamine neurotransmitters (dopamine, norepinephrine, and serotonin), the inhibitory neurotransmitter gamma-aminobutyric acid (GABA), and the excitatory neurotransmitter glutamate (Haleem, 2012; A. Higgins, 2018; McElroy et al., 2010; S. L. Murray & Holton, 2021; Pruccoli et al., 2021; Södersten et al., 2016). Here we focus mainly on the monoamine neurotransmitters. Current consensus is that dopamine and serotonin are implicated in anorexia, with norepinephrine also playing a role (A. Higgins, 2018; Hildebrandt & Downey, 2013). For bulimia, many view the main culprit as serotonin (Hildebrandt & Downey, 2013), although dopamine plays a notable role in binge eating (Y. Yu et al., 2022). ARFID is a new diagnosis, so there is little research on its neurochemistry (G. K. W. Frank et al., 2019; J. Steinglass et al., 2016).

Serotonin

A lot of anorexia and bulimia research has focused on serotonin. Some but not all suggests that serotonin levels are decreased in people with active symptoms of bulimia (Jimerson et al., 1997; W. Kaye, 2008; W. H. Kaye et al., 1998; Krzystanek & Pałasz, 2020). Decreased serotonin levels are also found (even more consistently than in bulimia) among active anorexics (Haleem, 2012; A. Higgins, 2018; Hildebrandt & Downey, 2013; W. H. Kaye et al., 2005, 2009, 2013). However, serotonin deficiencies may be the result of anorexia and bulimia rather than their cause. Here's why: When people don't eat, they fail to take in an essential amino acid obtained from food called **tryptophan** (Haleem, 2012; A. Higgins, 2018; W. Kaye, 2008). The body requires tryptophan to make serotonin. Therefore, someone who isn't eating properly lacks enough tryptophan to make serotonin. Consequently, serotonin levels drop (Haleem, 2012; A. Higgins, 2018; W. Kaye, 2008). This may explain why recovering anorexics and bulimics whose eating returns to normal show surges in serotonin levels (Hildebrandt & Downey, 2013). They finally have sufficient tryptophan necessary to produce serotonin again. Thus, many patients show decreased serotonin levels during anorexia or bulimia, but increased serotonin levels once recovered (W. Kaye, 2008; W. H. Kaye et al., 1991; Phillipou et al., 2014). While this suggests that low serotonin levels result

> **Tryptophan:** Amino acid obtained from food that is required to produce the neurotransmitter serotonin.

from (rather than cause) eating disorders, additional research on anorexia and bulimia implies that dysregulation of the serotonin system may predispose people to developing symptoms in the first place and persist even after recovery (Haleem, 2012; A. Higgins, 2018; Hildebrandt & Downey, 2013; Phillipou et al., 2014).

Dopamine

Dopamine, a neurotransmitter important to both appetite and reward, appears to play a part in eating problems, especially anorexia. Dopamine levels tend to be lower than normal in non-recovered anorexic patients, but—as with serotonin—they increase in recovered patients (Brambilla et al., 2001; W. H. Kaye, Ebert, Gwirtsman, et al., 1984; W. H. Kaye, Ebert, Raleigh, et al., 1984; Phillipou et al., 2014). Notably, this pattern is more consistent in the binge-purge subtype of anorexia than the restricting subtype (W. H. Kaye et al., 1999; Phillipou et al., 2014). In addition to dopamine levels, dopamine receptor sensitivity may be decreased among anorexic patients (Hildebrandt & Downey, 2013; Phillipou et al., 2014).

Dopamine has also been implicated in binge eating but with inconsistent results. Some studies find increased dopamine activity, but others find decreased activity—leading to suspicions that dopamine dysfunction varies in different stages of binge eating (Y. Yu et al., 2022). Unfortunately, research on dopamine's role in binge eating hasn't consistently defined "rewards." Does it refer to motivation to eat, enjoyment of eating, or reinforcement of eating (Salamone & Correa, 2013)? While dopamine's exact role remains unclear, it appears important in understanding bingeing due to its involvement in eating behavior, decision-making, and emotional response to "rewards" (W. Kaye, 2008; Y. Yu et al., 2022).

Psychopharmacology for Eating Problems
Antidepressants

SSRIs and other antidepressants are prescribed for anorexia, bulimia, BED, and ARFID—not surprising given the comorbidity of eating issues with other problems tied to serotonin, notably depression and OCD. For anorexia, SSRIs do not work very well (Bodell & Keel, 2010; Flament et al., 2012; A. S. Kaplan & Howlett, 2010; J. Lock & Kirz, 2008; Muratore & Attia, 2022; Powers & Bruty, 2009; Rossi et al., 2007; K. J. Steffen et al., 2014; J. Steinglass et al., 2016). This might be because starving anorexics lack enough tryptophan to produce the serotonin that SSRIs act upon (Powers & Bruty, 2009). Until patients with anorexia increase their eating, SSRIs do little for them. SSRIs and other antidepressants work better for bulimia, with *fluoxetine* (trade names Prozac and Sarafem) generally considered the "gold standard" (Broft et al., 2010; Muratore & Attia, 2022; J. R. Shapiro et al., 2007). However, these drugs are not a bulimia cure-all. They only mildly improve symptoms and relapse remains a problem (Luzier et al., 2019; McElroy et al., 2010, 2019; Milano & Capasso, 2019; J. E. Mitchell et al., 2013). Further, bulimia dosages need to be higher than for other problems, increasing side effects and noncompliance (Flament et al., 2012; J. E. Mitchell et al., 2013; Powers & Bruty, 2009). Similarly, antidepressants improve symptoms of BED but rarely result in full remission (Bodell & Devlin, 2010; Flament et al., 2012; Goracci et al., 2015; J. E. Mitchell et al., 2007; Reas & Grilo, 2014). As for ARFID, early evidence suggests SSRIs might reduce symptoms, especially comorbid depression and anxiety (Mahr et al., 2022; Spettigue et al., 2018). However, there is not much research yet and randomized controlled trials (RCTs) are needed (Spettigue et al., 2018; J. Steinglass et al., 2016).

Marta

Marta might be prescribed an SSRI for her anorexia. However, for the drug to help, Marta would first need to improve her food intake to insure she had enough tryptophan in her system. Therefore, other interventions—such as psychotherapy or, under dire circumstances, forced feeding—might be necessary first. Even so, because SSRIs aren't especially effective for anorexia, Marta might not benefit much from taking them.

Antipsychotics

In addition to antidepressants, antipsychotics—which typically target dopamine—are also prescribed for eating problems. Anorexic patients are periodically given atypical antipsychotics; *olanzapine* is the most researched and prescribed, but *risperidone, quetiapine, aripiprazole,* and *ziprasadone* are sometimes used too (Çöpür & Çöpür, 2020; A. S. Kaplan & Howlett, 2010; McElroy et al., 2010; Milano & Capasso, 2019; J. Steinglass et al., 2016). These drugs reduce depression and aggression, and induce weight gain—something desirable when treating anorexia (Milano & Capasso, 2019). Still, their effectiveness for anorexia is unclear, and their side effects are significant (Dold et al., 2015; J. Hagman et al., 2011; Halmi, 2013; Kishi et al., 2012; McElroy et al., 2019; Newman-Toker, 2000; Powers & Bruty, 2009; J. Steinglass et al., 2016). Thus, antipsychotics are typically used cautiously with anorexia (Milano & Capasso, 2019).

Marta

If the goal was weight gain, our anorexic case study client Marta might be prescribed an antipsychotic such as olanzapine. The antipsychotic would be instead of or in addition to any SSRI she was taking. Of course, Marta would need to be monitored for potential side effects. Ideally, the antipsychotic would help her regain lost weight, though it isn't guaranteed to work.

There is little research on using antipsychotics for bulimia, BED, or ARFID. Atypical antipsychotics may be contraindicated for bulimia and BED, as they can make symptoms worse (McElroy et al., 2010, 2019). Their utility for ARFID isn't clear either because research in this area is currently lacking (Muratore & Attia, 2022; J. Steinglass et al., 2016).

Other Drugs

The only drug approved in the United States for BED is *lisdexamfetamine* (trade name Vyvanse), a stimulant that reduces bingeing and weight—perhaps by affecting brain regions related to appetite, rewards, and cognitive processing (E. Schneider et al., 2021). Other drugs prescribed for eating problems include mood stabilizers, anticonvulsants, and benzodiazepines. The evidence for mood stabilizers such as *lamotrigine* is limited but encouraging (Bodell & Devlin, 2010, 2010; M. J. Kaplan, 2014; Powers & Bruty, 2009; Rossi et al., 2007; Trunko et al., 2017). Further, the anticonvulsant *topiramate* (a GABA/glutamate receptor antagonist) shows promise for reducing bingeing and purging (McElroy et al., 2019; Milano & Capasso, 2019). Finally, benzodiazepines (which enhance activity of the inhibitory neurotransmitter GABA; see Chapter 6) are used to reduce apprehension before meals in anorexia and ARFID patients, though it is not clear how well they work (J. Steinglass et al., 2016).

Psychopharmacology for Feeding Problems

The causes of pica and rumination are not clear. There are few randomized controlled trials on how to treat these problems (A. S. Hartmann et al., 2012; Martinez et al., 2021; H. B. Murray et al., 2019). SSRIs, tricyclics, and bupropion have all been used to treat to pica (Baheretibeb et al., 2008; Bhatia & Gupta, 2009; Ginsberg, 2006; Gundogar et al., 2003; Hergüner et al., 2008; Schreier, 1990). This is probably because some clinicians conceptualize pica as a variant of obsessive-compulsive disorder—and OCD is often treated with antidepressants (see Chapter 5) (Bharti et al., 2015; Gundogar et al., 2003; Hergüner et al., 2008; Schreier, 1990). When it comes to rumination, evidence suggests that *baclofen*, a skeletal muscle relaxant, can reduce regurgitation (Martinez et al., 2021; H. B. Murray et al., 2019).

Alastair

Our pica client, Alastair, might be given an SSRI to prevent him from eating things he isn't supposed to. Prescribing it would be wholly at the discretion of the doctor, who would have little research on which to base her decision.

> **Simone**
> *For her rumination symptoms, a doctor might prescribe Simon baclofen because research suggests it can reduce regurgitation.*

9.8 Brain Structure and Function Perspectives

The Hypothalamus and the HPA Axis

Given its roles in regulating involuntary sensations like hunger, the hypothalamus may play a major role in eating problems (J. H. Jennings et al., 2013; Krasne, 1962). It is part of the hypothalamic-pituitary-adrenal (HPA) axis (mentioned in several previous chapters), which produces cortisol, an anti-inflammatory stress hormone. People with anorexia often show elevated cortisol levels, suggesting hyperactivity of the HPA axis (Connan et al., 2007; Hildebrandt & Downey, 2013; Licinio et al., 1996; Lo Sauro et al., 2008; Luz Neto et al., 2019). However, it is unclear whether HPA dysfunction is a cause or result of anorexia; it could be due to starvation and weight loss (Bou Khalil et al., 2017). This might explain why cortisol levels increase less in bulimia than anorexia (Lo Sauro et al., 2008), though admittedly there is less data on bulimia from which to draw conclusions (Luz Neto et al., 2019).

While more responsive in anorexia and bulimia, the HPA axis is less responsive in binge eating (N. Rosenberg et al., 2013). One explanation for this is that binge eaters experience chronic stress. This is important because while short-term stress is correlated with increased HPA axis activity and more cortisol, chronic stress results in decreased HPA activity and less cortisol—something also common in posttraumatic stress (see Chapter 7). Thus, it makes sense that eating disorders and posttraumatic stress often co-occur (Brewerton, 2007; Ferrell et al., 2022). Eating issues might be one way of responding to posttraumatic stress. This could be why, despite generally being overactive in anorexia, the HPA axis sometimes appears underactive (Het et al., 2015; Marciello et al., 2020). There might be childhood trauma or chronic stress in such cases.

Keep in mind that existing research on the HPA axis and eating problems is correlational, not causal. Does stress lead to altered eating, which then impacts the HPA axis? Or does HPA axis dysfunction lead to stress, which then yields altered eating? Hopefully, future research will address these questions.

Reward Pathway Disturbances

Some suspect eating problems are a type of addiction because the same brain systems affected by substance abuse (see Chapter 11) are also impacted in anorexia, bulimia, and BED—with anorexics unresponsive to rewards and bulimics, binge eaters, and obese individuals too responsive to them (Colaianni & Festini, 2021; Hauck et al., 2020; W. H. Kaye et al., 2013; O'Hara et al., 2015; R. J. Park et al., 2014; Schreiber et al., 2013; D. G. Smith & Robbins, 2013; Volkow et al., 2013; R. A. Wise, 2013). Dopamine, already mentioned for its relevance to eating problems, is involved in this as part of the brain's *reward pathway* (i.e., **mesolimbic pathway**; again, see Chapter 11). In cases of binge eating and obesity, dysfunctional dopamine transmission along the mesolimbic pathway is suspected of causing addiction to food (Morales & Berridge, 2020; D. G. Smith & Robbins, 2013; Volkow et al., 2013; Y. Yu et al., 2022). Precisely what goes wrong in the mesolimbic pathway continues being researched.

Mesolimbic pathway: Brain pathway important in responding to rewards.

Other Brain Correlates
Ventricle Size and Brain Volume

Symptomatic anorexic patients often have larger brain ventricles (cavities containing cerebrospinal fluid), as well as less gray and white matter, which indicates brain volume reduction (Alfano et al., 2020; Bär et al., 2015; Friederich et al., 2012; Fujisawa et al., 2015; Hildebrandt & Downey, 2013; Phillipou et al., 2014, 2018; Suchan et al., 2010; Titova et al., 2013). Most brain volume reductions reverse as patients regain weight (Friederich et al., 2012; Frintrop et al., 2019;

Hildebrandt & Downey, 2013; Lambe et al., 1997; Roberto et al., 2011; J. Seitz et al., 2018). Similar patterns are found in bulimia, although gray matter volume might not decrease as much (Amianto et al., 2013; Donnelly et al., 2018; Schäfer et al., 2010).

Anterior Insula

The *anterior insula*—important in regulating autonomic activities such as hunger—is another brain structure implicated in eating problems (Hildebrandt & Downey, 2013; Miranda-Olivos et al., 2021). Anterior insula activity correlates with feelings of disgust among anorexics, possibly explaining their lack of interest in food (Aharoni & Hertz, 2012; L. M. Anderson et al., 2021; Hildebrandt & Downey, 2013). Whereas anterior insula impairment may keep anorexics from identifying when they're hungry, it could provide too strong a hunger signal in bulimia and BED (Oberndorfer et al., 2013). More research is needed.

9.9 Genetic Perspectives

Family and Twin Studies

Family studies find that relatives of people diagnosed with anorexia or bulimia are more likely to develop their own eating issues (Bulik et al., 2019; Hudson et al., 1987; Lilenfield et al., 1998; D. Stein et al., 1999; Strober et al., 2000). However, family studies don't control for shared environment. People with eating problems might have inherited problematic eating habits, been raised in a way that fostered such habits, or both.

Twin studies suggest that eating issues are indeed influenced by genetics (Fairweather-Schmidt & Wade, 2015; Javaras et al., 2008; Kendler et al., 1991; Klump et al., 2001; Mazzeo & Bulik, 2009; Munn-Chernoff et al., 2013; T. L. Root et al., 2010; Wade et al., 2008). However, the extent of this influence is disputed, with some researchers warning that twin and other genetic studies overrate the role of genes (Bulik et al., 2000; Ross, 2006). This possibly explains the wide variation in heritability estimates for eating disorders—anywhere between 48 percent and 88 percent for anorexia and 28 percent and 83 percent for bulimia (A. E. Becker et al., 2004; Hinney & Volckmar, 2013). Despite this wide variation, many researchers settle on heritability estimates in the low to mid 50 percent range for anorexia, bulimia, and BED (Bulik et al., 2006; Culbert et al., 2015; Javaras et al., 2008). If such estimates are accepted, it means that a little more than 50 percent of differences in anorexia, bulimia, and binge eating respectively can be attributed to genes. The remaining differences would be due to environment. Given the wide range of heritability estimates, many researchers simply conclude that genes and environment interact in complex ways to shape the development of eating problems, with the precise contribution of each unclear at this time (A. E. Becker et al., 2004; Culbert et al., 2015; Fairweather-Schmidt & Wade, 2015; Mazzeo & Bulik, 2009).

Genetic Marker Research

In genetic marker studies, many different gene indicators have been correlated with eating problems (Klump & Culbert, 2007; Peñas-Lledó et al., 2012; Slof-Op 't Landt et al., 2011, 2014, 2013; Wade et al., 2013). Given the suspected importance of serotonin and dopamine in disordered eating, it isn't surprising that serotonergic and dopaminergic genes have been the focus of candidate gene studies (first discussed in Chapter 5), which test whether specific genes correlate with particular disorders or symptoms (Munn-Chernoff & Baker, 2016). Some serotonergic and dopaminergic candidate gene studies have yielded significant findings (Lee & Lin, 2010; Munn-Chernoff & Baker, 2016). However, the results of candidate gene studies to date are considered inconsistent and inconclusive (Brandys et al., 2015; Munn-Chernoff & Baker, 2016; Munn-Chernoff et al., 2012; Trace et al., 2013).

The same is true of genome-wide association studies (GWAS, introduced in Chapter 4), which include all the genes of the genome rather than only candidate genes suspected of being relevant to a given disorder (Munn-Chernoff & Baker, 2016). Because they are testing every possible gene there is, GWAS research requires an enormous number of participants to find significant results. Not surprisingly then, GWAS investigations of eating problems haven't yielded much in terms of significant results, but they have identified promising genes worthy of attention (Boraska et al., 2012,

2014; Brandys et al., 2015; Munn-Chernoff & Baker, 2016). Based on the inconclusive findings of genetic association studies, it is hard to infer which genes are most important in eating problems.

Despite the uncertainty, it is easy to see why genetic association studies hold great appeal. In one intriguing study, the Met allele on the COMT gene was associated with symptoms of bulimia (Donofry et al., 2014). This is noteworthy because, as you may recall from Chapter 6, the Met allele has also been associated with obsessive-compulsive disorder (OCD) in females (S. Taylor, 2013). This suggests that OCD and eating problems could have similar biological origins. Even though a lot more research is needed to test such a hypothesis, the idea that we might find common genetic underpinnings for different disorders is precisely the kind of thing that motivates Research Domain Criteria (RDoC) researchers interested in building a diagnostic system based on biological markers (such as genes!) rather than behavioral symptoms. It is also what makes genetic association studies appealing. Still, it is important to keep in mind the correlational (rather than causal) nature of these studies. Just because a gene is associated with a particular disorder doesn't mean that it causes that disorder.

9.10 Evolutionary Perspectives

Evolutionary Explanations of Anorexia and Bulimia

Sexual competition hypothesis: Eating problems occur because women must compete to attract men by maintaining a "nubile" hourglass shape; even greater emphasis on thin shape emerges in industrial societies with less familial help to secure women mates.

The **sexual competition hypothesis** proposes that eating problems like anorexia and bulimia emerge because women must compete with one another to attract men (Abed, 1998; Faer et al., 2005; Mealey, 2000). This evolutionary hypothesis claims that women attract men by maintaining a desirable body shape—the "nubile" hourglass shape with a low waist to hip ratio (Abed, 1998; Kardum et al., 2008). Anorexia and bulimia, with their focus on thinness, help females achieve this sort of body shape. Not only does the sexual competition hypothesis argue that eating problems are caused by female competition to be thin and attract mates, but it also tries to explain the increase in eating disorders in industrialized societies by pointing out how—in industrial (compared with preindustrial) societies—families are less involved in helping their daughters obtain mates. Without things like dowries and prearranged marriages, women are required to secure mates on their own without much family assistance. This places extra pressure on women to maintain a desirably thin shape so they can successfully attract men. There are several drawbacks of the sexual competition hypothesis: (a) it assumes there are universal ideals of female attractiveness (mainly, being thin); (b) it doesn't explain what specific events trigger eating disorders; and (c) it doesn't account for eating disorders in men (Abed, 1998; Kardum et al., 2008).

Reproductive suppression hypothesis: Anorexia is a female strategy for maximizing long-term productive success by shutting down reproductive capacity through self-starvation during times when conditions are not optimal for having babies.

The **reproductive suppression hypothesis** was first developed to explain animal mating behavior, but was later used to understand anorexia in women (Condit, 1990; Kardum et al., 2008; Salmon & Crawford, 2012; Salmon et al., 2008; Voland & Voland, 1989; Wasser & Barash, 1983). It holds that anorexia is a female strategy for maximizing long-term reproductive success. According to this hypothesis, anorexic behaviors, which shut down a woman's reproductive capacity, are adaptive when current conditions aren't optimal for having babies. How so? Research suggests that girls who reach sexual maturity sooner are more likely to marry early, have children early, and be of lower socioeconomic status (SES) (probably because rather than going to school and gaining the education necessary to improve their economic standing, they are raising babies) (Condit, 1990). Teenage girls who hit puberty sooner may benefit from anorexia because the loss of menstruation that often accompanies it prevents them from carrying a baby to term. The reproductive suppression hypothesis predicts that anorexic behaviors will decrease later in life as anorexic girls grow into economically secure women who are now in a better situation to have and raise kids. While compelling in some ways, this hypothesis has been criticized for not explaining why (a) anorexics experience distorted body image and hyperactivity; (b) less costly means for inducing amenorrhea didn't evolve instead; (c) anorexia disproportionately affects wealthy girls at low risk for economic problems; and (d) men and postmenopausal women sometimes develop anorexia (Guisinger, 2003; Kardum et al., 2008).

Adapted to flee famine hypothesis: Anorexia evolved to assist those facing famine; anorexic symptoms of feeling energetic and restless while remaining in denial about weight loss encourages migration to new locations in search of food.

The **adapted to flee famine hypothesis** argues that anorexia evolved to assist those facing famine (Guisinger, 2003). It hypothesizes that anorexia's symptoms are adaptive because they lead people to feel energetic and restless (i.e., "hyperactive") while remaining in denial about their extreme weight loss. This makes it easier for them to migrate to new locations in search of food.

The main drawback of this explanation is that it while it might account for anorexic behaviors under famine conditions, it doesn't really explain why anorexics refuse to eat when plenty of food is available (Kardum et al., 2008).

Evolution and Binge Eating

When it comes to binge eating and obesity, evolutionary explanations contend that ancestral humans didn't have as much access to food as we do today. Therefore, eating as much as possible was adaptive because it wasn't known when food would next be available (Kardum et al., 2008; Pinel et al., 2000). Today we still eat as if such scarcity exists, even when there is plenty of food. Further, the snacks we eat today (e.g., energy drinks, granola bars) have a lot more calories in them than the snacks ancient humans ate (e.g., wild berries and seeds), but people don't naturally take this into account by adjusting their non-snack food intake (de Graaf, 2006). This therefore fosters overeating and obesity.

Critique of Evolutionary Perspectives

Evolutionary explanations of eating problems are intriguing. However, they are difficult to study because they rely on theoretical assumptions about what ancestral life was like for humans. Further, critics contend that they don't account for sociocultural factors very well. Sociologists have complained that evolutionary psychology "offers an impoverished view of culture" (S. Jackson & Rees, 2007, p. 920). How so? By reducing "the entirety of human social life … to the heterosexual, reproductive imperative: the drive to pass on our genes to the next generation" (S. Jackson & Rees, 2007, p. 918). According to such critics, complex human problems like eating and feeding difficulties are better explained sociologically and cannot be understood exclusively in evolutionary terms. Whether you find this critique sensible or not likely reflects the extent to which you are sympathetic to evolutionary psychological perspectives.

9.11 Immune System Perspectives

There is substantial evidence that anorexia is tied to increased levels of inflammatory cytokines, the small proteins produced by the immune system (Dalton et al., 2018; D. Gibson & Mehler, 2019). Evidence for increased cytokines in bulimia is less clear (Corcos et al., 2003; Dalton et al., 2018; Tabasi et al., 2020). However, a small body of research has linked the loss of control over eating that is characteristic of bingeing to elevated cytokine levels (Y. Yu et al., 2021). These findings are intriguing given that cytokines—as part of the immune system's response to invading foreign bodies—produce not only fever, but also decreased appetite and food intake (Marcos, 2000). Because eating problems often co-occur with depression, it is noteworthy that depression also involves immune system inflammation (see Chapter 5) (Felger & Lotrich, 2013; C.-H. Lee & Giuliani, 2019; N. A. L. Ruiz et al., 2022; J. J. Young et al., 2014). However, it isn't clear that increased cytokines cause or are caused by eating problems. When eating returns to normal, so do cytokine levels (Corcos et al., 2003).

Immune-system research also suggests that people with anorexia and bulimia are resistant to infections (R. F. Brown et al., 2008; Golla et al., 1981; Marcos, 2000; Marcos et al., 2003). However, this puzzling finding hasn't been consistently replicated and remains controversial (DeSarbo & DeSarbo, 2020). Beyond infections, people diagnosed with anorexia, bulimia, or BED are at increased risk for autoimmune diseases (A. Hedman et al., 2019; Raevuori et al., 2014). Finally, gut microbiota appear important in eating disorders because they influence neurotransmitter levels via the gut–brain axis (T. Liu et al., 2020). As these findings illustrate, the immune system is important in eating issues, even if there is much to learn.

9.12 Evaluating Biological Perspectives

Biological research on eating issues has mostly been correlational. We must therefore be careful not to incorrectly make causal inferences. All we currently know is that certain biological differences are related to problematic eating. Precisely how requires further investigation.

Biological explanations focus mainly on physiological aspects of eating problems, such as understanding the brain's role in hunger. This makes them helpful in identifying neurotransmitters and brain structures implicated in appetite and eating behavior. However, biological perspectives have little to say about the psychological components of eating problems. For instance, why do people with anorexia and bulimia experience distorted body image issues? Why are they so fearful about becoming overweight? For such questions, we may need to look beyond biological explanations.

Finally, biological perspectives frequently minimize or overlook sociocultural factors. Yet eating habits always develop within a cultural context. Many researchers feel the wider culture is equally or more important than biology in shaping problematic and non-problematic eating habits and how people experience their bodies—especially in Western industrialized societies that place extraordinary value on thinness.

PSYCHOLOGICAL PERSPECTIVES

9.13 Psychodynamic Perspectives

Personality Factors Associated with Eating Problems

Psychological perspectives often stress the importance of personality factors in eating issues. *Perfectionism* and *negative emotionality* (frequently experiencing anxiety, sadness, stress, and anger) strongly correlate with all eating disorders (Dahlenburg et al., 2019a; Farstad et al., 2016; Franco-Paredes et al., 2005). However, *impulsivity* is associated specifically with binge eating (M. M. Carr et al., 2021; Farstad et al., 2016; M. Howard et al., 2020). Therapies targeting perfectionism might improve problematic eating, but more research is needed (Galloway et al., 2022; M. Goldstein et al., 2014; Lloyd et al., 2015; K. Robinson & Wade, 2021).

Early Psychoanalytic Conceptualizations of Anorexia

Classic psychoanalysis traced anorexia back to oral stage conflicts. The anorexic patient was viewed as having a weak ego that was unable to manage strong oral id impulses—especially the unconscious desire for oral impregnation (defined earlier as yearning to become pregnant by oral means) (Caparrotta & Ghaffari, 2006; J. Lock & Kirz, 2008). Anorexia was seen as a way to manage unacceptable oral impregnation wishes and reassert control (Zerbe, 2010). By starving themselves and keeping their bodies from developing and becoming sexualized, anorexic girls were thought to reject these inappropriate impulses (V. V. McIntosh et al., 2000). Oral impregnation strikes many people today as sexist and outdated. It is no longer an accepted psychoanalytic explanation. However, seeing anorexia as a way to exert control over frightening and overwhelming feelings (sexual or otherwise) remains central to modern psychodynamic conceptualizations (Winston, 2012).

Early psychodynamic explanations also often portrayed anorexia as a type of hysteria (Zerbe, 2010). So even though DSM distinguishes eating disorders from somatic symptom disorders (discussed in Chapter 8), psychodynamic perspectives don't always abide by this distinction. They often view eating disorders as types of somatic symptom disorders. This makes sense because anorexia and bulimia involve somatic symptoms, often related to problematic eating (e.g., gastritis, stomach pain, nausea, indigestion, osteoporosis, and dental issues) (Erdur et al., 2012; Weigel et al., 2019).

Modern Psychodynamic Approaches

Modern psychodynamic perspectives shift from classic psychoanalytic drive theory to relationship-focused explanations of eating problems. Many of them are rooted in object relations therapy and attachment theory (see Chapter 2) (Clinton, 2006; G. A. Tasca & Balfour, 2014, 2019). What they generally share is the view that eating problems can be traced back to early parent–child interactions. Specifically, eating issues arise when caregivers resist their children's attempts to establish independence and autonomy (Bruch, 1978/2001; Zerbe, 2010). Instead of providing the love and support needed to make their children feel safe and secure, caregivers react anxiously, angrily, or indifferently. In response, the children feel pressure to be "perfect" by complying with (rather than establishing autonomy from) their parents' expectations and demands (Bruch, 1978/2001). Eating (or refusing to) becomes a way for such children to comfort themselves and feel a sense of control in response to having been mistreated (Zerbe, 2010). Though their perfectionism makes them seem perfect to others, patients with eating disorders live "in continuous fear of not being loved and acknowledged" (Bruch, 1978/2001, p. 53). Their problematic eating expresses an unfulfilled desire for "independence, autonomy, and age-appropriate dependence on other people" (Zerbe, 2010, p. 342). A growing body of evidence affirms the suspected link between attachment insecurity and problematic eating (Cortés-García et al., 2019; Faber et al., 2018; Forsén Mantilla et al., 2019).

Psychodynamic therapies for disordered eating help patients (a) gain insight into past relationship patterns, and (b) replace them with more functional ways of interacting (G. A. Tasca & Balfour, 2019). The therapist points out how the patient's dysfunctional patterns play out in session, as well as with people in the patient's life. Therapy provides a corrective emotional experience (see Chapter 2)—a caring, safe, and secure relationship with the therapist very different from what was experienced in the past. As new relationship patterns are learned, eating disorder symptoms disappear because they are no longer needed to cope. Research on psychodynamic therapy for eating problems holds promise, but there is not much of it and there are few randomized controlled trials (Abbate-Daga et al., 2016; Abbate-Daga & Marzola, 2017; Stefini et al., 2017; Zipfel et al., 2014).

Marta

If Marta sought psychodynamic therapy for her anorexia, she would begin projecting her conflicted feelings about being controlled and criticized by others onto her therapist. She might even come to feel controlled and criticized by him—even if he wasn't treating her in a controlling or critical manner. The therapist would openly discuss Marta's dysfunctional relationship patterns with her, providing her insight into how others experience her. She would start seeing how she feels obliged to go along with what she assumes those around her want—such as pursuing ballet throughout her childhood because her mother wanted her to be a dancer. Therapy would provide Marta with a "corrective emotional experience." She would realize that just because her mother is controlling and critical doesn't mean all relationships must be like that. As Marta came to learn new and healthier ways of relating to her therapist, her anorexic symptoms—which served as a way for her to assert control in situations where she felt she didn't have any—would dissipate. She would also begin generalizing her new relational patterns to others besides her therapist.

Interpersonal Therapy (IPT)

Interpersonal therapy (IPT) is a brief therapy influenced by interpersonal theorists like Harry Stack Sullivan. As noted in Chapter 5, IPT was originally developed to alleviate depression (Klerman et al., 1984). Like more traditional psychodynamic perspectives, IPT helps patients address interpersonal deficits. However, it is briefer and somewhat narrower in focus. As with depression, IPT for eating problems specifically emphasizes *role transitions*, *interpersonal conflicts*, and *grief* as they relate to symptoms (Apple, 1999; N. L. Burke et al., 2018; V. V. McIntosh et al., 2000; R. Murphy et al., 2012; Tanofsky-Kraff & Wilfley, 2010). In IPT, eating disorder symptoms are viewed as ways to avoid dealing with pressing interpersonal issues. For instance, "a female patient who avoids intimacy with her husband may attribute her avoidance to body dissatisfaction related to her obesity. She may wish to discuss her body concerns at great length to circumvent actual difficulties in communication with her husband" (Tanofsky-Kraff & Wilfley, 2010, p. 282). To avoid this sort of pitfall, IPT therapists don't spend much time talking with patients about their eating independent of its connection to dysfunctional relational patterns. Instead, IPT highlights how eating symptoms serve a purpose in interpersonal relationships—for instance, they can be a way to avoid grief or intimacy. Studies of IPT for eating problems generally find it to be a solid alternative to CBT (discussed below), with some evidence it might be as effective as CBT for anorexia and binge eating (Agras & Bohon, 2021; Miniati et al., 2018).

9.14 Cognitive-Behavioral Perspectives

Behavioral Interventions

Anorexia, Bulimia, and Binge Eating

Exposure therapies (introduced in Chapter 2; revisited in Chapters 6–7) expose clients to feared objects and situations to condition new emotional responses. ***In vivo* food exposure** is a type of *in vivo* exposure used to change the eating habits in anorexia, bulimia, and binge eating (Koskina et al., 2013; Reilly et al., 2017). It is *in vivo* because it is exposure done in real life. In *exposure plus response prevention of purging*, patients are prevented from purging after bingeing. This decreases their conditioned fear about overeating by showing them that nothing terrible happens if they don't purge (Koskina et al., 2013). In *exposure plus response prevention of bingeing*, patients are exposed to foods they usually binge on but are then prevented from doing so. This reconditions these foods so they no longer are conditioned stimuli for bingeing (Koskina et al., 2013). Finally, in *food exposure for anorexia*, patients are gradually exposed to food to reduce fear of food and food avoidance (Koskina et al., 2013; J. E. Steinglass et al., 2011).

The evidence for exposure therapies for bingeing and purging is mixed, with more studies needed (R. M. Butler & Heimberg, 2020). There are also calls for further research on exposure therapies for anorexia, though the small body of existing research suggests it can be helpful (R. M. Butler & Heimberg, 2020). From a practical standpoint, reluctant anorexia patients might be more open to virtual reality than *in vivo* exposure (R. M. Butler & Heimberg, 2020). Perhaps due to logistical difficulties and the meager research evidence to date, exposure therapies aren't often used for eating problems (Koskina et al., 2013; J. E. Steinglass et al., 2011).

Avoidant-Restrictive Food Intake

Behavioral parent-training is a psychoeducational approach that teaches parents behavioral techniques for reducing symptoms of avoidant-restrictive food intake in their children (J. Murphy & Zlomke, 2016). Appropriate parenting behaviors are modeled, and parents are taught to differentially reinforce desirable eating behaviors. Preliminary evidence suggests behavioral parent-training decreases avoidant-restrictive eating (J. Murphy & Zlomke, 2016). It can be used with other eating problems, too. However, further research on using it for avoidant-restrictive food intake issues is needed given that ARFID is a new disorder (it first appeared in DSM-5) that currently lacks evidence-based interventions (Bryant-Waugh et al., 2021).

> **Wendy**
>
> *Were Wendy's parents to pursue behavioral parent-training to address her avoidant-restrictive eating, they would learn techniques for reinforcing desired eating behaviors. For instance, Wendy's parents would be taught to smile and respond positively when Wendy tried new foods and ate appropriately but to ignore her whining and complaining when she didn't like a food. They would also be taught how to work with Wendy to develop a hierarchy of feared foods (from least to most frightening) for Wendy to try. For each food Wendy ate a bite of, she would receive a reward. For instance, if she ate a piece of carrot, she might receive a half hour of access to her mother's iPad. Over time, Wendy would be reinforced for better eating behaviors and hopefully her eating habits would become less restrictive.*

Pica

A range of behavioral interventions are employed to reduce pica (Mishori & McHale, 2014; Moline et al., 2021). Common techniques include (a) **aversion therapies**, in which patients are punished for eating things they shouldn't (e.g., by squirting them in the face with water or in the mouth with lemon juice); (b) differentially reinforcing desired behaviors incompatible with pica; (c) enriching the person's environment with toys and other engaging stimuli that reinforce behaviors that don't involve eating non-nutritive items; and (d) **overcorrection**, in which an undesired behavior

---

In vivo food exposure: Behavioral technique in which *in vivo* exposure is used to change the eating habits of people diagnosed with eating disorders.

Aversion therapies: Behavior therapy in which undesired behaviors are reduced or eliminated by associating them with something unpleasant (e.g., tastes, smells, pain).

Overcorrection: Behavioral technique in which an undesired behavior is punished by requiring the person to repeatedly engage in an opposite kind of behavior.

is punished by requiring repeated engagement in an opposite kind of behavior (e.g., brushing teeth and using mouthwash after eating something inappropriate such as feces) (McAdam et al., 2004). Research supports most behavioral interventions for pica (N. A. Call et al., 2015; McAdam et al., 2004; Moline et al., 2021). However, some clinicians disapprove of aversive techniques, viewing them as inflicting pain or humiliation on clients. Their use remains controversial (Fredericks et al., 1998; Kirby, 2021).

Alastair

How could aversion therapy reduce Alastair's pica? Every time he attempted to eat something inappropriate, he might be sprayed in the face with water. This would punish him for eating non-nutritive substances. In addition to aversion, Alastair might also be provided with interesting toys. The enjoyment he received from playing with these toys would reinforce non-pica behaviors.

Rumination

Behavioral conceptualizations of rumination focus on how regurgitating, re-chewing, and re-swallowing food is reinforced because it provides oral satisfaction (Lang et al., 2011). Aversion therapy gives ruminators electric shocks or puts something bad tasting in their mouths, but often isn't used due to ethical objections (Fredericks et al., 1998). Non-aversive behavioral interventions replace rumination with other satisfying oral activities, such as gum chewing (Fredericks et al., 1998; Lang et al., 2011). Other behavioral interventions include **diaphragmatic breathing** (a form of "belly breathing" that, when engaged in, prevents regurgitation) and **satiation techniques** (in which patients' regular meals are supplemented with additional food to reduce hunger and make rumination less rewarding) (Absah et al., 2017; Fredericks et al., 1998; Halland et al., 2016; Lang et al., 2011; Sharp et al., 2012). Diaphragmatic breathing appears to have the strongest research support for treating rumination (Halland et al., 2016; H. B. Murray et al., 2019).

Diaphragmatic breathing: Breathing technique that fully engages the diaphragm; used as a behavioral intervention for rumination disorder.

Satiation techniques: Behavioral technique in which regular meals are supplemented with additional food; because rumination often occurs when hungry, it discourages rumination by making the patient less hungry.

Simone

In behavioral therapy for her rumination, Simone might be taught to chew gum instead of regurgitating and re-chewing her food. She also might be given snacks between meals. This would decrease reinforcement for rumination, which often serves to satisfy hunger. Finally, she would be taught diaphragmatic breathing, which is incompatible with regurgitation.

Enhanced Cognitive-Behavioral Therapy (CBT-E)

Enhanced cognitive-behavioral therapy (CBT-E) (also called the *transdiagnostic model*) maintains that there is a "core psychopathology" behind all eating disorders—one in which people base their self-worth not on their achievements, but on their ability to control body weight and shape (Z. Cooper & Grace, 2017; Dudek et al., 2014; Fairburn et al., 1999, 2003; R. Murphy et al., 2010). CBT-E is transdiagnostic because it challenges dividing eating problems into anorexia, bulimia, and binge-eating diagnoses, arguing that people don't neatly fit these categories. According to CBT-E, the core psychopathology across eating disorders is a tendency to cognitively evaluate self-worth in terms of weight and body shape. CBT-E doesn't use traditional cognitive techniques, such as the Daily Record of Dysfunctional Thoughts (DRDT) and challenging core beliefs, because these techniques don't seem to work (Dalle Grave et al., 2013). Instead, psychoeducation is the primary technique employed. Patients are taught how to monitor their eating patterns and identify cognitive distortions that maintain these patterns—especially all-or-nothing thinking and selective attention (Dalle Grave et al., 2013).

Research finds CBT-E effective in reducing eating disorder symptoms, although it works better for bulimia and binge eating than anorexia (which is notoriously difficult to treat) (M. E. Atwood & Friedman, 2020; Dahlenburg et al., 2019b; de Jong et al., 2018). It is unclear if CBT-E is superior to other commonly used therapies for eating disorders (especially over the long-term),

Enhanced cognitive-behavioral therapy (CBT-E): Attributes a "core psychopathology" to all eating disorders, in which self-worth is based not on achievements but on the ability to control body weight and shape; also called the *transdiagnostic model*.

Daemyn

If Daemyn seeks CBT-E for his binge eating, his therapist would zero in on the "core psychopathology" common to all eating issues, namely Daemyn's tendency to base his sense of self on his weight and body shape. The therapist would help Daemyn see how he selectively attends to negative events (e.g., eating too much) while overlooking times he eats properly. Therapy would also raise Daemyn's awareness of his other accomplishments (e.g., his successful career as a computer programmer) so that his weight isn't the main means by which he evaluates his self-worth.

Photo 9.4 The popular podcast *Maintenance Phase* sets out to "debunk the junk science behind health fads, wellness scams and nonsensical nutrition advice," and features frank conversations around the body, eating issues, and their relationships to society. This is a great resource for more information on the issues discussed in this chapter.

SHVETS production/Pexels.

Cognitive-behavioral therapy for ARFID (CBT-AR): CBT treatment for ARFID that uses exposure therapy and psychoeducation to reduce aversion to feared foods.

Cognitive defusion: Acceptance and commitment therapy (ACT) technique in which clients dispassionately observe their thoughts and recognize that they are just thoughts, not absolutes; this lets them separate from and be less influenced by their thoughts.

Thought parade exercise: Acceptance and commitment therapy (ACT) technique in which clients calmly imagine a parade in which people carry signs reproducing their negative thoughts; detached observation of thoughts reduces their influence.

but it is nevertheless considered a highly effective therapy for eating issues (M. E. Atwood & Friedman, 2020). Aspects of CBT-E (as well as other therapy approaches) have even been incorporated into increasingly popular smartphone apps, which can be freely downloaded (S. B. Goldberg et al., 2022; A. S. Juarascio et al., 2015; Wasil et al., 2021).

Cognitive-Behavioral Therapy for ARFID (CBT-AR)

Cognitive-behavioral therapy for ARFID (CBT-AR) holds that some people are highly sensitive to sensory stimulation; they may also fear unpleasant consequences and/or not find food and eating especially interesting (J. J. Thomas et al., 2018). This predisposes them to negative reactions to the odor, texture, and taste of many foods, resulting in restricted eating. CBT-AR is a twenty-session intervention administered over six to twelve months. It combines in-session exposure to feared foods with psychoeducation about CBT, ARFID, and nutritional deficiencies. As ARFID was only added to DSM in 2013, CBT-AR is relatively new, but research on it so far is promising (J. J. Thomas et al., 2020, 2021).

Acceptance and Commitment Therapy (ACT)

Acceptance and commitment therapy (ACT), discussed in Chapters 6 and 7, is used with many presenting problems, including eating issues. The main premise of ACT is that people's thoughts about events—especially their desire to avoid these thoughts—are at the root of emotional distress (Dudek et al., 2014; S. C. Hayes, 2004; S. C. Hayes & Pankey, 2002; Heffner et al., 2002; Manlick et al., 2013; Sandoz et al., 2010; K. G. Wilson & Roberts, 2002). People often experience *fusion* with their thoughts (Dudek et al., 2014; Sandoz et al., 2010). They mistake their private thoughts for absolute truths, merging with these thoughts in upsetting ways that interfere with their openness to other interpretations. Those with eating problems avoid their distressing thoughts by focusing instead on controlling their food intake and weight.

Rather than directly challenging negative thoughts or asking clients to change them, ACT teaches **cognitive defusion**, in which clients dispassionately observe their thoughts and recognize that they are just thoughts, not absolutes (Dudek et al., 2014; S. C. Hayes & Pankey, 2002; Heffner et al., 2002; Manlick et al., 2013; Sandoz et al., 2010; K. G. Wilson & Roberts, 2002). Moment-to-moment awareness lets people separate from and be less influenced by their thoughts. Cognitive defusion allows an event to be experienced "fully for its complexity, without certain emotions or cognitions about the event dominating the experience" (Sandoz et al., 2010, p. 85). The **thought parade exercise** is a good example of a defusion technique. Clients calmly imagine a parade in which people carry signs reproducing their negative thoughts (Heffner et al., 2002). Research suggests ACT reduces eating disorder symptoms and body dissatisfaction, but more and better studies are needed (Fogelkvist et al., 2020; C. Griffiths et al., 2018; M. L. Hill et al., 2020; A. Juarascio et al., 2013; Linardon et al., 2019; Nicolaou et al., 2022).

Zayna

If Zayna sought acceptance and commitment therapy for her bulimia, she might engage in a "thought parade" exercise. Zayna would visualize herself watching a parade in which people held up signs repeating her negative thoughts (e.g., "I look like a pear!" "If I can't control my eating, I'm worthless."). She also might keep track of her weight-related thoughts and behaviors, as well as how much she is able to accept these thoughts and behaviors. The more Zayna can accept her thoughts, the less likely she is to binge and purge.

9.15 Humanistic Perspectives

Emotion-Focused Therapy (EFT)

Humanistic perspectives see eating problems as meaningful solutions to psychological distress. Emotion-focused therapy (EFT) for eating issues helps clients get in touch with negative emotions such as anger, shame, disgust, fear, and sadness (Dolhanty, 2006; Dolhanty & Greenberg, 2009; Ivanova & Watson, 2014). From an EFT perspective, people who restrict food intake tend to suppress negative emotions (especially anger and sadness), while those who binge and purge do so as a way to dissociate from upsetting emotions (Ivanova & Watson, 2014). The EFT perspective (discussed in Chapters 5 and 6) holds that people who experience anorexia, bulimia, and binge eating have been raised in environments where emotions were "dismissed, avoided, or … expressed in unpredictable and uncontrollable ways," leading them to suffer "from an impaired capacity to access, identify, and be guided by adaptive emotions" (Ivanova & Watson, 2014, p. 283). Emotion-focused therapists help clients with eating problems better identify and feel comfortable with their emotions (Dolhanty, 2006; Dolhanty & Greenberg, 2009). By empathically understanding clients' feelings (a typical humanistic therapy goal) and educating clients about how these feelings serve a useful purpose (e.g., by providing important information about their needs), EFT practitioners help clients to deal with feelings more effectively and stop using problematic eating as a way to avoid such feelings (Ivanova & Watson, 2014). EFT for eating problems can be conducted with individuals, but it has also been adapted to group and family formats (Brennan et al., 2015; Dolhanty & Lafrance, 2019; A. L. Robinson et al., 2015). Research evidence to date on EFT for eating issues is encouraging but limited (Glisenti et al., 2021; Osoro et al., 2022).

Marta

If EFT was used to help Marta address her anorexia, emphasis would be on helping her to identify and experience (rather than avoid) her emotions—especially ones she finds frightening, such as anger and sadness. The therapist would empathically reflect Marta's experiences back to her to make sure he understood what Marta was going through. As Marta became better at expressing her feelings, the therapist would educate Marta about the importance of acknowledging and listening to these feelings. Rather than ignoring her anger at her mother for pressuring her to take dance lessons, Marta might come to identify the anger as a sign that she probably doesn't want to dance and perhaps should tell this to her mother. EFT would be successful if Marta became better able to identify and act on her emotions. This would make her anorexic behaviors—the avoidant ways she has dealt with these feelings—less necessary.

Narrative Therapy

Narrative therapy (introduced in Chapter 2 and discussed in several other chapters) focuses on the *problem-saturated stories* that people tell themselves. One of the main techniques in narrative therapy is externalizing the problem, in which problems are talked about as entities outside people that get the best of them (Chimpén-López & Arriazu Muñoz, 2021; Maisel et al., 2004; N. Scott et al., 2013). This directly contradicts the medical model in which things like anorexia and bulimia are spoken of as disorders that reside inside individuals (Lainson, 2019; A. Lock et al., 2005). By recasting anorexia, bulimia, or binge eating as independent entities, narrative therapists help clients change the stories they tell about themselves and pinpoint *exceptions*—times when they were able to resist the pernicious influence of their eating problems (Chimpén-López & Arriazu Muñoz, 2021; A. Lock et al., 2002; Maisel et al., 2004; N. Scott et al., 2013). This allows clients to identify solutions for overcoming the influence of eating issues.

Narrative therapists have been slow to conduct traditional empirical research on their approach (J. Chang & Nylund, 2013). However, one small study in a group setting suggested narrative therapy may be effective with eating problems (M. Weber et al., 2006). While attractive to many clinicians, a lot more research on narrative therapy, EFT, and other humanistic approaches to eating issues is necessary for them to catch up to CBT-E and IPT in the empirical-evidence department.

Zayna

Imagine narrative therapy with Zayna. Instead of treating bulimia as a disease that Zayna "has," her therapist would externalize it. She might ask Zayna "How and when does bulimia get the best of you?" Zayna might reply that bulimia tells her she is worthless and ugly; she might also note that bulimia is most influential when she encounters stressful challenges in her life—such as exams in school. The therapist would then look for exceptions: "Can you think of times when bulimia had less of an influence over you? What did you do differently during those times?" Zayna might share how she is better able to resist the influence of bulimia when she gets sufficient rest, confides in close friends about her worries, and doesn't keep junk food at home. The therapist would then help Zayna recognize how these are strategies she can use going forward to counteract bulimia's insidious influence.

9.16 Evaluating Psychological Perspectives

CBT for eating issues currently has the largest and most robust research base, but IPT has also fared well in many studies (M. E. Atwood & Friedman, 2020; Fairburn et al., 2015; Moberg et al., 2021). Though effective, therapy doesn't benefit as many patients as we would like. A conservative estimate suggests between 30 percent and 50 percent of patients don't achieve remission after completing CBT-E (meaning they still have eating disorder symptoms), and these numbers are worse for interpersonal and psychodynamic therapies (M. E. Atwood & Friedman, 2020; Fairburn et al., 2015; Moberg et al., 2021). Nonetheless, there is compelling evidence supporting CBT, IPT, and even psychodynamic therapies for eating issues. By comparison, there is only a small body of research on emotion-focused therapy and even less on narrative therapy.

Inadvertently, some studies find **specialist supportive clinical management (SSCM)**—a non-theoretical approach to managing eating disorder symptoms originally devised as a control comparison in research studies on CBT and IPT—to be just as effective as more theoretically driven interventions for anorexia (J. Jordan et al., 2020; Kiely et al., 2022; V. V. W. McIntosh et al., 2022). In SSCM, clinicians work with patients to help them target problematic eating behaviors. They also provide nutritional advice while teaching clients to establish a proper diet, monitor their weight, and establish a realistic weight goal. Finally, SSCM provides patients with basic guidance and suggestions on life problems that may be impacting their eating. The effectiveness of a non-theoretical approach like SSCM suggests common factors might cut across different therapies and explain why they help.

Specialist supportive clinical management (SSCM): Non-theoretical approach to anorexia devised as a control comparison for research on other therapies but found effective in its own right; targets problematic eating, emphasizes proper diet, monitors weight, establishes realistic weight goals, and addresses life problems affecting eating.

SOCIOCULTURAL PERSPECTIVES

9.17 Cross-Cultural and Social Justice Perspectives

The Western Ideal of Thinness

As noted, eating disorders are generally thought to be much more common in Western industrialized countries (Makino et al., 2004; Qian et al., 2013, 2022; Swami, 2015). However, this may be changing, especially as other cultures come into closer contact with the **Western ideal of thinness** in which female bodies with small waists and minimal body fat are venerated (Sepúlveda & Calado, 2012; C. S. Warren & Akoury, 2020). Eating disorder diagnoses are increasing in countries around the

Western ideal of thinness: Beauty ideal in many Western cultures that values thin female bodies with small wastes and minimal body fat; when internalized, might contribute to eating disorders.

globe, with recent studies documenting growing prevalence and/or incidence throughout the middle east, Asia, and Latin America (Alfalahi et al., 2021; Azzeh et al., 2022; Banna et al., 2021; Chaudhury & Mujawar, 2019; Galmiche et al., 2019; Holenstein, 2020; Kolar et al., 2016; Z. Li et al., 2021; Nakai et al., 2021; Pike & Dunne, 2015; Santomauro et al., 2021; A. E. van Eeden et al., 2021; J. Wu et al., 2020). Even with the increases, people in Western countries still tend to have some of the highest rates of eating disorders. For instance, compared with people in Asian countries, Westerners' lifetime prevalence is twice as great for BED, 7.3 times as great for bulimia, and 21 times as great for anorexia (Qian et al., 2022). Does this mean eating disorders are culture-bound syndromes unique to Western and Western-influenced industrialized cultures that value thinness? Perhaps, but only some people in Western societies develop eating disorders, suggesting individual factors beyond culture also play a role (J. D. Brown & Witherspoon, 2002; Keel & Klump, 2003; López-Guimerà et al., 2010; Pike et al., 2013).

Photo 9.5 On September 27, 2020 a body positive catwalk was organized by the collective "The All Sizes Catwalk" in Paris. Five hundred models of all sizes and backgrounds were invited to parade, to show the beauty of all bodies, and to counter the "thin-ideal" of the media and fashion industries. *NurPhoto/Getty Images.*

Socioeconomic Status

Eating disorders used to be considered primarily a problem of middle- and upper-middle-class white females. This view is changing. Although some studies find an association between eating disorders and measures of higher socioeconomic status (SES) (Weissman, 2019), overall evidence linking eating disorders to higher SES is mixed (Assari & DeFreitas, 2018; Huryk et al., 2021). Interestingly, higher SES individuals are more likely to perceive a need for treatment and to receive it (Sonneville & Lipson, 2018). This implies that eating disorder prevalence might not differ by SES, but that being wealthier affords better access to mental health information and services.

Socioeconomic status is also relevant in thinking about obesity. Research often finds a negative correlation between income and obesity, at least in wealthy industrialized countries like the United States where sufficient food is available (Ameye & Swinnen, 2019; Mathieu-Bolh, 2022). That is, in rich countries where food is in abundance, people of lower socioeconomic status (SES) are more likely to be overweight. Why? Perhaps they consume more fast food and junk food because they cannot afford or do not have access to healthier options (Food Research & Action Center, 2015). They also might be less educated about healthy eating. The pattern is just the opposite in poorer developing countries. In these nations, SES positively correlates with obesity (Ameye & Swinnen, 2019; Mathieu-Bolh, 2022). This makes sense. In countries where food is scarce, rather than becoming obese on nutritionally deficient food, poor people simply go hungry. Importantly, social justice advocates contend that obesity and hunger are primarily attributable to economic rather than psychological causes. They see addressing inequality as the best way to alleviate mental distress tied to obesity and food scarcity (Arena et al., 2021). Notably, not only is obesity associated with being poor in wealthy industrialized countries but being obese also predicts lower future earnings

(T. J. Kim & Knesebeck, 2018). To the extent that this is attributable to prejudice against overweight people, it too can be considered a social justice issue (McPhail & Orsini, 2021).

Race and Ethnicity

When it comes to race and ethnicity, the evidence is a bit murky. Some research finds eating disorder prevalence lower among people of Black and Hispanic/Latino origin compared with white people, with those of Asian descent sometimes at higher and other times lower risk (Assari & DeFreitas, 2018; C. A. Levinson & Brosof, 2016; Lipson & Sonneville, 2017; Udo & Grilo, 2018). However, not all research finds prevalence differences across ethnic groups (Z. H. Cheng et al., 2019; K. M. Jennings et al., 2015). We do not know if this is because there are no differences or research is not capturing them. Complicating matters, race and ethnicity prevalence might be influenced by *acculturation* (how effectively people from ethnic and racial minority groups navigate multiple cultures) (Rodgers et al., 2018; C. S. Warren & Akoury, 2020). The exact role of acculturation remains unclear, but disordered eating and internalization of the thinness ideal might be tied to how psychologically difficult one finds the acculturation process (Rodgers et al., 2018; C. S. Warren & Akoury, 2020). More research is needed.

Gender and the Media

Gender and the media are two of the most important sociocultural factors talked about when discussing eating disorders. Women are at higher risk than men for anorexia, bulimia, and BED (American Psychiatric Association, 2022). Is the media to blame? Those who say yes point to research showing that exposure to media images of thin-ideal models increases body dissatisfaction in females (J. D. Brown & Witherspoon, 2002; Derenne & Beresin, 2006; Groesz et al., 2002; Spettigue & Henderson, 2004; Terhoeven et al., 2020). Television, films, magazines, the Internet, and social media are examples of media influences linked to increased eating disorder risk. However, their impact is debated because (a) not everyone exposed to thin-ideal media images is negatively affected by them, and (b) the media can positively impact eating if used for health promotion and prevention (Ferguson, 2013; Ferguson et al., 2014; A. M. Morris & Katzman, 2003). A hot topic among eating disorder researchers these days is the influence of social media (the newest form of media). See the "In Depth" box for more.

In Depth: Social Media and Eating Disorders

A burgeoning research literature points to small but significant positive correlations between social media use and problematic eating/weight-related behavior (O. Clark et al., 2021; Guo et al., 2022; G. Holland & Tiggemann, 2016; Ioannidis et al., 2021; B. R. Kim & Mackert, 2022; Padín et al., 2021; Patrícia et al., 2022; Uchôa et al., 2019; J. Zhang, Wang, Li, et al., 2021). This fits with findings that viewing idealized images on social media increases body dissatisfaction (Fioravanti et al., 2022). None of this is surprising. Most of us have experienced how social media encourages "frequent social comparisons" that can "aggravate the conflicts between the glamorous social images that people see displayed on their homepages and their perceptions of themselves" (J. Zhang, Wang, Li, et al., 2021, p. 10). Put simply, social media platforms make it easy to propagate the *thin ideal*. When this occurs, the "unrealistic beauty standards" shared by celebrities and online influencers encourage users to pursue "a body image that they can never achieve" (Patrícia et al., 2022, p. 2). Research on social media and eating disorders often identifies Instagram as "the most dangerous social media ... followed by Facebook and Twitter, due to the instant satisfaction of having positive peer reviews" (Fardouly & Vartanian, 2015; Patrícia et al., 2022, p. 2).

Importantly, the amount of social media use matters. Spending more time on sites like Facebook is "associated with increased body surveillance, greater endorsement of the thin ideal, more frequent appearance comparisons, and decreased weight satisfaction among younger girls and adolescent women" (Holland & Tiggemann, 2016, p. 102). There is even evidence that spending as little as twenty minutes on Facebook can increase body dissatisfaction (G. Holland & Tiggemann, 2016; Mabe et al., 2014)! However, the problem may not simply be the amount of time spent on social media, but how people use it. Posting more pictures of oneself, as well as "liking" and making a lot of comments on other people's posts, correlates with body-image dissatisfaction and a striving for thinness (Holland & Tiggemann, 2016). Personality factors might also play a role, with those susceptible to non-planned impulsiveness at greater risk for eating disorders (Z. He & Yang, 2022).

Of course, social media isn't all bad. It can benefit health by providing "peer-support, information-sharing, and normalization of various experiences" (R. J. Marks et al., 2020, p. 2). However, using it for this purpose poses its own perils. One of social media's more insidious impacts occurs when influencers broadcast problematic ideas as "health and wellness" advise: "Problematically, as most influencers are not trained as physicians (nor do they hold medical qualifications), explicit and implicit messages about health conveyed on the platform are rife with false assumptions that users are seldom aware of" (R. J. Marks et al., 2020, p. 3). Questionable health and wellness assumptions found on social media—including those propagated by the pro-eating disorders movement, which controversially encourages positive attitudes toward eating issues (Sukunesan et al., 2021)—include the following:

(1) the content is inspiring and positive for wellbeing, (2) shame is an effective motivator, (3) individuals will comply with health advice, (4) stress drives positive health behaviors, (5) the athletic ideal is an attainable goal, (6) dieting improves physical health, and (7) being overweight increases mortality risk.

(R. J. Marks et al., 2020, p. 3)

Despite the potential hazards of social media, some view it as a valuable recovery resource for those with eating disorders. While not all researchers recommend patients use social media in their recovery, several "best practices" have been identified for those who do so: (1) Be honest; (2) deemphasize physical changes (e.g., avoid posting "before" and "after" weight loss photos); (3) engage in constructive discussion (i.e., provide helpful feedback to others but avoid trolling); (4) have a therapist or trusted person to help you process your online interactions; and (5) unfollow or block triggering accounts (Willsky, 2022). For better or worse, social media is part of today's eating disorder landscape. Future research should further explore its risks and benefits.

Critical Thinking Questions

1. Given that social media may place people at greater risk for developing disordered eating, should children, teens, and other vulnerable groups have their social media use limited? Why or why not?
2. Should social media sites be regulated or held responsible when their users develop eating disorders? Explain your stance.
3. How comfortable are you with social media as health and wellness resource? Would you advise people to use it or avoid it as an eating disorder recovery resource? How come?

Objectification Theory

One theoretical model used to understand the connection between media portrayals and eating problems in women is **objectification theory** (Fredrickson & Roberts, 1997). According to this theory, media images (on television, in films, in magazines, and online) present women as sexual objects to be judged based on their looks. This results in *objectification*, in which the female body is "looked at and evaluated, primarily on the basis of appearance" (Tiggemann, 2013, p. 36). According to objectification theory, *self-objectification* occurs when girls and women internalize media messages that judge them based on their appearance and then begin to appraise their own worth based on these messages (Fredrickson & Roberts, 1997; Moradi & Huang, 2008; Tiggemann, 2013). Research supports the contention that self-objectification predicts disordered eating (Schaefer & Thompson, 2018). Evidence is accruing that this generalizes to ethnic minorities, sexual minority women, women who have suffered sexual harassment, mothers, men, homosexual men, and children (Beech et al., 2020; Brewster et al., 2019; Comiskey et al., 2020; S. Hayes et al., 2021; Jongenelis & Pettigrew, 2020; Kilpela et al., 2019; Moradi & Tebbe, 2022; Strübel & Petrie, 2020).

Objectification theory: Media images present women as sexual objects to be judged based on their looks (*objectification*), which leads women to objectify their bodies (*self-objectification*) and makes them vulnerable to body image and eating issues.

Zayna

When Zayna was a teenager, she began comparing her own developing body to those she saw on television and in fashion magazines. They were so much skinnier than she was. No matter how much dieting and exercising she did, Zayna couldn't get her body to look like the actresses and models she admired. She came to believe that being thin was equal to being happy and successful. When she looked in the mirror, Zayna judged herself a failure because she could never achieve the body shape she desired.

Muscle Dysmorphia

Women aren't alone in being influenced by media images that may lead to disordered eating. There is also evidence that men are affected by media portrayals that demand they have a "bulked up" and muscular body (J. D. Brown & Witherspoon, 2002; Dryer et al., 2016; Sepúlveda & Calado, 2012). **Muscle dysmorphia** (alluded to in Chapter 6), a subtype of body dysmorphic disorder (BDD) in which (mostly) males obsessively worry that they aren't muscular enough, may be influenced by such media portrayals. This is in keeping with research suggesting that people perceive anorexia as a "female" problem and muscle dysmorphia as a "male" problem (S. Griffiths et al., 2014). In light of this finding, it makes sense that men who display symptoms of anorexia are perceived as having

Muscle dysmorphia: Body dysmorphia in which (mostly) males obsessively worry that they aren't muscular enough.

more feminine characteristics (S. Griffiths et al., 2014). Because muscle dysmorphia is associated with eating disorder symptoms (Badenes-Ribera et al., 2019), muscle dysmorphic men who wish to be seen as masculine may, ironically, be viewed as feminine if they exhibit symptoms of anorexia.

Social Justice Efforts to Change Media Messages

Let's close this discussion with a provocative quote that indicts the media for not only emphasizing the thin ideal, but for spreading problematic values that potentially foster eating disorders:

Western media do not merely propagate a thin ideal, which is internalized by individuals in non-Western sites. Rather, Western media present a concoction of values that go beyond the idealization of thinness and that includes consumerism, the idealization of youthfulness, the veneration of beauty in and for itself, the notion that physical selves are malleable, and that work on the body is both healthy and required. (Swami, 2015, p. 47)

Clinicians and researchers operating from social justice perspectives work to change these kinds of societal values, which they see as destructively encouraging disordered eating habits. Those who agree with them probably share their view that social action challenging problematic social values is essential in addressing eating problems (Sepúlveda & Calado, 2012). But what kind of social interventions are needed? Some have suggested that we place warnings on objectionable media thought to place people at risk for eating disorders. The "Controversial Question" feature delves deeper into this issue.

Controversial Question: Should There Be Warning Labels on Unrealistic Images in Fashion Magazines and on Social Media?

Fashion magazines and social media are filled with unrealistic photos. These snapshots are digitally altered, airbrushed, and tweaked to present an idealized (and often unattainable) image of the perfect body. Because exposure to images that celebrate unrealistically thin bodies is positively correlated with body dissatisfaction and eating disorders, it has been suggested that warning labels be added to them to educate people about their damaging impact. Unfortunately, there is little evidence this works. Research consistently finds that warning labels or disclaimers on unrealistic fashion magazine images are ineffective in reducing body dissatisfaction—and sometimes might even make things worse (Bury et al., 2017; Di Gesto et al., 2022; Fardouly & Holland, 2018; Kwan et al., 2018; Naderer et al., 2022; Tiggemann & Brown, 2018; S. Weber et al., 2022). Studies on warning labels exemplify how research can test whether commonsense ideas hold up to scrutiny. Disclaimers on altered media sound like they should work, but they don't. For better or worse, most researchers have reluctantly concluded that warning labels are ineffective at countering the negative impact of unrealistic images in magazines and on social media—and that it is time to explore and assess other solutions.

Critical Thinking Questions

1. Are you surprised by the results of research on warning labels? Why or why not?
2. Irrespective of the effectiveness of warning labels, is it ethical for advertisers to digitally alter ads? Should they be prevented from doing so?
3. What other interventions might we develop to reduce the negative impact of unrealistic magazine and social media images? How might you go about testing their effectiveness?

Cultural Pica

Pica is often rooted in cultural practices. In rural India, pregnant women often eat "mud, clay, ash, lime, charcoal, and brick in response to cravings," while in parts of Africa pica plays a role in fertility and reproduction rituals (E. J. Fawcett et al., 2016; Stiegler, 2005, p. 27). As another example, tribes in Peru and Bolivia eat clay to ward off toxins in their primary food, potatoes (Stiegler, 2005). DSM-5-TR warns that pica shouldn't be diagnosed when eating non-food substances is part of a group's usual cultural practices (American Psychiatric Association, 2022). However, it's been argued that "DSM should more clearly explicate the construct of a culturally sanctioned practice because overall pica prevalence would likely decrease considerably if it was only diagnosed in regions or cultures where the practice violates cultural norms." (E. J. Fawcett et al., 2016, p. 282).

9.18 Service User Perspectives

Stigma

Being diagnosed with an eating disorder carries significant stigma, as does being overweight (Brelet et al., 2021; Foran et al., 2020; Vartanian & Porter, 2016). Compared with people diagnosed with other mental or physical disorders, those with eating disorders "provoke fewer positive reactions in both the general population and healthcare professionals" (Brelet et al., 2021, p. 10). This stigma has serious implications for people with eating disorders. It is associated with low self-esteem, depressive symptoms, alienation, social withdrawal, and poor physical health (Foran et al., 2020). Not surprisingly then, service users with eating disorders often think others see them as weak or having a character flaw (O'Connor et al., 2021). They struggle not to be reduced to their diagnosis: "I find it difficult to distinguish … what is me and what is the eating disorder" (Smith, as cited in Wetzler et al., 2020, p. 11). When it comes to recovery, service users identify several key factors—including the importance of supportive relationships, establishing meaning and purpose, gaining a sense of empowerment, self-compassion, and rebuilding identity so that their "sense of self in not contingent" on having an eating disorder (Wetzler et al., 2020, p. 11).

Levels of Care

The level of intervention for eating issues varies based on the severity of each case (Muhlheim, 2022; National Eating Disorders Association, 2020). The least restrictive level of care is *outpatient treatment*, in which patients live at home while attending weekly therapy sessions and regular appointments with a nutritionist. In *intensive outpatient treatment (IOP)*, patients still live at home but receive more concentrated and lengthy treatment several days per week. *Partial hospitalization*, the next level of intervention, involves attending a treatment center full-time at least five days a week while still living at home. *Residential treatment* is similar but offers around-the-clock care—including supervision of all meals. Finally, *medical hospitalization* is for patients who need continuous monitoring because their eating behavior has placed their health at risk; intravenous fluids or even involuntary tube feeding are more likely at this level of care. Determining level of care can be difficult, and the ethics of force-feeding patients whose eating patterns endanger their health is debated—with some viewing it as a lifesaving measure and others as a paternalistic violation of service user rights (Hawkins, 2021; Radden, 2021; Szmukler, 2021). Regardless of your stance on this issue, there is no doubt about the demand for services. The COVID-19 pandemic only made things worse. It corresponded with a sharp increase in inpatient admissions for eating disorders (Hartman-Munick et al., 2022).

9.19 Systems Perspectives

Psychosomatic Families

In Chapter 8, we discussed how Salvador Minuchin's (1974) structural family therapy viewed somatic symptoms as developing in *psychosomatic families*, which are characterized by *enmeshment*, *overprotectiveness*, *rigidity*, *conflict avoidance*, and *difficulty resolving conflict* (Minuchin et al., 1978). Minuchin and colleagues argued that anorexia is also a product of psychosomatic families. In such families, boundaries between members are blurred. The family acts in lockstep while being overprotective and downplaying disagreement among members. Minuchin contended that anorexia-prone psychosomatic families are

typically child-oriented. The child grows up carefully protected by parents who focus on her well-being. Parental concern is expressed in hypervigilance of the child's movements and intense observation of her psychological needs. Since the child experiences family members as focusing on her actions and commenting on them, she develops vigilance over her own actions. Since the evaluation of what she does is another's domain, the child develops an obsessive concern for perfection. (Minuchin et al., 1978, p. 59)

Although sometimes criticized for blaming families for causing anorexia, the notion of psychosomatic families was revolutionary because it attributed anorexia to dysfunctional family dynamics rather than individual pathology. Instead of conceptualizing the anorexic child as a "'sick' and helpless victim," anorexia was reframed as an "interpersonal problem in which all family members were involved"

Family meal:

Technique originated in structural family therapy—and used also in family-based treatment (FBT)—in which the therapist observes a family meal to directly observe dysfunctional family patterns.

(Dodge, 2016, p. 221). The goal of therapy wasn't simply a changed individual, but a more functional family system (Minuchin et al., 1978). Through a variety of family therapy techniques—including the **family meal**, during which the therapist observed the anorexic family having a meal together in order to directly observe dysfunctional family patterns—structural family therapists worked to understand (and counter) family dynamics that perpetuated anorexia (Dodge, 2016; Minuchin et al., 1978).

Despite being influential, the concept of psychosomatic families is not well supported. Many researchers have concluded that there isn't a clear pattern characterizing the families of those diagnosed with anorexia and other eating disorders (Dodge, 2016; Eisler, 2005; Erriu et al., 2020; Holtom-Viesel & Allan, 2014; Kog & Vandereycken, 1985; Lyke & Matsen, 2013). Rather, there is a great deal of variability across these families. The psychosomatic family approach is no longer a first-line family therapy for eating disorders, but the notion that family dynamics are important in understanding eating issues remains influential.

Family-Based Treatment (FBT) for Anorexia and Bulimia

Family-based treatment (FBT):

Manualized therapy for anorexia and bulimia that focuses on weight restoration and/or the establishment of healthy eating while not blaming parents; the family is encouraged to work together to help address the family member's eating disorder; also called the Maudsley approach.

Family-based treatment (FBT) is a manualized approach to anorexia and bulimia in teens that typically consists of twenty family therapy sessions spread over a year (K. K. Fitzpatrick, 2011; Rienecke, 2017). It is also called the *Maudsley approach*, after the hospital in London where it was developed. FBT differs from Minuchin's approach in that it doesn't assume eating disorders are caused by family dynamics. Instead, it tends to see anorexia and bulimia as diseases in which family patterns serve to influence and maintain symptoms.

In *Phase 1 (renourishment)* of FBT, weekly sessions focus on weight restoration and/or establishing healthy eating (Eisler et al., 2010; K. K. Fitzpatrick, 2011; Le Grange & Lock, 2010; J. Lock & Nicholls, 2020; Rienecke, 2017). Minuchin's family meal technique is used to identify problematic family patterns around eating and coach the family on how to remedy them. Because anorexic patients tend to be younger and at greater health risk than bulimic patients due to their self-starvation, their parents are given a great deal of authority in weight restoration. With bulimic patients, a more collaborative approach is used to negotiate appropriate rules for eating. Importantly, Phase 1 absolves parents of responsibility for their child's eating disorder (Eisler et al., 2010; K. K. Fitzpatrick, 2011; Le Grange, 2005; Le Grange & Lock, 2010; Rienecke, 2017). This is done to empower them as they work to improve their children's eating habits.

Phase 2 (autonomy over eating) begins when patients have reached a healthy body weight and are no longer struggling to eat normally (Eisler et al., 2010; K. K. Fitzpatrick, 2011; Le Grange & Lock, 2010; Rienecke, 2017). Session frequency decreases to every other week and patients are given greater autonomy over their eating and exercise habits. That is, "parents are encouraged to 'test the water'" of their child's readiness to eat in an age-appropriate way without parental monitoring (Eisler et al., 2010, p. 165).

Phase 3 (normal adolescence) occurs when the teen's eating and weight have returned to normal (Eisler et al., 2010; K. K. Fitzpatrick, 2011; Le Grange & Lock, 2010; Rienecke, 2017). Sessions occur only once per month and focus mainly on supporting the teen with normal developmental issues (schoolwork, dating, peer pressure, and ordinary worries about body height, size, and shape). Any concerns that the parents or teen have about the possibility of relapse are also addressed.

FBT is effective at reducing symptoms of anorexia and bulimia, especially in first-time non-chronic cases (Bentz et al., 2021; Le Grange, 2005; Le Grange et al., 2015; J. Lock, 2011). Roughly two-thirds of families respond well to it (Dalle Grave et al., 2019). However, it doesn't help everyone—especially given that 15 percent to 30 percent of families can't or won't participate in family therapy (K. K. Fitzpatrick, 2011). Even among families that benefit from it, symptoms completely remit less 40 percent of the time (Dalle Grave et al., 2019). FBT works, but not fully for everyone.

Marta

If Marta underwent FBT for her anorexia, weekly family sessions would initially focus on helping her regain weight. The therapist would observe a family meal and realize that Marta's parents often contradict one another, with mom telling Marta she needn't eat everything on her plate and dad insisting the plate must be emptied. Subsequent therapy sessions would teach Marta's parents to work together in setting appropriate expectations for Marta's eating. As Marta's eating (and weight) improved, she would be given greater autonomy and less supervision over her eating.

9.20 Evaluating Sociocultural Perspectives

Sociocultural factors are seen as playing a central role in fostering and maintaining eating problems. In cultures where thinness is venerated and women are judged by their looks, it makes sense that eating issues are common. Research clearly shows that media can influence body image and that people who spend more time taking in such media run a higher risk for engaging in problematic eating. Turning to family perspectives, family-based treatment (FBT) appears to be an effective therapy for anorexia and bulimia. It does well in studies comparing it with CBT and IPT. In fact, for anorexia some consider it the treatment of choice (A. E. Kass et al., 2013). Overall, there is less evidence for FBT's effectiveness for bulimia (Hay, 2013; Le Grange, 2010), but one recent randomized controlled trial of FBT for bulimia did find it superior to CBT (Le Grange et al., 2015). Some researchers are encouraging the combination of FBT and CBT-E in treating bulimia (Hurst et al., 2015).

CLOSING THOUGHTS

9.21 Are Feeding and Eating Problems Culture-Bound?

Eating habits are intimately intertwined with not only our biology and psychology but also with social norms and practices. What we eat, when we eat, with whom we eat, and how we eat are shaped by cultural customs that we usually take for granted. At the same time, eating is an activity with biological and psychological bases. Thus, when discussing feeding and eating disorders a formidable question arises: Are feeding and eating disorders culture-bound syndromes tied to our current historical era? Or are they universal disorders, rooted in underlying biological and psychological dysfunctions, that are merely influenced by sociocultural factors? While it may be some of each, most of us lean one way or the other on this issue. Theorists who view eating disorders as culture-bound syndromes embrace *cultural relativism*, in which "abnormality" is relative to social norms (Isaac, 2013); eating is only "disordered" within a social context that defines it as such. In contrast, theorists who view eating disorders as independent of culture and context come adopt *cultural universalism*; eating disorder behaviors might vary somewhat by or historical period or culture, but the disorders themselves cut across time and place (Florsheim, 2020; Isaac, 2013). The universalist–relativist debate can be applied to every presenting problem in this book. However, because eating behavior is so clearly rooted in biological, psychological, and social processes, our uncertainty over the universality of feeding and eating disorders is especially noticeable.

CHAPTER SUMMARY

Overview
- *Feeding problems* involve concern over food preferences.
- *Eating problems* are characterized by disturbed body image.

Diagnostic Perspectives
- DSM-5-TR and ICD-11 identify three eating disorders (*anorexia nervosa*, *bulimia nervosa*, and *binge-eating disorder*) and three feeding disorders (*avoidant/restrictive food intake disorder*, *pica*, and *rumination disorder*).
- PDM-2 links eating disorders to the psychological need for care and affection, HiTOP locates them on its "Somatoform" spectrum, and PTMF reframes them as responses to mistreatment and trauma.

Historical Perspectives
- The term "anorexia" has Greek origins and means "without appetite" and was first used to describe patients in 1873.
- Bulimia was first described in the 1950s but did not gain attention until the 1970s.

Biological Perspectives
- *Serotonin* deficiencies have been linked to anorexia and bulimia; when anorexic patients lack *tryptophan* from not eating, their brains cannot make serotonin.

- *Dopamine's* role in appetite and rewards is a target of interest in eating disorders.
- *Antidepressants* are prescribed for eating disorders, with mixed results.
- The *hypothalamus, HPA axis,* and the *mesolimbic pathway* are being studied for their role in eating disorders—along with ventricle size, brain volume, and the anterior insula.
- Complex gene–environment interactions are seen as playing a role in eating and feeding disorders. Various genetic markers are targets of ongoing research.
- Several evolutionary hypotheses have been devised to explain the development of eating disorders.
- Immune inflammation has been linked to eating disorders.

Psychological Perspectives

- Perfectionism and negative emotionality predict all eating disorders; impulsivity is linked to binge eating.
- Modern psychodynamic perspectives tie eating disorders to early attachment relationships; psychodynamic therapies encourage insight into and alteration of these patterns.
- Behavior therapists use *in vivo food exposure* and other behavioral techniques to treat eating disorders. *Aversion therapy* and *overcorrection* are often used with pica; *diaphragmatic breathing* and *satiation techniques* are used with rumination.
- *Enhanced CBT-E* sees all eating disorders as due to mistakenly evaluating self-worth based on body weight and shape.
- *Acceptance and commitment therapy (ACT)* teaches *cognitive defusion* to treat eating disorders.
- *Emotion-focused therapy (EFT)* helps people with eating disorders identify and be comfortable with difficult emotions.
- Narrative therapy externalizes eating disorders to help people identify solutions for dealing with their eating issues.
- *Specialist supportive clinical management (SSCM)* started as a control comparison in CBT and IPT eating disorder research, but it has proved effective on its own.

Sociocultural Perspectives

- Sociocultural theorists attribute eating disorders to the *Western ideal of thinness.*
- Socioeconomic status, race, and ethnicity are important factors in understanding eating issues.
- *Objectification theory* studies how women internalize societal ideals and media images about body shape and size.
- Eating disorders are highly stigmatizing, with many people attributing them to weakness or character flaws.
- Structural family therapy attributes eating disorders to psychosomatic families.
- *Family-based treatment (FBT)* is a twenty-session manualized therapy that treats eating disorders as illnesses but works with patients and their parents to improve eating habits.

Closing Thoughts

- Whether eating disorders are culturally relative or universal continues to be debated.

NEW VOCABULARY

1. Adapted to flee famine hypothesis
2. Anorexia nervosa
3. Aversion therapies
4. Avoidant/restrictive food intake disorder (ARFID)
5. Binge eating
6. Binge-eating disorder (BED)
7. Bulimia nervosa
8. Cognitive defusion
9. Cognitive-behavioral therapy for ARFID (CBT-AR)
10. Compensatory behavior
11. Diaphragmatic breathing
12. Eating problems
13. Enhanced cognitive-behavioral therapy (CBT-E)
14. Family-based treatment (FBT)
15. Family meal
16. Feeding problems
17. Geophagia
18. *In vivo* food exposure
19. Mercyism
20. Mesolimbic pathway
21. Muscle dysmorphia
22. Obesity
23. Objectification theory
24. Oral impregnation
25. Orthorexia nervosa
26. Other specified feeding or eating disorder
27. Overcorrection
28. Pica
29. Reproductive suppression hypothesis
30. Rumination disorder
31. Satiation techniques
32. Sexual competition hypothesis
33. Specialist supportive clinical management (SSCM)
34. Thought parade exercise
35. Tryptophan
36. Western ideal of thinness

SEXUAL FUNCTIONING AND GENDER IDENTITY

Photo 10.1
Yan Krukau/Pexels.

LEARNING OBJECTIVES

After reading this chapter, you should be able to:

1. Define basic sex and gender terms and discuss the role of values in discussing sex and gender.

2. Outline sexual dysfunction, paraphilia, and gender dysphoria diagnoses in DSM and ICD, as well as explain controversies concerning these diagnoses.

3. Describe historical trends in the history of understanding sex, gender, and mental distress—as well as identify significant figures from this history.

4. Explain biological perspectives on sexuality, gender, and mental distress, including those emphasizing brain chemistry, brain structure, genes, evolution, and the immune system.

5. Distinguish psychodynamic, cognitive-behavioral, and humanistic conceptualizations and interventions for sexual complaints and gender-related concerns.

6. Overview cross-cultural, social justice, and community-based program approaches to assessing and addressing sexual complaints and gender-related concerns.

OVERVIEW

10.1 Getting Started: What Is "Normal" Sexual Behavior?

Case Examples

Elena
Elena is a 30-year-old married woman who seeks therapy because she has lost all interest in sex. "No matter how hard my husband Hector tries to arouse me, I just can't seem to get turned on," she complains.

Ahmed
Ahmed, a 65-year-old man, has a new boyfriend, Mark. Ahmed finds Mark very attractive but is unable to get an erection. This is interfering with their sex life and relationship.

Bolin
Bolin, a 22-year-old male, seeks therapy because he is not getting along with his girlfriend, May. He reluctantly admits that sex with May isn't very good because "I cum too fast." Bolin is deeply embarrassed by this but hopes therapy might help.

Linnea

Linnea is a 48-year-old married woman who seeks medical attention because she experiences vaginal pain whenever she has sex with her husband Phillip. "I get very anxious anytime he wants to have sex because I know it's going to hurt," she says.

Lou

Lou is a 35-year-old married man who comes to therapy with his wife, Ruth. They have been arguing over Lou's insistence on wearing Ruth's undergarments when they have sex. In fact, Lou has difficulty getting aroused unless he wears women's clothes. Because Ruth finds this to be a big turnoff, she has increasingly avoided sex with Lou.

William

William is a 42-year-old man who has just been arrested for having child pornography on his computer. He admits to being turned on by pictures of naked children but swears that he has never actually touched a real child in a sexual manner. He goes on trial soon and is likely to be labeled as a sex offender.

Juana

Juana, a 30-year-old high school teacher, recently began identifying as a trans woman. She seeks therapy to help her navigate the coming out process. Juana just started hormone therapy and is considering gender affirmation surgery. "I want my outside to match what I know I am inside," she says. Nonetheless, Juana is struggling with how people will respond to her transitioning. She is especially concerned about job security. "The school where I teach isn't in a trans-friendly district," she laments. "What if coming out gets me fired?"

Sex, Gender, and Values

Don't be surprised if you have strong reactions to this chapter, especially if you recognize yourself in the material discussed. Covering sexual problems and gender-related concerns in a book such as this risks implying that they come in "normal" and "abnormal" varieties—a position worthy of skepticism. Nonetheless, people who experience sexual problems and gender-related concerns often seek mental health services, so knowledge of how clinicians conceptualize and address these issues is important. As you read this chapter, remember that "ideas about what is considered to be normal sexual behavior vary considerably over time" and "atypical sexual activity is not a *de facto* indicator of mental illness" (Kamens, 2011, p. 40).

Sex and Gender: Basic Terms

One of the challenges in discussing sex and gender is sorting out what people mean when they use different terms. This task is difficult because terms that some people find appropriate, others object to—which is why accepted terms change over time. Key terms related to sex and gender are reviewed below. See Table 10.1 for additional terminology.

Sex and Gender

Sex: One's biological status as male, female, or intersex.

Gender: Attitudes, feelings, and behaviors a culture associates with a person's biological sex.

Sex refers to one's biological status as male or female (American Psychiatric Association, n.d.-b; American Psychological Association, n.d.-f). It is determined by physical factors such as sex chromosomes, gonads, and reproductive organs. **Gender** has to do with cultural attitudes, feelings, and behaviors associated with biological sex. According to the American Psychological Association (n.d.-c), "sex usually refers to the biological aspects of maleness or femaleness, whereas gender implies the psychological, behavioral, social, and cultural aspects of being male or female (i.e., masculinity or femininity)." Sex is rooted in biology, but gender is a product of culture. This is a handy, if somewhat oversimplified, distinction (Mascolo, 2019).

Gender Identity

Gender identity: One's persistent sense of belonging to a male, female, or non-binary gender category.

Gender identity is one's sense of "belonging or not belonging to a particular gender, whether male, female or a non-binary alternative" (American Psychiatric Association, n.d.-b). People's clothes, haircuts, ways of speaking, and body language (among other indicators) communicate their

Table 10.1 Sex and Gender Terminology: General Definitions

- **Bisexual:** A person who is attracted to both people of their own gender and other genders.
- **Cisgender:** Individuals whose current gender identity is the same as the sex they were assigned at birth
- **Gay:** A person who is attracted primarily to members of the same gender. Gay is most frequently used to describe men who are attracted primarily to other men, although it can be used for men and women.
- **Gender:** The cultural roles, behaviors, activities, and attributes expected of people based on their sex.
- **Gender Expression:** How an individual chooses to present their gender to others through physical appearance and behaviors, such as style of hair or dress, voice, or movement.
- **Gender Identity:** An individual's sense of their self as man, woman, transgender, or something else.
- **Gender Minority:** Individuals whose gender identity (man, women, other) or expression (masculine, feminine, other) is different from their sex (male, female) assigned at birth.
- **Gender Nonbinary:** Individuals who do not identify their gender as man or woman. Other terms to describe this identity include genderqueer, agender, bigender, gender creative, etc.
- **Gender Nonconforming:** The state of one's physical appearance or behaviors not aligning with societal expectations of their gender (a feminine boy, a masculine girl, etc.).
- **Heterosexual or Straight:** A man who is primarily attracted to women or a woman who is primarily attracted to men.
- **Intersex:** Persons with variations in physical sex characteristics, including variations in anatomy, hormones, chromosomes or other traits, that differ from expectations generally associated with male and female bodies.
- **Lesbian:** A woman who is primarily attracted to other women.
- **LGBTQ:** Acronym that refers to the lesbian, gay, bisexual, transgender, and queer/questioning community.
- **Queer:** An umbrella term sometimes used to refer to the entire LGBT community.
- **Questioning:** For some, the process of exploring and discovering one's own sexual orientation, gender identity, or gender expression.
- **Sex:** An individual's biological status as male, female, or something else. Sex is assigned at birth and associated with physical attributes, such as anatomy and chromosomes.
- **Sexual Minority:** Individuals who identify as gay, lesbian, or bisexual, or who are attracted to or have sexual contact with people of the same gender.
- **Sexual Orientation:** Refers to a person's sexual and emotional attraction to another person and the behavior and/or social affiliation that may result from this attraction (lesbian, gay, bisexual, etc.).
- **SGM:** Acronym for sexual and gender minorities.
- **SGMY**: Acronym for sexual and gender minority youth.
- **SMY:** Acronym for sexual minority youth.
- **Transgender:** Individuals whose current gender identity differs from the sex they were assigned at birth.

Source: Reprinted from Centers for Disease Control and Prevention (2022e), https://www.cdc.gov/healthyyouth/terminology/sexual-and-gender-identity-terms.htm

gender identities to others; they are forms of *gender expression*. **Transgender** (shorthand "trans") is a term for "people whose gender identity is different from the gender they were thought to be when they were born" (National Center for Transgender Equality, 2016).

To treat a transgender person with respect, you treat them according to their gender identity, not their sex at birth. So, someone who lives as a woman today is called a transgender woman *and should be referred to as "she" and "her." A* transgender man *lives as a man today and should be referred to as "he" and "him." (National Center for Transgender Equality, 2016)*

The word **cisgender** (shorthand "cis") describes individuals whose gender identity matches their sex assigned at birth (UCSF Lesbian, Gay, Bisexual, and Transgender Resource Center, n.d.). The cisgender label distinguishes "people who do not identify themselves as transgender" without implying that the opposite of transgender is "normal" (Markman, 2011, p. 315). Later in the chapter, we discuss whether DSM and ICD pathologize transgender identities.

Transgender: Term for people whose gender identity, expression, or behavior is different from what is typically associated with their birth-assigned sex; shorthand: "trans."

Cisgender: Term for people whose gender identity and birth sex match; shorthand: "cis."

Juana

Juana has often experienced dissonance concerning her gender identity, gender expression, and birth-assigned sex. Much of this is due to prejudice and discrimination directed at those who don't conform to society's gender expectations.

Sexual Orientation

Sexual orientation refers to "one's enduring sexual attraction to male partners, female partners, or both" (American Psychological Association, n.d.-g). A person's sexual orientation can be "heterosexual, same sex (gay or lesbian), or bisexual" (American Psychological Association, n.d.-g). *Heterosexuals* are attracted to a gender other than their own, *homosexuals* are attracted to the same gender, *bisexuals* are attracted to multiple (but not all) genders, *pansexuals* are attracted to all genders and sexes, and *asexuals* do not feel sexual attraction or wish to sexually partner (UCSF Lesbian, Gay, Bisexual, and Transgender Resource Center, n.d.). People who identify as *queer* use it as an umbrella term to signify being out of the mainstream (i.e., not heterosexual or cisgender). The term *gay* describes male or female homosexuals, but some women prefer the term *lesbian*, which refers to female homosexuals (UCSF Lesbian, Gay, Bisexual, and Transgender Resource Center, n.d.). Importantly, sexual orientation is probably not as either/or as the categorical terms we use to describe it suggest. Although often viewed as consistent, sexual orientation may be fluid across time and the usual categories may be contested or not account for everyone (M. W. Ross et al., 2012).

Coming Out

Coming out is the ongoing process by which people accept and publicly declare their sexual orientation or gender identity (American Psychological Association, n.d.-b). This process can be very difficult due to **heterosexism**, a term for prejudice against any form of non-heterosexuality (American Psychological Association, n.d.-d). Gay men, lesbians, and people with nonconforming gender identities face a great deal of heterosexism when they come out. Heterosexual and cisgender individuals, who don't have to come out because their identities are assumed and taken for granted, are often oblivious to just how difficult coming out can be. Being an **ally** involves confronting heterosexism to support sexual minority persons (UCSF Lesbian, Gay, Bisexual, and Transgender Resource Center, n.d.).

Photo 10.2 Trans community leader "Mother Martha Nubia Sanchez" demonstrates during the "Yo Marcho Trans" transgender community pride parade in Bogota, Colombia on July 15, 2022. *NurPhoto/Getty Images.*

DIAGNOSTIC PERSPECTIVES

10.2 DSM and ICD

In a significant break with DSM, ICD-11 no longer classifies sexual dysfunctions and gender incongruence as mental disorders. Instead, it now considers them "conditions related to sexual health." This potentially decreases stigma by reframing such concerns in less psychological terms, but it also runs the risk of over-medicalizing them (Parameshwaran & Chandra, 2019). Some see moving sex and gender diagnoses out of the mental disorders section of ICD as an effort to overcome the mind/body separation that often ensnares understanding of these issues (G. M. Reed et al., 2016). Whatever the reasons or outcome, it is a big change—one that DSM, which only lists mental disorders, cannot make if it wishes to retain these diagnoses in its manual. Presently, DSM-5-TR includes separate chapters on "sexual dysfunctions," "paraphilic disorders," and "gender dysphoria"—a change from DSM-IV-TR, which grouped these problems together (Downing, 2015; C. A. Ross, 2015). The only sex-related diagnoses that ICD still deems mental disorders are paraphilias.

Sexual Dysfunctions

DSM-5-TR defines **sexual dysfunctions** as disturbances "in a person's ability to respond sexually or to experience sexual pleasure" (American Psychiatric Association, 2022, p. 477). Sexual dysfunction diagnoses aren't mutually exclusive; a person can have more than one. While clinical judgment is involved in diagnosing sexual dysfunctions, these disorders all require distress over the symptoms.

> **Sexual dysfunctions:** Defined by DSM and ICD as disturbances in responding sexually or experiencing sexual pleasure.

Disorders of Desire and Arousal

DSM-5-TR lists three disorders of desire and arousal, one for women and two for men (see Diagnostic Box 10.1). These diagnoses involve lack of sexual interest and/or difficulty becoming sexually aroused. **Female sexual interest/arousal disorder** is diagnosed in women who show little or no interest in or arousal from sexual activity. They rarely or never initiate sex and don't experience pleasure from it when they do engage in it. The problem is quite prevalent, with DSM-5-TR indicating that "approximately 30% of women experience chronic low desire" (American Psychiatric Association, 2022, p. 491).

> **Female sexual interest/arousal disorder:** DSM diagnosis for women who show little or no interest in or arousal from sexual activity.

Elena

Elena, our case example client who is unresponsive to her husband's sexual advances, might be diagnosed with female sexual interest/arousal disorder.

DSM's **male hypoactive sexual desire disorder** describes men who show minimal interest in sex. Such men have few sexual fantasies and don't easily become aroused. Men seem to suffer from lack of desire much less than women, according to DSM. Although sexual desire complaints in men increase with age, only 6 percent show symptoms for six months or longer and just 2 percent experience significant distress over it (American Psychiatric Association, 2022).

> **Male hypoactive sexual desire disorder:** DSM diagnosis for men who show minimal interest in sex.

Finally, **erectile disorder** is diagnosed in men who repeatedly have trouble obtaining or maintaining erections during sexual activity. DSM-5-TR notes that the lifetime prevalence of erectile disorder isn't known, but that roughly 13 percent to 21 percent of men between ages 40 and 80 occasionally have trouble obtaining or maintaining erections. The issue often becomes more significant with age.

> **Erectile disorder:** DSM disorder diagnosed in men who repeatedly have trouble obtaining or maintaining erections during sexual activity; called *male erectile dysfunction* in ICD.

Ahmed

Erectile disorder might be diagnosed in case example client Ahmed, who is unable to obtain an erection when engaging in sexual activity with his boyfriend, Mark.

Hypoactive sexual desire dysfunction: ICD diagnosis for men and women who have absent or reduced sexual thoughts, fantasies, or desires.

Female sexual arousal dysfunction: ICD diagnosis for women who show little or no arousal from sexual activity.

ICD-11 classifies sexual desire and arousal disorders a bit differently from DSM-5-TR. Instead of DSM-5-TR's single female sexual interest/arousal disorder, ICD contains two diagnoses—one for desire issues (**hypoactive sexual desire dysfunction**) and one for arousal issues (**female sexual arousal dysfunction**). Because the first of these can be diagnosed in men or women, ICD doesn't require a separate male hypoactive desire diagnosis (as DSM does). ICD and DSM are more in sync regarding erectile disorder, a diagnosis that is basically the same in both manuals except that ICD-11 calls it *male erectile dysfunction*. See Diagnostic Box 10.1.

Diagnostic Box 10.1 Disorders of Desire and Arousal

DSM-5-TR

- **Female Sexual Interest/Arousal Disorder**: For at least six months, absence or decrease in at least three of these: (1) sexual activity; (2) sexual thoughts/fantasies; (3) initiation of sex or responsiveness to partner initiating sex; (4) sexual responsiveness (in 75%–100% of sexual encounters); (5) responsiveness to sexual cues/signals; (6) arousal (in 75%–100% of sexual encounters).
- **Male Hypoactive Sexual Desire Disorder**: Absent or decreased sexual thoughts, fantasies, or desire for six months or more; symptoms accompanied by distress.
- **Erectile Disorder**: At least one of these 75%–100% of the time during sexual activity: (1) getting an erection; (2) keeping an erection; (3) maintaining erectile rigidity.

ICD-11

- **Female Sexual Arousal Dysfunction**: Diagnosable only in females and characterized by absent or minimal sexual arousal, even during masturbation.
- **Hypoactive Sexual Desire Dysfunction**: Diagnosable in males or females and characterized by absent or decreased sexual thoughts, fantasies, or desire for several months or more; the symptoms cause the person distress.
- **Male Erectile Dysfunction**: Characterized by inability to obtain or keep an erection long enough for sexual activity despite desire and sufficient stimulation; equivalent to DSM-5-TR's *erectile disorder*.

Information from American Psychiatric Association (2022, pp. 481–482, 489, 498–499) and World Health Organization (2022a).

Female orgasmic disorder: DSM diagnosis for women who rarely or never experience orgasms.

Anorgasmia: ICD diagnosis for men and women who experience absent, infrequent, or diminished orgasms.

Premature (early) ejaculation: DSM and ICD diagnosis for men who ejaculate too soon.

Delayed ejaculation: DSM and ICD diagnosis for men who show a delay in (or inability to) ejaculate despite being stimulated and wanting to ejaculate more quickly.

Disorders of Orgasm

Female orgasmic disorder is a DSM diagnosis for women who rarely or never experience orgasms. Even when these women do have orgasms, they are often of reduced intensity. DSM-5-TR reports that difficulties experiencing orgasm affect anywhere between 8 percent and 72 percent of women. They even estimate that 10 percent of women never experience an orgasm. However, these statistics don't tease out how many women experience distress over the issue, which is required for a diagnosis.

The ICD-11 equivalent to female orgasmic disorder is called **anorgasmia**. However, a significant difference between ICD-11's anorgasmia and DSM-5-TR's female orgasmic disorder is that anorgasmia can be diagnosed in males, with ICD-11 distinguishing between a man's physical ability to ejaculate and his subjective experience of orgasm (G. M. Reed et al., 2016). Although diagnosable in both men and women, anorgasmia is believed to be more common in women. Refer to Diagnostic Box 10.2 for more on female orgasmic disorder and anorgasmia.

There are two male orgasmic disorders (again, see Diagnostic Box 10.2). In DSM-5-TR, **premature (early) ejaculation** is diagnosed in men who ejaculate within one minute of vaginal penetration, while **delayed ejaculation** is diagnosed in men who show a delay in (or inability to) ejaculate despite being adequately stimulated and wanting to ejaculate more quickly. The ICD-11 versions of these diagnoses are similar to those in DSM, despite minor ICD name differences (*male early ejaculation* and *male delayed ejaculation*). DSM-5-TR estimates that 1 percent to 3 percent of men suffer from premature ejaculation, while 1 percent to 5 percent suffer from delayed ejaculation.

Diagnostic Box 10.2 Disorders of Orgasm

DSM-5-TR

- **Female Orgasmic Disorder**: For at least six months, one or more of these symptoms 75%–100% of the time during sexual activity: (1) delayed, infrequent, or no orgasm; (2) reduced intensity of orgasm; a diagnosis exclusive to women.
- **Premature (Early) Ejaculation**: For at least six months, 75%–100% of the time male ejaculation occurs within one minute of vaginal penetration and earlier than the person wants.
- **Delayed Ejaculation**: Delayed, infrequent, or absent ejaculation at least 75%–100% of the time during sex with a partner.

ICD-11

- **Anorgasmia**: Characterized by orgasms that are absent, infrequent, or of diminished intensity; a diagnosis more common in, but not exclusive to, women.
- **Male Early Ejaculation**: Ejaculation that occurs prior to or very soon after vaginal penetration; equivalent to DSM-5-TR's *premature (early) ejaculation.*
- **Male Delayed Ejaculation**: Inability to ejaculate or excessive delay in ejaculation despite sufficient sexual stimulation; equivalent to DSM-5-TR's *delayed ejaculation.*

Information from American Psychiatric Association (2022, pp. 478–479, 485–486, 501–502) and World Health Organization (2022a).

Bolin

Bolin, who complains "I cum too fast," might receive a premature (early) ejaculation diagnosis if he consistently ejaculates within one minute of vaginal penetration.

Disorders Involving Pain during Intercourse

Genito-pelvic pain/ penetration disorder:
DSM diagnosis for women who experience difficulties with vaginal penetration (often due to tightening of pelvic floor muscles), pain during penetration, or fear of painful penetration.

Sexual pain disorders used to be divided into two types: *vaginismus* and *dyspareunia*. Vaginismus was diagnosed when the pain was due to spasms in the muscles around the vagina during intercourse, whereas dyspareunia was diagnosed when the pain was attributed to either physical or psychological causes (Lamont, 2011). Vaginismus is no longer in DSM or ICD, and dyspareunia is now in ICD-11's reproductive and urinary tract disorder section, where it is assumed to have organic causes. Nonetheless, shades of these old diagnoses are reflected in the new ones that replaced them—both of which are diagnosed exclusively in women. The current DSM-5-TR sexual pain diagnosis is called **genito-pelvic pain/penetration disorder**. It is characterized by vaginal pain (or anxiety

Photo 10.3 Netflix's show *Sex Education* has been praised for raising awareness about various sexual health issues, including vaginismus.
TOLGA AKMEN/Getty Images.

about pain) during intercourse. The ICD-11 version is known as **sexual pain-penetration disorder**. It is comparable to DSM's genito-pelvic pain/penetration disorder, but it explicitly excludes ICD's dyspareunia diagnosis, implying its cause isn't considered strictly biological. DSM-5-TR says the prevalence of genito-pelvic pain/penetration disorder is unknown but that 10 percent to 28 percent of reproductive-age women in the United States regularly experience pain during intercourse.

Linnea

Assuming no organic basis for it can be found, Linnea's recurrent pain during intercourse would likely be diagnosed as genito-pelvic pain/penetration disorder (if using DSM-5-TR) and as sexual pain-penetration disorder (if using ICD-11).

Diagnostic Box 10.3 Pain during Intercourse

DSM-5-TR: Genito-Pelvic Pain/Penetration Disorder
- Difficulty with: (1) vaginal penetration; (2) pain during vaginal intercourse or penetration; (3) fear of pain before, during, or because of penetration; or (4) pelvic floor muscles tightening during penetration.

ICD-11: Sexual Pain-Penetration Disorder
- Difficulties with (1) vaginal penetration, in some cases due to tightening of pelvic floor muscles, (2) pain during penetration, or (3) fear of pain before, during, or as a consequence of penetration.
- Must rule out the reproductive and urinary tract disorder, *dyspareunia* (genital pain before, during, or after vaginal intercourse caused by physical determinants other than lack of lubrication).

Information from American Psychiatric Association (2022, pp. 493–494) and World Health Organization (2022a).

Paraphilias and Paraphilic Disorders

According to DSM-5-TR, **paraphilias** are sexual impulses, fantasies, and behaviors directed toward unusual (and sometimes socially taboo) objects and situations, while **paraphilic disorders** are paraphilias that cause "distress and impairment to the individual" or "personal harm, or risk of harm, to others" (American Psychiatric Association, 2022, p. 780). This means that DSM and ICD only consider paraphilias to be disordered when they cause distress to those experiencing them or harm to others (Downing, 2015). ICD-11 went so far as to remove masochism, fetishism, and transvestism as stand-alone diagnoses because they involve solitary or consensual behavior (Gosselin & Bombardier, 2020b; Tozdan & Briken, 2021). However, somewhat confusingly, these and similar issues can still be diagnosed as **paraphilic disorder involving solitary behavior or consenting individuals**. Diagnostic Box 10.4 presents DSM-5-TR and ICD-11 paraphilic disorders.

The prevalence of paraphilic disorders isn't known, but paraphilic interest is highly prevalent. In a Czech study, 31.3 percent of men and 13.6 percent of women divulged at least one paraphilic preference (Bártová et al., 2021), while Canadian researchers found that 45.6 percent of people surveyed wanted to engage in paraphilic behavior—and 33.9 percent already had (Joyal & Carpentier, 2017)! Similarly, a UK study found 40 percent to 70 percent of men and women had fantasies related to bondage, discipline, dominance, submission, and sadomasochism (BDSM), with 20 percent saying they had engaged in it (A. Brown et al., 2020). In considering these numbers, recall the distinction between paraphilias and paraphilic disorders. While paraphilias (which don't involve distress or harm) are common, the prevalence of paraphilic disorders (which do) remains unknown.

Lou and William

The cases of Lou and William provide examples of paraphilias. The difference between them is that Lou's cross-dressing for sexual arousal doesn't involve criminal behavior, whereas William's pedophilia does. Using DSM and ICD criteria, William suffers from pedophilic disorder. His use of child pornography harms the children exploited to obtain the photos. Whether Lou has a paraphilic disorder is less clear. His cross-dressing doesn't hurt anyone. DSM and ICD only consider it disordered if Lou is distressed by it.

Diagnostic Box 10.4 Paraphilic Disorders

DSM-5-TR DIAGNOSIS	ICD-11 DIAGNOSIS	DEFINITION
Exhibitionistic disorder	Exhibitionistic disorder	Sexual fantasies, urges, or behaviors related to exposing one's genitals to unsuspecting people.
Fetishistic disorder	Paraphilic disorder involving solitary behavior or consenting individuals	Sexual fantasies, urges, or behaviors related to non-living objects or non-genital body parts.
Frotteuristic disorder	Paraphilic disorder involving solitary behavior or consenting individuals	Sexual fantasies, urges, or behaviors related to touching or rubbing against a non-consenting person.
Pedophilic disorder	Pedophilic disorder	Sexual fantasies, urges, or behaviors related to sexual involvement with preteen children.
Sexual masochism disorder	Paraphilic disorder involving solitary behavior or consenting individuals	Sexual fantasies, urges, or behaviors related to being humiliated or made to suffer.
Sexual sadism disorder	Coercive sexual sadism disorder	Sexual fantasies, urges, or behaviors related to the physical or emotional suffering of another person.
Transvestic disorder	Paraphilic disorder involving solitary behavior or consenting individuals	Sexual fantasies, urges, or behaviors related to cross-dressing (DSM's transvestic disorder) and/or other solitary or consenting behaviors (ICD's paraphilic disorder involving solitary behavior or consenting individuals).
Voyeuristic disorder	Voyeuristic disorder	Sexual fantasies, urges, or behaviors related to observing an unsuspecting person naked.

- *Duration*: Fantasies, urges, or behaviors must last at least six months in DSM-5-TR. No minimum duration required in ICD-11.
- *For paraphilias involving potential criminal behavior (exhibitionism, frotteurism, pedophilia, sexual sadism, and voyeurism)*: DSM-5-TR and ICD-11 require the sexual urges to be acted upon or cause the person distress.
- *For paraphilias involving solitary behavior or consenting others*: DSM-5-TR and ICD-11 only require the sexual urges cause the person distress (regardless of whether acted upon).
- Other paraphilias are diagnosed as "other specified paraphilia" (DSM-5-TR) or "paraphilic disorder involving solitary behavior or consenting individuals" (ICD). Examples include sexual fantasies, urges, or behaviors involving dead bodies (*necrophilia*), animals (*zoophilia*), feces (*coprophilia*), urine (*urophilia*), enemas (*klismaphilia*), or making obscene phone calls (*scatalogia*).

Information from American Psychiatric Association (2022, pp. 779–801) and World Health Organization (2022a).

Fetishistic disorder: DSM paraphilic disorder involving distress over sexual fantasies, urges, or behaviors related to non-living objects or non-genital body parts.

Transvestic disorder: DSM paraphilic disorder involving distress over sexual fantasies, urges, or behaviors related to cross-dressing.

Frotteuristic disorder: DSM paraphilic disorder involving sexual fantasies, urges, or behaviors related to touching or rubbing against a nonconsenting person; must cause the individual distress if not acted upon.

Pedophilic disorder: DSM and ICD paraphilic disorder involving sexual fantasies, urges, or behaviors related to sexual involvement with preteen children; must cause the individual distress if not acted upon.

Sexual masochism disorder: DSM paraphilic disorder involving distress over sexual fantasies, urges, or behaviors related to being humiliated or made to suffer.

Sexual sadism disorder: DSM and ICD paraphilic disorder involving sexual fantasies, urges, or behaviors related to the physical or emotional suffering of another person; must cause the individual distress if not acted upon; called **coercive sexual sadism disorder** in ICD.

Voyeuristic disorder: DSM and ICD paraphilic disorder involving sexual fantasies, urges, or behaviors related to observing an unsuspecting person naked; must cause the individual distress if not acted upon.

Gender Dysphoria/Incongruence

Gender dysphoria is DSM-5-TR's diagnosis for people who show "a marked incongruence between the gender to which they have been assigned (usually based on phenotypic sex at birth, referred to as *birth-assigned gender*) and their experienced/expressed gender" (American Psychiatric Association, 2022, p. 513). It can be diagnosed in adolescents and adults or in children (the diagnostic criteria and codes are different for children). ICD-11 uses the term **gender incongruence** rather than gender dysphoria. Though gender dysphoria and incongruence are similar diagnoses, DSM-5-TR only requires incongruent gender feelings last six months before a childhood diagnosis can be made, whereas ICD-11 requires such feelings last roughly two years (see Diagnostic Box 10.5). Estimated prevalence of gender dysphoria in children and adolescents is between 0.6 percent and 1.7 percent, with the number of children and adolescents seeking help for it rapidly rising (Claahsen-van der Grinten et al., 2021). Importantly, gender dysphoria is not a synonym for transgender (Moleiro & Pinto, 2015). It is a diagnosis only for people experiencing stress and conflict over their gender identity. Those who identify as non-binary, for instance, make up only 10 percent of those diagnosed with gender dysphoria (Claahsen-van der Grinten et al., 2021). Being trans and experiencing gender incongruence aren't the same (Davy & Toze, 2018; Faheem et al., 2022).

Juana

Juana was assigned male at birth but was never comfortable with this. For instance, when she was a child and her parents dressed her in a suit for a family wedding, she yearned to wear a dress and be recognized as a girl. From childhood to early adulthood, the inconsistency between Juana's assigned and experienced genders caused her a great deal of distress. Until then, she was deeply conflicted over her gender identity—that is, she struggled with gender incongruence.

Diagnostic Box 10.5 Gender Dysphoria and Gender Incongruence

DSM-5-TR: Gender Dysphoria

- *Adolescents and adults*: Two or more for at least six months: (1) incongruence between experienced gender and birth-assigned gender; (2) wish to eliminate sex characteristics of incongruent gender; (3) wish for the sex characteristics of the other gender; (4) wish to change genders; (5) wish to be treated as the other gender; (6) conviction that one's feelings/responses are consistent with the other gender.
- *Children*: For at least six months, incongruence between experienced gender and birth-assigned gender, with one or more of the following: (1) wish to be the other gender or assertion that one is the other gender (or some alternative gender); (2) a strong preference for wearing the clothes and/or simulating the appearance of the other gender; (3) takes on cross-gender roles during play; (4) prefers toys, games, and activities stereotypical of the other gender; (5) prefers other-gender playmates; (6) rejects activities traditionally associated with one's birth sex; (7) shows distaste for one's sexual anatomy; (8) wishes for the physical sex characteristics of one's experienced gender.

ICD-11: Gender Incongruence

- *Adolescents and adults*: Incongruence between experienced gender and birth-assigned sex with desire to "transition" to, live as, and be accepted as the other sex.
- *Children*: For roughly two years, incongruence between experienced gender and birth-assigned gender; includes wish to be another gender, distaste for or desire to change one's sexual anatomy, preference for toys/games/activities stereotypical of the other gender.

Information from American Psychiatric Association (2022, pp. 512–513) and World Health Organization (2022a).

Gender dysphoria was called "gender identity disorder" in DSM-IV, but DSM-5 removed "disorder" from the name to destigmatize it (Faheem et al., 2022). This reflects an important clinical fact: In accepted professional practice, clinicians don't change people's gender identities to align them with birth-assigned gender (American Psychological Association, 2021a). Rather, gender dysphoria and incongruence diagnoses are made to help adults—and, more controversially, children and teens (Bazelon, 2022)—gain access to hormone treatments, gender-reassignment procedures, and other services that bring their physical bodies into sync with their experienced or expressed gender (American Psychiatric Association, n.d.-a; American Psychological Association, 2021b). In other words, these diagnoses are used to aid in the transitioning process as part of providing gender affirming care (American Psychological Association, 2021a).

Compulsive Sexual Disorder

ICD-11 includes a mental disorder called **compulsive sexual behavior disorder (CSBD)**, which it groups as an impulse-control disorder (see Chapter 13). As Diagnostic Box 10.6 shows, people diagnosed with CSBD seem unable to control their sexual appetites. They repeatedly engage in sexual behavior to such an extent that it interferes with their work, family, and health. DSM has considered adding a similar diagnosis called **hypersexual disorder**. It is akin to "sex addiction," a problem that has received attention from the media and public in recent years. Despite a formal proposal (defining it as a preoccupation with and excessive engagement in sexual activities, often as a coping mechanism) and some evidence of diagnostic reliability (Kafka, 2013; Reid et al., 2012), hypersexual disorder wasn't added to DSM out of concern that it included too many normal sexual variations, required more research, and was too controversial (Halpern, 2011; Kafka, 2014; Kingston, 2018). Some clinicians want it added to future diagnostic manuals but others remain opposed (Halpern, 2011; Kafka, 2014; Kingston, 2018). Meanwhile, research on it continues (Bőthe et al., 2018; Elrafei & Jamali, 2022).

Compulsive sexual behavior disorder (CSBD): ICD disorder diagnosed in people who seem unable to control their sexual appetites.

Hypersexual disorder: Proposed DSM disorder involving preoccupation with and excessive engagement in sexual activities.

Diagnostic Box 10.6 Compulsive Sexual Behavior Disorder (CSBD)

DSM-5-TR
- This diagnosis is not included.

ICD-11
- Recurring sexual urges that lead to repeated sexual behavior that involves one or more: (1) neglecting self-care, interests, activities, and responsibilities, (2) unable to reduce or control the behavior, (3) keep doing it despite negative consequences, (4) keep doing it even though it is no longer enjoyable.
- Causes distress and impaired functioning.
- Occurs over an extended duration (e.g., six months or more).

   Information from World Health Organization (2022a).

Evaluating DSM and ICD Perspectives
Pathologizing Normal Variations in Sexual Behavior?

One of the criticisms lodged against DSM and ICD is that they pathologize normal variations in human sexual interest, identity, and behavior. Detractors contend that "that there is little justification for granting a psychiatric manual the authority to define normal sexual function" (Kamens, 2011, p. 41). When it comes to sexual dysfunctions specifically, they note that "conditions such as delayed ejaculation, vaginismus or erectile dysfunction (ED) … may be variations of ordinary sexual responses which represent transient alterations in normal sexual activities" (Sungur & Gunduz, 2013, p. 114). Deciding what constitutes "normal sexual activities" is difficult and not everyone agrees with current diagnostic definitions. How long should it take for a man to ejaculate during intercourse? How often should a woman experience orgasm? How interested in sex should men and women be? The ways that DSM and ICD answer these questions can appear arbitrary. Given the lack of clear scientific data, some conclude that diagnostic categories for sexual dysfunctions, paraphilias, and gender dysphoria simply reflect social or professional norms (Faheem et al., 2022; Goldhill, 2015; Moser & Kleinplatz, 2020; C. A. Ross, 2015; Sungur & Gunduz, 2013). In other words, "given the malleability of human sexuality and the creativity of human beings in pursuing and amplifying sexual pleasure, it remains a debated question as to what justifies the classification of a source of sexual pleasure or a type of sexual activity as a mental disorder" (J. C. Wakefield, 2011, p. 195).

Should Gender Dysphoria Be a Disorder?

As transgender people have become more accepted in many countries, gender dysphoria diagnoses have become increasingly controversial. Some critics question whether gender dysphoria should be a disorder (Ashley, 2021; Daley & Mulé, 2014; Davy, 2015; Davy & Toze, 2018; Drescher et al., 2012; Drescher, 2015b; Faheem et al., 2022; Markman, 2011; Sennott, 2011). They maintain that gender incongruence among transgender people is a normal response to widespread social discrimination, not a sign of pathology. In their view, gender dysphoria and incongruence diagnoses reflect the questionable but common belief that sex, gender, and sexuality are fixed biological givens rather than fluid cultural constructs (Daley & Mulé, 2014; Markman, 2011). Based on these arguments, critics argue that gender dysphoria and incongruence should be removed from DSM and ICD. However, not all transgender activists agree with this view. Some wish to retain these diagnoses as part of gender-affirming care, even if they don't see gender dysphoria and incongruence as disordered. At least in the United States, a gender dysphoria or incongruence diagnosis is typically required for insurance coverage of costly hormone treatments and gender-reassignment procedures (Drescher, 2015b; Ducar, 2022). For this reason alone, many transgender advocates—including the World Professional Association for Transgender Health (WPATH)—support (albeit, sometimes reluctantly) gender dysphoria and incongruence remaining in DSM and ICD (Ashley, 2021; E. Coleman et al., 2022; Daley & Mulé, 2014; Davy, 2015; De Cuypere et al., 2011; Drescher et al., 2012; Drescher, 2015b). They are pleased that ICD reclassified gender incongruence as a sexual health condition, which they feel destigmatizes it (E. Coleman et al., 2022; Faheem et al., 2022). However, those who don't see it as either a mental or physical disorder remain dissatisfied. They would rather see insurers stop requiring a diagnosis before covering gender-affirming interventions (Ducar, 2022). Debate over these issues is ongoing.

10.3 Other Diagnostic Perspectives

PDM-2

PDM-2 notes that people experiencing sexual dysfunctions often exhibit anxiety and depression. They tend to lack self-confidence and are preoccupied with "inadequacy or compensatory fantasies of power, or both" (Lingiardi & McWilliams, 2017, p. 220). PDM-2 says people with a paraphilia are prone to obsessing about it and often feel anxiety, depression, or guilt. As for gender incongruence, PDM-2 indicates that preoccupation with gender is common, typically accompanied by depressed mood and, in some cases, suicidal ideation.

HiTOP and RDoC

Sexual problems fall on HiTOP's "Internalizing" spectra dimension. HiTOP researchers point to evidence of "cognitive inflexibility and/or behavioral inhibition" among those with sexual disorders while recommending improved assessment measures and additional research (D. Watson, Levin-Aspenson, et al., 2022). Like HiTOP, RDoC moves away from DSM's and ICD's descriptive categories. For example, to develop reliable diagnostic markers for problematic pornography use, RDoC researchers are studying individual factors (e.g., neurochemistry, brain circuits, and behavior) and social factors (e.g., toxic masculinity and gender roles) (Alves & Cavalhieri, 2020).

PTMF

According to PTMF, when people are physically or sexually abused, sexualized behavior is a common threat response. Further, PTMF says that what DSM and ICD consider female sexual dysfunctions are well-established distress responses to gender discrimination in which women are "treated as inferior or secondary" (Johnstone & Boyle, 2018, p. 222). As it does for all presenting problems, PTMF views sexual complaints and gender dysphoria as meaningful threat responses to social adversity. The idea that women's sexuality is unfairly medicalized and pathologized is revisited when discussing the New View campaign later in the chapter.

HISTORICAL PERSPECTIVES

10.4 The Medicalization of Sexual Deviance

The Bible's Old Testament not only prohibited homosexuality, but also condemned anal sex, cross-dressing, and masturbation (De Block & Adriaens, 2013; H. Gordon, 2008). Such religious attitudes influenced how medical doctors later defined sexual deviance. However, over the last two centuries there has been a shift from religious to medical perspectives. Recall from Chapter 1 how the eighteenth-century Swiss physician S. A. D. Tissot (1728–1797) declared masturbation (which he called onanism) to be a mental disorder (Bullough, 2002). Tissot wasn't alone in this assessment. Many eighteenth-century Enlightenment thinkers saw masturbation and other non-reproductive sex acts as dangerous to mind and body (Bullough, 2002; De Block & Adriaens, 2013). Tissot's identifying masturbation as a disease is an early example of the medicalization of sexual deviance.

The Sexual Instinct

The consensus among many historians is that the medicalization of sexual deviance occurred most fully between the mid-1800s and mid-1900s (De Block & Adriaens, 2013). It was during this time that doctors began hypothesizing about a **sexual instinct**, "thought of as a reproductive instinct, or an instinct for the propagation of the species" (De Block & Adriaens, 2013, p. 278). Sexual deviations were attributed to degeneration of the sexual instinct. According to nineteenth-century French physician Paul Moreau de Tours (1844–1908), the sexual instinct could be too weak, too strong, or absent entirely—which potentially explained differences in sexual interest and activity (De Block & Adriaens, 2013). However, the sexual instinct could also be misdirected—as in paraphilias and other "sexual perversions" where the instinct was believed to deviate "from its natural aim" (i.e., reproduction) (De Block & Adriaens, 2013, p. 279).

Sexual instinct: A reproductive instinct for the propagation of the species; proposed by early doctors as part of the process of medicalizing sexual deviance.

Krafft-Ebing's Psychopathia Sexualis

Medical explanations encouraged a shift from seeing deviant sexual behavior as sinful or criminal to viewing it as having biological and psychological origins. This culminated in the publication of Austrian-German psychiatrist Richard von Krafft-Ebing's (1840–1902) influential book *Psychopathia Sexualis* (Krafft-Ebing, 1894). In this book, which went through multiple editions, Krafft-Ebing used vivid case studies to illustrate what he defined as sexual pathology. He identified four basic kinds of sexual deviance: *anaesthesia* (lack of sexual desire), *hyperaesthesia* (excessive sexual desire), *paradoxia* (sexual excitement during an inappropriate time of life, such as childhood or old age), and *paraesthesia* (desire directed at non-reproductive sexual ends) (De Block & Adriaens, 2013; Krafft-Ebing, 1894; "Richard Freiherr von Krafft-Ebing," 2008). He introduced terms such as *sadism* and *masochism* (revisit Diagnostic Box 10.4), which are still used in DSM and ICD (De Block & Adriaens, 2013; Krafft-Ebing, 1894; Oosterhuis, 2012). He was also among the first to study *transsexualism* (a historical but no longer used term for transgender) (De Block & Adriaens, 2013; Krafft-Ebing, 1894; Oosterhuis, 2012).

Krafft-Ebing's work greatly influenced the medicalization of sexual deviance (Cacchioni, 2015). He presented homosexuality and masturbation as biological and psychological dysfunctions (Cacchioni, 2015; Oosterhuis, 2012). This shifted understandings of sexual deviance in a medical direction (De Block & Adriaens, 2013)—even if it continued the religious tradition of viewing such acts negatively. This is evidenced in the works of physicians such as Havelock Ellis (1859–1939) and Magnus Hirschfeld (1868–1935), who wrote extensively about sexual deviance in Britain and Germany, respectively, during the early twentieth century. Like Krafft-Ebing, Ellis and Hirschfeld argued that homosexuality and masturbation are best viewed as medical entities, not sinful vices (H. Ellis, 1927/2004; M. Hirschfeld, 1948). Despite Krafft-Ebing's medical orientation, by the end of his career he softened his stance on homosexuality, acknowledging "that his earlier views on the immoral and pathological nature of homosexuality had been one-sided and that there was truth in the point of view of many of his homosexual correspondents who asked for sympathy and compassion" (Oosterhuis, 2012, p. 137). Still, it would be another seventy years before homosexuality was officially declassified as a mental disorder. See the "In Depth" feature for the dramatic story of homosexuality's removal from DSM.

In Depth: Removing Homosexuality from DSM

Homosexuality was listed as a mental disorder in DSM-I (1952) and DSM-II (1968). Back then it was common for clinicians to engage in *conversion therapy* (also known as *reparative therapy*), which tried to turn homosexuals into heterosexuals (Socarides, 1978/1989). However, as social attitudes toward homosexuality became more tolerant during the 1960s and 1970s, psychiatry began questioning whether homosexuality should be considered a disorder. During the DSM-III revision process in the early 1970s, those who wanted homosexuality declassified as a mental disorder protested at American Psychiatric Association (APA) conventions (Drescher, 2015a, 2015c; Kirk & Kutchins, 1992). This produced one of the most controversial events in DSM history: the supposed "voting out" of homosexuality from DSM.

What happened? Many DSM-III task force members—including its leader, psychiatrist Robert Spitzer, concluded that if homosexuality didn't cause subjective distress, it shouldn't be considered a mental disorder. Numerous APA committees concurred with Spitzer and, in December 1973, the APA's Board of Trustees voted to remove homosexuality from DSM (Drescher, 2015a, 2015c; Kirk & Kutchins, 1992). Psychiatrists opposing the decision petitioned to have the entire APA membership vote on whether they agreed with the Board of Trustees. Half of APA's 20,000 members voted, with 58 percent of them supporting the Board (Drescher, 2015a, 2015c). Thus, homosexuality was officially removed from DSM.

Critics see this vote as proof that DSM is ruled by politics, not science (Kirk & Kutchins, 1992). After all, would we ever consider voting illnesses like diabetes or cancer out of existence? If a disorder is real, these critics claim, voting cannot change that. However, others challenge this argument (Drescher, 2015a, 2015c; Zachar & Kendler, 2012). They say human decisions about how to define and classify things are part of all scientific endeavors. For instance, when astronomers were debating what constitutes a planet, they voted on Pluto's status (and, controversially, decided it isn't one) (Zachar & Kendler, 2012). DSM defenders contend that science always requires social consensus (whether evaluating planets or mental disorders), and that the evolving consensus among psychiatrists in the 1970s was that being gay is not an illness.

But the issue didn't end there. DSM-III (1980) removed homosexuality but included a new diagnosis called *ego-dystonic homosexuality* for people who were gay and psychologically upset about it (Drescher, 2015a, 2015c). Critics saw this as backsliding and a way to pacify those who wished to continue diagnosing and treating homosexuality. Why, argued these critics, was there an ego-dystonic homosexuality category but not an ego-dystonic heterosexuality diagnosis? Couldn't one be straight and conflicted about it, too? In response to these criticisms, ego-dystonic homosexuality wasn't included in DSM-III-R (1987), DSM-IV (1994), or DSM-IV-TR (2000). However, these manuals allowed distress over sexual orientation to be diagnosed using the sexual disorder not otherwise specified (SDNOS) category (Drescher, 2015b). Critics continued to object, arguing that persistent distress about being gay or lesbian is due to social disapproval rather than mental disorder. Homosexuality was finally completely removed from DSM in 2013 when DSM-5 was published (Drescher, 2015b).

Although most of the controversy about homosexuality as a mental disorder has focused on DSM, ICD has generally followed in DSM's footsteps. Homosexuality was a mental disorder from ICD-6 (1948) through ICD-9 (1975) (Drescher, 2015b). ICD-10 echoed DSM-III's ego-dystonic homosexuality with a category called *ego-dystonic sexual orientation* (Drescher, 2015b). Today, ICD-11 and DSM-5-TR exclude homosexuality entirely (Drescher, 2015b; Robles et al., 2021). Further, many professional organizations consider conversion therapy ineffective and unethical (American Psychiatric Association, 2000b; American Psychological Association, 2021b; British Psychological Society, 2014, 2017b; Canadian Psychological Association, n.d.; Drescher et al., 2016; *Memorandum of Understanding on Conversion Therapy in the UK, Version 2*, 2021). It has been banned in four countries—Brazil, Ecuador, Germany, and Malta (Mendos, 2020; Wareham, 2021). There is no federal ban in the United States, but roughly half of the fifty states partially or completely ban conversion therapy for minors (Movement Advancement Project, 2022). However, the repudiation of homosexuality as a mental disorder is not universal. Despite objections from other professional organizations, the Indonesian Psychiatric Association considers homosexuality a mental disorder and endorses conversion therapy (Lamb, 2017; Moran, 2016; Nortajuddin, 2021; Yosephine, 2016). Thus, in some parts of the world, homosexuality remains pathologized.

Critical Thinking Questions

1. Was the removal of homosexuality from DSM influenced more by politics or science?
2. When it comes to deciding whether something is a disorder, can political considerations be eliminated? Explain.
3. Conversion therapy is increasingly prohibited. If you were a psychotherapist, what would you tell clients requesting it?

10.5 Asking People about Their Sex Lives

The Kinsey Reports

The American biologist Alfred Kinsey (1894–1956) is often identified as the first *sexologist* (a scientist who studies human sexual behavior). Kinsey shed light on human sexual activity and normalized sexual acts previously considered atypical and/or pathological. How? By asking people about their sex lives; something no scientist before him had really done. Kinsey and his colleagues famously interviewed Americans about their sex lives and reported their results in two volumes that became known as the Kinsey Reports (Kinsey et al., 1948, 1953). The Kinsey Reports contradicted many long-held assumptions. For instance, in Kinsey's day, women were believed to be disinterested in sex and to not enjoy it—but Kinsey's research contradicted this (Kinsey et al., 1953). His research also found that masturbation, considered a sign of pathology until that time (Bullough, 2002), was extremely common—as was oral sex. Finally, Kinsey's research challenged the predominant view of homosexuality and heterosexuality as mutually exclusive categories (Kinsey, 1941; Kinsey et al., 1948). On the contrary, he found it difficult to classify many people as homosexuals or heterosexuals due to their diverse sexual experiences. Consequently, Kinsey discouraged either/or identifications of sexual orientation. Instead, he advocated rating people using a six-point homosexuality–heterosexuality scale (Kinsey et al., 1948, 1953). His argument against homosexual and heterosexual categories anticipated current debates over dimensional versus categorical approaches to diagnosis (see Chapter 3). Kinsey memorably (and forcefully) made his point:

It is a fundamental of taxonomy that nature rarely deals with discrete categories. Only the human mind invents categories and tries to force facts into separated pigeon-holes. The living world is a continuum in each and every one of its aspects. The sooner we learn this concerning human sexual behavior the sooner we shall reach a sound understanding of the realities of sex. (Kinsey et al., 1948, p. 639)

Kinsey was criticized for not using representative samples, which called into question the generalizability of his results (Clausen, 1954; W. G. Cochran et al., 1953; Drucker, 2012). Nonetheless, the Kinsey Reports are historically important because they used research to identify common sexual behaviors and showed that human sexual behavior was much more diverse and expansive than previously believed. In fact, Kinsey grew skeptical of the idea that some forms of sex were disordered or unnatural, allegedly once remarking that "the only unnatural sex act is that which one cannot perform" (H. L. Call, 1963, p. 12). The Kinsey Reports became bestsellers and greatly influenced changing social and medical attitudes about sex and sexuality (Drucker, 2012).

The Hite and Janus Reports

In the 1970s and early 1980s, Shere Hite (1942–2020) followed in Kinsey's footsteps, publishing reports on the sexual behavior of American women and men (Hite, 1976, 1981). Surveying over 1,800 women, Hite found that most of them didn't typically experience orgasm during vaginal intercourse, even though 95 percent of them did when masturbating. This suggested that, in most cases, lack of female orgasm during sex wasn't reducible to physical causes. In the 1990s, psychologist Samuel Janus (1930–2011) and gynecologist Cynthia Janus gathered survey data to report on the sex lives of over 2,600 Americans (Janus & Janus, 1993). Among the Janus Report's findings: People over age 65 were highly interested in sex, 17 percent of women and 22 percent of men reported a homosexual experience, and 23 percent of women and 11 percent of men indicated being sexually abused as children. Like Kinsey, the Hite and Janus Reports were criticized for non-representative samples, not using inferential statistics, and making sweeping generalizations (C. Davis, 1993; Irvine, 2005). But, also like Kinsey, these reports were bestsellers.

10.6 Masters and Johnson on the Sexual Response Cycle

In 1966, gynecologist William H. Masters (1915–2001) and sexologist Virginia E. Johnson (1925–2013) published their famous work, *Human Sexual Response*. In it, they outlined a four-phase **sexual response cycle** for both men and women (Wylie, 2022). This model has been highly influential in defining, conceptualizing, and treating DSM and ICD sexual dysfunctions. Masters and Johnson's (1966) four sexual response cycle phases are:

1. *Excitement/arousal*: Sensual stimuli such as kissing, touching, and erotic imagery trigger arousal and excitement; *vasocongestion* (swelling of body tissue due to vascular blood flow) often occurs.
2. *Plateau*: Sexual pleasure peaks; heart rate and respiration increase.
3. *Orgasm*: Pelvic muscles around the sexual organs involuntarily contract; in men, ejaculation usually occurs, while in women the vagina's outer walls contract.
4. *Resolution*: After orgasm, blood pressure drops, and the body relaxes; men often experience a *refractory period* during which they cannot have another orgasm.

Sexual response cycle: In Masters and Johnson's original formulation, involved four phases: *excitement/arousal, plateau, orgasm, resolution*. Revised by Kaplan to consist of *desire, arousal/excitement, orgasm,* and *resolution* phases.

Despite its historical importance and influence, Masters and Johnson's sexual response cycle has faced criticism. Some say the plateau phase is misleading because the peak of sexual pleasure occurs during the orgasm phase, not the plateau phase. To address this, Helen Singer Kaplan (1929–1995) revised the sexual response cycle. She absorbed the plateau phase into the excitement phase and added a *desire* phase that could account for psychological factors such as sexual interests, fantasies, thoughts, and feelings (or the lack thereof). Kaplan's (1995) revised sexual response cycle consists of *desire, arousal/excitement, orgasm*, and *resolution* phases.

Some feel Masters and Johnson focused too much on the physical components of sex while overlooking psychological aspects (Levin, 2008). Others contend sexual response isn't so linear and propose circular models (Basson, 2001; ter Kuile et al., 2010). Finally, people have questioned whether the sexual response cycle is universal regardless of gender, social class, and individual differences (Tiefer, 1991). Despite criticisms and revisions, the sexual response cycle continues to influence modern conceptions of sexual dysfunction (Wylie, 2022).

BIOLOGICAL PERSPECTIVES

10.7 Brain Chemistry (and Hormonal) Perspectives

Sexual Dysfunctions

Hormones vs. Neurotransmitters

Both hormones and neurotransmitters are implicated in sexual dysfunctions. Recall from Chapter 5 that hormones are chemical messengers of the endocrine system, a collection of glands important in regulating sexual functioning, sleep, mood, and metabolism. Hormones are produced by endocrine glands and secreted directly into the bloodstream. This contrasts with neurotransmitters, which are part of the nervous system. As described in Chapter 2, neurotransmitters are chemical messengers produced by neurons in the brain that are critical to neural communication. Many hormones are chemically distinct from neurotransmitters, although the neurotransmitters norepinephrine and dopamine also function as endocrine system hormones; norepinephrine in the endocrine system is usually called **noradrenaline**.

Noradrenaline: Name of norepinephrine when it is secreted as a hormone in the endocrine system.

Hormones and Sexual Dysfunction

Testosterone and **estrogen**, the primary male and female sex hormones, are often implicated in sexual dysfunction (Meana, 2012; Rowland, 2012). Men and women have both these sex hormones, with men higher in testosterone and women higher in estrogen. Testosterone is an **androgen**, a type of hormone responsible for the development of male characteristics. For men, low levels of testosterone are correlated with low sexual interest and difficulty with erections (Corona et al., 2016; Kataoka & Kimura, 2017; Tsujimura, 2013). Testosterone's role in female sexual dysfunction is less clear (C. A. Graham, 2010; B. G. Reed et al., 2016; Wåhlin-Jacobsen et al., 2017; R. V. Weiss et al., 2019). Testosterone is administered to men (and sometimes women) experiencing low sexual interest or sexual performance difficulties—with more compelling results in men than in women (M. S. Allen & Walter, 2019; Corona et al., 2016; Kataoka & Kimura, 2017; Parish et al., 2021; B. G. Reed et al., 2016; Rizk et al., 2017; R. V. Weiss et al., 2019).

Testosterone: Primary male sex hormone.

Estrogen: Primary female sex hormone.

Androgen: Type of hormone responsible for the development of male characteristics; testosterone is the most well-known androgen.

Estrogen is also implicated in sexual dysfunction. Research suggests that low estrogen levels are related to reduced sexual desire in women—especially after *menopause*, the time in life when a woman's menstrual cycle ends (usually in her forties or fifties) and estrogen levels decrease (Fait, 2019; Wylie & Malik, 2009). Estrogen, androgens, and *progestin* (a synthetic hormone with effects like *progesterone*, an endogenous sex hormone important in menstruation) are sometimes prescribed to women experiencing low sexual desire, despite limited evidence (Fait, 2019; Hertlein & Weeks, 2009; Santoro et al., 2016). These drugs are used with both pre- and postmenopausal women. With the latter they are known as **hormone replacement therapy (HRT)** because the drugs replace depleted estrogen levels suspected of decreasing sexual interest and performance (Harper-Harrison & Shanahan, 2022; Wylie & Malik, 2009). HRT used to be popular, but research linking it to breast cancer, stroke, and some cardiovascular diseases has changed attitudes about it (J.-E. Kim et al.,

Hormone replacement therapy (HRT): Therapy in which postmenopausal women are given female sex hormones to replace depleted hormone levels.

2020; Vinogradova et al., 2020; X.-P. Yang & Reckelhoff, 2011). Some argue for a reconsideration of HRT, believing its benefits have been overlooked and its risks exaggerated (Dominus, 2023). For now, disagreement over HRT's safety continues.

Linnea

The pain during intercourse that our 48-year-old case study client Linnea experiences may be due to low estrogen levels associated with menopause. Lack of estrogen can lead to lubrication issues. Hormone replacement therapy (HRT) might improve Linnea's sexual interest, but its risks might lead her doctor to recommend other treatments instead.

Neurotransmitter and Non-Neurotransmitter-Focused Drug Treatments

Dopamine and norepinephrine play roles in sexual interest and arousal (Calabrò et al., 2019; Graf et al., 2019; Kingsberg & Simon, 2020; Pfaus, 2009). The antidepressant *bupropion* is sometimes prescribed for low sexual desire because it is a norepinephrine-dopamine reuptake inhibitor (NDRI) that boosts norepinephrine and dopamine. Therefore, it should increase sexual interest—at least in theory. In practice, bupropion hasn't proven especially effective for sexual desire issues (Bolduan & Haas, 2015).

Unlike dopamine and norepinephrine, serotonin typically reduces sexual interest, arousal, and orgasm (Calabrò et al., 2019; Kingsberg & Simon, 2020; La Torre et al., 2013; Uphouse, 2014). This is why SSRIs, which make more serotonin available, can interfere with sexual desire and functioning. The drug **flibanserin** (marketed as *Addyi*) aims to increase female sexual desire by reducing serotonin while enhancing dopamine and norepinephrine (Armitage, 2015; Caruso & Di Pasqua, 2019; Stahl et al., 2011). It was approved in the United States in 2015 (Joffe et al., 2016). However, some researchers have called into question the drug's effectiveness, safety, and approval process (Bueter & Jukola, 2020; Mintzes et al., 2021; J. Z. Segal, 2018). Studies suggest flibanserin yields only small improvements in sexual satisfaction and performance, accompanied by side effects like dizziness, sleepiness, nausea, fatigue, and possible drug interactions with alcohol (Jaspers et al., 2016; U.S. Food and Drug Administration, 2020b; Woloshin & Schwartz, 2016). Concerns about efficacy and side effects might be why flibanserin has yet to be approved in the UK. (L. Clark, 2015; Nast, 2021).

Flibanserin: Drug that aims to increase female sexual desire by reducing serotonin and increasing norepinephrine; marketed as Addyi.

Elena

Elena, who experiences low sexual desire and difficulty becoming aroused, lives in the United States. Upon learning of her sexual complaints, her doctor prescribes flibanserin.

In 2020, the United States approved another drug for low sexual desire: **bremelanotide** (trade name *Vyleesi*) (U.S. Food and Drug Administration, 2020a). Instead of taking a pill daily (as with flibanserin), women inject bremelanotide into their thighs forty-five minutes prior to having sex. This activates melanocortin receptors, though why this improves sexual interest isn't understood. Like flibanserin, unimpressive effectiveness data for bremelanotide has led to skepticism about its approval and use (Mintzes et al., 2021; Spielmans, 2021).

Bremelanotide: Drug women inject into their thigh forty-five minutes prior to having sex to increase sexual desire; marketed as Vyleesi.

Flibanserin is often called the "female Viagra" (Armitage, 2015; Baid & Agarwal, 2018). However, it is very different from the erectile dysfunction pill *Viagra* (chemical name **sildenafil**) (Kedia et al., 2020). Whereas flibanserin alters brain neurochemistry to enhance a woman's psychological experience of sexual desire, sildenafil works directly on sex organs. Sildenafil and similar drugs like *tadalafil* and *vardenafil* (tradenames *Cialis* and *Levitra*) are *phosphodiesterase type-5 inhibitors*. They reduce levels of the enzyme *phosphodiesterase type-5 (PDE5)*. PDE5 breaks down *cyclic guanosine monophosphate (cGMP)*, a chemical that increases blood flow to sex organs. Inhibiting PDE5 means more cGMP and a greater chance of sexual arousal. In men (to whom they are mainly given), PDE5 inhibitors increase blood flow to the penis and physically cause erections (Ghofrani et al., 2006; Kedia et al., 2020).

Sildenafil: A phosphodiesterase type-5 (PDE5) inhibitor used to increase blood flow to sex organs; given mainly to men to generate blood flow to penis necessary for erections; marketed as Viagra.

Ahmed

Ahmed, who suffers from difficulty becoming aroused, might be given sildenafil to physically stimulate erections.

Importantly, flibanserin doesn't directly stimulate sex organs. It increases arousal circuitously by altering neurotransmitter levels. By contrast, sildenafil doesn't target brain neurochemistry. Instead, it directly causes erections by increasing blood flow to the penis. Does this mean female sexual arousal is more rooted in mood and brain neurochemistry, while male arousal is a purely mechanical issue involving sex organ malfunction? This is a contentious question with no clear answer. What do you think?

Drug-Induced Sexual Dysfunctions

Sexual dysfunctions are a common side effect of medications for other presenting problems. Antidepressants, antipsychotics, mood stabilizers, and anxiolytics are all linked to them (García-Blanco et al., 2020; Hosseinzadeh Zoroufchi et al., 2021; Rothmore, 2020; Trinchieri et al., 2021). So are anticonvulsants (used to treat seizures and as mood stabilizers or anxiolytics) and antihypertensives like beta blockers (prescribed for high blood pressure and sometimes for anxiety) (Manolis et al., 2020; Yasmeen et al., 2021). Because medication side effects are easily overlooked, clinicians should rule them out before initiating other interventions for sexual complaints.

Paraphilias

Paraphilic disorders are notoriously difficult to eliminate (Assumpção et al., 2014). They have been linked to monoamine neurotransmitters (norepinephrine, dopamine, and serotonin)—which might be why Parkinson's disease drugs, which boost dopamine, sometimes induce paraphilic behavior (Gosselin & Bombardier, 2020b). Regarding pharmacotherapy, drugs are usually combined with psychotherapy. Two of the more common paraphilia drug treatments are SSRIs and antiandrogens (Assumpção et al., 2014; J. V. Becker et al., 2014; Gosselin & Bombardier, 2020b; Thibaut et al., 2020). These drugs are often used with sex offenders, regardless of whether a paraphilic disorder has been diagnosed.

SSRIs

SSRIs are hypothesized to decrease paraphilic interest by raising serotonin levels (Assumpção et al., 2014; Guay, 2009). While they haven't shown consistent effectiveness (Gosselin & Bombardier, 2020b), there is some evidence that they work, especially with milder paraphilias such as exhibitionism, compulsive masturbation, and pedophilia without acting out (Assumpção et al., 2014; Thibaut et al., 2020; Winder et al., 2019). Research on SSRIs for paraphilias has produced few double-blind controlled studies (in which both patients and doctors in the study are unaware of whether patients are receiving SSRIs or placebos) (Assumpção et al., 2014; Thibaut et al., 2020). Therefore, its conclusions should be taken cautiously.

Antiandrogens

Antiandrogens are drugs that reduce levels of male sex hormones such as testosterone, thereby decreasing sexual interest (Darjee & Quinn, 2020; Thibaut et al., 2020; Winder et al., 2019). Different antiandrogens work in chemically different ways, but all reduce androgen levels. Prescribing antiandrogens to sex offenders is controversially referred to as **chemical castration** because it brings testosterone to levels as low as those found in people who have been surgically castrated (J. V. Becker et al., 2014; K. Jordan et al., 2011). Chemical castration is a less severe alternative than **surgical castration**, which involves removing a man's testicles (*orchiectomy*) or a woman's ovaries (*oophorectomy*) (K. Harrison, 2007; Winder et al., 2019). Chemical castration is used across the globe, but the legality and ethics of chemically castrating sex offenders involuntarily is contentious and fiercely debated (T. Douglas et al., 2013; J. Y. Lee & Cho, 2013; Nour, 2020; Vincent et al., 2020). The effectiveness of antiandrogens in reducing paraphilias remains promising but uncertain due to limitations of existing research (Darjee & Quinn, 2020; Thibaut et al., 2020).

Antiandrogens: Drugs that reduce levels of male sex hormones such as testosterone, thereby decreasing sexual interest.

Chemical castration: Use of antiandrogens to bring testosterone levels as low as those found in people who have been surgically castrated.

Surgical castration: Removing a man's testicles (*orchiectomy*) or a woman's ovaries (*oophorectomy*).

Gender Dysphoria/Incongruence

Prenatal Sex Hormones

Some researchers hypothesize that gender dysphoria originates in exposure to atypical levels of prenatal sex hormones such as testosterone (Gosselin & Bombardier, 2020a). However, others believe that studying whether the brains of people experiencing gender dysphoria are more like their birth-assigned sex or experienced gender merely stigmatizes non-binary people (H. B. Nguyen et al., 2019). To further complicate matters, everyone's brain is a "mosaic" of "maleness" and "femaleness" (H. B. Nguyen et al., 2019). That is, "the distinction between the female and male brain is not always clear-cut, as brain regions may be more or less programmed by androgens and estrogens leading to greater or lesser masculinization of various brain regions during prenatal development" (H. B. Nguyen et al., 2019, p. 23). Although research on hormonal differences between trans and cisgender people has the potential to "bring broader cultural acceptance of transgender issues and help ensure equal treatment for all gender groups" by grounding gender identity in biology, it also risks reinforcing notions of gender dysphoria as due to pathological "prenatal sexual differentiation of the brain" (Gosselin & Bombardier, 2020a, p. 526).

Gender-Affirming Treatments and Procedures

Many trans people seek gender-affirming treatments and procedures to align their physical bodies with their experienced gender. One of the most common treatments is **gender affirmative hormone therapy (GAHT)**, in which masculinizing or feminizing hormones (androgens, estrogens, and antiandrogens) are prescribed that alter secondary sex characteristics to better match gender identity (Gosselin & Bombardier, 2020a; M. S. Harris et al., 2022; G. Meyer et al., 2020; H. B. Nguyen et al., 2019). Some people combine hormone treatment with **gender-affirming surgeries**. For trans women, this can involve removing the penis and crafting a vagina, breasts, clitoris and labia (Deutsche, 2016). For trans men, the uterus and breasts can be removed and a penis and scrotum crafted (usually using material from the clitoris and labia to do so) (Deutsche, 2016). After gender-affirming surgeries, patients continue taking hormones. Other procedures used in the transitioning process include "facial hair removal, interventions for the modification of speech and communication, and behavioral adaptations such as genital tucking or packing, or chest binding" (Deutsche, 2016, p. 23). In cases of preadolescent gender dysphoria, **puberty blockers** can be prescribed. These drugs—usually *gonadotropin-releasing hormone (GnRH)*—delay the onset of puberty and the development of secondary sex characteristics. This doesn't eliminate gender dysphoria but reduces psychological distress while providing trans preteens and teens time (often called a "pause") to explore whether they wish to transition (Rew et al., 2020). A possible side effect of puberty blockers is decreased bone density, but those who recommend them believe their psychological benefits outweigh any health risks (Twohey & Jewett, 2022). Nonetheless, a growing number of U.S. states have banned puberty blockers and other forms of transgender care for those under the age of 18 (Spencer, 2023). This has only exacerbated distress among trans youth, with 86 percent reporting that these bans (and the contentious policy debates surrounding them) have negatively impacted their mental health (Trevor News, 2023).

> **Gender affirmative hormone therapy (GAHT):** Administration of sex hormones (androgens, estrogens, and antiandrogens) to align secondary sex characteristics with gender identity. (10)
>
> **Gender-affirming surgeries:** Surgeries that alter the physical body to match gender identity. (10)
>
> **Puberty blockers:** Drugs to delay puberty in preadolescents experiencing gender dysphoria. (10)

10.8 Brain Structure and Function (and Anatomical) Perspectives

Sexual Dysfunctions

Many brain structures are implicated in sexual desire, arousal, and performance. They include the orbitofrontal cortex (believed to play a role in assessing the sexual relevance of faces), parietal cortex (significant in the cognitive elements of sexual desire), amygdala (tied to arousal and pleasurable emotions), hippocampus (important in memory, including memory of past sexual experiences), thalamus (important in erections), and hypothalamus (associated with sexual arousal) (Baird et al., 2007; Calabrò et al., 2019; Fonteille & Stoléru, 2011; Georgiadis, 2011; Georgiadis & Kringelbach, 2012; Pfaus, 2009; Ruesink & Georgiadis, 2017). Brain scan research into the relationship between brain areas and sexual function remains in its infancy (Georgiadis & Kringelbach, 2012; Ruesink & Georgiadis, 2017). A lot of promising data has been collected, but "it can be difficult to get a grip on the wealth of often complex results" (Ruesink & Georgiadis, 2017, p. 183).

Anatomically, erectile dysfunction is sometimes conceptualized as a problem with *tumescence*—increased blood flow leading to swelling of the sexual organs. When penile tumescence is poor, men have difficulty getting erections. To remedy this, they are often prescribed sildenafil (discussed earlier). When sildenafil doesn't work, doctors sometimes treat erection problems with **intracavernous injection therapy (ICI)**, which involves injecting chemicals into the penis that increase blood flow (Bar-Chama et al., 1997). ICI is effective (Bearelly et al., 2020). However, regular penile injections can be unpleasant. Further, some critics worry that medical doctors sometimes prescribe these injections even when erectile problems appear strictly psychological (J. D. Atwood, 2015).

Intracavernous injection therapy (ICI): Injection of drugs into the penis to increase blood flow and remedy erectile problems.

Paraphilias

The neurobiology behind paraphilias is relatively unknown. Research has found that lesions in the temporal and frontal lobes can lead to disinhibited sexual behavior (Bradford & Fedoroff, 2009; Gosselin & Bombardier, 2020b; Saleh et al., 2021). This is an intriguing finding given that people with paraphilias have irresistible sexual urges. Unfortunately, frontal and temporal lobe damage correlates with disinhibition generally and therefore isn't specific to sexual disinhibition (Bradford & Fedoroff, 2009; Gosselin & Bombardier, 2020b).

Gender Dysphoria/Incongruence

There is evidence of similarities between white matter in the brains of trans and cis women. Likewise, the white matter of trans men may be like that of cis men (Guillamón et al., 2016; Kreukels & Guillamon, 2016). Research is also exploring differences in gray matter and cortical thickness between trans and cis individuals (Baldinger-Melich et al., 2020; Guillamón et al., 2016; E. S. Smith et al., 2015), as well as disparities in brain connectivity (Uribe et al., 2020). For example, investigators suspect that lower gray matter volume impacts body perception and contributes to gender dysphoria (Spizzirri et al., 2018). Overall, numerous researchers note that "people with gender dysphoria have a brain structure more comparable to the gender to which they identify" (Boucher & Chinnah, 2020). However, others warn that the "idea of a 'female' or 'male' brain" is "simplistic" (Baldinger-Melich et al., 2020, p. 1353).

10.9 Genetic Perspectives

Sexual Dysfunction

Female sexual dysfunctions appear to be influenced by gene–environment interactions (A. Burri & Ogata, 2018; Jannini et al., 2015). Candidate genes related to dopamine, serotonin, estrogen, and testosterone (among others) have been implicated (A. V. Burri et al., 2009). Heritability has been estimated at 44 percent, which means over half the variability in female sexual complaints is attributable to environment (A. Burri, 2013; A. Burri et al., 2011, 2013; A. Burri & Ogata, 2018). In fact, once genes are controlled for, environmental factors—particularly relationship satisfaction—are the best predictors of female problems with arousal, desire, and lubrication (A. Burri et al., 2013). Nonetheless, genes play a role, as evidenced by research on other sexual dysfunctions. For instance, one recent genome-wide association study identified seventeen genes linked to erectile dysfunction (Kazemi et al., 2021).

Paraphilias

There isn't much research on the genetics of paraphilias. Men with an extra male (Y) chromosome (*XYY syndrome*) may be at higher risk for unconventional sexual behaviors and fantasies compared with men with an extra female (X) chromosome (*Klinefelter syndrome*) and men with no extra sex chromosomes (Ngun et al., 2014; Schiavi et al., 1988). More broadly, people with extra sex chromosomes are at higher risk for cognitive and behavioral difficulties in general—although the evidence base for this conclusion remains small (Leggett et al., 2010).

Of the paraphilias, pedophilia has the largest body of genetic research. Pedophilia and sex offending tend to run in families (Gaffney et al., 1984; Labelle et al., 2012; Långström et al., 2015). However, heritability of pedophilic interest is estimated at only 14.6 percent, suggesting environment is the main influence (Alanko et al., 2013; Tenbergen et al., 2015). Nevertheless, genes related to androgen, estrogen, prolactin, corticotrophin, serotonin, and oxytocin have all been linked to pedophilic interest or activity (Alanko et al., 2016; Jahn et al., 2022). Even so, reliable genetic biomarkers for pedophilia and sex offending remain elusive (Jakubczyk et al., 2017; K. Jordan et al., 2020).

Gender Dysphoria/Incongruence

Gender dysphoria-related heritability estimates range from .11 to .77, with most somewhere in the middle (Boucher & Chinnah, 2020; A. Burri et al., 2011; Coolidge et al., 2002; Klink & Den Heijer, 2014; Knafo et al., 2005; van Beijsterveldt et al., 2006). A twin study with a small sample size found 39.1 percent concordance for gender dysphoria among female identical twins, compared with 0 percent for non-identical twins (Heylens et al., 2012). This suggests a strong genetic component. However, in the few candidate gene studies on gender dysphoria to date, no single gene strongly correlates with it (Boucher & Chinnah, 2020; Fernández et al., 2014, 2015; Foreman et al., 2019; Klink & Den Heijer, 2014). Several candidate genes hold promise, but more research is needed.

10.10 Evolutionary Perspectives

Evolutionary theory defines disorder as that which interferes with reproduction. By this definition, pedophilia is the only paraphilia that clearly qualifies "because the targets of pedophilic behaviors are pre-reproductive individuals" (Quinsey, 2012, p. 219). From an evolutionary viewpoint, other paraphilias are only dysfunctional if they make passing on genes less likely. It is not clear whether DSM and ICD meet the evolutionary definition by requiring paraphilic disorders to cause distress or harm. What do you think of the evolutionary definition?

10.11 Immune System Explanations

Many illnesses can negatively impact sexual interest and performance. As one example, people with autoimmune diseases are highly susceptible to sexual dysfunction—including those with *rheumatoid arthritis* (in which inflammation progressively destroys joints) and *Addison's Disease* (in which the immune system attacks the endocrine system's adrenal glands) (Frikha et al., 2021; Granata et al., 2013; J. Hill et al., 2003; Tristano, 2009, 2014). When it comes to rheumatoid diseases, sexual impairment can result from many factors—including pain, stiffness, anxiety, depression, hormonal imbalances, reduced sex drive, medication, and negative body image (Frikha et al., 2021; Tristano, 2009). Perhaps because talking about sex is uncomfortable to many people, doctors often don't ask their rheumatoid patients about their sexual functioning (Frikha et al., 2021; J. Hill et al., 2003; Tristano, 2014). Doing so would bring sexual issues to light so they can be addressed.

10.12 Evaluating Biological Perspectives

There is limited research evidence on treating sexual dysfunctions, especially in women (Gonsalves et al., 2020). This problem isn't limited to biological interventions. It is "a recurrent theme, concerning pharmacological as well as psychological treatment methods" (Almås, 2016, p. 60). Beyond concerns about effectiveness, critics complain that biological perspectives medicalize sex and gender. They contend that medicalization yields a narrow definition of sexual "normalcy" (especially for women), unfairly pathologizing sexual experiences that don't emphasize genital arousal and orgasm (Tiefer, 2002). Over-medicalizing sexual complaints leads to a preoccupation with "curing" them via pharmaceuticals (e.g., "Female Viagra") instead of relationally addressing them through couples counseling, sex therapy, and sex education (Tiefer, 2002). Of course, medicalization can be justified when there is a clear biological basis. Seeing erectile dysfunction as a penile blood flow issue (rather than due to psychological conflicts) strikes many as progress (Ghofrani et al., 2006). Unfortunately, the biological basis of sexual complaints is often difficult to pinpoint.

What about the medicalization of sexual orientation and gender identity? Is being homosexual or transgender better understood biologically or socially? Does medicalizing sexual orientation and gender identity pathologize sexual minorities? Maybe but not necessarily. Mental health professionals have long been aware of biological differences between homosexuals and heterosexuals but the mental health professions do not see homosexuality as disordered anymore (LeVay, 1991, 2011). Difference isn't the same as dysfunction (Epting et al., 1994; L. Hoffman & Lincoln, 2011).

Paraphilic coercive disorder (PCD):
Proposed but rejected DSM paraphilic disorder involving distressing fantasies about or repeated acts of rape.

Still, the significant time we spend investigating the biology of transgender and gay people is telling. We rarely ask about the biological causes of being a cisgender heterosexual. What does that tell us?

The "Controversial Question" feature examines medicalization in an area that some people may find difficult to read about. It asks whether rape is a mental disorder. **Paraphilic coercive disorder (PCD)** has been repeatedly proposed for but never added to DSM. Should it have been? Read on to decide.

Controversial Question: Are Rapists Mentally Ill?

Is the urge to rape a mental disorder? Mental health professionals have long debated whether to add *paraphilic coercive disorder (PCD)* to DSM (Dodd, 2015; Marecek & Gavey, 2013). PCD, previously called *paraphilic rapism*, has been repeatedly proposed and rejected for inclusion in the manual. When DSM-5 was developed, the issue became so contentious that PCD wasn't even listed as a criteria set for further study (Agalaryan & Rouleau, 2014; First, 2014).

Various definitions of PCD have been proposed, all focusing on rape as a paraphilia (Thornton, 2010). Proposed DSM-5 criteria required (a) "recurrent, intense sexually arousing fantasies or sexual urges focused on sexual coercion" lasting six months; (b) distress over these urges, or actually having acted on them at least three separate times; and (c) not having a sexual sadism diagnosis (P. Stern, 2010, p. 1444). If added to DSM, PCD would be diagnosed almost entirely in men who repeatedly rape or are disturbed and upset about their desire to do so.

Arguments about PCD have focused on science and politics. Scientifically, can PCD be differentiated from other disorders? Research in this area relies on the *penile plethysmograph (PPG)*, a device that gauges sexual arousal by measuring blood flow to the penis. If PPG studies can identify men aroused by rape-related imagery, then we potentially have an objective basis for diagnosing PCD—a development that would please those seeking quantifiable biomarkers for diagnosing mental disorders (such as RDoC researchers; see Chapter 3). Unfortunately, although rapists are aroused by coercive imagery and fantasies, PPG studies haven't yielded definitive results (R. A. Knight, 2010; Thornton, 2010).

Politically, those who believe rape is a mental illness argue that identifying it as a paraphilic disorder will let us reduce recidivism by medically treating paraphilic rapists whose disorders lead to their crimes (P. Stern, 2010). PCD opponents counter that making rape a mental disorder merely excuses rapists from criminal responsibility (Dodd, 2015). They also worry that PCD would unfairly classify too many people as sexual predators, justifying lengthy or indefinite institutionalizations (J. C. Wakefield, 2012). Finally, PCP opponents argue that considering rape a mental disorder inappropriately transforms it from a social to medical problem (Dodd, 2015; Scully & Marolla, 1985). They contend that rape isn't an illness but rather an all-too-common act committed by "normal" men in a society that condones violence against women. When casting rape as an individual disorder, we ignore societal values that perpetuate it.

Though previously proposed PCD criteria excluded a sadism diagnosis, in the aftermath of PCD being rejected as a diagnosis, rape was subsumed into recalibrated DSM and ICD criteria for sexual sadism (Mokros et al., 2019). However, sexual sadism disorder is a controversial diagnosis (A. Liu et al., 2022). It requires acting on or being distressed by urges for sexual activity with nonconsenting persons—criteria that clearly include rape. ICD-11 even uses the name *coercive sexual sadism disorder*. Considered highly prevalent in sex offenders (including serial rapists) (R. B. Krueger et al., 2017; G. M. Reed et al., 2016), DSM and ICD's versions of coercive sexual sadism open a new front in the ongoing battle over whether rape and other sexual offenses are not just crimes, but also—in at least some cases—expressions of mental disorder.

Critical Thinking Questions

1. How do those wishing to make PCD a mental disorder espouse a medical model?
2. How do those opposing making PCD as mental disorder espouse a social justice model?
3. Should PCD be added to future revisions of DSM and ICD? Why or why not?
4. Are rape and other sex crimes sometimes best understood as sexual sadism disorders?

PSYCHOLOGICAL PERSPECTIVES

10.13 Psychodynamic Perspectives

Classic Freud

Psychoanalytic perspectives view sexual dysfunctions and paraphilias as expressions of unconscious conflicts. Freud (1905/1962) believed that sexual "perversions" (today called paraphilias) indicate fixation at one or more of the psychosexual stages. For instance, a fetish might originate in castration anxiety at the phallic stage, while vaginismus might be a response to unresolved penis envy (J. D. Atwood, 2015; Gabbard, 2014). As a result of such fixations, the sexual instinct becomes misdirected away from the "normal" aim of sexual intercourse (i.e., reproduction) and towards the paraphilic activity. While Freud's stance may sound regressive by modern standards, he challenged the idea that "perversions" only occur in seriously disturbed individuals (H. Wood, 2003). He believed everyone is at least somewhat "perverted." Said Freud: "No healthy person, it appears, can fail to make some addition that might be called perverse to the normal sexual aim; and the universality of this finding is in itself enough to show how inappropriate it is to use the word perversion as a term of reproach" (Freud, 1905/1962, p. 51). Here Freud didn't firmly distinguish "normal" from "abnormal" sexuality. Only when "perversions" interfere with our lives or cause harm to others did he feel psychoanalysis was necessary to address them.

Paraphilias as Hostile Fantasies

Even though the term "paraphilia" replaced "perversion" by the 1970s and 1980s, psychoanalyst Robert Stoller (1985, 1976/1986) preferred the word "perversion" because he considered it more powerful and less sanitized (Delcea, 2020). "I want to retain the word *perversion* just *because* of its nasty connotations," he provocatively explained. "*Perversion* is a sturdy word, throbbing with assumptions, while *paraphilia* is a wet noodle" (Stoller, 1985, p. 6). Stoller argued that "perverts" unconsciously feel guilty because their sexual urges and behaviors are motivated not by a desire for sexual intimacy, but by hostility. To Stoller, **perversions** (which he said occur mostly in men) are traceable to profound humiliation during childhood—including but not limited to being repeatedly demeaned, bullied, and abused (usually with the implication of not being masculine enough). Perversions, as responses to this mistreatment, are acts of revenge, according to Stoller. Degrading others fulfills a need to relive the past shame, but in the role of victor rather than victim. In this respect, perversions involve *identification with the aggressor*, in which people identity with those who have mistreated them and adopt their characteristics. This prevents genuine intimacy. Rather than engaging with their partners as whole persons, people suffering from perversions use them to extract vengeance for past humiliations.

Perversions: Old-fashioned term for paraphilias preferred by psychodynamic therapist Robert Stoller, who saw them as acts of revenge intended to compensate for profound humiliation during childhood.

Lou

Imagine psychodynamic therapy with Lou for his transvestism. During therapy, Lou recalls how his mother humiliated him when he misbehaved as a young child by making him wear his sister's clothes. His masculinity was deeply threatened. In therapy, Lou gains insight into how his women's clothes fetish is tied to this past humiliation. He comes to see how wearing women's clothes while overpowering his wife during sex lets him relive his shame and get vengeance for it. As Lou understands and works through this issue, he finds he no longer must wear women's clothes to get sexually aroused. Sex with Ruth (even when it still sometimes involves cross-dressing) becomes about emotional intimacy instead of about Lou trying to resolve past humiliation.

Importantly, it is the psychodynamics behind a sex act—rather than the act itself—that makes it "perverted" or not: "To label someone 'perverse' says something about his or her psychodynamics, especially about a *fantasy* of harming" (Stoller, 1985, p. 41). Psychodynamic therapy fosters insight into how past humiliations restrict genuine sexual intimacy. When perversions violate others' rights (e.g., pedophilia, exhibitionism, frotteurism, voyeurism, and some cases of sadomasochism), they require legal as well as psychological interventions (Stoller, 1985, 1976/1986). Unfortunately, there is very little research on whether psychodynamic therapy for paraphilias is effective (Yakeley & Wood, 2014).

Interpersonal Therapy (IPT) for Transgender Clients

Interpersonal therapy (IPT) (refer to Chapter 5) has been adapted for use with transgender clients (Barbisan et al., 2020; Budge, 2013). IPT addresses the *interpersonal role transitions*, *interpersonal role disputes*, *grief*, and *interpersonal sensitivity* that often accompany the transitioning process. When it comes to role transitions, IPT holds that trans clients must grieve the loss of the old gender role, develop a positive view of the new gender role, gain comfort and confidence with the new role, and develop an accepting social support system (Barbisan et al., 2020; Budge, 2013). There is little research on IPT for trans clients, but a case study with a 32-year-old trans woman reported it helped her with the transitioning process (Barbisan et al., 2020).

10.14 Cognitive-Behavioral Perspectives

Behavioral Perspectives on Sexual Dysfunctions and Paraphilias
Habituation and Conditioning

Habituation:
Behavioral term for when responsiveness to a stimulus decreases after repeated exposure to it.

Behaviorists explain sexual disorders and paraphilias in terms of habituation, classical conditioning, and operant conditioning (Plaud & Holm, 1998). **Habituation** is when responsiveness to a stimulus decreases after repeated exposure to it (Plaud & Holm, 1998).

Elena
Elena's loss of interest in sex with her husband Hector might be a product of habituation. If sex is the same every time (e.g., always at night, always in the missionary position, always in bed), then Elena's responsiveness likely has decreased due to the repetitious nature of their sexual interactions. Consequently, what previously aroused Elena no longer does. Behavior therapy would encourage Elena and Hector to experiment with different sexual times, positions, and locations whose novelty might excite her.

In classical conditioning (see Chapter 2) of sexual problems, neutral stimuli become conditioned stimuli after repeatedly being paired with inherently arousing stimuli (Bolling et al., 2006). Operant conditioning, also discussed in Chapter 2, focuses on how sexual behavior is shaped by its consequences (Bolling et al., 2006).

Lou
According to classical conditioning, Lou's arousal from cross-dressing resulted from repeatedly pairing women's clothes (a neutral stimulus) with sexual arousal until women's clothes became a conditioned stimulus for arousal. By contrast, operant conditioning holds that Lou's cross-dressing is maintained through reinforcement.

Sexual Dysfunctions

Sensate focus: Masters and Johnson technique for arousal and orgasm issues; partners engage in sensual touching but not(Gosselin & Bombardier, 2020b) intercourse, removing pressure to perform.

Spectatoring: Observing and negatively evaluating one's sexual performance as if one were a third person watching it.

Behavioral interventions use conditioning techniques to improve sexual performance. **Sensate focus**—originally developed by Masters and Johnson (1970)—is often considered an *in vivo* behavioral technique to elicit sexual arousal and orgasms. It accomplishes this by reducing performance pressure (Gosselin & Bombardier, 2020b; Metz et al., 2017; L. Weiner & Avery-Clark, 2014). Clients are instructed to engage in sensual touching with their partners without it leading to intercourse. This reduces **spectatoring**, the tendency to observe and negatively evaluate one's sexual performance (Masters & Johnson, 1970; Metz et al., 2017; L. Weiner & Avery-Clark, 2014). Because sensate focus removes pressure to perform and discourages spectatoring, clients ironically often "fail" the assignment by becoming aroused, engaging in intercourse, and even having orgasms. It is a well-regarded sex therapy technique, but its varied use across many types of therapy has made it difficult to judge when it is most effective (Linschoten et al., 2016; L. Weiner, 2022).

Elena and Ahmed
Elena (who isn't interested in sex with husband Hector) and Ahmed (who is unable to get an erection despite finding his boyfriend Mark very attractive) might benefit from sensate focus exercises.

For premature ejaculation, Masters and Johnson (1970) developed the **squeeze technique** in which the ridge at the top of the penis is repeatedly squeezed during sexual activity in order to delay ejaculation (Gosselin & Bombardier, 2020b; InformedHealth.org, 2019). Another technique is the **stop-start method**, where men learn to stop intercourse prior to ejaculating and to begin again only after arousal decreases (InformedHealth.org, 2019; H. S. Kaplan, 1974). The squeeze technique and the stop-start method condition men to not ejaculate so quickly.

Bolin

The squeeze technique or stop-start method would teach Bolin, who experiences premature ejaculation, to orgasm less quickly during intercourse with his girlfriend, May.

Pelvic floor rehabilitation is another behavioral technique to improve sexual interest. It improves pelvic floor muscle weaknesses associated with sexual pain in women, as well as premature ejaculation and erectile dysfunction in men. Patients are assigned *Kegel exercises*, which involve tightening and relaxing pelvic floor muscles to strengthen them (ter Kuile et al., 2010; van Lankveld et al., 2006; Yaacov et al., 2022). Pelvic floor rehabilitation is sometimes supplemented with biofeedback (patients are provided feedback on muscle strength in digital games/exercises and then reinforced for improving it) or systematic desensitization (anxiety about sex is reduced by having people practice relaxation while imagining increasingly stressful sexual situations). Pelvic floor muscle strength is linked to sexual dysfunctions and rehabilitation exercises show promise, but more research is needed (K. Cooper et al., 2015; Ghaderi et al., 2019; T. Y. Rosenbaum, 2007; Yaacov et al., 2022).

Paraphilias

Behavioral techniques are also used to curtail paraphilias. *Aversion therapies* (discussed in Chapter 9) reduce undesirable sexual interests and behaviors by associating them with aversive (unpleasant) events (Gaither et al., 1998; Ware et al., 2021). As examples, a client might self-administer an unpleasant odor during the undesired sexual activity (*olfactory aversion*) or be given an electric shock during it (*electrical aversive therapy*). Aversion techniques rely on punishment. **Covert sensitization** combines the operant conditioning aspects of aversion therapy with elements of classical conditioning. It involves presenting an unpleasant image (*in vivo* or imaginally) while the client focuses on the paraphilic interest (Miner & Munns, 2021; Ware et al., 2021). This reduces paraphilic behavior by associating it with the unpleasant image. For example, a client might imagine being scolded by the woman he exposed himself to and having his wife divorce him because of his exhibitionism (Gaither et al., 1998). Another technique, **masturbatory satiation**, eliminates undesirable sexual behaviors by associating them with boredom and fatigue rather than arousal. (Miner & Munns, 2021). This is accomplished by asking clients to masturbate to their deviant fantasies for longer than is pleasurable so they become associated with tediousness rather than arousal (Gaither et al., 1998; Miner & Munns, 2021).

William

Covert satiation with William, who is aroused by child pornography, would have him focus on sexually arousing thoughts about children while being reminded of the consequences of being caught with child pornography: social embarrassment, ridicule, and possibly prison. This will hopefully condition William to associate child porn with negative outcomes. William also might be asked to masturbate at home for two hours while engaged in pedophilic fantasies. Because two hours is a long time, William will eventually get bored and—if all goes well—his fantasies about children will become associated with this boredom and lose their allure.

Squeeze technique: Top of the penis is repeatedly squeezed during sexual activity to delay ejaculation; conditions men to not ejaculate so quickly.

Stop-start method: Men stop intercourse prior to ejaculating and start again only after arousal decreases; conditions men to not ejaculate so quickly.

Pelvic floor rehabilitation: Behavioral technique that improves sexual interest via physical exercises (e.g., Kegel exercises) that strengthen weak pelvic floor muscles associated with sexual pain in women, as well as premature ejaculation and erectile dysfunction in men.

Covert sensitization: Aversion therapy in which undesired behavior is eliminated by presenting unpleasant images (*in vivo* or imaginally) while the client imagines engaging in the behavior.

Masturbatory satiation: Behavioral technique in which clients masturbate to paraphilic imagery for much longer than is pleasurable to associate the paraphilia with boredom.

Cognitive Perspectives on Sexual Dysfunctions and Paraphilias
CBT for Sexual Dysfunctions

Cognitive-behavioral therapy (CBT) for sexual dysfunctions supplements behavioral techniques by addressing problematic thinking. Cognitive restructuring, in which reason and argument are used to replace dysfunctional beliefs with rational ones, has been found effective for sexual dysfunctions (J. Carvalho et al., 2013; J. Carvalho & Nobre, 2010; Géonet et al., 2013; Metz et al., 2017; Nobre & Pinto-Gouveia, 2006). Among women, examples of dysfunctional beliefs are that women should always be able to have orgasms during intercourse, sexual desire is sinful, morally upstanding women (especially older ones) shouldn't be sexual, women lose sexual interest with age, and postmenopausal women don't like sex (J. Carvalho et al., 2013; Gosselin & Bombardier, 2020b; Nobre & Pinto-Gouveia, 2006). Comparable problematic beliefs common to men include "real men" have sex often, difficulty getting an erection is a personal failure, impotent men aren't masculine, and a woman's sexual satisfaction is determined by the quality of a man's erection (Gosselin & Bombardier, 2020b; Nobre & Pinto-Gouveia, 2006). CBT interventions encourage more realistic assessments of sexual performance (M. P. Carey, 1998; Meana, 2012).

Bolin
With Bolin, who worries about ejaculating too quickly, cognitive therapy would help him revise his core belief that his worth as a man and his attractiveness as a boyfriend are tied exclusively to how long he lasts in bed.

CBT for Paraphilias

Cognitive restructuring is most relevant when paraphilias endanger others. When they don't, other options might be preferable. For instance, clients like Lou who find cross-dressing arousing might be better off seeking "alternative options to treatment, such as joining a transvestite club where they can crossdress free from social disapproval" (Marshall & Fernandez, 1998, p. 285). For paraphilias that do violate others' rights (voyeurism, pedophilia, frotteurism, and exhibitionism), cognitive restructuring challenges cognitive distortions that rationalize sex offenses (M. S. Kaplan & Krueger, 2012). It targets problematic beliefs, such as: children are sexual beings; sex isn't harmful to kids; sex is a right one is entitled to; social rules about sex are optional; and women are deceitful, manipulative, and bad (Schaffer et al., 2010). Cognitive restructuring confronts the ways that sex offenders justify, rationalize, excuse, minimize, and deny the negative effects of their actions. It also works to enhance empathy (because offenders often don't understand the impact of their behavior on others) and improve interpersonal skills (because many offenders struggle to establish intimate relationships and build support networks) (W. L. Marshall & Fernandez, 1998; Schaffer et al., 2010). Research finds CBT effective at reducing sex offender *recidivism rates* (i.e., how often additional crimes are committed) (J. L. Harrison et al., 2020; B. Kim et al., 2016; Mpofu et al., 2018).

Transgender-Affirmative CBT

Transgender-affirmative CBT (TA-CBT): Form of CBT that helps transgender clients cope with anxiety and depression due to transphobia; negative internalized beliefs about being transgender are examined and changed.

Transgender-affirmative CBT (TA-CBT) uses CBT techniques to help transgender clients understand how their thoughts and feelings about themselves are adversely affected by *transphobia* (social prejudice directed at transgender people) (A. Austin et al., 2017; A. Austin & Craig, 2015, 2019). In both individual and group modalities, TA-CBT targets "negative self-beliefs and cognitive biases that do not necessarily reflect the 'truthfulness' of reality (e.g., internalized homophobia/ transphobia, self-stigma, and shame-related thoughts)" (S. A. Carvalho et al., 2022, p. 5). Coping skills are emphasized (for dealing with prejudice, stigma, the coming out process, etc.), as is developing identity-affirming relationships (A. Austin & Craig, 2015, 2019; S. A. Carvalho et al., 2022). TA-CBT is relatively new, but early research is encouraging (A. Austin et al., 2018; S. L. Craig & Austin, 2016).

Juana

TA-CBT with Juana would address her internalized negative beliefs about being transgender. It would target dysfunctional cognitions influenced by prejudicial societal attitudes about trans people (e.g., "Nobody will love or accept me for who I truly am."). Juana would replace these beliefs with more functional ones (e.g., "Even if some people don't accept me, there are those who will love me for who I am."). This should improve Juana's emotional outlook and help her build relationships with people who accept her for who she is.

10.15 Humanistic Perspectives

Critique of Medicalization of Sexuality

Humanistic psychotherapists lament what they see as the excessive medicalization of sexuality (T. Szasz, 1991; Tiefer, 2006, 2012). To them, what we commonly identify as sexually disordered is rarely disordered at all, but usually just atypical or socially unacceptable. Humanistic clinicians believe labeling unusual sexual acts or interests as disordered unfairly pathologizes personally meaningful variations in sexual activity and experience (L. L. Armstrong, 2006; Bridges & New, 2019; Gunst, 2012; Kleinplatz, 1996, 2014; S. M. Peters, 2021; Tiefer, 2006). To their sensibility, sexual acts, interests, and complaints are meaningful efforts at personal growth to be respected and understood, not disorders to be eradicated:

Whether it is the rape victim's flashbacks and nightmares, the intense anxiety of the man reporting erectile dysfunction, the pain of the woman with vaginismus, or the paraphiliac's fantasies … distressing symptoms are never to be eliminated without attention to their value, meaning, purpose and clinical usefulness. (Kleinplatz, 2014, p. 205)

Photo 10.4 Experiential sex therapy focuses not just on sex but on personality and relationships. This transforms clients' entire lives, including sex.
Shingi Rice/Unsplash.

Experiential Sex Therapy

Experiential sex therapy, an outgrowth of experiential psychotherapy (Mahrer, 1996), humanistically focuses on the meaning of sex rather than on "fixing" broken parts or eliminating "dysfunctional" interests and activities (Kleinplatz, 1996, 2007, 2014). Its goal "is to allow the individual to fulfill—rather than contain—his or her sexual, and other, potentials" (Kleinplatz, 2014, p. 204). Importantly, "there is no attempt to target behaviors—sexual or otherwise, deviant or normophilic" (Kleinplatz, 2014, p. 204). Instead, the focus is on personality change. When this occurs, changes in "sexual and other desires, wishes, fantasies and behavior, intimate relationships and bodily phenomena" naturally follow (Kleinplatz, 2014, p. 204). Experiential sex therapy encourages clients to identify and explore strong feelings (which may not be directly related to sex). This provides access to important inner experiences that suggest new possibilities for living and being. By allowing these newly discovered inner experiences to inform how they go about life, clients undergo personal growth that lets them live in more self-consistent ways. This transforms all aspects of their lives, including their sex lives.

Experiential sex therapy can be used for erectile dysfunction, premature ejaculation, difficulties with orgasm, paraphilias, and other sexual problems (Gunst, 2012; Kleinplatz, 1998, 2004, 2007, 2010, 2014). However, because this approach resists viewing sexuality as disordered, its effectiveness with specific diagnoses isn't easy to assess (Kleinplatz, 2014). For better or worse, sex therapy research typically emphasizes outcomes for specific problems over more comprehensive (but harder to measure) personality transformation.

Experiential sex therapy: Humanistic approach that views sexual problems as personally meaningful; fosters personal growth that transforms and improves clients' lives, indirectly leading to the resolution of sexual issues.

Elena and Hector

Experiential sex therapy would not try to "fix" Elena's lack of sexual interest in Hector. Instead, it would help Elena identify strong emotion—perhaps her powerful desire to say "to hell with everyone else." Therapy would trace this feeling to past hurts Elena experienced when told she was "too aggressive" and "not feminine enough" and how she compensated for this by becoming interpersonally passive and sexually compliant with men she dated (including Hector). Her therapist would ask what her life would look like if she did say "to hell with everyone else." In response, Elena might express a desire to be more assertive at work and with Hector—including in bed. To her surprise, Elena would find that Hector welcomes such changes. Therapy would encourage her to act like the assertive person she feels she is. As she does so, she would experience changes in her life. Her interpersonal relationships at home and work would improve. She also might find herself aroused by the prospect of being more sexually assertive with Hector.

10.16 Evaluating Psychological Perspectives

Sexual Dysfunctions

Unfortunately, many people are reluctant to share their sexual problems with their doctors, so they don't receive therapy for them (Gosselin & Bombardier, 2020b). Among psychological interventions, CBT (including Kegel exercises, exposure therapies, and biofeedback) has received the most research attention (J. M. Weinberger et al., 2019). However, more research is needed on both psychological and biological interventions (Almås, 2016; J. M. Weinberger et al., 2019). Consistent with this, the World Health Organization found that professional association guidelines on treating sexual dysfunctions relied more on expert opinion than objective evaluation of evidence (Gonsalves et al., 2020). A longstanding tension in the field is to what extent sexual dysfunctions are biological versus psychological problems. It's likely a bit of both, but whether you find yourself rooting for the biological or psychological perspective in this debate tells you about your own theoretical commitments.

Paraphilic Disorders and Sex Offenders

People with paraphilic issues tend not to seek therapy because they don't see their behavior as problematic, they are embarrassed by it, or they hide it because it is illegal (Gosselin & Bombardier, 2020b). Consequently, the samples in paraphilia therapy research tend to be unrepresentative, consisting of people who have been arrested and mandated to undergo therapy. Unfortunately, "these individuals are usually highly motivated to report that the treatment has worked, but may not necessarily be motivated to change" (Gosselin & Bombardier, 2020b, p. 321). This makes assessing therapy for paraphilias difficult. Further, much of the research focuses on therapy effectiveness for sex offenders—a group that overlaps with, but isn't identical to, people with paraphilias. Overall, the effectiveness of psychotherapy for sex offenders and paraphilias remains unclear. Research results are mixed, with few randomized controlled trials and a tendency toward unrepresentative samples (Chaudhary & Garg, 2019).

SOCIOCULTURAL PERSPECTIVES

10.17 Cross-Cultural and Social Justice Perspectives

Prevalence rates for sexual dysfunctions, paraphilias, and gender dysphoria differ across cultures. For instance, DSM-5-TR notes that the prevalence of low sexual desire varies across the world, ranging from 26 percent to 43 percent. This makes sense from a cross-cultural perspective, which holds that what counts as sexually deviant differs by culture, so we must be careful before assuming DSM and ICD disorders are universal. Social justice-oriented therapists and researchers challenge the idea that sexual disorders are culture-free categories. Instead, they emphasize how gender, ethnicity, economic status, and other social issues shape understandings of sexual difficulties.

The New View Critique and Reconceptualization of Sexual Dysfunctions

From 2000 to 2016, feminist and humanistic mental health advocates conducted the **New View campaign**, which challenged seeing women's sexual dysfunctions as strictly medical (rather than interpersonal and social) problems (McHugh, 2006; New View Campaign, 2018; Tiefer, 2001b, 2002, 2010). The New View held that traditional medical approaches to sexual difficulties incorrectly assume that men and women are physiologically equivalent in their sexual functioning (Tiefer, 2001a). This overlooks important gender differences (e.g., women often don't distinguish between desire and arousal). The medical view also problematically conceptualizes women's desire and arousal complaints as signs of sickness, rather than as responses to relationship dissatisfaction and gender discrimination. After all, it's hard to maintain interest in sex if you feel abused by your partner and discriminated against in the wider world. Finally, the medical view minimizes individual and situational differences, assuming that certain levels of desire, interest, and activity are "normal" for all women—regardless of factors such as personality, economic status, and relationship satisfaction (World Association of Sexual Health, 2014). One target of the New View's ire was the DSM:

The American Psychiatric Association's DSM approach bypasses relational aspects of women's sexuality, which often lie at the root of sexual satisfactions and problems—e.g., desires for intimacy, wishes to please a partner, or, in some cases, wishes to avoid offending, losing, or angering a partner. The DSM takes an exclusively individual approach to sex, and assumes that if the sexual parts work, there is no problem; and if the parts don't work, there is a problem. But many women do not define their sexual difficulties this way. The DSM's reduction of "normal sexual function" to physiology implies, incorrectly, that one can measure and treat genital and physical difficulties without regard to the relationship in which sex occurs. (Tiefer, 2001a, p. 94)

In contrast to DSM, the New View proposed dividing sexual problems into four types: (1) *sexual problems due to sociocultural, political or economic factors*; (2) *sexual problems relating to partner and relationship*; (3) *sexual problems due to psychological factors*; and (4) *sexual problems due to medical factors* (Tiefer, 2001a, p. 94). This refocused attention on social, political, psychological, and relational factors, while leaving room for some sexual issues to be medical. Note how the New View spoke of sexual *problems* rather than sexual *disorders*—a clear shift from a strictly medical model (Iasenza, 2001; Kleinplatz, 2012; McHugh, 2006; Ogden, 2001; Tiefer, 2001b; S. P. Williams, 2001). There wasn't much research on the New View classification but one qualitative study found it effectively accounted for 98 percent of women's sexual complaints—with 65 percent of these complaints identified as relational, 20 percent as sociocultural/political/economic, 8 percent as psychological, and 7 percent as medical (Nicholls, 2008). Whether the New View classification will continue to garner attention now that the wider New View campaign has ended remains to be seen.

Elena

Rather than diagnosing Elena with female sexual interest/arousal disorder and treating it as a strictly medical problem involving faulty body parts, a New View therapist would consider additional explanations for Elena's lack of sexual interest. Exploring socioeconomic, political, and economic factors, Elena's therapist might learn that Elena has been sexually harassed at work and is paid less than men with comparable education and experience. The resulting stress could be negatively affecting her sexual interest. A New View therapist would also be interested in the quality of Elena's relationship with her husband Hector. Perhaps she isn't sexually interested because she feels estranged from him. Finally, psychological factors would be considered. If Elena is a survivor of past abuse, she might experience sex as a traumatic chore rather than an intimate way to connect with Hector. Therapy would focus on these issues to help Elena address them.

Transgender Affirmative Therapists: Gatekeepers or Advocates?

Should transgender people need permission from mental health professionals before receiving hormone therapy or gender affirmation surgeries? Those who say yes believe in **gatekeeping**, an approval process in which medical and mental health professionals assess the psychological and

New View campaign: Challenged privileging medical model view of female sexual problems and proposed four types: (1) *sexual problems due to sociocultural, political, or economic factors*; (2) *sexual problems relating to partner and relationship*; (3) *sexual problems due to psychological factors*; and (4) *sexual problems due to medical factors*.

Gatekeeping: Approval process conducted by medical and mental health professionals to keep people with gender dysphoria/incongruence who are deemed psychologically unfit from making irreversible gender-altering decisions.

physical readiness of those seeking to transition. WPATH, an interdisciplinary professional and educational organization devoted to transgender health, recommends that before undergoing gender-affirming medical and surgical procedures, adult patients should have to obtain a referral letter from a qualified professional attesting that they (a) have been diagnosed with gender incongruence, (b) are able to make informed decisions about treatment, and (c) have significant medical or mental health issues under control (E. Coleman et al., 2022). WPATH previously required two letters but reduced it to one in 2022, arguing that "limited research in the area indicates two opinions are largely unnecessary" (E. Coleman et al., 2022, p. S40).

Critics view gatekeeping as paternalistic and oppressive (Ashley, 2019; Feola, 2021; Jalopy, 2020). They say it interferes with trans people receiving urgently needed medical interventions. As one trans woman put it: "When I decided that I wanted to take hormones to feminise my body, the last thing I wanted to do was to go in front of a psychologist to justify my decision" (Ashley, 2019, p. 480). Consequently, there has been a shift—even within WPATH—from seeing psychotherapists as gatekeepers to viewing them as *advocates* who assist clients in overcoming obstacles to transitioning (Burnes et al., 2010; A. A. Singh & Burnes, 2010; A. A. Singh & Dickey, 2016). Believing that gatekeeping reflects cisgender bias, many transgender-affirmative therapists contend it is time to do away with it entirely. They argue that a mental health requirement for transitioning "punishes trans people for an adaptive human response to oppression and bars them from accessing gender-affirming medical interventions that could alleviate mental health symptoms" (Feola, 2021, para. 11). Nonetheless, some mental health professionals continue to believe that assessment and therapy should be prerequisites for transitioning (Saad et al., 2019)—at the very least among children and adolescents (Edwards-Leeper & Anderson, 2021). Debate over these issues is intense and unlikely to be resolved soon.

10.18 Service User Perspectives

Programs for Sexual Offenders

Rooted in CBT, classic **relapse prevention (RP)** programs help sex offenders identify environmental and cognitive factors that contribute to relapse (Pithers et al., 1988). Offenders learn to avoid high-risk situations, correct problematic thinking, develop coping skills, be aware of (and resist) urges for instant gratification, and manage relapses. They self-monitor their thoughts, feelings, and fantasies to identify triggers associated with reoffending. Further, they learn to estimate their responses to high-risk situations and develop strategies for handling them. RP with sexual offenders integrates cognitive and behavioral techniques, as well as relaxation training. Original RP has been critiqued for its shortcomings and lack of research support, although some studies find it beneficial (Laws, 2017; J. K. Marques et al., 2005; W. L. Marshall & Marshall, 2021). RP's limitations have led to the development of other approaches.

The **risk-need-responsivity (RNR) model** infers the *need* for intervention based on assessments of the *risk* of reoffending (based on personality factors, substance use, social support, attitudes, recreational activities, etc.) (D. A. Andrews & Bonta, 2010; Bonta & Andrews, 2007). Its *responsivity* principle says recidivism is best prevented by correctly matching risk with need to provide each offender appropriate interventions (D. A. Andrews & Bonta, 2010; Bonta & Andrews, 2007). For instance, an antisocial substance abuser and gambler who believes women "ask" to be raped by dressing provocatively poses a greater risk and needs intervention more than someone who gets along well with others, doesn't use substances, and holds respectful attitudes toward women. Research on RNR programs is encouraging even if overall effectiveness remains unclear, in part because these programs are implemented differently across studies, making results hard to compare (W. L. Marshall & Marshall, 2021; Olver & Wong, 2013).

The **good lives model (GLM)** adds a humanistic component to sex offender rehabilitation, arguing that reducing risk and avoiding problematic thoughts and behaviors isn't sufficient. GLM programs emphasize personal growth and fulfillment (Ward et al., 2007; Ward & Brown, 2004; Ward & Marshall, 2004; Ward & Stewart, 2003). They help offenders identify and pursue *primary goods* (intrinsically beneficial goals such as being independent, excelling at work, and fostering intimate relationships). Unfortunately, there isn't much controlled research on GLM. One case study with a

Relapse prevention (RP): CBT technique that prevents relapse by teaching those in recovery how to handle high-risk situations that tempt them to engage in the problematic activity again; used with sexual offenders, substance users, and behavioral addictions.

Risk-need-responsivity model (RNR): CBT program for offenders that tailors interventions to each offender by assessing *risk* and *need* in order determine *responsivity* (the appropriate kind and level of intervention needed to prevent repeat offenses).

Good lives model (GLM): Humanistic program for offenders emphasizing personal growth and fulfillment; identifies *primary goods* (intrinsically beneficial goals such as independence, excelling at work, and fostering intimate relationships) that guide rehabilitation.

violent (non-sex) offender found it beneficial (P. R. Whitehead et al., 2007). A qualitative study with (again, non-sex) offenders did not test the GLM specifically, but did find that offenders in general valued person-centered interventions (Barnao et al., 2015). Importantly, GLM's primary goods do seem related to adolescent well-being, so addressing primary goods could improve offenders' lives and decrease recidivism (Serie et al., 2021).

Transgender Support and Advocacy Groups

There are many transgender support and advocacy groups. Some of these groups focus exclusively on transgender concerns. Others are broader, offering services for anyone identifying as *LGBTQ* (an abbreviation that stands for *lesbian, gay, bisexual, transgender, and queer or questioning*) (The Welcoming Project, n.d.). Table 10.2 lists some of the more prominent consumer groups that provide education, online support, counseling information or services, and political advocacy for transgender people and others identifying under the LGBTQ umbrella. See "The Lived Experience" for a first-hand account of the joys and challenges of being trans.

Table 10.2 Transgender and Other LGBQT Support and Advocacy Groups

UNITED STATES AND CANADA	
Trans Lifeline http://www.translifeline.org	Non-profit organization in United States and Canada focused on the well-being of transgender people; runs a hotline for transgender people staffed by transgender people.
The Trevor Project http://www.thetrevorproject.org	Crisis intervention and suicide prevention services to LGBTQ people ages 13–24.
PFLAG https://www.pflag.org	Offers support, education, and advocacy for the LGBTQ community.
It Gets Better Project http://www.itgetsbetter.org	Non-profit organization to uplift, empower, and connect LGBTQ youth across the globe.
National Center for Transgender Equality https://transequality.org	Advocates for understanding and acceptance of transgender people.
Transgender Law Center https://transgenderlawcenter.org/	Works to change law, policy, and attitudes so all people can safely express their gender identities.

UNITED KINGDOM AND EUROPE	
Beaumont Society http://www.beaumontsociety.org.uk	Self-help body run by and for the transgender community.
Gender Trust http://gendertrust.org.uk	Registered charity that helps transgender people and those affected by issues related to gender identity.
Mermaids http://www.mermaidsuk.org.uk	Supports trans, non-binary, and gender-diverse children, young people, and their families.
Transgender Europe (TGEU) http://tgeu.org	Transgender support and advocacy group with 195 member organizations in 48 countries.
LGBT Foundation http://lgbt.foundation	Offers advice, support, and services to the LGBTQ communities.

AUSTRALIA	
The Gender Center https://gendercentre.org.au	Provides support services to the gender diverse in New South Wales, as well as their partners, families, and friends.
Transgender Victoria https://tgv.org.au	Engages in gender-diverse advocacy and training in Victoria.

Transcend http://www.transcendsupport.com.au	Parent-led peer support network and information hub for transgender children and their families.
QLife https://qlife.org.au	Anonymous peer support and referral services for lesbian, gay, bisexual, trans, and/or intersex people.

SOUTH AFRICA	
Gender DynamiX http://genderdynamix.org.za	Defends and promotes rights of trans and gender-diverse people in South Africa, Africa, and the world.
Same Love Toti http://pflagsouthafrica.org	Based in Amanzimtoti and provides support and resources to the LGBTQ communities in the Durban and South Coast areas.

The Lived Experience: On Being Trans

Photo 10.5 For transgender people like Evelyn, it is vital to have trans representation in the media and in positions of authority. Pictured are actor Ian Alexander and DJ/activist Nico Craig, both transgender, attending the annual Human Rights Campaign National Dinner in 2022.
STEFANI REYNOLDS/Getty Images.

I didn't want to be trans. I had seen how difficult life could be for trans people. The disgust and mockery they faced. How messy and extensive transitioning was. I didn't want to deal with that. My life wasn't too bad. I could tough it out.

I wasn't sure that I was trans, not for a long time. I had an idea of what trans people were in my head, and I didn't fit it. I had lots of typically male hobbies, male friends, male clothes, male voice. I had nothing that made me seem trans—if you ignored everything that did.

Most importantly, I wasn't trans. You had to be trans to be trans, and I wasn't trans. Therefore, I wasn't trans. Obviously.

I had the idea that being trans was transitioning, and because I wasn't transitioning, I wasn't trans. Then when I accepted that (maybe) I had some characteristics that could (perhaps) make me seem like a trans person, I still thought that if I didn't transition, I wouldn't be trans—and that my life would be easier, and therefore happier, and I could just forget.

My life didn't get easier, it didn't get happier, and I didn't forget.

I saw being trans as a losing game, and I thought that the only way to win was not to play. I hadn't considered that by playing, I might actually win. When I started looking at pictures of trans people that had been transitioning for years, and who looked so confident and beautiful and happy, I knew I wanted that. I wanted it more than I'd ever wanted anything. I wanted to win.

I texted a couple of my closest friends at college, who'd both been out as nonbinary for years, and asked if they'd mind trying out some new pronouns for me. If they hadn't reacted so enthusiastically and stripped away so much shame and doubt by being genuinely excited for me, I don't know where I'd be right now. The first few months of my social transition were colored by joy and discovery because of those friends and that conversation.

I enjoy the little pieces of my life so much more now. I like talking. I like walking. I like putting outfits together. I like shopping. I like smiling. I like having my picture taken. I like being seen. I like laughing.

I love catching a glimpse of myself in the mirror, highlighting the high silhouette of my hair and the depth of my eyes. I love seeing the delighted reaction of friends who haven't seen me in years. I love waking up and feeling so, so lucky.

Before transitioning, these were things that I tolerated or avoided. So much of my life is made up of these small pieces, and being able to enjoy them makes enjoying my life as a whole much, much easier.

I didn't want to be trans. I can't say that I always do now. Would I have struggled less and been happier for it? Or would I have been less fulfilled for not having struggled? Would I have fewer issues if I wasn't trans, or would they just be replaced by cis issues?

I have friends that are close to me because we're both trans. I have clothes and hobbies and stories that are precious to me because of my transition. My voice is a product of my birth and my actions.

If I wasn't trans, I don't know who I'd be. I love who I am now. That's enough for me.

By Evelyn. Reprinted with permission.

10.19 Systems Perspectives

Sexual Complaints as Expressions of Couple and Family Dynamics

Family systems perspectives view sexual problems as reflections of couple and family dynamics rather than as individual maladies. A systems view "stresses that sexual disorders do not exist in a vacuum but are often related to problems in the couple's emotional relationship, such as poor communication, hostility and competitiveness, and sex role problems" (J. D. Atwood, 2015, p. 452). Systems therapies disrupt family and relationship dynamics that perpetuate sexual problems. That doesn't mean all sexual complaints originate relationally, but "even in cases in which the sexual disorder is not related to relationship problems, the couple's emotional relationship is often damaged by the sexual problem and feelings of guilt, inadequacy, and frustration that usually accompany the sexual disorder" (J. D. Atwood, 2015, p. 452).

Elena

Elena's lack of sexual interest may be understood systemically as reflecting relational problems in her marriage. She and her husband Hector are both from conflict-avoidant families and have continued this pattern in their relationship—with each quietly nursing unaddressed grievances about the other. If systems-oriented couple therapy helps Elena and Hector communicate more effectively, then Elena's sexual interest may return.

Family Systems Approaches with Sexual Minority Youth

Sexual minority youth regularly encounter resistance when they come out, which can be exacerbated by problematic family dynamics (Doyle, 2018). Family systems therapy promotes more effective family communication. This is important because "parents may be more likely to provide permission for gender-affirming medical care for their child when communication is open and anxiety levels in the family are lowered" (Healy & Allen, 2020, p. 409). Family systems therapies for sexual minority youth are not yet widely developed or researched but potentially ease the coming out process by promoting emotional interconnectedness and healthy boundaries (Doyle, 2018; Healy & Allen, 2020).

10.20 Evaluating Sociocultural Perspectives

Sociocultural perspectives remind us that judgments about sexual behavior are influenced by culture and context. They often challenge the medical model, which in its pure form sees sexual disorders as culturally universal diseases rather than as socially and relationally defined problems. Sociocultural perspectives also emphasize how social values lead to discrimination against sexual minorities. They view advocacy and support groups as important social supports necessary to overcome such discrimination. When it comes to addressing sexual problems and gender dysphoria, sociocultural perspectives intervene at the social, rather than individual, level. Their main weakness is that in some cases sexual problems may be better attributed to biological and psychological (rather than social) causes. However, even then the social still matters.

Ahmed

The sexual problems of Ahmed—the 65-year-old who has trouble with erections—may be due to biological (age-related) factors effectively addressed via drugs. However, sociocultural advocates might counter that even in cases like Ahmed's, the problem isn't free of social influences. After all, Ahmed may be distressed over his biologically based erectile dysfunction because he lives in a culture that equates erections with manhood. In a different cultural context, his erectile issues might not bother him as much.

CLOSING THOUGHTS

10.21 Sexuality as Socially Constructed?

Attitudes about what constitutes normal sexual activity change over time. Some people argue that conceptions of sexuality—including ideas about love, desire, sexual orientation, sexual identity, sexual response, sexual dysfunction, and gender—are socially constructed (DeLamater & Hude, 1998; Foucault, 1978; Halperin, 1989; Nussbaum, 1997; Tiefer, 1991). As noted in Chapter 2, a social construction is any communal way of defining, talking about, and understanding something that brings into being certain shared social realities, which in turn influence how people come to comprehend themselves (Burr, 2015; Gergen, 2015). Social constructions about sexuality shape how people understand themselves sexually (Billings & Urban, 1982; De Block & Adriaens, 2013; Fausto-Sterling, 2000; Fishman & Mamo, 2001; D. F. Greenberg, 1988; Lavie-Ajayi, 2005; Tiefer, 2003). For instance, without the socially constructed distinction between homosexuality and heterosexuality, people could not come to experience themselves as gay or straight (Burr, 2015; D. F. Greenberg, 1988). Likewise, they could not see themselves as having sexual dysfunctions without having internalized socially agreed upon ideas about how much interest they should have in sex, how often they should engage in it, and what constitutes "proper" performance at it (Lavie-Ajayi, 2005; Tiefer, 2003).

If past and current understandings of sexuality and gender are socially constructed, then how might people one hundred years from now view current perspectives on sex and gender problems? How similar will these views be to our present understandings? Are there universal truths about sex and gender that transcend time, place, and culture? Or will ideas about them a century from now be utterly different? These questions can be asked about any presenting problem in this book but seem especially pertinent when thinking about sex and gender because notions about them have changed so rapidly and significantly over the past century.

CHAPTER SUMMARY

Overview

- *Sex* refers to one's biological status as male or female, while *gender* refers to cultural values, feelings, and behaviors having to do with sex.
- *Transgender* and *cisgender* are important terms in understanding *gender identity*.
- *Sexual orientation* involves who one is sexually attracted to; *heterosexism* can make *coming out* difficult.

Diagnostic Perspectives

- DSM and ICD sexual dysfunctions are organized into *desire and arousal disorders, orgasmic disorders,* and *sexual pain disorders.* The manuals define and name some of these disorders differently from one another.
- *Paraphilic disorders* involve unusual sexual interests that cause harm to others or distress to the person engaging in them or fantasizing about them.
- *Gender dysphoria* (DSM) and *gender incongruence* (ICD) are diagnosed in people distressed by discrepancies between their assigned and experienced genders.
- DSM and ICD have been criticized for pathologizing normal variations in sexual behavior.
- PDM links sexual problems to other issues like anxiety and depression. HiTOP and RDoC are researching dimensional ways to comprehend and diagnose sexual issues. PTMF sees sexual complaints and gender dysphoria as understandable and non-pathological threat responses to social adversity.

Historical Perspectives

- Sexuality has become increasingly medicalized in Western cultures.
- Starting with Kinsey in the 1940s and 1950s, researchers began asking people about their sex lives.
- Masters and Johnson's conducted seminal research on the sexual response cycle.

Biological Perspectives

- *Hormones* and *neurotransmitters* play important roles in sexual problems and inform many of the drug treatments that are used.
- Numerous brain regions are suspected of playing roles in sexual problems (e.g., *orbitofrontal cortex, parietal cortex, amygdala, hippocampus, thalamus,* and *hypothalamus*).
- Efforts to identify "male" and "female" brain differences have provided some insights into understanding gender dysphoria but run the risk of oversimplifying things.
- Gene–environment interactions appear important in sexual dysfunctions. Little is known about the genetics of paraphilias.
- Gender dysphoria seems to be heritable, but research on candidate genes is in its infancy.
- Evolutionary perspectives attribute sexual dysfunctions to evolution not keeping up with societal changes. They see paraphilias as only qualifying as disorders when they interfere with reproduction (thus only pedophilia clearly is disordered).
- Illnesses, including autoimmune diseases, contribute to sexual dysfunctions.

Psychological Perspectives

- Psychodynamic approaches view sexual dysfunctions as expressions of unconscious conflicts. Paraphilias (i.e., "perversions") can be viewed as acts of revenge for past humiliations.
- Interpersonal therapy helps trans clients with *interpersonal role transitions, interpersonal role disputes, grief,* and *interpersonal sensitivity* that accompany transitioning.
- Behavioral techniques for sexual dysfunctions include *sensate focus, squeeze technique, stop-start method,* and *pelvic floor rehabilitation*.
- *Aversion therapies, covert sensitization,* and *masturbatory satiation* are behavioral techniques used to eliminate paraphilias.
- CBT supplements behavioral techniques with cognitive interventions to change problematic beliefs related to sex.
- *Transgender-affirmative CBT (TA-CBT)* helps transgender clients revise thoughts and feelings that are unduly influenced by *transphobia,* while supporting them in coming out and/or transitioning.
- *Experiential sex therapy* is a humanistic approach that focuses on the meaning of sex rather than on "fixing" broken parts or eliminating "dysfunctional" interests and activities.

Sociocultural Perspectives

- The *New View campaign* challenged the medicalization of female sexual complaints, reframing them as due to socioeconomic factors, relationship dissatisfaction, gender discrimination.
- *Gatekeeping* is the controversial process in which trans people must be deemed psychologically ready by their medical and mental health professionals to receive hormone therapy or gender-affirming surgeries.
- *Relapse prevention (RP)* and the *risk-need-responsivity model (RNR)* are CBT programs used to prevent recidivism among sex offenders. The *good lives model (GLM)* adds humanistic elements in trying to prevent recidivism.
- Transgender support and advocacy groups offer information, assistance, and services to the LGBTQ community.
- Family systems perspectives attribute sexual problems to couple and family dynamics.
- Family systems therapists aim to improve family communication as they support and advocate for transgender clients.

Closing Thoughts

- Conceptions of sexuality can be viewed as social constructions that change over time.

NEW VOCABULARY

1. Ally
2. Androgen
3. Anorgasmia
4. Antiandrogens
5. Bremelanotide
6. Chemical castration
7. Cisgender
8. Coming out
9. Compulsive sexual behavior disorder (CSBD)
10. Covert sensitization
11. Delayed ejaculation
12. Erectile disorder
13. Estrogen
14. Exhibitionistic disorder
15. Experiential sex therapy
16. Female orgasmic disorder
17. Female sexual arousal dysfunction
18. Female sexual interest/arousal disorder
19. Fetishistic disorder
20. Flibanserin
21. Frotteuristic disorder
22. Gatekeeping
23. Gender
24. Gender affirmative hormone therapy (GAHT)
25. Gender-affirming surgeries
26. Gender dysphoria
27. Gender identity
28. Gender incongruence
29. Genito-pelvic pain/penetration disorder
30. Good lives model (GLM)
31. Habituation
32. Heterosexism
33. Hormone replacement therapy (HRT)
34. Hypersexual disorder
35. Hypoactive sexual desire dysfunction
36. Intracavernous injection therapy (ICI)
37. Male hypoactive sexual desire disorder
38. Masturbatory satiation
39. New View campaign
40. Noradrenaline
41. Paraphilias
42. Paraphilic coercive disorder (PCD)
43. Paraphilic disorder involving solitary behavior or consenting individuals
44. Paraphilic disorders
45. Pedophilic disorder
46. Pelvic floor rehabilitation
47. Perversions
48. Premature (early) ejaculation
49. Puberty blockers
50. Relapse prevention (RP)
51. Risk-need-responsivity model (RNR)
52. Sexual masochism disorder
53. Sexual sadism disorder
54. Sensate focus
55. Sex
56. Sexual dysfunctions
57. Sexual instinct
58. Sexual orientation
59. Sexual pain-penetration disorder
60. Sexual response cycle
61. Sildenafil
62. Spectatoring
63. Squeeze technique
64. Stop-start technique
65. Surgical castration
66. Testosterone
67. Transgender
68. Transgender-affirmative CBT (TA-CBT)
69. Transvestic disorder
70. Voyeuristic disorder

SUBSTANCE USE AND ADDICTION

LEARNING OBJECTIVES

After reading this chapter, you should be able to:

1. Define basic terms such as addiction, abuse, and dependence.

2. Identify different classes of drugs and describe their physiological and psychological effects.

3. Summarize DSM and ICD diagnoses related to substance use and behavioral addictions, as well as explain differences among and controversies over these diagnoses.

4. Discuss how ideas about addiction have changed across history.

5. Describe biological perspectives on substance use and behavioral addictions, including those pertaining to brain chemistry, brain structure, genes, evolution, and the immune system.

6. Summarize psychodynamic, cognitive-behavioral, and humanistic perspectives on substance use and addictions.

7. Outline sociocultural perspectives on substance use and behavioral addictions, especially the importance of socioeconomic factors.

8. Describe self-help, community treatment, and family approaches to substance use and behavioral addictions.

Photo 11.1
Anna Shvets/Pexels.

OVERVIEW

11.1 Getting Started: Substance Use and Other Behaviors as Addictive?

Case Examples

Walter

Walter is a 35-year-old businessman who seeks therapy at the insistence of his wife Margaret. Since his university days, he has considered himself the "life of the party." However, Margaret has grown frustrated with Walter's drinking. "He's drunk all the time," she complains. "He drinks all day, every day. He's more interested in his next beer than me and the kids." Walter admits he enjoys alcohol and drinks it often but denies that he's an alcoholic. "I don't drink as much as Margaret says I do. Besides, I could stop anytime," he insists. When it's pointed out that Margaret demanded he seek therapy because he was recently arrested for drunk driving, Walter dismisses it as "Bad luck that could happen to anyone."

Ayesha

Ayesha, a 22-year-old woman, is arrested while wandering the streets in a daze. She tells the police that, until recently, she was a graduate student in anthropology at the local university. However, she was kicked out of school for not paying her tuition. She says she's been down on her luck economically since her parents threw her out of the house. When asked why they kicked her out, she says she isn't sure. Further inquiry reveals Ayesha has been addicted to opioids for the past year, after initially being prescribed OxyContin to manage back pain. Her parents initially tried to help her but grew increasingly alarmed by Ayesha's behavior. They were upset when she used her tuition money to buy heroin, but the final straw was when she stole their debit card and withdrew $2,000 from their bank account. As Ayesha sits in jail waiting to be arraigned, she trembles, sweats, and feels sick to her stomach.

Pedro

Pedro is a 28-year-old bartender who seeks counseling for his chronic gambling. Pedro regularly bets on sporting events online. He also spends many weekends at a nearby casino or attending high stakes poker tournaments. Pedro began gambling in high school, when he and his friends wagered small sums on card games. By college, he was playing poker regularly, but only if money was involved. "Without something at stake, where's the fun in it?" Pedro asks. In recent years, his father has stepped in to pay off Pedro's debts, in one case saving him from an angry bookmaker. Pedro admits that when he gambles, he doesn't know when to stop: "If I lose, I keep going back for more. I always think the next bet is going to make up for the one before."

Liam

Liam is a 15-year-old high school student whose parents take him to therapy because they worry that he spends too much time playing video games. "He cares more about the characters and stories in these games than he does about his real life!" his mother exclaims. Liam says his parents are overreacting: "Sure, I like video games and play them a lot. First, they're interactive, not passive—unlike when my parents watch TV. Second, what's the harm if I enjoy it?" Liam's grades in school have dropped, but he says that has nothing to do with gaming. His parents wish he'd socialize with friends in the neighborhood. Liam says he prefers the people he games with online, even though he's never met them in person.

Deanna

Deanna is a 55-year-old woman whose partner, Leslie, brings her to psychotherapy because—in Leslie's words—she's a "shopaholic." Leslie says Deanna regularly rings up huge credit card bills at the mall and while shopping online. She is unable to pay these bills and is carrying a large credit card balance, in one case even exceeding her credit limit. "I enjoy the things I buy. Is that so wrong?" Deanna replies. Leslie says she may end their relationship if Deanna doesn't get her shopping under control.

Basic Terms: Addiction, Abuse, and Dependence
Addiction

Addiction: A non-diagnostic term describing lack of control over doing, taking, or using something despite potentially harmful consequences.

    Addiction is "a loaded term" that has "different meanings to different people" (Petry, 2016b, p. 1). It used to be reserved for drug use (A. Goodman, 1990), but it now includes excessive gambling, shopping, Internet use, and sexual activity (Barrilleaux, 2016; M. Clark, 2011; de Alarcón et al., 2019; Derbyshire & Grant, 2015; Niedermoser et al., 2021; Petry, 2016b; Potenza et al., 2019; K. Young, 2015). Addiction is often defined as "a treatable, chronic medical disease involving complex interactions among brain circuits, genetics, the environment, and an individual's life experiences" (American Society of Addiction Medicine, 2019, para. 1). However, not everyone embraces the disease model so fully. The UK's National Health Service (2021, para. 1) simply defines addiction as "not having control over doing, taking or using something to the point where it could be harmful to you." Perhaps due to difficulties defining it, ICD and DSM use the term sparingly (and not in the names of disorders). Though the lay public often speaks of addiction, professional consensus over its meaning and usage remains elusive.

Abuse vs. Dependence

When it comes to drug use, many but not all mental health professionals distinguish **abuse vs. dependence**. Abuse is the ongoing misuse of a substance, whereas dependence is physically or psychologically needing the substance to function (W. L. White, 2007). Substance abusers fail to meet school, work, and family obligations. Their substance use leads to irresponsible or dangerous behavior that damages relationships (e.g., driving under the influence). However, they aren't necessarily dependent on the substance. Dependence requires *tolerance* (needing more of a drug to produce the same effects) and *withdrawal* (unpleasant psychological and physical symptoms when the drug stops being taken) (W. L. White, 2007). For example, cigarette smokers dependent on nicotine must smoke more cigarettes to achieve the same effects (tolerance) but feel nauseous and groggy when prevented from smoking (withdrawal). As another example, many university students abuse alcohol. They drink too much, do foolish things, and perhaps even get in trouble. That's substance abuse. However, after graduation, most stop drinking to excess and behave more responsibly. Only those unable to stop are considered dependent. As a well-known addiction treatment center succinctly put it, "abuse is too much, too often" and "dependence is the inability to quit" (Hazelden Betty Ford Foundation, 2016, para. 2). The abuse–dependence distinction is sometimes clearer in theory than practice. As we shall see, ICD continues to make it but DSM does not.

Abuse vs. dependence: Abuse is the ongoing misuse of a substance; dependence is physically or psychologically needing the substance to function, as evidenced by *tolerance* (needing more of the substance for the same effect) and *withdrawal* (unpleasant psychological and physical symptoms when the drug stops being taken).

Photo 11.2 The film *Trainspotting* is an extremely well-known depiction of drug dependence, which examines the societal and economic factors linked to addiction. This portrayal of drug users has been both praised and critiqued heavily, revealing the controversy and discomfort around many types of addiction in Western society.

Lorenzo Agius/Getty Images.

11.2 Types of Drugs Common in Substance Use Issues

Depressants

Depressants are drugs that slow the central nervous system (CNS). They decrease brain function, reduce breathing rate, and lower blood pressure. Dizziness, slurred speech, drowsiness, and sedation also occur. Depressants are usually ingested orally.

Depressants: Drugs that slow the central nervous system (CNS).

Alcohol

Alcohol (also called *ethanol* or *ethyl alcohol*) is among the most used drugs, contained in many of our most popular beverages (National Institute on Drug Abuse, n.d.). People have been drinking alcohol for many millennia—as far back as 9,000 years ago (American Addiction Centers, 2022; Barceloux, 2012; Oei & Hashing, 2013). Alcohol content varies by drink. Beer contains roughly

Alcohol: A depressant drug in many popular beverages (also called *ethanol* or *ethyl alcohol*).

5 percent alcohol, wine 12–17 percent, and liquors typically 24–40 percent (National Institute on Alcohol Abuse and Alcoholism, n.d.-b). Alcohol is absorbed through the gastrointestinal tract, entering the bloodstream and slowing the central nervous system. It affects various neurotransmitter systems, such as GABA, dopamine, serotonin, and glutamate (Barceloux, 2012; Oei & Hashing, 2013). Alcohol enhances GABA activity while diminishing the effects of glutamate. Because GABA is inhibitory and glutamate excitatory, the result is relaxation. Alcohol also increases dopamine levels in the brain's reward center (Barceloux, 2012; Oei & Hashing, 2013).

Alcohol's status as a depressant can seem counterintuitive because in small amounts alcohol has a stimulant effect. As most of us know, having a drink or two can produce an enjoyable "buzz." The person loosens up (i.e., experiences *disinhibition*) and feels good. However, when the person drinks too much and gets drunk, alcohol's depressant effects become more obvious: slurred speech, decreased physical coordination, slowed reaction time, impaired judgment, and in some instances emotional outbursts. Extreme drunkenness produces the most intense depressant effects—things like not feeling pain, vomiting, and unconsciousness (Foundation for a Drug Free World, n.d.-b). Alcohol can be deadly, usually when a person's *blood alcohol content* (the percentage of alcohol in the blood stream) reaches 0.35 percent or higher (Sussman & Ames, 2008). For most people, it takes about an hour for their bodies to process a single drink (Sussman & Ames, 2008). Processing time is affected by weight and sex—because women usually have less body water than men, their blood alcohol levels increase more quickly (National Institute on Alcohol Abuse, 1999). Interestingly, how much alcohol counts as a single (i.e., standard) drink varies by country (see Table 11.1). U.S. standards are in Figure 11.1.

Alcohol is ubiquitous and plays a large role in many societies (Barceloux, 2012; National Institute on Drug Abuse, n.d.). In 2019, 65.8 million Americans age 12 or older reported **binge drinking** in the past month (Substance Abuse and Mental Health Services Administration, 2020). Binge drinking is drinking four or more drinks (if female) or five or more drinks (if male) in roughly two hours (National Institute on Alcohol Abuse and Alcoholism, n.d.-a). Americans aren't alone in this. In a survey between 2018 and 2020, nearly one in five Europeans age 15 or older said they drank heavily (60 grams of alcohol, or roughly six drinks) at least once a month in the previous year (Eurostat: Statistics Explained, 2021). Although drinking is often considered less serious than using other drugs, its social costs are enormous. Alcohol accounts for 5.1 percent of the global burden of disease and injury (World Health Organization, 2022c). It is responsible for 3 million deaths per year

Binge drinking: Drinking four or more drinks (if female) or five or more drinks (if male) in roughly two hours.

Table 11.1 One Standard Drink by Country. What is considered a "single drink" varies by country. There is no agreed-upon international standard.

Nutrientsreview.com

One Standard Drink by Country
(grams and milliliters of alcohol)

Australia	10 g	13 mL
Canada	13.6 g	17 mL
Ireland	10 g	13 mL
New Zealand	10 g	13 mL
UK	8 g	10 mL
USA	14 g	18 mL

A Standard Drink in the U.S.

= 18 mL or 14g of alcohol

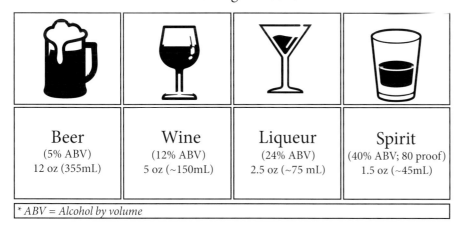

Beer	Wine	Liqueur	Spirit
(5% ABV)	(12% ABV)	(24% ABV)	(40% ABV; 80 proof)
12 oz (355mL)	5 oz (~150mL)	2.5 oz (~75 mL)	1.5 oz (~45mL)

* ABV = Alcohol by volume

Figure 11.1 Not all drinks are created equal. Thus, when imbibing it is important to pay attention to serving sizes of different types of drinks.
Source: Nutrientsreview.com

and 13.5 percent of deaths among people ages 20–39 (World Health Organization, 2022c). Alcohol is also a factor in many suicides, homicides, firearm injuries, motor vehicle accidents, occupational and machine injuries, drownings, and rapes (H. R. Alpert et al., 2022; de Bruijn & de Graaf, 2016; Gravelin et al., 2019; Hamilton et al., 2018; Lorenz & Ullman, 2016; M. F. Tomlinson et al., 2016; Tomsen, 2018; World Health Organization, 2022c).

Walter

Walter's arrest for drunk driving and his deteriorating marriage are attributable to his ongoing abuse of alcohol.

Alcohol abuse takes a huge toll on families. Children raised by parents who drink excessively often have the emotional and physical scars to prove it (S. Park & Schepp, 2015; Raitasalo et al., 2019; Rossow et al., 2016). Unborn children of pregnant women who drink are at risk too. They can be born with **fetal alcohol syndrome (FAS)** (Spohr, 2018; Vorgias & Bernstein, 2022). Children with FAS are usually identified by three characteristics: (a) retarded growth, falling under the tenth percentile of normal height and weight for their age; (b) developmental delays and impaired cognitive performance; and (c) atypical facial features: small heads (*microencephaly*), small eyes (*microphthalmia*), thin upper lips with lack of vertical indentation in the middle, and flat upper jaw bones (Khoury et al., 2015; J. J. Smith & Graden, 1998; Spohr, 2018).

The term *alcoholic* describes people who struggle to manage their alcohol use. It isn't a DSM or ICD diagnostic term, so—like addiction—its lacks a precise definition. Alcoholics typically experience tolerance and withdrawal. In roughly 3–5 percent of cases, their alcohol withdrawal is highly dramatic, inducing an intense syndrome known as **delirium tremens (DTs)** during which they become delirious, experience intense body tremors, and have terrifying hallucinations (S. Grover & Ghosh, 2018; Rahman & Paul, 2021). Chronic excessive alcohol use often causes irreversible scarring of the liver, known as **cirrhosis** (Roerecke et al., 2019; Starr & Raines, 2011). It can also lead to **Korsakoff syndrome**, characterized by serious deterioration in short- and long-term memory, as well as an inability to recall new information (Arts et al., 2017; Isenberg-Grzeda et al., 2012; Kopelman et al., 2009). To compensate for their memory problems, many Korsakoff patients engage in *confabulation*, wherein they invent explanations (which they themselves believe) to account for their gaps in recall (Arts et al., 2017; Isenberg-Grzeda et al., 2012; Kopelman et al., 2009). Korsakoff syndrome occurs when chronic alcohol use creates a *thiamine* (vitamin B-1) deficiency. Thiamine is a chemical compound that helps the brain convert sugar into energy. Chronic drinking decreases

Fetal alcohol syndrome (FAS): Syndrome in children of mothers who drink excessively during pregnancy; characterized by retarded growth, developmental delays, and atypical facial features (small heads [*microencephaly*], small eyes [*microphthalmia*], thin upper lips with no ventromedial indentation in the middle, and flat upper jaw bones).

Delirium tremens (DTs): Syndrome in extreme cases of alcohol withdrawal in which the person becomes delirious, experiences intense body tremors, and has terrifying hallucinations.

Cirrhosis: Irreversible scarring of the liver, often due to chronic excessive alcohol use.

Korsakoff syndrome: Syndrome characterized by serious deterioration in short- and long-term memory, as well as inability to recall new information; caused by a *thiamine* (Vitamin B-1) deficiency, usually from chronic excessive alcohol use.

thiamine levels and—over time—leads to Korsakoff symptoms (Arts et al., 2017; Isenberg-Grzeda et al., 2012; Kopelman et al., 2009).

Sedative-Hypnotics

Sedative-hypnotics:
A class of depressants sometimes simply called *sedatives*; barbiturates and benzodiazepines are types of sedative-hypnotic drugs.

Barbiturates: Highly addictive sedative-hypnotic drugs such as *secobarbital* and *pentobarbital*; previously used as anti-anxiety drugs but have generally been replaced by benzodiazepines.

Sedative-hypnotics (sometimes just called *sedatives*) are another class of depressants. **Barbiturates** are one of the most well-known sedative-hypnotics (Barceloux, 2012; Skibiski & Abdijadid, 2021). They go by slightly different names in the United States versus the rest of the world—ending in "al" or "one," respectively (Barceloux, 2012). Thus, *barbital* in the United States is *barbitone* elsewhere; likewise, *secobarbital* is *secorbarbitone* and *pentobarbital* is *pentobarbitone*. To further confuse things, these three drugs are also referred to by their respective trade names: Veronal, Seconal, and Nembutal (Barceloux, 2012; Sussman & Ames, 2008). First introduced as prescription drugs in the early twentieth century, barbiturates served as sedatives, anticonvulsants, anesthetics, headache remedies, and anxiolytics (anti-anxiety drugs). However, their strong addictive qualities created problems, so they are rarely prescribed today. Barbiturates effects are similar to alcohol: slurred speech, decreased physical coordination, cognitive impairment and judgment issues, disinhibition, and mental confusion (Barceloux, 2012). Like alcohol, barbiturates enhance the effects of the inhibitory neurotransmitter GABA (Barceloux, 2012; Skibiski & Abdijadid, 2021; Snozek, 2020). They are cardiorespiratory depressants, meaning that they slow respiration and movement of the diaphragm. Thus, at high doses barbiturates can cause extreme drowsiness, coma, breathing failure, and death (Barceloux, 2012; Snozek, 2020).

Benzodiazepines largely replaced barbiturates. Also known as minor tranquilizers (and mentioned in many other chapters), they are prescribed as anti-anxiety drugs, sedatives, and sleep aids. Benzodiazepines include *diazepam* (Valium), *chlordiazepoxide* (Librium), *chlorazepate* (Tranxene), *alprazolam* (Xanax), and *lorazepram* (Ativan). On the street, they are known as "benzos," "downers," "nerve pills," or "tranks" (Drug Enforcement Administration, 2019). While habit-forming, benzodiazepines are significantly less addictive than barbiturates (A. V. Horwitz, 2013). Like barbiturates and alcohol, they enhance GABA responsiveness (Snozek, 2020). In low doses, they reduce anxiety and improve sleep. However, at high doses they produce effects similar to alcohol and barbiturates—including tolerance, withdrawal, and other signs of dependence. Benzodiazepines cause less drowsiness than barbiturates. Overdoses are less deadly because benzodiazepines impact respiration more modestly. Although prescribed regularly and considered safe, doctors limit patient time on benzodiazepines to prevent abuse and dependence.

Let's briefly mention major tranquilizers—antipsychotic drugs such as *olanzapine* (Zyprexa), *quetiapine* (Seroquel), and *haloperidol* (Haldol). Like minor tranquilizers, major tranquilizers are depressants with sedative-like effects (Foundation for a Drug Free World, n.d.-a). They play a huge role in managing psychosis by decreasing dopamine transmission (see Chapter 4). Unlike benzodiazepines, antipsychotics aren't generally considered addictive, but they do produce withdrawal symptoms when people stop taking them (Brandt et al., 2020).

Stimulants

Stimulants: Drugs that speed up the central nervous system (CNS).

Whereas depressants slow down the central nervous system, **stimulants**—which can be taken orally, sniffed, smoked, or injected—speed it up (Sussman & Ames, 2008). Stimulants cause people to feel euphoric, alert, energetic, confident, and hypersensitive to their surroundings (Drug Enforcement Administration, 2020; Eaddy, 2013). Restlessness, loss of appetite, increased heart rate and blood pressure, irritability, and paranoia are additional effects (Sussman & Ames, 2008).

Cocaine

Cocaine: Stimulant made South American coca plant leaves that produces euphoria, excessive confidence, and tremendously high energy levels.

Cocaine, made from South American coca plant leaves, is one of the most powerful stimulants, producing euphoria, excessive confidence, and tremendously high energy levels. It does this by stimulating the release of dopamine, while also enhancing serotonin and norepinephrine levels (Barceloux, 2012; Goertz et al., 2015; Matsui & Alvarez, 2018; Nestler, 2005; Sussman & Ames, 2008). In powder form, cocaine can be "snorted" through the nose or dissolved in water and injected; in crystal form (called *crack*), it can be smoked (Drug Enforcement Administration, 2020). Crack is created by *freebasing*, the process of chemically separating the pure cocaine from sugars and other impurities. This makes crack more powerful and faster acting (Samokhvalov & Rehm, 2013).

In 2020, 21.5 million people were believed to use cocaine at least once, with trends suggesting an overall increase over the last decade (United Nations Office on Drugs and Crime, 2022). Like a lot of drugs, cocaine use rose during the early days of the COVID-19 pandemic but returned to pre-pandemic levels by 2021 (United Nations Office on Drugs and Crime, 2022). Figure 11.2 shows variations in estimated cocaine use around the world for 2020.

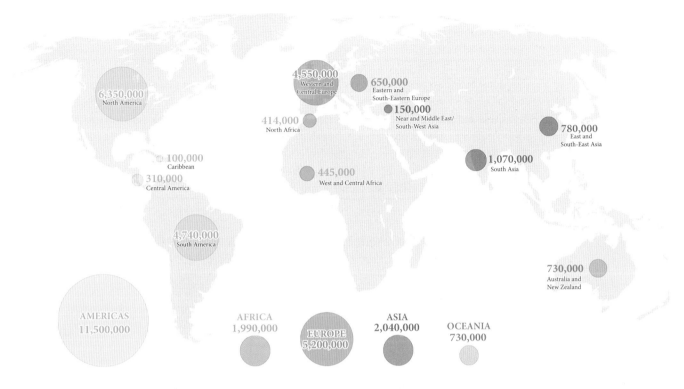

Figure 11.2 Estimated Number of People Who Used Cocaine in the Past Year, by Subregion, 2020.
United Nations Office on Drugs and Crime (2022, Booklet 4, p. 31).

Amphetamines

Amphetamines, such as *amphetamine* (Benzedrine) and *dextroamphetamine* (Dexedrine), are laboratory-manufactured stimulants. Like cocaine, they provide an "amped up" energetic feeling by enhancing dopamine, serotonin, and norepinephrine levels, but they remain in the bloodstream longer (D. Martin & Le, 2021; Sussman & Ames, 2008). As with all stimulants, amphetamines increase heart rate and respiration while reducing the need for sleep (Sussman & Ames, 2008). They enhance alertness and improve performance on mental and athletic tasks. Amphetamines are commonly ingested as pills but can also be injected or turned into crystal form and smoked. Other notable amphetamines include *methamphetamine* (trade name *Methedrine*, but street names include *speed*, *crystal meth*, *ice*, and *crank*) and *3,4-methylenedioxymethamphetamine* (*MDMA*, also known as or *Ecstasy* or *Molly*) (Drug Enforcement Administration, 2020; McKetin et al., 2013; Ramo et al., 2013; Sussman & Ames, 2008).

Because they increase dopamine activity, amphetamines can induce altered reality perception at high doses (i.e., amphetamine psychosis, discussed in Chapter 4). However, MDMA, which affects serotonin more than dopamine (Ramo et al., 2013), has especially strong hallucinogenic properties (Drug Enforcement Administration, 2020; S. S. Martins et al., 2013). People on Ecstasy mostly show stimulant effects: increased heart rate, decreased appetite, enhanced mood and energy, feelings of well-being along with lessened anxiety, and a sense of intimacy with others (Ramo et al., 2013). However, they also experience perceptual changes, such as sensitivity to light and touch. This is why MDMA is sometimes classified as a hallucinogen. Long popular as a "club drug," chronic MDMA use can cause permanent damage to the brain's serotonin neurons (Barceloux, 2012; Ramo et al., 2013; Sussman & Ames, 2008).

Despite their dangers, amphetamines have important medical and mental health uses. For instance, amphetamine-based drugs are prescribed for attention-deficit hyperactivity disorder (see

Amphetamines:

Laboratory-manufactured stimulants; include *amphetamine* (trade name *Benzedrine*), *dextroamphetamine* (trade name *Dexedrine*), and *methamphetamine* (trade name *Methedrine*).

Chapter 13) (Castells et al., 2018; Punja et al., 2016). Likewise, MDMA is increasingly incorporated into psychedelic-assisted psychotherapy for posttraumatic stress disorder (see Chapter 7) (Almond & Allan, 2019; Monson et al., 2020; A. C. Wagner et al., 2019).

Nicotine

Nicotine: A stimulant found in tobacco leaves that makes users feel alert and calm.

Some stimulants are common, easily obtained, and widely used—such as **nicotine**, found in tobacco leaves. Nicotine can be smoked in cigarettes, cigars, or pipes. In liquid form, it can be vaped in electronic cigarettes (e-cigarettes), e-cigars, e-pipes, vapes, vaporizers, vape pens, or hookah pens (Sussman & Ames, 2008; U.S. Food and Drug Administration, 2022a, 2022b). Chewing tobacco, tobacco-based chewing gum, and snuff (dried tobacco inhaled by nose) are other delivery methods (Sussman & Ames, 2008). Nicotine functions as a stimulant and a relaxant, making users feel alert and calm. It enhances neurotransmission of dopamine, glutamate, and **acetylcholine** (important in muscle movement, arousal, memory, and learning) (Benowitz, 2009; Sussman & Ames, 2008). Unfortunately, besides being habit-forming, nicotine and tobacco are linked to cancer (Grando, 2014; Khani et al., 2018). Smoking tobacco (or being exposed to it secondhand) is also associated with heart disease, chronic obstructive pulmonary disease (COPD), and complications during pregnancy (Centers for Disease Control and Prevention, 2020b).

Acetylcholine: Neurotransmitter important in muscle movement, arousal, memory, and learning.

Caffeine

Caffeine: A mild and commonly used stimulant found in many plants, including those used to make coffee, tea, chocolate, and soft drinks; increases alertness and energy while providing a sense of well-being.

Caffeine is the most widely used stimulant in the world, consumed daily by 85 percent of the U.S. population (D. C. Mitchell et al., 2014). It is found in over sixty different kinds of plants, including those used to make coffee, tea, chocolate, and soft drinks (G. N. Scott, 2013; A. P. Smith, 2013). Caffeine is a mild stimulant and not usually considered dangerous or harmful. In fact, it might have health benefits when taken in moderation (Alasmari, 2020; Poole et al., 2017). Caffeine blocks *adenosine*, an inhibitory neurotransmitter, while also affecting dopamine, glutamate, and GABA systems (Alasmari, 2020). It increases alertness and energy while providing a sense of well-being (Barceloux, 2012). However, it can negatively affect sleep (I. Clark & Landolt, 2017; Riera-Sampol et al., 2022). People develop tolerance to caffeine and experience withdrawal (e.g., headaches and drowsiness) when they stop taking it (Sajadi-Ernazarova et al., 2022; A. P. Smith, 2013). If you haven't had your usual cup of tea, coffee, or hot cocoa this morning and are feeling lousy, you know what I mean.

Opioids

Opioids: Natural, synthetic, or semisynthetic drugs that depress the central nervous system and serve as powerful painkillers; highly addictive, they mimic endogenous opioids created by our bodies (also called *opiates* and *narcotics*).

Opioids (also known as *opiates* or *narcotics*) are powerful painkillers, with mostly depressant, but also some stimulant, effects. They can be *natural* (found in nature), *semisynthetic* (derived from natural opiates), or *synthetic* (made entirely in the laboratory). As painkillers, opioid drugs mimic the central nervous system's *endogenous opioids* (also known as *endorphins*), created naturally by our bodies. Endogenous opioids serve as chemical messengers, reducing pain and calming us down. Opioid drugs have much the same effect as endogenous opioids. Euphoria and drowsiness accompanied by impaired memory, attention, and social functioning are common symptoms of opioid intoxication (Eaddy, 2013).

Opium: A natural opioid found in the sap of opium poppy plants.

Natural opioids are derived directly from **opium**—an addictive psychoactive substance found in the sap of opium poppy plants (Albertson, 2012). As far back as 3000 BC, opium was used to relieve pain (Barceloux, 2012). Eventually, advances in chemistry allowed us to break opium into its component alkaloids—*morphine* (a more powerful painkiller than opium that remains highly addictive), *codeine* (a milder opioid used as a pain reliever and cough medicine), and *thebaine* (which has more stimulant than depressive effects) (Barceloux, 2012; Sussman & Ames, 2008; WHO Advisory Group, 1980). Morphine, codeine, and thebaine are used to create semisynthetic opioid drugs such as heroin and oxycontin.

Heroin: A highly addictive semisynthetic opioid to which dependence develops quickly; tolerance and withdrawal are especially severe.

Heroin is a highly addictive semisynthetic opioid. People can become physically dependent on it in just two to three days (Barceloux, 2012). Tolerance develops quickly and withdrawal is severe. Withdrawal symptoms include restlessness, insomnia, irritability, high blood pressure, tachycardia (heart rate over 100 beats per minute), teary eyes, runny nose, sweating, dilated pupils, goose bumps on the skin, abdominal cramps, vomiting, diarrhea, and fever (Barceloux, 2012; Hartney, 2020; Samokhvalov & Rehm, 2013). Chronic users must keep increasing their heroin doses simply to avoid withdrawal. Heroin is illegal or tightly controlled in most countries.

Oxycodone is another semisynthetic opioid. Used as a pain reliever, it is the main ingredient in drugs marked under names like Percocet and OxyContin. Although a controlled rather than illegal substance, oxycodone is very habit-forming. Sadly, the aggressive marketing of OxyContin and other opioids in the U.S. has contributed to an epidemic of opioid addiction (DeWeerdt, 2019).

Finally, some opioids are completely synthetic. They aren't derived from opium at all. Instead, they are made in the laboratory. *Meperidine* (trade name *Demerol*), *fentanyl*, and *pentazocine* are synthetic opioids used as painkillers and anesthetics. As with benzodiazepines, doctors prescribing opioids must monitor patients for signs of abuse and dependence. Figures 11.3 and 11.4 illustrate the alarming increase in opioid overdose deaths in the U.S. between 1999 and 2020.

Oxycodone: A semisynthetic opioid used as a pain reliever in prescription drugs marketed under names like Percocet and OxyContin.

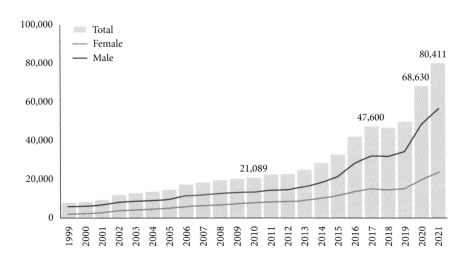

*Among deaths with drug overdose as the underlying cause, the "any opioid" subcategory was determined by the following ICD-10 multiple cause-of-death codes: natural and semi-synthetic opioids (T40.2), methadone (T40.3), other synthetic opioids(other than methadone) (T40.4), or heroin (T40.1). Source: Centers for Disease Control and Prevention, National Center for Health Statistics. Multiple Cause of Death 1999-2021 on CDC WONDER Online Database, released 1/2023.

Figure 11.3 U.S. Overdose Deaths Involving Any Opioid—Number among All Ages, by Gender, 1999–2021.
Source: National Institute on Drug Abuse (2023), Drug overdose death rates.

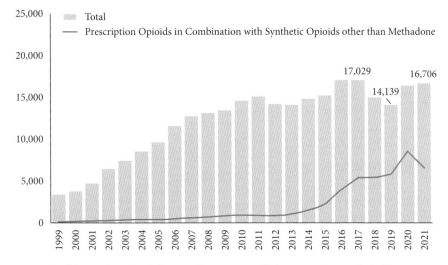

*Among deaths with drug overdose as the underlying cause, the prescription opioid subcategory was determined by the following ICD-10 multiple cause-of-death codes: natural and semi-synthetic opioids (T40.2) or methadone (T40.3). Source: Centers for Disease Control and Prevention, National Center for Health Statistics. Multiple Cause of Death 1999–2021 on CDC WONDER Online Database, Released 1/2023.

Figure 11.4 U.S. Overdose Deaths Involving Prescription Opioids, by Other Opioid Involvement—Number among All Ages, 1999–2021.
Source: National Institute on Drug Abuse (2023), Drug overdose death rates.

Ayesha

The trembling, sweating, and nausea that our case study client Ayesha experiences while sitting in her jail cell are symptoms of opioid withdrawal.

Hallucinogens

Hallucinogens (also known as *psychedelics*) are drugs that induce hallucinations, altered thinking and perceptions, out-of-body experiences, and sometimes paranoia (S. S. Martins et al., 2013; Sussman & Ames, 2008). They can also lead to *drug-induced synesthesia*, a mixing of sensory experiences in which stimulation of one sensory mode spawns perceptual responses from another sensory mode (Sinke et al., 2012). For instance, listening to music might trigger not only auditory stimulation (i.e., hearing the notes), but also visual imagery (i.e., seeing random colors and images). There are over 100 different hallucinogenic drugs and their mechanisms of action vary (Sussman & Ames, 2008). Let's review three types.

Indoleamine Hallucinogens

Indoleamine hallucinogens like *LSD* (lysergic acid diethylamide) harken back to 1960s counterculture and songs like The Beatles' "Lucy the Sky with Diamonds." These drugs work by activating serotonin receptors in the brain's medial prefrontal cortex and anterior cingulate cortex (Halberstadt, 2015; Halberstadt & Geyer, 2011; Sussman & Ames, 2008). This induces hallucinations and heightens emotional sensitivity. LSD was originally synthesized in 1938, and during the 1950s and 60s, investigators studied its psychedelic effects and its utility as a treatment for psychosis, alcoholism, sexual problems, and autism (Barceloux, 2012). However, this research ceased for many years after LSD became negatively associated with countercultural excess. Besides LSD, *DMT* (N,N-dimethyltryptamine), and *psilocybin* (4-phosphoryloxy-N,N-dimethyltryptamine; a.k.a., "magic mushrooms") are other indoleamine hallucinogens (Sussman & Ames, 2008). Though potentially dangerous when taken illicitly, LSD and psilocybin (as well as MDMA, discussed earlier) are increasingly being used in psychedelic-assisted therapy for depression, trauma (see "In Depth" feature in Chapter 5) (Tullis, 2021). Research on psilocybin as a treatment for alcohol use and

Photo 11.3 The Beatles' psychedelic album, *Yellow Submarine.*
Minha Baek/Unsplash.

smoking cessation shows promise (M. W. Johnson, 2022). New evidence also reaffirms older studies showing LSD to be an effective alcoholism intervention (Fuentes et al., 2020).

Within an hour two of taking it, people on an LSD "trip" experience an enhanced sense of perception. They often become highly attuned to physical and psychological changes in their bodies. Their heightened responsiveness may also lead to preoccupation with minute aspects of their surroundings, such as stripes on a necktie or individual hairs on their arms. Physical and psychological responses to LSD and other hallucinogens vary. Some users report a sense of peaceful bliss and enlightenment, but others experience terror and intense horror—a "bad trip." Because people build tolerance to LSD, doses must be steadily increased to produce the same effects. Unfortunately, as doses and frequency of use increase, so do the risks of frightening **drug flashbacks** (sometimes called *hallucinogen persisting perception disorder*), in which users unexpectedly re-experience perceptual disturbances of past drug trips (Martinotti et al., 2018; F. Müller et al., 2022).

Phenylalkylamine Hallucinogens

Phenylalkylamine hallucinogens produce both hallucinogenic and stimulant effects by affecting norepinephrine, dopamine, and serotonin receptors (Obreshkova et al., 2017). *Mescaline* (peyote and trimethoxy-phenethlamine) and *DOM* (2,5-dimethoxy- 4-methylamphetamine STP) are phenylalkyalimine hallucinogens (Obreshkova et al., 2017). Mescaline is derived from the peyote cactus found in the southwestern United States. According to research using radioactive carbon dating, Native Americans were using peyote for medicinal and religious purposes as far back as 5,700 years ago (El-Seedi et al., 2005). Because of their addictive qualities, drugs like mescaline are illegal or tightly regulated in many countries.

Phencyclidine (PCP)

Phencyclidine (PCP) is another type of hallucinogen. It is known by various street names, most famously *angel dust*. PCP reduces the influence of glutamate while enhancing dopamine and norepinephrine production (Barceloux, 2012; Bey & Patel, 2007). It is usually classified as a hallucinogen, but also has significant depressant and some stimulant properties (Barceloux, 2012). PCP is therefore sometimes considered a depressant. This makes sense considering it was developed in the 1950s as a surgical anesthetic and later used as an animal tranquilizer (tradename *Sernyl*) (Sussman & Ames, 2008). Despite its depressant effects, DSM-5-TR classifies PCP as a hallucinogen, probably because it can produce delirium, disorientation, agitation, paranoid delusions, and hallucinations (Barceloux, 2012; Bey & Patel, 2007). Due to its addictive and hallucinogenic properties, PCP is not very useful medically (Barceloux, 2012).

Interestingly, the anesthetic drug ketamine (discussed in Chapter 5 as an antidepressant) is a derivative of PCP (Barceloux, 2012). Ketamine is considered safer than PCP but still addictive. A common "club drug" taken in capsule, powder, crystal, tablet, or solution forms, ketamine goes by street names such as *K*, *Jet*, *Super Acid*, *Vitamin K*, and *Special K* (Ramo et al., 2013). Chronic use can damage the gastrointestinal system and urinary tract (Bokor & Anderson, 2014; Kamaya & Krishna, 1987; S. Ross, 2008; Y.-C. Wang et al., 2010; Winstock et al., 2012). Ketamine's addictive properties should be monitored when using it to treat depression, but evidence so far suggests low risk when carefully administered under medical supervision (McIntyre et al., 2021).

Cannabis

Cannabis refers to drugs made from the flowers, dried leaves, and extracts of assorted varieties of the *hemp plant* (*cannabis sativa*) (Barceloux, 2012; K. W. Grover et al., 2013). It contains chemical substances called *cannabinoids*, the main ones being *tetrahydrocannabinol (THC)* and *cannabidiol (CBD)*. THC is responsible for the stimulant, depressant, and psychedelic effects of cannabis (i.e., its "high"). The more THC, the greater the potency. While hemp leaves and buds both contain THC, the highest concentration is found in the plant's flower tops. Types of cannabis include *marijuana* (consisting of hemp leaves, flowers, and buds), *ganja* (derived from small cannabis leaves), *bhang* (a drink made from cannabis leaf extract), and *hashish* (a highly potent form of cannabis made from hemp plant flowers) (Barceloux, 2012). The percentage of THC in cannabis products has steadily increased, making them more potent and increasing addiction risk (Pennypacker et al., 2022; Stuyt, 2018).

Drug flashbacks: The unexpected re-experiencing perceptual disturbances of past drug trips (sometimes called *hallucinogen persisting perception disorder*).

Phenylalkylamine hallucinogens: Produce hallucinogenic and stimulant effects by affecting norepinephrine, dopamine, and serotonin receptors; *mescaline* and *DOM* are phenylalkylamine hallucinogens.

Phencyclidine (PCP): A hallucinogen with hallucinogenic, depressant, and some stimulant properties; reduces influence of glutamate while enhancing dopamine and norepinephrine production.

Cannabis: Drugs derived from the hemp plant, containing *cannabinoids* like *tetrahydrocannabinol (THC)* and *cannabidiol (CBD)*; cannabis "high" is caused by THC and includes feeling relaxed and content, losing track of time, perceptual distortions, and heightened awareness; cannabis types: *marijuana*, *ganja*, *bhang*, and *hashish*.

Cannabis can be inhaled (smoked or vaped), ingested in food or drink, or applied topically to the skin (Bruni et al., 2018; Sublime, 2021). It reduces GABA and glutamate while increasing dopamine (Barceloux, 2012; Borowicz et al., 2014). Cannabis intoxication tends to be mild and brief. It includes increased pulse, blood pressure, and appetite, along with bloodshot eyes, dizziness, impaired cognitive and motor performance on complex tasks, and sometimes sleepiness; (K. W. Grover et al., 2013). Responses to cannabis depend on many factors, including setting, mood, and personality (Barceloux, 2012). At low doses, many people report feeling relaxed and content. They lose track of time and experience perceptual distortions and heightened awareness (K. W. Grover et al., 2013). Others, however, become irritable and paranoid (K. W. Grover et al., 2013). At high doses, intense paranoia is common, with hallucinations, depersonalization, and even psychosis possible (Barceloux, 2012; N. T. Pearson & Berry, 2019; Sussman & Ames, 2008).

Students often ask whether cannabis is addictive. As already noted, addiction is not a clinically specific term. However, if the question is whether people can develop cannabis dependence, the answer is yes. Regular cannabis users experience tolerance and withdrawal (Bahji et al., 2020; Connor et al., 2021; Olivine, 2022). Withdrawal symptoms include irritability, anxiety, trouble sleeping, loss of appetite/weight, and depressed mood (Bahji et al., 2020; Bonnet & Preuss, 2017). Although cannabis tends to be seen as less harmful than many other drugs (Bonomo et al., 2019; Lachenmeier & Rehm, 2015; Memedovich et al., 2018), cannabis use issues are expected to rise in prevalence as more countries legalize recreational use (Connor et al., 2021). The Controversial Question feature explores the legalization of marijuana.

Controversial Question: Should We Be Legalizing Marijuana?

The legalization of marijuana use is occurring at a rapid pace. As of July 2022, thirty-eight U.S. states had legalized it for medical purposes and nineteen for recreational use, while several others were in the process of legalizing it (D. Avery, 2022; C. Hansen et al., 2022; M. Zhang & Demko, 2022). Cannabis is also legal in Uruguay, Canada, and South Africa (Nast, 2022). The liberalization of cannabis laws is consistent with public attitudes: 69 percent of Americans favor recreational legalization and 92 percent support medical legalization (SSRS, 2022). Pro-marijuana advocates contend that strict regulation interferes with researching and using cannabis for legitimate health purposes. Though more studies are needed, they point to evidence that cannabis is effective in treating chronic pain, cancer, AIDS, glaucoma, and inflammatory bowel disease (Doppen et al., 2022; MacMillan et al., 2019; McDonagh et al., 2022; Perisetti et al., 2020; M. Pratt et al., 2019; L. Wang et al., 2021). Supporters also cite data that cannabis is less dangerous than alcohol or tobacco (Bonomo et al., 2019; Lachenmeier & Rehm, 2015; Memedovich et al., 2018). Thus, they believe prosecuting recreational users wastes precious resources (Farley & Orchowsky, 2019; K. Jaeger, 2022; Krane, 2020). For these reasons, they celebrate the trend toward legalization.

However, not everyone is so enthusiastic. Some urge caution and point to studies suggesting that car accidents, hospitalizations, and emergency room visits rise after marijuana is legalized (Bechard et al., 2022; Nazif-Munoz et al., 2020; O'Brien et al., 2022; Steinemann et al., 2018; Tolan et al., 2022; Vozoris et al., 2022; G. S. Wang et al., 2018, 2021; M. E. M. Yeung et al., 2021). Others worry about marijuana's demonstrated negative effects on adolescent development (Albaugh et al., 2021; W. Hall et al., 2020). Along these lines, growing use among teens has been linked to their steadily higher rates of depression, anxiety, and suicidality (Gobbi et al., 2019). Further, many people worry that legalizing cannabis fosters its role as a "gateway" drug that precedes and encourages more serious drug use, although most people who use marijuana do not progress to harder drugs (National Institute on Drug Abuse, 2020). In fact, some believe that legalized cannabis leads to less opioid use—a big deal in countries like the United States, where opioids are a major problem. The assumption here is that when marijuana is legal and accessible, people tend to choose it over opioids for pain relief. Indeed, there is evidence that opioid use drops after cannabis legalization (Drake et al., 2021; G. Hsu & Kovács, 2021; M. D. Livingston et al., 2017; Sabia et al., 2021). However, not everyone is confident in these findings (Caputi & Sabet, 2018). One skeptic even estimated that opioid use increases over the long term when marijuana is legalized (Mathur & Ruhm, 2022). Additional studies are needed.

Science is an important tool in assessing the impact of legalizing cannabis, but it cannot tell us what to do. Allowing or denying access to drugs—even when the risks and benefits are informed by science—inevitably requires moral and political judgments. When it comes to cannabis, the current consensus is that the benefits outweigh the risks. What do you think?

Critical Thinking Questions

1. Given the research on cannabis' benefits and harms, do you think it should be legal?
2. In deciding whether cannabis should be legal, how much credence do you give to evidence that easier access is associated with increased health and injury risks?
3. If there are legal restrictions on cannabis, should there also be legal restrictions on alcohol—which, as noted earlier in the chapter, also has enormous health and financial costs? What (if any) legal restrictions would you support and why?

11.3 Polydrug Use: Using More than One Drug

Polydrug Use

Drug users often take more than one substance. This is known as **polydrug use** (Crummy et al., 2020; Ives & Ghelani, 2006). Polydrug use occurs in many different situations, ranging from mild to severe drug use. It can involve taking more than one drug simultaneously or transitioning over time from one drug to another (Ives & Ghelani, 2006). Polydrug use is common and problematic. For example, among people with opioid use issues, just over 57 percent were polydrug users, according to one study (Hassan & Le Foll, 2019). Alarmingly, roughly half of all 2019 overdose deaths in the United States involved polysubstance use (Centers for Disease Control and Prevention, 2022a). This statistic is even more worrisome given evidence that polydrug use is widely underreported (Walderhaug et al., 2019).

Polydrug use: When drug users take more than one substance.

Cross-Tolerance

Polydrug use can lead to **cross-tolerance**. In cross-tolerance, tolerance for one drug transfers to other drugs with similar chemical effects on the brain (United Nations Office on Drugs and Crime, 2016). Thus, regular users of a drug may find themselves highly tolerant of not just that drug, but also of other drugs—even ones they haven't previously used. For instance, a chronic drinker who runs out of alcohol might resort to taking a friend's benzodiazepines. In so doing, this person staves off going into alcohol withdrawal. Another example would be substituting illegally purchased heroin for fentanyl prescribed for post-surgical pain.

Cross-tolerance: When tolerance for one drug transfers to other drugs with similar chemical effects on the brain.

Synergistic Effects

Drugs taken together can also produce **synergistic effects** in which combining them amplifies their impact (United Nations Office on Drugs and Crime, 2016). Some drug combinations have cumulative synergistic effects. Taken at the same time, their effect multiplies, provoking a much more intense drug response. For instance, combining alcohol and barbiturates—both depressants—enhances the effects of both. It also greatly increases the risk of overdose.

Rather than enhancing one another, other synergistic drugs elicit opposite effects, cancelling each other out when used together. For instance, taking stimulants like cocaine or amphetamines with opioids—a process known as **speedballing**—provides the highs of both drugs while reducing their negative effects (United Nations Office on Drugs and Crime, 2016). However, it's also quite dangerous. For instance, heroin and cocaine produce intense synergistic effects, boosting dopamine a whopping 1,000 percent when taken together versus 70 percent and 350 percent, respectively, when taken separately (Duvauchelle et al., 1998; R. D. Goodwin et al., 2021; Leri et al., 2003). This makes overdoses much more likely. As one tragic example, violin prodigy Katya Tsukanova died in 2020 after taking a new speedball combination called "Calvin Klein (CK)," which combines cocaine and ketamine (M. S. Gold et al., 2020). To further illustrate the risks of polydrug, note how many of the famous people on this list of overdose deaths died from combining multiple drugs: https://en.wikipedia.org/wiki/List_of_drug-related_deaths.

Synergistic effects: Effect from taking drugs together; some combinations enhance the effects of both drugs, while other combinations cancel some of the effects of both drugs.

Speedballing: Combining drugs (usually stimulants and opioids) to produce a synergistic effect in which the highs of both drugs are experienced but the negative effects are reduced; increases risk of overdose.

11.4 Beyond Substances: Behavioral Addictions

Since 1990, the concept of addictions has expanded beyond substance use to include **behavioral addictions** (I. Marks, 1990). Like substance addictions, behavioral addictions can be difficult to define. They typically involve an activity like excessive gambling, sex, or shopping that meets the following criteria:

(1) disrupts personal, family, social, or vocational pursuits; (2) causes significant personal distress to self or others; (3) has risk or potential for significant physical or emotional harm to self or others; (4) is uncontrollable or resistant to change (e.g., patient feels out of control or unable to reduce or change the behavior), and (5) is not better accounted for by an alternate psychiatric diagnosis. (Fong et al., 2012, p. 280)

Failure to resist engaging in the behavior is an especially important criterion (Grant et al., 2010; Petry, 2016b)—although knowing when people can control their behavior isn't easy to determine. Beyond the

Behavioral addictions: Addictions involving behaviors rather than substances (e.g., excessive gambling, gaming, sex, eating, and shopping).

long-recognized issue of problem gambling, other behaviors have been proposed as addictive: shopping, working, eating, exercising, sexual activity, television watching, video game playing, Internet use, cell phone use, social networking, airline flying, and even tango dancing (Adams, 2013; Andreassen, 2013; Black, 2016; Carbonell et al., 2013; S. A. Cohen et al., 2011; Echeburúa, 2013; Fong et al., 2012; M. D. Griffiths et al., 2014; Q. Jiang et al., 2013; Q. Jiang & Huang, 2013; D. L. King & Delfabbro, 2013; Lejoyeux & Weinstein, 2013; Sussman & Moran, 2013; Targhetta et al., 2013; Toneatto, 2013). But where do we draw the line? Are these problems really addictions? Maybe they are better classified as obsessive-compulsive or impulse-control disorders (Fong et al., 2012)? Or perhaps they aren't disorders at all and we are simply pathologizing normal variations in behavior? In this vein, some clinicians and researchers worry that behavioral addictions lack evidence and risk becoming too broad and inclusive (Billieux et al., 2015; Fong et al., 2012; Sassover & Weinstein, 2020). One expert put it this way:

Surely not everyone should have a psychiatric condition, and if many excessive behavioral patterns are deemed psychiatric disorders most everyone would be diagnosed with a mental illness. This concern is particularly relevant to the construct of behavioral addictions. Excessive chocolate eating, even if it is causing weight gain and some distress, does not constitute a psychiatric disorder. (Petry, 2016b, pp. 2–3)

Do you agree that eating too much chocolate is not a behavioral addiction? The authors of DSM and ICD seem to. DSM only includes one behavioral addiction (gambling), while ICD limits itself to two (gambling and gaming). We turn to DSM and ICD perspectives next.

DIAGNOSTIC PERSPECTIVES

11.5 DSM and ICD

The DSM-5-TR and ICD-11 house substance use disorders and behavioral addictions together. This is a change from the past, when gambling was listed as an impulse-control (rather than addictive) disorder (Petry, 2016a).

Abuse vs. Dependence: A Distinction only ICD Still Makes
ICD-11: Harmful Use vs. Dependence

In classifying substance disorders, ICD-11 includes both harmful use (the ICD term for abuse) and dependence. In so doing, it abides by the long-time distinction between abuse and dependence. ICD-11's **harmful use** diagnosis involves ongoing misuse of a substance, while its **dependence** diagnosis requires tolerance and withdrawal. See Diagnostic Box 11.1.

Harmful use: ICD diagnosis that involves ongoing misuse of a substance leading to physical or mental health problems, adverse social consequences, and criticism from others; also called *substance abuse.*

Dependence: ICD diagnosis in which use of a substance takes on a higher priority than it once had; involves things like feeling compelled to take a substance, difficulty controlling use, tolerance, and withdrawal.

Diagnostic Box 11.1 Harmful Use and Dependence in ICD-11

Harmful Use
- Use that harms the physical or mental health of the user or the health of others.
- Can apply to a single *episode of use* or a recurrent *pattern of use.*
- If there is a recurrent pattern of use, it must be evident for twelve months or more (if use is periodic) or one month or more (if use is continuous).

Dependence
- Recurrent or continuous substance use that is difficult to control and which takes priority over other activities despite negative consequences.
- Symptoms of tolerance and withdrawal.
- Dependence occurs for twelve months or more, or for a minimum of three months if use occurs every day or almost every day.
- Specify *early full remission* if no substance use for one to twelve months, *sustained partial remission* if significant reduction in use for over twelve months, and *sustained full remission* if no substance use for over twelve months.

Information from World Health Organization (2022a).

DSM-5-TR: Substance Use Disorder

DSM decided (controversially) to eliminate the abuse–dependence distinction. It merged abuse and dependence into a single diagnosis called **substance use disorder**. To counter concerns about lumping minor and extreme cases together, DSM substance use disorders are assessed as mild, moderate, or severe based on how many diagnostic criteria a person meets. Diagnostic Box 11.2 lists DSM-5-TR criteria.

Substance use disorder: DSM diagnosis that combines symptoms of abuse and dependence; assessed based on type of drug being used and severity of use.

Diagnostic Box 11.2 Substance Use Disorder in DSM-5-TR

- Two or more of the following during a twelve-month period: (1) larger amounts of the substance taken for longer than planned; (2) wishes to or tries to reduce or control use; (3) lots of time spent getting, using, or recovering from using the substance; (4) desire or compulsion to use the substance; (5) consistently fails to meet obligations; (6) keeps using despite the substance causing or exacerbating interpersonal conflicts; (7) gives up other nonsubstance-related interests; (8) uses substance even when physically endangered by doing so; (9) keeps using even when knows substance is causing problems or making them worse; (10) tolerance; (11) withdrawal.
- Specify severity: *mild* (2–3 symptoms), *moderate* (4–5 symptoms), or *severe* (6 or more symptoms)
- Specify *early remission* if no symptoms for three to twelve months, or *sustained remission* if no symptoms for twelve or more months.

Information from American Psychiatric Association (2022, pp. 553–554).

Walter and Ayesha

Walter's drinking behavior, which involves abuse (e.g., drunk driving) and dependence (e.g., tolerance and withdrawal) of alcohol, meets criteria for alcohol use disorder. Similarly, Ayesha's abuse of opioids (including stealing money to purchase heroin) and her withdrawal symptoms in jail (trembling and sweating) qualify her for an opioid use disorder diagnosis.

There are different types of DSM substance use disorders. For each type, the kind of drug is substituted for the word "substance." Thus, DSM-5-TR includes diagnoses for alcohol use disorder, hallucinogen use disorder, opioid use disorder, and so forth. The diagnostic criteria are the same, but the specific drug type determines the disorder name and diagnostic codes used. The same is true for ICD-11. It includes both harmful use and dependence diagnoses for various substances (e.g., cocaine, alcohol, inhalants, and nicotine). Each diagnosis uses the same harmful use and dependence guidelines, but has its own name and codes. Tables 11.2 and 11.3 list DSM-5-TR and ICD-11 substance-related disorders. Note the ability to diagnose *intoxication* (being under the influence of the substance at the time of assessment), *remission* (no longer displaying signs of difficulty with the substance; sometimes referred to as being *in recovery*), and withdrawal. Also observe that there is no caffeine use disorder in DSM-5-TR or caffeine dependence in ICD-11. Despite inducing tolerance and withdrawal, regular caffeine use is not viewed as warranting these diagnoses (American Psychiatric Association, 2022; World Health Organization, 2022a).

Prevalence for substance use and substance use disorders varies by country and drug. Table 11.4 lists the most prevalent substances in 2021 among 19–30-year-olds and 35–60-year-olds in the United States. Unsurprisingly, substance use disorders often accompany other presenting problems. They are comorbid with mood disorders, anxiety disorders, eating disorders, posttraumatic stress disorder, personality disorders, and attention-deficit hyperactivity disorder (Bahji et al., 2019; Castillo-Carniglia et al., 2019; Crunelle et al., 2018; G. E. Hunt et al., 2018, 2020; Parmar & Kaloiya, 2018).

Gambling Disorder and Gaming Disorder

Gambling disorder is the only behavioral addiction in DSM-5-TR and one of two in ICD-11. It is characterized by recurrent gambling that leads to impairment and distress (see Diagnostic

Gambling disorder: DSM and ICD behavioral addiction characterized by recurrent problem gambling that leads to impairment and distress. (11)

Table 11.2 Types of DSM-5-TR Substance Disorders

Alcohol-Related Disorders: alcohol use disorder; alcohol intoxication; alcohol withdrawal; other alcohol-induced disorders; unspecified alcohol-related disorder

Caffeine-Related Disorders*: caffeine intoxication; caffeine withdrawal; other caffeine-induced disorders; unspecified caffeine-related disorder

Cannabis-Related Disorders: cannabis use disorder; cannabis intoxication; cannabis withdrawal; other cannabis-induced disorders; unspecified cannabis-related disorder

Hallucinogen-Related Disorders: phencyclidine use disorder; other hallucinogen use disorder; phencyclidine intoxication; other hallucinogen intoxication; hallucinogen persisting perception disorder; other phencyclidine-induced disorders; other hallucinogen-induced disorders; unspecified phencyclidine-related disorders; unspecified hallucinogen-related disorder

Inhalant-Related Disorders: inhalant use disorder; inhalant intoxication; other inhalant-induced disorders; unspecified inhalant-related disorder

Opioid-Related Disorders: opioid use disorder; opioid intoxication; opioid withdrawal; other opioid-induced disorders; unspecified opioid-related disorder

Sedative-, Hypnotic-, or Anxiolytic-Related Disorders: sedative, hypnotic, or anxiolytic use disorder; sedative, hypnotic, or anxiolytic intoxication; sedative, hypnotic, or anxiolytic withdrawal; other sedative-, hypnotic-, or anxiolytic-induced disorders, unspecified sedative-, hypnotic-, or anxiolytic-related disorder

Stimulant-Related Disorders: stimulant use disorder; stimulant intoxication; stimulant withdrawal; other stimulant-induced disorders; unspecified stimulant-related disorder

Tobacco-Related Disorders: tobacco use disorder; tobacco withdrawal; unspecified tobacco-related disorder

Other (or Unknown) Substance-Related Disorders: other (or unknown) substance use disorder; other (or unknown) substance intoxication; other (or unknown) substance withdrawal; other (or unknown) substance-induced disorders; unspecified other (or unknown) substance-related disorder

* DSM-5-TR does not include a caffeine use disorder diagnosis.

Table 11.3 Types of ICD-11 Substance Disorders

The following diagnoses can be given for the substances below: *episode of harmful use, pattern of harmful use, dependence, intoxication, withdrawal, substance induced-delirium,* and *substance induced-psychosis:*

- Alcohol
- Cannabis
- Synthetic cannabinoids
- Opioids
- Sedatives, hypnotics, anxiolytics
- Cocaine
- Stimulants, including amphetamines, methamphetamine, and methcathinone
- Synthetic cathinone
- Caffeine*
- Hallucinogens

- Nicotine
- Volatile inhalants
- MDMA or related drugs, including MDA**
- Dissociative drugs, including ketamine and phencyclidine (PCP)
- Other specified or multiple specified psychoactive substances
- Unknown or unspecified psychoactive substances
- Non-psychoactive substances

* ICD-11 does not include a caffeine dependence diagnosis.
** MDA is 3,4-Methylenedioxyamphetamine (MDA), a drug closely related to MDMA that goes by the street names "Sally," "Sass," or "Sassafras."

Box 11.3). DSM-5-TR estimates lifetime U.S. prevalence for gambling disorder at 0.4 percent to 1 percent, with men at greater risk (0.6 percent) than women (0.2 percent). The ICD-11 contains a second behavioral addiction, **gaming disorder**. It is a diagnosis for people who addictively play digital or video games (see Diagnostic Box 11.4). DSM-5-TR lists a similar diagnosis, *internet gaming disorder*, in its Section III as a potential future diagnosis in need of further study.

Gaming disorder: ICD behavioral addiction for those who compulsively play digital or video games.

Table 11.4 Most Prevalent Substances among Adults Ages 19–30 and 35–50 in the United States, 2021

ADULTS AGES 19–30		
	Past 12 months	*Past 30 days*
Alcohol	81.8%	66.3%
Marijuana	42.6%	28.5%
Vaping Nicotine	21.8%	16.1%
Vaping Marijuana	18.7%	12.4%
Cigarettes	18.6%	9.0%
Other Drugs*	18.3%	7.5%
ADULTS AGES 35–50		
	Past 12 months	*Past 30 days*
Alcohol	84.8%	71.4%
Marijuana	24.9%	15.8%
Cigarettes	14.5%	10.4%
Other Drugs*	11.2%	5.5%

* Includes hallucinogens (including LSD), cocaine, amphetamines, sedatives (barbiturates), tranquilizers, and narcotics (including heroin).
Source: Adapted from Patrick et al. (2022, pp. 10, 22).

Diagnostic Box 11.3 Gambling Disorder

DSM-5-TR
- Persistent and repeated gambling.
- Over twelve months, at least four of these: (1) must gamble larger sums for same excitement; (2) when tries to stop or reduce gambling, becomes impatient and short-tempered; (3) unsuccessfully tries to reduce or stop gambling; (4) absorbed in and focused on gambling much of the time; (5) gambles when upset; (6) tries to recoup losses by gambling more; (7) dishonest about degree of gambling; (8) risks or loses jobs, relationships, or other life prospects due to gambling; (9) relies on others to relieve financial problems caused by gambling.
- Specify severity: *mild* (4–5 symptoms), *moderate* (6–7 symptoms), or *severe* (8–9 symptoms).
- Specify *early remission* if no symptoms for three to twelve months, or *sustained remission* if no symptoms for twelve or more months.

ICD-11
- Persistent repeated gambling.
- Difficulty controlling gambling; gambling given priority over other activities and interests; keeps gambling despite negative consequences.
- Symptoms last for an extended period (e.g., twelve months).

Information from American Psychiatric Association (2022, p. 661) and World Health Organization (2022a).

Diagnostic Box 11.4 Gaming Disorder in ICD-11

- Persistent repeated online or offline digital game or videogame playing.
- Difficulty controlling gaming; gaming given priority over other activities and interests; keeps gaming despite negative consequences.
- Symptoms last for an extended period (e.g., twelve months).

Information from World Health Organization (2022a).

Pedro and Liam
Pedro engages in daily online sports betting and wagers large sums in poker games at the local casino. As he relentlessly "chases his losses," he incurs ever more debt. Liam does not gamble but remains in his room playing online games most days. He recently started visiting Facebook's Metaverse, with his only complaint being how difficult it is to charge the headgear without taking a break. Pedro's father believes he has gambling disorder, while Liam's parents are convinced that he suffers from gaming disorder.

Evaluating DSM and ICD Perspectives
Harmful Use and Dependence vs. Substance Use Disorder

ICD has retained both harmful use and dependence distinction, while DSM has collapsed them into a combined substance use disorder diagnosis (First et al., 2021). Which is preferable? Defenders of the DSM approach contend that the abuse versus dependence distinction is more easily made in theory than practice, so merging these diagnoses into a single category enhances diagnostic reliability (Denis et al., 2015; Hasin et al., 2013; Regier et al., 2013). Opponents counter that DSM's combined substance use disorder improperly pathologizes lots of people who only show milder symptoms (T. Chung et al., 2012; K. D. Jones et al., 2012; S. M. Kelly et al., 2014). Consistent with this, research indicates that many individuals who meet DSM criteria for substance use disorder do not qualify for an ICD diagnosis of substance dependence (Degenhardt et al., 2019). Whether you prefer the DSM or ICD approach, you can see how the manuals differing so greatly here might be problematic. Which manual is closer to being right?

Should DSM and ICD Include More Behavioral Addictions?

The notion of behavioral addictions has stirred controversy. Some worry that too many behaviors can easily (and inappropriately) be classified as behavioral addictions (Billieux et al., 2015). So far, DSM has erred on the side of caution by only including one behavioral addiction, gambling disorder. Not everyone appreciates this conservatism, arguing many other behaviors are addictive (e.g., sex, shopping, the Internet). Is ICD-11's addition of gaming disorder the first step in expanding the number of behavioral addictions? If so, is this a good or bad trend?

11.6 HiTOP

Substance users tend to score high on HiTOP's disinhibited externalizing spectrum. Disinhibited externalizing behavior entails "tendencies to act on impulse, without consideration for potential consequences," and this includes "the use of psychoactive substances to excess" (R. F. Krueger et al., 2021, p. 172). HiTOP clinicians assess patients with instruments like the Externalizing Spectrum Inventory (ESI), which measures aspects of externalizing, including disinhibition characteristic of substance users (R. F. Krueger et al., 2021).

11.7 PTMF

Rather than viewing substance misuse as an illness, PTMF sees it as a common response to social exclusion, one strongly correlated with adverse childhood experiences. Substance abuse becomes a way to meet emotional needs and self-soothe. From a PTMF perspective, clinician and service user should explore the service user's circumstances to determine how substance use developed into a meaningful strategy for coping with threat.

HISTORICAL PERSPECTIVES

11.8 Drug Use throughout Human History

Drug use is found throughout human history. There is evidence of alcohol being traded as far back as late prehistorical times, as well as hints that nearly all preliterate societies used psychoactive substances (Westermeyer, 2005). North and South American tribal societies used coca leaf, tobacco leaf, coffee bean, and peyote; African and Middle Eastern ethnic groups produced stimulants like qat, as well as cannabis; and across Asia, opium was prevalent (Westermeyer, 2005). Within particular cultures, economic and social sects didn't always use the same substances: "For example, one group in India consumed alcohol but not cannabis, whereas an adjacent group consumed cannabis but not alcohol" (Westermeyer, 2005, p. 18). Across religions, drugs were used differently, as well. Wine has traditionally been part of Jewish, Catholic, and other Christian rituals, but alcohol use is forbidden by many Muslim, Hindu, Buddhist, and fundamentalist Christian groups (Westermeyer, 2005).

11.9 Moral vs. Illness Models of Addiction

A distinction between the **moral versus illness models of addiction** recurs throughout history. The moral model predates the term "addiction," which first appeared in the sixteenth century and derives from the Latin word *addictionem* ("a devoting") (Westermeyer, 2013). In the moral model, addictive behavior is viewed as a vice of the morally weak (M. Clark, 2011; Pickard, 2020; Westermeyer, 2013). This model sees drug use as a crime to be prosecuted rather than a sickness to treat. The moral model remains influential today, as evidenced by widespread drug laws and societal disapproval of excessive drug use, gambling, or gaming. However, after the sixteenth century, the illness model (also called the *medical model of addiction*) grew in influence. First developed in Asia, Europe, and North America, the illness model views addiction as a disease (Clark, 2011; Westermeyer, 2013). As one historical example, Dr. Benjamin Rush (1746–1813)—the "Father of American Psychiatry"—advanced a medical model of alcoholism in the late 1700s and early 1800s, when drinking in the United States was more pervasive and widespread than today. Rush came to see extreme drinking not as a moral defect, but as a sickness. He argued that alcoholism is a disease, for which the only cure is total abstinence (Freed, 2012; B. Rush, 1784/1823). Rush urged compassion rather than condemnation for those he believed were sick: "Let us not, then, pass by the prostrate sufferer from strong drink, but administer the same relief, we would afford to a fellow creature, in a similar state, from an accidental and innocent cause" (B. Rush, 1784/1823, p. 29).

The illness model greatly influenced the nineteenth-century U.S. and European temperance movements, which saw eliminating alcohol from society as the best way to "cure" drunkenness (Freed, 2012; H. G. Levine, 1978; van der Stel, 2015). It is also reflected in early interventions for substance abuse, which increasingly adopted a medical stance. For instance, during the latter nineteenth century in the United States, chronic drunkards and excessive cocaine and opium users were diagnosed with *inebriety* and committed to asylums for treatment (Freed, 2012). During the twentieth century, biometrician E. M. Jellinek (1890–1963) and early female member of Alcoholics Anonymous Marty Mann (1904–1980) advanced the illness model (Freed, 2012; G. Glaser, 2015; H. G. Levine, 1978; Straussner & Attia, 2002). In order to "publicize the medical 'facts' about alcohol addiction," they opened "information centers nationwide to advertise alcoholism as an illness" (Freed, 2012, p. 35). Their efforts largely succeeded. The illness model of addiction remains predominant today.

11.10 The Founding of Alcoholics Anonymous

Another important twentieth-century development was the establishment of **12-step programs** for addiction. The original and most famous of these groups is **Alcoholics Anonymous (AA)**, cofounded by William Griffith Wilson (1895–1971). Wilson (more famously known as "Bill W." at AA meetings) was a chronic drinker who—in keeping with the illness model of addiction—viewed alcoholism as a

Moral versus illness models of drug addiction: The moral model views addiction as a vice, whereas the illness model (or medical model) views it as a disease.

12-step programs: Self-help groups such as Alcoholics Anonymous that see addiction as disease; by following the 12-steps, group members recover from their addictions.

Alcoholics Anonymous (AA): The largest and most well-known 12-step group for recovering alcoholics.

disease, not a moral weakness. However, he believed the best "cure" for alcoholism wasn't intervention by medical professionals, but encouragement and fellowship provided by other alcoholics. At weekly meetings, AA attendees acknowledge their powerlessness over alcohol and support each other in abstaining from drink (Freed, 2012). Doctors' initial response to AA's self-help model was quite negative. They criticized it "as 'a curious combination of organizing propaganda and religious exhortation … [with] no scientific merit or interest'" (Freed, 2012, p. 33). Similar tensions between 12-step programs and medical professionals periodically flare to this day (L. Dodes & Dodes, 2015; Peele, 1989). AA and other 12-step programs are discussed further under "Sociocultural Perspectives."

BIOLOGICAL PERSPECTIVES

11.11 Brain Chemistry Perspectives

Dopamine Hypotheses of Addiction

Dopamine is central to many biological perspectives on addiction. It plays a crucial role in the mesolimbic dopamine pathway (the brain's major reward pathway, introduced in Chapter 4 and discussed in this chapter again under brain structure perspectives). **Dopamine hypotheses of addiction** hold that addictive drugs increase brain dopamine levels (R. A. Wise & Jordan, 2021; R. A. Wise & Robble, 2020). Two examples are *reward deficiency syndrome theory (RDS)* and *incentive-sensitization theory*. RDS theory sees dopamine as producing pleasure and posits that addicted people take drugs to compensate for having too little dopamine or being insufficiently responsive to it (Blum et al., 1996, 2014, 2015). In other words, most people's dopamine levels increase naturally in response to pleasant events. The levels of people suffering from a reward deficiency do not. This places them at risk for addiction because when they take drugs, their dopamine levels are artificially raised—something they can't otherwise achieve. Incentive-sensitization theory proposes something a bit different, namely that drugs cause people to seek them out by increasing sensitivity to dopamine (Berridge, 2007, 2022; Berridge & Kringelbach, 2008; Littrell, 2010, 2015). Increased dopamine sensitivity results in people being more alert and on the lookout for drugs. In this model of addiction, drugs hijack the dopamine system by literally changing the brain (Littrell, 2010, 2015; Nestler & Malenka, 2004). The enduring nature of these brain changes may explain why relapse can occur long after drug use stops. The addicted person's brain remains altered. It therefore continues to be vulnerable to drug-related cues that trigger dopamine activity (Berridge, 2022; Kalivas & Volkow, 2005; Littrell, 2010, 2015).

Dopamine theories of addiction have become enormously influential, but a lot remains unanswered. First, the relationship between dopamine and reward is more complicated than initially believed (Pariyadath et al., 2013). Second, most dopamine studies have used stimulants (which directly increase dopamine), but not all drugs affect dopamine the way stimulants do; opiates and alcohol are good examples of this (Badiani et al., 2011; D. J. Nutt et al., 2015). Third, some drugs that increase dopamine turn out not to be addictive (D. J. Nutt et al., 2015). Fourth, dopamine theories haven't yielded new addiction treatments (D. J. Nutt et al., 2015).

Other Neurotransmitters

Besides dopamine, neurotransmitters such as glutamate are implicated in substance addiction. Ethanol, a type of alcohol, inhibits glutamate receptor activity, while withdrawal increases it (Fritz et al., 2022). Further, glutamate is implicated in relapse, with alcoholics showing lower glutamate levels than non-alcoholics when exposed to drinking cues (H. Cheng et al., 2018). Serotonin, norepinephrine, and GABA are also being researched as neurotransmitters involved in rewards, motivation, and addiction (S. L. Foster & Weinshenker, 2019; C. P. Müller & Homberg, 2015; Shyu et al., 2022). When it comes to substance use issues, different neurotransmitters interact in complex ways. Our grasp of these interactions is increasing, but there is much we still don't know.

Comparable Neurochemistry in Behavioral vs. Substance Addictions?

Research suggests that the neurochemistry of gambling and other behavioral addictions is remarkably like what occurs in substance addictions. For instance, reward deficiency syndrome is being applied to understand the role of dopamine and related neurotransmitters in gambling and

Dopamine hypotheses of addiction: Theorize that addictive drugs and behaviors increase dopamine; examples: *reward deficiency syndrome theory (RDS)* (which says people take drugs to compensate for too little dopamine) and *incentive-sensitization theory* (which says drugs hijack the brain by increasing dopamine sensitivity).

other behavioral addictions (Blum et al., 2014, 2021, 2022; Fauth-Bühler et al., 2016). This research fits within the Research Domain Criteria (RDoC) perspective introduced in Chapter 3. RDoC says disorders should be identified by shared brain abnormalities, not differences in behavior. If it turns out that substance users, compulsive shoppers, obsessive tan-seekers, and binge eaters all show the same neurotransmitter patterns in their brain reward centers, then perhaps they all have the same disease.

Drug Interventions for Addiction

Detoxification is the physical process of weaning addicted individuals from the drugs they are addicted to (Center for Substance Abuse Treatment, 2006). When removed from drugs all at once (going "cold turkey"), patients can experience intense physical and psychological withdrawal symptoms. However, if drug doses are decreased gradually, detoxification can be done with far less discomfort (J. R. McKay et al., 2015). Detoxification usually occurs in clinics or hospitals, although in some cases it can be accomplished in an outpatient setting. It is "often confused with treatment, but in reality detoxification is, at best, the first step in treatment" (J. R. McKay et al., 2015, p. 764). Detoxification generally occurs prior to other interventions.

Drugs to Treat Addiction and Prevent Relapse

Following detoxification, **antagonist drugs for substance abuse** prevent relapse by interfering with the addictive substance's effects (see Table 11.5). *Opioid blockers* are antagonist drugs that inhibit the body's pleasurable response to addictive substances like alcohol and opioids (Littrell, 2015; Niciu & Arias, 2013; Stahl, 2018; Theriot et al., 2022a). They are used to ward off cravings (J. R. McKay et al., 2015; Theriot et al., 2022b). Other antagonist drugs, such as *acamprosate* (trade name *Campral*) and *N-acetylcysteine (NAC)*, diminish cravings by blocking glutamate (Kalk & Lingford-Hughes, 2014; J. R. McKay et al., 2015; Tomko et al., 2018). Somewhat differently, *disulfiram* (trade name *Antabuse*) stops the enzyme *acetaldehyde* from breaking down alcohol, so that people taking it become sick when they drink (e.g., nausea, vomiting, and dizziness) (Kleczkowska, 2021; Stokes & Abdijadid, 2021). Unfortunately, to avoid this, many alcoholics simply stop taking it (Brewer et al., 2000; R. K. Fuller et al., 1986). Beyond antagonist drugs, the anticonvulsant *topiramate* reduces the desire for alcohol and cocaine by decreasing GABA and enhancing glutamate (J. R. McKay et al., 2015; Shinn & Greenfield, 2010). SSRIs are also occasionally prescribed (especially to alcohol users, who are believed to have low serotonin levels), but evidence for their effectiveness is mixed (J. R. McKay et al., 2015).

Drugs for nicotine dependence include SSRIs, the atypical antidepressant *bupropion* (marketed for smoking cessation as *Zyban*), and the tricyclic antidepressant *nortriptyline* (trade name *Pamelor*). However, none are as effective as *varenicline* (trade name *Chantix*), which makes cigarettes less enjoyable and decreases withdrawal symptoms by partially blocking nicotine receptors (Karam-Hage et al., 2021; Khunrong & Sittipunt, 2016; J. R. McKay et al., 2015; Rigotti, 2022; D. Singh & Saadabadi, 2022). Controversially, varenicline and bupropion used to carry a suicide risk warning in the United States, but it was removed in 2016 (Center for Drug Evaluation and Research, 2016; DeNoon, 2009).

Drug Replacement Therapies

Drug replacement therapies involve either changing the delivery method of a drug or exchanging one addictive drug for another. Sometimes the goal is to wean people off drugs. Other times it is to sustain them on similar but less dangerous drugs. Nicotine replacement therapy exemplifies the former and methadone maintenance therapy the latter. In **nicotine replacement therapy (NRT)**, the method of nicotine delivery is changed to ease people off it (Karam-Hage et al., 2021). *Nicotine gums*, *nasal sprays*, *lozenges*, *tablets*, *inhalers*, *patches*, and *e-cigarettes* are alternative delivery methods to help people stop smoking. Ideally, use decreases over time until the person is nicotine-free. Research finds NRT effective, although the quality of the evidence isn't as strong as it could be (Klemperer et al., 2022). E-cigarettes may be preferable to other methods (Hajek et al., 2019; J. Li, Hajek, et al., 2020), but many teens and young adults use them for pleasure rather than to quit smoking (Karam-Hage et al., 2021).

Methadone maintenance therapy (MMT) replaces more problematic opioids (e.g., heroin or fentanyl) with less problematic but chemically similar ones (usually *methadone* or *buprenorphine*)

Detoxification: Physical process of weaning addicted individuals from the drugs they are addicted to.

Antagonist drugs for substance abuse: Drugs that prevent relapse by interfering with an addictive substance's effects; *opioid blockers* (*naloxone, naltrexone,* and *nalmefene*), *acamprosate, N-acetylcysteine (NAC)*, and *disulfiram* are antagonist drugs.

Drug replacement therapies: Changes the delivery method of a drug or exchanges one drug for a chemically similar one, with the goal of weaning people off drugs or sustaining them on similar but less dangerous drugs.

Nicotine replacement therapy (NRT): Drug replacement therapy for smoking cessation in which the delivery method is changed to make weaning off nicotine easier; gum, patches, lozenges, and e-cigarettes are examples of alternative delivery methods.

Methadone maintenance therapy (MMT): Drug replacement therapy that replaces more problematic opioids (e.g., heroin or fentanyl) with less problematic but chemically similar ones (usually *methadone* or *buprenorphine*).

Table 11.5 Drugs to Treat Addiction and Prevent Relapse

DRUG	MECHANISM OF ACTION
Acamprosate (trade name *Campral*)	Blocks glutamate
N-acetylcysteine (NAC)	Blocks glutamate
Disulfiram (trade name *Antabuse*)	Prevents alcohol breakdown
Naltrexone (trade name *Vivitrol*)	Opioid blocker
Naloxone (trade name *Narcan*)	Opioid blocker
Nalmefene (trade name *Selincro*)	Opioid blocker
Topiramate	Anticonvulsant
SSRIs	Block serotonin reuptake

(Bromley et al., 2021; Mattick et al., 2009, 2014; World Health Organization, 2009). The synthetic replacement opioids are still addictive but provide less extreme highs, last longer (requiring fewer administrations), and can be safely and effectively given in inpatient or outpatient medical settings (Çakıcı et al., 2019; E. Day & Strang, 2011). The goal isn't necessarily for patients to stop using addictive opioids because—given the power of opioid addiction, especially its intense withdrawal symptoms—that may not be feasible. Instead, MMT assumes that long-term medically administered maintenance on methadone or buprenorphine is preferable to unsupervised opioid use because it is associated with less criminal behavior, higher social functioning, and (although the evidence isn't clear) reduced chance of death (Durand et al., 2021; Mattick et al., 2009, 2014). MMT is usually supplemented with naltrexone or naloxone to reduce cravings. Sometimes buprenorphine and naloxone are combined into a single drug (marketed as *Buprenex*, *Suboxone*, and *Subutex*).

Methadone is usually more effective than buprenorphine (especially with severe cases), but its withdrawal symptoms are worse and overdose risk greater (Çakıcı et al., 2019; Gowing et al., 2017; Mattick et al., 2014). Thus, methadone is limited to clinic settings, whereas buprenorphine can be taken at home (Çakıcı et al., 2019). MMT's main drawback is very high dropout rates. A 2021 study found only 46 percent of participants failed to drop out for at least a while during MMT (Durand et al., 2021). This echoes past research that consistently found people drop out of MMT at alarmingly high rates (Khue et al., 2017; Nosyk et al., 2010; K. Zhou & Zhuang, 2014). Additionally, not everyone is comfortable with MMT keeping people on opioids indefinitely, believing the goal of treatment should be getting people off opioids entirely (J. J. Sanders et al., 2013; Winstock et al., 2011). However, patients who find MMT helpful paint a different picture: "MMT allowed me to trade in the 26-hours a day, every day hustle of illegal heroin use, for the highly imperfect and overly difficult, but crucially-legal and therefore stable, strategy of obtaining my opioids through a methadone clinic" (D. Frank, 2020, p. 2).

Ayesha

If Ayesha underwent MMT for her opioid problem, she might regularly be administered methadone at a clinic. This would keep her off the streets and help her avoid using dirty needles that could carry the HIV virus and other illnesses. Ayesha would only need methadone every other day, compared with every few hours when doing heroin. Because MMT attrition rates are high, psychotherapy to prevent drop out would be important.

11.12 Brain Structure Perspectives

Neurochemical explanations of addiction often focus on neurotransmission in the brain's reward system. This reward system involves interactions among numerous brain areas, including the *medial prefrontal cortex, amygdala, ventral striatum, ventral tegmental area*, and *hippocampus* (A. Beck et al., 2011; Popescu et al., 2021). One part of the brain's reward system studied in addiction research is the

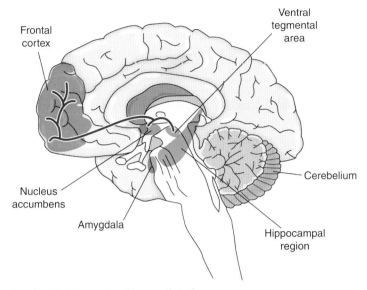

Figure 11.5 The Mesolimbic Dopamine (Reward) Pathway.
Source: Kalsi, G., Prescott, C. A., Kendler, K. S., & Riley, B. P. (2009). Unraveling the molecular mechanisms of alcohol dependence. Trends in Genetics, 25(1), 49–55. https://doi.org/10.1016/j.tig.2008.10.005

mesolimbic dopamine pathway (see Chapter 4 and Figure 11.5). This pathway connects the *ventral tegmental area (VTA)* (important in rewards and motivation) to the nucleus accumbens (which plays a role in reward processing). The mesolimbic dopamine pathway's importance in addiction fits with dopamine theories that say addictive drugs boost dopamine transmission (R. A. Wise & Jordan, 2021; R. A. Wise & Robble, 2020). Many researchers argue that habit-forming drugs directly or indirectly activate the mesolimbic dopamine pathway and that addiction is a disease of the brain's reward system (Pariyadath et al., 2013; Popescu et al., 2021).

11.13 Genetic Perspectives

Heritability of Addiction

The heritability of addiction is estimated to be between 40 and 60 percent (Popescu et al., 2021). If correct, this means about half the variation in people with substance use issues is due to genes and the rest due to environment. Specific heritability estimates for alcohol (29–51 percent), nicotine (59–71 percent), cocaine (42–79 percent), hallucinogens (25–39 percent), opioids (43–60 percent), cannabis (29–51 percent), and gaming disorder (50–60 percent) are roughly consistent with this (da Silva e Silva & de Araújo Moreira, 2021; Yau et al., 2021). Further, first-degree relatives of those with substance use disorders are 4.5 times as likely to also suffer from one (da Silva e Silva & de Araújo Moreira, 2021). Genes are important, even if environment also plays a role (da Silva e Silva & de Araújo Moreira, 2021; Deak & Johnson, 2021; Popescu et al., 2021; Yau et al., 2021).

Candidate Genes

Many different genes have been implicated in substance use issues, though results are hard to replicate (as is typical in genetic research). Among the genes linked to alcohol use disorders are dopamine genes and genes important in processing and breaking down alcohol (Deak & Johnson, 2021; Hatoum et al., 2022). Acetylcholine genes have been tied to nicotine and cannabis use disorders, while opioid receptor genes have been correlated with opioid use disorders (J. Chen et al., 2020; Crist et al., 2019; Deak & Johnson, 2021; Hatoum et al., 2022). Despite a lot of enthusiasm, genetic research has been criticized for defining addiction imprecisely and overstating the degree to which genes "cause" substance use issues (D. Moore, 2014). Some people also worry that should genetic diagnosis of addictions become a reality, having the genetic risk markers will be stigmatizing (Ostergren et al., 2015).

11.14 Evolutionary Perspectives

Chapter 1 introduced the *harmful internal dysfunction* model, which defined mental disorders as consisting of mental mechanisms that fail to function as evolutionarily designed, which then causes harm (J. C. Wakefield, 1992b). Generalizing from this, the **harmful dysfunction model of addiction** says addiction occurs when substances (like alcohol) and stimuli (like the Internet) coopt the human brain's reward system, which evolved before ever encountering them; thus, when exposed to them, the brain is unable to effectively respond (J. C. Wakefield, 2020). The result? Harmful use, abuse, and dependence. In other words, "addiction comes about due to evolutionarily novel inputs to the brain that cause a true harmful psychological dysfunction of choice mechanisms that were not designed for these inputs" (J. C. Wakefield, 2020, p. 7). In this model, although addiction is a medical disorder, humans are only vulnerable to it because their brains are not evolutionarily adapted to handle certain drugs or environmental triggers. Like many evolutionary explanations, the harmful dysfunction model is theoretical, though it does draw on previously discussed research into how addictions "hijack" the brain's reward system.

Harmful dysfunction model of addiction:
Addiction results when substances or stimuli coopt the brain's reward system, which cannot respond effectively because it has not evolved the ability to cope with them.

11.15 Immune System Perspectives

Substance use affects the immune system—including gut bacteria and *microglia* brain cells important in immune response (A. G. McGrath & Briand, 2019; Meredith et al., 2021; Qin et al., 2021). Consequently, prolonged substance use increases vulnerability to illness. For example, excessive drinking weakens immune functioning and has been linked to pneumonia, respiratory difficulties, liver problems, and some cancers (Meredith et al., 2021; Sarkar et al., 2015; G. Y. Trivedi & Saboo, 2020). Because substance use disorders are associated with immune inflammation, anti-inflammatory drugs such as *phosphodiesterase (PDE) inhibitors* (among others) are being studied as alcoholism treatments (E. K. Erickson et al., 2019; Meredith et al., 2021). Consistent with this, researchers are also investigating whether existing drug treatments for substance issues (e.g., naltrexone, nalmefene, and NAC) work by reducing inflammation (E. K. Erickson et al., 2019; Meredith et al., 2021). As for gut bacteria, disruptions in *gut microbiome* (see Chapter 6) appear to both result from and increase vulnerability to substance use disorders (Calleja-Conde et al., 2021; Jerlhag, 2019; Lucerne et al., 2021; Qamar et al., 2019; Qin et al., 2021; Ren & Lotfipour, 2020). Given the many connections between regular substance use and the immune system, it is no surprise that use increases vulnerability to COVID-19—ironic given how many people relieved pandemic stress by turning to drugs (Calina et al., 2021; Da et al., 2020; D. McKay & Asmundson, 2020; Y. Wei & Shah, 2020).

11.16 Evaluating Biological Perspectives

The main objection to biological perspectives is that they insist addiction is a "chronic, relapsing brain disease" (Campbell, 2010, p. 90), but not everyone agrees with this (Hall et al., 2015). The addiction-as-brain-disease assumption is so prevalent that many students are surprised anyone questions it. However, some people argue that although addictive behavior involves difficulties with self-control and choice, it is not a disease (C. E. Fisher, 2022; Kerr, 1996; Schaler, 2000, 2002). In the words of one medical model critic: "Chemical rewards have no power to compel—although this notion of compulsion may be a cherished part of clinicians' folklore. I am rewarded every time I eat chocolate cake, but I often eschew this reward" (Schaler, 2002). Defenders of the medical model counter that the capacity for choice doesn't rule out brain disease: "Pre-existing vulnerabilities and persistent drug use lead to a vicious circle of substantive disruptions in the brain that impair and undermine choice capacities for adaptive behavior, but do not annihilate them" (Heilig et al., 2021, p. 1720). This is reminiscent of the illness–moral model debate. If you agree with the first argument, you side with the moral model. If you prefer the second, you lean toward the illness model.

Critics also assert that reducing addiction to biology overlooks the social. A few examples: A person can't be an "alcoholic" without socially shared ideas about how much drinking is too much; "compulsive buying" makes little sense outside of capitalist environments that celebrate (yet also worry about excessive) consumer consumption; and "Internet addiction" wasn't a "thing" until we invented the Internet and began worrying about how much time online is okay. Social context matters a lot in what "counts" as addiction. Still, brain disease defenders say their model "does not deny the influence of social, environmental, developmental, or socioeconomic processes, but rather proposes that the brain is the underlying material substrate upon which those factors impinge and from which the responses originate" (Heilig et al., 2021, p. 1719). What do you think?

PSYCHOLOGICAL PERSPECTIVES

11.17 Psychodynamic Perspectives

The Self-Medication Hypothesis

Psychodynamic perspectives see compulsive drug use as a symptom of unconscious conflicts and early attachment issues (L. M. Dodes & Khantzian, 2005; K. Fletcher et al., 2015). The **self-medication hypothesis** views substance abuse as a defensive strategy to avoid upset and despair traceable to childhood maltreatment (K. Fletcher et al., 2015; Gottdiener & Suh, 2015; Khantzian, 1985, 1997, 2012, 2021). Self-medicators tend to have difficulty recognizing and regulating their emotions, making them susceptible to drug use as a mechanism for coping with emotional problems. They might use alcohol to manage constricted or repressed emotions, opiates to deal with anger, or cocaine to relieve boredom or fill the need for sensation-seeking. Like those who somaticize, substance abusers often exhibit *alexithymia* (difficulty naming and describing their feelings; see Chapter 8) (Suh et al., 2008). Research supports the self-medication hypothesis, despite some methodological limitations (Hawn et al., 2020). Psychodynamic therapies help substance issues identify avoidant relational patterns and share emotions more productively (L. M. Dodes & Khantzian, 2005; Gregory, 2019; Khantzian, 2012). As patients become more emotionally expressive and self-aware (i.e., less alexithymic), they no longer need drugs to escape their feelings. The extremely small body of research on psychodynamic therapy for substance issues suggests effectiveness for opiate dependence but not cocaine dependence (Leichsenring & Steinert, 2019).

When it comes to behavioral addictions, psychodynamic therapists attribute problem gambling to early losses and deprivation, an unconscious need to lose, the desire for approval, and unconscious feelings of not being good enough (López Viets & Miller, 1997; Rosenthal & Rugle, 1994). They explain compulsive shopping as an unconscious need for nurturing, an effort to deny death, and as a repressed need for sexual adventure (Black, 2016). There is little research on psychodynamic therapy for behavioral addictions, but a pilot study found it helped patients with gambling and compulsive addictions who had not responded to CBT (Mooney et al., 2019).

Self-medication hypothesis: Psychodynamic hypothesis that substance abuse is a defense used by those who have difficulty recognizing and regulating their emotions; this avoidance strategy is traceable to adverse childhood events.

Pedro

In psychodynamic therapy, Pedro's therapist would explore unconscious attachment issues tied to his gambling. Pedro might gain insight into his unconscious desire for his father's approval and how he never felt good enough: "I wanted my dad to recognize me and pay attention to me, but he was busy at work. He never had time for me, except when I got in trouble for gambling." As Pedro works through past emotional injuries and develops new ways of relating and being attached to others that don't require being a "screw up" to get attention, his gambling will likely decrease.

The Addictive Personality

Early psychoanalytic theorists posited an **addictive personality**, a set of traits that predispose people to addiction and reflect oral stage conflicts (B. Johnson, 2003). While popular, many researchers believe the notion of an addictive personality has been debunked and that no constellation of personality traits predicts addiction (Amodeo, 2015; Berglund et al., 2011; Kerr, 1996; Nathan, 1988; D. L. Roberts, 2019; Szalavitz, 2015). However, others counter that even without a singular personality pattern, certain characteristics are associated with addiction—including impulsivity, anxiety, depression, social discomfort, social alienation, sensation seeking, tolerance of deviance, nonconformity, and high stress combined with poor coping skills (Favennec et al., 2021; D. L. Roberts, 2019). Opponents still say the addictive personality idea should be retired because it

Addictive personality: Hotly debated notion that a specific set of personality traits predisposes people to addiction.

reinforces a stigmatizing and pessimistic view of substance abusers as having broken personalities that make recovery unlikely (Amodeo, 2015). Debate is likely to continue.

11.18 Cognitive-Behavioral Perspectives

Behaviorally, drugs serve as reinforcers—initially as positive reinforcers that make people feel good, and later as negative reinforcers that relieve unpleasant withdrawal symptoms (S. Edwards, 2016). Behaviorally speaking, then, prescribing disulfiram to addicts serves as a form of aversive conditioning by turning drugs from reinforcers to punishers (Lejuez et al., 1998). The nausea disulfiram induces punishes drug taking, but—as noted earlier—many patients stop taking it to avoid this. Like substance addictions, the persistence of behavioral addictions can be attributed to classical and operant conditioning contingencies (James & Tunney, 2017; I. Marks, 1990). Cognitively, substance use problems and behavioral addictions are about dysfunctional thinking and poor problem-solving (J. S. Beck et al., 2005; Grant et al., 2010). If people alter their thinking, behavior change follows. Let's review several CBT interventions for addiction.

Contingency Management

Contingency management (CM):
Operant conditioning behavioral technique in which abstinence and other desired behaviors are positively reinforced to strengthen them.

Contingency management (CM) is a behavioral technique that rewards abstinence and other desired behaviors. Rooted in the principles of operant conditioning, it positively reinforces sobriety (S. T. Higgins & Petry, 1999; Silva et al., 2021; Stitzer & Petry, 2006). CM program patients take regular drug tests. Those who pass are given rewards such as food, clothes, shelter, employment, and prizes. In some cases, they are given vouchers that can later be exchanged for rewards. Besides abstinence, contingency management is used to reward medication adherence and attendance at treatment meetings (M. W. Lewis, 2008). There is substantial evidence that CM works (H. D. Brown & DeFulio, 2020; D. R. Davis et al., 2016; T. Zhu, 2022). However, it is most effective while patients remain in the program (Rash et al., 2017). Once the program is finished and regular reinforcement ends, many people revert to earlier substance use (Guenzel & McChargue, 2022). Because of this, CM is often used in conjunction with other interventions (such as drug treatments, AA, and cognitive therapy) (Blonigen et al., 2015). However, supplementing CM with psychotherapy doesn't necessarily improve its effectiveness (Rains et al., 2020).

Social Skills Training

Drug abuse is often a means of compensating for poor social skills (J. J. Platt & Husband, 1993). In social skills training (SST; see Chapter 4), substance abusers are taught how to start social interactions, convey thoughts and feelings, handle criticism, and manage challenging interpersonal situations (Blonigen et al., 2015; P. M. Monti et al., 1994; P. M. Monti & O'Leary, 1999; J. J. Platt & Husband, 1993). SST teaches concrete behavioral strategies for interacting with others (e.g., how to start and carry conversations, how to politely disagree with others, how to appropriately share feelings). It is considered an effective intervention for substance issues (Amini Pozveh & Saleh, 2020; Blonigen et al., 2015; Limberger & Andretta, 2018; M. F. Wagner et al., 2021).

Relapse Prevention

Relapse prevention (RP), a CBT technique discussed in Chapter 10 as an intervention for sex offenders, is also used with substance abusers. RP prevents relapse by teaching those in recovery how to handle high-risk situations that tempt them to begin using again (D. Donovan & Witkiewitz, 2012; Marlatt & Donovan, 2005; Marlatt & George, 1984; Witkiewitz & Marlatt, 2004). High-risk situations involve people, places, and events associated with past drug use (Witkiewitz & Marlatt, 2004). They are often encountered unintentionally, usually by making insignificant everyday decisions—for example, inadvertently walking by a bar.

Ayesha
While in recovery from her opioid addiction, Ayehsa visits the beach and accidentally runs into her old drug dealer. This is a high-risk situation because it exposes Ayesha to cues (in this case her drug dealer) that tempt her start using drugs again.

To cope with high-risk situations, clients are taught behaviors like walking away from the situation or declining invitations to use the substance. They are also encouraged to develop a social support system because having one helps people avoid relapse. Finally, cognitive expectancies are evaluated to help recovering substance users feel more optimistic about their ability to navigate high-risk scenarios. In other words, *self-efficacy* (confidence one can succeed at a task) matters because negative expectations make failure more likely. Research supports RP for alcohol, tobacco, cocaine, and polysubstance use (D. Donovan & Witkiewitz, 2012; Hendershot et al., 2011; Witkiewitz & Marlatt, 2004).

Cognitive Therapy

The central focus of cognitive therapy for substance addiction is how people's belief systems impact drug use (J. S. Beck et al., 2005). Clients' automatic thoughts, intermediate beliefs, core beliefs, and schemas (all discussed in Chapter 2) influence how substance users respond to situations and why they resort to drugs as a coping strategy. Cognitive therapy for substance abuse helps clients identify and alter dysfunctional thoughts and behavior patterns that lead to drug use. Cognitive therapy often incorporates other CBT techniques, such as skills training and relapse prevention (D. Donovan & Witkiewitz, 2012; Ritvo et al., 2003).

Walter

Dysfunctional thoughts play a central role in Walter's drinking. He often has automatic thoughts about not being likable or interesting (e.g., "Nobody will like me if I'm not the life of the party" and "Unless I drink, everyone will see how boring I am"). These are tied to one of his core beliefs: "I'm not lovable." The goal in cognitive therapy would be to help Walter revise his belief system. He also might be taught social skills for interacting more effectively with others. Finally, Walter would learn to identify high-risk situations that tempt him to fall off the wagon (e.g., hanging out with his beer-drinking buddies or going to work-related cocktail parties).

11.19 Humanistic Perspectives

Influenced by Carl Rogers' person-centered therapy, **motivational interviewing (MI)** is a goal-directed, focused, and brief intervention (one to four sessions) that facilitates change by empathizing with clients, accepting them, and not pressing them to change before they are ready (W. R. Miller & Rollnick, 2002; W. R. Miller & Wilbourne, 2002). MI highlights inconsistencies between clients' goals and behavior so clients can decide whether to do something about them (Miller & Rollnick, 1991, 2002). It does not demand clients change but believes they can if they choose to (Miller & Rollnick, 1991, 2002). Though it integrates some CBT concepts (such as self-efficacy), MI's humanistic foundation is reflected in its refusal to label clients as "alcoholics" or "addicts." Its humanism is also seen in its five therapy strategies, best remembered by the acronym *OARS* (use *open questions*, *affirm*, *reflect*, and *summarize*) (Ingersoll, 2022). In practice, MI is often combined with the **transtheoretical model of change**, which says change occurs across five stages: (1) *precontemplation* (no awareness of a problem and no intention of changing), (2) *contemplation* (awareness of a problem, but not committed to change), (3) *preparation* (intends to change and makes small changes), (4) *action* (makes decisive changes), and (5) *maintenance* (works to prevent relapse) (DiClemente & Velasquez, 2002; Prochaska et al., 1992). Low to moderate quality research supports MI as an intervention for substance issues (Ingersoll, 2022; Smedslund et al., 2011).

11.20 Evaluating Psychological Perspectives

Contingency management, motivational interviewing, and CBT all have substantial bodies of research support for use with substance issues (Leonardi et al., 2021; J. R. McKay, 2022; Njoroge, 2018). Most behavioral or psychological interventions are equally effective to one another, while also working just as well as pharmacological interventions (Witkiewitz et al., 2019). Of course, when evaluating therapies for addiction, an important but often overlooked question is "what counts as success?" Typically, total abstinence has been the goal, but some researchers and therapists increasingly believe that helping people reduce or moderate their drug use can also be a good outcome. For more on **controlled drinking** and **harm reduction**, see the "In Depth" feature.

Motivational interviewing (MI): Humanistic technique rooted in person-centered theory that helps people recognize and do something about pressing problems.

Transtheoretical model of change: Model of therapeutic change that identifies five stages clients go through during the change process (*precontemplation, contemplation, preparation, action,* and *maintenance*).

Controlled drinking: Treatments that help people reduce their drinking to acceptable levels and moderate alcohol's role in their lives, but without demanding abstinence (e.g., *Moderation Management (MM)*, a controlled drinking support group alternative to AA).

Harm reduction: Intervention strategies for reducing individual and societal harm caused by drug and alcohol use; examples include needle exchange programs, adding thiamine to beer, and providing late-night public transportation.

Liam

Photo 11.4
ELLA DON/Unsplash.

Liam, the 15-year-old whose parents think he has a video gaming addiction, undergoes MI. He meets four times with a therapist, who empathizes when Liam insists "It's my parents who have a problem, not me!" The therapist avoids arguing with Liam and trying to convince him he's addicted to video games. However, she also helps Liam identify discrepancies between his goals and behavior. Liam admits that meeting most of his social needs via online gaming is lonely and unsatisfying; he confesses he'd like to develop deeper friendships with kids at school. His therapist empathically reflects this discrepancy: "You want to get out more and have more friends, but you're spending most of your time alone in your room playing games." After four MI sessions, Liam better understands what he wants. He cuts back on gaming and reallocates that time to after-school activities where he can make new friends.

In Depth: Controlled Drinking versus Total Abstinence

Must people with alcohol problems totally abstain from drinking or can they learn to control their alcohol use? While most approaches preach abstinence, controlled drinking and harm reduction perspectives argue otherwise. *Controlled drinking* treatments aim to help people reduce their drinking to acceptable levels and moderate alcohol's role in their lives, but without demanding abstinence (H. Rosenberg & Melville, 2005; Sobell & Sobell, 1995). Moderation can be achieved using both professional and self-help interventions (Witkiewitz & Alan Marlatt, 2006). *Moderation Management (MM)* is a controlled drinking self-help group whose members generally don't identify as alcoholics. In contrast to Alcoholics Anonymous, Moderation Management sees drinking as a learned behavior, not a disease. Thus, MM promotes controlled drinking over abstinence as an appropriate goal for many problem drinkers (Klaw & Humphreys, 2000; Lembke & Humphreys, 2012).

The objective in most controlled drinking approaches is *harm reduction*—reducing individual and societal harm caused by drug and alcohol use (Heather, 2006; Marlatt, 1996; Sodelli, 2021; Witkiewitz & Alan Marlatt, 2006). Harm reduction focuses less on stopping people from using substances and more on minimizing risk when they do. Examples of harm reduction strategies include needle exchange programs (to ensure that drug users avoid HIV by having clean needles), adding thiamine to beer (to prevent Korsakoff syndrome), and providing late-night public transportation (to decrease incidents of drunk driving) (Heather, 2006). Supporters of harm reduction argue that because many people will inevitably drink or take drugs, we should make sure they do so as safely as possible (Sodelli, 2021). Opponents, on the other hand, worry that such strategies encourage substance use (O'Loughlin, 2007).

Controlled drinking and harm reduction perspectives challenge both the moral and illness models of addiction (Marlatt, 1996). They deemphasize the moral model's insistence on criminalizing and punishing substance users and instead focus on health and safety issues. They also question the illness model, which in their view leans too heavily on the assumption that drinking is a disease and abstinence the only viable cure. As for research evidence, a 2021 review and meta-analysis found controlled drinking worked as well as total abstinence (Henssler et al., 2020). This was true regardless of drinking severity. This finding contradicts the conventional wisdom that moderation is only possible in less serious cases, but it fits with evidence that patient outcomes are better when patients choose treatment goals (in this case, abstinence or moderation) (Henssler et al., 2020). Abstinence remains the most common goal in drug treatment, especially in the United States (Ambrogne, 2002; Klingemann & Rosenberg, 2009; H. Rosenberg & Davis, 2014). Still, controlled drinking approaches encourage us to consider whether abstinence is the only option.

Critical Thinking Questions

1. Do you think controlled drinking is a realistic goal for problem alcohol and drug use? Explain your reasoning.
2. Does harm reduction implicitly promote drug use? Why or why not?
3. Some controlled drinking advocates believe that the illness model sets people up for repeated relapses by seeing them as having a lifelong disease. What do you think?

SOCIOCULTURAL PERSPECTIVES

11.21 Cross-Cultural and Social Justice Perspectives

Poverty, Discrimination, and Substance Use

Sociocultural factors influence when, why, and how often people use drugs. This may explain differences in drug popularity around the world (see Figure 11.6). Unfortunately, we often overlook social determinants of substance issues. Poverty and discrimination are associated with increased vulnerability to drug use and abuse—not surprising given that they add stress to people's lives (Amaro et al., 2021). For example, stress linked to social disadvantage likely contributed to the larger increases in substance issues during the COVID pandemic among lower socioeconomic status (SES) individuals and racial/ethnic minority groups (Czeisler et al., 2020; McKnight-Eily et al., 2021). However, poverty and discrimination don't just contribute to substance use problems. They also add to treatment disparities for people of color, who have less access and worse outcomes (Burlew et al., 2021; B. Lewis et al., 2018; Mennis & Stahler, 2016). Social justice advocates argue that reducing social inequality is key to more effectively addressing substance use issues.

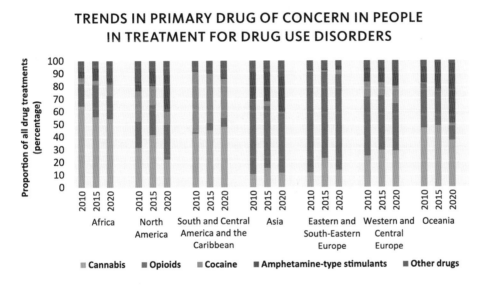

Figure 11.6 Trends in Primary Drug of Concern in People in Treatment for Drug Use Disorders.
Note: Oceania includes Australasia, Melanesia, Micronesia, and Polynesia.
Source: United Nations Office on Drugs and Crime (2022, Booklet 1, p. 41).

Prevention and Early Intervention Programs

Prevention and early intervention programs thwart the development of substance abuse or behavioral addictions and, if they develop, intervene early to keep them from snowballing into larger problems. Prevention efforts include drug screenings, drug testing, restricting availability, taxation or minimum pricing, banning advertising, and media campaigns to educate people about risks (Stockings et al., 2016). Methods that emphasize skill development work much better than those that merely provide information (Stockings et al., 2016). Early intervention programs include ones based on CBT or motivational interviewing (Botvin et al., 1984; Dusenbury et al., 1989; Foxcroft et al., 2016; Sussman & Ames, 2008). The *Reclaiming Futures* program in the United States exemplifies an early intervention program rooted in social justice (Curry-Stevens & Nissen, 2011; Nissen, 2007, 2014; Nissen & Pearce, 2011). It was designed for juveniles arrested on drug-related charges (many of them minority group members of low SES). The program is integrated into juvenile drug courts to provide easy access to treatment, mentorship programs, and community-based social supports (M. Dennis et al., 2016; A. Greene et al., 2016). Social inequalities are acknowledged and addressed to improve access to services and tailor them to the needs of juveniles in the program. Through nurturing and supportive means, *Reclaiming Futures* helps youth who have had drug-related run-ins with the law

Prevention and early intervention programs: Programs designed to prevent or intervene in the early stages of substance use.

turn their lives around before substance use becomes a lifelong problem. More research is needed, but evidence to date suggests the program improves outcomes, provides economic benefits (e.g., by reducing crime and mental health costs), and is well regarded by participating clinicians (M. Dennis et al., 2016; Korchmaros et al., 2016, 2017; McCollister et al., 2018; Nissen & Merrigan, 2011).

Therapeutic Communities

Therapeutic communities (TCs):
Residential or day treatment programs that provide an array of services and help participants develop new life skills; used for problems like addiction and psychosis.

Therapeutic communities (TCs) offer residential or day treatment to people with serious mental health problems such as substance addiction. They treat the whole person by providing an array of services, including "medical, mental health, vocational, educational, family counseling, fiscal, administrative, and legal" (De Leon, 2015a, p. 511). Drug abuse is viewed as a byproduct of social deficits, such as having trouble delaying gratification, resistance to authority, difficulty managing feelings, poor communication skills, and irresponsibility in meeting social obligations (De Leon, 2015a; De Leon & Unterrainer, 2020). Treatment communities re-socialize residents, helping them develop the life skills needed to eventually return to society and live more effectively. Patients not only receive treatment, but—reminiscent of the community care models for alleviating psychosis discussed in Chapter 4—are also expected to participate in the daily operation of the community (things like cooking, cleaning, and minor repair work) (De Leon, 2015a). Overall results are mixed, but there is some evidence that residential treatment reduces substance use and improves mental health (de Andrade et al., 2019). Interestingly, supporters question whether it is fair to assess therapeutic communities using randomized controlled trials (RCTs) because such communities involve complex interventions over an extended period that are not easily tested via traditional experimental designs (De Leon, 2015b).

Ayesha

After opioid detoxification, Ayesha enters a residential therapeutic community. She has her own room and is assigned household responsibilities. She is initially angry about having to assist in household tasks and attend individual and group therapy sessions. Nonetheless, Ayesha reluctantly attends these sessions and, over time, begins to acknowledge her issues. In therapy, she learns how to handle overwhelming negative feelings, which she had previously avoided by getting high. Besides individual and group therapy, Ayesha attends family therapy with her parents, in which they repair their relationship and work through dysfunctional family patterns. Through these various forms of therapy and having to navigate relationships with other residents of the community, Ayesha learns how to talk about her feelings and communicate them to others. In addition to psychotherapy, Ayesha is given financial and legal advice; the former allows her to develop the skills necessary to function economically once she gets out of treatment, and the latter helps her resolve lingering legal issues stemming from her drug arrest. As Ayesha improves, she becomes more cooperative, responsible, and respectful of house rules. She performs ever-more effectively in completing her chores and moves up the hierarchy in the residence. Ayesha is eventually put in charge of the kitchen and—with her newfound interpersonal communication skills— takes it upon herself to mentor several new residents, just as other members of the community had previously mentored her. After six months, Ayesha leaves the residence and begins her life anew.

11.22 Service User Perspectives

Stigma

Addiction is highly stigmatized (J. D. Avery & Avery, 2019). People with substance use issues are viewed as *reckless, unreliable, inadequate,* and *threatening* (because they are believed to cheat and lie) (Nieweglowski et al., 2019). Sadly, substance abusers internalize stigmatized ideas about themselves (S. Matthews et al., 2017; Volkow, 2020). This is problematic because some studies link internalized stigma to worse treatment outcomes (Crapanzano et al., 2018). Behavioral addictions also carry stigma. Compared with substance use problems, people are more likely to blame behavioral addictions on character flaws (Konkolÿ Thege et al., 2015). People believe gamblers and gamers can control their behavior, so they get angry with them, blame them, and don't want to be near them (S. C. Peter et al., 2019).

Deanna

Deanna concealed her compulsive shopping as long as she could. She didn't tell her partner, Leslie, about her online buying binges. Leslie only found out when the credit card bills arrived. Nor did Deanna confide in anyone else about her problem. In therapy, Deanna expressed shame for being a "bad person" with "low morals" who "selfishly shops when she can't afford it." Her therapist, who sees compulsive shopping as no less of an addiction than substance use disorders, works to shift Deanna's thinking. "You have a disease," he tells her, "It's no more your fault than if you had cancer or diabetes." Still, Deanna's partner Leslie remains skeptical: "Deanna just needs to stop it. She isn't 'required' to shop!"

Alcoholics Anonymous and Other 12-Step Programs

Alcoholics Anonymous (AA) and other 12-step programs such as Narcotics Anonymous, Cocaine Anonymous, Gamblers Anonymous, Heroin Anonymous, Marijuana Anonymous, and Nicotine Anonymous are self-help groups in which people struggling with drug and behavioral addictions meet regularly to support one another in their recovery (D. Greene, 2021). These groups are founded locally by addicts themselves. As such, they are organized and run entirely by non-professionals: "No therapists, psychologists or physicians can attend AA meetings unless they, too, have drinking problems" (Lilienfeld & Arkowitz, 2011, para. 3).

What is the 12-step philosophy? In a nutshell, it "emphasizes the importance of accepting addiction as a disease that can be arrested but never eliminated, enhancing individual maturity and spiritual growth, minimizing self-centeredness, and providing help to other individuals who are addicted" (D. M. Donovan et al., 2013, p. 315). These goals are accomplished by following the twelve steps in Table 11.6. These steps require addicts to admit their powerlessness over their addiction, accept the influence of God or a higher power in their recovery, and make amends for past wrongs (D. M. Donovan et al., 2013; D. Greene, 2021). The goal is total abstinence, achieved through regular attendance at meetings where members receive support and guidance from other recovering addicts (D. M. Donovan et al., 2013; D. Greene, 2021). AA has approximately 2 million members worldwide, with 123,000 groups spread across roughly 180 countries (Alcoholics Anonymous, n.d.). A 2014 demographic survey of 6,000 U.S. and Canadian AA members found that 62 percent were male and 89 percent were white; average member age was 50 and average length of sobriety was ten years (Alcoholics Anonymous, 2014).

Table 11.6 The Twelve Steps of Alcoholics Anonymous

1. We admitted we were powerless over alcohol—that our lives had become unmanageable.
2. Came to believe that a Power greater than ourselves could restore us to sanity.
3. Made a decision to turn our will and our lives over to the care of God as we understood Him.
4. Made a searching and fearless moral inventory of ourselves.
5. Admitted to God, to ourselves, and to another human being the exact nature of our wrongs.
6. Were entirely ready to have God remove all these defects of character.
7. Humbly asked Him to remove our shortcomings.
8. Made a list of all persons we had harmed, and became willing to make amends to them all.
9. Made direct amends to such people wherever possible, except when to do so would injure them or others.
10. Continued to take personal inventory and when we were wrong promptly admitted it.
11. Sought through prayer and meditation to improve our conscious contact with God as we understood Him, praying only for knowledge of His will for us and the power to carry that out.
12. Having had a spiritual awakening as the result of these steps, we tried to carry this message to alcoholics, and to practice these principles in all our affairs.

Assessing the effectiveness of 12-step groups is difficult because members are anonymous and not readily tracked. Further, 12-step programs don't systematically study their own outcomes—not surprising given that they are run by recovering addicts, not researchers. Nonetheless, a comprehensive review found AA and 12-step programs are highly effective—and actually superior to other treatments in producing continuous abstinence and remission (J. F. Kelly et al., 2020; J. F. Kelly & Abry, 2021). Nonetheless, AA and 12-step groups continue to have critics. Some are uncomfortable with the spiritual and religious emphasis of these groups (Ferentzy et al., 2010; Flanagin, 2014; M. Sharma & Branscum, 2010). Others question the disease model (M. Lewis, 2015). Still others worry about AA's predominantly white male demographic, with one female alcoholic concluding that "any program that tells us to renounce power that we have never had poses the threat of making us sicker" (H. Whitaker, 2019, para. 9). Finally, there are those who believe the evidence for 12-step programs is lacking (L. Dodes & Dodes, 2015). However, the authors of the research review that found AA effective think critics are too hard on 12-step programs. They acknowledge these programs aren't for everyone but argue critics should give them another chance: "For decades, AA has often been dismissed as superstitious, backwards and lacking in evidence of effectiveness. Our review indicates that it is time to turn the clock forward and leave those prejudices behind" (J. F. Kelly & Abry, 2021, p. 380). The debate over 12-step programs is likely to continue. However, one thing nobody doubts is that for some people, these programs are profoundly life altering. See "The Lived Experience" box for an example.

The Lived Experience: Stu W's Story of Recovery

The memory of my first cocktail is well ingrained in my consciousness. It was at my friend's Bar Mitzvah. A gray-haired woman walked away from the bar and left half of a whiskey sour. Curiously and almost instinctively, I grabbed the glass, turned it so the lipstick smudges wouldn't touch my lips, and downed the fruity beverage. What happened next would be a sensation that I would seek in almost all the high school teen dances, college fraternity parties, twenty-something-social mixers, romantic dates, and business-related functions I attended years later. I enjoyed alcohol like everyone else did. I loved the feelings it produced in me. It made me more relaxed and sociable. It made me laugh and helped me come out of my shell of shyness. It made me feel confident and "comfortable in my skin," which I never did. What I didn't realize is that, while I was drinking "normally" as others did, the internal reaction I had was different.

So, in the aftermath of my failed marriage, career challenges, lopsided custody situation and accompanying resentment and depression, I sought out situations and people where I blended in and drank to numb painful feelings. Alcohol seemed to have a different effect on me, but I didn't notice or care about it back then. After a night of enjoying too many cocktails to count, when others called a cab, I always insisted on driving. I drove as fast as my car would go. A lot. Thankfully and luckily, I never crashed or hurt anyone. Somehow, I never got caught. I engaged in many high-risk activities, spent money as if it were Monopoly currency, and ended up in places and with people that I *never ever* would have chosen to be with if I had been sober—and I did this repeatedly. When I had time with my son, I was sober and present, but the rest of the time, I sought out parties and booze to numb out.

So, on October 28, 2006, with all of this "wreckage," a feeling of hollowness in my gut, an aching heart, and an anxious mind, I took the longest walk of my life into my first 12-step recovery meeting. It was a Sunday morning in Newport Beach, California. I saw a large gathering of about 100 people on the beach about halfway between the boardwalk and the ocean. I stepped onto the sand and started the walk. What was just a few hundred feet seemed like it was a quarter mile. When I got to the circle, I sat on the periphery. About ten minutes into the meeting, I started to sob. I did not plan to break down in front of so many complete strangers. It caught me totally by surprise, but something moved in me, and I couldn't hold it back. The man sitting next to me reached over, put his arm around me, and whispered in my ear: "It's going to be okay. I'm glad you are here. Let's talk after the meeting." That man's name is Paul and every year for the last ten years, I have driven to Newport Beach to that meeting to thank him. Each year, he tells me the same thing: "Just pay it forward."

Paul sent me home with the suggestion to go to a meeting in San Diego that night, which I did. Halfway through the meeting, it happened again. I started sobbing. I was just so broken inside. The people at that meeting huddled around me and hugged me and gave me books and pamphlets and meeting schedules and phone numbers. They told me to "keep coming back" and to "call anytime day or night." I was so scared and numb with bewilderment. I didn't know anyone. I didn't know how I ended up in those meetings with those people. I had never even heard of those meetings, but there they were, right smack in the middle of the town where I worked and spent so many happy hours. In that teeny church's kindergarten classroom, a whole society of recovering people gathered on a regular basis. At the time, I had no idea that those meetings were everywhere across Southern California, with hundreds offered weekly.

Consumed with anxiety, I attended another meeting the next day. With my head down, still in shock, and once again on the verge of tears, this time the leader of the meeting called on me to share. In between sobs, I choked out some words of despair. The room was dead silent. When I was done, people clapped. Slips of paper started to get passed to me from all directions. On them were the phone numbers of men offering their support and help. To this day, almost eleven years later, I still carry a card in my wallet that has the names and numbers of ten of those men on it.

Despite the things I did when drinking, I was initially confused about whether I belonged at these meetings. I didn't drink like the other attendees had. I never sat at a bar for hours and then fell off my bar stool. I never got kicked off an airplane for being intoxicated, never went to jail, never had a DUI, and never went to a "detox" facility, let alone rehab. I certainly didn't see myself trading late night parties, with bikini-clad women-in-heels and copious amounts of booze and drugs, for 12-step meetings. I was never going to become one of those people drinking endless cups of bad coffee, and chain-smoking cigarettes. But my view shifted as I started to hear stories that sounded like mine. I began to see that I did fit in ... and I still do.

Virtually friendless, alone, nearly broke, and scared, I went to two and even three meetings every day. When I stopped consuming the mind-altering elixir that soothed my nerves (and masked my pain) the underlying feelings of being irritable, depressed, ashamed, resentful, and afraid set in ... and they didn't go away. I didn't know why I was feeling that way and I didn't know how to make it stop, but those people said they knew how—and they were laughing and happy. Anyway, when I shared my pain, something changed. All I know is that for the last ten years and ten months, I have been on a journey of recovery, which continues to this day. Whereas once, full of guilt and shame from the double-life I was living, I couldn't look my 4-year-old son in the eyes when he came to see me on Father's Day, I now have an amazingly close, emotionally open relationship with him. Back then, I was consumed with profound sadness and grief at the loss of my marriage, as well as intense resentment toward my now former wife. Now, I have an amicable relationship with her and her new husband.

Recovery, and the resulting Divine Power I discovered in the process, keep me sober today. I have replaced all-night parties with bottomless Jack and Cokes to a daily routine of spiritual practices and ongoing service work for others in need. But the wreckage from my partying years has left its toll. I lost two of my closest friends. I lost huge amounts of money. I lost my direction. I lost a piece of my soul. Except for the friendships, my recovery has helped me to establish balance in my life. I now have a more simplistic yet satisfying lifestyle. I am comfortable in my skin and can go anywhere and not be tempted to drink. That's the miracle of recovery.

So, with the intervention of a Power Greater than Myself, a program of recovery, and many supportive recovering friends around me, I am sober today. As I live my life, clean and sober, I now have the great responsibility and humble honor of being that man who can put his arm around another scared, suffering soul when he takes that long walk out on the sand and sits on the periphery of that circle. I am now qualified to say to him, "It's going to be okay. I'm glad you're here. Let's talk after the meeting."

By Stuart Weintraub. Reprinted with permission.

11.23 Systems Perspectives

Family systems perspectives emphasize the role of family functioning in fostering and sustaining substance abuse (Hogue et al., 2017; Kimball et al., 2020; C. L. Rowe, 2012). Family systems therapies address drug abuse by changing what they see as the problematic family dynamics behind it. Many different family systems therapies for substance abuse have been developed (Kimball et al., 2020). Here we review one: **multidimensional family therapy (MDFT)**. MDFT is specifically designed to treat adolescent substance issues. It focuses on individual, family, and environmental factors that contribute to ongoing drug use (Liddle, 2009, 2010; C. Rowe et al., 2002). MDFT works with the adolescent drug users themselves, as well as their parents, other family members, and social systems such as schools and the courts (Liddle, 2009, 2010; C. Rowe et al., 2002). Many interventions are used, which is what makes it "multidimensional." Individual and family psychotherapy sessions with adolescents and their families address personal and relational issues (e.g., adolescent feelings of alienation and isolation, parental disengagement, and patterns of ongoing family conflict). However, MDFT also includes a therapist assistant who functions like a case manager, communicating with external systems and overseeing aspects of treatment that occur outside of individual and family therapy sessions (e.g., psychosocial interventions such as tutoring, after-school programs, and court appointments) (C. Rowe et al., 2002). Research supports MDFT as an intervention for both drug use and Internet gaming (Filges et al., 2018; Liddle et al., 2004, 2018; Rigter et al., 2010, 2013; Schaub et al., 2014; T. M. van der Pol et al., 2018, 2021).

Multidimensional family therapy (MDFT): Family therapy for adolescents with substance issues that intervenes at individual, family, and social levels.

11.24 Evaluating Sociocultural Perspectives

Sociocultural perspectives draw attention to social and cultural aspects of substance use and behavioral addictions. Socioeconomic deprivation, cultural values, problems within families, and other social stressors affect how, when, and why people drink too much, shop too much, work too much, seek out porn on the Internet, get lost in video games, or snort cocaine. We must not forget that environmental factors (e.g., different triggers at work and home) influence how and

Photo 11.5 In many countries, student culture is almost synonymous with drinking. However, this environmental stimuli does not mean that all students develop addictions to alcohol. *Elevate/Unsplash.*

when specific drugs are used (Badiani, 2013). That said, not everyone facing the same environmental stimuli or social circumstances develops an addiction. To many, this means that sociocultural perspectives don't tell the whole story. Biological and psychological processes specific to individuals remain important, even when taking sociocultural factors into account.

CLOSING THOUGHTS

11.25 How Do I Know If I'm Addicted?

Most of us know someone with an addiction: a family member, friend, partner, boss, or colleague. Some of us may even wonder about whether we, ourselves, have a problem. The *Alcohol Use Disorders Identification Test (AUDIT)* is one way of evaluating this. Originally produced by the World Health Organization, the AUDIT is a 10-item self-report inventory to assess problem drinking and alcohol dependence (Babor et al., 2001). It has been adapted for use in countries around the globe—including a revised version for use in the United States (Babor et al., 2016). Several shortened versions for quicker administration have also been devised. You can complete the 3-item USAUDIT-C by consulting Figure 11.7. If concerned about your score, consult your instructor, a doctor, or a mental health practitioner.

Instructions: Alcohol can affect your health, medications, and treatments, so we ask patients the following questions. Your answers will remain confidential. Place an x in one box to answer. Think about your drinking in the past year. A drink means one beer, one small glass of wine (5 oz.), or one mixed drink containing one shot (1.5 oz.) of spirits.

Questions	0	1	2	3	4	5	6	Score
1. How often do you have a drink containing alcohol?	Never	Less than monthly	Monthly	Weekly	2-3 times a week	4-6 times a week	Daily	
2. How many drinks containing alcohol do you have on a typical day when you are drinking?	1 drink	2 drinks	3 drinks	4 drinks	5-6 drinks	7-9 drinks	10 or more drinks	
3. How often do you have X or more drinks a day (5 for men; 4 for women and men over age 65)?	Never	Less than monthly	Monthly	Weekly	2-3 times a week	4-6 times a week	Daily	
							Total →	

Figure 11.7 The USAUDIT-C. Scores of 7 or higher (women and men over age 65) and 8 or higher (men under age 65) suggest a health risk from drinking.
Source: Reproduced from Babor et al. (2016, p. 18).

CHAPTER SUMMARY

Overview

- *Addiction* refers to lack of control over doing, taking, or using something.
- *Abuse* is misusing a drug, whereas *dependence* requires *tolerance* and *withdrawal*.
- *Depressants, stimulants, opioids, hallucinogens,* and *cannabis* are types of drugs common in substance use issues.
- Taking multiple substances is *polysubstance use*. It can lead to *cross-tolerance* and have *synergistic effects*.
- *Behavioral addictions* involve excessive and compulsive behavior (gambling, gaming, sex, eating, shopping, etc.).

Diagnostic Perspectives

- ICD distinguishes *harmful use* from *dependence*, but DSM has merged them into a single *substance use disorder* category.
- DSM and ICD contain *gambling disorder* but only ICD officially includes *gaming disorder*.
- Substance users score high on HiTOP's disinhibited externalizing spectrum.
- PTMF sees substance use as a response to social exclusion, especially adverse childhood experiences.

Historical Perspectives

- Drug use has occurred throughout human history, with *moral versus illness models of addiction* being common perspectives for understanding it.
- *Alcoholics Anonymous (AA)* was the first *12-step program*, founded in the twentieth century.

Biological Perspectives

- *Dopamine hypotheses of addiction* say addictive drugs and behaviors increase dopamine and contribute to dopamine dysregulation. Glutamate may be involved in relapse. Serotonin, norepinephrine, and GABA are also implicated in addiction.
- Weaning people off addictive drugs is called *detoxification. Antagonist drugs for substance abuse* and *drug replacement therapies* are pharmacological treatments for substance issues.
- The *mesolimbic dopamine (reward) pathway* is implicated in addiction and involves numerous structures important to the brain's reward system.
- Addiction heritability is estimated at 40–60 percent. Genes tied to dopamine, acetylcholine, and opioid receptors are among those linked to substance issues.
- The *harmful dysfunction model of addiction* says the human brain gets "hijacked" by substances to which it has not evolved an effective response.
- Substance use leads to immune system vulnerability, and immune system vulnerability contributes to substance use problems.

Psychological Perspectives

- The *self-medication hypothesis* says substance use is a defense against upset traceable to childhood maltreatment.
- The *addictive personality* is set of traits that are believed to predispose people to addiction; whether there is such a thing as an addictive personality is controversial.
- *Contingency management (CM), social skills training (SST), relapse prevention,* and *cognitive therapy* are CBT interventions for substance issues and behavioral addictions.
- *Motivational interviewing (MI)* is a brief and focused humanistic intervention to motivate clients to address substance issues or behavioral addictions without pressing them to do so. It is often combined with the *transtheoretical model of change*.

Sociocultural Perspectives

- Social determinants of substance issues are often overlooked.
- *Prevention and early intervention programs* stop substance issues from developing or intervene early enough to keep them from becoming larger problems.
- *Therapeutic communities (TCs)* are residential or day treatment programs for people with serious mental health issues like substance addiction.

- Addiction is highly stigmatized.
- 12-step programs such as AA are self-help groups for people in recovery.
- *Multidimensional family therapy (MDFT)* is a systems intervention for adolescent substance abusers and their families. It intervenes at individual, family, and social levels.

Closing Thoughts

- The *Alcohol Use Disorders Identification Test (AUDIT)* is an instrument to quickly assess whether someone has a problem with alcohol.

NEW VOCABULARY

1. 12-step programs
2. Abuse vs. dependence
3. Acetylcholine
4. Addiction
5. Addictive personality
6. Alcohol
7. Alcoholics Anonymous (AA)
8. Amphetamines
9. Antagonist drugs for substance abuse
10. Barbiturates
11. Behavioral addictions
12. Binge drinking
13. Caffeine
14. Cannabis
15. Cirrhosis
16. Cocaine
17. Contingency management (CM)
18. Controlled drinking
19. Cross-tolerance
20. Delirium tremens (DTs)
21. Dependence
22. Depressants
23. Detoxification
24. Dopamine hypothesis of addiction
25. Drug flashbacks
26. Drug replacement therapies
27. Fetal alcohol syndrome (FAS)
28. Gambling disorder
29. Gaming disorder
30. Hallucinogens
31. Harm reduction
32. Harmful dysfunction model of addiction
33. Harmful use
34. Heroin
35. Indoleamine hallucinogens
36. Korsakoff syndrome
37. Methadone maintenance therapy (MMT)
38. Moderation Management (MM)
39. Moral versus illness models of addiction
40. Motivational interviewing (MI)
41. Multidimensional family therapy (MDFT)
42. Nicotine
43. Nicotine replacement therapy (NRT)
44. Opioids
45. Opium
46. Oxycodone
47. Phencyclidine
48. Phenylalkylamine hallucinogens
49. Polydrug use
50. Prevention and early intervention programs
51. Sedative-hypnotics
52. Self-medication hypothesis
53. Speedballing
54. Stimulants
55. Substance use disorder
56. Synergistic effects
57. Therapeutic communities (TCs)
58. Transtheoretical model of change

PERSONALITY ISSUES

Photo 12.1
cottonbro studio/Pexels.

LEARNING OBJECTIVES

After reading this chapter, you should be able to:

1. Define basic terms such as personality, traits, temperament, and personality disorder.

2. Describe what the five-factor model (FFM) of personality is and how it is relevant to thinking about personality disorder.

3. Outline the difference between categorical and dimensional models of personality disorder, summarize DSM and ICD models, and explain the debates about the strengths and weaknesses of these models.

4. Discuss historical ideas about personality and personality issues.

5. Explain how mental health professionals using brain chemistry, brain structure, genetic, evolutionary, and immune system perspectives conceptualize and treat personality issues.

6. Summarize psychodynamic, cognitive-behavioral, and humanistic approaches to thinking about and addressing personality issues.

7. Explain how sociocultural perspectives see gender bias, trauma, socioeconomic disadvantage, and racism as critical to understanding personality issues.

8. Describe systems approaches to personality issues.

OVERVIEW

12.1 Getting Started: What Is Personality?

Case Examples

Harvey

Harvey is a 23-year-old African American male in prison for attempted murder. He has a long history of being in trouble with the law, starting at age 15 when he was arrested for dealing drugs in the inner-city neighborhood where he grew up. Harvey was overseeing a small drug ring by the age of 18. His associates found him intimidating. He often lied to them or threatened them with physical harm. Sometimes he acted on his threats, violently assaulting them without provocation. On such occasions, Harvey rarely (if ever) seemed to feel remorse. In prison, Harvey regularly gets into fights. The severe punishments he is subjected to for these fights (including time in solitary confinement) do little to deter him or change his unruly conduct. When asked about his recurrent bad behavior, Harvey scowls and says "It ain't my fault. Everyone's against me."

Megan

Megan is a 25-year-old white female referred to therapy after attempting suicide by overdosing on antidepressants. She has a history of impulsive behavior: outrageous shopping sprees, abruptly quitting jobs, and vandalizing the car of an ex-boyfriend. She reports feeling sad and "empty" much of the time. In session, Megan's intense emotions abruptly shift. She is clingy one minute, angry the next, and despondent after that. In one therapy session, she ingratiatingly tells her therapist how kind and compassionate he is, then asks if he would extend sessions by fifteen minutes. When the therapist politely declines this request, Megan's mood quickly changes. She expresses rage at his insensitivity and says she knew he was pretending to care about her all along. She also remarks that if she doesn't get more time in sessions, she can't promise what might happen to her. When the therapist asks Megan if this is a veiled suicide threat, she shrugs and looks away. Megan's therapist finds her difficult to work with and often feels highly stressed by their sessions. "You never know from moment to moment what she's going to be like," he thinks to himself.

Defining and Measuring Personality

Personality: Stable and characteristic patterns of thinking, feeling, behaving, and interacting with others (often thought of as consisting of distinguishing qualities, or *traits*).

Can you define **personality**? It isn't as easy as it seems. According to the American Psychological Association, personality is "the enduring configuration of characteristics and behavior that comprises an individual's unique adjustment to life, including major traits, interests, drives, values, self-concept, abilities, and emotional patterns" (American Psychological Association, n.d.-e). It is customarily seen as consisting of enduring *traits*—internal characteristics that people "have," such as a tendency toward happiness, anxiousness, or aggression (American Psychological Association, n.d.-i). *Trait theories* tend to view traits as originating in biology and innate *temperament*, the automatic ways of responding to emotional stimuli that produce consistent habits and moods (Cloninger, 1994). While personality is often treated as synonymous with traits and temperament, it can also be viewed as emerging from how traits and temperament are molded by environmental experiences (Angleitner & Ostendorf, 1994). There isn't always agreement on how to differentiate personality, temperament, and traits. We do our best despite these terms' fuzzy boundaries.

Traits and Personality Disorder

Personality disorder (PD): Constellation of personality traits that consistently leads to interpersonal conflict and difficulty in daily functioning.

Trait theories view personality as relatively stable across settings (Markon & Jonas, 2015). For example, people high in the trait of "angry hostility" are expected to be confrontational and antagonistic whether at home, work, or out bowling with friends. In other words, people display enduring and universal traits that they have in greater or lesser amounts. Personality consists of any given person's constellation of traits. People are diagnosed with a **personality disorder (PD)** when their constellations of personality traits consistently lead to interpersonal conflict and difficulty in daily functioning (Hertz & Hertz, 2016). As you read this chapter, pay attention to how often the trait view of personality is taken for granted. How much you accept or question the trait view may inform which perspectives on personality problems appeal to you.

The Five-Factor Model of Personality

Five-factor model (FFM): Proposes that personality can be mapped along five trait dimensions: *extraversion, agreeableness, conscientiousness, neuroticism,* and *openness.*

Most trait theories see personality as consisting of one to five *trait factors*, which are traits distinguished from one another in research studies. The term "factor" is used because trait factor research relies on a statistical technique called *factor analysis*, which involves identifying patterns in how people respond to different items on self-report personality inventories. When responses to items are highly correlated, we infer that they are measuring the same thing—and therefore constitute a single "factor." Looking at the correlated items, we might decide they all involve how much one likes to socialize with others. Thus, we might name the factor "extraversion." The goal of factor analytic personality research is to statistically identify core factors (or traits) that account for individual differences.

Factor analytic techniques have yielded a variety of trait factor theories. However, over the past several decades, the **five-factor model (FFM)** has reigned supreme. This model, which has generated an enormous body of research, proposes that personality is culturally universal and can be mapped along five trait dimensions: *extraversion*, *agreeableness*, *conscientiousness*, *neuroticism*, and *openness* (Digman, 1990; L. R. Goldberg, 1993; McCrae, 2017; McCrae & John, 1992). These dimensions are sometimes referred to as the Big Five (see Chapter 3). The five-factor model has greatly influenced DSM and ICD perspectives on personality disorder (Pires et al., 2021; Suzuki et al., 2016; Trull, 2012; Widiger & Costa, 2012; Widiger & Crego, 2019). However, it has also been subject to intense criticism by humanistic and sociocultural theorists (Kroger & Wood, 1993; McCrae & John, 1992; Nilsson, 2014). Though the Big Five are linked to mental health issues like psychosis, emotional regulation, and personality disorders (Barańczuk, 2019; Shi et al., 2018; Widiger & McCabe, 2020), debate continues over whether they hold up cross-culturally or with different age groups (E. D. Beck et al., 2022; Gurven et al., 2013; Laajaj et al., 2019).

DIAGNOSTIC PERSPECTIVES

12.2 DSM and ICD

Consistent with trait theories, DSM and ICD see personality disorders as involving rigid and unbending patterns of relating to others that cause interpersonal difficulties and emotional distress. These patterns are stable and originate early in life. Personality disorders are broad and all-encompassing. They involve fundamental problems in the structure of an individual's personality and style of relating to others. When it comes to diagnosing personality disorders, DSM and ICD do so very differently. DSM-5-TR retains longstanding diagnostic categories, whereas ICD-11 eliminated these categories in favor of a fully dimensional approach. This shift by ICD marks one of the biggest changes to DSM or ICD in a long time. Let's review traditional DSM categories first, then turn to ICD's dimensional approach.

DSM-5-TR's Ten Personality Disorder Categories

DSM-5-TR officially recognizes ten personality disorders. It divides them into three types: *odd or eccentric personality disorders* (Cluster A), *dramatic, emotional, or erratic personality disorders* (Cluster B), and *anxious or fearful personality disorders* (Cluster C). Each is described below, with criteria summarized in Diagnostic Boxes 12.1 (odd or eccentric), 12.2 (dramatic, emotional, or erratic), and 12.3 (anxious or fearful).

Paranoid Personality Disorder

People diagnosed with **paranoid personality disorder** are unjustifiably suspicious. They have difficulty trusting people and worry about being exploited, harmed, or deceived. These individuals tend to be critical, humorless, and argumentative. They hold grudges and see conspiracies everywhere. Because of their combative and suspicious manner, they don't work and play well with others—further confirming their sense that people are out to get them. DSM-5-TR cites a median prevalence of 3.2 percent but says up to 23 percent of people in forensic settings may qualify for a diagnosis. Of course, clinicians must be careful before diagnosing socially marginalized people (e.g., minority group members), whose justified anger, frustration, fear, and hypervigilance can be misinterpreted as paranoia.

Schizoid Personality Disorder

Schizoid personality disorder is characterized by utter disinterest in relationships and people. Individuals with this diagnosis have no desire to engage with others and prefer to be alone. Characteristically, they have no close friends and don't care what others think about them. They show little emotion, have few interests, and have minimal or no desire for sexual experiences with others. People view them as emotionally cold, and they appear aloof and disconnected from their surroundings. DSM-5-TR reports prevalence rates between 1.3 percent and 4.9 percent. It might be slightly more common in men than women.

Schizotypal Personality Disorder

The key features of **schizotypal personality disorder (STPD)** are eccentric thoughts, perceptions, and behaviors accompanied by difficulty forming close relationships. People with this diagnosis strike others as strange. Not only do they appear suspicious and paranoid, but their thinking seems

Paranoid personality disorder: DSM diagnosis for people who are unjustifiably superstitious, have difficulty trusting others, and worry others are trying to exploit, harm, or deceive them.

Schizoid personality disorder: DSM diagnosis characterized by disinterest in relationships and people, with no desire to engage with others and a preference to be alone.

Schizotypal personality disorder (STPD): DSM diagnosis for people with eccentric thoughts, perceptions, and behaviors accompanied by difficulty forming close relationships; equivalent to ICD's psychotic disorder diagnosis, *schizotypal disorder*.

bizarre or magical. For instance, they might believe they have telepathic powers or can clairvoyantly predict the future. Their emotional reactions seem constricted or inappropriate, as well. Put bluntly, these individuals seem odd and peculiar. Consequently, they lack social connections and have few close friends. Prevalence estimates cited in DSM-5-TR range from 0.6 percent to 3.9 percent. Slightly more men than women qualify for this diagnosis. As discussed in Chapter 4, schizotypal personality disorder is grouped with personality disorder in DSM but with psychotic disorders in ICD-11, where it is simply called *schizotypal disorder*.

Diagnostic Box 12.1 DSM-5-TR Odd or Eccentric Personality Disorders

- **Paranoid Personality Disorder**: Ongoing pattern of suspiciousness and lack of trust; unjustifiably suspects others are conspiring against him/her or are out to cause harm; tends not to confide in others due to doubts about their trustworthiness.
- **Schizoid Personality Disorder**: Ongoing pattern of disengagement from others and limited ability to express a range of emotions; does not like or desire close relationships and displays poor social skills; has few interests and prefers solitary activities.
- **Schizotypal Personality Disorder**: Ongoing pattern of poor social skills and difficulty establishing intimate relationships, accompanied by odd and eccentric thoughts, perceptions, and behaviors. NOTE: Called "schizotypal disorder" in ICD and grouped with psychotic disorders.

Information from American Psychiatric Association (2022, pp. 737–738, 741–742, and 744–745).

Antisocial personality disorder (ASPD): DSM diagnosis for people who consistently manipulate and exploit others with little or no remorse; they consistently lie, deceive, break the law, and disregard social norms.

Psychopathy versus sociopathy: Both involve exploiting and disregarding the rights of others, lack of empathy, lack of guilt and remorse, being deceitful and manipulative, poor impulse control, and grandiosity—but psychopathy is mainly attributed to biological origins and sociopathy to environmental influences.

Antisocial Personality Disorder

Antisocial personality disorder (ASPD) describes people who consistently violate the rights of others. Such people are deceitful, disregard social norms, and often break the law. They are impulsive, reckless, irresponsible, and (in some cases) violent. They regularly manipulate and exploit others. People diagnosed with ASPD show little remorse for their actions and lack empathy for those they hurt. DSM-5-TR cites a median ASPD prevalence of 3.6 percent, but says prevalence jumps to more than 70 percent among men in substance abuse clinics, prisons, and forensic settings. ASPD is closely related (but not identical) to psychopathy and sociopathy, which is why people diagnosed with ASPD are often described as psychopaths or sociopaths. See the "In Depth" feature for more on **psychopathy versus sociopathy**.

Harvey
Harvey, who is in prison for attempted murder and has a long history of violent behavior without remorse, might be diagnosed with antisocial personality disorder.

In Depth: Psychopathy and Sociopathy

Students often want to know what DSM and ICD have to say about psychopaths and sociopaths. They are surprised to learn that neither diagnostic system uses these terms. The closest equivalents are antisocial personality disorder in DSM-5-TR and the dissociality trait dimension in ICD-11. However, some clinicians see this as inadequate. They lament that *psychopathy* and *sociopathy* are not included in DSM or ICD (Hare, 1996; Lykken, 2018; P. M. MacKenzie, 2014; Pemment, 2013). Let's examine them in depth to see if you agree.

Psychopathy is conceptualized as originating in biology (Lykken, 2018; Viding et al., 2014). Psychopaths "fail to become socialized primarily because of a genetic peculiarity, usually a peculiarity of temperament" (Lykken, 2018, p. 23). These individuals exhibit *emotional/interpersonal symptoms* (Hare, 1996; Hare et al., 2012; D. F. Thompson et al., 2014). They are glib, superficial, egocentric, and grandiose. They are also deceitful, manipulative, and display shallow emotions. When they wrong others, psychopaths lack remorse, guilt, and empathy. In addition to their emotional/interpersonal issues, psychopaths are also *socially deviant* (Hare, 1996; Hare et al., 2012; D. F. Thompson et al., 2014). They are impulsive and irresponsible, with a constant need for excitement and stimulation. Their symptoms start early in life and continue into adulthood (Hare, 1996; Hare et al., 2012; D. F. Thompson et al., 2014).

Sociopathy is distinguished from psychopathy by being attributed more to social causes, not biology (Lykken, 2018; P. M. MacKenzie, 2014). In other words, "psychopaths are born as psychopaths whereas sociopaths are the product of one's developmental environment" (P. M. MacKenzie, 2014). Unlike psychopaths, sociopaths do sometimes feel empathy. Yes, they violate others' rights, but they have a conscience—albeit one inconsistent with accepted cultural norms and practices (Pemment, 2013). Considering the subtle differences between them, some say psychopathy and sociopathy should be included in DSM as subtypes of antisocial personality disorder (P. M. MacKenzie, 2014).

Although psychopathy is viewed as physiologically based, in some cases the environment is cast in a supporting role. *Primary psychopathy* is defined as psychopathy rooted entirely in biology, whereas *secondary psychopathy* is viewed as psychopathy that results when a biologically innate predisposition is brought out by environmental factors (P. M. MacKenzie, 2014). An additional distinction is made between *successful psychopaths* and *unsuccessful psychopaths,* with the former effectively navigating the world and avoiding punishment and the latter being criminals likely to be incarcerated (Benning et al., 2018; D. F. Thompson et al., 2014). Ruthless but influential politicians and businesspeople might be successful psychopaths, whereas serial killers in prison are unsuccessful psychopaths.

Proposed distinctions notwithstanding, it is not clear whether psychopathy is truly distinct from sociopathy, or if the terms reflect preferences for biological versus social explanations of antisocial behavior. Biological researchers are searching for ways to distinguish psychopathy using biological brain markers (Blair et al., 2018; Pemment, 2013; D. F. Thompson et al., 2014; Y. Yang & Raine, 2018). However, others downplay the psychopathy–sociopathy distinction by either using the terms interchangeably or discarding them both in favor of less theoretically loaded DSM and ICD conceptions of antisocial/dissocial personality.

Critical Thinking Questions

1. Should DSM and ICD include psychopathy and sociopathy?
2. Can people be "born bad," as the concept of psychopathy implies?
3. Do you think psychopathy can be distinguished from sociopathy in clinical settings? In research settings? If yes, how? If no, why not?

Borderline Personality Disorder

Photo 12.2 The character of Bruce Banner/The Hulk can be interpreted as a metaphorical representation of BPD. He is impulsive and rapidly shifts emotional states—with his explosive anger and rage dissociated from his other feelings.
Moviestore Collection Ltd/Alamy Stock Photo.

Borderline personality disorder (BPD) describes people who show instability in their relationships, sense of self, and emotions. They have a difficult time regulating their own emotions, especially negative ones like anger and sadness. Their feelings about themselves and others shift rapidly depending on the circumstances. One minute they might idealize others, then the next

Borderline personality disorder (BPD): DSM diagnosis describing people who show instability in their relationships, sense of self, and emotions due to fear of abandonment and difficulty regulating emotions about self and others.

Parasuicidal behavior: Self-harm inflicted less because one wants to die and more to manipulate others, communicate distress, or regulate emotions.

minute disparage them. Such rapid shifts (the "unstable" aspect of being "borderline") stem from intense and often unrealistic fears of abandonment. Their emotional lability makes borderline clients difficult to deal with, even for therapists. Other challenging characteristics of BPD are impulsive behavior (substance abuse and behavioral addictions are common), chronic feelings of emptiness, and **parasuicidal behavior**—self-harm inflicted to manipulate others, communicate distress, or regulate emotions (Kreitman, 1977; Linehan, 1993). Unfortunately, the behavior of BPD clients leads others to reject or avoid them—the very outcomes they most fear. DSM-5-TR estimates median prevalence at 2.7 percent overall but 10 percent in outpatient mental health clinics and 20 percent in inpatient psychiatric settings. The manual says prevalence does not differ by gender, despite women in clinical samples receiving the diagnosis more often than men.

Megan

Megan meets criteria for BPD. One minute she thanks her therapist profusely for being supportive and caring, then the next minute becomes furious, angry, and insulting toward him when he declines her request to extend sessions by fifteen minutes. Megan's abrupt shift is a desperate and manipulative attempt to deal with feeling abandoned.

Histrionic personality disorder: DSM diagnosis for excessively dramatic and emotional individuals who crave being the center of attention and strike others as shallow and overly theatrical, shifting from one exaggerated emotional display to another.

Photo 12.3 Clark Gable as Rhett Butler and Vivien Leigh as Scarlett O'Hara in *Gone with the Wind*, 1939.
Clarence Sinclair Bull/Getty Images.

Histrionic Personality Disorder

Histrionic personality disorder is diagnosed in excessively dramatic and emotional individuals who crave being the center of attention. They strike others as shallow and overly theatrical, shifting rapidly from one exaggerated emotional display to another. Their style of speech is often vague and impressionistic. They can also be inappropriately flirtatious and seductive. People with this diagnosis are often disparagingly dismissed as "drama queens." Scarlett O'Hara in the classic movie *Gone with the Wind* exhibits many symptoms of histrionic personality disorder: "Her flair for the overly dramatic, the constant demand for attention, the quick foolish decisions, and emphasis on provocative clothing even during her impoverished years is typical histrionic" (Hammond, 2016, para. 4). Moira from the TV show *Schitt's Creek* is another (more recent) character who displays histrionic behavior. DSM-5-TR cites a median prevalence of 0.9 percent. Even though the diagnosis is more frequent in women, prevalence may be comparable across men and women.

Narcissistic personality disorder (NPD): DSM diagnosis characterized by an inflated sense of self (*grandiosity*) and a desperate need for admiration.

Narcissistic Personality Disorder

People meeting criteria for **narcissistic personality disorder (NPD)** exhibit *grandiosity* (see Chapter 5) in that they think of themselves as extremely important. This disorder is characterized by an inflated sense of self and a desperate need for admiration. Individuals diagnosed with NPD have an exaggerated sense of *entitlement*, the unreasonable expectation that they deserve special treatment or attention. In their minds, the usual rules don't apply to them. Thus, a narcissistic individual might expect his professor to give him an extension on a late paper despite a strictly enforced "no extensions" policy. NPD clients tend to be arrogant and preoccupied with fantasies of unlimited power. DSM-5-TR cites a median prevalence of 1.6 percent while noting that 50 percent to 75 percent of those diagnosed are men.

Avoidant personality disorder: DSM diagnosis for those who want guaranteed acceptance from others and actively avoid social interactions because they are excessively worried about criticism or rejection.

Avoidant Personality Disorder

People diagnosed with **avoidant personality disorder** avoid social interactions because they are excessively worried about criticism or rejection. These individuals want guaranteed acceptance. Without it, they are too frightened of disapproval to socially engage. Therefore, they steer clear of people to avoid being hurt. DSM-5-TR cites median prevalence rates of 2.1 percent, with the disorder slightly more common in women than in men. Avoidant personality disorder gets confused with schizoid personality disorder because, in both cases, those diagnosed avoid dealing with people. However, their reasons for doing so differ. People deemed schizoid don't care what others think of

Photo 12.4 Psychologist Dan McAdams has argued that former U.S. President Donald Trump is a quintessential example of narcissistic personality disorder: "Highly narcissistic people are always trying to draw attention to themselves. Repeated and inordinate self-reference is a distinguishing feature of their personality" (McAdams, 2016, para. 52). However, others warn against psychologists pathologizing people they have not personally interviewed or assessed.
Jon Tyson/Unsplash.

Diagnostic Box 12.2 DSM-5-TR Dramatic, Emotional, or Erratic Personality Disorders

- **Antisocial Personality Disorder**: Ongoing pattern of ignoring and violating other people's rights; tends to disregard social norms and other people's feelings, lies and manipulates others, acts out impulsively or aggressively, becomes easily frustrated, blames others, and shows lack of concern or remorse when injures others.
- **Borderline Personality Disorder**: Ongoing pattern of rapidly shifting and unstable relationships, sense of self, and emotions, along with impulsive behavior; typically tries to desperately avoid abandonment (real or imagined), alternates between idealizing and devaluing others, has a rapidly shifting self-image, feels empty inside, has difficulty controlling anger, and behaves impulsively (often including threats of self-harm).
- **Histrionic Personality Disorder**: Ongoing pattern of extreme emotionality and behavior intended to garner attention; often feels upset when not the center of attention, displays shallow and rapidly changing feelings, describes things in an impressionistic way, is dramatic or theatrical, overly focused on physical appearance, is inappropriately flirtatious, and believes relationships with others are deeper than they are.
- **Narcissistic Personality Disorder**: Ongoing pattern of grandiosity, a need to be admired, and a lack of empathy for others; tends to demand recognition, be overly focused on own importance (as powerful, beautiful, intelligent, successful, etc.), believes they are special or of high status, feels entitled, jealous of others, and exploits others for own gain.

Information from American Psychiatric Association (2022, pp. 748, 752–753, 757, and 760).

them and dodge social contact because they have no interest in relationships. By contrast, people considered avoidant desperately want relationships and care too much about what others think of them; they are so afraid of criticism or rejection that they refuse to take the risks necessary to connect with others. Avoidant personality disorder is also sometimes confused with antisocial personality disorder—mainly because in everyday language "antisocial" is a synonym for avoidant. However, DSM defines antisocial as violating others' rights and avoidant as not socializing due to fear of rejection.

Dependent Personality Disorder

Dependent personality disorder describes those who desperately want to be cared for. Lacking confidence in their own abilities, they regularly seek advice and reassurance. They are deferent,

Dependent personality disorder: DSM disorder describing those who desperately want to be cared for, lack confidence in their own abilities, and regularly seek advice and reassurance from others.

submissive, and emotionally needy. This results in them allowing others to make major life decisions for them. People with this diagnosis lack self-confidence and don't feel able to take care of themselves. Hence, they desperately cling to others because they are terrified of being left to their own devices. DSM-5-TR cites a median prevalence of just 0.4 percent for dependent personality disorder. The diagnosis is made more often in women than in men.

Obsessive-Compulsive Personality Disorder

People with **obsessive-compulsive personality disorder (OCPD)** are disproportionately focused on orderliness, rules, and control. They are excessively perfectionistic and rigid. Struggling to see the forest through the trees, these individuals often don't complete projects because they get lost in details and nothing is ever good enough. Although they sometimes co-occur, OCPD differs from OCD (obsessive-compulsive disorder; see Chapter 6). Unlike OCD, OCPD doesn't involve obsessions (intrusive thoughts) or compulsions (acts one feels compelled to do). Rather, OCPD is about control, orderliness, rigidity, and perfectionism. In this respect, its use of the phrase "obsessive-compulsive" is misleading. To avoid confusion, think of OCD as involving obsessions and compulsions and OCPD as describing an exceptionally controlling, rigid, and perfectionistic personality. DSM-5-TR says the median prevalence of OCPD is 4.7 percent and cites a large study suggesting it occurs equally in men and women.

Obsessive-compulsive personality disorder (OCPD): DSM diagnosis for excessively perfectionistic and rigid people disproportionately focused on orderliness, rules, and control.

Diagnostic Box 12.3 DSM-5-TR Anxious or Fearful Personality Disorders

- **Avoidant Personality Disorder**: Ongoing pattern of feeling socially inhibited, inadequate, and overly fearful of criticism or rejection by others; tends to avoid interactions with others due to fear of being judged or not receiving unconditional approval and to be socially inhibited because feels inadequate.
- **Dependent Personality Disorder**: Ongoing pattern of submissiveness, clinginess, fear of being alone, and a wish to be cared for; tends to be deferent, to have difficulty making decisions, to need excessive reassurance, to desperately seek relationships to avoid being alone, and to bend over backwards to receive support (even agreeing to do unpleasant things).
- **Obsessive-Compulsive Personality Disorder**: Ongoing pattern of being overly focused on control, orderliness, and perfectionism; tends to excessively focus on details (rules, lists, schedules, organization, etc.), be perfectionistic to the point being unable to finish tasks, be overly conscientious and rigid, be inflexible and self-righteous, and value productivity over relationships.

Information from American Psychiatric Association (2022, pp. 764–765, 768, and 771–772).

DSM-5-TR alternative model for personality disorders (AMPD): Proposed alternative to the DSM-5 categorical model of personality disorders that combines dimensional and categorical assessment in diagnosing personality disorders; also called the *hybrid trait model*.

Personality disorder-trait specified: Proposed diagnosis in the DSM-5 alternative model for personality disorders (AMPD); for people who don't meet trait-based criteria for any of the other six AMPD personality disorder categories but still show personality pathology in one or more trait domain.

DSM-5-TR's Alternative Model of Personality Disorders (AMPD)

DSM personality disorder categories suffer from poor diagnostic reliability and validity (Flory, 2020). They overlap with one another and are comorbid with other mental disorders. To remedy this, researchers have advocated for *dimensional* approaches that map personality disorders using Big Five and similar personality models (DeYoung et al., 2016; Widiger, 2015; Widiger & Costa, 2012; Widiger & Presnall, 2013). In this vein, let's consider the proposed **DSM-5-TR alternative model of personality disorders (AMPD)** (American Psychiatric Association, 2022; Waugh et al., 2022). The AMPD combines dimensional and categorical assessment. It is a proposal because it has not yet been adopted to replace DSM's ten traditional personality disorder categories.

Instead of the usual DSM procedure of comparing behavior with diagnostic criteria, the AMPD relies on dimensional assessment to assign patients to one of seven personality disorder categories—six "classic" personality disorders (*antisocial, avoidant, borderline, narcissistic, obsessive-compulsive,* and *schizotypal*) plus a new **personality disorder-trait specified** category. A personality disorder diagnosis is made by using DSM-devised personality measures to assess patients along five *trait domains* that roughly correspond to the Big Five (see Diagnostic Box 12.4). Trait domains are further divided into twenty-five narrower *trait facets* (also in Diagnostic Box 12.4) (American Psychiatric Association, n.d.-c, 2022). Depending on which trait facets patients score high on, they are assigned to one of the six "classic" personality disorder categories or, if they don't qualify for a classic category but still show personality pathology, to the personality-trait specified category. See Diagnostic Box 12.5.

Diagnostic Box 12.4 DSM-5-TR Alternative Model of Personality Disorders (AMPD): Five Trait Domains

TRAIT DOMAIN	DOMAIN DESCRIPTION	TRAIT FACETS
Negative Affectivity (vs. Emotional Stability)	Frequent experience of a wide range of negative emotions	1. Emotional lability (instability of mood) 2. Anxiousness 3. Separation insecurity 4. Submissiveness 5. Hostility 6. Perseveration (continuing behavior that has proven ineffective)
Detachment (vs. Extraversion)	Withdrawal from interpersonal interactions and restricted emotionality	7. Withdrawal 8. Intimacy avoidance 9. Anhedonia (lack of enjoyment from life) 10. Depressivity 11. Restricted emotionality 12. Suspiciousness
Antagonism (vs. Agreeableness)	Behaviors that place one at odds with other people	13. Manipulativeness 14. Deceitfulness 15. Grandiosity 16. Attention seeking 17. Callousness
Disinhibition (vs. Conscientiousness)	Orientation toward immediate gratification, leading to impulsiveness	18. Irresponsibility 19. Impulsivity 20. Distractibility 21. Risk taking 22. (Lack of) rigid perfectionism
Psychoticism (vs. Lucidity)	Displaying a wide range of odd, eccentric, or unusual behaviors and cognitions	23. Unusual beliefs and experiences 24. Eccentricity 25. Cognitive and perceptual dysregulation (including dissociation)

Information from American Psychiatric Association (2022, pp. 899–901).

Diagnostic Box 12.5 DSM-5-TR Alternative Model of Personality Disorders (AMPD): Diagnostic Criteria

DISORDER	TRAIT DOMAINS/FACETS REQUIRED FOR A DIAGNOSIS
Antisocial Personality Disorder	Pathological scores on 6 of the 7 trait facets from these trait domains: • **Antagonism** (4 facets: manipulativeness, callousness, deceitfulness, hostility) • **Deceitfulness** (3 facets: risk taking, impulsivity, irresponsibility)
Avoidant Personality Disorder	Pathological scores on 3 of the 4 trait facets from these trait domains: • **Negative Affectivity** (1 facet: anxiousness) • **Detachment** (3 facets: withdrawal, anhedonia, intimacy avoidance)
Borderline Personality Disorder	Pathological scores on 4 of the 7 trait facets from these trait domains (at least one must be *): • **Negative Affectivity** (4 facets: emotional lability, anxiousness, separation insecurity, depressivity) • **Disinhibition** (2 facets: impulsivity*, risk taking*) • **Antagonism** (1 facet: hostility*)

Narcissistic Personality Disorder	Pathological scores on the following two facets from this trait domain: • **Antagonism** (2 facets: grandiosity, attention seeking)
Obsessive-Compulsive Personality Disorder	Pathological scores on 3 of the 4 trait facets from these trait domains (one must be *): • **Conscientiousness** [opposite of **disinhibition**] (1 facet: rigid perfectionism*) • **Negative Affectivity** (1 facet: perseveration) • **Detachment** (2 facets: intimacy avoidance, restricted affectivity)
Schizotypal Personality Disorder	Pathological scores on 4 of the 6 trait facets from these trait domains: • **Psychoticism** (3 facets: cognitive/perceptual dysregulation, unusual beliefs/experiences; eccentricity) • **Detachment** (3 facets: restricted affectivity, withdrawal, suspiciousness)
Personality Disorder-Trait Specified	Pathological scores on one or more these trait domains or in specific facets of these domains: **Negative Affectivity, Detachment, Antagonism, Disinhibition,** and **Psychoticism**

Information from American Psychiatric Association (2022, pp. 881–890).

ICD-11's Complete Overhaul: A Fully Dimensional Approach

ICD-11 model of personality disorder: Dimensional approach to personality disorders that employs one diagnostic category (*personality disorder*), assessed using five trait domains (*negative affect, detachment, dissocial features, disinhibition,* and *anankastic features*) and distinguished by severity (*mild, moderate, or severe*).

The **ICD-11 model of personality disorders** goes further than the AMPD in two ways. First, its dimensional reconceptualization of personality disorders isn't merely a proposal for further study; it is the official ICD approach. Second, it discards traditional personality disorder categories entirely—something the AMPD does not do (J. S. Porter & Risler, 2014; Tyrer et al., 2019). In ICD-11, personality disorders are diagnosed completely dimensionally. Old categories (antisocial, histrionic, paranoid, etc.) are no longer recognized. Instead, ICD-11 restricts itself to just one personality disorder diagnosis, simply called *personality disorder*. Those who receive this diagnosis are evaluated in two areas: severity of symptoms and pathological traits. Regarding severity of symptoms, an ICD-11 personality disorder is diagnosed as *mild, moderate,* or *severe*; for cases below the disorder threshold, a *personality difficulty* diagnosis is available (Tyrer et al., 2019; World Health Organization, 2022a). Regarding pathological traits, ICD-11 relies on five trait domains: *negative affectivity, detachment, dissociality* (i.e., antisocial), *disinhibition,* and *anankastia* (i.e., obsessive-compulsive) (see Diagnostic Box 12.6). These are comparable to those of the Big Five and the AMPD, except they include an obsessive-compulsive dimension instead of a psychoticism dimension. When making a diagnosis, clinicians can opt to list one of the five traits as most prominent. Importantly, unlike the AMPD, ICD-11 doesn't require assessment before diagnosing a personality disorder. This keeps the process simple. It lets practitioners quickly make a diagnosis when personality issues are apparent, but details are lacking. After the diagnosis is made, mental health professionals can conduct a thorough assessment to map the full personality pattern.

Diagnostic Box 12.6 ICD-11 Model of Personality Disorders: Five Trait Domains plus Borderline Pattern Specifier

Assign the diagnostic label *personality disorder* (mild, moderate, or severe) and then assess the patient using the following five trait domains or assign the borderline pattern specifier.

TRAIT DOMAIN	DOMAIN DESCRIPTION
Negative affectivity	Tendency to manifest a broad range of distressing emotions including anxiety, anger, self-loathing, irritability, vulnerability, depression, and other negative emotional states, often in response to even relatively minor actual or perceived stressors.

Detachment	Emotional and interpersonal distance, manifested in marked social withdrawal and/or indifference to people, isolation with very few or no attachment figures, including avoidance of not only intimate relationships but also close friendships. Traits include aloofness or coldness, reserve, passivity and lack of assertiveness, and reduced experience and expression of emotion, especially positive emotions, to the point of a diminished capacity to experience pleasure.
Dissociality	Disregard for social obligations and conventions and the rights and feelings of others. Traits include callousness, lack of empathy, hostility and aggression, ruthlessness, and inability or unwillingness to maintain prosocial behavior, often manifested in an overly positive view of the self, entitlement, and a tendency to be manipulative and exploitative of others.
Disinhibition	Tendency to act impulsively in response to immediate internal or environmental stimuli without consideration of longer-term consequences. Traits include irresponsibility, impulsivity without regard for risks or consequences, distractibility, and recklessness.
Anankastia	A narrow focus on the control and regulation of one's own and others' behavior to ensure that things conform to the individual's particularistic ideal. Traits include perfectionism, perseveration, emotional and behavioral constraint, stubbornness, deliberativeness, orderliness, and concern with following rules and meeting obligations.
Borderline Pattern*	Pervasive instability in relationships, self-image, and emotion. Characterized by impulsive behavior, efforts to avoid abandonment, intense relationships, unstable self-image, repeated self-harm, reactive mood, feelings of emptiness, anger issues

Information from World Health Organization (2022a).

*Not a trait domain; a specifier one can use instead.

EVALUATING DSM AND ICD PERSPECTIVES

Although DSM-5-TR still officially classifies personality disorders categorically, the categorical approach appears on its way out. As noted, research consistently finds personality disorder categories overlap or co-occur (i.e., they are comorbid), making them difficult for clinicians to differentiate (Flory, 2020). This raises the issue of poor interrater reliability—a big problem in clinical practice. After all, the entire diagnostic process is suspect if clinicians consistently arrive at different diagnoses. Comorbidity also calls into question the validity of personality disorder categories. Do they really exist as distinct entities?

Efforts to improve reliability and validity have encouraged the steady move toward dimensional models of personality disorder (L. C. Morey, 2019; Mulder, 2021). Though most researchers support this shift, some oppose eliminating familiar categories—most notably borderline personality disorder (Herpertz et al., 2017). To address this issue, a "borderline pattern" specifier was added to ICD-11 at the last minute to "ease the transition for patients who have already been granted support or treatment based on a borderline diagnosis" (Bach et al., 2021, p. 3). This addition was made even though "the trait model was considered by the ICD-11 Working Group to fully account for maladaptive personality structure, including the borderline traits" (G. A. McCabe & Widiger, 2020, p. 73). Balancing politics with science is no easy task.

Are dimensional models on stronger scientific footing than categorical ones? The jury is still out, but there is preliminary evidence that the AMPD's and the ICD-11's dimensional models perform better than traditional categories in distinguishing personality disorder (R. F. Krueger & Hobbs, 2020; G. A. McCabe & Widiger, 2020; Oltmanns & Widiger, 2019; Pires et al., 2021; Widiger & Hines, 2022). Which model is better, AMPD or ICD? That is not clear, but the ICD-11 model has three advantages (G. A. McCabe & Widiger, 2020). First, it is official, not a proposal. Second, by eliminating old PD categories, it is simpler. Third, the ICD's worldwide influence makes countries likely to adopt something that conforms to its model.

Mental health professionals appreciate the AMPD and ICD-11 models, despite apprehension about using them (Bach et al., 2022; S. J. Hansen et al., 2019; Herpertz et al., 2017; Tracy et al., 2021). Their uneasiness may be because the clinical utility of these models is unclear. For the ICD-11 model, for example, we need to "further investigate whether practitioners find the severity classification and the trait domain specifiers helpful for case formulation, treatment planning, and intervention as suggested by initial research" (Bach et al., 2022, p. 8). When it comes to diagnosing personality disorders, the dimensions versus categories debate continues. Where do you stand?

12.3 HiTOP

HiTOP emphasizes dimensional assessment across the board, not just for personality disorders (C. C. Conway et al., 2022). HiTOP's spectra domains (detachment, antagonistic externalizing, disinhibited externalizing, thought disorder, internalizing, and somatoform) overlap extensively with the Big Five and the AMPD and ICD-11 model trait domains (Widiger et al., 2019). In other words, HiTOP fits with trends in personality disorder research because "the structure of general personality provides a fundamental base for the HiTOP dimensional model of psychopathology" (Widiger et al., 2019, p. 86). With that in mind, HiTOP researchers are developing inventories for dimensionally assessing paranoid, antisocial, obsessive-compulsive, schizoid, and other personality patterns (L. de F. Carvalho, 2021; L. de F. Carvalho et al., 2020; L. de F. Carvalho & Machado, 2021; Pianowski et al., 2019). Some contend HiTOP could encourage development of new therapies for personality problems that its spectra assess—including antagonism, introversion, and low conscientiousness (Widiger et al., 2019).

12.4 PDM-2

As with HiTOP, personality assessment is central to PDM diagnosis, which makes sense given the key role of personality in psychodynamic theories. PDM-2 assesses personality on one of its three central diagnostic axes, the P-Axis. This axis consists of twelve *personality syndromes* and is summarized in Table 12.1 (also see Table 3.5 in Chapter 3). For the most part, these syndromes have DSM equivalents (Lingiardi & McWilliams, 2017; Meehan & Levy, 2015; Sperry, 2016). The P-Axis differs from DSM in excluding schizotypal personality (which, like ICD, it groups with the psychoses) and including three personalities not in DSM: depressive, somatizing, and sadistic (Lingiardi & McWilliams, 2017). Again, see Table 12.1.

The importance of personality functioning in PDM cannot be overstated. In requiring P-Axis assessment of all patients, PDM ensures that personality issues aren't artificially separated from other types of psychological maladjustment. Personality functioning is evaluated regardless of whether other (non-personality) disorders are diagnosed. This reflects PDM's strong psychodynamic conviction that "all people have personality styles" and that personality issues naturally co-occur with other presenting problems, including "anxiety, depression, eating disorders, somatic symptoms, addictions, phobias, self-harm, trauma, and relationship problems" (Lingiardi & McWilliams, 2017, p. 17). Further, even in cases where no personality disorder is present, PDM contends that assessing overall personality functioning on the P-Axis provides crucial clinical information. From a PDM-perspective, "there is no hard and fast distinction between a personality *type* or *style* and a personality *disorder*" except that people identified as having personality disorders (or those who must interact with them) experience significantly higher levels of distress (Lingiardi & McWilliams, 2017, p. 17).

To differentiate higher from lower functioning personality styles, PDM distinguishes four **levels of personality organization**: *healthy, neurotic, borderline,* and *psychotic* (see Table 12.2). People at the healthy level are consistently flexible and adaptable, whereas those at the neurotic level function well most of the time but become rigid under challenging circumstances. Individuals at the borderline level display even more serious difficulties regulating emotion when stressed. (Confusingly, the borderline level of functioning is distinct from the borderline personality syndrome, even though they both use the term "borderline.") Finally, psychotic level functioning is the most pathological, exemplified by extremely poor reality testing and a diffuse sense of self. Someone "who stalks his love object in the conviction that this person 'really' loves him, despite all of the person's protestations to the contrary," would score at the psychotic level of personality organization (Lingiardi & McWilliams, 2017, p. 23).

Levels of personality organization:
Component of the P-Axis in PMD-2 diagnosis; patients are rated on a 10-point scale assessing their level of personality functioning, with "10" being most healthy and "1" being least healthy: *healthy level (9–10), neurotic level (6–8), borderline level (3–5),* and *psychotic level (1–2).*

Table 12.1 PDM-2 P-Axis Personality Syndromes and their Closest DSM-5-TR Equivalents

SYNDROME	TENSION/PREOCCUPATION	NEAREST DSM-5-TR PERSONALITY DISORDER EQUIVALENT	OTHER RELEVANT DSM-5-TR DISORDERS
Depressive	Self-critical, self-punishing, overly concerned with relatedness and/or loss	—	Mood disorders
Dependent	Maintaining relationships	Dependent personality disorder	
Anxious-avoidant and phobic	Staying safe vs. avoiding danger	Avoidant personality disorder	Anxiety disorders
Obsessive-compulsive	Submitting to vs. rebelling against the control or authority of others.	Obsessive-compulsive personality disorder	
Schizoid	Fearing intimacy vs. wanting intimacy	Schizoid personality disorder	
Somatizing	Integrity vs. fragmentation of the physical body	—	Somatic symptom and related disorders
Hysteric-histrionic	Unconscious devaluing of own gender while being envious and fearful of opposite gender	Histrionic personality disorder	
Narcissistic	Inflating vs. deflating self-esteem	Narcissistic personality disorder	
Paranoid	Attacking vs. being attacked by others	Paranoid personality disorder	
Psychopathic	Manipulating others vs. being manipulated by them	Antisocial personality disorder	
Sadistic	Suffering humiliation vs. imposing humiliation	—	Sexual sadism disorder
Borderline	Coherent vs. fragmented sense of self; enmeshed attachment vs. despair at abandonment	Borderline personality disorder	

NOTE: DSM-5-TR's schizotypal personality disorder has no equivalent PDM-2 personality syndrome, but PDM-2 assesses psychotic-like symptoms using P-Axis levels of personality organization (see Table 12.2).

Table 12.2 PDM-2 Levels of Personality Organization

The Psychodiagnostic Chart below can be used to rate levels of personality organization on a 1–10 scale, with 1 most pathological and 10 least pathological.

- *Psychotic level* (1–2): Break with reality; poor sense of identity; highly defensive; difficulty distinguishing fantasy and reality.
- *Borderline level* (3–5): Have difficulty with emotional regulation; often overwhelmed by intense depression, anxiety, and rage.
- *Neurotic level* (6–8): Respond to certain stressors with rigidity, despite having many functional capacities overall.
- *Healthy level* (9–10): Have preferred coping style, but it is flexible enough to accommodate challenges of everyday life.

Source: Levels of Personality Organization scale adapted from Gordon, R. M. & Bornstein, R. F. (2018). Construct validity of the Psychodiagnostic Chart: A transdiagnostic measure of personality organization, personality syndromes, mental functioning, and symptomatology. Psychoanalytic Psychology, http://dx.doi.org/10.1037/pap0000142

There is limited research on PDM diagnosis of personality, some of it promising. In one study, *concurrent validity* (when a new measure compares favorably to established measures) of the P-Axis was good in relation to other measures of personality disturbance, including traditional DSM categories and the APMD (R. M. Gordon, 2019). However, another study found poor diagnostic agreement across PDM, traditional DSM categories, and the AMPD (Huprich et al., 2019). Further research to evaluate PDM is needed, but clinicians who see personality patterns as a key aspect of psychopathology appreciate the PDM.

12.5 PTMF

From a PTMF perspective, the very notion of personality disorder is disparaging and problematic (Caulfield, 2021; Johnstone et al., 2018). PTMF rejects seeing personalities as "disordered" or "pathological." Instead, it says problematic interpersonal patterns develop when people encounter societal maltreatment, feel threatened, and make meaning of the experience in problem-causing ways. For example, PTMF reconceptualizes "borderline personality" (which it views as a disparaging and stigmatizing label) as an understandable reaction to physical or emotional abandonment (Caulfield, 2021). Thus, in a PTMF model, personality is never "disordered," but adverse circumstances lead to the development of problematic interpersonal patterns. Research on PTMF is limited but its appeal is understandable given the weak scientific status of traditional personality disorder categories (Livesley, 2021).

HISTORICAL PERSPECTIVES

12.6 Personality and Bodily Humors

The idea of personality as stable and enduring is found throughout history. For instance, ancient Chinese medicine attributed differences in temperament to a person's "blood and vital essence," which starts out fluid during early life, hardens into a stable personality during adulthood, and loosens again in old age (Crocq, 2013, p. 148). History is also replete with systems for distinguishing personality types. In ancient Greece, the philosopher Theophrastus (*c.* 371–*c.* 287 BCE) identified twelve character types, including the *thankless character* (who sees the negative in everything and is unable to enjoy life) and the *suspicious character* (who, like today's paranoid personality, doesn't trust others) (Crocq, 2013). More famously, the Greek physician Galen used the four bodily humors (see Chapter 1) proposed by Hippocrates (460–367 BCE) to articulate an early classification of personality types and personality disturbance (Merenda, 1987; Tyrer et al., 2015). See Table 12.3 for details.

Table 12.3 Bodily Humor Personality Types

HUMOR	PERSONALITY TYPE	PERSONALITY CHARACTERISTICS
Blood	*Sanguine*	Optimistic, hopeful, impulsive, pleasure-seeking
Black bile	*Melancholic*	Introverted, thoughtful, sad, and depressed
Yellow bile	*Choleric*	Ambitious, persevering, easily angered and irritable
Phlegm	*Phlegmatic*	Relaxed, quiet, apathetic

Mania without delusion: Philippe Pinel's term for patients who showed no overt symptoms of madness (they weren't hallucinatory, delusional, or incoherent), but who were prone to emotional outbursts such as fits of temper or impulsive violence; *manie sans délire* in the original French.

Moral insanity: James Cowles Prichard's eighteenth-century precursor to DSM-5's antisocial personality disorder, characterized by impulsive, violent, and depraved behavior, but without more florid symptoms of madness.

12.7 Moral Insanity and Psychopathic Personalities

The French physician Philippe Pinel (1745–1826), who famously unchained the inmates at Bicêtre Hospital (again, see Chapter 1), was one of the first to identify patterns of behavior that today would likely be diagnosed as personality disorders. He spoke of *manie sans délire* (**mania without delusion**), a term for patients who showed no overt symptoms of madness (Ekselius, 2018). They weren't hallucinatory, delusional, or incoherent. Instead, they were prone to emotional outbursts such as fits of temper or impulsive violence (Crocq, 2013). In many cases, Pinel attributed their personality problems to an improper upbringing, such as having a weak and undisciplined mother (Crocq, 2013). Pinel's work likely influenced James Cowles Prichard (1786–1848), who introduced the concept of **moral insanity**, a precursor to DSM's antisocial personality disorder. Moral insanity was characterized by impulsive, violent, and depraved behavior, but without more florid symptoms of madness (Coolidge & Segal, 1998). Prichard (1835, p. 6) vividly described it as a madness "consisting in a morbid perversion of the natural feelings, affections, inclinations, temper, habits, moral dispositions, and natural impulses, without any remarkable disorder or defect of the intellect or knowing and reasoning faculties, and particularly without any insane illusion or hallucination."

Prichard's work impacted that of Emil Kraepelin (1856–1926), who (as discussed in Chapter 3) developed one of the first psychiatric classification systems. In that system he included **psychopathic personalities**, which he believed were lifelong pathologies caused by inborn "defects" (Crocq, 2013). Kraepelin's notion of "psychopathic personalities" was broader than our current use of the term "psychopathy." He identified four specific psychopathic personalities: *born criminals, the weak-willed, pathological liars/swindlers,* and *the paranoid* (Crocq, 2013). Kraepelin's ideas about psychopathic personalities were in turn further expanded by Kurt Schneider (1887–1967). Schneider "defined 'psychopathic' personalities as those individuals who suffer, or cause society to suffer, because of their personality traits" (Crocq, 2013, p. 151). Like Kraepelin, he felt psychopathic personalities were mostly innate but influenced by environmental factors (Crocq, 2013). Schneider identified ten types of psychopathic personality: *depressive, insecure, fanatical, recognition-seeking, explosive, emotionally blunted, weak-willed, asthenic* (those lacking in energy), *hyperthymic* (those with exceptionally positive moods), and *labile* (those with rapidly changing moods) (Crocq, 2013). Schneider's ten "psychopathic personalities" profoundly influenced DSM and ICD personality disorders (Ekselius, 2018; Tyrer et al., 2015). Interestingly, Schneider was an early advocate of dimensional assessment because he felt personality couldn't be broken into discrete categories (Crocq, 2013). Thus, his work continues to influence modern conceptions of personality disorder.

Psychopathic personalities: Emil Kraepelin's term for people with one of four pathological personality types: *born criminals, the weak-willed, pathological liars/swindlers,* and *the paranoid*; Kurt Schneider later identified ten types of psychopathic personalities, which influenced DSM and ICD.

BIOLOGICAL PERSPECTIVES

12.8 Brain Chemistry Perspectives

Neurotransmitters and Personality Disorders
Serotonin in ASPD and BPD

Both antisocial personality disorder (ASPD) and borderline personality disorder (BPD) have been linked to low serotonin activity (Amad et al., 2014; Calati et al., 2013; Fanning et al., 2014; Moul et al., 2013; Soloff et al., 2014; Yildirim & Derksen, 2013). This makes sense given that reduced serotonin is associated with impulsive and aggressive behavior (da Cunha-Bang & Knudsen, 2021), both of which are common in ASPD and BPD. However, the research is mainly correlational and low serotonin is not unique to antisocial and borderline patients; it is correlated with many presenting problems.

Dopamine in STPD

Because schizotypal personality disorder (STPD) is often considered a mild form of psychosis, interest in the role of dopamine is understandable. The dopamine hypothesis of schizophrenia (see Chapter 4) attributes schizophrenia and other psychoses to too much dopamine. Excessive dopamine is suspected in STPD too. Research studies tend to support this (Attademo et al., 2021; Rössler et al., 2019; J. L. Thompson et al., 2020). It has been hypothesized that STPD has milder symptoms than schizophrenia because the brains of STPD patients compensate better for dopamine dysregulation (Perez-Rodriguez et al., 2013; Siever & Davis, 2004).

Polypharmacy and Non-Specificity of Drug Treatments

Many different types of drugs are used to treat personality disorders—including antidepressants, mood stabilizers, anticonvulsants, and antipsychotics (K. J. Nelson, 2021; Nicolò et al., 2021; Paolini et al., 2017; Paris, 2011). Often patients are prescribed multiple drugs at the same time, an approach known as **polypharmacy** (K. J. Nelson, 2021; Paolini et al., 2017; Riffer et al., 2019). For example, an antidepressant might be used to help ease sadness, a mood stabilizer or anticonvulsant given to reduce aggression and impulsivity, and an antipsychotic prescribed to address paranoia and odd thoughts or perceptions. Why do we use the same drugs for all PDs rather than targeting each with a drug specific to its neurochemistry? Because we currently lack the knowledge to do so. As one prominent psychologist bluntly but optimistically explained:

Polypharmacy: The practice of prescribing multiple drugs at the same time.

We do not know whether personality disordered patients have a "chemical imbalance", as so many seem to believe, without much supporting evidence. It is possible that any drug with strong sedating properties can reduce anger and impulsivity. Non-specific effects of this kind can still be useful, but we need to develop more specific agents …. Thus drugs for personality disorder are non-specific "stop-gaps" that will eventually be replaced by better and more precise alternatives. (Paris, 2011, p. 305)

Harvey and Megan
Harvey is prescribed an antipsychotic, an anticonvulsant, and an antidepressant for his ASPD, while Megan is given an antidepressant and a benzodiazepine for her BPD.

Medication for Personality Disorders: Debate over Effectiveness and Use

Given that drug treatments for personality disorders are non-specific, it makes sense that the limited research on their effectiveness has yielded disappointing results (K. J. Nelson, 2021). Medication does not appear to be especially effective, although it sometimes improves specific symptoms or comorbid issues like anxiety or depression (K. J. Nelson, 2021; J. D. Parker & Naeem, 2019; Stoffers-Winterling et al., 2021). Nonetheless, large numbers of people diagnosed with personality disorders—around 90 percent, in some instances—are prescribed one or more medication (Bridler et al., 2015; Paton et al., 2015; Riffer et al., 2019). This is astonishing considering that research casts doubt on these drugs' effectiveness. While most clinicians don't see drugs as a panacea, they use them to manage the challenging emotions and behaviors that people with personality disorders display—despite little evidence for doing so (K. J. Nelson, 2021; Paris, 2011; Stoffers-Winterling et al., 2021).

12.9 Brain Structure Perspectives

Brain Volume in Antisocial, Borderline, and Obsessive-Compulsive PDs

Total brain volume is often decreased in antisocial and borderline personality disorders (G. Davies, 2020; S. Kaya, 2020; O'Neill & Frodl, 2012; Sampedro et al., 2021). In BPD research, the hippocampus (important in memory) and amygdala (important in basic emotions) are often smaller (Cattane et al., 2017; G. Davies, 2020; Nunes et al., 2009; O'Neill & Frodl, 2012; Sampedro et al., 2021). It is suspected that adverse childhood circumstances such as abuse or neglect are linked to shrinkage of these regions (Cattane et al., 2017; O'Neill & Frodl, 2012). Similar volume reductions occur in OCPD and ASPD (Gurok et al., 2019; Tully et al., 2022). However, when it comes to specific brain regions and ASPD, volume differences vary widely from case to case (Tully et al., 2022). Why this is remains unknown.

Harvey and Megan
From a biological perspective, Harvey's antisocial behavior and Megan's emotional intensity might be linked to volume changes in the hippocampus, amygdala, and other brain regions. These changes might contribute to their symptoms but also be influenced by past abuse.

Schizotypal Personality Disorder

Many of the brain structure anomalies found in schizophrenia (including enlarged brain ventricles) are sometimes found in schizotypal personality disorder (STPD), albeit to a lesser degree (Attademo et al., 2021; Ettinger et al., 2014; Perez-Rodriguez et al., 2013). This isn't surprising given that both diagnoses involve psychotic symptoms, although STPD is milder. However, there are also brain differences between STPD and schizophrenia. For example, while some studies find similar frontal volume reductions in both STPD and schizophrenia, others find total brain volume increases in STPD that do not occur in schizophrenia (Attademo et al., 2021; Ettinger et al., 2014; Fervaha & Remington, 2013). The reason for these STPD brain volume increases is not known, but some speculate it is the brain's way of warding off full-blown psychosis—something the brains of those who develop schizophrenia may be unable to do (Attademo et al., 2021; Ettinger et al., 2014; Fervaha & Remington, 2013).

12.10 Genetic Perspectives

Heritability of Personality Disorders

Heritability estimates aim to tell us what percentage of a person's phenotypic variability (differences in displayed traits) is due to genes versus environment. For the Big Five personality traits, twin and family studies have yielded heritability estimates between 40 percent and 50 percent (South, 2015). This suggests that genes and environment contribute nearly equally to personality. For personality disorders, heritability estimates vary a lot, with one study citing median heritability of 61 percent and a range between 28 percent and 79 percent (Roussos & Siever, 2012; Torgersen et al., 2000). On the lower end, Cluster A heritability is estimated to be between 21 percent and 28 percent and Cluster C between 27 percent and 35 percent (Kendler et al., 2006; Reichborn-Kjennerud et al., 2007; Roussos & Siever, 2012). On the higher end, we find heritability estimates of 55–72 percent for Cluster A, 63–71 percent for Cluster B, 64 percent for avoidant PD, and 66 percent for dependent PD (Gjerde et al., 2012; Kendler et al., 2007; Torgersen et al., 2012). As these differing estimates make clear, the relative influence of genes (in terms of innate temperament) and environment (in terms of adverse experiences) on the development of personality issues remains contested.

Candidate Genes

To date, research on candidate genes has provided many leads but few definitive answers. Among the genes implicated in personality disorders are the DRD2, DRD3, and DRD4 dopamine genes (the first usually linked to Cluster A, the second two to Clusters B and C), the MAOA gene (linked to Cluster B), and the 5-HTTLPR serotonin gene (linked to both Clusters B and C) (Bulbena-Cabre et al., 2018; Reichborn-Kjennerud, 2010). Because impulsivity and aggression are common antisocial and borderline symptoms, a lot of Cluster B research focuses on the genetics of violent and impulsive behavior. Many different genes have been identified as potentially relevant, with the MAOA and 5-HTTLPR genes often mentioned (Beaver et al., 2018; Bulbena-Cabre et al., 2018; Ficks & Waldman, 2014; Fontaine & Viding, 2008; Hayden, 2013; Moul et al., 2015; Reichborn-Kjennerud, 2010; South, 2015; M. Yang et al., 2012, 2014).

Despite these tantalizing findings, not everyone is persuaded by research on the genetics of violence and criminality. Critics argue that (a) it is difficult to precisely define what counts as criminal behavior, (b) environmental and genetic influences can't be readily separated, and (c) many different genes, not just a few, contribute to violent behavior (Hayden, 2013). More broadly, critics feel that genetics research minimizes social influences on impulsive and violent behavior while overemphasizing genes and biology (J. Joseph, 2004; Wachbroit, 2001).

12.11 Evolutionary Perspectives

Evolutionary perspectives ask whether personality traits commonly identified as disordered are, in fact, adaptive and advantageous (Durisko et al., 2016; R. M. Nesse, 2005a; Nettle, 2006). For example, the **frequency-dependent selection hypothesis** holds that certain traits (such as psychopathy) are evolutionarily adaptive so long as their frequency in the population is low (K. N. Barr & Quinsey, 2004; Ene et al., 2022; Glenn et al., 2011; Jurjako, 2019; Mealey, 1995). Apparently, exploiting the human tendency to trust and cooperate is only effective if few people do it. When too many of us prey on others, people stop trusting and become more cautious, taking away psychopathy's reproductive advantage. Similarly, the **obsessive trait complex hypothesis** holds that obsessive-compulsive personality disorder traits are innate, not learned (Hertler, 2015a, 2015b). It hypothesizes that the inherited traits common to OCPD (e.g., anxiety, compulsive conscientiousness, miserliness, and an ever-present sense of urgency) are what allowed early humans who migrated to colder and more inhospitable climates to survive (Hertler, 2015a, 2015b).

Frequency-dependent selection hypothesis: Says traits like psychopathy are evolutionarily adaptive so long as their frequency in the population is low.

Obsessive trait complex hypothesis: Holds that obsessive-compulsive personality disorder traits (e.g., anxiety, compulsive conscientiousness, miserliness, and an ever-present sense of urgency) allowed early human to survive in inhospitable climates.

Traditional medical model adherents remain skeptical. They aren't convinced that problematic personality traits (such as psychopathy and obsessiveness) are evolved adaptations functioning normally. Instead, they say personality disorders are demonstrable brain disorders (Gurok et al., 2019; Nummenmaa et al., 2021; D. J. Stein, 1997). Evolutionary hypotheses are hard to test, making it difficult to resolve debate over them (Crusio, 2004).

12.12 Immune System Perspectives

As discussed in other chapters, stress and trauma are associated with immune system inflammation. People who have experienced abuse, neglect, and deprivation early in life are more likely to behave aggressively—and behavioral aggression is a consistent predictor of immune system inflammation (Blaney et al., 2020; R. Castle et al., 2021; Fanning et al., 2015). Because both early life trauma and aggressive behavior are common in personality disorders, researchers are studying the relationship between these disorders and immune system inflammation. Evidence does suggest a link. Levels of cytokines (the small proteins produced by immune system cells that cause swelling in large amounts) and other inflammatory markers tend to be higher in people with personality disorder diagnoses (Blaney et al., 2020; Coccaro et al., 2015b, 2015a; Fanning et al., 2015; Saccaro et al., 2021).

Of course, almost all presenting problems are associated with past stress of some kind. Thus, inflammation is common to most psychiatric diagnoses and not specific to personality disorders. Nonetheless, this link between trauma and personality issues (particularly aggressive tendencies) suggests a complex interaction between environmental conditions and immunological processes that warrants further examination.

12.13 Evaluating Biological Perspectives

Biological perspectives haven't yielded much in terms of treatment for personality issues. Despite widespread use, medications remain minimally effective. Scientifically speaking, genetic explanations of personality disorder are usually considered the strongest of the biological approaches, built on a compelling and extensive (if occasionally contested) body of research (Bulbena-Cabre et al., 2018; Kendler et al., 2019; South, 2015). Nonetheless, biological perspectives on personality difficulties are criticized for (a) minimizing social and contextual factors, and (b) relying on circular reasoning about traits. When it comes to social and contextual factors, it has long been argued that human behavior is influenced not just by innate biological traits, but also by situations and how people make sense of them (Mischel, 1973, 2009; Mischel & Shoda, 1995). Critics also contend that attributing behavior to inborn personality traits or disorders amounts to a non-explanation, one relying on a concept (traits) that can't be empirically verified (Boag, 2011).

Harvey

Maybe Harvey behaves angrily not because he has an innately "angry personality," but because he finds himself in situations he interprets as hostile. Further, the "angry personality" explanation relies on circular reasoning. How do we know that Harvey has innate antisocial personality traits? Because he behaves aggressively. And why does Harvey behave aggressively? Because of his innate antisocial personality traits!

Such circular reasoning is clearly problematic. It treats personality traits (an abstract concept) as physically real and then circularly uses them to explain behavior, even though the very behaviors that personality traits explain are simultaneously offered as "proof" that these traits exist in the first place (Boag, 2011).

PSYCHOLOGICAL PERSPECTIVES

12.14 Psychodynamic Perspectives

Psychodynamic perspectives stress how personality is shaped by early relationships with caregivers. When people experience neglect or abuse in early relationships, rigid personality styles (i.e., personality disorders) develop (Fonagy et al., 2020; Town & Driessen, 2013). As examples, consider narcissistic, borderline, and obsessive-compulsive personality problems. Many psychodynamic therapists consider narcissism a self-protective response to defend against feelings of shame tied to parental rejection and mistreatment; narcissistic individuals compensate for these negative feelings by convincing themselves they are wonderful and seeking admiration and approval from others (Kernberg, 2001; Ronningstam, 2011). Borderline personality, on the other hand, is viewed as involving the dissociation (or splitting into "good" and "bad" parts; see Chapter 2) of incompatible ego states (Clarkin et al., 2006; Kernberg et al., 1989). This allows the person to keep contradictory emotions separate. Splitting feelings of hurt and rejection from those of idealization and love is how borderline clients cope with perceived slights. These slights are experienced as intensely as the original childhood abuse and mistreatment that led them to rely on splitting as a defense in the first place (Clarkin et al., 2006; Kernberg et al., 1989). Finally, classic psychodynamic conceptions often see obsessive-compulsive personality disorder as related to anal stage conflicts tied to toilet training, while interpersonally oriented psychodynamic perspectives view it as either an attempt to establish autonomy from dominating parents or as a way to overcome anxiety, insecurity, and helplessness by controlling one's surroundings (Mallinger, 2009; Pollak, 1987; M. C. Wells et al., 1990). While specific psychodynamic explanations vary, they all focus on how childrearing contributes to rigid personality patterns.

Attachment and Object Relations Approaches

Attachment theory (discussed in previous chapters) holds that early experiences with caregivers lead to secure or insecure attachments (Bowlby, 1980, 1988). Securely attached babies have reliable parents who soothe and console them when they encounter stress (Ainsworth et al., 1978). Such babies grow up to be emotionally resilient, feeling good about themselves and safe with and connected to others. Insecurely attached babies, on the other hand, struggle to modulate feelings of frustration, fear, and rage (Ainsworth et al., 1978). In response to their parents' inconsistent warmth and attention, they learn that others are unreliable. As adults, they worry about being abandoned and have difficulty handling negative emotions that arise during stressful situations. Through a psychodynamically oriented attachment theory lens, then, personality disorders are viewed as problematic patterns of relating tied to difficulties with early attachment. Object relations therapy (see Chapter 2) is like attachment theory in emphasizing the importance of early caregiving. Both approaches maintain that people who experience abusive, inconsistent, or indifferent parenting develop rigid and problematic patterns of relating to others—in other words, disordered personality functioning (Blatt & Levy, 2003; Caligor & Clarkin, 2010; De Bei & Dazzi, 2014; Fonagy & Luyten, 2012; J. Holmes, 2015a; Kernberg et al., 1989; K. N. Levy & Blatt, 1999; Meehan & Levy, 2015). These dysfunctional personality patterns may have worked for coping with difficult caregivers during childhood, but they have serious limitations when relied on in adult relationships.

Object relations therapies assume that patients require a *corrective emotional experience* in which they learn new patterns of relating to others (Alexander & French, 1946). In these therapies, transference and countertransference take center stage. Transference occurs when patients project feelings about past relationships onto their therapists and then defend against these feelings by engaging in their usual problematic patterns of relating. Countertransference, on the other hand, can take two forms: a useful kind and a not-so-useful kind. The not-so-useful kind is when therapists project their own issues onto patients (Cashdan, 1988; Clarkin et al., 2006; Kernberg et al., 1989). This clouds therapists' ability to clearly understand patients. The useful kind is when therapists are induced to act and feel certain ways in response to patient behavior (Cashdan, 1988; Clarkin et al., 2006; Kernberg et al., 1989). For example, a patient who projects dependency and neediness might evoke feelings of omnipotence in her therapist, while also leading the therapist to feel pressured to solve her problems. By contrast, a narcissistic patient might elicit feelings of boredom and frustration from his therapist, who grows weary of the expectation to endlessly praise and be impressed by the patient. Corrective emotional experiences occur when therapists share their countertransference feelings, encouraging patients to relate to them without relying on their usual rigid and defensive patterns. By using the therapist–patient relationship to help patients gain insight into longstanding personality patterns, patients develop more effective and flexible ways of interacting—initially with their therapists, and eventually with others (A. Abbass, 2016; A. A. Abbass & Town, 2013; Caligor et al., 2007; Caligor & Clarkin, 2010; Cashdan, 1988; Clarkin et al., 2006; Davanloo, 1999; Eizirik & Fonagy, 2009; Fonagy et al., 2020; Kernberg et al., 1989; Levenson, 2017; Yeomans et al., 2015).

Megan

In psychodynamic therapy, when Megan insists that the therapist doesn't care for her because he won't extend session times, the therapist might use this as an opportunity to explore his relationship with Megan. He would examine how Megan felt during their interactions and link her frantic efforts to avoid his rejection to her previous experiences with rejection while growing up. By patiently providing a safe and secure relationship, one in which emotionally charged topics could be openly discussed (such as Megan feeling abandoned), the therapy would offer an emotionally corrective experience. It might take Megan time to feel safe enough to not rely on her "borderline" manipulations in session, but over time she would hopefully begin feeling like she didn't need to resort to such measures because she had developed faith and trust that the therapist cared for her and wouldn't abandon her. Ultimately, the goal would be to help Megan develop similar secure relationships outside of therapy in which borderline-style behaviors were no longer necessary.

Research on Structured Psychodynamic Therapies

Various **structured psychodynamic therapies for personality disorders** have been developed, including *transference-focused psychotherapy (TFP)* (Fonagy et al., 2020; Yeomans et al., 2015; Yeomans & Delaney, 2017; Yeomans & Diamond, 2010), *mentalization-based treatment (MBT)* (A. Bateman & Fonagy, 2013; A. W. Bateman & Fonagy, 2012; Fonagy et al., 2020; Fonagy & Luyten, 2009), and *intensive short-term dynamic psychotherapy (ISTDP)* (A. Abbass, 2016; A. Abbass et al., 2008; Davanloo, 1999). These therapies usually last a year or two, making them brief by psychodynamic standards. Their conceptualizations of personality problems vary somewhat, but all emphasize using the relationship between client and therapist to help rectify rigid and ineffective patterns of interaction learned in early childhood. Some psychoanalytic traditionalists remain skeptical, arguing that many of the more structured relational therapies do not sufficiently attend to sexual drives and unconscious conflicts (Fonagy & Campbell, 2015). However, advocates of these more structured psychodynamic interventions contend that they are accruing a compelling evidence base, even if further research is needed (A. Abbass, 2016; A. Bateman et al., 2016; Fonagy et al., 2020; Haskayne et al., 2014; Leichsenring & Steinert, 2018, 2019; Rocco et al., 2021; Taubner & Volkert, 2019; Town et al., 2013; Town & Driessen, 2013; Vogt & Norman, 2019).

Psychodynamic perspectives on personality disturbances have been criticized for being vague and overemphasizing the importance of upbringing. One critic urged psychodynamic therapists to acknowledge the importance of heritability and stop insisting that personality problems are mostly forged during childrearing (Hertler, 2014a). Of course, this returns us to earlier debates about how much personality is inherited versus shaped by environment. Suffice to say, even when they acknowledge genetic influences, psychodynamic clinicians remain committed to the idea that early life attachments are central to personality problems.

12.15 Cognitive-Behavioral Perspectives

Cognitive-behavioral therapies (CBT) attribute personality issues to learning and thinking (A. T. Beck et al., 2015; David & Freeman, 2015; K. M. Davidson, 2017; Leahy & McGinn, 2012; Linehan, 1993; Lobbestael & Arntz, 2012). CBT perspectives agree with psychodynamic approaches

Structured psychodynamic therapies for personality disorders: Psychodynamic therapies for personality disorders with a more prescribed structure and shorter timeframe (1–2 years) than traditional psychodynamic approaches. Examples: *transference-focused psychotherapy (TFP)*, *mentalization-based treatment (MBT)*, and *intensive short-term dynamic psychotherapy (ISTDP)*.

that what happens to you in early childhood matters. However, a CBT view emphasizes behavioral conditioning and the development of unhelpful but fixed beliefs about self, others, and relationships. Cognitively speaking, each personality disorder is associated with certain main beliefs developed early in life (see Table 12.4). When people stubbornly cling to such beliefs, their interpersonal relationships are disrupted, and they tend to get diagnosed with personality disorders. Cognitive therapy targets inflexible beliefs to foster greater latitude in thinking, feeling, and behaving. Below, two well-established CBT approaches to personality disorders are presented: *schema therapy* and *dialectical behavior therapy*.

Table 12.4 Main Beliefs Associated with Specific Personality Disorders

PERSONALITY DISORDER	MAIN BELIEF
Paranoid	I cannot trust people
Schizotypal	It's better to be isolated from others
Schizoid	Relationships are messy, undesirable
Histrionic	People are there to serve or admire me
Narcissistic	Since I am special, I deserve special rules
Borderline	I deserve to be punished
Antisocial	I am entitled to break rules
Avoidant	If people know the "real" me, they will reject me
Dependent	I need people to survive, be happy
Obsessive-compulsive	People should do better, try harder

Note: The main beliefs listed here are just some examples; this table should not be considered a complete list of main beliefs associated with the specific personality disorders.

Source: Adapted from Table 3.1: PBQ Beliefs Most Strongly Associated with Specific Personality Disorders in Beck, A. T., Davis, D. D., & Freeman, A. (2015). Cognitive therapy of personality disorders (3rd ed.). Guilford Press, p. 61.

Schema Therapy

Schema therapy (also called *schema-focused therapy*) places the cognitive concept of schemas front and center (Arntz et al., 2009; Arntz & Van Genderen, 2021; Farrell et al., 2014; Fassbinder & Arntz, 2021; Nysæter & Nordahl, 2008; J. E. Young, 1999; J. E. Young et al., 2003). Chapter 2 introduced schemas, the mental structures or scripts we use to organize information and guide our behavior. Schema therapy maintains that people diagnosed with personality disorders develop extremely rigid relationship schemas early in life due to abuse or neglect. These inflexible schemas dating to childhood are called *early maladaptive schemas (EMSs)*, and they reflect stable and dysfunctional life themes (Nysæter & Nordahl, 2008; J. E. Young et al., 2003). EMSs make people vulnerable to problematic interpersonal patterns. Among the many EMSs that contribute to problematic personality functioning are *abandonment* (the belief others will leave you in the lurch), *defectiveness* (the view that you are fundamentally broken), *insufficient control* (the assumption that others are trying to dominate you), *entitlement* (the belief that others owe you special treatment), and *mistrust/abuse* (the belief that others will mistreat you) (Nysæter & Nordahl, 2008; J. E. Young et al., 2003).

When EMSs are activated, people enter cognitive, emotional, and behavioral states known as *dysfunctional schema modes* (Arntz et al., 2009; Farrell et al., 2014; Nysæter & Nordahl, 2008; Young et al., 2003). Examples of dysfunctional schema modes are the *vulnerable child mode* (you feel helpless, weak, and unable to get your needs met), *angry/impulsive child mode* (you feel angry and impulsively lash out), *avoidant protector mode* (you disconnect from yourself and others to protect yourself from painful feelings), *compliant surrender mode* (you go along with other's demands to keep others from getting angry), and *punitive parent mode* (you punish yourself for expressing needs, making mistakes, or disappointing people) (Aalbers et al., 2021; Arntz et al., 2009; Farrell et al., 2014; Nysæter & Nordahl, 2008; J. E. Young et al., 2003). Dysfunctional schema modes contrast with *healthy and functional schema modes*, consisting of adaptive states of thinking, feeling, and behaving.

Schema therapy: Attributes personality disorders to *early maladaptive schemas (EMSs)* tied to childhood abuse and neglect; encourages awareness of situations that trigger *dysfunctional schema modes* and the development of healthier and more functional alternative responses.

The *healthy adult mode* (productive thoughts and feelings lead you to feel skilled and capable) and *healthy child mode* (you feel playful and can engage others in enjoyable activities) constitute the two healthy and functional schema modes (Aalbers et al., 2021; Arntz et al., 2009; Farrell et al., 2014; Nysæter & Nordahl, 2008; J. E. Young et al., 2003).

Schema therapy replaces dysfunctional schema modes with healthy and functional ones. EMSs and schema modes are explained to clients, and they are encouraged to pay attention to how these operate in their daily lives. If all goes as planned, over time clients become increasingly aware of how emotionally challenging situations trigger their EMSs and dysfunctional schema modes. This allows them to get better at identifying and resisting dysfunctional schemas and to develop more healthy and functional alternative schemas. As in psychodynamic therapies, the therapeutic relationship is important in schema therapy. It provides clients a secure relationship through which they develop more adaptive interpersonal schemas (Arntz & Van Genderen, 2021; Dadomo et al., 2018). There is not a great deal of research on schema therapy for personality disorders, but the literature that does exist tends to find it effective (Bamelis et al., 2014; Giesen-Bloo et al., 2006; Jacob & Arntz, 2013; Nordahl & Nysæter, 2005; Sempértegui et al., 2013; Thiel et al., 2016).

Dialectical Behavior Therapy (DBT)

Dialectical behavior therapy (DBT):
CBT-influenced therapy developed for borderline personality disorder that combines CBT skill-training with an emphasis on dialectics.

Marsha Linehan's **dialectical behavior therapy (DBT)** is a CBT-influenced approach that incorporates Zen Buddhist mindfulness. DBT was originally developed for borderline personality disorder but is also used with other presenting problems (Dimeff et al., 2021; Heard & Linehan, 1994; Linehan, 1993, 2015; Swales et al., 2000). Usually lasting a year, DBT helps borderline clients address poor self-related boundaries, impulsive behavior, difficulty regulating emotions, and interpersonal anxiety and conflict (Dimeff et al., 2021; Linehan, 1993, 2015). DBT combines skills training (CBT interventions such as reinforcement, exposure, problem-solving, behavioral rehearsal, contingency management, and cognitive restructuring) with an emphasis on *dialectics*, the rational process of reconciling opposites. As people with borderline personalities often struggle to integrate conflicting thoughts and feelings, learning to think dialectically can be beneficial.

Outpatient DBT is typically divided into three treatment modes administered simultaneously: (1) weekly individual DBT sessions; (2) weekly skills training group sessions; and (3) between session telephone consultations with the individual DBT therapist, as needed (Dimeff et al., 2021; Heard & Linehan, 1994; Linehan, 1993, 2015). DBT group skills training is explicitly cognitive-behavioral. It uses modeling and direct instruction to teach skills, behavioral rehearsal and feedback to strengthen skills, and homework assignments to help clients generalize skills beyond the therapy room (Linehan, 1993). Skills training is broken into distinct modules that focus on *core mindfulness skills* (observing and accepting, rather than avoiding, negative emotions) *interpersonal effectiveness skills* (productively interacting with others), *emotion regulation skills* (managing and regulating upsetting feelings), and *distress tolerance skills* (enduring distress without being overwhelmed by it) (Linehan, 2015). Individual sessions are more relationally focused than group sessions, emphasizing insight into behavior patterns that impair functioning. Individual therapy helps clients think in more integrated ways, incorporate the coping skills they are learning in group sessions into their everyday lives, and

Megan

If Megan undertook DBT for her borderline personality issues, her therapist would target specific problem behaviors—such as suicidal threats, drug use, and explosive emotional outbursts. Megan might be asked to log her thoughts, feelings, drug use, and other problematic behaviors on a diary card and identify links among them. This would reveal that Megan relies on alcohol to deal with feelings of misery. Megan would be encouraged to use skills she is learning in her skills training group to cope more effectively. For instance, she would apply core mindfulness skills to the emotions causing her misery by mindfully remaining aware of them, rather than avoiding, resisting, or impulsively reacting to them. As Megan becomes more mindful of painful feelings (such as rage and fear), she should be better able to accept them without being ruled by them—improving her ability to regulate feelings and tolerate emotional distress. Problematic behaviors (suicidal overtures, drug use, angry outbursts) would likely decrease or stop entirely.

accept themselves and their emotions (Heard & Linehan, 1994; Linehan, 2015). Several randomized controlled trials support using DBT for borderline personality issues, with research finding it effective in addressing suicidal behavior, self-harm, therapy drop-outs, hospital admission rates, reliance on prescription drugs, anger, anxiety, and depression (Andreasson et al., 2016; Barnicot et al., 2014; Binks et al., 2006; J. Birt et al., 2022; Kliem et al., 2010; Linehan et al., 1991, 2006; May et al., 2016; O'Connell & Dowling, 2014; Panos et al., 2014; Priebe et al., 2012; Stoffers et al., 2012; van den Bosch et al., 2005). Some studies suffer from small sample sizes and other methodological shortcomings, so further research has been recommended (Stoffers et al., 2012).

12.16 Humanistic Perspectives

Humanistic perspectives on personality disorders receive less attention than psychodynamic and CBT perspectives (Quinn, 2011). This may be because humanistic clinicians often reject medical model diagnosis (Comerford, 2018). Consequently, they dislike labels like "personality disorder," which they see as pejorative, demeaning, and mistakenly equating human distress with brain disease (Gunn & Potter, 2015; T. S. Szasz, 1987, 1970/1991). The "Controversial Question" box builds on this by asking whether some or all personality disorders are moral evaluations masquerading as medical diagnoses. Given their skepticism about diagnostic labels, many humanistic therapists would answer "yes." What do you think?

Recasting "Personality Disorders" as Fragile Process

In keeping with the humanistic perspective's non-pathologizing, anti-diagnostic view, psychotherapist Margaret Warner (2014; 2013) reframes "personality disorders" as examples of **difficult process**. She explains difficult process by supplementing Carl Rogers' person-centered therapy (PCT; see Chapter 2) with Bowlby's attachment theory. Difficult process emerges in people who don't receive Rogers' core conditions (empathy, genuineness, and unconditional positive regard) during infancy. This leads to insecure attachments with caregivers. Consequently, such people have trouble establishing the supportive relationships necessary for emotional growth and self-actualization, the humanistic motivation to fulfill one's potential.

Difficult process:
Non-pathologizing and anti-diagnostic humanistic term for mental distress that attributes it to lack of core conditions in early life relationships, which leads to insecure attachments, impaired emotional growth, and inability to self-actualize.

Controversial Question: Are Personality Disorders Merely Moral Judgments?

The late philosopher and bioethicist Louis Charland (1958–2021) argued that the Cluster B personality disorders (antisocial, borderline, histrionic, and narcissistic—the "dramatic, emotional, and erratic" disorders) aren't disorders at all. Instead, they reflect moral judgments about people who behave in socially unacceptable ways (Charland, 2004, 2006, 2010). Those with Cluster B diagnoses lie, cheat, manipulate, and emotionally carry on in ways others find morally reprehensible. However, just because behavior is immoral doesn't mean it is disordered. Charland's ideas may remind you of psychiatric gadfly Thomas Szasz, discussed in Chapter 1. Szasz (1987, 1970/1991) felt that DSM and ICD turn moral problems into medical ones. This medicalizes personality conflicts, allowing people whose behavior ethically offends or annoys to be labeled as ill. Rule breakers become "psychopaths," those we find emotionally manipulative become "borderlines," and those we feel demand too much attention for themselves become "narcissists." But what we have here, thinkers like Charland and Szasz maintain, aren't "personality disorders" afflicting the offending parties, but ethical conflicts between the offending parties and those who take offense. While Charland's critique of moral conflicts masquerading as mental disorders is limited to Cluster B personality disorders, Szasz's view extends to all mental disorder diagnoses. Those who reject Szasz's and Charland's ideas counter that while personality disorders do have a moral component, morally objectionable behavior may sometimes be caused by illness (Zachar, 2011; Zachar & Potter, 2010a, 2010b). Still, critiques of personality disorders as moral judgments remain compelling to those skeptical of DSM and ICD diagnosis.

Critical Thinking Questions

1. Do you agree with Charland that Cluster B personality disorders are moral judgments disguised as medical diagnoses? Explain why or why not.

2. Do you think Charland is correct in limiting his critique to Cluster B personality disorders? Or are you more partial to Szasz's argument that all mental disorder diagnoses are moral judgments? Explain your thinking.

3. Can mental disorders involve morally objectionable behavior while still being genuine disorders? If yes, what kind of evidence would one need to distinguish purely moral conflicts from mental disorders that also involve morally problematic behavior?

Fragile process: In humanistic theory, a type of *difficult process* found in those often diagnosed as "narcissistic" or "borderline," characterized by poor emotional regulation, difficulty taking other people's perspectives, and feeling invalidated.

From a difficult process perspective, "narcissistic" and "borderline" clients don't have mental disorders. Rather, due to their insecure attachments and failure to receive core conditions needed for positive self-development, they experience a specific type of difficult process called **fragile process**. Fragile process clients have difficulty regulating their emotions, struggle to see others' viewpoints, and feel overwhelmed and negated by people. Non-directive person-centered therapy provides these clients with a caring and empathic relationship. From a PCT viewpoint, more directive therapies for fragile process are risky because "attempts to direct or explain or to teach different ways of being with these experiences often backfire" (M. S. Warner, 2013, p. 355). Thus, PCT assumes that genuinely empathizing with and unconditionally accepting fragile process clients (despite their difficult and at times off-putting behavior) is what they require: "When therapists can stay with client experiences, clients become more and more able to stay connected to these experiences themselves. This allows experiences to process and resolve themselves" (M. S. Warner, 2013, p. 355).

Research Evidence for Person-Centered Therapy

There is very little research on person-centered therapy for personality issues (A. Quinn, 2011). In one study, PCT was effective for personality disorders, regardless of whether medication was used (and in some cases, most effective without medication) (Teusch et al., 2001). In a second study, PCT was equivalent to cognitive therapy in reducing self-harm, suicidality, depression, anxiety, and—over the long haul—hopelessness (Cottraux et al., 2009). Finally, a third study found PCT as effective as DBT in addressing impulsivity, anger, and depression but less effective at reducing suicidal and other self-harm behaviors (R. M. Turner, 2000). This last finding calls into question Warner's assertion that more directive fragile process interventions (such as skills training) often backfire. Supplementing PCT with more structured techniques may provide additional benefits (E. Steffen, 2013). The limited research on PCT for personality issues makes it difficult to draw conclusions.

12.17 Evaluating Psychological Perspectives

Psychotherapy is often recommended for personality issues. Both inpatient and outpatient delivery appear to be helpful (Antonsen et al., 2014; Horn et al., 2015). Most psychotherapy effectiveness research has focused on Cluster B disorders ("dramatic, emotional, and erratic")—especially borderline personality disorder (Dixon-Gordon et al., 2011). The evidence base for Clusters A ("odd and eccentric") and C ("anxious and fearful") is more meager, especially Cluster A (Dixon-Gordon et al., 2011). For BPD, the therapies with the most support are DBT, schema therapy, and mentalization-based (Choi-Kain et al., 2017; Cristea et al., 2017; Rameckers et al., 2021). Among these therapies, DBT has the most substantial evidence base. Even though the impact of these therapies is sometimes modest, they consistently perform better than medication at improving borderline symptoms (Choi-Kain et al., 2017).

SOCIOCULTURAL PERSPECTIVES

12.18 Cross-Cultural and Social Justice Perspectives

Personality Disorders: Culturally Universal or Culturally Relative?

How much is personality attributable to individual differences and how much to culture? Big Five research does find personality differences across cultures. For example, Americans and Europeans are more extraverted and open to experience (but less agreeable) than their Asian and African counterparts (Allik, 2005). Similarly, Polish students are more agreeable and open to experience than Ukrainian students (Tychmanowicz et al., 2021). The meaning of such findings is unclear, as they raise the issue of cultural relativism versus cultural universalism discussed in Chapter 9 (Calliess et al., 2008). Are the Big Five (and the very notion of personality) culturally universal or culture-bound? Can *acculturation* (acquiring the characteristics of a culture one moves to) change personality traits (Allik, 2005)? If so, does this make "personality" more a product of culture than genes? And if personality is strongly affected by culture, then are "personality disorders" truly individual afflictions in the same way that culturally universal diseases like diabetes and cancer seem to be? Or are they reified social constructions that tell us more about our cultural values than who is ill (Epstein, n.d.-b; Ta, 2019)? As another example, people in Western countries score higher on measures of narcissism than those in Eastern countries (Twenge, 2011). Why? Does this mean that Westerners suffer more from "narcissistic personality disorder"? Or does it mean cultural values influence how self-focused people are? Is that friend of yours whom you describe as "narcissistic" mentally ill or the victim of cultural indoctrination that celebrates a "Me First" mentality?

Cultural differences influence how personality disorders are conceptualized in different societies. For instance, people diagnosed with borderline personality disorder vary by country. American and British patients identified as borderline differ in terms of drug use, drug-related psychoses, aversion to dependency, and derealization/depersonalization symptoms (Jani et al., 2016). Do such differences reflect cultural variations in the expression of a universal disorder? Or is the term "borderline personality disorder" being used to describe different things in different cultures? And what about countries that don't recognize BPD? The *Chinese Classification of Mental Disorders (CCMD)* rejected BPD as a diagnosis and instead includes *impulsive personality disorder*. Why? Because two of BPD's central symptoms (fear of abandonment and feelings of emptiness) are alien to Chinese culture, which is more communally focused (Jani et al., 2016). Is China's impulsive personality disorder different from what other countries call borderline personality disorder? Further, if personality disorders vary by culture, are they truly universal disorders? These difficult debates remain unresolved.

Gender Bias, Trauma, Socioeconomic Disadvantage, and Racism

Many feminists and social justice advocates view personality issues not as disorders, but as expectable responses to sexism, abuse, and economic disadvantage. Feminist theorists view the personal as political, seeing individual problems as originating in sociopolitical circumstances (L. S. Brown, 1994; Hanisch, 1970/2006; Root, 1992). **Relational-cultural theory** exemplifies the feminist/social justice critique of personality disorders. It "challenges many of the traditional psychological theories of personality in terms of their emphasis on the growth of a separate self, their exclusive focus on intrapsychic phenomenon, and their espousal of enduring internal traits" (J. V. Jordan, 2004, p. 120). According to relational-cultural theorists, individualistic conceptions of personality disorder like those in DSM, ICD, and PDM improperly attribute mental distress to internal psychopathology rather than societal influences such as chronic social disconnection (J. V. Jordan, 2004; Nabar, 2009). They fail to consider "the importance of context beyond the traditional nuclear family and often beyond the influence of the early mother–infant relationship," mistakenly locating the source of emotional suffering "in the individual" (J. V. Jordan, 2004, p. 125). The unfortunate result is that "social conditions and the relational failures emanating from these social conditions are rarely examined as the source of the problem" (J. V. Jordan, 2004, p. 125). From relational-cultural and other social justice perspectives, those diagnosed with personality disorders aren't ill. Rather, they are struggling to deal with oppressive conditions such as gender bias, trauma, socioeconomic disadvantage, and racism (Epstein, 2006; Moane, 2014)—each briefly discussed below.

Relational-cultural theory: Holds that mental distress is often incorrectly attributed to internal psychopathology rather than social alienation.

Megan

A relational-cultural therapist would reject the idea that Megan "has" borderline personality disorder and instead look for ways in which Megan's mental distress is tied to factors like social isolation, gender bias, and traumatic abuse. The therapist would help Megan understand how adverse social conditions have contributed to her upset, while assisting her to develop a support system to aid her in overcoming and rectifying these oppressive social influences.

Gender Bias

From a feminist viewpoint, personality disorder categories are gender biased, mistaking socialized gender roles for psychopathology (B. Berger, 2014; L. S. Brown, 1992; Epstein, n.d.-b; M. Kaplan, 1983; C. Shaw & Proctor, 2005; Wirth-Cauchon, 2000). Feminists argue that histrionic and borderline PDs are diagnosed more in females because both involve "excessive" emotionality—thus unfairly targeting women, who are socialized to express feelings more readily than men (M. Kaplan,

Photo 12.5 Ursula in *The Little Mermaid* provides a great example of "excessive" emotionality, portrayed as grotesque and terrifying through her flamboyant femininity. We could view Ursula's deceitfulness, recklessness, and irresponsible behavior as evidence of a personality disorder, but we could also view this as a sexist potrayal of male fears of female excess, defined as evil and shunned by society.

Allstar Picture Library Limited./Alamy Stock Photo.

1983). Equating emotional expression with being histrionic (or "hysterical") goes all the way back to ancient Greek medicine, which—as noted in Chapter 1—attributed such symptoms to a wandering womb (Ng, 1999; Novais et al., 2015; Palis et al., 1985, 1985; C. Tasca et al., 2012). Histrionic and borderline aren't the only personality disorders deemed sexist. Some see dependent personality disorder as pathologizing women by treating their learned tendencies toward deference and support-seeking as signs of disorder. However, feminists believe "dependent personalities" are better explained in social terms: In cultures where women lack socioeconomic equality, many are—quite literally—dependent on men! When this leads to emotional distress, they are improperly labeled as mentally ill (L. S. Brown, 1992; M. Kaplan, 1983). Instead of attributing their distress to socially oppressive gender expectations, mental health professionals mistakenly diagnose dependent personality disorder.

Four decades ago, psychologist Marcie Kaplan (1983) famously proposed two fictitious diagnoses to illustrate her belief that personality disorders are sexist—*independent personality disorder* and *restricted personality disorder*. The former is characterized by putting work above relationships and not considering others when making decisions; "e.g., expects spouse and children to re-locate to another city because of individual's career plans" (M. Kaplan, 1983, p. 790). The latter involves excessive emotional restraint and avoidance; "e.g., absence of crying at sad moments" and "engages others (especially spouse) to perform emotional behaviors such as writing the individual's thank-you notes or telephoning to express the individual's concern" (M. Kaplan, 1983, p. 790). Kaplan's point was that these behaviors, because they are traditionally masculine, aren't identified as disorders, but that comparable female behaviors are:

In other words, whereas behaving in a feminine stereotyped manner alone will earn a … diagnosis (e.g., Dependent or Histrionic Personality Disorder), behaving in a masculine stereotyped manner alone will not. A masculine stereotyped individual, to be diagnosed, cannot just be remarkably masculine. Masculinity alone is not clinically suspect; femininity alone is. (M. Kaplan, 1983, p. 791)

Research does show gender differences in personality disorder diagnosis, but whether this is due to bias or genuine prevalence disparities is debatable. One research review found women are diagnosed more often as borderline (three times as often!), histrionic, and dependent, while men are more commonly diagnosed as antisocial, narcissistic, schizoid, and schizotypal (Schulte Holthausen & Habel, 2018). Another review partly confirmed this, finding gender bias in the diagnosis of histrionic and antisocial PDs but not borderline PD (Garb, 2021). Those concerned about gender biased personality disorder categories believe that ICD-11's dimensional model "poses a new chance" to rectify this issue (Schulte Holthausen & Habel, 2018, p. 107).

Trauma

Research has linked childhood trauma to many personality disorders, including antisocial, avoidant, borderline, histrionic, narcissistic, obsessive-compulsive, and schizotypal (Ashiq et al., 2018; Cotter et al., 2015; Eikenaes et al., 2015; Frías et al., 2016; Hageman et al., 2015; J. P. Klein et al., 2015; MacIntosh et al., 2015; Quidé et al., 2018; Schimmenti et al., 2015; Stepp et al., 2016; Velikonja et al., 2019; Yalch et al., 2021). The Collaborative Longitudinal Personality Disorders Study found that 73 percent of people diagnosed with personality disorders reported abuse and 82 percent reported neglect (Battle et al., 2004). Given this connection to childhood trauma, some believe complex PTSD (see Chapter 7) is a more accurate and less stigmatizing diagnosis than borderline personality disorder (J. D. Ford & Courtois, 2021; Herman, 2015). They prefer complex PTSD because it "frames the root problem of personal difficulties as victimization instead of personality deficiency" (Nicki, 2016, p. 219). Some counter that complex PTSD and BPD are distinct (if comorbid) disorders, so replacing the latter with the former is not always appropriate (J. D. Ford & Courtois, 2021). Nonetheless, feminist social justice advocates remain concerned that personality disorders such as BPD too often blame the victim.

Socioeconomic Disadvantage and Racism

Like trauma, socioeconomic status (SES) often predicts personality issues. Residing in a low SES neighborhood has been linked to lower overall functioning and higher rates of symptoms among those with personality disorder diagnoses (Walsh et al., 2013). When it comes to specific personality disorders, low SES is associated with antisocial, borderline, dependent, paranoid, and schizotypal personality issues (P. Cohen, Chen, et al., 2008; Harper, 2011; Y. Pan et al., 2022; Piotrowska et al., 2015; Zwaanswijk et al., 2018). SES isn't the only factor tied to paranoid and antisocial behavior. There is also a link to race. In the United States, some evidence suggests that Black patients are more likely to be diagnosed as paranoid than white patients (Harper, 2011; Loring & Powell, 1988; Raza et al., 2014; Whaley, 2004). Low SES and past trauma are both associated with paranoid personality symptoms among Black Americans, especially low SES (Iacovino et al., 2014). Race bias might also explain higher rates of antisocial PD diagnoses among Black compared with white patients (Garb, 2021). Can you hypothesize how?

Harvey

Harvey's antisocial behavior might be due to economic oppression and racism. Raised in an environment that provided poor Black youth few options, Harvey grew up feeling angry and acted out in the only ways he felt he could. His idea that everyone is out to get him might be better understood as a legitimate response to discrimination and economic restrictions rather than as symptomatic of paranoid personality. From a social justice viewpoint, social change is the key to helping Harvey. Medicating him or offering him therapy to adjust him to his conditions merely propagates an oppressive social system.

Although research on SES and race is mostly correlational, it supports the assertion that oppressive social conditions are a major culprit in personality issues. It makes sense that someone from a discriminated against group who grows up in poverty would be more likely to act out or be suspicious of others. Again, the great debate surrounds whether gender, race, and socioeconomic factors influence personality disorders, or whether personality disorders are a way of blaming people (rather than social ills) for their problems.

12.19 Service User Perspectives

Stigma

Personality disorders are among the most stigmatized of psychiatric diagnoses. People with personality disorder diagnoses are seen as manipulative, difficult, and responsible for their misbehavior (L. Sheehan et al., 2016). These views are not limited to the lay public. Mental health professionals also hold quite negative attitudes about personality disorders (L. Sheehan et al., 2016). A PD label is a red flag that screams "difficult" patient. Stigma appears to be a problem for all personality disorders, but especially borderline personality disorder—with mental health professionals viewing patients with BPD diagnoses more negatively than those with other diagnoses (Appel et al., 2020; J. Baker & Beazley, 2022; N. J. S. Day et al., 2018; Dickens et al., 2016; Lanfredi et al., 2019; K. McKenzie et al., 2022; Ociskova et al., 2017). Such patients are seen as manipulative, threatening, and rule-breaking (R. Lester et al., 2020)—though they are blamed less for this when labeled as "borderline" (as opposed to no diagnosis) (Masland & Null, 2022). Still, mental health professionals often dislike BPD patients. In describing psychiatric nurses' attitudes toward them, one study used the memorable (if unflattering) term "destructive whirlwind" (Woollaston & Hixenbaugh, 2008). When a mental health professional calls a patient "borderline," it may tell us as much about the clinician's feelings about the patient as it does the patient's clinical condition!

The stigma of personality disorders is so great that in some cases, mental health professionals are reluctant to inform patients when they diagnose them with BPD (Brauser, 2021; Lequesne & Hersh, 2004; R. Lester et al., 2020; Sisti et al., 2016). They withhold this information due to worry that "such a diagnosis would have deleterious effects on the patient's health and morale" (Lequesne & Hersh, 2004, p. 172). Even when they do tell patients, they often delay doing so or do it in a manner that can be alienating (R. Lester et al., 2020). One patient described the surreal experience this way:

I actually hadn't been told until that day that I had the diagnosis of borderline. And she sat there, the psychologist, and she just talked to the advocate, she didn't talk to me. And she goes "oh this is typical behaviour for someone with borderline personality disorder." And I'm going what? And when I left I went straight to the library to find out what on earth she was meaning. (Veysey, 2014, p. 26)

While it may be ethically dubious not to tell patients their diagnoses (Brauser, 2021), concerns over stigmatization may be justified because personality disorder labels can affect patients. That is, in response to the stigma and discrimination they face, people with personality disorders may engage in **self-stigmatization**. This means they internalize the negative attitudes espoused by their doctors, as well as by the media (M. L. Bowen, 2016). Consequently, they come to see themselves as others do, in a distinctly unfavorable light (Grambal et al., 2016; Koivisto et al., 2022; L. Sheehan et al., 2016). Patients diagnosed with personality disorders often feel powerless, perhaps because the culture has imposed a pathologizing diagnosis on them without understanding their point of view (Bonnington & Rose, 2014). They also feel dismissed, with many reporting that they have been subtly routed away from receiving care because their doctors view them as difficult (Sulzer, 2015). Thus, people with personality issues are often both stigmatized and denied much-needed help.

Self-stigmatization:
The process of internalizing negative attitudes about oneself espoused by others.

Service User/Survivor Perspectives

Perhaps because of the stigmatizing impact of diagnostic labels and the often less-than-humane treatment that some patients report, members of the service user/survivor movement (see Chapter 2) reject conventional mental health approaches to personality disorders (Capes-Ivy, 2010; Epstein, n.d.-b, n.d.-a, 2006). Themselves former patients, they argue that the mental health system does great harm when it assigns personality disorder labels to people. They contend that scientifically suspect and stigmatizing personality disorder diagnoses are unhelpful and that much of the "treatment" those who get them receive is more damaging than beneficial. From the service user/survivor perspective, a diagnosis like borderline personality disorder is "a 'sophisticated insult'" levied at trauma survivors by mental health professionals—one that adds to rather than relieves the trauma (Viera, 2016, para. 5). While not everyone who receives a personality disorder diagnosis finds it damaging, the fact that many do is worthy of attention. "The Lived Experience" feature examines both positive and negative experiences of being labeled as borderline.

The Lived Experience: Being Labeled as "Borderline"

What is it like to be labeled as "borderline?" For people like Laura, age 21, it is liberating:

I was diagnosed with it in 2017, after being in psychiatric hospital for a while. When I first heard about BPD, I went online and printed out a load of information on it and highlighted almost the whole of each page. It suddenly made so much sense. All the things I hadn't wanted to talk about, all the feelings that didn't make sense to me, things I couldn't put my finger on—they were all there on a few pages. Although the information said just 1.6% of us share this experience, it still made me feel so much less alone than I had. (YoungMinds, 2020, para. 2)

However, others have a much more negative reaction to being diagnosed:

It [being diagnosed] was such a shock, such a fucking slap in the face. It really was an insult actually. [The psychiatrist] invested no time in me whatsoever, and it was just like I was a naughty, dirty person ... it was like I should be ashamed of myself ... it was like being marked out differently. I'd struggled for so long not knowing who I was and then suddenly "here's a label." Well, what does that tell me then? Am I not part of humanity? ... it's made me very insecure about my worth as a person, who I am, because I used to be so capable and now I'm a nothing, a nobody. It's taken everything away from me. (Bonnington & Rose, 2014, p. 11)

Those who find the diagnosis helpful use it to make sense of their experience. For Gabby, age 22, her diagnosis was a first step in comprehending and sharing what she goes through:

My awful self-talk can spiral into intense suicidal thoughts and solid beliefs that everyone would be better off without me. When I'm struggling to manage my BPD, I can display people-pleasing and self-sacrificing behaviours. And I always feel worse for it because no matter how comforting someone is, they'll never fulfil my chronically unmet needs. (Rethink Mental Illness, 2021, para. 5)

However, due to intense stigma, others hesitate to disclose their BPD—even to medical professionals, who sometimes use the diagnosis pejoratively as a label for patients they find difficult and unlikable (Ociskova et al., 2017). As a client named Sarah explained:

Really, I mean [if I disclose it], the interaction always turns like I am the source of all problems. From then on, they interact with me with kind of a psycho attitude, you know, in a way you interact with a nutcase ... The diagnosis is more like a burden ... you're branded on your forehead, and you're treated accordingly. And the mental diagnosis will then be emphasized in all sorts of irrelevant contexts. (Koivisto et al., 2022, p. 11)

As these quotes make clear, the experience of receiving a BPD diagnosis varies widely—and is sometimes impacted by how the diagnosis is communicated to patients by health professionals (R. Lester et al., 2020). Some patients find the diagnosis helpful, but others do not. Regardless, it isn't going away anytime soon, despite concerns about diagnostic reliability and validity. Recall that ICD-11 included a "borderline pattern" specifier in its dimensional PD diagnostic system—a somewhat controversial late addition (Bach et al., 2022; G. A. McCabe & Widiger, 2020; Mulder, 2021). Considering the quotes above and what you have learned in this chapter, does the borderline diagnosis help more than it harms? Why or why not?

12.20 Systems Perspectives

Family Systems and Personality Issues

From a systems perspective, personality issues arise within the context of relationships—with the family system most often the focus of attention. As noted, many (if not most) people diagnosed with borderline or other personality disorders have experienced early life trauma—and this trauma has often occurred within the family (H. Choi, 2018; Sansone & Sansone, 2009). Thus, thinking systemically, people with difficult personalities developed them within family systems characterized by mistreatment or neglect. For example, many of the violent behaviors found in people with antisocial personality disorder diagnoses may be attributable to family dynamics (e.g., lack of parental warmth, harsh discipline, and witnessing parental violence) (Marzilli et al., 2021; K. H. Rosen, 1998).

Harvey

Harvey, who is in prison for attempted murder, was raised in a family where he regularly witnessed his father's explosive temper. Harvey's father rarely expressed affection but displayed much anger and hostility. Physical violence in the family was common. Harvey's father often hit Harvey, his siblings, and Harvey's mother. Once, during an especially intense family argument, Harvey saw his father threaten his mother with a knife. When Harvey was 15, his father was sentenced to prison for assault during an armed robbery. Sadly, his father's prison time anticipated the fate that befell Harvey.

Substantial attention has been paid to the families of borderline clients. It's been argued that **borderline families** are characterized by interpersonal chaos in which family members don't know how to nurture or support one another (Sperry, 2011). This may be because many of the family members qualify for other diagnoses themselves, such as substance use disorder, conduct disorder, bipolar disorder, and schizoaffective disorder (Sansone & Sansone, 2009; Sperry, 2011). Three kinds of borderline families have been identified (E. G. Goldstein, 1990; P. E. Marcus, 1993). *Enmeshed or overinvolved families* have poor boundaries between members, are intense, and display lots of

Borderline families:
Families characterized by interpersonal chaos in which members do not know how to nurture or support one another; three kinds of borderline families: *enmeshed or overinvolved*, *alienated or rejecting*, and *idealizing or denying*.

hostile conflict that the client who is later diagnosed as borderline gets caught in; one parent tends to be overprotective of the client while the other is dismissive and devaluing. *Alienated or rejecting families* see the client as different, unwelcome, bad, or the enemy; in these families, the parents are closely aligned with one another and exclude the client, who is blamed for family problems. Finally, in *idealizing or denying families* the family members see each other as perfect and downplay both the client's difficulties and other family conflicts.

Couples and Family DBT for Borderline Personality

Dialectical behavior therapy (DBT), described previously, has been adapted for use with families and couples in which borderline personality patterns are an issue (Fruzzetti et al., 2021; Fruzzetti & Payne, 2015). DBT with families helps partners and family members eliminate problematic ways of engaging one another typical of borderline personality (things like avoidance, withdrawal, and expressing destructive anger). Instead, constructive family communication skills are fostered, in which feelings are conveyed in a non-threatening way and each person openly receives feedback. Couple and family interactions are often video recorded so that family members and therapists can gain insight into problematic interpersonal patterns. Couples and families work with the therapist to track their dealings with one another, break the "chain" of old thinking-feeling-behavior patterns, and reinforce appropriate interpersonal skills (Fruzzetti et al., 2021; Fruzzetti & Payne, 2020). There is preliminary evidence that DBT reduces problematic family behaviors, but more studies are needed (Ekdahl et al., 2014; M. L. Miller & Skerven, 2017).

12.21 Evaluating Sociocultural Perspectives

Sociocultural perspectives are criticized for overlooking biological and psychological components of personality issues. In such critiques, contextual factors such as gender, race, and SES) are important but don't replace other influences—especially genetic predispositions to certain personality traits (Hertler, 2014b). Critics of sociocultural perspectives wonder whether doing away with personality disorders and instead diagnosing less pathologizing and more reliable disorders (such as depression and complex PTSD) is wise. First, they argue that depression and complex PTSD might overlap with a personality disorder like BPD but are not identical to it (J. D. Ford & Courtois, 2021). Second, they question whether switching to these diagnoses really reduces stigma (Paris, 2007). Critics contend that the stigma of personality disorders isn't carried solely by diagnostic labeling, but also reflects the disturbing and difficult ways that clients so labeled behave when dealing with others. For example, when it comes to clients diagnosed as borderline, "stigma cannot be removed by reclassification" because "patients who are chronically suicidal and who do not form strong treatment alliances will continue to be just as difficult, even under a different diagnostic label" (Paris, 2007, p. 36). This begs the question: Are diagnostic labels are causes or effects of negative attitudes? Criticisms notwithstanding, sociocultural perspectives contextualize personality issues and keep us attuned to factors beyond the individual that influence challenging interpersonal behavior.

CLOSING THOUGHTS

12.22 Can Personality Be Disordered?

Is "personality disorder" a legitimate concept? Your answer may depend on how you feel about the notion of personality, a notion that—despite its ubiquity in Western culture—remains fuzzy. As alluded to earlier, psychologist Walter Mischel famously challenged the idea that human behavior is best explained by attributing it to a stable and enduring personality (Mischel, 1973, 2009; Mischel & Shoda, 1995). He argued that people do not behave consistently across situations. For example, how you act with your friends is probably very different from how you act with your family. To Mischel, what we call "personality" is a function of situational factors and how people make sense of things, rather than an innate set of immutable traits. Extending this view, some critics contend that personality is a social construction. That is, it's "a concept that we use in our everyday lives in order to try to make sense of the things that other people and ourselves do … a theory for explaining human behaviour" (Burr, 2015, p. 40). But how good of a theory is it? As noted, some critics complain that attributing something to personality (or, by implication, a personality disorder) is circular and not much of an explanation at all:

> *Imagine that someone observes Jane acting in a consistently outgoing and friendly fashion and asks, "Why does Jane behave this way?" If the answer is that she has an "extraverted personality" by observing that she is generally outgoing and friendly, this is a tautological, pseudo-explanation.* (Fowler et al., 2007, p. 6)

Do you agree with this critique, or does it seem unfair? Whether we approve of the concept of personality disorders, most of us concur that many people do rely on recurrent ways of relationally engaging people that consistently create difficulties for them and others. Exactly why this is so remains an open question. Hopefully, this chapter has offered you a variety of perspectives to consider in reaching your own conclusions.

CHAPTER SUMMARY

Overview

- *Personality* refers to stable patterns of thought, emotion, and behavior. It is often measured along the five trait dimensions of the *Five-Factor Model (FFM)*.
- *Personality disorders* are diagnosed when personality traits result in interpersonal conflict.

Diagnostic Perspectives

- DSM-5-TR officially recognizes ten categories of personality disorder but is considering a proposed hybrid trait *alternative model of personality disorders (AMPD)*.
- ICD-11 has moved to a fully dimensional model of personality disorders that does away with traditional categories and replace them with a general category of "personality disorder" that is mapped along five trait domains.
- HiTOP and PDM both incorporate assessment of personality into their diagnostic systems, with HiTOP spectra dimensions overlapping with the Big Five and PDM-2 making the assessment of twelve personality syndromes a key element of its approach.
- PTMF rejects the idea of pathological personalities and instead attributes problematic interpersonal patterns to adverse social circumstances.

Historical Perspectives

- The notion of a stable personality is found throughout human history.
- Historical terms like *mania without delusion* and *moral insanity* anticipate later notions of personality disorder.
- Prichard and Schneider developed early classifications of *psychopathic personalities*.

Biological Perspectives

- Serotonin is linked to ASPD and BPD, while dopamine is implicated in STPD.
- Polypharmacy is common in treating personality disorders, despite evidence that drug treatments are not very effective.
- Brain volume changes are being studied across numerous personality disorders.
- Personality disorder heritability is debated but estimated at 40–50 percent. There are numerous candidate genes (including genes related to dopamine, monoamine oxidase, and serotonin).
- The *frequency-dependent selection* and *obsessive trait complex* hypotheses explain psychopathy and OCPD, respectively, in evolutionary terms.
- PDs are associated with immune inflammation, which is common in those who face adverse experiences.
- Biological explanations of personality disorders have yielded few treatments and are criticized for offering circular arguments.

Psychological Perspectives

- Psychodynamic perspectives view PDs as originating in abusive/neglectful early life relationships that result in insecure attachments. Psychodynamic therapies, including *structured psychodynamic therapies for personality disorders*, provide a corrective emotional experience.
- *Schema therapy* and *dialectical behavior therapy (DBT)* are CBT therapies for personality disorders. The former targets maladaptive relationship schemas and the latter combines mindfulness training, skills training, and an emphasis on dialectics.
- Humanistic therapies recast "personality disorders" as a type of *difficult process* called *fragile process*. It provides person-centered therapy's core conditions to foster client change.
- Psychotherapy is recommended for personality issues. There is modest evidence that several psychotherapies improve borderline relationship patterns, but further research is needed.

Sociocultural Perspectives

- Sociocultural perspectives question whether personality and personality disorders are culturally universal.
- *Relational-cultural theory* attributes mental distress to social alienation (including that which gets diagnosed as personality disorder).
- Social justice perspectives trace the behaviors that result in PD diagnoses to gender bias, trauma, socioeconomic disadvantage, and racism.
- Stigma, including *self-stigmatization*, are major issues affecting people diagnosed with personality disorders.
- Service users/survivors view personality disorder diagnoses as damaging to those who receive them.
- Family systems perspectives see personality issues as originating in family dynamics. The interpersonal chaos of *borderline families* is viewed as critical to fostering borderline behaviors and experiences.
- Couples and family therapies (such as DBT with families) foster family communication for addressing borderline and other personality patterns.
- Sociocultural perspectives are criticized for overlooking biological and psychological elements of personality issues and recasting them in exclusively social terms.

Closing Thoughts

- Debate continues as to whether personality is a cultural universal or a social construction.
- The legitimacy of the concept of personality disorders remains controversial.

NEW VOCABULARY

1. Antisocial personality disorder (ASPD)
2. Avoidant personality disorder
3. Borderline families
4. Borderline personality disorder (BPD)
5. Dependent personality disorder
6. Dialectical behavior therapy (DBT)
7. Difficult process
8. DSM-5-TR alternative model of personality disorders (AMPD)
9. Five-factor model (FFM)
10. Fragile process
11. Frequency-dependent selection hypothesis
12. Histrionic personality disorder
13. ICD-11 model of personality disorders
14. Levels of personality organization
15. Mania without delusion
16. Moral insanity
17. Narcissistic personality disorder (NPD)
18. Obsessive-compulsive personality disorder (OCPD)
19. Obsessive trait complex hypothesis
20. Paranoid personality disorder
21. Parasuicidal behavior
22. Personality
23. Personality disorder (PD)
24. Personality disorder-trait specified
25. Polypharmacy
26. Psychopathic personalities
27. Psychopathy versus sociopathy
28. Relational-cultural theory
29. Schema therapy
30. Schizoid personality disorder
31. Schizotypal personality disorder (STPD)
32. Self-stigmatization
33. Structured psychodynamic therapies for personality disorders

DISRUPTIVE BEHAVIOR AND ATTACHMENT

13

Photo 13.1
Tom Penpark/Getty Images.

LEARNING OBJECTIVES

After reading this chapter, you should be able to:

1. Distinguish externalizing from internalizing behaviors.

2. Outline DSM and ICD disruptive behavior diagnoses and social connection/attachment diagnoses, as well as discuss critiques of these diagnoses.

3. Describe historical perspectives on attention-deficit hyperactivity disorder (ADHD) and autism.

4. Summarize brain chemistry, brain structure, genetic, evolutionary, and immune system perspectives on disruptive behavior and autism.

5. Explain psychodynamic, cognitive-behavioral, and humanistic psychological perspectives on disruptive behavior and autism.

6. Outline sociocultural and systems perspectives on developmental issues, including how gender, race, socioeconomic status, and stigma influence such issues.

OVERVIEW

13.1 Getting Started: How Do Developmental Problems Impact Behavior?

Case Examples

Mark

Mark is a 9-year-old boy referred for psychological assessment by his school because of disruptive behavior in class. Mark has trouble staying in his seat and regularly interrupts his teacher. He bothers the other kids, finds it difficult to pay attention to his work, and often forgets to do his homework. Mark's parents aren't concerned, although Mark has some of the same problems at home—he fails to complete his chores and is often loud and unruly. "Boys will be boys!" says his father. The school, however, is demanding that something be done.

Sumiko

Sumiko is a 15-year-old girl whose parents take her to therapy. "She's insufferable!" exclaims her mother. "Anything we say, she says the opposite!" Sumiko regularly talks back, refuses to complete chores, and neglects her homework because it is "boring." Like her parents, Sumiko's teachers are flummoxed by her behavior. "She's got a quick temper and argues with me and other kids in the class," says one of her teachers. While Sumiko is perceived as obnoxious, she doesn't skip school, doesn't do drugs, and has never had a run-in with the law. When pressed about her challenging behavior, Sumiko admits that she feels sad and lonely much of the time and has a hard time sleeping.

Michael

Michael is a 15-year-old teen living in a poor part of town. He is repeatedly in trouble. Last month, he was suspended from school for assaulting another student. This month, he was arrested for stealing a car. Despite surveillance video showing him breaking into the car, Michael insists that it wasn't him. Since he was 9 years old, Michael has had little in the way of regular parental supervision. Michael's father is in prison for attempted murder and his mother works two jobs to support Michael and his three younger siblings.

Hernando

Hernando is a 3-year-old boy whose parents take him for a medical evaluation because they are concerned about his development. He rarely makes eye contact, gets extremely agitated if you touch him, and hasn't learned to speak. Hernando's only interest seems to be his collection of toy cars, which he spends hours meticulously arranging and rearranging in neat little rows. Whenever Hernando's daily routine is disrupted, he becomes extremely upset. His parents aren't sure what to do and worry that he won't be ready to enter pre-school in the fall.

Externalizing and Internalizing Behaviors

Externalizing versus internalizing behaviors: Externalizing behavior involve acting out in response to mental distress (e.g., poor impulse-control, rule breaking, physical or verbal aggression); internalizing behaviors do not involve acting out, so are harder to spot (e.g., social withdrawal, loneliness, depression, anxiety, difficulty concentrating).

Disruptive behavior and attachment issues are considered developmental problems because they often first appear in children or adolescents. Their symptoms are typically divided into **externalizing versus internalizing behaviors** (Achenbach, 1966; Achenbach et al., 2016; Bauminger et al., 2010; Samek & Hicks, 2014). *Externalizing behaviors* take internal thoughts and feelings and direct them externally at the environment. They are characterized by poor impulse-control, rule breaking, and physical or verbal aggression. *Internalizing behaviors* are less overt and therefore easier to overlook. They involve emotional experiences like social withdrawal, loneliness, depression, anxiety, and difficulty concentrating. Internalizing behaviors intrude less on others, but this doesn't mean those displaying them are less distressed than externalizers who blatantly act out.

DIAGNOSTIC PERSPECTIVES

13.2 DSM and ICD

Disruptive Behavior

In DSM-5-TR, most disruptive behavior issues (oppositional defiant disorder, conduct disorder, intermittent explosive disorder, pyromania, and kleptomania) are classified as "Disruptive, Impulse-Control, and Conduct Disorders." However, attention-deficit/hyperactivity disorder (ADHD) is grouped with "Neurodevelopmental Disorders" because DSM conceptualizes it as developing in childhood and being neurologically based. Similarly, ICD-11 places ADHD in its "neurodevelopmental disorders" section, oppositional defiant disorder and conduct disorder in its "disruptive behavior and dissocial disorders" section, and pyromania and kleptomania in its "impulse control disorders" section.

Oppositional Defiant Disorder and Conduct Disorder

Oppositional defiant disorder (ODD): DSM and ICD diagnosis for children and adolescents who are angry, argumentative, defiant, and vindictive.

Oppositional defiant disorder (ODD) is diagnosed in children and adolescents who are angry, argumentative, defiant, and vindictive. People with this diagnosis consistently argue with authority figures and disobey rules. They are touchy, quick to anger, and blame others for their own mistakes. ICD-11 includes an "ODD with chronic irritability-anger" subtype, in lieu of a stand-alone disruptive mood dysregulation disorder diagnosis (as found in DSM; see Chapter 5).

Photo 13.2 The Umbrella Project is an art installation in Liverpool, England. The project raises awareness of ADHD, autism, and other DSM and ICD diagnoses grouped under the neurodevelopmental umbrella.
Christopher Furlong/Getty Images.

Conduct disorder (CD) (called *conduct-dissocial disorder* in ICD-11) is more severe than ODD because it also involves serious violations of other people's rights. People considered ODD are merely disobedient and angry, but those diagnosed with conduct disorder engage in more worrisome and frightening behaviors, preying on others in often violent ways. They are physically aggressive, destroy property, lie, steal, and engage in significant rule violations.

Sumiko and Michael

Sumiko might get diagnosed with ODD because she is argumentative and disobeys authority figures. She wouldn't receive a conduct disorder diagnosis because she isn't physically aggressive and doesn't engage in destructive or criminal behavior. Michael, on the other hand, does qualify for conduct disorder because he repeatedly breaks rules and engages in violent behaviors that violate others' rights.

How readily ODD and CD can be differentiated is debated, though they are typically considered distinct disorders (Ghosh et al., 2017; Loeber et al., 2000; Norberg, 2010; R. Rowe et al., 2002). It is often believed that ODD can progress into conduct disorder, but how common this is remains unclear (Husby & Wichstrøm, 2016; R. Rowe et al., 2010). Conduct disorder is not only linked to ODD but also to antisocial personality disorder (ASPD; see Chapter 12). When CD continues past age 18, the diagnosis is often changed to ASPD. Diagnostic Boxes 13.1 and 13.2 contain criteria and guidelines for ODD and CD.

Conduct disorder (CD): DSM and ICD diagnosis for children and adolescents who engage in serious violations of other people's rights (e.g., physical aggression, destroying property, lying, stealing, and engaging in serious rule violations); called *conduct-dissocial disorder* in ICD.

Diagnostic Box 13.1 Oppositional Defiant Disorder (ODD)

DSM-5-TR
- Anger, irritability, and defiance for six months or more, as exemplified by things like losing temper, becoming annoyed easily, being angry and resentful, resisting authority, blaming others, and behaving spitefully or vindictively.
- Symptoms occur daily if under age 5 and at least weekly if over age 5.
- Symptoms can be *mild* (occur in one setting); *moderate* (occur in two settings), or *severe* (occur in three settings or more)

ICD-11
- Uncooperative, defiant, and disobedient behavior that lasts six months or more, as exemplified by things like arguing with adults/authority figures or refusing to obey rules, requests, or instructions.

- May also be irritable, angry, blame others, act vindictively, express resentment, purposely annoy people, behave rudely, or have trouble getting along with others.
- Two subtypes: *without chronic irritability-anger* and *with chronic irritability-anger* (can use the latter as equivalent to DSM-5-TR's "disruptive mood dysregulation disorder").

Information from American Psychiatric Association (2022, pp. 522–523) and World Health Organization (2022).

Diagnostic Box 13.2 Conduct Disorder (CD)

DSM-5-TR: Conduct Disorder
- For at least twelve months, regularly violates others' rights or breaks age-related social norms, as exemplified by aggression toward people or animals (e.g., frequent fights, cruelty to others, or use of weapons), destroying property (e.g., vandalism or fire-setting), lying and/or stealing (e.g., breaking and entering), and regular rule breaking (e.g., running away or cutting school).
- Don't diagnose in people over age 18 who qualify for antisocial personality disorder.
- Specify *mild, moderate,* or *severe.*
- Specify *with limited prosocial emotions* if lacking remorse, empathy, or concern about school or work performance.

ICD-11: Conduct-Dissocial Disorder
- Regularly violates others' rights or breaks age-related social norms, as exemplified by aggression toward people or animals (e.g., frequent fights, cruelty to others, or use of weapons), destroying property (e.g., vandalism or fire-setting), lying and/or stealing (e.g., breaking and entering), and regular rule breaking (e.g., running away or cutting school).
- Occurs over an extended period (e.g., twelve months).

Information from American Psychiatric Association (2022, pp. 530–532) and World Health Organization (2022).

Intermittent explosive disorder: DSM and ICD diagnosis characterized by recurrent aggressive outbursts that are verbal, physical, or both.

Pyromania: DSM and ICD impulse-control disorder that involves purposeful fire-setting that provides pleasure, gratification, or emotional relief but is not done for personal gain.

Kleptomania: DSM and ICD impulse-control disorder that involves impulsive stealing that provides pleasure, gratification, or emotional relief but is not done for personal gain.

Attention-deficit/ hyperactivity disorder (ADHD): DSM and ICD neurodevelopmental disorder involving difficulty sustaining attention, being revved-up and full of excessive energy, and impulsive behavior.

DSM-5-TR cites ODD prevalence estimates ranging from 1 percent to 11 percent with an average of 3.3 percent. Before adolescence, boys are diagnosed a bit more than girls, but after adolescence the prevalence is roughly equal (American Psychiatric Association, 2022). For conduct disorder, worldwide prevalence for children and adolescents is estimated at 8 percent, with higher prevalence among boys (11 percent) than girls (7 percent) (Mohammadi et al., 2021).

Intermittent Explosive Disorder, Pyromania, and Kleptomania

Intermittent explosive disorder is characterized by recurrent aggressive outbursts—verbal, physical, or both. People with this diagnosis become explosively angry when upset. DSM-5-TR reports lifetime prevalence of 4 percent. Onset typically occurs in late childhood or adolescence and very rarely after age 40 (American Psychiatric Association, 2022).

Pyromania and **kleptomania** are two other impulse-control diagnoses in DSM and ICD. The former is characterized by purposeful fire-setting, while the latter involves impulsive stealing. These activities aren't undertaken for monetary gain, vengeance, or to make a political statement. They are performed because they provide a sense of pleasure, gratification, or relief. According to DSM-5-TR, the prevalence for pyromania is unknown. As for kleptomania, it occurs in 4 percent to 24 percent of people arrested for shoplifting but its overall prevalence is rare (0.3–0.6 percent) (American Psychiatric Association, 2022). DSM-5-TR notes that pyromania and kleptomania often emerge during adolescence. It also reports kleptomania being three times more common in women than men. Diagnostic Box 13.3 displays criteria and guidelines.

Attention-Deficit/Hyperactivity Disorder (ADHD)

The hallmark features of **attention-deficit/hyperactivity disorder (ADHD)** are difficulty sustaining attention, being revved-up and full of excessive energy, and impulsive behavior. People with this diagnosis are divided into three types: those whose issue is mainly inattention, those whose issue is mainly hyperactivity-impulsivity, and those who struggle with both inattention and hyperactivity-impulsivity. To meet DSM-5-TR criteria for ADHD, symptoms must be present

Diagnostic Box 13.3 Intermittent Explosive Disorder, Pyromania, and Kleptomania

Intermittent Explosive Disorder
- **DSM-5-TR**: Trouble controlling disproportionate and unjustified aggressive impulses, as exemplified by verbal or physical aggression (at least twice a week for three months or, when directed at people or animals, at least three times in twelve months); usually must be at least age 6 for a diagnosis.
- **ICD-11**: Difficulty controlling aggressive impulses that leads to verbal or physical aggression.

Pyromania
- **DSM-5-TR**: Multiple instances of intentionally setting fires accompanied by emotional arousal before doing so, preoccupation with fire, enjoyment of or relief from fire-setting; no financial or other gain from setting fires, and no psychotic symptoms or judgment issues that lead to setting fires.
- **ICD-11**: Intentionally and repeatedly sets or tries to set fires without a clear motive such as financial gain, revenge, or political goals; preoccupation with fire and strong urges to set fires that are hard to resist or control, along with arousal before lighting fires and relief after doing so.

Kleptomania
- **DSM-5-TR**: Impulsively steals objects one has no need for, with tension right beforehand and enjoyment/relief afterwards; not motivated by anger, revenge, hallucinations, or delusions; must eliminate conduct disorder, mania, or antisocial personality disorder as causes for the stealing.
- **ICD-11**: Intentionally and repeatedly steals objects not wanted for personal use or financial gain; strong urges to steal, along with arousal before doing so and pleasure or relief after doing so.

Information from American Psychiatric Association (2022, pp. 527, 537, 539) and World Health Organization (2022).

before age 12 and occur in at least two settings. Therefore, if a child only displays inattention and hyperactivity at school or if symptoms didn't appear until adolescence or adulthood, then ADHD shouldn't be diagnosed. This is important given concerns about overdiagnosis, discussed more below. DSM-5-TR reports that ADHD occurs worldwide in about 7.2 percent of children and 2.5 percent of adults. Rates among U.S. children are higher (between 8.2 percent and 9.6 percent) and have been increasing since 2000 (Bitsko, 2022). ADHD did not appear in ICD until ICD-11, adopting guidelines that mirror DSM-5-TR criteria (Sklepníková & Slezáčková, 2022). See Diagnostic Box 13.4 for diagnostic details.

Mark
Reexamine the description of our 9-year-old case example client, Mark. Do you think he qualifies for an ADHD diagnosis? Why or why not?

Diagnostic Box 13.4 Attention-Deficit/Hyperactivity Disorder (ADHD)

DSM-5-TR
- Inattention and/or hyperactivity-impulsivity in more than one setting that develops before age 12 and lasts for six months or more.
- *Inattention* involves six of these (five if age 17 or older): (1) inattention to details or careless mistakes; (2) difficulty paying attention; (3) difficulty listening; (4) trouble following instructions or completing work; (5) disorganized; (6) avoids/doesn't like work requiring prolonged mental effort; (7) loses things needed to complete work; (8) easily distracted; (9) forgets to complete chores and errands.
- *Hyperactivity/impulsivity* involves six of these (five if age 17 or older): (1) fidgets or squirms; (2) has trouble staying seated; (3) runs or climbs inappropriately; (4) cannot play quietly; (5) always in motion (6) talks excessively; (7) answers before questions are finished; (8) cannot await turn; (9) interrupts or intrudes on conversations or activities.

Social Connection and Attachment Issues
Autism Spectrum Disorder

Autism spectrum disorder (ASD):
DSM and ICD neurodevelopmental disorder characterized by deficits in communication, social interaction, and comprehending relationships.

Autism spectrum disorder (ASD) is a DSM-5-TR and ICD-11 diagnosis for people who struggle with social interactions, have difficulties with verbal and nonverbal communication, and engage in repetitive and ritualistic behaviors (see Diagnostic Box 13.5). ASD is considered a neurodevelopmental disorder because it first appears in early childhood. According to DSM-5-TR, symptoms typically become noticeable in the second year of life. ASD is diagnosed on a *spectrum* because degree of impairment varies widely. DSM-5-TR specifies one of three levels of severity in social communication and restricted/repetitive behaviors: *requiring support*, *requiring substantial support*, and *requiring very substantial support*. ICD-11 goes further, providing diagnostic codes to distinguish whether there is a co-occurring intellectual disability (which is common in ASD). Global prevalence of ASD is estimated at 0.6 percent (Salari et al., 2022). However, U.S. prevalence is higher (1–2 percent) (American Psychiatric Association, 2022). According to DSM-5-TR, boys are diagnosed with ASD three to four times more often than girls, but girls with ASD are more likely to also show intellectual disabilities (see Chapter 14). ASD is regularly comorbid with other mental disorders—especially anxiety, depression, and ADHD (American Psychiatric Association, 2022). People with ASD are also more likely to identify as transgender or gender diverse (Warrier et al., 2020).

Hernando
Hernando, the 3-year-old boy who doesn't speak, withdraws from social contact, and repetitively lines up his toy cars for hours at a time, would likely be diagnosed with autism spectrum disorder.

Diagnostic Box 13.5 Autism Spectrum Disorder

Social (Pragmatic) Communication Disorder (SPCD)

In addition to ASD, DSM-5-TR includes a relatively new disorder called **social (pragmatic) communication disorder (SPCD)**. This diagnosis applies to individuals who develop difficulties communicating with others early in life. They struggle with basic verbal interactions, such as greeting people and sharing information in a socially appropriate manner. They find it hard to calibrate their communication style to the situation (e.g., speaking too loudly in class or failing to adjust language level when talking to children instead of adults). Following the rules of storytelling, making inferences based on what people say, and understanding subtleties of conversation such as humor, metaphors, and multiple meanings are difficult for them. Basically, SPCD is a diagnosis for people who show social communication problems but not the restricted and repetitive behavior required for ASD (Salari et al., 2022). SPCD is considered a communication disorder, not a form of autism. DSM-5-TR doesn't provide prevalence estimates for SPCD, but other research suggests it is more common than ASD. One study found social-pragmatic skill deficits in 6.1–10.5 percent of children (Saul et al., 2021). ICD-11 includes an analogous but somewhat narrower diagnosis than SPCD called **developmental language disorder with impairment of mainly pragmatic language**. Unlike SPCD, it can only be diagnosed if autism spectrum disorder is ruled out. Nonetheless, the two diagnoses cover many of the same patients. See Diagnostic Box 13.6 for details.

Social (pragmatic) communication disorder (SPCD): DSM-5 neurodevelopmental disorder involving difficulties communicating with others but not restricted/repetitive behavior.

Developmental language disorder with impairment of mainly pragmatic language: ICD-11 disorder characterized by development of communication difficulties early in life; analogous to DSM-5-TR's social (pragmatic) communication disorder (SPCD).

Diagnostic Box 13.6 Disorders of Social (Pragmatic) Communication

DSM-5-TR: Social (Pragmatic) Communication Disorder

- Verbal and nonverbal communication difficulties that begin in early childhood.
- Has hard time with social communication, matching communication to the situation, telling stories, following conversational rules, and inferring what isn't explicitly said.

ICD-11: Developmental Language Disorder with Impairment of Mainly Pragmatic Language

- Ongoing language impairment characterized by things like difficulty making inferences, comprehending humor, or understanding verbally ambiguity.
- Typically develops during childhood.
- Must rule out a diagnosis of autism spectrum disorder.

Information from American Psychiatric Association (2022, p. 54) and World Health Organization (2022).

Evaluating DSM and ICD Perspectives

Pathologizing Rebelliousness and Social Resistance?

Critics argue that diagnoses like ODD, CD, and ADHD improperly turn normal adolescent rebellion and anti-authoritarianism into mental disorders (D. A. Edwards, 2008; Enright, 2022; B. E. Levine, 2005, 2008; Whitley, 2021; Worley, 2014). Had DSM and ICD been around in the past, such critics contend, many important historical figures who resisted authority or didn't pay attention to ideas they found limiting—people like Albert Einstein, Thomas Paine, and Malcom X—might have been wrongly diagnosed with disruptive behavior disorders (B. E. Levine, 2012). For these critics, when social rebellion is treated as an indicator of mental disorder, adaptive and appropriate resistance to oppression is mistakenly pathologized and social change is potentially stifled (D. A. Edwards, 2008; B. E. Levine, 2005, 2008, 2012). They provocatively ask: "Do we really want to diagnose and medicate everyone with 'deficits in rule-governed behavior'" (B. E. Levine, 2012, para. 9)? Whether you think this is a fair question or not tells you something about your take on this issue.

ADHD: Lowered Diagnostic Threshold?

DSM has been criticized for loosening ADHD diagnostic criteria, qualifying more people for a diagnosis (Batstra & Frances, 2012; A. Frances, 2015; Paris et al., 2015; S. Sanders et al., 2019). It did this by raising the age limit for the first appearance of symptoms. In DSM-IV, onset of symptoms had to occur by age 7. However, in DSM-5 and 5-TR, symptoms can begin any time before age 12. In addition to relaxing the age threshold, the number of symptoms required for an adult diagnosis was reduced from six to five (Whitely, 2015). Whether increases in ADHD prevalence are attributable to these criteria changes is unclear. The looser DSM criteria took effect in 2013, but prevalence was steadily rising long before that (see Figure 13.1). However, several studies examining DSM criteria changes suggest that they boosted prevalence anywhere from 11 percent to 65 percent (Ghanizadeh, 2013; Matte et al., 2015; Rigler et al., 2016; Vitola et al., 2017). One recent investigation faulted DSM for not fully researching the impact of looser ADHD criteria, arguing that "changing the definition of health conditions places many people at risk of unnecessary diagnosis and treatment" (S. Sanders et al., 2019, p. 6). Not everyone thinks such criticisms are fair and some provide evidence that the altered criteria have not had much effect (Vande Voort et al., 2014). Clearly, this debate remains unresolved.

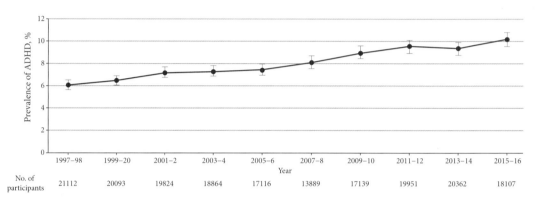

Figure 13.1 Prevalence of Diagnosed Attention-Deficit/Hyperactivity Disorder (ADHD) in U.S. Children and Adolescents, 1997–2016.

Source: Xu, G., Strathearn, L., Liu, B., Yang, B., & Bao, W. (2018). Twenty-year trends in diagnosed attention-deficit/hyperactivity disorder among US children and adolescents, 1997–2016. JAMA Network Open, 1(4), Article e181471.

Is ADHD a Valid Disorder?

Supporters of the ADHD diagnosis cite evidence of its reliability and validity. DSM-5 field trials rated the interrater reliability of ADHD as "good" or "very good" (Regier et al., 2013). Further, a group of prominent practitioners and researchers signed an international consensus statement in 2002 attesting to the validity of ADHD (Barkley, 2002), a sentiment they reiterated in 2021 (S. V. Faraone et al., 2021). Nonetheless, some critics object to the ADHD diagnosis, seeing it as lacking diagnostic validity. They question whether ADHD is a legitimate disorder and contend that it is a scientifically suspect diagnosis unfairly used to justify drugging children who irritate their teachers and parents (T. Armstrong, 1995; M. Quinn & Lynch, 2016; Timimi, 2004, 2015, 2018; Timimi & Leo, 2009; Visser & Jehan, 2009; Whitely, 2015). As one critic explained it, "ADHD is perhaps nothing more than an example of the 'medicalisation' of behaviours in children which are the most annoying and problematic for adults to control" (M. Quinn & Lynch, 2016, p. 62). Another critic put it even more strongly, arguing that "the rapid expansion in the use of culturally constructed diagnoses like ADHD, together with giving children powerful stimulant medications to control their behaviour, is a damning indictment of the position of children in neo-liberal cultures, rather than an indication of scientific progress" (Timimi, 2015, p. 575).

Not all critics have been so adamant. DSM-IV chair turned DSM-5 critic Allen Frances agreed that DSM defines ADHD too loosely and this risks improperly diagnosing some people with it (A. Frances, 2010b, 2012). However, he opposed rejecting ADHD entirely: "We need to tame the epidemic of ADHD, not eliminate the ADHD diagnosis" (A. Frances, 2015, p. 577). This position is echoed in arguments that the real problem is the failure of many doctors to conduct a thorough assessment before diagnosing ADHD, resulting in many careless and incorrect diagnoses (Hinshaw & Scheffler, 2014; Sparrow & Erhardt, 2014). Debate is ongoing between those who question ADHD's validity and those who say ADHD is valid but overdiagnosed. The "In Depth" feature explores another validity issue that plagues ADHD and other developmental diagnoses—namely, the problem of comorbidity.

In Depth: If You Have One Developmental Diagnosis, You Just Might Qualify for Another

Developmental issues consistently co-occur. In other words, they have high degrees of comorbidity. For instance, it has been estimated that 60 percent to 100 percent of ADHD patients are diagnosable with at least one other mental disorder (Gnanavel et al., 2019). Common diagnoses comorbid with ADHD include conduct disorder, oppositional defiant disorder, learning disorders, intellectual disabilities, depression, bipolar disorder, anxiety disorders, disruptive mood dysregulation disorder, tic disorders, and autism spectrum disorder (Bélanger et al., 2018; Gnanavel et al., 2019; Yüce et al., 2015). One review concluded that 42 percent of children with ASD qualify for an ADHD diagnosis, and 30 percent to 50 percent of children with ADHD meet criteria for conduct disorder or oppositional defiant disorder (Gnanavel et al., 2019). Another review cited even higher ADHD comorbidity with ODD and CD—as high as 90 percent (Bélanger et al., 2018)!

What to make of these high comorbidity rates? From the Research Domain Criteria (RDoC) perspective (see Chapter 3), the problem may be that existing developmental diagnostic categories rely on behavior (rather than biological and other rigorously measurable criteria) for making diagnoses and that many of these behavioral criteria overlap or are highly *heterogeneous* (i.e., varied and diverse)—resulting in high comorbidity rates (Cuthbert & Kozak, 2013; Katzman et al., 2017; Musser & Raiker, 2019). Thus, familiar diagnostic categories like ASD, ODD, and ADHD may not reflect the actual disorders that brain research ultimately discovers. Discussing autism, one RDoC researcher remarked: "Under the RDoC framework, the current definition of ASD is a somewhat arbitrary and ill-defined clustering of symptoms that are not necessarily closely related in terms of biology" (Damiano et al., 2014, p. 835). RDoC aims to remedy this problem with research on basic brain processes, from which we might eventually arrive at more valid diagnostic categories defined and assessed using reliable physiological and cognitive assessment measures rather than relying so heavily on observed behaviors, as DSM and ICD currently do (Baroni & Castellanos, 2015; Damiano et al., 2014; F. Levy, 2014).

Critical Thinking Questions

1. Do you think ADHD, ASD, and disruptive behavior disorders are distinct from one another, despite how often they co-occur? Why or why not?

2. If it turns out that 90 percent of children with ADHD also meet criteria for ODD or conduct disorder, then does this mean that kids with ADHD suffer from other behavior disorders at a very high rate, or does it suggest our diagnostic categories are unreliable and/or inadequate? Explain your reasoning.

3. Do you believe the RDoC initiative will produce physiological indicators (i.e., biomarkers) to make developmental diagnoses? If yes, why? If no, why not?

Objections to Eliminating Asperger's

DSM-5 combined three distinct DSM-IV disorders (*autistic disorder*, *Asperger's disorder*, and *pervasive developmental disorder-not otherwise specified [PDD-NOS]*) into today's ASD diagnosis (Cushing, 2018). Some people still lament the elimination of **Asperger's disorder**, which was characterized by milder symptoms than autism proper (L. J. Rudy, 2021). Asperger's involved less impairment in social and cognitive functioning and did not include problems with language acquisition (American Psychiatric Association, 2000a). After it was added to DSM-IV in 1994, prevalence skyrocketed—up to 32.5 million cases by 2015 (T. Vos et al., 2016). A lot of people—including psychiatrist Allen Frances, who oversaw DSM-IV's development—concluded that Asperger's had been defined too loosely, resulting in many false diagnoses (A. Frances, 2010a, 2010b; Steinberg, 2012). This influenced the DSM-5's decision to collapse three unreliable diagnoses (autistic disorder, Asperger's, and PDD-NOS) into one diagnosis, autism spectrum disorder (Cushing, 2018). An extra benefit of this move was that ASD's levels of severity fit the dimensional diagnosis zeitgeist (Happé & Frith, 2020).

Nevertheless, deleting Asperger's from DSM proved highly controversial, especially among those with the diagnosis (L. J. Rudy, 2021). To address this, DSM-5 included a "grandfather clause" that automatically gave ASD diagnoses to people previously diagnosed with Asperger's or PDD-NOS, even if ASD criteria weren't met (Amoretti et al., 2021; I. C. Smith et al., 2015). Consequently, "an individual that would now have no diagnosis at all (because she meets neither the ASD criteria nor the SPCD ones), would still be diagnosed with ASD if she had a DSM-IV diagnosis of Asperger's Disorder or PDD-NOS" (Amoretti et al., 2021, p. 17). This created quite an uproar. Imagine a new discovery changed our understanding of cancer. Would we "grandfather in" people who already had cancer and only apply our fresh knowledge to diagnosing new cases? Unlikely. Is this a fair analogy? You'll have to decide for yourself.

Asperger's disorder: Disorder removed from DSM and ICD that was characterized by impaired social skills, poor communication skills, and restricted interests that develops in early childhood; milder than autism, without significant deficits in language acquisition or cognitive functioning.

Defenders of the grandfather clause say they were balancing science with the practical benefits of allowing people with existing diagnoses to keep them. However, critics believe this has led to unequal treatment, with those grandfathered into an ASD diagnosis able to access autism services unavailable to new patients with the same symptoms but no diagnosis (Amoretti et al., 2021). What to do with past Asperger's and PDD-NOS cases notwithstanding, DSM-5's more stringent ASD criteria promised better diagnostic accuracy and reduced future prevalence. Unfortunately, this promise might not have been fulfilled. Despite DSM-5's more restrictive criteria, ASD prevalence continues to rise. In 2018, 1 in 44 U.S. children were estimated to have ASD (Centers for Disease Control and Prevention, 2022b). It isn't certain whether steadily higher prevalence rates are because increased awareness and improved assessment have yielded more accurate ASD counts, or because autism continues to be overdiagnosed (Happé & Frith, 2020; Kulage et al., 2020). What is clear is that many people continue using "Asperger's" to describe themselves, despite its removal from DSM-5-TR and ICD-11 (Juntti, 2022; L. J. Rudy, 2021). "The Lived Experience" box offers a first-hand account of someone previously diagnosed with Asperger's disorder but who today would be diagnosed with mild autism spectrum disorder.

The Lived Experience: Living with Autism Spectrum Disorder: Anita's Story

Anita Lesko is a nurse anesthetist and a champion for people living with autism spectrum disorder (ASD). Anita is herself an adult living with Asperger disorder who did not receive her diagnosis until she was 50 years old. Read more to learn more about Anita's unique story and what it means to be an adult living with ASD.

A Late Diagnosis

I had never suspected *anything!* I went the first 50 years of my life not knowing why I'm so different, never fit in, wasn't able to make friends, had difficulties with every social interaction, and had "unusual" sensory issues no one else seemed to have.

When I was 50, a co-worker's son was diagnosed with Asperger disorder. I had never heard of Asperger disorder, so I asked her what it was. She handed me some papers about it. The top one showed a list of 12 symptoms, and it said if you have 10 out of 12, then you have Asperger disorder. I had 12 out of 12. It was that exact moment when all the pieces of the puzzle of my life fell into place to create the whole picture. I stopped at the bookstore that very night on my way home from work and purchased every book they had on Asperger disorder. I stayed up all night reading, and by daybreak there was no question in my mind that I had Asperger disorder. Several weeks later, I received my formal diagnosis from a neuropsychologist. It was the greatest gift I had ever received, to *finally* know the answers to the mystery of my life.

Impact of ASD on Daily Life

A specific challenge is coping with change. We LOVE routine! Any deviation from the normal routine used to be unbearable. Since meeting and marrying my husband Abraham (who has ASD), we both have significantly overcome our adversity to change. I am much better able to deal with small changes, and even big changes far greater than ever before.

Another challenge is sensory issues. My extreme sensitivities to light, sound, touch, etc. have greatly improved over my lifetime, but still exist in many forms. I try to have control over them where I can. For example, I will avoid loud restaurants, or ask to be seated in a dimmer area of a restaurant. I have learned to advocate for myself and always encourage others to do the same for themselves.

Unique Advantages of Living with ASD

My gift of Asperger disorder gives me the ability to have what I call my "laser focus." It's the ability to stay focused on a project for extreme periods of time with total focus and concentration. For example, once while in the emergency room for a broken wrist, the anesthesiologist who came to give me sedation started talking to me as we waited. He asked what I was studying in college, to which I replied "nursing." He suggested I become a certified registered nurse anesthetist. My "laser focus" took over, and a year later after receiving my Bachelor of Science in Nursing, I was accepted at Columbia University in their master's degree program for nurse anesthesia. I graduated, passed my board exam, and have been working full time ever since!

People with ASD are also well-noted for having "special interests." I've had several special interests that have taken me to very lofty heights. The most spectacular one is getting a flight in an F-15 fighter jet. I saw the movie "Top Gun" for the first time in 1995, and by the end of the movie I decided I wanted a flight in a fighter jet. I spent the next 7 years working my way to becoming an internationally published military aviation photojournalist. On December 2, 2006, my dream was realized. I received a flight in an F-15 Strike Eagle! It was the most thrilling moment of my life!

Reprinted from https://www.cdc.gov/ncbddd/autism/features/living-with-autism-spectrum-disorder-anita.html

13.3 Other Diagnostic Perspectives on Disruptive Behavior and Attachment Issues

HiTOP and RDoC

HiTOP and RDoC move away from DSM's and ICD's highly comorbid disruptive behavior and attachment categories and instead assess these difficulties dimensionally. HiTOP maps developmental problems like ADHD, conduct disorder, and autism along its externalizing spectrum dimension, consisting of two sub-spectra: *disinhibited externalizing* (impulsive tendencies) and *antagonistic externalizing* (conflictual and hostile behavior) (R. F. Krueger et al., 2021). Importantly, "the HiTOP approach underscores a growing consensus that clinically significant externalizing problems lie on a continuum with normative functioning and maladaptive traits" (R. F. Krueger et al., 2021, p. 185). RDoC research echoes this dimensional emphasis but with a somewhat more biological focus. For example, two RDoC domains (cognitive systems and positive valence; see Chapter 3) are being used to organize understandings of how children with ADHD process information and respond to rewards (Musser & Raiker, 2019). Similarly, all five RDoC domains are being incorporated into brain research on autism, shedding new light on brain structures like the amygdala (Hennessey et al., 2018; K. Ibrahim & Sukhodolsky, 2018). RDoC has not generated much autism research to date, but it is regarded as having a great deal of potential for understanding autism (Mandy, 2018).

PDM

PDM-2 focuses on relational aspects of disruptive behavior and attachment problems. It views ADHD as characterized by self-centeredness and poor insight, oppositional defiant disorder as involving a desire for attention accompanied by feelings such as resentment and self-hatred, and conduct disorder as exemplified by relational indifference to others and impulsivity. PDM's emphasis on subjective experience extends to its discussion of autism. It highlights how "children with ASD are confronted with difficult challenges as they enter adolescence. Separation from the family, construction of a personal identity, opening to social relationships, and access to sexuality are particularly challenging to them" (Lingiardi & McWilliams, 2017, p. 433).

PTMF

PTMF looks at disruptive behavior and attachment problems as meaningful responses to oppressive social circumstances. While it has yet to be widely researched or adopted, some agencies are using it. One, a non-profit youth mental health organization in Ireland, appreciates PTMF's shift from psychiatric to sociocultural explanations: "For young people in general, it was deemed helpful that the PTMF looks at mental health difficulties as related to communities and societies as a whole, rather than being specifically located in the individual" (Aherne et al., 2019, p. 5). Another, an autism and learning disability team in the UK, liked how PTMF's question "What did you have to do to survive?" reframed *autism spectrum condition* (its preferred term for ASD) in terms of meaningful responses to threat:

For example, a person concerned about difficulties taking the perspective of others reframed their recent arguments about politicians excluding minorities as meaningfully related to a personal history of bullying and a lifetime of messages about being different. This formulation connected them with their values for inclusivity and fairness. The PTMF questions helped us to reframe "rigidity" on this subject as an act of creative resistance in response to power. (Flynn & Polak, 2019, p. 43)

HISTORICAL PERSPECTIVES

13.4 History of ADHD

Eighteenth Century: Identifying "Lack of Attention" as a Medical Condition

The German physician Melchior Adam Weikard (1742–1803) is credited with one of the earliest references anticipating ADHD (Schwarz, 2016). In 1775, he identified a condition he called "lack of attention" (*attentio volubilis* in Latin), describing sufferers as "unwary, careless, flighty and bacchanal" (Barkley & Peters, 2012, p. 627). Some treatments Weikard prescribed for lack of attention seem silly today (cold baths, sour milk, steel powder, and horseback riding), but he also recommended exercise, which doctors still encourage (Barkley & Peters, 2012). Two decades later, in 1798, the Scottish physician Sir Alexander Crichton (1763–1856) published a more extensive account of attention difficulties (Schwarz, 2016). Crichton (1798) posited that people can be born with or develop diseases of attention. He felt most children outgrow attention issues by adulthood, an idea that remained popular until the 1990s (K. W. Lange et al., 2010).

Nineteenth Century: Hoffman's "Fidgety Philip"

Numerous historians believe that the German physician and obstetrician Heinrich Hoffmann (1809–1894) was describing ADHD in his 1845 children's book, *Struwwelpeter* (J. Davidson, 2018; K. W. Lange et al., 2010; Schwarz, 2016; Sparrow & Erhardt, 2014; Thome & Jacobs, 2004). Two of the stories, "Fidgety Philip" and "Johnny Look-in-the-Air," portray restless and inattentive boys. However, historians remain divided over whether Hoffman was using the stories to depict attention-deficit problems or whether he was just telling amusing children's parables (K. W. Lange et al., 2010). As one skeptical historian remarked, "textbook histories of hyperactivity show how history can be exploited by interested parties to shape the understanding of a disorder" (M. Smith, 2012, p. 28). That is, we often interpret history through our current prism, imposing present conceptions on past events. See Figure 13.2 for more on Fidgety Philip's unfortunate mealtime predicament.

Early Twentieth Century: Attention Disorders, Lack of Moral Control, and Hyperkinetic Disease

At the turn of the twentieth century, the Scottish physician Thomas Clouston (1840–1915) wrote about what he called attention disorders (M. Smith, 2012). Unlike later notions of ADHD as lifelong, Clouston believed attention disorders generally lasted just a few months. However, anticipating later medical conceptions of ADHD, he believed these disorders were caused by dysfunctions in the cerebral cortex and he treated them with *bromides* (chemical compounds used as sedatives during that era) (M. Smith, 2012).

Die Geschichte vom Zappel-Philipp.

"Let me see if Philip can
Be a little gentleman;
Let me see if he is able
To sit still for once at table."
Thus spoke, in earnest tone,
The father to his son;
And the mother looked very grave
To see Philip so misbehave.
But Philip he did not mind
His father who was so kind.
He wriggled
And giggled,
And then, I declare,
Swung backward and forward
And tilted his chair,

Just like any rocking horse;-
"Philip! I am getting cross!"
See the naughty, restless child,
Growing still more rude and wild,
Till his chair falls over quite.
Philip screams with all his might,
Catches at the cloth, but then
That makes matters worse again.
Down upon the ground they fall,
Glasses, bread, knives forks and all.
How Mamma did fret and frown,
When she saw them tumbling down!
And Papa made such a face!
Philip is in sad disgrace.

Figure 13.2 The Story of "Fidgety Philip" from Heinrich Hoffmann's *Struwwelpeter.*
Source: Culture Club/Getty Images.

British physician Sir George F. Still's (1868–1941) 1902 lectures are viewed as the scientific starting point for modern understandings of ADHD (K. W. Lange et al., 2010). Still described children who suffered from "defects of moral control" (K. W. Lange et al., 2010; Rafalovich, 2004; M. Smith, 2012; Still, 2006). Admittedly, Still's notion of defective moral control was broader than modern ADHD. Many of his cases would be diagnosed with ODD or conduct disorder today, not ADHD (K. W. Lange et al., 2010). Nonetheless, Still's work established that disruptive behavior might be caused by an underlying medical condition. Thirty years later, the German physicians Franz Kramer (1878–1967) and Hans Pollnow (1902–1943) identified a "hyperkinetic disease" in infants and children characterized by extreme physical restlessness (K. W. Lange et al., 2010). Kramer's and Pollnow's work anticipated DSM's and ICD's use of the term "hyperkinetic disorder." It also influenced current descriptions of ADHD, especially the DSM criterion of acting as if "driven by a motor" (K. W. Lange et al., 2010; M. Smith, 2012; Still, 2006).

Discovery of Stimulant Medication to Treat Attention Problems

In 1937, American physician Charles Bradley (1902–1979) gave stimulant medications to neurologically impaired children to treat headaches. The drugs didn't cure the headaches, but—to Bradley's surprise—they improved the children's behavior in school (K. W. Lange et al., 2010; M. Smith, 2012). Bradley found that children with the shortest attention spans benefitted most. In 1954, the stimulant *methylphenidate* was first marketed under the name **Ritalin** (Coghill, 2022). To this day, it remains the most widely used ADHD drug (K. W. Lange et al., 2010; Wenthur, 2016). We revisit stimulant drugs when discussing biological perspectives.

Ritalin: Name under which the stimulant *methylphenidate* is marketed as a treatment for attention-deficit/hyperactivity disorder.

Latter Twentieth Century: From Hyperkinetic Reaction to Attention Deficit Disorder

By the 1960s and 1970s, researchers were studying hyperkinetic (i.e., hyperactive) behavior of children. Hyperactivity was attributed to minimal brain dysfunction that didn't affect overall intelligence but did impact the ability to regulate attention and activity—a hypothesis later criticized for being too broad and lacking evidence (K. W. Lange et al., 2010; M. Smith, 2012). By 1968, DSM-II included *hyperkinetic reaction of childhood*, which became *attention deficit disorder* (*ADD*) in DSM-III. ADD could be diagnosed "with or without hyperactivity" (K. W. Lange et al., 2010). The current diagnostic term, attention-deficit/hyperactivity disorder, was introduced in 1987's DSM-III-R. In the 1990s, the long-held assumption that people outgrew attention problems fell by the wayside. Doctors began diagnosing the disorder in adults as well as children (K. W. Lange et al., 2010; M. Smith, 2012). Thus, adult ADHD is a relatively recent diagnosis.

13.5 History of Autism

Leo Kanner and Autism

The Austrian-American psychiatrist Leo Kanner (1894–1981) is credited with first identifying "infantile autism" (J. P. Baker, 2013; Olmsted & Blaxill, 2016; Verhoeff, 2013; Volkmar & McPartland, 2014; S. Wolff, 2004). He described eleven children whose ability to socially engage was deeply impaired (Kanner, 1943). These children were socially unresponsive and cut off from others. They reacted negatively to changes in their environment and insisted on maintaining sameness. Some of the children also had difficulty with language and communication. Kanner felt autism was often misdiagnosed as schizophrenia. His use of the term "autism" didn't help in this regard because it originally referred to schizophrenia symptoms involving disordered thinking and a retreat from reality (J. P. Baker, 2013; Volkmar & McPartland, 2014). Confusion with schizophrenia notwithstanding, Kanner's description of autism was remarkably astute and continues to influence current conceptions (Verhoeff, 2013; Volkmar & McPartland, 2014).

Hans Asperger and Asperger's Syndrome

The Austrian pediatrician Hans Asperger (1906–1980) wrote a doctoral dissertation on "autistic psychopathy" in children. It was published in 1944, shortly after Kanner's seminal 1943 paper (Lyons & Fitzgerald, 2007). The children Asperger described were often quite capable in math and science but had difficulty with social relationships. They were extremely sensitive, struggled with empathy, engaged in repetitive and ritualistic behaviors, and were clumsy. Learning language wasn't a problem for them, but they often spoke in odd or idiosyncratic ways (Asperger, 1991; S. Wolff, 2004). Asperger believed these symptoms were innate, lifelong, and distinct from autism (Barahona-Corrêa & Filipe, 2016).

Although Kanner and Asperger were contemporaries, they don't seem to have been (at least initially) aware of one another despite numerous coincidences about their work (Barahona-Corrêa & Filipe, 2016). Both men were born in Austria and published on autism within a year of each other, but they never met (Barahona-Corrêa & Filipe, 2016; Lyons & Fitzgerald, 2007). Kanner gets most of the credit for discovering autism, perhaps because he wrote in English and was more systematic in his descriptions (Barahona-Corrêa & Filipe, 2016; S. Wolff, 2004). Asperger's ideas didn't gain widespread attention until popularized by English psychiatrist Lorna Wing (1928–2014), who introduced the term "Asperger's syndrome" in 1981 (Wing, 1981). The term caught on and within a decade or so was added to ICD and DSM. However, as discussed, its reign as a disorder was brief. Incidentally, Hans Asperger's character has been tarnished in recent years by allegations he collaborated with the Nazis during the Second World War (Czech, 2018).

The Refrigerator Mother Theory of Autism

Refrigerator mother theory of autism: Attributed autism to cold and aloof parenting.

In the mid-twentieth century, the **refrigerator mother theory of autism** was popular. Famously advanced by psychoanalyst Bruno Bettelheim (1903–1990), this theory attributed autism to cold and aloof parenting (Bettelheim, 1967). Other prominent figures also promoted the refrigerator theory—including Leo Kanner, although he eventually returned to his original belief that autistic children were born that way (J. P. Baker, 2013; Kanner, 1943, 1949; Kanner & Eisenberg, 1957; M. Waltz, 2013; M. M. Waltz, 2015; S. Wolff, 2004). In 1964, psychologist Bernard Rimland (1928–2006) debunked the refrigerator theory, replacing it with a neurological perspective on autism (Rimland, 1964). The refrigerator hypothesis is almost universally rejected and in disrepute today—as is the reputation of Bruno Bettelheim who, it was posthumously revealed, had faked his educational credentials, plagiarized some of his work, and physically abused emotionally troubled children at the group home he ran at The University of Chicago (Pollack, 1997). Although the refrigerator theory has been discredited, a few psychotherapists—especially in France—still adhere to it. We revisit this under psychodynamic perspectives.

BIOLOGICAL PERSPECTIVES

13.6 Brain Chemistry Perspectives

Disruptive Behavior
The Dopamine Hypothesis of ADHD

Dopamine hypothesis of ADHD: ADHD is caused by impaired dopamine transmission.

The **dopamine hypothesis of ADHD** attributes ADHD to deficits in the transmission of dopamine, the neurotransmitter associated with pleasure, motivation, and attention (F. Levy, 1991; F. Levy & Swanson, 2001; Tripp & Wickens, 2008, p. 2008; Volkow et al., 2009). Researchers favoring the dopamine hypothesis of ADHD note that stimulant medications for ADHD boost dopamine levels (Bukstin, 2022; Connolly et al., 2015; Daughton & Kratochvil, 2009). Thus, even though it is counterintuitive, stimulants are the drug of choice for hyperactivity. However, dopamine isn't the only catecholamine neurotransmitter linked to ADHD; so is norepinephrine (Arnsten, 2006; del Campo et al., 2011; K. E. Knight, 2013). Stimulants prescribed for ADHD increase both dopamine and norepinephrine (Daughton & Kratochvil, 2009; del Campo et al., 2011; F. Levy, 2009). Thus, the dopamine hypothesis of ADHD is sometimes framed more broadly as the **catecholamine hypothesis of ADHD** (del Campo et al., 2011; R. D. Hunt, 2006; Quist & Kennedy, 2001). Critics note that stimulants improve attention and vigilance in everyone, not just people diagnosed with ADHD—making it difficult to know whether the drugs prescribed are correcting a dopamine issue in ADHD patients (Gonon, 2009). Although research on its role has produced inconsistent results, dopamine remains central in ongoing efforts to understand the neurochemistry of ADHD (del Campo et al., 2011, 2013).

Catecholamine hypothesis of ADHD: ADHD is caused by deficits in dopamine and norepinephrine

Drugs Prescribed for ADHD

As noted, stimulants are the most used ADHD medications. However, sometimes other drugs that affect dopamine and norepinephrine are prescribed instead of or in addition to stimulants—especially if stimulants do not work or the patient has a substance use problem (Weyandt et al., 2014). Atomoxetine (trade name *Strattera*), a norepinephrine reuptake inhibitor, is a well-known example of a non-stimulant ADHD drug (Weyandt et al., 2014). See Table 13.1 for a list of common stimulant and non-stimulant ADHD medications. Given their widespread use, do these drugs improve symptoms? In the short-term, yes—with stimulants generally performing better than non-stimulants for both children and adults (Cortese et al., 2018; Pringsheim et al., 2015; Punja et al., 2016). Long-term effectiveness is less clear (Z. Chang et al., 2019; E. Taylor, 2019). There are not many studies of prolonged ADHD medication use, but existing data provides mixed results, with evidence suggesting that many people stop taking their medication and that stimulant effectiveness ebbs after several years (E. Taylor, 2019). Drug side effects like difficulty sleeping, loss of appetite, and stomach pain can also be problems (Castells et al., 2011; Punja et al., 2016; Storebø et al., 2015).

Mark
Nine-year-old Mark is likely to be prescribed Ritalin or another stimulant drug for his diagnosis of ADHD.

Table 13.1 Drugs Commonly Prescribed for ADHD

DRUG(S)	DRUG TYPE	COMMON TRADE NAME(S)
Methylphenidate	Stimulant	Ritalin, Methylin, Concerta, Ritalin, Metadate
Dextroamphetamine (dexamfetamine)	Stimulant	Dexedrine, Adderall*
Lisdexamfetamine	Stimulant	Vyvanse, Elvanse
Atomoxetine	Norepinephrine reuptake inhibitor	Strattera
Guanfacine	Alpha agonist	Tenex, Intuiv
Clonadine	Alpha agonist	Catapres
Bupropion†	Norepinephrine-dopamine reuptake inhibitor antidepressant	Wellbutrin
Desipramine†	Tricyclic antidepressant	Norpramin
Imipramine†	Tricyclic antidepressant	Tofranil
Nortriptyline†	Tricyclic antidepressant	Aventyl, Pamelor

* Adderall contains both dextroamphetamine and amphetamine.
† Not an approved medication for ADHD, but often prescribed "off label."

Are stimulants for ADHD overprescribed? Those who say yes point to the steady increase in ADHD prescriptions around the globe, particularly in the United States (Coghill, 2022; Raman et al., 2018; Sørensen et al., 2022). They also cite misdeeds, like when the mental healthcare company Cerebral became embroiled in scandal for overprescribing ADHD medication (K. Jennings, 2022; B. Miller, 2022). Those who do not think there is an overprescription problem say cases like Cerebral are anecdotal (Children and Adults with Attention-Deficit/Hyperactivity Disorder, 2017). Regardless, ADHD medication is controversial, in part because stimulant drugs are habit-forming (see Chapter 11)—even at the doses used for ADHD (Daughton & Kratochvil, 2009). However, these drugs might not lead to addiction in ADHD patients. Indeed, research suggests ADHD patients who take medication are less prone to substance abuse than those who do not (Z. Chang et al., 2014; P. D. Quinn et al., 2017). Nevertheless, misuse of ADHD drugs is widespread: "Among people aged 12 or older in 2020, 1.8 percent (or 5.1 million people) misused prescription stimulants in the past year" (Substance Abuse and Mental Health Services Administration, 2021, p. 17). For example, many people "borrow" ADHD drugs from friends and family to "cognitively enhance" their performance at school or work (Aikins, 2019; Plumber et al., 2021; Wilens & Kaminski, 2019). The takeaway message is that stimulant use for ADHD and related concerns remains hotly contested (Coghill, 2022).

Conduct Problems

Low serotonin levels seem to play a role in conduct disorder—just as they do in antisocial personality disorder, the adult diagnosis linked to CD (Junewicz & Billick, 2020). Serotonin deficiencies have been tied to aggression more broadly, though results are mixed and the relationship appears more complicated than initially believed (Runions et al., 2019; Tricklebank & Petrinovic, 2019). If low serotonin does contribute to aggression, then people with diagnoses like intermittent explosive disorder and conduct disorder are good candidates for selective-serotonin reuptake inhibitors (SSRIs), especially when their symptoms are accompanied by anxiety and depression (Cremers et al., 2016; Fairchild et al., 2019; Nevels et al., 2010). However, SSRIs pose complications when conduct problems are comorbid with ADHD because SSRIs aren't that helpful for ADHD, especially attention issues (Buoli et al., 2016; Popper, 1997).

Besides SSRIs, stimulants and the norepinephrine-dopamine reuptake inhibitor (NDRI) *bupropion* (see Chapter 9) are frequently prescribed to children and teens with conduct problems; mood stabilizers, anticonvulsants, and antipsychotics are used too (Fairchild et al., 2019; Sarteschi, 2014; Searight et al., 2001; Vaudreuil et al., 2021). However, administering mood stabilizers and antipsychotics to children is controversial due to their potency and side effects (J. S. Bell & Richards, 2021; Nevels et al., 2010; Sparks & Duncan, 2012; R. Whitaker, 2012). Additionally, with the possible exception of the atypical antipsychotic *risperidone*, evidence of their effectiveness is lacking (Gorman et al., 2015; Hambly et al., 2016; Pisano & Masi, 2020; Pringsheim et al., 2015; Sarteschi, 2014). Even risperidone is usually recommended only in the most severe cases (Pringsheim et al., 2015).

> **Michael**
> *Should Michael, the 15-year-old with a conduct disorder diagnosis and a history of aggressive and violent behavior, be prescribed risperidone? Why or why not?*

Autism

Excitatory-Inhibitory Imbalance (E/I) Model of Autism

Excitatory-inhibitory (E/I) imbalance model of autism: Attributes autism to increased ratios of GABA-glutamate neuronally activity. (13)

The **excitatory-inhibitory (E/I) imbalance model of autism** attributes ASD to dysregulation of GABA and glutamate, the brain's respective inhibitory and excitatory neurotransmitters (see Chapter 2). This model hypothesizes that autism is related to an increased ratio of GABA and glutamate activity. Impaired GABA potentially explains why people with autism feel overwhelmed by sensory information. Without sufficient inhibitory GABA signaling, their brains become overstimulated. Research support for the E/I model has been accruing, but many questions remain—including whether increased GABA-glutamate balance can sometimes be protective rather maladaptive (Antoine et al., 2019; Culotta & Penzes, 2020; Gonçalves et al., 2017; S. Maier et al., 2022; Oliveira et al., 2018; Port et al., 2019; Siegel-Ramsay et al., 2021).

Drugs Prescribed for Autism

Drugs interventions for ASD aim to improve behavioral symptoms like temper tantrums, aggression, self-injury, speech issues, lack of attention, and lethargy. As with ADHD, stimulants are used most often (D. M. Coleman et al., 2019). Atypical antipsychotics like risperidone (mentioned previously) and *aripiprazole* are also commonly prescribed (Accordino et al., 2016; Fieiras et al., 2022; Fung et al., 2016; Ghanizadeh et al., 2015; Hirsch & Pringsheim, 2016; Mano-Sousa et al., 2021). Anticonvulsants, mood stabilizers, and SSRIs are other drugs often given to ASD patients (Accordino et al., 2016; D. M. Coleman et al., 2019). Because most of these drugs have significant side effects, many worry about prescribing them to children. For instance, although risperidone and aripiprazole improve ASD symptoms, they also cause weight gain, sedation, drooling, and tremors (Alsayouf et al., 2022; D. M. Coleman et al., 2019; Fieiras et al., 2022; Hirsch & Pringsheim, 2016; Mano-Sousa et al., 2021). Thus, the UK's National Institute for Health and Care Excellence (2021) recommends prescribing antipsychotics for behavioral issues in ASD children only when psychosocial interventions are insufficient. Despite being approved in the United States and the UK for autism, use of atypical antipsychotics in children remains controversial. More broadly, all drugs used for ASD have a mix of benefits and side effects that complicates when and whether to prescribe them (D. M. Coleman et al., 2019).

Hernando

Would you prescribe atypical antipsychotics to 6-year-old Hernando, who is diagnosed with autism spectrum disorder?

To address social withdrawal in autism, investigators are exploring the role of **oxytocin**, an amino acid produced by the hypothalamus that functions as both a neurotransmitter and a hormone. Oxytocin is implicated in prosocial behavior (Geschwind, 2021; Neumann, 2008), with some studies linking low levels of it in children to ASD (John & Jaeggi, 2021; Moerkerke et al., 2021). If so, administering oxytocin might minimize social deficits in ASD. Thus, oxytocin nasal sprays have been developed to reduce social withdrawal in autism. Unfortunately, they have performed somewhat disappointingly in effectiveness studies, though researchers hold out hope for improving them through additional research on ASD and oxytocin (Geschwind, 2021; Y. Huang et al., 2021; D. Martins et al., 2022; Mayer et al., 2021; Sikich et al., 2021).

Oxytocin: An amino acid produced by the hypothalamus that functions as both a neurotransmitter and a hormone; important in sex and reproduction (by stimulating labor and breastfeeding) and in social behavior; administered via nasal spray for ASD.

13.7 Brain Structure Perspectives

Disruptive Behavior

Attention Issues

The precise neuroanatomy of ADHD is unknown (Kimonis et al., 2020; Thapar & Cooper, 2016). However, several findings are worth noting. People with ADHD seem to have smaller total brain volumes, as well as in areas like the prefrontal cortex, cerebellum, corpus callosum, and basal ganglia (Kimonis et al., 2020; T. R. Mehta et al., 2019). Many brain structures have been implicated in ADHD, with some overactive and others underactive. For example, the prefrontal cortex seems to be underactive and also matures later in ADHD patients (Kimonis et al., 2020; T. R. Mehta et al., 2019; Miao et al., 2017). Prefrontal cortex problems make sense given this brain region's central role in *executive functioning* (attention, planning, decision-making, and goal-directed behavior), an area where ADHD patients struggle. Despite promising advances, brain research on ADHD has been criticized methodologically for its small sample sizes and failure to account for use of stimulant medications by study participants (Visdómine-Lozano, 2019). Further, RDoC researchers contend that because ADHD consists of at least two kinds of impairment (inattention and hyperactivity-impulsivity), it should be broken into specific symptom domains and research conducted on the neural basis of each (Baroni & Castellanos, 2015; Musser & Raiker, 2019). This might better identify biological measures for diagnosing attention and impulsivity issues. However, while brain researchers have many leads they consider promising, there are currently no known biological markers for diagnosing ADHD (Thapar & Cooper, 2016).

Conduct Problems

People diagnosed with conduct disorder show reduced activity in brain areas involved in emotional processing activities such as emotional regulation and empathy (Fairchild et al., 2019). This might be because their autonomic nervous systems (which control heart rate, blood pressure, and emotional arousal; see Chapter 7) are under-responsive to fear conditioning (Matthys et al., 2013). If so, this implies that they aren't afraid of punishment and don't learn from it. However, autonomic nervous system differences have not been reliably borne out by research (Oldenhof et al., 2019; Prätzlich et al., 2019). Similarly inconsistent results plague investigations into the stress hormone cortisol. ODD and CD patients having blunted cortisol levels would imply they do not find aversive situations stressful (Cappadocia et al., 2009; Matthys et al., 2013). However, low cortisol, while present in some studies, has not been consistently found (Bernhard et al., 2021; Fairchild et al., 2019; Schoorl et al., 2016). Finally, two brain regions important in emotion and stress—the amygdala and the hypothalamic-pituitary-adrenal (HPA) axis—often (but not always) show decreased or impaired functioning (Cappadocia et al., 2009; Fairchild et al., 2019; Matthys et al., 2013).

Autism

The **early overgrowth hypothesis of autism** links ASD to excessive brain growth during the first two years of development, followed by arrested growth and normal brain volume later (Courchesne, 2004). Research robustly supports the first part of this hypothesis. The brains of young children with ASD are consistently larger than those of their peers (J. K. Lee et al., 2021; Prigge et al., 2021). However, whether the brains of older children and adults return to normal size is less clear (J. K. Lee et al., 2021; Yankowitz et al., 2020).

ASD has long been suspected of being multiple disorders—*autisms* rather than *autism* (Happé & Frith, 2020; Heijden et al., 2021; H. R. Park et al., 2016). If so, this might explain why it has various biological correlates. For instance, the cerebellum—implicated in movement, attention, and language (see Chapter 2), as well as social communication and cognition—appears to develop abnormally in children with autism (Fatemi, Aldinger, et al., 2012; Heijden et al., 2021; Mapelli et al., 2022; T. D. Rogers et al., 2013). The amygdala also seems to play a part, affecting two types of social withdrawal seen in autism: inability to maintain eye contact and difficulty processing faces (Kolevzon et al., 2013; Neuhaus et al., 2010; H. R. Park et al., 2016; Weston, 2019). Other brain regions with possible connections to autism include the caudate nucleus (important in goal-directed activity; see Chapter 4), prefrontal cortex (executive functioning), nucleus accumbens (social rewards), orbitofrontal cortex (decision-making), and insula (basic emotions, self-awareness, and body awareness) (E. Kelly et al., 2020; H. R. Park et al., 2016, 2017; Weston, 2019).

13.8 Genetic Perspectives

Disruptive Behavior

Those who believe ADHD is strongly genetic point to family, twin, and adoption studies. Parents and sibling of children with ADHD are two to eight times more likely to also qualify for a diagnosis (S. V. Faraone & Biederman, 2013). Consistent with this, twin studies have yielded heritability estimates between .70 and .80, making ADHD one of the most heritable mental disorders (Brikell et al., 2015; S. V. Faraone & Biederman, 2013; S. V. Faraone & Larsson, 2019; Thapar & Cooper, 2016). As a quick comparison, the heritability of conduct disorder is around .50—less heritable than ADHD but still considered highly heritable (Salvatore & Dick, 2018).

Genetic markers for ADHD have been difficult to identify. The first genome-wide association study (GWAS) to find significant results appeared in 2019, with a follow-up study currently under review (Demontis et al., 2019, 2022). GWAS research on conduct disorder has yielded similarly meager results, with few studies and only one that identified genetic markers (Tielbeek et al., 2017). More broadly, genes related to dopamine and serotonin are being studied as potentially contributing to externalizing, conduct-related problems (Chhangur et al., 2015; Gard et al., 2019; Janssens et al., 2015). However, a lot more research is needed.

Autism

Twin study concordance rates for autism have varied but generally been high, ranging from 36 percent to 96 percent for identical twins and 0 percent to 23 percent for fraternal twins (Castelbaum et al., 2020; Ronald & Hoekstra, 2014; R. E. Rosenberg et al., 2009). Differences in these estimates may depend on whether autism is defined narrowly or broadly (to include less severe cases) (Ronald & Hoekstra, 2014). Further, even when concordance is high, symptom severity across identical twin pairs varies a lot, suggesting that environment influences how genetic predispositions toward autism are expressed (Castelbaum et al., 2020). This is consistent with recent heritability estimates around .80 (D. Bai et al., 2019; Sandin et al., 2017; Tick et al., 2016). Such estimates suggest a strong genetic component to autism but still mean 20 percent of phenotypic variation is due to environment. As for specific genes, many have been identified as potentially important in autism, though—as with many disorders—results are difficult to replicate (Mpoulimari & Zintzaras, 2022; S. Nisar et al., 2019; Rylaarsdam & Guemez-Gamboa, 2019; Torrico et al., 2017; Z. Wang et al., 2019; Yousaf et al., 2020). ASD appears to have genetic links to other neurodevelopmental disorders, as well as to schizophrenia, anxiety, depression, and immune system functioning (Anney et al., 2017; Arenella et al., 2022; Ghirardi et al., 2021).

13.9 Evolutionary Perspectives

Attention-Deficits and Hyperactivity

Several evolutionary theories of ADHD have been advanced. **Mismatch theories of ADHD** hold that hyperactive-impulsive traits that were advantageous in ancestral times are counterproductive today (Swanepoel et al., 2017). That is, ADHD results from a mismatch between evolved traits and our modern environment. There are numerous examples of mismatch theories. *Hunter-farmer theory* hypothesizes that ADHD traits evolved because they were adaptive for hunters and farmers, who needed to be vigilant (to protect crops) and able to quickly shift gears (to chase prey) (T. Hartmann, 1997; Thagaard et al., 2016). Similarly, *response readiness theory* proposes that short attention spans and hyperactivity-impulsivity were necessary in ancestral environments where threats to safety were extreme and food was scarce (Jensen et al., 1997; Thagaard et al., 2016). *Wader theory* says humans evolved to have less body hair so they could better wade into water in search of food; this lack of hair made clinging to mothers for protection less adaptive, so children able to get maternal attention through hyperactive behaviors were more likely to be breastfed (Shelley-Tremblay & Rosén, 1996; Thagaard et al., 2016). Finally, *fighter theory* holds that hyperactivity and aggression evolved to help early humans battle Neanderthals (Shelley-Tremblay & Rosén, 1996; Thagaard et al., 2016). Mismatch theories are interesting because they reframe hyperactivity and impulsivity as adaptive rather than disordered. Although more studies of mismatch theory are needed (Thagaard et al., 2016), an analysis of genetic markers concluded that "natural selection has been acting against current ADHD-risk alleles for a long time" (Esteller-Cucala et al., 2020, p. 4).

Mismatch theories of ADHD: View hyperactive-impulsive traits as adaptive in ancestral times but not modern industrial societies; *hunter-farmer theory, response-readiness theory, wader theory,* and *fighter theory* are mismatch theories of ADHD.

Autism

It has been hypothesized that people with autism experience **mindblindness** in that they lack the evolved capacity for *theory of mind*, the ability to attribute thoughts and feelings to others by viewing the world through their eyes (see Chapter 4) (Baron-Cohen, 1995). Building on this idea, **extreme male brain (EMB) theory** posits that people with autism are better at *systemizing* than *empathizing* (Baron-Cohen, 2002, 2009; D. M. Greenberg & Baron-Cohen, 2020). Systemizers feel compelled to analyze and construct systems for organizing, predicting, and understanding; empathizers monitor others' behavior and try to respond in an emotionally appropriate way (Baron-Cohen, 2009; D. M. Greenberg & Baron-Cohen, 2020). EMB theory holds that men evolved a tendency toward systemizing (to aid in hunting and developing weapons) over empathizing (which would detract from their ability to kill enemies); women, by contrast, evolved strong empathizing skills (to help them navigate family relationships and childrearing) (Baron-Cohen, 2002, 2009; D. M. Greenberg & Baron-Cohen, 2020; Lindeman, 2020). Critics contend EMB theory perpetuates sexist gender stereotypes and greatly overestimates male–female brain differences (Hauth et al., 2014; Krahn & Fenton, 2012; Kung et al., 2016; Nadler et al., 2019; Perrykkad & Hohwy, 2019). EMB researchers vigorously disagree, arguing that a strong body of evidence supports their theory (D. M. Greenberg et al., 2018; D. M. Greenberg & Baron-Cohen, 2020).

Mindblindness: Idea that people with autism don't have the evolved capacity for *theory of mind*, the ability to view the world through others' eyes and to attribute thoughts and feelings to them.

Extreme male brain (EMB) theory: Posits that people with autism are better at systemizing (a trait more evolved in males) than empathizing (a trait more evolved in females).

13.10 Immune System Perspectives

Inflammation in ADHD and ASD

An increasing number of studies implicate the immune system in ADHD and autistic spectrum disorder. Immune inflammation has been linked to both ADHD and ASD (Misiak et al., 2022; Robinson-Agramonte et al., 2022; Siniscalco et al., 2018; R.-Y. Zhou et al., 2017). One focus of research in this area is the relationship between inflammation and altered gut microbiota. Findings could potentially explain why gastrointestinal symptoms are common in ADHD and ASD (Cenit et al., 2017; Doenyas, 2018; Kalenik et al., 2021; Richarte et al., 2021; M. Xu et al., 2019). We revisit this later when discussing diets for ADHD and ASD. Overall, more evidence is needed, but our understanding of inflammation's role in ADHD and ASD continues to grow (Kalenik et al., 2021; Leffa et al., 2018).

One highly contentious topic related to the immune system is the purported relationship between the measles-mumps-rubella (MMR) vaccine and autism. Does getting the MMR vaccine or other vaccines increase the chances of autism? The "Controversial Question" feature tackles this extremely polarizing issue.

Controversial Question: Do Vaccines Cause Autism?

A 1998 study in the leading medical journal *The Lancet* found a link between the measles-mumps-rubella (MMR) vaccine (typically administered between twelve and fifteen months of age) and the development of autism (A. J. Wakefield et al., 1998). This contributed to the widespread belief that vaccines cause autism. However, the study has been utterly refuted on scientific grounds, with research consistently finding no evidence that the MMR vaccine leads to autism (Demicheli et al., 2012; DeStefano, 2002; DeStefano & Shimabukuro, 2019; Hviid et al., 2019; Jain et al., 2015; Mohammed et al., 2022; L. E. Taylor et al., 2014). Further, the study was retracted by *The Lancet* following allegations that its lead author, Dr. Andrew Wakefield, and several of his co-authors manipulated their data (T. S. S. Rao & Andrade, 2011; "Retraction—Ileal-Lymphoid-Nodular Hyperplasia," 2010). It was also alleged that Wakefield had a financial conflict of interest because he received funding from a group seeking evidence to sue vaccine manufacturers (Deer, 2004; Godlee et al., 2011). In the aftermath of the controversy, Wakefield's medical license was revoked (Boseley, 2010; General Medical Council, 2010).

Despite being fraudulent, Wakefield's study received a lot of media attention, and vaccine skepticism has increased since its appearance (Motta & Stecula, 2021). Health professionals are deeply concerned about this. They warn that when vaccination rates go down, health and financial costs go up (Bruns et al., 2021; C. King & Leask, 2017; A. Norton, 2021; Ransing et al., 2021). Measles alone used to kill hundreds of children every year. A 1964–65 U.S. outbreak of rubella (German measles) was especially bad. It caused 12.5 million infections, 11,000 miscarriages, and the deaths of 2,100 babies (Centers for Disease Control and Prevention, 2020c). Nonetheless, anti-vaccine sentiment remains strong and extends beyond the MMR vaccine, as vividly illustrated by heated debate over the COVID-19 vaccine (Q. Chen & Crooks, 2022; F. K. Cheng, 2022; Pullan & Dey, 2021). As more parents have declined to vaccinate their children, previously vanquished diseases like measles and polio have begun reappearing (Dimala et al., 2021; H. Larkin, 2022; Locklear, 2022; Mandavilli, 2022; National Institute of Allergy and Infectious Diseases, 2019; Rochford, 2022). Still, many people—including prominent celebrities and social media influencers—remain apprehensive about vaccines (Benoit & Mauldin, 2021; D. Cohen, 2022; Dickson, 2019; Gravelle et al., 2022). Controversy over vaccines is unlikely to end any time soon. However, when it comes to the MMR vaccine and autism, researchers are confident that there is no connection.

Critical Thinking Questions

1. Why, despite so much evidence against the vaccine–autism connection and the debunking of the original study showing such a link, do you think that some people continue to believe the MMR vaccine can cause autism?
2. Has the media perpetuated the vaccine–autism link, as some researchers believe?
3. Is the controversy over the MMR vaccine and autism to blame for hesitancy about other vaccines, such as those for polio and COVID-19?
4. Is it fair to compare debunked evidence about the MMR vaccine and autism to more recent debates about the safety of the COVID-19 vaccine? Why or why not?

Autoimmune disease hypothesis: Proposes a link between autoimmune diseases and neurodevelopmental disorders like ADHD and ASD.

Autoimmune Issues in ADHD and ASD

The inflammatory hypothesis is deeply entwined with research on the **autoimmune disease hypothesis**, which proposes that there is a connection between a family history of autoimmune disease and neurodevelopmental disorders like ADHD and ASD. Some studies support this, finding ADHD and ASD patients and their family members are more likely to have autoimmune conditions such as rheumatoid arthritis, type 1 diabetes, celiac disease, ulcerative colitis, asthma, eczema, and allergies (Hegvik et al., 2022; Hughes et al., 2018; Keil et al., 2010; Schans et al., 2017; S. Wu et al., 2015). Due to the correlational nature much of this research, the precise role of autoimmune issues in ADHD and ASD remains unclear.

Viral theory of autism: Children with autism are more likely to have had mothers who had a (usually severe) viral or bacterial infection during pregnancy.

Viral Theory of ASD

The **viral theory of autism** proposes that children with autism are more likely to have mothers who had a (usually severe) viral or bacterial infection during pregnancy (Hisle-Gorman et al., 2018; Jash & Sharma, 2022; H. Jiang et al., 2016; Ornoy et al., 2016; H. R. Park et al., 2016; Shuid et al.,

2021; Zawadzka et al., 2021). This hypothesis is reminiscent of the viral theory of schizophrenia (see Chapter 4), which linked schizophrenia to maternal viral infections. The fact that investigators are studying similar viral theories for both autism and schizophrenia is interesting given that some symptoms of autism and schizophrenia overlap (Chisholm et al., 2015; Volkmar & Cohen, 1991). Because ASD risk is mostly tied to maternal infections requiring hospitalization, some worry that the COVID-19 pandemic (and the severe illness it often causes) will result in more women birthing children with ASD (Askham, 2022).

While most research to date has focused on autism, the viral theory has also been extended to other neurodevelopmental disorders like ADHD (Magnus et al., 2022). Notably, infections during pregnancy are not the only prenatal factors linked to ASD in offspring. Substance abuse and prescription medication use are also implicated (Hisle-Gorman et al., 2018). Maternal immune activation of any kind seems to increase the risk of the mother's proinflammatory cytokines crossing the placenta and affecting the fetus (Zawadzka et al., 2021).

13.11 Evaluating Biological Perspectives

Biological perspectives provide intriguing ways of thinking about developmental issues, but they aren't without critics. One challenge for biological perspectives is that biomarkers for making diagnoses have yet to be discovered. For example, there is no specific test for ADHD (Mayo Clinic, n.d.). According to one biological perspective detractor, "no child labeled as ADHD has met a medical standard that confirms the existence of a specific pathology connoting the disease. It can't be done because no such standard exists" (Olsen, 2012, p. 53). In other words, despite much tantalizing brain research, we currently cannot diagnose ADHD and other disruptive behavior issues biologically. Perhaps because of this, some critics worry that we too often inappropriately attribute such problems to biology (Ophir, 2019, 2021; Worley, 2014).

Similarly, while developmental problems are suspected of being highly heritable, some believe the evidence is frequently overstated. For example, one prominent critic contends that ADHD twin studies improperly make the *equal environments assumption* (see Chapter 4), erroneously assuming monozygotic and dizygotic twins experience identical environments even though identical twins (who look the same) are more likely to be treated similarly than fraternal twins (who don't) (J. Joseph, 2000). In ignoring this, we minimize environmental factors and overestimate genetic ones (J. Joseph, 2000). In a similar vein, this same critic concludes heritability estimates for autism are grossly inflated and should only be estimated at 37 percent (Joseph, 2012),

Finally, a lot of biological perspective research is correlational. We have not yet identified precise causal connections between physiological factors and developmental problems. Thus, critics assert that when it comes to problems like ADHD, biological viewpoints tend to overstate the belief that it is primarily biological (Gonon et al., 2011; Ophir, 2019, 2021). Criticisms notwithstanding, biological hypotheses are highly compelling and will continue to influence how we conceptualize and treat developmental issues.

PSYCHOLOGICAL PERSPECTIVES

13.12 Psychodynamic Perspectives

Disruptive Behavior

From a psychodynamic perspective, disruptive behavior reflects unconscious conflicts and/or attachment difficulties. Oppositional defiance, conduct issues, and other disruptive behavior problems have been linked to poor early childhood attachment relationships (J. P. Allen et al., 1996; S. G. Craig et al., 2021; Ding et al., 2020; Esmaeilpour et al., 2016; Guttmann-Steinmetz & Crowell, 2006; Madigan et al., 2007; M. Nowak et al., 2013; Theule et al., 2016; Waters et al., 1993). In other words, children who lack secure attachments to caregivers are more likely to develop disruptive behavior problems.

Regarding ADHD specifically, some psychodynamic conceptions are consistent with attachment perspectives. For instance, relational psychodynamic therapies view ADHD as tied to disturbed early parent–child interactions and attachment trauma (F. Conway, 2012, 2014, 2015; F. Conway et al., 2019; Laidlaw & Howcroft, 2015; Salomonsson, 2004; Sapountzis, 2020). In a slightly different vein, other psychodynamic approaches to ADHD emphasize ego functioning. Recall that in psychoanalytic theory, the ego is governed by the reality principle; the ego tries to fulfill id impulses based on what's practical and possible. From an ego psychology perspective, ADHD is attributable to a dysfunctional ego—which is why executive functioning is impaired (F. Conway, 2012; K. Gilmore, 2000, 2002). In psychodynamic therapies, therapists work with transference and countertransference issues in session (F. Conway, 2014, 2015; Laidlaw & Howcroft, 2015; Salomonsson, 2004; Sapountzis, 2020).

A psychodynamic case study provides a vivid example of interpreting transference (F. Conway, 2014). Jason, a 10-year-old boy diagnosed with ADHD, begins climbing on the furniture. When he nearly falls, the therapist asks him to stop climbing. Jason responds that she is no fun, to which the therapist replies, "Being expected to follow the rules when you are feeling the need to do something about your 'boredom' may seem to benefit me more than you" (F. Conway, 2014, p. 108). When Jason agrees, the therapist responds by saying "I believe I now understand how difficult it has been for you" (F. Conway, 2014, p. 108), then adds "Can you describe other times that you have experienced being bored and how you handled it?" This is a nice example of the therapist using the dynamic between herself and Jason to explore how Jason feels and behaves in other relationships. Transference issues are explored to help Jason share his own feelings, which reduces his need to express those feelings through disruptive behavior. Evidence for psychodynamic therapies for disruptive behavior mainly consists of case studies like this one. However, a small number of experimental studies also provide support for them (Gatta et al., 2019; Laezer, 2015; Stavrou, 2019). Additional research would be helpful.

Autism

Given their past tendency to blame "refrigerator mothers," psychodynamic perspectives on autism remain controversial. Not surprisingly then, psychoanalysis for autism is rare. One place where it remains influential is France (Bishop & Swendsen, 2021; Borelle et al., 2019; Houzel, 2018). However, there has been a strong backlash against this—with parents, autism advocacy groups, and behavior therapists lambasting psychoanalysis' continued use with autistic patients (Bishop & Swendsen, 2021; Castel, 2022; Chrisafis, 2018; Houzel, 2018; Schofield, 2012). Some psychoanalysts counter that viewing ASD strictly as a brain dysfunction to be managed through medication and behavioral conditioning overlooks key relational conflicts underlying the disturbance (Castel, 2022; Houzel, 2018). Others take a more moderate stance, accepting ASD as a neurodevelopmental brain disorder but viewing parent–child interactions as important in how it develops (Emanuel, 2015; Giannopolou et al., 2019; Sherkow et al., 2014). They use psychoanalysis to help ASD patients become more relationally attuned, thus improving perspective-taking and social skills. Rather than blaming parents, these psychoanalysts tend to see themselves as "sensitive translators" who decode and convey to parents what ASD children are thinking and feeling (Emanuel, 2015; Giannopolou et al., 2019; Grinberg & Zahavi, 2020; Sherkow et al., 2014). There is little research on psychoanalysis for autism, mostly case studies. Thus, psychodynamic perspectives remain controversial and on the fringes of autism treatment.

13.13 Cognitive-Behavioral Perspectives

Disruptive Behavior

Behavior Therapy for ADHD

Behavior therapies are probably the most well-regarded interventions for ADHD. Behavior modification techniques such as contingency management (see Chapter 11) are often used, which involve analyzing and then altering the environment to reinforce desired behaviors and ignore or discourage undesired ones (Waschbusch & Waxmonsky, 2015). In school settings, this might involve "developing specific and concrete rules for the child to follow, developing a system for tracking rule adherence and rule violations, and developing positive and negative consequences that are contingent on the child's performance during school" (Waschbusch & Waxmonsky, 2015, p. 399). Behavior therapies for ADHD have fared well in studies examining their effectiveness, resulting in them being recommended as empirically supported interventions (Fabiano et al., 2009; Hodgson et al., 2014; Staff et al., 2021; Vallerand et al., 2014; Waschbusch & Waxmonsky, 2015). While beneficial in the short term, it is not clear how well they work in the long term (Rajeh et al., 2017; Waschbusch & Waxmonsky, 2015). Further, not all kids respond to behavior therapies, though this might be because they are often poorly implemented (Waschbusch & Waxmonsky, 2015). Still, behavior therapies are considered highly effective for ADHD, perhaps equally or more effective than medication (S. Baldwin, 1999; Pelham et al., 2014, 2016; Rajeh et al., 2017).

CBT for ADHD

Cognitive-behavioral therapy (CBT) for ADHD combines cognitive and behavioral techniques. Common interventions include social skills training (teaching clients to read social cues and respond accordingly), **problem-solving skills training** (teaching planning, organization, and management skills), psychoeducation (teaching clients about how ADHD influences them so they can better implement cognitive strategies for overcoming it), and cognitive restructuring (helping clients better identify and reduce automatic, negative thoughts and cognitive distortions) (J. A. He & Antshel, 2016; Knouse & Fleming, 2016; J. T. Mitchell et al., 2013; Puente & Mitchell, 2016; J. R. Ramsay, 2017; Sprich et al., 2010; Storebø et al., 2011). Research suggests classic CBT improves ADHD symptoms (Fullen et al., 2020; Z. Young et al., 2020). There is also evidence (though less of it) that dialectical behavior therapy and mindfulness interventions are effective with ADHD (Fullen et al., 2020).

> **Problem-solving skills training:** Type of behavioral skills training that teaches planning, organization, and management skills.

CBT and Other Disruptive Behaviors

There is minimal research on using CBT to treat ODD, kleptomania, pyromania, and intermittent explosive disorder. The small body of existing evidence is encouraging but highly preliminary (Battagliese et al., 2015; A. M. Costa et al., 2018; R. S. Johnson & Netherton, 2016; Kohn, 2014). More research is needed.

Autism

Applied Behavior Analysis (ABA)

Applied behavior analysis (ABA) uses behavioral principles to understand how, on a case by case basis, environmental stimuli condition behavior in patients with developmental disabilities (Vismara & Rogers, 2010). The goal of ABA, which is often implemented in school or residential settings, is to condition alternative behaviors. **Discrete trial training (DTT)** is a highly structured type of ABA used for autism. It teaches concrete skills in a step-by-step manner using reinforcement and other behavioral techniques (Sigafoos et al., 2019). When DTT is used with patients under age 5, it is called **early and intensive behavioral intervention (EIBI)** (Klintwall & Eikeseth, 2014; Vismara & Rogers, 2010). As its name implies, EIBI aims to intervene early in the child's life (before age 5) and intensively (twenty to forty hours per week) (Vismara & Rogers, 2010).

DTT and EIBI involve taking complex skills that people with autism often struggle with and dividing them into concrete subskills, which are then intensively taught to patients using behavioral learning strategies. For example, social skills training might be employed in which social interactions are broken into specific skills, such as making eye contact, listening to what the other person says, and speaking in turn. Children are reinforced for mastering these subskills and combining them into more complex behaviors. For children with more limited language skills, the **Picture Exchange Communication System (PECS)** can be used, in which the child learns to communicate using picture cards (Bondy & Frost, 2002; Vismara & Rogers, 2010). The number of controlled studies isn't that large and some have methodological shortcomings, but research does suggest DTT, EIBI, PECS, social skills training, and other ABA interventions are effective in treating autism (Almurashi et al., 2022; Klintwall & Eikeseth, 2014; Reichow et al., 2018; Sigafoos et al., 2019; D. P. Smith et al., 2021; T. Smith & Iadarola, 2015; Virues-Ortega et al., 2022). Nonetheless, ABA methods are occasionally criticized for putting ASD children through demanding and unpleasant drills that try to change them (DeVita-Raeburn, 2016). Opponents believe ABA pathologizes ASD instead of encouraging self-acceptance (DeVita-Raeburn, 2016; McGill & Robinson, 2020; Wilkenfeld & McCarthy, 2020). Do you agree with these criticisms or think ABA teaches ASD children necessary life functioning skills?

> **Applied behavior analysis (ABA):** Uses behavioral principles to understand how environmental stimuli have conditioned a given individual's behavior, with the resulting knowledge used to change the environment and condition alternative behaviors.

> **Discrete trial training (DTT):** Applied behavior analysis (ABA) technique for working with developmental issues that teaches concrete skills in a step-by-step manner using reinforcement and other behavioral techniques.

> **Early and intensive behavioral intervention (EIBI):** Version of discrete trial training (DTT) used with patients under age 5.

> **Picture Exchange Communication System (PECS):** Applied behavior analysis (ABA) technique for children with communication difficulties in which the children learn to communicate using picture cards.

Hernando

Hernando, the 3-year-old ASD patient, undergoes EIBI until he turns 5, when he enrolls in a special school for autistic children. He then begins DTT. During his DTT sessions, approved forms of communication and social interaction are positively reinforced, while problematic behaviors are ignored. For instance, when Hernando averts his gaze from his DTT instructor, the instructor asks him to look at her. When he does, the therapist positively reinforces this by praising him and giving him a Cheerio to eat. Over the course of many DTT sessions, Hernando's social interaction skills improve.

Cognitive-Behavioral Therapy (CBT)

CBT is employed to reduce anxiety and depression in people with autism. It is often adapted for ASD patients and used to help them overcome communication difficulties, problems with tolerating change and uncertainty, and alexithymia (difficulty identifying and expressing emotions; see Chapter 8) (Spain et al., 2015; Spain & Happé, 2020). CBT perspectives often try to account for **weak central coherence theory**, which holds that people with ASD prefer focusing on parts, not wholes (Happé & Frith, 2006). This anxiety-provoking cognitive emphasis on details over the more global picture helps explain why those with ASD often struggle to see the forest through the trees (Happé & Frith, 2006). To reduce depression and anxiety, CBT teaches ASD patients to minimize cognitive distortions, while also behaviorally emphasizing concrete skill development. CBT improves anxiety symptoms in ASD but the strength and duration of its effects are unclear (Perihan et al., 2020). Interestingly, ASD children undergoing CBT rate it as less beneficial than do their parents and therapists (S. Sharma et al., 2021).

13.14 Humanistic Perspectives

Person-Centered Perspectives
Child-Centered Play Therapy for Externalizing and Internalizing Problems

Child-centered play therapy (CCPT), also called *person-centered play therapy*, is used for both externalizing and internalizing childhood problems, including disruptive behavior issues and autism (J. L. Cochran et al., 2010, 2011; Paone & Douma, 2009; Ray et al., 2012; VanFleet et al., 2010). Pioneered by psychologist Virginia Axline (1947a, 1947b, 1950, 1964), it adapts Carl Rogers' (1951, 1959) non-directive person-centered therapy (PCT) for use with children (see Chapter 2 for a refresher on PCT). Child-centered play therapists rely on carefully selected toys, games, sandboxes, arts and crafts, and other play activities as the means for children to express feelings and work through issues (Ray et al., 2013). Consistent with the person-centered tradition, the child-centered play therapist provides core conditions for change by being genuine, empathic, and unconditionally accepting of the child (Behr et al., 2013; Bratton et al., 2009; Ray & Jayne, 2016; VanFleet et al., 2010). This is believed to promote the child's innate tendency toward growth and self-actualization (Behr et al., 2013; Ray & Jayne, 2016). This description of therapy with a 6-year-old autistic boy named Andrew captures how different CCPT is compared with behavioral interventions:

Andrew's increased desire to be in relationship with the play therapist was not the result of being rewarded for staying on task or demonstrating particular play behaviors but because he was open to receiving the acceptance and unconditional positive regard offered by the play therapist, demonstrating his intrinsic motivation. (Ray et al., 2012, p. 172)

Humanistic therapists are skeptical of diagnostic labels like ADHD, oppositional defiant disorder, conduct disorder, intermittent explosive disorder, and even autism—which they see as judgmental and often scientifically unsupported diagnoses reflecting the medicalization of human conflicts and differences (J. E. Davis, 2021; Dowling, 2006; D. A. Edwards, 2008; B. E. Levine, 2005; M. Quinn & Lynch, 2016; Rutten, 2014; Worley, 2014). Instead, child-centered play therapy relies on a nonjudgmental relationship that accepts children for who they are and assumes that providing core conditions will naturally foster change (Axline, 1947b; Behr et al., 2013; Ray & Jayne, 2016). Research

---

Weak central coherence theory:
Holds that people with autism prefer focusing on parts, not wholes; thus, they cognitively emphasize details over the more global picture.

Child-centered play therapy (CCPT):
Combines play and person-centered therapy's core conditions for change (genuineness, empathy, and unconditional positive regard) to address children's developmental issues; also called *person-centered play therapy*.

on CCPT in educational and clinical settings points to its effectiveness for disruptive behavior problems and autism (Bratton et al., 2013; Dillman Taylor et al., 2021; Faramarzi, 2021; Hillman, 2018; M. M. Parker et al., 2021; Ray et al., 2015). However, as with other humanistic therapies, the body of research is small and further studies are needed (Hillman, 2018; M. M. Parker et al., 2021).

Hernando

Photo 13.3
cottonbro studio/Pexels.

Child-centered play therapy with 5-year-old ASD client, Hernando, would involve the therapist trying to enter and understand Hernando's world. Although Hernando might not initially engage much with the therapist, she would use reflective listening to empathize with him. If Hernando neatly lined up his toy cars in a row, she could say, "now they're just how you want them." If Hernando handed her several of his toy cars, she might respond, "you want me to play, too." The goal would be to help Hernando tap into his innate need for connection and personal growth by accepting him as he is.

From "Autism" to "Autistic Process"

Humanistic therapists caution against seeing autism as something unacceptable that must be changed (Ray et al., 2012; Rutten, 2014). Many prefer to speak of **autistic process**, not autism spectrum disorder (A. Robinson & Elliott, 2017; A. Robinson & Kalawski, 2022; Rutten, 2014). In this line of thinking, people with autistic process experience the world differently from *neurotypicals* (people without autism or other neurodevelopmental diagnoses), but they are not broken or ill: "If we view autism through a lens of deficit, dysfunction and impairment, we run the risk of being dismissive of parts of autism that the person appreciates or values" (Olinger, 2021b, p. 47). Humanistically speaking, although "clients with autism may have a qualitatively different process, there is nothing 'wrong' with that and it does not need 'fixing'" (Rutten, 2014, p. 84). Because they do not see autistic process as disordered, humanistic therapists do not try to cure it. Rather, they foster emotional awareness, self-understanding, and self-acceptance in autistic process clients (A. Robinson & Elliott, 2017; A. Robinson & Kalawski, 2022; Rutten, 2014). When more severe communication difficulties are present, pre-therapy (a variant of person-centered therapy used for psychosis; see Chapter 4) can be used (Rutten, 2014; P. M. Whitehead & Purvis, 2021). Research on person-centered approaches to autistic process remains underdeveloped (Rutten, 2014).

Autistic process:
Term used by those who see autism as a way of processing and responding to the world but not a disorder.

Narrative Therapy

Narrative therapy (see Chapter 2) emphasizes externalizing the problem, in which clients reframe problems as entities outside themselves that sometimes get the best of them (M. White & Epston, 1990). Identifying times when they resisted the problem highlights solutions for coping with it. Narrative therapy can be used to assist those with developmental diagnoses like ADHD, oppositional-defiant disorder, conduct-disorder, and autism (Cashin, 2008; Cashin et al., 2013; P. Douglas & Rice, 2021; Ingamells & Epston, 2014; J. Johnson, 2012; McGuinty et al., 2012; Monteiro, 2021; Nylund & Corsiglia, 1996; Olinger, 2021b, 2021a). For example, a case study of Justin, an Asperger's client with an explosive temper, described how he externalized his anger as "the bang" (Cashin, 2008). Justin was asked to keep a diary in which he mapped times when "the bang" snuck up on him. He and his therapist then wrote a letter to the school asking them to assist Justin in keeping "the bang" in check. As Justin and his school cooperated in finding exceptions (times they outsmarted "the bang" and kept it from influencing Justin), Justin's angry outbursts decreased. Though there is very little research on narrative therapy for disruptive behavior, one study showed it improved the school behavior of 9- to 11-year-old girls diagnosed with ADHD (Yoosefi Looyeh et al., 2012). It has also been found to enhance children's social and emotional skills (Beaudoin et al., 2016, 2017). Additional research would be helpful.

13.15 Evaluating Psychological Perspectives

Behavior Therapy versus Drugs for ADHD

Among psychological interventions for ADHD, cognitive-behavior therapies have the most research support (Anastopoulos et al., 2020; Champ et al., 2021; Fabiano et al., 2015; López-Pinar et al., 2018; Waschbusch & Waxmonsky, 2015). Many consider them a viable alternative to medication, especially those concerned about giving stimulant medications to children. There is evidence that behavior therapies for ADHD are equally as effective, or more so, than drugs (S. Baldwin, 1999; Pelham et al., 2014; M. Weiss et al., 2012). In fact, providing behavioral treatment prior to medication may be better than starting with medication (Pelham et al., 2016). It might make lower doses of medication necessary (Coles et al., 2020). Further, some studies suggest CBT alone works as well as CBT with medication (Weiss et al., 2012). However, other studies find drugs more effective or that psychological interventions do not add much (E. Chan et al., 2016; Corbisiero et al., 2018; Sonuga-Barke et al., 2013). Behavior therapies are more time-consuming and complicated to administer, so medications have the advantage of being quick and easy to provide. Still, for those who disapprove of prescribing stimulants to kids, behavior interventions are preferable. You will need to resolve the therapy versus drugs debate for yourself. Whatever you conclude, remember that neither is a cure-all. When withdrawn, symptoms tend to return (Waschbusch & Waxmonsky, 2015). Therapy might have an advantage here. After therapy ends, improvements last for a year, but how well they last beyond that is unclear (López-Pinar et al., 2018).

Psychological Therapies for Autism

Most research on psychological interventions for autism focuses on ABA and CBT approaches. While these interventions can be beneficial, the research base remains small (Bishop-Fitzpatrick et al., 2013; Klintwall & Eikeseth, 2014; Kodak & Grow, 2011; Reichow et al., 2018; Virues-Ortega et al., 2022). One promising study found that the effects of EIBI with young children last until adolescence (D. P. Smith et al., 2021). As with many psychological interventions for ASD, more studies are needed.

SOCIOCULTURAL PERSPECTIVES

13.16 Cross-Cultural and Social Justice Perspectives

Cultural and Social Influences
Culture Bias, Gender Bias, and Inequality

Sociocultural theorists are interested in how factors like gender, race, culture, and economic inequality influence or lead to the developmental issues many children face. They ask a variety of provocative questions challenging conventional understandings that overlook social influences on childhood issues. Some examples:

- Why are boys diagnosed with ADHD, conduct problems, and autism more than girls? Is this due to prevalence differences or gender bias in diagnosis (Abell & Dauphin, 2009; Haney, 2016; Slobodin & Davidovitch, 2019)?
- Why is ASD more common among those from socially deprived or immigrant backgrounds (Delobel-Ayoub et al., 2015; Morinaga et al., 2021; Sohn, 2017)?
- Why are racial and ethnic minorities less likely to have their autism identified (Burkett et al., 2015; Schmengler et al., 2021)?
- Why are rates of ADHD higher and steadily increasing in the United States (Bitsko, 2022; Bluth, 2018; G. Xu et al., 2018)? Are U.S. youth intrinsically more hyperactive or does American culture affect ADHD diagnostic rates?

Sociocultural perspectives argue that biological and psychological approaches, while useful and important, downplay the extent to which developmental issues are impacted by or reflect social customs and cultural values. One suspected social factor? A short-attention span culture that discourages patience and prolonged attention by operating at an increasingly frenetic pace while simultaneously demanding enhanced performance, attention, and productivity (T. Armstrong, 1995; Schwarz, 2016). Other suspected social factors include problematic parenting, boring classrooms, lack of physical activity, sleep issues, too much screen time, the rise of social media, and a breakdown in social hierarchies (T. Armstrong, 1995; Hari, 2022; M. M. Hill et al., 2020; P. S. Tandon et al., 2019). To a sociocultural sensibility, addressing these social issues would result in fewer internalizing and externalizing problems.

Reframing Developmental Disorders as Social Constructions

Unlike those who accept biological and psychological conceptions but want social factors to be weighted more heavily, other sociocultural theorists push in a more thoroughly social direction. Some of these theorists see developmental disorders not as biological or psychological givens, but as social constructions—socially shared ways of defining, talking about, and understanding things that establish how people experience them (see Chapter 2). In the social constructionist view, medicalized childhood diagnoses like ADHD, ODD, conduct disorder, and ASD are contestable culturally rooted social inventions, not universal disorders (Chiri et al., 2022; Danforth & Navarro, 2001; Mallett, 2006; Rafalovich, 2004; M. Smith, 2012; Timimi & Timimi, 2015). When children behave in ways deemed "disruptive," we rely on taken-for-granted Western social constructions that attribute problematic behaviors to something biologically or psychologically broken inside people. The result? Socially constructed diagnostic categories are treated as universally true things, rather than culturally derived understandings that reflect the social and political commitments of those who invented them. For example, many Western societies are committed to the Protestant work ethic, in which people are expected to direct focused time and energy toward reaching high levels of achievement. Such societies "might well be expected to define deviance in terms of distractibility, impulsiveness, and lack of motivation," making the socially constructed notion of ADHD "a means through which our society attempts to preserve its underlying value system" (T. Armstrong, 1995, p. 27). From a social justice viewpoint, when social constructions are mistaken for universal truths, oppression often results. Disruptive behavior problems are conceptualized as illnesses, rather than interpersonal or political conflicts (Rafalovich, 2004). Consequently, the individual unfairly becomes the target of intervention instead of social problems like poor parenting, bad schools, and a short attention-span culture. As one stern critic of medical models of ADHD and other disruptive behavior problems explained it, "what better way to maintain the status quo than to view inattention, anger, anxiety, and depression as biochemical problems of those who are mentally ill rather than normal reactions to an increasingly authoritarian society" (B. E. Levine, 2012, para. 18)?

Sumiko and Michael

A social justice perspective might conceptualize Sumiko's "ODD" as a socially constructed label that reflects cultural biases against girls who are assertive rather than compliant. Sumiko's refusal to do as she is told might be her way of resisting social norms that demand deference. Similarly, a social justice perspective might deconstruct 15-year-old Michael's "conduct disorder," viewing the diagnosis as a convenient way to lay blame on Michael rather than on broader social forces such as racism and economic inequality that have denied Michael the support he needs to develop in more prosocial ways. Social justice-oriented therapy with Sumiko and Michael would help them better understand—and resist—oppressive social norms and restrictions while challenging the idea that their problems are strictly due to individual deficits.

Environmental Factors
Environmental Toxins

Environmental toxin hypotheses posit that developmental difficulties like ADHD, conduct disorder, and ASD are associated with exposure to pollution and other environmental toxins (Dietrich, 2010; Lanphear, 2015; Pugsley et al., 2022). For example, ADHD has been linked to a variety of

Environmental toxin hypotheses: Attribute developmental difficulties in children to pollution and other environmental toxins.

toxins—such as lead, Bisphenol A (a synthetic compound in some plastics), phthalates (chemicals that make plastics durable), flame retardants, pesticides, mercury, and polycyclic aromatic hydrocarbons (chemicals given off when burning coal, oil, gas, wood, garbage, and tobacco) (S. Moore et al., 2022; J. R. Roberts et al., 2019). ASD has also been linked to toxins, including air pollution, herbicides, and heavy metals like lead and mercury (C.-K. Lin et al., 2021; Modabbernia et al., 2017; Pugsley et al., 2022). Environmental toxin research has methodological limitations, is difficult to replicate, and is correlational so causes cannot be inferred (Braun et al., 2014; Hamblin, 2016; Modabbernia et al., 2017; van Wijngaarden et al., 2017). Still, if environmental pollutants do contribute to developmental issues, then we face a social justice issue in which preventing toxin exposure might reduce the prevalence of internalizing and externalizing problems (Koger et al., 2005). Economic inequality is also important here because environmental toxin exposure appears greater among people of low socioeconomic status (Brailsford et al., 2018; Padula et al., 2018; Tyrrell et al., 2013).

Diet

Food additives hypothesis: Food additives lead to ADHD; the *Feingold Diet* eliminates food additives to reduce ADHD symptoms.

Excessive sugar-intake hypothesis: ADHD symptoms are caused or made worse by too much intake of refined sugars.

Polyunsaturated fatty acids (PUFA) hypothesis: ADHD is caused or exacerbated by polyunsaturated fat deficiencies.

A variety of dietary hypotheses about ADHD have been proposed. The **food additives hypothesis** contends that additives in food, such as synthetic food coloring, lead to ADHD (M. Smith, 2011, 2019). Thus, in the *Feingold Diet*, food additives are eliminated from the diets of children diagnosed with ADHD (Schnoll et al., 2003; M. Smith, 2011, 2019). In a similar vein, the **excessive sugar-intake hypothesis** holds that ADHD symptoms are caused or made worse by eating too much refined sugar (Schnoll et al., 2003). Diets based on this hypothesis restrict sugar consumption. Finally, the **polyunsaturated fatty acids (PUFA) hypothesis** proposes that ADHD is caused or exacerbated by PUFA deficiencies (Gillies et al., 2012; Hawkey & Nigg, 2014). Thus, the dietary solution is to increase PUFA intake. The evidence base for these diets is mixed. Some investigations connect food additives to ADHD but others conclude the link is tenuous (Kirkland et al., 2022; K. W. Lange et al., 2022; Rambler et al., 2022; Sambu et al., 2022). Similarly, certain studies tie sugar consumption to childhood and adolescent ADHD and conduct problems, while others do not (Del-Ponte et al., 2019; Ghanizadeh & Haddad, 2015; R. J. Johnson et al., 2021; Y. Kim & Chang, 2011; Lien et al., 2006; C.-J. Yu et al., 2016). Finally, some but not all studies suggest PUFA diets improve ADHD symptoms (Banaschewski et al., 2018; J. P.-C. Chang et al., 2018, 2019; Gillies et al., 2012; Hawkey & Nigg, 2014; Millichap, 2014; Sonuga-Barke et al., 2013; Stevenson et al., 2014).

> **Mark**
> *Should Mark's parents have concerns about stimulant medication, they could explore whether dietary changes might reduce his ADHD symptoms.*

Gluten/casein-free diet hypothesis: A diet low in *gluten* (proteins in wheat) and *casein* (a protein in milk) can reduce autism symptoms.

Regarding autism, the **gluten/casein-free diet hypothesis** maintains that a diet low in *gluten* (proteins in wheat) and *casein* (a protein in milk) can reduce ASD symptoms (Baspinar & Yardimci, 2020; Elder, 2008). This hypothesis posits that when the gut fails to fully breakdown foods high in gluten and casein, high levels of opioid peptides result. These peptides enter the bloodstream, cross the blood–brain barrier, and negatively affect neural transmission, leading to autism symptoms (Baspinar & Yardimci, 2020; Elder, 2008). Researchers disagree about the effectiveness of a gluten/casein-free diet for ASD, but skepticism outweighs enthusiasm (Baspinar & Yardimci, 2020; Piwowarczyk et al., 2020; Quan et al., 2022). The PUFA diet used for ADHD is also sometimes used for autism, but—as with ADHD—there is not much research support for it (De Crescenzo et al., 2020; Veselinović et al., 2021). Despite their weak evidence base, many parents of children diagnosed with ASD swear by these diets.

13.17 Service User Perspectives

Stigma

People diagnosed with developmental issues often experience stigma (Bisset et al., 2022; Botha et al., 2022; Ferrie et al., 2020; E. Han et al., 2022; Turnock et al., 2022). Their parents and families often feel stigmatized, too (Broady et al., 2017; Liao et al., 2019; P. T. Nguyen & Hinshaw, 2020). This is called **courtesy stigma** (or *associative stigma*) and it involves being stigmatized simply by being associated with a family member with a developmental issue or other stigmatized problem (Alareeki et al., 2019; Dikeç et al., 2022; Mitter et al., 2019; P. T. Nguyen & Hinshaw, 2020; Thibodeau & Finley, 2016). For example, the parents of autistic children often feel judged, rejected, and unsupported (Broady et al., 2017). As one parent put it, "we lost a lot of friends because no one wants to hang out with people with a baby that's screaming and yelling and bashing against the wall" (Broady et al., 2017, p. 229). When it comes to developmental issues, stigma is often a family affair. However, developmental diagnoses do not always have purely negative consequences. They can also provoke self-discovery by providing a framework for understanding one's experiences (Botha et al., 2022; Linton, 2014).

Courtesy stigma: Stigma or disapproval due to being associated with a stigmatized individual; also called *associative stigma*.

Identity and Asperger's

When DSM-5 removed Asperger's in 2013, many self-declared "Aspies" were upset (Annear, 2013; S. Jones, 2020; Rosin, 2014). The diagnosis had helped them create a large and supportive community: "With an Asperger's diagnosis, people felt enormous relief at finally being understood, and many don't want to give up that identity" (Cohen Marill, 2019, para. 15). Opponents of eliminating the diagnosis "worry that some people with Asperger's-like attributes will return to the ambiguous space they once occupied—too well-functioning to be diagnosed on the autism spectrum, but still in need of significant support" (Cohen Marill, 2019, para. 8). Despite its removal from DSM and ICD, the term continues to provide many people a sense of identity. For instance, six years after Asperger's was removed from DSM, climate activist Greta Thunberg tweeted: "I have Aspergers and that means I'm sometimes a bit different from the norm. And—given the right circumstances—being different is a superpower" (Cohen Marill, 2019; Thunberg, 2019). To what extent should communal identification with a diagnosis influence its scientific status? Is determining the validity of disorders like Asperger's the exclusive purview of psychiatric researchers or do the views of service users count, too?

13.18 Systems Perspectives

Systems perspectives attribute disruptive behavior less to individual mental disorders and more to social systems. As one representative example, **multisystemic therapy (MST)** has been used to address externalizing behaviors. MST was developed for juvenile offenders and is used for oppositional, conduct, and other externalizing behavior problems (Zajac et al., 2015). It sees disruptive behaviors as determined by the multiple social systems in which children and adolescents function: home, school, peer groups, and neighborhoods (Henggeler, 2011; Swenson et al., 2005; Zajac et al., 2015). MST identifies factors in these social systems that contribute to (i.e., are "drivers" of) disruptive behaviors. Clients and families are encouraged to devise ways of altering each system so that disruptive behaviors are reduced (Henggeler & Borduin, 1990; Swenson et al., 2005; Zajac et al., 2015). Because different systems require different solutions, MST employs a variety of interventions. It uses CBT to target problematic family member behaviors and intensive family therapy to remedy troublesome family dynamics, with clients frequently visited at home to make it easier for them to receive services. More systemically, MST incorporates *neighborhood-based projects* to address community issues that contribute to disruptive behavior. Neighborhood-based projects involve working with local politicians, community and business-leaders, the police, and community members to collaboratively identify and address neighborhood issues that contribute to disruptive behavior (Swenson et al., 2005). Thus, MST intervenes on individual, family, and community levels to reduce disruptive behaviors. A comprehensive review found some support for MST but concluded the evidence was inconsistent across studies (Littell et al., 2021).

Multisystemic therapy (MST): Sees disruptive behavior problems as determined by multiple social systems (home, school, peer groups, and neighborhoods) and uses individual, family, and community-level interventions to remedy them.

Michael

MST for Michael, the 15-year-old diagnosed with conduct disorder, would involve his entire family. An MST therapist would make regular visits to Michael's house and would work with him, his mother, and his siblings. His mother might be taught parenting skills to help her parent more effectively. Family therapy might help Michael and his family alter problematic family dynamics that have contributed to Michael's conduct problems. More broadly, the MST therapy team might initiate a neighborhood-based project that brings all the major stakeholders together to address issues in the schools and larger community that contribute to conduct problems like Michael's. The project might identify ways to improve community–police relations, while also developing an after-school program for at-risk youth that give children and adolescents somewhere to go after school when their parents are still at work.

13.19 Evaluating Sociocultural Perspectives

Sociocultural perspectives emphasize the importance of culture, gender, socioeconomic conditions, family dynamics, and social stigma in developmental issues. Still, critics argue such perspectives underestimate individual factors such as genetics. Sure, social factors influence how we understand problems like ADHD and autism, but heritability estimates for these diagnoses are consistently high, implying a strong genetic component (Grimm et al., 2020; S. Nisar et al., 2019; Rylaarsdam & Guemez-Gamboa, 2019; Salvatore & Dick, 2018). To critics of purely social explanations, this establishes ADHD and autism as more than just social constructions.

When it comes to treatment effectiveness, few healthcare professionals believe that addressing dietary, environmental, and family influences alone is sufficient for alleviating developmental issues. From a biological perspective, psychosocial interventions (e.g., social advocacy, stigma-reduction, individual therapy, and family therapy) merely help manage what are neurological disorders. In this critique, psychosocial approaches play second fiddle to biological ones. They offer beneficial support services that supplement brain-based explanations. Nonetheless, those from a sociocultural viewpoint continue to argue that developmental issues emerge from a social context and that paying attention to social factors is critically important.

CLOSING THOUGHTS

13.20 Neurodiversity

Neurodiversity: Emphasizes that those carrying diagnoses like autism and ADHD are neurologically different, not disordered.

How do we know what constitutes "normal" development? When do worrisome childhood behaviors—such as resisting authority, breaking rules, being socially uncommunicative, struggling to pay attention, or feeling overwhelmed by environmental stimulation—reflect underlying disorders rather than socially unacceptable behavior (i.e., deviance)? Even when deviant childhood behaviors can be tied to neurological factors, how do we know what is neurologically normal? In recent years, there has been a growing emphasis on **neurodiversity**—the idea that those carrying diagnoses like autism and ADHD are neurologically different, not disordered. Neurodiversity advocates stress appreciating (rather than changing) those whose brains function differently. To them, conditions like autism and ADHD are better thought of as gifts, not disorders (Honos-Webb, 2005; S. Silberman, 2015). They argue that "instead of viewing this gift as an error of nature … society should regard it as a valuable part of humanity's genetic legacy" (S. Silberman, 2015, p. 470). There are efforts to integrate neurodiversity and medical model perspectives, based on the idea that we should treat disabling aspects of autism, ADHD, and other neurological differences but avoid pathologizing people:

Photo 13.4 Deviant childhood behaviors don't necessarily reflect underlying disorders or "abnormality," and many people see neurodivergence as positive.
Keren Fedida/Unsplash.

What is attractive about the neurodiversity model is that it doesn't pathologize and focus disproportionately on what the person struggles with, and instead takes a more balanced view, to give equal attention to what the person can do .... But to encompass the breadth of the autism spectrum, we need to make space for the medical model too. (Baron-Cohen, 2019, p. 32)

To what extent do you prefer a neurodiversity versus disorder orientation, and is it possible to balance these contrasting ways of thinking about developmental issues?

CHAPTER SUMMARY

Overview

- *Externalizing behaviors* direct thoughts and feelings at the environment.
- *Internalizing behaviors* involve privately experienced emotions like depression or anxiety.

Diagnostic Perspectives

- DSM-5-TR and ICD-11 consider *oppositional defiant disorder (ODD)*, *conduct disorder (CD)*, *intermittent explosive disorder*, *pyromania*, and *kleptomania* as disruptive behavior disorders.
- *Attention-deficit/hyperactivity disorder (ADHD)* and *autism spectrum disorder (ASD)* are grouped as neurodevelopmental disorders in DSM-5-TR and ICD-11. DSM also includes *social (pragmatic) communication disorder (SPCD)*, while ICD contains a similar diagnosis called *developmental language disorder with impairment of mainly pragmatic language*.
- DSM and ICD are criticized for pathologizing rebelliousness, making ADHD too inclusive, and eliminating Asperger's disorder.
- HiTOP and RDoC are developing dimensional measures to address comorbidity issues among DSM and ICD developmental diagnoses.
- PDM emphasizes relational issues in diagnosing childhood disorders, while PTMF depathologizes childhood problems by emphasizing sociocultural context.

Historical Perspectives

- The earliest Western references to "lack of attention" as a disorder are traceable to the late eighteenth and nineteenth centuries.
- During the twentieth century, amphetamines were discovered as a treatment for lack of attention and medical conceptions evolved from "lack of moral control" to "hyperkinetic disease" to current notions of ADHD.
- Leo Kanner and Hans Asperger were the first to describe children who today would be placed on the autism spectrum.
- The *refrigerator mother theory of autism* was popular during the first half of the twentieth century but has been largely replaced by neurological explanations.

Biological Perspectives

- Dopamine and catecholamine hypotheses have been put forward for ADHD. Stimulants and other drugs that affect dopamine and norepinephrine are commonly prescribed.
- Low serotonin is implicated in CD and aggression more generally and various drugs are prescribed to improve symptoms.
- Glutamate-GABA dysregulation is suspected of playing a part in ASD. Drugs are often used to curb aggressive behavior and/or improve prosocial behavior.
- Brain volume is often diminished in ADHD and the prefrontal cortex (responsible for executive functioning) is believed to be underactive. CD is linked to reduced activity of brain areas tied to emotional regulation and empathy.
- The *early overgrowth hypothesis of autism* says ASD is tied to excessive brain growth during the first two years of life.
- ADHD and ASD appear highly heritable, though genetic markers are difficult to identify.
- *Mismatch theories* are evolutionary theories to explain ADHD, whereas *extreme male brain (EMB) theory* offers an evolutionary explanation of autism.
- Inflammation, autoimmune disorders, and maternal viral infections are being studied for possible links to ADHD and ASD.

Psychological Perspectives

- Psychodynamic perspectives see disruptive behaviors as expressions of unconscious conflicts and use relational therapy techniques to help children and adolescents resolve such conflicts.
- Psychodynamic approaches to ASD are rare today, though still popular in France.
- CBT approaches address developmental issues using behavior modification techniques and cognitive interventions, with *problem-solving skills training* one example. *Applied behavior analysis* is commonly used to treat ASD.
- *Weak central coherence theory* says people with ASD focus on parts, not wholes.
- *Child-centered play therapy (CCPT)* and *narrative therapy* are humanistic interventions used with disruptive behavior issues and autism.
- There is disagreement about whether drugs or therapy are preferable for ADHD.

Sociocultural Perspectives

- The roles of culture bias, gender bias, and inequality in developmental issues are often overlooked.
- Sociocultural perspectives often reframe developmental disorders as social constructions.
- Environmental toxins and dietary factors are suspected of playing significant roles in developmental issues like ADHD and ASD.
- Developmental issues carry stigma for those diagnosed with them, as well as *courtesy stigma* for the family and friends of those diagnosed with them.
- Although Asperger's was eliminated from DSM and ICD, the diagnosis still provides many people with a strong sense of identity.
- *Multisystemic therapy (MST)* combines individual, family, and community-level interventions to alter systems that foster and propagate disruptive behavior.

Closing Thoughts

- *Neurodiversity* is the idea that people with neurodevelopmental diagnoses are different, not disordered.
- Efforts to integrate neurodiversity perspectives with medical model understandings are ongoing but difficult.

NEW VOCABULARY

1. Applied behavior analysis (ABA)
2. Asperger's Disorder
3. Attention-deficit/hyperactivity disorder (ADHD)
4. Autism spectrum disorder (ASD)
5. Autistic process
6. Autoimmune disease hypothesis
7. Catecholamine hypothesis of ADHD
8. Child-centered play therapy (CCPT)
9. Conduct disorder (CD)
10. Courtesy stigma
11. Developmental language disorder with impairment of mainly pragmatic language
12. Discrete trial training (DTT)
13. Dopamine hypothesis of ADHD
14. Early and intensive behavioral intervention (EIBI)
15. Early overgrowth hypothesis of autism
16. Environmental toxin hypotheses
17. Excessive sugar-intake hypothesis
18. Excitatory-inhibitory (E/I) imbalance model of autism
19. Externalizing versus internalizing behaviors
20. Extreme male brain (EMB) theory
21. Food additives hypothesis
22. Gluten/casein-free diet hypothesis
23. Intermittent explosive disorder
24. Kleptomania
25. Mindblindness
26. Mismatch theories of ADHD
27. Multisystemic therapy (MST)
28. Neurodiversity
29. Oppositional defiant disorder (ODD)
30. Oxytocin
31. Picture Exchange Communication System (PECS)
32. Polyunsaturated fatty acids (PUFA) hypothesis
33. Problem-solving skills training
34. Pyromania
35. Refrigerator mother theory of autism
36. Ritalin
37. Social (pragmatic) communication disorder (SPCD)
38. Viral theory of autism
39. Weak central coherence theory

COGNITIVE, COMMUNICATION, AND MOTOR PROBLEMS

Photo 14.1
Jason Leung/Unsplash.

LEARNING OBJECTIVES

After reading this chapter, you should be able to:

1. Distinguish DSM and ICD definitions of intellectual and learning disabilities, as well as the history of intellectual disabilities.

2. Summarize biological, psychological, and sociocultural perspectives on intellectual and learning disabilities.

3. Identify DSM and ICD motor disorder diagnoses and discuss the history of Tourette's syndrome.

4. Describe these perspectives on Tourette's syndrome: biological (genetics, immune system dysfunction, and treatments), psychological (behavior and cognitive therapies), and sociocultural (the impact of stigma).

5. Describe DSM and ICD communication disorder diagnoses.

6. Explain these perspectives on stuttering: biological (the roles of genes, dopamine, and drug interventions), psychological (cognitive-behavioral and constructivist therapies), and sociocultural (the impact of stigma).

7. Summarize DSM and ICD perspectives on delirium and dementia, as well as the history of Alzheimer's disease.

8. For Alzheimer's dementia, outline biological perspectives (the Amyloid hypothesis, genetic influences, and drugs used), psychological perspectives (cognitive and behavioral therapies), and sociocultural perspectives (day care and long-term care plus cultural factors).

OVERVIEW

14.1 Getting Started: Neurodevelopmental and Neurocognitive Issues

This chapter examines presenting problems that DSM and ICD consider "neurodevelopmental" or "neurocognitive." Neurodevelopmental issues begin in infancy or childhood, whereas neurocognitive ones typically occur as people grow older. Some of the developmental and attachment issues from Chapter 13 are considered neurodevelopmental (e.g., ADHD, autism spectrum disorder). This chapter covers additional problems that DSM and ICD classify as neurodevelopmental (intellectual and learning difficulties, motor problems, and communication problems), as well as ones identified as neurocognitive (delirium and dementia).

INTELLECTUAL AND LEARNING DIFFICULTIES

Case Examples: Intellectual and Learning Difficulties

Yolanda

Yolanda is a 22-year-old female born with Down syndrome. Her intellectual functioning is much lower than most people her age. She has an IQ of 48, according to a standardized intelligence assessment, which is significantly below the average of roughly 100. Yolanda lives with her parents, but they worry about what will become of her when they grow old and are no longer physically or financially able to care for her.

Alfred

Alfred is a 10-year-old boy who struggles in school. He dislikes reading and isn't good at it. Standardized assessments find that his reading proficiency is well below where it should be for a boy his age. The kids in school tease him for being "stupid" and his teachers worry about his increasingly angry and disruptive classroom behavior. Despite his poor reading skills, Alfred's IQ is in the average range. He functions well outside of school, as evidenced by the fact that he was chosen captain of his travel football team.

Photo 14.2
Adrià Crehuet Cano/Unsplash.

14.2 DSM and ICD Perspectives on Intellectual and Learning Difficulties

Intellectual Development Disorder

Intellectual development disorder (IDD): DSM and ICD diagnosis involving deficits in intellectual and adaptive functioning that emerge early in development; also called *intellectual disability.*

In DSM-5-TR and ICD-11, **intellectual development disorder (IDD)** is characterized by deficits in intellectual and adaptive functioning that emerge early in a child's development. IDD is diagnosed by assessing intelligence (using intelligence tests; see Chapter 3), as well as by evaluating impairment in everyday functioning. Typically, children qualify for IDD if their intelligence quotient (IQ) is below 70, which is substantially lower than the average IQ of 100 (two standard deviations lower, for those of you with knowledge of statistics). See Chapter 3 for more on IQ score ranges. IDD is divided into four types: *mild* (IQ 50–69), *moderate* (IQ 35–49), *severe* (IQ 20–34), and *profound* (IQ less than 20) (Bhaumik et al., 2016). Both IQ score and level of adaptive functioning are used to determine severity. Individuals with mild and moderate IDD are usually able to live on their own and hold down skilled or semiskilled jobs. People with severe IDD require daily supervision and assistance, while those with profound IDD need help with the basic tasks like feeding themselves, walking, talking, and getting dressed. DSM-5-TR estimates that 10 out of every 1,000 people suffer from IDD. See Diagnostic Box 14.1 for criteria and guidelines. Note that DSM-5-TR recognizes *intellectual disability* as another name for IDD but no longer uses the term *mental retardation* because of its derogatory connotations (Martínez & Nellis, 2020).

Specific learning disorder (SLD): DSM diagnosis involving lower than expected academic performance in reading, writing, spelling, or math that begins during early school years and is not due to intellectual development disorder; called *developmental learning disorder* in ICD.

Yolanda

Yolanda's IQ of 48 combined with her inability to live independently of her parents or other adult supervision qualify her for an intellectual development disorder diagnosis.

Diagnostic Box 14.1 Intellectual Developmental Disorder (DSM-5-TR)/Disorder of Intellectual Development (ICD-11)

- Intellectual deficits.
  - Struggles to problem-solve, think abstractly, plan effectively, make sound judgments, perform in school, and learn from mistakes.
  - Functioning is two or more standard deviations below average.
- Diminished adaptability to everyday demands.
- Onset occurs early in development.
- Specify: *mild, moderate, severe,* or *profound.*
- DSM-5-TR notes this disorder is also referred to as *intellectual disability.*

Information from American Psychiatric Association (2022, pp. 37–38) and World Health Organization (2022a).

Learning Disorders

Specific learning disorder (SLD) is the DSM-5-TR diagnosis for children who exhibit difficulty learning and performing in school (see Diagnostic Box 14.2). It is called *developmental learning disorder* in ICD-11. Children who qualify for SLD diagnoses have trouble with reading, writing, spelling, and math. Their academic performance is substantially below expectations for their age. Importantly, SLD differs from IDD in that SLD does not involve deficits in intellectual and adaptive functioning. DSM and ICD list three main types of SLD: *with impairment in reading, with impairment in writing,* and *with impairment in mathematics.* People diagnosed with the impaired reading type show problems with comprehension; or they struggle to decode (i.e., recognize, decipher, or spell) words—a problem known as **dyslexia** (Adlof & Hogan, 2018; Shaywitz, 1996; Snowling & Hulme, 2012; Tunmer & Greaney, 2010). The impairment in math type, characterized by difficulty processing and calculating numbers, is often called **dyscalculia** (G. R. Price & Ansari, 2013). As for prevalence, DSM-5-TR says learning disorders affect 5 percent to 15 percent of school-age children. Reading, writing, and math SLDs are highly comorbid with one another, as well as with developmental diagnoses like ADHD and autism (Crisci et al., 2021; I. Ibrahim, 2020; Moll et al., 2014; Morsanyi et al., 2018; Willcutt et al., 2019). To what extent this is because learning disorders are better conceptualized dimensionally rather than categorically or because terms like dyslexia are used imprecisely remains unclear (Gibbs & Elliott, 2020; L. Peters & Ansari, 2019). The "Controversial Question" feature examines how best to assess learning disorders.

Dyslexia: Learning disorder that involves difficulty decoding information when reading; characterized by trouble recognizing, deciphering, or spelling words.

Dyscalculia: Learning disorder that involves impairment with mathematics; difficulty processing and calculating numbers.

Diagnostic Box 14.2 Specific Learning Disorder (DSM-5-TR)/Developmental Learning Disorder (ICD-11)

- Difficulties with learning or academic skills, as evidenced by academic skills that are significantly below what is expected for one's age and that interfere with performance at work, school, or in everyday life.
- The problem develops during school years but may not become apparent until academic demands exceed skills.
- Cannot be due to an intellectual disability, uncorrected vision or hearing problem, other mental/neurological disorders, socioeconomic adversity, lack of proficiency with language used in school, or poor-quality schooling.
- Duration:
  - **DSM-5-TR**: One or more for six months or longer: (1) incorrect or slow reading requiring extensive effort; (2) trouble with reading comprehension; (3) poor spelling; (4) poor writing; (5) trouble with understanding or calculating numbers; (6) difficulty solving math problems.
  - **ICD-11**: No duration specified; academic limitations can be limited to one skill or affect all reading, writing, and math skills.
- Specify:
  - **DSM-5-TR**: *with impairment in reading, with impairment in written expression,* or *with impairment in mathematics.*
  - **ICD-11**: *with impairment in reading, with impairment in written expression, with impairment in mathematics,* or *other specified impairment in learning.*

Information from American Psychiatric Association (2022, pp. 76–78) and World Health Organization (2022a).

IQ-achievement discrepancy model: Uses discrepancies between IQ scores and achievement scores to diagnose learning disorders.

Alfred

Alfred, the 9-year-old boy who struggles in school with reading, but who has an average IQ, might be diagnosed with specific learning disorder with impairment in reading.

Controversial Question: How Should We Diagnose Learning Disorders?

Diagnosing learning disorders has long been controversial. Starting in the late 1970s in the United States, diagnoses were often made using the **IQ-achievement discrepancy model**. This model relies on discrepancies between IQ scores and achievement scores (Cakiroglu, 2015; Martínez & Nellis, 2020; Vellutino, 2018). When children's IQ scores (thought to assess natural ability) are significantly higher than their performance on achievement tests (which measure mastery of material), the discrepancy is used to infer the presence of a learning disorder. Though IQ-achievement discrepancy was long the predominant way to diagnose learning disorders, the model has received extensive criticism. Many have questioned its validity, arguing that it fails to accurately distinguish who has a learning disorder (Humphries & Bone, 1993; Restori et al., 2009; Stuebing et al., 2002; Vellutino, 2018). Further, it is considered a "wait-to-fail" model because it delays making learning disorder diagnoses until a record of poor school performance relative to IQ is established (Cakiroglu, 2015; Martínez & Nellis, 2020).

Since the mid-2000s, the **response-to-intervention model (RTI)** has provided an alternative to the discrepancy model. RTI's main idea is "to identify the academic difficulties of students as early as possible to provide the necessary supplemental educational services" (Cakiroglu, 2015, p. 171). Rather than leaning so heavily on IQ scores, RTI evaluates each child's prior year school performance. One of the most common ways to do so is via a three-tier approach (Cakiroglu, 2015; Fuchs et al., 2003; Martínez & Nellis, 2020). Kids who meet grade-level standards (most children) are placed in *Tier 1*. Those who don't are moved to *Tier 2* and provided academic assistance in small groups for nine to twelve weeks. Tier 2 children who respond to this intervention are returned to Tier 1, but those who continue to struggle are moved to *Tier 3*, where they receive more intensive academic assistance over a longer period. Tier 3 also includes individualized assessment to rule out other possible causes of poor academic performance (e.g., intellectual disabilities, autism, vision or hearing impairments). Children who respond to Tier 3 interventions are reintegrated into Tiers 2 and 1, but those who don't are placed into special education programs (Cakiroglu, 2015; Fuchs et al., 2003).

RTI skeptics complain that it has worse, not better, validity than the discrepancy model. Why? Because RTI blurs the line between learning and intellectual disabilities by no longer using IQ discrepancy to identify learning disorders (Kavale & Spaulding, 2008; R. G. McKenzie, 2009). Thus, any student who does poorly in school, regardless of IQ, potentially qualifies for a learning disorder. Detractors therefore contend that RTI is ineffective as a diagnostic procedure and is better used as a form of prevention (Kavale & Spaulding, 2008). From this vantagepoint, only once a child fails to respond at Tier 3 should efforts to diagnose a learning disorder begin, using both IQ-achievement discrepancy and other relevant data. However, critics have also noted that the process of determining learning tier is not always clear or consistent (Fuchs & Fuchs, 2017). The takeaway from all this? Discrepancy versus RTI models of learning disorders continue to be hotly debated in the field of special education.

Critical Thinking Questions

1. Do you prefer the IQ-achievement discrepancy model of the response-to-intervention model? Why?
2. Can you think of ways to move beyond the discrepancy-RTI debate and more adequately conceptualize learning disorders?
3. To what extent are the ways we assess learning disorders intertwined with the priorities and values of the educational system?

Response-to-intervention model (RTI): Preventative approach that identifies and intervenes with children performing below grade level; if responsive, the children are reintegrated into the normal classroom, but if not, they are assigned to a special education classroom.

14.3 Historical Perspectives on Intellectual and Learning Difficulties

Attitudes toward people with intellectual disabilities have changed a lot over the last century or so. During the early twentieth century, the **eugenics movement** took hold in many countries (Diekema, 2003). It held that intelligence and other traits are primarily inherited. Eugenicists felt humanity could be improved by encouraging selective breeding of people with "desirable" traits while preventing reproduction among those with "undesirable" traits. At various points during the twentieth century countries like the United States, Canada, Australia, Germany, Japan, Denmark, and Iceland allowed the legal sterilization of intellectually disabled and other "mentally defective" people against their will (Diekema, 2003; A. Roy et al., 2012; Stefánsdóttir, 2014). Involuntary sterilization still occasionally occurs today, but the practice has fallen out of favor as attitudes toward people with intellectual disabilities have become less negative. Still, this history reminds us of the potential harm that helping professionals can inflict.

14.4 Biological Perspectives on Intellectual and Learning Difficulties

Intellectual Disabilities

Some intellectual disabilities are attributable to heritable diseases. For instance, **phenylketonuria (PKU)** is a rare recessive gene-linked illness. Babies born with PKU lack the liver enzyme, *phenylalanine hydroxylase*. Their bodies cannot break down phenylalanine and phenylpyruvic acid. This can lead to brain damage and intellectual impairment, along with physical characteristics such as small heads (R. A. Williams et al., 2008). Luckily, a lifetime diet low in phenylalanine combined with nutritional supplements to ensure sufficient protein intake can prevent intellectual impairment in PKU patients (C. S. Brown & Lichter-Konecki, 2016).

Other intellectual disabilities result from chromosomal abnormalities. For instance, **Down syndrome** is caused by an extra copy of the chromosome *trisomy 21* (Bull, 2020). Besides intellectual deficits, signs and symptoms include eyes that slant upwards; short, stocky bodies; flat faces and noses; small heads, ears, and mouths; and poor muscle tone (Bull, 2020). As another example, **Fragile X syndrome** is linked to a mutation in the *FMR1* gene on the *X chromosome* (Hagerman et al., 2017; Maenner et al., 2013). People with fragile X develop thin faces, long ears, large heads, prominent foreheads, flat feet, and extremely flexible joints (I. Newman et al., 2015). Fragile X is more common in boys than girls, but women usually carry the recessive gene that causes it (Hagerman et al., 2017; Maenner et al., 2013). Down syndrome and fragile X syndrome are comorbid with aggression and disruptive behavior problems such as ADHD (Ekstein et al., 2011; I. Newman et al., 2015; Wheeler et al., 2016; Yahia et al., 2014)(Newman et al., 2015; Wheeler, Raspa, Bishop, & Bailey, 2016). Autism symptoms such as sensitivity to noise and bright lights, speech and language difficulties, and intense anxiety in unfamiliar situations are also common (Bull, 2020; Hagerman et al., 2017). Could these disorders share genetic links to disorders with which they commonly co-occur?

Besides genetics, intellectual disabilities are linked to other biological factors. They can be caused by *problems during pregnancy* (e.g., maternal drug use, infections, and malnutrition, *complications during childbirth* (e.g., a baby's brain being denied oxygen), *illnesses during childhood* (e.g., whooping cough, meningitis, or the measles), and *brain injuries* (e.g., car accidents, exposure to environmental toxins) (Bhaumik et al., 2016). Other than genetic syndromes and chromosomal abnormalities, severe intellectual disabilities are most often tied to "congenital brain malformations, congenital central nervous system infections, inborn errors of metabolism, maternal disease during pregnancy, in utero exposure to toxins, and birth injury" (D. R. Patel et al., 2020, p. S26).

Yolanda

Yolanda's intellectual disability is linked to her having Down syndrome.

Learning Disorders

Dyslexia appears to be highly heritable, with numerous candidate genes associated with it (Erbeli et al., 2022). There is less research on the genetics of dyscalculia, and although genes are believed to play a role, it has been difficult to distinguish genetic from environmental influences in any given case (M. R. S. Carvalho & Haase, 2019). Brain regions implicated in dyslexia include the *temporoparietal area* (important in speech processing) and the *occipitotemporal area* (implicated in processing visual information), both of which are less active in dyslexia (Kearns et al., 2019; Shaywitz & Shaywitz, 2005). Provocatively, some critics argue that dyslexic brain differences do not reflect brain dysfunctions (Protopapas & Parrila, 2018). To them dyslexia, like autism and other neurodevelopmental diagnoses, is a form of neurodiversity (see Chapter 13). Therefore, it should not be viewed as disordered. Do you agree with this view? Why or why not?

Eugenics movement: Twentieth-century movement that believed intelligence and other traits were inherited and encouraged breeding between those with "desirable" traits while preventing it among those with "undesirable" traits.

Phenylketonuria (PKU): Genetic disease involving deficiency in the liver enzyme, phenylalanine hydroxylase, resulting in the inability to break down phenylalanine and phenylpyruvic acid; can lead to brain damage and intellectual impairment.

Down syndrome: Caused by an extra copy of the chromosome trisomy 21 and characterized by intellectual disability, stocky body, short stature, flat face and nose, small head, small ears, small mouth, and poor muscle tone.

Fragile X syndrome: Mutation on the X chromosome that leads to intellectual disability and physical signs like thin face, long ears, large head, prominent forehead, flat feet, and extremely flexible joints; more common in boys than girls.

14.5 Psychological Perspectives on Intellectual and Learning Difficulties

Intellectual Disabilities

Early interventions rooted in applied behavior analysis (ABA) (see Chapter 13) are commonly used to treat intellectual disabilities, along with CBT techniques like cognitive skills training that teaches how to complete everyday tasks by breaking them down into manageable steps (P. Cooney et al., 2018; Luiselli, 2016). ABA seems to work for IDD (Hassiotis et al., 2011; Haymes et al., 2013; Luiselli, 2016). There is some evidence for cognitive interventions, though the effectiveness of skills training has yet to be established (P. Cooney et al., 2018).

> **Yolanda**
> *As a child, Yolanda underwent ABA and cognitive skills training. She learned to complete basic tasks such as bathing, getting dressed, and making her bed. As she got older, more complex tasks (e.g., taking the bus, ordering in a restaurant, and paying bills online) were taught to her in a step-by-step way using skills training and reinforcement of desired responses.*

Learning Disorders

Music education:
Dyslexia treatment that reduces reading problems by improving musical skills; based on the idea that phonological awareness correlates with musical abilities.

Psychological interventions that emphasize *reading skills* and *phonological awareness* can improve reading performance in children diagnosed with dyslexia, but they are not always effective (Duff et al., 2014; Hulme & Snowling, 2016; Snowling & Hulme, 2012). *Oral language interventions* that teach speaking skills, listening skills, narrative skills, and vocabulary boost vocabulary but do not necessarily impact reading skills (Snowling & Hulme, 2012). Interestingly, **music education** is sometimes used to treat dyslexia. Rooted in the idea that phonological awareness correlates with musical abilities, the goal is to treat dyslexia by cultivating rhythmic awareness. Evidence supports the notion that people with dyslexia often struggle to maintain a beat (Groß et al., 2022; Reifinger, 2019). However, this may be a consequence rather than cause of reading issues (Rathcke & Lin, 2021). Nonetheless, a small body of evidence suggests that rhythm training improves reading skills (Bouloukou et al., 2021; Flaugnacco et al., 2015; Reifinger, 2019).

14.6 Sociocultural Perspectives on Intellectual and Learning Difficulties

Intellectual Disabilities
Socioeconomic Inequality

People living in poverty are at risk for intellectual disabilities, perhaps because they have less access to resources that foster intellectual development and are more likely to be exposed to toxins and other environmental hazards (Ahmed et al., 2016; Emerson, 2007). In addition to poverty increasing vulnerability to intellectual disabilities, intellectual disabilities also foster poverty (Emerson, 2007; Emerson et al., 2010). People with IDD and other developmental disabilities receive less education and lack earning potential (Queirós et al., 2015). IDD is also economically draining. Care is expensive, thus families with a member who is intellectually disabled often slide down the socioeconomic ladder. Making matters worse, IDD correlates with poor health outcomes and lower life expectancy (Gleason et al., 2021; Landes et al., 2021; Reppermund et al., 2020). This became crystal clear in recent years, when IDD became "the strongest independent risk factor for having a Covid-19 diagnosis among a large patient population in the United States" (Gleason et al., 2021, p. 9). Social justice advocates recommend remediating social inequality to prevent intellectual disabilities and assist those with them (Emerson & Parish, 2010).

Yolanda

Yolanda's parents have found it difficult to make ends meet given the costs Yolanda's intellectual disability incurs (medication, schooling, therapies, etc.).

Group Homes

When circumstances do not permit people with IDD to live on their own or with family members, residential treatment in **group homes** is a common alternative (Independent Living Association, 2021). Group homes typically house a small number of residents, providing them with medical care and live-in aids who assist them in their daily routines. Group homes let residents live in the community rather than in more institutional settings like hospitals or nursing homes. To ensure resident security and freedom, group homes should maintain cohesive, respectful, and inclusive cultures (Bigby & Beadle-Brown, 2016; Shipton & Lashewicz, 2017).

Yolanda

Yolanda might eventually move to a group home that lets her live independently in the community while receiving necessary social support. The challenge is finding high-quality group homes that are adequately funded and staffed.

Learning Disorders

A social constructionist perspective views current definitions of learning disorder (and strategies for "fixing" it) as culturally derived products of a Western worldview that attributes learning problems to individual defects (Dudley-Marling, 2004; Katchergin, 2014, 2016). Social constructionists hold that socially invented and taken-for-granted "learning disability" categories favor the privileged: "Students are rank-ordered and classified for instruction such that those from advantaged social groups tend to be prepared for the better jobs, while those from disadvantaged backgrounds tend to be channeled into low pay, low status work" (Sleeter, 1986, p. 48). Social constructionism questions whether learning disabilities are context-free disorders and reframes learning problems in more social and relational terms. It asks why learning disorders are more common among racial and ethnic minorities, *language minorities* (whose first language is not used in school), and boys (Shifrer et al., 2011). To a social constructionist way of thinking, sociocultural factors are minimized and individual factors overemphasized in how we talk about children who experience trouble learning. As such, learning problems are as much a social justice issue as a medical one.

MOTOR PROBLEMS

Case Example: Motor Problems

Greta

Greta is a 6-year-old girl who exhibits vocal and motor tics. She recurrently blinks, grunts, and makes odd clicking noises with her tongue. Previously an outgoing child and good student, Greta's school performance has deteriorated since the tics began.

14.7 DSM and ICD Perspectives on Motor Problems

DSM-5-TR and ICD-11 include several motor disorders. **Developmental coordination disorder** is diagnosed in children who show motor coordination skills well below what is expected for their age. They are excessively clumsy and bad at activities requiring physical coordination (e.g., catching a ball, using scissors, riding a bike, writing with a pen, or playing sports). **Stereotypic movement disorder** involves repetitive and purposeless movements that begin

Group homes: Typically house a small number of adult residents with special needs, providing them with medical care and live-in aids who assist with their daily routines.

Developmental coordination disorder: DSM disorder diagnosed in children who show motor coordination skills well below what is expected given their age; called *developmental motor coordination disorder* in ICD.

Stereotypic movement disorder: DSM disorder involving repetitive and purposeless movements that begin early in development and which the child seems driven to perform (e.g., waving one's hands, rocking back and forth, banging one's head, and biting or hitting oneself); called *stereotyped movement disorder* in ICD.

early in development, which the child seems driven to perform—things like waving one's hands, rocking back and forth, banging one's head, and biting or hitting oneself. Finally, **tic disorders** are characterized by abrupt and repetitive motor or vocal movements (i.e., *tics*). Tics can be divided into motor and verbal tics:

- *Simple motor tics* (the most common type) are simple repetitive movements like eye-blinking, shoulder-shrugging, or head-jerking, whereas *complex motor tics* are composed of more coordinated and purposeful movements such as hopping, skipping, tapping, stepping in certain patterns, and touching specific objects.
- *Simple vocal tics* involve brief utterances or sounds like repetitive throat clearing, coughing, sniffling, grunting, gurgling, and spitting. By comparison, *complex vocal tics* are characterized by repeating words, sounds, and phrases; for example, repeating one's own words (*palilalia*), repeating others' words (*echolalia*; see Chapter 4), and involuntary cursing (*coprolalia*).

The most well-known DSM tic disorder is **Tourette's disorder**, which involves both motor and vocal tics that have persisted for over a year. DSM-5-TR also includes two less severe tic disorders: **persistent (chronic) motor or vocal tic disorder** (in which the patient displays either motor or vocal tics—but not both—for over a year) and **provisional tic disorder** (in which the patient displays motor and/or verbal tics, but for less than one year). To qualify for any of these tic disorders, symptoms must begin before age 18. ICD-11 organizes things slightly differently. It includes Tourette's (which it calls *Tourette syndrome*). However, it divides DSM's persistent (chronic) motor or vocal tic disorder into two separate diagnoses, *chronic motor tic disorder* and *chronic phonic tic disorder*. Finally, ICD's *transient motor tics* diagnosis is equivalent to DSM's provisional tic disorder but diverges from it somewhat by not including verbal tics (these can be diagnosed using "other specified" or "unspecified" codes). Notably, ICD groups tic disorders with diseases of the nervous system rather than mental disorders. Diagnostic Box 14.3 shows criteria and guidelines for motor disorders. Herein, we focus on tic disorders, mainly Tourette's.

Photo 14.3 Internationally renowned soccer star Tim Howard has been outspoken about his struggle with Tourette syndrome. He has said that the stress of a big game causes his tics to flare.
Shaun Clark/Getty Images.

Greta

Our case example client, Greta, probably would be diagnosed with provisional tic disorder until her tics persist for more than a year. Once they do, her diagnosis would change to Tourette's disorder because she exhibits both motor and verbal tics.

DSM-5-TR estimates that 5 percent to 8 percent of children ages 5–11 suffer from developmental coordination disorder, with boys two to seven times more likely than girls to be affected by it. As for stereotypic movement disorder, it is especially prevalent among children in residential facilities diagnosed with intellectual disabilities; 10 percent to 15 percent of such children may qualify for a diagnosis, according to DSM-5-TR. When it comes to tic disorders, Tourette's disorder is estimated to occur in 3 percent to 9 percent of children worldwide but is more common in males than females. It is also comorbid with many other disorders, including OCD, ADHD, disruptive behavior disorders, autism spectrum disorder, major depressive disorder, bipolar disorder, personality disorders, learning disorders, sleep disorders, and epilepsy (Cravedi et al., 2017; Eapen et al., 2016; Ferreira et al., 2014; Goto et al., 2019; Kalyva et al., 2016; Robertson et al., 2015; L. C. Wong et al., 2016).

Diagnostic Box 14.3 Motor Disorders

Developmental Coordination Disorder (DSM-5-TR)/Developmental Motor Coordination Disorder (ICD-11)
- Delayed acquisition of motor skills that results in clumsy and uncoordinated motor behavior.
- Motor skills well below what is expected for the person's age.
- Begins in early development.

Stereotypic Movement Disorder (DSM-5-TR)/Stereotyped Movement Disorder (ICD-11)
- Repetitive and purposeless motor behavior (e.g., hand waving, body rocking, biting self, hitting self, head banging) that one seems driven to perform.
- Begins early in development.
- Specify: *with injurious behavior* or *without injurious behavior*.

Tic Disorders
- Characterized by abrupt and repetitive motor or vocal movements (i.e., tics).
- DSM-5-TR:
  - **Provisional tic disorder**: One or more motor and/or vocal tics for less than one year, starting before age 18.
  - **Persistent (chronic) motor or vocal tic disorder**: Either motor or vocal tics (but not both) for more than twelve months, starting before age 18.
  - **Tourette's disorder**: Multiple motor tics and at least one vocal tic (though not necessarily at the same time) for more than twelve months, starting before age 18.
- ICD-11:
  - **Transient motor tics**: Motor tics for less than twelve months.
  - **Chronic motor tic disorder**: Motor tics for at least twelve months, starting at an early age.
  - **Chronic phonic tic disorder**: Vocal tics for at least twelve months, starting at an early age.
  - **Tourette syndrome**: Both motor and vocal tics for at least twelve months (though not necessarily at the same time), starting at an early age.

Information from American Psychiatric Association (2022, pp. 85–86, 89, 93) and World Health Organization (2022a).

14.8 Historical Perspectives on Motor Problems

Tourette's syndrome is named after Georges Albert Édouard Brutus Gilles de la Tourette (1857–1904), a French physician and student of the famous neurologist Jean-Martin Charcot (1825–1893). In 1885, Gilles de la Tourette described nine patients who had vocal and motor tics (Kushner, 1999, 2000; McNaught, 2010). One case that Gilles de la Tourette wrote about was that of the Marquise de Dampierre, a French noblewoman who, despite being highly educated and sophisticated, was infamous for publicly shouting curse words in the middle of conversations. Gilles de la Tourette named the syndrome *maladie des tics*, but Charcot renamed it Tourette's syndrome in honor of the man who described it (McNaught, 2010).

Charcot and Gilles de la Tourette viewed Tourette's syndrome as an incurable brain disease. As Gilles de la Tourette put it, "once a ticcer, always a ticcer" (Kushner, 2000, p. 76). However, throughout much of the twentieth century, psychodynamic theories held sway. For example, psychoanalyst Margaret Mahler (1897–1985) believed Tourette's only developed in biologically susceptible children when there were repressed psychological conflicts tied to family dynamics (Kushner, 1999; Mahler & Rangell, 1943). Psychodynamic interventions for Tourette's were not very effective. However, they were far less invasive than lobotomies (see Chapter 1), which were sometimes performed in severe cases despite their damage to overall mental functioning (Hashemiyoon et al., 2017). The influence of psychodynamic therapy for treating tics did not wane until the antipsychotic drug *haloperidol* showed more promise and began being used instead during the 1960s. This led to the reemergence of genetic and other biological theories of tic disorders, discussed next.

14.9 Biological Perspectives on Motor Problems

Genetics, Brain Chemistry, and Brain Structure in Tic Disorders

The precise causes of tic disorders remain unknown (Jankovic, 2022; Z. A. Shaw & Coffey, 2014). Genetics researchers believe them to be moderately to highly heritable, though existing research is deemed relatively modest (Motlagh et al., 2012; Pagliaroli et al., 2016; Pauls et al., 2014; Z. A. Shaw & Coffey, 2014; Zilhao et al., 2017). There have been few genome-wide association studies of Tourette's and other tic disorders. Though results can be difficult to replicate, a variety of genes have been implicated (Pagliaroli et al., 2016; J. M. Scharf et al., 2013; D. Yu et al., 2019).

Given that candidate genes related to dopamine have been implicated, the **dopamine hypothesis of Tourette's disorder** holds that too much dopamine activity contributes to the disorder (Gloor & Walitza, 2016; Maia & Conceição, 2018). Specifically, dopamine dysregulation in the *basal ganglia* and associated *corticostriatothalamocortical circuits* (both important in movement) is suspected to have a central role (Gloor & Walitza, 2016; Jankovic, 2022). Other neurotransmitters such as serotonin, GABA, glutamate, acetylcholine, and histamine may also be relevant (Paschou et al., 2013).

Dopamine hypothesis of Tourette's disorder: Too much dopamine activity in the basal ganglia plays a role in Tourette's disorder.

Tics and Immune System Dysfunction

PANDAS is an acronym for *pediatric autoimmune neuropsychiatric disorders associated with streptococcal infection hypothesis*. The **PANDAS hypothesis** holds that tics or childhood OCD develop in genetically susceptible individuals who contract strep or other viruses (C.-J. Hsu et al., 2021; J. Leon et al., 2018; Martino et al., 2009; Swedo et al., 1998). This hypothesis continues to be researched and debated (C.-J. Hsu et al., 2021). Not everyone accepts it, and it may not apply to all tic disorder cases (Hoekstra et al., 2013).

PANDAS hypothesis: Holds that tics develop in genetically susceptible individuals who contract strep throat or other viruses; the full name of this hypothesis is the *Pediatric Autoimmune Neuropsychiatric Disorders Associated with Streptococcal Infection hypothesis*.

Biological Interventions
Drugs Prescribed

When it comes to drug treatments for Tourette's disorder, antipsychotics are commonly prescribed given the suspected role of extreme dopamine sensitivity in the basal ganglia (Nomura, 2022; Pringsheim et al., 2019). Aripiprazole, risperidone, and haloperidol all seem to reduce tics—with aripiprazole often preferred because, as a third-generation antipsychotic, it is believed to cause less severe side effects (Pringsheim et al., 2019; Roessner et al., 2022). Though antipsychotics are used most often, drugs affecting histamine, acetylcholine, GABA, glutamate, and norepinephrine are all receiving attention as treatments for tic disorders, as are antiepileptic drugs and cannabis (A. Hartmann et al., 2016; Roessner et al., 2022; C. Yang et al., 2016). This is consistent with speculation that many neurotransmitters interact in causing tics (Paschou et al., 2013; Roessner et al., 2013, 2022).

Deep Brain Stimulation (DBS)

When other interventions prove inadequate, deep brain stimulation (DBS) is sometimes used to treat Tourette's (Martino et al., 2021). DBS involves permanently implanting electrodes in the brain and then delivering low levels of electrical current using a transmitter the person wears (see Chapter 5). DBS appears to reduce tics and is growing in popularity because it is preferable to more invasive brain surgeries (Martinez-Ramirez et al., 2018; Pringsheim et al., 2019). However, it is still more invasive than drugs or cognitive-behavioral interventions and can cause side effects such as *dysarthria* (difficulty controlling the muscles needed to speak) and *paresthesia* (tingling or prickling sensations, often described as "pins and needles") (Martinez-Ramirez et al., 2018). It is debatable whether DBS should be used with children, whose tics often improve or disappear during adolescence or early adulthood (W. Xu et al., 2020). However, the risks of DBS must be weighed against the benefits of reducing tics during childhood, when social ostracism can negatively impact emotional and social development (W. Xu et al., 2020).

14.10 Psychological Perspectives on Motor Problems

Behavior Therapies

Behavior therapies, the most researched and used psychological interventions for Tourette's and other tic disorders, are often tried before or in combination with medication. Perhaps the most well-known approach is **habit reversal training (HRT)**. In HRT, the patient is trained to recognize sensory experiences that indicate the onset of a tic. Patients then engage in a behavioral response (breathing or movement) that is incompatible with the tic (Flessner, 2011; Hartmann et al., 2016; Verdellen et al., 2011). When HRT is supplemented with relaxation training and a functional analysis of environmental factors sustaining tics, it is known as **comprehensive behavioral intervention for tics (CBIT)** (Woods et al., 2008). HRT and CBIT are effective behavioral interventions for reducing tics (Andrén et al., 2022; Blount et al., 2018; Dreison & Lagges, 2017; Essoe et al., 2019; K. M. Kim et al., 2021; Pilcher et al., 2020; L. Yu et al., 2020).

> #### Greta
> *In HRT, Greta would learn to identify when her repeated blinking tic is about to begin by paying attention to sensations that typically precede it. She would be encouraged to engage in a competing response, such as keeping her eyes wide open until the urge to blink passes.*

Despite a less extensive evidence base than HRT and CBIT, exposure plus response prevention (described in Chapter 6) is another effective behavioral treatment for tics (Andrén et al., 2022; Essoe et al., 2019; K. M. Kim et al., 2021; Yan et al., 2022). After learning to be aware of sensations that predict when tics are about to begin, patients are asked to resist engaging in the tic to prevent the tic response. In so doing, they become habituated to the sensations that precede the tic, eventually causing these sensations to no longer function as conditioned stimuli that trigger the tic.

> #### Greta
> *In exposure plus response prevention, Greta would be taught to identify sensations preceding her tics, then actively resist doing them for as long as possible. With practice, she should begin to habituate to sensations that come before the tics and no longer feel a strong urge to engage in them.*

Cognitive Therapies

Cognitive restructuring, acceptance and commitment therapy (ACT) and mindfulness-based cognitive therapy (MBCT) are sometimes added to behavioral interventions (A. Hartmann et al., 2016). The goal is to help patients accept their experience and not judge themselves too harshly when they have tics. Negative beliefs surrounding tics are examined and in-the-moment acceptance and awareness of unpleasant feelings and experiences is encouraged. There is not much research yet on acceptance and mindfulness approaches to tics, but initial results are encouraging (Andrén et al., 2022; A. Hartmann et al., 2016).

14.11 Sociocultural Perspectives on Motor Problems

Tic disorders carry a great deal of social stigma (Malli et al., 2016; Malli & Forrester-Jones, 2022; H. Smith et al., 2015). People with frequent tics often feel others do not understand their condition, blame them for their tics, or see it as acceptable to treat them as the target of jokes: "You know you see jokes, memes like 'Never laugh at other people's disabilities, unless you have Tourette's because how can you not?' How can we be taken seriously?" (Malli & Forrester-Jones, 2022, p. 881). One tic sufferer described being socially excluded at school: "I feel like I somehow get left out of all the games, and I feel like I'm a dork and that stuff, and I don't really have much friends … and mostly I get picked on at school" (H. Smith et al., 2015, p. 625). Another reported feeling highly self-conscious: "In class I felt embarrassed, I couldn't pay attention because I heard a laugh and I thought my colleagues were laughing at me and I always kept an eye on what my colleagues thought, said, or did and I had a bad

---

Habit reversal training (HRT): Behavior therapy technique to reduce or eliminate undesired repetitive behaviors; patients are taught to recognize sensory experiences that precede the behavior and then engage in an incompatible behavioral response.

Comprehensive behavioral intervention for tics (CBIT): Combines *habit reversal training (HRT)* with additional behavioral techniques (e.g., relaxation training, functional analysis of behavior) to reduce or eliminate tics.

time" (H. Smith et al., 2015, p. 623). Like everyone, tic sufferers simply want positive and supportive relationships: "I can't control my tics but I want to be taken as I am for myself" (H. Smith et al., 2015, p. 625). For a powerful account of what it is like to have Tourette's, see "The Lived Experience" feature.

The Lived Experience: Real Stories from People Living with Tourette Syndrome: Mike

My name is Mike Higgins and I am a father, a pastor, a husband, a dean of students of a seminary, a minister, a full colonel in the United States Army, and I have Tourette syndrome.

The first time I heard the word, "Tourette syndrome," from the doctor I had no idea what he was talking about. I had never heard of it. I didn't know anybody who had ever heard of it before. There were a lot of days as a 12-year-old when I would lay in bed and think about what was happening to me that I could not control. It caused me to wonder, "Why was I born like this?"

I think that I was not diagnosed until I was 28 years old because our family doctors didn't know about Tourette syndrome. I had been training for three weeks in Death Valley, California, and I was really hot, really dirty, really tired, and my tics were all over the place. My battalion commander noticed and ordered me to get checked out. Finally, I met a neurologist who asked me if anybody in my family had ever had this. I told him that my grandfather did. And he said, "I think I know what you have."

I didn't think that I was ever going to be married because it seemed like it was hard enough to just be single with Tourette syndrome. But in my family life now, it's just who I am. I think that my wife Renee is such a spiritually mature woman and I still look up to her because she's been my champion in all of this, helping me along, and has really been there by my side. She has never treated me as a victim and refuses to let me be a victim.

The churches that I've been in have very celebratory worship styles. When I'm preaching, I don't tic a lot; sometimes not at all. It seems like there's a grace period I get when I'm focused on something that I'm passionate about. If we can educate the ministers, pastors, and religious leaders about Tourette's, then they can go on to educate folks in their congregations, families of children with Tourette's, and also folks who don't understand Tourette's.

I don't think Tourette's takes away your dreams. I just think that it may put an extra wall or two between you and accomplishing your dreams. But you can get over the walls. As I say, "You may have Tourette syndrome, but it doesn't have to have you."

Reprinted with permission from https://www.cdc.gov/ncbddd/tourette/stories/mike.html.

Speech-sound disorder: DSM and ICD diagnosis in which speech is understood but hard to generate due to difficulty making speech sounds; called *developmental speech-sound disorder* in ICD.

Language disorder: DSM and ICD diagnosis made in children who have trouble acquiring and using language; called *developmental language disorder* in ICD.

Childhood-onset fluency disorder (stuttering): DSM and ICD diagnosis in which sounds are repeated or consonants or vowels prolonged; called *developmental speech fluency disorder* in ICD.

COMMUNICATION PROBLEMS

14.12 DSM and ICD Perspectives on Communication Problems

Case Example: Communication Problems

Among the DSM an ICD neurodevelopmental disorders are several language disorders beside social (pragmatic) communication disorder (discussed in Chapter 13). People with **speech-sound disorder** comprehend and can generate speech, but their speech is hard to understand due to difficulty making speech sounds. By contrast, **language disorder** is diagnosed in children who have trouble acquiring and using language. They struggle with speaking and writing because they have difficulty understanding language and forming spoken sentences. For many with this diagnosis, conducting conversations is extremely difficult. Finally, **childhood-onset fluency disorder (stuttering)** is characterized by repeating sounds or prolonging consonants or vowels. People who stutter sometimes substitute different words to avoid words that are hard to say. They also tend to repeat one-syllable words. Stuttering not only interferes with speech fluency, but also results in much anxiety about speaking. ICD-11 uses slightly different names for these disorders. It also divides language disorders into three types: *with impairment of mainly expressive language*, *with impairment of receptive and expressive language*, and *with impairment of mainly pragmatic language* (this last one being social [pragmatic] communication disorder in DSM; again, see Chapter 13). Diagnostic Box 14.4 summarizes communication disorders, but we limit our discussion to stuttering.

Bobby
Bobby's speech fluency difficulties qualify him for a stuttering diagnosis.

14.13 Biological Perspectives on Communication Problems

Genetics and Stuttering

Stuttering seems to run in families, with high concordance rates in twin studies and estimated heritability in the .80 range (Frigerio-Domingues & Drayna, 2017; Kraft & Yairi, 2012; Yairi et al., 1996). This implies that genes play a major role, but environment matters too (Frigerio-Domingues & Drayna, 2017). Four genes (GNPTAB, GNPTG NAGPA, and AP4E1) have been linked to stuttering, and genome-wide association studies are identifying other possible genetic markers (Frigerio-Domingues & Drayna, 2017; T.-U. Han et al., 2019; C. Kang, 2021; Polikowsky et al., 2022; D. M. Shaw et al., 2021). However, results have been hard to replicate, and the four genes identified only account for 10 percent of persistent stuttering cases (C. Kang, 2021).

Bobby
Bobby suspects he was genetically predisposed to stuttering. He has several relatives, including his maternal grandfather, who also stuttered.

Dopamine and Drug Treatments

The **dopamine hypothesis of stuttering**, like the dopamine hypothesis of Tourette's, proposes that stuttering is related to excessive dopamine transmission in the basal ganglia (Alm, 2004; Maguire et al., 2012; J. C. Wu et al., 1997). Thus, it makes sense that—even though no drug is currently approved in the United States for stuttering—haloperidol and other antipsychotics are often prescribed (Bothe et al., 2006; A. Boyd et al., 2011; Maguire et al., 2020). They are somewhat effective, but their serious side effects limit their utility (Maguire et al., 2020). Antidepressants and the alpha agonist *clonidine* are other drugs used to treat stuttering, but they do not work very well (Maguire et al., 2020).

Dopamine hypothesis of stuttering: Stuttering is related to excessive dopamine transmission in the basal ganglia. (14)

> **Bobby**
>
> *When Bobby was 9 years old, he was briefly placed on an antipsychotic medication. It reduced his stuttering somewhat, but Bobby's parents took him off the drug due to its highly unpleasant side effects.*

14.14 Psychological Perspectives on Communication Problems

Cognitive-Behavioral Therapy
The Lidcombe Program

Lidcombe Program: Behavioral program for children whose stuttering starts before age 5; parents work with their children to reinforce fluency and acknowledge/correct stuttering.

The most well-known and researched behavioral intervention for stuttering is the **Lidcombe Program**, named after the Sydney, Australia suburb where it was developed (Blomgren, 2013). Aimed at children aged 5 and younger, this program consists of two stages. In *Stage 1*, the child's stuttering is assessed. Parents learn to evaluate the severity of their child's stuttering and how to positively reinforce stutter-free speech using *praise* (e.g., "that was lovely smooth talking"), *acknowledgment* (e.g., "that was smooth"), and *requests for self-evaluation* (e.g., "was that smooth?") (Onslow, 2021, pp. 4–5). When the child stutters, parents are taught to use *acknowledgment* (e.g., "that was a stuck word") and make *requests for self-correction* (e.g., "can you say it again?") (Onslow, 2021, pp. 5–6). In *Stage 2*, visits to the speech clinic become less frequent while the parents continue to implement the program at home. The goal is to prevent relapse, a common problem in stuttering treatment (Onslow, 2021). Studies consistently find the Lidcombe Program to be effective, though more high-quality evidence is sought (Arnott et al., 2014; Femrell et al., 2012; M. Jones et al., 2005; Nye et al., 2013; O'Brian et al., 2013; Shafiei et al., 2019; Sjøstrand et al., 2021).

CBT

Many people who stutter experience intense anxiety about speaking to others (A. Craig & Tran, 2014). To address worry about being negatively evaluated by others, cognitive interventions that challenge negative beliefs and expectations are combined with behavioral techniques for managing and reducing anxiety. Systematic desensitization, behavioral experiments, relaxation training, mindfulness-based interventions, acceptance and commitment therapy (ACT), and dialectical behavior therapy (DBT) are all used to manage stuttering (Blomgren, 2013; Kelman & Wheeler, 2015; Mongia et al., 2019). While there is evidence for CBT interventions, further research into their effectiveness for stuttering is needed (Kelman & Wheeler, 2015; Mongia et al., 2019).

> **Bobby**
>
> *Imagine Bobby seeks CBT for the anxiety that accompanies his stuttering. Cognitive restructuring might be used. Bobby's negative beliefs—such as "Everyone thinks I'm stupid because of how I talk" and "Nobody will like me if I can't speak properly"—would be challenged and replaced with more rational beliefs, such as "Some people can see past difficulties with speaking" and "Those who truly care about you love you no matter how you talk." As Bobby's beliefs change, he should experience less anxiety about talking to people, making it easier for him to speak more fluently.*

Constructivist Therapy and Stuttering Relapse

Constructivist perspectives focus on how people construct meaningful ways of understanding themselves and the world (see Chapter 2). From their point of view, stuttering relapse occurs when lack of fluency is construed as central to one's sense of self (DiLollo et al., 2002, 2003; DiLollo & Neimeyer, 2008, 2022; Fransella, 1987). As a person who stutters put it, "I often feel that when I'm fluent and people like me, I feel like it's a façade … like they're gonna find out I'm not what they thought I was. I'm an imposter" (DiLollo & Neimeyer, 2008, p. 167). Individuals like this relapse because they have not integrated being a fluent speaker into their sense of who they are. In other words, "for the person who stutters, despite experiencing fluent speech (for example, following successful behavioral therapy), it is likely that the experience will not be meaningful, and, thus, behavior will likely revert back to that which is compatible with the dominant construct system based on stuttering" (DiLollo et al., 2003, p. 180).

Constructivist therapy for stuttering focuses not simply on correcting speech, but also on having clients incorporate being fluent into their core sense of self. One way of accomplishing this is through the narrative therapy technique of externalizing the problem (introduced in Chapter 2 and revisited in other chapters) (DiLollo et al., 2002; DiLollo & Neimeyer, 2008, 2022; F. Ryan et al., 2015). Clients are asked to talk about the problem (in this case stuttering) as something outside themselves that sometimes gets the best of them. They identify exceptions—times when stuttering did not triumph, and fluent speech occurred instead. Separating the problem ("stuttering") from sense of self is important because people who construe stuttering as part of their core identity struggle to achieve fluency (DiLollo et al., 2002; DiLollo & Neimeyer, 2022; Fransella, 1987). While a promising approach, there aren't any published outcome studies yet on using narrative therapy as a stuttering intervention (F. Ryan et al., 2015).

14.15 Sociocultural Perspectives on Communication Problems

People who stutter are viewed negatively (S. Erickson & Block, 2013; Ip et al., 2012; Przepiorka et al., 2013; S. R. Seitz & Choo, 2022; St. Louis et al., 2016). In other words, stuttering is stigmatizing. This can detrimentally impact quality of life, with those who stutter reporting worse physical and emotional well-being than those who do not (Kasbi et al., 2015). How best to reduce the stigma of stuttering? As with many types of stigma, contact and education decrease people's negative attitudes toward those who stutter (M. P. Boyle et al., 2016). As people learn about stuttering and have face-to-face interactions with people who stutter, they become less likely to view stuttering in negative and stigmatizing ways (M. P. Boyle et al., 2016).

DELIRIUM AND DEMENTIA

Case Example: Delirium and Dementia

Sanjay

Sanjay, a 74-year-old man, has experienced memory difficulties the past few years. Initially, these problems were mild—forgetting words, losing track of where he left things, or becoming momentarily disoriented. Sanjay dismissed these occurrences as normal forgetfulness. "My senior moments," he laughingly called them. However, Sanjay's memory problems have steadily worsened. Sometimes he cannot remember how to drive home from the store. Other times, he is unable to recall the names of friends and family members. Increasingly, he struggles with basic household tasks like operating the vacuum cleaner and washer-dryer. The day that Sanjay did not recognize his grandchildren was the day his wife, Marsha, demanded he see a doctor.

14.16 DSM and ICD Perspectives on Delirium and Dementia

DSM-5-TR and ICD-11 define **delirium** as diminished attention to and awareness of one's surroundings. It involves memory problems, impaired perceptual functioning, and an overall state of confusion and disorientation. Delirium usually develops quickly (over a few hours or days) and fluctuates in severity. DSM criteria require a biological reason for it (e.g., a medical condition, drug intoxication, or drug withdrawal). See Diagnostic Box 14.5. Depending on its cause, delirium either lifts all together or comes and goes. According to DSM-5-TR, 1 percent to 2 percent of the total population suffers from delirium, with prevalence much higher among older people (8 percent to 17 percent).

Delirium can be difficult to distinguish from **dementia**, which is characterized by a permanent and usually progressive cognitive decline in functioning due to a specific brain disease or injury (see Diagnostic Box 14.5). Alzheimer's disease, Parkinson's disease, vascular disease, traumatic

Constructivist therapy for stuttering: Reduces stuttering by helping clients incorporate being fluent into their core constructions of self.

Delirium: DSM and ICD diagnosis describing a cognitive disturbance that fluctuates in severity and involves diminished attention to and awareness of one's surroundings.

Dementia: Permanent and usually progressive cognitive decline in functioning because of a specific brain disease or injury; ICD still uses this term as a diagnosis.

Mild neurocognitive disorder: DSM and ICD term for mild dementia, characterized by modest cognitive decline.

Major neurocognitive disorder: DSM term for severe dementia, characterized by significant cognitive decline; called *dementia* in ICD.

brain injury, Huntington's disease, and other brain diseases and injuries listed in Table 14.1 can cause dementia; the diagnostic code assigned varies, accordingly. Importantly, DSM has replaced the term dementia with *neurocognitive disorder (NCD)*, which it divides into two diagnoses: **mild neurocognitive disorder** (for cases of mild cognitive decline) and **major neurocognitive disorder** (for cases of severe cognitive decline). ICD-11 has partly followed suit. It uses the name mild neurocognitive disorder for less severe dementia but still refers to more serious cases as dementia, not major neurocognitive disorder.

Diagnostic Box 14.5 Delirium and Dementia

Delirium (DSM-5- TR and ICD-11)

- Disturbed attention to and awareness of the environment that develops over a short period (hours or days) and changes throughout the day.
- Involves disrupted cognition (memory problems, confusion, communication issues, perception difficulties).
- Not due to another neurocognitive disorder.
- **DSM-5-TR**: Biologically attributable to another medical condition or drug use/withdrawal.
- **ICD-11**: Must determine whether delirium is *substance or medication-induced, due to causes other than substances including medications, due to multiple etiologies,* or *due to unknown etiologies.*

Mild Neurocognitive Disorder (DSM-5- TR and ICD-11)

- Cognitive deterioration in one or more of these areas: attention, language, perception, social cognition, executive function, or learning and memory.
- Evidence of cognitive deterioration is based on: (a) reports of the patient, the clinician, or someone who knows the patient well, and (b) impaired mental functioning documented by observation and assessment.
- The person's ability to function is mildly impaired (e.g., can live independently and does not significantly interfere with daily living).

Major Neurocognitive Disorder (DSM-5-TR)/Dementia (ICD-11)

- Same as *mild neurocognitive disorder* except more severe.
- Three levels of severity:
  - *Mild*: Some difficulties with tasks like housework and managing finances.
  - *Moderate*: Requires support for many daily tasks like dressing and eating.
  - *Severe*: Unable to care for self; dependent on others.

Information from American Psychiatric Association (2022, pp. 672–674, 689–693) and World Health Organization (2022a).

According to DSM-5-TR, the prevalence of NCD increases with age, with it affecting 1–2 percent of 65-year-olds and as many as 30 percent of 85-year-olds. Consistent with this, a 2022 U.S. study found that 10 percent of those over age 65 had dementia, while another 22 percent had mild cognitive impairment (Manly et al., 2022). In light of these startling numbers, it is worth noting that some critics see the mild NCD diagnosis as vague (Bermejo-Pareja et al., 2020). They believe it unnecessarily pathologizes normal cognitive declines that occur with age (Kamens et al., 2017; Stokin et al., 2015). Whether one sees cognitive decline as pathological or part of normal aging, clearly many older people experience it. We revisit this debate throughout our examination of dementia below, which focuses mostly on dementia due to Alzheimer's disease.

Table 14.1 Common Dementia-Inducing Brain Diseases and Injuries

- *Alzheimer's disease*
- *Frontotemporal degeneration (Pick's disease)*
- *Human immunodeficiency virus (HIV)*
- *Huntington's disease*
- *Lewy body disease*
- *Parkinson's disease*
- *Prion disease (includes Creutzfeldt-Jakob disease)*
- *Traumatic brain injury*
- *Substance/medication use*
- *Vascular Disease*

14.17 Historical Perspectives on Delirium and Dementia

The term "dementia" derives from Latin words for "off" (*de*) and "mind" (*mens*) (Assal, 2019; G. Cipriani et al., 2011). The first historical reference to dementia has been attributed to the ancient Egyptian Prince Ptah-Hotep around 3000 BCE (Vatanabe et al., 2020). In the early Roman Empire (first and second centuries CE), Greek physicians like Galen and Aretheus of Cappadocia distinguished temporary cognitive declines (delirium) from more permanent ones (dementia) (Vatanabe et al., 2020). Many centuries later, Philippe Pinel (1745–1826)—famous for unchaining the inmates at Bicêtre Hospital in France (revisit Chapter 1)—provided extensive descriptions of patients with dementia; his student and colleague, Jean-Étienne-Dominique Esquirol (1772–1840), also wrote about dementia and speculated about its causes (G. Cipriani et al., 2011; Vatanabe et al., 2020).

The early twentieth-century discovery of **Alzheimer's disease** is attributed to the German physician Alois Alzheimer (1864–1915) (G. Cipriani et al., 2011; Dahm, 2006; N. S. Ryan et al., 2015; Toodayan, 2016; Vatanabe et al., 2020). Dr. Alzheimer worked with a 51-year-old female patient named Auguste Deter, who exhibited severe and progressive cognitive decline; she was confused, disoriented, and had extensive memory problems. After Deter died, Alzheimer examined her brain and identified **senile plaques** (the sticky buildup of *beta-amyloid protein* in the area surrounding neurons) and **neurofibrillary tangles** (the twisting of *tau protein fibers*, which help neurons keep their shape and allow them to transmit nutrients) (Vatanabe et al., 2020). Dr. Alzheimer's discovery greatly influenced modern ideas about Alzheimer's disease: Plaques and tangles are still considered biomarkers of the disease (M. W. Weiner et al., 2015; Zvěřová, 2019). See the "In Depth" feature to learn more about Auguste Deter.

Alzheimer's disease: Dementia linked to *senile plaques* and *neurofibrillary tangles* in the brain; *early-onset Alzheimer's* occurs before age 65 and mostly runs in families, while *late-onset Alzheimer's* occurs after age 65 and is tied to both genes and environment.

Senile plaques: Sticky buildup of beta-amyloid protein in the areas surrounding neurons that is implicated in Alzheimer's disease; also called *amyloid plaques*.

Neurofibrillary tangles: Twisting of tau protein fibers that help neurons keep their shape and allow them to transmit nutrients; common in Alzheimer's patients.

In Depth: The First Documented Case of Alzheimer's Disease

Auguste Deter was the first fully documented case of what became known as Alzheimer's disease. She came under the care of Dr. Alois Alzheimer in 1901 in Frankfurt, Germany. Her primary symptoms were mental confusion, agitation, and difficulty communicating. Her condition steadily worsened, and she eventually died. Here are two excerpts from Alzheimer's medical notes on the case of "Auguste D," recorded November 26, 1901. Dr. Alzheimer's questions are in regular font, while Auguste's responses are in italics. These exchanges provide a harrowing glimpse into the experience of Alzheimer's dementia.

Exchange 1

What year is it? *Eighteen hundred.* Are you ill? *Second month.* What are the names of the patients? She answers quickly and correctly. What month is it now? *The 11th.* What is the name of the 11th month? *The last one, if not the last one.* Which one? *I don't know.* What colour is snow? *White.* Soot? *Black.* The sky? *Blue.* Meadows? *Green.* How many fingers do you have? *5.* Eyes? *2.* Legs? *2.* (Maurer et al., 1997, p. 1547)

Exchange 2

If you buy 6 eggs, at 7 dimes each, how much is it? *Differently.* On what street do you live? *I can tell you, I must wait a bit.* What did I ask you? *Well, this is Frankfurt am Main.* On what street do you live? *Waldemarstreet, not, no ....* When did you marry? *I don't know at present. The woman lives on the same floor.* Which woman? *The woman where we are living.* The patient calls Mrs G, Mrs G, here a step deeper, she lives .... I show her a key, a pencil and a book and she names them correctly. What did I show you? *I don't know, I don't know.* It's difficult isn't it? *So anxious, so anxious.* I show her 3 fingers; how many fingers? *3.* Are you still anxious *Yes.* How many fingers did I show you? *Well this is Frankfurt am Main.* (Maurer et al., 1997, p. 1547)

Although Dr. Alzheimer provided a great deal of information about Auguste's cognitive decline, some complain that historical accounts typically prioritize the postmortem examination of her brain over her life as a working-class woman in Imperial Germany, and that this betrays social and gender biases that still plague dementia care today (and which we revisit when discussing sociocultural perspectives) (I. R. Jones, 2017):

There has arguably been more attention given to Auguste after death than when she was alive, and it seems that her value as a person has never been particularly regarded. It is therefore poignant to recall that [when] in an early interview with Alzheimer she was asked to write her own name and could not recall it, Auguste commented: I have, so to speak, lost myself. (Page & Fletcher, 2006, p. 581)

Photo 14.4 Auguste Deter.
Wikimedia Commons.

Critical Thinking Questions

1. Alzheimer's disease remains unsettling today, long after its identification as a disorder. What do you think it must have been like for people suffering from this disease, as well as their friends and families, before Dr. Alzheimer identified it?
2. Postmortem diagnosis of the brains of Alzheimer's patients remains the only sure way to confirm someone had it. What challenges does this pose for doctors and patients?
3. To fully appreciate the case of Auguste Deter, how important is it to understand the sociohistorical context in which she lived and the details of her life, many of which are lost to history?

14.18 Biological Perspectives on Delirium and Dementia

The Amyloid Hypothesis of Alzheimer's Disease

Consistent with the pioneering work of Alois Alzheimer, senile plaques and neurofibrillary tangles are found in various brain regions in Alzheimer's patients, including the hippocampus (important in memory and, as noted in Chapter 2, often decreased in volume in Alzheimer's patients and others experiencing cognitive decline) (T. Berger et al., 2020; Dawe et al., 2020; D. L. G. Hill et al., 2014; Wolz et al., 2014; L. N. Zhao et al., 2014). The **amyloid hypothesis** holds that—more than anything else—it is the senile plaques that are most critical (Karran & De Strooper, 2022; Makin, 2018). According to this hypothesis, the senile plaques (also called *amyloid plaques* because they consist of beta-amyloid proteins) trigger tau protein malfunctioning. This, in turn, produces neurofibrillary tangles. As the plaques and tangles impair brain functioning, many neurons die, and the brain literally shrinks. At the same time, the patient's cognitive functioning progressively gets worse. Despite the amyloid hypothesis, why plaques and tangles produce Alzheimer's isn't entirely understood; other brain mechanisms likely also play a role. The exact relationship between plaques and tau protein problems remains unclear (Makin, 2018). Neurological and cognitive assessments are still a big part of diagnosing Alzheimer's, but numerous biological measures (e.g., brain imaging, cerebrospinal fluid tests, blood tests, and genetic tests) have been developed over the past decade or so (Atri, 2019; Porsteinsson et al., 2021; Zagorski, 2022). While helpful, no single test can diagnose Alzheimer's because we still don't fully understand its etiology (Atri, 2019; Dubois et al., 2021).

Amyloid hypothesis:
Senile plaques are critical to Alzheimer's disease.

Genetics of Alzheimer's

Why do some people develop senile plaques and neurofibrillary tangles? Most researchers suspect that genes play a central role. Alzheimer's disease is believed to have a strong genetic component, with heritability estimated to be .79 (Gatz et al., 2006). Genes seem especially important in early-onset cases, roughly 10 percent of which are believed to be *autosomal dominant* (meaning if the gene is passed to you by one of your parents, you will develop the disorder) (Wingo et al., 2012). However, early-onset Alzheimer's only makes up about 5–6 percent of total cases (X.-C. Zhu et al., 2015). Some have challenged the early–late onset distinction—but regardless, genes are important in Alzheimer's (Reitz et al., 2020). However, also environment matters, especially in later onset cases. According to the **cognitive reserve hypothesis**, education and intelligence provide a buffer against Alzheimer's and other forms of dementia (Y. Stern, 2012). Studies that support this hypothesis have linked higher IQ scores and (to a lesser degree) more education to lower Alzheimer's and dementia risk (E. L. Anderson et al., 2020; R. Boyle et al., 2021; Contador et al., 2017; Rodriguez & Lachmann, 2020; W. Xu et al., 2016).

Early-onset Alzheimer's has been linked to three genes: *amyloid precursor protein (APP)*, *presenilin 1 (PSEN1)*, and *presenilin 2 (PSEN2)*. These genes are important in the brain's production of the beta-amyloid protein, as well as another protein called *presenilin* (Khanahmadi et al., 2015; Sherva & Kowall, 2022). Late-onset cases have most often been linked to the *apolipoprotein E (APOE)* gene, though various other genes are also attracting attention (Bellenguez et al., 2020, 2022; Mol et al., 2022; Sherva & Kowall, 2022). As with all genetics research, results aren't always replicated. Nonetheless, research continues in the hope of eventually understanding how genetic and environmental factors contribute to Alzheimer's.

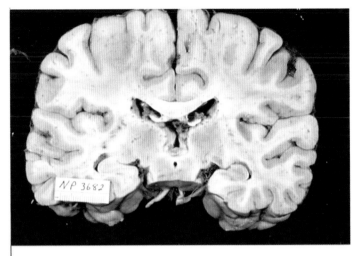

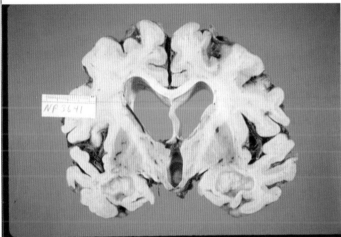

Figure 14.1 The Atrophying Brain in Alzheimer's Disease

Top: A normal adult brain. Bottom: The brain of an adult with Alzheimer's disease, reflecting the brain shrinkage commonly associated with the disorder.

Source: Bird, T. D. (2008). Genetic aspects of Alzheimer disease. Genetics in Medicine, 10(4), 231–239. https://doi.org/10.1097/GIM.0b013e31816b64dc

Cognitive reserve hypothesis: Intelligence and education provide a buffer against Alzheimer's and other forms of dementia.

Drugs Prescribed for Alzheimer's

There is currently no cure for Alzheimer's disease. However, new intravenous drugs are being developed to target and reduce amyloid plaques. There is a lot of excitement about one drug newly approved in the U.S., *lecanemab*, which performed well in early studies (Biogen, 2022; Swanson et al., 2021; U.S. Food and Drug Administration, 2023; van Dyck et al., 2023). However, its predecessor, *aducanumab*, did not live up to the hype. Its poor performance (and high price in the United States) led many to question its FDA approval (A. Park & Law, 2021).

In the meantime, many patients rely on older drugs to slow down or relieve dementia symptoms. Those based on the **cholinergic hypothesis of Alzheimer's** aim to improve memory by boosting levels of the neurotransmitter acetylcholine (P.-P. Liu et al., 2019). Another dementia drug called *memantine* is believed to slow cognitive decline by blocking glutamate (Kuns et al., 2022; R. Wang & Reddy, 2017). Unfortunately, these drugs only slow dementia progression, and their side effects can be unpleasant (Liu et al., 2019; McShane et al., 2019).

Rather than staving off Alzheimer's dementia once it starts, certain drugs are used to prevent it in the first place. To decrease the chances of developing Alzheimer's disease, some doctors recommend the female sex hormone estrogen or nonsteroidal anti-inflammatory drugs (NSAIDs) such as *aspirin*, *ibuprofen* (trade names *Advil*, *Motrin*, *Nuprin*), and *naproxen* (trade names *Aleve*

Cholinergic hypothesis of Alzheimer's: Enhancing acetylcholine transmission reduces memory problems and staves off the progression of Alzheimer's dementia.

and *Naprosyn*). There is some evidence for these drugs as dementia preventatives, although their effectiveness is debated and more research is needed (Benito-León et al., 2019; Birge, 1997; H. Kim et al., 2022; Rivers-Auty et al., 2020; Song et al., 2020).

Finally, sometimes drugs are used to reduce the agitation and aggression that often accompany dementia. Antidepressants and antipsychotics can help in this regard (Calsolaro et al., 2019). However, their serious side effects (especially in older patients) make their use controversial (Calsolaro et al., 2019). For a list of various dementia drugs, consult Table 14.2.

Sanjay

Sanjay is prescribed donezepil for his Alzheimer's dementia. It slows down Sanjay's mental deterioration but can't stop it. Over time, Sanjay loses the ability to communicate and experiences a shift in temperament. He had always been a pleasant and gentle man, but as his Alzheimer's advances, he becomes increasingly angry and sometimes violent. His doctor recommends antipsychotics to manage Sanjay's outbursts. Sanjay's wife, Marsha, reluctantly agrees despite the health risks such drugs pose. "I don't know how else to manage him," she laments.

Table 14.2 Dementia Drugs

DRUG	MECHANISM OF ACTION (GOAL)
Lecanemab (in clinical trials)	Anti-amyloid monoclonal antibody (slow memory loss)
Aducanumab (trade name Aduhelm)	Anti-amyloid monoclonal antibody (slow memory loss)
Donezepil (trade name Aricept)	Enhances acetylcholine transmission (slow memory loss)
Galantamine (trade name Razadyne)	Enhances acetylcholine transmission (slow memory loss)
Rivastigmine (trade name Exelon)	Enhances acetylcholine transmission (slow memory loss)
Memantine (trade name Namenda)	Blocks glutamate (slow memory loss)
NSAIDs (aspirin, ibuprofen, naproxen)	Reduce inflammation (prevent dementia)
Antipsychotics	Block dopamine (reduce agitation/aggression)
Antidepressants	Boost serotonin/norepinephrine (reduce agitation)

14.19 Psychological Perspectives on Delirium and Dementia

Cognitive and Behavioral Interventions for Alzheimer's Disease

Cognitive enhancement therapies assume that cognitively engaging with one's surroundings slows dementia progression (Choi & Twamley, 2013; Clare, 2003). The rationale behind these therapies is that cognitive engagement fosters brain changes that counteract or delay the course of dementia. There are three well-known types of cognitive enhancement therapy: *cognitive stimulation*, *cognitive training*, and *cognitive rehabilitation* (J. Choi & Twamley, 2013; Clare, 2003; Clare & Woods, 2004). Their exact strategies vary, but all three engage patients in exercises to improve cognitive functioning. Patients might be asked to recall names, faces, or events; play word games; practice situation-specific tasks; or organize everyday tasks (such as paying bills or going grocery shopping) to make them easier to remember and complete (J. Choi & Twamley, 2013). The severity of a patient's dementia affects which cognitive exercises can be used. Cognitive enhancement therapies are somewhat effective, though—like drugs—they slow, rather than stop, the impact of dementia (Bahar-Fuchs et al., 2019; Gavelin et al., 2020; Martin-Lopez et al., 2021).

Sanjay

Early in Sanjay's Alzheimer's disease, he undergoes cognitive interventions to counteract his memory deterioration. He is shown pictures of famous people and family members and asked to name them. He also is encouraged to play "Words with Friends" on his iPhone and to practice everyday tasks like heating food in the microwave. For a while, Sanjay's cognitive functioning improves a bit. Over time, however, it worsens until he is no longer able to participate in cognitive enhancement therapy.

Other Interventions: Physical Activity, Pre-Therapy, and Person-Centered Care

Behaviorally, physical activity is encouraged to prevent dementia or counter its advance. Older people who engage in such activity (e.g., walking, biking, household chores, games, sports, and exercise) are less likely to show cognitive and physical decline (Bamidis et al., 2014; M. Y. Cui et al., 2018; Su et al., 2022; J. Zhu et al., 2022). In a different vein, humanistic therapists employ pre-therapy with patients experiencing dementia (Dodds et al., 2014). As discussed in Chapter 4, pre-therapy is a more structured version of person-centered therapy that tries to make emotional contact with patients who are difficult to reach—such as those isolated by the experiences of psychosis, autistic process, or dementia. Pre-therapy cannot reverse dementia, but it provides patients with necessary, but often overlooked, emotional and relational support. Pre-therapy is consistent with a broader emphasis on **person-centered care**, which applies person-centered therapy principles to dementia care by providing a caring and nurturing environment and relationships to patients and their families (Fazio et al., 2018). Research suggests that person-centered care alleviates depression and agitation while improving quality of life (S. K. Kim & Park, 2017).

Person-centered care: Incorporates person-centered therapy concepts into dementia care to provide a supportive and caring environment to patients and their families.

14.20 Sociocultural Perspectives on Delirium and Dementia

Social Factors and Dementia

Social Connectedness

Various social factors are linked to dementia. As noted, education is suspected of protecting against it (W. Xu et al., 2016). The same goes for engaging in leisure activities and attending cultural events (Delfa-Lobato et al., 2021; Su et al., 2022). More broadly, social connectedness predicts lower dementia risk, while loneliness predicts greater risk (Gardener et al., 2021; Ilinca & Suzuki, 2021; Salinas et al., 2022). This contextualizes the association between dementia and mid-life hearing loss (G. Livingston et al., 2020). Hearing impairments socially isolate people, increasing vulnerability to cognitive decline. But hearing loss, loneliness, and lack of social engagement are *modifiable risk factors* that can be addressed or changed (H. Wang, 2020). Enhancing social connectedness (e.g., via easy access to lifelong learning and leisure activities) could mitigate dementia risk. So could healthcare initiatives that offer regular hearing checks and affordable hearing aids. From a social justice standpoint, policies that enhance people's *social reserves* protect or improve their cognitive reserves (Sachdev, 2022). This can potentially reduce rates of dementia and their emotional and financial costs.

Gender

Women appear to be at significantly higher risk for dementia than men (Alzheimer's Association, 2022). Roughly two-thirds of U.S. dementia cases are diagnosed in women (Sindi et al., 2021). The exact reasons for this are unknown, but one explanation is that women tend to live longer than men. Given that dementia is more likely with age, this places women at increased risk (Alzheimer's Association, 2022). Gender inequality is also suspected of playing a role by taxing women's cognitive reserves, making them more susceptible to Alzheimer's dementia (Ilinca & Suzuki, 2021). Besides being more likely than men to be afflicted with dementia, women are also more likely to be caregivers for relatives who develop it. Not only are women estimated to constitute two-thirds of dementia caregivers, but they make up 73 percent of caregivers providing

Photo 14.5 Intellectual stimulation and social connectedness both decrease dementia risk, and could both be found in this chess club. On the contrary, loneliness predicts a greater risk of dementia.

Юлія Вівчарик/Unsplash.

care over forty hours per week (Alzheimer's Association, 2022). Thus, even when women don't directly suffer from dementia, they are more vulnerable to the physical and psychological burdens associated with caring for someone who does.

Stress and Socioeconomic Status

Two other social factors associated with dementia are stress and socioeconomic status and stress. People who experience chronic or posttraumatic stress are at enhanced risk for dementia (Alzheimer's Society, 2017; Ávila-Villanueva et al., 2020; M. S. Greenberg et al., 2014). So are people who come from lower socioeconomic classes (Ilinca & Suzuki, 2021). Of course, stress and socioeconomic status may be related; those from poorer backgrounds may experience more stress in daily life as they struggle to get by. Some researchers suspect that prolonged stress directly contributes to dementia—with high levels of the immune system stress hormone cortisol possibly leading to dysfunctions in the hypothalamic-pituitary-adrenal (HPA) axis and hippocampus (Alzheimer's Society, 2017; Ávila-Villanueva et al., 2020; M. S. Greenberg et al., 2014). Further research examining these important social factors' relationship to dementia is called for.

Day Care and Long-Term Care

Day care programs:
Outpatient programs for people with dementia and other cognitive difficulties that provide interventions to patients and a respite to caregivers.

Long-term care:
Ongoing care in a hospital, nursing home, or assisted-living facility.

Day care programs are outpatient programs for people with dementia and other cognitive difficulties (J. S. M. Curran, 1995; R. L. Moore, 2019). Patients attend these programs during the day and then go home at night. Ideally, such programs provide helpful interventions for patients, improving their moods and reducing their risk of additional psychiatric problems. Day care centers also provide a respite for family caretakers, lifting some of their burden (Tretteteig et al., 2016, 2017). The evidence base is somewhat lacking but suggests adult day care programs benefit patients and their families, though questions about affordability and access remain (L. Duncan et al., 2016; Ellen et al., 2017; Lunt et al., 2021; Maffioletti et al., 2019). **Long-term care** in a hospital, nursing home, or assisted-living facility is also an option. Because it is expensive, comprehensive dementia care programs that allow people to remain in the community might be economically and socially preferable (L. A. Jennings et al., 2019). When long-term care is necessary, racial and ethnic disparities in access to and quality of care can be issues (Rivera-Hernandez et al., 2022).

Sanjay

For a while, Sanjay participates in a day care program. The program includes a variety of activities—exercise and cognitive therapy, for example—to mentally stimulate Sanjay. The day care program provides a break for Sanjay's wife Marsha, his primary caretaker. As Sanjay's functioning deteriorates and it becomes too difficult for Marsha to care for him at home, Sanjay enters a nursing home where he receives long-term care.

Culture, Context, and Dementia

Sociocultural perspectives look at how culture and context shape our understanding of presenting problems. When it comes to dementia, some sociocultural theorists believe that industrialized Western countries overly medicalize and stigmatize cognitive decline in old age, but not all cultures do (G. Cipriani & Borin, 2015). As one example, Native American culture often views psychosis and other cognitively atypical experiences common to dementia not as pathological, but as ways of connecting with the afterlife as "part of an elder's transition to the next world" (G. Cipriani & Borin, 2015, p. 200). As another example, in less individualistic cultures where family is more valued (such as Hispanic/Latino culture), dementia is regarded less negatively. Instead of treating it as a dreaded disease, these cultures see it as an expected component of aging. Within Western cultures, this would require shifting from seeing people with dementia as experiencing a "living death" to viewing them as active citizens who can advocate for themselves and participate in their communities (L. Birt et al., 2017). Part of what makes this shift difficult is the extensive stigma that surrounds dementia (T. Nguyen & Li, 2020).

CLOSING THOUGHTS

14.21 The Growing Prevalence of Dementia

The worldwide prevalence of dementia is increasing as more people live longer. It is estimated that 55 million people suffer from dementia, with almost 10 million new cases each year (World Health Organization, 2022d). The World Health Organization (2017b) has published a global action plan to address the growing number of dementia cases. It includes making dementia a public health priority, raising awareness about dementia, providing support for dementia caregivers, improving diagnosis and treatment of dementia, and sponsoring dementia research. It also emphasizes *dementia friendliness*, which promotes "an inclusive and accessible community environment that optimizes opportunities for health, participation and security for all people" (World Health Organization, 2017b, p. 14). The goal is to "ensure quality of life and dignity for people with dementia," as well as their caretakers and families.

CHAPTER SUMMARY

Intellectual and Learning Difficulties

- DSM-5-TR and ICD-11 distinguish *intellectual development disorders* from *learning disorders*.
- The *eugenics movement* saw intelligence as inherited, and it encouraged policies that only allowed those considered "intelligent" to reproduce.
- Numerous genetically inherited disorders can lead to intellectual and learning difficulties.
- *Applied behavior analysis (ABA)* is commonly used with children diagnosed with intellectual disabilities.
- *Music education* and related interventions aim to improve reading skills and phonological awareness among children with learning disorder diagnoses.
- Socioeconomic inequality is linked to intellectual disabilities.
- *Group homes* serve people with IDD unable to live on their own or with family.
- Social constructionist perspectives contend that the concept of learning disorder emerges from individualistic and pathologizing cultural discourses.

Motor Problems

- *Developmental coordination disorder, stereotypic movement disorder,* and *tic disorders* are DSM-5-TR and ICD-11 motor disorders.
- Gilles de la Tourette is credited with first describing Tourette syndrome.
- The *dopamine hypothesis of Tourette's disorder* links it to too much dopamine, while the *PANDAS hypothesis* attributes tics to contracting strep throat or other viruses in childhood.
- Biological interventions for tic disorders include *prescribing antipsychotic drugs* and *deep brain stimulation*.
- *Comprehensive behavioral intervention for tics (CBIT)* treats tics by combining relaxation training and functional analyses of behavior with *habit reversal training (HRT)*.
- Tic disorders carry a great deal of social stigma.

Communication Problems

- *Speech-sound disorder, language disorder,* and *childhood-onset fluency disorder (stuttering)* are DSM and ICD communication disorders.
- Stuttering runs in families and has been tied to several genes.
- The *dopamine hypothesis of stuttering* holds that excessive dopamine in the basal ganglia is related to stuttering.
- The *Lidcombe Program* is a behavioral intervention for stuttering. It, along with other CBT interventions, is commonly used as a stuttering treatment.
- *Constructivist therapy for stuttering* tries to reduce stuttering by incorporating being fluent into the client's core sense of self.
- Stuttering is stigmatizing and can negatively impact quality of life.

Delirium and Dementia

- *Delirium* and *dementia* involve memory problems and other forms of impaired cognitive functioning; DSM and ICD see the former as transient and the latter as progressive and permanent (and tied to a specific brain disease or injury).
- Historical accounts of dementia go back to the ancient Egyptians. In the early twentieth century, Alzheimer's dementia was identified by Dr. Alois Alzheimer, who discovered *senile plaques* and *neurofibrillary tangles* in the brains of his dementia patients.
- The *amyloid hypothesis* maintains that senile plaques in the brain are the main cause of Alzheimer's disease.
- Many cases of early Alzheimer's are inherited via autosomal dominant genes; late onset cases seem to have both genetic and environmental antecedents.
- Numerous drugs are prescribed for Alzheimer's, but they can only slow it or curb aggressive behavior.
- *Cognitive enhancement therapies* use engagement with one's surroundings to slow the progression of dementia.
- *Behavior therapies* encourage physical activity to slow dementia, while *person-centered care* applied person-centered therapy principles to helping dementia patients and their families to cope.
- Various social factors (e.g., social connectedness, more education, engagement in leisure activities) can mitigate dementia risk.
- Women are diagnosed with dementia significantly more often than men.
- Stress and lower socioeconomic status are both predictive of higher dementia rates.
- *Day care programs* and *long-term care* are used to aid dementia patients and their families.
- Cultural ideas about dementia can influence how people experience it.

Closing Thoughts

- The prevalence of dementia is increasing as more people live to old age, requiring a global action plan to address the mounting number of cases.

NEW VOCABULARY

1. Alzheimer's disease
2. Amyloid hypothesis
3. Childhood-onset fluency disorder (stuttering)
4. Cholinergic hypothesis of Alzheimer's
5. Cognitive enhancement therapies
6. Cognitive reserve hypothesis
7. Comprehensive behavioral intervention for tics (CBIT)
8. Constructivist therapy for stuttering
9. Day care programs
10. Delirium
11. Dementia
12. Developmental coordination disorder
13. Dopamine hypothesis of stuttering
14. Dopamine hypothesis of Tourette's disorder
15. Down syndrome
16. Eugenics movement
17. Fragile X syndrome
18. Group homes
19. Habit reversal training (HRT)
20. Intellectual development disorder (IDD)
21. IQ-achievement discrepancy model
22. Language disorder
23. Lidcombe Program
24. Long-term care
25. Major neurocognitive disorder
26. Mild neurocognitive disorder
27. Music education
28. Neurofibrillary tangles
29. PANDAS hypothesis
30. Person-centered care
31. Persistent (chronic) motor or vocal tic disorder
32. Phenylketonuria (PKU)
33. Provisional tic disorder
34. Response-to-intervention model (RTI)
35. Senile plaques
36. Specific learning disorder (SLD)
37. Stereotypic movement disorder
38. Tic disorders
39. Tourette's disorder

SLEEP AND ELIMINATION DIFFICULTIES

Photo 15.1
Taisiia Shestopal/Unsplash.

OVERVIEW

15.1 Getting Started: Introducing Sleep and Elimination Issues

This chapter discusses sleep difficulties, something we all have encountered at some point. It also examines elimination issues, which often occur during sleep. Sleep and sleep-related issues cause a great deal of mental distress. But when do they rise to the level of pathology? Not everyone agrees. Let's explore these issues so you can decide what you think.

SLEEP DISTURBANCES

Case Examples: Sleep Disturbances

Cassandra
Cassandra is a 46-year-old business executive for a large corporation who is married with three young children. For the past six months, she has had difficulty sleeping. Although tired when she gets in bed at night, Cassandra finds herself unable to sleep and often worries about work or family issues instead. When she does fall asleep, she sleeps poorly, waking up in the middle of the night or very early the next morning. She feels exhausted during the day but still struggles to sleep at night.

Hubert

Hubert is a 30-year-old man who has begun experiencing sudden periods of extreme sleepiness for no apparent reason: "Out of the blue, I'll just fall asleep." When this happens, his muscles often go limp, then he collapses. Not only is it embarrassing, but Hubert worries he might fall and injure himself during one of these episodes.

15.2 DSM and ICD Perspectives on Sleep Disturbances

As with disorders related to sexual health, ICD-11 has moved sleep disorders out of its mental disorders section. However, sleep disorders remain mental disorders in DSM-5-TR simply by being included in the manual, which—unlike ICD—is restricted to mental disorders. Sleep disturbances can be divided into *insomnia disorders*, *hypersomnia disorders*, *parasomnias*, and *breathing-related sleep disorders*. Below we discuss the first three types.

Insomnia, Hypersomnia, and Narcolepsy

Photo 15.2 "I couldn't sleep for six months. With insomnia, nothing seems real. Everything seems far away." *Fight Club* (1999) is one of the most well-known depictions of insomnia. Do the protagonist's symptoms fit with the diagnostic criteria discussed in this chapter?
Photo 12/Alamy Stock Photo.

Insomnia disorders: Sleep problems involving difficulty falling or staying asleep.

Hypersomnolence disorders: Sleep problems involving feeling perpetually tired and sometimes falling asleep despite getting sufficient sleep.

Narcolepsy: Sleep problem characterized by periods of unexpected and uncontrollable sleepiness and abrupt lapses into sleep; often accompanied by *cataplexy* (temporary loss of muscle tone).

Insomnia disorders are characterized by difficulty falling or staying asleep. By contrast, **hypersomnolence disorders** (types of *hypersomnia*) involve feeling excessively sleepy despite sufficient sleep. **Narcolepsy** is an especially dramatic form of hypersomnia, in which there are abrupt lapses into sleep and, in many instances, a sudden but temporary loss of muscle tone—a symptom called *cataplexy*. See Diagnostic Box 15.1. Regarding prevalence, insomnia is extremely common. DSM-5-TR reports that one-third of adults show symptoms and roughly 10 percent qualify for an insomnia disorder diagnosis. Middle-aged and older people are at greater risk, as are women and people with other medical and psychiatric diagnoses. Hypersomnia is less common than insomnia, with DSM-5-TR estimating that 1 percent of Americans and Europeans meet diagnostic criteria. Narcolepsy is rare. DSM-5-TR reports occurrence in just 0.02–0.05 percent of the global population. "The Lived Experience" feature provides a personal account of life with narcolepsy.

Diagnostic Box 15.1 Insomnia, Hypersomnia, and Narcolepsy

Insomnia

- Trouble falling asleep, staying asleep, or waking up early and being unable to go back to sleep not caused by drugs, a medical condition, or another sleep–wake disorder.
- Symptom duration:
  - **DSM-5-TR**: At least three nights per week for three months or longer (*insomnia disorder*).
  - **ICD-11**: Several nights per week for three months or longer (*chronic insomnia*) or for less than three months (*short-term insomnia*).

Hypersomnia

- Excessive sleepiness or napping during the day, despite sufficient nighttime sleep.
- Symptom duration:
  - **DSM-5-TR**: At least three times per week for three months or longer (*hypersomnolence disorder*).
  - **ICD-11**: Lasts for several months (*idiopathic insomnia*).

Narcolepsy

- Excessive sleepiness with abrupt lapses into sleep during the day, sometimes with *cataplexy* (muscle weakness).
- Disturbed/decreased REM sleep patterns.

Information from American Psychiatric Association (2022, pp. 409–410, 417–418, 422–423) and World Health Organization (2022a).

Cassandra and Hubert

Cassandra, who struggles to sleep at night, suffers from insomnia. Hubert, who suddenly and unexpectedly falls asleep during the day, is experiencing narcolepsy.

The Lived Experience: What I Wish People Knew About Living With Narcolepsy

Just before my 21st birthday, I was walking through an art museum in Milan with my mom. She was visiting me during my college semester abroad, where I was studying Italian fashion, culture, and of course, food.

We were mid conversation when my eyes started to get *really* heavy, as they often do. My mom said something to me and then was startled to see me stumble a bit. I had literally fallen asleep while I was walking.

Since I was an otherwise healthy teenager; for years my family, my doctor, and me (for the most part) chalked my fatigue and exhaustion up to a side effect of anxiety, which I have lived with since around age 15. My doctors ran blood panels to test for low iron and other deficiencies that may have potentially caused my lack of energy, but nothing came back abnormal. Not knowing why I was constantly needing to take naps to get through the day not only put stress on me, but also increased my anxiety.

It wasn't until halfway through my senior year of college that I finally took proactive measures to figure out why I couldn't sit through a forty-five-minute lecture without dozing off, or why sometimes, I woke up in the middle of the night feeling like I couldn't move my body. After staying overnight for a sleep study at a sleep center in my hometown, I was diagnosed with narcolepsy Type 1.

Wait, What's Narcolepsy Again?

Narcolepsy is a chronic sleep disorder that causes overwhelming daytime drowsiness and sudden attacks of sleep. The exact cause is unknown, but those with Type 1 have low levels of hypocretin, a neurochemical in the brain that helps regulate wakefulness and REM sleep.

Type 2 narcolepsy is characterized by excessive daytime sleepiness without cataplexy, which is the sudden loss of muscle tone when a person is awake. This can lead to weakness and a loss of voluntary muscle control.

When I tell people I have narcolepsy, often they initially think I'm simply exaggerating the fact that I'm tired all the time (which is fair, I *am* a very dramatic person). Still though, once I clarify that I actually have been diagnosed, I find that people make somewhat of a joke of it—treating the disorder as some sort of spectacle.

They'll say things like:

"Woah, so you just fall asleep randomly?"

"Oh, like that dog in the YouTube video (https://youtu.be/X0h2nleWTwI)?" *No, not like that.*

And my personal favorite: "That's kind of lucky—I wish I could fall asleep that quickly." *No, I promise you don't.*

I've never met anyone else with narcolepsy, and I'm certainly not an expert (although I *am* the only person I know that can fall asleep in 30 seconds). But the disorder has had a rather significant impact on my life, and I've had enough conversations with friends and family over the years to have crafted a running list of things I wish others knew about living with narcolepsy as a 24-year-old woman. Here are some of the biggies:

1. It's not a "blessing in disguise."

I realize that not being able to fall asleep at night can be extremely frustrating and upsetting—not to mention have a negative impact on the following day. The ability to fall sound asleep quickly would definitely be nice if it were something I could control.

Instead, I've fallen asleep in the middle of an exam, at a stoplight in my car, during a meeting a work, and in other public places where 1. It's not socially acceptable to be sleeping and 2. I absolutely do not want to be checked out mentally and 3. I am putting myself (and potentially others) in serious danger (i.e. falling asleep at the wheel)!

2. My "normal" is exhausted.

You know that feeling when you're the most exhausted you think you've ever been in your life—your eyes are so heavy that it would take physically holding them open with your fingers to keep yourself awake? Your mind is elsewhere and foggy and your body is begging you for sleep ...

That's how I feel every single day, several times a day. I am prescribed a stimulant by my sleep doctor, which I take daily (sometimes twice) to allow myself to be at a "normal" that is more in line with those around me. On the days that I don't take my medicine, I'll fall asleep at any given time—sitting at a table, on the train home, visiting with my roommates, you name it.

A daily routine that comes naturally for most people is tough for me to get through, which is both disheartening and frustrating. Quite frankly, it's exhausting being this exhausted.

3. I sleep often, but not well.

I could sleep more than 12 hours and still wake up feeling tired. According to the National Institute of Neurological Disorder and Stroke, narcolepsy affects the brain's ability to control sleep-wake cycles. I fall asleep as quickly as 30 seconds, and because of the disorder, I enter REM sleep almost immediately.

However, the rest of my night is filled with sleep disruptions caused by vivid nightmares, hallucinations, and sleep paralysis. During an episode of sleep paralysis, I'm unable to move my body or speak just before waking up or falling asleep, and let me tell you—it is terrifying. Enough to make this 24-year-old woman want to crawl in bed with her mom. Add hallucinations of someone standing over me, touching me, or sitting on my bed, and a good night's sleep is *absolutely* out of the question.

4. It affects every aspect of my life.

I've done poorly on exams, been late to important events, and completely missed plans I was committed to (and excited for) because of my sleep disorder. It's not something that lives in my subconscious—if I'm in the middle of a meeting, out to dinner with friends, or waiting for my dinner to finish cooking and one of my sleep attacks hit, it's nearly impossible for me to keep from falling asleep. Trust me, I've tried.

5. There's no cure (yet).

Though there isn't a cure for narcolepsy, medication and certain lifestyle changes help manage symptoms of the disorder. For example, I know that during a wave of sleepiness during the day, I will feel refreshed if I get up and move my body. Some days that means taking a walk around the block outside of work. When the weather isn't ideal, I'll take a few laps around my floor—get some cold water, say hi to a co-worker, and focus on something other than feeling like I'm going to fall asleep.

Some days are definitely tougher than others—like when I have had a particularly restless night or forget to take my medicine in the morning. As with everything in life, though, it's a learning process. I'm sure as the years go on, I'll identify more effective ways to manage my narcolepsy, and I hope to learn from others, too, along the way.

By Maya McDowell.

Reprinted from https://www.prevention.com/health/sleep-energy/a29011949/living-with-narcolepsy-personal-story/.

Parasomnias

Parasomnias involve undesired events or experiences during sleep. In DSM-5-TR's **non-rapid eye movement (NREM) sleep arousal disorder**, deep sleep is disrupted by either *sleepwalking* (getting out of bed and walking around while still asleep) or *sleep terrors* (episodes of intense terror that abruptly awaken one from deep sleep). Unlike DSM-5-TR, ICD-11 lists **sleepwalking disorder** and **sleep terrors** as separate diagnoses rather than as subtypes of a single non-REM sleep arousal disorder. It also includes a **sleep-related eating disorder** diagnosis for people who eat during sleepwalking episodes. Prevalence estimates for NREM sleep arousal disorders vary widely. For instance, DSM-5-TR reports lifetime prevalence of sleepwalking to range from 6.9 percent to 29.2 percent. Notably, both sleepwalking and sleep terrors (also called *night terrors*) are more common in children than adults.

Other DSM-5-TR and ICD-11 parasomnias include **rapid eye movement (REM) sleep behavior disorder** (acting out the dreams one experiences during REM sleep), **nightmare disorder** (recurrent vivid and upsetting dreams in which safety, security, or survival is at risk), and **restless legs syndrome** (irresistible urge to move one's legs while resting or trying to sleep). ICD-11 technically classifies restless leg syndrome as a sleep-related movement disorder, but DSM-5-TR considers it a parasomnia. More on parasomnias in Diagnostic Box 15.2.

Diagnostic Box 15.2 Parasomnias

Non-Rapid Eye Movement (NREM) Sleep Arousal Disorder
- **DSM-5-TR**: Partial awakening, usually during first third of sleep, that involves either:
  - *Sleepwalking* (getting out of bed and walking around, usually with a blank face and lack of responsiveness to others), or
  - *Sleep terrors* (abrupt arousal from sleep, typically accompanied by a panicked scream, rapid breathing, excessive heart rate, and perspiration).
- **ICD-11**: Divided into three disorders: "sleepwalking disorder," "sleep terrors," and "sleep-related eating disorder."

Rapid Eye Movement (REM) Sleep Behavior Disorder
- Arousal during REM sleep characterized by talking or physical movement.

Nightmare Disorder
- Repeated vivid and upsetting dreams of a frightening nature that usually involve threats to safety, security, or survival that usually occur during second half of sleep and result in abruptly waking up.

Restless Legs Syndrome
- Irresistible desire to move one's legs that gets worse when resting or trying to sleep.
- Symptoms improve when walking.
- NOTE: Classified as a "sleep-related movement disorder" in ICD-11.

Information from American Psychiatric Association (2022, pp. 452, 457, 461, 464–465) and World Health Organization (2022a).

Evaluating DSM and ICD Perspectives on Sleep Disturbances

As mentioned, sleep disorders are highly comorbid with other mental and physical disorders. This makes sense. Think of how your own sleep is affected when you feel anxious, sad, sick, or are having difficulties breathing. So, is insomnia a disorder in and of itself or a sign of some other problem? DSM and ICD classify it as a disorder all its own, but some people question this. They wonder how insomnia can be a discrete disorder if there are so many potentially different causes for it. Nonetheless, mental health professionals must be familiar with sleep problems because so many clients present with them.

Parasomnias: Sleep disturbances involving undesired events or experiences during sleep (e.g., sleepwalking, sleep terrors, nightmares, or acting out dreams).

Non-rapid eye movement (NREM) sleep arousal disorder: DSM parasomnia in which sleep is disrupted by sleepwalking or sleep terrors.

Sleepwalking disorder: ICD parasomnia characterized by getting out of bed and walking around while still asleep; the sleepwalker has a blank expression, in unresponsive to others, and is difficult to awaken; also called *somnambulism*.

Sleep terrors: ICD disorder involving episodes of intense terror that jerk a person abruptly from deep sleep, often with a panicked scream and a scramble to escape the room.

Sleep-related eating disorder: ICD diagnosis for people who eat while sleepwalking.

Rapid eye movement (REM) sleep behavior disorder: DSM and ICD parasomnia characterized by acting out the dreams one experiences during REM sleep.

Nightmare disorder: DSM and ICD parasomnia involving regularly having intense dreams in which one's safety or survival is threatened.

Restless legs syndrome: DSM and ICD disorder involving overwhelming desire to move one's legs while resting or going to sleep.

15.3 Historical Perspectives on Sleep Disturbances

Both sleep habits and ideas about what is normal sleep have changed across history. Early hunter-gatherers (*c.* 8000 BCE) likely slept in the fetal position in shallow pits next to cave walls (Bulger, 2016). The ancient Egyptians revered sleep as a near-death state, but the later Romans didn't focus much on sleep—possibly seeing it as a distraction from building roads, aqueducts, and the Coliseum (Bulger, 2016). People experiencing tough times in Europe during the Middle Ages huddled together to stay warm while they slept, so sleep wasn't especially comfortable or private (Bulger, 2016). It was during the Renaissance that Europeans began focusing on comfort during sleep. Mattresses were made more comfortable by placing them on ropes weaved back and forth across bed frames; some historians even attribute the phrase "sleep tight" to the fact that these ropes had to be tightened each evening before bed (T. Fisher, 2011). Prior to the advent of nighttime lighting, people usually went to sleep for several hours after sunset, then woke in the middle of the night to pray, talk, or have sex; after that, they went back to sleep for several hours before rising at dawn (Ekirch, 2005). The notion of an uninterrupted night's sleep is a modern conception that influences current ideas about normal sleep habits.

15.4 Biological Perspectives on Sleep Disturbances

The Sleep Cycle

Sleep cycle: Cycle a person goes through four to five times during a normal night's sleep, consisting of four distinct stages; the first three are *non-rapid eye movement (NREM) sleep* (involving little or no eye movement or dreaming) and the fourth is *rapid eye movement (REM) sleep* (involving rapid eye movement, muscle paralysis, and dreaming).

Using a machine called an electroencephalogram (*EEG*) to record the brain's electrical activity, researchers have identified different patterns of activity (i.e., *brain waves*) that occur during sleep and wakefulness. The **sleep cycle** consists of four stages. The first three involve *non-rapid eye movement (NREM) sleep*, in which there is little or no eye movement and dreaming is extremely rare (Suni, 2022). The final stage is *rapid eye movement (REM) sleep*, characterized by rapid eye movement, muscle paralysis, and dreaming (Suni, 2022). During an eight-hour night of sleep, older children and adults go through the sleep cycle four to five times (Suni, 2022). See Figures 15.1 and 15.2.

Biological Explanations and Drugs for Sleep Disturbances
Hyperarousal and Insomnia

Hyperarousal theory of insomnia: Some people are genetically predisposed to arousal and easily become conditioned to associate hyperarousal with sleep-related stimuli, making it difficult for them to fall or stay sleep.

The **hyperarousal theory of insomnia** proposes that people with chronic insomnia are genetically vulnerable to chronic hyperarousal (Riemann et al., 2010; I. Vargas et al., 2020). Through classical conditioning, this hyperarousal becomes associated with things like worrying or lying in bed at night (Riemann et al., 2010; I. Vargas et al., 2020). People with insomnia remain in a hyperaroused physiological state much of the time, making sleep difficult.

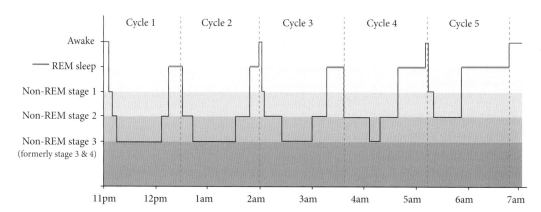

Figure 15.1 The Sleep Cycle during an Eight-Hour Night of Sleep. Most people go through the sleep cycle five times during a typical night's sleep, as illustrated by this hypnogram.
Source: Reprinted with permission from Luke Mastin. Available from: http://www.howsleepworks.com/types_cycles.html [accessed February 22, 2018]

Duration of Sleep Stages

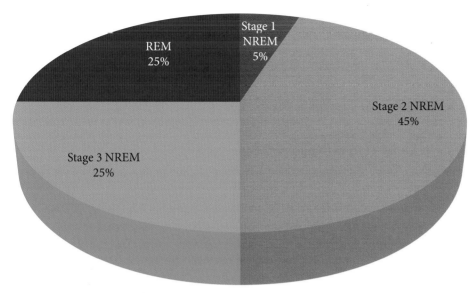

Figure 15.2 Percentage of Sleep Spent in Each of the Sleep Stages. Most time asleep is spent in NREM stages.

Source: Reprinted with permission from Luke Mastin. Available from: http://www.howsleepworks.com/types_cycles.html [accessed February 22, 2018]

Cassandra

According to hyperarousal theory, Cassandra's insomnia results from a genetic predisposition to hyperarousal—so much so that stimuli that should evoke rest, such as her bed, have become associated with an aroused physiological state.

Drug Treatments for Insomnia

Many different types of drugs are prescribed for insomnia. Benzodiazepines (see Chapter 6) and **non-benzodiazepine receptor antagonists** (or *Z-drugs*) are popular sleep aids (Monkmeyer et al., 2022). They improve sleep by targeting GABA, the inhibitory neurotransmitter that reduces anxiety (Monkmeyer et al., 2022). Benzodiazepines can be addictive, so less habit-forming Z-drugs are often used instead. Common Z-drugs include *zolpidem* (trade names *Ambien, Edular, ZolpiMist, Intermezzo*), *eszopiclone* (trade name *Lunesta*), and *zapelon* (trade name *Sonata*) (Monkmeyer et al., 2022). However, the newest drugs for insomnia are **orexin-receptor antagonists**—*suvoxerant* (trade name *Belsomra*), *lemborexant* (trade name *Dayvigo*), and *daridorexant* (trade name *Quuviq*). They block orexin, the neurotransmitter implicated in arousal and wakefulness (Monkmeyer et al., 2022). This decreases arousal and makes sleep more likely. Research finds benzodiazepines, Z-drugs, and orexin-receptor antagonists to be effective for insomnia, although side effects and safety remain challenges (De Crescenzo et al., 2022). Beyond these drugs, other sleep aids include *antihistamines* (which inhibit *histamine*, another wake-promoting neurotransmitter), *melatonin* (a hormone important in regulating sleep-wake cycles), tricyclic antidepressants (which induce drowsiness), and even antipsychotics (which have a tranquilizing effect) (Monkmeyer et al., 2022). No insomnia drug is a panacea. Prolonged use is generally discouraged due to side effects and long-term effectiveness is questionable (D. H. Solomon et al., 2021).

Non-benzodiazepine receptor antagonists: Enhance GABA activity and promote sleep; sometimes referred to as *Z-drugs*, they are used to treat insomnia.

Orexin-receptor antagonists: Insomnia drugs that block the wake-promoting neurotransmitter orexin, thereby promoting sleep.

Cassandra

Cassandra could be prescribed benzodiazepines for her insomnia. However, because of these drugs' potential for addiction, it might be better to try a non-benzodiazepine sleep aid such as zolpidem. Another possibility would be to prescribe her the newest sleep aid drug, suvoxerant. Regardless of which drug she used, it's likely to help only so long as she continues to take it.

Orexin and Narcolepsy

Orexin: Neurotransmitter important in regulating wakefulness and appetite.

Narcolepsy is associated with too little **orexin** (also called *hypocretin*), a neurotransmitter secreted by the lateral hypothalamus (Howell, 2012; Mahoney et al., 2019). Orexin—which comes in two varieties, orexin-A and orexin-B (Mahoney et al., 2019)—regulates wakefulness and appetite. Narcolepsy, including cataplexy, is linked to orexin cell loss (Mahoney et al., 2019; E. Mignot et al., 2021). Orexin is also linked to diseases involving neurological degeneration, including Parkinson's disease, Alzheimer's disease, and dementia with Lewy bodies (all implicated in dementia, discussed later), as well amyotrophic lateral sclerosis (ALS) (F. Gao et al., 2021; Howell, 2012).

Drug Treatments for Hypersomnia and Narcolepsy

Modafinil: A non-amphetamine stimulant drug used to treat insomnia.

Sodium oxybate: A central nervous system depressant prescribed to treat cataplexy; also known as *gamma-hydroxybutyrate (GHB)*.

For those who sleep too much or struggle to stay awake, amphetamines are often prescribed (Chervin, 2022; E. J. M. Mignot, 2012; M. S. Wise et al., 2007). These drugs inhibit sleep by stimulating the central nervous system. **Modafinil** (U.S. trade name, *Provogil*), a non-amphetamine stimulant, is often prescribed because it has fewer side effects than other sleep aid drugs (Chervin, 2022). Modafinil is sometimes supplemented with **sodium oxybate**, a depressant used to treat cataplexy (Chervin, 2022). Sodium oxybate is controversial not only due to its habit-forming qualities but also because of its well-publicized misuse. Also known as *gamma-hydroxybutyrate (GHB)*, it has been slipped into the drinks of unsuspecting people to sedate them against their wishes, resulting in media references to it as the "date-rape drug" (Krahn, 2003). Besides these drugs, antidepressants are sometimes prescribed for narcolepsy because they suppress REM sleep and reduce cataplexy.

Hubert

To treat his narcolepsy, Hubert could be prescribed amphetamines. However, given concerns about their addictive potential, he might be prescribed modafinil instead. While modafinil is likely to keep Hubert awake during the day, his cataplexy might be more responsive to sodium oxybate. Of course, his doctor will need to monitor Hubert closely to make sure the sodium oxybate doesn't become habit-forming.

15.5 Psychological Perspectives on Sleep Disturbances

Psychodynamic Theory and Nightmares

Psychodynamic perspectives focus more on dreams than sleep. In classic psychoanalysis, every dream is a wish fulfillment. The wishes expressed in dreams are often unconscious and unacceptable (Freud, 1900/1965). Psychodynamic therapies focus on the unconscious meanings of nightmares and sleep terrors and help patients work through the corresponding emotional conflicts (Lansky & Bley, 1995; Novellino, 2012). There is minimal research on psychodynamic perspectives on nightmares and night terrors, but many people remain convinced that nightmares (and dreams in general) are unconscious communications that must be analyzed and understood.

Cognitive-Behavioral Therapy for Insomnia (CBT-I)

Cognitive-behavioral therapy for insomnia (CBT-I): CBT insomnia treatment that uses cognitive therapy and relaxation training along with *stimulus control therapy, sleep restriction,* and *sleep hygiene education.*

Cognitive-behavioral therapy for insomnia (CBT-I) uses various CBT interventions to target dysfunctional cognitions and behaviors responsible for sleep difficulties (Baron et al., 2017; Edinger & Means, 2005; Rossman, 2019; Rybarczyk et al., 2013). Besides traditional cognitive therapy and relaxation training, one of the main CBT-I techniques is *stimulus control*, which reconditions bedtime and the bedroom to be associated with sleep rather than wakefulness. This is accomplished by having clients only go to bed when tired, get out of bed when they cannot sleep (so bed is not associated with being awake), and only use the bedroom for sleeping (so it is not associated with other activities, like reading or watching TV). Another technique is *sleep restriction*, in which total time in bed is steadily restricted so that it eventually matches the amount of time needed for sleep. This trains the person to remain in bed only so long as necessary to sleep. Finally, in *sleep* *hygiene education*, the client is taught habits conducive to getting a good night's sleep, including the importance of regular exercise, having a small snack before bed, keeping the bedroom dark and noise-free, and avoiding caffeine, alcohol, and nicotine before bed. Though it can take time to work and not everyone adheres to it because it is labor intensive, CBT-I is effective and less expensive than drug treatments (Ashworth et al., 2015; J. R. Davidson et al., 2019; E. E. Matthews et al., 2013; M. D. Mitchell et al., 2012; Natsky et al., 2020; Rybarczyk et al., 2013). It can even be administered digitally via a smartphone app (Erten Uyumaz et al., 2021). Unfortunately, doctors do not always screen for sleep issues or know about CBT-I, so it is an underutilized intervention (Koffel et al., 2018; Rossman, 2019).

Cassandra

In CBT-I for her insomnia, Cassandra's therapist would ask her to keep a sleep log to better understand when, where, and how often she sleeps. If Cassandra typically sleeps six hours per night, he might restrict her to no more than six and a half hours in bed per night. He also might have her avoid non-sleeping activities in bed—including reading, eating, thinking, watching TV, or even having sex with her husband ("Find another room in the house for that!"). The goal is to recondition the bedroom as a place associated solely with sleep and rest. Any irrational thoughts Cassandra might have, such as "I must get eight hours of sleep every night or I won't be able to function" or "I am incapable of sleeping through the night," would be challenged using cognitive therapy. Finally, the therapist would educate Cassandra about proper sleeping habits so that she engages in sleep-promoting behaviors like keeping her bedroom dark at night while avoiding sleep-impairing actions like drinking caffeinated drinks that stimulate wakefulness.

15.6 Sociocultural Perspectives on Sleep Disturbances

Culturally driven habits that we tend to overlook are sometimes associated with sleep problems. Caffeine intake and online screen time are two prominent examples (Hale et al., 2018; Kaldenbach et al., 2022; Maurya et al., 2022; Tomanic et al., 2022). Asking people with sleep issues about their screen time (especially before bed) and their daily intake of coffee, tea, carbonated beverages, and energy drinks can mitigate the need to prescribe sleep aids.

From a social justice perspective, sleep disturbances are often due to social injustice. For instance, *organizational injustice* (in which workplace conditions are unfair or oppressive) creates stress that can affect employees' sleep. Reduced pay, workplace inequality, workplace stress, working two jobs, working long hours, and spending a lot of time commuting all predict inadequate sleep (Basner et al., 2014; J. W. Brown, 2017; Elovainio et al., 2009; J. Greenberg, 2006). More broadly, socioeconomic disadvantage or belonging to a racial/ethnic minority group are also predictive of sleep difficulties (X. Chen et al., 2015; Grandner, 2017; Grandner et al., 2016; Stamatakis et al., 2007; N. Williams et al., 2019; W. Wu et al., 2018; T. Yip et al., 2022). Why does this matter? Because sleep issues are associated with poorer physical and mental health (Hale, 2014; Medic et al., 2017). From a social justice perspective, sleep loss is often not a sign of mental disorder, but of inequality. If we addressed poverty, discrimination, and other social issues that predict inadequate sleep, might we improve people's sleep and, in turn, their health? Social justice advocates believe that casting sleep issues exclusively as individual disorders results in overlooking broader societal inequalities requiring attention and reform.

Photo 15.3 Reduced pay, workplace inequality, working long hours, and belonging to a racial/ethnic minority group have all been linked to sleep difficulties.
Surface/Unsplash.

In Depth: Racial and Ethnic Disparities in Sleep

Many Americans don't get enough sleep, a problem that the COVID-19 pandemic only exacerbated (Neculicioiu et al., 2022; Partinen et al., 2021; C. M. Sheehan et al., 2019). However, lack of sleep varies noticeably by race and ethnicity. These disparities are both striking and alarming. As Figure 15.3 illustrates, research consistently finds Black, Native American, Asian American, and Hispanic individuals get less sleep than their white counterparts (D. A. Johnson et al., 2019; C. M. Sheehan et al., 2019; J. P. Smith et al., 2019; T. Yip et al., 2020). How come? Some researchers suspect that racial and ethnic groups face systemic disadvantages that negatively impact sleep, such as discrimination, being socioeconomically less well off, having to work more hours, and having less access to healthcare (D. A. Johnson et al., 2019; C. M. Sheehan et al., 2019; J. P. Smith et al., 2019; T. Yip et al., 2020). However, racial/ethnic differences in sleep remain even after controlling for socioeconomic status, behavioral differences, and clinical factors (D. A. Johnson et al., 2019). Hopefully, future research to understand why can help us reduce or eliminate this disparity.

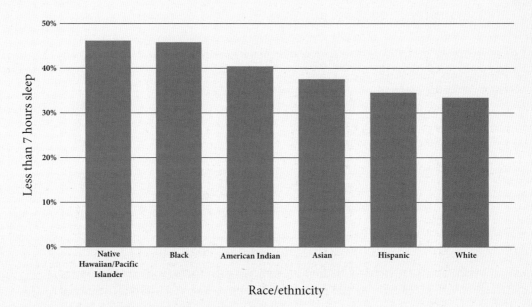

Figure 15.3 Insufficient Sleep by Race and Ethnicity.
Source: Reproduced from https://www.sleepfoundation.org/how-sleep-works/sleep-facts-statistics

Critical Thinking Questions

1. What factors do you believe are most important in explaining racial/ethnic disparities in sleep? Why?
2. Think of a time when your own sleep was disrupted. To what extent do you think racial or ethnic considerations played a role?

ELIMINATION ISSUES

Case Examples: Elimination Issues

Maribel

Maribel, age 8, began regularly wetting her bed six months ago. Her parents are upset and confused and upset by this. Maribel is embarrassed by her bedwetting and hopes her friends from school do not find out.

Arjun

Arjun, a 6-year-old boy, regularly defecates in his pants. Even worse, he sometimes "plays" with his stool, smearing it on the wall on several occasions. His parents are extremely worried. They acknowledge that Arjun has experienced problems with constipation in the past. Arjun avoids going to the toilet because defecating while constipated is painful and anxiety-provoking.

15.7 DSM and ICD Perspectives on Elimination Issues

Enuresis and Encopresis

In DSM-5-TR and ICD-11, **enuresis** is diagnosed in people five years or older who wet their beds or clothes, whereas **encopresis** is diagnosed in people four years or older who repeatedly have bowel movements in inappropriate places, such as in their pants or on the floor. For diagnostic details, see Diagnostic Box 15.3. According to DSM-5-TR, encopresis affects 1–4 percent of children in high-income countries; it occurs in 5–10 percent of 5-year-olds, 3–5 percent of 10-year-olds, and 1 percent of people 15 years old or older. Both diagnoses are more common in boys than girls. There is more research on enuresis than encopresis, so enuresis receives greater attention below. "The Lived Experience" box offers a vivid personal account of adult enuresis.

Enuresis: DSM and ICD diagnosis given to children who wet their beds or clothes; also known as *bedwetting.*

Encopresis: DSM and ICD diagnosis given to children who repeatedly have bowel movements in inappropriate places, such as on the floor.

Diagnostic Box 15.3 Elimination Disorders

Enuresis

- Unintentionally or intentionally urinates into bed or clothes.
- Must be at least 5 years old or at equivalent developmental level.
- Not caused by drugs or another medical condition.
- Symptom duration:
  - **DSM-5-TR**: At least twice weekly for three months.
  - **ICD-11**: Several times weekly for several months.

Encopresis

- Unintentionally or intentionally placing bowel movements in inappropriate places (e.g., in pants or on floor).
- Must be at least 4 years old or at equivalent developmental level.
- Not caused by drugs or another medical condition besides constipation.
- Symptom duration:
  - **DSM-5-TR**: At least once a month for three months.
  - **ICD-11**: At least once per month for several months.

Information from American Psychiatric Association (2022, pp. 399, 402) and World Health Organization (2022a).

Maribel and Arjun

Maribel qualifies for an enuresis diagnosis and Arjun for encopresis.

The Lived Experience: Not Everybody "Outgrows" Bedwetting

Matt* (name changed) has shared his story:

I used to consider my bedwetting the most shameful secret I had to carry. I'm 32 years old now, and in my 20s I did everything I could to make sure no one else worked it out. There were definitely giveaways. For one, I was a young guy living in a share house and washing my bed linens twice a week ...

Years later, anybody who knows me well is aware that I still wet the bed. Keeping my incontinence a secret is a ship that sailed a long time ago.

The fact is that some people wet the bed while others don't. Some people grow out of it, and others don't. I just happen to be one of the ones that didn't. It goes without saying that I've tried everything I can to stop wetting the bed.

For a long time, I thought it was normal and that most people had occasional bedwetting problems. It only happened about four times a year, so as a young teen, I didn't really think about it. I tried to ignore it and continued with the "bury my head in the sand" approach until a girlfriend brought it to my attention. By then, it was getting more and more frequent.

Seeking Treatment

I didn't see anybody for my issue until I was 18. I had treatment for a suspected infection but that didn't stop the bedwetting. Afterwards, I didn't go back to the doctor until age 21. That time, I really wanted to get help. The doctor referred me to a urologist, but I will never forget how silly and small I felt when I called to make an appointment. "We only deal with children," they said. As though I needed more reminding that this was something I was supposed to have "grown out of."

Hiding It

Growing up, I obeyed the unwritten rule in my household that this wasn't something to discuss. I just wish the approach had been different. If my kid was wetting the bed, I wouldn't try and ignore it. At night, I transformed into a mouse that changed the sheets silently at 3am or stayed awake during sleepovers with friends so that I wouldn't fall asleep and have an accident.

My biggest fear was my friends finding out. Eventually when I was 17, they did, and the taunts and bullying started. That period of my life damaged me for good. I was so hurt that people were having a laugh at my expense. It made me stronger though. I often think that if I could cop that and come through relatively unscathed, I don't need to worry.

Mental Health

Incontinence is certainly something that makes people uncomfortable. I have anxiety and depression and I speak freely about my mental health. But when you mention wetting the bed, people get this "look"—almost like they must react that way so everybody can see they don't have incontinence.

I have experienced incredibly cruel actions from people who just don't understand incontinence or think it's something to laugh about. A few years ago, my housemate's partner took a photo of me after I had wet the bed and posted it to Facebook. It made me feel incredibly vulnerable and never want to live in a share house again. What gave me a little bit of comfort—and hope—was that people who I didn't even know were defending me online and saying what she did wasn't cool.

Dating

My condition makes dating and relationships difficult. In fairness, it really is a lot to ask of anybody. These days I'm very upfront and tell a new partner that I may wet the bed but have prepared adequately with continence products like plastic sheets and a pull-up.

Yes, I'm a 32-year-old man and wear a pull-up to bed. Deal with it.

Sharing My Story

I've found that telling others about my incontinence can make a difference. I was working with a woman and after I was honest with her about my bedwetting, she actually told me that she had the same issue. I was one of the first people that she told. I really want to be a person that people can trust to confide in. That's a good way to see yourself.

I'm choosing to share my story with anybody who wants to read it. Anyone who is going through the same thing will understand on a totally different level. My message to you is to keep calm and carry on. You're a soldier. The people who judge have no idea what you go through daily.

This story was first published in *Bridge* magazine. Reprinted from https://www.continence.org.au/news/not-everybody-outgrows-bedwetting-matts-story.

Criticisms of DSM and ICD Perspectives

Some believe DSM and ICD define enuresis too broadly, failing to distinguish between nighttime bedwetting (which is always involuntary) and daytime bedwetting (which can be intentional or unintentional) (von Gontard, 2013a). There is also substantial comorbidity between enuresis and other presenting problems—especially ADHD but oppositional defiant disorder, anxiety disorders, and mood disorders, as well (Ferrara et al., 2019; R. Pole et al., 2022; Tsai et al., 2017; von Gontard & Equit, 2015). Physical and intellectual disabilities are also common in children with enuresis (Gontkovsky, 2011; L. D. Nair et al., 2015; von Gontard, 2013b). The high comorbidity raises the question of whether elimination issues are independent problems or symptoms of other issues.

15.8 Historical Perspectives on Elimination Issues

The first known reference to nocturnal enuresis was made by the ancient Egyptians around 1550 BCE (Glicklich, 1951; McDonald & Trepper, 1977; Salmon, 1975). During Roman times, the philosopher and naturalist Pliny the Elder (23–79 CE) proposed various interventions to prevent incontinence, including feeding children boiled mice (Salmon, 1975). The Persian physician Rhazes (*c.* 865–925 CE) explained enuresis in ways that seem quite modern. He said that it could be caused by deep sleep, drinking too much before bed, small bladder capacity, and delayed development (Changizi Ashtiyani et al., 2013). Later European views are more befuddling. In 1545, the English pediatrician Thomas Phaire recommended enuresis be treated by burning the windpipe of a cock or the testicles of a hedgehog into a powder having patients ingest it two or three times a day (Salmon, 1975). By the seventeenth and eighteenth centuries, enuresis became increasingly medicalized. Fluid restriction, enemas, alarm clocks, and cold or warm baths were all prescribed (Hurl, 2011; Salmon, 1975). There are nineteenth-century accounts of various devices being attached to the penis (including some that delivered electric shocks when urine was detected) or—even more invasively—the urethra being sealed to prevent urination (Hurl, 2011; Salmon, 1975). As you can see, there have been many explanations for enuresis throughout history, yet "no method or treatment has ever fully contained this elusive condition" and "no analysis has sufficiently defined its causes" (Hurl, 2011, p. 49).

15.9 Biological Perspectives on Elimination Issues

Genetics and Enuresis

Enuresis appears to run in families. Twin studies report higher concordance rates among identical twins than fraternal twins, although this finding applies more to boys than girls (R. J. Butler, 2004; M. B. Scharf et al., 1987; von Gontard et al., 2011). Further, potential genetic markers for enuresis have been identified (Eiberg et al., 1995; Jørgensen et al., 2021; von Gontard et al., 1997, 2001). However, more studies are needed.

Maribel

Maribel's mother was also a bed wetter growing up, as were several of Maribel's cousins on her mother's side. "We have a long history of weak bladders in our family," Maribel's mother awkwardly jokes. Whether this is due to genetics or shared family environment isn't clear.

Drug Treatments for Enuresis

The most common drug to treat enuresis is **desmopressin**—a synthetic version of *vasopressin*, a hormone that reduces urine production. Marketed under the trade name *DDAVP*, desmopressin decreases urine production to reduce or eliminate nighttime bedwetting. It is effective in treating bedwetting but only so long as it is taken (Glazener et al., 2004; Glazener & Evans, 2002; McCarty & Shah, 2022). Its side effects include headaches, stomach aches, and—most dangerously—*water intoxication*, in which a child taking it gets extremely thirsty, drinks too many fluids, and experiences symptoms ranging from dizziness and fatigue to seizures and even death (Thurber, 2017). Although water intoxication can be avoided by monitoring fluid intake, some parents remain hesitant about desmopressin.

Desmopressin: Synthetic form of the hormone *vasopressin*, prescribed to decrease urine production in the treatment of nighttime bedwetting.

Sometimes desmopressin is supplemented with anticholinergic medications such as *oxybutynin* and *tolterodine*, which block the activity of the neurotransmitter *acetylcholine* (important in activating muscles and regulating attention and memory) (Arda et al., 2016; Tranel et al., 2020; Tu & Baskin, 2022). This sometimes improves outcomes, although when used alone anticholinergic agents have a mixed track record (Tu & Baskin, 2022). If desmopressin fails, tricyclic antidepressants like imipramine are prescribed for nocturnal bedwetting (Caldwell et al., 2016; Tu & Baskin, 2022). Tricyclics, which stimulate vasopressin, reduce enuresis symptoms but have more serious side effects than desmopressin (Caldwell et al., 2016; Tu & Baskin, 2022).

Maribel

Maribel's pediatrician prescribes desmopressin for her nocturnal bedwetting. Maribel takes the medication for six months and her enuresis all but disappears. However, because the desmopressin gives Maribel stomach aches, her parents agree to let her stop taking it. Unfortunately, once Maribel goes off the desmopressin, her bedwetting returns.

15.10 Psychological Perspectives on Elimination Issues

Behavior Therapy for Enuresis

Enuresis alarm: Battery-operated alarm used for enuresis that sounds when urine is detected during the night, conditioning the child to go to the toilet; also called the *bell and pad method.*

The **enuresis alarm** (also called the *bell and pad method*) is a well-established behavioral intervention for nocturnal bedwetting in children (Michaels, 1939; Mowrer & Mowrer, 1938; Shapira & Dahlen, 2010; Thurber, 2017). During the night, a battery-operated alarm is attached to the child's underwear or to a pad placed on the bed. The alarm sounds when urine is detected. This wakes up the child, who can then get out of bed and go to the toilet. The enuresis alarm classically conditions an association between the alarm and having a full bladder, so that a full bladder becomes a conditioned stimulus that awakens the child (M. L. Brown et al., 2011; Keeley et al., 2009). Operant conditioning is also involved: Waking up and going to the toilet is negatively reinforced by allowing the child to avoid something unpleasant, namely wetting the bed (Keeley et al., 2009). The enuresis alarm is a highly effective intervention for nocturnal bedwetting (Alqannad et al., 2021; Kiddoo, 2011, 2015; Thurber, 2017). Though frequently combined with desmopressin, it is considered superior to it because it produces longer-lasting changes (Alqannad et al., 2021; Kiddoo, 2015; Perrin et al., 2015; Thurber, 2017).

Dry-bed training: Behavior therapy for enuresis in which children are awakened during the night and praised or punished depending on whether they have wet the bed.

Sometimes the enuresis alarm is combined with **dry-bed training**, a behavioral intervention in which parents wake up children during the night, praise them when they have not wet the bed, and punish them when they have (often by making them wash their bedding) (Azrin & Foxx, 1974; Thurber, 2017). Adding dry-bed training to an enuresis alarm can improve outcomes, though the evidence is mixed (M. L. Brown et al., 2011; Kiddoo, 2015; B. Zhou et al., 2019). Further, due to the punitive and potentially humiliating nature of making children wash their bedding, the UK's National Institute for Health Care and Clinical Excellence (NICE) advises against the use of dry-bed training (National Clinical Guideline Centre, 2010).

Despite extensive research support, behavioral techniques for enuresis are highly demanding and time-consuming (Keeley et al., 2009; Kiddoo, 2015). Consequently, many parents and their kids do not get up during the night to follow through with them. Such families prefer desmopressin and other drug interventions because they are far less labor intensive.

Maribel

After taking her off desmopressin, Maribel's parents try an enuresis alarm. Every night when Maribel goes to sleep, her parents attach the alarm to a pad on her bed. The alarm wakes Maribel whenever it detects urine on the pad. Because Maribel's parents must get up early for work, they initially struggle to implement the enuresis alarm, either sleeping through it or forgetting to turn it on before Maribel goes to sleep. However, when they become more diligent about turning on the alarm and arising to assist Maribel when it sounds, they notice a definite decrease in her bedwetting.

Cognitive-Behavioral Therapy (CBT) for Encopresis

Cognitive-behavioral therapy (CBT) is used for encopresis with constipation. Laxatives and enemas are given to empty the patient's bowels, then patients are placed on non-constipating high fiber and high fluid diets (L. T. Hardy, 2009; Kapalu & Christophersen, 2019; van Dijk et al., 2007). The CBT part of the intervention involves psychoeducation (to teach constipated children and their parents the biology of constipation), a behavior plan (to increase desired and decrease undesired toilet behaviors), and skills training (in which the constipated child learns techniques for properly expelling stool) (Kapalu & Christophersen, 2019). Research support for CBT for encopresis is encouraging but limited (K. A. Freeman et al., 2014; Kapalu & Christophersen, 2019).

Arjun

Arjun's family undergoes CBT for his encopresis. His parents are taught techniques for reinforcing Arjun when he goes to the toilet. Whenever Arjun defecates on the toilet, he gets a sticker and praise from his parents. Arjun is taught techniques for defecating that reduce pain. Negative cognitions that he and his parents hold are also examined, with the idea of getting them to see Arjun's problem as a learned habit that can be changed rather than a sign that they and Arjun are "seriously disturbed."

Psychodynamic and Humanistic Alternatives

Organic cases of enuresis and encopresis have medical/genetic causes, while *functional* cases are attributable to psychological conflicts. Psychodynamic and humanistic therapists focus on the latter, conceptualizing enuresis and encopresis as expressions of underlying mental distress. They believe that addressing this distress in therapy, rather than simply changing bathroom behavior, is critical to eliminating enuresis and encopresis. From a psychodynamic perspective, elimination issues express unconscious conflicts (G. Goodman, 2013; Mishne, 1993; Protinsky & Dillard, 1983). For instance, enuresis might reflect a child's fear of separation from a parent, or it could involve coping with stressful events by regressing to a less anxiety-provoking earlier stage of development (Mishne, 1993). Similarly, encopresis potentially distracts a child from painful emotions due to insecure attachments (G. Goodman, 2013). Though there is little research on psychodynamic therapies specifically, frequent bedwetting has been linked to stressful events in early childhood (Joinson et al., 2016).

Elimination issues have received significant attention from narrative therapists. As discussed in other chapters, narrative therapy "externalizes" problems by recasting them as independent entities that get the best of clients, rather than as disorders they "have" (M. White & Epston, 1990). The most famous example of externalizing the problem was a case of encopresis, in which a little boy named Nick kept smearing his poo on the walls, creating much dissension in his family. Nick and his parents Ron and Sue externalized the problem as "Sneaky Poo." They each came to understand the "requirements" of the problem (i.e., how Sneaky Poo affected them). Ron avoided others out of shame, Sue became depressed, and Nick played with his excrement. Once each family member understood the influence of Sneaky Poo, moments when Sneaky Poo's demands were successfully resisted were identified. Nick recognized times when Sneaky Poo didn't convince him to play with his feces, Sue identified occasions when she listened to music rather than letting Sneaky Poo depress her, and Ron recalled instances where he socially engaged despite Sneaky Poo's demands to the contrary. Understanding exceptions (times they didn't go along with Sneaky Poo) gave the family insights into effective strategies for sidestepping the problem, which they implemented over the course of therapy.

15.11 Sociocultural Perspectives on Elimination Issues

Culture, Stigma, and Socioeconomic Impact

Bedwetting has not always been regarded as a major problem across cultures. Historically, Native Americans were not especially concerned about it, and West Africans considered it a "cute" and curable childhood problem (McDonald & Trepper, 1977). However, in Western cultures, bedwetting is accompanied by stigma, shame, and embarrassment (R. J. Butler, 2004; Cendron, 2002). It is also expensive. The costs of laundering soiled clothes and sheets and eliminating bad odors in the home are often underestimated (Schulpen, 1997). The economic impact is potentially worsened because lower socioeconomic status (SES) has sometimes (but not always) been linked to enuresis (Bilal et al., 2020; R. J. Butler, 2004; Dolgun et al., 2012; Kamal & Mahrous, 2019; Kessel et al., 2017; Van Hoecke et al., 2003).

Arjun

Arjun's parents live on a limited income and most months they barely make ends meet. Arjun's constant soiling of his clothes and bedding has forced his mother to go to the laundromat daily. The cost of this is putting additional stress on Arjun's family.

Sociocultural perspectives examine how cultural factors affect the development of enuresis. The "Controversial Question" feature examines debate over the potential role of one well-known cultural practice, the use of disposable diapers.

Family Systems Approaches

Structural family therapy (introduced in Chapter 2) conceptualizes the child with enuresis as the *identified patient*—the member of the family whose outward symptoms represent the problem (Protinsky & Dillard, 1983). However, the problem isn't seen as specific to the child, but as a

Controversial Question: Does Using Disposable Diapers Predict Bedwetting?

Over the past two decades, several studies have linked the prolonged use of disposable diapers to higher rates of enuresis (X. Li, Wen, et al., 2020; J. L. Simon & Thompson, 2006; Tarbox et al., 2004; X. Z. Wang et al., 2019). Some researchers hypothesize that "bedwetting may be due to years of practice sleeping with disposable diapers, which conditions the brain to ignore the bladder" (X. Li, Wen, et al., 2020, p. 3). Past studies found children and adults with enuresis less likely to wet the bed when wearing underwear versus diapers (J. L. Simon & Thompson, 2006; Tarbox et al., 2004). Ongoing use of diapers may inadvertently propagate enuresis, even though the bedwetting that occurs understandably leads to continued diaper use.

But how strong is the evidence that wearing diapers contributes to bedwetting? A systematic review concluded that existing studies do suggest a connection between diaper use and enuresis (Breinbjerg et al., 2021). However, there are not many studies (only eight at the time of the review). Further, these studies are not very strong methodologically (Breinbjerg et al., 2021). So, while we cannot rule out that extended diaper use plays a role in enuresis, a lot more research is needed before we can reasonably infer causal connections between wearing diapers and wetting the bed.

Photo 15.4
kevin liang/Unsplash.

Critical Thinking Questions

1. What challenges do researchers face in designing experiments to test the hypothesis that diaper use causes enuresis?
2. Do you predict that future research will confirm the suspected link between diaper use and enuresis? Why or why not?

problem in the relational dynamics of the family (T. B. Fletcher, 2000; Protinsky & Dillard, 1983). For instance, the child's bedwetting might distract the family from unresolved parental conflicts. Family systems therapy treats enuresis (and the family conflicts it masks) by shifting usual patterns of family interaction. There is not much research on systems approaches to elimination issues, but many people nonetheless find them compelling.

Maribel

From a family systems perspective, Maribel's bedwetting distracts from marital tension between her parents. Maribel is enmeshed with her mother, which pushes her father to increasingly disengage. Family therapy would disrupt the usual dynamics, perhaps by placing Maribel's father in charge of her enuresis. This would force the family to approach Maribel's bedwetting in a new way, changing ingrained patterns. As Maribel's bedwetting decreased, attention could turn to marital conflict between her parents.

Alternative Therapies

Acupuncture: Ancient Chinese treatment for various health issues in which needles or lasers are used to stimulate designated points on the body.

Alternative therapies such as acupuncture, hypnosis, chiropractic, and massage have been used to treat enuresis (B. Zhou et al., 2019). **Acupuncture** is one of the more promising alternative approaches, with a small and imperfect but encouraging base of support (Alsharnoubi et al., 2017; Kiddoo, 2015; Lv et al., 2015; Moursy et al., 2014; B. Zhou et al., 2019). It is an ancient Chinese technique in which designated points on the body are stimulated by needles or lasers (Pearl & Schrollinger, 1999). The precise mechanism of action in acupuncture is unknown, but it is suspected of affecting desmopressin and other hormones linked to bladder function (B. Zhou et al., 2019). Further research on it as an enuresis treatment is called for.

CLOSING THOUGHTS

15.12 Infinite Variety in Presenting Problems

A recurring challenge that mental health professionals face is the co-occurrence of more than one presenting problem at a time—the often-discussed issue of comorbidity. Problems are comorbid because, despite our best efforts to organize them into discrete categories, people do not come in neat little packages. Nonetheless, the need to distinguish certain things as issues worthy of attention is important in determining how to assist people. To what extent would you expect to see the sleep issues reviewed in this chapter comorbid with other presenting problems? What would the implications of this be for clinical practice? Regardless of whether you conceptualize sleep issues as signs of other disorders or as disorders themselves, inquiring about a patient's sleep habits can provide critically important information.

CHAPTER SUMMARY

Sleep Disturbances

- DSM-5-TR and ICD-11 divide sleep disturbances into *insomnia disorders, hypersomnia disorders, parasomnias,* and *breathing-related sleep disorders.*
- Ideas about sleep—including the modern notion of an uninterrupted night's sleep—have evolved throughout history.
- Knowledge of the *sleep cycle* is important to understanding sleep disturbances.
- Biological perspectives, including the *hyperarousal theory of insomnia,* view sleep problems as tied to genes and brain chemistry; drug treatments are often informed by these perspectives.
- Psychodynamic perspectives see dreams as wish fulfillments, whereas CBT approaches aim to address sleep issues by altering dysfunctional cognitions and behaviors.
- Sociocultural perspectives emphasize how factors like *organizational injustice* contribute to sleep difficulties.

Elimination Issues

- DSM and ICD identify *enuresis* and *encopresis* as elimination issues. These issues have become increasingly medicalized throughout history.
- Biological perspectives emphasize how enuresis runs in families and rely on drug interventions such as *desmopressin.*
- Behavior therapies for enuresis include the *enuresis alarm* and *dry-bed training.*
- CBT for encopresis combines psychoeducation with a behavior plan and skills training.
- Psychodynamic and humanistic therapists view elimination issues as functional expressions of mental distress. Narrative therapies rely on the technique of externalizing the problem.
- Sociocultural perspectives examine cultural differences is attitudes toward bedwetting.
- Family systems therapy conceptualizes the child experiencing enuresis as the *identified patient* whose bedwetting behavior masks family conflicts.
- *Acupuncture* is a common alternative therapy for enuresis.

Closing Thoughts

- Comorbidity remains a challenge for the problems in this and other chapters because people's presenting problems do not always correspond to existing diagnostic categories.

NEW VOCABULARY

1. Acupuncture
2. Cognitive-behavioral therapy for insomnia (CBT-I)
3. Desmopressin
4. Dry-bed training
5. Encopresis
6. Enuresis
7. Enuresis alarm
8. Hyperarousal theory of insomnia
9. Hypersomnolence disorders
10. Insomnia disorders
11. Modafinil
12. Narcolepsy
13. Nightmare disorder
14. Non-benzodiazepine receptor antagonists
15. Non-rapid eye movement (NREM) sleep arousal disorder
16. Orexin
17. Orexin-receptor antagonists
18. Parasomnias
19. Rapid eye movement (REM) sleep behavior disorder
20. Restless legs syndrome
21. Sleep cycle
22. Sleep terrors
23. Sleep-related eating disorder
24. Sleepwalking disorder
25. Sodium oxybate
26. Speech-sound disorder

SUICIDE, ETHICS, AND LAW

16

Photo 16.1
Zennie/Getty Images.

OVERVIEW

16.1 Getting Started: Self-Harm and Other Ethical and Legal Dilemmas

Presenting problems always occur in a social context governed by ethical and legal principles. The latter half of this chapter explores ethical and legal perspectives on mental distress. However, first we examine suicide, which—besides accompanying almost every presenting problem—has many ethical and legal implications. Suicide poses complex dilemmas for clients, their families, and mental health professionals. At the same time, suicide is increasingly viewed not just as an ethically and legally challenging act that accompanies other presenting problems, but as a presenting problem all its own. Due to its many ethical and legal implications, suicide segues nicely into an examination of ethical and legal dilemmas—hence the inclusion of these topics side by side in our final chapter.

PERSPECTIVES ON SUICIDE

16.2 Suicide: Definition, Types, and Prevalence

Case Example

Dahlia

Dahlia is a 24-year-old woman who calls a suicide-prevention hotline feeling extremely depressed. She was recently laid off at work and is now struggling to pay her bills. "I think about dying most of the time and have tried to kill myself several times before—most recently about six months ago by swallowing the entire bottle of antidepressants my doctor prescribed me," she reluctantly admits. Dahlia also reports that she has little family support because her mother died when she was 9 years old, and the rest of her family stopped speaking to her when she came out to them as a lesbian several years ago. "Life just seems too pointless and painful," she laments, "and when it comes to getting my family to talk to me again, I'd rather be dead than violate who I am." When asked if she has the means to kill herself, Dahlia responds elusively and declines to answer directly.

Defining Suicide

Suicide: Intentionally ending one's own life; Shneidman's types: *death seekers* (wish to die and actively seek death), *death initiators* (kill themselves because they believe death is imminent), *death ignorers* (kill themselves because they view death as an escape/something new), and *death darers* (ambivalent about death, so take risks that could kill them).

Suicide involves intentionally ending one's own life. It is "the human act of self-inflicted, self-intentioned cessation" (Shneidman, 1981b, p. 198). Understandably, the notion of people killing themselves provokes strong feelings in most of us, making suicide one of the more difficult topics we discuss. Further, when clients present with suicidal thoughts and feelings, a myriad of ethical and legal issues arise. The late clinical psychologist and suicide researcher Edwin S. Shneidman (1918–2009) attributed suicide to intense psychological hurt, pain, and anguish—which he called *psychache* (Shneidman, 1993, 1998). Importantly, he argued that not all suicides are alike (Shneidman, 1981a, 1985). He posited four types of suicide:

- *Death seekers* attempt suicide because they actively seek their own deaths. They wish to die, although this desire waxes and wanes. Death seekers make multiple suicide attempts, with many ultimately succeeding in killing themselves.

Dahlia

Dahlia thinks about dying most of the time and has tried to kill herself several times before. Therefore, she can be classified as a death seeker.

- *Death initiators* believe the process of dying is already underway. Many, but not all, suffer from fatal illnesses. They kill themselves to accelerate the inevitability of imminent death. A terminal cancer patient who takes her own life to "get this over with" is a death initiator.
- *Death ignorers* view death as a beginning rather than an ending. They think death marks the start of something new. Some believe in an afterlife, seeing death as an escape to a better and more peaceful place. Others (such as young children who kill themselves) think of death as temporary or reversible.
- *Death darers* are ambivalent about wanting to die, which leads them to take risks that could cause death. For example, they might play "Russian roulette" or overdose on drugs but then call for help. In many instances, they engage in parasuicidal behavior (see Chapter 12), using self-harm to manipulate others, express distress, or regulate feelings (rather than because they wish to die).

Subintentional Death (Indirect Suicide)

Shneidman distinguished suicide proper from **subintentional death** (or *indirect suicide*), in which an unconscious wish to die leads to reckless or negligent actions. Subintentional deaths aren't overt suicide attempts because there isn't an active effort to kill oneself. However, at some level, there is an unrecognized desire to die (Shneidman, 1981a, 1985). Shneidman distinguished *four types of subintentional death*:

Photo 16.2 As of July 16, 2022, dialing 988 connects U.S.-based callers with a suicide prevention hotline. Kathleen Marchi is CEO and President of Samaritans Inc., one of five agencies that will be running the line.
Boston Globe/Getty Images.

- *Death chancers* take unnecessary risks to see what will happen. They might cross the street without looking or rock climb without safety gear. They take chances but are consciously unaware of a desire to die.
- *Death hasteners* engage in unhealthy lifestyles that hasten their deaths. They mistreat their bodies by doing things like taking drugs, eating poorly, or not getting enough sleep. Again, no overtly suicidal feelings or behaviors occur.
- *Death capitulators* give in to death. Their anxiety and depression lead them to psychologically capitulate, making death more likely. A person who psychologically gives up after having a stroke is a death capitulator.
- *Death experimenters* don't actively try to end their lives, but instead experiment with living in a continuously altered and foggy state. Substance users who regularly take drugs to remain chronically altered can be considered death experimenters.

Because they are less overt than suicides, subintentional deaths can be hard to identify. This makes it difficult to estimate how many deaths are subintentional. A lot more people may die subintentional deaths than we realize.

Subintentional death: Deaths due to an unconscious desire to die that yields reckless or negligent behavior; Shneidman's types: *death chancers* (take risks to see what will happen), *death hasteners* (engage in unhealthy lifestyles), *death capitulators* (give in to death due to depression/anxiety), and *death experimenters* (live in a perpetually altered state—e.g., drug haze); also called *indirect suicide*.

How Many People Die by Suicide?

There were more than 700,000 deaths by suicide in 2019, accounting for 1.3 percent of deaths worldwide (World Health Organization, 2021c). See Figure 16.1 for a breakdown by country. Among 15–29-year-olds, suicide was the fourth leading cause of death (World Health Organization, 2021b). In the United States alone in 2020, 44,834 people died by suicide, but way more made suicide plans (3.2 million) or attempted suicide (1.2 million) (Substance Abuse and Mental Health Services Administration, 2021). The most common methods of suicide in the United States between 2000 and 2018 were firearms, suffocation, and poisoning (Centers for Disease Control and Prevention, 2020a). As bad as these numbers seem, the COVID-19 pandemic made things worse: 21 percent of adults over age 18 who made suicide plans in 2020 said they did so because of the pandemic (Substance Abuse and Mental Health Services Administration, 2021). All these suicide statistics convey the widespread prevalence of suicidal ideation and behavior. However, although shocking, they might underestimate the problem because people do not always report suicide attempts. Further complicating prevalence estimates, self-harm is not always an attempt to end one's life. Nonetheless, suicide is clearly a widespread and daunting problem.

16.3 Historical Perspectives on Suicide

Ideas about suicide have changed over time. In ancient Greece, "suicide was viewed as a moral response to disgrace and an appropriate method of making a political statement" (Pridmore, 2011, p. 78). However, by the fourth century, St. Augustine (AD 354–430) saw suicide as a sinful act; and by AD 693, the Catholic Church was excommunicating those who attempted suicide (Shneidman, 1981b). Consistent with this position, more than 500 years later St. Thomas Aquinas (1225–1274) argued that "suicide was a mortal sin in that it usurped God's power over man's life and death"

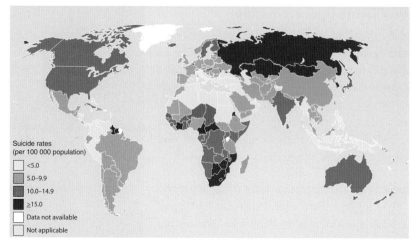

Figure 16.1 Age-Standardized Suicide Rates (per 100,000 Population), Both Sexes, 2019.
Source: World Health Organization (2021b, p. 4).

(Shneidman, 1981b, p. 202). However, when Renaissance Humanism took hold in Europe, thinkers like Jean-Jacques Rousseau (1712–1778) and David Hume (1711–1776) began challenging the "sin" model of suicide (Hume, 1783; J. J. Rousseau, 1810; Shneidman, 1981b; T. Szasz, 2011). Rousseau blamed suicide not on individuals, but on an oppressive society that prevents people from meeting their needs; whereas Hume argued that "suicide is not a transgression of our duties to God, to our fellow citizens, or to ourselves" (Shneidman, 1981b, p. 202). The nineteenth-century French psychiatrist Jean-Étienne Esquirol (1772–1840)—mentioned in Chapters 6 and 14—shifted further away from the sin model by conceptualizing suicide in medical terms. He was one of the first to gather epidemiological data on suicide, cataloging common methods people used to kill themselves and comparing suicide rates in different countries (Esquirol, 2015). Since Esquirol, it has been common to treat suicide as a medical problem (Pridmore, 2011). DSM and ICD exemplify medical conceptions of suicide.

16.4 DSM and ICD Perspectives on Suicide

Suicidal behavior disorder (SBD):
Proposed DSM disorder for those who have attempted suicide in the last two years.

Nonsuicidal self-injury disorder (NSSI):
Proposed DSM disorder involving intentional self-injury without suicidal intent.

DSM-5-TR includes proposals for two disorders related to suicide and self-harm. These proposals are for further study and not yet official diagnoses. **Suicidal behavior disorder (SBD)** would be diagnosed in anyone who has attempted suicide in the last two years—unless the attempt was for political or religious reasons, or due to delirium or mental confusion. All other suicide attempts would qualify a person for this disorder. **Nonsuicidal self-injury disorder (NSSI)** would be diagnosed in people without suicidal intent who intentionally injure their bodies to escape negative thoughts and feelings (e.g., depression or anxiety), cope with interpersonal conflicts, or comfort themselves. Most common among adolescents, NSSI self-harming activities include self-cutting (repeatedly cutting oneself with a sharp object), scratching, burning, hitting, stabbing, and excessive rubbing (American Psychiatric Association, 2022). Diagnostic Boxes 16.1 and 16.2 provide criteria for these two proposed disorders. ICD-11 considers neither a full-fledged mental disorder, but instead codes them as mental or behavioral signs or symptoms that can accompany other disorders.

Diagnostic Box 16.1 Suicidal Behavior Disorder

Proposed DSM-5-TR Disorder
- A suicide attempt within the last two years.
- Must rule out nonsuicidal self-injury and suicidal ideation (thoughts and preparation for the suicide attempt).
- The attempt is not due to a political act, a religious act, delirium, or mental confusion.
- Specify if *current* (no more than one year since last attempt) or *in early remission* (one to two years since last attempt).

Based on American Psychiatric Association (2022, p. 920).

Diagnostic Box 16.2 Nonsuicidal Self Injury (NSSI)

Proposed DSM-5-TR Disorder

- Intentional self-inflicted damage to the surface of one's body during at least five days over the past year (e.g., cutting, burning, stabbing, hitting, excessive rubbing) without any intent of suicide.
- The self-injury is intended to accomplish at least one of these: (a) reduce negative thoughts and feelings; (b) address interpersonal conflict; (c) produce a state of positive feeling.
- The self-injury is related to at least one of these: (a) interpersonal conflicts or negative thoughts and feelings (e.g., depression, anxiety, tension, anger, self-criticism, or emotional upset) that occur immediately prior to the self-injury; (b) being preoccupied with the self-injurious behavior before doing it; (c) recurrent thoughts about the self-injury, whether acted on or not.
- The self-injury isn't socially approved (e.g., a tattoo, body piercing, or religious ritual) and is more serious than just picking a scab or biting one's nails.
- The behavior isn't due to delirium, psychosis, substance use, or substance withdrawal; it also isn't better explained by another disorder (e.g., autism spectrum disorder, stereotypic movement disorder, or hair-pulling disorder).

ICD-11

- Intentional self-injury (e.g., cutting, scraping, burning, biting, or hitting).
- The self-injuring person expects no significant harm from the self-injury.

Information from American Psychiatric Association (2022, pp. 923–924) and World Health Organization (2022a).

Dahlia

Although not an official DSM disorder, Dahlia meets the criteria for suicidal behavior disorder because she has tried to kill herself within the last two years.

Proponents of SBD argue that it is a reliable and valid new diagnosis that encourages thorough integration of suicide assessment into everyday practice (Fehling & Selby, 2021; Oquendo & Baca-Garcia, 2014). However, critics counter that suicidal behavior is not a disorder in its own right, but rather a symptom of other disorders or a response to life stressors (Malhi & Bell, 2019; Obegi, 2019; Oquendo & Baca-Garcia, 2014). They note that *suicidal ideation* (a technical term for suicidal thoughts and feelings) is highly comorbid with other mental disorders (e.g., mood disorders, borderline personality disorder and other personality disorders, substance use disorders, and anxiety disorders), calling into question the wisdom of viewing suicidal behavior as a discrete disorder (Fehling & Selby, 2021; Nock et al., 2010). Other critics go further, bristling at the medicalization of suicide (Pridmore, 2011; T. Szasz, 2010). They see suicide as a moral act, not a medical one (T. Szasz, 2010; T. S. Szasz, 1999). Once suicide is conceptualized in medical terms, they ask, how long before homicide is transformed from a crime into a disorder and people are excused for it (Oquendo & Baca-Garcia, 2014)? Are such concerns about overly medicalizing suicidal behavior warranted?

Like SBD, NSSI's status as a stand-alone disorder is debated, with some pointing out its high comorbidity with other mental disorders (e.g., PTSD, panic disorder, borderline personality disorder, mood disorders, and anxiety disorders) (Bentley et al., 2015; Cipriano et al., 2017; J. D. Ford & Gómez, 2015). NSSI is also comorbid with suicidal behavior (Hamza et al., 2012; Preyde et al., 2014; Stewart et al., 2017). That is, even though NSSI patients are not typically viewed as wanting to die, there is evidence that NSSI and suicidal behavior are related. The implications are confusing given that NSSI is usually conceptualized as distinct from suicidality. Does the link between them point to a relationship between two separate problems? Or does it suggest that NSSI isn't distinguishable from suicidality and other mental disorder diagnoses? These issues are unresolved, and the relationship (if any) between NSSI and suicidal behavior is complex (X. Huang et al., 2020). NSSI's status as a discrete and reliable diagnostic category remains the subject of ongoing research and discussion (Ghinea et al., 2020; Malhi & Bell, 2020; Selby et al., 2015; Zetterqvist, 2015).

16.5 Biological Perspectives on Suicide

The Search for Suicide Biomarkers

Genes

Biological researchers are hunting for biomarkers to predict suicidal behavior, including genetic markers—perhaps because a predisposition to suicide seems to run in families (Docherty et al., 2020; A. C. Edwards et al., 2021; Pedersen & Fiske, 2010; Petersen et al., 2014; Ruderfer et al., 2020). As one set of enthusiastic researchers put it, "the likelihood of suicide is partly heritable. Our fates are not sealed … but are influenced by inborn factors" (D. Goldman, 2020, p. 881). Given that heritability estimates for suicidal behavior range from 17 percent to 55 percent, environmental factors obviously are very important, too (Docherty et al., 2020). That said, many candidate genes for suicidality have been identified, though—as is common in genetic research—findings are inconsistent (Docherty et al., 2020; González-Castro et al., 2017; Kimbrel et al., 2018; Mirza et al., 2022; Mullins et al., 2019; K. A. Sullivan et al., 2022). Do you think we will eventually be able to predict suicidal behavior based on genetic markers? Why or why not?

HPA Axis

Besides genes, overactivity of the hypothalamic-pituitary-adrenal (HPA) axis (important in responding to stress) is suspected of playing a role in suicidal behavior (Berardelli et al., 2020; Johnston et al., 2022). Consistent with this, suicidal individuals—like those who are depressed—experience immune system inflammation, a sign of prolonged stress (Bergmans et al., 2019; Brundin et al., 2015, 2017). They often fail the *dexamethasone suppression test (DST)*, which measures levels of the stress hormone cortisol in the bloodstream (Berardelli et al., 2020; Blasco-Fontecilla & Oquendo, 2016; Dogra & Vijayashankar, 2022; Johnston et al., 2022). Failing this test suggests that suicidal people are unable to suppress their stress response, which may explain their high cortisol levels even after taking dexamethasone, a synthetic steroid that decreases cortisol. Brain researchers consider DST results promising in seeking biomarkers for suicidal behavior (Blasco-Fontecilla & Oquendo, 2016; Johnston et al., 2022).

Serotonin and Other Possible Biomarkers

Low serotonin levels have been linked to suicidal behavior (Blasco-Fontecilla & Oquendo, 2016; Johnston et al., 2022). This makes sense given that serotonin deficiencies, as noted in Chapters 12 and 13, are often associated with impulsivity, aggression, and violence (Runions et al., 2019; Tricklebank & Petrinovic, 2019). Low serotonin is also implicated in depression (see Chapter 5), a presenting problem long tied to suicide (Hillhouse & Porter, 2015). Beyond serotonin, low levels of *lipids* (fats in the body) are potential suicide biomarkers; low cholesterol (fat in the bloodstream) and a diet lacking polyunsaturated fatty acids (PUFAs; see Chapter 13) have been linked to mood problems and suicidal behavior (Daray et al., 2018; Johnston et al., 2022). *Endocannabinoids*, lipid-based neurotransmitters that interact with the HPA axis and which are important in regulating memory, pleasure, and mood (among other things) are also suspected of being tied to suicidal activity—potentially explaining why chronic use of marijuana (a cannabinoid drug) is associated with depression and suicide risk (Thippaiah et al., 2021). Despite the wide-ranging search for biomarkers, we presently cannot differentiate depression, suicidality, impulsivity, and aggression from one another biologically. Do you think we will be able to some day?

Photo 16.3 In 2020, more than 4 per cent of the global population aged 15–64 (209 million people) used cannabis. More than a quarter of users reported greater amounts and greater frequency of cannabis use than before the pandemic, according to the World Drug Report (United Nations Office on Drugs and Crime, 2022). What could this mean for rates of suicidality?

Thought Catalog/Unsplash.

Medication for Suicide Prevention

Because suicidal behavior is associated with low serotonin, antidepressants that boost serotonin (usually SSRIs) are prescribed to reduce self-harm (Hawton et al., 2015; Naguy & AlAwadhi, 2018). However, given ongoing controversy over SSRIs and suicide risk (see Chapter 5), not everyone recommends this. Mood stabilizers (like lithium) and antipsychotics (usually clozapine) are also used to reduce suicidality (Limandri, 2019b). Why? Because mood stabilizers increase serotonin in some brain regions, while antipsychotics bind with 5-HT-2A serotonin receptors (counterintuitively, this blocks serotonin but sometimes reduces depression) (Mann & Currier, 2012). Other drugs suspected of anti-suicidal properties include ketamine and esketamine (antidepressants that inhibit glutamate), buprenorphine (an opioid), and psilocybin (a hallucinogen that reduces serotonin and is administered as part of psychedelic therapy) (Limandri, 2019b; Naguy & AlAwadhi, 2018; Rajkumar, 2022).

Dahlia
After her first suicide attempt, Dahlia's doctor prescribed her an SSRI antidepressant. However, it had little effect on her suicidal ideation. He is considering referring her for esketamine treatment and, if that doesn't work, recommending her for an upcoming psychedelic therapy trial.

16.6 Psychological Perspectives on Suicide

Psychodynamic Perspectives

Sigmund Freud and the early psychoanalysts conceptualized suicide as a response to anger toward others that is internalized and then redirected at oneself (D. Lester, 1994). As Freud explained it, "no neurotic harbours thoughts of suicide which he has not turned back upon himself from murderous impulses against others" (Freud, 1917/1953, p. 252). Later in his career, Freud theorized that people have a built-in **death instinct** (or *Thanatos*), which he contrasted with the **life instinct** (or *Eros*). Freud used the death instinct to explain why people are driven to behave in self-destructive ways. Though usually directed outwardly toward the world, sometimes the death instinct is turned against the self, which results in suicidal thoughts and actions. As a historical footnote, some historians believe that Freud, in severe pain at age 83 while dying from cancer of the mouth, ended his life via assisted suicide (L. Cohen, 2014; Lacoursiere, 2008). If so, this makes him a death initiator, one of Shneidman's four types of suicidal people.

Modern psychodynamic theories are more relational than classic Freud. They attribute suicidal ideation to early life losses, such as parental death or divorce (Goldblatt, 2014; Kaslow et al., 1998). From this perspective, "behind every suicidal gesture, even the most superficial one, there is always a tragedy" (Mikhailova, 2005, p. 42). Psychodynamic therapies for suicidal patients use the therapeutic relationship to identify and work through problematic attachment and interpersonal patterns (D. Lester, 1994). Evidence suggests that psychodynamic approaches are effective in preventing further suicide attempts (Sobanski et al., 2021).

> **Death instinct:** Unconscious instinct proposed by Freud that drives people to behave in self-destructive ways, including self-harm and suicide; also called *Thanatos*.

> **Life instinct:** Unconscious instinct proposed by Freud that drives people to survive and seek pleasure; also called *Eros*.

Dahlia
Dahlia's mother died when Dahlia was 9 years old. In psychodynamic therapy, Dahlia would work to uncover and work through her powerful (and often unconscious) feelings about losing her mother at such an early age.

Cognitive-Behavioral (CBT) Perspectives

From a CBT perspective, suicidal ideation stems from distorted and rigid thinking (the cognitive component) and inadequate environmental reinforcement of one's initiatives (the behavioral component) (Bryan & Rudd, 2018; D. Lester, 1994; B. Stanley et al., 2009; Wenzel & Beck, 2008). The result is learned helplessness, the belief that one's actions have no effect on one's surroundings (see Chapter 5). People experiencing learned helplessness may see suicide as the only way to escape situations that they believe cannot be changed (Bano et al., 2019).

Cognitive-behavioral therapy for suicide prevention (CBT-SP) alleviates suicidality by targeting problematic cognitions and behaviors (Bryan, 2019; Bryan & Rudd, 2018). CBT-SP is a brief intervention (usually ten to twelve sessions) that begins with *crisis response planning* and *means safety counseling* to mitigate immediate risks of self-harm by identifying environmental risks (e.g., access

> **Cognitive-behavioral therapy for suicide prevention (CBT-SP):** Targets dysfunctional cognitions and conditioned thoughts/behaviors that lead to suicidal behavior.

Photo 16.4 Actress Olivia Munn has been very public about her struggles with suicidal thoughts. "The pain is really tough," she said. "But if I had ended my life when I wanted to, there is so much I would have missed. And that's worth staying for." https://www.yahoo.com/lifestyle/olivia-munn-depression-171821200.html

Taylor Hill/Getty Images.

to guns or pills) and generating plans for staying safe (e.g., activities and social supports that decrease the likelihood of self-harm). Next come *emotion regulation skills training* and *cognitive flexibility skills training*. The former teaches clients to recognize and manage difficult emotions (e.g., sadness and anger), while the latter helps them to revise rigid beliefs contributing to suicidal ideation (e.g., shifting from "it's utterly hopeless" to "things may not be as bad as they seem"). CBT-SP also uses *relapse prevention*, in which clients recall past suicidal episodes and visualize themselves effectively using the skills learned in therapy to manage them. Research generally supports CBT-SP for suicide prevention, especially when the focus is explicitly on suicidal thoughts and behaviors (Hawton et al., 2016; Mewton & Andrews, 2016; Rudd et al., 2015; Sobanski et al., 2021).

Dahlia

Dahlia experiences learned helplessness, believing that no matter what she does, her life will not get better. CBT-SP would begin by helping Dahlia make an immediate plan to stay safe—perhaps by getting rid of pills she might use to overdose and seeking out supportive friends. She would be taught how to recognize and name upsetting emotions (e.g., sadness about being unemployed, anxiety about familial conflicts over her sexual orientation, grief about the death of her mother). It would also challenge rigid beliefs. Her assumptions that she is "unemployable" and that "nobody will ever accept her for who she is" would be subject to scrutiny and, hopefully, revision. As Dahlia learns to regulate her feelings and think more flexibly, her suicidal feelings should decrease.

Dialectical behavior therapy (DBT), a type of CBT developed for people diagnosed with personality disorders (see Chapter 12), is also used to reduce suicidal and other self-harming behaviors. It combines individual therapy that addresses self-harm with skills training groups that teach emotional regulation (Linehan, 1993, 2015). Many but not all studies conclude that DBT is an effective suicide prevention intervention (DeCou et al., 2019; McCauley et al., 2018; Sobanski et al., 2021).

Humanistic Perspectives

In a humanistic/existential vein, suicide is a personal and meaningful reaction to humiliation, anger, hurt, and loss (G. A. Kelly, 1961; R. A. Neimeyer, 1983; J. R. Rogers et al., 2007; J. R. Rogers & Soyka, 2004). Humanistically speaking, suicide is not an irrational act. It is a purposeful act in response to mental distress. Suicide can be a means of remaining self-consistent ("I'd rather be dead than violate who I am"). It can also be a way to exert control when one feels humiliated, angry, hurt, or dominated by others (J. R. Rogers et al., 2007). Rather than focusing on getting clients to agree not to hurt themselves (which calms therapists but alienates and demeans some clients), humanistic clinicians stress empathically understanding the meaning behind suicidal thoughts and acts (S. J. Fitzpatrick & River, 2018; J. R. Rogers & Soyka, 2004). In doing so, they treat suicide not as a disorder or brain disease, but as a personally meaningful response to psychological conflict and pain. However, because psychotherapists are understandably anxious about client self-harm and feel pressure to actively intervene, they are often reluctant to adopt less interventionist humanistic approaches with suicidal clients (S. J. Fitzpatrick & River, 2018; D. Lester, 1994). Should they be less reluctant? Why or why not?

16.7 Sociocultural Perspectives on Suicide

Durkheim and the Sociology of Suicide

Durkheim's sociological model of suicide: Focuses on social and cultural factors in suicide and proposes different types: *egoistic suicide* (social alienation and rejection), *altruistic suicide* (sacrificing self for greater good), *anomic suicide* (let down by society), and *fatalistic suicide* (overwhelmed by social rules/demands).

In 1897, Emile Durkheim (1858–1917) published a seminal book on the sociology of suicide (Durkheim, 1897/2002). Rather than emphasizing individual influences (like biological and psychological perspectives do), **Durkheim's sociological model of suicide** stresses the importance of social and cultural factors in why people end their lives. Durkheim argued that two social factors are most important in explaining suicide: *social integration* and *social regulation*. Social integration is a person's sense of being socially included and accepted, while social regulation concerns communal rules used to monitor, influence, and control people's behavior. Using the concepts of integration and regulation, Durkheim proposed different types of suicide:

- *Egoistic suicide* is a product of *low social integration*, which is characterized by feelings of alienation and not belonging. For example, gay, lesbian, and transgender people—who face social rejection and discrimination—are at higher risk for suicide and nonsuicidal self-injury (Berona et al., 2020; A. G. Horwitz et al., 2020; R. T. Liu et al., 2019). Feeling excluded or ostracized makes egoistic suicide more likely.
- *Altruistic suicide* is attributable to *high social integration*. Some people are so well integrated into society that they willingly sacrifice themselves for the greater good. A soldier who jumps on a grenade, a parent who takes a bullet for her child, or a protestor willing to die for a cause are altruistic suicides. Highly integrated cultures, where honor and serving the collective good are valued, foster altruistic suicides.
- *Anomic suicide* is a response to *low social regulation*, when society fails to provide dependable social structures for its members. Lack of adequate community support (from family, church, school, workplace, or government) lead to isolation and disappointment. For instance, war veterans who return home but don't receive necessary assistance run a higher risk of suicide (Bullman & Schneiderman, 2021; Wilks et al., 2019).
- *Fatalistic suicide* occurs due to *high social regulation*. Rules, expectations, and social demands are so great that death feels like the only way out. Enslaved or imprisoned people killing themselves to escape their fate exemplify fatalistic suicide, as do people who end their lives because they feel trapped by the demands of work, school, or home.

Durkheim's view diverges from biological and psychological perspectives by explaining suicide in social rather than individual terms. Of course, not everyone who faces challenging social circumstances attempts suicide—but then again, not everyone with specific genes or psychological experiences does, either! Ultimately, both individual and social factors inform our understanding of suicide. Below let's highlight several salient social factors.

Demographic Factors and Suicide

Gender and Age

Women attempt suicide more, but men succeed at it more. In fact, one review found that among adolescents and young adults, women attempted suicide twice as often as men, but men were almost three times as likely to die by suicide than women (Miranda-Mendizabal et al., 2019). Conveyed another way, men made up just 49 percent of the U.S. population in 2020 but accounted for 80 percent of the suicides (Centers for Disease Control and Prevention, 2022c). This suicide "gender paradox" is often attributed to men picking more lethal means of self-harm than women (Canetto & Sakinofsky, 1998). It might also be because men tend to display mental distress via externalizing problems (e.g., conduct issues, substance abuse, acting out), while women lean toward internalizing problems (e.g., depression and anxiety) (Miranda-Mendizabal et al., 2019). How would you explain this gender paradox?

Although males die by suicide more than females across all age groups, age is another important factor in suicide rates. People under age 15 are least likely to kill themselves, while those over age 75 are most likely to kill themselves (Curtin & Ahmad, 2022). However, because there are many more younger people than older people, the total number of suicides among younger age groups is higher than older age groups. Figure 16.2 illustrates this by presenting age-related suicide data in two ways: per every 100,000 people and in terms of total deaths.

People have been especially concerned in recent years about adolescent suicide rates, with intense debate over whether cell phones are contributing to them. Critics says cell phones lead teens to spend less time socializing and dating and more time alone with phones and other electronic devices (Twenge, 2017). This has purportedly left many adolescents isolated and depressed, interfering with their ability to develop the emotional resilience necessary to handle adversity and keep suicidal ideation at bay. The cell phone argument is compelling and there is some evidence to support it (Abi-Jaoude et al., 2020; Twenge, 2020). However, not everyone is convinced (Cavanagh, 2017; Orben & Przybylski, 2019, 2020).

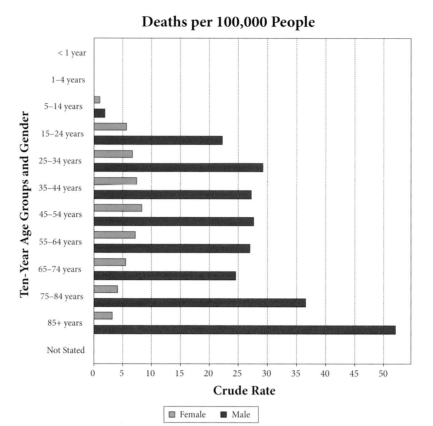

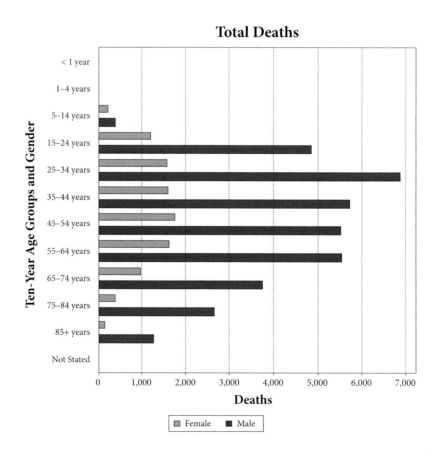

Figure 16.2 U.S. Intentional Self-Harm Deaths by Age and Gender, 2020.

Source: Centers for Disease Control and Prevention, National Center for Health Statistics. National Vital Statistics System, Mortality 1999–2020 on CDC WONDER Online Database, released in 2021. Data are from the Multiple Cause of Death Files, 1999–2020, as compiled from data provided by the 57 vital statistics jurisdictions through the Vital Statistics Cooperative Program. [Accessed at http://wonder.cdc.gov/ucd-icd10.html on Oct 28, 2022.]

What is clearer is that the COVID-19 pandemic coincided with a surge in suicidal behavior among teens. Hospital visits for suspected suicide attempts by adolescents aged 15–17 jumped from early 2019 (before the pandemic) to early 2021 (during the pandemic) (Yard, 2021). The increase was especially stark for girls (+50.6 percent), though it also affected boys (+3.7 percent). This matches the trend of sharper adolescent suicide increases among U.S. girls than boys between 2007 and 2017—a period with alarming increases for both (+50 percent for girls and +30 percent for boys, among those aged 15–19) (L. Holmes, 2017; R. Lewis, 2017). But suicide rates have not just gone up among teens. In the United States, they increased 36 percent between 2000 and 2018 before decreasing 5 percent between 2018 and 2020 (Centers for Disease Control and Prevention, 2022c). However, they bounced up again in 2021 (2 percent for females, 4 percent for males, and 4 percent total) (Curtin & Ahmad, 2022). Why rates went up after starting to come down isn't known. Could the COVID pandemic, economic instability, and political polarization in the United States have undercut progress to reverse longstanding increases in suicidal behavior?

Race/Ethnicity, Socioeconomic Status, and Other Demographic Factors

Like age and gender, suicide varies by race and ethnicity. In the United States, Native Americans are the only racial/ethnic group with higher suicide rates than white Americans. Hispanic Americans, Black Americans, and Asian Americans/Pacific Islanders all have lower suicide rates than whites (Centers for Disease Control and Prevention, 2022d). This is puzzling considering that racial and ethnic minorities face discrimination and socioeconomic inequality—factors both linked to suicide. Some wonder whether the number of Black suicides is underreported—although this would not fully explain the disparity (Frakt, 2020). Others point to Black Americans' higher rates of church attendance, noting that religious engagement predicts lower rates of suicidal behavior (but not ideation) (Lawrence et al., 2016). These are working hypotheses. We don't really know why suicide rates are higher for white Americans than most American racial and ethnic minority groups.

Several other demographic variables are worth mentioning. As alluded to, socioeconomic status (SES) is negatively correlated with suicide. As SES goes down, suicide risk goes up (Lorant et al., 2021; Machado et al., 2015; Näher et al., 2020). Other factors linked to suicide include being a veteran, having a disability, and (as noted when discussing egoistic suicide) being a sexual minority (Centers for Disease Control and Prevention, 2022d). Each of these factors is accompanied by stress, so perhaps that is the common denominator.

Social Contagion and Suicide

Is suicide socially "contagious"—meaning can one suicide influence others to do the same? Some argue yes, pointing to evidence of the **Werther effect**, which is the tendency for suicide rates to go up following a highly publicized suicide (D. P. Phillips, 1974). The Werther effect is named after the lead character who kills himself in Johann Wolfgang von Goethe's 1774 novel, *The Sorrows of Young Werther*. Following the book's publication, people noticed an uptick in suicides. Research since then has examined the Werther effect, and it often finds that the more publicity a suicide receives, the more suicide rates increase (Domaradzki, 2021; D. P. Phillips, 1974). It has been suggested that the Werther effect results from social modeling. People learn about a suicide from the media, then imitate it. But only some people are inspired to kill themselves after a highly publicized suicide, so who is most vulnerable? Unsurprisingly, experiencing depressed mood enhances susceptibility to contagion effects (Ma-Kellams et al., 2016). How a suicide is portrayed in the news (e.g., is coverage sensationalized, excessive, or detailed?) also appears to make a difference (Domaradzki, 2021). Media guidelines for reporting on suicide have been published, but their effectiveness in reducing contagion remains contested (Domaradzki, 2021; Sinyor et al., 2018; Stack, 2020).

16.8 Preventing Suicide

Suicide Prevention Programs

Suicide prevention programs, which began in the United States during the 1950s, aim to prevent self-harm before it occurs (Office of the U.S. Surgeon General, 2012). Such programs, developed nationally and locally (often through public–private sector partnerships), are implemented in a variety

Werther effect: The tendency for suicide rates to go up following a highly publicized suicide.

Suicide prevention programs: Programs implemented on local or national levels that work to reduce suicides using education, hotlines, crisis intervention, safety planning, method restriction, and hospitalization.

Photo 16.5 Jessica Curry speaks at the Santa Monica Out of the Darkness Walk organized by the American Foundation for Suicide Prevention on October 22, 2022.

Chelsea Guglielmino/Getty Images.

Suicide awareness education: Element of suicide prevention programs that prevents suicide by educating people about it.

of settings—including schools, workplaces, prisons, hospitals, and community mental health centers. Education, hotlines, crisis intervention, safety planning, method restriction, and hospitalization are common elements of suicide prevention programs. They are described next.

Education

Suicide awareness education teaches people about suicide, its risks, and its prevention. It ranges from local education initiatives (e.g., brochures about suicide prevention in a school or workplace) to *mass media campaigns* that "deliver messages across multiple media platforms, including print media, television, billboards, and posters" (Torok et al., 2017, p. 2). Suicide awareness education conveys a variety of messages—such as the importance of openly discussing suicide, the value of the suicidal person's life, the suffering that suicidal people experience, and the incredible anguish of those left behind after a completed suicide (Ftanou et al., 2017). Media campaigns work best when incorporated into a broader suicide prevention strategy (Pirkis et al., 2019; Torok et al., 2017). The U.S. National Institute of Mental Health's signs of suicide flyer (Figure 16.3) is an excellent example of suicide awareness education. It helps correct common myths about suicide listed in Table 16.1. Suicide education is intended not only to teach people about suicide, but also to overcome taboos against openly discussing it.

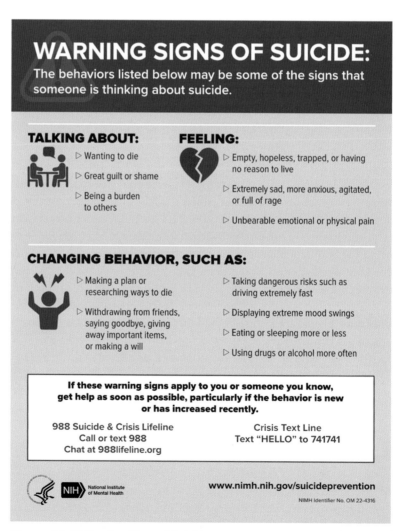

Figure 16.3 Warning Signs of Suicide.
Source: National Institute of Mental Health (n.d.-b)

Table 16.1 Myths about Suicide

Myth #1: Suicide only affects people with mental health conditions.
Feeling suicidal doesn't mean you have a mental disorder. Lots of people who are suicidal don't meet the criteria for a mental disorder. Others who are diagnosed with a mental disorder don't ever feel suicidal.

Myth #2: Once suicidal, always suicidal.
Suicidal feelings are often temporary and specific to the situation. Someone feeling suicidal is unlikely to always feel that way and can usually go on to live a long life.

Myth #3: Suicides usually happen suddenly with no warning.
While some suicides do occur without warning, most have clear warning signs. Suicidal people often say or do things that suggest suicide is on their minds.

Myth #4: Suicidal people want to die and are selfishly taking the easy way out.
Suicidal people are often ambivalent about dying. They may do something rash that ends their lives, but this doesn't mean they were determined to die or are taking the "easy way" out. Many suicide attempts are cries for help in which the person is communicating a genuine sense of intense unhappiness.

Myth #5: Talking about suicide encourages suicide.
Talking about it gives the suicidal person a chance to discuss difficult feelings and consider alternatives to suicide.

Source: Based on Fuller (2020).

Hotlines and Crisis Intervention

Suicide hotlines originated in 1961, when Anglican priest Bernard Mayes (1929–2014) placed advertisements on city buses in San Francisco that said "Thinking of ending it all? Call Bruce, PR1-0450, San Francisco Suicide Prevention" (Yardley, 2014). Today's hotlines are not just for calls. They also offer text and chat options. Some are national (e.g., the 988 Suicide and Crisis Line in the United States), while others are local (e.g., college campus crisis hotlines). Research on the effectiveness of suicide hotlines remains limited, though in one study crisis chat users reported being less distressed after using the service (Gould et al., 2021; Hoffberg et al., 2020). This fits with evidence that hotlines reduce immediate suicide risk and might help users marshal resources to address their difficulties (Hvidt et al., 2016; Menon et al., 2018). However, more research is sorely needed.

> **Suicide hotlines:** Offer 24-hour call, text, and chat options for those in crisis or feeling suicidal.

Hotlines are staffed by professional counselors or laypersons who have undergone **crisis intervention** training to identify and counsel suicidal individuals (Flannery & Everly Jr, 2000). Beyond using basic listening skills, crisis intervention includes assessing suicidal risk. That is, how likely does it seem that the client will eventually self-harm? To make such determinations, the crisis counselor asks directly about suicidal ideation: "Have you had thoughts of killing yourself?" "If yes, have you thought about how you'd kill yourself?" "Do you have a specific plan for killing yourself?" "Have you in any way acted to advance the plan?" The goal is to estimate suicide risk. People likely to encounter suicidal individuals (teachers, peers, school/office support staff, etc.) can be taught crisis intervention skills and then serve as gatekeepers who identify and take initial steps to address suicidal ideation (Hawgood et al., 2021; Menon et al., 2018).

> **Crisis intervention:** Techniques (e.g., listening skills, assessing risk) for assisting those in crisis, including suicidal individuals.

Safety Planning

Safety planning can be a part of crisis intervention. It is a brief clinical technique in which the counselor and suicidal client devise a comprehensive plan for keeping the client safe (G. K. Brown & Stanley, 2009; B. Stanley & Brown, 2008, 2012). Coping strategies to deal with suicidal feelings are generated (e.g., watching a favorite TV show, taking a walk, going to Starbucks to be around other people). A list is also created of social supports to rely on when upset or in crisis (family members, friends, urgent care services, crisis hotlines, and medical/mental health professionals). Finally, the client learns to identify warning signs (upsetting thoughts, moods, images, or behaviors) that should trigger implementation of the plan. The full plan is often written on an index card (called a *coping card*) that the client carries between sessions and refers to as needed (Y. Wang et al., 2016). As you can see, safety plans are comprehensive and detailed strategies for handling a suicidal crisis. Research supports using them, especially compared to *no-suicide contracts*, an older intervention that asks

> **Safety planning:** Suicide-prevention technique in which clients generate and utilize concrete steps for coping with suicidal ideation.

clients to promise they will not hurt themselves for an agreed-upon amount of time (Bryan et al., 2017; Nuij et al., 2021). One reason that safety plans might work better than no-suicide contracts is that—unlike no-suicide contracts—they explicitly lay out concrete steps the client will take to prevent self-harm.

Method Restriction

Method restriction: Suicide prevention strategy in which access to means of suicide is restricted.

Another approach to suicide prevention is **method restriction**, in which access to common ways that people kill themselves is curtailed or made more difficult (Menon et al., 2018). Gun control, regulating the availability of pesticides, detoxifying gasoline used in motor vehicles, and curbing access to alcohol and other drugs are types of method restriction. Other examples include altering the physical environment to make suicides more difficult (e.g., placing barriers at sites where people might hang themselves or jump to their deaths), prescribing fewer barbiturates and tricyclic antidepressants (which suicidal people often use to overdose), and using "safe rooms" in prisons and hospitals (built to make it much harder for people to harm themselves). There is research support for means restriction, though future studies should better tease apart what does and does not work (Eddleston & Gunnell, 2020; Lim et al., 2021; Okolie, Hawton, et al., 2020; Okolie, Wood, et al., 2020; P. S. F. Yip et al., 2012).

Hospitalization

"Thank you" theory of involuntary commitment: Holds that actively suicidal individuals will thank us later for hospitalizing them to prevent self-harm.

Suicidal people deemed an imminent threat to themselves can be hospitalized using civil commitment procedures (discussed later). The **"thank you" theory of involuntary commitment** holds that people who threaten or attempt suicide will thank us later for having them hospitalized. Once recovered, they will appreciate that we intervened—and this, rather than a mental health professional's limited ability to judge how dangerous they are, is the best legal justification for committing them (J. C. Beck & Golowka, 1988; A. A. Stone, 1975). Some civil libertarians take a very different view. They argue that not only is involuntary hospitalization a violation of people's freedom, but that even if we disapprove of suicide, people have a legal right to it (T. Szasz, 1986, 2011; T. S. Szasz, 1999). What are your thoughts on this contentious question? Do we do more harm than good by coercively stopping individuals from hurting themselves? Or do we provide an invaluable service by preventing people from taking actions they may later regret?

Can We Predict Suicide?

Although numerous factors—things like past suicide attempts, a family history of suicide, prior treatment for a serious presenting problem, depression, hopelessness, and general maladjustment—provide some information about who might attempt suicide, they aren't consistently strong predictors of suicide (although the more of them present, the better the predictions) (Franklin et al., 2017; Ribeiro et al., 2018). Perhaps because of this, mental health professionals are not that good at determining who will or won't self-harm (Franklin et al., 2017; Ribeiro et al., 2018). This difficulty is likely compounded because people don't always tell the truth about whether they're planning suicide. However, even if we account for client deception, it is still very difficult for people—even trained clinicians—to predict future behavior.

To remedy this, artificial intelligence (AI) is being employed to predict suicide attempts. While AI is not perfect, its ability to weigh many variables often gives it an advantage over people at forecasting behavior—including self-harm (Balbuena et al., 2022; D'Hotman & Loh, 2020; V. Kumar et al., 2022; Macalli et al., 2021; Nock et al., 2022). Suicide-predicting algorithms can be incorporated into electronic health records to identify suicidal patients. Social media sites like Facebook use them to identify at-risk individuals (Meta, 2022; Muriello et al., 2018). However, questions abound. Is AI's ability to foresee suicidality as good as advertised? That depends on how we evaluate it: "For example, using accuracy as a metric can be misleading if the dataset is unbalanced. A model can achieve 99% accuracy by always predicting there will be no risk of suicide if only 1% of the patients in the dataset are high risk" (Early, 2022, para. 8). Further, ethical concerns about privacy are paramount. What else is being done with the suicide-predicting data derived from our texts, online posts, and web searches—and who has access to it (Celedonia et al., 2021; D'Hotman et al., 2021)? As the case of AI in suicide prevention illustrates, identifying and assisting those experiencing mental distress raises many complex ethical and legal issues. It is to some of these ethical and legal concerns that we turn next.

ETHICAL PERSPECTIVES

16.9 Professional Ethics Codes

Psychologists, psychiatrists, counselors, couples and family therapists, social workers, and psychiatric nurses all have ethics codes designed to protect the service users with whom they work. The American Psychological Association's (2017b) ethics code is representative of such codes. It contains five general principles to guide professional research and practice (Table 16.2), as well as specific ethical standards psychologists are expected to uphold. Table 16.3 provides links to the ethics codes of selected psychological associations around the globe. These codes guide mental health professionals working in clinical and research capacities. Several issues addressed by ethics codes are examined below.

Table 16.2 General Principles of the Ethics Code of the American Psychological Association

Principle A: Beneficence and Nonmaleficence	Psychologists strive to benefit those with whom they work and take care to do no harm.
Principle B: Fidelity and Responsibility	Psychologists establish relationships of trust with those with whom they work. They are aware of their professional and scientific responsibilities to society and to the specific communities in which they work.
Principle C: Integrity	Psychologists seek to promote accuracy, honesty, and truthfulness in the science, teaching, and practice of psychology.
Principle D: Justice	Psychologists recognize that fairness and justice entitle all persons to access to and benefit from the contributions of psychology and to equal quality in the processes, procedures, and services being conducted by psychologists.
Principle E: Respect for People's Rights and Dignity	Psychologists respect the dignity and worth of all people, and the rights of individuals to privacy, confidentiality, and self-determination.

Source: American Psychological Association. (2017b). Ethical principles of psychologists and code of conduct (2002, amended effective June 1, 2010, and January 1, 2017). http://www.apa.org/ethics/code/index.html

Table 16.3 Ethics Codes in Psychology

PSYCHOLOGY
• American Psychological Association (APA): http://www.apa.org/ethics/code/
• Australian Psychological Society (APS): https://www.psychology.org.au/about/ethics/
• British Psychological Society (BPS): https://www.bps.org.uk/guideline/code-ethics-and-conduct
• Canadian Psychological Society (CPS): http://www.cpa.ca/aboutcpa/committees/ethics/codeofethics/
• European Federation of Psychologists' Associations (EFPA): https://www.efpa.eu/about-us/ethics
• New Zealand Psychological Society (NZPsS): https://www.psychology.org.nz/members/professional-resources/code-ethics
• Psychological Society of South Africa (PsySSA): https://www.psyssa.com/ethics

16.10 Informed Consent

Throughout this book, we have regularly cited research studies, many of them using participants who were vulnerable due to their debilitating presenting problem. It is important to study such people. However, professional ethics demands that people never be required to participate in a study or be misled to secure their participation. Study participants must always consent based on a full understanding of what they are getting themselves into. **Informed consent** is the process of providing prospective research participants sufficient information about a study—including why it is being conducted, as well as the risks and benefits of participating.

The importance of informed consent in protecting research participants may seem obvious, but the history of medical and psychological research is marred by gross violations in which consent was not obtained. Nazi doctors during the Second World War conducted horrible experiments on nonconsenting subjects. After the war, Nazi researchers accused of war crimes were tried by an international tribunal in what is now known as the Nuremberg trials. Most of the researchers tried were "physicians accused of murder and torture in the conduct of medical experiments on concentration-camp inmates" (Shuster, 1997, p. 1437). To protect human subjects, the tribunal issued the *Nuremburg Code*, "a sophisticated set of 10 research principles centered not on the physician but on the research subject" (Shuster, 1997, p. 1439). Informed consent was the first principle outlined in this code. Informed consent was further codified in 1964 when the World Health Association (WHA) approved the *Declaration of Helsinki*, a set of periodically revised ethical principles to govern medical research, including that with human subjects (World Medical Association, 2022).

Unfortunately, Nazi doctors aren't the only ones to violate participants' rights before or since the Nuremburg Code and the Declaration of Helsinki. The infamous *Tuskegee study*, which continued for forty years (1932–1972), was undertaken by the United States Public Health Service to study the natural course of syphilis (Chadwick, 1997; Heintzelman, 2003). Without obtaining informed consent, roughly 400 African American men were infected with (and then not treated for) syphilis—even though safe antibiotic treatments became readily available by the 1940s. Similarly, between the 1940s and 1970s, the U.S. government conducted experiments in which they exposed people to harmful radiation to see its effects, with no clear medical knowledge to be gleaned (by the 1950s and 1960s, the effects of radiation were already known) and often without informed consent (Chadwick, 1997; Kass & Sugarman, 1996; Subcommittee on Energy Conservation and Power, 1986). According to a report by the U.S. House of Representatives, "in some cases, the human subjects were captive audiences or populations that experimenters might frighteningly have considered 'expendable': the elderly, prisoners, hospital patients suffering from terminal diseases or who might not have retained their full faculties for informed consent" (Subcommittee on Energy Conservation and Power, 1986, p. 1).

Informed consent is always important, but when working with vulnerable populations, extra care is needed. Special attention is required when participants' ability to comprehend the study and appropriately consent is in doubt. Psychosis researchers, for instance, have developed strategies to evaluate whether prospective participants diagnosed with schizophrenia can give informed consent and—when they can—how to explain studies to them so that they can make informed decisions to participate (or not!) (K. K. Anderson & Mukherjee, 2007; Beebe & Smith, 2010; Jr. Carpenter William T. et al., 2000; S. Y. H. Kim et al., 2007; S. E. Morris & Heinssen, 2014; B. W. Palmer, 2006).

16.11 Confidentiality and Privilege

Case Example

Hugo

Hugo, a married father of five, seeks therapy after being arrested for soliciting male sex in the bathroom of a local coffee house. He is distraught and embarrassed, both about the arrest and about his wife, Jennifer, finding out.

Confidentiality

Have you ever shared something personal with a friend, assuming what you confided would be kept private, only to have that person tell others what you said? This likely discouraged you from confiding in that person again. Treating personal information with reverence and care is key for psychotherapists and other helping professionals, especially because most clients are experiencing emotionally painful and difficult problems that they may wish to keep private. Thus, professional ethics codes demand that practicing clinicians maintain client **confidentiality**—the requirement that they not disclose what clients tell them unless they have permission to do so (Adames et al., 2023). In other words, confidentiality is a professional duty of mental health professionals, one that demands they protect clients by avoiding the unauthorized release of information about them. It "is the key to most models of effective psychotherapy. Without this privacy, clients cannot be expected to reveal embarrassing, sometimes personally damaging, information in treatment" (Younggren & Harris, 2008, p. 589).

While confidentiality is a core ethical commitment of all mental health professions, there are several important situations in which clinicians can or must violate it. Clinicians accused of malpractice, for instance, are permitted to disclose information to defend themselves in court. Also, when people are considered dangerous to self or others, therapists are legally obligated to break confidentiality as part of their duty to protect the public (an issue discussed later in the chapter). Though circumstances requiring clinicians to break confidentiality are uncommon, they place clinicians in a difficult quandary because deciding to break confidentiality is never easy. The violation of trust that occurs can have negative consequences for clients, even when breaking confidentiality is justified (Winters, 2013).

> #### Hugo
> *Hugo is hesitant to share his arrest, or his long-time attraction to men, with his new therapist. "It's a small town, and you might run into Jenny," he says. The therapist explains that unless Hugo is a danger to himself or others, she is ethically required to keep what he shares in session confidential. He is relieved to learn this and becomes more comfortable confiding in her.*

Confidentiality applies not just to clinical practice, but also to research. Researchers are ethically obliged to keep participant data protected so that participants' identities and responses cannot be identified. Additionally, there is an ethical duty to protect research participants by storing their data safely and securely. When data is shared, all identifying information must be removed to protect participant confidentiality.

Privilege

Privilege is distinct from, but related to, confidentiality. It is a legal right that belongs to clients and protects their confidentiality (Adames et al., 2023). Privilege holds that certain relationships are protected, meaning that those in them are exempt from being legally compelled to share what was confided in the context of that relationship. Traditionally, communications between married people, clergy and their parishioners, lawyers and their clients, and doctors and their patients (including psychotherapists and their clients) are privileged (Konrad & Bath, 2014; Smith-Bell & Winslade, 1994). By designating confidential client communications as privileged, the legal system permits mental health professionals to withhold confidential information that they would otherwise be legally bound to share if asked.

> #### Hugo
> *The attorneys prosecuting Hugo for solicitation subpoena his therapist to release details about what he has disclosed in therapy. The therapist asserts that she is ethically obligated to protect Hugo's confidentiality, so she cannot share their discussions. That is, she asserts that this information is privileged and—unlike other witnesses being subpoenaed—she is legally protected from having to divulge what she knows. The judge concurs, ruling that communications between Hugo and his therapist are privileged.*

Confidentiality: The ethical requirement that practicing clinicians not disclose what clients tell them unless their clients grant them permission to do so.

Privilege: Legal right that protects communications confided within certain relationships (e.g., between married people, clergy and their parishioners, lawyers and their clients, and healthcare providers and their patients).

The difference between confidentiality and privilege can be confusing. A handy way to keep the distinction clear is to remember that "confidentiality is a professional duty to refrain from speaking about certain matters, while privilege is a relief from the duty to speak in a court proceeding about certain matters" (Smith-Bell & Winslade, 1994, p. 184). Depending on laws in specific jurisdictions, the courts may rule that certain communications between clients and their therapists aren't covered by privilege. When this happens, therapists must make a difficult choice between obeying the court and upholding their professional commitment to client confidentiality.

16.12 Competence

Competence: Ethical principle that clinicians only conduct therapies, assessments, and research when properly trained and competent to do so.

The ethical principle of **competence** holds that clinicians only conduct therapies, assessments, and research when they are properly trained and competent to do so (American Psychological Association, 2017b). Knowing the limits of one's expertise is critical for ethical practice. For example, psychologists, counselors, couple and family therapists, and social workers should not give medication advice to their clients because these professionals typically lack the medical training or authority to do so—just as psychiatrists who lack training and experience in psychotherapy should refer patients requesting such services. As another example, therapists trained only in cognitive-behavioral therapy (CBT) should not conduct psychodynamic therapy without appropriate training and supervision ensuring they can do so competently. Similarly, if conducting assessment (see Chapter 3), clinicians should stick to assessment instruments that they are trained to use. For instance, it is unethical to administer, score, and interpret the Minnesota Multiphasic Personality Inventory (MMPI) without appropriate training. As one last example, when clients present with problems outside a clinician's area of expertise, the clinician has a duty to obtain the training necessary to competently provide clinical services or make a referral.

16.13 Conflicts of Interest

Conflicts of interest: Situations in which a clinician or researcher has a professional, legal, financial, or other interest that might impair objectivity, competence, or effectiveness or that could lead to exploitation or harm.

Ethical professionals avoid **conflicts of interest**. They refrain from accepting professional roles if there are "personal, scientific, professional, legal, financial, or other interests or relationships" with the potential to "(1) impair their objectivity, competence, or effectiveness in performing their functions as psychologists or (2) expose the person or organization with whom the professional relationship exists to harm or exploitation" (American Psychological Association, 2017b, Standard 3.06). There are many potential conflicts of interest that clinicians and researchers must attend to. Having a dual role with a client could pose a conflict of interest. If I am your psychology professor and have grading power over you, I probably shouldn't also see you as a therapy client—especially if your student evaluations of me could influence whether my teaching contract is renewed! Similarly, I shouldn't see friends, family members, or people with whom I have a business relationship in therapy because I may have a vested interest in the decisions that they make, which could affect my clinical judgment. Financial conflicts are something ethical clinicians must especially pay heed to. The "In Depth" feature examines debate over alleged conflicts of interest in a particularly contentious area, namely whether psychiatrists' financial ties to pharmaceutical companies have compromised their work.

In Depth: Financial Conflicts of Interest in Professional Practice

Do psychiatrists and other mental health professionals with financial ties to pharmaceutical companies have a conflict of interest? Psychologist Lisa Cosgrove and colleagues contend they do, and they have been regularly publishing research documenting these financial ties for years. For instance, they found that 56 percent of DSM-IV committee members had at least one financial association with a drug company, with that percentage jumping to 100 percent for those on the mood disorder and schizophrenia committees (Cosgrove et al., 2006). They later found that in thirteen research trials overseen by DSM-5 committee members to test psychiatric drugs for new DSM-5 disorders, financial conflicts of interest occurred in all but one—with examples being "research grants, consultation, honoraria, speakers bureau participation, and/or stock" (Cosgrove et al., 2014, p. 110). Such conflicts extend beyond DSM. Cosgrove and colleagues found that 57 percent of clinical practice guidelines for depression had panel members with drug company connections (Cosgrove et al., 2017). Not even textbooks are safe from potentially pernicious conflicts of interest. Cosgrove discovered that 24 percent of psychopharmacology textbook authors had received $75,000 USD or more from the pharmaceutical industry (Cosgrove et al., 2022). Might this influence the content of their books?

When Cosgrove began publishing these studies, defenders of DSM and psychiatry countered that nothing sinister was going on, and that pharmaceutical ties do not indicate conflicts of interest. Having such ties made sense, they argued, because DSM panel members are prominent researchers connected to drug companies working on treatments for DSM disorders. In the words of David Kupfer and Darrel Regier, who oversaw DSM-5, Cosgrove and her co-authors "seem not to appreciate or understand how the collaborative relationships among government, academia, and industry are vital to the current and future development of pharmacological treatments for mental disorders" (Kupfer & Regier, 2009, para. 5). Further, they pointed to limits on how much psychiatrists could accept from drug companies—no more than $10,000 per year, $50,000 in stock, and $10,000 in annual dividends. Critics remained unconvinced, noting that $50,000 in stock and $10,000 in dividends is still a lot of money—surely enough to influence decision-making. To Cosgrove, "the APA's efforts at creating a conflict of interest (COI) policy have failed to ensure that the process for revising diagnostic and therapeutic guidelines is one that the public can trust" (Cosgrove & Bursztajn, 2009, para. 1).

Critical Thinking Questions

1. Does Cosgrove's research convince you that psychiatrists sometimes have financial conflicts of interest? Explain your reasoning.
2. Even if there was a conflict of interest, do you see evidence that DSM decisions were influenced by these conflicts?
3. Do you think the limits that the American Psychiatric Association established for how much money a DSM-5 committee member could receive from pharmaceutical companies were reasonable? Explain.
4. Cosgrove's critics counter that ties between government, academia, and industry are necessary to advance psychiatric knowledge and that suggesting these ties imply conflicts of interest is unfair. Do you agree with this statement and why?

16.14 Access to Care

Effective interventions for presenting problems only benefit people if they have access to them. This raises the ethical issue of **access to care**. Access to care can be defined as "the opportunity to reach and obtain appropriate healthcare services in situations of perceived need for care" (Levesque et al., 2013, p. 4). Providing access is key to ensuring physical, social, and psychological well-being.

Access to care: Extent to which people can obtain medical, psychological, and social services and are helped by doing so.

Barriers to Care

Unfortunately, not everyone has equal access to care. Barriers to access include:

1. *Financial barriers.* Many people can't afford help for their problems (Cunningham, 2018; Heath, 2021, 2022). This may be especially true in the United States, where there is no nationalized health insurance. Although at an all-time low, 9 percent of Americans remain uninsured (A. Seitz, 2022). Consequently, many delay seeking care because they cannot afford it, boosting the long-term price because healthcare expenses rise as people's conditions worsen. Ironically, this impacts not just uninsured and underinsured patients, but the healthcare system overall—by one estimate, adding $320 billion per year to U.S. healthcare spending (Dhar et al., 2022). Lack of access for some is costly to all.

2. *Insufficient services available.* Sometimes people lack access due to a scarcity of services. In the United States and Canada, there are not enough mental health providers available, especially in rural areas (USAFacts, 2021; T. Yun et al., 2022). As of September 30, 2022, only 27.7 percent of the need for mental health services in the United States was being met (Kaiser Family Foundation, 2022). A survey of psychologists in the fall of 2022 found that six in ten did not have openings for new patients (American Psychological Association, 2022b). Similarly, the wait time to see a psychiatrist in the UK's National Health Service in 2021 was a staggering eighteen weeks (Royal College of Psychiatrists, 2021). The shortage has only been exacerbated by the COVID-19 pandemic, when demand for services increased: "Many say that they are languishing on waiting lists, making call after call only to be turned away, with affordable options tough to find. Providers, who have long been in short supply, are stretched thin" (Caron, 2021).

3. *Racial and cultural barriers.* Being from a racial or ethnic minority group predicts poorer access to care. In the United States, Black, Hispanic/Latino, and Native Americans experience greater barriers to timely healthcare than whites (Caraballo et al., 2022; Radley et al., 2021). Discrimination and cultural miscommunication likely contribute to this problem. When surveyed, a majority of Black Americans (56 percent) reported negative experiences with healthcare providers (such as

not having their concerns taken seriously), and 40 percent recalled times when they had to assert themselves to receive proper care (Funk, 2022).

4. *Language barriers.* Language barriers overlap with racial and cultural barriers. Research indicates a link between lack of native language proficiency and underutilization of psychiatric services (Ohtani et al., 2015). Thus, increasing the number of bilingual providers and interpreters might improve access to care.

5. *Age-related barriers.* Older adults do not avail themselves of mental health services as readily as younger adults, often because they have more negative attitudes about doing so (E.-M. Kessler et al., 2015). Further, depressed or anxious older people often present with physical symptoms rather than psychological complaints, making them less likely to be offered mental health services (National Collaborating Centre for Mental Health, 2011).

6. *Stigma.* Mental health stigma is a major barrier to care for everyone, but it is especially prominent among men and members of racial and ethnic minority groups (Butkus et al., 2020; Chatmon, 2020; Knaak et al., 2017). Stigma makes people less likely to seek help for mental distress. Reducing it could increase access to care by making help-seeking more socially acceptable.

Enhancing Access via E-Mental Health

E-mental health:
Mental health services provided at a distance via telecommunication and information technologies.

Teletherapy: Uses real-time videoconferencing to provide psychotherapy and psychiatric consultations.

One way to improve access to care is through **e-mental health**, in which the Internet and related technologies are used to provide or enhance the delivery of services (Lal, 2019). This allows people to receive services without the time and travel expenses involved in visiting a clinic or office. **Teletherapy** is a form of telehealth in which psychotherapy or psychiatric consultations are conducted live over the Internet through videoconferencing. The COVID-19 pandemic hastened a massive shift toward teletherapy (L. A. Ellis et al., 2021). One study found that two months into the pandemic, family therapists were conducting 88 percent of their clinical work by teletherapy compared with just under 8 percent before the pandemic—not surprising given the stay-at-home guidelines implemented at that time (McKee et al., 2022). However, even after the pandemic's end, the therapists in this study predicted that 36.5 percent of their sessions would remain online rather than in person. This suggests the shift toward teletherapy may be permanent. In-person formats may never again be the dominant modality for therapy. While teletherapy has the potential to expand access to care, it could also propagate unequal access. To that end, we must better understand and address why some clients (notably those of lower SES) appear less likely than others to continue using teletherapy after the pandemic (Gangamma et al., 2022).

Not all forms of e-mental health are delivered live in the immediate moment (i.e., *synchronously*). Instead, many e-mental health interventions are administered via alternating interactions that occur at times convenient to the participants (i.e., *asynchronously*) (K. Myers & Vander Stoep, 2017). Email, social media, online discussion boards, and smartphone apps are examples of asynchronous e-mental health technologies used in e-mental health. Some e-mental health smartphone apps offer professional services via phone conversations and instant messaging, while others help people to manage depression, anxiety, and other issues on their own (Rice & Pedersen, 2022; Tzeses, 2021). The e-mental health landscape is rapidly evolving as technologies grow and develop. Because e-mental health remains relatively new, its uses, advantages, and limitations are just beginning to be understood and articulated. However, the impact of technology—especially social media—on the mental health field is rapidly expanding. The Controversial Question examines one divisive trend, the explosion of people diagnosing themselves with mental disorders via TikTok.

Controversial Question: Can TikTok Tell Me If I Have a Mental Disorder?

Teens are increasingly using social media sites to diagnose themselves with mental disorders—especially TikTok (M. Martin, 2022; Pugle, 2022). For instance, after spending hours watching TikTok videos about depersonalization disorder while isolated during the early days of the COVID-19 pandemic, a tenth grader named Kianna became convinced she had it (Caron, 2022). Kianna is not alone, and researchers are starting to document this trend (R. Gilmore et al., 2022). They point to an "increase in teens and young adults using TikTok to self-diagnose conditions such as autism, attention deficit hyperactivity disorder (ADHD), borderline personality disorder, dissociative identity disorder (DID), obsessive-compulsive disorder (OCD), and Tourette syndrome, among others" (Pugle, 2022, para. 3). Although mental health professionals are pleased to see mental distress being talked about openly on social media, many worry about people using TikTok videos to diagnose themselves. For one thing, there is a lot of misinformation on social media. Many of the videos that people turn to for diagnostic advice are misleading or wrong. For another thing, identifying DSM disorders is not as simple as TikTok makes it seem: "'It's incredibly easy to misdiagnose,' said Mitch Prinstein, the chief science officer of the American Psychological Association" (Caron, 2022, para. 16). A little knowledge can be a dangerous thing.

Why are so many young people turning to TikTok for mental health diagnoses? Some say it is for a sense of belongingness and community. They use "their current struggle with mental health symptoms as a way to find like-minded people, sometimes wearing their symptoms as a badge of pride or a shorthand way to explain themselves to others" (Caron, 2022, para. 26). Others believe teens turn to TikTok because they face so many barriers to accessing actual mental health services (Radez et al., 2021). These barriers include "stigma toward mental health issues, lack of trust in healthcare professionals, not knowing where to turn for help, and believing their problems aren't serious enough to warrant help" (Pugle, 2022, para. 8). The shortage of available mental health providers poses an additional impediment. Those who want appointments are often unable to get them (M. Martin, 2022). Thus, even though mental health professionals recommend consulting a professional rather than self-diagnosing via TikTok, the barriers to the former can see seem insurmountable. In this respect, perhaps "TikTok is a symptom of the broader problem instead of TikTok is necessarily causing the problem" (Pugle, 2022, para. 15).

Critical Thinking Questions

1. Do you agree or disagree with mental health professionals who believe it is dangerous for people to self-diagnose using TikTok? Explain your reasoning.
2. Should TikTok videos that encourage self-diagnosis be removed or screened to make sure they do not contain misinformation? Why or why not?
3. Can mental health professionals compete with the influence of social media? If access to mental health services was made easier, do you think self-diagnosing on TikTok would become less popular?

LEGAL PERSPECTIVES

Sometimes mental distress brings people into contact with the legal system. Below we examine four examples of this: the insanity defense, competency to stand trial, civil commitment, and duties to warn and protect. The legal and mental health systems often conceptualize these issues quite differently, which can pose challenges when they come into contact.

16.15 The Insanity Defense

Insanity and the Insanity Defense as Legal Terms

Insanity is a legal term, not a psychiatric one—which is why there is no "insanity" diagnosis in the DSM (R. Howes, 2009). The legal system defines insanity as "mental illness of such a severe nature that a person cannot distinguish fantasy from reality, cannot conduct her/his affairs due to psychosis, or is subject to uncontrollable impulsive behavior" ("Insanity," n.d., para. 1). Legal definitions of insanity are important to the **insanity defense**, in which criminal defendants claim to have been legally insane at the time of their crimes and therefore ask to be judged *not guilty by reason of insanity*. If their insanity pleas are successful, they are usually committed to mental hospitals for treatment (rather than sent to prison) and only released when deemed recovered. Below we examine the history, use, and arguments for and against the insanity defense.

Historical Origins of the Insanity Defense

The insanity defense as a legal tactic has mainly developed over the past two and a half centuries, but the notion existed in some form before that. The ancient Greek philosopher Plato, for instance, argued that mentally disturbed individuals should not be held responsible or punished for their crimes (R. J. Simon & Ahn-Redding, 2006). Further, precursors to the insanity defense can be found in both ancient Jewish and Islamic law (R. J. Simon & Ahn-Redding, 2006). Modern versions of the insanity

Insanity: Legal term for a mental illness so severe that it prevents distinguishing fantasy from reality, conducting daily affairs due to psychosis, or exerting control over behavior.

Insanity defense: A legal plea that challenges criminal responsibility by arguing that a defendant is not responsible for crimes committed as the result of a mental disorder.

Wild beast test:
Pre-cursor to the insanity defense developed in 1265 in the UK that compared defendants who did not understand their crimes to wild beasts.

defense grew out of British common law (law based mainly on precedents from judicial rulings rather than from codified statutes). For instance, in 1265, the British jurist Lord Bracton proposed the **wild beast test**, which "likened the defendant to a wild beast due to his complete lack of understanding" (R. J. Simon & Ahn-Redding, 2006, p. 6). Thus, even before modern legal tests of insanity developed, the idea of not holding people responsible for crimes due to their mental state was percolating.

Legal Tests of Insanity
M'Naghten Test

M' Naghten test:
Legal test of insanity that says defendants can be acquitted if, at the time their crimes, they were suffering from a disease of the mind that prevented them from understanding the nature of their acts or that these acts were wrong.

The first broadly established (and still used, in many places) test of insanity is the **M'Naghten test**. This test was developed in the aftermath of a landmark 1843 British murder case (*M'Naghten's Case*, 1843). In this famous case, a jury acquitted Scotsman Daniel M'Naghten by reason of insanity in the murder of Edwin Drummond, the secretary to British Prime Minister Robert Peel. M'Naghten (actually "McNaughton," but the judgment spelled his name wrong) had shot and killed Drummond, whom he'd mistaken for Peel (Allnutt et al., 2007). At trial, several witnesses testified that M'Naghten was delusional at the time of the murder. Nonetheless, his acquittal provoked public uproar, leading the House of Lords to clarify criteria for an insanity defense verdict. This became the M'Naghten test:

It must be clearly proved that at the time of commiting [sic] the act the party accused was labouring under such a defect of reason, from disease of the mind, as not to know the nature and quality of the act he was doing, or as not to know that what he was doing was wrong. (M'Naghten's Case, 1843)

The key question in the M'Naghten test is: At the time of the crime, was there a mental disorder that made the defendant unable to understand the actions taken or that these actions were wrong? The M'Naghten test remains widely used. It is still employed in the UK and in half of U.S. states ("The Insanity Defense among the States," 2019).

Irresistible Impulse Test

Irresistible impulse test: Legal test of insanity that says defendants can be acquitted when their crimes are attributable to impulses that they could not resist.

Whereas the M'Naghten test asks whether defendants understand their actions, the **irresistible impulse test** asks whether they can control those actions. Under the irresistible impulse test, people are deemed legally insane when a mental disease causes them to lose their free will, making them not responsible for their crimes. When first developed, the irresistible impulse test was sometimes used in addition to the M'Naghten test, but other times it was used instead of it ("The Irresistible Impulse Test," 2019). Either way, it came in for extensive criticism ("The Irresistible Impulse Test," 2019). The main objection was that it offered no way to decide who could or couldn't control their behavior. How can lack of control over behavior be proved or disproved—beyond each side in a trial bringing in dueling experts to plead their case? Because of its problems, the irresistible impulse test is used only in conjunction with the stricter M'Naghten rule in the four U.S. states where it remains on the books (Colorado, New Mexico, Texas, and Virginia) ("The Insanity Defense among the States," 2019).

Durham Test

Durham test: Legal test of insanity that says defendants can be acquitted when their illegal behavior was caused by a mental disorder.

The **Durham test** is the most inclusive test of insanity, requiring that criminal behavior merely be caused by a mental disorder. In other words, "a criminal defendant cannot be convicted of a crime if the act was the result of a mental disease or defect at the time of the incident" ("The 'Durham Rule,'" 2019, para. 3). The test originated in New Hampshire in 1871 but was more commonly implemented after the federal trial of Monte Durham, a troubled 26-year-old arrested for breaking and entering. Durham had a long history of emotional difficulties, including at least two suicide attempts (R. J. Simon & Ahn-Redding, 2006). His acquittal on the grounds that his crimes were caused by a mental disorder firmly established the Durham test, which the United States used at the federal level between 1954 and 1972. However, the Durham test was ultimately rejected for being overly inclusive. Under it, anyone who claimed a mental defect could plead insanity—even those able to understand and control their actions ("The 'Durham Rule,'" 2019). The Durham test was also criticized for being too dependent on mental health professionals to determine whether a defendant has a mental disorder. Today, New Hampshire is the only state that still uses it ("The 'Durham Rule,'" 2019; "The Insanity Defense among the States," 2019).

Model Penal Code Test

In the United States, twenty-one states use the **model penal code test**, which combines aspects of the M'Naghten and irresistible impulse rules ("The Insanity Defense among the States," 2019). Also known as the *American Law Institute test*, or *ALI test* (because it was proposed in 1955 by the American Law Institute), this test holds that defendants can be acquitted by reason of insanity if at the time of their crimes they had a mental disorder that prevented them from (a) having substantial capacity to appreciate the wrongfulness of their actions, or (b) controlling their behavior ("The 'Model Penal Code' Test for Legal Insanity," 2019). In other words, people can qualify for insanity in two ways (*either* not understanding actions *or* not being able to control behavior). Thus, the model penal code is more inclusive than the M'Naghten or irresistible impulse tests. Perhaps for this reason, it came under fire following John Hinckley, Jr.'s attempted assassination of President Ronald Reagan in 1981 (Rolf, 2006; R. J. Simon & Ahn-Redding, 2006). Hinckley's motivation for shooting Reagan? He was trying to impress the actress Jodie Foster, whom he had been stalking. Under the model penal code test, Hinckley—who pleaded insanity after being diagnosed with schizophrenia—was acquitted. Afterwards, the public was outraged and efforts were made to abolish or curtail use of the insanity defense in the United States (Rolf, 2006; R. J. Simon & Ahn-Redding, 2006).

Model penal code test: Legal test of insanity that acquits defendants if they lacked substantial capacity to appreciate the wrongfulness of their actions or could not control their behavior; also called the *American Law Institute test* or *ALI test.*

Insanity Defense Reform Act

In the aftermath of the Hinckley verdict, the U.S. Congress passed the **Insanity Defense Reform Act (IDRA)**, which adopted strict federal standards in insanity defense cases (D. N. Robinson, 1996; Rolf, 2006; Simon & Ahn-Redding, 2006). Under this act, the insanity defense is limited to instances where the mental defect or disorder is "severe." Psychosis is still included, but milder diagnoses typically no longer qualify. In addition, the irresistible impulse component of the model penal code was eliminated, while the M'Naghten component was narrowed (instead of merely lacking "substantial capacity to appreciate" wrongfulness, defendants must be "unable to appreciate" it). Finally, the burden of proof was shifted from the prosecution to the defense. Rather than prosecutors having to prove defendants sane, defense lawyers now must prove their clients insane. For better or worse (something you must judge for yourself), IDRA reforms make it more difficult for federal defendants to successfully plead insanity.

Insanity Defense Reform Act (IDRA): U.S. law that implemented strict federal standards in insanity defense cases, limiting it to cases where the mental defect or disorder was "severe."

Guilty But Mentally Ill

Four U.S. states (Idaho, Kansas, Montana, and Utah) have eliminated the insanity defense ("The Insanity Defense among the States," 2019). All of them except Kansas employ a **guilty but mentally ill (GBMI)** plea instead ("The Insanity Defense among the States," 2019). GMBI aims to hold people responsible for their crimes while also treating their mental disorders. If convicted under GBMI, the offender is concurrently sent to prison and treatment. However, critics say GMBI confuses jurors and that people convicted under GBMI don't consistently receive the treatment they are supposed to (Bloom & Kirkorsky, 2021; Melville & Naimark, 2002; C. A. Palmer & Hazelrigg, 2000; Plaut, 1983). To further confuse matters, GMBI is not exclusive to states with no insanity defense. Alaska, Arizona, and Georgia have both GMBI and insanity pleas.

Guilty but mentally ill (GBMI): Alternative to the insanity defense in which offenders, after being convicted, concurrently receive treatment along with a prison sentence.

The Insanity Defense Around the World

The M'Naghten test has influenced the insanity defense in many countries—including Germany, Brazil, Israel, and parts of Australia (R. J. Simon & Ahn-Redding, 2006). By comparison, France's insanity defense leans heavily on the irresistible impulse test, allowing defendants to avoid criminal responsibility if able to show their behavior resulted from a mental disorder that destroyed judgment or the ability to control actions (Simon & Ahn-Redding, 2006). The insanity pleas in countries like South Africa and parts of Australia emphasize both inability to understand and conform behavior, which is reminiscent of the model penal code. Interestingly, Australia and Canada do not use the stigmatizing term "insanity" ("The insanity defense," n.d.). In Australia, the insanity defense is called the *mental illness defense*, while in Canada it is the *not criminally responsible on account of mental disorder (NCR)* defense (CBC News, 2011; Nedim, 2015; R. J. Simon & Ahn-Redding, 2006). NCR emphasizes appreciating the nature of one's actions or knowing they were wrong (like the model penal code) but ability to control one's action isn't considered (like M'Naghten). This makes the NCR defense narrower than the model penal code but broader than M'Naghten.

Like the four U.S. states mentioned earlier, not all countries have an insanity defense. Sweden, Denmark, Norway, and The Netherlands do not (R. J. Simon & Ahn-Redding, 2006). In these countries, offenders deemed mentally ill by the courts are convicted but not punished. Instead, they are typically required to receive treatment. Though many consider this more humane, mandatory treatments can be experienced as punishment. More on this below.

Evaluating the Insanity Defense

Letting People Get Away with Crimes?

The insanity defense is extremely controversial. Many people feel that it lets people get away with crimes. But does it? First, the insanity defense is rare and usually unsuccessful. A classic study found that only 1 percent of defendants plead insanity and, of those, only 26 percent are acquitted (L. A. Callahan et al., 1991). Second, when acquitted, defendants are not simply set free. Instead, they are typically confined to mental hospitals until judged well enough to be released ("Insanity Defense in Criminal Cases," 2022). Some critics object to the insanity defense for this very reason. They don't like that insanity acquittals lead to indefinite stays in psychiatric facilities (L. Coleman, 1984; T. S. Szasz, 1963). In fact, people acquitted by reason of insanity are, on average, incarcerated almost twice as long as those sent to prison for similar offenses (Perlin, 2017b). While hospitalization is typically preferable to prison time, people acquitted by reason of insanity are not necessarily going unpunished. Insanity defense critics note that most of us would find being involuntarily detained—even in a hospital—quite punishing (Coleman, 1984; Szasz, 1963).

Can Experts Truly Determine Who Is Insane?

Opponents of the insanity defense question whether it is possible to validly distinguish "sane" from "insane" (L. Coleman, 1984; T. S. Szasz, 1963). Most legal definitions of insanity do not specify what counts as a "disease of the mind." Therefore, expert testimony from mental health professionals is required. Critics complain that this leads to "battles of the experts" in which each side in a trial lines up professionals to say whatever they are paid to say (Bergman, 2009). Others counter that the "battle of experts" idea is a myth and point to data that prosecution and defense reach consensus 80 percent to 90 percent of the time on whether an insanity plea is warranted (Perlin, 2017b). Even if trials aren't dominated by dueling experts, insanity defense detractors contend that we shouldn't place so much stock in expert testimony because mental health professionals lack the scientific knowledge necessary to determine when crimes are attributable to "mental defects" (Coleman, 1984; Szasz, 1963).

Free Will vs. Determinism

The insanity defense challenges the belief that people freely choose their actions and therefore warrant punishment for bad choices. Instead, it embraces a more deterministic stance, attributing erratic behavior to biological, psychological, or sociocultural causes. Does it make sense to hold people responsible for actions caused by their brains, psychological processes, or social determinants? Once we shift to a deterministic view, the wisdom of holding people accountable for their actions—even when not ascribed to mental disorder—becomes less clear. Ultimately, attitudes toward the insanity defense are greatly influenced by assumptions about free will versus determinism (Corrado, 2017).

16.16 Competence to Stand Trial

Case Example

Niki

Niki, a 35-year-old woman, was recently arrested for physically assaulting a neighbor. Mr. B, the attorney assigned to defend Niki in court, finds her difficult to communicate with when they discuss her case. When Mr. B asks Niki if she wants to plead innocent or guilty, Niki stares at the ceiling and keeps repeating: "It's a conspiracy! The water supply is laced with truth serum!" Unsure about whether Niki comprehends what he is telling her or the circumstances she faces, Mr. B considers requesting a court-appointed psychologist to assess her competency to stand trial.

What Is Competence to Stand Trial?

Whereas the insanity defense has to do with mental state at the time of a crime, **competence to stand trial** is about the capacity to participate in one's own defense. Courts have grappled with defendants unable or unwilling to participate in their own defenses for centuries—but not always sensitively. As far back as 1583 in England, "juries were appointed by courts to determine whether someone was mute by malice or by visitation of God" (Mudathikundan et al., 2014, p. 135). However, rather than suspending such trials, mentally impaired defendants were pressured to participate. Food was withheld or they were literally "pressed"—placed under a gradually increasing weight—until they either entered a plea or died. Such practices continued until the 1700s (Mudathikundan et al., 2014; A. Shah, 2012).

Today there are protections to prevent courts from forging ahead with trials of those who lack the mental capacity to participate. In the United States, these protections are traceable to a 1960 Supreme Court ruling, *Dusky v. United States*. The defendant, Milton Dusky, was convicted of kidnapping a girl and assisting two teens who raped her (Stork, 2013). His attorney appealed, arguing that a pretrial psychiatric evaluation found Dusky to have schizophrenia that prevented him from participating in his defense. The Supreme Court agreed. It overturned the conviction and remanded the case for a new trial (*Dusky v. United States*, 1960). The Dusky ruling established that competence to stand trial requires being able to (a) comprehend the proceedings, (b) participate in one's own defense, and (c) consult with legal counsel (Wall et al., 2018).

In the United States, defendants suspected of being incompetent to stand trial are referred for psychological assessment. Those declared incompetent have their trials suspended while they undergo mandatory *competence restoration* treatment in inpatient or outpatient settings (American Psychological Association, 2022a; Palermo, 2015). Treatment duration varies, with the expectation that it will return defendants to legal competence, at which point their trials can resume. In cases where recovery isn't adequate, there are limits to how long defendants may be kept in treatment (especially when involuntarily hospitalized). If not restored to competence within a certain period, they are released from treatment without a trial and either let go or civilly committed (a process discussed later). Certain jurisdictions limit how long defendants can be hospitalized for competency restoration (e.g., up to five years), but others do not despite a 1972 Supreme Court ruling limiting restoration to a "reasonable period" (*Jackson v. Indiana*, 1972).

Niki

At her attorney's request, Niki undergoes a competency evaluation, which yields a schizoaffective disorder diagnosis. Niki's court case is suspended, and she is referred to the local mental hospital for treatment. Because the hospital has a lengthy wait list for beds, it is several months before Niki is admitted—during which time she remains in jail. After three months of eventual treatment in the hospital, Niki still shows some psychotic symptoms. However, she is deemed sufficiently recovered for her trial to resume. She is convicted and sent to prison.

Competence to Stand Trial: Practical and Ethical Challenges

In some parts of the world (e.g., Canada, the UK, Australia, New Zealand, and Scotland), competency to stand trial is called *fitness to plead* and there are not that many cases—perhaps because ability to communicate with one's attorney is emphasized (Mackay, 2007; O'Shaughnessy, 2007). However, in the United States, where decisional competence is the key factor, the legal system is swamped with competency evaluations—between 19,000 and 94,000 annually, making them the most common psychological assessments requested by U.S. courts (Cochrane & Lloyd, 2020; N. P. Morris et al., 2021). Overwhelmed hospitals and community mental health agencies are expected to restore large numbers of incompetent patients to mental health so they can participate in their own defenses, but these institutions lack the resources to do so. Consequently, many defendants go untreated for long periods. This leads to complaints that too many people wind up with neither treatment nor a trial. Despite efforts to fund more treatment options—including innovative outpatient competency restoration programs—the system remains strained and there are ongoing calls for reform (Bloom et al., 2022; L. Callahan & Pinals, 2020; DeAngelis, 2022; Fader-Towe & Pinals, 2021).

Competence to stand trial: Legal standard used in the United States that says those charged with a crime must be able to (a) comprehend the proceedings, (b) participate in his or her own defense, and (c) consult with legal counsel.

The competency process faces other challenges, too. It has been criticized for being inconsistent, with widely different rulings from case to case and a lack of clarity about when competency is an issue (T. P. Rogers et al., 2008; A. Shah, 2012). Another concern is that being declared incompetent has adverse consequences for defendants (Stork, 2013). Many are sent to mental hospitals and forced to take medication so they can be restored to competence and tried (Bullock, 2002). After a potentially lengthy hospital stay with no clear discharge date, they could wind up incarcerated again if later convicted and sentenced to prison (Schug & Fradella, 2015; Stork, 2013). This can prove challenging for defense attorneys:

A defense attorney who has a potentially incompetent client faces a difficult situation. If the client has been charged with a misdemeanor, a finding of incompetency could easily keep him in a criminal psychiatric hospital for longer than he would have been in prison if he had been convicted (which could be zero days in jail since many misdemeanors only result in a fine). (Stork, 2013, p. 966)

Some people contend the competence to stand trial process infringes on civil liberties. They point to a 2006 United Nations General Assembly resolution on the rights of persons with disabilities that says "the existence of a disability shall in no case justify a deprivation of liberty" (United Nations General Assembly, 2006, Article 14b). Incarcerating people in mental hospitals after they are declared incompetent might violate this principle by involuntarily committing mentally disabled people without a trial. However, defenders of the competency system counter that we are obligated to restore people to competency before trying them, lest we violate their due process rights (Perlin, 2017a). What are your thoughts on this difficult issue?

16.17 Civil Commitment

Case Example

Marta

Marta, a 21-year-old woman studying at the local university, has begun seeing and hearing things that alarm her psychotherapist, Dr. Y. During sessions, she keeps saying the university president monitors her via the thermostats in campus classrooms. Marta's appearance has deteriorated in recent weeks. She has lost weight, looks gaunt, and appears to be getting little sleep. Marta's lack of grooming also concerns Dr. Y. Her hair is unkempt and tangled, and she hasn't been bathing regularly. Dr. Y begins to wonder if Marta is currently able to properly care for herself.

So far, we have been talking about **criminal commitment**, which involves placing people in mental hospitals for criminal behavior. Both the insanity defense and being declared incompetent to stand trial result in criminal commitment. However, another equally controversial form of commitment is **civil commitment** (also known as *involuntary commitment*; or, in the U.K., *sectioning* or *detaining*). In civil commitment, people considered harmful to themselves (or others) are treated against their will, either in hospital or outpatient settings (Substance Abuse and Mental Health Services Administration, 2019). Civilly committed individuals haven't broken the law, but their behavior frightens and appears dangerous to others. They act in ways that place themselves or others at risk, or they appear to desperately need treatment but refuse it.

Temporary Commitment

The basis for civil commitment stems from two forms of government power: police power (the state's authority to confine people who pose a danger to society) and *parens patriae* (the state's authority to restrict the freedom of children and the mentally incompetent; Latin for "state as parent") (Substance Abuse and Mental Health Services Administration, 2019). Using these two forms of power, how does civil commitment occur? In most jurisdictions, family members, the police, or medical/mental health professionals can initiate short-term psychiatric hospitalizations of those they believe pose a danger to self or others. This is known as **temporary commitment** (or *emergency commitment*) and it happens in crisis situations (Menninger, 2001). For example,

Criminal commitment: Placing people in mental hospitals because of crimes they committed.

Civil commitment: When people deemed dangerous to self or others or in serious need of treatment are treated against their will, either in hospital or outpatient settings; also known as *involuntary commitment*; or, in the UK, *sectioning* or *detaining*.

Temporary commitment: Short-term psychiatric hospitalization of those considered dangerous to self or others; also called *emergency commitment*.

highly suicidal individuals or those in the throes of psychosis might be placed in the hospital by the police or by doctors, usually with little or no legal approval required. This allows leeway to quickly intervene in emergencies. However, because so little approval is necessary, temporary commitment is typically limited to just a few days.

Marta

Dr. Y's concerns about Marta are confirmed when the police find her wandering the streets alone one cold winter evening wearing only her pajamas. After a brief evaluation in the local emergency room, Marta is temporarily committed for forty-eight hours.

Extended Commitment

Until the mid-twentieth century, there was no distinction between temporary and longer-term commitment. People hospitalized for psychiatric reasons had little recourse and often spent years (sometimes their whole lives) involuntarily committed to mental hospitals (Schug & Fradella, 2015). In the United States, sweeping reforms in the 1950s and 1960s—as well as the development of antipsychotics to quell erratic behavior—led to the widespread deinstitutionalization of many long-term mental patients (see Chapter 1) and the establishment of more extensive due process rights for those wishing to challenge their hospitalization (Schug & Fradella, 2015). Thus, civilly committing people for longer periods is now known as **extended commitment** and requires a legal proceeding to convince a court that hospitalization is the least restrictive treatment available (Menninger, 2001; Policy Surveillance Program, n.d.; Schug & Fradella, 2015).

Still, civil commitment proceedings do not provide as many due process protections as criminal trials, even though both can lead to involuntary incarceration (Schug & Fradella, 2015). While the burden of proof in civil commitment cases is higher than for civil lawsuits, it is lower than for criminal cases. Criminal trials employ the *beyond a reasonable doubt* standard, which requires jurors be all-but-certain of a defendant's guilt (the 90 percent certain rule). By contrast, civil lawsuits use a much lower standard because they don't result in anyone's confinement. They merely require *preponderance of the evidence*, in which the evidence just needs to lean slightly in one direction (the 50 percent rule). However, a 1979 Supreme Court ruling established an intermediary standard for civil commitment, *clear and convincing proof* (the 75 percent rule) (*Addington v. Texas*, 1979). The Court held that because psychiatry is an inexact science, predicting risk beyond a reasonable doubt is too burdensome and prevents proper care of those who require hospitalization (Testa & West, 2010; Tsesis, 2011). Critics of clear and convincing proof disagree. If the need for commitment is so "clear," they ask, why is beyond a reasonable doubt too high a bar (Caspar & Joukov, 2020)?

The goals of extended civil commitment are to (a) rehabilitate people diagnosed with mental illnesses, and (b) protect the public from such people (Schug & Fradella, 2015). Extended commitment typically requires that the person be judged *dangerous*, *gravely disabled*, or in *need of treatment* (Menninger, 2001; Substance Abuse and Mental Health Services Administration, 2019). In determining dangerousness, courts look at the type of danger (harm to self, others, or property?), its immediacy (when is it expected to occur?), and its likelihood (what are the chances of it occurring?). Of course, in some instances the danger isn't because of what people do, but what they don't do. In such cases, individuals can be committed for being *gravely disabled*, which means they are deemed unable to take care of their basic needs (for food, clothes, shelter, health, and safety). Dangerousness and being gravely disabled have increasingly taken precedence over need for treatment (which can be harder to agree on) in making extended commitment decisions (Menninger, 2001).

> **Extended commitment:** Civilly committing people for longer periods; *dangerousness*, *grave disability*, and *need for treatment* are the criteria used to make extended commitment decisions.

Marta

The psychiatrists at the hospital wish to extend Marta's civil commitment beyond the forty-eight-hour temporary window because they believe she is gravely disabled and in need of ongoing treatment, including antipsychotic drugs. Over Marta's strenuous objections, they go to court and get approval for this. Marta remains hospitalized for several months.

Involuntary outpatient commitment (IOC):
Legally mandated treatment in a community setting; also called *outpatient civil commitment, compulsory community treatment, assisted outpatient treatment, or community treatment orders.*

Involuntary Outpatient Commitment (IOC)

Not all civil commitment involves inpatient hospitalization. **Involuntary outpatient commitment (IOC)** (also called *compulsory community treatment, outpatient civil commitment, assisted outpatient treatment,* or *community treatment orders*) involves legally mandating treatment in a community, rather than hospital, setting (B. G. Moore & Weisman, 2016; A. J. O'Brien et al., 2009; Saks, 2003). IOC is a less restrictive form of civil commitment: "In contrast to inpatient civil commitment, which involves separation of a mentally ill person from society through placement behind a locked door, outpatient civil commitment allows people suffering from mental disorders to remain in their communities" (Testa & West, 2010, p. 37). IOC originated in the 1960s during the early deinstitutionalization movement (see Chapter 1), but was not implemented widely in the United States until the 1980s and 1990s (A. J. O'Brien et al., 2009). Today, all but three U.S. states (Connecticut, Maryland, and Massachusetts) use some form of it (Dailey et al., 2020). Other countries—including Canada, the UK, Australia, New Zealand, and Israel—have adopted it, too (Kisely et al., 2017; Mikellides et al., 2019). When used, IOC can serve as an alternative to hospitalization, as a condition of being released from a hospital following more intensive treatment, or as a preventative measure to avert the need for hospitalization (A. J. O'Brien et al., 2009; Saks, 2003).

Debate over Civil Commitment

Civil commitment is controversial. Those in favor of it believe it protects people with mental illnesses who are dangerous, gravely disabled, or in need of treatment. Thus, by forcing people into treatment, it helps those who cannot help themselves. Patient advocacy groups like the National Alliance on Mental Illness (NAMI) and prominent psychiatrists like E. Fuller Torrey are long-time advocates of civil commitment. As Torrey put it:

Most people will agree on the necessity of treating people who are a danger to themselves or others. Many disagree on treating people who are "in need of treatment." I personally am inclined to give people who are not aware of their illness a shot at treatment and would hospitalize them at least briefly and involuntarily to give them an attempt at medication to see if it does improve things. (D. Miller & Hanson, 2016, p. 23)

Opponents of civil commitment vigorously disagree with such sentiments. Psychiatric survivor groups such as MindFreedom International (see Chapter 2) and antipsychiatry groups like the Citizens Commission on Human Rights (CCHR; cofounded by the late psychiatrist Thomas Szasz and the Church of Scientology) wish to see civil commitment abolished. They argue that civil commitment not only incarcerates people who haven't committed crimes, but unfairly forces them to take psychiatric drugs (D. Miller & Hanson, 2016). Civil commitment, its most vocal critics argue, is a form of unjust punishment rather than a humane treatment. Thomas Szasz, perhaps the most well-known critic of civil commitment, contended that "whether we admit it or not, we have a choice between caring for others coercively and caring for them only with their consent" (T. Szasz, 1994, p. 205). He continued:

It is dishonest to pretend that caring coercively for the mentally ill invariably helps him, and that abstaining from such coercion is tantamount to "withholding treatment" from him. Every social policy entails benefits as well as harms. Although our ideas about benefits and harms vary from time to time, all history teaches us to beware of benefactors who deprive their beneficiaries of liberty. (T. Szasz, 1994, p. 205)

Civil libertarians like Szasz note that in some countries such as China and the former Soviet Union, civil commitment has been used as a form of social control or to punish political dissidents (S. Faraone, 1982; Safeguard Defenders, 2022; X. Zhao & Dawson, 2014). They worry that even in countries with greater civil liberties, declaring people mentally ill can be used to justify taking away their rights. Even if we don't wish to abolish civil commitment, its effectiveness is unclear because mental health professionals cannot reliably predict dangerousness (Monahan & Shah, 1989). Further, the threat of involuntary treatment discourages some people from seeking mental health services (D. Miller & Hanson, 2016; O'Reilly, 2004). To help you reach your own conclusions about civil commitment, Table 16.4 summarizes major arguments for and against it, while "The Lived Experience" feature presents a psychiatrist's reflections on using it.

Table 16.4 Some Arguments for and Against Civil Commitment

ARGUMENTS FOR	ARGUMENTS AGAINST
Society has an obligation to care for those who can't care for themselves and must commit those in desperate need of help.	Society has an obligation to protect individual rights and should never force people into treatment.
Civil commitment protects people from themselves.	Civil commitment violates people's civil rights.
Mentally ill people often don't know they are mentally ill, requiring that we overlook their opposition to civil commitment and involuntary treatment.	People who resist being committed are justified in not wanting to be incarcerated against their will and forced to take psychiatric drugs with serious side effects.
Many of those civilly committed might otherwise end up in jail or homeless, which are worse fates.	Civil commitment isn't fundamentally different from jail because, like jail, it involves restriction of freedom.
Civil commitment is the most effective way to intervene in situations where people are dangerous to self or others.	Voluntary community services, which are currently underfunded and difficult to access, are preferable to civil commitment.
People who are civilly committed will thank us when they are recovered and can better understand why we had to intervene and treat them.	Coercion, however well intentioned, inevitably causes people to fear and avoid the mental health system.

The Lived Experience: Involuntary Hospitalization

Dr. Sederer, former Chief Medical Officer of the New York State Office of Mental Health, describes his experience involuntarily hospitalizing patients.

When I have personally committed a patient of mine for what I believed to be a life threatening mental illness the result was that short-term safety was achieved—but at an unwelcome price.

... An intervention may be necessary but it may not be helpful—for more than the moment. People who are subject to loss of liberty, to the deeply unsettling experience of having the police intervene, of being transported in restraints, and of being put behind a locked hospital door never forget the experience. Some come to terms with it and a few even come to understand (even if they don't forgive). But this is a traumatic experience and a normal response to it is to not want to put yourself back into an environment, like a mental health clinic or hospital, where that could happen again.

Would I do what I did again should circumstances reach crisis and life-threatening proportions? I don't know what other responsible thing there would be to do. Thus, good answers seem to lie with solutions that avoid the use of coercion and loss of liberty, whenever possible. These are solutions, I believe, that require that mental health interventions be made more humane while we also work to reengineer services to intervene earlier and more effectively in the course of a person's illness.

We owe people with mental illness what has been called "patient centered" care—not as a slogan but as a standard of practice. What this would look like would include open access to an appointment where, instead of waiting for days or weeks, people in crisis could come to a clinic the same day they want to be seen. There would be the ability for clinicians to meet with patients (and families) outside the four walls of a clinic, in settings more natural and less stigmatizing (this is particularly necessary for younger people). Special attention needs to be paid to what is needed to keep youth in school and adults in work, or on a path to work. Shared decision-making where patients are made partners in their care is an important way to engage and retain people in treatment. The use of medications needs to be highly judicious and attentive to managing the side effects that frequently discourage patients from taking them. We need to enlist the help of families who can serve as an early warning system for problems in their loved ones. Most often (though not always) families are the most important and enduring source of support for a person with a medical illness, including mental disorders .... What I describe here is not new but it calls for changes that will take leadership and relentless persistence since change is hard, even when clearly needed.

We also owe people with mental illness and our communities an alternative to the demoralizing experience of a condition advancing to a severe, persistent and even dangerous state that makes involuntary commitment almost inescapable. This requires giving people with mental illness, their families and communities, and our mental health system the means to identify problems early, typically in adolescence, and new methods of engaging people with illness in effective treatments that also support their families .... This is the kind of overhaul the mental health system needs. This is the kind of overhaul that could provide more effective care with dignity and probably save lives and money.

Humane, patient centered services and early intervention are paths out of coercion. Imagine their impact on people with mental illness, their families and communities, and doctors who may not need to find themselves in situations such as I have described. Achieving these goals would be something to be proud of.

By Lloyd I. Sederer, MD. Reprinted with permission. Excerpted from Sederer (2013).

16.18 Right to Refuse Treatment

Why Might a Patient Refuse Treatment?

Sometimes civilly committed patients refuse treatment, usually psychiatric drugs. There are many reasons why they might do so. Sometimes they refuse due to problems in the doctor-patient relationship (Wettstein, 1999). Their doctors may have poorly explained the benefits of treatment or struggled to establish doctor-patient rapport, leading patients to reject treatment recommendations. Patients also refuse treatment due to side effects—like those that accompany psychiatric drugs and electroconvulsive therapy (ECT) (Wettstein, 1999). Further complicating matters, some patients may decide against treatment to resist or accommodate the wishes of family and friends (Wettstein, 1999). Additional reasons why patients refuse treatment include religious objections, the stigma that accompanies a psychiatric diagnosis, or legal motivations (such as wanting to appear sicker in court to help win a case) (Wettstein, 1999).

What Happens when a Patient Refuses Treatment?

Right to refuse treatment: Legal right to decline treatment unless judged incompetent to make such a decision.

If treatment is voluntary, then the patient has the right to decline. Someone who checks into a hospital voluntarily is legally entitled to reject the interventions offered—or to leave the hospital entirely. However, when treatment is involuntary (as in civil or criminal commitment), things get more complicated. However, U.S. courts have generally upheld that, unless judged to be legally incompetent, patients have a **right to refuse treatment** (R. Lewis, 2019). This is consistent with the growing emphasis on dangerousness over need for treatment in involuntarily commitment decisions. Ironically, the right to refuse treatment can lead to patients being involuntarily hospitalized for being dangerous but not receiving treatment because it is refused (Sederer, 2013).

> **Marta**
> *During Marta's extended commitment, she is prescribed antipsychotic drugs. However, she refuses to take them. The hospital staff are frustrated by this and view it as unfortunate, but Marta feels justified: "I have a right not to take that poison."*

Debate Surrounding Right to Refuse Treatment

Critics of the right to refuse treatment maintain that mentally disordered people often don't understand their situations well enough to make informed choices to decline treatment. These critics contend that when non-mentally disordered patients refuse treatment for, let's say, cancer or diabetes, they have a legal right to do so because they are rational agents capable of deciding. By contrast, patients diagnosed with severe mental disorders are often deemed unable to make rational decisions—which calls into question whether they should be allowed to reject treatment. Further, critics insist that involuntarily treated patients will be appreciative once recovered. According to the "thank you" test introduced when discussing suicide, clients will "thank the clinician afterward for treating them against their objections, thereby proving that the ostensible refusals were based on mental pathology rather than on principle or rational analysis" (Kapp, 1994, p. 228).

Conversely, those skeptical of involuntary interventions defend the right to refuse treatment and argue that mental health professionals are too often paternalistic and don't respect patient rights: "Although the underlying sentiments are honorable and sincere, in many cases beneficence or concern for patient well-being has been overextended into the sort of parentalistic 'doctor knows best' attitude that helped to inspire external oversight in the first place" (Kapp, 1994, p. 228). Right-to-refuse treatment defenders insist that regardless of the psychological issues involved, patients should always have a say in accepting or declining treatments that impact their lives, especially when those interventions have serious and sometimes debilitating side effects. But critics remain unconvinced. Like many topics in this chapter, the right to refuse treatment remains contentious and ethically fraught.

16.19 Right to Treatment

Involuntarily committed patients not only have a right to refuse treatment in some instances, but they also have a **right to treatment** because, according to some court decisions, failing to provide it renders hospitals indistinguishable from jails (Schwitzgebel, 1974). For example, U.S. legal rulings have found that it isn't acceptable simply to keep patients hospitalized (Schwitzgebel, 1974; Subedi, 2014). In the case of *Wyatt v. Stickney* (1971), "a federal court in Alabama held for the first time that people who are involuntarily committed to state institutions because of mental illness or developmental disabilities have a constitutional right to treatment that will afford them a realistic opportunity to return to society" (Disability Justice, n.d., para. 1).

This means that people who are involuntarily hospitalized are entitled to treatment, as opposed to simply being warehoused. The ruling held that civilly committed patients are legally entitled to minimal care (*Wyatt v. Stickney*, 1971). This includes "(1) a humane psychological and physical environment; (2) qualified staff in numbers sufficient to administer adequate treatment; and (3) individualized treatment plans" (Subedi, 2014, p. 52).

Right to treatment: Legal right of individuals to receive appropriate treatment while involuntarily committed.

16.20 Duty to Protect

Case Example

Norman

Dr. S has a new psychotherapy patient, Norman, a 35-year-old man seeking therapy for "scary thoughts" he is having about his 22-year-old neighbor, Belinda. Norman reports fantasies in which he violently murders Belinda. Norman has a history of impulse-control issues and did once spend a night in jail following a fist fight in a bar. When asked directly by Dr. S if he plans to follow through on his violent fantasies, Norman looks away and mutters, "Not if I can help it." Dr. S wonders if he needs to break confidentiality to protect Belinda from possible harm.

The Tarasoff Case and Duty to Protect

When their clients pose a safety threat to others, therapists in most jurisdictions are expected to take preventative action (Adi & Mathbout, 2018; Gorshkalova & Munakomi, 2022). This **duty to protect** originates in the famous case of *Tarasoff v. Regents of the University of California*. The case concerned a student from India named Prosenjit Poddar who was studying at the University of California at Berkeley in 1969. After a New Year's Eve kiss with a female student named Tatiana Tarasoff, Poddar expected a romantic relationship to develop. However, Tarasoff said she was dating other men and wasn't interested in a relationship. Despondent, Poddar's schoolwork suffered, and his behavior became erratic. During an outpatient therapy session at the university hospital, he told his therapist that he planned to kill Tarasoff. Nobody warned Tarasoff about the threat and, shortly thereafter, Poddar stabbed her to death. The subsequent lawsuit brought by Tarasoff's family surrounded whether Poddar's therapist had a *duty to warn* Tarasoff about the threat to her life. The case went all the way to the California Supreme Court, which held that therapists do indeed have a duty to protect potential victims against threats made against them by patients, even if this means breaking confidentiality (*Tarasoff v. Regents of the University of California*, 1976). Depending on the circumstances, therapists must warn threatened individuals, notify the police, or take other reasonable protective steps. The Tarasoff ruling applied only to California, but in North America most U.S. states and Canadian provinces have since established their own duty to protect laws (National Conference of State Legislatures, 2022). Some are *mandatory* and others *permissive* (APA Practice Organization, 2013). Mandatory laws require therapists to report imminent threats or potentially be held liable. Permissive laws grant therapists broader permission to break confidentiality when harm is predicted but without imposing liability.

Critics contend that therapists can't predict dangerousness very accurately, so imposing a duty to protect on them is unfairly burdensome (M. Thomas, 2009). Of course, difficulty predicting threat can cut both ways: "Lack of predictive certainty poses a disconcerting dilemma, whereby

Duty to protect: Legal and/or ethical duty of therapists to break confidentiality when necessary to protect their clients or other people threatened by their clients.

overestimation of a client's dangerousness may unnecessarily jeopardize the therapeutic relationship, yet on the other hand, underestimation could lead to potentially preventable harm" (Zachariades & Cabrera, 2012, p. 2). Beyond the challenge of predicting dangerousness, some worry that the duty to protect turns therapists from confidants into informants, increasing client reluctance to honestly share in session lest their therapists break confidentiality (Bollas & Sundelson, 1995). Finally, others complain that imposing a duty to protect on therapists makes them preoccupied with being sued (E. Henderson, 2015). Consequently, they operate defensively to protect themselves rather than in the best interests of their clients. Still, those in favor of the duty to protect counter that clinicians have ethical and legal obligations to safeguard the public, even if that means occasionally breaking confidentiality. What do you think?

Norman

Dr. S decides that protecting Belinda takes precedence over maintaining Norman's confidentiality. He shares what Norman told him in session with the police, who initiate emergency commitment procedures. Norman is briefly hospitalized and prescribed antipsychotic drugs. He stops having homicidal fantasies about Belinda but is furious with Dr. S for "ratting" him out. When released from the hospital, he does not return to Dr. S for further therapy.

CLOSING THOUGHTS

16.21 Ethical and Legal Dilemmas: The Case of Suicide

Let's conclude our discussion of suicide, ethics, and law by highlighting how suicide provides a vivid example (among others touched on in this chapter) of ethical and legal dilemmas in clinical practice. Looking back at the general ethical principles of the American Psychological Association (revisit Table 16.2), you can see that psychologists face a predicament with suicidal clients. Invoking the principle of beneficence and nonmaleficence, it can be argued that there is an ethical duty to involuntarily commit suicidal clients for their own protection. At the same time, appealing to the principle of respecting people's rights and dignity, an alternative argument can be made that hospitalization should be a last resort (or rejected entirely) due to clients' rights to privacy, confidentiality, and self-determination—which involuntary commitment violates. Thus, psychologists working with suicidal clients must make difficult ethical decisions about which reasonable people often disagree.

To further confuse matters, whatever ethical determinations a clinician makes inevitably occur within the confines of the broader legal system. A clinician who chooses safety planning over involuntary hospitalization out of respect for a client's rights and dignity may come into conflict with the legal system should the client later complete suicide—even if the therapist explains the ethical rationale for her actions. Ethical and legal perspectives do not always align. To add one more layer of complication, professional ethics codes and societal laws may not only conflict with each other, but also with the ethical beliefs of clients. Even when therapists and judges agree on a particular remedy, this does not necessarily mean that clients affected by such decisions also concur. A client might strongly assert a right to suicide, but professional ethics codes and legal statutes might say

Photo 16.6 Yukio Shige, 76, operates suicide prevention patrols in Tojinbo, Japan. Yukio began patrolling the cliffs in retirement after growing frustrated at the failure of the authorities to address the number of suicides there. He now runs a small team of volunteers who walk the cliffs several times a day looking for vulnerable people, who they assist by offering long-term help including accommodation and dispute resolution.

Carl Court/Getty Images.

otherwise. Whenever clinical practice, the legal system, and client ethical beliefs come into contact, disagreements are inevitable.

EPILOGUE

We have, at last, reached the end of our journey together. Most students find psychopathology and mental distress to be a fascinating, yet contentious, field of study. This is because there are so many ways to conceptualize the topic. Diagnostic, biological, psychological, and sociocultural perspectives offer different ideas on what constitute problems, what causes them, and how best to remedy them—something evident throughout this book.

Of course, when it comes to different perspectives, "contrasting" does not necessarily mean "incompatible." There are countless efforts to integrate perspectives. For instance, the biopsychosocial model from Chapter 4 says that because presenting problems "span the social, psychological, and biological," reducing them to one of these factors is simplistic and counterproductive (Engel, 1977, p. 133). This model, which became popular in the 1980s and 1990s (with even DSM espousing it) aims to move past longstanding conflicts among seemingly irreconcilable perspectives.

Integration at last, you say? Not so fast. If you've learned anything from this text, it is that there is always a contrasting point of view. Critics of the biopsychosocial model complain about its philosophical limitations, with some concluding that it yields a mindless eclecticism (S. N. Ghaemi, 2009; G. Henriques, 2015; O'Leary, 2021). **Eclecticism** is an approach to practice in which clinicians draw from multiple theories depending on what is useful in the moment. To critics, eclecticism fosters an unreflective (and therefore dangerous) pluralism in which clinicians pick whatever intervention they prefer without thinking things through (S. N. Ghaemi, 2009, 2010; G. Henriques, 2015). This "borders on anarchy" because "one can emphasise the 'bio' if one wishes, or the 'psycho', or the 'social'" without a rationale as to "why one heads in one direction or the other in deciding what interventions to use" (N. Ghaemi, 2014, p. 3).

Not everyone has given up on the biopsychosocial approach. Some wish to revive it and better incorporate both medical and humanistic threads (A. Frances, 2014; R. McKay et al., 2012). We aren't going to resolve disputes over the biopsychosocial model here, but they serve as one final reminder that—despite ongoing efforts at integration—contrasting perspectives on psychopathology and mental distress remain the norm. Hopefully, this book has whetted your appetite to further explore contrasting perspectives, even if your journey doesn't lead to simple and singular answers.

In closing, twentieth-century American psychologist George Kelly (1955/1991a, 1955/1991b), whose personal construct psychology was mentioned in previous chapters, once remarked that the questions we ask are often more important than the answers we give them. When it comes to the study of mental distress, learning to live with ambiguity and uncertainty is par for the course. Sometimes the more you know, the less you know for sure. Hopefully, your knowledge of psychopathology and mental distress has expanded sufficiently to make you keenly aware of how many questions remain to be asked and how many answers have yet to be generated.

Eclecticism: An approach to practice in which clinicians draw from multiple theories depending on what is useful in the moment.

CHAPTER SUMMARY

Overview

- Presenting problems occur within social and legal contexts. Suicide is an issue where these contexts sometimes collide.

Perspectives on Suicide

- Suicide is intentionally ending one's life. Shneidman identified four types.
- Subintentional death is form of indirect suicide. Shneidman identified four types.
- Suicide statistics illustrate that suicidal behavior and ideation are significant problems around the globe.
- Historically, attitudes about suicide have been shifting from a sin model to social and medical models.
- DSM includes proposals for *suicidal behavior disorder (SBD)* and *nonsuicidal self-injury disorder (NSSI)*.

- Genes, the HPA axis, and lack of serotonin have been linked to suicidal behavior. Antidepressants, mood stabilizers, and antipsychotics are sometimes prescribed.
- Classic psychoanalysis saw suicide as about anger turned inward, whereas modern psychodynamic perspectives attribute it to early life losses.
- *Cognitive-behavioral therapy for suicide prevention (CBT-SP)* addresses suicidality by targeting problematic cognitions and behaviors.
- Humanistic perspectives treat suicide as a meaningful response to humiliation, anger, hurt, and loss (rather than as a disorder).
- *Durkheim's sociological model of suicide* emphasizes the importance of social integration and regulation in suicide.
- There are important demographic differences in suicidality pertaining to gender, age, race/ethnicity, and socioeconomic status (SES).
- The *Werther effect* is the tendency for suicide rates to increase after a highly publicized suicide.
- *Suicide prevention programs* curb suicide via *suicide awareness education, suicide hotlines, crisis intervention, safety planning, method restriction,* and *hospitalization.*
- Predicting suicide can be very difficult. Artificial intelligence may predict better than people.

Ethical Perspectives

- Ethics codes help mental health professionals in research and practice.
- *Informed consent* requires research participants be given sufficient information to decide whether to participate in a study. Risks and benefits of participation must be made known.
- *Confidentiality* is the ethical requirement that mental health professionals not disclose what clients tell them, whereas *privilege* involves the legal protection of communications made in certain relationships, including clinician-client.
- *Competence* is an ethical principle that limits clinicians to only conducting assessments or interventions for which they are trained.
- Ethically, mental health professionals must avoid *conflicts of interest.*
- *Access to care* is the extent to which people can obtain services; there are often barriers to it.

Legal Perspectives

- The *insanity defense* allows criminal defendants to argue that they were legally *insane* at the time of their crimes and should not be held responsible for them.
- There are different tests for insanity (*M'Naghten, irresistible impulse, Durham, model penal code*), depending on the jurisdiction. There is sometimes a *guilty but mentally ill* verdict, as well.
- The insanity defense is controversial, with numerous arguments for and against it.
- *Competence to stand trial* concerns whether one is mentally capable to participating in one's own defense.
- Competency evaluations are the most requested mental health evaluations requested by U.S. courts.
- *Civil commitment* involves involuntarily hospitalizing/treating those deemed dangerous to self/others or in need of treatment. It differs from *criminal commitment* in which people are hospitalized/treated following crimes.
- *Temporary commitment* allows those who pose an imminent danger to be easily hospitalized. Court approval is required for *extended commitment.* Sometimes *involuntary outpatient commitment (IOC)* is used as an alternative to commitment in a hospital setting.
- Civil commitment pits protecting people from harm against depriving them of freedom.
- Civilly committed patients usually have a *right to refuse treatment*, as well as a *right to treatment.*
- The *duty to protect* involves violating confidentiality to prevent potential harm. It poses a difficult ethical dilemma for therapists.

Epilogue

- *Eclecticism* involves drawing from different perspectives in choosing client interventions.
- The biopsychosocial model marks an effort to integrate perspectives on mental distress.
- The field of "abnormal psychology" has many more questions than answers, and different perspectives continue to compete.

NEW VOCABULARY

1. Access to care
2. Civil commitment
3. Cognitive-behavioral therapy for suicide prevention (CBT-SP)
4. Competence
5. Competence to stand trial
6. Confidentiality
7. Conflicts of interest
8. Criminal commitment
9. Crisis intervention
10. Death instinct
11. Durham test
12. Durkheim's sociological model of suicide
13. Duty to protect
14. Eclecticism
15. E-mental health
16. Extended commitment
17. Guilty but mentally ill (GBMI)
18. Informed consent
19. Insanity
20. Insanity defense
21. Insanity Defense Reform Act (IDRA)
22. Involuntary outpatient commitment (IOC)
23. Irresistible impulse test
24. Life instinct
25. M'Naghten test
26. Method restriction
27. Moral penal code test
28. Nonsuicidal self-injury disorder (NSSI)
29. Privilege
30. Right to refuse treatment
31. Right to treatment
32. Safety planning
33. Subintentional death
34. Suicidal behavior disorder (SBD)
35. Suicide
36. Suicide awareness education
37. Suicide hotlines
38. Suicide prevention programs
39. Teletherapy
40. Temporary commitment
41. "Thank you" theory of involuntary commitment
42. Werther effect
43. Wild beast test

APPENDIX: DIAGNOSING THE CASE EXAMPLES

Below are the DSM-5-TR diagnoses assigned to case examples in the presenting problem chapters (4–16). Remember that mental health professionals sometimes disagree about which diagnosis is most appropriate for a case. Revisit the case examples in each chapter. Do you think the diagnoses below are justified or appropriate? Why or why not? How would other approaches (ICD, HiTOP, PDM, or PTMF) conceptualize these cases instead?

CHAPTER	CASE EXAMPLE	DSM-5-TR DIAGNOSIS
4	Luke	Schizophrenia
5	Shirley	Major depression
5	Don	Bipolar disorder
6	Gary Steadman	Obsessive-compulsive disorder
6	Theresa Steadman	Generalized anxiety disorder/social anxiety disorder
6	Tammy Steadman	Separation anxiety disorder
7	Joe	Posttraumatic stress disorder
7	Marigold	Prolonged grief disorder
8	Lauren	Dissociative identity disorder
8	Paul	Somatic symptom disorder
8	Tiiu	Functional neurological symptom (conversion) disorder
8	Isabel	Psychological factors affecting other medical conditions
9	Marta	Anorexia nervosa
9	Zayna	Bulimia nervosa
9	Daemyn	Binge-eating disorder
9	Wendy	Avoidant/restrictive food intake disorder (ARFID)
9	Alastair	Pica
9	Simone	Rumination disorder
10	Elena	Female sexual interest/arousal disorder
10	Ahmed	Erectile disorder
10	Bolin	Premature (early) ejaculation
10	Linnea	Genito-pelvic pain/penetration disorder
10	Lou	Transvestic disorder
10	William	Paraphilic disorder
10	Juana	Gender dysphoria
11	Walter	Alcohol use disorder
11	Ayesha	Opioid use disorder
11	Pedro	Gambling disorder
11	Liam	Gaming disorder
11	Deanna	No diagnosis[1]
12	Harvey	Antisocial personality disorder
12	Megan	Borderline personality disorder
13	Mark	ADHD
13	Sumiko	Oppositional defiant disorder
13	Michael	Conduct disorder
13	Hernando	Autism spectrum disorder

CHAPTER	CASE EXAMPLE	DSM-5-TR DIAGNOSIS
14	Yolanda	Intellectual development disorder
14	Alfred	Specific learning disorder, impairment in reading
14	Greta	Tourette's disorder
14	Bobby	Childhood-onset fluency disorder (stuttering)
14	Sanjay	Major neurocognitive disorder (due to Alzheimer's disease)
15	Cassandra	Insomnia
15	Hubert	Narcolepsy
15	Maribel	Enuresis
15	Arjun	Encopresis
16	Dahlia	Suicidal behavior disorder
16	Hugo	No diagnosis[2]
16	Niki	Schizoaffective disorder
16	Marta	Schizophrenia
16	Norman	Unknown[3]

1 Deanna shows symptoms of what some consider the behavioral addiction of "compulsive shopping," but compulsive shopping is not an official DSM diagnosis.

2 Hugo was arrested for soliciting homosexual sex in a public restroom. This behavior, while illegal, does not qualify him for a DSM diagnosis.

3 Norman is experiencing violent fantasies about harming his neighbor, but there is not enough information provided about him to make a DSM diagnosis.

GLOSSARY

NOTE: Numbers in parentheses refer to the chapter where the term is first introduced or most fully defined; use the index to track additional references to terms.

4P model of case formulation: Model of formulation in which clinicians gather information about four areas: (1) preconditions; (2) precipitating factors; (3) perpetuating factors; and (4) protective factors. (3)

12-step programs: Self-help groups such as Alcoholics Anonymous that see addiction as disease; by following the 12-steps, group members recover from their addictions. (11)

ABCDE model: REBT model of how psychological problems originate and how to fix them; A = <u>a</u>ctivating event; B = <u>b</u>eliefs; C = emotional <u>c</u>onsequences of beliefs; D = <u>d</u>isputing beliefs; and E = more <u>e</u>ffective beliefs that replace those that were disputed. (2)

Aberrant salience hypothesis: Ascribes psychosis to over activity of the *mesolimbic dopamine pathway*; this results in excess dopamine, which leads to over-attributing meaning (i.e., salience) to extraneous and irrelevant events. (4)

Abnormal motor behavior: A symptom of psychosis in which the person seems physically agitated/restless or catatonic (unresponsive to surroundings). (4)

Abnormal psychology: Alternative name for the study of psychopathology and mental distress that is increasingly considered pejorative. (1)

Abuse vs. dependence: Abuse is the ongoing misuse of a substance; dependence is physically or psychologically needing the substance to function, as evidenced by *tolerance* (needing more of the substance for the same effect) and *withdrawal* (unpleasant psychological and physical symptoms when the drug stops being taken). (11)

Acceptance and commitment therapy (ACT): CBT intervention designed to help people stay focused and in touch with the present moment; acceptance of negative emotions encouraged as a method to defuse them. (6)

Access to care: Extent to which people can obtain medical, psychological, and social services and are helped by doing so. (16)

Accommodation: Process by which patients' relatives or significant others collude with them to help them avoid anxiety-provoking situations or repeatedly reassure them that everything is okay; associated with poorer patient outcomes. (6)

Acetylcholine: Neurotransmitter important in muscle movement, arousal, memory, and learning. (11)

Action potential: When an electrical impulse is sent along a neuron's axis; occurs when neurotransmitters bond with receptors on a neuron's dendrites, causing the electrical charge in the neuron to shift from negative to positive; central process in neural communication. (2)

Acupuncture: Ancient Chinese treatment for various health issues in which needles or lasers are used to stimulate designated points on the body. (15)

Acute stress: DSM and ICD term for PTSD-like symptoms that do not last long enough for a PTSD diagnosis; considered a disorder in DSM ("acute stress disorder") but normal and expected in ICD ("acute stress reaction"). (7)

Adaptationist versus dysregulation models: Adaptationist models say depression serves adaptive purposes (e.g., avoiding social risks, minimizing losses, conserving energy, soliciting assistance), whereas dysregulation models say the adaptive mechanism behind normal sadness is broken and runs amok in severe and recurrent depression. (5)

Adapted to flee famine hypothesis: Anorexia evolved to assist those facing famine; anorexic symptoms of feeling energetic and restless while remaining in denial about weight loss encourages migration to new locations in search of food. (9)

Addiction: A non-diagnostic term describing lack of control over doing, taking, or using something despite potentially harmful consequences. (11)

Addictive personality: Hotly debated notion that a specific set of personality traits predisposes people to addiction. (11)

Adjustment disorders: DSM and ICD diagnoses used to identify emotional reactions to ongoing stressors. (7)

Adoption studies: Compare rates of traits or disorders among siblings adopted early in life and reared in separate environments. (4)

Agoraphobia: DSM and ICD disorder diagnosed in people who fear being in situations where they may have an intense and embarrassing fear reaction (such as a panic attack) and won't be able to escape. (6)

Alcohol: A depressant drug in many popular beverages (also called *ethanol* or *ethyl alcohol*). (11)

Alcoholics Anonymous (AA): The largest and most well-known 12-step group for recovering alcoholics. (11)

Alexithymia: Difficulty naming, describing, or expressing emotions verbally. (8)

Ally: Someone who confronts heterosexism to support sexual minority persons. (10)

Alzheimer's disease: Dementia linked to senile plaques and neurofibrillary tangles in the brain; *early-onset Alzheimer's* occurs before age 65 and mostly runs in families, while *late-onset Alzheimer's* occurs after age 65 and is tied to both genes and environment. (14)

Amnesia: Memory gaps; sometimes occurs in dissociation. (7)

Amphetamines: Laboratory-manufactured stimulants; include *amphetamine* (trade name *Benzedrine*), *dextroamphetamine* (trade name *Dexedrine*), and *methamphetamine* (trade name *Methedrine*). (11)

Amyloid hypothesis: Senile plaques are critical to Alzheimer's disease. (14)

Anaclitic depression: Historically used to describe depression in young children, but now refers to attachment-related depression in adults who are clingy, helpless, dependent, and fear abandonment. (5)

Analogue experiment: Uses laboratory scenarios similar (*analogous*) to situations that cannot be practically studied; *animal studies*, which use animals as analogues for humans, are an example. (1)

Androgen: Type of hormone responsible for the development of male characteristics; testosterone is the most well-known androgen. (10)

Anorexia nervosa: DSM and ICD disorder involving seriously low body weight due to restricted food intake. (9)

Anorgasmia: ICD diagnosis for men and women who experience absent, infrequent, or diminished orgasms. (10)

Antagonist drugs for substance abuse: Drugs that prevent relapse by interfering with an addictive substance's effects; *opioid blockers* (*naloxone*, *naltrexone*, and *nalmefene*), *acamprosate, N-acetylcysteine (NAC)*, and *disulfiram* are antagonist drugs. (11)

Antiandrogens: Drugs that reduce levels of male sex hormones such as testosterone, thereby decreasing sexual interest. (10)

Anticonvulsants: Drugs initially developed to treat seizures, but also used for various psychiatric conditions; they enhance GABA activity. (5)

Antidepressants: Drugs used to alleviate depression and many other presenting problems; they work by affecting monoamine neurotransmitters in the brain. (5)

Antipsychiatry: Movement that challenged the medical model of psychiatry, arguing that mental illnesses are better viewed as everyday problems in living. (1)

Antipsychotics: Drugs used to alleviate psychotic symptoms; *first-generation antipsychotics* reduce dopamine transmission, while *second-* and *third-generation antipsychotics* reduce dopamine and serotonin transmission; also called *neuroleptics* and *major tranquilizers*. (4)

Antisocial personality disorder (ASPD): DSM diagnosis for people who consistently manipulate and exploit others with little or no remorse; they consistently lie, deceive, break the law, and disregard social norms. (12)

Anxiety: Emotion characterized by feelings of tension, worried thoughts, and physical changes like increased blood pressure; involves cognitive appraisals related to more basic fear responses. (6)

Anxiolytics: Drugs used to relieve anxiety; usually refers to benzodiazepines. (6)

Applied behavior analysis (ABA): Uses behavioral principles to understand how environmental stimuli have conditioned a given individual's behavior, with the resulting knowledge used to change the environment and condition alternative behaviors. (13)

Asperger's disorder: Disorder removed from DSM and ICD that was characterized by impaired social skills, poor communication skills, and restricted interests that develops in early childhood; milder than autism, without significant deficits in language acquisition or cognitive functioning. (13)

Assertive community treatment (ACT): A way to organize services for those diagnosed with schizophrenia and other severe psychological disorders in which team members from a variety of professions work together to coordinate services for outpatients with schizophrenia and other chronic mental disorder diagnoses. (4)

Assessment: Gathering information to understand or diagnose a person's difficulties. (3)

Attachment-based family therapy: Integrates attachment theory into family therapy to strengthen parent–child attachment relationships in depressed and suicidal adolescents. (5)

Attention-deficit/hyperactivity disorder (ADHD): DSM and ICD neurodevelopmental disorder involving difficulty sustaining attention, being revved-up and full of excessive energy, and impulsive behavior. (13)

Attenuated psychosis syndrome (APS): Proposed DSM diagnosis characterized by odd or eccentric behavior that does not qualify as full-blown psychosis. (4)

Atypical antidepressants: Antidepressants that are chemically unrelated to the four main types of antidepressants (SSRIs, SNRIs, MAOIs, and tricyclics). *Bupropion, trazadone*, and *mirtazapine* are examples. (5)

Autism spectrum disorder (ASD): DSM and ICD neurodevelopmental disorder characterized by deficits in communication, social interaction, and comprehending relationships. (13)

Autistic process: Term used by those who see autism as a way of processing and responding to the world but not a disorder. (13)

Autoimmune disease hypothesis: Proposes a link between autoimmune diseases and neurodevelopmental disorders like ADHD and ASD. (13)

Autonomic nervous system (ANS): Regulates automatic biological functions affected by stress; consists of *sympathetic nervous system* (during times of stress, activates increased breathing and heart rate, pupil dilation, inhibition of appetite, and higher blood pressure) and *parasympathetic nervous systems* (following stress, slows down breathing and heart rates, normalizes pupils, reestablishes hunger, and lowers blood pressure). (7)

Aversion therapies: Behavior therapies in which undesired behaviors are reduced or eliminated by associating them with something unpleasant (e.g., tastes, smells, pain). (9)

Avoidant personality disorder: DSM diagnosis for those who want guaranteed acceptance from others and actively avoid social interactions because they are excessively worried about criticism or rejection. (12)

Avoidant/restrictive food intake disorder (ARFID): DSM and ICD disorder characterized by extremely picky eating and failure to eat enough to meet basic nutritional needs. (9)

Barbiturates: Highly addictive sedative-hypnotic drugs such as *secobarbital* and *pentobarbital*; previously used as anti-anxiety drugs but have generally been replaced by benzodiazepines. (11)

Beck Depression Inventory (BDI): 21-item self-administered inventory for measuring depression. (5)

Behavioral activation: Behavioral technique in which client schedules activities that bring positive reinforcement. (5)

Behavioral addictions: Addictions involving behaviors rather than substances (e.g., excessive gambling, gaming, sex, eating, and shopping). (11)

Behavioral assessment: Identifies conditions in the environment that sustain undesirable behaviors; uses techniques such as behavioral observation, clinical interviews, and self-reports. (3)

Behavioral perspectives: View mental distress as caused by environmental conditioning and social learning, not internal psychopathology. (2)

Behavioral rehearsal: Behavioral technique in which the client role-plays how to act in specific social situations. (4)

Bender Visual Motor Gestalt Test: Neuropsychological test consisting of nine cards with geometrical designs; test-takers are asked to examine the designs and draw them from memory; difficulty doing so is often interpreted as an indicator of brain damage. (3)

Benzodiazepines: Anxiolytic drugs that enhance the functioning of the inhibitory neurotransmitter GABA to reduce anxiety; sometimes also used as mood stabilizers. (6)

Bereavement: The situation of having recently lost a significant person through death. (7)

Bereavement exclusion: DSM-IV criterion for major depressive disorder that discouraged clinicians from diagnosing major depression in people grieving the loss of a loved one; removed starting with DSM-5. (5)

Beta blockers: Blood pressure reducing drugs that block norepinephrine receptors; used to relieve anxiety. (6)

Big Five: The five traits measured by the Five-Factor Model (FFM) of personality: *extraversion*, *agreeableness*, *conscientiousness*, *neuroticism*, and *openness*. (3)

Binge drinking: Drinking four or more drinks (if female) or five or more drinks (if male) in roughly two hours. (11)

Binge eating: Overeating in which a huge amount of food is eaten in a single sitting—much more than most people would eat during a comparable period. (9)

Binge-eating disorder (BED): DSM and ICD disorder characterized by recurrent binge eating. (9)

Bioenergetics exercises: Breathing and other exercises intended to enhance bodily awareness. (8)

Biofeedback: Technique that provides patients feedback on one or more biological functions (e.g., heart rate, breathing rate, muscle tension, or temperature) and reinforces them for desired changes to these functions. (8)

Biological perspectives: Attribute mental distress to illnesses that afflict people. (1)

Biopsychosocial model: Holds that presenting problems arise from an interaction among biological, psychological, and social factors. (4)

Bipolar I disorder: DSM and ICD disorder diagnosed in those who experience one or more manic episodes. (5)

Bipolar II disorder: DSM and ICD disorder diagnosed in those who have experienced hypomanic and depressive episodes but have never had a manic episode. (5)

Bodily distress disorder: ICD disorder characterized by physical symptoms that the person finds distressing and pays excessive attention to; roughly equivalent to the DSM's *somatic symptom disorder*. (8)

Bodily humors: Four biological substances identified by the Ancient Greeks and long considered important in understanding mental distress; the four humors were *black bile*, *yellow bile*, *phlegm*, and *blood*. (1)

Body dysmorphic disorder (BDD): DSM and ICD disorder in which people display obsessional preoccupation with one or more perceived physical flaws in their appearance. (6)

Body-oriented psychotherapies: Incorporate dance, meditation, martial arts, yoga, and awareness through movement techniques into the therapeutic encounter. (8)

Borderline families: Families characterized by interpersonal chaos in which members do not know how to nurture or support one another; three kinds of borderline families: *enmeshed or overinvolved*, *alienated or rejecting*, and *idealizing or denying*. (12)

Borderline personality disorder (BPD): DSM diagnosis describing people who show instability in their relationships, sense of self, and emotions due to fear of abandonment and difficulty regulating emotions about self and others. (12)

Brain chemistry perspectives: Biological approaches to psychopathology that focus on neurotransmitters (chemicals in brain) and how they influence cognition, emotion, and behavior. (2)

Brain structure and function perspectives: Biological approaches that stress how the functioning (or malfunctioning) of different brain regions influences psychopathology. (2)

Bremelanotide: Drug women inject into their thigh forty-five minutes prior to having sex to increase sexual desire; marketed as Vyleesi. (10)

Brief psychotic disorder: DSM disorder in which psychotic symptoms only last a short time (one day to one month); called *acute and transient psychotic disorder (ATPD)* in ICD and can last longer (up to three months). (4)

Bulimia nervosa: DSM and ICD disorder characterized by binge eating followed by compensatory behavior. (9)

Buspirone: An anti-anxiety drug that decreases serotonin levels, but not by blocking serotonin reuptake; thus, it is not classified as an SSRI. (6)

Caffeine: A mild and commonly used stimulant found in many plants, including those used to make coffee, tea, chocolate, and soft drinks; increases alertness and energy while providing a sense of well-being. (11)

Cannabis: Drugs derived from the hemp plant, containing *cannabinoids* like *tetrahydrocannabinol (THC)* and *cannabidiol (CBD)*; cannabis "high" is caused by THC and includes feeling relaxed and content, losing track of time, perceptual distortions, and heightened awareness; cannabis types: *marijuana*, *ganja*, *bhang*, and *hashish*. (11)

Case study: Qualitative design that examines a specific instance of something in depth; its focus can be a person, small group, organization, partnership, community, relationship, decision, or project. (1)

Catastrophic misinterpretation model of panic disorder: People prone to recurrent, unexpected panic attacks catastrophically misinterpret certain bodily sensations; the more they interpret sensations in an anxious way, the stronger the sensations become—eventually resulting in a full-blown panic attack. (6)

Catatonia: Form of abnormal motor behavior that sometimes occurs in psychosis; characterized by decreased responsiveness to one's surroundings as evidenced by reduced movement, holding oneself in a rigid posture, or a *catatonic stupor* (ceasing to respond verbally or physically). (4)

Catecholamine hypothesis of ADHD: ADHD is caused by deficits in dopamine and norepinephrine. (13)

Character armor: Physical postures (how one walks, talks, breathes, and carries oneself) that provide insight into one's psychological functioning; also called *body armor*. (8)

Chemical castration: Use of antiandrogens to bring testosterone levels as low as those found in people who have been surgically castrated. (10)

Child-centered play therapy (CCPT): Combines play and person-centered therapy's core conditions for change (genuineness, empathy, and unconditional positive regard) to address children's developmental issues; also called *person-centered play therapy*. (13)

Childhood-onset fluency disorder (stuttering): DSM and ICD diagnosis in which sounds are repeated or consonants or vowels prolonged; called *developmental speech fluency disorder* in ICD. (14)

Cholinergic hypothesis of Alzheimer's: Enhancing acetylcholine transmission reduces memory problems and staves off the progression of Alzheimer's dementia. (14)

Cirrhosis: Irreversible scarring of the liver, often due to chronic excessive alcohol use. (11)

Cisgender: Term for people whose gender identity and birth sex match; shorthand: "cis." (10)

Civil commitment. When people deemed dangerous to self or others or in serious need of treatment are treated against their will, either in hospital or outpatient settings; also known as *involuntary commitment*; or, in the UK, *sectioning* or *detaining*. (16)

Classical conditioning: An *unconditioned stimulus* (no learning required) is paired with a *neutral stimulus*, which turns the neutral stimulus into a *conditioned stimulus* that evokes the same response as the unconditioned stimulus, even when the unconditioned stimulus isn't present. (2)

Cliff-edge fitness theory: Proposes psychosis occurs when theory of mind ability shifts from exceedingly sensitive to over interpretive. (4)

Clinical interview: Assessment procedure in which clinician talks to client to gather information about the presenting problem; can be *structured* (clinician employs a clearly defined and predetermined set of questions) or *unstructured* (clinician asks client open-ended questions). (3)

Cocaine: Stimulant made South American coca plant leaves that produces euphoria, excessive confidence, and tremendously high energy levels. (11)

Cognitive defusion: Acceptance and commitment therapy (ACT) technique in which clients dispassionately observe their thoughts and recognize that they are just thoughts, not absolutes; this lets them separate from and be less influenced by their thoughts. (9)

Cognitive distortions: Errors in thinking that lead to emotional distress. (2)

Cognitive enhancement therapies: Assume that the progression of Alzheimer's and other forms of dementia can be slowed by boosting patients' cognitive engagement with their surroundings. (14)

Cognitive models of anxiety: Hold that anxiety results from faulty thinking processes; besides Beck's model, other well-known cognitive models include the *avoidance model of worry*, the *intolerance of uncertainty model*, the *metacognitive model*, and the *emotional dysregulation model*. (6)

Cognitive models of OCD: Maintain that everyone periodically has intrusive thoughts, but obsessive patients overestimate the importance of such thoughts—especially during times of stress. (6)

Cognitive perspectives: Emphasize thoughts and beliefs as the root causes of mental distress. (2)

Cognitive processing therapy (CPT): Cognitive therapy for PTSD that combines exposure therapy with a more primary focus on having clients examine and revise their cognitions about the traumatic event. (7)

Cognitive reserve hypothesis: Intelligence and education provide a buffer against Alzheimer's and other forms of dementia. (14)

Cognitive therapy: Aaron Beck's therapy approach, which focuses on correcting the client's dysfunctional thoughts; focuses on four levels of cognition: *automatic thoughts*, *intermediate beliefs*, *core beliefs*, and *schemas*. (2)

Cognitive therapy for PTSD: Therapy for PTSD that works to (1) eliminate *negative appraisals* that produce an ongoing sense of threat, (2) reduce re-experiencing of the trauma by helping people elaborate memories of it and identify triggers, and (3) eliminate dysfunctional cognitive and behavioral strategies used by trauma survivors. (7)

Cognitive triad: Negative beliefs about self, experience, and future that cognitive therapists believe result in depression. (5)

Cognitive-behavioral conjoint therapy (CBCT): Fifteen-session manualized PTSD treatment for couples and families in which cognitive therapy techniques are used to teach conflict management. (7)

Cognitive-behavioral therapy (CBT): Therapy that combines elements of *cognitive therapy* and *behavior therapy*. (2)

Cognitive-behavioral therapy for ARFID (CBT-AR): CBT treatment for ARFID that uses exposure therapy and psychoeducation to reduce aversion to feared foods. (9)

Cognitive-behavioral therapy for insomnia (CBT-I): CBT insomnia treatment that uses cognitive therapy and relaxation training along with *stimulus control*, *sleep restriction*, and *sleep hygiene education*. (15)

Cognitive-behavioral therapy for psychosis (CBTp): Uses cognitive and behavioral therapy techniques (e.g., *Socratic questioning*, *evidential analysis*, *normalization*, and *behavioral experiments*) to challenge the psychotic patient's perceptions and behavior. (4)

Cognitive-behavioral therapy for suicide prevention (CBT-SP): Targets dysfunctional cognitions and conditioned thoughts/behaviors that lead to suicidal behavior. (16)

Coming out: Process by which people accept and publicly declare their sexual orientation or gender identity. (10)

Common criteria of "abnormality": *Statistical deviation, violation of social norms and values, behavior that disturbs others, harmfulness to self or others, emotional suffering, and misperception of reality*; used to make judgments of "abnormality." (1)

Community care: Care that integrates people with chronic mental health issues into the social environment, often by housing them in group homes or other shared living situations; emphasizes continuity of care, encouraging independence, and advocacy that ensures patients receive necessary services and are treated properly. (4)

Comorbidity: When multiple disorders co-occur (i.e., are diagnosed at the same time). (3)

Compensatory behavior: Behavior a person engages in to counteract having binged; includes *purging, fasting*, and *excessive exercise*. (9)

Competence: Ethical principle that clinicians only conduct therapies, assessments, and research when properly trained and competent to do so. (16)

Competence to stand trial: Legal standard used in the United States that says those charged with a crime must be able to (a) comprehend the proceedings, (b) participate in his or her own defense, and (c) consult with legal counsel. (16)

Complex PTSD: ICD diagnosis for PTSD patients who have difficulties managing emotions, negative beliefs about themselves as worthless, and trouble maintaining relationships. (7)

Comprehensive behavioral intervention for tics (CBIT): Combines *habit reversal training (HRT)* with additional behavioral techniques (e.g., relaxation training, functional analysis of behavior) to reduce or eliminate tics. (14)

Compulsions: Behaviors or mental acts that a person feels driven to perform. (6)

Compulsive sexual behavior disorder (CSBD): ICD disorder diagnosed in people who seem unable to control their sexual appetites. (10)

Concordance rates: Percentage of time both twins in a pair develop a trait or disorder. (4)

Conduct disorder (CD): DSM and ICD diagnosis for children and adolescents who engage in serious violations of other people's rights (e.g., physical aggression, destroying property, lying, stealing, and engaging in serious rule violations); called *conduct-dissocial disorder* in ICD. (13)

Confidentiality: The ethical requirement that practicing clinicians not disclose what clients tell them unless their clients grant them permission to do so. (16)

Conflicts of interest: Situations in which a clinician or researcher has a professional, legal, financial, or other interest that might impair objectivity, competence, or effectiveness or that could lead to exploitation or harm. (16)

Confounding variable: Any variable in an experiment that interferes with the independent variable manipulation. (1)

Constructivist perspectives: Emphasize how people create meaningful ways of understanding themselves, their world, and their relationships, which they use to guide their lives; difficulties occur when unhelpful constructions are mistaken for reality itself. (2)

Constructivist therapy for stuttering: Reduces stuttering by helping clients incorporate being fluent into their core constructions of self. (14)

Consumer movement: Movement of consumers of psychiatric services that accepts psychiatric views of mental disorder and often finds traditional treatments helpful; largely directed toward reducing stigma and increasing access to services. (2)

Contingency management (CM): Operant conditioning behavioral technique in which abstinence and other desired behaviors are positively reinforced to strengthen them. (11)

Control group: A group of experimental participants who do not receive the treatment; gives us something with which to compare the treatment group. (1)

Controlled drinking: Treatments that help people reduce their drinking to acceptable levels and moderate alcohol's role in their lives, but without demanding abstinence (e.g., *Moderation Management (MM)*, a controlled drinking support group alternative to AA). (11)

Conversion disorder: See *functional neurological symptom disorder*. (8)

Correlation: When two variables are related; changes in one systematically are associated

with changes in the other; correlations can be *positive* (as one variable increases, so does the other) or *negative* (as one variable increases, the other decreases). (1)

Correlational research: Looks at the relationship between two variables to see whether changes in one are systematically tied to changes in the other. (1)

Cortico-striatal-thalamo-cortical loop (CBGTC) hypothesis: OCD involves dysfunction in the circuitry linking the *orbitofrontal cortex* (important in goal-directed behavior), *anterior cingulate cortex* (implicated in decision-making, anticipating rewards, emotion, and impulse control), *thalamus* (relays sensory information), *striatum* (part of the brain's reward system), and *basal ganglia* (important in voluntary motor movement). (6)

Cortisol: Primary stress hormone of the *endocrine system*; high levels correlated with problems like depression and mania, while low levels may occur in response to posttraumatic stress. (5)

Courtesy stigma: Stigma or disapproval due to being associated with a stigmatized individual; also called *associative stigma*. (13)

Covert sensitization: Aversion therapy in which undesired behavior is eliminated by presenting unpleasant images (*in vivo* or imaginally) while the client imagines engaging in the behavior. (10)

Criminal commitment: Placing people in mental hospitals because of crimes they committed. (16)

Crisis intervention: Techniques (e.g., listening skills, assessing risk) for assisting those in crisis, including suicidal individuals. (16)

Critical incident stress debriefing (CISD): Extended single session post-trauma intervention during which trauma victims are asked to recall the event in vivid detail shortly after it occurs; controversial because some research suggests CISD can be harmful. (7)

Cross-tolerance: When tolerance for one drug transfers to other drugs with similar chemical effects on the brain. (11)

Cultural adaptations: Modifying empirically supported treatments to account for cultural differences. (7)

Culture bias: Occurs when diagnostic, formulation, or assessment approaches reflect

the cultural assumptions of those devising them. (3)

Cyclothymic disorder: DSM and ICD diagnosis for those with hypomanic and depressive symptoms that do not rise to the level of hypomanic and depressive episodes. (5)

Daily Record of Dysfunctional Thoughts (DRDT): A form used by cognitive therapists to help clients track events, their emotional reactions, their automatic thoughts, their behavioral response, and their errors in logic. (5)

Dark therapy: Treatment sometimes combined with light therapy for bipolar disorder; patient kept in the dark for several hours to correct circadian rhythm disruptions suspected of causing mania. (5)

Day care programs: Outpatient programs for people with dementia and other cognitive difficulties that provide interventions to patients and a respite to caregivers. (14)

Death instinct: Unconscious instinct proposed by Freud that drives people to behave in self-destructive ways, including self-harm and suicide; also called *Thanatos*. (16)

Deep brain stimulation (DBS): Treatment in which electrodes are permanently implanted in the brain and then low levels of electrical current are sent to these electrodes using a transmitter the person wears; used to treat Parkinson's disease and Tourette's syndrome, as well as chronic depression that does not respond to antidepressants. (5)

Defense mechanisms: In psychodynamic theories, partly unconscious mental processes used to ward off or reduce anxiety and cope with emotionally upsetting experiences. (2)

Deinstitutionalization: Release of patients from mental hospitals; widespread in the latter twentieth century at mental institutions across North America and Europe. (1)

Delayed ejaculation: DSM and ICD diagnosis for men who show a delay in (or inability to) ejaculate despite being stimulated and wanting to ejaculate more quickly. (10)

Delirium: DSM and ICD diagnosis describing a cognitive disturbance that fluctuates in severity and involves diminished attention to and awareness of one's surroundings. (14)

Delirium tremens (DTs): Syndrome in extreme cases of alcohol withdrawal in which the person becomes delirious, experiences intense body tremors, and has terrifying hallucinations. (11)

Delusional disorder: DSM and ICD disorder characterized by delusional thinking. (4)

Delusions: False beliefs that a person won't give up, despite overwhelming evidence against them; specific types include *bizarre delusions, erotomanic delusions, grandiose delusions, jealous delusions, non-bizarre delusions, persecutory delusions,* and *somatic delusions.* (4)

Dementia: Permanent and usually progressive cognitive decline in functioning because of a specific brain disease or injury; ICD still uses this term as a diagnosis. (14)

Dementia praecox: Early term used to describe what is today called schizophrenia; it means "premature dementia." (4)

Demonological perspective: Views abnormal behavior as due to possession by evil spirits; also called the *supernatural perspective.* (1)

Dependence: ICD diagnosis in which use of a substance takes on a higher priority than it once had; involves things like feeling compelled to take a substance, difficulty controlling use, tolerance, and withdrawal. (11)

Dependent personality disorder: DSM disorder describing those who desperately want to be cared for, lack confidence in their own abilities, and regularly seek advice and reassurance from others. (12)

Dependent variable: Variable that depends on the manipulation of the independent variable; the observed result in an experiment. (1)

Depersonalization: Form of dissociation characterized by disconnecting from self and emotions; the self seems unreal or changed. (7)

Depersonalization/derealization disorder: DSM and ICD dissociative disorder diagnosed in those who experience *depersonalization* (disconnection from self), *derealization* (disconnection from world), or both. (8)

Depressants: Drugs that slow the central nervous system (CNS). (11)

Depressive episode: In DSM and ICD, at least two weeks of intense sadness and depressed mood or loss of interest in daily activities; other symptoms include change in appetite, sleep disturbance, tiredness, indecisiveness, feelings of worthlessness, lethargy or restlessness, and suicidal feelings. (5)

Derealization: Form of dissociation characterized by disconnecting from one's surroundings; the world seems remote, altered, or unreal. (7)

Desmopressin: Synthetic form of the hormone *vasopressin*, prescribed to decrease urine production in the treatment of nighttime bedwetting. (15)

Detoxification: Physical process of weaning addicted individuals from the drugs they are addicted to. (11)

Developmental coordination disorder: DSM disorder diagnosed in children who show motor coordination skills well below what is expected given their age; called *developmental motor coordination disorder* in ICD. (14)

Developmental language disorder with impairment of mainly pragmatic language: ICD-11 disorder characterized by development of communication difficulties early in life; analogous to DSM-5-TR's social (pragmatic) communication disorder (SPCD). (13)

Deviance: Behavior that violates social norms and values. (1)

Diagnosis: In medical terms, a procedure for determining the nature and circumstances of a diseased condition; in psychological and social terms, seeking the cause or nature of a problem or situation. (3)

***Diagnostic and Statistical Manual of Mental Disorders* (DSM)**: Diagnostic manual of the American Psychiatric Association. (3)

Diagnostic code: An alphanumeric key assigned to disorder categories. (3)

Diagnostic criteria: Symptom lists used to make DSM diagnoses; they tend to be strict and discourage clinical judgment. (3)

Diagnostic guidelines: Descriptors used to make ICD diagnoses; written broadly for diagnostic flexibility, they include *essential features* of each diagnosis. (3)

Dialectical behavior therapy (DBT): CBT-influenced therapy developed for borderline personality disorder that combines CBT skill-training with an emphasis on dialectics. (12)

Diaphragmatic breathing: Breathing technique that fully engages the diaphragm; used as a behavioral intervention for rumination disorder. (9)

Diathesis-stress model of psychosomatic illness: Psychosomatic illness emerges from a combination of *diathesis* (a predisposing biological vulnerability) and *stress.* (8)

Difficult process: Non-pathologizing and anti-diagnostic humanistic term for mental distress that attributes it to lack of core conditions in early life relationships, which leads to insecure attachments, impaired emotional growth, and inability to self-actualize. (12)

Discontinuation syndrome: Occurs when antidepressants are discontinued; includes flu-like symptoms, dizziness, insomnia, nausea, diarrhea, irritability, nightmares, and depressive symptoms due to stopping the drug. (5)

Discrete trial training (DTT): Applied behavior analysis (ABA) technique for working with developmental issues that teaches concrete skills in a step-by-step manner using reinforcement and other behavioral techniques. (13)

Disinhibited social engagement disorder: DSM and ICD diagnosis given to children who have experienced severe environmental neglect and show a lack of reticence and/or overly familiar behavior around adult strangers. (7)

Disorganized thinking: Thinking pattern in psychosis characterized by disturbances in the form of thought; loose associations (leaping from topic to topic during conversation) and tangential responding (responding to something other than what was asked) are common, as is incoherent or disrupted language use (e.g., *word salad*); also called *formal thought disorder.* (4)

Disruptive mood dysregulation disorder (DMDD): DSM disorder diagnosed in children and adolescents who show depressive symptoms combined with temper outbursts. (5)

Dissociation: Detaching from or compartmentalizing experience; involves experiences such as *amnesia, depersonalization, derealization, identity confusion,* and *identity alteration.* (7)

Dissociative amnesia: DSM and ICD dissociative disorder that involves difficulty recalling important autobiographical information; diagnosed as *dissociative amnesia with dissociative fugue* if there is intentional travel or confused wandering from home. (8)

Dissociative identity disorder (DID): DSM and ICD dissociative disorder describing people who have two or more distinct "personalities" (or *alters*"); ICD-11 includes *partial dissociative identity disorder* for cases where the non-dominant personalities are intrusive but don't seize executive control. (8)

Dissociative neurological symptom disorder: ICD disorder in which there is lost or altered sensory, motor, or cognitive functioning inconsistent with any known disease or health condition; DSM equivalent is *functional neurological symptom disorder*. (8)

Dopamine: An inhibitory neurotransmitter implicated in memory, motivation, and reward/pleasure; too much is associated with psychosis. (2)

Dopamine hypotheses of addiction: Theorize that addictive drugs and behaviors increase dopamine; examples: *reward deficiency syndrome theory (RDS)* (which says people take drugs to compensate for too little dopamine) and *incentive-sensitization theory* (which says drugs hijack the brain by increasing dopamine sensitivity). (11)

Dopamine hypothesis of ADHD: ADHD is caused by impaired dopamine transmission. (13)

Dopamine hypothesis of schizophrenia: Hypothesis that schizophrenia results from too much of the brain neurotransmitter dopamine. (4)

Dopamine hypothesis of stuttering: Stuttering is related to excessive dopamine transmission in the basal ganglia. (14)

Dopamine hypothesis of Tourette's disorder: Too much dopamine activity in the basal ganglia plays a role in Tourette's disorder. (14)

Double bind: Occurs when someone is placed in a situation where there are two contradictory demands, neither of which can be satisfied or avoided; children in families where double binds are the norm have been hypothesized to be at greater risk for schizophrenia. (4)

Double-blind studies: Experiments in which neither the participants nor the researchers testing them know which treatment group participants belong to. (1)

Double dissociation: Term to explain how African Americans (and other marginalized groups) often experience themselves in two distinct but incompatible ways (positively and through the prejudiced views of the dominant culture). (8)

Down syndrome: Caused by an extra copy of the chromosome trisomy 21 and characterized by intellectual disability, stocky body, short stature, flat face and nose, small head, small ears, small mouth, and poor muscle tone. (14)

Drug flashbacks: The unexpected re-experiencing perceptual disturbances of past drug trips (sometimes called *hallucinogen persisting perception disorder*). (11)

Drug replacement therapies: Changes the delivery method of a drug or exchanges one drug for a chemically similar one, with the goal of weaning people off drugs or sustaining them on similar but less dangerous drugs. (11)

Dry-bed training: Behavior therapy for enuresis in which children are awakened during the night and praised or punished depending on whether they have wet the bed. (15)

DSM: See *Diagnostic and Statistical Manual of Mental Disorders* (DSM).

DSM-5-TR alternative model for personality disorders (AMPD): Proposed alternative to the DSM-5 categorical model of personality disorders that combines dimensional and categorical assessment in diagnosing personality disorders; also called the *hybrid trait model*. (12)

Durham test: Legal test of insanity that says defendants can be acquitted when their illegal behavior was caused by a mental disorder. (16)

Durkheim's sociological model of suicide: Focuses on social and cultural factors in suicide and proposes different types: *egoistic suicide* (social alienation and rejection), *altruistic suicide* (sacrificing self for greater good), *anomic suicide* (let down by society), and *fatalistic suicide* (overwhelmed by social rules/demands). (16)

Duty to protect: Legal and/or ethical duty of therapists to break confidentiality when necessary to protect their clients or other people threatened by their clients. (16)

Dyscalculia: Learning disorder that involves impairment with mathematics; difficulty processing and calculating numbers. (14)

Dyslexia: Learning disorder that involves difficulty decoding information when reading; characterized by trouble recognizing, deciphering, or spelling words. (14)

Dysthymic disorder: ICD disorder for ongoing depression lasting two years or more that is milder than a depressive episode; related to but different in important respects from DSM's *persistent depressive disorder*. (5)

E-mental health: Mental health services provided at a distance via telecommunication and information technologies. (16)

Early and intensive behavioral intervention (EIBI): Version of discrete trial training (DTT) used with patients under age 5. (13)

Early overgrowth hypothesis of autism: Autism spectrum disorder is linked to larger brain growth and volume in early child development but normal growth and volume later. (13)

Eating problems: Characterized by disturbed body image; involve concerns about being overweight or experiencing one's body negatively or in ways that appear distorted. (9)

Eclecticism: An approach to practice in which clinicians draw from multiple theories depending on what is useful in the moment. (16)

Ego: Partly conscious/partly unconscious psychoanalytic personality structure that tries to satisfy id impulses while considering superego demands and constraints in the external environment; motivated by the *reality principle* (what is practical and possible). (2)

Electroconvulsive therapy (ECT): Treatment in which electrical volts are delivered to the brain to produce a seizure; used mainly for treatment-resistant depression, but sometimes also used for bipolar disorder and psychosis. (5)

Emotion-focused therapy (EFT): Brief humanistic psychotherapy that combines person-centered, Gestalt, and constructivist ideas. (5)

Emotionally focused couples therapy (EFCT): Combines humanistic, narrative, attachment, interpersonal, and family systems elements into a therapy for trauma survivors and their partners. (7)

Emotional processing theory: Cognitive theory that attributes trauma, fear, and anxiety responses to dysfunctional *fear structures*; contends that for exposure therapy to be most effective, fear structures must be activated during exposure. (7)

Empirically supported treatments (ESTs): Treatments that have been found effective for specific presenting problems in randomized controlled trials. (1)

Encopresis: DSM and ICD diagnosis given to children who repeatedly have bowel movements in inappropriate places, such as in their pants or on the floor. (15)

Enhanced cognitive behavioral therapy (CBT-E): Attributes a "core psychopathology" to all eating disorders, in which self-worth is based not on achievements but on the ability to control body weight and shape; also called the *transdiagnostic model*. (9)

Enuresis: DSM and ICD diagnosis given to children who wet their beds or clothes; also known as *bedwetting*. (15)

Enuresis alarm: Battery-operated alarm used for enuresis that sounds when urine is detected during the night, conditioning the child to go to the toilet; also called the *bell and pad method*. (15)

Environmental toxin hypotheses: Attribute developmental difficulties in children to pollution and other environmental toxins. (13)

Epidemiological research: Form of correlational research used to study the prevalence and incidence of disorders. (1)

Erectile disorder: DSM disorder diagnosed in men who repeatedly have trouble obtaining or maintaining erections during sexual activity; called *male erectile dysfunction* in ICD. (10)

Estrogen: Primary female sex hormone. (10)

Eugenics movement: Twentieth-century movement that believed intelligence and other traits were inherited and encouraged breeding between those with "desirable" traits while preventing it among those with "undesirable" traits. (14)

Evolutionary perspectives: Use Darwin's evolutionary theory to understand how presenting problems evolved, seeing them as both genetically inherited and adaptive in early human history. (2)

Excessive sugar-intake hypothesis: ADHD symptoms are caused or made worse by too much intake of refined sugars. (13)

Excitatory-inhibitory (E/I) imbalance model of autism: Attributes autism to increased ratios of GABA-glutamate neuronally activity. (13)

Excoriation (skin-picking disorder): DSM and ICD disorder that involves compulsive picking of the skin. (6)

Exhibitionistic disorder: DSM and ICD paraphilic disorder involving sexual fantasies, urges, or behaviors related to exposing one's genitals to unsuspecting people; must cause the individual distress if not acted upon. (10)

Existential anxiety: Normal and expected anxiety that motivates people to construct meaningful lives for themselves; emerges from the four basic existential givens: death, freedom, isolation, and meaninglessness. (6)

Existential psychotherapies: Focus on people living authentically by creating their own meanings and accepting responsibility for these meanings and their life choices. (2)

Experiential sex therapy: Humanistic approach that views sexual problems as personally meaningful; fosters personal growth that transforms and improves clients' lives, indirectly leading to the resolution of sexual issues. (10)

Experiments: Research studies in which controlled variables are manipulated to identify causal relationships among variables. (1)

Exposure plus response prevention: Exposure technique in which client is thrust into contact with the conditioned stimulus and prevented from leaving the situation; client learns nothing bad happens when in contact with the stimulus; also called *flooding and response prevention*. (6)

Exposure therapies: Behavior therapy techniques in which the client is placed in the presence of the conditioned stimulus to extinguish the old response and condition a new one. (2)

Expressed emotion: Degree to which family members respond to a patient in a hostile, critical, or emotionally overinvolved way; associated with poorer patient outcomes. (4)

Extended commitment: Civilly committing people for longer periods; *dangerousness*, *grave disability*, and *need for treatment* are the criteria used to make extended commitment decisions. (16)

External validity: The extent to which experimental results can be generalized to everyday life. (1)

Externalizing the problem: Narrative therapy technique in which clients are asked to talk about their problems as something separate from them that sometimes gets the best of them (as opposed to disorders they "have"). (2)

Externalizing versus internalizing behaviors: *Externalizing behaviors* involve acting out in response to mental distress (e.g., poor impulse-control, rule breaking, physical or verbal aggression); *internalizing behaviors* do not involve acting out, so are harder to spot (e.g., social withdrawal, loneliness, depression, anxiety, difficulty concentrating). (13)

Extinction: When a conditioned stimulus is no longer paired with an unconditioned stimulus, the conditioned stimulus stops eliciting a conditioned response. (2)

Extrapyramidal side effects: Side effects of antipsychotic drugs that include muscle tremors, a shuffling gait, and drooling. (4)

Extreme male brain (EMB) theory: Posits that people with autism are better at systemizing (a trait more evolved in males) than empathizing (a trait more evolved in females). (13)

Eye movement desensitization and reprocessing (EMDR): Therapy technique in which people imagine anxiety-provoking or traumatic events while engaging in bilateral stimulation. (7)

Factitious disorder: DSM and ICD diagnosis for people who physically tamper with themselves or otherwise exaggerate or simulate symptoms to produce signs of illness and convince others they are sick, with the goal being to get medical attention; can also be done to others; also called *Munchausen's syndrome* (self-tampering) or *Munchausen's syndrome by proxy* (tampering with others). (8)

Family-based treatment (FBT): Manualized therapy for anorexia and bulimia that focuses on weight restoration and/or the establishment of healthy eating while not blaming parents; the family is encouraged to work together to help address the family member's eating disorder; also called the *Maudsley approach*. (9)

Family-focused grief therapy: Ten-session therapy that teaches families to communicate and share emotions more effectively to help with the mourning process. (7)

Family-focused therapy (FFT): Family therapy approach emphasizing psychoeducation, improving communication skills, and problem-solving. (5)

Family meal: Technique originated in structural family therapy—and used also in family-based treatment (FBT)—in which the therapist observes a family meal to directly observe dysfunctional family patterns. (9)

Family studies: Study how often the relatives of those with a trait or disorder also develop it. (4)

Fear: Basic emotional response to something specific that is perceived as dangerous with distinct physiological symptoms that are universal, automatic, and brief. (6)

Feeding problems: Characterized by concern over food preferences; involve fussy or faddish eating habits in which certain foods are avoided or refused because of taste, texture, or a basic dislike for them. (9)

Female orgasmic disorder: DSM diagnosis for women who rarely or never experience orgasms. (10)

Female sexual arousal dysfunction: ICD diagnosis for women who show little or no arousal from sexual activity. (10)

Female sexual interest/arousal disorder: DSM diagnosis for women who show little or no interest in or arousal from sexual activity. (10)

Feminist therapy: Holds that patriarchy (the structuring of society so that men are in charge) is the root cause of many problems labeled as mental disorders; sees therapy as a collaborative relationship between therapist and client, one in which both work for social reform. (2)

Fetal alcohol syndrome (FAS): Syndrome in children of mothers who drink excessively during pregnancy; characterized by retarded growth, developmental delays, and atypical facial features (small heads [*microencephaly*], small eyes [*microphthalmia*], thin upper lips with no ventromedial indentation in the middle, and flat upper jaw bones). (11)

Fetishistic disorder: DSM paraphilic disorder involving distress over sexual fantasies, urges, or behaviors related to non-living objects or non-genital body parts. (10)

Fight or flight response: Controlled by the sympathetic nervous system; process by which organism decides whether to flee from danger, engage it, or freeze. (7)

Five-factor model (FFM): Proposes that personality can be mapped along five trait dimensions: *extraversion*, *agreeableness*, *conscientiousness*, *neuroticism*, and *openness*. (12)

Five-stage theory of grief: Kübler-Ross's theory of grief in which a mourner progresses through discrete stages of *denial*, *anger*, *bargaining*, *depression*, and *acceptance*. (7)

Flibanserin: Drug that aims to increase female sexual desire by reducing serotonin and increasing norepinephrine; marketed as Addyi. (10)

Food additives hypothesis: Food additives lead to ADHD; the *Feingold Diet* eliminates food additives to reduce ADHD symptoms. (13)

Formulation: A hypothesis about a person's difficulties, which draws from psychological theory. (3)

Four P model of case formulation: See *4P model of case formulation*.

Fragile process: In humanistic theory, a type of *difficult process* found in those often diagnosed as "narcissistic" or "borderline," characterized by poor emotional regulation, difficulty taking other people's perspectives, and feeling invalidated. (12)

Fragile X syndrome: Mutation on the X chromosome that leads to intellectual disability and physical signs like thin face, long ears, large head, prominent forehead, flat feet, and extremely flexible joints; more common in boys than girls. (14)

Frequency-dependent selection hypothesis: Says traits like psychopathy are evolutionarily adaptive so long as their frequency in the population is low. (12)

Frontal lobe: Brain region important in executing behavior. (5)

Frotteuristic disorder: DSM paraphilic disorder involving sexual fantasies, urges, or behaviors related to touching or rubbing against a nonconsenting person; must cause the individual distress if not acted upon. (10)

Functional neurological symptom disorder: DSM diagnosis that involves physical loss or alteration for which there is no known neurological or medical explanation; also called *conversion disorder* or, in ICD, *dissociative neurological symptom disorder*. (8)

Functional relaxation: Body-oriented relaxation technique to increase body awareness. (8)

Gambling disorder: DSM and ICD behavioral addiction characterized by recurrent problem gambling that leads to impairment and distress. (11)

Gaming disorder: ICD behavioral addiction for those who compulsively play digital or video games. (11)

Gamma-aminobutyric acid (GABA): The brain's primary inhibitory neurotransmitter. (2)

Gatekeeping: Approval process conducted by medical and mental health professionals to keep people with gender dysphoria/incongruence who are deemed psychologically unfit from making irreversible gender-altering decisions. (10)

Gender: Attitudes, feelings, and behaviors a culture associates with a person's biological sex. (10)

Gender affirmative hormone therapy (GAHT): Administration of sex hormones (androgens, estrogens, and antiandrogens) to align secondary sex characteristics with gender identity. (10)

Gender dysphoria: DSM diagnosis for children, adolescents, and adults who display incongruence between their assigned and experienced/expressed gender; see also *gender incongruence* (ICD). (10)

Gender identity: One's persistent sense of belonging to a male, female, or non-binary gender category. (10)

Gender incongruence: ICD diagnosis for children, adolescents, and adults who display incongruence between their assigned and experienced/expressed gender; see also *gender dysphoria* (DSM). (10)

Gender-affirming surgeries: Surgeries that alter the physical body to match gender identity. (10)

General adaptation syndrome (GAS): Defines stress in terms of three stages: alarm, resistance, and exhaustion. (7)

Generalized anxiety disorder (GAD): DSM and ICD diagnosis characterized by excessive and consistent worry that is global rather than specific. (6)

Genetic association studies: Aim to identify genetic markers (DNA sequences on chromosomes) associated with the disorder or trait being studied; *candidate gene studies* focus on specific genes while *genome-wide association studies (GWAS)* analyze the entire genome. (4)

Genetic perspectives: Focus on the role of genes in explaining the origins of presenting problems. (2)

Genito-pelvic pain/penetration disorder: DSM diagnosis for women who experience difficulties with vaginal penetration (often due to tightening of pelvic floor muscles), pain during penetration, or fear of painful penetration. (10)

Geophagia: Form of pica in which a person intentionally eats dirt, soil, or clay. (9)

Germ theories: Hypothesize that psychological disorders can be caused by viruses, bacteria, fungi, or parasites that attack the immune system. (2)

Glutamate: The brain's main excitatory neurotransmitter. (2)

Glutamate hypothesis of depression: Proposes that depression is associated with high levels of glutamate, the brain's main excitatory neurotransmitter. (5)

Glutamate hypothesis of OCD: Contends that obsessive-compulsive disorder (OCD) results from excess glutamate. (6)

Glutamate hypothesis of schizophrenia: Hypothesizes that deficient glutamate transmission is behind many symptoms of schizophrenia. (4)

Gluten/casein-free diet hypothesis: A diet low in *gluten* (proteins in wheat) and *casein* (a protein in milk) can reduce autism symptoms. (13)

Good lives model (GLM): Humanistic program for offenders emphasizing personal growth and fulfillment; identifies *primary goods* (intrinsically beneficial goals such as independence, excelling at work, and fostering intimate relationships) that guide rehabilitation. (10)

Grief: Primary emotional response to bereavement, consisting of emotional and physical reactions. (7)

Grounded theory methods: Qualitative methods that attempt to help researchers develop *grounded theories*—conceptual theoretical models of the topics they study; data collected via participant observation, interviewing, and reviewing documents/archives, and then qualitatively coded. (1)

Group homes: Typically house a small number of adult residents with special needs, providing them with medical care and live-in aids who assist with their daily routines. (14)

Group selection theory of OCD: OCD behaviors developed via group selection; having some group members partake in time-consuming behaviors (e.g., checking, cleaning, and hoarding) benefits the entire group without everyone needing to expend energy on them. (6)

Guilty but mentally ill (GBMI): Alternative to the insanity defense in which offenders, after being convicted, concurrently receive treatment along with a prison sentence. (16)

Gut–brain axis: System of biochemical connections between the *gut* (or *gastrointestinal tract*) and brain; imbalances in gut bacteria (*gut microbiome*) are suspected of playing roles in anxiety, OCD, depression, autism, psychosis, and other presenting problems. (6)

Habit reversal training (HRT): Behavior therapy technique to reduce or eliminate undesired repetitive behaviors; patients are taught to recognize sensory experiences that precede the behavior and then engage in an incompatible behavioral response. (14)

Habituation: Behavioral term for when responsiveness to a stimulus decreases after repeated exposure to it. (10)

Hair-pulling disorder: See *Trichtotillomania*.

Hallucinations: Sensory experiences in the absence of sensory stimulation; can be auditory (hearing things), visual (seeing things), olfactory (smelling things), gustatory (tasting things), or tactile (feeling things touching you). (4)

Hallucinogens: Drugs that induce hallucinations, altered thinking and perceptions, out-of-body experiences, and sometimes paranoia; also known as *psychedelics*. (11)

Halstead-Reitan Neuropsychological Test Battery (HRB): Neuropsychological battery that assesses visual, auditory, and tactile functioning; verbal communication; spatial and sequential perception; ability to analyze information; motor ability; and attention, concentration, and memory. (3)

Harm reduction: Intervention strategies for reducing individual and societal harm caused by drug and alcohol use; examples include needle exchange programs, adding thiamine to beer, and providing late-night public transportation. (11)

Harmful dysfunction model of addiction: Addiction results when substances or stimuli coopt the brain's reward system, which cannot respond effectively because it has not evolved the ability to cope with them. (11)

Harmful internal dysfunction: Definition of mental disorder that has two components: (a) a mental mechanism that fails to operate according to its naturally designed function (i.e., an internal dysfunction), and (b) behavior that society deems harmful which is caused by the internal dysfunction. (1)

Harmful use: ICD diagnosis that involves ongoing misuse of a substance leading to physical or mental health problems, adverse social consequences, and criticism from others; also called *substance abuse*. (11)

Harmfulness to self or others: Criterion that identifies those whose behavior is harmful to self or others as abnormal. Judgments often differ about how much harm is acceptable and what counts as a harmful behavior. (1)

Herbal remedies for depression: Herbs used to treat depression that are not approved by mainstream medicine; most notably *St. John's wort* and *Rhodiola rosea*. (5)

Heritability: Percentage of phenotypic variation attributed to genes, as opposed to environment; *heritability estimates* (scores from 0.0 to 1.0) estimate the degree to which a trait is genetic (e.g., .60 attributes 60 percent of phenotypic variation to genes and 40 percent to environment). (2)

Heroin: A highly addictive semisynthetic opioid to which dependence develops quickly; tolerance and withdrawal are especially severe. (11)

Heterosexism: Prejudice against any form of non-heterosexuality. (10)

Hierarchical Taxonomy of Psychopathology (HiTOP): Offers a dimensional (rather than categorical) approach to diagnosing mental disorders. (3)

Histrionic personality disorder: DSM diagnosis for excessively dramatic and emotional individuals who crave being the center of attention and strike others as shallow and overly theatrical, shifting from one exaggerated emotional display to another. (12)

Hoarding disorder: DSM and ICD diagnosis for people who have a hard time giving up possessions, even when they have too many or the possessions are no longer useful or valuable. (6)

Hopelessness theory: Predicts that people who make stable, global, and internal attributions will experience depression. (5)

Hormone replacement therapy (HRT): Therapy in which postmenopausal women are given female sex hormones to replace depleted hormone levels. (10)

Hormones: Chemical messengers of the endocrine systems. (5)

Humanistic perspectives: See people as proactive meaning-makers who strive to develop their full potential; include humanistic, existential, and constructivist perspectives. (2)

Hyperarousal theory of insomnia: Some people are genetically predisposed to arousal and easily become conditioned to associate hyperarousal with sleep-related stimuli, making it difficult for them to fall or stay sleep. (15)

Hyperassociativity: Cognitive tendency in dissociation in which upsetting memories readily activate other tangentially related (and often emotionally out-of-sync) memories. (8)

Hypersexual disorder: Proposed DSM disorder involving preoccupation with and excessive engagement in sexual activities. (10)

Hypersomnolence disorders: Sleep problems involving feeling perpetually tired and sometimes falling asleep despite getting sufficient sleep. (15)

Hypnosis: Combines deep relaxation (a *trance* state) with suggestion (requests that hypnotic subjects can follow if they wish to). (8)

Hypoactive sexual desire dysfunction: ICD diagnosis for men and women who have absent or reduced sexual thoughts, fantasies, or desires. (10)

Hypochondriasis: ICD diagnosis describing excessive worry about being physically ill, traditionally with the assumption that there is little or no basis for such concern; *illness anxiety disorder* is its closest DSM equivalent. (8)

Hypomanic episode: In DSM and ICD, a shorter and milder version of a manic episode, lasting just a few days. (5)

Hypothalamic-pituitary-adrenal (HPA) axis: Interconnected brain structures that play a role in managing stress and releasing cortisol (the primary stress hormone). (5)

Hypothesis: A prediction we make about how variables will affect one another. (1)

Hysteria: A malady involving numerous psychological and physical symptoms that the ancient Greeks diagnosed exclusively in women. (1)

Iatrogenic condition: A condition or disorder induced when mental health professionals subtly (and usually inadvertently) encourage their patients that they have it. (8)

ICD-11 model of personality disorders: Dimensional approach to personality disorders that employs one diagnostic category (*personality disorder*), assessed using five trait domains (*negative affect, detachment, dissocial features, disinhibition,* and *anankastic features*) and distinguished by severity (*mild, moderate,* or *severe*). (12)

Id: Unconscious psychoanalytic personality structure consisting of the infant's aggressive, selfish, and sexual desires; motivated by the *pleasure principle* (desire for immediate pleasure/gratification). (2)

Identity alteration: Form of dissociation that sometimes accompanies identity confusion, in which a person establishes a new identity in lieu of the old one. (8)

Identity confusion: Form of dissociation in which there is confusion about or difficulty recalling one's identity. (8)

Illness anxiety disorder: DSM somatic symptom diagnosis for people who worry about having one or more physical illnesses; differs from ICD's *hypochondriasis* by not requiring that those diagnosed aren't sick. (8)

Imaginal exposure: Exposure technique in which client is asked to imagine the feared scenario to condition a new, non-anxious response to it. (6)

Immune system perspectives: Emphasize the importance of the immune system (cells and biological processes to fight off pathogens) in understanding psychopathology. (2)

***In vivo* exposure**: Exposure technique in which client is exposed to the actual anxiety-provoking object or situation to condition a new, non-anxious response to it. (6)

***In vivo* food exposure**: Behavioral technique in which *in vivo* exposure is used to change the eating habits of people diagnosed with eating disorders. (9)

Incidence: The number of new cases of a mental disorder that are diagnosed within a specified period. (1)

Independent variable: Variable the researcher controls; its manipulation should cause the result in the dependent variable. (1)

Indoleamine hallucinogens: Drugs such as *LSD, DMT,* and *psilocybin* that induce hallucinations and heighten emotional sensitivity by activating serotonin receptors in the prefrontal cortex and anterior cingulate cortex. (11)

Inflammatory hypothesis: Postulates that many psychiatric disorders (psychosis, anxiety, mood problems, etc.) are tied to immune system inflammation. (4)

Informed consent: The process of providing prospective research participants sufficient information about a study, including why it is being conducted and the risks and benefits of participating. (16)

Insanity: Legal term for a mental illness so severe that it prevents distinguishing

fantasy from reality, conducting daily affairs due to psychosis, or exerting control over behavior. (16)

Insanity defense: A legal plea that challenges criminal responsibility by arguing that a defendant is not responsible for crimes committed as the result of a mental disorder. (16)

Insanity Defense Reform Act (IDRA): U.S. law that implemented strict federal standards in insanity defense cases, limiting it to cases where the mental defect or disorder was "severe." (16)

Insomnia disorders: Sleep problems involving difficulty falling or staying asleep. (15)

Integrative evidence-based case formulation: Four-step model of formulation in which the steps are: (1) create a problem list; (2) make a diagnosis; (3) develop an explanatory hypothesis; and (4) plan treatment. (3)

Intellectual development disorder (IDD): DSM and ICD diagnosis involving deficits in intellectual and adaptive functioning that emerge early in development; also called *intellectual disability*. (14)

Intelligence quotient (IQ): Mental age (a score reflecting level of performance on an intelligence test) divided by chronological age (how old one is) multiplied by 100. (3)

Intelligence tests: Assessment measures used to evaluate intelligence. (3)

Intensive short-term dynamic psychotherapy (ISTDP): Short-term psychodynamic therapy that helps patients identify anxiety and defenses that interfere with the experience of hidden emotions; used for depression and other presenting problems. (5)

Intermittent explosive disorder: DSM and ICD diagnosis characterized by recurrent aggressive outbursts that are verbal, physical, or both. (13)

Internal family systems therapy (IFS): Offers a systemic conceptualization of internal psychological functioning; sees human personality as a series of "parts" that relate to one another. (8)

Internal validity: The degree to which experimental results are caused by the manipulation of the independent variable. (1)

***International Classification of Diseases* (ICD)**: Diagnostic manual of the World Health Organization. (3)

Interpersonal and social rhythm therapy (IPSRT): Short-term therapy for bipolar symptoms that uses interpersonal therapy (IPT) techniques to help clients regulate sleep habits and overcome suspected circadian rhythm disruptions. (5)

Interpersonal PTSD groups/PTSD process groups: Emphasize helping group members gain awareness of their feelings and patterns of relating to others; the group setting provides an excellent forum for members to give one another interpersonal feedback. (7)

Interpersonal therapy (IPT): Short-term therapy that focuses on improving relationships to alleviate depression and other presenting problems. (5)

Intracavernous injection therapy (ICI): Injection of drugs into the penis to increase blood flow and remedy erectile problems. (10)

Involuntary outpatient commitment (IOC): Legally mandated treatment in a community setting; also called *outpatient civil commitment*, *compulsory community treatment*, *assisted outpatient treatment*, or *community treatment orders*. (16)

IQ-achievement discrepancy model: Uses discrepancies between IQ scores and achievement scores to diagnose learning disorders. (14)

Irresistible impulse test: Legal test of insanity that says defendants can be acquitted when their crimes are attributable to impulses that they could not resist. (16)

Ketamine: Anesthetic drug that inhibits glutamate and has antidepressant and antianxiety effects; ketamine and a derivative of it, *esketamine*, are used to treat depression. (5)

Kleptomania: DSM and ICD impulse control disorder that involves impulsive stealing that provides pleasure, gratification, or emotional relief but is not done for personal gain. (13)

Korsakoff syndrome: Syndrome characterized by serious deterioration in short- and long-term memory, as well as inability to recall new information; caused by a *thiamine* (Vitamin B-1) deficiency, usually from chronic excessive alcohol use. (11)

Language disorder: DSM and ICD diagnosis made in children who have trouble acquiring and using language; called *developmental language disorder* in ICD. (14)

Learned helplessness: Conditioned response in which an organism learns its behavior has no effect on its environment so it stops engaging in behavior and endures unpleasant situations—even when they can be avoided. (5)

Levels of personality organization: Component of the P-Axis in PMD-2 diagnosis; patients are rated on a 10-point scale assessing their level of personality functioning, with "10" being most healthy and "1" being least healthy: *healthy level* (9–10), *neurotic level* (6–8), *borderline level* (3–5), and *psychotic level* (1–2). (12).

Lidcombe Program: Behavioral program for children whose stuttering starts before age 5; parents work with their children to reinforce fluency and acknowledge/correct stuttering. (14)

Life instinct: Unconscious instinct proposed by Freud that drives people to survive and seek pleasure; also called *Eros*. (16)

Light therapy: Therapy for seasonal affective disorder in which patient sits next to a box that projects bright light. (5)

Lithium: Metallic mineral salt used as a mood stabilizer. (5)

Lobotomy: Historical form of *psychosurgery* used mainly for schizophrenia in which the prefrontal cortex was surgically disconnected from the rest of the brain; also called a *leucotomy*. (1)

Logotherapy: Existential treatment method developed by Victor Frankl that emphasizes helping clients find meaning in life. (6)

Long-term care: Ongoing care in a hospital, nursing home, or assisted-living facility. (14)

Luria-Nebraska Neuropsychological Battery (LNNB): Neuropsychological inventory consisting of clinical scales assessing areas such as reading, writing, math, memory, language, and motor function. (3)

Lymphocytes: White blood cells important in fighting off illness; *natural killer (NK) cells*, *B cells*, and *T cells* are lymphocytes. (8)

M'Naghten test: Legal test of insanity that says defendants can be acquitted if, at the time their crimes, they were suffering from a disease of the mind that prevented them from understanding the nature of their acts or that these acts were wrong. (16)

Magnetic resonance imaging (MRI): Neuroimaging technique that creates an x-ray-like picture of the brain using the magnetic activity of hydrogen atoms; one kind, the fMRI (functional MRI), tracks oxygen levels in the brain's hemoglobin, allowing assessment of blood flow in various brain areas while the person is thinking, feeling, or completing a task. (3)

Major depressive disorder (MDD): DSM disorder diagnosed in those who experience one or more major depressive episodes; divided into *single episode depressive disorder* and *recurrent depressive disorder* in ICD. (5)

Major neurocognitive disorder: DSM term for severe dementia, characterized by significant cognitive decline; called *dementia* in ICD. (14)

Male hypoactive sexual desire disorder: DSM diagnosis for men who show minimal interest in sex. (10)

Malleus Maleficarum: Popular book during the Middle Ages that examined witchcraft and demonic possession; reflected a demonological perspective. (1)

Mania without delusion: Philippe Pinel's term for patients who showed no overt symptoms of madness (they weren't hallucinatory, delusional, or incoherent), but who were prone to emotional outbursts such as fits of temper or impulsive violence; *manie sans délire* in the original French. (12)

Manic episode: In DSM and ICD, one week or more of persistently elevated mood accompanied by high energy and intense goal-directed activity; often involves inflated self-esteem, grandiosity, decreased need for sleep, extreme talkativeness, racing thoughts, distractibility, and impulsive/risky behavior. (5)

MAO inhibitors (MAOIs): Antidepressants that work by inhibiting monoamine oxidase (MAO), a brain enzyme that breaks down excess monoamine neurotransmitters; this leaves more monoamine neurotransmitters available. (5)

Masturbatory satiation: Behavioral technique in which clients masturbate to paraphilic imagery for much longer than is pleasurable to associate the paraphilia with boredom. (10)

Medical model: Views psychiatric problems as categorical syndromes reflecting underlying biological illnesses that must be accurately diagnosed before they can be effectively treated. (1)

Medicalization: Inappropriately classifying non-medical problems as medical. (1)

Mental disorder: Defined by the American Psychiatric Association as a syndrome characterized by clinically significant disturbance in a person's cognition, emotional regulation, or behavior reflecting a dysfunction in psychological, biological, or developmental processes. (1)

Mental distress: Cognitive and/or emotional upset, sometimes accompanied by physical symptoms; considered expected/normal in some cases and a sign of psychopathology in others. (1)

Mental illness: Defined by the American Psychiatric Association as an illness affecting or located in a person's brain that affects how a person thinks, behaves, and interacts with other people. (1)

Mental status exam: Structured clinical interview to assess current mental status; data is gathered about appearance, attitude, and activity; mood and affect; speech and language; thought processes, thought content, and perception; cognition; and insight and judgment. (3)

Mercyism: Another name for ruminations in humans; used in past historic eras. (9)

Mesolimbic pathway: Brain pathway important in responding to rewards. (9)

Methadone maintenance therapy (MMT): Drug replacement therapy that replaces more problematic opioids (e.g., heroin or fentanyl) with less problematic but chemically similar ones (usually *methadone* or *buprenorphine*). (11)

Method restriction: Suicide prevention strategy in which access to means of suicide is restricted. (16)

Mild neurocognitive disorder: DSM and ICD term for mild dementia, characterized by modest cognitive decline. (14)

Mindblindness: Idea that people with autism don't have the evolved capacity for *theory of mind*, the ability to view the world through others' eyes and to attribute thoughts and feelings to them. (13)

Mindfulness-based cognitive therapy (MBCT): Therapy that combines *mindfulness training* (learning to observe and be aware of thoughts) with *cognitive therapy*. (5)

Mindfulness-based stress reduction (MBSR): Variation of mindfulness-based cognitive therapy that facilitates awareness of one's thoughts without trying to influence or stop them. (8)

Minnesota Multiphasic Personality Inventory (MMPI): Objective self-report personality inventory; contains clinical scales plus validity scales to determine if test-taker is faking good or bad. (3)

Mismatch theories of ADHD: View hyperactive-impulsive traits as adaptive in ancestral times but not modern industrial societies; *hunter-farmer theory*, *response readiness theory*, *wader theory*, and *fighter theory* are mismatch theories of ADHD. (13)

Mixed anxiety and depressive disorder: Proposed DSM and official ICD diagnosis for people who display symptoms of both depression and anxiety for two weeks or more, but whose symptoms don't qualify them for other mood or anxiety disorders. (6)

Mixed episode: ICD-only mood episode in which manic and depressive symptoms rapidly alternate or co-occur for at least two weeks; replaced with "with mixed features" specifier in DSM. (5)

Mixed methods: Combine qualitative and quantitative methods to study a specific issue. (1)

Modafinil: A non-amphetamine stimulant drug used to treat insomnia. (15)

Model penal code test: Legal test of insanity that acquits defendants if they lacked substantial capacity to appreciate the wrongfulness of their actions or could not control their behavior; also called the *American Law Institute test* or *ALI test*. (16)

Modeling: Indirect form of exposure in which the therapist models the aversive behavior for the client, demonstrating that the fear is unjustified. (4)

Monoamine hypothesis: Hypothesis that depression is due to a shortage of the monoamine neurotransmitters serotonin, norepinephrine, and dopamine. (5)

Monoamine oxidase (MAO) inhibitors: See *MAO inhibitors*.

Mood stabilizers: Various types of drugs used to treat mania. (5)

Moral insanity: James Cowles Prichard's eighteenth-century precursor to DSM-5's antisocial personality disorder, characterized by impulsive, violent, and depraved behavior, but without more florid symptoms of madness. (12)

Moral therapy: An early treatment for mental distress in which providing a warm and nurturing environment was used to help people overcome madness. (1)

Moral versus illness models of drug addiction: The moral model views addiction as a vice, whereas the illness model (or medical model) views it as a disease. (11)

Motivational interviewing (MI): Humanistic technique rooted in person-centered theory that helps people recognize and do something about pressing problems. (11)

MRI: See *magnetic resonance imaging (MRI)*.

Multicultural perspectives: Hold that what is considered psychopathology is often a function of culture and that clinicians must be aware of how cultural differences impact their work with clients. (2)

Multidimensional family therapy (MDFT): Family therapy for adolescents with substance issues that intervenes at individual, family, and social levels. (11)

Multigenerational family therapy: Bowen's approach to family therapy, which stresses how families pass dysfunctional patterns down across generations. (2)

Multisystemic therapy (MST): Sees disruptive behavior problems as determined by multiple social systems (home, school, peer groups, and neighborhoods) and uses individual, family, and community-level interventions to remedy them. (13)

Muscle dysmorphia: Body dysmorphia in which (mostly) males obsessively worry that they aren't muscular enough. (9)

Music education: Dyslexia treatment that reduces reading problems by improving musical skills; based on the idea that phonological awareness correlates with musical abilities. (14)

Narcissistic personality disorder (NPD): DSM diagnosis characterized by an inflated sense of self (*grandiosity*) and a desperate need for admiration. (12)

Narcolepsy: Sleep problem characterized by periods of unexpected and uncontrollable sleepiness and abrupt lapses into sleep; often accompanied by *cataplexy* (temporary loss of muscle tone). (15)

Narrative therapy: Constructivist therapy in which clients are asked to examine and revise the stories they tell about their lives. (2)

NAVIGATE program: Community intervention program for psychosis that stresses individualized medication management, psychoeducation, resilience-focused psychotherapy, and employment training. (4)

Negative symptoms: Subtracted from the personality in psychosis; symptoms such as *diminished emotional expression*, *flattened affect*, *avolition* (decreased motivation), *alogia* (poverty of speech), *anhedonia* (loss of pleasure), and *asociality* (disinterest in social contact). (4)

Neurodiversity: Emphasizes that those carrying diagnoses like autism and ADHD are neurologically different, not disordered. (13)

Neurofibrillary tangles: Twisting of tau protein fibers that help neurons keep their shape and allow them to transmit nutrients; common in Alzheimer's patients. (14)

Neurological tests: Physiological tests that measure brain functioning directly. (3)

Neuropsychological tests: Psychological tests used to evaluate perceptual, cognitive, and motor skills; often used to infer underlying brain dysfunction. (3)

Neurotic anxiety: Pathological anxiety that occurs in people who refuse to acknowledge existential givens that demand they invest their lives with meaning. (6)

Neurotransmitters: Brain chemicals involved in neural communication. (2)

New View campaign: Challenged privileging medical model view of female sexual problems and proposed four types: (1) *sexual problems due to sociocultural, political, or economic factors*; (2) *sexual problems relating to partner and relationship*; (3) *sexual problems due to psychological factors*; and (4) *sexual problems due to medical factors*. (10)

Nicotine: A stimulant found in tobacco leaves that makes users feel alert and calm. (11)

Nicotine replacement therapy (NRT): Drug replacement therapy for smoking cessation in which the delivery method is changed to make weaning off nicotine easier; gum, patches, lozenges, and e-cigarettes are examples of alternative delivery methods. (11)

Nightmare disorder: DSM and ICD parasomnia involving regularly having intense dreams in which one's safety or survival is threatened. (15)

Non-benzodiazepine receptor antagonists: Enhance GABA activity and promote sleep; sometimes referred to as *Z-drugs*, they are used to treat insomnia. (15)

Non-rapid eye movement (NREM) sleep arousal disorder: DSM parasomnia in which sleep is disrupted by sleepwalking or sleep terrors. (15)

Nonsteroidal anti-inflammatory drugs (NSAIDs): Anti-inflammatory pain relief drugs such as aspirin and ibuprofen. (5)

Nonsuicidal self-injury disorder (NSSI): Proposed DSM disorder involving intentional self-injury without suicidal intent. (16)

Noradrenaline: Name of norepinephrine when it is secreted as a hormone in the endocrine system. (10)

Norepinephrine: An excitatory neurotransmitter associated with anxiety and depression. (2)

Obesity: According to the World Health Organization, extremely high body mass index (greater than 30). (9)

Object relations therapy: Refers to a loose cluster of psychodynamic therapies that emphasize how early attachment relationships with caregivers lead to psychologically internalized expectations, which result in recurring patterns of interacting with others later in life; the goal is to provide a *corrective emotional experience* in which these patterns are worked through and changed using the patient–therapist relationship. (2)

Objectification theory: Media images present women as sexual objects to be judged based on their looks (*objectification*), which leads women to objectify their bodies (*self-objectification*) and makes them vulnerable to body image and eating issues. (9)

Objective test: Test that uses standardized items with limited response choices (e.g., multiple-choice, "true/false," or "yes/no"); *self-report personality inventories* are objective tests. (3)

Obsessions: Persistent thoughts, images, or urges that are hard to dismiss or stop thinking about. (6)

Obsessive trait complex hypothesis: Holds that obsessive-compulsive personality disorder traits (e.g., anxiety, compulsive conscientiousness, miserliness, and an ever-present sense of urgency) allowed early human to survive in inhospitable climates. (12)

Obsessive-compulsive disorder (OCD): DSM and ICD disorder marked by the presence of obsessions and compulsions. (6)

Obsessive-compulsive personality disorder (OCPD): DSM diagnosis for excessively perfectionistic and rigid people disproportionately focused on orderliness, rules, and control. (12)

Open Dialogue: A community-care approach rooted in narrative and dialogical theories that aims to create a support network that can intervene and assist the person experiencing psychosis. (4)

Operant conditioning: Behavioral approach focused on how the consequences of behavior (reinforcement of punishment) influence whether it is likely to be repeated. (2)

Opioid antagonists: Drugs used to treat substance addiction and dissociation; they bond to opioid receptors, preventing other opioid substances (such as heroin) from doing the same; examples include *naloxone* (trade names *Narcan* an *Evzio*) and *naltrexone* (trade names *Vivitrol* and *Revia*). (8)

Opioids: Natural, synthetic, or semisynthetic drugs that depress the central nervous system and serve as powerful painkillers; highly addictive, they mimic endogenous opioids created by our bodies (also called *opiates* and *narcotics*). (11)

Opium: A natural opioid found in the sap of opium poppy plants. (11)

Oppositional defiant disorder (ODD): DSM and ICD diagnosis for children and adolescents who are angry, argumentative, defiant, and vindictive. (13)

Oral impregnation: Psychodynamic conceptualization of eating disorders in which patients have an unconscious Oedipal wish to become pregnant by oral means. (9)

Orexin: Neurotransmitter important in regulating wakefulness and appetite. (15)

Orexin-receptor antagonists: Insomnia drugs that block the wake-promoting neurotransmitter orexin, thereby promoting sleep. (15)

Orthorexia nervosa: Proposed mental disorder characterized by a preoccupation with healthy eating. (9)

Other specified feeding or eating disorder (OSFED): DSM and ICD diagnosis for those who don't meet criteria for other feeding or eating disorders but warrant a diagnosis; used to diagnose *purging disorder*, *night eating syndrome*, *atypical anorexia*, and *atypical bulimia*. (9)

Overcorrection: Behavioral technique in which an undesired behavior is punished by requiring the person to repeatedly engage in an opposite kind of behavior. (9)

Oxycodone: A semisynthetic opioid used as a pain reliever in prescription drugs marketed under names like Percocet and OxyContin. (11)

Oxytocin: An amino acid produced by the hypothalamus that functions as both a neurotransmitter and a hormone; important in sex and reproduction (by stimulating labor and breastfeeding) and in social behavior; administered via nasal spray for ASD. (13)

PANDAS hypothesis: Holds that tics develop in genetically susceptible individuals who contract strep throat or other viruses; the full name of this hypothesis is the *Pediatric Autoimmune Neuropsychiatric Disorders Associated with Streptococcal Infection hypothesis*. (14)

Panic attack: Intense and sudden anxiety reaction; symptoms include pounding heart, trembling, shortness of breath, chest pain, nausea, dizziness, feeling chilled or hot, tingling sensations, and detachment from self or world. (6)

Panic disorder: DSM and ICD disorder characterized by recurrent and unexpected panic attacks. (6)

Paranoid personality disorder: DSM diagnosis for people who are unjustifiably superstitious, have difficulty trusting others, and worry others are trying to exploit, harm, or deceive them. (12)

Paraphilias: Sexual impulses, fantasies, and behaviors directed toward unusual (and sometimes socially taboo) objects and situations. (10)

Paraphilic coercive disorder (PCD): Proposed but rejected DSM paraphilic disorder involving distressing fantasies about or repeated acts of rape. (10)

Paraphilic disorder involving solitary behavior or consenting individuals: ICD paraphilic disorder diagnosis for all paraphilias involving distress over solitary or consenting sexual fantasies, urges, or behaviors. (10)

Paraphilic disorders: DSM and ICD paraphilia diagnoses; must impair or distress the person engaging in or fantasizing about the paraphilia, or cause (or risk causing) harm. (10)

Parasomnias: Sleep disturbances involving undesired events or experiences during sleep (e.g., sleepwalking, sleep terrors, nightmares, or acting out dreams). (15)

Parasuicidal behavior: Self-harm inflicted less because one wants to die and more to manipulate others, communicate distress, or regulate emotions. (12)

Participant modeling: Variety of modeling wherein the client is invited to partake in anxiety-provoking the activity with the therapist. (6)

Pedophilic disorder: DSM and ICD paraphilic disorder involving sexual fantasies, urges, or behaviors related to sexual involvement with preteen children; must cause the individual distress if not acted upon. (10)

Pelvic floor rehabilitation: Behavioral technique that improves sexual interest via physical exercises (e.g., Kegel exercises) that strengthen weak pelvic floor muscles associated with sexual pain in women, as well as premature ejaculation and erectile dysfunction in men. (10)

Persistent (chronic) motor or vocal tic disorder: DSM disorder in which a person displays either motor or vocal tics—but not both—for over a year; divided into two disorders in ICD (*chronic motor tic disorder* and *chronic phonic tic disorder*). (14)

Persistent depressive disorder (PDD): DSM disorder for chronic depression that lasts two years or more, either with or without also meeting criteria for a depressive episode; related to but different in important respects from ICD's *dysthymic disorder*. (5)

Person-centered care: Incorporates person-centered therapy concepts into dementia care to provide a supportive and caring environment to patients and their families. (14)

Person-centered play therapy: See *client-centered play therapy*.

Person-centered therapy: Rogers' humanistic and non-directive therapy in which therapists provide core conditions for change (empathy, genuineness, and unconditional positive regard) to get clients back on a path toward self-actualization. (2)

Personality: Stable and characteristic patterns of thinking, feeling, behaving, and interacting with others (often thought of as consisting of distinguishing qualities, or *traits*). (12)

Personality disorder (PD): Constellation of personality traits that consistently leads to interpersonal conflict and difficulty in daily functioning. (12)

Personality disorder-trait specified: Proposed diagnosis in the DSM-5 alternative model for personality disorders (AMPD); for people who don't meet trait-based criteria for any of the other six AMPD personality disorder categories but still show personality pathology in one or more trait domain. (12)

Personality test: Any test that measures emotions, interpersonal relationship patterns, levels of motivation and interest, and attitudes; includes self-report inventories and projective tests. (3)

Perversions: Old-fashioned term for paraphilias preferred by psychodynamic therapist Robert Stoller, who saw them as acts of revenge intended to compensate for profound humiliation during childhood. (10)

PET scan: See *positron-emission topography (PET scan)*.

Phencyclidine (PCP): A hallucinogen with hallucinogenic, depressant, and some stimulant properties; reduces influence of glutamate while enhancing dopamine and norepinephrine production. (11)

Phenomenological methods: Qualitative research approaches in which the goal is to describe the essence of something by setting aside one's biases and preconceptions and studying conscious experience; requires bracketing preconceptions and allowing the world to "present" itself to us so we can interpretively describe and make sense of it. (1)

Phenylalkylamine hallucinogens: Produce hallucinogenic and stimulant effects by affecting norepinephrine, dopamine, and serotonin receptors; *mescaline* and *DOM* are phenylalkylamine hallucinogens. (11)

Phenylketonuria (PKU): Genetic disease involving deficiency in the liver enzyme, phenylalanine hydroxylase, resulting in the inability to break down phenylalanine and phenylpyruvic acid; can lead to brain damage and intellectual impairment. (14)

Pica: DSM and ICD disorder involving the eating of nonfood substances. (9)

Picture Exchange Communication System (PECS): Applied behavior analysis (ABA) technique for children with communication difficulties in which the children learn to communicate using picture cards. (13)

Placebo control group: A control group that gets an activity that is comparable to the treatment, but is not the treatment. (1)

Placebo effect: When a placebo control group activity induces results like those expected from a treatment group. (1)

Polydrug use: When drug users take more than one substance. (11)

Polypharmacy: The practice of prescribing multiple drugs at the same time. (12)

Polyunsaturated fatty acids (PUFA) hypothesis: ADHD is caused or exacerbated by polyunsaturated fat deficiencies. (13)

Population: All people of a given class; for instance, all people suffering from depression. (1)

Positive symptoms: Additions to the personality that occur in psychosis; hallucinations and delusions are examples. (4)

Positron emission topography (PET scan): Neuroimaging technique in which radioactive isotopes are placed in the bloodstream and gamma rays used to generate images reflecting changes in cerebral blood flow; identifies brain areas active during a given task. (3)

Postpartum depression: Depression that develops in women who are pregnant or have given birth within the last four weeks. (5)

Posttraumatic Growth (PTG): Positive changes following crises, traumas, losses, and other stressful events. (7)

Posttraumatic model: Links somatic and dissociative symptoms to stress or trauma; also called the *traumagenic position*. (8)

Posttraumatic stress disorder (PTSD): DSM and ICD disorder diagnosed in people who experience significant psychological difficulty for an extended period following a traumatic event. (7)

Power threat meaning framework (PTMF): Psychosocial alternative to traditional diagnosis, which attributes distress to economic and social injustice, not individual disorders; emphasizes *power* (what happened to a person), *threat* (response to what happened), and *meaning* (sense made of what happened). (3)

Pre-therapy: Version of person-centered therapy for use with psychotic individuals; goal is to make *psychological contact* with the psychotic client as a pre-condition for effective therapy. (4)

Premature (early) ejaculation: DSM and ICD diagnosis for men who ejaculate too soon. (10)

Premenstrual dysphoric disorder (PMDD): DSM and ICD disorder diagnosed in women who show depressive symptoms during the week before their menstrual periods. (5)

Prepared conditioning: Conditioning that is easier to accomplish because the organism is evolutionarily predisposed to it. (6)

Presenting problems: The problems that clients request help for when consulting with mental health professionals. Presenting problems may or may not ultimately be the primary focus of treatment. (1)

Prevalence: Percentage of people in the population believed to currently suffer from a specific mental disorder. (1)

Prevention and early intervention programs: Programs designed to prevent or intervene in the early stages of substance use. (11)

Primary gain: The reason for a symptom; the central (or *primary*) conflict the symptom is intended to address. (8)

Privilege: Legal right that protects communications confided within certain relationships (e.g., between married people, clergy and their parishioners, lawyers and their clients, and healthcare providers and their patients). (16)

Problem-solving skills training: Type of behavioral skills training that teaches planning, organization, and management skills. (13)

Problem-solving therapy: Cognitive-behavioral therapy (CBT) approach in which therapist helps client define specific problems and then generate solutions that can be implemented. (5)

Projective test: Uses responses to artistic representation to infer aspects of psychological functioning. (3)

Prolonged grief disorder: DSM and ICD diagnosis for people who experience intense and disruptive grief for an extended period following the loss of a loved one. (7)

Provisional tic disorder: DSM diagnosis in which a person displays motor and/or verbal tics, but for less than one year; limited to *transient motor tics* in ICD. (14)

Psychedelic-assisted therapy: Combines hallucinogenic drugs like psilocybin, MDMA, or LSD with talk therapy for issues like depression and trauma. (5)

Psychoanalysis: Freud's original therapy in which patients lie on couch facing away from analyst; employs *free association* (patient says whatever comes to mind), *dream analysis* (unconscious wish fulfillments expressed in dreams are identified), and examination of *transference* (ways patients transfer feelings about important others onto their analysts); *catharsis* (emotional release) and *working through* (psychological integration of what has been made conscious) are goals. (2)

Psychodynamic Diagnostic Manual (PDM): Diagnostic manual of the American Psychoanalytic Association. (3)

Psychodynamic PTSD groups: Aim to make members' traumatic memories conscious so feelings about them can be worked through in the group setting. (7)

Psychodynamic perspectives: Theories that trace their origins to Freud's work; early life attachments and unconscious processes are emphasized. (2)

Psychoeducation: Technique in which clients are taught about the problem they are diagnosed with to help them better cope with it.

Psychological factors affecting other medical conditions: DSM diagnosis for people who have a known medical symptom that is brought on or made worse by ongoing psychological stress. Called *psychological or behavioral factors affecting disorders or diseases classified elsewhere* in ICD. (8)

Psychological first aid (PFA): Less invasive intervention than CISD that builds on research showing most people are resilient in the face of trauma; offers help to victims in the aftermath of a traumatic event in a non-intrusive way. (7)

Psychological or behavioral factors affecting disorders or diseases classified elsewhere: ICD equivalent to the DSM diagnosis of *psychological factors affecting other medical conditions*. (8)

Psychological perspectives: Attribute mental distress to psychological conflicts involving problematic thoughts, feelings, and behaviors. (1)

Psychoneuroimmunology (PNI): Discipline that studies how psychological stress influences the central nervous system, endocrine system, and immune system. (8)

Psychopathic personalities: Emil Kraepelin's term for people with one of four pathological personality types: *born criminals*, *the weak-willed*, *pathological liars/swindlers*, and *the paranoid*; Kurt Schneider later identified ten types of psychopathic personalities, which influenced DSM and ICD. (12)

Psychopathology: Attributes mental distress to internal dysfunction or sickness inside the individual. (1)

Psychopathy versus sociopathy: Both involve exploiting and disregarding the rights of others, lack of empathy, lack of guilt and remorse, being deceitful and manipulative, poor impulse control, and grandiosity—but psychopathy is mainly attributed to biological origins and sociopathy to environmental influences. (12)

Psychosexual stages: Developmental stages that determine id, ego, superego patterns in adult personality; the stages are *oral* (birth to 1½ years old), *anal* (1½ to 3 years old, ego develops), *phallic* (3 to 5 years old, superego develops via Oedipal/Electra complexes), *latency* (6 years old to pre-adolescence), and *genital* (adolescence onward); *fixation* at one or more of the first three stages leads to symptoms at the genital stage. (2)

Psychosis: A broad term used to describe people whose thoughts, behaviors, and perceptions are so strange that they appear to have lost contact with reality. (4)

Psychosomatic: Term for when prolonged psychological stress results in or exacerbates a real medical condition; sometimes also referred to as *psychophysiological*. (8)

Psychosomatic families: Families in which there is a great deal of enmeshment, rigidity, overprotectiveness, and difficulty with conflict resolution; in such families, somatic symptoms and eating disorders are believed to be more likely; sometimes called *psychosomatogenic families*. (8)

PTSD: See *Posttraumatic stress disorder (PTSD)*.

Puberty blockers: Drugs to delay puberty in preadolescents experiencing gender dysphoria. (10)

Punishment: Consequences that decrease the likelihood of the behavior they follow; can be *positive* (add something undesirable) or *negative* (remove something desirable). (2)

Purposive sampling: Sampling technique in which participants are recruited to participate in a study because they have characteristics that allow the research question to be examined in depth; often used in grounded theory research. (1)

Pyromania: DSM and ICD impulse control disorder that involves purposeful fire-setting

that provides pleasure, gratification, or emotional relief but is not done for personal gain. (13)

Q-sort: Person-centered assessment in which 100 cards with descriptors written on them are sorted into piles to describe client personality using everyday language. (3)

Qualitative methods: Research methods in which accounts of subjective experiences or sociocultural phenomena are collected, with the goal of comprehending worldviews about what is being studied. (1)

Quantitative methods: Research methods in which numerical data and statistical analyses are used to test hypotheses. (1)

Quasi-experiment: Variation on an experiment in which the researchers are unable to randomly assign participants to groups; often uses *matched-control groups* in which control participants are selected who are demographically comparable to the experimental group. (1)

Random assignment: The practice of assigning an experiment's participants to different independent variable conditions at random. (1)

Random sample: A sample that is chosen arbitrarily from the population; choosing participants randomly gives us the best chance that the sample will be representative of the larger population. (1)

Randomized controlled trial (RCT): A kind of experiment designed to compare different therapies' effectiveness in treating specific presenting problems. (1)

Rapid eye movement (REM) sleep behavior disorder: DSM and ICD parasomnia characterized by acting out the dreams one experiences during REM sleep. (15)

Rational emotive behavior therapy (REBT): Albert Ellis' cognitive therapy, which focuses on disputing clients' irrational beliefs. (2)

RDoC: See *Research Domain Criteria (RDoC)*.

Reactive attachment disorder: DSM and ICD diagnosis given to children who have experienced severe environmental neglect and do not develop the ability to form attachments; they are withdrawn and inhibited around caregivers. (7)

Refrigerator mother theory of autism: Attributed autism to cold and aloof parenting. (13)

Reinforcement: Consequences that increase the likelihood of the behavior they follow; can be *positive* (add something desirable) or *negative* (remove something undesirable). (2)

Relapse prevention (RP): CBT technique that prevents relapse by teaching those in recovery how to handle high-risk situations that tempt them to engage in the problematic activity again; used with sexual offenders, substance users, and behavioral addictions. (10)

Relational-cultural theory: Holds that mental distress is often incorrectly attributed to internal psychopathology rather than social alienation. (12)

Reliability: Regarding diagnosis, the degree to which a diagnostic system yields similar results each time it is used; *interrater reliability* is high when different clinicians independently arrive at the same diagnosis much of the time. (3)

Repression: Unacceptable ideas and impulses are pushed out of awareness (i.e., made unconscious). (2)

Reproductive suppression hypothesis: Anorexia is a female strategy for maximizing long term productive success by shutting down reproductive capacity through self-starvation during times when conditions are not optimal for having babies. (9)

Research Domain Criteria (RDoC): U.S. National Institute of Mental Health (NIMH) research initiative to devise a diagnostic system that uses biological measures (i.e., biomarkers) to diagnose mental disorders. (3)

Response-to-intervention model (RTI): Preventative approach that identifies and intervenes with children performing below grade level; if responsive, the children are reintegrated into the normal classroom, but if not, they are assigned to a special education classroom. (14)

Restless legs syndrome: DSM and ICD disorder involving overwhelming desire to move one's legs while resting or going to sleep. (15)

Right to refuse treatment: Legal right to decline treatment unless judged incompetent to make such a decision. (16)

Right to treatment: Legal right of individuals to receive appropriate treatment while involuntarily committed. (16)

Risk-need-responsivity model (RNR): CBT program for offenders that tailors interventions to each offender by assessing *risk* and *need* in order determine *responsivity* (the appropriate kind and level of intervention needed to prevent repeat offenses). (10)

Ritalin: Name under which the stimulant *methylphenidate* is marketed as a treatment for attention-deficit/hyperactivity disorder. (13)

Role construct repertory test (rep test): Personality test in which a client's *personal constructs* (bipolar dimensions of meaning created by the client) are elicited and their relationships mapped; allows for an assessment using the client's personal meanings rather than the clinician's diagnostic categories. (3)

Rorschach Inkblot Method (RIM): Projective assessment technique in which test-taker responds to ten inkblots. (3)

Rumination disorder: DSM disorder characterized by re-chewing, re-swallowing, or spitting out food after intentionally regurgitating it; called *rumination and regurgitation disorder* in ICD. (9)

Safety planning: Suicide-prevention technique in which clients generate and utilize concrete steps for coping with suicidal ideation. (16)

Sample: Members of a population chosen to participate in a study. (1)

Satiation techniques: Behavioral technique in which regular meals are supplemented with additional food; because rumination often occurs when hungry, it discourages rumination by making the patient less hungry. (9)

Schizoaffective disorder: DSM and ICD disorder in which the person displays aspects of psychosis and depression. (4)

Schizoid personality disorder: DSM diagnosis characterized by disinterest in relationships and people, with no desire to engage with others and a preference to be alone. (12)

Schizophrenia: The best known and perhaps most severe psychotic disorder in the DSM and ICD; characterized by hallucinations, delusions, and disorganized speech. (4)

Schizophreniform disorder: DSM disorder that shows same basic symptoms as schizophrenia, but they don't last as long; not in ICD. (4)

Schizophrenogenic mothers: Fromm-Reichmann's term for cold, demanding, and domineering mothers whose parenting style she blamed for their children's schizophrenia. (4)

Schizotypal disorder: ICD psychotic disorder diagnosis for people with eccentric thoughts, perceptions, and behaviors accompanied by difficulty forming close relationships; equivalent to DSM's *schizotypal personality disorder (STPD)*. (4)

Schizotypal personality disorder (STPD): DSM diagnosis for people with eccentric thoughts, perceptions, and behaviors accompanied by difficulty forming close relationships; equivalent to ICD's psychotic disorder diagnosis, *schizotypal disorder*. (12)

Seasonal affective disorder (SAD): Depression that occurs during the winter months when there are fewer hours of daylight. (5)

Secondary gain: Any other advantages a symptom provides beyond the original unconscious conflict that it expresses. (8)

Sedative-hypnotics: A class of depressants sometimes simply called *sedatives*; barbiturates and benzodiazepines are types of sedative-hypnotic drugs. (11)

Selective mutism: DSM and ICD disorder diagnosed mainly in children who fail to speak in social situations in which it is expected. (6)

Selective serotonin reuptake inhibitors (SSRIs): Antidepressants that prevent reuptake or reabsorption of serotonin by neurons that release it; this leaves more serotonin available. (5)

Self-hypnosis: Ability to enter a hypnotic trance one one's own without guidance from others. (8)

Self-medication hypothesis: Psychodynamic hypothesis that substance abuse is a defense used by those who have difficulty recognizing and regulating their emotions; this avoidance strategy is traceable to adverse childhood events. (11)

Self-stigmatization: The process of internalizing negative attitudes about oneself espoused by others. (12)

Senile plaques: Sticky buildup of beta-amyloid protein in the areas surrounding neurons that is implicated in Alzheimer's disease; also called *amyloid plaques*. (14)

Sensate focus: Masters and Johnson technique for arousal and orgasm issues; partners engage in sensual touching but not intercourse, removing pressure to perform. (10)

Separation anxiety disorder: DSM and ICD disorder in which one shows excessive anxiety about being separated from significant attachment figures. (6)

Serotonin: An inhibitory neurotransmitter associated with depression and anxiety. (2)

Serotonin and norepinephrine reuptake inhibitors (SNRIs): Antidepressants that block reuptake of serotonin and norepinephrine, leaving more of both available. (5)

Service user perspectives: Focus on the experience and concerns of people receiving psychiatric services. (2)

Service user/survivor movement: Rejects mainstream psychiatric perspectives, contending that many interventions—especially prescription drugs and involuntary treatments—are often inhumane and abusive; also called the *psychiatric survivor movement*. (2)

Sex: One's biological status as male, female, or intersex. (10)

Sexual competition hypothesis: Eating problems occur because women must compete to attract men by maintaining a "nubile" hourglass shape; even greater emphasis on thin shape emerges in industrial societies with less familial help to secure women mates. (9)

Sexual dysfunctions: Defined by DSM and ICD as disturbances in responding sexually or experiencing sexual pleasure. (10)

Sexual instinct: A reproductive instinct for the propagation of the species; proposed by early doctors as part of the process of medicalizing sexual deviance. (10)

Sexual masochism disorder: DSM paraphilic disorder involving distress over sexual fantasies, urges, or behaviors related to being humiliated or made to suffer. (10)

Sexual orientation: Types of people one is attracted to (one's own gender, a different gender, all genders/sexes, no genders/sexes, etc.). (10)

Sexual pain-penetration disorder: ICD equivalent to DSM's genito-pelvic pain/penetration disorder, except it excludes dyspareunia. (10)

Sexual response cycle: In Masters and Johnson's original formulation, involved four phases: *excitement/arousal, plateau, orgasm, resolution*. Revised by Kaplan to consist of *desire, arousal/excitement, orgasm*, and *resolution* phases. (10)

Sexual sadism disorder: DSM and ICD paraphilic disorder involving sexual fantasies, urges, or behaviors related to the physical or emotional suffering of another person; must cause the individual distress if not acted upon; called *coercive sexual sadism disorder* in ICD. (10)

Short-term dynamic therapy of stress response syndromes: Psychodynamic therapy that addresses five phases of trauma and grief: (a) initial outcry; (b) denial and numbness; (c) intrusive thoughts and feelings; (d) "working through;" and (e) completion. (7)

Sildenafil: A phosphodiesterase type-5 (PDE5) inhibitor used to increase blood flow to sex organs; given mainly to men to generate blood flow to penis necessary for erections; marketed as Viagra. (10)

Silencing the self (STS) theory: Sees depression as a product of deeply rooted cultural assumptions that direct women to silence or suppress certain thoughts or feelings to satisfy the demands of a male-centered world. (5)

Single-subject experiment: Experiment conducted on just one person; most common type is the ABAB design, which alternates between presenting and removing the independent variable manipulation to see its effect on the single participant. (1)

Sixteen Personality Factor (16PF) Questionnaire: Multiple-choice self-report personality inventory yielding scores on sixteen primary personality factors (*warmth, reasoning, emotional stability, dominance, liveliness, rule-consciousness, social boldness, sensitivity, vigilance, abstractedness, privateness, apprehension, openness to change, self-reliance, perfectionism*, and *tension*), plus the "Big-Five" global personality traits (*extraversion, anxiety, tough-mindedness, independence*, and *self-control*). (3)

Sleep cycle: Cycle a person goes through four to five times during a normal night's sleep, consisting of four distinct stages; the first three are *non-rapid eye movement (NREM) sleep* (involving little or no eye movement or dreaming) and the fourth is *rapid eye movement (REM) sleep* (involving rapid eye movement, muscle paralysis, and dreaming). (15)

Sleep terrors: ICD disorder involving episodes of intense terror that jerk a person abruptly from deep sleep, often with a panicked scream and a scramble to escape the room. (15)

Sleep-related eating disorder: ICD diagnosis for people who eat while sleepwalking. (15)

Sleepwalking disorder: ICD parasomnia characterized by getting out of bed and walking

around while still asleep; the sleepwalker has a blank expression, in unresponsive to others, and is difficult to awaken; also called *somnambulism*. (15)

Snowball sampling: Sampling technique in which additional participants are recruited by asking initial participants if they know anyone else with similar experiences; often used in grounded theory research. (1)

SNRI: See *serotonin and norepinephrine reuptake inhibitors*.

Social anxiety disorder: DSM and ICD disorder diagnosed in people who become anxious and fear embarrassing or humiliating themselves in social situations where they might be scrutinized. (6)

Social drift: Tendency of those diagnosed with severe mental disorders such as schizophrenia to slide (or drift) down the socioeconomic ladder. (4)

Social justice perspectives: View mental distress as the product of social inequality; aim to reduce mental distress by eliminating oppressive social conditions. (2)

Social learning theory: Behavioral approach that focuses on how observation and modeling contribute to learning. (2)

Social oppression: Unjust social conditions, which lead to mental distress. (1)

Social (pragmatic) communication disorder (SPCD): DSM-5 neurodevelopmental disorder involving difficulties communicating with others but not restricted/repetitive behavior. (13)

Social skills training (SST): CBT technique in which complicated social scenarios (e.g., making friends, dating, ordering food in a restaurant, or going for a job interview) are broken down into discrete steps and taught to clients. (4)

Sociocognitive model: Maintains there is no such thing as dissociative identity disorder; media accounts and therapists who believe in DID iatrogentically induce it; also known as the *fantasy model* and the *iatrogenic position*. (8)

Sociocultural perspectives: Attribute mental distress to social causes (e.g., socioeconomic conditions, cultural influences, and social oppression). (1)

Sociodevelopmental-cognitive model of schizophrenia: Says schizophrenia emerges

from a circular and mutually influencing interaction among biological, cognitive, and sociocultural factors; genetic vulnerability and social disadvantage/adversity lead to dopamine dysregulation, which produces cognitive misattributions of salience, which yields psychosocial stress, which further impacts dopamine transmission, and so on in an ongoing cycle. (4)

Sodium oxybate: A central nervous system depressant prescribed to treat cataplexy; also known as *gamma-hydroxybutyrate (GHB)*. (15)

Somatic complaint: Presenting problem that involves experiencing or worrying about physical symptoms. (8)

Somatic symptom disorder (SSD): DSM diagnosis for people who have one or more somatic symptoms that they think and worry about excessively; roughly equivalent to *bodily distress disorder* in ICD. (8)

Somatization: The process of expressing psychological problems in physical terms. (8)

Soteria model: A community-based approach to schizophrenia that applies humanistic-existential ideas to therapeutic communities for people diagnosed with schizophrenia. (4)

Specialist supportive clinical management (SSCM): Non-theoretical approach to anorexia devised as a control comparison for research on other therapies but found effective in its own right; targets problematic eating, emphasizes proper diet, monitors weight, establishes realistic weight goals, and addresses life problems affecting eating. (9)

Specific learning disorder (SLD): DSM diagnosis involving lower than expected academic performance in reading, writing, spelling, or math that begins during early school years and is not due to intellectual development disorder; called *developmental learning disorder* in ICD. (14)

Specific phobia: DSM and ICD disorder characterized by the fear associated with a given object or situation; the fear is focused on something specific. (6)

Spectatoring: Observing and negatively evaluating one's sexual performance as if one were a third person watching it. (10)

Speech-sound disorder: DSM and ICD diagnosis in which speech is understood but hard to generate due to difficulty making speech sounds; called *developmental speech sound disorder* in ICD. (14)

Speedballing: Combining drugs (usually stimulants and opioids) to produce a synergistic effect in which the highs of both drugs are experienced but the negative effects are reduced; increases risk of overdose. (11)

Squeeze technique: Top of the penis is repeatedly squeezed during sexual activity to delay ejaculation; conditions men to not ejaculate so quickly. (10)

SSRI: See *selective serotonin reuptake inhibitors.*

State-dependent learning: People's ability to recall something is affected by their psychological or emotional state. (8)

Statistical deviation: Defines abnormality as what is statistically atypical. Whether what is atypical is abnormal in the sense of being psychopathological is often debated. (1)

Stereotypic movement disorder: DSM disorder involving repetitive and purposeless movements that begin early in development and which the child seems driven to perform (e.g., waving one's hands, rocking back and forth, banging one's head, and biting or hitting oneself); called *stereotyped movement disorder* in ICD. (14)

Stimulants: Drugs that speed up the central nervous system (CNS). (11)

Stop-start method: Men stop intercourse prior to ejaculating and start again only after arousal decreases; conditions men to not ejaculate so quickly. (10)

Stress: A feeling of being overwhelmed, worried, or run-down. (7)

Stress inoculation training (SIT): Uses CBT techniques to decrease avoidance and anxiety (e.g., education, relaxation training, breathing retraining, role playing, covert modeling, guided self-dialogue, graduated *in vivo* exposure, and thought stopping). (7)

Stress-vulnerability-coping skills model: Says a *biological vulnerability* to psychosis is triggered by *environmental stress*; the degree to which someone has sufficient cognitive coping skills influences whether stress triggers the biological vulnerability or, once triggered, allows the resulting psychotic symptoms to be dealt with effectively. (4)

Structural family therapy: Minuchin's family therapy, which emphasizes how the structure of a family system—including its rules,

boundaries, coalitions, and power hierarchies—contributes to its dysfunction. (2)

Structured Clinical Interview for DSM Disorders (SCID): Semi-structured interview for making DSM diagnoses. (3)

Structured psychodynamic therapies for personality disorders: Psychodynamic therapies for personality disorders with a more prescribed structure and shorter timeframe (1–2 years) than traditional psychodynamic approaches. Examples: *transference-focused psychotherapy (TFP)*, *mentalization-based treatment (MBT)*, and *intensive short-term dynamic psychotherapy (ISTDP)*. (12)

Stuttering: See *Childhood-onset fluency disorder.*

Subintentional death: Deaths due to an unconscious desire to die that yields reckless or negligent behavior; Shneidman's types: *death chancers* (take risks to see what will happen), *death hasteners* (engage in unhealthy lifestyles), *death capitulators* (give in to death due to depression/anxiety), and *death experimenters* (live in a perpetually altered state—e.g., drug haze); also called *indirect suicide*. (16)

Substance use disorder: DSM diagnosis that combines symptoms of abuse and dependence; assessed based on type of drug being used and severity of use. (11)

Suicidal behavior disorder (SBD): Proposed DSM disorder for those who have attempted suicide in the last two years. (16)

Suicide: Intentionally ending one's own life; Shneidman's types: *death seekers* (wish to die and actively seek death), *death initiators* (kill themselves because they believe death is imminent), *death ignorers* (kill themselves because they view death as an escape/something new), and *death darers* (ambivalent about death, so take risks that could kill them). (16)

Suicide awareness education: Element of suicide prevention programs that prevents suicide by educating people about it. (16)

Suicide hotlines: Offer 24-hour call, text, and chat options for those in crisis or feeling suicidal. (16)

Suicide prevention programs: Programs implemented on local or national levels that work to reduce suicides using education, hotlines, crisis intervention, safety planning, method restriction, and hospitalization. (16)

Superego: Partly conscious/partly unconscious psychoanalytic personality structure that houses moral beliefs. (2)

Supportive PTSD groups: Group members provide each other with emotional support and encouragement; by fostering supportive relationships, those coping with trauma assist one another. (7)

Surgical castration: Removing a man's testicles (*orchiectomy*) or a woman's ovaries (*oophorectomy*). (10)

Synergistic effects: Effect from taking drugs together; some combinations enhance the effects of both drugs, while other combinations cancel some of the effects of both drugs. (11)

Systematic desensitization: Exposure technique that combines *relaxation training* and use of a *fear hierarchy* (ranking potential experiences with the feared object or situation and from least to most scary); the client is gradually exposed to the conditioned stimulus while in a relaxed state, with the goal of conditioning a new response. (6)

Systems perspectives: Look at how individuals are influenced by and function within "systems" of relationships. (2)

Tardive dyskinesia: Irreversible syndrome from prolonged use of antipsychotics; involves repetitive and involuntary muscle movements; symptoms such as lip smacking, tongue wagging, and repeated eye blinking are common. (4)

Teletherapy: Uses real-time videoconferencing to provide psychotherapy and psychiatric consultations. (16)

Temporary commitment: Short-term psychiatric hospitalization of those considered dangerous to self or others; also called *emergency commitment*. (16)

Testosterone: Primary male sex hormone. (10)

"Thank you" theory of involuntary commitment: Holds that actively suicidal individuals will thank us later for hospitalizing them to prevent self-harm. (16)

Thematic Apperception Test (TAT): Projective assessment technique in which test-taker tells stories about pictures on twenty cards (determined by age and gender). (3)

Theory of mind: Evolved human ability to view the world through others' eyes and generate interpretations of why others behave as they do, as well as to infer and comprehend one's own mental states and behavior. (4)

Therapeutic communities (TCs): Residential or day treatment programs that provide an array of services and help participants develop new life skills; used for problems like addiction and psychosis. (11)

Thought parade exercise: Acceptance and commitment therapy (ACT) technique in which clients calmly imagine a parade in which people carry signs reproducing their negative thoughts; detached observation of thoughts reduces their influence. (9)

Thought stopping: CBT technique in which clients are taught to stop their thoughts, often by saying or thinking "Stop!" whenever an intrusive thought occurs. (6)

Tic disorders: DSM and ICD disorders involving abrupt and repetitive motor or vocal movements known as *tics*. (14)

Time-limited dynamic psychotherapy (TLDP): Short-term psychodynamic therapy that shares object relations therapy's emphasis on using therapy to identify and revise problematic interpersonal patterns (*cyclical maladaptive patterns*) but does so more quickly by establishing clear therapeutic goals and addressing them in twenty to twenty-five sessions. (2)

Tourette's disorder: DSM and ICD disorder that involves motor and vocal tics that have persisted for over a year; called *Tourette's syndrome* in ICD. (14)

Transcranial magnetic stimulation (TMS): Treatment for depression and sometimes bipolar symptoms in which magnetic energy is sent through the brain via electromagnetic coils placed on the scalp. (5)

Transgender: Term for people whose gender identity, expression, or behavior is different from what is typically associated with their birth-assigned sex; shorthand: "trans." (10)

Transgender-affirmative CBT (TA-CBT): Form of CBT that helps transgender clients cope with anxiety and depression due to transphobia; negative internalized beliefs about being transgender are examined and changed. (10)

Transtheoretical model of change: Model of therapeutic change that identifies five stages clients go through during the change process (*precontemplation, contemplation, preparation, action,* and *maintenance*). (11)

Transvestic disorder: DSM paraphilic disorder involving distress over sexual fantasies, urges, or behaviors related to cross-dressing. (10)

Trauma: Exposure to actual or threatened death, serious injury, or sexual violence. (7)

Trauma-focused CBT (TF-CBT): Brief trauma therapy for children and adolescents that combines behavioral techniques (e.g., exposure therapy and relaxation) with cognitive techniques (e.g., cognitive restructuring, affect modulation skill training, trauma narration, and psychoeducation about the effects of trauma). (7)

Trauma-focused cognitive-behavioral groups: Structured group approach that educates members about trauma and uses exposure and relaxation techniques to address anxiety. (7)

Trepanation: Prehistoric treatment of abnormal behavior in which holes were drilled in the skull to free evil spirits; also called *trephination.* (1)

Trichotillomania (hair-pulling disorder): DSM and ICD disorder describing those who compulsively pull out their own hair. (6)

Tricyclics: Antidepressants that mainly affect norepinephrine and serotonin (usually with more impact of norepinephrine); they work by inhibiting reabsorption of these neurotransmitters, leaving more available. (5)

Trustworthiness: Characteristic of good qualitative research; evaluated by looking at the study's social validity, whether it acknowledges its biases, and whether it provides adequate data. (1)

Tryptophan: Amino acid obtained from food that is required to produce the neurotransmitter serotonin. (9)

Twelve-step programs: See *12-step programs.*

Twin studies: Studies in which identical twins, who are genetically the same, are compared to see if both develop a trait or disorder. (4)

Unified psychodynamic therapy protocol for anxiety disorders (UPP-ANXIETY): Psychodynamic protocol for all anxiety disorders; therapy is broken into concrete steps (or "modules"), each with empirical support for its effectiveness. (6)

Validity: Degree to which a diagnostic system or assessment instrument measures what it claims to; types include *descriptive validity* (does a measure accurately describe what is being observed?), *face validity* (on the face of it, does a measure seem accurate?), *predictive validity* (does a measure predict outcomes?), *construct validity* (does a measure correlate with other measures measuring the same thing?), and *concurrent validity* (are a measure's results consistent with other measures given at the same time?). (3)

Variables: Aspects of the world that can change; measured in correlational and experimental research studies. (1)

Viral theory of autism: Children with autism are more likely to have had mothers who had a (usually severe) viral or bacterial infection during pregnancy. (13)

Viral theory of schizophrenia: People whose mothers had a virus while pregnant with them are at higher risk for schizophrenia. (4)

Virtual reality exposure: Exposure technique in which client is exposed to the anxiety-provoking object or situation using computer-generated virtual reality experiences to condition a new, non-anxious response to it. (6)

Voyeuristic disorder: DSM and ICD paraphilic disorder involving sexual fantasies, urges, or behaviors related to observing an unsuspecting person naked; must cause the individual distress if not acted upon. (10)

Wandering womb theory: The ancient Greek physician Hippocrates' biological theory that attributed hysteria to a woman's uterus detaching from its natural location and wandering around her body. (1)

Weak central coherence theory: Holds that people with autism prefer focusing on parts, not wholes; thus, they cognitively emphasize details over the more global picture. (13)

Werther effect: The tendency for suicide rates to go up following a highly publicized suicide. (16)

Western ideal of thinness: Beauty ideal in many Western cultures that values thin female bodies with small wastes and minimal body fat; when internalized, might contribute to eating disorders. (9)

Wild beast test: Pre-cursor to the insanity defense developed in 1265 in the UK that compared defendants who did not understand their crimes to wild beasts. (16)

REFERENCES

Aalbers, G., Engels, T., Haslbeck, J. M. B., Borsboom, D., & Arntz, A. (2021). The network structure of schema modes. *Clinical Psychology & Psychotherapy*, 28(5), 1065–1078. https://doi.org/10.1002/cpp.2577

Aaltonen, J., Seikkula, J., & Lehtinen, K. (2011). The comprehensive open-dialogue approach in Western Lapland: I. The incidence of non-affective psychosis and prodromal states. *Psychosis: Psychological, Social and Integrative Approaches*, 3(3), 179–191. https://doi.org/10.1080/17522439.2011.601750

Abbass, A. (2016). The emergence of psychodynamic psychotherapy for treatment resistant patients: Intensive short-term dynamic psychotherapy. *Psychodynamic Psychiatry*, 44(2), 245–280. https://doi.org/10.1521/pdps.2016.44.2.245

Abbass, A. A., & Town, J. M. (2013). Key clinical processes in intensive short-term dynamic psychotherapy. *Psychotherapy*, 50(3), 433–437. https://doi.org/10.1037/a0032166

Abbass, A., Sheldon, A., Gyra, J., & Kalpin, A. (2008). Intensive short-term dynamic psychotherapy for DSM-IV personality disorders: A randomized controlled trial. *Journal of Nervous and Mental Disease*, 196(3), 211–216. https://doi.org/10.1097/NMD.0b013e3181662ff0

Abbass, A., Town, J., Holmes, H., Luyten, P., Cooper, A., Russell, L., Lumley, M. A., Schubiner, H., Allinson, J., Bernier, D., De Meulemeester, C., Kroenke, K., & Kisely, S. (2020). Short-term psychodynamic psychotherapy for functional somatic disorders: A meta-analysis of randomized controlled trials. *Psychotherapy and Psychosomatics*, 89(6), 363–370. https://doi.org/10.1159/000507738

Abbate-Daga, G., & Marzola, E. (2017). Psychodynamic psychotherapies for bulimia nervosa: Trend and perspectives. *Eating and Weight Disorders*, 22(3), 557–558. https://doi.org/10.1007/s40519-017-0423-8

Abbate-Daga, G., Marzola, E., Amianto, F., & Fassino, S. (2016). A comprehensive review of psychodynamic treatments for eating disorders. *Eating and Weight Disorders*, 21(4), 553–580. https://doi.org/10.1007/s40519-016-0265-9

Abé, C., Ching, C. R. K., Liberg, B., Lebedev, A. V., Agartz, I., Akudjedu, T. N., Alda, M., Alnæs, D., Alonso-Lana, S., Benedetti, F., Berk, M., Bøen, E., Bonnin, C. del M., Breuer, F., Brosch, K., Brouwer, R. M., Canales-Rodríguez, E. J., Cannon, D. M., Chye, Y., … Landén, M. (2021). Longitudinal structural brain changes in bipolar disorder: A multicenter neuroimaging study of 1232 individuals by the ENIGMA Bipolar Disorder Working Group. *Biological Psychiatry*. https://doi.org/10.1016/j.biopsych.2021.09.008

Abed, R. T. (1998). The sexual competition hypothesis for eating disorders. *British Journal of Medical Psychology*, 71(4), 525–547. doi:10.1111/j.2044-8341.1998.tb01007.x

Abell, S., & Dauphin, B. (2009). The perpetuation of patriarchy: The hidden factor of gender bias in the diagnosis and treatment of children. *Clinical Child Psychology and Psychiatry*, 14(1), 117–133. https://doi.org/10.1177/1359104508096773

Abi-Jaoude, E., Naylor, K. T., & Pignatiello, A. (2020). Smartphones, social media use and youth mental health. *Canadian Medical Association Journal*, 192(6), E136–E141. https://doi.org/10.1503/cmaj.190434

Abramowitz, J. S., & Jacoby, R. J. (2014a). The use and misuse of exposure therapy for obsessive-compulsive and related disorders. *Current Psychiatry Reviews*, 10(4), 277–283. https://doi.org/10.2174/1573400510666140714171934

Abramowitz, J. S., Fabricant, L. E., Taylor, S., Deacon, B. J., McKay, D., & Storch, E. A. (2014). The relevance of analogue studies for understanding obsessions and compulsions. *Clinical Psychology Review*, 34(3), 206–217. https://doi.org/10.1016/j.cpr.2014.01.004

Abramowitz, J. S., & Jacoby, R. J. (2014b). Obsessive-compulsive disorder in the DSM-5. *Clinical Psychology: Science and Practice*, 21(3), 221–235. https://doi.org/10.1111/cpsp.12076

Abramson, L. Y., Metalsky, G. I., & Alloy, L. B. (1989). Hopelessness depression: A theory-based subtype of depression. *Psychological Review*, 96(2), 358–372. https://doi.org/10.1037/0033-295X.96.2.358

Abramson, L. Y., Seligman, M. E., & Teasdale, J. D. (1978). Learned helplessness in humans: Critique and reformulation. *Journal of Abnormal Psychology*, 87(1), 49–74. https://doi.org/10.1037/0021-843X.87.1.49

Abreu, T., & Bragança, M. (2015). The bipolarity of light and dark: A review on bipolar disorder and circadian cycles. *Journal of Affective Disorders*, 185, 219–229. https://doi.org/10.1016/j.jad.2015.07.017

Absah, I., Rishi, A., Talley, N. J., Katzka, D., & Halland, M. (2017). Rumination syndrome: Pathophysiology, diagnosis, and treatment. *Neurogastroenterology and Motility: The Official Journal of the European Gastrointestinal Motility Society*, 29(4). https://doi.org/10.1111/nmo.12954

Accordino, R. E., Kidd, C., Politte, L. C., Henry, C. A., & McDougle, C. J. (2016). Psychopharmacological interventions in autism spectrum disorder. *Expert Opinion on Pharmacotherapy*, 17(7), 937–952. https://doi.org/10.1517/14656566.2016.1154536

Achenbach, T. M. (1966). The classification of children's psychiatric symptoms: A factor-analytic study. *Psychological Monographs: General and Applied*, 80(7), 1–37. https://doi.org/10.1037/h0093906

Achenbach, T. M., Ivanova, M. Y., Rescorla, L. A., Turner, L. V., & Althoff, R. R. (2016). Internalizing/externalizing problems: Review and recommendations for clinical and research applications. *Journal of the American Academy of Child & Adolescent Psychiatry*, 55(8), 647–656. https://doi.org/10.1016/j.jaac.2016.05.012

Adame, A. L. (2014). "There needs to be a place in society for madness": The psychiatric survivor movement and new directions in mental health care. *Journal of Humanistic Psychology*, 54(4), 456–475. https://doi.org/10.1177/0022167813510207

Adames, H. Y., Chavez-Dueñas, N. Y., Vasquez, M. J. T., & Pope, K. S. (2023). *Succeeding as a therapist: How to create a thriving practice in a changing world*. American Psychological Association. https://doi.org/10.1037/0000321-000

Adams, J. (2013). Exercise dependence. In P. M. Miller, S. A. Ball, M. E. Bates, A. W. Blume, K. M. Kampman, D. J. Kavanagh, M. E. Larimer, N. M. Petry, & P. De Witte (Eds.), *Comprehensive addictive behaviors and disorders, Vol. 1: Principles of addiction* (pp. 827–835). Elsevier Academic Press.

Addington v. Texas, 441 U.S. 418 (1979). https://supreme.justia.com/cases/federal/us/441/418/

Adi, A., & Mathbout, M. (2018). The duty to protect: Four decades after *Tarasoff*. *American Journal of Psychiatry: Residents' Journal*, 13(4), 6–8. https://doi.org/10.1176/appi.ajp-rj.2018.130402

Adlof, S. M., & Hogan, T. P. (2018). Understanding dyslexia in the context of developmental language disorders. *Language, Speech, and Hearing Services in Schools*, 49(4), 762–773. https://doi.org/10.1044/2018_LSHSS-DYSLC-18-0049

Adriaens, P. R. (2008). Debunking evolutionary psychiatry's schizophrenia paradox. *Medical Hypotheses*, 70(6), 1215–1222. https://doi.org/10.1016/j.mehy.2007.10.014

Adriaens, P. R., & De Block, A. (2010). The evolutionary turn in psychiatry: A historical overview. *History of Psychiatry*, 21(2), 131–143. https://doi.org/10.1177/0957154X10370632

Agalaryan, A., & Rouleau, J.-L. (2014). Paraphilic coercive disorder: An unresolved issue. *Archives of Sexual Behavior*, 43(7), 1253–1256. https://doi.org/10.1007/s10508-014-0372-5

Agras, W. S., & Bohon, C. (2021). Cognitive behavioral therapy for the eating disorders. *Annual Review of Clinical Psychology*, 17, 417–438. https://doi.org/10.1146/annurev-clinpsy-081219-110907

Aharoni, R., & Hertz, M. M. (2012). Disgust sensitivity and anorexia nervosa. *European Eating Disorders Review*, 20(2), 106–110. https://doi.org/10.1002/erv.1124

Aherne, C., Moloney, O., & O'Brien, G. (2019, January). Youth mental health and the Power Threat Meaning Framework: Jigsaw's systems perspective. *Clinical Psychology Forum*, 313, 3–8.

Ahmed, S., Sanauddin, N., & Sajjid, I. A. (2016). Do socio-economic dynamics matter in intellectual disability among children? *Humanities and Social Sciences*, 23, 10.

Ahmed-Leitao, F., Spies, G., van den Heuvel, L., & Seedat, S. (2016). Hippocampal and amygdala volumes in adults with posttraumatic stress disorder secondary to childhood abuse or maltreatment: A systematic review. *Psychiatry Research: Neuroimaging*, 256, 33–43. https://doi.org/10.1016/j.pscychresns.2016.09.008

Aikins, R. (2019). "The white version of cheating?" Ethical and social equity concerns of cognitive enhancing drug users in higher education. *Journal of Academic Ethics*, 17(2), 111–130. https://doi.org/10.1007/s10805-018-9320-7

Ainsworth, M. D. S., Blehar, M. C., Waters, E., & Wall, S. (1978). *Patterns of attachment: A psychological study of the strange situation*. Lawrence Erlbaum.

Akbari, M., Seydavi, M., Zamani, E., Nikčević, A. V., & Spada, M. M. (2021). The Persian COVID-19 Anxiety Syndrome Scale (C-19ASS): Psychometric properties in a general community sample of Iranians. *Clinical Psychology & Psychotherapy*, cpp.2686. https://doi.org/10.1002/cpp.2686

Aktaş, S., Gülen, M., & Sevi, O. M. (2019). Mindfulness therapies for medically unexplained somatic symptoms: A systematic review. *Psikiyatride Güncel Yaklaşımlar*, 11(3), 271–283. https://doi.org/10.18863/pgy.540852

Akyurek, G., Sezer, K. S., Kaya, L., & Temucin, K. (2019). Stigma in obsessive compulsive disorder. In N. Kocabasoglu & H. Bingol Caglayan (Eds.), *Anxiety disorders—From childhood to adulthood* (pp. 87–112). IntechOpen. https://doi.org/10.5772/intechopen.83642

Alam, N., Ali, S., Akbar, N., Ilyas, M., Ahmed, H., Mustafa, A., Khurram, S., Sajid, Z., Ullah, N., Qayyum, S., Rahim, T., Usman, M. S., Ali, N., Khan, I., Pervez, K., Sumaira, B., Ali, N., Sultana, N., Tanoli, A. Y., & Islam, M. (2021). Association study of six candidate genes with major depressive disorder in the North-Western population of Pakistan. *PLOS ONE*, 16(8), e0248454. https://doi.org/10.1371/journal.pone.0248454

Alanko, K., Gunst, A., Mokros, A., & Santtila, P. (2016). Genetic variants associated with male pedophilic sexual interest. *Journal of Sexual Medicine*, 13(5), 835–842. https://doi.org/10.1016/j.jsxm.2016.02.170

Alanko, K., Salo, B., Mokros, A., & Santtila, P. (2013). Evidence for heritability of adult men's sexual interest in youth under age 16 from a population-based extended twin design. *Journal of Sexual Medicine*, 10(4), 1090–1099. https://doi.org/10.1111/jsm.12067

Alareeki, A., Lashewicz, B., & Shipton, L. (2019). "Get your child in order:" Illustrations of courtesy stigma from fathers raising both autistic and non-autistic children. *Disability Studies Quarterly*, 39(4), Article 4. https://doi.org/10.18061/dsq.v39i4.6501

Alasmari, F. (2020). Caffeine induces neurobehavioral effects through modulating neurotransmitters. *Saudi Pharmaceutical Journal*, 28(4), 445–451. https://doi.org/10.1016/j.jsps.2020.02.005

Albaugh, M. D., Ottino-Gonzalez, J., Sidwell, A., Lepage, C., Juliano, A., Owens, M. M., Chaarani, B., Spechler, P., Fontaine, N., Rioux, P., Lewis, L., Jeon, S., Evans, A., D'Souza, D., Radhakrishnan, R., Banaschewski, T., Bokde, A. L. W., Quinlan, E. B., Conrod, P., … IMAGEN Consortium. (2021). Association of cannabis use during adolescence with neurodevelopment. *JAMA Psychiatry*, 78(9), 1031. https://doi.org/10.1001/jamapsychiatry.2021.1258

Albertson, T. E. (2012). Opiates and opioids. In K. R. Olson (Ed.), *Poisoning & Drug Overdose* (6th ed.). The McGraw Hill Companies.

Albery, I. P., Spada, M. M., & Nikčević, A. V. (2021). The COVID-19 anxiety syndrome and selective attentional bias towards COVID-19-related stimuli in UK residents during the 2020–2021 pandemic. *Clinical Psychology & Psychotherapy*, 28(6), 1367–1378. https://doi.org/10.1002/cpp.2639

Albus, C. (2010). Psychological and social factors in coronary heart disease. *Annals of Medicine*, 42(7), 487–494. https://doi.org/10.3109/07853890.2010.515605

Alcoholics Anonymous. (n.d.). *A.A. around the world*. Retrieved August 31, 2022, from https://www.aa.org/aa-around-the-world

Alcoholics Anonymous. (2014). *2014 membership survey*. http://www.aa.org/assets/en_US/p-48_membership-survey.pdf

Alda, M. (2015). Lithium in the treatment of bipolar disorder: Pharmacology and pharmacogenetics. *Molecular Psychiatry*, 20(6), 661–670. https://doi.org/10.1038/mp.2015.4

Aldarondo, E. (2007). *Advancing social justice through clinical practice*. Lawrence Erlbaum.

Alexander, F., & French, T. (1946). *Psychoanalytic therapy: Principles and applications*. Ronald Press.

Alfalahi, M., Mahadevan, S., Balushi, R. al, Chan, M. F., Saadon, M. A., Al-Adawi, S., & Qoronfleh, M. W. (2021). Prevalence of eating disorders and disordered eating in Western Asia: A systematic review and meta-Analysis. *Eating Disorders*, 0(0), 1–30. https://doi.org/10.1080/10640266.2021.1969495

Alfano, V., Mele, G., Cotugno, A., & Longarzo, M. (2020). Multimodal neuroimaging in anorexia nervosa. *Journal of Neuroscience Research*, 98(11), 2178–2207. https://doi.org/10.1002/jnr.24674

Allen, B. (2016). A RADical idea: A call to eliminate "attachment disorder" and "attachment therapy" from the clinical lexicon. *Evidence-Based Practice in Child and Adolescent Mental Health*, 1(1), 60–71. https://doi.org/10.1080/23794925.2016.1117958

Allen, J. G., & Smith, W. H. (1993). Diagnosing dissociative disorders. *Bulletin of the Menninger Clinic*, 57(3), 328–343.

Allen, J. P., Hauser, S. T., & Borman-Spurrell, E. (1996). Attachment theory as a framework for understanding sequelae of severe adolescent psychopathology: An 11-year follow-up study. *Journal of Consulting and Clinical Psychology*, 64(2), 254–263. https://doi.org/10.1037/0022-006X.64.2.254

Allen, L. A., & Woolfolk, R. L. (2010). Cognitive behavioral therapy for somatoform disorders. *Psychiatric Clinics of North America*, 33(3), 579–593. https://doi.org/10.1016/j.psc.2010.04.014

Allen, M. S., & Walter, E. E. (2019). Erectile dysfunction: An umbrella review of meta-analyses of risk-factors, treatment, and prevalence outcomes. *The Journal of Sexual Medicine*, 16(4), 531–541. https://doi.org/10.1016/j.jsxm.2019.01.314

Allen, N. B., & Badcock, P. B. T. (2006). Darwinian models of depression: A review of evolutionary accounts of mood and mood disorders. *Progress in Neuro-Psychopharmacology & Biological Psychiatry*, 30(5), 815–826. https://doi.org/10.1016/j.pnpbp.2006.01.007

Allen, S. J., Bharadwaj, R., Hyde, T. M., & Kleinman, J. E. (2021). Genetic neuropathology revisited: Gene expression in psychosis. In C. A. Tamminga, E. I. Ivleva, U. Reininghaus, & J. van Os (Eds.), *Psychotic disorders: Comprehensive conceptualization and treatments* (pp. 163–168). Oxford University Press.

Allik, J. (2005). Personality dimensions across cultures. *Journal of Personality Disorders*, 19(3), 212–232. https://doi.org/10.1521/pedi.2005.19.3.212

Allnutt, S., Samuels, A., & O'Driscoll, C. (2007). The insanity defence: From wild beasts to M'Naghten. *Australasian Psychiatry*, 15(4), 292–299. https://doi.org/10.1080/10398560701352181

Alm, P. A. (2004). Stuttering and the basal ganglia circuits: A critical review of possible relations. *Journal of Communication Disorders*, 37(4), 325–369. https://doi.org/10.1016/j.jcomdis.2004.03.001

Almås, E. (2016). Psychological treatment of sexual problems. Thematic analysis of guidelines and recommendations on a systematic literature review 2001–2010. *Sexual and Relationship Therapy*, 31(1), 54–69. https://doi.org/10.1080/14681994.2015.1086739

Almeida, H. S., Mitjans, M., Arias, B., Vieta, E., Ríos, J., & Benabarre, A. (2020). Genetic differences between bipolar disorder subtypes: A systematic review focused in bipolar disorder type II. *Neuroscience & Biobehavioral Reviews*, 118, 623–630. https://doi.org/10.1016/j.neubiorev.2020.07.033

Almli, L. M., Fani, N., Smith, A. K., & Ressler, K. J. (2014). Genetic approaches to understanding post-traumatic stress disorder. *International Journal of Neuropsychopharmacology*, 17(2), 355–370. https://doi.org/10.1017/S1461145713001090

Almohammed, O. A., Alsalem, A. A., Almangour, A. A., Alotaibi, L. H., Yami, M. S. A., & Lai, L. (2022). Antidepressants and health-related quality of life (HRQoL) for patients with depression: Analysis of the medical expenditure panel survey from the United States. *PLOS ONE*, 17(4), e0265928. https://doi.org/10.1371/journal.pone.0265928

Almond, K., & Allan, R. (2019). Incorporating MDMA as an adjunct in emotionally focused couples therapy with clients impacted by trauma or PTSD. *The Family Journal*, 27(3), 293–299. https://doi.org/10.1177/1066480719852360

Almurashi, H., Bouaziz, R., Alharthi, W., Al-Sarem, M., Hadwan, M., & Kammoun, S. (2022). Augmented reality, serious games and picture exchange communication system for people with ASD: Systematic literature review and future directions. *Sensors*, 22(3), Article 3. https://doi.org/10.3390/s22031250

Alpert, E., Hayes, A. M., Yasinski, C., Webb, C., & Deblinger, E. (2021). Processes of change in trauma-focused cognitive behavioral therapy for youth: An emotional processing theory informed approach. *Clinical Psychological Science: A Journal of the Association for Psychological Science*, 9(2), 270–283. https://doi.org/10.1177/2167702620957315

Alpert, H. R., Slater, M. E., Yoon, Y.-H., Chen, C. M., Winstanley, N., & Esser, M. B. (2022). Alcohol consumption and 15 causes of fatal injuries: A systematic review and meta-analysis. *American Journal of Preventive Medicine*, 63(2), 286–300. https://doi.org/10.1016/j.amepre.2022.03.025

Al-Qahtani, A. M., Shaikh, M. A. K., & Shaikh, I. A. (2018). Exercise as a treatment modality for depression: A narrative review. *Alexandria Journal of Medicine*, 54(4), 429–435. https://doi.org/10.1016/j.ajme.2018.05.004

Alqannad, E. M., Alharbi, A. S., Almansour, R. A., & Alghamdi, M. S. (2021). Alarm therapy in the treatment of enuresis in children: Types and efficacy review. *Cureus*, 13(8), Article e17358. https://doi.org/10.7759/cureus.17358

Alsayouf, H. A., Talo, H., & Biddappa, M. L. (2022). Core signs and symptoms in children with autism spectrum disorder improved after starting risperidone and aripiprazole in combination with standard

supportive therapies: A large, single-center, retrospective case series. *Brain Sciences*, 12(5). https://doi.org/10.3390/brainsci12050618

Alsharnoubi, J., Sabbour, A. A., Shoukry, A. I., & Abdelazeem, A. M. (2017). Nocturnal enuresis in children between laser acupuncture and medical treatment: A comparative study. *Lasers In Medical Science*, 32, 95–99. https://doi.org/10.1007/s10103-016-2090-9

Altemus, M. (2006). Sex differences in depression and anxiety disorders: Potential biological determinants. *Hormones and Behavior*, 50(4), 534–538. https://doi.org/10.1016/j.yhbeh.2006.06.031

Altemus, M., Sarvaiya, N., & Epperson, C. N. (2014). Sex differences in anxiety and depression clinical perspectives. *Frontiers in Neuroendocrinology*, 35(3), 320–330. https://doi.org/10.1016/j.yfrne.2014.05.004

Alvarez, R. P., Kirlic, N., Misaki, M., Bodurka, J., Rhudy, J. L., Paulus, M. P., & Drevets, W. C. (2015). Increased anterior insula activity in anxious individuals is linked to diminished perceived control. *Translational Psychiatry*, 5(6), e591–e591. https://doi.org/10.1038/tp.2015.84

Alves, C. D. B., & Cavalhieri, K. E. (2020). Self-perceived problematic pornography use: An integrative model from a research domain criteria and ecological perspective. *Sexuality & Culture: An Interdisciplinary Quarterly*, 24(5), 1619–1640. https://doi.org/10.1007/s12119-019-09680-w

Alzheimer's Association. (2022). 2022 Alzheimer's disease facts and figures. *Alzheimer's & Dementia*, 18(4), 700–789. https://doi.org/10.1002/alz.12638

Alzheimer's Society. (2017, April 15). *Can stress cause dementia?* https://www.alzheimers.org.uk/blog/can-stress-cause-dementia

Amad, A., Ramoz, N., Thomas, P., Jardri, R., & Gorwood, P. (2014). Genetics of borderline personality disorder: Systematic review and proposal of an integrative model. *Neuroscience & Biobehavioral Reviews*, 40, 6–19. https://doi.org/10.1016/j.neubiorev.2014.01.003

Amaresha, A. C., & Venkatasubramanian, G. (2012). Expressed emotion in schizophrenia: An overview. *Indian Journal of Psychological Medicine*, 34(1), 12–20. https://doi.org/10.4103/0253-7176.96149

Amaro, H., Sanchez, M., Bautista, T., & Cox, R. (2021). Social vulnerabilities for substance use: Stressors, socially toxic environments, and discrimination and racism. *Neuropharmacology*, 188, 108518. https://doi.org/10.1016/j.neuropharm.2021.108518

Ambrogne, J. A. (2002). Reduced-risk drinking as a treatment goal: What clinicians need to know. *Journal of Substance Abuse Treatment*, 22(1), 45–53. https://doi.org/10.1016/S0740-5472(01)00210-0

American Academy of Professional Coders. (2019, August 16). *US gets the ball rolling on ICD-11*. AAPC Knowledge Center. https://www.aapc.com/blog/48275-us-gets-the-ball-rolling-on-icd-11/

American Addiction Centers. (2022, July 18). *The history of alcohol throughout the world*. Recovery.Org. https://recovery.org/alcohol-addiction/history/

American Psychiatric Association. (n.d.-a). *A guide for working with transgender and gender nonconforming patients: Medical treatment and surgical interventions*. Psychiatry.Org. Retrieved July 15, 2022, from https://psychiatry.org/psychiatrists/cultural-competency/transgender-and-gender-nonconforming-patients/gender-affirming-therapy

American Psychiatric Association. (n.d.-b). *A guide for working with transgender and gender nonconforming patients: Terminology*. Psychiatry.Org. Retrieved July 15, 2022, from https://psychiatry.org/psychiatrists/diversity/education/transgender-and-gender-nonconforming-patients/terminology

American Psychiatric Association. (n.d.-c). *DSM-5-TR online assessment measures*. Retrieved September 4, 2022, from https://psychiatry.org:443/psychiatrists/practice/dsm/educational-resources/assessment-measures

American Psychiatric Association. (n.d.-d). *What is psychiatry?* https://www.psychiatry.org/patients-families/what-is-psychiatry

American Psychiatric Association. (1952). *Diagnostic and statistical manual of mental disorders*. Author.

American Psychiatric Association. (1980). *Diagnostic and statistical manual of mental disorders* (3rd ed.). Author.

American Psychiatric Association. (1987). *Diagnostic and statistical manual of mental disorders* (3rd ed., revised). Author.

American Psychiatric Association. (1994). *Diagnostic and statistical manual of mental disorders* (4th ed.). Author.

American Psychiatric Association. (1998). *Position statement on psychiatric treatment and sexual orientation*. Author.

American Psychiatric Association. (2000a). *Diagnostic and statistical manual of mental disorders* (4th ed., text revision). Author.

American Psychiatric Association. (2000b). Position statement on therapies focused on attempts to change sexual orientation (reparative or conversion therapies). *The American Journal of Psychiatry, 157*(10), 1719–1721.

American Psychiatric Association. (2013). *Diagnostic and statistical manual of mental disorders* (5th ed.). https://dx.doi.org/10.1176/appi.books.9780890425596

American Psychiatric Association. (2018). *What is mental illness?* https://www.psychiatry.org/patients-families/what-is-mental-illness

American Psychiatric Association. (2022). *Diagnostic and statistical manual of mental disorders* (5th ed., text revision). https://doi.org/10.1176/appi.books.9780890425787

American Psychological Association. (n.d.-a). *Anxiety*. http://www.apa.org/topics/anxiety

American Psychological Association. (n.d.-b). Coming out. In *APA Dictionary of psychology*. Retrieved July 15, 2022, from https://dictionary.apa.org/coming-out

American Psychological Association. (n.d.-c). Gender. In *APA Dictionary of psychology*. Retrieved July 15, 2022, from https://dictionary.apa.org/gender

American Psychological Association. (n.d.-d). Heterosexism. In *APA Dictionary of psychology*. Retrieved July 15, 2022, from https://dictionary.apa.org/heterosexism

American Psychological Association. (n.d.-e). Personality. In *APA Dictionary of psychology*. Retrieved September 2, 2022, from https://dictionary.apa.org/personality

American Psychological Association. (n.d.-f). Sex. In *APA Dictionary of psychology*. Retrieved July 15, 2022, from https://dictionary.apa.org/sex

American Psychological Association. (n.d.-g). Sexual orientation. In *APA Dictionary of psychology*. Retrieved July 15, 2022, from https://dictionary.apa.org/sexual-orientation

American Psychological Association. (n.d.-h). Stress. In *APA Dictionary of psychology*. Retrieved March 23, 2022, from https://dictionary.apa.org/stress

American Psychological Association. (n.d.-i). Trait theories. In *APA Dictionary of psychology*. Retrieved September 2, 2022, from https://dictionary.apa.org/

American Psychological Association. (2012). Guidelines for psychological practice with lesbian, gay, and bisexual clients. *American Psychologist, 67*, 10–42. https://doi.org/10.1037/a0024659

American Psychological Association. (2017a). *Multicultural guidelines: An ecological approach to context, identity, and intersectionality*. American Psychological Association. https://doi.org/10.1037/e501962018-001

American Psychological Association. (2017b, March). *Ethical principles of psychologists and code of conduct*. https://www.apa.org/ethics/code

American Psychological Association. (2017c, March 23). *The hierarchical taxonomy of psychopathology (HiTOP)*. https://www.apa.org/pubs/highlights/spotlight/issue-88

American Psychological Association. (2020). *Stress in America™ 2020: A national mental health crisis*. https://www.apa.org/news/press/releases/stress/2020/sia-mental-health-crisis.pdf

American Psychological Association. (2021a). *APA resolution on gender identity change efforts*. https://www.apa.org/about/policy/resolution-gender-identity-change-efforts.pdf

American Psychological Association. (2021b). *Guidelines for psychological practice with sexual minority persons*. https://www.apa.org/about/policy/psychological-sexual-minority-persons.pdf

American Psychological Association. (2022a, June 1). What does it mean to be "incompetent to stand trial"? *Monitor on Psychology, 53*(4), 64.

American Psychological Association. (2022b, November 15). *Psychologists struggle to meet demand amid mental health crisis: 2022 COVID-19 practitioner impact survey*. https://www.apa.org/pubs/reports/practitioner/2022-covid-psychologist-workload

American Psychological Association Guideline Development Panel for the Treatment of PTSD in Adults. (2017). *Clinical practice guideline for the treatment of posttraumatic stress disorder (PTSD) in adults*. American Psychological Association. https://doi.org/10.1037/e501872017-001

American Society of Addiction Medicine. (2019, September 15). *Definition of addiction*. https://www.asam.org/quality-care/definition-of-addiction

Ameye, H., & Swinnen, J. (2019). Obesity, income and gender: The changing global relationship. *Global Food Security, 23*, 267–281. https://doi.org/10.1016/j.gfs.2019.09.003

Amianto, F., Caroppo, P., D'Agata, F., Spalatro, A., Lavagnino, L., Caglio, M., Righi, D., Bergui, M., Abbate-Daga, G., Rigardetto, R., Mortara, P., & Fassino, S. (2013). Brain volumetric abnormalities in patients with anorexia and bulimia nervosa: A voxel-based morphometry study. *Psychiatry Research: Neuroimaging, 213*(3), 210–216. https://doi.org/10.1016/j.pscychresns.2013.03.010

Amini Pozveh, Z., & Saleh, Z. (2020). The role of social skills in the prevention of drug addiction in adolescents. *Advanced Biomedical Research, 9*, 41. https://doi.org/10.4103/abr.abr_99_20

Amodeo, M. (2015). The addictive personality. *Substance Use & Misuse, 50*(8–9), 1031–1036. https://doi.org/10.3109/10826084.2015.1007646

Amoretti, M. C., Lalumera, E., & Serpico, D. (2021). The DSM-5 introduction of the Social (Pragmatic) Communication Disorder as a new mental disorder: A philosophical review. *History and Philosophy of the Life Sciences, 43*(4), Article 108. https://doi.org/10.1007/s40656-021-00460-0

Amos, T., Stein, D. J., & Ipser, J. C. (2014). Pharmacological interventions for preventing post-traumatic stress disorder (PTSD). *Cochrane Database of Systematic Reviews, 2014*(7), Article CD006239. https://doi.org/10.1002/14651858.CD006239.pub2

Anand, A., Mathew, S. J., Sanacora, G., Murrough, J. W., Goes, F. S., Altinay, M., Aloysi, A. S., Asghar-Ali, A. A., Barnett, B. S., Chang, L. C., Collins, K. A., Costi, S., Iqbal, S., Jha, M. K., Krishnan, K., Malone, D. A., Nikayin, S., Nissen, S. E., Ostroff, R. B., … Hu, B. (2023). Ketamine versus ECT for nonpsychotic treatment-resistant major depression. *New England Journal of Medicine*. Advance online publication. https://doi.org/10.1056/NEJMoa2302399

Anastasi, A., & Urbina, S. (1997). *Psychological testing* (7th ed.). Prentice Hall.

Anastopoulos, A. D., King, K. A., Besecker, L. H., O'Rourke, S. R., Bray, A. C., & Supple, A. J. (2020). Cognitive-behavioral therapy for college students with ADHD: Temporal stability of improvements in functioning following active treatment. *Journal of Attention Disorders, 24*(6), 863–874. https://doi.org/10.1177/1087054717749932

Anders, S., Tanaka, M., & Kinney, D. K. (2013). Depression as an evolutionary strategy for defense against infection. *Brain, Behavior, and Immunity, 31*, 9–22. https://doi.org/10.1016/j.bbi.2012.12.002

Anderson, E. L., Howe, L. D., Wade, K. H., Ben-Shlomo, Y., Hill, W. D., Deary, I. J., Sanderson, E. C., Zheng, J.,

Korologou-Linden, R., Stergiakouli, E., Davey Smith, G., Davies, N. M., & Hemani, G. (2020). Education, intelligence and Alzheimer's disease: Evidence from a multivariable two-sample Mendelian randomization study. *International Journal of Epidemiology, 49*(4), 1163–1172. https://doi.org/10.1093/ije/dyz280

Anderson, I. M. (2021). Electroconvulsive therapy (ECT) versus sham ECT for depression: Do study limitations invalidate the evidence (and mean we should stop using ECT)? *BJPsych Advances, 27*(5), 285–291. https://doi.org/10.1192/bja.2021.23

Anderson, K. K., & Mukherjee, S. D. (2007). The need for additional safeguards in the informed consent process in schizophrenia research. *Journal of Medical Ethics: Journal of the Institute of Medical Ethics, 33*(11), 647–650. https://doi.org/10.1136/jme.2006.017376

Anderson, K. N., Jeon, A. B., Blenner, J. A., Wiener, R. L., & Hope, D. A. (2015). How people evaluate others with social anxiety disorder: A comparison to depression and general mental illness stigma. *American Journal of Orthopsychiatry, 85*(2), 131–138. https://doi.org/10.1037/ort0000046

Anderson, L. M., Berg, H., Brown, T. A., Menzel, J., & Reilly, E. E. (2021). The role of disgust in eating disorders. *Current Psychiatry Reports, 23*(2), 4. https://doi.org/10.1007/s11920-020-01217-5

Anderson, R. E., McKenny, M., Mitchell, A., Koku, L., & Stevenson, H. C. (2018). EMBRacing racial stress and trauma: Preliminary feasibility and coping responses of a racial socialization intervention. *Journal of Black Psychology, 44*(1), 25–46. https://doi.org/10.1177/0095798417732930

Andersson, G., & Ghaderi, A. (2006). Overview and analysis of the behaviourist criticism of the *Diagnostic and statistical manual of mental disorders* (DSM). *Clinical Psychologist, 10*(2), 67–77. https://doi.org/10.1080/13284200600690461

Andreasen, N. C. (2010). Posttraumatic stress disorder: A history and a critique. *Annals of the New York Academy of Sciences, 1208*, 67–71. https://doi.org/10.1111/j.1749-6632.2010.05699.x

Andreassen, C. S. (2013). Work addiction. In P. M. Miller, S. A. Ball, M. E. Bates, A. W. Blume, K. M. Kampman, D. J. Kavanagh, M. E. Larimer, N. M. Petry, & P. De Witte (Eds.), *Comprehensive addictive behaviors and disorders: Vol. 1. Principles of addiction* (pp. 837–845). Elsevier Academic Press.

Andreasson, K., Krogh, J., Wenneberg, C., Jessen, H. K. L., Krakauer, K., Gluud, C., Thomsen, R. R., Randers, L., & Nordentoft, M. (2016). Effectiveness of dialectical behavior therapy versus collaborative assessment and management of suicidality treatment for reduction of self-harm in adults with borderline personality traits and disorder—A randomized observer-blinded clinical trial. *Depression and Anxiety, 33*(6), 520–530. https://doi.org/10.1002/da.22472

Andrén, P., Jakubovski, E., Murphy, T. L., Woitecki, K., Tarnok, Z., Zimmerman-Brenner, S., van de Griendt, J., Debes, N. M., Viefhaus, P., Robinson, S., Roessner, V., Ganos, C., Szejko, N., Müller-Vahl, K. R., Cath, D., Hartmann, A., & Verdellen, C. (2022). European clinical guidelines for Tourette syndrome and other tic disorders—version 2.0. Part II: Psychological interventions. *European Child & Adolescent Psychiatry, 31*(3), 403–423. https://doi.org/10.1007/s00787-021-01845-z

Andrews, D. A., & Bonta, J. (2010). Rehabilitating criminal justice policy and practice. *Psychology, Public Policy, and Law, 16*(1), 39–55. https://doi.org/10.1037/a0018362

Andrews, G., Bell, C., Boyce, P., Gale, C., Lampe, L., Marwat, O., Rapee, R., & Wilkins, G. (2018). Royal Australian and New Zealand College of Psychiatrists clinical practice guidelines for the treatment of panic disorder, social anxiety disorder and generalised anxiety disorder. *Australian & New Zealand Journal of Psychiatry, 52*(12), 1109–1172. https://doi.org/10.1177/0004867418799453

Andrews, J. (2007a). The (un)dress of the mad poor in England, c.1650-1850. Part 1. *History of Psychiatry, 18*(1), 5–24. https://doi.org/10.1177/0957154X07067245

Andrews, J. (2007b). The (un)dress of the mad poor in England, c.1650-1850. Part 2. *History of Psychiatry, 18*(2), 131–156. https://doi.org/10.1177/0957154X06067246

Andrews, P. W., & Thomson, J. A. (2009). The bright side of being blue: Depression as an adaptation for analyzing complex problems. *Psychological Review, 116*(3), 620–654. https://doi.org/10.1037/a0016242

Angell, B., Cooke, A., & Kovac, K. (2005). First-person accounts of stigma. In P. W. Corrigan (Ed.), *On the stigma of mental illness: Practical strategies for research and social change* (pp. 69–98). American Psychological Association.

Angier, N. (2003, June 22). Short men, short shrift. Are drugs the answer? *The New York Times.*

Angleitner, A., & Ostendorf, F. (1994). Temperament and the Big Five factors of personality. In Jr. Halverson Charles F., G. A. Kohnstamm, & R. P. Martin (Eds.), *The developing structure of temperament and personality from infancy to adulthood* (pp. 69–90). Lawrence Erlbaum.

Anglin, D. M., Ereshefsky, S., Klaunig, M. J., Bridgwater, M. A., Niendam, T. A., Ellman, L. M., DeVylder, J., Thayer, G., Bolden, K., Musket, C. W., Grattan, R. E., Lincoln, S. H., Schiffman, J., Lipner, E., Bachman, P., Corcoran, C. M., Mota, N. B., & van der Ven, E. (2021). From womb to neighborhood: A racial analysis of social determinants of psychosis in the United States. *American Journal of Psychiatry, 178*(7), 599–610. https://doi.org/10.1176/appi.ajp.2020.20071091

Anglin, R., Moayyedi, P., & Leontiadis, G. I. (2015). Anti-inflammatory intervention in depression: Comment. *JAMA Psychiatry, 72*(5), 512–512. https://doi.org/10.1001/jamapsychiatry.2014.3246

Angst, J., Ajdacic-Gross, V., & Rössler, W. (2020). Bipolar disorders in ICD-11: Current status and strengths. *International Journal of Bipolar Disorders, 8*(1), 3. https://doi.org/10.1186/s40345-019-0165-9

Angus, L. (2012). Toward an integrative understanding of narrative and emotion processes in emotion-focused therapy of depression: Implications for theory, research and practice. *Psychotherapy Research, 22*(4), 367–380. https://doi.org/10.1080/10503307.2012.683988

Angus, L., Watson, J. C., Elliott, R., Schneider, K., & Timulak, L. (2015). Humanistic psychotherapy research 1990–2015: From methodological innovation to evidence-supported treatment outcomes and beyond. *Psychotherapy Research, 25*(3), 330–347. https://doi.org/10.1080/10503307.2014.989290

Annear, K. (2013, May 27). *The disorder formerly known as Asperger's.* http://www.abc.net.au/rampup/articles/2013/05/24/3766915.htm

Anney, R. J. L., Ripke, S., Anttila, V., Grove, J., Holmans, P., Huang, H., Klei, L., Lee, P. H., Medland, S. E., Neale, B., Robinson, E., Weiss, L. A., Zwaigenbaum, L., Yu, T. W., Wittemeyer, K., Willsey, A. J., Wijsman, E. M., Werge, T., Wassink, T. H., … The Autism Spectrum Disorders Working Group of The Psychiatric Genomics Consortium. (2017). Meta-analysis of GWAS of over 16,000 individuals with autism spectrum disorder highlights a novel locus at 10q24.32 and a significant overlap with schizophrenia. *Molecular Autism, 8*(1), 21. https://doi.org/10.1186/s13229-017-0137-9

Antoine, M. W., Langberg, T., Schnepel, P., & Feldman, D. E. (2019). Increased excitation-inhibition ratio stabilizes synapse and circuit excitability in four autism mouse models. *Neuron, 101*(4), 648-661.e4. https://doi.org/10.1016/j.neuron.2018.12.026

Antonsen, B. T., Klungsøyr, O., Kamps, A., Hummelen, B., Johansen, M. S., Pedersen, G., Urnes, Ø., Kvarstein, E. H., Karterud, S., & Wilberg, T. (2014). Step-down versus outpatient psychotherapeutic treatment for personality disorders: 6-year follow-up of the Ulleväl personality project. *BMC Psychiatry, 14.* https://doi.org/10.1186/1471-244X-14-119

APA Practice Organization. (2013, Fall). Duty to protect. *Good Practice, 2–5.*

Apaydin, E. A., Maher, A. R., Shanman, R., Booth, M. S., Miles, J. N. V., Sorbero, M. E., & Hempel, S. (2016). A systematic review of St. John's wort for major depressive disorder. *Systematic Reviews, 5*(1), 148. https://doi.org/10.1186/s13643-016-0325-2

Appel, G., Zaidi, S. R., Han, B. H., Avery, J. J., & Avery, J. D. (2020). A call for increased psychiatric training in emergency medicine: Physician attitudes toward substance use disorders and co-occurring borderline personality disorder. *The Primary Care Companion for CNS Disorders, 22*(4), 26579. https://doi.org/10.4088/PCC.20br02674

Apple, R. F. (1999). Interpersonal therapy for bulimia nervosa. *Journal of Clinical Psychology, 55*(6), 715–725. https://doi.org/10.1002/(SICI)1097-4679(199906)55:63.0.CO;2-B

Archer, J. (2001). Grief from an evolutionary perspective. In M. S. Stroebe, R. O. Hansson, W. Stroebe, & H. Schut (Eds.), *Handbook of bereavement research: Consequences, coping, and care* (pp. 263–283). American Psychological Association. https://doi.org/10.1037/10436-011

Arda, E., Cakiroglu, B., & Thomas, D. T. (2016). Primary nocturnal enuresis: A review. *Nephro-Urology Monthly, 8*(4), Article e35809. https://doi.org/10.5812/numonthly.35809

Arena, R., Laddu, D., Severin, R., Hall, G., & Bond, S. (2021). Healthy living and social justice: Addressing the current syndemic in underserved communities. *Journal of Cardiopulmonary Rehabilitation and Prevention, 41*(3), E5–E6. https://doi.org/10.1097/HCR.0000000000000612

Arenella, M., Cadby, G., De Witte, W., Jones, R. M., Whitehouse, A. J., Moses, E. K., Fornito, A., Bellgrove, M. A., Hawi, Z., Johnson, B., Tiego, J., Buitelaar, J. K., Kiemeney, L. A., Poelmans, G., & Bralten, J. (2022). Potential role for immune-related genes in autism spectrum disorders: Evidence from genome-wide association meta-analysis of autistic traits. *Autism, 26*(2), 361–372. https://doi.org/10.1177/13623613211019547

Arimitsu, K., Hitokoto, H., Kind, S., & Hofmann, S. G. (2019). Differences in compassion, well-being, and social anxiety between Japan and the USA. *Mindfulness, 10*(5), 854–862. https://doi.org/10.1007/s12671-018-1045-6

Aring, C. D. (1974). The Gheel experience: Eternal spirit of the chainless mind. *JAMA: Journal of the American Medical Association, 230*(7), 998–1001. https://doi.org/10.1001/jama.230.7.998

Arizmendi, B. J., & O'Connor, M.-F. (2015). What is "normal" in grief? *Australian Critical Care, 28*(2), 58–62. https://doi.org/10.1016/j.aucc.2015.01.005

Arkhipov, V. I. (1999). Memory dissociation: The approach to the study of retrieval processes. *Behavioural Brain Research, 106*(1–2), 39–46. https://doi.org/10.1016/S0166-4328(99)00090-X

Armando, M., Pontillo, M., & Vicari, S. (2015). Psychosocial interventions for very early and early-onset schizophrenia: A review of treatment efficacy. *Current Opinion in Psychiatry, 28*(4), 312–323. https://doi.org/10.1097/YCO.0000000000000165

Armitage, H. (2015, August 24). How does the new "female Viagra" work? *Science.* http://www.sciencemag.org/news/2015/08/how-does-new-female-viagra-work

Armon, G. (2014). Personality and serum lipids: Does lifestyle account for their concurrent and long-term relationships. *European Journal of Personality, 28*(6), 550–559. https://doi.org/10.1002/per.1943

Armstrong, L. L. (2006). Barriers to intimate sexuality: Concerns and meaning-based therapy approaches. *The Humanistic Psychologist, 34*(3), 281–298. https://doi.org/10.1207/s15473333thp3403_5

Armstrong, T. (1995). *The myth of the A.D.D. child: 50 ways to improve your child's attention span without drugs, labels, or coercion.* Plume.

Arnedo, J., Svrakic, D. M., Del Val, C., Romero-Zaliz, R., Hernández-Cuervo, H., Fanous, A. H., Pato, M. T., Pato, C. N., de Erausquin, G. A., Cloninger, R., & Zwir, I. (2015). Uncovering the hidden risk architecture of the schizophrenias: Confirmation in three independent genome-wide association studies. *The American Journal of Psychiatry, 172*(2), 139–153. https://doi.org/10.1176/appi.ajp.2014.14040435

Arnone, D., McIntosh, A. M., Ebmeier, K. P., Munafò, M. R., & Anderson, I. M. (2012). Magnetic resonance imaging studies in unipolar depression: Systematic review and meta-regression analyses. *European Neuropsychopharmacology, 22*(1), 1–16. https://doi.org/10.1016/j.euroneuro.2011.05.003

Arnott, S., Onslow, M., O'Brian, S., Packman, A., Jones, M., & Block, S. (2014). Group Lidcombe Program treatment for early stuttering: A randomized controlled trial. *Journal of Speech, Language, and Hearing Research, 57*(5), 1606–1618. https://doi.org/10.1044/2014_JSLHR-S-13-0090

Arnsten, A. F. T. (2006). Fundamentals of attention-deficit/hyperactivity disorder: Circuits and pathways. *The Journal of Clinical Psychiatry, 67*(Suppl. 8), 7–12.

Arntz, A., & van Genderen, H. (2021). *Schema therapy for borderline personality disorder* (2nd ed.). Wiley-Blackwell.

Arntz, A., van Genderen, H., Drost, J., Sendt, K., & Baumgarten-Kustner, S. (2009). *Schema therapy for borderline personality disorder.* Wiley-Blackwell.

Aromaa, E., Tolvanen, A., Tuulari, J., & Wahlbeck, K. (2011). Personal stigma and use of mental health services among people with depression in a general population in Finland. *BMC Psychiatry, 11.* https://doi.org/10.1186/1471-244X-11-52

Arts, N. J., Walvoort, S. J., & Kessels, R. P. (2017). Korsakoff's syndrome: A critical review. *Neuropsychiatric Disease and Treatment, 13*, 2875–2890. https://doi.org/10.2147/NDT.S130078

Asami, T., Hyuk Lee, S., Bouix, S., Rathi, Y., Whitford, T. J., Niznikiewicz, M., Nestor, P., McCarley, R. W., Shenton, M. E., & Kubicki, M. (2014). Cerebral white matter abnormalities and their associations with negative but not positive symptoms of schizophrenia. *Psychiatry Research: Neuroimaging, 222*(1–2), 52–59. https://doi.org/10.1016/j.pscychresns.2014.02.007

Asher, M., Asnaani, A., & Aderka, I. M. (2017). Gender differences in social anxiety disorder: A review. *Clinical Psychology Review, 56*, 1–12. https://doi.org/10.1016/j.cpr.2017.05.004

Ashiq, A., Riaz, M. N., & Riaz, M. A. (2018). Direct and indirect effect of childhood traumatic experiences on cluster-b personality disorders in adults. *Pakistan Journal of Medical Research, 5.*

Ashley, F. (2019). Gatekeeping hormone replacement therapy for transgender patients is dehumanising. *Journal of Medical Ethics, 45*(7), 480–482. https://doi.org/10.1136/medethics-2018-105293

Ashley, F. (2021). The misuse of gender dysphoria: Toward greater conceptual clarity in transgender health. *Perspectives on Psychological Science, 16*(6), 1159–1164. https://doi.org/10.1177/1745691619872987

Ashworth, D. K., Sletten, T. L., Junge, M., Simpson, K., Clarke, D., Cunnington, D., & Rajaratnam, S. M. W. (2015). A randomized controlled trial of cognitive behavioral therapy for insomnia: An effective treatment for comorbid insomnia and depression. *Journal of Counseling Psychology, 62*(2), 115–123. https://doi.org/10.1037/cou0000059

Ask, H., Cheesman, R., Jami, E. S., Levey, D. F., Purves, K. L., & Weber, H. (2021). Genetic contributions to anxiety disorders: Where we are and where we are heading. *Psychological Medicine, 51*(13), 2231–2246. https://doi.org/10.1017/S0033291720005486

Ask, H., Waaktaar, T., Seglem, K. B., & Torgersen, S. (2016). Common etiological sources of anxiety, depression, and somatic complaints in adolescents: A multiple rater twin study. *Journal of Abnormal Child Psychology*, *44*(1), 101–114. https://doi.org/10.1007/s10802-015-9977-y

Askham, A. V. (2022, March 2). As the pandemic wanes, will autism diagnoses rise in its wake? *Spectrum: Autism Research News*. https://www.spectrumnews. org/news/as-the-pandemic-wanes-will-autism-diagnoses-rise-in-its-wake/

Asmundson, G. J. G., Taylor, S., & Smits, J. A. J. (2014). Panic disorder and agoraphobia: An overview and commentary on DSM-5 changes. *Depression and Anxiety*, *31*(6), 480–486. https://doi.org/10.1002/da.22277

Asperger, H. (1991). Autistic psycopathy in childhood. In U. Frith (Ed.), *Autism and asperger syndrome*. Cambridge University Press. https://doi.org/10.1017/cbo9780511526770.002

Assal, F. (2019). History of dementia. *Frontiers of Neurology and Neuroscience*, *44*, 118–126. https://doi.org/10.1159/000494959

Assari, S., & DeFreitas, M. R. (2018). Ethnic variations in psychosocial and health correlates of eating disorders. *Healthcare (Basel, Switzerland)*, *6*(2), E38. https://doi.org/10.3390/healthcare6020038

Assumpção, A. A., Garcia, F. D., Garcia, H. D., Bradford, J. M. W., & Thibaut, F. (2014). Pharmacologic treatment of paraphilias. *Psychiatric Clinics of North America*, *37*(2), 173–181. https://doi.org/10.1016/j.psc.2014.03.002

Astbury, J. (2010). The social causes of women's depression: A question of rights violated? In D. C. Jack & A. Ali (Eds.), *Silencing the self across cultures: Depression and gender in the social world* (pp. 19–45). Oxford University Press.

Astill Wright, L., Sijbrandij, M., Sinnerton, R., Lewis, C., Roberts, N. P., & Bisson, J. I. (2019). Pharmacological prevention and early treatment of post-traumatic stress disorder and acute stress disorder: A systematic review and meta-analysis. *Translational Psychiatry*, *9*(1), 1–10. https://doi.org/10.1038/s41398-019-0673-5

Atri, A. (2019). The Alzheimer's disease clinical spectrum: Diagnosis and management. *Medical Clinics*, *103*(2), 263–293. https://doi.org/10.1016/j.mcna.2018.10.009

Attademo, L., Bernardini, F., & Verdolini, N. (2021). Neural correlates of schizotypal personality disorder: A systematic review of neuroimaging and EEG studies. *Current Medical Imaging*, *17*(11), 1283–1298. https://doi.org/10.2174/1573405617666210114142206

Attia, E., Becker, A. E., Bryant-Waugh, R., Hoek, H. W., Kreipe, R. E., Marcus, M. D., Mitchell, J. E., Striegel, R. H., Walsh, B. T., Wilson, G. T., Wolfe, B. E., & Wonderlich, S. (2013). Feeding and eating disorders in DSM-5. *The American Journal of Psychiatry*, *170*(11), 1237–1239. https://doi.org/10.1176/appi.ajp.2013.13030326

Attia, E., & Roberto, C. A. (2009). Should amenorrhea be a diagnostic criterion for anorexia nervosa? *International Journal of Eating Disorders*, *42*(7), 581–589. https://doi.org/10.1002/eat.20720

Atwood, J. D. (2015). Sexual disorders and sex therapy. In J. L. Wetchler & L. L. Hecker (Eds.), *An introduction to marriage and family therapy* (2nd ed., pp. 431–467). Routledge.

Atwood, M. E., & Friedman, A. (2020). A systematic review of enhanced cognitive behavioral therapy (CBT-E) for eating disorders. *International Journal of Eating Disorders*, *53*(3), 311–330. https://doi.org/10.1002/eat.23206

Aucott, C., & Soni, A. (2016). Reflections on the use of critical incident stress debriefing in schools. *Educational Psychology in Practice*, *32*(1), 85–99. https://doi.org/10.1080/02667363.2015.1112257

Austin, A., & Craig, S. L. (2015). Transgender affirmative cognitive behavioral therapy: Clinical considerations and applications. *Professional Psychology: Research and Practice*, *46*(1), 21–29. https://doi.org/10.1037/a0038642

Austin, A., & Craig, S. L. (2019). Transgender affirmative cognitive-behavioral therapy. In J. E. Pachankis & S.

A. Safren (Eds.), *Handbook of evidence-based mental health practice with sexual and gender minorities* (pp. 74–96). Oxford University Press. https://doi.org/10.1093/med-psych/9780190669300.003.0004

Austin, A., Craig, S. L., & Alessi, E. J. (2017). Affirmative cognitive behavior therapy with transgender and gender nonconforming adults. *Psychiatric Clinics of North America*, *40*(1), 141–156. https://doi.org/10.1016/j.psc.2016.10.003

Austin, A., Craig, S. L., & D'Souza, S. A. (2018). An AFFIRMative cognitive behavioral intervention for transgender youth: Preliminary effectiveness. *Professional Psychology: Research and Practice*, *49*(1), 1–8. https://doi.org/10.1037/pro0000154

Austin, D. W., & Richards, J. C. (2001). The catastrophic misinterpretation model of panic disorder. *Behaviour Research and Therapy*, *39*(11), 1277–1291. https://doi.org/10.1016/S0005-7967(00)00095-4

Avery, D. (2022, August 8). *Marijuana laws in all 50 states*. CNET. https://www.cnet.com/news/politics/marijuana-laws-in-every-state/

Avery, J. D., & Avery, J. J. (Eds.). (2019). *The stigma of addiction: An essential guide*. Springer. https://doi.org/10.1007/978-3-030-02580-9

Ávila-Villanueva, M., Gómez-Ramírez, J., Maestú, F., Venero, C., Ávila, J., & Fernández-Blázquez, M. A. (2020). The role of chronic stress as a trigger for the Alzheimer disease continuum. *Frontiers in Aging Neuroscience*, *12*, Article 561504. https://doi.org/10.3389/fnagi.2020.561504

Awad, G. H., Kia-Keating, M., & Amer, M. M. (2019). A model of cumulative racial–ethnic trauma among Americans of Middle Eastern and North African (MENA) descent. *American Psychologist*, *74*(1), 76–87. https://doi.org/10.1037/amp0000344

Axline, V. M. (1947a). Nondirective therapy for poor readers. *Journal of Consulting Psychology*, *11*(2), 61–69. https://doi.org/10.1037/h0063079

Axline, V. M. (1947b). *Play therapy; the inner dynamics of childhood* (1948-00732-000). Houghton Mifflin.

Axline, V. M. (1950). Play therapy experiences as described by child participants. *Journal of Consulting Psychology*, *14*(1), 53–63. https://doi.org/10.1037/h0056179

Axline, V. M. (1964). *Dibs: In search of self*. Ballantine Books.

Aydogmus, M. E. (2020). Social stigma towards people with medically unexplained symptoms: The somatic symptom disorder. *Psychiatric Quarterly*, *91*(2), 349–361. https://doi.org/10.1007/s11126-019-09704-6

Ayling, K., Jia, R., Coupland, C., Chalder, T., Massey, A., Broadbent, E., & Vedhara, K. (2022). Psychological predictors of self-reported COVID-19 outcomes: Results from a prospective cohort study. *Annals of Behavioral Medicine*, kaab106. https://doi.org/10.1093/abm/kaab106

Azibo, D. A. (2014). The Azibo Nosology II: Epexegesis and 25th anniversary update: 55 culture-focused mental disorders suffered by African descent people. *The Journal of Pan African Studies*, *7*(5), 32–145.

Azibo, D. A. (2016). Thomas Szasz on psychiatric slavery vis-à-vis restoring the African personality: Exposing and clarifying ethical clashing. *Journal of Humanistic Psychology*, *56*(6), 665–693. https://doi.org/10.1177/0022167815613885

Azibo, D. A. ya. (2013). Unmasking materialistic depression as a mental health problem: Its effect on depression and materialism in an African–United States undergraduate sample. *Journal of Affective Disorders*, *150*(2), 623–628. https://doi.org/10.1016/j.jad.2013.03.001

Azrin, N. H., & Foxx, R. M. (1974). *Toilet training in less than a day*. Pocket Books.

Azzeh, M., Peachey, G., & Loney, T. (2022). Prevalence of high-risk disordered eating amongst adolescents and young adults in the middle east: A scoping review. *International Journal of Environmental Research and Public Health*, *19*(9), 5234. https://doi.org/10.3390/ijerph19095234

Azzone, P. (2013). *Depression as a psychoanalytic problem*. University Press of America.

Babor, T. F., Higgins-Biddle, J. C., & Robaina, K. (2016). *The Alcohol Use Disorders Identification Test, adapted for use in the United States: A guide for primary care practitioners*. Substance Abuse and Mental Health Services Administration.

Babor, T. F., Higgins-Biddle, J. C., Saunders, J. B., & Monteiro, M. G. (2001). *AUDIT: The Alcohol Use Disorders Identification Test: Guidelines for use in primary care* (2nd ed.). World Health Organization.

Bach, B., Kramer, U., Doering, S., Di Giacomo, E., Hutsebaut, J., Kaera, A., De Panfilis, C., Schmahl, C., Swales, M., Taubner, S., & Renneberg, B. (2022). The ICD-11 classification of personality disorders: A European perspective on challenges and opportunities. *Borderline Personality Disorder and Emotion Dysregulation*, *9*(1), 12. https://doi.org/10.1186/s40479-022-00182-0

Bach, B., Somma, A., & Keeley, J. W. (2021). Editorial: Entering the brave new world of icd-11 personality disorder diagnosis. *Frontiers in Psychiatry*, *12*, Article 793133. https://doi.org/10.3389/fpsyt.2021.793133

Bachmann, S. (2018). Epidemiology of suicide and the psychiatric perspective. *International Journal of Environmental Research and Public Health*, *15*(7), Article 7. https://doi.org/10.3390/ijerph15071425

Badcock, P. B., Davey, C. G., Whittle, S., Allen, N. B., & Friston, K. J. (2017). The depressed brain: An evolutionary systems theory. *Trends in Cognitive Sciences*, *21*(3), 182–194. https://doi.org/10.1016/j.tics.2017.01.005

Badenes-Ribera, L., Rubio-Aparicio, M., Sánchez-Meca, J., Fabris, M. A., & Longobardi, C. (2019). The association between muscle dysmorphia and eating disorder symptomatology: A systematic review and meta-analysis. *Journal of Behavioral Addictions*, *8*(3), 351–371. https://doi.org/10.1556/2006.8.2019.44

Badiani, A. (2013). Substance-specific environmental influences on drug use and drug preference in animals and humans. *Current Opinion in Neurobiology*, *23*(4), 588–596. https://doi.org/10.1016/j.conb.2013.03.010

Badiani, A., Belin, D., Epstein, D., Calu, D., & Shaham, Y. (2011). Opiate versus psychostimulant addiction: The differences do matter. *Nature Reviews Neuroscience*, *12*(11), 685–700. https://doi.org/10.1038/nrn3104

Baer, R. A. (2003). Mindfulness training as a clinical intervention: A conceptual and empirical review. *Clinical Psychology: Science and Practice*, *10*(2), 125–143.

Bafiti, T. V. (2001). The function of the parental family system and the sense of coherence as factors related to psychosomatic health. *Psychology: The Journal of the Hellenic Psychological Society*, *8*(2), 249–266.

Bagby, R. M., & Widiger, T. A. (2020). Assessment of the ICD-11 dimensional trait model: An introduction to the special section. *Psychological Assessment*, *32*(1), 1–7. https://doi.org/10.1037/pas0000785

Bahar-Fuchs, A., Martyr, A., Goh, A. M., Sabates, J., & Clare, L. (2019). Cognitive training for people with mild to moderate dementia. *Cochrane Database of Systematic Reviews*, *2019*(3), Article CD013069. https://doi.org/10.1002/14651858.CD013069.pub2

Baheretibeb, Y., Law, S., & Pain, C. (2008). The girl who ate her house–Pica as an obsessive-compulsive disorder: A case report. *Clinical Case Studies*, *7*(1), 3–11. https://doi.org/10.1177/1534650106298917

Bahji, A., Mazhar, M. N., Hudson, C. C., Nadkarni, P., MacNeil, B. A., & Hawken, E. (2019). Prevalence of substance use disorder comorbidity among individuals with eating disorders: A systematic review and meta-analysis. *Psychiatry Research*, *273*, 58–66. https://doi.org/10.1016/j.psychres.2019.01.007

Bahji, A., Stephenson, C., Tyo, R., Hawken, E. R., & Seitz, D. P. (2020). Prevalence of cannabis withdrawal symptoms among people with regular or dependent use of cannabinoids: A systematic review and meta-analysis. *JAMA Network Open*, *3*(4), e202370. https://doi.org/10.1001/jamanetworkopen.2020.2370

Bai, D., Yip, B. H. K., Windham, G. C., Sourander, A., Francis, R., Yoffe, R., Glasson, E., Mahjani, B., Suominen, A., Leonard, H., Gissler, M., Buxbaum, J. D., Wong, K., Schendel, D., Kodesh, A., Breshnahan, M., Levine, S. Z., Parner, E. T., Hansen, S. N., … Sandin, S. (2019). Association of genetic and environmental factors with autism in a 5-country cohort. *JAMA Psychiatry, 76*(10), 1035–1043. https://doi.org/10.1001/jamapsychiatry.2019.1411

Bai, S., Guo, W., Feng, Y., Deng, H., Li, G., Nie, H., Guo, G., Yu, H., Ma, Y., Wang, J., Chen, S., Jing, J., Yang, J., Tang, Y., & Tang, Z. (2020). Efficacy and safety of anti-inflammatory agents for the treatment of major depressive disorder: A systematic review and meta-analysis of randomised controlled trials. *Journal of Neurology, Neurosurgery & Psychiatry, 91*(1), 21–32. https://doi.org/10.1136/jnnp-2019-320912

Baid, R., & Agarwal, R. (2018). Flibanserin: A controversial drug for female hypoactive sexual desire disorder. *Industrial Psychiatry Journal, 27*(1), 154–157. https://doi.org/10.4103/ipj.ipj_20_16

Baird, A. D., Wilson, S. J., Bladin, P. F., Saling, M. M., & Reutens, D. C. (2007). Neurological control of human sexual behaviour: Insights from lesion studies. *Journal of Neurology, Neurosurgery & Psychiatry, 78*(10), 1042–1049. https://doi.org/10.1136/jnnp.2006.107193

Baker, C. (2004). *Behavioral genetics: An introduction to how genes and environments interact through development to shape differences in mood, personality, and intelligence.* American Association for the Advancement of Science and The Hastings Center.

Baker, J., & Beazley, P. I. (2022). Judging personality disorder: A systematic review of clinician attitudes and responses to borderline personality disorder. *Journal of Psychiatric Practice*, 28(4), 275–293. https://doi.org/10.1097/PRA.0000000000000642

Baker, J. P. (2013). Autism at 70—Redrawing the boundaries. *The New England Journal of Medicine, 369*(12), 1089–1091. https://doi.org/10.1056/NEJMp1306380

Baker, K. G. (2015). Bowen family systems couple coaching. In A. S. Gurman, J. L. Lebow, & D. K. Snyder (Eds.), *Clinical handbook of couple therapy* (5th ed., pp. 246–267). Guilford Press.

Baker, R. W., & Trzepacz, P. T. (2013). Conducting a mental status examination. In G. P. Koocher, J. C. Norcross, & B. A. Greene (Eds.), *Psychologists' desk reference* (3rd ed., pp. 17–22). Oxford University Press.

Baker, T. B., McFall, R. M., & Shoham, V. (2008). Current status and future prospects of clinical psychology: Toward a scientifically principled approach to mental and behavioral health care. *Psychological Science in the Public Interest, 9*(2), 67–103. https://doi.org/10.1111/j.1539-6053.2009.01036.x

Bakker, G. M. (2009). In defence of thought stopping. *Clinical Psychologist, 13*(2), 59–68. https://doi.org/10.1080/13284200902810452

Balbuena, L. D., Baetz, M., Sexton, J. A., Harder, D., Feng, C. X., Boctor, K., LaPointe, C., Letwiniuk, E., Shamloo, A., Ishwaran, H., John, A., & Brantsæter, A. L. (2022). Identifying long-term and imminent suicide predictors in a general population and a clinical sample with machine learning. *BMC Psychiatry, 22*(1), 120. https://doi.org/10.1186/s12888-022-03702-y

Baldessarini, R. J., Pérez, J., Salmtore, P., Trede, K., & Maggini, C. (2015). History of bipolar manic-depressive disorder. In A. Yildiz, P. Ruiz, & C. B. Nemeroff (Eds.), *The bipolar book: History, neurobiology, and treatment* (pp. 3–19). Oxford University Press.

Baldessarini, R. J., Vieta, E., Calabrese, J. R., Tohen, M., & Bowden, C. L. (2010). Bipolar depression: Overview and commentary. *Harvard Review of Psychiatry, 18*(3), 143–157. https://doi.org/10.3109/10673221003747955

Baldinger-Melich, P., Urquijo Castro, M. F., Seiger, R., Ruef, A., Dwyer, D. B., Kranz, G. S., Klöbl, M., Kambeitz, J., Kaufmann, U., Windischberger, C., Kasper, S., Falkai, P., Lanzenberger, R., & Koutsouleris, N. (2020). Sex matters: A multivariate pattern analysis of sex- and gender-related neuroanatomical differences in cis- and transgender individuals using structural magnetic resonance imaging. *Cerebral Cortex, 30*(3), 1345–1356. https://doi.org/10.1093/cercor/bhz170

Baldwin, D. V. (2013). Primitive mechanisms of trauma response: An evolutionary perspective on trauma-related disorders. *Neuroscience and Biobehavioral Reviews, 37*(8), 1549–1566. https://doi.org/10.1016/j.neubiorev.2013.06.004

Baldwin, M. L., & Marcus, S. C. (2007). Labor market outcomes of persons with mental disorders. *Industrial Relations: A Journal of Economy & Society, 46*(3), 481–510. https://doi.org/10.1111/j.1468-232X.2007.00478.x

Baldwin, S. (1999). Applied behavior analysis in the treatment of ADHD: A review and rapprochement. *Ethical Human Sciences & Services, 1*(1), 35–59. https://doi.org/10.1891/1523-150X.1.1.35

Baldwin, S. A., Williams, D. C., & Houts, A. C. (2004). The creation, expansion, and embodiment of posttraumatic stress disorder: A case study in historical critical psychopathology. *The Scientific Review of Mental Health Practice, 3*(1). http://www.srmhp.org/0301/hcp.html

Baller, E. B., & Ross, D. A. (2019). Premenstrual dysphoric disorder: From Plato to petri dishes. *Biological Psychiatry, 85*(12), e63–e65. https://doi.org/10.1016/j.biopsych.2019.04.018

Balon, R., & Starcevic, V. (2020). Role of benzodiazepines in anxiety disorders. *Advances in Experimental Medicine and Biology, 1191*, 367–388. https://doi.org/10.1007/978-981-32-9705-0_20

Balsam, R. H. (2013). Appreciating difference: Roy Schafer on psychoanalysis and women. *The Psychoanalytic Quarterly, 82*(1), 23–38. https://doi.org/10.1002/j.2167-4086.2013.00003.x

Balsikci, A., Uzun, O., Erdem, M., Doruk, A., Cansever, A., & Ates, M. A. (2014). Side effects that cause noncompliance to antidepressant medications in the course of outpatient treatment. *Klinik Psikofarmakoloji Bülteni-Bulletin of Clinical Psychopharmacology, 24*(1), 69–75. https://doi.org/10.5455/bcp.20120827114140

Bamelis, L. L. M., Evers, S. M. A. A., Spinhoven, P., & Arntz, A. (2014). Results of a multicenter randomized controlled trial of the clinical effectiveness of schema therapy for personality disorders. *American Journal of Psychiatry, 171*(3), 305–322. https://doi.org/10.1176/appi.ajp.2013.12040518

Bamidis, P. D., Vivas, A. B., Styliadis, C., Frantzidis, C., Klados, M., Schlee, W., Siountas, A., & Papageorgiou, S. G. (2014). A review of physical and cognitive interventions in aging. *Neuroscience and Biobehavioral Reviews, 44*, 206–220. https://doi.org/10.1016/j.neubiorev.2014.03.019

Banaschewski, T., Belsham, B., Bloch, M. H., Ferrin, M., Johnson, M., Kustow, J., Robinson, S., & Zuddas, A. (2018). Supplementation with polyunsaturated fatty acids (PUFAs) in the management of attention deficit hyperactivity disorder (ADHD). *Nutrition and Health, 24*(4), 279–284. https://doi.org/10.1177/0260106018772170

Bandelow, B., Lichte, T., Rudolf, S., Wiltink, J., & Beutel, M. E. (2014). The diagnosis of and treatment recommendations for anxiety disorders. *Deutsches Ärzteblatt International, 111*(27–28), 473–480.

Bandelow, B., & Michaelis, S. (2015). Epidemiology of anxiety disorders in the 21st century. *Dialogues in Clinical Neuroscience, 17*(3), 327–335.

Bandelow, B., Reitt, M., Röver, C., Michaelis, S., Görlich, Y., & Wedekind, D. (2015). Efficacy of treatments for anxiety disorders: A meta-analysis. *International Clinical Psychopharmacology, 30*(4), 183–192. https://doi.org/10.1097/YIC.0000000000000078

Bandelow, B., Reitt, M., & Wedekind, D. (2012). Selective serotonin reuptake inhibitors, reversible inhibitors of monoamine oxidase-A, and buspirone. In S. G. Hofmann (Ed.), *Psychobiological approaches for anxiety disorders: Treatment combination strategies* (pp. 61–74). Wiley-Blackwell. https://doi.org/10.1002/9781119945901.ch4

Bandelow, B., Werner, A. M., Kopp, I., Rudolf, S., Wiltink, J., & Beutel, M. E. (2021). The German Guidelines for the treatment of anxiety disorders: First revision. *European Archives of Psychiatry and Clinical Neuroscience.* https://doi.org/10.1007/s00406-021-01324-1

Bandini, J. (2015). The medicalization of bereavement: (Ab)normal grief in the DSM-5. *Death Studies, 39*(6), 347–352. https://doi.org/10.1080/07481187.2014.951498

Bandura, A. (1965). Influence of models' reinforcement contingencies on the acquisition of imitative responses. *Journal of Personality and Social Psychology, 1*(6), 589–595. https://doi.org/10.1037/h0022070

Bandura, A., Jeffrey, R. W., & Wright, C. L. (1974). Efficacy of participant modeling as a function of response induction aids. *Journal of Abnormal Psychology, 83*(1), 56–64.

Bandura, A., Ross, D., & Ross, S. A. (1961). Transmission of aggression through imitation of aggressive models. *The Journal of Abnormal and Social Psychology, 63*(3), 575–582. https://doi.org/10.1037/h0045925

Bandura, A., Ross, D., & Ross, S. A. (1963a). A comparative test of the status envy, social power, and secondary reinforcement theories of identificatory learning. *The Journal of Abnormal and Social Psychology, 67*(6), 527–534. https://doi.org/10.1037/h0046546

Bandura, A., Ross, D., & Ross, S. A. (1963b). Imitation of film-mediated aggressive models. *The Journal of Abnormal and Social Psychology, 66*(1), 3–11. https://doi.org/10.1037/h0048687

Bandura, A., Ross, D., & Ross, S. A. (1963c). Vicarious reinforcement and imitative learning. *The Journal of Abnormal and Social Psychology, 67*(6), 601–607. https://doi.org/10.1037/h0045550

Banna, M. H. A., Dewan, M. F., Tariq, M. R., Sayeed, A., Kundu, S., Disu, T. R., Akter, S., Sahrin, S., & Khan, M. S. I. (2021). Prevalence and determinants of eating disorder risk among Bangladeshi public university students: A cross-sectional study. *Health Psychology Research, 9*(1), 24837. https://doi.org/10.52965/001c.24837

Bano, Z., Aslam, H., & Naz, I. (2019). Learned helplessness and suicidality: Role of cognitive behavior therapy. *Rawal Medical Journal, 44*(3), 569–572.

Bär, K.-J., de la Cruz, F., Berger, S., Schultz, C. C., & Wagner, G. (2015). Structural and functional differences in the cingulate cortex relate to disease severity in anorexia nervosa. *Journal of Psychiatry & Neuroscience, 40*(4), 269–278. https://doi.org/10.1503/jpn.140193

Barahona-Corrêa, J. B., & Filipe, C. N. (2016). A concise history of Asperger Syndrome: The short reign of a troublesome diagnosis. *Frontiers In Psychology, 6*, 2024–2024. https://doi.org/10.3389/fpsyg.2015.02024

Barańczuk, U. (2019). The five factor model of personality and emotion regulation: A meta-analysis. *Personality and Individual Differences, 139*, 217–227. https://doi.org/10.1016/j.paid.2018.11.025

Barbisan, G. K., Moura, D. H., Lobato, M. I. R., & da Rocha, N. S. (2020). Interpersonal psychotherapy for gender dysphoria in a transgender woman. *Archives of Sexual Behavior, 49*(2), 787–791. https://doi.org/10.1007/s10508-019-01601-0

Barceloux, D. G. (2012). *Medical toxicology of drug abuse: Synthesized chemicals and psychoactive plants.* John Wiley.

Bar-Chama, N., Zaslau, S., & Gribetz, M. (1997). Intracavernosal injection therapy and other treatment options for erectile dysfunction. *Endocrine Practice, 3*(1), 54–59.

Barendse, M. E. A., Byrne, M. L., Flournoy, J. C., McNeilly, E. A., Guazzelli Williamson, V., Barrett, A.-M. Y., Chavez, S. J., Shirtcliff, E. A., Allen, N. B., & Pfeifer, J. H. (2022). Multimethod assessment of pubertal timing and associations with internalizing psychopathology in early adolescent girls. *Journal of Psychopathology and Clinical Science, 131*(1), 14–25. https://doi.org/10.1037/abn0000721

Barker, R. (2015). Using pre-therapy in forensic settings. In A. Meaden & A. Fox (Eds.), *Innovations in psychosocial interventions for psychosis: Working with the hard to reach* (pp. 22–37). Routledge.

Barkham, M., Saxon, D., Hardy, G. E., Bradburn, M., Galloway, D., Wickramasekera, N., Keetharuth, A. D., Bower, P., King, M., Elliott, R., Gabriel, L., Kellett, S., Shaw, S., Wilkinson, T., Connell, J., Harrison, P., Ardern, K., Bishop-Edwards, L., Ashley, K., … Brazier, J. E. (2021). Person-centred experiential therapy versus cognitive behavioural therapy delivered in the English Improving Access to Psychological Therapies service for the treatment of moderate or severe depression (PRaCTICED): A pragmatic, randomised, non-inferiority trial. *The Lancet Psychiatry, 8*(6), 487–499. https://doi.org/10.1016/S2215-0366(21)00083-3

Barkley, R. A. (2002). International consensus statement on ADHD. *Journal of the American Academy of Child & Adolescent Psychiatry, 41*(12), 1389–1389. https://doi.org/10.1097/00004583-200212000-00001

Barkley, R. A., & Peters, H. (2012). The earliest reference to ADHD in the medical literature? Melchior Adam Weikard's description in 1775 of "attention deficit" (Mangel der aufmerksamkeit, attentio volubilis). *Journal of Attention Disorders, 16*(8), 623–630. https://doi.org/10.1177/1087054711432309

Barlow, D. H., Farchione, T. J., Bullis, J. R., Gallagher, M. W., Murray-Latin, H., Sauer-Zavala, S., Bentley, K. H., Thompson-Hollands, J., Conklin, L. R., Boswell, J. F., Ametaj, A., Carl, J. R., Boettcher, H. T., & Cassiello-Robbins, C. (2017). The unified protocol for transdiagnostic treatment of emotional disorders compared with diagnosis-specific protocols for anxiety disorders: A randomized clinical trial. *JAMA Psychiatry, 74*(9), 875–884. https://doi.org/10.1001/jamapsychiatry.2017.2164

Barlow, M. R., & Freyd, J. J. (2009). Adaptive dissociation: Information processing and response to betrayal. In P. F. Dell & J. A. O'Neil (Eds.), *Dissociation and the dissociative disorders: DSM-V and beyond* (pp. 93–105). Routledge.

Barnao, M., Ward, T., & Casey, S. (2015). Looking beyond the illness: Forensic service users' perceptions of rehabilitation. *Journal of Interpersonal Violence, 30*(6), 1025–1045. https://doi.org/10.1177/0886260514539764

Barnby, J. M., & Mehta, M. A. (2018). Psilocybin and mental health–don't lose control. *Frontiers in Psychiatry, 9*, Article 293. https://doi.org/10.3389/fpsyt.2018.00293

Barnes, M. A., & Caltabiano, M. L. (2017). The interrelationship between orthorexia nervosa, perfectionism, body image and attachment style. *Eating and Weight Disorders, 22*(1), 177–184. https://doi.org/10.1007/s40519-016-0280-x

Barnicot, K., Savill, M., Bhatti, N., & Priebe, S. (2014). A pragmatic randomised controlled trial of dialectical behaviour therapy: Effects on hospitalisation and post-treatment follow-up. *Psychotherapy and Psychosomatics, 83*(3), 192–193. https://doi.org/10.1159/000357365

Baron, K. G., Perlis, M. L., Nowakowski, S., Smith, Jr., Michael T., Jungquist, C. R., & Orff, H. J. (2017). Cognitive behavioral therapy for insomnia. In H. P. Attarian (Ed.), *Clinical handbook of insomnia* (pp. 75–96). Humana Press. https://doi.org/10.1007/978-3-319-41400-3_6

Baron-Cohen, S. (1995). *Mindblindness: An essay on autism and theory of mind*. The MIT Press.

Baron-Cohen, S. (2002). The extreme male brain theory of autism. *Trends in Cognitive Sciences, 6*(6), 248–254. https://doi.org/10.1016/s1364-6613(02)01904-6

Baron-Cohen, S. (2009). Autism: The empathizing-systemizing (E-S) theory. *Annals of the New York Academy of Sciences, 1156*, 68–80. https://doi.org/10.1111/j.1749-6632.2009.04467.x

Baron-Cohen, S. (2019). The concept of neurodiversity is dividing the autism community. *Scientific American Mind, 30*(4), 30–32.

Baroni, A., & Castellanos, F. X. (2015). Neuroanatomic and cognitive abnormalities in attention-deficit/hyperactivity disorder in the era of "high definition" neuroimaging. *Current Opinion in Neurobiology, 30*, 1–8. https://doi.org/10.1016/j.conb.2014.08.005

Barr, K. N., & Quinsey, V. L. (2004). Is psychopathy pathology or a life strategy? Implications for social policy. In C. Crawford & C. Salmon (Eds.), *Evolutionary psychology, public policy and personal decisions* (pp. 293–317). Lawrence Erlbaum.

Barr, R., & Abernethy, V. (1977). Conversion reaction: Differential diagnosis in the light of biofeedback research. *Journal of Nervous and Mental Disease, 164*(4), 287–292. https://doi.org/10.1097/00005053-197704000-00010

Barrilleaux, J. C. (2016). Sexual addiction: Definitions and interventions. *Journal of Social Work Practice in the Addictions, 16*(4), 421–438. https://doi.org/10.1080/1533256X.2016.1235425

Barry, E. (2022, March 18). How long should it take to grieve? Psychiatry has come up with an answer. *The New York Times*. https://www.nytimes.com/2022/03/18/health/prolonged-grief-disorder.html

Bártová, K., Androvičová, R., Krejčová, L., Weiss, P., & Klapilová, K. (2021). The prevalence of paraphilic interests in the Czech population: Preference, arousal, the use of pornography, fantasy, and behavior. *The Journal of Sex Research, 58*(1), 86–96. https://doi.org/10.1080/00224499.2019.1707468

Bas-Hoogendam, J. M., & Westenberg, P. M. (2020). Imaging the socially-anxious brain: Recent advances and future prospects. *F1000Research, 9*, F1000 Faculty Rev-230. https://doi.org/10.12688/f1000research.21214.1

Basner, M., Spaeth, A. M., & Dinges, D. F. (2014). Sociodemographic characteristics and waking activities and their role in the timing and duration of sleep. *Sleep, 37*(12), 1889–1906. https://doi.org/10.5665/sleep.4238

Baspinar, B., & Yardimci, H. (2020). Gluten-free casein-free diet for autism spectrum disorders: Can it be effective in solving behavioural and gastrointestinal problems? *The Eurasian Journal of Medicine, 52*(3), 292–297. https://doi.org/10.5152/eurasianjmed.2020.19230

Bass, C., & Halligan, P. (2014). Factitious disorders and malingering: Challenges for clinical assessment and management. *The Lancet, 383*(9926), 1422–1432. https://doi.org/10.1016/S0140-6736(13)62186-8

Bassett, A. M., & Baker, C. (2015). Normal or abnormal? "Normative uncertainty" in psychiatric practice. *Journal of Medical Humanities, 36*(2), 89–111. https://doi.org/10.1007/s10912-014-9324-2

Bassman, R. (2001). Whose reality is it anyway? Consumers/survivors/ex-patients can speak for themselves. *Journal of Humanistic Psychology, 41*(4), 11–35. https://doi.org/10.1177/0022167801414002

Basson, R. (2001). Human sex-response cycles. *Journal of Sex & Marital Therapy, 27*(1), 33–44. https://doi.org/10.1080/00926230152035831

Bastian, B., Jetten, J., & Ferris, L. J. (2014). Pain as social glue: Shared pain increases cooperation. *Psychological Science, 25*(11), 2079–2085. https://doi.org/10.1177/0956797614545886

Bateman, A., & Fonagy, P. (2013). Mentalization-based treatment. *Psychoanalytic Inquiry, 33*(6), 595–613. https://doi.org/10.1080/07351690.2013.835170

Bateman, A., O'Connell, J., Lorenzini, N., Gardner, T., & Fonagy, P. (2016). A randomised controlled trial of mentalization-based treatment versus structured clinical management for patients with comorbid borderline personality disorder and antisocial personality disorder. *BMC Psychiatry, 16*, Article 304. https://doi.org/10.1186/s12888-016-1000-9

Bateman, A. W., & Fonagy, P. (2012). Mentalization-based treatment of borderline personality disorder. In T. A. Widiger (Ed.), *The Oxford handbook of personality disorders* (pp. 767–784). Oxford

University Press. https://doi.org/10.1093/oxfordhb/9780199735013.013.0036

Bateson, G., Jackson, D. D., Haley, J., & Weakland, J. (1956). Toward a theory of schizophrenia. *Behavioral Science, 1*, 251–264. https://doi.org/10.1002/bs.3830010402

Batstra, L., & Frances, A. (2012). DSM-5 further inflates attention deficit hyperactivity disorder. *Journal of Nervous and Mental Disease, 200*(6), 486–488. https://doi.org/10.1097/NMD.0b013e318257c4b6

Battagliese, G., Caccetta, M., Luppino, O. I., Baglioni, C., Cardi, V., Mancini, F., & Buonanno, C. (2015). Cognitive-behavioral therapy for externalizing disorders: A meta-analysis of treatment effectiveness. *Behaviour Research and Therapy, 75*, 60–71. https://doi.org/10.1016/j.brat.2015.10.008

Batterham, P. J., Griffiths, K. M., Barney, L. J., & Parsons, A. (2013). Predictors of generalized anxiety disorder stigma. *Psychiatry Research, 206*(2–3), 282–286. https://doi.org/10.1016/j.psychres.2012.11.018

Battle, C. L., Shea, M. T., Johnson, D. M., Yen, S., Zlotnick, C., Zanarini, M. C., Sanislow, C. A., Skodol, A. E., Gunderson, J. G., Grilo, C. M., McGlashan, T. H., & Morey, L. C. (2004). Childhood maltreatment associated with adult personality disorders: Findings from the collaborative longitudinal personality disorders study. *Journal of Personality Disorders, 18*(2), 193–211. https://doi.org/10.1521/pedi.18.2.193.32777

Bauer, M., & Dinan, T. (2015). Hypothalamic-pituitary-adrenal axis and hypothalamic-pituitary-thyroid axis and their treatment impact. In A. Yildiz, P. Ruiz, & C. B. Nemeroff (Eds.), *The bipolar book: History, neurobiology, and treatment* (pp. 137–148). Oxford University Press.

Bauer, M., Pfennig, A., Severus, E., Whybrow, P. C., Angst, J., & Möller, H.-J. (2013). World Federation of Societies of Biological Psychiatry (WFSBP) guidelines for biological treatment of unipolar depressive disorders, Part 1: Update 2013 on the acute and continuation treatment of unipolar depressive disorders. *The World Journal of Biological Psychiatry, 14*(5), 334–385. https://doi.org/10.3109/15622975.2013.804195

Bauer, M., Severus, E., Köhler, S., Whybrow, P. C., Angst, J., & Möller, H.-J. (2015). World Federation of Societies of Biological Psychiatry (WFSBP) guidelines for biological treatment of unipolar depressive disorders. Part 2: Maintenance treatment of major depressive disorder-update 2015. *The World Journal of Biological Psychiatry, 16*(2), 76–95. https://doi.org/10.3109/15622975.2014.1001786

Baum, M. (1970). Extinction of avoidance responding through response prevention (flooding). *Psychological Bulletin, 74*(4), 276–284. https://doi.org/10.1037/h0029789

Bauminger, N., Solomon, M., & Rogers, S. J. (2010). Externalizing and internalizing behaviors in ASD. *Autism Research, 3*(3), 101–112. https://doi.org/10.1002/aur.131

Baune, B. T., Sampson, E., Louise, J., Hori, H., Schubert, K. O., Clark, S. R., Mills, N. T., & Fourrier, C. (2021). No evidence for clinical efficacy of adjunctive celecoxib with vortioxetine in the treatment of depression: A 6-week double-blind placebo controlled randomized trial. *European Neuropsychopharmacology, 53*, 34–46. https://doi.org/10.1016/j.euroneuro.2021.07.092

Bayliss, P., & Holttum, S. (2015). Experiences of antidepressant medication and cognitive–behavioural therapy for depression: A grounded theory study. *Psychology and Psychotherapy: Theory, Research and Practice, 88*(3), 317–334. https://doi.org/10.1111/papt.12040

Bazelon, E. (2022, June 15). The battle over gender therapy. *The New York Times*. https://www.nytimes.com/2022/06/15/magazine/gender-therapy.html

Beahrs, J. O. (1994). Dissociative identity disorder: Adaptive deception of self and others. *Bulletin of the American Academy of Psychiatry & the Law, 22*(2), 223–237.

Bear, T. L. K., Dalziel, J. E., Coad, J., Roy, N. C., Butts, C. A., & Gopal, P. K. (2020). The role of the gut microbiota in dietary interventions for depression and anxiety. *Advances in Nutrition, 11*(4), 890–907. https://doi.org/10.1093/advances/nmaa016

Beard, G. (1869). Neurasthenia, or nervous exhaustion. *Boston Medical & Surgical Journal, 3*(13), 217–221.

Bearelly, P., Phillips, E. A., Pan, S., O&, K., apos, Brien, Asher, K., Martinez, D., & Munarriz, R. (2020). Long-term intracavernosal injection therapy: Treatment efficacy and patient satisfaction. *International Journal of Impotence Research, 32*(3), 345–352. https://doi.org/10.1038/s41443-019-0186-z

Beaudoin, M.-N., Moersch, M., & Evare, B. S. (2016). The effectiveness of narrative therapy with children's social and emotional skill development: An empirical study of 813 problem-solving stories. *Journal of Systemic Therapies, 35*(3), 42–59. https://doi.org/10.1521/jsyt.2016.35.3.42

Beaudoin, M.-N., Tan, A., Gannon, C., & Moersch, M. (2017). A comparative study of the effects of 6, 12, and 16 weeks of narrative therapy on social and emotional skills: An empirical analysis of 722 children's problem-solving accounts. *Journal of Systemic Therapies, 36*(4), 57–73. https://doi.org/10.1521/jsyt.2017.36.4.57

Beaver, K. M., Connolly, E. J., Nedelec, J. L., & Schwartz, J. A. (2018). *On the genetic and genomic basis of aggression, violence, and antisocial behavior* (R. L. Hopcroft, Ed.; Vol. 1). Oxford University Press. https://doi.org/10.1093/oxfordhb/9780190299323.013.15

Bebbington, P. (2013). The classification and epidemiology of unipolar depression. In M. Power (Ed.), *The Wiley-Blackwell handbook of mood disorders* (2nd ed., pp. 3–37). Wiley-Blackwell.

Bechard, M., Cloutier, P., Lima, I., Salamatmanesh, M., Zemek, R., Bhatt, M., Suntharalingam, S., Kurdyak, P., Baker, M., & Gardner, W. (2022). Cannabis-related emergency department visits by youths and their outcomes in Ontario: A trend analysis. *Canadian Medical Association Open Access Journal, 10*(1), E100–E108. https://doi.org/10.9778/cmajo.20210142

Beck, A., Grace, A. A., & Heinz, A. (2011). Reward processing. In B. Adinoff & E. A. Stein (Eds.), *Neuroimaging in addiction* (pp. 107–129). Wiley-Blackwell. https://doi.org/10.1002/9781119998938.ch5

Beck, A. T., Davis, D. D., & Freeman, A. (2015). *Cognitive therapy of personality disorders* (3rd ed.). Guilford Press.

Beck, A. T., & Rector, N. A. (2000). Cognitive therapy of schizophrenia: A new therapy for the new millennium. *American Journal of Psychotherapy, 54*(3), 291–300. https://doi.org/10.1176/appi.psychotherapy.2000.54.3.291

Beck, A. T., Rush, A. J., Shaw, B. F., & Emery, G. (1979). *Cognitive therapy of depression*. The Guilford Press.

Beck, E. D., Condon, D., & Jackson, J. (2022). Interindividual age differences in personality structure. *European Journal of Personality*. https://doi.org/10.1177/08902070221084862

Beck, J. (2016, March 11). "Americanitis": The disease of living too fast. *The Atlantic*.

Beck, J. C., & Golowka, E. A. (1988). A study of enforced treatment in relation to Stone's "thank you" theory. *Behavioral Sciences & the Law, 6*(4), 559–566. https://doi.org/10.1002/bsl.2370060411

Beck, J. G., & Sloan, D. M. (2014). Group treatments for PTSD: What do we know and what do we need to know? In M. J. Friedman, T. M. Keane, & P. A. Resick (Eds.), *Handbook of PTSD: Science and practice* (2nd ed., pp. 466–481). Guilford Press.

Beck, J. S. (2011). *Cognitive behavior therapy: Basics and beyond* (2nd ed.). Guilford Press.

Beck, J. S., Liese, B. S., & Najavits, L. M. (2005). Cognitive therapy. In R. J. Frances, S. I. Miller, & A. H. Mack (Eds.), *Clinical textbook of addictive disorders* (3rd ed., pp. 474–501). Guilford Publications.

Becker, A. E., Keel, P., Anderson-Fye, E. P., & Thomas, J. J. (2004). Genes and/or jeans?: Genetic and socio-cultural contributions to risk for eating disorders. *Journal of Addictive Diseases, 23*(3), 81–103. doi:10.1300/J069v23n03_07

Becker, C. B., Zayfert, C., & Anderson, E. (2004). A survey of psychologists' attitudes towards and utilization of exposure therapy for PTSD. *Behaviour Research and Therapy, 42*(3), 277–292. https://doi.org/10.1016/S0005-7967(03)00138-4

Becker, J. V., Johnson, B. R., & Perkins, A. (2014). Paraphilic disorders. In R. E. Hales, S. C. Yudofsky, & L. W. Roberts (Eds.), *The American Psychiatric Publishing textbook of psychiatry* (6th ed., pp. 895–925). American Psychiatric Publishing.

Becker-Blease, K. A., Deater-Deckard, K., Eley, T., Freyd, J. J., Stevenson, J., & Plomin, R. (2004). A genetic analysis of individual differences in dissociative behaviors in childhood and adolescence. *Journal of Child Psychology and Psychiatry, 45*(3), 522–532. https://doi.org/10.1111/j.1469-7610.2004.00242.x

Beebe, L. H., & Smith, K. (2010). Informed consent to research in persons with schizophrenia spectrum disorders. *Nursing Ethics, 17*(4), 425–434. https://doi.org/10.1177/0969733010364581

Beech, O. D., Kaufmann, L., & Anderson, J. (2020). A systematic literature review exploring objectification and motherhood. *Psychology of Women Quarterly, 44*(4), 521–538. https://doi.org/10.1177/0361684320949810

Beer, M. D. (1996). Psychosis: A history of the concept. *Comprehensive Psychiatry, 37*(4), 273–291. https://doi.org/10.1016/S0010-440X(96)90007-3

Beevers, C. G., Wenzlaff, R. M., Hayes, A. M., & Scott, W. D. (1999). Depression and the ironic effects of thought suppression: Therapeutic strategies for improving mental control. *Clinical Psychology: Science and Practice, 6*(2), 133–148. https://doi.org/10.1093/clipsy.6.2.133

Behar, E., DiMarco, I. D., Hekler, E. B., Mohlman, J., & Staples, A. M. (2009). Current theoretical models of generalized anxiety disorder (GAD): Conceptual review and treatment implications. *Journal of Anxiety Disorders, 23*(8), 1011–1023. https://doi.org/10.1016/j.janxdis.2009.07.006

Behr, M., Nuding, D., & McGinnis, S. (2013). Person-centred psychotherapy and counselling with children and young people. In M. Cooper, M. O'Hara, P. F. Schmid, & A. C. Bohart (Eds.), *The handbook of person-centred psychotherapy and counselling* (pp. 266–281). Palgrave Macmillan.

Bélanger, S. A., Andrews, D., Gray, C., & Korczak, D. (2018). ADHD in children and youth: Part 1—Etiology, diagnosis, and comorbidity. *Paediatrics & Child Health, 23*(7), 447–453. https://doi.org/10.1093/pch/pxy109

Bell, A. C., & D'Zurilla, T. J. (2009). Problem-solving therapy for depression: A meta-analysis. *Clinical Psychology Review, 29*(4), 348–353. https://doi.org/10.1016/j.cpr.2009.02.003

Bell, J. S., & Richards, G. C. (2021). Off-label medicine use: Ethics, practice and future directions. *Australian Journal of General Practice, 50*(5), 329–331. https://doi.org/10.3316/informit.764436296999704

Bellenguez, C., Grenier-Boley, B., & Lambert, J.-C. (2020). Genetics of Alzheimer's disease: Where we are, and where we are going. *Current Opinion in Neurobiology, 61*, 40–48. https://doi.org/10.1016/j.conb.2019.11.024

Bellenguez, C., Küçükali, F., Jansen, I. E., Kleineidam, L., Moreno-Grau, S., Amin, N., Naj, A. C., Campos-Martin, R., Grenier-Boley, B., Andrade, V., Holmans, P. A., Boland, A., Damotte, V., van der Lee, S. J., Costa, M. R., Kuulasmaa, T., Yang, Q., de Rojas, I., Bis, J. C., … Lambert, J.-C. (2022). New insights into the genetic etiology of Alzheimer's disease and related dementias. *Nature Genetics, 54*(4), Article 4. https://doi.org/10.1038/s41588-022-01024-z

Belvederi Murri, M., Prestia, D., Mondelli, V., Pariante, C., Patti, S., Olivieri, B., Arzani, C., Masotti, M., Respino, M., Antonioli, M., Vassallo, L., Serafini, G., Perna, G., Pompili, M., & Amore, M. (2016). The HPA axis in bipolar disorder: Systematic review and meta-analysis. *Psychoneuroendocrinology, 63*, 327–342. https://doi.org/10.1016/j.psyneuen.2015.10.014

Benedetti, F., Aggio, V., Pratesi, M. L., Greco, G., & Furlan, R. (2020). Neuroinflammation in bipolar depression. *Frontiers in Psychiatry, 11*, Article 71. https://doi.org/10.3389/fpsyt.2020.00071

Benish, S. G., Imel, Z. E., & Wampold, B. E. (2008). The relative efficacy of bona fide psychotherapies for treating post-traumatic stress disorder: A meta-analysis of direct comparisons. *Clinical Psychology Review, 28*(5), 746–758. https://doi.org/10.1016/j.cpr.2007.10.005

Benito-León, J., Contador, I., Vega, S., Villarejo-Galende, A., & Bermejo-Pareja, F. (2019). Non-steroidal anti-inflammatory drugs use in older adults decreases risk of Alzheimer's disease mortality. *PLOS ONE, 14*(9), Article e0222505. https://doi.org/10.1371/journal.pone.0222505

Benjet, C., Bromet, E., Karam, E. G., Kessler, R. C., McLaughlin, K. A., Ruscio, A. M., Shahly, V., Stein, D. J., Petukhova, M., Hill, E., Alonso, J., Atwoli, L., Bunting, B., Bruffaerts, R., Caldas-de-almeida, J. M., de Girolamo, G., Florescu, S., Gureje, O., Huang, Y., … Koenen, K. C. (2016). The epidemiology of traumatic event exposure worldwide: Results from the World Mental Health Survey Consortium. *Psychological Medicine, 46*(2), 327–343. https://doi.org/10.1017/S0033291715001981

Benning, S. D., Venables, N. C., & Hall, J. R. (2018). Successful psychopathy. In C. J. Patrick (Ed.), *Handbook of psychopathy* (2nd ed., pp. 585–608). The Guilford Press.

Benoit, S. L., & Mauldin, R. F. (2021). The "anti-vax" movement: A quantitative report on vaccine beliefs and knowledge across social media. *BMC Public Health, 21*(1), 2106. https://doi.org/10.1186/s12889-021-12114-8

Benowitz, N. L. (2009). Pharmacology of nicotine: Addiction, smoking-induced disease, and therapeutics. *Annual Review of Pharmacology and Toxicology, 49*, 57–71. https://doi.org/10.1146/annurev.pharmtox.48.113006.094742

Ben-Porath, Y. S., Sellbom, M., & Suhr, J. A. (2020). Minnesota Multiphasic Personality Inventory-2-Restructured Form (MMPI-2-RF). In J. A. Suhr & M. Sellbom (Eds.), *The Cambridge handbook of clinical assessment and diagnosis* (pp. 208–230). Cambridge University Press. https://doi.org/10.1017/9781108235433.016

Ben-Porath, Y. S., & Tellegen, A. (2020). *MMPI-3: Manual for administration, scoring, and interpretation*. Pearson.

Benros, M. E., Nielsen, P. R., Nordentoft, M., Eaton, W. W., Dalton, S. O., & Mortensen, P. B. (2011). Autoimmune diseases and severe infections as risk factors for schizophrenia: A 30-year population-based register study. *The American Journal of Psychiatry, 168*(12), 1303–1310. https://doi.org/10.1176/appi.ajp.2011.11030516

Ben-Shahar, A. R. (2014). *Touching the relational edge: Body psychotherapy*. Karnac Books.

Benson, E. (2003, February). Intelligent intelligence testing: Psychologists are broadening the concept of intelligence and how to test it. *Monitor on Psychology, 34*(2), 48.

Bentall, R. (2013). Understanding psychotic symptoms: Cognitive and integrative models. In J. Read & J. Dillon (Eds.), *Models of madness: Psychological, social and biological approaches to psychosis* (2013-19717-023; 2nd ed., pp. 220–237). Routledge/Taylor & Francis Group.

Bentall, R. P. (2013). Would a rose, by any other name, smell sweeter? *Psychological Medicine, 43*(7), 1560–1562. https://doi.org/10.1017/S0033291713000925

Bentall, R. P., Jackson, H. F., & Pilgrim, D. (1988). Abandoning the concept of "schizophrenia": Some implications of validity arguments for psychological research into psychotic phenomena. *British Journal of Clinical Psychology, 27*(4), 303–324. https://doi.org/10.1111/j.2044-8260.1988.tb00795.x

Bentley, K. H., Cassiello-Robbins, C. F., Vittorio, L., Sauer-Zavala, S., & Barlow, D. H. (2015). The association between nonsuicidal self-injury and the emotional disorders: A meta-analytic review. *Clinical Psychology Review, 37*, 72–88. https://doi.org/10.1016/j.cpr.2015.02.006

Bentz, M., Pedersen, S. H., & Moslet, U. (2021). An evaluation of family-based treatment for restrictive-type eating disorders, delivered as standard care in a public mental health service. *Journal of Eating Disorders, 9*(1), 141. https://doi.org/10.1186/s40337-021-00498-2

Benvenuto, S. (2018). The silent fog. *American Imago, 75*(1), 1–23. https://doi.org/10.1353/aim.2018.0000

Berardelli, I., Serafini, G., Cortese, N., Fiaschè, F., O'Connor, R. C., & Pompili, M. (2020). The involvement of hypothalamus–pituitary–adrenal (HPA) axis in suicide risk. *Brain Sciences, 10*(9), 653. https://doi.org/10.3390/brainsci10090653

Berger, B. (2014). Power, selfhood, and identity: A feminist critique of borderline personality disorder. *Advocates' Forum: A Publication by Students of The University of Chicago School of Social Service Administration*, 1–8.

Berger, T., Lee, H., Young, A. H., Aarsland, D., & Thuret, S. (2020). Adult hippocampal neurogenesis in major depressive disorder and Alzheimer's disease. *Trends in Molecular Medicine, 26*(9), 803–818. https://doi.org/10.1016/j.molmed.2020.03.010

Berglund, K., Roman, E., Balldin, J., Berggren, U., Eriksson, M., Gustavsson, P., & Fahlke, C. (2011). Do men with excessive alcohol consumption and social stability have an addictive personality? *Scandinavian Journal of Psychology, 52*(3), 257–260. https://doi.org/10.1111/j.1467-9450.2010.00872.x

Bergman, S. (2009, July 13). The farce of dueling psychiatrists. *Boston Globe*. http://archive.boston.com/bostonglobe/editorial_opinion/oped/articles/2009/07/13/the_farce_of_dueling_psychiatrists/

Bergmans, R. S., Kelly, K. M., & Mezuk, B. (2019). Inflammation as a unique marker of suicide ideation distinct from depression syndrome among U.S. adults. *Journal of Affective Disorders, 245*, 1052–1060. https://doi.org/10.1016/j.jad.2018.11.046

Bergström, T., Seikkula, J., Alakare, B., Mäki, P., Köngäs-Saviaro, P., Taskila, J. J., Tolvanen, A., & Aaltonen, J. (2018). The family-oriented open dialogue approach in the treatment of first-episode psychosis: Nineteen–year outcomes. *Psychiatry Research, 270*, 168–175. https://doi.org/10.1016/j.psychres.2018.09.039

Bergström, T., Seikkula, J., Holma, J., Köngäs-Saviaro, P., Taskila, J. J., & Alakare, B. (2021). Retrospective experiences of first-episode psychosis treatment under Open Dialogue-Based services: A qualitative study. *Community Mental Health Journal*. https://doi.org/10.1007/s10597-021-00895-6

Berlim, M. T., van den Eynde, F., Tovar-Perdomo, S., & Daskalakis, Z. J. (2014). Response, remission and drop-out rates following high-frequency repetitive transcranial magnetic stimulation (rTMS) for treating major depression: A systematic review and meta-analysis of randomized, double-blind and sham-controlled trials. *Psychological Medicine, 44*(2), 225–239. https://doi.org/10.1017/S0033291713000512

Bermejo-Pareja, F., Contador, I., Del Ser, T., Olazarán, J., Llamas-Velasco, S., Vega, S., & Benito-León, J. (2020). Predementia constructs: Mild cognitive impairment or mild neurocognitive disorder? A narrative review. *International Journal of Geriatric Psychiatry*. https://doi.org/10.1002/gps.5474

Bernhard, A., Mayer, J. S., Fann, N., & Freitag, C. M. (2021). Cortisol response to acute psychosocial stress in ADHD compared to conduct disorder and major depressive disorder: A systematic review. *Neuroscience & Biobehavioral Reviews, 127*, 899–916. https://doi.org/10.1016/j.neubiorev.2021.06.005

Berona, J., Horwitz, A. G., Czyz, E. K., & King, C. A. (2020). Predicting suicidal behavior among lesbian, gay, bisexual, and transgender youth receiving psychiatric emergency services. *Journal of Psychiatric Research, 122*, 64–69. https://doi.org/10.1016/j.jpsychires.2019.12.007

Berridge, K. C. (2007). The debate over dopamine's role in reward: The case for incentive salience. *Psychopharmacology, 191*(3), 391–431. https://doi.org/10.1007/s00213-006-0578-x

Berridge, K. C. (2022). Is addiction a brain disease? The incentive-sensitization view. In N. Heather, M. Field, A. C. Moss, & S. Satel (Eds.), *Evaluating the brain disease model of addiction* (1st ed., pp. 74–86). Routledge. https://doi.org/10.4324/9781003032762-8

Berridge, K. C., & Kringelbach, M. L. (2008). Affective neuroscience of pleasure: Reward in humans and animals. *Psychopharmacology, 199*(3), 457–480. https://doi.org/10.1007/s00213-008-1099-6

Berzoff, J. (2003). Psychodynamic theories in grief and bereavement. *Smith College Studies in Social Work, 73*(3), 273–298. https://doi.org/10.1080/00377310309517686

Bettelheim, B. (1967). *The empty fortress*. Free Press.

Beucke, J. C., Simon, D., Sepulcre, J., Talukdar, T., Feusner, J. D., Kaufmann, C., & Kathmann, N. (2020). Heightened degree connectivity of the striatum in obsessive-compulsive disorder induced by symptom provocation. *Journal of Affective Disorders, 276*, 1069–1076. https://doi.org/10.1016/j.jad.2020.07.062

Beurel, E., Toups, M., & Nemeroff, C. B. (2020). The bidirectional relationship of depression and inflammation: Double trouble. *Neuron, 107*(2), 234–256. https://doi.org/10.1016/j.neuron.2020.06.002

Bey, T., & Patel, A. (2007). Phencyclidine intoxication and adverse effects: A clinical and pharmacological review of an illicit drug. *The California Journal of Emergency Medicine, 8*(1), 9–14.

Bharti, A., Mishra, A. K., Sinha, V., Anwar, Z., Kumar, V., & Mitra, S. (2015). Paper eating: An unusual obsessive-compulsive disorder dimension. *Industrial Psychiatry Journal, 24*(2), 189–191. https://doi.org/10.4103/0972-6748.181713

Bhatia, M. S., & Gupta, R. (2009). Pica responding to SSRI: An OCD spectrum disorder? *The World Journal of Biological Psychiatry, 10*(4 Pt 3), 936–938. https://doi.org/10.1080/15622970701308389

Bhattacharya, A., Cooper, M., McAdams, C., Peebles, R., & Timko, C. A. (2022). Cultural shifts in the symptoms of anorexia nervosa: The case of orthorexia nervosa. *Appetite, 170*, 105869. https://doi.org/10.1016/j.appet.2021.105869

Bhaumik, S., Kiani, R., Michael, D. M., Gangavati, S., Khan, S., Torales, J., Javate, K. R., & Ventriglio, A. (2016). World Psychiatric Association (WPA) report on mental health issues in people with intellectual disability. Paper 1: Intellectual disability and mental health: An overview. *International Journal of Culture and Mental Health, 9*(4), 417–429. https://doi.org/10.1080/17542863.2016.1228687

Bhola, P., & Chaturvedi, S. K. (2020). Neurasthenia: Tracing the journey of a protean malady. *International Review of Psychiatry, 32*(5–6), 491–499. https://doi.org/10.1080/09540261.2020.1758638

Bienemann, B., Ruschel, N. S., Campos, M. L., Negreiros, M. A., & Mograbi, D. C. (2020). Self-reported negative outcomes of psilocybin users: A quantitative textual analysis. *PLOS ONE, 15*(2), e0229067. https://doi.org/10.1371/journal.pone.0229067

Bigby, C., & Beadle-Brown, J. (2016). Culture in better group homes for people with intellectual disability at severe levels. *Intellectual and Developmental Disabilities, 54*(5), 316–331. https://doi.org/10.1352/1934-9556-54.5.316

Bilal, M., Haseeb, A., Saeed, A., Saeed, A., Sarwar, T., Ahmed, S., Ishaque, A., & Raza, M. (2020). Prevalence of nocturnal enuresis among children dwelling in rural areas of Sindh. *Cureus, 12*(8). https://doi.org/10.7759/cureus.9590

Billieux, J., Schimmenti, A., Khazaal, Y., Maurage, P., & Heeren, A. (2015). Are we overpathologizing everyday life? A tenable blueprint for behavioral addiction research. *Journal of Behavioral Addictions, 4*(3), 119–123. https://doi.org/10.1556/2006.4.2015.009

Billings, D. B., & Urban, T. (1982). The socio-medical construction of transsexualism: An interpretation and critique. *Social Problems, 29*(3), 266–282. https://doi.org/10.1525/sp.1982.29.3.03a00050

Binks, C., Fenton, M., McCarthy, L., Lee, T., Adams, C. E., & Duggan, C. (2006). Psychological therapies for people with borderline personality disorder (Review). *Cochrane Database of Systematic Reviews, 2006* (1), Article CD005652. https://doi.org/10.1002/14651858.CD005653

Biogen. (2022, September 27). *Lecanemab confirmatory phase 3 clarity ad study met primary endpoint, showing highly statistically significant reduction of clinical decline in large global clinical study of 1,795 participants with early Alzheimer's disease.* https://investors.biogen.com/news-releases/news-release-details/lecanemab-confirmatory-phase-3-clarity-ad-study-met-primary

Bird, T. D. (2008). Genetic aspects of Alzheimer disease. *Genetics in Medicine, 10*(4), 231–239. https://doi.org/10.1097/GIM.0b013e31816b64dc

Birge, S. J. (1997). The role of estrogen in the treatment of Alzheimer's disease. *Neurology, 48*(5Suppl. 7), 36S–41S. https://doi.org/10.1212/WNL.48.5_Suppl_7.36S

Birt, J., Thacher, A., Steinberg, H., Weiler, R., Poplawski, R., Dobbs-Marsh, J., Robinson, A., & Zack, S. (2022). Effectiveness of DBT skills training in outpatient men: A naturalistic study. *Psychological Services*. https://doi.org/10.1037/ser0000686

Birt, L., Poland, F., Csipke, E., & Charlesworth, G. (2017). Shifting dementia discourses from deficit to active citizenship. *Sociology of Health & Illness, 39*(2), 199–211. https://doi.org/10.1111/1467-9566.12530

Bishop, D. V. M., & Swendsen, J. (2021). Psychoanalysis in the treatment of autism: Why is France a cultural outlier? *BJPsych Bulletin, 45*(2), 89–93. https://doi.org/10.1192/bjb.2020.138

Bishop-Fitzpatrick, L., Minshew, N. J., & Eack, S. M. (2013). A systematic review of psychosocial interventions for adults with autism spectrum disorders. *Journal of Autism and Developmental Disorders, 43*(3), 687–694. https://doi.org/10.1007/s10803-012-1615-8

Bisset, M., Winter, L., Middeldorp, C. M., Coghill, D., Zendarski, N., Bellgrove, M. A., & Sciberras, E. (2022). Recent attitudes toward ADHD in the broader community: A systematic review. *Journal of Attention Disorders, 26*(4), 537–548. https://doi.org/10.1177/10870547211003671

Bisson, J. I., Ehlers, A., Matthews, R., Pilling, S., Richards, D., & Turner, S. (2007). Psychological treatments for chronic post-traumatic stress disorder: Systematic review and meta-analysis. *The British Journal of Psychiatry, 190*(2), 97–104. https://doi.org/10.1192/bjp.bp.106.021402

Bisson, J. I., McFarlane, A. C., Rose, S., Ruzek, J. I., & Watson, P. J. (2009). Psychological debriefing for adults. In E. B. Foa, T. M. Keane, M. J. Friedman, & J. A. Cohen (Eds.), *Effective treatments for PTSD: Practice guidelines from the International Society for Traumatic Stress Studies* (2nd ed., pp. 83–105). Guilford Press.

Bitsko, R. H. (2022). Mental health surveillance among children—United States, 2013–2019. *MMWR Supplements, 71*(Suppl. 2), 1–42. https://doi.org/10.15585/mmwr.su7102a1

Black, D. W. (2016). Compulsive shopping as a behavioral addiction. In N. M. Petry (Ed.), *Behavioral addictions: DSM-5® and beyond* (pp. 125–156). Oxford University Press.

Blair, R. J. R., Meffert, H., Hwang, S., & White, S. F. (2018). Psychopathy and brain function: Insights from neuroimaging research. In C. J. Patrick (Ed.), *Handbook of psychopathy* (2nd ed., pp. 401–421). The Guilford Press.

Blaney, C., Sommer, J., El-Gabalawy, R., Bernstein, C., Walld, R., Hitchon, C., Bolton, J., Sareen, J., Patten, S., Singer, A., Lix, L., Katz, A., Fisk, J., Marrie, R. A., & CIHR Team in Defining the Burden and Managing the Impact of Psychiatric Comorbidity in Immune-Mediated Inflammatory Disease. (2020). Incidence and temporal trends of co-occurring personality disorder diagnoses in immune-mediated inflammatory diseases. *Epidemiology and Psychiatric Sciences*, 29, e84. https://doi.org/10.1017/S2045796019000854

Blasco-Fontecilla, H., & Oquendo, M. A. (2016). Biomarkers of suicide: Predicting the predictable? In P. Courtet (Ed.), *Understanding suicide: From diagnosis to personalized treatment* (pp. 77–83). Springer.

Blashfield, R. K., Keeley, J. W., Flanagan, E. H., & Miles, S. R. (2014). The cycle of classification: DSM-I through DSM-5. *Annual Review of Clinical Psychology*, 10, 25–51. https://doi.org/10.1146/annurev-clinpsy-032813-153639

Blatt, S. J., & Homann, E. (1992). Parent-child interaction in the etiology of dependent and self-critical depression. *Clinical Psychology Review*, 12(1), 47–91. https://doi.org/10.1016/0272-7358(92)90091-L

Blatt, S. J., & Levy, K. N. (2003). Attachment theory, psychoanalysis, personality development, and psychopathology. *Psychoanalytic Inquiry*, 23(1), 102–150. https://doi.org/10.1080/07351692309349028

Bledsoe, B. E. (2003). Critical incident stress management (CISM): Benefit or risk for emergency services? *Prehospital Emergency Care*, 7(2), 272–279.

Bleichhardt, G., Timmer, B., & Rief, W. (2004). Cognitive-behavioural therapy for patients with multiple somatoform symptoms—a randomised controlled trial in tertiary care. *Journal of Psychosomatic Research*, 56(4), 449–454. https://doi.org/10.1016/S0022-3999(03)00630-5

Blewett, A., & Bottéro, A. (1995). L.-V. Marcé and the psychopathology of eating disorders. *History of Psychiatry*, 6(21, Pt 1), 69–85. https://doi.org/10.1177/0957154X9500602104

Blihar, D., Delgado, E., Buryak, M., Gonzalez, M., & Waechter, R. (2020). A systematic review of the neuroanatomy of dissociative identity disorder. *European Journal of Trauma & Dissociation*, 4(3), 100148. https://doi.org/10.1016/j.ejtd.2020.100148

Bliss, E. L. (1984). Spontaneous self-hypnosis in multiple personality disorder. *Psychiatric Clinics of North America*, 7(1), 135–148.

Bloch-Atefi, A., & Smith, J. (2015). The effectiveness of body-oriented psychotherapy: A review of the literature. *Psychotherapy and Counselling Journal of Australia*, 3(1). https://pacja.org.au/2015/07/the-effectiveness-of-body-oriented-psychotherapy-a-review-of-the-literature/

Block, J. (2008). *The Q-Sort in character appraisal*. American Psychological Association.

Blomgren, M. (2013). Behavioral treatments for children and adults who stutter: A review. *Psychology Research and Behavior Management*, 6, 9–19. https://doi.org/10.2147/PRBM.S31450

Blomstedt, P., Sjöberg, R. L., Hansson, M., Bodlund, O., & Hariz, M. I. (2011). Deep brain stimulation in the treatment of depression. *Acta Psychiatrica Scandinavica*, 123(1), 4–11. https://doi.org/10.1111/j.1600-0447.2010.01625.x

Blonigen, D. M., Finney, J. W., Wilbourne, P. L., & Moos, R. H. (2015). Psychosocial treatments for substance use disorders. In P. E. Nathan & J. M. Gorman (Eds.), *A guide to treatments that work* (4th ed., pp. 731–761). Oxford University Press.

Bloom, J. D., Hansen, T. E., & Blekic, A. (2022). Competency to stand trial, civil commitment, and Oregon State Hospital. *Journal of the American Academy of Psychiatry and the Law Online*, 50(1), 67–73. https://doi.org/10.29158/JAAPL.210055-21

Bloom, J. D., & Kirkorsky, S. E. (2021). *Mens rea*, competency to stand trial, and guilty but mentally ill. *Journal of the American Academy of Psychiatry and the Law*, 49(2), 241–245. https://doi.org/10.29158/JAAPL.200105-20

Bloomfield, M. A. P., & Howes, O. D. (2021). Dopaminergic mechanisms underlying psychosis. In C. A. Tamminga, E. I. Ivleva, U. Reininghaus, & J. van Os (Eds.), *Psychotic disorders: Comprehensive conceptualization and treatments* (pp. 277–286). Oxford University Press. https://doi.org/10.1093/med/9780190653279.003.0031

Blount, T. H., Raj, J. J., & Peterson, A. L. (2018). Intensive outpatient comprehensive behavioral intervention for tics: A clinical replication series. *Cognitive and Behavioral Practice*, 25(1), 156–167. https://doi.org/10.1016/j.cbpra.2017.02.001

Blum, K., Bowirrat, A., Braverman, E. R., Baron, D., Cadet, J. L., Kazmi, S., Elman, I., Thanos, P. K., Badgaiyan, R. D., Downs, W. B., Bagchi, D., Llanos-Gomez, L., & Gold, M. S. (2021). Reward deficiency syndrome (RDS): A cytoarchitectural common neurobiological trait of all addictions. *International Journal of Environmental Research and Public Health*, 18(21), 11529. https://doi.org/10.3390/ijerph182111529

Blum, K., Cull, J. G., Braverman, E. R., & Comings, D. E. (1996). Reward deficiency syndrome. *American Scientist*, 84(2), 132–145.

Blum, K., Febo, M., McLaughlin, T., Cronjé, F. J., Han, D., & Gold, M. S. (2014). Hatching the behavioral addiction egg: Reward Deficiency Solution System (RDSS)™ as a function of dopaminergic neurogenetics and brain functional connectivity linking all addictions under a common rubric. *Journal of Behavioral Addictions*, 3(3), 149–156. https://doi.org/10.1556/JBA.3.2014.019

Blum, K., Hauser, M., Agan, G., Giordano, J., Fratantonio, J., Badgaiyan, R. D., & Febo, M. (2015). Understanding the importance of dopaminergic deficit in Reward Deficiency Syndrome (RDS): Redeeming joy overcoming "darkness" in recovery. *Psychology*, 6(4), 435–439. https://doi.org/10.4236/psych.2015.64040

Blum, K., McLaughlin, T., Bowirrat, A., Modestino, E. J., Baron, D., Gomez, L. L., Ceccanti, M., Braverman, E. R., Thanos, P. K., Cadet, J. L., Elman, I., Badgaiyan, R. D., Jalali, R., Green, R., Simpatico, T. A., Gupta, A., & Gold, M. S. (2022). Reward deficiency syndrome (RDS) surprisingly Is evolutionary and found everywhere: Is It "Blowin' in the Wind"? *Journal of Personalized Medicine*, 12(2), 321. https://doi.org/10.3390/jpm12020321

Bluth, R. (2018, September 10). ADHD numbers are rising, and scientists are trying to understand why. *Washington Post*. https://www.washingtonpost.com/national/health-science/adhd-numbers-are-rising-and-scientists-are-trying-to-understand-why/2018/09/07/a918d0f4-b07e-11e8-a20b-5f4f84429666_story.html

Boag, S. (2011). Explanation in personality psychology: "Verbal magic" and the five-factor model. *Philosophical Psychology*, 24(2), 223–243. https://doi.org/10.1080/09515089.2010.548319

Bockoven, J. S. (1972). *Moral treatment in community mental health*. Springer Publishing.

Bodell, L. P., & Devlin, M. J. (2010). Pharmacotherapy for binge-eating disorder. In C. M. Grilo & J. E. Mitchell (Eds.), *The treatment of eating disorders: A clinical handbook* (pp. 402–413). Guilford Press.

Bodell, L. P., & Keel, P. K. (2010). Current treatment for anorexia nervosa: Efficacy, safety, and adherence. *Psychology Research and Behavior Management*, 2010(3), 91-108. https://doi.org/10.2147/PRBM.S13814

Bodenmann, G., & Randall, A. (2013). Marital therapy for dealing with depression. In M. Power (Ed.), *The Wiley-Blackwell handbook of mood disorders* (2nd ed., pp. 215–227). Wiley-Blackwell.

Boelen, P. A., de Keijser, J., van den Hout, M. A., & van den Bout, J. (2007). Treatment of complicated grief: A comparison between cognitive-behavioral therapy and supportive counseling. *Journal of Consulting and Clinical Psychology*, 75(2), 277–284. https://doi.org/10.1037/0022-006X.75.2.277

Boelen, P. A., van den Hout, M., & van den Bout, J. (2013). Prolonged grief disorder: Cognitive-behavioral theory and therapy. In M. Stroebe, H. Schut, & J. van den Bout (Eds.), *Complicated grief: Scientific foundations for health care professionals* (pp. 221–234). Routledge.

Boeree, C. G. (2006). *Victor Frankl*. http://webspace.ship.edu/cgboer/frankl.html

Bögels, S. M., Wijts, P., Oort, F. J., & Sallaerts, S. J. M. (2014). Psychodynamic psychotherapy versus cognitive behavior therapy for social anxiety disorder: An efficacy and partial effectiveness trial. *Depression and Anxiety*, 31(5), 363–373. https://doi.org/10.1002/da.22246

Bogowicz, P., Curtis, H. J., Walker, A. J., Cowen, P., Geddes, J., & Goldacre, B. (2021). Trends and variation in antidepressant prescribing in English primary care: A retrospective longitudinal study. *BJGP Open*, 5(4), BJGPO.2021.0020. https://doi.org/10.3399/BJGPO.2021.0020

Bohman, M., Cloninger, C. R., von Knorring, A.-L., & Sigvardsson, S. (1984). An adoption study of somatoform disorders: III. Cross-fostering analysis and genetic relationship to alcoholism and criminality. *Archives of General Psychiatry*, 41(9), 872–878. https://doi.org/10.1001/archpsyc.1984.01790200054007

Bokor, G., & Anderson, P. D. (2014). Ketamine: An update on its abuse. *Journal of Pharmacy Practice*, 27(6), 582–586. https://doi.org/10.1177/0897190014525754

Boksa, P. (2008). Maternal infection during pregnancy and schizophrenia. *Journal of Psychiatry & Neuroscience*, 33(3), 183–185.

Boku, S., Nakagawa, S., Toda, H., & Hishimoto, A. (2018). Neural basis of major depressive disorder: Beyond monoamine hypothesis. *Psychiatry and Clinical Neurosciences*, 72(1), 3–12. https://doi.org/10.1111/pcn.12604

Bola, J. R., Lehtinen, K., Aaltonen, J., Räkköläinen, V., Syvälahti, E., & Lehtinen, V. (2006). Predicting medication-free treatment response in acute psychosis: Cross-validation from the Finnish need-adapted project. *Journal of Nervous and Mental Disease*, 194(10), 732–739. https://doi.org/10.1097/01.nmd.0000243080.90255.88

Bola, J. R., & Mosher, L. R. (2003). Treatment of acute psychosis without neuroleptics: Two-year outcomes from the Soteria project. *Journal of Nervous and Mental Disease*, 191(4), 219–229. https://doi.org/10.1097/00005053-200304000-00002

Bolduan, A. J., & Haas, D. M. (2015). A systematic review of the use of bupropion for hypoactive sexual desire disorder in premenopausal women. *Journal of Woman's Reproductive Health*, 1(1), 14–23. https://doi.org/10.14302/issn.2381-862X.jwrh-14-546

Bollas, C., & Sundelson, D. (1995). *The new informants: The betrayal of confidentiality in psychoanalysis and psychotherapy*. Jason Aronson.

Bolling, M. Y., Terry, C. M., & Kohlneberg, R. J. (2006). Behavioral therapies. In J. C. Thomas & D. L. Segel (Eds.), *Comprehensive handbook of personality and psychopathology: Vol. 1. Personality and everyday functioning* (pp. 142–172). John Wiley.

Bolton, J. W. (2014). Case formulation after Engel—The 4P model: A philosophical case conference. *Philosophy, Psychiatry, & Psychology*, 21(3), 179–189. https://doi.org/10.1353/ppp.2014.0027

Bomba, J., & Cichocki, Ł. (2009). Will neuroscience account for the psychotherapeutic outcome in schizophrenia? *Archives of Psychiatry and Psychotherapy*, 11(3), 11–16.

Bonanno, G. A., Galea, S., Bucciarelli, A., & Vlahov, D. (2007). What predicts psychological resilience after disaster? The role of demographics, resources, and life stress. *Journal of Consulting and Clinical Psychology*, 75(5), 671–682. https://doi.org/10.1037/0022-006X.75.5.671

Bonanno, G. A., Papa, A., Lalande, K., Zhang, N., & Noll, J. G. (2005). Grief processing and deliberate grief avoidance: A prospective comparison of bereaved spouses and parents in the United States and the People's Republic of China. *Journal of Consulting and Clinical Psychology*, 73(1), 86–98. https://doi.org/10.1037/0022-006X.73.1.86

Bond, K., & Anderson, I. M. (2015). Psychoeducation for relapse prevention in bipolar disorder: A systematic review of efficacy in randomized controlled trials. *Bipolar Disorders*, 17(4), 349–362. https://doi.org/10.1111/bdi.12287

Bondy, A., & Frost, L. (2002). *A picture's worth: PECS and other visual communication strategies in autism*. Woodbine House.

Bonfils, K. A., Lysaker, P. H., Minor, K. S., & Salyers, M. P. (2016). Affective empathy in schizophrenia: A meta-analysis. *Schizophrenia Research*, 175(1–3), 109–117. https://doi.org/10.1016/j.schres.2016.03.037

Bonnet, U., & Preuss, U. W. (2017). The cannabis withdrawal syndrome: Current insights. *Substance Abuse and Rehabilitation*, 8, 9–37. https://doi.org/10.2147/SAR.S109576

Bonnington, O., & Rose, D. (2014). Exploring stigmatisation among people diagnosed with either bipolar disorder or borderline personality disorder: A critical realist analysis. *Social Science & Medicine*, 123, 7–17. https://doi.org/10.1016/j.socscimed.2014.10.048

Bonomo, Y., Norman, A., Biondo, S., Bruno, R., Daglish, M., Dawe, S., Egerton-Warburton, D., Karro, J., Kim, C., Lenton, S., Lubman, D. I., Pastor, A., Rundle, J., Ryan, J., Gordon, P., Sharry, P., Nutt, D., & Castle, D. (2019). The Australian drug harms ranking study. *Journal of Psychopharmacology*, 33(7), 759–768. https://doi.org/10.1177/0269881119841569

Bonta, J., & Andrews, D. A. (2007). Risk-need-responsivity model for offender assessment and rehabilitation. *Rehabilitation*, 6, 1–22.

Bora, E., Yucel, M., & Pantelis, C. (2009). Theory of mind impairment in schizophrenia: Meta-analysis. *Schizophrenia Research*, 109(1–3), 1–9. https://doi.org/10.1016/j.schres.2008.12.020

Boraska, V., Davis, O. S. P., Cherkas, L. F., Helder, S. G., Harris, J., Krug, I., … Zeggini, E. (2012). Genome-wide association analysis of eating disorder-related symptoms, behaviors, and personality traits. *American Journal of Medical Genetics*. Part B, Neuropsychiatric Genetics: The Official Publication of The International Society of Psychiatric Genetics, 159B(7), 803–811. doi:10.1002/ajmg.b.32087

Boraska, V., Franklin, C. S., Floyd, J. A. B., Thornton, L. M., Huckins, L. M., Southam, L., … Tortorella, A. (2014). A genome-wide association study of anorexia nervosa. *Molecular Psychiatry*, 19(10), 1085–1094. doi:10.1038/mp.2013.187

Border, R., Johnson, E. C., Evans, L. M., Smolen, A., Berley, N., Sullivan, P. F., & Keller, M. C. (2019). No support for historical candidate gene or candidate gene-by-interaction hypotheses for major depression across multiple large samples. *American Journal of Psychiatry*, 176(5), 376–387. https://doi.org/10.1176/appi.ajp.2018.18070881

Borelle, C., Eideliman, J.-S., Fansten, M., Planche, M., & Turlais, A. (2019). Against the tide: Psychodynamic approaches to agitated childhood in France, between crisis and resistance. *Saúde e Sociedade*, 28, 27–39. https://doi.org/10.1590/S0104-12902019181114

Borghans, L., Golsteyn, B. H. H., Heckman, J. J., & Humphries, J. E. (2016). What grades and achievement tests measure. *Proceedings of the National Academy of Sciences*, 113(47), 13354–13359. https://doi.org/10.1073/pnas.1601135113

Borkovec, T. D., Alcaine, O. M., & Behar, E. (2004). Avoidance theory of worry and generalized anxiety disorder. In R. G. Heimberg, C. L. Turk, & D. S. Mennin (Eds.), *Generalized anxiety disorder: Advances in research and practice* (pp. 77–108). Guilford Press.

Bornstein, R. F. (2011). From symptom to process: How the PDM alters goals and strategies in psychological assessment. *Journal of Personality Assessment*, 93(2), 142–150. https://doi.org/10.1080/00223891.2011.542714

Bornstein, R. F., Denckla, C. A., & Chung, W.-J. (2013). Psychodynamic models of personality. In H. Tennen & J. Suls (Eds.), *Handbook of psychology: Vol. 5. Personality and social psychology* (2nd ed., pp. 43–64). John Wiley & Sons.

Borowicz, K. K., Kaczmarska, P., & Barbara, S. (2014). Medical uses of marijuana. *Archives of Physiotherapy and Global Researches*, 18(4), 13–17. https://doi.org/10.15442/apgr.18.1.20

Boschloo, L., Bekhuis, E., Weitz, E. S., Reijnders, M., DeRubeis, R. J., Dimidjian, S., Dunner, D. L., Dunlop, B. W., Hegerl, U., Hollon, S. D., Jarrett, R. B., Kennedy, S. H., Miranda, J., Mohr, D. C., Simons, A. D., Parker, G., Petrak, F., Herpertz, S., Quilty, L. C., … Cuijpers, P. (2019). The symptom-specific efficacy of antidepressant medication vs. cognitive behavioral therapy in the treatment of depression: Results from an individual patient data meta-analysis. *World Psychiatry*, 18(2), 183–191. https://doi.org/10.1002/wps.20630

Boseley, S. (2010, May 24). Andrew Wakefield struck off register by General Medical Council. *The Guardian*. https://www.theguardian.com/society/2010/may/24/andrew-wakefield-struck-off-gmc

Bosker, F. J., Tanke, M. A. C., Jongsma, M. E., Cremers, T. I. F. H., Jagtman, E., Pietersen, C. Y., van der Hart, M. G. C., Gladkevich, A. V., Kema, I. P., Westerink, B. H. C., Korf, J., & den Boer, J. A. (2010). Biochemical and behavioral effects of long-term citalopram administration and discontinuation in rats: Role of serotonin synthesis. *Neurochemistry International*, 57(8), 948–957. https://doi.org/10.1016/j.neuint.2010.10.001

Boss, J. M. (1979). The seventeenth-century transformation of the hysteric affection, and Sydenham's Baconian medicine. *Psychological Medicine*, 9(2), 221–234. https://doi.org/10.1017/S0033291700030725

Botha, M., Dibb, B., & Frost, D. M. (2022). "Autism is me": An investigation of how autistic individuals make sense of autism and stigma. *Disability & Society*, 37(3), 427–453. https://doi.org/10.1080/09687599.2020.1822782

Bothe, A. K., Davidow, J. H., Bramlett, R. E., Franic, D. M., & Ingham, R. J. (2006). Stuttering treatment research 1970-2005: II. Systematic review incorporating trial quality assessment of pharmacological approaches. *American Journal of Speech-Language Pathology*, 15(4), 342–352. https://doi.org/10.1044/1058-0360(2006/032)

Bőthe, B., Bartók, R., Tóth-Király, I., Reid, R. C., Griffiths, M. D., Demetrovics, Z., & Orosz, G. (2018). Hypersexuality, gender, and sexual orientation: A large-scale psychometric survey study. *Archives of Sexual Behavior*, 47(8), 2265–2276. https://doi.org/10.1007/s10508-018-1201-z

Botvin, G. J., Baker, E., Renick, N. L., Filazzola, A. D., & Botvin, E. M. (1984). A cognitive-behavioral approach to substance abuse prevention. *Addictive Behaviors*, 9(2), 137–147. https://doi.org/10.1016/0306-4603(84)90051-0

Bou Khalil, R., Souaiby, L., & Farès, N. (2017). The importance of the hypothalamo-pituitary-adrenal axis as a therapeutic target in anorexia nervosa. *Physiology & Behavior*, 171, 13–20. https://doi.org/10.1016/j.physbeh.2016.12.035

Bouchard, T. J., & McGue, M. (1981). Familial studies of intelligence: A review. *Science*, 212(4498), 1055–1059. https://doi.org/10.1126/science.7195071

Boucher, F. J. O., & Chinnah, T. I. (2020). Gender dysphoria: A review investigating the relationship between genetic influences and brain development. *Adolescent Health, Medicine and Therapeutics*, 11, 89–99. https://doi.org/10.2147/AHMT.S259168

Boulet, C., Lopez-Castroman, J., Mouchabac, S., Olié, E., Courtet, P., Thouvenot, E., Abbar, M., & Conejero, I. (2022). Stress response in dissociation and conversion disorders: A systematic review. *Neuroscience & Biobehavioral Reviews*, 132, 957–967. https://doi.org/10.1016/j.neubiorev.2021.10.049

Bouloukou, F., Marin-Diaz, V., & Jimenez-Fanjul, N. (2021). Effects of an interventional music program on learning skills of primary-school students with dyslexia. *International Journal of Education and Practice*, 9(3), Article 3. https://doi.org/10.18488/journal.61.2021.93.456.467

Bouman, T. K. (2014). Cognitive and behavioral models and cognitive-behavioral and related therapies for health anxiety and hypochondriasis. In V. Starcevic & Jr. Noyes Russell (Eds.), *Hypochondriasis and health anxiety: A guide for clinicians* (pp. 149–198). Oxford University Press.

Bourke, E., Barker, C., & Fornells-Ambrojo, M. (2021). Systematic review and meta-analysis of therapeutic alliance, engagement, and outcome in psychological therapies for psychosis. *Psychology and Psychotherapy: Theory, Research and Practice*, 94(3), 822–853. https://doi.org/10.1111/papt.12330

Bowcut, J. C., & Weiser, M. (2018). Inflammation and schizophrenia. *Psychiatric Annals*, 48(5), 237–243. https://doi.org/10.3928/00485713-20180416-01

Bowen, M. (1978). *Family therapy in clinical practice*. Jason Aronson.

Bowen, M. L. (2016). Stigma: Content analysis of the representation of people with personality disorder in the UK popular press, 2001–2012. *International Journal of Mental Health Nursing*. https://doi.org/10.1111/inm.12213

Bower, G. (1994). Temporary emotional states act like multiple personalities. In R. M. Klein & B. K. Doane (Eds.), *Psychological concepts and dissociative disorders* (pp. 207–234). Lawrence Erlbaum.

Bower, G. H. (1981). Mood and memory. *American Psychologist*, 36(2), 129–148. https://doi.org/10.1037/0003-066X.36.2.129

Bowl, R. (1996). Legislating for user involvement in the United Kingdom: Mental health services and the NHS and Community Care Act 1990. *International Journal of Social Psychiatry*, 42(3), 165–180.

Bowlby, J. (1980). *Attachment and loss*. Basic Books.

Bowlby, J. (1988). *A secure base: Parent-child attachment and healthy human development*. Basic Books.

Boyd, A., Dworzynski, K., & Howell, P. (2011). Pharmacological agents for developmental stuttering in children and adolescents: A systematic review. *Journal of Clinical Psychopharmacology*, 31(6), 740–744. https://doi.org/10.1097/JCP.0b013e318234ee3b

Boyd, J. E., Lanius, R. A., & McKinnon, M. C. (2018). Mindfulness-based treatments for posttraumatic stress disorder: A review of the treatment literature and neurobiological evidence. *Journal of Psychiatry & Neuroscience*, 43(1), 7–25. https://doi.org/10.1503/jpn.170021

Boyle, M. (2002). *Schizophrenia: A scientific delusion?* (2nd ed.). Routledge.

Boyle, M. (2022). Power in the power threat meaning framework. *Journal of Constructivist Psychology*, 35(1), 27–40. https://doi.org/10.1080/10720537.2020.1773357

Boyle, M. P., Dioguardi, L., & Pate, J. E. (2016). A comparison of three strategies for reducing the public stigma associated with stuttering. *Journal of Fluency Disorders*, 50, 44–58. https://doi.org/10.1016/j.jfludis.2016.09.004

Boyle, R., Knight, S. P., De Looze, C., Carey, D., Scarlett, S., Stern, Y., Robertson, I. H., Kenny, R. A., & Whelan, R. (2021). Verbal intelligence is a more robust cross-sectional measure of cognitive reserve than level of education in healthy older adults. *Alzheimer's Research & Therapy*, 2021 (13), Article 128. https://doi.org/10.1186/s13195-021-00870-z

Bozkurt, H., Mutluer, T. D., Kose, C., & Zoroglu, S. (2015). High psychiatric comorbidity in adolescents with dissociative disorders. *Psychiatry and Clinical Neurosciences*, 69(6), 369–374. https://doi.org/10.1111/pcn.12256

Bradford, J. M., & Fedoroff, J. P. (2009). The neurobiology of sexual behavior and the paraphilias. In F. M. Saleh, Jr. Grudzinskas Albert J., J. M. Bradford, & D. J. Brodsky (Eds.), *Sex offenders: Identification, risk assessment, treatment, and legal issues* (pp. 36–46). Oxford University Press.

Brailsford, J. M., Hill, T. D., Burdette, A. M., & Jorgenson, A. K. (2018). Are socioeconomic inequalities in physical health mediated by embodied environmental toxins? *Socius: Sociological Research for a Dynamic World*, 4, 1-9. https://doi.org/10.1177/2378023118771462

Brambilla, F., Bellodi, L., Arancio, C., Ronchi, P., & Limonta, D. (2001). Central dopaminergic function in Anorexia and Bulimia Nervosa: A psychoneuroendocrine approach. *Psychoneuroendocrinology*, 26(4), 393–409. https://doi.org/10.1016/s0306-4530(00)00062-7

Brand, B. L. (2012). What we know and what we need to learn about the treatment of dissociative disorders. *Journal of Trauma & Dissociation*, 13(4), 387–396. https://doi.org/10.1080/15299732.2012.672550

Brand, B. L., Classen, C. C., McNary, S. W., & Zaveri, P. (2009). A review of dissociative disorders treatment studies. *Journal of Nervous and Mental Disease*, 197(9), 646–654. https://doi.org/10.1097/NMD.0b013e3181b3afaa

Brand, B. L., Lanius, R., Vermetten, E., Loewenstein, R. J., & Spiegel, D. (2012). Where are we going? An update on assessment, treatment, and neurobiological research in dissociative disorders as we move toward the DSM-5. *Journal of Trauma & Dissociation*, 13(1), 9–31. https://doi.org/10.1080/15299732.2011.620687

Brand, B. L., Loewenstein, R. J., & Spiegel, D. (2014). Dispelling myths about dissociative identity disorder treatment: An empirically based approach. *Psychiatry: Interpersonal and Biological Processes*, 77(2), 169–189. https://doi.org/10.1521/psyc.2014.77.2.169

Brand, B., Loewenstein, R. J., & Spiegel, D. (2013). Disinformation about dissociation: Dr Joel Paris's notions about dissociative identity disorder. *Journal of Nervous and Mental Disease*, 201(4), 354–356. https://doi.org/10.1097/NMD.0b013e318288d2ee

Brando, F., Giordano, G. M., Bucci, P., Palumbo, D., Piegari, G., Mucci, A., & Galderisi, S. (2021). Effectiveness of social skills training conducted in a group of subjects with first-episode psychosis. *European Psychiatry*, 64(S1), S505–S505. https://doi.org/10.1192/j.eurpsy.2021.1352

Brandt, L., Bschor, T., Henssler, J., Müller, M., Hasan, A., Heinz, A., & Gutwinski, S. (2020). Antipsychotic withdrawal symptoms: A systematic review and meta-analysis. *Frontiers in Psychiatry*, 11, Article 569912. https://doi.org/10.3389/fpsyt.2020.569912

Brandys, M. K., de Kovel, C. G. F., Kas, M. J., van Elburg, A. A., & Adan, R. A. H. (2015). Overview of genetic research in anorexia nervosa: The past, the present and the future. *International Journal of Eating Disorders*, 48(7), 814–825. doi:10.1002/eat.22400

Branitsky, A., Longden, E., & Corstens, D. (2021). Hearing voices groups. In C. A. Tamminga, E. I. Ivleva, U. Reininghaus, & J. van Os (Eds.), *Psychotic disorders: Comprehensive conceptualization and treatments* (pp. 555–564). Oxford University Press.

Bransfield & Friedman. (2019). Differentiating psychosomatic, somatopsychic, multisystem illnesses, and medical uncertainty. *Healthcare*, 7(4), 114. https://doi.org/10.3390/healthcare7040114

Bratman, S. (n.d.). *The health food eating disorder*. https://www.beyondveg.com/bratman-s/hfj/hf-junkie-1a.shtml (Previously published in *Yoga Journal*, October 1997, pp. 42–50)

Bratton, S. C., Ceballos, P. L., Sheely-Moore, A. I., Meany-Walen, K., Pronchenko, Y., & Jones, L. D. (2013). Head start early mental health intervention: Effects of child-centered play therapy on disruptive behaviors. *International Journal of Play Therapy*, 22(1), 28–42. https://doi.org/10.1037/a0030318

Bratton, S. C., Ray, D. C., Edwards, N. A., & Landreth, G. (2009). Child-centered play therapy (CCPT): Theory, research, and practice. *Person-Centered and Experiential Psychotherapies*, 8(4), 266–281. https://doi.org/10.1080/14779757.2009.9688493

Braun, J. M., Froehlich, T., Kalkbrenner, A., Pfeiffer, C. M., Fazili, Z., Yolton, K., & Lanphear, B. P. (2014). Brief report: Are autistic-behaviors in children related to prenatal vitamin use and maternal whole blood folate concentrations? *Journal of Autism and Developmental Disorders*, 44(10), 2602–2607. https://doi.org/10.1007/s10803-014-2114-x

Brauser, D. (2021, March 22). BPD diagnosis: To tell or not to tell your patient? *Medscape*. https://www.medscape.com/viewarticle/947850

Breathnach, C. S. (1998). Richard Morton's *Phthisiologia*. *Journal of the Royal Society of Medicine*, 91(10), 551–552. https://doi.org/10.1177/014107689809101021

Bredström, A. (2019). Culture and context in mental health diagnosing: Scrutinizing the DSM-5 revision. *Journal of Medical Humanities*, 40(3), 347–363. https://doi.org/10.1007/s10912-017-9501-1

Breggin, P. R. (2007). ECT damages the brain: Disturbing news for patients and shock doctors alike. *Ethical Human Psychology and Psychiatry: An International Journal of Critical Inquiry*, 9(2), 83–86. https://doi.org/10.1891/152315007782021196

Breggin, P. R. (2009). Electroshock forced on children and involuntary adults. *Ethical Human Psychology and Psychiatry: An International Journal of Critical Inquiry*, 11(2), 80–82. https://doi.org/10.1891/1559-4343.11.2.80

Breggin, P. R. (2010). The FDA should test the safety of ECT machines. *Ethical Human Psychology and Psychiatry: An International Journal of Critical Inquiry*, 12(2), 139–143. https://doi.org/10.1891/1559-4343.12.2.139

Breggin, P. R. (2019). Extreme psychospiritual states versus organic brain disease: Bringing together science and the human factor. *Journal of Humanistic Psychology*, 59(5), 686–696. https://doi.org/10.1177/0022167818761975

Breinbjerg, A., Rittig, S., & Kamperis, K. (2021). Does the development and use of modern disposable diapers affect bladder control? A systematic review. *Journal of Pediatric Urology*, 17(4), 463–471. https://doi.org/10.1016/j.jpurol.2021.05.007

Breitborde, N. J. K., López, S. R., & Nuechterlein, K. H. (2010). Expressed emotion and the course of schizophrenia: The role of human agency. *Directions in Psychiatry*, 30(1), 29–40.

Breitenfeld, T., Jurasic, M. J., & Breitenfeld, D. (2014). Hippocrates: The forefather of neurology. *Neurological Sciences*, 35(9), 1349–1352. https://doi.org/10.1007/s10072-014-1869-3

Brelet, L., Flaudias, V., Désert, M., Guillaume, S., Llorca, P.-M., & Boirie, Y. (2021). Stigmatization toward people with anorexia nervosa, bulimia nervosa, and binge eating disorder: A scoping review. *Nutrients*, 13, Article 8. https://doi.org/10.3390/nu13082834

Bremner, J. D. (1999). Does stress damage the brain? *Biological Psychiatry*, 45(7), 797–805. https://doi.org/10.1016/S0006-3223(99)00009-8

Bremner, J. D., Mishra, S., Campanella, C., Shah, M., Kasher, N., Evans, S., Fani, N., Shah, A. J., Reiff, C., Davis, L. L., Vaccarino, V., & Carmody, J. (2017). A pilot study of the effects of mindfulness-based stress reduction on post-traumatic stress disorder symptoms and brain response to traumatic reminders of combat in Operation Enduring Freedom/Operation Iraqi Freedom combat veterans with post-traumatic stress disorder. *Frontiers in Psychiatry*, 8, Article 157. https://www.doi.org/10.3389/fpsyt.2017.00157

Brennan, M. A., Emmerling, M. E., & Whelton, W. J. (2015). Emotion-focused group therapy: Addressing self-criticism in the treatment of eating disorders. *Counselling & Psychotherapy Research*, 15(1), 67–75.

Bresch, A., Rullmann, M., Luthardt, J., Arelin, K., Becker, G. A., Patt, M., Lobsien, D., Baldofski, S., Drabe, M., Zeisig, V., Regenthal, R., Blüher, M., Hilbert, A., Sabri, O., & Hesse, S. (2016). In-vivo serotonin transporter availability and somatization in healthy subjects. *Personality and Individual Differences*, 94, 354–359. https://doi.org/10.1016/j.paid.2016.01.042

Breuer, J., & Freud, S. (2013). *Studies on hysteria* (J. Strachey, Trans.). Forgotten Books. (Original work published 1893–1895.)

Brew, B. K., Lundholm, C., Caffrey Osvald, E., Chambers, G., Öberg, S., Fang, F., & Almqvist, C. (2022). Early-life adversity due to bereavement and inflammatory diseases in the next generation: A population study in transgenerational stress exposure. *American Journal of Epidemiology*, 191(1), 38–48. https://doi.org/10.1093/aje/kwab236

Brewer, C., Meyers, R. J., & Johnsen, J. (2000). Does disulfiram help to prevent relapse in alcohol abuse? *CNS Drugs*, 14(5), 329–341. https://doi.org/10.2165/00023210-200014050-00001

Brewerton, T. D. (2007). Eating disorders, trauma, and comorbidity: Focus on PTSD. *Eating Disorders*, 15(4), 285–304. https://doi.org/10.1080/10640260701454311

Brewin, C. R., Andrews, B., & Valentine, J. D. (2000). Meta-analysis of risk factors for posttraumatic stress disorder in trauma-exposed adults. *Journal of Consulting and Clinical Psychology*, 68(5), 748–766. https://doi.org/10.1037/0022-006X.68.5.748

Brewin, C. R., & Holmes, E. A. (2003). Psychological theories of posttraumatic stress disorder. *Clinical Psychology Review*, 23(3), 339–376. https://doi.org/10.1016/S0272-7358(03)00033-3

Brewster, M. E., Velez, B. L., Breslow, A. S., & Geiger, E. F. (2019). Unpacking body image concerns and disordered eating for transgender women: The roles of sexual objectification and minority stress. *Journal of Counseling Psychology*, 66(2), 131–142. https://doi.org/10.1037/cou0000333

Bridges, S. K., & New, C. M. (2019). Humanistic perspectives on sexuality. In L. Hoffman, H. Cleare-Hoffman, N. Granger, & D. St. John (Eds.), *Humanistic Approaches to Multiculturalism and Diversity* (pp. 167–177). Routledge.

Bridler, R., Häberle, A., Müller, S. T., Cattapan, K., Grohmann, R., Toto, S., Kasper, S., & Greil, W. (2015). Psychopharmacological treatment of 2195 in-patients with borderline personality disorder: A comparison with other psychiatric disorders. *European Neuropsychopharmacology*, 25(6), 763–772. https://doi.org/10.1016/j.euroneuro.2015.03.017

Brikell, I., Kuja-Halkola, R., & Larsson, H. (2015). Heritability of attention-deficit hyperactivity disorder in adults. *American Journal of Medical Genetics Part B: Neuropsychiatric Genetics*, 168(6), 406–413. https://doi.org/10.1002/ajmg.b.32335

British Psychological Society. (2011). *Response to the American Psychiatric Association: DSM-5 development* (pp. 1–26).

British Psychological Society. (2014). *Conversion therapy: Consensus statement*. http://www.bps.org.uk/system/files/Public%20files/conversion_therapy_final_version.pdf

British Psychological Society. (2017a). *Understanding psychosis and schizophrenia* (Rev. ed.). https://www.bps.org.uk/what-psychology/understanding-psychosis-and-schizophrenia

British Psychological Society. (2017b). *UK organisations unite against conversion therapy*. https://beta.bps.org.uk/news-and-policy/uk-organisations-unite-against-conversion-therapy

Britnell, S. R., Jackson, A. D., Brown, J. N., & Capehart, B. P. (2017). Aripiprazole for post-traumatic stress disorder: A systematic review. *Clinical Neuropharmacology*, 40(6), 273–278. https://doi.org/10.1097/WNF.0000000000000251

Broady, T. R., Stoyles, G. J., & Morse, C. (2017). Understanding carers' lived experience of stigma: The voice of families with a child on the autism spectrum. *Health & Social Care in the Community*, 25(1), 224–233. https://doi.org/10.1111/hsc.12297

Brockman, R., & Murrell, E. (2015). What are the primary goals of cognitive behavior therapy for psychosis? A theoretical and empirical review. *Journal of Cognitive Psychotherapy*, 29(1), 45–67. https://doi.org/10.1891/0889-8391.29.1.45

Brody, D. J., & Gu, Q. (2020). *Antidepressant use among adults: United States, 2015–2018* (No. 377; NCHS Data Brief). National Center for Health Statistics. https://www.cdc.gov/nchs/products/databriefs/db377.htm

Broft, A., Berner, L. A., & Walsh, B. T. (2010). Pharmacotherapy for bulimia nervosa. In C. M. Grilo & J. E. Mitchell (Eds.), *The treatment of eating disorders: A clinical handbook* (pp. 388–401). Guilford Press.

Bromley, L., Kahan, M., Regenstreif, L., Srivastava, A., & Wyman, J. (2021). *Methadone treatment for people who use fentanyl: Recommendations*. META:PHI. http://www.metaphi.ca/

Brooks, M. (2022, August 22). *FDA approves "rapid-acting" oral drug for major depression*. https://www.medscape.com/viewarticle/979568

Brown, A., Barker, E. D., & Rahman, Q. (2020). A systematic scoping review of the prevalence, etiological, psychological, and interpersonal factors associated with BDSM. *The Journal of Sex Research, 57*(6), 781–811. https://doi.org/10.1080/00224499.2019.1665619

Brown, A. S. (2011). The environment and susceptibility to schizophrenia. *Progress in Neurobiology, 93*(1), 23–58. https://doi.org/10.1016/j.pneurobio.2010.09.003

Brown, A. S., & Derkits, E. J. (2010). Prenatal infection and schizophrenia: A review of epidemiologic and translational studies. *The American Journal of Psychiatry, 167*(3), 261–280. https://doi.org/10.1176/appi.ajp.2009.09030361

Brown, C. S., & Lichter-Konecki, U. (2016). Phenylketonuria (PKU): A problem solved? *Molecular Genetics and Metabolism Reports, 6*, 8–12. https://doi.org/10.1016/j.ymgmr.2015.12.004

Brown, G. K., & Stanley, B. (2009). *Safety planning guide: A quick guide for clinicians*. Suicide Prevention Resource Center. https://sprc.org/resources-programs/safety-planning-guide-quick-guide-clinicians

Brown, H. D., & DeFulio, A. (2020). Contingency management for the treatment of methamphetamine use disorder: A systematic review. *Drug and Alcohol Dependence, 216*, 108307. https://doi.org/10.1016/j.drugalcdep.2020.108307

Brown, J. D., & Witherspoon, E. M. (2002). The mass media and American adolescents' health. *Journal of Adolescent Health, 31*(Suppl. 6), 153–170. https://doi.org/10.1016/S1054-139X(02)00507-4

Brown, J. W. (2017). The effect of justice and injustice on sleep quality [Doctoral dissertation, State University of New York at Albany]. In *ProQuest Dissertations and Theses*. http://www.proquest.com/docview/1892810416/abstract/2CEB-549585864166PQ/1

Brown, L. S. (1992). A feminist critique of the personality disorders. In L. S. Brown & M. Ballou (Eds.), *Personality and psychopathology: Feminist reappraisals* (pp. 206–228). Guilford Press.

Brown, L. S. (1994). *Subversive dialogues: Theory in feminist therapy*. Basic Books.

Brown, L. S. (1997). The private practice of subversion: Psychology as Tikkun Olam. *American Psychologist, 52*(4), 449–462. https://doi.org/10.1037/0003-066X.52.4.449

Brown, M. L., Pope, A. W., & Brown, E. J. (2011). Treatment of primary nocturnal enuresis in children: A review. *Child: Care, Health and Development, 37*(2), 153–160. https://doi.org/10.1111/j.1365-2214.2010.01146.x

Brown, R. F., Bartrop, R., & Birmingham, C. L. (2008). Immunological disturbance and infectious disease in anorexia nervosa: A review. *Acta Neuropsychiatrica, 20*(3), 117–128. https://doi.org/10.1111/j.1601-5215.2008.00286.x

Brown, R. J. (2006). Different types of "dissociation" have different psychological mechanisms. *Journal of Trauma & Dissociation, 7*(4), 7–28. https://doi.org/10.1300/J229v07n04_02

Brown, T. A., Holland, L. A., & Keel, P. K. (2014). Comparing operational definitions of DSM-5 anorexia nervosa for research contexts. *International Journal of Eating Disorders, 47*(1), 76–84. https://doi.org/10.1002/eat.22184

Brown, T. J. (1998). *Dorothea Dix: New England reformer*. Harvard University Press.

Browne, H. A., Gair, S. L., Scharf, J. M., & Grice, D. E. (2014). Genetics of obsessive-compulsive disorder and related disorders. *The Psychiatric Clinics of North America, 37*(3), 319–335. https://doi.org/10.1016/j.psc.2014.06.002

Browne, T. K. (2015). Is premenstrual dysphoric disorder really a disorder? *Journal of Bioethical Inquiry, 12*(2), 313–330. https://doi.org/10.1007/s11673-014-9567-7

Browning, M., Paul Fletcher, Dp., & Sharpe, M. (2011). Can neuroimaging help us to understand and classify somatoform disorders? A systematic and critical review. *Psychosomatic Medicine, 73*(2), 173–184. https://doi.org/10.1097/PSY.0b013e31820824f6

Bruch, H. (1962). Perceptual and conceptual disturbances in anorexia nervosa. *Psychosomatic Medicine, 24*(2), 187–194.

Bruch, H. (1963). Disturbed communication in eating disorders. *American Journal of Orthopsychiatry, 33*(1), 99–104. https://doi.org/10.1111/j.1939-0025.1963.tb00363.x

Bruch, H. (1971). Family transactions in eating disorders. *Comprehensive Psychiatry, 12*(3), 238–248. https://doi.org/10.1016/0010-440X(71)90021-6

Bruch, H. (2001). *The golden cage: The enigma of anorexia nervosa*. Harvard University Press. (Original work published 1978.)

Brühl, A. B., Delsignore, A., Komossa, K., & Weidt, S. (2014). Neuroimaging in social anxiety disorder—A meta-analytic review resulting in a new neurofunctional model. *Neuroscience and Biobehavioral Reviews, 47*, 260–280. https://doi.org/10.1016/j.neubiorev.2014.08.003

Brundin, L., Bryleva, E. Y., & Thirtamara Rajamani, K. (2017). Role of inflammation in suicide: From mechanisms to treatment. *Neuropsychopharmacology, 42*(1), 271–283. https://doi.org/10.1038/npp.2016.116

Brundin, L., Erhardt, S., Bryleva, E. Y., Achtyes, E. D., & Postolache, T. T. (2015). The role of inflammation in suicidal behaviour. *Acta Psychiatrica Scandinavica, 132*(3), 192–203. https://doi.org/10.1111/acps.12458

Brüne, M. (2004). Schizophrenia—An evolutionary enigma? *Neuroscience and Biobehavioral Reviews, 28*(1), 41–53. https://doi.org/10.1016/j.neubiorev.2003.10.002

Brüne, M. (2005). "Theory of mind" in schizophrenia: A review of the literature. *Schizophrenia Bulletin, 31*(1), 21–42. https://doi.org/10.1093/schbul/sbi002

Brüne, M., & Brüne-Cohrs, U. (2006). Theory of mind—Evolution, ontogeny, brain mechanisms and psychopathology. *Neuroscience and Biobehavioral Reviews, 30*(4), 437–455. https://doi.org/10.1016/j.neubiorev.2005.08.001

Brunet, A., Saumier, D., Liu, A., Streiner, D. L., Tremblay, J., & Pitman, R. K. (2018). Reduction of PTSD symptoms with pre-reactivation propranolol therapy: A randomized controlled trial. *American Journal of Psychiatry, 175*(5), 427–433. https://doi.org/10.1176/appi.ajp.2017.17050481

Bruni, N., Della Pepa, C., Oliaro-Bosso, S., Pessione, E., Gastaldi, D., & Dosio, F. (2018). Cannabinoid delivery systems for pain and inflammation treatment. *Molecules: A Journal of Synthetic Chemistry and Natural Product Chemistry, 23*(10), Article 2478. https://doi.org/10.3390/molecules23102478

Bruns, H., Hosangadi, D., Trotochaud, M., & Sell, K. (2021). *COVID-19 vaccine misinformation and disinformation costs an estimated $50 to $300 million each day*. The Johns Hopkins Center for Health Security.

Brus, M., Novakovic, V., & Friedberg, A. (2012). Psychotherapy for schizophrenia: A review of modalities and their evidence base. *Psychodynamic Psychiatry, 40*(4), 609–616. https://doi.org/10.1521/pdps.2012.40.4.609

Bruty, H. R., Emslie, G. J., & Croarkin, P. (2012). Novel (atypical) antidepressants. In D. R. Rosenberg & S. Gershon (Eds.), *Pharmacotherapy of child and adolescent psychiatric disorders* (3rd ed., pp. 155–179). Wiley-Blackwell. https://doi.org/10.1002/9781119958338.ch9

Bryan, C. J. (2019). Cognitive behavioral therapy for suicide prevention (CBT-SP): Implications for meeting standard of care expectations with suicidal patients. *Behavioral Sciences & the Law, 37*(3), 247–258. https://doi.org/10.1002/bsl.2411

Bryan, C. J., Mintz, J., Clemans, T. A., Leeson, B., Burch, T. S., Williams, S. R., Maney, E., & Rudd, M. D. (2017). Effect of crisis response planning vs. contracts for safety on suicide risk in U.S. Army Soldiers: A randomized clinical trial. *Journal of Affective Disorders, 212*, 64–72. https://doi.org/10.1016/j.jad.2017.01.028

Bryan, C. J., & Rudd, M. D. (2018). *Brief cognitive-behavioral therapy for suicide prevention*. Guilford Press.

Bryant, R. A. (2019). Post-traumatic stress disorder: A state-of-the-art review of evidence and challenges. *World Psychiatry, 18*(3), 259–269. https://doi.org/10.1002/wps.20656

Bryant, R. A., Felmingham, K. L., Falconer, E. M., Pe Benito, L., Dobson-Stone, C., Pierce, K. D., & Schofield, P. R. (2010). Preliminary evidence of the short allele of the serotonin transporter gene predicting poor response to cognitive behavior therapy in posttraumatic stress disorder. *Biological Psychiatry, 67*(12), 1217–1219. https://doi.org/10.1016/j.biopsych.2010.03.016

Bryant, R. A., Kenny, L., Joscelyne, A., Rawson, N., Maccallum, F., Cahill, C., Hopwood, S., Aderka, I., & Nickerson, A. (2014). Treating prolonged grief disorder: A randomized clinical trial. *JAMA Psychiatry, 71*(12), 1332. https://doi.org/10.1001/jamapsychiatry.2014.1600

Bryant, R. A., Kenny, L., Joscelyne, A., Rawson, N., Maccallum, F., Cahill, C., Hopwood, S., & Nickerson, A. (2017). Treating prolonged grief disorder: A 2-year follow-up of a randomized controlled trial. *The Journal of Clinical Psychiatry, 78*(9), 1363–1368. https://doi.org/10.4088/JCP.16m10729

Bryant-Waugh, R., Loomes, R., Munuve, A., & Rhind, C. (2021). Towards an evidence-based out-patient care pathway for children and young people with avoidant restrictive food intake disorder. *Journal of Behavioral and Cognitive Therapy, 31*(1), 15–26. https://doi.org/10.1016/j.jbct.2020.11.001

Bryant-Waugh, R., Markham, L., Kreipe, R. E., & Walsh, B. T. (2010). Feeding and eating disorders in childhood. *International Journal of Eating Disorders, 43*(2), 98–111.

Brymer, M., Layne, C., Jacobs, A., Pynoos, R., Ruzek, J., Steinberg, A., Vernberg, E., & Watson, P. (2006). *Psychological first aid: Field operations guide* (2nd ed.). National Child Traumatic Stress Network and National Center for PTSD.

Brytek-Matera, A. (2012). Orthorexia nervosa—An eating disorder, obsessive-compulsive disorder or disturbed eating habit? *Archives of Psychiatry and Psychotherapy, 14*(1), 55–60.

Buchanan, R. W., Freedman, R., Javitt, D. C., Abi-Dargham, A., & Lieberman, J. A. (2007). Recent advances in the development of novel pharmacological agents for the treatment of cognitive impairments in schizophrenia. *Schizophrenia Bulletin, 33*(5), 1120–1130. https://doi.org/10.1093/schbul/sbm083

Buck, K., Zekri, S., Nguyen, L., & Ogar, U. J. (2019). Cognitive behavior therapy for postpartum depression. *American Family Physician, 100*(4), 244–245.

Budge, S. L. (2013). Interpersonal psychotherapy with transgender clients. *Psychotherapy, 50*(3), 356–359. https://doi.org/10.1037/a0032194

Bueter, A., & Jukola, S. (2020). Sex, drugs, and how to deal with criticism: The case of flibanserin. In A. LaCaze & B. Osimani (Eds.), *Uncertainty in pharmacology: Epistemology, methods, and decisions* (Vol. 338, pp.

451–470). Springer International Publishing. https://doi.org/10.1007/978-3-030-29179-2

Bugental, J. F. T. (1987). *The art of the psychotherapist.* Norton.

Bui, E., Nadal-Vicens, M., & M. Simon, N. (2012). Pharmacological approaches to the treatment of complicated grief: Rationale and a brief review of the literature. *Dialogues in Clinical Neuroscience, 14*(2), 149–157.

Buizza, C., Candini, V., Ferrari, C., Ghilardi, A., Saviotti, F. M., Turrina, C., Nobili, G., Sabaudo, M., & de Girolamo, G. (2019). The long-term effectiveness of psychoeducation for bipolar disorders in mental health services. A 4-year follow-up study. *Frontiers in Psychiatry, 10*, Article 873. https://www.doi.org/10.3389/fpsyt.2019.00873

Bukstin, O. (2022, April 7). *Pharmacotherapies for attention deficit hyperactivity disorder in adults.* UpToDate. https://www.uptodate.com/contents/pharmacotherapies-for-attention-deficit-hyperactivity-disorder-in-adults

Bulbena-Cabre, A., Bassir Nia, A., & Perez-Rodriguez, M. M. (2018). Current knowledge on gene-environment interactions in personality disorders: An update. *Current Psychiatry Reports, 20*(9), Article 74. https://doi.org/10.1007/s11920-018-0934-7

Bulger, A. (2016, November 11). A brief history of how we slept, from 8,000 BCE to today. *Van Winkle's.* http://vanwinkles.com/how-humans-slept-through-out-history-hint-it-mostly-sucked

Bulik, C. M., Blake, L., & Austin, J. (2019). Genetics of eating disorders: What the clinician needs to know. *Psychiatric Clinics, 42*(1), 59–73. https://doi.org/10.1016/j.psc.2018.10.007

Bulik, C. M., Sullivan, P. F., Wade, T. D., & Kendler, K. S. (2000). Twin studies of eating disorders: A review. *International Journal of Eating Disorders, 27*(1), 1–20.

Bulik, C. M., Sullivan, P. F., Tozzi, F., Furberg, H., Lichtenstein, P., & Pedersen, N. L. (2006). Prevalence, heritability, and prospective risk factors for anorexia nervosa. *Archives of General Psychiatry, 63*(3), 305–312. doi:10.1001/archpsyc.63.3.305

Bull, M. J. (2020). Down syndrome. *The New England Journal of Medicine, 382*(24), 2344–2352. https://doi.org/10.1056/NEJMra1706537

Bullman, T., & Schneiderman, A. (2021). Risk of suicide among U.S. veterans who deployed as part of Operation Enduring Freedom, Operation Iraqi Freedom, and Operation New Dawn. *Injury Epidemiology, 8*(1), Article 40. https://doi.org/10.1186/s40621-021-00332-y

Bullock, J. L. (2002). Involuntary treatment of defendants found incompetent to stand trial. *Journal of Forensic Psychology Practice, 2*(4), 1–33. https://doi.org/10.1300/J158v02n04_01

Bullough, V. L. (2002). Masturbation: A historical overview. *Journal of Psychology and Human Sexuality, 14*(2/3), 17–33.

Buoli, M., Serati, M., & Cahn, W. (2016). Alternative pharmacological strategies for adult ADHD treatment: A systematic review. *Expert Review of Neurotherapeutics, 16*(2), 131–144. https://doi.org/10.1586/14737175.2016.1135735

Burchill, C. N. (2019). Critical incident stress debriefing: Helpful, harmful, or neither? *Journal of Emergency Nursing, 45*(6), 611–612. https://doi.org/10.1016/j.jen.2019.08.006

Burgess, A. W. (1983). Rape trauma syndrome. *Behavioral Sciences & the Law, 1*(3), 97–113. https://doi.org/10.1002/bsl.2370010310

Burgess, A. W., & Holmstrom, L. L. (1974). Rape trauma syndrome. *The American Journal of Psychiatry, 131*(9), 981–986.

Burke, H. M., Davis, M. C., Otte, C., & Mohr, D. C. (2005). Depression and cortisol responses to psychological stress: A meta-analysis. *Psychoneuroendocrinology, 30*(9), 846–856. https://doi.org/10.1016/j.psyneuen.2005.02.010

Burke, N. L., Karam, A. M., Tanofsky-Kraff, M., & Wilfley, D. E. (2018). Interpersonal psychotherapy for the treatment of eating disorders. In W. S. Agras & A. Robinson (Eds.), *The Oxford handbook of eating disorders* (2nd ed., pp. 287–318). Oxford University Press.

Burke, R. J. (1985). Beliefs and fears underlying Type A behavior: Correlates of time urgency and hostility. *The Journal of General Psychology, 112*(2), 133–145.

Burkett, K., Morris, E., Manning-Courtney, P., Anthony, J., & Shambley-Ebron, D. (2015). African American families on autism diagnosis and treatment: The influence of culture. *Journal of Autism and Developmental Disorders, 45*(10), 3244–3254. https://doi.org/10.1007/s10803-015-2482-x

Burlew, K., McCuistian, C., & Szapocznik, J. (2021). Racial/ethnic equity in substance use treatment research: The way forward. *Addiction Science & Clinical Practice, 16*(1), 50. https://doi.org/10.1186/s13722-021-00256-4

Burnes, T. R., Singh, A. A., Harper, A. J., Harper, B., Maxon-Kann, W., Pickering, D. L., Moundas, S., Scofield, T. R., Roan, A., & Hosea, J. (2010). American Counseling Association: Competencies for counseling with transgender clients. *Journal of LGBT Issues in Counseling, 4*(3–4), 135–159.

Burns, J. K. (2006). Psychosis: A costly by-product of social brain evolution in Homo sapiens. *Progress in Neuro-Psychopharmacology & Biological Psychiatry, 30*(5), 797–814. https://doi.org/10.1016/j.pnpbp.2006.01.006

Burns, J. K. (2009). Reconciling "the new epidemiology" with an evolutionary genetic basis for schizophrenia. *Medical Hypotheses, 72*(3), 353–358. https://doi.org/10.1016/j.mehy.2008.09.046

Burokas, A., Arboleya, S., Moloney, R. D., Peterson, V. L., Murphy, K., Clarke, G., Stanton, C., Dinan, T. G., & Cryan, J. F. (2017). Targeting the microbiota-gut-brain axis: Prebiotics have anxiolytic and antidepressant-like effects and reverse the impact of chronic stress in mice. *Biological Psychiatry, 82*(7), 472–487. https://doi.org/10.1016/j.biopsych.2016.12.031

Burr, V. (2015). *Social constructionism* (3rd ed.). Routledge.

Burri, A. (2013). Bringing sex research into the 21st century: Genetic and epigenetic approaches on female sexual function. *Journal of Sex Research, 50*(3–4), 318–328. https://doi.org/10.1080/00224499.2012.753027

Burri, A., Cherkas, L., Spector, T., & Rahman, Q. (2011). Genetic and environmental influences on female sexual orientation, childhood gender typicality and adult gender identity. *Plos One, 6*(7), e21982–e21982. https://doi.org/10.1371/journal.pone.0021982

Burri, A., & Ogata, S. (2018). Stability of genetic and environmental influences on female sexual functioning. *Journal of Sexual Medicine, 15*(4), 550–557. https://doi.org/10.1016/j.jsxm.2018.01.020

Burri, A., Spector, T., & Rahman, Q. (2013). A discordant monozygotic twin approach to testing environmental influences on sexual dysfunction in women. *Archives of Sexual Behavior, 42*(6), 961–972. https://doi.org/10.1007/s10508-013-0089-x

Burri, A. V., Cherkas, L. M., & Spector, T. D. (2009). The genetics and epidemiology of female sexual dysfunction: A review. *Journal of Sexual Medicine, 6*(3), 646–657. https://doi.org/10.1111/j.1743-6109.2008.01144.x

Burstow, B. (2005). A critique of posttraumatic stress disorder and the DSM. *Journal of Humanistic Psychology, 45*(4), 429–445. https://doi.org/10.1177/0022167805280265

Bury, B., Tiggemann, M., & Slater, A. (2017). Disclaimer labels on fashion magazine advertisements: Does timing of digital alteration information matter? *Eating Behaviors, 25*, 18–22. https://doi.org/10.1016/j.eatbeh.2016.08.010

Busch, F. N., & Milrod, B. L. (2015). Psychodynamic treatment for separation anxiety in a treatment nonresponder. *Journal of the American Psychoanalytic Association, 63*(5), 893–919. https://doi.org/10.1177/0003065115607491

Busch, F. N., Milrod, B. L., & Shear, K. (2010). Psychodynamic concepts of anxiety. In D. J. Stein, E. Hollander, & B. O. Rothbaum (Eds.), *Textbook of anxiety disorders* (2nd ed., pp. 117–128). American Psychiatric Publishing.

Butkus, R., Rapp, K., Cooney, T. G., & Engel, L. S. (2020). Envisioning a better U.S. health care system for all: Reducing barriers to care and addressing social determinants of health. *Annals of Internal Medicine, 172*(Suppl. 2), S50–S59. https://doi.org/10.7326/M19-2410

Butler, A. C., Chapman, J. E., Forman, E. M., & Beck, A. T. (2006). The empirical status of cognitive-behavioral therapy: A review of meta-analyses. *Clinical Psychology Review, 26*(1), 17–31. https://doi.org/10.1016/j.cpr.2005.07.003

Butler, L. D. (2004). The dissociations of everyday life. *Journal of Trauma & Dissociation, 5*(2), 1–11. https://doi.org/10.1300/J229v05n02_01

Butler, L. D. (2006). Normative dissociation. *Psychiatric Clinics of North America, 29*(1), 45–62. https://doi.org/10.1016/j.psc.2005.10.004

Butler, M. I., Mörkl, S., Sandhu, K. V., Cryan, J. F., & Dinan, T. G. (2019). The gut microbiome and mental health: What should we tell our patients? *Canadian Journal of Psychiatry, 64*(11), 747–760. https://doi.org/10.1177/0706743719874168

Butler, R. J. (2004). Childhood nocturnal enuresis: Developing a conceptual framework. *Clinical Psychology Review, 24*(8), 909–931. https://doi.org/10.1016/j.cpr.2004.07.001

Butler, R. M., & Heimberg, R. G. (2020). Exposure therapy for eating disorders: A systematic review. *Clinical Psychology Review, 78*, Article 101851. https://doi.org/10.1016/j.cpr.2020.101851

Butterworth, P., Olesen, S. C., & Leach, L. S. (2012). The role of hardship in the association between socio-economic position and depression. *Australian and New Zealand Journal of Psychiatry, 46*(4), 364–373. https://doi.org/10.1177/0004867411433215

Butts, H. F. (2002). The black mask of humanity: Racial/ethnic discrimination and post-traumatic stress disorder. *Journal of the American Academy of Psychiatry and the Law, 30*(3), 336–339.

Buus, N., Ong, B., Einboden, R., Lennon, E., Mikes-Liu, K., Mayers, S., & McCloughen, A. (2021). Implementing Open Dialogue approaches: A scoping review. *Family Process.* https://doi.org/10.1111/famp.12695

Buwalda, F. M., Bouman, T. K., & van Duijn, M. A. J. (2007). Psychoeducation for hypochondriasis: A comparison of a cognitive-behavioural approach and a problem-solving approach. *Behaviour Research and Therapy, 45*(5), 887–899. https://doi.org/10.1016/j.brat.2006.08.004

Bystritsky, A. (2004). Current pharmacological treatments for obsessive-compulsive disorder. *Essential Psychopharmacology, 5*(4), 22.

Cacchioni, T. (2015). The medicalization of sexual deviance, reproduction, and functioning. In J. DeLamater & R. F. Plante (Eds.), *Handbook of the sociology of sexualities* (pp. 435–452). Springer International Publishing. https://doi.org/10.1007/978-3-319-17341-2_24

Cahalan, S. (2019). *The great pretender.* Grand Central Publishing.

Cahill, S. P., Rothbaum, B. O., Resick, P. A., & Follette, V. M. (2009). Cognitive-behavioral therapy for adults. In E. B. Foa, T. M. Keane, M. J. Friedman, & J. A. Cohen (Eds.), *Effective treatments for PTSD: Practice guidelines from the International Society for Traumatic Stress Studies* (2nd ed., pp. 139–222). Guilford Press.

Cahn, W., Rais, M., Stigter, F. P., van Haren, N. E. M., Caspers, E., Pol, H. E. H., Xu, Z., Schnack, H. G., & Kahn, R. S. (2009). Psychosis and brain volume changes during the first five years of schizophrenia. *European Neuropsychopharmacology, 19*(2), 147–151. https://doi.org/10.1016/j.euroneuro.2008.10.006

Cai, H., Xie, X.-M., Zhang, Q., Cui, X., Lin, J.-X., Sim, K., Ungvari, G. S., Zhang, L., & Xiang, Y.-T. (2021).

Prevalence of suicidality in major depressive disorder: A systematic review and meta-analysis of comparative studies. *Frontiers in Psychiatry, 12*, Article 690130. https://www.doi.org/10.3389/fpsyt.2021.690130

Cain, D. J. (2010). *Person-centered psychotherapies.* American Psychological Association.

Cakiroglu, O. (2015). Response to intervention: Early identification of students with learning disabilities. *International Journal of Early Childhood Special Education, 7*(1), 170–182.

Çakıcı, M., Araz, D., Aksoy, E., & Gökyiğit, A. (2019). Comparison of methadone and buprenorphine. *Anatolian Journal of Psychiatry, 20*(Special Issue 1), 119–121. https://doi.org/10.5455/apd.302644875

Calabrò, R. S., Cacciola, A., Bruschetta, D., Milardi, D., Quattrini, F., Sciarrone, F., la Rosa, G., Bramanti, P., & Anastasi, G. (2019). Neuroanatomy and function of human sexual behavior: A neglected or unknown issue? *Brain and Behavior, 9*(12), Article e01389. https://doi.org/10.1002/brb3.1389

Calati, R., Gressier, F., Balestri, M., & Serretti, A. (2013). Genetic modulation of borderline personality disorder: Systematic review and meta-analysis. *Journal of Psychiatric Research, 47*(10), 1275–1287. https://doi.org/10.1016/j.jpsychires.2013.06.002

Caldwell, P. H., Sureshkumar, P., & Wong, W. C. (2016). Tricyclic and related drugs for nocturnal enuresis in children. *Cochrane Database of Systematic Reviews, 2016*(1), Article CD002117. https://doi.org/10.1002/14651858.CD002117.pub2

Calhoun, L. G., & Tedeschi, R. G. (2006). The foundations of posttraumatic growth: An expanded framework. In L. G. Calhoun & R. G. Tedeschi (Eds.), *Handbook of posttraumatic growth: Research and practice* (pp. 3–23). Lawrence Erlbaum.

Caligor, E., & Clarkin, J. F. (2010). An object relations model of personality and personality pathology. In J. F. Clarkin, P. Fonagy, & G. O. Gabbard (Eds.), *Psychodynamic psychotherapy for personality disorders: A clinical handbook* (pp. 3–35). American Psychiatric Publishing.

Caligor, E., Kernberg, O. F., & Clarkin, J. F. (2007). *Handbook of dynamic psychotherapy for higher level personality pathology.* American Psychiatric Publishing.

Calina, D., Hartung, T., Mardare, I., Mitroi, M., Poulas, K., Tsatsakis, A., Rogoveanu, I., & Docea, A. O. (2021). COVID-19 pandemic and alcohol consumption: Impacts and interconnections. *Toxicology Reports, 8*, 529–535. https://doi.org/10.1016/j.toxrep.2021.03.005

Call, C., Walsh, B. T., & Attia, E. (2013). From DSM-IV to DSM-5: Changes to eating disorder diagnoses. *Current Opinion in Psychiatry, 26*(6), 532–536.

Call, H. L. (1963, August). *The hypocrisy of sexual morality.* http://outhistory.org/items/show/4290

Call, N. A., Simmons, C. A., Mevers, J. E. L., & Alvarez, J. P. (2015). Clinical outcomes of behavioral treatments for pica in children with developmental disabilities. *Journal of Autism and Developmental Disorders, 45*(7), 2105–2114. https://doi.org/10.1007/s10803-015-2375-z

Callahan, L. A., Steadman, H. J., McGreevy, M. A., & Robbins, P. C. (1991). The volume and characteristics of insanity defense pleas: An eight-state study. *Bulletin of the American Academy of Psychiatry and the Law, 19*(4), 331–338.

Callahan, L., & Pinals, D. A. (2020). Challenges to reforming the competence to stand trial and competence restoration system. *Psychiatric Services, 71*(7), 691–697. https://doi.org/10.1176/appi.ps.201900483

Calleja-Conde, J., Echeverry-Alzate, V., Bühler, K.-M., Durán-González, P., Morales-García, J. Á., Segovia-Rodríguez, L., Rodríguez de Fonseca, F., Giné, E., & López-Moreno, J. A. (2021). The immune system through the lens of alcohol intake and gut microbiota. *International Journal of Molecular Sciences, 22*(14), Article 14. https://doi.org/10.3390/ijms22147485

Calliess, I. T., Sieberer, M., Machleidt, W., & Ziegenbein, M. (2008). Personality disorders in a cross-cultural perspective: Impact of culture and migration on diagnosis and etiological aspects. *Current Psychiatry Reviews, 4*(1), 39–47. https://doi.org/10.2174/157340008783743776

Calsolaro, V., Antognoli, R., Okoye, C., & Monzani, F. (2019). The use of antipsychotic drugs for treating behavioral symptoms in Alzheimer's disease. *Frontiers in Pharmacology, 10*, Article 1465. https://doi.org/10.3389/fphar.2019.01465

Calton, T., Ferriter, M., Huband, N., & Spandler, H. (2008). A systematic review of the Soteria paradigm for the treatment of people diagnosed with schizophrenia. *Schizophrenia Bulletin, 34*(1), 181–192. https://doi.org/10.1093/schbul/sbm047

Campbell, D. T., & Stanley, J. C. (1963). *Experimental and quasi-experimental designs for research.* Houghton Mifflin Company.

Campbell, P. (2013). Service users and survivors. In J. Cromby, D. Harper, & P. Reavey (Eds.), *Psychology, mental health and distress* (pp. 139–157). Palgrave Macmillan.

Campbell, P. D., Miller, A. M., & Woesner, M. E. (2017). Bright light therapy: Seasonal affective disorder and beyond. *The Einstein Journal of Biology and Medicine, 32*, E13–E25.

Canadian Psychological Association. (n.d.). *CPA policy statement on conversion/reparative therapy for sexual orientation.* http://www.cpa.ca/docs/File/Position/SOGII%20Policy%20Statement%20-%20LGB%20Conversion%20Therapy%20FINALAPPROVED2015.pdf

Canetto, S. S., & Sakinofsky, I. (1998). The gender paradox in suicide. *Suicide & Life-Threatening Behavior, 28*(1), 1–23.

Cano, R. L. E., & Lopera, H. D. E. (2013). Introduction to T and B lymphocytes. In J.-M. Anaya, Y. Shoenfeld, A. Rojas-Villarraga, R. A. Levy, & R. Cervera (Eds.), *Autoimmunity: From bench to bedside* (pp. 77–95). El Rosario University Press. https://www.ncbi.nlm.nih.gov/books/NBK459471/

Cantor, C. (2009). Post-traumatic stress disorder: Evolutionary perspectives. *The Australian and New Zealand Journal of Psychiatry, 43*(11), 1038–1048. https://doi.org/10.3109/00048670903270407

Cantu, L., & Thomas, L. (2020). Baseline well-being, perceptions of critical incidents, and openness to debriefing in community hospital emergency department clinical staff before COVID-19, a cross-sectional study. *BMC Emergency Medicine, 20*(1), 82. https://doi.org/10.1186/s12873-020-00372-5

Caparrotta, L., & Ghaffari, K. (2006). A historical overview of the psychodynamic contributions to the understanding of eating disorders. *Psychoanalytic Psychotherapy, 20*(3), 175–196. https://doi.org/10.1080/02668730600868807

Capes-Ivy, Q. (2010, June 11). Borderline personality disorder—A feminist critique. *The F-Word.* https://thefword.org.uk/2010/06/borderline_pers/

Caplan, P. J. (1995). *They say you're crazy: How the world's most powerful psychiatrists decide who's normal.* Addison-Wesley/Addison-Wesley Longman.

Caplan, P. J., & Watson, J. (2020, February 15). Why must people pathologize eating problems? *Mad in the UK.* https://www.madintheuk.com/2020/02/why-pathologize-eating-problems/

Cappadocia, M. C., Desrocher, M., Pepler, D., & Schroeder, J. H. (2009). Contextualizing the neurobiology of conduct disorder in an emotion dysregulation framework. *Clinical Psychology Review, 29*(6), 506–518. https://doi.org/10.1016/j.cpr.2009.06.001

Cappetta, K., Beyer, C., Johnson, J. A., & Bloch, M. H. (2018). Meta-analysis: Risk of dry mouth with second generation antidepressants. *Progress in Neuro-Psychopharmacology and Biological Psychiatry, 84*, 282–293. https://doi.org/10.1016/j.pnpbp.2017.12.012

Caputi, T. L., & Sabet, K. A. (2018). Population-level analyses cannot tell us anything about individual-level marijuana-opioid substitution. *American Journal of Public Health, 108*(3), e12–e12. https://doi.org/10.2105/AJPH.2017.304253

Caraballo, C., Ndumele, C. D., Roy, B., Lu, Y., Riley, C., Herrin, J., & Krumholz, H. M. (2022). Trends in racial and ethnic disparities in barriers to timely medical care among adults in the US, 1999 to 2018. *JAMA Health Forum, 3*(10), Article e223856. https://doi.org/10.1001/jamahealthforum.2022.3856

Carbonell, X., Oberst, U., & Beranuy, M. (2013). The cell phone in the twenty-first century: A risk for addiction or a necessary tool? In P. M. Miller, S. A. Ball, M. E. Bates, A. W. Blume, K. M. Kampman, D. J. Kavanagh, M. E. Larimer, N. M. Petry, & P. De Witte (Eds.), *Comprehensive addictive behaviors and disorders: Vol. 1. Principles of addiction* (pp. 901–909). Elsevier Academic Press.

Carboni, E., Carta, A. R., Carboni, E., & Novelli, A. (2021). Repurposing ketamine in depression and related disorders: Can this enigmatic drug achieve success? *Frontiers in Neuroscience, 15*, Article 657714. https://www.doi.org/10.3389/fnins.2021.657714

Cardno, A. G., & Gottesman, I. I. (2000). Twin studies of schizophrenia: From bow-and-arrow concordances to Star Wars Mx and functional genomics. *American Journal of Medical Genetics, 97*, 12–17.

Carey, M. P. (1998). Cognitive-behavioral treatment of sexual dysfunctions. In V. E. Caballo (Ed.), *International handbook of cognitive and behavioural treatments for psychological disorders* (pp. 251–280). Pergamon/Elsevier Science. https://doi.org/10.1016/B978-008043433-9/50011-0

Carey, T. A., & Stiles, W. B. (2015). Some problems with randomized controlled trials and some viable alternatives. *Clinical Psychology & Psychotherapy.* https://doi.org/10.1002/cpp.1942

Carhart-Harris, R. L., Bolstridge, M., Day, C. M. J., Rucker, J., Watts, R., Erritzoe, D. E., Kaelen, M., Giribaldi, B., Bloomfield, M., Pilling, S., Rickard, J. A., Forbes, B., Feilding, A., Taylor, D., Curran, H. V., & Nutt, D. J. (2018). Psilocybin with psychological support for treatment-resistant depression: Six-month follow-up. *Psychopharmacology, 235*(2), 399–408. https://doi.org/10.1007/s00213-017-4771-x

Carleton, R. N. (2012). The intolerance of uncertainty construct in the context of anxiety disorders: Theoretical and practical perspectives. *Expert Review of Neurotherapeutics, 12*(8), 937–947. https://doi.org/10.1586/ern.12.82

Carleton, R. N. (2016). Into the unknown: A review and synthesis of contemporary models involving uncertainty. *Journal of Anxiety Disorders, 39*, 30–43. https://doi.org/10.1016/j.janxdis.2016.02.007

Carlsson, A. (1999). The discovery of the SSRIs: A milestone In neuropsychopharmacology and rational drug design. In S. C. Stanford (Ed.), *Selective serotonin reuptake inhibitors (SSRIs): Past, present, and future* (pp. 1–7). R. G. Landes Company. https://web.archive.org/web/20141020125440/https://www.landesbioscience.com/pdf/Stanford1.pdf#

Carnahan, K. T., & Jha, A. (2022). *Factitious disorder.* StatPearls Publishing. https://www.ncbi.nlm.nih.gov/books/NBK557547/

Caron, C. (2021, February 17). "Nobody has openings": Mental health providers struggle to meet demand. *The New York Times.* https://www.nytimes.com/2021/02/17/well/mind/therapy-appointments-shortages-pandemic.html

Caron, C. (2022, October 29). Teens turn to TikTok in search of a mental health diagnosis. *The New York Times.* https://www.nytimes.com/2022/10/29/well/mind/tiktok-mental-illness-diagnosis.html

Carona, C., Handford, C., & Fonseca, A. (2021). Socratic questioning put into clinical practice. *BJPsych Advances, 27*(6), 424–426. https://doi.org/10.1192/bja.2020.77

Carpenter, Jr., William T., Gold, J. M., Lahti, A. C., Queern, C. A., Conley, R. R., Bartko, J. J., Kovnick, J., & Appelbaum, P. S. (2000). Decisional capacity for informed consent in schizophrenia research. *Archives of General Psychiatry, 57*(6), 533–538. https://doi.org/10.1001/archpsyc.57.6.533

Carpenter, W. T. (2013). RDoC and DSM-5: What's the fuss? *Schizophrenia Bulletin, 39*(5), 945–946. https://doi.org/10.1093/schbul/sbt101

Carpenter, W. T. (2020). Classification is essential for the attenuated psychosis syndrome. *Biological Psychiatry, 88*(4), 289–290. https://doi.org/10.1016/j.biopsych.2019.08.013

Carpenter, W. T., & Buchanan, R. W. (2002). Commentary on the Soteria project: Misguided therapeutics. *Schizophrenia Bulletin, 28*(4), 577–581.

Carpenter, W. T., & Davis, J. M. (2012). Another view of the history of antipsychotic drug discovery and development. *Molecular Psychiatry, 17*(12), 1168–1173. https://doi.org/10.1038/mp.2012.121

Carpenter, W. T., Regier, D., & Tandon, R. (2014). Misunderstandings about Attenuated Psychosis Syndrome in the DSM-5. *Schizophrenia Research, 152*(1), 303–303.

Carpenter, W. T., & van Os, J. (2011). Should attenuated psychosis syndrome be a DSM-5 diagnosis? *The American Journal of Psychiatry, 168*(5), 460–463. https://doi.org/10.1176/appi.ajp.2011.10121816

Carr, A. (2014). The evidence base for family therapy and systemic interventions for child-focused problems. *Journal of Family Therapy, 36*(2), 107–157. https://doi.org/10.1111/1467-6427.12032

Carr, E. R., McKernan, L. C., Hillbrand, M., & Hamlett, N. (2018). Expanding traditional paradigms: An integrative approach to the psychotherapeutic treatment of psychosis. *Journal of Psychotherapy Integration, 28*(2), 154–170. https://doi.org/10.1037/int0000083

Carr, M. M., Wiedemann, A. A., Macdonald-Gagnon, G., & Potenza, M. N. (2021). Impulsivity and compulsivity in binge eating disorder: A systematic review of behavioral studies. *Progress in Neuro-Psychopharmacology & Biological Psychiatry, 110*, Article 110318. https://doi.org/10.1016/j.pnpbp.2021.110318

Carroll, B. J. (2013). Biomarkers in DSM-5: Lost in translation. *Australian and New Zealand Journal of Psychiatry, 47*(7), 676–678. https://doi.org/10.1177/0004867413491162

Carter, R. T. (2007). Racism and psychological and emotional injury: Recognizing and assessing race-based traumatic stress. *The Counseling Psychologist, 35*(1), 13–105. https://doi.org/10.1177/0011000006292033

Cartwright, S. A. (1851). Diseases and peculiarities of the Negro race. *DeBow's Review, 11*. https://www.pbs.org/wgbh/aia/part4/4h3106t.html

Caruso, S., & Di Pasqua, S. (2019). Update on pharmacological management of female sexual dysfunctions. *Sexologies, 28*(2), e1–e5. https://doi.org/10.1016/j.sexol.2019.02.002

Carvalho, J., & Nobre, P. (2010). Predictors of women's sexual desire: The role of psychopathology, cognitive-emotional determinants, relationship dimensions, and medical factors. *Journal of Sexual Medicine, 7*(2, Pt 2), 928–937. https://doi.org/10.1111/j.1743-6109.2009.01568.x

Carvalho, J., Veríssimo, A., & Nobre, P. J. (2013). Cognitive and emotional determinants characterizing women with persistent genital arousal disorder. *Journal of Sexual Medicine, 10*(6), 1549–1558. https://doi.org/10.1111/jsm.12122

Carvalho, L. de F. (2021). Measuring pathological traits of the schizotypal personality disorder through the HiTOP model. *Scandinavian Journal of Psychology, 62*(6), 839–845. https://doi.org/10.1111/sjop.12761

Carvalho, L. de F., Ferraz, A. S., & Otoni, F. (2020). Development of the Dimensional Clinical Personality Inventory—Avoidant version based on the HiTOP. *Avaliação Psicológica, 19*(1), 29–37. https://doi.org/10.15689/ap.2020.1901.17046.04

Carvalho, L. de F., & Machado, G. M. (2021). Proposal for an HiTOP-based evaluation scale of traits of the Paranoid Personality Disorder. *Archives of Psychiatry and Psychotherapy*, 25–33.

Carvalho, M. R. S., & Haase, V. G. (2019). Genetics of dyscalculia 1: In search of genes. In A. Fritz, V. G. Haase, & P. Räsänen (Eds.), *International handbook of mathematical learning difficulties: From the laboratory to the classroom* (pp. 329–343). Springer International Publishing. https://doi.org/10.1007/978-3-319-97148-3_21

Carvalho, S. A., Castilho, P., Seabra, D., Salvador, C., Rijo, D., & Carona, C. (2022). Critical issues in cognitive behavioural therapy (CBT) with gender and sexual minorities (GSMs). *The Cognitive Behaviour Therapist, 15*, Article e3. https://doi.org/10.1017/S1754470X21000398

Casale, A. D., Ferracuti, S., Barbetti, A. S., Bargagna, P., Zega, P., Iannuccelli, A., Caggese, F., Zoppi, T., Luca, G. P. D., Parmigiani, G., Berardelli, I., & Pompili, M. (2022). Grey matter volume reductions of the left hippocampus and amygdala in PTSD: A coordinate-based meta-analysis of magnetic resonance imaging studies. *Neuropsychobiology, 81*(4), 257–264. https://doi.org/10.1159/000522003

Caselli, I., Ielmini, M., Bellini, A., Zizolfi, D., & Callegari, C. (2023). Efficacy of short-term psychodynamic psychotherapy (STPP) in depressive disorders: A systematic review and meta-analysis. *Journal of Affective Disorders, 325*, 169–176. https://doi.org/10.1016/j.jad.2022.12.161

Casey, P. (2001). Multiple personality disorder. *Primary Care Psychiatry, 7*(1), 7–11. https://doi.org/10.1185/135525701750167447

Casey, P., & Bailey, S. (2011). Adjustment disorders: The state of the art. *World Psychiatry, 10*(1), 11–18. https://doi.org/10.1002/j.2051-5545.2011.tb00003.x

Cashdan, S. (1988). *Object relations therapy: Using the relationship*. Norton.

Cashin, A. (2008). Narrative therapy: A psychotherapeutic approach in the treatment of adolescents with Asperger's disorder. *Journal of Child and Adolescent Psychiatric Nursing, 21*(1), 48–56. https://doi.org/10.1111/j.1744-6171.2008.00128.x

Cashin, A., Browne, G., Bradbury, J., & Mulder, A. (2013). The effectiveness of narrative therapy with young people with autism. *Journal of Child and Adolescent Psychiatric Nursing, 26*(1), 32–41. https://doi.org/10.1111/jcap.12020

Caspar, S. M., & Joukov, A. M. (2020). Worse than punishment: How the involuntary commitment of persons with mental illness violates the United States Constitution. *Hastings Constitutional Law Quarterly, 47*(4), Article 3.

Caspi, A., Sugden, K., Moffitt, T. E., Taylor, A., Craig, I. W., Harrington, H., McClay, J., Mill, J., Martin, J., Braithwaite, A., & Poulton, R. (2003). Influence of life stress on depression: Moderation by a polymorphism in the 5-HTT gene. *Science, 301*(5631), 386–389. https://doi.org/10.1126/science.1083968

Castel, P.-H. (2022). Autism: The French debate. In L. Tarsia & K. Valendinova (Eds.), *Treating autism today: Lacanian perspectives* (pp. 103–113). Routledge/Taylor & Francis Group. https://doi.org/10.4324/9781003221487-9

Castelbaum, L., Sylvester, C. M., Zhang, Y., Yu, Q., & Constantino, J. N. (2020). On the nature of monozygotic twin concordance and discordance for autistic trait severity: A quantitative analysis. *Behavior Genetics, 50*(4), 263–272. https://doi.org/10.1007/s10519-019-09987-2

Castells, X., Blanco-Silvente, L., & Cunill, R. (2018). Amphetamines for attention deficit hyperactivity disorder (ADHD) in adults. *Cochrane Database of Systematic Reviews, 2018*(8), Article CD007813. https://doi.org/10.1002/14651858.cd007813.pub3

Castells, X., Ramos-Quiroga, J. A., Bosch, R., Nogueira, M., & Casas, M. (2011). Amphetamines for attention deficit hyperactivity disorder (ADHD) in adults. *Cochrane Database of Systematic Reviews, 2011*(6), Article CD007813. https://doi.org/10.1002/14651858.CD007813.pub2

Castillo-Carniglia, A., Keyes, K. M., Hasin, D. S., & Cerdá, M. (2019). Psychiatric comorbidities in alcohol use disorder. *The Lancet. Psychiatry, 6*(12), 1068–1080. https://doi.org/10.1016/S2215-0366(19)30222-6

Castle, D., Beilharz, F., Phillips, K. A., Brakoulias, V., Drummond, L. M., Hollander, E., Ioannidis, K., Pallanti, S., Chamberlain, S. R., Rossell, S. L., Veale, D., Wilhelm, S., Van Ameringen, M., Dell'Osso, B., Menchon, J. M., & Fineberg, N. A. (2021). Body dysmorphic disorder: A treatment synthesis and consensus on behalf of the International College of Obsessive-Compulsive Spectrum Disorders and the Obsessive Compulsive and Related Disorders Network of the European College of Neuropsychopharmacology. *International Clinical Psychopharmacology, 36*(2), 61–75. https://doi.org/10.1097/YIC.0000000000000342

Castle, R., Bushell, W. C., Mills, P. J., Williams, M. A., Chopra, D., & Rindfleisch, J. A. (2021). Global correlations between chronic inflammation and violent incidents: Potential behavioral consequences of inflammatory illnesses across socio-demographic levels. *International Journal of General Medicine, 14*, 6677–6691. https://doi.org/10.2147/IJGM.S324367

Cath, D. C., Zilhão, N. R., Smit, D. J. A., & Boomsma, D. I. (2019). Family and twin studies of obsessive-compulsive and related disorders. In L. F. Fontenelle & M. Yücel (Eds.), *A transdiagnostic approach to obsessions, compulsions and related phenomena* (pp. 19–28). Cambridge University Press. https://doi.org/10.1017/9781108164313.004

Cattane, N., Rossi, R., Lanfredi, M., & Cattaneo, A. (2017). Borderline personality disorder and childhood trauma: Exploring the affected biological systems and mechanisms. *BMC Psychiatry, 17*(1), 221. https://doi.org/10.1186/s12888-017-1383-2

Cattell, H. E. P. (2004). The Sixteen Personality Factor (16PF) Questionnaire. In M. J. Hilsenroth & D. L. Segal (Eds.), *Comprehensive handbook of psychological assessment: Vol. 2. Personality assessment* (pp. 39–49). John Wiley.

Caulfield, S. (2021, November 24). "Who hurt you?": A reformulation of Borderline Personality Disorder. *Clinical Psychology Today*. https://clinicalpsychology-today.wordpress.com/2021/11/24/who-hurt-you-a-re-formulation-of-borderline-personality-disorder/

Causadias, J. M. (2013). A roadmap for the integration of culture into developmental psychopathology. *Development and Psychopathology, 25*(4, Pt 2), 1375–1398. https://doi.org/10.1017/S0954579413000679

Cavanagh, S. R. (2017, August 6). No, smartphones are not destroying a generation [Psychology Today]. *Once More, With Feeling*. https://www.psychologytoday.com/us/blog/once-more-feeling/201708/no-smart-phones-are-not-destroying-generation

Čavojová, V., & Mikušková, E. B. (2015). Does intelligence predict academic achievement? Two case studies. *Procedia - Social and Behavioral Sciences, 174*, 3462–3469. https://doi.org/10.1016/j.sbspro.2015.01.1019

CBC News. (2011). *What does "not criminally responsible" really mean?* http://www.cbc.ca/news/canada/what-does-not-criminally-responsible-really-mean-1.1012505

Ceccarini, J., Liu, H., Van Laere, K., Morris, E. D., & Sander, C. Y. (2020). Methods for quantifying neurotransmitter dynamics in the living brain with PET imaging. *Frontiers in Physiology, 11*, Article 792. https://doi.org/10.3389/fphys.2020.00792

Cechnicki, A., Bielańska, A., Hanuszkiewicz, I., & Daren, A. (2013). The predictive validity of expressed emotions (EE) in schizophrenia. A 20-year prospective study. *Journal of Psychiatric Research, 47*(2), 208–214. https://doi.org/10.1016/j.jpsychires.2012.10.004

Celedonia, K. L., Corrales Compagnucci, M., Minssen, T., & Lowery Wilson, M. (2021). Legal, ethical, and wider implications of suicide risk detection systems in social media platforms. *Journal of Law and the*

Biosciences, 8(1), 1–11. https://doi.org/10.1093/jlb/lsab021

Cendron, M. (2002). Removing the stigma: Helping reduce the psychosocial impact of bedwetting. *Urologic Nursing, 22*(4), 286–287.

Cenit, M. C., Nuevo, I. C., Codoñer-Franch, P., Dinan, T. G., & Sanz, Y. (2017). Gut microbiota and attention deficit hyperactivity disorder: New perspectives for a challenging condition. *European Child & Adolescent Psychiatry, 26*(9), 1081–1092. https://doi.org/10.1007/s00787-017-0969-z

Center for Drug Evaluation and Research. (2016). FDA Drug Safety Communication: FDA revises description of mental health side effects of the stop-smoking medicines Chantix (varenicline) and Zyban (bupropion) to reflect clinical trial findings. *FDA.* https://www.fda.gov/drugs/drug-safety-and-availability/fda-drug-safety-communication-fda-revises-description-mental-health-side-effects-stop-smoking

Center for Substance Abuse Treatment. (2006). *Detoxification and substance abuse treatment: A treatment improvement protocol* (Treatment Improvement Protocol [TIP] Series, No. 45, HHS Publication No. [SMA] 15-4131). Center for Substance Abuse Treatment.

Centers for Disease Control and Prevention. (2020a). QuickStats: Age-adjusted suicide Rates, by sex and three most common methods — United States, 2000–2018. *Morbidity and Mortality Weekly Report, 69*(9), 249. https://doi.org/10.15585/mmwr.mm6909a7

Centers for Disease Control and Prevention. (2020b, April 28). *Health effects of smoking and tobacco use.* https://www.cdc.gov/tobacco/basic_information/health_effects/index.htm

Centers for Disease Control and Prevention. (2020c, December 31). *Rubella in the U.S.* https://www.cdc.gov/rubella/about/in-the-us.html

Centers for Disease Control and Prevention. (2022a, February 23). *Polysubstance use facts.* https://www.cdc.gov/stopoverdose/polysubstance-use/index.html

Centers for Disease Control and Prevention. (2022b, March 2). *Data and statistics on autism spectrum disorder.* https://www.cdc.gov/ncbddd/autism/data.html

Centers for Disease Control and Prevention. (2022c, June 28). *Suicide data and statistics.* https://www.cdc.gov/suicide/suicide-data-statistics.html

Centers for Disease Control and Prevention. (2022d, October 11). *Disparities in suicide.* https://www.cdc.gov/suicide/facts/disparities-in-suicide.html

Centers for Disease Control and Prevention. (2022e, December 23). *Terminology | DASH | CDC.* https://www.cdc.gov/healthyyouth/terminology/sexual-and-gender-identity-terms.htm

Cerezuela, G. P., Tejero, P., Chóliz, M., Chisvert, M., & Monteagudo, M. J. (2004). Wertheim's hypothesis on "highway hypnosis": Empirical evidence from a study on motorway and conventional road driving. *Accident Analysis and Prevention, 36*(6), 1045–1054. https://doi.org/10.1016/j.aap.2004.02.002

Ceruso, A., Martínez-Cengotitabengoa, M., Peters-Corbett, A., Diaz-Gutierrez, M. J., & Martínez-Cengotitabengoa, M. (2020). Alterations of the HPA axis observed in patients with major depressive disorder and their relation to early life stress: A systematic review. *Neuropsychobiology, 79*(6), 417–427. https://doi.org/10.1159/000506484

Chadwick, G. L. (1997). Historical perspective: Nuremberg, Tuskegee, and the radiation experiments. *Journal of the International Association of Physicians in AIDS Care, 3*(1), 27–28.

Chahine, G., Diekhof, E. K., Tinnermann, A., & Gruber, O. (2015). On the role of the anterior prefrontal cortex in cognitive "branching": An fMRI study. *Neuropsychologia, 77*, 421–429. https://doi.org/10.1016/j.neuropsychologia.2015.08.018

Chalavi, S., Vissia, E. M., Giesen, M. E., Nijenhuis, E. R. S., Draijer, N., Cole, J. H., Dazzan, P., Pariante, C. M., Madsen, S. K., Rajagopalan, P., Thompson, P. M., Toga, A. W., Veltman, D. J., & Reinders, A. A. T. S. (2015). Abnormal hippocampal morphology in dissociative identity disorder and post-traumatic stress disorder correlates with childhood trauma and dissociative symptoms. *Human Brain Mapping, 36*(5), 1692–1704. https://doi.org/10.1002/hbm.22730

Chalder, M., Wiles, N. J., Campbell, J., Hollinghurst, S. P., Haase, A. M., Taylor, A. H., Fox, K. R., Costelloe, C., Searle, A., Baxter, H., Winder, R., Wright, C., Turner, K. M., Calnan, M., Lawlor, D. A., Peters, T. J., Sharp, D. J., Montgomery, A. A., & Lewis, G. (2012). Facilitated physical activity as a treatment for depressed adults: Randomised controlled trial. *BMJ: British Medical Journal, 344*, e2758. https://doi.org/10.1136/bmj.e2758

Chambless, D. L. (2012). Adjunctive couple and family intervention for patients with anxiety disorders. *Journal of Clinical Psychology, 68*(5), 536–547. https://doi.org/10.1002/jclp.21851

Chambless, D. L., Bryan, A. D., Aiken, L. S., Steketee, G., & Hooley, J. M. (2001). Predicting expressed emotion: A study with families of obsessive–compulsive and agoraphobic outpatients. *Journal of Family Psychology, 15*(2), 225–240. https://doi.org/10.1037/0893-3200.15.2.225

Chambless, D. L., Floyd, F. J., Rodebaugh, T. L., & Steketee, G. S. (2007). Expressed emotion and familial interaction: A study with agoraphobic and obsessive-compulsive patients and their relatives. *Journal of Abnormal Psychology, 116*(4), 754–761. https://doi.org/10.1037/0021-843X.116.4.754

Champ, R. E., Adamou, M., & Tolchard, B. (2021). The impact of psychological theory on the treatment of attention deficit hyperactivity disorder (ADHD) in adults: A scoping review. *PLoS ONE, 16*(12). https://doi.org/10.1371/journal.pone.0261247

Chan, E., Fogler, J. M., & Hammerness, P. G. (2016). Treatment of attention-deficit/hyperactivity disorder in adolescents: A systematic review. *JAMA: Journal of the American Medical Association, 315*(18), 1997–2008. https://doi.org/10.1001/jama.2016.5453

Chan, Z. C. Y., Fung, Y., & Chien, W. (2013). Bracketing in phenomenology: Only undertaken in the data collection and analysis process? *The Qualitative Report, 18*, 1–9.

Chang, J., & Nylund, D. (2013). Narrative and solution-focused therapies: A twenty-year retrospective. *Journal of Systemic Therapies, 32*(2), 72–88.

Chang, J. P.-C., Su, K.-P., Mondelli, V., & Pariante, C. M. (2018). Omega-3 polyunsaturated fatty acids in youths with attention deficit hyperactivity disorder: A systematic review and meta-analysis of clinical trials and biological studies. *Neuropsychopharmacology, 43*(3), Article 3. https://doi.org/10.1038/npp.2017.160

Chang, J. P.-C., Su, K.-P., Mondelli, V., Satyanarayanan, S. K., Yang, H.-T., Chiang, Y.-J., Chen, H.-T., & Pariante, C. M. (2019). High-dose eicosapentaenoic acid (EPA) improves attention and vigilance in children and adolescents with attention deficit hyperactivity disorder (ADHD) and low endogenous EPA levels. *Translational Psychiatry, 9*(1), Article 1. https://doi.org/10.1038/s41398-019-0633-0

Chang, Z., Ghirardi, L., Quinn, P. D., Asherson, P., D'Onofrio, B. M., & Larsson, H. (2019). Risks and benefits of ADHD medication on behavioral and neuropsychiatric outcomes: A qualitative review of pharmacoepidemiology studies using linked prescription databases. *Biological Psychiatry, 86*(5), 335–343. https://doi.org/10.1016/j.biopsych.2019.04.009

Chang, Z., Lichtenstein, P., Halldner, L., D'Onofrio, B., Serlachius, E., Fazel, S., Långström, N., & Larsson, H. (2014). Stimulant ADHD medication and risk for substance abuse. *Journal of Child Psychology and Psychiatry, and Allied Disciplines, 55*(8), 878–885. https://doi.org/10.1111/jcpp.12164

Changizi Ashtiyani, S., Shamsi, M., Cyrus, A., & Tabatabayei, S. M. (2013). Rhazes, a genius physician in the diagnosis and treatment of nocturnal enuresis in medical history. *Iranian Red Crescent Medical Journal, 15*(8), 633–638. https://doi.org/10.5812/ircmj.5017

Chao, L. L., Yaffe, K., Samuelson, K., & Neylan, T. C. (2014). Hippocampal volume is inversely related to PTSD duration. *Psychiatry Research: Neuroimaging, 222*(3), 119–123. https://doi.org/10.1016/j.pscychresns.2014.03.005

Chard, K. M., Ricksecker, E. G., Healy, E. T., Karlin, B. E., & Resick, P. A. (2012). Dissemination and experience with cognitive processing therapy. *Journal of Rehabilitation Research and Development, 49*(5), 667–678. https://doi.org/10.1682/jrrd.2011.10.0198

Charland, L. C. (2004). Character: Moral treatment and the personality disorders. In J. Radden (Ed.), *The philosophy of psychiatry: A companion* (pp. 64–77). Oxford University Press.

Charland, L. C. (2006). Moral nature of the DSM-IV Cluster B personality disorders. *Journal of Personality Disorders, 20*(2), 116–125. https://doi.org/10.1521/pedi.2006.20.2.116

Charland, L. C. (2007). Benevolent theory: Moral treatment at the York Retreat. *History of Psychiatry, 18*(1), 61–80. https://doi.org/10.1177/0957154X07070320

Charland, L. C. (2010). Medical or moral kinds? Moving beyond a false dichotomy. *Philosophy, Psychiatry, & Psychology, 17*(2), 119–125. https://doi.org/10.1353/ppp.0.0292

Charmaz, K. (2014). *Constructing grounded theory* (2nd ed.). SAGE.

Chatmon, B. N. (2020). Males and mental health stigma. *American Journal of Men's Health, 14*(4), 1557988320949322. https://doi.org/10.1177/1557988320949322

Chaudhary, S., & Garg, B. (2019). Management of paraphilias: Guidelines, challenges and options. *Indian Journal of Health, Sexuality & Culture, 5*(2), 27–41.

Chaudhury, S., & Mujawar, S. (2019). Eating disorders in developing countries. *Online Journal of Neurology and Brain Disorders, 2*(4), 181–182. https://doi.org/10.32474/OJNBD.2019.02.000144

Chavez-Dueñas, N. Y., Adames, H. Y., Perez-Chavez, J. G., & Salas, S. P. (2019). Healing ethno-racial trauma in Latinx immigrant communities: Cultivating hope, resistance, and action. *American Psychologist, 74*(1), 49–62. https://doi.org/10.1037/amp0000289

Chen, J., Loukola, A., Gillespie, N. A., Peterson, R., Jia, P., Riley, B., Maes, H., Dick, D. M., Kendler, K. S., Damaj, M. I., Miles, M. F., Zhao, Z., Li, M. D., Vink, J. M., Minica, C. C., Willemsen, G., Boomsma, D. I., Qaiser, B., Madden, P. A. F., … Chen, X. (2020). Genome-wide meta-analyses of FTND and TTFC phenotypes. *Nicotine & Tobacco Research, 22*(6), 900–909. https://doi.org/10.1093/ntr/ntz099

Chen, L. W., Sun, D., Davis, S. L., Haswell, C. C., Dennis, E. L., Swanson, C. A., Whelan, C. D., Gutman, B., Jahanshad, N., Iglesias, J. E., Thompson, P., Wagner, H. R., Saemann, P., LaBar, K. S., & Morey, R. A. (2018). Smaller hippocampal CA1 subfield volume in posttraumatic stress disorder. *Depression and Anxiety, 35*(11), 1018–1029. https://doi.org/10.1002/da.22833

Chen, Q., & Crooks, A. (2022). Analyzing the vaccination debate in social media data Pre- and Post-COVID-19 pandemic. *International Journal of Applied Earth Observation and Geoinformation, 110*, 102783. https://doi.org/10.1016/j.jag.2022.102783

Chen, T., Wang, Y., Zhang, J., Wang, Z., Xu, J., Yang, Z., & Liu, D. (2017). Abnormal concentration of GABA and glutamate in the prefrontal cortex in schizophrenia.-An in vivo 1H-MRS study. *Shanghai Archives of Psychiatry, 29*(5), 277–286. https://doi.org/10.11919/j.issn.1002-0829.217004

Chen, X., Wang, R., Zee, P., Lutsey, P. L., Javaheri, S., Alcántara, C., Jackson, C. L., Williams, M. A., & Redline, S. (2015). Racial/ethnic differences in sleep disturbances: The Multi-Ethnic Study of Atherosclerosis (MESA). *SLEEP.* https://doi.org/10.5665/sleep.4732

Chen, Z., Ying, J., Ingles, J., Zhang, D., Rajbhandari-Thapa, J., Wang, R., Emerson, K. G., & Feng, Z. (2020). Gender differential impact of bereavement on health outcomes: Evidence from the China Health and

Retirement Longitudinal Study, 2011–2015. *BMC Psychiatry*, *20*(1), 514. https://doi.org/10.1186/s12888-020-02916-2

Cheng, F., & Jones, P. B. (2013). Drug treatments for schizophrenia: Pragmatism in trial design shows lack of progress in drug design. *Epidemiology and Psychiatric Sciences*, *22*(3), 223–233. https://doi.org/10.1017/S204579601200073X

Cheng, F. K. (2022). Debate on mandatory COVID-19 vaccination. *Ethics, Medicine, and Public Health*, *21*, 100761. https://doi.org/10.1016/j.jemep.2022.100761

Cheng, H., Kellar, D., Lake, A., Finn, P., Rebec, G. V., Dharmadhikari, S., Dydak, U., & Newman, S. (2018). Effects of alcohol cues on MRS glutamate levels in the anterior cingulate. *Alcohol and Alcoholism*, *53*(3), 209–215. https://doi.org/10.1093/alcalc/agx119

Cheng, Z. H., Perko, V. L., Fuller-Marashi, L., Gau, J. M., & Stice, E. (2019). Ethnic differences in eating disorder prevalence, risk factors, and predictive effects of risk factors among young women. *Eating Behaviors*, *32*, 23–30. https://doi.org/10.1016/j.eatbeh.2018.11.004

Cherian, A. V., Pandian, D., Math, S. B., Kandavel, T., & Janardhan Reddy, Y. C. (2014). Family accommodation of obsessional symptoms and naturalistic outcome of obsessive–compulsive disorder. *Psychiatry Research*, *215*(2), 372–378. https://doi.org/10.1016/j.psychres.2013.11.017

Chervin, R. D. (2022, January 31). *Idiopathic hypersomnia*. UpToDate. https://www.uptodate.com/contents/idiopathic-hypersomnia

Chhangur, R. R., Overbeek, G., Verhagen, M., Weeland, J., Matthys, W., & Engels, R. C. M. E. (2015). DRD4 and DRD2 genes, parenting, and adolescent delinquency: Longitudinal evidence for a gene by environment interaction. *Journal of Abnormal Psychology*, *124*(4), 791–802. https://doi.org/10.1037/abn0000091

Chiari, G., & Nuzzo, M. L. (2010). *Constructivist psychotherapy: A narrative hermeneutic approach*. Routledge.

Chicayban, L. de M., & Malagris, L. E. N. (2014). Breathing and relaxation training for patients with hypertension and stress. *Estudos de Psicologia (Campinas)*, *31*(1), 115–126. https://doi.org/10.1590/0103-166X2014000100012

Children and Adults with Attention-Deficit/Hyperactivity Disorder. (2017, November 2). Why does the idea persist that ADHD meds are over-prescribed? *CHADD*. https://chadd.org/adhd-weekly/why-does-the-idea-persist-that-adhd-meds-are-over-prescribed/

Chimpén-López, C., & Arriazu Muñoz, R. (2021). Narrative therapy for anorexia nervosa: Using documents of resistance. *Australian and New Zealand Journal of Family Therapy*, *42*(3), 276–291. https://doi.org/10.1002/anzf.1459

Chiodo, G. T., Tolle, S. W., & Bevan, L. (2000). Placebo-controlled trials: Good science or medical neglect? *Western Journal of Medicine*, *172*(4), 271–273.

Chiri, G., Bergey, M., & Mackie, T. I. (2022). Deserving but not entitled: The social construction of autism spectrum disorder in federal policy. *Social Science & Medicine*, *301*, 114974. https://doi.org/10.1016/j.socscimed.2022.114974

Chisholm, K., Lin, A., Abu-Akel, A., & Wood, S. J. (2015). The association between autism and schizophrenia spectrum disorders: A review of eight alternate models of co-occurrence. *Neuroscience and Biobehavioral Reviews*, *55*, 173–183. https://doi.org/10.1016/j.neubiorev.2015.04.012

Choi, H. (2018). Family systemic approaches for borderline personality disorder in acute adult mental health care settings. *Australian and New Zealand Journal of Family Therapy*, *39*(2), 155–173. https://doi.org/10.1002/anzf.1308

Choi, J., & Twamley, E. W. (2013). Cognitive rehabilitation therapies for Alzheimer's disease: A review of methods to improve treatment engagement and self-efficacy. *Neuropsychology Review*, *23*(1), 48–62. https://doi.org/10.1007/s11065-013-9227-4

Choi-Kain, L. W., Finch, E. F., Masland, S. R., Jenkins, J. A., & Unruh, B. T. (2017). What works in the treatment of borderline personality disorder. *Current Behavioral Neuroscience Reports*, *4*(1), 21–30. https://doi.org/10.1007/s40473-017-0103-z

Chrisafis, A. (2018, February 8). "France is 50 years behind": The "state scandal" of French autism treatment. *The Guardian*. https://www.theguardian.com/world/2018/feb/08/france-is-50-years-behind-the-state-scandal-of-french-autism-treatment

Chrisler, J. C., & Erchull, M. J. (2011). The treatment of evolutionary psychology in social psychology textbooks. *Sex Roles*, *64*(9–10), 754–757. https://doi.org/10.1007/s11199-010-9783-5

Christiansen, D. M. (2015). Examining sex and gender differences in anxiety disorders. In F. Durbano (Ed.), *A fresh look at anxiety disorders* (pp. 17–49). IntechOpen. https://doi.org/10.5772/60662

Christopher, M. (2004). A broader view of trauma: A biopsychosocial-evolutionary view of the role of the traumatic stress response in the emergence of pathology and/or growth. *Clinical Psychology Review*, *24*(1), 75–98. https://doi.org/10.1016/j.cpr.2003.12.003

Chuang, J.-Y., Murray, G. K., Metastasio, A., Segarra, N., Tait, R., Spencer, J., Ziauddeen, H., Dudas, R. B., Fletcher, P. C., & Suckling, J. (2014). Brain structural signatures of negative symptoms in depression and schizophrenia. *Frontiers in Psychiatry*, *5*, Article 116. https://doi.org/10.3389/fpsyt.2014.00116

Chung, R. C.-Y., & Bemak, F. P. (2012). *Social justice counseling: The next steps beyond multiculturalism*. SAGE.

Chung, T., Martin, C. S., Maisto, S. A., Cornelius, J. R., & Clark, D. B. (2012). Greater prevalence of proposed DSM-5 nicotine use disorder compared to DSM-IV nicotine dependence in treated adolescents and young adults. *Addiction*, *107*(4), 810–818. https://doi.org/10.1111/j.1360-0443.2011.03722.x

Cicero, D. C., Jonas, K. G., Chmielewski, M., Martin, E. A., Docherty, A. R., Berzon, J., Haltigan, J. D., Reininghaus, U., Caspi, A., Graziolplene, R. G., & Kotov, R. (2022). Development of the thought disorder measure for the Hierarchical Taxonomy of Psychopathology. *Assessment*, *29*(1), 46–61. https://doi.org/10.1177/107319112110153

Cipriani, A., Furukawa, T. A., Salanti, G., Chaimani, A., Atkinson, L. Z., Ogawa, Y., Leucht, S., Ruhe, H. G., Turner, E. H., Higgins, J. P. T., Egger, M., Takeshima, N., Hayasaka, Y., Imai, H., Shinohara, K., Tajika, A., Ioannidis, J. P. A., & Geddes, J. R. (2018). Comparative efficacy and acceptability of 21 antidepressant drugs for the acute treatment of adults with major depressive disorder: A systematic review and network meta-analysis. *The Lancet*, *391*(10128), 1357–1366. https://doi.org/10.1016/S0140-6736(17)32802-7

Cipriani, G., & Borin, G. (2015). Understanding dementia in the sociocultural context: A review. *International Journal of Social Psychiatry*, *61*(2), 198–204. https://doi.org/10.1177/0020764014560357

Cipriani, G., Dolciotti, C., Picchi, L., & Bonuccelli, U. (2011). Alzheimer and his disease: A brief history. *Neurological Sciences*, *32*(2), 275–279. https://doi.org/10.1007/s10072-010-0454-7

Cipriano, A., Cella, S., & Cotrufo, P. (2017). Nonsuicidal self-injury: A systematic review. *Frontiers in Psychology*, *8*, Article 1946. https://doi.org/10.3389/fpsyg.2017.01946

Claahsen-van der Grinten, H., Verhaak, C., Steensma, T., Middelberg, T., Roeffen, J., & Klink, D. (2021). Gender incongruence and gender dysphoria in childhood and adolescence—Current insights in diagnostics, management, and follow-up. *European Journal of Pediatrics*, *180*(5), 1349–1357. https://doi.org/10.1007/s00431-020-03906-y

Claes, L., Bijttebier, P., Van Den Eynde, F., Mitchell, J. E., Faber, R., de Zwaan, M., & Mueller, A. (2010). Emotional reactivity and self-regulation in relation to compulsive buying. *Personality and Individual Differences*, *49*(5), 526–530. https://doi.org/10.1016/j.paid.2010.05.020

Clare, L. (2003). Cognitive training and cognitive rehabilitation for people with early-stage dementia. *Reviews in Clinical Gerontology*, *13*(1), 75–83. https://doi.org/10.1017/S0959259803013170

Clare, L., & Woods, R. T. (2004). Cognitive training and cognitive rehabilitation for people with early-stage Alzheimer's disease: A review. *Neuropsychological Rehabilitation*, *14*(4), 385–401. https://doi.org/10.1080/09602010443000074

Claréus, B., & Renström, E. A. (2019). Physicians' gender bias in the diagnostic assessment of medically unexplained symptoms and its effect on patient-physician relations. *Scandinavian Journal of Psychology*, *60*(4), 338–347. https://doi.org/10.1111/sjop.12545

Clark, D. A. (1995). Perceived limitations of standard cognitive therapy: A consideration of efforts to revise Beck's theory and therapy. *Journal of Cognitive Psychotherapy*, *9*(3), 153–172.

Clark, D. A., & Beck, A. T. (2010). *Cognitive therapy of anxiety disorders: Science and practice*. Guilford Press.

Clark, D. M. (1986). A cognitive approach to panic. *Behaviour Research and Therapy*, *24*(4), 461–470. https://doi.org/10.1016/0005-7967(86)90011-2

Clark, D. M., & Ehlers, A. (1993). An overview of the cognitive theory and treatment of panic disorder. *Applied & Preventive Psychology*, *2*(3), 131–139. https://doi.org/10.1016/S0962-1849(05)80119-2

Clark, D. M., & Salkovskis, P. (2009). *Panic disorder: Manual for Improving Access to Psychological Therapy (IAPT) high intensity CBT therapists*. https://oxcadatresources.com/wp-content/uploads/2018/06/Cognitive-Therapy-for-Panic-Disorder_IAPT-Manual.pdf

Clark, I., & Landolt, H.-P. (2017). Coffee, caffeine, and sleep: A systematic review of epidemiological studies and randomized controlled trials. *Sleep Medicine Reviews*, *31*. https://doi.org/10.1016/j.smrv.2016.01.006

Clark, L. (2015, August 19). Why "female viagra" approved in the US isn't coming to the UK. *Wired*. http://www.wired.co.uk/article/female-viagra-fda-approval

Clark, M. (2011). Conceptualising addiction: How useful is the construct? *International Journal of Humanities and Social Science*, *1*(13), 55–64.

Clark, O., Lee, M. M., Jingree, M. L., O'Dwyer, E., Yue, Y., Marrero, A., Tamez, M., Bhupathiraju, S. N., & Mattei, J. (2021). Weight stigma and social media: Evidence and public health solutions. *Frontiers in Nutrition*, *8*, Article 739056. https://www.doi.org/10.3389/fnut.2021.739056

Clark, P. R., Polivka, B., Zwart, M., & Sanders, R. (2019). Pediatric emergency department staff preferences for a critical incident stress debriefing. *Journal of Emergency Nursing*, *45*(4), 403–410. https://doi.org/10.1016/j.jen.2018.11.009

Clarke, D. E., Narrow, W. E., Regier, D. A., Kuramoto, S. J., Kupfer, D. J., Kuhl, E. A., Greiner, L., & Kraemer, H. C. (2013). DSM-5 field trials in the United States and Canada, part I: Study design, sampling strategy, implementation, and analytic approaches. *The American Journal of Psychiatry*, *170*(1), 43–58. https://doi.org/10.1176/appi.ajp.2012.12070998

Clarkin, J. F., Yeomans, F. E., & Kernberg, O. F. (2006). *Psychotherapy for borderline personality: Focusing on object relations*. American Psychiatric Publishing.

Clausen, J. A. (1954). Biological bias and methodological limitations in the Kinsey studies. *Social Problems*, *1*(4), 126–133. https://doi.org/10.2307/799383

Cleare, A. J., & Rane, L. J. (2013). Biological models of unipolar depression. In M. Power (Ed.), *The Wiley-Blackwell handbook of mood disorders* (2nd ed., pp. 39–67). Wiley-Blackwell.

Clem, R. L., & Huganir, R. L. (2010). Calcium-permeable AMPA receptor dynamics mediate fear memory erasure. *Science (New York, NY)*, *330*(6007), 1108–1112. https://doi.org/10.1126/science.1195298

Clinton, D. (2006). Affect regulation, object relations and the central symptoms of eating disorders. *European*

Eating Disorders Review, *14*(4), 203–211. https://doi.org/10.1002/erv.710

Cloninger, C. R. (1994). Temperament and personality. *Current Opinion in Neurobiology*, *4*, 266–273.

Coccaro, E. F., Lee, R., & Coussons-Read, M. (2015a). Cerebrospinal fluid and plasma C-reactive protein and aggression in personality-disordered subjects: A pilot study. *Journal of Neural Transmission*, *122*(2), 321–326. https://doi.org/10.1007/s00702-014-1263-6

Coccaro, E. F., Lee, R., & Coussons-Read, M. (2015b). Cerebrospinal fluid inflammatory cytokines and aggression in personality disordered subjects. *International Journal of Neuropsychopharmacology*, *18*(7), 1–7. https://doi.org/10.1093/ijnp/pyv001

Cochran, J. L., Cochran, N. H., Cholette, A., & Nordling, W. J. (2011). Limits and relationship in child-centered play therapy: Two case studies. *International Journal of Play Therapy*, *20*(4), 236–251. https://doi.org/10.1037/a0025425

Cochran, J. L., Cochran, N. H., Nordling, W. J., McAdam, A., & Miller, D. T. (2010). Two case studies of child-centered play therapy for children referred with highly disruptive behavior. *International Journal of Play Therapy*, *19*(3), 130–143. https://doi.org/10.1037/a0019119

Cochran, W. G., Mosteller, F., & Tukey, J. W. (1953). Statistical problems of the Kinsey report. *Journal of the American Statistical Association*, *48*, 673–716. https://doi.org/10.2307/2281066

Cochrane, R. E., & Lloyd, K. P. (2020). Competency to stand trial. In A. B. Batastini & M. J. Vitacco (Eds.), *Forensic mental health evaluations in the digital age* (pp. 49–82). Springer International Publishing. https://doi.org/10.1007/978-3-030-33908-1_3

Coe, C. L., & Laudenslager, M. L. (2007). Psychosocial influences on immunity, including effects on immune maturation and senescence. *Brain, Behavior, and Immunity*, *21*(8), 1000–1008. https://doi.org/10.1016/j.bbi.2007.06.015

Coghill, D. (2022). The benefits and limitations of stimulants in treating ADHD. In S. C. Stanford & E. Sciberras (Eds.), *New discoveries in the behavioral neuroscience of attention-deficit hyperactivity disorder* (Vol. 57, pp. 51–77). Springer International Publishing. https://doi.org/10.1007/7854_2022_331

Coglan, L., & Otasowie, J. (2019). Avoidant/restrictive food intake disorder: What do we know so far? *BJPsych Advances*, *25*(2), 90–98. https://doi.org/10.1192/bja.2018.48

Cohen, D. (2022, February 2). Anti-vaxx celebrities are still coming out of the woodwork. *The Cut*. https://www.thecut.com/2022/02/anti-vaxx-celebrities-are-coming-out-of-the-woodwork.html

Cohen, J. A., Deblinger, E., & Mannarino, A. P. (2018). Trauma-focused cognitive behavioral therapy for children and families. *Psychotherapy Research*, *28*(1), 47–57. https://doi.org/10.1080/10503307.2016.1208375

Cohen, J. A., & Mannarino, A. P. (2015). Trauma-focused cognitive behavioral therapy for traumatized children and families. *Child and Adolescent Psychiatric Clinics of North America*, *24*(3), 557–570. https://doi.org/10.1016/j.chc.2015.02.005

Cohen, L. (2014). How Sigmund Freud wanted to die. In *The Atlantic*. https://www.theatlantic.com/health/archive/2014/09/how-sigmund-freud-wanted-to-die/380322/

Cohen, M., Granger, S., & Fuller-Thomson, E. (2015). The association between bereavement and biomarkers of inflammation. *Behavioral Medicine*, *41*(2), 49–59. https://doi.org/10.1080/08964289.2013.866539

Cohen, P., Chen, H., Gordon, K., Johnson, J., Brook, J., & Kasen, S. (2008). Socioeconomic background and the developmental course of schizotypal and borderline personality disorder symptoms. *Development and Psychopathology*, *20*(2), 633–650. https://doi.org/10.1017/S095457940800031X

Cohen, P., Rogol, A. D., Deal, C. L., Saenger, P., Reilter, E. O., Ross, J. L., Chernausek, S. D., Savage, M. O.,

& Wit, J. M. (2008). Consensus statement on the diagnosis and treatment of children with idiopathic short stature: A summary of the Growth Hormone Research Society, the Lawson Wilkins Pediatric Endocrine Society, and the European Society for Paediatric Endocrinology Workshop. *Journal of Clinical Endocrinology & Metabolism*, *93*(11), 4210–4217. https://doi.org/10.1210/jc.2008-0509

Cohen, R. J., & Swerdlik, M. E. (2018). *Psychological testing and assessment* (9th ed.). McGraw Hill Education.

Cohen, S. A., Higham, J. E. S., & Cavaliere, C. T. (2011). Binge flying. *Annals of Tourism Research*, *38*(3), 1070–1089. https://doi.org/10.1016/j.annals.2011.01.013

Cohen Marill, M. (2019, November 7). The enduring power of Asperger's, even as a non-diagnosis. *Wired*. https://www.wired.com/story/the-enduring-power-of-aspergers-even-as-a-non-diagnosis/

Colaianni, A., & Festini, S. B. (2021). Exploring the potential shared pathology of eating disorders and addiction: A behavioral neuroscience approach. *Acta Spartae*, *5*(1), 1–5.

Colameco, S., Becker, L. A., & Simpson, M. (1983). Sex bias in the assessment of patient complaints. *The Journal of Family Practice*, *16*(6), 1117–1121.

Coleman, D. M., Adams, J. B., Anderson, A. L., & Frye, R. E. (2019). Rating of the effectiveness of 26 psychiatric and seizure medications for autism spectrum disorder: Results of a national survey. *Journal of Child and Adolescent Psychopharmacology*, *29*(2), 107–123. https://doi.org/10.1089/cap.2018.0121

Coleman, E., Radix, A. E., Bouman, W. P., Brown, G. R., de Vries, A. L. C., Deutsch, M. B., Ettner, R., Fraser, L., Goodman, M., Green, J., Hancock, A. B., Johnson, T. W., Karasic, D. H., Knudson, G. A., Leibowitz, S. F., Meyer-Bahlburg, H. F. L., Monstrey, S. J., Motmans, J., Nahata, L., … Arcelus, J. (2022). Standards of care for the health of transgender and gender diverse people, version 8. *International Journal of Transgender Health*, *23*(Suppl. 1), S1–S259. https://doi.org/10.1080/26895269.2022.2100644

Coleman, J. R. I., Gaspar, H. A., Bryois, J., Breen, G., Byrne, E. M., Forstner, A. J., Holmans, P. A., de Leeuw, C. A., Mattheisen, M., McQuillin, A., Whitehead Pavlides, J. M., Pers, T. H., Ripke, S., Stahl, E. A., Steinberg, S., Trubetskoy, V., Trzaskowski, M., Wang, Y., Abbott, L., … Wray, N. R. (2020). The genetics of the mood disorder spectrum: Genome-wide association analyses of more than 185,000 cases and 439,000 controls. *Biological Psychiatry*, *88*(2), 169–184. https://doi.org/10.1016/j.biopsych.2019.10.015

Coleman, L. (1984). *The reign of error: Psychiatry, authority, and law*. Beacon Press.

Coles, E. K., Pelham, W. E., Fabiano, G. A., Gnagy, E. M., Burrows-MacLean, L., Wymbs, B. T., Chacko, A., Walker, K. S., Wymbs, F., Robb Mazzant, J., Garefino, A., Hoffman, M. T., Massetti, G. M., Page, T. F., Waschbusch, D. A., Waxmonsky, J. G., & Pelham, W. E. (2020). Randomized trial of first-line behavioral intervention to reduce need for medication in children with ADHD. *Journal of Clinical Child and Adolescent Psychology*, *49*(5), 673–687. https://doi.org/10.1080/15374416.2019.1630855

Comas-Díaz, L., Hall, G. N., & Neville, H. A. (2019). Racial trauma: Theory, research, and healing: Introduction to the special issue. *American Psychologist*, *74*(1), 1. https://doi.org/10.1037/amp0000442

Combs, D. R., & Tiegreen, J. (2007). The use of behavioral experiments to modify delusions and paranoia: Clinical guidelines and recommendations. *International Journal of Behavioral Consultation and Therapy*, *3*(1), 30–37. https://doi.org/10.1037/h0100177

Comerford, P. (2018). Response to Eugene McHugh's "A conversation on DSM-5 and its usefulness in counselling and psychotherapy"–The Rogerian perspective. *The Irish Journal of Counselling and Psychotherapy*, *18*(4), 4–9.

Comiskey, A., Parent, M. C., & Tebbe, E. A. (2020). An inhospitable world: Exploring a model of objectification theory with trans women. *Psychology*

of Women Quarterly, *44*(1), 105–116. https://doi.org/10.1177/0361684319889595

COMPASS Pathways. (2021, November 9). *COMPASS Pathways announces positive topline results from groundbreaking phase IIb trial of investigational COMP360 psilocybin therapy for treatment-resistant depression | Compass Pathways*. Https://Compass-pathways.Com/. https://compasspathways.com/positive-topline-results/

Condit, V. K. (1990). Anorexia nervosa: Levels of causation. *Human Nature*, *1*(4), 391–413. doi:10.1007/BF02734052

Connan, F., Lightman, S. L., Landau, S., Wheeler, M., Treasure, J., & Campbell, I. C. (2007). An investigation of hypothalamic-pituitary-adrenal axis hyperactivity in anorexia nervosa: The role of CRH and AVP. *Journal of Psychiatric Research*, *41*(1–2), 131–143. https://doi.org/10.1016/j.jpsychires.2005.12.005

Connolly, J., Glessner, J., Elia, J., & Hakonarson, H. (2015). ADHD & pharmacogenomic: Past, present and future. *Therapeutic Innovation & Regulatory Science*, *49*(5), 632–642. https://doi.org/10.1177/2168479015599811

Connor, J. P., Stjepanović, D., Le Foll, B., Hoch, E., Budney, A. J., & Hall, W. D. (2021). Cannabis use and cannabis use disorder. *Nature Reviews Disease Primers*, *7*(1), Article 16. https://doi.org/10.1038/s41572-021-00247-4

Conradi, H. J., Dingemanse, P., Noordhof, A., Finkenauer, C., & Kamphuis, J. H. (2018). Effectiveness of the "Hold me Tight" relationship enhancement program in a self-referred and a clinician-referred sample: An emotionally focused couples therapy-based approach. *Family Process*, *57*(3), 613–628. https://doi.org/10.1111/famp.12305

Contador, I., Del Ser, T., Llamas, S., Villarejo, A., Benito-León, J., & Bermejo-Pareja, F. (2017). Impact of literacy and years of education on the diagnosis of dementia: A population-based study. *Journal of Clinical and Experimental Neuropsychology*, *39*(2), 112–119. https://doi.org/10.1080/13803395.2016.1204992

Conway, C. C., Forbes, M. K., South, S. C., & HiTOP Consortium. (2022). A hierarchical taxonomy of psychopathology (HiTOP) primer for mental health researchers. *Clinical Psychological Science*, *10*(2), 236–258. https://doi.org/10.1177%2F21677026211017834

Conway, C. C., & Krueger, R. F. (2021). Rethinking the diagnosis of mental disorders: Data-driven psychological dimensions, not categories, as a framework for mental-health research, treatment, and training. *Current Directions in Psychological Science*, *30*(2), 151–158. https://doi.org/10.1177/0963721421990353

Conway, F. (2012). Psychodynamic psychotherapy of ADHD: A review of the literature. *Psychotherapy*, *49*(3), 404–417. https://doi.org/10.1037/a0027344

Conway, F. (2014). The use of empathy and transference as interventions in psychotherapy with attention deficit hyperactive disorder latency-aged boys. *Psychotherapy*, *51*(1), 104–109. https://doi.org/10.1037/a0032596

Conway, F. (2015). Current research and future directions in psychodynamic treatment of ADHD: Is empathy the missing link? *Journal of Infant, Child & Adolescent Psychotherapy*, *14*(3), 280–287. https://doi.org/10.1080/15289168.2015.1069235

Conway, F., Lyon, S., Silber, M., & Donath, S. (2019). Cultivating compassion ADHD project: A mentalization informed psychodynamic psychotherapy approach. *Journal of Infant, Child & Adolescent Psychotherapy*, *18*(3), 212–222. https://doi.org/10.1080/15289168.2019.1654271

Cook, B. G., & Rumrill, P. D. (2005). Using and interpreting analogue designs. *Work: Journal of Prevention, Assessment & Rehabilitation*, *24*(1), 93–97.

Cooke, A. (Ed.). (2017). *Understanding psychosis and schizophrenia: Why people sometimes hear voices, believe things that others find strange, or appear out of touch with reality, and what can help* (Report by the Division of Clinical Psychology; Rev. ed.).

British Psychological Society. https://www.bps.org.uk/what-psychology/understanding-psychosis-and-schizophrenia

Cooke, A., & Kinderman, P. (2018). "But what about real mental illnesses?" Alternatives to the disease model approach to "schizophrenia." *Journal of Humanistic Psychology, 58*(1), 47–71. https://doi.org/10.1177/0022167817745621

Coolidge, F. L., & Segal, D. L. (1998). Evolution of personality disorder diagnosis in the *Diagnostic and statistical manual of mental disorders. Clinical Psychology Review, 18*(5), 585–599. https://doi.org/10.1016/S0272-7358(98)00002-6

Coolidge, F. L., Thede, L. L., & Young, S. E. (2002). The heritability of gender identity disorder in a child and adolescent twin sample. *Behavior Genetics, 32*(4), 251–257.

Cooney, G. M., Dwan, K., Greig, C. A., Lawlor, D. A., Rimer, J., Waugh, F. R., McMurdo, M., & Mead, G. E. (2013). Exercise for depression. *Cochrane Database of Systematic Reviews, 2013*(9), Article CD004366. https://doi.org/10.1002/14651858.CD004366.pub6

Cooney, P., Tunney, C., & O'Reilly, G. (2018). A systematic review of the evidence regarding cognitive therapy skills that assist cognitive behavioural therapy in adults who have an intellectual disability. *Journal of Applied Research in Intellectual Disabilities, 31*(1), 23–42. https://doi.org/10.1111/jar.12365

Cooper, D., & Gupta, V. (2022). Lumateperone. In *StatPearls*. StatPearls Publishing. http://www.ncbi.nlm.nih.gov/books/NBK560844/

Cooper, K., Martyn-St James, M., Kaltenthaler, E., Dickinson, K., Cantrell, A., Wylie, K., Frodsham, L., & Hood, C. (2015). Behavioral therapies for management of premature ejaculation: A systematic review. *Sexual Medicine, 3*(3), 174–188. https://doi.org/10.1002/sm2.65

Cooper, M. (2003). *Existential therapies*. SAGE.

Cooper, R. (2014). *Diagnosing the Diagnostic and statistical manual of mental disorders*. Karnac.

Cooper, R. E., Laxhman, N., Crellin, N., Moncrieff, J., & Priebe, S. (2020). Psychosocial interventions for people with schizophrenia or psychosis on minimal or no antipsychotic medication: A systematic review. *Schizophrenia Research, 225*, 15–30. https://doi.org/10.1016/j.schres.2019.05.020

Cooper, Z., & Grace, R. D. (2017). Eating disorders: Transdiagnostic theory and treatment. In S. Hofmann & G. J. G. Asmundson (Eds.), *The science of cognitive behavioral therapy* (pp. 337–357). Elsevier Science & Technology. http://dx.doi.org/10.1016/B978-0-12-803457-6.00014-3

Çöpür, S., & Çöpür, M. (2020). Olanzapine in the treatment of anorexia nervosa: A systematic review. *The Egyptian Journal of Neurology, Psychiatry and Neurosurgery, 56*(1), 60. https://doi.org/10.1186/s41983-020-00195-y

Corbisiero, S., Bitto, H., Newark, P., Abt-Mörstedt, B., Elsässer, M., Buchli-Kammermann, J., Künne, S., Nyberg, E., Hofecker-Fallahpour, M., & Stieglitz, R.-D. (2018). A comparison of cognitive-behavioral and pharmacotherapy vs. Pharmacotherapy alone in adults with attention-deficit/hyperactivity disorder (ADHD)—A randomized controlled trial. *Frontiers in Psychiatry, 9*, Article 571. https://doi.org/10.3389/fpsyt.2018.00571

Corcos, M., Guilbaud, O., Paterniti, S., Moussa, M., Chambry, J., Chaouat, G., Consoli, S. M., & Jeammet, P. (2003). Involvement of cytokines in eating disorders: A critical review of the human literature. *Psychoneuroendocrinology, 28*(3), 229–249. https://doi.org/10.1016/S0306-4530(02)00021-5

Cordaro, M., Grigsby, T. J., Howard, J. T., Deason, R. G., Haskard-Zolnierek, K., & Howard, K. (2021). Pandemic-specific factors related to generalized anxiety disorder during the initial COVID-19 protocols in the United States. *Issues in Mental Health Nursing, 42*(8), 747–757. https://doi.org/10.1080/01612840.2020.1867675

Corley, C. (2015, July 2). Coping while black: A season of traumatic news takes a psychological toll. *NPR*. http://www.npr.org/sections/codeswitch/2015/07/02/419462959/coping-while-black-a-season-of-traumatic-news-takes-a-psychological-toll

Cornwall, M. W. (Ed.). (2019a). Humanistic perspectives on understanding and responding to extreme states: Part 1 [Special issue]. In *Journal of Humanistic Psychology* (Vol. 59).

Cornwall, M. W. (2019b). Merciful love can help relieve the emotional suffering of extreme states. *Journal of Humanistic Psychology, 59*(5), 665–671. https://doi.org/10.1177/0022167818773467

Corona, G., Isidori, A. M., Aversa, A., Burnett, A. L., & Maggi, M. (2016). Endocrinologic control of men's sexual desire and arousal/erection. *Journal of Sexual Medicine, 13*(3), 317–337. https://doi.org/10.1016/j.jsxm.2016.01.007

Corponi, F., Bonassi, S., Vieta, E., Albani, D., Frustaci, A., Ducci, G., Landi, S., Boccia, S., Serretti, A., & Fabbri, C. (2019). Genetic basis of psychopathological dimensions shared between schizophrenia and bipolar disorder. *Progress in Neuro-Psychopharmacology and Biological Psychiatry, 89*, 23–29. https://doi.org/10.1016/j.pnpbp.2018.08.023

Corradi, R. B. (2011). Schizophrenia as a human process. *Journal of the American Academy of Psychoanalysis & Dynamic Psychiatry, 39*(4), 717–736. https://doi.org/10.1521/jaap.2011.39.4.717

Corrado, M. L. (2017). Insanity and free will: The humanitarian argument for abolition. In M. D. White (Ed.), *The insanity defense: Multidisciplinary views on its history, trends, and controversies* (pp. 243–270). Praeger.

Corrigan, P. W. (2005). *On the stigma of mental illness: Practical strategies for research and social change*. American Psychological Association.

Corrigan, P. W., & Kleinlein, P. (2005). The impact of mental illness stigma. In P. W. Corrigan (Ed.), *On the stigma of mental illness: Practical strategies for research and social change* (pp. 11–44). American Psychological Association.

Cortese, S., Adamo, N., Giovane, C. D., Mohr-Jensen, C., Hayes, A. J., Carucci, S., Atkinson, L. Z., Tessari, L., Banaschewski, T., Coghill, D., Hollis, C., Simonoff, E., Zuddas, A., Barbui, C., Purgato, M., Steinhausen, H.-C., Shokraneh, F., Xia, J., & Cipriani, A. (2018). Comparative efficacy and tolerability of medications for attention-deficit hyperactivity disorder in children, adolescents, and adults: A systematic review and network meta-analysis. *The Lancet Psychiatry, 5*(9), 727–738. https://doi.org/10.1016/S2215-0366(18)30269-4

Cortés-García, L., Takkouche, B., Seoane, G., & Senra, C. (2019). Mediators linking insecure attachment to eating symptoms: A systematic review and meta-analysis. *PLoS ONE, 14*(3). https://doi.org/10.1371/journal.pone.0213099

Coryell, W. (2009). Maintenance treatment in bipolar disorder: A reassessment of lithium as the first choice. *Bipolar Disorders, 11*(Suppl. 2), 77–83. https://doi.org/10.1111/j.1399-5618.2009.00712.x

Cosci, F., & Chouinard, G. (2019). The monoamine hypothesis of depression revisited: Could it mechanistically novel antidepressant strategies? In J. Quevedo, A. F. Carvalho, & C. A. Zarate (Eds.), *Neurobiology of depression* (pp. 63–73). Academic Press. https://doi.org/10.1016/B978-0-12-813333-0.00007-X

Cosgrove, L., & Bursztajn, H. J. (2009). Toward credible conflict of interest policies in clinical psychiatry. In *Psychiatric Times* (Vol. 26, Issue 1). http://www.psychiatrictimes.com/articles/toward-credible-conflict-interest-policies-clinical-psychiatry

Cosgrove, L., Herrawi, F., & Shaughnessy, A. F. (2022). Conflicts of interest in psychopharmacology textbooks. *Community Mental Health Journal, 58*(4), 619–623. https://doi.org/10.1007/s10597-021-00906-6

Cosgrove, L., Krimsky, S., Vijayaraghavan, M., & Schneider, L. (2006). Financial ties between DSM-IV panel members and the pharmaceutical industry. *Psychotherapy and Psychosomatics, 75*(3), 154–160. https://doi.org/10.1159/000091772

Cosgrove, L., Krimsky, S., Wheeler, E. E., Kaitz, J., Greenspan, S. B., & DiPentima, N. L. (2014). Tripartite conflicts of interest and high stakes patent extensions in the DSM-5. *Psychotherapy and Psychosomatics, 83*(2), 106–113. https://doi.org/10.1159/000357499

Cosgrove, L., Krimsky, S., Wheeler, E. E., Peters, S. M., Brodt, M., & Shaughnessy, A. F. (2017). Conflict of interest policies and industry relationships of guideline development group members: A cross-sectional study of clinical practice guidelines for depression. *Accountability in Research, 24*(2), 99–115. https://doi.org/10.1080/08989621.2016.1251319

Costa, A. M., Medeiros, G. C., Redden, S., Grant, J. E., Tavares, H., & Seger, L. (2018). Cognitive-behavioral group therapy for intermittent explosive disorder: Description and preliminary analysis. *Brazilian Journal of Psychiatry, 40*(3), 316–319. https://doi.org/10.1590/1516-4446-2017-2262

Costa, L. da S., Alencar, Á. P., Neto, P. J. N., Santos, M. do S. V. dos, da Silva, C. G. L., Pinheiro, S. de F. L., Teixeira Silveira, R., Bianco, B. A. V., Pinheiro Júnior, R. F. F., de Lima, M. A. P., Reis, A. O. A., & Neto, M. L. R. (2015). Risk factors for suicide in bipolar disorder: A systematic review. *Journal of Affective Disorders, 170*, 237–254. https://doi.org/10.1016/j.jad.2014.09.003

Costello, S. J. (2011). An existential analysis of anxiety: Frankl, Kierkegaard, Voegelin. *International Forum for Logotherapy, 34*(2), 65–71.

Cotter, J., Kaess, M., & Yung, A. R. (2015). Childhood trauma and functional disability in psychosis, bipolar disorder and borderline personality disorder: A review of the literature. *Irish Journal of Psychological Medicine, 32*(Spec Iss1), 21–30. https://doi.org/10.1017/ipm.2014.74

Cottraux, J., Note, I. D., Boutitie, F., Milliery, M., Genouihlac, V., Yao, S. N., Note, B., Mollard, E., Bonasse, F., Gaillard, S., Djamoussian, D., de Mey Guillard, C., Culem, A., & Gueyffier, F. (2009). Cognitive therapy versus Rogerian supportive therapy in borderline personality disorder: Two-year follow-up of a controlled pilot study. *Psychotherapy and Psychosomatics, 78*(5), 307–316. https://doi.org/10.1159/000229769

Coulon, S. M. (2015). *A bioecological approach to understanding the interaction of environmental stress and genetic susceptibility in influencing cortisol and blood pressure in African American adults* [Doctoral dissertation, University of South Carolina]. https://scholarcommons.sc.edu/etd/2798/

Courcha, P. (2015). "She's talking to me!" Training home carers to use Pre-Therapy contact reflections: An action research study. *Person-Centered and Experiential Psychotherapies, 14*(4), 285–299. https://doi.org/10.1080/14779757.2015.1058291

Courchesne, E. (2004). Brain development in autism: Early overgrowth followed by premature arrest of growth. *Mental Retardation and Developmental Disabilities Research Reviews, 10*(2), 106–111. https://doi.org/10.1002/mrdd.20020

Craig, A., & Tran, Y. (2014). Trait and social anxiety in adults with chronic stuttering: Conclusions following meta-analysis. *Journal of Fluency Disorders, 40*, 35–43. https://doi.org/10.1016/j.jfludis.2014.01.001

Craig, S. G., Sierra Hernandez, C., Moretti, M. M., & Pepler, D. J. (2021). The mediational effect of affect dysregulation on the association between attachment to parents and oppositional defiant disorder symptoms in adolescents. *Child Psychiatry & Human Development, 52*(5), 818–828. https://doi.org/10.1007/s10578-020-01059-5

Craig, S. L., & Austin, A. (2016). The AFFIRM open pilot feasibility study: A brief affirmative cognitive behavioral coping skills group intervention for sexual and gender minority youth. *Children and Youth Services*

Review, 64, 136–144. https://doi.org/10.1016/j.childyouth.2016.02.022

Craig, T. K. J., Cox, A. D., & Klein, K. (2002). Intergenerational transmission of somatization behaviour: A study of chronic somatizers and their children. *Psychological Medicine, 32*(5), 805–816. https://doi.org/10.1017/S0033291702005846

Cramer, P. (1999). Future directions for the Thematic Apperception Test. *Journal of Personality Assessment, 72*(1), 74–92. https://doi.org/10.1207/s15327752jpa7201_5

Crapanzano, K. A., Hammarlund, R., Ahmad, B., Hunsinger, N., & Kullar, R. (2018). The association between perceived stigma and substance use disorder treatment outcomes: A review. *Substance Abuse and Rehabilitation, 10*, 1–12. https://doi.org/10.2147/SAR.S183252

Craske, M. G. (2017). *Cognitive-behavioral therapy* (2nd ed.). American Psychological Association.

Cravedi, E., Deniau, E., Giannitelli, M., Xavier, J., Hartmann, A., & Cohen, D. (2017). Tourette syndrome and other neurodevelopmental disorders: A comprehensive review. *Child and Adolescent Psychiatry and Mental Health, 11*(1), 59. https://doi.org/10.1186/s13034-017-0196-x

Cremers, H., Lee, R., Keedy, S., Phan, K. L., & Coccaro, E. (2016). Effects of escitalopram administration on face processing in intermittent explosive disorder: An fMRI study. *Neuropsychopharmacology, 41*(2), 590–597. https://doi.org/10.1038/npp.2015.187

Creswell, J. W., & Creswell, J. D. (2018). *Research design: Qualitative, quantitative, and mixed methods approaches* (5th ed.). SAGE.

Crichton, A. (1798). *An inquiry into the nature and origin of mental derangement: Comprehending a concise system of the physiology and pathology of the human mind and a history of the passions and their effects* (Vol. 2). T. Cadell, Jr., and W. Davies. https://books.google.com/books?hl=en&lr=&id=x-HVJAAAAYAAJ&oi=fnd&pg=PR2&dq=An+inquiry+into+the+nature+and+origin+of+mental+derangement:+Comprehending+a+concise+system+of+the+physiol-+ogy+and+pathology+of+the+human+mind+and+a+history+of+the+passions+and+their+effects&ots=mHoexMWtp2&sig=bk-O64OXovqPwM8H-uUFFWye-f8#v=onepage&q=An%20inquiry%20into%20the%20nature%20and%20origin%20of%20mental%20derangement%3A%20Comprehending%20a%20concise%20system%20of%20the%20physiol-%20ogy%20and%20pathology%20of%20the%20human%20mind%20and%20a%20history%20of%20the%20passions%20and%20their%20effects&f=false

Crisci, G., Caviola, S., Cardillo, R., & Mammarella, I. C. (2021). Executive functions in neurodevelopmental disorders: Comorbidity overlaps between attention deficit and hyperactivity disorder and specific learning disorders. *Frontiers in Human Neuroscience, 15*, Article 594234. https://doi.org/10.3389/fnhum.2021.594234

Crist, R. C., Reiner, B. C., & Berrettini, W. H. (2019). A review of opioid addiction genetics. *Current Opinion in Psychology, 27*, 31–35. https://doi.org/10.1016/j.copsyc.2018.07.014

Cristea, I. A., Gentili, C., Cotet, C. D., Palomba, D., Barbui, C., & Cuijpers, P. (2017). Efficacy of psychotherapies for borderline personality disorder: A systematic review and meta-analysis. *JAMA Psychiatry, 74*(4), 319–328. https://doi.org/10.1001/jamapsychiatry.2016.4287

Criswell, E., & Serlin, I. A. (2015). Humanistic psychology, mind-body medicine, and whole-person health care. In K. J. Schneider, J. F. Pierson, & J. F. T. Bugental (Eds.), *The handbook of humanistic psychology: Theory, research, and practice* (pp. 653–666). SAGE Publications.

Crocq, M.-A. (2013). Milestones in the history of personality disorders. *Dialogues in Clinical Neuroscience, 15*(2), 147–153.

Crocq, M.-A., & Crocq, L. (2000). From shell shock and war neurosis to posttraumatic stress disorder: A history of psychotraumatology. *Dialogues in Clinical Neuroscience, 2*(1), 47–55.

Cromby, J. (2022). Meaning in the power threat meaning framework. *Journal of Constructivist Psychology, 35*(1), 41–53. https://doi.org/10.1080/10720537.2020.1773355

Cronin, E., Brand, B. L., & Mattanah, J. F. (2014). The impact of the therapeutic alliance on treatment outcome in patients with dissociative disorders. *European Journal of Psychotraumatology, 5*.

Crossley, N. (2004). Not being mentally ill: Social movements, system survivors and the oppositional habitus. *Anthropology & Medicine, 11*(2), 161–180. https://doi.org/10.1080/1364847041000167668

Crow, T. J. (1988). The viral theory of schizophrenia. *The British Journal of Psychiatry, 153*, 564–566.

Crowell, A. L., Riva-Posse, P., Holtzheimer, P. E., Garlow, S. J., Kelley, M. E., Gross, R. E., Denison, L., Quinn, S., & Mayberg, H. S. (2019). Long-term outcomes of subcallosal cingulate deep brain stimulation for treatment-resistant depression. *American Journal of Psychiatry, 176*(11), 949–956. https://doi.org/10.1176/appi.ajp.2019.18121427

Crumeyrolle-Arias, M., Jaglin, M., Bruneau, A., Vancassel, S., Cardona, A., Daugé, V., Naudon, L., & Rabot, S. (2014). Absence of the gut microbiota enhances anxiety-like behavior and neuroendocrine response to acute stress in rats. *Psychoneuroendocrinology, 42*, 207–217. https://doi.org/10.1016/j.psyneuen.2014.01.014

Crummy, E. A., O'Neal, T. J., Baskin, B. M., & Ferguson, S. M. (2020). One is not enough: Understanding and modeling polysubstance use. *Frontiers in Neuroscience, 14*, Article 569. https://doi.org/10.3389/fnins.2020.00569

Crunelle, C. L., van den Brink, W., Moggi, F., Konstenius, M., Franck, J., Levin, F. R., van de Glind, G., Demetrovics, Z., Coetzee, C., Luderer, M., Schellekens, A., Consensus Group, I., & Matthys, F. (2018). International consensus statement on screening, diagnosis and treatment of substance use disorder patients with comorbid attention deficit/hyperactivity disorder. *European Addiction Research, 24*(1), 43–51. https://doi.org/10.1159/000487767

Crusio, W. E. (2004). The sociobiology of sociopathy: An alternative hypothesis. *Behavioral and Brain Sciences, 27*(1), 154–155. doi:10.1017/S0140525X04220040

Cui, D., Guo, Y., Cao, W., Gao, W., Qiu, J., Su, L., Jiao, Q., & Lu, G. (2020). Correlation between decreased amygdala subnuclei volumes and impaired cognitive functions in pediatric bipolar disorder. *Frontiers in Psychiatry, 11*, Article 612. https://doi.org/10.3389/fpsyt.2020.00612

Cui, M. Y., Lin, Y., Sheng, J. Y., Zhang, X., & Cui, R. J. (2018). Exercise intervention associated with cognitive improvement in Alzheimer's disease. *Neural Plasticity, 2018*, e9234105. https://doi.org/10.1155/2018/9234105

Cui, Y., Fang, H., Bao, C., Geng, W., Yu, F., & Li, X. (2022). Efficacy of transcranial magnetic stimulation for reducing suicidal ideation in depression: A meta-analysis. *Frontiers in Psychiatry, 12*, Article 764183. https://doi.org/10.3389/fpsyt.2021.764183

Cuijpers, P., Berking, M., Andersson, G., Quigley, L., Kleiboer, A., & Dobson, K. S. (2013). A meta-analysis of cognitive-behavioural therapy for adult depression, alone and in comparison with other treatments. *The Canadian Journal of Psychiatry/La Revue Canadienne de Psychiatrie, 58*(7), 376–385.

Cuijpers, P., Donker, T., Weissman, M. M., Ravitz, P., & Cristea, I. A. (2016). Interpersonal psychotherapy for mental health problems: A comprehensive meta-analysis. *American Journal of Psychiatry, 173*(7), 680–687. https://doi.org/10.1176/appi.ajp.2015.15091141

Cuijpers, P., Geraedts, A. S., van Oppen, P., Andersson, G., Markowitz, J. C., & van Straten, A. (2011). Interpersonal psychotherapy for depression: A meta-analysis. *The American Journal of Psychiatry, 168*(6), 581–592. https://doi.org/10.1176/appi.ajp.2010.10101411

Cuijpers, P., Karyotaki, E., Weitz, E., Andersson, G., Hollon, S. D., & van Straten, A. (2014). The effects of psychotherapies for major depression on remission, recovery and improvement: A meta-analysis. *Journal of Affective Disorders, 159*, 118–126. https://doi.org/10.1016/j.jad.2014.02.026

Cuijpers, P., van Straten, A., & Warmerdam, L. (2007). Problem solving therapies for depression: A meta-analysis. *European Psychiatry, 22*(1), 9–15. https://doi.org/10.1016/j.eurpsy.2006.11.001

Cuijpers, P., van Veen, S. C., Sijbrandij, M., Yoder, W., & Cristea, I. A. (2020). Eye movement desensitization and reprocessing for mental health problems: A systematic review and meta-analysis. *Cognitive Behaviour Therapy, 49*(3), 165–180. https://doi.org/10.1080/16506073.2019.1703801

Čukić, I., & Bates, T. C. (2015). The association between neuroticism and heart rate variability is not fully explained by cardiovascular disease and depression. *PLoS ONE, 10*(5), e0125882. https://doi.org/10.1371/journal.pone.0125882

Cukor, J., Spitalnick, J., Difede, J., Rizzo, A., & Rothbaum, B. O. (2009). Emerging treatments for PTSD. *Clinical Psychology Review, 29*(8), 715–726. https://doi.org/10.1016/j.cpr.2009.09.001

Culbert, K. M., Racine, S. E., & Klump, K. L. (2015). Research review: What we have learned about the causes of eating disorders—A synthesis of sociocultural, psychological, and biological research. *Journal of Child Psychology and Psychiatry, 56*(11), 1141–1164. doi:10.1111/jcpp.12441

Culotta, L., & Penzes, P. (2020). Exploring the mechanisms underlying excitation/inhibition imbalance in human iPSC-derived models of ASD. *Molecular Autism, 11*(1), 32. https://doi.org/10.1186/s13229-020-00339-0

Cummings, C. M., Caporino, N. E., & Kendall, P. C. (2014). Comorbidity of anxiety and depression in children and adolescents: 20 years after. *Psychological Bulletin, 140*(3), 816–845. https://doi.org/10.1037/a0034733

Cunningham, P. J. (2018, September 27). *Why even healthy low-income people have greater health risks than higher-income people.* The Commonwealth Fund. https://doi.org/10.26099/y2gb-wa98

Curcio, C., & Corboy, D. (2020). Stigma and anxiety disorders: A systematic review. *Stigma and Health, 5*(2), 125–137. https://doi.org/10.1037/sah0000183

Curran, G., & Ravindran, A. (2014). Lithium for bipolar disorder: A review of the recent literature. *Expert Review of Neurotherapeutics, 14*(9), 1079–1098. https://doi.org/10.1586/14737175.2014.947965

Curran, J. S. M. (1995). Current provision and effectiveness of day care services for people with dementia. *Reviews in Clinical Gerontology, 5*(3), 313–320. https://doi.org/10.1017/S0959259800004354

Curry-Stevens, A., & Nissen, L. B. (2011). Reclaiming Futures considers an anti-oppressive frame to decrease disparities. *Children and Youth Services Review, 33*(Suppl. 1), S54–S59. https://doi.org/10.1016/j.childyouth.2011.06.013

Curtin, S. C., & Ahmad, F. B. (2022). *Provisional numbers and rates of suicide by month and demographic characteristics: United States, 2021* (No. 24; Vital Statistics Rapid Release). National Center for Health Statistics, Centers for Disease Control. https://www.cdc.gov/nchs/data/vsrr/vsrr024.pdf

Cusack, K., Jonas, D. E., Forneris, C. A., Wines, C., Sonis, J., Middleton, J. C., Feltner, C., Brownley, K. A., Olmsted, K. R., Greenblatt, A., Weil, A., & Gaynes, B. N. (2016). Psychological treatments for adults with posttraumatic stress disorder: A systematic review and meta-analysis. *Clinical Psychology Review, 43*, 128–141. https://doi.org/10.1016/j.cpr.2015.10.003

Cushing, S. (2018). Has autism changed? In M. Dos Santos & J.-F. Pelletier (Eds.), *The social constructions and experiences of madness* (pp. 75–94). Brill Rodopi. https://doi.org/10.1163/9789004361898_005

Cuthbert, B. N. (2014). The RDoC framework: Facilitating transition from ICD/DSM to dimensional approaches that integrate neuroscience and psychopathology. *World Psychiatry, 13*(1), 28–35. https://doi.org/10.1002/wps.20087

Cuthbert, B. N. (2022). Research domain criteria (RDoC): Progress and potential. *Current Directions in Psychological Science, 31*(2), 107–114. https://doi.org/10.1177/09637214211051363

Cuthbert, B. N., & Kozak, M. J. (2013). Constructing constructs for psychopathology: The NIMH research domain criteria. *Journal of Abnormal Psychology, 122*(3), 928–937. https://doi.org/10.1037/a0034028

Cuthbert, B. N., & Morris, S. E. (2021). Evolving concepts of the schizophrenia spectrum: A Research Domain Criteria perspective. *Frontiers in Psychiatry, 12*, Article 641319. https://doi.org/10.3389/fpsyt.2021.641319

Czarnecki, K., Jones, D. T., Burnett, M. S., Mullan, B., & Matsumoto, J. Y. (2011). SPECT perfusion patterns distinguish psychogenic from essential tremor. *Parkinsonism & Related Disorders, 17*(5), 328–332. https://doi.org/10.1016/j.parkreldis.2011.01.012

Czech, H. (2018). Hans Asperger, National Socialism, and "race hygiene" in Nazi-era Vienna. *Molecular Autism, 9*(1), 29. https://doi.org/10.1186/s13229-018-0208-6

Czeisler, M. É., Lane, R. I., Petrosky, E., Wiley, J. F., Christensen, A., Njai, R., Weaver, M. D., Robbins, R., Facer-Childs, E. R., Barger, L. K., Czeisler, C. A., Howard, M. E., & Rajaratnam, S. M. W. (2020). Mental health, substance use, and suicidal ideation during the COVID-19 pandemic—United States, June 24–30, 2020. *Morbidity and Mortality Weekly Report, 69*(32), 1049–1057. https://doi.org/10.15585/mmwr.mm6932a1

Da, B. L., Im, G. Y., & Schiano, T. D. (2020). Coronavirus disease 2019 hangover: A rising tide of alcohol use disorder and alcohol-associated liver disease. *Hepatology, 72*(3), 1102–1108. https://doi.org/10.1002/hep.31307

da Cunha-Bang, S., & Knudsen, G. M. (2021). The modulatory role of serotonin on human impulsive aggression. *Biological Psychiatry, 90*(7), 447–457. https://doi.org/10.1016/j.biopsych.2021.05.016

da Mota Gomes, M., & Engelhardt, E. (2014a). A neurological bias in the history of hysteria: From the womb to the nervous system and Charcot. *Arquivos de Neuro-Psiquiatria, 72*(12), 972–975. https://doi.org/10.1590/0004-282X20140149

da Mota Gomes, M., & Engelhardt, E. (2014b). Hysteria to conversion disorders: Babinski's contributions. *Arquivos de Neuro-Psiquiatria, 72*(4), 318–321. https://doi.org/10.1590/0004-282x20130229

da Silva E Silva, D., & de Araújo Moreira, F. (2021). Genetic aspects of substance use disorders. In D. De Micheli, A. L. M. Andrade, R. A. Reichert, E. A. da Silva, B. de O. Pinheiro, & F. M. Lopes (Eds.), *Drugs and human behavior: Biopsychosocial aspects of psychotropic substances use* (pp. 85–94). Springer International Publishing. https://doi.org/10.1007/978-3-030-62855-0_6

Dadomo, H., Panzeri, M., Caponcello, D., Carmelita, A., & Grecucci, A. (2018). Schema therapy for emotional dysregulation in personality disorders: A review. *Current Opinion in Psychiatry, 31*(1), 43–49. https://doi.org/10.1097/YCO.0000000000000380

D'Agostino, A., English, C. D., & Rey, J. A. (2015). Vortioxetine (Brintellix): A New Serotonergic Antidepressant. *Pharmacy and Therapeutics, 40*(1), 36–40.

Dahlenburg, S. C., Gleaves, D. H., & Hutchinson, A. D. (2019a). Anorexia nervosa and perfectionism: A meta-analysis. *International Journal of Eating Disorders, 52*(3), 219–229. https://doi.org/10.1002/eat.23009

Dahlenburg, S. C., Gleaves, D. H., & Hutchinson, A. D. (2019b). Treatment outcome research of enhanced cognitive behaviour therapy for eating disorders: A systematic review with narrative and meta-analytic

synthesis. *Eating Disorders: The Journal of Treatment & Prevention, 27*(5), 482–502. https://doi.org/10.1080/10640266.2018.1560240

Dahm, R. (2006). Alzheimer's discovery. *Current Biology, 16*(21), R906–R910. https://doi.org/10.1016/j.cub.2006.09.056

Dailey, L., Gray, M., Johnson, B., Muhammad, S., & Sinclair, E. (2020). *Grading the states: An analysis of involuntary psychiatric treatment laws.* Treatment Advocacy Center. https://www.treatmentadvocacycenter.org/grading-the-states

Dalenberg, C. J., Brand, B. L., Gleaves, D. H., Dorahy, M. J., Loewenstein, R. J., Cardeña, E., Frewen, P. A., Carlson, E. B., & Spiegel, D. (2012). Evaluation of the evidence for the trauma and fantasy models of dissociation. *Psychological Bulletin, 138*(3), 550–588. https://doi.org/10.1037/a0027447

Dalenberg, C. J., Brand, B. L., Loewenstein, R. J., Gleaves, D. H., Dorahy, M. J., Cardeña, E., Frewen, P. A., Carlson, E. B., & Spiegel, D. (2014). Reality versus fantasy: Reply to Lynn et al (2014). *Psychological Bulletin, 140*(3), 911–920. https://doi.org/10.1037/a0036685

Daley, A., & Mulé, N. J. (2014). LGBTQs and the DSM-5: A critical queer response. *Journal of Homosexuality, 61*(9), 1288–1312. https://doi.org/10.1080/00918369.2014.926766

Dalgleish, T., Black, M., Johnston, D., & Bevan, A. (2020). Transdiagnostic approaches to mental health problems: Current status and future directions. *Journal of Consulting and Clinical Psychology, 88*(3), 179–195. https://doi.org/10.1037/ccp0000482

Dalle Grave, R., Calugi, S., Doll, H. A., & Fairburn, C. G. (2013). Enhanced cognitive behaviour therapy for adolescents with anorexia nervosa: An alternative to family therapy? *Behaviour Research and Therapy, 51*(1), R9–R12. https://doi.org/10.1016/j.brat.2012.09.008

Dalle Grave, R., Eckhardt, S., Calugi, S., & Le Grange, D. (2019). A conceptual comparison of family-based treatment and enhanced cognitive behavior therapy in the treatment of adolescents with eating disorders. *Journal of Eating Disorders, 7*, Article 42. https://doi.org/10.1186/s40337-019-0275-x

Dallos, R., & Stedmon, J. (2014). Systemic formulation: Mapping the family dance. In L. Johnstone & R. Dallos (Eds.), *Formulation in psychology and psychotherapy: Making sense of people's problems* (2nd ed., pp. 67–95). Routledge.

Dalton, B., Bartholdy, S., Robinson, L., Solmi, M., Ibrahim, M. A. A., Breen, G., Schmidt, U., & Himmerich, H. (2018). A meta-analysis of cytokine concentrations in eating disorders. *Journal of Psychiatric Research, 103*, 252–264. https://doi.org/10.1016/j.jpsychires.2018.06.002

Damiano, C. R., Mazefsky, C. A., White, S. W., & Dichter, G. S. (2014). Future directions for research in autism spectrum disorders. *Journal of Clinical Child and Adolescent Psychology, 43*(5), 828–843. https://doi.org/10.1080/15374416.2014.945214

Dandekar, M. P., Fenoy, A. J., Carvalho, A. F., Soares, J. C., & Quevedo, J. (2018). Deep brain stimulation for treatment-resistant depression: An integrative review of preclinical and clinical findings and translational implications. *Molecular Psychiatry, 23*(5), Article 5. https://doi.org/10.1038/mp.2018.2

Danese, A., & Lewis, S. J. (2017). Psychoneuroimmunology of early-life stress: The hidden wounds of childhood trauma? *Neuropsychopharmacology, 42*(1), Article 1. https://doi.org/10.1038/npp.2016.198

Danforth, S., & Navarro, V. (2001). Hyper talk: Sampling the social construction of ADHD in everyday language. *Anthropology & Education Quarterly, 32*(2), 167–190.

Dang, A. B., Giles, S., Fuller-Tyszkiewicz, M., Kiropoulos, L., & Krug, I. (2022). A systematic review and meta-analysis on the DSM–5 severity ratings for eating disorders. *Clinical Psychology: Science and Practice.* https://doi.org/10.1037/cps0000078

Daniel, A. E., Burn, R. J., & Horarik, S. (1999). Patients' complaints about medical practice. *The Medical Journal of Australia, 170*(12), 598–602.

Daray, F. M., Mann, J. J., & Sublette, M. E. (2018). How lipids may affect risk for suicidal behavior. *Journal of Psychiatric Research, 104*, 16–23. https://doi.org/10.1016/j.jpsychires.2018.06.007

Darjee, R., & Quinn, A. (2020). Pharmacological treatment of sexual offenders. In J. Proulx, F. Cortoni, L. A. Craig, & E. J. Letourneau (Eds.), *The Wiley handbook of what works with sexual offenders: Contemporary perspectives in theory, assessment, treatment, and prevention* (pp. 217–245). Wiley-Blackwell. https://doi.org/10.1002/9781119439325.ch13

Darwin, C. (2021). *The origin of species by means of natural selection* (6th ed.). Project Gutenberg. https://www.gutenberg.org/files/2009/2009-h/2009-h.htm (Original work published 1872.)

Dattani, S., Ritchie, H., & Roser, M. (2021). Mental health. *Our World in Data.* https://ourworldindata.org/mental-health

Daughton, J. M., & Kratochvil, C. J. (2009). Review of ADHD pharmacotherapies: Advantages, disadvantages, and clinical pearls. *Journal of the American Academy of Child & Adolescent Psychiatry, 48*(3), 240–248. https://doi.org/10.1097/CHI.0b013e3181977481

Dauphin, V. B. (2020). A critique of the American Psychological Association clinical practice guideline for the treatment of posttraumatic stress disorder (PTSD) in Adults. *Psychoanalytic Psychology, 37*(2), 117–127. https://doi.org/10.1037/pap0000253

Davanloo, H. (1995). *Unlocking the unconscious: Selected papers of Habib Davanloo.* John Wiley & Sons.

Davanloo, H. (1999). Intensive short-term dynamic psychotherapy—Central dynamic sequence: Head-on collision with resistance. *International Journal of Intensive Short-Term Dynamic Psychotherapy, 13*(4), 263–282. https://doi.org/10.1002/(SICI)1099-1182(199912)13:43.0.CO;2-E

David, D. O., & Freeman, A. (2015). Overview of cognitive-behavioral therapy of personality disorder. In A. T. Beck, D. D. Davis, & A. Freeman (Eds.), *Cognitive therapy of personality disorders* (2014-50109-001; 3rd ed., pp. 3–18). Guilford Press.

Davidson, J. (2015). Vintage treatments for PTSD: A reconsideration of tricyclic drugs. *Journal of Psychopharmacology, 29*(3), 264–269. doi:10.1177/0269881114565143

Davidson, J. (2018). Struwwelpeter by Heinrich Hoffmann—psychiatry in literature. *The British Journal of Psychiatry, 212*(3), 174–174. https://doi.org/10.1192/bjp.2017.55

Davidson, J. R., Dawson, S., & Krsmanovic, A. (2019). Effectiveness of group cognitive behavioral therapy for Insomnia (CBT-I) in a primary care setting. *Behavioral Sleep Medicine, 17*(2), 191–201. https://doi.org/10.1080/15402002.2017.1318753

Davidson, K. M. (2017). Cognitive therapy for personality disorders. In B. Stanley & A. New (Eds.), *Borderline Personality Disorder* (pp. 307–324). Oxford University Press. https://doi.org/10.1093/med/9780199997510.003.0017

Davies, G. (2020). A systematic review of structural MRI investigations within borderline personality disorder: Identification of key psychological variables of interest going forward. *Psychiatry Research, 286*(2020), Article 112864. https://doi.org/10.1016/j.psychres.2020.112864

Davies, L. M., Lewis, S., Jones, P. B., Barnes, T. R. E., Gaughran, F., Hayhurst, K., Markwick, A., & Lloyd, H. (2007). Cost-effectiveness of first- v. Second-generation antipsychotic drugs: Results from a randomised controlled trial in schizophrenia responding poorly to previous therapy. *The British Journal of Psychiatry, 191*, 14–22. https://doi.org/10.1192/bjp.bp.106.028654

Davies, M. N., Verdi, S., Burri, A., Trzaskowski, M., Lee, M., Hettema, J. M., Jansen, R., Boomsma, D. I., & Spector, T. D. (2015). Generalised anxiety disorder—A twin study of genetic architecture, genome-wide association and differential gene expression. *PLoS ONE, 10*(8). https://doi.org/10.1371/journal.pone.0134865

Davis, A. K., Barrett, F. S., May, D. G., Cosimano, M. P., Sepeda, N. D., Johnson, M. W., Finan, P. H., & Griffiths, R. R. (2021). Effects of psilocybin-assisted therapy on major depressive disorder: A randomized clinical trial. *JAMA Psychiatry, 78*(5), 481–489. https://doi.org/10.1001/jamapsychiatry.2020.3285

Davis, C. (1993). Review of the book, A reader's guide to the Janus report. *Journal of Sex Research, 30*(4), 336–338.

Davis, D. R., Kurti, A. N., Skelly, J. M., Redner, R., White, T. J., & Higgins, S. T. (2016). A review of the literature on contingency management in the treatment of substance use disorders, 2009–2014. *Preventive Medicine, 92*, 36–46. https://doi.org/10.1016/j.ypmed.2016.08.008

Davis, E. B., & Strawn, B. D. (2010). The *Psychodynamic diagnostic manual*: An adjunctive tool for diagnosis, case formulation, and treatment. *Journal of Psychology and Christianity, 29*(2), 109–115.

Davis, J. E. (2021, Fall). All pathology, all the time. *The New Atlantis, 66*, 55–65.

Davis, L. L., Frazier, E. C., Williford, R. B., & Newell, J. M. (2006). Long-term pharmacotherapy for post-traumatic stress disorder. *CNS Drugs, 20*(6), 465–476. https://doi.org/10.2165/00023210-200620060-00003

Davis, L. W., Luedtke, B., Monson, C., Siegel, A., Daggy, J. K., Yang, Z., Bair, M. J., Brustuen, B., & Ertl, M. (2021). Testing adaptations of cognitive-behavioral conjoint therapy for PTSD: A randomized controlled pilot study with veterans. *Couple and Family Psychology: Research and Practice, 10*(2), 71–86. https://doi.org/10.1037/cfp0000148

Davy, Z. (2015). The DSM-5 and the politics of diagnosing transpeople. *Archives of Sexual Behavior, 44*(5), 1165–1176. https://doi.org/10.1007/s10508-015-0573-6

Davy, Z., & Toze, M. (2018). What is gender dysphoria? A critical systematic narrative review. *Transgender Health, 3*(1), 159–169. https://doi.org/10.1089/trgh.2018.0014

Dawe, R. J., Yu, L., Arfanakis, K., Schneider, J. A., Bennett, D. A., & Boyle, P. A. (2020). Late-life cognitive decline is associated with hippocampal volume, above and beyond its associations with traditional neuropathologic indices. *Alzheimer's & Dementia, 16*(1), 209–218. https://doi.org/10.1002/alz.12009

Dawson, C. T., Wu, W., Fennie, K. P., Ibañez, G., Cano, M. Á., Pettit, J. W., & Trepka, M. J. (2019). Parental-perceived neighborhood characteristics and adolescent depressive symptoms: A multilevel moderation analysis. *Journal of Community Psychology, 47*(7), 1568–1590. https://doi.org/10.1002/jcop.22205

Day, E., & Strang, J. (2011). Outpatient versus inpatient opioid detoxification: A randomized controlled trial. *Journal of Substance Abuse Treatment, 40*(1), 56–66. https://doi.org/10.1016/j.jsat.2010.08.007

Day, N. J. S., Hunt, A., Cortis-Jones, L., & Grenyer, B. F. S. (2018). Clinician attitudes towards borderline personality disorder: A 15-year comparison. *Personality and Mental Health, 12*(4), 309–320. https://doi.org/10.1002/pmh.1429

de Alarcón, R., de la Iglesia, J. I., Casado, N. M., & Montejo, A. L. (2019). Online porn addiction: What we know and what we don't—a systematic review. *Journal of Clinical Medicine, 8*(1), Article 1. https://doi.org/10.3390/jcm8010091

de Andrade, D., Elphinston, R. A., Quinn, C., Allan, J., & Hides, L. (2019). The effectiveness of residential treatment services for individuals with substance use disorders: A systematic review. *Drug and Alcohol Dependence, 201*, 227–235. https://doi.org/10.1016/j.drugalcdep.2019.03.031

De Bei, F., & Dazzi, N. (2014). Attachment and relational psychoanalysis: Bowlby according to Mitchell.

Psychoanalytic Dialogues, 24(5), 562–577. https://doi.org/10.1080/10481885.2014.949492

De Berardis, D., Campanella, D., Serroni, N., Gambi, F., Carano, A., La Rovere, R., Nardella, E., Pizzorno, A. M., Cotellessa, C., Salerno, R. M., & Ferro, F. M. (2008). Insight and perceived expressed emotion among adult outpatients with obsessive-compulsive disorder. *Journal of Psychiatric Practice, 14*(3), 154–159. https://doi.org/10.1097/01.pra.0000320114.38434.5f

De Block, A., & Adriaens, P. R. (2013). Pathologizing sexual deviance: A history. *Journal of Sex Research, 50*(3–4), 276–298. https://doi.org/10.1080/00224499.2012.738259

de Bruijn, D. M., & de Graaf, I. M. (2016). The role of substance use in same-day intimate partner violence: A review of the literature. *Aggression and Violent Behavior*. https://doi.org/10.1016/j.avb.2016.02.010

De Crescenzo, F., D'Alò, G. L., Morgano, G. P., Minozzi, S., Mitrova, Z., Saulle, R., Cruciani, F., Fulceri, F., Davoli, M., Scattoni, M. L., Nardocci, F., Schünemann, H. J., Amato, L., Nardocci, F., & on behalf of the ISACA guideline working group. (2020). Impact of polyunsaturated fatty acids on patient-important outcomes in children and adolescents with autism spectrum disorder: A systematic review. *Health and Quality of Life Outcomes, 18*(1), 28. https://doi.org/10.1186/s12955-020-01284-5

De Crescenzo, F., D'Alò, G. L., Ostinelli, E. G., Ciabattini, M., Franco, V. D., Watanabe, N., Kurtulmus, A., Tomlinson, A., Mitrova, Z., Foti, F., Giovane, C. D., Quested, D. J., Cowen, P. J., Barbui, C., Amato, L., Efthimiou, O., & Cipriani, A. (2022). Comparative effects of pharmacological interventions for the acute and long-term management of insomnia disorder in adults: A systematic review and network meta-analysis. *The Lancet, 400*(10347), 170–184. https://doi.org/10.1016/S0140-6736(22)00878-9

De Cuypere, G., Knudson, G., & Bockting, W. (2011). Second response of the World Professional Association for Transgender Health to the proposed revision of the diagnosis of gender dysphoria for DSM 5. *International Journal of Transgenderism, 13*(2), 51–53. https://doi.org/10.1080/15532739.2011.624047

De Graaf, C. (2006). Effects of snacks on energy intake: An evolutionary perspective. *Appetite, 47*(1), 18–23. doi:http://dx.doi.org/10.1016/j.appet.2006.02.007

De Gucht, V., & Fischler, B. (2002). Somatization: A critical review of conceptual and methodological issues. *Psychosomatics, 43*(1), 1–9. https://doi.org/10.1176/appi.psy.43.1.1

de Jong, M., Schoorl, M., & Hoek, H. W. (2018). Enhanced cognitive behavioural therapy for patients with eating disorders: A systematic review. *Current Opinion in Psychiatry, 31*(6), 436–444. https://doi.org/10.1097/YCO.0000000000000452

de Jonge, P., Roest, A. M., Lim, C. C. W., Levinson, D., & Scott, K. M. (2018). Panic disorder and panic attacks. In D. J. Stein, K. M. Scott, P. de Jonge, & R. C. Kessler (Eds.), *Mental disorders around the world: Facts and figures from the WHO world mental health surveys* (pp. 93–105). Cambridge University Press. https://doi.org/10.1017/9781316536168.007

de Jonghe, F., de Maat, S., Van, R., Hendriksen, M., Kool, S., van Aalst, G., & Dekker, J. (2013). Short-term psychoanalytic supportive psychotherapy for depressed patients. *Psychoanalytic Inquiry, 33*(6), 614–625. https://doi.org/10.1080/07351690.2013.835184

de Kloet, C. S., Vermetten, E., Geuze, E., Kavelaars, A., Heijnen, C. J., & Westenberg, H. G. M. (2006). Assessment of HPA-axis function in posttraumatic stress disorder: Pharmacological and non-pharmacological challenge tests, a review. *Journal of Psychiatric Research, 40*(6), 550–567. https://doi.org/10.1016/j.jpsychires.2005.08.002

De la Rosa-Cáceres, A., Stasik-O'Brien, S., Rojas, A. J., Sanchez-Garcia, M., Lozano, O. M., & Díaz-Batanero, C. (2020). Spanish adaptation of the inventory of

depression and anxiety symptoms (IDAS-II) and a study of its psychometric properties. *Journal of Affective Disorders, 271*, 81–90. https://doi.org/10.1016/j.jad.2020.03.187

de Lange, F. P., Toni, I., & Roelofs, K. (2010). Altered connectivity between prefrontal and sensorimotor cortex in conversion paralysis. *Neuropsychologia, 48*(6), 1782–1788. https://doi.org/10.1016/j.neuropsychologia.2010.02.029

De Leon, G. (2015a). Therapeutic communities. In M. Galanter, H. D. Kleber, & K. T. Brady (Eds.), *The American Psychiatric Publishing textbook of substance abuse treatment* (5th ed., pp. 511–530). American Psychiatric Publishing.

De Leon, G. (2015b). "The gold standard" and related considerations for a maturing science of substance abuse treatment. Therapeutic communities; a case in point. *Substance Use & Misuse, 50*(8–9), 1106–1109. https://doi.org/10.3109/10826084.2015.1012846

De Leon, G., & Unterrainer, H. F. (2020). The therapeutic community: A unique social psychological approach to the treatment of addictions and related disorders. *Frontiers in Psychiatry, 11*, Article 786. https://doi.org/10.3389/fpsyt.2020.00786

de Mello, M. F., de Jesus Mari, J., Bacaltchuk, J., Verdeli, H., & Neugebauer, R. (2005). A systematic review of research findings on the efficacy of interpersonal therapy for depressive disorders. *European Archives of Psychiatry and Clinical Neuroscience, 255*(2), 75–82. https://doi.org/10.1007/s00406-004-0542-x

De Peri, L., Traber, R., Bolla, E., & Vita, A. (2021). Are Schizophrenic disorders with or without early cannabis use neurobiologically distinct disease entities? A meta-analysis of magnetic resonance imaging studies. *Psychiatry Research, 297*, 113731. https://doi.org/10.1016/j.psychres.2021.113731

de Ruiter, M. B., Veltman, D. J., Phaf, R. H., & van Dyck, R. (2007). Negative words enhance recognition in nonclinical high dissociators: An fMRI study. *Neuroimage, 37*(1), 323–334. https://doi.org/10.1016/j.neuroimage.2007.04.064

Deacon, B. J. (2013). The biomedical model of mental disorder: A critical analysis of its validity, utility, and effects on psychotherapy research. *Clinical Psychology Review, 33*(7), 846–861.

Deacon, M. (2015). Personal experience: Being depressed is worse than having advanced cancer. *Journal of Psychiatric and Mental Health Nursing, 22*(6), 457–459. https://doi.org/10.1111/jpm.12219

Deak, J. D., & Johnson, E. C. (2021). Genetics of substance use disorders: A review. *Psychological Medicine, 51*(13), 2189–2200. https://doi.org/10.1017/S0033291721000969

Dean, C. E. (2021). *The skeptical professional's guide to psychiatry: On the risks and benefits of antipsychotics, antidepressants, psychiatric diagnoses, and neuromania.* Routledge.

Dean, R. L., Hurducas, C., Hawton, K., Spyridi, S., Cowen, P. J., Hollingsworth, S., Marquardt, T., Barnes, A., Smith, R., McShane, R., Turner, E. H., & Cipriani, A. (2021). Ketamine and other glutamate receptor modulators for depression in adults with unipolar major depressive disorder. *Cochrane Database of Systematic Reviews, 2021*(9), Article CD011612. https://doi.org/10.1002/14651858.CD011612.pub3

DeAngelis, T. (2022, June 1). Standing tall: A new stage for incompetency cases. *Monitor on Psychology, 53*(4), 56.

Decker, H. S. (2013). *The making of DSM-III.* Oxford University Press.

DeCou, C. R., Comtois, K. A., & Landes, S. J. (2019). Dialectical behavior therapy is effective for the treatment of suicidal behavior: A meta-analysis. *Behavior Therapy, 50*(1), 60–72. https://doi.org/10.1016/j.beth.2018.03.009

Dedovic, K., & Ngiam, J. (2015). The cortisol awakening response and major depression: Examining the evidence. *Neuropsychiatric Disease and Treatment, 11*.

Deer, B. (2004, February 22). Revealed: MMR research scandal. *The Sunday Times*. http://briandeer.com/mmr/lancet-deer-1.htm

Degenhardt, L., Bharat, C., Bruno, R., Glantz, M. D., Sampson, N. A., Lago, L., Aguilar-Gaxiola, S., Alonso, J., Andrade, L. H., Bunting, B., Caldas-de-almeida, J. M., Cia, A. H., Gureje, O., Karam, E. G., Khalaf, M., McGrath, J. J., Moskalewicz, J., Lee, S., Mneimneh, Z., … Kessler, R. C. (2019). Concordance between the diagnostic guidelines for alcohol and cannabis use disorders in the draft ICD-11 and other classification systems: Analysis of data from the WHO's World Mental Health Surveys. *Addiction*, 114(3), 534–552. https://doi.org/10.1111/add.14482

Degerlund Maldi, K., Asellus, P., Myléus, A., & Norström, F. (2021). Cost-utility analysis of esketamine and electroconvulsive therapy in adults with treatment-resistant depression. *BMC Psychiatry*, 21. https://doi.org/10.1186/s12888-021-03601-8

del Campo, N., Chamberlain, S. R., Sahakian, B. J., & Robbins, T. W. (2011). The roles of dopamine and noradrenaline in the pathophysiology and treatment of attention-deficit/hyperactivity disorder. *Biological Psychiatry*, 69(12), e145–e157. https://doi.org/10.1016/j.biopsych.2011.02.036

del Campo, N., Fryer, T. D., Hong, Y. T., Smith, R., Brichard, L., Acosta-Cabronero, J., Chamberlain, S. R., Tait, R., Izquierdo, D., Regenthal, R., Dowson, J., Suckling, J., Baron, J.-C., Aigbirhio, F. I., Robbins, T. W., Sahakian, B. J., & Müller, U. (2013). A positron emission tomography study of nigro-striatal dopaminergic mechanisms underlying attention: Implications for ADHD and its treatment. *Brain*, 136(11), 3252–3270. https://doi.org/10.1093/brain/awt263

Del Casale, A., Sorice, S., Padovano, A., Simmaco, M., Ferracuti, S., Lamis, D. A., Rapinesi, C., Sani, G., Girardi, P., Kotzalidis, G. D., & Pompili, M. (2019). Psychopharmacological treatment of obsessive-compulsive disorder (OCD). *Current Neuropharmacology*, 17(8), 710–736. https://doi.org/10.2174/1570159X16666180813155017

Del Giudice, M. (2014). An evolutionary life history framework for psychopathology. *Psychological Inquiry*, 25(3–4), 261–300. https://doi.org/10.1080/1047840X.2014.884918

Delaloye, S., & Holtzheimer, P. E. (2014). Deep brain stimulation in the treatment of depression. *Dialogues in Clinical Neuroscience*, 16(1), 83–91.

DeLamater, J. D., & Hude, J. S. (1998). Essentialism vs. Social constructionism in the study of human sexuality. *Journal of Sex Research*, 35(1), 10–18. https://doi.org/10.1080/00224499809551913

Delcea, C. (2020). Psychodynamic formulations of paraphilias. *International Journal of Advanced Studies in Sexology*, 2(1). https://doi.org/10.46388/ijass.2020.13.20

Delfa-Lobato, L., Guàrdia-Olmos, J., & Feliu-Torruella, M. (2021). Benefits of cultural activities on people with cognitive impairment: A systematic review. *Frontiers in Psychology*, 12, Article 762392. https://doi.org/10.3389/fpsyg.2021.762392

Dell, P. F. (2013). The weakness of the sociocognitive model of dissociative identity disorder. *Journal of Nervous and Mental Disease*, 201(5), 483–483.

Dell'Osso, L., Abelli, M., Carpita, B., Pini, S., Castellini, G., Carmassi, C., & Ricca, V. (2016). Historical evolution of the concept of anorexia nervosa and relationships with orthorexia nervosa, autism, and obsessive–compulsive spectrum. *Neuropsychiatric Disease and Treatment*, 12, 1651–1660. https://doi.org/10.2147/NDT.S108912

Delobel-Ayoub, M., Ehlinger, V., Klapouszczak, D., Maffre, T., Raynaud, J.-P., Delpierre, C., & Arnaud, C. (2015). Socioeconomic disparities and prevalence of autism spectrum disorders and intellectual disability. *PLoS ONE*, 10(11), e0141964. https://doi.org/10.1371/journal.pone.0141964

Del-Ponte, B., Anselmi, L., Assunção, M. C. F., Tovo-Rodrigues, L., Munhoz, T. N., Matijasevich, A., Rohde, L. A., & Santos, I. S. (2019). Sugar consumption and attention-deficit/hyperactivity disorder (ADHD): A birth cohort study. *Journal of Affective Disorders*, 243, 290–296. https://doi.org/10.1016/j.jad.2018.09.051

Deltito, J., & Beyer, D. (1998). The scientific, quasi-scientific and popular literature on the use of St. John's Wort in the treatment of depression. *Journal of Affective Disorders*, 51(3), 345–351. https://doi.org/10.1016/S0165-0327(99)00008-7

DeLuca, N. L., Moser, L. L., & Bond, G. R. (2008). Assertive community treatment. In K. T. Mueser & D. V. Jeste (Eds.), *Clinical handbook of schizophrenia* (pp. 329–338). Guilford Press.

Demicheli, V., Rivetti, A., Debalini, M. G., & Di Pietrantonj, C. (2012). Vaccines for measles, mumps and rubella in children. *Cochrane Database of Systematic Reviews*, 2012(2), Article CD004407. https://doi.org/10.1002/14651858.CD004407.pub3

Demontis, D., Walters, G. B., Athanasiadis, G., Walters, R., Therrien, K., Farajzadeh, L., Voloudakis, G., Bendl, J., Zeng, B., Zhang, W., Grove, J., Als, T. D., Duan, J., Satterstrom, F. K., Bybjerg-Grauholm, J., Bækved-Hansen, M., Gudmundsson, O. O., Magnusson, S. H., Baldursson, G., … Børglum, A. D. (2022). *Genome-wide analyses of ADHD identify 27 risk loci, refine the genetic architecture and implicate several cognitive domains* (p. 2022.02.14.22270780). medRxiv. https://doi.org/10.1101/2022.02.14.22270780

Demontis, D., Walters, R. K., Martin, J., Mattheisen, M., Als, T. D., Agerbo, E., Baldursson, G., Belliveau, R., Bybjerg-Grauholm, J., Bækvad-Hansen, M., Cerrato, F., Chambert, K., Churchhouse, C., Dumont, A., Eriksson, N., Gandal, M., Goldstein, J. I., Grasby, K. L., Grove, J., … Neale, B. M. (2019). Discovery of the first genome-wide significant risk loci for attention deficit/hyperactivity disorder. *Nature Genetics*, 51(1), Article 1. https://doi.org/10.1038/s41588-018-0269-7

Deng, W., Hu, D., Xu, S., Liu, X., Zhao, J., Chen, Q., Liu, J., Zhang, Z., Jiang, W., Ma, L., Hong, X., Cheng, S., Liu, B., & Li, X. (2019). The efficacy of virtual reality exposure therapy for PTSD symptoms: A systematic review and meta-analysis. *Journal of Affective Disorders*, 257, 698–709. https://doi.org/10.1016/j.jad.2019.07.086

Denis, C. M., Gelernter, J., Hart, A. B., & Kranzler, H. R. (2015). Inter-observer reliability of DSM-5 substance use disorders. *Drug and Alcohol Dependence*, 153, 229–235. https://doi.org/10.1016/j.drugalcdep.2015.05.019

Denney, D. R., Sullivan, B. J., & Thiry, M. R. (1977). Participant modeling and self-verbalization training in the reduction of spider fears. *Journal of Behavior Therapy and Experimental Psychiatry*, 8(3), 247–253. https://doi.org/10.1016/0005-7916(77)90062-3

Dennis, H., Eisma, M. C., & Breen, L. J. (2022). Public stigma of prolonged grief disorder: An experimental replication and extension. *Journal of Nervous & Mental Disease*, 210(3), 199–205. https://doi.org/10.1097/NMD.0000000000001427

Dennis, M., Baumer, P., & Stevens, S. (2016). The concurrent evolution and intertwined nature of juvenile drug courts and Reclaiming Futures approaches to juvenile justice reform. *Drug Court Review*, 10(1), 6–30.

DeNoon, D. J. (2009, July 1). *Warning on stop-smoking drugs Chantix, Zyban*. WebMD. https://www.webmd.com/smoking-cessation/news/20090701/warning-on-stop-smoking-drugs-chantix-zyban

Derbyshire, K. L., & Grant, J. E. (2015). Compulsive sexual behavior: A review of the literature. *Journal of Behavioral Addictions*, 4(2), 37–43. https://doi.org/10.1556/2006.4.2015.003

Derenne, J. L., & Beresin, E. V. (2006). Body image, media, and eating disorders. *Academic Psychiatry*, 30(3), 257–261. https://doi.org/10.1176/appi.ap.30.3.257

DeRosse, P., Nitzburg, G. C., Kompancaril, B., & Malhotra, A. K. (2014). The relation between childhood maltreatment and psychosis in patients with schizophrenia and non-psychiatric controls. *Schizophrenia Research*, 155(1–3), 66–71. https://doi.org/10.1016/j.schres.2014.03.009

DeRubeis, R. J., Siegle, G. J., & Hollon, S. D. (2008). Cognitive therapy vs. Medications for depression: Treatment outcomes and neural mechanisms. *Nature Reviews. Neuroscience*, 9(10), 788–796. https://doi.org/10.1038/nrn2345

DeSarbo, J. R., & DeSarbo, L. (2020). Anorexia nervosa and COVID-19. *Current Psychiatry*, 19(8). https://doi.org/10.12788/cp.0011

DeStefano, F. (2002). MMR vaccine and autism: A review of the evidence for a causal association. *Molecular Psychiatry*, 7(Suppl. 2), S51–S52. https://doi.org/10.1038/sj.mp.4001181

DeStefano, F., & Shimabukuro, T. T. (2019). The MMR vaccine and autism. *Annual Review of Virology*, 6(1), 585–600. https://doi.org/10.1146/annurev-virology-092818-015515

Deutsche, M. B. (2016). *Guidelines for the primary and gender-affirming care of transgender and gender nonbinary people* (2nd ed.). UCSF Center of Excellence for Transgender Health. https://transcare.ucsf.edu/guidelines

DeVita-Raeburn, E. (2016, August 10). The controversy over autism's most common therapy. *Spectrum: Autism Research News*. https://www.spectrumnews.org/features/deep-dive/controversy-autisms-common-therapy/

Devlin, M. (2014). *10 crazy facts from Bedlam, history's most notorious asylum*. Retrieved from https://listverse.com/2014/04/02/10-crazy-facts-from-bedlam-historys-most-notorious-asylum/

DeVylder, J. E., Oh, H. Y., Yang, L. H., Cabassa, L. J., Chen, F., & Lukens, E. P. (2013). Acculturative stress and psychotic-like experiences among Asian and Latino immigrants to the United States. *Schizophrenia Research*, 150(1), 223–228. https://doi.org/10.1016/j.schres.2013.07.040

DeWeerdt, S. (2019). Tracing the US opioid crisis to its roots. *Nature*, 573(7773), S10–S12. https://doi.org/10.1038/d41586-019-02686-2

DeYoung, C. G., Carey, B. E., Krueger, R. F., & Ross, S. R. (2016). Ten aspects of the Big Five in the Personality Inventory for DSM–5. *Personality Disorders: Theory, Research, and Treatment*, 7(2), 113–123. https://doi.org/10.1037/per0000170

Dhabhar, F. S. (2014). Effects of stress on immune function: The good, the bad, and the beautiful. *Immunologic Research*, 58(2–3), 193–210. https://doi.org/10.1007/s12026-014-8517-0

Dhar, A., Bhatt, J., Batra, N., & Rush, B. (2022, June 22). *US health care can't afford health inequities*. Deloitte Insights. https://www2.deloitte.com/us/en/insights/industry/health-care/economic-cost-of-health-disparities.html

D'Hotman, D., & Loh, E. (2020). AI enabled suicide prediction tools: A qualitative narrative review. *BMJ Health & Care Informatics*, 27(3), Article e100175. https://doi.org/10.1136/bmjhci-2020-100175

D'Hotman, D., Loh, E., & Savulescu, J. (2021). AI-enabled suicide prediction tools: Ethical considerations for medical leaders. *BMJ Leader*, 5(2), 102–107. https://doi.org/10.1136/leader-2020-000275

Di Benedetto, B., Rupprecht, R., & Rammes, G. (2010). Beyond the monoamine hypothesis: The quest for an integrative etiology of depression and new therapeutic strategies. In J. T. Van Leeuwen (Ed.), *Antidepressants: Types, efficiency and possible side effects* (pp. 155–167). Nova Science Publishers.

Di Gesto, C., Matera, C., Policardo, G. R., & Nerini, A. (2022). Instagram as a digital mirror: The effects of Instagram likes and disclaimer labels on self-awareness, body dissatisfaction, and social physique anxiety among young Italian women. *Current Psychology*. https://doi.org/10.1007/s12144-021-02675-7

Diamond, G. M. (2014). Attachment-based family therapy interventions. *Psychotherapy*, 51(1), 15–19. https://doi.org/10.1037/a0032689

Dibben, C. R. M., Khandaker, G. M., Underwood, B. R., O'Loughlin, C., Keep, C., Mann, L., & Jones, P. B. (2016). First-generation antipsychotics: Not gone but forgotten. *BJPsych Bulletin*, 40(2), 93–96. https://doi.org/10.1192pb.bp.115.050708

Dickens, G. L., Lamont, E., & Gray, S. (2016). Mental health nurses' attitudes, behaviour, experience and knowledge regarding adults with a diagnosis of borderline personality disorder: Systematic, integrative literature review. *Journal of Clinical Nursing*, 25(13–14), 1848–1875. https://doi.org/10.1111/jocn.13202

Dickerson, F. B. (2000). Cognitive behavioral psychotherapy for schizophrenia: A review of recent empirical studies. *Schizophrenia Research*, 43(2–3), 71–90. https://doi.org/10.1016/S0920-9964(99)00153-X

Dickerson, F. B. (2004). Update on cognitive behavioral psychotherapy for schizophrenia: Review of recent studies. *Journal of Cognitive Psychotherapy*, 18(3), 189–205. https://doi.org/10.1891/jcop.18.3.189.65654

Dickerson, F. B., & Lehman, A. F. (2011). Evidence-based psychotherapy for schizophrenia. *Journal of Nervous and Mental Disease*, 199(8), 520–526. https://doi.org/10.1097/NMD.0b013e318225ee78

Dickson, E. J. (2019, June 14). A guide to 17 anti-vaccination celebrities. *Rolling Stone*. https://www.rollingstone.com/culture/culture-features/celebrities-anti-vaxxers-jessica-biel-847779/

DiClemente, C. C., & Velasquez, M. M. (2002). Motivational interviewing and the stages of change. In W. R. Miller & S. Rollnick (Eds.), *Motivational interviewing: Preparing people for change* (2nd ed., pp. 201–216). The Guilford Press.

Dictionary.com. (n.d.-a). *Bedlam*. Retrieved December 11, 2021, from https://www.dictionary.com/browse/bedlam

Dictionary.com. (n.d.-b). *Diagnosis*. Retrieved December 11, 2021, from https://www.dictionary.com/browse/diagnosis

Diekema, D. S. (2003). Involuntary sterilization of persons with mental retardation: An ethical analysis. *Mental Retardation and Developmental Disabilities Research Reviews*, 9(1), 21–26. https://doi.org/10.1002/mrdd.10053

Dietrich, K. N. (2010). Environmental toxicants. In K. O. Yeates, M. D. Ris, H. G. Taylor, B. F. Pennington, K. O. Yeates, M. D. Ris, H. G. Taylor, & B. F. Pennington (Eds.), *Pediatric neuropsychology: Research, theory, and practice* (2nd ed., pp. 211–264). Guilford Press.

Digman, J. M. (1990). Personality structure: Emergence of the five-factor model. *Annual Review of Psychology*, 41, 417–440. https://doi.org/10.1146/annurev.ps.41.020190.002221

Dijkstra-Kersten, S. M. A., Biesheuvel-Leliefeld, K. E. M., van der Wouden, J. C., Penninx, B. W. J. H., & van Marwijk, H. W. J. (2015). Associations of financial strain and income with depressive and anxiety disorders. *Journal of Epidemiology and Community Health*, 69(7), 660–665. https://doi.org/10.1136/jech-2014-205088

Dikeç, G., Bilaç, Ö., Kardelen, C., & Sapmaz, Ş. Y. (2022). Do we learn to internalize stigma from our parents? Comparison of internalized stigmatization in adolescents diagnosed with ADHD and their parents. *Adolescents*, 2(4), Article 4. https://doi.org/10.3390/adolescents2040034

Dillman Taylor, D., Purswell, K., Cornett, N., & Bratton, S. C. (2021). Effects of child-centered play therapy (CCPT) on disruptive behavior of at-risk preschool children in Head Start. *International Journal of Play Therapy*, 30(2), 86–97. https://doi.org/10.1037/pla0000125

DiLollo, A., Manning, W. H., & Neimeyer, R. A. (2003). Cognitive anxiety as a function of speaker role for fluent speakers and persons who stutter. *Journal of Fluency Disorders*, 28(3), 167–186. https://doi.org/10.1016/S0094-730X(03)00043-3

DiLollo, A., & Neimeyer, R. A. (2008). Talking back to stuttering: Constructivist contributions to stuttering treatment. In J. D. Raskin & S. K. Bridges (Eds.), *Studies in meaning 3: Constructivist psychotherapy in the real world* (pp. 165–181). Pace University Press.

DiLollo, A., & Neimeyer, R. A. (2022). *Counseling in speech-language pathology and audiology: Reconstructing personal narratives* (2nd ed.). Plural Publishing.

DiLollo, A., Neimeyer, R. A., & Manning, W. H. (2002). A personal construct psychology view of relapse: Indications for a narrative therapy component to stuttering treatment. *Journal of Fluency Disorders*, 27(1), 19–42. https://doi.org/10.1016/S0094-730X(01)00109-7

Dimala, C. A., Kadia, B. M., Nji, M. A. M., & Bechem, N. N. (2021). Factors associated with measles resurgence in the United States in the post-elimination era. *Scientific Reports*, 11(1), Article 1. https://doi.org/10.1038/s41598-020-80214-3

DiMauro, J., Carter, S., Folk, J. B., & Kashdan, T. B. (2014). A historical review of trauma-related diagnoses to reconsider the heterogeneity of PTSD. *Journal of Anxiety Disorders*, 28(8), 774–786. https://doi.org/10.1016/j.janxdis.2014.09.002

Dimeff, L. A., Rizvi, S. L., & Koerner, K. (Eds.). (2021). *Dialectical behavior therapy in clinical practice* (2nd ed.). Guilford.

Dimsdale, J. E., Creed, F., Escobar, J., Sharpe, M., Wulsin, L., Barsky, A., Lee, S., Irwin, M. R., & Levenson, J. (2013). Somatic symptom disorder: An important change in DSM. *Journal of Psychosomatic Research*, 75(3), 223–228. https://doi.org/10.1016/j.jpsychores.2013.06.033

Ding, W., Meza, J., Lin, X., He, T., Chen, H., Wang, Y., & Qin, S. (2020). Oppositional defiant disorder symptoms and children's feelings of happiness and depression: Mediating roles of interpersonal relationships. *Child Indicators Research*, 13(1), 215–235. https://doi.org/10.1007/s12187-019-09685-9

Direk, N., Williams, S., Smith, J. A., Ripke, S., Air, T., Amare, A. T., Amin, N., Baune, B. T., Bennett, D. A., Blackwood, D. H. R., Boomsma, D., Breen, G., Buttenschøn, H. N., Byrne, E. M., Børglum, A. D., Castelao, E., Cichon, S., Clarke, T.-K., Cornelis, M. C., … Sullivan, P. F. (2017). An analysis of two genome-wide association meta-analyses identifies a new locus for broad depression phenotype. *Biological Psychiatry*, 82(5), 322–329. https://doi.org/10.1016/j.biopsych.2016.11.013

Disability Justice. (n.d.). *Wyatt v. Stickney*. http://disabilityjustice.org/wyatt-v-stickney/

Division of Clinical Psychology. (2010). *Understanding bipolar disorder*.

Dix, D. (2006). "I tell what I have seen": The reports of asylum reformer Dorothea Dix. *American Journal of Public Health*, 96(4), 622–625. https://doi.org/10.2105/AJPH.96.4.622 (Original work published 1843.)

Dixon, L., Perkins, D., & Calmes, C. (2009). *Guideline watch (September, 2009): Practice guideline for the treatment of patients with schizophrenia*. American Psychiatric Association.

Dixon-Gordon, K. L., Turner, B. J., & Chapman, A. L. (2011). Psychotherapy for personality disorders. *International Review of Psychiatry*, 23(3), 282–302. https://doi.org/10.3109/09540261.2011.586992

Dmytriw, A. A. (2015). Gender and sex manifestations in hysteria across medicine and the arts. *European Neurology*, 73(1–2), 44–50. https://doi.org/10.1159/000367891

Docherty, A. R., Shabalin, A. A., DiBlasi, E., Monson, E., Mullins, N., Adkins, D. E., Bacanu, S.-A., Bakian, A. V., Crowell, S., Chen, D., Darlington, T. M., Callor, W. B., Christensen, E. D., Gray, D., Keeshin, B.,

Klein, M., Anderson, J. S., Jerominski, L., Hayward, C., … Coon, H. (2020). Genome-wide association study of suicide death and polygenic prediction of clinical antecedents. *American Journal of Psychiatry*, 177(10), 917–927. https://doi.org/10.1176/appi.ajp.2020.19101025

Dockery, L., Jeffery, D., Schauman, O., Williams, P., Farrelly, S., Bonnington, O., Gabbidon, J., Lassman, F., Szmukler, G., Thornicroft, G., & Clement, S. (2015). Stigma- and non-stigma-related treatment barriers to mental healthcare reported by service users and caregivers. *Psychiatry Research*, 228(3), 612–619. https://doi.org/10.1016/j.psychres.2015.05.044

Dodd, J. (2015). "The name game": Feminist protests of the DSM and diagnostic labels in the 1980s. *History of Psychology*, 18(3), 312–323. https://doi.org/10.1037/a0039520

Dodds, P., Bruce-Hay, P., & Stapleton, S. (2014). Pre-therapy and dementia—The opportunity to put Person-Centred theory into everyday practice. In P. Pearce & L. Sommerbeck (Eds.), *Person-centred practice at the difficult edge* (pp. 102–118). PCCS Books.

Dodes, L., & Dodes, Z. (2015). *The sober truth: Debunking the bad science behind 12-step programs and the rehab industry*. Beacon Press.

Dodes, L. M., & Khantzian, E. J. (2005). Individual psychodynamic psychotherapy. In R. J. Frances, S. I. Miller, & A. H. Mack (Eds.), *Clinical textbook of addictive disorders* (3rd ed., pp. 457–473). Guilford Publications.

Dodge, E. (2016). Forty years of eating disorder-focused family therapy—The legacy of "psychosomatic families." *Advances in Eating Disorders*, 4(2), 219–227. https://doi.org/10.1080/21662630.2015.1099452

Dodgson, G., & Gordon, S. (2009). Avoiding false negatives: Are some auditory hallucinations an evolved design flaw? *Behavioural and Cognitive Psychotherapy*, 37(3), 325–334. https://doi.org/10.1017/S1352465809005244

Doenyas, C. (2018). Gut microbiota, inflammation, and probiotics on neural development in autism spectrum disorder. *Neuroscience*, 374, 271–286. https://doi.org/10.1016/j.neuroscience.2018.01.060

Doering, B. K., & Eisma, M. C. (2016). Treatment for complicated grief: State of the science and ways forward. *Current Opinion in Psychiatry*, 29(5), 286–291. https://doi.org/10.1097/YCO.0000000000000263

Dogan, B., Ertekin, E., Turkdogan, F. T., Memis, C. O., & Sevincok, L. (2019). Cortico-thalamo-striatal circuit components' volumes and their correlations differ significantly among patients with obsessive–compulsive disorder: A case–control MRI study. *Psychiatry and Clinical Psychopharmacology*, 29(2), 162–170. https://doi.org/10.1080/24750573.2019.1583481

Dogra, P., & Vijayashankar, N. P. (2022). Dexamethasone suppression test. In *StatPearls [Internet]*. StatPearls Publishing. https://www.ncbi.nlm.nih.gov/books/NBK542317/

Dold, M., Aigner, M., Klabunde, M., Treasure, J., & Kasper, S. (2015). Second-generation antipsychotic drugs in anorexia nervosa: A meta-analysis of randomized controlled trials. *Psychotherapy and Psychosomatics*, 84(2), 110–116. https://doi.org/10.1159/000369978

Dolgun, G., Savaser, S., Balci, S., & Yazici, S. (2012). Prevalence of nocturnal enuresis and related factors in children aged 5-13 in Istanbul. *Iranian Journal of Pediatrics*, 22(2), 205–212.

Dolhanty, J. (2006). *Emotion-focused therapy for eating disorders*. http://nedic.ca/emotion-focused-therapy-eating-disorders

Dolhanty, J., & Greenberg, L. S. (2009). Emotion-focused therapy in a case of anorexia nervosa. *Clinical Psychology & Psychotherapy*, 16(4), 366–382. https://doi.org/10.1002/cpp.624

Dolhanty, J., & Lafrance, A. (2019). Emotion-focused family therapy for eating disorders. In L. S. Greenberg & R. N. Goldman (Eds.), *Clinical handbook of emotion-focused therapy* (pp. 403–423).

American Psychological Association. https://doi.org/10.1037/0000112-018

Domaradzki, J. (2021). The Werther effect, the Papageno effect or no effect? A literature review. *International Journal of Environmental Research and Public Health*, 18(5), Article 5. https://doi.org/10.3390/ijerph18052396

Domhardt, M., & Baumeister, H. (2018). Psychotherapy of adjustment disorders: Current state and future directions. *The World Journal of Biological Psychiatry*, 19(sup1), S21–S35. https://doi.org/10.1080/15622975.2018.1467041

Dominus, S. (2023, February 1). Women have been misled about menopause. *The New York Times*. https://www.nytimes.com/2023/02/01/magazine/menopause-hot-flashes-hormone-therapy.html

Domozych, W., & Dragan, W. Ł. (2016). Genetic and environmental basis of the relationship between dissociative experiences and Cloninger's temperament and character dimensions – pilot study. *Polish Psychological Bulletin*, 47(4), 412–420. https://doi.org/10.1515/ppb-2016-0048

Dong, C., Yang, Q., Liang, J., Seger, C. A., Han, H., Ning, Y., Chen, Q., & Peng, Z. (2020). Impairment in the goal-directed corticostriatal learning system as a biomarker for obsessive–compulsive disorder. *Psychological Medicine*, 50(9), 1490–1500. https://doi.org/10.1017/S0033291719001429

Donnelly, B., Touyz, S., Hay, P., Burton, A., Russell, J., & Caterson, I. (2018). Neuroimaging in bulimia nervosa and binge eating disorder: A systematic review. *Journal of Eating Disorders*, 6(1), 3. https://doi.org/10.1186/s40337-018-0187-1

Donofry, S. D., Roecklein, K. A., Wildes, J. E., Miller, M. A., Flory, J. D., & Manuck, S. B. (2014). COMT met allele differentially predicts risk versus severity of aberrant eating in a large community sample. *Psychiatry Research*, 220(1–2), 513–518. doi:10.1016/j.psychres.2014.08.037

Donovan, D. M., Ingalsbe, M. H., Benbow, J., & Daley, D. C. (2013). 12-step interventions and mutual support programs for substance use disorders: An overview. *Social Work in Public Health*, 28, 313–332. https://doi.org/10.1080/19371918.2013.774663

Donovan, D., & Witkiewitz, K. (2012). Relapse prevention: From radical idea to common practice. *Addiction Research & Theory*, 20(3), 204–217. https://doi.org/10.3109/16066359.2011.647133

Doppen, M., Kung, S., Maijers, I., John, M., Dunphy, H., Townsley, H., Eathorne, A., Semprini, A., & Braithwaite, I. (2022). Cannabis in palliative care: A systematic review of current evidence. *Journal of Pain and Symptom Management*. https://doi.org/10.1016/j.jpainsymman.2022.06.002

Dorahy, M. J. (2006). The dissociative processing style: A cognitive organization activated by perceived or actual threat in clinical dissociators. *Journal of Trauma & Dissociation*, 7(4), 29–53. https://doi.org/10.1300/J229v07n04_03

Dorahy, M. J., Brand, B. L., Sar, V., Krüger, C., Stavropoulos, P., Martínez-Taboas, A., Lewis-Fernández, R., & Middleton, W. (2014). Dissociative identity disorder: An empirical overview. *The Australian and New Zealand Journal of Psychiatry*, 48(5), 402–417. https://doi.org/10.1177/0004867414527523

Dorahy, M. J., & van der Hart, O. (2006). Fable or fact? Did Janet really come to repudiate his dissociation theory? *Journal of Trauma & Dissociation*, 7(2), 29–37. https://doi.org/10.1300/J229v07n02_03

Doron, G., Mikulincer, M., Kyrios, M., & Sar-Ei, D. (2015). Obsessive-compulsive disorder. In P. Luyten, L. C. Mayes, P. Fonagy, M. Target, & S. J. Blatt (Eds.), *Handbook of psychodynamic approaches to psychopathology* (pp. 199–215). Guilford Press.

Dougherty, J. W., Ettensohn, M. F., & Levine, S. P. (2018). Beyond depression: Ketamine and glutamatergic agents for PTSD, OCD, and other potential applications. *Psychiatric Annals*, 48(4), 184–188. https://doi.org/10.3928/00485713-20180312-03

Douglas, P., & Rice, C. (2021). Re-storying autism: An interview with Patty Douglas and Carla Rice. *The International Journal of Narrative Therapy and Community Work*, 2021(2), 23–31.

Douglas, T., Bonte, P., Focquaert, F., Devolder, K., & Sterckx, S. (2013). Coercion, incarceration, and chemical castration: An argument from autonomy. *Journal of Bioethical Inquiry*, 10(3), 393–405. https://doi.org/10.1007/s11673-013-9465-4

Dowbiggin, I. R. (2009). High anxieties: The social construction of anxiety disorders. *The Canadian Journal of Psychiatry/La Revue Canadienne de Psychiatrie*, 54(7), 429–436.

Dowling, T. (2006, June 7). Who are you calling angry? *The Guardian*. https://www.theguardian.com/lifeandstyle/2006/jun/08/healthandwellbeing.health

Downing, L. (2015). Heteronormativity and repronormativity in sexological "perversion theory" and the DSM-5's "paraphilic disorder" diagnoses. *Archives of Sexual Behavior*, 44(5), 1139–1145. https://doi.org/10.1007/s10508-015-0536-y

Doyle, J. (2018). A new family systems therapeutic approach for parents and families of sexual minority youth. *Issues in Law & Medicine*, 33(2), 223–234.

Dozios, D. J. A., & Covin, R. (2004). The Beck Depression Inventory (BDI-II), Beck Hopelessness Scale, and Beck Scale for Suicide Ideation. In M. J. Hilsenroth & D. L. Segal (Eds.), *Comprehensive handbook of psychological assessment: Vol. 2. Personality assessment* (pp. 50–69). John Wiley.

Drake, C., Wen, J., Hinde, J., & Wen, H. (2021). *Recreational cannabis laws and opioid-related emergency department visit rates*. 30, 2595–2605. https://doi.org/10.1002/hec.4377

Dreher, D. E. (2013). Abnormal psychology in the Renaissance. In T. G. Plante (Ed.), *Abnormal psychology across the ages: Vol. 1. History and conceptualizations* (pp. 33–50). Praeger/ABC-CLIO.

Dreison, K. C., & Lagges, A. M. (2017). Effectiveness of the Comprehensive Behavioral Intervention for Tics (CBIT) in a pediatric psychiatry clinic: A retrospective chart review. *Clinical Practice in Pediatric Psychology*, 5(2), 180–185. https://doi.org/10.1037/cpp0000189

Drescher, J. (2012). The removal of homosexuality from the DSM: Its impact on today's marriage equality debate. *Journal of Gay & Lesbian Mental Health*, 16(2), 124–135. https://doi.org/10.1080/19359705.2012.653255

Drescher, J. (2015a). Can sexual orientation be changed? *Journal of Gay & Lesbian Mental Health*, 19(1), 84–93. https://doi.org/10.1080/19359705.2014.944460

Drescher, J. (2015b). Queer diagnoses revisited: The past and future of homosexuality and gender diagnoses in DSM and ICD. *International Review of Psychiatry*, 27(5), 386–395. https://doi.org/10.3109/09540261.2015.1053847

Drescher, J. (2015c). Out of DSM: Depathologizing homosexuality. *Behavioral Sciences*, 5(4), 565–575. https://doi.org/10.3390/bs5040565

Drescher, J., Cohen-Kettenis, P., & Winter, S. (2012). Minding the body: Situating gender identity diagnoses in the ICD-11. *International Review of Psychiatry*, 24(6), 568–577. https://doi.org/10.3109/09540261.2012.741575

Drescher, J., Schwartz, A., Casoy, F., McIntosh, C. A., Hurley, B., Ashley, K., Barber, M., Goldenberg, D., Herbert, S. E., Lothwell, L. E., Mattson, M. R., McAfee, S. G., Pula, J., Rosario, V., & Tompkins, D. A. (2016). The growing regulation of conversion therapy. *Journal of Medical Regulation*, 102(2), 7–12.

Driessen, J., Blom, J. D., Muris, P., Blashfield, R. K., & Molendijk, M. L. (2020). Anxiety in children with selective mutism: A meta-analysis. *Child Psychiatry & Human Development*, 51(2), 330–341. https://doi.org/10.1007/s10578-019-00933-1

Drobisz, D., & Damborská, A. (2019). Deep brain stimulation targets for treating depression. *Behavioural Brain Research*, 359, 266–273. https://doi.org/10.1016/j.bbr.2018.11.004

Drozdick, L. W., & Puig, J. (2020). Intellectual Assessment. In J. A. Suhr & M. Sellbom (Eds.), *The Cambridge handbook of clinical assessment and diagnosis* (pp. 135–159). Cambridge University Press. https://doi.org/10.1017/9781108235433.012

Drucker, D. J. (2012). "A most interesting chapter in the history of science": Intellectual responses to Alfred Kinsey's *Sexual behavior in the human male*. *History of the Human Sciences*, 25(1), 75–98. https://doi.org/10.1177/0952695111432523

Drug Enforcement Administration. (2019). *Benzodiazepines*. U.S. Department of Justice. https://www.deadiversion.usdoj.gov/drug_chem_info/benzo.pdf

Drug Enforcement Administration. (2020). *Drugs of abuse: A DEA resource guide (2020 edition)*. Drug Enforcement Administration, U.S. Department of Justice.

Dryden, W., & Ellis, A. (2001). Rational emotive behavior therapy. In K. S. Dobson (Ed.), *Handbook of cognitive-behavioral therapies* (2nd ed., pp. 295–348). Guilford.

Dryer, R., Farr, M., Hiramatsu, I., & Quinton, S. (2016). The role of sociocultural influences on symptoms of muscle dysmorphia and eating disorders in men, and the mediating effects of perfectionism. *Behavioral Medicine*, 42(3), 174–182. https://doi.org/10.1080/08964289.2015.1122570

du Plessis, S., Scheffler, F., Luckhoff, H., Asmal, L., Kilian, S., Phahladira, L., & Emsley, R. (2020). Childhood trauma and hippocampal subfield volumes in first-episode schizophrenia and healthy controls. *Schizophrenia Research*, 215, 308–313. https://doi.org/10.1016/j.schres.2019.10.009

Dubois, B., Villain, N., Frisoni, G. B., Rabinovici, G. D., Sabbagh, M., Cappa, S., Bejanin, A., Bombois, S., Epelbaum, S., Teichmann, M., Habert, M.-O., Nordberg, A., Blennow, K., Galasko, D., Stern, Y., Rowe, C. C., Salloway, S., Schneider, L. S., Cummings, J. L., & Feldman, H. H. (2021). Clinical diagnosis of Alzheimer's disease: Recommendations of the International Working Group. *The Lancet Neurology*, 20(6), 484–496. https://doi.org/10.1016/S1474-4422(21)00066-1

Ducar, D. (2022, March 11). Giving gender-affirming care: "Gender dysphoria" diagnosis should not be required. *STAT*. https://www.statnews.com/2022/03/11/giving-gender-affirming-care-gender-dysphoria-diagnosis-should-not-be-required/

Dückers, M. L. A., Alisic, E., & Brewin, C. R. (2016). A vulnerability paradox in the cross-national prevalence of post-traumatic stress disorder. *The British Journal of Psychiatry*, 209(4), 300–305. https://doi.org/10.1192/bjp.bp.115.176628

Dückers, M. L. A., & Brewin, C. R. (2016). A paradox in individual versus national mental health vulnerability: Are higher resource levels associated with higher disorder prevalence? *Journal of Traumatic Stress*, 29(6), 572–576. https://doi.org/10.1002/jts.22144

Dückers, M. L. A., & Olff, M. (2017). Does the vulnerability paradox in PTSD apply to women and men? An exploratory study. *Journal of Traumatic Stress*. https://doi.org/10.1002/jts.22173

Duckworth, K. (2015, April 10). *Science meets the human experience: Integrating the medical and recovery models*. NAMI: National Alliance on Mental Illness. https://www.nami.org/blogs/nami-blog/april-2015/science-meets-the-human-experience-integrating-th

Dudek, J., Paweł, O., & Stanisław, M. (2014). Transdiagnostic models of eating disorders and therapeutic methods: The example of Fairburn's cognitive behavior therapy and acceptance and commitment therapy. *Rockzniki Psychologiczne/Annals of Psychology*, 17(1), 25–39.

Dudley, R., Dodgson, G., Sarll, G., Halhead, R., Bolas, H., & McCarthy-Jones, S. (2014). The effect of arousal on auditory threat detection and the relationship to auditory hallucinations. *Journal of Behavior Therapy and Experimental Psychiatry*, 45(3), 311–318. https://doi.org/10.1016/j.jbtep.2014.02.002

Dudley-Marling, C. (2004). The social construction of learning disabilities. *Journal of Learning Disabilities*, *37*(6), 482–489. https://doi.org/10.1177/00222194040370060201

Duff, F. J., Hulme, C., Grainger, K., Hardwick, S. J., Miles, J. N. V., & Snowling, M. J. (2014). Reading and language intervention for children at risk of dyslexia: A randomised controlled trial. *Journal of Child Psychology and Psychiatry*, *55*(11), 1234–1243. https://doi.org/10.1111/jcpp.12257

Duffy, F., Sharpe, H., & Schwannauer, M. (2019). Review: The effectiveness of interpersonal psychotherapy for adolescents with depression – a systematic review and meta-analysis. *Child and Adolescent Mental Health*, *24*(4), 307–317. https://doi.org/10.1111/camh.12342

Dugas, M. J., Freeston, M. H., & Ladouceur, R. (1997). Intolerance of uncertainty and problem orientation in worry. *Cognitive Therapy and Research*, *21*(6), 593–606. https://doi.org/10.1023/A:1021890322153

Duggins, R., & Veitch, P. (2013). Evaluating the impact of an embedded psychodynamic psychotherapist in an early intervention in psychosis service. *Journal of Psychiatric and Mental Health Nursing*, *20*(9), 853–856.

Dumont, M. P., & Dumont, D. M. (2008). Deinstitutionalization in the United States and Italy: A historical survey. *International Journal of Mental Health*, *37*(4), 61–70. https://doi.org/10.2753/IMH0020-7411370405

Duncan, L., Bowla, J., & Tanis, R. (2016). Evaluating the effectiveness of adult day care on alleviating caregiver stress/burden. *Florida Public Health Review*, *13*, Article 2.

Duncan, L. E., Ostacher, M., & Ballon, J. (2019). How genome-wide association studies (GWAS) made traditional candidate gene studies obsolete. *Neuropsychopharmacology*, *44*(9), 1518–1523. https://doi.org/10.1038/s41386-019-0389-5

Duncan, L. E., Ratanatharathorn, A., Aiello, A. E., Almli, L. M., Amstadter, A. B., Ashley-Koch, A. E., Baker, D. G., Beckham, J. C., Bierut, L. J., Bisson, J., Bradley, B., Chen, C.-Y., Dalvie, S., Farrer, L. A., Galea, S., Garrett, M. E., Gelernter, J. E., Guffanti, G., Hauser, M. A., … Koenen, K. C. (2018). Largest GWAS of PTSD (N=20 070) yields genetic overlap with schizophrenia and sex differences in heritability. *Molecular Psychiatry*, *23*(3), 666–673. https://doi.org/10.1038/mp.2017.77

Dunlop, J., & Brandon, N. J. (2015). Schizophrenia drug discovery and development in an evolving era: Are new drug targets fulfilling expectations? *Journal of Psychopharmacology*, *29*(2), 230–238. https://doi.org/10.1177/0269881114565806

Dunlop, K., Woodside, B., Olmsted, M., Colton, P., Giacobbe, P., & Downar, J. (2016). Reductions in cortico-striatal hyperconnectivity accompany successful treatment of obsessive-compulsive disorder with dorsomedial prefrontal rTMS. *Neuropsychopharmacology*, *41*(5), Article 5. https://doi.org/10.1038/npp.2015.292

Dunn, E. C., Brown, R. C., Dai, Y., Rosand, J., Nugent, N. R., Amstadter, A. B., & Smoller, J. W. (2015). Genetic determinants of depression: Recent findings and future directions. *Harvard Review of Psychiatry*, *23*(1), 1–18. https://doi.org/10.1097/HRP.0000000000000054

Dunn, T. M., & Bratman, S. (2016). On orthorexia nervosa: A review of the literature and proposed diagnostic criteria. *Eating Behaviors*, *21*, 11–17. https://doi.org/10.1016/j.eatbeh.2015.12.006

Durand, L., Boland, F., O'Driscoll, D., Bennett, K., Barry, J., Keenan, E., Fahey, T., & Cousins, G. (2021). Factors associated with early and later dropout from methadone maintenance treatment in specialist addiction clinics: A six-year cohort study using proportional hazards frailty models for recurrent treatment episodes. *Drug and Alcohol Dependence*, *219*, Article 108466. https://doi.org/10.1016/j.drugalcdep.2020.108466

Durisko, Z., Mulsant, B. H., & Andrews, P. W. (2015). An adaptationist perspective on the etiology of depression. *Journal of Affective Disorders*, *172*, 315–323. https://doi.org/10.1016/j.jad.2014.09.032

Durisko, Z., Mulsant, B. H., McKenzie, K., & Andrews, P. W. (2016). Using evolutionary theory to guide mental health research. *The Canadian Journal of Psychiatry*, *61*(3), 159–165. https://doi.org/10.1177/0706743716632517

Durkheim, E. (2002). *Suicide: A study in sociology* (G. Simpson, Ed.; J. A. Spaulding & G. Simpson, Trans.). Routledge Classics. https://archive.org/details/DurkheimEmileSuicideAStudyInSociology2005/page/n3/mode/2up (Original work published 1897.)

Dusek, J. A., Hibberd, P. L., Buczynski, B., Chang, B.-H., Dusek, K. C., Johnston, J. M., Wohlhueter, A. L., Benson, H., & Zusman, R. M. (2008). Stress management versus lifestyle modification on systolic hypertension and medication elimination: A randomized trial. *The Journal of Alternative and Complementary Medicine*, *14*(2), 129–138. https://doi.org/10.1089/acm.2007.0623

Dusenbury, L., Botvin, G. J., & James-Ortiz, S. (1989). The primary prevention of adolescent substance abuse through the promotion of personal and social competence. *Prevention in Human Services*, *7*(1), 201–224. https://doi.org/10.1300/J293v07n01_10

Dusky v. United States, 362 U.S. 402 (1960). https://supreme.justia.com/cases/federal/us/362/402/

Dutta, A., McKie, S., & Deakin, J. F. W. (2015). Ketamine and other potential glutamate antidepressants. *Psychiatry Research*, *225*(1–2), 1–13. https://doi.org/10.1016/j.psychres.2014.10.028

Duvauchelle, C. L., Sapoznik, T., & Kornetsky, C. (1998). The synergistic effects of combining cocaine and heroin ("speedball") using a progressive-ratio schedule of drug reinforcement. *Pharmacology Biochemistry and Behavior*, *61*(3), 297–302. https://doi.org/10.1016/S0091-3057(98)00098-7

Dx Revision Watch. (2019, June 17). *World Health Assembly adopts ICD-11: When will member states start using the new edition?* https://dxrevisionwatch.com/2019/06/17/world-health-assembly-adopts-icd-11-when-will-member-states-start-using-the-new-edition/

Eaddy, J. L. (2013). Prescription and over-the-counter medications. In P. M. Miller, S. A. Ball, M. E. Bates, A. W. Blume, K. M. Kampman, D. J. Kavanagh, M. E. Larimer, N. M. Petry, & P. De Witte (Eds.), *Comprehensive addictive behaviors and disorders: Vol. 1. Principles of addiction* (pp. 755–766). Elsevier Academic Press.

Eagle, M. N. (2011). *From classical to contemporary psychoanalysis: A critique and integration*. Routledge.

Eapen, V., Cavanna, A. E., & Robertson, M. M. (2016). Comorbidities, social impact, and quality of life in Tourette syndrome. *Frontiers in Psychiatry*, *7*, Article 97. https://doi.org/10.3389/fpsyt.2016.00097

Early, J. (2022, October 2). *AI could help predict suicides—But rushing the technology could lead to big mistakes*. The Conversation. http://theconversation.com/ai-could-help-predict-suicides-but-rushing-the-technology-could-lead-to-big-mistakes-192266

Ebdrup, B. H., Glenthøj, B., Rasmussen, H., Aggernaes, B., Langkilde, A. R., Paulson, O. B., Lublin, H., Skimminge, A., & Baaré, W. (2010). Hippocampal and caudate volume reductions in antipsychotic-naive first-episode schizophrenia. *Journal of Psychiatry & Neuroscience*, *35*(2), 95–104. https://doi.org/10.1503/jpn.090049

Ebigbo, P. O., Elekwachi, C. L., & Nweze, F. C. (2017). Brain fag syndrome. In B. A. Sharpless (Ed.), *Unusual and rare psychological disorders: A handbook for clinical practice and research* (pp. 196–207). Oxford University Press.

Echeburúa, E. (2013). Overuse of social networking. In P. M. Miller, S. A. Ball, M. E. Bates, A. W. Blume, K. M. Kampman, D. J. Kavanagh, M. E. Larimer, N. M. Petry, & P. De Witte (Eds.), *Comprehensive addictive behaviors and disorders: Vol. 1. Principles of addiction* (pp. 911–920). Elsevier Academic Press.

Eddleston, M., & Gunnell, D. (2020). Preventing suicide through pesticide regulation. *The Lancet Psychiatry*, *7*(1), 9–11. https://doi.org/10.1016/S2215-0366(19)30478-X

Edinger, J. D., & Means, M. K. (2005). Cognitive-behavioral therapy for primary insomnia. *Clinical Psychology Review*, *25*(5), 539–558. https://doi.org/10.1016/j.cpr.2005.04.003

Edvardsen, J., Torgersen, S., Røysamb, E., Lygren, S., Skre, I., Onstad, S., & Øien, P. A. (2008). Heritability of bipolar spectrum disorders. Unity or heterogeneity? *Journal of Affective Disorders*, *106*(3), 229–240. https://doi.org/10.1016/j.jad.2007.07.001

Edwards, A. C., Ohlsson, H., Mościcki, E., Crump, C., Sundquist, J., Lichtenstein, P., Kendler, K. S., & Sundquist, K. (2021). On the genetic and environmental relationship between suicide attempt and death by suicide. *American Journal of Psychiatry*, *178*(11), 1060–1069. https://doi.org/10.1176/appi.ajp.2020.20121705

Edwards, D. A. (2008). *Opposition and defiance: A critical-theoretical approach to understanding subjugation and control through pathologizing hope: Vol. Doctoral dissertation* [Doctoral dissertation]. The Chicago School of Professional Psychology.

Edwards, S. (2016). Reinforcement principles for addiction medicine; from recreational drug use to psychiatric disorder. In H. Ekhtiari & M. Paulus (Eds.), *Progress in brain research* (Vol. 223, pp. 63–76). Elsevier. https://doi.org/10.1016/bs.pbr.2015.07.005

Edwards-Leeper, L., & Anderson, E. (2021, November 24). The mental health establishment is failing trans kids. *The Washington Post*. https://www.washingtonpost.com/outlook/2021/11/24/trans-kids-therapy-psychologist/

Eels, T. D. (2015). *Psychotherapy case formulation*. American Psychological Association.

Efran, J., & Fauber, R. (2015). Spitting in the client's soup: Don't overthink your interventions. *Psychotherapy Networker*.

Egerton, A., Grace, A. A., Stone, J., Bossong, M. G., Sand, M., & McGuire, P. (2020). Glutamate in schizophrenia: Neurodevelopmental perspectives and drug development. *Schizophrenia Research*, *223*, 59–70. https://doi.org/10.1016/j.schres.2020.09.013

Egerton, A., Modinos, G., Ferrera, D., & McGuire, P. (2017). Neuroimaging studies of GABA in schizophrenia: A systematic review with meta-analysis. *Translational Psychiatry*, *7*(6), e1147. https://doi.org/10.1038/tp.2017.124

Egerton, A., Murphy, A., Donocik, J., Anton, A., Barker, G. J., Collier, T., Deakin, B., Drake, R., Eliasson, E., Emsley, R., Gregory, C. J., Griffiths, K., Kapur, S., Kassoumeri, L., Knight, L., Lambe, E. J. B., Lawrie, S. M., Lees, J., Lewis, S., … Howes, O. D. (2021). Dopamine and glutamate in antipsychotic-responsive compared with antipsychotic-nonresponsive psychosis: A multicenter positron emission tomography and magnetic resonance spectroscopy study (STRATA). *Schizophrenia Bulletin*, *47*(2), 505–516. https://doi.org/10.1093/schbul/sbaa128

Ehlers, A. (2006). Understanding and treating complicated grief: What can we learn from posttraumatic stress disorder? *Clinical Psychology: Science and Practice*, *13*(2), 135–140. https://doi.org/10.1111/j.1468-2850.2006.00015.x

Ehlers, A., Bisson, J., Clark, D. M., Creamer, M., Pilling, S., Richards, D., Schnurr, P. P., Turner, S., & Yule, W. (2010). Do all psychological treatments really work the same in posttraumatic stress disorder? *Clinical Psychology Review*, *30*(2), 269–276. https://doi.org/10.1016/j.cpr.2009.12.001

Ehlers, A., & Clark, D. M. (2000). A cognitive model of posttraumatic stress disorder. *Behaviour Research and Therapy*, *38*(4), 319–345. https://doi.org/10.1016/S0005-7967(99)00123-0

Ehlers, A., Clark, D. M., Hackmann, A., McManus, F., & Fennell, M. (2005). Cognitive therapy for post-traumatic stress disorder: Development and evaluation.

Behaviour Research and Therapy, 43(4), 413–431. https://doi.org/10.1016/j.brat.2004.03.006

Ehlers, A., Hackmann, A., Grey, N., Wild, J., Liness, S., Albert, I., Deale, A., Stott, R., & Clark, D. M. (2014). A randomized controlled trial of 7-day intensive and standard weekly cognitive therapy for PTSD and emotion-focused supportive therapy. *The American Journal of Psychiatry, 171*(3), 294–304. https://doi.org/10.1176/appi.ajp.2013.13040552

Eiberg, H., Berendt, I., & Mohr, J. (1995). Assignment of dominant inherited nocturnal enuresis (ENUR1) to chromosome 13q. *Nature Genetics, 10*(3), 354–356. https://doi.org/10.1038/ng0795-354

Eikenaes, I., Egeland, J., Hummelen, B., & Wilberg, T. (2015). Avoidant personality disorder versus social phobia: The significance of childhood neglect. *PLOS ONE, 10*(3), e0122846. https://doi.org/10.1371/journal.pone.0122846

Eisler, I. (2005). The empirical and theoretical base of family therapy and multiple family day therapy for adolescent anorexia nervosa. *Journal of Family Therapy, 27*(2), 104–131. https://doi.org/10.1111/j.1467-6427.2005.00303.x

Eisler, I., Lock, J., & le Grange, D. (2010). Family-based treatments for adolescents with anorexia nervosa: Single-family and multifamily approaches. In C. M. Grilo & J. E. Mitchell (Eds.), *The treatment of eating disorders: A clinical handbook* (pp. 150–174). Guilford Press.

Eisma, M. C. (2018). Public stigma of prolonged grief disorder: An experimental study. *Psychiatry Research, 261*, 173–177. https://doi.org/10.1016/j.psychres.2017.12.064

Eisma, M. C., te Riele, B., Overgaauw, M., & Doering, B. K. (2019). Does prolonged grief or suicide bereavement cause public stigma? A vignette-based experiment. *Psychiatry Research, 272*, 784–789. https://doi.org/10.1016/j.psychres.2018.12.122

Eizirik, M., & Fonagy, P. (2009). Mentalization-based treatment for patients with borderline personality disorder: An overview. *Revista Brasileira de Psiquiatria, 31*(1), 72–75. https://doi.org/10.1590/S1516-44462009000100016

Ekdahl, S., Idvall, E., & Perseius, K.-I. (2014). Family skills training in dialectical behaviour therapy: The experience of the significant others. *Archives of Psychiatric Nursing, 28*(4), 235–241. https://doi.org/10.1016/j.apnu.2014.03.002

Ekirch, A. R. (2005). *At day's close: Night in times past.* Norton.

Ekselius, L. (2018). Personality disorder: A disease in disguise. *Upsala Journal of Medical Sciences, 123*(4), 194–204. https://doi.org/10.1080/03009734.2018.1526235

Ekstein, S., Glick, B., Weill, M., Kay, B., & Berger, I. (2011). Down syndrome and attention-deficit/hyperactivity disorder (ADHD). *Journal of Child Neurology, 26*(10), 1290–1295. https://doi.org/10.1177/0883073811405201

Elder, J. H. (2008). The gluten-free, casein-free diet in autism: An overview with clinical implications. *Nutrition in Clinical Practice, 23*(6), 583–588. https://doi.org/10.1177/0884533608326061

Elkins, D. N. (2016). *The human elements of psychotherapy: A nonmedical model of emotional healing.* American Psychological Association.

Ellen, M. E., Demaio, P., Lange, A., & Wilson, M. G. (2017). Adult day center programs and their associated outcomes on clients, caregivers, and the health system: A scoping review. *The Gerontologist, 57*(6), e85–e94. https://doi.org/10.1093/geront/gnw165

Ellenhorn, R. (2015). Assertive community treatment: A "living-systems" alternative to hospital and residential care. *Psychiatric Annals, 45*(3), 120–125. https://doi.org/10.3928/00485713-20150304-06

Elliott, A. (2015). *Psychoanalytic theory: An introduction* (3rd ed.). Palgrave Macmillan.

Elliott, R. (2013). Person-centered/experiential psychotherapy for anxiety difficulties: Theory, research and

practice. *Person-Centered and Experiential Psychotherapies, 12*(1), 16–32. https://doi.org/10.1080/14779757.2013.767750

Elliott, R. (2016). Research on person-centred/experiential psychotherapy and counselling: Summary of the main findings. In C. Lago & D. Charura (Eds.), *The person-centred counselling and psychotherapy handbook* (pp. 223–232). McGraw Hill.

Elliott, R., Greenberg, Watson, Timulak, L., & Freire, E. (2013). Research on humanistic-experiential psychotherapies. In M. J. Lambert (Ed.), *Bergin and Garfield's handbook of psychotherapy and behavior Change* (6th ed., pp. 495–538). Wiley.

Ellis, A., & Ellis, D. J. (2019). *Rational emotive behavior therapy* (2nd ed.). American Psychological Association.

Ellis, H. (2004). *Studies in the psychology of sex: Vol. 2. Sexual inversion* (3rd ed.). Project Gutenberg. https://www.gutenberg.org/files/13611/13611-h/13611-h.htm (Original work published 1927.)

Ellis, L. A., Meulenbroeks, I., Churruca, K., Pomare, C., Hatem, S., Harrison, R., Zurynski, Y., & Braithwaite, J. (2021). The application of e-mental health in response to COVID-19: Scoping review and bibliometric analysis. *JMIR Mental Health, 8*(12), Article e32948. https://doi.org/10.2196/32948

Elofsson, U. O. E., von Schèele, B., Theorell, T., & Söndergaard, H. P. (2008). Physiological correlates of eye movement desensitization and reprocessing. *Journal of Anxiety Disorders, 22*(4), 622–634. https://doi.org/10.1016/j.janxdis.2007.05.012

Elovainio, M., Ferrie, J. E., Gimeno, D., Vogli, R. D., Shipley, M., Brunner, E. J., Kumari, M., Vahtera, J., Marmot, M. G., & Kivimäki, M. (2009). Organizational justice and sleeping problems: The Whitehall II study. *Psychosomatic Medicine, 71*(3), 334–340. https://doi.org/10.1097/PSY.0b013e3181960665

Elrafei, H., & Jamali, Q. (2022). Assessment and treatment of hypersexuality: A review. *BJPsych Advances, 28*(3), 198–205. https://doi.org/10.1192/bja.2021.68

El-Sayed, M., Steen, R. G., Poe, M. D., Bethea, T. C., Gerig, G., Lieberman, J., & Sikich, L. (2010). Brain volumes in psychotic youth with schizophrenia and mood disorders. *Journal of Psychiatry & Neuroscience, 35*(4), 229–236. https://doi.org/10.1503/jpn.090051

El-Seedi, H. R., De Smet, P. A. G. M., Beck, O., Possnert, G., & Bruhn, J. G. (2005). Prehistoric peyote use: Alkaloid analysis and radiocarbon dating of archaeological specimens of Lophophora from Texas. *Journal of Ethnopharmacology, 101*(1–3), 238–242. https://doi.org/10.1016/j.jep.2005.04.022

Emanuel, C. (2015). An accidental Pokemon expert: Contemporary psychoanalysis on the autism spectrum. *International Journal of Psychoanalytic Self Psychology, 10*(1), 53–68. https://doi.org/10.1080/15551024.2015.977485

Emerson, E. (2007). Poverty and people with intellectual disabilities. *Mental Retardation and Developmental Disabilities Research Reviews, 13*(2), 107–113. https://doi.org/10.1002/mrdd.20144

Emerson, E., & Parish, S. (2010). Intellectual disability and poverty: Introduction to the special section. *Journal of Intellectual and Developmental Disability, 35*(4), 221–223. https://doi.org/10.3109/13668250.2010.525869

Emerson, E., Shahtahmasebi, S., Lancaster, G., & Berridge, D. (2010). Poverty transitions among families supporting a child with intellectual disability. *Journal of Intellectual and Developmental Disability, 35*(4), 224–234. https://doi.org/10.3109/13668250.2010.518562

Enatescu, V. R., Cozma, D., Tint, D., Enatescu, I., Simu, M., Giurgi-Oncu, C., Lazar, M. A., & Mornos, C. (2021). The relationship between Type D personality and the complexity of coronary artery disease. *Neuropsychiatric Disease and Treatment, Volume 17*, 809–820. https://doi.org/10.2147/NDT.S303644

Endleman, R. (1990). *Deviance and psychopathology: The sociology and psychology of outsiders.* Krieger.

Endler, N. S. (1988). The origins of electroconvulsive therapy (ECT). *Convulsive Therapy, 4*(1), 5–23.

Ene, I., Wong, K. K.-Y., & Salali, G. D. (2022). Is it good to be bad? An evolutionary analysis of the adaptive potential of psychopathic traits. *Evolutionary Human Sciences, 4*, e37. https://doi.org/10.1017/ehs.2022.36

Engel, G. L. (1977). The need for a new medical model: A challenge for biomedicine. *Science (New York, NY), 196*(4286), 129–136. https://doi.org/10.1126/science.847460

Ennis, N., Shorer, S., Shoval-Zuckerman, Y., Freedman, S., Monson, C. M., & Dekel, R. (2020). Treating posttraumatic stress disorder across cultures: A systematic review of cultural adaptations of trauma-focused cognitive behavioral therapies. *Journal of Clinical Psychology, 76*(4), 587–611. https://doi.org/10.1002/jclp.22909

Enright, J. (2022, May 1). O.D.D. does not exist. *Fourth Wave.* https://medium.com/fourth-wave/o-d-d-does-not-exist-4cca512e27ec

Epstein, M. (n.d.-a). *Borderline personality disorder: Getting some action at a national level—The lament of a tired campaigner.* Merinda Epstein - A Consumer Activist's Guide To Mental Health In Australia. Retrieved September 13, 2022, from http://www.takver.com/epstein/articles/borderline_personality_disorder.htm

Epstein, M. (n.d.-b). *Let s face it! She s just too f*****d the politics of borderline personality disorder.* Retrieved September 10, 2022, from https://docplayer.net/8363170-Let-s-face-it-she-s-just-too-f-d-the-politics-of-borderline-personality-disorder.html

Epstein, M. (2006). *The emperor's new clothes: On being invisible and neglected within the mental health system—A gendered perspective from a "borderline pioneer."* 16th Annual Conference of the Mental Health Services (theMHS), Townsville, Australia. http://www.takver.com/epstein/articles/emperors_new_clothes_themhs_2006%20.pdf

Epting, F. R., Raskin, J. D., & Burke, T. B. (1994). Who is a homosexual? A critique of the heterosexual-homosexual dimension. *The Humanistic Psychologist, 22*, 353–370. https://doi.org/10.1080/08873267.1994.9976959

Erard, R. E., Meyer, G. J., & Viglione, D. J. (2014). Setting the record straight: Comment on Gurley, Piechowski, Sheehan, and Gray (2014) on the admissibility of the Rorschach Performance Assessment System (R-PAS) in court. *Psychological Injury and Law, 7*(2), 165–177. https://doi.org/10.1007/s12207-014-9195-x

Erb, S. J., Schappi, J. M., & Rasenick, M. M. (2016). Antidepressants accumulate in lipid rafts independent of monoamine transporters to modulate redistribution of the G protein, Gαs. *Journal of Biological Chemistry, 291*(38), 19725–19733. https://doi.org/10.1074/jbc.M116.727263

Erbeli, F., Rice, M., & Paracchini, S. (2022). Insights into dyslexia genetics research from the last two decades. *Brain Sciences, 12*(1), Article 1. https://doi.org/10.3390/brainsci12010027

Erdur, L., Kallenbach-Dermutz, B., Lehmann, V., Zimmermann-Viehoff, F., Köpp, W., Weber, C., & Deter, H.-C. (2012). Somatic comorbidity in anorexia nervosa: First results of a 21-year follow-up study on female inpatients. *Biopsychosocial Medicine, 6*, 4. https://doi.org/10.1186/1751-0759-6-4

Erickson, E. K., Grantham, E. K., Warden, A. S., & Harris, R. A. (2019). Neuroimmune signaling in alcohol use disorder. *Pharmacology Biochemistry and Behavior, 177*, 34–60. https://doi.org/10.1016/j.pbb.2018.12.007

Erickson, S., & Block, S. (2013). The social and communication impact of stuttering on adolescents and their families. *Journal of Fluency Disorders, 38*(4), 311–324. https://doi.org/10.1016/j.jfludis.2013.09.003

Erriu, M., Cimino, S., & Cerniglia, L. (2020). The role of family relationships in eating disorders in adolescents: A narrative review. *Behavioral Sciences, 10*(4), Article 4. https://doi.org/10.3390/bs10040071

Erskine, R. (2015). Meeting Vincent: Reconnections from behind the wall—Pre-Therapy in a psychiatric unit context. *Person-Centered and Experiential Psychotherapies*, 14(4), 300–309. https://doi.org/10.1080/14779757.2015.1073608

Erten Uyumaz, B., Feijs, L., & Hu, J. (2021). A review of digital cognitive behavioral therapy for insomnia (CBT-I apps): Are they designed for engagement? *International Journal of Environmental Research and Public Health*, 18(6), Article 6. https://doi.org/10.3390/ijerph18062929

Esan, O. B., Ojagbemi, A., & Gureje, O. (2012). Epidemiology of schizophrenia—An update with a focus on developing countries. *International Review of Psychiatry*, 24(5), 387–392.

Eshuis, L. V., van Gelderen, M. J., van Zuiden, M., Nijdam, M. J., Vermetten, E., Olff, M., & Bakker, A. (2021). Efficacy of immersive PTSD treatments: A systematic review of virtual and augmented reality exposure therapy and a meta-analysis of virtual reality exposure therapy. *Journal of Psychiatric Research*, 143, 516–527. https://doi.org/10.1016/j.jpsychires.2020.11.030

Esmaeilpour, K., Mir, A., & Zareei, A. (2016). Relationship between attachment problems and symptoms of oppositional defiant disorder in children. *Quarterly Journal of Child Mental Health*, 3(3), 73–83.

Espinoza Oyarce, D. A., Shaw, M. E., Alateeq, K., & Cherbuin, N. (2020). Volumetric brain differences in clinical depression in association with anxiety: A systematic review with meta-analysis. *Journal of Psychiatry & Neuroscience*, 45(6), 406–429. https://doi.org/10.1503/jpn.190156

Espiridion, E. D., & Kerbel, S. A. (2020). A systematic literature review of the association between somatic symptom disorder and antisocial personality disorder. *Cureus*. https://doi.org/10.7759/cureus.9318

Espirito-Santo, H., & Pio-Abreu, J. L. (2009). Psychiatric symptoms and dissociation in conversion, somatization and dissociative disorders. *Australian and New Zealand Journal of Psychiatry*, 43(3), 270–276. https://doi.org/10.1080/00048670802653307

Esquirol, J.-É. D. (2015, May 24). *Jean-Étienne-Dominique Esquirol (1772-1840) from* Mental maladies: A treatise on insanity. The Ethics of Suicide Digital Archive. https://ethicsofsuicide.lib.utah.edu/selections/esquirol/

Essoe, J. K.-Y., Grados, M. A., Singer, H. S., Myers, N. S., & McGuire, J. F. (2019). Evidence-based treatment of Tourette's disorder and chronic tic disorders. *Expert Review of Neurotherapeutics*, 19(11), 1103–1115. https://doi.org/10.1080/14737175.2019.1643236

Esteller-Cucala, P., Maceda, I., Børglum, A. D., Demontis, D., Faraone, S. V., Cormand, B., & Lao, O. (2020). Genomic analysis of the natural history of attention-deficit/hyperactivity disorder using Neanderthal and ancient Homo sapiens samples. *Scientific Reports*, 10(1), Article 1. https://doi.org/10.1038/s41598-020-65322-4

Esterling, B. A., Kiecolt-Glaser, J. K., Bodnar, J. C., & Glaser, R. (1994). Chronic stress, social support, and persistent alterations in the natural killer cell response to cytokines in older adults. *Health Psychology*, 13(4), 291–298. https://doi.org/10.1037/0278-6133.13.4.291

Etherton, J. L., & Farley, R. (2020). Behavioral activation for PTSD: A meta-analysis. *Psychological Trauma: Theory, Research, Practice, and Policy*. https://doi.org/10.1037/tra0000566

Etkin, A. (2012). Neurobiology of anxiety: From neural circuits to novel solutions? *Depression and Anxiety*, 29(5), 355–358. https://doi.org/10.1002/da.21957

Etkin, A., & Wager, T. D. (2007). Functional neuroimaging of anxiety: A meta-analysis of emotional processing in PTSD, social anxiety disorder, and specific phobia. *The American Journal of Psychiatry*, 164(10), 1476–1488. https://doi.org/10.1176/appi.ajp.2007.07030504

Ettinger, U., Meyhöfer, I., Steffens, M., Wagner, M., & Koutsouleris, N. (2014). Genetics, cognition, and neurobiology of schizotypal personality: A review of the overlap with schizophrenia. *Frontiers in Psychiatry*, 5, Article 18. https://doi.org/10.3389/fpsyt.2014.00018

Ettman, C. K., Cohen, G. H., Abdalla, S. M., Sampson, L., Trinquart, L., Castrucci, B. C., Bork, R. H., Clark, M. A., Wilson, I., Vivier, P. M., & Galea, S. (2022). Persistent depressive symptoms during COVID-19: A national, population-representative, longitudinal study of U.S. adults. *The Lancet Regional Health – Americas*, 5. https://doi.org/10.1016/j.lana.2021.100091

Etzi, J. (2014). The *Psychodynamic diagnostic manual* M axis: Toward an articulation of what it can assess. *Psychoanalytic Psychology*, 31(1), 119–133. https://doi.org/10.1037/a0031907

Eubanks, C. F., & Hunter, E. B. (2020). HiTOP and psychotherapy integration: Promising potential. *Journal of Psychotherapy Integration*, 30(4), 498–505. https://doi.org/10.1037/int0000254

European Society of Preventative Medicine. (n.d.). *Stress and psychology*. Retrieved March 23, 2022, from http://www.esprevmed.org/lifestyle-health/stress-and-psychology/

Eurostat: Statistics Explained. (2021, July). *Alcohol consumption statistics*. https://ec.europa.eu/eurostat/statistics-explained/index.php?title=Alcohol_consumption_statistics

Ewing, D. L., Monsen, J. J., Thompson, E. J., Cartwright-Hatton, S., & Field, A. (2015). A meta-analysis of transdiagnostic cognitive behavioural therapy in the treatment of child and young person anxiety disorders. *Behavioural and Cognitive Psychotherapy*, 43(5), 562–577. https://doi.org/10.1017/S1352465813001094

Ewing, E. S. K., Diamond, G., & Levy, S. (2015). Attachment-based family therapy for depressed and suicidal adolescents: Theory, clinical model and empirical support. *Attachment & Human Development*, 17(2), 136–156. https://doi.org/10.1080/14616734.2015.1006384

Express Scripts. (2020, April). *America's state of mind report*. https://www.express-scripts.com/corporate/americas-state-of-mind-report

Faber, A., Dubé, L., & Knäuper, B. (2018). Attachment and eating: A meta-analytic review of the relevance of attachment for unhealthy and healthy eating behaviors in the general population. *Appetite*, 123, 410–438. https://doi.org/10.1016/j.appet.2017.10.043

Fabiano, G. A., Pelham, W. E., Jr., Coles, E. K., Gnagy, E. M., Chronis-Tuscano, A., & O'Connor, B. C. (2009). A meta-analysis of behavioral treatments for attention-deficit/hyperactivity disorder. *Clinical Psychology Review*, 29(2), 129–140. https://doi.org/10.1016/j.cpr.2008.11.001

Fabiano, G. A., Schatz, N. K., Aloe, A. M., Chacko, A., & Chronis-Tuscano, A. (2015). A systematic review of meta-analyses of psychosocial treatment for attention-deficit/hyperactivity disorder. *Clinical Child and Family Psychology Review*, 18(1), 77–97. https://doi.org/10.1007/s10567-015-0178-6

Fader-Towe, H., & Pinals, D. A. (2021). Data on evaluations as a foundation for states rethinking competency to stand trial. *The Journal of the American Academy of Psychiatry and the Law*, 49(4), 540–544. https://doi.org/10.29158/JAAPL.210108-21

Faer, L. M., Hendriks, A., Abed, R. T., & Figueredo, A. J. (2005). The evolutionary psychology of eating disorders: Female competition for mates or for status? *Psychology and Psychotherapy: Theory, Research and Practice*, 78(3), 397–417. doi:10.1348/147608305X42929

Fagundes, C., Brown, R. L., Chen, M. A., Murdock, K. W., Saucedo, L., LeRoy, A., Wu, E. L., Garcini, L. M., Shahane, A. D., Baameur, F., & Heijnen, C. (2019). Grief, depressive symptoms, and inflammation in the spousally bereaved. *Psychoneuroendocrinology*, 100, 190–197. https://doi.org/10.1016/j.psyneuen.2018.10.006

Fagundes, C. P., Murdock, K. W., LeRoy, A., Baameur, F., Thayer, J. F., & Heijnen, C. (2018). Spousal bereavement is associated with more pronounced ex vivo cytokine production and lower heart rate variability: Mechanisms underlying cardiovascular risk? *Psychoneuroendocrinology*, 93, 65–71. https://doi.org/10.1016/j.psyneuen.2018.04.010

Faheem, A., Balasubramanian, I., & Menon, V. (2022). Gender dysphoria in adults: Concept, critique, and controversies. *Journal of Current Research in Scientific Medicine*, 8(1), 8.

Fairburn, C. G., Bailey-Straebler, S., Basden, S., Doll, H. A., Jones, R., Murphy, R., O'Connor, M. E., & Cooper, Z. (2015). A transdiagnostic comparison of enhanced cognitive behaviour therapy (CBT-E) and interpersonal psychotherapy in the treatment of eating disorders. *Behaviour Research and Therapy*, 70, 64–71. https://doi.org/10.1016/j.brat.2015.04.010

Fairburn, C. G., Cooper, Z., & Shafran, R. (2003). Cognitive behaviour therapy for eating disorders: A "transdiagnostic" theory and treatment. *Behaviour Research and Therapy*, 41(5), 509–528. https://doi.org/10.1016/S0005-7967(02)00088-8

Fairburn, C. G., Shafran, R., & Cooper, Z. (1999). A cognitive behavioural theory of anorexia nervosa. *Behaviour Research and Therapy*, 37(1), 1–13. https://doi.org/10.1016/S0005-7967(98)00102-8

Fairchild, G., Hawes, D. J., Frick, P. J., Copeland, W. E., Odgers, C. L., Franke, B., Freitag, C. M., & De Brito, S. A. (2019). Conduct disorder. *Nature Reviews Disease Primers*, 5(1), 43. https://doi.org/10.1038/s41572-019-0095-y

Fairweather-Schmidt, A. K., & Wade, T. D. (2015). Changes in genetic and environmental influences on disordered eating between early and late adolescence: A longitudinal twin study. *Psychological Medicine*, 45(15), 3249–3258. doi:10.1017/S0033291715001257

Fait, T. (2019). Menopause hormone therapy: Latest developments and clinical practice. *Drugs in Context*, 8, 212551. https://doi.org/10.7573/dic.212551

Fallon, B. A. (2004). Pharmacotherapy of somatoform disorders. *Journal of Psychosomatic Research*, 56(4), 455–460. https://doi.org/10.1016/S0022-3999(03)00631-7

Fang, A., Matheny, N. L., & Wilhelm, S. (2014). Body dysmorphic disorder. *The Psychiatric Clinics of North America*, 37(3), 287–300. https://doi.org/10.1016/j.psc.2014.05.003

Fanning, J. R., Berman, M. E., Guillot, C. R., Marsic, A., & McCloskey, M. S. (2014). Serotonin (5-HT) augmentation reduces provoked aggression associated with primary psychopathy traits. *Journal of Personality Disorders*, 28(3), 449–461. https://doi.org/10.1521/pedi_2012_26_065

Fanning, J. R., Lee, R., Gozal, D., Coussons-Read, M., & Coccaro, E. F. (2015). Childhood trauma and parental style: Relationship with markers of inflammation, oxidative stress, and aggression in healthy and personality disordered subjects. *Biological Psychology*, 112, 56–65. https://doi.org/10.1016/j.biopsycho.2015.09.003

Fanous, A. H. (2015). Can genomics help usher schizophrenia into the age of RDoC and DSM-6? *Schizophrenia Bulletin*, 41(3), 535–541. https://doi.org/10.1093/schbul/sbv029

Faramarzi, F. (2021). The effectiveness of child-centered play therapy in aggression of children with oppositional defiant disorder. *International Journal of Medical Investigation*, 10(4), 83–93.

Faraone, S. (1982). Psychiatry and political repression in the Soviet Union. *American Psychologist*, 37(10), 1105–1112. https://doi.org/10.1037/0003-066X.37.10.1105

Faraone, S. V., Banaschewski, T., Coghill, D., Zheng, Y., Biederman, J., Bellgrove, M. A., Newcorn, J. H., Gignac, M., Al Saud, N. M., Manor, I., Rohde, L. A., Yang, L., Cortese, S., Almagor, D., Stein, M. A., Albatti, T. H., Aljoudi, H. F., Alqahtani, M. M. J., Asherson, P., … Wang, Y. (2021). The World Federation of ADHD International Consensus Statement: 208 evidence-based conclusions about the disorder. *Neuroscience & Biobehavioral Reviews, 128,* 789–818. https://doi.org/10.1016/j.neubiorev.2021.01.022

Faraone, S. V., & Biederman, J. (2013). Neurobiology of attention deficit/hyperactivity disorder. In D. S. Charney, J. D. Buxbaum, P. Sklar, E. J. Nestler, D. S. Charney, J. D. Buxbaum, P. Sklar, & E. J. Nestler (Eds.), *Neurobiology of mental illness* (4th ed., pp. 1034–1047). Oxford University Press. https://doi.org/10.1093/med/9780199934959.003.0078

Faraone, S. V., & Larsson, H. (2019). Genetics of attention deficit hyperactivity disorder. *Molecular Psychiatry, 24*(4), Article 4. https://doi.org/10.1038/s41380-018-0070-0

Fardouly, J., & Holland, E. (2018). Social media is not real life: The effect of attaching disclaimer-type labels to idealized social media images on women's body image and mood. *New Media & Society, 20*(11), 4311–4328. https://doi.org/10.1177/1461444818771083

Fardouly, J., & Vartanian, L. R. (2015). Negative comparisons about one's appearance mediate the relationship between Facebook usage and body image concerns. *Body Image, 12,* 82–88. https://doi.org/10.1016/j.bodyim.2014.10.004

Farley, E. J., & Orchowsky, S. (2019). *Measuring the criminal justice system impacts of marijuana legalization and decriminalization using state data.* Justice Research and Statistics Association. https://www.ojp.gov/ncjrs/virtual-library/abstracts/measuring-criminal-justice-system-impacts-marijuana-legalization-0

Farrell, J. M., Reiss, N., Shaw, I. A., & Finkelmeier, B. (2014). *The schema therapy clinician's guide: A complete resource for building and delivering individual, group and integrated schema mode treatment programs.* Wiley-Blackwell. https://doi.org/10.1002/9781118510018

Farrelly, S., Jeffery, D., Rüsch, N., Williams, P., Thornicroft, G., & Clement, S. (2015). The link between mental health-related discrimination and suicidality: Service user perspectives. *Psychological Medicine, 45*(10), 2013–2022. https://doi.org/10.1017/S0033291714003158

Farstad, S. M., McGeown, L. M., & von Ranson, K. M. (2016). Eating disorders and personality, 2004–2016: A systematic review and meta-analysis. *Clinical Psychology Review, 46,* 91–105. https://doi.org/10.1016/j.cpr.2016.04.005

Fassbinder, E., & Arntz, A. (2021). Schema therapy. In A. Wenzel (Ed.), *Handbook of cognitive behavioral therapy: Overview and approaches., Vol. 1* (pp. 493–537). American Psychological Association. https://doi.org/10.1037/0000218-017

Fatemi, S. H., Aldinger, K. A., Ashwood, P., Bauman, M. L., Blaha, C. D., Blatt, G. J., Chauhan, A., Chauhan, V., Dager, S. R., Dickson, P. E., Estes, A. M., Goldowitz, D., Heck, D. H., Kemper, T. L., King, B. H., Martin, L. A., Millen, K. J., Mittleman, G., Mosconi, M. W., … Welsh, J. P. (2012). Consensus paper: Pathological role of the cerebellum in autism. *The Cerebellum, 11*(3), 777–807. https://doi.org/10.1007/s12311-012-0355-9

Fatemi, S. H., Folsom, T. D., Rooney, R. J., Mori, S., Kornfield, T. E., Reutiman, T. J., Kneeland, R. E., Liesch, S. B., Hua, K., Hsu, J., & Patel, D. H. (2012). The viral theory of schizophrenia revisited: Abnormal placental gene expression and structural changes with lack of evidence for H1N1 viral presence in placentae of infected mice or brains of exposed offspring. *Neuropharmacology, 62*(3), 1290–1298. https://doi.org/10.1016/j.neuropharm.2011.01.011

Faucher, L. (2016). Darwinian blues: Evolutionary psychiatry and depression. In J. C. Wakefield & S. Demazeux (Eds.), *Sadness or depression? International perspectives on the depression epidemic and its meaning.* (2016-01677-006; Vol. 15, pp. 69–94). Springer Science + Business Media. https://doi.org/10.1007/978-94-017-7423-9_6

Faure, K., & Forbes, M. K. (2021). Clarifying the placement of obsessive-compulsive disorder in the empirical structure of psychopathology. *Journal of Psychopathology and Behavioral Assessment, 43*(3), 671–685. https://doi.org/10.1007/s10862-021-09868-1

Fausto-Sterling, A. (2000). *Sexing the body: Gender politics and the construction of sexuality.* Basic Books.

Fauth-Bühler, M., Mann, K., & Potenza, M. N. (2016). Pathological gambling: A review of the neurobiological evidence relevant for its classification as an addictive disorder. *Addiction Biology.* https://doi.org/10.1111/adb.12378

Fava, G. A., Benasi, G., Lucente, M., Offidani, E., Cosci, F., & Guidi, J. (2018). Withdrawal symptoms after serotonin-noradrenaline reuptake inhibitor discontinuation: Systematic review. *Psychotherapy and Psychosomatics, 87*(4), 195–203. https://doi.org/10.1159/000491524

Fava, G. A., Gatti, A., Belaise, C., Guidi, J., & Offidani, E. (2015). Withdrawal symptoms after selective serotonin reuptake inhibitor discontinuation: A systematic review. *Psychotherapy and Psychosomatics, 84*(2), 72–81. https://doi.org/10.1159/000370338

Favennec, M., Bronsard, G., Guillou, M., Le Reste, J.-Y., & Planche, P. (2021). Addictive behaviours in young people—An international comparative study of the construction of an addictive personality (France, Switzerland, Quebec). *Psychology, 12*(7), 1153–1170. https://doi.org/10.4236/psych.2021.127071

Fawcett, E. J., Fawcett, J. M., & Mazmanian, D. (2016). A meta-analysis of the worldwide prevalence of pica during pregnancy and the postpartum period. *International Journal of Gynaecology and Obstetrics, 133*(3), 277–283. https://doi.org/10.1016/j.ijgo.2015.10.012

Fawcett, J., Cameron, R. P., & Schatzberg, A. F. (2010). Mixed anxiety-depressive disorder: An undiagnosed and undertreated severity spectrum? In D. J. Stein, E. Hollander, & B. O. Rothbaum (Eds.), *Textbook of anxiety disorders* (2nd ed., pp. 241–257). American Psychiatric Publishing.

Fayed, M. (2021, November 15). *Health & wellness: Beyond PTSD: Moral injury in first responders.* Firehouse. https://www.firehouse.com/safety-health/article/21241509/health-wellness-beyond-ptsd-moral-injury-in-first-responders

Fazio, S., Pace, D., Flinner, J., & Kallmyer, B. (2018). The fundamentals of person-centered care for individuals with dementia. *The Gerontologist, 58*(suppl_1), S10–S19. https://doi.org/10.1093/geront/gnx122

Fehling, K. B., & Selby, E. A. (2021). Suicide in DSM-5: Current evidence for the proposed suicide behavior disorder and other possible improvements. *Frontiers in Psychiatry, 11,* Article 499980. https://doi.org/10.3389/fpsyt.2020.499980

Feigenson, K. A., Kusnecov, A. W., & Silverstein, S. M. (2014). Inflammation and the two-hit hypothesis of schizophrenia. *Neuroscience and Biobehavioral Reviews, 38,* 72–93. https://doi.org/10.1016/j.neubiorev.2013.11.006

Feinstein, R. E. (2021). Crisis intervention psychotherapy in the age of COVID-19. *Journal of Psychiatric Practice, 27*(3), 152–163. https://doi.org/10.1097/PRA.0000000000000542

Feiring, C., Cleland, C. M., & Simon, V. A. (2010). Abuse-specific self-schemas and self-functioning: A prospective study of sexually abused youth. *Journal of Clinical Child and Adolescent Psychology, 39*(1), 35–50. https://doi.org/10.1080/15374410903401112

Felger, J. C., & Lotrich, F. E. (2013). Inflammatory cytokines in depression: Neurobiological mechanisms and therapeutic implications. *Neuroscience, 246,* 199–229. https://doi.org/10.1016/j.neuroscience.2013.04.060

Femrell, L., Åvall, M., & Lindström, E. (2012). Two-year follow-up of the Lidcombe Program in ten Swedish-speaking children. *Folia Phoniatrica et Logopaedica:International Journal of Phoniatrics, Speech Therapy and Communication Pathology, 64*(5), 248–253. https://doi.org/10.1159/000342149

Fennell, D., & Boyd, M. (2014). Obsessive-compulsive disorder in the media. *Deviant Behavior, 35*(9), 669–686. https://doi.org/10.1080/01639625.2013.872526

Feola, H. (2021, November 8). It's time to stop gatekeeping medical transition. *American Scientist.* https://www.americanscientist.org/blog/macroscope/its-time-to-stop-gatekeeping-medical-transition

Ferentzy, P., Skinner, W., & Antze, P. (2010). The Serenity Prayer: Secularism and spirituality in Gamblers Anonymous. *Journal of Groups in Addiction & Recovery, 5*(2), 124–144. https://doi.org/10.1080/1556035100376615

Ferguson, C. J. (2013). In the eye of the beholder: Thin-ideal media affects some, but not most, viewers in a meta-analytic review of body dissatisfaction in women and men. *Psychology of Popular Media Culture, 2*(1), 20–37. https://doi.org/10.1037/a0030766

Ferguson, C. J., Muñoz, M. E., Garza, A., & Galindo, M. (2014). Concurrent and prospective analyses of peer, television and social media influences on body dissatisfaction, eating disorder symptoms and life satisfaction in adolescent girls. *Journal of Youth and Adolescence, 43*(1), 1–14. https://doi.org/10.1007/s10964-012-9898-9

Fernández, R., Cortés-Cortés, J., Esteva, I., Gómez-Gil, E., Almaraz, M. C., Lema, E., Rumbo, T., Haro-Mora, J.-J., Roda, E., Guillamón, A., & Pásaro, E. (2015). The CYP17 MspA1 polymorphism and the gender dysphoria. *The Journal of Sexual Medicine, 12*(6), 1329–1333. https://doi.org/10.1111/jsm.12895

Fernández, R., Esteva, I., Gómez-Gil, E., Rumbo, T., Almaraz, M. C., Roda, E., Haro-Mora, J., Guillamón, A., & Pásaro, E. (2014). The (CA)n polymorphism of ERβ gene is associated with FtM transsexualism. *Journal of Sexual Medicine, 11*(3), 720–728. https://doi.org/10.1111/jsm.12398

Fernández-Álvarez, H., Consoli, A. J., & Gómez, B. (2016). Integration in psychotherapy: Reasons and challenges. *American Psychologist, 71*(8), 820–830. https://doi.org/10.1037/amp0000100

Ferrando, C., & Selai, C. (2021). A systematic review and meta-analysis on the effectiveness of exposure and response prevention therapy in the treatment of obsessive-compulsive disorder. *Journal of Obsessive-Compulsive and Related Disorders, 31,* 100684. https://doi.org/10.1016/j.jocrd.2021.100684

Ferrara, P., Autuori, R., Dosa, F., Di Lucia, A., Gatto, A., & Chiaretti, A. (2019). Medical comorbidity of nocturnal enuresis in children. *Indian Journal of Nephrology, 29*(5), 345–352. https://doi.org/10.4103/ijn.IJN_319_18

Ferreira, B. R., Pio-Abreu, J. L., & Januário, C. (2014). Tourette's syndrome and associated disorders: A systematic review. *Trends in Psychiatry and Psychotherapy, 36*(3), 123–133. https://doi.org/10.1590/2237-6089-2014-1003

Ferrell, E. L., Russin, S. E., & Flint, D. D. (2022). Prevalence estimates of comorbid eating disorders and posttraumatic stress disorder: A quantitative synthesis. *Journal of Aggression, Maltreatment & Trauma, 31*(2), 264–282. https://doi.org/10.1080/10926771.2020.1832168

Ferrie, J., Miller, H., & Hunter, S. C. (2020). Psychosocial outcomes of mental illness stigma in children and adolescents: A mixed-methods systematic review. *Children and Youth Services Review, 113,* 104961. https://doi.org/10.1016/j.childyouth.2020.104961

Ferrier, I. N., Waite, J., & Sivasanker, V. (2021). Recent advances in electroconvulsive therapy and physical treatments for depression. *BJPsych Advances, 27*(5), 295–302. https://doi.org/10.1192/bja.2021.18

Fervaha, G., & Remington, G. (2013). Neuroimaging findings in schizotypal personality disorder: A systematic review. *Progress in Neuro-Psychopharmacology & Biological Psychiatry, 43,* 96–107. https://doi.org/10.1016/j.pnpbp.2012.11.014

Fett, A.-K. J., Lemmers-Jansen, I. L. J., & Krabbendam, L. (2019). Psychosis and urbanicity: A review of the recent literature from epidemiology to neurourban-ism. *Current Opinion in Psychiatry, 32*(3), 232–241. https://doi.org/10.1097/YCO.0000000000000486

Fetters, M. D., Curry, L. A., & Creswell, J. W. (2013). Achieving integration in mixed methods designs—Principles and practices. *Health Services Research, 48*(6, Pt2), 2134–2156. https://doi.org/10.1111/1475-6773.12117

Feygin, D. L., Swain, J. E., & Leckman, J. F. (2006). The normalcy of neurosis: Evolutionary origins of obsessive compulsive disorder and related behaviors. *Progress in Neuro-Psychopharmacology & Biological Psychiatry, 30*(5), 854–864. https://doi.org/10.1016/j.pnpbp.2006.01.009

Ficks, C. A., & Waldman, I. D. (2014). Candidate genes for aggression and antisocial behavior: A meta-analysis of association studies of the 5HTTLPR and MAOA-uVNTR. *Behavior Genetics, 44*(5), 427–444. https://doi.org/10.1007/s10519-014-9661-y

Fieiras, C., Chen, M. H., Liquitay, C. M. E., Meza, N., Rojas, V., Franco, J. V. A., & Madrid, E. (2022). Risperidone and aripiprazole for autism spectrum disorder in children: An overview of systematic reviews. *BMJ Evidence-Based Medicine*. https://doi.org/10.1136/bmjebm-2021-111804

Fields, A. J. (2010). Multicultural research and practice: Theoretical issues and maximizing cultural exchange. *Professional Psychology: Research and Practice, 41*(3), 196–201. https://doi.org/10.1037/a0017938

Fife, S. T. (2020). Theory: The heart of systemic family therapy. In *The Handbook of systemic family therapy* (pp. 293–316). John Wiley & Sons. https://doi.org/10.1002/9781119790181.ch13

Filatova, E. V., Shadrina, M. I., & Slominsky, P. A. (2021). Major depression: One brain, one disease, one set of intertwined processes. *Cells, 10*(6), 1283. https://doi.org/10.3390/cells10061283

Filges, T., Andersen, D., & Jørgensen, A.-M. K. (2018). Effects of multidimensional family therapy (MDFT) on nonopioid drug abuse: A systematic review and meta-analysis. *Research on Social Work Practice, 28*(1), 68–83. https://doi.org/10.1177/1049731515608241

Fink, M. (2009). *Electroconvulsive therapy: A guide for professionals and their patients*. Oxford University Press.

Fioravanti, G., Bocci Benucci, S., Ceragioli, G., & Casale, S. (2022). How the exposure to beauty ideals on social networking sites influences body image: A systematic review of experimental studies. *Adolescent Research Review*. https://doi.org/10.1007/s40894-022-00179-4

First, M. B. (2014). DSM-5 and paraphilic disorders. *Journal of the American Academy of Psychiatry and the Law, 42*(2), 191–201.

First, M. B. (2015). Structured clinical interview for the DSM (SCID). In *The encyclopedia of clinical psychology* (pp. 1–6). American Cancer Society. https://doi.org/10.1002/9781118625392.wbecp351

First, M. B., Gaebel, W., Maj, M., Stein, D. J., Kogan, C. S., Saunders, J. B., Poznyak, V. B., Gureje, O., Lewis-Fernández, R., Maercker, A., Brewin, C. R., Cloitre, M., Claudino, A., Pike, K. M., Baird, G., Skuse, D., Krueger, R. B., Briken, P., Burke, J. D., … Reed, G. M. (2021). An organization- and category-level comparison of diagnostic requirements for mental disorders in ICD -11 and DSM -5. *World Psychiatry, 20*(1), 34–51. https://doi.org/10.1002/wps.20825

First, M. B., & Gibbon, M. (2004). The structured clinical interview for *DSM-IV* axis 1 disorders (SCID-I) and the structured clinical interview for *DSM-IV* axis II disorders (SCID-II). In M. J. Hilsenroth & D. L. Segal (Eds.), *Comprehensive handbook of psychological assessment: Vol. 2. Personality assessment* (pp. 134–143). John Wiley.

First, M. B., Reed, G. M., Hyman, S. E., & Saxena, S. (2015). The development of the ICD-11 Clinical descriptions and diagnostic guidelines for mental and behavioural disorders. *World Psychiatry, 14*(1), 82–90. https://doi.org/10.1002/wps.20189

Fishbain, D. A. (1994). Secondary gain concept: Definition problems and its abuse in medical practice. *APS Journal, 3*(4), 264–273. https://doi.org/10.1016/S1058-9139(05)80274-8

Fisher, C. E. (2022, January 15). It's misleading to call addiction a disease. *The New York Times*. https://www.nytimes.com/2022/01/15/opinion/addiction-disease.html

Fisher, H. L., Jones, P. B., Fearon, P., Craig, T. K., Dazzan, P., Morgan, K., Hutchinson, G., Doody, G. A., McGuffin, P., Leff, J., Murray, R. M., & Morgan, C. (2010). The varying impact of type, timing and frequency of exposure to childhood adversity on its association with adult psychotic disorder. *Psychological Medicine, 40*(12), 1967–1978. https://doi.org/10.1017/S0033291710000231

Fisher, P. L., & Wells, A. (2011). Conceptual models of generalized anxiety disorder. *Psychiatric Annals, 41*(2), 127–132.

Fisher, T. (2011). The surprising origins of "sleep tight" and other common phrases. In *Van Winkle's*. http://vanwinkles.com/how-we-talk-about-sleep

Fishman, J. R., & Mamo, L. (2001). What's in a disorder: A cultural analysis of medical and pharmaceutical constructions of male and female sexual dysfunction. *Women & Therapy, 24*(1–2), 179–193. https://doi.org/10.1300/J015v24n01_20

Fitzgerald, P. B. (2019). Is maintenance repetitive transcranial magnetic stimulation for patients with depression a valid therapeutic strategy? *Clinical Pharmacology & Therapeutics, 106*(4), 723–725. https://doi.org/10.1002/cpt.1566

Fitzpatrick, K. K. (2011). Family-based therapy for adolescent anorexia: The nuts and bolts of empowering families to renourish their children. *Adolescent Psychiatry, 1*(4), 267–276. https://doi.org/10.2174/2210676741101040267

Fitzpatrick, S. J., & River, J. (2018). Beyond the medical model: Future directions for suicide intervention services. *International Journal of Health Services, 48*(1), 189–203. https://doi.org/10.1177/0020731417716086

Fjorback, L. O., Arendt, M., Ørnbøl, E., Walach, H., Rehfeld, E., Schröder, A., & Fink, P. (2013). Mindfulness therapy for somatization disorder and functional somatic syndromes—Randomized trial with one-year follow-up. *Journal of Psychosomatic Research, 74*(1), 31–40. https://doi.org/10.1016/j.jpsychores.2012.09.006

Flament, M. F., Bissada, H., & Spettigue, W. (2012). Evidence-based pharmacotherapy of eating disorders. *International Journal of Neuropsychopharmacology, 15*(2), 189–207. https://doi.org/10.1017/S1461145711000381

Flament, M. F., Buchholz, A., Henderson, K., Obeid, N., Maras, D., Schubert, N., Paterniti, S., & Goldfield, G. (2015). Comparative distribution and validity of DSM-IV and DSM-5 diagnoses of eating disorders in adolescents from the community. *European Eating Disorders Review, 23*(2), 100–110. https://doi.org/10.1002/erv.2339

Flanagin, J. (2014, March 25). The surprising failures of 12 steps. *The Atlantic*. https://www.theatlantic.com/health/archive/2014/03/the-surprising-failures-of-12-steps/284616/

Flannery, R. B., & Everly Jr, G. S. (2000). Crisis intervention: A review. *International Journal of Emergency Mental Health, 2*(2), 119–126.

Flaskerud, J. H. (2007). Neurasthenia: Here and there, now and then. *Issues in Mental Health Nursing, 28*(6), 657–659. https://doi.org/10.1080/01612840701354638

Flaugnacco, E., Lopez, L., Terribili, C., Montico, M., Zoia, S., & Schön, D. (2015). Music training increases phonological awareness and reading skills in developmental dyslexia: A randomized control trial. *PLOS ONE, 10*(9), e0138715. https://doi.org/10.1371/journal.pone.0138715

Fleming, M. P., & Martin, C. R. (2011). Genes and schizophrenia: A pseudoscientific disenfranchisement of the individual. *Journal of Psychiatric and Mental Health Nursing, 18*(6), 469–478. https://doi.org/10.1111/j.1365-2850.2011.01690.x

Flessner, C. A. (2011). Cognitive-behavioral therapy for childhood repetitive behavior disorders: Tic disorders and trichotillomania. *Child and Adolescent Psychiatric Clinics of North America, 20*(2), 319–328. doi:10.1016/j.chc.2011.01.007

Fletcher, K., Nutton, J., & Brend, D. (2015). Attachment, a matter of substance: The potential of attachment theory in the treatment of addictions. *Clinical Social Work Journal, 43*(1), 109–117. https://doi.org/10.1007/s10615-014-0502-5

Fletcher, T. B. (2000). Primary nocturnal enuresis: A structural and strategic family systems approach. *Journal of Mental Health Counseling, 22*(1), 32–44.

Flor, H., Birbaumer, N., Schugens, M. M., & Lutzenberger, W. (1992). Symptom-specific psychophysiological responses in chronic pain patients. *Psychophysiology, 29*(4), 452–460. https://doi.org/10.1111/j.1469-8986.1992.tb01718.x

Flor, H., Birbaumer, N., & Turk, D. C. (1990). The psychobiology of chronic pain. *Advances in Behaviour Research & Therapy, 12*(2), 47–84. https://doi.org/10.1016/0146-6402(90)90007-D

Flor, H., & Turk, D. C. (1989). Psychophysiology of chronic pain: Do chronic pain patients exhibit symptom-specific psychophysiological responses? *Psychological Bulletin, 105*(2), 215–259. https://doi.org/10.1037/0033-2909.105.2.215

Florsheim, D. B. (2020). Psychopathology and absolutisms: Universalism, objectivism and foundationalism in mental health. *Psicologia Em Estudo, 25*, e45334. https://doi.org/10.4025/psicolestud.v25i0.45334

Flory, J. D. (2020). Categorical assessment of personality disorders: Considerations of reliability and validity. In C. W. Lejuez & K. L. Gratz (Eds.), *The Cambridge handbook of personality disorders* (pp. 356–364). Cambridge University Press. https://doi.org/10.1017/9781108333931.062

Fluitman, S., Denys, D., Vulink, N., Schutters, S., Heijnen, C., & Westenberg, H. (2010). Lipopolysaccharide-induced cytokine production in obsessive–compulsive disorder and generalized social anxiety disorder. *Psychiatry Research, 178*(2), 313–316. https://doi.org/10.1016/j.psychres.2009.05.008

Flynn, A., & Polak, N. (2019, January). Incorporating the Power Threat Meaning Framework into an autism and learning disability team. *Clinical Psychology Forum, 313*, 42–46.

Foa, E. B., Huppert, J. D., & Cahill, S. P. (2006). Emotional processing theory: An update. In B. O. Rothbaum (Ed.), *Pathological anxiety: Emotional processing in etiology and treatment* (pp. 3–24). Guilford Press.

Foa, E. B., & Kozak, M. J. (1991). Emotional processing: Theory, research, and clinical implications for anxiety disorders. In J. D. Safran & L. S. Greenberg (Eds.), *Emotion, psychotherapy, and change* (pp. 21–49). Guilford Press.

Foa, E. B., & McLean, C. P. (2016). The efficacy of exposure therapy for anxiety-related disorders and its underlying mechanisms: The case of OCD and PTSD. *Annual Review of Clinical Psychology, 12*(1), 1–28. https://doi.org/10.1146/annurev-clinpsy-021815-093533

Foa, E. B., Steketee, G., & Grayson, J. B. (1985). Imaginal and in vivo exposure: A comparison with obsessive-compulsive checkers. *Behavior Therapy, 16*(3), 292–302. https://doi.org/10.1016/S0005-7894(85)80017-4

Fodor, L. A., Coteț, C. D., Cuijpers, P., Szamoskozi, Ștefan, David, D., & Cristea, I. A. (2018). The effectiveness of virtual reality based interventions for symptoms of anxiety and depression: A meta-analysis. *Scientific Reports, 8*(1), Article 1. https://doi.org/10.1038/s41598-018-28113-6

Fogelkvist, M., Gustafsson, S. A., Kjellin, L., & Parling, T. (2020). Acceptance and commitment therapy to reduce eating disorder symptoms and body image problems in patients with residual eating disorder symptoms: A randomized controlled trial. *Body Image*, 32, 155–166. https://doi.org/10.1016/j.bodyim.2020.01.002

Follette, V. M., La Bash, H. A. J., & Sewell, M. T. (2010). Adult disclosure of a history of childhood sexual abuse: Implications for behavioral psychotherapy. *Journal of Trauma & Dissociation*, 11(2), 228–243. https://doi.org/10.1080/15299730903502953

Fonagy, P. (2001). *Attachment theory and psychoanalysis*. Karnac.

Fonagy, P., Bateman, A., Luyten, P., Allison, E., & Campbell, C. (2020). Psychoanalytic/psychodynamic approaches to personality disorders. In C. W. Lejuez & K. L. Gratz (Eds.), *The Cambridge handbook of personality disorders* (pp. 427–439). Cambridge University Press. https://doi.org/10.1017/9781108333931.075

Fonagy, P., & Campbell, C. (2015). Bad blood revisited: Attachment and psychoanalysis, 2015. *British Journal of Psychotherapy*, 31(2), 229–250. https://doi.org/10.1111/bjp.12150

Fonagy, P., & Luyten, P. (2009). A developmental, mentalization-based approach to the understanding and treatment of borderline personality disorder. *Development and Psychopathology*, 21(4), 1355–1381. https://doi.org/10.1017/S0954579409990198

Fonagy, P., & Luyten, P. (2012). Psychodynamic models of personality disorders. In T. A. Widiger (Ed.), *The Oxford handbook of personality disorders* (pp. 345–371). Oxford University Press. https://doi.org/10.1093/oxfordhb/9780199735013.013.0017

Fond, G., Lançon, C., Korchia, T., Auquier, P., & Boyer, L. (2020). The role of inflammation in the treatment of schizophrenia. *Frontiers in Psychiatry*, 11, Article 160. https://doi.org/10.3389/fpsyt.2020.00160

Fone, D., White, J., Farewell, D., Kelly, M., John, G., Lloyd, K., Williams, G., & Dunstan, F. (2014). Effect of neighborhood deprivation and social cohesion on mental health inequality: A multilevel population-based longitudinal study. *Psychological Medicine*, 44(11), 2449–2460. https://doi.org/10.1017/S0033291713003255

Fong, T. W., Reid, R. C., & Parhami, I. (2012). Behavioral addictions: Where to draw the lines? *Psychiatric Clinics of North America*, 35(2), 279–296. https://doi.org/10.1016/j.psc.2012.03.001

Fontaine, N., & Viding, E. (2008). Genetics of personality disorders. *Psychiatry*, 7(3), 137–141. https://doi.org/10.1016/j.mppsy.2008.01.002

Fonteille, V., & Stoléru, S. (2011). The cerebral correlates of sexual desire: Functional neuroimaging approach. *Sexologies*, 20(3), 142–148. https://doi.org/10.1016/j.sexol.2010.03.011

Food Research & Action Center. (2015). *Understanding the connections: Food insecurity and obesity*. https://frac.org/wp-content/uploads/frac_brief_understanding_the_connections.pdf

Foran, A., O'Donnell, A. T., & Muldoon, O. T. (2020). Stigma of eating disorders and recovery-related outcomes: A systematic review. *European Eating Disorders Review*, 28(4), 385–397. https://doi.org/10.1002/erv.2735

Forbes, J., & Sashidharan, S. P. (1997). User involvement in services—Incorporation or challenge? *British Journal of Social Work*, 27(4), 481–498. https://doi.org/10.1093/oxfordjournals.bjsw.a011237

Ford, C. V., & Folks, D. G. (1985). Conversion disorders: An overview. *Psychosomatics: Journal of Consultation and Liaison Psychiatry*, 26(5), 371–383. https://doi.org/10.1016/S0033-3182(85)72845-9

Ford, J. D., & Courtois, C. A. (2021). Complex PTSD and borderline personality disorder. *Borderline Personality Disorder and Emotion Dysregulation*, 8(1), Article 16. https://doi.org/10.1186/s40479-021-00155-9

Ford, J. D., & Gómez, J. M. (2015). The relationship of psychological trauma and dissociative and posttraumatic stress disorders to nonsuicidal self-injury and suicidality: A review. *Journal of Trauma & Dissociation*, 16(3), 232–271. https://doi.org/10.1080/15299732.2015.989563

Foreman, M., Hare, L., York, K., Balakrishnan, K., Sánchez, F. J., Harte, F., Erasmus, J., Vilain, E., & Harley, V. R. (2019). Genetic link between gender dysphoria and sex hormone signaling. *The Journal of Clinical Endocrinology & Metabolism*, 104(2), 390–396. https://doi.org/10.1210/jc.2018-01105

Fornaro, M., Anastasia, A., Valchera, A., Carano, A., Orsolini, L., Vellante, F., Rapini, G., Olivieri, L., Di Natale, S., Perna, G., Martinotti, G., Di Giannantonio, M., & De Berardis, D. (2019). The FDA "black box" warning on antidepressant suicide risk in young adults: More harm than benefits? *Frontiers in Psychiatry*, 10, Article 294. https://doi.org/10.3389/fpsyt.2019.00294

Forsén Mantilla, E., Clinton, D., & Birgegård, A. (2019). The unsafe haven: Eating disorders as attachment relationships. *Psychology and Psychotherapy: Theory, Research and Practice*, 92(3), 379–393. https://doi.org/10.1111/papt.12184

Forster, G. L., Simons, R. M., & Baugh, L. A. (2017). Revisiting the role of the amygdala in posttraumatic stress disorder. In B. Ferry (Ed.), *The amygdala*. IntechOpen. https://doi.org/10.5772/67585

Forstner, A. J., Awasthi, S., Wolf, C., Maron, E., Erhardt, A., Czamara, D., Eriksson, E., Lavebratt, C., Allgulander, C., Friedrich, N., Becker, J., Hecker, J., Rambau, S., Conrad, R., Geiser, F., McMahon, F. J., Moebus, S., Hess, T., Buerfent, B. C., … Schumacher, J. (2021). Genome-wide association study of panic disorder reveals genetic overlap with neuroticism and depression. *Molecular Psychiatry*, 26(8), 4179–4190. https://doi.org/10.1038/s41380-019-0590-2

Fortuna, L. R., Porche, M. V., & Padilla, A. (2018). A treatment development study of a cognitive and mindfulness-based therapy for adolescents with co-occurring post-traumatic stress and substance use disorder. *Psychology and Psychotherapy: Theory, Research and Practice*, 91(1), 42–62. https://doi.org/10.1111/papt.12143

Fosse, R., Joseph, J., & Richardson, K. (2015). A critical assessment of the equal-environment assumption of the twin method for schizophrenia. *Frontiers in Psychiatry*, 6, Article 62. https://doi.org/10.3389/fpsyt.2015.00062

Foster, J. A., & McVey Neufeld, K.-A. (2013). Gut–brain axis: How the microbiome influences anxiety and depression. *Trends in Neurosciences*, 36(5), 305–312. https://doi.org/10.1016/j.tins.2013.01.005

Foster, R. G. (2020). Sleep, circadian rhythms and health. *Interface Focus*, 10(3), 20190098. https://doi.org/10.1098/rsfs.2019.0098

Foster, S. L., & Weinshenker, D. (2019). The role of norepinephrine in drug addiction: Past, present, and future. In M. Torregrossa (Ed.), *Neural mechanisms of addiction* (pp. 221–236). Academic Press. https://doi.org/10.1016/B978-0-12-812202-0.00015-4

Foucault, M. (1978). *The history of sexuality: Vol. 1. An introduction*. Pantheon Books.

Foundation for a Drug Free World. (n.d.-a). *Depressants*. http://www.drugfreeworld.org/drugfacts/prescription/depressants.html

Foundation for a Drug Free World. (n.d.-b). *What is alcohol?* http://www.drugfreeworld.org/drugfacts/alcohol.html

Fountoulakis, K. N., & Möller, H.-J. (2011). Efficacy of antidepressants: A re-analysis and re-interpretation of the Kirsch data. *The International Journal of Neuropsychopharmacology*, 14(3), 405–412. https://doi.org/10.1017/S1461145710000957

Fountoulakis, K. N., Veroniki, A. A., Siamouli, M., & Möller, H.-J. (2013). No role for initial severity on the efficacy of antidepressants: Results of a multi-meta-analysis. *Annals of General Psychiatry*, 12(1), 26. https://doi.org/10.1186/1744-859X-12-26

Fowler, K. A., O'Donohue, W., & Lilienfeld, S. O. (2007). Introduction: Personality disorders in perspective. In W. O'Donohue, K. A. Fowler, & S. O. Lilienfeld (Eds.), *Personality disorders: Toward the DSM-V* (pp. 1–19). SAGE Publications.

Foxcroft, D. R., Coombes, L., Wood, S., Allen, D., & Almeida Santimano, M. T., N. M. L. Moreira. (2016). Motivational interviewing for the prevention of alcohol misuse in young adults (Review). *Cochrane Database of Systematic Reviews*, 2016(7), Article CD007025. https://doi.org/10.1002/14651858.CD008063.pub2

Frakt, A. (2020, December 30). What can be learned from differing rates of suicide among groups. *The New York Times*. https://www.nytimes.com/2020/12/30/upshot/suicide-demographic-differences.html

France, C. M., Lysaker, P. H., & Robinson, R. P. (2007). The "chemical imbalance" explanation for depression: Origins, lay endorsement, and clinical implications. *Professional Psychology: Research and Practice*, 38(4), 411–420. https://doi.org/10.1037/0735-7028.38.4.411

Frances, A. (2010a). Will DSM5 contain or worsen the epidemic of autism? [Psychology Today]. *DSM5 in Distress*. https://www.psychologytoday.com/blog/dsm5-in-distress/201003/will-dsm5-contain-or-worsen-the-epidemic-autism

Frances, A. (2010b, July 6). Normality is an endangered species: Psychiatric fads and overdiagnosis. *Psychiatric Times*. http://www.psychiatrictimes.com/dsm-5/normality-endangered-species-psychiatric-fads-and-overdiagnosis

Frances, A. (2012, December 3). DSM-5 is a guide, not a bible: Simply ignore its 10 worst changes. *Huffington Post*. http://www.huffingtonpost.com/allen-frances/dsm-5_b_2227626.html

Frances, A. (2013a). *Saving normal: An insider's revolt against out-of-control psychiatric diagnosis, DSM-5, big pharma, and the medicalization of ordinary life*. Morrow.

Frances, A. (2013b). The new somatic symptom disorder in DSM-5 risks mislabeling many people as mentally ill. *BMJ: British Medical Journal (Online)*, 346. https://doi.org/10.1136/bmj.f1580

Frances, A. (2013c, November 26). Psychosis risk syndrome is back. *Psychiatric Times*.

Frances, A. (2014). Resuscitating the biopsychosocial model. *The Lancet Psychiatry*, 1(7), 496–497. https://doi.org/10.1016/S2215-0366(14)00058-3

Frances, A. (2015). Don't throw out the baby with the bath water. *Australian and New Zealand Journal of Psychiatry*, 49(6), 577. https://doi.org/10.1177/0004867415579467

Frances, A. (2018). Commentary on the *Psychodynamic diagnostic manual*, 2nd edition: The PDM-2 as an effort to enhance the psychiatric diagnosis. *Psychoanalytic Psychology*, 35(3), 296–298. https://doi.org/10.1037/pap0000189

Frances, A., & Chapman, S. (2013). DSM-5 somatic symptom disorder mislabels medical illness as mental disorder. *Australian and New Zealand Journal of Psychiatry*, 47(5), 483–484. https://doi.org/10.1177/0004867413484525

Frances, A. J., & Nardo, J. M. (2013). ICD-11 should not repeat the mistakes made by DSM-5. *The British Journal of Psychiatry*, 203(1), 1–2.

Frances, A. J., & Widiger, T. (2012). Psychiatric diagnosis: Lessons from the DSM-IV past and cautions for the DSM-5 future. *Annual Review of Clinical Psychology*, 8, 109–130. https://doi.org/10.1146/annurev-clinpsy-032511-143102

Franco-Paredes, K., Mancilla-Díaz, J. M., Vázquez-Arévalo, R., López-Aguilar, X., & Álvarez-Rayón, G. (2005). Perfectionism and eating disorders: A review of the literature. *European Eating Disorders Review*, 13(1), 61–70. https://doi.org/10.1002/erv.605

Frank, D. (2020). Methadone maintenance treatment is swapping one drug for another, and that's why it works: Towards a treatment-based critique of the war on drugs. *International Journal of Drug Policy*, 83, Article 102844. https://doi.org/10.1016/j.drugpo.2020.102844

Frank, E. (2007). Interpersonal and social rhythm therapy: A means of improving depression and preventing relapse in bipolar disorder. *Journal of Clinical*

Psychology, 63(5), 463–473. https://doi.org/10.1002/jclp.20371

Frank, G. K. W., Shott, M. E., & DeGuzman, M. C. (2019). The neurobiology of eating disorders. *Child and Adolescent Psychiatric Clinics of North America*, 28(4), 629–640. https://doi.org/10.1016/j.chc.2019.05.007

Frankenburg, F. R., & Baldessarini, R. J. (2008). Neurosyphilis, malaria, and the discovery of antipsychotic agents. *Harvard Review of Psychiatry*, 16(5), 299–307. https://doi.org/10.1080/10673220802432350

Frankl, V. E. (1959). *Man's search for meaning* (I. Lasch, Trans.). Pocket Books.

Frankl, V. E. (1968). *The doctor and the soul: From psychotherapy to logotherapy* (R. Winston, Trans.). Alfred A. Knopf.

Franklin, J. C., Ribeiro, J. D., Fox, K. R., Bentley, K. H., Kleiman, E. M., Huang, X., Musacchio, K. M., Jaroszewski, A. C., Chang, B. P., & Nock, M. K. (2017). Risk factors for suicidal thoughts and behaviors: A meta-analysis of 50 years of research. *Psychological Bulletin*, 143(2), 187–232. https://doi.org/10.1037/bul0000084

Fransella, F. (1987). Stuttering to fluency via reconstruing. In R. A. Neimeyer & G. J. Neimeyer (Eds.), *Personal construct therapy casebook* (pp. 290–308). Springer.

Frazier, P., Tennen, H., Gavian, M., Park, C., Tomich, P., & Tashiro, T. (2009). Does self-reported posttraumatic growth reflect genuine positive change? *Psychological Science*, 20(7), 912–919. https://doi.org/10.1111/j.1467-9280.2009.02381.x

Fredericks, D. W., Carr, J. E., & Larry Williams, W. (1998). Overview of the treatment of rumination disorder for adults in a residential setting. *Journal of Behavior Therapy and Experimental Psychiatry*, 29(1), 31–40. https://doi.org/10.1016/S0005-7916(98)00002-0

Fredrickson, B. L., & Roberts, T.-A. (1997). Objectification theory: Toward understanding women's lived experiences and mental health risks. *Psychology of Women Quarterly*, 21(2), 173–206. https://doi.org/10.1111/j.1471-6402.1997.tb00108.x

Freed, C. R. (2012). Historical perspectives on addiction. In H. J. Shaffer, D. A. LaPlante, & S. E. Nelson (Eds.), *APA addiction syndrome handbook, Vol. 1: Foundations, influences, and expressions of addiction* (pp. 27–47). American Psychological Association. https://doi.org/10.1037/13751-002

Freedman, R., Lewis, D. A., Michels, R., Pine, D. S., Schultz, S. K., Tamminga, C. A., Gabbard, G. O., Gau, S. S.-F., Javitt, D. C., Oquendo, M. A., Shrout, P. E., Vieta, E., & Yager, J. (2013). The initial field trials of DSM-5: New blooms and old thorns. *The American Journal of Psychiatry*, 170(1), 1–5.

Freeman, A. M., Tribe, R. H., Stott, J. C. H., & Pilling, S. (2019). Open Dialogue: A review of the evidence. *Psychiatric Services*, 70(1), 46–59. https://doi.org/10.1176/appi.ps.201800236

Freeman, A., Tyrovolas, S., Koyanagi, A., Chatterji, S., Leonardi, M., Ayuso-Mateos, J. L., Tobiasz-Adamczyk, B., Koskinen, S., Rummel-Kluge, C., & Haro, J. M. (2016). The role of socio-economic status in depression: Results from the COURAGE (aging survey in Europe). *BMC Public Health*, 16, 1098. https://doi.org/10.1186/s12889-016-3638-0

Freeman, K. A., Riley, A., Duke, D. C., & Fu, R. (2014). Systematic review and meta-analysis of behavioral interventions for fecal incontinence with constipation. *Journal of Pediatric Psychology*, 39(8), 887–902. https://doi.org/10.1093/jpepsy/jsu039

Freizinger, M., Recto, M., Jhe, G., & Lin, J. (2022). Atypical anorexia in youth: Cautiously bridging the treatment gap. *Children*, 9(6), 837. https://doi.org/10.3390/children9060837

Freud, S. (1914). *The psychopathology of everyday life* (A. A. Brill, Trans.). Macmillan.

Freud, S. (1953). Mourning and melancholia. In J. Strachey, A. Freud, A. Strachey, & A. Tyson (Eds.), & J. Strachey (Trans.), *The standard edition of the complete psychological works of Sigmund Freud* (Vol.

14, pp. 243–258). Hogarth Press & The Institute of Psycho-analysis. (Original work published 1917)

Freud, S. (1955a). Analysis of a phobia in a five-year-old boy. In J. Strachey, A. Freud, A. Strachey, & A. Tyson (Eds.), & J. Strachey (Trans.), *The standard edition of the complete psychological works of Sigmund Freud* (Vol. 10, pp. 3–149). Hogarth Press & The Institute of Psycho-analysis. (Original work published 1909.)

Freud, S. (1955b). Notes upon a case of obsessional neurosis. In J. Strachey, A. Freud, A. Strachey, & A. Tyson (Eds.), & J. Strachey (Trans.), *The standard edition of the complete psychological works of Sigmund Freud* (Vol. 10, pp. 153–326). Hogarth Press & The Institute of Psycho-analysis. (Original work published 1909.)

Freud, S. (1959). Neurosis and psychosis. In J. Riviere (Trans.), *Collected papers* (Vol. 2, pp. 250–254). Basic Books. (Original work published 1924.)

Freud, S. (1960). *The ego and the id*. Norton. (Original work published 1923.)

Freud, S. (1962). *Three essays on the theory of sexuality* (J. Strachey, Trans.). Avon Books. (Original work published 1905.)

Freud, S. (1965). *New introductory lectures on psychoanalysis* (J. Strachey, Trans.). Norton. (Original work published 1933.)

Freud, S. (1965). *The interpretation of dreams* (J. Strachey, Trans.). Avon Books. (Original work published 1900.)

Frías, Á., Palma, C., Farriols, N., & González, J. (2016). Sexuality-related issues in borderline personality disorder: A comprehensive review. *Personality and Mental Health*, 10(3), 216–231. https://doi.org/10.1002/pmh.1330

Friedan, J. (2015). Don't like ICD-10? Don't worry—ICD-11 Is on the horizon. *MedPage Today*.

Friederich, H. C., Walther, S., Bendszus, M., Biller, A., Thomann, P., Zeigermann, S., Katus, T., Brunner, R., Zastrow, A., & Herzog, W. (2012). Grey matter abnormalities within cortico-limbic-striatal circuits in acute and weight-restored anorexia nervosa patients. *NeuroImage*, 59. https://doi.org/10.1016/j.neuroimage.2011.09.042

Friedman, M. (1977). Type A behavior pattern: Some of its pathophysiological components. *Bulletin of the New York Academy of Medicine*, 53(7), 593–604.

Friedman, M., & Rosenman, R. H. (1959). Association of specific overt behavior pattern with blood and cardiovascular findings; blood cholesterol level, blood clotting time, incidence of arcus senilis, and clinical coronary artery disease. *Journal of the American Medical Association*, 169(12), 1286–1296. https://doi.org/10.1001/jama.1959.03000290012005

Friedman, M. J. (2018). Eradicating traumatic memories: Implications for PTSD treatment. *American Journal of Psychiatry*, 175(5), 391–392. https://doi.org/10.1176/appi.ajp.2018.18010106

Friedman, M. J., & Davidson, J. R. T. (2014). Pharmacotherapy for PTSD. In M. J. Friedman, T. M. Keane, & P. A. Resick (Eds.), *Handbook of PTSD: Science and practice* (2nd ed., pp. 482–501). New York, NY: Guilford Press.

Friedman, R. (2013). The book stops here. *The New York Times*. https://www.nytimes.com/2013/05/21/health/the-dsm-5-as-a-guide-not-a-bible.html?_r=0

Friedman, R. A. (2014). Antidepressants' black-box warning—10 years later. *New England Journal of Medicine*, 371(18), 1666–1668. https://doi.org/10.1056/NEJMp1408480

Frigerio-Domingues, C., & Drayna, D. (2017). Genetic contributions to stuttering: The current evidence. *Molecular Genetics & Genomic Medicine*, 5(2), 95–102. https://doi.org/10.1002/mgg3.276

Frikha, F., Masmoudi, J., Salah, R. B., Ghribi, M., & Bahloul, Z. (2021). Sexual function and dysfunction among patients with systemic and auto-immune diseases. *Annals of Clinical and Medical Case Reports*, 05, Article 11. https://doi.org/10.47829/ACM-CR.2021.51104

Frintrop, L., Trinh, S., Liesbrock, J., Leunissen, C., Kempermann, J., Etdöger, S., Kas, M. J., Tolba, R.,

Heussen, N., Neulen, J., Konrad, K., Päfgen, V., Kiessling, F., Herpertz-Dahlmann, B., Beyer, C., & Seitz, J. (2019). The reduction of astrocytes and brain volume loss in anorexia nervosa—The impact of starvation and refeeding in a rodent model. *Translational Psychiatry*, 9(1), 159. https://doi.org/10.1038/s41398-019-0493-7

Frith, C. D. (2004). Schizophrenia and theory of mind. *Psychological Medicine*, 34(3), 385–389. https://doi.org/10.1017/S0033291703001326

Frith, C. D., & Corcoran, R. (1996). Exploring "theory of mind" in people with schizophrenia. *Psychological Medicine*, 26(3), 521–530. https://doi.org/10.1017/S0033291700035601

Fritz, M., Klawonn, A. M., & Zahr, N. M. (2022). Neuroimaging in alcohol use disorder: From mouse to man. *Journal of Neuroscience Research*, 100(5), 1140–1158. https://doi.org/10.1002/jnr.24423

Fromm, M. (2004). *Introduction to the repertory grid interview*. Waxmann Münster.

Fromm-Reichmann, F. (1939). Transference problems in schizophrenics. *The Psychoanalytic Quarterly*, 8, 412–426.

Fromm-Reichmann, F. (1948). Notes on the development of treatment of schizophrenics by psychoanalytic therapy. *Psychiatry: Journal for the Study of Interpersonal Processes*, 11, 263–273.

Fromm-Reichmann, F. (1954). Psychotherapy of schizophrenia. *The American Journal of Psychiatry*, 111, 410–419.

Frost, N. (2011). *Qualitative research methods in psychology: Combining core approaches*. McGraw Hill/Open University Press.

Frost, R. O., Steketee, G., & Tolin, D. F. (2011). Comorbidity in hoarding disorder. *Depression and Anxiety*, 28(10), 876–884. https://doi.org/10.1002/da.20861

Frostadottir, A. D., & Dorjee, D. (2019). Effects of mindfulness based cognitive therapy (MBCT) and compassion focused therapy (CFT) on symptom change, mindfulness, self-compassion, and rumination in clients with depression, anxiety, and stress. *Frontiers in Psychology*, 10, Article 1099. https://www.doi.org/10.3389/fpsyg.2019.01099

Fruzzetti, A. E., & Payne, L. (2015). Couple therapy and borderline personality disorder. In A. S. Gurman, J. L. Lebow, & D. K. Snyder (Eds.), *Clinical handbook of couple therapy* (5th ed., pp. 606–634). Guilford Press.

Fruzzetti, A. E., & Payne, L. (2020). Assessment of parents, couples, and families in dialectical behavior therapy. *Cognitive and Behavioral Practice*, 27(1), 39–49. https://doi.org/10.1016/j.cbpra.2019.10.006

Fruzzetti, A. E., Payne, L. G., & Hoffman, P. D. (2021). DBT with families. In L. A. Dimeff, S. L. Rizvi, & K. Koerner (Eds.), *Dialectical behavior therapy in clinical practice: Applications across disorders and settings* (2nd ed., pp. 366–387). The Guilford Press.

Frysh, P. (2022, January 4). A long, strange trip: Magic mushrooms, MDMA, and the promise of psychedelic-assisted therapy. *WebMD*. https://st-0066173.stprod.webmd.com/mental-health/story/psychedelic-assisted-therapy

Ftanou, M., Cox, G., Nicholas, A., Spittal, M. J., Machlin, A., Robinson, J., & Pirkis, J. (2017). Suicide prevention public service announcements (PSAs): Examples from around the world. *Health Communication*, 32(4), 493–501. https://doi.org/10.1080/10410236.2016.1140269

Fu, X., Zhang, F., Liu, F., Yan, C., & Guo, W. (2019). Editorial: Brain and somatization symptoms in psychiatric disorders. *Frontiers in Psychiatry*, 10, Article 146. https://doi.org/10.3389/fpsyt.2019.00146

Fuchs, D., & Fuchs, L. S. (2017). Critique of the national evaluation of response to intervention: A case for simpler frameworks. *Exceptional Children*, 83(3), 255–268. https://doi.org/10.1177/0014402917693580

Fuchs, D., Mock, D., Morgan, P. L., & Young, C. L. (2003). Responsiveness-to-intervention: Definitions, evidence, and implications for the learning disabilities construct. *Learning Disabilities Research & Practice*,

18(3), 157–171. https://doi.org/10.1111/1540-5826.00072

Fuentes, J. J., Fonseca, F., Elices, M., Farré, M., & Torrens, M. (2020). Therapeutic use of LSD in psychiatry: A systematic review of randomized-controlled clinical trials. *Frontiers in Psychiatry, 10*, Article 943. https://doi.org/10.3389/fpsyt.2019.00943

Fujisawa, T. X., Yatsuga, C., Mabe, H., Yamada, E., Masuda, M., & Tomoda, A. (2015). Anorexia nervosa during adolescence is associated with decreased gray matter volume in the inferior frontal gyrus. *PLoS ONE, 10*(6), e0128548. https://doi.org/10.1371/journal.pone.0128548

Fullen, T., Jones, S. L., Emerson, L. M., & Adamou, M. (2020). Psychological treatments in adult ADHD: A systematic review. *Journal of Psychopathology and Behavioral Assessment, 42*(3), 500–518. https://doi.org/10.1007/s10862-020-09794-8

Fuller, K. (2020, September 30). *5 common myths about suicide debunked.* National Alliance on Mental Illness. https://www.nami.org/Blogs/NAMI-Blog/September-2020/5-Common-Myths-About-Suicide-Debunked

Fuller, R. K., Branchey, L., Brightwell, D. R., Derman, R. M., Emrick, C. D., Iber, F. L., James, K. E., Lacoursiere, R. B., Lee, K. K., & Lowenstam, I. (1986). Disulfiram treatment of alcoholism. A Veterans Administration cooperative study. *JAMA, 256*(11), 1449–1455.

Fung, L. K., Mahajan, R., Nozzolillo, A., Bernal, P., Krasner, A., Jo, B., Coury, D., Whitaker, A., Veenstra-Vanderweele, J., & Hardan, A. Y. (2016). Pharmacologic treatment of severe irritability and problem behaviors in autism: A systematic review and meta-analysis. *Pediatrics, 137*(Suppl. 2), S124–S135. https://doi.org/10.1542/peds.2015-2851K

Funk, C. (2022, April 7). 3. Black Americans' views about health disparities, experiences with health care. *Pew Research Center Science & Society.* https://www.pewresearch.org/science/2022/04/07/black-americans-views-about-health-disparities-experiences-with-health-care/

Furtado, M., & Katzman, M. A. (2015). Neuroinflammatory pathways in anxiety, posttraumatic stress, and obsessive compulsive disorders. *Psychiatry Research, 229*(1–2), 37–48. https://doi.org/10.1016/j.psychres.2015.05.036

Fusar-Poli, P., Raballo, A., & Parnas, J. (2017). What Is an attenuated psychotic symptom? On the importance of the context. *Schizophrenia Bulletin, 43*(4), 687–692. https://doi.org/10.1093/schbul/sbw182

Fusar-Poli, P., Smieskova, R., Kempton, M. J., Ho, B. C., Andreasen, N. C., & Borgwardt, S. (2013). Progressive brain changes in schizophrenia related to antipsychotic treatment? A meta-analysis of longitudinal MRI studies. *Neuroscience and Biobehavioral Reviews, 37*(8), 1680–1691. https://doi.org/10.1016/j.neubiorev.2013.06.001

Fusar-Poli, P., & Yung, A. R. (2012). Should attenuated psychosis syndrome be included in DSM-5? *The Lancet, 379*(9816), 591–592. https://doi.org/10.1016/S0140-6736(11)61507-9

Gabbard, G. O. (2014). *Psychodynamic psychiatry in clinical practice* (5th ed.). American Psychiatric Publishing.

Gable, R. A., Quinn, M. M., Rutherford, R. B., Howell, K. W., & Hoffman, C. C. (1999). *Addressing student problem behavior-part II: Conducting a functional behavioral assessment.* American Institutes for Research.

Gacono, C. B., & Smith, J. M. (2021). Issues to consider prior to using the R-PAS in a forensic context. *Journal of Projective Psychology & Mental Health, 28*(1), 4–13. https://doi.org/10.13140/RG.2.2.20515.68649

Gaebel, W., Zielasek, J., & Falkai, P. (2015). Psychotic disorders in ICD-11. *Die Psychiatrie: Grundlagen & Perspektiven, 12*(2), 71–76.

Gaffney, G. R., Lurie, S. F., & Berlin, F. S. (1984). Is there familial transmission of pedophilia? *Journal of Nervous and Mental Disease, 172*(9), 546–548. https://doi.org/10.1097/00005053-198409000-00006

Gahlsdorf, T., Krause, R., & Beal, M. W. (2007). Efficacy of St. John's wort for treating mild to moderate depression. *Complementary Health Practice Review, 12*(3), 184–195.

Gaither, G. A., Rosenkranz, R. R., & J., P. J. (1998). Sexual disorders. In J. J. Plaud & G. H. Eifert (Eds.), *From behavior theory to behavior therapy* (pp. 152–171). Allyn & Bacon.

Gałecki, P., & Talarowska, M. (2017). The evolutionary theory of depression. *Medical Science Monitor: International Medical Journal of Experimental and Clinical Research, 23*, 2267–2274. https://doi.org/10.12659/MSM.901240

Galli, S., Tatu, L., Bogousslavsky, J., & Aybek, S. (2018). Conversion, factitious disorder and malingering: A distinct pattern or a continuum? *Frontiers of Neurology and Neuroscience, 42*, 72–80. https://doi.org/10.1159/000475699

Galloway, R., Watson, H., Greene, D., Shafran, R., & Egan, S. J. (2022). The efficacy of randomised controlled trials of cognitive behaviour therapy for perfectionism: A systematic review and meta-analysis. *Cognitive Behaviour Therapy, 51*(2), 170–184. https://doi.org/10.1080/16506073.2021.1952302

Galmiche, M., Déchelotte, P., Lambert, G., & Tavolacci, M. P. (2019). Prevalence of eating disorders over the 2000–2018 period: A systematic literature review. *The American Journal of Clinical Nutrition, 109*(5), 1402–1413. https://doi.org/10.1093/ajcn/nqy342

Gambini, B. (2017, March 23). *Research consortium develops evidence-based diagnostic model for mental illness.* https://www.buffalo.edu/news/releases/2017/03/044.html

Gambrill, E. (2014). The *Diagnostic and statistical manual of mental disorders* as a major form of dehumanization in the modern world. *Research on Social Work Practice, 24*(1), 13–36. https://doi.org/10.1177/1049731513499411

Gandra, S. S. A., D Almeida, A. L., & Teixeira, Z. M. (2019). Benzodiazepines dependence: Addiction to legally prescribed substances. *Journal of Forensic Psychology, 04*(02). https://doi.org/10.35248/2475-319X.19.4.149

Gangamma, R., Walia, B., Luke, M., & Lucena, C. (2022). Continuation of teletherapy after the COVID-19 pandemic: Survey study of licensed mental health professionals. *JMIR Formative Research, 6*(6), Article e32419. https://doi.org/10.2196/32419

Gannon, L. (2002). A critique of evolutionary psychology. *Psychology, Evolution & Gender, 4*(2), 173–218. https://doi.org/10.1080/1461666031000063665

Ganz, M. B., Rasmussen, H. F., McDougall, T. V., Corner, G. W., Black, T. T., & De Los Santos, H. F. (2022). Emotionally focused couple therapy within VA healthcare: Reductions in relationship distress, PTSD, and depressive symptoms as a function of attachment-based couple treatment. *Couple and Family Psychology: Research and Practice, 11*(1), 15–32. https://doi.org/10.1037/cfp0000210

Gao, F., Liu, T., Tuo, M., & Chi, S. (2021). The role of orexin in Alzheimer disease: From sleep-wake disturbance to therapeutic target. *Neuroscience Letters, 765*, 136247. https://doi.org/10.1016/j.neulet.2021.136247

Gao, K., Wu, R., Grunze, H., & Calabrese, J. R. (2015). Pharmacological treatment bipolar depression. In A. Yildiz, P. Ruiz, & C. B. Nemeroff (Eds.), *The bipolar book: History, neurobiology, and treatment* (pp. 281–297). Oxford University Press.

Gara, M. A., Minsky, S., Silverstein, S. M., Miskimen, T., & Strakowski, S. M. (2019). A naturalistic study of racial disparities in diagnoses at an outpatient behavioral health clinic. *Psychiatric Services, 70*(2), 130–134. https://doi.org/10.1176/appi.ps.201800223

Garakani, A., Murrough, J. W., Freire, R. C., Thom, R. P., Larkin, K., Buono, F. D., & Iosifescu, D. V. (2020). Pharmacotherapy of anxiety disorders: Current and emerging treatment options. *Frontiers in Psychiatry, 11*, Article 595584. https://doi.org/10.3389/fpsyt.2020.595584

Garb, H. N. (1998). Recommendations for training in the use of the Thematic Apperception Test (TAT). *Professional Psychology: Research and Practice, 29*(6), 621–622. https://doi.org/10.1037/0735-7028.29.6.621.b

Garb, H. N. (2021). Race bias and gender bias in the diagnosis of psychological disorders. *Clinical Psychology Review, 90*, 102087. https://doi.org/10.1016/j.cpr.2021.102087

García-Blanco, A., García-Portilla, M. P., Fuente-Tomás, L. de la, Batalla, M., Sánchez-Autet, M., Arranz, B., Safont, G., Arqués, S., Livianos, L., & Sierra, P. (2020). Sexual dysfunction and mood stabilizers in long-term stable patients with bipolar disorder. *The Journal of Sexual Medicine, 17*(5), 930–940. https://doi.org/10.1016/j.jsxm.2020.01.032

García-Campayoa, J., Fayed, N., Serrano-Blanco, A., & Roca, M. (2009). Brain dysfunction behind functional symptoms: Neuroimaging and somatoform, conversive, and dissociative disorders. *Current Opinion in Psychiatry, 22*(2), 224–231. https://doi.org/10.1097/YCO.0b013e3283252d43

Gard, A. M., Dotterer, H. L., & Hyde, L. W. (2019). Genetic influences on antisocial behavior: Recent advances and future directions. *Current Opinion in Psychology, 27*, 46–55. https://doi.org/10.1016/j.copsyc.2018.07.013

Gardener, H., Levin, B., DeRosa, J., Rundek, T., Wright, C. B., Elkind, M. S. V., & Sacco, R. L. (2021). Social connectivity is related to mild cognitive impairment and dementia. *Journal of Alzheimer's Disease, 84*(4), 1811–1820. https://doi.org/10.3233/JAD-210519

Garety, P. A., Fowler, D. G., Freeman, D., Bebbington, P., Dunn, G., & Kuipers, E. (2008). Cognitive-behavioural therapy and family intervention for relapse prevention and symptom reduction in psychosis: Randomised controlled trial. *The British Journal of Psychiatry, 192*(6), 412–423. https://doi.org/10.1192/bjp.bp.107.043570

Garlipp, P. (2017). Koro—A genital retraction syndrome. In B. A. Sharpless (Ed.), *Unusual and rare psychological disorders: A handbook for clinical practice and research* (pp. 167–176). Oxford University Press.

Garrett, A., & Chang, K. (2008). The role of the amygdala in bipolar disorder development. *Development and Psychopathology, 20*(4), 1285–1296. https://doi.org/10.1017/S0954579408000618

Gasquoine, P. G. (2020). Railway spine: The advent of compensation for concussive symptoms. *Journal of the History of the Neurosciences, 29*(2), 234–245. https://doi.org/10.1080/0964704X.2019.1711350

Gatta, M., Miscioscia, M., Svanellini, L., Spoto, A., Difronzo, M., de Sauma, M., & Ferruzza, E. (2019). Effectiveness of brief psychodynamic therapy with children and adolescents: An outcome study. *Frontiers in Pediatrics, 7*, Article 501. https://doi.org/10.3389/fped.2019.00501

Gatz, M., Reynolds, C. A., Fratiglioni, L., Johansson, B., Mortimer, J. A., Berg, S., Fiske, A., & Pedersen, N. L. (2006). Role of genes and environments for explaining Alzheimer disease. *Archives of General Psychiatry, 63*(2), 168–174. https://doi.org/10.1001/archpsyc.63.2.168

Gautam, M., Tripathi, A., Deshmukh, D., & Gaur, M. (2020). Cognitive behavioral therapy for depression. *Indian Journal of Psychiatry, 62*(Suppl. 2), S223–S229. https://doi.org/10.4103/psychiatry.IndianJPsychiatry_772_19

Gavelin, H. M., Lampit, A., Hallock, H., Sabatés, J., & Bahar-Fuchs, A. (2020). Cognition-oriented treatments for older adults: A systematic overview of systematic reviews. *Neuropsychology Review, 30*(2), 167–193. https://doi.org/10.1007/s11065-020-09434-8

Gayle, M. C., & Raskin, J. D. (2017). *DSM-5*: Do counselors really want an alternative? *Journal of Humanistic Psychology, 57*(6), 650–666. https://doi.org/10.1177/0022167817696839

GBD 2019 Mental Disorders Collaborators. (2022). Global, regional, and national burden of 12 mental disorders in 204 countries and territories, 1990–2019: A systematic analysis for the Global Burden of Disease Study 2019. *The Lancet Psychiatry, 9*(2), 137–150. https://doi.org/10.1016/S2215-0366(21)00395-3

Gbemudu, A. O. (2021, April 1). *Benzodiazepines,* RxList. http://www.rxlist.com/benzodiazepines/drugs-condition.htm

Geddes, J. R., & Miklowitz, D. J. (2013). Treatment of bipolar disorder. *The Lancet, 381*(9878), 1672–1682. https://doi.org/10.1016/S0140-6736(13)60857-0

Gee, B. A., Hood, H. K., & Antony, M. M. (2013). Anxiety disorders—A historical perspective. In T. G. Plante (Ed.), *Abnormal psychology across the ages: Vol. 2. Disorders and treatments* (pp. 31–47). Praeger/ABC-CLIO.

Gejman, P., Sanders, A., & Duan, J. (2010). The role of genetics in the etiology of schizophrenia. *The Psychiatric Clinics of North America, 33*(1), 35–66. https://doi.org/10.1016/j.psc.2009.12.003

General Medical Council. (2010). *General Medical Council, Fitness to Practise Panel Hearing, 24 May 2010, Andrew Wakefield, determination of serious professional misconduct.* https://briandeer.com/solved/gmc-wakefield-sentence.pdf

Gentile, J. P., Dillon, K. S., & Gillig, P. M. (2013). Psychotherapy and pharmacotherapy for patients with dissociative identity disorder. *Innovations in Clinical Neuroscience, 10*(2), 22–29.

Gentile, J. P., Snyder, M. P. M. G., & Gillig, P. M. (2014). Stress and trauma: Psychotherapy and pharmacotherapy for depersonalization/derealization disorder. *Innovations in Clinical Neuroscience, 11*(7–8), 37–41.

Géonet, M., De Sutter, P., & Zech, E. (2013). Cognitive factors in female hypoactive sexual desire disorder. *Sexologies: European Journal of Sexology and Sexual Health/Revue Européenne de Sexologie et de Santé Sexuelle, 22*(1), e9–e15. https://doi.org/10.1016/j.sexol.2012.01.011

George, B., & Klijn, A. (2013). A modern name for schizophrenia (PSS) would diminish self-stigma. *Psychological Medicine, 43*(7), 1555–1557. https://doi.org/10.1017/S0033291713000895

Georgiadis, J. R. (2011). Exposing orgasm in the brain: A critical eye. *Sexual and Relationship Therapy, 26*(4), 342–355. https://doi.org/10.1080/14681994.2011.647904

Georgiadis, J. R., & Kringelbach, M. L. (2012). The human sexual response cycle: Brain imaging evidence linking sex to other pleasures. *Progress in Neurobiology, 98*(1), 49–81. https://doi.org/10.1016/j.pneurobio.2012.05.004

Gergen, K. J. (2015). *An invitation to social construction* (3rd ed.). SAGE.

Gergen, K. J., & McNamee, S. (2000). From disordering discourse to transformative dialogue. In R. A. Neimeyer & J. D. Raskin (Eds.), *Constructions of disorder: Meaning-making frameworks for psychotherapy* (pp. 333–349). American Psychological Association. https://doi.org/10.1037/10368-014

Geschwind, D. H. (2021). Oxytocin for autism spectrum disorder—Down, but not out. *The New England Journal of Medicine, 385*(16), 1524–1525. https://doi.org/10.1056/NEJMe2110158

Ghaderi, F., Bastani, P., Hajebrahimi, S., Jafarabadi, M. A., & Berghmans, B. (2019). Pelvic floor rehabilitation in the treatment of women with dyspareunia: A randomized controlled clinical trial. *International Urogynecology Journal, 30*(11), 1849–1855. https://doi.org/10.1007/s00192-019-04019-3

Ghaemi, N. (2014). Psychopathology for what purpose? *Acta Psychiatrica Scandinavica, 129*(1), 78–79. https://doi.org/10.1111/acps.12198

Ghaemi, S. N. (2009). The rise and fall of the biopsychosocial model. *The British Journal of Psychiatry, 195*(1), 3–4. https://doi.org/10.1192/bjp.bp.109.063859

Ghaemi, S. N. (2010). *The rise and fall of the biopsychosocial model: Reconciling art and science in psychiatry.* Johns Hopkins University Press.

Ghaemi, S. N., & Vöhringer, P. A. (2011). The heterogeneity of depression: An old debate renewed. *Acta Psychiatrica Scandinavica, 124*(6), 497–497. https://doi.org/10.1111/j.1600-0447.2011.01746.x

Ghaemi, S. N., Vöhringer, P. A., & Whitham, E. A. (2013). Antidepressants from a public health perspective. Re-examining effectiveness, suicide, and carcinogenicity. *Acta Psychiatrica Scandinavica, 127*(2), 89–93. https://doi.org/10.1111/acps.12059

Ghanizadeh, A. (2013). Agreement between *Diagnostic and statistical manual of mental disorders,* fourth edition, and the proposed DSM-V attention deficit hyperactivity disorder diagnostic criteria: An exploratory study. *Comprehensive Psychiatry, 54*(1), 7–10. https://doi.org/10.1016/j.comppsych.2012.06.001

Ghanizadeh, A., & Haddad, B. (2015). The effect of dietary education on ADHD, a randomized controlled clinical trial. *Annals of General Psychiatry, 14.* https://doi.org/10.1186/s12991-015-0050-6

Ghanizadeh, A., Tordjman, S., & Jaafari, N. (2015). Aripiprazole for treating irritability in children and adolescents with autism: A systematic review. *The Indian Journal of Medical Research, 142*(3), 269–275. https://doi.org/10.4103/0971-5916.166584

Ghinea, D., Edinger, A., Parzer, P., Koenig, J., Resch, F., & Kaess, M. (2020). Non-suicidal self-injury disorder as a stand-alone diagnosis in a consecutive help-seeking sample of adolescents. *Journal of Affective Disorders, 274,* 1122–1125. https://doi.org/10.1016/j.jad.2020.06.009

Ghirardi, L., Kuja-Halkola, R., Butwicka, A., Martin, J., Larsson, H., D'Onofrio, B. M., Lichtenstein, P., & Taylor, M. J. (2021). Familial and genetic associations between autism spectrum disorder and other neurodevelopmental and psychiatric disorders. *Journal of Child Psychology and Psychiatry, 62*(11), 1274–1284. https://doi.org/10.1111/jcpp.13508

Ghochani, M., Saffarian Toosi, M., & Khoynezhad, G. (2020). A comparison between the effectiveness of the combined couple therapy and emotionally focused therapy for couples on the improvement of intimacy and PTSD. *Learning and Motivation, 71,* 101637. https://doi.org/10.1016/j.lmot.2020.101637

Ghofrani, H. A., Osterloh, I. H., & Grimminger, F. (2006). Sildenafil: From angina to erectile dysfunction to pulmonary hypertension and beyond. *Nature Reviews. Drug Discovery, 5*(8), 689–702. https://doi.org/10.1038/nrd2030

Ghosh, A., Ray, A., & Basu, A. (2017). Oppositional defiant disorder: Current insight. *Psychology Research and Behavior Management, 10,* 353–367. https://doi.org/10.2147/PRBM.S120582

Giacomantonio, S. G. (2012). Three problems with the theory of cognitive therapy. *American Journal of Psychotherapy, 66*(4), 375–390. https://doi.org/10.1176/appi.psychotherapy.2012.66.4.375

Giannopolou, I., Lazaratou, H., Economou, M., & Dikeos, D. (2019). Converging psychoanalytic and neurobiological understanding of autism: Promise for integrative therapeutic approaches. *Psychodynamic Psychiatry, 47*(3), 275–290. https://doi.org/10.1521/pdps.2019.47.3.275

Gibbs, S. J., & Elliott, J. G. (2020). The dyslexia debate: Life without the label. *Oxford Review of Education, 46*(4), 487–500. https://doi.org/10.1080/03054985.2020.1747419

Gibney, P. (2006). The double bind theory: Still crazy-making after all these years. *Psychotherapy in Australia, 12*(3), 48–55.

Gibson, A. (2014). Insulin coma therapy. *The Psychiatric Bulletin, 38*(4), 198–198. https://doi.org/10.1192/pb.38.4.198

Gibson, D., & Mehler, P. S. (2019). Anorexia nervosa and the immune system—A narrative review. *Journal of Clinical Medicine, 8*(11), 1915. https://doi.org/10.3390/jcm8111915

Gibson, S., Brand, S. L., Burt, S., Boden, Z. V. R., & Benson, O. (2013). Understanding treatment non-adherence in schizophrenia and bipolar disorder: A survey of what service users do and why. *BMC Psychiatry, 13.*

Giesen-Bloo, J., van Dyck, R., Spinhoven, P., van Tilburg, W., Dirksen, C., van Asselt, T., Kremers, I., Nadort, M., & Arntz, A. (2006). Outpatient psychotherapy for borderline personality disorder: Randomized trial of schema-focused therapy vs transference-focused psychotherapy. *Archives of General Psychiatry, 63*(6), 649–658. https://doi.org/10.1001/archpsyc.63.6.649

Gigante, A. D., Lafer, B., & Yatham, L. N. (2012). Long-acting injectable antipsychotics for the maintenance treatment of bipolar disorder. *CNS Drugs, 26*(5), 403–420. https://doi.org/10.2165/11631310-000000000-00000

Gilbertson, M. W., Shenton, M. E., Ciszewski, A., Kasai, K., Lasko, N. B., Orr, S. P., & Pitman, R. K. (2002). Smaller hippocampal volume predicts pathologic vulnerability to psychological trauma. *Nature Neuroscience, 5*(11), 1242–1247. https://doi.org/10.1038/nn958

Gill, J. H., DeWitt, J. R., & Nielson, H. C. (1986). Dissociation of maze performance in the original learning state following drugged-state feeding. *Physiological Psychology, 14*(3–4), 104–110.

Gilleland, J., Suveg, C., Jacob, M. L., & Thomassin, K. (2009). Understanding the medically unexplained: Emotional and familial influences on children's somatic functioning. *Child: Care, Health and Development, 35*(3), 383–390. https://doi.org/10.1111/j.1365-2214.2009.00950.x

Gillespie, N. A., Zhu, G., Heath, A. C., Hickie, I. B., & Martin, N. G. (2000). The genetic aetiology of somatic distress. *Psychological Medicine, 30*(5), 1051–1061. https://doi.org/10.1017/S0033291799002640

Gillies, D., Sinn, J. K., Lad, S. S., Leach, M. J., & Ross, M. J. (2012). Polyunsaturated fatty acids (PUFA) for attention deficit hyperactivity disorder (ADHD) in children and adolescents. *Cochrane Database of Systematic Reviews, 2012*(7), CD007986. https://doi.org/10.1002/14651858.CD007986.pub2

Gilmore, K. (2000). A psychoanalytic perspective on attention-deficit/hyperactivity disorder. *Journal of the American Psychoanalytic Association, 48*(4), 1259–1293. https://doi.org/10.1177/00030651000480040901

Gilmore, K. (2002). Diagnosis, dynamics, and development: Considerations in the psychoanalytic assessment of children with AD/HD. *Psychoanalytic Inquiry, 22*(3), 372–390. https://doi.org/10.1080/07351692209348993

Gilmore, R., Beezhold, J., Selwyn, V., Howard, R., Bartolome, I., & Henderson, N. (2022). Is TikTok increasing the number of self-diagnoses of ADHD in young people? *European Psychiatry, 65*(Suppl. 1), S571. https://doi.org/10.1192/j.eurpsy.2022.1463

Ginsberg, D. L. (2006). Bupropion SR for nicotine-craving pica in a developmentally disabled adult. *Primary Psychiatry, 13*(12), 27–28.

Giorgi, A. (1970). *Psychology as a human science: A phenomenologically based approach.* Harper & Row.

Giorgi, A. (1997). The theory, practice, and evaluation of the phenomenological method as a qualitative research procedure. *Journal of Phenomenological Psychology, 28*(2), 235–260. https://doi.org/10.1163/156916297X00103

Gipps, R. G. T. (2013). Cognitive behavior therapy: A philosophical appraisal. In K. W. M. Fulford, M. Davies, R. G. T. Gipps, G. Graham, J. Z. Sadler, G. Stanghellini, & T. Thornton (Eds.), *The Oxford handbook of philosophy and psychiatry* (pp. 1245–1263). Oxford University Press.

Gipps, R. G. T. (2017). Does the cognitive therapy of depression rest on a mistake? *BJPsych Bulletin, 41*(5), 267–271. https://doi.org/10.1192/pb.bp.115.052936

Gitlin, M. (2016). Lithium side effects and toxicity: Prevalence and management strategies. *International Journal of Bipolar Disorders, 4,* 27. https://doi.org/10.1186/s40345-016-0068-y

Gjerde, L. C., Czajkowski, N., Røysamb, E., Ørstavik, R. E., Knudsen, G. P., Østby, K., Torgersen, S., Myers, J., Kendler, K. S., & Reichborn-Kjennerud, T. (2012). The heritability of avoidant and dependent personality disorder assessed by personal interview and questionnaire. *Acta Psychiatrica Scandinavica, 126*(6), 448–457. https://doi.org/10.1111/j.1600-0447.2012.01862.x

Glaser, G. (2015). The irrationality of Alcoholics Anonymous. In *The Atlantic.* http://www.theatlantic.com/magazine/archive/2015/04/the-irrationality-of-alcoholics-anonymous/386255/

Glaser, R. (2005). Stress-associated immune dysregulation and its importance for human health: A personal history of psychoneuroimmunology. *Brain, Behavior, and Immunity, 19*(1), 3–11. https://doi.org/10.1016/j.bbi.2004.06.003

Glasersfeld, E. von. (1984). An introduction to radical constructivism. In P. Watzlawick (Ed.), *The invented reality: How do we know what we believe we know? Contributions to constructivism* (pp. 17–40). Norton.

Glass, D. J. (2012). Evolutionary clinical psychology, broadly construed: Perspectives on obsessive-compulsive disorder. *Journal of Social, Evolutionary, and Cultural Psychology, 6*(3), 292–308. https://doi.org/10.1037/h0099250

Glatt, S. J. (2008). Genetics. In K. T. Mueser & D. V. Jeste (Eds.), *Clinical handbook of schizophrenia* (pp. 55–64). Guilford Press.

Glazener, C. M. A., & Evans, J. H. C. (2002). Desmopressin for nocturnal enuresis in children. *Cochrane Database of Systematic Reviews, 2002*(3), Article CD002112. https://doi.org/10.1002/14651858.CD002112

Glazener, C. M. A., Evans, J. H. C., & Peto, R. E. (2004). Treating nocturnal enuresis in children: Review of evidence. *Journal of Wound, Ostomy, and Continence Nursing, 31*(4), 223–234. https://doi.org/10.1097/00152192-200407000-00013

Gleason, J., Boehmler, W., Fossi, A., Blonsky, H., Alexander, J., & Stephens, M. (2021). The devastating impact of Covid-19 on individuals with intellectual disabilities in the United States. *NEJM Catalyst Innovations in Care Delivery.* https://doi.org/10.1056/CAT.21.0051

Gleaves, D. H. (1996). The sociocognitive model of dissociative identity disorder: A reexamination of the evidence. *Psychological Bulletin, 120*(1), 42–59. https://doi.org/10.1037/0033-2909.120.1.42

Gleaves, D. H., May, M. C., & Cardeña, E. (2001). An examination of the diagnostic validity of dissociative identity disorder. *Clinical Psychology Review, 21*(4), 577–608. https://doi.org/10.1016/S0272-7358(99)00073-2

Glenn, A. L., Kurzban, R., & Raine, A. (2011). Evolutionary theory and psychopathy. *Aggression and Violent Behavior, 16*(5), 371–380. https://doi.org/10.1016/j.avb.2011.03.009

Glicklich, L. B. (1951). Special reviews: An historical account of enuresis. *Pediatrics, 8*(6), 859–876. https://doi.org/10.1542/peds.8.6.859

Glisenti, K., Strodl, E., King, R., & Greenberg, L. (2021). The feasibility of emotion-focused therapy for binge-eating disorder: A pilot randomised wait-list control trial. *Journal of Eating Disorders, 9*(1), 2. https://doi.org/10.1186/s40337-020-00358-5

Gloor, F. T., & Walitza, S. (2016). Tic disorders and Tourette syndrome: Current concepts of etiology and treatment in children and adolescents. *Neuropediatrics, 47*(2), 84–96. https://doi.org/10.1055/s-0035-1570492

Glue, P., Medlicott, N. J., Harland, S., Neehoff, S., Anderson-Fahey, B., Le Nedelec, M., Gray, A., & McNaughton, N. (2017). Ketamine's dose-related effects on anxiety symptoms in patients with treatment refractory anxiety disorders. *Journal of Psychopharmacology, 31*(10), 1302–1305. https://doi.org/10.1177/0269881117705089

Glue, P., Neehoff, S. M., Medlicott, N. J., Gray, A., Kibby, G., & McNaughton, N. (2018). Safety and efficacy

of maintenance ketamine treatment in patients with treatment-refractory generalised anxiety and social anxiety disorders. *Journal of Psychopharmacology (Oxford, England), 32*(6), 663–667. https://doi.org/10.1177/0269881118762073

Gnanavel, S., Sharma, P., Kaushal, P., & Hussain, S. (2019). Attention deficit hyperactivity disorder and comorbidity: A review of literature. *World Journal of Clinical Cases, 7*(17), 2420–2426. https://doi.org/10.12998/wjcc.v7.i17.2420

Gobbi, G., Atkin, T., Zytynski, T., Wang, S., Askari, S., Boruff, J., Ware, M., Marmorstein, N., Cipriani, A., Dendukuri, N., & Mayo, N. (2019). Association of cannabis use in adolescence and risk of depression, anxiety, and suicidality in young adulthood: A systematic review and meta-analysis. *JAMA Psychiatry, 76*(4), 426–434. https://doi.org/10.1001/jamapsychiatry.2018.4500

Goday, P. S., Huh, S. Y., Silverman, A., Lukens, C. T., Dodrill, P., Cohen, S. S., Delaney, A. L., Feuling, M. B., Noel, R. J., Gisel, E., Kenzer, A., Kessler, D. B., Kraus de Camargo, O., Browne, J., & Phalen, J. A. (2019). Pediatric feeding disorder. *Journal of Pediatric Gastroenterology and Nutrition, 68*(1), 124–129. https://doi.org/10.1097/MPG.0000000000002188

Godlee, F., Smith, J., & Marcovitch, H. (2011). Wakefield's article linking MMR vaccine and autism was fraudulent. *BMJ (Clinical Research Ed.), 342*, c7452–c7452. https://doi.org/10.1136/bmj.c7452

Goertz, R. B., Wanat, M. J., Gomez, J. A., Brown, Z. J., Phillips, P. E., & Paladini, C. A. (2015). Cocaine increases dopaminergic neuron and motor activity via midbrain α1 adrenergic signaling. *Neuropsychopharmacology, 40*(5), Article 5. https://doi.org/10.1038/npp.2014.296

Gold, A. K., & Kinrys, G. (2019). Treating circadian rhythm disruption in bipolar disorder. *Current Psychiatry Reports, 21*(3), 14. https://doi.org/10.1007/s11920-019-1001-8

Gold, M. S., Cadet, J. L., Baron, D., Badgaiyan, R. D., & Blum, K. (2020). Calvin Klein (CK) designer cocktail, new "Speedball" is the "grimm [sic] reaper": Brain dopaminergic surge a potential death sentence. *Journal of Systems and Integrative Neuroscience, 7*, 10.15761/JSIN.1000227. https://doi.org/10.15761/JSIN.1000227

Gold, S. M., Köhler-Forsberg, O., Moss-Morris, R., Mehnert, A., Miranda, J. J., Bullinger, M., Steptoe, A., Whooley, M. A., & Otte, C. (2020). Comorbid depression in medical diseases. *Nature Reviews Disease Primers, 6*(1), 69. https://doi.org/10.1038/s41572-020-0200-2

Goldberg, J. S., Bell, C. E., & Pollard, D. A. (2014). Revisiting the monoamine hypothesis of depression: A new perspective. *Perspectives in Medicinal Chemistry, 6*, 1–8. https://doi.org/10.4137/PMC.S11375

Goldberg, L. R. (1993). The structure of phenotypic personality traits. *American Psychologist, 48*(1), 26–34. https://doi.org/10.1037/0003-066X.48.1.26

Goldberg, S. B., Lam, S. U., Simonsson, O., Torous, J., & Sun, S. (2022). Mobile phone-based interventions for mental health: A systematic meta-review of 14 meta-analyses of randomized controlled trials. *PLOS Digital Health, 1*(1), e0000002. https://doi.org/10.1371/journal.pdig.0000002

Goldberg, S. B., Pace, B. T., Nicholas, C. R., Raison, C. L., & Hutson, P. R. (2020). The experimental effects of psilocybin on symptoms of anxiety and depression: A meta-analysis. *Psychiatry Research, 284*, 112749. https://doi.org/10.1016/j.psychres.2020.112749

Goldblatt, M. J. (2014). Psychodynamics of suicide. In M. K. Nock (Ed.), *The Oxford handbook of suicide and self-injury* (pp. 255–264). Oxford University Press. https://doi.org/10.1093/oxfordhb/9780195388565.013.0014

Goldhill, S. (2015). The imperialism of historical arrogance: Where is the past in the DSM's idea of sexuality? *Archives of Sexual Behavior, 44*(5), 1099–1108. https://doi.org/10.1007/s10508-015-0556-7

Goldman, D. (2020). Predicting suicide. *The American Journal of Psychiatry, 177*(10), 881–883. MEDLINE with Full Text. https://doi.org/10.1176/appi.ajp.2020.20071138

Goldman, R. N., & Greenberg, L. S. (2015a). *Case formulation in emotion-focused psychotherapy: Co-creating clinical maps for change.* American Psychological Association.

Goldman, R. N., & Greenberg, L. S. (2015b). Fundamentals of emotion-focused therapy. In R. Goldman & L. S. Greenberg (Eds.), *Case formulation in emotion-focused therapy: Co-creating clinical maps for change* (pp. 21–42). American Psychological Association.

Goldsmith, L. P., Lewis, S. W., Dunn, G., & Bentall, R. P. (2015). Psychological treatments for early psychosis can be beneficial or harmful, depending on the therapeutic alliance: An instrumental variable analysis. *Psychological Medicine, 45*(11), 2365–2373. https://doi.org/10.1017/S003329171500032X

Goldstein, E. G. (1990). *Borderline disorders: Clinical models and techniques.* Guilford Press.

Goldstein, G. (2017). Halstead Reitan Battery: An opinionated history. In W. B. Barr & L. A. Bieliauskas (Eds.), *The Oxford handbook of history of clinical neuropsychology.* https://doi.org/10.1093/oxfordhb/9780199765683.013.34

Goldstein, J. L., & Godemont, M. M. L. (2003). The legend and lessons of Geel, Belgium: A 1500-year-old legend, a 21st-century model. *Community Mental Health Journal, 39*(5), 441–458. https://doi.org/10.1023/A:1025813003347

Goldstein, M., Peters, L., Thornton, C. E., & Touyz, S. W. (2014). The treatment of perfectionism within the eating disorders: A pilot study. *European Eating Disorders Review, 22*(3), 217–221. https://doi.org/10.1002/erv.2281

Golla, J. A., Larson, L. A., Anderson, C. F., Lucas, A. R., Wilson, W. R., & Tomasi, T. B. (1981). An immunological assessment of patients with anorexia nervosa. *The American Journal of Clinical Nutrition, 34*(12), 2756–2762. https://doi.org/10.1093/ajcn/34.12.2756

Gollaher, D. (1995). *Voice for the mad: The life of Dorothea Dix.* The Free Press.

Gonçalves, J., Violante, I. R., Sereno, J., Leitão, R. A., Cai, Y., Abrunhosa, A., Silva, A. P., Silva, A. J., & Castelo-Branco, M. (2017). Testing the excitation/inhibition imbalance hypothesis in a mouse model of the autism spectrum disorder: In vivo neurospectroscopy and molecular evidence for regional phenotypes. *Molecular Autism, 8*(1), 47. https://doi.org/10.1186/s13229-017-0166-4

Gonon, F. (2009). The dopaminergic hypothesis of attention-deficit/hyperactivity disorder needs re-examining. *Trends in Neurosciences, 32*(1), 2–8. https://doi.org/10.1016/j.tins.2008.09.010

Gonon, F., Bezard, E., & Boraud, T. (2011). What should be said to the lay public regarding ADHD etiology. *American Journal of Medical Genetics Part B: Neuropsychiatric Genetics, 156*(8), 989–991. https://doi.org/10.1002/ajmg.b.31236

Gonsalves, L., Cottler-Casanova, S., VanTreeck, K., & Say, L. (2020). Results of a World Health Organization scoping of sexual dysfunction–related guidelines: What exists and what is needed. *The Journal of Sexual Medicine, 17*(12), 2518–2521. https://doi.org/10.1016/j.jsxm.2020.08.022

Gonschor, J., Eisma, M. C., Barke, A., & Doering, B. K. (2020). Public stigma towards prolonged grief disorder: Does diagnostic labeling matter? *PLoS ONE, 15*(9), e0237021. https://doi.org/10.1371/journal.pone.0237021

Gontkovsky, S. T. (2011). Prevalence of enuresis in a community sample of children and adolescents referred for outpatient clinical psychological evaluation: Psychiatric comorbidities and association with intellectual functioning. *Journal of Child and Adolescent Mental Health, 23*(1), 53–58. https://doi.org/10.2989/17280583.2011.594253

González-Castro, T. B., Hernandez-Diaz, Y., Juárez-Rojop, I. E., López-Narváez, L., Tovilla-Zárate, C. A., Rodriguez-Perez, J. M., & Sánchez-de la Cruz, J. P. (2017). The role of the Cys23Ser (rs6318) polymorphism of the HTR2C gene in suicidal behavior: Systematic review and meta-analysis. *Psychiatric Genetics*, 27(6), 199–209. https://doi.org/10.1097/YPG.0000000000000184

Goodheart, C. D. (2014). *A primer for ICD-10-CM users: Psychological and behavioral conditions*. American Psychological Association.

Goodman, A. (1990). Addiction: Definition and implications. *British Journal of Addiction*, 85(11), 1403–1408. https://doi.org/10.1111/j.1360-0443.1990.tb01620.x

Goodman, G. (2013). Encopresis happens: Theoretical and treatment considerations from an attachment perspective. *Psychoanalytic Psychology*, 30(3), 438–455. https://doi.org/10.1037/a0030894

Goodman, L. A., Liang, B., Helms, J. E., Latta, R. E., Sparks, E., & Weintraub, S. R. (2004). Training counseling psychologists as social justice agents: Feminist and multicultural principles in action. *The Counseling Psychologist*, 32, 793–837. https://doi.org/10.1177/0011000004268802

Goodman, W. K., Grice, D. E., Lapidus, K. A. B., & Coffey, B. J. (2014). Obsessive-compulsive disorder. *The Psychiatric Clinics of North America*, 37(3), 257–267. https://doi.org/10.1016/j.psc.2014.06.004

Goodman, W. K., Storch, E. A., & Sheth, S. A. (2021). Harmonizing the neurobiology and treatment of obsessive-compulsive disorder. *American Journal of Psychiatry*, 178(1), 17–29. https://doi.org/10.1176/appi.ajp.2020.20111601

Goodwin, G. M., Aaronson, S. T., Alvarez, O., Arden, P. C., Baker, A., Bennett, J. C., Bird, C., Blom, R. E., Brennan, C., Brusch, D., Burke, L., Campbell-Coker, K., Carhart-Harris, R., Cattell, J., Daniel, A., DeBattista, C., Dunlop, B. W., Eisen, K., Feifel, D., … Malievskaia, E. (2022). Single-dose psilocybin for a treatment-resistant episode of major depression. *New England Journal of Medicine*, 387(18), 1637–1648. https://doi.org/10.1056/NEJMoa2206443

Goodwin, R. D., Moeller, S. J., Zhu, J., Yarden, J., Ganzhorn, S., & Williams, J. M. (2021). The potential role of cocaine and heroin co-use in the opioid epidemic in the United States. *Addictive Behaviors*, 113, 106680. https://doi.org/10.1016/j.addbeh.2020.106680

Goracci, A., Casamassima, F., Iovieno, N., Di Volo, S., Benbow, J., Bolognesi, S., & Fagiolini, A. (2015). Binge eating disorder: From clinical research to clinical practice. *Journal of Addiction Medicine*, 9(1), 20–24. https://doi.org/10.1097/ADM.0000000000000085

Gordon, H. (2008). Editorial: The treatment of paraphilias: An historical perspective. *Criminal Behaviour and Mental Health*, 18(2), 79–87. https://doi.org/10.1002/cbm.687

Gordon, R. A. (2010). Drugs don't talk: Do medication and biological psychiatry contribute to silencing the self? In D. C. Jack & A. Ali (Eds.), *Silencing the self across cultures: Depression and gender in the social world* (pp. 47–72). Oxford University Press.

Gordon, R. M. (2009). Reactions to the *Psychodynamic diagnostic manual* (PDM) by psychodynamic, CBT and other non-psychodynamic psychologists. *Issues in Psychoanalytic Psychology*, 31(1), 53–59.

Gordon, R. M. (2019). A concurrent validity study of the PDM-2 personality syndromes. *Current Psychology: A Journal for Diverse Perspectives on Diverse Psychological Issues*, 38(3), 698–704. https://doi.org/10.1007/s12144-017-9644-2

Gordon, R. M., & Bornstein, R. F. (2018). Construct validity of the psychodiagnostic chart: A transdiagnostic measure of personality organization, personality syndromes, mental functioning, and symptomatology. *Psychoanalytic Psychology*, 35(2), 280–288. https://doi.org/10.1037/pap0000142

Gorman, D. A., Gardner, D. M., Murphy, A. L., Feldman, M., Bélanger, S. A., Steele, M. M., Boylan, K., Cochrane-Brink, K., Goldade, R., Soper, P. R., Ustina,

J., & Pringsheim, T. (2015). Canadian guidelines on pharmacotherapy for disruptive and aggressive behaviour in children and adolescents with attention-deficit hyperactivity disorder, oppositional defiant disorder, or conduct disorder. *The Canadian Journal of Psychiatry*, 60(2), 62–76. https://doi.org/10.1177/070674371506000204

Gornall, J. (2013). DSM-5: A fatal diagnosis? *BMJ*, 346, 18–20. https://doi.org/10.1136/bmj.f3256

Gorshkalova, O., & Munakomi, S. (2022). Duty to warn. In *StatPearls [Internet]*. StatPearls Publishing. https://www.ncbi.nlm.nih.gov/books/NBK542236/

Gosselin, J. T., & Bombardier, M. (2020a). Gender dysphoria. In J. E. Maddux & B. A. Winstead (Eds.), *Psychopathology: Foundations for a contemporary understanding* (5th ed., pp. 521–535). Routledge.

Gosselin, J. T., & Bombardier, M. (2020b). Sexual dysfunctions and paraphilic disorders. In J. E. Maddux & B. A. Winstead (Eds.), *Psychopathology: Foundations for a contemporary understanding* (5th ed., pp. 305–339). Routledge.

Gotlib, I. H., & LeMoult, J. (2014). The "ins" and "outs" of the depressive disorders section of DSM-5. *Clinical Psychology: Science and Practice*, 21(3), 193–207. https://doi.org/10.1111/cpsp.12072

Goto, R., Fujio, M., Matsuda, N., Fujiwara, M., Nobuyoshi, M., Nonaka, M., Kono, T., Kojima, M., Skokauskas, N., & Kano, Y. (2019). The effects of comorbid Tourette symptoms on distress caused by compulsive-like behavior in very young children: A cross-sectional study. *Child and Adolescent Psychiatry and Mental Health*, 13(1), 28. https://doi.org/10.1186/s13034-019-0290-3

Gottdiener, W. H., & Suh, J. J. (2015). Substance use disorders. In P. Luyten, L. C. Mayes, P. Fonagy, M. Target, & S. J. Blatt (Eds.), *Handbook of psychodynamic approaches to psychopathology* (pp. 216–233). Guilford Press.

Gottesman, I. I. (1991). *Schizophrenia genesis: The origins of madness*. Freeman.

Gottesman, I. I., Laursen, T. M., Bertelsen, A., & Mortensen, P. B. (2010). Severe mental disorders in offspring with 2 psychiatrically ill parents. *Archives of General Psychiatry*, 67(3), 252–257. https://doi.org/10.1001/archgenpsychiatry.2010.1

Gottlieb, J. F., Benedetti, F., Geoffroy, P. A., Henriksen, T. E. G., Lam, R. W., Murray, G., Phelps, J., Sit, D., Swartz, H. A., Crowe, M., Etain, B., Frank, E., Goel, N., Haarman, B. C. M., Inder, M., Kallestad, H., Jae Kim, S., Martiny, K., Meesters, Y., … Chen, S. (2019). The chronotherapeutic treatment of bipolar disorders: A systematic review and practice recommendations from the ISBD task force on chronotherapy and chronobiology. *Bipolar Disorders*, 21(8), 741–773. https://doi.org/10.1111/bdi.12847

Gould, M. S., Chowdhury, S., Lake, A. M., Galfalvy, H., Kleinman, M., Kuchuk, M., & McKeon, R. (2021). National Suicide Prevention Lifeline crisis chat interventions: Evaluation of chatters' perceptions of effectiveness. *Suicide and Life-Threatening Behavior*, 51(6), 1126–1137. https://doi.org/10.1111/sltb.12795

Gowing, L., Ali, R., White, J. M., & Mbewe, D. (2017). Buprenorphine for managing opioid withdrawal. *Cochrane Database of Systematic Reviews*, 2017(2), Article CD002025. https://doi.org/10.1002/14651858.CD002025.pub5

Graf, H., Malejko, K., Metzger, C. D., Walter, M., Grön, G., & Abler, B. (2019). Serotonergic, dopaminergic, and noradrenergic modulation of erotic stimulus processing in the male human brain. *Journal of Clinical Medicine*, 8(3), 363. https://doi.org/10.3390/jcm8030363

Graham, C. A. (2010). The DSM diagnostic criteria for female sexual arousal disorder. *Archives of Sexual Behavior*, 39(2), 240–255. https://doi.org/10.1007/s10508-009-9535-1

Graham, J. R. (2011). *MMPI-2: Assessing personality and psychopathology*. Oxford.

Grambal, A., Prasko, J., Kamaradova, D., Latalova, K., Holubova, M., Marackova, M., Ociskova, M., & Slepecky, M. (2016). Self-stigma in borderline personality disorder—Cross-sectional comparison with schizophrenia spectrum disorder, major depressive disorder, and anxiety disorders. *Neuropsychiatric Disease and Treatment*, 12. https://doi.org/10.2147/NDT.S114671

Granata, A., Tirabassi, G., Pugni, V., Arnaldi, G., Boscaro, M., Carani, C., & Balercia, G. (2013). Sexual dysfunctions in men affected by autoimmune Addison's disease before and after short-term gluco- and mineralocorticoid replacement therapy. *Journal of Sexual Medicine*, 10(8), 2036–2043. https://doi.org/10.1111/j.1743-6109.2012.02673.x

Grande, G., Romppel, M., & Barth, J. (2012). Association between type D personality and prognosis in patients with cardiovascular diseases: A systematic review and meta-analysis. *Annals of Behavioral Medicine*, 43(3), 299–310. https://doi.org/10.1007/s12160-011-9339-0

Grandner, M. A. (2017). Sleep, health, and society. *Sleep Medicine Clinics*, 12(1), 1–22. https://doi.org/10.1016/j.jsmc.2016.10.012

Grandner, M. A., Williams, N. J., Knutson, K. L., Roberts, D., & Jean-Louis, G. (2016). Sleep disparity, race/ethnicity, and socioeconomic position. *Sleep Medicine*, 18, 7–18. https://doi.org/10.1016/j.sleep.2015.01.020

Grando, S. A. (2014). Connections of nicotine to cancer. *Nature Reviews Cancer*, 14(6), Article 6. https://doi.org/10.1038/nrc3725

Granek, L. (2017). Is grief a disease? The medicalization of grief by the psy-disciplines in the twenty-first century. In N. Thompson & G. R. Cox (Eds.), *Handbook of the sociology of death, grief, and bereavement: A guide to theory and practice* (pp. 264–277). Taylor & Francis.

Granholm, E., Twamley, E. W., Mahmood, Z., Keller, A. V., Lykins, H. C., Parrish, E. M., Thomas, M. L., Perivoliotis, D., & Holden, J. L. (2022). Integrated cognitive-behavioral social skills training and compensatory cognitive training for negative symptoms of psychosis: Effects in a pilot randomized controlled trial. *Schizophrenia Bulletin*, 48(2), 359–370. https://doi.org/10.1093/schbul/sbab126

Grant, J. E., Potenza, M. N., Weinstein, A., & Gorelick, D. A. (2010). Introduction to behavioral addictions. *The American Journal of Drug and Alcohol Abuse*, 36(5), 233–241. https://doi.org/10.3109/00952990.2010.491884

Gravelin, C. R., Biernat, M., & Bucher, C. E. (2019). Blaming the victim of acquaintance rape: Individual, situational, and sociocultural factors. *Frontiers in Psychology*, 9, Article 2422. https://www.doi.org/10.3389/fpsyg.2018.02422

Gravelle, T. B., Phillips, J. B., Reifler, J., & Scotto, T. J. (2022). Estimating the size of "anti-vax" and vaccine hesitant populations in the US, UK, and Canada: Comparative latent class modeling of vaccine attitudes. *Human Vaccines & Immunotherapeutics*, 18(1), Article e2008214. https://doi.org/10.1080/21645515.2021.2008214

Gray, C., Calderbank, A., Adewusi, J., Hughes, R., & Reuber, M. (2020). Symptoms of posttraumatic stress disorder in patients with functional neurological symptom disorder. *Journal of Psychosomatic Research*, 129, 109907. https://doi.org/10.1016/j.jpsychores.2019.109907

Green, M. F. (2001). *Schizophrenia revealed: From neurons to social interactions*. Norton.

Greenberg, D. F. (1988). *The construction of homosexuality*. The University of Chicago Press.

Greenberg, D. M., & Baron-Cohen, S. (2020). Empathizing-systemizing theory: Past, present, and future. In V. Zeigler-Hill & T. K. Shackelford (Eds.), *Encyclopedia of personality and individual differences* (pp. 1348–1352). Springer International Publishing. https://doi.org/10.1007/978-3-319-24612-3_893

Greenberg, D. M., Warrier, V., Allison, C., & Baron-Cohen, S. (2018). Testing the empathizing–systemizing theory of sex differences and the Extreme Male Brain Theory of autism in half a million people. *Proceedings of the National Academy of Sciences*, 115(48), 12152–12157. https://doi.org/10.1073/pnas.1811032115

Greenberg, G. (2013). *The book of woe: The DSM and the unmaking of psychiatry*. Plume.

Greenberg, J. (2006). Losing sleep over organizational injustice: Attenuating insomniac reactions to underpayment inequity with supervisory training in interactional justice. *Journal of Applied Psychology*, 91(1), 58–69. https://doi.org/10.1037/0021-9010.91.1.58

Greenberg, L. S., & Goldman, R. (2006). Case formulation in emotion-focused therapy. In T. D. Eels (Ed.), *Handbook of psychotherapy case formulation* (pp. 379–411). Guilford.

Greenberg, L. S., & Watson, J. C. (2006). *Emotion-focused therapy for depression*. American Psychological Association.

Greenberg, M. S., Tanev, K., Marin, M.-F., & Pitman, R. K. (2014). Stress, PTSD, and dementia. *Alzheimer's & Dementia*, 10(3), S155–S165. https://doi.org/10.1016/j.jalz.2014.04.008

Greene, A., Ostlie, E., Kagen, R., & Davis, M. (2016). The process of integrating practices: The juvenile drug court and reclaiming futures logic model. *Drug Court Review*, 10(1), 31–59.

Greene, D. (2021). Revisiting 12-step approaches: An evidence-based perspective. In W. M. Meil (Ed.), *Addictions: Diagnosis and treatment*. IntechOpen. https://doi.org/10.5772/intechopen.95985

Greenman, P. S., & Johnson, S. M. (2012). United we stand: Emotionally focused therapy for couples in the treatment of posttraumatic stress disorder. *Journal of Clinical Psychology*, 68(5), 561–569. https://doi.org/10.1002/jclp.21853

Greeven, A., van Balkom, A. J. L. M., van der Leeden, R., Merkelbach, J. W., van den Heuvel, O. A., & Spinhoven, P. (2009). Cognitive behavioral therapy versus paroxetine in the treatment of hypochondriasis: An 18-month naturalistic follow-up. *Journal of Behavior Therapy and Experimental Psychiatry*, 40(3), 487–496. https://doi.org/10.1016/j.jbtep.2009.06.005

Gregory, R. J. (2019). Dynamic deconstructive psychotherapy for substance use disorders co-occurring with personality disorders. In D. Kealy & J. S. Ogrodniczuk (Eds.), *Contemporary psychodynamic psychotherapy: Evolving clinical practice* (pp. 163–175). Academic Press. https://doi.org/10.1016/B978-0-12-813373-6.00011-8

Greiner, T., Haack, B., Toto, S., Bleich, S., Grohmann, R., Faltraco, F., Heinze, M., & Schneider, M. (2020). Pharmacotherapy of psychiatric inpatients with adjustment disorder: Current status and changes between 2000 and 2016. *European Archives of Psychiatry and Clinical Neuroscience*, 270(1), 107–117. https://doi.org/10.1007/s00406-019-01058-1

Gressier, F., Rotenberg, S., Cazas, O., & Hardy, P. (2015). Postpartum electroconvulsive therapy: A systematic review and case report. *General Hospital Psychiatry*, 37(4), 310–314. https://doi.org/10.1016/j.genhosppsych.2015.04.009

Griebel, G., & Holmes, A. (2013). 50 years of hurdles and hope in anxiolytic drug discovery. *Nature Reviews. Drug Discovery*, 12(9), 667–687. https://doi.org/10.1038/nrd4075

Griffiths, A. (2019, January). Reflections on using the Power Threat Meaning Framework in peer-led systems. *Clinical Psychology Forum*, 313, 25–32.

Griffiths, C., Williamson, H., Zucchelli, F., Paraskeva, N., & Moss, T. (2018). A systematic review of the effectiveness of acceptance and commitment therapy (ACT) for body image dissatisfaction and weight self-stigma in adults. *Journal of Contemporary Psychotherapy*, 48(4), 189–204. https://doi.org/10.1007/s10879-018-9384-0

Griffiths, M. D., Kuss, D. J., & Demetrovics, Z. (2014). Social networking addiction. In N. Petry (Ed.), *Behavioral addictions: DSM-5® and beyond* (pp. 119–141). Elsevier. https://doi.org/10.1016/B978-0-12-407724-9.00006-9

Griffiths, S., Mond, J. M., Murray, S. B., & Touyz, S. (2014). Young peoples' stigmatizing attitudes and beliefs about anorexia nervosa and muscle dysmorphia. *International Journal of Eating Disorders*, 47(2), 189–195. https://doi.org/10.1002/eat.22220

Grimm, O., Kranz, T. M., & Reif, A. (2020). Genetics of ADHD: What should the clinician know? *Current Psychiatry Reports*, 22(4), 18. https://doi.org/10.1007/s11920-020-1141-x

Grinberg, H., & Zahavi, A. (2020). Becoming the little prince: Autism within a psychoanalytic environment. *Psychoanalytic Inquiry*, 40(7), 529–535. https://doi.org/10.1080/07351690.2020.1810527

Grob, G. N. (1994). *The mad among us: A history of the care of America's mentally ill*. The Free Press.

Groesz, L. M., Levine, M. P., & Murnen, S. K. (2002). The effect of experimental presentation of thin media images on body satisfaction: A meta-analytic review. *International Journal of Eating Disorders*, 31(1), 1–16. https://doi.org/10.1002/eat.10005

Gropalis, M., Bleichhardt, G., Hiller, W., & Witthöft, M. (2013). Specificity and modifiability of cognitive biases in hypochondriasis. *Journal of Consulting and Clinical Psychology*, 81(3), 558–565. https://doi.org/10.1037/a0028493

Groß, C., Serrallach, B. L., Möhler, E., Pousson, J. E., Schneider, P., Christiner, M., & Bernhofs, V. (2022). Musical performance in adolescents with ADHD, ADD and dyslexia—Behavioral and neurophysiological aspects. *Brain Sciences*, 12(2), Article 2. https://doi.org/10.3390/brainsci12020127

Grossman, P., Niemann, L., Schmidt, S., & Walach, H. (2004). Mindfulness-based stress reduction and health benefits: A meta-analysis. *Journal of Psychosomatic Research*, 57(1), 35–43. https://doi.org/10.1016/S0022-3999(03)00573-7

Grover, K. W., Zvolensky, M. J., Bonn-Miller, M. O., Kosiba, J., & Hogan, J. (2013). Marijuana use and abuse. In P. M. Miller, S. A. Ball, M. E. Bates, A. W. Blume, K. M. Kampman, D. J. Kavanagh, M. E. Larimer, N. M. Petry, & P. De Witte (Eds.), *Comprehensive addictive behaviors and disorders: Vol. 1. Principles of addiction* (pp. 679–687). Elsevier Academic Press.

Grover, S., & Ghosh, A. (2018). Delirium tremens: Assessment and management. *Journal of Clinical and Experimental Hepatology*, 8(4), 460–470. https://doi.org/10.1016/j.jceh.2018.04.012

Grover, S., Sahoo, S., Rabha, A., & Koirala, R. (2019). ECT in schizophrenia: A review of the evidence. *Acta Neuropsychiatrica*, 31(3), 115–127. https://doi.org/10.1017/neu.2018.32

Grubaugh, A. L. (2014). Trauma and stressor-related disorders: Posttraumatic stress disorder, acute stress disorder, and adjustment disorders. In D. C. Beidel, B. C. Frueh, & M. Hersen (Eds.), *Adult psychopathology and diagnosis* (7th ed., pp. 387–406). John Wiley & Sons.

Grünblatt, E., Hauser, T. U., & Walitza, S. (2014). Imaging genetics in obsessive-compulsive disorder: Linking genetic variations to alterations in neuroimaging. *Progress In Neurobiology*, 121, 114–124. https://doi.org/10.1016/j.pneurobio.2014.07.003

Grzywacz, J. G., Almeida, D. M., Neupert, S. D., & Ettner, S. L. (2004). Socioeconomic status and health: A micro-level analysis of exposure and vulnerability to daily stressors. *Journal of Health and Social Behavior*, 45(1), 1–16. https://doi.org/10.1177/002214650404500101

Guang, Y., Lei, Z., Nan, X., Hui, L., Soufu, X., & Junting, X. (2014). Analysis of quantitative genetic characteristics of schizophrenia using combined allele frequency as a genetic marker. *Psychiatry Research*, 220(1–2), 722–722. https://doi.org/10.1016/j.psychres.2014.08.038

Guay, D. R. P. (2009). Drug treatment of paraphilic and nonparaphilic sexual disorders. *Clinical Therapeutics: The International Peer-Reviewed Journal of Drug Therapy*, 31(1), 1–31. https://doi.org/10.1016/j.clinthera.2009.01.009

Guenzel, N., & McChargue, D. (2022). Addiction relapse prevention. In *StatPearls [Internet]*. StatPearls Publishing. https://www.ncbi.nlm.nih.gov/books/NBK551500/

Guglielmo, R., Miskowiak, K. W., & Hasler, G. (2021). Evaluating endophenotypes for bipolar disorder. *International Journal of Bipolar Disorders*, 9(1), 17. https://doi.org/10.1186/s40345-021-00220-w

Guideline Development Panel for the Treatment of Depressive Disorders. (2019). *APA clinical practice guideline for the treatment of depression across three age cohorts* [Data set]. American Psychological Association. https://doi.org/10.1037/e505892019-001

Guillamón, A., Junqué, C., & Gómez-Gil, E. (2016). A review of the status of brain structure research in transsexualism. *Archives of Sexual Behavior*. https://doi.org/10.1007/s10508-016-0768-5

Guina, J., Rossetter, S. R., Derhodes, B. J., Nahhas, R. W., & Welton, R. S. (2015). Benzodiazepines for PTSD: A systematic review and meta-analysis. *Journal of Psychiatric Practice*, 21(4), 281–303. https://doi.org/10.1097/PRA.0000000000000091

Guisinger, S. (2003). Adapted to flee famine: Adding an evolutionary perspective on anorexia nervosa. *Psychological Review*, 110(4), 745–761. doi:10.1037/0033-295X.110.4.745

Gukasyan, N., Davis, A. K., Barrett, F. S., Cosimano, M. P., Sepeda, N. D., Johnson, M. W., & Griffiths, R. R. (2022). Efficacy and safety of psilocybin-assisted treatment for major depressive disorder: Prospective 12-month follow-up. *Journal of Psychopharmacology*, 36(2), 151–158. https://doi.org/10.1177/02698811211073759

Gull, W. W. (1954). Anorexia nervosa (apepsia hysterica, anorexia hysterica). *Bulletin of the Isaac Ray Medical Library*, 2, 173–181. (Original work published 1874.)

Gumber, S., & Stein, C. H. (2013). Consumer perspectives and mental health reform movements in the United States: 30 years of first-person accounts. *Psychiatric Rehabilitation Journal*, 36(3), 187–194. https://doi.org/10.1037/prj0000003

Gundogar, D., Demir, S. B., & Eren, I. (2003). Is pica in the spectrum of obsessive-compulsive disorders? *General Hospital Psychiatry*, 25(4), 293–294. https://doi.org/10.1016/S0163-8343(03)00039-2

Gunn, J. S., & Potter, B. (2015). *Borderline personality disorder: New perspectives on a stigmatizing and overused diagnosis*. Praeger.

Gunst, E. (2012). Experiential psychotherapy with sex offenders: Experiencing as a way to change, to live more fulfilling lives, to desist from offending. *Person-Centered and Experiential Psychotherapies*, 11(4), 321–334. https://doi.org/10.1080/14779757.2012.740324

Gunter, R. W., & Bodner, G. E. (2008). How eye movements affect unpleasant memories: Support for a working-memory account. *Behaviour Research and Therapy*, 46(8), 913–931. https://doi.org/10.1016/j.brat.2008.04.006

Guo, L., & Ash, J. (2020). Anxiety and attachment styles: A systematic review. *Advances in Social Science, Education and Humanities Research*, 466, 1005–1012. https://doi.org/10.2991/assehr.k.200826.207

Guo, L., Gu, L., Peng, Y., Gao, Y., Mei, L., Kang, Q., Chen, C., Hu, Y., Xu, W., & Chen, J. (2022). Online media exposure and weight and fitness management app use correlate with disordered eating symptoms: Evidence from the mainland of China. *Journal of Eating Disorders*, 10(1), 58. https://doi.org/10.1186/s40337-022-00577-y

Gupta, N., & Singh, R. A. (2019). Role of materialism in influencing self-esteem. *Journal of Projective Psychology & Mental Health*, 26(1), 51–55.

Gupta, P. (2020). Efficacy of stress inoculation training on coping with pain and impact of tension type headache. *Indian Journal of Clinical Psychology*, 47(1), 64–72.

Gureje, O., & Reed, G. M. (2016). Bodily distress disorder in ICD-11: Problems and prospects. *World Psychiatry*, 15(3), 291–292. https://doi.org/10.1002/wps.20353

Gurley, J. R. (2017). *Essentials of Rorschach assessment: Comprehensive system and R-PAS (2016-52143-000)*. John Wiley & Sons.

Gurley, J. R., Sheehan, B. L., Piechowski, L. D., & Gray, J. (2014). The admissibility of the R-PAS in court. *Psychological Injury and Law, 7*(1), 9–17. https://doi.org/10.1007/s12207-014-9182-2

Gurok, M. G., Korucu, T., Kilic, M. C., Yildirim, H., & Atmaca, M. (2019). Hippocampus and amygdalar volumes in patients with obsessive-compulsive personality disorder. *Journal of Clinical Neuroscience, 64*, 259–263. https://doi.org/10.1016/j.jocn.2019.03.060

Gurven, M., von Rueden, C., Massenkoff, M., Kaplan, H., & Lero Vie, M. (2013). How universal is the Big Five? Testing the five-factor model of personality variation among forager–farmers in the Bolivian Amazon. *Journal of Personality and Social Psychology, 104*(2), 354–370. https://doi.org/10.1037/a0030841

Guss, J., Krause, R., & Sloshower, J. (2020). *Yale manual for psilocybin-assisted therapy of depression*. http://doi.org/10.31234/osf.io/u6v9y

Guttmann-Steinmetz, S., & Crowell, J. A. (2006). Attachment and externalizing disorders: A developmental psychopathology perspective. *Journal of the American Academy of Child & Adolescent Psychiatry, 45*(4), 440–451. https://doi.org/10.1097/01.chi.0000196422.42599.63

Guze, S. B., Cloninger, C. R., Martin, R. L., & Clayton, P. J. (1986). A follow-up and family study of Briquet's syndrome. *The British Journal of Psychiatry, 149*, 17–23. https://doi.org/10.1192/bjp.149.1.17

Guze, S. B., Woodruff, R. A., & Clayton, P. J. (1972). Sex, age, and the diagnosis of hysteria (Briquet's syndrome). *The American Journal of Psychiatry, 129*(6), 745–748. https://doi.org/10.1176/ajp.129.6.745

Gygi, J. T., Hagmann-von Arx, P., Schweizer, F., & Grob, A. (2017). The predictive validity of four intelligence tests for school grades: A small sample longitudinal study. *Frontiers in Psychology, 8*, Article 375. https://doi.org/10.3389/fpsyg.2017.00375

Hadaway, S. M., & Brue, A. W. (2016). *Practitioner's guide to functional behavioral assessment: Process, purpose, planning, and prevention*. Springer International Publishing.

Hadjistavropoulos, T., Craig, K. D., Duck, S., Cano, A., Goubert, L., Jackson, P. L., Mogil, J. S., Rainville, P., Sullivan, M. J. L., de C. Williams, A. C., Vervoort, T., & Fitzgerald, T. D. (2011). A biopsychosocial formulation of pain communication. *Psychological Bulletin, 137*(6), 910–939. https://doi.org/10.1037/a0023876

Haeffel, G. J., Jeronimus, B. F., Kaiser, B. N., Weaver, L. J., Soyster, P. D., Fisher, A. J., Vargas, I., Goodson, J. T., & Lu, W. (2022). Folk classification and factor rotations: Whales, sharks, and the problems with the Hierarchical Taxonomy of Psychopathology (HiTOP). *Clinical Psychological Science, 10*(2), 259–278. https://doi.org/10.1177/21677026211002500

Hageman, T. K., Francis, A. J. P., Field, A. M., & Carr, S. N. (2015). Links between childhood experiences and avoidant personality disorder symptomatology. *International Journal of Psychology & Psychological Therapy, 15*(1), 101–116.

Hagen, E. H. (2011). Evolutionary theories of depression: A critical review. *The Canadian Journal of Psychiatry, 56*(12), 716–725.

Hagerman, R. J., Berry-Kravis, E., Hazlett, H. C., Bailey, D. B., Moine, H., Kooy, R. F., Tassone, F., Gantois, I., Sonenberg, N., Mandel, J. L., & Hagerman, P. J. (2017). Fragile X syndrome. *Nature Reviews Disease Primers, 3*(1), 17065. https://doi.org/10.1038/nrdp.2017.65

Hagman, G. (2001). Beyond decathexis: Toward a new psychoanalytic understanding and treatment of mourning. In R. A. Neimeyer (Ed.), *Meaning reconstruction and the experience of loss* (pp. 13–31). American Psychological Association. https://doi.org/10.1037/10397-001

Hagman, J., Gralla, J., Sigel, E., Ellert, S., Dodge, M., Gardner, R., O'Lonergan, T., Frank, G., & Wamboldt, M. Z. (2011). A double-blind, placebo-controlled study of risperidone for the treatment of adolescents and young adults with anorexia nervosa: A pilot study. *Journal of the American Academy of Child & Adolescent Psychiatry, 50*(9), 915–924. https://doi.org/10.1016/j.jaac.2011.06.009

Haijma, S. V., Van Haren, N., Cahn, W., Koolschijn, P. C. M. P., Pol, H. E. H., & Kahn, R. S. (2013). Brain volumes in schizophrenia: A meta-analysis in over 18,000 subjects. *Schizophrenia Bulletin, 39*(5), 1129–1138. https://doi.org/10.1093/schbul/sbs118

Haimerl, J., Finke, J., & Luderer, H.-J. (2009). Person-centered and experiential therapy of depression. *International Journal of Psychotherapy, 13*(2), 18–25.

Hajek, P., Phillips-Waller, A., Przulj, D., Pesola, F., Myers Smith, K., Bisal, N., Li, J., Parrott, S., Sasieni, P., Dawkins, L., Ross, L., Goniewicz, M., Wu, Q., & McRobbie, H. J. (2019). A randomized trial of e-cigarettes versus nicotine-replacement therapy. *New England Journal of Medicine, 380*(7), 629–637. https://doi.org/10.1056/NEJMoa1808779

Halaris, A., Cantos, A., Johnson, K., Hakimi, M., & Sinacore, J. (2020). Modulation of the inflammatory response benefits treatment-resistant bipolar depression: A randomized clinical trial. *Journal of Affective Disorders, 261*, 145–152. https://doi.org/10.1016/j.jad.2019.10.021

Halberstadt, A. L. (2015). Recent advances in the neuropsychopharmacology of serotonergic hallucinogens. *Behavioural Brain Research, 277*, 99–120. https://doi.org/10.1016/j.bbr.2014.07.016

Halberstadt, A. L., & Geyer, M. A. (2011). Multiple receptors contribute to the behavioral effects of indoleamine hallucinogens. *Neuropharmacology, 61*(3), 364–381. https://doi.org/10.1016/j.neuropharm.2011.01.017

Hale, L. (2014). Inadequate sleep duration as a public health and social justice problem: Can we truly trade off our daily activities for more sleep? *Sleep: Journal of Sleep and Sleep Disorders Research, 37*(12), 1879–1880. https://doi.org/10.5665/sleep.4228

Hale, L., Kirschen, G. W., LeBourgeois, M. K., Gradisar, M., Garrison, M. M., Montgomery-Downs, H., Kirschen, H., McHale, S. M., Chang, A.-M., & Buxton, O. M. (2018). Youth screen media habits and sleep: Sleep-friendly screen-behavior recommendations for clinicians, educators, and parents. *Child and Adolescent Psychiatric Clinics of North America, 27*(2), 229–245. https://doi.org/10.1016/j.chc.2017.11.014

Hale, L., Strauss, C., & Taylor, B. L. (2013). The effectiveness and acceptability of mindfulness-based therapy for obsessive compulsive disorder: A review of the literature. *Mindfulness, 4*(4), 375–382. https://doi.org/10.1007/s12671-012-0137-y

Haleem, D. J. (2012). Serotonin neurotransmission in anorexia nervosa. *Behavioural Pharmacology, 23*(5–6), 478–495. https://doi.org/10.1097/FBP.0b013e328357440d

Hall, L. R., Sanchez, K., da Graca, B., Bennett, M. M., Powers, M., & Warren, A. M. (2021). Income differences and COVID-19: Impact on daily life and mental health. *Population Health Management*. https://doi.org/10.1089/pop.2021.0214

Hall, W., Leung, J., & Lynskey, M. (2020). The effects of cannabis use on the development of adolescents and young adults. *Annual Review of Developmental Psychology, 2*(1), 461–483. https://doi.org/10.1146/annurev-devpsych-040320-084904

Halland, M., Parthasarathy, G., Bharucha, A. E., & Katzka, D. A. (2016). Diaphragmatic breathing for rumination syndrome: Efficacy and mechanisms of action. *Neurogastroenterology and Motility, 28*(3), 384–391. https://doi.org/10.1111/nmo.12737

Halmi, K. A. (2013). Perplexities of treatment resistance in eating disorders. *BMC Psychiatry, 13*. https://doi.org/10.1186/1471-244X-13-292

Halperin, D. M. (1989). Is there a history of sexuality? *History and Theory, 28*(3), 257–274. https://doi.org/10.2307/2505179

Halpern, A. L. (2011). The proposed diagnosis of hypersexual disorder for inclusion in DSM-5: Unnecessary and harmful. *Archives of Sexual Behavior, 40*(3), 487–488. https://doi.org/10.1007/s10508-011-9727-3

Halstead-Reitan Battery. (n.d.). In *Encyclopedia of mental disorders*. http://www.minddisorders.com/Flu Inv/Halstead-Reitan-Battery.html

Halter, M. J., Rolin-Kenny, D., & Grund, F. (2013). DSM-5 historical perspectives. *Journal of Psychosocial Nursing and Mental Health Services, 51*(4), 22–29. https://doi.org/10.3928/02793695-20130226-03

Hamad, R., Penko, J., Kazi, D. S., Coxson, P., Guzman, D., Wei, P. C., Mason, A., Wang, E. A., Goldman, L., Fiscella, K., & Bibbins-Domingo, K. (2020). Association of low socioeconomic status with premature coronary heart disease in US adults. *JAMA Cardiology, 5*(8), 899–908. https://doi.org/10.1001/jamacardio.2020.1458

Hamblen, J. L., Norman, S. B., Sonis, J. H., Phelps, A. J., Bisson, J. I., Nunes, V. D., Megnin-Viggars, O., Forbes, D., Riggs, D. S., & Schnurr, P. P. (2019). A guide to guidelines for the treatment of posttraumatic stress disorder in adults: An update. *Psychotherapy, 56*(3), 359–373. https://doi.org/10.1037/pst0000231

Hamblin, J. (2016, May 12). Concerns about folate causing autism are premature. *The Atlantic*. https://www.theatlantic.com/science/archive/2016/05/on-folate-and-autism/482307/

Hambly, J. L., Khan, S., McDermott, B., Bor, W., & Haywood, A. (2016). Pharmacotherapy of conduct disorder: Challenges, options and future directions. *Journal of Psychopharmacology, 30*(10), 967–975. https://doi.org/10.1177/0269881116658985

Hamby, C. (2023, February 20). A fraught new frontier in telehealth: Ketamine. *The New York Times*. https://www.nytimes.com/2023/02/20/us/ketamine-telemedicine.html

Hamed, S. A. (2017). The effect of antiepileptic drugs on the kidney function and structure. *Expert Review of Clinical Pharmacology, 10*(9), 993–1006. https://doi.org/10.1080/17512433.2017.1353418

Hameed, S., Kumar, M., Puri, P., Sapna, F. N. U., & Athwal, P. S. S. (2020). Consequences of a missed history: A case of antidepressant discontinuation syndrome. *Cureus, 12*(10), e10950. https://doi.org/10.7759/cureus.10950

Hamilton, K., Keech, J. J., Peden, A. E., & Hagger, M. S. (2018). Alcohol use, aquatic injury, and unintentional drowning: A systematic literature review. *Drug and Alcohol Review, 37*(6), 752–773. https://doi.org/10.1111/dar.12817

Hamlin, A., & Oakes, P. (2008). Reflections on deinstitutionalization in the United Kingdom. *Journal of Policy and Practice in Intellectual Disabilities, 5*(1), 47–55. https://doi.org/10.1111/j.1741-1130.2007.00139.x

Hamm, J. A., Hasson-Ohayon, I., Kukla, M., & Lysaker, P. H. (2013). Individual psychotherapy for schizophrenia: Trends and developments in the wake of the recovery movement. *Psychology Research and Behavior Management, 6*.

Hammond, C. (2016, March 18). *Understanding histrionic personality disorder*. Psych Central. https://psychcentral.com/pro/exhausted-woman/2016/03/understanding-histrionic-personality-disorder

Hamza, C. A., Stewart, S. L., & Willoughby, T. (2012). Examining the link between nonsuicidal self-injury and suicidal behavior: A review of the literature and an integrated model. *Clinical Psychology Review, 32*(6), 482–495. https://doi.org/10.1016/j.cpr.2012.05.003

Han, E., Scior, K., Avramides, K., & Crane, L. (2022). A systematic review on autistic people's experiences of stigma and coping strategies. *Autism Research, 15*(1), 12–26. https://doi.org/10.1002/aur.2652

Han, T.-U., Root, J., Reyes, L. D., Huchinson, E. B., Hoffmann, J. du, Lee, W.-S., Barnes, T. D., & Drayna, D. (2019). Human GNPTAB stuttering mutations engineered into mice cause vocalization deficits and astrocyte pathology in the corpus callosum. *Proceedings of the National Academy of Sciences,*

116(35), 17515–17524. https://doi.org/10.1073/pnas.1901480116

Haney, J. L. (2016). Autism, females, and the DSM-5: Gender bias in autism diagnosis. *Social Work in Mental Health, 14*(4), 396–407. https://doi.org/10.1080/15332985.2015.1031858

Hanisch, C. (2006). *The personal is political.* http://www.carolhanisch.org/CHwritings/PersonalIsPol.pdf (Original work published 1970.)

Hansen, C., Alas, H., & Davis, Jr., E. (2022, July 27). *Where is marijuana legal? A guide to marijuana legalization.* US News & World Report. https://www.usnews.com/news/best-states/articles/where-is-marijuana-legal-a-guide-to-marijuana-legalization

Hansen, S. J., Christensen, S., Kongerslev, M. T., First, M. B., Widiger, T. A., Simonsen, E., & Bach, B. (2019). Mental health professionals' perceived clinical utility of the *ICD-10* vs. *ICD-11* classification of personality disorders. *Personality and Mental Health, 13*(2), 84–95. https://doi.org/10.1002/pmh.1442

Hanwella, R. (2020). Lithium: The wonder drug of psychiatry. *Sri Lanka Journal of Psychiatry, 11*(2), Article 2. https://doi.org/10.4038/sljpsyc.v11i2.8272

Happé, F., & Frith, U. (2006). The weak coherence account: Detail-focused cognitive style in autism spectrum disorders. *Journal of Autism and Developmental Disorders, 36*(1), 5–25. https://doi.org/10.1007/s10803-005-0039-0

Happé, F., & Frith, U. (2020). Annual research review: Looking back to look forward – changes in the concept of autism and implications for future research. *Journal of Child Psychology & Psychiatry, 61*(3), 218–232. https://doi.org/10.1111/jcpp.13176

Hardy, L. T. (2007). Attachment theory and reactive attachment disorder: Theoretical perspectives and treatment implications. *Journal of Child and Adolescent Psychiatric Nursing, 20*(1), 27–39.

Hardy, L. T. (2009). Encopresis: A guide for psychiatric nurses. *Archives of Psychiatric Nursing, 23*(5), 351–358. https://doi.org/10.1016/j.apnu.2008.09.002

Hardy, S., Bastick, L., O'Neill-Kerr, A., Sabesan, P., Lankappa, S., & Palaniyappan, L. (2016). Transcranial magnetic stimulation in clinical practice. *BJPsych Advances, 22*(6), 373–379. https://doi.org/10.1192/apt.bp.115.015206

Hare, R. D. (1996). Psychopathy and antisocial personality disorder: A case of diagnostic confusion. *Psychiatric Times, 13*(2). https://www.psychiatrictimes.com/view/psychopathy-and-antisocial-personality-disorder-case-diagnostic-confusion

Hare, R. D., Neumann, C. S., & Widiger, T. A. (2012). Psychopathy. In T. A. Widiger (Ed.), *The Oxford handbook of personality disorders* (pp. 478–504). Oxford University Press. https://doi.org/10.1093/oxfordhb/9780199735013.013.0022

Hari, J. (2022, January 2). Your attention didn't collapse. It was stolen. *The Observer.* https://www.theguardian.com/science/2022/jan/02/attention-span-focus-screens-apps-smartphones-social-media

Harlow, H. F. (1958). The nature of love. *American Psychologist, 13*(12), 673–685. https://doi.org/10.1037/h0047884

Harlow, H. F., & Suomi, S. J. (1974). Induced depression in monkeys. *Behavioral Biology, 12*(3), 273–296. https://doi.org/10.1016/S0091-6773(74)91475-8

Harlow, J. M. (1848). Passage of an iron rod through the head. *Boston Medical and Surgical Journal, 39*, 389–393.

Harney, P. A., & Harvey, M. R. (1999). Group psychotherapy: An overview. In B. H. Young & D. D. Blake (Eds.), *Group treatments for post-traumatic stress disorder* (pp. 1–14). Brunner/Mazel.

Harper, D. J. (2011). Social inequality and the diagnosis of paranoia. *Health Sociology Review, 20*(4), 423–436. https://doi.org/10.5172/hesr.2011.20.4.423

Harper, D. J., & Cromby, J. (2022). From "what's wrong with you?" to "what's happened to you?": An introduction to the special issue on the Power Threat Meaning Framework. *Journal of Constructivist*

Psychology, 35(1), 1–6. https://doi.org/10.1080/10720537.2020.1773362

Harper-Harrison, G., & Shanahan, M. M. (2022). Hormone replacement therapy. In *StatPearls [Internet].* StatPearls Publishing. https://www.ncbi.nlm.nih.gov/books/NBK493191/

Harrington, A. (2019). *Mind fixers: Psychiatry's troubled search for the biology of mental illness.* Norton.

Harris, B. (1979). Whatever happened to little Albert? *American Psychologist, 34*(2), 151–160. https://doi.org/10.1037/0003-066X.34.2.151

Harris, J. C. (2003). A rake's progress: "Bedlam." *Archives of General Psychiatry, 60*(4), 338–339. https://doi.org/10.1001/archpsyc.60.4.338

Harris, M. S., Goodrum, B. A., & Krempasky, C. N. (2022). An introduction to gender-affirming hormone therapy for transgender and gender-nonbinary patients. *The Nurse Practitioner, 47*(3), 18–28. https://doi.org/10.1097/01.NPR.0000819612.24729.c7

Harrison, J. L., O'Toole, S. K., Ammen, S., Ahlmeyer, S., Harrell, S. N., & Hernandez, J. L. (2020). Sexual offender treatment effectiveness within cognitive-behavioral programs: A meta-analytic investigation of general, sexual, and violent recidivism. *Psychiatry, Psychology, and Law, 27*(1), 1–25. https://doi.org/10.1080/13218719.2018.1485526

Harrison, K. (2007). The high-risk sex offender strategy in England and Wales: Is chemical castration an option? *The Howard Journal of Criminal Justice, 46*(1), 16–31. https://doi.org/10.1111/j.1468-2311.2007.00451.x

Harrison, P. J. (2015). Recent genetic findings in schizophrenia and their therapeutic relevance. *Journal of Psychopharmacology (Oxford, England), 29*(2), 85–96. https://doi.org/10.1177/0269881114553647

Hartman-Munick, S. M., Lin, J. A., Milliren, C. E., Braverman, P. K., Brigham, K. S., Fisher, M. M., Golden, N. H., Jary, J. M., Lemly, D. C., Matthews, A., Ornstein, R. M., Roche, A., Rome, E. S., Rosen, E. L., Sharma, Y., Shook, J. K., Taylor, J. L., Thew, M., Vo, M., … Richmond, T. K. (2022). Association of the COVID-19 pandemic with adolescent and young adult eating disorder care volume. *JAMA Pediatrics, 176*(12), 1225–1232. https://doi.org/10.1001/jamapediatrics.2022.4346

Hartmann, A., Martino, D., & Murphy, T. (2016). Gilles de la Tourette syndrome—A treatable condition? *Revue Neurologique, 172*(8–9), 446–454. https://doi.org/10.1016/j.neurol.2016.07.004

Hartmann, A. S., Becker, A. E., Hampton, C., & Bryant-Waugh, R. (2012). Pica and rumination disorder in DSM-5. *Psychiatric Annals, 42*(11), 426–430. https://doi.org/10.3928/00485713-20121105-09

Hartmann, T. (1997). *Attention deficit disorder: A different perception* (2nd ed.). Underwood Books.

Hartney, E. (2020, March 24). *What to expect from heroin withdrawal.* Verywell Mind. https://www.verywellmind.com/what-to-expect-from-heroin-withdrawal-22049

Hartwell, C. E. (1996). The schizophrenogenic mother concept in American psychiatry. *Psychiatry: Interpersonal and Biological Processes, 59*(3), 274–297.

Harvey, B. H., & Slabbert, F. N. (2014). New insights on the antidepressant discontinuation syndrome. *Human Psychopharmacology: Clinical and Experimental, 29*(6), 503–516. https://doi.org/10.1002/hup.2429

Harvey, P. D. (2017). Inflammation in schizophrenia: What it means and how to treat it. *The American Journal of Geriatric Psychiatry, 25*(1), 62–63. https://doi.org/10.1016/j.jagp.2016.10.012

Harvey, S. B., Øverland, S., Hatch, S. L., Wessely, S., Mykletun, A., & Hotopf, M. (2018). Exercise and the prevention of depression: Results of the HUNT cohort study. *American Journal of Psychiatry, 175*(1), 28–36. https://doi.org/10.1176/appi.ajp.2017.16111223

Hashemi, A. H., & Cochrane, R. (1999). Expressed emotion and schizophrenia: A review of studies across cultures. *International Review of Psychiatry, 11*(2–3), 219–224. https://doi.org/10.1080/09540269974401

Hashemiyoon, R., Kuhn, J., & Visser-Vandewalle, V. (2017). Putting the pieces together in Gilles de la Tourette syndrome: Exploring the link between clinical observations and the biological basis of dysfunction. *Brain Topography, 30*(1), 3–29. https://doi.org/10.1007/s10548-016-0525-z

Hashimoto, K. (2009). Emerging role of glutamate in the pathophysiology of major depressive disorder. *Brain Research Reviews, 61*(2), 105–123. https://doi.org/10.1016/j.brainresrev.2009.05.005

Hasin, D. S., O'Brien, C. P., Auriacombe, M., Borges, G., Bucholz, K., Budney, A., Compton, W. M., Crowley, T., Ling, W., Petry, N. M., Schuckit, M., & Grant, B. F. (2013). DSM-5 criteria for substance use disorders: Recommendations and rationale. *American Journal of Psychiatry, 170*(8), 834–851. https://doi.org/doi:10.1176/appi.ajp.2013.12060782

Hasin, D. S., Sarvet, A. L., Meyers, J. L., Saha, T. D., Ruan, W. J., Stohl, M., & Grant, B. F. (2018). Epidemiology of adult *DSM-5* major depressive disorder and its specifiers in the United States. *JAMA Psychiatry, 75*(4), 336–346. https://doi.org/10.1001/jamapsychiatry.2017.4602

Haskayne, D., Hirschfeld, R., & Larkin, M. (2014). The outcome of psychodynamic psychotherapies with individuals diagnosed with personality disorders: A systematic review. *Psychoanalytic Psychotherapy, 28*(2), 115–138. https://doi.org/10.1080/02668734.2014.888675

Hassan, A. N., & Le Foll, B. (2019). Polydrug use disorders in individuals with opioid use disorder. *Drug and Alcohol Dependence, 198*, 28–33. https://doi.org/10.1016/j.drugalcdep.2019.01.031

Hasse, T. D., & Fuller, K. (2017, April 3). A true story of living with obsessive-compulsive disorder [Psychology Today]. *Happiness Is a State of Mind.* https://www.psychologytoday.com/us/blog/happiness-is-state-mind/201704/true-story-living-obsessive-compulsive-disorder

Hassiotis, A., Canagasabey, A., Robotham, D., Marston, L., Romeo, R., & King, M. (2011). Applied behaviour analysis and standard treatment in intellectual disability: 2-year outcomes. *The British Journal of Psychiatry, 198*(6), 490–491. https://doi.org/10.1192/bjp.bp.109.076646

Hatoum, A. S., Colbert, S. M. C., Johnson, E. C., Huggett, S. B., Deak, J. D., Pathak, G., Jennings, M. V., Paul, S. E., Karcher, N. R., Hansen, I., Baranger, D. A. A., Edwards, A., Grotzinger, A., Consortium, S. U. D. W. G. of the P. G., Tucker-Drob, E. M., Kranzler, H. R., Davis, L. K., Sanchez-Roige, S., Polimanti, R., … Agrawal, A. (2022). *Multivariate genome-wide association meta-analysis of over 1 million subjects identifies loci underlying multiple substance use disorders.* medRxiv. https://doi.org/10.1101/2022.01.06.22268753

Hauck, C., Cook, B., & Ellrott, T. (2020). Food addiction, eating addiction and eating disorders. *Proceedings of the Nutrition Society, 79*(1), 103–112. https://doi.org/10.1017/S0029665119001162

Haukvik, U. K., Gurholt, T. P., Nerland, S., Elvsåshagen, T., Akudjedu, T. N., Alda, M., Alnæs, D., Alonso-Lana, S., Bauer, J., Baune, B. T., Benedetti, F., Berk, M., Bettella, F., Bøen, E., Bonnín, C. M., Brambilla, P., Canales-Rodríguez, E. J., Cannon, D. M., Caseras, X., … ENIGMA Bipolar Disorder Working Group. (2022). In vivo hippocampal subfield volumes in bipolar disorder—A mega-analysis from The Enhancing Neuro Imaging Genetics through Meta-Analysis Bipolar Disorder Working Group. *Human Brain Mapping, 43*(1), 385–398. https://doi.org/10.1002/hbm.25249

Hauth, I., de Bruijn, Y. G. E., Staal, W., Buitelaar, J. K., & Rommelse, N. N. (2014). Testing the extreme male brain theory of autism spectrum disorder in a familial design. *Autism Research, 7*(4), 491–500. https://doi.org/10.1002/aur.1384

Havens, L. L. (1966). Charcot and hysteria. *Journal of Nervous and Mental Disease, 141*(5), 505–516. https://doi.org/10.1097/00005053-196511000-00003

Hawgood, J., Woodward, A., Quinnett, P., & De Leo, D. (2021). Gatekeeper training and minimum standards of competency: Essentials for the suicide prevention workforce. *Crisis: The Journal of Crisis Intervention and Suicide Prevention*. https://doi.org/10.1027/0227-5910/a000794

Hawkey, E., & Nigg, J. T. (2014). Omega−3 fatty acid and ADHD: Blood level analysis and meta-analytic extension of supplementation trials. *Clinical Psychology Review*, 34(6), 496–505. https://doi.org/10.1016/j.cpr.2014.05.005

Hawkins, J. (2021). Why even a liberal can justify limited paternalistic intervention in anorexia nervosa. *Philosophy, Psychiatry & Psychology*, 28(2), 155–158.

Hawn, S. E., Cusack, S. E., & Amstadter, A. B. (2020). A systematic review of the self-medication hypothesis in the context of posttraumatic stress disorder and comorbid problematic alcohol use. *Journal of Traumatic Stress*, 33(5), 699–708. https://doi.org/10.1002/jts.22521

Hawn, S. E., Sheerin, C. M., Lind, M. J., Hicks, T. A., Marraccini, M. E., Bountress, K., Bacanu, S.-A., Nugent, N. R., & Amstadter, A. B. (2019). GxE effects of FKBP5 and traumatic life events on PTSD: A meta-analysis. *Journal of Affective Disorders*, 243, 455–462. https://doi.org/10.1016/j.jad.2018.09.058

Hawton, K., Witt, K. G., Taylor Salisbury, T. L., Arensman, E., Gunnell, D., Hazell, P., Townsend, E., & van Heeringen, K. (2015). Pharmacological interventions for self-harm in adults. *Cochrane Database of Systematic Reviews*, 2015(7), Article CD011777. https://doi.org/10.1002/14651858.CD011777

Hawton, K., Witt, K. G., Taylor Salisbury, T. L., Arensman, E., Gunnell, D., Hazell, P., Townsend, E., & van Heeringen, K. (2016). Psychosocial interventions for self-harm in adults. *Cochrane Database of Systematic Reviews*, 2016(5), Article CD012189. https://doi.org/10.1002/14651858.CD012189

Hay, P. (2013). A systematic review of evidence for psychological treatments in eating disorders: 2005–2012. *International Journal of Eating Disorders*, 46(5), 462–469.

Hayden, E. C. (2013). Taboo genetics. *Nature*, 502(7469), 26–28. https://doi.org/10.1038/502026a

Hayes, S. C. (2004). Acceptance and commitment therapy, relational frame theory, and the third wave of behavioral and cognitive therapies. *Behavior Therapy*, 35(4), 639–665. https://doi.org/10.1016/S0005-7894(04)80013-3

Hayes, S. C., & Pankey, J. (2002). Experiential avoidance, cognitive fusion, and an ACT approach to anorexia nervosa. *Cognitive and Behavioral Practice*, 9(3), 243–247. https://doi.org/10.1016/S1077-7229(02)80055-4

Hayes, S., Linardon, J., Kim, C., & Mitchison, D. (2021). Understanding the relationship between sexual harassment and eating disorder psychopathology: A systematic review and meta-analysis. *International Journal of Eating Disorders*, 54(5), 673–689. https://doi.org/10.1002/eat.23499

Haymes, L. K., Storey, K., Maldonado, A., Post, M., & Montgomery, J. (2013). Using applied behavior analysis and smart technology for meeting the health needs of individuals with intellectual disabilities. *Developmental Neurorehabilitation*, 18(6), 407–419. https://doi.org/10.3109/17518423.2013.850750

Haynes, S. N. (1998). The changing nature of behavioral assessment. In A. S. Bellack & M. Hersen (Eds.), *Behavioral assessment: A practical handbook* (2nd ed., pp. 1–21). Allyn and Bacon.

Hazelden Betty Ford Foundation. (2016, July 24). *What is the difference between alcohol abuse & dependence?* https://www.hazeldenbettyford.org/articles/what-is-the-difference-between-alcohol-abuse-and-dependence

Hazlett-Stevens, H., & Craske, M. G. (2008). Live (in vivo) exposure. In W. T. O'Donohue & J. E. Fisher (Eds.), *Cognitive behavior therapy: Applying empirically supported techniques in your practice*

(2009-02306-038; 2nd ed., pp. 309–316). John Wiley & Sons.

He, J. A., & Antshel, K. M. (2016). Cognitive behavioral therapy for attention-deficit/hyperactivity disorder in college students: A review of the literature. *Cognitive and Behavioral Practice*. https://doi.org/10.1016/j.cbpra.2016.03.010

He, Z., & Yang, W. (2022). Impulsiveness as potential moderators of the relation between social media dependence and eating disorders risk. *BMC Psychology*, 10, Article 120. https://doi.org/10.1186/s40359-022-00830-8

Head, L. S., & Gross, A. M. (2008). Systematic desensitization. In W. T. O'Donohue & J. E. Fisher (Eds.), *Cognitive behavior therapy: Applying empirically supported techniques in your practice* (2009-02306-069; 2nd ed., pp. 542–549). John Wiley & Sons.

Healy, R. W., & Allen, L. R. (2020). Bowen family systems therapy with transgender minors: A case study. *Clinical Social Work Journal*, 48(4), 402–411. https://doi.org/10.1007/s10615-019-00704-4

Heard, H. L., & Linehan, M. M. (1994). Dialectical behavior therapy: An integrative approach to the treatment of borderline personality disorder. *Journal of Psychotherapy Integration*, 4(1), 55–82. https://doi.org/10.1037/h0101147

Hearing Voices Network. (2022). *Basic Information about voices & visions*. https://www.hearing-voices.org/voices-visions/

Hearing Voices Network USA. (n.d.). *Hearing Voices Network USA: Voices, visions & other unusual or extreme experiences*. Retrieved November 9, 2022, from http://www.hearingvoicesusa.org/

Hearon, B. A., & Otto, M. W. (2012). Benzodiazepines. In S. G. Hofmann (Ed.), *Psychobiological approaches for anxiety disorders: Treatment combination strategies* (pp. 25–39). Wiley-Blackwell. https://doi.org/10.1002/9781119945901.ch2

Heath, S. (2021, December 14). *More patients cite out-of-pocket costs as care access barrier*. Patient Engagement HIT. https://patientengagementhit.com/news/more-patients-cite-out-of-pocket-costs-as-care-access-barrier

Heath, S. (2022, February 22). *Top challenges impacting patient access to healthcare*. Patient Engagement HIT. https://patientengagementhit.com/news/top-challenges-impacting-patient-access-to-healthcare

Heather, N. (2006). Controlled drinking, harm reduction and their roles in the response to alcohol-related problems. *Addiction Research & Theory*, 14(1), 7–18. https://doi.org/10.1080/16066350500489170

Hecker, J. E. (1990). Emotional processing in the treatment of simple phobia: A comparison of imaginal and in vivo exposure. *Behavioural Psychotherapy*, 18(1), 21–34. https://doi.org/10.1017/S0141347300017961

Heckers, S., Barch, D. M., Bustillo, J., Gaebel, W., Gur, R., Malaspina, D., Owen, M. J., Schultz, S., Tandon, R., Tsuang, M., Van Os, J., & Carpenter, W. (2013). Structure of the psychotic disorders classification in DSM-5. *Schizophrenia Research*, 150(1), 11–14. https://doi.org/10.1016/j.schres.2013.04.039

Hedman, A., Breithaupt, L., Hübel, C., Thornton, L. M., Tillander, A., Norring, C., Birgegård, A., Larsson, H., Ludvigsson, J. F., Sävendahl, L., Almqvist, C., & Bulik, C. M. (2019). Bidirectional relationship between eating disorders and autoimmune diseases. *Journal of Child Psychology and Psychiatry*, 60(7), 803–812. https://doi.org/10.1111/jcpp.12958

Hedman, E., Axelsson, E., Andersson, E., Lekander, M., & Ljótsson, B. (2016). Exposure-based cognitive–behavioural therapy via the internet and as bibliotherapy for somatic symptom disorder and illness anxiety disorder: Randomised controlled trial. *The British Journal of Psychiatry*, 209(5), 407–413. https://doi.org/10.1192/bjp.bp.116.181396

Hedman, E., Lekander, M., Karshikoff, B., Ljótsson, B., Axelsson, E., & Axelsson, J. (2016). Health anxiety in a disease-avoidance framework: Investigation of

anxiety, disgust and disease perception in response to sickness cues. *Journal of Abnormal Psychology*, 125(7), 868–878. https://doi.org/10.1037/abn0000195

Heffner, M., Sperry, J., Eifert, G. H., & Detweiler, M. (2002). Acceptance and commitment therapy in the treatment of an adolescent female with anorexia nervosa: A case example. *Cognitive and Behavioral Practice*, 9(3), 232–236. https://doi.org/10.1016/S1077-7229(02)80053-0

Hegvik, T.-A., Chen, Q., Kuja-Halkola, R., Klungsøyr, K., Butwicka, A., Lichtenstein, P., Almqvist, C., Faraone, S. V., Haavik, J., & Larsson, H. (2022). Familial co-aggregation of attention-deficit/hyperactivity disorder and autoimmune diseases: A cohort study based on Swedish population-wide registers. *International Journal of Epidemiology*, 51(3), 898–909. https://doi.org/10.1093/ije/dyab151

Heiby, E. M., & Haynes, S. N. (2004). Introduction to behavioral assessment. In S. N. Haynes & E. M. Heiby (Eds.), *Comprehensive handbook of psychological assessment: Vol. 3. Behavioral assessment* (pp. 3–18). John Wiley.

Heijden, M. E. van Der, Gill, J. S., & Sillitoe, R. V. (2021). Abnormal cerebellar development in autism spectrum disorders. *Developmental Neuroscience*, 43(3–4), 181–190. https://doi.org/10.1159/000515189

Heilig, M., MacKillop, J., Martinez, D., Rehm, J., Leggio, L., & Vanderschuren, L. J. M. J. (2021). Addiction as a brain disease revised: Why it still matters, and the need for consilience. *Neuropsychopharmacology*, 46(10), Article 10. https://doi.org/10.1038/s41386-020-00950-y

Heim, G., & Bühler, K.-E. (2006). Psychological trauma and fixed ideas in Pierre Janet's conception of dissociative disorders. *American Journal of Psychotherapy*, 60(2), 111–127. https://doi.org/10.1176/appi.psychotherapy.2006.60.2.111

Heintzelman, C. A. (2003). *The Tuskegee syphilis study and its implications for the 21st century* (Vol. 10, Issue 4). Retrieved from http://www.socialworker.com/feature-articles/ethics-articles/The_Tuskegee_Syphilis_Study_and_Its_Implications_for_the_21st_Century/

Heir, T., Bonsaksen, T., Grimholt, T., Ekeberg, Ø., Skogstad, L., Lerdal, A., & Schou-Bredal, I. (2019). Serious life events and post-traumatic stress disorder in the Norwegian population. *BJPsych Open*, 5(5), e82. https://doi.org/10.1192/bjo.2019.62

Helms, J. E., Nicolas, G., & Green, C. E. (2012). Racism and ethnoviolence as trauma: Enhancing professional and research training. *Traumatology*, 18(1), 65–74. https://doi.org/10.1177/1534765610396728

Hendershot, C. S., Witkiewitz, K., George, W. H., & Marlatt, G. A. (2011). Relapse prevention for addictive behaviors. *Substance Abuse Treatment, Prevention, and Policy*, 6(1), 17. https://doi.org/10.1186/1747-597X-6-17

Henderson, E. (2015). Potentially dangerous patients: A review of the duty to warn. *Journal of Emergency Nursing*, 41(3), 193–200. https://doi.org/10.1016/j.jen.2014.08.012

Henderson, R. (2021, March 23). *Update on America's state of mind – 4 Key takeaways*. Evernorth. https://www.evernorth.com/articles/www.evernorth.com/articles/americas-state-of-mind-update-on-covid-19-and-mental-health

Henderson, S. W., & Martin, A. (2014). Case formulation and integration of information in child and adolescent mental health. In J. M. Rey (Ed.), *IACAPAP e-textbook of child and adolescent mental health* (pp. 1–20). International Association for Child and Adolescent Psychiatry and Allied Professions.

Hengartner, M. P., Kawohl, W., Haker, H., Rössler, W., & Ajdacic-Gross, V. (2016). Big five personality traits may inform public health policy and preventive medicine: Evidence from a cross-sectional and a prospective longitudinal epidemiologic study in a Swiss community. *Journal of Psychosomatic Research*, 84, 44–51. https://doi.org/10.1016/j.jpsychores.2016.03.012

Henggeler, S. W. (2011). Efficacy studies to large-scale transport: The development and validation of multi-systemic therapy programs. *Annual Review of Clinical Psychology*, 7, 351–381. https://doi.org/10.1146/annurev-clinpsy-032210-104615

Henggeler, S. W., & Borduin, C. M. (1990). *Family therapy and beyond: A multisystemic approach to treating behavior problems of children and adolescents*. Brooks/Cole.

Henken, H. T., Kupka, R. W., Draisma, S., Lobbestael, J., van den Berg, K., Demacker, S. M. A., & Regeer, E. J. (2020). A cognitive behavioural group therapy for bipolar disorder using daily mood monitoring. *Behavioural and Cognitive Psychotherapy*, 48(5), 515–529. https://doi.org/10.1017/S1352465820000259

Hennemann, S., Böhme, K., Kleinstäuber, M., Baumeister, H., Küchler, A.-M., Ebert, D. D., & Witthöft, M. (2022). Internet-based CBT for somatic symptom distress (iSOMA) in emerging adults: A randomized controlled trial. *Journal of Consulting and Clinical Psychology*, 90(4), 353–365. https://doi.org/10.1037/ccp0000707

Hennessey, T., Andari, E., & Rainnie, D. G. (2018). RDoC-based categorization of amygdala functions and its implications in autism. *Neuroscience and Biobehavioral Reviews*, 90, 115–129. https://doi.org/10.1016/j.neubiorev.2018.04.007

Henriksen, M. G., Nordgaard, J., & Jansson, L. B. (2017). Genetics of schizophrenia: Overview of methods, findings and limitations. *Frontiers in Human Neuroscience*, 11, Article 322. https://doi.org/10.3389/fnhum.2017.00322

Henriques, G. (2015). *The biopsychosocial model and its limitations*. [Psychology Today]. https://www.psychologytoday.com/blog/theory-knowledge/201510/the-biopsychosocial-model-and-its-limitations

Henriques, G. R. (2002). The harmful dysfunction analysis and the differentiation between mental disorder and disease. *The Scientific Review of Mental Health Practice: Objective Investigations of Controversial and Unorthodox Claims in Clinical Psychology, Psychiatry, and Social Work*, 1(2), 157–173.

Henssler, J., Brandt, L., Müller, M., Liu, S., Montag, C., Sterzer, P., & Heinz, A. (2020). Migration and schizophrenia: Meta-analysis and explanatory framework. *European Archives of Psychiatry and Clinical Neuroscience*, 270(3), 325–335. https://doi.org/10.1007/s00406-019-01028-7

Herbert, J. D., Lilienfeld, S. O., Lohr, J. M., Montgomery, R. W., O'Donohue, W. T., Rosen, G. M., & Tolin, D. F. (2000). Science and pseudoscience in the development of eye movement desensitization and reprocessing: Implications for clinical psychology. *Clinical Psychology Review*, 20(8), 945–971. https://doi.org/10.1016/S0272-7358(99)00017-3

Herbert, R. (2013). An empirical study of normative dissociation in musical and non-musical everyday life experiences. *Psychology of Music*, 41(3), 372–394. https://doi.org/10.1177/0305735611430080

Hergüner, S., Özyıldırım, İ., & Tanıdır, C. (2008). Is pica an eating disorder or an obsessive-compulsive spectrum disorder? *Progress in Neuro-Psychopharmacology & Biological Psychiatry*, 32(8), 2010–2011. https://doi.org/10.1016/j.pnpbp.2008.09.011

Herman, J. (2015). *Trauma and recovery: The aftermath of violence—From domestic abuse to political terror*. Basic Books.

Herpertz, S. C., Huprich, S. K., Bohus, M., Chanen, A., Goodman, M., Mehlum, L., Moran, P., Newton-Howes, G., Scott, L., & Sharp, C. (2017). The challenge of transforming the diagnostic system of personality disorders. *Journal of Personality Disorders*, 31(5), 577–589.

Hertlein, K. M., & Weeks, G. R. (2009, March/April). Sexual health. *Family Therapy Magazine*, 48–58.

Hertler, S. C. (2014a). A review and critique of obsessive-compulsive personality disorder etiologies. *Europe's Journal of Psychology*, 10(1), 168–184.

Hertler, S. C. (2014b). The continuum of conscientiousness: The antagonistic interests among obsessive and antisocial personalities. *Polish Psychological Bulletin*, 45(1), 52–63. https://doi.org/10.2478/ppb-2014-0008

Hertler, S. C. (2015a). Obsessive compulsive personality disorder as an adaptive anachronism: The operation of phylogenetic inertia upon obsessive populations in Western modernity. *Psihologijske Teme*, 24(2), 207–232.

Hertler, S. C. (2015b). The evolutionary logic of the obsessive trait complex: Obsessive compulsive personality disorder as a complementary behavioral syndrome. *Psychological Thought*, 8(1), 18. https://doi.org/10.5964/psyct.v8i1.125

Hertz, P. (2016). The psychoses, with a special emphasis on schizophrenia spectrum disorders. In J. Berzoff, L. M. Flanagan, & P. Hertz (Eds.), *Inside out and outside in: Psychodynamic clinical theory and psychopathology in contemporary multicultural contexts* (4th ed., pp. 330–362). Rowman & Littlefield.

Hertz, P., & Hertz, M. (2016). Personality disorders, with a special emphasis on borderline and narcissistic syndromes. In J. Berzoff, L. M. Flanagan, & P. Hertz (Eds.), *Inside out and outside in: Psychodynamic clinical theory and psychopathology in contemporary multicultural contexts* (4th ed., pp. 363–411). Rowman & Littlefield.

Hervey, N. (1986). Advocacy or folly: The Alleged Lunatics' Friend Society, 1845-63. *Medical History*, 30(3), 245–275.

Het, S., Vocks, S., Wolf, J. M., Hammelstein, P., Herpertz, S., & Wolf, O. T. (2015). Blunted neuroendocrine stress reactivity in young women with eating disorders. *Journal of Psychosomatic Research*, 78(3), 260–267. https://doi.org/10.1016/j.jpsychores.2014.11.001

Hettema, J. M., Neale, M. C., & Kendler, K. S. (2001). A review and meta-analysis of the genetic epidemiology of anxiety disorders. *The American Journal of Psychiatry*, 158(10), 1568–1578. https://doi.org/10.1176/appi.ajp.158.10.1568

Hewson, H. (2015). A narrative approach to individuals with psychosis. In A. Meaden & A. Fox (Eds.), *Innovations in psychosocial interventions for psychosis: Working with the hard to reach* (pp. 146–163). Routledge.

Heylens, G., De Cuypere, G., Zucker, K. J., Schelfaut, C., Elaut, E., Vanden Bossche, H., De Baere, E., & T'Sjoen, G. (2012). Gender identity disorder in twins: A review of the case report literature. *Journal of Sexual Medicine*, 9(3), 751–757. https://doi.org/10.1111/j.1743-6109.2011.02567.x

Heyvaert, M., Maes, B., & Onghena, P. (2013). Mixed methods research synthesis: Definition, framework, and potential. *Quality & Quantity: International Journal of Methodology*, 47(2), 659–676. https://doi.org/10.1007/s11135-011-9538-6

Hezel, D. M., & Simpson, H. B. (2019). Exposure and response prevention for obsessive-compulsive disorder: A review and new directions. *Indian Journal of Psychiatry*, 61(Suppl. 1), S85–S92. https://doi.org/10.4103/psychiatry.IndianJPsychiatry_516_18

Hieronymus, F., Lisinski, A., Nilsson, S., & Eriksson, E. (2018). Efficacy of selective serotonin reuptake inhibitors in the absence of side effects: A mega-analysis of citalopram and paroxetine in adult depression. *Molecular Psychiatry*, 23(8), Article 8. https://doi.org/10.1038/mp.2017.147

Higbee, M., Wright, E. R., & Roemerman, R. M. (2022). Conversion therapy in the southern United States: Prevalence and experiences of the survivors. *Journal of Homosexuality*, 69(4), 612–631. https://doi.org/10.1080/00918369.2020.1840213

Higgins, A. (2018). The neurobiology of anorexia nervosa. In H. Himmerich & I. Jáuregui-Lobera (Eds.), *Anorexia and bulimia nervosa*. IntechOpen. https://doi.org/10.5772/intechopen.82751

Higgins, S. T., & Petry, N. M. (1999). Contingency management: Incentives for sobriety. *Alcohol Research & Health*, 23(2), 122–127.

Hildebrandt, T. B., & Downey, A. (2013). The neurobiology of eating disorders. In D. S. Charney, J. D. Buxbaum, P. Sklar, & E. J. Nestler (Eds.), *Neurobiology of mental illness* (4th ed., pp. 1171–1185). Oxford University Press. https://doi.org/10.1093/med/9780199934959.003.0089

Hill, D. L. G., Schwarz, A. J., Isaac, M., Pani, L., Vamvakas, S., Hemmings, R., Carrillo, M. C., Yu, P., Sun, J., Beckett, L., Boccardi, M., Brewer, J., Brumfield, M., Cantillon, M., Cole, P. E., Fox, N., Frisoni, G. B., Jack, C., Kelleher, T., … Stephenson, D. (2014). Coalition against major diseases/European medicines agency biomarker qualification of hippocampal volume for enrichment of clinical trials in predementia stages of Alzheimer's disease. *Alzheimer's & Dementia: The Journal of the Alzheimer's Association*, 10(4), 421–429. https://doi.org/10.1016/j.jalz.2013.07.003

Hill, J., Bird, H., & Thorpe, R. (2003). Effects of rheumatoid arthritis on sexual activity and relationships. *Rheumatology*, 42(2), 280–286.

Hill, M. L., Schaefer, L. W., Spencer, S. D., & Masuda, A. (2020). Compassion-focused acceptance and commitment therapy for women with restrictive eating and problematic body-checking: A multiple baseline across participants study. *Journal of Contextual Behavioral Science*, 16, 144–152. https://doi.org/10.1016/j.jcbs.2020.04.006

Hill, M. M., Gangi, D., Miller, M., Rafi, S. M., & Ozonoff, S. (2020). Screen time in 36-month-olds at increased likelihood for ASD and ADHD. *Infant Behavior & Development*, 61, 101484. https://doi.org/10.1016/j.infbeh.2020.101484

Hill, S. K., Bishop, J. R., Palumbo, D., & Sweeney, J. A. (2010). Effect of second-generation antipsychotics on cognition: Current issues and future challenges. *Expert Review of Neurotherapeutics*, 10(1), 43–57. https://doi.org/10.1586/ern.09.143

Hillhouse, T. M., & Porter, J. H. (2015). A brief history of the development of antidepressant drugs: From monoamines to glutamate. *Experimental and Clinical Psychopharmacology*, 23(1), 1–21. https://doi.org/10.1037/a0038550

Hillman, H. (2018). Child-centered play therapy as an intervention for children with autism: A literature review. *International Journal of Play Therapy*, 27(4), 198–204. https://doi.org/10.1037/pla0000083

Hinney, A., & Volckmar, A.-L. (2013). Genetics of eating disorders. *Current Psychiatry Reports*, 15(12), 423–423. doi:10.1007/s11920-013-0423-y

Hinshaw, S. P., & Scheffler, R. M. (2014). *The ADHD explosion: Myths, medicine, money, and today's push for performance*. Oxford University Press.

Hirsch, L. E., & Pringsheim, T. (2016). Aripiprazole for autism spectrum disorders (ASD). *Cochrane Database of Systematic Reviews*, 2016(6), Article CD009043. https://doi.org/10.1002/14651858.CD009043.pub3

Hirschfeld, M. (1948). *Sexual anomalies: The origins, nature, and treatment of sexual disorders* (Rev. ed.). Emerson Books.

Hirschfeld, R. M. (2000). History and evolution of the monoamine hypothesis of depression. *The Journal of Clinical Psychiatry*, 61(Suppl. 6), 4–6.

Hirschfeld, R. M. A. (2001). The comorbidity of major depression and anxiety disorders: Recognition and management in primary care. *Primary Care Companion to the Journal of Clinical Psychiatry*, 3(6), 244–254.

Hirschowitz, J., Kolevzon, A., & Garakani, A. (2010). The pharmacological treatment of bipolar disorder: The question of modern advances. *Harvard Review of Psychiatry*, 18(5), 266–278. https://doi.org/10.3109/10673229.2010.507042

Hisle-Gorman, E., Susi, A., Stokes, T., Gorman, G., Erdie-Lalena, C., & Nylund, C. M. (2018). Prenatal, perinatal, and neonatal risk factors of autism spectrum disorder. *Pediatric Research*, 84(2), 190–198. https://doi.org/10.1038/pr.2018.23

Hite, S. (1976). *The Hite report: A nationwide study on female sexuality*. Macmillan.

Hite, S. (1981). *The Hite report on male sexuality*. Alfred A. Knopf.

Hiyoshi, A., Fall, K., Netuveli, G., & Montgomery, S. (2015). Remarriage after divorce and depression risk. *Social Science & Medicine*, *141*, 109–114. https://doi.org/10.1016/j.socscimed.2015.07.029

Hjelmervik, H., Craven, A. R., Johnsen, E., Kompus, K., Kroken, R. A., Løberg, E.-M., & Hugdahl, K. (2018). F184. Testing the GABA-glutamate hypothesis for schizophrenia in relation to auditory hallucinations—Preliminary results. *Schizophrenia Bulletin*, *44*(suppl_1), S292–S293. https://doi.org/10.1093/schbul/sby017.715

Ho, C., & Adcock, L. (2017). *Short-term psychodynamic psychotherapy for the treatment of mental illness: A review of clinical effectiveness and guidelines* (CADTH Rapid Response Report: Summary with Critical Appraisal). Canadian Agency for Drugs and Technologies in Health. https://www.ncbi.nlm.nih.gov/books/NBK525874/

Ho, M. S. K., & Lee, C. W. (2012). Cognitive behaviour therapy versus eye movement desensitisation and reprocessing for post-traumatic disorder—Is it all in the homework then? *European Review of Applied Psychology/Revue Européenne de Psychologie Appliquée*, *62*(4), 253–260. https://doi.org/10.1016/j.erap.2012.08.001

Ho, P., & Ross, D. A. (2017). More than a gut feeling: The implications of the gut microbiota in psychiatry. *Biological Psychiatry*, *81*(5), e35–e37. https://doi.org/10.1016/j.biopsych.2016.12.018

Ho, T. C., Gutman, B., Pozzi, E., Grabe, H. J., Hosten, N., Wittfeld, K., Völzke, H., Baune, B., Dannlowski, U., Förster, K., Grotegerd, D., Redlich, R., Jansen, A., Kircher, T., Krug, A., Meinert, S., Nenadic, I., Opel, N., Dinga, R., ... Schmaal, L. (2022). Subcortical shape alterations in major depressive disorder: Findings from the ENIGMA major depressive disorder working group. *Human Brain Mapping*, *43*(1), 341–351. https://doi.org/10.1002/hbm.24988

Hodgson, K., Hutchinson, A. D., & Denson, L. (2014). Nonpharmacological treatments for ADHD: A meta-analytic review. *Journal of Attention Disorders*, *18*(4), 275–282. https://doi.org/10.1177/1087054712444732

Hoebel, J., Maske, U. E., Zeeb, H., & Lampert, T. (2017). Social inequalities and depressive symptoms in adults: The role of objective and subjective socioeconomic status. *PLOS ONE*, *12*(1), e0169764. https://doi.org/10.1371/journal.pone.0169764

Hoekstra, P. J., Dietrich, A., Edwards, M. J., Elamin, I., & Martino, D. (2013). Environmental factors in Tourette syndrome. *Neuroscience & Biobehavioral Reviews*, *37*(6), 1040–1049. https://doi.org/10.1016/j.neubiorev.2012.10.010

Hoertel, N., Sánchez-Rico, M., Vernet, R., Beeker, N., Jannot, A.-S., Neuraz, A., Salamanca, E., Paris, N., Daniel, C., Gramfort, A., Lemaitre, G., Bernaux, M., Bellamine, A., Lemogne, C., Airagnes, G., Burgun, A., & Limosin, F. (2021). Association between antidepressant use and reduced risk of intubation or death in hospitalized patients with COVID-19: Results from an observational study. *Molecular Psychiatry*, *26*(9), Article 9. https://doi.org/10.1038/s41380-021-01021-4

Hoffberg, A. S., Stearns-Yoder, K. A., & Brenner, L. A. (2020). The effectiveness of crisis line services: A systematic review. *Frontiers in Public Health*, *7*, Article 399. https://doi.org/10.3389/fpubh.2019.00399

Hoffman, I. Z. (2009). Doublethinking our way to "scientific" legitimacy: The desiccation of human experience. *Journal of the American Psychoanalytic Association*, *57*(5), 1043–1069. https://doi.org/10.1177/0003065109343925

Hoffman, L., & Lincoln, J. (2011). Science, interpretation, and identity in the sexual orientation debate: What does finger length have to do with understanding a person? *PsycCRITIQUES*, *56*(15). https://doi.org/10.1037/a0023178

Hofmann, S. G., Asnaani, A., & Hinton, D. E. (2010). Cultural aspects in social anxiety and social anxiety disorder. *Depression and Anxiety*, *27*(12), 1117–1127. https://doi.org/10.1002/da.20759

Hofmann, S. G., Asnaani, A., Vonk, I. J. J., Sawyer, A. T., & Fang, A. (2012). The efficacy of cognitive behavioral therapy: A review of meta-analyses. *Cognitive Therapy and Research*, *36*(5), 427–440. https://doi.org/10.1007/s10608-012-9476-1

Hofmann, S. G., & Gómez, A. F. (2017). Mindfulness-based interventions for anxiety and depression. *The Psychiatric Clinics of North America*, *40*(4), 739–749. https://doi.org/10.1016/j.psc.2017.08.008

Hofmann, S. G., & Hinton, D. E. (2014). Cross-cultural aspects of anxiety disorders. *Current Psychiatry Reports*, *16*(6), 450. https://doi.org/10.1007/s11920-014-0450-3

Hofmann, S. G., Moscovitch, D. A., & Heinrichs, N. (2002). Evolutionary mechanisms of fear and anxiety. *Journal of Cognitive Psychotherapy*, *16*(3), 317–330. https://doi.org/10.1891/jcop.16.3.317.52519

Hoge, E. A., Bui, E., Mete, M., Dutton, M. A., Baker, A. W., & Simon, N. M. (2022). Mindfulness-based stress reduction vs escitalopram for the treatment of adults with anxiety disorders: A randomized clinical trial. *JAMA Psychiatry*. https://doi.org/10.1001/jamapsychiatry.2022.3679

Hogue, A., Bobek, M., Dauber, S., Henderson, C. E., McLeod, B. D., & Southam-Gerow, M. A. (2017). Distilling the core elements of family therapy for adolescent substance use: Conceptual and empirical solutions. *Journal of Child & Adolescent Substance Abuse*, *26*(6), 437–453. https://doi.org/10.1080/1067828X.2017.1322020

Holenstein, N. (2020, September 12). Looking at eating disorders in developing countries. *Borgen Magazine*. https://www.borgenmagazine.com/eating-disorders-in-developing-countries/

Holland, G., & Tiggemann, M. (2016). A systematic review of the impact of the use of social networking sites on body image and disordered eating outcomes. *Body Image*, *17*, 100–110. https://doi.org/10.1016/j.bodyim.2016.02.008

Holland, J. M., Rozalski, V., Thompson, K. L., Tiongson, R. J., Schatzberg, A. F., O'Hara, R., & Gallagher-Thompson, D. (2014). The unique impact of late-life bereavement and prolonged grief on diurnal cortisol. *The Journals of Gerontology: Series B: Psychological Sciences and Social Sciences*, *69B*(1), 4–11. https://doi.org/10.1093/geronb/gbt051

Holliday, K. L., Macfarlane, G. J., Nicholl, B. I., Creed, F., Thomson, W., & McBeth, J. (2010). Genetic variation in neuroendocrine genes associates with somatic symptoms in the general population: Results from the EPIFUND study. *Journal of Psychosomatic Research*, *68*(5), 469–474. https://doi.org/10.1016/j.jpsychores.2010.01.024

Holliday, S. B., Dubowitz, T., Haas, A., Ghosh-Dastidar, B., DeSantis, A., & Troxel, W. M. (2020). The association between discrimination and PTSD in African Americans: Exploring the role of gender. *Ethnicity & Health*, *25*(5), 717–731. https://doi.org/10.1080/13557858.2018.1444150

Hölling, I. (2001). About the impossibility of a single (ex-)user and survivor of psychiatry position. *Acta Psychiatrica Scandinavica. Supplementum*, *104*(Suppl. 410), 102–106. https://doi.org/10.1034/j.1600-0447.2001.1040s2102.x

Hollon, S. D. (2006). Randomized clinical trials. In J. C. Norcross, L. E. Beutler, & R. F. Levant (Eds.), *Evidenced-based practices in mental health* (pp. 96–105). American Psychological Association.

Holmes, E. A., Brown, R. J., Mansell, W., Fearon, R. P., Hunter, E. C. M., Frasquilho, F., & Oakley, D. A. (2005). Are there two qualitatively distinct forms of dissociation? A review and some clinical implications. *Clinical Psychology Review*, *25*(1), 1–23. https://doi.org/10.1016/j.cpr.2004.08.006

Holmes, J. (2015a). Attachment theory in clinical practice: A personal account. *British Journal of Psychotherapy*, *31*(2), 208–228. https://doi.org/10.1111/bjp.12151

Holmes, J. (2015b, August 24). The case for teaching ignorance. *The New York Times*. https://www.nytimes.com/2015/08/24/opinion/the-case-for-teaching-ignorance.html

Holmes, L. (2017). *Suicide rates for teen boys and girls are climbing*. http://www.huffingtonpost.com/entry/suicide-rates-teen-girls_us_59848b64e4b0cb15b1be13f4

Holper, L., & Hengartner, M. P. (2020). Comparative efficacy of placebos in short-term antidepressant trials for major depression: A secondary meta-analysis of placebo-controlled trials. *BMC Psychiatry*, *20*(1), 437. https://doi.org/10.1186/s12888-020-02839-y

Holster, J., Hawks, E. M., & Ostermeyer, B. (2017). Somatic symptom and related disorders. *Psychiatric Annals*, *47*(4), 184–191. http://dx.doi.org/10.3928/00485713-20170308-03

Holtom-Viesel, A., & Allan, S. (2014). A systematic review of the literature on family functioning across all eating disorder diagnoses in comparison to control families. *Clinical Psychology Review*, *34*(1), 29–43. https://doi.org/10.1016/j.cpr.2013.10.005

Honos-Webb, L. (2005). *The gift of ADHD: How to transform your child's problems into strengths* (pp. vi, 204). New Harbinger Publications.

Hopf, D., Eckstein, M., Aguilar-Raab, C., Warth, M., & Ditzen, B. (2020). Neuroendocrine mechanisms of grief and bereavement: A systematic review and implications for future interventions. *Journal of Neuroendocrinology*, *32*(8), e12887. https://doi.org/10.1111/jne.12887

Hoppen, T. H., Lindemann, A. S., & Morina, N. (2022). Safety of psychological interventions for adult post-traumatic stress disorder: Meta-analysis on the incidence and relative risk of deterioration, adverse events and serious adverse events. *The British Journal of Psychiatry*, 1–10. https://doi.org/10.1192/bjp.2022.111

Hopwood, T. L., & Schutte, N. S. (2017). A meta-analytic investigation of the impact of mindfulness-based interventions on post traumatic stress. *Clinical Psychology Review*, *57*, 12–20. https://doi.org/10.1016/j.cpr.2017.08.002

Horesh, D., Lowe, S. R., Galea, S., Aiello, A. E., Uddin, M., & Koenen, K. C. (2017). An in-depth look into PTSD-depression comorbidity: A longitudinal study of chronically-exposed Detroit residents. *Journal of Affective Disorders*, *208*, 653–661. https://doi.org/10.1016/j.jad.2016.08.053

Horn, E. K., Bartak, A., Meerman, A. M. M. A., Rossum, B. V., Ziegler, U. M., Thunnissen, M., Soons, M., Andrea, H., Hamers, E. F. M., Emmelkamp, P. M. G., Stijnen, T., Busschbach, J. J. V., & Verheul, R. (2015). Effectiveness of psychotherapy in personality disorders not otherwise specified: A comparison of different treatment modalities. *Clinical Psychology & Psychotherapy*, *22*(5), 426–442. https://doi.org/10.1002/cpp.1904

Horney, K. (1924). On the genesis of the castration complex in women. *The International Journal of Psychoanalysis*, *5*, 50–65.

Horowitz, M. J. (1973). Phase oriented treatment of stress response syndromes. *American Journal of Psychotherapy*, *27*(4), 506–515. https://doi.org/10.1176/appi.psychotherapy.1973.27.4.506

Horowitz, M. J. (1991). Short-term dynamic therapy of stress response syndromes. In P. Crits-Christoph & J. P. Barber (Eds.), *Handbook of short-term dynamic psychotherapy* (pp. 166–198). Basic Books.

Horowitz, M. J. (2014). Grieving: The role of self-reorganization. *Psychodynamic Psychiatry*, *42*(1), 89–97. https://doi.org/10.1521/pdps.2014.42.1.89

Horowitz, M. J., Wilner, N., Kaltreider, N., & Alvarez, W. (1980). Signs and symptoms of posttraumatic stress disorder. *Archives of General Psychiatry*, *37*(1), 85–92. https://doi.org/10.1001/archpsyc.1980.01780140087010

Horowitz, M. J., Wilner, N., Marmar, C., & Krupnick, J. (1980). Pathological grief and the activity of latent self-images. *The American Journal of Psychiatry*, *137*(10), 1157–1162.

Horowitz, R. (2002). Psychotherapy and schizophrenia: The mirror of countertransference. *Clinical Social Work Journal*, *30*(3), 235–244. https://doi.org/10.1023/A:1016041330728

Horwitz, A. G., Berona, J., Busby, D. R., Eisenberg, D., Zheng, K., Pistorello, J., Albucher, R., Coryell, W., Favorite, T., Walloch, J. C., & King, C. A. (2020). Variation in suicide risk among subgroups of sexual and gender minority college students. *Suicide and Life-Threatening Behavior*, *50*(5), 1041–1053. https://doi.org/10.1111/sltb.12637

Horwitz, A. V. (2013). *Anxiety: A short history*. The Johns Hopkins University Press.

Horwitz, A. V. (2021). *DSM: A history of psychiatry's bible*. Johns Hopkins University Press.

Horwitz, A. V., & Wakefield, J. C. (2007). *The loss of sadness: How psychiatry transformed normal sadness into depressive disorder*. Oxford University Press.

Horwitz, B. N., Marceau, K., Narusyte, J., Ganiban, J., Spotts, E. L., Reiss, D., Lichtenstein, P., & Neiderhiser, J. M. (2015). Parental criticism is an environmental influence on adolescent somatic symptoms. *Journal of Family Psychology*, *29*(2), 283–289. https://doi.org/10.1037/fam0000065

Hoskins, M. D., Bridges, J., Sinnerton, R., Nakamura, A., Underwood, J. F. G., Slater, A., Lee, M. R. D., Clarke, L., Lewis, C., Roberts, N. P., & Bisson, J. I. (2021). Pharmacological therapy for post-traumatic stress disorder: A systematic review and meta-analysis of monotherapy, augmentation and head-to-head approaches. *European Journal of Psychotraumatology*, *12*(1). https://doi.org/10.1080/20008198.2020.1802920

Hoskins, M., Pearce, J., Bethell, A., Dankova, L., Barbui, C., Tol, W. A., van Ommeren, M., de Jong, J., Seedat, S., Chen, H., & Bisson, J. I. (2015). Pharmacotherapy for post-traumatic stress disorder: Systematic review and meta-analysis. *The British Journal of Psychiatry*, *206*(2), 93–100. https://doi.org/10.1192/bjp.bp.114.148551

Hossain, M., Pearson, R. J., McAlpine, A., Bacchus, L. J., Spangaro, J., Muthuri, S., Muuo, S., Franchi, G., Hess, T., Bangha, M., & Izugbara, C. (2021). Gender-based violence and its association with mental health among Somali women in a Kenyan refugee camp: A latent class analysis. *Journal of Epidemiology and Community Health*, *75*(4), 327–334. https://doi.org/10.1136/jech-2020-214086

Hosseinzadeh Zoroufchi, B., Doustmohammadi, H., Mokhtari, T., & Abdollahpour, A. (2021). Benzodiazepines related sexual dysfunctions: A critical review on pharmacology and mechanism of action. *Revista Internacional de Andrología*, *19*(1), 62–68. https://doi.org/10.1016/j.androl.2019.08.003

Hotopf, M., Hardy, R., & Lewis, G. (1997). Discontinuation rates of SSRIs and tricyclic antidepressants: A meta-analysis and investigation of heterogeneity. *The British Journal of Psychiatry*, *170*(2), 120–127. https://doi.org/10.1192/bjp.170.2.120

Hou, R., & Baldwin, D. S. (2012). A neuroimmunological perspective on anxiety disorders. *Human Psychopharmacology: Clinical and Experimental*, *27*(1), 6–14. https://doi.org/10.1002/hup.1259

Hou, R., Garner, M., Holmes, C., Osmond, C., Teeling, J., Lau, L., & Baldwin, D. S. (2017). Peripheral inflammatory cytokines and immune balance in Generalised Anxiety Disorder: Case-controlled study. *Brain, Behavior, and Immunity*, *62*, 212–218. https://doi.org/10.1016/j.bbi.2017.01.021

Hourani, L., Tueller, S., Kizakevich, P., Lewis, G., Strange, L., Weimer, B., Bryant, S., Bishop, E., Hubal, R., & Spira, J. (2016). Toward preventing post-traumatic stress disorder: Development and testing of a pilot predeployment stress inoculation training program. *Military Medicine*, *181*(9), 1151–1160. https://doi.org/10.7205/MILMED-D-15-00192

Houts, A. C. (1996). Harmful dysfunction and the search for value neutrality in the definition of mental disorder: Response to Wakefield, part 2. *Behaviour Research and Therapy*, *39*, 1099–1132. https://doi.org/10.1016/S0005-7967(01)00053-5

Houzel, D. (2018). Autism and psychoanalysis in the French context. *International Journal of Psychoanalysis*, *99*(3), 725–745. https://doi.org/10.1080/00207578.2018.1468220

Howard, C. (2016). Understanding the difference between a feeding and eating disorder in your child. In *Eating Disorder Hope*. http://www.eatingdisorderhope.com/blog/understanding-the-difference-between-a-feeding-and-eating-disorder-in-your-child

Howard, D. M., Adams, M. J., Clarke, T.-K., Hafferty, J. D., Gibson, J., Shirali, M., Coleman, J. R. I., Hagenaars, S. P., Ward, J., Wigmore, E. M., Alloza, C., Shen, X., Barbu, M. C., Xu, E. Y., Whalley, H. C., Marioni, R. E., Porteous, D. J., Davies, G., Deary, I. J., … McIntosh, A. M. (2019). *Genome-wide meta-analysis of depression identifies 102 independent variants and highlights the importance of the prefrontal brain regions*. 33.

Howard, D. M., Adams, M. J., Shirali, M., Clarke, T.-K., Marioni, R. E., Davies, G., Coleman, J. R. I., Alloza, C., Shen, X., Barbu, M. C., Wigmore, E. M., Gibson, J., Hagenaars, S. P., Lewis, C. M., Ward, J., Smith, D. J., Sullivan, P. F., Haley, C. S., Breen, G., … McIntosh, A. M. (2018a). Addendum: Genome-wide association study of depression phenotypes in UK Biobank identifies variants in excitatory synaptic pathways. *Nature Communications*, *9*(1), 3578. https://doi.org/10.1038/s41467-018-05310-5

Howard, D. M., Adams, M. J., Shirali, M., Clarke, T.-K., Marioni, R. E., Davies, G., Coleman, J. R. I., Alloza, C., Shen, X., Barbu, M. C., Wigmore, E. M., Gibson, J., Hagenaars, S. P., Lewis, C. M., Ward, J., Smith, D. J., Sullivan, P. F., Haley, C. S., Breen, G., … McIntosh, A. M. (2018b). Genome-wide association study of depression phenotypes in UK Biobank identifies variants in excitatory synaptic pathways. *Nature Communications*, *9*(1), 1470. https://doi.org/10.1038/s41467-018-03819-3

Howard, M., Gregertsen, E. C., Hindocha, C., & Serpell, L. (2020). Impulsivity and compulsivity in anorexia and bulimia nervosa: A systematic review. *Psychiatry Research*, *293*, 113354. https://doi.org/10.1016/j.psychres.2020.113354

Howard, S., & Hughes, B. M. (2013). Type D personality is associated with a sensitized cardiovascular response to recurrent stress in men. *Biological Psychology*, *94*(2), 450–455. https://doi.org/10.1016/j.biopsycho.2013.09.001

Howe, A. S., Buttenschøn, H. N., Bani-Fatemi, A., Maron, E., Otowa, T., Erhardt, A., Binder, E. B., Gregersen, N. O., Mors, O., Woldbye, D. P., Domschke, K., Reif, A., Shlik, J., Kõks, S., Kawamura, Y., Miyashita, A., Kuwano, R., Tokunaga, K., Tanii, H., … De Luca, V. (2016). Candidate genes in panic disorder: Meta-analyses of 23 common variants in major anxiogenic pathways. *Molecular Psychiatry*, *21*(5), 665–679. https://doi.org/10.1038/mp.2015.138

Howe, L., Tickle, A., & Brown, I. (2014). "Schizophrenia is a dirty word": Service users' experiences of receiving a diagnosis of schizophrenia. *The Psychiatric Bulletin*, *38*(4), 154–158. https://doi.org/10.1192/pb.bp.113.045179

Howell, M. J. (2012). Parasomnias: An updated review. *Neurotherapeutics*, *9*(4), 753–775. https://doi.org/10.1007/s13311-012-0143-8

Howes, O. D., Hird, E. J., Adams, R. A., Corlett, P. R., & McGuire, P. (2020). Aberrant salience, information processing, and dopaminergic signaling in people at clinical high risk for psychosis. *Biological Psychiatry*, *88*(4), 304–314. https://doi.org/10.1016/j.biopsych.2020.03.012

Howes, O. D., McCutcheon, R., & Stone, J. (2015). Glutamate and dopamine in schizophrenia: An update for the 21st century. *Journal of Psychopharmacology*, *29*(2), 97–115. https://doi.org/10.1177/0269881114563634

Howes, O. D., & Murray, R. M. (2014). Schizophrenia: An integrated sociodevelopmental-cognitive model. *The Lancet*, *383*(9929), 1677–1687. https://doi.org/10.1016/S0140-6736(13)62036-X

Howes, O. D., & Nour, M. M. (2016). Dopamine and the aberrant salience hypothesis of schizophrenia. *World Psychiatry*, *15*(1), 3–4. https://doi.org/10.1002/wps.20276

Howes, R. (2009). The definition of insanity. In *In Therapy*. https://www.psychologytoday.com/blog/in-therapy/200907/the-definition-insanity-is

Hsu, C.-J., Wong, L.-C., & Lee, W.-T. (2021). Immunological dysfunction in Tourette syndrome and related disorders. *International Journal of Molecular Sciences*, *22*(2), 853. https://doi.org/10.3390/ijms22020853

Hsu, G., & Kovács, B. (2021). Association between county level cannabis dispensary counts and opioid related mortality rates in the United States: Panel data study. *BMJ*, *372*, m4957. https://doi.org/10.1136/bmj.m4957

Hu, J., Ferguson, L., Adler, K., Farah, C. A., Hastings, M. H., Sossin, W. S., & Schacher, S. (2017). Selective erasure of distinct forms of long-term synaptic plasticity underlying different forms of memory in the same postsynaptic neuron. *Current Biology*, *27*(13), 1888–1899. https://doi.org/10.1016/j.cub.2017.05.081

Hu, M. X., Turner, D., Generaal, E., Bos, D., Ikram, M. K., Ikram, M. A., Cuijpers, P., & Penninx, B. W. J. H. (2020). Exercise interventions for the prevention of depression: A systematic review of meta-analyses. *BMC Public Health*, *20*(1), 1255. https://doi.org/10.1186/s12889-020-09323-y

Hu, S., Tucker, L., & Yang, L. (2020). Beneficial effects of exercise on depression and anxiety during the Covid-19 pandemic: A narrative review. *Frontiers in Psychiatry*, *11*, Article 587557. https://doi.org/10.3389/fpsyt.2020.587557

Hu, T., Zhang, D., & Yang, Z. (2015). The relationship between attributional style for negative outcomes and depression: A meta-analysis. *Journal of Social and Clinical Psychology*, *34*(4), 304–321. https://doi.org/10.1521/jscp.2015.34.4.304

Huang, L., Zhao, Y., Qiang, C., & Fan, B. (2018). Is cognitive behavioral therapy a better choice for women with postnatal depression? A systematic review and meta-analysis. *PLoS ONE*, *13*(10), e0205243. https://doi.org/10.1371/journal.pone.0205243

Huang, X., Ribeiro, J. D., & Franklin, J. C. (2020). The differences between individuals engaging in nonsuicidal self-injury and suicide attempt are complex (vs. Complicated or simple). *Frontiers in Psychiatry*, *11*, Article 239. https://doi.org/10.3389/fpsyt.2020.00239

Huang, Y., Huang, X., Ebstein, R. P., & Yu, R. (2021). Intranasal oxytocin in the treatment of autism spectrum disorders: A multilevel meta-analysis. *Neuroscience & Biobehavioral Reviews*, *122*, 18–27. https://doi.org/10.1016/j.neubiorev.2020.12.028

Huang, Z.-D., Zhao, Y.-F., Li, S., Gu, H.-Y., Lin, L.-L., Yang, Z.-Y., Niu, Y.-M., Zhang, C., & Luo, J. (2020). Comparative efficacy and acceptability of pharmaceutical management for adults with post-traumatic stress disorder: A systematic review and meta-analysis. *Frontiers in Pharmacology*, *11*, Article 559. https://doi.org/10.3389/fphar.2020.00559

Huda, A. S. (2021). The medical model and its application in mental health. *International Review of Psychiatry*, *33*(5), 463–470. https://doi.org/10.1080/09540261.2020.1845125

Hudson, J. I., Pope, H. G., Jonas, J. M., Yurgelun-Todd, D., & Frankenburg, F. R. (1987). A controlled family history study of bulimia. *Psychological Medicine*, *17*(4), 883–890. https://doi.org/10.1017/S0033291700000684

Hughes, H. K., Mills Ko, E., Rose, D., & Ashwood, P. (2018). Immune dysfunction and autoimmunity as pathological mechanisms in autism spectrum disorders. *Frontiers in Cellular Neuroscience*, *12*, Article 405. https://www.doi.org/10.3389/fncel.2018.00405

Hulgaard, D., Dehlholm-Lambertsen, G., & Rask, C. U. (2019). Family-based interventions for children and adolescents with functional somatic symptoms: A systematic review. *Journal of Family Therapy*, 41(1), 4–28. https://doi.org/10.1111/1467-6427.12199

Hulme, C., & Snowling, M. J. (2016). Reading disorders and dyslexia. *Current Opinion in Pediatrics*, 28(6), 731–735. https://doi.org/10.1097/MOP.0000000000000411

Hume, D. (1783). *Essays on suicide and the immortality of the soul: The complete 1783 edition*. http://www.geocities.ws/iloveselfinjury/ebooks/essaysonsuicide.pdf

Humphreys, C. L., Rubin, J. S., Knudson, R. M., & Stiles, W. B. (2005). The assimilation of anger in a case of dissociative identity disorder. *Counselling Psychology Quarterly*, 18(2), 121–132. https://doi.org/10.1080/09515070500136488

Humphries, T., & Bone, J. (1993). Validity of IQ-achievement discrepancy criteria for identifying learning disabilities. *Canadian Journal of School Psychology*, 9(2), 181–191. https://doi.org/10.1177/082957359400900206

Hunger, C., Hilzinger, R., Klewinghaus, L., Deusser, L., Sander, A., Mander, J., Bents, H., Ditzen, B., & Schweitzer, J. (2020). Comparing cognitive behavioral therapy and systemic therapy for social anxiety disorder: Randomized controlled pilot trial (SOPHO-CBT/ST). *Family Process*, 59(4), 1389–1406. https://doi.org/10.1111/famp.12492

Hunt, G. E., Large, M. M., Cleary, M., Lai, H. M. X., & Saunders, J. B. (2018). Prevalence of comorbid substance use in schizophrenia spectrum disorders in community and clinical settings, 1990–2017: Systematic review and meta-analysis. *Drug and Alcohol Dependence*, 191, 234–258. https://doi.org/10.1016/j.drugalcdep.2018.07.011

Hunt, G. E., Malhi, G. S., Lai, H. M. X., & Cleary, M. (2020). Prevalence of comorbid substance use in major depressive disorder in community and clinical settings, 1990–2019: Systematic review and meta-analysis. *Journal of Affective Disorders*, 266, 288–304. https://doi.org/10.1016/j.jad.2020.01.141

Hunt, R. D. (2006, March 9). Functional roles of norepinephrine and dopamine in ADHD. Medscape. http://www.medscape.org/viewarticle/523887

Hunter, M. D., & Woodruff, P. W. R. (2005). History, aetiology and symptomatology of schizophrenia. *Psychiatry*, 4(10), 2–6. https://doi.org/10.1383/psyt.2005.4.10.2

Huprich, S. K., Jowers, C., & Nelson, S. (2019). Comparing DSM–5-Hybrid, SWAP, and PDM prototype models of personality disorders: Convergent and divergent findings. *Personality Disorders: Theory, Research, and Treatment*, 10(4), 376–382. https://doi.org/10.1037/per0000340

Hurl, C. (2011). Urine trouble: A social history of bedwetting and its regulation. *History of the Human Sciences*, 24(2), 48–64. https://doi.org/10.1177/0952695111400957

Hurst, K., Read, S., & Holtham, T. (2015). Bulimia nervosa in adolescents: A new therapeutic frontier. *Journal of Family Therapy*. doi:10.1111/1467-6427.12095

Huryk, K. M., Drury, C. R., & Loeb, K. L. (2021). Diseases of affluence? A systematic review of the literature on socioeconomic diversity in eating disorders. *Eating Behaviors*, 43, 101548. https://doi.org/10.1016/j.eatbeh.2021.101548

Husain, M. I., Chaudhry, I. B., Khoso, A. B., Husain, M. O., Hodsoll, J., Ansari, M. A., Naqvi, H. A., Minhas, F. A., Carvalho, A. F., Meyer, J. H., Deakin, B., Mulsant, B. H., Husain, N., & Young, A. H. (2020). Minocycline and celecoxib as adjunctive treatments for bipolar depression: A multicentre, factorial design randomised controlled trial. *The Lancet Psychiatry*, 7(6), 515–527. https://doi.org/10.1016/S2215-0366(20)30138-3

Husby, S. M., & Wichstrøm, L. (2016). Interrelationships and continuities in symptoms of oppositional defiant and conduct disorders from age 4 to 10 in the community. *Journal of Abnormal Child Psychology*. https://doi.org/10.1007/s10802-016-0210-4

Husted, J. A., Ahmed, R., Chow, E. W. C., Brzustowicz, L. M., & Bassett, A. S. (2010). Childhood trauma and genetic factors in familial schizophrenia associated with the NOS1AP gene. *Schizophrenia Research*, 121(1–3), 187–192. https://doi.org/10.1016/j.schres.2010.05.021

Husted, J. A., Ahmed, R., Chow, E. W. C., Brzustowicz, L. M., & Bassett, A. S. (2012). Early environmental exposures influence schizophrenia expression even in the presence of strong genetic predisposition. *Schizophrenia Research*, 137(1–3), 166–168. https://doi.org/10.1016/j.schres.2012.02.009

Hvidt, E. A., Ploug, T., & Holm, S. (2016). The impact of telephone crisis services on suicidal users: A systematic review of the past 45 years. *Mental Health Review Journal*, 21(2), 141–160. https://doi.org/10.1108/MHRJ-07-2015-0019

Hviid, A., Hansen, J. V., Frisch, M., & Melbye, M. (2019). Measles, mumps, rubella vaccination and autism: A nationwide cohort study. *Annals of Internal Medicine*, 170(8), 513–520. https://doi.org/10.7326/M18-2101

Hyman, S. (2014). Mental health: Depression needs large human-genetics studies. *Nature*, 515(7526), 189–191. https://doi.org/10.1038/515189a

Hypericum Depression Trial Study, G. (2002). Effect of hypericum perforatum (St. John's wort) in major depressive disorder: A randomized controlled trial. *JAMA*, 287(14), 1807–1814. https://doi.org/10.1001/jama.287.14.1807

Iacovino, J. M., Jackson, J. J., & Oltmanns, T. F. (2014). The relative impact of socioeconomic status and childhood trauma on Black-White differences in paranoid personality disorder symptoms. *Journal of Abnormal Psychology*, 123(1), 225–230. https://doi.org/10.1037/a0035258

Iacovou, S. (2011). What is the difference between existential anxiety and so called neurotic anxiety? "The sine qua non of true vitality" an examination of the difference between existential anxiety and neurotic anxiety. *Existential Analysis*, 22(2), 356–367.

Iannitelli, A., Parnanzone, S., Pizziconi, G., Riccobono, G., & Pacitti, F. (2019). Psychodynamically oriented psychopharmacotherapy: Towards a necessary synthesis. *Frontiers in Human Neuroscience*, 13, Article 15. https://doi.org/10.3389/fnhum.2019.00015

Iasenza, S. (2001). Sex therapy with "A New View." *Women & Therapy*, 24(1–2), 43–46. https://doi.org/10.1300/J015v24n01_08

Ibrahim, I. (2020). Specific learning disorder in children with autism spectrum disorder: Current issues and future implications. *Advances in Neurodevelopmental Disorders*, 4(2), 103–112. https://doi.org/10.1007/s41252-019-00141-x

Ibrahim, K., & Sukhodolsky, D. (2018). RDoC and autism. In F. R. Volkmar (Ed.), *Encyclopedia of autism spectrum disorders* (pp. 1–2). https://doi.org/10.1007/978-1-4614-6435-8_102261-1

ICD vs. DSM. (2009, October). *Monitor on Psychology*, 40(9), 63.

Iglewicz, A. M. D., Seay, K. B. S., Vigeant, S. B. S., Jouhal, S. K. M. D., & Zisook, S. M. D. (2013). The bereavement exclusion: The truth between pathology and politics. *Psychiatric Annals*, 43(6), 261–266. https://doi.org/10.3928/00485713-20130605-05

Iglewicz, A., Shear, M. K., Reynolds, C. F. I., Simon, N., Lebowitz, B., & Zisook, S. (2020). Complicated grief therapy for clinicians: An evidence-based protocol for mental health practice. *Depression and Anxiety*, 37(1), 90–98. https://doi.org/10.1002/da.22965

Ilieva, K., Atanasova, M., Atanasova, D., Kortenska, L., & Tchekalarova, J. (2021). Chronic agomelatine treatment alleviates icvAβ-induced anxiety and depressive-like behavior through affecting Aβ metabolism in the hippocampus in a rat model of Alzheimer's disease. *Physiology & Behavior*, 239. https://doi.org/10.1016/j.physbeh.2021.113525

Ilinca, S., & Suzuki, E. (2021). Gender and socioeconomic differences in modifiable risk factors for Alzheimer's disease and other types of dementia throughout the life course. In M. T. Ferretti, A. S. Dimech, & A. S. Chadha (Eds.), *Sex and gender differences in Alzheimer's disease* (pp. 333–360). Academic Press. https://doi.org/10.1016/B978-0-12-819344-0.00004-1

Indelli, P., Landeira-Fernandez, J., & Mograbi, D. C. (2018). In search of connection: Towards a transdiagnostic view of dissociative phenomena through research domain criteria (RDoC) framework. *Psicologia Clínica*, 30(3), 509–540.

Independent Living Association. (2021, January 25). *Home is where the heart is: Group homes for intellectually and developmentally disabled adults*. https://ilaonline.org/home-is-where-the-heart-is-group-homes-for-intellectually-and-developmentally-disabled-adults/

Inder, M. L., Crowe, M. T., Luty, S. E., Carter, J. D., Moor, S., Frampton, C. M., & Joyce, P. R. (2015). Randomized, controlled trial of interpersonal and social rhythm therapy for young people with bipolar disorder. *Bipolar Disorders*, 17(2), 128–138. https://doi.org/10.1111/bdi.12273

InformedHealth.org. (2019). Premature ejaculation: What can I do on my own? In *InformedHealth.org* [Internet]. Institute for Quality and Efficiency in Health Care (IQWiG). https://www.ncbi.nlm.nih.gov/books/NBK547551/

Ingamells, K., & Epston, D. (2014). Love is not all you need: A revolutionary approach to parental abuse. *Australian and New Zealand Journal of Family Therapy*, 35(3), 364–382. https://doi.org/10.1002/anzf.1069

Ingersoll, K. (2022, March 1). *Motivational interviewing for substance use disorders*. UpToDate. https://www.uptodate.com/contents/motivational-interviewing-for-substance-use-disorders

Ingle, M. (2019, September 11). *How does the Soteria House heal?* Mad In America. https://www.madinamerica.com/2019/09/soteria-house-heal/

Insanity. (n.d.). In *The Free Dictionary*. Retrieved October 31, 2022, from https://legal-dictionary.thefreedictionary.com/insanity

Insanity defense in criminal cases. (2022, October). *Justia*. https://www.justia.com/criminal/defenses/insanity/

Insel, T. (2013, April 29). Transforming diagnosis. *National Institute of Mental Health*. http://psychrights.org/2013/130429NIMHTransformingDiagnosis.htm

Insel, T., Cuthbert, B., Garvey, M., Heinssen, R., Pine, D. S., Quinn, K., Sanislow, C., & Wang, P. (2010). Research domain criteria (RDoC): Toward a new classification framework for research on mental disorders. *The American Journal of Psychiatry*, 167(7), 748–751. https://doi.org/10.1176/appi.ajp.2010.09091379

International Society for the Study of Trauma and Dissociation. (2011). Guidelines for treating dissociative identity disorder in adults, third revision: Summary version. *Journal of Trauma & Dissociation*, 12(2), 188–212. https://doi.org/10.1080/15299732.2011.537248

Inzaghi, E., Reiter, E., & Cianfarani, S. (2019). The challenge of defining and investigating the causes of idiopathic short stature and finding an effective therapy. *Hormone Research in Paediatrics*, 92(2), 71–83. https://doi.org/10.1159/000502901

Ioannidis, K., Taylor, C., Holt, L., Brown, K., Lochner, C., Fineberg, N. A., Corazza, O., Chamberlain, S. R., Roman-Urrestarazu, A., & Czabanowska, K. (2021). Problematic usage of the internet and eating disorder and related psychopathology: A multifaceted, systematic review and meta-analysis. *Neuroscience & Biobehavioral Reviews*, 125, 569–581. https://doi.org/10.1016/j.neubiorev.2021.03.005

Iosifescu, D. V., Jones, A., O'Gorman, C., Streicher, C., Feliz, S., Fava, M., & Tabuteau, H. (2022). Efficacy and safety of AXS-05 (dextromethorphan-bupropion) in patients with major depressive disorder: A phase 3 randomized clinical trial (GEMINI). *The Journal of Clinical Psychiatry*, 83(4), 41226. https://doi.org/10.4088/JCP.21m14345

Ip, M. L., St. Louis, K. O., Myers, F. L., & Xue, S. A. (2012). Stuttering attitudes in Hong Kong and adjacent Mainland China. *International Journal of Speech-Language Pathology*, 14(6), 543–556. https://doi.org/10.3109/17549507.2012.712158

Iranpour, S., Sabour, S., Koohi, F., & Saadati, H. M. (2022). The trend and pattern of depression prevalence in the U.S.: Data from National Health and Nutrition Examination Survey (NHANES) 2005 to 2016. *Journal of Affective Disorders*, 298, 508–515. https://doi.org/10.1016/j.jad.2021.11.027

Ironson, G., Cruess, D., & Kumar, M. (2007). Immune and neuroendocrine alterations in post-traumatic stress disorder. In R. Ader (Ed.), *Psychoneuroimmunology* (Vol. 1, pp. 531–547). Elsevier Academic Press.

Irvine, J. (2005). *Disorders of desire: Sexuality and gender in modern American sexology* (revised and expanded). Temple University Press. https://books.google.com/books?id=uIJXT7ZCTCsC&pg=PA112&lpg=PA112&dq=hite+report+critique&source=bl&ots=kUGF5hmmUj&sig=BPB1Jpye9m-2VUS5SfD-bVpzl2oE&hl=en&sa=X&ved=0ahUKEwiLqfuCnrzOAhWJBcAKHTdXAiE4ChDoAQg-4MAU#v=snippet&q=Hite%20Report&f=false

Isaac, D. (2013). Culture-bound syndromes in mental health: A discussion paper. *Journal of Psychiatric and Mental Health Nursing*, 20(4), 355–361. https://doi.org/10.1111/jpm.12016

Isenberg-Grzeda, E., Kutner, H. E., & Nicolson, S. E. (2012). Wernicke-Korsakoff-syndrome: Under-recognized and under-treated. *Psychosomatics*, 53(6), 507–516. https://doi.org/10.1016/j.psym.2012.04.008

Ito, M., Horikoshi, M., Kato, N., Oe, Y., Fujisato, H., Yamaguchi, K., Nakajima, S., Miyamae, M., Toyota, A., Okumura, Y., & Takebayashi, Y. (2022). Efficacy of the unified protocol for transdiagnostic cognitive-behavioral treatment for depressive and anxiety disorders: A randomized controlled trial. *Psychological Medicine*, 1–12. https://doi.org/10.1017/S0033291721005067

Itoi, K., & Sugimoto, N. (2010). The brainstem noradrenergic systems in stress, anxiety and depression. *Journal of Neuroendocrinology*, 22(5), 355–361. https://doi.org/10.1111/j.1365-2826.2010.01988.x

Ivanova, I., & Watson, J. (2014). Emotion-focused therapy for eating disorders: Enhancing emotional processing. *Person-Centered and Experiential Psychotherapies*, 13(4), 278–293. https://doi.org/10.1080/14779757.2014.910132

Ives, R., & Ghelani, P. (2006). Polydrug use (the use of drugs in combination): A brief review. *Drugs: Education, Prevention & Policy*, 13(3), 225–232. https://doi.org/10.1080/09687630600655596

Jablensky, A. (2010). The diagnostic concept of schizophrenia: Its history, evolution, and future prospects. *Dialogues in Clinical Neuroscience*, 12(3), 271–287.

Jack, D. C. (1991). *Silencing the self: Women and depression*. HarperCollins.

Jack, D. C., & Ali, A. (2010). *Silencing the self across cultures: Depression and gender in the social world*. Oxford University Press.

Jackson, M. R. (2015). Resistance to qual/quant parity: Why the "paradigm" discussion can't be avoided. *Qualitative Psychology*, 2(2), 181–198. https://doi.org/10.1037/qup0000031

Jackson, S., Baity, M. R., Bobb, K., Swick, D., & Giorgio, J. (2019). Stress inoculation training outcomes among veterans with PTSD and TBI. *Psychological Trauma: Theory, Research, Practice, and Policy*, 11(8), 842–850. https://doi.org/10.1037/tra0000432

Jackson, S., & Rees, A. (2007). The appalling appeal of nature: The popular influence of evolutionary psychology as a problem for sociology. *Sociology*, 41(5), 917–930. doi:10.1177/0038038507080445

Jackson v. Indiana, 406 U.S. 715 (1972). https://supreme.justia.com/cases/federal/us/406/715/

Jacob, G. A., & Arntz, A. (2013). Schema therapy for personality disorders—A review. *International Journal of Cognitive Therapy*, 6(2), 171–185. https://doi.org/10.1521/ijct.2013.6.2.171

Jacobs, Y. (2019). Soteria: Reflections on "Being with" finding ones way through psychosis. *Journal of Humanistic Psychology*, 59(5), 681–685. https://doi.org/10.1177/0022167818763201

Jaeger, J. A., Echiverri, A., Zoellner, L. A., Post, L., & Feeny, N. C. (2010). Factors associated with choice of exposure therapy for PTSD. *International Journal of Behavioral Consultation and Therapy*, 5(3–4), 294–310. https://doi.org/10.1037/h0100890

Jaeger, K. (2022, March 31). Federal marijuana legalization bill would add billions in revenue and reduce prison costs, Congressional Budget Office says. *Marijuana Moment*. https://www.marijuanamoment.net/federal-marijuana-legalization-bill-would-add-billions-in-revenue-and-reduce-prison-costs-congressional-budget-office-says/

Jahn, K., Kurz, B., Sinke, C., Kneer, J., Riemer, O., Ponseti, J., Walter, M., Beier, K. M., Walter, H., Frieling, H., Schiffer, B., & Kruger, T. H. C. (2022). Serotonin system-associated genetic and epigenetic changes in pedophilia and child sexual offending. *Journal of Psychiatric Research*, 145, 60–69. https://doi.org/10.1016/j.jpsychires.2021.11.042

Jain, A., Marshall, J., Buikema, A., Bancroft, T., Kelly, J. P., & Newschaffer, C. J. (2015). Autism occurrence by MMR vaccine status among US children with older siblings with and without autism. *JAMA: Journal of the American Medical Association*, 313(15), 1534–1540. https://doi.org/10.1001/jama.2015.3077

Jakšić, N., Brajković, L., Ivezić, E., Topić, R., & Jakovljević, M. (2012). The role of personality traits in posttraumatic stress disorder (PTSD). *Psychiatria Danubina*, 24(3), 256–266.

Jakubczyk, A., Krasowska, A., Bugaj, M., Kopera, M., Klimkiewicz, A., Łoczewska, A., Michalska, A., Majewska, A., Szejko, N., Podgórska, A., Sołowiej, M., Markuszewski, L., Jakima, S., Płoski, R., Brower, K., & Wojnar, M. (2017). Paraphilic sexual offenders do not differ from control subjects with respect to dopamine- and serotonin-related genetic polymorphisms. *The Journal of Sexual Medicine*, 14(1), 125–133. https://doi.org/10.1016/j.jsxm.2016.11.309

Jakupcak, M., Wagner, A., Paulson, A., Varra, A., & McFall, M. (2010). Behavioral activation as a primary care-based treatment for PTSD and depression among returning veterans. *Journal of Traumatic Stress*, 23(4), 491–495. https://doi.org/10.1002/jts.20543

Jalopy, R. K. (2020, December 29). Transgender trouble: 40 years of gender essentialism and gatekeeping. *Current Affairs*. https://www.currentaffairs.org/2020/12/transgender-trouble-40-years-of-gender-essentialism-and-gatekeeping

James, R. J. E., & Tunney, R. J. (2017). The need for a behavioural analysis of behavioural addictions. *Clinical Psychology Review*, 52, 69–76. https://doi.org/10.1016/j.cpr.2016.11.010

Jamison, D. (2014). Daudi Azibo: Defining and developing africana psychological theory, research and practice. *The Journal of Pan African Studies*, 7(5), 2–18.

Janca, A., Isaac, M., Bennett, L. A., & Tacchini, G. (1995). Somatoform disorders in different cultures: A mail questionnaire survey. *Social Psychiatry and Psychiatric Epidemiology*, 30(1), 44–48. https://doi.org/10.1007/BF00784434

Janet, P. (1886). *Unconscious acts and the doubling of personality during provoked somnambulism* (Vol. 22, pp. 577–592). Retrieved from https://sites.google.com/site/psychiatryfootnotes/translations/unconscious-acts

Jang, K. L., Paris, J., Zweig-Frank, H., & Livesley, W. J. (1998). Twin study of dissociative experience. *Journal of Nervous and Mental Disease*, 186(6), 345–351. https://doi.org/10.1097/00005053-199806000-00004

Jani, S., Johnson, R. S., Banu, S., & Shah, A. (2016). Cross-cultural bias in the diagnosis of borderline personality disorder. *Bulletin of the Menninger Clinic*, 80(2), 146–165. https://doi.org/10.1521/bumc.2016.80.2.146

Janicak, P. G., & Carpenter, L. (2014). The efficacy of transcranial magnetic stimulation for major depression: A review of the evidence. *Psychiatric Annals*, 44(6), 284–292. https://doi.org/10.3928/00485713-20140609-06

Janiri, D., Kotzalidis, G. D., Di Luzio, M., Giuseppin, G., Simonetti, A., Janiri, L., & Sani, G. (2021). Genetic neuroimaging of bipolar disorder: A systematic 2017–2020 update. *Psychiatric Genetics*, 31(2), 50–64. https://doi.org/10.1097/YPG.0000000000000274

Jankovic, J. (2022, June 13). *Tourette syndrome: Pathogenesis, clinical features, and diagnosis*. UpToDate. https://www.uptodate.com/contents/tourette-syndrome-pathogenesis-clinical-features-and-diagnosis

Jankowicz, D. (2003). *The easy guide to repertory grids*. John Wiley.

Jankowski, K. (2016). *PTSD and physical health* (Issue February 23). http://www.ptsd.va.gov/professional/co-occurring/ptsd-physical-health.asp

Jannini, E. A., Burri, A., Jern, P., & Novelli, G. (2015). Genetics of human sexual behavior: Where we are, where we are going. *Sexual Medicine Reviews*, 3(2), 65–77. https://doi.org/10.1002/smrj.46

Jansen, J. E., Wøldike, P. M., Haahr, U. H., & Simonsen, E. (2015). Service user perspectives on the experience of illness and pathway to care in first-episode psychosis: A qualitative study within the TOP project. *Psychiatric Quarterly*, 86(1), 83–94. https://doi.org/10.1007/s11126-014-9332-4

Janssens, A., Van Den Noortgate, W., Goossens, L., Verschueren, K., Colpin, H., De Laet, S., Claes, S., & Van Leeuwen, K. (2015). Externalizing problem behavior in adolescence: Dopaminergic genes in interaction with peer acceptance and rejection. *Journal of Youth and Adolescence*, 44(7), 1441–1456. https://doi.org/10.1007/s10964-015-0304-2

Janus, S. S., & Janus, C. L. (1993). *The Janus report on sexual behavior*. John Wiley.

Jasbi, M., Sadeghi Bahmani, D., Karami, G., Omidbeygi, M., Peyravi, M., Panahi, A., Mirzaee, J., Holsboer-Trachsler, E., & Brand, S. (2018). Influence of adjuvant mindfulness-based cognitive therapy (MBCT) on symptoms of post-traumatic stress disorder (PTSD) in veterans—Results from a randomized control study. *Cognitive Behaviour Therapy*, 47(5), 431–446. https://doi.org/10.1080/16506073.2018.1445773

Jash, S., & Sharma, S. (2022). Viral infections and temporal programming of autism spectrum disorders in the mother's womb. *Frontiers in Virology*, 2, Article 863202. https://doi.org/10.3389/fviro.2022.863202

Jaspers, L., Feys, F., Bramer, W. M., Franco, O. H., Leusink, P., & Laan, E. T. M. (2016). Efficacy and safety of flibanserin for the treatment of hypoactive sexual desire disorder in women: A systematic review and meta-analysis. *JAMA Internal Medicine*, 176(4), 453–462. https://doi.org/10.1001/jamainternmed.2015.8565

Jauhar, S., McKenna, P. J., Radua, J., Fung, E., Salvador, R., & Laws, K. R. (2014). Cognitive-behavioural therapy for the symptoms of schizophrenia: Systematic review and meta-analysis with examination of potential bias. *The British Journal of Psychiatry*, 204(1), 20–29. https://doi.org/10.1192/bjp.bp.112.116285

Javaras, K. N., Laird, N. M., Reichborn-Kjennerud, T., Bulik, C. M., Pope, H. G., Jr., & Hudson, J. I. (2008). Familiality and heritability of binge eating disorder: Results of a case-control family study and a twin study. *International Journal of Eating Disorders*, 41(2), 174–179. doi:10.1002/eat.20484

Javitt, D. C. (2021). Glutamate in the pathophysiology of schizophrenia. In C. A. Tamminga, E. I. Ivleva, U. Reininghaus, & J. van Os (Eds.), *Psychotic disorders: Comprehensive conceptualization and treatments*. (pp. 287–296). Oxford University Press. https://doi.org/10.1093/med/9780190653279.003.0032

Jeffries, F. W., & Davis, P. (2013). What is the role of eye movements in eye movement desensitization and reprocessing (EMDR) for post-traumatic stress disorder (PTSD)? A review. *Behavioural and Cognitive Psychotherapy*, *11*(3), 290–300. https://doi.org/10.1017/S1352465812000793

Jelovac, A., Kolshus, E., & McLoughlin, D. M. (2013). Relapse following successful electroconvulsive therapy for major depression: A meta-analysis. *Neuropsychopharmacology*, *38*(12), 2467–2474. https://doi.org/10.1038/npp.2013.149

Jennings, J. H., Rizzi, G., Stamatakis, A. M., Ung, R. L., & Stuber, G. D. (2013). The inhibitory circuit architecture of the lateral hypothalamus orchestrates feeding. *Science*, *341*(6153), 1517–1521. https://doi.org/10.1126/science.1241812

Jennings, K. (2022, May 4). *Mental health startup Cerebral to stop ADHD prescriptions for new patients*. Forbes. https://www.forbes.com/sites/katiejennings/2022/05/04/mental-health-startup-cerebral-to-stop-adhd-prescriptions-for-new-patients/

Jennings, K. M., Kelly-Weeder, S., & Wolfe, B. E. (2015). Binge eating among racial minority groups in the United States: An integrative review. *Journal of the American Psychiatric Nurses Association*, *21*(2), 117–125. https://doi.org/10.1177/1078390315581923

Jennings, L. A., Laffan, A. M., Schlissel, A. C., Colligan, E., Tan, Z., Wenger, N. S., & Reuben, D. B. (2019). Health care utilization and cost outcomes of a comprehensive dementia care program for Medicare beneficiaries. *JAMA Internal Medicine*, *179*(2), 161–166. https://doi.org/10.1001/jamainternmed.2018.5579

Jensen, P. S., Mrazek, D., Knapp, P. K., Steinberg, L., Pfeffer, C., Schowalter, J., & Shapiro, T. (1997). Evolution and revolution in child psychiatry: ADHD as a disorder of adaptation. *Journal of the American Academy of Child & Adolescent Psychiatry*, *36*(12), 1672–1681. https://doi.org/10.1097/00004583-199712000-00015

Jeppesen, R., & Benros, M. E. (2019). Autoimmune diseases and psychotic disorders. *Frontiers in Psychiatry*, *10*, Article 131. https://www.doi.org/10.3389/fpsyt.2019.00131

Jerlhag, E. (2019). Gut-brain axis and addictive disorders: A review with focus on alcohol and drugs of abuse. *Pharmacology & Therapeutics*, *196*, 1–14. https://doi.org/10.1016/j.pharmthera.2018.11.005

Jewell, J. S. (2003). American nervousness: Its causes and consequences A supplement to nervous exhaustion (neurasthenia). *Journal of Nervous and Mental Disease*, *191*(1), 56–56. https://doi.org/10.1097/00005053-200301000-00010

Jiang, H., Xu, L., Shao, L., Xia, R., Yu, Z., Ling, Z., Yang, F., Deng, M., & Ruan, B. (2016). Maternal infection during pregnancy and risk of autism spectrum disorders: A systematic review and meta-analysis. *Brain, Behavior, and Immunity*, *58*, 165–172. https://doi.org/10.1016/j.bbi.2016.06.005

Jiang, Q., & Huang, X. (2013). Internet: Immersive virtual worlds. In P. M. Miller, S. A. Ball, M. E. Bates, A. W. Blume, K. M. Kampman, D. J. Kavanagh, M. E. Larimer, N. M. Petry, & P. De Witte (Eds.), *Comprehensive addictive behaviors and disorders: Vol. 1. Principles of addiction* (pp. 881–890). Elsevier Academic Press.

Jiang, Q., Huang, X., & Tao, R. (2013). Internet addiction: Cybersex. In P. M. Miller, S. A. Ball, M. E. Bates, A. W. Blume, K. M. Kampman, D. J. Kavanagh, M. E. Larimer, N. M. Petry, & P. De Witte (Eds.), *Comprehensive addictive behaviors and disorders: Vol. 1. Principles of addiction* (pp. 809–818). Elsevier Academic Press.

Jimerson, D. C., Wolfe, B. E., Metzger, E. D., Finkelstein, D. M., Cooper, T. B., & Levine, J. M. (1997). Decreased serotonin function in bulimia nervosa. *Archives of General Psychiatry*, *54*(6), 529–534. https://doi.org/10.1001/archpsyc.1997.01830180043005

Joas, E., Bäckman, K., Karanti, A., Sparding, T., Colom, F., Pålsson, E., & Landén, M. (2020). Psychoeducation for bipolar disorder and risk of recurrence and hospitalization – a within-individual analysis using registry data. *Psychological Medicine*, *50*(6), 1043–1049. https://doi.org/10.1017/S0033291719001053

Joensen, B. H., Harrington, M. O., Berens, S. C., Cairney, S, A., Gaskell, M. G., & Horner, A. J. (2022). Targeted memory reactivation during sleep can induce forgetting of overlapping memories. *Learning & Memory*, *29*(11), 401–411. https://doi.org/10.1101/lm.053594.122

Joffe, H. V., Chang, C., Sewell, C., Easley, O., Nguyen, C., Dunn, S., Lehrfeld, K., Lee, L., Kim, M.-J., Slagle, A. F., & Beitz, J. (2016). FDA approval of flibanserin—Treating hypoactive sexual desire disorder. *The New England Journal of Medicine*, *374*(2), 101–104. https://doi.org/10.1056/NEJMp1513686

Johansson, V., Kuja-Halkola, R., Cannon, T. D., Hultman, C. M., & Hedman, A. M. (2019). A population-based heritability estimate of bipolar disorder – In a Swedish twin sample. *Psychiatry Research*, *278*, 180–187. https://doi.org/10.1016/j.psychres.2019.06.010

John, S., & Jaeggi, A. V. (2021). Oxytocin levels tend to be lower in autistic children: A meta-analysis of 31 studies. *Autism*, *25*(8), 2152–2161. https://doi.org/10.1177/13623613211034375

Johnson, B. (2003). Psychological addiction, physical addiction, addictive character, and addictive personality disorder: A nosology of addictive disorders. *Canadian Journal of Psychoanalysis*, *11*(1), 135–160.

Johnson, D. A., Jackson, C. L., Williams, N. J., & Alcántara, C. (2019). Are sleep patterns influenced by race/ethnicity – a marker of relative advantage or disadvantage? Evidence to date. *Nature and Science of Sleep*, *11*, 79–95. https://doi.org/10.2147/NSS.S169312

Johnson, E. C., Border, R., Melroy-Greif, W. E., de Leeuw, C. A., Ehringer, M. A., & Keller, M. C. (2017). No evidence that schizophrenia candidate genes are more associated with schizophrenia than noncandidate genes. *Biological Psychiatry*, *82*(10), 702–708. https://doi.org/10.1016/j.biopsych.2017.06.033

Johnson, J. (2012). Using externalization as a means to regulate emotion in children with autism spectrum disorders. *Journal of Family Psychotherapy*, *23*(2), 163–168. https://doi.org/10.1080/08975353.2012.679906

Johnson, J. (2014). *American lobotomy: A rhetorical history*. University of Michigan Press.

Johnson, M. W. (2022). Classic psychedelics in addiction treatment: The case for psilocybin in tobacco smoking cessation. In F. S. Barrett & K. H. Preller (Eds.), *Disruptive psychopharmacology* (pp. 213–227). Springer International Publishing. https://doi.org/10.1007/7854_2022_327

Johnson, R. J., Wilson, W. L., Bland, S. T., & Lanaspa, M. A. (2021). Fructose and uric acid as drivers of a hyperactive foraging response: A clue to behavioral disorders associated with impulsivity or mania? *Evolution and Human Behavior*, *42*(3), 194–203. https://doi.org/10.1016/j.evolhumbehav.2020.09.006

Johnson, R. S., & Netherton, E. (2016). Fire setting and the impulse-control disorder of pyromania. *American Journal of Psychiatry Residents' Journal*, *11*(7), 14–16. https://doi.org/10.1176/appi.ajp-rj.2016.110707

Johnson, S. (2001). Family therapy saves the planet: Messianic tendencies in the family systems literature. *Journal of Marital and Family Therapy*, *27*(1), 3–11. https://doi.org/10.1111/j.1752-0606.2001.tb01132.x

Johnson, S. M. (2002). *Emotionally focused couple therapy with trauma survivors: Strengthening attachment bonds* (2002-00570-000). Guilford Press.

Johnston, J. N., Campbell, D., Caruncho, H. J., Henter, I. D., Ballard, E. D., & Zarate, C. A. (2022). Suicide biomarkers to predict risk, classify diagnostic subtypes, and identify novel therapeutic targets: 5 years of promising research. *International Journal of Neuropsychopharmacology*, *25*(3), 197–214. https://doi.org/10.1093/ijnp/pyab083

Johnstone, L. (2014). Controversies and debates about formulation. In L. Johnstone & R. Dallos (Eds.), *Formulation in psychology and psychotherapy* (2nd ed., pp. 260–289). Routledge.

Johnstone, L. (2020). Does COVID-19 pose a challenge to the diagnoses of anxiety and depression? A psychologist's view. *BJPsych Bulletin*, *45*(5), 278–281. https://doi.org/10.1192/bjb.2020.101

Johnstone, L. (2022). General patterns in the power threat meaning framework – principles and practice. *Journal of Constructivist Psychology*, *35*(1), 16–26. https://doi.org/10.1080/10720537.2020.1773358

Johnstone, L., & Boyle, M. (2018). The Power Threat Meaning Framework: An alternative nondiagnostic conceptual system. *Journal of Humanistic Psychology*. Advance online publication. https://doi.org/10.1177/0022167818793289

Johnstone, L., Boyle, M., Cromby, J., Dillon, J., Harper, D., Kinderman, P., Longden, E., Pilgrim, D., & Read, J. (2019, January). Reflections on responses to the Power Threat Meaning Framework one year on. *Clinical Psychology Forum*, *313*, 47–54.

Johnstone, L., Boyle, M. (with Cromby, J., Dillon, J., Harper, D., Kinderman, P., Longden, E., Pilgrim, D., & Read, J. (2018). *The Power Threat Meaning Framework: Towards the identification of patterns in emotional distress, unusual experiences and troubled or troubling behaviour, as an alternative to functional psychiatric diagnosis.* British Psychological Society.

Johnstone, L., & Dallos, R. (2014a). *Formulation in psychology and psychotherapy* (2nd ed.). Routledge.

Johnstone, L., & Dallos, R. (2014b). Introduction to formulation. In L. Johnstone & R. Dallos (Eds.), *Formulation in psychology and psychotherapy* (2nd ed., pp. 1–17). Routledge.

Joinson, C., Sullivan, S., von Gontard, A., & Heron, J. (2016). Stressful events in early childhood and developmental trajectories of bedwetting at school age. *Journal of Pediatric Psychology*, *41*(9), 1002–1010. https://doi.org/10.1093/jpepsy/jsw025

Jokela, M., Pulkki-Råback, L., Elovainio, M., & Kivimäki, M. (2014). Personality traits as risk factors for stroke and coronary heart disease mortality: Pooled analysis of three cohort studies. *Journal of Behavioral Medicine*, *37*(5), 881–889. https://doi.org/10.1007/s10865-013-9548-z

Jonathan, L. J., Chee, K.-T., & Ng, B.-Y. (2013). Schizoaffective disorder—An issue of diagnosis. *ASEAN Journal of Psychiatry*, *14*(1), 76–81.

Jones, B., & Jacobsen, P. (2021). Mental health professionals' attitudes and knowledge about hearing voices groups. *Psychosis*, 1–9. https://doi.org/10.1080/17522439.2021.1936142

Jones, C., Hacker, D., Cormac, I., Meaden, A., & Irving, C. B. (2012). Cognitive behavior therapy versus other psychosocial treatments for schizophrenia. *Schizophrenia Bulletin*, *38*(5), 908–910. https://doi.org/10.1093/schbul/sbs090

Jones, E., & Wessely, S. (2007). A paradigm shift in the conceptualization of psychological trauma in the 20th century. *Journal of Anxiety Disorders*, *21*(2), 164–175. https://doi.org/10.1016/j.janxdis.2006.09.009

Jones, I. R. (2017). Social class, dementia and the fourth age. *Sociology of Health & Illness*, *39*(2), 303–317. https://doi.org/10.1111/1467-9566.12520

Jones, K. D. (2010). The unstructured clinical interview. *Journal of Counseling & Development*, *88*(2), 220–226. https://doi.org/10.1002/j.1556-6678.2010.tb00013.x

Jones, K. D. (2012). A critique of the DSM-5 field trials. *Journal of Nervous and Mental Disease*, *200*(6), 517–519.

Jones, K. D., Gill, C., & Ray, S. (2012). Review of the proposed DSM-5 substance use disorder. *Journal of Addictions & Offender Counseling*, *33*(2), 115–123. https://doi.org/10.1002/j.2161-1874.2012.00009.x

Jones, M., Onslow, M., Packman, A., Williams, S., Ormond, T., Schwarz, I., & Gebski, V. (2005). Randomised controlled trial of the Lidcombe programme of early stuttering intervention. *BMJ: British Medical Journal*, *331*(7518), 659–659. https://doi.org/10.1136/bmj.38520.451840.E0

Jones, S. (2020, May 19). How the loss of Asperger syndrome has lasting repercussions. *Spectrum: Autism Research News*. https://www.spectrumnews.org/opinion/viewpoint/how-the-loss-of-asperger-syndrome-has-lasting-repercussions/

Jongenelis, M. I., & Pettigrew, S. (2020). Body image and eating disturbances in children: The role of self-objectification. *Psychology of Women Quarterly, 44*(3), 393–402. https://doi.org/10.1177/0361684320923294

Jordan, A. H., & Litz, B. T. (2014). Prolonged grief disorder: Diagnostic, assessment, and treatment considerations. *Professional Psychology: Research and Practice, 45*(3), 180–187. https://doi.org/10.1037/a0036836

Jordan, J., McIntosh, V. V. W., & Bulik, C. M. (2020). Specialist Supportive Clinical Management for anorexia nervosa: What it is (and what it is not). *Australasian Psychiatry, 28*(2), 156–159. https://doi.org/10.1177/1039856219875024

Jordan, J. V. (2004). Personality disorder or relational disconnection? In J. J. Magnavita & J. J. Magnavita (Eds.), *Handbook of personality disorders: Theory and practice* (pp. 120–134). John Wiley & Sons.

Jordan, K., Fromberger, P., Stolpmann, G., & Müller, J. L. (2011). The role of testosterone in sexuality and paraphilia—A neurobiological approach. Part II: Testosterone and paraphilia. *Journal of Sexual Medicine, 8*(11), 3008–3029. https://doi.org/10.1111/j.1743-6109.2011.02393.x

Jordan, K., Wild, T. S. N., Fromberger, P., Müller, I., & Müller, J. L. (2020). Are there any biomarkers for pedophilia and sexual child abuse? A review. *Frontiers in Psychiatry, 10*, Article 940. https://doi.org/10.3389/fpsyt.2019.00940

Jørgensen, C. S., Horsdal, H. T., Rajagopal, V. M., Grove, J., Als, T. D., Kamperis, K., Nyegaard, M., Walters, G. B., Eðvarðsson, V. Ö., Stefánsson, H., Nordentoft, M., Hougaard, D. M., Werge, T., Mors, O., Mortensen, P. B., Agerbo, E., Rittig, S., Stefánsson, K., Børglum, A. D., … Christensen, J. H. (2021). Identification of genetic loci associated with nocturnal enuresis: A genome-wide association study. *The Lancet Child & Adolescent Health, 5*(3), 201–209. https://doi.org/10.1016/S2352-4642(20)30350-3

Joseph, A. J. (2015). The necessity of an attention to Eurocentrism and colonial technologies: An addition to critical mental health literature. *Disability & Society, 30*(7), 1021–1041. https://doi.org/10.1080/09687599.2015.1067187

Joseph, J. (2000). Not in their genes: A critical view of the genetics of attention-deficit hyperactivity disorder. *Developmental Review, 20*(4), 539–567. https://doi.org/10.1006/drev.2000.0511

Joseph, J. (2004). *The gene illusion: Genetic research in psychiatry and psychology under the microscope.* Algora Publishing.

Joseph, J. (2012). The "missing heritability" of psychiatric disorders: Elusive genes or non-existent genes? *Applied Developmental Science, 16*(2), 65–83. https://doi.org/10.1080/10888691.2012.667343

Joseph, J. (2013). The use of the classical twin method in the social and behavioral sciences: The fallacy continues. *The Journal of Mind and Behavior, 34*(1), 1–40.

Joseph, J. (2015). *The trouble with twin studies: A reassessment of twin research in the social and behavioral sciences* (2014-54797-000). Routledge/Taylor & Francis Group.

Joseph, S., & Linley, P. A. (2006). Growth following adversity: Theoretical perspectives and implications for clinical practice. *Clinical Psychology Review, 26*(8), 1041–1053. https://doi.org/10.1016/j.cpr.2005.12.006

Joshi, S., Mooney, S. J., Rundle, A. G., Quinn, J. W., Beard, J. R., & Cerdá, M. (2017). Pathways from neighborhood poverty to depression among older adults. *Health & Place, 43*, 138–143. https://doi.org/10.1016/j.healthplace.2016.12.003

Joyal, C. C., & Carpentier, J. (2017). The prevalence of paraphilic interests and behaviors in the general population: A provincial survey. *The Journal of Sex Research, 54*(2), 161–171. https://doi.org/10.1080/00224499.2016.1139034

Joyce, P. R. (1980). The medical model—Why psychiatry is a branch of medicine. *Australian and New Zealand Journal of Psychiatry, 14*(4), 269–278.

Juarascio, A. S., Manasse, S. M., Goldstein, S. P., Forman, E. M., & Butryn, M. L. (2015). Review of smartphone applications for the treatment of eating disorders. *European Eating Disorders Review, 23*(1), 1–11. https://doi.org/10.1002/erv.2327

Juarascio, A., Shaw, J., Forman, E., Timko, C. A., Herbert, J., Butryn, M., Bunnell, D., Matteucci, A., & Lowe, M. (2013). Acceptance and commitment therapy as a novel treatment for eating disorders: An initial test of efficacy and mediation. *Behavior Modification, 37*(4), 459–489. https://doi.org/10.1177/0145445513478633

Junewicz, A., & Billick, S. B. (2020). Conduct disorder: Biology and developmental trajectories. *Psychiatric Quarterly, 91*(1), 77–90. https://doi.org/10.1007/s11126-019-09678-5

Juntti. (2022, July 21). *It's time to stop calling autism "Asperger's."* Fatherly. https://www.fatherly.com/health/aspergers-vs-autism-and-hans-asperger

Jurjako, M. (2019). Is psychopathy a harmful dysfunction? *Biology & Philosophy, 34*(1), 5. https://doi.org/10.1007/s10539-018-9668-5

Juuhl-Langseth, M., Hartberg, C. B., Holmén, A., Thormodsen, R., Groote, I. R., Rimol, L. M., Emblem, K. E., Agartz, I., & Rund, B. R. (2015). Impaired verbal learning is associated with larger caudate volumes in early onset schizophrenia spectrum disorders. *PLoS ONE, 10*(7).

Kaczkurkin, A. N., & Foa, E. B. (2015). Cognitive-behavioral therapy for anxiety disorders: An update on the empirical evidence. *Dialogues in Clinical Neuroscience, 17*(3), 337–346.

Kafka, M. P. (2013). The development and evolution of the criteria for a newly proposed diagnosis for DSM-5: Hypersexual disorder. *Sexual Addiction & Compulsivity, 20*(1–2), 19–26.

Kafka, M. P. (2014). What happened to hypersexual disorder? *Archives of Sexual Behavior, 43*(7), 1259–1261. https://doi.org/10.1007/s10508-014-0326-y

Kaiser Family Foundation. (2022, October 21). Mental health care health professional shortage areas (HPSAS). *KFF*. https://www.kff.org/other/state-indicator/mental-health-care-health-professional-shortage-areas-hpsas/

Kaldenbach, S., Leonhardt, M., Lien, L., Bjærtnes, A. A., Strand, T. A., & Holten-Andersen, M. N. (2022). Sleep and energy drink consumption among Norwegian adolescents – a cross-sectional study. *BMC Public Health, 22*(1), Article 534. https://doi.org/10.1186/s12889-022-12972-w

Kalenik, A., Kardaś, K., Rahnama, A., Sirojć, K., & Wolańczyk, T. (2021). Gut microbiota and probiotic therapy in ADHD: A review of current knowledge. *Progress in Neuro-Psychopharmacology and Biological Psychiatry, 110*, 110277. https://doi.org/10.1016/j.pnpbp.2021.110277

Kalin, N. H. (2020). The critical relationship between anxiety and depression. *American Journal of Psychiatry, 177*(5), 365–367. https://doi.org/10.1176/appi.ajp.2020.20030305

Kalivas, P. W., & Volkow, N. D. (2005). The neural basis of addiction: A pathology of motivation and choice. *The American Journal of Psychiatry, 162*(8), 1403–1413. https://doi.org/10.1176/appi.ajp.162.8.1403

Kalk, N. J., & Lingford-Hughes, A. R. (2014). The clinical pharmacology of acamprosate: The clinical pharmacology of acamprosate. *British Journal of Clinical Pharmacology, 77*(2), 315–323. https://doi.org/10.1111/bcp.12070

Kaloeti, D. V. S., Manalu, R., Kristiana, I. F., & Bidzan, M. (2021). The role of social media use in peer bullying victimization and onset of anxiety among Indonesian elementary school children. *Frontiers in Psychology, 12*, Article 635725. https://www.doi.org/10.3389/fpsyg.2021.635725

Kalsi, G., Prescott, C. A., Kendler, K. S., & Riley, B. P. (2009). Unraveling the molecular mechanisms of alcohol dependence. *Trends in Genetics, 25*(1), 49–55. https://doi.org/10.1016/j.tig.2008.10.005

Kalyva, E., Kyriazi, M., Vargiami, E., & Zafeiriou, D. I. (2016). A review of co-occurrence of autism spectrum disorder and Tourette syndrome. *Research in Autism Spectrum Disorders, 24*, 39–51. https://doi.org/10.1016/j.rasd.2016.01.007

Kamal, N. N., & Mahrous, D. M. (2019). The epidemiology and factors associated with nocturnal enuresis among primary school children in Minia City, Egypt. *The Egyptian Journal of Community Medicine, 37*(1), 63–71. https://doi.org/10.21608/ejcm.2019.28133

Kamaya, H., & Krishna, P. R. (1987). Ketamine addiction. *Anesthesiology, 67*(5), 861–862. https://doi.org/10.1097/00000542-198711000-00054

Kamens, S. R. (2011). On the proposed sexual and gender identity diagnoses for DSM-5: History and controversies. *The Humanistic Psychologist, 39*(1), 37–59. https://doi.org/10.1080/08873267.2011.539935

Kamens, S. R. (2014, August 5). *Attenuated psychosis syndrome was not actually removed from DSM-5.* Global Summit on Diagnostic Alternatives, Washington, DC.

Kamens, S. R., Elkins, D. N., & Robbins, B. D. (2017). Open letter to the DSM-5. *Journal of Humanistic Psychology, 57*(6), 675–687. https://doi.org/10.1177/0022167817698261

Kanayama, N., Sato, A., & Ohira, H. (2008). Dissociative experience and mood-dependent memory. *Cognition and Emotion, 22*(5), 881–896. https://doi.org/10.1080/02699930701541674

Kane, J. M., Robinson, D. G., Schooler, N. R., Mueser, K. T., Penn, D. L., Rosenceck, R. A., Addington, J., Brunette, M. F., Correll, C. U., Estroff, S. E., Marcy, P., Robinson, J., Meyer-Kalos, P. S., Gottlieb, J. D., Glynn, S. M., Lynde, D. W., Pipes, R., Kurian, B. T., Miller, A. L., … Heinssen, R. K. (2016). Comprehensive versus usual community care for first-episode psychosis: 2-year outcomes from the NIMH RAISE Early Treatment Program. *American Journal of Psychiatry, 173*(4), 362–372. https://doi.org/10.1176/appi.ajp.2015.15050632

Kang, C. (2021). *Progress, challenges, and future perspectives in genetic researches of stuttering. 18*(2), 75–82. https://doi.org/10.5734/JGM.2021.18.2.75

Kang, H.-J., Kim, S.-Y., Bae, K.-Y., Kim, S.-W., Shin, I.-S., Yoon, J.-S., & Kim, J.-M. (2015). Comorbidity of depression with physical disorders: Research and clinical implications. *Chonnam Medical Journal, 51*(1), 8–18. https://doi.org/10.4068/cmj.2015.51.1.8

Kanner, L. (1943). Autistic disturbance of affective contact. *Nervous Child, 2*, 217–250.

Kanner, L. (1949). Problems of nosology and psychodynamics of early infantile autism. *American Journal of Orthopsychiatry, 19*(3), 416–426. https://doi.org/10.1111/j.1939-0025.1949.tb05441.x

Kanner, L., & Eisenberg, L. (1957). Early infantile autism, 1943-1955. *Psychiatric Research Reports, 7*, 55–65. https://doi.org/10.4159/harvard.9780674367012.c2

Kantrowitz, R. E., & Ballou, M. (1992). A feminist critique of cognitive-behavioral therapy. In L. S. Brown & M. Ballou (Eds.), *Personality and psychopathology: Feminist reappraisals* (pp. 70–87). The Guilford Press.

Kapalu, C. M. L., & Christophersen, E. R. (2019). Cognitive behavioral therapy for encopresis. In R. D. Friedberg & J. K. Paternostro (Eds.), *Handbook of cognitive behavioral therapy for pediatric medical conditions* (pp. 239–259). Springer Nature Switzerland AG. https://doi.org/10.1007/978-3-030-21683-2_16

Kaplan, A. S., & Howlett, A. (2010). Pharmacotherapy for anorexia nervosa. In C. M. Grilo & J. E. Mitchell (Eds.), *The treatment of eating disorders: A clinical handbook* (pp. 175–186). Guilford Press.

Kaplan, H. S. (1974). *The new sex therapy: Active treatment of sexual dysfunctions.* Brunner/Mazel.

Kaplan, H. S. (1995). *The sexual desire disorders: Dysfunctional regulation of sexual motivation.* Brunner/Mazel.

Kaplan, J. S., & Tolin, D. F. (2011). Exposure therapy for anxiety disorders. *Psychiatric Times*, 28(9). http://www.psychiatrictimes.com/anxiety/exposure-therapy-anxiety-disorders

Kaplan, M. (1983). A woman's view of DSM-III. *American Psychologist*, 38(7), 786–792. https://doi.org/10.1037/0003-066X.38.7.786

Kaplan, M. J. (2014). A psychodynamic perspective on treatment of patients with conversion and other somatoform disorders. *Psychodynamic Psychiatry*, 42(4), 593–615. https://doi.org/10.1521/pdps.2014.42.4.593

Kaplan, M. S., & Krueger, R. B. (2012). *Cognitive-behavioral treatment of paraphilias* (Vol. 49, Issue 4, pp. 291–296). http://doctorsonly.co.il/wp-content/uploads/2013/03/08_-Cognitive-behavioral-treatment.pdf

Kaplan, R. M. (2013). A history of insulin coma therapy in Australia. *Australasian Psychiatry*, 21(6), 587–591. https://doi.org/10.1177/1039856213500361

Kapp, M. B. (1994). Treatment and refusal rights in mental health: Therapeutic justice and clinical accommodation. *American Journal of Orthopsychiatry*, 64(2), 223–234. https://doi.org/10.1037/h0079524

Kapulsky, L., Christos, P., Ilagan, J., & Kocsis, J. (2021). The effects of ibuprofen consumption on the incidence of postpartum depression. *Clinical Neuropharmacology*, 44(4), 117–122. https://doi.org/10.1097/WNF.0000000000000448

Kapur, S. (2003). Psychosis as a state of aberrant salience: A framework linking biology, phenomenology, and pharmacology in schizophrenia. *The American Journal of Psychiatry*, 160(1), 13–23. https://doi.org/10.1176/appi.ajp.160.1.13

Kapur, S. (2004). How antipsychotics become anti-"psychotic" – from dopamine to salience to psychosis. *Trends in Pharmacological Sciences*, 25(8), 402–406. https://doi.org/10.1016/j.tips.2004.06.005

Kapur, S., Mizrahi, R., & Li, M. (2005). From dopamine to salience to psychosis—Linking biology, pharmacology and phenomenology of psychosis. *Schizophrenia Research*, 79(1), 59–68. https://doi.org/10.1016/j.schres.2005.01.003

Karabulut, S., Taşdemir, İ., Akcan, U., Küçükali, C. İ., Tüzün, E., & Çakir, S. (2019). Inflammation and neurodegeneration in patients with early-stage and chronic bipolar disorder. *Türk Psikiyatri Dergisi*, 30(2), 1–7.

Karam, E. G., Tabet, C. C., & Itani, L. A. (2013). The bereavement exclusion: Findings from a field study. *Psychiatric Annals*, 43(6), 267–271. https://doi.org/10.3928/00485713-20130605-06

Karam-Hage, M., Gonzalez, R., & Damaj, M. I. (2021). Pharmacotherapy for smoking cessation: Overview of medications including over-the-counter nicotine replacement therapy, bupropion, and varenicline. In F. G. Moeller & M. Terplan (Eds.), *Substance use disorders*. Oxford University Press.

Karanti, A., Kardell, M., Lundberg, U., & Landén, M. (2016). Changes in mood stabilizer prescription patterns in bipolar disorder. *Journal of Affective Disorders*, 195, 50–56. https://doi.org/10.1016/j.jad.2016.01.043

Kardiner, A., & Spiegel, H. (1947). *War stress and neurotic illness* (2nd ed.). P. B. Hoeber.

Kardum, I., Gračanin, A., & Hudek-Knežević, J. (2008). Evolutionary explanations of eating disorders. *Psihologijske Teme*, 17(2), 247–263.

Karl, T., & Arnold, J. C. (2014). Schizophrenia: A consequence of gene-environment interactions? *Frontiers in Behavioral Neuroscience*, 8, Article 435. https://doi.org/10.3389/fnbeh.2014.00435

Karon, B. P. (1992). The fear of understanding schizophrenia. *Psychoanalytic Psychology*, 9(2), 191–211. https://doi.org/10.1037/h0079355

Karon, B. P. (2000). The clinical interpretation of the Thematic Apperception Test, Rorschach, and other clinical data: A reexamination of statistical versus clinical prediction. *Professional Psychology:*

Research and Practice, 31(2), 230–233. https://doi.org/10.1037/0735-7028.31.2.230

Karon, B. P. (2003). The tragedy of schizophrenia without psychotherapy. *Journal of the American Academy of Psychoanalysis*, 31(1), 89–119. https://doi.org/10.1521/jaap.31.1.89.21931

Karon, B. P. (2008a). An "incurable" schizophrenic: The case of Mr. X. *Pragmatic Case Studies in Psychotherapy*, 4(1), 1–24.

Karon, B. P. (2008b). Psychotherapy of schizophrenia works. *Pragmatic Case Studies in Psychotherapy*, 4(1), 55–61.

Karow, A., Reimer, J., König, H.-H., Heider, D., Bock, T., Huber, C., Schöttle, D., Meister, K., Rietschel, L., Ohm, G., Schulz, H., Naber, D., Schimmelmann, B. G., & Lambert, M. (2012). Cost-effectiveness of 12-month assertive community treatment as part of integrated care versus standard care in patients with schizophrenia treated with quetiapine immediate release (ACCESS Trial). *Journal of Clinical Psychiatry*, 73(3), e402–e408. https://doi.org/10.4088/JCP.11m06875

Karran, E., & De Strooper, B. (2022). The amyloid hypothesis in Alzheimer disease: New insights from new therapeutics. *Nature Reviews Drug Discovery*, 21(4), Article 4. https://doi.org/10.1038/s41573-022-00391-w

Kasbi, F., Mokhlesin, M., Maddah, M., Noruzi, R., Monshizadeh, L., & Khani, M. M. M. (2015). Effects of stuttering on quality of life in adults who stutter. *Middle East Journal of Rehabilitation and Health*, 2(1), Article 1. https://doi.org/10.17795/mejrh-25314

Kaslow, N. J., Reviere, S. L., Chance, S. E., Rogers, J. H., Hatcher, C. A., Wasserman, F., Smith, L., Jessee, S., James, M. E., & Seelig, B. (1998). An empirical study of the psychodynamics of suicide. *Journal of the American Psychoanalytic Association*, 46(3), 777–796. https://doi.org/10.1177/00030651980460030701

Kass, A. E., Kolko, R. P., & Wilfley, D. E. (2013). Psychological treatments for eating disorders. *Current Opinion in Psychiatry*, 26(6), 549–555. doi:10.1097/YCO.0b013e328365a30e

Kass, N. E., & Sugarman, J. (1996). Are research subjects adequately protected? A review and discussion of studies conducted by the Advisory Committee on Human Radiation Experiments. *Kennedy Institute of Ethics Journal*, 6(3), 271–282. https://doi.org/10.1353/ken.1996.0026

Kataoka, T., & Kimura, K. (2017). Testosterone and erectile function: A review of evidence from basic research. In G. Drevenšek (Ed.), *Sex hormones in neurodegenerative processes and diseases* (pp. 257–272). IntechOpen. https://doi.org/10.5772/intechopen.72935

Katchergin, O. (2014). "Learning disabilities" as a "black box": On the different conceptions and constructions of a popular clinical entity in Israel. *Culture, Medicine, and Psychiatry: An International Journal of Cross-Cultural Health Research*, 38(4), 669–699. https://doi.org/10.1007/s11013-014-9398-3

Katchergin, O. (2016). The DSM and learning difficulties: Formulating a genealogy of the learning-disabled subject. *History of Psychiatry*, 27(2), 190–207. https://doi.org/10.1177/0957154X16633406

Katzman, M. A., Bilkey, T. S., Chokka, P. R., Fallu, A., & Klassen, L. J. (2017). Adult ADHD and comorbid disorders: Clinical implications of a dimensional approach. *BMC Psychiatry*, 17, 302. https://doi.org/10.1186/s12888-017-1463-3

Katzman, M. A., Bleau, P., Blier, P., Chokka, P., Kjernisted, K., Van Ameringen, M., & the Canadian Anxiety Guidelines Initiative Group on behalf of the Anxiety Disorders Association of Canada/Association Canadienne des troubles anxieux and McGill University. (2014). Canadian clinical practice guidelines for the management of anxiety, posttraumatic stress and obsessive-compulsive disorders. *BMC Psychiatry*, 14(1), S1. https://doi.org/10.1186/1471-244X-14-S1-S1

Kaufer, D. I. (2007). The dorsolateral and cingulate cortex. In B. L. Miller & J. L. Cummings (Eds.), *The human frontal lobes: Functions and disorders* (2nd ed., pp. 44–58). Guilford Press.

Kavalali, E. T., & Monteggia, L. M. (2015). How does ketamine elicit a rapid antidepressant response? *Current Opinion in Pharmacology*, 20, 35–39. https://doi.org/10.1016/j.coph.2014.11.005

Kavale, K. A., & Spaulding, L. S. (2008). Is response to intervention good policy for specific learning disability? *Learning Disabilities Research & Practice*, 23(4), 169–179. https://doi.org/10.1111/j.1540-5826.2008.00274.x

Kawa, S., & Giordano, J. (2012). A brief historicity of the *Diagnostic and statistical manual of mental disorders*: Issues and implications for the future of psychiatric canon and practice. *Philosophy, Ethics, and Humanities in Medicine*, 7(1), Article 2. https://doi.org/10.1186/1747-5341-7-2

Kaya, F., Juntune, J., & Stough, L. (2015). Intelligence and its relationship to achievement. *İlköğretim Online*, 14(3). https://doi.org/10.17051/io.2015.25436

Kaya, S. (2020). Reduced hippocampus and amygdala volumes in antisocial personality disorder. *Journal of Clinical Neuroscience*, 75, 199–203. https://doi.org/10.1016/j.jocn.2020.01.048

Kaye, W. (2008). Neurobiology of anorexia and bulimia nervosa. *Physiology & Behavior*, 94(1), 121–135. https://doi.org/10.1016/j.physbeh.2007.11.037

Kaye, W. H., Ebert, M. H., Gwirtsman, H. E., & Weiss, S. R. (1984). Differences in brain serotonergic metabolism between nonbulimic and bulimic patients with anorexia nervosa. *The American Journal of Psychiatry*, 141(12), 1598–1601. https://doi.org/10.1176/ajp.141.12.1598

Kaye, W. H., Ebert, M. H., Raleigh, M., & Lake, R. (1984). Abnormalities in CNS monoamine metabolism in anorexia nervosa. *Archives of General Psychiatry*, 41(4), 350–355. https://doi.org/10.1001/archpsyc.1984.01790150040007

Kaye, W. H., Frank, G. K., Bailer, U. F., Henry, S. E., Meltzer, C. C., Price, J. C., Mathis, C. A., & Wagner, A. (2005). Serotonin alterations in anorexia and bulimia nervosa: New insights from imaging studies. *Physiology & Behavior*, 85(1), 73–81. https://doi.org/10.1016/j.physbeh.2005.04.013

Kaye, W. H., Frank, G. K. W., & McConaha, C. (1999). Altered dopamine activity after recovery from restricting-type anorexia nervosa. *Neuropsychopharmacology*, 21(4), 503–506. https://doi.org/10.1016/S0893-133X(99)00053-6

Kaye, W. H., Fudge, J. L., & Paulus, M. (2009). New insights into symptoms and neurocircuit function of anorexia nervosa. *Nature Reviews Neuroscience*, 10(8), 573–584. https://doi.org/10.1038/nrn2682

Kaye, W. H., Gendall, K., & Strober, M. (1998). Serotonin neuronal function and selective serotonin reuptake inhibitor treatment in anorexia and bulimia nervosa. *Biological Psychiatry*, 44(9), 825–838. https://doi.org/10.1016/S0006-3223(98)00195-4

Kaye, W. H., Gwirtsman, H. E., George, D. T., & Ebert, M. H. (1991). Altered serotonin activity in anorexia nervosa after long-term weight restoration: Does elevated cerebrospinal fluid 5-hydroxyindoleacetic acid level correlate with rigid and obsessive behavior? *Archives of General Psychiatry*, 48(6), 556–562. https://doi.org/10.1001/archpsyc.1991.01810300068010

Kaye, W. H., Wierenga, C. E., Bailer, U. F., Simmons, A. N., Wagner, A., & Bischoff-Grethe, A. (2013). Does a shared neurobiology for foods and drugs of abuse contribute to extremes of food ingestion in anorexia and bulimia nervosa? *Biological Psychiatry*, 73(9), 836–842. https://doi.org/10.1016/j.biopsych.2013.01.002

Kaysen, D., Resick, P. A., & Wise, D. (2003). Living in danger: The impact of chronic traumatization and the traumatic context on posttraumatic stress disorder.

Trauma, Violence, & Abuse, 4(3), 247–264. https://doi.org/10.1177/1524838003004003004

Kazemi, E., Zargooshi, J., Kaboudi, M., Heidari, P., Kahrizi, D., Mahaki, B., Mohammadian, Y., Khazaei, H., & Ahmed, K. (2021). A genome-wide association study to identify candidate genes for erectile dysfunction. *Briefings in Bioinformatics, 22*(4), bbaa338. https://doi.org/10.1093/bib/bbaa338

Kearns, D. M., Hancock, R., Hoeft, F., Pugh, K. R., & Frost, S. J. (2019). The neurobiology of dyslexia. *TEACHING Exceptional Children, 51*(3), 175–188. https://doi.org/10.1177/0040059918820051

Keck, P. E., McElroy, S. L., & Yildiz, A. (2015). Treatment of mania. In A. Yildiz, P. Ruiz, & C. B. Nemeroff (Eds.), *The bipolar book: History, neurobiology, and treatment* (pp. 263–279). Oxford University Press.

Kedia, G. T., Ückert, S., Tsikas, D., Becker, A. J., Kuczyk, M. A., & Bannowsky, A. (2020). The use of vasoactive drugs in the treatment of male erectile dysfunction: Current concepts. *Journal of Clinical Medicine, 9*(9), 2987. https://doi.org/10.3390/jcm9092987

Keel, P. K., & Klump, K. L. (2003). Are eating disorders culture-bound syndromes? Implications for conceptualizing their etiology. *Psychological Bulletin, 129*(5), 747–769. https://doi.org/10.1037/0033-2909.129.5.747

Keeley, M. L., Graziano, P., & Geffken, G. R. (2009). Nocturnal enuresis and encopresis: Empirically supported approaches for refractory cases. In D. McKay & E. A. Storch (Eds.), *Cognitive-behavior therapy for children: Treating complex and refractory cases* (pp. 445–473). Springer.

Keil, A., Daniels, J. L., Forssen, U., Hultman, C., Cnattingius, S., Söderberg, K. C., Feychting, M., & Sparen, P. (2010). Parental autoimmune diseases associated with autism spectrum disorders in offspring. *Epidemiology, 21*(6), 805–808. https://doi.org/10.1097/EDE.0b013e-3181f26e3f

Kelleher, I., Jenner, J. A., & Cannon, M. (2010). Psychotic symptoms in the general population—An evolutionary perspective. *The British Journal of Psychiatry, 197*(3), 167–169. https://doi.org/10.1192/bjp.bp.109.076018

Kellner, C. H., & Fink, M. (2015). Electroconvulsive therapy versus pharmacotherapy for bipolar depression. *The American Journal of Psychiatry, 172*(3), 295–295. https://doi.org/10.1176/appi.ajp.2014.14101284

Kellner, C. H., Obbels, J., & Sienaert, P. (2020). When to consider electroconvulsive therapy (ECT). *Acta Psychiatrica Scandinavica, 141*(4), 304–315. https://doi.org/10.1111/acps.13134

Kellner, R. (1994). Psychosomatic syndromes, somatization and somatoform disorders. *Psychotherapy and Psychosomatics, 61*(1–2), 4–24. https://doi.org/10.1159/000288868

Kelly, E., Meng, F., Fujita, H., Morgado, F., Kazemi, Y., Rice, L. C., Ren, C., Escamilla, C. O., Gibson, J. M., Sajadi, S., Pendry, R. J., Tan, T., Ellegood, J., Basson, M. A., Blakely, R. D., Dindot, S. V., Golzio, C., Hahn, M. K., Katsanis, N., … Tsai, P. T. (2020). Regulation of autism-relevant behaviors by cerebellar–prefrontal cortical circuits. *Nature Neuroscience, 23*(9), 1102–1110. https://doi.org/10.1038/s41593-020-0665-z

Kelly, G. A. (1961). Suicide: The personal construct point of view. In N. L. Farberow & E. S. Shneidman (Eds.), *The cry for help.* McGraw Hill.

Kelly, G. A. (1991a). *The psychology of personal constructs: Vol. 1. A theory of personality.* Routledge. (Original work published 1955.)

Kelly, G. A. (1991b). *The psychology of personal constructs: Vol. 2. Clinical diagnosis and psychotherapy.* Routledge. (Original work published 1955.)

Kelly, J. F., & Abry, A. W. (2021). Leave the past behind by recognizing the effectiveness and cost-effectiveness of 12-step facilitation and Alcoholics Anonymous. *Alcohol and Alcoholism (Oxford, Oxfordshire), 56*(4), 380–382. https://doi.org/10.1093/alcalc/agab010

Kelly, J. F., Humphreys, K., & Ferri, M. (2020). Alcoholics Anonymous and other 12-step programs for alcohol use disorder. *Cochrane Database of Systematic Reviews, 2020*(3), Article CD012880. https://doi.org/10.1002/14651858.CD012880.pub2

Kelly, S. M., Gryczynski, J., Mitchell, S. G., Kirk, A., O'Grady, K. E., & Schwartz, R. P. (2014). Concordance between DSM-5 and DSM-IV nicotine, alcohol, and cannabis use disorder diagnoses among pediatric patients. *Drug and Alcohol Dependence, 140*, 213–216. https://doi.org/10.1016/j.drugalcdep.2014.03.034

Kelman, E., & Wheeler, S. (2015). Cognitive Behaviour Therapy with children who stutter. *Procedia—Social and Behavioral Sciences, 193*, 165–174. https://doi.org/10.1016/j.sbspro.2015.03.256

Kelsven, S., de la Fuente-sandoval, C., Achim, C. L., Reyes-Madrigal, F., Mirzakhanian, H., Domingues, I., & Cadenhead, K. (2020). Immuno-inflammatory changes across phases of early psychosis: The impact of antipsychotic medication and stage of illness. *Schizophrenia Research, 226*, 13–23. https://doi.org/10.1016/j.schres.2020.01.003

Kemeny, M. E., & Schedlowski, M. (2007). Understanding the interaction between psychosocial stress and immune-related diseases: A stepwise progression. *Brain, Behavior, and Immunity, 21*(8), 1009–1018. https://doi.org/10.1016/j.bbi.2007.07.010

Kendler, K. S., Aggen, S. H., Gillespie, N., Krueger, R. F., Czajkowski, N., Ystrom, E., & Reichborn-Kjennerud, T. (2019). The structure of genetic and environmental influences on normative personality, abnormal personality traits, and personality disorder symptoms. *Psychological Medicine, 49*(8), 1392–1399. https://doi.org/10.1017/S0033291719000047

Kendler, K. S., Czajkowski, N., Tambs, K., Torgersen, S., Aggen, S. H., Neale, M. C., & Reichborn-Kjennerud, T. (2006). Dimensional representations of DSM-IV Cluster A personality disorders in a population-based sample of Norwegian twins: A multivariate study. *Psychological Medicine, 36*(11), 1583–1591. https://doi.org/10.1017/S0033291706008609

Kendler, K. S., MacLean, C., Neale, M., Kessler, R. C., Heath, A., & Eaves, L. (1991). The genetic epidemiology of bulimia nervosa. *The American Journal of Psychiatry, 148*(12), 1627–1637.

Kendler, K. S., Myers, J., Torgersen, S., Neale, M. C., & Reichborn-Kjennerud, T. (2007). The heritability of cluster A personality disorders assessed by both personal interview and questionnaire. *Psychological Medicine, 37*(05), 655. https://doi.org/10.1017/S0033291706009755

Kendler, K. S., & Schaffner, K. F. (2011). The dopamine hypothesis of schizophrenia: An historical and philosophical analysis. *Philosophy, Psychiatry, & Psychology, 18*(1), 41–63. https://doi.org/10.1353/ppp.2011.0005

Kendler, K. S., Walters, E. E., Truett, K. R., Heath, A. C., Neale, M. C., Martin, N. G., & Eaves, L. J. (1995). A twin-family study of self-report symptoms of panic-phobia and somatization. *Behavior Genetics, 25*(6), 499–515. https://doi.org/10.1007/BF02327574

Kennair, L. E. O., Kleppestø, T. H., Larsen, S. M., & Jørgensen, B. E. G. (2017). Depression: Is rumination really adaptive? In T. K. Shackelford & V. Zeigler-Hill (Eds.), *The evolution of psychopathology* (pp. 73–92). Springer International Publishing. https://doi.org/10.1007/978-3-319-60576-0_3

Kennedy, J. J., & Bush, A. J. (1985). *An introduction to the design and analysis of experiments.* University Press of America.

Kennedy, K. (2017, July 14). *Before sloth meant laziness, it was the spiritual sin of acedia.* Atlas Obscura. http://www.atlasobscura.com/articles/desert-fathers-sins-acedia-sloth

Kennerley, H. (1996). Cognitive therapy of dissociative symptoms associated with trauma. *British Journal of Clinical Psychology, 35*(3), 325–340. https://doi.org/10.1111/j.2044-8260.1996.tb01188.x

Kernberg, O. F. (2001). Object relations, affects, and drives: Toward a new synthesis. *Psychoanalytic Inquiry, 21*(5), 604–619. https://doi.org/10.1080/07351692109348963

Kernberg, O. F., Selzer, M. A., Koenigsberg, H. W., Carr, A. C., & Appelbaum, A. H. (1989). *Psychodynamic psychotherapy of borderline patients.* Basic Books.

Kerr, J. S. (1996). Two myths of addiction: The addictive personality and the issue of free choice. *Human Psychopharmacology: Clinical and Experimental, 11*(Suppl. 1), S9–S13. https://doi.org/10.1002/(SICI)1099-1077(199602)11:1+3.0.CO;2-6

Kersting, A., Kroker, K., Horstmann, J., Baune, B. T., Hohoff, C., Mortensen, L. S., Neumann, L. C., Arolt, V., & Domschke, K. (2007). Association of MAO-A variant with complicated grief in major depression. *Neuropsychobiology, 56*(4), 191–196. https://doi.org/10.1159/000120624

Keshavan, M. S., Tandon, R., Boutros, N. N., & Nasrallah, H. A. (2008). Schizophrenia, "just the facts": What we know in 2008: Part 3: Neurobiology. *Schizophrenia Research, 106*(2–3), 89–107. https://doi.org/10.1016/j.schres.2008.07.020

Kessel, E. M., Allmann, A. E. S., Goldstein, B., Finsaas, M., Dougherty, L. R., Bufferd, S. J., Carlson, G. A., & Klein, D. N. (2017). Predictors and outcomes of childhood primary enuresis. *Journal of the American Academy of Child and Adolescent Psychiatry, 56*(3), 250–257. https://doi.org/10.1016/j.jaac.2016.12.007

Kessler, E.-M., Agines, S., & Bowen, C. E. (2015). Attitudes towards seeking mental health services among older adults: Personal and contextual correlates. *Aging & Mental Health, 19*(2), 182–191. https://doi.org/10.1080/13607863.2014.920300

Kessler, R. C., Berglund, P., Demler, O., Jin, R., Koretz, D., Merikangas, K. R., Rush, A. J., Walters, E. E., & Wang, P. S. (2003). The epidemiology of major depressive disorder: Results from the National Comorbidity Survey Replication (NCS-R). *JAMA, 289*(23), 3095–3105.

Kessler, R. C., Birnbaum, H. G., Shahly, V., Bromet, E., Hwang, I., McLaughlin, K. A., Sampson, N., Andrade, L. H., de Girolamo, G., Demytteenaere, K., Haro, J. M., Karam, A. N., Kostyuchenko, S., Kovess, V., Lara, C., Levinson, D., Matschinger, H., Nakane, Y., Browne, M. O., … Stein, D. J. (2010). Age differences in the prevalence and co-morbidity of DSM-IV major depressive episodes: Results from the WHO World Mental Health Survey Initiative. *Depression and Anxiety, 27*(4), 351–364. https://doi.org/10.1002/da.20634

Kety, S. S. (1988). Schizophrenic illness in the families of schizophrenic adoptees: Findings from the Danish national sample. *Schizophrenia Bulletin, 14*(2), 217–222.

Keuthen, N. J., Tung, E. S., Reese, H. E., Raikes, J., Lee, L., & Mansueto, C. S. (2015). Getting the word out: Cognitive-behavioral therapy for trichotillomania (hair-pulling disorder) and excoriation (skin-picking) disorder. *Annals of Clinical Psychiatry, 27*(1), 10–15.

Keynan, I., & Keynan, J. (2016). War trauma, politics of recognition and purple heart: PTSD or PTSI? *Social Sciences, 5*(4), Article 57. https://doi.org/10.3390/socsci5040057

Khanahmadi, M., Farhud, D. D., & Malmir, M. (2015). Genetic of Alzheimer's disease: A narrative review article. *Iranian Journal of Public Health, 44*(7), 892–901.

Khani, Y., Pourgholam-Amiji, N., Afshar, M., Otroshi, O., Sharifi-Esfahani, M., Sadeghi-Gandomani, H., Vejdani, M., & Salehiniya, H. (2018). Tobacco smoking and cancer types: A review. *Biomedical Research and Therapy, 5*(4), Article 4. https://doi.org/10.15419/bmrat.v5i4.428

Khantzian, E. J. (1985). The self-medication hypothesis of addictive disorders: Focus on heroin and cocaine dependence. *The American Journal of Psychiatry, 142*(11), 1259–1264. https://doi.org/10.1176/ajp.142.11.1259

Khantzian, E. J. (1997). The self-medication hypothesis of substance use disorders: A reconsideration and recent applications. *Harvard Review of Psychiatry*, 4(5), 231–244. https://doi.org/10.3109/10673229709030550

Khantzian, E. J. (2012). Reflections on treating addictive disorders: A psychodynamic perspective. *The American Journal on Addictions*, 21(3), 274–279. https://doi.org/10.1111/j.1521-0391.2012.00234.x

Khantzian, E. J. (2021). Commentary: It is not about supply, it is about demand: Why the self-medication hypotheses is still so important. *American Journal on Addictions*, 30(4), 301–304. https://doi.org/10.1111/ajad.13111

Kharrazian, D. (2011). Non-validity and clinical relevance of neurotransmitter testing. *Functional Neurology, Rehabilitation, and Ergonomics*, 1(3), 501–508.

Khayyam-Nekouei, Z., Neshatdoost, H., Yousefy, A., Sadeghi, M., & Manshaee, G. (2013). Psychological factors and coronary heart disease. *ARYA Atherosclerosis*, 9(1), 102–111.

Khazan, I. Z. (2013). *The clinical handbook of biofeedback: A step-by-step guide for training and practice with mindfulness*. Wiley-Blackwell. https://doi.org/10.1002/9781118485309

Khoury, J. E., Milligan, K., & Girard, T. A. (2015). Executive functioning in children and adolescents prenatally exposed to alcohol: A meta-analytic review. *Neuropsychology Review*, 25(2), 149–170. https://doi.org/10.1007/s11065-015-9289-6

Khue, P. M., Tham, N. T., Thanh Mai, D. T., Thuc, P. V., Thuc, V. M., Han, P. V., & Lindan, C. (2017). A longitudinal and case-control study of dropout among drug users in methadone maintenance treatment in Haiphong, Vietnam. *Harm Reduction Journal*, 14, 59. https://doi.org/10.1186/s12954-017-0185-7

Khunrong, P., & Sittipunt, C. (2016). Comparison of efficacy of varenicline and nortriptyline– Short-term smoking cessation in outpatient setting. *European Respiratory Journal*, 48(suppl 60). https://doi.org/10.1183/13993003.congress-2016.PA4601

Khusid, M. A., & Vythilingam, M. (2016). The emerging role of mindfulness meditation as effective self-management strategy, Part 1: Clinical implications for depression, post-traumatic stress disorder, and anxiety. *Military Medicine*, 181(9), 961–968. https://doi.org/10.7205/MILMED-D-14-00677

Kida, S. (2019). Reconsolidation/destabilization, extinction and forgetting of fear memory as therapeutic targets for PTSD. *Psychopharmacology*, 236(1), 49–57. https://doi.org/10.1007/s00213-018-5086-2

Kiddoo, D. (2011). Nocturnal enuresis. *BMJ Clinical Evidence*, 2011, Article 305.

Kiddoo, D. (2015). Nocturnal enuresis: Non-pharmacological treatments. *BMJ Clinical Evidence*, 2015, Article 305.

Kiecolt-Glaser, J. K., & Glaser, R. (1992). Psychoneuroimmunology: Can psychological interventions modulate immunity? *Journal of Consulting and Clinical Psychology*, 60(4), 569–575. https://doi.org/10.1037/0022-006X.60.4.569

Kiely, L., Touyz, S., Conti, J., & Hay, P. (2022). Conceptualising specialist supportive clinical management (SSCM): Current evidence and future directions. *Journal of Eating Disorders*, 10(1), 32. https://doi.org/10.1186/s40337-022-00557-2

Kienle, J., Rockstroh, B., Bohus, M., Fiess, J., Huffziger, S., & Steffen-Klatt, A. (2017). Somatoform dissociation and posttraumatic stress syndrome – two sides of the same medal? A comparison of symptom profiles, trauma history and altered affect regulation between patients with functional neurological symptoms and patients with PTSD. *BMC Psychiatry*, 17(1), 248. https://doi.org/10.1186/s12888-017-1414-z

Kihlstrom, J. F., Glisky, M. L., & Angiulo, M. J. (1994). Dissociative tendencies and dissociative disorders. *Journal of Abnormal Psychology*, 103(1), 117–124. https://doi.org/10.1037/0021-843X.103.1.117

Kilpela, L. S., Calogero, R., Wilfred, S. A., Verzijl, C. L., Hale, W. J., & Becker, C. B. (2019). Self-objectification and eating disorder pathology in an ethnically diverse sample of adult women: Cross-sectional

and short-term longitudinal associations. *Journal of Eating Disorders*, 7(1), 45. https://doi.org/10.1186/s40337-019-0273-z

Kim, B., Benekos, P. J., & Merlo, A. V. (2016). Sex offender recidivism revisited: Review of recent meta-analyses on the effects of sex offender treatment. *Trauma, Violence, & Abuse*, 17(1), 105–117. https://doi.org/10.1177/1524838014566719

Kim, B., Kim, H., Kim, S., & Hwang, Y. (2021). A brief review of non-invasive brain imaging technologies and the near-infrared optical bioimaging. *Applied Microscopy*, 51(1), 9. https://doi.org/10.1186/s42649-021-00058-7

Kim, B. R., & Mackert, M. (2022). Social media use and binge eating: An integrative review. *Public Health Nursing*, 39(5), 1134–1141. https://doi.org/10.1111/phn.13069

Kim, H., Yoo, J., Han, K., Lee, D.-Y., Fava, M., Mischoulon, D., & Jeon, H. J. (2022). Hormone therapy and the decreased risk of dementia in women with depression: A population-based cohort study. *Alzheimer's Research & Therapy*, 14(1), 83. https://doi.org/10.1186/s13195-022-01026-3

Kim, J.-E., Chang, J.-H., Jeong, M.-J., Choi, J., Park, J., Baek, C., Shin, A., Park, S. M., Kang, D., & Choi, J.-Y. (2020). A systematic review and meta-analysis of effects of menopausal hormone therapy on cardiovascular diseases. *Scientific Reports*, 10(1), Article 1. https://doi.org/10.1038/s41598-020-77534-9

Kim, K. M., Bae, E., Lee, J., Park, T.-W., & Lim, M. H. (2021). A review of cognitive and behavioral interventions for tic disorder. *Journal of the Korean Academy of Child and Adolescent Psychiatry*, 32(2), 51–62. https://doi.org/10.5765/jkacap.200042

Kim, S. K., & Park, M. (2017). Effectiveness of person-centered care on people with dementia: A systematic review and meta-analysis. *Clinical Interventions in Aging*, 12, 381–397. https://doi.org/10.2147/CIA.S117637

Kim, S. Y. H., Appelbaum, P. S., Swan, J., Stroup, T. S., McEvoy, J. P., Goff, D. C., Jeste, D. V., Lamberti, J. S., Leibovici, A., & Caine, E. D. (2007). Determining when impairment constitutes incapacity for informed consent in schizophrenia research. *The British Journal of Psychiatry*, 191, 38–43. https://doi.org/10.1192/bjp.bp.106.033324

Kim, T. J., & Knesebeck, O. von dem. (2018). Income and obesity: What is the direction of the relationship? A systematic review and meta-analysis. *BMJ Open*, 8(1), e019862. https://doi.org/10.1136/bmjopen-2017-019862

Kim, Y., & Chang, H. (2011). Correlation between attention deficit hyperactivity disorder and sugar consumption, quality of diet, and dietary behavior in school children. *Nutrition Research and Practice*, 5(3), 236–245. https://doi.org/10.4162/nrp.2011.5.3.236

Kimball, T. G., Shumway, S. T., Bradshaw, S. D., & Soloski, K. L. (2020). A systemic understanding of addiction formation and the recovery process. In *The handbook of systemic family therapy* (pp. 325–355). John Wiley & Sons. https://doi.org/10.1002/9781119438519.ch95

Kimbrel, N. A., Garrett, M. E., Dennis, M. F., Hauser, M. A., Ashley-Koch, A. E., & Beckham, J. C. (2018). A genome-wide association study of suicide attempts and suicidal ideation in U.S. military veterans. *Psychiatry Research*, 269, 64–69. https://doi.org/10.1016/j.psychres.2018.07.017

Kimerling, R., Weitlauf, J. C., Iverson, K. M., Karpenko, J. A., & Jain, S. (2014). Gender issues in PTSD. In M. J. Friedman, T. M. Keane, & P. A. Resick (Eds.), *Handbook of PTSD: Science and practice* (2nd ed., pp. 313–330). Guilford Press.

Kimonis, E. R., Frick, P. J., & Fleming, G. E. (2020). Externalizing disorders of childhood and adolescence. In J. E. Maddux & B. A. Winstead (Eds.), *Psychopathology: Foundations for a contemporary understanding* (2015-46288-019; 5th ed., pp. 427–458). Routledge/Taylor & Francis Group.

Kinderman, P. (2014a). *A prescription for psychiatry: Why we need a whole new approach to mental health and wellbeing*. Palgrave Macmillan.

Kinderman, P. (2014b, August 18). *Shh ... Just whisper it, but there might just be a revolution underway*. https://www.madinamerica.com/2014/08/shh-just-whisper-might-just-revolution-underway/

Kinderman, P. (2017). A manifesto for psychological health and wellbeing. In J. Davies (Ed.), *The sedated society: The causes and harms of our psychiatric drug epidemic* (pp. 271–301). Palgrave Macmillan.

Kinderman, P., & Cooke, A. (2017). Responses to the publication of the American Psychiatric Association's DSM-5. *Journal of Humanistic Psychology*, 57(6), 625–649. https://doi.org/10.1177/0022167817698262

Kinderman, P., Schwannauer, M., Pontin, E., & Tai, S. (2013). Psychological processes mediate the impact of familial risk, social circumstances and life events on mental health. *PLoS ONE*, 8(10). https://doi.org/10.1371/journal.pone.0076564

King, C., & Leask, J. (2017). The impact of a vaccine scare on parental views, trust and information needs: A qualitative study in Sydney, Australia. *BMC Public Health*, 17(1), 106. https://doi.org/10.1186/s12889-017-4032-2

King, D. L., & Delfabbro, P. H. (2013). Issues for DSM-5: Video-gaming disorder? *Australian and New Zealand Journal of Psychiatry*, 47(1), 20–22. https://doi.org/10.1177/0004867412464065

Kingsberg, S. A., & Simon, J. A. (2020). Female hypoactive sexual desire disorder: A practical guide to causes, clinical diagnosis, and treatment. *Journal of Women's Health*, 29(8), 1101–1112. https://doi.org/10.1089/jwh.2019.7865

Kingston, D. A. (2018). Hypersexuality: Fact or fiction? *The Journal of Sexual Medicine*, 15(5), 613–615. https://doi.org/10.1016/j.jsxm.2018.02.015

Kinsey, A. C. (1941). Homosexuality; criteria for a hormonal explanation of the homosexual. *Journal of Clinical Endocrinology*, 1, 424–428. https://doi.org/10.1210/jcem-1-5-424

Kinsey, A. C., Pomeroy, W. B., & Martin, C. E. (1948). *Sexual behavior in the human male*. Saunders.

Kinsey, A. C., Pomeroy, W. B., Martin, C. E., & Gebhard, P. H. (1953). *Sexual behavior in the human female*. Saunders.

Kirby, M. (2021, July 10). Debate over "aversive therapy" goes on. *The Sun Chronicle*. https://www.thesunchronicle.com/opinion/columns/mike-kirby-debate-over-aversive-therapy-goes-on/article_92968f32-2b7b-5c77-8e3b-d0f90a67eef6.html

Kirk, S. A., & Kutchins, H. (1992). *The selling of DSM: The rhetoric of science in psychiatry*. Aldine de Gruyter.

Kirkland, A. E., Langan, M. T., & Holton, K. F. (2022). Artificial food coloring affects EEG power and ADHD symptoms in college students with ADHD: A pilot study. *Nutritional Neuroscience*, 25(1), 159–168. https://doi.org/10.1080/1028415X.2020.1730614

Kirkner, R. M. (2015). *On ICD-10, the empire strikes back*. https://www.managedcaremag.com/archives/2015/3/icd-10-empire-strikes-back

Kirsch, I. (2010). *The emperor's new drugs: Exploding the antidepressant myth*. Basic Books.

Kirsch, I. (2014). Antidepressants and the placebo effect. *Zeitschrift Für Psychologie*, 222(3), 128–134. https://doi.org/10.1027/2151-2604/a000176

Kirsch, I. (2019). Placebo effect in the treatment of depression and anxiety. *Frontiers in Psychiatry*, 10, Article 407. https://doi.org/10.3389/fpsyt.2019.00407

Kische, H., Ollmann, T. M., Voss, C., Hoyer, J., Rückert, F., Pieper, L., Kirschbaum, C., & Beesdo-Baum, K. (2021). Associations of saliva cortisol and hair cortisol with generalized anxiety, social anxiety, and major depressive disorder: An epidemiological cohort study in adolescents and young adults. *Psychoneuroendocrinology*, 126, 105167. https://doi.org/10.1016/j.psyneuen.2021.105167

Kisely, S. R., Campbell, L. A., & O'Reilly, R. (2017). Compulsory community and involuntary outpatient treatment for people with severe mental disorders. *Cochrane Database of Systematic Reviews*, *2017*(3), Article CD004408. https://doi.org/10.1002/14651858.CD004408.pub5

Kishi, T., Kafantaris, V., Sunday, S., Sheridan, E. M., & Correll, C. U. (2012). Are antipsychotics effective for the treatment of anorexia nervosa? Results from a systematic review and meta-analysis. *Journal of Clinical Psychiatry*, *73*(6), e757–e766. https://doi.org/10.4088/JCP.12r07691

Kissane, D. W., & Lichtenthal, W. G. (2008). Family focused grief therapy: From palliative care into bereavement. In M. S. Stroebe, R. O. Hansson, H. Schut, & W. Stroebe (Eds.), *Handbook of bereavement research and practice: Advances in theory and intervention* (pp. 485–510). American Psychological Association. https://doi.org/10.1037/14498-023

Kissane, D. W., McKenzie, M., Block, S., Moskowitz, C., McKenzie, D. P., & O'Neill, I. (2006). Family focused grief therapy: A randomized, controlled trial in palliative care and bereavement. *The American Journal of Psychiatry*, *163*(7), 1208–1218. https://doi.org/10.1176/appi.ajp.163.7.1208

Klaw, E., & Humphreys, K. (2000). Life stories of Moderation Management mutual help group members. *Contemporary Drug Problems: An Interdisciplinary Quarterly*, *27*(4), 779–803. https://doi.org/10.1177/009145090002700404

Kleczkowska, P. (2021). Advantages and disadvantages of disulfiram coadministered with popular addictive substances. *European Journal of Pharmacology*, *904*, Article 174143. https://doi.org/10.1016/j.ejphar.2021.174143

Klein, J. P., Roniger, A., Schweiger, U., Späth, C., & Brodbeck, J. (2015). The association of childhood trauma and personality disorders with chronic depression: A cross-sectional study in depressed outpatients. *The Journal of Clinical Psychiatry*, *76*(6), e794–e801. https://doi.org/10.4088/JCP.14m09158

Klein, M., Heimann, P., Isaacs, S., & Riviere, J. (1952). *Developments in psychoanalysis* (J. Riviere, Ed.). Karnac.

Klein Hofmeijer-Sevink, M., Batelaan, N. M., van Megen, H. J. G. M., Penninx, B. W., Cath, D. C., van den Hout, M. A., & van Balkom, A. J. L. M. (2012). Clinical relevance of comorbidity in anxiety disorders: A report from the Netherlands Study of Depression and Anxiety (NESDA). *Journal of Affective Disorders*, *137*(1–3), 106–112. https://doi.org/10.1016/j.jad.2011.12.008

Kleinman, A. M. (1977). Depression, somatization and the new cross-cultural psychiatry. *Social Science & Medicine*, *11*(1), 3–10. https://doi.org/10.1016/0037-7856(77)90138-X

Kleinplatz, P. J. (1996). Transforming sex therapy: Integrating erotic potential. *The Humanistic Psychologist*, *24*(2), 190–202. https://doi.org/10.1080/08873267.1996.9986850

Kleinplatz, P. J. (1998). Sex therapy for vaginismus: A review, critique, and humanistic alternative. *Journal of Humanistic Psychology*, *38*(2), 41–81. https://doi.org/10.1177/00221678980382004

Kleinplatz, P. J. (2004). Beyond sexual mechanics and hydraulics: Humanizing the discourse surrounding erectile dysfunction. *Journal of Humanistic Psychology*, *44*(2), 215–242. https://doi.org/10.1177/0022167804263130

Kleinplatz, P. J. (2007). Coming out of the sex therapy closet: Using experiential psychotherapy with sexual problems and concerns. *American Journal of Psychotherapy*, *61*(3), 333–348. https://doi.org/10.1176/appi.psychotherapy.2007.61.3.333

Kleinplatz, P. J. (2010). "Desire disorders" or opportunities for optimal erotic intimacy? In S. R. Leiblum (Ed.), *Treating sexual desire disorders: A clinical casebook* (pp. 92–113). Guilford Press.

Kleinplatz, P. J. (2012). Is that all there is? A new critique of the goals of sex therapy. In P. J. Kleinplatz (Ed.), *New directions in sex therapy: Innovations and alternatives* (2nd ed., pp. 101–118). Routledge.

Kleinplatz, P. J. (2014). The paraphilias: An experiential approach to "dangerous" desires. In Y. M. Binik & K. S. K. Hall (Eds.), *Principles and practice of sex therapy* (5th ed., pp. 195–218). Guilford Press.

Kleinstäuber, M., Allwang, C., Bailer, J., Berking, M., Brünahl, C., Erkic, M., Gitzen, H., Gollwitzer, M., Gottschalk, J.-M., Heider, J., Hermann, A., Lahmann, C., Löwe, B., Martin, A., Rau, J., Schröder, A., Schwabe, J., Schwarz, J., Stark, R., … Rief, W. (2019). Cognitive behaviour therapy complemented with emotion regulation training for patients with persistent physical symptoms: A randomised clinical trial. *Psychotherapy and Psychosomatics*, *88*(5), 287–299. https://doi.org/10.1159/000501621

Kleinstäuber, M., Witthöft, M., Steffanowski, A., Marwijk, H. van, Hiller, W., & Lambert, M. J. (2014). Pharmacological interventions for somatoform disorders in adults. *Cochrane Database of Systematic Reviews*, *2014*(11), Article CD010628. https://doi.org/10.1002/14651858.CD010628.pub2

Klemperer, E. M., Streck, J. M., Lindson, N., West, J. C., Su, A., Hughes, J. R., & Carpenter, M. J. (2022). A systematic review and meta-analysis of interventions to induce attempts to quit tobacco among adults not ready to quit. *Experimental and Clinical Psychopharmacology*. https://doi.org/10.1037/pha0000583

Klerman, G. L., Weissman, M. M., Rounsaville, B. J., & Chevron, E. S. (1984). *Interpersonal psychotherapy of depression: A brief, focused, specific strategy*. Jason Aronson.

Klest, B. (2012). Childhood trauma, poverty, and adult victimization. *Psychological Trauma: Theory, Research, Practice, and Policy*, *4*(3), 245–251. https://doi.org/10.1037/a0024468

Klest, B., Freyd, J. J., & Foynes, M. M. (2013). Trauma exposure and posttraumatic symptoms in Hawaii: Gender, ethnicity, and social context. *Psychological Trauma: Theory, Research, Practice, and Policy*, *5*(5), 409–416. https://doi.org/10.1037/a0029336

Klest, B., Freyd, J. J., Hampson, S. E., & Dubanoski, J. P. (2013). Trauma, socioeconomic resources, and self-rated health in an ethnically diverse adult cohort. *Ethnicity & Health*, *18*(1), 97–113. https://doi.org/10.1080/13557858.2012.700916

Kliem, S., Kröger, C., & Kosfelder, J. (2010). Dialectical behavior therapy for borderline personality disorder: A meta-analysis using mixed-effects modeling. *Journal of Consulting and Clinical Psychology*, *78*(6), 936–951. https://doi.org/10.1037/a0021015

Klingemann, H., & Rosenberg, H. (2009). Acceptance and therapeutic practice of controlled drinking as an outcome goal by Swiss alcohol treatment programmes. *European Addiction Research*, *15*(3), 121–127. https://doi.org/10.1159/000210041

Klink, D., & Den Heijer, M. (2014). Genetic aspects of gender identity development and gender dysphoria. In B. P. C. Kreukels, T. D. Steensma, & A. L. C. de Vries (Eds.), *Gender dysphoria and disorders of sex development: Progress in care and knowledge* (pp. 25–51). Springer Science + Business Media. https://doi.org/10.1007/978-1-4614-7441-8_2

Klintwall, L., & Eikeseth, S. (2014). Early and intensive behavioral intervention (EIBI) in autism. In V. B. Patel, V. R. Preedy, & C. R. Martin (Eds.), *Comprehensive guide to autism* (pp. 117–137). Springer New York. https://doi.org/10.1007/978-1-4614-4788-7_129

Kluft, R. P. (2000). The psychoanalytic psychotherapy of dissociative identity disorder in the context of trauma therapy. *Psychoanalytic Inquiry*, *20*(2), 259–286. https://doi.org/10.1080/07351692009348887

Kluge, M., Schüssler, P., Künzel, H. E., Dresler, M., Yassouridis, A., & Steiger, A. (2007). Increased nocturnal secretion of ACTH and cortisol in obsessive compulsive disorder. *Journal of Psychiatric Research*, *41*(11), 928–933. https://doi.org/10.1016/j.jpsychires.2006.08.005

Klump, K. L., & Culbert, K. M. (2007). Molecular genetic studies of eating disorders: Current

status and future directions. *Current Directions in Psychological Science*, *16*(1), 37–41. doi:10.1111/j.1467-8721.2007.00471.x

Klump, K. L., Miller, K. B., Keel, P. K., McGue, M., & Iacono, W. G. (2001). Genetic and environmental influences on anorexia nervosa syndromes in a population-based twin sample. *Psychological Medicine*, *31*(4), 737–740. doi:10.1017/S0033291701003725

Knaak, S., Mantler, E., & Szeto, A. (2017). Mental illness-related stigma in healthcare. *Healthcare Management Forum*, *30*(2), 111–116. https://doi.org/10.1177/0840470416679413

Knafo, A., Iervolino, A. C., & Plomin, R. (2005). Masculine girls and feminine boys: Genetic and environmental contributions to atypical gender development in early childhood. *Journal of Personality and Social Psychology*, *88*(2), 400–412. https://doi.org/10.1037/0022-3514.88.2.400

Knapp, C. (2019). That's how the light gets in. *Journal of Humanistic Psychology*, *59*(5), 730–741. https://doi.org/10.1177/0022167818761998

Knapp, M., Beecham, J., McDaid, D., Matosevic, T., & Smith, M. (2011). The economic consequences of deinstitutionalisation of mental health services: Lessons from a systematic review of European experience. *Health & Social Care in the Community*, *19*(2), 113–125.

Kneeland, R. E., & Fatemi, S. H. (2013). Viral infection, inflammation and schizophrenia. *Progress in Neuro-Psychopharmacology & Biological Psychiatry*, *42*, 35–48. https://doi.org/10.1016/j.pnpbp.2012.02.001

Knight, K. E. (2013). Attention deficit hyperactivity disorder (ADHD) in adolescents: An investigative study of dopamine and norepinephrine systems [University of Arizona]. In *Department of Psychology: Vol. Doctoral dissertation* (2013-99180-456). http://arizona.openrepository.com/arizona/bitstream/10150/247278/1/azu_etd_12403_sip1_m.pdf

Knight, R. A. (2010). Is a diagnostic category for paraphilic coercive disorder defensible? *Archives of Sexual Behavior*, *39*(2), 419–426. https://doi.org/10.1007/s10508-009-9571-x

Knouse, L. E., & Fleming, A. P. (2016). Applying cognitive-behavioral therapy for ADHD to emerging adults. *Cognitive and Behavioral Practice*. https://doi.org/10.1016/j.cbpra.2016.03.008

Kodak, T., & Grow, L. L. (2011). Behavioral treatment of autism. In W. W. Fisher, C. C. Piazza, & H. S. Roane (Eds.), *Handbook of applied behavior analysis* (pp. 402–416). Guilford Press.

Koehler, B., Silver, A.-L., & Karon, B. (2013). Psychodynamic approaches to understanding psychosis: Defenses against terror. In J. Read & J. Dillon (Eds.), *Models of madness: Psychological, social and biological approaches to psychosis* (2nd ed., pp. 238–248). Routledge/Taylor & Francis Group.

Koehler, B., & Silver, A.-L. S. (2009). Psychodynamic treatment of psychosis in the USA: Promoting development beyond biological reductionism. In Y. O. Alanen, M. González de Chávez, A.-L. S. Silver, & B. Martindale (Eds.), *Psychotherapeutic approaches to schizophrenic psychoses* (pp. 215–232). Routledge.

Koelen, J. A., Houtveen, J. H., Abbass, A., Luyten, P., Eurelings-Bontekoe, E. H. M., Van Broeckhuysen-Kloth, S. A. M., Bühring, M. E. F., & Geenen, R. (2014). Effectiveness of psychotherapy for severe somatoform disorder: Meta analysis. *The British Journal of Psychiatry*, *204*(1), 12–19. https://doi.org/10.1192/bjp.bp.112.121830

Koenders, L., Machielsen, M. W. J., van der Meer, F. J., van Gasselt, A. C. M., Meijer, C. J., van den Brink, W., Koeter, M. W. J., Caan, M. W. A., Cousijn, J., den Braber, A., van 't Ent, D., Rive, M. M., Schene, A. H., van de Giessen, E., Huyser, C., de Kwaasteniet, B. P., Veltman, D. J., & de Haan, L. (2015). Brain volume in male patients with recent onset schizophrenia with and without cannabis use disorders. *Journal of Psychiatry & Neuroscience*, *40*(3), 197–206.

Koenen, K. C., Amstadter, A. B., & Nugent, N. R. (2009). Gene-environment interaction in posttraumatic stress disorder: An update. *Journal of Traumatic Stress*, 22(5), 416–426. https://doi.org/10.1002/jts.20435

Koenen, K. C., Nugent, N. R., & Amstadter, A. B. (2008). Gene-environment interaction in posttraumatic stress disorder. *European Archives of Psychiatry and Clinical Neuroscience*, 258(2), 82–96. https://doi.org/10.1007/s00406-007-0787-2

Koenen, K. C., Ratanatharathorn, A., Ng, L., McLaughlin, K. A., Bromet, E. J., Stein, D. J., Karam, E. G., Meron Ruscio, A., Benjet, C., Scott, K., Atwoli, L., Petukhova, M., Lim, C. C. W., Aguilar-Gaxiola, S., Al-Hamzawi, A., Alonso, J., Bunting, B., Ciutan, M., de Girolamo, G., … Kessler, R. C. (2017). Posttraumatic stress disorder in the World Mental Health Surveys. *Psychological Medicine*, 47(13), 2260–2274. https://doi.org/10.1017/S0033291717000708

Koenigs, M., & Grafman, J. (2009). Posttraumatic stress disorder: The role of medial prefrontal cortex and amygdala. *The Neuroscientist*, 15(5), 540–548. https://doi.org/10.1177/1073858409333072

Koffel, E., Bramoweth, A. D., & Ulmer, C. S. (2018). Increasing access to and utilization of cognitive behavioral therapy for insomnia (CBT-I): A narrative review. *Journal of General Internal Medicine*, 33(6), 955–962. https://doi.org/10.1007/s11606-018-4390-1

Kog, E., & Vandereycken, W. (1985). Family characteristics of anorexia nervosa and bulimia: A review of the research literature. *Clinical Psychology Review*, 5(2), 159–180. https://doi.org/10.1016/0272-7358(85)90020-0

Kog, E., Vandereycken, W., & Vertommen, H. (1985). The psychosomatic family model: A critical analysis of family interaction concepts. *Journal of Family Therapy*, 7(1), 31–44. https://doi.org/10.1046/j..1985.00663.x

Koger, S. M., Schettler, T., & Weiss, B. (2005). Environmental toxicants and developmental disabilities: A challenge for psychologists. *American Psychologist*, 60(3), 243–255. https://doi.org/10.1037/0003-066X.60.3.243

Koh, K. B., Choi, E. H., Lee, Y., & Han, M. (2011). Serotonin-related gene pathways associated with undifferentiated somatoform disorder. *Psychiatry Research*, 189(2), 246–250. https://doi.org/10.1016/j.psychres.2011.04.002

Kohlenberg, R. J. (1973). Behavioristic approach to multiple personality: A case study. *Behavior Therapy*, 4(1), 137–140. https://doi.org/10.1016/S0005-7894(73)80086-3

Kohler, C. G., Walker, J. B., Martin, E. A., Healey, K. M., & Moberg, P. J. (2010). Facial emotion perception in schizophrenia: A meta-analytic review. *Schizophrenia Bulletin*, 36(5), 1009–1019. https://doi.org/10.1093/schbul/sbn192

Köhler-Forsberg, O., N Lydholm, C., Hjorthøj, C., Nordentoft, M., Mors, O., & Benros, M. E. (2019). Efficacy of anti-inflammatory treatment on major depressive disorder or depressive symptoms: Meta-analysis of clinical trials. *Acta Psychiatrica Scandinavica*, 139(5), 404–419. https://doi.org/10.1111/acps.13016

Kohn, C. S. (2014). Conceptualization and treatment of kleptomania behaviors using cognitive and behavioral strategies. *International Journal of Behavioral Consultation and Therapy*, 2(4), 553. https://doi.org/10.1037/h0101007

Koivisto, M., Melartin, T., & Lindeman, S. (2022). Self-invalidation in borderline personality disorder: A content analysis of patients' verbalizations. *Psychotherapy Research*, 1–14. https://doi.org/10.1080/10503307.2022.2025627

Kolar, D. R., Rodriguez, D. L. M., Chams, M. M., & Hoek, H. W. (2016). Epidemiology of eating disorders in Latin America: A systematic review and meta-analysis. *Current Opinion in Psychiatry*, 29(6), 363–371. https://doi.org/10.1097/YCO.0000000000000279

Kolesar, T. A., Bilevicius, E., Wilson, A. D., & Kornelsen, J. (2019). Systematic review and meta-analyses of neural structural and functional differences in generalized anxiety disorder and healthy controls using magnetic resonance imaging. *NeuroImage: Clinical*, 24, 102016. https://doi.org/10.1016/j.nicl.2019.102016

Kolevzon, A., Wang, A. T., Grodberg, D., & Buxbaum, J. D. (2013). Autism spectrum disorders. In D. S. Charney, J. D. Buxbaum, P. Sklar, E. J. Nestler, D. S. Charney, J. D. Buxbaum, P. Sklar, & E. J. Nestler (Eds.), *Neurobiology of mental illness* (4th ed., pp. 1022–1033). Oxford University Press. https://doi.org/10.1093/med/9780199934959.003.0077

Konkolÿ Thege, B., Colman, I., el-Guebaly, N., Hodgins, D. C., Patten, S. B., Schopflocher, D., Wolfe, J., & Wild, T. C. (2015). Social judgments of behavioral versus substance-related addictions: A population-based study. *Addictive Behaviors*, 42, 24–31. https://doi.org/10.1016/j.addbeh.2014.10.025

Konrad, S. S., & Bath, E. (2014). Confidentiality and privilege. In E. Ford & M. Rotter (Eds.), *Landmark cases in forensic psychiatry* (pp. 3–9). Oxford University Press.

Konstantinos, F., & Heun, R. (2020). The effects of Rhodiola Rosea supplementation on depression, anxiety and mood – A systematic review. *Global Psychiatry*, 3(1), 72–82. https://doi.org/10.2478/gp-2019-0022

Koopmans, M. (2001). From Double Bind to N-Bind: Toward a new theory of schizophrenia and family interaction. *Nonlinear Dynamics, Psychology, and Life Sciences*, 5(4), 289–323. https://doi.org/10.1023/A:1009518729645

Kopelman, M. D., Thomson, A. D., Guerrini, I., & Marshall, E. J. (2009). The Korsakoff syndrome: Clinical aspects, psychology and treatment. *Alcohol and Alcoholism*, 44(2), 148–154. https://doi.org/10.1093/alcalc/agn118

Korchmaros, J. D., Baumer, P. C., & Valdez, E. S. (2016). Critical components of adolescent substance use treatment programs—The impact of juvenile drug court: Strategies in practice and elements of Reclaiming Futures. *Drug Court Review*, 10(1), 80–115.

Korchmaros, J. D., Thompson-Dyck, K., & Haring, R. C. (2017). Professionals' perceptions of and recommendations for matching juvenile drug court clients to services. *Children and Youth Services Review*, 73, 149–164. https://doi.org/10.1016/j.childyouth.2016.12.005

Koskina, A., Campbell, I. C., & Schmidt, U. (2013). Exposure therapy in eating disorders revisited. *Neuroscience and Biobehavioral Reviews*, 37(2), 193–208. https://doi.org/10.1016/j.neubiorev.2012.11.010

Kotapati, V. P., Khan, A. M., Dar, S., Begum, G., Bachu, R., Adnan, M., Zubair, A., & Ahmed, R. A. (2019). The effectiveness of selective serotonin reuptake inhibitors for treatment of obsessive-compulsive disorder in adolescents and children: A systematic review and meta-analysis. *Frontiers in Psychiatry*, 10, Article 523. https://doi.org/10.3389/fpsyt.2019.00523

Kothgassner, O. D., Goreis, A., Kafka, J. X., Van Eickels, R. L., Plener, P. L., & Felnhofer, A. (2019). Virtual reality exposure therapy for posttraumatic stress disorder (PTSD): A meta-analysis. *European Journal of Psychotraumatology*, 10(1). https://doi.org/10.1080/20008198.2019.1654782

Kotov, R., Jonas, K. G., Carpenter, W. T., Dretsch, M. N., Eaton, N. R., Forbes, M. K., Forbush, K. T., Hobbs, K., Reininghaus, U., Slade, T., South, S. C., Sunderland, M., Waszczuk, M. A., Widiger, T. A., Wright, A. G. C., Zald, D. H., Krueger, R. F., Watson, D., & Workgroup, H. U. (2020). Validity and utility of Hierarchical Taxonomy of Psychopathology (HiTOP): I. Psychosis superspectrum. *World Psychiatry*, 19(2), 151–172. https://doi.org/10.1002/wps.20730

Kotov, R., Krueger, R. F., Watson, D., Achenbach, T. M., Althoff, R. R., Bagby, R. M., Brown, T. A., Carpenter, W. T., Caspi, A., Clark, L. A., Eaton, N. R., Forbes, M. K., Forbush, K. T., Goldberg, D., Hasin, D., Hyman, S. E., Ivanova, M. Y., Lynam, D. R., Markon, K., … Zimmerman, M. (2017). The Hierarchical Taxonomy of Psychopathology (HiTOP): A dimensional alternative to traditional nosologies. *Journal of Abnormal Psychology*, 126(4), 454–477. https://doi.org/10.1037/abn0000258

Kotov, R., Krueger, R. F., Watson, D., Cicero, D. C., Conway, C. C., DeYoung, C. G., Eaton, N. R., Forbes, M. K., Hallquist, M. N., Latzman, R. D., Mullins-Sweatt, S. N., Ruggero, C. J., Simms, L. J., Waldman, I. D., Waszczuk, M. A., & Wright, A. G. C. (2021). The Hierarchical Taxonomy of Psychopathology (HiTOP): A quantitative nosology based on consensus of evidence. *Annual Review of Clinical Psychology*, 17, 83–108. https://doi.org/10.1146/annurev-clinpsy-081219-093304

Kotsiubinskii, A. P. (2002). A biopsychosocial model of schizophrenia. *International Journal of Mental Health*, 31(2), 51–60.

Koven, N. S., & Abry, A. W. (2015). The clinical basis of orthorexia nervosa: Emerging perspectives. *Neuropsychiatric Disease and Treatment*, 11, 385–394. https://doi.org/10.2147/NDT.S61665

Kowitt, S. D., Aiello, A. E., Callahan, L. F., Fisher, E. B., Gottfredson, N. C., Jordan, J. M., & Muessig, K. E. (2020). Associations among neighborhood poverty, perceived neighborhood environment, and depressed mood are mediated by physical activity, perceived individual control, and loneliness. *Health & Place*, 62, 102278. https://doi.org/10.1016/j.healthplace.2019.102278

Kozak, M. J., & Cuthbert, B. N. (2016). The NIMH Research Domain Criteria initiative: Background, issues, and pragmatics. *Psychophysiology*, 53(3), 286–297. https://doi.org/10.1111/psyp.12518

Kozloff, N., Foussias, G., Durbin, J., Sockalingam, S., Addington, J., Addington, D., Ampofo, A., Anderson, K. K., Barwick, M., Bromley, S., Cunningham, J. E. A., Dahrouge, S., Duda, L., Ford, C., Gallagher, S., Haltigan, J. D., Henderson, J., Jaouich, A., Miranda, D., … Voineskos, A. N. (2020). Early Psychosis Intervention-Spreading Evidence-based Treatment (EPI-SET): Protocol for an effectiveness-implementation study of a structured model of care for psychosis in youth and emerging adults. *BMJ Open*, 10(6), e034280. https://doi.org/10.1136/bmjopen-2019-034280

Kozlowska, K., English, M., & Savage, B. (2013). Connecting body and mind: The first interview with somatising patients and their families. *Clinical Child Psychology and Psychiatry*, 18(2), 224–245. https://doi.org/10.1177/1359104512447314

Kozlowska, K., Griffiths, K. R., Foster, S. L., Linton, J., Williams, L. M., & Korgaonkar, M. S. (2017). Grey matter abnormalities in children and adolescents with functional neurological symptom disorder. *NeuroImage: Clinical*, 15, 306–314. https://doi.org/10.1016/j.nicl.2017.04.028

Kraemer, H. C., Kupfer, D. J., Clarke, D. E., Narrow, W. E., & Regier, D. A. (2012). "Standards for DSM-5 reliability": Reply. *The American Journal of Psychiatry*, 169(5), 537–538.

Krafft-Ebing, R. von. (1894). *Psychopathia sexualis, with special reference to contrary sexual instinct: A medico-legal study* (C. G. Chaddock, Trans.; 7th ed.). F. A. Davis. https://archive.org/details/PsychopathiaSexualis1000006945

Kraft, S. J., & Yairi, E. (2012). Genetic bases of stuttering: The state of the art, 2011. *Folia Phoniatrica et Logopaedica:International Journal of Phoniatrics, Speech Therapy and Communication Pathology*, 64(1), 34–47. https://doi.org/10.1159/000331073

Krahn, L. E. (2003). Sodium oxybate: A new way to treat narcolepsy. *Current Psychiatry*, 2(8), 65–69.

Krahn, T. M., & Fenton, A. (2012). The extreme male brain theory of autism and the potential adverse effects for boys and girls with autism. *Journal of Bioethical Inquiry*, 9(1), 93–103. https://doi.org/10.1007/s11673-011-9350-y

Kramer, H., Sprenger, J., & Summers, M. (2021). *The malleus maleficarum*. http://www.malleusmaleficarum.org (Original work published 1486.)

Kramer, P. (2011, July 10). In defense of antidepressants. *The New York Times*.

Krane, K. (2020, May 26). Cannabis legalization is key to economic recovery, much like ending alcohol prohibition helped us out of the Great Depression. *Forbes*. https://www.forbes.com/sites/kriskrane/2020/05/26/cannabis-legalization-is-key-to-economic-recovery-much-like-ending-alcohol-prohibition-helped-us-out-of-the-great-depression/

Krasne, F. B. (1962). General disruption resulting from electrical stimulus of ventromedial hypothalamus. *Science*, 138(3542), 822–823. https://doi.org/10.1126/science.138.3542.822

Kratzer, L., Knefel, M., Haselgruber, A., Heinz, P., Schennach, R., & Karatzias, T. (2021). Co-occurrence of severe PTSD, somatic symptoms and dissociation in a large sample of childhood trauma inpatients: A network analysis. *European Archives of Psychiatry and Clinical Neuroscience*. https://doi.org/10.1007/s00406-021-01342-z

Kredlow, M. A., Fenster, R. J., Laurent, E. S., Ressler, K. J., & Phelps, E. A. (2022). Prefrontal cortex, amygdala, and threat processing: Implications for PTSD. *Neuropsychopharmacology*, 47(1), 247–259. https://doi.org/10.1038/s41386-021-01155-7

Kreitman, N. (1977). *Parasuicide*. John Wiley.

Kreukels, B. P. C., & Guillamon, A. (2016). Neuroimaging studies in people with gender incongruence. *International Review of Psychiatry*, 28(1), 120–128. https://doi.org/10.3109/09540261.2015.1113163

Krieg, R. G. (2001). An interdisciplinary look at the deinstitutionalization of the mentally ill. *The Social Science Journal*, 38(3), 367–380. https://doi.org/10.1016/S0362-3319(01)00136-7

Krigbaum, G. (2013). Abnormal psychology in a multicultural context. In T. G. Plante (Ed.), *Abnormal psychology across the ages: Vol. 3. Trends and future directions* (pp. 231–241). Praeger/ABC-CLIO.

Krivinko, J. M., Koppel, J., Savonenko, A., & Sweet, R. A. (2020). Animal models of psychosis in Alzheimer disease. *The American Journal of Geriatric Psychiatry*, 28(1), 1–19. https://doi.org/10.1016/j.jagp.2019.05.009

Kroenke, K. (2003). Patients presenting with somatic complaints: Epidemiology, psychiatric comorbidity and management. *International Journal of Methods in Psychiatric Research*, 12(1), 34–43. https://doi.org/10.1002/mpr.140

Kroenke, K. (2007). Efficacy of treatment for somatoform disorders: A review of randomized controlled trials. *Psychosomatic Medicine*, 69(9), 881–888. https://doi.org/10.1097/PSY.0b013e31815b00c4

Kroger, R. O., & Wood, L. A. (1993). Reification, "faking," and the Big Five. *American Psychologist*, 48(12), 1297–1298. https://doi.org/10.1037/0003-066X.48.12.1297

Krogh, J., Hjorthøj, C., Speyer, H., Gluud, C., & Nordentoft, M. (2017). Exercise for patients with major depression: A systematic review with meta-analysis and trial sequential analysis. *BMJ Open*, 7(9), e014820. https://doi.org/10.1136/bmjopen-2016-014820

Krueger, R. B., Reed, G. M., First, M. B., Marais, A., Kismodi, E., & Briken, P. (2017). Proposals for paraphilic disorders in the international classification of diseases and related health problems, eleventh revision (ICD-11). *Archives of Sexual Behavior*. https://doi.org/10.1007/s10508-017-0944-2

Krueger, R. F., & Hobbs, K. A. (2020). An overview of the DSM-5 alternative model of personality disorders. *Psychopathology*, 53(3), 126–132. https://doi.org/10.1159/000508538

Krueger, R. F., Hobbs, K. A., Conway, C. C., Dick, D. M., Dretsch, M. N., Eaton, N. R., Forbes, M. K., Forbush, K. T., Keyes, K. M., Latzman, R. D., Michelini, G., Patrick, C. J., Sellbom, M., Slade, T., South, S. C., Sunderland, M., Tackett, J., Waldman, I., Waszczuk,

M. A., … Workgroup, H. U. (2021). Validity and utility of Hierarchical Taxonomy of Psychopathology (HiTOP): II. Externalizing superspectrum. *World Psychiatry*, 20(2), 171–193. https://doi.org/10.1002/wps.20844

Krüger, C. (2020). Culture, trauma and dissociation: A broadening perspective for our field. *Journal of Trauma & Dissociation*, 21(1), 1–13. https://doi.org/10.1080/15299732.2020.1675134

Krupnick, J. L. (2002). Brief psychodynamic treatment of PTSD. *Journal of Clinical Psychology*, 58(8), 919–932. https://doi.org/10.1002/jclp.10067

Krycka, K. C. (2010). Multiplicity: A first-person exploration of dissociative experiencing. *Person-Centered and Experiential Psychotherapies*, 9(2), 143–156. https://doi.org/10.1080/14779757.2010.9688514

Krystal, J. H., Sanacora, G., & Duman, R. S. (2013). Rapid-acting glutamatergic antidepressants: The path to ketamine and beyond. *Biological Psychiatry*, 73(12), 1133–1141. https://doi.org/10.1016/j.biopsych.2013.03.026

Krzystanek, M., & Pałasz, A. (2020). The role of blocking serotonin 2C receptor by fluoxetine in the treatment of bulimia. *Pharmacotherapy in Psychiatry and Neurology*, 36(2), 135–141. https://doi.org/10.33450/fpn.2020.07.001

Kübler-Ross, E. (1970). *On death and dying*. Collier Books/Macmillan.

Kübler-Ross, E., Wessler, S., & Avioli, L. V. (1972). On death and dying. *JAMA*, 221(2), 174–179.

Kubota, Y., Sato, W., Kochiyama, T., Uono, S., Yoshimura, S., Sawada, R., & Toichi, M. (2019). Corticostriatal-limbic correlates of sub-clinical obsessive-compulsive traits. *Psychiatry Research: Neuroimaging*, 285, 40–46. https://doi.org/10.1016/j.pscychresns.2019.01.012

Kudler, H. S., Krupnick, J. L., Blank, Jr., Arthur S., Herman, J. L., & Horowitz, M. J. (2009). Psychodynamic therapy for adults. In E. B. Foa, T. M. Keane, M. J. Friedman, & J. A. Cohen (Eds.), *Effective treatments for PTSD: Practice guidelines from the International Society for Traumatic Stress Studies* (2nd ed., pp. 346–369). Guilford Press.

Kugler, J., Andresen, F. J., Bean, R. C., & Blais, R. K. (2019). Couple-based interventions for PTSD among military veterans: An empirical review. *Journal of Clinical Psychology*, 75(10), 1737–1755. https://doi.org/10.1002/jclp.22822

Kulaga, S. S., & Miller, C. W. T. (2021). Viral respiratory infections and psychosis: A review of the literature and the implications of COVID-19. *Neuroscience & Biobehavioral Reviews*, 127, 520–530. https://doi.org/10.1016/j.neubiorev.2021.05.008

Kulage, K. M., Goldberg, J., Usseglio, J., Romero, D., Bain, J. M., & Smaldone, A. M. (2020). How has DSM-5 affected autism diagnosis? A 5-year follow-up systematic literature review and meta-analysis. *Journal of Autism and Developmental Disorders*, 50(6), 2102–2127. https://doi.org/10.1007/s10803-019-03967-5

Kumar, R. M. (2021). The many faces of grief: A systematic literature review of grief during the COVID-19 pandemic. *Illness, Crisis & Loss*, 10541373211038084. https://doi.org/10.1177/10541373211038084

Kumar, V., Sznajder, K. K., & Kumara, S. (2022). Machine learning based suicide prediction and development of suicide vulnerability index for US counties. *Npj Mental Health Research*, 1(1), Article 1. https://doi.org/10.1038/s44184-022-00002-x

Kumari, V., Fannon, D., Peters, E. R., Ffytche, D. H., Sumich, A. L., Premkumar, P., Anilkumar, A. P., Andrew, C., Phillips, M. L., Williams, S. C. R., & Kuipers, E. (2011). Neural changes following cognitive behaviour therapy for psychosis: A longitudinal study. *Brain*, 134(8), 2396–2407. https://doi.org/10.1093/brain/awr154

Kung, K. T. F., Spencer, D., Pasterski, V., Neufeld, S., Glover, V., O'Connor, T. G., Hindmarsh, P. C., Hughes, I. A., Acerini, C. L., & Hines, M. (2016). No relationship between prenatal androgen exposure and autistic

traits: Convergent evidence from studies of children with congenital adrenal hyperplasia and of amniotic testosterone concentrations in typically developing children. *Journal of Child Psychology and Psychiatry*, 57(12), 1455–1462. https://doi.org/10.1111/jcpp.12602

Kuns, B., Rosani, A., & Varghese, D. (2022). Memantine. In *StatPearls* [Internet]. StatPearls Publishing. https://www.ncbi.nlm.nih.gov/books/NBK500025/

Kupfer, D. J., & Regier, D. A. (2009). Counterpoint: Toward credible conflict of interest policies in clinical psychiatry. In *Psychiatric Times* (Vol. 26, Issue 1). http://www.psychiatrictimes.com/articles/toward-credible-conflict-interest-policies-clinical-psychiatry/page/0/2

Kupper, N., & Denollet, J. (2018). Type D personality as a risk factor in coronary heart disease: A review of current evidence. *Current Cardiology Reports*, 20(11), 104. https://doi.org/10.1007/s11886-018-1048-x

Kusalaruk, P., Saipanish, R., & Hiranyatheb, T. (2015). Attitudes of psychiatrists toward obsessive–compulsive disorder patients. *Neuropsychiatric Disease and Treatment*, 11.

Kushner, H. I. (1999). *A cursing brain? The histories of Tourette's syndrome*. Harvard University Press.

Kushner, H. I. (2000). A brief history of Tourette syndrome. *Revista Brasileira de Psiquiatria*, 22, 76–79. https://doi.org/10.1590/S1516-44462000000020008

Kwan, M. Y., Haynos, A. F., Blomquist, K. K., & Roberto, C. A. (2018). Warning labels on fashion images: Short- and longer-term effects on body dissatisfaction, eating disorder symptoms, and eating behavior. *International Journal of Eating Disorders*, 51(10), 1153–1161. https://doi.org/10.1002/eat.22951

Kwate, N. O. A. (2005). The heresy of African-centered psychology. *Journal of Medical Humanities*, 26(4), 215–235. https://doi.org/10.1007/s10912-005-7698-x

Kymalainen, J. A., & Weisman de Mamani, A. G. (2008). Expressed emotion, communication deviance, and culture in families of patients with schizophrenia: A review of the literature. *Cultural Diversity and Ethnic Minority Psychology*, 14(2), 85–91. https://doi.org/10.1037/1099-9809.14.2.85

La Torre, A., Conca, A., Duffy, D., Giupponi, G., Pompili, M., & Grözinger, M. (2013). Sexual dysfunction related to psychotropic drugs: A critical review. Part II: Antipsychotics. *Pharmacopsychiatry*, 46(6), 201–208. https://doi.org/10.1055/s-0033-1347177

Laajaj, R., Macours, K., Pinzon Hernandez, D. A., Arias, O., Gosling, S. D., Potter, J., Rubio-Codina, M., & Vakis, R. (2019). Challenges to capture the Big Five personality traits in non-WEIRD populations. *Science Advances*, 5(7), eaaw5226. https://doi.org/10.1126/sciadv.aaw5226

Labelle, A., Bourget, D., Bradford, J. M. W., Alda, M., & Tessier, P. (2012). Familial paraphilia: A pilot study with the construction of genograms. *ISRN Psychiatry*, 2012, 692813–692813. https://doi.org/10.5402/2012/692813

Lacasse, J. R. (2014). After DSM-5: A critical mental health research agenda for the 21st century. *Research on Social Work Practice*, 24(1), 5–10. https://doi.org/10.1177/1049731513510048

Lachenmeier, D. W., & Rehm, J. (2015). Comparative risk assessment of alcohol, tobacco, cannabis and other illicit drugs using the margin of exposure approach. *Scientific Reports*, 5, 8126. https://doi.org/10.1038/srep08126

Lacoursiere, R. B. (2008). Freud's death: Historical truth and biographical fictions. *American Imago*, 65(1), 107–128. https://doi.org/10.1353/aim.0.0003

Laezer, K. L. (2015). Effectiveness of psychoanalytic psychotherapy and behavioral therapy treatment in children with attention deficit hyperactivity disorder and oppositional defiant disorder. *Journal of Infant, Child & Adolescent Psychotherapy*, 14(2), 111–128. https://doi.org/10.1080/15289168.2015.1014991

Lahmann, C., Nickel, M., Schuster, T., Sauer, N., Ronel, J., Noll-Hussong, M., Tritt, K., Nowak, D., Röhricht, F.,

& Loew, T. (2009). Functional relaxation and guided imagery as complementary therapy in asthma: A randomized controlled clinical trial. *Psychotherapy and Psychosomatics*, 78(4), 233–239. https://doi.org/10.1159/000214445

Lahmann, C., Röhricht, F., Sauer, N., Noll-Hussong, M., Ronel, J., Henrich, G., von Arnim, A., & Loew, T. (2010). Functional relaxation as complementary therapy in irritable bowel syndrome: A randomized, controlled clinical trial. *The Journal of Alternative and Complementary Medicine*, 16(1), 47–52. https://doi.org/10.1089/acm.2009.0084

Laidlaw, C., & Howcroft, G. (2015). Encountering a cartwheeling princess: Relational psychoanalytic therapy of a child with attachment difficulties and ADHD. *Journal of Child & Adolescent Mental Health*, 27(3), 227–245. https://doi.org/10.2989/17280583.2015.1067620

Laing, R. D. (1965). *The divided self*. Penguin.

Laing, R. D. (1967). *The politics of experience*. Ballantine Books.

Lainson, K. (2019). Narrative therapy, neuroscience and anorexia: A reflection on practices, problems and possibilities. *The International Journal of Narrative Therapy and Community Work*, 2019(3), 80–95.

Lal, S. (2019). E-mental health: Promising advancements in policy, research, and practice. *Healthcare Management Forum*, 32(2), 56–62. https://doi.org/10.1177/0840470418818583

Lalonde, J. K., Hudson, J. I., Gigante, R. A., & Pope, Jr., Harrison G. (2001). Canadian and American psychiatrists' attitudes toward dissociative disorders diagnoses. *The Canadian Journal of Psychiatry*, 46(5), 407–412. https://doi.org/10.1177/070674370104600504

Lam, C., & Chung, M.-H. (2021). A meta-analysis of the effect of interpersonal and social rhythm therapy on symptom and functioning improvement in patients with bipolar disorders. *Applied Research in Quality of Life*, 16(1), 153–165. https://doi.org/10.1007/s11482-019-09740-1

Lam, R. W., Teng, M. Y., Jung, Y.-E., Evans, V. C., Gottlieb, J. F., Chakrabarty, T., Michalak, E. E., Murphy, J. K., Yatham, L. N., & Sit, D. K. (2020). Light therapy for patients with bipolar depression: Systematic review and meta-analysis of randomized controlled trials. *The Canadian Journal of Psychiatry*, 65(5), 290–300. https://doi.org/10.1177/0706743719892471

Lamb, K. (2017). *Why LGBT hatred suddenly spiked in Indonesia*. https://www.theguardian.com/global-development-professionals-network/2017/feb/22/why-lgbt-hatred-suddenly-spiked-in-indonesia

Lambe, E. K., Katzman, D. K., Mikulis, D. J., Kennedy, S. H., & Zipursky, R. B. (1997). Cerebral gray matter volume deficits after weight recovery from anorexia nervosa. *Archives of General Psychiatry*, 54. https://doi.org/10.1001/archpsyc.1997.01830180055006

Lamberty, G. J. (2007). *Understanding somatization in the practice of clinical neuropsychology*. Oxford University Press.

Lamers, F., Vogelzangs, N., Merikangas, K. R., de Jonge, P., Beekman, A. T. F., & Penninx, B. W. J. H. (2013). Evidence for a differential role of HPA-axis function, inflammation and metabolic syndrome in melancholic versus atypical depression. *Molecular Psychiatry*, 18(6), 692–699.

Lamont, J. A. (2011). *Dyspareunia and vaginismus*. https://doi.org/10.3843/GLOWM.10430

Landes, S. D., Stevens, J. D., & Turk, M. A. (2021). Cause of death in adults with intellectual disability in the United States. *Journal of Intellectual Disability Research*, 65(1), 47–59. https://doi.org/10.1111/jir.12790

Landin-Romero, R., Moreno-Alcazar, A., Pagani, M., & Amann, B. L. (2018). How does eye movement desensitization and reprocessing therapy work? A systematic review on suggested mechanisms of action. *Frontiers in Psychology*, 9, Article 1395. https://doi.org/10.3389/fpsyg.2018.01395

Landy, L. N., Schneider, R. L., & Arch, J. J. (2015). Acceptance and commitment therapy for the treatment of anxiety disorders: A concise review. *Current Opinion in Psychology*, 2, 70–74. https://doi.org/10.1016/j.copsyc.2014.11.004

Lanfredi, M., Ridolfi, M. E., Occhialini, G., Pedrini, L., Ferrari, C., Lasalvia, A., Gunderson, J. G., Black, D. W., & Rossi, R. (2019). Attitudes of mental health staff toward patients with borderline personality disorder: An Italian cross-sectional multisite study. *Journal of Personality Disorders*, 1–16. https://doi.org/10.1521/pedi_2019_33_421

Lang, R., Mulloy, A., Giesbers, S., Pfeiffer, B., Delaune, E., Didden, R., Sigafoos, J., Lancioni, G., & O'Reilly, M. (2011). Behavioral interventions for rumination and operant vomiting in individuals with intellectual disabilities: A systematic review. *Research in Developmental Disabilities*, 32(6), 2193–2205. https://doi.org/10.1016/j.ridd.2011.06.011

Lange, K. W., Nakamura, Y., & Reissmann, A. (2022). Diet and food in attention-deficit hyperactivity disorder. *Journal of Future Foods*, 2(2), 112–118. https://doi.org/10.1016/j.jfutfo.2022.03.008

Lange, K. W., Reichl, S., Lange, K. M., Tucha, L., & Tucha, O. (2010). The history of attention deficit hyperactivity disorder. *ADHD Attention Deficit and Hyperactivity Disorders*, 2(4), 241–255. https://doi.org/10.1007/s12402-010-0045-8

Langer, E. (1989). *Mindfulness*. Addison-Wesley.

Långström, N., Babchishin, K. M., Fazel, S., Lichtenstein, P., & Frisell, T. (2015). Sexual offending runs in families: A 37-year nationwide study. *International Journal of Epidemiology*, 44(2), 713–720. https://doi.org/10.1093/ije/dyv029

Lanius, R. A. (2015). Trauma-related dissociation and altered states of consciousness: A call for clinical, treatment, and neuroscience research. *European Journal of Psychotraumatology*, 6, 10.3402/ejpt.v6.27905. https://doi.org/10.3402/ejpt.v6.27905

Lanovaz, M. J., Argumedes, M., Roy, D., Duquette, J. R., & Watkins, N. (2013). Using ABC narrative recording to identify the function of problem behavior: A pilot study. *Research in Developmental Disabilities*, 34(9), 2734–2742. https://doi.org/10.1016/j.ridd.2013.05.038

Lanphear, B. P. (2015). The impact of toxins on the developing brain. *Annual Review of Public Health*, 36(1), 211–230. https://doi.org/10.1146/annurev-publhealth-031912-114413

Lansky, M. R., & Bley, C. R. (1995). *Posttraumatic nightmares: Psychodynamic explorations*. Analytic Press.

Larkin, H. (2022). What all physicians need to know about the polio resurgence in new york state. *JAMA*, 328(11), 1020–1022. https://doi.org/10.1001/jama.2022.15171

Larkin, M. (2018, May 22). On the Power Threat Meaning Framework. *Imperfect Cognitions*.

Larroya, A., Pantoja, J., Codoñer-Franch, P., & Cenit, M. C. (2021). Towards tailored gut microbiome-based and dietary interventions for promoting the development and maintenance of a healthy brain. *Frontiers in Pediatrics*, 9, Article 705859. https://doi.org/10.3389/fped.2021.705859

Larsen, T. K. (2009). Biological and psychological treatments for psychosis: An overdue alliance? In J. F. M. Gleeson, E. Killackey, & H. Krstev (Eds.), *Psychotherapies for the psychoses: Theoretical, cultural and clinical integration* (pp. 75–88). Routledge.

Larson, D. G. (2013). A person-centred approach to grief counselling. In M. Cooper, M. O'Hara, P. F. Schmid, & A. C. Bohart (Eds.), *The handbook of person-centred psychotherapy and counselling* (2013-20423-021; 2nd ed., pp. 313–326). Palgrave Macmillan/Springer Nature. https://doi.org/10.1007/978-1-137-32900-4_21

Lasalvia, A., Vita, A., Bellomo, A., Tusconi, M., Favaretto, G., Bonetto, C., Zanalda, E., Mencacci, C., & Carpiniello, B. (2021). Renaming schizophrenia? A survey among psychiatrists, mental health service users and family members in Italy. *Schizophrenia Research*, 228, 502–509. https://doi.org/10.1016/j.schres.2020.03.047

Lavie-Ajayi, M. (2005). "Because all real women do": The construction and deconstruction of "female orgasmic disorder." *Sexualities, Evolution & Gender*, 7(1), 57–72. https://doi.org/10.1080/14616660500123664

Lavretsky, H. (2008). History of schizophrenia as a psychiatric disorder. In K. T. Mueser & D. V. Jeste (Eds.), *Clinical handbook of schizophrenia* (pp. 3–13). Guilford Press.

Law, R. (2011). Interpersonal psychotherapy for depression. *Advances in Psychiatric Treatment*, 17(1), 23–31.

Lawlor, C. (2012). *From melancholia to Prozac: A history of depression*. Oxford University Press.

Lawrence, R. E., Oquendo, M. A., & Stanley, B. (2016). Religion and suicide risk: A systematic review. *Archives of Suicide Research*, 20(1), 1–21. https://doi.org/10.1080/13811118.2015.1004494

Laws, D. R. (2017). The rise and fall of relapse prevention: An update. In D. P. Boer, A. R. Beech, T. Ward, L. A. Craig, M. Rettenberger, L. E. Marshall, & W. L. Marshall (Eds.), *The Wiley handbook on the theories, assessment, and treatment of sexual offending: Vol. 3: Treatment* (pp. 1299–1312). Wiley-Blackwell.

Lawson, C., Calicchia, J., & Lawson, J. (2021). Efficacy of treatment for reactive attachment disorder: A follow-up study. *North American Journal of Psychology*, 23(4), 639–652.

Lazaridou, F., & Heinz, A. (2021). Cultivating environments of belonging in psychiatry, clinical psychology and the allied mental health fields. In E. Guerrero (Ed.), *Effective elimination of structural racism*. IntechOpen. https://doi.org/10.5772/intechopen.99925

Le Grange, D. (2005). The Maudsley family-based treatment for adolescent anorexia nervosa. *World Psychiatry*, 4(3), 142–146.

Le Grange, D. (2010). Family-based treatment for adolescents with bulimia nervosa. *Australian and New Zealand Journal of Family Therapy*, 31(2), 165–175. doi:10.1375/anft.31.2.165

Le Grange, D., & Lock, J. (2010). Family-based treatment for adolescents with bulimia nervosa. In C. M. Grilo & J. E. Mitchell (Eds.), *The treatment of eating disorders: A clinical handbook* (pp. 372–387). Guilford Press.

Le Grange, D., Lock, J., Agras, W. S., Bryson, S. W., & Jo, B. (2015). Randomized clinical trial of family-based treatment and cognitive-behavioral therapy for adolescent bulimia nervosa. *Journal of the American Academy of Child & Adolescent Psychiatry*, 54(11), 886–894. https://doi.org/10.1016/j.jaac.2015.08.008

Leahy, R. L., & McGinn, L. K. (2012). Cognitive therapy for personality disorders. In T. A. Widiger (Ed.), *The Oxford handbook of personality disorders* (pp. 727–750). Oxford University Press. https://doi.org/10.1093/oxfordhb/9780199735013.013.0034

Leahy, R. L., & Rego, S. A. (2012). Cognitive restructuring. In W. T. O'Donohue & J. E. Fisher (Eds.), *Cognitive behavior therapy: Core principles for practice* (pp. 133–158). John Wiley.

LeBlanc, A. (2001). The origins of the concept of dissociation: Paul Janet, his nephew Pierre, and the problem of post-hypnotic suggestion. *History of Science*, 39(1), 57–69. https://doi.org/10.1177/007327530103900103

Lebowitz, E., Woolston, J., Bar-Haim, Y., Calvocoressi, L., Dauser, C., Warnick, E., Scahill, L., Chakir, A., Shechner, T., Hermes, H., Vitulano, L., King, R., & Leckman, J. (2013). Family accommodation in pediatric anxiety disorders. *Depression and Anxiety*, 30. https://doi.org/10.1002/da.21998

Lebowitz, E. R., Panza, K. E., & Bloch, M. H. (2016). Family accommodation in obsessive-compulsive and anxiety disorders: A five-year update. *Expert Review of Neurotherapeutics*, 16(1), 45–53. https://doi.org/10.1586/14737175.2016.1126181

Lebowitz, E. R., Panza, K. E., Su, J., & Bloch, M. H. (2012). Family accommodation in obsessive-compulsive disorder. *Expert Review of Neurotherapeutics*, 12(2), 229–238. https://doi.org/10.1586/ern.11.200

Leboyer, M., Oliveira, J., Tamouza, R., & Groc, L. (2016). Is it time for immunopsychiatry in psychotic disorders? *Psychopharmacology*, 233(9), 1651–1660. https://doi.org/10.1007/s00213-016-4266-1

LeDoux, J. (2015). *Anxious: Using the brain to understand and treat fear and anxiety*. Penguin Books.

Lee, C. C., Liem, S. K., Leung, J., Young, V., Wu, K., Kenny, K. K. W., Yuen, S. K., Lee, W. F., Leung, T., Shum, M., Kwong, P., & Lo, W. (2015). From deinstitutionalization to recovery-oriented assertive community treatment in Hong Kong: What we have achieved. *Psychiatry Research*, 228(3), 243–250. https://doi.org/10.1016/j.psychres.2015.05.106

Lee, C.-H., & Giuliani, F. (2019). The role of inflammation in depression and fatigue. *Frontiers in Immunology*, 10, Article 1696. https://doi.org/10.3389/fimmu.2019.01696

Lee, D. J., Schnitzlein, C. W., Wolf, J. P., Vythilingam, M., Rasmusson, A. M., & Hoge, C. W. (2016). Psychotherapy versus pharmacotherapy for posttraumatic stress disorder: Systemic review and meta-analyses to determine first-line treatments. *Depression and Anxiety*, 33(9), 792–806. https://doi.org/10.1002/da.22511

Lee, E. E., Hong, S., Martin, A. S., Eyler, L. T., & Jeste, D. V. (2017). Inflammation in schizophrenia: Cytokine levels and their relationships to demographic and clinical variables. *The American Journal of Geriatric Psychiatry*, 25(1), 50–61. https://doi.org/10.1016/j.jagp.2016.09.009

Lee, H. S., Min, D., Baik, S. Y., Kwon, A., Jin, M. J., & Lee, S.-H. (2022). *Association between dissociative symptoms and morning cortisol levels in patients with post-traumatic stress disorder*. 20(2), 292–299. https://doi.org/10.9758/cpn.2022.20.2.292

Lee, J. K., Andrews, D. S., Ozonoff, S., Solomon, M., Rogers, S., Amaral, D. G., & Nordahl, C. W. (2021). Longitudinal evaluation of cerebral growth across childhood in boys and girls with autism spectrum disorder. *Biological Psychiatry*, 90(5), 286–294. https://doi.org/10.1016/j.biopsych.2020.10.014

Lee, J. Y., & Cho, K. S. (2013). Chemical castration for sexual offenders: Physicians' views. *Journal of Korean Medical Science*, 28(2), 171–172. https://doi.org/10.3346/jkms.2013.28.2.171

Lee, S. T. H. (2020). Inflammation, depression, and anxiety disorder: A population-based study examining the association between Interleukin-6 and the experiencing of depressive and anxiety symptoms. *Psychiatry Research*, 285, 112809. https://doi.org/10.1016/j.psychres.2020.112809

Lee, Y., & Lin, P.-Y. (2010). Association between serotonin transporter gene polymorphism and eating disorders: A meta-analytic study. *International Journal of Eating Disorders*, 43(6), 498–504. doi:10.1002/eat.20732

Leffa, D. T., Torres, I. L. S., & Rohde, L. A. (2018). A review on the role of inflammation in attention-deficit/hyperactivity disorder. *Neuroimmunomodulation*, 25(5–6), 328–333. https://doi.org/10.1159/000489635

Leggett, V., Jacobs, P., Nation, K., Scerif, G., & Bishop, D. V. M. (2010). Neurocognitive outcomes of individuals with a sex chromosome trisomy: XXX, XYY, or XXY: A systematic review*: Systematic Review. *Developmental Medicine & Child Neurology*, 52(2), 119–129. https://doi.org/10.1111/j.1469-8749.2009.03545.x

Lehrer-Small, A. (2021, December 22). "Their whole sky has fallen": 1 in 450 youth have lost a parent or caregiver to COVID. *The 74*. https://www.the74million.org/article/their-whole-sky-has-fallen-1-in-450-youth-have-lost-a-parent-or-caregiver-to-covid/

Lehrner, A., Daskalakis, N., & Yehuda, R. (2016). Cortisol and the hypothalamic–pituitary–adrenal axis in PTSD. In *Posttraumatic Stress Disorder* (pp. 265–290). John Wiley & Sons. https://doi.org/10.1002/9781118356142.ch11

Leichsenring, F., & Salzer, S. (2014). A unified protocol for the transdiagnostic psychodynamic treatment of anxiety disorders: An evidence-based approach. *Psychotherapy*, 51(2), 224–245. https://doi.org/10.1037/a0033815

Leichsenring, F., & Steinert, C. (2018). Towards an evidence-based unified psychodynamic protocol for emotional disorders. *Journal of Affective Disorders*, 232, 400–416. https://doi.org/10.1016/j.jad.2017.11.036

Leichsenring, F., & Steinert, C. (2019). The efficacy of psychodynamic psychotherapy: An up-to-date review. In D. Kealy & J. S. Ogrodniczuk (Eds.), *Contemporary psychodynamic psychotherapy: Evolving clinical practice* (pp. 49–74). Academic Press. https://doi.org/10.1016/B978-0-12-813373-6.00004-0

Leichtman, M. (2004). Projective tests: The nature of the task. In M. J. Hilsenroth & D. L. Segal (Eds.), *Comprehensive handbook of psychological assessment: Vol. 2. Personality assessment* (pp. 297–314). John Wiley.

Leigh, H. (2015). Dissociative disorders. In H. Leigh & J. Strltzer (Eds.), *Handbook of consultation-liaison psychiatry* (2nd ed., pp. 259–264). Springer Science + Business Media. https://doi.org/10.1007/978-3-319-11005-9_18

Lejoyeux, M., & Weinstein, A. (2013). Shopping addiction. In P. M. Miller, S. A. Ball, M. E. Bates, A. W. Blume, K. M. Kampman, D. J. Kavanagh, M. E. Larimer, N. M. Petry, & P. De Witte (Eds.), *Comprehensive addictive behaviors and disorders: Vol. 1. Principles of addiction* (pp. 847–853). Elsevier Academic Press.

Lejuez, C. W., Schaal, D. W., & O'Donnell, J. (1998). Behavioral pharmacology and the treatment of substance abuse. In J. J. Plaud & G. H. Eifert (Eds.), *From behavior theory to behavior therapy* (pp. 116–135). Allyn & Bacon.

Lembke, A., & Humphreys, K. (2012). Moderation management: A mutual-help organization for problem drinkers who are not alcohol-dependent. *Journal of Groups in Addiction & Recovery*, 7(2–4), 130–141. https://doi.org/10.1080/1556035X.2012.705657

Lemma, A., Target, M., & Fonagy, P. (2010). The development of a brief psychodynamic protocol for depression: Dynamic interpersonal therapy (DIT). *Psychoanalytic Psychotherapy*, 24(4), 329–346. https://doi.org/10.1080/02668734.2010.513547

Lemmens, L. H. J. M., Arntz, A., Peeters, F., Hollon, S. D., Roefs, A., & Huibers, M. J. H. (2015). Clinical effectiveness of cognitive therapy v. Interpersonal psychotherapy for depression: Results of a randomized controlled trial. *Psychological Medicine*, 45(10), 2095–2110. https://doi.org/10.1017/S0033291715000033

Lemogne, C., Delaveau, P., Freton, M., Guionnet, S., & Fossati, P. (2012). Medial prefrontal cortex and the self in major depression. *Journal of Affective Disorders*, 136(1–2), e1–e11. https://doi.org/10.1016/j.jad.2010.11.034

Lemogne, C., Mayberg, H., Bergouignan, L., Volle, E., Delaveau, P., Lehéricy, S., Allilaire, J.-F., & Fossati, P. (2010). Self-referential processing and the prefrontal cortex over the course of depression: A pilot study. *Journal of Affective Disorders*, 124(1–2), 196–201. https://doi.org/10.1016/j.jad.2009.11.003

Lener, M. S., & Iosifescu, D. V. (2015). In pursuit of neuroimaging biomarkers to guide treatment selection in major depressive disorder: A review of the literature. *Annals of the New York Academy of Sciences*, 1344, 50–65. https://doi.org/10.1111/nyas.12759

Leo, R. J., & Narendran, R. (1999). Anticonvulsant use in the treatment of bipolar disorder: A primer for primary care physicians. *Primary Care Companion to The Journal of Clinical Psychiatry*, 1(3), 74–84.

Leon, A. C. (2007). The revised warning for antidepressants and suicidality: Unveiling the black box of statistical analyses. *The American Journal of Psychiatry*, 164(12), 1786–1789.

Leon, J., Hommer, R., Grant, P., Farmer, C., D'Souza, P., Kessler, R., Williams, K., Leckman, J. F., & Swedo, S. (2018). Longitudinal outcomes of children with pediatric autoimmune neuropsychiatric disorder associated with streptococcal infections (PANDAS). *European Child & Adolescent Psychiatry*, 27(5), 637–643. https://doi.org/10.1007/s00787-017-1077-9

Leonardi, J. L., Josua, J., & Gomes, C. (2021). Evidence-based psychotherapy for substance use disorder. In D. De Micheli, A. L. M. Andrade, R.

A. Reichert, E. A. da Silva, B. de O. Pinheiro, & F. M. Lopes (Eds.), *Drugs and human behavior: Biopsychosocial aspects of psychotropic substances use* (pp. 193–204). Springer International Publishing. https://doi.org/10.1007/978-3-030-62855-0_13

Leong, K., Tham, J. C. W., Scamvougeras, A., & Vila-Rodriguez, F. (2015). Electroconvulsive therapy treatment in patients with somatic symptom and related disorders. *Neuropsychiatric Disease and Treatment*, 11, 2565–2572. https://doi.org/10.2147/NDT.S90969

Leopold, R., & Backenstrass, M. (2015). Neuropsychological differences between obsessive-compulsive washers and checkers: A systematic review and meta-analysis. *Journal of Anxiety Disorders*, 30, 48–58. https://doi.org/10.1016/j.janxdis.2014.12.016

Lequesne, E. R., & Hersh, R. G. (2004). Disclosure of a diagnosis of borderline personality disorder. *Journal of Psychiatric Practice*, 10(3), 170–176. https://doi.org/10.1097/00131746-200405000-00005

Leri, F., Bruneau, J., & Stewart, J. (2003). Understanding polydrug use: Review of heroin and cocaine co-use. *Addiction*, 98(1), 7–22. https://doi.org/10.1046/j.1360-0443.2003.00236.x

Lerner, P. M. (1998). *Psychoanalytic perspectives on the Rorschach*. The Analytic Press.

Lester, D. (1994). Psychotherapy for suicidal clients. *Death Studies*, 18(4), 361–374. https://doi.org/10.1080/07481189408252363

Lester, R., Prescott, L., McCormack, M., Sampson, M., & North West Boroughs Healthcare, NHS Foundation Trust. (2020). Service users' experiences of receiving a diagnosis of borderline personality disorder: A systematic review. *Personality and Mental Health*, 14(3), 263–283. https://doi.org/10.1002/pmh.1478

Leucht, S., Cipriani, A., & Furukawa, T. A. (2021). Pharmacological approaches to treatment. In C. A. Tamminga, E. I. Ivleva, U. Reininghaus, & J. van Os (Eds.), *Psychotic disorders: Comprehensive conceptualization and treatments* (pp. 487–495). Oxford University Press. https://doi.org/10.1093/med/9780190653279.003.0054

Leucht, S., Leucht, C., Huhn, M., Chaimani, A., Mavridis, D., Helfer, B., Samara, M., Rabaioli, M., Bächer, S., Cipriani, A., Geddes, J. R., Salanti, G., & Davis, J. M. (2017). Sixty years of placebo-controlled antipsychotic drug trials in acute schizophrenia: Systematic review, Bayesian meta-analysis, and meta-regression of efficacy predictors. *American Journal of Psychiatry*, 174(10), 927–942. https://doi.org/10.1176/appi.ajp.2017.16121358

LeVay, S. (1991). A difference in hypothalamic structure between heterosexual and homosexual men. *Science*, 253(5023), 1034–1037. https://doi.org/10.1126/science.1887219

LeVay, S. (2011). *Gay, straight, and the reason why: The science of sexual orientation*. Oxford University Press.

Levenson, H. (2017). *Brief dynamic therapy* (2nd ed.). American Psychological Association.

Levesque, J.-F., Harris, M. F., & Russell, G. (2013). Patient-centred access to health care: Conceptualising access at the interface of health systems and populations. *International Journal for Equity in Health*, 12(1), Article 18. https://doi.org/10.1186/1475-9276-12-18

Levi King, D. (2021, June 23). Ketamine and the return of the party-state. *Palladium*. https://palladiummag.com/2021/06/23/ketamine-and-the-return-of-the-party-state/

Levi, O., Bar-Haim, Y., Kreiss, Y., & Fruchter, E. (2016). Cognitive–behavioural therapy and psychodynamic psychotherapy in the treatment of combat-related post-traumatic stress disorder: A comparative effectiveness study. *Clinical Psychology & Psychotherapy*, 23(4), 298–307. https://doi.org/10.1002/cpp.1969

Levi, O., Shoval-Zuckerman, Y., Fruchter, E., Bibi, A., Bar-Haim, Y., & Wald, I. (2017). Benefits of a psychodynamic group therapy (PGT) model for treating veterans with PTSD. *Journal of Clinical Psychology*, 73(10), 1247–1258. https://doi.org/10.1002/jclp.22443

Levin, R. J. (2008). Critically revisiting aspects of the human sexual response cycle of Masters and Johnson: Correcting errors and suggesting modifications. *Sexual and Relationship Therapy, 23*(4), 393–399. https://doi.org/10.1080/14681990802488816

Levin-Aspenson, H. F., Watson, D., Ellickson-Larew, S., Stanton, K., & Stasik-O'Brien, S. M. (2021). Beyond distress and fear: Differential psychopathology correlates of PTSD symptom clusters. *Journal of Affective Disorders, 284*, 9–17. https://doi.org/10.1016/j.jad.2021.01.090

Levine, B. E. (2005). Mental illness or rebellion? *Ethical Human Psychology and Psychiatry, 7*(2), 125–129. https://doi.org/10.1891/1559-4343.7.2.125

Levine, B. E. (2008, January 28). How teenage rebellion has become a mental illness. *AlterNet.* https://www.alternet.org/2008/01/how_teenage_rebellion_has_become_a_mental_illness/

Levine, B. E. (2012, February 26). Why anti-authoritarians are diagnosed as mentally ill. *Mad in America.* https://www.madinamerica.com/2012/02/why-anti-authoritarians-are-diagnosed-as-mentally-ill/

Levine, H. G. (1978). The discovery of addiction: Changing conceptions of habitual drunkenness in America. *Journal of Studies on Alcohol, 39*(1), 143–174. https://doi.org/10.15288/jsa.1978.39.143

Levinson, C. A., & Brosof, L. C. (2016). Cultural and ethnic differences in eating disorders and disordered eating behaviors. *Current Psychiatry Reviews, 12*(2), 163–174. https://doi.org/10.2174/1573400512666160216234238

Levinson, D. F., & Mowry, B. J. (2000). Genetics of schizophrenia. In D. W. Pfaff, W. H. Berrettini, T. H. Joh, & S. C. Maxson (Eds.), *Genetic influences on neural and behavioral functions* (pp. 47–82). CRC Press.

Levitt, H. M. (2016). Qualitative methods. In J. C. Norcross, G. R. VandenBos, D. K. Freedheim, & B. O. Olatunji (Eds.), *APA handbook of clinical psychology: Volume 2. Clinical psychology: Theory and research* (pp. 335–348). American Psychological Association.

Levitt, H. M. (2021). *Essentials of critical-constructivist grounded theory research.* American Psychological Association.

Levy, F. (1991). The dopamine theory of attention deficit hyperactivity disorder (ADHD). *Australian and New Zealand Journal of Psychiatry, 25*(2), 277–283. https://doi.org/10.3109/00048679109077746

Levy, F. (2009). Dopamine vs noradrenaline: Inverted-U effects and ADHD theories. *Australian and New Zealand Journal of Psychiatry, 43*(2), 101–108. https://doi.org/10.1080/00048670802607238

Levy, F. (2014). DSM-5, ICD-11, RDoC and ADHD diagnosis. *Australian and New Zealand Journal of Psychiatry, 48*(12), 1163–1164. https://doi.org/10.1177/0004867414557527

Levy, F., & Swanson, J. M. (2001). Timing, space and ADHD: The dopamine theory revisited. *Australian and New Zealand Journal of Psychiatry, 35*(4), 504–511. https://doi.org/10.1046/j.1440-1614.2001.00923.x

Levy, K. N., & Blatt, S. J. (1999). Attachment theory and psychoanalysis: Further differentiation within insecure attachment patterns. *Psychoanalytic Inquiry, 19*(4), 541–575. https://doi.org/10.1080/07351699909534266

Lewis, A. J. (2008). Neuropsychological deficit and psychodynamic defence models of schizophrenia: Towards an integrated psychotherapeutic model. In J. F. M. Gleeson, E. Killackey, & H. Krstev (Eds.), *Psychotherapies for the psychoses: Theoretical, cultural and clinical integration* (pp. 52–69). Routledge.

Lewis, B., Hoffman, L., Garcia, C. C., & Nixon, S. J. (2018). Race and socioeconomic status in substance use progression and treatment entry. *Journal of Ethnicity in Substance Abuse, 17*(2), 150–166. https://doi.org/10.1080/15332640.2017.1336959

Lewis, C. M., & Knight, J. (2012). Introduction to genetic association studies. *Cold Spring Harbor Protocols, 2012*(3), pdb.top068163. https://doi.org/10.1101/pdb.top068163

Lewis, D. A. (2011). Antipsychotic medications and brain volume: Do we have cause for concern? *Archives of General Psychiatry, 68*(2), 126–127. https://doi.org/10.1001/archgenpsychiatry.2010.187

Lewis, M. (2015, July 12). *Addiction is not a disease: How AA and 12-step programs erect barriers while attempting to relieve suffering.* Salon. https://www.salon.com/2015/07/11/addiction_is_not_a_disease_how_aa_and_12_step_programs_erect_barriers_while_attempting_to_relieve_suffering/

Lewis, M. W. (2008). Application of contingency management-prize reinforcement to community practice with alcohol and drug problems: A critical examination. *Behavior and Social Issues, 17*(2), 119–138. https://doi.org/10.5210/bsi.v17i2.2038

Lewis, R. (2017). Suicide rate for teen girls hits 40-year high. In *Time.* http://time.com/4887282/teen-suicide-rate-cdc/

Lewis, R. (2019). Right to refuse treatment. In M. Rotter, J. Colley, H. E. Cucolo, M. Rotter, H. Cucolo, & J. Colley (Eds.), *Landmark Cases in Forensic Psychiatry* (pp. 79–84). Oxford University Press. https://doi.org/10.1093/med/9780190914424.003.0010

Lewis, S. W., & Buchanan, R. W. (2002). *Schizophrenia* (2nd ed.). Health Press.

Lewis-Fernández, R., Hinton, D. E., Laria, A. J., Patterson, E. H., Hofmann, S. G., Craske, M. G., Stein, D. J., Asnaani, A., & Liao, B. (2010). Culture and the anxiety disorders: Recommendations for DSM-V. *Depression and Anxiety, 27*(2), 212–229. https://doi.org/10.1002/da.20647

Lewis-Fernández, R., Martínez-Taboas, A., Sar, V., Patel, S., & Boatin, A. (2007). The cross-cultural assessment of dissociation. In J. P. Wilson & C. S. Tang (Eds.), *Cross-cultural assessment of psychological trauma and PTSD* (pp. 279–317). Springer Science + Business Media. https://doi.org/10.1007/978-0-387-70990-1_12

Leza, J. C., García-Bueno, B., Bioque, M., Arango, C., Parellada, M., Do, K., O'Donnell, P., & Bernardo, M. (2015). Inflammation in schizophrenia: A question of balance. *Neuroscience and Biobehavioral Reviews, 55*, 612–626. https://doi.org/10.1016/j.neubiorev.2015.05.014

Li, C.-T., Yang, K.-C., & Lin, W.-C. (2019). Glutamatergic dysfunction and glutamatergic compounds for major psychiatric disorders: Evidence from clinical neuroimaging studies. *Frontiers in Psychiatry, 9*, Article 767. https://doi.org/10.3389/fpsyt.2018.00767

Li, J., Hajek, P., Pesola, F., Wu, Q., Phillips-Waller, A., Przulj, D., Myers Smith, K., Bisal, N., Sasieni, P., Dawkins, L., Ross, L., Goniewicz, M. L., McRobbie, H., & Parrott, S. (2020). Cost-effectiveness of e-cigarettes compared with nicotine replacement therapy in stop smoking services in England (TEC study): A randomized controlled trial. *Addiction, 115*(3), 507–517. https://doi.org/10.1111/add.14829

Li, J.-M., Zhang, Y., Su, W.-J., Liu, L.-L., Gong, H., Peng, W., & Jiang, C.-L. (2018). Cognitive behavioral therapy for treatment-resistant depression: A systematic review and meta-analysis. *Psychiatry Research, 268*, 243–250. https://doi.org/10.1016/j.psychres.2018.07.020

Li, K., Zhou, G., Xiao, Y., Gu, J., Chen, Q., Xie, S., & Wu, J. (2022). Risk of suicidal behaviors and antidepressant exposure among children and adolescents: A meta-analysis of observational studies. *Frontiers in Psychiatry, 13*, Article 880496. https://doi.org/10.3389/fpsyt.2022.880496

Li, L., Wu, M., Liao, Y., Ouyang, L., Du, M., Lei, D., Chen, L., Yao, L., Huang, X., & Gong, Q. (2014). Grey matter reduction associated with posttraumatic stress disorder and traumatic stress. *Neuroscience & Biobehavioral Reviews, 43*, 163–172. https://doi.org/10.1016/j.neubiorev.2014.04.003

Li, M., Liu, S., D'Arcy, C., Gao, T., & Meng, X. (2020). Interactions of childhood maltreatment and genetic variations in adult depression: A systematic review. *Journal of Affective Disorders, 276*, 119–136. https://doi.org/10.1016/j.jad.2020.06.055

Li, M., Yao, X., Sun, L., Zhao, L., Xu, W., Zhao, H., Zhao, F., Zou, X., Cheng, Z., Li, B., Yang, W., & Cui, R. (2020). Effects of electroconvulsive therapy on depression and Its potential mechanism. *Frontiers in Psychology, 11*, Article 80. https://doi.org/10.3389/fpsyg.2020.00080

Li, N.-X., Hu, Y.-R., Chen, W.-N., & Zhang, B. (2022). Dose effect of psilocybin on primary and secondary depression: A preliminary systematic review and meta-analysis. *Journal of Affective Disorders, 296*, 26–34. https://doi.org/10.1016/j.jad.2021.09.041

Li, Q., Xiao, Y., Li, Y., Li, L., Lu, N., Xu, Z., Mou, X., Mao, S., Wang, W., & Yuan, Y. (2016). Altered regional brain function in the treatment-naive patients with somatic symptom disorder: A resting-state fMRI study. *Brain and Behavior, 6*(10). https://doi.org/10.1002/brb3.521

Li, X., Wen, J. G., Shen, T., Yang, X. Q., Peng, S. X., Wang, X. Z., Xie, H., Wu, X. D., & Du, Y. K. (2020). Disposable diaper overuse is associated with primary enuresis in children. *Scientific Reports, 10*(1), Article 14407. https://doi.org/10.1038/s41598-020-70195-8

Li, Z., Wang, L., Guan, H., Han, C., Cui, P., Liu, A., & Li, Y. (2021). Burden of eating disorders in China, 1990-2019: An updated systematic analysis of the Global Burden of Disease Study 2019. *Frontiers in Psychiatry, 12*, Article 632418. https://doi.org/10.3389/fpsyt.2021.632418

Liao, X., Lei, X., & Li, Y. (2019). Stigma among parents of children with autism: A literature review. *Asian Journal of Psychiatry, 45*, 88–94. https://doi.org/10.1016/j.ajp.2019.09.007

Licinio, J., Wong, M.-L., & Gold, P. W. (1996). The hypothalamic-pituitary-adrenal axis in anorexia nervosa. *Psychiatry Research, 62*(1), 75–83. https://doi.org/10.1016/0165-1781(96)02991-5

Liddle, H. A. (2009). Multidimensional family therapy: A science-based treatment system for adolescent drug abuse. In J. H. Bray & M. Stanton (Eds.), *The Wiley-Blackwell handbook of family psychology* (pp. 341–354). Blackwell Publishing. https://doi.org/10.1002/9781444310238.ch23

Liddle, H. A. (2010). Multidimensional family therapy: A science-based treatment system for adolescent drug abuse. *Sucht: Zeitschrift Für Wissenschaft Und Praxis, 56*(1), 43–50. https://doi.org/10.1024/0939-5911/a000011

Liddle, H. A., Dakof, G. A., Rowe, C. L., Henderson, C., Greenbaum, P., Wang, W., & Alberga, L. (2018). Multidimensional family therapy as a community-based alternative to residential treatment for adolescents with substance use and co-occurring mental health disorders. *Journal of Substance Abuse Treatment, 90*, 47–56. https://doi.org/10.1016/j.jsat.2018.04.011

Liddle, H. A., Rowe, C. L., Dakof, G. A., Ungaro, R. A., & Henderson, C. E. (2004). Early intervention for adolescent substance abuse: Pretreatment to posttreatment outcomes of a randomized clinical trial comparing multidimensional family therapy and peer group treatment. *Journal of Psychoactive Drugs, 36*(1), 49–63. https://doi.org/10.1080/02791072.2004.10399723

Lieberman, J. (2015, April 30). *From fever cure to coma therapy: Psychiatric treatments through time.* https://www.sciencefriday.com/articles/from-fever-cure-to-coma-therapy-psychiatric-treatments-through-time/

Liebers, D. T., Pirooznia, M., Ganna, A., & Goes, F. S. (2021). Discriminating bipolar depression from major depressive disorder with polygenic risk scores. *Psychological Medicine, 51*(9), 1451–1458. https://doi.org/10.1017/S003329172000015X

Lieblich, S. M., Castle, D. J., Pantelis, C., Hopwood, M., Young, A. H., & Everall, I. P. (2015). High heterogeneity and low reliability in the diagnosis of major depression will impair the development of new drugs. *British Journal of Psychiatry Open, 1*(2), e5–e7.

Liebman, L. S., Ahle, G. M., Briggs, M. C., & Kellner, C. H. (2015). Electroconvulsive therapy and bipolar disorder. In A. Yildiz, P. Ruiz, & C. B. Nemeroff (Eds.), *The bipolar book: History, neurobiology, and treatment* (pp. 367–375). Oxford University Press.

Lien, L., Lien, N., Heyerdahl, S., Thoresen, M., & Bjertness, E. (2006). Consumption of soft drinks and hyperactivity, mental distress, and conduct problems among adolescents in Oslo, Norway. *American Journal of Public Health*, 96(10), 1815–1820. https://doi.org/10.2105/AJPH.2004.059477

Lilenfeld, L. R., Kaye, W. H., Greeno, C. G., Merikangas, K. R., Plotnicov, K., Pollice, C., Rao, R., Strober, M., Bulik, C. M., & Nagy, L. (1998). A controlled family study of anorexia nervosa and bulimia nervosa: Psychiatric disorders in first-degree relatives and effects of proband comorbidity. *Archives of General Psychiatry*, 55(7), 603–610. https://doi.org/10.1001/archpsyc.55.7.603

Lilienfeld, S. O., & Arkowitz, H. (2011). Does Alcoholics Anonymous work? *Scientific American*. https://www.scientificamerican.com/article/does-alcoholics-anonymous-work/

Lilienfeld, S. O., Kirsch, I., Sarbin, T. R., Lynn, S. J., Chaves, J. F., Ganaway, G. K., & Powell, R. A. (1999). Dissociative identity disorder and the sociocognitive model: Recalling the lessons of the past. *Psychological Bulletin*, 125(5), 507–523. https://doi.org/10.1037/0033-2909.125.5.507

Lilienfeld, S. O., & Marino, L. (1995). Mental disorder as a Roschian concept: A critique of Wakefield's "harmful dysfunction" analysis. *Journal of Abnormal Psychology*, 104(3), 411–420. https://doi.org/10.1037/0021-843X.104.3.411

Lilienfeld, S. O., & Marino, L. (1999). Essentialism revisited: Evolutionary theory and the concept of mental disorder. *Journal of Abnormal Psychology*, 108(3), 400–411. https://doi.org/10.1037/0021-843X.108.3.400

Lilienfeld, S. O., McKay, D., & Hollon, S. D. (2018). Why randomised controlled trials of psychological treatments are still essential. *The Lancet Psychiatry*, 5(7), 536–538. https://doi.org/10.1016/S2215-0366(18)30045-2

Lilienfeld, S. O., & Treadway, M. T. (2016). Clashing diagnostic approaches: DSM-ICD versus RDoC. *Annual Review of Clinical Psychology*, 12, 435–463. https://doi.org/10.1146/annurev-clinpsy-021815-093122

Lilienfeld, S. O., Wood, J. M., & Garb, H. N. (2000). The scientific status of projective techniques. *Psychological Science in the Public Interest*, 1, 27–66.

Lim, J. S., Buckley, N. A., Chitty, K. M., Moles, R. J., & Cairns, R. (2021). Association between means restriction of poison and method-specific suicide rates: A systematic review. *JAMA Health Forum*, 2(10), Article e213042. https://doi.org/10.1001/jamahealthforum.2021.3042

Limandri, B. J. (2019a). Clinical use of dopamine modulators as third-generation antipsychotic agents. *Journal of Psychosocial Nursing and Mental Health Services*, 57(2), 7–11. https://doi.org/10.3928/02793695-20190116-02

Limandri, B. J. (2019b). Psychopharmacology of suicide. *Journal of Psychosocial Nursing & Mental Health Services*, 57(12), 9–14. https://doi.org/10.3928/02793695-20191112-02

Limberger, J., & Andretta, I. (2018). Social skills training for drug users under treatment: A pilot study with follow-up. *Psicologia: Reflexão e Crítica*, 31(1), 29. https://doi.org/10.1186/s41155-018-0109-9

Lin, C.-K., Chang, Y.-T., Lee, F.-S., Chen, S.-T., & Christiani, D. (2021). Association between exposure to ambient particulate matters and risks of autism spectrum disorder in children: A systematic review and exposure-response meta-analysis. *Environmental Research Letters*, 16(6), Article 063003. https://doi.org/10.1088/1748-9326/abfcf7

Lin, L. A., Rosenheck, R., Sugar, C., & Zbrozek, A. (2015). Comparing antipsychotic treatments for schizophrenia: A health state approach. *Psychiatric Quarterly*, 86(1), 107–121. https://doi.org/10.1007/s11126-014-9326-2

Lin, P., Li, L., Wang, Y., Zhao, Z., Liu, G., Chen, W., Tao, H., & Gao, X. (2018). Type D personality, but not

Type A behavior pattern, is associated with coronary plaque vulnerability. *Psychology, Health & Medicine*, 23(2), 216–223. https://doi.org/10.1080/13548506.2017.1344254

Lin, Y., Mojtabai, R., Goes, F. S., & Zandi, P. P. (2020). Trends in prescriptions of lithium and other medications for patients with bipolar disorder in office-based practices in the United States: 1996–2015. *Journal of Affective Disorders*, 276, 883–889. https://doi.org/10.1016/j.jad.2020.07.063

Linardon, J., Gleeson, J., Yap, K., Murphy, K., & Brennan, L. (2019). Meta-analysis of the effects of third-wave behavioural interventions on disordered eating and body image concerns: Implications for eating disorder prevention. *Cognitive Behaviour Therapy*, 48(1), 15–38. https://doi.org/10.1080/16506073.2018.1517389

Lincoln, T., & Brabban, A. (2021). Cognitive-behavioral therapy. In C. A. Tamminga, E. I. Ivleva, U. Reininghaus, & J. van Os (Eds.), *Psychotic disorders: Comprehensive conceptualization and treatments* (pp. 514–523). Oxford University Press. https://doi.org/10.1093/med/9780190653279.003.0057

Lincoln, T. M., & Pedersen, A. (2019). An overview of the evidence for psychological interventions for psychosis: Results from meta-analyses. *Clinical Psychology in Europe*, 1(1), Article 1. https://doi.org/10.32872/cpe.v1i1.31407

Linde, K., Berner, M., Egger, M., & Mulrow, C. (2005). St John's wort for depression. *The British Journal of Psychiatry*, 186(2), 99.

Lindegaard, T., Berg, M., & Andersson, G. (2020). Efficacy of internet-delivered psychodynamic therapy: Systematic review and meta-analysis. *Psychodynamic Psychiatry*, 48(4), 437–454. https://doi.org/10.1521/pdps.2020.48.4.437

Lindeman, M. (2020). Empathizing-systemizing theory. In V. Zeigler-Hill & T. K. Shackelford (Eds.), *Encyclopedia of personality and individual differences* (pp. 1346–1347). Springer International Publishing. https://doi.org/10.1007/978-3-319-28099-8_1129-1

Linden, S. C., & Jones, E. (2014). "Shell shock" revisited: An examination of the case records of the national hospital in London. *Medical History*, 58(4), 519–545. https://doi.org/10.1017/mdh.2014.51

Lindgren, I., Hogstedt, M. F., & Cullberg, J. (2006). Outpatient vs. Comprehensive first-episode psychosis services, a 5-year follow-up of Soteria Nacka. *Nordic Journal of Psychiatry*, 60(5), 405–409. https://doi.org/10.1080/08039480600937686

Lindsay, D. S. (1998). Recovered memories and social justice. *American Psychologist*, 53(4), 486–487. https://doi.org/10.1037/0003-066X.53.4.486

Lindsley, O. R. (1956). Operant conditioning methods applied to research in chronic schizophrenia. *Psychiatric Research Reports*, 5, 118–139.

Lindsley, O. R. (1960). Characteristics of the behavior of chronic psychotics as revealed by free-operant conditioning methods. *Diseases of the Nervous System*, 21(Suppl. 2), 66–78.

Linehan, M. M. (1993). *Cognitive-behavioral treatment of borderline personality disorder*. Guilford Press.

Linehan, M. M. (2015). *DBT skills training manual* (2nd ed.). Guilford Press.

Linehan, M. M., Armstrong, H. E., Suarez, A., Allmon, D., & Heard, H. L. (1991). Cognitive-behavioral treatment of chronically parasuicidal borderline patients. *Archives of General Psychiatry*, 48(12), 1060–1064. https://doi.org/10.1001/archpsyc.1991.01810360024003

Linehan, M. M., Comtois, K. A., Murray, A. M., Brown, M. Z., Gallop, R. J., Heard, H. L., Korslund, K. E., Tutek, D. A., Reynolds, S. K., & Lindenboim, N. (2006). Two-year randomized controlled trial and follow-up of dialectical behavior therapy vs therapy by experts for suicidal behaviors and borderline personality disorder. *Archives of General Psychiatry*, 63(7), 757–766. https://doi.org/10.1001/archpsyc.63.7.757

Ling Young, S., Taylor, M., & Lawrie, S. M. (2015). "First do no harm." A systematic review of the prevalence

and management of antipsychotic adverse effects. *Journal of Psychopharmacology*, 29(4), 353–362. https://doi.org/10.1177/0269881114562090

Lingiardi, V., & McWilliams, N. (2017). *Psychodynamic diagnostic manual* (2nd ed.). The Guilford Press.

Lingiardi, V., McWilliams, N., Bornstein, R. F., Gazzillo, F., & Gordon, R. M. (2015). The *Psychodynamic diagnostic manual* Version 2 (PDM-2): Assessing patients for improved clinical practice and research. *Psychoanalytic Psychology*, 32(1), 94–115. https://doi.org/10.1037/a0038546

Linsambarth, S., Moraga-Amaro, R., Quintana-Donoso, D., Rojas, S., & Stehberg, J. (2017). The amygdala and anxiety. In B. Ferry (Ed.), *The amygdala—Where emotions shape perception, learning and memories* (pp. 139–171). IntechOpen. https://doi.org/10.5772/intechopen.68618

Linschoten, M., Weiner, L., & Avery-Clark, C. (2016). Sensate focus: A critical literature review. *Sexual and Relationship Therapy*, 31(2), 230–247. https://doi.org/10.1080/14681994.2015.1127909

Linton, K. F. (2014). Clinical diagnoses exacerbate stigma and improve self-discovery according to people with autism. *Social Work in Mental Health*, 12(4), 330–342. https://doi.org/10.1080/15332985.2013.861383

Lipowski, Z. J. (1987). Somatization: The experience and communication of psychological distress as somatic symptoms. *Psychotherapy and Psychosomatics*, 47(3–4), 160–167. https://doi.org/10.1159/000288013

Lipsitt, D. R. (2019). Is today's 21st century burnout 19th century's neurasthenia? *Journal of Nervous and Mental Disease*, 207(9), 773–777. https://doi.org/10.1097/NMD.0000000000001014

Lipson, S., & Sonneville, K. (2017). Eating disorder symptoms among undergraduate and graduate students at 12 U.S. colleges and universities. *Eating Behaviors*, 24, 81–88. https://doi.org/10.1016/j.eatbeh.2016.12.003

Lisanby, S. H. (2007). Electroconvulsive therapy for depression. *The New England Journal of Medicine*, 357(19), 1939–1945.

Lisik, M. Z. (2014). Molecular aspects of autism spectrum disorders. *Psychiatria Polska*, 48(4), 689–700.

Littell, J. H., Pigott, T. D., Nilsen, K. H., Green, S. J., & Montgomery, O. L. K. (2021). Multisystemic Therapy® for social, emotional, and behavioural problems in youth age 10 to 17: An updated systematic review and meta-analysis. *Campbell Systematic Reviews*, 17(4), e1158. https://doi.org/10.1002/cl2.1158

Littrell, J. (2010). Perspectives emerging from neuroscience on how people become addicted and what to do about it. *Journal of Social Work Practice in the Addictions*, 10(3), 229–256. https://doi.org/10.1080/1533256X.2010.498741

Littrell, J. (2015). *Neuroscience for psychologists and other mental health professionals*. Springer.

Litz, B. T., Gray, M. J., Bryant, R. A., & Adler, A. B. (2002). Early intervention for trauma: Current status and future directions. *Clinical Psychology: Science and Practice*, 9(2), 112–134. https://doi.org/10.1093/clipsy/9.2.112

Liu, A., Zhang, E., Leroux, E. J., & Benassi, P. (2022). Sexual sadism disorder and coercive paraphilic disorder: A scoping review. *The Journal of Sexual Medicine*, 19(3), 496–506. https://doi.org/10.1016/j.jsxm.2022.01.002

Liu, J., Gill, N. S., Teodorczuk, A., Li, Z., & Sun, J. (2019). The efficacy of cognitive behavioural therapy in somatoform disorders and medically unexplained physical symptoms: A meta-analysis of randomized controlled trials. *Journal of Affective Disorders*, 245, 98–112. https://doi.org/10.1016/j.jad.2018.10.114

Liu, L., Wang, L., Cao, C., Cao, X., Zhu, Y., Liu, P., Luo, S., & Zhang, J. (2018). Serotonin transporter 5-HTTLPR genotype is associated with intrusion and avoidance symptoms of DSM-5 posttraumatic stress disorder (PTSD) in Chinese earthquake survivors. *Anxiety, Stress, and Coping*, 31(3), 318–327. https://doi.org/10.1080/10615806.2017.1420174

Liu, P.-P., Xie, Y., Meng, X.-Y., & Kang, J.-S. (2019). History and progress of hypotheses and clinical trials for Alzheimer's disease. *Signal Transduction and Targeted Therapy*, 4(1), Article 1. https://doi.org/10.1038/s41392-019-0063-8

Liu, Q., He, H., Yang, J., Feng, X., Zhao, F., & Lyu, J. (2020). Changes in the global burden of depression from 1990 to 2017: Findings from the Global Burden of Disease study. *Journal of Psychiatric Research*, 126, 134–140. https://doi.org/10.1016/j.jpsychires.2019.08.002

Liu, R. T., Kleiman, E. M., Nestor, B. A., & Cheek, S. M. (2015). The hopelessness theory of depression: A quarter-century in review. *Clinical Psychology: Science and Practice*, 22(4), 345–365. https://doi.org/10.1111/cpsp.12125

Liu, R. T., Sheehan, A. E., Walsh, R. F. L., Sanzari, C. M., Cheek, S. M., & Hernandez, E. M. (2019). Prevalence and correlates of non-suicidal self-injury among lesbian, gay, bisexual, and transgender individuals: A systematic review and meta-analysis. *Clinical Psychology Review*, 74, 101783. https://doi.org/10.1016/j.cpr.2019.101783

Liu, T., Feenstra, K. A., Heringa, J., & Huang, Z. (2020). Influence of gut microbiota on mental health via neurotransmitters: A review. *Journal of Artificial Intelligence for Medical Sciences*, 1(1–2), 1. https://doi.org/10.2991/jaims.d.200420.001

Liu, Y., Zhao, J., Fan, X., & Guo, W. (2019). Dysfunction in serotonergic and noradrenergic systems and somatic symptoms in psychiatric disorders. *Frontiers in Psychiatry*, 10, Article 286. https://doi.org/10.3389/fpsyt.2019.00286

Livesley, W. J. (2021). Why is an evidence-based classification of personality disorder so elusive? *Personality and Mental Health*, 15(1), 8–25. https://doi.org/10.1002/pmh.1471

Livingston, G., Huntley, J., Sommerlad, A., Ames, D., Ballard, C., Banerjee, S., Brayne, C., Burns, A., Cohen-Mansfield, J., Cooper, C., Costafreda, S. G., Dias, A., Fox, N., Gitlin, L. N., Howard, R., Kales, H. C., Kivimäki, M., Larson, E. B., Ogunniyi, A., … Mukadam, N. (2020). Dementia prevention, intervention, and care: 2020 report of the *Lancet* Commission. *The Lancet*, 396(10248), 413–446. https://doi.org/10.1016/S0140-6736(20)30367-6

Livingston, M. D., Barnett, T. E., Delcher, C., & Wagenaar, A. C. (2017). Recreational cannabis legalization and opioid-related deaths in Colorado, 2000–2015. *American Journal of Public Health*, 107(11), 1827–1829. https://doi.org/10.2105/AJPH.2017.304059

Lloyd, S., Schmidt, U., Khondoker, M., & Tchanturia, K. (2015). Can psychological interventions reduce perfectionism? A systematic review and meta-analysis. *Behavioural and Cognitive Psychotherapy*, 43(6), 705–731. https://doi.org/10.1017/S1352465814000162

Lo Sauro, C., Ravaldi, C., Cabras, P. L., Faravelli, C., & Ricca, V. (2008). Stress, hypothalamic-pituitary-adrenal axis and eating disorders. *Neuropsychobiology*, 57(3), 95–115. https://doi.org/10.1159/000138912

Lobbestael, J., & Arntz, A. (2012). Cognitive contributions to personality disorders. In T. A. Widiger (Ed.), *The Oxford handbook of personality disorders* (pp. 325–344). Oxford University Press. https://doi.org/10.1093/oxfordhb/9780199735013.013.0016

Lobel, D. S. (2013). History of psychosis. In T. G. Plante (Ed.), *Abnormal psychology across the ages: Vol. 2. Disorders and treatments* (pp. 15–29). Praeger/ABC-CLIO.

Lochner, C., Roos, A., & Stein, D. J. (2017). Excoriation (skin-picking) disorder: A systematic review of treatment options. *Neuropsychiatric Disease and Treatment*, 13, 1867–1872. https://doi.org/10.2147/NDT.S121138

Lochner, C., Seedat, S., Hemmings, S. M. J., Moolman-Smook, J. C., Kidd, M., & Stein, D. J. (2007). Investigating the possible effects of trauma experiences and 5-HTT on the dissociative experiences of patients with OCD using path analysis and multiple

regression. In *Neuropsychobiology* (Vol. 56, Issue 1, pp. 6–13). https://doi.org/10.1159/000109971

Lock, A., Epston, D., & Maisel, R. (2002, October 2). Countering that which is called anorexia. *Narrative Inquiry*. http://www.narrativeapproaches.com/resources/anorexia-bulimia-archives-of-resistance/836-2/

Lock, A., Epston, D., Maisel, R., & de Faria, N. (2005). Resisting anorexia/bulimia: Foucauldian perspectives in narrative therapy. *British Journal of Guidance & Counselling*, 33(3), 315–332. https://doi.org/10.1080/03069880500179459

Lock, J. (2011). Evaluation of family treatment models for eating disorders. *Current Opinion in Psychiatry*, 24(4), 274–279. https://doi.org/10.1097/YCO.0b013e-328346f71e

Lock, J., & Kirz, N. (2008). Eating disorders: Anorexia nervosa. In W. E. Craighead, D. J. Miklowitz, & L. W. Craighead (Eds.), *Psychopathology: History, diagnosis, and empirical foundations* (pp. 467–494). John Wiley & Sons.

Lock, J., & Nicholls, D. (2020). Toward a greater understanding of the ways family-based treatment addresses the full range of psychopathology of adolescent anorexia nervosa. *Frontiers in Psychiatry*, 10, Article 968. https://doi.org/10.3389/fpsyt.2019.00968

Locklear, M. (2022, January 4). *Another vaccine crisis: Rise in missed doses may portend return of measles*. YaleNews. https://news.yale.edu/2022/01/04/another-vaccine-crisis-rise-missed-doses-may-portend-return-measles

Loeber, R., Burke, J. D., Lahey, B. B., Winters, A., & Zera, M. (2000). Oppositional defiant and conduct disorder: A review of the past 10 years, Part I. *Journal of the American Academy of Child & Adolescent Psychiatry*, 39(12), 1468–1484. https://doi.org/10.1097/00004583-200012000-00007

Loew, T. H., Sohn, R., Martus, P., Tritt, K., & Rechlin, T. (2000). Functional relaxation as a somatopsychotherapeutic intervention: A prospective controlled study. *Alternative Therapies in Health and Medicine*, 6(6), 70–75.

Loewenstein, R. J. (2005). Psychopharmacologic treatments for dissociative identity disorder. *Psychiatric Annals*, 35(8), 666–673. https://doi.org/10.3928/00485713-20050801-08

Loewenstein, R. J. (2018). Dissociation debates: Everything you know is wrong. *Dialogues in Clinical Neuroscience*, 20(3), 229–242.

Loewenstein, R. J., & Ross, D. R. (1992). Multiple personality and psychoanalysis: An introduction. *Psychoanalytic Inquiry*, 12(1), 3–48. https://doi.org/10.1080/07351699209533881

Loftus, E. F. (1979). The malleability of human memory: Information introduced after we view an incident can transform memory. *American Scientist*, 67(3), 312–320.

Loftus, E. F. (2005). Planting misinformation in the human mind: A 30-year investigation of the malleability of memory. *Learning & Memory*, 12(4), 361–366. https://doi.org/10.1101/lm.94705

Loftus, E. F. (2011). Crimes of memory: False memories and societal justice. In M. A. Gernsbacher, R. W. Pew, L. M. Hough, & J. R. Pomerantz (Eds.), *Psychology and the real world: Essays illustrating fundamental contributions to society* (pp. 83–88). Worth Publishers.

Loftus, E. F., & Ketcham, K. (1994). *The myth of repressed memory: False memories and allegations of sexual abuse*. St. Martin's Press.

Lohr, J. M., Lilienfeld, S. O., Tolin, D. F., & Herbert, J. D. (1999). Eye movement desensitization and reprocessing: An analysis of specific versus nonspecific treatment factors. *Journal of Anxiety Disorders*, 13(1–2), 185–207. https://doi.org/10.1016/S0887-6185(98)00047-4

Lohr, J. M., Tolin, D. F., & Lilienfeld, S. O. (1998). Efficacy of eye movement desensitization and reprocessing: Implications for behavior therapy. *Behavior Therapy*,

29(1), 123–156. https://doi.org/10.1016/S0005-7894(98)80035-X

Lombardo, T. W., & Turner, S. M. (1979). Thought-stopping in the control of obsessive ruminations. *Behavior Modification*, 3(2), 267–272. https://doi.org/10.1177/014544557932008

Longden, E. (2017). Listening to the voices people hear: Auditory hallucinations beyond a diagnostic framework. *Journal of Humanistic Psychology*, 57(6), 573–601. https://doi.org/10.1177/0022167817696838

Longden, E., Read, J., & Dillon, J. (2018). Assessing the impact and effectiveness of Hearing Voices Network self-help groups. *Community Mental Health Journal*, 54(2), 184–188. https://doi.org/10.1007/s10597-017-0148-1

Looper, K. J., & Kirmayer, L. J. (2004). Perceived stigma in functional somatic syndromes and comparable medical conditions. *Journal of Psychosomatic Research*, 57(4), 373–378. https://doi.org/10.1016/j.jpsychores.2004.03.005

López, S. R., & Guarnaccia, P. J. (2020). Cultural dimensions of psychopathology: The social world's impact on mental disorders. In J. E. Maddux & B. A. Winstead (Eds.), *Psychopathology: Foundations for a contemporary understanding* (5th ed., pp. 67–84). Routledge.

López-Guimerà, G., Levine, M. P., Sánchez-Carracedo, D., & Fauquet, J. (2010). Influence of mass media on body image and eating disordered attitudes and behaviors in females: A review of effects and processes. *Media Psychology*, 13(4), 387–416. https://doi.org/10.1080/15213269.2010.525737

López-Jaramillo, C., Vargas, C., Díaz-Zuluaga, A. M., Palacio, J. D., Castrillón, G., Bearden, C., & Vieta, E. (2017). Increased hippocampal, thalamus and amygdala volume in long-term lithium-treated bipolar I disorder patients compared with unmedicated patients and healthy subjects. *Bipolar Disorders*, 19(1), 41–49. https://doi.org/10.1111/bdi.12467

López-López, J. A., Davies, S. R., Caldwell, D. M., Churchill, R., Peters, T. J., Tallon, D., Dawson, S., Wu, Q., Li, J., Taylor, A., Lewis, G., Kessler, D. S., Wiles, N., & Welton, N. J. (2019). The process and delivery of CBT for depression in adults: A systematic review and network meta-analysis. *Psychological Medicine*, 49(12), 1937–1947. https://doi.org/10.1017/S003329171900120X

López-Muñoz, F., & Alamo, C. (2009). Monoaminergic neurotransmission: The history of the discovery of antidepressants from 1950s until today. *Current Pharmaceutical Design*, 15(14), 1563–1586. https://doi.org/10.2174/138161209788168001

López-Muñoz, F., Álamo, C., & García-García, P. (2011). The discovery of chlordiazepoxide and the clinical introduction of benzodiazepines: Half a century of anxiolytic drugs. *Journal of Anxiety Disorders*, 25(4), 554–562. https://doi.org/10.1016/j.janxdis.2011.01.002

López-Pinar, C., Martínez-Sanchís, S., Carbonell-Vayá, E., Fenollar-Cortés, J., & Sánchez-Meca, J. (2018). Long-term efficacy of psychosocial treatments for adults with attention-deficit/hyperactivity disorder: A meta-analytic review. *Frontiers in Psychology*, 9, Article 638. https://doi.org/10.3389/fpsyg.2018.00638

López-Solà, C., Bui, M., Hopper, J. L., Fontenelle, L. F., Davey, C. G., Pantelis, C., Alonso, P., van den Heuvel, O. A., & Harrison, B. J. (2018). Predictors and consequences of health anxiety symptoms: A novel twin modeling study. *Acta Psychiatrica Scandinavica*, 137(3), 241–251. https://doi.org/10.1111/acps.12850

Lorant, V., Kapadia, D., Perelman, J., & Group, the D. study. (2021). Socioeconomic disparities in suicide: Causation or confounding? *PLOS ONE*, 16(1), e0243895. https://doi.org/10.1371/journal.pone.0243895

Lorenz, K., & Ullman, S. E. (2016). Alcohol and sexual assault victimization: Research findings and future directions. *Aggression and Violent Behavior*. https://doi.org/10.1016/j.avb.2016.08.001

Lorenzetti, V., Allen, N. B., Fornito, A., & Yücel, M. (2009). Structural brain abnormalities in major depressive disorder: A selective review of recent MRI studies. *Journal of Affective Disorders*, 117(1–2), 1–17. https://doi.org/10.1016/j.jad.2008.11.021

Loring, M., & Powell, B. (1988). Gender, race, and DSM-III: A study of the objectivity of psychiatric diagnostic behavior. *Journal of Health and Social Behavior*, 29(1), 1–22. https://doi.org/10.2307/2137177

Louch, P., Goodman, C., & Greenhalgh, T. (2005). Involving service users in the evaluation and redesign of primary care services for depression: A qualitative study. *Primary Care & Community Psychiatry*, 10(3), 109–117. https://doi.org/10.1185/135525706X56682

Lovas, D. A., & Schuman-Olivier, Z. (2018). Mindfulness-based cognitive therapy for bipolar disorder: A systematic review. *Journal of Affective Disorders*, 240, 247–261. https://doi.org/10.1016/j.jad.2018.06.017

Löwe, B., Levenson, J., Depping, M., Hüsing, P., Kohlmann, S., Lehmann, M., Shedden-Mora, M., Toussaint, A., Uhlenbusch, N., & Weigel, A. (2022). Somatic symptom disorder: A scoping review on the empirical evidence of a new diagnosis. *Psychological Medicine*, 52(4), 632–648. https://doi.org/10.1017/S0033291721004177

Lowe, G. (1983). Alcohol and state-dependent learning. *Substance & Alcohol Actions/Misuse*, 4(4), 273–282.

Lowen, A. (1971). *The language of the body*. Collier.

Lu, S. (2015). Erasing bad memories. In *Monitor on Psychology*. http://www.apa.org/monitor/2015/02/bad-memories.aspx

Lucerne, K. E., Osman, A., Meckel, K. R., & Kiraly, D. D. (2021). Contributions of neuroimmune and gut-brain signaling to vulnerability of developing substance use disorders. *Neuropharmacology*, 192, 108598. https://doi.org/10.1016/j.neuropharm.2021.108598

Luiselli, J. K. (2016). Intellectual disability. In C. M. Nezu & A. M. Nezu (Eds.), *The Oxford handbook of cognitive and behavioral therapies* (pp. 401–418). Oxford University Press.

Lukoff, D. (2019). Spirituality and extreme states. *Journal of Humanistic Psychology*, 59(5), 754–761. https://doi.org/10.1177/0022167818767511

Lundorff, M., Holmgren, H., Zachariae, R., Farver-Vestergaard, I., & O'Connor, M. (2017). Prevalence of prolonged grief disorder in adult bereavement: A systematic review and meta-analysis. *Journal of Affective Disorders*, 212, 138–149. https://doi.org/10.1016/j.jad.2017.01.030

Lunt, C., Dowrick, C., & Lloyd-Williams, M. (2021). What is the impact of day care on older people with long-term conditions: A systematic review. *Health & Social Care in the Community*, 29(5), 1201–1221. https://doi.org/10.1111/hsc.13245

Luo, Y., Kataoka, Y., Ostinelli, E. G., Cipriani, A., & Furukawa, T. A. (2020). National prescription patterns of antidepressants in the treatment of adults with major depression in the US between 1996 and 2015: A population representative survey based analysis. *Frontiers in Psychiatry*, 11, Article 35. https://doi.org/10.3389/fpsyt.2020.00035

Luo, Y., Zhang, L., He, P., Pang, L., Guo, C., & Zheng, X. (2019). Individual-level and area-level socioeconomic status (SES) and schizophrenia: Cross-sectional analyses using the evidence from 1.9 million Chinese adults. *BMJ Open*, 9(9), e026532. https://doi.org/10.1136/bmjopen-2018-026532

Luoni, C., Agosti, M., Crugnola, S., Rossi, G., & Termine, C. (2018). Psychopathology, dissociation and somatic symptoms in adolescents who were exposed to traumatic experiences. *Frontiers in Psychology*, 9, Article 2390. https://www.doi.org/10.3389/fpsyg.2018.02390

Luria-Nebraska Neuropsychological Battery. (n.d.). In *Encyclopedia of mental disorders*. http://www.minddisorders.com/Kau-Nu/Luria-Nebraska-Neuropsychological-Battery.html

Luszczynska, A., Scholz, U., & Schwarzer, R. (2005). The general self-efficacy scale: Multicultural validation studies. *The Journal of Psychology: Interdisciplinary and Applied*, 139(5), 439–457. https://doi.org/10.3200/JRLP.139.5.439-457

Luyten, P., De Meulemeester, C., & Fonagy, P. (2019). Psychodynamic therapy in patients with somatic symptom disorder. In D. Kealy & J. S. Ogrodniczuk (Eds.), *Contemporary psychodynamic psychotherapy: Evolving clinical practice* (pp. 191–206). Elsevier Academic Press. https://doi.org/10.1016/B978-0-12-813373-6.00013-1

Luyten, P., & Fonagy, P. (2020). Psychodynamic psychotherapy for patients with functional somatic disorders and the road to recovery. *American Journal of Psychotherapy*, 73(4), 125–130. https://doi.org/10.1176/appi.psychotherapy.20200010

Luz Neto, L. M., Vasconcelos, F. M. N. de, Silva, J. E. da, Pinto, T. C. C., Sougey, É. B., & Ximenes, R. C. C. (2019). Differences in cortisol concentrations in adolescents with eating disorders: A systematic review. *Jornal de Pediatria*, 95, 18–26. https://doi.org/10.1016/j.jped.2018.02.007

Luzier, J., Rached, K., & Talley, J. (2019). Relapse prevention and selective serotonin reuptake inhibitor medication in two adolescents with anorexia nervosa. *International Journal of Eating Disorders*, 52(7), 863–867. https://doi.org/10.1002/eat.23092

Lv, Z.-T., Song, W., Wu, J., Yang, J., Wang, T., Wu, C.-H., Gao, F., Yuan, X.-C., Liu, J.-H., & Li, M. (2015). Efficacy of acupuncture in children with nocturnal enuresis: A systematic review and meta-analysis of randomized controlled trials. *Evidence-Based Complementary and Alternative Medicine*, 2015, 320701–320701. https://doi.org/10.1155/2015/320701

Lyke, J., & Matsen, J. (2013). Family functioning and risk factors for disordered eating. *Eating Behaviors*, 14(4), 497–499. https://doi.org/10.1016/j.eatbeh.2013.08.009

Lykken, D. T. (2018). Psychopathy, sociopathy, and antisocial personality disorder. In C. J. Patrick (Ed.), *Handbook of psychopathy* (2nd ed., pp. 22–38). The Guilford Press.

Lynch, D., Laws, K. R., & McKenna, P. J. (2010). Cognitive behavioural therapy for major psychiatric disorder: Does it really work? A meta-analytical review of well-controlled trials. *Psychological Medicine*, 40(1), 9–24. https://doi.org/10.1017/S003329170900590X

Lynn, S. J., Knox, J. A., Fassler, O., Lilienfeld, S. O., & Loftus, E. F. (2004). Memory, trauma, and dissociation. In G. M. Rosen (Ed.), *Posttraumatic stress disorder: Issues and controversies* (pp. 163–186). John Wiley & Sons. https://doi.org/10.1002/9780470713570.ch9

Lynn, S. J., Lilienfeld, S. O., Merckelbach, H., Giesbrecht, T., & van der Kloet, D. (2012). Dissociation and dissociative disorders: Challenging conventional wisdom. *Current Directions in Psychological Science*, 21(1), 48–53. https://doi.org/10.1177/0963721411429457

Lynn, S. J., Lilienfeld, S. O., Merckelbach, H., Maxwell, R., Aksen, D., Baltman, J., & Giesbrecht, T. (2020). Dissociative disorders. In J. E. Maddux & B. A. Winstead (Eds.), *Psychopathology: Foundations for a contemporary understanding* (5th ed., pp. 298–317). Routledge.

Lynn, S. J., Maxwell, R., Merckelbach, H., Lilienfeld, S. O., Kloet, D. van der, & Miskovic, V. (2019). Dissociation and its disorders: Competing models, future directions, and a way forward. *Clinical Psychology Review*, 73, 101755. https://doi.org/10.1016/j.cpr.2019.101755

Lyons, V., & Fitzgerald, M. (2007). Asperger (1906-1980) and Kanner (1894-1981), the two pioneers of autism. *Journal of Autism & Developmental Disorders*, 37, 2022–2023. https://doi.org/10.1007/s10803-007-0383-3

Lysaker, P. H., Buck, K. D., Fogley, R. L., Ringer, J., Harder, S., Hasson-Ohayon, I., Olesek, K., Grant, M. L. A., & Dimaggio, G. (2013). The mutual development of intersubjectivity and metacognitive capacity in the psychotherapy for persons with schizophrenia. *Journal of Contemporary Psychotherapy*, 43(2), 63–72. https://doi.org/10.1007/s10879-012-9218-4

Lysaker, P. H., Clements, C. A., Plascak-Hallberg, C. D., Knipscheer, S. J., & Wright, D. E. (2002). Insight and personal narratives of illness in schizophrenia. *Psychiatry: Interpersonal and Biological Processes*, 65(3), 197–206. https://doi.org/10.1521/psyc.65.3.197.20174

Lysaker, P. H., Glynn, S. M., Wilkniss, S. M., & Silverstein, S. M. (2010). Psychotherapy and recovery from schizophrenia: A review of potential applications and need for future study. *Psychological Services*, 7(2), 75–91. https://doi.org/10.1037/a0019115

Lysaker, P. H., Kukla, M., Leonhardt, B. L., Hamm, J. A., Schnakenberg Martin, A., Zalzala, A. B., Gagen, E. C., & Hasson-Ohayon, I. (2020). Meaning, integration, and the self in serious mental illness: Implications of research in metacognition for psychiatric rehabilitation. *Psychiatric Rehabilitation Journal*, 43(4), 275–283. https://doi.org/10.1037/prj0000436

Lysaker, P. H., & Lysaker, J. T. (2006). A typology of narrative impoverishment in schizophrenia: Implications for understanding the processes of establishing and sustaining dialogue in individual psychotherapy. *Counselling Psychology Quarterly*, 19(1), 57–68. https://doi.org/10.1080/09515070600673703

Lysaker, P. H., Lysaker, J. T., & Lysaker, J. T. (2001). Schizophrenia and the collapse of the dialogical self: Recovery, narrative and psychotherapy. *Psychotherapy: Theory, Research, Practice, Training*, 38(3), 252–261. https://doi.org/10.1037/0033-3204.38.3.252

Lysaker, P. H., Wickett, A. M., Campbell, K., & Buck, K. D. (2003). Movement towards coherence in the psychotherapy of schizophrenia: A method for assessing narrative transformation. *Journal of Nervous and Mental Disease*, 191(8), 538–541. https://doi.org/10.1097/01.nmd.0000082182.77891.89

Lysaker, P. H., Zalzala, A. B., Ladegaard, N., Buck, B., Leonhardt, B. L., & Hamm, J. A. (2019). A disorder by any other name: Metacognition, schizophrenia, and diagnostic practice. *Journal of Humanistic Psychology*, 59(1), 26–47. https://doi.org/10.1177/0022167818787881

Lyssenko, L., Schmahl, C., Bockhacker, L., Vonderlin, R., Bohus, M., & Kleindienst, N. (2018). Dissociation in psychiatric disorders: A meta-analysis of studies using the dissociative experiences scale. *American Journal of Psychiatry*, 175(1), 37–46. https://doi.org/10.1176/appi.ajp.2017.17010025

Maass, U., Kühne, F., Maas, J., Unverdross, M., & Weck, F. (2020). Psychological interventions for health anxiety and somatic symptoms: A systematic review and meta-analysis. *Zeitschrift Für Psychologie*, 228(2), 68–80. https://doi.org/10.1027/2151-2604/a000400

Mabe, A. G., Forney, K. J., & Keel, P. K. (2014). Do you "like" my photo? Facebook use maintains eating disorder risk. *International Journal of Eating Disorders*, 47(5), 516–523. https://doi.org/10.1002/eat.22254

Macalli, M., Navarro, M., Orri, M., Tournier, M., Thiébaut, R., Côté, S. M., & Tzourio, C. (2021). A machine learning approach for predicting suicidal thoughts and behaviours among college students. *Scientific Reports*, 11(1), Article 1. https://doi.org/10.1038/s41598-021-90728-z

MacDonald, A. W., III, Goodman, S. H., & Watson, D. (2021). The Journal of Psychopathology and Clinical Science is the future of the Journal of Abnormal Psychology: An editorial. *Journal of Abnormal Psychology*, 130(1), 1. https://doi.org/10.1037/abn0000665

MacGill, M. (2018, December 14). What is a randomized controlled trial in medical research? *Medical News Today*. https://www.medicalnewstoday.com/articles/280574

Machado, D. B., Rasella, D., & Dos Santos, D. N. (2015). Impact of income inequality and other social determinants on suicide rate in Brazil. *PLOS ONE*, 10(4), e0124934. https://doi.org/10.1371/journal.pone.0124934

MacIntosh, H. B., Godbout, N., & Dubash, N. (2015). Borderline personality disorder: Disorder of trauma or personality, a review of the empirical literature.

Canadian Psychology/Psychologie Canadienne, 56(2), 227–241. https://doi.org/10.1037/cap0000028

Mackay, R. D. (2007). AAPL practice guideline for the forensic psychiatric evaluation of competence to stand trial. An English legal perspective. *Journal of the American Academy of Psychiatry and the Law, 35*(4), 501–504.

MacKenzie, M. B., Abbott, K. A., & Kocovski, N. L. (2018). Mindfulness-based cognitive therapy in patients with depression: Current perspectives. *Neuropsychiatric Disease and Treatment, 14*, 1599–1605. https://doi.org/10.2147/NDT.S160761

MacKenzie, P. M. (2014). *Psychopathy, antisocial personality & sociopathy: The basics a history review.* https://www.all-about-forensic-psychology.com/support-files/psychopathy-antisocial-personality-and-sociopathy.pdf

MacLean, P. D. (1985). Evolutionary psychiatry and the triune brain. *Psychological Medicine, 15*(2), 219–221. https://doi.org/10.1017/S0033291700023485

MacLeod, A. K. (2013). Suicide and attempted suicide. In M. Power (Ed.), *The Wiley-Blackwell handbook of mood disorders* (2nd ed., pp. 413–431). Wiley-Blackwell.

MacLeod, R., Elliott, R., & Rodgers, B. (2012). Process-experiential/emotion-focused therapy for social anxiety: A hermeneutic single-case efficacy design study. *Psychotherapy Research, 22*(1), 67–81. https://doi.org/10.1080/10503307.2011.626805

MacMillan, K. M., Keddy, A., & Furlong, J. (2019). Cannabis and glaucoma: A literature review. *DALHOUSIE MEDICAL JOURNAL, 46*(1). https://doi.org/10.15273/dmj.Vol46No1.9830

Macul Ferreira de Barros, P., Polga, N., Szejko, N., Miguel, E. C., Leckman, J. F., Silverman, W. K., & Lebowitz, E. R. (2020). Family accommodation mediates the impact of childhood anxiety on functional impairment. *Journal of Anxiety Disorders, 76*, 102318. https://doi.org/10.1016/j.janxdis.2020.102318

Maddux, J. E., Gosselin, J. T., & Winstead, B. A. (2020). Conceptions of psychopathology: A social constructionist perspective. In J. E. Maddux & B. A. Winstead (Eds.), *Psychopathology: Foundations for a contemporary understanding* (5th ed., pp. 3–18). Routledge.

Madigan, S. (2019). *Narrative therapy* (2nd ed.). American Psychological Association. https://doi.org/10.1037/0000131-000

Madigan, S., Moran, G., Schuengel, C., Pederson, D. R., & Otten, R. (2007). Unresolved maternal attachment representations, disrupted maternal behavior and disorganized attachment in infancy: Links to toddler behavior problems. *Journal of Child Psychology and Psychiatry, 48*(10), 1042–1050. https://doi.org/10.1111/j.1469-7610.2007.01805.x

Madison, A. A., Shrout, M. R., Renna, M. E., & Kiecolt-Glaser, J. K. (2021). Psychological and behavioral predictors of vaccine efficacy: Considerations for COVID-19. *Perspectives on Psychological Science, 16*(2), 191–203. https://doi.org/10.1177/1745691621989243

Madonna, D., Delvecchio, G., Soares, J. C., & Brambilla, P. (2019). Structural and functional neuroimaging studies in generalized anxiety disorder: A systematic review. *Brazilian Journal of Psychiatry, 41*, 336–362. https://doi.org/10.1590/1516-4446-2018-0108

Maeng, L. Y., & Milad, M. R. (2015). Sex differences in anxiety disorders: Interactions between fear, stress, and gonadal hormones. *Hormones and Behavior, 76*, 106–117. https://doi.org/10.1016/j.yhbeh.2015.04.002

Maenner, M. J., Baker, M. W., Broman, K. W., Tian, J., Barnes, J. K., Atkins, A., McPherson, A., Hong, J., Brilliant, M. H., & Mailick, M. R. (2013). FMR1 CGG expansions: Prevalence and sex ratios. *American Journal of Medical Genetics Part B: Neuropsychiatric Genetics, 162*(5), 466–473. https://doi.org/10.1002/ajmg.b.32176

Maercker, A., Brewin, C. R., Bryant, R. A., Cloitre, M., van Ommeren, M., Jones, L. M., Humayan, A., Kagee, A., Llosa, A. E., Rousseau, C., Somasundaram,

D. J., Souza, R., Suzuki, Y., Weissbecker, I., Wessely, S. C., First, M. B., & Reed, G. M. (2013). Diagnosis and classification of disorders specifically associated with stress: Proposals for ICD-11. *World Psychiatry, 12*(3), 198–206. https://doi.org/10.1002/wps.20057

Maffioletti, V. L. R., Baptista, M. A. T., Santos, R. L., Rodrigues, V. M., & Dourado, M. C. N. (2019). Effectiveness of day care in supporting family caregivers of people with dementia: A systematic review. *Dementia & Neuropsychologia, 13*(3), 268–283. https://doi.org/10.1590/1980-57642018dn13-030003

Magnus, W., Nazir, S., Anilkumar, A. C., & Shaban, K. (2022). Attention deficit hyperactivity disorder. In *StatPearls [Internet].* StatPearls Publishing. https://www.ncbi.nlm.nih.gov/books/NBK441838/

Mago, R., Borra, D., & Mahajan, R. (2014). Role of adverse effects in medication nonadherence in bipolar disorder. *Harvard Review of Psychiatry, 22*(6), 363–366. https://doi.org/10.1097/HRP.0000000000000017

Maguire, G. A., Nguyen, D. L., Simonson, K. C., & Kurz, T. L. (2020). The pharmacologic treatment of stuttering and its neuropharmacological basis. *Frontiers in Neuroscience, 14*, Article 158. https://doi.org/10.3389/fnins.2020.00158

Maguire, G. A., Yeh, C. Y., & Ito, B. S. (2012). Overview of the diagnosis and treatment of stuttering. *Journal of Experimental & Clinical Medicine, 4*(2), 92–97. https://doi.org/10.1016/j.jecm.2012.02.001

Mahase, E. (2019). Esketamine is approved in Europe for treating resistant major depressive disorder. *BMJ, 367*, l7069. https://doi.org/10.1136/bmj.l7069

Mahler, M. S., & Rangell, L. (1943). A psychosomatic study of maladie des tics (Gilles de la Tourette's disease). *Psychiatric Quarterly, 17*, 579–603. https://doi.org/10.1007/BF01561841

Mahoney, C. E., Cogswell, A., Koralnik, I. J., & Scammell, T. E. (2019). The neurobiological basis of narcolepsy. *Nature Reviews. Neuroscience, 20*(2), 83–93. https://doi.org/10.1038/s41583-018-0097-x

Mahr, F., Billman, M., Essayli, J. H., & Lane Loney, S. E. (2022). Selective serotonin reuptake inhibitors and hydroxyzine in the treatment of avoidant/restrictive food intake disorder in children and adolescents: Rationale and evidence. *Journal of Child and Adolescent Psychopharmacology, 32*(2), 117–121. https://doi.org/10.1089/cap.2021.0038

Mahrer, A. R. (1996). *The complete guide to experiential psychotherapy.* John Wiley & Sons.

Mai, F. M. (1983). Pierre Briquet: 19th Century savant with 20th Century ideas. *The Canadian Journal of Psychiatry, 28*(6), 418–421. https://doi.org/10.1177/070674378302800602

Mai, F. M., & Merskey, H. (1980). Briquet's treatise on hysteria: A synopsis and commentary. *Archives of General Psychiatry, 37*(12), 1401–1405. https://doi.org/10.1001/archpsyc.1980.01780250087010

Mai, F. M., & Merskey, H. (1981). Briquet's concept of hysteria: An historical perspective. *The Canadian Journal of Psychiatry, 26*(1), 57–63. https://doi.org/10.1177/070674378102600112

Maia, T. V., & Conceição, V. A. (2018). Dopaminergic disturbances in Tourette syndrome: An integrative account. *Biological Psychiatry, 84*(5), 332–344. https://doi.org/10.1016/j.biopsych.2018.02.1172

Maia, T. V., Cooney, R. E., & Peterson, B. S. (2008). The neural bases of obsessive-compulsive disorder in children and adults. *Development and Psychopathology, 20*(4), 1251–1283. https://doi.org/10.1017/S0954579408000606

Maier, S., Düppers, A. L., Runge, K., Dacko, M., Lange, T., Fangmeier, T., Riedel, A., Ebert, D., Endres, D., Domschke, K., Perlov, E., Nickel, K., & Tebartz van Elst, L. (2022). Increased prefrontal GABA concentrations in adults with autism spectrum disorders. *Autism Research, 15*(7), 1222–1236. https://doi.org/10.1002/aur.2740

Maier, S. F., & Seligman, M. E. (1976). Learned helplessness: Theory and evidence. *Journal of Experimental Psychology: General, 105*(1), 3–46. https://doi.org/10.1037/0096-3445.105.1.3

Maina, G., Rosso, G., Rigardetto, S., Chiadò Piat, S., & Bogetto, F. (2010). No effect of adding brief dynamic therapy to pharmacotherapy in the treatment of obsessive-compulsive disorder with concurrent major depression. *Psychotherapy and Psychosomatics, 79*(5), 295–302. https://doi.org/10.1159/000318296

Maisel, R., Epston, D., & Borden, A. (2004). *Biting the hand that starves you: Inspiring resistance to anorexia/bulimia.* Norton.

Maj, M. (2013). Mood disorders in ICD-11 and DSM-5: A brief overview. *Die Psychiatrie: Grundlagen & Perspektiven, 10*(1), 24–29.

Maj, M. (2015). The media campaign on the DSM-5: Recurring comments and lessons for the future of diagnosis in psychiatric practice. *Epidemiology and Psychiatric Sciences, 24*(3), 97–202. https://doi.org/10.1017/S2045796014000572

Maji, S., & Dixit, S. (2019). Self-silencing and women's health: A review. *International Journal of Social Psychiatry, 65*(1), 3–13. https://doi.org/10.1177/0020764018814271

Mak, L., Streiner, D. L., & Steiner, M. (2015). Is serotonin transporter polymorphism (5-HTTLPR) allele status a predictor for obsessive-compulsive disorder? A meta-analysis. *Archives of Women's Mental Health, 18*(3), 435–445. https://doi.org/10.1007/s00737-015-0526-z

Ma-Kellams, C., Baek, J. H., & Or, F. (2016). Suicide contagion in response to widely publicized celebrity deaths: The roles of depressed affect, death-thought accessibility, and attitudes. *Psychology of Popular Media Culture.* https://doi.org/10.1037/ppm0000115

Makin, S. (2018). The amyloid hypothesis on trial. *Nature, 559*(7715), S4–S7. https://doi.org/10.1038/d41586-018-05719-4

Makino, M., Tsuboi, K., & Dennerstein, L. (2004). Prevalence of eating disorders: A comparison of Western and non-Western countries. *Medscape General Medicine, 6*(3), 49.

Malchow, B., Hasan, A., Schneider-Axmann, T., Jatzko, A., Gruber, O., Schmitt, A., Falkai, P., & Wobrock, T. (2013). Effects of cannabis and familial loading on subcortical brain volumes in first-episode schizophrenia. *European Archives of Psychiatry and Clinical Neuroscience, 263*(Suppl. 2), S155–S168. https://doi.org/10.1007/s00406-013-0451-y

Maldonado, J. R., & Spiegel, D. (2014). Dissociative disorders. In R. E. Hales, S. C. Yudofsky, & L. W. Roberts (Eds.), *The American Psychiatric Publishing textbook of psychiatry* (6th ed., pp. 499–530). American Psychiatric Publishing. https://doi.org/10.1176/appi.books.9781585625031.rh15

Maletic, V., & Raison, C. (2014). Integrated neurobiology of bipolar disorder. *Frontiers in Psychiatry, 5*, Article 98.

Malhi, G. S., & Bell, E. (2019). Make news: Suicidal behaviour disorder—A "diagnosis" with good intentions? *Australian and New Zealand Journal of Psychiatry, 53*(9), 927–931. https://doi.org/10.1177/0004867419872533

Malhi, G. S., & Bell, E. (2020). Make news: Is non-suicidal self-injury a harmful diagnosis? *Australian and New Zealand Journal of Psychiatry, 54*(9), 943–946. https://doi.org/10.1177/0004867420950544

Malhi, G. S., Hitching, R., Berk, M., Boyce, P., Porter, R., & Fritz, K. (2013). Pharmacological management of unipolar depression. *Acta Psychiatrica Scandinavica, 127*(Suppl 443), 6–23. https://doi.org/10.1111/acps.12122

Malhi, G. S., Tanious, M., Das, P., Coulston, C. M., & Berk, M. (2013). Potential mechanisms of action of lithium in bipolar disorder: Current understanding. *CNS Drugs, 27*(2), 135–153. https://doi.org/10.1007/s40263-013-0039-0

Maljanen, T., Härkänen, T., Virtala, E., Lindfors, O., Tillman, P., & Knekt, P. (2014). The cost-effectiveness of short-term psychodynamic psychotherapy and solution-focused therapy in the treatment of depressive and anxiety disorders during a three-year follow. *Open Journal of Psychiatry, 4*, 238–250. https://doi.org/10.13140/2.1.3992.6404

Mallett, C. A. (2006). Behaviorally-based disorders: The historical social construction of youths' most prevalent psychiatric diagnoses. *History of Psychiatry, 17*(4), 437–460. https://doi.org/10.1177/0957154X06063760

Malli, M. A., & Forrester-Jones, R. (2022). Stigma and adults with Tourette's syndrome: "Never laugh at other people's disabilities, unless they have Tourette's—because how can you not?" *Journal of Developmental and Physical Disabilities, 34*(5), 871–897. https://doi.org/10.1007/s10882-021-09829-2

Malli, M. A., Forrester-Jones, R., & Murphy, G. (2016). Stigma in youth with Tourette's syndrome: A systematic review and synthesis. *European Child & Adolescent Psychiatry, 25*(2), 127–139. https://doi.org/10.1007/s00787-015-0761-x

Mallinger, A. (2009). The myth of perfection: Perfectionism in the obsessive personality. *American Journal of Psychotherapy, 63*(2), 103–131. https://doi.org/10.1176/appi.psychotherapy.2009.63.2.103

Malykhin, N. V., & Coupland, N. J. (2015). Hippocampal neuroplasticity in major depressive disorder. *Neuroscience, 309*, 200–213. https://doi.org/10.1016/j.neuroscience.2015.04.047

Mancini, A. D., Griffin, P., & Bonanno, G. A. (2012). Recent trends in the treatment of prolonged grief. *Current Opinion in Psychiatry, 25*(1), 46–51. https://doi.org/10.1097/YCO.0b013e32834de48a

Mandavilli, A. (2022, August 18). Polio was almost eradicated. This year it staged a comeback. *The New York Times.* https://www.nytimes.com/2022/08/18/health/polio-new-york-malawi.html

Mandy, W. (2018). The Research Domain Criteria: A new dawn for neurodiversity research? *Autism, 22*(6), 642–644. https://doi.org/10.1177/1362361318782586

Manjula, M., & Sudhir, P. M. (2019). New-wave behavioral therapies in obsessive-compulsive disorder: Moving toward integrated behavioral therapies. *Indian Journal of Psychiatry, 61*(Suppl. 1), S104–S113. https://doi.org/10.4103/psychiatry.IndianJPsychiatry_531_18

Manlick, C. F., Cochran, S. V., & Koon, J. (2013). Acceptance and commitment therapy for eating disorders: Rationale and literature review. *Journal of Contemporary Psychotherapy, 43*(2), 115–122. https://doi.org/10.1007/s10879-012-9223-7

Manly, J. J., Jones, R. N., Langa, K. M., Ryan, L. H., Levine, D. A., McCammon, R., Heeringa, S. G., & Weir, D. (2022). Estimating the prevalence of dementia and mild cognitive impairment in the US: The 2016 health and retirement study Harmonized Cognitive Assessment Protocol project. *JAMA Neurology, 79*(12), 1242–1249. https://doi.org/10.1001/jamaneurol.2022.3543

Mann, J. J., & Currier, D. (2012). Medication in suicide prevention Insights from neurobiology of suicidal behavior. In Y. Dwivedi (Ed.), *The neurobiological basis of suicide.* CRC Press/Taylor & Francis. https://www.ncbi.nlm.nih.gov/books/NBK107195/

Manolis, A., Doumas, M., Ferri, C., & Mancia, G. (2020). Erectile dysfunction and adherence to antihypertensive therapy: Focus on β-blockers. *European Journal of Internal Medicine, 81*, 1–6. https://doi.org/10.1016/j.ejim.2020.07.009

Mano-Sousa, B. J., Pedrosa, A. M., Alves, B. C., Fernandes Galduróz, J. C., Belo, V. S., Chaves, V. E., & Duarte-Almeida, J. M. (2021). Effects of risperidone in autistic children and young adults: A systematic review and meta-analysis. *Current Neuropharmacology, 19*(4), 538–552. https://doi.org/10.2174/1570159X18666200529151741

Manzoni, M., Fernandez, I., Bertella, S., Tizzoni, F., Gazzola, E., Molteni, M., & Nobile, M. (2021). Eye movement desensitization and reprocessing: The state of the art of efficacy in children and adolescent with post traumatic stress disorder. *Journal of Affective Disorders, 282*, 340–347. https://doi.org/10.1016/j.jad.2020.12.088

Mao, J. J., Xie, S. X., Zee, J., Soeller, I., Li, Q. S., Rockwell, K., & Amsterdam, J. D. (2015). Rhodiola rosea versus sertraline for major depressive disorder: A randomized placebo-controlled trial. *Phytomedicine, 22*(3), 394–399. https://doi.org/10.1016/j.phymed.2015.01.010

Mao, R., Zhang, C., Chen, J., Zhao, G., Zhou, R., Wang, F., Xu, J., Yang, T., Su, Y., Huang, J., Wu, Z., Cao, L., Wang, Y., Hu, Y., Yuan, C., Yi, Z., Hong, W., Wang, Z., Peng, D., & Fang, Y. (2018). Different levels of pro- and anti-inflammatory cytokines in patients with unipolar and bipolar depression. *Journal of Affective Disorders, 237*, 65–72. https://doi.org/10.1016/j.jad.2018.04.115

Mapelli, L., Soda, T., D'Angelo, E., & Prestori, F. (2022). The cerebellar involvement in autism spectrum disorders: From the social brain to mouse models. *International Journal of Molecular Sciences, 23*(7), Article 7. https://doi.org/10.3390/ijms23073894

Marazziti, D., Mucci, F., Lombardi, A., Falaschi, V., & Dell'Osso, L. (2015). The cytokine profile of OCD: Pathophysiological insights. *International Journal of Interferon, Cytokine and Mediator Research, 7*, 35–42. https://doi.org/10.2147/IJICMR.S76710

Marc, D. T., Ailts, J. W., Campeau, D. C. A., Bull, M. J., & Olson, K. L. (2011). Neurotransmitters excreted in the urine as biomarkers of nervous system activity: Validity and clinical applicability. *Neuroscience & Biobehavioral Reviews, 35*(3), 635–644. https://doi.org/10.1016/j.neubiorev.2010.07.007

Marciello, F., Cascino, G., Patriciello, G., Pellegrino, F., Fiorenza, G., & Monteleone, P. (2020). Early traumatic experiences and eating disorders: A focus on the endogenous stress response system. *Journal of Psychopathology, 26*(1), 77–84. https://doi.org/10.36148/2284-0249-364

Marcos, A. (2000). Eating disorders: A situation of malnutrition with peculiar changes in the immune system. *European Journal of Clinical Nutrition, 54*(Suppl. 1), S61–S64. https://doi.org/10.1038/sj.ejcn.1600987

Marcos, A., Nova, E., & Montero, A. (2003). Changes in the immune system are conditioned by nutrition. *European Journal of Clinical Nutrition, 57*(Suppl. 1), S66–S69. https://doi.org/10.1038/sj.ejcn.1601819

Marcus, D. K., Gurley, J. R., Marchi, M. M., & Bauer, C. (2007). Cognitive and perceptual variables in hypochondriasis and health anxiety: A systematic review. *Clinical Psychology Review, 27*(2), 127–139. https://doi.org/10.1016/j.cpr.2006.09.003

Marcus, P. E. (1993). Borderline families. In C. S. Fawcett (Ed.), *Family psychiatric nursing* (pp. 328–341). C. V. Mosby.

Marecek, J., & Gavey, N. (2013). DSM-5 and beyond: A critical feminist engagement with psychodiagnosis. *Feminism & Psychology, 23*(1), 3–9. https://doi.org/10.1177/0959353512467962

Markert, C., Gomm, C., Ehlert, U., Gaab, J., & Nater, U. M. (2019). Effects of cognitive-behavioral stress management training in individuals with functional somatic symptoms – an exploratory randomized controlled trial. *Stress, 22*(6), 696–706. https://doi.org/10.1080/10253890.2019.1625329

Markman, E. R. (2011). Gender identity disorder, the gender binary, and transgender oppression: Implications for ethical social work. *Smith College Studies in Social Work, 81*(4), 314–327. https://doi.org/10.1080/00377317.2011.616839

Markon, K. E., & Jonas, K. G. (2015). The role of traits in describing, assessing, and understanding personality pathology. In S. K. Huprich (Ed.), *Personality disorders: Toward theoretical and empirical integration in diagnosis and assessment* (pp. 63–84). American Psychological Association. https://doi.org/10.1037/14549-004

Markowitz, J. C. (2013). Interpersonal psychotherapy of depression. In M. Power (Ed.), *The Wiley-Blackwell handbook of mood disorders* (2nd ed., pp. 193–214). Wiley-Blackwell.

Marks, I. (1990). Behavioural (non-chemical) addictions. *British Journal of Addiction, 85*(11), 1389–1394. https://doi.org/10.1111/j.1360-0443.1990.tb01618.x

Marks, I. M., & Nesse, R. M. (1994). Fear and fitness: An evolutionary analysis of anxiety disorders. *Ethology & Sociobiology, 15*(5–6), 247–261. https://doi.org/10.1016/0162-3095(94)90002-7

Marks, R. J., De Foe, A., & Collett, J. (2020). The pursuit of wellness: Social media, body image and eating disorders. *Children and Youth Services Review, 119*, 105659. https://doi.org/10.1016/j.childyouth.2020.105659

Marksberry, K. (n.d.). What is stress? *The American Institute of Stress.* Retrieved March 23, 2022, from https://www.stress.org/what-is-stress

Marlatt, G. A. (1996). Harm reduction: Come as you are. *Addictive Behaviors, 21*(6), 779–788. https://doi.org/10.1016/0306-4603(96)00042-1

Marlatt, G. A., & Donovan, D. M. (Eds.). (2005). *Relapse prevention: Maintenance strategies in the treatment of addictive behaviors* (2nd ed). Guilford Press.

Marlatt, G. A., & George, W. H. (1984). Relapse prevention: Introduction and overview of the model. *British Journal of Addiction, 79*, 261–273.

Marlock, G., & Weiss, H. (2015). *The handbook of body psychotherapy & somatic psychology.* North Atlantic Books.

Maron, E., Hettema, J. M., & Shlik, J. (2010). Advances in molecular genetics of panic disorder. *Molecular Psychiatry, 15*(7), 681–701. https://doi.org/10.1038/mp.2009.145

Marques, A. A., Bevilaqua, M. C. do N., da Fonseca, A. M. P., Nardi, A. E., Thuret, S., & Dias, G. P. (2016). Gender differences in the neurobiology of anxiety: Focus on adult hippocampal neurogenesis. *Neural Plasticity, 2016*, e5026713. https://doi.org/10.1155/2016/5026713

Marques, J. K., Wiederanders, M., Day, D. M., Nelson, C., & van Ommeren, A. (2005). Effects of a relapse prevention program on sexual recidivism: Final results from California's Sex Offender Treatment and Evaluation Project (SOTEP). *Sexual Abuse: Journal of Research and Treatment, 17*(1), 79–107. https://doi.org/10.1177/107906320501700108

Marshall, R. D., Spitzer, R., & Liebowitz, M. R. (1999). Review and critique of the new DSM-IV diagnosis of acute stress disorder. *The American Journal of Psychiatry, 156*(11), 1677–1685.

Marshall, W. L., & Fernandez, Y. M. (1998). Cognitive-behavioral approaches to the treatment of the paraphilias: Sexual offenders. In V. E. Caballo (Ed.), *International handbook of cognitive and behavioural treatments for psychological disorders* (pp. 281–312). Pergamon/Elsevier Science. https://doi.org/10.1016/B978-008043433-9/50012-2

Marshall, W. L., & Marshall, L. E. (2021). Empirically based psychological approaches to the treatment of sex offenders. In F. M. Saleh, J. M. Bradford, & D. J. Brodsky (Eds.), *Sex offenders: Identification, risk assessment, treatment, and legal issues* (2nd ed., pp. 276–291). Oxford University Press.

Martell, C. R., Dimidjian, S., & Herman-Dunn, R. (2022). *Behavioral activation for depression: A clinician's guide* (2nd ed.). Guilford Press.

Martin, D., & Le, J. K. (2021). Amphetamine. In *StatPearls [Internet].* StatPearls Publishing. https://www.ncbi.nlm.nih.gov/books/NBK556103/

Martin, M. (2022, January 23). *Why the nature of TikTok could exacerbate a worrisome social media trend* [Radio broadcast]. All Things Considered. https://www.npr.org/2022/01/23/1075216842/why-the-nature-of-tiktok-could-exacerbate-a-worrisome-social-media-trend

Martin, W. E., & Bridgmon, K. D. (2012). *Quantitative and statistical research methods: From hypothesis to results.* Jossey-Bass.

Martinez, M., Rathod, S., Friesen, H. J., Rosen, J. M., Friesen, C. A., & Schurman, J. V. (2021). Rumination syndrome in children and adolescents: A mini review.

Frontiers in Pediatrics, 9, Article 709326. https://doi.org/10.3389/fped.2021.709326

Martínez, R. S., & Nellis, L. M. (2020). Learning disorders of childhood and adolescence. In J. E. Maddux & B. A. Winstead (Eds.), *Psychopathology: Foundations for a contemporary understanding* (5th ed., pp. 481–493). Routledge/Taylor & Francis Group.

Martinez-Ramirez, D., Jimenez-Shahed, J., Leckman, J. F., Porta, M., Servello, D., Meng, F.-G., Kuhn, J., Huys, D., Baldermann, J. C., Foltynie, T., Hariz, M. I., Joyce, E. M., Zrinzo, L., Kefalopoulou, Z., Silburn, P., Coyne, T., Mogilner, A. Y., Pourfar, M. H., Khandhar, S. M., … Okun, M. S. (2018). Efficacy and safety of deep brain stimulation in Tourette syndrome: The International Tourette Syndrome Deep Brain Stimulation Public Database and Registry. *JAMA Neurology, 75*(3), 353–359. https://doi.org/10.1001/jamaneurol.2017.4317

Martin-Lopez, J. E., Molina-Linde, J. M., Isabel-Gomez, R., Castro, J. L., & Blasco-Amaro, J. A. (2021). Cognitive training for people with mild to moderate dementia: A systematic review and meta-analysis of cognitive effects. *Advances in Neurology and Neuroscience Research, 2*, Article 100015. https://doi.org/10.51956/ANNR.100015

Martino, D., Deeb, W., Jimenez-Shahed, J., Malaty, I., Pringsheim, T. M., Fasano, A., Ganos, C., Wu, W., & Okun, M. (2021). The 5 pillars in Tourette syndrome deep brain stimulation patient selection: Present and future. *Neurology, 96*(14), 664–676. https://doi.org/10.1212/WNL.0000000000011704

Martino, D., Defazio, G., & Giovannoni, G. (2009). The PANDAS subgroup of tic disorders and childhood-onset obsessive–compulsive disorder. *Journal of Psychosomatic Research, 67*(6), 547–557. https://doi.org/10.1016/j.jpsychores.2009.07.004

Martinotti, G., Santacroce, R., Pettorruso, M., Montemitro, C., Spano, M. C., Lorusso, M., Di Giannantonio, M., & Lerner, A. G. (2018). Hallucinogen persisting perception disorder: Etiology, clinical features, and therapeutic perspectives. *Brain Sciences, 8*(3), Article 3. https://doi.org/10.3390/brainsci8030047

Martins, D., Brodmann, K., Veronese, M., Dipasquale, O., Mazibuko, N., Schuschnig, U., Zelaya, F., Fotopoulou, A., & Paloyelis, Y. (2022). "Less is more": A dose-response account of intranasal oxytocin pharmacodynamics in the human brain. *Progress in Neurobiology, 211*, 102239. https://doi.org/10.1016/j.pneurobio.2022.102239

Martins, S. S., Lee, G. P., Sanchez, Z. M., Harrell, P., Ghandour, L. A., & Storr, C. L. (2013). Hallucinogens. In P. M. Miller, S. A. Ball, M. E. Bates, A. W. Blume, K. M. Kampman, D. J. Kavanagh, M. E. Larimer, N. M. Petry, & P. De Witte (Eds.), *Comprehensive addictive behaviors and disorders: Vol. 1. Principles of addiction* (pp. 699–709). Elsevier Academic Press.

Martín-Santos, R., Navinés, R., & Valdés, M. (2017). Dhat syndrome. In B. A. Sharpless (Ed.), *Unusual and rare psychological disorders: A handbook for clinical practice and research* (pp. 223–241). Oxford University Press.

Marzilli, E., Cerniglia, L., & Cimino, S. (2021). Antisocial personality problems in emerging adulthood: The role of family functioning, impulsivity, and empathy. *Brain Sciences, 11*(6), 687. https://doi.org/10.3390/brainsci11060687

Mascolo, M. (2019, July 31). Time to move beyond "gender is socially constructed" [Psychology Today]. *Old-School Parenting for Modern-Day Families*. https://www.psychologytoday.com/us/blog/old-school-parenting-modern-day-families/201907/time-move-beyond-gender-is-socially-constructed

Masland, S. R., & Null, K. E. (2022). Effects of diagnostic label construction and gender on stigma about borderline personality disorder. *Stigma and Health, 7*(1), 89–99. https://doi.org/10.1037/sah0000320

Maslow, A. H. (1968). *Toward a psychology of being* (2nd ed.). Van Nostrand Reinhold.

Masson, J. M. (1984). *The assault on truth: Freud's suppression of the seduction theory*. Farrar, Straus and Giroux.

Masters, W. H., & Johnson, V. E. (1966). *Human sexual response*. Little, Brown, and Company.

Masters, W. H., & Johnson, V. E. (1970). *Human sexual inadequacy*. Little, Brown, and Company.

Mataix-Cols, D. (2006). Deconstructing obsessive-compulsive disorder: A multidimensional perspective. *Current Opinion in Psychiatry, 19*(1), 84–89. https://doi.org/10.1097/01.yco.0000194809.98967.49

Mataix-Cols, D., Wooderson, S., Lawrence, N., Brammer, M. J., Speckens, A., & Phillips, M. L. (2004). Distinct neural correlates of washing, checking, and hoarding symptom dimensions in obsessive-compulsive disorder. *Archives of General Psychiatry, 61*(6), 564–576. https://doi.org/10.1001/archpsyc.61.6.564

Matheny, K. B., Brack, G. L., McCarthy, C. J., & Penick, J. M. (1996). The effectiveness of cognitively-based approaches in treating stress-related symptoms. *Psychotherapy: Theory, Research, Practice, Training, 33*(2), 305–320. https://doi.org/10.1037/0033-3204.33.2.305

Mathieu-Bolh, N. (2022). The elusive link between income and obesity. *Journal of Economic Surveys, 36*(4), 935–968. https://doi.org/10.1111/joes.12458

Mathur, N. K., & Ruhm, C. J. (2022). *Marijuana legalization and opioid deaths* (NBER Working Paper No. 29802). National Bureau of Economic Research. http://www.nber.org/papers/w29802

Matsuda, Y., Makinodan, M., Morimoto, T., & Kishimoto, T. (2019). Neural changes following cognitive remediation therapy for schizophrenia. *Psychiatry and Clinical Neurosciences, 73*(11), 676–684. https://doi.org/10.1111/pcn.12912

Matsui, A., & Alvarez, V. A. (2018). Cocaine inhibition of synaptic transmission in the ventral pallidum is pathway-specific and mediated by serotonin. *Cell Reports, 23*(13), 3852–3863. https://doi.org/10.1016/j.celrep.2018.05.076

Mattar, S. (2011). Educating and training the next generations of traumatologists: Development of cultural competencies. *Psychological Trauma: Theory, Research, Practice, and Policy, 3*(3), 258–265. https://doi.org/10.1037/a0024477

Matte, B., Anselmi, L., Salum, G. A., Kieling, C., Gonçalves, H., Menezes, A., Grevet, E. H., & Rohde, L. A. (2015). ADHD in DSM-5: A field trial in a large, representative sample of 18- to 19- year-old adults. *Psychological Medicine, 45*(2), 361–373. https://doi.org/10.1017/S0033291714001470

Matthews, E. E., Arnedt, J. T., McCarthy, M. S., Cuddihy, L. J., & Aloia, M. S. (2013). Adherence to cognitive behavioral therapy for insomnia: A systematic review. *Sleep Medicine Reviews, 17*(6), 453–464. https://doi.org/10.1016/j.smrv.2013.01.001

Matthews, J. R., & Matthews, L. H. (2013). Influences of the Greeks and Romans. In T. G. Plante (Ed.), *Abnormal psychology across the ages: Vol. 1. History and conceptualizations* (pp. 1–14). Praeger/ABC-CLIO.

Matthews, S., Dwyer, R., & Snoek, A. (2017). Stigma and self-stigma in addiction. *Journal of Bioethical Inquiry, 14*(2), 275–286. https://doi.org/10.1007/s11673-017-9784-y

Matthys, W., Vanderschuren, L. J. M. J., & Schutter, D. J. L. G. (2013). The neurobiology of oppositional defiant disorder and conduct disorder: Altered functioning in three mental domains. *Development and Psychopathology, 25*(1), 193–207. https://doi.org/10.1017/S0954579412000272

Mattick, R. P., Breen, C., Kimber, J., & Davoli, M. (2009). Methadone maintenance therapy versus no opioid replacement therapy for opioid dependence. *Cochrane Database of Systematic Reviews, 2009*(3), Article CD002209. https://doi.org/10.1002/14651858.CD002209.pub2

Mattick, R. P., Breen, C., Kimber, J., & Davoli, M. (2014). Buprenorphine maintenance versus placebo or methadone maintenance for opioid dependence. *Cochrane Database of Systematic Reviews, 2014*(2), Article CD002207. https://doi.org/10.1002/14651858.CD002207.pub4

Maturana, H. R., & Varela, F. J. (1992). *The tree of knowledge: The biological roots of human understanding* (R. Paolucci, Trans.; Rev. ed.). Shambhala.

Maurer, K., Volk, S., & Gerbaldo, H. (1997). Auguste D and Alzheimer's disease. *The Lancet, 349*(9064), 1546–1549. https://doi.org/10.1016/S0140-6736(96)10203-8

Maurya, C., Muhammad, T., Maurya, P., & Dhillon, P. (2022). The association of smartphone screen time with sleep problems among adolescents and young adults: Cross-sectional findings from India. *BMC Public Health, 22*(1), 1686. https://doi.org/10.1186/s12889-022-14076-x

Mavranezouli, I., Link to external site, this link will open in a new window, Megnin-Viggars, O., Daly, C., Dias, S., Welton, N. J., Stockton, S., Bhutani, G., Grey, N., Leach, J., Greenberg, N., Katona, C., El-Leithy, S., & Pilling, S. (2020). Psychological treatments for post-traumatic stress disorder in adults: A network meta-analysis. *Psychological Medicine, 50*(4), 542–555. https://doi.org/10.1017/S0033291720000070

May, J. M., Richardi, T. M., & Barth, K. S. (2016). Dialectical behavior therapy as treatment for borderline personality disorder. *The Mental Health Clinician, 6*(2), 62–67. https://doi.org/10.9740/mhc.2016.03.62

Maydych, V., Claus, M., Dychus, N., Ebel, M., Damaschke, J., Diestel, S., Wolf, O. T., Kleinsorge, T., & Watzl, C. (2017). Impact of chronic and acute academic stress on lymphocyte subsets and monocyte function. *PLoS ONE, 12*(11), e0188108. https://doi.org/10.1371/journal.pone.0188108

Mayer, A. V., Wermter, A.-K., Stroth, S., Alter, P., Haberhausen, M., Stehr, T., Paulus, F. M., Krach, S., & Kamp-Becker, I. (2021). Randomized clinical trial shows no substantial modulation of empathy-related neural activation by intranasal oxytocin in autism. *Scientific Reports, 11*(1), Article 1. https://doi.org/10.1038/s41598-021-94407-x

Mayo Clinic. (n.d.). *Attention-deficit/hyperactivity disorder (ADHD) in children—Diagnosis and treatment—Mayo Clinic*. Retrieved September 23, 2022, from https://www.mayoclinic.org/diseases-conditions/adhd/diagnosis-treatment/drc-20350895

Mazzeo, S. E., & Bulik, C. M. (2009). Environmental and genetic risk factors for eating disorders: What the clinician needs to know. *Child and Adolescent Psychiatric Clinics of North America, 18*(1), 67–82. doi:10.1016/j.chc.2008.07.003

Mazzucchelli, T., Kane, R., & Rees, C. (2009). Behavioral activation treatments for depression in adults: A meta-analysis and review. *Clinical Psychology: Science and Practice, 16*(4), 383–411. https://doi.org/10.1111/j.1468-2850.2009.01178.x

McAdam, D. B., Sherman, J. A., Sheldon, J. B., & Napolitano, D. A. (2004). Behavioral interventions to reduce the pica of persons with developmental disabilities. *Behavior Modification, 28*(1), 45–72. https://doi.org/10.1177/0145445503259219

McAdams, D. P. (2016, May 17). The mind of Donald Trump. *The Atlantic*. https://www.theatlantic.com/magazine/archive/2016/06/the-mind-of-donald-trump/480771/

McCabe, G. A., & Widiger, T. A. (2020). A comprehensive comparison of the ICD-11 and DSM-5 section III personality disorder models. *Psychological Assessment, 32*(1), 72–84. https://doi.org/10.1037/pas0000772

McCabe, R. E., Miller, J. L., Laugesen, N., Antony, M. M., & Young, L. (2010). The relationship between anxiety disorders in adults and recalled childhood teasing. *Journal of Anxiety Disorders, 24*(2), 238–243. https://doi.org/10.1016/j.janxdis.2009.11.002

McCarty, T. S., & Shah, A. D. (2022). Desmopressin. In *StatPearls [Internet]*. StatPearls Publishing. https://www.ncbi.nlm.nih.gov/books/NBK554582/

McCauley, E., Berk, M. S., Asarnow, J. R., Adrian, M., Cohen, J., Korslund, K., Avina, C., Hughes, J., Harned,

M., Gallop, R., & Linehan, M. M. (2018). Efficacy of dialectical behavior therapy for adolescents at high risk for suicide: A randomized clinical trial. *JAMA Psychiatry*, 75(8), 777–785. https://doi.org/10.1001/jamapsychiatry.2018.1109

McClelland, L. (2014). Reformulating the impact of social inequalities: Power and social justice. In L. Johnstone & R. Dallos (Eds.), *Formulation in psychology and psychotherapy: Making sense of people's problems* (2nd ed., pp. 121–144). Routledge.

McClintock, S. M., Brandon, A. R., Husain, M. M., & Jarrett, R. B. (2011). A systematic review of the combined use of electroconvulsive therapy and psychotherapy for depression. *The Journal of ECT*, 27(3), 236–243. https://doi.org/10.1097/YCT.0b013e-3181faaeca

McCollister, K., Baumer, P., Davis, M., Greene, A., Stevens, S., & Dennis, M. (2018). Economic evaluation of the juvenile drug court/Reclaiming Futures (JDC/RF) model. *The Journal of Behavioral Health Services & Research*, 45(3), 321–339. https://doi.org/10.1007/s11414-018-9606-y

McConnell, J. V. (1990). Negative reinforcement and positive punishment. *Teaching of Psychology*, 17(4), 247–249. https://doi.org/10.1207/s15328023top1704_10

McCrae, R. R. (2017). The Five-Factor Model across cultures. In A. T. Church (Ed.), *The Praeger handbook of personality across cultures: Trait psychology across cultures* (Vol. 1, pp. 47–71). Praeger/ABC-CLIO.

McCrae, R. R., & John, O. P. (1992). An introduction to the five-factor model and its applications. *Journal of Personality*, 60(2), 175–215. https://doi.org/10.1111/j.1467-6494.1992.tb00970.x

McCullumsmith, C. B., & Ford, C. V. (2011). Simulated illness: The factitious disorders and malingering. *Psychiatric Clinics of North America*, 34(3), 621–641. https://doi.org/10.1016/j.psc.2011.05.013

McDonagh, M. S., Morasco, B. J., Wagner, J., Ahmed, A. Y., Fu, R., Kansagara, D., & Chou, R. (2022). Cannabis-based products for chronic pain. *Annals of Internal Medicine*, 175(8), 1143–1153. https://doi.org/10.7326/M21-4520

McDonald, J. E., & Trepper, T. (1977). Enuresis: An historical, cultural, and contemporary account of etiology and treatment. *Psychology in the Schools*, 14(3), 308–314. https://doi.org/10.1002/1520-6807(197707)14:33.0.CO;2-1

McElroy, S. L., Guerdjikova, A. I., Mori, N., & Romo-Nava, F. (2019). Progress in developing pharmacologic agents to treat bulimia nervosa. *CNS Drugs*, 33(1), 31–46. https://doi.org/10.1007/s40263-018-0594-5

McElroy, S. L., Guerdjikova, A. I., O'Melia, A. M., Mori, N., & Keck, J. P. E. (2010). Pharmacotherapy of the eating disorders. In W. S. Agras (Ed.), *The Oxford handbook of eating disorders* (pp. 417–451). Oxford University Press.

McEvoy, P. M., Nathan, P., & Norton, P. J. (2009). Efficacy of transdiagnostic treatments: A review of published outcome studies and future research directions. *Journal of Cognitive Psychotherapy*, 23(1), 20–33.

McGill, O., & Robinson, A. (2020). "Recalling hidden harms": Autistic experiences of childhood applied behavioural analysis (ABA). *Advances in Autism*, 7(4), 269–282. https://doi.org/10.1108/AIA-04-2020-0025

McGrath, A. G., & Briand, L. A. (2019). A potential role for microglia in stress- and drug-induced plasticity in the nucleus accumbens: A mechanism for stress-induced vulnerability to substance use disorder. *Neuroscience and Biobehavioral Reviews*, 107, 360–369. https://doi.org/10.1016/j.neubiorev.2019.09.007

McGrath, J. J. (2005). Myths and plain truths about schizophrenia epidemiology—The NAPE lecture 2004. *Acta Psychiatrica Scandinavica*, 111(1), 4–11.

McGregor, B. A., Murphy, K. M., Albano, D. L., & Ceballos, R. M. (2016). Stress, cortisol, and B-lymphocytes: A novel approach to understanding academic stress and immune function. *Stress (Amsterdam, Netherlands)*, 19(2), 185–191. https://doi.org/10.3109/10253890.2015.1127913

McGuffin, P., Alsabban, S., & Uher, R. (2011). The truth about genetic variation in the serotonin transporter gene and response to stress and medication. *The British Journal of Psychiatry*, 198(6), 424–427.

McGuinty, E., Armstrong, D., Nelson, J., & Sheeler, S. (2012). Externalizing metaphors: Anxiety and high-externalizing autism. *Journal of Child and Adolescent Psychiatric Nursing*, 25(1), 9–16. https://doi.org/10.1111/j.1744-6171.2011.00305.x

McGuire, T. M., Lee, C. W., & Drummond, P. D. (2014). Potential of eye movement desensitization and reprocessing therapy in the treatment of post-traumatic stress disorder. *Psychology Research and Behavior Management*, 7.

McHenry, J., Carrier, N., Hull, E., & Kabbaj, M. (2014). Sex differences in anxiety and depression: Role of testosterone. *Frontiers in Neuroendocrinology*, 35(1), 42–57. https://doi.org/10.1016/j.yfrne.2013.09.001

McHugh, M. C. (2006). What do women want? A new view of women's sexual problems. *Sex Roles*, 54(5–6), 361–369. https://doi.org/10.1007/s11199-006-9006-2

McIntosh, V. V., Bulik, C. M., McKenzie, J. M., Luty, S. E., & Jordan, J. (2000). Interpersonal psychotherapy for anorexia nervosa. *International Journal of Eating Disorders*, 27(2), 125–139. https://doi.org/10.1002/(SICI)1098-108X(200003)27:23.0.CO;2-4

McIntosh, V. V. W., Carter, J. D., Jordan, J., & Loughlin, A. (2022). Specialist supportive clinical management for anorexia nervosa: Analysis of therapy content and relation to outcome. *International Journal of Eating Disorders*. https://doi.org/10.1002/eat.23697

McIntyre, R. S., Rosenblat, J. D., Nemeroff, C. B., Sanacora, G., Murrough, J. W., Berk, M., Brietzke, E., Dodd, S., Gorwood, P., Ho, R., Iosifescu, D. V., Lopez Jaramillo, C., Kasper, S., Kratiuk, K., Lee, J. G., Lee, Y., Lui, L. M. W., Mansur, R. B., Papakostas, G. I., … Stahl, S. (2021). Synthesizing the evidence for ketamine and esketamine in treatment-resistant depression: An international expert opinion on the available evidence and implementation. *American Journal of Psychiatry*, 178(5), 383–399. https://doi.org/10.1176/appi.ajp.2020.20081251

McKay, D. (2011). Methods and mechanisms in the efficacy of psychodynamic psychotherapy. *American Psychologist*, 66(2), 147–148. https://doi.org/10.1037/a0021195

McKay, D., & Asmundson, G. J. G. (2020). Substance use and abuse associated with the behavioral immune system during COVID-19: The special case of healthcare workers and essential workers. *Addictive Behaviors*, 110, 106522. https://doi.org/10.1016/j.addbeh.2020.106522

McKay, D., & Lilienfeld, S. O. (2017, November 26). Clinical practice guidelines: A clear public good, the doubters notwithstanding [Psychology Today]. *Your Fears and Anxieties*. https://www.psychologytoday.com/us/blog/your-fears-and-anxieties/201711/clinical-practice-guidelines

McKay, J. R. (2022, July 25). *Psychotherapies for substance use disorders*. UpToDate. https://www.uptodate.com/contents/psychotherapies-for-substance-use-disorders

McKay, J. R., Kranzler, H. R., Kampman, K. M., Ashare, R. L., & Schnoll, R. A. (2015). Psychopharmacological treatments for substance use disorders. In P. E. Nathan & J. M. Gorman (Eds.), *A guide to treatments that work* (4th ed., pp. 763–800). Oxford University Press.

McKay, R., McDonald, R., Lie, D., & McGowan, H. (2012). Reclaiming the best of the biopsychosocial model of mental health care and "recovery" for older people through a "person-centred" approach. *Australasian Psychiatry*, 20(6), 492–495. https://doi.org/10.1177/1039856212460286

McKee, G. B., Pierce, B. S., Tyler, C. M., Perrin, P. B., & Elliott, T. R. (2022). The COVID-19 pandemic's influence on family systems therapists' provision of teletherapy. *Family Process*, 61(1), 155–166. https://doi.org/10.1111/famp.12665

McKenna, P., & Kingdon, D. (2014). Has cognitive behavioural therapy for psychosis been oversold? *BMJ (Clinical Research Ed.)*, 348, g2295–g2295. https://doi.org/10.1136/bmj.g2295

McKenzie, K., Gregory, J., & Hogg, L. (2022). Mental health workers' attitudes towards individuals with a diagnosis of borderline personality disorder: A systematic literature review. *Journal of Personality Disorders*, 36(1), 70–98. https://doi.org/10.1521/pedi_2021_35_528

McKenzie, R. G. (2009). Obscuring vital distinctions: The oversimplification of learning disabilities within RTI. *Learning Disability Quarterly*, 32(4), 203–215. https://doi.org/10.2307/27740373

McKetin, R., Kaye, S. S., Clemens, K. J., & Hermens, D. (2013). Methamphetamine addiction. In P. M. Miller, S. A. Ball, M. E. Bates, A. W. Blume, K. M. Kampman, D. J. Kavanagh, M. E. Larimer, N. M. Petry, & P. De Witte (Eds.), *Comprehensive addictive behaviors and disorders: Vol. 1. Principles of addiction* (pp. 689–698). Elsevier Academic Press.

McKnight-Eily, L. R., Okoro, C. A., Strine, T. W., Verlenden, J., Hollis, N. D., Njai, R., Mitchell, E. W., Board, A., Puddy, R., & Thomas, C. (2021). Racial and ethnic disparities in the prevalence of stress and worry, mental health conditions, and increased substance use among adults during the COVID-19 pandemic—United States, April and May 2020. *Morbidity and Mortality Weekly Report*, 70(5), 162–166. https://doi.org/10.15585/mmwr.mm7005a3

McLaren, N. (2011). Cells, circuits, and syndromes: A critical commentary on the NIMH Research Domain Criteria project. *Ethical Human Psychology and Psychiatry*, 13(3), 229–236. https://doi.org/10.1891/1559-4343.13.3.229

McLaughlin, A. P., Pariante, C. M., & Mondelli, V. (2021). Inflammatory mechanisms in psychosis. In C. A. Tamminga, E. I. Ivleva, U. Reininghaus, & J. van Os (Eds.), *Psychotic disorders: Comprehensive conceptualization and treatments* (pp. 351–360). Oxford University Press.

McLaughlin, K. A., Breslau, J., Green, J. G., Lakoma, M. D., Sampson, N. A., Zaslavsky, A. M., & Kessler, R. C. (2011). Childhood socio-economic status and the onset, persistence, and severity of DSM-IV mental disorders in a US national sample. *Social Science & Medicine*, 73(7), 1088–1096. https://doi.org/10.1016/j.socscimed.2011.06.011

McLean, C. P., Asnaani, A., Litz, B. T., & Hofmann, S. G. (2011). Gender differences in anxiety disorders: Prevalence, course of illness, comorbidity and burden of illness. *Journal of Psychiatric Research*, 45(8), 1027–1035. https://doi.org/10.1016/j.jpsychires.2011.03.006

McLean, C. P., Levy, H. C., Miller, M. L., & Tolin, D. F. (2022). Exposure therapy for PTSD: A meta-analysis. *Clinical Psychology Review*, 91, 102115. https://doi.org/10.1016/j.cpr.2021.102115

McLean, C. P., Yeh, R., Rosenfield, D., & Foa, E. B. (2015). Changes in negative cognitions mediate PTSD symptom reductions during client-centered therapy and prolonged exposure for adolescents. *Behaviour Research and Therapy*, 68, 64–69. https://doi.org/10.1016/j.brat.2015.03.008

McLoughlin, G. (2002). Is depression normal in human beings? A critique of the evolutionary perspective. *International Journal of Mental Health Nursing*, 11(3), 170–173. https://doi.org/10.1046/j.1440-0979.2002.00244.x

McManus, F., Shafran, R., & Cooper, Z. (2010). What does a "transdiagnostic" approach have to offer the treatment of anxiety disorders? *British Journal of Clinical Psychology*, 49(4), 491–505. https://doi.org/10.1348/014466509X476567

McNaught, K. St. P. (2010). *125 years of Tourette syndrome: The discovery, early history and future of the disorder*. https://www.tourette.org/resource/125-years-tourette-syndrome-discovery-early-history-future-disorder/

McPhail, D., & Orsini, M. (2021). Fat acceptance as social justice. *CMAJ*, 193(35), E1398–E1399. https://doi.org/10.1503/cmaj.210772

McWilliams, N. (2011). The *Psychodynamic diagnostic manual*: An effort to compensate for the limitations of descriptive psychiatric diagnosis. *Journal of Personality Assessment*, 93(2), 112–122. https://doi.org/10.1080/00223891.2011.542709

Mead, M. (1974). On Freud's view of female psychology. In J. Strouse (Ed.), *Women and analysis: Dialogues on psychoanalytic views of femininity* (pp. 95–106). Dell.

Mealey, L. (1995). The sociobiology of sociopathy: An integrated evolutionary model. *Behavioral and Brain Sciences*, 18(3), 523–599. https://doi.org/10.1017/S0140525X00039595

Mealey, L. (2000). Anorexia: A "losing" strategy? *Human Nature*, 11(1), 105–116. doi:10.1007/s12110-000-1005-3

Meana, M. (2012). *Sexual dysfunction in women*. Hogrefe.

Medco. (2010). *America's state of mind*. http://apps.who.int/medicinedocs/documents/s19032en/s19032en.pdf

Medda, E., Fagnani, C., Alessandri, G., Baracchini, C., Hernyes, A., Lucatelli, P., Pucci, G., Tarnoki, A. D., Tarnoki, D. L., & Stazi, M. A. (2020). Association between personality profile and subclinical atherosclerosis: The role of genes and environment. *International Journal of Cardiology*, 316, 236–239. https://doi.org/10.1016/j.ijcard.2020.05.034

Medic, G., Wille, M., & Hemels, M. E. (2017). Short- and long-term health consequences of sleep disruption. *Nature and Science of Sleep*, 9, 151–161. https://doi.org/10.2147/NSS.S134864

Meehan, K. B., & Levy, K. N. (2015). Personality disorders. In P. Luyten, L. C. Mayes, P. Fonagy, M. Target, & S. J. Blatt (Eds.), *Handbook of psychodynamic approaches to psychopathology* (pp. 311–333). Guilford Press.

Meewisse, M.-L., Reitsma, J. B., De Vries, G.-J., Gersons, B. P. R., & Olff, M. (2007). Cortisol and post-traumatic stress disorder in adults. *The British Journal of Psychiatry*, 191(5), 387–392.

Meganck, R. (2017). Beyond the impasse – Reflections on dissociative identity disorder from a Freudian–Lacanian perspective. *Frontiers in Psychology*, 8, Article 789. https://doi.org/10.3389/fpsyg.2017.00789

Mehta, D., & Binder, E. B. (2012). Gene × environment vulnerability factors for PTSD: The HPA-axis. *Neuropharmacology*, 62(2), 654–662. https://doi.org/10.1016/j.neuropharm.2011.03.009

Mehta, T. R., Monegro, A., Nene, Y., Fayyaz, M., & Bollu, P. C. (2019). Neurobiology of ADHD: A review. *Current Developmental Disorders Reports*, 6(4), 235–240. https://doi.org/10.1007/s40474-019-00182-w

Mehta, U. M., Thirthalli, J., Basavaraju, R., Gangadhar, B. N., & Pascual-Leone, A. (2014). Reduced mirror neuron activity in schizophrenia and its association with theory of mind deficits: Evidence from a transcranial magnetic stimulation study. *Schizophrenia Bulletin*, 40(5), 1083–1094. https://doi.org/10.1093/schbul/sbt155

Mei, L., Gao, Y., Chen, M., Zhang, X., Yue, W., Zhang, D., & Yu, H. (2022). Overlapping common genetic architecture between major depressive disorders and anxiety and stress-related disorders. *Progress in Neuro-Psychopharmacology and Biological Psychiatry*, 113, Article 110450. https://doi.org/10.1016/j.pnpbp.2021.110450

Meichenbaum, D. (2007). Stress inoculation training: A preventative and treatment approach. In P. M. Lehrer, R. L. Woolfolk, & W. E. Sime (Eds.), *Principles and practice of stress management* (3rd ed., pp. 497–516). The Guilford Press.

Meichenbaum, D. (2019). Stress inoculation training: A resilience-engendering intervention. In B. A. Moore & W. E. Penk (Eds.), *Treating PTSD in military personnel: A clinical handbook* (2nd ed., pp. 136–150). The Guilford Press.

Meloni, E. G., Gillis, T. E., Manoukian, J., & Kaufman, M. J. (2014). Xenon impairs reconsolidation of fear memories in a rat model of post-traumatic stress disorder (PTSD). *PLOS One*, 9(8), Article e106189. https://doi.org/10.1371/journal.pone.0106189

Meltzer, M., & Blum, D. (2022, March 11). A ketamine clinic treads the line between health care and a "spa day for your brain." *The New York Times*. https://www.nytimes.com/2022/03/11/well/mind/wellness-ketamine-mental-health.html

Melville, J. D., & Naimark, D. (2002). Punishing the insane: The verdict of guilty but mentally ill. *Journal of the American Academy of Psychiatry and the Law*, 30(4), 553–555.

Memedovich, K. A., Dowsett, L. E., Spackman, E., Noseworthy, T., & Clement, F. (2018). The adverse health effects and harms related to marijuana use: An overview review. *Canadian Medical Association Open Access Journal*, 6(3), E339–E346. https://doi.org/10.9778/cmajo.20180023

Memorandum of understanding on conversion therapy in the UK, Version 2. (2021). https://www.psychotherapy.org.uk/media/cptnc5qm/mou2.pdf

Mencacci, C., & Salvi, V. (2021). Expected effects of COVID-19 outbreak on depression incidence in Italy. *Journal of Affective Disorders*, 278, 66–67. https://doi.org/10.1016/j.jad.2020.09.043

Mendos, L. R. (2020). *Curbing deception 2020: A world survey on legal regulation of so-called "conversion therapies."* International Lesbian, Gay, Bisexual, Trans and Intersex Association. https://ilga.org/Conversion-therapy-report-ILGA-World-Curbing-Deception

Mennin, D. S., Turk, C. L., Heimberg, R. G., & Carmin, C. N. (2004). Regulation of emotion in generalized anxiety disorder. In M. A. Reinecke & D. A. Clark (Eds.), *Cognitive therapy across the lifespan* (1st ed., pp. 60–89). Cambridge University Press. https://doi.org/10.1017/CBO9781139087094.005

Menninger, J. A. (2001). Involuntary treatment: Hospitalization and medications. In J. L. Jacobson & A. M. Jacobson (Eds.), *Psychiatric secrets* (2nd ed., pp. 477–484). Hanley & Belfus.

Mennis, J., & Stahler, G. J. (2016). Racial and ethnic disparities in outpatient substance use disorder treatment episode completion for different substances. *Journal of Substance Abuse Treatment*, 63, 25–33. https://doi.org/10.1016/j.jsat.2015.12.007

Menon, V., Subramanian, K., Selvakumar, N., & Kattimani, S. (2018). Suicide prevention strategies: An overview of current evidence and best practice elements. *International Journal of Advanced Medical and Health Research*, 5(2), 43–51.

Mental Health America. (n.d.). *Atypical antidepressants*. MHA Screening. Retrieved February 9, 2022, from https://screening.mhanational.org/content/atypical-antidepressants/

Mental Health Foundation. (n.d.). *Schizophrenia: The facts*. https://www.mentalhealth.org.uk/sites/default/files/schizophrenia-factsheet.pdf

Mental Health Foundation. (2015, August 7). *Stress*. Mental Health Foundation. https://www.mentalhealth.org.uk/a-to-z/s/stress

Menzies, L., Chamberlain, S. R., Laird, A. R., Thelen, S. M., Sahakian, B. J., & Bullmore, E. T. (2008). Integrating evidence from neuroimaging and neuropsychological studies of obsessive-compulsive disorder: The orbitofronto-striatal model revisited. *Neuroscience & Biobehavioral Reviews*, 32(3), 525–549. https://doi.org/10.1016/j.neubiorev.2007.09.005

Mercadante, A. A., & Tadi, P. (2022). Neuroanatomy, gray matter. In *StatPearls*. StatPearls Publishing. http://www.ncbi.nlm.nih.gov/books/NBK553239/

Meredith, L. R., Burnette, E. M., Grodin, E. N., Irwin, M. R., & Ray, L. A. (2021). Immune treatments for alcohol use disorder: A translational framework. *Brain, Behavior, and Immunity*, 97, 349–364. https://doi.org/10.1016/j.bbi.2021.07.023

Merenda, P. F. (1987). Toward a four-factor theory of temperament and/or personality. *Journal of Personality Assessment*, 51(3), 367–374. https://doi.org/10.1207/s15327752jpa5103_4

Merriam-Webster Dictionary. (n.d.). *Nomenclature*. https://www.merriam-webster.com/dictionary/nomenclature

Merz, J., Schwarzer, G., & Gerger, H. (2019). Comparative efficacy and acceptability of pharmacological, psychotherapeutic, and combination treatments in adults with posttraumatic stress disorder: A network meta-analysis. *JAMA Psychiatry*, 76(9), 904. https://doi.org/10.1001/jamapsychiatry.2019.0951

Mesholam-Gately, R. I., Varca, N., Spitzer, C., Parrish, E. M., Hogan, V., Behnke, S. H., Larson, L., Rosa-Baez, C., Schwirian, N., Stromeyer, C., Williams, M. J., Saks, E. R., & Keshavan, M. S. (2021). Are we ready for a name change for schizophrenia? A survey of multiple stakeholders. *Schizophrenia Research*, 238, 152–160. https://doi.org/10.1016/j.schres.2021.08.034

Messer, S. B. (2001). Introduction to the special issue on assimilative integration. *Journal of Psychotherapy Integration*, 11(1), 1–4. doi:10.1023/A:1026619423048

Meta. (2022). *Suicide prevention*. Safety Center, Facebook. https://www.facebook.com/safetyv2

Metz, M. E., Epstein, N. B., & McCarthy, B. (2017). *Cognitive-behavioral therapy for sexual dysfunction*. Taylor & Francis/Routledge. https://www.taylorfrancis.com/books/mono/10.4324/9780203863459/cognitive-behavioral-therapy-sexual-dysfunction-michael-metz-norman-epstein-barry-mccarthy

Metzak, P. D., Devoe, D. J., Iwaschuk, A., Braun, A., & Addington, J. (2020). Brain changes associated with negative symptoms in clinical high risk for psychosis: A systematic review. *Neuroscience & Biobehavioral Reviews*, 118, 367–383. https://doi.org/10.1016/j.neubiorev.2020.07.041

Mewton, L., & Andrews, G. (2016). Cognitive behavioral therapy for suicidal behaviors: Improving patient outcomes. *Psychology Research and Behavior Management*, 21. https://doi.org/10.2147/PRBM.S84589

Meyer, E. C., Zimering, R. T., Knight, J., Morissette, S. B., Kamholz, B. W., Coe, E., Carpenter, T. P., Keane, T. M., Kimbrel, N. A., & Gulliver, S. B. (2020). Negative emotionality interacts with trauma exposure to prospectively predict posttraumatic stress disorder symptoms during firefighters' first 3 years of service. *Journal of Traumatic Stress*. https://doi.org/10.1002/jts.22632

Meyer, G. J., & Eblin, J. J. (2012). An overview of the Rorschach Performance Assessment System (R-PAS). *Psychological Injury and Law*, 5(2), 107–121. https://doi.org/10.1007/s12207-012-9130-y

Meyer, G., Mayer, M., Mondorf, A., Flügel, A. K., Herrmann, E., & Bojunga, J. (2020). Safety and rapid efficacy of guideline-based gender-affirming hormone therapy: An analysis of 388 individuals diagnosed with gender dysphoria. *European Journal of Endocrinology*, 182(2), 149–156. https://doi.org/10.1530/EJE-19-0463

Meyer, U. (2013). Developmental neuroinflammation and schizophrenia. *Progress in Neuro-Psychopharmacology & Biological Psychiatry*, 42, 20–34. https://doi.org/10.1016/j.pnpbp.2011.11.003

Miao, S., Han, J., Gu, Y., Wang, X., Song, W., Li, D., Liu, Z., Yang, J., & Li, X. (2017). Reduced prefrontal cortex activation in children with attention-deficit/hyperactivity disorder during go/no-go task: A functional near-infrared spectroscopy study. *Frontiers in Neuroscience*, 11, Article 367. https://doi.org/10.3389/fnins.2017.00367

Michaels, J. J. (1939). Enuresis—A method for its study and treatment: O. H. Mowrer and Willie Mae Mowrer: A critique. *American Journal of Orthopsychiatry*, 9(3), 629–634. https://doi.org/10.1111/j.1939-0025.1939.tb05632.x

Michelini, G., Palumbo, I. M., DeYoung, C. G., Latzman, R. D., & Kotov, R. (2021). Linking RDoC and HiTOP: A new interface for advancing psychiatric nosology and neuroscience. *Clinical Psychology Review*, 86. https://doi.org/10.1016/j.cpr.2021.102025

Michopoulos, V., & Jovanovic, T. (2015). Chronic inflammation: A new therapeutic target for post-traumatic stress disorder? *The Lancet Psychiatry*, 2(11), 954–955. https://doi.org/10.1016/S2215-0366(15)00355-7

Mignot, E. J. M. (2012). A practical guide to the therapy of narcolepsy and hypersomnia syndromes. *Neurotherapeutics*, 9(4), 739–752. https://doi.org/10.1007/s13311-012-0150-9

Mignot, E., Zeitzer, J., Pizza, F., & Plazzi, G. (2021). Sleep problems in narcolepsy and the role of hypocretin/orexin deficiency. *Frontiers of Neurology and Neuroscience*, 45, 103–116. https://doi.org/10.1159/000514959

Mihura, J. L., & Meyer, G. J. (2018). *Using the Rorschach Performance Assessment System® (R-PAS®)*. Guilford Press.

Mikellides, G., Stefani, A., & Tantele, M. (2019). Community treatment orders: International perspective. *BJPsych International*, 16(4), 83–86. https://doi.org/10.1192/bji.2019.4

Mikhailova, O. (2005). Suicide in psychoanalysis. *Psychoanalytic Social Work*, 12(2), 19–45. https://doi.org/10.1300/J032v12n02_02

Miklowitz, D. J., Efthimiou, O., Furukawa, T. A., Scott, J., McLaren, R., Geddes, J. R., & Cipriani, A. (2021). Adjunctive psychotherapy for bipolar disorder: A systematic review and component network meta-analysis. *JAMA Psychiatry*, 78(2), 141–150. https://doi.org/10.1001/jamapsychiatry.2020.2993

Miklowitz, D. J., Schneck, C. D., George, E. L., Taylor, D. O., Sugar, C. A., Birmaher, B., Kowatch, R. A., DelBello, M. P., & Axelson, D. A. (2014). Pharmacotherapy and family-focused treatment for adolescents with bipolar I and II disorders: A 2-year randomized trial. *The American Journal of Psychiatry*, 171(6), 658–667. https://doi.org/10.1176/appi.ajp.2014.13081130

Milano, W., & Capasso, A. (2019). Psychopharmacological options in the multidisciplinary and multidimensional treatment of eating disorders. *The Open Neurology Journal*, 13(1). https://doi.org/10.2174/1874205X01913010022

Miller, B. (2022, May 23). The Cerebral scandal brings ADHD overprescription into the spotlight. *Lown Institute*. https://lowninstitute.org/the-cerebral-scandal-brings-adhd-overprescription-into-the-spotlight/

Miller, B. J., Buckley, P., Seabolt, W., Mellor, A., & Kirkpatrick, B. (2011). Meta-analysis of cytokine alterations in schizophrenia: Clinical status and antipsychotic effects. *Biological Psychiatry*, 70(7), 663–671. https://doi.org/10.1016/j.biopsych.2011.04.013

Miller, B. J., Culpepper, N., Rapaport, M. H., & Buckley, P. (2013). Prenatal inflammation and neurodevelopment in schizophrenia: A review of human studies. *Progress in Neuro-Psychopharmacology & Biological Psychiatry*, 42, 92–100. https://doi.org/10.1016/j.pnpbp.2012.03.010

Miller, B. J., Gassama, B., Sebastian, D., Buckley, P., & Mellor, A. (2013). Meta-analysis of lymphocytes in schizophrenia: Clinical status and antipsychotic effects. *Biological Psychiatry*, 73(10), 993–999. https://doi.org/10.1016/j.biopsych.2012.09.007

Miller, D., & Hanson, A. (2016). *Committed: The battle over involuntary psychiatric care*. Johns Hopkins University Press.

Miller, E. W., Shoup, D. S., & Recktenwald, E. W. (2019). Real-world and clinical trial efficacy of selective serotonin-reuptake inhibitors in the treatment of obsessive-compulsive disorder measured by survey and meta-analysis. *Journal of Obsessive-Compulsive and Related Disorders*, 23, 100456. https://doi.org/10.1016/j.jocrd.2019.100456

Miller, F. G., & Rosenstein, D. L. (2006). The nature and power of the placebo effect. *Journal of Clinical Epidemiology*, 59(4), 331–335. https://doi.org/10.1016/j.jclinepi.2005.12.001

Miller, J. J. (2022). Hope for the New Year. *Psychiatric Times*, 39(1). https://www.psychiatrictimes.com/view/hope-for-the-new-year

Miller, J. S. (2004). The Child Abuse Potential (CAP) Inventory. In M. J. Hilsenroth & D. L. Segal (Eds.), *Comprehensive handbook of psychological assessment: Vol. 2. Personality assessment* (pp. 237–246). John Wiley.

Miller, M. L., & Skerven, K. (2017). Family skills: A naturalistic pilot study of a family-oriented dialectical behavior therapy program. *Couple and Family Psychology: Research and Practice*, 6(2), 79–93. https://doi.org/10.1037/cfp0000076

Miller, M. W. (2003). Personality and the etiology and expression of PTSD: A three-factor model perspective. *Clinical Psychology: Science and Practice*, 10(4), 373–393. https://doi.org/10.1093/clipsy/bpg040

Miller, M. W., Wolf, E. J., & Keane, T. M. (2014). Posttraumatic stress disorder in DSM-5: New criteria and controversies. *Clinical Psychology: Science and Practice*, 21(3), 208–220. https://doi.org/10.1111/cpsp.12070

Miller, M. W., Wolf, E. J., Reardon, A., Greene, A., Ofrat, S., & McInerney, S. (2012). Personality and the latent structure of PTSD comorbidity. *Journal of Anxiety Disorders*, 26(5), 599–607. https://doi.org/10.1016/j.janxdis.2012.02.016

Miller, R. B. (2015). *Not so abnormal psychology*. American Psychological Association.

Miller, W. R., & Rollnick, S. (2002). *Motivational interviewing: Preparing people for change*. The Guilford Press.

Miller, W. R., & Wilbourne, P. L. (2002). Mesa Grande: A methodological analysis of clinical trials of treatment for alcohol use disorders. *Addiction*, 97(3), 265–277. https://doi.org/10.1046/j.1360-0443.2002.00019.x

Millichap, J. (2014). PUFA supplement in ADHD: Meta analysis. *Pediatric Neurology Briefs*, 28(4), Article 4. https://doi.org/10.15844/pedneurbriefs-28-4-9

Milling, L. S., & Breen, A. (2003). Mediation and moderation of hypnotic and cognitive-behavioural pain reduction. *Contemporary Hypnosis*, 20(2), 81–97. https://doi.org/10.1002/ch.268

Millon, T. (2004). *Masters of the mind: Exploring the story of mental illness from ancient times to the new millennium*. John Wiley.

MindFreedom International. (n.d.). About MFI. *Mind-Freedom International* (*MFI*). Retrieved November 9, 2022, from https://mindfreedom.org/about-mfi

Mineka, S., & Öhman, A. (2002). Phobias and preparedness: The selective, automatic, and encapsulated nature of fear. *Biological Psychiatry*, 52(10), 927–937. https://doi.org/10.1016/S0006-3223(02)01669-4

Miner, M. H., & Munns, R. (2021). Psychological treatments for paraphilias and compulsive sexual behavior. In L. A. Craig & R. M. Bartels (Eds.), *Sexual deviance: Understanding and managing deviant sexual interests and paraphilic disorders* (pp. 253–267). John Wiley & Sons. https://doi.org/10.1002/9781119771401.ch16

Miniati, M., Callari, A., Maglio, A., & Calugi, S. (2018). Interpersonal psychotherapy for eating disorders: Current perspectives. *Psychology Research and Behavior Management*, 11, 353–369. https://doi.org/10.2147/PRBM.S120584

Minihan, E., Gavin, B., Kelly, B. D., & McNicholas, F. (2020). COVID-19, mental health and psychological first aid. *Irish Journal of Psychological Medicine*, 37(4), 259–263. https://doi.org/10.1017/ipm.2020.41

Mintzes, B., Tiefer, L., & Cosgrove, L. (2021). Bremelanotide and flibanserin for low sexual desire in women: The fallacy of regulatory precedent. *Drug and Therapeutics Bulletin*, 59(12), 185–188. https://doi.org/10.1136/dtb.2021.000020

Minuchin, S. (1974). *Families and family therapy*. Harvard University Press.

Minuchin, S., Baker, L., Rosman, B. L., Liebman, R., Milman, L., & Todd, T. C. (1975). A conceptual model of psychosomatic illness in children: Family organization and family therapy. *Archives of General Psychiatry*, 32(8), 1031–1038. https://doi.org/10.1001/archpsyc.1975.01760260095008

Minuchin, S., Rosman, B. L., & Baker, L. (1978). *Psychosomatic families: Anorexia nervosa in context*. Harvard University Press.

Miranda-Mendizabal, A., Castellví, P., Parés-Badell, O., Alayo, I., Almenara, J., Alonso, I., Blasco, M. J., Cebrià, A., Gabilondo, A., Gili, M., Lagares, C., Piqueras, J. A., Rodríguez-Jiménez, T., Rodríguez-Marín, J., Roca, M., Soto-Sanz, V., Vilagut, G., & Alonso, J. (2019). Gender differences in suicidal behavior in adolescents and young adults: Systematic review and meta-analysis of longitudinal studies. *International Journal of Public Health*, 64(2), 265–283. https://doi.org/10.1007/s00038-018-1196-1

Miranda-Olivos, R., Steward, T., Martínez-Zalacaín, I., Mestre-Bach, G., Juaneda-Seguí, A., Jiménez-Murcia, S., Fernández-Formoso, J. A., Vilarrasa, N., Heras, M. V. de las, Custal, N., Virgili, N., Lopez-Urdiales, R., Menchón, J. M., Granero, R., Soriano-Mas, C., & Fernandez-Aranda, F. (2021). The neural correlates of delay discounting in obesity and binge eating disorder. *Journal of Behavioral Addictions*, 10(3), 498–507. https://doi.org/10.1556/2006.2021.00023

Mirza, S., Docherty, A. R., Bakian, A., Coon, H., Soares, J. C., Walss-Bass, C., & Fries, G. R. (2022). Genetics and epigenetics of self-injurious thoughts and behaviors: Systematic review of the suicide literature and methodological considerations. *American Journal of Medical Genetics. Part B, Neuropsychiatric Genetics*, 189(7–8), 221–246. https://doi.org/10.1002/ajmg.b.32917

Mischel, W. (1973). Toward a cognitive social learning reconceptualization of personality. *Psychological Review*, 80(4), 252–283. https://doi.org/10.1037/h0035002

Mischel, W. (2009). From *Personality and Assessment* (1968) to personality science, 2009. *Journal of Research in Personality*, 43(2), 282–290. https://doi.org/10.1016/j.jrp.2008.12.037

Mischel, W., & Shoda, Y. (1995). A cognitive-affective system theory of personality: Reconceptualizing situations, dispositions, dynamics, and invariance in personality structure. *Psychological Review*, 102(2), 246–268. https://doi.org/10.1037/0033-295X.102.2.246

Mischoulon, D. (2018). Popular herbal and natural remedies used in psychiatry. *FOCUS*, 16(1), 2–11. https://doi.org/10.1176/appi.focus.20170041

Mishne, J. M. (1993). Primary nocturnal enuresis: A psychodynamic clinical perspective. *Child & Adolescent Social Work Journal*, 10(6), 469–495. https://doi.org/10.1007/BF00757431

Mishori, R., & McHale, C. (2014). Pica: An age-old eating disorder that's often missed. *The Journal of Family Practice*, 63(7), E1–E4.

Misiak, B., Wójta-Kempa, M., Samochowiec, J., Schiweck, C., Aichholzer, M., Reif, A., Samochowiec, A., & Stańczykiewicz, B. (2022). Peripheral blood inflammatory markers in patients with attention deficit/hyperactivity disorder (ADHD): A systematic review and meta-analysis. *Progress in Neuro-Psychopharmacology and Biological Psychiatry*, 118, 110581. https://doi.org/10.1016/j.pnpbp.2022.110581

Missori, P., Currà, A., Paris, H. S., Peschillo, S., Fattapposta, F., Paolini, S., & Domenicucci, M. (2015). Reconstruction of skull defects in the Middle Ages and Renaissance. *The Neuroscientist*, 21(3), 322–328. https://doi.org/10.1177/1073858414559252

Mitchell, A. M., Sakraida, T. J., & Kameg, K. (2003). Critical incident stress debriefing: Implications for best practice. *Disaster Management & Response*, 1(2), 46–51. https://doi.org/10.1016/s1540-2487(03)00008-7

Mitchell, D. C., Knight, C. A., Hockenberry, J., Teplansky, R., & Hartman, T. J. (2014). Beverage caffeine intakes in the U.S. *Food and Chemical Toxicology*, 63, 136–142. https://doi.org/10.1016/j.fct.2013.10.042

Mitchell, G. (2015). *Bertalanffy's general systems theory*. https://trans4mind.com/mind-development/systems.html

Mitchell, J. E., Agras, S., & Wonderlich, S. (2007). Treatment of bulimia nervosa: Where are we and where are we going? *International Journal of Eating Disorders*, 40(2), 95–101. https://doi.org/10.1002/eat.20343

Mitchell, J. E., Roerig, J., & Steffen, K. (2013). Biological therapies for eating disorders. *International Journal of Eating Disorders*, 46(5), 470–477. https://doi.org/10.1002/eat.22104

Mitchell, J. M. (2022, February). A psychedelic may soon go to the FDA for approval to treat trauma. *Scientific American*, 326(2), 56–61. https://doi.org/10.1038/scientificamerican0222-56

Mitchell, J. T. (1983). When disaster strikes … the critical incident stress debriefing process. *JEMS: A Journal of Emergency Medical Services*, 8(1), 36–39.

Mitchell, J. T., Benson, J. W., Knouse, L. E., Kimbrel, N. A., & Anastopoulos, A. D. (2013). Are negative automatic thoughts associated with ADHD in adulthood? *Cognitive Therapy and Research*, 37(4), 851–859. https://doi.org/10.1007/s10608-013-9525-4

Mitchell, M. D., Gehrman, P., Perlis, M., & Umscheid, C. A. (2012). Comparative effectiveness of cognitive behavioral therapy for insomnia: A systematic review. *BMC Family Practice*, 13, 40–40. https://doi.org/10.1186/1471-2296-13-40

Mitra, P., & Jain, A. (2021). Dissociative identity disorder. In *StatPearls [Internet]*. StatPearls Publishing. https://www.ncbi.nlm.nih.gov/books/NBK568768/

Mittal, D., Drummond, K. L., Blevins, D., Curran, G., Corrigan, P., & Sullivan, G. (2013). Stigma associated with PTSD: Perceptions of treatment seeking combat veterans. *Psychiatric Rehabilitation Journal*, 36(2), 86–92. https://doi.org/10.1037/h0094976

Mitter, N., Ali, A., & Scior, K. (2019). Stigma experienced by families of individuals with intellectual disabilities and autism: A systematic review. *Research in Developmental Disabilities*, 89, 10–21. https://doi.org/10.1016/j.ridd.2019.03.001

Miura, T., Noma, H., Furukawa, T. A., Mitsuyasu, H., Tanaka, S., Stockton, S., Salanti, G., Motomura, K., Shimano-Katsuki, S., Leucht, S., Cipriani, A., Geddes, J. R., & Kanba, S. (2014). Comparative efficacy and tolerability of pharmacological treatments in the maintenance treatment of bipolar disorder: A systematic review and network meta-analysis. *The Lancet Psychiatry*, 1(5), 351–359. https://doi.org/10.1016/S2215-0366(14)70314-1

Miziou, S., Tsitsipa, E., Moysidou, S., Karavelas, V., Dimelis, D., Polyzoidou, V., & Fountoulakis, K. N. (2015). Psychosocial treatment and interventions for bipolar disorder: A systematic review. *Annals of General Psychiatry*, 14. https://doi.org/10.1186/s12991-015-0057-z

M'Naghten's Case, House of Lords United Kingdom (1843). https://law.justia.com/cases/foreign/united-kingdom/8-eng-rep-718.html

Moane, G. (2014). Liberation psychology, feminism, and social justice psychology. In C. V. Johnson, H. L. Friedman, J. Diaz, Z. Franco, & B. K. Nastasi (Eds.), *The Praeger handbook of social justice and psychology: Vol. 1. Fundamental issues and special populations* (pp. 115–132). Praeger/ABC-CLIO.

Moberg, L. T., Solvang, B., Sæle, R. G., & Myrvang, A. D. (2021). Effects of cognitive-behavioral and psychodynamic-interpersonal treatments for eating disorders: A meta-analytic inquiry into the role of patient characteristics and change in eating disorder-specific and general psychopathology in remission. *Journal of Eating Disorders*, 9(1), 74. https://doi.org/10.1186/s40337-021-00430-8

Modabbernia, A., Velthorst, E., & Reichenberg, A. (2017). Environmental risk factors for autism: An evidence-based review of systematic reviews and meta-analyses. *Molecular Autism*, 8, Article 13. https://doi.org/10.1186/s13229-017-0121-4

Moerkerke, M., Peeters, M., de Vries, L., Daniels, N., Steyaert, J., Alaerts, K., & Boets, B. (2021). Endogenous oxytocin levels in autism—A meta-analysis. *Brain Sciences*, 11(11), Article 11. https://doi.org/10.3390/brainsci11111545

Moghadam, S., Kazemi, R., Taklavi, S., & Naeim, M. (2020). Comparing the effectiveness of eye movement desensitization reprocessing and cognitive behavioral therapy in reducing post traumatic stress disorder. *Health Psychology Report*, 8(1), 31–37. https://doi.org/10.5114/hpr.2019.92305

Mohammadi, M.-R., Salmanian, M., & Keshavarzi, Z. (2021). The global prevalence of conduct disorder: A systematic review and meta-analysis. *Iranian Journal of Psychiatry*, 16(2), 205–225. https://doi.org/10.18502/ijps.v16i2.5822

Mohammed, S. A., Rajashekar, S., Giri Ravindran, S., Kakarla, M., Ausaja Gambo, M., Yousri Salama, M., Haidar Ismail, N., Tavalla, P., Uppal, P., & Hamid, P. (2022). Does vaccination increase the risk of autism spectrum disorder? *Cureus*. https://doi.org/10.7759/cureus.27921

Möhler, H. (2013). Differential roles of GABA receptors in anxiety. In D. S. Charney, J. D. Buxbaum, P. Sklar, & E. J. Nestler (Eds.), *Neurobiology of mental illness* (4th ed., pp. 567–579). Oxford University Press.

Mokros, A., Wessels, J., Hofmann, M., & Nitschke, J. (2019). Coercive sexual sadism: A systematic qualitative review. *Current Psychiatry Reports*, 21(12), 135. https://doi.org/10.1007/s11920-019-1118-9

Mol, M. O., van der Lee, S. J., Hulsman, M., Pijnenburg, Y. A. L., Scheltens, P., Seelaar, H., van Swieten, J. C., Kaat, L. D., Holstege, H., van Rooij, J. G. J., & Netherlands Brain Bank. (2022). Mapping the genetic landscape of early-onset Alzheimer's disease in a cohort of 36 families. *Alzheimer's Research & Therapy*, 14(1), 77. https://doi.org/10.1186/s13195-022-01018-3

Moleiro, C., & Pinto, N. (2015). Sexual orientation and gender identity: Review of concepts, controversies and their relation to psychopathology classification systems. *Frontiers in Psychology*, 6, Article 1511. https://doi.org/10.3389/fpsyg.2015.01511

Moline, R., Hou, S., Chevrier, J., & Thomassin, K. (2021). A systematic review of the effectiveness of behavioural treatments for pica in youths. *Clinical Psychology & Psychotherapy*, 28(1), 39–55. https://doi.org/10.1002/cpp.2491

Moll, K., Kunze, S., Neuhoff, N., Bruder, J., & Schulte-Körne, G. (2014). Specific learning disorder: Prevalence and gender differences. *PLoS ONE*, 9(7). https://doi.org/10.1371/journal.pone.0103537

Moncrieff, J. (2009). A critique of the dopamine hypothesis of schizophrenia and psychosis. *Harvard Review of Psychiatry*, 17(3), 214–225. https://doi.org/10.1080/10673220902979896

Moncrieff, J., Cooper, R. E., Stockmann, T., Amendola, S., Hengartner, M. P., & Horowitz, M. A. (2022). The serotonin theory of depression: A systematic umbrella review of the evidence. *Molecular Psychiatry*. https://doi.org/10.1038/s41380-022-01661-0

Moncrieff, J., & Leo, J. (2010). A systematic review of the effects of antipsychotic drugs on brain volume. *Psychological Medicine*, 40(9), 1409–1422. https://doi.org/10.1017/S0033291709992297

Moncrieff-Boyd, J. (2016). Anorexia nervosa (apepsia hysterica, anorexia hysterica), Sir William Gull, 1873. *Advances in Eating Disorders: Theory, Research and Practice*, 4(1), 112–117. https://doi.org/10.1080/21662630.2015.1079694

Mondelli, V., & Howes, O. (2014). Inflammation: Its role in schizophrenia and the potential anti-inflammatory effects of antipsychotics. *Psychopharmacology*, 231(2), 317–318. https://doi.org/10.1007/s00213-013-3383-3

Mongan, D., Ramesar, M., Föcking, M., Cannon, M., & Cotter, D. (2020). Role of inflammation in the pathogenesis of schizophrenia: A review of the evidence, proposed mechanisms and implications for treatment. *Early Intervention in Psychiatry*, 14(4), 385–397. https://doi.org/10.1111/eip.12859

Mongia, M., Gupta, A. K., Vijay, A., & Sadhu, R. (2019). Management of stuttering using cognitive behavior therapy and mindfulness meditation. *Industrial Psychiatry Journal*, 28(1), 4–12. https://doi.org/10.4103/ipj.ipj_18_19

Monk, G., Winslade, J., Crocket, K., & Epston, D. (1997). *Narrative therapy in practice: The archaeology of hope*. Jossey-Bass.

Monkmeyer, N., Thomas, S. V., Hilleman, D. E., & Malesker, M. A. (2022). Insomnia treatment update with a focus on orexin receptor antagonists. *U.S. Pharmacist*, 47(5), 43–48.

Monson, C. M., Fitzpatrick, S., Wagner, A. C., Valela, R., Whitfield, K. M., Varma, S., Landy, M. S. H., Di Bartolomeo, A., Crenshaw, A. O., Fulham, L., Morland, L., Knopp, K., Proctor, D. W., Toller, A., Webster, K., & Doss, B. D. (2021). The development of Couple HOPES: A guided online intervention for PTSD and relationship satisfaction enhancement. *European Journal of Psychotraumatology*, 12(1). https://doi.org/10.1080/20008198.2021.1917879

Monson, C. M., & Fredman, S. J. (2019). *Cognitive-behavioral conjoint therapy for PTSD: Harnessing the healing power of relationships*. Guilford Press.

Monson, C. M., Wagner, A. C., Crenshaw, A. O., Whitfield, K. M., Newnham, C. M., Valela, R., Varma, S., Di Bartolomeo, A. A., Fulham, L., Collins, A., Donkin, V., Mensah, D. H., Landy, M. S. H., Samonas, C., Morland, L., Doss, B. D., & Fitzpatrick, S. (2022). An uncontrolled trial of couple HOPES: A guided online couple intervention for PTSD and relationship enhancement. *Journal of Family Psychology*. https://doi.org/10.1037/fam0000976

Monson, C. M., Wagner, A. C., Mithoefer, A. T., Liebman, R. E., Feduccia, A. A., Jerome, L., Yazar-Klosinski, B., Emerson, A., Doblin, R., & Mithoefer, M. C. (2020). MDMA-facilitated cognitive-behavioural conjoint therapy for posttraumatic stress disorder: An uncontrolled trial. *European Journal of Psychotraumatology*, 11(1). https://doi.org/10.1080/20008198.2020.1840123

Monteiro, M. J. (2021). Narrative therapy and the autism spectrum: A model for clinicians. *Human Systems*, 1(2–3), 150–164. https://doi.org/10.1177/26344041211049763

Monti, F., Tonetti, L., & Bitti, P. E. R. (2014). Comparison of cognitive-behavioural therapy and psychodynamic therapy in the treatment of anxiety among university students: An effectiveness study. *British Journal of Guidance & Counselling*, 42(3), 233–244. https://doi.org/10.1080/03069885.2013.878018

Monti, P. M., Gulliver, S. B., & Myers, M. G. (1994). Social skills training for alcoholics: Assessment and treatment. *Alcohol and Alcoholism*, 29(6), 627–637.

Monti, P. M., & O'Leary, T. A. (1999). Coping and social skills training for alcohol and cocaine dependence. *Psychiatric Clinics of North America*, 22(2), 447–470. https://doi.org/10.1016/S0193-953X(05)70086-1

Mooney, A., Roberts, A., Bayston, A., & Bowden-Jones, H. (2019). The piloting of a brief relational psychodynamic protocol (psychodynamic addiction model) for problem gambling and other compulsive addictions: A retrospective analysis. *Counselling and Psychotherapy Research*, 19(4), 484–496. https://doi.org/10.1002/capr.12251

Moore, B. G., & Weisman, R. L. (2016). Involuntary outpatient treatment. *Journal of the American Academy of Psychiatry and the Law Online*, 44(2), 272–274.

Moore, D. (2014). Reflections on the enduring value of critical scholarship. *Drug and Alcohol Review*, 33(6), 577–580. https://doi.org/10.1111/dar.12190

Moore, R. L. (2019). *What is adult day care?* National Caregivers Library. https://www.caregiverslibrary.org/Caregivers-Resources/GRP-Caring-For-Yourself/HSGRP-Support-Systems/What-Is-Adult-Day-Care-Article

Moore, S., Paalanen, L., Melymuk, L., Katsonouri, A., Kolossa-Gehring, M., & Tolonen, H. (2022). The association between ADHD and environmental chemicals—A scoping review. *International Journal of Environmental Research and Public Health*, 19(5), 2849. https://doi.org/10.3390/ijerph19052849

Moore, T. O. (2005). A Fanonian perspective on double consciousness. *Journal of Black Studies*, 35(6), 751–762. https://doi.org/10.1177/0021934704263839

Moorey, S. (2017). The cognitive therapy of depression rests on substantial theoretical, empirical and clinical foundations: A reply to Dr Gipps. *BJPsych Bulletin*, 41(5), 272–275. https://doi.org/10.1192/pb.bp.116.055616

Moradi, B., & Huang, Y.-P. (2008). Objectification theory and psychology of women: A decade of advances and future directions. *Psychology of Women Quarterly*, 32(4), 377–398. https://doi.org/10.1111/j.1471-6402.2008.00452.x

Moradi, B., & Tebbe, E. (2022). A test of objectification theory with sexual minority women. *Psychology of Women Quarterly*, 46(2), 226–240. https://doi.org/10.1177/03616843211052525

Moral treatment in America's lunatic asylums. (1976). *Hospital & Community Psychiatry*, 27(7), 468–470.

Morales, I., & Berridge, K. C. (2020). "Liking" and "wanting" in eating and food reward: Brain mechanisms and clinical implications. *Physiology & Behavior*, 227, 113152. https://doi.org/10.1016/j.physbeh.2020.113152

Moran, M. (2012, March 2). DSM-5 emphasizes diagnostic reliability. *Psychiatric News*. https://doi.org/10.1176/pn.47.5.psychnews_47_5_1-a

Moran, M. (2016). APA responds to Indonesian psychiatrists for stance against LGBT individuals. *Psychiatrics News*. https://doi.org/10.1176/appi.pn.2016.4a10

Moreno, J. L., Kurita, M., Holloway, T., López, J., Cadagan, R., Martínez-Sobrido, L., García-Sastre, A., & González-Maeso, J. (2011). Maternal influenza viral infection causes schizophrenia-like alterations of 5-HT$_2$A and mGlu$_2$ receptors in the adult offspring. *The Journal of Neuroscience*, 31(5), 1863–1872. https://doi.org/10.1523/JNEUROSCI.4230-10.2011

Moreno-Agostino, D., Wu, Y.-T., Daskalopoulou, C., Hasan, M. T., Huisman, M., & Prina, M. (2021). Global trends in the prevalence and incidence of depression: A systematic review and meta-analysis. *Journal of Affective Disorders*, 281, 235–243. https://doi.org/10.1016/j.jad.2020.12.035

Moretti, R. J., & Rossini, E. D. (2004). The Thematic Apperception Test (TAT). In M. J. Hilsenroth & D. L. Segal (Eds.), *Comprehensive handbook of psychological assessment: Vol. 2. Personality assessment* (pp. 356–371). John Wiley.

Morey, L. C. (2019). Interdiagnostician reliability of the *DSM-5* Section II and Section III alternative model criteria for borderline personality disorder. *Journal of Personality Disorders*, 33(6), 721-S18. https://doi.org/10.1521/pedi_2019_33_362

Morey, R. A., Gold, A. L., LaBar, K. S., Beall, S. K., Brown, V. M., Haswell, C. C., Nasser, J. D., Wagner, H. R., & McCarthy, G. (2012). Amygdala volume changes in posttraumatic stress disorder in a large case-controlled veterans group. *JAMA Psychiatry*, 69(11), 1169–1178.

Morgan, J. D., Laungani, P., & Palmer, S. (2009). *Death and bereavement around the world: Vol. 5. Reflective essays*. Baywood Publishing.

Morgan, M. A., Kelber, M. S., Workman, D. E., Beech, E. H., Garvey Wilson, A. L., Edwards-Stewart, A., Belsher, B. E., Evatt, D. P., Otto, J., Skopp, N. A., Bush, N. E., & Campbell, M. (2021). Adjustment disorders: A research gaps analysis. *Psychological Services*. https://doi.org/10.1037/ser0000517

Morinaga, M., Rai, D., Hollander, A.-C., Petros, N., Dalman, C., & Magnusson, C. (2021). Migration or ethnic minority status and risk of autism spectrum disorders and intellectual disability: Systematic review. *European Journal of Public Health*, 31(2), 304–312. https://doi.org/10.1093/eurpub/ckaa108

Morishita, T., Fayad, S. M., Higuchi, M., Nestor, K. A., & Foote, K. D. (2014). Deep brain stimulation for treatment-resistant depression: Systematic review of clinical outcomes. *Neurotherapeutics*, 11(3), 475–484. https://doi.org/10.1007/s13311-014-0282-1

Morris, A. M., & Katzman, D. K. (2003). The impact of the media on eating disorders in children and adolescents. *Paediatrics & Child Health*, 8(5), 287–289.

Morris, N. P., McNiel, D. E., & Binder, R. L. (2021). Estimating annual numbers of competency to stand trial evaluations across the United States. *Journal of the American Academy of Psychiatry and the Law Online*. https://doi.org/10.29158/JAAPL.200129-20

Morris, S. E., & Heinssen, R. K. (2014). Informed consent in the psychosis prodrome: Ethical, procedural, and cultural considerations. *Philosophy, Ethics, and Humanities in Medicine*, 9(1), Article 19. https://doi.org/10.1186/1747-5341-9-19

Morris, S. E., Pacheco, J., & Sanislow, C. A. (2021). Applying Research Domain Criteria (RDoC) dimensions to psychosis. In C. A. Tamminga, E. I. Ivleva, U. Reininghaus, & J. van Os (Eds.), *Psychotic disorders: Comprehensive conceptualization and treatments* (pp. 29–37). Oxford University Press. https://doi.org/10.1093/med/9780190653279.003.0004

Morrison, A. P. (2001). Cognitive-behavioral therapy. In K. T. Mueser & D. V. Jeste (Eds.), *Clinical handbook of schizophrenia* (pp. 226–239). Guilford Press.

Morrison, A. P., Hutton, P., Wardle, M., Spencer, H., Barratt, S., Brabban, A., Callcott, P., Christodoulides, T., Dudley, R., French, P., Lumley, V., Tai, S. J., & Turkington, D. (2012). Cognitive therapy for people with a schizophrenia spectrum diagnosis not taking antipsychotic medication: An exploratory trial. *Psychological Medicine*, 42(5), 1049–1056. https://doi.org/10.1017/S0033291711001899

Morrison, A. P., Law, H., Carter, L., Sellers, R., Emsley, R., Pyle, M., French, P., Shiers, D., Yung, A. R., Murphy, E. K., Holden, N., Steele, A., Bowe, S. E., Palmier-Claus, J., Brooks, V., Byrne, R., Davies, L., & Haddad, P. M. (2018). Antipsychotic drugs versus cognitive behavioural therapy versus a combination of both in people with psychosis: A randomised controlled pilot and feasibility study. *The Lancet Psychiatry*, 5(5), 411–423. https://doi.org/10.1016/S2215-0366(18)30096-8

Morrison, A. P., Shryane, N., Fowler, D., Birchwood, M., Gumley, A. I., Taylor, H. E., French, P., Stewart, S. L. K., Jones, P. B., Lewis, S. W., & Bentall, R. P. (2015). Negative cognition, affect, metacognition and dimensions of paranoia in people at ultra-high risk of psychosis: A multi-level modelling analysis. *Psychological Medicine*, 45(12), 2675–2684. https://doi.org/10.1017/S0033291715000689

Morrison, A. P., Turkington, D., Pyle, M., Spencer, H., Brabban, A., Dunn, G., Christodoulides, T., Dudley, R., Chapman, N., Callcott, P., Grace, T., Lumley, V., Drage, L., Tully, S., Irving, K., Cummings, A., Byrne, R., Davies, L. M., & Hutton, P. (2014). Cognitive therapy for people with schizophrenia spectrum disorders not taking antipsychotic drugs: A single-blind randomised controlled trial. *The Lancet*, 383(9926), 1395–1403. https://doi.org/10.1016/S0140-6736(13)62246-1

Morrison, M. (2015). Growth hormone, enhancement and the pharmaceuticalisation of short stature. *Social Science & Medicine*, 131, 305–312. https://doi.org/10.1016/j.socscimed.2014.10.015

Morrow, S. L. (2005). Quality and trustworthiness in qualitative research in counseling psychology. *Journal of Counseling Psychology*, 52(2), 250–260. https://doi.org/10.1037/0022-0167.52.2.250

Morrow, S. L., & Beckstead, A. L. (2004). Conversion therapies for same-sex attracted clients in religious conflict: Context, predisposing factors, experiences, and implications for therapy. *The Counseling Psychologist*, 32, 641–650. https://doi.org/10.1177/0011000004268877

Morrow, S. L., Castañeda-Sound, C. L., & Abrams, E. M. (2012). Counseling psychology research methods: Qualitative approaches. In N. A. Fouad, J. A. Carter, & L. M. Subich (Eds.), *APA handbook of counseling psychology: Vol. 1. Theories, research, and methods* (pp. 93–117). American Psychological Association.

Morrow, S. L., Hawxhurst, D. M., Montes de Vegas, A. Y., Abousleman, T. M., & Castañeda, C. L. (2006). Toward a radical feminist multicultural therapy: Renewing a commitment to activism. In R. L. Toporek, L. H. Gerstein, N. Fouad, G. Roysircar, & T. Israel (Eds.), *Handbook for social justice in counseling psychology: Leadership, vision, and action* (pp. 231–247). SAGE.

Morsanyi, K., van Bers, B. M. C. W., McCormack, T., & McGourty, J. (2018). The prevalence of specific learning disorder in mathematics and comorbidity with other developmental disorders in primary school-age children. *British Journal of Psychology*, 109(4), 917–940. https://doi.org/10.1111/bjop.12322

Mortimer, A. M., Singh, P., Shepherd, C. J., & Puthiryackal, J. (2010). Clozapine for treatment-resistant schizophrenia: National Institute of Clinical Excellence (NICE) guidance in the real world. *Clinical Schizophrenia & Related Psychoses*, 4(1), 49–55. https://doi.org/10.3371/CSRP.4.1.4

Morton, R. (2011). *Phthisiologia, or, a treatise of consumptions* (Vol. 3). Text Creation Partnership. http://name.umdl.umich.edu/A51415.0001.001 (Original work published 1694)

Moser, C., & Kleinplatz, P. J. (2020). Conceptualization, history, and future of the paraphilias. *Annual Review of Clinical Psychology*, 16(1), 379–399. https://doi.org/10.1146/annurev-clinpsy-050718-095548

Mosher, L. (2015). Treating madness without hospitals: Soteria and its successors. In K. J. Schneider, J. F. Pierson, & J. F. T. Bugental (Eds.), *The handbook of humanistic psychology: Theory, research, and practice* (2nd ed., pp. 491–504). SAGE.

Mosher, L., Gosden, R., & Beder, S. (2013). Drug companies and "schizophrenia": Unbridled capitalism meets madness. In J. Read & J. Dillon (Eds.), *Models of madness: Psychological, social and biological approaches to psychosis* (2nd ed., pp. 125–139). Routledge.

Mosher, L. R. (1991). Soteria: A therapeutic community for psychotic persons. *International Journal of Therapeutic Communities*, 12(1), 53–67.

Mosher, L. R. (1999). Soteria and other alternatives to acute psychiatric hospitalization: A personal and professional review. *Journal of Nervous and Mental Disease*, 187(3), 142–149. https://doi.org/10.1097/00005053-199903000-00003

Mosher, L. R., Menn, A., & Matthews, S. M. (1975). Soteria: Evaluation of a home-based treatment for schizophrenia. *American Journal of Orthopsychiatry*, 45(3), 455–467. https://doi.org/10.1111/j.1939-0025.1975.tb02556.x

Mosher, L. R., Vallone, R., & Menn, A. (1995). The treatment of acute psychosis without neuroleptics: Six-week psychopathology outcome data from the Soteria project. *International Journal of Social Psychiatry*, 41(3), 157–173. https://doi.org/10.1177/002076409504100301

Mosley, P. E., Marsh, R., & Carter, A. (2015). Deep brain stimulation for depression: Scientific issues and future directions. *The Australian and New Zealand Journal of Psychiatry*.

Moss, D. (2015). The roots and genealogy of humanistic psychology. In K. J. Schneider, J. F. Pierson, & J. F. T. Bugental (Eds.), *The handbook of humanistic psychology: Theory, research, and practice* (2nd ed., pp. 3–18). SAGE Publications.

Motlagh, M. G., Fernandez, T. V., & Leckman, J. F. (2012). Genetics of Tourette syndrome and related disorders. In J. I. Nurnberger, Jr. & W. H. Berrettini (Eds.), *Principles of psychiatric genetics* (pp. 336–346). Cambridge University Press. https://doi.org/10.1017/CBO9781139025997.029

Motta, M., & Stecula, D. (2021). Quantifying the effect of Wakefield et al (1998) on skepticism about MMR vaccine safety in the US. *PLoS ONE*, 16(8). https://doi.org/10.1371/journal.pone.0256395

Moul, C., Dobson-Stone, C., Brennan, J., Hawes, D., & Dadds, M. (2013). An exploration of the serotonin system in antisocial boys with high levels of callous-unemotional traits. *PLoS ONE*, 8(2), e56619. https://doi.org/10.1371/journal.pone.0056619

Moul, C., Dobson-Stone, C., Brennan, J., Hawes, D. J., & Dadds, M. R. (2015). Serotonin 1B receptor gene (HTR1B) methylation as a risk factor for callous-unemotional traits in antisocial boys. *Plos One*, 10(5), e0126903–e0126903. https://doi.org/10.1371/journal.pone.0126903

Moursy, E. E. S., Kamel, N. F., & Kaseem, A. F. (2014). Combined laser acupuncture and desmopressin for treating resistant cases of monosymptomatic nocturnal enuresis: A randomized comparative study. *Scandinavian Journal of Urology*, 48(6), 559–564. https://doi.org/10.3109/21681805.2014.922609

Movement Advancement Project. (2022, July 13). *Conversion "therapy" laws*. https://www.lgbtmap.org/equality-maps/conversion_therapy

Mowrer, O. H. (1939). A stimulus-response analysis of anxiety and its role as a reinforcing agent. *Psychological Review*, 46(6), 553–565. https://doi.org/10.1037/h0054288

Mowrer, O. H. (1947). On the dual nature of learning—A re-interpretation of "conditioning" and "problem-solving." *Harvard Educational Review*, 17, 102–148.

Mowrer, O. H. (1956). Two-factor learning theory reconsidered, with special reference to secondary reinforcement and the concept of habit. *Psychological Review*, 63(2), 114–128. https://doi.org/10.1037/h0040613

Mowrer, O. H. (1960). *Learning theory and behavior*. Wiley.

Mowrer, O. H., & Mowrer, W. M. (1938). Enuresis—A method for its study and treatment. *American Journal of Orthopsychiatry*, 8(3), 436–459. https://doi.org/10.1111/j.1939-0025.1938.tb06395.x

Moynihan, J. A., & Santiago, F. M. (2007). Brain behavior and immunity: Twenty years of T cells. *Brain, Behavior, and Immunity*, 21(7), 872–880. https://doi.org/10.1016/j.bbi.2007.06.010

Mpofu, E., Athanasou, J. A., Rafe, C., & Belshaw, S. H. (2018). Cognitive-behavioral therapy efficacy for reducing recidivism rates of moderate- and high-risk sexual offenders: A scoping systematic literature review. *International Journal of Offender Therapy and Comparative Criminology*, 62(1), 170–186. https://doi.org/10.1177/0306624X16644501

Mpoulimari, I., & Zintzaras, E. (2022). Synthesis of genetic association studies on autism spectrum disorders using a genetic model-free approach. *Psychiatric Genetics*, 32(3), 91–104. https://doi.org/10.1097/YPG.0000000000000316

Mudathikundan, F., Chao, O., & Forrester, A. (2014). Mental health and fitness to plead proposals in England and Wales. *International Journal of Law and Psychiatry*, 37(2), 135–141. https://doi.org/10.1016/j.ijlp.2013.11.008

Mueller, A., Mitchell, J. E., Peterson, L. A., Faber, R. J., Steffen, K. J., Crosby, R. D., & Claes, L. (2011). Depression, materialism, and excessive Internet use in relation to compulsive buying. *Comprehensive Psychiatry*, 52(4), 420–424. https://doi.org/10.1016/j.comppsych.2010.09.001

Mueser, K. T., Gingerich, S., Addington, J., Brunette, M. F., Cather, C., Gottlieb, J. D., Lynde, D. W., & Penn, D. L. (2014). *The NAVIGATE team members' guide* (National Institute of Mental Health, Trans.).

Mueser, K. T., Meyer-Kalos, P. S., Glynn, S. M., Lynde, D. W., Robinson, D. G., Gingerich, S., Penn, D. L., Cather, C., Gottlieb, J. D., Marcy, P., Wiseman, J. L., Potretzke, S., Brunette, M. F., Schooler, N. R., Addington, J., Rosenheck, R. A., Estroff, S. E., & Kane, J. M. (2019). Implementation and fidelity assessment of the NAVIGATE treatment program for first episode psychosis in a multi-site study. *Schizophrenia Research*, 204, 271–281. https://doi.org/10.1016/j.schres.2018.08.015

Mueser, K. T., Penn, D. L., Addington, J., Brunette, M. F., Gingerich, S., Glynn, S. M., Lynde, D. W., Gottlieb, J. D., Meyer-Kalos, P., McGurk, S. R., Cather, C., Saade, S., Robinson, D. G., Schooler, N. R., Rosenheck, R. A., & Kane, J. M. (2015). The NAVIGATE program for first-episode psychosis: Rationale, overview, and description of psychosocial components. *Psychiatric Services*, 66(7), 680–690. https://doi.org/10.1176/appi.ps.201400413

Muesser, K. T. (1998). Cognitive behavioral treatment of schizophrenia. In V. E. Caballo (Ed.), *International handbook of cognitive and behavioural treatments for psychological disorders* (pp. 551–570). Pergamon.

Mugisha, J., Muyinda, H., Wandiembe, P., & Kinyanda, E. (2015). Prevalence and factors associated with posttraumatic stress disorder seven years after the conflict in three districts in northern Uganda (The Wayo-Nero Study). *BMC Psychiatry*, 15, 170. https://doi.org/10.1186/s12888-015-0551-5

Muhlheim, L. (2022, April 7). *Which level of eating disorder treatment is right for me?* Verywell Mind. https://www.verywellmind.com/levels-of-eating-disorder-treatment-4134267

Mulder, R. T. (2021). ICD-11 personality disorders: Utility and implications of the new model. *Frontiers in Psychiatry*, 12, Article 655548. https://doi.org/10.3389/fpsyt.2021.655548

Mulick, P. S., Landes, S. J., & Kanter, J. W. (2011). Contextual behavior therapies in the treatment of PTSD: A review. *International Journal of Behavioral Consultation and Therapy*, 7(1), 23–31. https://doi.org/10.1037/h0100923

Müller, C. P., & Homberg, J. R. (2015). The role of serotonin in drug use and addiction. *Behavioural Brain Research*, 277, 146–192. https://doi.org/10.1016/j.bbr.2014.04.007

Müller, F., Kraus, E., Holze, F., Becker, A., Ley, L., Schmid, Y., Vizeli, P., Liechti, M. E., & Borgwardt, S. (2022). Flashback phenomena after administration of LSD and psilocybin in controlled studies with healthy participants. *Psychopharmacology*, 239(6), 1933–1943. https://doi.org/10.1007/s00213-022-06066-z

Müller, T., Mannel, M., Murck, H., & Rahlfs, V. W. (2004). Treatment of somatoform disorders with St John's wort: A randomized, double-blind and placebo-controlled trial. *Psychosomatic Medicine*, 66(4), 538–547. https://doi.org/10.1097/01.psy.0000128900.13711.5b

Mullins, N., Bigdeli, T. B., Børglum, A. D., Coleman, J. R. I., Demontis, D., Mehta, D., Power, R. A., Ripke, S., Stahl, E. A., Starnawska, A., Anjorin, A., Corvin, A., Sanders, A. R., Forstner, A. J., Reif, A., Koller, A. C., Świątkowska, B., Baune, B. T., Müller-Myhsok, B., … Lewis, C. M. (2019). GWAS of suicide attempt in psychiatric disorders and association with major depression polygenic risk scores. *American Journal of Psychiatry*, 176(8), 651–660. https://doi.org/10.1176/appi.ajp.2019.18080957

Mundo, E., Zanoni, S., & Altamura, A. C. (2006). Genetic issues in obsessive-compulsive disorder and related disorders. *Psychiatric Annals*, 36(7), 495–512.

Muñiz-Velázquez, J. A., Gomez-Baya, D., & Lopez-Casquete, M. (2017). Implicit and explicit assessment of materialism: Associations with happiness and depression. *Personality and Individual Differences*, 116, 123–132. https://doi.org/10.1016/j.paid.2017.04.033

Munkholm, K., Paludan-Müller, A. S., & Boesen, K. (2019). Considering the methodological limitations in the evidence base of antidepressants for depression: A reanalysis of a network meta-analysis. *BMJ Open*, 9(6), e024886. https://doi.org/10.1136/bmjopen-2018-024886

Munn-Chernoff, M. A., & Baker, J. H. (2016). A primer on the genetics of comorbid eating disorders and substance use disorders. *European Eating Disorders Review*, 24(2), 91–100. doi:10.1002/erv.2424

Munn-Chernoff, M. A., Duncan, A. E., Grant, J. D., Wade, T. D., Agrawal, A., Bucholz, K. K., … Heath, A. C. (2013). A twin study of alcohol dependence, binge eating, and compensatory behaviors. *Journal of Studies on Alcohol and Drugs*, 74(5), 664–673.

Munn-Chernoff, M. A., McQueen, M. B., Stetler, G. L., Haberstick, B. C., Rhee, S. H., Sobik, L. E., … Stallings, M. C. (2012). Examining associations between disordered eating and serotonin transporter gene polymorphisms. *International Journal of Eating Disorders*, 45(4), 556–561. doi:10.1002/eat.22001

Münzel, T., Hahad, O., Sørensen, M., Lelieveld, J., Duerr, G. D., Nieuwenhuijsen, M., & Daiber, A. (2022). Environmental risk factors and cardiovascular diseases: A comprehensive expert review. *Cardiovascular Research*, 118(14), 2880–2902. https://doi.org/10.1093/cvr/cvab316

Muratore, A. F., & Attia, E. (2022). Psychopharmacologic management of eating disorders. *Current Psychiatry Reports*. https://doi.org/10.1007/s11920-022-01340-5

Muriello, D., Donahue, L., Ben-David, D., Ozertem, U., & Shilon, R. (2018, February 21). *Under the hood: Suicide prevention tools powered by AI*. Meta AI. https://ai.facebook.com/blog/under-the-hood-suicide-prevention-tools-powered-by-ai/

Murphy, D. (2019). *Person-centred experiential counselling for depression* (2019-61318-000; 2nd ed.). SAGE Publications.

Murphy, D., Hunt, E., Luzon, O., & Greenberg, N. (2014). Exploring positive pathways to care for members of the UK Armed Forces receiving treatment for PTSD: A qualitative study. *European Journal of Psychotraumatology*, 5. https://doi.org/10.3402/ejpt.v5.21759

Murphy, D., & Joseph, S. (2016). Person-centered therapy: Past, present, and future orientations. In D. J. Cain, K. Keenan, & S. Rubin (Eds.), *Humanistic psychotherapies: Handbook of research and practice* (2nd ed., pp. 185–218). American Psychological Association. https://doi.org/10.1037/14775-007

Murphy, D., & Woolfolk, R. L. (2000). The harmful dysfunction analysis of mental disorder. *Philosophy, Psychiatry, & Psychology*, 7(4), 241–252.

Murphy, J., & Zlomke, K. R. (2016). A behavioral parent-training intervention for a child with avoidant/restrictive food intake disorder. *Clinical Practice in Pediatric Psychology*, 4(1), 23–34. https://doi.org/10.1037/cpp0000128

Murphy, R., Straebler, S., Basden, S., Cooper, Z., & Fairburn, C. G. (2012). Interpersonal psychotherapy for eating disorders. *Clinical Psychology & Psychotherapy*, 19(2), 150–158. https://doi.org/10.1002/cpp.1780

Murphy, R., Straebler, S., Cooper, Z., & Fairburn, C. G. (2010). Cognitive behavioral therapy for eating disorders. *The Psychiatric Clinics of North America*, 33(3), 611–627. https://doi.org/10.1016/j.psc.2010.04.004

Murray, H. B., Juarascio, A. S., Lorenzo, C. D., Drossman, D. A., & Thomas, J. J. (2019). Diagnosis and treatment of rumination syndrome: A critical review. *The American Journal of Gastroenterology*, 114(4), 562–578. https://doi.org/10.14309/ajg.0000000000000060

Murray, R. M., & Lewis, S. W. (1987). Is schizophrenia a neurodevelopmental disorder? *British Medical Journal*, 295, 681–682.

Murray, S. L., & Holton, K. F. (2021). Post-traumatic stress disorder may set the neurobiological stage for eating disorders: A focus on glutamatergic dysfunction. *Appetite*, 167, 105599. https://doi.org/10.1016/j.appet.2021.105599

Musa, Z. A., Kim Lam, S., Binti Mamat @ Mukhtar, F., Kwong Yan, S., Tajudeen Olalekan, O., & Kim Geok, S. (2020). Effectiveness of mindfulness-based cognitive therapy on the management of depressive disorder: Systematic review. *International Journal of Africa Nursing Sciences*, 12, 100200. https://doi.org/10.1016/j.ijans.2020.100200

Musazzi, L., Treccani, G., & Popoli, M. (2012). Glutamate hypothesis of depression and its consequences for antidepressant treatments. *Expert Review of Neurotherapeutics*, 12(10), 1169–1172. https://doi.org/10.1586/ern.12.96

Musser, E. D., & Raiker, J. S. (2019). Attention-deficit/hyperactivity disorder: An integrated developmental psychopathology and Research Domain Criteria (RDoC) approach. *Comprehensive Psychiatry*, 90, 65–72. https://doi.org/10.1016/j.comppsych.2018.12.016

Myers, K., & Vander Stoep, A. (2017). i-therapy: Asynchronous telehealth expands access to mental health care and challenges tenets of the therapeutic process. *Journal of the American Academy of Child*

& *Adolescent Psychiatry, 56*(1), 5–7. https://doi.org/10.1016/j.jaac.2016.11.001

Myers, L. L., & Wiman, A. M. (2014). Binge eating disorder: A review of a new DSM diagnosis. *Research on Social Work Practice, 24*(1), 86–95. https://doi.org/10.1177/1049731513507755

Myrick, A. C., Webermann, A. R., Langeland, W., Putnam, F. W., & Brand, B. L. (2017). Treatment of dissociative disorders and reported changes in inpatient and outpatient cost estimates. *European Journal of Psychotraumatology, 8*(1). https://doi.org/10.1080/20008198.2017.1375829

Myrick, A. C., Webermann, A. R., Loewenstein, R. J., Lanius, R., Putnam, F. W., & Brand, B. L. (2017). Six-year follow-up of the treatment of patients with dissociative disorders study. *European Journal of Psychotraumatology, 8*(1). https://doi.org/10.1080/20008198.2017.1344080

Na, P. J., Tsai, J., Southwick, S. M., & Pietrzak, R. H. (2021). Factors associated with post-traumatic growth in response to the COVID-19 pandemic: Results from a national sample of U.S. military veterans. *Social Science & Medicine, 289*, 114409. https://doi.org/10.1016/j.socscimed.2021.114409

Nabar, K. K. (2009). *Individualistic ideology as contained in the "Diagnostic & Statistical Manual of Mental Disorders-Fourth Edition-Text Revision" personality disorders: A relational-cultural critique* [Doctoral dissertation]. The Chicago School of Professional Psychology.

Naderer, B., Peter, C., & Karsay, K. (2022). This picture does not portray reality: Developing and testing a disclaimer for digitally enhanced pictures on social media appropriate for Austrian tweens and teens. *Journal of Children and Media, 16*(2), 149–167. https://doi.org/10.1080/17482798.2021.1938619

Nadkarni, A., & Santhouse, A. (2012). *Diagnostic and statistical manual of mental disorders* (DSM): A culture bound syndrome? *Asian Journal of Psychiatry, 5*(1), 118–119. https://doi.org/10.1016/j.ajp.2012.01.002

Nadler, A., Camerer, C. F., Zava, D. T., Ortiz, T. L., Watson, N. V., Carré, J. M., & Nave, G. (2019). Does testosterone impair men's cognitive empathy? Evidence from two large-scale randomized controlled trials. *Proceedings of the Royal Society B: Biological Sciences, 286*(1910), 20191062. https://doi.org/10.1098/rspb.2019.1062

Naeem, F., Khoury, B., Munshi, T., Ayub, M., Lecomte, T., Kingdon, D., & Farooq, S. (2016). Brief cognitive behavioral therapy for psychosis (CBTp) for schizophrenia: Literature review and meta-analysis. *International Journal of Cognitive Therapy, 9*(1), 73–86. https://doi.org/10.1521/ijct_2016_09_04

Nagar, S., Mehta, S., Bhatara, V., & Aparasu, R. (2010). Health care consequences of black-box warnings for antidepressants in the United States and Canada. *Research in Social & Administrative Pharmacy, 6*(1), 78–84. https://doi.org/10.1016/j.sapharm.2009.02.005

Nagata, D. K., Kim, J. H. J., & Wu, K. (2019). The Japanese American wartime incarceration: Examining the scope of racial trauma. *American Psychologist, 74*(1), 36–48. https://doi.org/10.1037/amp0000303

Naguy, A., & AlAwadhi, D. (2018). Psychopharmacology of suicide. *Asian Journal of Psychiatry, 36*, 100–101. https://doi.org/10.1016/j.ajp.2018.07.007

Näher, A.-F., Rummel-Kluge, C., & Hegerl, U. (2020). Associations of suicide rates with socioeconomic status and social isolation: Findings from longitudinal register and census data. *Frontiers in Psychiatry, 10*, Article 898. https://doi.org/10.3389/fpsyt.2019.00898.

Nair, L. D., Sagayaraj, B., Rajan, V. T. T., & Kumar, R. (2015). Incontinence in intellectual disability: An under recognized cause. *Journal of Clinical and Diagnostic Research: JCDR, 9*(9), SD01–SD02. https://doi.org/10.7860/JCDR/2015/14019.6448

Nair, N. P., & Sharma, M. (1989). Neurochemical and receptor theories of depression. *Psychiatric Journal of the University of Ottawa, 14*(2), 328–341.

Najjar, S., Pearlman, D. M., Alper, K., Najjar, A., & Devinsky, O. (2013). Neuroinflammation and psychiatric illness. *Journal of Neuroinflammation, 10*(1), 816. https://doi.org/10.1186/1742-2094-10-43

Nakai, Y., Nin, K., & Goel, N. J. (2021). The changing profile of eating disorders and related sociocultural factors in Japan between 1700 and 2020: A systematic scoping review. *International Journal of Eating Disorders, 54*(1), 40–53. https://doi.org/10.1002/eat.23439

Nanke, A., & Rief, W. (2004). Biofeedback in somatoform disorders and related syndromes. *Current Opinion in Psychiatry, 17*(2), 133–138. https://doi.org/10.1097/00001504-200403000-00011

Narrow, W. E., Clarke, D. E., Kuramoto, S. J., Kraemer, H. C., Kupfer, D. J., Greiner, L., & Regier, D. A. (2013). DSM-5 field trials in the United States and Canada, part III: Development and reliability testing of a cross-cutting symptom assessment for DSM-5. *The American Journal of Psychiatry, 170*(1), 71–82. https://doi.org/10.1176/appi.ajp.2012.12071000

Nash, J., & Nutt, D. (2007). Psychopharmacology of anxiety. *Psychiatry, 6*(4), 143–148. https://doi.org/10.1016/j.mppsy.2007.02.001

Nasir, M., Trujillo, D., Levine, J., Dwyer, J. B., Rupp, Z. W., & Bloch, M. H. (2020). Glutamate systems in DSM-5 anxiety disorders: Their role and a review of glutamate and GABA psychopharmacology. *Frontiers in Psychiatry, 11*, Article 548505. https://doi.org/10.3389/fpsyt.2020.548505

Nast, C. (2021, August 6). *Is there a female equivalent of Viagra? And if so, does it actually work?* Glamour UK. https://www.glamourmagazine.co.uk/article/viagra-women

Nast, C. (2022, June 14). *These are the countries where marijuana is legal.* Condé Nast Traveller India. https://www.cntraveller.in/story/these-are-the-countries-where-marijuana-is-legal/

Natha, F., & Daiches, A. (2014). The effectiveness of EMDR in reducing psychological distress in survivors of natural disasters: A review. *Journal of EMDR Practice and Research, 8*(3), 157–170. https://doi.org/10.1891/1933-3196.8.3.157

Nathan, P. E. (1988). The addictive personality is the behavior of the addict. *Journal of Consulting and Clinical Psychology, 56*(2), 183–188. https://doi.org/10.1037/0022-006X.56.2.183

National Center for Biotechnology Information. (2019). Anticonvulsants. In *LiverTox: Clinical and research information on drug-induced liver injury.* National Institute of Diabetes and Digestive and Kidney Diseases. http://www.ncbi.nlm.nih.gov/books/NBK548365/

National Center for Transgender Equality. (2016, July 9). *Understanding transgender people: The basics.* https://transequality.org/issues/resources/understanding-transgender-people-the-basics

National Clinical Guideline Centre. (2010). *Nocturnal enuresis: The management of bedwetting in children and young people.* The Royal College of Physicians. https://www.ncbi.nlm.nih.gov/books/NBK62712/pdf/Bookshelf_NBK62712.pdf

National Collaborating Centre for Mental Health. (2011). *Common mental health disorders: Identification and pathways to care.* British Psychological Society & The Royal College of Psychiatrists. https://www.ncbi.nlm.nih.gov/books/NBK92265/

National Conference of State Legislatures. (2022, March 16). *Mental health professionals' duty to warn.* https://www.ncsl.org/research/health/mental-health-professionals-duty-to-warn.aspx

National Eating Disorders Association. (2020, November 16). *Levels of care* [NADA]. National Eating Disorders Association. https://www.nationaleatingdisorders.org/treatment/levels-care

National Health Service. (2021, June 9). *Addiction: What is it?* Nhs.Uk. https://www.nhs.uk/live-well/addiction-support/addiction-what-is-it/

National Institute for Health and Care Excellence. (2021, June 14). *Autism spectrum disorder in under 19s:*

Support and management. https://www.nice.org.uk/guidance/cg170/chapter/Recommendations

National Institute of Allergy and Infectious Diseases. (2019, April 18). *Decline in measles vaccination is causing a preventable global resurgence of the disease.* National Institutes of Health. https://www.nih.gov/news-events/news-releases/decline-measles-vaccination-causing-preventable-global-resurgence-disease

National Institute of Mental Health. (n.d.-a). *Development and definitions of the RDoC domains and constructs.* Retrieved December 26, 2021, from https://www.nimh.nih.gov/research/research-funded-by-nimh/rdoc/development-and-definitions-of-the-rdoc-domains-and-constructs

National Institute of Mental Health. (n.d.-b). *Warning signs of suicide.* Retrieved November 8, 2022, from https://www.nimh.nih.gov/health/publications/warning-signs-of-suicide

National Institute on Alcohol Abuse. (1999). Are women more vulnerable to alcohol's effects? *Alcohol Alert, 46.* https://pubs.niaaa.nih.gov/publications/aa46.htm

National Institute on Alcohol Abuse and Alcoholism. (n.d.-a). *Drinking levels defined.* Retrieved August 15, 2022, from https://www.niaaa.nih.gov/alcohol-health/overview-alcohol-consumption/moderate-binge-drinking

National Institute on Alcohol Abuse and Alcoholism. (n.d.-b). *What is a standard drink?* Retrieved August 15, 2022, from https://www.niaaa.nih.gov/alcohols-effects-health/overview-alcohol-consumption/what-standard-drink

National Institute on Drug Abuse. (n.d.). *Alcohol.* Retrieved August 15, 2022, from https://nida.nih.gov/research-topics/alcohol

National Institute on Drug Abuse. (2020). *Is marijuana a gateway drug?* https://nida.nih.gov/publications/research-reports/marijuana/marijuana-gateway-drug

National Institute on Drug Abuse. (2023, February 9). *Drug overdose death rates.* https://nida.nih.gov/research-topics/trends-statistics/overdose-death-rates

National Library of Medicine. (2021, October 9). *Germs and hygiene* [Text]. National Library of Medicine. https://medlineplus.gov/germsandhygiene.html

Natsky, A. N., Vakulin, A., Chai-Coetzer, C. L., Lack, L., McEvoy, R. D., Lovato, N., Sweetman, A., Gordon, C. J., Adams, R. J., & Kaambwa, B. (2020). Economic evaluation of cognitive behavioural therapy for insomnia (CBT-I) for improving health outcomes in adult populations: A systematic review. *Sleep Medicine Reviews, 54*, 101351. https://doi.org/10.1016/j.smrv.2020.101351

Nazif-Munoz, J. I., Oulhote, Y., & Ouimet, M. C. (2020). The association between legalization of cannabis use and traffic deaths in Uruguay. *Addiction, 115*(9), 1697–1706. https://doi.org/10.1111/add.14994

Neculicioiu, V. S., Colosi, I. A., Costache, C., Sevastre-Berghian, A., & Clichici, S. (2022). Time to sleep?—A review of the impact of the COVID-19 pandemic on sleep and mental health. *International Journal of Environmental Research and Public Health, 19*(6), 3497. https://doi.org/10.3390/ijerph19063497

Nedim, U. (2015). *The mental illness defence in criminal trials.* http://nswcourts.com.au/articles/the-mental-illness-defence-in-criminal-trials/

Neimeyer, G. J., Taylor, J. M., Wear, D. M., & Buyukgoze-Kavas, A. (2011). How special are the specialties? Workplace settings in counseling and clinical psychology in the United States. *Counselling Psychology Quarterly, 24*(1), 43–53. https://doi.org/10.1080/09515070.2011.558343

Neimeyer, R. A. (1983). Toward a personal construct conceptualization of depression and suicide. *Death Education, 7*(2–3), 127–173. https://doi.org/10.1080/07481188308252160

Neimeyer, R. A. (Ed.). (2001a). *Meaning reconstruction and the experience of loss.* American Psychological Association. https://doi.org/10.1037/10397-000

Neimeyer, R. A. (2001b). The language of loss: Grief therapy as a process of meaning reconstruction. In

R. A. Neimeyer (Ed.), *Meaning reconstruction and the experience of loss* (pp. 261–292). American Psychological Association. https://doi.org/10.1037/10397-014

Neimeyer, R. A. (2005). Complicated grief and the quest for meaning: A constructivist contribution. *Omega-Journal of Death and Dying, 52*(1), 37–52. https://doi.org/10.2190/EQL1-LN3V-KNYR-18TF

Neimeyer, R. A. (2009). *Constructivist psychotherapy: Distinctive features.* Routledge.

Neimeyer, R. A. (2019). Meaning reconstruction in bereavement: Development of a research program. *Death Studies, 43*(2), 79–91. https://doi.org/10.1080/07481187.2018.1456620

Neimeyer, R. A., Klass, D., & Dennis, M. R. (2014). A social constructionist account of grief: Loss and the narration of meaning. *Death Studies, 38*(8), 485–498. https://doi.org/10.1080/07481187.2014.913454

Neimeyer, R. A., & Mahoney, M. J. (1995). *Constructivism in psychotherapy.* American Psychological Association. https://doi.org/10.1037/10170-000

Neimeyer, R. A., & Raskin, J. D. (Eds.). (2000). *Constructions of disorder: Meaning-making frameworks for psychotherapy.* American Psychological Association. https://doi.org/10.1037/10368-000

Neimeyer, R. A., Steffen, E. M., Milman, E., & Neimeyer, R. A. (2023). Grief therapy as a quest for meaning. In *The handbook of grief therapies* (pp. 53–67). SAGE.

Nelemans, S. A., Boks, M., Lin, B., Oldehinkel, T., van Lier, P., Branje, S., & Meeus, W. (2021). Polygenic risk for major depression interacts with parental criticism in predicting adolescent depressive symptom development. *Journal of Youth and Adolescence, 50*(1), 159–176. https://doi.org/10.1007/s10964-020-01353-4

Nelson, B. (2014). Attenuated psychosis syndrome: Don't jump the gun. *Psychopathology, 47*(5), 292–296. https://doi.org/10.1159/000365291

Nelson, K. J. (2021, July 21). *Pharmacotherapy for personality disorders.* UpToDate. https://www.uptodate.com/contents/pharmacotherapy-for-personality-disorders

Neng, J. M. B., & Weck, F. (2015). Attribution of somatic symptoms in hypochondriasis. *Clinical Psychology & Psychotherapy, 22*(2), 116–124. https://doi.org/10.1002/cpp.1871

Neria, Y., Nandi, A., & Galea, S. (2008). Post-traumatic stress disorder following disasters: A systematic review. *Psychological Medicine, 38*(4), 467–480. https://doi.org/10.1017/S0033291707001353

Nesic, M. J., Stojkovic, B., & Maric, N. P. (2019). On the origin of schizophrenia: Testing evolutionary theories in the post-genomic era. *Psychiatry and Clinical Neurosciences, 73*(12), 723–730. https://doi.org/10.1111/pcn.12933

Nesse, R. M. (2000). Is depression an adaptation? *Archives of General Psychiatry, 57*(1), 14–20. https://doi.org/10.1001/archpsyc.57.1.14

Nesse, R. M. (2004). Cliff-edged fitness functions and the persistence of schizophrenia. *Behavioral and Brain Sciences, 27*, 862–863.

Nesse, R. M. (2005a). Evolutionary psychology and mental health. In D. M. Buss (Ed.), *The handbook of evolutionary psychology* (pp. 903–927). John Wiley & Sons. https://doi.org/10.1002/9780470939376.ch32

Nesse, R. M. (2005b). An evolutionary framework for understanding grief. In D. Carr & R. M. Nesse (Eds.), *Spousal bereavement in late life* (pp. 195–226). Springer.

Nestler, E. J. (2005). The neurobiology of cocaine addiction. *Science & Practice Perspectives, 3*(1), 4–10.

Nestler, E. J., & Malenka, R. C. (2004). The addicted brain. *Scientific American, 290*(3), 78–85. https://doi.org/10.1038/scientificamerican0304-78

Nettle, D. (2004). Evolutionary origins of depression: A review and reformulation. *Journal of Affective Disorders, 81*(2), 91–102. https://doi.org/10.1016/j.jad.2003.08.009

Nettle, D. (2006). The evolution of personality variation in humans and other animals. *American Psychologist, 61*(6), 622–631. https://doi.org/10.1037/0003-066X.61.6.622

Neuhaus, E., Beauchaine, T. P., & Bernier, R. (2010). Neurobiological correlates of social functioning in autism. *Clinical Psychology Review, 30*(6), 733–748. https://doi.org/10.1016/j.cpr.2010.05.007

Neumann, I. D. (2008). Brain oxytocin: A key regulator of emotional and social behaviours in both females and males. *Journal of Neuroendocrinology, 20*(6), 858–865. https://doi.org/10.1111/j.1365-2826.2008.01726.x

Nevels, R. M., Dehon, E. E., Alexander, K., & Gontkovsky, S. T. (2010). Psychopharmacology of aggression in children and adolescents with primary neuropsychiatric disorders: A review of current and potentially promising treatment options. *Experimental and Clinical Psychopharmacology, 18*(2), 184–201. https://doi.org/10.1037/a0018059

Nevéus, T. (2011). Nocturnal enuresis—Theoretic background and practical guidelines. *Pediatric Nephrology, 26*(8), 1207–1214. https://doi.org/10.1007/s00467-011-1762-8

New View Campaign. (2018). *The New View manifesto.* http://www.newviewcampaign.org/manifesto5.asp

Newby, J. M., & McElroy, E. (2020). The impact of internet-delivered cognitive behavioural therapy for health anxiety on cyberchondria. *Journal of Anxiety Disorders, 69*, 102150. https://doi.org/10.1016/j.janxdis.2019.102150

Newby, J. M., Smith, J., Uppal, S., Mason, E., Mahoney, A. E. J., & Andrews, G. (2018). Internet-based cognitive behavioral therapy versus psychoeducation control for illness anxiety disorder and somatic symptom disorder: A randomized controlled trial. *Journal of Consulting and Clinical Psychology, 86*(1), 89–98. https://doi.org/10.1037/ccp0000248

Newman, I., Leader, G., Chen, J. L., & Mannion, A. (2015). An analysis of challenging behavior, comorbid psychopathology, and attention-deficit/hyperactivity disorder in Fragile X syndrome. *Research in Developmental Disabilities, 38*, 7–17. https://doi.org/10.1016/j.ridd.2014.11.003

Newman, J. B. (2013). Heart disease: From psychosocial to pathophysiological to treatment with biofeedback—An overview. *Biofeedback, 41*(1), 39–42. https://doi.org/10.5298/1081-5937-41.1.03

Newman, M. G., Llera, S. J., Erickson, T. M., Przeworski, A., & Castonguay, L. G. (2013). Worry and generalized anxiety disorder: A review and theoretical synthesis of evidence on nature, etiology, mechanisms, and treatment. *Annual Review of Clinical Psychology, 9*, 275–297. https://doi.org/10.1146/annurev-clinpsy-050212-185544

Newman-Toker, J. (2000). Risperidone in anorexia nervosa. *Journal of the American Academy of Child & Adolescent Psychiatry, 39*(8), 941–942. https://doi.org/10.1097/00004583-200008000-00002

Neylan, T. C., & O'Donovan, A. (2019). Inflammation and PTSD. *PTSD Research Quarterly, 29*(4), 1–10.

Nezu, A. M., & Nezu, C. M. (2008). The "devil is in the details": Recognizing and dealing with threats to validity in randomized controlled trials. In A. M. Nezu & C. M. Nezu (Eds.), *Evidence-based outcome research: A practical guide to conducting randomized controlled trials for psychosocial interventions* (pp. 3–24). Oxford University Press.

Ng, B.-Y. (1999). Hysteria: A cross-cultural comparison of its origins and history. *History of Psychiatry, 10*(39, Pt 3), 287–301. https://doi.org/10.1177/0957154X9901003901

Ngun, T. C., Ghahramani, N. M., Creek, M. M., Williams-Burris, S. M., Barseghyan, H., Itoh, Y., Sánchez, F. J., McClusky, R., Sinsheimer, J. S., Arnold, A. P., & Vilain, E. (2014). Feminized behavior and brain gene expression in a novel mouse model of Klinefelter Syndrome. *Archives of Sexual Behavior, 43*(6), 1043–1057. https://doi.org/10.1007/s10508-014-0316-0

Nguyen, H. B., Loughead, J., Lipner, E., Hantsoo, L., Kornfield, S. L., & Epperson, C. N. (2019). What has sex got to do with it? The role of hormones in the transgender brain. *Neuropsychopharmacology, 44*(1), 22–37. https://doi.org/10.1038/s41386-018-0140-7

Nguyen, P. T., & Hinshaw, S. P. (2020). Understanding the stigma associated with ADHD: Hope for the future? *The ADHD Report, 28*(5), 1–10,12. https://doi.org/10.1521/adhd.2020.28.5.1

Nguyen, T., & Li, X. (2020). Understanding public-stigma and self stigma in the context of dementia: A systematic review of the global literature. *Dementia, 19*(2), 148–181. https://doi.org/10.1177/1471301218800122

NICE Guidance. (2019, July 26). *Generalised anxiety disorder and panic disorder in adults: Management.* National Institute for Health Care Excellence (NICE). https://www.nice.org.uk/guidance/cg113

Nicholls, L. (2008). Putting the new view classification scheme to an empirical test. *Feminism & Psychology, 18*(4), 515–526. https://doi.org/10.1177/0959353508096180

Nichols, C. (2009). Is there an evolutionary advantage of schizophrenia? *Personality and Individual Differences, 46*(8), 832–838. https://doi.org/10.1016/j.paid.2009.01.013

Niciu, M. J., & Arias, A. J. (2013). Targeted opioid receptor antagonists in the treatment of alcohol use disorders. *CNS Drugs, 27*(10), 777–787. https://doi.org/10.1007/s40263-013-0096-4

Nickel, M., Cangoez, B., Bachler, E., Muehlbacher, M., Lojewski, N., Mueller-Rabe, N., Mitterlehner, F. O., Egger, C., Leiberich, P., Rother, N., Buschmann, W., Kettler, C., Gil, F. P., Lahmann, C., Fartacek, R., Rother, W. K., Loew, T. H., & Nickel, C. (2006). Bioenergetic exercises in inpatient treatment of Turkish immigrants with chronic somatoform disorders: A randomized, controlled study. *Journal of Psychosomatic Research, 61*(4), 507–513. https://doi.org/10.1016/j.jpsychores.2006.01.004

Nicki, A. (2016). Borderline personality disorder, discrimination, and survivors of chronic childhood trauma. *International Journal of Feminist Approaches to Bioethics, 9*(1), 218–245.

Nicolaou, P., Merwin, R. M., & Karekla, M. (2022). Acceptability and feasibility of a gamified digital eating disorder early-intervention program (AcceptME) based on Acceptance and Commitment Therapy (ACT). *Journal of Contextual Behavioral Science, 25*, 26–34. https://doi.org/10.1016/j.jcbs.2022.06.001

Nicolini, H., Arnold, P., Nestadt, G., Lanzagorta, N., & Kennedy, J. L. (2009). Overview of genetics and obsessive-compulsive disorder. *Psychiatry Research, 170*(1), 7–14. https://doi.org/10.1016/j.psychres.2008.10.011

Nicolò, G., Procacci, M., & Carcione, A. (2021). Pharmacological treatment of patients with personality disorders. In A. Carcione, G. Nicolo, & A. Semerari (Eds.), *Complex cases of personality disorders: Metacognitive interpersonal therapy* (pp. 209–220). Springer. https://doi.org/10.1007/978-3-030-70455-1_12

Niedermoser, D. W., Petitjean, S., Schweinfurth, N., Wirz, L., Ankli, V., Schilling, H., Zueger, C., Meyer, M., Poespodihardjo, R., Wiesbeck, G., & Walter, M. (2021). Shopping addiction: A brief review. *Practice Innovations, 6*(3), 199–207. https://doi.org/10.1037/pri0000152

Nielsen, J., Jensen, S. O. W., Friis, R. B., Valentin, J. B., & Correll, C. U. (2015). Comparative effectiveness of risperidone long-acting injectable vs first-generation antipsychotic long-acting injectables in schizophrenia: Results from a nationwide, retrospective inception cohort study. *Schizophrenia Bulletin, 41*(3), 627–636. https://doi.org/10.1093/schbul/sbu128

Nievergelt, C. M., Maihofer, A. X., Klengel, T., Atkinson, E. G., Chen, C.-Y., Choi, K. W., Coleman, J. R. I., Dalvie, S., Duncan, L. E., Gelernter, J., Levey, D. F., Logue, M. W., Polimanti, R., Provost, A. C., Ratanatharathorn, A., Stein, M. B., Torres, K., Aiello, A. E., Almli, L. M., … Koenen, K. C. (2019). International meta-analysis of PTSD genome-wide association studies identifies sex- and ancestry-specific genetic risk loci. *Nature Communications, 10*(1), Article 1. https://doi.org/10.1038/s41467-019-12576-w

Nieweglowski, K., Dubke, R., Mulfinger, N., Sheehan, L., & Corrigan, P. W. (2019). Understanding the factor structure of the public stigma of substance use disorder. *Addiction Research & Theory*, 27(2), 156–161. https://doi.org/10.1080/16066359.2018.1474205

Nijenhuis, E. R. S., & den Boer, J. A. (2009). Psychobiology of traumatization and trauma-related structural dissociation of the personality. In P. F. Dell & J. A. O'Neil (Eds.), *Dissociation and the dissociative disorders: DSM-V and beyond* (pp. 337–365). Routledge.

Nijenhuis, E. R. S., & van der Hart, O. (2011). Dissociation in trauma: A new definition and comparison with previous formulations. *Journal of Trauma & Dissociation*, 12(4), 416–445. https://doi.org/10.1080/15299732.2011.570592

Nijenhuis, E., van der Hart, O., & Steele, K. (2010). Trauma-related structural dissociation of the personality. *Activitas Nervosa Superior*, 52(1), 1–23.

Nikčević, A. V., Marino, C., Kolubinski, D. C., Leach, D., & Spada, M. M. (2021). Modelling the contribution of the Big Five personality traits, health anxiety, and COVID-19 psychological distress to generalised anxiety and depressive symptoms during the COVID-19 pandemic. *Journal of Affective Disorders*, 279, 578–584. https://doi.org/10.1016/j.jad.2020.10.053

Nikčević, A. V., & Spada, M. M. (2020). The COVID-19 anxiety syndrome scale: Development and psychometric properties. *Psychiatry Research*, 292, 113322. https://doi.org/10.1016/j.psychres.2020.113322

Nilsson, A. (2014). A non-reductive science of personality, character, and well-being must take the person's worldview into account. *Frontiers in Psychology*, 5, Article 961. https://doi.org/10.3389/fpsyg.2014.00961

Nisar, H., & Srivastava, R. (2018). Fundamental concept of psychosomatic disorders: A review. *Psychosomatic Disorders*, 3(1), 12–18.

Nisar, S., Hashem, S., Bhat, A. A., Syed, N., Yadav, S., Azeem, M. W., Uddin, S., Bagga, P., Reddy, R., & Haris, M. (2019). Association of genes with phenotype in autism spectrum disorder. *Aging (Albany NY)*, 11(22), 10742–10770. https://doi.org/10.18632/aging.102473

Nissen, L. B. (2007). Reclaiming futures: Communities helping teens overcome drugs, alcohol and crime–A new practice framework for juvenile justice. *Journal of Psychoactive Drugs*, 39(1), 51–58. https://doi.org/10.1080/02791072.2007.10399864

Nissen, L. B. (2014). *Strengthening a social justice lens for addictions practice: Exploration, reflections, possibilities, and a challenge to promote recovery among the most vulnerable.* Retrieved from http://www.attcnetwork.org/find/news/attcnews/epubs/addmsg/August2014article.asp

Nissen, L. B., & Merrigan, D. (2011). The development and evolution of Reclaiming Futures at the ten-year mark: Reflections and recommendations. *Children and Youth Services Review*, 33(Suppl 1), S9–S15. https://doi.org/10.1016/j.childyouth.2011.06.007

Nissen, L. B., & Pearce, J. (2011). Exploring the implementation of justice-based alcohol and drug intervention strategies with juvenile offenders: Reclaiming Futures, enhanced adolescent substance abuse treatment, and juvenile drug courts. *Children and Youth Services Review*, 33(Suppl. 1), S60–S65. https://doi.org/10.1016/j.childyouth.2011.06.014

Niyonambaza, S. D., Kumar, P., Xing, P., Mathault, J., De Koninck, P., Boisselier, E., Boukadoum, M., & Miled, A. (2019). A review of neurotransmitters sensing methods for neuro-engineering research. *Applied Sciences (2076-3417)*, 9(21), 4719–4719. https://doi.org/10.3390/app9214719

Niznikiewicz, M. A., Kubicki, M., & Shenton, M. E. (2003). Recent structural and functional imaging findings in schizophrenia. *Current Opinion in Psychiatry*, 16(2), 123–147. https://doi.org/10.1097/00001504-200303000-00002

Njoroge, M. W. (2018). Review on treatment of substance use disorders. *Journal of Addiction Research & Therapy*, 9(1), Article 1000353. https://doi.org/10.4172/2155-6105.1000353

Nobre, P. J., & Pinto-Gouveia, J. (2006). Dysfunctional sexual beliefs as vulnerability factors for sexual dysfunction. *Journal of Sex Research*, 43(1), 68–75. https://doi.org/10.1080/00224490609552300

Nock, M. K., Hwang, I., Sampson, N. A., & Kessler, R. C. (2010). Mental disorders, comorbidity and suicidal behavior: Results from the National Comorbidity Survey replication. *Molecular Psychiatry*, 15(8), 868–876. https://doi.org/10.1038/mp.2009.29

Nock, M. K., Millner, A. J., Ross, E. L., Kennedy, C. J., Al-Suwaidi, M., Barak-Corren, Y., Castro, V. M., Castro-Ramirez, F., Lauricella, T., Murman, N., Petukhova, M., Bird, S. A., Reis, B., Smoller, J. W., & Kessler, R. C. (2022). Prediction of suicide attempts using clinician assessment, patient self-report, and electronic health records. *JAMA Network Open*, 5(1), Article e2144373. https://doi.org/10.1001/jamanetworkopen.2021.44373

Nolan, M., Roman, E., Nasa, A., Levins, K. J., O'Hanlon, E., O'Keane, V., & Willian Roddy, D. (2020). Hippocampal and amygdalar volume changes in major depressive disorder: A targeted review and focus on stress. *Chronic Stress*, 4, 2470547020944553. https://doi.org/10.1177/2470547020944553

Nomura, Y. (2022). Pharmacological therapy for Tourette syndrome: What medicine can do and cannot do. *Biomedical Journal*, 45(2), 229–239. https://doi.org/10.1016/j.bj.2021.09.002

Norberg, J. (2010). *The historical foundations of conduct disorders: Historical context, theoretical explanations, and interventions* [Master's thesis, University of Oslo]. In *Educational Psychology: Vol. Master's thesis*. https://core.ac.uk/download/pdf/30900501.pdf

Norcross, J. C. (2000). Clinical versus counseling psychology: What's the diff? *Eye on Psi Chi*, 5(1). https://doi.org/10.24839/1092-0803.Eye5.1.20

Norcross, J. C., Beutler, L. E., & Levant, R. F. (2006). *Evidence-based practices in mental health: Debate and dialogue on the fundamental questions.* American Psychological Association. https://doi.org/10.1037/11265-000

Nordahl, H. M., & Nysæter, T. E. (2005). Schema therapy for patients with borderline personality disorder: A single case series. *Journal of Behavior Therapy and Experimental Psychiatry*, 36(3), 254–264. https://doi.org/10.1016/j.jbtep.2005.05.007

Norman, J. (2004). Gender bias in the diagnosis and treatment of depression. *International Journal of Mental Health*, 33(2), 32–43.

Normann, C., & Buttenschøn, H. N. (2020). Gene–environment interactions between HPA-axis genes and childhood maltreatment in depression: A systematic review. *Acta Neuropsychiatrica*, 32(3), 111–121. https://doi.org/10.1017/neu.2020.1

Nortajuddin, A. (2021, February 22). *Indonesia's controversial conversion therapy.* The ASEAN Post. https://theaseanpost.com/article/indonesias-controversial-conversion-therapy

North, C. S. (2015). The classification of hysteria and related disorders: Historical and phenomenological considerations. *Behavioral Sciences*, 5(4), 496–517. https://doi.org/10.3390/bs5040496

Norton, A. (2021, March 12). *Driven by anti-vaxxers, measles outbreaks cost everyone money.* Consumer Health News | HealthDay. https://consumer.healthday.com/3-12-driven-by-anti-vaxxers-measles-outbreaks-cost-everyone-money-2650924860.html

Norton, A. R., Abbott, M. J., Norberg, M. M., & Hunt, C. (2015). A systematic review of mindfulness and acceptance-based treatments for social anxiety disorder. *Journal of Clinical Psychology*, 71(4), 283–301. https://doi.org/10.1002/jclp.22144

Norton, P. J., & Paulus, D. J. (2017). Transdiagnostic models of anxiety disorder: Theoretical and empirical underpinnings. *Clinical Psychology Review*, 56, 122–137. https://doi.org/10.1016/j.cpr.2017.03.004

Norton, P. J., & Roberge, P. (2017). Transdiagnostic therapy. *The Psychiatric Clinics of North America*, 40(4), 675–687. https://doi.org/10.1016/j.psc.2017.08.003

Nosyk, B., Marsh, D. C., Sun, H., Schechter, M. T., & Anis, A. H. (2010). Trends in methadone maintenance treatment participation, retention, and compliance to dosing guidelines in British Columbia, Canada: 1996–2006. *Journal of Substance Abuse Treatment*, 39(1), 22–31. https://doi.org/10.1016/j.jsat.2010.03.008

Nour, A. (2020). Chemical castration of the sexual offender versus human fundamental rights and freedoms. *Scholars International Journal of Law, Crime and Justice*, 3(5), 144–148. https://doi.org/10.36348/sijlcj.2020.v03i05.002

Novais, F., Araújo, A., & Godinho, P. (2015). Historical roots of histrionic personality disorder. *Frontiers in Psychology*, 6, Article 1463. https://doi.org/10.3389/fpsyg.2015.01463

Novellino, M. (2012). The shadow and the demon: The psychodynamics of nightmares. *Transactional Analysis Journal*, 42(4), 277–284. https://doi.org/10.1177/036215371204200406

Novick, D. M., & Swartz, H. A. (2019). Evidence-based psychotherapies for bipolar disorder. *FOCUS*, 17(3), 238–248. https://doi.org/10.1176/appi.focus.20190004

Nowak, D. A., & Fink, G. R. (2009). Psychogenic movement disorders: Aetiology, phenomenology, neuroanatomical correlates and therapeutic approaches. *NeuroImage*, 47(3), 1015–1025. https://doi.org/10.1016/j.neuroimage.2009.04.082

Nowak, M., Gawęda, A., Jelonek, I., & Janas-Kozik, M. (2013). The disruptive behavior disorders and the coexisting deficits in the context of theories describing family relations. *Archives of Psychiatry and Psychotherapy*, 15(1), 61–65.

Nuij, C., van Ballegooijen, W., de Beurs, D., Juniar, D., Erlangsen, A., Portzky, G., O'Connor, R. C., Smit, J. H., Kerkhof, A., & Riper, H. (2021). Safety planning-type interventions for suicide prevention: Meta-analysis. *The British Journal of Psychiatry*, 219(2), 419–426. https://doi.org/10.1192/bjp.2021.50

Nummenmaa, L., Lukkarinen, L., Sun, L., Putkinen, V., Seppälä, K., Karjalainen, T., Karlsson, H. K., Hudson, M., Venetjoki, N., Salomaa, M., Rautio, P., Hirvonen, J., Lauerma, H., & Tiihonen, J. (2021). Brain basis of psychopathy in criminal offenders and general population. *Cerebral Cortex*, 31(9), 4104–4114. https://doi.org/10.1093/cercor/bhab072

Nunes, P. M., Wenzel, A., Borges, K. T., Porto, C. R., Caminha, R. M., & de Oliveira, I. R. (2009). Volumes of the hippocampus and amygdala in patients with borderline personality disorder: A meta-analysis. *Journal of Personality Disorders*, 23(4), 333–345.

Nuss, P. (2015). Anxiety disorders and GABA neurotransmission: A disturbance of modulation. *Neuropsychiatric Disease and Treatment*, 11.

Nussbaum, M. C. (1997). Constructing love, desire, and care. In M. C. Nussbaum & D. M. Estlund (Eds.), *Sex, preference, and family: Essays on law and nature* (pp. 17–43). Oxford University Press.

Nutt, D., Argyropoulos, S., Hood, S., & Potokar, J. (2006). Generalized anxiety disorder: A comorbid disease. *European Neuropsychopharmacology*, 16(Suppl. 2), S109–S118. https://doi.org/10.1016/j.euroneuro.2006.04.003

Nutt, D. J., Lingford-Hughes, A., Erritzoe, D., & Stokes, P. R. A. (2015). The dopamine theory of addiction: 40 years of highs and lows. *Nature Reviews Neuroscience*, 16(5), 305–312. https://doi.org/10.1038/nrn3939

Nydegger, R. (2013). Somatoform disorders. In T. G. Plante (Ed.), *Abnormal psychology across the ages: Vol. 2. Disorders and treatments* (pp. 49–65). Praeger/ABC-CLIO.

Nye, C., Vanryckeghem, M., Schwartz, J. B., Herder, C., Turner, I., Herbert M., & Howard, C. (2013). Behavioral stuttering interventions for children and adolescents: A systematic review and meta-analysis. *Journal of Speech, Language, and Hearing Research*,

56(3), 921–932. https://doi.org/10.1044/1092-4388(2012/12-0036)

Nylund, D., & Corsiglia, V. (1996). From deficits to special abilities: Working narratively with children labeled "ADHD." In M. F. Hoyt (Ed.), *Constructive therapies* (Vol. 2, pp. 163–183). Guilford Press.

Nysæter, T. E., & Nordahl, H. M. (2008). Principles and clinical application of schema therapy for patients with borderline personality disorder. *Nordic Psychology*, 60(3), 249–263. https://doi.org/10.1027/1901-2276.60.3.249

Oaks, D. (2006). The evolution of the consumer movement: Comment. *Psychiatric Services*, 57(8), 1212. https://doi.org/10.1176/appi.ps.57.8.1212

Obegi, J. H. (2019). Rethinking suicidal behavior disorder. *Crisis*, 40(3), 209–219. https://doi.org/10.1027/0227-5910/a000543

Oberling, P., Rocha, B., Di Scala, G., & Sandner, G. (1993). Evidence for state-dependent retrieval in conditioned place aversion. *Behavioral & Neural Biology*, 60(1), 27–32. https://doi.org/10.1016/0163-1047(93)90677-A

Oberndorfer, T. A., Frank, G. K. W., Simmons, A. N., Wagner, A., McCurdy, D., Fudge, J. L., Yang, T. T., Paulus, M. P., & Kaye, W. H. (2013). Altered insula response to sweet taste processing after recovery from anorexia and bulimia nervosa. *The American Journal of Psychiatry*, 170(10), 1143–1151. https://doi.org/10.1176/appi.ajp.2013.11111745

Obiols, J. E. (2012). DSM 5: Precedents, present and prospects. *International Journal of Clinical and Health Psychology*, 12(2), 281–290.

Obreshkova, D., Kandilarov, I., Angelova, V., Iliev, Y., Atanasov, P., & Fotev, P. (2017). Pharmaco-toxicological aspects and analysis of phenylalkylamine and indolylalllkylamine hallucinogens (Review). *Pharmacia*, 64(1), 32–47.

O'Brian, S., Iverach, L., Jones, M., Onslow, M., Packman, A., & Menzies, R. (2013). Effectiveness of the Lidcombe Program for early stuttering in Australian community clinics. *International Journal of Speech-Language Pathology*, 15(6), 593–603. https://doi.org/10.3109/17549507.2013.783112

O'Brien, A. (2016). Comparing the risk of tardive dyskinesia in older adults with first-generation and second-generation antipsychotics: A systematic review and meta-analysis. *International Journal of Geriatric Psychiatry*, 31(7), 683–693. https://doi.org/10.1002/gps.4399

O'Brien, A. J., McKenna, B. G., & Kydd, R. R. (2009). Compulsory community mental health treatment: Literature review. *International Journal of Nursing Studies*, 46(9), 1245–1255. https://doi.org/10.1016/j.ijnurstu.2009.02.006

O'Brien, M., Rogers, P., & Smith, E. (2022). A chart review of emergency department visits following implementation of the Cannabis Act in Canada. *Canadian Journal of Medicine*, 4(1), 13–21. https://doi.org/10.33844/cjm.2022.6016

Ochberg, F. (2013, March–April). An injury not a disorder. *Military Review*, 96–99.

Ociskova, M., Prasko, J., Latalova, K., Sedlackova, Z., Kamaradova, D., Sandoval, A., & Grambal, A. (2017). *F*ck your care if you label me! Borderline personality disorder, stigma, and self-stigma.* 59(1), 16–22.

Ociskova, M., Prasko, J., Vrbova, K., Kasalova, P., Holubova, M., Grambal, A., & Machu, K. (2018). Self-stigma and treatment effectiveness in patients with anxiety disorders – a mediation analysis. *Neuropsychiatric Disease and Treatment*, 14, 383–392. https://doi.org/10.2147/NDT.S152208

O'Connell, B., & Dowling, M. (2014). Dialectical behaviour therapy (DBT) in the treatment of borderline personality disorder. *Journal of Psychiatric and Mental Health Nursing*, 21(6), 518–525. https://doi.org/10.1111/jpm.12116

O'Connor, C., McNamara, N., O'Hara, L., McNicholas, M., & McNicholas, F. (2021). How do people with eating disorders experience the stigma associated with their condition? A mixed-methods systematic review. *Journal of Mental Health*, 30(4), 454–469. https://doi.org/10.1080/09638237.2019.1685081

O'Connor, M.-F., Schultze-Florey, C. R., Irwin, M. R., Arevalo, J. M. G., & Cole, S. W. (2014). Divergent gene expression responses to complicated grief and non-complicated grief. *Brain, Behavior, and Immunity*, 37, 78–83. https://doi.org/10.1016/j.bbi.2013.12.017

O'Doherty, D. C. M., Chitty, K. M., Saddiqui, S., Bennett, M. R., & Lagopoulos, J. (2015). A systematic review and meta-analysis of magnetic resonance imaging measurement of structural volumes in posttraumatic stress disorder. *Psychiatry Research: Neuroimaging*, 232(1), 1–33. https://doi.org/10.1016/j.pscychresns.2015.01.002

O'Donnell, M. L., Agathos, J. A., Metcalf, O., Gibson, K., & Lau, W. (2019). Adjustment disorder: Current developments and future directions. *International Journal of Environmental Research and Public Health*, 16(14). https://doi.org/10.3390/ijerph16142537

O'Donnell, M. L., Metcalf, O., Watson, L., Phelps, A., & Varker, T. (2018). A systematic review of psychological and pharmacological treatments for adjustment disorder in adults. *Journal of Traumatic Stress*, 31(3), 321–331. https://doi.org/10.1002/jts.22295

O'Driscoll, C., Sener, S. B., Angmark, A., & Shaikh, M. (2019). Caregiving processes and expressed emotion in psychosis, a cross-cultural, meta-analytic review. *Schizophrenia Research*, 208, 8–15. https://doi.org/10.1016/j.schres.2019.03.020

Oei, T. P. S., & Hashing, P. A. (2013). Alcohol use disorders. In P. M. Miller, S. A. Ball, M. E. Bates, A. W. Blume, K. M. Kampman, D. J. Kavanagh, M. E. Larimer, N. M. Petry, & P. De Witte (Eds.), *Comprehensive addictive behaviors and disorders: Vol. 1. Principles of addiction* (pp. 647–655). Elsevier Academic Press.

Office of the U.S. Surgeon General. (2012). Brief history of suicide prevention in the United States. In *2012 National strategy for suicide prevention: Goals and objectives for action: A report of the U.S. Surgeon General and of the National Action Alliance for Suicide Prevention.* U.S. Department of Health & Human Services. https://www.ncbi.nlm.nih.gov/books/NBK109918/

Offman, A., & Kleinplatz, P. J. (2004). Does PMDD belong in the DSM? Challenging the medicalization of women's bodies. *Canadian Journal of Human Sexuality*, 13(1), 17–27.

Ogden, G. (2001). The taming of the screw: Reflections on "A New View of women's sexual problems." *Women & Therapy*, 24(1–2), 17–21. https://doi.org/10.1300/J015v24n01_03

Ogrodniczuk, J. S., & Oliffe, J. L. (2011). Men and depression. *Canadian Family Physician*, 57(2), 153–155.

Oh, H., Yang, L. H., Anglin, D. M., & DeVylder, J. E. (2014). Perceived discrimination and psychotic experiences across multiple ethnic groups in the United States. *Schizophrenia Research*, 157(1–3), 259–265. https://doi.org/10.1016/j.schres.2014.04.036

O'Hara, C. B., Campbell, I. C., & Schmidt, U. (2015). A reward-centred model of anorexia nervosa: A focussed narrative review of the neurological and psychophysiological literature. *Neuroscience and Biobehavioral Reviews*, 52, 131–152. https://doi.org/10.1016/j.neubiorev.2015.02.012

Öhlund, L., Ott, M., Oja, S., Bergqvist, M., Lundqvist, R., Sandlund, M., Salander Renberg, E., & Werneke, U. (2018). Reasons for lithium discontinuation in men and women with bipolar disorder: A retrospective cohort study. *BMC Psychiatry*, 18(1), 37. https://doi.org/10.1186/s12888-018-1622-1

Ohst, B., & Tuschen-Caffier, B. (2018). Catastrophic misinterpretation of bodily sensations and external events in panic disorder, other anxiety disorders, and healthy subjects: A systematic review and meta-analysis. *PLoS ONE*, 13(3), e0194493. https://doi.org/10.1371/journal.pone.0194493

Ohst, B., & Tuschen-Caffier, B. (2020). Are catastrophic misinterpretations of bodily sensations typical for patients with panic disorder? An experimental study of patients with panic disorder or other anxiety disorders and healthy controls. *Cognitive Therapy and Research*, 44(6), 1106–1115. https://doi.org/10.1007/s10608-020-10141-0

Ohtani, A., Suzuki, T., Takeuchi, H., & Uchida, H. (2015). Language barriers and access to psychiatric care: A systematic review. *Psychiatric Services*, 66(8), 798–805. https://doi.org/10.1176/appi.ps.201400351

Okolie, C., Hawton, K., Lloyd, K., Price, S. F., Dennis, M., & John, A. (2020). Means restriction for the prevention of suicide on roads. *Cochrane Database of Systematic Reviews*, 2020(9), Article CD013728. https://doi.org/10.1002/14651858.CD013738

Okolie, C., Wood, S., Hawton, K., Kandalama, U., Glendenning, A. C., Dennis, M., Price, S. F., Lloyd, K., & John, A. (2020). Means restriction for the prevention of suicide by jumping. *Cochrane Database of Systematic Reviews*, 2020(2), Article CD013543. https://doi.org/10.1002/14651858.CD013543

Olatunji, B. O., Kauffman, B. Y., Meltzer, S., Davis, M. L., Smits, J. A. J., & Powers, M. B. (2014). Cognitive-behavioral therapy for hypochondriasis/health anxiety: A meta-analysis of treatment outcome and moderators. *Behaviour Research and Therapy*, 58, 65–74. https://doi.org/10.1016/j.brat.2014.05.002

Oldenhof, H., Prätzlich, M., Ackermann, K., Baker, R., Batchelor, M., Baumann, S., Bernhard, A., Clanton, R., Dikeos, D., Dochnal, R., Fehlbaum, L. V., Fernández-Rivas, A., de Geus, E., Gonzalez, K., de Artaza-lavesa, M. G., Guijarro, S., Gundlach, M., Herpertz-Dahlmann, B., Hervas, A., … Popma, A. (2019). Baseline autonomic nervous system activity in female children and adolescents with conduct disorder: Psychophysiological findings from the FemNAT-CD study. *Journal of Criminal Justice*, 65, 101564. https://doi.org/10.1016/j.jcrimjus.2018.05.011

O'Leary, A. (1990). Stress, emotion, and human immune function. *Psychological Bulletin*, 108(3), 363–382. https://doi.org/10.1037/0033-2909.108.3.363

O'Leary, D. (2021). How to be a holist who rejects the biopsychosocial model. *European Journal of Analytic Philosophy*, 17(2), 5–20. https://doi.org/10.31820/ejap.17.2.5

Olff, M. (2017). Sex and gender differences in post-traumatic stress disorder: An update. *European Journal of Psychotraumatology*, 8(sup4), 1351204. https://doi.org/10.1080/20008198.2017.1351204

Olff, M., Güzelcan, Y., de Vries, G.-J., Assies, J., & Gersons, B. P. R. (2006). HPA- and HPT-axis alterations in chronic posttraumatic stress disorder. *Psychoneuroendocrinology*, 31(10), 1220–1230. https://doi.org/10.1016/j.psyneuen.2006.09.003

Olinger, C. (2021a). Narrative practices and autism: Part 1: Theory and engagement: Shedding ableism from therapy. *The International Journal of Narrative Therapy and Community Work*, 2021(2), 32–41.

Olinger, C. (2021b). Part 2: Expanding on understandings of autism. *The International Journal of Narrative Therapy and Community Work*, 2021(2), 42–49.

Oliva, F., Versino, E., Gammino, L., Colombi, N., Ostacoli, L., Carletto, S., Furlan, P. M., & Picci, R. L. (2016). Type D personality and essential hypertension in primary care: A cross-sectional observational study within a cohort of patients visiting general practitioners. *The Journal of Nervous and Mental Disease*, 204(1), 43–48. https://doi.org/10.1097/NMD.0000000000000421

Oliveira, B., Mitjans, M., Nitsche, M. A., Kuo, M.-F., & Ehrenreich, H. (2018). Excitation-inhibition dysbalance as predictor of autistic phenotypes. *Journal of Psychiatric Research*, 104, 96–99. https://doi.org/10.1016/j.jpsychires.2018.06.004

Olivine, A. (2022, February 17). *Is marijuana addictive? Possibly, but it depends.* Verywell Health. https://www.verywellhealth.com/is-marijuana-addictive-5215991

Ollendick, T. H., Alvarez, H. K., & Greene, R. W. (2004). Behavioral assessment: History of underlying concepts. In S. N. Haynes & E. M. Heiby (Eds.), *Comprehensive handbook of psychological assessment: Vol. 3. Behavioral assessment* (pp. 19–34). John Wiley.

Olmsted, D., & Blaxill, M. (2016). Leo Kanner's mention of 1938 in his report on autism refers to his first patient. *Journal of Autism & Developmental Disorders, 46*(1), 340–341. https://doi.org/10.1007/s10803-015-2541-3

O'Loughlin, P. (2007). Is it harm reduction–or harm continuation? In *The Journal of Global Drug Policy and Practice* (Vol. 1, Issue 2). https://www.dfaf.org/archive/

Olsen, G. (2012). The marketing of madness and psychotropic drugs to children. In S. Olfman, B. D. Robbins, S. Olfman, & B. D. Robbins (Eds.), *Drugging our children: How profiteers are pushing antipsychotics on our youngest, and what we can do to stop it* (pp. 52–77). Praeger/ABC-CLIO.

Olson, M. (2019, February 1). *Olson: A history of the Open Dialogue approach in the US.* New York Association of Rehabilitative Services. https://www.nyaprs.org/e-news-bulletins/2019/2/1/olson-a-history-of-the-open-dialogue-approach-in-the-us

Oltmanns, J. R., & Widiger, T. A. (2019). Evaluating the assessment of the ICD-11 personality disorder diagnostic system. *Psychological Assessment, 31*(5), 674–684. https://doi.org/10.1037/pas0000693

Olver, M. E., & Wong, S. C. P. (2013). Treatment programs for high risk sexual offenders: Program and offender characteristics, attrition, treatment change and recidivism. *Aggression and Violent Behavior, 18*(5), 579–591. https://doi.org/10.1016/j.avb.2013.06.002

O'Malley, K. J., Cook, K. F., Price, M. D., Wildes, K. R., Hurdle, J. F., & Ashton, C. M. (2005). Measuring diagnoses: ICD code accuracy. *Health Services Research, 40*(5, Pt 2), 1620–1639. https://doi.org/10.1111/j.1475-6773.2005.00444.x

O'Neill, A., & Frodl, T. (2012). Brain structure and function in borderline personality disorder. *Brain Structure and Function, 217*(4), 767–782. https://doi.org/10.1007/s00429-012-0379-4

Online Etymology Dictionary. (n.d.). *Diagnosis.* https://www.etymonline.com/word/diagnosis

Onslow, M. (2021). *Lidcombe Program treatment guide: Version 1.3.* Lidcombe Program Trainers Consortium. https://www.lidcombeprogram.org/download/1609/

Oosterhuis, H. (2012). Sexual modernity in the works of Richard von Krafft-Ebing and Albert Moll. *Medical History, 56*(2), 133–155. https://doi.org/10.1017/mdh.2011.30

Opheim, E., Andersen, P. N., Jakobsen, M., Aasen, B., & Kvaal, K. (2019). Poor quality in systematic reviews on PTSD and EMDR – An examination of search methodology and reporting. *Frontiers in Psychology, 10*, Article 1558. https://doi.org/10.3389/fpsyg.2019.01558

Ophir, Y. (2019, September 12). ADHD is not an illness, and Ritalin is not a cure. *Haaretz.* https://www.haaretz.com/israel-news/2019-09-12/ty-article-magazine/.premium/adhd-is-not-an-illness-and-ritalin-is-not-a-cure/0000017f-e3ef-d75c-a7ff-ffeff8260000

Ophir, Y. (2021). Evidence that the diagnosis of ADHD does not reflect a chronic bio-medical disease. *Ethical Human Psychology and Psychiatry, 2*, 100–126. https://doi.org/10.1891/EHPP-2021-0001

Oquendo, M. A., & Baca-Garcia, E. (2014). Suicidal behavior disorder as a diagnostic entity in the DSM-5 classification system: Advantages outweigh limitations. *World Psychiatry, 13*(2), 128–130. https://doi.org/10.1002/wps.20116

Oram, S., Khalifeh, H., & Howard, L. M. (2017). Violence against women and mental health. *The Lancet Psychiatry, 4*(2), 159–170. https://doi.org/10.1016/S2215-0366(16)30261-9

Orben, A., & Przybylski, A. K. (2019). The association between adolescent well-being and digital technology use. *Nature Human Behaviour, 3*(2), 173–182. https://doi.org/10.1038/s41562-018-0506-1

Orben, A., & Przybylski, A. K. (2020). Reply to: Underestimating digital media harm. *Nature Human Behaviour, 4*(4), 349–351. https://doi.org/10.1038/s41562-020-0840-y

O'Reilly, R. (2004). Why are community treatment orders controversial? *The Canadian Journal of Psychiatry, 49*(9), 579–584. https://doi.org/10.1177/070674370404900902

Oren, E., & Solomon, R. (2012). EMDR therapy: An overview of its development and mechanisms of action. *European Review of Applied Psychology/Revue Européenne de Psychologie Appliquée, 62*(4), 197–203. https://doi.org/10.1016/j.erap.2012.08.005

Oriuwa, C., Mollica, A., Feinstein, A., Giacobbe, P., Lipsman, N., Perez, D. L., & Burke, M. J. (2022). Neuromodulation for the treatment of functional neurological disorder and somatic symptom disorder: A systematic review. *Journal of Neurology, Neurosurgery & Psychiatry, 93*(3), 280–290. https://doi.org/10.1136/jnnp-2021-327025

Ormel, J., Hartman, C. A., & Snieder, H. (2019). The genetics of depression: Successful genome-wide association studies introduce new challenges. *Translational Psychiatry, 9*, Article 1. https://doi.org/10.1038/s41398-019-0450-5

Ornoy, A., Weinstein- Fudim, L., & Ergaz, Z. (2016). Genetic syndromes, maternal diseases and antenatal factors associated with autism spectrum disorders (ASD). *Frontiers in Neuroscience, 10*, Article 316. https://doi.org/10.3389/fnins.2016.00316

Orsillo, S. M., & Batten, S. V. (2005). Acceptance and commitment therapy in the treatment of posttraumatic stress disorder. *Behavior Modification, 29*(1), 95–129. https://doi.org/10.1177/0145445504270876

Orsolini, L., De Berardis, D., & Volpe, U. (2020). Up-to-date expert opinion on the safety of recently developed antipsychotics. *Expert Opinion on Drug Safety, 19*(8), 981–998. https://doi.org/10.1080/14740338.2020.1795126

Osborn, E., Wittkowski, A., Brooks, J., Briggs, P. E., & O'Brien, P. M. S. (2020). Women's experiences of receiving a diagnosis of premenstrual dysphoric disorder: A qualitative investigation. *BMC Women's Health, 20*(1), 242. https://doi.org/10.1186/s12905-020-01100-8

O'Shaughnessy, R. J. (2007). AAPL practice guideline for the forensic psychiatric evaluation of competence to stand trial: A Canadian legal perspective. *Journal of the American Academy of Psychiatry and the Law, 35*(4), 505–508.

Osimo, E. F., Baxter, L. J., Lewis, G., Jones, P. B., & Khandaker, G. M. (2019). Prevalence of low-grade inflammation in depression: A systematic review and meta-analysis of CRP levels. *Psychological Medicine, 49*(12), 1958–1970. https://doi.org/10.1017/S0033291719001454

Oskotsky, T., Marić, I., Tang, A., Oskotsky, B., Wong, R. J., Aghaeepour, N., Sirota, M., & Stevenson, D. K. (2021). Mortality risk among patients with covid-19 prescribed selective serotonin reuptake inhibitor antidepressants. *JAMA Network Open, 4*(11), e2133090. https://doi.org/10.1001/jamanetworkopen.2021.33090

Osório, C., Jones, N., Fertout, M., & Greenberg, N. (2013). Perceptions of stigma and barriers to care among UK military personnel deployed to Afghanistan and Iraq. *Anxiety, Stress & Coping: An International Journal, 26*(5), 539–557. https://doi.org/10.1080/10615806.2012.725470

Osoro, A., Villalobos, D., & Tamayo, J. A. (2022). Efficacy of emotion-focused therapy in the treatment of eating disorders: A systematic review. *Clinical Psychology & Psychotherapy, 29*(3), 815–836. https://doi.org/10.1002/cpp.2690

Öst, L.-G., Havnen, A., Hansen, B., & Kvale, G. (2015). Cognitive behavioral treatments of obsessive–compulsive disorder. A systematic review and meta-analysis of studies published 1993–2014. *Clinical Psychology Review, 40*, 156–169. https://doi.org/10.1016/j.cpr.2015.06.003

Ostergren, J. E., Dingel, M. J., McCormick, J. B., & Koenig, B. A. (2015). Unwarranted optimism in media portrayals of genetic research on addiction overshadows critical ethical and social concerns. *Journal of Health Communication, 20*(5), 555–565. https://doi.org/10.1080/10810730.2014.999895

Otero-López, J. M., & Villardefrancos, E. (2013). Materialism and addictive buying in women: The mediating role of anxiety and depression. *Psychological Reports, 113*(1), 328–344. https://doi.org/10.2466/18.02.PR0.113x11z9

Otgaar, H., Howe, M. L., Patihis, L., Merckelbach, H., Lynn, S. J., Lilienfeld, S. O., & Loftus, E. F. (2019). The return of the repressed: The persistent and problematic claims of long-forgotten trauma. *Perspectives on Psychological Science, 14*(6), 1072–1095. https://doi.org/10.1177/1745691619862306

Otgaar, H., Wang, J., Dodier, O., Howe, M. L., Lilienfeld, S. O., Loftus, E. F., Lynn, S. J., Merckelbach, H., & Patihis, L. (2020). Skirting the issue: What does believing in repression mean? *Journal of Experimental Psychology: General, 149*(10), 2005–2006. https://doi.org/10.1037/xge0000982

Otten, M., & Meeter, M. (2015). Hippocampal structure and function in individuals with bipolar disorder: A systematic review. *Journal of Affective Disorders, 174*, 113–125. https://doi.org/10.1016/j.jad.2014.11.001

Ou, Y., Buchanan, A. M., Witt, C. E., & Hashemi, P. (2019). Frontiers in electrochemical sensors for neurotransmitter detection: Towards measuring neurotransmitters as chemical diagnostics for brain disorders. *Analytical Methods, 11*(21), 2738–2755. https://doi.org/10.1039/C9AY00055K

Oud, M., Winter, L. de, Vermeulen-Smit, E., Bodden, D., Nauta, M., Stone, L., Heuvel, M. van den, Taher, R. A., Graaf, I. de, Kendall, T., Engels, R., & Stikkelbroek, Y. (2019). Effectiveness of CBT for children and adolescents with depression: A systematic review and meta-regression analysis. *European Psychiatry, 57*, 33–45. https://doi.org/10.1016/j.eurpsy.2018.12.008

Overholser, J. C., & Beale, E. E. (2019). Neurasthenia: Modern malady or historical relic? *Journal of Nervous and Mental Disease, 207*(9), 731–739. https://doi.org/10.1097/NMD.0000000000000943

Overmier, J. B., & Seligman, M. E. (1967). Effects of inescapable shock upon subsequent escape and avoidance responding. *Journal of Comparative and Physiological Psychology, 63*(1), 28–33. https://doi.org/10.1037/h0024166

Ozkiris, A., Essizoglu, A., Gulec, G., & Aksaray, G. (2015). The relationship between insight and the level of expressed emotion in patients with obsessive–compulsive disorder. *Nordic Journal of Psychiatry, 69*(3), 204–209. https://doi.org/10.3109/08039488.2014.959996

Pace, T. W. W., & Heim, C. M. (2011). A short review on the psychoneuroimmunology of posttraumatic stress disorder: From risk factors to medical comorbidities. *Brain, Behavior, and Immunity, 25*(1), 6–13. https://doi.org/10.1016/j.bbi.2010.10.003

Pack, M. J. (2013). Critical incident stress management: A review of the literature with implications for social work. *International Social Work, 56*(5), 608–627. https://doi.org/10.1177/0020872811435371

Packard, M. G., & Teather, L. A. (1999). Dissociation of multiple memory systems by posttraining intracerebral injections of glutamate. *Psychobiology, 27*(1), 40–50.

Padín, P. F., González-Rodríguez, R., Verde-Diego, C., & Vázquez-Pérez, R. (2021). Social media and eating disorder psychopathology: A systematic review. *Cyberpsychology: Journal of Psychosocial Research on Cyberspace, 15*(3), Article 3. https://doi.org/10.5817/CP2021-3-6

Padula, A. M., Huang, H., Baer, R. J., August, L. M., Jankowska, M. M., Jellife-Pawlowski, L. L., Sirota, M., & Woodruff, T. J. (2018). Environmental pollution and social factors as contributors to preterm birth in Fresno County. *Environmental Health*, 17(1), 70. https://doi.org/10.1186/s12940-018-0414-x

Page, S., & Fletcher, T. (2006). Auguste D: One hundred years on: "The person" not "the case." *Dementia*, 5(4), 571–583. https://doi.org/10.1177/1471301206069939

Pagliaroli, L., Vető, B., Arányi, T., & Barta, C. (2016). From genetics to epigenetics: New perspectives in tourette syndrome research. *Frontiers in Neuroscience*, 10, Article 277, https://doi.org/10.3389/fnins.2016.00277

Pai, A., Suris, A., & North, C. (2017). Posttraumatic stress disorder in the DSM-5: Controversy, change, and conceptual considerations. *Behavioral Sciences*, 7(1), 7.

Paintain, E., & Cassidy, S. (2018). First-line therapy for post-traumatic stress disorder: A systematic review of cognitive behavioural therapy and psychodynamic approaches. *Counselling & Psychotherapy Research*, 18(3), 237–250. https://doi.org/10.1002/capr.12174

Pais, S. (2009). A systemic approach to the treatment of dissociative identity disorder. *Journal of Family Psychotherapy*, 20(1), 72–88. https://doi.org/10.1080/08975350802716566

Palamar, J. J., Rutherford, C., & Keyes, K. M. (2021). Trends in ketamine use, exposures, and seizures in the United States up to 2019. *American Journal of Public Health*, 111(11), 2046–2049. https://doi.org/10.2105/AJPH.2021.306486

Palermo, G. B. (2015). Dusky is here to stay—For now. *International Journal of Offender Therapy and Comparative Criminology*, 59(14), 1503–1504. https://doi.org/10.1177/0306624X15616656

Palis, J., Rossopoulos, E., & Triarhou, L. C. (1985). The Hippocratic concept of hysteria: A translation of the original texts. *Integrative Psychiatry*, 3(3), 226–228.

Palmer, B. W. (2006). Informed consent for schizophrenia research: What is an investigator (or IRB) to do? *Behavioral Sciences & the Law*, 24(4), 447–452. https://doi.org/10.1002/bsl.695

Palmer, C. A., & Hazelrigg, M. (2000). The guilty but mentally ill verdict: A review and conceptual analysis of intent and impact. *Journal of the American Academy of Psychiatry and the Law*, 28(1), 47–54.

Pan, X., Kaminga, A. C., Wen, S. W., & Liu, A. (2018). Catecholamines in post-traumatic stress disorder: A systematic review and meta-analysis. *Frontiers in Molecular Neuroscience*, 11, Article 450. https://doi.org/10.3389/fnmol.2018.00450

Pan, Y., Aierken, A., Ding, X., Chen, Y., & Li, Y. (2022). Socioeconomic status association with dependency from objective and subjective assessments: A cross-sectional study. *Frontiers in Psychiatry*, 13, Article 898686. https://doi.org10.3389/fpsyt.2022.898686.

Panos, P. T., Jackson, J. W., Hasan, O., & Panos, A. (2014). Meta-analysis and systematic review assessing the efficacy of Dialectical Behavior Therapy (DBT). *Research on Social Work Practice*, 24(2), 213–223. https://doi.org/10.1177/1049731513503047

Panossian, A., Hamm, R., Wikman, G., & Efferth, T. (2014). Mechanism of action of Rhodiola, salidroside, tyrosol and triandrin in isolated neuroglial cells: An interactive pathway analysis of the downstream effects using RNA microarray data. *Phytomedicine*, 21(11), 1325–1348. https://doi.org/10.1016/j.phymed.2014.07.008

Paolini, E., Mezzetti, F. A. F., Pierri, F., & Moretti, P. (2017). Pharmacological treatment of borderline personality disorder: A retrospective observational study at inpatient unit in Italy. *International Journal of Psychiatry in Clinical Practice*, 21(1), 75–79. https://doi.org/10.1080/13651501.2016.1235202

Paone, T. R., & Douma, K. B. (2009). Child-centered play therapy with a seven-year-old boy diagnosed with intermittent explosive disorder. *International Journal of Play Therapy*, 18(1), 31–44. https://doi.org/10.1037/a0013938

Papanastasiou, E., Stone, J. M., & Shergill, S. (2013). When the drugs don't work: The potential of glutamatergic antipsychotics in schizophrenia. *The British Journal of Psychiatry*, 202(2), 91–93. https://doi.org/10.1192/bjp.bp.112.110999

Papiasvili, E. D., & Mayers, L. A. (2013). Perceptions, thoughts, and attitudes in the Middle Ages. In T. G. Plante (Ed.), *Abnormal psychology across the ages: Vol. 1. History and conceptualizations* (pp. 15–31). Praeger/ABC-CLIO.

Papiol, S., Schulze, T. G., & Alda, M. (2018). Genetics of lithium response in bipolar disorder. *Pharmacopsychiatry*, 51(5), 206–211. https://doi.org/10.1055/a-0590-4992

Paradies, Y., Ben, J., Denson, N., Elias, A., Priest, N., Pieterse, A., Gupta, A., Kelaher, M., & Gee, G. (2015). Racism as a determinant of health: A systematic review and meta-analysis. *PLoS ONE*, 10(9), e0138511. https://doi.org/10.1371/journal.pone.0138511

Parameshwaran, S., & Chandra, P. S. (2018). Will the DSM-5 and ICD-11 "Make-over" really make a difference to women's mental health? *Indian Journal of Social Psychiatry*, 34(5), 79–85. https://doi.org/10.4103/ijsp.ijsp_34_18

Parameshwaran, S., & Chandra, P. S. (2019). The new avatar of female sexual dysfunction in ICD-11—Will it herald a better future? *Journal of Psychosexual Health*, 1(2), 111–113. https://doi.org/10.1177/2631831819862408

Paris, J. (2007). Why psychiatrists are reluctant to diagnose: Borderline personality disorder. *Psychiatry*, 4(1), 35–39.

Paris, J. (2011). Pharmacological treatments for personality disorders. *International Review of Psychiatry*, 23(3), 303–309. https://doi.org/10.3109/09540261.2011.586993

Paris, J. (2012). The rise and fall of dissociative identity disorder. *Journal of Nervous and Mental Disease*, 200(12), 1076–1079. https://doi.org/10.1097/NMD.0b013e318275d285

Paris, J. (2015). *The intelligent clinician's guide to the DSM-5* (2nd ed.). Oxford University Press.

Paris, J. (2019). Dissociative identity disorder: Validity and use in the criminal justice system. *BJPsych Advances*, 25(05), 287–293. https://doi.org/10.1192/bja.2019.12

Paris, J., Bhat, V., & Thombs, B. (2015). Is adult attention-deficit hyperactivity disorder being overdiagnosed? *The Canadian Journal of Psychiatry*, 60(7), 324–328. https://doi.org/10.1177/070674371506000705

Parish, S. J., Simon, J. A., Davis, S. R., Giraldi, A., Goldstein, I., Goldstein, S. W., Kim, N. N., Kingsberg, S. A., Morgentaler, A., Nappi, R. E., Park, K., Stuenkel, C. A., Traish, A. M., & Vignozzi, L. (2021). International Society for the Study of Women's Sexual Health clinical practice guideline for the use of systemic testosterone for hypoactive sexual desire disorder in women. *The Journal of Sexual Medicine*, 18(5), 849–867. https://doi.org/10.1016/j.jsxm.2020.10.009

Pariyadath, V., Paulus, M. P., & Stein, E. A. (2013). Brain, reward, and drug addiction. In D. S. Charney, J. D. Buxbaum, P. Sklar, & E. J. Nestler (Eds.), *Neurobiology of mental illness* (4th ed., pp. 732–741). Oxford University Press. https://doi.org/10.1093/med/9780199934959.003.0055

Park, A., & Law, T. (2021, August 5). Doctors remain divided over first drug to treat Alzheimer's, but patients are eager to try it. *Time*. https://time.com/6081333/biogen-alzheimers-drug-aduhelm-fda-controversy/

Park, H. R., Kim, I. H., Kang, H., Lee, D. S., Kim, B.-N., Kim, D. G., & Paek, S. H. (2017). Nucleus accumbens deep brain stimulation for a patient with self-injurious behavior and autism spectrum disorder: Functional and structural changes of the brain: report of a case and review of literature. *Acta Neurochirurgica*, 159(1), 137–143. https://doi.org/10.1007/s00701-016-3002-2

Park, H. R., Lee, J. M., Moon, H. E., Lee, D. S., Kim, B.-N., Kim, J., Kim, D. G., & Paek, S. H. (2016). A short review on the current understanding of autism spectrum disorders. *Experimental Neurobiology*, 25(1), 1–13. https://doi.org/10.5607/en.2016.25.1.1

Park, R. J., Godier, L. R., & Cowdrey, F. A. (2014). Hungry for reward: How can neuroscience inform the development of treatment for Anorexia Nervosa? *Behaviour Research and Therapy*, 62, 47–59. https://doi.org/10.1016/j.brat.2014.07.007

Park, S., & Schepp, K. G. (2015). A systematic review of research on children of alcoholics: Their inherent resilience and vulnerability. *Journal of Child and Family Studies*, 24(5), 1222–1231. https://doi.org/10.1007/s10826-014-9930-7

Parker, J. D., & Naeem, A. (2019). Pharmacologic treatment of borderline personality disorder. *American Family Physician*, 99(5), 333A-333B.

Parker, M. M., Hunnicutt Hollenbaugh, K. M., & Kelly, C. T. (2021). Exploring the impact of child-centered play therapy for children exhibiting behavioral problems: A meta-analysis. *International Journal of Play Therapy*, 30(4), 259–271. https://doi.org/10.1037/pla0000128

Parkes, C. M., Laungani, P., & Young, W. (Eds.). (2015). *Death and bereavement across cultures* (2nd ed.). Routledge.

Parmar, A., & Kaloiya, G. (2018). Comorbidity of personality disorder among substance use disorder patients: A narrative review. *Indian Journal of Psychological Medicine*, 40(6), 517–527. https://doi.org/10.4103/IJPSYM.IJPSYM_164_18

Parry, M. S. (2006). Dorothea Dix (1802-1887). *American Journal of Public Health*, 96(4), 624–625.

Parry-Jones, B. (1994). Merycism or rumination disorder: A historical investigation and current assessment. *The British Journal of Psychiatry*, 165(3), 303–314. https://doi.org/10.1192/bjp.165.3.303

Parry-Jones, B., & Parry-Jones, W. L. (1992). Pica: Symptom or eating disorder? A historical assessment. *The British Journal of Psychiatry*, 160, 341–354. https://doi.org/10.1192/bjp.160.3.341

Parsons, A. (1970). Is the Oedipus complex universal? In W. Muensterberger (Ed.), *Man and his culture* (pp. 331–385). Taplinger Publishing.

Parsons, C., Roberts, R., & Mills, N. T. (2020). Review: Inflammation and anxiety-based disorders in children and adolescents – a systematic review and meta-analysis. *Child and Adolescent Mental Health*. https://doi.org/10.1111/camh.12434

Partinen, M., Holzinger, B., Morin, C. M., Espie, C., Chung, F., Penzel, T., Benedict, C., Bolstad, C. J., Cedernaes, J., Chan, R. N. Y., Dauvilliers, Y., Gennaro, L. D., Han, F., Inoue, Y., Matsui, K., Leger, D., Cunha, A. S., Merikanto, I., Mota-Rolim, S., … Bjorvatn, B. (2021). Sleep and daytime problems during the COVID-19 pandemic and effects of coronavirus infection, confinement and financial suffering: A multinational survey using a harmonised questionnaire. *BMJ Open*, 11 (12), Article e050672. https://doi.org/10.1136/bmjopen-2021-050672

Paschou, P., Fernandez, T. V., Sharp, F., Heiman, G. A., & Hoekstra, P. J. (2013). Genetic susceptibility and neurotransmitters in Tourette syndrome. In D. Martino & A. E. Cavanna (Eds.), *International Review of Neurobiology* (Vol. 112, pp. 155–177). Academic Press. https://doi.org/10.1016/B978-0-12-411546-0.00006-8

Passos, I. C., Vasconcelos-Moreno, M. P., Costa, L. G., Kunz, M., Brietzke, E., Quevedo, J., Salum, G., Magalhães, P. V., Kapczinski, F., & Kauer-Sant'Anna, M. (2015). Inflammatory markers in post-traumatic stress disorder: A systematic review, meta-analysis, and meta-regression. *The Lancet Psychiatry*, 2(11), 1002–1012. https://doi.org/10.1016/S2215-0366(15)00309-0

Patel, D. R., Cabral, M. D., Ho, A., & Merrick, J. (2020). A clinical primer on intellectual disability.

Translational Pediatrics, 9(Suppl. 1), S23–S35. https://doi.org/10.21037/tp.2020.02.02

Patel, S., Khan, S., M, S., & Hamid, P. (2020). The association between cannabis use and schizophrenia: Causative or curative? A systematic review. *Cureus, 12*(7), Article e9309. https://doi.org/10.7759/cureus.9309

Patil, T., & Giordano, J. (2010). On the ontological assumptions of the medical model of psychiatry: Philosophical considerations and pragmatic tasks. *Philosophy, Ethics, and Humanities in Medicine, 5*, 3.

Paton, C., Crawford, M. J., Bhatti, S. F., Patel, M. X., & Barnes, T. R. E. (2015). The use of psychotropic medication in patients with emotionally unstable personality disorder under the care of UK mental health services. *The Journal of Clinical Psychiatry, 76*(4), e512-518. https://doi.org/10.4088/JCP.14m09228

Patrícia, A.-M., Nataniel, O. F., Paula, C. F., Rizzo, de Souza, D. T., Diogo, P., & Ágata, A. (2022). *Influence of social media on body dissatisfaction in adolescents and increasing risk of developing eating disorders: A systematic review. 7*, Article 2144.

Patrick, M. E., Schulenberg, J. E., Miech, R. A., Johnston, L. D., O'Malley, P. M., & Bachman, J. G. (2022). *Monitoring the Future Panel Study annual report: National data on substance use among adults ages 19 to 60, 1976-2021* (Monitoring the Future Monograph Series). University of Michigan Institute for Social Research. https://doi.org/10.7826/ISRUM.06.585140.002.07.0001.2022

Patten, S. B. (2015). Medical models and metaphors for depression. *Epidemiology and Psychiatric Sciences, 24*(4), 303–308. https://doi.org/10.1017/S2045796015000153

Pauls, D. L. (2012). The genetics of obsessive-compulsive disorder: Current status. In J. Zohar (Ed.), *Obsessive compulsive disorder: Current science and clinical practice* (pp. 277–299). Wiley-Blackwell. https://doi.org/10.1002/9781119941125.ch11

Pauls, D. L., Fernandez, T. V., Mathews, C. A., State, M. W., & Scharf, J. M. (2014). The inheritance of tourette disorder: A review. *Journal of Obsessive-Compulsive and Related Disorders, 3*(4), 380–385. https://doi.org/10.1016/j.jocrd.2014.06.003

Pearce, J. M. S. (2004). Richard Morton: Origins of anorexia nervosa. *European Neurology, 52*(4), 191–192. https://doi.org/10.1159/000082033

Pearce, J., Rafiq, S., Simpson, J., & Varese, F. (2019). Perceived discrimination and psychosis: A systematic review of the literature. *Social Psychiatry and Psychiatric Epidemiology, 54*(9), 1023–1044. https://doi.org/10.1007/s00127-019-01729-3

Pearce, N. (2012). Classification of epidemiological study designs. *International Journal of Epidemiology, 41*(2), 393–397. https://doi.org/doi: 10.1093/ije/dys049

Pearl, D., & Schrollinger, E. (1999). Acupuncture: Its use in medicine. *The Western Journal of Medicine, 171*(3), 176–180.

Pearson, M., R. Egglestone, S., & Winship, G. (2023). The biological paradigm of psychosis in crisis: A Kuhnian analysis. *Nursing Philosophy*, Article e12418. https://doi.org/10.1111/nup.12418

Pearson, N. T., & Berry, J. H. (2019). Cannabis and psychosis through the lens of DSM-5. *International Journal of Environmental Research and Public Health, 16*, Article 4149. https://doi.org/10.3390/ijerph16214149

Pedersen, N. L., & Fiske, A. (2010). Genetic influences on suicide and nonfatal suicidal behavior: Twin study findings. *European Psychiatry, 25*(5), 264–267. https://doi.org/10.1016/j.eurpsy.2009.12.008

Peele, S. (1989). *Diseasing of America: Addiction treatment out of control.* Houghton Mifflin.

Pelham, W. E., Burrows-MacLean, L., Gnagy, E. M., Fabiano, G. A., Coles, E. K., Wymbs, B. T., Chacko, A., Walker, K. S., Wymbs, F., Garefino, A., Hoffman, M. T., Waxmonsky, J. G., & Waschbusch, D. A. (2014). A dose-ranging study of behavioral and pharmacological treatment in social settings for children with ADHD. *Journal of Abnormal Child Psychology, 42*(6), 1019–1031. https://doi.org/10.1007/s10802-013-9843-8

Pelham, W. E., Fabiano, G. A., Waxmonsky, J. G., Greiner, A. R., Gnagy, E. M., Pelham, W. E., Coxe, S., Verley, J., Bhatia, I., Hart, K., Karch, K., Konijnendijk, E., Tresco, K., Nahum-Shani, I., & Murphy, S. A. (2016). Treatment sequencing for childhood ADHD: A multiple-randomization study of adaptive medication and behavioral interventions. *Journal of Clinical Child and Adolescent Psychology, 45*(4), 396–415. https://doi.org/10.1080/15374416.2015.1105138

Peluso, M. J., Lewis, S. W., Barnes, T. R. E., & Jones, P. B. (2012). Extrapyramidal motor side-effects of first- and second-generation antipsychotic drugs. *British Journal of Psychiatry, 200*(5), 387–392. https://doi.org/10.1192/bjp.bp.111.101485

Pemment, J. (2013). Psychopathy versus sociopathy: Why the distinction has become crucial. *Aggression and Violent Behavior, 18*(5), 458–461. https://doi.org/10.1016/j.avb.2013.07.001

Peñas-Lledó, E. M., Dorado, P., Agüera, Z., Gratacós, M., Estivill, X., Fernández-Aranda, F., & Llerena, A. (2012). CYP2D6 polymorphism in patients with eating disorders. *The Pharmacogenomics Journal, 12*(2), 173–175. doi:10.1038/tpj.2010.78

Penninx, B. W., Pine, D. S., Holmes, E. A., & Reif, A. (2021). Anxiety disorders. *The Lancet, 397*(10277), 914–927. https://doi.org/10.1016/S0140-6736(21)00359-7

Pennypacker, S. D., Cunnane, K., Cash, M. C., & Romero-Sandoval, E. A. (2022). Potency and therapeutic THC and CBD ratios: U.S. cannabis markets overshoot. *Frontiers in Pharmacology, 13*, Article 921493. https://www.doi.org/10.3389/fphar.2022.921493

Pereira, L. P., Köhler, C. A., Stubbs, B., Miskowiak, K. W., Morris, G., de Freitas, B. P., Thompson, T., Fernandes, B. S., Brunoni, A. R., Maes, M., Pizzagalli, D. A., & Carvalho, A. F. (2018). Imaging genetics paradigms in depression research: Systematic review and meta-analysis. *Progress in Neuro-Psychopharmacology and Biological Psychiatry, 86*, 102–113. https://doi.org/10.1016/j.pnpbp.2018.05.012

Pérez de Mendiola, X., Hidalgo-Mazzei, D., Vieta, E., & González-Pinto, A. (2021). Overview of lithium's use: A nationwide survey. *International Journal of Bipolar Disorders, 9*(1), 10. https://doi.org/10.1186/s40345-020-00215-z

Pérez-López, F. R., Chedraui, P., Pérez-Roncero, G., López-Baena, M. T., & Cuadros-López, J. L. (2009). Premenstrual syndrome and premenstrual dysphoric disorder: Symptoms and cluster influences. *The Open Psychiatry Journal, 3.*

Perez-Rodriguez, M. M., New, A. S., & Siever, L. J. (2013). The neurobiology of personality disorders: The shift to DSM-5. In D. S. Charney, J. D. Buxbaum, P. Sklar, & E. J. Nestler (Eds.), *Neurobiology of mental illness* (4th ed., pp. 1089–1102). Oxford University Press. https://doi.org/10.1093/med/9780199934959.003.0084

Perihan, C., Burke, M., Bowman-Perrott, L., Bicer, A., Gallup, J., Thompson, J., & Sallese, M. (2020). Effects of cognitive behavioral therapy for reducing anxiety in children with high functioning ASD: A systematic review and meta-analysis. *Journal of Autism and Developmental Disorders, 50*(6), 1958–1972. https://doi.org/10.1007/s10803-019-03949-7

Peris, T. S., Sugar, C. A., Bergman, R. L., Chang, S., Langley, A., & Piacentini, J. (2012). Family factors predict treatment outcome for pediatric obsessive-compulsive disorder. *Journal of Consulting and Clinical Psychology, 80*(2), 255–263. https://doi.org/10.1037/a0027084

Peris, T. S., Yadegar, M., Asarnow, J. R., & Piacentini, J. (2012). Pediatric obsessive compulsive disorder: Family climate as a predictor of treatment outcome. *Journal of Obsessive-Compulsive and Related Disorders, 1*(4), 267–273. https://doi.org/10.1016/j.jocrd.2012.07.003

Perisetti, A., Rimu, A. H., Khan, S. A., Bansal, P., & Goyal, H. (2020). Role of cannabis in inflammatory bowel diseases. *Annals of Gastroenterology, 33*(2), 134–144. https://doi.org/10.20524/aog.2020.0452

Perkins, B. R., & Rouanzoin, C. C. (2002). A critical evaluation of current views regarding eye movement desensitization and reprocessing (EMDR): Clarifying points of confusion. *Journal of Clinical Psychology, 58*(1), 77–97. https://doi.org/10.1002/jclp.1130

Perkins, K. M., & Cross, Jr., W. E. (2014). False consciousness and the maintenance of injustice. In C. V. Johnson, H. L. Friedman, J. Diaz, Z. Franco, & B. K. Nastasi (Eds.), *The Praeger handbook of social justice and psychology: Vol. 1. Fundamental issues and special populations* (pp. 97–114). Praeger.

Perlin, M. L. (2017a). "God said to Abraham/kill me a son": Why the insanity defense and the incompetency status are compatible with and required by the Convention on the Rights of Persons with Disabilities and basic principles of therapeutic jurisprudence. *American Criminal Law Review, 54*(2), 477–519.

Perlin, M. L. (2017b). The insanity defense: Nine myths that will not go away. In M. D. White (Ed.), *The insanity defense: Multidisciplinary views on its history, trends, and controversies* (pp. 3–22). Praeger.

Perlis, R. H. (2015). The emerging genetics of bipolar disorder. In A. Yildiz, P. Ruiz, & C. B. Nemeroff (Eds.), *The bipolar book: History, neurobiology, and treatment* (pp. 181–188). Oxford University Press.

Perrin, N., Sayer, L., & While, A. (2015). The efficacy of alarm therapy versus desmopressin therapy in the treatment of primary mono-symptomatic nocturnal enuresis: A systematic review. *Primary Health Care Research and Development, 16*(1), 21–31. https://doi.org/10.1017/S146342361300042X

Perrykkad, K., & Hohwy, J. (2019). When big data aren't the answer. *Proceedings of the National Academy of Sciences, 116*(28), 13738–13739. https://doi.org/10.1073/pnas.1902050116

Pertusa, A., Fullana, M. A., Singh, S., Alonso, P., Menchón, J. M., & Mataix-Cols, D. (2008). Compulsive hoarding: OCD symptom, distinct clinical syndrome, or both? *The American Journal of Psychiatry, 165*(10), 1289–1298. https://doi.org/10.1176/appi.ajp.2008.07111730

Pescosolido, B. A., Halpern-Manners, A., Luo, L., & Perry, B. (2021). Trends in public stigma of mental illness in the US, 1996-2018. *JAMA Network Open, 4*(12), e2140202. https://doi.org/10.1001/jamanetworkopen.2021.40202

Peter, S. C., Li, Q., Pfund, R. A., Whelan, J. P., & Meyers, A. W. (2019). Public stigma across addictive behaviors: Casino gambling, eSports gambling, and Internet gaming. *Journal of Gambling Studies, 35*(1), 247–259. https://doi.org/10.1007/s10899-018-9775-x

Peters, B. M. (2013). Evolutionary psychology: Neglecting neurobiology in defining the mind. *Theory & Psychology, 23*(3), 305–322. https://doi.org/10.1177/0959354313480269

Peters, L., & Ansari, D. (2019). Are specific learning disorders truly specific, and are they disorders? *Trends in Neuroscience and Education, 17*, 100115. https://doi.org/10.1016/j.tine.2019.100115

Peters, S. M. (2021). Demedicalizing the aftermath of sexual assault: Toward a radical humanistic approach. *Journal of Humanistic Psychology, 61*(6), 939–961. https://doi.org/10.1177/0022167819831526

Petersen, L., Sørensen, T. I. A., Andersen, P. K., Mortensen, P. B., & Hawton, K. (2014). Genetic and familial environmental effects on suicide attempts: A study of Danish adoptees and their biological and adoptive siblings. *Journal of Affective Disorders, 155*, 273–277. https://doi.org/10.1016/j.jad.2013.11.012

Peterson, B. S. (2015). Research Domain Criteria (RDoC): A new psychiatric nosology whose time has not yet come. *Journal of Child Psychology and Psychiatry*, *56*(7), 719–722. https://doi.org/10.1111/jcpp.12439

Peterson, D. L., Webb, C. A., Keeley, J. W., Gaebel, W., Zielasek, J., Rebello, T. J., Robles, R., Matsumoto, C., Kogan, C. S., Kulygina, M., Farooq, S., Green, M. F., Falkai, P., Hasan, A., Galderisi, S., Larach, V., Krasnov, V., & Reed, G. M. (2019). The reliability and clinical utility of ICD-11 schizoaffective disorder: A field trial. *Schizophrenia Research*, *208*, 235–241. https://doi.org/10.1016/j.schres.2019.02.011

Petry, N. M. (2016a). Gambling disorder: The first officially recognized behavioral addiction. In N. M. Petry (Ed.), *Behavioral addictions: DSM-5® and beyond* (pp. 7–41). Oxford University Press.

Petry, N. M. (2016b). Introduction to behavioral addictions. In N. M. Petry (Ed.), *Behavioral addictions: DSM-5® and beyond* (pp. 1–5). Oxford University Press.

Peyrot, W. J., Van der Auwera, S., Milaneschi, Y., Dolan, C. V., Madden, P. A. F., Sullivan, P. F., Strohmaier, J., Ripke, S., Rietschel, M., Nivard, M. G., Mullins, N., Montgomery, G. W., Henders, A. K., Heat, A. C., Fisher, H. L., Dunn, E. C., Byrne, E. M., Air, T. A., Baune, B. T., ... Sullivan, P. F. (2018). Does childhood trauma moderate polygenic risk for depression? A meta-analysis of 5765 subjects from the psychiatric genomics consortium. *Biological Psychiatry*, *84*(2), 138–147. https://doi.org/10.1016/j.biopsych.2017.09.009

Pfaus, J. G. (2009). Pathways of sexual desire. *Journal of Sexual Medicine*, *6*(6), 1506–1533. https://doi.org/10.1111/j.1743-6109.2009.01309.x

Phelps, B. J. (2000). Dissociative identity disorder: The relevance of behavior analysis. *The Psychological Record*, *50*(2), 235–249.

Phillipou, A., Carruthers, S. P., Di Biase, M. A., Zalesky, A., Abel, L. A., Castle, D. J., Gurvich, C., & Rossell, S. L. (2018). White matter microstructure in anorexia nervosa. *Human Brain Mapping*, *39*(11), 4385–4392. https://doi.org/10.1002/hbm.24279

Phillipou, A., Rossell, S. L., & Castle, D. J. (2014). The neurobiology of anorexia nervosa: A systematic review. *Australian and New Zealand Journal of Psychiatry*, *48*(2), 128–152. https://doi.org/10.1177/0004867413509693

Phillips, D. P. (1974). The influence of suggestion on suicide: Substantive and theoretical implications of the Werther effect. *American Sociological Review*, *39*(3), 340–354. https://doi.org/10.2307/2094294

Phillips, G., & Raskin, J. D. (2021). A primer for clinicians on alternatives to the *Diagnostic and statistical manual of mental disorders*. *Professional Psychology: Research and Practice*, *52*(2), 91–103. https://doi.org/10.1037/pro0000327

Pianowski, G., Carvalho, L. de F., & Miguel, F. K. (2019). Investigating the Spectra constellations of the Hierarchical Taxonomy of Psychopathology (HiTOP) model for personality disorders based on empirical data from a community sample. *Brazilian Journal of Psychiatry*, *41*, 148–152. https://doi.org/10.1590/1516-4446-2018-0015

Pickard, H. (2020). What we're not talking about when we talk about addiction. *Hastings Center Report*, *50*(4), 37–46. https://doi.org/10.1002/hast.1172

Pickup, G. J., & Frith, C. D. (2001). Theory of mind impairments in schizophrenia: Symptomatology, severity and specificity. *Psychological Medicine*, *31*(2), 207–220. https://doi.org/10.1017/S0033291701003385

Pieper, S., Out, D., Bakermans-Kranenburg, M. J., & van Ijzendoorn, M. H. (2011). Behavioral and molecular genetics of dissociation: The role of the serotonin transporter gene promoter polymorphism (5-HTTLPR). *Journal of Traumatic Stress*, *24*(4), 373–380. https://doi.org/10.1002/jts.20659

Pies, R. W. (2014). The bereavement exclusion and DSM-5: An update and commentary. *Innovations in Clinical Neuroscience*, *11*(7–8), 19–22.

Pike, K. M., & Dunne, P. E. (2015). The rise of eating disorders in Asia: A review. *Journal of Eating Disorders*, *3*(1), 33. https://doi.org/10.1186/s40337-015-0070-2

Pike, K. M., Dunne, P. E., & Addai, E. (2013). Expanding the boundaries: Reconfiguring the demographics of the "typical" eating disordered patient. *Current Psychiatry Reports*, *15*(11), 411–411. https://doi.org/10.1007/s11920-013-0411-2

Pilcher, F., Seri, S., & Cavanna, A. E. (2020). Initial treatment retention for habit reversal training in adults with Tourette syndrome. *Journal of Psychopathology*, 1. https://doi.org/10.36148/2284-0249-368

Pilecki, B., Luoma, J. B., Bathje, G. J., Rhea, J., & Narloch, V. F. (2021). Ethical and legal issues in psychedelic harm reduction and integration therapy. *Harm Reduction Journal*, *18*(1), 40. https://doi.org/10.1186/s12954-021-00489-1

Pilkington, K., Boshnakova, A., & Richardson, J. (2006). St John's wort for depression: Time for a different perspective? *Complementary Therapies in Medicine*, *14*(4), 268–281. https://doi.org/10.1016/j.ctim.2006.01.003

Pincott, J. (2012, March 13). Slips of the tongue. *Psychology Today*. https://www.psychologytoday.com/intl/articles/201203/slips-the-tongue

Pinel, J. P. J., Assanand, S., & Lehman, D. R. (2000). Hunger, eating, and ill health. *American Psychologist*, *55*(10), 1105–1116. doi:10.1037/0003-066X.55.10.1105

Piotrowska, P. J., Stride, C. B., Croft, S. E., & Rowe, R. (2015). Socioeconomic status and antisocial behaviour among children and adolescents: A systematic review and meta-analysis. *Clinical Psychology Review*, *35*, 47–55. https://doi.org/10.1016/j.cpr.2014.11.003

Piper, A., & Merskey, H. (2004a). The persistence of folly: A critical examination of dissociative identity disorder. Part I. The excesses of an improbable concept. *The Canadian Journal of Psychiatry*, *49*(9), 592–600. https://doi.org/10.1177/070674370404900904

Piper, A., & Merskey, H. (2004b). The persistence of folly: Critical examination of dissociative identity disorder. Part II. The defence and decline of multiple personality or dissociative identity disorder. *The Canadian Journal of Psychiatry*, *49*(10), 678–683. https://doi.org/10.1177/070674370404901005

Pires, R., Henriques-Calado, J., Sousa Ferreira, A., Bach, B., Paulino, M., Gama Marques, J., Ribeiro Moreira, A., Grácio, J., & Gonçalves, B. (2021). The utility of ICD-11 and DSM-5 traits for differentiating patients with personality disorders from other clinical groups. *Frontiers in Psychiatry*, *12*, Article 633882. https://doi.org/10.3389/fpsyt.2021.633882

Pirkis, J., Rossetto, A., Nicholas, A., Ftanou, M., Robinson, J., & Reavley, N. (2019). Suicide prevention media campaigns: A systematic literature review. *Health Communication*, *34*(4), 402–414. https://doi.org/10.1080/10410236.2017.1405484

Pisano, S., & Masi, G. (2020). Recommendations for the pharmacological management of irritability and aggression in conduct disorder patients. *Expert Opinion on Pharmacotherapy*, *21*(1), 5–7. https://doi.org/10.1080/14656566.2019.1685498

Pithers, W. D., Kashima, K. M., Cumming, G. F., Beal, L. S., & Buell, M. M. (1988). Relapse prevention of sexual aggression. *Annals of the New York Academy of Sciences*, *528*(1), 244–260. https://doi.org/10.1111/j.1749-6632.1988.tb50868.x

Pittenger, C., & Bloch, M. H. (2014). Pharmacological treatment of obsessive-compulsive disorder. *The Psychiatric Clinics of North America*, *37*(3), 375–391. https://doi.org/10.1016/j.psc.2014.05.006

Pittig, A., Kotter, R., & Hoyer, J. (2019). The struggle of behavioral therapists with exposure: Self-reported practicability, negative beliefs, and therapist distress about exposure-based interventions. *Behavior Therapy*, *50*(2), 353–366. https://doi.org/10.1016/j.beth.2018.07.003

Pittman, J. P. (2016). Double consciousness. In E. N. Zalta (Ed.), *The Stanford Encyclopedia of Philosophy* (Summer 2016). Metaphysics Research Lab, Stanford University. https://plato.stanford.edu/archives/sum2016/entries/double-consciousness/

Piwowarczyk, A., Horvath, A., Pisula, E., Kawa, R., & Szajewska, H. (2020). Gluten-free diet in children with autism spectrum disorders: A randomized, controlled, single-blinded trial. *Journal of Autism and Developmental Disorders*, *50*(2), 482–490. https://doi.org/10.1007/s10803-019-04266-9

Platt, J. J., & Husband, S. D. (1993). An overview of problem-solving and social skills approaches in substance abuse treatment. *Psychotherapy: Theory, Research, Practice, Training*, *30*(2), 276–283. https://doi.org/10.1037/0033-3204.30.2.276

Platt, J., Keyes, K. M., & Koenen, K. C. (2014). Size of the social network versus quality of social support: Which is more protective against PTSD? *Social Psychiatry and Psychiatric Epidemiology*, *49*(8), 1279–1286. https://doi.org/10.1007/s00127-013-0798-4

Plaud, J. J., & Holm, J. E. (1998). Sexual dysfunctions. In J. J. Plaud & G. H. Eifert (Eds.), *Bollin* (pp. 136–151). Allyn & Bacon.

Plaut, V. L. (1983). Punishment versus treatment of the guilty but mentally ill. *Journal of Criminal Law & Criminology*, *74*(2), 428–456. https://doi.org/10.2307/1143083

Ploog, D. W. (2003). The place of the triune brain in psychiatry. *Physiology & Behavior*, *79*(3), 487–493. https://doi.org/10.1016/S0031-9384(03)00154-9

Plumber, N., Majeed, M., Ziff, S., Thomas, S. E., Bolla, S. R., & Gorantla, V. R. (2021). Stimulant usage by medical students for cognitive enhancement: A systematic review. *Cureus*, *13*(5), e15163. https://doi.org/10.7759/cureus.15163

Pohar, R., & Argáez, C. (2017). *Acceptance and commitment therapy for post-traumatic stress disorder, anxiety, and depression: A review of clinical effectiveness*. Canadian Agency for Drugs and Technologies in Health. https://www.ncbi.nlm.nih.gov/books/NBK525684/

Pol, H. E. H., van Baal, G. C. M., Schnack, H. G., Brans, R. G. H., van der Schot, A. C., Brouwer, R. M., van Haren, N. E. M., Lepage, C., Collins, D. L., Evans, A. C., Boomsma, D. I., Nolen, W., & Kahn, R. S. (2012). Overlapping and segregating structural brain abnormalities in twins with schizophrenia or bipolar disorder. *Archives of General Psychiatry*, *69*(4), 349–359. https://doi.org/10.1001/archgenpsychiatry.2011.1615

Pole, N., Best, S. R., Metzler, T., & Marmar, C. R. (2005). Why are Hispanics at greater risk for PTSD? *Cultural Diversity and Ethnic Minority Psychology*, *11*(2), 144–161. https://doi.org/10.1037/1099-9809.11.2.144

Pole, R., Vankar, G., & Ghogare, A. (2022). A clinical review of enuresis and its associated psychiatric comorbidities. *Annals of Indian Psychiatry*, *6*(1), 4–14. https://doi.org/10.4103/aip.aip_102_21

Policy Surveillance Program. (n.d.). *Long-term involuntary commitment laws*. Retrieved November 3, 2022, from https://lawatlas.org/datasets/long-term-involuntary-commitment-laws

Polikowsky, H. G., Shaw, D. M., Petty, L. E., Chen, H.-H., Pruett, D. G., Linklater, J. P., Viljoen, K. Z., Beilby, J. M., Highland, H. M., Levitt, B., Avery, C. L., Mullan Harris, K., Jones, R. M., Below, J. E., & Kraft, S. J. (2022). Population-based genetic effects for developmental stuttering. *Human Genetics and Genomics Advances*, *3*(1), Article 100073. https://doi.org/10.1016/j.xhgg.2021.100073

Polimeni, J., Reiss, J. P., & Sareen, J. (2005). Could obsessive-compulsive disorder have originated as a group-selected adaptive trait in traditional societies? *Medical Hypotheses*, *65*(4), 655–664.

Pollack, R. (1997). *The creation of Dr. B: A biography of Bruno Bettelheim*. Simon & Schuster.

Pollak, J. (1987). Obsessive-compulsive personality: Theoretical and clinical perspectives and recent research findings. *Journal of Personality Disorders*, 1(3), 248–262. https://doi.org/10.1521/pedi.1987.1.3.248

Pollan, M. (2019, May 10). Not so fast on psychedelic mushrooms. *The New York Times*. https://www.nytimes.com/2019/05/10/opinion/denver-mushrooms-psilocybin.html

Polusny, M. A., Erbes, C. R., Thuras, P., Moran, A., Lamberty, G. J., Collins, R. C., Rodman, J. L., & Lim, K. O. (2015). Mindfulness-based stress reduction for posttraumatic stress disorder among veterans: A randomized clinical trial. *JAMA*, 314(5), 456. https://doi.org/10.1001/jama.2015.8361

Polychronis, P. D., & Keyes, L. N. (2022). A case for using the *Psychodynamic diagnostic manual-2* instead of the *Diagnostic and statistical manual of mental disorders*-5 in university and college counseling centers. *Journal of College Student Psychotherapy*, 36(1), 83–94. https://doi.org/10.1080/87568225.2020.1760161

Pontillo, M., Tata, M. C., Averna, R., Demaria, F., Gargiullo, P., Guerrera, S., Pucciarini, M. L., Santonastaso, O., & Vicari, S. (2019). Peer victimization and onset of social anxiety disorder in children and adolescents. *Brain Sciences*, 9(6), Article 6. https://doi.org/10.3390/brainsci9060132

Ponzini, G. T., & Steinman, S. A. (2022). A systematic review of public stigma attributes and obsessive–compulsive disorder symptom subtypes. *Stigma and Health*, 7(1), 14–26. https://doi.org/10.1037/sah0000310

Poole, R., Kennedy, O. J., Roderick, P., Fallowfield, J. A., Hayes, P. C., & Parkes, J. (2017). Coffee consumption and health: Umbrella review of meta-analyses of multiple health outcomes. *BMJ*, 359, j5024. https://doi.org/10.1136/bmj.j5024

Pope, Jr., Harrison G., Barry, S., Bodkin, A., & Hudson, J. I. (2006). Tracking scientific interest in the dissociative disorders: A study of scientific publication output 1984-2003. *Psychotherapy and Psychosomatics*, 75(1), 19–24. https://doi.org/10.1159/000089223

Pope, Jr., Harrison G., Oliva, P. S., Hudson, J. I., Bodkin, J. A., & Gruber, A. J. (1999). Attitudes toward DSM-IV dissociative disorders diagnoses among board-certified American psychiatrists. *The American Journal of Psychiatry*, 156(2), 321–323. https://doi.org/10.1176/ajp.156.2.321

Popescu, A., Marian, M., Drăgoi, A. M., & Costea, R.-V. (2021). Understanding the genetics and neurobiological pathways behind addiction (Review). *Experimental and Therapeutic Medicine*, 21(5), 1–10. https://doi.org/10.3892/etm.2021.9976

Popolo, R., Dimaggio, G., Luther, L., Vinci, G., Salvatore, G., & Lysaker, P. H. (2016). Theory of mind in schizophrenia: Associations with clinical and cognitive insight controlling for levels of psychopathology. *Journal of Nervous and Mental Disease*, 204(3), 240–243. https://doi.org/10.1097/NMD.0000000000000454

Popovic, D., Schmitt, A., Kaurani, L., Senner, F., Papiol, S., Malchow, B., Fischer, A., Schulze, T. G., Koutsouleris, N., & Falkai, P. (2019). Childhood trauma in schizophrenia: Current findings and research perspectives. *Frontiers in Neuroscience*, 13, Article 274. https://doi.org/10.3389/fnins.2019.00274

Popovic, D., Scott, J., & Colom, F. (2015). Cognitive behavioral therapy and psychoeducation. In A. Yildiz, P. Ruiz, & C. B. Nemeroff (Eds.), *The bipolar book: History, neurobiology, and treatment* (pp. 435–444). Oxford University Press.

Popper, C. W. (1997). Antidepressants in the treatment of attention-deficit/hyperactivity disorder. *The Journal of Clinical Psychiatry*, 58(Suppl. 14), 14–29.

Porsteinsson, A. P., Isaacson, R. S., Knox, S., Sabbagh, M. N., & Rubino, I. (2021). Diagnosis of early Alzheimer's disease: Clinical practice in 2021. *The Journal of Prevention of Alzheimer's Disease*, 8(3), 371–386. https://doi.org/10.14283/jpad.2021.23

Port, R. G., Oberman, L. M., & Roberts, T. P. (2019). Revisiting the excitation/inhibition imbalance hypothesis of ASD through a clinical lens. *The British Journal of Radiology*, 92(1101), 20180944. https://doi.org/10.1259/bjr.20180944

Porter, J. S., & Risler, E. (2014). The new alternative DSM-5 model for personality disorders: Issues and controversies. *Research on Social Work Practice*, 24(1), 50–56. https://doi.org/10.1177/1049731513500348

Porter, R. (2002). *Madness: A brief history*. Oxford University Press.

Portnow, L. H., Vaillancourt, D. E., & Okun, M. S. (2013). The history of cerebral PET scanning: From physiology to cutting-edge technology. *Neurology*, 80(10), 952–956. https://doi.org/10.1212/WNL.0b013e318285c135

Potenza, M. N., Balodis, I. M., Derevensky, J., Grant, J. E., Petry, N. M., Verdejo Garcia, A., & Yip, S. W. (2019). Gambling disorder (Primer). *Nature Reviews: Disease Primers*. https://doi.org/10.1038/s41572-019-0099-7

Potvin, S., Stip, E., Sepehry, A. A., Gendron, A., Bah, R., & Kouassi, E. (2008). Inflammatory cytokine alterations in schizophrenia: A systematic quantitative review. *Biological Psychiatry*, 63(8), 801–808. https://doi.org/10.1016/j.biopsych.2007.09.024

Power, M. (2013). CBT for depression. In M. Power (Ed.), *The Wiley-Blackwell handbook of mood disorders* (2nd ed., pp. 173–191). Wiley-Blackwell.

Powers, P. S., & Bruty, H. (2009). Pharmacotherapy for eating disorders and obesity. *Child and Adolescent Psychiatric Clinics of North America*, 18(1), 175–187. https://doi.org/10.1016/j.chc.2008.07.009

Prata, D. P., Costa-Neves, B., Cosme, G., & Vassos, E. (2019). Unravelling the genetic basis of schizophrenia and bipolar disorder with GWAS: A systematic review. *Journal of Psychiatric Research*, 114, 178–207. https://doi.org/10.1016/j.jpsychires.2019.04.007

Pratt, L. A., Brody, D. J., & Gu, Q. (2017, August). Antidepressant use among persons aged 12 and over: United States, 2011-2014. *NCHS Data Brief*.

Pratt, M., Stevens, A., Thuku, M., Butler, C., Skidmore, B., Wieland, L. S., Clemons, M., Kanji, S., & Hutton, B. (2019). Benefits and harms of medical cannabis: A scoping review of systematic reviews. *Systematic Reviews*, 8(1), 320. https://doi.org/10.1186/s13643-019-1243-x

Prätzlich, M., Oldenhof, H., Steppan, M., Ackermann, K., Baker, R., Batchelor, M., Baumann, S., Bernhard, A., Clanton, R., Dikeos, D., Dochnal, R., Fehlbaum, L. V., Fernández-Rivas, A., González de Artaza-Lavesa, M., Gonzalez-Madruga, K., Guijarro, S., Gundlach, M., Herpertz-Dahlmann, B., Hervas, A., … Stadler, C. (2019). Resting autonomic nervous system activity is unrelated to antisocial behaviour dimensions in adolescents: Cross-sectional findings from a European multi-centre study. *Journal of Criminal Justice*, 65, 101536. https://doi.org/10.1016/j.jcrimjus.2018.01.004

Prescod, M. C. (2020, November 28). *PTSD is a normal reaction to extreme trauma ~ just as bleeding is a normal reaction to being stabbed*. The Center. https://www.thecenter4counseling.com/post/ptsd-is-a-normal-reaction-to-extreme-trauma-~-just-as-bleeding-is-a-normal-reaction-to-being-stabbed

Prescott, C. A., & Gottesman, I. I. (1993). Genetically mediated vulnerability to schizophrenia. *Psychiatric Clinics of North America*, 16(2), 245–267.

Pressman, D. L., & Bonanno, G. A. (2007). With whom do we grieve? Social and cultural determinants of grief processing in the United States and China. *Journal of Social and Personal Relationships*, 24(5), 729–746. https://doi.org/10.1177/0265407507081458

Preyde, M., Vanderkooy, J., Msw, P. C., Heintzman, J., Msw, A. W., & Barrick, K. (2014). The psychosocial characteristics associated with NSSI and suicide attempt of youth admitted to an in-patient psychiatric unit. 23(2), 100–110.

Price, G. R., & Ansari, D. (2013). Dyscalculia: Characteristics, causes, and treatments. *Numeracy: Advancing Education in Quantitative Literacy*, 6(1), 1–16. https://doi.org/10.5038/1936-4660.6.1.2

Price, J. S. (2013). In F. Durbano (Ed.), *New insights into anxiety disorders* (pp. 3–20). IntechOpen. https://doi.org/10.5772/52902

Prichard, J. C. (1835). *A treatise on insanity and other disorders affecting the mind*. Sherwood, Gilbert, and Piper.

Pridmore, S. (2011). Medicalisation of suicide. *The Malaysian Journal of Medical Sciences*, 18(4), 78–83.

Priebe, S., Bhatti, N., Barnicot, K., Bremner, S., Gaglia, A., Katsakou, C., Molosankwe, I., McCrone, P., & Zinkler, M. (2012). Effectiveness and cost-effectiveness of dialectical behaviour therapy for self-harming patients with personality disorder: A pragmatic randomised controlled trial. *Psychotherapy and Psychosomatics*, 81(6), 356–365. https://doi.org/10.1159/000338897

Priest, J. B. (2013). Emotionally focused therapy as treatment for couples with generalized anxiety disorder and relationship distress. *Journal of Couple & Relationship Therapy*, 12(1), 22–37. https://doi.org/10.1080/15332691.2013.749763

Priest, J. B. (2015). A Bowen family systems model of generalized anxiety disorder and romantic relationship distress. *Journal of Marital and Family Therapy*, 41(3), 340–353. https://doi.org/10.1111/jmft.12063

Prigerson, H. G., Boelen, P. A., Xu, J., Smith, K. V., & Maciejewski, P. K. (2021). Validation of the new DSM-5-TR criteria for prolonged grief disorder and the PG-13-Revised (PG-13-R) scale. *World Psychiatry*, 20(1), 96–106. https://doi.org/10.1002/wps.20823

Prigerson, H. G., Kakarala, S., Gang, J., & Maciejewski, P. K. (2021). History and status of prolonged grief disorder as a psychiatric diagnosis. *Annual Review of Clinical Psychology*, 17(1), 109–126. https://doi.org/10.1146/annurev-clinpsy-081219-093600

Prigge, M. B. D., Lange, N., Bigler, E. D., King, J. B., Dean, D. C., Adluru, N., Alexander, A. L., Lainhart, J. E., & Zielinski, B. A. (2021). A 16-year study of longitudinal volumetric brain development in males with autism. *NeuroImage*, 236, 118067. https://doi.org/10.1016/j.neuroimage.2021.118067

Prilleltensky, I. (1999). Critical psychology foundations for the promotion of mental health. *Annual Review of Critical Psychology*, 1(100–118).

Prilleltensky, I., Dokecki, P., Frieden, G., & Ota Wang, V. (2007). Counseling for wellness and justice: Foundations and ethical dilemmas. In E. Aldarondo (Ed.), *Advancing social justice through clinical practice* (pp. 19–42). Lawrence Erlbaum.

Pringsheim, T., Hirsch, L., Gardner, D., & Gorman, D. A. (2015). The pharmacological management of oppositional behaviour, conduct problems, and aggression in children and adolescents with attention-deficit hyperactivity disorder, oppositional defiant disorder, and conduct disorder: A systematic review and meta-analysis. Part 1: Psychostimulants, alpha-2 agonists, and atomoxetine. *The Canadian Journal of Psychiatry*, 60(2), 42–51. https://doi.org/10.1177/070674371506000202

Pringsheim, T., Holler-Managan, Y., Okun, M. S., Jankovic, J., Piacentini, J., Cavanna, A. E., Martino, D., Müller-Vahl, K., Woods, D. W., Robinson, M., Jarvie, E., Roessner, V., & Oskoui, M. (2019). Comprehensive systematic review summary: Treatment of tics in people with Tourette syndrome and chronic tic disorders. *Neurology*, 92(19), 907–915. https://doi.org/10.1212/WNL.0000000000007467

Prior, A., Fenger-Grøn, M., Davydow, D. S., Olsen, J., Li, J., Guldin, M.-B., & Vestergaard, M. (2018). Bereavement, multimorbidity and mortality: A population-based study using bereavement as an indicator of mental stress. *Psychological Medicine*, 48(9), 1437–1443. https://doi.org/10.1017/S0033291717002380

Prochaska, J. O., DiClemente, C. C., & Norcross, J. C. (1992). In search of how people change: Applications to addictive behaviors. *American Psychologist*, 47(9), 1102–1114. https://doi.org/10.1037/0003-066X.47.9.1102

Prochazka, J., Parilakova, K., Rudolf, P., Bruk, V., Jung-wirthova, R., Fejtova, S., Masaryk, R., & Vaculik, M. (2022). Pain as social glue: A preregistered direct replication of experiment 2 of Bastian et al. (2014). *Psychological Science*, 33(3), 463–473. https://doi.org/10.1177/09567976211040745

Procter, H., & Winter, D. (2020). *Personal and relational construct psychotherapy*. Palgrave Macmillan. https://doi.org/10.1007/978-3-030-52177-6

Protinsky, H., & Dillard, C. (1983). Enuresis: A family therapy model. *Psychotherapy: Theory, Research & Practice*, 20(1), 81–89. https://doi.org/10.1037/h0088482

Protopapas, A., & Parrila, R. (2018). Is dyslexia a brain disorder? *Brain Sciences*, 8(4), 61. https://doi.org/10.3390/brainsci8040061

Prouty, G. (1994). *Theoretical evolutions in person-centered/experiential therapy*. Praeger.

Prouty, G. (2002). Humanistic psychotherapy for people with schizophrenia. In D. J. Cain (Ed.), *Humanistic psychotherapies: Handbook of research and practice* (pp. 579–601). American Psychological Association.

Prouty, G. (2007). Pre-therapy: The application of contact reflections. *American Journal of Psychotherapy*, 61(3), 285–295. https://doi.org/10.1176/appi.psychotherapy.2007.61.3.285

Pruccoli, J., Parmeggiani, A., Cordelli, D., & Lanari, M. (2021). The role of the noradrenergic system in eating disorders: A systematic review. *International Journal of Molecular Sciences*, 22(20), 11086. https://doi.org/10.3390/ijms222011086

Pruthi, G. K. (2018). Managing dissociative disorder with cognitive behaviour therapy: A case study. *The International Journal of Indian Psychology*, 6(6), 31–37. https://doi.org/10.25215/0604.004

Przepiorka, A. M., Blachnio, A., St. Louis, K. O., & Wozniak, T. (2013). Public attitudes toward stuttering in Poland. *International Journal of Language & Communication Disorders*, 48(6), 703–714. https://doi.org/10.1111/1460-6984.12041

Przeworski, A., Zoellner, L. A., Franklin, M. E., Garcia, A., Freeman, J., March, J. S., & Foa, E. B. (2012). Maternal and child expressed emotion as predictors of treatment response in pediatric obsessive–compulsive disorder. *Child Psychiatry and Human Development*, 43(3), 337–353. https://doi.org/10.1007/s10578-011-0268-8

Public Health England. (2020, December 3). *Prescribed medicines review: Summary*. GOV.UK. https://www.gov.uk/government/publications/prescribed-medicines-review-report/prescribed-medicines-review-summary

Puente, A. N., & Mitchell, J. T. (2016). Cognitive-behavioral therapy for adult ADHD: A case study of multi-method assessment of executive functioning in clinical practice and manualized treatment adaptation. *Clinical Case Studies*, 15(3), 198–211. https://doi.org/10.1177/1534650115614098

Pugle, M. (2022, February 28). *TikTok trend alert: Is self-diagnosing a mental disorder safe?* Everyday-Health.Com. https://www.everydayhealth.com/emotional-health/young-people-are-using-tiktok-to-diagnose-themselves-with-serious-mental-health-disorders/

Pugsley, K., Scherer, S. W., Bellgrove, M. A., & Hawi, Z. (2022). Environmental exposures associated with elevated risk for autism spectrum disorder may augment the burden of deleterious de novo mutations among probands. *Molecular Psychiatry*, 27(1), Article 1. https://doi.org/10.1038/s41380-021-01142-w

Pukay-Martin, N. D., Torbit, L., Landy, M. S. H., Macdonald, A., & Monson, C. M. (2017). Present- and trauma-focused cognitive–behavioral conjoint therapy for posttraumatic stress disorder: A case study. *Couple and Family Psychology: Research and Practice*, 6(2), 61–78. https://doi.org/10.1037/cfp0000071

Pukay-Martin, N. D., Torbit, L., Landy, M. S. H., Wanklyn, S. G., Shnaider, P., Lane, J. E. M., & Monson, C.

M. (2015). An uncontrolled trial of a present-focused cognitive-behavioral conjoint therapy for posttraumatic stress disorder. *Journal of Clinical Psychology*, 71(4), 302–312. https://doi.org/10.1002/jclp.22166

Pulkki-Råback, L., Ahola, K., Elovainio, M., Kivimäki, M., Hintsanen, M., Isometsä, E., Lönnqvist, J., & Virtanen, M. (2012). Socio-economic position and mental disorders in a working-age Finnish population: The Health 2000 Study. *European Journal of Public Health*, 22(3), 327–332. https://doi.org/10.1093/eurpub/ckr127

Pullan, S., & Dey, M. (2021). Vaccine hesitancy and anti-vaccination in the time of COVID-19: A Google Trends analysis. *Vaccine*, 39(14), 1877–1881. https://doi.org/10.1016/j.vaccine.2021.03.019

Punja, S., Shamseer, L., Hartling, L., Urichuk, L., Vandermeer, B., Nikles, J., & Vohra, S. (2016). Amphetamines for attention deficit hyperactivity disorder (ADHD) in children and adolescents. *Cochrane Database of Systematic Reviews*, 2016(2), CD009996. https://doi.org/10.1002/14651858.CD009996.pub2

Purves-Tyson, T. D., Weber-Stadlbauer, U., Richetto, J., Rothmond, D. A., Labouesse, M. A., Polesel, M., Robinson, K., Shannon Weickert, C., & Meyer, U. (2021). Increased levels of midbrain immune-related transcripts in schizophrenia and in murine offspring after maternal immune activation. *Molecular Psychiatry*, 26(3), 849–863. https://doi.org/10.1038/s41380-019-0434-0

Qamar, N., Castano, D., Patt, C., Chu, T., Cottrell, J., & Chang, S. L. (2019). Meta-analysis of alcohol induced gut dysbiosis and the resulting behavioral impact. *Behavioural Brain Research*, 376, 112196. https://doi.org/10.1016/j.bbr.2019.112196

Qian, J., Hu, Q., Wan, Y., Li, T., Wu, M., Ren, Z., & Yu, D. (2013). Prevalence of eating disorders in the general population: A systematic review. *Shanghai Archives of Psychiatry*, 25(4), 212–222. https://doi.org/10.3969/j.issn.1002-0829.2013.04.003

Qian, J., Wu, Y., Liu, F., Zhu, Y., Jin, H., Zhang, H., Wan, Y., Li, C., & Yu, D. (2022). An update on the prevalence of eating disorders in the general population: A systematic review and meta-analysis. *Eating and Weight Disorders - Studies on Anorexia, Bulimia and Obesity*, 27(2), 415–428. https://doi.org/10.1007/s40519-021-01162-z

Qin, C., Hu, J., Wan, Y., Cai, M., Wang, Z., Peng, Z., Liao, Y., Li, D., Yao, P., Liu, L., Rong, S., Bao, W., Xu, G., & Yang, W. (2021). Narrative review on potential role of gut microbiota in certain substance addiction. *Progress in Neuro-Psychopharmacology and Biological Psychiatry*, 106, 110093. https://doi.org/10.1016/j.pnpbp.2020.110093

Quan, L., Xu, X., Cui, Y., Han, H., Hendren, R. L., Zhao, L., & You, X. (2022). A systematic review and meta-analysis of the benefits of a gluten-free diet and/or casein-free diet for children with autism spectrum disorder. *Nutrition Reviews*, 80(5), 1237–1246. https://doi.org/10.1093/nutrit/nuab073

Queirós, F. C., Wehby, G. L., & Halpern, C. T. (2015). Developmental disabilities and socioeconomic outcomes in young adulthood. *Public Health Reports*, 130(3), 213–221.

Quidé, Y., Cohen-Woods, S., O'Reilly, N., Carr, V. J., Elzinga, B. M., & Green, M. J. (2018). Schizotypal personality traits and social cognition are associated with childhood trauma exposure. *British Journal of Clinical Psychology*, 57(4), 397–419. https://doi.org/10.1111/bjc.12187

Quinn, A. (2008). A person-centered approach to the treatment of combat veterans with post-traumatic stress disorder. *Journal of Humanistic Psychology*, 48(4), 458–476. https://doi.org/10.1177/0022167808316247

Quinn, A. (2011). A person-centered approach to the treatment of borderline personality disorder. *Journal of Humanistic Psychology*, 51(4), 465–491. https://doi.org/10.1177/0022167811399764

Quinn, M., & Lynch, A. (2016). Is ADHD a "real" disorder? *Support for Learning*, 31(1), 59–70. https://doi.org/10.1111/1467-9604.12114

Quinn, P. D., Chang, Z., Hur, K., Gibbons, R. D., Lahey, B. B., Rickert, M. E., Sjölander, A., Lichtenstein, P., Larsson, H., & D'Onofrio, B. M. (2017). ADHD medication and substance-related problems. *American Journal of Psychiatry*, 174(9), 877–885. https://doi.org/10.1176/appi.ajp.2017.16060686

Quinsey, V. L. (2012). Pragmatic and Darwinian views of the paraphilias. *Archives of Sexual Behavior*, 41(1), 217–220. https://doi.org/10.1007/s10508-011-9872-8

Quist, J. F., & Kennedy, J. L. (2001). Genetics of childhood disorders: XXIII. ADHD, part 7: The serotonin system. *Journal of the American Academy of Child & Adolescent Psychiatry*, 40(2), 253–256. https://doi.org/10.1097/00004583-200102000-00022

Qureshi, N. A., & Al-Bedah, A. M. (2013). Mood disorders and complementary and alternative medicine: A literature review. *Neuropsychiatric Disease and Treatment*, 9.

Rabeea, S. A., Merchant, H. A., Khan, M. U., Kow, C. S., & Hasan, S. S. (2021). Surging trends in prescriptions and costs of antidepressants in England amid COVID-19. *DARU Journal of Pharmaceutical Sciences*, 29(1), 217–221. https://doi.org/10.1007/s40199-021-00390-z

Rachman, S. (1997). A cognitive theory of obsessions. *Behaviour Research and Therapy*, 35(9), 793–802. https://doi.org/10.1016/S0005-7967(97)00040-5

Rachman, S. (1998). A cognitive theory of obsessions: Elaborations. *Behaviour Research and Therapy*, 36(4), 385–401. https://doi.org/10.1016/s0005-7967(97)10041-9

Radden, J. H. (2021). Food refusal, anorexia and soft paternalism: What's at stake? *Philosophy, Psychiatry & Psychology*, 28(2), 141–150.

Radez, J., Reardon, T., Creswell, C., Lawrence, P. J., Evdoka-Burton, G., & Waite, P. (2021). Why do children and adolescents (not) seek and access professional help for their mental health problems? A systematic review of quantitative and qualitative studies. *European Child & Adolescent Psychiatry*, 30(2), 183–211. https://doi.org/10.1007/s00787-019-01469-4

Radley, D. C., Baumgartner, J. C., Collins, S. R., Zephyrin, L., & Schneider, E. C. (2021, November 18). *Achieving racial and ethnic equity in U.S. health care*. The Commonwealth Fund. https://doi.org/10.26099/ggmq-mm33

Radulescu, E., Ganeshan, B., Shergill, S. S., Medford, N., Chatwin, C., Young, R. C. D., & Critchley, H. D. (2014). Grey-matter texture abnormalities and reduced hippocampal volume are distinguishing features of schizophrenia. *Psychiatry Research: Neuroimaging*, 223(3), 179–186. https://doi.org/10.1016/j.pscychresns.2014.05.014

Radulovic, J., Lee, R., & Ortony, A. (2018). State-dependent memory: Neurobiological advances and prospects for translation to dissociative amnesia. *Frontiers in Behavioral Neuroscience*, 12, Article 259. https://doi.org/10.3389/fnbeh.2018.00259

Raevuori, A., Haukka, J., Vaarala, O., Suvisaari, J. M., Gissler, M., Grainger, M., Linna, M. S., & Suokas, J. T. (2014). The increased risk for autoimmune diseases in patients with eating disorders. *Plos One*, 9(8), e104845–e104845. https://doi.org/10.1371/journal.pone.0104845

Rafalovich, A. (2004). *Framing ADHD children: A critical examination of the history, discourse, and everyday experience of attention deficit/hyperactivity disorder*. Lexington Books.

Rafiq, S., Batool, Z., Liaquat, L., & Haider, S. (2020). Blockade of muscarinic receptors impairs reconsolidation of older fear memory by decreasing cholinergic neurotransmission: A study in rat model of PTSD. *Life Sciences*, 256, 118014. https://doi.org/10.1016/j.lfs.2020.118014

Raguram, R., & Weiss, M. (2004). Stigma and soma-tisation. *The British Journal of Psychiatry*, 185(2), 174–174. https://doi.org/10.1192/bjp.185.2.174

Raguram, R., Weiss, M. G., Channabasavanna, S. M., & Devins, G. M. (1996). Stigma, depression, and soma-tization in South India. *The American Journal of Psy-chiatry*, 153(8), 1043–1049. https://doi.org/10.1176/ajp.153.8.1043

Rahman, A., & Paul, M. (2021). *Delirium tremens*. StatPearls Publishing. https://www.ncbi.nlm.nih.gov/books/NBK482134/

Rains, L. S., Steare, T., Mason, O., & Johnson, S. (2020). Improving substance misuse outcomes in contingency management treatment with adjunctive formal psychotherapy: A systematic review and meta-analysis. *BMJ Open*, 10(10), e034735. https://doi.org/10.1136/bmjopen-2019-034735

Raitasalo, K., Holmila, M., Jääskeläinen, M., & Santalahti, P. (2019). The effect of the severity of parental alcohol abuse on mental and behavioural disorders in chil-dren. *European Child & Adolescent Psychiatry*, 28(7), 913–922. https://doi.org/10.1007/s00787-018-1253-6

Rajeh, A., Amanullah, S., Shivakumar, K., & Cole, J. (2017). Interventions in ADHD: A comparative review of stimulant medications and behavioral therapies. *Asian Journal of Psychiatry*, 25, 131–135. https://doi.org/10.1016/j.ajp.2016.09.005

Rajendram, R., Kronenberg, S., Burt, C. L., & Arnold, P. D. (2017). Glutamate genetics in obsessive-com-pulsive disorder: A review. *Journal of the Canadian Academy of Child and Adolescent Psychiatry*, 26(3), 205–213.

Rajkumar, R. P. (2022). Pharmacological strategies for suicide prevention based on the social pain model: A scoping review. *Psych*, 4(3), Article 3. https://doi.org/10.3390/psych4030038

Ralph, S., & Cooper, M. (2022). Brief humanistic counselling with an adolescent client experiencing obsessive-compulsive difficulties: A theory-building case study. *Counselling and Psychotherapy Research*, 22(3), 748–759. https://doi.org/10.1002/capr.12499

Raman, S. R., Man, K. K. C., Bahmanyar, S., Berard, A., Bilder, S., Boukhris, T., Bushnell, G., Crystal, S., Furu, K., KaoYang, Y.-H., Karlstad, Ø., Kieler, H., Kubota, K., Lai, E. C.-C., Martikainen, J. E., Maura, G., Moore, N., Montero, D., Nakamura, H., … Wong, I. C. K. (2018). Trends in attention-deficit hyperactivity dis-order medication use: A retrospective observational study using population-based databases. *The Lancet Psychiatry*, 5(10), 824–835. https://doi.org/10.1016/S2215-0366(18)30293-1

Rambler, R. M., Rinehart, E., Boehmler, W., Gait, P., Moore, J., Schlenker, M., & Kashyap, R. (2022). A review of the association of blue food coloring with attention deficit hyperactivity disorder symptoms in children. *Cureus*, 14(9). https://doi.org/10.7759/cureus.29241

Rameckers, S. A., Verhoef, R. E. J., Grasman, R. P. P. P., Cox, W. R., van Emmerik, A. A. P., Engelmoer, I. M., & Arntz, A. (2021). Effectiveness of psychological treatments for borderline personality disorder and predictors of treatment outcomes: A multivariate multilevel meta-analysis of data from all design types. *Journal of Clinical Medicine*, 10(23), 5622. https://doi.org/10.3390/jcm10235622

Ramnani, N., & Owen, A. M. (2004). Anterior prefrontal cortex: Insights into function from anatomy and neuroimaging. *Nature Reviews Neuroscience*, 5(3), 184–194. https://doi.org/10.1038/nrn1343

Ramo, D. E., Grov, C., & Parsons, J. T. (2013). Ecstasy/MDMA. In P. M. Miller, S. A. Ball, M. E. Bates, A. W. Blume, K. M. Kampman, D. J. Kavanagh, M. E. Larimer, N. M. Petry, & P. De Witte (Eds.), *Comprehensive addictive behaviors and disorders: Vol. 1. Principles of addiction* (pp. 711–721). Elsevier Academic Press.

Ramsay, J. R. (2017). The relevance of cognitive distor-tions in the psychosocial treatment of adult ADHD. *Professional Psychology: Research and Practice*, 48(1), 62–69. https://doi.org/10.1037/pro0000101

Ramsay, M. C., & Reynolds, C. R. (2004). Relations between intelligence and achievement tests. In G. Goldstein & S. R. Beers (Eds.), *Comprehensive hand-book of psychological assessment: Vol. 1. Intellectual and neuropsychological assessment* (pp. 25–50). John Wiley.

Randløv, C., Mehlsen, J., Thomsen, C. F., Hedman, C., von Fircks, H., & Winther, K. (2006). The efficacy of St. John's Wort in patients with minor depressive symptoms or dysthymia – a double-blind place-bo-controlled study. *Phytomedicine*, 13(4), 215–221. https://doi.org/10.1016/j.phymed.2005.11.006

Ransing, R., Dashi, E., Rehman, S., Chepure, A., Mehta, V., & Kundadak, G. K. (2021). COVID-19 anti-vac-cine movement and mental health: Challenges and the way forward. *Asian Journal of Psychiatry*, 58, 102614. https://doi.org/10.1016/j.ajp.2021.102614

Ranta, K., Kaltiala-Heino, R., Pelkonen, M., & Marttunen, M. (2009). Associations between peer victimization, self-reported depression and social phobia among adolescents: The role of comorbidity. *Journal of Adolescence*, 32(1), 77–93. https://doi.org/10.1016/j.adolescence.2007.11.005

Rantala, M. J., Luoto, S., Krams, I., & Karlsson, H. (2018). Depression subtyping based on evolutionary psychi-atry: Proximate mechanisms and ultimate functions. *Brain, Behavior, and Immunity*, 69, 603–617. https://doi.org/10.1016/j.bbi.2017.10.012

Rao, N. P., Venkatasubramanian, G., Ravi, V., Kalmady, S., Cherian, A., & Yc, J. R. (2015). Plasma cytokine abnormalities in drug-naïve, comorbidity-free obsessive-compulsive disorder. *Psychiatry Research*, 229(3), 949–952. https://doi.org/10.1016/j.psy-chres.2015.07.009

Rao, T. S. S., & Andrade, C. (2011). The MMR vaccine and autism: Sensation, refutation, retraction, and fraud. *Indian Journal of Psychiatry*, 53(2), 95–96. https://doi.org/10.4103/0019-5545.82529

Rapp, C., Walter, A., Studerus, E., Bugra, H., Tamagni, C., Röthlisberger, M., Borgwardt, S., Aston, J., & Riecher-Rössler, A. (2013). Cannabis use and brain structural alterations of the cingulate cortex in early psychosis. *Psychiatry Research: Neuroimaging*, 214(2), 102–108. https://doi.org/10.1016/j.pscychres-ns.2013.06.006

Rash, C. J., Stitzer, M., & Weinstock, J. (2017). Contingen-cy management: New directions and remaining chal-lenges for an evidence-based intervention. *Journal of Substance Abuse Treatment*, 72, 10–18. https://doi.org/10.1016/j.jsat.2016.09.008

Raskin, J. D. (2013, January 4). *Can evolutionary theory help us define mental disorder?* [New Existential-ists]. https://www.saybrook.edu/newexistentialists/posts/01-04-13

Raskin, J. D. (2014). A critical look at social justice ideology in counseling and psychotherapy. In C. V. Johnson, H. L. Friedman, J. Diaz, Z. Franco, & B. K. Nastasi (Eds.), *The Praeger handbook of social justice and psychology: Vol. 1. Fundamental issues and special populations* (pp. 51–64). Praeger/ABC-CLIO.

Raskin, J. D. (2021). Power threat meaning framework (PTMF). In J. N. Lester & M. O'Reilly (Eds.), *The Palgrave encyclopedia of critical perspectives on mental health*. Palgrave Macmillan. https://doi.org/10.1007/978-3-030-12852-4_46-1

Raskin, J. D. (in press). *Constructive psychotherapies*. American Psychological Association.

Raskin, J. D., & Gayle, M. C. (2016). *DSM-5*: Do psychologists really want an alternative? *Journal of Humanistic Psychology*, 56(5), 439–456. https://doi.org/10.1177/0022167815577897

Raskin, J. D., Maynard, D., & Gayle, M. C. (2022). Psy-chologist attitudes toward DSM-5 and its alternatives. *Professional Psychology: Research and Practice*, 53(6), 553–563. https://doi.org/10.1037/pro0000480

Rathcke, T., & Lin, C.-Y. (2021). Towards a comprehen-sive account of rhythm processing issues in develop-mental dyslexia. *Brain Sciences*, 11 (10), Article 10. https://doi.org/10.3390/brainsci11101303

Rauch, S. A. M., Eftekhari, A., & Ruzek, J. I. (2012). Re-view of exposure therapy: A gold standard for PTSD treatment. *Journal of Rehabilitation Research and Development*, 49(5), 679–687.

Rauch, S., & Foa, E. (2006). Emotional processing theory (EPT) and exposure therapy for PTSD. *Journal of Contemporary Psychotherapy*, 36(2), 61–65. https://doi.org/10.1007/s10879-006-9008-y

Raven, M., & Parry, P. (2012). Psychotropic marketing practices and problems: Implications for DSM-5. *Journal of Nervous and Mental Disease*, 200(6), 512–516.

Ray, D. C., Armstrong, S. A., Balkin, R. S., & Jayne, K. M. (2015). Child-centered play therapy in the schools: Review and meta-analysis. *Psychology in the Schools*, 52(2), 107–123. https://doi.org/10.1002/pits.21798

Ray, D. C., & Jayne, K. M. (2016). Humanistic psycho-therapy with children. In D. J. Cain, K. Keenan, S. Rubin, D. J. Cain, K. Keenan, & S. Rubin (Eds.), *Humanistic psychotherapies: Handbook of research and practice* (2nd ed., pp. 387–417). American Psycholog-ical Association. https://doi.org/10.1037/14775-013

Ray, D. C., Lee, K. R., Meany-Walen, K. K., Carlson, S. E., Carnes-Holt, K. L., & Ware, J. N. (2013). Use of toys in child-centered play therapy. *International Journal of Play Therapy*, 22(1), 43–57. https://doi.org/10.1037/a0031430

Ray, D. C., Sullivan, J. M., & Carlson, S. E. (2012). Rela-tional intervention: Child-centered play therapy with children on the autism spectrum. In L. Gallo-Lopez & L. C. Rubin (Eds.), *Play-based interventions for chil-dren and adolescents with autism spectrum disorders* (pp. 159–175). Routledge/Taylor & Francis Group.

Raymond, R. R. (2019, August 14). Extreme inequality is driving anxiety and depression in the US. *Truthout*. https://truthout.org/articles/extreme-inequal-ity-is-driving-anxiety-and-depression-in-the-u-s/

Raza, G. T., DeMarce, J. M., Lash, S. J., & Parker, J. D. (2014). Paranoid personality disorder in the United States: The role of race, illicit drug use, and income. *Journal of Ethnicity in Substance Abuse*, 13(3), 247–257. https://doi.org/10.1080/15332640.2013.850463

Read, J. (2013a). Childhood adversity and psychosis. In J. Read & J. Dillon (Eds.), *Models of madness: Psycho-logical, social and biological approaches to psychosis* (2013-19717-023; 2nd ed., pp. 249–275). Routledge/Taylor & Francis Group.

Read, J. (2013b). Does "schizophrenia" exist? Reliability and validity. In J. Read & J. Dillon (Eds.), *Models of madness: Psychological, social and biological ap-proaches to psychosis* (2nd ed., pp. 47–61). Routledge.

Read, J. (2019). Making sense of, and responding sensibly to, psychosis. *Journal of Humanistic Psychology*, 59(5), 672–680. https://doi.org/10.1177/0022167818761918

Read, J., & Arnold, C. (2017). Is electroconvulsive therapy for depression more effective than placebo? A sys-tematic review of studies since 2009. *Ethical Human Psychology and Psychiatry*, 19(1), 5–23. https://doi.org/10.1891/1559-4343.19.1.5

Read, J., & Dillon, J. (2013). *Models of madness: Psycholog-ical, social and biological approaches to psychosis* (2nd ed.). Routledge.

Read, J., & Harper, David. J. (2022). The power threat meaning framework: Addressing adversity, challeng-ing prejudice and stigma, and transforming services. *Journal of Constructivist Psychology*, 35(1), 54–67. https://doi.org/10.1080/10720537.2020.1773356

Reas, D. L., & Grilo, C. M. (2014). Current and emerging drug treatments for binge eating disorder. *Expert Opinion on Emerging Drugs*, 19(1), 99–142. https://doi.org/10.1517/14728214.2014.879291

Reddy, Y. C. J., & Arumugham, S. S. (2020). Are current pharmacotherapeutic strategies effective in treating OCD? *Expert Opinion on Pharmacotherapy*, 21(8), 853–856. https://doi.org/10.1080/14656566.2020.1735355

Redondo, R. L., Kim, J., Arons, A. L., Ramirez, S., Liu, X., & Tonegawa, S. (2014). Bidirectional switch of the valence associated with a hippocampal contextual memory engram. *Nature, 513*(7518), 426–430. https://doi.org/10.1038/nature13725

Reed, B. G., Nemer, L. B., & Carr, B. R. (2016). Has testosterone passed the test in premenopausal women with low libido? A systematic review. *International Journal of Women's Health, 8,* 599–607. https://doi.org/10.2147/IJWH.S116212

Reed, G. M. (2010). Toward ICD-11: Improving the clinical utility of WHO's international classification of mental disorders. *Professional Psychology: Research and Practice, 41*(6), 457–464. https://doi.org/19.1037/a0021701

Reed, G. M., Drescher, J., Krueger, R. B., Atalla, E., Cochran, S. D., First, M. B., Cohen-Kettenis, P. T., Arango-de Montis, I., Parish, S. J., Cottler, S., Briken, P., & Saxena, S. (2016). Disorders related to sexuality and gender identity in the ICD-11: Revising the ICD-10 classification based on current scientific evidence, best clinical practices, and human rights considerations. *World Psychiatry, 15*(3), 205–221. https://doi.org/10.1002/wps.20354

Reed, G. M., Ritchie, P. L.-J., Maercker, A., & Rebello, T. (Eds.). (2022). *A psychological approach to diagnosis: Using the ICD-11 as a framework.* American Psychological Association.

Reed, G. M., Sharan, P., Rebello, T. J., Keeley, J. W., Elena Medina-Mora, M., Gureje, O., Luis Ayuso-Mateos, J., Kanba, S., Khoury, B., Kogan, C. S., Krasnov, V. N., Maj, M., de Jesus Mari, J., Stein, D. J., Zhao, M., Akiyama, T., Andrews, H. F., Asevedo, E., Cheour, M., … Pike, K. M. (2018). The ICD-11 developmental field study of reliability of diagnoses of high-burden mental disorders: Results among adult patients in mental health settings of 13 countries. *World Psychiatry, 17*(2), 174–186. https://doi.org/10.1002/wps.20524

Regier, D. A., Narrow, W. E., Clarke, D. E., Kraemer, H. C., Kuramoto, S. J., Kuhl, E. A., & Kupfer, D. J. (2013). DSM-5 field trials in the United States and Canada, part II: Test-retest reliability of selected categorical diagnoses. *The American Journal of Psychiatry, 170*(1), 59–70. https://doi.org/10.1176/appi.ajp.2012.12070999

Reich, W. (1945). *Character analysis* (3rd ed.). Farar, Straus and Giroux.

Reichborn-Kjennerud, T. (2010). The genetic epidemiology of personality disorders. *Dialogues in Clinical Neuroscience, 12*(1), 103–114. https://doi.org/10.31887/DCNS.2010.12.1/trkjennerud

Reichborn-Kjennerud, T., Czajkowski, N., Neale, M. C., Ørstavik, R. E., Torgersen, S., Tambs, K., Røysamb, E., Harris, J. R., & Kendler, K. S. (2007). Genetic and environmental influences on dimensional representations of DSM-IV cluster C personality disorders: A population-based multivariate twin study. *Psychological Medicine, 37*(5), 645–653. https://doi.org/10.1017/S0033291706009548

Reichow, B., Hume, K., Barton, E. E., & Boyd, B. A. (2018). Early intensive behavioral intervention (EIBI) for young children with autism spectrum disorders (ASD). *Cochrane Database of Systematic Reviews, 2018*(5), Article CD009260. https://doi.org/10.1002/14651858.CD009260.pub3

Reid, R. C., Carpenter, B. N., Hook, J. N., Garos, S., Manning, J. C., Gilliland, R., Cooper, E. B., McKittrick, H., Davtian, M., & Fong, T. (2012). Report of findings in a DSM-5 field trial for hypersexual disorder. *Journal of Sexual Medicine, 9*(11), 2868–2877. https://doi.org/10.1111/j.1743-6109.2012.02936.x

Reifinger, J. L. (2019). Dyslexia in the music classroom: A review of literature. *Update: Applications of Research in Music Education, 38*(1), 9–17. https://doi.org/10.1177/8755123319831736

Reilly, E. E., Anderson, L. M., Gorrell, S., Schaumberg, K., & Anderson, D. A. (2017). Expanding exposure-based interventions for eating disorders. *The International Journal of Eating Disorders, 50*(10), 1137–1141. https://doi.org/10.1002/eat.22761

Reilly-Harrington, N. A., Roberts, S., & Sylvia, L. G. (2015). Family-focused therapy, interpersonal and

social rhythm therapy, and dialectical behavioral therapy. In A. Yildiz, P. Ruiz, & C. B. Nemeroff (Eds.), *The bipolar book: History, neurobiology, and treatment* (pp. 445–453). Oxford University Press.

Reinares, M., Sánchez-Moreno, J., & Fountoulakis, K. N. (2014). Psychosocial interventions in bipolar disorder: What, for whom, and when. *Journal of Affective Disorders, 156,* 46–55. https://doi.org/10.1016/j.jad.2013.12.017

Reinders, A. A. T. S. (2008). Cross-examining dissociative identity disorder: Neuroimaging and etiology on trial. *Neurocase, 14*(1), 44–53. https://doi.org/10.1080/13554790801992768

Reinecke, M. A., & Freeman, A. (2003). Cognitive therapy. In A. S. Gurman & S. B. Messer (Eds.), *Essential psychotherapies: Theory and practice* (2nd ed., pp. 224–271). Guilford.

Reininghaus, U., Priebe, S., & Bentall, R. P. (2013). Testing the psychopathology of psychosis: Evidence for a general psychosis dimension. *Schizophrenia Bulletin, 39*(4), 884–895. https://doi.org/10.1093/schbul/sbr182

Reis, M., Dinelli, S., & Elias, L. (2019, January). Surviving prison: Using the Power Threat Meaning Framework to explore the impact of long-term imprisonment. *Clinical Psychology Forum, 313,* 25–32.

Reis, S., & Grenyer, B. F. S. (2002). Pathways to anaclitic and introjective depression. *Psychology and Psychotherapy: Theory, Research and Practice, 75*(4), 445–459. https://doi.org/10.1348/147608302321151934

Reitan, R. M., & Wolfson, D. (2004). Theoretical, methodological, and validational bases of the Halstead-Reitan Neuropsychological Test Battery. In G. Goldstein & S. R. Beers (Eds.), *Comprehensive handbook of psychological assessment: Vol. 1. Intellectual and neuropsychological assessment* (pp. 105–131). John Wiley.

Reitz, C., Rogaeva, E., & Beecham, G. W. (2020). Late-onset vs nonmendelian early-onset Alzheimer disease: A distinction without a difference? *Neurology Genetics, 6*(5). https://doi.org/10.1212/NXG.0000000000000512

Ren, M., & Lotfipour, S. (2020). The role of the gut microbiome in opioid use. *Behavioural Pharmacology, 31*(2-#000263), 113–121. https://doi.org/10.1097/FBP.0000000000000538

Reppermund, S., Srasuebkul, P., Dean, K., & Trollor, J. N. (2020). Factors associated with death in people with intellectual disability. *Journal of Applied Research in Intellectual Disabilities, 33*(3), 420–429. https://doi.org/10.1111/jar.12684

Resick, P. A., Monson, C. M., & Chard, K. M. (2017). *Cognitive processing therapy for PTSD: A comprehensive manual.* Guilford Press. https://www.guilford.com/books/Cognitive-Processing-Therapy-for-PTSD/Resick-Monson-Chard/9781462528646

Resick, P. A., & Schnicke, M. K. (1992). Cognitive processing therapy for sexual assault victims. *Journal of Consulting and Clinical Psychology, 60*(5), 748–756. https://doi.org/10.1037/0022-006X.60.5.748

Restori, A. F., Katz, G. S., & Lee, H. B. (2009). A critique of the IQ/achievement discrepancy model for identifying specific learning disabilities. *Europe's Journal of Psychology, 5*(4), Article 4. https://doi.org/10.5964/ejop.v5i4.244

Rethink Mental Illness. (2021, May 25). *"BPD impacts my life in every way"—Gabby's story.* "BPD Impacts My Life in Every Way." https://www.rethink.org/news-and-stories/blogs/2021/05/bpd-impacts-my-life-in-every-way-gabby-s-story/

Retraction—Ileal-lymphoid-nodular hyperplasia, non-specific colitis, and pervasive developmental disorder in children. (2010). *The Lancet, 375*(9713), 445–445. https://doi.org/10.1016/S0140-6736(10)60175-4

Rew, L., Young, C. C., Monge, M., & Bogucka, R. (2020). Review: Puberty blockers for transgender and gender diverse youth—a critical review of the literature. *Child and Adolescent Mental Health.* https://doi.org/10.1111/camh.12437

Reynaud, E., Guedj, E., Trousselard, M., El Khoury-Malhame, M., Zendjidjian, X., Fakra, E., Souville, M.,

Nazarian, B., Blin, O., Canini, F., & Khalfa, S. (2015). Acute stress disorder modifies cerebral activity of amygdala and prefrontal cortex. *Cognitive Neuroscience, 6*(1), 39–43. https://doi.org/10.1080/17588928.2014.996212

Reynolds, T., Winegard, B. M., Baumeister, R. F., & Maner, J. K. (2015). The long goodbye: A test of grief as a social signal. *Evolutionary Behavioral Sciences, 9*(1), 20–42. https://doi.org/10.1037/ebs0000032

Ribeiro, J. D., Huang, X., Fox, K. R., & Franklin, J. C. (2018). Depression and hopelessness as risk factors for suicide ideation, attempts and death: Meta-analysis of longitudinal studies. *British Journal of Psychiatry, 212*(5), 279–286. https://doi.org/10.1192/bjp.2018.27

Rice, C., & Pedersen, T. (2022, March 8). *Top 10 free mental health apps in 2022.* Psych Central. https://psychcentral.com/blog/top-10-free-mental-health-apps

Richard Freiherr von Krafft-Ebing. (2008). In *New world encyclopedia.* https://www.newworldencyclopedia.org/entry/Richard_Freiherr_von_Krafft-Ebing

Richards, D. G. (1990). Dissociation and transformation. *Journal of Humanistic Psychology, 30*(3), 54–83. https://doi.org/10.1177/0022167890303004

Richardson, F. C., & Manaster, G. J. (2003). Social interest, emotional well-being, and the quest for civil society. *The Journal of Individual Psychology, 59*(2), 123–135.

Richarte, V., Sánchez-Mora, C., Corrales, M., Fadeuilhe, C., Vilar-Ribó, L., Arribas, L., Garcia, E., Rosales-Ortiz, S. K., Arias-Vasquez, A., Soler-Artigas, M., Ribasés, M., & Ramos-Quiroga, J. A. (2021). Gut microbiota signature in treatment-naïve attention-deficit/hyperactivity disorder. *Translational Psychiatry, 11*(1), Article 1. https://doi.org/10.1038/s41398-021-01504-6

Ridenour, J. M., Hamm, J. A., & Czaja, M. (2019). A review of psychotherapeutic models and treatments for psychosis. *Psychosis, 11*(3), 248–260. https://doi.org/10.1080/17522439.2019.1615111

Ridley, M., Rao, G., Schilbach, F., & Patel, V. (2020). Poverty, depression, and anxiety: Causal evidence and mechanisms. *Science, 370* (6522), eaay0214. https://doi.org/10.1126/science.aay0214

Rief, W., Pilger, F., Lhle, D., Verkerkd, R., Scharpe, S., & Maes, M. (2004). Psychobiological aspects of somatoform disorders: Contributions of monoaminergic transmitter systems. *Neuropsychobiology, 49*(1), 24–29. https://doi.org/10.1159/000075335

Riemann, D., Spiegelhalder, K., Feige, B., Voderholzer, U., Berger, M., Perlis, M., & Nissen, C. (2010). The hyperarousal model of insomnia: A review of the concept and its evidence. *Sleep Medicine Reviews, 14*(1), 19–31. https://doi.org/10.1016/j.smrv.2009.04.002

Rienecke, R. D. (2017). Family-based treatment of eating disorders in adolescents: Current insights. *Adolescent Health, Medicine and Therapeutics, 8,* 69–79. https://doi.org/10.2147/AHMT.S115775

Riera-Sampol, A., Rodas, L., Martínez, S., Moir, H. J., & Tauler, P. (2022). Caffeine intake among undergraduate students: Sex differences, sources, motivations, and associations with smoking status and self-reported sleep quality. *Nutrients, 14*(8), 1661. https://doi.org/10.3390/nu14081661

Riffer, F., Farkas, M., Streibl, L., Kaiser, E., & Sprung, M. (2019). Psychopharmacological treatment of patients with borderline personality disorder: Comparing data from routine clinical care with recommended guidelines. *International Journal of Psychiatry in Clinical Practice, 23*(3), 178–188. https://doi.org/10.1080/13651501.2019.1576904

Rigler, T., Manor, I., Kalansky, A., Shorer, Z., Noyman, I., & Sadaka, Y. (2016). New DSM-5 criteria for ADHD—Does it matter? *Comprehensive Psychiatry, 68,* 56–59. https://doi.org/10.1016/j.comppsych.2016.03.008

Rigotti, N. A. (2022, April 12). *Pharmacotherapy for smoking cessation in adults.* UpToDate. https://www.

uptodate.com/contents/pharmacotherapy-for-smoking-cessation-in-adults

Rigter, H., Henderson, C. E., Pelc, I., Tossmann, P., Phan, O., Hendriks, V., Schaub, M., & Rowe, C. L. (2013). Multidimensional family therapy lowers the rate of cannabis dependence in adolescents: A randomised controlled trial in Western European outpatient settings. *Drug and Alcohol Dependence*, *130*(1–3), 85–93. https://doi.org/10.1016/j.drugalcdep.2012.10.013

Rigter, H., Pelc, I., Tossmann, P., Phan, O., Grichting, E., Hendriks, V., & Rowe, C. (2010). INCANT: A transnational randomized trial of Multidimensional Family Therapy versus treatment as usual for adolescents with cannabis use disorder. *BMC Psychiatry*, *10*. https://doi.org/10.1186/1471-244X-10-28

Rimland, B. (1964). *Infantile autism: The syndrome and its implications for a neural theory of behavior.* Appleton-Century-Crofts.

Ringuette, E. L. (1982). Double binds, schizophrenics, and psychological theory: Letters from mothers of schizophrenic and nonschizophrenic patients. *Psychological Reports*, *51*(3, Pt 1), 693–694. https://doi.org/10.2466/pr0.1982.51.3.693

Ripke, S., O'Dushlaine, C., Chambert, K., Moran, J. L., Kähler, A. K., Akterin, S., Bergen, S. E., Collins, A. L., Crowley, J. J., Fromer, M., Kim, Y., Lee, S. H., Magnusson, P. K. E., Sanchez, N., Stahl, E. A., Williams, S., Wray, N. R., Xia, K., Bettella, F., … Sullivan, P. F. (2013). Genome-wide association analysis identifies 13 new risk loci for schizophrenia. *Nature Genetics*, *45*(10), 1150–1159. https://doi.org/10.1038/ng.2742

Rissmiller, D. J., & Rissmiller, J. H. (2006). Evolution of the antipsychiatry movement into mental health consumerism. *Psychiatric Services*, *57*(6), 863–866. https://doi.org/10.1176/appi.ps.57.6.863

Ritter, B. (1968). Effect of contact desensitization on avoidance behavior, fear ratings, and self-evaluative statements. *Proceedings of the Annual Convention of the American Psychological Association*, *3*, 527–528.

Ritvo, P., Lewis, M. D., Irvine, J., Brown, L., Matthew, A., & Shaw, B. F. (2003). The application of cognitive-behavioral therapy in the treatment of substance abuse. *Primary Psychiatry*, *10*(5), 72–77.

Rivera-Hernandez, M., Kumar, A., Roy, I., Fashaw-Walters, S., & Baldwin, J. A. (2022). Quality of care and outcomes among a diverse group of long-term care residents with Alzheimer's disease and related dementias. *Journal of Aging and Health*, *34*(2), 283–296. https://doi.org/10.1177/08982643211043319

Rivers-Auty, J., Mather, A. E., Peters, R., Lawrence, C. B., & Brough, D. (2020). Anti-inflammatories in Alzheimer's disease—Potential therapy or spurious correlate? *Brain Communications*, *2*(2), Article fcaa109. https://doi.org/10.1093/braincomms/fcaa109

Rizk, P. J., Kohn, T. P., Pastuszak, A. W., & Khera, M. (2017). Testosterone therapy improves erectile function and libido in hypogonadal men. *Current Opinion in Urology*, *27*(6), 511–515. https://doi.org/10.1097/MOU.0000000000000442

Rizkalla, M., Kowalkowski, B., & Prozialeck, W. C. (2020). Antidepressant discontinuation syndrome: A common but underappreciated clinical problem. *Journal of Osteopathic Medicine*, *120*(3), 174–178. https://doi.org/10.7556/jaoa.2020.030

Rizvi, S., & Khan, A. M. (2019). Use of transcranial magnetic stimulation for depression. *Cureus*, *11*(5), e4736. https://doi.org/10.7759/cureus.4736

Robbins, B. D., Kamens, S. R., & Elkins, D. N. (2017). DSM-5 reform efforts by the Society for Humanistic Psychology. *Journal of Humanistic Psychology*, *57*(6), 602–624. https://doi.org/10.1177/0022167817698617

Robbins, T. W., Vaghi, M. M., & Banca, P. (2019). Obsessive-compulsive disorder: Puzzles and prospects. *Neuron*, *102*(1), 27–47. https://doi.org/10.1016/j.neuron.2019.01.046

Roberto, C. A., Mayer, L. E., Brickman, A. M., Barnes, A., Muraskin, J., Yeung, L. K., Steffener, J., Sy, M., Hirsch, J., & Stern, Y. (2011). Brain tissue volume changes following weight gain in adults with anorexia nervosa.

International Journal of Eating Disorders, *44*. https://doi.org/10.1002/eat.20840

Roberts, D. L. (2019). The addictive personality: Myth or cornerstone of prevention and treatment? *Psychological Applications and Trends 2019*, 328–331. https://doi.org/10.36315/2019inpact085

Roberts, J. R., Dawley, E. H., & Reigart, J. R. (2019). Children's low-level pesticide exposure and associations with autism and ADHD: A review. *Pediatric Research*, *85*(2), 234–241. https://doi.org/10.1038/s41390-018-0200-z

Roberts, M. C., & Evans, S. C. (2013). Using the *International classification of diseases* system (*ICD-10*). In G. P. Koocher, J. C. Norcross, & B. A. Greene (Eds.), *Psychologists' desk reference* (3rd ed., pp. 71–76). Oxford University Press.

Roberts, N. P., Roberts, P. A., Jones, N., & Bisson, J. I. (2015). Psychological interventions for post-traumatic stress disorder and comorbid substance use disorder: A systematic review and meta-analysis. *Clinical Psychology Review*, *38*, 25–38. https://doi.org/10.1016/j.cpr.2015.02.007

Robertson, M. M., Cavanna, A. E., & Eapen, V. (2015). Gilles de la Tourette syndrome and disruptive behavior disorders: Prevalence, associations, and explanation of the relationships. *The Journal of Neuropsychiatry and Clinical Neurosciences*, *27*(1), 33–41. https://doi.org/10.1176/appi.neuropsych.13050112

Robins, E., & Guze, S. B. (1970). Establishment of diagnostic validity in psychiatric illness: Its application to schizophrenia. *The American Journal of Psychiatry*, *126*(7), 983–986.

Robinson, A., & Elliott, R. (2017). Emotion-focused therapy for clients with autistic process. *Person-Centered and Experiential Psychotherapies*, *16*(3), 215–235. https://doi.org/10.1080/14779757.2017.1330700

Robinson, A., & Kalawski, J. P. (2022). Experiences of the step-out technique in emotion-focused therapy for clients with autistic process. *Person-Centered & Experiential Psychotherapies*, 1–18. https://doi.org/10.1080/14779757.2022.2115941

Robinson, A. L., Dolhanty, J., & Greenberg, L. (2015). Emotion-focused family therapy for eating disorders in children and adolescents: Emotion-focused family therapy for eating disorders. *Clinical Psychology & Psychotherapy*, *22*(1), 75–82. https://doi.org/10.1002/cpp.1861

Robinson, J. S., Larson, C. L., & Cahill, S. P. (2014). Relations between resilience, positive and negative emotionality, and symptoms of anxiety and depression. *Psychological Trauma: Theory, Research, Practice, and Policy*, *6*(Suppl. 1), S92–S98. https://doi.org/10.1037/a0033733

Robinson, K., & Wade, T. D. (2021). Perfectionism interventions targeting disordered eating: A systematic review and meta-analysis. *International Journal of Eating Disorders*, *54*(4), 473–487. https://doi.org/10.1002/eat.23483

Robinson-Agramonte, M. de los A., Noris García, E., Fraga Guerra, J., Vega Hurtado, Y., Antonucci, N., Semprún-Hernández, N., Schultz, S., & Siniscalco, D. (2022). Immune dysregulation in autism spectrum disorder: What do we know about it? *International Journal of Molecular Sciences*, *23*(6), Article 6. https://doi.org/10.3390/ijms23063033

Robles, R., Ребека, Р., Real, T., Таня, Р., Reed, G. M., & М, Р. Д. (2021). Depathologizing sexual orientation and transgender identities in psychiatric classifications. *Consortium Psychiatricum*, *2*(2), Article 2. https://doi.org/10.17816/CP61

Rocco, D., Calvo, V., Agrosi, V., Bergami, F., Busetto, L. M., Marin, S., Pezzetta, G., Rossi, L., Zuccotti, L., & Abbass, A. (2021). Intensive short-term dynamic psychotherapy provided by novice psychotherapists: Effects on symptomatology and psychological structure in patients with anxiety disorders. *Research in Psychotherapy: Psychopathology, Process, and Outcome*, *24*(1), 503. https://doi.org/10.4081/ripppo.2021.503

Rochford, R. (2022, September 7). *Fears of a polio resurgence in the US have health officials on high alert – a virologist explains the history of this dreaded disease.* The Conversation. http://theconversation.com/fears-of-a-polio-resurgence-in-the-us-have-health-officials-on-high-alert-a-virologist-explains-the-history-of-this-dreaded-disease-189107

Roddy, D. W., Farrell, C., Doolin, K., Roman, E., Tozzi, L., Frodl, T., O'Keane, V., & O'Hanlon, E. (2019). The hippocampus in depression: More than the sum of its parts? Advanced hippocampal substructure segmentation in depression. *Biological Psychiatry*, *85*(6), 487–497. https://doi.org/10.1016/j.biopsych.2018.08.021

Rodgers, R. F., Berry, R., & Franko, D. L. (2018). Eating disorders in ethnic minorities: An update. *Current Psychiatry Reports*, *20*(10), 90. https://doi.org/10.1007/s11920-018-0938-3

Rodriguez, F. S., & Lachmann, T. (2020). Systematic review on the impact of intelligence on cognitive decline and dementia risk. *Frontiers in Psychiatry*, *11*, Article 658. https://doi.org/10.3389/fpsyt.2020.00658

Roerecke, M., Vafaei, A., Hasan, O. S., Chrystoja, B. R., Cruz, M., Lee, R., Neuman, M. G., & Rehm, J. (2019). Alcohol consumption and risk of liver cirrhosis: A systematic review and meta-analysis. *The American Journal of Gastroenterology*, *114*(10), 1574–1586. https://doi.org/10.14309/ajg.0000000000000340

Roessner, V., Eichele, H., Stern, J. S., Skov, L., Rizzo, R., Debes, N. M., Nagy, P., Cavanna, A. E., Termine, C., Ganos, C., Münchau, A., Szejko, N., Cath, D., Müller-Vahl, K. R., Verdellen, C., Hartmann, A., Rothenberger, A., Hoekstra, P. J., & Plessen, K. J. (2022). European clinical guidelines for Tourette syndrome and other tic disorders—version 2.0. Part III: Pharmacological treatment. *European Child & Adolescent Psychiatry*, *31*(3), 425–441. https://doi.org/10.1007/s00787-021-01899-z

Roessner, V., Schoenefeld, K., Buse, J., Bender, S., Ehrlich, S., & Münchau, A. (2013). Pharmacological treatment of tic disorders and Tourette Syndrome. *Neuropharmacology*, *68*, 143–149. https://doi.org/10.1016/j.neuropharm.2012.05.043

Rogers, C. R. (1951). *Client-centered therapy*. Constable.

Rogers, C. R. (1959). A theory of therapy, personality, and interpersonal relationships, as developed in the client-centered framework. In S. Koch (Ed.), *Psychology: A study of science: Vol. 3. Formulations of the person and the social contact* (pp. 184–256). McGraw Hill.

Rogers, C. R. (1961). *On becoming a person*. Houghton Mifflin.

Rogers, C. R. (1967). *The therapeutic relationship and its impact: A study of psychotherapy with schizophrenics*. University of Wisconsin Press.

Rogers, J. R., Bromley, J. L., McNally, C. J., & Lester, D. (2007). Content analysis of suicide notes as a test of the motivational component of the existential-constructivist model of suicide. *Journal of Counseling & Development*, *85*(2), 182–188. https://doi.org/10.1002/j.1556-6678.2007.tb00461.x

Rogers, J. R., & Soyka, K. M. (2004). "One size fits all": An existential-constructivist perspective on the crisis intervention approach with suicidal individuals. *Journal of Contemporary Psychotherapy*, *34*(1), 7–22. https://doi.org/10.1023/B:JOCP.0000010910.74165.3a

Rogers, M. A., Yamasue, H., & Kasai, K. (2016). Antidepressant medication may moderate the effect of depression duration on hippocampus volume. *Journal of Psychophysiology*, *30*(1), 1–8. https://doi.org/10.1027/0269-8803/a000148

Rogers, T. D., McKimm, E., Dickson, P. E., Goldowitz, D., Blaha, C. D., & Mittleman, G. (2013). Is autism a disease of the cerebellum? An integration of clinical and pre-clinical research. *Frontiers in Systems Neuroscience*, *7*, Article 15. https://doi.org/10.3389/fnsys.2013.00015

Rogers, T. P., Blackwood, N. J., Farnham, F., Pickup, G. J., & Watts, M. J. (2008). Fitness to plead and competence to stand trial: A systematic review of the constructs and their application. *Journal of Forensic Psychiatry & Psychology*, 19(4), 576–596. https://doi.org/10.1080/14789940801947909

Rohlof, H. G., Knipscheer, J. W., & Kleber, R. J. (2014). Somatization in refugees: A review. *Social Psychiatry and Psychiatric Epidemiology*, 49(11), 1793–1804. https://doi.org/10.1007/s00127-014-0877-1

Röhricht, F. (2009). Body oriented psychotherapy. The state of the art in empirical research and evidence-based practice: A clinical perspective. *Body, Movement and Dance in Psychotherapy*, 4(2), 135–156. https://doi.org/10.1080/17432970902857263

Röhricht, F. (2015). Body psychotherapy for the treatment of severe mental disorders—An overview. *Body, Movement and Dance in Psychotherapy*, 10(1), 51–67. https://doi.org/10.1080/17432979.2014.962093

Röhricht, F., & Elanjithara, T. (2014). Management of medically unexplained symptoms: Outcomes of a specialist liaison clinic. *The Psychiatric Bulletin*, 38(3), 102–107. https://doi.org/10.1192/pb.bp.112.040733

Röhricht, F., Gallagher, S., Geuter, U., & Hutto, D. D. (2014). Embodied cognition and body psychotherapy: The construction of new therapeutic environments. *Sensoria: A Journal of Mind, Brain & Culture*, 10(1), 11–20. https://doi.org/10.7790/sa.v10i1.389

Röhricht, F., Sattel, H., Kuhn, C., & Lahmann, C. (2019). Group body psychotherapy for the treatment of somatoform disorder—A partly randomised-controlled feasibility pilot study. *BMC Psychiatry*, 19. https://doi.org/10.1186/s12888-019-2095-6

Roiser, J. P., Stephan, K. E., den Ouden, H. E. M., Barnes, T. R. E., Friston, K. J., & Joyce, E. M. (2009). Do patients with schizophrenia exhibit aberrant salience? *Psychological Medicine*, 39(2), 199–209. https://doi.org/10.1017/S0033291708003863

Rolf, C. (2006). *From M'Naghten to Yates – Transformation of the insanity defense in the United States – Is it still viable?* (Vol. 2, Issue 1). Retrieved from https://www.rivier.edu/journal/ROAJ-2006-Spring/J41-ROLF.pdf

Rolls, G. (2015). *Classic case studies in psychology* (3rd ed.). Routledge.

Romanelli, R. J., Wu, F. M., Gamba, R., Mojtabai, R., & Segal, J. B. (2014). Behavioral therapy and serotonin reuptake inhibitor pharmacotherapy in the treatment of obsessive-compulsive disorder: A systematic review and meta-analysis of head-to-head randomized controlled trials. *Depression & Anxiety (1091-4269)*, 31(8), 641–652. https://doi.org/10.1002/da.22232

Ronald, A., & Hoekstra, R. (2014). Progress in understanding the causes of autism spectrum disorders and autistic traits: Twin studies from 1977 to the present day. In S. H. Rhee & A. Ronald (Eds.), *Behavior genetics of psychopathology* (pp. 33–65). Springer Science + Business Media. https://doi.org/10.1007/978-1-4614-9509-3_2

Ronningstam, E. (2011). Psychoanalytic theories on narcissism and narcissistic personality. In W. K. Campbell & J. D. Miller (Eds.), *The handbook of narcissism and narcissistic personality disorder: Theoretical approaches, empirical findings, and treatments* (pp. 41–55). John Wiley & Sons.

Root, M. P. P. (1992). Reconstructing the impact of trauma on personality. In L. S. Brown & M. Ballou (Eds.), *Personality and psychopathology: Feminist reappraisals* (pp. 229–265). Guilford Press.

Root, T. L., Thornton, L. M., Lindroos, A. K., Stunkard, A. J., Lichtenstein, P., Pedersen, N. L., … Bulik, C. M. (2010). Shared and unique genetic and environmental influences on binge eating and night eating: A Swedish twin study. *Eating Behaviors*, 11(2), 92–98. doi:10.1016/j.eatbeh.2009.10.004

Rosa, P. G. P., Schaufelberger, M. S., Uchida, R. R., Duran, F. L. S., Lappin, J. M., Menezes, P. R., Scazufca, M., McGuire, P. K., Murray, R. M., & Busatto, G. F. (2010). Lateral ventricle differences between first-episode schizophrenia and first-episode psychotic bipolar disorder: A population-based morphometric MRI study. *The World Journal of Biological Psychiatry*,

11(7–8), 873–887. https://doi.org/10.3109/15622975.2010.486042

Rose, S. P. R. (2006). Commentary: Heritability estimates—Long past their sell-by date. *International Journal of Epidemiology*, 35(3), 525–527. https://doi.org/10.1093/ije/dyl064

Rosen, G. M., & Lilienfeld, S. O. (2008). Posttraumatic stress disorder: An empirical evaluation of core assumptions. *Clinical Psychology Review*, 28(5), 837–868. https://doi.org/10.1016/j.cpr.2007.12.002

Rosen, K. H. (1998). The family roots of aggression and violence: A life span perspective. In L. L'Abate (Ed.), *Family psychopathology: The relational roots of dysfunctional behavior* (pp. 333–357). Guilford Press.

Rosenbaum, B. (2019). Psychosis and individual psychodynamic psychotherapy. In D. Kealy & J. S. Ogrodniczuk (Eds.), *Contemporary psychodynamic psychotherapy: Evolving clinical practice* (pp. 177–189). Elsevier Academic Press. https://doi.org/10.1016/B978-0-12-813373-6.00012-X

Rosenbaum, B., Harder, S., Knudsen, P., Køster, A., Lajer, M., Lindhardt, A., Valbak, K., & Winther, G. (2012). Supportive psychodynamic psychotherapy versus treatment as usual for first-episode psychosis: Two-year outcome. *Psychiatry: Interpersonal and Biological Processes*, 75(4), 331–341. https://doi.org/10.1521/psyc.2012.75.4.331

Rosenbaum, J. F. (2020). Benzodiazepines: A perspective. *American Journal of Psychiatry*, 177(6), 488–490. https://doi.org/10.1176/appi.ajp.2020.20040376

Rosenbaum, T. Y. (2007). Pelvic floor involvement in male and female sexual dysfunction and the role of pelvic floor rehabilitation in treatment: A literature review. *Journal of Sexual Medicine*, 4(1), 4–13. https://doi.org/10.1111/j.1743-6109.2006.00393.x

Rosenberg, H., & Davis, A. K. (2014). Differences in the acceptability of non-abstinence goals by type of drug among American substance abuse clinicians. *Journal of Substance Abuse Treatment*, 46(2), 214–218. https://doi.org/10.1016/j.jsat.2013.07.005

Rosenberg, H., & Melville, J. (2005). Controlled drinking and controlled drug use as outcome goals in British treatment services. *Addiction Research & Theory*, 13(1), 85–92. https://doi.org/10.1080/16066350412331314894

Rosenberg, N., Bloch, M., Ben Avi, I., Rouach, V., Schreiber, S., Stern, N., & Greenman, Y. (2013). Cortisol response and desire to binge following psychological stress: Comparison between obese subjects with and without binge eating disorder. *Psychiatry Research*, 208(2), 156–161. https://doi.org/10.1016/j.psychres.2012.09.050

Rosenberg, R. E., Law, J. K., Yenokyan, G., McGready, J., Kaufmann, W. E., & Law, P. A. (2009). Characteristics and concordance of autism spectrum disorders among 277 twin pairs. *Archives of Pediatrics & Adolescent Medicine*, 163(10), 907–914. https://doi.org/10.1001/archpediatrics.2009.98

Rosenblat, J. D., Brietzke, E., Mansur, R. B., Maruschak, N. A., Lee, Y., & McIntyre, R. S. (2015). Inflammation as a neurobiological substrate of cognitive impairment in bipolar disorder: Evidence, pathophysiology and treatment implications. *Journal of Affective Disorders*, 188, 149–159. https://doi.org/10.1016/j.jad.2015.08.058

Rosenblat, J. D., Cha, D. S., Mansur, R. B., & McIntyre, R. S. (2014). Inflamed moods: A review of the interactions between inflammation and mood disorders. *Progress in Neuro-Psychopharmacology and Biological Psychiatry*, 53, 23–34. https://doi.org/10.1016/j.pnpbp.2014.01.013

Rosenblat, J. D., Kakar, R., Berk, M., Kessing, L. V., Vinberg, M., Baune, B. T., Mansur, R. B., Brietzke, E., Goldstein, B. I., & McIntyre, R. S. (2016). Anti-inflammatory agents in the treatment of bipolar depression: A systematic review and meta-analysis. *Bipolar Disorders*, 18(2), 89–101. https://doi.org/10.1111/bdi.12373

Rosenblatt, P. C. (2008). Grief across cultures: A review and research agenda. In M. S. Stroebe, R. O. Hansson, H. Schut, & W. Stroebe (Eds.), *Handbook of bereavement research and practice: Advances in theory and intervention* (pp. 207–222). American Psychological Association. https://doi.org/10.1037/14498-010

Rosenblum, A., Marsch, L. A., Joseph, H., & Portenoy, R. K. (2008). Opioids and the treatment of chronic pain: Controversies, current status, and future directions. *Experimental and Clinical Psychopharmacology*, 16(5), 405–416. https://doi.org/10.1037/a0013628

Rosenhan, D. L. (1973). On being sane in insane places. *Science*, 179(4070), 250–258. https://doi.org/10.1126/science.179.4070.250

Rosenheck, R. (2013). Second generation antipsychotics: Evolution of scientific knowledge or uncovering fraud. *Epidemiology and Psychiatric Sciences*, 22(3), 235–237. https://doi.org/10.1017/S2045796012000662

Rosenman, R. H., & Friedman, M. (1961). Association of specific behavior pattern in women with blood and cardiovascular findings. *Circulation*, 24, 1173–1184. https://doi.org/10.1161/01.CIR.24.5.1173

Roshanaei-Moghaddam, B., Pauly, M. C., Atkins, D. C., Baldwin, S. A., Stein, M. B., & Roy-Byrne, P. (2011). Relative effects of CBT and pharmacotherapy in depression versus anxiety: Is medication somewhat better for depression, and CBT somewhat better for anxiety? *Depression and Anxiety*, 28(7), 560–567. https://doi.org/10.1002/da.20829

Rosin, H. (2014, March). Letting go of Asperger's. *The Atlantic*. Retrieved from http://www.theatlantic.com/magazine/archive/2014/03/letting-go-of-aspergers/357563/

Ross, C. A. (2008). Dissociative schizophrenia. In A. Moskowitz, I. Schäfer, & M. J. Dorahy (Eds.), *Psychosis, trauma and dissociation: Emerging perspectives on severe psychopathology* (pp. 281–294). Wiley-Blackwell. https://doi.org/10.1002/9780470699652.ch20

Ross, C. A. (2009). Errors of logic and scholarship concerning dissociative identity disorder. *Journal of Child Sexual Abuse: Research, Treatment, & Program Innovations for Victims, Survivors, & Offenders*, 18(2), 221–231. https://doi.org/10.1080/10538710902743982

Ross, C. A. (2013a). Biology and genetics in DSM-5. *Ethical Human Psychology and Psychiatry: An International Journal of Critical Inquiry*, 15(3), 195–198. https://doi.org/10.1891/1559-4343.15.3.195

Ross, C. A. (2013b). "The rise and persistence of dissociative identity disorder": Comment. *Journal of Trauma & Dissociation*, 14(5), 584–588. https://doi.org/10.1080/15299732.2013.785464

Ross, C. A. (2014). The equal environments assumption in schizophrenia genetics. *Psychosis: Psychological, Social and Integrative Approaches*, 6(2), 189–191. https://doi.org/10.1080/17522439.2013.773365

Ross, C. A. (2015). Commentary: Problems with the sexual disorders sections of DSM-5. *Journal of Child Sexual Abuse*, 24(2), 195–201. https://doi.org/10.1080/10538712.2015.997411

Ross, C. A., & Margolis, R. L. (2019). Research Domain Criteria: Strengths, weaknesses, and potential alternatives for future psychiatric research. *Complex Psychiatry*, 5(4), 218–236. https://doi.org/10.1159/000501797

Ross, D. M. (1984). Thought-stopping: A coping strategy for impending feared events. *Issues in Comprehensive Pediatric Nursing*, 7(2–3), 83–89. https://doi.org/10.3109/01460868409009046

Ross, M. J., & Berger, R. S. (1996). Effects of stress inoculation training on athletes' postsurgical pain and rehabilitation after orthopedic injury. *Journal of Consulting and Clinical Psychology*, 64(2), 406–410. https://doi.org/10.1037/0022-006X.64.2.406

Ross, M. W., Daneback, K., & Månsson, S.-A. (2012). Fluid versus fixed: A new perspective on bisexuality as a fluid sexual orientation beyond gender. *Journal of Bisexuality*, 12(4), 449–460. https://doi.org/10.1080/15299716.2012.702609

Ross, S. (2008). Ketamine and addiction. *Primary Psychiatry*, 15(9), 61–69.

Rossi, G., Balottin, U., Rossi, M., Chiappedi, M., Fazzi, E., & Lanzi, G. (2007). Pharmacological treatment of anorexia nervosa: A retrospective study in preadolescents and adolescents. *Clinical Pediatrics*, 46(9), 806–811. https://doi.org/10.1177/0009922807303929

Rossini, E. D., & Moretti, R. J. (1997). Thematic Apperception Test (TAT) interpretation: Practice recommendations from a survey of clinical psychology doctoral programs accredited by the American Psychological Association. *Professional Psychology: Research and Practice*, 28(4), 393–398. https://doi.org/10.1037/0735-7028.28.4.393

Rössler, E., Unterassner, L., Wyss, T., Haker, H., Brugger, P., Rössler, W., & Wotruba, D. (2019). Schizotypal traits are linked to dopamine-induced striato-cortical decoupling: A randomized double-blind placebo-controlled study. *Schizophrenia Bulletin*, 45(3), 680–688. https://doi.org/10.1093/schbul/sby079

Rossman, J. (2019). Cognitive-behavioral therapy for insomnia: An effective and underutilized treatment for insomnia. *American Journal of Lifestyle Medicine*, 13(6), 544–547. https://doi.org/10.1177/1559827619867677

Rossow, I., Felix, L., Keating, P., & McCambridge, J. (2016). Parental drinking and adverse outcomes in children: A scoping review of cohort studies. *Drug and Alcohol Review*, 35(4), 397–405. https://doi.org/10.1111/dar.12319

Rost, F. (2021). Q-sort methodology: Bridging the divide between qualitative and quantitative An introduction to an innovative method for psychotherapy research. *Counselling & Psychotherapy Research*, 21(98–106). https://doi.org/10.1002/capr.12367

Rothmore, J. (2020). Antidepressant-induced sexual dysfunction. *Medical Journal of Australia*, 212(7), 329–334. https://doi.org/10.5694/mja2.50522

Rousseau, J. J. (1810). *On suicide*. http://www.sophia-project.org/uploads/1/3/9/5/13955288/rousseau_suicide.pdf

Rousseau, S., Grietens, H., Vanderfaeillie, J., Ceulemans, E., Hoppenbrouwers, K., Desoete, A., & Van Leeuwen, K. (2014). The distinction of "psychosomatogenic family types" based on parents' self reported questionnaire information: A cluster analysis. *Families, Systems, & Health*, 32(2), 207–218. https://doi.org/10.1037/fsh0000031

Roussos, P., & Siever, L. J. (2012). Neurobiological contributions. In T. A. Widiger (Ed.), *The Oxford handbook of personality disorders* (pp. 299–324). Oxford University Press. https://doi.org/10.1093/oxfordhb/9780199735013.013.0015

Rowe, C. L. (2012). Family therapy for drug abuse: Review and updates 2003–2010. *Journal of Marital and Family Therapy*, 38(1), 59–81. https://doi.org/10.1111/j.1752-0606.2011.00280.x

Rowe, C., Liddle, H. A., McClintic, K., & Quille, T. J. (2002). Integrative treatment development: Multidimensional family therapy for adolescent substance abuse. In F. W. Kaslow (Ed.), *Comprehensive handbook of psychotherapy: Integrative/eclectic* (Vol. 4, pp. 133–161). John Wiley.

Rowe, R., Costello, E. J., Angold, A., Copeland, W. E., & Maughan, B. (2010). Developmental pathways in Oppositional Defiant Disorder and Conduct Disorder. *Journal of Abnormal Psychology*, 119(4), 726–738. https://doi.org/10.1037/a0020798

Rowe, R., Maughan, B., Pickles, A., Costello, E. J., & Angold, A. (2002). The relationship between DSM-IV oppositional defiant disorder and conduct disorder: Findings from the Great Smoky Mountains Study. *Journal of Child Psychology and Psychiatry*, 43(3), 365–373. https://doi.org/10.1111/1469-7610.00027

Rowland, D. L. (2012). *Sexual dysfunction in men*. Hogrefe.

Roy, A., Roy, A., & Roy, M. (2012). The human rights of women with intellectual disability. *Journal of the Royal Society of Medicine*, 105(9), 384–389. https://doi.org/10.1258/jrsm.2012.110303

Roy, M. J., Costanzo, M. E., Blair, J. R., & Rizzo, A. A. (2014). Compelling evidence that exposure therapy for PTSD normalizes brain function. *Annual Review of CyberTherapy and Telemedicine*, 12, 61–65.

Royal College of Psychiatrists. (2021, October 6). *Workforce shortages in mental health cause "painfully" long waits for treatment*. https://www.rcpsych.ac.uk/news-and-features/latest-news/detail/2021/10/06/workforce-shortages-in-mental-health-cause-painfully-long-waits-for-treatment

Roy-Byrne, P. P., Craske, M. G., & Stein, M. B. (2006). Panic disorder. *The Lancet*, 368(9540), 1023–1032. https://doi.org/10.1016/S0140-6736(06)69418-X

Roydeva, M. I., & Reinders, A. A. T. S. (2021). Biomarkers of pathological dissociation: A systematic review. *Neuroscience & Biobehavioral Reviews*, 123, 120–202. https://doi.org/10.1016/j.neubiorev.2020.11.019

Rubin, M., Shvil, E., Papini, S., Chhetry, B. T., Helpman, L., Markowitz, J. C., Mann, J. J., & Neria, Y. (2016). Greater hippocampal volume is associated with PTSD treatment response. *Psychiatry Research: Neuroimaging*, 252, 36–39. https://doi.org/10.1016/j.pscychresns.2016.05.001

Ruby, E., Rothman, K., Corcoran, C., Goetz, R. R., & Malaspina, D. (2017). Influence of early trauma on features of schizophrenia. *Early Intervention in Psychiatry*, 11(4), 322–333. https://doi.org/10.1111/eip.12239

Rucker, J. J., & Young, A. H. (2021). Psilocybin: From serendipity to credibility? *Frontiers in Psychiatry*, 12, Article 659044. https://doi.org/10.3389/fpsyt.2021.659044

Rudd, M. D., Bryan, C. J., Wertenberger, E. G., Peterson, A. L., Young-mccaughan, S., Mintz, J., Williams, S. R., Arne, K. A., Breitbach, J., Delano, K., Wilkinson, E., & Bruce, T. O. (2015). Brief cognitive-behavioral therapy effects on post-treatment suicide attempts in a military sample: Results of a randomized clinical trial with 2-year follow-up. *The American Journal of Psychiatry*, 172(5), 441–449. https://doi.org/10.1176/appi.ajp.2014.14070843

Ruderfer, D. M., Walsh, C. G., Aguirre, M. W., Tanigawa, Y., Ribeiro, J. D., Franklin, J. C., & Rivas, M. A. (2020). Significant shared heritability underlies suicide attempt and clinically predicted probability of attempting suicide. *Molecular Psychiatry*, 25(10), 2422–2430. https://doi.org/10.1038/s41380-018-0326-8

Rudy, B. M., Storch, E. A., & Lewin, A. B. (2015). When families won't play ball: A case example of the effect of family accommodation on anxiety symptoms and treatment. *Journal of Child and Family Studies*, 24(7), 2070–2078. https://doi.org/10.1007/s10826-014-0008-3

Rudy, L. J. (2021, May 20). *Asperger syndrome is no longer an official diagnosis*. Verywell Health. https://www.verywell.com/does-asperger-syndrome-still-exist-259944

Ruesink, G. B., & Georgiadis, J. R. (2017). Brain imaging of human sexual response: Recent developments and future directions. *Current Sexual Health Reports*, 9(4), 183–191. https://doi.org/10.1007/s11930-017-0123-4

Ruggero, C. J., Kotov, R., Hopwood, C. J., First, M., Clark, L. A., Skodol, A. E., Mullins-Sweatt, S. N., Patrick, C. J., Bach, B., Cicero, D. C., Docherty, A., Simms, L. J., Bagby, R. M., Krueger, R. F., Callahan, J. L., Chmielewski, M., Conway, C. C., De Clercq, B., Dornbach-Bender, A., … Zimmermann, J. (2019). Integrating the Hierarchical Taxonomy of Psychopathology (HiTOP) into clinical practice. *Journal of Consulting and Clinical Psychology*, 87(12), 1069–1084. https://doi.org/10.1037/ccp0000452

Ruiz, M. T., & Verbrugge, L. M. (1997). A two way view of gender bias in medicine. *Journal of Epidemiology and Community Health*, 51(2), 106–109. https://doi.org/10.1136/jech.51.2.106

Ruiz, N. A. L., Del Ángel, D. S., Brizuela, N. O., Peraza, A. V., Olguín, H. J., Soto, M. P., & Guzmán, D. C. (2022). Inflammatory process and immune system in major depressive disorder. *International Journal of Neuropsychopharmacology*, 25(1), 46–53. https://doi.org/10.1093/ijnp/pyab072

Runions, K. C., Morandini, H. a. E., Rao, P., Wong, J. W. Y., Kolla, N. J., Pace, G., Mahfouda, S., Hildebrandt, C. S., Stewart, R., & Zepf, F. D. (2019). Serotonin and aggressive behaviour in children and adolescents: A systematic review. *Acta Psychiatrica Scandinavica*, 139(2), 117–144. https://doi.org/10.1111/acps.12986

Ruscio, A. M., Hallion, L. S., Lim, C. C. W., Aguilar-Gaxiola, S., Al-Hamzawi, A., Alonso, J., Andrade, L. H., Borges, G., Bromet, E. J., Bunting, B., Caldas de Almeida, J. M., Demyttenaere, K., Florescu, S., de Girolamo, G., Gureje, O., Haro, J. M., He, Y., Hinkov, H., Hu, C., … Scott, K. M. (2017). Cross-sectional comparison of the epidemiology of DSM-5 generalized anxiety disorder across the globe. *JAMA Psychiatry*, 74(5), 465–475. https://doi.org/10.1001/jamapsychiatry.2017.0056

Rush, A. J., & Beck, A. T. (1978). Cognitive therapy of depression and suicide. *American Journal of Psychotherapy*, 32(2), 201–219.

Rush, A. J., Trivedi, M. H., Wisniewski, S. R., Nierenberg, A. A., Stewart, J. W., Warden, D., Niederehe, G., Thase, M. E., Lavori, P. W., Lebowitz, B. D., McGrath, P. J., Rosenbaum, J. F., Sackeim, H. A., Kupfer, D. J., Luther, J., & Fava, M. (2006). Acute and longer-term outcomes in depressed outpatients requiring one or several treatment steps: A STAR*D report. *The American Journal of Psychiatry*, 163(11), 1905–1917. https://doi.org/10.1176/appi.ajp.163.11.1905

Rush, B. (1823). *An inquiry into the effects of ardent spirits on the human body and mind* (8th ed.). James Loring. https://books.google.com/books?id=-6UoAAAAYAAJ&printsec=frontcover&dq=An+Inquiry+into+the+Effects+of+Ardent+Spirits+on+the+Human+Body+and+Mind&hl=en&sa=X&ved=0ahUKEwj5zK2at8vPAhVDax4KHSHTC3sQ6AEIHjAA#v=onepage&q=An%20Inquiry%20into%20the%20Effects%20of%20Ardent%20Spirits%20on%20the%20Human%20Body%20and%20Mind&f=false (Original work published 1784.)

Russell, G. (1979). Bulimia nervosa: An ominous variant of anorexia nervosa. *Psychological Medicine*, 9(3), 429–448. https://doi.org/10.1017/S0033291700031974

Russell, G. F. M. (2004). Thoughts on the 25th anniversary of bulimia nervosa. *European Eating Disorders Review*, 12(3), 139–152. https://doi.org/10.1002/erv.575

Rutherford, A. (2003). Skinner boxes for psychotics: Operant conditioning at Metropolitan State Hospital. *The Behavior Analyst*, 26(2), 267–279.

Rutsch, A., Kantsjö, J. B., & Ronchi, F. (2020). The gut-brain axis: How microbiota and host inflammasome influence brain physiology and pathology. *Frontiers in Immunology*, 11, Article 604179. https://doi.org/10.3389/fimmu.2020.604179

Rutten, A. (2014). A person-centred approach to counselling clients with autistic process. In P. Pearce, L. Sommerbeck, P. Pearce, & L. Sommerbeck (Eds.), *Person-centred practice at the difficult edge* (pp. 74–87). PCCS Books.

Ryan, F., O'Dwyer, M., & Leahy, M. M. (2015). Separating the problem and the person: Insights from narrative therapy with people who stutter. *Topics in Language Disorders*, 35(3), 267–274. https://doi.org/10.1097/TLD.0000000000000062

Ryan, N. S., Rossor, M. N., & Fox, N. C. (2015). Alzheimer's disease in the 100 years since Alzheimer's death. *Brain: A Journal of Neurology*, 138(Pt 12), 3816–3821. https://doi.org/10.1093/brain/awv316

Rybak, A. (2015). Organic and nonorganic feeding disorders. *Annals of Nutrition and Metabolism*, 66(Suppl. 5), 16–22. https://doi.org/10.1159/000381373

Rybakowski, J. K. (2018). Challenging the negative perception of lithium and optimizing its long-term administration. *Frontiers in Molecular Neuroscience*, 11, Article 349. https://doi.org/10.3389/fnmol.2018.00349

Rybarczyk, B., Lund, H. G., Garroway, A. M., & Mack, L. (2013). Cognitive behavioral therapy for insomnia in older adults: Background, evidence, and overview of treatment protocol. *Clinical Gerontologist*, 36(1), 70–93. https://doi.org/10.1080/07317115.2012.731478

Rylaarsdam, L., & Guemez-Gamboa, A. (2019). Genetic causes and modifiers of autism spectrum disorder. *Frontiers in Cellular Neuroscience*, 13, Article 385. https://doi.org/10.3389/fncel.2019.00385

Ryman, F. V. M., Cesuroglu, T., Bood, Z. M., & Syurina, E. V. (2019). Orthorexia nervosa: Disorder or not? Opinions of Dutch health professionals. *Frontiers in Psychology*, 10, Article 555. https://doi.org/10.3389/fpsyg.2019.00555

Saad, T. C., Link to external site, this link will open in a new window, Blackshaw, B. P., Link to external site, this link will open in a new window, & Rodger, D. (2019). Hormone replacement therapy: Informed consent without assessment? *Journal of Medical Ethics*, 45(12), 824. https://doi.org/10.1136/medethics-2019-105611

Sabia, J. J., Dave, D. M., Alotaibi, F., & Rees, D. I. (2021). *Is recreational marijuana a gateway to harder drug use and crime?* (NBER Working Paper No. 29038). National Bureau of Economic Research. http://www.nber.org/papers/w29038

Saccaro, L. F., Schilliger, Z., Dayer, A., Perroud, N., & Piguet, C. (2021). Inflammation, anxiety, and stress in bipolar disorder and borderline personality disorder: A narrative review. *Neuroscience & Biobehavioral Reviews*, 127, 184–192. https://doi.org/10.1016/j.neubiorev.2021.04.017

Sachdev, P. S. (2022). Social health, social reserve and dementia. *Current Opinion in Psychiatry*, 35(2), 111–117. https://doi.org/10.1097/YCO.0000000000000779

Sacher, J., Neumann, J., Fünfstück, T., Soliman, A., Villringer, A., & Schroeter, M. L. (2012). Mapping the depressed brain: A meta-analysis of structural and functional alterations in major depressive disorder. *Journal of Affective Disorders*, 140(2), 142–148. https://doi.org/10.1016/j.jad.2011.08.001

Sadeh, N., Miller, M. W., Wolf, E. J., & Harkness, K. L. (2015). Negative emotionality and disconstraint influence PTSD symptom course via exposure to new major adverse life events. *Journal of Anxiety Disorders*, 31, 20–27. https://doi.org/10.1016/j.janxdis.2015.01.003

Sadler, J. Z., & Agich, G. J. (1995). Diseases, functions, values, and psychiatric classification. *Philosophy, Psychiatry, & Psychology*, 2(3), 219–231.

Safeguard Defenders. (2022, August 16). *Mental torture: China is locking up critics in psychiatric facilities.* https://safeguarddefenders.com/en/blog/mental-torture-china-locking-critics-psychiatric-facilities

Sajadi-Ernazarova, K. R., Anderson, J., Dhakal, A., & Hamilton, R. J. (2022). Caffeine withdrawal. In *StatPearls [Internet]*. StatPearls Publishing. https://www.ncbi.nlm.nih.gov/books/NBK430790/

Saks, E. R. (2003). Involuntary outpatient commitment. *Psychology, Public Policy, and Law*, 9(1–2), 94–106. https://doi.org/10.1037/1076-8971.9.1-2.94

Saks, E. R. (2021). Psychoanalytic treatment of psychosis. In C. A. Tamminga, E. I. Ivleva, U. Reininghaus, & J. Van Os (Eds.), *Psychotic disorders: Comprehensive conceptualization and treatments* (pp. 509–513). Oxford University Press. https://doi.org/10.1093/med/9780190653279.003.0056

Sala, M., Perez, J., Soloff, P., Di Nemi, S. U., Caverzasi, E., Soares, J. C., & Brambilla, P. (2004). Stress and hippocampal abnormalities in psychiatric disorders. *European Neuropsychopharmacology*, 14(5), 393–405. https://doi.org/10.1016/j.euroneuro.2003.12.005

Salamone, J. D., & Correa, M. (2013). Dopamine and food addiction: Lexicon badly needed. *Biological Psychiatry*, 73(9), e15–e24. https://doi.org/10.1016/j.biopsych.2012.09.027

Salari, N., Rasoulpoor, S., Rasoulpoor, S., Shohaimi, S., Jafarpour, S., Abdoli, N., Khaledi-Paveh, B., & Mohammadi, M. (2022). The global prevalence of autism spectrum disorder: A comprehensive systematic review and meta-analysis. *Italian Journal of Pediatrics*, 48(1), 112. https://doi.org/10.1186/s13052-022-01310-w

Salazar de Pablo, G., Catalan, A., & Fusar-Poli, P. (2020). Clinical validity of *DSM-5* attenuated psychosis syndrome: Advances in diagnosis, prognosis, and treatment. *JAMA Psychiatry*, 77(3), 311. https://doi.org/10.1001/jamapsychiatry.2019.3561

Salcedo, S., Gold, A. K., Sheikh, S., Marcus, P. H., Nierenberg, A. A., Deckersbach, T., & Sylvia, L. G. (2016). Empirically supported psychosocial interventions for bipolar disorder: Current state of the research. *Journal of Affective Disorders*, 201, 203–214. https://doi.org/10.1016/j.jad.2016.05.018

Saleem, F. T., Anderson, R. E., & Williams, M. (2020). Addressing the "myth" of racial trauma: Developmental and ecological considerations for youth of color. *Clinical Child and Family Psychology Review*, 23(1), 1–14. https://doi.org/10.1007/s10567-019-00304-1

Saleh, F. M., Bradford, J. M., Taylor, J., & Fedoroff, J. P. (2021). The neurobiology of sexual behavior and the paraphilias. In F. M. Saleh, J. M. Bradford, & D. J. Brodsky (Eds.), *Sex offenders: Identification, risk assessment, treatment, and legal issues* (2nd ed., pp. 61–79). Oxford University Press.

Salik, I., & Marwaha, R. (2022). Electroconvulsive therapy. In *StatPearls*. StatPearls Publishing. http://www.ncbi.nlm.nih.gov/books/NBK538266/

Salinas, J., Beiser, A. S., Samra, J. K., O'Donnell, A., DeCarli, C. S., Gonzales, M. M., Aparicio, H. J., & Seshadri, S. (2022). Association of loneliness with 10-year dementia risk and early markers of vulnerability for neurocognitive decline. *Neurology*, 98(13), e1337–e1348. https://doi.org/10.1212/WNL.0000000000200039

Salkovskis, P. M. (1985). Obsessional-compulsive problems: A cognitive-behavioural analysis. *Behaviour Research and Therapy*, 23(5), 571–583. https://doi.org/10.1016/0005-7967(85)90105-6

Salkovskis, P. M. (2007). Cognitive-behavioural treatment for panic. *Psychiatry*, 6(5), 193–197. https://doi.org/10.1016/j.mppsy.2007.03.002

Salkovskis, P. M., Forrester, E., & Richards, C. (1998). Cognitive–behavioural approach to understanding obsessional thinking. *The British Journal of Psychiatry*, 173(S35), 53–63. https://doi.org/10.1192/S0007125000297900

Sallis, H. M., Croft, J., Havdahl, A., Jones, H. J., Dunn, E. C., Davey Smith, G., Zammit, S., & Munafò, M. R. (2021). Genetic liability to schizophrenia is associated with exposure to traumatic events in childhood. *Psychological Medicine*, 51(11), 1814–1821. https://doi.org/10.1017/S0033291720000537

Salmon, C., & Crawford, C. (2012). When intersexual conflict leads to intrasexual competition: The reproductive suppression hypothesis. In T. K. Shackelford & A. T. Goetz (Eds.), The Oxford handbook of sexual conflict in humans (pp. 134–147). Oxford University Press.

Salmon, C., Crawford, C., Dane, L., & Zuberbier, O. (2008). Ancestral mechanisms in modern environments: Impact of competition and stressors on body image and dieting behavior. Human Nature, 19(1), 103–117. doi:10.1007/s12110-008-9030-8

Salmon, M. A. (1975). An historical account of nocturnal enuresis and its treatment. *Proceedings of the Royal Society of Medicine*, 68(7), 443–445.

Salomon, C., & Hamilton, B. (2014). Antipsychotic discontinuation syndromes: A narrative review of the evidence and its integration into Australian mental health nursing textbooks. *International Journal of Mental Health Nursing*, 23(1), 69–78. https://doi.org/10.1111/j.1447-0349.2012.00889.x

Salomon, R. M., Miller, H. L., Krystal, J. H., Heninger, G. R., & Charney, D. S. (1997). Lack of behavioral effects of monoamine depletion in healthy subjects. *Biological Psychiatry*, 41(1), 58–64. https://doi.org/10.1016/0006-3223(95)00670-2

Salomonsson, B. (2004). Some psychoanalytic viewpoints on neuropsychiatric disorders in children. *The International Journal of Psychoanalysis*, 85(1), 117–136. https://doi.org/10.1516/BQYA-14CN-LA29-C4H8

Salvatore, J. E., & Dick, D. M. (2018). Genetic influences on conduct disorder. *Neuroscience and Biobehavioral Reviews*, 91, 91–101. https://doi.org/10.1016/j.neubiorev.2016.06.034

Salzberg, S. L. (2018). Open questions: How many genes do we have? *BMC Biology*, 16(1), 94. https://doi.org/10.1186/s12915-018-0564-x

Samaran, R., & Vivek, R. (2020). Concept of psychosomatic disorders in homoeopathy: A review. *International Journal of Homoeopathic Sciences*, 4(2), 150–155.

Sambu, S., Hemaram, U., Murugan, R., & Alsofi, A. A. (2022). Toxicological and teratogenic effect of various food additives: An updated review. *BioMed Research International*, 2022, e6829409. https://doi.org/10.1155/2022/6829409

Samek, D. R., & Hicks, B. M. (2014). Externalizing disorders and environmental risk: Mechanisms of gene-environment interplay and strategies for intervention. *Clinical Practice*, 11(5), 537–547. https://doi.org/10.2217/CPR.14.47

Samokhvalov, A. V., & Rehm, J. (2013). Heroin addiction. In P. M. Miller, S. A. Ball, M. E. Bates, A. W. Blume, K. M. Kampman, D. J. Kavanagh, M. E. Larimer, N. M. Petry, & P. De Witte (Eds.), *Comprehensive addictive behaviors and disorders: Vol. 1. Principles of addiction* (pp. 657–667). Elsevier Academic Press.

Sampedro, F., Farrés, C. C. i, Soler, J., Elices, M., Schmidt, C., Corripio, I., Domínguez-Clavé, E., Pomarol-Clotet, E., Salvador, R., & Pascual, J. C. (2021). Structural brain abnormalities in borderline personality disorder correlate with clinical severity and predict psychotherapy response. *Brain Imaging and Behavior*, 15(5), 2502–2512. https://doi.org/10.1007/s11682-021-00451-6

Sanacora, G., Frye, M. A., McDonald, W., Mathew, S. J., Turner, M. S., Schatzberg, A. F., Summergrad, P., & Nemeroff, C. B. (2017). A consensus statement on the use of ketamine in the treatment of mood disorders. *JAMA Psychiatry*. https://doi.org/10.1001/jamapsychiatry.2017.0080

Sanacora, G., Treccani, G., & Popoli, M. (2012). Towards a glutamate hypothesis of depression: An emerging frontier of neuropsychopharmacology for mood disorders. *Neuropharmacology*, 62(1), 63–77. https://doi.org/10.1016/j.neuropharm.2011.07.036

Sanders, J. J., Roose, R. J., Lubrano, M. C., & Lucan, S. C. (2013). Meaning and methadone: Patient perceptions of methadone dose and a model to promote adherence to maintenance treatment. *Journal of Addiction Medicine*, 7(5), 307–313. https://doi.org/10.1097/ADM.0b013e318297021e

Sanders, J. L. (2011). A distinct language and a historic pendulum: The evolution of the *Diagnostic and statistical manual of mental disorders*. *Archives of Psychiatric Nursing*, 25(6), 394–403.

Sanders, S., Thomas, R., Glasziou, P., & Doust, J. (2019). A review of changes to the attention deficit/hyperactivity disorder age of onset criterion using the checklist for modifying disease definitions. *BMC Psychiatry*, 19(1), Article 357. https://doi.org/10.1186/s12888-019-2337-7

Sandin, S., Lichtenstein, P., Kuja-Halkola, R., Hultman, C., Larsson, H., & Reichenberg, A. (2017). The heritability of autism spectrum disorder. *JAMA*, 318(12), 1182–1184. https://doi.org/10.1001/jama.2017.12141

Sandoz, E., Wilson, K., & DuFrene, T. (2010). *Acceptance and commitment therapy for eating disorders: A process-focused guide to treating anorexia and bulimia.* New Harbinger Publications.

Sani, G., Gualtieri, I., Paolini, M., Bonanni, L., Spinazzola, E., Maggiora, M., Pinzone, V., Brugnoli, R., Angeletti, G., Girardi, P., Rapinesi, C., & Kotzalidis, G. D. (2019). Drug treatment of trichotillomania (hair-pulling disorder), excoriation (skin-picking) disorder, and nail-biting (onychophagia). *Current Neuropharmacology*, *17*(8), 775–786. https://doi.org/10.2174/1570159X17666190320164223

Sani, G., Tondo, L., Undurraga, J., Vázquez, G. H., Salvatore, P., & Baldessarini, R. J. (2020). Melancholia: Does this ancient concept have contemporary utility? *International Review of Psychiatry*, *32*(5–6), 466–470. https://doi.org/10.1080/09540261.2019.1708708

Sansone, R. A., & Sansone, L. A. (2009). The families of borderline patients: The psychological environment revisited. *Psychiatry (Edgmont)*, *6*(2), 19–24.

Sansone, R. A., & Sansone, L. A. (2014). Serotonin norepinephrine reuptake inhibitors: A pharmacological comparison. *Innovations in Clinical Neuroscience*, *11*(3–4), 37–42.

Santarsieri, D., & Schwartz, T. L. (2015). Antidepressant efficacy and side-effect burden: A quick guide for clinicians. *Drugs in Context*, *4*, 212290. https://doi.org/10.7573/dic.212290

Santomauro, D. F., Mantilla Herrera, A. M., Shadid, J., Zheng, P., Ashbaugh, C., Pigott, D. M., Abbafati, C., Adolph, C., Amlag, J. O., Aravkin, A. Y., Bang-Jensen, B. L., Bertolacci, G. J., Bloom, S. S., Castellano, R., Castro, E., Chakrabarti, S., Chattopadhyay, J., Cogen, R. M., Collins, J. K., … Ferrari, A. J. (2021). Global prevalence and burden of depressive and anxiety disorders in 204 countries and territories in 2020 due to the COVID-19 pandemic. *The Lancet*, *398*(10312), 1700–1712. https://doi.org/10.1016/S0140-6736(21)02143-7

Santoro, N., Worsley, R., Miller, K. K., Parish, S. J., & Davis, S. R. (2016). Role of estrogens and estrogen-like compounds in female sexual function and dysfunction. *The Journal of Sexual Medicine*, *13*(3), 305–316. https://doi.org/10.1016/j.jsxm.2015.11.015

Santos, M. A. O., Bezerra, L. S., Carvalho, A. R. M. R., & Brainer-Lima, A. M. (2018). Global hippocampal atrophy in major depressive disorder: A meta-analysis of magnetic resonance imaging studies. *Trends in Psychiatry and Psychotherapy*, *40*(4), 369–378. https://doi.org/10.1590/2237-6089-2017-0130

Sapolsky, R. M. (2000). Glucocorticoids and hippocampal atrophy in neuropsychiatric disorders. *Archives of General Psychiatry*, *57*(10), 925–935. https://doi.org/10.1001/archpsyc.57.10.925

Sapolsky, R. M. (2001). Depression, antidepressants, and the shrinking hippocampus. *Proceedings of the National Academy of Sciences of the United States of America*, *98*(22), 12320–12322. https://doi.org/10.1073/pnas.231475998

Sapountzis, I. (2020). From Jackson Pollock to psychic blades: Climbing the semiotic ladder in working with children with attention-deficit/hyperactivity disorder. *Psychoanalytic Psychology*, *37*(4), 305–312. https://doi.org/10.1037/pap0000296

Sar, V. (2011). Epidemiology of dissociative disorders: An overview. *Epidemiology Research International*, 1–8. https://doi.org/10.1155/2011/404538

Şar, V. (2014). The many faces of dissociation: Opportunities for innovative research in psychiatry. *Clinical Psychopharmacology and Neuroscience*, *12*(3), 171–179. https://doi.org/10.9758/cpn.2014.12.3.171

Şar, V., Akyüz, G., & Doğan, O. (2007). Prevalence of dissociative disorders among women in the general population. *Psychiatry Research*, *149*(1–3), 169–176. https://doi.org/10.1016/j.psychres.2006.01.005

Sar, V., Önder, C., Kilincaslan, A., Zoroglu, S. S., & Alyanak, B. (2014). Dissociative identity disorder among adolescents: Prevalence in a university psychiatric outpatient unit. *Journal of Trauma & Dissociation*, *15*(4), 402–419. https://doi.org/10.1080/15299732.2013.864748

Sarkar, D., Jung, M. K., & Wang, H. J. (2015). Alcohol and the immune system. *Alcohol Research: Current Reviews*, *37*(2), 153–155.

Sarma, S., Ranjith, S., & Abeysundera, H. (2021). Remission of somatic symptom disorder with comorbid severe major depressive disorder after treatment with electroconvulsive therapy. *The Journal*

of ECT, *37*(4), e40–e41. https://doi.org/10.1097/YCT.0000000000000795

Sarris, J., Panossian, A., Schweitzer, I., Stough, C., & Scholey, A. (2011). Herbal medicine for depression, anxiety and insomnia: A review of psychopharmacology and clinical evidence. *European Neuropsychopharmacology*, *21*(12), 841–860. https://doi.org/10.1016/j.euroneuro.2011.04.002

Sarteschi, C. M. (2014). Randomized controlled trials of psychopharmacological interventions of children and adolescents with conduct disorder: A descriptive analysis. *Journal of Evidence-Based Social Work*, *11*(4), 350–359. https://doi.org/10.1080/10911359.2014.897105

Sartre, J.-P. (2007). *Existentialism is a humanism* (C. Macomber, Trans.). Yale University Press. (Original work published 1947.)

Sassover, E., & Weinstein, A. (2020). Should compulsive sexual behavior (CSB) be considered as a behavioral addiction? A debate paper presenting the opposing view. *Journal of Behavioral Addictions*, *11*(2), 166–179. https://doi.org/10.1556/2006.2020.00055

Sauer-Zavala, S., Gutner, C. A., Farchione, T. J., Boettcher, H. T., Bullis, J. R., & Barlow, D. H. (2017). Current definitions of "transdiagnostic" in treatment development: A search for consensus. *Behavior Therapy*, *48*(1), 128–138. https://doi.org/10.1016/j.beth.2016.09.004

Saul, J., Griffiths, S. L., & Norbury, C. (2021). *Prevalence and functional impact of social (pragmatic) communication disorders*. PsyArXiv. https://doi.org/10.31234/osf.io/yms6f

Saxena, S., Bota, R. G., & Brody, A. L. (2001). Brain-behavior relationships in obsessive-compulsive disorder. *Seminars in Clinical Neuropsychiatry*, *6*(2), 82–101. https://doi.org/10.1053/scnp.2001.21833

Sayo, A., Jennings, R. G., & Van Horn, J. D. (2012). Study factors influencing ventricular enlargement in schizophrenia: A 20 year follow-up meta-analysis. *NeuroImage*, *59*(1), 154–167. https://doi.org/10.1016/j.neuroimage.2011.07.011

Sbarra, D. A., Emery, R. E., Beam, C. R., & Ocker, B. L. (2014). Marital dissolution and major depression in midlife: A propensity score analysis. *Clinical Psychological Science*, *2*(3), 249–257. https://doi.org/10.1177/2167702613498727

Schaefer, L. M., & Thompson, J. K. (2018). Self-objectification and disordered eating: A meta-analysis. *The International Journal of Eating Disorders*, *51*(6), 483–502. https://doi.org/10.1002/eat.22854

Schäfer, A., Vaitl, D., & Schienle, A. (2010). Regional grey matter volume abnormalities in bulimia nervosa and binge-eating disorder. *NeuroImage*, *50*(2), 639–643. https://doi.org/10.1016/j.neuroimage.2009.12.063

Schaffer, M., Jeglic, E. L., Moster, A., & Wnuk, D. (2010). Cognitive-behavioral therapy in the treatment management of sex offenders. *Journal of Cognitive Psychotherapy*, *24*(2), 92–103. https://doi.org/10.1891/0889-8391.24.2.92

Schaler, J. A. (2000). *Addiction is a choice*. Open Court Publishing Co.

Schaler, J. A. (2002). Addiction is a choice. In *Psychiatric Times* (Vol. 19, Issue 10). http://www.psychiatrictimes.com/addiction/addiction-choice

Schalkwyk, G. I. van, & Leckman, J. F. (2017). Evolutionary perspectives on OCD. In C. Pittenger (Ed.), *Obsessive-compulsive disorder: Phenomenology, pathophysiology, and treatment* (pp. 683–688). Oxford University Press. https://oxfordmedicine.com/view/10.1093/med/9780190228163.001.0001/med-9780190228163-chapter-61

Schanche, E., Vøllestad, J., Visted, E., Svendsen, J. L., Osnes, B., Binder, P. E., Franer, P., & Sørensen, L. (2020). The effects of mindfulness-based cognitive therapy on risk and protective factors of depressive relapse – a randomized wait-list controlled trial. *BMC Psychology*, *8*(1), 57. https://doi.org/10.1186/s40359-020-00417-1

Schans, J. van der, Çiçek, R., de Vries, T. W., Hak, E., & Hoekstra, P. J. (2017). Association of atopic diseases and attention-deficit/hyperactivity disorder: A systematic review and meta-analyses. *Neuroscience & Biobehavioral Reviews*, *74*, 139–148. https://doi.org/10.1016/j.neubiorev.2017.01.011

Scharf, J. M., Yu, D., Mathews, C. A., Neale, B. M., Stewart, S. E., Fagerness, J. A., Evans, P., Gamazon, E., Edlund, C. K., Service, S. K., Tikhomirov, A., Osiecki, L., Illmann, C., Pluzhnikov, A., Konkashbaev, A., Davis, L. K., Han, B., Crane, J., Moorjani, P., … Pauls, D. L. (2013). Genome-wide association study of Tourette's syndrome. *Molecular Psychiatry*, *18*(6), 721–728. https://doi.org/10.1038/mp.2012.69

Scharf, M. B., Pravda, M. F., Jennings, S. W., Kauffman, R., & Ringel, J. (1987). Childhood enuresis: A comprehensive treatment program. *Psychiatric Clinics of North America*, *10*(4), 655–666.

Schaub, M. P., Henderson, C. E., Pelc, I., Tossmann, P., Phan, O., Hendriks, V., Rowe, C., & Rigter, H. (2014). Multidimensional family therapy decreases the rate of externalising behavioural disorder symptoms in cannabis abusing adolescents: Outcomes of the INCANT trial. *BMC Psychiatry*, *14*. https://doi.org/10.1186/1471-244X-14-26

Scheepers, F. E., de Mul, J., Boer, F., & Hoogendijk, W. J. (2018). Psychosis as an evolutionary adaptive mechanism to changing environments. *Frontiers in Psychiatry*, *9*, Article 237. https://doi.org/10.3389/fpsyt.2018.00237

Scheff, T. J. (1999). *Being mentally ill: A sociological theory* (3rd ed.). Aldine.

Scheffler, F., Du Plessis, S., Asmal, L., Kilian, S., Phahladira, L., Luckhoff, H. K., & Emsley, R. (2021). Cannabis use and hippocampal subfield volumes in males with a first episode of a schizophrenia spectrum disorder and healthy controls. *Schizophrenia Research*, *231*, 13–21. https://doi.org/10.1016/j.schres.2021.02.017

Scher, L. M., Knudsen, P., & Leamon, M. (2014). Somatic symptom and related disorders. In R. E. Hales, S. C. Yudofsky, & L. W. Roberts (Eds.), *The American Psychiatric Publishing textbook of psychiatry* (6th ed., pp. 531–556). American Psychiatric Publishing. https://doi.org/10.1176/appi.books.9781585625031.rh16

Schiavi, R. C., Theilgaard, A., Owen, D. R., & White, D. (1988). Sex chromosome anomalies, hormones, and sexuality. *Archives of General Psychiatry*, *45*(1), 19–24. https://doi.org/10.1001/archpsyc.1988.01800250023004

Schimmenti, A., Di Carlo, G., Passanisi, A., & Caretti, V. (2015). Abuse in childhood and psychopathic traits in a sample of violent offenders. *Psychological Trauma: Theory, Research, Practice and Policy*, *7*(4), 340–347. https://doi.org/10.1037/tra0000023

Schlax, J., Jünger, C., Beutel, M. E., Münzel, T., Pfeiffer, N., Wild, P., Blettner, M., Kerahrodi, J. G., Wiltink, J., & Michal, M. (2019). Income and education predict elevated depressive symptoms in the general population: Results from the Gutenberg health study. *BMC Public Health*, *19*(1), 430. https://doi.org/10.1186/s12889-019-6730-4

Schlax, J., Wiltink, J., Beutel, M. E., Münzel, T., Pfeiffer, N., Wild, P., Blettner, M., Ghaemi Kerahrodi, J., & Michal, M. (2020). Symptoms of depersonalization/derealization are independent risk factors for the development or persistence of psychological distress in the general population: Results from the Gutenberg health study. *Journal of Affective Disorders*, *273*, 41–47. https://doi.org/10.1016/j.jad.2020.04.018

Schmengler, H., Cohen, D., Tordjman, S., & Melchior, M. (2021). Autism spectrum and other neurodevelopmental disorders in children of immigrants: A brief review of current evidence and implications for clinical practice. *Frontiers in Psychiatry*, *12*, Article 566368. https://doi.org/10.3389/fpsyt.2021.566368

Schmidt, C. K., Khalid, S., Loukas, M., & Tubbs, R. S. (2018). Neuroanatomy of anxiety: A brief review. *Cureus*, *10*(1). https://doi.org/10.7759/cureus.2055

Schmidt, N. B., & Lerew, D. R. (1998). Prospective evaluation of psychological risk factors as predictors of functional impairment during acute stress. *Journal of Occupational Rehabilitation, 8*(3), 199–212. https://doi.org/10.1023/A: 1021378523582

Schmidt, U. (2015). A plea for symptom-based research in psychiatry. *European Journal of Psychotraumatology, 6,* Article 27660. https://doi.org/10.3402/ejpt.v6.27660

Schmidt, U., & Vermetten, E. (2018). Integrating NIMH Research Domain Criteria (RDoC) into PTSD research. *Current Topics in Behavioral Neurosciences, 38,* 69–91. https://doi.org/10.1007/7854_2017_1

Schneider, E., Higgs, S., & Dourish, C. T. (2021). Lisdexamfetamine and binge-eating disorder: A systematic review and meta-analysis of the preclinical and clinical data with a focus on mechanism of drug action in treating the disorder. *European Neuropsychopharmacology, 53,* 49–78. https://doi.org/10.1016/j.euroneuro.2021.08.001

Schneider, M. R., DelBello, M. P., McNamara, R. K., Strakowski, S. M., & Adler, C. M. (2012). Neuroprogression in bipolar disorder. *Bipolar Disorders, 14*(4), 356–374. https://doi.org/10.1111/j.1399-5618.2012.01024.x

Schnoll, R., Burshteyn, D., & Cea-Aravena, J. (2003). Nutrition in the treatment of attention-deficit hyperactivity disorder: A neglected but important aspect. *Applied Psychophysiology and Biofeedback, 28*(1), 63–75. https://doi.org/10.1023/A:1022321017467

Schofield, H. (2012, April 2). France's autism treatment "shame." *BBC.* http://www.bbc.com/news/magazine-17583123

Scholz, U., Doña, B. G., Sud, S., & Schwarzer, R. (2002). Is general self-efficacy a universal construct? Psychometric findings from 25 countries. *European Journal of Psychological Assessment, 18*(3), 242–251. https://doi.org/10.1027//1015-5759.18.3.242

School Psychologist Files. (2021). *Understanding test scores.* Retrieved December 26, 2021 from https://schoolpsychologistfiles.com/testscores/

Schoorl, J., Rijn, S. van, Wied, M. de, van Goozen, S., & Swaab, H. (2016). The role of anxiety in cortisol stress response and cortisol recovery in boys with oppositional defiant disorder/conduct disorder. *Psychoneuroendocrinology, 73,* 217–223. https://doi.org/10.1016/j.psyneuen.2016.08.007

Schoot, T. S., Molmans, T. H. J., Grootens, K. P., & Kerckhoffs, A. P. M. (2020). Systematic review and practical guideline for the prevention and management of the renal side effects of lithium therapy. *European Neuropsychopharmacology, 31,* 16–32.

Schreiber, L. R. N., Odlaug, B. L., & Grant, J. E. (2013). The overlap between binge eating disorder and substance use disorders: Diagnosis and neurobiology. *Journal of Behavioral Addictions, 2*(4), 191–198. https://doi.org/10.1556/JBA.2.2013.015

Schreier, H. A. (1990). OCD and tricyclics. *Journal of the American Academy of Child & Adolescent Psychiatry, 29*(4), 668–669. https://doi.org/10.1097/00004583-199007000-00027

Schröder, A., Heider, J., Zaby, A., & Göllner, R. (2013). Cognitive behavioral therapy versus progressive muscle relaxation training for multiple somatoform symptoms: Results of a randomized controlled trial. *Cognitive Therapy and Research, 37*(2), 296–306. https://doi.org/10.1007/s10608-012-9474-3

Schröder, T., Cooper, A., Naidoo, R., Tickle, A., & Rennoldson, M. (2016). Intensive short-term dynamic psychotherapy (ISTDP). In D. Dawson & N. Moghaddam (Eds.), *7. Intensive short-term dynamic psychotherapy (ISTDP)* (pp. 99–122). De Gruyter Open Poland. https://doi.org/10.1515/9783110471014-009

Schug, R. A., & Fradella, H. F. (2015). *Mental illness and crime.* SAGE Publications.

Schuham, A. I. (1967). The double-bind hypothesis a decade later. *Psychological Bulletin, 68*(6), 409–416. https://doi.org/10.1037/h0020188

Schulpen, T. W. (1997). The burden of nocturnal enuresis. *Acta Paediatrica, 86*(9), 981–984. https://doi.org/10.1111/j.1651-2227.1997.tb15183.x

Schulte Holthausen, B., & Habel, U. (2018). Sex differences in personality disorders. *Current Psychiatry Reports, 20*(12), 107. https://doi.org/10.1007/s11920-018-0975-y

Schultz, W. M., Kelli, H. M., Lisko, J. C., Varghese, T., Shen, J., Sandesara, P., Quyyumi, A. A., Taylor, H. A., Gulati, M., Harold, J. G., Mieres, J. H., Ferdinand, K. C., Mensah, G. A., & Sperling, L. S. (2018). Socioeconomic status and cardiovascular outcomes. *Circulation, 137*(20), 2166–2178. https://doi.org/10.1161/CIRCULATIONAHA.117.029652

Schultze-Florey, C. R., Martínez-Maza, O., Magpantay, L., Breen, E. C., Irwin, M. R., Gündel, H., & O'Connor, M.-F. (2012). When grief makes you sick: Bereavement induced systemic inflammation is a question of genotype. *Brain, Behavior, and Immunity, 26*(7), 1066–1071. https://doi.org/10.1016/j.bbi.2012.06.009

Schumacher, J., Kristensen, A. S., Wendland, J. R., Nöthen, M. M., Mors, O., & McMahon, F. J. (2011). The genetics of panic disorder. *Journal of Medical Genetics, 48*(6), 361–368. https://doi.org/10.1136/jmg.2010.086876

Schure, M. B., Simpson, T. L., Martinez, M., Sayre, G., & Kearney, D. J. (2018). Mindfulness-based processes of healing for veterans with post-traumatic stress disorder. *The Journal of Alternative and Complementary Medicine, 24*(11), 1063–1068. https://doi.org/10.1089/acm.2017.0404

Schwannauer, M. (2013). Cognitive behavioral therapy for bipolar affective disorders. In M. Power (Ed.), *The Wiley-Blackwell handbook of mood disorders* (2nd ed., pp. 361–381). Wiley-Blackwell.

Schwartz, C. (2015, July 23). A neuroscientist argues that everybody Is misunderstanding fear and anxiety. *New York Magazine.* http://nymag.com/scienceofus/2015/07/everybody-misunderstanding-fear-and-anxiety.html

Schwartz, E. K., Docherty, N. M., Najolia, G. M., & Cohen, A. S. (2019). Exploring the racial diagnostic bias of schizophrenia using behavioral and clinical-based measures. *Journal of Abnormal Psychology, 128*(3), 263–271. https://doi.org/10.1037/abn0000409

Schwartz, R. C., & Blankenship, D. M. (2014). Racial disparities in psychotic disorder diagnosis: A review of empirical literature. *World Journal of Psychiatry, 4*(4), 133–140. https://doi.org/10.5498/wjp.v4.i4.133

Schwartz, R. C., Schwartz, M. F., & Galperin, L. (2009). Internal family systems therapy. In C. A. Courtois & J. D. Ford (Eds.), *Treating complex traumatic stress disorders: An evidence-based guide* (pp. 353–370). The Guilford Press.

Schwartze, D., Barkowski, S., Strauss, B., Knaevelsrud, C., & Rosendahl, J. (2019). Efficacy of group psychotherapy for posttraumatic stress disorder: Systematic review and meta-analysis of randomized controlled trials. *Psychotherapy Research, 29*(4), 415–431. https://doi.org/10.1080/10503307.2017.1405168

Schwarz, A. (2016). *ADHD nation: Children, doctors, Big Pharma, and the making of an American epidemic* (2016-46155-000). Scribner/Simon & Schuster.

Schwitzgebel, R. K. (1974). The right to effective mental treatment. *California Law Review, 62*(3), 936–956. https://doi.org/10.15779/Z385J2N

Scott, G. N. (2013). *Which plants contain caffeine?* (Issue March 13). http://www.medscape.com/viewarticle/780334

Scott, N., Hanstock, T. L., & Patterson-Kane, L. (2013). Using narrative therapy to treat eating disorder not otherwise specified. *Clinical Case Studies, 12*(4), 307–321. https://doi.org/10.1177/1534650113486184

Scully, D., & Marolla, J. (1985). "Riding the bull at Gilley's": Convicted rapists describe the rewards of rape. *Social Problems, 32*(3), 251–263. https://doi.org/10.1525/sp.1985.32.3.03a00070

Searight, H. R., Rottnek, F., & Abby, S. L. (2001). Conduct disorder: Diagnosis and treatment in primary care. *American Family Physician, 63*(8), 1579–1589.

Searles, H. F. (2013). Scorn, disillusionment and adoration in the psychotherapy of schizophrenia. *Psychoanalytic Review, 100*(2), 338 359.

Searls, D. (2017). *The inkblots: Hermann Rorschach, his iconic test, and the power of seeing.* Crown.

Sederer, L. I. (2013, October 8). Involuntary psychiatric hospitalization [Psychology Today]. *Therapy. It's More than Just Talk.* https://www.psychologytoday.com/us/blog/therapy-it-s-more-just-talk/201310/involuntary-psychiatric-hospitalization

Sedláková, H., & Říháček, T. (2019). The incorporation of a spiritual emergency experience Into a client's worldview: A grounded theory. *Journal of Humanistic Psychology, 59*(6), 877–897. https://doi.org/10.1177/0022167816668114

Seedat, S., Stein, D. J., & Carey, P. D. (2005). Post-traumatic stress disorder in women: Epidemiological and treatment issues. *CNS Drugs, 19*(5), 411–427. https://doi.org/10.2165/00023210-200519050-00004

Seeley, J. R., Farmer, R. F., Kosty, D. B., & Gau, J. M. (2019). Prevalence, incidence, recovery, and recurrence of alcohol use disorders from childhood to age 30. *Drug and Alcohol Dependence, 194,* 45–50. https://doi.org/10.1016/j.drugalcdep.2018.09.012

Seeman, M. V. (2011). Canada: Psychosis in the immigrant Caribbean population. *International Journal of Social Psychiatry, 57*(5), 462–470. https://doi.org/10.1177/0020764010365979

Seeman, M. V., & Seeman, P. (2014). Is schizophrenia a dopamine supersensitivity psychotic reaction? *Progress in Neuro-Psychopharmacology & Biological Psychiatry, 48,* 155–160. https://doi.org/10.1016/j.pnpbp.2013.10.003

Seeman, P. (2011). All roads to schizophrenia lead to dopamine supersensitivity and elevated dopamine D2High receptors. *CNS Neuroscience & Therapeutics, 17*(2), 118–132. https://doi.org/10.1111/j.1755-5949.2010.00162.x

Seeman, P. (2013). Schizophrenia and dopamine receptors. *European Neuropsychopharmacology, 23*(9), 999–1009. https://doi.org/10.1016/j.euroneuro.2013.06.005

Segal, J. Z. (2018). Sex, drugs, and rhetoric: The case of flibanserin for "female sexual dysfunction." *Social Studies of Science, 48*(4), 459–482. https://doi.org/10.1177/0306312718778802

Segal, Z. V., Dimidjian, S., Beck, A., Boggs, J. M., Vanderkruik, R., Metcalf, C. A., Gallop, R., Felder, J. N., & Levy, J. (2020). Outcomes of online mindfulness-based cognitive therapy for patients with residual depressive symptoms: A randomized clinical trial. *JAMA Psychiatry, 77*(6), 563–573. https://doi.org/10.1001/jamapsychiatry.2019.4693

Segal, Z. V., Teasdale, J. D., & Williams, J. M. G. (2004). Mindfulness-based cognitive therapy: Theoretical rationale and empirical status. In S. C. Hayes, V. M. Follette, & M. M. Linehan (Eds.), *Mindfulness and acceptance: Expanding the cognitive-behavioral tradition* (pp. 45–65). Guilford Press.

Segal, Z. V., Williams, J. M. G., & Teasdale, J. D. (2013). *Mindfulness-based cognitive therapy for depression* (2nd ed.). Guilford Press.

Segerstrom, S. C., & Miller, G. E. (2004). Psychological stress and the human immune system: A meta-analytic study of 30 years of inquiry. *Psychological Bulletin, 130*(4), 601–630. https://doi.org/10.1037/0033-2909.130.4.601

Seikkula, J., Aaltonen, J., Alakare, B., Haarakangas, K., Keränen, J., & Lehtinen, K. (2006). Five-year experience of first-episode nonaffective psychosis in open-dialogue approach: Treatment principles, follow-up outcomes, and two case studies. *Psychotherapy Research, 16*(2), 214–228. https://doi.org/10.1080/10503300500268490

Seikkula, J., Alakare, B., & Aaltonen, J. (2001a). Open dialogue in psychosis I: An introduction and case illustration. *Journal of Constructivist Psychology*, 14(4), 247–265. https://doi.org/10.1080/107205301750433397

Seikkula, J., Alakare, B., & Aaltonen, J. (2001b). Open dialogue in psychosis II: A comparison of good and poor outcome cases. *Journal of Constructivist Psychology*, 14(4), 267–284. https://doi.org/10.1080/107205301750433405

Seikkula, J., Alakare, B., & Aaltonen, J. (2011). The comprehensive open-dialogue approach in Western Lapland: II. Long-term stability of acute psychosis outcomes in advanced community care. *Psychosis: Psychological, Social and Integrative Approaches*, 3(3), 192–204. https://doi.org/10.1080/17522439.2011.595819

Seiler, A., Fagundes, C. P., & Christian, L. M. (2020). The impact of everyday stressors on the immune system and health. In A. Choukèr (Ed.), *Stress challenges and immunity in space: From mechanisms to monitoring and preventive strategies* (pp. 71–92). Springer International Publishing. https://doi.org/10.1007/978-3-030-16996-1_6

Seiler, A., von Känel, R., & Slavich, G. M. (2020). The psychobiology of bereavement and health: A conceptual review from the perspective of social signal transduction theory of depression. *Frontiers in Psychiatry*, 11, Article 565239. https://doi.org/10.3389/fpsyt.2020.565239

Seitz, A. (2022, August 2). Number of uninsured Americans drops to record low. *AP News*. https://apnews.com/article/biden-health-us-department-of-and-human-services-government-politics-24684188cb-67c576ed00d01b2f53c09c

Seitz, J., Konrad, K., & Herpertz-Dahlmann, B. (2018). Extend, pathomechanism and clinical consequences of brain volume changes in anorexia nervosa. *Current Neuropharmacology*, 16(8), 1164–1173. https://doi.org/10.2174/1570159X15666171109145651

Seitz, S. R., & Choo, A. L. (2022). Stuttering: Stigma and perspectives of (dis)ability in organizational communication. *Human Resource Management Review*, 32(4), 100875. https://doi.org/10.1016/j.hrmr.2021.100875

Selby, E. A., Kranzler, A., Fehling, K. B., & Panza, E. (2015). Nonsuicidal self-injury disorder: The path to diagnostic validity and final obstacles. *Clinical Psychology Review*, 38, 79–91. https://doi.org/10.1016/j.cpr.2015.03.003

Seligman, M. E., & Maier, S. F. (1967). Failure to escape traumatic shock. *Journal of Experimental Psychology*, 74(1), 1–9. https://doi.org/10.1037/h0024514

Seligman, M. E., Maier, S. F., & Geer, J. H. (1968). Alleviation of learned helplessness in the dog. *Journal of Abnormal Psychology*, 73(3, Pt.1), 256–262. https://doi.org/10.1037/h0025831

Seligman, M. E. P. (1971). Phobias and preparedness. *Behavior Therapy*, 2(3), 307–320. https://doi.org/10.1016/S0005-7894(71)80064-3

Sellbom, M., Forbush, K. T., Gould, S. R., Markon, K. E., Watson, D., & Witthöft, M. (2022). HiTOP assessment of the somatoform spectrum and eating disorders. *Assessment*, 29(1), 62–74. https://doi.org/10.1177/10731911211020825

Sellbom, M., Kremyar, A. J., & Wygant, D. B. (2021). Mapping MMPI-3 scales onto the hierarchical taxonomy of psychopathology. *Psychological Assessment*. https://doi.org/10.1037/pas0001049

Selye, H. (1950). Stress and the general adaptation syndrome. *British Medical Journal*, 1(4667), 1383–1392.

Semkovska, M., Keane, D., Babalola, O., & McLoughlin, D. M. (2011). Unilateral brief-pulse electroconvulsive therapy and cognition: Effects of electrode placement, stimulus dosage and time. *Journal of Psychiatric Research*, 45(6), 770–780. https://doi.org/10.1016/j.jpsychires.2010.11.001

Sempértegui, G. A., Karreman, A., Arntz, A., & Bekker, M. H. J. (2013). Schema therapy for borderline personality disorder: A comprehensive review of its empirical foundations, effectiveness and implementation

possibilities. *Clinical Psychology Review*, 33(3), 426–447. https://doi.org/10.1016/j.cpr.2012.11.006

Sennott, S. L. (2011). Gender disorder as gender oppression: A transfeminist approach to rethinking the pathologization of gender non-conformity. *Women & Therapy*, 34(1–2), 93–113. https://doi.org/10.1080/02703149.2010.532683

Sepúlveda, A. R., & Calado, M. (2012). *Westernization: The role of mass media on body image and eating disorders* (Issue 3, pp. 47–64). InTech. https://doi.org/10.5772/31307

Serie, C. M. B., Van Damme, L., Pleysier, S., De Ruiter, C., & Put, J. (2021). The relationship between primary human needs of the Good Lives Model (GLM) and subjective well-being in adolescents: A multi-level meta-analysis. *Aggression and Violent Behavior*, 61, Article 101651. https://doi.org/10.1016/j.avb.2021.101651

Setterberg, S. R., Ernst, M., Rao, U., Campbell, M., Carlson, G. A., Shaffer, D., & Staghezza, B. M. (1991). Child psychiatrists' views of DSM-III—R: A survey of usage and opinions. *Journal of the American Academy of Child & Adolescent Psychiatry*, 30(4), 652–658. https://doi.org/10.1097/00004583-199107000-00019

Settle, E. C. (1998). Antidepressant drugs: Disturbing and potentially dangerous adverse effects. *Journal of Clinical Psychiatry*, 59(Suppl. 16), 25–30.

Severance, E. G., Yolken, R. H., & Eaton, W. W. (2016). Autoimmune diseases, gastrointestinal disorders and the microbiome in schizophrenia: More than a gut feeling. *Schizophrenia Research*, 176(1), 23–35. https://doi.org/10.1016/j.schres.2014.06.027

Sewell, K. W., & Williams, A. M. (2001). Construing stress: A constructivist therapeutic approach to posttraumatic stress reactions. In R. A. Neimeyer (Ed.), *Meaning reconstruction and the experience of loss* (pp. 293–310). American Psychological Association. https://doi.org/10.1037/10397-015

Shadrina, M., Bondarenko, E. A., & Slominsky, P. A. (2018). Genetics factors in major depression disease. *Frontiers in Psychiatry*, 9, Article 334. https://doi.org/10.3389/fpsyt.2018.00334

Shafiei, B., Faramarzi, S., Abedi, A., Dehqan, A., & Scherer, R. C. (2019). Effects of the Lidcombe Program and parent-child interaction therapy on stuttering reduction in preschool children. *Folia Phoniatrica et Logopaedica*, 71(1), 29–41. https://doi.org/10.1159/000493915

Shafter, R. (1989). Women and madness: A social historical perspective. *Issues in Ego Psychology*, 12(1), 77–82.

Shah, A. (2012). Making fitness to plead fit for purpose. *International Journal of Criminology and Sociology*, 1, 176–197.

Shah, A. A., & Han, J. Y. (2015). Anxiety. *CONTINUUM: Lifelong Learning in Neurology*, 21(3), 772–782.

Shahar, B. (2014). Emotion-focused therapy for the treatment of social anxiety: An overview of the model and a case description. *Clinical Psychology & Psychotherapy*, 21(6), 536–547.

Shahar, B., Bar-Kalifa, E., & Alon, E. (2017). Emotion-focused therapy for social anxiety disorder: Results from a multiple-baseline study. *Journal of Consulting and Clinical Psychology*, 85(3), 238–249. https://doi.org/10.1037/ccp0000166

Shahar, B., Carlin, E. R., Engle, D. E., Hegde, J., Szepsenwol, O., & Arkowitz, H. (2012). A pilot investigation of emotion-focused two-chair dialogue intervention for self-criticism. *Clinical Psychology & Psychotherapy*, 19(6), 496–507. https://doi.org/10.1002/cpp.762

Shapira, B. E., & Dahlen, P. (2010). Therapeutic treatment protocol for enuresis using an enuresis alarm. *Journal of Counseling & Development*, 88(2), 246–252. https://doi.org/10.1002/j.1556-6678.2010.tb00017.x

Shapiro, E. (2012). EMDR and early psychological intervention following trauma. *Revue Européenne de Psychologie Appliquée/European Review of Applied Psychology*, 62(4), 241–251. https://doi.org/10.1016/j.erap.2012.09.003

Shapiro, F. (2012). EMDR therapy: An overview of current and future research. *Revue Européenne de Psychologie Appliquée/European Review of Applied Psychology*, 62(4), 193–195. https://doi.org/10.1016/j.erap.2012.09.005

Shapiro, F., & Maxfield, L. (2002). Eye movement desensitization and reprocessing (EMDR): Information processing in the treatment of trauma. *Journal of Clinical Psychology*, 58(8), 933–946. https://doi.org/10.1002/jclp.10068

Shapiro, J. R., Berkman, N. D., Brownley, K. A., Sedway, J. A., Lohr, K. N., & Bulik, C. M. (2007). Bulimia nervosa treatment: A systematic review of randomized controlled trials. *International Journal of Eating Disorders*, 40(4), 321–336. https://doi.org/10.1002/eat.20372

Shapiro, R., & Brown, L. S. (2019). Eye movement desensitization and reprocessing therapy and related treatments for trauma: An innovative, integrative trauma treatment. *Practice Innovations*, 4(3), 139–155. https://doi.org/10.1037/pri0000092

Sharma, M., & Branscum, P. (2010). Is Alcoholics Anonymous effective? *Journal of Alcohol and Drug Education*, 54(3), 3–6.

Sharma, S., Hucker, A., Matthews, T., Grohmann, D., & Laws, K. R. (2021). Cognitive behavioural therapy for anxiety in children and young people on the autism spectrum: A systematic review and meta-analysis. *BMC Psychology*, 9(1), 151. https://doi.org/10.1186/s40359-021-00658-8

Sharp, R. A., Phillips, K. J., & Mudford, O. C. (2012). Comparisons of interventions for rumination maintained by automatic reinforcement. *Research in Autism Spectrum Disorders*, 6(3), 1107–1112. https://doi.org/10.1016/j.rasd.2012.03.002

Shaw, C., & Proctor, G. (2005). Women at the margins: A critique of the diagnosis of borderline personality disorder. *Feminism & Psychology*, 15(4), 483–490. https://doi.org/10.1177/0959-353505057620

Shaw, D. M., Polikowsky, H. P., Pruett, D. G., Chen, H.-H., Petty, L. E., Viljoen, K. Z., Beilby, J. M., Jones, R. M., Kraft, S. J., & Below, J. E. (2021). Phenome risk classification enables phenotypic imputation and gene discovery in developmental stuttering. *American Journal of Human Genetics*, 108(12), 2271–2283. https://doi.org/10.1016/j.ajhg.2021.11.004

Shaw, Z. A., & Coffey, B. J. (2014). Tics and Tourette syndrome. *The Psychiatric Clinics of North America*, 37(3), 269–286. https://doi.org/10.1016/j.psc.2014.05.001

Shaywitz, S. E. (1996). Dyslexia. *Scientific American*, 275(5), 98–104.

Shaywitz, S. E., & Shaywitz, B. A. (2005). Dyslexia (specific reading disability). *Biological Psychiatry*, 57(11), 1301–1309. https://doi.org/10.1016/j.biopsych.2005.01.043

Shea, M. T., McDevitt-Murphy, M., Ready, D. J., & Schnurr, P. P. (2009). Group therapy. In E. B. Foa, T. M. Keane, M. J. Friedman, & J. A. Cohen (Eds.), *Effective treatments for PTSD: Practice guidelines from the International Society for Traumatic Stress Studies* (2nd ed., pp. 306–326). Guilford Press.

Shean, G. D. (2004). *Understanding and treating schizophrenia: Contemporary research, theory, and practice*. Haworth Clinical Practice Press.

Shear, M. K., & Mulhare, E. (2008). Complicated grief. *Psychiatric Annals*, 38(10), 662–670. https://doi.org/10.3928/00485713-20081001-10

Shedler, J. (2017, November 19). Selling bad therapy to trauma victims [Psychology Today]. *Psychologically Minded*. https://www.psychologytoday.com/us/blog/psychologically-minded/201711/selling-bad-therapy-trauma-victims

Sheehan, C. M., Frochen, S. E., Walsemann, K. M., & Ailshire, J. A. (2019). Are U.S. adults reporting less sleep?: Findings from sleep duration trends in the National Health Interview Survey, 2004–2017. *Sleep*, 42(2), zsy221. https://doi.org/10.1093/sleep/zsy221

Sheehan, L., Nieweglowski, K., & Corrigan, P. (2016). The stigma of personality disorders. *Current Psychiatry*

Reports, 18(1), Article 11. https://doi.org/10.1007/s11920-015-0654-1

Sheerin, C. M., Kovalchick, L. V., Overstreet, C., Rappaport, L. M., Williamson, V., Vladimirov, V., Ruggiero, K. J., & Amstadter, A. B. (2019). Genetic and environmental predictors of adolescent PTSD symptom trajectories following a natural disaster. *Brain Sciences, 9*(6), Article 6. https://doi.org/10.3390/brainsci9060146

Sheffler, Z. M., & Abdijadid, S. (2022). Antidepressants. In *StatPearls*. StatPearls Publishing. http://www.ncbi.nlm.nih.gov/books/NBK538182/

Shelley-Tremblay, J. F., & Rosén, L. A. (1996). Attention deficit hyperactivity disorder: An evolutionary perspective. *The Journal of Genetic Psychology: Research and Theory on Human Development, 157*(4), 443–453. https://doi.org/10.1080/00221325.1996.9914877

Shepard, P. D. (2014). Basic science, RDoC, and Schizophrenia Bulletin. *Schizophrenia Bulletin, 40*(4), 717–718. https://doi.org/10.1093/schbul/sbu077

Sherer, M., Maddux, J. E., Mercandante, B., Prentice-Dunn, S., Jacobs, B., & Rogers, R. W. (1982). The self-efficacy scale: Construction and validation. *Psychological Reports, 51*(2), 663–671.

Sheridan, K. (2017, March 15). Rich countries are more anxious than poorer countries. *STAT.* https://www.statnews.com/2017/03/15/anxiety-rich-country-poor-country/

Sherin, J. E., & Nemeroff, C. B. (2011). Post-traumatic stress disorder: The neurobiological impact of psychological trauma. *Dialogues In Clinical Neuroscience, 13*(3), 263–278.

Sherkow, S. P., Harrison, A. M., & Singletary, W. M. (2014). *Autism spectrum disorder: Perspectives from psychoanalysis and neuroscience* (2013-42984-000). Jason Aronson.

Sherman, J. A. (2001). Evolutionary origin of bipolar disorder (EOBD). *Psycoloquy, 12*(28).

Sherman, J. A. (2006). Bipolar disorder evolved as an adaptation to severe climate. *Behavioral and Brain Sciences, 29*(4), 421–422. https://doi.org/10.1017/S0140525X06399098

Sherman, J. A. (2012). Evolutionary origin of bipolar disorder-revised: EOBD-R. *Medical Hypotheses, 78*(1), 113–122. https://doi.org/10.1016/j.mehy.2011.10.005

Sherva, R., & Kowall, N. W. (2022, May 19). *Genetics of Alzheimer disease.* UpToDate. https://www.uptodate.com/contents/genetics-of-alzheimer-disease

Shi, J., Yao, Y., Zhan, C., Mao, Z., Yin, F., & Zhao, X. (2018). The relationship between big five personality traits and psychotic experience in a large non-clinical youth sample: The mediating role of emotion regulation. *Frontiers in Psychiatry, 9*, Article 648. https://doi.org/10.3389/fpsyt.2018.00648

Shifrer, D., Muller, C., & Callahan, R. (2011). Disproportionality and learning disabilities: Parsing apart race, socioeconomic status, and language. *Journal of Learning Disabilities, 44*(3), 246–257. doi:10.1177/0022219410374236

Shimada-Sugimoto, M., Otowa, T., & Hettema, J. M. (2015). Genetics of anxiety disorders: Genetic epidemiological and molecular studies in humans. *Psychiatry and Clinical Neurosciences, 69*(7), 388–401. https://doi.org/10.1111/pcn.12291

Shimshoni, Y., Shrinivasa, B., Cherian, A. V., & Lebowitz, E. R. (2019). Family accommodation in psychopathology: A synthesized review. *Indian Journal of Psychiatry, 61*(Suppl. 1), S93. https://doi.org/10.4103/psychiatry.IndianJPsychiatry_530_18

Shin, L. M., Rauch, S. L., & Pitman, R. K. (2006). Amygdala, medial prefrontal cortex, and hippocampal function in PTSD. *Annals of the New York Academy of Sciences, 1071*, 67–79.

Shin, L. M., Wright, C. I., Cannistraro, P. A., Wedig, M. M., McMullin, K., Martis, B., Macklin, M. L., Lasko, N. B., Cavanagh, S. R., Krangel, T. S., Orr, S. P., Pitman, R. K., Whalen, P. J., & Rauch, S. L. (2005). A functional magnetic resonance imaging study of amygdala and medial prefrontal cortex responses

to overtly presented fearful faces in posttraumatic stress disorder. *Archives of General Psychiatry, 62*(3), 273–281. https://doi.org/10.1001/archpsyc.62.3.273

Shinn, A. K., & Greenfield, S. F. (2010). Topiramate in the treatment of substance related disorders: A critical review of the literature. *The Journal of Clinical Psychiatry, 71*(5), 634–648. https://doi.org/10.4088/JCP.08r04062gry

Shipton, L., & Lashewicz, B. M. (2017). Quality group home care for adults with developmental disabilities and/or mental health disorders: Yearning for understanding, security and freedom. *Journal of Applied Research in Intellectual Disabilities, 30*(5), 946–957. https://doi.org/10.1111/jar.12289

Shirotsuki, K., Nonaka, Y., Takano, J., Abe, K., Adachi, S., Adachi, S., & Nakao, M. (2017). Brief internet-based cognitive behavior therapy program with a supplement drink improved anxiety and somatic symptoms in Japanese workers. *BioPsychoSocial Medicine, 11.*

Shnaider, P., Pukay-Martin, N. D., Fredman, S. J., Macdonald, A., & Monson, C. M. (2014). Effects of cognitive–behavioral conjoint therapy for PTSD on partners' psychological functioning. *Journal of Traumatic Stress, 27*(2), 129–136. https://doi.org/10.1002/jts.21893

Shneidman, E. S. (1981a). Orientations toward death: Subintentioned death and indirect suicide. *Suicide and Life-Threatening Behavior, 11*(4), 232–253. https://doi.org/10.1111/j.1943-278X.1981.tb01004.x

Shneidman, E. S. (1981b). Suicide. *Suicide and Life-Threatening Behavior, 11*(4), 198–220. https://doi.org/10.1111/j.1943-278X.1981.tb01002.x

Shneidman, E. S. (1985). *Definition of suicide.* John Wiley & Sons.

Shneidman, E. S. (1993). Commentary: Suicide as psychache. *Journal of Nervous and Mental Disease, 181*(3), 145–147. https://doi.org/10.1097/00005053-199303000-00001

Shneidman, E. S. (1998). Perspectives on suicidology: Further reflections on suicide and psychache. *Suicide and Life-Threatening Behavior, 28*(3), 245–250.

Shorter, E. (1997). *A history of psychiatry: From the era of the asylum to the age of Prozac.* John Wiley.

Shorter, E. (2009). *Before Prozac: The troubled history of mood disorders in psychiatry.* Oxford University Press.

Shorter, E. (2013). The history of DSM. In J. Paris & J. Phillips (Eds.), *Making the DSM-5* (pp. 3–19). Springer.

Shorter, E. (2019). Bipolar disorder in historical perspective. In G. Parker (Ed.), *Bipolar II disorder: Modelling, measuring and managing* (2018-43393-002; 3rd ed., pp. 6–15). Cambridge University Press. https://doi.org/10.1017/9781108333252.003

Shuid, A. N., Jayusman, P. A., Shuid, N., Ismail, J., Kamal Nor, N., & Mohamed, I. N. (2021). Association between viral infections and risk of autistic disorder: An overview. *International Journal of Environmental Research and Public Health, 18*(6), 2817. https://doi.org/10.3390/ijerph18062817

Shumaker, D. (2012). An existential–integrative treatment of anxious and depressed adolescents. *Journal of Humanistic Psychology, 52*(4), 375–400. https://doi.org/10.1177/0022167811422947

Shuster, E. (1997). Fifty years later: The significance of the Nuremberg Code. *New England Journal of Medicine, 337*(20), 1436–1440. https://doi.org/10.1056/nejm199711133372006

Shyu, C., Chavez, S., Boileau, I., & Foll, B. L. (2022). Quantifying GABA in addiction: A review of proton magnetic resonance spectroscopy studies. *Brain Sciences, 12*(7), Article 7. https://doi.org/10.3390/brainsci12070918

Sibbald, B., & Roland, M. (1998). Understanding controlled trials: Why are randomised controlled trials important? *BMJ, 316*(7126), 201. https://doi.org/10.1136/bmj.316.7126.201

Siber, K. (2022, October 18). "You don't look anorexic." *The New York Times.* https://www.nytimes.com/2022/10/18/magazine/anorexia-obesity-eating-disorder.html

Sibrava, N. J., Bjornsson, A. S., Pérez Benítez, A. C. I., Moitra, E., Weisberg, R. B., & Keller, M. B. (2019). Posttraumatic stress disorder in African American and Latino adults: Clinical course and the role of racial and ethnic discrimination. *The American Psychologist, 74*(1), 101–116. https://doi.org/10.1037/amp0000339

Siefert, C. J., Stein, M. B., Slavin-Mulford, J., Sinclair, S. J., Haggerty, G., & Blais, M. A. (2016). Estimating the effects of Thematic Apperception Test card content on SCORS–G ratings: Replication with a nonclinical sample. *Journal of Personality Assessment, 98*(6), 598–607. https://doi.org/10.1080/00223891.2016.1167696

Siegel-Ramsay, J. E., Romaniuk, L., Whalley, H. C., Roberts, N., Branigan, H., Stanfield, A. C., Lawrie, S. M., & Dauvermann, M. R. (2021). Glutamate and functional connectivity—Support for the excitatory-inhibitory imbalance hypothesis in autism spectrum disorders. *Psychiatry Research: Neuroimaging, 313*, 111302. https://doi.org/10.1016/j.pscychresns.2021.111302

Siesser, W. B., Sachs, B. D., Ramsey, A. J., Sotnikova, T. D., Beaulieu, J.-M., Zhang, X., Caron, M. G., & Gainetdinov, R. R. (2012). Chronic SSRI treatment exacerbates serotonin deficiency in humanized Tph2 mutant mice. *ACS Chemical Neuroscience, 4*(1), 84–88. https://doi.org/10.1021/cn300127h

Siever, L. J., & Davis, K. L. (2004). The pathophysiology of schizophrenia disorders: Perspectives from the spectrum. *The American Journal of Psychiatry, 161*(3), 398–413. https://doi.org/10.1176/appi.ajp.161.3.398

Sigafoos, J., Carnett, A., O'Reilly, M. F., & Lancioni, G. E. (2019). Discrete trial training: A structured learning approach for children with ASD. In S. G. Little & A. Akin-Little (Eds.), *Behavioral interventions in schools: Evidence-based positive strategies* (2nd ed., pp. 227–243). American Psychological Association. https://doi.org/10.1037/0000126-013

Sikes, C., & Sikes, V. (2003). EMDR: Why the controversy? *Traumatology, 9*(3), 169–182. https://doi.org/10.1177/153476560300900304

Sikich, L., Kolevzon, A., King, B. H., McDougle, C. J., Sanders, K. B., Kim, S.-J., Spanos, M., Chandrasekhar, T., Trelles, M. D. P., Rockhill, C. M., Palumbo, M. L., Witters Cundiff, A., Montgomery, A., Siper, P., Minjarez, M., Nowinski, L. A., Marler, S., Shuffrey, L. C., Alderman, C., … Veenstra-VanderWeele, J. (2021). Intranasal oxytocin in children and adolescents with autism spectrum disorder. *New England Journal of Medicine, 385*(16), 1462–1473. https://doi.org/10.1056/NEJMoa2103583

Silberman, E., Balon, R., Starcevic, V., Shader, R., Cosci, F., Fava, G. A., Nardi, A. E., Salzman, C., & Sonino, N. (2021). Benzodiazepines: It's time to return to the evidence. *The British Journal of Psychiatry, 218*(3), 125–127. https://doi.org/10.1192/bjp.2020.164

Silberman, E. K., Putnam, F. W., Weingartner, H., Braun, B. G., & Post, R. M. (1985). Dissociative states in multiple personality disorder: A quantitative study. *Psychiatry Research, 15*(4), 253–260. https://doi.org/10.1016/0165-1781(85)90062-9

Silberman, S. (2015). *NeuroTribes: The legacy of autism and the future of neurodiversity.* Avery.

Silote, G. P., de Oliveira, S. F. S., Ribeiro, D. E., Machado, M. S., Andreatini, R., Joca, S. R. L., & Beijamini, V. (2020). Ketamine effects on anxiety and fear-related behaviors: Current literature evidence and new findings. *Progress in Neuro-Psychopharmacology & Biological Psychiatry, 100.* https://doi.org/10.1016/j.pnpbp.2020.109878

Silva, K. de S., Miguel, A. de Q. C., & Sampaio, A. A. S. (2021). Contingency management as intervention for substance abuse. In A. L. M. Andrade, D. De Micheli, E. Aparecida da Silva, F. M. Lopes, B. de O. Pinheiro, & R. A. Reichert (Eds.), *Psychology of substance abuse: Psychotherapy, clinical management and social intervention* (pp. 275–287). Springer. https://doi.org/10.1007/978-3-030-62106-3_19

Silver, A.-L. S., & Stedman, L. (2009). United States of America: Psychodynamic developments, 1940s to the present. In Y. O. Alanen, M. González de Chávez, A.-L. S. Silver, & B. Martindale (Eds.), *Psychotherapeutic approaches to schizophrenic psychoses* (pp. 67–77). Routledge.

Silverman, J. A. (1987). Robert Whytt, 1714–1766: Eighteenth century limner of anorexia nervosa and bulimia: An essay. *International Journal of Eating Disorders*, 6(1), 143–146. https://doi.org/10.1002/1098-108X(198701)6:13.0.CO;2-I

Silverman, J. A. (1989). Louis-Victor Marcé, 1828-1864: Anorexia nervosa's forgotten man. *Psychological Medicine*, 19(4), 833–835. https://doi.org/10.1017/S0033291700005547

Simeon, D. (2001). Hypothalamic-pituitary-adrenal axis dysregulation in depersonalization disorder. *Neuropsychopharmacology*, 25(5), 793–795. https://doi.org/10.1016/S0893-133X(01)00288-3

Simeon, D., Knutelska, M., Yehuda, R., Putnam, F., Schmeidler, J., & Smith, L. M. (2007). Hypothalamic-pituitary-adrenal axis function in dissociative disorders, post-traumatic stress disorder, and healthy volunteers. *Biological Psychiatry*, 61(8), 966–973. https://doi.org/10.1016/j.biopsych.2006.07.030

Simon, A. E., Riecher-Rössler, A., Lang, U. E., & Borgwardt, S. (2013). The attenuated psychosis syndrome in DSM-5. *Schizophrenia Research*, 151(1–3), 295. https://doi.org/10.1016/j.schres.2013.09.019

Simon, J. L., & Thompson, R. H. (2006). The effects of undergarment type on the urinary continence of toddlers. *Journal of Applied Behavior Analysis*, 39(3), 363–368. https://doi.org/10.1901/jaba.2006.124-05

Simon, N. M. (2013). Treating complicated grief. *JAMA: Journal of the American Medical Association*, 310(4), 416–423. https://doi.org/10.1001/jama.2013.8614

Simon, N., Roberts, N. P., Lewis, C. E., van Gelderen, M. J., & Bisson, J. I. (2019). Associations between perceived social support, posttraumatic stress disorder (PTSD) and complex PTSD (CPTSD): Implications for treatment. *European Journal of Psychotraumatology*, 10(1), 1573129. https://doi.org/10.1080/20008198.2019.1573129

Simon, R. J., & Ahn-Redding, H. (2006). *The insanity defense, the world over.* Rowman & Littlefield.

Simon, S. S., Cordás, T. A., & Bottino, C. M. C. (2015). Cognitive behavioral therapies in older adults with depression and cognitive deficits: A systematic review. *International Journal of Geriatric Psychiatry*, 30(3), 223–233. https://doi.org/10.1002/gps.4239

Sinason, V., & Silver, A.-L. S. (2008). Treating dissociative and psychotic disorders psychodynamically. In A. Moskowitz, I. Schäfer, & M. J. Dorahy (Eds.), *Psychosis, trauma and dissociation: Emerging perspectives on severe psychopathology* (pp. 239–253). Wiley-Blackwell. https://doi.org/10.1002/9780470699652.ch17

Sindi, S., Toopchiani, S., Barbera, M., Håkansson, K., Lehtisalo, J., Rosenberg, A., Stephen, R., Udeh-Momoh, C., & Kivipelto, M. (2021). Sex and gender differences in genetic and lifestyle risk and protective factors for dementia. In M. T. Ferretti, A. S. Dimech, & A. S. Chadha (Eds.), *Sex and gender differences in Alzheimer's disease* (pp. 269–308). Academic Press. https://doi.org/10.1016/B978-0-12-819344-0.00013-2

Singh, A. A., & Burnes, T. R. (2010). Shifting the counselor role from gatekeeping to advocacy: Ten strategies for using the Competencies for counseling with transgender clients for individual and social change. *Journal of LGBT Issues in Counseling*, 4(3–4), 241–255. https://doi.org/10.1080/15538605.2010.525455

Singh, A. A., & Dickey, L. M. (2016). Implementing the APA guidelines on psychological practice with transgender and gender nonconforming people: A call to action to the field of psychology. *Psychology of Sexual Orientation and Gender Diversity*, 3(2), 195–200. https://doi.org/10.1037/sgd0000179

Singh, A., & Kar, S. K. (2017). How electroconvulsive therapy works?: Understanding the neurobiological mechanisms. *Clinical Psychopharmacology and Neuroscience*, 15(3), 210–221. https://doi.org/10.9758/cpn.2017.15.3.210

Singh, D., & Saadabadi, A. (2022). Varenicline. In *StatPearls [Internet]*. StatPearls Publishing. https://www.ncbi.nlm.nih.gov/books/NBK534846/

Singh, I. (2003). Boys will be boys: Fathers' perspectives on ADHD symptoms, diagnosis, and drug treatment. *Harvard Review of Psychiatry*, 11(6), 308–316. https://doi.org/10.1080/714044393

Singh, I. (2004). Doing their jobs: Mothering with Ritalin in a culture of mother-blame. *Social Science & Medicine*, 59(6), 1193–1205. https://doi.org/10.1016/j.socscimed.2004.01.011

Singh, N., & Reece, J. (2014). Psychotherapy, pharmacotherapy, and their combination for adolescents with major depressive disorder: A meta-analysis. *The Australian Educational and Developmental Psychologist*, 31(1), 47–65. https://doi.org/10.1017/edp.2013.20

Siniscalco, D., Schultz, S., Brigida, A. L., & Antonucci, N. (2018). Inflammation and neuro-immune dysregulations in autism spectrum disorders. *Pharmaceuticals*, 11(2), Article 2. https://doi.org/10.3390/ph11020056

Sinke, C., Halpern, J. H., Zedler, M., Neufeld, J., Emrich, H. M., & Passie, T. (2012). Genuine and drug-induced synesthesia: A comparison. *Consciousness and Cognition*, 21(3), 1419–1434. https://doi.org/10.1016/j.concog.2012.03.009

Sinyor, M. (2012). Evolutionary approach highly informative but should not be overstated. *The Canadian Journal of Psychiatry*, 57(5), 336–336.

Sinyor, M., Schaffer, A., Heisel, M. J., Picard, A., Adamson, G., Cheung, C. P., Katz, L. Y., Jetly, R., & Sareen, J. (2018). Media guidelines for reporting on suicide: 2017 update of the Canadian Psychiatric Association policy paper. *The Canadian Journal of Psychiatry*, 63(3), 182–196. https://doi.org/10.1177/0706743717753147

Sirri, L., & Fava, G. A. (2014). Clinical manifestations of hypochondriasis and related conditions. In V. Starcevic & Jr. Noyes Russell (Eds.), *Hypochondriasis and health anxiety: A guide for clinicians* (pp. 8–27). Oxford University Press.

Sisti, D., Segal, A. G., Siegel, A. M., Johnson, R., & Gunderson, J. (2016). Diagnosing, disclosing, and documenting borderline personality disorder: A survey of psychiatrists' practices. *Journal of Personality Disorders*, 30(6), 848–856. https://doi.org/10.1521/pedi201529228

Sjøstrand, Å., Kefalianos, E., Hofslundsengen, H., Guttormsen, L. S., Kirmess, M., Lervåg, A., Hulme, C., & Bottegaard Næss, K.-A. (2021). Non-pharmacological interventions for stuttering in children six years and younger. *Cochrane Database of Systematic Reviews*, 2021(9), Article CD013489. https://doi.org/10.1002/14651858.CD013489.pub2

Skewes, M. C., & Blume, A. W. (2019). Understanding the link between racial trauma and substance use among American Indians. *American Psychologist*, 74(1), 88–100. https://doi.org/10.1037/amp0000331

Skibiski, J., & Abdijadid, S. (2021). Barbiturates. In *StatPearls [Internet]*. StatPearls Publishing. https://www.ncbi.nlm.nih.gov/books/NBK539731/

Skinner, B. F. (1954). A new method for the experimental analysis of the behavior of psychotic patients. *Journal of Nervous and Mental Disease*, 120, 403–406.

Skinner, B. F. (1985). Cognitive science and behaviourism. *British Journal of Psychology*, 76(3), 291–301. https://doi.org/10.1111/j.2044-8295.1985.tb01953.x

Skinner, B. F. (1987). Whatever happened to psychology as the science of behavior? *American Psychologist*, 42(8), 780–786. https://doi.org/10.1037/0003-066X.42.8.780

Skinner, B. F. (1990). Can psychology be a science of mind? *American Psychologist*, 45(11), 1206–1210. https://doi.org/10.1037/0003-066X.45.11.1206

Sklepníková, J., & Slezáčková, A. (2022). Evolution of the ADHD concept and its relation to the hyperkinetic disorders: Narrative review. *Československá Psychologie*, 66(3), Article 3. https://doi.org/10.51561/cspsych.66.3.255

Skolnick, P., Popik, P., & Trullas, R. (2009). Glutamate-based antidepressants: 20 years on. *Trends in Pharmacological Sciences*, 30(11), 563–569. https://doi.org/10.1016/j.tips.2009.09.002

Skre, I., Onstad, S., Torgersen, S., Lygren, S., & Kringlen, E. (1993). A twin study of DSM-III–R anxiety disorders. *Acta Psychiatrica Scandinavica*, 88(2), 85–92. https://doi.org/10.1111/j.1600-0447.1993.tb03419.x

Slavich, G. M. (2020). Psychoneuroimmunology of stress and mental health. In K. L. Harkness & E. P. Hayden (Eds.), *The Oxford handbook of stress and mental health* (pp. 518–546). Oxford University Press. https://doi.org/10.1093/oxfordhb/9780190681777.013.24

Sleeter, C. E. (1986). Learning disabilities: The social construction of a special education category. *Exceptional Children*, 53(1), 46–54. https://doi.org/10.1177/001440298605300105

Slobodin, O., & Davidovitch, M. (2019). Gender differences in objective and subjective measures of ADHD among clinic-referred children. *Frontiers in Human Neuroscience*, 13, Article 441. https://doi.org/10.3389/fnhum.2019.00441

Slof-Op't Landt, M. C. T., Bartels, M., Middeldorp, C. M., van Beijsterveldt, C. E. M., Slagboom, P. E., Boomsma, D. I., … Meulenbelt, I. (2013). Genetic variation at the TPH2 gene influences impulsivity in addition to eating disorders. *Behavior Genetics*, 43(1), 24–33. doi:10.1007/s10519-012-9569-3

Slof-Op't Landt, M. C. T., Meulenbelt, I., Bartels, M., Suchiman, E., Middeldorp, C. M., Houwing-Duistermaat, J. J., … Slagboom, P. E. (2011). Association study in eating disorders: TPH2 associates with anorexia nervosa and self-induced vomiting. *Genes, Brain, and Behavior*, 10(2), 236–243. doi:10.1111/j.1601-183X.2010.00660.x

Slof-Op't Landt, M. C. T., van Furth, E. F., Meulenbelt, I., Bartels, M., Hottenga, J. J., Slagboom, P. E., & Boomsma, D. I. (2014). Association study of the estrogen receptor I gene (ESR1) in anorexia nervosa and eating disorders: No replication found. *The International Journal of Eating Disorders*, 47(2), 211–214. doi:10.1002/eat.22228

Slomski, A. (2021). Thousands of us youths cope with the trauma of losing parents to COVID-19. *JAMA*, 326(21), 2117–2119. https://doi.org/10.1001/jama.2021.20846

Smedslund, G., Berg, R. C., Hammerstrøm, K. T., Steiro, A., Leiknes, K. A., Dahl, H. M., & Karlsen, K. (2011). Motivational interviewing for substance abuse. *Campbell Systematic Reviews*, 7(1), 1–126. https://doi.org/10.4073/csr.2011.6

Šmigelskas, K., Žemaitienė, N., Julkunen, J., & Kauhanen, J. (2015). Type A behavior pattern is not a predictor of premature mortality. *International Journal of Behavioral Medicine*, 22(2), 161–169. https://doi.org/10.1007/s12529-014-9435-1

Smigielski, L., Jagannath, V., Rössler, W., Walitza, S., & Grünblatt, E. (2020). Epigenetic mechanisms in schizophrenia and other psychotic disorders: A systematic review of empirical human findings. *Molecular Psychiatry*, 25(8), 1718–1748. https://doi.org/10.1038/s41380-019-0601-3

Smith, A. P. (2013). Caffeine and caffeinated energy drinks. In P. M. Miller, S. A. Ball, M. E. Bates, A. W. Blume, K. M. Kampman, D. J. Kavanagh, M. E. Larimer, N. M. Petry, & P. De Witte (Eds.), *Comprehensive addictive behaviors and disorders: Vol. 1. Principles of addiction* (pp. 777–785). Elsevier Academic Press.

Smith, D. (2012). *It's still the "age of anxiety." Or is it?* http://opinionator.blogs.nytimes.com/2012/01/14/its-still-the-age-of-anxiety-or-is-it/?_r=0

Smith, D. G., & Robbins, T. W. (2013). The neurobiological underpinnings of obesity and binge eating: A rationale for adopting the food addiction model. *Biological Psychiatry*, 73(9), 804–810. https://doi.org/10.1016/j.biopsych.2012.08.026

Smith, D. P., Hayward, D. W., Gale, C. M., Eikeseth, S., & Klintwall, L. (2021). Treatment gains from early and intensive behavioral intervention (EIBI) are maintained 10 years later. *Behavior Modification*, 45(4), 581–601. https://doi.org/10.1177/0145445519882895

Smith, E. S., Junger, J., Derntl, B., & Habel, U. (2015). The transsexual brain—A review of findings on the neural basis of transsexualism. *Neuroscience and Biobehavioral Reviews*, 59, 251–266. https://doi.org/10.1016/j.neubiorev.2015.09.008

Smith, H., Fox, J. R. E., & Trayner, P. (2015). The lived experiences of individuals with Tourette syndrome or tic disorders: A meta-synthesis of qualitative studies. *British Journal of Psychology*, 106(4), 609–634. https://doi.org/10.1111/bjop.12118

Smith, I. C., Reichow, B., & Volkmar, F. R. (2015). The effects of DSM-5 criteria on number of individuals diagnosed with autism spectrum disorder: A systematic review. *Journal of Autism and Developmental Disorders*, 45(8), 2541–2552. https://doi.org/10.1007/s10803-015-2423-8

Smith, J. J., & Graden, J. L. (1998). Fetal alcohol syndrome. In L. Phelps (Ed.), *Health-related disorders in children and adolescents: A guidebook for understanding and educating* (pp. 291–298). American Psychological Association. https://doi.org/10.1037/10300-040

Smith, J. P., Hardy, S. T., Hale, L. E., & Gazmararian, J. A. (2019). Racial disparities and sleep among preschool aged children: A systematic review. *Sleep Health*, 5(1), 49–57. https://doi.org/10.1016/j.sleh.2018.09.010

Smith, J. R., Workneh, A., & Yaya, S. (2020). Barriers and facilitators to help-seeking for individuals with posttraumatic stress disorder: A systematic review. *Journal of Traumatic Stress*, 33(2), 137–150. https://doi.org/10.1002/jts.22456

Smith, M. (2011). *An alternative history of hyperactivity: Food additives and the Feingold Diet*. Rutgers University Press.

Smith, M. (2012). *Hyperactive: The controversial history of ADHD*. Reaktion Books.

Smith, M. (2019). Explaining the emergence of attention deficit hyperactivity disorder: Children, childhood, and historical change. *Journal of Disease Prevention and Health Promotion*, 3, 16–20. https://doi.org/10.5283/mnhd.14

Smith, M. L., & Glass, G. V. (1987). *Research and evaluation in education and the social sciences*. Prentice Hall.

Smith, M., & Segal, J. (2021, November). Finding a therapist who can help you heal. *HelpGuide*. https://www.helpguide.org/articles/mental-health/finding-a-therapist-who-can-help-you-heal.htm

Smith, S. D., Reynolds, C. A., & Rovnak, A. (2009). A critical analysis of the social advocacy movement in counseling. *Journal of Counseling & Development*, 87(4), 483–491. https://doi.org/10.1002/j.1556-6678.2009.tb00133.x

Smith, T., & Iadarola, S. (2015). Evidence base update for autism spectrum disorder. *Journal of Clinical Child and Adolescent Psychology*, 44(6), 897–922. https://doi.org/10.1080/15374416.2015.1077448

Smith-Bell, M., & Winslade, W. J. (1994). Privacy, confidentiality, and privilege in psychotherapeutic relationships. *American Journal of Orthopsychiatry*, 64(2), 180–193. https://doi.org/10.1037/h0079520

Snorrason, I., Berlin, G. S., & Lee, H.-J. (2015). Optimizing psychological interventions for trichotillomania (hair-pulling disorder): An update on current empirical status. *Psychology Research and Behavior Management*, 8, 105–113. https://doi.org/10.2147/PRBM.S53977

Snowling, M. J., & Hulme, C. (2012). Interventions for children's language and literacy difficulties. *International Journal of Language & Communication Disorders*, 47(1), 27–34. https://doi.org/10.1111/j.1460-6984.2011.00081.x

Snozek, C. L. H. (2020). CNS depressants: Benzodiazepines and barbiturates. In H. Ketha & U. Garg (Eds.), *Toxicology cases for the clinical and forensic laboratory* (pp. 209–217). Academic Press. https://doi.org/10.1016/B978-0-12-815846-3.00013-2

Sobanski, T., Josfeld, S., Peikert, G., & Wagner, G. (2021). Psychotherapeutic interventions for the prevention of suicide re-attempts: A systematic review. *Psychological Medicine*, 51(15), 2525–2540. https://doi.org/10.1017/S0033291721003081

Sobell, M. B., & Sobell, L. C. (1995). Controlled drinking after 25 years: How important was the great debate? *Addiction*, 90(9), 1149–1153. https://doi.org/10.1111/j.1360-0443.1995.tb01077.x

Socarides, C. W. (1989). *Homosexuality: Psychoanalytic therapy*. Aronson. (Original work published 1978.)

Society of Counseling Psychology. (n.d.). *What is counseling psychology?* Society of Counseling Psychology – American Psychological Association Division 17. Retrieved from https://www.div17.org

Sodelli, M. (2021). Harm reduction in the prevention of risk use and drug dependence at school. In D. De Micheli, A. L. M. Andrade, R. A. Reichert, E. Aparecida da Silva, B. de O. Pinheiro, & F. M. Lopes (Eds.), *Drugs and human behavior: Biopsychosocial aspects of psychotropic substances use* (pp. 393–398). Springer Nature Switzerland AG. https://doi.org/10.1007/978-3-030-62855-0_28

Söderstén, P., Bergh, C., Leon, M., & Zandian, M. (2016). Dopamine and anorexia nervosa. *Neuroscience & Biobehavioral Reviews*, 60, 26–30. https://doi.org/10.1016/j.neubiorev.2015.11.003

Soh, N., Walter, G., Robertson, M., & Malhi, G. S. (2010). Charles Lasègue (1816-1883): Beyond anorexie hystérique. *Acta Neuropsychiatrica*, 22(6), 300–301. https://doi.org/10.1111/j.1601-5215.2010.00499.x

Sohn, E. (2017, November 29). Why autism seems to cluster in some immigrant groups. *Spectrum: Autism Research News*. https://www.spectrumnews.org/features/deep-dive/why-autism-seems-to-cluster-in-some-immigrant-groups/

Soloff, P. H., Chiappetta, L., Mason, N. S., Becker, C., & Price, J. C. (2014). Effects of serotonin-2A receptor binding and gender on personality traits and suicidal behavior in borderline personality disorder. *Psychiatry Research*, 222(3), 140–148. https://doi.org/10.1016/j.pscychresns.2014.03.008

Solomon, D. H., Ruppert, K., Habel, L. A., Finkelstein, J. S., Lian, P., Joffe, H., & Kravitz, H. M. (2021). Prescription medications for sleep disturbances among midlife women during 2 years of follow-up: A SWAN retrospective cohort study. *BMJ Open*, 11(5), e045074. https://doi.org/10.1136/bmjopen-2020-045074

Solomon, R. M. (2018). EMDR treatment of grief and mourning. *Clinical Neuropsychiatry: Journal of Treatment Evaluation*, 15(3), 173–186.

Solomon, R. M., & Hensley, B. J. (2020). EMDR therapy treatment of grief and mourning in times of COVID-19 (coronavirus). *Journal of EMDR Practice and Research*, 14(3), 162–174. https://doi.org/10.1891/EMDR-D-20-00031

Solomon, R. M., & Rando, T. A. (2007). Utilization of EMDR in the treatment of grief and mourning. *Journal of EMDR Practice and Research*, 1(2), 109–117. https://doi.org/10.1891/1933-3196.1.2.109

Somani, A., & Kar, S. K. (2019). Efficacy of repetitive transcranial magnetic stimulation in treatment-resistant depression: The evidence thus far. *General Psychiatry*, 32(4), e100074. https://doi.org/10.1136/gpsych-2019-100074

Somashekar, B., Jainer, A., & Wuntakal, B. (2013). Psychopharmacotherapy of somatic symptoms disorders. *International Review of Psychiatry*, 25(1), 107–115. https://doi.org/10.3109/09540261.2012.729758

Somma, A., Krueger, R. F., Markon, K. E., Gialdi, G., Boscaro, L., & Fossati, A. (2022). Post-traumatic disorder symptom severity in the perspective of hierarchical taxonomy of psychopathology spectra and dysfunctional personality domains among trauma-exposed community-dwelling women. *Personality and Mental Health*, 16(1), 47–58. https://doi.org/10.1002/pmh.1525

Sommers-Flanagan, J., Johnson, V. I., & Rides At The Door, M. (2020). Clinical Interviewing. In J. A. Suhr & M. Sellbom (Eds.), *The Cambridge handbook of clinical assessment and diagnosis* (pp. 113–122). Cambridge University Press. https://doi.org/10.1017/9781108235433.010

Song, Y., Li, S., Li, X., Chen, X., Wei, Z., Liu, Q., & Cheng, Y. (2020). The effect of estrogen replacement therapy on Alzheimer's disease and Parkinson's disease in postmenopausal women: A meta-analysis. *Frontiers in Neuroscience*, 14, Article 157. https://doi.org/10.3389/fnins.2020.00157

Sonis, J., & Cook, J. M. (2019). Medication versus trauma-focused psychotherapy for adults with posttraumatic stress disorder: A systematic review and meta-analysis. *Psychiatry Research*, 282, 112637. https://doi.org/10.1016/j.psychres.2019.112637

Sonneville, K. R., & Lipson, S. K. (2018). Disparities in eating disorder diagnosis and treatment according to weight status, race/ethnicity, socioeconomic background, and sex among college students. *International Journal of Eating Disorders*, 51(6), 518–526. https://doi.org/10.1002/eat.22846

Sonuga-Barke, E. J. S., Brandeis, D., Cortese, S., Daley, D., Ferrin, M., Holtmann, M., Stevenson, J., Danckaerts, M., van der Oord, S., Döpfner, M., Dittmann, R. W., Simonoff, E., Zuddas, A., Banaschewski, T., Buitelaar, J., Coghill, D., Hollis, C., Konofal, E., Lecendreux, M., … Sergeant, J. (2013). Nonpharmacological interventions for ADHD: Systematic review and meta-analyses of randomized controlled trials of dietary and psychological treatments. *The American Journal of Psychiatry*, 170(3), 275–289. https://doi.org/10.1176/appi.ajp.2012.12070991

Sørensen, A. M. S., Wesselhöft, R., Andersen, J. H., Reutfors, J., Cesta, C. E., Furu, K., Hartz, I., & Rasmussen, L. (2022). Trends in use of attention deficit hyperactivity disorder medication among children and adolescents in Scandinavia in 2010–2020. *European Child & Adolescent Psychiatry*. https://doi.org/10.1007/s00787-022-02034-2

South, S. C. (2015). Biological bases of personality disorders. In S. K. Huprich (Ed.), *Personality disorders: Toward theoretical and empirical integration in diagnosis and assessment* (pp. 163–201). American Psychological Association. https://doi.org/10.1037/14549-008

Southwick, S. M., Paige, S., Morgan, 3rd, C. A., Bremner, J. D., Krystal, J. H., & Charney, D. S. (1999). Neurotransmitter alterations in PTSD: Catecholamines and serotonin. *Seminars In Clinical Neuropsychiatry*, 4(4), 242–248.

Spain, D., & Happé, F. (2020). How to optimise cognitive behaviour therapy (CBT) for people with autism spectrum disorders (ASD): A Delphi study. *Journal of Rational-Emotive & Cognitive-Behavior Therapy*, 38(2), 184–208. https://doi.org/10.1007/s10942-019-00335-1

Spain, D., Sin, J., Chalder, T., Murphy, D., & Happé, F. (2015). Cognitive behaviour therapy for adults with autism spectrum disorders and psychiatric co-morbidity: A review. *Research in Autism Spectrum Disorders*, 9, 151–162. https://doi.org/10.1016/j.rasd.2014.10.019

Spanos, N. P. (1994). Multiple identity enactments and multiple personality disorder: A sociocognitive perspective. *Psychological Bulletin*, 116(1), 143–165. https://doi.org/10.1037/0033-2909.116.1.143

Sparks, J. A., & Duncan, B. L. (2012). Pediatric antipsychotics: A call for ethical care. In S. Olfman, B. D. Robbins, S. Olfman, & B. D. Robbins (Eds.), *Drugging our children: How profiteers are pushing antipsychotics on our youngest, and what we can do to stop it* (pp. 81–98). Praeger/ABC-CLIO.

Sparks, J. A., & Duncan, B. L. (2013). Outside the black box: Re-assessing pediatric antidepressant prescription. *Journal of the Canadian Academy of Child and Adolescent Psychiatry*, 22(3), 240–246.

Sparrow, E. P., & Erhardt, D. (2014). *Essentials of ADHD assessment for children and adolescents* (2014-14182-000). John Wiley & Sons.

Speer, K. E., Semple, S., Naumovski, N., D'Cunha, N. M., & McKune, A. J. (2019). HPA axis function and diurnal cortisol in post-traumatic stress disorder: A systematic review. *Neurobiology of Stress, 11*, 100180. https://doi.org/10.1016/j.ynstr.2019.100180

Spencer, S. (2023, June 18). "We're gonna have to live in fear": The fight over medical care for transgender youth. CBS News. https://www.cbsnews.com/news/fight-over-medical-care-for-transgender-youth-gender-dysphoria/

Spermon, D., Darlington, Y., & Gibney, P. (2010). Psychodynamic psychotherapy for complex trauma: Targets, focus, applications, and outcomes. *Psychology Research and Behavior Management, 3*, 119–127. https://doi.org/10.2147/PRBM.S10215

Sperry, L. (2011). Family therapy with personality-disordered individuals and families: Understanding and treating the borderline family. *The Journal of Individual Psychology, 67*(3), 222–231.

Sperry, L. (2016). *Handbook of diagnosis and treatment of DSM-5 personality disorders* (3rd ed.). Routledge. https://doi.org/10.4324/9780203427088

Spettigue, W., & Henderson, K. A. (2004). Eating disorders and the role of the media. *The Canadian Child and Adolescent Psychiatry Review, 13*(1), 16–19.

Spettigue, W., Norris, M. L., Santos, A., & Obeid, N. (2018). Treatment of children and adolescents with avoidant/restrictive food intake disorder: A case series examining the feasibility of family therapy and adjunctive treatments. *Journal of Eating Disorders, 6*(1), 20. https://doi.org/10.1186/s40337-018-0205-3

Spiegel, D., Lewis-Fernández, R., Lanius, R., Vermetten, E., Simeon, D., & Friedman, M. (2013). Dissociative disorders in DSM-5. *Annual Review of Clinical Psychology, 9*, 299–326. https://doi.org/10.1146/annurev-clinpsy-050212-185531

Spielberger, C. D., & Reheiser, E. C. (2004). Measuring anxiety, anger, depression, and curiosity as emotional states and personality states with the STAI, STAXI, and STPI. In M. J. Hilsenroth & D. L. Segal (Eds.), *Comprehensive handbook of psychological assessment: Vol. 2. Personality assessment* (pp. 70–86). John Wiley.

Spielmans, G. I. (2021). Re-analyzing Phase III bremelanotide trials for "hypoactive sexual desire disorder" in women. *The Journal of Sex Research, 58*(9), 1085–1105. https://doi.org/10.1080/00224499.2021.1885601

Spielmans, G. I., Spence-Sing, T., & Parry, P. (2020). Duty to warn: Antidepressant black box suicidality warning is empirically justified. *Frontiers in Psychiatry, 11*, Article 18. https://doi.org/10.3389/fpsyt.2020.00018

Spitzer, R. L., Williams, J. B. W., & Endicott, J. (2012). Standards for DSM-5 reliability. *The American Journal of Psychiatry, 169*(5), 537–537.

Spivak, S., Mojtabai, R., Green, C., Firth, T., Sater, H., & Cullen, B. A. (2019). Distribution and correlates of assertive community treatment (ACT) and ACT-like programs: Results from the 2015 N-MHSS. *Psychiatric Services, 70*(4), 271–278. https://doi.org/10.1176/appi.ps.201700561

Spizzirri, G., Duran, F. L. S., Chaim-Avancini, T. M., Serpa, M. H., Cavallet, M., Pereira, C. M. A., Santos, P. P., Squarzoni, P., da Costa, N. A., Busatto, G. F., & Abdo, C. H. N. (2018). Grey and white matter volumes either in treatment-naïve or hormone-treated transgender women: A voxel-based morphometry study. *Scientific Reports, 8* (1), Article 1. https://doi.org/10.1038/s41598-017-17563-z

Spohr, H.-L. (2018). *Fetal alcohol syndrome: A lifelong challenge* (B. M. van Noort, H. Wolter, & H.-L. Spohr, Trans.). De Gruyter. https://doi.org/10.1515/9783110436563

Sprich, S. E., Knouse, L. E., Cooper-Vince, C., Burbridge, J., & Safren, S. A. (2010). Description and demonstration of CBT for ADHD in adults. *Cognitive and Behavioral Practice, 17*(1), 9–15. https://doi.org/10.1016/j.cbpra.2009.09.002

Springer, K. S., Levy, H. C., & Tolin, D. F. (2018). Remission in CBT for adult anxiety disorders: A meta-analysis. *Clinical Psychology Review, 61*, 1–8. https://doi.org/10.1016/j.cpr.2018.03.002

SSRS. (2022, April 20). *In the weeds: Marijuana and the American public 2022*. https://ssrs.com/in-the-weeds-marijuana-and-the-american-public-2022/

St. Louis, K. O., Sønsterud, H., Junuzović-Žunić, L., Tomaiuoli, D., Del Gado, F., Caparelli, E., Theiling, M., Flobakk, C., Helmen, L. N., Heitmann, R. R., Kvenseth, H., Nilsson, S., Wetterling, T., Lundström, C., Daly, C., Leahy, M., Tyrrell, L., Ward, D., & Węsierska, M. (2016). Public attitudes toward stuttering in Europe: Within-country and between-country comparisons. *Journal of Communication Disorders, 62*, 115–130. https://doi.org/10.1016/j.jcomdis.2016.05.010

Stack, S. (2020). Media guidelines and suicide: A critical review. *Social Science & Medicine, 262*, Article 112690. https://doi.org/10.1016/j.socscimed.2019.112690

Stack, S., & Scourfield, J. (2015). Recency of divorce, depression, and suicide risk. *Journal of Family Issues, 36*(6), 695–715. https://doi.org/10.1177/0192513X13494824

Staff, A. I., van den Hoofdakker, B. J., van der Oord, S., Hornstra, R., Hoekstra, P. J., Twisk, J. W. R., Oosterlaan, J., & Luman, M. (2021). Effectiveness of specific techniques in behavioral teacher training for childhood ADHD: A randomized controlled microtrial. *Journal of Clinical Child & Adolescent Psychology, 50*(6), 763–779. https://doi.org/10.1080/15374416.2020.1846542

Stahl, S. M. (2018). Antagonist treatment is just as effective as replacement therapy for opioid addiction but neither is used often enough. *CNS Spectrums, 23*(2), 113–116. https://doi.org/10.1017/S1092852918000858

Stahl, S. M., Grady, M. M., Moret, C., & Briley, M. (2005). SNRIs: The pharmacology, clinical efficacy, and tolerability in comparison with other classes of antidepressants. *CNS Spectrums, 10*(9), 732–747.

Stahl, S. M., Sommer, B., & Allers, K. A. (2011). Multifunctional pharmacology of flibanserin: Possible mechanism of therapeutic action in hypoactive sexual desire disorder. *Journal of Sexual Medicine, 8*(1), 15–27. https://doi.org/10.1111/j.1743-6109.2010.02032.x

Stam, H. J. (1987). The psychology of control: A textual critique. In H. J. Stam, T. B. Rogers, & K. J. Gergen (Eds.), *The analysis of psychological theory: Metapsychological perspectives* (pp. 131–156). Hemisphere Publishing.

Stamatakis, K. A., Kaplan, G. A., & Roberts, R. E. (2007). Short sleep duration across income, education, and race/ethnic groups: Population prevalence and growing disparities during 34 years of follow-up. *Annals of Epidemiology, 17*(12), 948–955. https://doi.org/10.1016/j.annepidem.2007.07.096

Stander, V. A., Thomsen, C. J., & Highfill-McRoy, R. M. (2014). Etiology of depression comorbidity in combat-related PTSD: A review of the literature. *Clinical Psychology Review, 34*(2), 87–98. https://doi.org/10.1016/j.cpr.2013.12.002

Staniloiu, A., & Markowitsch, H. J. (2014). Dissociative amnesia. *The Lancet Psychiatry, 1*(3), 226–241. https://doi.org/10.1016/S2215-0366(14)70279-2

Staniute, M., Brozaitiene, J., Burkauskas, J., Kazukauskiene, N., Mickuviene, N., & Bunevicius, R. (2015). Type D personality, mental distress, social support and health-related quality of life in coronary artery disease patients with heart failure: A longitudinal observational study. *Health and Quality of Life Outcomes, 13*, Article 1. https://doi.org/10.1186/s12955-014-0204-2

Stanley, B., & Brown, G. K. (2008). *Safety plan treatment manual to reduce suicide risk: Veteran version* (p. 20). Suicide Prevention Resource Center. https://www.sprc.org/resources-programs/safety-plan-treatment-manual-reduce-suicide-risk-veteran-version

Stanley, B., & Brown, G. K. (2012). Safety planning intervention: A brief intervention to mitigate suicide risk.

Cognitive and Behavioral Practice, 19(2), 256–264. https://doi.org/10.1016/j.cbpra.2011.01.001

Stanley, B., Brown, G., Brent, D., Wells, K., Curry, J., Kennard, B. D., Wagner, A., Cwik, M., Klomek, A. B., Goldstein, T., Vitiello, B., Barnett, S., Daniel, S., & Hughes, J. (2009). Cognitive behavior therapy for suicide prevention (CBT-SP): Treatment model, feasibility and acceptability. *Journal of the American Academy of Child and Adolescent Psychiatry, 48*(10), 1005–1013. https://doi.org/10.1097/CHI.0b013e3181b5dbfe

Stanley, C. M., & Raskin, J. D. (2002). Abnormality: Does it define us or do we define it? In J. D. Raskin & S. K. Bridges (Eds.), *Studies in meaning: Exploring constructivist psychology* (pp. 123–142). Pace University Press.

Stanley, I. H., Hom, M. A., Chu, C., Dougherty, S. P., Gallyer, A. J., Spencer-Thomas, S., Shelef, L., Fruchter, E., Comtois, K. A., Gutierrez, P. M., Sachs-Ericsson, N. J., & Joiner, T. E. (2019). Perceptions of belongingness and social support attenuate PTSD symptom severity among firefighters: A multi-study investigation. *Psychological Services, 16*(4), 543–555. https://doi.org/10.1037/ser0000240

Starr, S. P., & Raines, D. (2011). Cirrhosis: Diagnosis, management, and prevention. *American Family Physician, 84*(12), 1353–1359.

Stavrou, P.-D. (2019). *Outcomes of psychodynamic psychotherapy with incorporated mentalization-focused approaches for children with ADHD and mentalization impairment*. 26.

Steardo, L., Luciano, M., Sampogna, G., Zinno, F., Saviano, P., Staltari, F., Garcia, C. S., De Fazio, P., & Fiorillo, A. (2020). Efficacy of the interpersonal and social rhythm therapy (IPSRT) in patients with bipolar disorder: Results from a real-world, controlled trial. *Annals of General Psychiatry, 19*, 1–7. https://doi.org/10.1186/s12991-020-00266-7

Steenkamp, M. M., Litz, B. T., Hoge, C. W., & Marmar, C. R. (2015). Psychotherapy for military-related PTSD: A review of randomized clinical trials. *JAMA: Journal of the American Medical Association, 314*(5), 489–500. https://doi.org/10.1001/jama.2015.8370

Stefánsdóttir, G. V. (2014). Sterilisation and women with intellectual disability in Iceland. *Journal of Intellectual and Developmental Disability, 39*(2), 188–197. https://doi.org/10.3109/13668250.2014.899327

Steffen, E. (2013). Both "being with" and "doing to": Borderline personality disorder and the integration of humanistic values in contemporary therapy practice. *Counselling Psychology Review, 28*(1), 64–71.

Steffen, K. J., Roerig, J. L., & Mitchell, J. E. (2014). Pharmacological treatment of eating disorders. In G. O. Gabbard (Ed.), *Gabbard's treatments of psychiatric disorders* (5th ed., pp. 549–559). American Psychiatric Publishing.

Stefini, A., Salzer, S., Reich, G., Horn, H., Winkelmann, K., Bents, H., Rutz, U., Frost, U., von Boetticher, A., Ruhl, U., Specht, N., & Kronmüller, K.-T. (2017). Cognitive-behavioral and psychodynamic therapy in female adolescents with bulimia nervosa: A randomized controlled trial. *Journal of the American Academy of Child & Adolescent Psychiatry, 56*(4), 329–335. https://doi.org/10.1016/j.jaac.2017.01.019

Stein, D. J. (1997). Sociopathy: Adaptation, abnormality, or both? *Behavioral and Brain Sciences, 20*(3), 531–532. https://doi.org/10.1017/S0140525X97231511

Stein, D. J. (2018). Pharmacotherapy of adjustment disorder: A review. *The World Journal of Biological Psychiatry, 19*(Suppl. 1), S46–S52. https://doi.org/10.1080/15622975.2018.1492736

Stein, D. J., & Bouwer, C. (1997). A neuro-evolutionary approach to the anxiety disorders. *Journal of Anxiety Disorders, 11*(4), 409–429. https://doi.org/10.1016/S0887-6185(97)00019-4

Stein, D. J., Lim, C. C. W., Roest, A. M., de Jonge, P., Aguilar-Gaxiola, S., Al-Hamzawi, A., Alonso, J., Benjet, C., Bromet, E. J., Bruffaerts, R., de Girolamo, G., Florescu, S., Gureje, O., Haro, J. M., Harris, M. G.,

He, Y., Hinkov, H., Horiguchi, I., Hu, C., … Scott, K. M. (2017). The cross-national epidemiology of social anxiety disorder: Data from the World Mental Health Survey Initiative. *BMC Medicine, 15*, 143. https://doi.org/10.1186/s12916-017-0889-2

Stein, D. J., Lund, C., & Nesse, R. M. (2013). Classification systems in psychiatry: Diagnosis and global mental health in the era of DSM-5 and ICD-11. *Current Opinion in Psychiatry, 26*(5), 493–497.

Stein, D. J., & Nesse, R. M. (2011). Threat detection, precautionary responses, and anxiety disorders. *Neuroscience and Biobehavioral Reviews, 35*(4), 1075–1079. https://doi.org/10.1016/j.neubiorev.2010.11.012

Stein, D. J., & Williams, D. (2010). Cultural and social aspects of anxiety disorders. In D. J. Stein, E. Hollander, & B. O. Rothbaum (Eds.), *Textbook of anxiety disorders* (2nd ed., pp. 717–729). American Psychiatric Publishing.

Stein, D., Lilenfeld, L. R., Plotnicov, K., Pollice, C., Rao, R., Strober, M., & Kaye, W. H. (1999). Familial aggregation of eating disorders: Results from a controlled family study of bulimia nervosa. *The International Journal of Eating Disorders, 26*(2), 211–215.

Stein, M. B., Chen, C.-Y., Ursano, R. J., Cai, T., Gelernter, J., Heeringa, S. G., Jain, S., Jensen, K. P., Maihofer, A. X., Mitchell, C., Nievergelt, C. M., Nock, M. K., Neale, B. M., Polimanti, R., Ripke, S., Sun, X., Thomas, M. L., Wang, Q., Ware, E. B., … Smoller, J. W. (2016). Genome-wide association studies of posttraumatic stress disorder in 2 cohorts of US Army soldiers. *JAMA Psychiatry, 73*(7), 695–704. https://doi.org/10.1001/jamapsychiatry.2016.0350

Stein, M. B., Levey, D. F., Cheng, Z., Wendt, F. R., Harrington, K., Pathak, G. A., Cho, K., Quaden, R., Radhakrishnan, K., Girgenti, M. J., Anne, Y.-L., Posner, D., Aslan, M., Duman, R. S., Zhao, H., Polimanti, R., Concato, J., Gelernter, J., Polimanti, R., & Ho, Y.-L. A. (2021). Genome-wide association analyses of post-traumatic stress disorder and its symptom subdomains in the Million Veteran Program. *Nature Genetics, 53*(2), 174-7, 184A-184F. https://doi.org/10.1038/s41588-020-00767-x

Stein, M. B., Slavin-Mulford, J., Siefert, C. J., Sinclair, S. J., Renna, M., Malone, J., Bello, I., & Blais, M. A. (2014). SCORS-G stimulus characteristics of select Thematic Apperception Test Cards. *Journal of Personality Assessment, 96*(3), 339–349. https://doi.org/10.1080/00223891.2013.823440

Stein, M. B., Slavin-Mulford, J., Siefert, C. J., Sinclair, S. J., Smith, M., Chung, W.-J., Liebman, R., & Blais, M. A. (2015). External validity of SCORS-G ratings of Thematic Apperception Test narratives in a sample of outpatients and inpatients. *Rorschachiana, 36*(1), 58–81. https://doi.org/10.1027/1192-5604/a000057

Stein, M., Hilsenroth, M. J., Slavin-Mulford, J., & Pinsker, J. (2011). *Social Cognition and Object Relations Scale: Global rating method (SCORS-G)*. Unpublished manuscript, Massachusetts General Hospital and Harvard Medical School, Boston, MA. http://www-personal.umd.umich.edu/~csiefert/docs/SCORSGlobalTrainingManual_4thEd_2011.pdf

Steinberg, P. (2012, January 31). Asperger's history of overdiagnosis. *The New York Times*. http://www.nytimes.com/2012/02/01/opinion/aspergers-history-of-over-diagnosis.html

Steinemann, S., Galanis, D., Nguyen, T., & Biffl, W. (2018). Motor vehicle crash fatalities and undercompensated care associated with legalization of marijuana. *Journal of Trauma and Acute Care Surgery, 85*(3), 566–571. https://doi.org/10.1097/TA.0000000000001983

Steinert, C., Hofmann, M., Kruse, J., & Leichsenring, F. (2014). Relapse rates after psychotherapy for depression – stable long-term effects? A meta-analysis. *Journal of Affective Disorders, 168*, 107–118. https://doi.org/10.1016/j.jad.2014.06.043

Steinert, C., Munder, T., Rabung, S., Hoyer, J., & Leichsenring, F. (2017). Psychodynamic therapy: As efficacious as other empirically supported treatments? A meta-analysis testing equivalence of outcomes. *American Journal of Psychiatry, 174*(10), 943–953. https://doi.org/10.1176/appi.ajp.2017.17010057

Steinglass, J. E., Sysko, R., Glasofer, D., Albano, A. M., Simpson, H. B., & Walsh, B. T. (2011). Rationale for the application of exposure response prevention to the treatment of anorexia nervosa. *The International Journal of Eating Disorders, 44*(2), 134–141. https://doi.org/10.1002/eat.20784

Steinglass, J., Mayer, L., & Attia, E. (2016). Treatment of restrictive eating and low-weight conditions, including anorexia nervosa and avoidant/restrictive food intake disorder. In B. T. Walsh, E. Attia, D. R. Glasofer, & R. Sysko (Eds.), *Handbook of assessment and treatment of eating disorders* (pp. 259–277). American Psychiatric Publishing.

Steketee, G., & Chambless, D. L. (2001). Does expressed emotion predict behaviour therapy outcome at follow-up for obsessive-compulsive disorder and agoraphobia? *Clinical Psychology & Psychotherapy, 8*(6), 389–399. https://doi.org/10.1002/cpp.307

Stepp, S. D., Lazarus, S. A., & Byrd, A. L. (2016). A systematic review of risk factors prospectively associated with borderline personality disorder: Taking stock and moving forward. *Personality Disorders: Theory, Research, and Treatment, 7*(4), 316–323. https://doi.org/10.1037/per0000186

Stern, D. B. (2009). Dissociation and unformulated experience: A psychoanalytic model of mind. In P. F. Dell & J. A. O'Neil (Eds.), *Dissociation and the dissociative disorders: DSM-V and beyond* (pp. 653–663). Routledge.

Stern, D. B. (2017). Unformulated experience, dissociation, and *Nachträglichkeit. The Journal of Analytical Psychology, 62*(4), 501–525. https://doi.org/10.1111/1468-5922.12334

Stern, D. B. (2020). Dissociative multiplicity and unformulated experience: Commentary on Diamond. *Journal of the American Psychoanalytic Association, 68*(5), 907–920. https://doi.org/10.1177/0003065120967741

Stern, P. (2010). Paraphilic coercive disorder in the DSM: The right diagnosis for the right reasons. *Archives of Sexual Behavior, 39*(6), 1443–1447. https://doi.org/10.1007/s10508-010-9645-9

Stern, Y. (2012). Cognitive reserve in ageing and Alzheimer's disease. *Lancet Neurology, 11*(11), 1006–1012. https://doi.org/10.1016/S1474-4422(12)70191-6

Stevenson, J., Buitelaar, J., Cortese, S., Ferrin, M., Konofal, E., Lecendreux, M., Simonoff, E., Wong, I. C. K., & Sonuga-Barke, E. (2014). Research review: The role of diet in the treatment of attention-deficit/hyperactivity disorder – An appraisal of the evidence on efficacy and recommendations on the design of future studies. *Journal of Child Psychology and Psychiatry, 55*(5), 416–427. https://doi.org/10.1111/jcpp.12215

Stewart, J. G., Esposito, E. C., Glenn, C. R., Gilman, S. E., Pridgen, B., Gold, J., & Auerbach, R. P. (2017). Adolescent self-injurers: Comparing non-ideators, suicide ideators, and suicide attempters. *Journal of Psychiatric Research, 84*, 105–112. https://doi.org/10.1016/j.jpsychires.2016.09.031

Stiegler, L. N. (2005). Understanding pica behavior: A review for clinical and education professionals. *Focus on Autism and Other Developmental Disabilities, 20*(1), 27–38. https://doi.org/10.1177/10883576050200010301

Still, G. F. (2006). Some abnormal psychical conditions in children: Excerpts from three lectures. *Journal of Attention Disorders, 10*(2), 126–136. https://doi.org/10.1177/1087054706288114

Stitzer, M., & Petry, N. (2006). Contingency management for treatment of substance abuse. *Annual Review of Clinical Psychology, 2*, 411–434. https://doi.org/10.1146/annurev.clinpsy.2.022305.095219

Stockemer, D. (2019). *Quantitative methods for the social sciences: A practical introduction with examples in SPSS and Stata*. Springer International Publishing.

Stockings, E., Hall, W. D., Lynskey, M., Morley, K. I., Reavley, N., Strang, J., Patton, G., & Degenhardt, L. (2016). Prevention, early intervention, harm reduction, and treatment of substance use in young people. *The Lancet Psychiatry, 3*(3), 280–296. https://doi.org/10.1016/S2215-0366(16)00002-X

Stoffers, J. M., Völlm, B. A., Rücker, G., Timmer, A., Huband, N., & Lieb, K. (2012). Psychological therapies for people with borderline personality disorder (Review). *Cochrane Database of Systematic Reviews, 2012*(2), Article CD005652. https://doi.org/10.1002/14651858.CD005652

Stoffers-Winterling, J., Völlm, B., & Lieb, K. (2021). Is pharmacotherapy useful for treating personality disorders? *Expert Opinion on Pharmacotherapy, 22*(4), 393–395. https://doi.org/10.1080/14656566.2021.1873277

Stojek, M. M., McSweeney, L. B., & Rauch, S. A. M. (2018). Neuroscience informed prolonged exposure practice: Increasing efficiency and efficacy through mechanisms. *Frontiers in Behavioral Neuroscience, 12*, Article 281. https://doi.org/10.3389/fnbeh.2018.00281

Stokes, M., & Abdijadid, S. (2021). Disulfiram. In *StatPearls [Internet]*. StatPearls Publishing. https://www.ncbi.nlm.nih.gov/books/NBK459340/

Stokin, G. B., Krell-Roesch, J., Petersen, R. C., & Geda, Y. E. (2015). Mild neurocognitive disorder: An old wine in a new bottle. *Harvard Review of Psychiatry, 23*(5), 368–376. https://doi.org/10.1097/HRP.0000000000000084

Stoller, R. J. (1985). *Observing the erotic imagination*. Yale University Press.

Stoller, R. J. (1986). *Perversion: The erotic form of hatred*. Karnac. (Original work published 1976)

Stone, A. A. (1975). *Mental health and law: A system in transition*. National Institute for Mental Health and Centers for Studies of Crime and Delinquency.

Stone, J. M. (2011). Glutamatergic antipsychotic drugs: A new dawn in the treatment of schizophrenia? *Therapeutic Advances In Psychopharmacology, 1*(1), 5–18. https://doi.org/10.1177/2045125311400779

Stone, J., Smyth, R., Carson, A., Warlow, C., & Sharpe, M. (2006). La belle indifférence in conversion symptoms and hysteria. *The British Journal of Psychiatry, 188*(3), 204–209.

Stone, M. H. (2010). History of anxiety disorders. In D. J. Stein, E. Hollander, & B. O. Rothbaum (Eds.), *Textbook of anxiety disorders* (2nd ed., pp. 3–15). American Psychiatric Publishing.

Stonecipher, A., Galang, R., & Black, J. (2006). Psychotropic discontinuation symptoms: A case of withdrawal neuroleptic malignant syndrome. *General Hospital Psychiatry, 28*(6), 541–543. https://doi.org/10.1016/j.genhosppsych.2006.07.007

Storebø, O. J., Ramstad, E., Krogh, H. B., Nilausen, T. D., Skoog, M., Holmskov, M., Rosendal, S., Groth, C., Magnusson, F. L., Moreira-Maia, C. R., Gillies, D., Buch Rasmussen, K., Gauci, D., Zwi, M., Kirubakaran, R., Forsbol, B., Simonsen, E., & Gluud, C. (2015). Methylphenidate for children and adolescents with attention deficit hyperactivity disorder (ADHD). *Cochrane Database of Systematic Reviews, 2015*(11), 1–774. https://doi.org/10.1002/14651858.CD009885.pub2

Storebø, O. J., Skoog, M., Damm, D., Thomsen, P. H., Simonsen, E., & Gluud, C. (2011). Social skills training for Attention Deficit Hyperactivity Disorder (ADHD) in children aged 5 to 18 years. *Cochrane Database of Systematic Reviews, 2011*(12), CD008223. https://doi.org/10.1002/14651858.CD008223.pub2

Stork, E. (2013). A competent competency standard: Should it require a mental disease or defect? *Columbia Human Rights Law Review, 44*(3), 927–969.

Strain, J. J., & Diefenbacher, A. (2008). The adjustment disorders: The conundrums of the diagnoses. *Comprehensive Psychiatry, 49*(2), 121–130. https://doi.org/10.1016/j.comppsych.2007.10.002

Strain, J. J., & Friedman, M. J. (2011). Considering adjustment disorders as stress response syndromes for DSM-5. *Depression and Anxiety, 28*(9), 818–823. https://doi.org/10.1002/da.20782

Straussner, S. L. A., & Attia, P. R. (2002). Women's addiction and treatment through a historical lens. In S. L. A. Straussner & S. Brown (Eds.), *The handbook of addiction treatment for women* (pp. 3–25). Jossey-Bass.

Strawbridge, R., Young, A. H., & Cleare, A. J. (2017). Biomarkers for depression: Recent insights, current challenges and future prospects. *Neuropsychiatric Disease and Treatment, 13*, 1245–1262. https://doi.org/10.2147/NDT.S114542

Striegel-Moore, R. H., & Franko, D. L. (2008). Should binge eating disorder be included in the DSM-V? A critical review of the state of the evidence. *Annual Review of Clinical Psychology, 4*, 305–324. https://doi.org/10.1146/annurev.clinpsy.4.022007.141149

Strober, M., Freeman, R., Lampert, C., Diamond, J., & Kaye, W. (2000). Controlled family study of anorexia nervosa and bulimia nervosa: Evidence of shared liability and transmission of partial syndromes. *The American Journal of Psychiatry, 157*(3), 393–401. https://doi.org/10.1176/appi.ajp.157.3.393

Stroebe, M., Schut, H., & Boerner, K. (2017). Cautioning health-care professionals: Bereaved persons are misguided through the stages of grief. *Omega: Journal of Death and Dying, 74*(4), 455–473. https://doi.org/10.1177/0030222817691870

Stroebe, M., Schut, H., & Stroebe, W. (2007). Health outcomes of bereavement. *The Lancet, 370*(9603), 1960–1973. https://doi.org/10.1016/S0140-6736(07)61816-9

Stroebe, W., Schut, H., & Stroebe, M. S. (2005). Grief work, disclosure and counseling: Do they help the bereaved? *Clinical Psychology Review, 25*(4), 395–414. https://doi.org/10.1016/j.cpr.2005.01.004

Strong, T. (2019). Brief report: A counselling-friendly alternative to the DSM-5? A review of the Power Threat Meaning Framework. *Canadian Journal of Counselling and Psychotherapy, 53*(3), Article 3.

Strosahl, K. D., & Linehan, M. M. (1986). Basic issues in behavioral assessment. In A. R. Ciminero, K. S. Calhoun, & H. E. Adams (Eds.), *Handbook of behavioral assessment* (2nd ed., pp. 12–46). John Wiley.

Stroud, J. B., Freeman, T. P., Leech, R., Hindocha, C., Lawn, W., Nutt, D. J., Curran, H. V., & Carhart-Harris, R. L. (2018). Psilocybin with psychological support improves emotional face recognition in treatment-resistant depression. *Psychopharmacology, 235*(2), 459–466. https://doi.org/10.1007/s00213-017-4754-y

Strübel, J., & Petrie, T. A. (2020). Sexual orientation, eating disorder classification, and men's psychosocial well-being. *Psychology of Men & Masculinities, 21*(2), 190–200. https://doi.org/10.1037/men0000224

Strupp, H. H. (1986). [Review of the book *Psychotherapy of schizophrenia: The treatment of choice*]. *Psychoanalytic Psychology, 3*(4), 385–388. https://doi.org/10.1037/h0085112

Stuebing, K. K., Fletcher, J. M., LeDoux, J. M., Lyon, G. R., Shaywitz, S. E., & Shaywitz, B. A. (2002). Validity of IQ-discrepancy classifications of reading disabilities: A meta-analysis. *American Educational Research Journal, 39*(2), 469–518. https://doi.org/10.3102/00028312039002469

Sturges, J. W. (2013). Biological views. In T. G. Plante (Ed.), *Abnormal psychology across the ages: Vol. 1. History and conceptualizations* (pp. 187–200). Praeger/ABC-CLIO.

Sturmey, P. (2009). Behavioral activation is an evidence-based treatment for depression. *Behavior Modification, 33*(6), 818–829. https://doi.org/10.1177/0145445509350094

Stuyt, E. (2018). The problem with the current high potency thc marijuana from the perspective of an addiction psychiatrist. *Missouri Medicine, 115*(6), 482–486.

Su, S., Shi, L., Zheng, Y., Sun, Y., Huang, X., Zhang, A., Que, J., Sun, X., Shi, J., Bao, Y., Deng, J., & Lu, L. (2022). Leisure activities and the risk of dementia: A systematic review and meta-analysis. *Neurology,* 99(15), e1651–e1663. https://doi.org/10.1212/WNL.0000000000200929

Subcommittee on Energy Conservation and Power. (1986). *American nuclear guinea pigs: Three decades of radiation experiments on U.S. citizens.* U.S. Government Printing Office. http://contentdm.library.unr.edu/cdm/singleitem/collection/conghear/id/102#metajump

Subedi, B. (2014). *Right to treatment* (pp. 51–53). Oxford University Press.

Sublime. (2021, March 4). *Cannabis delivery systems and their unique pros and cons.* Sublime Fuzzies. https://sublimefuzzies.com/2021/03/04/cannabis-delivery-systems-and-their-unique-pros-and-cons/

Substance Abuse and Mental Health Services Administration. (2019). *Civil commitment and the mental health care continuum: Historical trends and principles for law and practice.* Office of the Chief Medical Officer, Substance Abuse and Mental Health Services Administration.

Substance Abuse and Mental Health Services Administration. (2020). *Key substance use and mental health indicators in the United States: Results from the 2019 National Survey on Drug Use and Health* (HHS Publication No. PEP20-07-01-001, NSDUH Series H-55). Center for Behavioral Health Statistics and Quality, Substance Abuse and Mental Health Services Administration. https://www.samhsa.gov/data/

Substance Abuse and Mental Health Services Administration. (2021). *Key substance use and mental health indicators in the United States: Results from the 2020 National Survey on Drug Use and Health* (HHS Publication No. PEP21-07-01-003, NSDUH Series H-56). Center for Behavioral Health Statistics and Quality, Substance Abuse and Mental Health Services Administration. https://www.samhsa.gov/data/

Suchan, B., Busch, M., Schulte, D., Gronemeyer, D., Herpertz, S., & Vocks, S. (2010). Reduction of gray matter density in the extrastriate body area in women with anorexia nervosa. *Behavioural Brain Research, 206.* https://doi.org/10.1016/j.bbr.2009.08.035

Sudak, D. M. (2011). *Combining CBT and medication.* John Wiley.

Sugranyes, G., de la Serna, E., Romero, S., Sanchez-Gistau, V., Calvo, A., Moreno, D., Baeza, I., Diaz-Caneja, C. M., Sanchez-Gutierrez, T., Janssen, J., Bargallo, N., & Castro-Fornieles, J. (2015). Gray matter volume decrease distinguishes schizophrenia from bipolar offspring during childhood and adolescence. *Journal of the American Academy of Child & Adolescent Psychiatry, 54*(8), 677–684. https://doi.org/10.1016/j.jaac.2015.05.003

Suh, J. J., Ruffins, S., Robins, C. E., Albanese, M. J., & Khantzian, E. J. (2008). Self-medication hypothesis: Connecting affective experience and drug choice. *Psychoanalytic Psychology, 25*(3), 518–532. https://doi.org/10.1037/0736-9735.25.3.518

Suhr, J. A., & Angers, K. (2020). Neuropsychological testing and assessment. In J. A. Suhr & M. Sellbom (Eds.), *The Cambridge handbook of clinical assessment and diagnosis* (pp. 191–207). Cambridge University Press. https://doi.org/10.1017/9781108235433.015

Sukel, K. (2019, August 1). Neurotransmitters. *Dana Foundation.* https://www.dana.org/article/neurotransmitters/

Sukunesan, S., Huynh, M., & Sharp, G. (2021). Examining the pro-eating disorders community on twitter via the hashtag #proana: Statistical modeling approach. *JMIR Mental Health, 8*(7), Article e24340. https://doi.org/10.2196/24340

Sullivan, H. S. (1962). *Schizophrenia as a human process.* Norton.

Sullivan, K. A., Lane, M., Cashman, M., Miller, J. I., Pavicic, M., Walker, A. M., Cliff, A., Romero, J., Qin, X., Lindquist, J., Mullins, N., Docherty, A., Coon, H., Ruderfer, D. M., International Suicide Genetics Consortium, VA Million Veteran Program, MVP Suicide Exemplar Workgroup, Garvin, M. R., Pestian, J. P., … Kainer, D. (2022). *Digging deeper into GWAS signal using GRIN implicates additional genes contributing to suicidal behavior* [Preprint]. Genetic and Genomic Medicine. https://doi.org/10.1101/2022.04.20.22273895

Sullivan, P. F., Neale, M. C., & Kendler, K. S. (2000). Genetic epidemiology of major depression: Review and meta-analysis. *American Journal of Psychiatry, 157*(10), 1552–1562. https://doi.org/10.1176/appi.ajp.157.10.1552

Sullivan, S., Bentall, R. P., Fernyhough, C., Pearson, R. M., & Zammit, S. (2013). Cognitive styles and psychotic experiences in a community sample. *PLoS ONE, 8*(11).

Sulzer, S. H. (2015). Does "difficult patient" status contribute to de facto demedicalization? The case of borderline personality disorder. *Social Science & Medicine, 142*, 82–89. https://doi.org/10.1016/j.socscimed.2015.08.008

Sumathipala, A. (2007). What is the evidence for the efficacy of treatments for somatoform disorders? A critical review of previous intervention studies. *Psychosomatic Medicine, 69*(9), 889–900. https://doi.org/10.1097/PSY.0b013e31815b5cf6

Summers, A., & Rosenbaum, B. (2013). Psychodynamic psychotherapy for psychosis: Empirical evidence. In J. Read & J. Dillon (Eds.), *Models of madness: Psychological, social and biological approaches to psychosis* (2013-19717-023; 2nd ed., pp. 336–344). Routledge/Taylor & Francis Group.

Sun, D., Gold, A. L., Swanson, C. A., Haswell, C. C., Brown, V. M., Stjepanovic, D., LaBar, K. S., & Morey, R. A. (2020). Threat-induced anxiety during goal pursuit disrupts amygdala–prefrontal cortex connectivity in posttraumatic stress disorder. *Translational Psychiatry, 10*(1), Article 1. https://doi.org/10.1038/s41398-020-0739-4

Sun, Y., Qu, Y., & Zhu, J. (2021). The relationship between inflammation and post-traumatic stress disorder. *Frontiers in Psychiatry, 12*, Article 707543. https://doi.org/10.3389/fpsyt.2021.707543

Sundararajan, L., Misra, G., & Marsella, A. J. (2013). Indigenous approaches to assessment, diagnosis, and treatment of mental disorders. In F. A. Paniagua & A.-M. Yamada (Eds.), *Handbook of multicultural mental health: Assessment and treatment of diverse populations* (2nd ed., pp. 69–87). Elsevier Academic Press. https://doi.org/10.1016/B978-0-12-394420-7.00004-7

Sungur, M. Z., & Gunduz, A. (2013). Critiques and challenges to old and recently proposed American Psychiatric Association's website DSM 5 diagnostic criteria for sexual dysfunctions. *Klinik Psikofarmakoloji Bülteni/Bulletin of Clinical Psychopharmacology, 23*(1), 113–128. https://doi.org/10.5455/bcp.20130416063859

Suni, E. (2022, August 29). *What happens when you sleep?* National Sleep Foundation. https://sleepfoundation.org/how-sleep-works/what-happens-when-you-sleep

Sussman, S., & Ames, S. L. (2008). *Drug abuse: Concepts, prevention, and cessation.* Cambridge University Press. https://doi.org/10.1017/CBO9780511500039

Sussman, S., & Moran, M. B. (2013). Hidden addiction: Television. *Journal of Behavioral Addictions, 2*(3), 125–132. https://doi.org/10.1556/JBA.2.2013.008

Sutar, R., & Sahu, S. (2019). Pharmacotherapy for dissociative disorders: A systematic review. *Psychiatry Research, 281*, Article 112529. https://doi.org/10.1016/j.psychres.2019.112529

Suzuki, T., Griffin, S. A., & Samuel, D. B. (2016). Capturing the DSM-5 alternative personality disorder model traits in the five-factor model's nomological net. *Journal of Personality.* https://doi.org/10.1111/jopy.12235

Svancer, P., & Spaniel, F. (2021). Brain ventricular volume changes in schizophrenia. A narrative review. *Neuroscience Letters, 759*, 136065. https://doi.org/10.1016/j.neulet.2021.136065

Swab, J. (2020). Critical incident stress management: Perspectives on its history, frequency of use, efficacy, and success. *Crisis, Stress, and Human Resilience: An International Journal*, 1(4), 215–226.

Swales, M., Heard, H. L., & Williams, M. G. (2000). Linehan's Dialectical Behaviour Therapy (DBT) for borderline personality disorder: Overview and adaptation. *Journal of Mental Health*, 9(1), 7–23. https://doi.org/10.1080/09638230016921

Swami, V. (2015). Cultural influences on body size ideals: Unpacking the impact of Westernization and modernization. *European Psychologist*, 20(1), 44–51. https://doi.org/10.1027/1016-9040/a000150

Swanepoel, A., Music, G., Launer, J., & Reiss, M. J. (2017). How evolutionary thinking can help us to understand ADHD. *BJPsych Advances*, 23(6), 410–418. https://doi.org/10.1192/apt.bp.116.016659

Swanson, C. J., Zhang, Y., Dhadda, S., Wang, J., Kaplow, J., Lai, R. Y. K., Lannfelt, L., Bradley, H., Rabe, M., Koyama, A., Reyderman, L., Berry, D. A., Berry, S., Gordon, R., Kramer, L. D., & Cummings, J. L. (2021). A randomized, double-blind, phase 2b proof-of-concept clinical trial in early Alzheimer's disease with lecanemab, an anti-Aβ protofibril antibody. *Alzheimer's Research & Therapy*, 13(1), 80. https://doi.org/10.1186/s13195-021-00813-8

Swanton, T. (2020). The dopamine, glutamate, and GABA hypotheses of schizophrenia: Glutamate may be the key. *ANU Undergraduate Research Journal*, 10(1), Article 1.

Swartz, H. A. (2014). Family-focused therapy study raises new questions. *The American Journal of Psychiatry*, 171(6), 603–606. https://doi.org/10.1176/appi.ajp.2014.14020217

Swartz, H. A., Levenson, J. C., & Frank, E. (2012). Psychotherapy for bipolar II disorder: The role of interpersonal and social rhythm therapy. *Professional Psychology: Research and Practice*, 43(2), 145–153. https://doi.org/10.1037/a0027671

Swartz, J. R., Knodt, A. R., Radtke, S. R., & Hariri, A. R. (2015). A neural biomarker of psychological vulnerability to future life stress. *Neuron*, 85(3), 505–511. https://doi.org/10.1016/j.neuron.2014.12.055

Swayze, V. W. (1995). Frontal leukotomy and related psychosurgical procedures in the era before antipsychotics (1935-1954): A historical overview. *The American Journal of Psychiatry*, 152(4), 505–515.

Swedo, S. E., Mittleman, B., & Lougee, L. (1998). Pediatric autoimmune neuropsychiatric disorders associated with streptococcal infections: Clinical description of the first 50 cases. *American Journal of Psychiatry*, 155(2), 264–271. https://doi.org/10.1176/ajp.155.2.264

Sweezy, M., & Ziskind, E. L. (2013). *Internal family systems therapy: New dimensions*. Routledge.

Swenson, C. C., Henggeler, S. W., Taylor, I. S., & Addison, O. W. (2005). *Multisystemic therapy and neighborhood partnerships: Reducing adolescent violence and substance abuse*. The Guilford Press.

Szalavitz, M. (2015). No more addictive personality. *Nature*, 522(7557), S48–S49. https://doi.org/10.1038/522S48a

Szasz, T. (1986). The case against suicide prevention. *American Psychologist*, 41(7), 806–812. https://doi.org/10.1037/0003-066X.41.7.806

Szasz, T. (1991). The medicalization of sex. *Journal of Humanistic Psychology*, 31(3), 34–42. https://doi.org/10.1177/0022167891313007

Szasz, T. (1994). *Cruel compassion: Psychiatric control of society's unwanted*. John Wiley & Sons.

Szasz, T. (2008). Debunking antipsychiatry: Laing, law, and largactil. *Current Psychology: A Journal for Diverse Perspectives on Diverse Psychological Issues*, 27(2), 79–101. https://doi.org/10.1007/s12144-008-9024-z

Szasz, T. (2010). The medicalization of suicide. In *The Freeman* (Vol. 8, Issue 1, pp. 13–14).

Szasz, T. (2011). *Suicide prohibition: The shame of medicine*. Syracuse University Press.

Szasz, T. S. (1963). *Law, liberty and psychiatry: An inquiry into the social uses of mental health practices*. Macmillan.

Szasz, T. S. (1974). *The myth of mental illness: Foundations of a theory of personal conduct* (Rev. ed.). Harper & Row.

Szasz, T. S. (1987). *Insanity: The idea and its consequences*. John Wiley.

Szasz, T. S. (1991). *Ideology and insanity: Essays on the psychiatric dehumanization of man*. Syracuse University Press. (Original work published 1970.)

Szasz, T. S. (1996). *The meaning of mind: Language, morality, and neuroscience*. Praeger.

Szasz, T. S. (1999). *Fatal freedom: The ethics and politics of suicide*. Praeger.

Szasz, T. S. (2004). *Schizophrenia: The sacred symbol of psychiarty*. Syracuse University Press. (Original work published 1976.)

Szmukler, G. (2021). Anorexia nervosa, lack of "coherence" with deeply held beliefs and values, and involuntary treatment. *Philosophy, Psychiatry & Psychology*, 28(2), 151–154.

Ta, L. D. (2019, November). The social construction of borderline personality disorder. *Bossy: The ANU Women's Department Magazine*, 5, 113–115.

Tabasi, M., Anbara, T., Siadat, S. D., Khezerloo, J. K., Elyasinia, F., Bayanolhagh, S., Safavi, S. A. S., Yazdannasab, M. R., Soroush, A., & Bouzari, S. (2020). Socio-demographic characteristics, biochemical and cytokine levels in bulimia nervosa candidates for sleeve gastrectomy. *Archives of Iranian Medicine*, 23(1), 23–30.

Tait, R. C., & Chibnall, J. T. (2014). Racial/ethnic disparities in the assessment and treatment of pain: Psychosocial perspectives. *American Psychologist*, 69(2), 131–141. https://doi.org/10.1037/a0035204

Takaesu, Y. (2018). Circadian rhythm in bipolar disorder: A review of the literature. *Psychiatry and Clinical Neurosciences*, 72(9), 673–682. https://doi.org/10.1111/pcn.12688

Tal, J. Z., & Primeau, M. (2015). Circadian rhythms, sleep, and their treatment impact. In A. Yildiz, P. Ruiz, & C. B. Nemeroff (Eds.), *The bipolar book: History, neurobiology, and treatment* (pp. 127–135). Oxford University Press.

Tan, G., Rintala, D. H., Jensen, M. P., Fukui, T., Smith, D., & Williams, W. (2015). A randomized controlled trial of hypnosis compared with biofeedback for adults with chronic low back pain. *European Journal of Pain*, 19(2), 271–280. https://doi.org/10.1002/ejp.545

Tan, K. R., Rudolph, U., & Lüscher, C. (2011). Hooked on benzodiazepines: GABAA receptor subtypes and addiction. *Trends in Neurosciences*, 34(4), 188–197. https://doi.org/10.1016/j.tins.2011.01.004

Tan, S.-Y., & Wong, T. K. (2012). Existential therapy: Empirical evidence and clinical applications from a Christian perspective. *Journal of Psychology and Christianity*, 31(3), 272–277.

Tandon, P. S., Sasser, T., Gonzalez, E. S., Whitlock, K. B., Christakis, D. A., & Stein, M. A. (2019). Physical activity, screen time, and sleep in children with ADHD. *Journal of Physical Activity and Health*, 16(6), 416–422. https://doi.org/10.1123/jpah.2018-0215

Tandon, R., Nasrallah, H. A., & Keshavan, M. S. (2010). Schizophrenia, "Just the Facts" 5. Treatment and prevention Past, present, and future. *Schizophrenia Research*, 122(1–3), 1–23. https://doi.org/10.1016/j.schres.2010.05.025

Tanofsky-Kraff, M., & Wilfley, D. E. (2010). Interpersonal psychotherapy for bulimia nervosa and binge-eating disorder. In C. M. Grilo & J. E. Mitchell (Eds.), *The treatment of eating disorders: A clinical handbook* (pp. 271–293). Guilford Press.

Tarasoff v. Regents of the University of California, 17 Cal.3d 425, 131 Cal. Rptr. 14, 551 P.2d 334 (1976). https://law.justia.com/cases/california/supreme-court/3d/17/425.html

Tarbox, R. S. F., Williams, W. L., & Friman, P. C. (2004). Extended diaper wearing: Effects on continence in and out of the diaper. *Journal of Applied Behavior Analysis*, 37(1), 97–100. https://doi.org/10.1901/jaba.2004.37-97

Targhetta, R., Nalpas, B., & Perney, P. (2013). Argentine tango: Another behavioral addiction? *Journal of Behavioral Addictions*, 2(3), 179–186. https://doi.org/10.1556/jba.2.2013.007

Tarsha, M. S., Park, S., & Tortora, S. (2020). Body-centered interventions for psychopathological conditions: A review. *Frontiers in Psychology*, 10, Article 2907. https://doi.org/10.3389/fpsyg.2019.02907

Tasca, C., Rapetti, M., Carta, M. G., & Fadda, B. (2012). Women and hysteria in the history of mental health. *Clinical Practice and Epidemiology in Mental Health*, 8, 110–119. https://doi.org/10.2174/1745017901208010110

Tasca, G. A., & Balfour, L. (2014). Eating disorders and attachment: A contemporary psychodynamic perspective. *Psychodynamic Psychiatry*, 42(2), 257–276. https://doi.org/10.1521/pdps.2014.42.2.257

Tasca, G. A., & Balfour, L. (2019). Psychodynamic treatment of eating disorders: An attachment-informed approach. In D. Kealy & J. S. Ogrodniczuk (Eds.), *Contemporary psychodynamic psychotherapy: Evolving clinical practice* (pp. 207–221). Elsevier Academic Press. https://doi.org/10.1016/B978-0-12-813373-6.00014-3

Taubner, S., & Volkert, J. (2019). Evidence-based psychodynamic therapies for the treatment of patients with borderline personality disorder. *Clinical Psychology in Europe*, 1(2), Article 2. https://doi.org/10.32872/cpe.v1i2.30639

Tavares, A. C. de S., Lima, R. F. F., & Tokumaru, R. S. (2021). Evolutionary theories of depression: Overview and perspectives. *Psicologia USP*, 32, e200003. https://doi.org/10.1590/0103-6564e200003

Taylor, C., & Nutt, D. (2004). Anxiolytics. *Psychiatry*, 3(7), 17–21. https://doi.org/10.1383/psyt.3.7.17.42874

Taylor, E. (2019). ADHD medication in the longer term. *Zeitschrift Für Kinder- Und Jugendpsychiatrie Und Psychotherapie*, 47(6), 542–546. https://doi.org/10.1024/1422-4917/a000664

Taylor, L. E., Swerdfeger, A. L., & Eslick, G. D. (2014). Vaccines are not associated with autism: An evidence-based meta-analysis of case-control and cohort studies. *Vaccine*, 32(29), 3623–3629. https://doi.org/10.1016/j.vaccine.2014.04.085

Taylor, R., Galvez, V., & Loo, C. (2018). Transcranial magnetic stimulation (TMS) safety: A practical guide for psychiatrists. *Australasian Psychiatry: Bulletin of Royal Australian and New Zealand College of Psychiatrists*, 26(2), 189–192. https://doi.org/10.1177/1039856217748249

Taylor, S. (2013). Molecular genetics of obsessive-compulsive disorder: A comprehensive meta-analysis of genetic association studies. *Molecular Psychiatry*, 18(7), 799–805. https://doi.org/10.1038/mp.2012.76

Taylor, S., Abramowitz, J. S., McKay, D., & Asmundson, G. J. G. (2010). Anxious traits and temperaments. In D. J. Stein, E. Hollander, & B. O. Rothbaum (Eds.), *Textbook of anxiety disorders* (2nd ed., pp. 73–86). American Psychiatric Publishing.

Taylor, S., Landry, C. A., Paluszek, M. M., Fergus, T. A., McKay, D., & Asmundson, G. J. G. (2020). Development and initial validation of the COVID Stress Scales. *Journal of Anxiety Disorders*, 72, 102232. https://doi.org/10.1016/j.janxdis.2020.102232

Teasdale, J. D. (2004). Mindfulness-based cognitive therapy. In J. Yiend (Ed.), *Cognition, emotion and psychopathology: Theoretical, empirical and clinical directions* (pp. 270–289). Cambridge University Press. https://doi.org/10.1017/CBO9780511521263.015

Tedeschi, R. G., & Calhoun, L. G. (2004). Posttraumatic growth: Conceptual foundations and empirical evidence. *Psychological Inquiry*, 15(1), 1–18. https://doi.org/10.1207/s15327965pli1501_01

Tehrani, N. (2004). *Workplace trauma: Concepts, assessments, and interventions*. Brunner-Routledge.

Teive, H. A. G., Germiniani, F. M. B., Munhoz, R. P., & de Paola, L. (2014). 126 hysterical years—The contribution of Charcot. *Arquivos de Neuro-Psiquiatria*, 72(8), 636–639. https://doi.org/10.1590/0004-282X20140068

Telles-Correia, D., & Marques, J. G. (2015). Melancholia before the twentieth century: Fear and sorrow or partial insanity? *Frontiers in Psychology*, 6, Article 81. https://doi.org/10.3389/fpsyg.2015.00081

Telman, L. G. E., Steensel, F. J. A., Maric, M., & Bögels, S. M. (2018). What are the odds of anxiety disorders running in families? A family study of anxiety disorders in mothers, fathers, and siblings of children with anxiety disorders. *European Child & Adolescent Psychiatry*, 27(5), 615–624. https://doi.org/10.1007/s00787-017-1076-x

Temple, M., & Gall, T. L. (2018). Working through existential anxiety toward authenticity: A spiritual journey of meaning making. *Journal of Humanistic Psychology*, 58(2), 168–193. https://doi.org/10.1177/0022167816629968

Tenbergen, G., Wittfoth, M., Frieling, H., Ponseti, J., Walter, M., Walter, H., Beier, K. M., Schiffer, B., & Kruger, T. H. C. (2015). The neurobiology and psychology of pedophilia: Recent advances and challenges. *Frontiers in Human Neuroscience*, 9, 344–344. https://doi.org/10.3389/fnhum.2015.00344

Tenesa, A., & Haley, C. S. (2013). The heritability of human disease: Estimation, uses and abuses. *Nature Reviews Genetics*, 14(2), 139–149. https://doi.org/10.1038/nrg3377

Tenhula, W. N., & Bellack, A. S. (2008). Social skills training. In K. T. Mueser & D. V. Jeste (Eds.), *Clinical handbook of schizophrenia* (pp. 240–248). Guilford Press.

ter Kuile, M. M., Both, S., & van Lankveld, J. J. D. M. (2010). Cognitive behavioral therapy for sexual dysfunctions in women. *Psychiatric Clinics of North America*, 33(3), 595–610. https://doi.org/10.1016/j.psc.2010.04.010

Terhoeven, V., Nikendei, C., Bärnighausen, T., Bountogo, M., Friederich, H.-C., Ouermi, L., Sié, A., & Harling, G. (2020). Eating disorders, body image and media exposure among adolescent girls in rural Burkina Faso. *Tropical Medicine & International Health: TM & IH*, 25(1), 132–141. https://doi.org/10.1111/tmi.13340

Testa, M., & West, S. G. (2010). Civil commitment in the United States. *Psychiatry*, 7(10), 30–40.

Teusch, L., Böhme, H., Finke, J., & Gastpar, M. (2001). Effects of client-centered psychotherapy for personality disorders alone and in combination with psychopharmacological treatment. *Psychotherapy and Psychosomatics*, 70(6), 328–336. https://doi.org/10.1159/000056273

Thagaard, M. S., Faraone, S. V., Sonuga-Barke, E. J., & Østergaard, S. D. (2016). Empirical tests of natural selection-based evolutionary accounts of ADHD: A systematic review. *Acta Neuropsychiatrica*, 28(5), 249–256. https://doi.org/10.1017/neu.2016.14

Thapar, A., & Cooper, M. (2016). Attention deficit hyperactivity disorder. *The Lancet*, 387(10024), 1240–1250. https://doi.org/10.1016/S0140-6736(15)00238-X

The "Durham Rule." (2019). In *FindLaw*. https://www.findlaw.com/criminal/criminal-procedure/the-durham-rule.html

The insanity defense among the states. (2019, January 23). *FindLaw*. https://www.findlaw.com/criminal/criminal-procedure/the-insanity-defense-among-the-states.html

The irresistible impulse test. (2019). In *FindLaw*. https://www.findlaw.com/criminal/criminal-procedure/the-irresistible-impulse-test.html

The "Model Penal Code" test for legal insanity. (2019). In *FindLaw*. https://www.findlaw.com/criminal/criminal-procedure/the-model-penal-code-test-for-legal-insanity.html

The Welcoming Project. (n.d.). *Terminology*. Retrieved August 11, 2022, from https://thewelcomingproject.org/terminology/

Theimer, K., & Hansen, D. J. (2018). Child sexual abuse: Stigmatization of victims and suggestions for clinicians. *The Behavior Therapist*, 41(4), 213–219.

TheOneInside Podcast (Director). (2021, November 11). *IFS and dissociation with Joanne Twombly*. https://www.youtube.com/watch?v=vULDIjUq75A

Theriot, J., Sabir, S., & Azadfard, M. (2022a). Opioid antagonists. In *StatPearls [Internet]*. StatPearls Publishing. https://www.ncbi.nlm.nih.gov/books/NBK537079/

Theriot, J., Sabir, S., & Azadfard, M. (2022b). Opioid antagonists. In *StatPearls [Internet]*. StatPearls Publishing. https://www.ncbi.nlm.nih.gov/books/NBK537079/

Theule, J., Germain, S. M., Cheung, K., Hurl, K. E., & Markel, C. (2016). Conduct disorder/oppositional defiant disorder and attachment: A meta-analysis. *Journal of Developmental and Life-Course Criminology*, 2(2), 232–255. https://doi.org/10.1007/s40865-016-0031-8

Thibaut, F., Cosyns, P., Fedoroff, J. P., Briken, P., Goethals, K., & Bradford, J. M. W. (2020). The World Federation of Societies of Biological Psychiatry (WFSBP) 2020 guidelines for the pharmacological treatment of paraphilic disorders. *The World Journal of Biological Psychiatry*, 21(6), 412–490. https://doi.org/10.1080/15622975.2020.1744723

Thibodeau, R., & Finley, J. R. (2016). On associative stigma: Implicit and explicit evaluations of a mother of a child with autism spectrum disorder. *Journal of Child and Family Studies*. https://doi.org/10.1007/s10826-016-0615-2

Thiel, N., Jacob, G. A., Tuschen-Caffier, B., Herbst, N., Külz, A. K., Hertenstein, E., Nissen, C., & Voderholzer, U. (2016). Schema therapy augmented exposure and response prevention in patients with obsessive–compulsive disorder: Feasibility and efficacy of a pilot study. *Journal of Behavior Therapy and Experimental Psychiatry*, 52, 59–67. https://doi.org/10.1016/j.jbtep.2016.03.006

Thippaiah, S. M., Iyengar, S. S., & Vinod, K. Y. (2021). Exo- and endo-cannabinoids in depressive and suicidal behaviors. *Frontiers in Psychiatry*, 12, Article 636228. https://doi.org/10.3389/fpsyt.2021.636228

Thomas, J. J., Becker, K. R., Breithaupt, L., Murray, H. B., Jo, J. H., Kuhnle, M. C., Dreier, M. J., Harshman, S., Kahn, D. L., Hauser, K., Slattery, M., Misra, M., Lawson, E. A., & Eddy, K. T. (2021). Cognitive-behavioral therapy for adults with avoidant/restrictive food intake disorder. *Journal of Behavioral and Cognitive Therapy*, 31(1), 47–55. https://doi.org/10.1016/j.jbct.2020.10.004

Thomas, J. J., Becker, K. R., Kuhnle, M. C., Jo, J. H., Harshman, S. G., Wons, O. B., Keshishian, A. C., Hauser, K., Breithaupt, L., Liebman, R. E., Misra, M., Wilhelm, S., Lawson, E. A., & Eddy, K. T. (2020). Cognitive-behavioral therapy for avoidant/restrictive food intake disorder (CBT-AR): Feasibility, acceptability, and proof-of-concept for children and adolescents. *International Journal of Eating Disorders*, 53(10), 1636–1646. https://doi.org/10.1002/eat.23355

Thomas, J. J., Eddy, K. T., Murray, H. B., Tromp, M. D. P., Hartmann, A. S., Stone, M. T., Levendusky, P. G., & Becker, A. E. (2015). The impact of revised DSM-5 criteria on the relative distribution and inter-rater reliability of eating disorder diagnoses in a residential treatment setting. *Psychiatry Research*, 229(1–2), 517–523. https://doi.org/10.1016/j.psychres.2015.06.017

Thomas, J. J., Wons, O., & Eddy, K. (2018). Cognitive-behavioral treatment of avoidant/restrictive food intake disorder. *Current Opinion in Psychiatry*, 31(6), 425–430. https://doi.org/10.1097/YCO.0000000000000454

Thomas, K. M., Hopwood, C. J., Donnellan, M. B., Wright, A. G. C., Sanislow, C. A., McDevitt-Murphy, M. E., Ansell, E. B., Grilo, C. M., McGlashan, T. H., Shea, M. T., Markowitz, J. C., Skodol, A. E., Zanarini, M. C., & Morey, L. C. (2014). Personality heterogeneity in PTSD: Distinct temperament and interpersonal typologies. *Psychological Assessment*, 26(1), 23–34. https://doi.org/10.1037/a0034318

Thomas, M. (2009). Expanded liability for psychiatrists: Tarasoff gone crazy? In *Journal of Mental Health Law* (pp. 45–56).

Thomas, N. (2015). What's really wrong with cognitive behavioral therapy for psychosis? *Frontiers in Psychology*, 6, Article 323. https://doi.org/10.3389/fpsyg.2015.00323

Thome, J., & Jacobs, K. A. (2004). Attention deficit hyperactivity disorder (ADHD) in a 19th century children's book. *European Psychiatry*, 19(5), 303–306. https://doi.org/10.1016/j.eurpsy.2004.05.004

Thompson, D. F., Ramos, C. L., & Willett, J. K. (2014). Psychopathy: Clinical features, developmental basis and therapeutic challenges. *Journal of Clinical Pharmacy and Therapeutics*, 39(5), 485–495. https://doi.org/10.1111/jcpt.12182

Thompson, I. A., de Vries, E. F. J., & Sommer, I. E. C. (2020). Dopamine D2 up-regulation in psychosis patients after antipsychotic drug treatment: *Current Opinion in Psychiatry*, 33(3), 200–205. https://doi.org/10.1097/YCO.0000000000000598

Thompson, J. L., Rosell, D. R., Slifstein, M., Xu, X., Rothstein, E. G., Modiano, Y. A., Kegeles, L. S., Koenigsberg, H. W., New, A. S., Hazlett, E. A., McClure, M. M., Perez-Rodriguez, M. M., Siever, L. J., & Abi-Dargham, A. (2020). Amphetamine-induced striatal dopamine release in schizotypal personality disorder. *Psychopharmacology*, 237(9), 2649–2659. https://doi.org/10.1007/s00213-020-05561-5

Thompson, M. (2011). *The disappearing "disorder": Why PTSD is becoming PTS*. http://nation.time.com/2011/06/05/the-disappearing-disorder-why-ptsd-is-becoming-pts/

Thompson, R. H., & Borrero, J. C. (2011). Direct observation. In W. W. Fisher, C. C. Piazza, & H. S. Roane (Eds.), *Handbook of applied behavior analysis* (pp. 191–205). Guilford Press.

Thompson-Hollands, J., Edson, A., Tompson, M. C., & Comer, J. S. (2014). Family involvement in the psychological treatment of obsessive–compulsive disorder: A meta-analysis. *Journal of Family Psychology*, 28(3), 287–298. https://doi.org/10.1037/a0036709

Thornicroft, G. (1994). The NHS and Community Care Act, 1990. *Psychiatric Bulletin*, 18, 13–17.

Thornton, D. (2010). Evidence regarding the need for a diagnostic category for a coercive paraphilia. *Archives of Sexual Behavior*, 39(2), 411–418. https://doi.org/10.1007/s10508-009-9583-6

Thunberg, G. [@gretathunberg]. (2019, August 31). *When haters go after your looks and differences, it means they have nowhere left to go. And then you know* [Tweet]. Twitter. https://twitter.com/gretathunberg/status/1167916177927991296

Thurber, S. (2017). Childhood enuresis: Current diagnostic formulations, salient findings, and effective treatment modalities. *Archives of Psychiatric Nursing*, 31(3), 319–323. https://doi.org/10.1016/j.apnu.2016.11.005

Tick, B., Bolton, P., Happé, F., Rutter, M., & Rijsdijk, F. (2016). Heritability of autism spectrum disorders: A meta-analysis of twin studies. *Journal of Child Psychology and Psychiatry, and Allied Disciplines*, 57(5), 585–595. https://doi.org/10.1111/jcpp.12499

Tickell, A., Ball, S., Bernard, P., Kuyken, W., Marx, R., Pack, S., Strauss, C., Sweeney, T., & Crane, C. (2020). The effectiveness of mindfulness-based cognitive therapy (MBCT) in real-world healthcare services. *Mindfulness*, 11(2), 279–290. https://doi.org/10.1007/s12671-018-1087-9

Tiefer, L. (1991). Historical, scientific, clinical and feminist criticisms of "the human sexual response cycle" model. *Annual Review of Sex Research*, 2(1), 1–23.

Tiefer, L. (2001a). A new view of women's sexual problems: Why new? Why now? *Journal of Sex Research*, 38(2), 89–96. https://doi.org/10.1080/00224490109552075

Tiefer, L. (2001b). Arriving at a "New View" of women's sexual problems: Background, theory, and activism. *Women & Therapy*, 24(1–2), 63–98. https://doi.org/10.1300/J015v24n01_12

Tiefer, L. (2002). Beyond the medical model of women's sexual problems: A campaign to resist the promotion of "female sexual dysfunction." *Sexual and*

Relationship Therapy, 17(2), 127–135. https://doi.org/10.1080/14681990220121248

Tiefer, L. (2003). Female sexual dysfunction (FSD): Witnessing social construction in action. *Sexualities, Evolution & Gender, 5*(1), 33–36. https://doi.org/10.1080/14616660310001594962

Tiefer, L. (2006). Sex therapy as a humanistic enterprise. *Sexual and Relationship Therapy, 21*(3), 359–375. https://doi.org/10.1080/14681990600740723

Tiefer, L. (2010). Activism on the medicalization of sex and female genital cosmetic surgery by the New View Campaign in the United States. *Reproductive Health Matters, 18*(35), 56–63. https://doi.org/10.1016/S0968-8080(10)35493-0

Tiefer, L. (2012). Medicalizations and demedicalizations of sexuality therapies. *Journal of Sex Research, 49*(4), 311–318. https://doi.org/10.1080/00224499.2012.678948

Tielbeek, J. J., Johansson, A., Polderman, T. J. C., Rautiainen, M.-R., Jansen, P., Taylor, M., Tong, X., Lu, Q., Burt, A. S., Tiemeier, H., Viding, E., Plomin, R., Martin, N. G., Heath, A. C., Madden, P. A. F., Montgomery, G., Beaver, K. M., Waldman, I., Gelernter, J., … for the Broad Antisocial Behavior Consortium collaborators. (2017). Genome-wide association studies of a broad spectrum of antisocial behavior. *JAMA Psychiatry, 74*(12), 1242–1250. https://doi.org/10.1001/jamapsychiatry.2017.3069

Tienari, P. J., Wahlberg, K.-E., & Wynne, L. C. (2006). Finnish adoption study of schizophrenia: Implications for family interventions. *Families, Systems, & Health, 24*(4), 442–451. https://doi.org/10.1037/1091-7527.24.4.442

Tiggemann, M. (2013). Objectification theory: Of relevance for eating disorder researchers and clinicians? *Clinical Psychologist, 17*(2), 35–45. https://doi.org/10.1111/cp.12010

Tiggemann, M., & Brown, Z. (2018). Labelling fashion magazine advertisements: Effectiveness of different label formats on social comparison and body dissatisfaction. *Body Image, 25*, 97–102. https://doi.org/10.1016/j.bodyim.2018.02.010

Timimi, S. (2004). A critique of the international consensus statement on ADHD. *Clinical Child and Family Psychology Review, 7*(1), 59–63. https://doi.org/10.1023/B:CCFP.0000020192.49298.7a

Timimi, S. (2015). Attention deficit hyperactivity disorder is an example of bad medicine. *Australian and New Zealand Journal of Psychiatry, 49*(6), 575–576. https://doi.org/10.1177/0004867415580820

Timimi, S. (2018). Attention-deficit hyperactivity disorder: A critique of the concept. *Irish Journal of Psychological Medicine, 35*(3), 257–259. https://doi.org/10.1017/ipm.2018.9

Timimi, S., & Leo, J. (Eds.). (2009). *Rethinking ADHD: From brain to culture.* Palgrave Macmillan.

Timimi, S., & Timimi, L. (2015). The social construction of attention deficit hyperactivity disorder. In M. O'Reilly & J. N. Lester (Eds.), *The Palgrave handbook of child mental health: Discourse and conversation studies* (pp. 139–157). Palgrave Macmillan. https://doi.org/10.1057/9781137428318_8

Timm, J. C. (2013). *PTSD is not a disorder, says Medal of Honor winner.* Retrieved from http://www.msnbc.com/morning-joe/ptsd-not-disorder-says-medal-honor

Timulak, L., & Keogh, D. (2020). Emotion-focused therapy: A transdiagnostic formulation. *Journal of Contemporary Psychotherapy, 50*(1), 1–13. https://doi.org/10.1007/s10879-019-09426-7

Timulak, L., & Keogh, D. (2022). *Transdiagnostic emotion-focused therapy: A clinical guide for transforming emotional pain.* American Psychological Association. https://www.apa.org/pubs/books/transdiagnostic-emotion-focused-therapy

Timulak, L., Keogh, D., Chigwedere, C., Wilson, C., Ward, F., Hevey, D., Griffin, P., Jacobs, L., Hughes, S., Vaughan, C., Beckham, K., & Mahon, S. (2022). A comparison of emotion-focused therapy and cognitive-behavioral therapy in the treatment of generalized anxiety disorder: Results of a feasibility randomized controlled trial. *Psychotherapy, 59*(1), 84–95. https://doi.org/10.1037/pst0000427

Timulak, L., & McElvaney, J. (2016). Emotion-focused therapy for generalized anxiety disorder: An overview of the model. *Journal of Contemporary Psychotherapy, 46*, 41–52. https://doi.org/10.1007/s10879-015-9310-7

Titova, O. E., Hjorth, O. C., Schiöth, H. B., & Brooks, S. J. (2013). Anorexia nervosa is linked to reduced brain structure in reward and somatosensory regions: A meta-analysis of VBM studies. *BMC Psychiatry, 13*(1), 1–11. https://doi.org/10.1186/1471-244x-13-110

Tobe, B. T. D., Crain, A. M., Winquist, A. M., Calabrese, B., Makihara, H., Zhao, W., Lalonde, J., Nakamura, H., Konopaske, G., Sidor, M., Pernia, C. D., Yamashita, N., Wada, M., Inoue, Y., Nakamura, F., Sheridan, S. D., Logan, R. W., Brandel, M., Wu, D., … Snyder, E. Y. (2017). Probing the lithium-response pathway in hiPSCs implicates the phosphoregulatory set-point for a cytoskeletal modulator in bipolar pathogenesis. *Proceedings of the National Academy of Sciences, 114*(22), E4462–E4471. https://doi.org/10.1073/pnas.1700111114

Tokita, K., Yamaji, T., & Hashimoto, K. (2012). Roles of glutamate signaling in preclinical and/or mechanistic models of depression. *Pharmacology Biochemistry and Behavior, 100*(4), 688–704. https://doi.org/10.1016/j.pbb.2011.04.016

Tolan, N. V., Terebo, T., Chai, P. R., Erickson, T. B., Hayes, B. D., Uljon, S. N., Petrides, A. K., Demetriou, C. A., & Melanson, S. E. F. (2022). Impact of marijuana legalization on cannabis-related visits to the emergency department. *Clinical Toxicology (Philadelphia, Pa.), 60*(5), 585–595. https://doi.org/10.1080/15563650.2021.2012576

Tolin, D. F. (2010). Is cognitive–behavioral therapy more effective than other therapies? A meta-analytic review. *Clinical Psychology Review, 30*(6), 710–720. https://doi.org/10.1016/j.cpr.2010.05.003

Tolin, D. F., & Foa, E. B. (2008). Sex differences in trauma and posttraumatic stress disorder: A quantitative review of 25 years of research. *Psychological Trauma: Theory, Research, Practice, and Policy, S*(1), 37–85. https://doi.org/10.1037/1942-9681.S.1.37

Tolin, D. F., Frost, R. O., Steketee, G., & Muroff, J. (2015). Cognitive behavioral therapy for hoarding disorder: A meta-analysis. *Depression and Anxiety, 32*(3), 158–166. https://doi.org/10.1002/da.22327

Tomanic, M., Paunovic, K., Lackovic, M., Djurdjevic, K., Nestorovic, M., Jakovljevic, A., & Markovic, M. (2022). Energy drinks and sleep among adolescents. *Nutrients, 14*(18), Article 3813. https://doi.org/10.3390/nu14183813

Tomasik, J., Rahmoune, H., Guest, P. C., & Bahn, S. (2016). Neuroimmune biomarkers in schizophrenia. *Schizophrenia Research, 176*(1), 3–13. https://doi.org/10.1016/j.schres.2014.07.025

Tomko, R. L., Jones, J. L., Gilmore, A. K., Brady, K. T., Back, S. E., & Gray, K. M. (2018). N-acetylcysteine: A potential treatment for substance use disorders. *Current Psychiatry, 17*(6), 30–55.

Tomlinson, M. F., Brown, M., & Hoaken, P. N. S. (2016). Recreational drug use and human aggressive behavior: A comprehensive review since 2003. *Aggression and Violent Behavior, 27*, 9–29. https://doi.org/10.1016/j.avb.2016.02.004

Tomlinson, W. C. (2006). Freud and psychogenic movement disorders. In M. Hallett, C. R. Cloninger, S. Fahn, J. Jankovic, A. E. Lang, & S. C. Yudofsky (Eds.), *Psychogenic movement disorders: Neurology and neuropsychiatry* (pp. 14–19). Lippincott Williams & Wilkins.

Tomm, K. (1989). Externalizing the problem and internalizing personal agency. *Journal of Strategic and Systemic Therapies, 8*(1), 54–59. https://doi.org/10.1521/jsst.1989.8.1.54

Tomsen, S. (2018). Homicides with direct and indirect links to the night-time economy: Homicide with links to the night-time economy. *Drug and Alcohol Review, 37*(6), 794–801. https://doi.org/10.1111/dar.12824

Tondo, L., Alda, M., Bauer, M., Bergink, V., Grof, P., Hajek, T., Lewitka, U., Licht, R. W., Manchia, M., Müller-Oerlinghausen, B., Nielsen, R. E., Selo, M., Simhandl, C., Baldessarini, R. J., & for the International Group for Studies of Lithium (IGSLi). (2019). Clinical use of lithium salts: Guide for users and prescribers. *International Journal of Bipolar Disorders, 7*(1), 16. https://doi.org/10.1186/s40345-019-0151-2

Toneatto, T. (2013). Gambling. In P. M. Miller, S. A. Ball, M. E. Bates, A. W. Blume, K. M. Kampman, D. J. Kavanagh, M. E. Larimer, N. M. Petry, & P. De Witte (Eds.), *Comprehensive addictive behaviors and disorders: Vol. 1. Principles of addiction* (pp. 797–807). Elsevier Academic Press.

Toodayan, N. (2016). Professor Alois Alzheimer (1864-1915): Lest we forget. *Journal of Clinical Neuroscience, 31*, 47–55. https://doi.org/10.1016/j.jocn.2015.12.032

Toporek, R. L., & Williams, R. A. (2006). Ethics and professional issues related to the practice of social justice in counseling psychology. In R. L. Toporek, L. H. Gerstein, N. Fouad, G. Roysircar, & T. Israel (Eds.), *Handbook for social justice in counseling psychology: Leadership, vision, and action* (pp. 17–34). SAGE.

Torgersen, S. (1986). Genetics of somatoform disorders. *Archives of General Psychiatry, 43*(5), 502–505. https://doi.org/10.1001/archpsyc.1986.01800050108014

Torgersen, S., Lygren, S., Øien, P. A., Skre, I., Onstad, S., Edvardsen, J., Tambs, K., & Kringlen, E. (2000). A twin study of personality disorders. *Comprehensive Psychiatry, 41*(6), 416–425. https://doi.org/10.1053/comp.2000.16560

Torgersen, S., Myers, J., Reichborn-Kjennerud, T., Røysamb, E., Kubarych, T. S., & Kendler, K. S. (2012). The heritability of cluster B personality disorders assessed both by personal interview and questionnaire. *Journal of Personality Disorders, 26*(6), 848–866. https://doi.org/10.1521/pedi.2012.26.6.848

Torok, M., Calear, A., Shand, F., & Christensen, H. (2017). A systematic review of mass media campaigns for suicide prevention: Understanding their efficacy and the mechanisms needed for successful behavioral and literacy change. *Suicide & Life-Threatening Behavior, 47*(6), 672–687. https://doi.org/10.1111/sltb.12324

Torrey, E. F. (1992). Are we overestimating the genetic contribution to schizophrenia? *Schizophrenia Bulletin, 18*(2), 159–170.

Torrey, E. F. (2013). *Surviving schizophrenia: A family manual* (6th ed.). Harper Collins.

Torrey, E. F. (2014). *American psychosis: How the federal government destroyed the mental illness treatment system.* Oxford University Press.

Torrey, E. F., & Simmons, W., & Yolken, R. H. (2015). Is childhood cat ownership a risk factor for schizophrenia later in life? *Schizophrenia Research, 165*(1), 1–2. https://doi.org/10.1016/j.schres.2015.03.036

Torrico, B., Chiocchetti, A. G., Bacchelli, E., Trabetti, E., Hervás, A., Franke, B., Buitelaar, J. K., Rommelse, N., Yousaf, A., Duketis, E., Freitag, C. M., Caballero-Andaluz, R., Martinez-Mir, A., Scholl, F. G., Ribasés, M., ITAN, Battaglia, A., Malerba, G., Delorme, R., … Toma, C. (2017). Lack of replication of previous autism spectrum disorder GWAS hits in European populations. *Autism Research, 10*(2), 202–211. https://doi.org/10.1002/aur.1662

Town, J. M., Abbass, A., & Bernier, D. (2013). Effectiveness and cost effectiveness of Davanloo's Intensive Short-Term Dynamic Psychotherapy: Does unlocking the unconscious make a difference? *American Journal of Psychotherapy, 67*(1), 89–108. https://doi.org/10.1176/appi.psychotherapy.2013.67.1.89

Town, J. M., Abbass, A., Stride, C., & Bernier, D. (2017). A randomised controlled trial of Intensive Short-Term Dynamic Psychotherapy for treatment resistant depression: The Halifax Depression Study. *Journal of Affective Disorders, 214*, 15–25. https://doi.org/10.1016/j.jad.2017.02.035

Town, J. M., Abbass, A., Stride, C., Nunes, A., Bernier, D., & Berrigan, P. (2020). Efficacy and cost-effectiveness of intensive short-term dynamic psychotherapy for treatment resistant depression: 18-Month follow-up of the Halifax depression trial. *Journal of Affective Disorders, 273*, 194–202. https://doi.org/10.1016/j.jad.2020.04.035

Town, J. M., & Driessen, E. (2013). Emerging evidence for intensive short-term dynamic psychotherapy with personality disorders and somatic disorders. *Psychiatric Annals, 43*(11), 502–507. https://doi.org/10.3928/00485713-20131105-05

Tozdan, S., & Briken, P. (2021). Paraphilias: Diagnostics, comorbidities, and treatment. In M. Lew-Starowicz, A. Giraldi, & T. H. C. Krüger (Eds.), *Psychiatry and Sexual Medicine* (pp. 407–416). Springer International Publishing. https://doi.org/10.1007/978-3-030-52298-8_27

Trace, S. E., Baker, J. H., Peñas-Lledó, E., & Bulik, C. M. (2013). The genetics of eating disorders. *Annual Review of Clinical Psychology, 9*, 589–620. doi:10.1146/annurev-clinpsy-050212-185546

Tracy, M., Tiliopoulos, N., Sharpe, L., & Bach, B. (2021). The clinical utility of the ICD-11 classification of personality disorders and related traits: A preliminary scoping review. *Australian & New Zealand Journal of Psychiatry, 55*(9), 849–862. https://doi.org/10.1177/0004867421025607

Tranel, D., Nikolas, M., & Markon, K. (2020). Psychopathology: A neurobiological perspective. In J. E. Maddux & B. A. Winstead (Eds.), *Psychopathology: Foundations for a contemporary understanding* (5th ed., pp. 19–56). Routledge/Taylor & Francis Group.

Traynor, W. (2019). *Person-centred therapy and pre-therapy for people who hear voices, have unusual experiences or psychotic processes, practitioner and client perceptions of helpful and unhelpful practice and perceived client changes* [Doctoral dissertation, University of Strathclyde]. University of Strathclyde Glasgow Repository. https://doi.org/10.48730/vq26-9m95

Traynor, W., Elliott, R., & Cooper, M. (2011). Helpful factors and outcomes in person-centered therapy with clients who experience psychotic processes: Therapists' perspectives. *Person-Centered and Experiential Psychotherapies, 10*(2), 89–104. https://doi.org/10.1080/14779757.2011.576557

Treadway, M. T., & Pizzagalli, D. A. (2014). Imaging the pathophysiology of major depressive disorder—From localist models to circuit-based analysis. *Biology of Mood & Anxiety Disorders, 4*, 5–5. https://doi.org/10.1186/2045-5380-4-5

Tretteteig, S., Vatne, S., & Rokstad, A. M. M. (2016). The influence of day care centres for people with dementia on family caregivers: An integrative review of the literature. *Aging & Mental Health, 20*(5), 450–462. https://doi.org/10.1080/13607863.2015.1023765

Tretteteig, S., Vatne, S., & Rokstad, A. M. M. (2017). The influence of day care centres designed for people with dementia on family caregivers – a qualitative study. *BMC Geriatrics, 17*, 5. https://doi.org/10.1186/s12877-016-0403-2

Trevor News. (2023, January 19). New poll emphasizes negative impacts of anti-LGBTQ policies on LGBTQ youth [Press release]. The Trevor Project. https://www.thetrevorproject.org/blog/new-poll-emphasizes-negative-impacts-of-anti-lgbtq-policies-on-lgbtq-youth/

Tricklebank, M. D., & Petrinovic, M. M. (2019). Serotonin and aggression. In M. D. Tricklebank & E. Daly (Eds.), *The serotonin system: History, neuropharmacology, and pathology* (pp. 155–180). Academic Press. https://doi.org/10.1016/B978-0-12-813323-1.00009-8

Trifu, S., Sevcenco, A., Stănescu, M., Drăgoi, A. M., & Cristea, M. B. (2021). Efficacy of electroconvulsive therapy as a potential firstchoice treatment in treatmentresistant depression (Review). *Experimental and Therapeutic Medicine, 22*(5), 1–8. https://doi.org/10.3892/etm.2021.10716

Trinchieri, M., Trinchieri, M., Perletti, G., Magri, V., Stamatiou, K., Cai, T., Montanari, E., & Trinchieri, A. (2021). Erectile and ejaculatory dysfunction associated with use of psychotropic drugs: A systematic review. *The Journal of Sexual Medicine, 18*(8), 1354–1363. https://doi.org/10.1016/j.jsxm.2021.05.016

Tripp, G., & Wickens, J. R. (2008). Dopamine transfer deficit: A neurobiological theory of altered reinforcement mechanisms in ADHD. *Journal of Child Psychology and Psychiatry, 49*(7), 691–704. https://doi.org/10.1111/j.1469-7610.2007.01851.x

Tristano, A. G. (2009). The impact of rheumatic diseases on sexual function. *Rheumatology International, 29*(8), 853–860. https://doi.org/10.1007/s00296-009-0850-6

Tristano, A. G. (2014). Impact of rheumatoid arthritis on sexual function. *World Journal of Orthopedics, 5*(2), 107–111. https://doi.org/10.5312/wjo.v5.i2.107

Trivedi, G. Y., & Saboo, B. (2020). The risk factors for immune system impairment and the need for lifestyle changes. *Journal of Social Health and Diabetes, 8*(1), 25–28. https://doi.org/10.1055/s-0040-1715778

Trivedi, M. H., Rush, A. J., Wisniewski, S. R., Nierenberg, A. A., Warden, D., Ritz, L., Norquist, G., Howland, R. H., Lebowitz, B., McGrath, P. J., Shores-Wilson, K., Biggs, M. M., Balasubramani, G. K., & Fava, M. (2006). Evaluation of outcomes with citalopram for depression using measurement-based care in STAR*D: Implications for clinical practice. *The American Journal of Psychiatry, 163*(1), 28–40. https://doi.org/10.1176/appi.ajp.163.1.28

Troubat, R., Barone, P., Leman, S., Desmidt, T., Cressant, A., Atanasova, B., Brizard, B., El Hage, W., Surget, A., Belzung, C., & Camus, V. (2021). Neuroinflammation and depression: A review. *The European Journal of Neuroscience, 53*(1), 151–171. https://doi.org/10.1111/ejn.14720

Trower, P., Casey, A., & Dryden, W. (1988). *Cognitive-behavioural counselling in action*. SAGE.

Trull, T. J. (2012). The Five-Factor Model of personality disorder and DSM-5. *Journal of Personality, 80*(6), 1697–1720. https://doi.org/10.1111/j.1467-6494.2012.00771.x

Trunko, M. E., Schwartz, T. A., Berner, L. A., Cusack, A., Nakamura, T., Bailer, U. F., Chen, J. Y., & Kaye, W. H. (2017). A pilot open series of lamotrigine in DBT-treated eating disorders characterized by significant affective dysregulation and poor impulse control. *Borderline Personality Disorder and Emotion Dysregulation, 4*(1), 21. https://doi.org/10.1186/s40479-017-0072-6

Tsai, J.-D., Wang, I. C., Chen, H.-J., Sheu, J.-N., Li, T.-C., Tsai, H. J., & Wei, C.-C. (2017). Trend of nocturnal enuresis in children with attention deficit/hyperactivity disorder: A nationwide population-based study in Taiwan. *Journal of Investigative Medicine, 65*, 370–375. https://doi.org/10.1136/jim-2016-000223

Tsesis, A. (2011). Due process in civil commitments. *Washington and Lee Law Review, 68*, 253–307.

Tsoi, D. T. Y., Hunter, M. D., & Woodruff, P. W. R. (2008). History, aetiology, and symptomatology of schizophrenia. *Psychiatry, 7*(10), 404–409. https://doi.org/10.1016/j.mppsy.2008.07.010

Tsuang, M. T., Van Os, J., Tandon, R., Barch, D. M., Bustillo, J., Gaebel, W., Gur, R. E., Heckers, S., Malaspina, D., Owen, M. J., Schultz, S., & Carpenter, W. (2013). Attenuated psychosis syndrome in DSM-5. *Schizophrenia Research, 150*(1), 31–35. https://doi.org/10.1016/j.schres.2013.05.004

Tsujimura, A. (2013). The relationship between testosterone deficiency and men's health. *The World Journal of Men's Health, 31*(2), 126–135. https://doi.org/10.5534/wjmh.2013.31.2.126

Tu, N. D., & Baskin, L. S. (2022, June 2). *Nocturnal enuresis in children: Management*. UpToDate. https://www.uptodate.com/contents/nocturnal-enuresis-in-children-management

Tueth, M. J. (1995). Schizophrenia: Emil Kraepelin, Adolph Meyer, and beyond. *The Journal of Emergency Medicine, 13*(6), 805–809. https://doi.org/10.1016/0736-4679(95)02022-5

Tufford, L., & Newman, P. (2012). Bracketing in qualitative research. *Qualitative Social Work: Research and Practice, 11*(1), 80–96. https://doi.org/10.1177/1473325010368316

Tullis, P. (2021). How ecstasy and psilocybin are shaking up psychiatry. *Nature, 589*(7843), 506–509. https://doi.org/10.1038/d41586-021-00187-9

Tully, J., Cross, B., Gerrie, B., Griem, J., Blackwood, N., Blair, J., & McCutcheon, R. (2022). *Variability and magnitude of brain volume abnormalities in disruptive behavior disorders, antisocial personality disorder, and psychopathy—A meta-analysi.* Research Square. https://doi.org/10.21203/rs.3.rs-1918461/v1

Tunmer, W., & Greaney, K. (2010). Defining dyslexia. *Journal of Learning Disabilities, 43*(3), 229–243. https://doi.org/10.1177/0022219409345009

Turk, D. C. (2002). A diathesis-stress model of chronic pain and disability following traumatic injury. *Pain Research and Management, 7*(1), 9–19. https://doi.org/10.1155/2002/252904

Turna, J., Grosman Kaplan, K., Anglin, R., & Van Ameringen, M. (2016). "What's bugging the gut in OCD?" A review of the gut microbiome in obsessive–compulsive disorder. *Depression and Anxiety, 33*(3), 171–178. https://doi.org/10.1002/da.22454

Turner, D. T., McGlanaghy, E., Cuijpers, P., van der Gaag, M., Karyotaki, E., & MacBeth, A. (2018). A meta-analysis of social skills training and related interventions for psychosis. *Schizophrenia Bulletin, 44*(3), 475–491. https://doi.org/10.1093/schbul/sbx146

Turner, R. M. (2000). Naturalistic evaluation of dialectical behavior therapy-oriented treatment for borderline personality disorder. *Cognitive and Behavioral Practice, 7*(4), 413–419. https://doi.org/10.1016/S1077-7229(00)80052-8

Turnock, A., Langley, K., & Jones, C. R. G. (2022). Understanding stigma in autism: A narrative review and theoretical model. *Autism in Adulthood, 4*(1), 76–91. https://doi.org/10.1089/aut.2021.0005

Twenge, J. M. (2011). Narcissism and culture. In W. K. Campbell & J. D. Miller (Eds.), *The handbook of narcissism and narcissistic personality disorder: Theoretical approaches, empirical findings, and treatments* (pp. 202–209). John Wiley & Sons.

Twenge, J. M. (2017). *Have smartphones destroyed a generation?* https://www.theatlantic.com/magazine/archive/2017/09/has-the-smartphone-destroyed-a-generation/534198/

Twenge, J. M. (2020). Increases in depression, self-harm, and suicide among U.S. adolescents after 2012 and links to technology use: Possible mechanisms. *Psychiatric Research and Clinical Practice, 2*(1), 19–25. https://doi.org/10.1176/appi.prcp.20190015

Twohey, M., & Jewett, C. (2022, November 14). They paused puberty, but is there a cost? *The New York Times*. https://www.nytimes.com/2022/11/14/health/puberty-blockers-transgender.html

Twombly, J. H. (2013). Integrating IFS with phase-oriented treatment of clients with dissociative disorder. In M. Sweezy & E. L. Ziskind (Eds.), *Internal family systems therapy: New dimensions* (pp. 72–89). Routledge.

Tychmanowicz, A., Filipiak, S., & Sprynska, Z. (2021). Extravert individualists or introvert collectivists? Personality traits and individualism and collectivism in students in Poland and Ukraine. *Current Psychology, 40*(12), 5947–5957. https://doi.org/10.1007/s12144-019-00480-x

Tyrer, P., Mulder, R., Kim, Y.-R., & Crawford, M. J. (2019). The development of the ICD-11 classification of personality disorders: An amalgam of science, pragmatism, and politics. *Annual Review of Clinical Psychology, 15*, 481–502. https://doi.org/10.1146/annurev-clinpsy-050718-095736

Tyrer, P., Reed, G. M., & Crawford, M. J. (2015). Classification, assessment, prevalence, and effect of personality disorder. *The Lancet, 385*(9969), 717–726. https://doi.org/10.1016/S0140-6736(14)61995-4

Tyrrell, J., Melzer, D., Henley, W., Galloway, T. S., & Osborne, N. J. (2013). Associations between socioeconomic status and environmental toxicant concentrations in adults in the USA: NHANES 2001-2010. *Environment International*, 59, 328–335. https://doi.org/10.1016/j.envint.2013.06.017

Tzeses, J. (2021, December 22). *Top mental health apps for 2021: An alternative to therapy?* PSYCOM. https://www.psycom.net/25-best-mental-health-apps

Uchôa, F. N. M., Uchôa, N. M., Daniele, T. M. da C., Lustosa, R. P., Garrido, N. D., Deana, N. F., Aranha, Á. C. M., & Alves, N. (2019). Influence of the mass media and body dissatisfaction on the risk in adolescents of developing eating disorders. *International Journal of Environmental Research and Public Health*, 16(9), 1508. https://doi.org/10.3390/ijerph16091508

UCSF Lesbian, Gay, Bisexual, and Transgender Resource Center. (n.d.). *General definitions*. LGBT Resource Center. Retrieved July 15, 2022, from https://lgbt.ucsf.edu/glossary-terms

Uddin, L. Q., Nomi, J. S., Hebert-Seropian, B., Ghaziri, J., & Boucher, O. (2017). Structure and function of the human insula. *Journal of Clinical Neurophysiology*, 34(4), 300–306. https://doi.org/10.1097/WNP.0000000000000377

Uddin, M., & Diwadkar, V. A. (2014). Inflammation and psychopathology: What we now know, and what we need to know. *Social Psychiatry and Psychiatric Epidemiology*, 49(10), 1537–1539. https://doi.org/10.1007/s00127-014-0934-9

Udo, T., & Grilo, C. M. (2018). Prevalence and correlates of DSM-5–defined eating disorders in a nationally representative sample of U.S. adults. *Biological Psychiatry*, 84(5), 345–354. https://doi.org/10.1016/j.biopsych.2018.03.014

Uher, R., Payne, J. L., Pavlova, B., & Perlis, R. H. (2014). Major depressive disorder in DSM-5: Implications for clinical practice and research of changes from DSM-IV. *Depression and Anxiety*, 31(6), 459–471. https://doi.org/10.1002/da.22217

Uher, R., & Rutter, M. (2012). Classification of feeding and eating disorders: Review of evidence and proposals for ICD-11. *World Psychiatry*, 11(2), 80–92. https://doi.org/10.1016/j.wpsyc.2012.05.005

Unger, R. (2019). Moving toward a wider perspective on psychosis. *Journal of Humanistic Psychology*, 59(5), 768–774. https://doi.org/10.1177/0022167818762204

United Nations General Assembly. (2006). *Convention on the rights of persons with disabilities*. http://www.un-documents.net/a61r106.htm

United Nations Office on Drugs and Crime. (2022). *World drug report 2022*. United Nations. www.unodc.org/unodc/en/data-and-analysis/world-drug-report-2022.html

United Nations Office on Drugs and Crime. (2016). *World drug report 2016*. http://www.unodc.org/wdr2016/

Unwin, H. J. T., Hillis, S., Cluver, L., Flaxman, S., Goldman, P. S., Butchart, A., Bachman, G., Rawlings, L., Donnelly, C. A., Ratmann, O., Green, P., Nelson, C. A., Blenkinsop, A., Bhatt, S., Desmond, C., Villaveces, A., & Sherr, L. (2022). Global, regional, and national minimum estimates of children affected by COVID-19-associated orphanhood and caregiver death, by age and family circumstance up to Oct 31, 2021: An updated modelling study. *The Lancet Child & Adolescent Health*, 6(4), 249–259. https://doi.org/10.1016/S2352-4642(22)00005-0

Uphoff, E., Ekers, D., Robertson, L., Dawson, S., Sanger, E., South, E., Samaan, Z., Richards, D., Meader, N., & Churchill, R. (2020). Behavioural activation therapy for depression in adults. *Cochrane Database of Systematic Reviews*, 2020(7), Article CD013305. https://doi.org/10.1002/14651858.cd013305.pub2

Uphouse, L. (2014). Pharmacology of serotonin and female sexual behavior. *Pharmacology Biochemistry and Behavior*, 121, 31–42. https://doi.org/10.1016/j.pbb.2013.11.008

Uribe, C., Junque, C., Gómez-Gil, E., Abos, A., Mueller, S. C., & Guillamon, A. (2020). Brain network interactions in transgender individuals with gender incongruence. *NeuroImage*, 211, 116613. https://doi.org/10.1016/j.neuroimage.2020.116613

U.S. Food and Drug Administration. (2019, March 5). *FDA approves new nasal spray medication for treatment-resistant depression; available only at a certified doctor's office or clinic*. FDA; FDA. https://www.fda.gov/news-events/press-announcements/fda-approves-new-nasal-spray-medication-treatment-resistant-depression-available-only-certified

U.S. Food and Drug Administration. (2020a, March 24). *FDA approves new treatment for hypoactive sexual desire disorder in premenopausal women*. FDA; FDA. https://www.fda.gov/news-events/press-announcements/fda-approves-new-treatment-hypoactive-sexual-desire-disorder-premenopausal-women

U.S. Food and Drug Administration. (2020b, March 24). *FDA orders important safety labeling changes for Addyi*. FDA; FDA. https://www.fda.gov/news-events/press-announcements/fda-orders-important-safety-labeling-changes-addyi

U.S. Food and Drug Administration. (2022a, April 28). *Cigarettes*. FDA; FDA. https://www.fda.gov/tobacco-products/products-ingredients-components/cigarettes

U.S. Food and Drug Administration. (2022b, June 29). *E-cigarettes, vapes, and other electronic nicotine delivery systems (ENDS)*. FDA. https://www.fda.gov/tobacco-products/products-ingredients-components/e-cigarettes-vapes-and-other-electronic-nicotine-delivery-systems-ends

U.S. Food and Drug Administration. (2023, July 7). *FDA converts novel Alzheimer's disease treatment to traditional approval*. FDA; FDA. https://www.fda.gov/news-events/press-announcements/fda-converts-novel-alzheimers-disease-treatment-traditional-approval

USAFacts. (2021, July 14). *Over one-third of Americans live in areas lacking mental health professionals*. https://usafacts.org/articles/over-one-third-of-americans-live-in-areas-lacking-mental-health-professionals/

Ussher, J. M. (2011). *The madness of women: Myth and experience*. Routledge.

Ussher, J. M. (2013). Diagnosing difficult women and pathologising femininity: Gender bias in psychiatric nosology. *Feminism & Psychology*, 23(1), 63–69. https://doi.org/10.1177/0959353512467968

Vadermeersch, P. (1994). "Les mythes d'origine" in the history of psychiatry. In M. S. Micale & R. Porter (Eds.), *Discovering the history of psychiatry* (pp. 219–231). Oxford University Press.

Vaessen, T., Rintala, A., Otsabryk, N., Viechtbauer, W., Wampers, M., Claes, S., & Myin-Germeys, I. (2021). The association between self-reported stress and cardiovascular measures in daily life: A systematic review. *PLOS ONE*, 16(11), e0259557. https://doi.org/10.1371/journal.pone.0259557

Vahia, I. V., & Cohen, C. I. (2008). Psychopathology. In K. T. Mueser & D. V. Jeste (Eds.), *Clinical handbook of schizophrenia* (pp. 82–90). Guilford Press.

Valenstein, E. S. (1998). *Blaming the brain: The truth about drugs and mental health*. The Free Press.

Vallerand, I. A., Kalenchuk, A. L., & McLennan, J. D. (2014). Behavioural treatment recommendations in clinical practice guidelines for attention-deficit/hyperactivity disorder: A scoping review. *Child and Adolescent Mental Health*, 19(4), 251–258. https://doi.org/10.1111/camh.12062

van Beijsterveldt, C. E. M., Hudziak, J. J., & Boomsma, D. I. (2006). Genetic and environmental influences on cross-gender behavior and relation to behavior problems: A study of Dutch twins at ages 7 and 10 years. *Archives of Sexual Behavior*, 35(6), 647–658. https://doi.org/10.1007/s10508-006-9072-0

van Bilsen, H. (2013). *Cognitive behaviour therapy in the real world: Back to basics*. Karnac Books.

van den Bosch, L. M. C., Koeter, M. W. J., Stijnen, T., Verheul, R., & van den Brink, W. (2005). Sustained efficacy of dialectical behaviour therapy for borderline personality disorder. *Behaviour Research and Therapy*, 43(9), 1231–1241. https://doi.org/10.1016/j.brat.2004.09.008

van den Heuvel, O. A., Remijnse, P. L., Mataix-Cols, D., Vrenken, H., Groenewegen, H. J., Uylings, H. B. M., van Balkom, A. J. L. M., & Veltman, D. J. (2009). The major symptom dimensions of obsessive-compulsive disorder are mediated by partially distinct neural systems. *Brain: A Journal of Neurology*, 132(4), 853–868. https://doi.org/10.1093/brain/awn267

van den Heuvel, O. A., Veale, D., & Stein, D. J. (2014). Hypochondriasis: Considerations for ICD-11. *Revista Brasileira de Psiquiatria*, 36, 21–27.

van den Hout, M. A., & Engelhard, I. M. (2012). How does EMDR work? *Journal of Experimental Psychopathology*, 3(5), 724–738. https://doi.org/10.5127/jep.028212

van der Feltz-cornelis, C. M., & van Dyck, R. (1997). The notion of somatization: An artefact of the conceptualization of body and mind. *Psychotherapy and Psychosomatics*, 66(3), 117–127. https://doi.org/10.1159/000289121

van der Hart, O. (2021). Trauma-related dissociation: An analysis of two conflicting models. *European Journal of Trauma & Dissociation*, 5(4), 100210. https://doi.org/10.1016/j.ejtd.2021.100210

van der Hart, O., & Horst, R. (1989). The dissociation theory of Pierre Janet. *Journal of Traumatic Stress*, 2(4), 397–412. https://doi.org/10.1002/jts.2490020405

van der Kolk, B. A. (2007). The history of trauma in psychiatry. In M. J. Friedman, T. M. Keane, & P. A. Resick (Eds.), *Handbook of PTSD: Science and practice* (pp. 19–36). Guilford Press.

van der Pol, T. M., Cohn, M. D., van Domburgh, L., Rigter, H., & Vermeiren, R. R. J. M. (2021). Assessing the effect of multidimensional family therapy in adolescents on police arrests against a background of falling crime rates. A randomised controlled trial with 7-year follow-up. *Journal of Experimental Criminology*, 17(4), 597–609. https://doi.org/10.1007/s11292-020-09431-0

van der Pol, T. M., Hendriks, V., Rigter, H., Cohn, M. D., Doreleijers, T. A. H., van Domburgh, L., & Vermeiren, R. R. J. M. (2018). Multidimensional family therapy in adolescents with a cannabis use disorder: Long-term effects on delinquency in a randomized controlled trial. *Child and Adolescent Psychiatry and Mental Health*, 12(1), 44. https://doi.org/10.1186/s13034-018-0248-x

van der Stel, J. (2015). Evolution of mental health and addiction care systems in Europe. In G. Dom & F. Moggi (Eds.), *Co-occurring addictive and psychiatric disorders: A practice-based handbook from a European perspective* (pp. 13–26). Springer-Verlag Publishing. https://doi.org/10.1007/978-3-642-45375-5_2

van Deurzen, E. (2012). *Existential counselling and psychotherapy in practice* (3rd ed.). SAGE.

van Dijk, M., Benninga, M. A., Grootenhuis, M. A., Nieuwenhuizen, A.-M. O., & Last, B. F. (2007). Chronic childhood constipation: A review of the literature and the introduction of a protocolized behavioral intervention program. *Patient Education and Counseling*, 67(1–2), 63–77. https://doi.org/10.1016/j.pec.2007.02.002

van Dis, E. A. M., van Veen, S. C., Hagenaars, M. A., Batelaan, N. M., Bockting, C. L. H., van den Heuvel, R. M., Cuijpers, P., & Engelhard, I. M. (2020). Long-term outcomes of cognitive behavioral therapy for anxiety-related disorders: A systematic review and meta-analysis. *JAMA Psychiatry*, 77(3), 265–273. https://doi.org/10.1001/jamapsychiatry.2019.3986

van Dyck, C. H., Swanson, C. J., Aisen, P., Bateman, R. J., Chen, C., Gee, M., Kanekiyo, M., Li, D., Reyderman, L., Cohen, S., Froelich, L., Katayama, S., Sabbagh, M., Vellas, B., Watson, D., Dhadda, S., Irizarry, M., Kramer, L. D., & Iwatsubo, T. (2023). Lecanemab in early

Alzheimer's disease. *New England Journal of Medicine*, 388, 9–21. https://doi.org/10.1056/NEJMoa2212948

van Eeden, A. E., van Hoeken, D., & Hoek, H. W. (2021). Incidence, prevalence and mortality of anorexia nervosa and bulimia nervosa. *Current Opinion in Psychiatry*, 34(6), 515–524. https://doi.org/10.1097/YCO.0000000000000739

van Eeden, W. A., El Filali, E., van Hemert, A. M., Carlier, I. V. E., Penninx, B. W. J. H., Lamers, F., Schoevers, R., & Giltay, E. J. (2021). Basal and LPS-stimulated inflammatory markers and the course of anxiety symptoms. *Brain, Behavior, and Immunity*, 98, 378–387. https://doi.org/10.1016/j.bbi.2021.09.001

van Egmond, J. J. (2003). The multiple meanings of secondary gain. *The American Journal of Psychoanalysis*, 63(2), 137–147. https://doi.org/10.1023/A:1024027131335

van Emmerik, A. A. P., Kamphuis, J. H., Hulsbosch, A. M., & Emmelkamp, P. M. G. (2002). Single session debriefing after psychological trauma: A meta-analysis. *The Lancet*, 360(9335), 766–771. https://doi.org/10.1016/S0140-6736(02)09897-5

van Erp, T. G. M., Greve, D. N., Rasmussen, J., Turner, J., Calhoun, V. D., Young, S., Mueller, B., Brown, G. G., McCarthy, G., Glover, G. H., Lim, K. O., Bustillo, J. R., Belger, A., McEwen, S., Voyvodic, J., Mathalon, D. H., Keator, D., Preda, A., Nguyen, D., … Potkin, S. G. (2014). A multi-scanner study of subcortical brain volume abnormalities in schizophrenia. *Psychiatry Research: Neuroimaging*, 222(1–2), 10–16. https://doi.org/10.1016/j.pscychresns.2014.02.011

Van Hoecke, E., Baeyens, D., Walle, J. V., Hoebeke, P., & Roeyers, H. (2003). Socioeconomic status as a common factor underlying the association between enuresis and psychopathology. *Journal of Developmental and Behavioral Pediatrics*, 24(2), 109–114. https://doi.org/10.1097/00004703-200304000-00006

van Lankveld, J. J. D. M., ter Kuile, M. M., de Groot, H. E., Melles, R., Nefs, J., & Zandbergen, M. (2006). Cognitive-behavioral therapy for women with lifelong vaginismus: A randomized waiting-list controlled trial of efficacy. *Journal of Consulting and Clinical Psychology*, 74(1), 168–178. https://doi.org/10.1037/0022-006X.74.1.168

van Minnen, A., Hendriks, L., & Olff, M. (2010). When do trauma experts choose exposure therapy for PTSD patients? A controlled study of therapist and patient factors. *Behaviour Research and Therapy*, 48(4), 312–320. https://doi.org/10.1016/j.brat.2009.12.003

van Minnen, A., & Tibben, M. (2021). A brief cognitive-behavioural treatment approach for PTSD and Dissociative Identity Disorder, a case report. *Journal of Behavior Therapy and Experimental Psychiatry*, 72, 101655. https://doi.org/10.1016/j.jbtep.2021.101655

van Os, J. (2009a). A salience dysregulation syndrome. *The British Journal of Psychiatry*, 194(2), 101–103. https://doi.org/10.1192/bjp.bp.108.054254

van Os, J. (2009b). "Salience syndrome" replaces "schizophrenia" in DSM-V and ICD-11: Psychiatry's evidence-based entry into the 21st century? *Acta Psychiatrica Scandinavica*, 120(5), 363–372. https://doi.org/10.1111/j.1600-0447.2009.01456.x

van Os, J., Rutten, B. P., Myin-Germeys, I., Delespaul, P., Viechtbauer, W., van Zelst, C., Bruggeman, R., Reininghaus, U., Morgan, C., Murray, R. M., Di Forti, M., McGuire, P., Valmaggia, L. R., Kempton, M. J., Gayer-Anderson, C., Hubbard, K., Beards, S., Stilo, S. A., Onyejiaka, A., … Baudin, G. et al. (2014). Identifying gene-environment interactions in schizophrenia: Contemporary challenges for integrated, large-scale investigations. *Schizophrenia Bulletin*, 40(4), 729–736. https://doi.org/10.1093/schbul/sbu069

van Reekum, E. A., & Watt, M. C. (2019). A pilot study of interpersonal process group therapy for PTSD in Canadian Veterans. *Journal of Military, Veteran and Family Health*, 5(2), 147–158. https://doi.org/10.3138/jmvfh.2018-0001

Van Rensburg, G. (2015). The adapted open dialogue approach. In A. Meaden & A. Fox (Eds.), *Innovations in psychosocial interventions for psychosis: Working with the hard to reach* (pp. 5–21). Routledge.

van Rooij, S. J. H., Kennis, M., Sjouwerman, R., van den Heuvel, M. P., Kahn, R. S., & Geuze, E. (2015). Smaller hippocampal volume as a vulnerability factor for the persistence of post-traumatic stress disorder. *Psychological Medicine*, 45(13), 2737–2746. https://doi.org/10.1017/S0033291715000707

Van Werde, D., & Prouty, G. (2013). Clients with contact-impaired functioning: Pre-therapy. In M. Cooper, M. O'Hara, P. F. Schmid, & A. C. Bohart (Eds.), *The handbook of person-centred psychotherapy and counselling* (2013-20423-022; 2nd ed., pp. 327–342). Palgrave Macmillan/Springer Nature. https://doi.org/10.1007/978-1-137-32900-4_22

van Wijngaarden, E., Thurston, S. W., Myers, G. J., Harrington, D., Cory-Slechta, D. A., Strain, J. J., Watson, G. E., Zareba, G., Love, T., Henderson, J., Shamlaye, C. F., & Davidson, P. W. (2017). Methyl mercury exposure and neurodevelopmental outcomes in the Seychelles Child Development Study main cohort at age 22 and 24years. *Neurotoxicology and Teratology*, 59, 35–42. https://doi.org/10.1016/j.ntt.2016.10.011

Vande Voort, J. L., He, J.-P., Jameson, N. D., & Merikangas, K. R. (2014). Impact of the DSM-5 attention-deficit/hyperactivity disorder age-of-onset criterion in the US adolescent population. *Journal of the American Academy of Child & Adolescent Psychiatry*, 53(7), 736–744. https://doi.org/10.1016/j.jaac.2014.03.005

Vandereycken, W., & Van Deth, R. (1989). Who was the first to describe anorexia nervosa: Gull or Lasègue? *Psychological Medicine*, 19(4), 837–845. https://doi.org/10.1017/S0033291700005559

Vanderminden, J., & Esala, J. J. (2019). Beyond symptoms: Race and gender predict anxiety disorder diagnosis. *Society and Mental Health*, 9(1), 111–125. https://doi.org/10.1177/2156869318811435

VanFleet, R., Sywulak, A. E., & Sniscak, C. C. (2010). *Child-centered play therapy* (2010-24672-000). Guilford Press.

Vanheule, S., Desmet, M., Meganck, R., Inslegers, R., Willemsen, J., De Schryver, M., & Devisch, I. (2014). Reliability in psychiatric diagnosis with the DSM: Old wine in new barrels. *Psychotherapy and Psychosomatics*, 83(5), 313–314. https://doi.org/10.1159/000358809

Varese, F., Douglas, M., Dudley, R., Bowe, S., Christodoulides, T., Common, S., Grace, T., Lumley, V., McCartney, L., Pace, S., Reeves, T., Morrison, A. P., & Turkington, D. (2021). Targeting dissociation using cognitive behavioural therapy in voice hearers with psychosis and a history of interpersonal trauma: A case series. *Psychology and Psychotherapy: Theory, Research and Practice*, 94(2), 247–265. https://doi.org/10.1111/papt.12304

Vargas, A. S., Luís, Â., Barroso, M., Gallardo, E., & Pereira, L. (2020). Psilocybin as a new approach to treat depression and anxiety in the context of life-threatening diseases—A systematic review and meta-analysis of clinical trials. *Biomedicines*, 8(9), 331. https://doi.org/10.3390/biomedicines8090331

Vargas, I., Nguyen, A. M., Muench, A., Bastien, C. H., Ellis, J. G., & Perlis, M. L. (2020). Acute and chronic insomnia: What has time and/or hyperarousal got to do with it? *Brain Sciences*, 10(2), Article 2. https://doi.org/10.3390/brainsci10020071

Varghese, F. P., & Brown, E. S. (2001). The hypothalamic-pituitary-adrenal axis in major depressive disorder: A brief primer for primary care physicians. *Primary Care Companion to the Journal of Clinical Psychiatry*, 3(4), 151–155.

Vartanian, L. R., & Porter, A. M. (2016). Weight stigma and eating behavior: A review of the literature. *Appetite*, 102, 3–14. https://doi.org/10.1016/j.appet.2016.01.034

Vasan, S., & Padhy, R. K. (2022). Tardive dyskinesia. In *StatPearls*. StatPearls Publishing. http://www.ncbi.nlm.nih.gov/books/NBK448207/

Vasile, C. (2020). CBT and medication in depression (Review). *Experimental and Therapeutic Medicine*, 20(4), 3513–3516. https://doi.org/10.3892/etm.2020.9014

Vasile, D., & Vasiliu, O. (2022). Orthorexia nervosa – A different lifestyle or a specific eating disorder? *Psihiatru.Ro*, 68(1), 8–15.

Vaskinn, A., Melle, I., Aas, M., & Berg, A. O. (2021). Sexual abuse and physical neglect in childhood are associated with affective theory of mind in adults with schizophrenia. *Schizophrenia Research: Cognition*, 23, Article 100189. https://doi.org/10.1016/j.scog.2020.100189

Vassend, O., Røysamb, E., & Nielsen, C. S. (2012). Neuroticism and self-reported somatic health: A twin study. *Psychology & Health*, 27(1), 1–12. https://doi.org/10.1080/08870446.2010.540665

Vatanabe, I. P., Manzine, P. R., & Cominetti, M. R. (2020). Historic concepts of dementia and Alzheimer's disease: From ancient times to the present. *Revue Neurologique*, 176(3), 140–147. https://doi.org/10.1016/j.neurol.2019.03.004

Vatne, S., & Holmes, C. (2006). Limit setting in mental health: Historical factors and suggestions as to its rationale. *Journal of Psychiatric and Mental Health Nursing*, 13(5), 588–597.

Vaudreuil, C., Farrell, A., & Wozniak, J. (2021). Psychopharmacology of treating explosive behavior. *Child and Adolescent Psychiatric Clinics of North America*, 30(3), 537–560. https://doi.org/10.1016/j.chc.2021.04.006

Veijola, J., Guo, J. Y., Moilanen, J. S., Jääskeläinen, E., Miettunen, J., Kyllönen, M., Haapea, M., Huhtaniska, S., Alaräisänen, A., Mäki, P., Kiviniemi, V., Nikkinen, J., Starck, T., Remes, J. J., Tanskanen, P., Tervonen, O., Wink, A.-M., Kehagia, A., Suckling, J., … Murray, G. K. (2014). Longitudinal changes in total brain volume in schizophrenia: Relation to symptom severity, cognition and antipsychotic medication. *PLoS ONE*, 9(7).

Velikonja, T., Velthorst, E., McClure, M. M., Rutter, S., Calabrese, W. R., Rosell, D., Koenigsberg, H. W., Goodman, M., New, A. S., Hazlett, E. A., & Perez-Rodriguez, M. M. (2019). Severe childhood trauma and clinical and neurocognitive features in schizotypal personality disorder. *Acta Psychiatrica Scandinavica*, 140(1), 50–64. https://doi.org/10.1111/acps.13032

Veling, W., & Susser, E. (2011). Migration and psychotic disorders. *Expert Review of Neurotherapeutics*, 11(1), 65–76. https://doi.org/10.1586/ern.10.91

Vellutino, F. R. (2018). Ability–achievement discrepancy. In B. B. Frey (Ed.), *The SAGE encyclopedia of educational research, measurement, and evaluation* (pp. 11–14). SAGE Publications. https://doi.org/10.4135/9781506326139

Verdellen, C., van de Griendt, J., Hartmann, A., & Murphy, T. (2011). European clinical guidelines for Tourette Syndrome and other tic disorders. Part III: Behavioural and psychosocial interventions. *European Child & Adolescent Psychiatry*, 20(4), 197–207. doi:10.1007/s00787-011-0167-3

Verdurmen, M. J. H., Videler, A. C., Kamperman, A. M., Khasho, D., & van der Feltz-cornelis, C. M. (2017). Cognitive behavioral therapy for somatic symptom disorders in later life: A prospective comparative explorative pilot study in two clinical populations. *Neuropsychiatric Disease and Treatment*, 13. https://doi.org/10.2147/NDT.S141208

Verhoeff, B. (2013). Autism in flux: A history of the concept from Leo Kanner to DSM-5. *History of Psychiatry*, 24(4), 442–458. https://doi.org/10.1177/0957154X13500584

Verkuil, B., Atasayi, S., & Molendijk, M. L. (2015). Workplace bullying and mental health: A meta-analysis on cross-sectional and longitudinal data. *PLOS ONE*, 10(8), e0135225. https://doi.org/10.1371/journal.pone.0135225

Vermetten, E., Schmahl, C., Lindner, S., Loewenstein, R. J., & Bremner, J. D. (2006). Hippocampal and amygdalar volumes in dissociative identity disorder.

The American Journal of Psychiatry, 163(4), 630–636. https://doi.org/10.1176/appi.ajp.163.4.630

Vermeulen, K. (2021). *Generation disaster: Coming of age post-9/11.* Oxford University Press.

Vernberg, E. M., Steinberg, A. M., Jacobs, A. K., Brymer, M. J., Watson, P. J., Osofsky, J. D., Layne, C. M., Pynoos, R. S., & Ruzek, J. I. (2008). Innovations in disaster mental health: Psychological first aid. *Professional Psychology: Research and Practice, 39*(4), 381–388. https://doi.org/10.1037/a0012663

Veselinović, A., Petrović, S., Zikić, V., Subotić, M., Jakovljević, V., Jeremić, N., & Vučić, V. (2021). Neuroinflammation in autism and supplementation based on omega-3 polyunsaturated fatty acids: A narrative review. *Medicina, 57*(9), 893. https://doi.org/10.3390/medicina57090893

Vesga-López, O., Schneier, F. R., Wang, S., Heimberg, R. G., Liu, S.-M., Hasin, D. S., & Blanco, C. (2008). Gender differences in generalized anxiety disorder: Results from the national epidemiologic survey on alcohol and related conditions (NESARC). *Journal of Clinical Psychiatry, 69*(10), 1606–1616. https://doi.org/10.4088/JCP.v69n1011

Vespia, K. M. (2009). Culture and psychotic disorders. In S. Eshun & R. A. R. Gurung (Eds.), *Culture and mental health: Sociocultural influences, theory, and practice* (pp. 245–272). Wiley-Blackwell.

Veysey, S. (2014). People with a borderline personality disorder diagnosis describe discriminatory experiences. *Kōtuitui: New Zealand Journal of Social Sciences Online, 9*(1), 20–35. https://doi.org/10.1080/1177083X.2013.871303

Vialou, V., Bagot, R. C., Cahill, M. E., Ferguson, D., Robison, A. J., Dietz, D. M., Fallon, B., Mazei-Robison, M., M. Ku, S., Harrigan, E., Winstanley, C. A., Joshi, T., Feng, J., Berton, O., & Nestler, E. J. (2014). Prefrontal cortical circuit for depression- and anxiety-related behaviors mediated by cholecystokinin: Role of ΔFosB. *The Journal of Neuroscience, 34*(11), 3878–3887. https://doi.org/10.1523/JNEUROSCI.1787-13.2014

Vickers, A. J., & de Craen, A. J. (2000). Why use placebos in clinical trials? A narrative review of the methodological literature. *Journal of Clinical Epidemiology, 53*(2), 157–161.

Viding, E., McCrory, E., & Seara-Cardoso, A. (2014). Psychopathy. *Current Biology, 24*(18), R871–R874. https://doi.org/10.1016/j.cub.2014.06.055

Viera, H. (2016, November 21). Healing the rifts between mental health workers and psychiatric survivors. *LSE Business Review.* https://blogs.lse.ac.uk/businessreview/2016/11/21/healing-the-rifts-between-mental-health-workers-and-psychiatric-survivors/

Villarreal, G., Hamilton, D. A., Petropoulos, H., Driscoll, I., Rowland, L. M., Griego, J. A., Kodituwakku, P. W., Hart, B. L., Escalona, R., & Brooks, W. M. (2002). Reduced hippocampal volume and total white matter volume in posttraumatic stress disorder. *Biological Psychiatry, 52*(2), 119–125. https://doi.org/10.1016/S0006-3223(02)01359-8

Vincent, N. A., Nadelhoffer, T., & McCay, A. (Eds.). (2020). Chemical castration as punishment. In K. L. Sifferd, *Neurointerventions and the law: Regulating human mental capacity* (pp. 293–318). Oxford University Press. https://doi.org/10.1093/oso/9780190651145.003.0013

Viney, W., & Bartsch, L. (1984). Dorothea Lynde Dix: Positive or negative influence on the development of treatment for the mentally ill. *The Social Science Journal, 21*(2), 71–82.

Vinogradova, Y., Coupland, C., & Hippisley-Cox, J. (2020). Use of hormone replacement therapy and risk of breast cancer: Nested case-control studies using the QResearch and CPRD databases. *BMJ, 371,* Article m3873. https://doi.org/10.1136/bmj.m3873

Virues-Ortega, J., Pérez-Bustamante, A., & Tarifa-Rodriguez, A. (2022). Evidence-based applied behavior analysis (ABA) autism treatments: An overview of comprehensive and focused meta-analyses. In J. L.

Matson & P. Sturmey (Eds.), *Handbook of autism and pervasive developmental disorder: Assessment, diagnosis, and treatment* (pp. 631–659). Springer International Publishing. https://doi.org/10.1007/978-3-030-88538-0_27

Visdómine-Lozano, J. C. (2019). The fallacy of the impaired brain in attention deficit/hyperactivity disorder (ADHD) continues: A critical review of recent neuroimaging studies. *The Journal of Mind and Behavior, 40*(1), 1–28.

Vismara, L. A., & Rogers, S. J. (2010). Behavioral treatments in autism spectrum disorder: What do we know? *Annual Review of Clinical Psychology, 6,* 447–468. https://doi.org/10.1146/annurev.clinpsy.121208.131151

Visser, J., & Jehan, Z. (2009). ADHD: A scientific fact or a factual opinion? A critique of the veracity of attention deficit hyperactivity disorder. *Emotional & Behavioural Difficulties, 14*(2), 127–140. https://doi.org/10.1080/13632750902921930

Vitola, E. S., Bau, C. H. D., Salum, G. A., Horta, B. L., Quevedo, L., Barros, F. C., Pinheiro, R. T., Kieling, C., Rohde, L. A., & Grevet, E. H. (2017). Exploring DSM-5 ADHD criteria beyond young adulthood: Phenomenology, psychometric properties and prevalence in a large three-decade birth cohort. *Psychological Medicine, 47*(4), 744–754. https://doi.org/10.1017/S0033291716002853

Vogel, E. A., Rose, J. P., Roberts, L. R., & Eckles, K. (2014). Social comparison, social media, and self-esteem. *Psychology of Popular Media Culture, 3*(4), 206–222. https://doi.org/10.1037/ppm0000047

Vogt, K. S., & Norman, P. (2019). Is mentalization-based therapy effective in treating the symptoms of borderline personality disorder? A systematic review. *Psychology and Psychotherapy: Theory, Research and Practice, 92*(4), 441–464. https://doi.org/10.1111/papt.12194

Voland, E., & Voland, R. (1989). Evolutionary biology and psychiatry: The case of anorexia nervosa. *Ethology & Sociobiology, 10*(4), 223–240. doi:10.1016/0162-3095(89)90001-0

Volkmann, C., Bschor, T., & Köhler, S. (2020). Lithium treatment over the lifespan in bipolar disorders. *Frontiers in Psychiatry, 11,* Article 377. https://doi.org/10.3389/fpsyt.2020.00377

Volkmar, F. R., & Cohen, D. J. (1991). Comorbid association of autism and schizophrenia. *The American Journal of Psychiatry, 148*(12), 1705–1707. https://doi.org/10.1176/ajp.148.12.1705

Volkmar, F. R., & McPartland, J. C. (2014). From Kanner to DSM-5: Autism as an evolving diagnostic concept. *Annual Review of Clinical Psychology, 10,* 193–212. https://doi.org/10.1146/annurev-clinpsy-032813-153710

Volkow, N. D. (2020). Stigma and the toll of addiction. *New England Journal of Medicine, 382*(14), 1289–1290. https://doi.org/10.1056/NEJMp1917360

Volkow, N. D., Wang, G.-J., Kollins, S. H., Wigal, T. L., Newcorn, J. H., Telang, F., Fowler, J. S., Zhu, W., Logan, J., Ma, Y., Pradhan, K., Wong, C., & Swanson, J. M. (2009). Evaluating dopamine reward pathway in ADHD: Clinical implications. *JAMA: Journal of the American Medical Association, 302*(10), 1084–1091. https://doi.org/10.1001/jama.2009.1308

Volkow, N. D., Wang, G.-J., Tomasi, D., & Baler, R. D. (2013). The addictive dimensionality of obesity. *Biological Psychiatry, 73*(9), 811–818. https://doi.org/10.1016/j.biopsych.2012.12.020

von Bertalanffy, L. (1969). General systems theory and psychiatry—an overview. In W. Gray, F. J. Duhl, & N. D. Rizzo (Eds.), *General systems theory and psychiatry* (pp. 33–46). Little, Brown and Company.

von Dem Knesebeck, O., Lehmann, M., Löwe, B., & Makowski, A. C. (2018). Public stigma towards individuals with somatic symptom disorders – Survey results from Germany. *Journal of Psychosomatic Research, 115,* 71–75. https://doi.org/10.1016/j.jpsychores.2018.10.014

von Glischinski, M., von Brachel, R., & Hirschfeld, G. (2019). How depressed is "depressed"? A systematic review and diagnostic meta-analysis of optimal cut points for the Beck Depression Inventory revised (BDI-II). *Quality of Life Research: An International Journal of Quality of Life Aspects of Treatment, Care & Rehabilitation, 28*(5), 1111–1118. https://doi.org/10.1007/s11136-018-2050-x

von Gontard, A. (2013a). The impact of DSM-5 and guidelines for assessment and treatment of elimination disorders. *European Child & Adolescent Psychiatry, 22*(Suppl. 1), 61–67. https://doi.org/10.1007/s00787-012-0363-9

von Gontard, A. (2013b). Urinary incontinence in children with special needs. *Nature Reviews. Urology, 10*(11), 667–674. https://doi.org/10.1038/nrurol.2013.213

von Gontard, A., & Equit, M. (2015). Comorbidity of ADHD and incontinence in children. *European Child & Adolescent Psychiatry, 24*(2), 127–140. https://doi.org/10.1007/s00787-014-0577-0

von Gontard, A., Heron, J., & Joinson, C. (2011). Family history of nocturnal enuresis and urinary incontinence: Results from a large epidemiological study. *The Journal of Urology, 185*(6), 2303–2307. https://doi.org/10.1016/j.juro.2011.02.040

von Gontard, A., Hollmann, E., Eiberg, H., Benden, B., Rittig, S., & Lehmkuhl, G. (1997). Clinical enuresis phenotypes in familial nocturnal enuresis. *Scandinavian Journal of Urology and Nephrology: Supplementum, 183,* 11–16.

von Gontard, A., Schaumburg, H., Hollmann, E., Eiberg, H., & Rittig, S. (2001). The genetics of enuresis: A review. *The Journal of Urology, 166*(6), 2438–2443. https://doi.org/10.1097/00005392-200112000-00117

von Peter, S., Aderhold, V., Cubellis, L., Bergström, T., Stastny, P., Seikkula, J., & Puras, D. (2019). Open Dialogue as a human rights-aligned approach. *Frontiers in Psychiatry, 10,* Article 387. https://doi.org/10.3389/fpsyt.2019.00387

Vorgias, D., & Bernstein, B. (2022). Fetal alcohol syndrome. In *StatPearls [Internet].* StatPearls Publishing. https://www.ncbi.nlm.nih.gov/books/NBK448178/

Vos, J. (2019). A review of research on existential-phenomenological therapies. In *The Wiley world handbook of existential therapy* (pp. 592–614). John Wiley & Sons. https://doi.org/10.1002/9781119167198.ch37

Vos, J., Craig, M., & Cooper, M. (2015). Existential therapies: A meta-analysis of their effects on psychological outcomes. *Journal of Consulting and Clinical Psychology, 83*(1), 115–128. https://doi.org/10.1037/a0037167

Vos, T., Allen, C., Arora, M., Barber, R. M., Bhutta, Z. A., Brown, A., Carter, A., Casey, D. C., Charlson, F. J., Chen, A. Z., Coggeshall, M., Cornaby, L., Dandona, L., Dicker, D. J., Dilegge, T., Erskine, H. E., Ferrari, A. J., Fitzmaurice, C., Fleming, T., … Murray, C. J. L. (2016). Global, regional, and national incidence, prevalence, and years lived with disability for 310 diseases and injuries, 1990–2015: A systematic analysis for the Global Burden of Disease Study 2015. *The Lancet, 388*(10053), 1545–1602. https://doi.org/10.1016/S0140-6736(16)31678-6

Vozoris, N. T., Zhu, J., Ryan, C. M., Chow, C.-W., & To, T. (2022). Cannabis use and risks of respiratory and all-cause morbidity and mortality: A population-based, data-linkage, cohort study. *BMJ Open Respiratory Research, 9*(1), e001216. https://doi.org/10.1136/bmjresp-2022-001216

Wachbroit, R. (2001). Understanding the genetics-of-violence controversy. In D. Wasserman & R. Wachbroit (Eds.), *Genetics and criminal behavior* (pp. 25–46). Cambridge University Press. https://doi.org/10.1017/CBO9781139173162.002

Wada, K. (2022). Medicalization of grief: Its developments and paradoxes. In J. N. Lester & M. O'Reilly (Eds.), *The Palgrave encyclopedia of critical perspectives on mental health.* Springer International Publishing. https://doi.org/10.1007/978-3-030-12852-4_36-1

Wade, T. D., Gordon, S., Medland, S., Bulik, C. M., Heath, A. C., Montgomery, G. W., & Martin, N. G. (2013). Genetic variants associated with disordered eating. *The International Journal of Eating Disorders*, 46(6), 594–608. doi:10.1002/eat.22133

Wade, T. D., Tiggemann, M., Bulik, C. M., Fairburn, C. G., Wray, N. R., & Martin, N. G. (2008). Shared temperament risk factors for anorexia nervosa: A twin study. *Psychosomatic Medicine*, 70(2), 239–244. doi:10.1097/PSY.0b013e31815c40f1

Wagner, A. C., Mithoefer, M. C., Mithoefer, A. T., & Monson, C. M. (2019). Combining cognitive-behavioral conjoint therapy for PTSD with 3, 4-methylenedioxymethamphetamine (MDMA): A case example. *Journal of Psychoactive Drugs*, 51(2), 166–173. https://doi.org/10.1080/02791072.2019.1589028

Wagner, M. F., da Silva Oliveira, M., & Andretta, I. (2021). Evaluation and training of social skills in alcohol an other drugs users. In A. L. M. Andrade, D. De Micheli, E. A. da Silva, F. M. Lopes, B. de O. Pinheiro, & R. A. Reichert (Eds.), *Psychology of substance abuse: Psychotherapy, clinical management and social intervention* (pp. 259–273). Springer. https://doi.org/10.1007/978-3-030-62106-3_18

Wåhlin-Jacobsen, S., Kristensen, E., Pedersen, A. T., Laessøe, N. C., Cohen, A. S., Hougaard, D. M., Lundqvist, M., & Giraldi, A. (2017). Androgens and psychosocial factors related to sexual dysfunctions in premenopausal women. *The Journal of Sexual Medicine*, 14(3), 366–379. https://doi.org/10.1016/j.jsxm.2016.12.237

Wainberg, M., Jacobs, G. R., Di Forti, M., & Tripathy, S. J. (2021). Cannabis, schizophrenia genetic risk, and psychotic experiences: A cross-sectional study of 109, 308 participants from the UK Biobank. *Translational Psychiatry*, 11(1), 1–9. https://doi.org/10.1038/s41398-021-01330-w

Wakefield, A. J., Murch, S. H., Anthony, A., Linnell, J., Casson, D. M., Malik, M., Berelowitz, M., Dhillon, A. P., Thomson, M. A., Harvey, P., Valentine, A., Davies, S. E., & Walker-Smith, J. A. (1998). RETRACTED: Ileal-lymphoid-nodular hyperplasia, non-specific colitis, and pervasive developmental disorder in children. *Lancet (London, England)*, 351(9103), 637–641.

Wakefield, J. C. (1992a). Disorder as harmful dysfunction: A conceptual critique of DSM-III-R's definition of mental disorder. *Psychological Review*, 99, 232–247.

Wakefield, J. C. (1992b). The concept of mental disorder: On the boundary between biological facts and social values. *American Psychologist*, 47, 373–388.

Wakefield, J. C. (1999). Evolutionary versus prototype analyses of the concept of disorder. *Journal of Abnormal Psychology*, 108, 374–399.

Wakefield, J. C. (2006). Is behaviorism becoming a pseudo-science?: Power versus scientific rationality in the eclipse of token economies by biological psychiatry in the treatment of schizophrenia. *Behavior and Social Issues*, 15(2), 202–221.

Wakefield, J. C. (2011). DSM-5 proposed diagnostic criteria for sexual paraphilias: Tensions between diagnostic validity and forensic utility. *International Journal of Law and Psychiatry*, 34(3), 195–209. https://doi.org/10.1016/j.ijlp.2011.04.012

Wakefield, J. C. (2012). The DSM-5's proposed new categories of sexual disorder: The problem of false positives in sexual diagnosis. *Clinical Social Work Journal*, 40(2), 213–223. https://doi.org/10.1007/s10615-011-0353-2

Wakefield, J. C. (2013a). DSM-5: An overview of changes and controversies. *Clinical Social Work Journal*, 41(2), 139–154. https://doi.org/10.1007/s10615-013-0445-2

Wakefield, J. C. (2013b). The DSM-5 debate over the bereavement exclusion: Psychiatric diagnosis and the future of empirically supported treatment. *Clinical Psychology Review*, 33(7), 825–845. https://doi.org/10.1016/j.cpr.2013.03.007

Wakefield, J. C. (2020). Addiction from the harmful dysfunction perspective: How there can be a mental disorder in a normal brain. *Behavioural Brain Research*,

389, Article 112665. https://doi.org/10.1016/j.bbr.2020.112665

Wakefield, J. C., & First, M. B. (2012). Validity of the bereavement exclusion to major depression: Does the empirical evidence support the proposal to eliminate the exclusion in DSM-5? *World Psychiatry*, 11(1), 3–10.

Walderhaug, E., Seim-Wikse, K. J., Enger, A., & Milin, O. (2019). Polydrug use – prevalence and registration. *Tidsskrift for Den Norske Legeforening*. https://doi.org/10.4045/tidsskr.19.0251

Waldman, I. D., Poore, H. E., Luningham, J. M., & Yang, J. (2020). Testing structural models of psychopathology at the genomic level. *World Psychiatry*, 19(3), 350–359. https://doi.org/10.1002/wps.20772

Walker, W. II., Walton, J. C., DeVries, A. C., & Nelson, R. J. (2020). Circadian rhythm disruption and mental health. *Translational Psychiatry*, 10(1), Article 1. https://doi.org/10.1038/s41398-020-0694-0

Wall, B. W., Ash, P., Keram, E., Pinals, D. A., & Thompson, C. R. (2018). AAPL practice resource for the forensic psychiatric evaluation of competence to stand trial. *Journal of the American Academy of Psychiatry and the Law Online*, 46(Suppl. 3), S4–S79. https://doi.org/10.29158/JAAPL.003778-18

Waller, J. (2009). A forgotten plague: Making sense of dancing mania. *The Lancet*, 373(9664), 624–625. https://doi.org/10.1016/S0140-6736(09)60386-X

Waller, N. G., & Ross, C. A. (1997). The prevalence and biometric structure of pathological dissociation in the general population: Taxometric and behavior genetic findings. *Journal of Abnormal Psychology*, 106(4), 499–510. https://doi.org/10.1037/0021-843X.106.4.499

Wallerstein, R. S. (2011). The *Psychodynamic diagnostic manual* (PDM): Rationale, conception, and structure. *Journal of the American Psychoanalytic Association*, 59(1), 153–164. https://doi.org/10.1177/0003065111402330

Wallis, J. (2012). Looking back: This fascinating and fatal disease. *The Psychologist*, 25(10), 790–791.

Walsh, Z., Mollaahmetoglu, O. M., Rootman, J., Golsof, S., Keeler, J., Marsh, B., Nutt, D. J., & Morgan, C. J. A. (2022). Ketamine for the treatment of mental health and substance use disorders: Comprehensive systematic review. *BJPsych Open*, 8(1). https://doi.org/10.1192/bjo.2021.1061

Walsh, Z., Shea, M. T., Yen, S., Ansell, E. B., Grilo, C. M., McGlashan, T. H., Stout, R. L., Bender, D. S., Skodol, A. E., Sanislow, C. A., Morey, L. C., & Gunderson, J. G. (2013). Socioeconomic-status and mental health in a personality disorder sample: The importance of neighborhood factors. *Journal of Personality Disorders*, 27(6), 820–831. https://doi.org/10.1521/pedi_2012_26_061

Waltz, M. (2013). *Autism: A social and medical history*. Palgrave Macmillan.

Waltz, M. M. (2015). Mothers and autism: The evolution of a discourse of blame. *AMA Journal of Ethics*, 17(4), 353–358.

Wampold, B. E., & Imel, Z. E. (2015). *The great psychotherapy debate: The evidence for what makes psychotherapy work* (2nd ed.). Routledge.

Wang, G. S., Buttorff, C., Wilks, A., Schwam, D., Tung, G., & Pacula, R. L. (2021). Changes in emergency department encounters for vomiting after cannabis legalization in Colorado. *JAMA Network Open*, 4(9), e2125063. https://doi.org/10.1001/jamanetworkopen.2021.25063

Wang, G. S., Davies, S. D., Halmo, L. S., Sass, A., & Mistry, R. D. (2018). Impact of marijuana legalization in Colorado on adolescent emergency and urgent care visits. *The Journal of Adolescent Health*, 63(2), 239–241. https://doi.org/10.1016/j.jadohealth.2017.12.010

Wang, H. (2020). Nexus between cognitive reserve and modifiable risk factors of dementia. *International Psychogeriatrics*, 32(5), 559–562. https://doi.org/10.1017/S1041610220000320

Wang, J., Zhao, H., & Girgenti, M. J. (2022). Posttraumatic stress disorder brain transcriptomics: Convergent genomic signatures across biological sex. *Biological Psychiatry*, 91(1), 6–13. https://doi.org/10.1016/j.biopsych.2021.02.012

Wang, L., Hong, P. J., May, C., Rehman, Y., Oparin, Y., Hong, C. J., Hong, B. Y., AminiLari, M., Gallo, L., Kaushal, A., Craigie, S., Couban, R. J., Kum, E., Shanthanna, H., Price, I., Upadhye, S., Ware, M. A., Campbell, F., Buchbinder, R., … Busse, J. W. (2021). Medical cannabis or cannabinoids for chronic non-cancer and cancer related pain: A systematic review and meta-analysis of randomised clinical trials. *BMJ*, n1034. https://doi.org/10.1136/bmj.n1034

Wang, L., Zhao, J., Wang, C., Hou, X., Ning, N., Sun, C., Guo, S., Yuan, Y., Li, L., Hölscher, C., & Wang, X. (2020). D-Ser2-oxyntomodulin ameliorated Aβ31-35-induced circadian rhythm disorder in mice. *CNS Neuroscience & Therapeutics*, 26(3), 343–354. https://doi.org/10.1111/cns.13211

Wang, Q., Shelton, R. C., & Dwivedi, Y. (2018). Interaction between early-life stress and FKBP5 gene variants in major depressive disorder and post-traumatic stress disorder: A systematic review and meta-analysis. *Journal of Affective Disorders*, 225, 422–428. https://doi.org/10.1016/j.jad.2017.08.066

Wang, R., & Reddy, P. H. (2017). Role of glutamate and NMDA receptors in Alzheimer's disease. *Journal of Alzheimer's Disease*, 57(4), 1041–1048. https://doi.org/10.3233/JAD-160763

Wang, S., Zhang, Z., Yao, L., Ding, N., Jiang, L., & Wu, Y. (2020). Bright light therapy in the treatment of patients with bipolar disorder: A systematic review and meta-analysis. *PLOS ONE*, 15(5), e0232798. https://doi.org/10.1371/journal.pone.0232798

Wang, X. Z., Wen, Y. B., Shang, X. P., Wang, Y. H., Li, Y. W., Li, T. F., Li, S. L., Yang, J., Liu, Y. J., Lou, X. P., Zhou, W., Li, X., Zhang, J. J., Song, C. P., Jorgensen, C. S., Rittig, S., Bauer, S., Mosiello, G., Wang, Q. W., & Wen, J. G. (2019). The influence of delay elimination communication on the prevalence of primary nocturnal enuresis—A survey from Mainland China. *Neurourology and Urodynamics*, 38(5), 1423–1429. https://doi.org/10.1002/nau.24002

Wang, Y., Chung, M. C., Wang, N., Yu, X., & Kenardy, J. (2021). Social support and posttraumatic stress disorder: A meta-analysis of longitudinal studies. *Clinical Psychology Review*, 85, 101998. https://doi.org/10.1016/j.cpr.2021.101998

Wang, Y., Hsieh, L., Wang, M., Chou, C., Huang, M., & Ko, H. (2016). Coping card usage can further reduce suicide reattempt in suicide attempter case management within 3-month intervention. *Suicide and Life-Threatening Behavior*, 46(1), 106–120. https://doi.org/10.1111/sltb.12177

Wang, Y.-C., Chen, S.-K., & Lin, C.-M. (2010). Breaking the drug addiction cycle is not easy in ketamine abusers. *International Journal of Urology*, 17(5), 496. https://doi.org/10.1111/j.1442-2042.2010.02491.x

Wang, Y.-P., & Gorenstein, C. (2013). Psychometric properties of the Beck Depression Inventory-II: A comprehensive review. *Brazilian Journal of Psychiatry*, 35, 416–431. https://doi.org/10.1590/1516-4446-2012-1048

Wang, Z., Zhang, J., Lu, T., Zhang, T., Jia, M., Ruan, Y., Zhang, D., Li, J., & Wang, L. (2019). Replication of previous GWAS hits suggests the association between rs4307059 near MSNP1AS and autism in a Chinese Han population. *Progress in Neuro-Psychopharmacology and Biological Psychiatry*, 92, 194–198. https://doi.org/10.1016/j.pnpbp.2018.12.016

Wang, Z.-J., Han, Y.-F., Zhao, F., Yang, G.-Z., Yuan, L., Cai, H.-Y., Yang, J.-T., Holscher, C., Qi, J.-S., & Wu, M.-N. (2020). A dual GLP-1 and Gcg receptor agonist rescues spatial memory and synaptic plasticity in APP/PS1 transgenic mice. *Hormones and Behavior*, 118, 104640. https://doi.org/10.1016/j.yhbeh.2019.104640

Waraan, L., Rognli, E. W., Czajkowski, N. O., Aalberg, M., & Mehlum, L. (2021). Effectiveness of attachment-based family therapy compared to treatment as usual for depressed adolescents in community mental health clinics. *Child & Adolescent Psychiatry & Mental Health*, 15(1), 1–14. https://doi.org/10.1186/s13034-021-00361-x

Waraan, L., Rognli, E. W., Czajkowski, N. O., Mehlum, L., & Aalberg, M. (2021). Efficacy of attachment-based family therapy compared to treatment as usual for suicidal ideation in adolescents with MDD. *Clinical Child Psychology and Psychiatry*, 26(2), 464–474. https://doi.org/10.1177/1359104520980776

Ward, T., & Brown, M. (2004). The Good Lives Model and conceptual issues in offender rehabilitation. *Psychology, Crime & Law*, 10(3), 243–257. https://doi.org/10.1080/10683160410001662744

Ward, T., Mann, R. E., & Gannon, T. A. (2007). The good lives model of offender rehabilitation: Clinical implications. *Aggression and Violent Behavior*, 12(1), 87–107. https://doi.org/10.1016/j.avb.2006.03.004

Ward, T., & Marshall, W. L. (2004). Good lives, aetiology and the rehabilitation of sex offenders: A bridging theory. *Journal of Sexual Aggression*, 10(2), 153–169. https://doi.org/10.1080/13552600412331290102

Ward, T., & Stewart, C. (2003). Criminogenic needs and human needs: A theoretical model. *Psychology, Crime & Law*, 9(2), 125–143. https://doi.org/10.1080/1068316031000116247

Wardenaar, K. J., Lim, C. C. W., Al-Hamzawi, A. O., Alonso, J., Andrade, L. H., Benjet, C., Bunting, B., de Girolamo, G., Demyttenaere, K., Florescu, S. E., Gureje, O., Hisateru, T., Hu, C., Huang, Y., Karam, E., Kiejna, A., Lepine, J. P., Navarro-Mateu, F., Browne, M. O., … de Jonge, P. (2017). The cross-national epidemiology of specific phobia in the World Mental Health Surveys. *Psychological Medicine*, 47(10), 1744–1760. https://doi.org/10.1017/S0033291717000174

Ware, J., McIvor, L., & Fernandez, Y. M. (2021). Behavioral control models in managing sexual deviance. In L. A. Craig & R. M. Bartels (Eds.), *Sexual deviance: Understanding and managing deviant sexual interests and paraphilic disorders* (pp. 311–323). John Wiley & Sons. https://doi.org/10.1002/9781119771401.ch20

Wareham, J. (2021, March 8). *This is where LGBTQ "conversion therapy" Is illegal*. Forbes. https://www.forbes.com/sites/jamiewareham/2021/03/08/this-is-where-lgbtq-conversion-therapy-is-illegal/

Warner, M. (2014). Client processes at the difficult edge. In P. Pearce & L. Sommerbeck (Eds.), *Person-centred practice at the difficult edge* (pp. 121–137). PCCS Books.

Warner, M. S. (1998). A client-centered approach to therapeutic work with dissociated and fragile process. In L. S. Greenberg, J. C. Watson, & G. Lietaer (Eds.), *Handbook of experiential psychotherapy* (pp. 368–387). Guilford Press.

Warner, M. S. (2013). Difficult client process. In M. Cooper, M. O'Hara, P. F. Schmid, & A. C. Bohart (Eds.), *The handbook of person-centred psychotherapy and counselling* (2nd ed., pp. 343–358). Palgrave Macmillan.

Warren, C. S., & Akoury, L. M. (2020). Emphasizing the "cultural" in sociocultural: A systematic review of research on thin-ideal internalization, acculturation, and eating pathology in US ethnic minorities. *Psychology Research and Behavior Management*, 13, 319–330. https://doi.org/10.2147/PRBM.S204274

Warren, R. (2020). Cognitive-behavior therapy for generalized anxiety disorder: Recent developments in theory and treatment. *Anxiety and Depression Journal*, 3(1), 122.

Warrier, V. (2020). Delineating the shared genetics across the mood disorders spectrum. *Biological Psychiatry*, 88(2), 134–135. https://doi.org/10.1016/j.biopsych.2020.04.017

Warrier, V., Greenberg, D. M., Weir, E., Buckingham, C., Smith, P., Lai, M.-C., Allison, C., & Baron-Cohen, S. (2020). Elevated rates of autism, other neurodevelopmental and psychiatric diagnoses, and autistic traits in transgender and gender-diverse individuals. *Nature Communications*, 11(1), 3959. https://doi.org/10.1038/s41467-020-17794-1

Waschbusch, D. A., & Waxmonsky, J. G. (2015). Empirically supported, promising, and unsupported treatments for attention-deficit/hyperactivity disorder. In S. O. Lilienfeld, S. J. Lynn, & J. M. Lohr (Eds.), *Science and pseudoscience in clinical psychology* (2014-57878-013; 2nd ed., pp. 391–430). Guilford Press.

Wasil, A. R., Patel, R., Cho, J. Y., Shingleton, R. M., Weisz, J. R., & DeRubeis, R. J. (2021). Smartphone apps for eating disorders: A systematic review of evidence-based content and application of user-adjusted analyses. *International Journal of Eating Disorders*, 54(5), 690–700. https://doi.org/10.1002/eat.23478

Wasser, S. K., & Barash, D. P. (1983). Reproductive suppression among female mammals: Implications for biomedicine and sexual selection theory. *The Quarterly Review of Biology*, 58(4), 513–538.

Waszczuk, M. A. (2021). The utility of hierarchical models of psychopathology in genetics and biomarker research. *World Psychiatry*, 20(1), 65–66. https://doi.org/10.1002/wps.20811

Waszczuk, M. A., Eaton, N. R., Krueger, R. F., Shackman, A. J., Waldman, I. D., Zald, D. H., Lahey, B. B., Patrick, C. J., Conway, C. C., Ormel, J., Hyman, S. E., Fried, E. I., Forbes, M. K., Docherty, A. R., Althoff, R. R., Bach, B., Chmielewski, M., DeYoung, C. G., Forbush, K. T., … Kotov, R. (2020). Redefining phenotypes to advance psychiatric genetics: Implications from hierarchical taxonomy of psychopathology. *Journal of Abnormal Psychology*, 129(2), 143–161. https://doi.org/10.1037/abn0000486

Waters, E., Posada, G., Crowell, J., & Keng-ling, L. (1993). Is attachment theory ready to contribute to our understanding of disruptive behavior problems? *Development and Psychopathology*, 5(1–2), 215–224. https://doi.org/10.1017/S0954579400004351

Watkins, L. E., Sprang, K. R., & Rothbaum, B. O. (2018). Treating PTSD: A review of evidence-based psychotherapy interventions. *Frontiers in Behavioral Neuroscience*, 12, Article 258. https://doi.org/10.3389/fnbeh.2018.00258

Watson, D. C. (2015). Materialism and the five-factor model of personality: A facet-level analysis. *North American Journal of Psychology*, 17(1), 133–150.

Watson, D., Forbes, M. K., Levin-Aspenson, H. F., Ruggero, C. J., Kotelnikova, Y., Khoo, S., Bagby, R. M., Sunderland, M., Patalay, P., & Kotov, R. (2022). The development of preliminary HiTOP internalizing spectrum scales. *Assessment*, 29(1), 17–33. https://doi.org/10.1177/10731911211003976

Watson, D., Levin-Aspenson, H. F., Waszczuk, M. A., Conway, C. C., Dalgleish, T., Dretsch, M. N., Eaton, N. R., Forbes, M. K., Forbush, K. T., Hobbs, K. A., Michelini, G., Nelson, B. D., Sellbom, M., Slade, T., South, S. C., Sunderland, M., Waldman, I., Witthöft, M., Wright, A. G. C., … Zinbarg, R. E. (2022). Validity and utility of hierarchical taxonomy of psychopathology (HiTOP): III. Emotional dysfunction superspectrum. *World Psychiatry*, 21(1), 26–54. https://doi.org/10.1002/wps.20943

Watson, J. B., & Rayner, R. (1920). Conditioned emotional reactions. *Journal of Experimental Psychology*, 3(1), 1–14. https://doi.org/10.1037/h0069608

Watson, P. J., & Andrews, P. W. (2002). Toward a revised evolutionary adaptationist analysis of depression: The social navigation hypothesis. *Journal of Affective Disorders*, 72(1), 1–14. https://doi.org/10.1016/S0165-0327(01)00459-1

Waugh, M. H., Ridenour, J. M., & Lewis, K. C. (2022). The alternative *DSM* model for personality disorders in psychological assessment and treatment. In S. K. Huprich (Ed.), *Personality disorders and pathology: Integrating clinical assessment and practice in the DSM-5 and ICD-11 era* (pp. 159–182). American Psychological Association. https://doi.org/10.1037/0000310-008

Weber, J., & Czarnetzki, A. (2001). Trepanationen im frühen Mittelalter im Südwesten von Deutschland—Indikationen, Komplikationen und Outcome [Trepanations from the early medieval period of southwestern Germany—Indications, complications and outcome]. *Central European Neurosurgery*, 62(1), 10–14. https://doi.org/10.1055/s-2001-16333

Weber, M., Davis, K., & McPhie, L. (2006). Narrative therapy, eating disorders and groups: Enhancing outcomes in rural NSW. *Australian Social Work*, 59(4), 391–405. https://doi.org/10.1080/03124070600985970

Weber, S., Hjelmervik, H., Craven, A. R., Johnsen, E., Kroken, R. A., Løberg, E.-M., Ersland, L., Kompus, K., & Hugdahl, K. (2021). Glutamate- and GABA-modulated connectivity in auditory hallucinations-A combined resting state fMRI and MR spectroscopy study. *Frontiers in Psychiatry*, 12, Article 643564. https://doi.org/10.3389/fpsyt.2021.643564

Weber, S., Messingschlager, T., & Stein, J.-P. (2022). This is an Insta-vention! Exploring cognitive countermeasures to reduce negative consequences of social comparisons on Instagram. *Media Psychology*, 25(3), 411–440. https://doi.org/10.1080/15213269.2021.1968440

Weck, F., Gropalis, M., Hiller, W., & Bleichhardt, G. (2015). Effectiveness of cognitive-behavioral group therapy for patients with hypochondriasis (health anxiety). *Journal of Anxiety Disorders*, 30, 1–7. https://doi.org/10.1016/j.janxdis.2014.12.012

Wegemer, C. M. (2020). Selflessness, depression, and neuroticism: An interactionist perspective on the effects of self-transcendence, perspective-taking, and materialism. *Frontiers in Psychology*, 11, Article 523950. https://doi.org/10.3389/fpsyg.2020.523950

Wegner, M., Amatriain-Fernández, S., Kaulitzky, A., Murillo-Rodriguez, E., Machado, S., & Budde, H. (2020). Systematic review of meta-analyses: Exercise effects on depression in children and adolescents. *Frontiers in Psychiatry*, 11, Article 81. https://doi.org/10.3389/fpsyt.2020.00081

Wei, D., Liu, Y., Zhuang, K., Lv, J., Meng, J., Sun, J., Chen, Q., Yang, W., & Qiu, J. (2020). Brain structures associated with individual differences in somatic symptoms and emotional distress in a healthy sample. *Frontiers in Human Neuroscience*, 14, Article 492990. https://doi.org/10.3389/fnhum.2020.492990

Wei, Y., & Shah, R. (2020). Substance use disorder in the COVID-19 pandemic: A systematic review of vulnerabilities and complications. *Pharmaceuticals*, 13(7), Article 7. https://doi.org/10.3390/ph13070155

Weigel, A., Löwe, B., & Kohlmann, S. (2019). Severity of somatic symptoms in outpatients with anorexia and bulimia nervosa. *European Eating Disorders Review*, 27(2), 195–204. https://doi.org/10.1002/erv.2643

Weinberger, D. R. (1987). Implications of normal brain development for the pathogenesis of schizophrenia. *Archives of General Psychiatry*, 44(7), 660–669.

Weinberger, J. M., Houman, J., Caron, A. T., & Anger, J. (2019). Female sexual dysfunction: A systematic review of outcomes across various treatment modalities. *Sexual Medicine Reviews*, 7(2), 223–250. https://doi.org/10.1016/j.sxmr.2017.12.004

Weiner, I. B. (2004). Rorschach assessment: Current status. In M. J. Hilsenroth & D. L. Segal (Eds.), *Comprehensive handbook of psychological assessment: Vol. 2. Personality assessment* (pp. 343–355). John Wiley.

Weiner, L. (2022). Sensate focus touch in sexual health and sex therapy: A critical literature review. *Journal of Sexual Medicine*, 19(5(Suppl. 2)), S152. https://doi.org/10.1016/j.jsxm.2022.03.350

Weiner, L., & Avery-Clark, C. (2014). Sensate focus: Clarifying the Masters and Johnson's model. *Sexual and Relationship Therapy*, 29(3), 307–319. https://doi.org/10.1080/14681994.2014.892920

Weiner, M. W., Veitch, D. P., Aisen, P. S., Beckett, L. A., Cairns, N. J., Cedarbaum, J., Green, R. C., Harvey, D., Jack, C. R., Jagust, W., Luthman, J., Morris, J. C., Petersen, R. C., Saykin, A. J., Shaw, L., Shen, L., Schwarz, A., Toga, A. W., & Trojanowski, J. Q. (2015).

2014 update of the Alzheimer's disease neuroimaging initiative: A review of papers published since its inception. *Alzheimer's & Dementia: The Journal of the Alzheimer's Association, 11*(6), e1–e120. https://doi.org/10.1016/j.jalz.2014.11.001

Weingarten, C. P., & Strauman, T. J. (2015). Neuroimaging for psychotherapy research: Current trends. *Psychotherapy Research, 25*(2), 185–213. https://doi.org/10.1080/10503307.2014.883088

Weiss, M., Murray, C., Wasdell, M., Greenfield, B., Giles, L., & Hechtman, L. (2012). A randomized controlled trial of CBT therapy for adults with ADHD with and without medication. *BMC Psychiatry, 12*. https://doi.org/10.1186/1471-244X-12-30

Weiss, R. V., Hohl, A., Athayde, A., Pardini, D., Gomes, L., Oliveira, M. de, Meirelles, R., Clapauch, R., & Spritzer, P. M. (2019). Testosterone therapy for women with low sexual desire: A position statement from the Brazilian Society of Endocrinology and Metabolism. *Archives of Endocrinology and Metabolism, 63*(3), 190–198. https://doi.org/10.20945/2359-3997000000152

Weiss, T., Skelton, K., Phifer, J., Jovanovic, T., Gillespie, C. F., Smith, A., Umpierrez, G., Bradley, B., & Ressler, K. J. (2011). Posttraumatic stress disorder is a risk factor for metabolic syndrome in an impoverished urban population. *General Hospital Psychiatry, 33*(2), 135–142. https://doi.org/10.1016/j.genhosppsych.2011.01.002

Weissman, R. S. (2019). The role of sociocultural factors in the etiology of eating disorders. *Psychiatric Clinics of North America, 42*(1), 121–144. https://doi.org/10.1016/j.psc.2018.10.009

Wells, A. (1995). Meta-cognition and worry: A cognitive model of generalized anxiety disorder. *Behavioural and Cognitive Psychotherapy, 23*(3), 301–320. https://doi.org/10.1017/S1352465800015897

Wells, A. (2010). Metacognitive theory and therapy for worry and generalized anxiety disorder: Review and status. *Journal of Experimental Psychopathology, 1*(1), jep.007910. https://doi.org/10.5127/jep.007910

Wells, M. C., Glickauf-Hughes, C., & Buzzell, V. (1990). Treating obsessive-compulsive personalities in psychodynamic/interpersonal group therapy. *Psychotherapy: Theory, Research, Practice, Training, 27*(3), 366–379. https://doi.org/10.1037/0033-3204.27.3.366

Wender, P. H., Rosenthal, D., Kety, S. S., Schulsinger, F., & Welner, J. (1974). Crossfostering: A research strategy for clarifying the role of genetic and experiential factors in the etiology of schizophrenia. *Archives of General Psychiatry, 30*(1), 121–128. https://doi.org/10.1001/archpsyc.1974.01760070097016

Wenthur, C. J. (2016). Classics in chemical neuroscience: Methylphenidate. *ACS Chemical Neuroscience, 7*(8), 1030–1040. https://doi.org/10.1021/acschemneuro.6b00199

Wenzel, A., & Beck, A. T. (2008). A cognitive model of suicidal behavior: Theory and treatment. *Applied and Preventive Psychology, 12*(4), 189–201. https://doi.org/10.1016/j.appsy.2008.05.001

Werneke, U., Ott, M., Renberg, E. S., Taylor, D., & Stegmayr, B. (2012). A decision analysis of long-term lithium treatment and the risk of renal failure. *Acta Psychiatrica Scandinavica, 126*(3), 186–197. https://doi.org/10.1111/j.1600-0447.2012.01847.x

Westen, D., Lohr, N., Silk, K. R., Gold, L., & Kerber, K. (1990). Object relations and social cognition in borderlines, major depressives, and normals: A Thematic Apperception Test analysis. *Psychological Assessment: A Journal of Consulting and Clinical Psychology, 2*(4), 355–364. https://doi.org/10.1037/1040-3590.2.4.355

Westermeyer, J. (2005). Historical and social context of psychoactive substance use disorders. In R. J. Frances, S. I. Miller, & A. H. Mack (Eds.), *Clinical textbook of addictive disorders* (3rd ed., pp. 16–34). Guilford Publications.

Westermeyer, J. (2013). Historical understandings of addiction. In P. M. Miller, S. A. Ball, M. E. Bates, A.

W. Blume, K. M. Kampman, D. J. Kavanagh, M. E. Larimer, N. M. Petry, & P. De Witte (Eds.), *Comprehensive addictive behaviors and disorders: Vol. 1. Principles of addiction* (pp. 3–12). Elsevier Academic Press.

Weston, C. S. E. (2019). Four social brain regions, their dysfunctions, and sequelae, extensively explain autism spectrum disorder symptomatology. *Brain Sciences, 9*(6), E130. https://doi.org/10.3390/brainsci9060130

Wetherell, J. L. (2012). Complicated grief therapy as a new treatment approach. *Dialogues in Clinical Neuroscience, 14*(2), 159–166.

Wettstein, R. M. (1999). The right to refuse psychiatric treatment. *Psychiatric Clinics of North America, 22*(1), 173–182. https://doi.org/10.1016/S0193-953X(05)70067-8

Wetzler, S., Hackmann, C., Peryer, G., Clayman, K., Friedman, D., Saffran, K., Silver, J., Swarbrick, M., Magill, E., Furth, E. F., & Pike, K. M. (2020). A framework to conceptualize personal recovery from eating disorders: A systematic review and qualitative meta-synthesis of perspectives from individuals with lived experience. *International Journal of Eating Disorders, 53*(8), 1188–1203. https://doi.org/10.1002/eat.23260

Weyandt, L., Oster, D., Marraccini, M. E., Gudmundsdottir, B., Munro, B., Martinez Zavras, B., & Kuhar, B. (2014). Pharmacological interventions for adolescents and adults with ADHD: Stimulant and nonstimulant medications and misuse of prescription stimulants. *Psychology Research and Behavior Management*, 223. https://doi.org/10.2147/PRBM.S47013

Whaley, A. L. (2004). Paranoia in African-American men receiving inpatient psychiatric treatment. *Journal of the American Academy of Psychiatry and the Law, 32*(3), 282–290.

Wheeler, A. C., Raspa, M., Bishop, E., & Bailey, D. B. (2016). Aggression in fragile X syndrome. *Journal of Intellectual Disability Research, 60*(2), 113–125. https://doi.org/10.1111/jir.12238

Whiston, A., Bockting, C. L. H., & Semkovska, M. (2019). Towards personalising treatment: A systematic review and meta-analysis of face-to-face efficacy moderators of cognitive-behavioral therapy and interpersonal psychotherapy for major depressive disorder. *Psychological Medicine, 49*(16), 2657–2668. https://doi.org/10.1017/S0033291719002812

Whitaker, H. (2019, December 27). The patriarchy of alcoholics anonymous. *The New York Times*. https://www.nytimes.com/2019/12/27/opinion/alcoholics-anonymous-women.html

Whitaker, R. (2002). *Mad in America: Bad science, bad medicine, and the enduring mistreatment of the mentally ill*. Perseus Publishing.

Whitaker, R. (2010). *Anatomy of an epidemic: Magic bullets, psychiatric drugs, and the astonishing rise of mental illness in America*. Broadway Paperbacks.

Whitaker, R. (2012). Weighing the evidence: What science has to say about prescribing atypical antipsychotics to children. In S. Olfman & B. D. Robbins (Eds.), *Drugging our children: How profiteers are pushing antipsychotics on our youngest, and what we can do to stop it* (pp. 3–16). Praeger/ABC-CLIO.

White, C., & Fessler, D. M. T. (2017). An evolutionary account of vigilance in grief. *Evolution, Medicine, and Public Health, 2018*(1), 34–42. https://doi.org/10.1093/emph/eox018

White, M., & Epston, D. (1990). *Narrative means to therapeutic ends*. Norton.

White, W. L. (2007). Addiction recovery: Its definition and conceptual boundaries. *Journal of Substance Abuse Treatment, 33*(3), 229–241. https://doi.org/10.1016/j.jsat.2007.04.015

Whitehead, P. M., & Purvis, K. (2021). Humanizing autism research and treatment: Facilitating individuation through person-centered therapy. *The Humanistic Psychologist*, No Pagination Specified-No Pagination Specified. https://doi.org/10.1037/hum0000249

Whitehead, P. R., Ward, T., & Collie, R. M. (2007). Time for a change: Applying the Good Lives Model of rehabilitation to a high-risk violent offender. *International Journal of Offender Therapy and Comparative Criminology, 51*(5), 578–598. https://doi.org/10.1177/0306624X06296236

Whitely, M. (2015). Attention deficit hyperactive disorder diagnosis continues to fail the reliability and validity tests. *Australian and New Zealand Journal of Psychiatry, 49*(6), 497–498. https://doi.org/10.1177/0004867415579921

Whitley, R. (2021). *Men's issues and men's mental health: An introductory primer*. Springer International Publishing. https://doi.org/10.1007/978-3-030-86320-3

WHO Advisory Group. (1980). The dependence potential of thebaine. *Bulletin on Narcotics, 32*(1), 45–54.

Widiger, T. A. (2015). Assessment of DSM-5 personality disorder. *Journal of Personality Assessment, 97*(5), 456–466. https://doi.org/10.1080/00223891.2015.1041142

Widiger, T. A. (2020). Classification and diagnosis: Historical development and contemporary issues. In J. E. Maddux & B. A. Winstead (Eds.), *Psychopathology: Foundations for a contemporary understanding* (5th ed., pp. 109–124). Routledge.

Widiger, T. A., & Costa Jr., Paul T. (2012). Integrating normal and abnormal personality structure: The Five-Factor Model. *Journal of Personality, 80*(6), 1471–1506. https://doi.org/10.1111/j.1467-6494.2012.00776.x

Widiger, T. A., & Crego, C. (2019). The Five Factor Model of personality structure: An update. *World Psychiatry, 18*(3), 271–272. https://doi.org/10.1002/wps.20658

Widiger, T. A., & Hines, A. (2022). The *Diagnostic and statistical manual of mental disorders, fifth edition* alternative model of personality disorder. *Personality Disorders: Theory, Research, and Treatment, 13*(4), 347–355. https://doi.org/10.1037/per0000524

Widiger, T. A., & McCabe, G. A. (2020). The alternative model of personality disorders (AMPD) from the perspective of the five-factor model. *Psychopathology, 53*(3), 149–156. https://doi.org/10.1159/000507378

Widiger, T. A., & Presnall, J. R. (2013). Clinical application of the Five-Factor Model. *Journal of Personality, 81*(6), 515–527. https://doi.org/10.1111/jopy.12004

Widiger, T. A., Sellbom, M., Chmielewski, M., Clark, L. A., DeYoung, C. G., Kotov, R., Krueger, R. F., Lynam, D. R., Miller, J. D., Mullins-Sweatt, S., Samuel, D. B., South, S. C., Tackett, J. L., Thomas, K. M., Watson, D., & Wright, A. G. C. (2019). Personality in a hierarchical model of psychopathology. *Clinical Psychological Science, 7*(1), 77–92. https://doi.org/10.1177/2167702618797105

Wignall, E. L., Dickson, J. M., Vaughan, P., Farrow, T. F. D., Wilkinson, Iain D., Hunter, M. D., & Woodruff, P. W. R. (2004). Smaller hippocampal volume in patients with recent-onset posttraumatic stress disorder. *Biological Psychiatry, 56*(11), 832–836. https://doi.org/10.1016/j.biopsych.2004.09.015

Wilens, T. E., & Kaminski, T. A. (2019). Prescription stimulants: From cognitive enhancement to misuse. *Pediatric Clinics of North America, 66*(6), 1109–1120. https://doi.org/10.1016/j.pcl.2019.08.006

Wiles, N. J., Thomas, L., Turner, N., Garfield, K., Kounali, D., Campbell, J., Kessler, D., Kuyken, W., Lewis, G., Morrison, J., Williams, C., Peters, T. J., & Hollinghurst, S. (2016). Long-term effectiveness and cost-effectiveness of cognitive behavioural therapy as an adjunct to pharmacotherapy for treatment-resistant depression in primary care: Follow-up of the CoBalT randomised controlled trial. *The Lancet Psychiatry, 3*(2), 137–144. https://doi.org/10.1016/S2215-0366(15)00495-2

Wilhelm, K. A. (2009). Men and depression. *Australian Family Physician, 38*(3), 102–105.

Wilkenfeld, D. A., & McCarthy, A. M. (2020). Ethical concerns with applied behavior analysis for autism spectrum "disorder." *Kennedy Institute of Ethics*

Journal, 30(1), 31–69. https://doi.org/10.1353/ken.2020.0000

Wilks, C. R., Morland, L. A., Dillon, K. H., Mackintosh, M.-A., Blakey, S. M., Wagner, H. R., & Elbogen, E. B. (2019). Anger, social support, and suicide risk in U.S. military veterans. Journal of Psychiatric Research, 109, 139–144. https://doi.org/10.1016/j.jpsychires.2018.11.026

Willcutt, E. G., McGrath, L. M., Pennington, B. F., Keenan, J. M., DeFries, J. C., Olson, R. K., & Wadsworth, S. J. (2019). Understanding comorbidity between specific learning disabilities. New Directions for Child and Adolescent Development, 2019(165), 91–109. https://doi.org/10.1002/cad.20291

Williams, D. R., Yu, Y., Jackson, J. S., & Anderson, N. B. (1997). Racial differences in physical and mental health: Socio-economic status, stress and discrimination. Journal of Health Psychology, 2(3), 335–351. https://doi.org/10.1177/135910539700200305

Williams, K., Lund, T. J., Liang, B., Mousseau, A. D., & Spencer, R. (2018). Associations between stress, psychosomatic complaints, and parental criticism among affluent adolescent girls. Journal of Child and Family Studies, 27(5), 1384–1393. https://doi.org/10.1007/s10826-017-0991-2

Williams, M., Malcoun, E., Sawyer, B., Davis, D., Nouri, L., & Bruce, S. (2014). Cultural adaptations of prolonged exposure therapy for treatment and prevention of posttraumatic stress disorder in African Americans. Behavioral Sciences, 4(2), 102–124. https://doi.org/10.3390/bs4020102

Williams, M. T., Davis, D. M., Powers, M., & Weissflog, L. O. (2014). Current trends in prescribing medications for obsessive-compulsive disorder: Best practices and new research. Directions in Psychiatry, 34(4), 247–259.

Williams, M. T., Metzger, I. W., Leins, C., & DeLapp, C. (2018). Assessing racial trauma within a DSM-5 framework: The UConn Racial/Ethnic Stress & Trauma Survey. Practice Innovations, 3(4), 242–260. https://doi.org/10.1037/pri0000076

Williams, M. T., Osman, M., Gran-Ruaz, S., & Lopez, J. (2021). Intersection of racism and PTSD: Assessment and treatment of racial stress and trauma. Current Treatment Options in Psychiatry, 8(4), 167–185. https://doi.org/10.1007/s40501-021-00250-2

Williams, N., Jean-Louis, G., Blanc, J., & Wallace, D. M. (2019). Race, socioeconomic position and sleep. In M. A. Grandner (Ed.), Sleep and health (pp. 57–76). Academic Press. https://doi.org/10.1016/B978-0-12-815373-4.00006-X

Williams, R. A., Mamotte, C. D. S., & Burnett, J. R. (2008). Phenylketonuria: An inborn error of phenylalanine metabolism. The Clinical Biochemist Reviews, 29(1), 31–41.

Williams, S. P. (2001). Reaching the hard to reach: Implications of the New View of women's sexual problems. Women & Therapy, 24(1–2), 39–42.

Williamson, J. B., Heilman, K. M., Porges, E. C., Lamb, D. G., & Porges, S. W. (2013). A possible mechanism for PTSD symptoms in patients with traumatic brain injury: Central autonomic network disruption. Frontiers In Neuroengineering, 6, Article 13. https://doi.org/10.3389/fneng.2013.00013

Willick, M. S. (2001). Psychoanalysis and schizophrenia: A cautionary tale. Journal of the American Psychoanalytic Association, 49(1), 27–56. https://doi.org/10.1177/00030651010490012001

Willsky, K. (2022, February 24). Sharing your eating disorder recovery online can be risky, experts say. Follow this advice. Washington Post. https://www.washingtonpost.com/wellness/2022/02/04/eating-disorder-recovery-social-media/

Wilson, D. M., Cohen, J., MacLeod, R., & Houttekier, D. (2018). Bereavement grief: A population-based foundational evidence study. Death Studies, 42(7), 463–469. https://doi.org/10.1080/07481187.2017.1382609

Wilson, G., Farrell, D., Barron, I., Hutchins, J., Whybrow, D., & Kiernan, M. D. (2018). The use of eye-movement desensitization reprocessing (EMDR) therapy in treating post-traumatic stress disorder—A systematic narrative review. Frontiers in Psychology, 9, Article 923. https://doi.org/10.3389/fpsyg.2018.00923

Wilson, K. G., & Roberts, M. (2002). Core principles in acceptance and commitment therapy: An application to anorexia. Cognitive and Behavioral Practice, 9(3), 237–243. https://doi.org/10.1016/S1077-7229(02)80054-2

Wilson, T. K., & Tripp, J. (2022). Buspirone. In StatPearls. StatPearls Publishing. http://www.ncbi.nlm.nih.gov/books/NBK531477/

Winder, B., Fedoroff, J. P., Grubin, D., Klapilová, K., Kamenskov, M., Tucker, D., Basinskaya, I. A., & Vvedensky, G. E. (2019). The pharmacologic treatment of problematic sexual interests, paraphilic disorders, and sexual preoccupation in adult men who have committed a sexual offence. International Review of Psychiatry, 31(2), 159–168. https://doi.org/10.1080/09540261.2019.1577223

Winegard, B. M., Reynolds, T., Baumeister, R. F., Winegard, B., & Maner, J. K. (2014). Grief functions as an honest indicator of commitment. Personality and Social Psychology Review, 18(2), 168–186. https://doi.org/10.1177/1088868314521016

Winerman, L. (2013, August). NIMH funding to shift away from DSM categories. Monitor on Psychology, 44(7), 10.

Wing, L. (1981). Asperger's syndrome: A clinical account. Psychological Medicine, 11(1), 115–129. https://doi.org/10.1017/S0033291700053332

Wingo, T. S., Lah, J. J., Levey, A. I., & Cutler, D. J. (2012). Autosomal recessive causes likely in early-onset Alzheimer disease. Archives of Neurology, 69(1), 59–64. https://doi.org/10.1001/archneurol.2011.221

Winstead, B. A., & Sanchez-Hucles, J. (2020). Gender, race, and class and their role in psychopathology. In J. E. Maddux & B. A. Winstead (Eds.), Psychopathology: Foundations for a contemporary understanding (5th ed., pp. 85–107). Routledge.

Winstock, A. R., Lintzeris, N., & Lea, T. (2011). "Should I stay or should I go?" Coming off methadone and buprenorphine treatment. International Journal of Drug Policy, 22(1), 77–81. https://doi.org/10.1016/j.drugpo.2010.08.001

Winstock, A. R., Mitcheson, L., Gillatt, D. A., & Cottrell, A. M. (2012). The prevalence and natural history of urinary symptoms among recreational ketamine users. BJU International, 110(11), 1762–1766. https://doi.org/10.1111/j.1464-410X.2012.11028.x

Winston, T. (2012). Psychodynamic approaches to eating disorders. In J. Fox & K. Goss (Eds.), Eating and its disorders (pp. 244–259). Wiley-Blackwell. https://doi.org/10.1002/9781118328910.ch17

Winters, N. (2013). Whether to break confidentiality: An ethical dilemma. Journal of Emergency Nursing, 39(3), 233–235. https://doi.org/10.1016/j.jen.2012.03.003

Winton-Brown, T. T., & Kapur, S. (2021). Aberrant salience attribution and psychosis. In C. A. Tamminga, E. I. Ivleva, U. Reininghaus, & J. van Os (Eds.), Psychotic disorders: Comprehensive conceptualization and treatments (pp. 442–450). Oxford University Press. https://doi.org/10.1093/med/9780190653279.003.0049

Wirth-Cauchon, J. (2000). A dangerous symbolic mobility: Narratives of borderline personality disorder. In D. Fee (Ed.), Pathology and the postmodern: Mental illness as discourse and experience (pp. 141–162). SAGE.

Wise, M. S., Arand, D. L., Auger, R. R., Brooks, S. N., & Watson, N. F. (2007). Treatment of narcolepsy and other hypersomnias of central origin: An American Academy of Sleep Medicine review. Sleep, 30(12), 1712–1727. https://doi.org/10.1093/sleep/30.12.1712

Wise, R. A. (2013). Dual roles of dopamine in food and drug seeking: The drive-reward paradox. Biological Psychiatry, 73(9), 819–826. https://doi.org/10.1016/j.biopsych.2012.09.001

Wise, R. A., & Jordan, C. J. (2021). Dopamine, behavior, and addiction. Journal of Biomedical Science, 28(1), 83. https://doi.org/10.1186/s12929-021-00779-7

Wise, R. A., & Robble, M. A. (2020). Dopamine and addiction. Annual Review of Psychology, 71(1), 79–106. https://doi.org/10.1146/annurev-psych-010418-103337

Witkiewitz, K., & Alan Marlatt, G. (2006). Overview of harm reduction treatments for alcohol problems. International Journal of Drug Policy, 17(4), 285–294. https://doi.org/10.1016/j.drugpo.2006.03.005

Witkiewitz, K., Litten, R. Z., & Leggio, L. (2019). Advances in the science and treatment of alcohol use disorder. Science Advances, 5(9), eaax4043. https://doi.org/10.1126/sciadv.aax4043

Witkiewitz, K., & Marlatt, G. A. (2004). Relapse prevention for alcohol and drug problems: That was Zen, this Is Tao. American Psychologist, 59(4), 224–235. https://doi.org/10.1037/0003-066X.59.4.224

Wittouck, C., Van Autreve, S., De Jaegere, E., Portzky, G., & van Heeringen, K. (2011). The prevention and treatment of complicated grief: A meta-analysis. Clinical Psychology Review, 31(1), 69–78. https://doi.org/10.1016/j.cpr.2010.09.005

Wolf, E. J., Rasmusson, A. M., Mitchell, K. S., Logue, M. W., Baldwin, C. T., & Miller, M. W. (2014). A genome-wide association study of clinical symptoms of dissociation in a trauma-exposed sample. Depression and Anxiety, 31(4), 352–360. https://doi.org/10.1002/da.22260

Wolf, N. J., & Hopko, D. R. (2008). Psychosocial and pharmacological interventions for depressed adults in primary care: A critical review. Clinical Psychology Review, 28(1), 131–161. https://doi.org/10.1016/j.cpr.2007.04.004

Wolff, M., Alsobrook, I., John P., & Pauls, D. L. (2000). Genetic aspects of obsessive-compulsive disorder. Psychiatric Clinics of North America, 23(3), 535–544. https://doi.org/10.1016/S0193-953X(05)70179-9

Wolff, M., Evens, R., Mertens, L. J., Koslowski, M., Betzler, F., Gründer, G., & Jungaberle, H. (2020). Learning to let go: A cognitive-behavioral model of how psychedelic therapy promotes acceptance. Frontiers in Psychiatry, 11, Article 5. https://doi.org/10.3389/fpsyt.2020.00005

Wolff, S. (2004). The history of autism. European Child & Adolescent Psychiatry, 13(4), 201–208. https://doi.org/10.1007/s00787-004-0363-5

Woloshin, S., & Schwartz, L. M. (2016). US Food and Drug Administration approval of flibanserin: Even the score does not add up. JAMA Internal Medicine, 176(4), 439–442. https://doi.org/10.1001/jamainternmed.2016.0073

Wolpe, J. (1961). The systematic desensitization treatment of neuroses. Journal of Nervous and Mental Disease, 132, 189–203. https://doi.org/10.1097/00005053-196103000-00001

Wolpe, J. (1968). Psychotherapy by reciprocal inhibition. Conditional Reflex: A Pavlovian Journal of Research & Therapy, 3(4), 234–240. https://doi.org/10.1007/BF03000093

Wolz, R., Schwarz, A. J., Yu, P., Cole, P. E., Rueckert, D., Jack, C. R., Raunig, D., & Hill, D. (2014). Robustness of automated hippocampal volumetry across magnetic resonance field strengths and repeat images. Alzheimer's & Dementia: The Journal of the Alzheimer's Association, 10(4), 430–438. https://doi.org/10.1016/j.jalz.2013.09.014

Wong, L. C., Huang, H.-L., Weng, W.-C., Jong, Y.-J., Yin, Y.-J., Chen, H.-A., Lee, W.-T., & Ho, S.-Y. (2016). Increased risk of epilepsy in children with Tourette syndrome: A population-based case-control study. Research in Developmental Disabilities, 51–52, 181–187. https://doi.org/10.1016/j.ridd.2015.10.005

Wong, S. E. (2006). Behavior analysis of psychotic disorders: Scientific dead end or casualty of the mental health political economy? Behavior and Social Issues, 15(2), 152–177.

Wong, S. E. (2014). A critique of the diagnostic construct schizophrenia. *Research on Social Work Practice, 24*(1), 132–141.

Wood, H. (2003). Psychoanalytic theories of perversion reformulated. In *Reformulation* (pp. 26–31).

Wood, J., & Ahmari, S. E. (2015). A framework for understanding the emerging role of corticolimbic-ventral striatal networks in OCD-associated repetitive behaviors. *Frontiers in Systems Neuroscience, 9*, Article 171. https://doi.org/10.3389/fnsys.2015.00171

Wood, J. M., Garb, H. N., Nezworski, M. T., Lilienfeld, S. O., & Duke, M. C. (2015). A second look at the validity of widely used Rorschach indices: Comment on Mihura, Meyer, Dumitrascu, and Bombel (2013). *Psychological Bulletin, 141*(1), 236–249. https://doi.org/10.1037/a0036005

Wood, J. M., & Lilienfeld, S. O. (1999). The Rorschach Inkblot Test: A case of overstatement? *Assessment, 6*(4), 341–351. https://doi.org/10.1177/107319119900600405

Wood, J. M., Nezworski, M. T., Garb, H. N., & Lilienfeld, S. O. (2001). The misperception of psychopathology: Problems with norms of the Comprehensive System for the Rorschach. *Clinical Psychology: Science and Practice, 8*(3), 350–373. https://doi.org/10.1093/clipsy/8.3.350

Wood, L., Birtel, M., Alsawy, S., Pyle, M., & Morrison, A. (2014). Public perceptions of stigma towards people with schizophrenia, depression, and anxiety. *Psychiatry Research, 220*(1–2), 604–608. https://doi.org/10.1016/j.psychres.2014.07.012

Wood, L., Williams, C., Billings, J., & Johnson, S. (2020). A systematic review and meta-analysis of cognitive behavioural informed psychological interventions for psychiatric inpatients with psychosis. *Schizophrenia Research, 222*, 133–144. https://doi.org/10.1016/j.schres.2020.03.041

Woods, D. W., Piacentini, J. C., Chang, S. W., Deckersbach, T., Ginsburg, G. S., Peterson, A. L., Scahill, L. D., Walkup, J. T., & Wilhelm, S. (2008). *Managing Tourette syndrome: A behavioral intervention for children and adults. Therapist guide*. University Press.

Woolfolk, R. L., & Allen, L. A. (2012). Cognitive behavioral therapy for somatoform disorders. In I. R. de Oliveira (Ed.), *Standard and innovative strategies in cognitive behavior therapy* (pp. 117–144). InTech. https://doi.org/10.5772/26800

Woollaston, K., & Hixenbaugh, P. (2008). "Destructive whirlwind": Nurses' perceptions of patients diagnosed with borderline personality disorder. *Journal of Psychiatric and Mental Health Nursing, 15*(9), 703–709. https://doi.org/10.1111/j.1365-2850.2008.01275.x

Woon, F. L., Sood, S., & Hedges, D. W. (2010). Hippocampal volume deficits associated with exposure to psychological trauma and posttraumatic stress disorder in adults: A meta-analysis. *Progress in Neuro-Psychopharmacology & Biological Psychiatry, 34*(7), 1181–1188. https://doi.org/10.1016/j.pnpbp.2010.06.016

Work Group on Major Depressive Disorder. (2010). *Practice guideline for the treatment of patients with major depressive disorder*. American Psychiatric Association.

World Association of Sexual Health. (2014). *Declaration of sexual rights* (Report; Rev. ed.). https://worldsexualhealth.net/resources/declaration-of-sexual-rights/

World Health Organization. (1992). *The ICD-10 classification of mental and behavioural disorders*. http://www.who.int/classifications/icd/en/bluebook.pdf

World Health Organization. (2009). Clinical guidelines for withdrawal management and treatment of drug dependence in closed settings. In *Clinical guidelines for withdrawal management and treatment of drug dependence in closed settings*. World Health Organization. https://www.ncbi.nlm.nih.gov/books/NBK310658/

World Health Organization. (2011, October 2). *Psychological first aid: Guide for field workers*. https://www.who.int/publications-detail-redirect/9789241548205

World Health Organization. (2014). *Preventing suicide: A global imperative* [Report]. https://apps.who.int/iris/bitstream/handle/10665/131056/9789241564779_eng.pdf;jsessionid=565B5F062DD0677BE-9FB73D777FFE42F?sequence=1

World Health Organization. (2017a). *Depression and other common mental disorders: Global health estimates*. https://www.who.int/publications-detail-redirect/depression-global-health-estimates

World Health Organization. (2017b, December 8). *Global action plan on the public health response to dementia 2017–2025*. https://www.who.int/publications-detail-redirect/9789241513487

World Health Organization. (2018, June 18). *WHO releases new International classification of diseases (ICD 11)*. https://www.who.int/news/item/18-06-2018-who-releases-new-international-classification-of-diseases-(icd-11)

World Health Organization. (2019, May 25). *World Health Assembly update, 25 May 2019*. https://www.who.int/news/item/25-05-2019-world-health-assembly-update

World Health Organization. (2021a, June 9). *Obesity and overweight*. https://www.who.int/en/news-room/fact-sheets/detail/obesity-and-overweight

World Health Organization. (2021b). *Suicide worldwide in 2019: Global health estimates*. https://www.who.int/publications-detail-redirect/9789240026643

World Health Organization. (2021c, June 17). *Suicide*. http://www.who.int/mediacentre/factsheets/fs398/en/

World Health Organization. (2021d, September 13). *Depression*. https://www.who.int/news-room/fact-sheets/detail/depression

World Health Organization. (2022a). *International statistical classification of diseases and related health problems* (11th ed.). https://icd.who.int/

World Health Organization. (2022b, February 11). *ICD-11 2022 release*. https://www.who.int/news/item/11-02-2022-icd-11-2022-release

World Health Organization. (2022c, May 9). *Alcohol*. https://www.who.int/news-room/fact-sheets/detail/alcohol

World Health Organization. (2022d, September 20). *Dementia*. https://www.who.int/news-room/fact-sheets/detail/dementia

World Medical Association. (2022, September). *WMA Declaration of Helsinki – ethical principles for medical research involving human subjects*. https://www.wma.net/policies-post/wma-declaration-of-helsinki-ethical-principles-for-medical-research-involving-human-subjects/

World Population Review. (n.d.). *Depression rates by country 2021*. Retrieved January 30, 2022, from https://worldpopulationreview.com/country-rankings/depression-rates-by-country

Worley, S. (2014). Conduct disorder: Pathologizing the normal? In C. Perring & L. A. Wells (Eds.), *Diagnostic dilemmas in child and adolescent psychiatry: Philosophical perspectives* (pp. 182–208). Oxford University Press.

Woywodt, A., & Kiss, A. (2002). Geophagia: The history of earth-eating. *Journal of The Royal Society of Medicine, 95*(3), 143–146. https://doi.org/10.1258/jrsm.95.3.143

Wray, N. R., Ripke, S., Mattheisen, M., Trzaskowski, M., Byrne, E. M., Abdellaoui, A., Adams, M. J., Agerbo, E., Air, T. M., Andlauer, T. M. F., Bacanu, S.-A., Bækvad-Hansen, M., Beekman, A. F. T., Bigdeli, T. B., Binder, E. B., Blackwood, D. R. H., Bryois, J., Buttenschøn, H. N., Bybjerg-Grauholm, J., … Sullivan, P. F. (2018). Genome-wide association analyses identify 44 risk variants and refine the genetic architecture of major depression. *Nature Genetics, 50*(5), 668-681, 681A-681D. https://doi.org/10.1038/s41588-018-0090-3

Wright, A., Reisig, A., & Cullen, B. (2020). Efficacy and cultural adaptations of narrative exposure therapy for trauma-related outcomes in refugees/asylum-seekers: A systematic review and meta-analysis. *Journal of Behavioral and Cognitive Therapy, 30*(4), 301–314. https://doi.org/10.1016/j.jbct.2020.10.003

Wright, K. (2013). Psychological theories of and therapies for bipolar disorder. In M. Power (Ed.), *The Wiley-Blackwell handbook of mood disorders* (2nd ed., pp. 325–342). Wiley-Blackwell.

Wu, J., Liu, J., Li, S., Ma, H., & Wang, Y. (2020). Trends in the prevalence and disability-adjusted life years of eating disorders from 1990 to 2017: Results from the Global Burden of Disease Study 2017. *Epidemiology and Psychiatric Sciences, 29*, e191. https://doi.org/10.1017/S2045796020001055

Wu, J. C., Maguire, G., Riley, G., Lee, A., Keator, D., Tang, C., Fallon, J., & Najafi, A. (1997). Increased dopamine activity associated with stuttering. *NeuroReport, 8*(3), 767–770. https://doi.org/10.1097/00001756-199702100-00037

Wu, S., Ding, Y., Wu, F., Li, R., Xie, G., Hou, J., & Mao, P. (2015). Family history of autoimmune diseases is associated with an increased risk of autism in children: A systematic review and meta-analysis. *Neuroscience and Biobehavioral Reviews, 55*, 322–332. https://doi.org/10.1016/j.neubiorev.2015.05.004

Wu, W., Wang, W., Dong, Z., Xie, Y., Gu, Y., Zhang, Y., Li, M., & Tan, X. (2018). Sleep quality and its associated factors among low-income adults in a rural area of China: A population-based study. *International Journal of Environmental Research and Public Health, 15*(9), Article 2055. https://doi.org/10.3390/ijerph15092055

Wu, Y., Kralj, C., Acosta, D., Guerra, M., Huang, Y., Jotheeswaran, A. T., Jimenez-Velazquez, I. Z., Liu, Z., Llibre Rodriguez, J. J., Salas, A., Sosa, A. L., Alkholy, R., Prince, M., & Prina, A. M. (2020). The association between, depression, anxiety, and mortality in older people across eight low- and middle-income countries: Results from the 10/66 cohort study. *International Journal of Geriatric Psychiatry, 35*(1), 29–36. https://doi.org/10.1002/gps.5211

Wu, Y., Mo, J., Sui, L., Zhang, J., Hu, W., Zhang, C., Wang, Y., Liu, C., Zhao, B., Wang, X., Zhang, K., & Xie, X. (2021). Deep brain stimulation in treatment-resistant depression: A systematic review and meta-analysis on efficacy and safety. *Frontiers in Neuroscience, 15*, Article 655412. https://doi.org/10.3389/fnins.2021.655412

Wyatt v. Stickney, 325 F. Supp. 781 (M.D. Ala. 1971). https://law.justia.com/cases/federal/district-courts/FSupp/325/781/2594259/

Wyatt, W. J., & Midkiff, D. M. (2006). Biological psychiatry: A practice in search of a science. *Behavior and Social Issues, 15*(2), 132–151. https://doi.org/10.5210/bsi.v15i2.372

Wylie, K. (2022). Masters & Johnson—their unique contribution to sexology. *BJPsych Advances, 28*(3), 163–165. https://doi.org/10.1192/bja.2021.53

Wylie, K., & Malik, F. (2009). Review of drug treatment for female sexual dysfunction. *International Journal of STD & AIDS, 20*(10), 671–674. https://doi.org/10.1258/ijsa.2009.009206

Xie, Y., Wu, Z., Sun, L., Zhou, L., Wang, G., Xiao, L., & Wang, H. (2021). The effects and mechanisms of exercise on the treatment of depression. *Frontiers in Psychiatry, 12*, Article 705559. https://doi.org/10.3389/fpsyt.2021.705559

Xu, G., Strathearn, L., Liu, B., Yang, B., & Bao, W. (2018). Twenty-year trends in diagnosed attention-deficit/hyperactivity disorder among us children and adolescents, 1997-2016. *JAMA Network Open, 1*(4), e181471. https://doi.org/10.1001/jamanetworkopen.2018.1471

Xu, M., Xu, X., Li, J., & Li, F. (2019). Association between gut microbiota and autism spectrum disorder: A systematic review and meta-analysis. *Frontiers in Psychiatry, 10*, Article 473. https://doi.org/10.3389/fpsyt.2019.00473

Xu, T., Gu, Q., Zhao, Q., Wang, P., Liu, Q., Fan, Q., Chen, J., & Wang, Z. (2021). Impaired cortico-striatal functional connectivity is related to trait impulsivity in unmedicated patients with obsessive-compulsive disorder. *Journal of Affective Disorders, 281*, 899–907. https://doi.org/10.1016/j.jad.2020.11.037

Xu, T., Magnusson Hanson, L. L., Lange, T., Starkopf, L., Westerlund, H., Madsen, I. E. H., Rugulies, R., Pentti, J., Stenholm, S., Vahtera, J., Hansen, Å. M., Virtanen, M., Kivimäki, M., & Rod, N. H. (2019). Workplace bullying and workplace violence as risk factors for cardiovascular disease: A multi-cohort study. *European Heart Journal, 40*(14), 1124–1134. https://doi.org/10.1093/eurheartj/ehy683

Xu, W., Tan, L., Wang, H.-F., Tan, M.-S., Tan, L., Li, J.-Q., Zhao, Q.-F., & Yu, J.-T. (2016). Education and risk of dementia: Dose-response meta-analysis of prospective cohort studies. *Molecular Neurobiology, 53*(5), 3113–3123. https://doi.org/10.1007/s12035-015-9211-5

Xu, W., Zhang, C., Deeb, W., Patel, B., Wu, Y., Voon, V., Okun, M. S., & Sun, B. (2020). Deep brain stimulation for Tourette's syndrome. *Translational Neurodegeneration, 9*(1), Article 4. https://doi.org/10.1186/s40035-020-0183-7

Xuan, R., Li, X., Qiao, Y., Guo, Q., Liu, X., Deng, W., Hu, Q., Wang, K., & Zhang, L. (2020). Mindfulness-based cognitive therapy for bipolar disorder: A systematic review and meta-analysis. *Psychiatry Research, 290*, 113116. https://doi.org/10.1016/j.psychres.2020.113116

Xue, C., Ge, Y., Tang, B., Liu, Y., Kang, P., Wang, M., & Zhang, L. (2015). A meta-analysis of risk factors for combat-related PTSD among military personnel and veterans. *PLoS ONE, 10*(3). https://doi.org/10.1371/journal.pone.0120270

Yaacov, D., Nelinger, G., & Kalichman, L. (2022). The effect of pelvic floor rehabilitation on males with sexual dysfunction: A narrative review. *Sexual Medicine Reviews, 10*(1), 162–167. https://doi.org/10.1016/j.sxmr.2021.02.001

Yager, J. (2019, October 18). Deep brain stimulation for treatment-resistant depression: Long-term results. *NEJM Journal Watch: Psychiatry.*

Yahia, S., El-Hadidy, M., El-Gilany, A.-H., Amdel-Hady, D., Wahba, Y., & Al-Haggar, M. (2014). Disruptive behavior in Down syndrome children: A cross-sectional comparative study. *Annals of Saudi Medicine, 34*(6), 517–521. https://doi.org/10.5144/0256-4947.2014.517

Yairi, E., Ambrose, N., & Cox, N. (1996). Genetics of stuttering: A critical review. *Journal of Speech & Hearing Research, 39*(4), 771–784. https://doi.org/10.1044/jshr.3904.771

Yakeley, J., & Wood, H. (2014). Paraphilias and paraphilic disorders: Diagnosis, assessment and management. *Advances in Psychiatric Treatment, 20*(3), 202–213. https://doi.org/10.1192/apt.bp.113.011197

Yalch, M. M., Stewart, A. M., & Dehart, R. M. (2021). Influence of betrayal trauma on antisocial personality disorder traits. *Journal of Trauma & Dissociation, 22*(1), 122–134. https://doi.org/10.1080/15299732.2020.1792025

Yalom, I. D. (1980). *Existential psychotherapy.* Basic Books.

Yan, J., Cui, L., Wang, M., Cui, Y., & Li, Y. (2022). The Efficacy and neural correlates of ERP-based therapy for OCD & TS: A systematic review and meta-analysis. *Journal of Integrative Neuroscience, 21*(3), 97. https://doi.org/10.31083/j.jin2103097

Yang, C., Hao, Z., Zhu, C., Guo, Q., Mu, D., & Zhang, L. (2016). Interventions for tic disorders: An overview of systematic reviews and meta analyses. *Neuroscience and Biobehavioral Reviews, 63*, 239–255. https://doi.org/10.1016/j.neubiorev.2015.12.013

Yang, E. V., & Glaser, R. (2002). Stress-induced immunomodulation and the implications for health. *International Immunopharmacology, 2*(2–3), 315–324. https://doi.org/10.1016/S1567-5769(01)00182-5

Yang, J.-J., & Jiang, W. (2020). Immune biomarkers alterations in post-traumatic stress disorder: A systematic review and meta-analysis. *Journal of Affective Disorders, 268*, 39–46. https://doi.org/10.1016/j.jad.2020.02.044

Yang, M., Kavi, V., Wang, W., Wu, Z., & Hao, W. (2012). The association of 5-HTR2A-1438A/G, COMTVal-158Met, MAOA-LPR, DATVNTR and 5-HTTVNTR gene polymorphisms and antisocial personality disorder in male heroin-dependent Chinese subjects. *Progress in Neuro-Psychopharmacology & Biological Psychiatry, 36*(2), 282–289. https://doi.org/10.1016/j.pnpbp.2011.11.009

Yang, M., Mamy, J., Wang, Q., Liao, Y.-H., Seewoobudul, V., Xiao, S.-Y., & Hao, W. (2014). The association of 5-HTR2A-1438A/G, COMTVal158Met, MAOA-LPR, DATVNTR and 5-HTTVNTR gene polymorphisms and borderline personality disorder in female heroin-dependent Chinese subjects. *Progress in Neuro-Psychopharmacology and Biological Psychiatry, 50*, 74–82. https://doi.org/10.1016/j.pnpbp.2013.12.005

Yang, X.-P., & Reckelhoff, J. F. (2011). Estrogen, hormonal replacement therapy and cardiovascular disease. *Current Opinion in Nephrology and Hypertension, 20*(2), 133–138. https://doi.org/10.1097/MNH.0b013e3283431921

Yang, Y., & Raine, A. (2018). The neuroanatomical bases of psychopathy: A review of brain imaging findings. In C. J. Patrick (Ed.), *Handbook of psychopathy* (2nd ed., pp. 380–400). The Guilford Press.

Yankowitz, L. D., Herrington, J. D., Yerys, B. E., Pereira, J. A., Pandey, J., & Schultz, R. T. (2020). Evidence against the "normalization" prediction of the early brain overgrowth hypothesis of autism. *Molecular Autism, 11*(1), 51. https://doi.org/10.1186/s13229-020-00353-2

Yard, E. (2021). Emergency department visits for suspected suicide attempts among persons aged 12–25 years before and during the COVID-19 pandemic—United States, January 2019–May 2021. *MMWR. Morbidity and Mortality Weekly Report, 70*(24), 888–894. https://doi.org/10.15585/mmwr.mm7024e1

Yardley, W. (2014, November 1). Bernard Mayes, 85, dies; Started first U.S. suicide hotline. *The New York Times.* https://www.nytimes.com/2014/11/02/us/bernard-mayes-85-dies-started-first-us-suicide-hotline.html

Yasmeen, R., Mobeen, N., Khan, M. A., Aslam, I., & Chaudhry, S. (2021). Intake of anti-epileptic drugs and their influences on sexual dysfunctions: Anti-epileptic drugs in sexual dysfunctions. *Pakistan BioMedical Journal, 3*(2). https://doi.org/10.52229/pbmj.v3i2.15

Yau, Y. H. C., Leeman, R. F., & Potenza, M. N. (2021). Biological underpinning of behavioral addictions and management implications. In N. el-Guebaly, G. Carrà, M. Galanter, & A. M. Baldacchino (Eds.), *Textbook of addiction treatment* (pp. 889–910). Springer International Publishing. https://doi.org/10.1007/978-3-030-36391-8_63

Yen, L.-L., Patrick, W. K., & Chie, W.-C. (1996). Comparison of relaxation techniques, routine blood pressure measurements, and self-learning packages in hypertension control. *Preventive Medicine: An International Journal Devoted to Practice and Theory, 25*(3), 339–345. https://doi.org/10.1006/pmed.1996.0064

Yeo, R. A., Martinez, D., Pommy, J., Ehrlich, S., Schulz, S. C., Ho, B.-C., Bustillo, J. R., & Calhoun, V. D. (2014). The impact of parent socio-economic status on executive functioning and cortical morphology in individuals with schizophrenia and healthy controls. *Psychological Medicine, 44*(6), 1257–1265. https://doi.org/10.1017/S0033291713001608

Yeomans, F. E., Clarkin, J. F., & Kernberg, O. F. (2015). *Transference-focused psychotherapy for borderline personality disorder: A clinical guide.* American Psychiatric Publishing.

Yeomans, F. E., & Delaney, J. C. (2017). Transference-focused psychotherapy: A psychodynamic treatment of personality disorders. In B. Stanley & A. New (Eds.), *Borderline personality disorder* (pp. 271–281). Oxford University Press. https://doi.org/10.1093/med/9780199997510.003.0015

Yeomans, F. E., & Diamond, D. (2010). Transference-focused psychotherapy and borderline personality

disorder. In J. F. Clarkin, P. Fonagy, & G. O. Gabbard (Eds.), *Psychodynamic psychotherapy for personality disorders: A clinical handbook* (pp. 209–238). American Psychiatric Publishing.

Yeomans, F. E., Clarkin, J. F., & Kernberg, O. F. (2015). *Transference-focused psychotherapy for borderline personality disorder: A clinical guide.* American Psychiatric Publishing.

Yeung, K. S., Hernandez, M., Mao, J. J., Haviland, I., & Gubili, J. (2018). Herbal medicine for depression and anxiety: A systematic review with assessment of potential psycho-oncologic relevance. *Phytotherapy Research, 32*(5), 865–891. https://doi.org/10.1002/ptr.6033

Yeung, M. E. M., Weaver, C. G., Hartmann, R., Haines-Saah, R., & Lang, E. (2021). Emergency department pediatric visits in alberta for cannabis after legalization. *Pediatrics, 148*(4), e2020045922. https://doi.org/10.1542/peds.2020-045922

Yildirim, B. O., & Derksen, J. J. L. (2013). Systematic review, structural analysis, and new theoretical perspectives on the role of serotonin and associated genes in the etiology of psychopathy and sociopathy. *Neuroscience and Biobehavioral Reviews, 37*(7), 1254–1296. https://doi.org/10.1016/j.neubiorev.2013.04.009

Yin, R. K. (2014). *Case study research: Design and methods.* SAGE.

Yip, A. G., & Carpenter, L. L. (2010). Transcranial magnetic stimulation for medication-resistant depression. *Journal of Clinical Psychiatry, 71*(4), 502–503. https://doi.org/10.4088/JCP.10ac06054blu

Yip, P. S. F., Yousuf, S., Chang, S.-S., Caine, E., Wu, K. C.-C., & Chen, Y.-Y. (2012). Means restriction for suicide prevention. *The Lancet, 379*(9834), 2393–2399. https://doi.org/10.1016/S0140-6736(12)60521-2

Yip, T., Cheon, Y. M., Wang, Y., Cham, H., Tryon, W., & El-Sheikh, M. (2020). Racial disparities in sleep: Associations with discrimination among ethnic/racial minority adolescents. *Child Development, 91*(3), 914–931. https://doi.org/10.1111/cdev.13234

Yip, T., Chung, K., & Chae, D. H. (2022). Vicarious racism, ethnic/racial identity, and sleep among Asian Americans. *Cultural Diversity and Ethnic Minority Psychology.* Advance online publication. https://doi.org/10.1037/cdp0000534

Yoosefi Looyeh, M., Kamali, K., & Shafieian, R. (2012). An exploratory study of the effectiveness of group narrative therapy on the school behavior of girls with attention-deficit/hyperactivity symptoms. *Archives of Psychiatric Nursing, 26*(5), 404–410. https://doi.org/10.1016/j.apnu.2012.01.001

Yosephine, L. (2016). Indonesian psychiatrists label LGBT as mental disorders. In *The Jakarta Post.* http://www.thejakartapost.com/news/2016/02/24/indonesian-psychiatrists-label-lgbt-mental-disorders.html

Young, B. H., & Blake, D. D. (1999). *Group treatments for post-traumatic stress disorder.* Brunner/Mazel.

Young, G. (2014). PTSD, endophenotypes, the RDoC, and the DSM-5. *Psychological Injury and Law, 7*(1), 75–91. https://doi.org/10.1007/s12207-014-9187-x

Young, J. E. (1999). *Cognitive therapy for personality disorders: A schema-focused approach* (3rd ed.). Professional Resource Press/Professional Resource Exchange.

Young, J. E., Klosko, J. S., & Weishaar, M. E. (2003). *Schema therapy: A practitioner's guide.* Guilford Press.

Young, J. J., Bruno, D., & Pomara, N. (2014). A review of the relationship between proinflammatory cytokines and major depressive disorder. *Journal of Affective Disorders, 169*, 15–20. https://doi.org/10.1016/j.jad.2014.07.032

Young, K. (2015). The evolution of Internet addiction disorder. In C. Montag & M. Reuter (Eds.), *Internet addiction: Neuroscientific approaches and therapeutical interventions* (pp. 3–17). Springer Science + Business Media. https://doi.org/10.1007/978-3-319-07242-5_1

Young, Z., Moghaddam, N., & Tickle, A. (2020). The efficacy of cognitive behavioral therapy for adults with ADHD: A systematic review and meta-analysis of randomized controlled trials. *Journal of Attention Disorders*, 24(6), 875–888. https://doi.org/10.1177/1087054716664413

Younggren, J. N., & Harris, E. A. (2008). Can you keep a secret? Confidentiality in psychotherapy. *Journal of Clinical Psychology*, 64(5), 589–600. https://doi.org/10.1002/jclp.20480

YoungMinds. (2020, November 23). *What I wish people knew about BPD*. https://www.youngminds.org.uk/young-person/blog/what-i-wish-people-knew-about-borderline-personality-disorder/

Yousaf, A., Waltes, R., Haslinger, D., Klauck, S. M., Duketis, E., Sachse, M., Voran, A., Biscaldi, M., Schulte-Rüther, M., Cichon, S., Nöthen, M., Ackermann, J., Koch, I., Freitag, C. M., & Chiocchetti, A. G. (2020). Quantitative genome-wide association study of six phenotypic subdomains identifies novel genome-wide significant variants in autism spectrum disorder. *Translational Psychiatry*, 10(1), Article 1. https://doi.org/10.1038/s41398-020-00906-2

Yousry Elnazer, H., & Baldwin, D. S. (2014). Investigation of cortisol levels in patients with anxiety disorders: A structured review. In C. M. Pariante & M. D. Lapiz-Bluhm (Eds.), *Behavioral neurobiology of stress-related disorders* (Vol. 18, pp. 191–216). Springer-Verlag Publishing. https://doi.org/10.1007/7854_2014_299

Yu, C.-J., Du, J.-C., Chiou, H.-C., Feng, C.-C., Chung, M.-Y., Yang, W., Chen, Y.-S., Chien, L.-C., Hwang, B., & Chen, M.-L. (2016). Sugar-sweetened beverage consumption Is adversely associated with childhood attention deficit/hyperactivity disorder. *International Journal of Environmental Research and Public Health*, 13(7). https://doi.org/10.3390/ijerph13070678

Yu, D., Sul, J. H., Tsetsos, F., Nawaz, M. S., Huang, A. Y., Zelaya, I., Illmann, C., Osiecki, L., Darrow, S. M., Hirschtritt, M. E., Greenberg, E., Muller-Vahl, K. R., Stuhrmann, M., Dion, Y., Rouleau, G., Aschauer, H., Stamenkovic, M., Schlögelhofer, M., Sandor, P., … Scharf, J. M. (2019). Interrogating the genetic determinants of Tourette's syndrome and other tic disorders through genome-wide association studies. *American Journal of Psychiatry*, 176(3), 217–227. https://doi.org/10.1176/appi.ajp.2018.18070857

Yu, L., Li, Y., Zhang, J., Yan, C., Wen, F., Yan, J., Wang, F., Liu, J., & Cui, Y. (2020). The therapeutic effect of habit reversal training for Tourette syndrome: A meta-analysis of randomized control trials. *Expert Review of Neurotherapeutics*, 20(11), 1189–1196. https://doi.org/10.1080/14737175.2020.1826933

Yu, Y., Fernandez, I. D., Meng, Y., Zhao, W., & Groth, S. W. (2021). Gut hormones, adipokines, and pro- and anti-inflammatory cytokines/markers in loss of control eating: A scoping review. *Appetite*, 166, 105442. https://doi.org/10.1016/j.appet.2021.105442

Yu, Y., Miller, R., & Groth, S. W. (2022). A literature review of dopamine in binge eating. *Journal of Eating Disorders*, 10(1), 11. https://doi.org/10.1186/s40337-022-00531-y

Yu, Z., Zhang, J., Zheng, Y., & Yu, L. (2020). Trends in antidepressant use and expenditure in six major cities in China from 2013 to 2018. *Frontiers in Psychiatry*, 11, Article 551. https://doi.org/10.3389/fpsyt.2020.00551

Yüce, M., Uçar, F., & Nur Say, G. (2015). Comorbid conditions in child and adolescent patients diagnosed with attention deficit/hyperactivity disorder. In J. M. Norvilitis (Ed.), *ADHD - New directions in diagnosis and treatment* (pp. 109–164). InTech. https://doi.org/10.5772/61112

Yüksel, C., McCarthy, J., Shinn, A., Pfaff, D. L., Baker, J. T., Heckers, S., Renshaw, P., & Öngür, D. (2012). Gray matter volume in schizophrenia and bipolar disorder with psychotic features. *Schizophrenia Research*, 138(2–3), 177–182. https://doi.org/10.1016/j.schres.2012.03.003

Yun, S., Yang, B., Anair, J. D., Martin, M. M., Fleps, S. W., Pamukcu, A., Yeh, N.-H., Contractor, A., Kennedy, A., & Parker, J. G. (2023). Antipsychotic drug efficacy

correlates with the modulation of D1 rather than D2 receptor-expressing striatal projection neurons. *Nature Neuroscience*. Advance online publication. https://doi.org/10.1038/s41593-023-01390-9

Yun, T. (2022, June 29). *"Crisis level": N.L. faces shortage of psychologists as they leave public system*. CTVNews. https://www.ctvnews.ca/health/crisis-level-n-l-faces-shortage-of-psychologists-as-they-leave-public-system-1.5967841

Yung, A. R., Woods, S. W., Ruhrmann, S., Addington, J., Schultze-Lutter, F., Cornblatt, B. A., Amminger, G. P., Bechdolf, A., Birchwood, M., Borgwardt, S., Cannon, T. D., de Haan, L., French, P., Fusar-Poli, P., Keshavan, M., Klosterkötter, J., Kwon, J. S., McGorry, P. D., McGuire, P., … McGlashan, T. H. (2012). Whither the attenuated psychosis syndrome? *Schizophrenia Bulletin*, 38(6), 1130–1134. https://doi.org/10.1093/schbul/sbs108

Zachar, P. (2009). Psychiatric comorbidity: More than a Kuhnian anomaly. *Philosophy, Psychiatry, & Psychology*, 16(1), 13–22. https://doi.org/10.1353/ppp.0.0212

Zachar, P. (2011). The clinical nature of personality disorders: Answering the neo-Szaszian critique. *Philosophy, Psychiatry, & Psychology*, 18(3), 191–202. https://doi.org/10.1353/ppp.2011.0038

Zachar, P., First, M. B., & Kendler, K. S. (2017). The bereavement exclusion debate in the *DSM-5*: A history. *Clinical Psychological Science*, 5(5), 890–906. https://doi.org/10.1177/2167702617711284

Zachar, P., & Kendler, K. S. (2012). *The removal of Pluto from the class of planets and homosexuality from the class of psychiatric disorders: A comparison* (Vol. 7, Issue 4). Retrieved from http://www.peh-med.com/content/7/1/4

Zachar, P., Link to external site, this link will open in a new window, First, M. B., & Kendler, K. S. (2020). The DSM-5 proposal for attenuated psychosis syndrome: A history. *Psychological Medicine*, 50(6), 920–926. https://doi.org/10.1017/S0033291720000653

Zachar, P., & Potter, N. N. (2010a). Personality disorders: Moral or medical kinds—Or both? *Philosophy, Psychiatry, & Psychology*, 17(2), 101–117. https://doi.org/10.1353/ppp.0.0290

Zachar, P., & Potter, N. N. (2010b). Valid moral appraisals and valid personality disorders. *Philosophy, Psychiatry, & Psychology*, 17(2), 131–142. https://doi.org/10.1353/ppp.0.0296

Zachariades, F., & Cabrera, C. (2012). The duty to warn revisited: Contemporary issues within the North American context. *Journal of Ethics in Mental Health*, 7, 1–5.

Zafiropoulou, M., & Pappa, E. (2002). The role of preparedness and social environment in developing social phobia. *Psychology: The Journal of the Hellenic Psychological Society*, 9(3), 365–377.

Zagorski, N. (2022). FDA clears first in vitro assay to improve Alzheimer's diagnosis. *Psychiatric News*. https://doi.org/10.1176/appi.pn.2022.08.7.15

Zai, G., Barta, C., Cath, D., Eapen, V., Geller, D., & Grünblatt, E. (2019). New insights and perspectives on the genetics of obsessive-compulsive disorder. *Psychiatric Genetics*, 29(5), 142–151. https://doi.org/10.1097/YPG.0000000000000230

Zainal, N. H., & Newman, M. G. (2022). Inflammation mediates depression and generalized anxiety symptoms predicting executive function impairment after 18 years. *Journal of Affective Disorders*, 296, 465–475. https://doi.org/10.1016/j.jad.2021.08.077

Zajac, K., Randall, J., & Swenson, C. C. (2015). Multisystemic therapy for externalizing youth. *Child and Adolescent Psychiatric Clinics of North America*, 24(3), 601–616. https://doi.org/10.1016/j.chc.2015.02.007

Zajkowska, Z., Gullett, N., Walsh, A., Zonca, V., Pedersen, G. A., Souza, L., Kieling, C., Fisher, H. L., Kohrt, B. A., & Mondelli, V. (2022). Cortisol and development of depression in adolescence and young adulthood—a systematic review and meta-analysis. *Psychoneuroendocrinology*, 136, 105625. https://doi.org/10.1016/j.psyneuen.2021.105625

Zakowski, S. G., McAllister, C. G., Deal, M., & Baum, A. (1992). Stress, reactivity, and immune function in healthy men. *Health Psychology*, 11(4), 223–232. https://doi.org/10.1037/0278-6133.11.4.223

Zalta, A. K., & Foa, E. B. (2012). Exposure therapy: Promoting emotional processing of pathological anxiety. In W. T. O'Donohue & J. E. Fisher (Eds.), *Cognitive behavior therapy: Core principles for practice* (pp. 75–104). John Wiley & Sons.

Zalta, A. K., Tirone, V., Orlowska, D., Blais, R. K., Lofgreen, A., Klassen, B., Held, P., Stevens, N. R., Adkins, E., & Dent, A. L. (2021). Examining moderators of the relationship between social support and self-reported PTSD symptoms: A meta-analysis. *Psychological Bulletin*, 147(1), 33–54. https://doi.org/10.1037/bul0000316

Zambrano-Vazquez, L., Levy, H. C., Belleau, E. L., Dworkin, E. R., Howard Sharp, K. M., Pittenger, S. L., Schumacher, J. A., & Coffey, S. F. (2017). Using the research domain criteria framework to track domains of change in comorbid PTSD and SUD. *Psychological Trauma: Theory, Research, Practice, and Policy*, 9(6), 679–687. https://doi.org/10.1037/tra0000257

Zandberg, L., Kaczkurkin, A. N., McLean, C. P., Rescorla, L., Yadin, E., & Foa, E. B. (2016). Treatment of adolescent PTSD: The impact of prolonged exposure versus client-centered therapy on co-occurring emotional and behavioral problems. *Journal of Traumatic Stress*, 29(6), 507–514. https://doi.org/10.1002/jts.22138

Zaroff, C. M., Davis, J. M., Chio, P. H., & Madhavan, D. (2012). Somatic presentations of distress in China. *Australian and New Zealand Journal of Psychiatry*, 46(11), 1053–1057.

Zawadzka, A., Cieślik, M., & Adamczyk, A. (2021). The role of maternal immune activation in the pathogenesis of autism: A review of the evidence, proposed mechanisms and implications for treatment. *International Journal of Molecular Sciences*, 22(21), Article 21. https://doi.org/10.3390/ijms222111516

Zecher, J. L. (2020, August 26). Acedia: The lost name for the emotion we're all feeling right now. *The Conversation*. https://theconversation.com/acedia-the-lost-name-for-the-emotion-were-all-feeling-right-now-144058

Zelviene, P., & Kazlauskas, E. (2018). Adjustment disorder: Current perspectives. *Neuropsychiatric Disease and Treatment*, 14, 375–381. https://doi.org/10.2147/NDT.S121072

Zerbe, K. J. (2010). Psychodynamic therapy for eating disorders. In C. M. Grilo & J. E. Mitchell (Eds.), *The treatment of eating disorders: A clinical handbook* (pp. 339–358). Guilford Press.

Zerbinati, L., Murri, M. B., Caruso, R., Nanni, M. G., Lam, W., De Padova, S., Sabato, S., Bertelli, T., Schillani, G., Giraldi, T., Fielding, R., & Grassi, L. (2021). Post-traumatic stress symptoms and serotonin transporter (5-HTTLPR) polymorphism in breast cancer patients. *Frontiers in Psychiatry*, 12, Article 632596. https://doi.org/10.3389/fpsyt.2021.632596

Zetterqvist, M. (2015). The DSM-5 diagnosis of nonsuicidal self-injury disorder: A review of the empirical literature. *Child and Adolescent Psychiatry and Mental Health*, 9, Article 31. https://doi.org/10.1186/s13034-015-0062-7

Zhang, F.-F., Peng, W., Sweeney, J. A., Jia, Z.-Y., & Gong, Q.-Y. (2018). Brain structure alterations in depression: Psychoradiological evidence. *CNS Neuroscience & Therapeutics*, 24(11), 994–1003. https://doi.org/10.1111/cns.12835

Zhang, H., Mellor, D., & Peng, D. (2018). Neuroimaging genomic studies in major depressive disorder: A systematic review. *CNS Neuroscience & Therapeutics*, 24(11), 1020–1036. https://doi.org/10.1111/cns.12829

Zhang, J., Wang, Y., Li, Q., & Wu, C. (2021). The relationship between SNS usage and disordered eating behaviors: A meta-analysis. *Frontiers in Psychology*, 12, Article 641919. https://doi.org/10.3389/fpsyg.2021.641919

Zhang, J., Wang, G., Yang, X., & Gao, K. (2021). Efficacy and safety of electroconvulsive therapy plus medication versus medication alone in acute mania: A meta-analysis of randomized controlled trials. *Psychiatry Research, 302*, Article 114019. https://doi.org/10.1016/j.psychres.2021.114019

Zhang, M., & Demko, P. (2022, August 3). Where cannabis legalization efforts stand across the country. *Politico.* https://www.politico.com/news/2022/08/03/cannabis-legalization-efforts-across-the-states-00049224

Zhao, L. N., Lu, L., Chew, L. Y., & Mu, Y. (2014). Alzheimer's disease—A panorama glimpse. *International Journal of Molecular Sciences, 15*(7), 12631–12650. https://doi.org/10.3390/ijms150712631

Zhao, M., Yang, J., Wang, W., Ma, J., Zhang, J., Zhao, X., Qiu, X., Yang, X., Qiao, Z., Song, X., Wang, L., Jiang, S., Zhao, E., & Yang, Y. (2017). Meta-analysis of the interaction between serotonin transporter promoter variant, stress, and posttraumatic stress disorder. *Scientific Reports, 7*(1), Article 1. https://doi.org/10.1038/s41598-017-15168-0

Zhao, Q., Xu, T., Wang, Y., Chen, D., Liu, Q., Yang, Z., & Wang, Z. (2021). Limbic cortico-striato-thalamo-cortical functional connectivity in drug-naïve patients of obsessive-compulsive disorder. *Psychological Medicine, 51*(1), 70–82. https://doi.org/10.1017/S0033291719002988

Zhao, X., & Dawson, J. (2014). The new Chinese mental health law. *Psychiatry, Psychology and Law, 21*(5), 669–686. https://doi.org/10.1080/13218719.2014.882248

Zhou, B., Lu, J., Shi, P., & An, Y. (2019). Advances in treatment of nocturnal enuresis in children. In R. Pang (Ed.), *Lower urinary tract dysfunction—From evidence to clinical practice.* IntechOpen. https://doi.org/10.5772/intechopen.89106

Zhou, K., & Zhuang, G. (2014). Retention in methadone maintenance treatment in mainland China, 2004–2012: A literature review. *Addictive Behaviors, 39*(1), 22–29. https://doi.org/10.1016/j.addbeh.2013.09.001

Zhou, R.-Y., Wang, J.-J., Sun, J.-C., You, Y., Ying, J.-N., & Han, X.-M. (2017). Attention deficit hyperactivity disorder may be a highly inflammation and immune-associated disease (Review). *Molecular Medicine Reports, 16*(4), 5071–5077. https://doi.org/10.3892/mmr.2017.7228

Zhu, H., & Zhou, X. (2020). Statistical methods for SNP heritability estimation and partition: A review. *Computational and Structural Biotechnology Journal, 18*, 1557–1568. https://doi.org/10.1016/j.csbj.2020.06.011

Zhu, J., Ge, F., Zeng, Y., Qu, Y., Chen, W., Yang, H., Yang, L., Fang, F., & Song, H. (2022). Physical and mental activity, disease susceptibility, and risk of dementia: A prospective cohort study based on UK biobank. *Neurology, 99*(8), e799–e813. https://doi.org/10.1212/WNL.0000000000200701

Zhu, J., Weiss, L. G., Prifitera, A., & Coalson, D. (2004). The Weschler Intelligence Scales for children and adults. In G. Goldstein & S. R. Beers (Eds.), *Comprehensive handbook of psychological assessment: Vol. 1. Intellectual and neuropsychological assessment* (pp. 51–75). John Wiley.

Zhu, T. (2022). Contingency management intervention in quitting substance abuse: A literature review. *Proceedings of the 2021 International Conference on Social Development and Media Communication (SDMC 2021), 631*, 703–706. https://doi.org/10.2991/assehr.k.220105.129

Zhu, X., Suarez-Jimenez, B., Lazarov, A., Helpman, L., Papini, S., Lowell, A., Durosky, A., Lindquist, M. A., Markowitz, J. C., Schneier, F., Wager, T. D., & Neria, Y. (2018). Exposure-based therapy changes amygdala and hippocampus resting-state functional connectivity in patients with PTSD. *Depression and Anxiety, 35*(10), 974–984. https://doi.org/10.1002/da.22816

Zhu, X., Yao, S., Dere, J., Zhou, B., Yang, J., & Ryder, A. G. (2014). The cultural shaping of social anxiety: Concerns about causing distress to others in Han Chinese and Euro-Canadian outpatients. *Journal of Social and Clinical Psychology, 33*(10), 906–917. https://doi.org/10.1521/jscp.2014.33.10.906

Zhu, X.-C., Tan, L., Wang, H.-F., Jiang, T., Cao, L., Wang, C., Wang, J., Tan, C.-C., Meng, X.-F., & Yu, J.-T. (2015). Rate of early onset Alzheimer's disease: A systematic review and meta-analysis. *Annals of Translational Medicine, 3*(3), Article 38. https://doi.org/10.3978/j.issn.2305-5839.2015.01.19

Zhuo, C., Xiao, B., Chen, C., Jiang, D., Li, G., Ma, X., Li, R., Wang, L., Xu, Y., Zhou, C., & Lin, X. (2020). Antipsychotic agents deteriorate brain and retinal function in schizophrenia patients with combined auditory and visual hallucinations: A pilot study and secondary follow-up study. *Brain and Behavior, 10*(6), e01611. https://doi.org/10.1002/brb3.1611

Zięba, M., Wiecheć, K., Biegańska-Banaś, J., & Mieleszczenko-Kowszewicz, W. (2019). Coexistence of post-traumatic growth and post-traumatic depreciation in the aftermath of trauma: Qualitative and quantitative narrative analysis. *Frontiers in Psychology, 10*, Article 687. https://doi.org/10.3389/fpsyg.2019.00687

Zilhao, N. R., Olthof, M. C., Smit, D. J. A., Cath, D. C., Ligthart, L., Mathews, C. A., Delucchi, K., Boomsma, D. I., & Dolan, C. V. (2017). Heritability of tic disorders: A twin-family study. *Psychological Medicine, 47*(6), 1085–1096. https://doi.org/10.1017/S0033291716002981

Zipfel, S., Wild, B., Groß, G., Friederich, H.-C., Teufel, M., Schellberg, D., Giel, K. E., de Zwaan, M., Dinkel, A., Herpertz, S., Burgmer, M., Löwe, B., Tagay, S., von Wietersheim, J., Zeeck, A., Schade-Brittinger, C., Schauenburg, H., & Herzog, W. (2014). Focal psychodynamic therapy, cognitive behaviour therapy, and optimised treatment as usual in outpatients with anorexia nervosa (ANTOP study): Randomised controlled trial. *The Lancet, 383*(9912), 127–137. https://doi.org/10.1016/S0140-6736(13)61746-8

Zipursky, R. B., Reilly, T. J., & Murray, R. M. (2013). The myth of schizophrenia as a progressive brain disease. *Schizophrenia Bulletin, 39*(6), 1363–1372. https://doi.org/10.1093/schbul/sbs135

Zisook, S., Corruble, E., Duan, N., Iglewicz, A., Karam, E. G., Lanuoette, N., Lebowitz, B., Pies, R., Reynolds, C., Seay, K., Shear, M. K., Simon, N., & Young, I. T. (2012). The bereavement exclusion and DSM-5. *Depression and Anxiety, 29*(5), 425–443. https://doi.org/10.1002/da.21927

Zoellner, L. A., Abramowitz, J. S., Moore, S. A., & Slagle, D. M. (2008). Flooding. In W. T. O'Donohue & J. E. Fisher (Eds.), *Cognitive behavior therapy: Applying empirically supported techniques in your practice* (2nd ed., pp. 202–210). John Wiley & Sons.

Zoellner, L. A., Rothbaum, B. O., & Feeny, N. C. (2011). PTSD not an anxiety disorder? DSM committee proposal turns back the hands of time. *Depression and Anxiety, 28*(10), 853–856. https://doi.org/10.1002/da.20899

Zoellner, T., & Maercker, A. (2006a). Posttraumatic growth and psychotherapy. In L. G. Calhoun & R. G. Tedeschi (Eds.), *Handbook of posttraumatic growth: Research & practice* (pp. 334–354). Lawrence Erlbaum.

Zoellner, T., & Maercker, A. (2006b). Posttraumatic growth in clinical psychology–A critical review and introduction of a two component model. *Clinical Psychology Review, 26*(5), 626–653. https://doi.org/10.1016/j.cpr.2006.01.008

Zorn, J. V., Schür, R. R., Boks, M. P., Kahn, R. S., Joëls, M., & Vinkers, C. H. (2017). Cortisol stress reactivity across psychiatric disorders: A systematic review and meta-analysis. *Psychoneuroendocrinology, 77*, 25–36. https://doi.org/10.1016/j.psyneuen.2016.11.036

Zou, R., Xu, X., Hong, X., & Yuan, J. (2020). Higher socioeconomic status predicts less risk of depression in adolescence: Serial mediating roles of social support and optimism. *Frontiers in Psychology, 11*, Article 1955. https://doi.org/10.3389/fpsyg.2020.01955

Zvěřová, M. (2019). Clinical aspects of Alzheimer's disease. *Clinical Biochemistry, 72*, 3–6. https://doi.org/10.1016/j.clinbiochem.2019.04.015

Zwaanswijk, W., van Geel, M., & Vedder, P. (2018). Socioeconomic status and psychopathic traits in a community sample of youth. *Journal of Abnormal Child Psychology, 46*(8), 1643–1649. https://doi.org/10.1007/s10802-018-0411-0

Zwicker, A., Denovan-Wright, E. M., & Uher, R. (2018). Gene–environment interplay in the etiology of psychosis. *Psychological Medicine, 48*(12), 1925–1936. https://doi.org/10.1017/S003329171700383X

NAME INDEX

SUBJECT INDEX

Note: Page numbers in *italics* refer to Figures and Tables; those in **bold** refer to terms in the Glossary